# Foreign Trade
## of the United States
Including State and Metro Area Export Data

First Edition, 1999

# Foreign Trade
## of the United States
Including State and Metro Area Export Data

First Edition, 1999

EDITOR
Courtenay M. Slater

ASSOCIATE EDITOR
James B. Rice

BERNAN PRESS
Washington, DC

© 1999 Bernan Press, an imprint of Bernan Associates, a division of the Kraus Organization Limited.

ISBN: 0-89059-160-1

ISSN: 1524-3931

Printed in the United States of America by Automated Graphic Systems, Inc., White Plains, MD, on acid-free paper that meets the American National Standards Institute Z39-48 standard.

2000    1999          4  3  2  1


Bernan Press
1130 Connecticut Avenue, NW
Suite 675
Washington, DC 20036
email: info@bernan.com

# Contents

# About the Editors

Courtenay M. Slater, Manager of Economic Publication at Bernan Press, has served as Chief Economist for the U.S. Department of Commerce and as a senior economist at both the President's Council of Economic Advisors and at the Joint Economic Committee of Congress. Throughout her career, Ms. Slater has specialized in the presentation and interpretation of economic data, including foreign trade data. At the Commerce Department her responsibilities included explaining foreign trade and balance of payments data to the press, as well as testifying before Congress on questions pertaining to such data. More recently, she served as a consultant to the Committee on National Statistics of the National Academy of Sciences in its examination of data on U.S. international trade and finance. Ms. Slater holds a Ph.D. in economics from American University, where she specialized in international economics.

James B. Rice, an economic analyst at Bernan Press, holds a B.S. in political science from University of Tennessee, Chattanooga and has done graduate work in economics at the University of Tennessee, Knoxville.

# Preface

International commerce has always been of vital importance to the United States. The Revolutionary War was fought, in part, to gain freedom from the restrictions imposed by Great Britain on trade to and from the colonies that were to become the United States. Yet never have U.S. international economic relations been more important than in today's increasingly integrated global economy. U.S. exports make a contribution to the economy of every state and every major metropolitan area. Imports bring consumers an astounding variety of goods and services and introduce price competition that helps restrain inflation, but they also impact employment and profitability in industries beset by foreign competition.

Given the importance of international commerce, it is surprising that, until now, the available wealth of basic statistical information about U.S. foreign trade has not been brought together in a single printed source. *Foreign Trade of the United States* from Bernan Press now accomplishes this. Bernan's innovative new publication provides ready access to data on U.S. imports and exports of both goods and services. These national data are followed by data on exports from each state and most major metropolitan areas. The export tables provide detail on countries of destination and on industrial classification of the products exported. Accompanying graphics highlight the five most important groups of manufactured goods exported in each state and in 43 major metropolitan areas.

Exports and imports of goods and services measure only one aspect of international economic transactions alough obviously an important one. Flows of direct and indirect investment, earnings on investments already made, remittances to family members in other countries—all of these contribute to the U.S. international financial position. Thus, this book includes a presentation of U.S. international transactions or, as these data are more familiarly known, the balance of payments. Complete annual data from 1960 through 1998 are provided.

Also included are data showing U.S. exports and imports as a percent of gross domestic product, perhaps the best summary measure of the contribution of foreign trade to the economy.

Exchange rates—that is, the dollar values of foreign currencies—affect prices of exports and imports. Understanding trade patterns requires knowledge of changes in exchange rates. This volume includes annual data for several indexes of the value of the dollar against groups of important foreign currencies and then gives a detailed listing of the exchange rates for individual national currencies.

Data on U.S. foreign trade and finance come from several major government sources. Estimates of trade in services are prepared by the Bureau of Economic Analysis (BEA) of the U.S. Department of Commerce. BEA also prepares the balance of payments tables.

Data on trade in goods are prepared by the Bureau of the Census, based on tallies supplied by the U.S. Customs Service. The International Trade Administration (ITA) of the U.S. Department of Commerce uses the Bureau of the Census data to prepare tables on exports by state and metropolitan area as well as summary tables of national trade highlights.

This diversity of source agencies, coupled with limitations on agency publication budgets, helps explain the lack of a single comprehensive reference volume. In particular, ITA lacks the resources to publish its state and metro area export data in printed form, although the data are available on its web site. And ITA's former publication *Foreign Trade Highlights*, containing national data, is now available only as a set of tables on the web. Bernan's *Foreign Trade of the United States* assembles the most important data from the various government sources into one convenient volume. Annual time series are provided in all cases, so that year-to-year changes can be observed. An introductory article analyzes trends in foreign trade, especially during the 1900s, and an appendix provides detailed notes on sources, definitions, and methodology.

All statistical data are subject to error arising from sampling variability, reporting and classification errors, incomplete coverage, imputation, and other causes. The responsibility of the editor and publisher of this volume is limited to reasonable care in the reproduction and presentation of data obtained from established sources.

It is the associate editor, James B. Rice, who has brought this book into being. He prepared the data tables and the background notes and coordinated the entire project. Others who assisted with table preparation, fact checking, and other aspects of preparation for publication include Richard Dodge and Carletta Cutchember. The editor is deeply grateful to all of them. Thanks also are due to the Bernan Press production department, in particular Benjamin Shupe, for managing the production aspects of this volume. Finally, we are greatful to those at the Bureau of the Census, BEA, ITA, and elsewhere in government who not only have been generous with assistance in obtaining and understanding their data, but who, through efforts extending over many years, have developed the statistical information that enables data users to better understand U.S. participation in the world economy.

Courtenay M. Slater

# USING THIS BOOK

*Foreign Trade of the United States* contains statistical information about U.S. exports and imports and related topics. The main body of the book is divided into five sections. Sections A, B, and C provide information for the United States as a whole; Section D provides statistics on the exports of each state by country or region of destination and by industry; Section E provides similar information for large metropolitan areas. Each section is described briefly below, with examples of the information found in that section.

The "Notes" section in the back of the book provides general information about sources and definitions and specific notes for each section. Refer to the notes to learn how terms are defined, where to go for additional information, what countries are included in the regional totals shown in some tables, and how to interpret any symbols and abbreviations used in the tables.

The data in this book are annual time series; that is, they provide data pertaining to each year within a specified time span. This type of information allows examination of individual year-to-year changes as well as trends over longer periods. Preliminary data for 1998 are included in most of the summary tables but were not available at press time for the more detailed tables.

## Part A. Highlights of U.S. International Transactions (pages 7–22)

Part A is an overview of U.S. trade in goods and services and of other U.S. international transactions. This summary section provides data for a longer historical period than is possible in the other sections of the book. Table A-1 covers the longest time period, showing the relationship of exports and imports to U.S. gross domestic product (GDP) each year from 1946 through 1998. Table A-2 summarizes exports, imports, and the trade balance from 1960 through 1998. Table A-3 presents the U.S. balance of payments from 1960 through 1998. This table provides a full picture of all U.S. international transactions, including earnings on foreign investments and capital flows to and from the United States as well as exports and imports of goods and services. Table A-4 shows the exchange value of the dollar against other foreign currencies during the past several years.

> Table A-1 includes columns showing exports and imports as percentages of GDP, thus documenting the growing importance of foreign trade in the U.S. economy. From 1950 through 1969, exports only rarely reached 5 percent of GDP; the same was true of imports. Since 1969, however, both exports and imports have been rising as a percentage of GDP; by 1998, exports were more than 11 percent of GDP and imports exceeded 13 percent.

### Table A-1. U.S. Gross Domestic Product, Exports, and Imports, 1946–1998 —*Continued*

| Year | Exports and imports as a percent of gross domestic product | | | | | | Net exports |
| | Exports | | | Imports | | | |
| | Total | Goods | Services | Total | Goods | Services | |
|---|---|---|---|---|---|---|---|
| 1950 | 4.18 | 3.46 | 0.71 | 3.94 | 3.09 | 0.85 | 0.24 |
| 1951 | 5.00 | 4.18 | 0.82 | 4.30 | 3.30 | 1.00 | 0.71 |
| 1952 | 4.55 | 3.74 | 0.81 | 4.27 | 3.01 | 1.25 | 0.28 |
| 1953 | 4.00 | 3.27 | 0.74 | 4.21 | 2.90 | 1.32 | -0.21 |
| 1954 | 4.12 | 3.38 | 0.73 | 4.04 | 2.73 | 1.34 | 0.08 |
| 1955 | 4.24 | 3.47 | 0.77 | 4.14 | 2.77 | 1.37 | 0.10 |
| 1956 | 4.84 | 4.02 | 0.82 | 4.32 | 2.92 | 1.39 | 0.53 |
| 1957 | 5.18 | 4.25 | 0.93 | 4.32 | 2.89 | 1.45 | 0.87 |
| 1958 | 4.37 | 3.51 | 0.86 | 4.28 | 2.78 | 1.52 | 0.09 |
| 1959 | 4.06 | 3.25 | 0.83 | 4.40 | 3.02 | 1.38 | -0.34 |
| 1960 | 4.80 | 3.89 | 0.91 | 4.33 | 2.89 | 1.44 | 0.46 |
| 1961 | 4.77 | 3.84 | 0.94 | 4.17 | 2.77 | 1.40 | 0.62 |
| 1962 | 4.68 | 3.71 | 0.97 | 4.27 | 2.89 | 1.38 | 0.41 |
| 1963 | 4.76 | 3.77 | 0.99 | 4.23 | 2.87 | 1.36 | 0.53 |
| 1964 | 5.07 | 4.03 | 0.95 | 4.24 | 2.93 | 1.31 | 0.83 |
| 1995 | 11.27 | 8.03 | 3.24 | 12.43 | 10.42 | 2.00 | -1.15 |
| 1996 | 11.40 | 8.07 | 3.33 | 12.60 | 10.56 | 2.04 | -1.19 |
| 1997 | 11.90 | 8.49 | 3.42 | 13.05 | 10.95 | 2.10 | -1.15 |
| 1998 (p) | 11.27 | 8.00 | 3.27 | 13.05 | 10.96 | 2.09 | -1.78 |

Table A-2 shows the increasing importance of U.S. trade in services. The value of service exports has more than doubled in the last ten years, rising from $111 billion in 1988 to $260 billion in 1998, when service exports exceeded service imports by $79 billion.

## Table A-2.  U.S. International Trade in Goods and Services, 1960–1998

(Balance of payments basis, billions of dollars.)

| Year | Exports | | | Imports | | | Trade balance | | |
|---|---|---|---|---|---|---|---|---|---|
| | Total | Goods | Services | Total | Goods | Services | Total | Goods | Services |
| | | | | | 368.4 | | -140.6 | -145.1 | 4.5 |
| 1987 | 348.8 | 250.2 | 98.6 | 502.1 | 409.8 | 92.3 | -153.3 | -159.6 | 6.2 |
| 1988 | 431.3 | 320.2 | 111.1 | 547.2 | 447.2 | 100.0 | -115.9 | -127.0 | 11.1 |
| 1989 | 489.4 | 362.1 | 127.2 | 581.6 | 477.4 | 104.2 | -92.2 | -115.2 | 23.0 |
| 1992 | 617.3 | 440.4 | 177.0 | 656.0 | 536.5 | 119.5 | -38.7 | -96.1 | 57.4 |
| 1993 | 643.2 | 456.8 | 186.4 | 715.2 | 589.4 | 125.7 | -71.9 | -132.6 | 60.7 |
| 1994 | 703.8 | 502.4 | 201.4 | 804.7 | 668.6 | 136.2 | -100.9 | -166.2 | 65.3 |
| 1995 | 795.6 | 575.8 | 219.8 | 895.5 | 749.6 | 146.0 | -99.9 | -173.7 | 73.8 |
| 1996 | 850.8 | 612.0 | 238.8 | 959.3 | 803.3 | 156.0 | -108.6 | -191.3 | 82.8 |
| 1997 | 937.6 | 679.3 | 258.3 | 1 047.8 | 877.3 | 170.5 | -110.2 | -198.0 | 87.7 |
| 1998 (p) | 931.4 | 671.1 | 260.4 | 1 100.5 | 919.0 | 181.5 | -169.1 | -248.0 | 78.9 |

The data in table A-3 often are called the "balance of payments." Unlike the other tables in this book, this table uses a minus sign to identify transactions that transfer dollars from U.S. to foreign governments, businesses, or individuals. Imports are one example: dollars are transferred to foreigners in payment. U.S. foreign investments are another example: the assets acquired are purchased from foreign entities. Earnings on past foreign investments are funds flowing back to the United States, however, and thus are a plus item in the accounts. The column headed "Income Receipts on U.S. Assets Abroad: Total" shows U.S. earnings on foreign investment (private and government combined) reaching $242,615 million (or $243 billion when rounded) in 1998, up more than 90 percent from five years earlier.

## Table A-3.  U.S. International Transactions, 1960–1998 —Continued

(Millions of dollars.)

| Year | Exports of services—Continued | | Income receipts on U.S. assets abroad | | | | Imports of goods, services, and income | |
|---|---|---|---|---|---|---|---|---|
| | Other private services | U.S. government miscellaneous services | Total | Direct investment receipts | Other private receipts | U.S. government receipts | Total | Goods, adjusted, excluding military |
| 1990 | 40 341 | 668 | 163 324 | 58 740 | 94 072 | 10 512 | -757 507 | -498 337 |
| 1991 | 47 821 | 690 | 141 408 | 52 198 | 81 186 | 8 023 | -732 068 | -490 981 |
| 1992 | 50 022 | 841 | 125 003 | 51 912 | 65 977 | 7 114 | -758 481 | -536 458 |
| 1993 | 53 975 | 883 | 126 702 | 61 241 | 60 353 | 5 108 | -817 910 | -589 441 |
| 1994 | 61 880 | 887 | 157 742 | 72 391 | 81 230 | 4 121 | -946 008 | -668 590 |
| 1995 | 65 555 | 818 | 203 844 | 93 164 | 105 967 | 4 713 | -1 080 107 | -749 574 |
| 1996 | 73 073 | 893 | 213 196 | 99 802 | 108 733 | 4 661 | -1 158 309 | -803 320 |
| 1997 | 84 465 | 784 | 241 787 | 109 407 | 128 845 | 3 535 | -1 294 904 | -877 279 |
| 1998 (p) | 90 729 | 788 | 242 615 | 100 447 | 138 600 | 3 568 | -1 365 648 | -919 040 |

Table A-4 illustrates how the foreign exchange value of the dollar has risen in the last few years. According to the "Broad" index in the top line, based on January 1997=100, the average value of the dollar against the currencies included in this broad group rose from an index value of 76.3 in 1992 to 104.5 in 1997. Taking the percent change from the first to the second of these numbers, the average value of the dollar rose 37 percent.

### Table A-4. Exchange Rates, 1992–1997

(Annual average, except as noted; units per U.S. dollar.)

| | 1992 | 1993 | 1994 | 1995 | 1996 | 1997 |
|---|---|---|---|---|---|---|
| **Trade-weighted exchange indexes** | | | | | | |
| Broad (January 1997=100) ............................. | 76.29 | 84.45 | 90.42 | 92.52 | 97.43 | 104.47 |
| Major Currency (March 1973=100) ...................... | 85.45 | 87.73 | 86.25 | 81.39 | 85.23 | 91.85 |
| Other Important Trading Partners (January 1997=100) ........ | 52.88 | 66.01 | 80.51 | 92.51 | 98.25 | 104.67 |
| G-10 (March 1973=100) ................................ | 86.64 | 93.17 | 91.32 | 84.25 | 87.34 | 96.38 |

## Part B. U.S. Foreign Trade in Services (pages 23–71)

Part B contains detailed information on U.S. international transactions in services. For services, the terms "exports" and "imports" do not refer to physical shipments of merchandise from or to the United States. Instead, they refer to services provided by U.S. governments, businesses, or individuals to residents of other countries and to similar services provided by foreigners to U.S. residents. (In this context, the term "resident" refers to businesses and other organizations as well as individuals.)

Important types of international service transactions are travel, transportation services, royalties and license fees, educational services, and business and professional services. Table B-1 summarizes U.S. receipts from (exports) and payments for (imports) of services by type of service. Table B-2 shows total trade in services by country or region. Only limited country detail is available for 1986 through 1991; much greater detail exists for 1992 and later years. Tables B-3 through B-12 provide additional detail on the different categories of trade in services.

All of the data in Section B refer to private services transactions. The U.S. government also makes international service transactions, primarily defense related. Totals for these government transactions can be found in Table A-3: U.S. International Transactions, 1960–98.

Table B-1 shows U.S. exports of private services reaching $239,215 million (or $239 billion when rounded) in 1997. Of this total, $73 billion (31 percent) was travel expenditure by foreign visitors to the United States, and $34 billion (14 percent) was royalties and license fees, such as those for use of U.S. patents and copyrights. Over the 12 years shown in the table, U.S. earnings from each of the major service categories have risen, some quite rapidly. Earnings from business, professional, and technical services have more than quadrupled.

### Table B-1. U.S. Private Service Transactions by Type, 1986–1997 —Continued

(Millions of dollars.)

| Type of service | Exports—Continued | | | | | |
|---|---|---|---|---|---|---|
| | 1992 | 1993 | 1994 | 1995 | 1996 | 1997 |
| **TOTAL PRIVATE SERVICES** ............................ | 163 754 | 172 031 | 187 760 | 204 229 | 224 213 | 239 215 |
| **Travel** ................................................ | 54 742 | 57 875 | 58 417 | 63 395 | 69 751 | 73 268 |
| Overseas ........................................... | 40 864 | 45 298 | 47 299 | 54 331 | 59 905 | 63 014 |
| Canada ............................................. | 8 182 | 7 458 | 6 252 | 6 207 | 6 842 | 6 824 |
| Freight ............................................. | 8 441 | | 9 | 11 2 | 11 146 | 11 |
| Port services ...................................... | 13 088 | 13 364 | 14 180 | 14 809 | 14 929 | 15 137 |
| **Royalties and License Fees** ......................... | 20 841 | 21 695 | 26 712 | 30 289 | 32 823 | 33 676 |
| Affiliated .......................................... | 15 658 | 15 688 | 20 275 | 22 859 | 24 710 | 25 515 |
| U.S. parents transactions ...................... | 14 925 | 14 936 | 19 250 | 21 399 | 22 781 | 23 457 |
| U.S. affiliates transactions ................... | 733 | 752 | 1 025 | 1 460 | 1 929 | 2 058 |
| Unaffiliated ....................................... | 5 | 6 007 | | 7 430 | | |
| Industrial | | | | | | |
| Business, professional, and technical services ............ | 11 722 | 12 958 | 15 330 | 16 064 | 19 678 | 21 304 |
| Accounting, auditing, and bookkeeping services ...... | 164 | 164 | 132 | 181 | 253 | 255 |
| Advertising ......................................... | 315 | 338 | 487 | 425 | 551 | 581 |
| Agricultural services ............................... | 54 | | 30 | 30 | 20 | 25 |
| Computer and data processing | | | | | | |

The country purchasing the most services from the United States throughout the years shown in table B-2 was Japan, and, in each year shown, the United States had a large surplus on its services trade with Japan: in 1997, for example, the United States exported $34 billion of services to Japan while purchasing only $14 billion of Japanese services.

### Table B-2.  U.S. Private Services Transactions by Region and Country, 1986–1997 —Continued

(Millions of dollars.)

| Country or region | Exports—Continued | | | | | |
|---|---|---|---|---|---|---|
| | 1992 | 1993 | 1994 | 1995 | 1996 | 1997 |
| ALL COUNTRIES | 163 754 | 172 031 | 187 760 | 204 229 | 224 213 | 239 215 |
| Canada | 17 454 | 17 040 | 17 314 | 18 032 | 19 938 | 20 501 |
| Mexico | 9 534 | 9 400 | 10 062 | 7 392 | 8 138 | 9 334 |
| Europe | 60 630 | 62 595 | 67 988 | 73 637 | 82 348 | 85 986 |
| China | 1 604 | 1 979 | 2 110 | 2 593 | 3 214 | 3 697 |
| Hong Kong | 2 259 | 2 365 | 2 831 | 3 049 | 3 368 | 3 689 |
| India | 1 105 | 1 152 | 1 240 | 1 335 | 1 528 | 1 649 |
| Indonesia | 788 | 907 | 888 | 1 175 | 1 430 | 1 787 |
| Japan | 25 635 | 26 878 | 29 056 | 33 346 | 33 657 | 34 002 |
| Malaysia | 611 | 690 | 905 | 1 047 | 1 295 | 1 215 |
| New Zealand | 768 | 800 | 840 | 998 | 1 174 | 1 262 |
| Philippines | 983 | 1 263 | 1 204 | 1 078 | 1 250 | 1 551 |
| Singapore | 2 157 | 2 416 | 2 657 | 3 159 | 3 906 | 4 008 |
| South Korea | 3 401 | 3 668 | 4 634 | 5 727 | 7 374 | 6 885 |
| Taiwan | 3 173 | 3 466 | 4 176 | 4 440 | 4 053 | 4 625 |
| Thailand | 764 | 1 030 | 1 034 | 1 202 | 1 236 | 1 259 |
| Other | 2 239 | 2 256 | 2 361 | 2 845 | 2 724 | 2 996 |

### Table B-2.  U.S. Private Services Transactions by Region and Country, 1986–1997 —Continued

(Millions of dollars.)

| Country or region | Imports—Continued | | | | | |
|---|---|---|---|---|---|---|
| | 1992 | 1993 | 1994 | 1995 | 1996 | 1997 |
| ALL COUNTRIES | 103 464 | 111 259 | 123 303 | 133 355 | 142 261 | 156 236 |
| Canada | 8 883 | 9 423 | 10 424 | 11 467 | 12 794 | 14 063 |
| Mexico | 9 501 | 9 781 | 10 576 | 10 780 | 11 769 | 13 120 |
| Europe | 39 946 | 44 676 | 49 464 | 53 247 | 54 280 | 61 847 |
| Asia and Pacific | 25 911 | | 31 726 | 34 | 36 634 | |
| Australia | 2 232 | 2 183 | 1 945 | 2 161 | 2 605 | 2 635 |
| China | 1 126 | 1 396 | 1 555 | 1 794 | 2 065 | 2 327 |
| Hong Kong | 1 429 | 1 346 | 1 917 | 1 933 | 2 957 | 3 038 |
| India | 662 | 719 | 792 | 884 | 1 138 | 1 249 |
| Indonesia | 449 | 437 | 446 | 452 | 575 | 564 |
| Japan | 10 653 | 11 840 | 12 708 | 13 599 | 13 009 | 14 253 |
| Malaysia | 273 | 308 | 368 | 462 | 467 | 535 |
| New Zealand | 527 | 540 | 568 | 602 | 671 | 682 |
| Philippines | 788 | 854 | 1 041 | 1 126 | 1 366 | 1 434 |
| Singapore | 687 | 942 | 1 196 | 1 265 | 1 850 | 2 062 |
| South Korea | 2 062 | 2 369 | | 3 618 | | |
| Taiwan | | 2 408 | | | | |
| Thailand | | | | | | |

As shown in B-11, the United States earned $4.1 billion in 1997 by supplying construction, engineering, architectural, and mining services to other countries. Of this $4.1 billion, $1.2 billion (almost 30 percent) came from the Middle East. Under Middle East, the "(D)" shown for Saudi Arabia and for "Other" indicates that, because some services were supplied by only a few large firms, the Bureau of Economic Analysis, the source agency for these data, has suppressed this information so that the data pertaining to an individual firm cannot be separately identified. Two data cells must be suppressed here so that the value for a suppressed cell cannot be obtained by subtracting the remaining numbers from the total.

### Table B-11.  U.S. Business, Professional, and Technical Service Receipts, 1994–1997 —Continued

(Unaffiliated transactions; millions of dollars.)

| Country or region | Legal services | | | | Construction, engineering, architectural, and mining services | | | | Industrial engineering | | | |
|---|---|---|---|---|---|---|---|---|---|---|---|---|
| | 1994 | 1995 | 1996 | 1997 | 1994 | 1995 | 1996 | 1997 | 1994 | 1995 | 1996 | 1997 |
| ALL COUNTRIES | 1 617 | 1 667 | 1 973 | 2 085 | 2 474 | 2 550 | 3 560 | 4 084 | 575 | 726 | 915 | 1 098 |
| Canada | 116 | 107 | 119 | 160 | 44 | 38 | 98 | 282 | 71 | 75 | (D) | 104 |
| Mexico | 29 | 26 | 32 | 28 | 72 | 43 | 86 | 139 | 26 | 24 | 18 | 23 |
| Middle East | 52 | 39 | 49 | 66 | 237 | 255 | 1 028 | 1 237 | (D) | 57 | 47 | 58 |
| Israel | 13 | 12 | 14 | 20 | 6 | 23 | 26 | 18 | 1 | (D) | 5 | 6 |
| Saudi Arabia | 17 | 12 | 11 | 14 | 119 | 122 | (D) | (D) | (D) | (D) | 39 | 51 |
| Other | 21 | 15 | 24 | 31 | 112 | 110 | (D) | (D) | (*) | (*) | 3 | 2 |
| Asia and Pacific | 442 | 480 | 618 | 634 | 977 | 1 156 | 1 166 | 1 244 | 143 | 346 | 384 | 507 |
| Australia | 22 | 26 | 33 | | 11 | 12 | | 15 | | | | |
| China | | 11 | | | | | | | | | | |

## Part C. U.S. Foreign Trade in Goods (pages 73–112)

Part C contains U.S. national totals for exports and imports of goods. The first three tables show three different ways of looking at the types of goods traded. The remaining two tables show total exports and imports by region and country. Table C-4 provides a one-page summary of trade by major geographic region. Table C-5 provides information by country as well as region. Almost 200 countries or country groups are included. The countries are arranged by geographic region, beginning with the Western Hemisphere and continuing through Europe, Asia, Australia and Oceania, and Africa. Within regions, the countries are arranged alphabetically. Some special regional groupings are found at the end of this table. Lists of the countries in each group are found in the "Notes" section in the back of the book.

In table C-1 total exports and imports of goods are divided into manufactured goods, agricultural products, mineral fuels, and other goods. In 1998, the United States exported $595.2 billion of manufactured goods, or 87 percent of total goods exports; manufactured goods also made up 87 percent of total goods imports. Imports of manufactured goods exceeded exports by $197.2 billion. In agricultural trade, however, the United States maintains a substantial surplus, about $16 billion in 1998. For mineral fuels (which includes crude oil), imports are far larger than exports. The dollar value of mineral fuel imports fell more than 25 percent from 1997 to 1998. This does not mean that fewer barrels of oil were imported; in fact, more barrels of oil were imported in 1998, but at a substantially lower price.

### Table C-1.  U.S. Foreign Trade in Goods, 1970–1998

(Census basis, billions of dollars.)

| Year | Exports | | | | | Imports | | | | |
|---|---|---|---|---|---|---|---|---|---|---|
| | Total goods | Manufactured goods | Agricultural products | Mineral fuels | Other goods | Total goods | Manufactured goods | Agricultural products | Mineral fuels | Other goods |
| 1970 | 43.8 | 31.7 | 7.3 | 1.6 | 3.1 | 40.4 | 27.3 | 5.8 | 3.1 | 4.2 |
| 1993 | 465.1 | 388.7 | 42.8 | 9.9 | 23.7 | 580.7 | 479.9 | 23.6 | 53.9 | 21.2 |
| 1994 | 512.6 | 431.1 | 45.9 | 9.0 | 26.7 | 663.3 | 557.3 | 26.0 | 56.4 | 23.6 |
| 1995 | 584.7 | 486.7 | 56.0 | 10.5 | 31.6 | 743.4 | 629.7 | 29.3 | 59.1 | 25.4 |
| 1996 | 625.1 | 524.7 | 60.6 | 12.4 | 27.4 | 795.3 | 658.8 | 32.6 | 78.1 | 25.8 |
| 1997 | 689.2 | 592.5 | 57.1 | 13.0 | 26.7 | 870.7 | 728.9 | 35.2 | 78.3 | 28.3 |
| 1998 (p) | 683.0 | 595.2 | 52.0 | 10.1 | 25.7 | 913.8 | 792.4 | 35.7 | 57.6 | 28.0 |

Table C-2 shows exports and imports by the type of use for which they are intended. Six major categories are shown, and a trade balance is given for each category. The United States maintains a large surplus on trade in capital goods, except automotive ($29.1 billion in 1998), while the largest deficit ($136 billion in 1998) is on consumer goods.

## Table C-2.  U.S. Foreign Trade in Goods by End-Use Category, 1978–1998

(Census basis, billions of dollars.)

| Year | Foods, feed, and beverages | | | Industrial supplies and materials | | | Capital goods, except automotive | | |
|---|---|---|---|---|---|---|---|---|---|
| | Exports | Imports | Balance | Exports | Imports | Balance | Exports | Imports | Balance |
| 1978 | 25.6 | 15.8 | 9.7 | 39.0 | 79.2 | -40.1 | 46.9 | 19.7 | 27.2 |
| 1979 | 30.3 | 18.0 | 12.3 | 57.3 | 102.6 | -45.3 | 58.8 | 24.9 | 33.9 |
| 1980 | 36.0 | 18.5 | 17.5 | 70.6 | 124.7 | -54.1 | 74.8 | 31.1 | 43.7 |
| 1981 | 38.6 | 18.5 | 20.1 | 67.7 | 130.7 | -63.0 | 82.5 | 37.0 | 45.5 |
| 1982 | 32.0 | 17.5 | 14.5 | 62.1 | 107.7 | -45.6 | 75.1 | 38.4 | 36.7 |
| 1983 | 30.7 | 18.5 | 12.2 | 57.4 | 105.3 | -47.8 | 70.6 | 39.4 | 31.2 |
| 1984 | 31.3 | 21.5 | 9.8 | 62.6 | 121.6 | -59.1 | 76.4 | 58.0 | 18.5 |
| 1985 | 24.1 | 22.3 | 1.8 | 59.2 | 114.1 | -54.9 | 78.9 | 62.4 | 16.4 |
| 1986 | 22.5 | 24.5 | -2.0 | 62.0 | 102.9 | -40.9 | 81.8 | 72.6 | 9.2 |
| 1987 | 24.3 | 26.8 | -2.6 | 66.7 | 117.3 | -50.6 | 86.2 | 87.0 | -0.8 |
| 1988 | 32.3 | 24.8 | 7.5 | 85.1 | 118.3 | -33.2 | 109.2 | 101.4 | 7.8 |
| 1989 | 37.2 | 25.1 | 12.1 | 99.3 | 132.3 | -33.0 | 138.8 | 113.3 | 25.5 |
| 1990 | 35.1 | 26.6 | 8.4 | 104.4 | 143.2 | -38.8 | 152.7 | 116.4 | 36.3 |
| 1991 | 35.7 | 26.5 | 9.2 | 109.7 | 131.6 | -21.9 | 166.7 | 120.7 | 45.9 |
| 1992 | 40.3 | 27.6 | 12.7 | 109.1 | 138.6 | -29.5 | 175.9 | 134.3 | 41.7 |
| 1993 | 40.6 | 27.9 | 12.8 | 111.8 | 145.6 | -33.8 | 181.7 | 152.4 | 29.3 |
| 1994 | 42.0 | 31.0 | 11.0 | 121.4 | 162.1 | -40.7 | 205.0 | 184.4 | 20.7 |
| 1995 | 50.5 | 33.2 | 17.3 | 146.2 | 181.8 | -35.6 | 233.0 | 221.4 | 11.6 |
| 1996 | 55.5 | 35.7 | 19.8 | 147.7 | 204.5 | -56.8 | 252.9 | 229.1 | 23.8 |
| 1997 | 51.5 | 39.7 | 11.8 | 158.2 | 213.8 | -55.5 | 294.5 | 254.2 | 40.3 |
| 1998 (p) | 46.4 | 41.2 | 5.1 | 147.9 | 200.4 | -52.5 | 299.5 | 270.4 | 29.1 |

| Year | Automotive vehicles, engines, and parts | | | Consumer goods, except automotive | | | Other goods | | |
|---|---|---|---|---|---|---|---|---|---|
| | Exports | Imports | Balance | Exports | Imports | Balance | Exports | Imports | Balance |
| 1978 | 14.6 | 25.9 | -11.3 | 11.1 | 29.6 | -18.5 | 8.6 | 3.1 | 5.5 |
| 1979 | 16.6 | 26.9 | -10.3 | 13.4 | 31.3 | -17.9 | 9.9 | 3.4 | 6.5 |
| 1980 | 16.0 | 28.2 | -12.1 | 17.2 | 34.3 | -17.2 | 11.1 | 4.6 | 6.5 |
| 19?? | 18.? | 30.? | 12.5 | 17.1 | 38.4 | -21.2 | 14.4 | 5.? | 8.8 |
| 1986 | 19.9 | 78.5 | -58.6 | 17.8 | 80.3 | -62.5 | 23.6 | 11.2 | 12.3 |
| 1987 | 24.6 | 87.5 | -62.8 | 17.7 | 93.6 | -76.0 | 34.6 | 12.2 | 22.4 |
| 1988 | 29.3 | 87.7 | -58.4 | 23.1 | 95.9 | -72.8 | 43.4 | 12.8 | 30.6 |
| 1989 | 34.8 | 86.1 | -51.3 | 36.4 | 102.9 | -66.4 | 17.2 | 13.6 | 3.6 |
| 1990 | 37.4 | 87.3 | -49.9 | 43.3 | 105.7 | -62.4 | 20.7 | 16.1 | 4.6 |
| 1991 | 40.0 | 85.7 | -45.6 | 45.9 | 108.0 | -62.1 | 23.7 | 15.9 | 7.7 |
| 1992 | 47.0 | 91.8 | -44.8 | 51.4 | 122.7 | -71.2 | 24.4 | 17.7 | 6.7 |
| 1993 | 52.4 | 102.4 | -50.0 | 54.7 | 134.0 | -79.4 | 23.9 | 18.4 | 5.5 |
| 1994 | 57.8 | 118.3 | -60.5 | 60.0 | 146.3 | -86.3 | 26.5 | 21.3 | 5.2 |
| 1995 | 61.8 | 123.8 | -62.0 | 64.4 | 159.9 | -95.5 | 28.7 | 23.4 | 5.3 |
| 1996 | 65.0 | 128.9 | -63.9 | 70.1 | 171.0 | -100.9 | 33.8 | 26.1 | 7.7 |
| 1997 | 74.0 | 140.8 | -66.8 | 77.4 | 192.9 | -115.5 | 33.5 | 29.3 | 4.2 |
| 1998 (p) | 72.7 | 150.7 | -78.0 | 79.5 | 215.5 | -136.0 | 37.0 | 35.6 | 1.4 |

The rows of table C-3 show U.S. goods trade by industrial category. Computers and office equipment, for example, accounted for $50 billion of exports in 1997 and $71 billion of imports. In this category, therefore, the United States had a large trade deficit ($21 billion). In the aircraft and parts classification, exports were $49 billion and imports $17 billion, for a surplus of $32 billion.

## Table C-3.  U.S. Foreign Trade in Goods by Industry, 1991–1997 —Continued

(Trade by Standard Industrial Classification [SIC] product codes; census basis; millions of dollars.)

| SIC description | SIC code | Exports | | | | | | |
|---|---|---|---|---|---|---|---|---|
| | | 1991 | 1992 | 1993 | 1994 | 1995 | 1996 | 1997 |
| Special industry machinery, except metalworking machinery | 355 | 5 220 | | 9 664 | 9 901 | | 10 195 | |
| General industrial machinery and equipment | 356 | 8 591 | 8 795 | 9 241 | 10 543 | 11 662 | 12 550 | 14 597 |
| Computers and office equipment | 357 | 28 298 | 29 858 | 30 297 | 34 363 | 40 711 | 44 766 | 50 475 |
| Refrigeration and service industry machinery | 358 | 3 427 | 3 900 | 4 214 | 4 513 | 5 180 | 5 581 | 6 194 |
| Miscellaneous industrial and commercial machinery and equipment | 359 | 2 205 | 2 321 | 2 700 | 2 965 | 3 772 | 3 861 | 4 762 |
| **Electronic and other electrical equipment except computers, total** | 36 | 47 802 | 52 938 | 60 831 | 73 949 | 90 377 | 94 880 | 108 276 |
| Electric transmission and distribution equipment | 361 | 670 | 747 | 798 | 855 | 996 | 1 139 | 1 378 |
| Electrical industrial apparatus | 362 | 3 393 | 3 840 | 4 065 | 4 421 | 5 169 | 5 323 | 6 105 |
| Household appliances | | | 2 603 | | | | | |
| Electronic components and accessories | 367 | 21 006 | 22 510 | 26 364 | 34 357 | 43 514 | 47 976 | 54 289 |
| Miscellaneous electrical machinery, equipment, and supplies | 369 | 6 521 | 7 026 | 7 771 | 8 687 | 9 495 | 10 497 | 11 343 |
| **Transportation equipment, total** | 37 | 77 765 | 84 652 | 82 492 | 88 159 | 85 752 | 96 568 | 112 259 |
| Motor vehicles and motor vehicle equipment | 371 | 32 410 | 37 473 | 41 286 | 47 128 | 49 524 | 52 138 | 58 342 |
| Aircraft and parts | 372 | 41 842 | 42 891 | 37 623 | 36 331 | 31 134 | 38 797 | 48 635 |
| Ship and boat building and repairing | 373 | 1 113 | 1 407 | 929 | 1 173 | 1 196 | 1 015 | 1 319 |
| Railroad equipment | 374 | 468 | 494 | 462 | 605 | 766 | 732 | 1 097 |
| Motorcycles, bicycles, and parts | 375 | 709 | 749 | 783 | 762 | 905 | 955 | 1 012 |
| Guided missiles, space vehicles, and parts | 376 | 27 | 36 | | 26 | 56 | | 16 |
| Miscellaneous transportation equipment | | | | | | | | |

## Table C-3.  U.S. Foreign Trade in Goods by Industry, 1991–1997 —Continued

(Trade by Standard Industrial Classification [SIC] product codes; census basis; millions of dollars.)

| SIC description | SIC code | Imports | | | | | | |
|---|---|---|---|---|---|---|---|---|
| | | 1991 | 1992 | 1993 | 1994 | 1995 | 1996 | 1997 |
| **Stone, clay, glass and concrete products, total** | 32 | 5 549 | 5 935 | 6 454 | 7 620 | 8 553 | 9 132 | 10 220 |
| Flat glass | 321 | 283 | 278 | 342 | 416 | 399 | 463 | 495 |
| Special industry machinery, except metalworking machinery | 355 | 5 326 | 6 716 | 6 513 | 7 585 | 90 | 8 717 | |
| General industrial machinery and equipment | 356 | 6 728 | 7 305 | 7 925 | 9 766 | 11 243 | 12 144 | 12 375 |
| Computers and office equipment | 357 | 26 962 | 32 759 | 39 232 | 47 612 | 57 916 | 62 934 | 71 325 |
| Refrigeration and service industry machinery | 358 | 1 776 | 1 917 | 2 042 | 2 446 | 2 677 | 2 954 | 2 893 |
| Miscellaneous industrial and commercial machinery and equipment | 359 | 1 453 | 1 517 | 1 700 | 1 990 | 2 498 | 2 469 | 2 670 |
| **Electronic and other electrical equipment except computers, total** | 36 | 61 992 | 69 917 | 79 161 | 96 678 | 116 198 | 115 277 | 122 571 |
| Electric transmission and distribution equipment | 361 | 695 | 807 | 936 | 990 | 1 231 | 1 276 | 1 493 |
| Electrical industrial apparatus | 362 | 3 316 | 3 777 | 4 334 | 5 367 | 6 145 | 6 476 | 7 268 |
| Household appliances | | | 4 292 | | | | | |
| Electronic components and accessories | 367 | 21 886 | 914 | 29 520 | 37 926 | 20 | 51 057 | |
| Miscellaneous electrical machinery, equipment, and supplies | 369 | 6 552 | 7 492 | 8 435 | 10 090 | 10 753 | 11 342 | 12 349 |
| **Transportation equipment, total** | 37 | 88 205 | 92 990 | 101 072 | 115 377 | 120 877 | 127 707 | 140 615 |
| Motor vehicles and motor vehicle equipment | 371 | 73 419 | 77 407 | 85 990 | 99 784 | 105 519 | 109 846 | 118 597 |
| Aircraft and parts | 372 | 12 422 | 12 930 | 11 532 | 11 728 | 10 958 | 13 138 | 17 256 |
| Ship and boat building and repairing | 373 | 212 | 270 | 920 | 750 | 765 | 974 | 824 |
| Railroad equipment | 374 | 532 | 595 | 587 | 969 | 1 088 | 1 128 | 1 158 |
| Motorcycles, bicycles, and parts | 375 | 1 370 | 1 574 | 1 759 | 1 801 | 2 179 | 2 046 | 2 117 |
| Guided missiles, space vehicles, and parts | 376 | 1 | 0 | 0 | 0 | 1 | 134 | 179 |
| Miscellaneous transportation equipment | | | 212 | | | | | |

Of the $689 billion total shown in table C-4 for goods exports in 1997, $223 billion (32 percent) went to North America, that is, to Canada and Mexico; almost as much, $214 billion, went to Asian destinations. The pattern is not the same in all years. From 1991 to 1993 and again in 1995 and 1996, Asia rather than North America was the most important destination region.

### Table C-4.  U.S. Foreign Trade in Goods, Summary by Regions, 1991–1997

(Millions of dollars.)

| Region | 1991 | 1992 | 1993 | 1994 | 1995 | 1996 | 1997 |
|---|---|---|---|---|---|---|---|
| **All destinations** | | | | | | | |
| Exports: All goods | 421 730 | 448 164 | 465 091 | 512 627 | 584 742 | 625 075 | 689 182 |
| Agriculture | 39 468 | 43 134 | 42 949 | 46 300 | 56 364 | 60 562 | 57 092 |
| **North America** | | | | | | | |
| Exports: All goods | 118 427 | 131 186 | 142 025 | 165 283 | 173 518 | 191 002 | 223 155 |
| Agriculture | 8 076 | 9 167 | 9 387 | 10 673 | 9 935 | 12 230 | 12 667 |
| Manufactures | 104 300 | 114 972 | 125 941 | 147 280 | 153 951 | 168 730 | 198 708 |
| **Asia** | | | | | | | |
| Exports: All goods | 130 629 | 138 262 | 146 726 | 160 995 | 197 402 | 207 328 | 213 547 |
| Agriculture | 16 104 | 17 393 | 17 576 | 20 121 | 27 360 | 27 641 | 24 694 |
| Manufactures | 98 462 | 104 949 | 113 551 | 125 095 | 151 612 | 162 859 | 174 465 |

## Part D. State Exports of Goods (pages 113–340) and
## Part E. Metropolitan Area Exports of Goods (pages 341–414)

Parts D and E are similar in their organization. The first table in each section provides totals by year for exports of goods from each state (Table D-1) or from each of more than 250 metropolitan areas (Table E-1). Subsequent tables provide detail by destination or by industry. Table D-3, the longest and most detailed in the book, shows the exports of each state by industrial classification and by destination. Ten individual country destinations are shown; these are the ten countries to which the United States as a whole sends the most exports. Several regional groupings also are shown. Table E-2, Metropolitan Area Exports of Goods by Industry, 1993–97, provides industry detail for the 43 large metropolitan areas for which such information is available.

Data by state or metropolitan area can be provided only for exports of goods. Neither exports of services nor imports of either goods or services can be systematically assigned to any particular geographic area within the United States.

The assignment of goods exports to a state or metropolitan area is based on the location of the exporter of record. Such assignment may or may not reflect the location where the goods were produced. And, even if the final products were produced in the state to which they were assigned, these products may use parts manufactured elsewhere. An airplane assembled in Washington State, for example, is likely to contain parts produced in other states or even in other countries. Thus, while the data in sections D and E provide a good general indication of the role of exports in a local economy, they should be interpreted as only rough approximations.

In 1998, total U.S. exports of goods shown in table D-1 dipped following several years of strong growth. The pattern varied by state, however. Exports from California were down almost 5 percent, reflecting weak Asian markets and falling world prices for computers and other electronic goods. In contrast, exports from Washington State were up almost 20 percent, reflecting, in part, strong world demand for aircraft.

### Table D-1.  State Exports of Goods, 1987 and 1991–1998

(Billions of dollars.)

| State | 1987 | 1991 | 1992 | 1993 | 1994 | 1995 | 1996 | 1997 | 1998 |
|---|---|---|---|---|---|---|---|---|---|
| **All States** | 244.4 | 420.0 | 447.5 | 464.9 | 512.4 | 583.0 | 622.8 | 687.6 | 683.0 |
| Arkansas | 0.4 | 0.8 | 1.1 | 1.1 | 1.5 | 1.8 | 2.0 | 2.2 | 1.9 |
| California | 32.9 | 59.0 | 66.7 | 68.1 | 78.2 | 92.0 | 98.6 | 103.8 | 98.8 |
| Virginia | 3.1 | 8.8 | 8.5 | 8.1 | 9.9 | 10.4 | 10.9 | 11.5 | 11.5 |
| Washington | 10.3 | 27.3 | 28.7 | 27.4 | 25.1 | 22.0 | 25.5 | 31.7 | 38.0 |
| West Virginia | 0.7 | 0.9 | 0.9 | 0.8 | 0.9 | 1.1 | 1.2 | 1.2 | 1.2 |

The pie chart preceding each state's data in table D-3 shows how the state's goods exports are divided into manufactures, agricultural and livestock products, and other commodities. For Alabama, like most states, manufactures make up the bulk of goods exports (93 percent in this case). The right-hand bar chart shows total exports of manufactures and the five top manufacturing industry groups. In Alabama's case electric and electronic equipment accounts for $1.1 billion of the total of $4.2 billion of manufactured exports. Industrial machinery and computers account for another $0.6 billion.

## ALABAMA: Exports of Goods, 1997

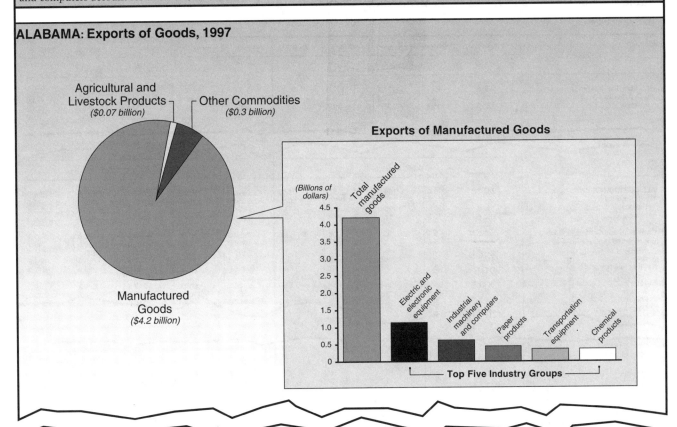

## Table D-3. State Exports of Goods by Destination and Industry, 1993–1997

### ALABAMA (Millions of dollars.)

| Industry | 1993 | 1994 | 1995 | 1996 | 1997 | 1993 | 1994 | 1995 | 1996 | 1997 |
|---|---|---|---|---|---|---|---|---|---|---|
| | All destinations | | | | | Canada | | | | |
| **ALL GOODS** | 2 504.3 | 3 115.4 | 3 587.1 | 3 702.4 | 4 537.2 | 621.7 | 789.0 | 988.5 | 1 177.4 | 1 251.1 |
| **Manufactured goods** | 2 173.1 | 2 796.6 | 3 167.0 | 3 359.9 | 4 207.7 | 591.4 | 745.6 | 939.9 | 1 118.6 | 1 199.4 |
| Food products | 33.5 | 32.4 | 49.6 | 40.9 | 52.1 | 27.7 | 26.6 | 41.3 | 31.0 | 37.8 |
| Tobacco products | 1.1 | 1.1 | 0.7 | 2.4 | 1.5 | ..... | ..... | ..... | ..... | ..... |
| Textile mill products | 49.4 | 66.0 | 83.9 | 86.0 | 122.4 | 23.8 | 35.9 | 34.6 | 25.1 | 32.2 |
| Apparel | 72.7 | 79.4 | 94.8 | 129.6 | 168.4 | 12.4 | 11.3 | 12.9 | 13.5 | 18.1 |
| Lumber and wood products | 126.3 | 129.9 | 143.1 | 140.2 | 143.6 | 5.0 | 6.9 | 5.4 | 7.3 | 20.9 |
| Furniture and fixtures | 28.0 | 32.2 | 25.6 | 21.9 | 27.5 | 19.7 | 22.0 | 21.0 | 15.3 | 20.5 |
| Paper products | 264.8 | 333.0 | 500.5 | 440.1 | 442.6 | 27.6 | 35.1 | 56.6 | 81.5 | 89.6 |
| Printing and publishing | 3.6 | 4.9 | 4.3 | 3.2 | 5.6 | 2.2 | 2.8 | 2.7 | 0.9 | 0.8 |
| Chemical products | 194.2 | 219.6 | 292.7 | 335.2 | 356.8 | 47.6 | 51.6 | 57.0 | 56.4 | 69.8 |
| Refined petroleum products | 0.2 | 0.8 | 1.5 | 9.4 | 3.1 | ..... | 0.2 | 0.2 | 8.1 | 1.4 |
| Rubber and plastic products | 56.4 | 61.3 | 56.6 | 64.8 | 82.5 | 31.2 | 31.4 | 24.1 | 24.3 | 42.5 |
| Leather products | 1.0 | 0.5 | 0.7 | 1.7 | 1.3 | 0.3 | 0.1 | 0.4 | 0.4 | 0.1 |
| Stone, clay and glass products | 39.9 | 42.3 | 49.5 | 46.2 | 47.8 | 8.7 | 9.6 | 10.2 | 12.1 | 13.4 |
| Primary metals | 114.7 | 140.5 | 187.9 | 146.5 | 199.0 | 32.8 | 40.0 | 50.0 | 48.0 | 82.8 |
| Fabricated metal products | 114.8 | 79.9 | 90.7 | 110.0 | 165.0 | 46.7 | 26.6 | 31.3 | 33.6 | 28.7 |
| Industrial machinery and computers | 358.6 | 393.9 | 457.6 | 457.0 | 625.6 | 79.8 | 92.6 | 106.6 | 109.0 | 111.6 |
| Electric and electronic equipment | 407.0 | 487.9 | 610.0 | 819.6 | 1 140.0 | 170.0 | 211.7 | 239.9 | 358.2 | 210.5 |
| Transportation equipment | 214.4 | 591.6 | 418.8 | 400.5 | 357.8 | 30.7 | 101.7 | 207.1 | 250.2 | 232.6 |
| Scientific and measuring instruments | 59.5 | 62.1 | 64.0 | 63.8 | 220.0 | 13.0 | 24.1 | 26.3 | 28.1 | 172.5 |
| Miscellaneous manufactures | 23.3 | 27.0 | 24.1 | 31.1 | 32.8 | 10.9 | 14.0 | 10.2 | 13.7 | 10.1 |
| Unidentified manufactures | 9.7 | 10.2 | 10.2 | 9.6 | 12.1 | 1.2 | 1.6 | 2.0 | 1.9 | 3.4 |
| **Agricultural and livestock products** | 36.6 | 69.2 | 125.4 | 64.7 | 69.5 | 16.4 | 21.3 | 25.8 | 30.7 | 22.3 |
| Agricultural products | 32.7 | 65.5 | 121.3 | 58.3 | 62.4 | 15.1 | 19.2 | 24.1 | 27.3 | 17.9 |
| Livestock and livestock products | 3.9 | 3.8 | 4.1 | 6.5 | 7.1 | 1.3 | 2.1 | 1.6 | 3.5 | 4.3 |

Table E-3 shows that exports from the Atlanta, Georgia metro area are distributed fairly evenly across regions: in 1997, 29 percent went to Europe, 24 percent to Asia, another 24 percent to North America, and the remainder to the other world regions. In contrast, Brownsville-Harlingen-San Benito, Texas, located on the Mexican border, sent 80 percent of its exports to Mexico. The metropolitan areas in this table are arranged in alphabetical order and the export destinations are listed alphabetically within major world region.

## Table E-3.  Metropolitan Area Exports of Goods by Destination, 1993–1997—Continued

(Millions of dollars.)

| Destination | 1993 | 1994 | 1995 | 1996 | 1997 | 1993 | 1994 | 1995 | 1996 | 1997 |
|---|---|---|---|---|---|---|---|---|---|---|
| | Anchorage, AK | | | | | Appleton - Oshkosh - Neenah, WI | | | | |
| ALL DESTINATIONS | 128.8 | 198.2 | 150.4 | 109.0 | 213.1 | 529.5 | 507.7 | 593.7 | 608.5 | 647.9 |
| North America | 23.1 | 15.9 | 32.4 | 19.8 | 141.1 | 330.6 | 357.7 | 402.8 | 363.1 | 374.8 |
| Canada | 23.0 | 15.8 | 32.4 | 19.7 | 141.1 | 278.7 | 320.2 | 367.5 | 339.9 | 343.0 |
| Mexico | 0.1 | 0.1 | 0.1 | 0.1 | ..... | 51.9 | 37.5 | 35.3 | 23.2 | 31.8 |
| | Asheville, NC | | | | | Atlanta, GA | | | | |
| ALL DESTINATIONS | 232.3 | 228.6 | 185.2 | 236.7 | 294.2 | 3 870.6 | 4 739.1 | 5 811.4 | 5 891.5 | 6 604.6 |
| North America | 157.8 | 171.8 | 130.7 | 168.2 | 202.2 | 960.7 | 1 260.3 | 1 300.5 | 1 373.6 | 1 578.5 |
| Canada | 150.0 | 160.5 | 116.5 | 152.3 | 177.2 | 755.9 | 903.3 | 1 004.5 | 1 010.2 | 1 024.2 |
| Mexico | 7.8 | 11.3 | 14.2 | 15.9 | 25.0 | 204.7 | 357.0 | 296.0 | 363.4 | 554.3 |
| Caribbean and Central America | 1.5 | 0.8 | 0.9 | 0.6 | 2.6 | 269.2 | 325.0 | 399.5 | 380.6 | 431.4 |
| South America | 4.1 | 5.7 | 7.8 | 5.2 | 7.6 | 336.5 | 534.1 | 708.5 | 650.0 | 748.0 |
| Argentina | 0.3 | 0.5 | 0.1 | 0.2 | 1.0 | 101.1 | 182.3 | 134.7 | 105.1 | 126.2 |
| Brazil | 2.2 | 3.1 | 4.8 | 2.3 | 4.1 | 48.8 | 113.3 | 287.3 | 248.8 | 304.8 |
| Other South America | 1.6 | 2.1 | 2.9 | 2.7 | 2.4 | 186.5 | 238.5 | 286.5 | 296.0 | 317.0 |
| Europe | 45.0 | 28.9 | 28.3 | 41.7 | 51.5 | 1 122.2 | 1 346.0 | 1 549.9 | 1 678.2 | 1 914.3 |
| Belgium | 0.5 | 0.7 | 1.4 | 2.6 | 2.8 | 89.1 | 100.1 | 83.7 | 78.9 | 202.0 |
| France | 1.5 | 1.0 | 2.8 | 1.9 | 2.5 | 118.0 | 8.4 | 116.6 | | |
| Germany | 27.8 | 6.6 | 3.7 | | | 213.7 | | | | |
| Netherlands | | | 5.5 | | | | | | | |
| Other Eastern Europe | 0.3 | ..... | 0.3 | 1.9 | 0.5 | 15.6 | 19.7 | 20.5 | 19.7 | 21.7 |
| Other Europe | 3.4 | 6.4 | 4.7 | 5.8 | 12.7 | 287.4 | 319.7 | 399.7 | 372.0 | 481.8 |
| Asia | 20.0 | 18.8 | 15.9 | 17.6 | 23.8 | 850.7 | 993.4 | 1 546.1 | 1 467.7 | 1 553.5 |
| Japan | 2.1 | 2.1 | 2.7 | 4.3 | 5.8 | 276.5 | 278.8 | 394.7 | 419.8 | 420.0 |
| China | 2.2 | 6.7 | 0.2 | 0.7 | 5.0 | 97.2 | 49.3 | 88.5 | 117.4 | 106.5 |
| Hong Kong | 0.3 | 2.1 | 2.9 | 1.1 | 1.6 | 94.0 | 137.0 | 200.5 | 220.3 | 242.1 |
| Taiwan | 0.7 | 0.7 | 0.9 | 0.8 | 1.4 | 110.5 | 114.8 | 119.6 | 99.2 | 109.9 |
| Singapore | 0.1 | 0.5 | 1.0 | 0.7 | 0.7 | 58.7 | 63.6 | 81.4 | | 170.0 |
| South Korea | | | 4.8 | | | | | | | |

## Table E-3.  Metropolitan Area Exports of Goods by Destination, 1993–1997—Continued

(Millions of dollars.)

| Destination | 1993 | 1994 | 1995 | 1996 | 1997 | 1993 | 1994 | 1995 | 1996 | 1997 |
|---|---|---|---|---|---|---|---|---|---|---|
| | Bloomington, IN | | | | | Boston, MA - NH | | | | |
| ALL DESTINATIONS | 113.6 | 115.7 | 127.6 | 198.8 | 166.8 | 6 472.5 | 7 095.3 | 7 902.7 | 8 715.8 | 9 570.6 |
| North America | 56.7 | 45.9 | 30.9 | 36.9 | 34.3 | 1 320.3 | 1 523.5 | 1 488.8 | 1 640.5 | 1 605.9 |
| Canada | 53.3 | 43.3 | 29.4 | 34.8 | 32.8 | 1 084.9 | 1 189.5 | 1 355.7 | 1 465.4 | 1 408.3 |
| Mexico | 3.4 | 2.6 | 1.5 | 2.1 | 1.5 | 235.4 | 334.1 | 133.1 | 175.1 | 197.6 |
| Middle East | 2.3 | 3.8 | 5.3 | 0.9 | 2.6 | 130.1 | 121.6 | 143.1 | 187.0 | 215.0 |
| Australia | 3.6 | 4.1 | 3.6 | 2.4 | 5.2 | 200.5 | 189.6 | 207.6 | 223.1 | 188.5 |
| Rest of World | ..... | ..... | ..... | ..... | ..... | 0.1 | 0.1 | | | ..... |
| | Bridgeport, CT | | | | | Brownsville - Harlingen - San Benito, TX | | | | |
| ALL DESTINATIONS | 1 125.9 | 918.8 | 952.9 | 788.6 | 981.4 | 1 904.4 | 2 113.4 | 2 245.9 | 2 612.6 | 2 697.1 |
| North America | 157.1 | 188.3 | 170.4 | 194.5 | 237.3 | 1 862.1 | 2 060.9 | 2 178.1 | 2 560.9 | 2 634.0 |
| Canada | 128.0 | 115.2 | 133.9 | 148.3 | 170.9 | 35.6 | 133.9 | 453.1 | 372.9 | 467.8 |
| Mexico | 29.1 | 73.1 | 36.5 | 46.2 | 66.4 | 1 826.5 | 1 927.0 | 1 725.0 | 2 188.0 | 2 166.3 |
| Caribbean and Central America | 44.7 | 48.7 | 70.8 | 78.3 | 186.5 | 10.4 | 19.0 | 21.6 | 13.6 | 14.3 |
| South America | 31.2 | 49.9 | 40.6 | 20.4 | 22.1 | 2.1 | 2.0 | 2.9 | 1.5 | 6.6 |
| Argentina | 6.4 | 19.1 | 3.4 | 2.1 | 1.1 | 0.7 | 0.1 | 0.2 | 0.2 | 0.4 |
| Brazil | 11.6 | 11.4 | 12.8 | 10.2 | 13.1 | 0.3 | 0.5 | 0.5 | 0.3 | 1.7 |
| Other South America | 13.2 | 19.3 | 24.4 | 8.1 | 7.9 | 1.1 | 1.4 | 2.3 | 1.0 | 4.5 |
| Europe | 538.3 | 364.2 | 409.0 | 281.3 | 278.5 | 16.2 | 7.3 | 6.4 | | |
| Belgium | 8.6 | 16.9 | 6.4 | | | | | | | |
| France | | | 13.5 | | | | | | | |

# U.S. Foreign Trade: An Overview

Exports make a contribution to the economy of every state and every major metropolitan area. Imports bring consumers a vast array of goods and services and introduce price competition that helps restrain inflation. Economists have preached the benefits of international trade ever since Adam Smith published *The Wealth of Nations* in 1776, and even long before. Yet the American public remains unconvinced. The threats to U.S. jobs and wages are more clearly perceived than the offsetting benefits. When asked in an NBC News/Wall Street Journal poll in December 1998 to choose between two statements, 58 percent of respondents agreed that "foreign trade has been bad for the U.S. economy, because cheap imports from abroad have hurt wages and cost jobs here at home." Only 32 percent chose the alternative, that "foreign trade has been good for the U.S. economy, because demand for U.S. products abroad has resulted in economic growth and jobs for Americans here at home."

Foreign trade has been a controversial topic ever since Americans fought a revolution to gain freedom from the trading restrictions imposed by Great Britain. The statistical tables in this volume present a balanced and complete picture of U.S. trade today—trade in services as well as trade in goods. A complete balance of payments table also is included so that trade can be analyzed in the context of investment and other financial flows to and from the United States. This overview provides additional context by highlighting some important aspects of the role of foreign trade in the U.S. economy.

## Trade and the U.S. Economy

The past half-century has witnessed remarkable growth in world trade, and this trade has taken on increased importance for the U.S. economy.

In the years immediately after World War II, U.S. materials and supplies were urgently needed to rebuild a war-shattered world. U.S. exports rose to 7.7 percent of gross domestic product (GDP) in 1947, while imports were only 3.2 percent (**Figure 1**). The resulting surplus (exports less imports) was 4.4 percent of GDP, a far higher percentage than in any subsequent year. (See Table A-1.) There was much discussion of the "dollar shortage," reflecting the world-wide hunger for dollars to pay for U.S. goods.

These were also the years during which new international economic institutions were established. In the 1930s, tariffs and other restrictions had devastated world trade and contributed to prolonged depression in the United States and elsewhere. Determined to avoid any repetition, major nations entered into agreements to establish the International Monetary Fund, the World Bank, and, most directly relevant to trade, the General Agreement on Tariffs and Trade (GATT).

**Figure 1. U.S. Exports and Imports as a Percentage of Gross Domestic Product, 1946–98**

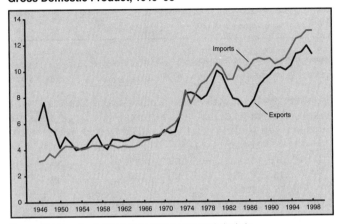

**Source**: U.S. Department of Commerce, Bereau of Economic Analysis

By 1950, with these institutions in place and world economic recovery under way, U.S. exports and imports returned more nearly to balance. During the 1950s and 1960s exports and imports grew along with the rest of the economy, remaining within a fairly narrow range of 4.0 to 5.5 percent of GDP. Trade was in surplus in most years, but the surpluses were small, averaging 0.3 percent of GDP from 1950 to 1970.

The further relaxation of trade barriers that began with the Kennedy Round of trade negotiations in the 1960s, together with improvements in international transportation and communication, led to strong expansion of U.S. trade beginning about 1970. Exports rose as a percentage of GDP, but imports rose even more rapidly, persistently exceeding exports. By 1986 and 1987, the trade deficit reached 3 percent of GDP.

Expansion of U.S. trade has continued, and even accelerated, in the 1990s, with strong export growth from 1994 to 1997 contradicting the typical cyclical pattern. Foreign trade has a strong cyclical component. That is, during periods of recession or slow growth, imports will tend to decline (or grow only slowly) as both business needs for materials and supplies and consumer purchases are restrained. Conversely, in periods of rapid economic growth, import demand will be strong and export growth may slow, as a larger share of production is diverted to meet domestic demand. This normal cyclical pattern was evident in U.S. trade during the early 1990s. Exports grew and imports dipped during the 1990-1991 recession, and, as recovery got under way, exports declined (as a percent of GDP) in 1993 and imports rose.

From 1994 through 1997, however—years of brisk U.S. economic expansion—exports boomed, rising from 10.4 percent of GDP in 1994 to 11.9 percent in 1997.

**Table 1. Exports and Imports of Advanced Technology Products, 1995–98**

(billions of dollars)

|  | Exports | Imports |
|---|---|---|
| 1995 ............................................. | 138.5 | 124.8 |
| 1996 ............................................. | 154.9 | 130.4 |
| 1997 ............................................. | 179.5 | 147.3 |
| 1998 ............................................. | 186.6 | 156.7 |

**Source**: U.S. Department of Commerce, Bereau of Economic Analysis

Imports grew a little less rapidly than exports. As a result, the trade deficit, while remaing a large absolute number, fell slightly relative to GDP, from 1.3 percent in 1994 to 1.2 percent in 1997. This pattern contrasts with that of previous expansionary periods, such as the late 1960s and the late 1980s, when trade surpluses declined or deficits increased relative to GDP. Thus, in the mid-1990s, U.S. goods and services proved themselves highly competitive in world markets, and exports contributed importantly to the expansion of the U.S. economy. This export growth was achieved despite a rising international value of the dollar from 1994 to 1997, a trend that tended to make U.S. exports more expensive and imports cheaper. Developments in 1998, when adverse world economic conditions damped the demand for U.S. exports, are discussed below in the section titled "Developments in 1998."

## The Changing Composition of U.S. Trade

Exports of services and of advanced technology products have become increasingly important to U.S. trade, while the relative importance of agricultural exports has declined.

Sales of services—items such as travel, royalties and license fees, and educational and business services—have come to constitute an increasingly important share of total U.S. exports over the past half-century. Their growth was especially marked during the early- and mid-1980s, when the services share of total trade rose from 19 percent in 1980 to more than 29.5 percent in 1987. Since 1987, with exports of both goods and services growing rapidly, the services share has remained in the vicinity of 29 percent.

The rapid growth of service exports has earned the United States increasingly large surpluses on trade in services, peaking at $88 billion in 1997. (See Table A-2.) Exports more than doubled from 1989 to 1997, while imports rose 64 percent. Spending by foreign travelers to the United States is the largest single source of these export earnings (**Figure 2**).[1] (See Table B-1.) Some of the most impressive trade growth was in business, professional, and technical services, where both exports and imports more than tripled. With exports starting from their larger base, net U.S. earnings on this category of service trade rose from $5 billion in 1989 to $15 billion

in 1997. Another major earnings category for the United States was royalties and license fees, with a $24 billion surplus in 1997.

Total U.S. exports of manufactured goods also more than doubled from 1989 to 1997. Export growth was particularly strong in 1997, when exports rose $68 billion, or 13 percent, reaching $593 billion. (See Table C-1.) During the same 1989 to 1997 period, however, U.S. imports rose 92 percent to $729 billion, increasing the U.S. trade deficit on manufactured goods to $136 billion in 1997.

Advanced technology products dominate the U.S. manufacturing export picture. Four commodity groups—industrial machinery, electronic equipment, chemicals, and instruments—accounted for more than one-half of U.S. manufactured exports in 1997. (See Table C-3). These are the groups that contain the large concentrations of high-tech goods. A more precise measure of advanced technology products is shown in **Table 1**. The totals in this table are an aggregation of about 500 of the 22,000 commodity classification codes used in reporting U.S. goods trade. Only classifications dominated by leading-edge technology in a recognized high-technology field are included. In 1997 the United States exported $179.5 billion of these advanced technology products.

Agricultural products have long been a strong factor in U.S. exports. With the more rapid growth of exports of manufactures, however, the agricultural share of total goods exports has diminished. Year-to-year fluctuations in foreign agricultural sales sometimes are large, reflecting changes in crop yields, world prices, and other highly variable factors. Comparing peak years, agricultural exports were 22.3 percent of total goods exports in 1974, 18.3 percent in 1981, and only 9.7 percent in 1996. In no year of the past quarter-century, however, has trade in agricultural products failed to produce a large U.S. surplus in this category.

The mineral fuels category includes petroleum and petroleum products. (See Table C-1). Here, imports greatly exceed exports, reflecting U.S. dependence on imported oil. This dependence has increased during the

**Figure 2. U.S. Trade in Private Services, 1997**
(Billions of dollars)

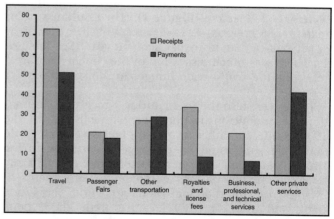

**Source**: U.S. Department of Commerce, Bereau of Economic Analysis

1990s as increases in domestic oil production have failed to keep pace with the energy consumption demands of a growing economy. Quantities imported rose at an average rate of 5.5 percent per year from 1991 to 1998. The cost of these imports held steady in the early 1990s as falling world prices offset increased quantities imported (**Table 2**). Costs leaped upward in 1996, reflecting a 20 percent jump in the price of crude petroleum. Then, in 1998, the lowest crude oil prices in many years brought a $20 billion drop in the cost of total petroleum product imports, even though the quantity imported rose nearly 8 percent.

## Trade by Country and Region

U.S. trade with individual countries and regions varies from year to year with fluctuations in economic conditions, shifts in relative exchange rates, and other factors. An underlying trend in the 1990s has been the increasing importance of trade within North America. For trade in goods, Canada has long been the most important U.S trading partner, and, in 1997, Mexico surpassed Japan as the second largest market for U.S. exports. (See Table C-5.) By 1997 these two North American countries accounted for 32 percent of U.S. goods exports and 29 percent of imports, up from 28 percent and 25 percent, respectively, in 1991. Although growth of trade among the North American countries was already well under way, the adoption of the North American Free Trade Agreement (NAFTA) in 1993 likely caused it to accelerate. As North American and other destinations have taken on increased importance, U.S. exports to Western Europe have become a lesser share of the total, falling from 28 percent in 1991 to less than 23 percent in 1997. U.S. exports to Asian destinations rose from 31 percent of total goods exports in 1991 to close to 34 percent in 1995 but fell back to 31 percent in 1997, reflecting, in part, a weak Japanese economy with a reduced demand for U.S. goods.

The geographic pattern of trade in services differs from that of goods. Three countries—Canada, Japan, and the United Kingdom—account for nearly one-third of U.S. trade in services, and that proportion has varied little since 1986. (See Table B-2.) Japan is the strongest export market; the Japanese purchased $34.0 billion of U.S. services in 1997. The United Kingdom is the leading U.S. import source, selling U.S. residents $21.2 billion of services in 1997. For all three countries, passenger fares and other spending by travelers to the United States are the dominant sources of U.S. service export earnings. In 1997, the Japanese spent $16.5 billion for these services, the British $9.3 billion, and the Canadians $8.2 billion. U.S. residents spent $7.9 billion in 1997 to travel to Britain or on British passenger carriers and $5.4 billion for Canadian travel and transportation, but only $3.7 billion for travel and related services to Japan.

## Trade and Local Economies

In a country as large and diverse as the United States, regions and localities may vary greatly in the relative volume of their exports, in the destinations to which they export, and in the types of products exported. Parts D and E of this book contain information on goods exports by state and metropolitan area. These data give an indication of the importance of exports to a particular area, but, for several reasons, they must be interpreted with caution. First, they pertain only to goods exports; comparable data about service exports are not available. Second, they identify the location (state or metropolitan area) of the seller of the export merchandise; often the merchandise is sold by the producer and the production occurs in the same state or metropolitan area as the sale, but this is not always the case. Third, even if the final product is produced in the state or metropolitan area to which it is assigned, the product likely contains parts produced elsewhere. Hence, these data give a general impression of the importance of export production to a local economy, but not a precise measure.

*States.* Every state except Hawaii experienced growth in its exports from 1987 to 1997. (See Table D-1.) In general, states in the South Atlantic, South Central, and

**Table 2. Imports of Petroleum and Petroleum Products, 1991–97**

| | Total energy-related petroleum products | | Crude petroleum | | | |
|---|---|---|---|---|---|---|
| | Quantity (millions of barrels) | Value (billions of dollars) | Quantity (millions of barrels) | | Value (billions of dollars) | Unit price (dollars per barrel) |
| | | | Total | Average per day | | |
| 1991 | 2 829.0 | 50.6 | 2 146.1 | 5.9 | 37.5 | 17.46 |
| 1992 | 2 947.6 | 50.5 | 2 294.6 | 6.3 | 38.6 | 16.80 |
| 1993 | 3 257.0 | 50.2 | 2 543.4 | 7.0 | 38.5 | 15.13 |
| 1994 | 3 416.0 | 49.5 | 2 704.2 | 7.4 | 38.5 | 14.23 |
| 1995 | 3 361.9 | 53.8 | 2 767.3 | 7.6 | 43.7 | 15.81 |
| 1996 | 3 622.4 | 70.2 | 2 893.6 | 7.9 | 54.9 | 18.98 |
| 1997 | 3 802.6 | 69.3 | 3 069.4 | 8.4 | 54.2 | 17.67 |
| 1998 | 4 101.8 | 49.4 | 3 257.7 | 8.9 | 37.5 | 11.52 |

**Source**: U.S. Department of Commerce, Bureau of the Census.

Southwest regions experienced the most rapid growth, but there are exceptions to this general pattern (**Figure 3**). New Mexico, Arizona, Texas, Kentucky, Arkansas, Tennessee, and Mississippi all had export growth well above the national average, but so did Illinois, Wisconsin, and Ohio.

California, Texas, and New York—the three states with the largest populations—each had even larger shares of exports. Together these states had 26 percent of the U.S. population in 1997 and 30 percent of exports. Florida, with the fourth largest population, has an export share below its population share, however, doubtless reflecting its large retired population and the relatively limited role of manufacturing in the Florida economy.

It is worth reiterating that these export data cover only goods exports; they do not measure the overall participation of a state in the international economy. Hawaii's goods exports may be small, but its earnings from spending by foreign visitors are a vital factor in its economy. Florida has seen rapid growth of its goods exports in the past 10 years, but more important may be Florida's popularity as an international tourist destination and its role as a transportation hub for movement of people and goods to Latin America.

*Metropolitan areas.* The two metropolitan areas with the most goods exports in 1997 were New York, New York, and San Jose, California, each with about $29 billion of exports. Other metropolitan areas with exports in excess of $20 billion in 1997 were Seattle-Bellevue-Everett, WA; Detroit, MI; Los Angeles-Long Beach, CA; and Chicago, IL. (See Table E-1.)

Although the totals are almost the same, the export patterns of San Jose and New York are a study in contrasts. San Jose's exports have grown rapidly—almost 80 percent from 1993 to 1997; New York's 1997 exports were only 3 percent above those of 1993, and they had

gone lower in the intervening years. San Jose's exports are heavily concentrated in computers, electronics, and other high-tech products; 95 percent of 1997 exports were in the SIC categories of industrial machinery, electronic equipment, and instruments—the three categories that contain the bulk of high-tech manufacturing. New York's exports were more diversified, but 15 percent were primary metals (iron, steel, and nonferrous metals), an industry group marked by declining employment and no net output growth over the past two decades. And even New York's high-tech exports have failed to experience the growth that San Jose has seen. (See Table E-2.) The two metropolitan areas also differ in the markets toward which their exports are directed. More than one-half of San Jose's exports went to Asian markets in 1997, including $4.8 billion to Japan and more than $2 billion each to Singapore, South Korea, and Taiwan. New York's exports are spread more broadly, with about 34 percent to Europe, a similar percentage to Asia, and the remainder to other regions. (See Table E-3.)

Among other large metropolitan areas, Phoenix-Mesa, Arizona, has experienced some of the most rapid export growth, with 1997 exports about two and one-half times as large as those in 1993. Again, the picture is one of concentration in high-tech goods and Asian markets. Of $11 billion of total exports in 1997, more than one-half went to Asia, including $1.7 billion to Japan and another $1 billion to Taiwan.

## Developments in 1998

In 1998 the "Asian crisis" became the "global crisis." The Asian crisis began with the collapse of the Thai currency in mid-1997 and spread rapidly to several other "miracle" economies of Asia, including South Korea and Indonesia. Failures of underdeveloped and poorly man-

**Figure 3. Growth of Exports by State, 1987–97**

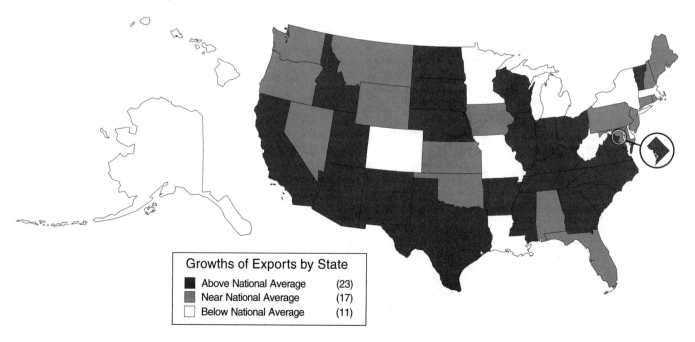

Growths of Exports by State

- ■ Above National Average    (23)
- ▨ Near National Average    (17)
- □ Below National Average    (11)

aged financial institutions in these nations may have brought on the crisis, but the financial problems were quickly translated into abrupt reversals of previously impressive economic growth. Japan, too, found itself in renewed recession in 1998; Russia devalued its currency in mid-1998, and Brazil was forced to do so early in 1999.

Among the worldwide impacts of these developments were export price cuts and sharp import reductions by the countries in crisis, leading to broad declines in world commodity prices. For the United States, this meant a stronger exchange value for the dollar, cheaper imports, and reduced demand and lower prices for many exports.

U.S. goods exports, which had risen 10 percent in 1997, fell about 1 percent in 1998. Manufactured goods registered a small gain, but this was more than offset by declines in earnings from exports of agricultural products and mineral fuels. (See Table C-1.) Import growth slowed from 9 percent in 1997 to only 5 percent in 1998, but, with exports not growing at all, the trade deficit widened substantially.

These trade results were heavily influenced by declining world prices. U.S. export prices fell 3.5 percent from December 1997 to December 1998 (**Table 3**). Thus, in volume terms, U.S. exports appear actually to have grown—the 1 percent drop in dollar value was more than offset by price declines. Import prices fell even more, about 6.3 percent. When the large drop in petroleum prices is excluded, however, prices of other imports fell 3.3 percent, or just about as much as export prices.

Declining export prices and weak overseas markets created difficulties for U.S. exporters, leading to declining profits and employment reductions in some industries. At the same time, lower import prices and abundant supplies of most raw materials were helpful in restraining inflation. Import prices for petroleum and petroleum products fell 59 percent from December 1997 to December 1998, a drop that meant major cost savings for both business and consumers.

Import prices for computers fell 11 percent, and export prices 13 percent. Compared to 1995, import prices were

down 50 percent and export prices 41 percent. Again, difficult times for producers but good news for consumers.

The agricultural sector was especially hard hit in 1998. Export prices for agricultural commodities were down 9 percent from December 1997 to December 1998. The impact of weak export markets was compounded by adverse weather conditions in many areas, leading to a $5 billion drop in export sales. Even so, the United States achieved a $16 billion surplus in agricultural trade in 1998.

The global financial crisis also brought a drop in U.S. net earnings from international service transactions, especially travel. With the value of their currencies lower against the dollar, foreign visitors cut back their spending on travel to the United States, while U.S. residents increased their travel spending abroad. The United States continued to have a large surplus on international travel in 1998, but it was down some 20 percent from 1997. Overall, exports of services showed little growth in 1998, compared to a roughly 8 percent gain in 1997. Imports grew about 6 percent, compared to more than 9 percent in 1997. The overall U.S. surplus on international trade in services was down almost 10 percent from 1997 but was still well above all years prior to 1996.

The impact of the global financial crisis on 1998 export performance varied greatly by state. California, with its Pacific Rim orientation and its concentration on high-tech goods, saw its exports drop by $5 billion (4.8 percent), thus erasing 1997s gains. Arizona's experience was similar but with larger percentage swings; exports were up 37.3 percent in 1997, then dropped 20.6 percent in 1998. Washington's export growth continued, however, with a nearly 20 percent 1998 gain coming on top of a 24 percent increase in 1997. Continued revival of the state's aircraft exports likely was a leading factor. Texas, the state that ranks second after California in export sales, had an export gain of $2.7 billion in 1998, but New York, the third ranking state, saw its exports drop $3.3 billion. The contrasts continue down the list of states.

**Table 3. Export and Import Price Indexes by End-Use Category, 1995–98**

(1995=100; data are for December)

| | Export price indexes | | | | Import price indexes | | | |
|---|---|---|---|---|---|---|---|---|
| | 1995 | 1996 | 1997 | 1998 | 1995 | 1996 | 1997 | 1998 |
| All commodities ................................................ | 100.5 | 99.3 | 98.2 | 94.8 | 100.4 | 101.9 | 96.6 | 90.5 |
| All commodities, except petroleum ......................... | ..... | ..... | ..... | ..... | 100.4 | 98.7 | 95.9 | 92.7 |
| Foods, feeds, and beverages ............................... | 109.9 | 102.7 | 99.3 | 91.2 | 98.1 | 96.8 | 98.1 | 95.1 |
| Industrial supplies and materials ........................... | 97.3 | 95.0 | 93.7 | 87.1 | 100.9 | 110.1 | 98.6 | 81.9 |
| Industrial supplies and materials, except petroleum ...... | ..... | ..... | ..... | ..... | 101.3 | 98.8 | 97.1 | 90.7 |
| Petroleum and products ...................................... | 102.7 | 125.7 | 115.8 | 88.8 | 100.7 | 134.7 | 100.4 | 59.4 |
| Capital goods ................................................. | 100.4 | 100.5 | 98.9 | 97.1 | 99.9 | 96.1 | 89.0 | 84.5 |
| Capital goods, except computers ........................... | 100.9 | 102.3 | 102.0 | 101.4 | 100.3 | 97.7 | 93.0 | 91.1 |
| Computers .................................................... | 94.7 | 79.8 | 65.0 | 56.3 | 95.2 | 75.0 | 53.6 | 47.6 |
| Automotive vehicles, parts, and engines .................. | 101.0 | 101.5 | 102.3 | 102.8 | 100.8 | 100.8 | 101.3 | 101.3 |
| Consumer goods, except automotive ....................... | 100.3 | 101.8 | 102.7 | 101.9 | 100.7 | 100.1 | 99.2 | 97.9 |

**Source**: U.S. Department of Labor, Bureau of Labor Statistics.

In summary, the impact of the global financial crisis on U.S. foreign trade varied industry by industry and state by state. On the whole, the U.S. economy demonstrated its strength and international competitiveness in 1998. Export levels for both goods and services were sustained under challenging circumstances. On the import side, the increase in imports helped meet the strong demands of a highly prosperous domestic economy and avoid the price increases that otherwise might have led to an interruption of the long expansion of the 1990s. U.S. gross national product grew an impressive 3.9 percent in 1998, surprising many observers. The unemployment rate fell to 4.5 percent, the lowest since 1969, and consumer prices rose only 1.6 percent.

As 1999 began, there were signs that the troubled economies of Asia were stabilizing and that some degree of calm had returned to world financial markets. Although the already large U.S. trade deficit was generally expected to grow somewhat larger in 1999, economic forecasters both within and outside the government saw this growth as no threat to continued U.S. economic growth and prosperity.

---

1. Spending by foreign travelers is divided into two categories in the statistical presentations. "Travel" encompasses purchases of goods and services such as food, lodging, and other items incidental to a foreign visit. Expenditures by foreign residents for travel on U.S. carriers, either for travel to and from the United States or for travel between foreign destinations, is included in "passenger fares."

# PART A.  Highlights of International Transactions

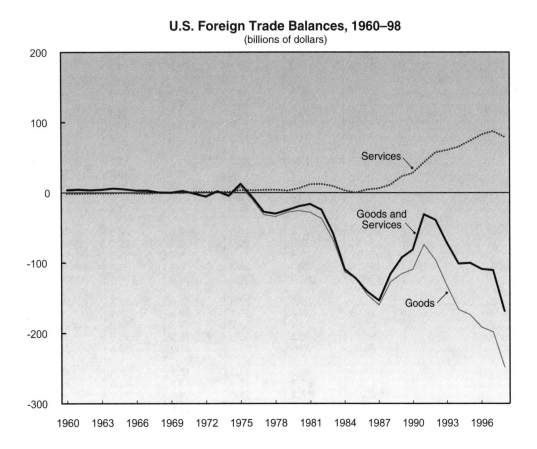

**U.S. Foreign Trade Balances, 1960–98**
(billions of dollars)

**Table A-1.  U.S. Gross Domestic Product, Exports, and Imports, 1946–1998**

| Year | Gross domestic product (GDP), exports, imports, and net exports (Billions of dollars) | | | | | | | |
| | GDP | Exports | | | Imports | | | Net exports |
| | | Total | Goods | Services | Total | Goods | Services | |
|---|---|---|---|---|---|---|---|---|
| 1946 | 222.6 | 14.1 | 11.8 | 2.3 | 7.0 | 5.1 | 1.9 | 7.1 |
| 1947 | 244.6 | 18.7 | 16.1 | 2.6 | 7.9 | 6.0 | 2.0 | 10.8 |
| 1948 | 269.7 | 15.5 | 13.3 | 2.2 | 10.1 | 7.6 | 2.5 | 5.4 |
| 1949 | 267.8 | 14.4 | 12.2 | 2.2 | 9.2 | 6.9 | 2.4 | 5.2 |
| 1950 | 294.6 | 12.3 | 10.2 | 2.1 | 11.6 | 9.1 | 2.5 | 0.7 |
| 1951 | 339.7 | 17.0 | 14.2 | 2.8 | 14.6 | 11.2 | 3.4 | 2.4 |
| 1952 | 358.6 | 16.3 | 13.4 | 2.9 | 15.3 | 10.8 | 4.5 | 1.0 |
| 1953 | 379.7 | 15.2 | 12.4 | 2.8 | 16.0 | 11.0 | 5.0 | -0.8 |
| 1954 | 381.3 | 15.7 | 12.9 | 2.8 | 15.4 | 10.4 | 5.1 | 0.3 |
| 1955 | 415.1 | 17.6 | 14.4 | 3.2 | 17.2 | 11.5 | 5.7 | 0.4 |
| 1956 | 438.0 | 21.2 | 17.6 | 3.6 | 18.9 | 12.8 | 6.1 | 2.3 |
| 1957 | 461.0 | 23.9 | 19.6 | 4.3 | 19.9 | 13.3 | 6.7 | 4.0 |
| 1958 | 467.3 | 20.4 | 16.4 | 4.0 | 20.0 | 13.0 | 7.1 | 0.4 |
| 1959 | 507.2 | 20.6 | 16.5 | 4.2 | 22.3 | 15.3 | 7.0 | -1.7 |
| 1960 | 526.6 | 25.3 | 20.5 | 4.8 | 22.8 | 15.2 | 7.6 | 2.4 |
| 1961 | 544.8 | 26.0 | 20.9 | 5.1 | 22.7 | 15.1 | 7.6 | 3.4 |
| 1962 | 585.2 | 27.4 | 21.7 | 5.7 | 25.0 | 16.9 | 8.1 | 2.4 |
| 1963 | 617.4 | 29.4 | 23.3 | 6.1 | 26.1 | 17.7 | 8.4 | 3.3 |
| 1964 | 663.0 | 33.6 | 26.7 | 6.3 | 28.1 | 19.4 | 8.7 | 5.5 |
| 1965 | 719.1 | 35.4 | 27.8 | 7.6 | 31.5 | 22.2 | 9.3 | 3.9 |
| 1966 | 787.8 | 38.9 | 30.7 | 8.2 | 37.1 | 26.3 | 10.7 | 1.9 |
| 1967 | 833.6 | 41.4 | 32.2 | 9.2 | 39.9 | 27.8 | 12.2 | 1.4 |
| 1968 | 910.6 | 45.3 | 35.3 | 10.0 | 46.6 | 33.9 | 12.6 | -1.3 |
| 1969 | 982.2 | 49.3 | 38.3 | 11.0 | 50.5 | 36.8 | 13.7 | -1.2 |
| 1970 | 1 035.6 | 57.0 | 44.5 | 12.4 | 55.8 | 40.9 | 14.9 | 1.2 |
| 1971 | 1 125.4 | 59.3 | 45.6 | 13.8 | 64.3 | 46.6 | 15.8 | -5.0 |
| 1972 | 1 237.3 | 66.2 | 51.8 | 14.4 | 74.2 | 56.9 | 17.3 | -8.0 |
| 1973 | 1 382.6 | 91.8 | 73.9 | 17.8 | 91.2 | 71.8 | 19.3 | 0.6 |
| 1974 | 1 496.9 | 124.3 | 101.0 | 23.3 | 127.5 | 104.5 | 22.9 | -3.2 |
| 1975 | 1 630.6 | 136.3 | 109.6 | 26.7 | 122.7 | 99.0 | 23.7 | 13.6 |
| 1976 | 1 819.0 | 148.9 | 117.8 | 31.1 | 151.1 | 124.6 | 26.5 | -2.2 |
| 1977 | 2 026.9 | 158.8 | 123.7 | 35.1 | 182.4 | 152.6 | 29.8 | -23.7 |
| 1978 | 2 291.4 | 186.1 | 145.4 | 40.7 | 212.3 | 177.4 | 34.8 | -26.2 |
| 1979 | 2 557.5 | 228.7 | 184.0 | 44.7 | 252.7 | 212.8 | 39.9 | -24.0 |
| 1980 | 2 784.2 | 278.9 | 225.8 | 53.2 | 293.8 | 248.6 | 45.3 | -14.9 |
| 1981 | 3 115.9 | 302.8 | 239.1 | 63.7 | 317.8 | 267.8 | 49.9 | -15.0 |
| 1982 | 3 242.1 | 282.6 | 215.0 | 67.6 | 303.2 | 250.5 | 52.6 | -20.6 |
| 1983 | 3 514.5 | 277.0 | 207.3 | 69.7 | 328.6 | 272.7 | 56.0 | -51.6 |
| 1984 | 3 902.4 | 303.1 | 225.6 | 77.5 | 405.1 | 336.3 | 68.8 | -102.0 |
| 1985 | 4 180.7 | 303.0 | 222.2 | 80.8 | 417.2 | 343.3 | 73.9 | -114.2 |
| 1986 | 4 422.2 | 320.7 | 226.0 | 94.7 | 452.2 | 370.0 | 82.2 | -131.5 |
| 1987 | 4 692.3 | 365.7 | 257.5 | 108.2 | 507.9 | 414.8 | 93.1 | -142.1 |
| 1988 | 5 049.6 | 447.2 | 325.8 | 121.4 | 553.2 | 452.1 | 101.1 | -106.1 |
| 1989 | 5 438.7 | 509.3 | 371.7 | 137.6 | 589.7 | 484.5 | 105.3 | -80.4 |
| 1990 | 5 743.8 | 557.3 | 398.5 | 158.8 | 628.6 | 508.0 | 120.6 | -71.3 |
| 1991 | 5 916.7 | 601.8 | 426.4 | 175.4 | 622.3 | 500.7 | 121.6 | -20.5 |
| 1992 | 6 244.4 | 639.4 | 448.7 | 190.7 | 669.0 | 544.9 | 124.1 | -29.5 |
| 1993 | 6 558.1 | 658.6 | 459.7 | 198.9 | 719.3 | 592.8 | 126.5 | -60.7 |
| 1994 | 6 947.0 | 721.2 | 509.6 | 211.6 | 812.1 | 676.8 | 135.3 | -90.9 |
| 1995 | 7 269.6 | 819.4 | 583.8 | 235.6 | 903.3 | 757.6 | 145.7 | -83.9 |
| 1996 | 7 661.6 | 873.8 | 618.3 | 255.5 | 965.0 | 809.0 | 156.0 | -91.2 |
| 1997 | 8 110.9 | 965.4 | 688.3 | 277.1 | 1 058.8 | 888.3 | 170.4 | -93.4 |
| 1998 (p) | 8 510.7 | 959.3 | 681.0 | 278.3 | 1 110.5 | 932.7 | 177.8 | -151.2 |

**Table A-1.  U.S. Gross Domestic Product, Exports, and Imports, 1946–1998** —*Continued*

| Year | Exports and imports as a percent of gross domestic product | | | | | | Net exports |
| | Exports | | | Imports | | | |
| | Total | Goods | Services | Total | Goods | Services | |
|---|---|---|---|---|---|---|---|
| 1946 | 6.33 | 5.30 | 1.03 | 3.14 | 2.29 | 0.85 | 3.19 |
| 1947 | 7.65 | 6.58 | 1.06 | 3.23 | 2.45 | 0.82 | 4.42 |
| 1948 | 5.75 | 4.93 | 0.82 | 3.74 | 2.82 | 0.93 | 2.00 |
| 1949 | 5.38 | 4.56 | 0.82 | 3.44 | 2.58 | 0.90 | 1.94 |
| 1950 | 4.18 | 3.46 | 0.71 | 3.94 | 3.09 | 0.85 | 0.24 |
| 1951 | 5.00 | 4.18 | 0.82 | 4.30 | 3.30 | 1.00 | 0.71 |
| 1952 | 4.55 | 3.74 | 0.81 | 4.27 | 3.01 | 1.25 | 0.28 |
| 1953 | 4.00 | 3.27 | 0.74 | 4.21 | 2.90 | 1.32 | -0.21 |
| 1954 | 4.12 | 3.38 | 0.73 | 4.04 | 2.73 | 1.34 | 0.08 |
| 1955 | 4.24 | 3.47 | 0.77 | 4.14 | 2.77 | 1.37 | 0.10 |
| 1956 | 4.84 | 4.02 | 0.82 | 4.32 | 2.92 | 1.39 | 0.53 |
| 1957 | 5.18 | 4.25 | 0.93 | 4.32 | 2.89 | 1.45 | 0.87 |
| 1958 | 4.37 | 3.51 | 0.86 | 4.28 | 2.78 | 1.52 | 0.09 |
| 1959 | 4.06 | 3.25 | 0.83 | 4.40 | 3.02 | 1.38 | -0.34 |
| 1960 | 4.80 | 3.89 | 0.91 | 4.33 | 2.89 | 1.44 | 0.46 |
| 1961 | 4.77 | 3.84 | 0.94 | 4.17 | 2.77 | 1.40 | 0.62 |
| 1962 | 4.68 | 3.71 | 0.97 | 4.27 | 2.89 | 1.38 | 0.41 |
| 1963 | 4.76 | 3.77 | 0.99 | 4.23 | 2.87 | 1.36 | 0.53 |
| 1964 | 5.07 | 4.03 | 0.95 | 4.24 | 2.93 | 1.31 | 0.83 |
| 1965 | 4.92 | 3.87 | 1.06 | 4.38 | 3.09 | 1.29 | 0.54 |
| 1966 | 4.94 | 3.90 | 1.04 | 4.71 | 3.34 | 1.36 | 0.24 |
| 1967 | 4.97 | 3.86 | 1.10 | 4.79 | 3.33 | 1.46 | 0.17 |
| 1968 | 4.97 | 3.88 | 1.10 | 5.12 | 3.72 | 1.38 | -0.14 |
| 1969 | 5.02 | 3.90 | 1.12 | 5.14 | 3.75 | 1.39 | -0.12 |
| 1970 | 5.50 | 4.30 | 1.20 | 5.39 | 3.95 | 1.44 | 0.12 |
| 1971 | 5.27 | 4.05 | 1.23 | 5.71 | 4.14 | 1.40 | -0.44 |
| 1972 | 5.35 | 4.19 | 1.16 | 6.00 | 4.60 | 1.40 | -0.65 |
| 1973 | 6.64 | 5.35 | 1.29 | 6.60 | 5.19 | 1.40 | 0.04 |
| 1974 | 8.30 | 6.75 | 1.56 | 8.52 | 6.98 | 1.53 | -0.21 |
| 1975 | 8.36 | 6.72 | 1.64 | 7.52 | 6.07 | 1.45 | 0.83 |
| 1976 | 8.19 | 6.48 | 1.71 | 8.31 | 6.85 | 1.46 | -0.12 |
| 1977 | 7.83 | 6.10 | 1.73 | 9.00 | 7.53 | 1.47 | -1.17 |
| 1978 | 8.12 | 6.35 | 1.78 | 9.27 | 7.74 | 1.52 | -1.14 |
| 1979 | 8.94 | 7.19 | 1.75 | 9.88 | 8.32 | 1.56 | -0.94 |
| 1980 | 10.02 | 8.11 | 1.91 | 10.55 | 8.93 | 1.63 | -0.54 |
| 1981 | 9.72 | 7.67 | 2.04 | 10.20 | 8.59 | 1.60 | -0.48 |
| 1982 | 8.72 | 6.63 | 2.09 | 9.35 | 7.73 | 1.62 | -0.64 |
| 1983 | 7.88 | 5.90 | 1.98 | 9.35 | 7.76 | 1.59 | -1.47 |
| 1984 | 7.77 | 5.78 | 1.99 | 10.38 | 8.62 | 1.76 | -2.61 |
| 1985 | 7.25 | 5.31 | 1.93 | 9.98 | 8.21 | 1.77 | -2.73 |
| 1986 | 7.25 | 5.11 | 2.14 | 10.23 | 8.37 | 1.86 | -2.97 |
| 1987 | 7.79 | 5.49 | 2.31 | 10.82 | 8.84 | 1.98 | -3.03 |
| 1988 | 8.86 | 6.45 | 2.40 | 10.96 | 8.95 | 2.00 | -2.10 |
| 1989 | 9.36 | 6.83 | 2.53 | 10.84 | 8.91 | 1.94 | -1.48 |
| 1990 | 9.70 | 6.94 | 2.76 | 10.94 | 8.84 | 2.10 | -1.24 |
| 1991 | 10.17 | 7.21 | 2.96 | 10.52 | 8.46 | 2.06 | -0.35 |
| 1992 | 10.24 | 7.19 | 3.05 | 10.71 | 8.73 | 1.99 | -0.47 |
| 1993 | 10.04 | 7.01 | 3.03 | 10.97 | 9.04 | 1.93 | -0.93 |
| 1994 | 10.38 | 7.34 | 3.05 | 11.69 | 9.74 | 1.95 | -1.31 |
| 1995 | 11.27 | 8.03 | 3.24 | 12.43 | 10.42 | 2.00 | -1.15 |
| 1996 | 11.40 | 8.07 | 3.33 | 12.60 | 10.56 | 2.04 | -1.19 |
| 1997 | 11.90 | 8.49 | 3.42 | 13.05 | 10.95 | 2.10 | -1.15 |
| 1998 (p) | 11.27 | 8.00 | 3.27 | 13.05 | 10.96 | 2.09 | -1.78 |

## Table A-2.  U.S. International Trade in Goods and Services, 1960–1998

(Balance of payments basis, billions of dollars.)

| Year | Exports | | | Imports | | | Trade balance | | |
|---|---|---|---|---|---|---|---|---|---|
| | Total | Goods | Services | Total | Goods | Services | Total | Goods | Services |
| 1960 | 25.9 | 19.7 | 6.3 | 22.4 | 14.8 | 7.7 | 3.5 | 4.9 | -1.4 |
| 1961 | 26.4 | 20.1 | 6.3 | 22.2 | 14.5 | 7.7 | 4.2 | 5.6 | -1.4 |
| 1962 | 27.7 | 20.8 | 6.9 | 24.4 | 16.3 | 8.1 | 3.4 | 4.5 | -1.2 |
| 1963 | 29.6 | 22.3 | 7.3 | 25.4 | 17.0 | 8.4 | 4.2 | 5.2 | -1.0 |
| 1964 | 33.3 | 25.5 | 7.8 | 27.3 | 18.7 | 8.6 | 6.0 | 6.8 | -0.8 |
| 1965 | 35.3 | 26.5 | 8.8 | 30.6 | 21.5 | 9.1 | 4.7 | 5.0 | -0.3 |
| 1966 | 38.9 | 29.3 | 9.6 | 36.0 | 25.5 | 10.5 | 2.9 | 3.8 | -0.9 |
| 1967 | 41.3 | 30.7 | 10.7 | 38.7 | 26.9 | 11.9 | 2.6 | 3.8 | -1.2 |
| 1968 | 45.5 | 33.6 | 11.9 | 45.3 | 33.0 | 12.3 | 0.2 | 0.6 | -0.4 |
| 1969 | 49.2 | 36.4 | 12.8 | 49.1 | 35.8 | 13.3 | 0.1 | 0.6 | -0.5 |
| 1970 | 56.6 | 42.5 | 14.2 | 54.4 | 39.9 | 14.5 | 2.3 | 2.6 | -0.3 |
| 1971 | 59.7 | 43.3 | 16.4 | 61.0 | 45.6 | 15.4 | -1.3 | -2.3 | 1.0 |
| 1972 | 67.2 | 49.4 | 17.8 | 72.7 | 55.8 | 16.9 | -5.4 | -6.4 | 1.0 |
| 1973 | 91.2 | 71.4 | 19.8 | 89.3 | 70.5 | 18.8 | 1.9 | 0.9 | 1.0 |
| 1974 | 120.9 | 98.3 | 22.6 | 125.2 | 103.8 | 21.4 | -4.3 | -5.5 | 1.2 |
| 1975 | 132.6 | 107.1 | 25.5 | 120.2 | 98.2 | 22.0 | 12.4 | 8.9 | 3.5 |
| 1976 | 142.7 | 114.7 | 28.0 | 148.8 | 124.2 | 24.6 | -6.1 | -9.5 | 3.4 |
| 1977 | 152.3 | 120.8 | 31.5 | 179.5 | 151.9 | 27.6 | -27.2 | -31.1 | 3.8 |
| 1978 | 178.4 | 142.1 | 36.4 | 208.2 | 176.0 | 32.2 | -29.8 | -33.9 | 4.2 |
| 1979 | 224.1 | 184.4 | 39.7 | 248.7 | 212.0 | 36.7 | -24.6 | -27.6 | 3.0 |
| 1980 | 271.8 | 224.3 | 47.6 | 291.2 | 249.8 | 41.5 | -19.4 | -25.5 | 6.1 |
| 1981 | 294.4 | 237.0 | 57.4 | 310.6 | 265.1 | 45.5 | -16.2 | -28.0 | 11.9 |
| 1982 | 275.2 | 211.2 | 64.1 | 299.4 | 247.6 | 51.7 | -24.2 | -36.5 | 12.3 |
| 1983 | 266.0 | 201.8 | 64.2 | 323.8 | 268.9 | 54.9 | -57.8 | -67.1 | 9.3 |
| 1984 | 290.9 | 219.9 | 71.0 | 400.1 | 332.4 | 67.7 | -109.2 | -112.5 | 3.3 |
| 1985 | 288.8 | 215.9 | 72.9 | 410.9 | 338.1 | 72.8 | -122.1 | -122.2 | 0.1 |
| 1986 | 309.7 | 223.3 | 86.4 | 450.3 | 368.4 | 81.8 | -140.6 | -145.1 | 4.5 |
| 1987 | 348.8 | 250.2 | 98.6 | 502.1 | 409.8 | 92.3 | -153.3 | -159.6 | 6.2 |
| 1988 | 431.3 | 320.2 | 111.1 | 547.2 | 447.2 | 100.0 | -115.9 | -127.0 | 11.1 |
| 1989 | 489.4 | 362.1 | 127.2 | 581.6 | 477.4 | 104.2 | -92.2 | -115.2 | 23.0 |
| 1990 | 537.2 | 389.3 | 147.9 | 618.4 | 498.3 | 120.0 | -81.1 | -109.0 | 27.9 |
| 1991 | 581.3 | 416.9 | 164.3 | 611.9 | 490.7 | 121.2 | -30.7 | -73.8 | 43.1 |
| 1992 | 617.3 | 440.4 | 177.0 | 656.0 | 536.5 | 119.6 | -38.7 | -96.1 | 57.4 |
| 1993 | 643.2 | 456.8 | 186.4 | 715.2 | 589.4 | 125.7 | -71.9 | -132.6 | 60.7 |
| 1994 | 703.8 | 502.4 | 201.4 | 804.7 | 668.6 | 136.2 | -100.9 | -166.2 | 65.3 |
| 1995 | 795.6 | 575.8 | 219.8 | 895.5 | 749.6 | 146.0 | -99.9 | -173.7 | 73.8 |
| 1996 | 850.8 | 612.0 | 238.8 | 959.3 | 803.3 | 156.0 | -108.6 | -191.3 | 82.8 |
| 1997 | 937.6 | 679.3 | 258.3 | 1 047.8 | 877.3 | 170.5 | -110.2 | -198.0 | 87.7 |
| 1998 (p) | 931.4 | 671.1 | 260.4 | 1 100.5 | 919.0 | 181.5 | -169.1 | -248.0 | 78.9 |

## Table A-3.  U.S. International Transactions, 1960–1998

(Millions of dollars.)

| Year | Exports of goods, services, and income | | | | | | | |
| | Total | Goods, adjusted, excluding military | Exports of services | | | | | |
| | | | Total | Transfers under U.S. military agency sales contracts | Travel | Passenger fares | Other transportation | Royalties and license fees |
|---|---|---|---|---|---|---|---|---|
| 1960 ..................... | 30 556 | 19 650 | 6 290 | 2 030 | 919 | 175 | 1 607 | 837 |
| 1961 ..................... | 31 402 | 20 108 | 6 295 | 1 867 | 947 | 183 | 1 620 | 906 |
| 1962 ..................... | 33 340 | 20 781 | 6 941 | 2 193 | 957 | 191 | 1 764 | 1 056 |
| 1963 ..................... | 35 776 | 22 272 | 7 348 | 2 219 | 1 015 | 205 | 1 898 | 1 162 |
| 1964 ..................... | 40 165 | 25 501 | 7 840 | 2 086 | 1 207 | 241 | 2 076 | 1 314 |
| 1965 ..................... | 42 722 | 26 461 | 8 824 | 2 465 | 1 380 | 271 | 2 175 | 1 534 |
| 1966 ..................... | 46 454 | 29 310 | 9 616 | 2 721 | 1 590 | 317 | 2 333 | 1 516 |
| 1967 ..................... | 49 353 | 30 666 | 10 667 | 3 191 | 1 646 | 371 | 2 426 | 1 747 |
| 1968 ..................... | 54 911 | 33 626 | 11 917 | 3 939 | 1 775 | 411 | 2 548 | 1 867 |
| 1969 ..................... | 60 132 | 36 414 | 12 806 | 4 138 | 2 043 | 450 | 2 652 | 2 019 |
| 1970 ..................... | 68 387 | 42 469 | 14 171 | 4 214 | 2 331 | 544 | 3 125 | 2 331 |
| 1971 ..................... | 72 384 | 43 319 | 16 358 | 5 472 | 2 534 | 615 | 3 299 | 2 545 |
| 1972 ..................... | 81 986 | 49 381 | 17 841 | 5 856 | 2 817 | 699 | 3 579 | 2 770 |
| 1973 ..................... | 113 050 | 71 410 | 19 832 | 5 369 | 3 412 | 975 | 4 465 | 3 225 |
| 1974 ..................... | 148 484 | 98 306 | 22 591 | 5 197 | 4 032 | 1 104 | 5 697 | 3 821 |
| 1975 ..................... | 157 936 | 107 088 | 25 497 | 6 256 | 4 697 | 1 039 | 5 840 | 4 300 |
| 1976 ..................... | 172 090 | 114 745 | 27 971 | 5 826 | 5 742 | 1 229 | 6 747 | 4 353 |
| 1977 ..................... | 184 655 | 120 816 | 31 485 | 7 554 | 6 150 | 1 366 | 7 090 | 4 920 |
| 1978 ..................... | 220 516 | 142 075 | 36 353 | 8 209 | 7 183 | 1 603 | 8 136 | 5 885 |
| 1979 ..................... | 287 965 | 184 439 | 39 692 | 6 981 | 8 441 | 2 156 | 9 971 | 6 184 |
| 1980 ..................... | 344 440 | 224 250 | 47 584 | 9 029 | 10 588 | 2 591 | 11 618 | 7 085 |
| 1981 ..................... | 380 928 | 237 044 | 57 354 | 10 720 | 12 913 | 3 111 | 12 560 | 7 284 |
| 1982 ..................... | 361 436 | 211 157 | 64 079 | 12 572 | 12 393 | 3 174 | 12 317 | 5 603 |
| 1983 ..................... | 351 306 | 201 799 | 64 307 | 12 524 | 10 947 | 3 610 | 12 590 | 5 778 |
| 1984 ..................... | 395 850 | 219 926 | 71 168 | 9 969 | 17 177 | 4 067 | 13 809 | 6 177 |
| 1985 ..................... | 382 749 | 215 915 | 73 155 | 8 718 | 17 762 | 4 411 | 14 674 | 6 678 |
| 1986 ..................... | 400 881 | 223 344 | 86 350 | 8 549 | 20 385 | 5 582 | 15 438 | 8 113 |
| 1987 ..................... | 449 312 | 250 208 | 98 593 | 11 106 | 23 563 | 7 003 | 17 027 | 10 183 |
| 1988 ..................... | 560 664 | 320 230 | 111 068 | 9 284 | 29 434 | 8 976 | 19 311 | 12 146 |
| 1989 ..................... | 643 012 | 362 120 | 127 233 | 8 564 | 36 205 | 10 657 | 20 526 | 13 818 |
| 1990 ..................... | 700 552 | 389 307 | 147 922 | 9 932 | 43 007 | 15 298 | 22 042 | 16 634 |
| 1991 ..................... | 722 653 | 416 913 | 164 333 | 11 135 | 48 385 | 15 854 | 22 631 | 17 819 |
| 1992 ..................... | 742 337 | 440 352 | 176 982 | 12 387 | 54 742 | 16 618 | 21 531 | 20 841 |
| 1993 ..................... | 769 919 | 456 832 | 186 385 | 13 471 | 57 875 | 16 528 | 21 958 | 21 695 |
| 1994 ..................... | 861 574 | 502 398 | 201 434 | 12 787 | 58 417 | 16 997 | 23 754 | 26 712 |
| 1995 ..................... | 999 491 | 575 845 | 219 802 | 14 755 | 63 395 | 18 909 | 26 081 | 30 289 |
| 1996 ..................... | 1 063 971 | 611 983 | 238 792 | 15 765 | 69 751 | 20 413 | 26 074 | 32 823 |
| 1997 ..................... | 1 179 380 | 679 325 | 258 268 | 18 269 | 73 268 | 20 895 | 26 911 | 33 676 |
| 1998 (p) ................ | 1 174 055 | 671 055 | 260 385 | 16 765 | 71 116 | 20 137 | 25 787 | 35 063 |

## Table A-3.  U.S. International Transactions, 1960–1998 —*Continued*

(Millions of dollars.)

| Year | Exports of goods, services, and income—*Continued* | | | | | | Imports of goods, services, and income | |
|---|---|---|---|---|---|---|---|---|
| | Exports of services—*Continued* | | Income receipts on U.S. assets abroad | | | | | |
| | Other private services | U.S. government miscellaneous services | Total | Direct investment receipts | Other private receipts | U.S. government receipts | Total | Goods, adjusted, excluding military |
| 1960 | 570 | 153 | 4 616 | 3 621 | 646 | 349 | -23 670 | -14 758 |
| 1961 | 607 | 164 | 4 999 | 3 823 | 793 | 383 | -23 453 | -14 537 |
| 1962 | 585 | 195 | 5 618 | 4 241 | 904 | 473 | -25 676 | -16 260 |
| 1963 | 613 | 236 | 6 157 | 4 636 | 1 022 | 499 | -26 970 | -17 048 |
| 1964 | 651 | 265 | 6 824 | 5 106 | 1 256 | 462 | -29 102 | -18 700 |
| 1965 | 714 | 285 | 7 437 | 5 506 | 1 421 | 510 | -32 708 | -21 510 |
| 1966 | 814 | 326 | 7 528 | 5 260 | 1 669 | 599 | -38 468 | -25 493 |
| 1967 | 951 | 336 | 8 021 | 5 603 | 1 781 | 636 | -41 476 | -26 866 |
| 1968 | 1 024 | 353 | 9 367 | 6 591 | 2 021 | 756 | -48 671 | -32 991 |
| 1969 | 1 160 | 343 | 10 913 | 7 649 | 2 338 | 925 | -53 998 | -35 807 |
| 1970 | 1 294 | 332 | 11 748 | 8 169 | 2 671 | 907 | -59 901 | -39 866 |
| 1971 | 1 546 | 347 | 12 707 | 9 160 | 2 641 | 906 | -66 414 | -45 579 |
| 1972 | 1 764 | 357 | 14 765 | 10 949 | 2 949 | 866 | -79 237 | -55 797 |
| 1973 | 1 985 | 401 | 21 808 | 16 542 | 4 330 | 936 | -98 997 | -70 499 |
| 1974 | 2 321 | 419 | 27 587 | 19 157 | 7 356 | 1 074 | -137 274 | -103 811 |
| 1975 | 2 920 | 446 | 25 351 | 16 595 | 7 644 | 1 112 | -132 745 | -98 185 |
| 1976 | 3 584 | 489 | 29 375 | 18 999 | 9 043 | 1 332 | -162 109 | -124 228 |
| 1977 | 3 848 | 557 | 32 354 | 19 673 | 11 057 | 1 625 | -193 764 | -151 907 |
| 1978 | 4 717 | 620 | 42 088 | 25 458 | 14 788 | 1 843 | -229 870 | -176 002 |
| 1979 | 5 439 | 520 | 63 834 | 38 183 | 23 356 | 2 295 | -281 657 | -212 007 |
| 1980 | 6 276 | 398 | 72 606 | 37 146 | 32 898 | 2 562 | -333 774 | -249 750 |
| 1981 | 10 250 | 517 | 86 529 | 32 549 | 50 300 | 3 680 | -364 196 | -265 067 |
| 1982 | 17 444 | 576 | 86 200 | 23 922 | 58 160 | 4 118 | -355 804 | -247 642 |
| 1983 | 18 192 | 666 | 85 200 | 26 950 | 53 418 | 4 832 | -377 573 | -268 901 |
| 1984 | 19 255 | 714 | 104 756 | 31 262 | 68 267 | 5 227 | -474 203 | -332 418 |
| 1985 | 20 035 | 878 | 93 679 | 30 547 | 57 633 | 5 499 | -484 037 | -338 088 |
| 1986 | 27 687 | 595 | 91 186 | 31 968 | 52 806 | 6 413 | -529 355 | -368 425 |
| 1987 | 29 186 | 526 | 100 511 | 39 608 | 55 592 | 5 311 | -593 416 | -409 765 |
| 1988 | 31 253 | 664 | 129 366 | 52 092 | 70 571 | 6 703 | -662 876 | -447 189 |
| 1989 | 36 875 | 587 | 153 659 | 55 368 | 92 638 | 5 653 | -720 189 | -477 365 |
| 1990 | 40 341 | 668 | 163 324 | 58 740 | 94 072 | 10 512 | -757 507 | -498 337 |
| 1991 | 47 821 | 690 | 141 408 | 52 198 | 81 186 | 8 023 | -732 068 | -490 981 |
| 1992 | 50 022 | 841 | 125 003 | 51 912 | 65 977 | 7 114 | -758 481 | -536 458 |
| 1993 | 53 975 | 883 | 126 702 | 61 241 | 60 353 | 5 108 | -817 910 | -589 441 |
| 1994 | 61 880 | 887 | 157 742 | 72 391 | 81 230 | 4 121 | -946 008 | -668 590 |
| 1995 | 65 555 | 818 | 203 844 | 93 164 | 105 967 | 4 713 | -1 080 107 | -749 574 |
| 1996 | 73 073 | 893 | 213 196 | 99 802 | 108 733 | 4 661 | -1 158 309 | -803 320 |
| 1997 | 84 465 | 784 | 241 787 | 109 407 | 128 845 | 3 535 | -1 294 904 | -877 279 |
| 1998 (p) | 90 729 | 788 | 242 615 | 100 447 | 138 600 | 3 568 | -1 365 648 | -919 040 |

**Table A-3. U.S. International Transactions, 1960–1998** —*Continued*

(Millions of dollars.)

| Year | Imports of goods, services, and income—*Continued* | | | | | | | |
|---|---|---|---|---|---|---|---|---|
| | Imports of services | | | | | | | |
| | Services | Direct defense expenditures | Travel | Passenger fares | Other transportation | Royalties and license fees | Other private services | U.S. government miscellaneous services |
| 1960 | -7 674 | -3 087 | -1 750 | -513 | -1 402 | -74 | -593 | -254 |
| 1961 | -7 671 | -2 998 | -1 785 | -506 | -1 437 | -89 | -588 | -268 |
| 1962 | -8 092 | -3 105 | -1 939 | -567 | -1 558 | -100 | -528 | -296 |
| 1963 | -8 362 | -2 961 | -2 114 | -612 | -1 701 | -112 | -493 | -370 |
| 1964 | -8 619 | -2 880 | -2 211 | -642 | -1 817 | -127 | -527 | -415 |
| 1965 | -9 111 | -2 952 | -2 438 | -717 | -1 951 | -135 | -461 | -457 |
| 1966 | -10 494 | -3 764 | -2 657 | -753 | -2 161 | -140 | -506 | -513 |
| 1967 | -11 863 | -4 378 | -3 207 | -829 | -2 157 | -166 | -565 | -561 |
| 1968 | -12 302 | -4 535 | -3 030 | -885 | -2 367 | -186 | -668 | -631 |
| 1969 | -13 322 | -4 856 | -3 373 | -1 080 | -2 455 | -221 | -751 | -586 |
| 1970 | -14 520 | -4 855 | -3 980 | -1 215 | -2 843 | -224 | -827 | -576 |
| 1971 | -15 400 | -4 819 | -4 373 | -1 290 | -3 130 | -241 | -956 | -592 |
| 1972 | -16 868 | -4 784 | -5 042 | -1 596 | -3 520 | -294 | -1 043 | -589 |
| 1973 | -18 843 | -4 629 | -5 526 | -1 790 | -4 694 | -385 | -1 180 | -640 |
| 1974 | -21 379 | -5 032 | -5 980 | -2 095 | -5 942 | -346 | -1 262 | -722 |
| 1975 | -21 996 | -4 795 | -6 417 | -2 263 | -5 708 | -472 | -1 551 | -789 |
| 1976 | -24 570 | -4 895 | -6 856 | -2 568 | -6 852 | -482 | -2 006 | -911 |
| 1977 | -27 640 | -5 823 | -7 451 | -2 748 | -7 972 | -504 | -2 190 | -951 |
| 1978 | -32 189 | -7 352 | -8 475 | -2 896 | -9 124 | -671 | -2 573 | -1 099 |
| 1979 | -36 689 | -8 294 | -9 413 | -3 184 | -10 906 | -831 | -2 822 | -1 239 |
| 1980 | -41 491 | -10 851 | -10 397 | -3 607 | -11 790 | -724 | -2 909 | -1 214 |
| 1981 | -45 503 | -11 564 | -11 479 | -4 487 | -12 474 | -650 | -3 562 | -1 287 |
| 1982 | -51 749 | -12 460 | -12 394 | -4 772 | -11 710 | -795 | -8 159 | -1 460 |
| 1983 | -54 973 | -13 087 | -13 149 | -6 003 | -12 222 | -943 | -8 001 | -1 568 |
| 1984 | -67 748 | -12 516 | -22 913 | -5 735 | -14 843 | -1 168 | -9 040 | -1 534 |
| 1985 | -72 862 | -13 108 | -24 558 | -6 444 | -15 643 | -1 170 | -10 203 | -1 735 |
| 1986 | -81 835 | -13 730 | -25 913 | -6 505 | -17 766 | -1 401 | -14 834 | -1 686 |
| 1987 | -92 349 | -14 950 | -29 310 | -7 283 | -19 010 | -1 857 | -18 047 | -1 893 |
| 1988 | -99 965 | -15 604 | -32 114 | -7 729 | -20 891 | -2 601 | -19 106 | -1 921 |
| 1989 | -104 185 | -15 313 | -33 416 | -8 249 | -22 172 | -2 528 | -20 636 | -1 871 |
| 1990 | -120 021 | -17 531 | -37 349 | -10 531 | -24 966 | -3 135 | -24 590 | -1 919 |
| 1991 | -121 196 | -16 409 | -35 322 | -10 012 | -24 975 | -4 035 | -28 328 | -2 116 |
| 1992 | -119 561 | -13 835 | -38 552 | -10 603 | -23 767 | -5 161 | -25 381 | -2 263 |
| 1993 | -125 715 | -12 202 | -40 713 | -11 410 | -24 524 | -5 032 | -29 580 | -2 255 |
| 1994 | -136 155 | -10 292 | -43 782 | -13 062 | -26 019 | -5 852 | -34 588 | -2 560 |
| 1995 | -145 964 | -9 986 | -44 916 | -14 663 | -27 034 | -6 919 | -39 823 | -2 623 |
| 1996 | -156 029 | -11 081 | -48 048 | -15 818 | -27 403 | -7 854 | -43 138 | -2 687 |
| 1997 | -170 520 | -11 488 | -51 220 | -18 235 | -28 949 | -9 411 | -48 421 | -2 796 |
| 1998 (p) | -181 514 | -12 693 | -53 728 | -18 851 | -30 285 | -10 654 | -52 470 | -2 833 |

## Table A-3.  U.S. International Transactions, 1960–1998 —*Continued*

(Millions of dollars.)

| Year | Imports of goods, services, and income—*Continued* | | | | Unilateral transfers, net | | | |
|---|---|---|---|---|---|---|---|---|
| | Income payments on foreign assets in the U.S. | | | | | | | |
| | Total | Direct investment payments | Other private payments | U.S. government payments | Total | U.S. government grants | U.S. government pensions and other transfers | Private remittances and other transfers |
| 1960 | -1 238 | -394 | -511 | -332 | -4 062 | -3 367 | -273 | -423 |
| 1961 | -1 245 | -432 | -535 | -278 | -4 127 | -3 320 | -373 | -434 |
| 1962 | -1 324 | -399 | -586 | -339 | -4 277 | -3 453 | -347 | -477 |
| 1963 | -1 560 | -459 | -701 | -401 | -4 392 | -3 479 | -339 | -575 |
| 1964 | -1 783 | -529 | -802 | -453 | -4 240 | -3 227 | -399 | -614 |
| 1965 | -2 088 | -657 | -942 | -489 | -4 583 | -3 444 | -463 | -677 |
| 1966 | -2 481 | -711 | -1 221 | -549 | -4 955 | -3 802 | -499 | -655 |
| 1967 | -2 747 | -821 | -1 328 | -598 | -5 294 | -3 844 | -571 | -879 |
| 1968 | -3 378 | -876 | -1 800 | -702 | -5 629 | -4 256 | -537 | -836 |
| 1969 | -4 869 | -848 | -3 244 | -777 | -5 735 | -4 259 | -537 | -939 |
| 1970 | -5 515 | -875 | -3 617 | -1 024 | -6 156 | -4 449 | -611 | -1 096 |
| 1971 | -5 435 | -1 164 | -2 428 | -1 844 | -7 402 | -5 589 | -696 | -1 117 |
| 1972 | -6 572 | -1 284 | -2 604 | -2 684 | -8 544 | -6 665 | -770 | -1 109 |
| 1973 | -9 655 | -1 610 | -4 209 | -3 836 | -6 913 | -4 748 | -915 | -1 250 |
| 1974 | -12 084 | -1 331 | -6 491 | -4 262 | -9 249 | -7 293 | -939 | -1 017 |
| 1975 | -12 564 | -2 234 | -5 788 | -4 542 | -7 075 | -5 101 | -1 068 | -906 |
| 1976 | -13 311 | -3 110 | -5 681 | -4 520 | -5 686 | -3 519 | -1 250 | -917 |
| 1977 | -14 217 | -2 834 | -5 841 | -5 542 | -5 226 | -2 990 | -1 378 | -859 |
| 1978 | -21 680 | -4 211 | -8 795 | -8 674 | -5 788 | -3 412 | -1 532 | -844 |
| 1979 | -32 961 | -6 357 | -15 481 | -11 122 | -6 593 | -4 015 | -1 658 | -920 |
| 1980 | -42 532 | -8 635 | -21 214 | -12 684 | -8 349 | -5 486 | -1 818 | -1 044 |
| 1981 | -53 626 | -6 898 | -29 415 | -17 313 | -11 702 | -5 145 | -2 041 | -4 516 |
| 1982 | -56 412 | -1 943 | -35 187 | -19 282 | -17 075 | -6 087 | -2 251 | -8 738 |
| 1983 | -53 700 | -4 206 | -30 501 | -18 993 | -17 718 | -6 469 | -2 207 | -9 043 |
| 1984 | -74 036 | -8 723 | -44 158 | -21 155 | -20 598 | -8 696 | -2 159 | -9 742 |
| 1985 | -73 087 | -7 213 | -42 745 | -23 129 | -22 700 | -11 268 | -2 138 | -9 295 |
| 1986 | -79 095 | -7 058 | -47 412 | -24 625 | -24 679 | -11 883 | -2 372 | -10 424 |
| 1987 | -91 302 | -7 425 | -57 659 | -26 218 | -23 909 | -10 309 | -2 409 | -11 192 |
| 1988 | -115 722 | -11 693 | -72 314 | -31 715 | -25 988 | -10 537 | -2 709 | -12 742 |
| 1989 | -138 639 | -6 507 | -93 768 | -38 364 | -26 963 | -10 911 | -2 744 | -13 308 |
| 1990 | -139 149 | -2 871 | -95 508 | -40 770 | -34 669 | -17 433 | -3 184 | -14 053 |
| 1991 | -119 891 | 3 433 | -82 452 | -40 872 | 5 032 | 24 160 | -3 730 | -15 399 |
| 1992 | -102 462 | -302 | -63 079 | -39 081 | -35 230 | -15 826 | -4 018 | -15 386 |
| 1993 | -102 754 | -5 574 | -57 804 | -39 376 | -38 142 | -16 821 | -4 081 | -17 240 |
| 1994 | -141 263 | -20 621 | -76 450 | -44 192 | -39 391 | -15 508 | -4 545 | -19 338 |
| 1995 | -184 569 | -30 195 | -97 004 | -57 370 | -34 638 | -11 170 | -3 433 | -20 035 |
| 1996 | -198 960 | -33 641 | -97 901 | -67 418 | -40 577 | -15 023 | -4 442 | -21 112 |
| 1997 | -247 105 | -45 674 | -113 959 | -87 472 | -39 691 | -12 090 | -4 193 | -23 408 |
| 1998 (p) | -265 094 | -45 796 | -128 560 | -90 738 | -41 855 | -12 492 | -4 304 | -25 059 |

## Table A-3.  U.S. International Transactions, 1960–1998 —*Continued*

(Millions of dollars.)

| Year | U.S. assets abroad, net | U.S. official reserve assets, net | | | | |
|---|---|---|---|---|---|---|
| | Total | Total | Gold | Special drawing rights | Reserve position in the International Monetary Fund | Foreign currencies |
| 1960 | -4 099 | 2 145 | 1 703 | ..... | 442 | ..... |
| 1961 | -5 538 | 607 | 857 | ..... | -135 | -115 |
| 1962 | -4 174 | 1 535 | 890 | ..... | 626 | 19 |
| 1963 | -7 270 | 378 | 461 | ..... | 29 | -112 |
| 1964 | -9 560 | 171 | 125 | ..... | 266 | -220 |
| 1965 | -5 716 | 1 225 | 1 665 | ..... | -94 | -346 |
| 1966 | -7 321 | 570 | 571 | ..... | 537 | -538 |
| 1967 | -9 757 | 53 | 1 170 | ..... | -94 | -1 023 |
| 1968 | -10 977 | -870 | 1 173 | ..... | -870 | -1 173 |
| 1969 | -11 585 | -1 179 | -967 | ..... | -1 034 | 822 |
| 1970 | -9 337 | 2 481 | 787 | -851 | 389 | 2 156 |
| 1971 | -12 475 | 2 349 | 866 | -249 | 1 350 | 382 |
| 1972 | -14 497 | -4 | 547 | -703 | 153 | -1 |
| 1973 | -22 874 | 158 | ..... | 9 | -33 | 182 |
| 1974 | -34 745 | -1 467 | ..... | -172 | -1 265 | -30 |
| 1975 | -39 703 | -849 | ..... | -66 | -466 | -317 |
| 1976 | -51 269 | -2 558 | ..... | -78 | -2 212 | -268 |
| 1977 | -34 785 | -375 | -118 | -121 | -294 | 158 |
| 1978 | -61 130 | 732 | -65 | 1 249 | 4 231 | -4 683 |
| 1979 | -66 054 | -1 133 | -65 | -1 136 | -189 | 257 |
| 1980 | -86 967 | -8 155 | ..... | -16 | -1 667 | -6 472 |
| 1981 | -114 147 | -5 175 | ..... | -1 824 | -2 491 | -861 |
| 1982 | -122 335 | -4 965 | ..... | -1 371 | -2 552 | -1 041 |
| 1983 | -61 573 | -1 196 | ..... | -66 | -4 434 | 3 304 |
| 1984 | -36 313 | -3 131 | ..... | -979 | -995 | -1 156 |
| 1985 | -39 889 | -3 858 | ..... | -897 | 908 | -3 869 |
| 1986 | -106 753 | 312 | ..... | -246 | 1 501 | -942 |
| 1987 | -72 617 | 9 149 | ..... | -509 | 2 070 | 7 588 |
| 1988 | -100 221 | -3 912 | ..... | 127 | 1 025 | -5 064 |
| 1989 | -168 744 | -25 293 | ..... | -535 | 471 | -25 229 |
| 1990 | -74 011 | -2 158 | ..... | -192 | 731 | -2 697 |
| 1991 | -57 881 | 5 763 | ..... | -177 | -367 | 6 307 |
| 1992 | -68 774 | 3 901 | ..... | 2 316 | -2 692 | 4 277 |
| 1993 | -194 537 | -1 379 | ..... | -537 | -44 | -797 |
| 1994 | -171 102 | 5 346 | ..... | -441 | 494 | 5 293 |
| 1995 | -327 453 | -9 742 | ..... | -808 | -2 466 | -6 468 |
| 1996 | -368 801 | 6 668 | ..... | 370 | -1 280 | 7 578 |
| 1997 | -478 502 | -1 010 | ..... | -350 | -3 575 | 2 915 |
| 1998 (p) | -305 385 | -6 784 | ..... | -149 | -5 118 | -1 517 |

## Table A-3.  U.S. International Transactions, 1960–1998 —*Continued*

(Millions of dollars.)

| Year | U.S. assets abroad, net—*Continued* | | | | | | | | |
| --- | --- | --- | --- | --- | --- | --- | --- | --- | --- |
| | U.S. government assets, other than official reserve assets, net | | | | U.S. private assets | | | | |
| | | | | | | | | U.S. claims | |
| | Total | U.S. credits and other long-term assets | Repayments on U.S. credits and other long-term assets | U.S. foreign currency holdings and U.S. short-term assets, net | Total | Direct investment | Foreign securities | on unaffiliated foreigners reported by U.S. non-banking concerns | reported by U.S. banks, not included elsewhere |
| 1960 | -1 100 | -1 214 | 642 | -528 | -5 144 | -2 940 | -663 | -394 | -1 148 |
| 1961 | -910 | -1 928 | 1 279 | -261 | -5 235 | -2 653 | -762 | -558 | -1 261 |
| 1962 | -1 085 | -2 128 | 1 288 | -245 | -4 623 | -2 851 | -969 | -354 | -450 |
| 1963 | -1 662 | -2 204 | 988 | -447 | -5 986 | -3 483 | -1 105 | 157 | -1 556 |
| 1964 | -1 680 | -2 382 | 720 | -19 | -8 050 | -3 760 | -677 | -1 108 | -2 505 |
| 1965 | -1 605 | -2 463 | 874 | -16 | -5 336 | -5 011 | -759 | 341 | 93 |
| 1966 | -1 543 | -2 513 | 1 235 | -265 | -6 347 | -5 418 | -720 | -442 | 233 |
| 1967 | -2 423 | -3 638 | 1 005 | 209 | -7 386 | -4 805 | -1 308 | -779 | -495 |
| 1968 | -2 274 | -3 722 | 1 386 | 62 | -7 833 | -5 295 | -1 569 | -1 203 | 233 |
| 1969 | -2 200 | -3 489 | 1 200 | 89 | -8 206 | -5 960 | -1 549 | -126 | -570 |
| 1970 | -1 589 | -3 293 | 1 721 | -16 | -10 229 | -7 590 | -1 076 | -596 | -967 |
| 1971 | -1 884 | -4 181 | 2 115 | 182 | -12 940 | -7 618 | -1 113 | -1 229 | -2 980 |
| 1972 | -1 568 | -3 819 | 2 086 | 165 | -12 925 | -7 747 | -618 | -1 054 | -3 506 |
| 1973 | -2 644 | -4 638 | 2 596 | -602 | -20 388 | -11 353 | -671 | -2 383 | -5 980 |
| 1974 | 366 | -5 001 | 4 826 | 541 | -33 643 | -9 052 | -1 854 | -3 221 | -19 516 |
| 1975 | -3 474 | -5 941 | 2 475 | -9 | -35 380 | -14 244 | -6 247 | -1 357 | -13 532 |
| 1976 | -4 214 | -6 943 | 2 596 | 133 | -44 498 | -11 949 | -8 885 | -2 296 | -21 368 |
| 1977 | -3 693 | -6 445 | 2 719 | 33 | -30 717 | -11 890 | -5 460 | -1 940 | -11 427 |
| 1978 | -4 660 | -7 470 | 2 941 | -131 | -57 202 | -16 056 | -3 626 | -3 853 | -33 667 |
| 1979 | -3 746 | -7 697 | 3 926 | 25 | -61 176 | -25 222 | -4 726 | -5 014 | -26 213 |
| 1980 | -5 162 | -9 860 | 4 456 | 242 | -73 651 | -19 222 | -3 568 | -4 023 | -46 838 |
| 1981 | -5 097 | -9 674 | 4 413 | 164 | -103 875 | -9 624 | -5 699 | -4 377 | -84 175 |
| 1982 | -6 131 | -10 063 | 4 292 | -360 | -111 239 | 991 | -7 983 | 6 823 | -111 070 |
| 1983 | -5 006 | -9 967 | 5 012 | -51 | -55 372 | -7 728 | -6 762 | -10 954 | -29 928 |
| 1984 | -5 489 | -9 599 | 4 490 | -379 | -27 694 | -12 344 | -4 756 | 533 | -11 127 |
| 1985 | -2 821 | -7 657 | 4 719 | 117 | -33 211 | -14 065 | -7 481 | -10 342 | -1 323 |
| 1986 | -2 022 | -9 084 | 6 089 | 973 | -105 044 | -19 025 | -4 271 | -21 773 | -59 975 |
| 1987 | 1 006 | -6 506 | 7 625 | -113 | -82 771 | -28 355 | -5 251 | -7 046 | -42 119 |
| 1988 | 2 967 | -7 680 | 10 370 | 277 | -99 275 | -16 175 | -7 980 | -21 193 | -53 927 |
| 1989 | 1 259 | -5 590 | 6 723 | 125 | -144 710 | -36 834 | -22 070 | -27 646 | -58 160 |
| 1990 | 2 307 | -8 430 | 10 867 | -130 | -74 160 | -29 950 | -28 765 | -27 824 | 12 379 |
| 1991 | 2 911 | -12 874 | 16 776 | -992 | -66 555 | -31 369 | -45 673 | 11 097 | -610 |
| 1992 | -1 657 | -7 398 | 5 807 | -66 | -71 018 | -42 640 | -49 166 | -387 | 21 175 |
| 1993 | -342 | -6 299 | 6 270 | -313 | -192 817 | -77 945 | -146 253 | 766 | 30 615 |
| 1994 | -389 | -5 272 | 5 068 | -185 | -176 059 | -75 214 | -60 309 | -36 336 | -4 200 |
| 1995 | -589 | -4 843 | 4 115 | 139 | -317 122 | -96 654 | -100 074 | -45 286 | -75 108 |
| 1996 | -708 | -5 011 | 4 197 | 106 | -374 761 | -81 072 | -115 801 | -86 333 | -91 555 |
| 1997 | 174 | -5 302 | 5 504 | -28 | -477 666 | -121 843 | -87 981 | -120 403 | -147 439 |
| 1998 (p) | -836 | -4 761 | 4 211 | -286 | -297 765 | -131 933 | -89 352 | -45 440 | -31 040 |

**Table A-3.   U.S. International Transactions, 1960–1998** —*Continued*

(Millions of dollars.)

| Year | | Foreign assets in the United States | | | | | | |
| | | Foreign official assets in the United States | | | | | | |
| | Total | Total | U.S. Government Securities | | | Other U.S. government liabilities | U.S. liabilities reported by U.S. banks, not included elsewhere | Other foreign official assets |
| | | | Total | U.S. Treasury securities | Other | | | |
|---|---|---|---|---|---|---|---|---|
| 1960 | 2 294 | 1 473 | 655 | 655 | ..... | 215 | 603 | ..... |
| 1961 | 2 705 | 765 | 233 | 233 | ..... | 25 | 508 | ..... |
| 1962 | 1 911 | 1 270 | 1 409 | 1 410 | -1 | 152 | -291 | ..... |
| 1963 | 3 217 | 1 986 | 816 | 803 | 12 | 429 | 742 | ..... |
| 1964 | 3 643 | 1 660 | 432 | 434 | -2 | 298 | 930 | ..... |
| 1965 | 742 | 134 | -141 | -134 | -7 | 65 | 210 | ..... |
| 1966 | 3 661 | -672 | -1 527 | -1 548 | 21 | 113 | 742 | ..... |
| 1967 | 7 379 | 3 451 | 2 261 | 2 222 | 39 | 83 | 1 106 | ..... |
| 1968 | 9 928 | -774 | -769 | -798 | 29 | -15 | 10 | ..... |
| 1969 | 12 702 | -1 301 | -2 343 | -2 269 | -74 | 251 | 792 | ..... |
| 1970 | 6 359 | 6 908 | 9 439 | 9 411 | 28 | -456 | -2 075 | ..... |
| 1971 | 22 970 | 26 879 | 26 570 | 26 578 | -8 | -510 | 819 | ..... |
| 1972 | 21 461 | 10 475 | 8 470 | 8 213 | 257 | 182 | 1 638 | 185 |
| 1973 | 18 388 | 6 026 | 641 | 59 | 582 | 936 | 4 126 | 323 |
| 1974 | 35 341 | 10 546 | 4 172 | 3 270 | 902 | 301 | 5 818 | 254 |
| 1975 | 17 170 | 7 027 | 5 563 | 4 658 | 905 | 1 517 | -2 158 | 2 104 |
| 1976 | 38 018 | 17 693 | 9 892 | 9 319 | 573 | 4 627 | 969 | 2 205 |
| 1977 | 53 219 | 36 816 | 32 538 | 30 230 | 2 308 | 1 400 | 773 | 2 105 |
| 1978 | 67 036 | 33 678 | 24 221 | 23 555 | 666 | 2 476 | 5 551 | 1 430 |
| 1979 | 40 852 | -13 665 | -21 972 | -22 435 | 463 | -40 | 7 213 | 1 135 |
| 1980 | 62 612 | 15 497 | 11 895 | 9 708 | 2 187 | 615 | -159 | 3 145 |
| 1981 | 86 232 | 4 960 | 6 322 | 5 019 | 1 303 | -338 | -3 670 | 2 646 |
| 1982 | 96 418 | 3 593 | 5 085 | 5 779 | -694 | 605 | -1 747 | -350 |
| 1983 | 88 780 | 5 845 | 6 496 | 6 972 | -476 | 602 | 545 | -1 798 |
| 1984 | 118 032 | 3 140 | 4 703 | 4 690 | 13 | 739 | 555 | -2 857 |
| 1985 | 146 383 | -1 119 | -1 139 | -838 | -301 | 844 | 645 | -1 469 |
| 1986 | 230 211 | 35 648 | 33 150 | 34 364 | -1 214 | 2 195 | 1 187 | -884 |
| 1987 | 248 383 | 45 387 | 44 802 | 43 238 | 1 564 | -2 326 | 3 918 | -1 007 |
| 1988 | 246 065 | 39 758 | 43 050 | 41 741 | 1 309 | -467 | -319 | -2 506 |
| 1989 | 224 390 | 8 503 | 1 532 | 149 | 1 383 | 160 | 4 976 | 1 835 |
| 1990 | 140 992 | 33 910 | 30 243 | 29 576 | 667 | 1 868 | 3 385 | -1 586 |
| 1991 | 109 641 | 17 389 | 16 147 | 14 846 | 1 301 | 1 367 | -1 484 | 1 359 |
| 1992 | 168 776 | 40 477 | 22 403 | 18 454 | 3 949 | 2 191 | 16 571 | -688 |
| 1993 | 279 671 | 71 753 | 53 014 | 48 952 | 4 062 | 1 313 | 14 841 | 2 585 |
| 1994 | 304 460 | 39 583 | 36 827 | 30 750 | 6 077 | 1 564 | 3 665 | -2 473 |
| 1995 | 465 449 | 109 768 | 72 712 | 68 977 | 3 735 | -217 | 34 008 | 3 265 |
| 1996 | 563 357 | 127 344 | 120 679 | 115 671 | 5 008 | -362 | 5 704 | 1 323 |
| 1997 | 733 441 | 15 817 | -2 936 | -7 270 | 4 334 | -2 521 | 21 928 | -654 |
| 1998 (p) | 542 482 | -22 112 | -3 614 | -9 946 | 6 332 | -2 506 | -12 515 | -3 477 |

## Table A-3.  U.S. International Transactions, 1960–1998 —*Continued*

(Millions of dollars.)

| Year | Foreign assets in the United States—*Continued* | | | | | | | Allocations of special drawing rights |
|---|---|---|---|---|---|---|---|---|
| | Other foreign assets in the United States | | | | | U.S. liabilities | | |
| | Total | Direct investment | U.S. Treasury securities | U.S. currency | U.S. securities other than U.S. Treasury securities | to unaffiliated foreigners reported by U.S. nonbanking concerns | reported by U.S. banks, not included elsewhere | |
| 1960 | 821 | 315 | -364 | ..... | 282 | -90 | 678 | ..... |
| 1961 | 1 939 | 311 | 151 | ..... | 324 | 226 | 928 | ..... |
| 1962 | 641 | 346 | -66 | ..... | 134 | -110 | 336 | ..... |
| 1963 | 1 231 | 231 | -149 | ..... | 287 | -37 | 898 | ..... |
| 1964 | 1 983 | 322 | -146 | ..... | -85 | 75 | 1 818 | ..... |
| 1965 | 607 | 415 | -131 | ..... | -358 | 178 | 503 | ..... |
| 1966 | 4 333 | 425 | -356 | ..... | 906 | 476 | 2 882 | ..... |
| 1967 | 3 928 | 698 | -135 | ..... | 1 016 | 584 | 1 765 | ..... |
| 1968 | 10 703 | 807 | 136 | ..... | 4 414 | 1 475 | 3 871 | ..... |
| 1969 | 14 002 | 1 263 | -68 | ..... | 3 130 | 792 | 8 886 | ..... |
| 1970 | -550 | 1 464 | 81 | ..... | 2 189 | 2 014 | -6 298 | 867 |
| 1971 | -3 909 | 367 | -24 | ..... | 2 289 | 369 | -6 911 | 717 |
| 1972 | 10 986 | 949 | -39 | ..... | 4 507 | 815 | 4 754 | 710 |
| 1973 | 12 362 | 2 800 | -216 | ..... | 4 041 | 1 035 | 4 702 | ..... |
| 1974 | 24 796 | 4 760 | 697 | 1 100 | 378 | 1 844 | 16 017 | ..... |
| 1975 | 10 143 | 2 603 | 2 590 | 1 500 | 2 503 | 319 | 628 | ..... |
| 1976 | 20 326 | 4 347 | 2 783 | 1 500 | 1 284 | -578 | 10 990 | ..... |
| 1977 | 16 403 | 3 728 | 534 | 1 900 | 2 437 | 1 086 | 6 719 | ..... |
| 1978 | 33 358 | 7 897 | 2 178 | 3 000 | 2 254 | 1 889 | 16 141 | ..... |
| 1979 | 54 516 | 11 877 | 4 060 | 3 000 | 1 351 | 1 621 | 32 607 | 1 139 |
| 1980 | 47 115 | 16 918 | 2 645 | 4 500 | 5 457 | 6 852 | 10 743 | 1 152 |
| 1981 | 81 272 | 25 195 | 2 927 | 3 200 | 6 905 | 917 | 42 128 | 1 093 |
| 1982 | 92 826 | 12 464 | 7 027 | 4 000 | 6 085 | -2 383 | 65 633 | ..... |
| 1983 | 82 934 | 10 457 | 8 689 | 5 400 | 8 164 | -118 | 50 342 | ..... |
| 1984 | 114 892 | 24 748 | 23 001 | 4 100 | 12 568 | 16 626 | 33 849 | ..... |
| 1985 | 147 501 | 20 010 | 20 433 | 5 200 | 50 962 | 9 851 | 41 045 | ..... |
| 1986 | 194 563 | 35 623 | 3 809 | 4 100 | 70 969 | 3 325 | 76 737 | ..... |
| 1987 | 202 996 | 58 219 | -7 643 | 5 400 | 42 120 | 18 363 | 86 537 | ..... |
| 1988 | 206 307 | 57 278 | 20 239 | 5 800 | 26 353 | 32 893 | 63 744 | ..... |
| 1989 | 215 887 | 67 736 | 29 618 | 5 900 | 38 767 | 22 086 | 51 780 | ..... |
| 1990 | 107 082 | 47 915 | -2 534 | 18 800 | 1 592 | 45 133 | -3 824 | ..... |
| 1991 | 92 253 | 22 004 | 18 826 | 15 400 | 35 144 | -3 115 | 3 994 | ..... |
| 1992 | 128 299 | 17 936 | 37 131 | 13 400 | 30 043 | 13 573 | 16 216 | ..... |
| 1993 | 207 918 | 48 993 | 24 381 | 18 900 | 80 092 | 10 489 | 25 063 | ..... |
| 1994 | 264 877 | 44 592 | 34 274 | 23 400 | 56 971 | 1 302 | 104 338 | ..... |
| 1995 | 355 681 | 57 653 | 99 548 | 12 300 | 96 367 | 59 637 | 30 176 | ..... |
| 1996 | 436 013 | 77 622 | 154 996 | 17 362 | 130 151 | 39 404 | 16 478 | ..... |
| 1997 | 717 624 | 93 449 | 146 710 | 24 782 | 196 845 | 107 779 | 148 059 | ..... |
| 1998 (p) | 564 594 | 196 229 | 48 060 | 16 622 | 217 312 | 43 803 | 42 568 | ..... |

**Table A-3.   U.S. International Transactions, 1960–1998** —*Continued*

(Millions of dollars.)

| Year | Statistical discrepancy | Balance on | | | | | | |
| | | Balance on goods | Balance on services | Balance on goods and services | Balance on investment income | Balance on goods, services, and income | Unilateral transfers, net | Balance on current account |
|---|---|---|---|---|---|---|---|---|
| 1960 ..................... | -1 019 | 4 892 | -1 385 | 3 508 | 3 379 | 6 886 | -4 062 | 2 824 |
| 1961 ..................... | -989 | 5 571 | -1 376 | 4 195 | 3 755 | 7 949 | -4 127 | 3 822 |
| 1962 ..................... | -1 124 | 4 521 | -1 151 | 3 370 | 4 294 | 7 664 | -4 277 | 3 387 |
| 1963 ..................... | -360 | 5 224 | -1 014 | 4 210 | 4 596 | 8 806 | -4 392 | 4 414 |
| 1964 ..................... | -907 | 6 801 | -779 | 6 022 | 5 041 | 11 063 | -4 240 | 6 823 |
| 1965 ..................... | -457 | 4 951 | -287 | 4 664 | 5 350 | 10 014 | -4 583 | 5 431 |
| 1966 ..................... | 629 | 3 817 | -877 | 2 940 | 5 047 | 7 987 | -4 955 | 3 031 |
| 1967 ..................... | -205 | 3 800 | -1 196 | 2 604 | 5 274 | 7 878 | -5 294 | 2 583 |
| 1968 ..................... | 438 | 635 | -385 | 250 | 5 990 | 6 240 | -5 629 | 611 |
| 1969 ..................... | -1 516 | 607 | -516 | 91 | 6 044 | 6 135 | -5 735 | 399 |
| 1970 ..................... | -219 | 2 603 | -349 | 2 254 | 6 233 | 8 486 | -6 156 | 2 331 |
| 1971 ..................... | -9 779 | -2 260 | 957 | -1 303 | 7 272 | 5 969 | -7 402 | -1 433 |
| 1972 ..................... | -1 879 | -6 416 | 973 | -5 443 | 8 192 | 2 749 | -8 544 | -5 795 |
| 1973 ..................... | -2 654 | 911 | 989 | 1 900 | 12 153 | 14 053 | -6 913 | 7 140 |
| 1974 ..................... | -2 558 | -5 505 | 1 213 | -4 292 | 15 503 | 11 210 | -9 249 | 1 962 |
| 1975 ..................... | 4 417 | 8 903 | 3 501 | 12 404 | 12 787 | 25 191 | -7 075 | 18 116 |
| 1976 ..................... | 8 955 | -9 483 | 3 401 | -6 082 | 16 063 | 9 982 | -5 686 | 4 295 |
| 1977 ..................... | -4 099 | -31 091 | 3 845 | -27 246 | 18 137 | -9 109 | -5 226 | -14 335 |
| 1978 ..................... | 9 236 | -33 927 | 4 164 | -29 763 | 20 408 | -9 355 | -5 788 | -15 143 |
| 1979 ..................... | 24 349 | -27 568 | 3 003 | -24 565 | 30 873 | 6 308 | -6 593 | -285 |
| 1980 ..................... | 20 886 | -25 500 | 6 093 | -19 407 | 30 073 | 10 666 | -8 349 | 2 317 |
| 1981 ..................... | 21 792 | -28 023 | 11 852 | -16 172 | 32 903 | 16 732 | -11 702 | 5 030 |
| 1982 ..................... | 37 359 | -36 485 | 12 329 | -24 156 | 29 788 | 5 632 | -17 075 | -11 443 |
| 1983 ..................... | 16 779 | -67 102 | 9 335 | -57 767 | 31 500 | -26 267 | -17 718 | -43 985 |
| 1984 ..................... | 17 231 | -112 492 | 3 419 | -109 073 | 30 720 | -78 353 | -20 598 | -98 951 |
| 1985 ..................... | 17 494 | -122 173 | 294 | -121 880 | 20 592 | -101 288 | -22 700 | -123 987 |
| 1986 ..................... | 29 696 | -145 081 | 4 515 | -140 566 | 12 091 | -128 475 | -24 679 | -153 154 |
| 1987 ..................... | -7 753 | -159 557 | 6 244 | -153 313 | 9 209 | -144 105 | -23 909 | -168 013 |
| 1988 ..................... | -17 644 | -126 959 | 11 103 | -115 856 | 13 644 | -102 212 | -25 988 | -128 201 |
| 1989 ..................... | 48 494 | -115 245 | 23 048 | -92 197 | 15 020 | -77 177 | -26 963 | -104 139 |
| 1990 ..................... | 24 643 | -109 030 | 27 901 | -81 129 | 24 174 | -56 955 | -34 669 | -91 624 |
| 1991 ..................... | -47 378 | -74 068 | 43 137 | -30 931 | 21 517 | -9 414 | 5 032 | -4 383 |
| 1992 ..................... | -48 628 | -96 106 | 57 421 | -38 685 | 22 541 | -16 144 | -35 230 | -51 374 |
| 1993 ..................... | 999 | -132 609 | 60 670 | -71 939 | 23 948 | -47 991 | -38 142 | -86 133 |
| 1994 ..................... | -9 533 | -166 192 | 65 279 | -100 913 | 16 479 | -84 434 | -39 391 | -123 825 |
| 1995 ..................... | -22 742 | -173 729 | 73 838 | -99 891 | 19 275 | -80 616 | -34 638 | -115 254 |
| 1996 ..................... | -59 641 | -191 337 | 82 763 | -108 574 | 14 236 | -94 338 | -40 577 | -134 915 |
| 1997 ..................... | -99 724 | -197 954 | 87 748 | -110 206 | -5 318 | -115 524 | -39 691 | -155 215 |
| 1998 (p) ............... | -3 649 | -247 985 | 78 871 | -169 114 | -22 479 | -191 593 | -41 855 | -233 448 |

## Table A-4. Exchange rates, 1992–1997

(Annual average, except as noted; units per U.S. dollar.)

| | 1992 | 1993 | 1994 | 1995 | 1996 | 1997 |
|---|---|---|---|---|---|---|
| **Trade-weighted exchange indexes** | | | | | | |
| Broad (January 1997=100) | 76.29 | 84.45 | 90.42 | 92.52 | 97.43 | 104.47 |
| Major Currency (March 1973=100) | 85.45 | 87.73 | 86.25 | 81.39 | 85.23 | 91.85 |
| Other Important Trading Partners (January 1997=100) | 52.88 | 66.01 | 80.51 | 92.51 | 98.25 | 104.67 |
| G-10 (March 1973=100) | 86.64 | 93.17 | 91.32 | 84.25 | 87.34 | 96.38 |
| **National currencies** | | | | | | |
| Afghanistan, Afghanis | 50.60 | 50.60 | 425.10 | 833.33 | 2 333.33 | 3 000.00 |
| Albania, Leks | 75.03 | 102.06 | 94.62 | 92.70 | 104.50 | 148.93 |
| Algeria, Algerian Dinars | 21.84 | 23.35 | 35.06 | 47.66 | 54.75 | 57.71 |
| Argentina, Pesos | 0.99 | 1.00 | 1.00 | 1.00 | 1.00 | 1.00 |
| Armenia, Dram | ..... | 9.11 | 288.65 | 405.91 | 414.04 | 490.85 |
| Aruba, Aruban Florins | 1.79 | 1.79 | 1.79 | 1.79 | 1.79 | 1.79 |
| Australia, Australian Dollar | 1.36 | 1.47 | 1.37 | 1.35 | 1.28 | 1.34 |
| Austria, Schillings | 10.99 | 11.63 | 11.42 | 10.08 | 10.59 | 12.20 |
| Azerbaijan, Manats | 54.20 | 99.98 | 1 570.23 | 4 413.54 | 4 301.26 | 3 985.38 |
| Bahamas, Bahamian Dollar | 1.23 | 1.23 | 1.23 | 1.23 | 1.23 | 1.23 |
| Bahrain, Dinars | 0.38 | 0.38 | 0.38 | 0.38 | 0.38 | 0.38 |
| Bangladesh, Taka | 38.95 | 39.57 | 40.21 | 40.28 | 41.79 | 43.89 |
| Barbados, Barbados Dollar | 2.00 | 2.00 | 2.00 | 2.00 | 2.00 | 2.00 |
| Belarus, Rubels | ..... | ..... | ..... | ..... | ..... | 25 964.00 |
| Belgium, Francs | 32.15 | 34.60 | 33.46 | 29.48 | 30.96 | 35.77 |
| Belize, Belize Dollars | 2.00 | 2.00 | 2.00 | 2.00 | 2.00 | 2.00 |
| Bhutan, Ngultrum | 25.92 | 30.49 | 31.37 | 32.43 | 35.43 | 36.31 |
| Bolivia, Bolivianos | 3.90 | 4.27 | 4.62 | 4.80 | 5.08 | 5.25 |
| Botswana, Pula | 2.11 | 2.42 | 2.69 | 2.77 | 3.32 | 3.65 |
| Brazil, Reais | 0.00 | 0.03 | 0.64 | 0.92 | 1.01 | 1.08 |
| Bulgaria, Leva | 23.34 | 27.59 | 54.13 | 67.17 | 177.89 | 1 681.88 |
| Burundi, Burundi Francs | 208.30 | 242.78 | 252.66 | 249.76 | 302.75 | 352.35 |
| Cambodia, Riels | 1 266.60 | 2 689.00 | 2 545.20 | 2 450.80 | 2 624.10 | 2 946.30 |
| Canada, Canadian Dollar | 1.21 | 1.29 | 1.37 | 1.37 | 1.36 | 1.39 |
| Cape Verde, Escudos | 68.02 | 80.43 | 81.89 | 76.85 | 82.59 | 93.18 |
| CFA Francs | 264.69 | 283.16 | 555.20 | 499.15 | 511.55 | 583.67 |
| Chile, Pesos | 362.59 | 404.35 | 420.08 | 396.78 | 412.27 | 419.30 |
| China, People's Republic, Yuan | 5.52 | 5.76 | 8.62 | 8.35 | 8.31 | 8.29 |
| Colombia, Pesos | 759.28 | 863.07 | 844.84 | 912.83 | 1 036.69 | 1 140.96 |
| Comoros, Comorian Francs | 264.69 | 283.16 | 416.40 | 374.36 | 383.66 | 437.75 |
| Congo, Democratic Republic of, New Zaires | 0.22 | 2.51 | 1 194.00 | 7 024.00 | ..... | 125 180.00 |
| Costa Rica, Colones | 134.51 | 142.17 | 157.07 | 179.73 | 207.69 | 232.60 |
| Croatia, Kuna | ..... | 3.58 | 6.00 | 5.23 | 5.43 | 6.10 |
| Cyprus, Cyprus Pounds | 0.45 | 0.50 | 0.49 | 0.45 | 0.47 | 0.51 |
| Czech Republic, Koruny | ..... | 29.15 | 28.79 | 26.54 | 27.15 | 31.70 |
| Denmark, Kroner | 6.04 | 6.48 | 6.36 | 5.60 | 5.80 | 6.60 |
| Djibouti, Djibouti Francs | 177.72 | 177.72 | 177.72 | 177.72 | 177.72 | 177.72 |
| Dominican Republic, Pesos | 12.77 | 12.68 | 13.16 | 13.60 | 13.78 | 14.27 |
| East Caribbean Dollars | 2.70 | 2.70 | 2.70 | 2.70 | 2.70 | 2.70 |
| Ecuador, Sucres | 1 533.96 | 1 919.10 | 2 196.73 | 2 564.49 | 3 189.50 | 3 998.30 |
| Egypt, Egyptian Pounds | 3.32 | 3.35 | 3.39 | 3.39 | 3.39 | 3.39 |
| El Salvador, Colones | 9.17 | 8.67 | 8.75 | 8.76 | 8.76 | 8.76 |
| Estonia, Krooni | ..... | 13.22 | 12.99 | 11.47 | 12.03 | 13.88 |
| Ethiopia, Birr | 2.80 | 5.00 | 5.47 | 6.16 | 6.35 | 6.71 |
| Fiji, Fiji Dollars | 1.50 | 1.54 | 1.46 | 1.41 | 1.40 | 1.44 |
| Finland, Markkaa | 4.48 | 5.71 | 5.22 | 4.37 | 4.59 | 5.19 |
| France, Francs | 5.29 | 5.66 | 5.55 | 4.99 | 5.12 | 5.84 |
| Gambia, Dalasis | 8.89 | 9.13 | 9.58 | 9.55 | 9.79 | 10.20 |
| Germany, Deutsche Mark | 1.56 | 1.65 | 1.62 | 1.43 | 1.51 | 1.73 |
| Ghana, Cedis | 437.09 | 649.06 | 956.71 | 1 200.43 | 1 637.23 | 2 050.17 |

## Table A-4. Exchange rates, 1992–1997—*Continued*

(Annual average, except as noted; units per U.S. dollar.)

| | 1992 | 1993 | 1994 | 1995 | 1996 | 1997 |
|---|---|---|---|---|---|---|
| Greece, Drachmas | 190.62 | 229.25 | 242.60 | 231.66 | 240.71 | 273.06 |
| Guatemala, Quetzales | 5.17 | 5.64 | 5.75 | 5.81 | 6.05 | 6.07 |
| Guinea, Francs | 902.00 | 955.49 | 976.64 | 991.41 | 1 004.00 | 1 095.30 |
| Guinea-Bissau, Francs | 106.68 | 155.10 | 198.34 | 278.04 | 405.75 | 583.67 |
| Guyana, Guyana Dollars | 125.00 | 126.73 | 138.29 | 141.99 | 140.40 | 142.40 |
| Haiti, Gourdes | 9.80 | 12.82 | 15.04 | 15.11 | 15.70 | 16.66 |
| Honduras, Lempiras | 5.50 | 6.47 | 8.41 | 9.71 | 11.71 | 13.00 |
| Hong Kong, Hong Kong Dollar | 7.74 | 7.74 | 7.73 | 7.74 | 7.73 | 7.74 |
| Hungary, Forint | 78.99 | 91.93 | 105.16 | 125.68 | 152.65 | 186.79 |
| Iceland, Kronur | 57.55 | 67.60 | 69.94 | 64.69 | 66.50 | 70.90 |
| India, Rupees | 25.92 | 30.49 | 31.37 | 32.43 | 35.43 | 36.31 |
| Indonesia, Rupiah | 2 029.92 | 2 087.10 | 2 160.75 | 2 248.61 | 2 342.30 | 2 909.40 |
| Iran, Rials | 65.55 | 1 267.77 | 1 748.75 | 1 748.00 | 1 750.76 | 1 752.92 |
| Iraq, Dinars | 0.31 | 0.31 | 0.31 | 0.31 | 0.31 | 0.31 |
| Ireland, Irish Pounds | 0.59 | 0.68 | 0.67 | 0.62 | 0.63 | 0.66 |
| Israel, New Sheqalim | 2.46 | 2.83 | 3.01 | 3.01 | 3.19 | 3.45 |
| Italy, Lire | 1 232.41 | 1 573.67 | 1 612.44 | 1 629.62 | 1 542.90 | 1 703.10 |
| Jamaica, Jamaica Dollars | 22.96 | 24.95 | 33.09 | 35.14 | 37.12 | 35.40 |
| Japan, Yen | 126.65 | 111.20 | 102.21 | 94.06 | 108.78 | 120.99 |
| Jordan, Dinars | 0.68 | 0.69 | 0.70 | 0.70 | 0.71 | 0.71 |
| Kazakstan, Tenge | ..... | ..... | 35.54 | 60.95 | 67.30 | 75.44 |
| Kenya, Kenya Shillings | 32.22 | 58.00 | 56.05 | 51.43 | 57.12 | 58.73 |
| Korea, Won | 780.65 | 802.67 | 803.45 | 771.27 | 804.45 | 951.29 |
| Kuwait, Dinars | 0.29 | 0.30 | 0.30 | 0.30 | 0.30 | 0.30 |
| Kyrgyz Republic, Soms | ..... | ..... | 10.84 | 10.82 | 12.81 | 17.36 |
| Lao People's Democratic Republic, Kip | 716.08 | 716.25 | 717.67 | 804.69 | 921.14 | 1 256.73 |
| Latvia, Lats | 0.74 | 0.68 | 0.56 | 0.53 | 0.55 | 0.58 |
| Lebanon, Lebanese Pounds | 1 712.79 | 1 741.36 | 1 680.07 | 1 621.41 | 1 571.40 | 1 539.50 |
| Lesotho, Loti | 2.85 | 3.27 | 3.55 | 3.63 | 4.30 | 4.61 |
| Liberia, Liberian Dollar | 1.00 | 1.00 | 1.00 | 1.00 | 1.00 | 1.00 |
| Libya, Libyan Dinars | 0.28 | 0.31 | 0.32 | 0.35 | 0.37 | 0.39 |
| Lithuania, Litai | 1.77 | 4.34 | 3.98 | 4.00 | 4.00 | 4.00 |
| Luxembourg, Francs | 32.15 | 34.60 | 33.46 | 29.48 | 30.96 | 35.77 |
| Macedonia, Denar | ..... | ..... | 43.26 | 37.88 | 39.98 | 50.00 |
| Madagascar, Malagasy Francs | 1 863.97 | 1 913.78 | 3 067.34 | 4 265.63 | 4 061.30 | 5 090.90 |
| Malawi, Kwacha | 3.60 | 4.40 | 8.74 | 15.28 | 15.31 | 16.81 |
| Malaysia, Ringgit | 2.55 | 2.57 | 2.62 | 2.50 | 2.52 | 2.81 |
| Maldives, Rufiyaa | 10.57 | 10.96 | 11.59 | 11.77 | 11.77 | 11.77 |
| Malta, Maltese Liri | 0.32 | 0.38 | 0.38 | 0.35 | 0.35 | 0.36 |
| Mauritania, Ouguiyas | 87.03 | 120.81 | 123.58 | 129.77 | 137.22 | 151.85 |
| Mauritius, Rupees | 15.56 | 17.65 | 17.96 | 17.39 | 17.95 | 20.56 |
| Mexico, New Pesos | 3.09 | 3.12 | 3.38 | 6.42 | 7.60 | 7.91 |
| Moldova, Lei | ..... | ..... | ..... | 4.50 | 4.61 | 4.62 |
| Mongolia, Tugriks | 42.56 | ..... | 412.72 | 448.61 | 548.40 | 789.99 |
| Morocco, Dirhams | 8.54 | 9.30 | 9.20 | 8.54 | 8.72 | 9.53 |
| Mozambique, Meticais | 2 516.50 | 3 874.20 | 6 038.60 | 9 024.30 | 11 293.80 | 11 543.60 |
| Myanmar, Kyats | 6.10 | 6.16 | 5.98 | 5.67 | 5.92 | 6.24 |
| Namibia, Namibia Dollars | 2.85 | 3.27 | 3.55 | 3.63 | 4.30 | 4.61 |
| Nepal, Rupees | 42.72 | 48.61 | 49.40 | 51.89 | 56.69 | 58.01 |
| Netherlands Antilles, Guilders | 1.79 | 1.79 | 1.79 | 1.79 | 1.79 | 1.79 |
| Netherlands, Guilders | 1.76 | 1.86 | 1.82 | 1.61 | 1.69 | 1.95 |
| New Zealand, New Zealand Dollar | 1.86 | 1.85 | 1.69 | 1.52 | 1.45 | 1.51 |
| Nicaragua, Cordobas | 5.00 | 5.62 | 6.72 | 7.55 | 8.44 | 9.45 |
| Nigeria, Naira | 17.30 | 22.07 | 22.00 | 21.90 | 21.88 | 21.89 |
| Norway, Kroner | 6.21 | 7.09 | 7.06 | 6.34 | 6.45 | 7.07 |

## Table A-4.  Exchange rates, 1992–1997—*Continued*

(Annual average, except as noted; units per U.S. dollar.)

| | 1992 | 1993 | 1994 | 1995 | 1996 | 1997 |
|---|---|---|---|---|---|---|
| Oman, Rials Omani | 0.38 | 0.39 | 0.39 | 0.39 | 0.39 | 0.39 |
| Pakistan, Rupees | 25.08 | 28.11 | 30.57 | 31.64 | 36.08 | 41.11 |
| Panama, Balboas | 1.00 | 1.00 | 1.00 | 1.00 | 1.00 | 1.00 |
| Papua New Guinea, Kina | 0.96 | 0.98 | 1.01 | 1.28 | 1.32 | 1.43 |
| Paraguay, Guaranies | 1 500.26 | 1 744.35 | 1 911.54 | 1 970.40 | 2 062.80 | 2 191.00 |
| Peru, Nuevos Soles | 1.25 | 1.99 | 2.20 | 2.25 | 2.45 | 2.66 |
| Philippines, Pesos | 25.51 | 27.12 | 26.42 | 25.71 | 26.22 | 29.47 |
| Poland, Zlotys | 1.36 | 1.81 | 2.27 | 2.43 | 2.70 | 3.28 |
| Portugal, Escudos | 135.00 | 160.80 | 165.99 | 151.11 | 154.24 | 175.31 |
| Qatar, Riyals | 3.64 | 3.64 | 3.64 | 3.64 | 3.64 | 3.64 |
| Romania, Lei | 307.95 | 760.05 | 1 655.10 | 2 033.30 | 3 084.22 | 7 167.94 |
| Russia, Rubles | ..... | 0.99 | 2.19 | 4.56 | 5.12 | 5.78 |
| Rwanda, Rwanda Francs | 133.35 | 144.31 | ..... | 262.20 | 306.82 | 301.53 |
| Samoa, Tala | 2.47 | 2.57 | 2.53 | 2.48 | 2.46 | 2.56 |
| Sao Tome and Principe, Dobras | 321.34 | 429.85 | 732.63 | 1 420.30 | 2 203.20 | 4 552.50 |
| Saudi Arabia, Riyals | 3.75 | 3.75 | 3.75 | 3.75 | 3.75 | 3.75 |
| Seychelles, Rupees | 5.12 | 5.18 | 5.06 | 4.76 | 4.97 | 5.03 |
| Sierra Leone, Leones | 499.44 | 567.46 | 586.74 | 755.22 | 920.73 | 967.72 |
| Singapore, Singapore Dollar | 1.63 | 1.62 | 1.53 | 1.42 | 1.41 | 1.49 |
| Slovak Republic, Koruny | ..... | 30.77 | 32.05 | 29.71 | 30.65 | 33.62 |
| Slovenia, Tolars | 81.29 | 113.24 | 128.81 | 118.52 | 135.36 | 159.69 |
| Solomon Islands, Solomon Island Dollar | 2.93 | 3.19 | 3.29 | 3.41 | 3.57 | 3.72 |
| South Africa, Rand | 2.85 | 3.27 | 3.55 | 3.63 | 4.30 | 4.61 |
| Spain, Pesetas | 102.38 | 127.26 | 133.96 | 124.69 | 126.66 | 146.41 |
| Sri Lanka, Rupees | 43.83 | 48.32 | 49.42 | 51.25 | 55.27 | 59.00 |
| Sudan, Sudanese Pounds | 97.43 | 159.31 | 289.61 | 580.87 | 1 250.79 | 1 575.74 |
| Suriname, Guilders | 1.79 | 1.79 | 134.12 | 442.23 | 401.26 | 401.00 |
| Swaziland, Langeni | 2.85 | 3.27 | 3.55 | 3.63 | 4.27 | 4.60 |
| Sweden, Kronor | 5.82 | 7.78 | 7.72 | 7.13 | 6.71 | 7.64 |
| Switzerland, Swiss Francs | 1.41 | 1.48 | 1.37 | 1.18 | 1.24 | 1.45 |
| Syrian Arab Republic, Syrian Pounds | 11.23 | 11.23 | 11.23 | 11.23 | 11.23 | 11.23 |
| Tajikistan, Tajik Rubles | 222.20 | 932.20 | 2 204.30 | ..... | ..... | ..... |
| Tanzania, Tanzania Shilli | 297.71 | 405.27 | 509.63 | 574.76 | 579.98 | 612.12 |
| Thailand, Baht | 25.40 | 25.32 | 25.15 | 24.91 | 25.34 | 31.36 |
| Tonga, Pa'anga | 1.35 | 1.38 | 1.32 | 1.27 | 1.23 | 1.26 |
| Trinidad and Tobago, TT Dollars | 4.25 | 5.35 | 5.93 | 5.95 | 6.01 | 6.25 |
| Tunisia, Dinars | 0.88 | 1.00 | 1.01 | 0.95 | 0.97 | 1.11 |
| Turkey, Liras | 6 872.40 | 10 984.60 | 29 608.70 | 45 845.10 | 81 405.00 | 151 865.00 |
| Uganda, Uganda Shilling | 1 133.83 | 1 195.02 | 979.45 | 968.92 | 1 046.10 | 10 830.00 |
| Ukraine, Hryvnias | ..... | 0.05 | 0.33 | 1.47 | 1.83 | 1.86 |
| United Arab Emirates, Dirhams | 3.67 | 3.67 | 3.67 | 3.67 | 3.67 | 3.67 |
| United Kingdom, Pounds Sterling | 0.57 | 0.67 | 0.65 | 0.63 | 0.64 | 0.64 |
| Uruguay, Pesos | 3.03 | 3.95 | 5.05 | 6.35 | 7.97 | 9.45 |
| Vanuatu, Vatu | 113.39 | 121.58 | 116.41 | 112.11 | 111.72 | 115.87 |
| Venezuela, Bolivares | 68.38 | 90.83 | 148.50 | 176.84 | 417.33 | 488.64 |
| Yemen, Republic of, Rials | 12.01 | 12.01 | 12.01 | 40.84 | 94.16 | 129.16 |
| Zambia, Kwacha | 172.21 | 452.76 | 669.37 | 857.23 | 1 203.71 | 1 333.81 |
| Zimbabwe, Zimbabwe Dollar | 5.10 | 6.48 | 8.15 | 8.67 | 9.92 | 11.89 |

# PART B.  U.S. Foreign Trade in Services

**U.S. Trade in Services, 1997**
(billions of dollars)

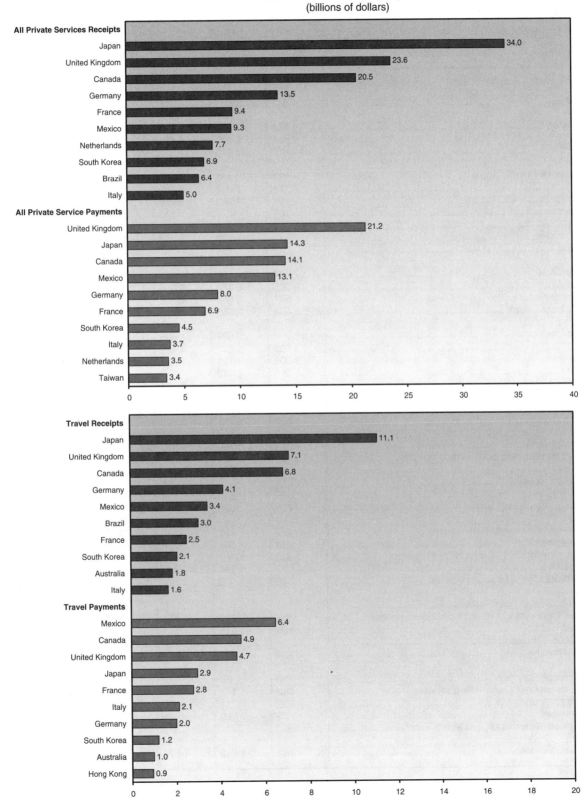

## Table B-1.　U.S. Private Service Transactions by Type, 1986–1997

(Millions of dollars.)

| Type of service | Exports | | | | | |
|---|---|---|---|---|---|---|
| | 1986 | 1987 | 1988 | 1989 | 1990 | 1991 |
| **TOTAL PRIVATE SERVICES** | 77 205 | 86 962 | 101 120 | 118 081 | 137 322 | 152 510 |
| **Travel** | 20 385 | 23 563 | 29 434 | 36 205 | 43 007 | 48 385 |
| Overseas | 15 650 | 18 044 | 22 314 | 26 939 | 30 806 | 34 518 |
| Canada | 2 701 | 3 309 | 4 150 | 5 340 | 7 093 | 8 500 |
| Mexico | 2 034 | 2 210 | 2 970 | 3 926 | 5 108 | 5 367 |
| **Passenger Fares** | 5 582 | 7 003 | 8 976 | 10 657 | 15 298 | 15 854 |
| **Other Transportation** | 15 438 | 17 027 | 19 311 | 20 526 | 22 042 | 22 631 |
| Freight | 4 864 | 5 452 | 6 491 | 7 209 | 8 379 | 8 651 |
| Port services | 10 574 | 11 575 | 12 820 | 13 318 | 13 662 | 13 979 |
| **Royalties and License Fees** | 8 113 | 10 183 | 12 146 | 13 818 | 16 634 | 17 819 |
| Affiliated | 6 174 | 7 897 | 9 501 | 10 961 | 13 250 | 14 106 |
| U.S. parents transactions | 5 994 | 7 668 | 9 238 | 10 612 | 12 867 | 13 523 |
| U.S. affiliates transactions | 180 | 229 | 263 | 349 | 383 | 583 |
| Unaffiliated | 1 939 | 2 286 | 2 646 | 2 857 | 3 384 | 3 712 |
| Industrial processes | ..... | 1 593 | 1 863 | 1 947 | 2 333 | 2 435 |
| Other | ..... | 694 | 782 | 910 | 1 052 | 1 277 |
| **Other Private Services** | 27 687 | 29 186 | 31 253 | 36 875 | 40 341 | 47 821 |
| Affiliated services | 8 385 | 8 494 | 9 568 | 12 296 | 13 622 | 14 539 |
| U.S. parents transactions | 5 577 | 5 658 | 6 808 | 9 117 | 9 532 | 9 976 |
| U.S. affiliates transactions | 2 808 | 2 836 | 2 760 | 3 179 | 4 090 | 4 563 |
| Unaffiliated services | 19 302 | 20 692 | 21 685 | 24 580 | 26 719 | 33 282 |
| Education | 3 495 | 3 821 | 4 142 | 4 575 | 5 126 | 5 679 |
| Financial services | 3 301 | 3 731 | 3 831 | 5 036 | 4 417 | 5 012 |
| Insurance, net | 1 385 | 1 573 | 847 | 103 | 230 | 491 |
| Premiums | 3 424 | 3 615 | 3 534 | 3 117 | 3 388 | 3 365 |
| Losses | 2 039 | 2 042 | 2 687 | 3 015 | 3 158 | 2 874 |
| Telecommunications | 1 827 | 2 111 | 2 196 | 2 519 | 2 735 | 3 291 |
| Business, professional, and technical services | 4 813 | 4 765 | 5 970 | 6 823 | 7 752 | 12 045 |
| Accounting, auditing, and bookkeeping services | 21 | 27 | 37 | 124 | 119 | 168 |
| Advertising | 94 | 109 | 145 | 145 | 130 | 274 |
| Agricultural services | 4 | 7 | 4 | 3 | 4 | 56 |
| Computer and data processing services | 985 | 649 | 1 198 | 978 | 1 031 | 1 738 |
| Construction, engineering, architectural, and mining services ... | 759 | 668 | 790 | 939 | 867 | 1 478 |
| Data base and other information services | 124 | 133 | 196 | 205 | 283 | 442 |
| Industrial engineering | 98 | 304 | 278 | 219 | 473 | 363 |
| Installation, maintenance, and repair of equipment | 1 033 | 1 087 | 1 276 | 1 717 | 2 031 | 2 574 |
| Legal services | 97 | 147 | 272 | 397 | 451 | 1 309 |
| Mailing, reproduction, and commercial art | 0 | 22 | 29 | 9 | 8 | 18 |
| Management of health care facilities | 1 | 0 | 0 | 0 | 0 | 22 |
| Management, consulting, and public relations services | 306 | 327 | 344 | 300 | 354 | 870 |
| Medical services | 490 | 516 | 541 | 588 | 630 | 672 |
| Miscellaneous disbursements | ..... | ..... | ..... | ..... | ..... | 89 |
| Operational leasing | 384 | 484 | 544 | 671 | 801 | 796 |
| Personnel supply services | 0 | 38 | 0 | 2 | 1 | 160 |
| Research, development, and testing services | 282 | 177 | 231 | 375 | 384 | 602 |
| Sports and performing arts | 32 | 11 | 0 | 43 | 47 | 71 |
| Training services | 73 | 60 | 54 | 109 | 138 | 345 |
| Other business, professional, and technical services | ..... | ..... | ..... | ..... | ..... | ..... |
| Other unaffiliated services | 4 482 | 4 692 | 4 699 | 5 524 | 6 459 | 6 765 |

**Table B-1.  U.S. Private Service Transactions by Type, 1986–1997** —*Continued*

(Millions of dollars.)

| Type of service | Exports—*Continued* | | | | | |
| --- | --- | --- | --- | --- | --- | --- |
| | 1992 | 1993 | 1994 | 1995 | 1996 | 1997 |
| **TOTAL PRIVATE SERVICES** .................................................. | 163 754 | 172 031 | 187 760 | 204 229 | 224 213 | 239 215 |
| **Travel** .......................................................................... | 54 742 | 57 875 | 58 417 | 63 395 | 69 751 | 73 268 |
| Overseas ..................................................................... | 40 864 | 45 298 | 47 299 | 54 331 | 59 905 | 63 014 |
| Canada ........................................................................ | 8 182 | 7 458 | 6 252 | 6 207 | 6 842 | 6 824 |
| Mexico ......................................................................... | 5 696 | 5 119 | 4 866 | 2 857 | 3 004 | 3 430 |
| **Passenger Fares** ....................................................... | 16 618 | 16 528 | 16 997 | 18 909 | 20 413 | 20 895 |
| **Other Transportation** ................................................ | 21 531 | 21 958 | 23 754 | 26 081 | 26 074 | 26 911 |
| Freight .......................................................................... | 8 441 | 8 594 | 9 575 | 11 273 | 11 146 | 11 773 |
| Port services ............................................................... | 13 088 | 13 364 | 14 180 | 14 809 | 14 929 | 15 137 |
| **Royalties and License Fees** .................................... | 20 841 | 21 695 | 26 712 | 30 289 | 32 823 | 33 676 |
| Affiliated ...................................................................... | 15 658 | 15 688 | 20 275 | 22 859 | 24 710 | 25 515 |
| U.S. parents transactions ...................................... | 14 925 | 14 936 | 19 250 | 21 399 | 22 781 | 23 457 |
| U.S. affiliates transactions .................................... | 733 | 752 | 1 025 | 1 460 | 1 929 | 2 058 |
| Unaffiliated .................................................................. | 5 183 | 6 007 | 6 437 | 7 430 | 8 113 | 8 161 |
| Industrial processes ............................................... | 2 525 | 2 820 | 3 026 | 3 513 | 3 488 | 3 272 |
| Other ......................................................................... | 2 657 | 3 187 | 3 411 | 3 917 | 4 625 | 4 889 |
| **Other Private Services** ............................................. | 50 022 | 53 975 | 61 880 | 65 555 | 75 152 | 84 465 |
| Affiliated services ...................................................... | 16 823 | 16 813 | 20 043 | 20 791 | 23 779 | 26 336 |
| U.S. parents transactions ...................................... | 10 479 | 10 902 | 13 530 | 13 341 | 14 772 | 16 164 |
| U.S. affiliates transactions .................................... | 6 344 | 5 911 | 6 513 | 7 450 | 9 007 | 10 172 |
| Unaffiliated services ................................................. | 33 199 | 37 162 | 41 838 | 44 764 | 51 374 | 58 128 |
| Education .................................................................. | 6 186 | 6 738 | 7 174 | 7 515 | 7 888 | 8 278 |
| Financial services .................................................... | 4 034 | 4 999 | 5 763 | 7 029 | 8 382 | 11 064 |
| Insurance, net .......................................................... | 682 | 1 020 | 1 676 | 1 296 | 1 971 | 2 391 |
| Premiums .............................................................. | 3 852 | 3 981 | 4 921 | 5 491 | 5 978 | 5 952 |
| Losses .................................................................. | 3 170 | 2 961 | 3 245 | 4 195 | 4 007 | 3 561 |
| Telecommunications ................................................ | 2 885 | 2 785 | 2 865 | 3 228 | 3 270 | 3 771 |
| Business, professional, and technical services ........ | 11 722 | 12 958 | 15 330 | 16 064 | 19 678 | 21 304 |
| Accounting, auditing, and bookkeeping services ...... | 164 | 164 | 132 | 181 | 253 | 255 |
| Advertising ........................................................... | 315 | 338 | 487 | 425 | 551 | 581 |
| Agricultural services ............................................. | 54 | 47 | 30 | 30 | 20 | 25 |
| Computer and data processing services ................ | 776 | 986 | 1 306 | 1 340 | 1 634 | 1 616 |
| Construction, engineering, architectural, and mining services ... | 1 935 | 2 407 | 2 474 | 2 550 | 3 560 | 4 084 |
| Data base and other information services ............. | 641 | 694 | 1 026 | 1 078 | 1 164 | 1 431 |
| Industrial engineering .......................................... | 212 | 268 | 575 | 726 | 915 | 1 098 |
| Installation, maintenance, and repair of equipment ... | 2 744 | 2 978 | 3 497 | 3 218 | 3 703 | 3 468 |
| Legal services ...................................................... | 1 358 | 1 442 | 1 617 | 1 667 | 1 973 | 2 085 |
| Mailing, reproduction, and commercial art ............ | 14 | 12 | 10 | 4 | 64 | 29 |
| Management of health care facilities .................... | 22 | 19 | 18 | 18 | 17 | 33 |
| Management, consulting, and public relations services ... | 728 | 826 | 1 134 | 1 489 | 1 680 | 2 139 |
| Medical services .................................................. | 708 | 750 | 794 | 841 | 872 | 888 |
| Miscellaneous disbursements .............................. | 97 | 222 | 222 | 251 | 338 | 362 |
| Operational leasing ............................................. | 854 | 834 | 925 | 978 | 1 281 | 1 422 |
| Personnel supply services ................................... | 127 | 113 | 85 | 95 | 101 | 63 |
| Research, development, and testing services ........ | 611 | 464 | 522 | 638 | 688 | 862 |
| Sports and performing arts .................................. | 43 | 77 | 86 | 116 | 152 | 174 |
| Training services .................................................. | 320 | 319 | 388 | 421 | 403 | 384 |
| Other business, professional, and technical services ... | ..... | ..... | ..... | ..... | 308 | 305 |
| Other unaffiliated services .................................... | 7 690 | 8 663 | 9 032 | 9 633 | 10 185 | 11 321 |

## Table B-1.  U.S. Private Service Transactions by Type, 1986–1997 —Continued

(Millions of dollars.)

| Type of service | Imports | | | | | |
|---|---|---|---|---|---|---|
| | 1986 | 1987 | 1988 | 1989 | 1990 | 1991 |
| **TOTAL PRIVATE SERVICES** | 66 419 | 75 507 | 82 441 | 87 001 | 100 571 | 102 672 |
| **Travel** | 25 913 | 29 310 | 32 114 | 33 416 | 37 349 | 35 322 |
| Overseas | 20 311 | 23 313 | 25 260 | 25 746 | 28 929 | 26 506 |
| Canada | 3 034 | 2 939 | 3 232 | 3 394 | 3 541 | 3 705 |
| Mexico | 2 568 | 3 058 | 3 622 | 4 276 | 4 879 | 5 111 |
| **Passenger Fares** | 6 505 | 7 283 | 7 729 | 8 249 | 10 531 | 10 012 |
| **Other Transportation** | 17 766 | 19 010 | 20 891 | 22 172 | 24 966 | 24 975 |
| Freight | 12 512 | 12 618 | 13 792 | 13 997 | 15 046 | 14 554 |
| Port services | 5 254 | 6 392 | 7 099 | 8 176 | 9 920 | 10 421 |
| **Royalties and License Fees** | 1 401 | 1 857 | 2 601 | 2 528 | 3 135 | 4 035 |
| Affiliated | 917 | 1 309 | 1 426 | 1 703 | 2 206 | 2 955 |
| U.S. parents transactions | 118 | 168 | 141 | 71 | 239 | 166 |
| U.S. affiliates transactions | 799 | 1 141 | 1 285 | 1 632 | 1 967 | 2 789 |
| Unaffiliated | 484 | 547 | 1 175 | 824 | 929 | 1 080 |
| Industrial processes | ..... | 435 | 488 | 568 | 666 | 796 |
| Other | ..... | 112 | 689 | 256 | 265 | 283 |
| **Other Private Services** | 14 834 | 18 047 | 19 106 | 20 636 | 24 590 | 28 328 |
| Affiliated services | 3 915 | 5 357 | 6 043 | 7 911 | 9 118 | 9 732 |
| U.S. parents transactions | 2 391 | 3 050 | 3 461 | 4 783 | 5 334 | 5 260 |
| U.S. affiliates transactions | 1 524 | 2 307 | 2 582 | 3 128 | 3 784 | 4 472 |
| Unaffiliated services | 10 919 | 12 691 | 13 063 | 12 725 | 15 472 | 18 596 |
| Education | 433 | 452 | 539 | 586 | 658 | 698 |
| Financial services | 1 769 | 2 077 | 1 656 | 2 056 | 2 475 | 2 669 |
| Insurance, net | 2 200 | 3 241 | 2 628 | 823 | 1 910 | 2 467 |
| Premiums | 7 217 | 8 538 | 8 954 | 9 909 | 10 222 | 11 207 |
| Losses | 5 017 | 5 297 | 6 326 | 9 086 | 8 312 | 8 740 |
| Telecommunications | 3 253 | 3 736 | 4 576 | 5 172 | 5 583 | 6 608 |
| Business, professional, and technical services | 1 303 | 1 367 | 1 926 | 2 059 | 2 093 | 3 015 |
| Accounting, auditing, and bookkeeping services | 29 | 37 | 31 | 22 | 57 | 89 |
| Advertising | 77 | 128 | 188 | 228 | 243 | 301 |
| Agricultural services | 5 | 7 | 4 | 2 | 0 | 22 |
| Computer and data processing services | 32 | 74 | 107 | 46 | 44 | 116 |
| Construction, engineering, architectural, and mining services ... | 301 | 163 | 307 | 443 | 170 | 315 |
| Data base and other information services | 23 | 25 | 39 | 31 | 54 | 51 |
| Industrial engineering | 75 | 103 | 133 | 53 | 74 | 30 |
| Installation, maintenance, and repair of equipment | 467 | 496 | 616 | 704 | 714 | 538 |
| Legal services | 40 | 56 | 98 | 81 | 111 | 244 |
| Mailing, reproduction, and commercial art | 12 | 9 | 9 | 8 | 8 | 38 |
| Management of health care facilities | 0 | 0 | 2 | 0 | 0 | 13 |
| Management, consulting, and public relations services | 60 | 67 | 73 | 143 | 135 | 271 |
| Medical services | ..... | ..... | ..... | ..... | ..... | ..... |
| Miscellaneous disbursements | ..... | ..... | ..... | ..... | ..... | 342 |
| Operational leasing | 50 | 48 | 78 | 88 | 202 | 229 |
| Personnel supply services | 25 | 7 | 10 | 10 | 5 | 15 |
| Research, development, and testing services | 76 | 114 | 182 | 133 | 210 | 241 |
| Sports and performing arts | 21 | 25 | 40 | 54 | 48 | 84 |
| Training services | 7 | 9 | 10 | 13 | 17 | 77 |
| Other business, professional, and technical services | ..... | ..... | ..... | ..... | ..... | ..... |
| Other unaffiliated services | 1 961 | 1 818 | 1 737 | 2 028 | 2 753 | 3 139 |

## Table B-1.  U.S. Private Service Transactions by Type, 1986–1997 —*Continued*

(Millions of dollars.)

| Type of service | Imports—*Continued* | | | | | |
| --- | --- | --- | --- | --- | --- | --- |
| | 1992 | 1993 | 1994 | 1995 | 1996 | 1997 |
| **TOTAL PRIVATE SERVICES** | 103 464 | 111 259 | 123 303 | 133 355 | 142 261 | 156 236 |
| **Travel** | 38 552 | 40 713 | 43 782 | 44 916 | 48 048 | 51 220 |
| Overseas | 29 838 | 31 862 | 34 534 | 35 281 | 37 406 | 39 876 |
| Canada | 3 554 | 3 692 | 3 914 | 4 319 | 4 670 | 4 901 |
| Mexico | 5 160 | 5 159 | 5 334 | 5 316 | 5 972 | 6 443 |
| **Passenger Fares** | 10 603 | 11 410 | 13 062 | 14 663 | 15 818 | 18 235 |
| **Other Transportation** | 23 767 | 24 524 | 26 019 | 27 034 | 27 403 | 28 949 |
| Freight | 13 571 | 14 518 | 16 006 | 16 455 | 16 539 | 17 644 |
| Port services | 10 197 | 10 005 | 10 013 | 10 579 | 10 864 | 11 305 |
| **Royalties and License Fees** | 5 161 | 5 032 | 5 852 | 6 919 | 7 854 | 9 411 |
| Affiliated | 3 396 | 3 386 | 3 934 | 5 257 | 5 506 | 7 087 |
| U.S. parents transactions | 189 | 234 | 420 | 583 | 766 | 955 |
| U.S. affiliates transactions | 3 207 | 3 152 | 3 514 | 4 674 | 4 740 | 6 132 |
| Unaffiliated | 1 766 | 1 646 | 1 919 | 1 663 | 2 347 | 2 324 |
| Industrial processes | 818 | 1 054 | 1 034 | 948 | 1 233 | 1 265 |
| Other | 948 | 592 | 884 | 714 | 1 115 | 1 060 |
| **Other Private Services** | 25 381 | 29 580 | 34 588 | 39 823 | 43 138 | 48 421 |
| Affiliated services | 9 640 | 10 677 | 12 924 | 14 215 | 16 668 | 18 324 |
| U.S. parents transactions | 5 355 | 5 721 | 7 012 | 7 443 | 8 089 | 9 407 |
| U.S. affiliates transactions | 4 285 | 4 956 | 5 912 | 6 772 | 8 579 | 8 917 |
| Unaffiliated services | 15 740 | 18 903 | 21 663 | 25 607 | 26 469 | 30 098 |
| Education | 767 | 857 | 972 | 1 125 | 1 247 | 1 347 |
| Financial services | 986 | 1 371 | 1 654 | 2 472 | 2 995 | 3 906 |
| Insurance, net | 1 324 | 3 095 | 4 034 | 5 360 | 3 773 | 5 208 |
| Premiums | 11 738 | 12 093 | 14 075 | 15 284 | 14 652 | 15 036 |
| Losses | 10 414 | 8 998 | 10 041 | 9 925 | 10 879 | 9 828 |
| Telecommunications | 6 052 | 6 365 | 6 928 | 7 305 | 8 304 | 8 113 |
| Business, professional, and technical services | 3 102 | 3 504 | 3 869 | 4 822 | 5 550 | 6 571 |
| Accounting, auditing, and bookkeeping services | 104 | 103 | 130 | 170 | 229 | 335 |
| Advertising | 450 | 646 | 728 | 833 | 976 | 863 |
| Agricultural services | 21 | 18 | 14 | 17 | 9 | 13 |
| Computer and data processing services | 71 | 101 | 83 | 126 | 139 | 270 |
| Construction, engineering, architectural, and mining services ... | 261 | 319 | 280 | 345 | 489 | 346 |
| Data base and other information services | 72 | 110 | 141 | 160 | 148 | 164 |
| Industrial engineering | 112 | 142 | 100 | 160 | 202 | 246 |
| Installation, maintenance, and repair of equipment | 191 | 175 | 164 | 160 | 247 | 355 |
| Legal services | 311 | 321 | 383 | 469 | 580 | 568 |
| Mailing, reproduction, and commercial art | 37 | 33 | 17 | 22 | 39 | 53 |
| Management of health care facilities | 13 | 11 | 12 | 16 | 23 | 43 |
| Management, consulting, and public relations services | 243 | 287 | 321 | 465 | 593 | 782 |
| Medical services | ..... | ..... | ..... | ..... | ..... | ..... |
| Miscellaneous disbursements | 395 | 371 | 538 | 843 | 813 | 1 075 |
| Operational leasing | 337 | 356 | 401 | 407 | 343 | 425 |
| Personnel supply services | 14 | 13 | 3 | 4 | 29 | 42 |
| Research, development, and testing services | 225 | 239 | 294 | 364 | 343 | 473 |
| Sports and performing arts | 145 | 156 | 122 | 120 | 154 | 210 |
| Training services | 101 | 101 | 137 | 145 | 152 | 269 |
| Other business, professional, and technical services | ..... | ..... | ..... | ..... | 41 | 39 |
| Other unaffiliated services | 3 510 | 3 712 | 4 206 | 4 524 | 4 600 | 4 952 |

## Table B-2.  U.S. Private Services Transactions by Region and Country, 1986–1997

(Millions of dollars.)

| Country or region | Exports | | | | | |
| --- | --- | --- | --- | --- | --- | --- |
| | 1986 | 1987 | 1988 | 1989 | 1990 | 1991 |
| **ALL COUNTRIES** | 77 205 | 86 962 | 101 120 | 118 081 | 137 322 | 152 510 |
| **Canada** | 8 536 | 9 450 | 10 770 | 13 390 | 15 753 | 17 827 |
| **Mexico** | 3 919 | 4 007 | 4 694 | 6 288 | 7 967 | 8 934 |
| **Europe** | 25 205 | 30 609 | 36 133 | 42 016 | 48 608 | 53 989 |
| Belgium and Luxembourg | 1 032 | 1 035 | 1 219 | 1 487 | 1 775 | 1 955 |
| France | 2 947 | 3 686 | 3 923 | 4 689 | 5 590 | 6 213 |
| Germany | 4 051 | 5 263 | 5 949 | 6 206 | 7 431 | 8 897 |
| Italy | 1 865 | 2 161 | 2 470 | 2 698 | 3 305 | 3 697 |
| Netherlands | 1 949 | 2 118 | 2 459 | 2 595 | 3 279 | 3 590 |
| Norway | ..... | ..... | ..... | ..... | ..... | ..... |
| Spain | ..... | ..... | ..... | ..... | ..... | ..... |
| Sweden | ..... | ..... | ..... | ..... | ..... | ..... |
| Switzerland | ..... | ..... | ..... | ..... | ..... | ..... |
| United Kingdom | 6 559 | 8 451 | 10 177 | 12 526 | 13 064 | 14 180 |
| Other | ..... | ..... | ..... | ..... | ..... | ..... |
| **Latin America and Other Western Hemisphere** [1] | 13 961 | 14 311 | 15 847 | 17 960 | 21 815 | 24 623 |
| South and Central America [1] | 11 166 | 11 592 | 13 123 | 15 174 | 18 216 | 20 890 |
| Argentina | ..... | ..... | ..... | ..... | ..... | ..... |
| Brazil | ..... | ..... | ..... | ..... | ..... | ..... |
| Chile | ..... | ..... | ..... | ..... | ..... | ..... |
| Venezuela | 934 | 839 | 923 | 1 038 | 1 283 | 1 576 |
| Other | ..... | ..... | ..... | ..... | ..... | ..... |
| Other Western Hemisphere | 2 795 | 2 718 | 2 723 | 2 785 | 3 600 | 3 733 |
| Bermuda | ..... | ..... | ..... | ..... | ..... | ..... |
| Other | ..... | ..... | ..... | ..... | ..... | ..... |
| **Africa, Middle East, and Asia and Pacific** | 25 980 | 28 665 | 33 758 | 39 815 | 45 822 | 51 704 |
| Africa | ..... | ..... | ..... | ..... | ..... | ..... |
| South Africa | ..... | ..... | ..... | ..... | ..... | ..... |
| Other | ..... | ..... | ..... | ..... | ..... | ..... |
| Middle East | ..... | ..... | ..... | ..... | ..... | ..... |
| Israel | ..... | ..... | ..... | ..... | ..... | ..... |
| Saudi Arabia | ..... | ..... | ..... | ..... | ..... | ..... |
| Other | ..... | ..... | ..... | ..... | ..... | ..... |
| Asia and Pacific | ..... | ..... | ..... | ..... | ..... | ..... |
| Australia | 1 626 | 1 873 | 2 343 | 2 864 | 3 303 | 3 257 |
| China | ..... | ..... | ..... | ..... | ..... | ..... |
| Hong Kong | ..... | ..... | ..... | ..... | ..... | ..... |
| India | ..... | ..... | ..... | ..... | ..... | ..... |
| Indonesia | ..... | ..... | ..... | ..... | ..... | ..... |
| Japan | 10 311 | 12 417 | 14 875 | 18 423 | 21 230 | 24 058 |
| Malaysia | ..... | ..... | ..... | ..... | ..... | ..... |
| New Zealand | ..... | ..... | ..... | ..... | ..... | ..... |
| Philippines | ..... | ..... | ..... | ..... | ..... | ..... |
| Singapore | ..... | ..... | ..... | ..... | ..... | ..... |
| South Korea | ..... | ..... | ..... | ..... | ..... | ..... |
| Taiwan | ..... | ..... | ..... | ..... | ..... | ..... |
| Thailand | ..... | ..... | ..... | ..... | ..... | ..... |
| Other | ..... | ..... | ..... | ..... | ..... | ..... |
| **International organizations and unallocated** | 3 523 | 3 927 | 4 612 | 4 900 | 5 324 | 4 367 |
| **European Union** | 20 946 | 25 507 | 29 710 | 34 601 | 39 438 | 44 450 |
| **Eastern Europe** | 327 | 342 | 452 | 745 | 1 008 | 1 187 |

1. Includes Mexico.

**Table B-2.  U.S. Private Services Transactions by Region and Country, 1986–1997** *—Continued*

(Millions of dollars.)

| Country or region | Exports—*Continued* | | | | | |
|---|---|---|---|---|---|---|
| | 1992 | 1993 | 1994 | 1995 | 1996 | 1997 |
| **ALL COUNTRIES** | 163 754 | 172 031 | 187 760 | 204 229 | 224 213 | 239 215 |
| **Canada** | 17 454 | 17 040 | 17 314 | 18 032 | 19 938 | 20 501 |
| **Mexico** | 9 534 | 9 400 | 10 062 | 7 392 | 8 138 | 9 334 |
| **Europe** | 60 630 | 62 595 | 67 988 | 73 637 | 82 348 | 85 986 |
| Belgium and Luxembourg | 2 319 | 2 221 | 2 798 | 2 865 | 2 924 | 2 896 |
| France | 7 047 | 6 865 | 6 749 | 8 022 | 8 965 | 9 438 |
| Germany | 10 946 | 11 422 | 11 668 | 12 793 | 13 579 | 13 488 |
| Italy | 4 515 | 4 100 | 4 286 | 4 557 | 4 913 | 5 015 |
| Netherlands | 3 766 | 4 130 | 5 499 | 6 143 | 7 165 | 7 650 |
| Norway | 1 127 | 1 251 | 1 167 | 1 219 | 1 415 | 1 359 |
| Spain | 2 458 | 2 262 | 2 695 | 3 008 | 3 117 | 3 216 |
| Sweden | 1 760 | 1 737 | 1 756 | 1 896 | 2 478 | 2 474 |
| Switzerland | 2 904 | 2 936 | 3 710 | 3 859 | 4 337 | 4 238 |
| United Kingdom | 15 825 | 17 261 | 17 971 | 18 748 | 20 433 | 23 630 |
| Other | 7 968 | 8 408 | 9 692 | 10 525 | 13 019 | 12 581 |
| **Latin America and Other Western Hemisphere** [1] | 26 322 | 28 760 | 32 150 | 32 240 | 35 129 | 42 154 |
| South and Central America [1] | 22 766 | 24 791 | 27 279 | 26 948 | 29 125 | 34 221 |
| Argentina | 1 845 | 2 207 | 2 544 | 2 464 | 2 807 | 3 388 |
| Brazil | 2 553 | 3 015 | 3 811 | 5 066 | 5 258 | 6 401 |
| Chile | 647 | 811 | 1 188 | 1 025 | 1 237 | 1 420 |
| Venezuela | 2 004 | 2 444 | 2 164 | 2 512 | 2 417 | 2 760 |
| Other | 6 190 | 6 915 | 7 513 | 8 492 | 9 269 | 10 920 |
| Other Western Hemisphere | 3 556 | 3 967 | 4 871 | 5 293 | 6 002 | 7 933 |
| Bermuda | 414 | 533 | 755 | 604 | 849 | 1 048 |
| Other | 3 138 | 3 434 | 4 118 | 4 688 | 5 154 | 6 886 |
| **Africa, Middle East, and Asia and Pacific** | 55 392 | 59 164 | 65 577 | 75 204 | 80 889 | 84 713 |
| Africa | 2 363 | 2 459 | 2 671 | 2 988 | 3 190 | 3 579 |
| South Africa | 475 | 505 | 637 | 806 | 862 | 1 039 |
| Other | 1 889 | 1 955 | 2 034 | 2 180 | 2 329 | 2 541 |
| Middle East | 4 036 | 4 224 | 5 132 | 5 893 | 6 801 | 7 512 |
| Israel | 920 | 1 134 | 1 513 | 1 669 | 1 928 | 1 917 |
| Saudi Arabia | 1 378 | 1 261 | 1 885 | 2 110 | 1 740 | 1 929 |
| Other | 1 739 | 1 829 | 1 732 | 2 113 | 3 135 | 3 664 |
| Asia and Pacific | 48 993 | 52 481 | 57 774 | 66 323 | 70 899 | 73 622 |
| Australia | 3 505 | 3 605 | 3 839 | 4 327 | 4 690 | 5 001 |
| China | 1 604 | 1 979 | 2 110 | 2 593 | 3 214 | 3 697 |
| Hong Kong | 2 259 | 2 365 | 2 831 | 3 049 | 3 368 | 3 689 |
| India | 1 105 | 1 152 | 1 240 | 1 335 | 1 528 | 1 649 |
| Indonesia | 788 | 907 | 888 | 1 175 | 1 430 | 1 787 |
| Japan | 25 635 | 26 878 | 29 056 | 33 346 | 33 657 | 34 002 |
| Malaysia | 611 | 690 | 905 | 1 047 | 1 295 | 1 215 |
| New Zealand | 768 | 800 | 840 | 998 | 1 174 | 1 262 |
| Philippines | 983 | 1 263 | 1 204 | 1 078 | 1 250 | 1 551 |
| Singapore | 2 157 | 2 416 | 2 657 | 3 159 | 3 906 | 4 008 |
| South Korea | 3 401 | 3 668 | 4 634 | 5 727 | 7 374 | 6 885 |
| Taiwan | 3 173 | 3 466 | 4 176 | 4 440 | 4 053 | 4 625 |
| Thailand | 764 | 1 030 | 1 034 | 1 202 | 1 236 | 1 259 |
| Other | 2 239 | 2 256 | 2 361 | 2 845 | 2 724 | 2 996 |
| **International organizations and unallocated** | 3 953 | 4 473 | 4 733 | 5 116 | 5 909 | 5 866 |
| **European Union** | 51 618 | 52 703 | 56 225 | 64 344 | 69 692 | 74 760 |
| **Eastern Europe** | 1 214 | 1 725 | 2 236 | 2 632 | 3 367 | 3 545 |

1. Includes Mexico.

## Table B-2.  U.S. Private Services Transactions by Region and Country, 1986–1997 —*Continued*

(Millions of dollars.)

| Country or region | Imports | | | | | |
|---|---|---|---|---|---|---|
| | 1986 | 1987 | 1988 | 1989 | 1990 | 1991 |
| **ALL COUNTRIES** | 66 419 | 75 507 | 82 441 | 87 001 | 100 571 | 102 672 |
| **Canada** | 6 440 | 6 989 | 8 499 | 8 801 | 9 307 | 9 939 |
| **Mexico** | 4 895 | 5 542 | 5 874 | 6 936 | 8 279 | 8 877 |
| **Europe** | 24 253 | 28 443 | 31 030 | 33 225 | 40 030 | 39 486 |
| Belgium and Luxembourg | 608 | 562 | 627 | 823 | 1 026 | 964 |
| France | 2 284 | 2 695 | 2 949 | 3 536 | 4 192 | 3 964 |
| Germany | 3 999 | 5 217 | 5 562 | 6 081 | 6 851 | 6 459 |
| Italy | 2 264 | 2 516 | 2 879 | 2 872 | 3 481 | 3 310 |
| Netherlands | 1 037 | 1 310 | 1 325 | 1 618 | 1 945 | 2 167 |
| Norway | ..... | ..... | ..... | ..... | ..... | ..... |
| Spain | ..... | ..... | ..... | ..... | ..... | ..... |
| Sweden | ..... | ..... | ..... | ..... | ..... | ..... |
| Switzerland | ..... | ..... | ..... | ..... | ..... | ..... |
| United Kingdom | 7 576 | 8 959 | 9 460 | 9 864 | 11 626 | 12 155 |
| Other | ..... | ..... | ..... | ..... | ..... | ..... |
| **Latin America and Other Western Hemisphere** [1] | 14 316 | 16 096 | 16 567 | 17 912 | 20 299 | 21 494 |
| South and Central America [1] | 8 755 | 10 131 | 11 074 | 12 166 | 14 305 | 15 104 |
| Argentina | ..... | ..... | ..... | ..... | ..... | ..... |
| Brazil | ..... | ..... | ..... | ..... | ..... | ..... |
| Chile | ..... | ..... | ..... | ..... | ..... | ..... |
| Venezuela | 487 | 528 | 621 | 490 | 662 | 586 |
| Other | ..... | ..... | ..... | ..... | ..... | ..... |
| Other Western Hemisphere | 5 561 | 5 966 | 5 493 | 5 745 | 5 994 | 6 390 |
| Bermuda | ..... | ..... | ..... | ..... | ..... | ..... |
| Other | ..... | ..... | ..... | ..... | ..... | ..... |
| **Africa, Middle East, and Asia and Pacific** | 19 493 | 22 163 | 23 821 | 24 481 | 28 224 | 29 679 |
| Africa | ..... | ..... | ..... | ..... | ..... | ..... |
| South Africa | ..... | ..... | ..... | ..... | ..... | ..... |
| Other | ..... | ..... | ..... | ..... | ..... | ..... |
| Middle East | ..... | ..... | ..... | ..... | ..... | ..... |
| Israel | ..... | ..... | ..... | ..... | ..... | ..... |
| Saudi Arabia | ..... | ..... | ..... | ..... | ..... | ..... |
| Other | ..... | ..... | ..... | ..... | ..... | ..... |
| Asia and Pacific | ..... | ..... | ..... | ..... | ..... | ..... |
| Australia | 1 169 | 1 510 | 1 650 | 1 756 | 2 300 | 2 394 |
| China | ..... | ..... | ..... | ..... | ..... | ..... |
| Hong Kong | ..... | ..... | ..... | ..... | ..... | ..... |
| India | ..... | ..... | ..... | ..... | ..... | ..... |
| Indonesia | ..... | ..... | ..... | ..... | ..... | ..... |
| Japan | 6 676 | 7 545 | 8 416 | 8 955 | 10 564 | 11 861 |
| Malaysia | ..... | ..... | ..... | ..... | ..... | ..... |
| New Zealand | ..... | ..... | ..... | ..... | ..... | ..... |
| Philippines | ..... | ..... | ..... | ..... | ..... | ..... |
| Singapore | ..... | ..... | ..... | ..... | ..... | ..... |
| South Korea | ..... | ..... | ..... | ..... | ..... | ..... |
| Taiwan | ..... | ..... | ..... | ..... | ..... | ..... |
| Thailand | ..... | ..... | ..... | ..... | ..... | ..... |
| Other | ..... | ..... | ..... | ..... | ..... | ..... |
| **International organizations and unallocated** | 1 917 | 1 816 | 2 524 | 2 582 | 2 711 | 2 074 |
| **European Union** | 20 507 | 24 063 | 25 939 | 28 222 | 33 552 | 33 084 |
| **Eastern Europe** | 350 | 482 | 515 | 594 | 815 | 1 074 |

1. Includes Mexico.

**Table B-2.   U.S. Private Services Transactions by Region and Country, 1986–1997** —*Continued*

(Millions of dollars.)

| Country or region | Imports—*Continued* | | | | | |
|---|---|---|---|---|---|---|
| | 1992 | 1993 | 1994 | 1995 | 1996 | 1997 |
| **ALL COUNTRIES** | 103 464 | 111 259 | 123 303 | 133 355 | 142 261 | 156 236 |
| **Canada** | 8 883 | 9 423 | 10 424 | 11 467 | 12 794 | 14 063 |
| **Mexico** | 9 501 | 9 781 | 10 576 | 10 780 | 11 769 | 13 120 |
| **Europe** | 39 946 | 44 676 | 49 464 | 53 247 | 54 280 | 61 847 |
| Belgium and Luxembourg | 1 032 | 1 053 | 1 282 | 1 518 | 1 553 | 1 776 |
| France | 4 604 | 4 980 | 5 811 | 6 012 | 5 977 | 6 883 |
| Germany | 6 406 | 6 840 | 7 357 | 7 662 | 7 812 | 8 015 |
| Italy | 3 187 | 3 155 | 3 459 | 3 769 | 3 549 | 3 720 |
| Netherlands | 2 489 | 2 222 | 2 635 | 3 220 | 3 263 | 3 549 |
| Norway | 1 038 | 1 419 | 1 187 | 1 167 | 1 284 | 1 280 |
| Spain | 1 275 | 1 086 | 1 151 | 1 114 | 1 312 | 1 479 |
| Sweden | 792 | 957 | 872 | 859 | 901 | 913 |
| Switzerland | 1 718 | 1 954 | 2 336 | 2 311 | 2 627 | 2 761 |
| United Kingdom | 10 594 | 13 696 | 14 850 | 16 224 | 16 424 | 21 246 |
| Other | 6 812 | 7 316 | 8 520 | 9 391 | 9 580 | 10 223 |
| **Latin America and Other Western Hemisphere** [1] | 22 418 | 23 016 | 25 591 | 27 189 | 30 001 | 32 509 |
| South and Central America [1] | 15 698 | 15 973 | 17 618 | 18 396 | 20 618 | 22 316 |
| Argentina | 22 418 | 15 973 | 580 | 578 | 783 | 844 |
| Brazil | 685 | 740 | 917 | 1 180 | 1 446 | 1 781 |
| Chile | 333 | 363 | 417 | 428 | 520 | 514 |
| Venezuela | 636 | 718 | 767 | 708 | 777 | 733 |
| Other | 4 093 | 3 907 | 4 367 | 4 723 | 5 319 | 5 321 |
| Other Western Hemisphere | 6 719 | 7 042 | 7 972 | 8 792 | 9 382 | 10 193 |
| Bermuda | 1 522 | 1 279 | 1 834 | 2 714 | 3 009 | 3 140 |
| Other | 5 197 | 5 760 | 6 138 | 6 078 | 6 375 | 7 050 |
| **Africa, Middle East, and Asia and Pacific** | 29 485 | 32 212 | 35 939 | 39 170 | 42 225 | 45 248 |
| Africa | 1 495 | 1 551 | 1 935 | 1 976 | 2 402 | 2 458 |
| South Africa | 201 | 231 | 299 | 404 | 547 | 684 |
| Other | 1 296 | 1 319 | 1 636 | 1 570 | 1 852 | 1 774 |
| Middle East | 2 079 | 2 200 | 2 274 | 2 696 | 3 189 | 3 093 |
| Israel | 1 024 | 1 078 | 1 201 | 1 184 | 1 381 | 1 450 |
| Saudi Arabia | 341 | 343 | 311 | 563 | 441 | 505 |
| Other | 712 | 779 | 761 | 949 | 1 367 | 1 138 |
| Asia and Pacific | 25 911 | 28 460 | 31 729 | 34 497 | 36 634 | 39 697 |
| Australia | 2 232 | 2 183 | 1 945 | 2 161 | 2 605 | 2 635 |
| China | 1 126 | 1 396 | 1 555 | 1 794 | 2 065 | 2 327 |
| Hong Kong | 1 429 | 1 346 | 1 917 | 1 933 | 2 957 | 3 038 |
| India | 662 | 719 | 792 | 884 | 1 138 | 1 249 |
| Indonesia | 449 | 437 | 446 | 452 | 575 | 564 |
| Japan | 10 653 | 11 840 | 12 708 | 13 599 | 13 009 | 14 253 |
| Malaysia | 273 | 308 | 368 | 462 | 467 | 535 |
| New Zealand | 527 | 540 | 568 | 602 | 671 | 682 |
| Philippines | 788 | 854 | 1 041 | 1 126 | 1 366 | 1 434 |
| Singapore | 687 | 942 | 1 196 | 1 265 | 1 850 | 2 062 |
| South Korea | 2 063 | 2 369 | 2 833 | 3 618 | 4 163 | 4 541 |
| Taiwan | 2 000 | 2 408 | 2 684 | 2 888 | 2 738 | 3 380 |
| Thailand | 395 | 383 | 483 | 686 | 851 | 782 |
| Other | 2 629 | 2 732 | 3 192 | 3 028 | 2 179 | 2 216 |
| **International organizations and unallocated** | 2 732 | 1 935 | 1 885 | 2 286 | 2 956 | 2 574 |
| **European Union** | 33 117 | 36 904 | 40 599 | 45 715 | 45 802 | 53 112 |
| **Eastern Europe** | 1 626 | 1 549 | 2 013 | 2 222 | 2 414 | 2 181 |

1. Includes Mexico.

## Table B-3.  U.S. Travel, Passenger Fare, and Other Transportation Receipts, 1994–1997

(Millions of dollars.)

| Country or region | Travel | | | | Passenger Fares | | | |
|---|---|---|---|---|---|---|---|---|
| | 1994 | 1995 | 1996 | 1997 | 1994 | 1995 | 1996 | 1997 |
| **ALL COUNTRIES** | 58 417 | 63 395 | 69 751 | 73 268 | 16 997 | 18 909 | 20 413 | 20 895 |
| **Canada** | 6 252 | 6 207 | 6 842 | 6 824 | 1 186 | 1 284 | 1 331 | 1 409 |
| **Mexico** | 4 866 | 2 857 | 3 004 | 3 430 | 733 | 515 | 761 | 859 |
| **Europe** | 18 669 | 20 665 | 23 171 | 23 287 | 5 737 | 6 192 | 6 866 | 6 807 |
| Belgium and Luxembourg | 442 | 486 | 557 | 514 | 218 | 272 | 294 | 294 |
| France | 1 639 | 2 063 | 2 327 | 2 485 | 825 | 976 | 954 | 929 |
| Germany | 3 577 | 4 212 | 4 403 | 4 142 | 1 297 | 1 592 | 1 714 | 1 366 |
| Italy | 1 219 | 1 344 | 1 691 | 1 647 | 437 | 483 | 461 | 613 |
| Netherlands | 756 | 782 | 1 141 | 972 | 132 | 161 | 222 | 188 |
| Norway | 246 | 251 | 336 | 405 | 39 | ..... | 1 | ..... |
| Spain | 659 | 753 | 831 | 964 | 408 | 452 | 366 | 339 |
| Sweden | 480 | 506 | 635 | 665 | 180 | 212 | 234 | 183 |
| Switzerland | 1 202 | 1 252 | 1 363 | 1 124 | 286 | 325 | 353 | 219 |
| United Kingdom | 6 119 | 6 662 | 6 450 | 7 090 | 1 580 | 1 456 | 1 804 | 2 191 |
| Other | 2 330 | 2 354 | 3 437 | 3 279 | 335 | 263 | 463 | 485 |
| **Latin America and Other Western Hemisphere** [1] | 14 122 | 13 482 | 14 984 | 18 113 | 3 366 | 3 584 | 4 098 | 4 713 |
| South and Central America [1] | 12 537 | 11 699 | 12 888 | 15 443 | 2 902 | 3 087 | 3 601 | 4 162 |
| Argentina | 1 096 | 1 072 | 1 224 | 1 536 | 447 | 388 | 485 | 634 |
| Brazil | 1 817 | 2 431 | 2 588 | 3 021 | 487 | 744 | 839 | 841 |
| Chile | 345 | 441 | 489 | 549 | 103 | 122 | 164 | 193 |
| Venezuela | 1 162 | 1 384 | 1 401 | 1 440 | 210 | 300 | 203 | 291 |
| Other | 3 251 | 3 514 | 4 182 | 5 467 | 922 | 1 018 | 1 149 | 1 344 |
| Other Western Hemisphere | 1 585 | 1 783 | 2 096 | 2 670 | 464 | 497 | 497 | 551 |
| Bermuda | 12 | 15 | 14 | 16 | 6 | 4 | 4 | 7 |
| Other | 1 573 | 1 768 | 2 082 | 2 654 | 458 | 493 | 493 | 544 |
| **Africa** | 607 | 699 | 766 | 1 054 | 55 | 33 | 77 | 65 |
| South Africa | 288 | 344 | 285 | 370 | 14 | 1 | 7 | ..... |
| Other | 319 | 355 | 481 | 684 | 41 | 32 | 70 | 65 |
| **Middle East** | 1 391 | 1 852 | 1 979 | 2 316 | 221 | 371 | 425 | 509 |
| Israel | 432 | 638 | 694 | 822 | 151 | 239 | 264 | 290 |
| Saudi Arabia | 383 | 523 | 454 | 558 | ..... | 4 | ..... | 11 |
| Other | 576 | 691 | 831 | 936 | 70 | 128 | 161 | 208 |
| **Asia and Pacific** | 17 376 | 20 490 | 22 009 | 21 674 | 6 432 | 7 445 | 7 616 | 7 392 |
| Australia | 1 431 | 1 639 | 1 709 | 1 839 | 428 | 431 | 540 | 621 |
| China | 369 | 406 | 807 | 1 101 | 9 | 18 | 100 | 142 |
| Hong Kong | 567 | 644 | 624 | 741 | 249 | 325 | 380 | 471 |
| India | 364 | 445 | 544 | 634 | 16 | 17 | 42 | 50 |
| Indonesia | 190 | 237 | 337 | 392 | 20 | 10 | 19 | 24 |
| Japan | 9 868 | 11 760 | 11 790 | 11 068 | 5 100 | 6 043 | 5 790 | 5 442 |
| Malaysia | 168 | 228 | 262 | 268 | ..... | ..... | ..... | ..... |
| New Zealand | 407 | 493 | 608 | 616 | 118 | 134 | 121 | 108 |
| Philippines | 318 | 325 | 476 | 585 | 86 | 83 | 82 | 84 |
| Singapore | 272 | 350 | 377 | 383 | 45 | 61 | 49 | 77 |
| South Korea | 1 417 | 1 798 | 2 345 | 2 056 | 149 | 91 | 308 | 132 |
| Taiwan | 1 468 | 1 559 | 1 370 | 1 287 | 119 | 120 | 84 | 114 |
| Thailand | 282 | 331 | 421 | 349 | ..... | 2 | 3 | 15 |
| Other | 255 | 275 | 339 | 355 | 93 | 110 | 98 | 112 |
| **International organizations and unallocated** | ..... | ..... | ..... | ..... | ..... | ..... | ..... | ..... |
| **European Union** | 15 219 | 18 293 | 20 004 | 20 246 | 5 051 | 5 803 | 6 390 | 6 416 |
| **Eastern Europe** | 558 | 691 | 1 213 | 1 249 | 94 | 57 | 104 | 144 |

1. Includes Mexico.

## Table B-3.   U.S. Travel, Passenger Fare, and Other Transportation Receipts, 1994–1997 —*Continued*

(Millions of dollars.)

| Country or region | Other Transportation | | | | | | | |
|---|---|---|---|---|---|---|---|---|
| | Total | | | | Freight | | | |
| | | | | | Total | | | |
| | 1994 | 1995 | 1996 | 1997 | 1994 | 1995 | 1996 | 1997 |
| ALL COUNTRIES ............................................ | 23 754 | 26 081 | 26 074 | 26 911 | 9 575 | 11 273 | 11 146 | 11 773 |
| Canada ........................................................ | 1 973 | 2 275 | 2 394 | 2 384 | 1 525 | 1 806 | 1 816 | 1 880 |
| Mexico ......................................................... | 567 | 420 | 549 | 576 | 263 | 160 | 186 | 241 |
| Europe ......................................................... | 7 867 | 8 228 | 8 138 | 8 146 | 2 344 | 2 777 | 2 842 | 2 999 |
| Belgium and Luxembourg ........................... | 343 | 355 | 326 | 350 | 193 | 234 | 270 | 300 |
| France ...................................................... | 393 | 410 | 417 | 577 | 195 | 226 | 241 | 266 |
| Germany ................................................... | 1 177 | 1 172 | 860 | 957 | 305 | 386 | 368 | 408 |
| Italy ......................................................... | 492 | 452 | 338 | 347 | 109 | 108 | 109 | 126 |
| Netherlands .............................................. | 788 | 914 | 883 | 761 | 326 | 391 | 395 | 384 |
| Norway ..................................................... | 496 | 535 | 503 | 360 | 10 | 13 | 20 | 21 |
| Spain ....................................................... | 209 | 170 | 195 | 174 | 114 | 97 | 90 | 98 |
| Sweden ..................................................... | 286 | 283 | 308 | 290 | 36 | 41 | 45 | 59 |
| Switzerland ............................................... | 248 | 240 | 311 | 228 | 34 | 35 | 40 | 64 |
| United Kingdom ........................................ | 1 077 | 1 229 | 1 359 | 1 715 | 495 | 547 | 599 | 694 |
| Other ........................................................ | 2 358 | 2 468 | 2 638 | 2 387 | 527 | 699 | 665 | 579 |
| Latin America and Other Western Hemisphere [1] ........ | 3 117 | 3 363 | 3 178 | 3 692 | 1 582 | 1 776 | 1 746 | 2 048 |
| South and Central America [1] ..................... | 2 641 | 2 778 | 2 598 | 3 142 | 1 403 | 1 508 | 1 504 | 1 823 |
| Argentina .............................................. | 197 | 157 | 152 | 204 | 105 | 86 | 84 | 113 |
| Brazil ................................................... | 466 | 480 | 290 | 631 | 134 | 198 | 217 | 330 |
| Chile .................................................... | 171 | 118 | 158 | 199 | 26 | 30 | 50 | 62 |
| Venezuela ............................................. | 162 | 168 | 159 | 203 | 89 | 101 | 116 | 166 |
| Other ................................................... | 1 078 | 1 435 | 1 290 | 1 329 | 786 | 933 | 851 | 911 |
| Other Western Hemisphere ....................... | 476 | 585 | 580 | 550 | 179 | 268 | 242 | 225 |
| Bermuda ............................................... | 5 | 7 | 4 | 4 | 5 | 7 | 4 | 4 |
| Other ................................................... | 471 | 578 | 576 | 546 | 174 | 261 | 238 | 221 |
| Africa .......................................................... | 534 | 568 | 450 | 389 | 411 | 347 | 215 | 191 |
| South Africa ............................................. | 34 | 84 | 84 | 132 | 12 | 16 | 18 | 17 |
| Other ........................................................ | 500 | 484 | 366 | 257 | 399 | 331 | 197 | 174 |
| Middle East ................................................. | 859 | 938 | 1 073 | 1 023 | 578 | 491 | 634 | 507 |
| Israel ........................................................ | 511 | 371 | 481 | 287 | 318 | 229 | 348 | 162 |
| Saudi Arabia ............................................. | 84 | 100 | 88 | 125 | 68 | 60 | 49 | 87 |
| Other ........................................................ | 264 | 467 | 504 | 611 | 192 | 202 | 237 | 258 |
| Asia and Pacific ......................................... | 9 128 | 10 339 | 10 312 | 10 745 | 3 136 | 4 071 | 3 875 | 4 134 |
| Australia ................................................... | 220 | 279 | 304 | 324 | 105 | 125 | 154 | 168 |
| China ....................................................... | 576 | 738 | 597 | 565 | 121 | 211 | 132 | 209 |
| Hong Kong ............................................... | 633 | 602 | 459 | 509 | 372 | 455 | 389 | 432 |
| India ........................................................ | 167 | 140 | 156 | 167 | 67 | 98 | 126 | 140 |
| Indonesia ................................................. | 35 | 64 | 86 | 91 | 24 | 58 | 41 | 50 |
| Japan ....................................................... | 3 049 | 3 270 | 3 190 | 3 231 | 1 097 | 1 351 | 1 329 | 1 290 |
| Malaysia ................................................... | 118 | 133 | 174 | 162 | 66 | 92 | 109 | 126 |
| New Zealand ............................................. | 81 | 123 | 130 | 177 | 10 | 36 | 30 | 25 |
| Philippines ............................................... | 318 | 269 | 227 | 253 | 106 | 111 | 93 | 136 |
| Singapore ................................................. | 688 | 672 | 626 | 684 | 219 | 221 | 220 | 272 |
| South Korea ............................................. | 1 315 | 1 534 | 2 339 | 2 040 | 217 | 286 | 374 | 340 |
| Taiwan ..................................................... | 1 223 | 1 313 | 1 115 | 1 491 | 311 | 371 | 283 | 268 |
| Thailand ................................................... | 147 | 151 | 127 | 142 | 103 | 112 | 95 | 96 |
| Other ........................................................ | 558 | 1 051 | 782 | 909 | 318 | 544 | 500 | 582 |
| International organizations and unallocated .............. | 276 | 370 | 529 | 532 | ..... | 4 | 16 | 14 |
| European Union ......................................... | 5 748 | 6 240 | 6 092 | 6 409 | 1 871 | 2 243 | 2 386 | 2 567 |
| Eastern Europe .......................................... | 445 | 535 | 475 | 442 | 296 | 383 | 302 | 292 |

1. Includes Mexico.

## Table B-3.  U.S. Travel, Passenger Fare, and Other Transportation Receipts, 1994–1997  —*Continued*

(Millions of dollars.)

| Country or region | Other Transportation— *Continued* | | | | | | | | | | | |
|---|---|---|---|---|---|---|---|---|---|---|---|---|
| | Freight—*Continued* | | | | | | | | | | | |
| | Ocean | | | | Air | | | | Other | | | |
| | 1994 | 1995 | 1996 | 1997 | 1994 | 1995 | 1996 | 1997 | 1994 | 1995 | 1996 | 1997 |
| ALL COUNTRIES .......................................... | 4 476 | 5 278 | 4 703 | 4 577 | 3 177 | 3 657 | 3 956 | 4 610 | 1 923 | 2 337 | 2 485 | 2 586 |
| Canada ............................................................ | 26 | 59 | 32 | 54 | 48 | 55 | 59 | 69 | 1 451 | 1 692 | 1 725 | 1 757 |
| Mexico ............................................................. | 133 | 98 | 96 | 97 | 94 | 58 | 86 | 95 | 36 | 4 | 4 | 49 |
| Europe ............................................................ | 1 351 | 1 608 | 1 522 | 1 450 | 968 | 1 089 | 1 226 | 1 445 | 25 | 80 | 94 | 104 |
| Belgium and Luxembourg ............................. | 139 | 181 | 204 | 222 | 52 | 49 | 61 | 72 | 2 | 4 | 5 | 6 |
| France .......................................................... | 45 | 54 | 59 | 54 | 148 | 166 | 176 | 205 | 2 | 6 | 6 | 7 |
| Germany ....................................................... | 141 | 157 | 132 | 153 | 160 | 217 | 223 | 240 | 4 | 12 | 13 | 15 |
| Italy .............................................................. | 62 | 54 | 40 | 51 | 46 | 51 | 64 | 70 | 1 | 3 | 5 | 5 |
| Netherlands .................................................. | 262 | 305 | 281 | 250 | 56 | 60 | 83 | 100 | 8 | 26 | 31 | 34 |
| Norway ......................................................... | 6 | 10 | 16 | 14 | 4 | 3 | 4 | 7 | ..... | ..... | ..... | ..... |
| Spain ............................................................ | 67 | 56 | 47 | 52 | 47 | 41 | 43 | 46 | ..... | ..... | ..... | ..... |
| Sweden ......................................................... | 21 | 21 | 18 | 23 | 15 | 20 | 27 | 36 | ..... | ..... | ..... | ..... |
| Switzerland .................................................. | ..... | ..... | ..... | 18 | 34 | 35 | 40 | 46 | ..... | ..... | ..... | ..... |
| United Kingdom ........................................... | 161 | 184 | 188 | 189 | 330 | 354 | 401 | 494 | 4 | 9 | 10 | 11 |
| Other ............................................................ | 447 | 586 | 537 | 424 | 76 | 93 | 104 | 129 | 4 | 20 | 24 | 26 |
| Latin America and Other Western Hemisphere [1] ........ | 717 | 869 | 661 | 727 | 644 | 667 | 799 | 1 013 | 221 | 240 | 286 | 308 |
| South and Central America [1] ...................... | 602 | 667 | 499 | 593 | 606 | 631 | 754 | 960 | 195 | 210 | 251 | 270 |
| Argentina .................................................. | 24 | 19 | 25 | 49 | 81 | 67 | 59 | 64 | ..... | ..... | ..... | ..... |
| Brazil ........................................................ | 36 | 59 | 63 | 111 | 98 | 139 | 154 | 219 | ..... | ..... | ..... | ..... |
| Chile ......................................................... | 16 | 6 | 28 | 35 | 10 | 24 | 22 | 27 | ..... | ..... | ..... | ..... |
| Venezuela ................................................. | 59 | 62 | 48 | 65 | 22 | 32 | 61 | 93 | 8 | 7 | 7 | 8 |
| Other ......................................................... | 334 | 423 | 239 | 236 | 301 | 311 | 372 | 462 | 151 | 199 | 240 | 213 |
| Other Western Hemisphere ......................... | 115 | 202 | 162 | 134 | 38 | 36 | 45 | 53 | 26 | 30 | 35 | 38 |
| Bermuda ................................................... | ..... | 2 | ..... | ..... | 5 | 5 | 4 | 4 | ..... | ..... | ..... | ..... |
| Other ......................................................... | 115 | 200 | 162 | 134 | 33 | 31 | 41 | 49 | 26 | 30 | 35 | 38 |
| Africa .............................................................. | 378 | 305 | 182 | 153 | 30 | 35 | 26 | 29 | 3 | 7 | 7 | 9 |
| South Africa ................................................ | 6 | 5 | 8 | 5 | 3 | 4 | 3 | 3 | 3 | 7 | 7 | 9 |
| Other ............................................................ | 372 | 300 | 174 | 148 | 27 | 31 | 23 | 26 | ..... | ..... | ..... | ..... |
| Middle East ..................................................... | 522 | 438 | 565 | 430 | 56 | 53 | 69 | 77 | ..... | ..... | ..... | ..... |
| Israel ............................................................ | 292 | 199 | 318 | 162 | 26 | 30 | 30 | ..... | ..... | ..... | ..... | ..... |
| Saudi Arabia ................................................ | 55 | 51 | 49 | 57 | 13 | 9 | ..... | 30 | ..... | ..... | ..... | ..... |
| Other ............................................................ | 175 | 188 | 198 | 211 | 17 | 14 | 39 | 47 | ..... | ..... | ..... | ..... |
| Asia and Pacific ............................................. | 1 482 | 1 995 | 1 725 | 1 749 | 1 431 | 1 758 | 1 777 | 1 977 | 223 | 318 | 373 | 408 |
| Australia ...................................................... | 3 | 2 | 14 | 4 | 82 | 88 | 99 | 119 | 20 | 35 | 41 | 45 |
| China ............................................................ | 89 | 110 | 76 | 120 | 32 | 101 | 56 | 89 | ..... | ..... | ..... | ..... |
| Hong Kong ................................................... | 144 | 184 | 139 | 157 | 228 | 271 | 250 | 275 | ..... | ..... | ..... | ..... |
| India ............................................................. | 64 | 91 | 119 | 128 | 3 | 7 | 7 | 12 | ..... | ..... | ..... | ..... |
| Indonesia ..................................................... | 19 | 46 | 33 | 35 | 5 | 12 | 8 | 15 | ..... | ..... | ..... | ..... |
| Japan ........................................................... | 490 | 583 | 522 | 470 | 557 | 694 | 720 | 725 | 50 | 74 | 87 | 95 |
| Malaysia ....................................................... | 15 | 25 | 23 | 25 | 51 | 67 | 86 | 101 | ..... | ..... | ..... | ..... |
| New Zealand ................................................ | 1 | 17 | 9 | ..... | 3 | 7 | 8 | 11 | 6 | 12 | 13 | 14 |
| Philippines ................................................... | 75 | 86 | 61 | 61 | 31 | 25 | 32 | 75 | ..... | ..... | ..... | ..... |
| Singapore ..................................................... | 50 | 56 | 39 | 57 | 169 | 165 | 181 | 215 | ..... | ..... | ..... | ..... |
| South Korea ................................................. | 99 | 150 | 238 | 231 | 118 | 136 | 136 | 109 | ..... | ..... | ..... | ..... |
| Taiwan .......................................................... | 194 | 239 | 183 | 101 | 117 | 132 | 100 | 167 | ..... | ..... | ..... | ..... |
| Thailand ....................................................... | 68 | 73 | 52 | 36 | 35 | 39 | 43 | 60 | ..... | ..... | ..... | ..... |
| Other ............................................................ | 171 | 333 | 217 | 324 | ..... | 14 | 51 | 4 | 147 | 197 | 232 | 254 |
| International organizations and unallocated ............... | ..... | 4 | 16 | 14 | ..... | ..... | ..... | ..... | ..... | ..... | ..... | ..... |
| European Union .............................................. | 974 | 1 172 | 1 156 | 1 127 | 875 | 1 001 | 1 148 | 1 350 | 22 | 70 | 82 | 90 |
| Eastern Europe ............................................... | 271 | 351 | 265 | 249 | 24 | 24 | 27 | 32 | 1 | 8 | 10 | 11 |

1. Includes Mexico.

## Table B-3.  U.S. Travel, Passenger Fare, and Other Transportation Receipts, 1994–1997  —Continued

(Millions of dollars.)

| Country or region | Other Transportation—Continued | | | | | | | | | | | |
|---|---|---|---|---|---|---|---|---|---|---|---|---|
| | Port Services | | | | | | | | | | | |
| | Total | | | | Ocean | | | | Air | | | |
| | 1994 | 1995 | 1996 | 1997 | 1994 | 1995 | 1996 | 1997 | 1994 | 1995 | 1996 | 1997 |
| ALL COUNTRIES | 14 180 | 14 809 | 14 929 | 15 137 | 7 898 | 8 298 | 7 799 | 7 626 | 6 135 | 6 361 | 6 971 | 7 359 |
| Canada | 448 | 469 | 578 | 504 | 28 | 29 | 60 | 64 | 275 | 291 | 358 | 287 |
| Mexico | 304 | 260 | 363 | 335 | 43 | 60 | 88 | 75 | 261 | 200 | 275 | 260 |
| Europe | 5 523 | 5 451 | 5 296 | 5 147 | 2 898 | 2 942 | 2 880 | 2 878 | 2 625 | 2 509 | 2 416 | 2 269 |
| Belgium and Luxembourg | 150 | 121 | 56 | 50 | 43 | 50 | 19 | 24 | 107 | 71 | 37 | 26 |
| France | 198 | 184 | 176 | 311 | 46 | 13 | 6 | 22 | 152 | 171 | 170 | 289 |
| Germany | 872 | 786 | 492 | 549 | 275 | 319 | 393 | 456 | 597 | 467 | 99 | 93 |
| Italy | 383 | 344 | 229 | 221 | 231 | 194 | 89 | 101 | 152 | 150 | 140 | 120 |
| Netherlands | 462 | 523 | 488 | 377 | 77 | 117 | 68 | 60 | 385 | 406 | 420 | 317 |
| Norway | 486 | 522 | 483 | 339 | 486 | 522 | 483 | 339 | ..... | ..... | ..... | ..... |
| Spain | 95 | 73 | 105 | 76 | ..... | ..... | ..... | ..... | 95 | 73 | 105 | 76 |
| Sweden | 250 | 242 | 263 | 231 | 148 | 151 | 167 | 135 | 102 | 91 | 96 | 96 |
| Switzerland | 214 | 205 | 271 | 164 | ..... | ..... | 45 | ..... | 214 | 205 | 226 | 164 |
| United Kingdom | 582 | 682 | 760 | 1 021 | 125 | 134 | 135 | 308 | 457 | 548 | 625 | 713 |
| Other | 1 831 | 1 769 | 1 973 | 1 808 | 1 467 | 1 442 | 1 475 | 1 433 | 364 | 327 | 498 | 375 |
| Latin America and Other Western Hemisphere [1] | 1 535 | 1 587 | 1 432 | 1 644 | 355 | 397 | 395 | 345 | 1 180 | 1 190 | 1 037 | 1 299 |
| South and Central America [1] | 1 238 | 1 270 | 1 094 | 1 319 | 279 | 305 | 275 | 236 | 959 | 965 | 819 | 1 083 |
| Argentina | 92 | 71 | 68 | 91 | 7 | 6 | 2 | 2 | 85 | 65 | 66 | 89 |
| Brazil | 332 | 282 | 73 | 301 | 16 | 43 | 16 | 10 | 316 | 239 | 57 | 291 |
| Chile | 145 | 88 | 108 | 137 | 63 | 44 | 68 | 50 | 82 | 44 | 40 | 87 |
| Venezuela | 73 | 67 | 43 | 37 | 50 | 50 | 26 | 20 | 23 | 17 | 17 | 17 |
| Other | 292 | 502 | 439 | 418 | 100 | 102 | 75 | 79 | 192 | 400 | 364 | 339 |
| Other Western Hemisphere | 297 | 317 | 338 | 325 | 76 | 92 | 120 | 109 | 221 | 225 | 218 | 216 |
| Bermuda | ..... | ..... | ..... | ..... | ..... | ..... | ..... | ..... | ..... | ..... | ..... | ..... |
| Other | 297 | 317 | 338 | 325 | 76 | 92 | 120 | 109 | 221 | 225 | 218 | 216 |
| Africa | 123 | 220 | 235 | 198 | 77 | 81 | 49 | 43 | 46 | 139 | 186 | 155 |
| South Africa | 22 | 67 | 66 | 115 | 2 | 2 | 3 | 5 | 20 | 65 | 63 | 110 |
| Other | 101 | 153 | 169 | 83 | 75 | 79 | 46 | 38 | 26 | 74 | 123 | 45 |
| Middle East | 281 | 447 | 439 | 516 | 72 | 159 | 147 | 157 | 209 | 288 | 292 | 359 |
| Israel | 193 | 142 | 133 | 125 | ..... | ..... | ..... | ..... | 193 | 142 | 133 | 125 |
| Saudi Arabia | 16 | 40 | 39 | 38 | ..... | ..... | ..... | ..... | 16 | 40 | 39 | 38 |
| Other | 72 | 265 | 267 | 353 | 72 | 159 | 147 | 157 | ..... | 106 | 120 | 196 |
| Asia and Pacific | 5 992 | 6 268 | 6 437 | 6 611 | 4 192 | 4 324 | 3 755 | 3 621 | 1 800 | 1 944 | 2 682 | 2 990 |
| Australia | 115 | 154 | 150 | 156 | 15 | 19 | 15 | 22 | 100 | 135 | 135 | 134 |
| China | 455 | 527 | 465 | 356 | 257 | 370 | 301 | 173 | 198 | 157 | 164 | 183 |
| Hong Kong | 261 | 147 | 70 | 77 | 258 | 147 | 69 | 75 | 3 | ..... | 1 | 2 |
| India | 100 | 42 | 30 | 27 | 88 | 34 | 11 | 5 | 12 | 8 | 19 | 22 |
| Indonesia | 11 | 6 | 45 | 41 | 5 | 4 | ..... | 3 | 6 | 2 | 45 | 38 |
| Japan | 1 952 | 1 919 | 1 861 | 1 941 | 1 413 | 1 377 | 1 175 | 1 114 | 539 | 542 | 686 | 827 |
| Malaysia | 52 | 41 | 65 | 36 | 12 | 9 | 28 | 3 | 40 | 32 | 37 | 33 |
| New Zealand | 71 | 87 | 100 | 152 | ..... | ..... | ..... | ..... | 71 | 87 | 100 | 152 |
| Philippines | 212 | 158 | 134 | 117 | 104 | 74 | 46 | 23 | 108 | 84 | 88 | 94 |
| Singapore | 469 | 451 | 406 | 412 | 305 | 310 | 258 | 264 | 164 | 141 | 148 | 148 |
| South Korea | 1 098 | 1 248 | 1 965 | 1 700 | 677 | 791 | 1 092 | 809 | 421 | 457 | 873 | 891 |
| Taiwan | 912 | 942 | 832 | 1 223 | 834 | 822 | 686 | 1 076 | 78 | 120 | 146 | 147 |
| Thailand | 44 | 39 | 32 | 46 | 4 | 10 | 1 | 4 | 40 | 29 | 31 | 42 |
| Other | 240 | 507 | 282 | 327 | 220 | 357 | 73 | 50 | 20 | 150 | 209 | 277 |
| International organizations and unallocated | 276 | 366 | 513 | 518 | 276 | 366 | 513 | 518 | ..... | ..... | ..... | ..... |
| European Union | 3 877 | 3 997 | 3 706 | 3 842 | 1 705 | 1 805 | 1 770 | 1 861 | 2 172 | 2 192 | 1 936 | 1 981 |
| Eastern Europe | 149 | 152 | 173 | 150 | 98 | 87 | 98 | 70 | 51 | 65 | 75 | 80 |

1. Includes Mexico.

## Table B-4.  U.S. Travel, Passenger Fare, and Other Transportation Payments, 1994–1997

(Millions of dollars.)

| Country or region | Travel | | | | Passenger Fares | | | |
|---|---|---|---|---|---|---|---|---|
| | 1994 | 1995 | 1996 | 1997 | 1994 | 1995 | 1996 | 1997 |
| **ALL COUNTRIES** ................................ | 43 782 | 44 916 | 48 048 | 51 220 | 13 062 | 14 663 | 15 818 | 18 235 |
| **Canada** ................................ | 3 914 | 4 319 | 4 670 | 4 901 | 302 | 306 | 391 | 470 |
| **Mexico** ................................ | 5 334 | 5 316 | 5 972 | 6 443 | 601 | 569 | 650 | 777 |
| **Europe** ................................ | 16 188 | 16 489 | 15 935 | 17 852 | 6 355 | 7 416 | 7 775 | 9 176 |
| Belgium and Luxembourg ......... | 295 | 312 | 268 | 236 | 98 | 106 | 149 | 221 |
| France ................................ | 2 511 | 2 615 | 2 427 | 2 752 | 460 | 537 | 524 | 615 |
| Germany ................................ | 2 458 | 2 247 | 2 013 | 1 984 | 760 | 845 | 939 | 1 225 |
| Italy ................................ | 1 651 | 1 927 | 1 843 | 2 107 | 458 | 530 | 515 | 440 |
| Netherlands ............................ | 380 | 442 | 495 | 670 | 556 | 699 | 688 | 865 |
| Norway ................................ | 146 | 124 | 140 | 235 | 36 | 50 | 26 | 36 |
| Spain ................................ | 638 | 563 | 671 | 832 | 131 | 137 | 155 | 136 |
| Sweden ................................ | 138 | 162 | 200 | 171 | 42 | 49 | 39 | 49 |
| Switzerland ............................ | 661 | 510 | 650 | 655 | 360 | 456 | 490 | 590 |
| United Kingdom ...................... | 4 375 | 4 304 | 3 788 | 4 703 | 2 253 | 2 616 | 2 756 | 3 209 |
| Other ................................ | 2 935 | 3 283 | 3 440 | 3 507 | 1 201 | 1 391 | 1 494 | 1 790 |
| **Latin America and Other Western Hemisphere** [1] ........ | 12 803 | 12 621 | 14 108 | 14 956 | 2 190 | 2 240 | 2 438 | 2 781 |
| South and Central America [1] ..... | 8 568 | 8 639 | 10 010 | 10 828 | 1 759 | 1 808 | 1 968 | 2 209 |
| Argentina ........................... | 304 | 245 | 352 | 426 | 99 | 128 | 134 | 143 |
| Brazil ............................... | 269 | 331 | 418 | 592 | 286 | 366 | 389 | 462 |
| Chile ................................ | 180 | 188 | 228 | 223 | 70 | 74 | 93 | 92 |
| Venezuela .......................... | 245 | 224 | 256 | 270 | 104 | 72 | 80 | 104 |
| Other ............................... | 2 236 | 2 335 | 2 784 | 2 874 | 599 | 599 | 622 | 631 |
| Other Western Hemisphere .......... | 4 235 | 3 982 | 4 098 | 4 128 | 431 | 432 | 470 | 572 |
| Bermuda ............................ | 393 | 323 | 312 | 394 | 1 | 1 | ..... | ..... |
| Other ............................... | 3 842 | 3 659 | 3 786 | 3 734 | 430 | 431 | 470 | 572 |
| **Africa** ................................ | 1 029 | 1 063 | 1 300 | 1 240 | 202 | 277 | 286 | 435 |
| South Africa .......................... | 141 | 198 | 268 | 267 | 77 | 119 | 124 | 239 |
| Other ................................ | 888 | 865 | 1 032 | 973 | 125 | 158 | 162 | 196 |
| **Middle East** ............................ | 881 | 1 058 | 1 227 | 1 136 | 391 | 396 | 447 | 399 |
| Israel ................................ | 506 | 439 | 446 | 481 | 215 | 214 | 261 | 253 |
| Saudi Arabia .......................... | 126 | 343 | 208 | 263 | 47 | 60 | 71 | 75 |
| Other ................................ | 249 | 276 | 573 | 392 | 129 | 122 | 115 | 71 |
| **Asia and Pacific** ...................... | 8 967 | 9 366 | 10 808 | 11 135 | 3 622 | 4 028 | 4 481 | 4 974 |
| Australia ............................. | 784 | 831 | 1 068 | 965 | 421 | 452 | 507 | 546 |
| China ................................ | 616 | 644 | 733 | 889 | 60 | 66 | 107 | 149 |
| Hong Kong ........................... | 812 | 776 | 1 101 | 924 | 349 | 414 | 480 | 421 |
| India ................................ | 380 | 414 | 502 | 583 | 96 | 134 | 120 | 135 |
| Indonesia ............................ | 256 | 256 | 276 | 287 | 43 | 47 | 62 | 66 |
| Japan ................................ | 2 917 | 2 754 | 2 905 | 2 939 | 543 | 613 | 712 | 757 |
| Malaysia ............................. | 130 | 212 | 202 | 220 | 64 | 64 | 66 | 75 |
| New Zealand ......................... | 293 | 273 | 300 | 247 | 164 | 198 | 193 | 217 |
| Philippines ........................... | 514 | 557 | 754 | 719 | 180 | 233 | 235 | 268 |
| Singapore ............................ | 264 | 341 | 474 | 544 | 263 | 234 | 309 | 249 |
| South Korea .......................... | 775 | 880 | 945 | 1 174 | 655 | 777 | 763 | 1 083 |
| Taiwan ............................... | 576 | 580 | 622 | 757 | 516 | 532 | 633 | 678 |
| Thailand ............................. | 249 | 403 | 440 | 380 | 69 | 64 | 81 | 111 |
| Other ................................ | 401 | 445 | 486 | 507 | 199 | 200 | 213 | 219 |
| **International organizations and unallocated** ............... | ..... | ..... | ..... | ..... | ..... | ..... | ..... | ..... |
| **European Union** ...................... | 13 545 | 14 379 | 13 158 | 15 104 | 5 499 | 6 477 | 6 848 | 8 051 |
| **Eastern Europe** ...................... | 1 021 | 1 080 | 1 223 | 946 | 224 | 299 | 250 | 317 |

1. Includes Mexico.

## Table B-4.   U.S. Travel, Passenger Fare, and Other Transportation Payments, 1994–1997   —*Continued*

(Millions of dollars.)

| Country or region | Other Transportation | | | | | | | |
|---|---|---|---|---|---|---|---|---|
| | Total | | | | Freight | | | |
| | | | | | Total | | | |
| | 1994 | 1995 | 1996 | 1997 | 1994 | 1995 | 1996 | 1997 |
| **ALL COUNTRIES** | 26 019 | 27 034 | 27 403 | 28 949 | 16 006 | 16 455 | 16 539 | 17 644 |
| **Canada** | 2 330 | 2 513 | 2 790 | 3 037 | 1 874 | 1 968 | 2 249 | 2 415 |
| **Mexico** | 476 | 481 | 525 | 800 | 59 | 88 | 106 | 118 |
| **Europe** | 9 536 | 9 416 | 9 753 | 10 556 | 5 916 | 5 828 | 5 768 | 6 331 |
| Belgium and Luxembourg | 394 | 426 | 445 | 454 | 129 | 149 | 119 | 132 |
| France | 661 | 632 | 706 | 687 | 183 | 156 | 163 | 226 |
| Germany | 1 416 | 1 489 | 1 545 | 1 748 | 752 | 809 | 776 | 924 |
| Italy | 637 | 517 | 422 | 467 | 429 | 350 | 246 | 336 |
| Netherlands | 595 | 676 | 700 | 707 | 250 | 314 | 297 | 282 |
| Norway | 849 | 863 | 958 | 881 | 846 | 860 | 957 | 876 |
| Spain | 45 | 44 | 99 | 105 | 7 | 26 | 28 | 41 |
| Sweden | 248 | 257 | 344 | 253 | 238 | 250 | 335 | 244 |
| Switzerland | 77 | 109 | 114 | 138 | 77 | 109 | 105 | 111 |
| United Kingdom | 1 529 | 1 450 | 1 605 | 2 205 | 455 | 473 | 481 | 786 |
| Other | 3 085 | 2 953 | 2 815 | 2 911 | 2 550 | 2 332 | 2 261 | 2 373 |
| **Latin America and Other Western Hemisphere** [1] | 2 126 | 2 279 | 2 253 | 2 464 | 776 | 806 | 811 | 761 |
| South and Central America [1] | 1 487 | 1 642 | 1 569 | 1 747 | 526 | 542 | 517 | 479 |
| Argentina | 33 | 23 | 22 | 28 | 15 | 13 | 8 | 10 |
| Brazil | 101 | 93 | 93 | 121 | 45 | 62 | 44 | 58 |
| Chile | 104 | 96 | 116 | 117 | 99 | 95 | 105 | 105 |
| Venezuela | 286 | 276 | 235 | 182 | 62 | 62 | 51 | 51 |
| Other | 487 | 673 | 578 | 499 | 246 | 222 | 203 | 137 |
| Other Western Hemisphere | 639 | 637 | 684 | 717 | 250 | 264 | 294 | 282 |
| Bermuda | ..... | 1 | ..... | ..... | ..... | ..... | ..... | ..... |
| Other | 639 | 636 | 684 | 717 | 250 | 264 | 294 | 282 |
| **Africa** | 276 | 183 | 177 | 148 | 119 | 79 | 86 | 54 |
| South Africa | 16 | 22 | 18 | 30 | 10 | 13 | 10 | 23 |
| Other | 260 | 161 | 159 | 118 | 109 | 66 | 76 | 31 |
| **Middle East** | 298 | 445 | 493 | 599 | 192 | 313 | 273 | 347 |
| Israel | 131 | 139 | 251 | 283 | 45 | 73 | 75 | 80 |
| Saudi Arabia | 27 | 41 | 22 | 51 | 19 | 26 | 20 | 23 |
| Other | 140 | 265 | 220 | 265 | 128 | 214 | 178 | 244 |
| **Asia and Pacific** | 10 814 | 11 327 | 10 959 | 11 052 | 6 492 | 6 590 | 6 374 | 6 644 |
| Australia | 215 | 258 | 308 | 229 | 49 | 53 | 51 | 62 |
| China | 486 | 650 | 611 | 636 | 451 | 596 | 557 | 516 |
| Hong Kong | 261 | 176 | 585 | 587 | 197 | 104 | 141 | 165 |
| India | 102 | 71 | 98 | 65 | 79 | 36 | 44 | 22 |
| Indonesia | 40 | 41 | 63 | 22 | 11 | 7 | 38 | 14 |
| Japan | 4 626 | 4 600 | 4 207 | 4 182 | 2 340 | 2 201 | 2 032 | 2 045 |
| Malaysia | 32 | 42 | 34 | 24 | 24 | 34 | 28 | 20 |
| New Zealand | 64 | 73 | 76 | 80 | 14 | 15 | 17 | 23 |
| Philippines | 117 | 96 | 128 | 128 | 93 | 65 | 61 | 59 |
| Singapore | 393 | 438 | 713 | 811 | 381 | 419 | 542 | 654 |
| South Korea | 974 | 1 462 | 1 950 | 1 762 | 938 | 1 412 | 1 690 | 1 502 |
| Taiwan | 1 312 | 1 408 | 1 112 | 1 528 | 1 202 | 1 282 | 912 | 1 368 |
| Thailand | 37 | 47 | 116 | 52 | 7 | 10 | 8 | 25 |
| Other | 2 155 | 1 965 | 958 | 946 | 706 | 356 | 253 | 169 |
| **International organizations and unallocated** | 639 | 871 | 978 | 1 093 | 639 | 871 | 978 | 1 093 |
| **European Union** | 6 865 | 7 045 | 7 456 | 8 141 | 3 563 | 3 763 | 3 773 | 4 235 |
| **Eastern Europe** | 363 | 367 | 317 | 272 | 242 | 239 | 201 | 171 |

1. Includes Mexico.

## Table B-4.  U.S. Travel, Passenger Fare, and Other Transportation Payments, 1994–1997  —*Continued*

(Millions of dollars.)

| Country or region | Other Transportation— *Continued* | | | | | | | | | | | |
| --- | --- | --- | --- | --- | --- | --- | --- | --- | --- | --- | --- | --- |
| | Freight—*Continued* | | | | | | | | | | | |
| | Ocean | | | | Air | | | | Other | | | |
| | 1994 | 1995 | 1996 | 1997 | 1994 | 1995 | 1996 | 1997 | 1994 | 1995 | 1996 | 1997 |
| **ALL COUNTRIES** | 11 371 | 11 514 | 11 258 | 11 896 | 2 913 | 3 113 | 3 201 | 3 542 | 1 724 | 1 828 | 2 080 | 2 207 |
| **Canada** | 98 | 88 | 112 | 131 | 54 | 54 | 60 | 80 | 1 722 | 1 826 | 2 077 | 2 204 |
| **Mexico** | 49 | 78 | 95 | 104 | 8 | 8 | 8 | 11 | 2 | 2 | 3 | 3 |
| **Europe** | 4 877 | 4 654 | 4 539 | 5 022 | 1 039 | 1 174 | 1 229 | 1 309 | ..... | ..... | ..... | ..... |
| Belgium and Luxembourg | 65 | 70 | 41 | 58 | 64 | 79 | 78 | 74 | ..... | ..... | ..... | ..... |
| France | 61 | 19 | 16 | 66 | 122 | 137 | 147 | 160 | ..... | ..... | ..... | ..... |
| Germany | 517 | 538 | 501 | 639 | 235 | 271 | 275 | 285 | ..... | ..... | ..... | ..... |
| Italy | 348 | 276 | 180 | 270 | 81 | 74 | 66 | 66 | ..... | ..... | ..... | ..... |
| Netherlands | 98 | 135 | 123 | 123 | 152 | 179 | 174 | 159 | ..... | ..... | ..... | ..... |
| Norway | 846 | 860 | 957 | 876 | ..... | ..... | ..... | ..... | ..... | ..... | ..... | ..... |
| Spain | ..... | ..... | ..... | 2 | 7 | 26 | 28 | 39 | ..... | ..... | ..... | ..... |
| Sweden | 216 | 218 | 299 | 204 | 22 | 32 | 36 | 40 | ..... | ..... | ..... | ..... |
| Switzerland | ..... | ..... | ..... | ..... | 77 | 109 | 105 | 111 | ..... | ..... | ..... | ..... |
| United Kingdom | 272 | 260 | 217 | 474 | 183 | 213 | 264 | 312 | ..... | ..... | ..... | ..... |
| Other | 2 454 | 2 278 | 2 205 | 2 310 | 96 | 54 | 56 | 63 | ..... | ..... | ..... | ..... |
| **Latin America and Other Western Hemisphere** [1] | 592 | 646 | 659 | 591 | 182 | 158 | 149 | 167 | 2 | 2 | 3 | 3 |
| South and Central America [1] | 365 | 391 | 374 | 317 | 159 | 149 | 140 | 159 | 2 | 2 | 3 | 3 |
| Argentina | 11 | 5 | 2 | 3 | 4 | 8 | 6 | 7 | ..... | ..... | ..... | ..... |
| Brazil | 18 | 34 | 22 | 11 | 27 | 28 | 22 | 47 | ..... | ..... | ..... | ..... |
| Chile | 79 | 59 | 73 | 56 | 20 | 36 | 32 | 49 | ..... | ..... | ..... | ..... |
| Venezuela | 60 | 60 | 50 | 51 | 2 | 2 | 1 | ..... | ..... | ..... | ..... | ..... |
| Other | 148 | 155 | 132 | 92 | 98 | 67 | 71 | 45 | ..... | ..... | ..... | ..... |
| Other Western Hemisphere | 227 | 255 | 285 | 274 | 23 | 9 | 9 | 8 | ..... | ..... | ..... | ..... |
| Bermuda | ..... | ..... | ..... | ..... | ..... | ..... | ..... | ..... | ..... | ..... | ..... | ..... |
| Other | 227 | 255 | 285 | 274 | 23 | 9 | 9 | 8 | ..... | ..... | ..... | ..... |
| **Africa** | 108 | 65 | 81 | 42 | 11 | 14 | 5 | 12 | ..... | ..... | ..... | ..... |
| South Africa | 6 | 8 | 5 | 15 | 4 | 5 | 5 | 8 | ..... | ..... | ..... | ..... |
| Other | 102 | 57 | 76 | 27 | 7 | 9 | ..... | 4 | ..... | ..... | ..... | ..... |
| **Middle East** | 115 | 198 | 178 | 228 | 77 | 115 | 95 | 119 | ..... | ..... | ..... | ..... |
| Israel | ..... | ..... | ..... | ..... | 45 | 73 | 75 | 80 | ..... | ..... | ..... | ..... |
| Saudi Arabia | ..... | ..... | ..... | ..... | 19 | 26 | 20 | 23 | ..... | ..... | ..... | ..... |
| Other | 115 | 198 | 178 | 228 | 13 | 16 | ..... | 16 | ..... | ..... | ..... | ..... |
| **Asia and Pacific** | 4 942 | 4 992 | 4 711 | 4 789 | 1 550 | 1 598 | 1 663 | 1 855 | ..... | ..... | ..... | ..... |
| Australia | 24 | 28 | 24 | 36 | 25 | 25 | 27 | 26 | ..... | ..... | ..... | ..... |
| China | 297 | 397 | 343 | 253 | 154 | 199 | 214 | 263 | ..... | ..... | ..... | ..... |
| Hong Kong | 194 | 104 | 139 | 162 | 3 | ..... | 2 | 3 | ..... | ..... | ..... | ..... |
| India | 62 | 23 | 35 | 14 | 17 | 13 | 9 | 8 | ..... | ..... | ..... | ..... |
| Indonesia | 5 | 2 | 34 | 8 | 6 | 5 | 4 | 6 | ..... | ..... | ..... | ..... |
| Japan | 1 766 | 1 630 | 1 482 | 1 467 | 574 | 571 | 550 | 578 | ..... | ..... | ..... | ..... |
| Malaysia | 8 | 6 | 7 | 7 | 16 | 28 | 21 | 13 | ..... | ..... | ..... | ..... |
| New Zealand | ..... | ..... | ..... | ..... | 14 | 15 | 17 | 23 | ..... | ..... | ..... | ..... |
| Philippines | 77 | 46 | 43 | 36 | 16 | 19 | 18 | 23 | ..... | ..... | ..... | ..... |
| Singapore | 316 | 328 | 426 | 519 | 65 | 91 | 116 | 135 | ..... | ..... | ..... | ..... |
| South Korea | 891 | 1 005 | 1 249 | 945 | 47 | 407 | 441 | 557 | ..... | ..... | ..... | ..... |
| Taiwan | 1 161 | 1 146 | 757 | 1 203 | 41 | 136 | 155 | 165 | ..... | ..... | ..... | ..... |
| Thailand | 3 | 5 | 2 | 8 | 4 | 5 | 6 | 17 | ..... | ..... | ..... | ..... |
| Other | 138 | 272 | 170 | 131 | 568 | 84 | 83 | 38 | ..... | ..... | ..... | ..... |
| **International organizations and unallocated** | 639 | 871 | 978 | 1 093 | ..... | ..... | ..... | ..... | ..... | ..... | ..... | ..... |
| **European Union** | 2 682 | 2 727 | 2 670 | 3 061 | 881 | 1 036 | 1 103 | 1 174 | ..... | ..... | ..... | ..... |
| **Eastern Europe** | 236 | 227 | 193 | 160 | 6 | 12 | 8 | 11 | ..... | ..... | ..... | ..... |

1. Includes Mexico.

## Table B-4.   U.S. Travel, Passenger Fare, and Other Transportation Payments, 1994–1997   —Continued

(Millions of dollars.)

| Country or region | Other Transportation— Continued | | | | | | | | | | | |
| --- | --- | --- | --- | --- | --- | --- | --- | --- | --- | --- | --- | --- |
| | Port Services | | | | | | | | | | | |
| | Total | | | | Ocean | | | | Air | | | |
| | 1994 | 1995 | 1996 | 1997 | 1994 | 1995 | 1996 | 1997 | 1994 | 1995 | 1996 | 1997 |
| ALL COUNTRIES | 10 013 | 10 579 | 10 864 | 11 305 | 2 325 | 2 555 | 2 231 | 2 186 | 7 609 | 7 947 | 8 551 | 9 034 |
| Canada | 456 | 545 | 541 | 622 | 141 | 197 | 131 | 165 | 238 | 271 | 328 | 373 |
| Mexico | 417 | 393 | 419 | 682 | 127 | 107 | 82 | 123 | 290 | 286 | 337 | 559 |
| Europe | 3 620 | 3 588 | 3 985 | 4 225 | 668 | 635 | 691 | 659 | 2 952 | 2 953 | 3 294 | 3 566 |
| Belgium and Luxembourg | 265 | 277 | 326 | 322 | 67 | 75 | 98 | 111 | 198 | 202 | 228 | 211 |
| France | 478 | 476 | 543 | 461 | 45 | 35 | 44 | 46 | 433 | 441 | 499 | 415 |
| Germany | 664 | 680 | 769 | 824 | 86 | 91 | 102 | 107 | 578 | 589 | 667 | 717 |
| Italy | 208 | 167 | 176 | 131 | 73 | 30 | 21 | 25 | 135 | 137 | 155 | 106 |
| Netherlands | 345 | 362 | 403 | 425 | 119 | 132 | 142 | 118 | 226 | 230 | 261 | 307 |
| Norway | 3 | 3 | 1 | 5 | 3 | 3 | 1 | 5 | ..... | ..... | ..... | ..... |
| Spain | 38 | 18 | 71 | 64 | 38 | 18 | 13 | 20 | ..... | ..... | 58 | 44 |
| Sweden | 10 | 7 | 9 | 9 | 10 | 7 | 9 | 9 | ..... | ..... | ..... | ..... |
| Switzerland | ..... | ..... | 9 | 27 | ..... | ..... | ..... | ..... | ..... | ..... | 9 | 27 |
| United Kingdom | 1 074 | 977 | 1 124 | 1 419 | 101 | 95 | 118 | 111 | 973 | 882 | 1 006 | 1 308 |
| Other | 535 | 621 | 554 | 538 | 126 | 149 | 143 | 107 | 409 | 472 | 411 | 431 |
| Latin America and Other Western Hemisphere [1] | 1 350 | 1 473 | 1 442 | 1 703 | 550 | 662 | 493 | 566 | 800 | 811 | 949 | 1 137 |
| South and Central America [1] | 961 | 1 100 | 1 052 | 1 268 | 407 | 553 | 397 | 450 | 554 | 547 | 655 | 818 |
| Argentina | 18 | 10 | 14 | 18 | 18 | 10 | 14 | 18 | ..... | ..... | ..... | ..... |
| Brazil | 56 | 31 | 49 | 63 | 56 | 31 | 29 | 43 | ..... | ..... | 20 | 20 |
| Chile | 5 | 1 | 11 | 12 | 5 | 1 | 11 | 12 | ..... | ..... | ..... | ..... |
| Venezuela | 224 | 214 | 184 | 131 | 123 | 114 | 66 | 126 | 101 | 100 | 118 | 5 |
| Other | 241 | 451 | 375 | 362 | 78 | 290 | 195 | 128 | 163 | 161 | 180 | 234 |
| Other Western Hemisphere | 389 | 373 | 390 | 435 | 143 | 109 | 96 | 116 | 246 | 264 | 294 | 319 |
| Bermuda | ..... | 1 | ..... | ..... | ..... | 1 | ..... | ..... | ..... | ..... | ..... | ..... |
| Other | 389 | 372 | 390 | 435 | 143 | 108 | 96 | 116 | 246 | 264 | 294 | 319 |
| Africa | 157 | 104 | 91 | 94 | 157 | 101 | 79 | 75 | ..... | 3 | 12 | 19 |
| South Africa | 6 | 9 | 8 | 7 | 6 | 6 | 4 | 2 | ..... | 3 | 4 | 5 |
| Other | 151 | 95 | 83 | 87 | 151 | 95 | 75 | 73 | ..... | ..... | 8 | 14 |
| Middle East | 106 | 132 | 220 | 252 | 106 | 132 | 146 | 82 | ..... | ..... | 74 | 170 |
| Israel | 86 | 66 | 176 | 203 | 86 | 66 | 107 | 57 | ..... | ..... | 69 | 146 |
| Saudi Arabia | 8 | 15 | 2 | 28 | 8 | 15 | ..... | 12 | ..... | ..... | 2 | 16 |
| Other | 12 | 51 | 42 | 21 | 12 | 51 | 39 | 13 | ..... | ..... | 3 | 8 |
| Asia and Pacific | 4 322 | 4 737 | 4 585 | 4 408 | 703 | 828 | 691 | 639 | 3 619 | 3 909 | 3 894 | 3 769 |
| Australia | 166 | 205 | 257 | 167 | 3 | 4 | 9 | 1 | 163 | 201 | 248 | 166 |
| China | 35 | 54 | 54 | 120 | 35 | 54 | 50 | 5 | ..... | ..... | 4 | 115 |
| Hong Kong | 64 | 72 | 444 | 422 | 64 | 72 | 65 | 51 | ..... | ..... | 379 | 371 |
| India | 23 | 35 | 54 | 43 | 23 | 35 | 46 | 43 | ..... | ..... | 8 | ..... |
| Indonesia | 29 | 34 | 25 | 8 | 29 | 34 | 25 | 8 | ..... | ..... | ..... | ..... |
| Japan | 2 286 | 2 399 | 2 175 | 2 137 | 213 | 220 | 177 | 165 | 2 073 | 2 179 | 1 998 | 1 972 |
| Malaysia | 8 | 8 | 6 | 4 | 8 | 8 | 6 | 4 | ..... | ..... | ..... | ..... |
| New Zealand | 50 | 58 | 59 | 57 | ..... | 1 | 2 | 1 | 50 | 57 | 57 | 56 |
| Philippines | 24 | 31 | 67 | 69 | 24 | 31 | 13 | 8 | ..... | ..... | 54 | 61 |
| Singapore | 12 | 19 | 171 | 157 | 12 | 19 | 6 | 10 | ..... | ..... | 165 | 147 |
| South Korea | 36 | 50 | 260 | 260 | 36 | 50 | 116 | 114 | ..... | ..... | 144 | 146 |
| Taiwan | 110 | 126 | 200 | 160 | 110 | 126 | 81 | 50 | ..... | ..... | 119 | 110 |
| Thailand | 30 | 37 | 108 | 27 | 30 | 37 | 19 | 5 | ..... | ..... | 89 | 22 |
| Other | 1 449 | 1 609 | 705 | 777 | 116 | 137 | 76 | 174 | 1 333 | 1 472 | 629 | 603 |
| International organizations and unallocated | ..... | ..... | ..... | ..... | ..... | ..... | ..... | ..... | ..... | ..... | ..... | ..... |
| European Union | 3 302 | 3 282 | 3 683 | 3 906 | 545 | 516 | 585 | 574 | 2 757 | 2 766 | 3 098 | 3 332 |
| Eastern Europe | 121 | 128 | 116 | 101 | 77 | 84 | 75 | 58 | 44 | 44 | 41 | 43 |

1. Includes Mexico.

## Table B-5.  U.S. Royalty and License Fee Receipts, 1994–1997

(Millions of dollars.)

| Country or region | Total | | | | Affiliated | | | | | | | |
| --- | --- | --- | --- | --- | --- | --- | --- | --- | --- | --- | --- | --- |
| | | | | | Total | | | | By U.S. parents from their foreign affiliates | | | |
| | 1994 | 1995 | 1996 | 1997 | 1994 | 1995 | 1996 | 1997 | 1994 | 1995 | 1996 | 1997 |
| ALL COUNTRIES | 26 712 | 30 289 | 32 823 | 33 676 | 20 275 | 22 859 | 24 710 | 25 515 | 19 250 | 21 399 | 22 781 | 23 457 |
| Canada | 1 466 | 1 387 | 1 541 | 1 561 | 1 227 | 1 162 | 1 279 | 1 333 | 1 189 | 1 124 | 1 229 | 1 283 |
| Mexico | 678 | 434 | 477 | 628 | 548 | (D) | (D) | 549 | 542 | 349 | 384 | 491 |
| Europe | 13 842 | 15 572 | 17 109 | 16 544 | 11 848 | 13 270 | 14 252 | 13 768 | 11 292 | 12 363 | 12 911 | 12 753 |
| Belgium and Luxembourg | 759 | 770 | 810 | 705 | 634 | 656 | 682 | 610 | 626 | 646 | 623 | 592 |
| France | 1 795 | 2 126 | 2 447 | 2 214 | 1 570 | 1 867 | 2 116 | 1 895 | 1 488 | 1 648 | 1 720 | 1 836 |
| Germany | 2 685 | 2 945 | 2 871 | 2 750 | 2 231 | 2 373 | 2 173 | 2 082 | 2 154 | 2 286 | 2 097 | 2 012 |
| Italy | 1 130 | 1 182 | 1 177 | 1 032 | 926 | 976 | 949 | 794 | 881 | 884 | 906 | 756 |
| Netherlands | 1 701 | 1 926 | 2 260 | 2 656 | 1 616 | 1 826 | (D) | 2 541 | 1 443 | 1 585 | 1 859 | 2 174 |
| Norway | 98 | 96 | 108 | 97 | 69 | (D) | 84 | 71 | 69 | 79 | 83 | 70 |
| Spain | 507 | 687 | 709 | 574 | 439 | 580 | 591 | 451 | 429 | 572 | 589 | 451 |
| Sweden | 289 | 367 | 552 | 398 | 202 | 216 | (D) | (D) | 200 | 215 | 244 | 219 |
| Switzerland | 562 | 597 | 634 | 667 | 485 | 517 | 510 | 561 | 474 | 506 | 471 | 467 |
| United Kingdom | 2 560 | 2 663 | 3 035 | 3 175 | 2 182 | 2 246 | 2 533 | 2 655 | 2 037 | 2 023 | 2 205 | 2 310 |
| Other | 1 756 | 2 211 | 2 504 | 2 274 | 1 495 | (D) | 2 150 | (D) | 1 493 | 1 919 | 2 114 | 1 866 |
| Latin America and Other Western Hemisphere [1] | 1 443 | 1 449 | 1 599 | 2 116 | 1 060 | 1 067 | 1 192 | 1 714 | 1 048 | 1 036 | 1 169 | 1 639 |
| South and Central America [1] | 1 352 | 1 315 | 1 459 | 1 749 | 994 | (D) | 1 093 | 1 377 | 984 | 950 | 1 074 | 1 307 |
| Argentina | 159 | 161 | 203 | 215 | 101 | 103 | 148 | 158 | 101 | 97 | 145 | 156 |
| Brazil | 222 | 355 | 416 | 489 | 158 | 269 | 301 | 371 | 154 | 269 | 301 | 367 |
| Chile | 47 | 38 | 46 | 53 | 23 | 15 | 22 | 27 | 23 | 15 | 20 | 26 |
| Venezuela | 92 | 112 | 114 | 127 | 66 | 82 | (D) | 95 | 66 | 82 | 82 | 95 |
| Other | 154 | 216 | 203 | 237 | 99 | (D) | 142 | 177 | 99 | 137 | 141 | 171 |
| Other Western Hemisphere | 91 | 135 | 140 | 367 | 66 | (D) | 99 | 337 | 64 | 86 | 95 | 332 |
| Bermuda | 46 | 89 | 83 | 77 | 42 | 76 | (D) | 76 | 42 | 76 | (D) | 76 |
| Other | 46 | 46 | 57 | 291 | 24 | (D) | (D) | 261 | 22 | 10 | (D) | 257 |
| Africa | 150 | 205 | 245 | 224 | 72 | 114 | 144 | 122 | 71 | 113 | 142 | 122 |
| South Africa | 102 | 151 | 168 | 151 | 47 | 85 | 102 | 98 | 45 | 84 | 102 | 98 |
| Other | 48 | 54 | 77 | 73 | 25 | 29 | 41 | 24 | 25 | 29 | 40 | 24 |
| Middle East | 255 | 254 | 118 | 155 | 32 | 25 | 32 | 40 | 28 | 24 | 28 | 35 |
| Israel | 58 | (D) | 59 | 63 | 17 | 12 | 19 | 18 | 16 | 12 | 19 | 18 |
| Saudi Arabia | 166 | (D) | 33 | 48 | 13 | 9 | 6 | 14 | 9 | 9 | 6 | 13 |
| Other | 31 | 21 | 27 | 44 | 2 | 4 | 7 | 8 | 2 | 4 | 4 | 3 |
| Asia and Pacific | 8 162 | 9 846 | 10 476 | 11 334 | 5 021 | 6 077 | 6 575 | 7 263 | 4 660 | 5 668 | 6 162 | 6 452 |
| Australia | 685 | 658 | 690 | 697 | (D) | 514 | 543 | 543 | 530 | 505 | 540 | 539 |
| China | 72 | 113 | 155 | 245 | 24 | 54 | 90 | 164 | 24 | 52 | 87 | 163 |
| Hong Kong | 328 | 342 | 328 | 352 | (D) | 269 | 260 | (D) | 243 | 266 | 257 | 281 |
| India | 51 | 56 | 67 | 78 | 19 | 18 | 19 | 19 | 19 | 18 | 19 | 19 |
| Indonesia | 69 | 72 | 85 | 87 | 31 | 28 | 32 | 39 | 30 | 28 | 31 | 38 |
| Japan | 5 008 | 5 889 | 5 991 | 6 643 | 3 030 | 3 600 | 3 587 | 4 136 | 2 708 | 3 239 | 3 224 | 3 392 |
| Malaysia | 93 | 109 | 128 | 138 | 62 | 70 | 72 | 80 | 61 | 69 | 71 | 76 |
| New Zealand | 73 | 64 | 80 | 95 | 57 | 46 | 57 | 69 | 57 | 46 | 57 | 69 |
| Philippines | 83 | 93 | 94 | 103 | 61 | 68 | 66 | 69 | 61 | 64 | 65 | 68 |
| Singapore | 688 | 1 074 | 1 475 | 1 404 | 580 | (D) | (D) | 1 321 | 571 | (D) | 1 369 | 1 302 |
| South Korea | 625 | 909 | 826 | 813 | 155 | 192 | (D) | (D) | 151 | 188 | 226 | 244 |
| Taiwan | 260 | 316 | 400 | 502 | 134 | (D) | 135 | 162 | 131 | (D) | 131 | 161 |
| Thailand | 119 | 136 | 135 | 160 | 74 | 82 | 83 | 96 | 74 | 82 | 83 | 96 |
| Other | 11 | 16 | 21 | 18 | 1 | 4 | 2 | 3 | 1 | 4 | 2 | 3 |
| International organizations and unallocated | 1 394 | 1 576 | 1 736 | 1 741 | 1 015 | 1 143 | 1 236 | 1 276 | 962 | 1 070 | 1 140 | 1 173 |
| European Union | 12 354 | 14 690 | 16 145 | 15 465 | 10 751 | 12 579 | 13 547 | 12 971 | 10 210 | 11 686 | 12 246 | 12 055 |
| Eastern Europe | 136 | 138 | 147 | 221 | 65 | 75 | 83 | 136 | 65 | 72 | 83 | 135 |

1. Includes Mexico.

## Table B-5.  U.S. Royalty and License Fee Receipts, 1994–1997 —*Continued*

(Millions of dollars.)

| Country or region | Affiliated—*Continued* By U.S. affiliates from their foreign parents | | | | Unaffiliated Total | | | | Unaffiliated Industrial processes | | | |
|---|---|---|---|---|---|---|---|---|---|---|---|---|
| | 1994 | 1995 | 1996 | 1997 | 1994 | 1995 | 1996 | 1997 | 1994 | 1995 | 1996 | 1997 |
| ALL COUNTRIES ................................................ | 1 025 | 1 460 | 1 929 | 2 058 | 6 437 | 7 430 | 8 113 | 8 161 | 3 026 | 3 513 | 3 488 | 3 272 |
| Canada .................................................................. | 38 | 38 | 50 | 49 | 239 | 225 | 261 | 229 | 54 | 55 | 81 | 82 |
| Mexico .................................................................. | 6 | (D) | (D) | 58 | 130 | (D) | (D) | 79 | 33 | 24 | 26 | 25 |
| Europe .................................................................. | 556 | 907 | 1 341 | 1 015 | 1 994 | 2 302 | 2 857 | 2 776 | 768 | 829 | 1 028 | 807 |
| Belgium and Luxembourg ................................. | 8 | 10 | 59 | 19 | 125 | 114 | 128 | 95 | 88 | 83 | 90 | 51 |
| France ............................................................. | 82 | 219 | 396 | 59 | 225 | 259 | 331 | 318 | 107 | 84 | 122 | 85 |
| Germany ......................................................... | 77 | 86 | 76 | 69 | 455 | 572 | 698 | 669 | 142 | 171 | 218 | 168 |
| Italy ................................................................ | 45 | 92 | 43 | 38 | 204 | 206 | 228 | 238 | 71 | 66 | 65 | 75 |
| Netherlands .................................................... | 173 | 242 | (D) | 367 | 85 | 100 | (D) | 114 | 30 | 36 | 80 | 41 |
| Norway ........................................................... | (*) | (D) | (*) | 1 | 30 | (D) | 24 | 27 | 15 | 5 | 3 | 2 |
| Spain .............................................................. | 10 | 9 | 1 | (*) | 68 | 106 | 119 | 123 | 18 | 31 | 28 | 26 |
| Sweden ........................................................... | 2 | 1 | (D) | (D) | 87 | 151 | (D) | (D) | 55 | 106 | 137 | 107 |
| Switzerland ..................................................... | 11 | 11 | 39 | 95 | 77 | 80 | 124 | 106 | 44 | 41 | 78 | 64 |
| United Kingdom .............................................. | 146 | 223 | 328 | 345 | 377 | 417 | 503 | 521 | 113 | 115 | 123 | 107 |
| Other .............................................................. | 2 | (D) | 36 | (D) | 260 | (D) | 355 | (D) | 85 | 90 | 85 | 82 |
| Latin America and Other Western Hemisphere [1] ........ | 13 | 31 | 24 | 75 | 383 | 382 | 406 | 402 | 86 | 88 | 83 | 69 |
| South and Central America [1] ..................................... | 10 | (D) | 19 | 70 | 358 | (D) | 366 | 372 | 83 | (D) | (D) | 69 |
| Argentina .................................................... | 0 | 6 | 3 | 1 | 59 | 58 | 55 | 58 | 13 | 9 | 4 | 5 |
| Brazil ......................................................... | 4 | 0 | 0 | 5 | 64 | 85 | 115 | 118 | 8 | 9 | 12 | 11 |
| Chile .......................................................... | (*) | 0 | 2 | 1 | 24 | 23 | 24 | 26 | 6 | 8 | 6 | 6 |
| Venezuela .................................................. | (*) | 0 | (D) | (*) | 26 | 30 | (D) | 31 | 8 | 9 | 12 | 10 |
| Other .......................................................... | (*) | (D) | 1 | 6 | 55 | (D) | 61 | 60 | 16 | (D) | (D) | 12 |
| Other Western Hemisphere ........................... | 2 | (D) | 4 | 5 | 25 | (D) | 40 | 30 | 3 | (D) | (D) | 1 |
| Bermuda ..................................................... | 0 | 0 | 0 | 0 | 4 | 13 | (D) | 1 | 1 | (D) | (D) | (*) |
| Other .......................................................... | 2 | (D) | 4 | 5 | 22 | (D) | (D) | 29 | 2 | 2 | (D) | (*) |
| Africa .................................................................... | 1 | 1 | 1 | 0 | 78 | 91 | 101 | 102 | 26 | 35 | 28 | 17 |
| South Africa .................................................... | 1 | 1 | 0 | 0 | 55 | 66 | 65 | 53 | 23 | 28 | 23 | 12 |
| Other .............................................................. | 0 | 0 | 1 | 0 | 22 | 25 | 36 | 49 | 2 | 7 | 5 | 5 |
| Middle East ........................................................... | 4 | 1 | 4 | 5 | 223 | 229 | 86 | 115 | 20 | 35 | 23 | 40 |
| Israel .............................................................. | 1 | (*) | 0 | 0 | 41 | (D) | 40 | 45 | 7 | 7 | 8 | (D) |
| Saudi Arabia ................................................... | 3 | 1 | (*) | (*) | 154 | (D) | 27 | 34 | 12 | 26 | 11 | 15 |
| Other .............................................................. | 0 | 0 | 4 | 4 | 28 | 17 | 19 | 37 | 1 | 2 | 3 | (D) |
| Asia and Pacific ................................................... | 361 | 410 | 413 | 811 | 3 141 | 3 768 | 3 901 | 4 071 | 2 063 | 2 462 | 2 238 | 2 249 |
| Australia ......................................................... | (D) | 8 | 2 | 4 | (D) | 144 | 148 | 154 | 37 | 34 | 35 | 32 |
| China .............................................................. | (*) | 2 | 3 | 1 | 47 | 59 | 65 | 81 | 33 | 31 | 43 | 48 |
| Hong Kong ...................................................... | (D) | 4 | 3 | (D) | (D) | 72 | 68 | (D) | 15 | 22 | 8 | (D) |
| India ............................................................... | 0 | 0 | 0 | 0 | 32 | 38 | 47 | 58 | 28 | 27 | 37 | 31 |
| Indonesia ........................................................ | (*) | (*) | 1 | (*) | 38 | 44 | 53 | 48 | 20 | 15 | 13 | 23 |
| Japan .............................................................. | 323 | 361 | 363 | 744 | 1 978 | 2 289 | 2 405 | 2 507 | 1 372 | 1 548 | 1 388 | 1 437 |
| Malaysia ......................................................... | (*) | (*) | 1 | 3 | 31 | 40 | 56 | 58 | 19 | (D) | (D) | (D) |
| New Zealand ................................................... | 0 | 0 | 0 | 0 | 15 | 17 | 23 | 26 | 3 | 3 | 5 | 4 |
| Philippines ...................................................... | 0 | 4 | 2 | 1 | 22 | 25 | 27 | 33 | 1 | 2 | 2 | 7 |
| Singapore ....................................................... | 10 | 19 | (D) | 19 | 108 | (D) | (D) | 83 | 73 | 34 | 30 | 44 |
| South Korea .................................................... | 4 | 4 | (D) | (D) | 470 | 717 | (D) | (D) | 396 | 607 | 478 | 391 |
| Taiwan ............................................................ | 3 | 7 | 4 | 1 | 126 | (D) | 265 | 340 | 39 | 80 | 129 | 148 |
| Thailand .......................................................... | 0 | 0 | 0 | 0 | 45 | 55 | 52 | 64 | 25 | (D) | 27 | 34 |
| Other .............................................................. | 0 | 0 | 0 | 0 | 9 | 12 | 19 | 14 | 2 | 4 | (D) | 3 |
| International organizations and unallocated .............. | 52 | 73 | 96 | 103 | 379 | 433 | 500 | 466 | 9 | 8 | 8 | 7 |
| European Union .................................................... | 541 | 893 | 1 301 | 917 | 1 603 | 2 111 | 2 598 | 2 494 | 598 | 756 | 930 | 724 |
| Eastern Europe ..................................................... | 0 | 3 | 0 | 1 | 71 | 63 | 63 | 85 | 30 | 21 | 11 | 12 |

1. Includes Mexico.

## Table B-5.  U.S. Royalty and License Fee Receipts, 1994–1997 —*Continued*

(Millions of dollars.)

| Country or region | Books, records, and tapes | | | | Broadcasting and recording of live events | | | | Franchise fees | | | |
|---|---|---|---|---|---|---|---|---|---|---|---|---|
| | 1994 | 1995 | 1996 | 1997 | 1994 | 1995 | 1996 | 1997 | 1994 | 1995 | 1996 | 1997 |
| ALL COUNTRIES | 276 | 275 | 325 | 339 | 172 | 218 | 315 | 267 | 342 | 400 | 425 | 463 |
| Canada | 20 | 15 | 15 | 15 | 9 | 13 | 12 | 13 | 34 | 33 | 36 | 18 |
| Mexico | 13 | 3 | 4 | 5 | 11 | 8 | 11 | 8 | 16 | 8 | 7 | 8 |
| Europe | 160 | 158 | 193 | 201 | 79 | 105 | 122 | 125 | 142 | 162 | 171 | 188 |
| Belgium and Luxembourg | 3 | 4 | 3 | 4 | 2 | 3 | 4 | 4 | 2 | 2 | 2 | 2 |
| France | 21 | 22 | 26 | 34 | 18 | 22 | 20 | 17 | 7 | 10 | 10 | 17 |
| Germany | 40 | 37 | 41 | 42 | (D) | 25 | 28 | 29 | 61 | 78 | 81 | 75 |
| Italy | 20 | 17 | 21 | 22 | 5 | 8 | 10 | 11 | 2 | 2 | 3 | 3 |
| Netherlands | 7 | 7 | 9 | 10 | 4 | 4 | 6 | (D) | 2 | 3 | 3 | 5 |
| Norway | 1 | 1 | 2 | 2 | 1 | 1 | 1 | 1 | 1 | 2 | 2 | 2 |
| Spain | 9 | 10 | 13 | 11 | 7 | 8 | 9 | 8 | 2 | 3 | 4 | 4 |
| Sweden | 3 | 4 | 5 | 5 | 2 | 4 | 5 | 2 | 13 | 4 | 4 | 5 |
| Switzerland | 4 | 5 | 5 | 5 | 2 | 3 | 3 | 3 | 2 | 2 | 2 | 2 |
| United Kingdom | 41 | 40 | 52 | 49 | 16 | 22 | (D) | (D) | 33 | 33 | 34 | 43 |
| Other | 11 | 12 | 17 | 17 | (D) | 6 | (D) | 14 | 16 | 22 | 24 | 30 |
| Latin America and Other Western Hemisphere [1] | 27 | 19 | 24 | 27 | 41 | 46 | 68 | 73 | 43 | 39 | 38 | 51 |
| South and Central America [1] | 26 | 18 | 23 | 26 | 39 | 43 | 60 | 63 | 35 | 28 | 26 | 36 |
| Argentina | 4 | 4 | 4 | 5 | (D) | (D) | 17 | 18 | 3 | 3 | 3 | 4 |
| Brazil | 6 | 6 | 11 | 12 | 7 | 10 | 19 | 21 | 2 | 3 | 2 | 3 |
| Chile | (*) | 1 | 1 | 1 | 2 | 4 | 5 | 5 | 3 | 3 | 2 | 3 |
| Venezuela | 1 | 2 | 1 | 1 | 1 | 1 | 2 | 2 | 2 | 1 | 1 | 1 |
| Other | 2 | 3 | 2 | 2 | (D) | (D) | 7 | 8 | 9 | 12 | 12 | 16 |
| Other Western Hemisphere | (*) | 1 | 1 | 1 | 2 | 3 | 8 | 9 | 8 | 11 | 12 | 15 |
| Bermuda | 0 | (*) | 0 | 0 | (*) | (*) | (*) | (*) | 1 | (*) | (*) | (*) |
| Other | (*) | 1 | 1 | 1 | 2 | 2 | 8 | 9 | 8 | 11 | 12 | 15 |
| Africa | 7 | 8 | 6 | 6 | 1 | 1 | 1 | 2 | 5 | 6 | 10 | 11 |
| South Africa | 6 | 8 | 6 | 5 | 1 | 1 | 1 | 1 | 2 | 2 | 3 | 4 |
| Other | (*) | (*) | 1 | 1 | 0 | (*) | (*) | (*) | 3 | 4 | 6 | 6 |
| Middle East | 3 | 7 | 7 | 8 | (*) | (*) | (*) | 1 | 15 | 24 | 25 | 29 |
| Israel | 2 | 3 | 4 | 4 | (*) | (*) | (*) | 1 | 4 | 6 | 8 | 8 |
| Saudi Arabia | 2 | 4 | 3 | 4 | (*) | (*) | 0 | 0 | (D) | 8 | 7 | 9 |
| Other | (*) | 1 | (*) | (*) | 0 | 0 | (*) | (*) | (D) | 10 | 9 | 12 |
| Asia and Pacific | 51 | 56 | 64 | 60 | 38 | 48 | (D) | 53 | 93 | 125 | 135 | 154 |
| Australia | 7 | 8 | 13 | 11 | 7 | 8 | 9 | 9 | 11 | 10 | 14 | 16 |
| China | 1 | 1 | 1 | 1 | (*) | 1 | 1 | 1 | 3 | 4 | 5 | 5 |
| Hong Kong | 6 | 3 | 2 | 2 | (D) | 3 | 4 | 4 | 8 | 10 | 10 | 11 |
| India | 1 | (*) | 1 | 1 | 0 | 0 | (*) | (*) | 1 | (*) | 1 | 4 |
| Indonesia | 3 | 4 | 4 | 4 | 1 | 2 | 3 | 3 | 5 | 8 | 8 | 8 |
| Japan | 25 | 28 | 30 | 29 | (D) | 25 | 30 | 22 | 31 | 40 | 41 | 46 |
| Malaysia | (*) | 1 | (*) | 1 | 1 | 1 | 2 | 2 | 3 | 8 | 8 | 9 |
| New Zealand | (*) | (*) | 1 | (*) | 1 | 1 | 2 | 2 | 3 | 3 | 3 | 4 |
| Philippines | 2 | 3 | 2 | 2 | 1 | 1 | 1 | 2 | 3 | 5 | 4 | 5 |
| Singapore | (*) | (*) | 3 | 2 | 1 | 1 | 1 | 1 | 3 | 4 | 8 | 5 |
| South Korea | 2 | 5 | 4 | 2 | 1 | 1 | 1 | 1 | 5 | 10 | 9 | 15 |
| Taiwan | 1 | 1 | 2 | 2 | 2 | 3 | (D) | 4 | 9 | 11 | 10 | 14 |
| Thailand | 2 | 1 | 1 | 2 | 2 | 2 | 1 | (*) | 6 | 7 | 10 | 10 |
| Other | 0 | (*) | (*) | (*) | (*) | (*) | 1 | 1 | 3 | 3 | 3 | 3 |
| International organizations and unallocated | 8 | 12 | 15 | 23 | 3 | 4 | (D) | 1 | 9 | 10 | 11 | 12 |
| European Union | 144 | 148 | 182 | 188 | 67 | 101 | 115 | 116 | 117 | 148 | 154 | 167 |
| Eastern Europe | 1 | 3 | 4 | 5 | (*) | 1 | 3 | 3 | 5 | 6 | 8 | 8 |

1. Includes Mexico.

## Table B-5.  U.S. Royalty and License Fee Receipts, 1994–1997 —Continued

(Millions of dollars.)

| Country or region | Unaffiliated—Continued | | | | | | | |
| --- | --- | --- | --- | --- | --- | --- | --- | --- |
| | Trademarks | | | | Other | | | |
| | 1994 | 1995 | 1996 | 1997 | 1994 | 1995 | 1996 | 1997 |
| ALL COUNTRIES | 794 | 930 | 991 | 1 001 | 1 827 | 2 094 | 2 569 | 2 818 |
| Canada | 23 | 34 | 35 | 32 | 98 | 74 | 83 | 69 |
| Mexico | 29 | (D) | (D) | 15 | 29 | 18 | 14 | 17 |
| Europe | 281 | 349 | 354 | 356 | 564 | 698 | 988 | 1 098 |
| Belgium and Luxembourg | 6 | 7 | (D) | 12 | 25 | 16 | (D) | 22 |
| France | 29 | 36 | 37 | 41 | 44 | 87 | 115 | 125 |
| Germany | (D) | 38 | 33 | 26 | 161 | 223 | 297 | 329 |
| Italy | 46 | 50 | 46 | 35 | 60 | 63 | 84 | 92 |
| Netherlands | 9 | 11 | (D) | 6 | 33 | 39 | 53 | (D) |
| Norway | 2 | (D) | 6 | 4 | 9 | 7 | 11 | 15 |
| Spain | 20 | 36 | 40 | 40 | 12 | 18 | 25 | 33 |
| Sweden | 4 | 7 | (D) | 6 | 10 | 25 | 27 | (D) |
| Switzerland | 10 | 11 | 8 | 5 | 15 | 18 | 29 | 26 |
| United Kingdom | 43 | 57 | (D) | 72 | 131 | 149 | 216 | (D) |
| Other | (D) | (D) | (D) | 108 | 64 | 54 | (D) | (D) |
| Latin America and Other Western Hemisphere [1] | 81 | 78 | 100 | 81 | 105 | 112 | 93 | 102 |
| South and Central America [1] | 80 | (D) | 97 | 78 | 94 | 107 | (D) | 101 |
| Argentina | (D) | (D) | 20 | 14 | 14 | 10 | 8 | 12 |
| Brazil | 17 | 19 | 30 | 21 | 25 | 38 | 41 | 49 |
| Chile | 4 | 6 | 8 | 8 | 8 | 2 | 2 | 3 |
| Venezuela | 6 | 6 | 7 | 8 | 8 | 11 | (D) | 10 |
| Other | (D) | (D) | (D) | 13 | 11 | 27 | (D) | 10 |
| Other Western Hemisphere | 1 | (D) | 3 | 3 | 10 | 5 | (D) | 1 |
| Bermuda | (*) | (D) | (*) | (*) | 1 | 1 | (D) | (*) |
| Other | 1 | (D) | 3 | 2 | 9 | 4 | (D) | 1 |
| Africa | 18 | 20 | 23 | 22 | 22 | 21 | 34 | 45 |
| South Africa | 12 | 13 | 13 | (D) | 11 | 14 | 19 | (D) |
| Other | 6 | 7 | 10 | (D) | 10 | 6 | 14 | (D) |
| Middle East | 7 | 8 | 13 | 11 | 176 | 154 | 19 | 27 |
| Israel | 2 | 3 | 7 | 6 | 25 | (D) | 13 | (D) |
| Saudi Arabia | (D) | 2 | 3 | 2 | (D) | (D) | 3 | 5 |
| Other | (D) | 3 | 3 | 3 | (D) | 2 | 3 | (D) |
| Asia and Pacific | 372 | 421 | 460 | 492 | 524 | 656 | (D) | 1 064 |
| Australia | (D) | 24 | 22 | 21 | 58 | 61 | 55 | 65 |
| China | 3 | 8 | 7 | 6 | 9 | 14 | 7 | 19 |
| Hong Kong | 21 | 22 | 31 | 25 | 17 | 13 | 14 | 14 |
| India | 1 | 4 | 3 | 11 | 2 | 6 | 6 | 11 |
| Indonesia | 7 | 10 | 15 | 3 | 3 | 5 | 10 | 7 |
| Japan | (D) | 290 | 313 | 362 | 271 | 357 | 602 | 610 |
| Malaysia | 3 | (D) | (D) | 2 | 5 | 4 | 8 | (D) |
| New Zealand | 5 | 5 | 5 | (D) | 4 | 5 | 8 | (D) |
| Philippines | 9 | 12 | 14 | 15 | 5 | 3 | 4 | 2 |
| Singapore | 3 | 3 | (D) | (D) | 27 | (D) | (D) | (D) |
| South Korea | 19 | 23 | (D) | 15 | 48 | 70 | 83 | (D) |
| Taiwan | 8 | 9 | (D) | 9 | 67 | (D) | (D) | 163 |
| Thailand | 3 | (D) | 8 | 7 | 7 | 6 | 5 | 11 |
| Other | 3 | 3 | (D) | 6 | 1 | 1 | 1 | 2 |
| International organizations and unallocated | 11 | 20 | 7 | 8 | 338 | 379 | (D) | 414 |
| European Union | 199 | 303 | 304 | 307 | 478 | 653 | 914 | 992 |
| Eastern Europe | 9 | 14 | 9 | (D) | 25 | 19 | 29 | (D) |

1. Includes Mexico.

## Table B-6.  U.S. Royalty and License Fee Payments, 1994–1997

(Millions of dollars.)

| Country or region | Total | | | | Affiliated | | | | | | | |
| --- | --- | --- | --- | --- | --- | --- | --- | --- | --- | --- | --- | --- |
| | | | | | Total | | | | By U.S. parents to their foreign affiliates | | | |
| | 1994 | 1995 | 1996 | 1997 | 1994 | 1995 | 1996 | 1997 | 1994 | 1995 | 1996 | 1997 |
| ALL COUNTRIES | 5 852 | 6 919 | 7 854 | 9 411 | 3 934 | 5 257 | 5 506 | 7 087 | 420 | 583 | 766 | 955 |
| Canada | 93 | 151 | 217 | 317 | 58 | 111 | 128 | 200 | 26 | 31 | 22 | 30 |
| Mexico | 39 | 52 | 60 | 117 | (D) | (D) | (D) | 109 | 15 | 6 | 11 | 21 |
| Europe | 3 909 | 4 561 | 4 896 | 5 917 | 2 788 | 3 529 | 3 782 | 4 518 | 271 | 400 | 542 | 682 |
| Belgium and Luxembourg | 92 | 121 | 123 | 138 | 63 | 73 | 80 | 100 | 11 | 9 | 10 | 23 |
| France | (D) | 374 | 445 | 723 | 148 | 170 | 210 | 287 | 27 | 28 | 31 | 28 |
| Germany | 631 | 714 | 731 | 904 | 462 | 527 | 543 | 689 | 43 | 54 | 60 | 69 |
| Italy | 55 | 98 | 143 | 116 | 40 | 61 | 92 | 79 | 20 | 20 | 18 | 27 |
| Netherlands | 312 | 459 | 448 | 498 | 272 | 411 | 414 | 454 | 15 | 12 | 16 | 18 |
| Norway | (D) | 9 | 12 | 12 | 2 | (D) | 4 | 2 | 1 | (D) | 1 | 1 |
| Spain | 29 | 26 | 16 | 21 | (D) | 23 | 13 | 12 | 5 | 8 | 11 | 10 |
| Sweden | (D) | 53 | 104 | 153 | 54 | 47 | 54 | (D) | 3 | 2 | 3 | 6 |
| Switzerland | 550 | 642 | 689 | 785 | 420 | 551 | 591 | 682 | 15 | 38 | 68 | 73 |
| United Kingdom | 1 445 | 1 846 | 1 914 | 2 116 | 1 164 | 1 506 | 1 590 | 1 791 | 59 | 119 | 165 | 257 |
| Other | 193 | 220 | 270 | 450 | (D) | (D) | 190 | (D) | 72 | (D) | 157 | 170 |
| Latin America and Other Western Hemisphere [1] | 85 | 91 | 173 | 187 | 55 | 67 | 125 | 149 | 22 | 14 | 26 | 41 |
| South and Central America [1] | 55 | 67 | 151 | 154 | (D) | (D) | (D) | 124 | 22 | 13 | (D) | 29 |
| Argentina | 1 | 4 | 38 | 9 | (*) | 3 | 37 | 7 | (*) | 3 | 4 | 1 |
| Brazil | 3 | 1 | 1 | 7 | (*) | 1 | (*) | 1 | 0 | 0 | 0 | 1 |
| Chile | 1 | 3 | (*) | 1 | (*) | (*) | (D) | 0 | (*) | (*) | (D) | 0 |
| Venezuela | (D) | 2 | 35 | 2 | 4 | 1 | (D) | 1 | 4 | 1 | 2 | 1 |
| Other | (D) | 6 | 16 | 18 | 2 | 2 | (D) | 5 | 2 | 2 | 2 | 4 |
| Other Western Hemisphere | 30 | 24 | 22 | 34 | (D) | (D) | (D) | 25 | 1 | 1 | (D) | 12 |
| Bermuda | (D) | 3 | 2 | 8 | (D) | 3 | 2 | 8 | 1 | 0 | (*) | 1 |
| Other | (D) | 21 | 20 | 26 | 5 | (D) | (D) | 17 | 0 | 1 | (D) | 11 |
| Africa | 6 | 2 | 6 | 13 | 4 | 1 | 1 | 5 | 4 | 1 | 1 | 5 |
| South Africa | 4 | 1 | 5 | 9 | 3 | (*) | 1 | 1 | 3 | (*) | 1 | 1 |
| Other | 2 | 1 | (*) | 4 | 1 | (*) | (*) | 4 | 1 | (*) | (*) | 4 |
| Middle East | 12 | 18 | 13 | 13 | 2 | 4 | 2 | 2 | 1 | (*) | (*) | 1 |
| Israel | 10 | 17 | 13 | 12 | 1 | 4 | 2 | 2 | (*) | (*) | (*) | 1 |
| Saudi Arabia | 1 | 1 | (*) | 1 | 1 | (*) | (*) | (*) | 1 | (*) | (*) | (*) |
| Other | 1 | (*) | (*) | (*) | 0 | 0 | 0 | 0 | 0 | 0 | 0 | 0 |
| Asia and Pacific | 1 112 | 1 666 | 1 626 | 2 325 | 798 | 1 248 | 1 158 | 1 814 | 70 | 103 | 133 | 143 |
| Australia | 23 | 22 | 32 | 85 | 14 | 13 | 18 | (D) | 9 | 8 | 11 | 10 |
| China | 8 | 1 | (D) | 41 | 1 | (*) | (*) | 1 | 1 | (*) | (*) | 1 |
| Hong Kong | 13 | (D) | 17 | 30 | 10 | 8 | 10 | (D) | 10 | 8 | 10 | 8 |
| India | 2 | 2 | (*) | 2 | 1 | 1 | 0 | (*) | 1 | 1 | 0 | (*) |
| Indonesia | 1 | 1 | 1 | 2 | 1 | 1 | 1 | 1 | 1 | 1 | 1 | 1 |
| Japan | 1 030 | 1 561 | 1 432 | 2 082 | 747 | 1 188 | 1 069 | 1 675 | 30 | 66 | 87 | 86 |
| Malaysia | 4 | (*) | (*) | 1 | 4 | 0 | 0 | 0 | 4 | 0 | 0 | 0 |
| New Zealand | 2 | 2 | 11 | 12 | 2 | (*) | (*) | (*) | 2 | 0 | (*) | 0 |
| Philippines | 2 | 2 | 2 | 2 | 1 | (*) | (*) | (*) | 1 | (*) | (*) | (*) |
| Singapore | 4 | 5 | (D) | 4 | 3 | 3 | (D) | (D) | 2 | 2 | 1 | (*) |
| South Korea | 11 | (D) | 47 | 38 | 5 | 9 | (D) | 22 | 4 | 8 | 10 | 16 |
| Taiwan | 10 | 24 | 15 | 19 | 8 | 23 | 14 | 16 | 4 | 8 | 11 | 15 |
| Thailand | 2 | 7 | 2 | 6 | 2 | 1 | 2 | 5 | 2 | 1 | 2 | 5 |
| Other | (*) | (*) | (*) | 1 | (*) | 0 | 0 | 1 | (*) | 0 | 0 | 1 |
| International organizations and unallocated | 635 | 431 | 923 | 639 | 229 | 297 | 311 | 399 | 27 | 34 | 43 | 53 |
| European Union | 3 004 | 3 875 | 4 131 | 5 035 | 2 221 | 2 970 | 3 180 | 3 829 | 188 | 356 | 467 | 603 |
| Eastern Europe | 18 | 8 | 12 | 15 | 7 | 5 | 6 | 4 | 6 | 3 | 5 | 3 |

1. Includes Mexico.

## Table B-6.  U.S. Royalty and License Fee Payments, 1994–1997 —*Continued*

(Millions of dollars.)

| Country or region | Affiliated—*Continued* By U.S. affiliates to their foreign parents | | | | Unaffiliated Total | | | | Industrial processes | | | |
|---|---|---|---|---|---|---|---|---|---|---|---|---|
| | 1994 | 1995 | 1996 | 1997 | 1994 | 1995 | 1996 | 1997 | 1994 | 1995 | 1996 | 1997 |
| **ALL COUNTRIES** .......................................... | 3 514 | 4 674 | 4 740 | 6 132 | 1 919 | 1 663 | 2 347 | 2 324 | 1 034 | 948 | 1 233 | 1 265 |
| **Canada** ...................................................... | 32 | 79 | 106 | 170 | 35 | 40 | 89 | 117 | 11 | 13 | 57 | 76 |
| **Mexico** ...................................................... | (D) | (D) | (D) | 88 | (D) | (D) | (D) | 8 | 1 | (D) | (*) | (D) |
| **Europe** ...................................................... | 2 518 | 3 130 | 3 240 | 3 837 | 1 120 | 1 032 | 1 114 | 1 399 | 712 | 572 | 765 | 774 |
| Belgium and Luxembourg ............................. | 52 | 64 | 70 | 78 | 28 | 48 | 43 | 38 | 27 | 30 | 36 | 32 |
| France ......................................................... | 121 | 142 | 180 | 259 | (D) | 204 | 234 | 437 | 92 | 121 | 192 | 199 |
| Germany ...................................................... | 420 | 473 | 483 | 620 | 169 | 187 | 189 | 215 | 113 | 110 | 148 | 148 |
| Italy ............................................................ | 21 | 42 | 74 | 51 | 15 | 37 | 51 | 38 | 7 | 9 | (D) | (D) |
| Netherlands ................................................. | 257 | 399 | 398 | 436 | 40 | 48 | 34 | 45 | 22 | 27 | 24 | 22 |
| Norway ........................................................ | 1 | (D) | 3 | 1 | (D) | (D) | 7 | 10 | (D) | (D) | 5 | 5 |
| Spain .......................................................... | (D) | 15 | 1 | 2 | (D) | 3 | 4 | 9 | (*) | 1 | 1 | 1 |
| Sweden ........................................................ | 50 | 45 | 51 | (D) | (D) | 6 | 50 | (D) | (D) | 3 | 49 | 55 |
| Switzerland .................................................. | 405 | 512 | 522 | 609 | 130 | 91 | 98 | 103 | 114 | 79 | 72 | 85 |
| United Kingdom ........................................... | 1 105 | 1 387 | 1 424 | 1 534 | 281 | 340 | 324 | 325 | 104 | 126 | 132 | 111 |
| Other ........................................................... | (D) | (D) | 33 | (D) | (D) | (D) | 80 | (D) | 54 | (D) | (D) | (D) |
| **Latin America and Other Western Hemisphere** [1] ........ | 33 | 53 | 98 | 108 | 29 | 25 | 48 | 38 | 15 | 14 | 11 | 8 |
| South and Central America [1] ......................... | (D) | (D) | 92 | 95 | (D) | (D) | (D) | 29 | (D) | (D) | (D) | 2 |
| Argentina ................................................. | 0 | 0 | 33 | 6 | (*) | (*) | 1 | 2 | 0 | 0 | 0 | 0 |
| Brazil ...................................................... | (*) | 1 | (*) | (*) | 2 | 1 | 1 | 5 | 2 | (*) | (*) | (*) |
| Chile ....................................................... | 0 | 0 | 0 | 0 | (*) | 2 | (D) | 1 | (*) | (*) | 0 | 0 |
| Venezuela ............................................... | 0 | 0 | (D) | 0 | (D) | (*) | (D) | 1 | (*) | (*) | 1 | (*) |
| Other ...................................................... | (*) | (*) | (D) | 1 | (D) | 4 | (D) | 13 | (D) | (*) | (D) | (D) |
| Other Western Hemisphere ......................... | (D) | (D) | 7 | 13 | (D) | (D) | (D) | 9 | (D) | (D) | (D) | 7 |
| Bermuda .................................................. | (D) | 3 | 1 | 7 | (D) | 0 | (*) | 0 | (D) | 0 | 0 | 0 |
| Other ...................................................... | 5 | (D) | 5 | 6 | (D) | (D) | (D) | 9 | (D) | (D) | (D) | 7 |
| **Africa** ........................................................ | 0 | 0 | 0 | 0 | 2 | 1 | 5 | 9 | 1 | (*) | 4 | 3 |
| South Africa ................................................ | 0 | 0 | 0 | 0 | 2 | 1 | 5 | 8 | 1 | (*) | 4 | 3 |
| Other ........................................................... | 0 | 0 | 0 | 0 | (*) | (*) | (*) | (*) | 0 | 0 | 0 | 0 |
| **Middle East** ............................................... | 1 | 4 | 2 | 1 | 11 | 14 | 10 | 11 | 9 | 13 | 10 | 9 |
| Israel .......................................................... | 1 | 4 | 2 | 1 | 9 | 13 | 10 | 10 | 9 | 13 | 10 | 9 |
| Saudi Arabia ............................................... | 0 | 0 | 0 | 0 | (*) | 1 | (*) | 1 | (*) | (*) | 0 | 0 |
| Other ........................................................... | 0 | 0 | 0 | 0 | 1 | (*) | (*) | (*) | 0 | 0 | 0 | 0 |
| **Asia and Pacific** ........................................ | 728 | 1 145 | 1 024 | 1 671 | 315 | 417 | 468 | 511 | 283 | 333 | 382 | 391 |
| Australia ...................................................... | 5 | 5 | 6 | (D) | 9 | 9 | 15 | (D) | 3 | 3 | 9 | 3 |
| China .......................................................... | 0 | 0 | 0 | 0 | 7 | 1 | (D) | 41 | 7 | (*) | (D) | (D) |
| Hong Kong .................................................. | 0 | 0 | 0 | (D) | 3 | (D) | 6 | (D) | 3 | (D) | (*) | (*) |
| India ........................................................... | (*) | (*) | 0 | 0 | 1 | 1 | (*) | 1 | (*) | (*) | 0 | (*) |
| Indonesia .................................................... | 0 | 0 | 0 | 0 | (*) | (*) | (*) | 1 | 0 | (*) | (*) | 0 |
| Japan .......................................................... | 717 | 1 122 | 982 | 1 590 | 283 | 373 | 363 | 407 | 262 | 307 | 305 | 334 |
| Malaysia ...................................................... | 0 | 0 | 0 | 0 | (*) | (*) | (*) | 1 | 0 | (*) | (*) | (*) |
| New Zealand ................................................ | (*) | (*) | (*) | (*) | (*) | 2 | 11 | 12 | (*) | 1 | (D) | (*) |
| Philippines .................................................. | 0 | 0 | 0 | 0 | 1 | 1 | 2 | 2 | (*) | (*) | (*) | (*) |
| Singapore .................................................... | 1 | 2 | (D) | (D) | 1 | 1 | (D) | (D) | (*) | (*) | (*) | 0 |
| South Korea ................................................ | (*) | 1 | (D) | 5 | 7 | (D) | (D) | 16 | 6 | (D) | (D) | (D) |
| Taiwan ........................................................ | 4 | 15 | 2 | 2 | 2 | 1 | 1 | 2 | 2 | (*) | (*) | (*) |
| Thailand ...................................................... | 0 | 0 | 0 | 0 | (*) | 5 | (*) | 1 | (*) | 5 | 0 | (*) |
| Other ........................................................... | 0 | 0 | 0 | 0 | (*) | (*) | (*) | (*) | 0 | (*) | (*) | 0 |
| **International organizations and unallocated** ............. | 202 | 263 | 268 | 346 | 406 | 134 | 612 | 240 | 3 | 3 | 3 | 3 |
| **European Union** ......................................... | 2 033 | 2 614 | 2 714 | 3 226 | 784 | 906 | 951 | 1 206 | 395 | 461 | 635 | 613 |
| **Eastern Europe** ......................................... | 1 | 1 | 1 | 1 | 11 | 3 | 6 | 12 | (*) | 1 | 4 | 4 |

1. Includes Mexico.

## Table B-6.  U.S. Royalty and License Fee Payments, 1994–1997 —*Continued*

(Millions of dollars.)

| Country or region | Books, records, and tapes | | | | Broadcasting and recording of live events | | | | Franchise fees | | | |
|---|---|---|---|---|---|---|---|---|---|---|---|---|
| | 1994 | 1995 | 1996 | 1997 | 1994 | 1995 | 1996 | 1997 | 1994 | 1995 | 1996 | 1997 |
| **ALL COUNTRIES** | 126 | 131 | 146 | 164 | 296 | 37 | 523 | 68 | 1 | 1 | 6 | 8 |
| **Canada** | 13 | 16 | 20 | 21 | 2 | 2 | 3 | 4 | (*) | (*) | 0 | 0 |
| **Mexico** | (D) | 1 | 3 | 3 | (*) | (*) | 1 | 1 | 0 | 0 | 0 | 0 |
| **Europe** | 95 | 97 | 94 | 1 120 | (D) | 34 | (D) | 60 | (*) | (*) | 6 | 8 |
| Belgium and Luxembourg | (*) | (*) | (*) | (*) | (*) | (*) | (*) | (*) | 0 | 0 | 0 | 0 |
| France | 5 | 4 | 6 | 6 | (*) | 4 | 4 | (D) | 0 | 0 | 0 | 0 |
| Germany | 3 | 3 | 4 | 5 | 1 | (*) | (*) | (*) | (*) | (*) | 0 | 0 |
| Italy | 7 | 6 | 2 | 2 | 1 | 1 | 1 | 1 | 0 | 0 | 0 | 0 |
| Netherlands | 1 | 2 | 2 | 3 | (*) | (*) | (*) | (*) | 0 | 0 | 0 | 0 |
| Norway | (*) | 0 | (*) | (*) | (D) | 0 | 0 | 1 | 0 | 0 | 0 | 0 |
| Spain | (D) | 1 | 1 | 2 | (*) | (*) | (*) | 1 | 0 | 0 | 0 | 0 |
| Sweden | 1 | 1 | 1 | 1 | (*) | 1 | (*) | (*) | 0 | 0 | 0 | 0 |
| Switzerland | 2 | 1 | 3 | 2 | 1 | (*) | (D) | 8 | 0 | 0 | 0 | 0 |
| United Kingdom | 73 | 76 | 71 | 87 | (D) | 28 | 33 | 39 | 0 | 0 | 0 | 0 |
| Other | (D) | 2 | 3 | 3 | 0 | (*) | (*) | (D) | 0 | (*) | 6 | 8 |
| **Latin America and Other Western Hemisphere** [1] | 8 | 5 | 6 | 5 | 1 | (*) | 1 | 1 | 1 | 1 | 0 | 0 |
| South and Central America [1] | 6 | 3 | 4 | 4 | 1 | (*) | 1 | 1 | 0 | 1 | 0 | 0 |
| Argentina | (*) | (*) | 1 | 1 | 0 | 0 | 0 | (*) | 0 | 0 | 0 | 0 |
| Brazil | (*) | (*) | (*) | (*) | (*) | (*) | (*) | (*) | 0 | 0 | 0 | 0 |
| Chile | (*) | 0 | 0 | 0 | 0 | 0 | 0 | (*) | 0 | 0 | 0 | 0 |
| Venezuela | (D) | (*) | (*) | (*) | (*) | (*) | (*) | (*) | 0 | 0 | 0 | 0 |
| Other | 2 | 1 | 1 | (*) | 0 | 0 | 0 | 0 | 0 | 1 | 0 | 0 |
| Other Western Hemisphere | 2 | 2 | 1 | 1 | 0 | 0 | 0 | 0 | 1 | 0 | 0 | 0 |
| Bermuda | 0 | 0 | 0 | 0 | 0 | 0 | 0 | 0 | 0 | 0 | 0 | 0 |
| Other | 2 | 2 | 1 | 1 | 0 | 0 | 0 | 0 | 1 | 0 | 0 | 0 |
| **Africa** | 1 | 1 | 1 | 1 | (*) | 0 | 0 | 1 | 0 | 0 | 0 | 0 |
| South Africa | 1 | 1 | 1 | 1 | 0 | 0 | 0 | 1 | 0 | 0 | 0 | 0 |
| Other | (*) | (*) | (*) | (*) | (*) | 0 | 0 | 0 | 0 | 0 | 0 | 0 |
| **Middle East** | (*) | (*) | (*) | (*) | 0 | (*) | 0 | 0 | 0 | 0 | 0 | 0 |
| Israel | (*) | (*) | (*) | (*) | 0 | (*) | 0 | 0 | 0 | 0 | 0 | 0 |
| Saudi Arabia | 0 | 0 | 0 | 0 | 0 | 0 | 0 | 0 | 0 | 0 | 0 | 0 |
| Other | 0 | 0 | 0 | 0 | 0 | 0 | 0 | 0 | 0 | 0 | 0 | 0 |
| **Asia and Pacific** | 6 | 7 | 20 | 20 | (*) | (*) | 1 | 1 | 0 | (*) | 0 | 0 |
| Australia | 2 | 2 | 4 | 4 | (*) | (*) | (*) | 1 | 0 | 0 | 0 | 0 |
| China | 0 | 0 | 0 | 0 | 0 | (*) | 0 | 0 | 0 | 0 | 0 | 0 |
| Hong Kong | (*) | (*) | 1 | 1 | 0 | 0 | 0 | 0 | 0 | 0 | 0 | 0 |
| India | 0 | 0 | 0 | 0 | 0 | 0 | 0 | 0 | 0 | 0 | 0 | 0 |
| Indonesia | 0 | 0 | (*) | (*) | 0 | 0 | 0 | 0 | 0 | 0 | 0 | 0 |
| Japan | 2 | 1 | 3 | 3 | (*) | (*) | (*) | (*) | 0 | 0 | 0 | 0 |
| Malaysia | (*) | 0 | 0 | 0 | 0 | 0 | 0 | 0 | 0 | 0 | 0 | 0 |
| New Zealand | (*) | 1 | (D) | 9 | 0 | 0 | 0 | 0 | 0 | 0 | 0 | 0 |
| Philippines | 1 | 1 | 1 | 2 | 0 | 0 | 0 | 0 | 0 | 0 | 0 | 0 |
| Singapore | (*) | 1 | (D) | 0 | 0 | 0 | 0 | 0 | 0 | 0 | 0 | 0 |
| South Korea | 1 | (*) | 0 | (*) | 0 | 0 | 0 | 0 | 0 | 0 | 0 | 0 |
| Taiwan | (*) | (*) | (*) | (*) | 0 | 0 | 0 | 0 | 0 | 0 | 0 | 0 |
| Thailand | 0 | 0 | 0 | 0 | 0 | 0 | 0 | 0 | 0 | (*) | 0 | 0 |
| Other | (*) | 0 | (*) | (*) | 0 | 0 | 0 | 0 | 0 | 0 | 0 | 0 |
| **International organizations and unallocated** | 3 | 4 | 5 | 5 | (D) | (*) | (D) | (*) | 0 | 0 | 0 | (*) |
| **European Union** | 91 | 94 | 89 | 107 | 25 | 34 | 38 | 51 | (*) | (*) | 6 | 8 |
| **Eastern Europe** | (D) | 2 | 2 | 2 | 0 | 0 | 0 | (*) | 0 | (*) | 0 | 0 |

1. Includes Mexico.

## Table B-6.   U.S. Royalty and License Fee Payments, 1994–1997 —Continued

(Millions of dollars.)

| Country or region | Unaffiliated—Continued | | | | | | | |
|---|---|---|---|---|---|---|---|---|
| | Trademarks | | | | Other | | | |
| | 1994 | 1995 | 1996 | 1997 | 1994 | 1995 | 1996 | 1997 |
| ALL COUNTRIES | 154 | 151 | 135 | 200 | 306 | 394 | 304 | 620 |
| Canada | 1 | 3 | 2 | 4 | 7 | 7 | 8 | 12 |
| Mexico | 1 | (*) | (*) | (*) | (*) | (*) | (D) | (D) |
| Europe | 110 | 107 | (D) | 84 | (D) | 221 | 127 | 361 |
| Belgium and Luxembourg | 1 | 1 | 1 | 2 | (*) | 16 | 5 | 3 |
| France | 1 | (D) | 3 | 6 | (D) | (D) | 29 | (D) |
| Germany | 24 | 13 | 10 | (D) | 28 | 61 | 27 | (D) |
| Italy | 1 | 1 | 1 | 1 | (*) | 20 | (D) | (D) |
| Netherlands | 7 | (*) | (*) | (D) | 9 | 18 | 8 | (D) |
| Norway | (*) | (*) | (*) | (*) | (*) | (*) | 2 | 3 |
| Spain | (*) | (*) | (*) | 1 | (*) | (*) | (*) | 5 |
| Sweden | 1 | 1 | (*) | 4 | (*) | (*) | (*) | (D) |
| Switzerland | 11 | 7 | (D) | 2 | 2 | 3 | (*) | 5 |
| United Kingdom | 63 | 78 | 43 | 45 | (D) | 31 | 44 | 45 |
| Other | (*) | (D) | (D) | (*) | (D) | (D) | (D) | 14 |
| Latin America and Other Western Hemisphere [1] | 1 | 1 | (D) | 1 | 3 | 4 | (D) | 22 |
| South and Central America [1] | 1 | 1 | (D) | 1 | (D) | 4 | (D) | 21 |
| Argentina | 0 | 0 | (*) | 0 | (*) | (*) | (*) | 1 |
| Brazil | (*) | (*) | (*) | (*) | (*) | (*) | (*) | 4 |
| Chile | 0 | 0 | 0 | 0 | 0 | 2 | (D) | 1 |
| Venezuela | (*) | (*) | (D) | (*) | (*) | (*) | (*) | (*) |
| Other | 0 | (*) | 1 | 1 | (D) | 1 | (D) | (D) |
| Other Western Hemisphere | 1 | 0 | 0 | 0 | (D) | (*) | (*) | 1 |
| Bermuda | 0 | 0 | 0 | 0 | (D) | 0 | (*) | 0 |
| Other | 1 | 0 | 0 | 0 | (D) | (*) | (*) | 1 |
| Africa | 0 | 0 | 0 | 0 | (*) | (*) | (*) | 3 |
| South Africa | 0 | 0 | 0 | 0 | (*) | (*) | (*) | 3 |
| Other | 0 | 0 | 0 | 0 | (*) | (*) | (*) | 0 |
| Middle East | (*) | (*) | (*) | (*) | 1 | 1 | (*) | 2 |
| Israel | (*) | (*) | (*) | (*) | (*) | (*) | (*) | 1 |
| Saudi Arabia | 0 | 0 | (*) | (*) | (*) | (*) | (*) | 1 |
| Other | 0 | 0 | 0 | 0 | 1 | (*) | (*) | (*) |
| Asia and Pacific | 10 | 9 | 15 | 12 | 15 | 68 | 51 | 87 |
| Australia | 2 | 1 | 1 | 2 | 2 | 2 | (*) | (D) |
| China | 0 | 0 | 0 | 0 | (*) | 1 | (*) | (D) |
| Hong Kong | (*) | 3 | 4 | 3 | (*) | (*) | 1 | (D) |
| India | 0 | 0 | 0 | 0 | 1 | 1 | (*) | 1 |
| Indonesia | 0 | 0 | 0 | 0 | (*) | (*) | (*) | 1 |
| Japan | 8 | 4 | 9 | 7 | 10 | 60 | 46 | 62 |
| Malaysia | 0 | 0 | 0 | 0 | (*) | (*) | (*) | 1 |
| New Zealand | (*) | 0 | (*) | (*) | (*) | (*) | (*) | 2 |
| Philippines | 0 | 0 | 0 | (*) | 1 | (*) | 1 | 1 |
| Singapore | (*) | 1 | (*) | 0 | (*) | (*) | 1 | (D) |
| South Korea | (*) | (*) | (*) | (*) | (*) | 1 | (*) | (D) |
| Taiwan | (*) | (*) | (*) | (*) | (*) | 1 | 1 | 2 |
| Thailand | 0 | (*) | 0 | 0 | (*) | (*) | (*) | (*) |
| Other | 0 | 0 | 0 | 0 | (*) | (*) | (*) | 0 |
| International organizations and unallocated | 32 | 32 | (D) | 98 | (D) | 94 | (D) | 133 |
| European Union | 98 | 99 | 59 | 81 | 174 | 218 | 124 | 345 |
| Eastern Europe | 0 | (*) | 0 | 0 | (*) | 1 | (*) | 6 |

1. Includes Mexico.

## Table B-7.  United States: Other Private Service Receipts, 1994–1997

(Millions of dollars.)

| Country or region | Total | | | | Affiliated | | | | | | | |
| --- | --- | --- | --- | --- | --- | --- | --- | --- | --- | --- | --- | --- |
| | | | | | Total | | | | Between U.S. parents and their foreign affiliates | | | |
| | 1994 | 1995 | 1996 | 1997 | 1994 | 1995 | 1996 | 1997 | 1994 | 1995 | 1996 | 1997 |
| **ALL COUNTRIES** | 61 880 | 65 555 | 75 152 | 84 465 | 20 043 | 20 791 | 23 779 | 26 336 | 13 530 | 13 341 | 14 772 | 16 164 |
| **Canada** | 6 437 | 6 879 | 7 830 | 8 323 | 3 254 | 3 558 | 4 092 | 4 314 | 2 540 | 2 623 | 2 630 | 2 813 |
| **Mexico** | 3 218 | 3 166 | 3 347 | 3 841 | 407 | 315 | 353 | 442 | 336 | 265 | 294 | 360 |
| **Europe** | 21 873 | 22 980 | 27 064 | 31 199 | 9 948 | 10 138 | 11 924 | 13 302 | 7 083 | 6 763 | 7 469 | 8 154 |
| Belgium and Luxembourg | 1 036 | 982 | 937 | 1 013 | 413 | 373 | 360 | 348 | 380 | 346 | 337 | 318 |
| France | 2 097 | 2 447 | 2 820 | 3 231 | 1 061 | 1 179 | 1 435 | 1 444 | 809 | 797 | 821 | 866 |
| Germany | 2 932 | 2 872 | 3 731 | 4 277 | 1 433 | 1 337 | 1 752 | 1 902 | 750 | 604 | 598 | 633 |
| Italy | 1 008 | 1 096 | 1 246 | 1 373 | 379 | 390 | 466 | 509 | 283 | 296 | 322 | 386 |
| Netherlands | 2 122 | 2 360 | 2 659 | 3 071 | 1 550 | 1 660 | 1 832 | 2 226 | 1 296 | 1 246 | 1 425 | 1 798 |
| Norway | 288 | 337 | 467 | 497 | 102 | 146 | 209 | 231 | 79 | 57 | 79 | 79 |
| Spain | 912 | (D) | (D) | (D) | 186 | (D) | (D) | (D) | 184 | 181 | 173 | 173 |
| Sweden | 521 | 528 | 749 | 938 | 180 | 115 | 276 | 438 | 61 | 44 | 46 | 51 |
| Switzerland | 1 412 | 1 445 | 1 676 | 2 000 | 835 | 801 | 929 | 1 110 | 531 | 581 | 617 | 663 |
| United Kingdom | 6 635 | 6 738 | 7 785 | 9 460 | 3 173 | 3 161 | 3 395 | 3 890 | 2 167 | 2 109 | 2 318 | 2 582 |
| Other | 2 913 | (D) | (D) | (D) | 637 | (D) | (D) | (D) | 544 | 503 | 733 | 604 |
| **Latin America and Other Western Hemisphere** [1] | 10 102 | 10 362 | 11 270 | 13 520 | 1 342 | 1 391 | 1 393 | 1 547 | 959 | 849 | 891 | 1 039 |
| South and Central America [1] | 7 847 | 8 069 | 8 579 | 9 725 | 869 | 803 | 893 | 1 043 | 659 | 581 | 668 | 832 |
| Argentina | 645 | 686 | 743 | 799 | 54 | 60 | 70 | 76 | 53 | 53 | 62 | 64 |
| Brazil | 819 | 1 056 | 1 125 | 1 419 | 117 | 188 | 167 | 186 | 76 | 102 | 128 | 171 |
| Chile | 522 | 306 | 380 | 426 | 36 | 36 | 27 | 29 | 35 | 34 | 27 | 25 |
| Venezuela | (D) | (D) | 540 | 699 | (D) | (D) | 58 | 82 | 69 | 49 | 51 | 73 |
| Other | (D) | (D) | 2 445 | 2 543 | (D) | (D) | 218 | 229 | 90 | 78 | 106 | 139 |
| Other Western Hemisphere | 2 255 | 2 293 | 2 689 | 3 795 | 473 | 588 | 501 | 504 | 300 | 269 | 223 | 207 |
| Bermuda | 686 | 489 | 744 | 944 | 215 | 332 | 260 | 218 | 115 | 79 | 80 | 70 |
| Other | 1 570 | 1 803 | 1 946 | 2 851 | 258 | 256 | 241 | 286 | 185 | 189 | 143 | 137 |
| **Africa** | (D) | 1 483 | 1 652 | 1 847 | (D) | 143 | 117 | 157 | 99 | 86 | 92 | 117 |
| South Africa | 199 | 226 | (D) | 386 | 16 | 19 | (D) | 36 | 16 | 16 | 17 | 32 |
| Other | (D) | 1 255 | (D) | 1 462 | (D) | 124 | (D) | 121 | 84 | 71 | 75 | 85 |
| **Middle East** | (D) | 2 478 | 3 206 | 3 508 | (D) | 334 | 299 | 217 | 87 | 101 | 105 | 88 |
| Israel | (D) | (D) | 430 | 455 | (D) | (D) | 25 | 28 | 7 | 2 | 9 | 16 |
| Saudi Arabia | (D) | (D) | (D) | (D) | (D) | (D) | (D) | (D) | 21 | 16 | 21 | 13 |
| Other | 792 | 806 | (D) | (D) | 83 | 101 | (D) | (D) | 60 | 83 | 75 | 60 |
| **Asia and Pacific** | 16 676 | 18 203 | 20 486 | 22 477 | 4 843 | 5 057 | 5 712 | 6 591 | 2 623 | 2 749 | 3 344 | 3 747 |
| Australia | 1 075 | 1 320 | 1 447 | 1 520 | 381 | 448 | 463 | 424 | 345 | 401 | 435 | 381 |
| China | 1 084 | 1 318 | 1 555 | 1 644 | 36 | 68 | 106 | 165 | 31 | 36 | 63 | 111 |
| Hong Kong | 1 054 | 1 136 | 1 577 | 1 616 | 403 | 409 | 630 | 701 | 360 | 364 | 570 | 619 |
| India | 642 | 677 | 719 | 720 | 1 | 7 | 18 | 24 | 1 | 7 | 18 | 23 |
| Indonesia | 574 | 792 | 903 | 1 193 | 119 | 135 | 90 | 98 | 118 | 128 | 84 | 89 |
| Japan | 6 031 | 6 384 | 6 896 | 7 618 | 2 688 | 2 705 | 2 874 | 3 434 | 663 | 736 | 860 | 968 |
| Malaysia | (D) | (D) | 731 | 647 | (D) | (D) | 108 | 156 | 111 | 95 | 103 | 152 |
| New Zealand | 161 | 184 | 235 | (D) | 25 | 41 | 39 | (D) | 24 | 39 | 38 | 29 |
| Philippines | 399 | 308 | 371 | 526 | 41 | 39 | 47 | 83 | 41 | 39 | 40 | 74 |
| Singapore | 964 | 1 002 | 1 379 | 1 460 | 627 | 637 | 899 | 935 | 577 | 560 | 802 | 889 |
| South Korea | 1 128 | (D) | 1 556 | (D) | 83 | (D) | 170 | (D) | 73 | 95 | 111 | 147 |
| Taiwan | 1 106 | 1 132 | 1 084 | 1 231 | 220 | 191 | 165 | 196 | 197 | 165 | 125 | 160 |
| Thailand | 486 | 582 | 550 | 593 | 58 | 64 | 80 | 87 | 57 | 63 | 73 | 76 |
| Other | (D) | 1 393 | 1 484 | 1 602 | (D) | 19 | 23 | 30 | 25 | 19 | 22 | 30 |
| **International organizations and unallocated** | 3 063 | 3 170 | 3 644 | 3 593 | 139 | 169 | 240 | 208 | 139 | 169 | 240 | 208 |
| **European Union** | 17 853 | 19 318 | 21 061 | 26 224 | 8 674 | 9 121 | 10 621 | 11 836 | 6 292 | 6 074 | 6 611 | 7 289 |
| **Eastern Europe** | 1 003 | 1 211 | 1 428 | 1 489 | 53 | 59 | 62 | 119 | 50 | 42 | 59 | 116 |

1. Includes Mexico.

## Table B-7.  United States: Other Private Service Receipts, 1994–1997 —Continued

(Millions of dollars.)

| Country or region | Affiliated—Continued Between U.S. affiliates and their foreign parents | | | | Unaffiliated Total | | | | Unaffiliated Education | | | |
|---|---|---|---|---|---|---|---|---|---|---|---|---|
| | 1994 | 1995 | 1996 | 1997 | 1994 | 1995 | 1996 | 1997 | 1994 | 1995 | 1996 | 1997 |
| ALL COUNTRIES | 6 513 | 7 450 | 9 007 | 10 172 | 41 838 | 44 764 | 51 374 | 58 128 | 7 174 | 7 515 | 7 888 | 8 278 |
| Canada | 715 | 935 | 1 462 | 1 502 | 3 183 | 3 321 | 3 738 | 4 009 | 383 | 403 | 425 | 443 |
| Mexico | 70 | 50 | 59 | 82 | 2 811 | 2 851 | 2 994 | 3 399 | 131 | 151 | 153 | 159 |
| Europe | 2 866 | 3 375 | 4 455 | 5 149 | 11 925 | 12 842 | 15 140 | 17 897 | 1 139 | 1 245 | 1 352 | 1 438 |
| Belgium and Luxembourg | 34 | 27 | 23 | 30 | 623 | 609 | 577 | 665 | 16 | 17 | 17 | 18 |
| France | 252 | 382 | 614 | 578 | 1 036 | 1 268 | 1 385 | 1 787 | 99 | 101 | 103 | 105 |
| Germany | 683 | 734 | 1 154 | 1 269 | 1 499 | 1 535 | 1 979 | 2 375 | 142 | 148 | 162 | 174 |
| Italy | 96 | 94 | 144 | 123 | 629 | 706 | 780 | 864 | 43 | 47 | 50 | 52 |
| Netherlands | 254 | 415 | 407 | 428 | 572 | 700 | 827 | 845 | 31 | 32 | 35 | 36 |
| Norway | 23 | 90 | 130 | 152 | 186 | 191 | 258 | 266 | 42 | 38 | 40 | 42 |
| Spain | 1 | (D) | (D) | (D) | 726 | 664 | 711 | 837 | 84 | 86 | 84 | 85 |
| Sweden | 119 | 71 | 230 | 387 | 341 | 413 | 473 | 500 | 55 | 61 | 70 | 78 |
| Switzerland | 304 | 221 | 312 | 447 | 577 | 644 | 747 | 890 | 27 | 29 | 30 | 31 |
| United Kingdom | 1 006 | 1 053 | 1 077 | 1 308 | 3 462 | 3 575 | 4 390 | 5 569 | 132 | 137 | 143 | 141 |
| Other | 93 | (D) | (D) | (D) | 2 276 | 2 537 | 3 014 | 3 279 | 469 | 550 | 619 | 676 |
| Latin America and Other Western Hemisphere [1] | 383 | 542 | 502 | 509 | 8 760 | 8 971 | 9 877 | 11 973 | 740 | 793 | 837 | 915 |
| South and Central America [1] | 210 | 223 | 225 | 212 | 6 978 | 7 266 | 7 686 | 8 682 | 569 | 606 | 643 | 697 |
| Argentina | 1 | 6 | 8 | 12 | 591 | 626 | 673 | 723 | 33 | 34 | 38 | 42 |
| Brazil | 41 | 87 | 39 | 15 | 702 | 868 | 958 | 1 233 | 81 | 84 | 97 | 109 |
| Chile | 2 | 2 | (*) | 4 | 486 | 270 | 353 | 397 | 15 | 15 | 18 | 20 |
| Venezuela | (D) | (D) | 7 | 9 | 468 | 491 | 482 | 617 | 61 | 69 | 79 | 92 |
| Other | (D) | (D) | 111 | 90 | 1 922 | 2 162 | 2 227 | 2 314 | 247 | 253 | 259 | 275 |
| Other Western Hemisphere | 173 | 319 | 278 | 297 | 1 782 | 1 705 | 2 188 | 3 291 | 171 | 187 | 194 | 218 |
| Bermuda | 100 | 252 | 180 | 148 | 471 | 157 | 484 | 726 | 10 | 10 | 11 | 12 |
| Other | 73 | 67 | 98 | 149 | 1 312 | 1 547 | 1 705 | 2 565 | 161 | 177 | 183 | 206 |
| Africa | (D) | 56 | 26 | 40 | 1 204 | 1 340 | 1 535 | 1 690 | 325 | 341 | 359 | 378 |
| South Africa | (*) | 3 | (D) | 4 | 183 | 207 | 295 | 350 | 31 | 34 | 35 | 36 |
| Other | (D) | 53 | (D) | 36 | 1 021 | 1 131 | 1 241 | 1 341 | 293 | 307 | 324 | 343 |
| Middle East | (D) | 233 | 193 | 128 | 2 012 | 2 144 | 2 907 | 3 291 | 351 | 355 | 363 | 374 |
| Israel | (D) | (D) | 16 | 12 | 335 | 360 | 405 | 427 | 46 | 44 | 45 | 47 |
| Saudi Arabia | (D) | (D) | (D) | (D) | 966 | 1 077 | 971 | 1 065 | 59 | 67 | 72 | 76 |
| Other | 23 | 18 | (D) | (D) | 709 | 705 | 1 532 | 1 799 | 246 | 244 | 245 | 251 |
| Asia and Pacific | 2 220 | 2 309 | 2 368 | 2 844 | 11 833 | 13 146 | 14 774 | 15 886 | 4 237 | 4 379 | 4 551 | 4 730 |
| Australia | 36 | 46 | 28 | 43 | 694 | 872 | 984 | 1 095 | 37 | 40 | 43 | 43 |
| China | 5 | 32 | 43 | 54 | 1 048 | 1 250 | 1 449 | 1 479 | 576 | 530 | 556 | 545 |
| Hong Kong | 43 | 45 | 60 | 81 | 651 | 727 | 947 | 915 | 178 | 174 | 169 | 164 |
| India | (*) | (*) | (*) | (*) | 641 | 670 | 701 | 696 | 451 | 451 | 446 | 442 |
| Indonesia | 1 | 6 | 6 | 9 | 455 | 657 | 813 | 1 095 | 152 | 160 | 180 | 195 |
| Japan | 2 025 | 1 969 | 2 015 | 2 467 | 3 343 | 3 679 | 4 022 | 4 185 | 701 | 745 | 785 | 835 |
| Malaysia | (D) | (D) | 5 | 5 | 391 | 389 | 623 | 491 | 178 | 183 | 197 | 206 |
| New Zealand | 1 | 2 | 1 | (D) | 136 | 143 | 196 | 237 | 14 | 15 | 15 | 15 |
| Philippines | (*) | (*) | 7 | 10 | 358 | 269 | 324 | 443 | 46 | 47 | 44 | 43 |
| Singapore | 51 | 77 | 97 | 46 | 337 | 365 | 480 | 525 | 63 | 60 | 58 | 55 |
| South Korea | 10 | (D) | 59 | (D) | 1 045 | 1 290 | 1 386 | 1 615 | 403 | 452 | 509 | 570 |
| Taiwan | 24 | 26 | 39 | 36 | 886 | 941 | 919 | 1 035 | 488 | 490 | 459 | 444 |
| Thailand | 1 | 1 | 7 | 11 | 428 | 518 | 470 | 506 | 124 | 146 | 171 | 200 |
| Other | (D) | 0 | 1 | 1 | 1 419 | 1 374 | 1 461 | 1 572 | 825 | 886 | 921 | 973 |
| International organizations and unallocated | 0 | 0 | 0 | 0 | 2 924 | 3 001 | 3 404 | 3 384 | 0 | 0 | 0 | 0 |
| European Union | 2 382 | 3 047 | 4 010 | 4 547 | 9 179 | 10 196 | 10 440 | 14 388 | 656 | 674 | 699 | 717 |
| Eastern Europe | 3 | 17 | 3 | 3 | 950 | 1 152 | 1 366 | 1 370 | 164 | 213 | 252 | 285 |

1. Includes Mexico.

## Table B-7.  United States: Other Private Service Receipts, 1994–1997 —*Continued*

(Millions of dollars.)

| Country or region | Unaffiliated—*Continued* | | | | | | | | | | | |
| --- | --- | --- | --- | --- | --- | --- | --- | --- | --- | --- | --- | --- |
| | Financial services | | | | Insurance | | | | | | | |
| | | | | | Net | | | | Premiums | | | |
| | 1994 | 1995 | 1996 | 1997 | 1994 | 1995 | 1996 | 1997 | 1994 | 1995 | 1996 | 1997 |
| ALL COUNTRIES | 5 763 | 7 029 | 8 382 | 11 064 | 1 676 | 1 296 | 1 971 | 2 391 | 4 921 | 5 491 | 5 978 | 5 952 |
| Canada | 389 | 580 | 599 | 571 | 391 | 373 | 343 | 353 | 1 027 | 1 106 | 1 062 | 1 013 |
| Mexico | 231 | 160 | 254 | 248 | 50 | 37 | 43 | 57 | 117 | 101 | 98 | 114 |
| Europe | 2 454 | 2 948 | 3 669 | 4 710 | 359 | 270 | 545 | 785 | 2 076 | 2 575 | 2 726 | 2 371 |
| Belgium and Luxembourg | 138 | 143 | 168 | 172 | 36 | 52 | 62 | 54 | 95 | 149 | 131 | 102 |
| France | 214 | 246 | 308 | 435 | 8 | 89 | 32 | 130 | 173 | 216 | 204 | 221 |
| Germany | 169 | 196 | 333 | 328 | 74 | 61 | 128 | 88 | 180 | 264 | 312 | 299 |
| Italy | 89 | 121 | 165 | 140 | 10 | 29 | 15 | 40 | 40 | 62 | 74 | 75 |
| Netherlands | 141 | 179 | 217 | 256 | 10 | 19 | -14 | -37 | 35 | 42 | 42 | 42 |
| Norway | 15 | 20 | 27 | 39 | 12 | 5 | 44 | 18 | 21 | 34 | 65 | 55 |
| Spain | 66 | 70 | 103 | 145 | 20 | 6 | 9 | 16 | 27 | 23 | 33 | 25 |
| Sweden | 41 | 51 | 90 | 91 | 8 | 8 | 16 | 14 | 22 | 33 | 42 | 30 |
| Switzerland | 237 | 303 | 351 | 395 | 7 | -45 | -43 | -13 | 104 | 89 | 84 | 53 |
| United Kingdom | 1 055 | 1 272 | 1 510 | 2 201 | 174 | 6 | 281 | 431 | 1 305 | 1 556 | 1 610 | 1 316 |
| Other | 287 | 346 | 397 | 508 | 1 | 40 | 14 | 45 | 73 | 108 | 129 | 154 |
| Latin America and Other Western Hemisphere [1] | 1 529 | 1 705 | 2 050 | 3 216 | 465 | 147 | 405 | 738 | 843 | 801 | 1 031 | 1 430 |
| South and Central America [1] | 694 | 679 | 924 | 1 253 | 226 | 210 | 217 | 189 | 457 | 470 | 553 | 603 |
| Argentina | 107 | 111 | 162 | 211 | 69 | 46 | 43 | 20 | 120 | 110 | 122 | 135 |
| Brazil | 106 | 122 | 173 | 280 | 9 | 8 | 5 | 5 | 12 | 14 | 22 | 23 |
| Chile | 56 | 42 | 57 | 70 | 12 | 19 | 26 | 24 | 32 | 44 | 65 | 84 |
| Venezuela | 40 | 60 | 74 | 139 | 11 | 9 | 7 | 16 | 19 | 17 | 26 | 28 |
| Other | 154 | 184 | 204 | 305 | 76 | 92 | 94 | 68 | 156 | 183 | 220 | 220 |
| Other Western Hemisphere | 835 | 1 027 | 1 126 | 1 963 | 240 | -63 | 187 | 549 | 386 | 330 | 478 | 827 |
| Bermuda | 174 | 184 | 293 | 487 | 203 | -139 | 109 | 163 | 321 | 198 | 350 | 372 |
| Other | 661 | 843 | 833 | 1 476 | 37 | 76 | 79 | 385 | 65 | 132 | 128 | 455 |
| Africa | 54 | 66 | 101 | 106 | -1 | 6 | 6 | 8 | 7 | 13 | 16 | 17 |
| South Africa | 14 | 20 | 27 | 35 | 2 | 3 | 1 | 3 | 2 | 5 | 7 | 7 |
| Other | 40 | 46 | 74 | 71 | -3 | 3 | 5 | 4 | 4 | 9 | 9 | 9 |
| Middle East | 178 | 206 | 249 | 265 | 8 | 21 | 7 | 14 | 30 | 36 | 45 | 52 |
| Israel | 56 | 54 | 62 | 75 | 3 | 7 | 7 | 1 | 16 | 19 | 25 | 35 |
| Saudi Arabia | 42 | 46 | 62 | 59 | 3 | 2 | 1 | 2 | 4 | 4 | 4 | 4 |
| Other | 80 | 106 | 125 | 131 | 2 | 11 | (*) | 11 | 9 | 13 | 16 | 13 |
| Asia and Pacific | 1 111 | 1 406 | 1 609 | 1 982 | 393 | 418 | 418 | 432 | 821 | 833 | 916 | 888 |
| Australia | 87 | 121 | 160 | 173 | 28 | 50 | 37 | 25 | 76 | 101 | 111 | 109 |
| China | 7 | 23 | 40 | 54 | -1 | 23 | (*) | 3 | 7 | 25 | 10 | 16 |
| Hong Kong | 157 | 191 | 264 | 281 | 26 | 26 | 10 | 12 | 44 | 47 | 53 | 36 |
| India | 32 | 29 | 31 | 36 | 2 | 4 | 3 | (*) | 2 | 6 | 7 | 7 |
| Indonesia | 31 | 83 | 59 | 93 | (*) | 5 | 4 | -1 | 3 | 9 | 16 | 15 |
| Japan | 382 | 482 | 471 | 597 | 246 | 241 | 324 | 314 | 471 | 461 | 524 | 483 |
| Malaysia | 29 | 36 | 42 | 41 | 12 | 5 | 2 | 4 | 18 | 14 | 14 | 13 |
| New Zealand | 11 | 13 | 23 | 19 | 11 | 14 | 7 | 10 | 15 | 19 | 15 | 13 |
| Philippines | 25 | 30 | 45 | 48 | 10 | 6 | -7 | 6 | 15 | 14 | 15 | 15 |
| Singapore | 96 | 105 | 171 | 188 | 16 | 3 | 12 | 20 | 38 | 28 | 25 | 30 |
| South Korea | 65 | 89 | 121 | 161 | 5 | 15 | 7 | 4 | 26 | 26 | 25 | 22 |
| Taiwan | 56 | 76 | 80 | 115 | 27 | 20 | 14 | 28 | 87 | 71 | 88 | 111 |
| Thailand | 29 | 36 | 46 | 43 | 10 | 5 | 5 | 8 | 16 | 8 | 12 | 14 |
| Other | 104 | 91 | 56 | 133 | 2 | 2 | (*) | (*) | 2 | 3 | (*) | 2 |
| International organizations and unallocated | 49 | 117 | 105 | 214 | 61 | 61 | 248 | 61 | 118 | 127 | 182 | 182 |
| European Union | 2 023 | 2 501 | 1 636 | 4 021 | 338 | 320 | 525 | 768 | 1 909 | 2 434 | 2 548 | 2 229 |
| Eastern Europe | 40 | 54 | 79 | 100 | 1 | -1 | 7 | 11 | 5 | 14 | 21 | 25 |

1. Includes Mexico.

## Table B-7.  United States: Other Private Service Receipts, 1994–1997 —*Continued*

(Millions of dollars.)

| Country or region | Insurance—Continued Losses 1994 | 1995 | 1996 | 1997 | Telecommunications 1994 | 1995 | 1996 | 1997 | Business, professional, and technical services 1994 | 1995 | 1996 | 1997 |
|---|---|---|---|---|---|---|---|---|---|---|---|---|
| ALL COUNTRIES | 3 245 | 4 195 | 4 007 | 3 561 | 2 865 | 3 228 | 3 270 | 3 771 | 15 330 | 16 064 | 19 678 | 21 304 |
| Canada | 636 | 734 | 719 | 660 | 244 | 299 | 295 | 272 | 1 376 | 1 241 | 1 639 | 1 943 |
| Mexico | 68 | 65 | 55 | 57 | 195 | 251 | 350 | 432 | 714 | 671 | 630 | 793 |
| Europe | 1 717 | 2 306 | 2 182 | 1 586 | 924 | 950 | 876 | 1 092 | 4 921 | 5 143 | 6 225 | 6 690 |
| Belgium and Luxembourg | 58 | 97 | 69 | 48 | 37 | 40 | 32 | 92 | 340 | 286 | 211 | 250 |
| France | 166 | 127 | 172 | 91 | 72 | 72 | 59 | 86 | 436 | 496 | 647 | 694 |
| Germany | 106 | 204 | 184 | 210 | 144 | 118 | 74 | 77 | 554 | 613 | 753 | 858 |
| Italy | 31 | 34 | 59 | 36 | 83 | 92 | 45 | 46 | 185 | 206 | 290 | 318 |
| Netherlands | 25 | 24 | 56 | 79 | 45 | 40 | 32 | 52 | 266 | 339 | 450 | 437 |
| Norway | 10 | 29 | 21 | 37 | 16 | 33 | 40 | 52 | 68 | 63 | 64 | 70 |
| Spain | 7 | 16 | 24 | 9 | 46 | 45 | 35 | 37 | 266 | 173 | 225 | 236 |
| Sweden | 14 | 25 | 26 | 15 | 28 | 24 | 20 | 27 | 147 | 191 | 216 | 230 |
| Switzerland | 97 | 133 | 127 | 67 | 46 | 44 | 37 | 47 | 205 | 262 | 326 | 376 |
| United Kingdom | 1 131 | 1 550 | 1 329 | 885 | 199 | 215 | 276 | 325 | 1 495 | 1 500 | 1 719 | 1 888 |
| Other | 73 | 68 | 115 | 109 | 208 | 227 | 228 | 251 | 959 | 1 013 | 1 324 | 1 332 |
| Latin America and Other Western Hemisphere [1] | 377 | 654 | 626 | 692 | 669 | 750 | 855 | 986 | 2 697 | 2 702 | 2 847 | 3 036 |
| South and Central America [1] | 231 | 261 | 336 | 414 | 547 | 633 | 736 | 869 | 2 398 | 2 388 | 2 414 | 2 735 |
| Argentina | 51 | 65 | 79 | 115 | 65 | 30 | 30 | 37 | 198 | 251 | 269 | 282 |
| Brazil | 3 | 6 | 17 | 18 | 46 | 86 | 86 | 103 | 319 | 372 | 401 | 534 |
| Chile | 20 | 26 | 40 | 59 | 19 | 27 | 35 | 49 | 321 | 102 | 148 | 162 |
| Venezuela | 8 | 8 | 20 | 13 | 43 | 39 | 40 | 44 | 268 | 264 | 225 | 264 |
| Other | 80 | 92 | 126 | 152 | 179 | 200 | 194 | 204 | 578 | 728 | 742 | 700 |
| Other Western Hemisphere | 146 | 393 | 290 | 278 | 121 | 117 | 118 | 118 | 299 | 314 | 433 | 300 |
| Bermuda | 118 | 337 | 241 | 209 | 22 | 13 | 15 | 15 | 58 | 86 | 53 | 45 |
| Other | 28 | 56 | 49 | 70 | 99 | 104 | 103 | 102 | 241 | 228 | 380 | 256 |
| Africa | 8 | 7 | 10 | 9 | 95 | 111 | 109 | 137 | 556 | 636 | 773 | 867 |
| South Africa | (*) | 1 | 6 | 4 | 17 | 28 | 51 | 54 | 77 | 76 | 107 | 133 |
| Other | 7 | 6 | 4 | 5 | 78 | 83 | 58 | 83 | 479 | 559 | 667 | 735 |
| Middle East | 22 | 15 | 38 | 37 | 172 | 171 | 162 | 197 | 1 166 | 1 242 | 1 965 | 2 274 |
| Israel | 13 | 11 | 18 | 34 | 60 | 66 | 52 | 73 | 114 | 124 | 169 | 162 |
| Saudi Arabia | 1 | 3 | 3 | 1 | 43 | 38 | 30 | 34 | 784 | 886 | 765 | 850 |
| Other | 7 | 1 | 16 | 2 | 68 | 67 | 80 | 90 | 267 | 231 | 1 031 | 1 262 |
| Asia and Pacific | 428 | 415 | 498 | 456 | 756 | 942 | 968 | 1 087 | 4 340 | 4 838 | 5 934 | 6 168 |
| Australia | 49 | 51 | 75 | 84 | 59 | 81 | 68 | 78 | 321 | 378 | 476 | 537 |
| China | 8 | 2 | 10 | 13 | 78 | 73 | 182 | 210 | 276 | 472 | 536 | 527 |
| Hong Kong | 19 | 21 | 43 | 25 | 58 | 64 | 67 | 71 | 217 | 249 | 406 | 344 |
| India | 1 | 2 | 4 | 7 | 58 | 59 | 52 | 59 | 74 | 102 | 142 | 132 |
| Indonesia | 3 | 4 | 12 | 17 | 21 | 19 | 23 | 26 | 217 | 348 | 504 | 737 |
| Japan | 225 | 220 | 200 | 169 | 212 | 306 | 216 | 221 | 1 511 | 1 590 | 1 860 | 1 796 |
| Malaysia | 6 | 8 | 12 | 9 | 14 | 27 | 14 | 22 | 138 | 114 | 343 | 190 |
| New Zealand | 4 | 5 | 8 | 3 | 14 | 14 | 13 | 16 | 51 | 51 | 90 | 125 |
| Philippines | 5 | 8 | 22 | 10 | 27 | 31 | 36 | 43 | 216 | 115 | 162 | 254 |
| Singapore | 22 | 25 | 12 | 10 | 19 | 28 | 36 | 41 | 129 | 149 | 183 | 195 |
| South Korea | 21 | 11 | 18 | 18 | 96 | 112 | 126 | 129 | 399 | 528 | 513 | 614 |
| Taiwan | 60 | 51 | 74 | 83 | 61 | 79 | 80 | 117 | 232 | 249 | 256 | 286 |
| Thailand | 6 | 3 | 7 | 6 | 15 | 21 | 24 | 26 | 222 | 273 | 184 | 185 |
| Other | 1 | 1 | (*) | 2 | 26 | 30 | 30 | 29 | 335 | 221 | 280 | 248 |
| International organizations and unallocated | 57 | 65 | -66 | 121 | 5 | 4 | 4 | 1 | 275 | 262 | 294 | 327 |
| European Union | 1 571 | 2 114 | 2 024 | 1 461 | 695 | 737 | 649 | 826 | 3 734 | 4 006 | 4 826 | 5 251 |
| Eastern Europe | 5 | 15 | 14 | 14 | 78 | 92 | 102 | 120 | 547 | 664 | 772 | 695 |

1. Includes Mexico.

## Table B-7.  United States: Other Private Service Receipts, 1994–1997 —*Continued*

(Millions of dollars.)

| Country or region | Unaffiliated—*Continued* Other services | | | | Addendum: film and tape rentals | | | |
|---|---|---|---|---|---|---|---|---|
| | 1994 | 1995 | 1996 | 1997 | 1994 | 1995 | 1996 | 1997 |
| ALL COUNTRIES | 9 032 | 9 633 | 10 185 | 11 321 | 4 354 | 4 775 | 5 028 | 6 175 |
| Canada | 400 | 425 | 436 | 427 | 282 | 348 | 344 | 300 |
| Mexico | 1 489 | 1 581 | 1 564 | 1 711 | 59 | 81 | 65 | 73 |
| Europe | 2 129 | 2 288 | 2 472 | 3 184 | 3 015 | 3 096 | 3 240 | 4 122 |
| Belgium and Luxembourg | 56 | 72 | 87 | 99 | 48 | 78 | 81 | 92 |
| France | 207 | 264 | 236 | 339 | 378 | 480 | 427 | 520 |
| Germany | 416 | 399 | 529 | 846 | 441 | 395 | 526 | 827 |
| Italy | 219 | 211 | 215 | 271 | 254 | 234 | 232 | 289 |
| Netherlands | 78 | 91 | 108 | 103 | 900 | 833 | 865 | 991 |
| Norway | 33 | 33 | 43 | 46 | 18 | 17 | 27 | 29 |
| Spain | 244 | 284 | 255 | 317 | 282 | 322 | 288 | 359 |
| Sweden | 62 | 78 | 61 | 60 | 64 | 85 | 68 | 63 |
| Switzerland | 55 | 51 | 46 | 53 | 42 | 36 | 29 | 34 |
| United Kingdom | 407 | 445 | 461 | 583 | 446 | 477 | 490 | 685 |
| Other | 352 | 361 | 432 | 467 | 140 | 141 | 207 | 236 |
| Latin America and Other Western Hemisphere [1] | 2 661 | 2 873 | 2 883 | 3 082 | 242 | 364 | 332 | 375 |
| South and Central America [1] | 2 545 | 2 750 | 2 752 | 2 939 | 230 | 350 | 315 | 357 |
| Argentina | 119 | 154 | 131 | 131 | 31 | 64 | 38 | 37 |
| Brazil | 140 | 196 | 197 | 202 | 67 | 124 | 113 | 139 |
| Chile | 63 | 65 | 69 | 72 | 14 | 15 | 17 | 19 |
| Venezuela | 45 | 50 | 58 | 62 | 23 | 28 | 35 | 38 |
| Other | 689 | 705 | 734 | 762 | 37 | 40 | 47 | 51 |
| Other Western Hemisphere | 117 | 123 | 131 | 143 | 12 | 14 | 16 | 17 |
| Bermuda | 4 | 3 | 3 | 3 | 5 | 3 | 4 | 3 |
| Other | 112 | 120 | 128 | 140 | 7 | 11 | 13 | 14 |
| Africa | 175 | 180 | 187 | 194 | 26 | 32 | 59 | 74 |
| South Africa | 42 | 47 | 74 | 89 | 25 | 29 | 55 | 69 |
| Other | 133 | 133 | 113 | 105 | 2 | 3 | 4 | 4 |
| Middle East | 137 | 149 | 161 | 167 | 22 | 30 | 38 | 41 |
| Israel | 56 | 65 | 69 | 70 | 13 | 19 | 22 | 21 |
| Saudi Arabia | 36 | 38 | 41 | 44 | 3 | 5 | 7 | 9 |
| Other | 45 | 46 | 50 | 54 | 5 | 7 | 9 | 11 |
| Asia and Pacific | 996 | 1 163 | 1 294 | 1 487 | 724 | 890 | 987 | 1 239 |
| Australia | 163 | 203 | 200 | 238 | 173 | 242 | 245 | 285 |
| China | 113 | 129 | 135 | 140 | 5 | 6 | 7 | 8 |
| Hong Kong | 14 | 23 | 31 | 43 | 14 | 24 | 33 | 43 |
| India | 24 | 25 | 27 | 28 | 1 | 1 | 2 | 2 |
| Indonesia | 34 | 42 | 43 | 45 | 13 | 21 | 21 | 23 |
| Japan | 290 | 315 | 366 | 422 | 374 | 404 | 454 | 539 |
| Malaysia | 20 | 24 | 25 | 28 | 6 | 9 | 10 | 12 |
| New Zealand | 35 | 39 | 48 | 53 | 25 | 29 | 37 | 42 |
| Philippines | 34 | 40 | 44 | 49 | 11 | 16 | 19 | 23 |
| Singapore | 14 | 20 | 20 | 26 | 11 | 17 | 17 | 56 |
| South Korea | 77 | 94 | 110 | 137 | 59 | 72 | 88 | 133 |
| Taiwan | 22 | 27 | 30 | 44 | 25 | 30 | 33 | 51 |
| Thailand | 28 | 37 | 41 | 44 | 8 | 16 | 19 | 22 |
| Other | 127 | 144 | 174 | 189 | 1 | 2 | 2 | 2 |
| International organizations and unallocated | 2 534 | 2 555 | 2 753 | 2 780 | 42 | 14 | 26 | 26 |
| European Union | 1 733 | 1 959 | 2 104 | 2 798 | 2 818 | 2 974 | 3 090 | 3 962 |
| Eastern Europe | 121 | 131 | 155 | 159 | 31 | 40 | 60 | 61 |

1. Includes Mexico.

## Table B-8. United States: Other Private Service Payments, 1994–1997

(Millions of dollars.)

| Country or region | Total | | | | Affiliated | | | | | | | |
| --- | --- | --- | --- | --- | --- | --- | --- | --- | --- | --- | --- | --- |
| | | | | | Total | | | | Between U.S. parents and their foreign affiliates | | | |
| | 1994 | 1995 | 1996 | 1997 | 1994 | 1995 | 199C | 1997 | 1994 | 1995 | 1996 | 1997 |
| ALL COUNTRIES | 34 588 | 39 823 | 43 138 | 48 421 | 12 924 | 14 215 | 16 668 | 18 324 | 7 012 | 7 443 | 8 089 | 9 407 |
| Canada | 3 785 | 4 178 | 4 726 | 5 338 | 1 797 | 1 930 | 2 587 | 2 796 | 556 | 507 | 585 | 814 |
| Mexico | 4 126 | 4 362 | 4 562 | 4 983 | 144 | 145 | 174 | 182 | 123 | 100 | 114 | 134 |
| Europe | 13 476 | 15 365 | 15 921 | 18 346 | 6 633 | 7 299 | 8 720 | 9 398 | 3 749 | 3 813 | 4 195 | 4 953 |
| Belgium and Luxembourg | 403 | 553 | 568 | (D) | 239 | 300 | 356 | (D) | 189 | 213 | 249 | (D) |
| France | 1 814 | 1 854 | 1 875 | 2 106 | 973 | 963 | 1 132 | 1 197 | 552 | 471 | 517 | 589 |
| Germany | 2 092 | 2 367 | 2 584 | 2 154 | 1 124 | 1 110 | 1 479 | 1 324 | 650 | 642 | 641 | 625 |
| Italy | 658 | 697 | 626 | 590 | 242 | 260 | 289 | 222 | 153 | 107 | 113 | 82 |
| Netherlands | 792 | 944 | 932 | 809 | 621 | 682 | 653 | 635 | 189 | 220 | 239 | 295 |
| Norway | 117 | 121 | 148 | 116 | 36 | 46 | 93 | 67 | 16 | 4 | 19 | 6 |
| Spain | 308 | (D) | 371 | (D) | 49 | (D) | 73 | (D) | 41 | 31 | 51 | 48 |
| Sweden | 247 | 338 | 214 | 287 | 138 | 140 | 168 | 188 | 36 | 39 | 28 | 26 |
| Switzerland | 688 | 594 | 684 | 593 | 572 | 502 | 636 | 548 | 169 | 150 | 138 | 200 |
| United Kingdom | 5 248 | 6 008 | 6 361 | 9 013 | 2 329 | 2 771 | 3 304 | 4 034 | 1 635 | 1 849 | 2 028 | 2 568 |
| Other | 1 106 | (D) | 1 561 | 1 565 | 308 | (D) | 538 | 604 | 119 | 86 | 173 | (D) |
| Latin America and Other Western Hemisphere [1] | 8 387 | 9 958 | 11 029 | 12 121 | 789 | 904 | 1 023 | 983 | 510 | 473 | 548 | 578 |
| South and Central America [1] | 5 749 | 6 240 | 6 920 | 7 378 | 275 | 372 | 458 | 408 | 200 | 250 | 263 | 335 |
| Argentina | 143 | 178 | 237 | 238 | 14 | 31 | 30 | 41 | 12 | 28 | 30 | 40 |
| Brazil | 258 | 389 | 545 | 599 | 49 | 125 | 145 | 137 | 38 | 81 | 87 | 125 |
| Chile | 62 | 67 | 83 | 81 | 1 | (*) | 3 | 2 | 1 | (*) | 1 | 1 |
| Venezuela | 127 | (D) | (D) | 175 | 15 | (D) | (D) | 19 | 12 | 16 | 10 | 12 |
| Other | 1 037 | (D) | (D) | 1 299 | 53 | (D) | (D) | 27 | 15 | 25 | 21 | 23 |
| Other Western Hemisphere | 2 637 | 3 717 | 4 108 | 4 742 | 513 | 532 | 565 | 575 | 310 | 223 | 286 | 242 |
| Bermuda | 1 431 | 2 386 | 2 695 | 2 738 | 283 | 256 | 274 | 289 | 206 | 147 | 160 | 101 |
| Other | 1 207 | 1 331 | 1 415 | 2 001 | 231 | 276 | 292 | 286 | 104 | 77 | 126 | 141 |
| Africa | (D) | 451 | 633 | (D) | (D) | 13 | 65 | (D) | 3 | 5 | 29 | 23 |
| South Africa | 61 | 64 | (D) | (D) | 7 | 5 | (D) | (D) | 1 | 3 | 24 | 20 |
| Other | (D) | 385 | (D) | 483 | (D) | 7 | (D) | 4 | 2 | 2 | 5 | 2 |
| Middle East | (D) | 779 | 1 009 | (D) | (D) | 150 | 175 | (D) | 114 | 138 | 161 | 207 |
| Israel | (D) | 375 | 410 | (D) | (D) | 123 | 148 | 194 | 87 | 116 | 138 | (D) |
| Saudi Arabia | 110 | (D) | 140 | 115 | 11 | (D) | 6 | 4 | 11 | (D) | 6 | 4 |
| Other | 242 | (D) | 459 | (D) | 22 | (D) | 21 | (D) | 17 | (D) | 17 | (D) |
| Asia and Pacific | 7 214 | 8 110 | 8 760 | 10 211 | 3 345 | 3 464 | 3 431 | 4 447 | 1 892 | 2 052 | 1 902 | 2 408 |
| Australia | 502 | 598 | 690 | 810 | 168 | 212 | 227 | 313 | 138 | 183 | 200 | 276 |
| China | 385 | 433 | 561 | 612 | 50 | 23 | 17 | 30 | 14 | 12 | 14 | 22 |
| Hong Kong | 482 | 553 | 774 | 1 076 | 292 | 343 | 435 | 598 | 241 | 289 | 317 | 530 |
| India | 212 | 263 | 418 | 464 | 10 | 11 | 12 | 28 | 8 | 8 | 6 | 9 |
| Indonesia | 106 | 107 | 173 | 187 | 15 | 14 | 29 | 22 | 15 | 13 | 26 | 21 |
| Japan | 3 592 | 4 071 | 3 753 | 4 293 | 2 383 | 2 443 | 2 272 | 2 789 | 1 187 | 1 287 | 1 063 | 1 119 |
| Malaysia | 138 | 144 | 165 | 215 | 49 | 59 | 66 | 128 | 47 | 55 | 53 | 87 |
| New Zealand | 45 | 56 | 91 | (D) | 6 | 10 | 27 | (D) | 3 | 6 | 25 | 36 |
| Philippines | 228 | 238 | 247 | 317 | 15 | 4 | 3 | 6 | 11 | 4 | 2 | 6 |
| Singapore | 272 | 247 | 340 | 454 | 181 | 138 | 189 | 291 | 151 | 113 | 118 | 202 |
| South Korea | 418 | 475 | 458 | (D) | 124 | 121 | 79 | (D) | 50 | 40 | 39 | 42 |
| Taiwan | 270 | 344 | 356 | 398 | 41 | 75 | 58 | 86 | 22 | 37 | 33 | 47 |
| Thailand | 126 | 165 | 212 | 233 | 10 | 9 | 15 | 14 | 6 | 2 | 3 | 9 |
| Other | 437 | 418 | 522 | 543 | 1 | 2 | 3 | 4 | 1 | 1 | 2 | 3 |
| International organizations and unallocated | 611 | 984 | 1 055 | 842 | 190 | 455 | 667 | 423 | 190 | 455 | 667 | 423 |
| European Union | 11 686 | 13 939 | 14 209 | 16 781 | 5 788 | 6 722 | 7 976 | 8 756 | 3 476 | 3 656 | 4 032 | 4 733 |
| Eastern Europe | 387 | 468 | 612 | 631 | 7 | 19 | 7 | 19 | 7 | 1 | 4 | 13 |

1. Includes Mexico.

## Table B-8. United States: Other Private Service Payments, 1994–1997 —Continued

(Millions of dollars.)

| Country or region | Affiliated—Continued Between U.S. affiliates and their foreign parents | | | | Unaffiliated Total | | | | Education | | | |
|---|---|---|---|---|---|---|---|---|---|---|---|---|
| | 1994 | 1995 | 1996 | 1997 | 1994 | 1995 | 1996 | 1997 | 1994 | 1995 | 1996 | 1997 |
| **ALL COUNTRIES** | 5 912 | 6 772 | 8 579 | 8 917 | 21 663 | 25 607 | 26 469 | 30 098 | 972 | 1 125 | 1 247 | 1 347 |
| **Canada** | 1 242 | 1 423 | 2 001 | 1 981 | 1 988 | 2 248 | 2 141 | 2 542 | 8 | 9 | 10 | 12 |
| **Mexico** | 20 | 45 | 60 | 48 | 3 982 | 4 217 | 4 388 | 4 801 | 112 | 119 | 158 | 178 |
| **Europe** | 2 884 | 3 487 | 4 525 | 4 445 | 6 843 | 8 066 | 7 201 | 8 948 | 574 | 650 | 708 | 761 |
| Belgium and Luxembourg | 50 | 87 | 107 | 206 | 164 | 253 | 212 | 218 | 9 | 8 | 9 | 10 |
| France | 420 | 492 | 615 | 608 | 841 | 891 | 743 | 909 | 85 | 90 | 93 | 99 |
| Germany | 474 | 468 | 838 | 699 | 968 | 1 257 | 1 105 | 830 | 38 | 40 | 42 | 45 |
| Italy | 89 | 152 | 176 | 140 | 416 | 437 | 337 | 368 | 69 | 81 | 94 | 100 |
| Netherlands | 432 | 463 | 413 | 339 | 171 | 262 | 279 | 175 | 7 | 8 | 8 | 9 |
| Norway | 21 | 41 | 74 | 61 | 81 | 75 | 55 | 49 | 0 | 0 | 0 | 0 |
| Spain | 8 | (D) | 22 | (D) | 259 | 286 | 298 | 315 | 81 | 93 | 103 | 114 |
| Sweden | 102 | 101 | 140 | 161 | 109 | 198 | 46 | 99 | 1 | 1 | 1 | 1 |
| Switzerland | 403 | 352 | 498 | 348 | 116 | 92 | 48 | 45 | 3 | 3 | 2 | 2 |
| United Kingdom | 695 | 922 | 1 276 | 1 465 | 2 919 | 3 238 | 3 056 | 4 979 | 191 | 226 | 244 | 262 |
| Other | 189 | (D) | 365 | (D) | 798 | 1 078 | 1 023 | 961 | 91 | 99 | 110 | 118 |
| **Latin America and Other Western Hemisphere** [1] | 279 | 431 | 475 | 406 | 7 598 | 9 051 | 10 005 | 11 137 | 255 | 305 | 362 | 408 |
| South and Central America [1] | 75 | 122 | 195 | 73 | 5 474 | 5 868 | 6 462 | 6 970 | 221 | 263 | 312 | 351 |
| Argentina | 2 | 3 | (*) | (*) | 129 | 147 | 207 | 197 | 7 | 7 | 8 | 9 |
| Brazil | 11 | 44 | 59 | 12 | 209 | 264 | 400 | 462 | 8 | 9 | 10 | 11 |
| Chile | 0 | (*) | 2 | 1 | 61 | 67 | 80 | 79 | 15 | 19 | 15 | 17 |
| Venezuela | 4 | (D) | (D) | 7 | 112 | 110 | 139 | 156 | 1 | 5 | 5 | 6 |
| Other | 38 | (D) | (D) | 4 | 984 | 1 063 | 1 246 | 1 272 | 77 | 104 | 116 | 130 |
| Other Western Hemisphere | 204 | 309 | 280 | 333 | 2 124 | 3 185 | 3 543 | 4 167 | 34 | 41 | 50 | 56 |
| Bermuda | 77 | 109 | 114 | 188 | 1 148 | 2 130 | 2 421 | 2 449 | 0 | 1 | 0 | 0 |
| Other | 127 | 200 | 165 | 145 | 976 | 1 055 | 1 123 | 1 715 | 34 | 40 | 50 | 56 |
| **Africa** | (D) | 8 | 36 | (D) | 382 | 438 | 568 | 569 | 17 | 22 | 25 | 25 |
| South Africa | 6 | 2 | (D) | (D) | 54 | 59 | 39 | 90 | 1 | 1 | 7 | 2 |
| Other | (D) | 6 | (D) | 1 | 328 | 378 | 25 | 479 | 16 | 21 | 18 | 23 |
| **Middle East** | (D) | 12 | 14 | (D) | 561 | 629 | 834 | 723 | 25 | 32 | 22 | 22 |
| Israel | (D) | 8 | 10 | (D) | 241 | 252 | 262 | 227 | 25 | 31 | 21 | 21 |
| Saudi Arabia | 0 | 0 | 0 | 0 | 99 | 111 | 134 | 111 | 0 | 0 | 0 | 0 |
| Other | 6 | 5 | 4 | 4 | 220 | 266 | 438 | 385 | 0 | 1 | 1 | 1 |
| **Asia and Pacific** | 1 453 | 1 412 | 1 529 | 2 039 | 3 869 | 4 646 | 5 329 | 5 764 | 92 | 107 | 120 | 120 |
| Australia | 30 | 29 | 27 | 37 | 334 | 387 | 464 | 497 | 26 | 36 | 37 | 42 |
| China | 36 | 10 | 2 | 8 | 335 | 410 | 544 | 582 | 5 | 6 | 9 | 8 |
| Hong Kong | 51 | 55 | 119 | 68 | 190 | 210 | 339 | 478 | 1 | 1 | 3 | 2 |
| India | 2 | 2 | 5 | 20 | 202 | 252 | 406 | 436 | 2 | 2 | 3 | 3 |
| Indonesia | 1 | 1 | 3 | 1 | 91 | 93 | 144 | 165 | 1 | 1 | 1 | 1 |
| Japan | 1 196 | 1 155 | 1 209 | 1 670 | 1 209 | 1 623 | 1 482 | 1 506 | 25 | 26 | 24 | 23 |
| Malaysia | 2 | 4 | 14 | 41 | 89 | 85 | 99 | 87 | 0 | 0 | 0 | 0 |
| New Zealand | 3 | 5 | 2 | (D) | 39 | 46 | 64 | 88 | 2 | 3 | 0 | 3 |
| Philippines | 5 | (*) | 1 | (*) | 213 | 234 | 244 | 311 | 0 | 0 | 0 | 0 |
| Singapore | 30 | 25 | 70 | 89 | 91 | 109 | 151 | 163 | 0 | 0 | 1 | 0 |
| South Korea | 74 | 81 | 39 | (D) | 294 | 354 | 379 | 383 | 2 | 2 | 3 | 2 |
| Taiwan | 19 | 38 | 25 | 39 | 229 | 269 | 298 | 312 | 1 | 1 | 1 | 1 |
| Thailand | 3 | 6 | 12 | 5 | 116 | 156 | 197 | 219 | 1 | 1 | 1 | 1 |
| Other | (*) | 1 | 1 | 1 | 436 | 416 | 519 | 539 | 26 | 30 | 38 | 33 |
| **International organizations and unallocated** | 0 | 0 | 0 | 0 | 421 | 531 | 389 | 419 | 0 | 0 | 0 | 0 |
| **European Union** | 2 312 | 3 066 | 3 943 | 4 023 | 5 898 | 7 216 | 6 233 | 8 024 | 507 | 579 | 633 | 681 |
| **Eastern Europe** | 0 | 18 | 3 | 6 | 380 | 449 | 605 | 613 | 31 | 34 | 39 | 43 |

1. Includes Mexico.

## Table B-8.   United States: Other Private Service Payments, 1994–1997  —*Continued*

(Millions of dollars.)

| Country or region | Financial services | | | | Unaffiliated—*Continued* Insurance Net | | | | Premiums | | | |
|---|---|---|---|---|---|---|---|---|---|---|---|---|
| | 1994 | 1995 | 1996 | 1997 | 1994 | 1995 | 1996 | 1997 | 1994 | 1995 | 1996 | 1997 |
| ALL COUNTRIES ............................... | 1 654 | 2 472 | 2 995 | 3 906 | 4 034 | 5 360 | 3 773 | 5 208 | 14 075 | 15 284 | 14 652 | 15 036 |
| Canada .................................... | 121 | 190 | 178 | 244 | 715 | 609 | 459 | 535 | 1 171 | 1 266 | 1 061 | 1 133 |
| Mexico ..................................... | 75 | 79 | 129 | 129 | 1 | -1 | -2 | -4 | 1 | 1 | 3 | 2 |
| Europe ..................................... | 860 | 1 413 | 1 704 | 2 385 | 1 661 | 1 855 | 305 | 1 028 | 6 663 | 6 995 | 6 542 | 6 428 |
| Belgium and Luxembourg ............. | 19 | 57 | 54 | 56 | 5 | 32 | 30 | 29 | 43 | 57 | 72 | 71 |
| France ................................. | 59 | 101 | 128 | 153 | 342 | 308 | 150 | 229 | 638 | 646 | 469 | 497 |
| Germany .............................. | 61 | 250 | 181 | 126 | 332 | 329 | 255 | 46 | 1 175 | 1 153 | 1 300 | 1 246 |
| Italy ................................... | 17 | 39 | 41 | 36 | 45 | 44 | -24 | -1 | 158 | 227 | 61 | 63 |
| Netherlands .......................... | 20 | 73 | 70 | 58 | -19 | -7 | -5 | -112 | 27 | 26 | 27 | 27 |
| Norway ................................ | 4 | 6 | 8 | 12 | 30 | 37 | 11 | 3 | 43 | 43 | 17 | 14 |
| Spain .................................. | 12 | 22 | 23 | 36 | 6 | 4 | 5 | 4 | 4 | 4 | 11 | 12 |
| Sweden ................................ | 16 | 33 | 26 | 31 | 22 | 84 | -51 | (*) | 88 | 130 | 54 | 69 |
| Switzerland ........................... | 51 | 98 | 120 | 165 | -68 | -154 | -271 | -324 | 659 | 684 | 684 | 545 |
| United Kingdom ....................... | 554 | 611 | 937 | 1 576 | 1 073 | 1 177 | 463 | 1 397 | 3 533 | 3 654 | 3 332 | 3 357 |
| Other .................................. | 47 | 125 | 116 | 136 | -108 | 1 | -256 | -236 | 296 | 371 | 513 | 526 |
| Latin America and Other Western Hemisphere [1] ........ | 223 | 259 | 398 | 587 | 1 659 | 2 691 | 2 953 | 3 406 | 5 595 | 6 292 | 6 480 | 6 968 |
| South and Central America [1] ........ | 157 | 173 | 279 | 350 | (*) | (D) | 41 | 24 | 21 | 16 | 91 | 48 |
| Argentina ............................. | 16 | 10 | 27 | 44 | -2 | -2 | 1 | -3 | (*) | (*) | 15 | 17 |
| Brazil .................................. | 21 | 30 | 65 | 86 | -9 | -9 | 35 | 5 | 4 | (*) | 46 | 1 |
| Chile .................................. | 3 | 5 | 8 | 8 | 2 | 1 | 2 | (*) | 2 | 2 | 2 | 1 |
| Venezuela ............................ | 28 | 12 | 9 | 31 | 2 | 2 | 6 | 8 | 2 | 2 | 6 | 8 |
| Other .................................. | 15 | 37 | 41 | 52 | -1 | -2 | (*) | 17 | 12 | 11 | 19 | 21 |
| Other Western Hemisphere ......... | 66 | 87 | 119 | 237 | 1 667 | 2 702 | 2 912 | 3 382 | 5 574 | 6 276 | 6 389 | 6 920 |
| Bermuda .............................. | 15 | 13 | 56 | 49 | 1 113 | 2 099 | 2 338 | 2 364 | 3 383 | 3 980 | 4 175 | 4 318 |
| Other .................................. | 51 | 74 | 63 | 188 | 554 | 603 | 574 | 1 017 | 2 191 | 2 296 | 2 214 | 2 602 |
| Africa ...................................... | 6 | 10 | 18 | 21 | 1 | 5 | 3 | 8 | 4 | 7 | 5 | 10 |
| South Africa .......................... | 3 | 5 | 7 | 9 | (*) | -1 | (*) | (*) | (*) | -1 | 1 | 1 |
| Other .................................. | 3 | 5 | 11 | 12 | 1 | 6 | 3 | 8 | 4 | 8 | 5 | 8 |
| Middle East ............................... | 4 | 12 | 11 | 11 | 7 | 7 | 18 | 20 | 15 | 16 | 11 | 10 |
| Israel .................................. | 1 | 2 | 4 | 6 | (*) | -2 | 12 | 11 | 2 | 1 | 2 | (*) |
| Saudi Arabia ......................... | 1 | 2 | 2 | 1 | (*) | (*) | (*) | (*) | (*) | (*) | (*) | (*) |
| Other .................................. | 2 | 8 | 5 | 4 | 6 | 8 | 6 | 8 | 12 | 14 | 9 | 9 |
| Asia and Pacific .......................... | 410 | 517 | 618 | 580 | -19 | 162 | 14 | 161 | 616 | 681 | 543 | 449 |
| Australia .............................. | 34 | 43 | 60 | 55 | 49 | 52 | 47 | 59 | 97 | 124 | 132 | 152 |
| China .................................. | 1 | 3 | 5 | 2 | (*) | -2 | 4 | -6 | 8 | 4 | 1 | 1 |
| Hong Kong ........................... | 68 | 78 | 73 | 79 | -68 | -91 | -85 | 19 | (D) | 63 | 80 | 6 |
| India ................................... | 3 | 7 | 15 | 16 | 1 | (*) | (*) | 2 | 3 | 5 | 4 | 3 |
| Indonesia ............................. | 8 | 13 | 16 | 25 | -2 | (*) | 3 | 4 | -3 | 1 | 3 | 4 |
| Japan .................................. | 169 | 248 | 276 | 199 | 10 | 191 | 20 | 68 | 434 | 457 | 279 | 248 |
| Malaysia .............................. | 35 | 36 | 40 | 26 | (*) | -1 | (*) | (*) | (*) | (*) | (*) | (*) |
| New Zealand ......................... | 9 | 6 | 12 | 9 | -1 | (*) | 7 | 7 | 1 | 1 | (D) | 10 |
| Philippines ........................... | 5 | 9 | 12 | 38 | (*) | (*) | 1 | -4 | (*) | (*) | 2 | 1 |
| Singapore ............................. | 27 | 22 | 34 | 38 | -1 | 1 | 3 | -3 | 1 | 3 | 5 | 2 |
| South Korea .......................... | 10 | 16 | 19 | 27 | -2 | 2 | 7 | 7 | (D) | 9 | 13 | 9 |
| Taiwan ................................ | 3 | 6 | 9 | 11 | 2 | 4 | 2 | 2 | 6 | 8 | 9 | 4 |
| Thailand .............................. | 15 | 18 | 17 | 13 | (*) | 3 | 2 | 3 | (*) | 3 | 2 | 5 |
| Other .................................. | 23 | 13 | 30 | 42 | 1 | 2 | 3 | 5 | 2 | 2 | (D) | 4 |
| International organizations and unallocated ............. | 30 | 71 | 68 | 78 | 10 | 31 | 21 | 51 | 11 | 28 | 10 | 39 |
| European Union ......................... | 757 | 1 246 | 1 498 | 2 144 | 1 658 | 1 968 | 556 | 1 337 | 5 768 | 6 261 | 5 833 | 5 861 |
| Eastern Europe ......................... | 1 | 15 | 19 | 36 | 2 | (*) | (*) | 1 | (*) | (*) | (*) | (*) |

1. Includes Mexico.

## Table B-8.  United States: Other Private Service Payments, 1994–1997 —*Continued*

(Millions of dollars.)

| Country or region | Insurance—*Continued* Losses | | | | Telecommunications | | | | Business, professional, and technical services | | | |
|---|---|---|---|---|---|---|---|---|---|---|---|---|
| | 1994 | 1995 | 1996 | 1997 | 1994 | 1995 | 1996 | 1997 | 1994 | 1995 | 1996 | 1997 |
| **ALL COUNTRIES** | 10 041 | 9 925 | 10 879 | 9 828 | 6 928 | 7 305 | 8 304 | 8 113 | 3 869 | 4 822 | 5 550 | 6 571 |
| **Canada** | 456 | 657 | 602 | 598 | 391 | 381 | 350 | 352 | 374 | 629 | 673 | 887 |
| **Mexico** | (*) | 2 | 5 | 6 | 966 | 1 067 | 1 162 | 1 130 | 105 | 102 | 96 | 264 |
| **Europe** | 5 002 | 5 139 | 6 236 | 5 400 | 1 603 | 1 561 | 1 378 | 1 252 | 1 683 | 2 066 | 2 576 | 2 955 |
| Belgium and Luxembourg | 38 | 25 | 42 | 43 | 57 | 57 | 41 | 31 | 62 | 84 | 63 | 76 |
| France | 296 | 338 | 320 | 268 | 111 | 120 | 99 | 94 | 189 | 215 | 208 | 274 |
| Germany | 843 | 824 | 1 046 | 1 200 | 237 | 215 | 118 | 111 | 239 | 348 | 436 | 416 |
| Italy | 113 | 184 | 84 | 64 | 176 | 158 | 107 | 96 | 82 | 85 | 92 | 104 |
| Netherlands | 46 | 33 | 33 | 139 | 47 | 55 | 52 | 42 | 79 | 100 | 120 | 144 |
| Norway | 13 | 6 | 7 | 11 | 16 | 14 | 11 | 9 | 26 | 13 | 21 | 20 |
| Spain | -2 | (*) | 6 | 8 | 101 | 101 | 75 | 63 | 44 | 57 | 81 | 88 |
| Sweden | 66 | 46 | 105 | 77 | 26 | 21 | 16 | 14 | 28 | 41 | 34 | 40 |
| Switzerland | 727 | 839 | 956 | 869 | 61 | 60 | 59 | 47 | 55 | 67 | 110 | 138 |
| United Kingdom | 2 460 | 2 477 | 2 870 | 1 960 | 291 | 275 | 268 | 286 | 697 | 802 | 1 008 | 1 296 |
| Other | 404 | 370 | 770 | 762 | 480 | 487 | 532 | 458 | 182 | 253 | 402 | 359 |
| **Latin America and Other Western Hemisphere** [1] | 3 936 | 3 601 | 3 527 | 3 562 | 2 361 | 2 527 | 2 981 | 2 920 | 269 | 305 | 342 | 595 |
| South and Central America [1] | 29 | 28 | 50 | 24 | 2 054 | 2 228 | 2 586 | 2 500 | 258 | 291 | 320 | 561 |
| Argentina | 3 | 2 | 14 | 19 | 81 | 99 | 133 | 99 | 22 | 29 | 32 | 42 |
| Brazil | 14 | 10 | 11 | -5 | 143 | 169 | 204 | 240 | 36 | 53 | 73 | 106 |
| Chile | (*) | 1 | 1 | (*) | 33 | 32 | 40 | 30 | 6 | 9 | 13 | 22 |
| Venezuela | (*) | (*) | (*) | (*) | 62 | 68 | 91 | 88 | 11 | 15 | 19 | 14 |
| Other | 12 | 13 | 19 | 4 | 769 | 793 | 955 | 912 | 78 | 84 | 86 | 113 |
| Other Western Hemisphere | 3 907 | 3 574 | 3 477 | 3 538 | 307 | 300 | 395 | 420 | 11 | 14 | 22 | 33 |
| Bermuda | 2 270 | 1 881 | 1 837 | 1 953 | 16 | 15 | 18 | 19 | 3 | 1 | 8 | 16 |
| Other | 1 637 | 1 693 | 1 641 | 1 585 | 292 | 284 | 378 | 401 | 7 | 13 | 14 | 17 |
| **Africa** | 3 | 3 | 2 | 1 | 210 | 234 | 346 | 328 | 123 | 138 | 147 | 156 |
| South Africa | (*) | 1 | (*) | 1 | (D) | 33 | 52 | 50 | 15 | 16 | 20 | 21 |
| Other | 3 | 2 | 1 | (*) | (D) | 201 | 294 | 278 | 108 | 122 | 127 | 136 |
| **Middle East** | 8 | 9 | -7 | -10 | 415 | 455 | 560 | 466 | 83 | 93 | 192 | 169 |
| Israel | 2 | 3 | -10 | -11 | 172 | 175 | 169 | 132 | 34 | 32 | 42 | 42 |
| Saudi Arabia | (*) | (*) | (*) | (*) | (D) | 88 | 109 | 83 | 14 | 17 | 19 | 20 |
| Other | 6 | 6 | 3 | 1 | (D) | 192 | 282 | 251 | 35 | 44 | 131 | 108 |
| **Asia and Pacific** | 635 | 519 | 529 | 288 | 1 684 | 1 876 | 2 445 | 2 570 | 1 225 | 1 484 | 1 619 | 1 809 |
| Australia | 48 | 72 | 85 | 93 | 66 | 70 | 85 | 114 | 131 | 153 | 204 | 194 |
| China | 16 | 7 | -3 | 8 | 211 | 246 | 356 | 385 | 34 | 38 | 48 | 68 |
| Hong Kong | (D) | 154 | 165 | -13 | 111 | 132 | 211 | 224 | 66 | 80 | 127 | 144 |
| India | 3 | 4 | 4 | 1 | 143 | (D) | 300 | 316 | 21 | 35 | 57 | 68 |
| Indonesia | (*) | 1 | (*) | (*) | 42 | 42 | 68 | 69 | 33 | 28 | 46 | 56 |
| Japan | 424 | 266 | 259 | 180 | 268 | 276 | 308 | 304 | 658 | 779 | 739 | 800 |
| Malaysia | (*) | (*) | (*) | (*) | 25 | 29 | 32 | 33 | 19 | 12 | 17 | 18 |
| New Zealand | 2 | 1 | (D) | 4 | 16 | 16 | 24 | 48 | 11 | 16 | 19 | 18 |
| Philippines | (*) | (*) | (*) | 5 | 178 | 179 | 184 | 211 | 25 | 41 | 43 | 62 |
| Singapore | 2 | 3 | 2 | 5 | 33 | 45 | 64 | 59 | 27 | 37 | 46 | 65 |
| South Korea | (D) | 8 | 6 | 2 | 210 | 227 | 238 | 225 | 45 | 71 | 79 | 85 |
| Taiwan | 3 | 4 | 7 | 3 | 151 | 183 | 189 | 187 | 45 | 49 | 74 | 89 |
| Thailand | (*) | (*) | (*) | 1 | 55 | 60 | 91 | 89 | 38 | 66 | 77 | 102 |
| Other | (*) | (*) | (D) | (*) | 174 | (D) | 294 | 307 | 71 | 78 | 45 | 39 |
| **International organizations and unallocated** | 1 | -4 | -11 | (D) | 265 | 270 | 245 | 226 | 113 | 107 | (*) | (*) |
| **European Union** | 4 110 | 4 293 | 5 277 | 4 525 | 1 185 | 1 175 | 927 | 872 | 1 442 | 1 846 | 2 216 | 2 551 |
| **Eastern Europe** | -2 | (*) | (*) | -1 | 207 | 232 | 295 | 251 | 85 | 116 | 195 | 220 |

1. Includes Mexico.

## Table B-8.  United States: Other Private Service Payments, 1994–1997 —*Continued*

(Millions of dollars.)

| Country or region | Unaffiliated—*Continued* Other services | | | | Addendum: film and tape rentals | | | |
|---|---|---|---|---|---|---|---|---|
| | 1994 | 1995 | 1996 | 1997 | 1994 | 1995 | 1996 | 1997 |
| ALL COUNTRIES ................................................. | 4 206 | 4 524 | 4 600 | 4 952 | 228 | 227 | 247 | 247 |
| Canada .......................................................................... | 380 | 428 | 470 | 513 | 55 | 59 | 90 | 108 |
| Mexico .......................................................................... | 2 723 | 2 850 | 2 846 | 3 105 | 6 | (D) | (*) | (*) |
| Europe ......................................................................... | 463 | 518 | 531 | 566 | 149 | 109 | 103 | 108 |
| Belgium and Luxembourg ............................................ | 12 | 15 | 15 | 16 | 5 | (*) | (*) | (*) |
| France ........................................................................... | 55 | 57 | 66 | 60 | 18 | 11 | 19 | 10 |
| Germany ........................................................................ | 62 | 75 | 73 | 85 | 8 | 11 | 2 | 10 |
| Italy .............................................................................. | 27 | 31 | 27 | 30 | 11 | 5 | 6 | 9 |
| Netherlands .................................................................. | 37 | 33 | 33 | 34 | 14 | 5 | 5 | 4 |
| Norway .......................................................................... | 5 | 4 | 4 | 4 | (*) | (*) | (*) | (*) |
| Spain ............................................................................ | 16 | 9 | 10 | 11 | 6 | (*) | (*) | (*) |
| Sweden ......................................................................... | 16 | 18 | 19 | 20 | (*) | (*) | (*) | (*) |
| Switzerland ................................................................... | 15 | 18 | 27 | 16 | 4 | 5 | 17 | 3 |
| United Kingdom ........................................................... | 113 | 146 | 137 | 163 | 71 | 67 | 50 | 70 |
| Other ............................................................................ | 106 | 113 | 119 | 126 | 11 | 1 | 1 | 1 |
| Latin America and Other Western Hemisphere [1] ........ | 2 832 | 2 965 | 2 968 | 3 220 | 8 | (D) | (D) | 5 |
| South and Central America [1] ..................................... | 2 793 | 2 923 | 2 922 | 3 183 | 8 | (D) | (D) | 4 |
| Argentina .................................................................. | 5 | 4 | 6 | 6 | (*) | (*) | (*) | (*) |
| Brazil ......................................................................... | 10 | 12 | 13 | 14 | 1 | 2 | 2 | 2 |
| Chile .......................................................................... | 1 | 1 | 1 | 1 | 0 | (*) | (*) | (*) |
| Venezuela .................................................................. | 8 | 8 | 9 | 9 | (*) | (*) | (D) | (*) |
| Other ......................................................................... | 47 | 47 | 48 | 48 | 1 | (D) | (D) | 0 |
| Other Western Hemisphere ........................................ | 39 | 42 | 46 | 37 | 1 | 1 | 1 | 1 |
| Bermuda .................................................................... | 1 | 1 | 1 | 1 | 1 | 1 | 1 | 1 |
| Other ......................................................................... | 38 | 41 | 45 | 35 | (*) | (*) | (*) | (*) |
| Africa .......................................................................... | 25 | 30 | 29 | 31 | (*) | 0 | 0 | 0 |
| South Africa ................................................................. | (D) | 7 | 7 | 9 | (*) | 0 | 0 | 0 |
| Other ............................................................................ | (D) | 23 | 21 | 22 | 0 | 0 | 0 | 0 |
| Middle East ................................................................ | 27 | 30 | 31 | 35 | (*) | (*) | (*) | (*) |
| Israel ............................................................................ | 9 | 14 | 14 | 15 | (*) | (*) | (*) | (*) |
| Saudi Arabia ................................................................ | (D) | 4 | 4 | 7 | 0 | 0 | 0 | 3 |
| Other ............................................................................ | (D) | 13 | 13 | 13 | 0 | 0 | 0 | 0 |
| Asia and Pacific ....................................................... | 478 | 500 | 514 | 524 | 15 | 34 | 29 | 17 |
| Australia ....................................................................... | 27 | 34 | 32 | 33 | 6 | 7 | 3 | 7 |
| China ............................................................................ | 92 | 119 | 122 | 126 | 0 | (*) | (*) | (*) |
| Hong Kong .................................................................... | 12 | 11 | 10 | 10 | 2 | 1 | 1 | 1 |
| India ............................................................................. | 32 | (D) | 31 | 31 | 0 | 0 | 0 | 0 |
| Indonesia ...................................................................... | 9 | 9 | 10 | 11 | 0 | 0 | 0 | 0 |
| Japan ............................................................................ | 79 | 105 | 115 | 112 | (*) | 13 | 22 | 8 |
| Malaysia ....................................................................... | 10 | 9 | 10 | 10 | 0 | (*) | (*) | (*) |
| New Zealand ................................................................. | 3 | 6 | 1 | 2 | 1 | 4 | 0 | 0 |
| Philippines .................................................................... | 4 | 5 | 4 | 4 | 1 | 1 | 0 | 0 |
| Singapore ..................................................................... | 5 | 4 | 3 | 3 | 1 | (*) | (*) | (*) |
| South Korea ................................................................. | 29 | 36 | 34 | 37 | (*) | 7 | 6 | 0 |
| Taiwan .......................................................................... | 28 | 26 | 23 | 22 | 0 | (*) | (*) | (*) |
| Thailand ........................................................................ | 7 | 8 | 9 | 11 | 0 | (*) | (*) | (*) |
| Other ............................................................................ | 141 | (D) | 109 | 113 | 0 | 0 | 0 | 0 |
| International organizations and unallocated .............. | 4 | 53 | 57 | 64 | 1 | (D) | (D) | 5 |
| European Union ........................................................... | 349 | 394 | 394 | 432 | 140 | 102 | 85 | 105 |
| Eastern Europe ........................................................... | 53 | 52 | 58 | 61 | 4 | (*) | (*) | (*) |

1. Includes Mexico.

## Table B-9.  U.S. Insurance Receipts, 1994–1997

(Unaffiliated transactions; millions of dollars.)

| Country or region | Total | | | | | | | | | | | |
|---|---|---|---|---|---|---|---|---|---|---|---|---|
| | Net | | | | Premiums received | | | | Losses paid | | | |
| | 1994 | 1995 | 1996 | 1997 | 1994 | 1995 | 1996 | 1997 | 1994 | 1995 | 1996 | 1997 |
| **ALL COUNTRIES** ........................ | 1 676 | 1 296 | 1 971 | 2 391 | 4 921 | 5 491 | 5 978 | 5 952 | 3 245 | 4 195 | 4 007 | 3 561 |
| **Canada** ........................ | 391 | 373 | 343 | 353 | 1 027 | 1 106 | 1 062 | 1 013 | 636 | 734 | 719 | 660 |
| **Mexico** ........................ | 49 | 37 | 43 | 57 | 117 | 101 | 98 | 114 | 68 | 65 | 55 | 57 |
| **Europe** ........................ | 359 | 270 | 545 | 785 | 2 076 | 2 575 | 2 726 | 2 371 | 1 717 | 2 306 | 2 182 | 1 586 |
| Belgium and Luxembourg ........................ | 37 | 52 | 62 | 54 | 95 | 149 | 131 | 102 | 58 | 97 | 69 | 48 |
| France ........................ | 7 | 89 | 32 | 130 | 173 | 216 | 204 | 221 | 166 | 127 | 172 | 91 |
| Germany ........................ | 74 | 61 | 128 | 88 | 180 | 264 | 312 | 299 | 106 | 204 | 184 | 210 |
| Italy ........................ | 9 | 29 | 15 | 40 | 40 | 62 | 74 | 75 | 31 | 34 | 59 | 36 |
| Netherlands ........................ | 11 | 19 | -14 | -37 | 35 | 42 | 42 | 42 | 25 | 24 | 56 | 79 |
| Norway ........................ | 12 | 5 | 44 | 18 | 21 | 34 | 65 | 55 | 10 | 29 | 21 | 37 |
| Spain ........................ | 20 | 6 | 9 | 16 | 27 | 23 | 33 | 25 | 7 | 16 | 24 | 9 |
| Sweden ........................ | 8 | 8 | 16 | 14 | 22 | 33 | 42 | 30 | 14 | 25 | 26 | 15 |
| Switzerland ........................ | 7 | -45 | -43 | -13 | 104 | 89 | 84 | 53 | 97 | 133 | 127 | 67 |
| United Kingdom ........................ | 174 | 6 | 281 | 431 | 1 305 | 1 556 | 1 610 | 1 316 | 1 131 | 1 550 | 1 329 | 885 |
| Other ........................ | 1 | 40 | 14 | 45 | 73 | 108 | 129 | 154 | 73 | 68 | 115 | 109 |
| **Latin America and Other Western Hemisphere** [1] ........ | 466 | 147 | 405 | 738 | 843 | 801 | 1 031 | 1 430 | 377 | 654 | 626 | 692 |
| South and Central America [1] ........................ | 226 | 210 | 217 | 189 | 457 | 470 | 553 | 603 | 231 | 261 | 336 | 414 |
| Argentina ........................ | 69 | 46 | 43 | 20 | 120 | 110 | 122 | 135 | 51 | 65 | 79 | 115 |
| Brazil ........................ | 9 | 8 | 5 | 5 | 12 | 14 | 22 | 23 | 3 | 6 | 17 | 18 |
| Chile ........................ | 12 | 19 | 26 | 24 | 32 | 44 | 65 | 84 | 20 | 26 | 40 | 59 |
| Venezuela ........................ | 11 | 9 | 7 | 16 | 19 | 17 | 26 | 28 | 8 | 8 | 20 | 13 |
| Other ........................ | 76 | 92 | 94 | 68 | 156 | 183 | 220 | 220 | 80 | 92 | 126 | 152 |
| Other Western Hemisphere ........................ | 240 | -63 | 187 | 549 | 386 | 330 | 478 | 827 | 146 | 393 | 290 | 278 |
| Bermuda ........................ | 203 | -139 | 109 | 163 | 321 | 198 | 350 | 372 | 118 | 337 | 241 | 209 |
| Other ........................ | 37 | 76 | 79 | 385 | 65 | 132 | 128 | 455 | 28 | 56 | 49 | 70 |
| **Africa** ........................ | -1 | 6 | 6 | 8 | 7 | 13 | 16 | 17 | 8 | 7 | 10 | 9 |
| South Africa ........................ | 2 | 3 | 1 | 3 | 2 | 5 | 7 | 7 | (*) | 1 | 6 | 4 |
| Other ........................ | -3 | 3 | 5 | 4 | 4 | 9 | 9 | 9 | 7 | 6 | 4 | 5 |
| **Middle East** ........................ | 8 | 21 | 7 | 14 | 30 | 36 | 45 | 52 | 22 | 15 | 38 | 37 |
| Israel ........................ | 3 | 7 | 7 | 1 | 16 | 19 | 25 | 35 | 13 | 11 | 18 | 34 |
| Saudi Arabia ........................ | 3 | 2 | 1 | 2 | 4 | 4 | 4 | 4 | 1 | 3 | 3 | 1 |
| Other ........................ | 2 | 11 | (*) | 11 | 9 | 13 | 16 | 13 | 7 | 1 | 16 | 2 |
| **Asia and Pacific** ........................ | 393 | 418 | 418 | 432 | 821 | 833 | 916 | 888 | 428 | 415 | 498 | 456 |
| Australia ........................ | 28 | 50 | 37 | 25 | 76 | 101 | 111 | 109 | 49 | 51 | 75 | 84 |
| China ........................ | -1 | 23 | (*) | 3 | 78 | 25 | 10 | 16 | (*) | 2 | 10 | 13 |
| Hong Kong ........................ | 26 | 26 | 10 | 12 | 44 | 47 | 53 | 36 | 19 | 21 | 43 | 25 |
| India ........................ | 2 | 4 | 3 | (*) | 2 | 6 | 7 | 7 | 1 | 2 | 4 | 7 |
| Indonesia ........................ | (*) | 5 | 4 | -1 | 3 | 9 | 16 | 15 | 3 | 4 | 12 | 17 |
| Japan ........................ | 246 | 241 | 324 | 314 | 471 | 461 | 524 | 483 | 225 | 220 | 200 | 169 |
| Malaysia ........................ | 12 | 5 | 2 | 4 | 18 | 14 | 14 | 13 | 6 | 8 | 12 | 9 |
| New Zealand ........................ | 11 | 14 | 7 | 10 | 15 | 19 | 15 | 13 | 4 | 5 | 8 | 3 |
| Philippines ........................ | 10 | 6 | -7 | 6 | 15 | 14 | 15 | 15 | 5 | 8 | 22 | 10 |
| Singapore ........................ | 16 | 3 | 12 | 20 | 38 | 28 | 25 | 30 | 22 | 25 | 12 | 10 |
| South Korea ........................ | 5 | 15 | 7 | 4 | 26 | 26 | 25 | 22 | 21 | 11 | 18 | 18 |
| Taiwan ........................ | 27 | 20 | 14 | 28 | 87 | 71 | 88 | 111 | 60 | 51 | 74 | 83 |
| Thailand ........................ | 10 | 5 | 5 | 8 | 16 | 8 | 12 | 14 | 6 | 3 | 7 | 6 |
| Other ........................ | 2 | 2 | (*) | (*) | 2 | 3 | (*) | 2 | 1 | 1 | (*) | 2 |
| **International organizations and unallocated** ............... | 61 | 61 | 248 | 61 | 118 | 127 | 182 | 182 | 57 | 65 | -66 | 121 |
| **European Union** ........................ | 338 | 320 | 525 | 768 | 1 909 | 2 434 | 2 548 | 2 229 | 1 571 | 2 114 | 2 024 | 1 461 |
| **Eastern Europe** ........................ | 1 | -1 | 7 | 11 | 5 | 14 | 21 | 25 | 5 | 15 | 14 | 14 |

1. Includes Mexico.

## Table B-9.   U.S. Insurance Receipts, 1994–1997 —*Continued*

(Unaffiliated transactions; millions of dollars.)

| Country or region | Primary insurance | | | | | | | | | | | |
|---|---|---|---|---|---|---|---|---|---|---|---|---|
| | Net | | | | Premiums received | | | | Losses paid | | | |
| | 1994 | 1995 | 1996 | 1997 | 1994 | 1995 | 1996 | 1997 | 1994 | 1995 | 1996 | 1997 |
| **ALL COUNTRIES** | 361 | 349 | 700 | 406 | 870 | 834 | 1 048 | 922 | 509 | 484 | 348 | 516 |
| **Canada** | 129 | 126 | 99 | 75 | 302 | 368 | 336 | 280 | 172 | 242 | 237 | 205 |
| **Mexico** | 19 | 10 | 19 | 20 | 26 | 16 | 26 | 29 | 7 | 6 | 7 | 9 |
| **Europe** | -59 | 36 | 199 | 152 | 128 | 136 | 292 | 221 | 186 | 100 | 93 | 69 |
| Belgium and Luxembourg | 2 | 2 | 5 | 2 | 5 | 6 | 8 | 5 | 3 | 5 | 3 | 3 |
| France | 5 | 4 | 12 | 8 | (D) | 15 | 20 | 14 | (D) | 11 | 8 | 6 |
| Germany | 9 | 13 | 16 | 8 | 18 | 27 | 25 | 15 | 9 | 14 | 9 | 7 |
| Italy | 2 | 2 | 6 | 3 | 5 | 7 | 9 | 5 | 3 | 5 | 3 | 2 |
| Netherlands | 2 | 5 | 5 | 2 | 2 | 5 | 6 | 5 | 1 | (*) | 1 | 3 |
| Norway | 1 | 2 | 17 | 13 | 4 | 8 | (D) | 18 | 3 | 7 | (D) | 5 |
| Spain | 2 | 1 | 5 | 2 | 5 | 6 | 8 | 5 | 3 | 5 | 3 | 2 |
| Sweden | 2 | 1 | 4 | 2 | 5 | 6 | 8 | 4 | 3 | 4 | 4 | 2 |
| Switzerland | 2 | 2 | 4 | 2 | 5 | 6 | 8 | 4 | 3 | 4 | 3 | 2 |
| United Kingdom | -91 | (*) | 119 | 108 | (D) | 36 | 162 | 134 | (D) | 36 | 43 | 26 |
| Other | 5 | 6 | 7 | 2 | (D) | 15 | (D) | 12 | (D) | 9 | (D) | 10 |
| **Latin America and Other Western Hemisphere** [1] | 131 | 109 | 118 | 125 | 184 | 155 | 175 | 185 | 54 | 46 | 57 | 59 |
| South and Central America [1] | 128 | 103 | 112 | 113 | 180 | 149 | 163 | 169 | 52 | 46 | 51 | 56 |
| Argentina | 57 | 37 | 38 | 39 | 83 | (D) | 51 | (D) | 26 | (D) | 12 | (D) |
| Brazil | 5 | 6 | 8 | 8 | 7 | 8 | 9 | 10 | 1 | 2 | 1 | 2 |
| Chile | 6 | 6 | 6 | 6 | 7 | 8 | 7 | 7 | (*) | 1 | 1 | 1 |
| Venezuela | 4 | 4 | 8 | 8 | 5 | 5 | 8 | 9 | 1 | 1 | 1 | 1 |
| Other | 36 | 39 | 33 | 32 | 53 | (D) | 62 | (D) | 17 | (D) | 29 | (D) |
| Other Western Hemisphere | 3 | 6 | 6 | 12 | 5 | 6 | 12 | 16 | 2 | (*) | 6 | 4 |
| Bermuda | (*) | 1 | -1 | 3 | 1 | 1 | 2 | 4 | 1 | (*) | 3 | 1 |
| Other | 2 | 5 | 7 | 9 | 4 | 5 | 11 | 12 | 2 | (*) | 4 | 3 |
| **Africa** | (*) | 2 | 3 | 2 | (*) | 3 | 4 | 4 | (*) | 2 | 1 | 2 |
| South Africa | (*) | (*) | 1 | 1 | (*) | (*) | 1 | 1 | 0 | 0 | (*) | (*) |
| Other | (*) | 1 | 2 | 2 | (*) | 3 | 3 | 4 | (*) | 2 | 1 | 2 |
| **Middle East** | 1 | 2 | 2 | 2 | 2 | 3 | 4 | 4 | 1 | 1 | 1 | 1 |
| Israel | (*) | 1 | 1 | 1 | 1 | 1 | 1 | 1 | 1 | (*) | (*) | (*) |
| Saudi Arabia | 1 | 1 | 1 | 1 | 1 | 1 | 1 | 1 | 1 | 1 | 1 | (*) |
| Other | (*) | (*) | (*) | 1 | (*) | 1 | 1 | 1 | 0 | (*) | 1 | 1 |
| **Asia and Pacific** | 116 | 31 | 50 | 24 | 156 | 57 | 80 | 82 | 40 | 26 | 30 | 58 |
| Australia | 7 | 6 | 7 | -4 | 14 | 12 | 20 | 19 | 8 | 6 | 13 | 23 |
| China | (*) | (*) | (*) | (*) | (*) | (*) | 1 | 1 | -1 | (*) | (*) | (*) |
| Hong Kong | 24 | 8 | 8 | 1 | (D) | (D) | 13 | (D) | (D) | (D) | 5 | (D) |
| India | (*) | (*) | (*) | -1 | (*) | 1 | 1 | 1 | (*) | 1 | (*) | 1 |
| Indonesia | (*) | 1 | 1 | 1 | (*) | 1 | 2 | 1 | 0 | (*) | (*) | 1 |
| Japan | 2 | 5 | 9 | 5 | 5 | 9 | 11 | 9 | 3 | 4 | 2 | 4 |
| Malaysia | 10 | 1 | (*) | 1 | (D) | 1 | 1 | 1 | (D) | 1 | (*) | (*) |
| New Zealand | (*) | (*) | 1 | 1 | (*) | 1 | 1 | 1 | (*) | (*) | (*) | (*) |
| Philippines | 7 | 2 | 1 | (*) | 9 | 3 | 2 | 2 | 2 | 1 | 1 | 2 |
| Singapore | 18 | 4 | 11 | 8 | (D) | (D) | (D) | (D) | (D) | (D) | (D) | (D) |
| South Korea | 6 | 2 | 2 | 1 | 9 | 3 | 3 | 4 | 3 | 1 | 1 | 4 |
| Taiwan | 32 | 2 | 8 | 9 | 40 | 6 | (D) | 12 | 8 | 5 | (D) | 3 |
| Thailand | 8 | (*) | 1 | 1 | (D) | (*) | 1 | 1 | (D) | (*) | (*) | (*) |
| Other | 2 | (*) | (*) | 1 | 2 | (*) | 1 | 1 | (*) | (*) | (*) | (*) |
| **International organizations and unallocated** | 43 | 43 | 229 | 24 | 98 | 111 | 156 | 146 | 55 | 67 | -73 | 122 |
| **European Union** | -64 | 32 | 177 | 137 | 112 | 119 | 261 | 195 | 177 | 87 | 85 | 58 |
| **Eastern Europe** | (*) | (*) | 1 | (*) | (*) | 1 | 2 | 2 | (*) | (*) | 1 | 1 |

1. Includes Mexico.

## Table B-9.  U.S. Insurance Receipts, 1994–1997 —*Continued*

(Unaffiliated transactions; millions of dollars.)

| Country or region | Reinsurance | | | | | | | | | | | |
|---|---|---|---|---|---|---|---|---|---|---|---|---|
| | Net | | | | Premiums received | | | | Losses paid | | | |
| | 1994 | 1995 | 1996 | 1997 | 1994 | 1995 | 1996 | 1997 | 1994 | 1995 | 1996 | 1997 |
| **ALL COUNTRIES** | 1 315 | 947 | 1 272 | 1 985 | 4 051 | 4 658 | 4 931 | 5 030 | 2 736 | 3 711 | 3 659 | 3 045 |
| **Canada** | 262 | 247 | 244 | 278 | 725 | 739 | 726 | 733 | 464 | 492 | 482 | 455 |
| **Mexico** | 30 | 26 | 23 | 37 | 92 | 85 | 72 | 85 | 61 | 58 | 49 | 48 |
| **Europe** | 418 | 234 | 346 | 633 | 1 949 | 2 439 | 2 434 | 2 150 | 1 531 | 2 205 | 2 088 | 1 517 |
| Belgium and Luxembourg | 34 | 50 | 57 | 53 | 89 | 142 | 123 | 97 | 55 | 92 | 66 | 45 |
| France | 2 | 86 | 19 | 122 | (D) | 201 | 184 | 207 | (D) | 116 | 164 | 85 |
| Germany | 65 | 48 | 112 | 80 | 162 | 237 | 287 | 284 | 98 | 190 | 175 | 204 |
| Italy | 7 | 27 | 10 | 37 | 35 | 55 | 65 | 70 | 28 | 29 | 55 | 33 |
| Netherlands | 9 | 14 | -19 | -40 | 33 | 38 | 36 | 37 | 24 | 24 | 55 | 76 |
| Norway | 10 | 3 | 28 | 5 | 17 | 25 | (D) | 37 | 7 | 22 | (D) | 32 |
| Spain | 18 | 5 | 4 | 14 | 22 | 17 | 25 | 20 | 4 | 12 | 21 | 6 |
| Sweden | 6 | 7 | 12 | 13 | 17 | 27 | 34 | 26 | 11 | 20 | 22 | 13 |
| Switzerland | 5 | -46 | -47 | -16 | 99 | 83 | 77 | 49 | 93 | 129 | 123 | 64 |
| United Kingdom | 265 | 7 | 162 | 323 | (D) | 1 520 | 1 448 | 1 182 | (D) | 1 513 | 1 286 | 859 |
| Other | -4 | 34 | 7 | 43 | (D) | 93 | (D) | 141 | (D) | 59 | (D) | 99 |
| **Latin America and Other Western Hemisphere** [1] | 335 | 38 | 287 | 612 | 658 | 645 | 856 | 1 245 | 323 | 608 | 569 | 633 |
| South and Central America [1] | 98 | 107 | 105 | 76 | 277 | 321 | 391 | 434 | 179 | 215 | 285 | 358 |
| Argentina | 12 | 8 | 5 | -20 | 38 | (D) | 71 | (D) | 25 | (D) | 66 | (D) |
| Brazil | 3 | 2 | -2 | -2 | 5 | 6 | 13 | 14 | 2 | 5 | 15 | 16 |
| Chile | 6 | 13 | 19 | 18 | 26 | 37 | 58 | 76 | 20 | 24 | 39 | 58 |
| Venezuela | 7 | 5 | -1 | 8 | 14 | 12 | 18 | 19 | 7 | 7 | 19 | 12 |
| Other | 40 | 53 | 61 | 36 | 103 | (D) | 158 | (D) | 63 | (D) | 97 | (D) |
| Other Western Hemisphere | 237 | -69 | 181 | 536 | 381 | 324 | 465 | 811 | 144 | 393 | 284 | 275 |
| Bermuda | 202 | -140 | 110 | 160 | 320 | 197 | 348 | 368 | 118 | 337 | 238 | 208 |
| Other | 35 | 71 | 72 | 376 | 61 | 127 | 117 | 443 | 26 | 56 | 46 | 67 |
| **Africa** | -1 | 5 | 3 | 5 | 6 | 10 | 11 | 12 | 8 | 5 | 9 | 7 |
| South Africa | 1 | 3 | (*) | 3 | 2 | 4 | 6 | 7 | (*) | 1 | 5 | 4 |
| Other | -3 | 2 | 2 | 2 | 4 | 6 | 6 | 6 | 7 | 4 | 3 | 3 |
| **Middle East** | 7 | 19 | 5 | 12 | 28 | 33 | 41 | 48 | 21 | 14 | 36 | 36 |
| Israel | 3 | 7 | 6 | (*) | 16 | 18 | 24 | 34 | 13 | 11 | 18 | 34 |
| Saudi Arabia | 2 | 1 | (*) | 1 | 3 | 3 | 3 | 3 | 1 | 2 | 2 | 1 |
| Other | 2 | 11 | -1 | 11 | 9 | 12 | 15 | 12 | 7 | 1 | 16 | 1 |
| **Asia and Pacific** | 278 | 387 | 368 | 408 | 665 | 775 | 836 | 806 | 388 | 388 | 468 | 399 |
| Australia | 21 | 44 | 30 | 29 | 62 | 89 | 92 | 89 | 41 | 46 | 62 | 61 |
| China | 7 | 23 | (*) | 2 | 8 | 25 | 9 | 15 | (*) | 2 | 10 | 13 |
| Hong Kong | 2 | 18 | 2 | 10 | (D) | (D) | 40 | (D) | (D) | (D) | 38 | (D) |
| India | 2 | 4 | 2 | 1 | 2 | 5 | 6 | 7 | 1 | 1 | 4 | 6 |
| Indonesia | (*) | 4 | 2 | -2 | 3 | 8 | 14 | 14 | 3 | 4 | 12 | 16 |
| Japan | 243 | 236 | 315 | 309 | 465 | 452 | 513 | 474 | 222 | 216 | 198 | 164 |
| Malaysia | 1 | 5 | 2 | 3 | (D) | 12 | 13 | 12 | (D) | 8 | 12 | 9 |
| New Zealand | 11 | 14 | 7 | 9 | 14 | 18 | 14 | 12 | 4 | 4 | 7 | 3 |
| Philippines | 3 | 4 | (*) | 5 | 6 | 11 | 13 | 13 | 3 | 7 | 21 | 8 |
| Singapore | -2 | -1 | 2 | 11 | (D) | (D) | (D) | (D) | (D) | (D) | (D) | (D) |
| South Korea | -1 | 13 | 5 | 3 | 17 | 24 | 22 | 18 | 18 | 10 | 17 | 15 |
| Taiwan | -4 | 18 | 6 | 19 | 47 | 65 | (D) | 99 | 52 | 47 | (D) | 80 |
| Thailand | 3 | 5 | 4 | 7 | (D) | 8 | 11 | 13 | (D) | 3 | 7 | 6 |
| Other | (*) | 2 | -1 | -1 | (*) | 3 | -1 | 1 | 1 | 1 | -1 | 2 |
| **International organizations and unallocated** | 18 | 18 | 19 | 37 | 20 | 16 | 26 | 36 | 2 | -2 | 7 | -1 |
| **European Union** | 402 | 288 | 348 | 631 | 1 796 | 2 314 | 2 287 | 2 034 | 1 394 | 2 026 | 1 939 | 1 403 |
| **Eastern Europe** | 1 | -1 | 6 | 11 | 5 | 13 | 19 | 23 | 4 | 14 | 13 | 12 |

1. Includes Mexico.

## Table B-10.   U.S. Insurance Payments, 1994–1997

(Unaffiliated transactions; millions of dollars.)

| Country or region | Total | | | | | | | | | | | |
|---|---|---|---|---|---|---|---|---|---|---|---|---|
| | Net | | | | Premiums paid | | | | Losses recovered | | | |
| | 1994 | 1995 | 1996 | 1997 | 1994 | 1995 | 1996 | 1997 | 1994 | 1995 | 1996 | 1997 |
| ALL COUNTRIES | 4 034 | 5 360 | 3 773 | 5 208 | 14 075 | 15 284 | 14 652 | 15 036 | 10 041 | 9 925 | 10 879 | 9 828 |
| Canada | 715 | 609 | 459 | 535 | 1 171 | 1 266 | 1 061 | 1 133 | 456 | 657 | 602 | 598 |
| Mexico | 1 | -1 | -2 | -4 | 1 | 1 | 3 | 2 | (*) | 2 | 5 | 6 |
| Europe | 1 661 | 1 855 | 305 | 1 028 | 6 663 | 6 995 | 6 542 | 6 428 | 5 002 | 5 139 | 6 236 | 5 400 |
| Belgium and Luxembourg | 5 | 32 | 30 | 29 | 43 | 57 | 72 | 71 | 38 | 25 | 42 | 43 |
| France | 342 | 308 | 150 | 229 | 638 | 646 | 469 | 497 | 296 | 338 | 320 | 268 |
| Germany | 332 | 329 | 255 | 46 | 1 175 | 1 153 | 1 300 | 1 246 | 843 | 824 | 1 046 | 1 200 |
| Italy | 45 | 44 | -24 | -1 | 158 | 227 | 61 | 63 | 113 | 184 | 84 | 64 |
| Netherlands | -19 | -7 | -5 | -112 | 27 | 26 | 27 | 27 | 46 | 33 | 33 | 139 |
| Norway | 30 | 37 | 11 | 3 | 43 | 43 | 17 | 14 | 13 | 6 | 7 | 11 |
| Spain | 6 | 4 | 5 | 4 | 4 | 4 | 11 | 12 | -2 | (*) | 6 | 8 |
| Sweden | 22 | 84 | -51 | (*) | 88 | 130 | 54 | 69 | 66 | 46 | 105 | 77 |
| Switzerland | -68 | -154 | -271 | -324 | 659 | 684 | 684 | 545 | 727 | 839 | 956 | 869 |
| United Kingdom | 1 073 | 1 177 | 463 | 1 397 | 3 533 | 3 654 | 3 332 | 3 357 | 2 460 | 2 477 | 2 870 | 1 960 |
| Other | -108 | 1 | -256 | -236 | 296 | 371 | 513 | 526 | 404 | 370 | 770 | 762 |
| Latin America and Other Western Hemisphere [1] | 1 659 | 2 691 | 2 953 | 3 406 | 5 595 | 6 292 | 6 480 | 6 968 | 3 936 | 3 601 | 3 527 | 3 562 |
| South and Central America [1] | (*) | (D) | 41 | 24 | 21 | 16 | 91 | 48 | 29 | 28 | 50 | 24 |
| Argentina | -2 | -2 | 1 | -3 | (*) | (*) | 15 | 17 | 3 | 2 | 14 | 19 |
| Brazil | -9 | -9 | 35 | 5 | 4 | (*) | 46 | 1 | 14 | 10 | 11 | -5 |
| Chile | 2 | 1 | 2 | (*) | 2 | 2 | 2 | 1 | (*) | 1 | 1 | (*) |
| Venezuela | 2 | 2 | 6 | 8 | 2 | 2 | 6 | 8 | (*) | (*) | (*) | (*) |
| Other | -1 | -2 | (*) | 17 | 12 | 11 | 19 | 21 | 12 | 13 | 19 | 4 |
| Other Western Hemisphere | 1 667 | 2 702 | 2 912 | 3 382 | 5 574 | 6 276 | 6 389 | 6 920 | 3 907 | 3 574 | 3 477 | 3 538 |
| Bermuda | 1 113 | 2 099 | 2 338 | 2 364 | 3 383 | 3 980 | 4 175 | 4 318 | 2 270 | 1 881 | 1 837 | 1 953 |
| Other | 554 | 603 | 574 | 1 017 | 2 191 | 2 296 | 2 214 | 2 602 | 1 637 | 1 693 | 1 641 | 1 585 |
| Africa | 1 | 5 | 3 | 8 | 4 | 7 | 5 | 10 | 3 | 3 | 2 | 1 |
| South Africa | (*) | -1 | (*) | (*) | (*) | -1 | 1 | 1 | (*) | 1 | (*) | 1 |
| Other | 1 | 6 | 3 | 8 | 4 | 8 | 5 | 8 | 3 | 2 | 1 | (*) |
| Middle East | 7 | 7 | 18 | 20 | 15 | 16 | 11 | 10 | 8 | 9 | -7 | -10 |
| Israel | (*) | -2 | 12 | 11 | 2 | 1 | 2 | (*) | 2 | 3 | -10 | -11 |
| Saudi Arabia | (*) | (*) | (*) | (*) | (*) | (*) | (*) | (*) | (*) | (*) | (*) | (*) |
| Other | 6 | 8 | 6 | 8 | 12 | 14 | 9 | 9 | 6 | 6 | 3 | 1 |
| Asia and Pacific | -19 | 162 | 14 | 161 | 616 | 681 | 543 | 449 | 635 | 519 | 529 | 288 |
| Australia | 49 | 52 | 47 | 59 | 97 | 124 | 132 | 152 | 48 | 72 | 85 | 93 |
| China | 8 | -2 | 4 | -6 | 16 | 4 | 1 | 1 | 5 | 7 | -3 | 8 |
| Hong Kong | -68 | -91 | -85 | 19 | (D) | 63 | 80 | 6 | (D) | 154 | 165 | -13 |
| India | 1 | (*) | (*) | 2 | 3 | 5 | 4 | 3 | 3 | 4 | 4 | 1 |
| Indonesia | -2 | (*) | 3 | 4 | -3 | 1 | 3 | 4 | (*) | 1 | (*) | (*) |
| Japan | 10 | 191 | 20 | 68 | 434 | 457 | 279 | 248 | 424 | 266 | 259 | 180 |
| Malaysia | (*) | -1 | (*) | (*) | (*) | (*) | (*) | (*) | (*) | (*) | (*) | (*) |
| New Zealand | -1 | (*) | 7 | 7 | 1 | 1 | (D) | 10 | 2 | 1 | (D) | 4 |
| Philippines | (*) | (*) | 1 | -4 | (*) | (*) | 2 | 1 | (*) | (*) | (*) | 5 |
| Singapore | -1 | 1 | 3 | -3 | 1 | 3 | 5 | 2 | 2 | 3 | 2 | 5 |
| South Korea | -2 | 2 | 7 | 7 | (D) | 9 | 13 | 9 | (D) | 8 | 6 | 2 |
| Taiwan | 2 | 4 | 2 | 2 | 6 | 8 | 9 | 4 | 3 | 4 | 7 | 3 |
| Thailand | (*) | 3 | 2 | 3 | (*) | 3 | 2 | 5 | (*) | (*) | (*) | 1 |
| Other | 1 | 2 | 3 | 5 | 2 | 2 | (D) | 4 | (*) | (*) | (D) | (*) |
| International organizations and unallocated | 10 | 31 | 21 | 51 | 11 | 28 | 10 | 39 | 1 | -4 | -11 | (D) |
| European Union | 1 658 | 1 968 | 556 | 1 337 | 5 768 | 6 261 | 5 833 | 5 861 | 4 110 | 4 293 | 5 277 | 4 525 |
| Eastern Europe | 2 | (*) | (*) | 1 | (*) | (*) | (*) | (*) | -2 | (*) | (*) | -1 |

1. Includes Mexico.

## Table B-10.  U.S. Insurance Payments, 1994–1997 —*Continued*

(Unaffiliated transactions; millions of dollars.)

| Country or region | Primary insurance | | | | | | | | | | | |
|---|---|---|---|---|---|---|---|---|---|---|---|---|
| | Net | | | | Premiums paid | | | | Losses recovered | | | |
| | 1994 | 1995 | 1996 | 1997 | 1994 | 1995 | 1996 | 1997 | 1994 | 1995 | 1996 | 1997 |
| **ALL COUNTRIES** | 1 769 | 1 520 | 1 299 | 1 485 | 1 980 | 1 845 | 1 518 | 1 630 | 211 | 325 | 219 | 145 |
| **Canada** | 130 | 102 | 61 | 223 | (D) | (D) | (D) | (D) | (D) | (D) | (D) | (D) |
| **Mexico** | (*) | (*) | (*) | (*) | (*) | (*) | 1 | (*) | 0 | 0 | (*) | (*) |
| **Europe** | 1 145 | 864 | 881 | 891 | 1 247 | 1 135 | 969 | 954 | 102 | 271 | 88 | 63 |
| Belgium and Luxembourg | 12 | 13 | 9 | 11 | 13 | (D) | 9 | 11 | 1 | (D) | (*) | (*) |
| France | 186 | 163 | 57 | 52 | (D) | 163 | (D) | 58 | (D) | (*) | (D) | 6 |
| Germany | 24 | 15 | 16 | 15 | 25 | (D) | 17 | 15 | 1 | (D) | (*) | (*) |
| Italy | 23 | 21 | 1 | 1 | (D) | (D) | 1 | 1 | (D) | (D) | (*) | (*) |
| Netherlands | 1 | 1 | (*) | (*) | 1 | 1 | (*) | (*) | 0 | 0 | (*) | (*) |
| Norway | 32 | 36 | 12 | 8 | 37 | 38 | (D) | 11 | 5 | 2 | (D) | 2 |
| Spain | 0 | 0 | (*) | (*) | 0 | 0 | (*) | 0 | 0 | 0 | (*) | (*) |
| Sweden | 4 | 10 | 1 | 1 | 5 | 10 | 2 | 2 | 1 | (*) | 1 | (*) |
| Switzerland | 40 | 53 | 16 | 29 | 40 | 53 | 16 | 29 | 0 | 0 | (*) | (*) |
| United Kingdom | 796 | 526 | 767 | 772 | 878 | 783 | 846 | 826 | 82 | 257 | 80 | 54 |
| Other | 27 | 27 | 1 | 1 | (D) | (D) | 1 | 1 | (D) | (D) | (*) | (*) |
| **Latin America and Other Western Hemisphere** [1] | 416 | 469 | 345 | 353 | 503 | 502 | 450 | (D) | 87 | 33 | 105 | (D) |
| South and Central America [1] | 13 | 11 | 18 | 28 | 13 | 11 | 18 | (D) | (*) | 0 | (*) | (D) |
| Argentina | (*) | (*) | (D) | (*) | (*) | (*) | (D) | (D) | 0 | 0 | (D) | (D) |
| Brazil | (*) | (*) | (*) | (*) | (*) | (*) | (D) | (*) | (*) | 0 | (D) | (*) |
| Chile | 2 | 2 | 2 | 1 | 2 | 2 | 2 | 1 | 0 | 0 | (*) | (*) |
| Venezuela | 1 | 0 | 5 | 8 | (D) | 0 | 5 | 8 | (D) | 0 | (*) | (*) |
| Other | 9 | 9 | (D) | 19 | (D) | 9 | (D) | (D) | (D) | 0 | (D) | (D) |
| Other Western Hemisphere | 403 | 458 | 327 | 325 | 489 | 491 | 432 | 391 | 87 | 33 | 105 | 65 |
| Bermuda | 378 | 436 | 313 | 305 | 465 | 469 | 418 | 369 | 87 | 33 | 105 | 64 |
| Other | 24 | 21 | 14 | 21 | 24 | 21 | 14 | 22 | 0 | 0 | (*) | 1 |
| **Africa** | 2 | 7 | 4 | 4 | 2 | 7 | 4 | 4 | 0 | 0 | (*) | (*) |
| South Africa | 0 | 0 | 0 | (*) | 0 | 0 | 0 | 0 | 0 | 0 | 0 | (*) |
| Other | 2 | 7 | 4 | 4 | 2 | 7 | 4 | 4 | 0 | 0 | (*) | (*) |
| **Middle East** | 9 | 11 | 8 | 6 | 9 | (D) | 8 | 7 | (*) | (D) | (*) | (*) |
| Israel | 2 | 1 | 2 | (*) | 2 | 1 | 2 | (*) | 0 | 0 | (*) | (*) |
| Saudi Arabia | (*) | (*) | (*) | (*) | (*) | (*) | (*) | 0 | 0 | 0 | (*) | (*) |
| Other | 7 | 10 | 6 | 6 | 7 | (D) | 6 | 6 | (*) | (D) | (*) | (*) |
| **Asia and Pacific** | 62 | 61 | 2 | 8 | 64 | 63 | (D) | 9 | 3 | 3 | (D) | 1 |
| Australia | 1 | 4 | (*) | -1 | 1 | 4 | (*) | 0 | 0 | 0 | 8 | 1 |
| China | 5 | 2 | 0 | (*) | 0 | 2 | 0 | (*) | -13 | 0 | 0 | (*) |
| Hong Kong | 2 | 3 | 4 | (D) | 2 | (D) | 4 | (D) | 0 | (D) | (*) | (D) |
| India | 0 | 0 | (*) | (*) | 0 | 0 | (*) | 0 | 0 | 0 | (*) | (*) |
| Indonesia | 0 | 1 | 2 | 2 | 0 | 1 | 2 | 2 | 0 | 0 | 0 | (*) |
| Japan | 54 | 51 | 2 | 1 | (D) | (D) | 2 | 2 | (D) | (D) | (*) | (*) |
| Malaysia | 0 | 0 | 0 | (*) | 0 | 0 | 0 | 0 | 0 | 0 | 0 | (*) |
| New Zealand | 0 | 0 | (*) | (D) | 0 | 0 | (*) | (D) | 0 | 0 | (*) | (D) |
| Philippines | (*) | (*) | (*) | (*) | (*) | (*) | (*) | (*) | 0 | 0 | (*) | (*) |
| Singapore | (*) | (*) | (*) | (*) | (*) | (*) | (*) | (*) | 0 | 0 | (*) | (*) |
| South Korea | 1 | 1 | (*) | (*) | (D) | 1 | (*) | (*) | (D) | 0 | (*) | (*) |
| Taiwan | 0 | (*) | (*) | (*) | 0 | (*) | (*) | (*) | 0 | 0 | (*) | (*) |
| Thailand | 0 | 0 | (*) | (*) | 0 | 0 | (*) | 0 | 0 | 0 | 0 | (*) |
| Other | (*) | (*) | 2 | 1 | (*) | (*) | (D) | 1 | 0 | 0 | (D) | (*) |
| **International organizations and unallocated** | 6 | 6 | 0 | (*) | (D) | 7 | 0 | (*) | (D) | 1 | 0 | 0 |
| **European Union** | 1 070 | 775 | 852 | 853 | 1 166 | 1 044 | 940 | 914 | 96 | 269 | 88 | 61 |
| **Eastern Europe** | (*) | (*) | (*) | (*) | (*) | (*) | (*) | (*) | 0 | 0 | (*) | (*) |

1. Includes Mexico.

## Table B-10.  U.S. Insurance Payments, 1994–1997 —*Continued*

(Unaffiliated transactions; millions of dollars.)

| Country or region | Reinsurance | | | | | | | | | | | |
|---|---|---|---|---|---|---|---|---|---|---|---|---|
| | Net | | | | Premiums paid | | | | Losses recovered | | | |
| | 1994 | 1995 | 1996 | 1997 | 1994 | 1995 | 1996 | 1997 | 1994 | 1995 | 1996 | 1997 |
| ALL COUNTRIES | 2 265 | 3 839 | 2 474 | 3 723 | 12 095 | 13 439 | 13 134 | 13 406 | 9 830 | 9 600 | 10 660 | 9 683 |
| Canada | 585 | 507 | 398 | 312 | (D) | (D) | (D) | (D) | (D) | (D) | (D) | (D) |
| Mexico | 1 | -1 | -3 | -4 | 1 | 1 | 2 | 2 | (*) | 2 | 5 | 6 |
| Europe | 516 | 991 | -575 | 137 | 5 417 | 5 860 | 5 573 | 5 474 | 4 900 | 4 869 | 6 148 | 5 337 |
| Belgium and Luxembourg | -7 | 20 | 21 | 18 | 30 | (D) | 63 | 61 | 37 | (D) | 42 | 43 |
| France | 156 | 145 | 92 | 177 | (D) | 483 | (D) | 439 | (D) | 338 | (D) | 262 |
| Germany | 308 | 314 | 239 | 31 | 1 150 | (D) | 1 284 | 1 231 | 842 | (D) | 1 045 | 1 200 |
| Italy | 22 | 23 | -24 | -1 | (D) | (D) | 60 | 63 | (D) | (D) | 84 | 64 |
| Netherlands | -19 | (*) | -5 | -112 | 26 | 26 | 27 | 27 | 46 | 33 | 33 | 139 |
| Norway | -2 | 1 | -1 | -5 | 6 | 5 | (D) | 4 | 8 | 4 | (D) | 9 |
| Spain | 6 | 4 | 5 | 4 | 4 | 4 | 11 | 12 | -2 | (*) | 6 | 8 |
| Sweden | 18 | 74 | -52 | -9 | 83 | 120 | 52 | 67 | 65 | 45 | 104 | 77 |
| Switzerland | -108 | -207 | -288 | -353 | 620 | 631 | 668 | 516 | 727 | 839 | 956 | 869 |
| United Kingdom | 277 | 651 | -304 | 625 | 2 655 | 2 871 | 2 486 | 2 530 | 2 378 | 2 220 | 2 790 | 1 906 |
| Other | -135 | -25 | -257 | -237 | (D) | (D) | 512 | 525 | (D) | (D) | 770 | 762 |
| Latin America and Other Western Hemisphere [1] | 1 243 | 2 222 | 2 608 | 3 053 | 5 093 | 5 790 | 6 030 | (D) | 3 849 | 3 568 | 3 422 | (D) |
| South and Central America [1] | -21 | -23 | 24 | -3 | 8 | 5 | 74 | (D) | 29 | 28 | 50 | (D) |
| Argentina | -2 | -2 | (D) | -3 | (*) | (*) | (D) | (D) | 3 | 2 | (D) | (D) |
| Brazil | -10 | -10 | 35 | 5 | 4 | (*) | (D) | (*) | 14 | 10 | (D) | -5 |
| Chile | (*) | (*) | -1 | (*) | (*) | (*) | (*) | (*) | (*) | 1 | 1 | (*) |
| Venezuela | (*) | 2 | 1 | (*) | (D) | 2 | 1 | (*) | (D) | (*) | (*) | (*) |
| Other | -10 | -11 | (D) | -2 | (D) | 1 | (D) | (D) | 13 | (D) | (D) | (D) |
| Other Western Hemisphere | 1 265 | 2 245 | 2 585 | 3 056 | 5 085 | 5 785 | 5 957 | 6 529 | 3 820 | 3 541 | 3 372 | 3 473 |
| Bermuda | 735 | 1 663 | 2 025 | 2 059 | 2 918 | 3 511 | 3 757 | 3 948 | 2 183 | 1 848 | 1 731 | 1 889 |
| Other | 530 | 582 | 560 | 997 | 2 167 | 2 275 | 2 200 | 2 581 | 1 637 | 1 693 | 1 640 | 1 584 |
| Africa | -1 | -2 | -1 | 4 | 2 | 1 | 1 | 6 | 3 | 3 | 2 | 1 |
| South Africa | (*) | -1 | (*) | (*) | (*) | -1 | 1 | 1 | (*) | 1 | (*) | 1 |
| Other | -1 | -1 | -1 | 4 | 2 | 1 | (*) | 5 | 3 | 2 | 1 | (*) |
| Middle East | -2 | -5 | 10 | 13 | 6 | (D) | 3 | 3 | 8 | (D) | -7 | -10 |
| Israel | -2 | -3 | 10 | 11 | (*) | (*) | (*) | (*) | 2 | 3 | -10 | -11 |
| Saudi Arabia | (*) | (*) | (*) | (*) | (*) | (*) | (*) | (*) | (*) | (*) | (*) | (*) |
| Other | (*) | -2 | (*) | 2 | 5 | (D) | 3 | 3 | 6 | (D) | 3 | 1 |
| Asia and Pacific | -81 | 101 | 12 | 153 | 552 | 617 | (D) | 440 | 633 | 516 | (D) | 287 |
| Australia | 49 | 48 | 56 | 59 | 97 | 120 | 132 | 152 | 48 | 72 | 77 | 92 |
| China | 4 | -4 | 4 | -6 | 16 | 3 | 1 | 1 | (D) | 7 | -3 | 8 |
| Hong Kong | -70 | -94 | -89 | (D) | (D) | (D) | 76 | (D) | (D) | (D) | 165 | (D) |
| India | 1 | (*) | (*) | 2 | 2 | 3 | 3 | 3 | 3 | 4 | 4 | 1 |
| Indonesia | -2 | -1 | 1 | 2 | -3 | (*) | 1 | 2 | (*) | 1 | (*) | (*) |
| Japan | -44 | 141 | 18 | 66 | (D) | (D) | 277 | 246 | (D) | (D) | 259 | 180 |
| Malaysia | (*) | -1 | (*) | (*) | (*) | (*) | (*) | (*) | (*) | (*) | (*) | (*) |
| New Zealand | -1 | (*) | 7 | (D) | 1 | 1 | (D) | (D) | 2 | 1 | (D) | (D) |
| Philippines | (*) | (*) | 1 | -4 | (*) | (*) | 1 | 1 | (*) | (*) | (*) | 4 |
| Singapore | -1 | 1 | 3 | -3 | 1 | 3 | 4 | 2 | 2 | 3 | 1 | 5 |
| South Korea | -3 | 1 | 7 | 7 | (D) | 9 | 13 | 9 | (D) | 8 | 6 | 2 |
| Taiwan | 2 | 4 | 2 | 2 | 6 | 8 | 9 | 4 | 3 | 4 | 7 | 3 |
| Thailand | (*) | 3 | 2 | 3 | (*) | 3 | 2 | 5 | (*) | (*) | (*) | 1 |
| Other | 1 | 2 | 1 | 3 | 2 | 2 | (D) | 3 | (*) | (*) | (D) | (*) |
| International organizations and unallocated | 4 | 25 | 21 | 51 | (D) | 20 | 10 | 39 | (D) | -4 | -11 | (D) |
| European Union | 589 | 1 193 | -296 | 483 | 4 602 | 5 216 | 4 893 | 4 947 | 4 013 | 4 024 | 5 190 | 4 464 |
| Eastern Europe | 2 | (*) | (*) | 1 | (*) | (*) | (*) | (*) | -2 | (*) | (*) | -1 |

1. Includes Mexico.

## Table B-11.  U.S. Business, Professional, and Technical Service Receipts, 1994–1997

(Unaffiliated transactions; millions of dollars.)

| Country or region | Total | | | | Advertising | | | | Computer and data processing services | | | |
|---|---|---|---|---|---|---|---|---|---|---|---|---|
| | 1994 | 1995 | 1996 | 1997 | 1994 | 1995 | 1996 | 1997 | 1994 | 1995 | 1996 | 1997 |
| ALL COUNTRIES | 15 330 | 16 064 | 19 678 | 21 304 | 487 | 425 | 551 | 581 | 1 306 | 1 340 | 1 634 | 1 616 |
| Canada | 1 376 | 1 241 | 1 639 | 1 943 | 207 | 80 | 101 | 100 | 241 | 179 | 225 | 183 |
| Mexico | 714 | 671 | 630 | 793 | 14 | 14 | 14 | 17 | 40 | 48 | 62 | 70 |
| Europe | 4 921 | 5 143 | 6 225 | 6 690 | 118 | 164 | 253 | 273 | 382 | 469 | 725 | 609 |
| Belgium and Luxembourg | 340 | 286 | 211 | 250 | 1 | 1 | (D) | (D) | 13 | 10 | 24 | 26 |
| France | 436 | 496 | 647 | 694 | 13 | 17 | 27 | 28 | 27 | 42 | 79 | 59 |
| Germany | 554 | 613 | 753 | 858 | 23 | 23 | 36 | 34 | 54 | 78 | 113 | 96 |
| Italy | 185 | 206 | 290 | 318 | 18 | 20 | 19 | 19 | 17 | 16 | 25 | 20 |
| Netherlands | 266 | 339 | 450 | 437 | 2 | 2 | 4 | 7 | 45 | 67 | 103 | 51 |
| Norway | 68 | 63 | 64 | 70 | (*) | (*) | 1 | (*) | 13 | 10 | 14 | 14 |
| Spain | 266 | 173 | 225 | 236 | 2 | 4 | 6 | 6 | 6 | 10 | 18 | 21 |
| Sweden | 147 | 191 | 216 | 230 | (D) | (D) | (D) | (D) | 12 | 30 | 36 | 31 |
| Switzerland | 205 | 262 | 326 | 376 | 5 | 7 | 13 | 16 | 34 | 41 | 51 | 30 |
| United Kingdom | 1 495 | 1 500 | 1 719 | 1 888 | 25 | 57 | 89 | 96 | 94 | 107 | 195 | 195 |
| Other | 959 | 1 013 | 1 324 | 1 332 | (D) | (D) | 8 | 11 | 66 | 59 | 69 | 65 |
| Latin America and Other Western Hemisphere [1] | 2 697 | 2 702 | 2 847 | 3 036 | 72 | 84 | 83 | 84 | 147 | 159 | 203 | 248 |
| South and Central America [1] | 2 398 | 2 388 | 2 414 | 2 735 | 40 | 53 | 41 | 44 | 133 | 152 | 191 | 236 |
| Argentina | 198 | 251 | 269 | 282 | 3 | 1 | 1 | 1 | 19 | 14 | 25 | 26 |
| Brazil | 319 | 372 | 401 | 534 | (D) | 5 | 3 | 4 | 37 | 57 | 65 | 91 |
| Chile | 321 | 102 | 148 | 162 | (*) | (*) | (D) | (D) | 11 | 3 | 8 | 9 |
| Venezuela | 268 | 264 | 225 | 264 | (*) | (D) | (*) | (*) | 11 | 17 | 12 | 16 |
| Other | 578 | 728 | 742 | 700 | (D) | (D) | (D) | (D) | 15 | 13 | 20 | 25 |
| Other Western Hemisphere | 299 | 314 | 433 | 300 | 33 | 32 | 42 | 41 | 14 | 7 | 12 | 12 |
| Bermuda | 58 | 86 | 53 | 45 | (D) | (D) | (D) | (D) | 2 | 2 | 3 | 2 |
| Other | 241 | 228 | 380 | 256 | (D) | (D) | (D) | (D) | 12 | 5 | 9 | 9 |
| Africa | 556 | 636 | 773 | 867 | 1 | 1 | 1 | 2 | 30 | 27 | 25 | 44 |
| South Africa | 77 | 76 | 107 | 133 | 1 | 1 | (*) | (*) | 16 | 18 | 15 | 32 |
| Other | 479 | 559 | 667 | 735 | (*) | (*) | (*) | 2 | 14 | 9 | 10 | 11 |
| Middle East | 1 166 | 1 242 | 1 965 | 2 274 | 3 | 3 | 5 | 5 | 243 | 213 | 40 | 60 |
| Israel | 114 | 124 | 169 | 162 | 2 | 2 | 3 | 3 | 35 | (D) | 11 | 13 |
| Saudi Arabia | 784 | 886 | 765 | 850 | 1 | 1 | 1 | 1 | (D) | (D) | 22 | 37 |
| Other | 267 | 231 | 1 031 | 1 262 | (*) | (*) | 1 | 1 | (D) | 3 | 8 | 11 |
| Asia and Pacific | 4 340 | 4 838 | 5 934 | 6 168 | 81 | 86 | 109 | 117 | 240 | 283 | 416 | 472 |
| Australia | 321 | 378 | 476 | 537 | 5 | 2 | 4 | 6 | 70 | 77 | 80 | 132 |
| China | 276 | 472 | 536 | 527 | 1 | (*) | 2 | 2 | 12 | 20 | 19 | 24 |
| Hong Kong | 217 | 249 | 406 | 344 | 17 | 23 | 33 | 32 | 24 | 17 | 23 | 30 |
| India | 74 | 102 | 142 | 132 | 1 | (*) | 2 | 2 | 3 | 8 | 11 | 14 |
| Indonesia | 217 | 348 | 504 | 737 | (*) | 2 | 2 | 2 | 4 | 6 | 7 | 13 |
| Japan | 1 511 | 1 590 | 1 860 | 1 796 | 39 | 39 | 42 | 55 | 61 | 83 | 164 | 114 |
| Malaysia | 138 | 114 | 343 | 190 | (*) | (*) | (*) | 1 | 8 | 5 | 11 | 15 |
| New Zealand | 51 | 51 | 90 | 125 | (*) | (*) | 1 | (*) | 6 | 6 | 8 | 10 |
| Philippines | 216 | 115 | 162 | 254 | 2 | (*) | 1 | 1 | 7 | 4 | 14 | 22 |
| Singapore | 129 | 149 | 183 | 195 | 3 | 3 | 6 | 6 | 8 | 9 | 10 | 17 |
| South Korea | 399 | 528 | 513 | 614 | 6 | 6 | 7 | 5 | 15 | 22 | 27 | 37 |
| Taiwan | 232 | 249 | 256 | 286 | 5 | 6 | 8 | 5 | 13 | 15 | 23 | 22 |
| Thailand | 222 | 273 | 184 | 185 | 2 | 1 | 2 | 2 | 10 | 9 | 17 | 19 |
| Other | 335 | 221 | 280 | 248 | 1 | 2 | (*) | (*) | 1 | 2 | 2 | 5 |
| International organizations and unallocated | 275 | 262 | 294 | 327 | 5 | 6 | (*) | (*) | 24 | 11 | (*) | (*) |
| European Union | 3 734 | 4 006 | 4 826 | 5 251 | 86 | 178 | 238 | 253 | 274 | 390 | 631 | 540 |
| Eastern Europe | 547 | 664 | 772 | 695 | (*) | 1 | 1 | 1 | 35 | 27 | 25 | 21 |

1. Includes Mexico.

## Table B-11.   U.S. Business, Professional, and Technical Service Receipts, 1994–1997 —Continued

(Unaffiliated transactions; millions of dollars.)

| Country or region | Database and other information services | | | | Research, development, and testing services | | | | Management, consulting, and public relations services | | | |
|---|---|---|---|---|---|---|---|---|---|---|---|---|
| | 1994 | 1995 | 1996 | 1997 | 1994 | 1995 | 1996 | 1997 | 1994 | 1995 | 1996 | 1997 |
| ALL COUNTRIES | 1 026 | 1 078 | 1 164 | 1 431 | 522 | 638 | 688 | 862 | 1 134 | 1 489 | 1 680 | 2 139 |
| Canada | 92 | 106 | 114 | 152 | 35 | 52 | 48 | 47 | 72 | 94 | 118 | 203 |
| Mexico | 30 | 30 | 32 | 51 | 6 | 10 | 9 | 7 | 52 | 39 | 51 | 53 |
| Europe | 517 | 531 | 570 | 677 | 183 | 268 | 238 | 337 | 394 | 605 | 692 | 907 |
| Belgium and Luxembourg | 17 | 22 | 17 | 24 | 7 | 8 | 10 | 14 | 7 | 12 | 16 | 16 |
| France | 72 | 72 | 75 | 83 | 15 | 28 | 30 | 37 | 18 | 20 | 31 | 47 |
| Germany | 89 | 84 | 74 | 86 | 32 | 29 | 40 | 62 | 47 | 69 | 69 | 88 |
| Italy | 47 | 64 | 70 | 94 | 15 | 9 | 10 | 29 | 24 | 13 | 18 | 23 |
| Netherlands | 28 | 26 | 27 | 30 | 9 | 13 | 13 | 9 | 23 | 20 | 30 | 29 |
| Norway | 5 | 4 | 5 | 5 | 1 | 2 | 2 | 1 | 2 | 5 | 1 | 2 |
| Spain | 18 | 17 | 16 | 20 | 6 | 21 | 5 | 5 | 7 | 3 | 7 | 8 |
| Sweden | 17 | 16 | 19 | 24 | 10 | 17 | 14 | 15 | 10 | 19 | 15 | 20 |
| Switzerland | 25 | 20 | 25 | 34 | 28 | 43 | 49 | 69 | 17 | 36 | 32 | 39 |
| United Kingdom | 134 | 141 | 171 | 165 | 51 | 81 | 48 | 56 | 128 | 144 | 224 | 334 |
| Other | 66 | 65 | 72 | 111 | 9 | 17 | 19 | 40 | 112 | 264 | 248 | 302 |
| Latin America and Other Western Hemisphere [1] | 81 | 82 | 83 | 137 | 15 | 26 | 23 | 24 | 152 | 190 | 189 | 249 |
| South and Central America [1] | 69 | 67 | 69 | 121 | 15 | 26 | 23 | 23 | 130 | 134 | 163 | 229 |
| Argentina | 6 | 7 | 7 | 11 | 1 | (*) | (*) | 2 | 6 | 7 | 10 | 12 |
| Brazil | 11 | 10 | 10 | 24 | 4 | 2 | 5 | 5 | 6 | 10 | 23 | 69 |
| Chile | 6 | 4 | 4 | 7 | (*) | 1 | (*) | (*) | 1 | 5 | 2 | 4 |
| Venezuela | 4 | 6 | 7 | 10 | 2 | 1 | 1 | 1 | 6 | 6 | 10 | 8 |
| Other | 12 | 10 | 8 | 19 | 3 | 12 | 8 | 9 | 58 | 67 | 67 | 84 |
| Other Western Hemisphere | 12 | 15 | 15 | 16 | (*) | 1 | (*) | 1 | 22 | 56 | 26 | 20 |
| Bermuda | 4 | 4 | 1 | 1 | (*) | (*) | (*) | (*) | 10 | 46 | 6 | 2 |
| Other | 8 | 11 | 14 | 15 | (*) | 1 | (*) | (*) | 11 | 10 | 20 | 18 |
| Africa | 21 | 34 | 39 | 45 | 32 | 29 | 14 | 19 | 110 | 140 | 158 | 152 |
| South Africa | 14 | 25 | (D) | (D) | (*) | 3 | 5 | 4 | 5 | 9 | 8 | 8 |
| Other | 6 | 9 | (D) | (D) | 32 | 26 | 9 | 15 | 105 | 132 | 150 | 144 |
| Middle East | 30 | 38 | (D) | 64 | 13 | 18 | 93 | 101 | 111 | 119 | 126 | 141 |
| Israel | 16 | 16 | 17 | 8 | 5 | 3 | (D) | (D) | 5 | 10 | 24 | 26 |
| Saudi Arabia | 4 | 10 | (D) | 22 | 5 | 13 | (D) | (D) | 77 | 82 | 69 | 71 |
| Other | 10 | 12 | (D) | 34 | 3 | 1 | (D) | (D) | 29 | 26 | 33 | 44 |
| Asia and Pacific | 283 | 282 | 307 | 356 | 228 | 235 | 269 | 330 | 275 | 317 | 394 | 444 |
| Australia | 67 | 71 | 74 | 78 | 12 | 21 | 24 | 32 | 41 | 44 | 78 | 84 |
| China | 5 | 5 | 5 | 6 | 4 | 2 | 4 | 5 | 7 | 9 | 11 | 11 |
| Hong Kong | 17 | 18 | 25 | 23 | 1 | 2 | 2 | 4 | 24 | 36 | 29 | 25 |
| India | 6 | 9 | 13 | 19 | 2 | 2 | 3 | 2 | 8 | 11 | 15 | 17 |
| Indonesia | 2 | 1 | 2 | 4 | (D) | 7 | 10 | 7 | 26 | 37 | 37 | 35 |
| Japan | 116 | 105 | 103 | 124 | 150 | 155 | 178 | 212 | 61 | 72 | 92 | 116 |
| Malaysia | 5 | 7 | 6 | 7 | 1 | 3 | 4 | 1 | 1 | 4 | 3 | 10 |
| New Zealand | 10 | 11 | 12 | 20 | (*) | 1 | (*) | 2 | 6 | 7 | 8 | 6 |
| Philippines | 3 | 3 | 3 | 5 | 1 | 2 | 2 | 3 | 18 | 23 | 22 | 31 |
| Singapore | 13 | 21 | 33 | 25 | (*) | 2 | 5 | 4 | 3 | 9 | 13 | 14 |
| South Korea | 17 | 13 | 13 | 19 | 12 | 15 | 20 | 26 | 11 | 9 | 11 | 9 |
| Taiwan | 10 | 6 | 6 | 11 | 19 | 11 | 9 | 14 | 11 | 8 | 9 | 8 |
| Thailand | 7 | 9 | 7 | 9 | 1 | 5 | 4 | 13 | 7 | 8 | 9 | 15 |
| Other | 3 | 4 | 4 | 7 | (D) | 6 | 4 | 6 | 51 | 40 | 57 | 63 |
| International organizations and unallocated | 3 | 4 | (*) | (*) | 16 | 8 | 1 | 4 | 21 | 24 | 2 | 43 |
| European Union | 442 | 492 | 524 | 595 | 136 | 216 | 182 | 255 | 260 | 313 | 427 | 585 |
| Eastern Europe | 6 | 7 | 7 | 30 | 6 | 7 | 4 | 11 | 98 | 244 | 216 | 261 |

1. Includes Mexico.

## Table B-11.  U.S. Business, Professional, and Technical Service Receipts, 1994–1997 —*Continued*

(Unaffiliated transactions; millions of dollars.)

| Country or region | Legal services | | | | Construction, engineering, architectural, and mining services | | | | Industrial engineering | | | |
|---|---|---|---|---|---|---|---|---|---|---|---|---|
| | 1994 | 1995 | 1996 | 1997 | 1994 | 1995 | 1996 | 1997 | 1994 | 1995 | 1996 | 1997 |
| **ALL COUNTRIES** | 1 617 | 1 667 | 1 973 | 2 085 | 2 474 | 2 550 | 3 560 | 4 084 | 575 | 726 | 915 | 1 098 |
| **Canada** | 116 | 107 | 119 | 160 | 44 | 38 | 98 | 282 | 71 | 75 | (D) | 104 |
| **Mexico** | 29 | 26 | 32 | 28 | 72 | 43 | 86 | 139 | 26 | 24 | 18 | 23 |
| **Europe** | 876 | 912 | 1 051 | 1 098 | 585 | 401 | 434 | 439 | 74 | 105 | 146 | 230 |
| Belgium and Luxembourg | 42 | 55 | 61 | 69 | (D) | 5 | (D) | 5 | (*) | (*) | 3 | 3 |
| France | 148 | 162 | 200 | 213 | 8 | 12 | 15 | 11 | 4 | 11 | 6 | 8 |
| Germany | 125 | 133 | 158 | 164 | 22 | 49 | 23 | 32 | 5 | 15 | 9 | 35 |
| Italy | 20 | 26 | 24 | 35 | 5 | 11 | (D) | 11 | 5 | 2 | 2 | 3 |
| Netherlands | 36 | 47 | 28 | 38 | 28 | 10 | 43 | 64 | 2 | 3 | (D) | 18 |
| Norway | 15 | 11 | 10 | 12 | 4 | 1 | 1 | 1 | 3 | 3 | 1 | 1 |
| Spain | 10 | 10 | 11 | 11 | 125 | 23 | 38 | 37 | 3 | 7 | (D) | (D) |
| Sweden | 16 | 18 | 26 | 19 | 5 | 6 | 3 | 3 | 7 | 10 | 10 | 12 |
| Switzerland | 30 | 34 | 37 | 47 | 5 | 3 | 7 | 5 | 5 | 8 | (D) | (D) |
| United Kingdom | 355 | 330 | 378 | 381 | 128 | 94 | 58 | 62 | 12 | 13 | 13 | 17 |
| Other | 78 | 84 | 118 | 110 | (D) | 187 | (D) | 209 | 27 | 32 | 50 | 67 |
| **Latin America and Other Western Hemisphere** [1] | 99 | 91 | 117 | 119 | 477 | 486 | 598 | 559 | (D) | 125 | 245 | 182 |
| South and Central America [1] | 71 | 69 | 79 | 89 | 397 | 391 | 417 | 508 | (D) | 125 | 242 | 174 |
| Argentina | 8 | 5 | 8 | 9 | 18 | 32 | 23 | 26 | 2 | 8 | 24 | 27 |
| Brazil | 12 | 10 | 14 | 15 | 3 | 14 | 61 | 72 | 4 | 1 | 7 | 17 |
| Chile | 5 | 2 | 6 | 8 | 5 | 6 | (D) | (D) | (D) | 1 | (D) | 25 |
| Venezuela | 9 | 11 | 7 | 12 | 163 | 121 | 100 | 97 | 3 | (D) | 21 | 47 |
| Other | 9 | 14 | 11 | 17 | 136 | 176 | (D) | (D) | 4 | (D) | (D) | 35 |
| Other Western Hemisphere | 27 | 23 | 38 | 30 | 80 | 95 | 181 | 51 | 2 | (*) | 3 | 8 |
| Bermuda | 15 | 12 | 20 | 14 | (*) | 1 | (*) | (*) | (*) | 0 | (*) | (*) |
| Other | 12 | 10 | 18 | 16 | 80 | 94 | 181 | 51 | 2 | (*) | 3 | 8 |
| **Africa** | 6 | 7 | 18 | 7 | 150 | 214 | 235 | 322 | 5 | 14 | (D) | 17 |
| South Africa | 3 | 3 | 8 | 5 | 15 | 3 | 10 | 13 | (*) | (*) | (D) | (D) |
| Other | 3 | 4 | 10 | 3 | 135 | 211 | 225 | 310 | 5 | 14 | 8 | (D) |
| **Middle East** | 52 | 39 | 49 | 66 | 237 | 255 | 1 028 | 1 237 | (D) | 57 | 47 | 58 |
| Israel | 13 | 12 | 14 | 20 | 6 | 23 | 26 | 18 | 1 | (D) | 5 | 6 |
| Saudi Arabia | 17 | 12 | 11 | 14 | 119 | 122 | (D) | (D) | (D) | (D) | 39 | 51 |
| Other | 21 | 15 | 24 | 31 | 112 | 110 | (D) | (D) | (*) | (*) | 3 | 2 |
| **Asia and Pacific** | 442 | 480 | 618 | 634 | 977 | 1 156 | 1 166 | 1 244 | 143 | 346 | 384 | 507 |
| Australia | 22 | 26 | 33 | 38 | 11 | 12 | 37 | 15 | 2 | 8 | 7 | 7 |
| China | 6 | 11 | 18 | 19 | 135 | 262 | 165 | 202 | 14 | 13 | 39 | 40 |
| Hong Kong | 45 | 47 | 79 | 69 | 40 | 18 | 3 | 6 | 2 | (D) | 1 | 1 |
| India | 1 | 1 | 3 | 2 | 21 | 29 | (D) | 19 | 4 | 14 | 25 | 23 |
| Indonesia | 2 | 5 | 7 | 9 | 107 | 134 | 248 | 424 | 3 | (D) | (D) | (D) |
| Japan | 322 | 328 | 381 | 382 | 97 | 117 | 178 | 73 | 55 | (D) | 104 | 130 |
| Malaysia | 1 | 1 | 2 | 2 | 60 | 28 | 183 | 55 | 7 | 2 | (D) | (D) |
| New Zealand | 2 | 2 | 3 | 4 | (*) | (*) | (*) | -1 | (*) | 1 | (*) | (D) |
| Philippines | 3 | 2 | 6 | 4 | 140 | 30 | 53 | 112 | 4 | 4 | 9 | (D) |
| Singapore | 5 | 7 | 8 | 12 | 29 | 16 | 14 | 20 | 4 | 9 | 13 | 18 |
| South Korea | 19 | 26 | 50 | 62 | 140 | 232 | 137 | 208 | 12 | 34 | 29 | 30 |
| Taiwan | 8 | 12 | 16 | 24 | 41 | 45 | 28 | 35 | 13 | 19 | 40 | 42 |
| Thailand | 1 | 2 | 3 | 4 | 121 | (D) | 49 | 50 | (D) | 2 | 10 | 7 |
| Other | 4 | 9 | 9 | 4 | 34 | (D) | (D) | 25 | (D) | (D) | (D) | 30 |
| **International organizations and unallocated** | 27 | 30 | 2 | (*) | 4 | 1 | 1 | 1 | 7 | 3 | (*) | 0 |
| **European Union** | 763 | 821 | 928 | 973 | 385 | 222 | 250 | 248 | 54 | 78 | 90 | 138 |
| **Eastern Europe** | 30 | 40 | 69 | 55 | 170 | 151 | 153 | 94 | 2 | 14 | 33 | (D) |

1. Includes Mexico.

**Table B-11.  U.S. Business, Professional, and Technical Service Receipts, 1994–1997** —*Continued*

(Unaffiliated transactions; millions of dollars.)

| Country or region | Installation, maintenance, and repair of equipment | | | | Other | | | |
|---|---|---|---|---|---|---|---|---|
| | 1994 | 1995 | 1996 | 1997 | 1994 | 1995 | 1996 | 1997 |
| **ALL COUNTRIES** | 3 497 | 3 218 | 3 703 | 3 468 | 2 690 | 2 934 | 3 810 | 3 941 |
| **Canada** | 252 | 258 | 267 | 251 | 246 | 253 | (D) | 461 |
| **Mexico** | 241 | 211 | 166 | 228 | 206 | 228 | 160 | 177 |
| **Europe** | 1 077 | 942 | 965 | 901 | 714 | 745 | 1 152 | 1 218 |
| Belgium and Luxembourg | 141 | 93 | 41 | 52 | (D) | 79 | (D) | (D) |
| France | 94 | 78 | 82 | 103 | 37 | 54 | 102 | 105 |
| Germany | 111 | 76 | 113 | 131 | 46 | 57 | 116 | 130 |
| Italy | 19 | 19 | 32 | 38 | 14 | 24 | (D) | 47 |
| Netherlands | 62 | 117 | 120 | 109 | 32 | 32 | (D) | 81 |
| Norway | 14 | 14 | 12 | 9 | 13 | 13 | 18 | 24 |
| Spain | 55 | 45 | 61 | 54 | 32 | 32 | (D) | (D) |
| Sweden | 24 | 29 | 39 | 32 | (D) | (D) | (D) | (D) |
| Switzerland | 29 | 40 | 40 | 37 | 28 | 30 | (D) | (D) |
| United Kingdom | 334 | 282 | 229 | 238 | 233 | 251 | 315 | 342 |
| Other | 195 | 147 | 196 | 98 | (D) | (D) | (D) | 320 |
| **Latin America and Other Western Hemisphere** [1] | 430 | 401 | 439 | 493 | (D) | 1 057 | 868 | 940 |
| South and Central America [1] | 382 | 379 | 392 | 450 | (D) | 993 | 798 | 861 |
| Argentina | 24 | 46 | 71 | 63 | 113 | 132 | 100 | 107 |
| Brazil | 25 | 18 | 50 | 59 | (D) | 244 | 163 | 179 |
| Chile | 15 | 8 | 17 | 16 | (D) | 71 | 37 | (D) |
| Venezuela | 33 | 55 | 24 | 28 | 37 | 37 | 41 | 46 |
| Other | 44 | 41 | 64 | 56 | (D) | 282 | 297 | (D) |
| Other Western Hemisphere | 48 | 22 | 47 | 43 | 61 | 64 | 70 | 79 |
| Bermuda | 5 | (*) | 1 | (*) | (D) | (D) | (D) | (D) |
| Other | 43 | 22 | 46 | 43 | (D) | (D) | (D) | (D) |
| **Africa** | 91 | 62 | 135 | 120 | 111 | 107 | (D) | 139 |
| South Africa | 16 | 9 | 8 | 16 | 7 | 5 | (D) | 14 |
| Other | 75 | 53 | 127 | 104 | 104 | 102 | (D) | 126 |
| **Middle East** | 400 | 434 | 446 | 460 | (D) | 66 | (D) | 82 |
| Israel | 13 | 13 | 32 | 29 | 20 | 23 | (D) | (D) |
| Saudi Arabia | 341 | 375 | 373 | 390 | (D) | 26 | (D) | 14 |
| Other | 46 | 46 | 42 | 42 | (D) | 17 | (D) | (D) |
| **Asia and Pacific** | 1 238 | 1 121 | 1 451 | 1 236 | 433 | 530 | 819 | 828 |
| Australia | 56 | 67 | 72 | 77 | 36 | 49 | 67 | 69 |
| China | 62 | 106 | 141 | 83 | 30 | 45 | 131 | 136 |
| Hong Kong | 20 | 33 | 104 | 36 | 26 | (D) | 106 | 119 |
| India | 13 | 13 | 13 | 9 | 14 | 13 | (D) | 24 |
| Indonesia | 31 | 21 | 63 | 43 | (D) | (D) | (D) | (D) |
| Japan | 440 | 382 | 431 | 453 | 170 | (D) | 187 | 138 |
| Malaysia | 42 | 47 | 75 | 38 | 13 | 15 | (D) | (D) |
| New Zealand | 20 | 16 | 14 | 18 | 7 | 7 | 44 | (D) |
| Philippines | 26 | 34 | 27 | 35 | 13 | 10 | 23 | (D) |
| Singapore | 56 | 65 | 66 | 65 | 6 | 8 | 13 | 14 |
| South Korea | 150 | 146 | 191 | 181 | 17 | 25 | 29 | 37 |
| Taiwan | 99 | 112 | 86 | 81 | 13 | 15 | 30 | 44 |
| Thailand | 59 | 48 | 72 | 55 | (D) | (D) | 12 | 11 |
| Other | 163 | 32 | 96 | 62 | (D) | 54 | 48 | 46 |
| **International organizations and unallocated** | 10 | (*) | (*) | 6 | 160 | 176 | 289 | 273 |
| **European Union** | 832 | 732 | 746 | 781 | 501 | 564 | 810 | 882 |
| **Eastern Europe** | (D) | 98 | 114 | 34 | (D) | 76 | 151 | (D) |

1. Includes Mexico.

## Table B-12.  U.S. Business, Professional, and Technical Service Payments, 1994–1997

(Unaffiliated transactions; millions of dollars.)

| Country or region | Total | | | | Advertising | | | | Computer and data processing services | | | |
|---|---|---|---|---|---|---|---|---|---|---|---|---|
| | 1994 | 1995 | 1996 | 1997 | 1994 | 1995 | 1996 | 1997 | 1994 | 1995 | 1996 | 1997 |
| ALL COUNTRIES | 3 869 | 4 822 | 5 550 | 6 571 | 728 | 833 | 976 | 863 | 83 | 126 | 139 | 270 |
| Canada | 374 | 629 | 673 | 887 | 47 | 49 | 47 | 51 | 25 | 27 | 33 | 71 |
| Mexico | 105 | 102 | 96 | 264 | 29 | 28 | 24 | 19 | 1 | 1 | 3 | 3 |
| Europe | 1 683 | 2 066 | 2 576 | 2 955 | 287 | 314 | 419 | 339 | 26 | 46 | 56 | 113 |
| Belgium and Luxembourg | 62 | 84 | 63 | 76 | 12 | 10 | 13 | 9 | 2 | 9 | 4 | 7 |
| France | 189 | 215 | 208 | 274 | 54 | 48 | 54 | 43 | 5 | 9 | 7 | (D) |
| Germany | 239 | 348 | 436 | 416 | 58 | 72 | 100 | 75 | 1 | 1 | 8 | 21 |
| Italy | 82 | 85 | 92 | 104 | 23 | 19 | 23 | 18 | 1 | 1 | 1 | 2 |
| Netherlands | 79 | 100 | 120 | 144 | 8 | 8 | 6 | 6 | 5 | 9 | 6 | 8 |
| Norway | 26 | 13 | 21 | 20 | 2 | 2 | 2 | 2 | (*) | (*) | 7 | 3 |
| Spain | 44 | 57 | 81 | 88 | 18 | 26 | 38 | 29 | (*) | 1 | 1 | 8 |
| Sweden | 28 | 41 | 34 | 40 | 5 | 5 | 7 | · 7 | (*) | 1 | 1 | 1 |
| Switzerland | 55 | 67 | 110 | 138 | 9 | 9 | 15 | 10 | 6 | 9 | 2 | 3 |
| United Kingdom | 697 | 802 | 1 008 | 1 296 | 77 | 91 | 136 | 123 | 4 | 6 | 16 | 46 |
| Other | 182 | 253 | 402 | 359 | 22 | 25 | 26 | 15 | 1 | 1 | 3 | (D) |
| Latin America and Other Western Hemisphere [1] | 269 | 305 | 342 | 595 | 51 | 46 | 59 | 59 | 3 | 9 | 8 | 8 |
| South and Central America [1] | 258 | 291 | 320 | 561 | 51 | 46 | 58 | 57 | 3 | 9 | 7 | 7 |
| Argentina | 22 | 29 | 32 | 42 | 6 | 3 | 6 | 3 | (*) | 1 | 1 | 1 |
| Brazil | 36 | 53 | 73 | 106 | 8 | 8 | 17 | 20 | 1 | 1 | 2 | 2 |
| Chile | 6 | 9 | 13 | 22 | 1 | 1 | 2 | 2 | (*) | (*) | (*) | (*) |
| Venezuela | 11 | 15 | 19 | 14 | 1 | 1 | 1 | 1 | (*) | 1 | 1 | 1 |
| Other | 78 | 84 | 86 | 113 | 7 | 4 | 8 | 12 | 1 | 5 | 1 | 1 |
| Other Western Hemisphere | 11 | 14 | 22 | 33 | (*) | (*) | 1 | 1 | (*) | (*) | 1 | 1 |
| Bermuda | 3 | 1 | 8 | 16 | (*) | (*) | (*) | (*) | (*) | 0 | (*) | 1 |
| Other | 7 | 13 | 14 | 17 | (*) | (*) | 1 | 1 | (*) | (*) | (*) | (*) |
| Africa | 123 | 138 | 147 | 156 | 2 | 3 | 6 | 5 | 2 | (*) | (*) | (*) |
| South Africa | 15 | 16 | 20 | 21 | 1 | 1 | 3 | 3 | (*) | (*) | (*) | (*) |
| Other | 108 | 122 | 127 | 136 | 1 | 2 | 3 | 2 | 1 | (*) | (*) | (*) |
| Middle East | 83 | 93 | 192 | 169 | 14 | 14 | 32 | 26 | 2 | 3 | 2 | 5 |
| Israel | 34 | 32 | 42 | 42 | 8 | 6 | 14 | 10 | (*) | 1 | 1 | 1 |
| Saudi Arabia | 14 | 17 | 19 | 20 | 4 | 5 | (*) | (D) | 1 | 2 | 1 | 3 |
| Other | 35 | 44 | 131 | 108 | 1 | 3 | 18 | (D) | (*) | (*) | (*) | (*) |
| Asia and Pacific | 1 225 | 1 484 | 1 619 | 1 809 | 317 | 401 | 413 | 384 | 21 | 33 | 40 | 73 |
| Australia | 131 | 153 | 204 | 194 | 23 | 19 | 25 | 26 | 9 | 9 | 11 | 11 |
| China | 34 | 38 | 48 | 68 | 3 | 2 | 4 | 4 | (*) | 2 | 1 | 1 |
| Hong Kong | 66 | 80 | 127 | 144 | 13 | 17 | 18 | 16 | 1 | 1 | 5 | 7 |
| India | 21 | 35 | 57 | 68 | (*) | (*) | 2 | 2 | 3 | 5 | 2 | 4 |
| Indonesia | 33 | 28 | 46 | 56 | 1 | 1 | 3 | 2 | 2 | 2 | 1 | 1 |
| Japan | 658 | 779 | 739 | 800 | 231 | 293 | 305 | 281 | 1 | 3 | 5 | 18 |
| Malaysia | 19 | 12 | 17 | 18 | 1 | 1 | 2 | 2 | (*) | (*) | (*) | 1 |
| New Zealand | 11 | 16 | 19 | 18 | 2 | 2 | 3 | 3 | (*) | 1 | (*) | 1 |
| Philippines | 25 | 41 | 43 | 62 | 2 | 1 | 2 | 2 | 2 | 2 | 6 | 10 |
| Singapore | 27 | 37 | 46 | 65 | 6 | (D) | 11 | 8 | 1 | (*) | 4 | 5 |
| South Korea | 45 | 71 | 79 | 85 | 20 | 27 | 21 | 17 | (*) | 4 | 2 | 3 |
| Taiwan | 45 | 49 | 74 | 89 | 9 | 13 | 11 | 16 | 2 | 2 | 3 | 8 |
| Thailand | 38 | 66 | 77 | 102 | 2 | 2 | 2 | 2 | (*) | 1 | 1 | 1 |
| Other | 71 | 78 | 45 | 39 | 3 | (D) | 4 | 3 | (*) | (*) | (*) | (*) |
| International organizations and unallocated | 113 | 107 | (*) | (*) | 10 | 6 | 0 | 0 | 4 | 8 | 0 | 0 |
| European Union | 1 442 | 1 846 | 2 216 | 2 551 | 260 | 302 | 395 | 323 | 19 | 37 | 46 | 105 |
| Eastern Europe | 85 | 116 | 195 | 220 | 5 | 1 | 4 | 3 | (*) | (*) | (*) | (*) |

1. Includes Mexico.

## Table B-12.  U.S. Business, Professional, and Technical Service Payments, 1994–1997 —Continued

(Unaffiliated transactions; millions of dollars.)

| Country or region | Database and other information services | | | | Research, development, and testing services | | | | Management, consulting, and public relations services | | | |
|---|---|---|---|---|---|---|---|---|---|---|---|---|
| | 1994 | 1995 | 1996 | 1997 | 1994 | 1995 | 1996 | 1997 | 1994 | 1995 | 1996 | 1997 |
| **ALL COUNTRIES** | 141 | 160 | 148 | 164 | 294 | 364 | 343 | 473 | 321 | 465 | 593 | 782 |
| **Canada** | 9 | 8 | 5 | 3 | 35 | 44 | 30 | 37 | 27 | 70 | 68 | 111 |
| **Mexico** | (*) | (*) | (*) | (*) | 3 | 5 | 4 | 4 | 4 | 5 | 8 | 20 |
| **Europe** | 96 | 114 | 113 | 129 | 143 | 198 | 211 | 316 | 153 | 187 | 278 | 342 |
| Belgium and Luxembourg | (*) | (*) | (*) | (*) | 4 | 15 | 5 | 6 | 4 | 5 | 6 | 11 |
| France | 6 | 8 | 8 | 14 | 13 | 14 | 11 | 22 | 9 | 9 | 24 | 30 |
| Germany | 8 | 13 | 11 | 3 | 14 | 28 | 35 | 34 | 18 | 24 | 39 | 56 |
| Italy | (*) | (*) | (*) | (*) | 4 | 5 | 2 | 3 | 7 | 8 | 7 | 8 |
| Netherlands | 7 | 16 | 20 | 21 | 7 | 10 | 10 | 20 | 5 | 5 | 7 | 12 |
| Norway | (*) | (*) | (*) | (*) | 3 | 2 | 3 | 4 | 2 | 2 | 1 | 1 |
| Spain | 1 | 2 | 2 | 8 | 3 | 2 | 3 | 3 | 4 | 4 | 5 | 6 |
| Sweden | (*) | (*) | (*) | (*) | 7 | 8 | 8 | 9 | 3 | (D) | 4 | 5 |
| Switzerland | 2 | 2 | 2 | 3 | 10 | 11 | 33 | 37 | 12 | 8 | 14 | 19 |
| United Kingdom | 65 | 68 | 65 | 70 | 54 | 68 | 70 | 96 | 67 | 74 | 137 | 158 |
| Other | 6 | 5 | 5 | 9 | 23 | 35 | 30 | 80 | 23 | (D) | 36 | 37 |
| **Latin America and Other Western Hemisphere** [1] | 1 | 2 | 2 | 2 | 12 | 29 | 34 | 38 | 26 | 40 | 44 | 86 |
| South and Central America [1] | 1 | 1 | (*) | 1 | 11 | 28 | 30 | 36 | 25 | 39 | 42 | 84 |
| Argentina | (*) | (*) | (*) | (*) | (*) | 2 | 2 | 3 | 3 | 6 | 5 | 3 |
| Brazil | (*) | (*) | (*) | (*) | 3 | 10 | 13 | 17 | 6 | 12 | 9 | 31 |
| Chile | (*) | 0 | (*) | (*) | (*) | 1 | 2 | 2 | 1 | 2 | 3 | 3 |
| Venezuela | (*) | (*) | (*) | (*) | (*) | (*) | (*) | (*) | 1 | 2 | 4 | 2 |
| Other | (*) | (*) | (*) | (*) | 4 | 9 | 9 | 10 | 9 | 12 | 14 | 25 |
| Other Western Hemisphere | 0 | 1 | 1 | 1 | 2 | 1 | 3 | 2 | 1 | 1 | 2 | 2 |
| Bermuda | 0 | 0 | (*) | (*) | 0 | (*) | (*) | 1 | (*) | (*) | 1 | 1 |
| Other | 0 | 1 | 1 | 1 | 2 | 1 | 3 | 1 | 1 | 1 | 1 | 2 |
| **Africa** | (*) | (*) | (*) | (*) | 13 | 22 | 25 | 27 | 22 | 27 | 35 | 30 |
| South Africa | (*) | (*) | (*) | (*) | 2 | 3 | 2 | 2 | 1 | 1 | 1 | 1 |
| Other | 0 | (*) | (*) | (*) | 11 | 19 | 23 | 25 | 22 | 27 | 35 | 28 |
| **Middle East** | (*) | (*) | (*) | (*) | 4 | 10 | 5 | 5 | 3 | 8 | 13 | 12 |
| Israel | (*) | (*) | (*) | (*) | 3 | 9 | 2 | 4 | 1 | 1 | 4 | 3 |
| Saudi Arabia | (*) | (*) | (*) | (*) | (*) | (*) | 2 | (*) | 1 | 2 | 3 | 3 |
| Other | 0 | (*) | (*) | (*) | 1 | 1 | (*) | (*) | 2 | 5 | 6 | 5 |
| **Asia and Pacific** | 32 | 33 | 29 | 30 | 75 | 52 | 38 | 51 | 71 | 113 | 154 | 200 |
| Australia | 2 | 2 | 1 | 1 | 5 | 5 | 6 | 4 | 6 | 16 | 19 | 24 |
| China | 2 | 1 | 1 | 3 | 2 | 1 | 2 | 2 | 5 | 4 | 6 | 9 |
| Hong Kong | (*) | 1 | 1 | 1 | 1 | 1 | (*) | 1 | 2 | 4 | 9 | 16 |
| India | 4 | 2 | (*) | 1 | (*) | 1 | 4 | 3 | 4 | 8 | 8 | 8 |
| Indonesia | 0 | (*) | (*) | (*) | 2 | 1 | 1 | 5 | 5 | 2 | 6 | 8 |
| Japan | 19 | 20 | 20 | 16 | 54 | 23 | 12 | 19 | 17 | 30 | 32 | 41 |
| Malaysia | 0 | 0 | (*) | (*) | (*) | (*) | (*) | (*) | 5 | 5 | 7 | 7 |
| New Zealand | (*) | (*) | (*) | (*) | 1 | 3 | 3 | 2 | 2 | (*) | 2 | 1 |
| Philippines | 3 | 5 | 3 | 3 | 1 | 1 | 1 | 1 | 5 | 12 | 14 | 28 |
| Singapore | 2 | (*) | (*) | 3 | (*) | (*) | 1 | 2 | 1 | 3 | 3 | 5 |
| South Korea | (*) | 1 | 1 | 1 | 1 | 5 | 2 | 5 | 3 | 9 | 15 | 19 |
| Taiwan | (*) | 1 | 1 | (*) | 4 | 6 | 1 | 3 | 3 | 5 | 4 | 4 |
| Thailand | 0 | (*) | (*) | (*) | 2 | 3 | 2 | 2 | 6 | (D) | (D) | (D) |
| Other | (*) | (*) | (*) | (*) | 2 | 1 | 2 | 2 | 7 | (D) | (D) | (D) |
| **International organizations and unallocated** | 3 | 3 | 0 | 0 | 11 | 8 | 0 | 0 | 19 | 20 | (*) | (*) |
| **European Union** | 88 | 112 | 111 | 123 | 112 | 166 | 162 | 217 | 120 | 150 | 236 | 294 |
| **Eastern Europe** | (*) | (*) | (*) | 3 | 6 | 18 | 13 | 56 | 13 | 22 | 25 | 25 |

1. Includes Mexico.

## Table B-12.  U.S. Business, Professional, and Technical Service Payments, 1994–1997 —*Continued*

(Unaffiliated transactions; millions of dollars.)

| Country or region | Legal services | | | | Construction, engineering, architectural, and mining services | | | | Industrial engineering | | | |
|---|---|---|---|---|---|---|---|---|---|---|---|---|
| | 1994 | 1995 | 1996 | 1997 | 1994 | 1995 | 1996 | 1997 | 1994 | 1995 | 1996 | 1997 |
| **ALL COUNTRIES** | 383 | 469 | 580 | 568 | 280 | 345 | 489 | 346 | 100 | 160 | 202 | 246 |
| **Canada** | 23 | 27 | 31 | 31 | 58 | 70 | 99 | 45 | 17 | 34 | 24 | 36 |
| **Mexico** | 12 | 13 | 13 | 13 | 7 | 9 | 4 | 9 | (*) | (*) | 2 | 1 |
| **Europe** | 196 | 240 | 302 | 291 | 72 | 133 | 179 | 122 | 28 | (D) | 76 | 75 |
| Belgium and Luxembourg | 5 | 7 | 8 | 7 | 3 | 3 | 5 | 4 | (*) | (*) | 1 | 1 |
| France | 13 | 16 | 22 | 21 | 5 | 8 | 12 | 6 | 3 | (D) | 7 | 6 |
| Germany | 38 | 46 | 60 | 54 | 5 | (D) | (D) | 12 | (D) | 4 | (D) | 9 |
| Italy | 6 | 6 | 9 | 8 | 4 | 1 | 1 | 1 | (*) | (*) | 3 | (D) |
| Netherlands | 8 | 8 | 9 | 7 | 10 | (D) | 19 | 14 | (*) | (*) | (*) | (*) |
| Norway | 3 | 5 | 5 | 4 | (*) | 1 | 1 | 1 | (D) | (*) | (*) | (*) |
| Spain | 6 | 8 | 10 | 10 | (*) | (*) | (*) | (*) | (*) | 2 | 2 | 2 |
| Sweden | 6 | 5 | 6 | 5 | (*) | 0 | (*) | (*) | (*) | (*) | (*) | (*) |
| Switzerland | 5 | 5 | 8 | 8 | 2 | 2 | 7 | 4 | 1 | (*) | (*) | (*) |
| United Kingdom | 82 | 106 | 126 | 129 | 28 | 25 | 24 | 76 | 9 | 23 | 26 | 19 |
| Other | 23 | 27 | 40 | 38 | 13 | 10 | (D) | 3 | 6 | (D) | (D) | (D) |
| **Latin America and Other Western Hemisphere** [1] | 33 | 41 | 51 | 54 | 32 | 21 | 11 | 26 | 1 | (*) | 4 | 4 |
| South and Central America [1] | 31 | 39 | 47 | 50 | 31 | 20 | 10 | 26 | 1 | (*) | 4 | 3 |
| Argentina | 4 | 5 | 7 | 8 | 1 | 2 | (*) | (D) | 0 | 0 | (*) | (*) |
| Brazil | 5 | 8 | 11 | 12 | (*) | (*) | (*) | 1 | 0 | 0 | 1 | (*) |
| Chile | 2 | 2 | 3 | 2 | (*) | (*) | 1 | (*) | (*) | (*) | 1 | 1 |
| Venezuela | 2 | 4 | 4 | 4 | 2 | 3 | 1 | (*) | (*) | (*) | (*) | (*) |
| Other | 6 | 7 | 10 | 11 | 20 | 6 | 5 | (D) | (*) | (*) | (*) | 1 |
| Other Western Hemisphere | 2 | 2 | 4 | 4 | 1 | 1 | 1 | (*) | 0 | (*) | (*) | 1 |
| Bermuda | 1 | (*) | 2 | 2 | 0 | 0 | (*) | (*) | 0 | 0 | (*) | 1 |
| Other | 1 | 1 | 2 | 2 | 1 | 1 | 1 | (*) | 0 | (*) | (*) | (*) |
| **Africa** | 3 | 4 | 6 | 5 | 26 | 25 | 31 | 28 | (*) | (*) | (*) | 3 |
| South Africa | 1 | 2 | 3 | 2 | (*) | (*) | (*) | (*) | 0 | 0 | 0 | (*) |
| Other | 2 | 2 | 3 | 3 | 26 | 24 | 31 | 28 | (*) | (*) | (*) | 3 |
| **Middle East** | 5 | 6 | 12 | 11 | 22 | 22 | (D) | (D) | 2 | (*) | 4 | 4 |
| Israel | 2 | 2 | 5 | 5 | (*) | (*) | (*) | (*) | 2 | (*) | (*) | (*) |
| Saudi Arabia | 1 | 1 | 3 | 2 | 1 | 1 | 2 | 1 | (*) | 0 | 3 | 4 |
| Other | 2 | 2 | 4 | 4 | 21 | 21 | (D) | (D) | 0 | 0 | (*) | (*) |
| **Asia and Pacific** | 90 | 118 | 178 | 176 | 65 | 72 | (D) | (D) | 52 | (D) | 94 | 125 |
| Australia | 11 | 14 | 20 | 24 | 8 | 11 | (D) | (D) | 1 | 1 | 2 | 2 |
| China | 4 | 5 | 8 | 7 | 7 | 9 | (*) | (*) | 1 | 1 | (D) | (D) |
| Hong Kong | 9 | 12 | 27 | 31 | 2 | 2 | (*) | (*) | (*) | (*) | (*) | (*) |
| India | 1 | 1 | 6 | 2 | (*) | (*) | (*) | (*) | 2 | (*) | 2 | 5 |
| Indonesia | 2 | 2 | 2 | 2 | 1 | 2 | (D) | (D) | 3 | 0 | 0 | (*) |
| Japan | 46 | 59 | 74 | 70 | 7 | 5 | 3 | 2 | (D) | (D) | (D) | (D) |
| Malaysia | 1 | 1 | 1 | 1 | (*) | (*) | (*) | (*) | (D) | 1 | (*) | (*) |
| New Zealand | 2 | 2 | 4 | 2 | (*) | 0 | (*) | (*) | (*) | 0 | (*) | (*) |
| Philippines | 1 | 1 | 2 | 2 | 7 | 14 | 7 | 6 | (*) | (*) | 2 | 2 |
| Singapore | 2 | 2 | 4 | 6 | 2 | 1 | 1 | 7 | (*) | 0 | (*) | 2 |
| South Korea | 7 | 10 | 16 | 17 | 1 | (*) | (*) | 1 | 0 | 0 | 1 | 1 |
| Taiwan | 5 | 5 | 9 | 8 | 6 | 2 | 1 | 1 | 1 | 1 | 1 | 1 |
| Thailand | 1 | 1 | 2 | 2 | (D) | 9 | 2 | 2 | (*) | 0 | (*) | (D) |
| Other | (*) | 1 | 3 | 2 | (D) | 16 | 10 | 3 | 0 | 0 | (D) | (D) |
| **International organizations and unallocated** | 32 | 33 | (*) | (*) | 4 | 3 | (*) | (*) | 1 | 1 | 0 | 0 |
| **European Union** | 165 | 216 | 267 | 257 | 56 | 126 | 128 | 114 | 23 | 46 | 52 | 47 |
| **Eastern Europe** | 9 | 10 | 18 | 18 | (D) | 2 | (D) | 2 | 1 | 1 | (D) | (D) |

1. Includes Mexico.

## Table B-12.  U.S. Business, Professional, and Technical Service Payments, 1994–1997 —Continued

(Unaffiliated transactions; millions of dollars.)

| Country or region | Installation, maintenance, and repair of equipment | | | | Other | | | |
|---|---|---|---|---|---|---|---|---|
| | 1994 | 1995 | 1996 | 1997 | 1994 | 1995 | 1996 | 1997 |
| **ALL COUNTRIES** | 164 | 160 | 247 | 355 | 1 375 | 1 742 | 1 832 | 2 504 |
| **Canada** | 141 | 312 | 30 | 75 | 118 | 269 | 305 | 427 |
| **Mexico** | 3 | 4 | 2 | 1 | 46 | 36 | 38 | 195 |
| **Europe** | 82 | 79 | 161 | 230 | 599 | (D) | 781 | 998 |
| Belgium and Luxembourg | 1 | 5 | 1 | 1 | 31 | 29 | 20 | 28 |
| France | (D) | 8 | 3 | (D) | (D) | (D) | 60 | 115 |
| Germany | 10 | 21 | 10 | 29 | (D) | (D) | 100 | 123 |
| Italy | 14 | 16 | 11 | (D) | 21 | 29 | 35 | 43 |
| Netherlands | 2 | 2 | 3 | 3 | 25 | (D) | 39 | 54 |
| Norway | (*) | (*) | (*) | 2 | (D) | 1 | 2 | 3 |
| Spain | 4 | 4 | 3 | 4 | 8 | 10 | 17 | 18 |
| Sweden | 1 | (*) | 2 | 2 | 4 | (D) | 5 | 10 |
| Switzerland | 1 | 1 | (*) | (*) | 8 | 18 | 29 | 52 |
| United Kingdom | 33 | 16 | (D) | 157 | 280 | 324 | (D) | 422 |
| Other | (D) | 5 | (D) | 7 | (D) | 105 | (D) | 130 |
| **Latin America and Other Western Hemisphere** [1] | 8 | 7 | 6 | 3 | 102 | 110 | 123 | 314 |
| South and Central America [1] | 8 | 7 | 6 | 3 | 97 | 103 | 115 | 293 |
| Argentina | 1 | 1 | 1 | (*) | 7 | 8 | 11 | (D) |
| Brazil | 2 | (*) | 3 | 2 | 9 | 13 | 18 | 21 |
| Chile | (*) | (*) | (*) | (*) | 2 | 2 | 2 | 12 |
| Venezuela | (*) | (*) | (*) | (*) | 5 | 5 | 8 | 5 |
| Other | 2 | 2 | (*) | (*) | 29 | 38 | 38 | (D) |
| Other Western Hemisphere | (*) | (*) | (*) | (*) | 4 | 7 | 8 | 21 |
| Bermuda | 0 | 0 | (*) | 0 | 3 | 1 | 4 | 11 |
| Other | (*) | (*) | (*) | (*) | 2 | 6 | 5 | 11 |
| **Africa** | 1 | 4 | 1 | 1 | 53 | 52 | 43 | 58 |
| South Africa | (*) | 2 | (*) | 1 | 9 | 8 | 11 | 11 |
| Other | 1 | 2 | 1 | 0 | 44 | 44 | 32 | 46 |
| **Middle East** | 2 | 4 | (D) | 3 | 29 | 27 | 29 | (D) |
| Israel | (*) | (*) | (*) | 1 | 17 | 11 | 16 | 18 |
| Saudi Arabia | 1 | 3 | 1 | 0 | 4 | 3 | 3 | (D) |
| Other | (*) | 1 | (D) | 3 | 8 | 12 | 10 | (D) |
| **Asia and Pacific** | 51 | 33 | (D) | 43 | 450 | (D) | 551 | (D) |
| Australia | (D) | (D) | (D) | (D) | (D) | (D) | 70 | 55 |
| China | 1 | (*) | (D) | (*) | 10 | 13 | 18 | (D) |
| Hong Kong | 4 | (*) | 1 | 1 | 34 | 41 | 65 | 71 |
| India | (*) | (*) | (*) | (*) | 7 | 18 | 32 | 42 |
| Indonesia | 2 | (*) | 1 | 1 | 16 | 17 | (D) | (D) |
| Japan | (D) | (D) | 10 | (D) | 234 | 266 | (D) | (D) |
| Malaysia | (*) | 3 | 2 | (*) | (D) | 2 | 4 | 6 |
| New Zealand | 1 | 2 | 1 | (*) | 2 | 5 | 6 | 8 |
| Philippines | (*) | (*) | 1 | (*) | 4 | 5 | 6 | 7 |
| Singapore | 1 | 1 | 2 | 3 | 12 | (D) | 20 | 24 |
| South Korea | 4 | 4 | 1 | 1 | 7 | 11 | 20 | 22 |
| Taiwan | 1 | (*) | 4 | 1 | 14 | 13 | 40 | 48 |
| Thailand | (*) | 2 | 1 | (*) | (D) | (D) | (D) | 69 |
| Other | (*) | (*) | (*) | 0 | (D) | 51 | 15 | (D) |
| **International organizations and unallocated** | 5 | 1 | 0 | 0 | 24 | 25 | 0 | (*) |
| **European Union** | 78 | 76 | 155 | 227 | 521 | 616 | 664 | 844 |
| **Eastern Europe** | 1 | 1 | 2 | (*) | (D) | 60 | 69 | (D) |

1. Includes Mexico.

# PART C.   U.S. Foreign Trade in Goods

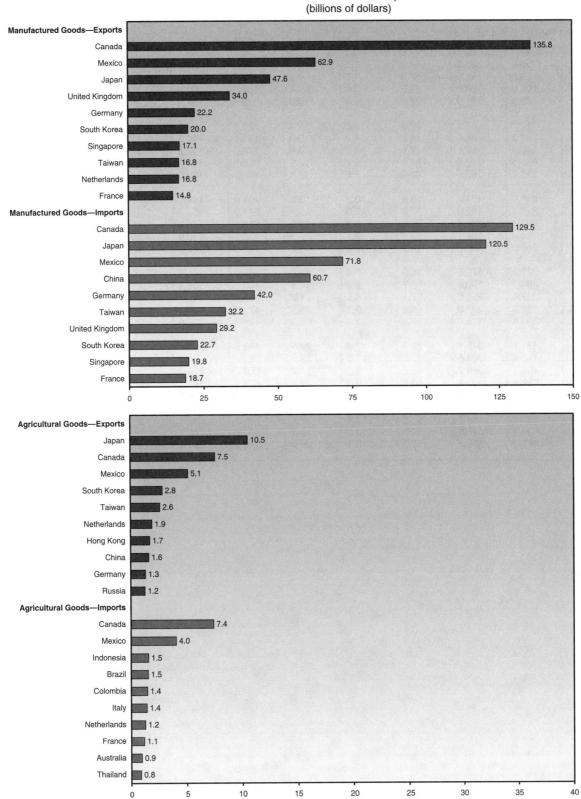

**U.S. Trade in Goods, 1997**
(billions of dollars)

## Table C-1.  U.S. Foreign Trade in Goods, 1970–1998

(Census basis, billions of dollars.)

| Year | Exports | | | | | Imports | | | | |
|---|---|---|---|---|---|---|---|---|---|---|
| | Total goods | Manufac- tured goods | Agricul- tural products | Mineral fuels | Other goods | Total goods | Manufac- tured goods | Agricul- tural products | Mineral fuels | Other goods |
| 1970 | 43.8 | 31.7 | 7.3 | 1.6 | 3.1 | 40.4 | 27.3 | 5.8 | 3.1 | 4.2 |
| 1971 | 44.7 | 32.9 | 7.8 | 1.5 | 2.5 | 46.2 | 32.1 | 5.8 | 3.7 | 4.6 |
| 1972 | 50.5 | 36.5 | 9.5 | 1.6 | 2.9 | 56.4 | 39.7 | 6.5 | 4.8 | 5.3 |
| 1973 | 72.5 | 48.5 | 17.9 | 1.7 | 4.5 | 70.5 | 47.1 | 8.5 | 8.2 | 6.7 |
| 1974 | 100.0 | 68.5 | 22.3 | 3.4 | 5.8 | 102.6 | 57.8 | 10.4 | 25.5 | 8.9 |
| 1975 | 109.3 | 76.9 | 22.1 | 4.5 | 5.9 | 98.5 | 54.0 | 9.5 | 26.5 | 8.6 |
| 1976 | 117.0 | 83.1 | 23.3 | 4.2 | 6.4 | 123.5 | 67.6 | 11.2 | 34.0 | 10.7 |
| 1977 | 123.2 | 88.9 | 24.2 | 4.2 | 5.9 | 151.0 | 80.5 | 13.6 | 47.2 | 9.8 |
| 1978 | 145.9 | 103.6 | 29.8 | 3.9 | 8.6 | 174.8 | 104.3 | 15.0 | 42.0 | 13.4 |
| 1979 | 186.5 | 132.7 | 35.2 | 5.7 | 12.9 | 209.5 | 117.1 | 16.9 | 59.9 | 15.5 |
| 1980 | 225.7 | 160.7 | 41.8 | 8.2 | 15.1 | 245.3 | 133.0 | 17.4 | 78.9 | 15.9 |
| 1981 | 238.7 | 171.7 | 43.8 | 10.3 | 12.8 | 261.0 | 149.8 | 17.2 | 81.2 | 12.8 |
| 1982 | 216.4 | 155.3 | 37.0 | 12.8 | 11.3 | 244.0 | 151.7 | 15.7 | 65.3 | 11.3 |
| 1983 | 205.6 | 148.7 | 36.1 | 9.8 | 11.0 | 258.0 | 170.9 | 16.0 | 57.8 | 13.4 |
| 1984 | 224.0 | 164.1 | 37.9 | 9.7 | 12.3 | 330.7 | 230.9 | 19.3 | 60.8 | 19.6 |
| 1985 | 218.8 | 168.0 | 29.3 | 10.3 | 11.2 | 336.5 | 257.5 | 19.5 | 53.7 | 5.9 |
| 1986 | 227.2 | 179.8 | 26.3 | 8.4 | 12.6 | 365.4 | 296.7 | 20.9 | 37.2 | 10.7 |
| 1987 | 254.1 | 199.9 | 28.7 | 8.0 | 17.5 | 406.2 | 324.4 | 20.3 | 44.1 | 17.4 |
| 1988 | 322.4 | 255.6 | 37.1 | 8.5 | 21.2 | 441.0 | 361.4 | 20.7 | 41.0 | 17.8 |
| 1989 | 363.8 | 287.0 | 41.6 | 9.9 | 25.3 | 473.2 | 379.4 | 21.1 | 52.6 | 20.0 |
| 1990 | 393.6 | 315.4 | 39.6 | 12.4 | 26.3 | 495.3 | 388.8 | 22.3 | 64.7 | 19.5 |
| 1991 | 421.7 | 345.1 | 39.4 | 12.3 | 24.9 | 488.5 | 392.4 | 22.1 | 54.1 | 19.8 |
| 1992 | 448.2 | 368.5 | 43.1 | 11.3 | 25.2 | 532.7 | 434.3 | 23.4 | 55.3 | 19.7 |
| 1993 | 465.1 | 388.7 | 42.8 | 9.9 | 23.7 | 580.7 | 479.9 | 23.6 | 55.9 | 21.2 |
| 1994 | 512.6 | 431.1 | 45.9 | 9.0 | 26.7 | 663.3 | 557.3 | 26.0 | 56.4 | 23.6 |
| 1995 | 584.7 | 486.7 | 56.0 | 10.5 | 31.6 | 743.4 | 629.7 | 29.3 | 59.1 | 25.4 |
| 1996 | 625.1 | 524.7 | 60.6 | 12.4 | 27.4 | 795.3 | 658.8 | 32.6 | 78.1 | 25.8 |
| 1997 | 689.2 | 592.5 | 57.1 | 13.0 | 26.7 | 870.7 | 728.9 | 35.2 | 78.3 | 28.3 |
| 1998 (p) | 683.0 | 595.2 | 52.0 | 10.1 | 25.7 | 913.8 | 792.4 | 35.7 | 57.6 | 28.0 |

**Table C-2. U.S. Foreign Trade in Goods by End-Use Category, 1978–1998**

(Census basis, billions of dollars.)

| Year | Foods, feed, and beverages | | | Industrial supplies and materials | | | Capital goods, except automotive | | |
|---|---|---|---|---|---|---|---|---|---|
| | Exports | Imports | Balance | Exports | Imports | Balance | Exports | Imports | Balance |
| 1978 | 25.6 | 15.8 | 9.7 | 39.0 | 79.2 | -40.1 | 46.9 | 19.7 | 27.2 |
| 1979 | 30.3 | 18.0 | 12.3 | 57.3 | 102.6 | -45.3 | 58.8 | 24.9 | 33.9 |
| 1980 | 36.0 | 18.5 | 17.5 | 70.6 | 124.7 | -54.1 | 74.8 | 31.1 | 43.7 |
| 1981 | 38.6 | 18.5 | 20.1 | 67.7 | 130.7 | -63.0 | 82.5 | 37.0 | 45.5 |
| 1982 | 32.0 | 17.5 | 14.5 | 62.1 | 107.7 | -45.6 | 75.1 | 38.4 | 36.7 |
| 1983 | 30.7 | 18.5 | 12.2 | 57.4 | 105.3 | -47.8 | 70.6 | 39.4 | 31.2 |
| 1984 | 31.3 | 21.5 | 9.8 | 62.6 | 121.6 | -59.1 | 76.4 | 58.0 | 18.5 |
| 1985 | 24.1 | 22.3 | 1.8 | 59.2 | 114.1 | -54.9 | 78.9 | 62.4 | 16.4 |
| 1986 | 22.5 | 24.5 | -2.0 | 62.0 | 102.9 | -40.9 | 81.8 | 72.6 | 9.2 |
| 1987 | 24.3 | 26.8 | -2.6 | 66.7 | 117.3 | -50.6 | 86.2 | 87.0 | -0.8 |
| 1988 | 32.3 | 24.8 | 7.5 | 85.1 | 118.3 | -33.2 | 109.2 | 101.4 | 7.8 |
| 1989 | 37.2 | 25.1 | 12.1 | 99.3 | 132.3 | -33.0 | 138.8 | 113.3 | 25.5 |
| 1990 | 35.1 | 26.6 | 8.4 | 104.4 | 143.2 | -38.8 | 152.7 | 116.4 | 36.3 |
| 1991 | 35.7 | 26.5 | 9.2 | 109.7 | 131.6 | -21.9 | 166.7 | 120.7 | 45.9 |
| 1992 | 40.3 | 27.6 | 12.7 | 109.1 | 138.6 | -29.5 | 175.9 | 134.3 | 41.7 |
| 1993 | 40.6 | 27.9 | 12.8 | 111.8 | 145.6 | -33.8 | 181.7 | 152.4 | 29.3 |
| 1994 | 42.0 | 31.0 | 11.0 | 121.4 | 162.1 | -40.7 | 205.0 | 184.4 | 20.7 |
| 1995 | 50.5 | 33.2 | 17.3 | 146.2 | 181.8 | -35.6 | 233.0 | 221.4 | 11.6 |
| 1996 | 55.5 | 35.7 | 19.8 | 147.7 | 204.5 | -56.8 | 252.9 | 229.1 | 23.8 |
| 1997 | 51.5 | 39.7 | 11.8 | 158.2 | 213.8 | -55.5 | 294.5 | 254.2 | 40.3 |
| 1998 (p) | 46.4 | 41.2 | 5.1 | 147.9 | 200.4 | -52.5 | 299.5 | 270.4 | 29.1 |

| Year | Automotive vehicles, engines, and parts | | | Consumer goods, except automotive | | | Other goods | | |
|---|---|---|---|---|---|---|---|---|---|
| | Exports | Imports | Balance | Exports | Imports | Balance | Exports | Imports | Balance |
| 1978 | 14.6 | 25.9 | -11.3 | 11.1 | 29.6 | -18.5 | 8.6 | 3.1 | 5.5 |
| 1979 | 16.6 | 26.9 | -10.3 | 13.4 | 31.3 | -17.9 | 9.9 | 3.4 | 6.5 |
| 1980 | 16.0 | 28.2 | -12.1 | 17.2 | 34.3 | -17.2 | 11.1 | 4.6 | 6.5 |
| 1981 | 18.3 | 30.7 | -12.5 | 17.1 | 38.4 | -21.2 | 14.4 | 5.7 | 8.8 |
| 1982 | 16.0 | 34.3 | -18.3 | 15.7 | 39.6 | -24.0 | 15.6 | 6.5 | 9.1 |
| 1983 | 15.4 | 42.1 | -26.7 | 16.2 | 46.3 | -30.1 | 15.3 | 6.5 | 8.8 |
| 1984 | 18.6 | 55.1 | -36.5 | 16.4 | 61.4 | -45.0 | 17.9 | 8.1 | 9.8 |
| 1985 | 20.6 | 66.6 | -46.0 | 15.8 | 69.9 | -54.1 | 20.7 | 10.0 | 10.7 |
| 1986 | 19.9 | 78.5 | -58.6 | 17.8 | 80.3 | -62.5 | 23.6 | 11.2 | 12.3 |
| 1987 | 24.6 | 87.5 | -62.8 | 17.7 | 93.6 | -76.0 | 34.6 | 12.2 | 22.4 |
| 1988 | 29.3 | 87.7 | -58.4 | 23.1 | 95.9 | -72.8 | 43.4 | 12.8 | 30.6 |
| 1989 | 34.8 | 86.1 | -51.3 | 36.4 | 102.9 | -66.4 | 17.2 | 13.6 | 3.6 |
| 1990 | 37.4 | 87.3 | -49.9 | 43.3 | 105.7 | -62.4 | 20.7 | 16.1 | 4.6 |
| 1991 | 40.0 | 85.7 | -45.6 | 45.9 | 108.0 | -62.1 | 23.7 | 15.9 | 7.7 |
| 1992 | 47.0 | 91.8 | -44.8 | 51.4 | 122.7 | -71.2 | 24.4 | 17.7 | 6.7 |
| 1993 | 52.4 | 102.4 | -50.0 | 54.7 | 134.0 | -79.4 | 23.9 | 18.4 | 5.5 |
| 1994 | 57.8 | 118.3 | -60.5 | 60.0 | 146.3 | -86.3 | 26.5 | 21.3 | 5.2 |
| 1995 | 61.8 | 123.8 | -62.0 | 64.4 | 159.9 | -95.5 | 28.7 | 23.4 | 5.3 |
| 1996 | 65.0 | 128.9 | -63.9 | 70.1 | 171.0 | -100.9 | 33.8 | 26.1 | 7.7 |
| 1997 | 74.0 | 140.8 | -66.8 | 77.4 | 192.9 | -115.5 | 33.5 | 29.3 | 4.2 |
| 1998 (p) | 72.7 | 150.7 | -78.0 | 79.5 | 215.5 | -136.0 | 37.0 | 35.6 | 1.4 |

## Table C-3. U.S. Foreign Trade in Goods by Industry, 1991–1997

(Trade by Standard Industrial Classification [SIC] product codes; census basis; millions of dollars.)

| SIC description | SIC code | Exports | | | | | | |
|---|---|---|---|---|---|---|---|---|
| | | 1991 | 1992 | 1993 | 1994 | 1995 | 1996 | 1997 |
| **ALL COMMODITIES, TOTAL** | 0 | 421 854 | 447 471 | 464 858 | 512 416 | 583 031 | 622 827 | 687 598 |
| **Agricultural products, total** | 1 | 21 704 | 23 206 | 22 222 | 22 915 | 30 161 | 33 134 | 28 290 |
| Cash grains and other crops | 11 | 13 799 | 15 296 | 14 991 | 13 988 | 19 909 | 23 966 | 18 564 |
| Field crops, except cash grains | 13 | 4 548 | 4 383 | 3 519 | 4 744 | 5 968 | 4 971 | 5 204 |
| Vegetables and melons | 16 | 862 | 906 | 1 007 | 1 073 | 1 111 | 1 040 | 1 132 |
| Fruits and tree nuts | 17 | 2 134 | 2 245 | 2 313 | 2 704 | 2 742 | 2 719 | 2 865 |
| Horticultural specialties | 18 | 361 | 375 | 393 | 406 | 430 | 438 | 526 |
| **Livestock and livestock products, total** | 2 | 1 000 | 928 | 847 | 980 | 962 | 998 | 1 150 |
| Livestock, except dairy and poultry | 21 | 265 | 268 | 207 | 289 | 175 | 194 | 312 |
| Dairy farms | 24 | 50 | 43 | 39 | 47 | 31 | 36 | 34 |
| Poultry and eggs | 25 | 204 | 207 | 214 | 225 | 227 | 226 | 238 |
| Animal specialties | 27 | 480 | 410 | 387 | 420 | 530 | 542 | 566 |
| **Forestry products, total** | 8 | 286 | 306 | 293 | 285 | 297 | 292 | 301 |
| Standing timber | 81 | 63 | 66 | 77 | 62 | 58 | 66 | 72 |
| Forestry products | 83 | 223 | 240 | 215 | 223 | 239 | 226 | 229 |
| **Commercial fishing, total** | 9 | 2 822 | 3 068 | 2 703 | 2 787 | 2 952 | 2 716 | 2 453 |
| **Metallic ores and concentrates, total** | 10 | 1 126 | 1 258 | 852 | 1 023 | 1 586 | 1 169 | 1 282 |
| Iron ore | 101 | 156 | 187 | 168 | 162 | 184 | 232 | 236 |
| Copper ore | 102 | 382 | 445 | 342 | 393 | 486 | 287 | 211 |
| Lead and zinc ores | 103 | 364 | 441 | 191 | 188 | 265 | 305 | 414 |
| Gold and silver ores | 104 | 4 | 5 | 3 | 16 | 9 | 10 | 22 |
| Ferroalloy ores, except vanadium | 106 | 148 | 136 | 102 | 218 | 580 | 264 | 327 |
| Miscellaneous metal ores | 109 | 71 | 45 | 45 | 46 | 61 | 71 | 71 |
| **Coal and lignite, total** | 12 | 4 628 | 4 242 | 3 092 | 2 859 | 3 574 | 3 697 | 3 408 |
| Bituminous coal and lignite | 122 | 4 593 | 4 210 | 3 062 | 2 826 | 3 523 | 3 646 | 3 362 |
| Anthracite mining | 123 | 35 | 31 | 30 | 33 | 50 | 51 | 45 |
| **Oil and gas extraction, total** | 13 | 693 | 741 | 591 | 586 | 734 | 1 214 | 1 674 |
| Crude petroleum and natural gas | 131 | 105 | 262 | 138 | 159 | 126 | 583 | 1 013 |
| Natural gas liquids | 132 | 588 | 479 | 453 | 426 | 607 | 632 | 661 |
| **Nonmetallic minerals, except fuels, total** | 14 | 1 148 | 1 159 | 1 116 | 1 208 | 1 303 | 1 322 | 1 402 |
| Dimension stone (includes granite, marble, etc.) | 141 | 70 | 57 | 48 | 60 | 58 | 63 | 74 |
| Crushed and broken limestone | 142 | 32 | 46 | 58 | 53 | 69 | 66 | 63 |
| Sand and gravel | 144 | 95 | 98 | 97 | 106 | 113 | 117 | 130 |
| Clay, ceramic, and refractory minerals | 145 | 571 | 634 | 635 | 706 | 757 | 770 | 808 |
| Chemical and fertilizer minerals | 147 | 154 | 92 | 73 | 71 | 88 | 87 | 102 |
| Nonmetallic minerals, except fuels | 149 | 227 | 232 | 204 | 211 | 218 | 220 | 226 |
| **Food and kindred products, total** | 20 | 17 726 | 20 059 | 20 847 | 23 459 | 26 401 | 27 568 | 29 109 |
| Meat products and meat packing products | 201 | 5 262 | 5 842 | 5 880 | 6 936 | 8 435 | 8 878 | 8 811 |
| Dairy products | 202 | 571 | 851 | 965 | 883 | 894 | 850 | 1 066 |
| Canned, frozen, and preserved fruits and vegetables | 203 | 2 019 | 2 272 | 2 339 | 2 603 | 2 885 | 3 015 | 3 202 |
| Grain mill products | 204 | 3 233 | 3 476 | 3 710 | 3 951 | 4 093 | 4 289 | 4 351 |
| Bakery products | 205 | 224 | 295 | 340 | 368 | 362 | 378 | 411 |
| Sugar and confectionery products | 206 | 1 452 | 1 532 | 1 700 | 1 868 | 1 919 | 2 160 | 2 015 |
| Fats and oils | 207 | 2 455 | 2 877 | 2 681 | 2 951 | 3 799 | 3 681 | 4 693 |
| Beverages and flavorings | 208 | 1 261 | 1 460 | 1 558 | 1 890 | 2 104 | 2 161 | 2 338 |
| Miscellaneous food preparations and kindred products | 209 | 1 249 | 1 454 | 1 674 | 2 008 | 1 910 | 2 155 | 2 222 |
| **Tobacco products, total** | 21 | 4 581 | 4 518 | 4 262 | 5 424 | 5 264 | 5 268 | 5 005 |
| Cigarettes | 211 | 4 239 | 4 200 | 3 934 | 5 011 | 4 812 | 4 765 | 4 456 |
| Cigars | 212 | 7 | 9 | 6 | 7 | 8 | 12 | 18 |
| Chewing and smoking tobacco, and snuff | 213 | 266 | 245 | 268 | 337 | 346 | 401 | 461 |
| Manufactured tobacco, including processed tobacco | 214 | 70 | 64 | 53 | 68 | 98 | 90 | 70 |
| **Textile mill products, total** | 22 | 4 215 | 4 583 | 4 809 | 5 270 | 5 830 | 6 315 | 7 225 |
| Cotton broad woven fabrics | 221 | 552 | 591 | 641 | 725 | 834 | 906 | 965 |
| Silk and manmade fiber broad woven fabrics | 222 | 816 | 922 | 1 007 | 1 076 | 1 127 | 1 235 | 1 330 |
| Wool broad woven fabrics | 223 | 66 | 104 | 88 | 90 | 118 | 122 | 140 |
| Narrow woven fabrics | 224 | 246 | 256 | 292 | 350 | 409 | 431 | 546 |
| Knit fabrics and hosiery | 225 | 441 | 519 | 585 | 625 | 759 | 829 | 1 038 |
| Carpets and rugs | 227 | 724 | 734 | 727 | 695 | 673 | 737 | 823 |
| Yarns and thread | 228 | 280 | 248 | 219 | 299 | 398 | 452 | 519 |
| Miscellaneous textile goods | 229 | 1 089 | 1 208 | 1 249 | 1 410 | 1 512 | 1 604 | 1 865 |

# Table C-3.  U.S. Foreign Trade in Goods by Industry, 1991–1997 —*Continued*

(Trade by Standard Industrial Classification [SIC] product codes; census basis; millions of dollars.)

| SIC description | SIC code | Imports | | | | | | |
|---|---|---|---|---|---|---|---|---|
| | | 1991 | 1992 | 1993 | 1994 | 1995 | 1996 | 1997 |
| **ALL COMMODITIES, TOTAL** | 0 | 488 873 | 532 017 | 580 469 | 663 830 | 743 505 | 791 315 | 870 213 |
| **Agricultural products, total** | 1 | 7 323 | 7 262 | 7 427 | 8 745 | 9 818 | 11 096 | 12 284 |
| Cash grains and other crops | 11 | 402 | 538 | 599 | 890 | 770 | 896 | 1 122 |
| Field crops, except cash grains | 13 | 1 344 | 1 281 | 1 310 | 1 209 | 1 081 | 1 955 | 1 779 |
| Vegetables and melons | 16 | 984 | 849 | 1 122 | 1 227 | 1 486 | 1 729 | 1 763 |
| Fruits and tree nuts | 17 | 3 944 | 3 878 | 3 617 | 4 584 | 5 490 | 5 396 | 6 428 |
| Horticultural specialties | 18 | 649 | 716 | 779 | 835 | 991 | 1 119 | 1 192 |
| **Livestock and livestock products, total** | 2 | 1 645 | 2 032 | 2 159 | 2 046 | 2 441 | 2 374 | 2 483 |
| Livestock, except dairy and poultry | 21 | 1 178 | 1 408 | 1 521 | 1 348 | 1 690 | 1 505 | 1 564 |
| Dairy farms | 24 | 10 | 28 | 26 | 16 | 23 | 25 | 16 |
| Poultry and eggs | 25 | 28 | 35 | 42 | 40 | 36 | 39 | 37 |
| Animal specialties | 27 | 428 | 561 | 571 | 643 | 693 | 806 | 865 |
| **Forestry products, total** | 8 | 847 | 956 | 1 068 | 1 208 | 1 932 | 1 809 | 1 625 |
| Standing timber | 81 | 30 | 31 | 29 | 30 | 34 | 36 | 40 |
| Forestry products | 83 | 817 | 925 | 1 039 | 1 179 | 1 898 | 1 773 | 1 585 |
| **Commercial fishing, total** | 9 | 4 587 | 4 570 | 4 797 | 5 515 | 5 615 | 5 525 | 6 479 |
| **Metallic ores and concentrates, total** | 10 | 1 500 | 1 435 | 1 243 | 1 379 | 1 535 | 1 597 | 1 523 |
| Iron ore | 101 | 437 | 396 | 415 | 510 | 486 | 556 | 551 |
| Copper ore | 102 | 67 | 107 | 42 | 126 | 137 | 76 | 67 |
| Lead and zinc ores | 103 | 204 | 248 | 116 | 90 | 102 | 162 | 118 |
| Gold and silver ores | 104 | 45 | 49 | 31 | 54 | 87 | 74 | 42 |
| Ferroalloy ores, except vanadium | 106 | 136 | 114 | 110 | 109 | 206 | 186 | 190 |
| Miscellaneous metal ores | 109 | 611 | 520 | 529 | 490 | 518 | 542 | 556 |
| **Coal and lignite, total** | 12 | 112 | 127 | 218 | 229 | 248 | 238 | 257 |
| Bituminous coal and lignite | 122 | 112 | 122 | 210 | 218 | 247 | 235 | 255 |
| Anthracite mining | 123 | 0 | 5 | 8 | 11 | 1 | 3 | 2 |
| **Oil and gas extraction, total** | 13 | 42 181 | 42 902 | 44 291 | 45 041 | 48 961 | 58 325 | 63 450 |
| Crude petroleum and natural gas | 131 | 39 487 | 40 949 | 41 685 | 42 381 | 46 046 | 54 500 | 59 501 |
| Natural gas liquids | 132 | 2 694 | 1 954 | 2 606 | 2 661 | 2 915 | 3 825 | 3 949 |
| **Nonmetallic minerals, except fuels, total** | 14 | 828 | 747 | 769 | 842 | 915 | 915 | 1 090 |
| Dimension stone (includes granite, marble, etc.) | 141 | 25 | 21 | 21 | 18 | 21 | 24 | 24 |
| Crushed and broken limestone | 142 | 32 | 43 | 52 | 61 | 71 | 72 | 95 |
| Sand and gravel | 144 | 9 | 9 | 8 | 8 | 7 | 9 | 11 |
| Clay, ceramic, and refractory minerals | 145 | 22 | 23 | 25 | 28 | 34 | 38 | 43 |
| Chemical and fertilizer minerals | 147 | 430 | 324 | 244 | 318 | 349 | 367 | 442 |
| Nonmetallic minerals, except fuels | 149 | 310 | 328 | 418 | 408 | 432 | 405 | 476 |
| **Food and kindred products, total** | 20 | 15 741 | 16 944 | 16 599 | 17 799 | 18 713 | 21 295 | 23 006 |
| Meat products and meat packing products | 201 | 3 182 | 3 020 | 3 092 | 2 971 | 2 692 | 2 684 | 3 036 |
| Dairy products | 202 | 701 | 807 | 785 | 860 | 1 058 | 1 218 | 1 158 |
| Canned, frozen, and preserved fruits and vegetables | 203 | 2 286 | 2 616 | 2 339 | 2 515 | 2 610 | 3 052 | 3 180 |
| Grain mill products | 204 | 567 | 653 | 706 | 863 | 893 | 1 101 | 1 196 |
| Bakery products | 205 | 376 | 419 | 468 | 540 | 599 | 658 | 706 |
| Sugar and confectionery products | 206 | 2 144 | 2 228 | 2 098 | 2 132 | 2 377 | 2 896 | 3 129 |
| Fats and oils | 207 | 942 | 1 182 | 1 193 | 1 388 | 1 524 | 1 874 | 1 883 |
| Beverages and flavorings | 208 | 3 639 | 4 096 | 4 025 | 4 387 | 4 625 | 5 338 | 6 015 |
| Miscellaneous food preparations and kindred products | 209 | 1 905 | 1 922 | 1 893 | 2 142 | 2 334 | 2 474 | 2 701 |
| **Tobacco products, total** | 21 | 221 | 360 | 607 | 163 | 184 | 280 | 497 |
| Cigarettes | 211 | 130 | 265 | 496 | 72 | 64 | 69 | 75 |
| Cigars | 212 | 45 | 45 | 52 | 64 | 94 | 188 | 403 |
| Chewing and smoking tobacco, and snuff | 213 | 46 | 50 | 59 | 27 | 25 | 19 | 14 |
| Manufactured tobacco, including processed tobacco | 214 | 0 | 0 | 0 | 0 | 1 | 3 | 5 |
| **Textile mill products, total** | 22 | 5 447 | 5 943 | 6 258 | 6 618 | 7 037 | 7 233 | 8 437 |
| Cotton broad woven fabrics | 221 | 1 282 | 1 493 | 1 554 | 1 499 | 1 634 | 1 535 | 1 712 |
| Silk and manmade fiber broad woven fabrics | 222 | 1 440 | 1 531 | 1 589 | 1 630 | 1 586 | 1 622 | 1 799 |
| Wool broad woven fabrics | 223 | 246 | 240 | 232 | 243 | 258 | 267 | 297 |
| Narrow woven fabrics | 224 | 179 | 193 | 226 | 265 | 291 | 307 | 346 |
| Knit fabrics and hosiery | 225 | 516 | 414 | 536 | 644 | 715 | 944 | 1 370 |
| Carpets and rugs | 227 | 586 | 705 | 662 | 743 | 845 | 824 | 932 |
| Yarns and thread | 228 | 298 | 363 | 381 | 437 | 458 | 478 | 583 |
| Miscellaneous textile goods | 229 | 901 | 1 003 | 1 078 | 1 157 | 1 251 | 1 256 | 1 397 |

## Table C-3.  U.S. Foreign Trade in Goods by Industry, 1991–1997 —*Continued*

(Trade by Standard Industrial Classification [SIC] product codes; census basis; millions of dollars.)

| SIC description | SIC code | Exports | | | | | | |
|---|---|---|---|---|---|---|---|---|
| | | 1991 | 1992 | 1993 | 1994 | 1995 | 1996 | 1997 |
| **Apparel and related products, total** | 23 | 3 866 | 4 806 | 5 603 | 6 350 | 7 428 | 8 400 | 9 654 |
| Suits and coats, mens and boys | 231 | 165 | 203 | 244 | 302 | 280 | 279 | 267 |
| Shirts, nightwear, underwear, mens and boys | 232 | 1 229 | 1 635 | 2 009 | 2 243 | 2 536 | 2 895 | 3 383 |
| Ladies outerwear (blouses, dresses, etc.) | 233 | 387 | 556 | 632 | 635 | 766 | 788 | 905 |
| Womens, girls, and infants undergarments | 234 | 363 | 416 | 479 | 533 | 676 | 675 | 845 |
| Headwear | 235 | 44 | 57 | 72 | 69 | 68 | 71 | 65 |
| Outerwear of textile materials | 236 | 472 | 639 | 718 | 936 | 1 293 | 1 766 | 2 038 |
| Fur goods | 237 | 71 | 77 | 61 | 66 | 78 | 78 | 96 |
| Miscellaneous apparel and accessories | 238 | 273 | 280 | 330 | 389 | 466 | 439 | 454 |
| Miscellaneous fabricated textile products | 239 | 812 | 903 | 1 015 | 1 149 | 1 239 | 1 382 | 1 577 |
| **Lumber and wood products, total** | 24 | 6 627 | 6 877 | 7 420 | 7 317 | 7 506 | 7 486 | 7 398 |
| Logs, pulpwood, and timber | 241 | 2 718 | 2 762 | 3 087 | 2 920 | 3 032 | 2 853 | 2 373 |
| Sawmill and planing mill products | 242 | 2 289 | 2 427 | 2 564 | 2 523 | 2 496 | 2 504 | 2 598 |
| Millwork, plywood, veneer, and structural wood products | 243 | 872 | 1 023 | 1 083 | 1 102 | 1 165 | 1 242 | 1 431 |
| Wood containers | 244 | 63 | 62 | 65 | 66 | 65 | 74 | 98 |
| Wood buildings and mobile homes | 245 | 202 | 77 | 60 | 88 | 91 | 112 | 119 |
| Miscellaneous wood products | 249 | 483 | 525 | 560 | 618 | 656 | 702 | 779 |
| **Furniture and fixtures, total** | 25 | 2 205 | 2 625 | 2 901 | 3 173 | 3 140 | 3 307 | 3 918 |
| Household furniture | 251 | 82 | 86 | 90 | 103 | 106 | 118 | 139 |
| Office furniture | 252 | 5 | 6 | 6 | 6 | 9 | 8 | 7 |
| Partitions, shelving, lockers, and office and store fixtures | 254 | 104 | 132 | 142 | 195 | 147 | 160 | 193 |
| Miscellaneous furniture and fixtures | 259 | 2 014 | 2 402 | 2 663 | 2 869 | 2 878 | 3 021 | 3 579 |
| **Paper and allied products, total** | 26 | 9 361 | 10 123 | 9 533 | 11 123 | 15 119 | 14 205 | 14 703 |
| Pulp mill products | 261 | 2 945 | 3 259 | 2 501 | 2 998 | 4 765 | 3 397 | 3 281 |
| Paper mill products | 262 | 4 107 | 4 299 | 4 212 | 4 841 | 6 478 | 6 416 | 6 615 |
| Paperboard | 263 | 0 | 0 | 0 | 0 | 1 | 1 | 2 |
| Paperboard containers and boxes | 265 | 597 | 697 | 786 | 918 | 1 152 | 1 288 | 1 405 |
| Converted paper and paperboard products, except boxes | 267 | 1 711 | 1 868 | 2 034 | 2 366 | 2 724 | 3 104 | 3 401 |
| **Printing, publishing, and allied industries, total** | 27 | 3 765 | 3 970 | 4 192 | 4 193 | 4 570 | 4 632 | 4 905 |
| Newspapers | 271 | 38 | 30 | 27 | 35 | 31 | 28 | 34 |
| Periodicals, unbound | 272 | 705 | 732 | 738 | 791 | 828 | 822 | 868 |
| Books and pamphlets | 273 | 1 542 | 1 689 | 1 739 | 1 785 | 1 846 | 1 864 | 1 958 |
| Miscellaneous publishing | 274 | 62 | 79 | 84 | 73 | 95 | 90 | 92 |
| Commercial printed matter | 275 | 1 209 | 1 205 | 1 363 | 1 226 | 1 384 | 1 396 | 1 482 |
| Manifold business forms | 276 | 14 | 13 | 13 | 17 | 16 | 15 | 15 |
| Greeting cards | 277 | 50 | 58 | 60 | 84 | 149 | 161 | 182 |
| Blankbooks and looseleaf binders | 278 | 90 | 103 | 110 | 119 | 142 | 174 | 195 |
| Printing blocks, cylinders, and plates | 279 | 55 | 60 | 58 | 64 | 78 | 83 | 79 |
| **Chemicals and allied products, total** | 28 | 42 159 | 42 829 | 43 493 | 49 735 | 58 813 | 59 590 | 66 397 |
| Industrial inorganic chemicals | 281 | 5 578 | 5 873 | 5 517 | 6 048 | 7 106 | 7 300 | 8 310 |
| Plastic materials and synthetic resins | 282 | 10 016 | 9 532 | 9 600 | 11 180 | 13 811 | 14 248 | 15 468 |
| Drugs | 283 | 5 843 | 6 912 | 7 370 | 7 737 | 8 212 | 9 168 | 10 695 |
| Soap, detergents, cleaners, perfumes, and cosmetics | 284 | 2 301 | 2 604 | 2 952 | 3 462 | 3 816 | 4 250 | 4 894 |
| Paints, varnishes, and allied products | 285 | 688 | 758 | 818 | 943 | 1 021 | 1 108 | 1 332 |
| Industrial organic chemicals | 286 | 10 375 | 10 344 | 10 702 | 12 729 | 16 063 | 14 608 | 15 978 |
| Agricultural chemicals | 287 | 4 685 | 4 147 | 3 654 | 4 704 | 5 489 | 5 376 | 5 743 |
| Miscellaneous chemicals | 289 | 2 673 | 2 660 | 2 881 | 2 933 | 3 296 | 3 532 | 3 978 |
| **Petroleum refining and related products, total** | 29 | 7 166 | 6 434 | 6 239 | 5 578 | 6 081 | 7 305 | 7 518 |
| Petroleum refinery products | 291 | 6 552 | 5 827 | 5 715 | 5 025 | 5 398 | 6 442 | 6 619 |
| Asphalt paving and roofing materials | 295 | 71 | 88 | 93 | 102 | 94 | 96 | 123 |
| Miscellaneous petroleum and coal products | 299 | 543 | 519 | 431 | 450 | 589 | 767 | 776 |
| **Rubber and miscellaneous plastics products, total** | 30 | 7 096 | 7 947 | 8 722 | 10 174 | 11 306 | 12 397 | 14 549 |
| Tires and inner tubes | 301 | 1 282 | 1 418 | 1 473 | 1 630 | 1 901 | 2 004 | 2 466 |
| Rubber and plastics footwear | 302 | 145 | 143 | 144 | 152 | 159 | 132 | 133 |
| Rubber and plastics hose and belting | 305 | 919 | 977 | 1 080 | 1 257 | 1 447 | 1 730 | 2 054 |
| Miscellaneous fabricated rubber products | 306 | 730 | 750 | 809 | 955 | 1 026 | 1 115 | 1 325 |
| Miscellaneous plastics products | 308 | 4 020 | 4 659 | 5 215 | 6 180 | 6 773 | 7 416 | 8 572 |
| **Leather and leather products, total** | 31 | 1 453 | 1 573 | 1 664 | 1 681 | 1 715 | 1 890 | 2 091 |
| Tanned and finished leather | 311 | 702 | 732 | 795 | 720 | 709 | 733 | 845 |
| Shoe and boot cut stock and findings | 313 | 124 | 139 | 152 | 158 | 182 | 273 | 315 |
| Footwear, except rubber | 314 | 371 | 399 | 393 | 433 | 425 | 447 | 446 |
| Leather gloves | 315 | 14 | 13 | 16 | 15 | 15 | 12 | 8 |
| Luggage | 316 | 119 | 146 | 150 | 180 | 191 | 250 | 276 |
| Handbags and other personal leather goods | 317 | 58 | 69 | 77 | 84 | 97 | 92 | 94 |
| Miscellaneous leather goods | 319 | 64 | 75 | 81 | 91 | 95 | 82 | 107 |

## Table C-3.  U.S. Foreign Trade in Goods by Industry, 1991–1997 —Continued

(Trade by Standard Industrial Classification [SIC] product codes; census basis; millions of dollars.)

| SIC description | SIC code | Imports | | | | | | |
|---|---|---|---|---|---|---|---|---|
| | | 1991 | 1992 | 1993 | 1994 | 1995 | 1996 | 1997 |
| **Apparel and related products, total** | 23 | 27 598 | 32 924 | 35 632 | 38 699 | 41 307 | 43 158 | 50 315 |
| Suits and coats, mens and boys | 231 | 679 | 793 | 826 | 955 | 1 044 | 1 135 | 1 319 |
| Shirts, nightwear, underwear, mens and boys | 232 | 7 602 | 9 405 | 10 393 | 11 548 | 13 323 | 14 124 | 16 822 |
| Ladies outerwear (blouses, dresses, etc.) | 233 | 6 348 | 7 327 | 7 834 | 8 100 | 8 600 | 9 132 | 10 015 |
| Womens, girls, and infants undergarments | 234 | 1 269 | 1 536 | 1 787 | 2 071 | 2 443 | 2 492 | 2 887 |
| Headwear | 235 | 407 | 576 | 663 | 679 | 693 | 739 | 704 |
| Outerwear of textile materials | 236 | 6 609 | 8 073 | 8 229 | 8 961 | 8 925 | 9 220 | 11 288 |
| Fur goods | 237 | 173 | 142 | 176 | 190 | 151 | 193 | 184 |
| Miscellaneous apparel and accessories | 238 | 2 140 | 2 468 | 2 582 | 2 737 | 2 561 | 2 500 | 2 902 |
| Miscellaneous fabricated textile products | 239 | 2 370 | 2 605 | 3 142 | 3 458 | 3 567 | 3 623 | 4 193 |
| **Lumber and wood products, total** | 24 | 5 311 | 6 766 | 8 919 | 10 547 | 10 400 | 12 205 | 13 553 |
| Logs, pulpwood, and timber | 241 | 199 | 219 | 265 | 273 | 293 | 291 | 323 |
| Sawmill and planing mill products | 242 | 2 855 | 3 723 | 5 279 | 6 277 | 5 745 | 7 066 | 7 597 |
| Millwork, plywood, veneer, and structural wood products | 243 | 984 | 1 251 | 1 531 | 1 738 | 1 789 | 2 109 | 2 528 |
| Wood containers | 244 | 44 | 50 | 49 | 55 | 72 | 91 | 145 |
| Wood buildings and mobile homes | 245 | 9 | 10 | 10 | 22 | 24 | 42 | 44 |
| Miscellaneous wood products | 249 | 1 222 | 1 514 | 1 785 | 2 182 | 2 477 | 2 605 | 2 916 |
| **Furniture and fixtures, total** | 25 | 5 069 | 5 567 | 6 265 | 7 525 | 8 307 | 9 325 | 11 013 |
| Household furniture | 251 | 375 | 465 | 495 | 579 | 672 | 769 | 986 |
| Office furniture | 252 | 13 | 13 | 12 | 9 | 13 | 12 | 16 |
| Partitions, shelving, lockers, and office and store fixtures | 254 | 96 | 118 | 131 | 166 | 194 | 216 | 265 |
| Miscellaneous furniture and fixtures | 259 | 4 586 | 4 971 | 5 626 | 6 771 | 7 429 | 8 330 | 9 745 |
| **Paper and allied products, total** | 26 | 10 517 | 10 467 | 10 897 | 11 782 | 16 771 | 14 798 | 14 852 |
| Pulp mill products | 261 | 2 142 | 2 104 | 1 868 | 2 285 | 3 745 | 2 601 | 2 572 |
| Paper mill products | 262 | 6 926 | 6 737 | 7 224 | 7 370 | 10 235 | 9 158 | 9 059 |
| Paperboard | 263 | 1 | 1 | 1 | 1 | 1 | 1 | 0 |
| Paperboard containers and boxes | 265 | 177 | 233 | 254 | 342 | 466 | 488 | 497 |
| Converted paper and paperboard products, except boxes | 267 | 1 272 | 1 392 | 1 550 | 1 784 | 2 324 | 2 551 | 2 723 |
| **Printing, publishing, and allied industries, total** | 27 | 1 892 | 2 058 | 2 217 | 2 424 | 2 904 | 2 999 | 3 211 |
| Newspapers | 271 | 48 | 53 | 52 | 9 | 9 | 9 | 9 |
| Periodicals, unbound | 272 | 121 | 134 | 194 | 209 | 222 | 217 | 204 |
| Books and pamphlets | 273 | 870 | 951 | 965 | 1 018 | 1 188 | 1 242 | 1 298 |
| Miscellaneous publishing | 274 | 52 | 45 | 50 | 51 | 64 | 61 | 69 |
| Commercial printed matter | 275 | 504 | 543 | 604 | 704 | 883 | 882 | 975 |
| Manifold business forms | 276 | 1 | 2 | 3 | 3 | 14 | 17 | 10 |
| Greeting cards | 277 | 46 | 54 | 59 | 103 | 109 | 121 | 136 |
| Blankbooks and looseleaf binders | 278 | 240 | 269 | 288 | 321 | 409 | 444 | 502 |
| Printing blocks, cylinders, and plates | 279 | 10 | 6 | 4 | 5 | 6 | 6 | 8 |
| **Chemicals and allied products, total** | 28 | 23 491 | 26 474 | 27 917 | 32 190 | 38 194 | 42 254 | 47 468 |
| Industrial inorganic chemicals | 281 | 4 743 | 4 671 | 4 546 | 5 232 | 6 153 | 6 573 | 6 769 |
| Plastic materials and synthetic resins | 282 | 3 036 | 3 507 | 4 207 | 5 218 | 6 172 | 6 260 | 6 948 |
| Drugs | 283 | 4 882 | 6 016 | 6 322 | 6 935 | 8 555 | 11 221 | 14 110 |
| Soap, detergents, cleaners, perfumes, and cosmetics | 284 | 1 221 | 1 491 | 1 636 | 1 855 | 2 147 | 2 294 | 2 495 |
| Paints, varnishes, and allied products | 285 | 141 | 184 | 197 | 261 | 343 | 393 | 440 |
| Industrial organic chemicals | 286 | 6 758 | 7 499 | 7 629 | 9 085 | 10 630 | 11 064 | 12 112 |
| Agricultural chemicals | 287 | 1 689 | 1 891 | 2 086 | 2 250 | 2 603 | 2 744 | 2 702 |
| Miscellaneous chemicals | 289 | 1 021 | 1 216 | 1 293 | 1 354 | 1 589 | 1 705 | 1 892 |
| **Petroleum refining and related products, total** | 29 | 11 510 | 10 990 | 10 355 | 10 018 | 9 022 | 13 548 | 13 464 |
| Petroleum refinery products | 291 | 11 362 | 10 831 | 10 191 | 9 789 | 8 816 | 13 312 | 13 205 |
| Asphalt paving and roofing materials | 295 | 84 | 88 | 103 | 123 | 124 | 138 | 132 |
| Miscellaneous petroleum and coal products | 299 | 65 | 71 | 61 | 107 | 82 | 98 | 127 |
| **Rubber and miscellaneous plastics products, total** | 30 | 10 360 | 11 870 | 13 225 | 14 566 | 16 181 | 17 097 | 18 513 |
| Tires and inner tubes | 301 | 2 275 | 2 470 | 2 685 | 2 985 | 3 095 | 3 030 | 3 370 |
| Rubber and plastics footwear | 302 | 2 381 | 2 693 | 3 101 | 3 006 | 3 240 | 3 442 | 3 728 |
| Rubber and plastics hose and belting | 305 | 952 | 1 109 | 1 217 | 1 480 | 1 663 | 1 819 | 1 990 |
| Miscellaneous fabricated rubber products | 306 | 885 | 1 127 | 1 343 | 1 576 | 1 829 | 2 015 | 2 065 |
| Miscellaneous plastics products | 308 | 3 867 | 4 470 | 4 879 | 5 520 | 6 354 | 6 790 | 7 360 |
| **Leather and leather products, total** | 31 | 10 352 | 10 911 | 11 818 | 13 056 | 13 708 | 14 285 | 15 562 |
| Tanned and finished leather | 311 | 582 | 644 | 751 | 869 | 954 | 921 | 1 004 |
| Shoe and boot cut stock and findings | 313 | 327 | 367 | 424 | 467 | 409 | 423 | 457 |
| Footwear, except rubber | 314 | 6 748 | 6 994 | 7 556 | 8 133 | 8 357 | 8 771 | 9 710 |
| Leather gloves | 315 | 171 | 193 | 216 | 259 | 290 | 294 | 309 |
| Luggage | 316 | 1 137 | 1 285 | 1 423 | 1 711 | 1 983 | 2 054 | 2 336 |
| Handbags and other personal leather goods | 317 | 1 247 | 1 270 | 1 281 | 1 421 | 1 485 | 1 583 | 1 548 |
| Miscellaneous leather goods | 319 | 140 | 158 | 168 | 195 | 229 | 239 | 198 |

## Table C-3. U.S. Foreign Trade in Goods by Industry, 1991–1997 —*Continued*

(Trade by Standard Industrial Classification [SIC] product codes; census basis; millions of dollars.)

| SIC description | SIC code | Exports | | | | | | |
|---|---|---|---|---|---|---|---|---|
| | | 1991 | 1992 | 1993 | 1994 | 1995 | 1996 | 1997 |
| **Stone, clay, glass and concrete products, total** | 32 | 3 464 | 3 751 | 3 978 | 4 393 | 4 921 | 5 229 | 5 988 |
| Flat glass | 321 | 500 | 502 | 588 | 632 | 697 | 806 | 825 |
| Glass and glassware, pressed or blown | 322 | 801 | 843 | 841 | 936 | 1 120 | 1 199 | 1 423 |
| Glass products, made of purchased glass | 323 | 374 | 424 | 484 | 537 | 555 | 595 | 818 |
| Cement, hydralulic | 324 | 47 | 51 | 49 | 47 | 56 | 60 | 61 |
| Structural clay products | 325 | 132 | 124 | 136 | 131 | 163 | 174 | 205 |
| Pottery and related products | 326 | 368 | 409 | 486 | 549 | 630 | 579 | 722 |
| Concrete, gypsum, and plaster products | 327 | 131 | 158 | 130 | 133 | 143 | 175 | 224 |
| Cut stone and stone products | 328 | 43 | 36 | 36 | 37 | 32 | 31 | 31 |
| Abrasive, asbestos, and miscellaneous nonmetallic mineral products | 329 | 1 068 | 1 203 | 1 227 | 1 392 | 1 525 | 1 612 | 1 679 |
| **Primary metal products, total** | 33 | 15 004 | 14 558 | 18 981 | 16 812 | 20 812 | 21 902 | 23 526 |
| Steel works, blast furnaces, and rolling and finishing mill products | 331 | 4 061 | 3 391 | 3 204 | 3 477 | 5 264 | 4 696 | 5 536 |
| Iron and steel foundry products | 332 | 301 | 365 | 310 | 314 | 410 | 478 | 484 |
| Smelted and refined nonferrous metals | 333 | 5 794 | 5 757 | 10 267 | 6 895 | 7 405 | 8 675 | 8 184 |
| Secondary smelting and refining of nonferrous metals | 334 | 10 | 9 | 12 | 18 | 20 | 20 | 26 |
| Rolled, drawn and extruded nonferrous metals | 335 | 4 615 | 4 834 | 4 960 | 5 854 | 7 336 | 7 697 | 8 889 |
| Nonferrous foundries (castings) | 336 | 64 | 38 | 45 | 52 | 78 | 87 | 95 |
| Miscellaneous primary metal products | 339 | 160 | 164 | 183 | 202 | 298 | 249 | 312 |
| **Fabricated metal products, except machinery, total** | 34 | 11 905 | 13 065 | 13 867 | 13 770 | 15 562 | 17 103 | 18 487 |
| Metal cans and shipping containers | 341 | 261 | 350 | 346 | 346 | 412 | 354 | 372 |
| Cutlery, handtools, and general hardware | 342 | 1 665 | 1 883 | 2 077 | 2 383 | 2 480 | 2 676 | 2 931 |
| Heating equipment except electric and warm air, and plumbing fixtures | 343 | 333 | 390 | 335 | 362 | 355 | 362 | 456 |
| Fabricated structural metal products | 344 | 1 358 | 1 506 | 1 745 | 1 844 | 2 114 | 2 368 | 2 934 |
| Bolts, nuts, screws, rivets and washers | 345 | 645 | 702 | 739 | 939 | 1 089 | 1 410 | 1 381 |
| Metal forgings and stampings | 346 | 1 464 | 1 734 | 1 882 | 609 | 523 | 531 | 581 |
| Ordnance and accessories, except vehicles and guided missiles | 348 | 2 422 | 2 558 | 2 391 | 2 229 | 2 687 | 2 649 | 2 428 |
| Miscellaneous fabricated metal products | 349 | 3 758 | 3 941 | 4 351 | 5 058 | 5 903 | 6 754 | 7 404 |
| **Industrial and commercial machinery and computer equipment, total** | 35 | 70 387 | 74 004 | 77 828 | 88 528 | 103 239 | 111 983 | 127 707 |
| Engines and turbines | 351 | 5 148 | 5 782 | 6 700 | 8 133 | 9 303 | 8 852 | 10 650 |
| Farm and garden machinery and equipment | 352 | 2 763 | 2 862 | 3 243 | 3 496 | 4 005 | 4 653 | 5 517 |
| Construction, mining, and materials handling machinery | 353 | 10 811 | 10 831 | 10 712 | 11 931 | 13 352 | 14 979 | 17 381 |
| Metalworking machinery and parts | 354 | 3 915 | 4 444 | 4 857 | 5 682 | 5 885 | 6 546 | 7 597 |
| Special industry machinery, except metalworking machinery | 355 | 5 228 | 5 211 | 5 864 | 6 901 | 9 369 | 10 193 | 10 534 |
| General industrial machinery and equipment | 356 | 8 591 | 8 795 | 9 241 | 10 543 | 11 662 | 12 550 | 14 597 |
| Computers and office equipment | 357 | 28 298 | 29 858 | 30 297 | 34 363 | 40 711 | 44 766 | 50 475 |
| Refrigeration and service industry machinery | 358 | 3 427 | 3 900 | 4 214 | 4 513 | 5 180 | 5 581 | 6 194 |
| Miscellaneous industrial and commercial machinery and equipment | 359 | 2 205 | 2 321 | 2 700 | 2 965 | 3 772 | 3 861 | 4 762 |
| **Electronic and other electrical equipment except computers, total** | 36 | 47 802 | 52 938 | 60 831 | 73 949 | 90 377 | 94 880 | 108 276 |
| Electric transmission and distribution equipment | 361 | 670 | 747 | 798 | 855 | 996 | 1 139 | 1 378 |
| Electrical industrial apparatus | 362 | 3 393 | 3 840 | 4 065 | 4 421 | 5 169 | 5 323 | 6 105 |
| Household appliances | 363 | 2 384 | 2 603 | 2 835 | 2 975 | 3 053 | 3 257 | 3 514 |
| Electric lighting and wiring equipment | 364 | 2 848 | 3 224 | 3 594 | 4 166 | 4 710 | 5 061 | 5 553 |
| Household audio and video equipment and audio recordings | 365 | 4 745 | 5 512 | 6 224 | 7 214 | 7 627 | 7 108 | 8 376 |
| Communications equipment | 366 | 6 235 | 7 476 | 9 179 | 11 275 | 13 814 | 14 520 | 17 719 |
| Electronic components and accessories | 367 | 21 006 | 22 510 | 26 364 | 34 357 | 45 514 | 47 976 | 54 289 |
| Miscellaneous electrical machinery, equipment, and supplies | 369 | 6 521 | 7 026 | 7 771 | 8 687 | 9 495 | 10 497 | 11 343 |
| **Transportation equipment, total** | 37 | 77 765 | 84 652 | 82 492 | 88 159 | 85 752 | 96 568 | 112 259 |
| Motor vehicles and motor vehicle equipment | 371 | 32 410 | 37 473 | 41 286 | 47 128 | 49 524 | 52 138 | 58 342 |
| Aircraft and parts | 372 | 41 842 | 42 891 | 37 623 | 36 331 | 31 134 | 38 797 | 48 635 |
| Ship and boat building and repairing | 373 | 1 113 | 1 407 | 929 | 1 173 | 1 196 | 1 015 | 1 319 |
| Railroad equipment | 374 | 468 | 494 | 462 | 605 | 766 | 732 | 1 097 |
| Motorcycles, bicycles, and parts | 375 | 709 | 749 | 783 | 762 | 905 | 955 | 1 012 |
| Guided missiles, space vehicles, and parts | 376 | 27 | 36 | 24 | 26 | 56 | 134 | 16 |
| Miscellaneous transportation equipment | 379 | 1 195 | 1 601 | 1 386 | 2 135 | 2 172 | 2 797 | 1 838 |
| **Scientific and professional instruments; photographic and optical goods, total** | 38 | 23 573 | 24 888 | 26 135 | 28 162 | 31 392 | 34 804 | 39 397 |
| Search, detection, navigation and guidance systems | 381 | 2 242 | 2 151 | 2 139 | 2 048 | 1 948 | 2 054 | 2 535 |
| Analytical, optical, measuring, and controlling instruments | 382 | 9 536 | 10 041 | 10 886 | 11 999 | 13 613 | 14 936 | 17 527 |
| Surgical, medical, and dental instruments and supplies | 384 | 7 009 | 7 860 | 8 331 | 9 166 | 10 281 | 11 669 | 12 777 |
| Opthalmic goods | 385 | 455 | 474 | 506 | 556 | 646 | 786 | 842 |
| Photographic equipment and supplies | 386 | 4 062 | 4 089 | 3 973 | 4 075 | 4 573 | 5 026 | 5 342 |
| Watches, clocks, clockwork operated devices and parts | 387 | 269 | 274 | 299 | 318 | 331 | 332 | 373 |

## Table C-3.   U.S. Foreign Trade in Goods by Industry, 1991–1997 —*Continued*

(Trade by Standard Industrial Classification [SIC] product codes; census basis; millions of dollars.)

| SIC description | SIC code | Imports | | | | | | |
|---|---|---|---|---|---|---|---|---|
| | | 1991 | 1992 | 1993 | 1994 | 1995 | 1996 | 1997 |
| **Stone, clay, glass and concrete products, total** | 32 | 5 549 | 5 935 | 6 454 | 7 620 | 8 553 | 9 132 | 10 220 |
| Flat glass | 321 | 283 | 278 | 342 | 416 | 399 | 463 | 495 |
| Glass and glassware, pressed or blown | 322 | 1 126 | 1 259 | 1 344 | 1 606 | 1 831 | 1 998 | 2 204 |
| Glass products, made of purchased glass | 323 | 352 | 376 | 412 | 526 | 613 | 692 | 698 |
| Cement, hydralulic | 324 | 335 | 251 | 284 | 444 | 542 | 596 | 753 |
| Structural clay products | 325 | 422 | 484 | 540 | 583 | 639 | 709 | 817 |
| Pottery and related products | 326 | 1 527 | 1 747 | 1 815 | 2 021 | 2 211 | 2 124 | 2 315 |
| Concrete, gypsum, and plaster products | 327 | 97 | 114 | 134 | 227 | 337 | 418 | 560 |
| Cut stone and stone products | 328 | 475 | 404 | 399 | 444 | 498 | 560 | 680 |
| Abrasive, asbestos, and miscellaneous nonmetallic mineral products | 329 | 932 | 1 022 | 1 184 | 1 353 | 1 483 | 1 571 | 1 698 |
| **Primary metal products, total** | 33 | 21 291 | 21 610 | 22 940 | 30 266 | 33 790 | 34 705 | 37 924 |
| Steel works, blast furnaces, and rolling and finishing mill products | 331 | 9 312 | 9 457 | 10 218 | 14 403 | 14 379 | 15 296 | 16 085 |
| Iron and steel foundry products | 332 | 215 | 200 | 218 | 301 | 411 | 397 | 403 |
| Smelted and refined nonferrous metals | 333 | 7 520 | 7 256 | 7 703 | 9 785 | 11 704 | 11 794 | 12 772 |
| Secondary smelting and refining of nonferrous metals | 334 | 623 | 820 | 703 | 764 | 895 | 873 | 1 184 |
| Rolled, drawn and extruded nonferrous metals | 335 | 3 388 | 3 633 | 3 835 | 4 730 | 6 044 | 5 981 | 6 987 |
| Nonferrous foundries (castings) | 336 | 39 | 43 | 38 | 47 | 65 | 45 | 59 |
| Miscellaneous primary metal products | 339 | 193 | 200 | 226 | 236 | 292 | 318 | 434 |
| **Fabricated metal products, except machinery, total** | 34 | 11 231 | 12 297 | 13 400 | 15 012 | 16 615 | 17 889 | 19 602 |
| Metal cans and shipping containers | 341 | 147 | 185 | 186 | 210 | 229 | 301 | 287 |
| Cutlery, handtools, and general hardware | 342 | 2 388 | 2 684 | 2 963 | 3 456 | 3 765 | 4 165 | 4 661 |
| Heating equipment except electric and warm air, and plumbing fixtures | 343 | 328 | 379 | 427 | 497 | 518 | 593 | 683 |
| Fabricated structural metal products | 344 | 640 | 566 | 644 | 792 | 1 036 | 1 386 | 1 369 |
| Bolts, nuts, screws, rivets and washers | 345 | 1 121 | 1 247 | 1 407 | 1 693 | 1 935 | 1 879 | 1 939 |
| Metal forgings and stampings | 346 | 1 076 | 1 159 | 1 159 | 737 | 772 | 747 | 643 |
| Ordnance and accessories, except vehicles and guided missiles | 348 | 501 | 568 | 682 | 762 | 649 | 608 | 578 |
| Miscellaneous fabricated metal products | 349 | 5 029 | 5 507 | 5 933 | 6 864 | 7 711 | 8 211 | 9 441 |
| **Industrial and commercial machinery and computer equipment, total** | 35 | 56 098 | 63 116 | 73 928 | 90 294 | 107 219 | 113 601 | 126 310 |
| Engines and turbines | 351 | 2 306 | 2 362 | 2 726 | 3 202 | 3 701 | 3 523 | 3 639 |
| Farm and garden machinery and equipment | 352 | 2 034 | 2 162 | 2 316 | 3 097 | 3 268 | 3 224 | 3 679 |
| Construction, mining, and materials handling machinery | 353 | 3 924 | 4 342 | 5 428 | 6 842 | 7 586 | 7 676 | 9 107 |
| Metalworking machinery and parts | 354 | 5 590 | 5 036 | 6 045 | 7 753 | 9 429 | 9 961 | 10 941 |
| Special industry machinery, except metalworking machinery | 355 | 5 326 | 5 716 | 6 513 | 7 585 | 8 900 | 8 717 | 9 681 |
| General industrial machinery and equipment | 356 | 6 728 | 7 305 | 7 925 | 9 766 | 11 243 | 12 144 | 12 375 |
| Computers and office equipment | 357 | 26 962 | 32 759 | 39 232 | 47 612 | 57 916 | 62 934 | 71 325 |
| Refrigeration and service industry machinery | 358 | 1 776 | 1 917 | 2 042 | 2 446 | 2 677 | 2 954 | 2 893 |
| Miscellaneous industrial and commercial machinery and equipment | 359 | 1 453 | 1 517 | 1 700 | 1 990 | 2 498 | 2 469 | 2 670 |
| **Electronic and other electrical equipment except computers, total** | 36 | 61 992 | 69 917 | 79 161 | 96 678 | 116 198 | 115 277 | 122 571 |
| Electric transmission and distribution equipment | 361 | 695 | 807 | 936 | 990 | 1 231 | 1 276 | 1 493 |
| Electrical industrial apparatus | 362 | 3 316 | 3 777 | 4 334 | 5 367 | 6 145 | 6 476 | 7 268 |
| Household appliances | 363 | 3 693 | 4 292 | 4 571 | 5 005 | 5 416 | 5 717 | 6 128 |
| Electric lighting and wiring equipment | 364 | 3 895 | 4 459 | 5 184 | 5 892 | 6 287 | 6 481 | 7 070 |
| Household audio and video equipment and audio recordings | 365 | 12 633 | 14 680 | 15 200 | 18 037 | 18 746 | 17 533 | 18 475 |
| Communications equipment | 366 | 9 321 | 9 896 | 10 982 | 13 372 | 14 300 | 15 396 | 16 538 |
| Electronic components and accessories | 367 | 21 886 | 24 514 | 29 520 | 37 926 | 53 320 | 51 057 | 53 250 |
| Miscellaneous electrical machinery, equipment, and supplies | 369 | 6 552 | 7 492 | 8 435 | 10 090 | 10 753 | 11 342 | 12 349 |
| **Transportation equipment, total** | 37 | 88 205 | 92 990 | 101 072 | 115 377 | 120 877 | 127 707 | 140 615 |
| Motor vehicles and motor vehicle equipment | 371 | 73 419 | 77 407 | 85 990 | 99 784 | 105 519 | 109 846 | 118 597 |
| Aircraft and parts | 372 | 12 422 | 12 930 | 11 532 | 11 728 | 10 958 | 13 138 | 17 256 |
| Ship and boat building and repairing | 373 | 212 | 270 | 920 | 750 | 765 | 974 | 824 |
| Railroad equipment | 374 | 532 | 595 | 587 | 969 | 1 088 | 1 128 | 1 158 |
| Motorcycles, bicycles, and parts | 375 | 1 370 | 1 574 | 1 759 | 1 801 | 2 179 | 2 046 | 2 117 |
| Guided missiles, space vehicles, and parts | 376 | 1 | 0 | 0 | 0 | 1 | 134 | 179 |
| Miscellaneous transportation equipment | 379 | 249 | 212 | 283 | 346 | 367 | 439 | 484 |
| **Scientific and professional instruments; photographic and optical goods, total** | 38 | 19 183 | 20 990 | 22 698 | 25 065 | 28 127 | 29 353 | 31 995 |
| Search, detection, navigation and guidance systems | 381 | 876 | 915 | 803 | 763 | 868 | 932 | 1 166 |
| Analytical, optical, measuring, and controlling instruments | 382 | 4 904 | 5 460 | 6 125 | 7 524 | 8 814 | 9 387 | 10 368 |
| Surgical, medical, and dental instruments and supplies | 384 | 4 181 | 4 618 | 4 923 | 4 946 | 5 564 | 5 975 | 6 610 |
| Opthalmic goods | 385 | 1 010 | 1 130 | 1 146 | 1 216 | 1 413 | 1 522 | 1 605 |
| Photographic equipment and supplies | 386 | 6 018 | 6 653 | 7 277 | 8 099 | 8 837 | 8 862 | 9 537 |
| Watches, clocks, clockwork operated devices and parts | 387 | 2 195 | 2 214 | 2 424 | 2 518 | 2 631 | 2 675 | 2 708 |

## Table C-3.  U.S. Foreign Trade in Goods by Industry, 1991–1997 —*Continued*

(Trade by Standard Industrial Classification [SIC] product codes; census basis; millions of dollars.)

| SIC description | SIC code | Exports | | | | | | |
|---|---|---|---|---|---|---|---|---|
| | | 1991 | 1992 | 1993 | 1994 | 1995 | 1996 | 1997 |
| **Miscellaneous manufactured goods, total** | 39 | 6 626 | 7 257 | 7 642 | 8 622 | 9 620 | 10 338 | 11 107 |
| Jewelry, silverware, and plated ware | 391 | 2 527 | 2 505 | 2 677 | 3 074 | 3 488 | 3 864 | 4 163 |
| Musical instruments | 393 | 309 | 346 | 369 | 401 | 425 | 447 | 446 |
| Dolls, toys, games, and sporting and athletic goods | 394 | 1 930 | 2 276 | 2 487 | 2 894 | 3 350 | 3 502 | 3 695 |
| Pens, pencils, and other artists materials | 395 | 550 | 586 | 587 | 641 | 696 | 766 | 889 |
| Costume jewelry, novelties, buttons, and miscellaneous notions | 396 | 249 | 274 | 289 | 304 | 294 | 309 | 381 |
| Miscellaneous manufactured products | 399 | 1 061 | 1 270 | 1 233 | 1 308 | 1 367 | 1 451 | 1 532 |
| **Manufactured commodities not identified by kind** | ..... | 11 588 | 11 769 | 11 800 | 13 023 | 14 182 | 15 408 | 16 328 |
| **Scrap and waste** | ..... | 4 050 | 3 311 | 3 452 | 4 300 | 6 251 | 4 684 | 4 414 |
| **Used or second-hand merchandise** | ..... | 2 965 | 2 582 | 2 653 | 2 470 | 2 218 | 2 286 | 2 725 |
| **U.S. goods exported and returned** | ..... | 1 090 | 1 222 | 1 418 | 1 592 | 1 661 | 2 032 | 2 378 |
| **Special classification provisions** | ..... | 2 007 | 2 222 | 2 382 | 2 515 | 2 301 | 2 707 | 2 573 |

**Table C-3.  U.S. Foreign Trade in Goods by Industry, 1991–1997** —*Continued*

(Trade by Standard Industrial Classification [SIC] product codes; census basis; millions of dollars.)

| SIC description | SIC code | Imports | | | | | | |
|---|---|---|---|---|---|---|---|---|
| | | 1991 | 1992 | 1993 | 1994 | 1995 | 1996 | 1997 |
| **Miscellaneous manufactured goods, total** | 39 | 19 759 | 22 714 | 25 272 | 26 910 | 28 765 | 31 164 | 35 648 |
| Jewelry, silverware, and plated ware | 391 | 7 536 | 8 007 | 9 387 | 10 357 | 10 765 | 11 607 | 13 025 |
| Musical instruments | 393 | 611 | 685 | 737 | 789 | 923 | 899 | 961 |
| Dolls, toys, games, and sporting and athletic goods | 394 | 7 841 | 9 622 | 10 446 | 10 570 | 11 440 | 13 013 | 15 598 |
| Pens, pencils, and other artists materials | 395 | 739 | 803 | 897 | 1 005 | 1 077 | 1 076 | 1 168 |
| Costume jewelry, novelties, buttons, and miscellaneous notions | 396 | 814 | 925 | 926 | 987 | 918 | 878 | 851 |
| Miscellaneous manufactured products | 399 | 2 217 | 2 671 | 2 878 | 3 202 | 3 642 | 3 690 | 4 043 |
| **Manufactured commodities not identified by kind** | ..... | ..... | ..... | ..... | ..... | ..... | ..... | ..... |
| **Scrap and waste** | ..... | 1 135 | 1 040 | 1 105 | 1 431 | 1 926 | 1 761 | 1 903 |
| **Used or second-hand merchandise** | ..... | 2 053 | 2 182 | 2 861 | 2 690 | 2 880 | 3 050 | 3 952 |
| **U.S. goods exported and returned** | ..... | 11 040 | 12 281 | 13 067 | 15 720 | 17 223 | 19 594 | 21 801 |
| **Special classification provisions** | ..... | 4 806 | 5 641 | 5 827 | 6 374 | 7 141 | 7 727 | 8 589 |

## Table C-4.  U.S. Foreign Trade in Goods, Summary by Regions, 1991–1997

(Millions of dollars.)

| Region | 1991 | 1992 | 1993 | 1994 | 1995 | 1996 | 1997 |
|---|---|---|---|---|---|---|---|
| **All destinations** | | | | | | | |
| Exports: All goods | 421 730 | 448 164 | 465 091 | 512 627 | 584 742 | 625 075 | 689 182 |
| Agriculture | 39 468 | 43 134 | 42 949 | 46 300 | 56 364 | 60 562 | 57 092 |
| Manufactures | 345 428 | 368 165 | 388 537 | 430 845 | 484 971 | 522 660 | 591 233 |
| Imports: All goods | 488 453 | 532 665 | 580 659 | 663 256 | 743 445 | 795 289 | 870 671 |
| Agriculture | 22 184 | 23 447 | 23 664 | 25 949 | 29 260 | 32 568 | 35 148 |
| Manufactures | 393 820 | 434 256 | 480 016 | 557 871 | 629 632 | 659 867 | 728 574 |
| Balance: All goods | -66 723 | -84 501 | -115 568 | -150 629 | -158 703 | -170 214 | -181 488 |
| **North America** | | | | | | | |
| Exports: All goods | 118 427 | 131 186 | 142 025 | 165 283 | 173 518 | 191 002 | 223 155 |
| Agriculture | 8 076 | 9 167 | 9 387 | 10 673 | 9 935 | 12 230 | 12 667 |
| Manufactures | 104 300 | 114 972 | 125 941 | 147 280 | 153 951 | 168 730 | 198 708 |
| Imports: All goods | 122 194 | 133 841 | 151 133 | 177 900 | 206 471 | 230 190 | 254 139 |
| Agriculture | 5 805 | 6 417 | 7 273 | 8 070 | 9 329 | 10 443 | 11 391 |
| Manufactures | 92 685 | 102 225 | 115 858 | 140 139 | 164 365 | 181 409 | 201 318 |
| Balance: All goods | -3 766 | -2 655 | -9 108 | -12 617 | -32 953 | -39 188 | -30 983 |
| **South and Central America, and the Caribbean** | | | | | | | |
| Exports: All goods | 29 659 | 34 785 | 36 170 | 41 127 | 49 095 | 51 870 | 62 088 |
| Agriculture | 2 605 | 2 797 | 3 141 | 3 474 | 4 350 | 4 901 | 5 090 |
| Manufactures | 24 356 | 29 381 | 30 578 | 35 127 | 41 706 | 43 713 | 53 608 |
| Imports: All goods | 31 306 | 33 518 | 34 433 | 38 443 | 42 429 | 49 505 | 53 657 |
| Agriculture | 5 475 | 5 668 | 5 310 | 6 015 | 6 373 | 7 243 | 8 110 |
| Manufactures | 12 478 | 14 329 | 15 398 | 18 583 | 19 984 | 21 077 | 23 938 |
| Balance: All goods | -1 647 | 1 267 | 1 737 | 2 684 | 6 666 | 2 365 | 8 430 |
| **Europe** | | | | | | | |
| Exports: All goods | 123 469 | 122 617 | 119 785 | 123 479 | 140 564 | 148 810 | 163 273 |
| Agriculture | 10 203 | 10 525 | 9 660 | 8 774 | 10 767 | 11 912 | 11 446 |
| Manufactures | 102 223 | 101 770 | 102 337 | 105 710 | 118 591 | 126 467 | 141 712 |
| Imports: All goods | 104 062 | 112 707 | 119 082 | 136 562 | 152 376 | 164 587 | 181 440 |
| Agriculture | 5 127 | 5 168 | 5 088 | 5 574 | 6 233 | 7 077 | 7 398 |
| Manufactures | 92 665 | 100 138 | 106 055 | 121 421 | 137 558 | 147 152 | 164 164 |
| Balance: All goods | 19 407 | 9 911 | 702 | -13 084 | -11 812 | -15 778 | -18 167 |
| **Asia** | | | | | | | |
| Exports: All goods | 130 629 | 138 262 | 146 726 | 160 995 | 197 402 | 207 328 | 213 547 |
| Agriculture | 16 104 | 17 393 | 17 576 | 20 121 | 27 360 | 27 641 | 24 694 |
| Manufactures | 98 462 | 104 949 | 113 551 | 125 095 | 151 612 | 162 859 | 174 465 |
| Imports: All goods | 210 207 | 233 130 | 256 424 | 291 318 | 321 647 | 326 611 | 354 997 |
| Agriculture | 3 212 | 3 710 | 3 647 | 4 065 | 5 103 | 5 392 | 5 635 |
| Manufactures | 191 633 | 213 227 | 238 203 | 272 402 | 302 014 | 304 103 | 332 063 |
| Balance: All goods | -79 578 | -94 868 | -109 698 | -130 322 | -124 245 | -119 282 | -141 450 |
| **Australia and Oceania** | | | | | | | |
| Exports: All goods | 9 797 | 10 682 | 9 938 | 11 687 | 12 794 | 14 087 | 14 450 |
| Agriculture | 379 | 378 | 455 | 522 | 485 | 463 | 525 |
| Manufactures | 8 960 | 9 904 | 9 074 | 10 812 | 11 920 | 13 170 | 13 474 |
| Imports: All goods | 5 337 | 5 097 | 4 752 | 4 914 | 5 085 | 5 601 | 6 465 |
| Agriculture | 1 902 | 1 895 | 1 724 | 1 559 | 1 528 | 1 511 | 1 718 |
| Manufactures | 2 032 | 1 939 | 1 848 | 2 322 | 2 410 | 2 771 | 3 257 |
| Balance: All goods | 4 460 | 5 585 | 5 186 | 6 773 | 7 709 | 8 485 | 7 986 |
| **Africa** | | | | | | | |
| Exports: All goods | 8 820 | 9 907 | 9 428 | 9 219 | 9 904 | 10 615 | 11 390 |
| Agriculture | 1 858 | 2 500 | 2 381 | 2 413 | 2 829 | 2 712 | 2 255 |
| Manufactures | 6 464 | 6 869 | 6 411 | 6 330 | 6 431 | 7 133 | 8 443 |
| Imports: All goods | 14 002 | 14 346 | 14 798 | 14 091 | 15 481 | 18 744 | 19 925 |
| Agriculture | 661 | 589 | 621 | 665 | 694 | 903 | 897 |
| Manufactures | 2 315 | 2 386 | 2 632 | 2 986 | 3 281 | 3 338 | 3 797 |
| Balance: All goods | -5 182 | -4 439 | -5 370 | -4 872 | -5 577 | -8 129 | -8 535 |

## Table C-5.  U.S. Trade in Goods by Country or Region, 1991–1997

(Millions of dollars.)

| Country or region | 1991 | 1992 | 1993 | 1994 | 1995 | 1996 | 1997 |
|---|---|---|---|---|---|---|---|
| **ALL DESTINATIONS** | | | | | | | |
| Exports: All goods | 421 730 | 448 164 | 465 091 | 512 627 | 584 742 | 625 075 | 689 182 |
| Agriculture | 39 468 | 43 134 | 42 949 | 46 300 | 56 364 | 60 562 | 57 092 |
| Manufactures | 345 428 | 368 165 | 388 537 | 430 845 | 484 971 | 522 660 | 591 233 |
| Imports: All goods | 488 453 | 532 665 | 580 659 | 663 256 | 743 445 | 795 289 | 870 671 |
| Agriculture | 22 184 | 23 447 | 23 664 | 25 949 | 29 260 | 32 568 | 35 148 |
| Manufactures | 393 820 | 434 256 | 480 016 | 557 871 | 629 632 | 659 867 | 728 574 |
| Balance: All goods | -66 723 | -84 501 | -115 568 | -150 629 | -158 703 | -170 214 | -181 488 |
| **WESTERN HEMISPHERE** | | | | | | | |
| Exports: All goods | 148 592 | 166 395 | 178 870 | 206 994 | 223 470 | 243 567 | 286 183 |
| Agriculture | 10 757 | 12 037 | 12 600 | 14 220 | 14 360 | 17 208 | 17 832 |
| Manufactures | 129 061 | 144 675 | 157 098 | 182 897 | 196 417 | 213 030 | 253 139 |
| Imports: All goods | 153 521 | 167 385 | 185 603 | 216 371 | 248 930 | 279 721 | 307 845 |
| Agriculture | 11 281 | 12 086 | 12 584 | 14 086 | 15 703 | 17 686 | 19 500 |
| Manufactures | 105 174 | 116 566 | 131 278 | 158 740 | 184 368 | 202 503 | 225 293 |
| Balance: All goods | -4 929 | -991 | -6 733 | -9 376 | -25 460 | -36 153 | -21 662 |
| **NORTH AMERICA** | | | | | | | |
| Exports: All goods | 118 427 | 131 186 | 142 025 | 165 283 | 173 518 | 191 002 | 223 155 |
| Agriculture | 8 076 | 9 167 | 9 387 | 10 673 | 9 935 | 12 230 | 12 667 |
| Manufactures | 104 300 | 114 972 | 125 941 | 147 280 | 153 951 | 168 730 | 198 708 |
| Imports: All goods | 122 194 | 133 841 | 151 133 | 177 900 | 206 471 | 230 190 | 254 139 |
| Agriculture | 5 805 | 6 417 | 7 273 | 8 070 | 9 329 | 10 443 | 11 391 |
| Manufactures | 92 685 | 102 225 | 115 858 | 140 139 | 164 365 | 181 409 | 201 318 |
| Balance: All goods | -3 766 | -2 655 | -9 108 | -12 617 | -32 953 | -39 188 | -30 983 |
| **Canada** | | | | | | | |
| Exports: All goods | 85 150 | 90 594 | 100 444 | 114 439 | 127 226 | 134 210 | 151 767 |
| Agriculture | 5 129 | 5 453 | 5 864 | 6 201 | 6 479 | 6 863 | 7 544 |
| Manufactures | 75 900 | 80 421 | 89 979 | 103 177 | 113 649 | 119 952 | 135 823 |
| Imports: All goods | 91 064 | 98 630 | 111 216 | 128 406 | 144 370 | 155 893 | 168 201 |
| Agriculture | 3 291 | 4 032 | 4 566 | 5 210 | 5 549 | 6 730 | 7 373 |
| Manufactures | 69 685 | 75 127 | 84 476 | 99 782 | 113 837 | 120 444 | 129 523 |
| Balance: All goods | -5 914 | -8 036 | -10 772 | -13 967 | -17 144 | -21 682 | -16 434 |
| **Mexico** | | | | | | | |
| Exports: All goods | 33 277 | 40 592 | 41 581 | 50 844 | 46 292 | 56 792 | 71 388 |
| Agriculture | 2 947 | 3 714 | 3 523 | 4 472 | 3 456 | 5 367 | 5 123 |
| Manufactures | 28 400 | 34 551 | 35 962 | 44 103 | 40 302 | 48 778 | 62 885 |
| Imports: All goods | 31 130 | 35 211 | 39 917 | 49 494 | 62 101 | 74 297 | 85 938 |
| Agriculture | 2 514 | 2 385 | 2 707 | 2 860 | 3 780 | 3 713 | 4 018 |
| Manufactures | 23 000 | 27 098 | 31 382 | 40 357 | 50 528 | 60 965 | 71 795 |
| Balance: All goods | 2 148 | 5 381 | 1 664 | 1 350 | -15 809 | -17 506 | -14 549 |
| **SOUTH AND CENTRAL AMERICA, AND CARIBBEAN** | | | | | | | |
| Exports: All goods | 29 659 | 34 785 | 36 170 | 41 127 | 49 095 | 51 870 | 62 088 |
| Agriculture | 2 605 | 2 797 | 3 141 | 3 474 | 4 350 | 4 901 | 5 090 |
| Manufactures | 24 356 | 29 381 | 30 578 | 35 127 | 41 706 | 43 713 | 53 608 |
| Imports: All goods | 31 306 | 33 518 | 34 433 | 38 443 | 42 429 | 49 505 | 53 657 |
| Agriculture | 5 475 | 5 668 | 5 310 | 6 015 | 6 373 | 7 243 | 8 110 |
| Manufactures | 12 478 | 14 329 | 15 398 | 18 583 | 19 984 | 21 077 | 23 938 |
| Balance: All goods | -1 647 | 1 267 | 1 737 | 2 684 | 6 666 | 2 365 | 8 430 |
| **CARIBBEAN** | | | | | | | |
| Exports: All goods | 6 184 | 6 341 | 6 784 | 7 173 | 8 259 | 8 608 | 9 962 |
| Agriculture | 961 | 950 | 1 010 | 996 | 1 275 | 1 402 | 1 496 |
| Manufactures | 4 502 | 4 763 | 5 085 | 5 533 | 6 331 | 6 474 | 7 703 |
| Imports: All goods | 5 252 | 5 720 | 5 910 | 6 471 | 6 721 | 7 676 | 8 188 |
| Agriculture | 368 | 338 | 347 | 416 | 387 | 495 | 587 |
| Manufactures | 2 946 | 3 321 | 3 665 | 4 209 | 4 681 | 4 744 | 5 289 |
| Balance: All goods | 932 | 621 | 874 | 702 | 1 538 | 932 | 1 774 |

**Table C-5.  U.S. Trade in Goods by Country or Region, 1991–1997** —*Continued*

(Millions of dollars.)

| Country or region | 1991 | 1992 | 1993 | 1994 | 1995 | 1996 | 1997 |
|---|---|---|---|---|---|---|---|
| **Bahamas** | | | | | | | |
| Exports: All goods ............................................... | 721 | 712 | 704 | 685 | 661 | 726 | 810 |
| Agriculture ................................................ | 111 | 112 | 137 | 120 | 118 | 135 | 114 |
| Manufactures ............................................ | 468 | 483 | 440 | 445 | 444 | 481 | 610 |
| Imports: All goods ............................................... | 469 | 605 | 328 | 203 | 157 | 165 | 155 |
| Agriculture ................................................ | 3 | 5 | 3 | 3 | 2 | 2 | 3 |
| Manufactures ............................................ | 348 | 404 | 202 | 79 | 78 | 87 | 83 |
| Balance: All goods ............................................. | 252 | 107 | 376 | 482 | 505 | 561 | 655 |
| **Barbados** | | | | | | | |
| Exports: All goods ............................................... | 166 | 128 | 145 | 161 | 186 | 223 | 281 |
| Agriculture ................................................ | 34 | 25 | 29 | 31 | 38 | 52 | 49 |
| Manufactures ............................................ | 118 | 90 | 104 | 120 | 133 | 155 | 205 |
| Imports: All goods ............................................... | 31 | 31 | 34 | 35 | 38 | 41 | 42 |
| Agriculture ................................................ | 2 | 1 | 0 | 0 | 0 | 1 | 1 |
| Manufactures ............................................ | 27 | 28 | 30 | 30 | 33 | 36 | 36 |
| Balance: All goods ............................................. | 135 | 97 | 111 | 127 | 148 | 181 | 239 |
| **Belize** | | | | | | | |
| Exports: All goods ............................................... | 114 | 117 | 136 | 115 | 100 | 107 | 115 |
| Agriculture ................................................ | 19 | 21 | 19 | 19 | 15 | 16 | 16 |
| Manufactures ............................................ | 89 | 91 | 107 | 90 | 80 | 86 | 89 |
| Imports: All goods ............................................... | 45 | 59 | 54 | 51 | 52 | 68 | 77 |
| Agriculture ................................................ | 18 | 30 | 20 | 20 | 17 | 31 | 35 |
| Manufactures ............................................ | 21 | 22 | 26 | 21 | 21 | 22 | 21 |
| Balance: All goods ............................................. | 69 | 58 | 82 | 64 | 48 | 39 | 38 |
| **Cayman Islands** | | | | | | | |
| Exports: All goods ............................................... | 117 | 282 | 164 | 202 | 180 | 208 | 270 |
| Agriculture ................................................ | 10 | 8 | 9 | 14 | 16 | 17 | 32 |
| Manufactures ............................................ | 97 | 245 | 154 | 179 | 155 | 179 | 219 |
| Imports: All goods ............................................... | 18 | 10 | 35 | 53 | 18 | 17 | 20 |
| Agriculture ................................................ | 0 | 0 | 0 | 0 | 0 | 0 | 0 |
| Manufactures ............................................ | 1 | 3 | 24 | 44 | 10 | 8 | 12 |
| Balance: All goods ............................................. | 99 | 272 | 130 | 150 | 162 | 191 | 251 |
| **Dominican Republic** | | | | | | | |
| Exports: All goods ............................................... | 1 743 | 2 100 | 2 350 | 2 799 | 3 015 | 3 191 | 3 924 |
| Agriculture ................................................ | 243 | 250 | 286 | 279 | 368 | 412 | 533 |
| Manufactures ............................................ | 1 408 | 1 754 | 1 965 | 2 391 | 2 509 | 2 637 | 3 221 |
| Imports: All goods ............................................... | 2 008 | 2 373 | 2 672 | 3 091 | 3 399 | 3 575 | 4 327 |
| Agriculture ................................................ | 286 | 240 | 244 | 309 | 298 | 369 | 451 |
| Manufactures ............................................ | 1 699 | 2 099 | 2 394 | 2 740 | 3 035 | 3 087 | 3 633 |
| Balance: All goods ............................................. | -265 | -273 | -322 | -292 | -384 | -384 | -403 |
| **Guyana** | | | | | | | |
| Exports: All goods ............................................... | 86 | 118 | 122 | 110 | 141 | 137 | 143 |
| Agriculture ................................................ | 11 | 17 | 18 | 20 | 26 | 29 | 28 |
| Manufactures ............................................ | 73 | 98 | 101 | 87 | 113 | 105 | 111 |
| Imports: All goods ............................................... | 83 | 101 | 91 | 98 | 107 | 110 | 113 |
| Agriculture ................................................ | 1 | 13 | 6 | 9 | 3 | 10 | 11 |
| Manufactures ............................................ | 10 | 10 | 12 | 29 | 47 | 39 | 36 |
| Balance: All goods ............................................. | 3 | 17 | 32 | 12 | 34 | 27 | 30 |
| **Haiti** | | | | | | | |
| Exports: All goods ............................................... | 395 | 209 | 228 | 205 | 550 | 475 | 499 |
| Agriculture ................................................ | 115 | 137 | 107 | 105 | 224 | 188 | 198 |
| Manufactures ............................................ | 258 | 75 | 110 | 98 | 289 | 248 | 275 |
| Imports: All goods ............................................... | 284 | 107 | 154 | 59 | 130 | 144 | 188 |
| Agriculture ................................................ | 11 | 0 | 6 | 3 | 9 | 6 | 10 |
| Manufactures ............................................ | 270 | 106 | 148 | 55 | 117 | 135 | 173 |
| Balance: All goods ............................................. | 111 | 102 | 74 | 146 | 420 | 331 | 311 |

**Table C-5.   U.S. Trade in Goods by Country or Region, 1991–1997** —*Continued*

(Millions of dollars.)

| Country or region | 1991 | 1992 | 1993 | 1994 | 1995 | 1996 | 1997 |
|---|---|---|---|---|---|---|---|
| **Jamaica** | | | | | | | |
| Exports: All goods ............................................. | 961 | 938 | 1 116 | 1 066 | 1 420 | 1 491 | 1 417 |
|     Agriculture ................................................ | 136 | 118 | 134 | 128 | 167 | 204 | 198 |
|     Manufactures ............................................. | 695 | 697 | 838 | 807 | 1 095 | 1 105 | 1 032 |
| Imports: All goods ............................................. | 576 | 599 | 720 | 747 | 847 | 838 | 738 |
|     Agriculture ................................................ | 32 | 31 | 43 | 45 | 36 | 48 | 47 |
|     Manufactures ............................................. | 304 | 335 | 471 | 525 | 622 | 589 | 541 |
| Balance: All goods ........................................... | 385 | 340 | 396 | 319 | 573 | 653 | 678 |
| **Leeward and Windward Islands** | | | | | | | |
| Exports: All goods ............................................. | 378 | 342 | 368 | 344 | 342 | 356 | 444 |
|     Agriculture ................................................ | 78 | 63 | 66 | 63 | 65 | 79 | 76 |
|     Manufactures ............................................. | 260 | 244 | 256 | 244 | 279 | 273 | 312 |
| Imports: All goods ............................................. | 67 | 79 | 104 | 89 | 71 | 61 | 108 |
|     Agriculture ................................................ | 4 | 5 | 13 | 5 | 4 | 2 | 8 |
|     Manufactures ............................................. | 55 | 70 | 89 | 80 | 84 | 78 | 81 |
| Balance: All goods ........................................... | 311 | 264 | 263 | 255 | 270 | 295 | 336 |
| **Netherlands Antilles and Aruba** | | | | | | | |
| Exports: All goods ............................................. | 861 | 766 | 785 | 795 | 751 | 764 | 714 |
|     Agriculture ................................................ | 95 | 95 | 98 | 100 | 105 | 111 | 109 |
|     Manufactures ............................................. | 533 | 486 | 463 | 525 | 475 | 491 | 475 |
| Imports: All goods ............................................. | 748 | 856 | 854 | 887 | 711 | 1 243 | 1 190 |
|     Agriculture ................................................ | 0 | 0 | 0 | 7 | 2 | 2 | 2 |
|     Manufactures ............................................. | 27 | 65 | 48 | 78 | 71 | 128 | 150 |
| Balance: All goods ........................................... | 114 | -90 | -69 | -92 | 41 | -479 | -476 |
| **Suriname** | | | | | | | |
| Exports: All goods ............................................. | 134 | 142 | 114 | 122 | 190 | 223 | 183 |
|     Agriculture ................................................ | 12 | 17 | 13 | 14 | 21 | 25 | 23 |
|     Manufactures ............................................. | 117 | 118 | 102 | 106 | 165 | 191 | 153 |
| Imports: All goods ............................................. | 52 | 46 | 58 | 43 | 100 | 97 | 92 |
|     Agriculture ................................................ | 0 | 0 | 0 | 0 | 0 | 0 | 1 |
|     Manufactures ............................................. | 1 | 2 | 5 | 10 | 43 | 14 | 7 |
| Balance: All goods ........................................... | 83 | 96 | 56 | 79 | 90 | 126 | 92 |
| **Trinidad and Tobago** | | | | | | | |
| Exports: All goods ............................................. | 468 | 448 | 529 | 541 | 689 | 666 | 1 106 |
|     Agriculture ................................................ | 94 | 82 | 91 | 98 | 108 | 132 | 116 |
|     Manufactures ............................................. | 352 | 350 | 426 | 417 | 565 | 486 | 950 |
| Imports: All goods ............................................. | 866 | 848 | 803 | 1 113 | 1 086 | 1 313 | 1 134 |
|     Agriculture ................................................ | 10 | 12 | 13 | 13 | 15 | 22 | 19 |
|     Manufactures ............................................. | 183 | 175 | 216 | 518 | 521 | 518 | 515 |
| Balance: All goods ........................................... | -398 | -400 | -274 | -573 | -397 | -648 | -28 |
| **Turks and Caicos Islands** | | | | | | | |
| Exports: All goods ............................................. | 40 | 38 | 22 | 29 | 34 | 44 | 59 |
|     Agriculture ................................................ | 3 | 4 | 3 | 3 | 4 | 4 | 5 |
|     Manufactures ............................................. | 34 | 33 | 17 | 25 | 29 | 37 | 51 |
| Imports: All goods ............................................. | 4 | 6 | 4 | 4 | 5 | 5 | 5 |
|     Agriculture ................................................ | 0 | 0 | 0 | 0 | 0 | 0 | 0 |
|     Manufactures ............................................. | 0 | 0 | 0 | 1 | 0 | 2 | 1 |
| Balance: All goods ........................................... | 36 | 32 | 18 | 25 | 29 | 38 | 53 |
| **CENTRAL AMERICA** | | | | | | | |
| Exports: All goods ............................................. | 4 265 | 5 403 | 5 964 | 6 628 | 7 412 | 7 742 | 8 999 |
|     Agriculture ................................................ | 534 | 583 | 725 | 764 | 880 | 1 024 | 1 069 |
|     Manufactures ............................................. | 3 237 | 4 262 | 4 763 | 5 417 | 5 999 | 6 143 | 7 275 |
| Imports: All goods ............................................. | 3 241 | 3 981 | 4 546 | 5 126 | 6 169 | 7 120 | 8 788 |
|     Agriculture ................................................ | 1 387 | 1 516 | 1 566 | 1 571 | 1 816 | 1 915 | 2 184 |
|     Manufactures ............................................. | 1 560 | 2 164 | 2 646 | 3 152 | 3 895 | 4 743 | 5 929 |
| Balance: All goods ........................................... | 1 023 | 1 422 | 1 419 | 1 502 | 1 243 | 622 | 210 |

**Table C-5.  U.S. Trade in Goods by Country or Region, 1991–1997** —*Continued*

(Millions of dollars.)

| Country or region | 1991 | 1992 | 1993 | 1994 | 1995 | 1996 | 1997 |
|---|---|---|---|---|---|---|---|
| **Costa Rica** | | | | | | | |
| Exports: All goods | 1 034 | 1 357 | 1 542 | 1 870 | 1 736 | 1 816 | 2 024 |
| Agriculture | 84 | 102 | 147 | 161 | 162 | 217 | 188 |
| Manufactures | 881 | 1 167 | 1 330 | 1 633 | 1 513 | 1 540 | 1 778 |
| Imports: All goods | 1 154 | 1 412 | 1 541 | 1 647 | 1 843 | 1 974 | 2 323 |
| Agriculture | 475 | 535 | 552 | 550 | 637 | 682 | 747 |
| Manufactures | 639 | 839 | 951 | 1 049 | 1 161 | 1 229 | 1 494 |
| Balance: All goods | -120 | -55 | 1 | 223 | -107 | -158 | -299 |
| **El Salvador** | | | | | | | |
| Exports: All goods | 534 | 742 | 873 | 931 | 1 111 | 1 075 | 1 400 |
| Agriculture | 106 | 116 | 143 | 130 | 173 | 192 | 230 |
| Manufactures | 374 | 575 | 685 | 754 | 870 | 821 | 1 088 |
| Imports: All goods | 303 | 384 | 488 | 609 | 812 | 975 | 1 346 |
| Agriculture | 130 | 134 | 134 | 92 | 88 | 101 | 154 |
| Manufactures | 157 | 233 | 332 | 493 | 694 | 931 | 1 158 |
| Balance: All goods | 231 | 358 | 386 | 322 | 298 | 99 | 54 |
| **Guatemala** | | | | | | | |
| Exports: All goods | 945 | 1 205 | 1 312 | 1 352 | 1 647 | 1 566 | 1 730 |
| Agriculture | 119 | 124 | 195 | 211 | 239 | 272 | 260 |
| Manufactures | 655 | 902 | 975 | 1 029 | 1 283 | 1 172 | 1 330 |
| Imports: All goods | 899 | 1 081 | 1 194 | 1 283 | 1 527 | 1 679 | 1 990 |
| Agriculture | 472 | 503 | 510 | 548 | 648 | 660 | 778 |
| Manufactures | 389 | 535 | 632 | 682 | 812 | 914 | 1 091 |
| Balance: All goods | 46 | 124 | 118 | 70 | 120 | -112 | -261 |
| **Honduras** | | | | | | | |
| Exports: All goods | 625 | 811 | 899 | 1 012 | 1 279 | 1 643 | 2 019 |
| Agriculture | 88 | 76 | 88 | 85 | 113 | 132 | 162 |
| Manufactures | 481 | 635 | 718 | 886 | 1 101 | 1 398 | 1 717 |
| Imports: All goods | 557 | 782 | 914 | 1 098 | 1 441 | 1 795 | 2 322 |
| Agriculture | 213 | 251 | 231 | 238 | 279 | 277 | 296 |
| Manufactures | 242 | 423 | 574 | 733 | 1 033 | 1 366 | 1 842 |
| Balance: All goods | 68 | 28 | -15 | -86 | -162 | -153 | -303 |
| **Nicaragua** | | | | | | | |
| Exports: All goods | 150 | 185 | 150 | 186 | 250 | 262 | 290 |
| Agriculture | 43 | 52 | 44 | 52 | 69 | 65 | 67 |
| Manufactures | 99 | 129 | 99 | 126 | 170 | 186 | 210 |
| Imports: All goods | 60 | 69 | 128 | 167 | 239 | 350 | 439 |
| Agriculture | 40 | 44 | 74 | 77 | 71 | 80 | 95 |
| Manufactures | 2 | 6 | 24 | 43 | 95 | 192 | 230 |
| Balance: All goods | 90 | 116 | 22 | 19 | 11 | -88 | -150 |
| **Panama** | | | | | | | |
| Exports: All goods | 978 | 1 103 | 1 187 | 1 277 | 1 390 | 1 381 | 1 536 |
| Agriculture | 95 | 113 | 108 | 127 | 124 | 148 | 162 |
| Manufactures | 748 | 854 | 956 | 989 | 1 061 | 1 026 | 1 152 |
| Imports: All goods | 269 | 254 | 280 | 322 | 307 | 346 | 367 |
| Agriculture | 58 | 50 | 65 | 65 | 93 | 115 | 115 |
| Manufactures | 131 | 128 | 133 | 152 | 99 | 110 | 114 |
| Balance: All goods | 709 | 850 | 908 | 955 | 1 082 | 1 034 | 1 169 |
| **SOUTH AMERICA** | | | | | | | |
| Exports: All goods | 19 210 | 23 041 | 23 422 | 27 326 | 33 424 | 35 520 | 43 127 |
| Agriculture | 1 110 | 1 264 | 1 406 | 1 714 | 2 195 | 2 475 | 2 525 |
| Manufactures | 16 617 | 20 356 | 20 730 | 24 177 | 29 376 | 31 096 | 38 630 |
| Imports: All goods | 22 813 | 23 817 | 23 977 | 26 846 | 29 539 | 34 709 | 36 681 |
| Agriculture | 3 720 | 3 814 | 3 397 | 4 028 | 4 170 | 4 833 | 5 339 |
| Manufactures | 7 972 | 8 844 | 9 087 | 11 222 | 11 408 | 11 590 | 12 720 |
| Balance: All goods | -3 602 | -776 | -556 | 480 | 3 885 | 811 | 6 446 |

**Table C-5. U.S. Trade in Goods by Country or Region, 1991–1997** *—Continued*

(Millions of dollars.)

| Country or region | 1991 | 1992 | 1993 | 1994 | 1995 | 1996 | 1997 |
|---|---|---|---|---|---|---|---|
| **Argentina** | | | | | | | |
| Exports: All goods | 2 045 | 3 223 | 3 776 | 4 462 | 4 189 | 4 517 | 5 810 |
| Agriculture | 43 | 89 | 81 | 109 | 122 | 157 | 344 |
| Manufactures | 1 900 | 3 009 | 3 559 | 4 188 | 3 893 | 4 213 | 5 305 |
| Imports: All goods | 1 287 | 1 256 | 1 206 | 1 725 | 1 761 | 2 279 | 2 228 |
| Agriculture | 568 | 487 | 392 | 417 | 475 | 730 | 686 |
| Manufactures | 531 | 481 | 602 | 986 | 841 | 652 | 848 |
| Balance: All goods | 758 | 1 967 | 2 570 | 2 736 | 2 428 | 2 238 | 3 582 |
| **Bolivia** | | | | | | | |
| Exports: All goods | 192 | 222 | 218 | 185 | 214 | 270 | 295 |
| Agriculture | 35 | 41 | 27 | 31 | 28 | 40 | 31 |
| Manufactures | 151 | 176 | 180 | 150 | 179 | 223 | 259 |
| Imports: All goods | 208 | 162 | 191 | 260 | 262 | 275 | 223 |
| Agriculture | 20 | 10 | 9 | 20 | 10 | 14 | 20 |
| Manufactures | 153 | 134 | 157 | 191 | 190 | 200 | 149 |
| Balance: All goods | -17 | 60 | 27 | -75 | -49 | -6 | 72 |
| **Brazil** | | | | | | | |
| Exports: All goods | 6 148 | 5 751 | 6 058 | 8 102 | 11 439 | 12 718 | 15 915 |
| Agriculture | 251 | 146 | 190 | 474 | 462 | 561 | 514 |
| Manufactures | 5 178 | 4 968 | 5 294 | 7 057 | 10 230 | 11 279 | 14 594 |
| Imports: All goods | 6 717 | 7 609 | 7 479 | 8 683 | 8 833 | 8 773 | 9 626 |
| Agriculture | 1 250 | 1 378 | 1 203 | 1 298 | 1 183 | 1 349 | 1 502 |
| Manufactures | 4 746 | 5 475 | 5 394 | 6 451 | 6 618 | 6 522 | 7 178 |
| Balance: All goods | -569 | -1 858 | -1 421 | -581 | 2 607 | 3 944 | 6 289 |
| **Chile** | | | | | | | |
| Exports: All goods | 1 839 | 2 466 | 2 599 | 2 774 | 3 615 | 4 140 | 4 368 |
| Agriculture | 69 | 91 | 107 | 98 | 164 | 128 | 123 |
| Manufactures | 1 673 | 2 260 | 2 384 | 2 544 | 3 244 | 3 766 | 4 006 |
| Imports: All goods | 1 302 | 1 388 | 1 462 | 1 821 | 1 931 | 2 262 | 2 293 |
| Agriculture | 444 | 497 | 457 | 534 | 545 | 753 | 747 |
| Manufactures | 629 | 634 | 653 | 819 | 790 | 885 | 875 |
| Balance: All goods | 537 | 1 078 | 1 137 | 953 | 1 684 | 1 877 | 2 075 |
| **Colombia** | | | | | | | |
| Exports: All goods | 1 952 | 3 286 | 3 235 | 4 064 | 4 624 | 4 714 | 5 197 |
| Agriculture | 119 | 216 | 218 | 302 | 456 | 609 | 523 |
| Manufactures | 1 732 | 2 970 | 2 923 | 3 671 | 4 040 | 3 907 | 4 471 |
| Imports: All goods | 2 736 | 2 837 | 3 032 | 3 171 | 3 791 | 4 424 | 4 737 |
| Agriculture | 784 | 881 | 811 | 1 021 | 1 134 | 1 121 | 1 426 |
| Manufactures | 647 | 798 | 860 | 908 | 1 055 | 1 064 | 1 077 |
| Balance: All goods | -784 | 449 | 203 | 893 | 833 | 291 | 460 |
| **Ecuador** | | | | | | | |
| Exports: All goods | 948 | 999 | 1 100 | 1 195 | 1 538 | 1 259 | 1 526 |
| Agriculture | 101 | 57 | 90 | 71 | 160 | 156 | 187 |
| Manufactures | 826 | 885 | 962 | 1 085 | 1 279 | 1 046 | 1 224 |
| Imports: All goods | 1 327 | 1 344 | 1 399 | 1 726 | 1 940 | 1 958 | 2 055 |
| Agriculture | 470 | 394 | 355 | 517 | 550 | 539 | 549 |
| Manufactures | 40 | 49 | 82 | 104 | 89 | 112 | 121 |
| Balance: All goods | -380 | -345 | -299 | -532 | -402 | -700 | -529 |
| **Paraguay** | | | | | | | |
| Exports: All goods | 374 | 415 | 521 | 788 | 992 | 898 | 913 |
| Agriculture | 10 | 13 | 17 | 21 | 24 | 33 | 31 |
| Manufactures | 307 | 348 | 444 | 719 | 915 | 821 | 833 |
| Imports: All goods | 43 | 35 | 50 | 80 | 55 | 42 | 41 |
| Agriculture | 8 | 5 | 10 | 6 | 14 | 9 | 12 |
| Manufactures | 35 | 30 | 39 | 72 | 40 | 32 | 28 |
| Balance: All goods | 331 | 380 | 471 | 708 | 937 | 855 | 873 |

### Table C-5. U.S. Trade in Goods by Country or Region, 1991–1997 —*Continued*

(Millions of dollars.)

| Country or region | 1991 | 1992 | 1993 | 1994 | 1995 | 1996 | 1997 |
|---|---|---|---|---|---|---|---|
| **Peru** | | | | | | | |
| Exports: All goods | 840 | 1 005 | 1 072 | 1 408 | 1 775 | 1 774 | 1 953 |
| Agriculture | 160 | 170 | 189 | 205 | 297 | 307 | 192 |
| Manufactures | 629 | 737 | 804 | 1 079 | 1 417 | 1 409 | 1 725 |
| Imports: All goods | 776 | 738 | 754 | 841 | 1 035 | 1 261 | 1 772 |
| Agriculture | 105 | 81 | 61 | 116 | 187 | 154 | 273 |
| Manufactures | 482 | 457 | 421 | 488 | 514 | 702 | 1 019 |
| Balance: All goods | 64 | 266 | 318 | 566 | 741 | 513 | 181 |
| **Uruguay** | | | | | | | |
| Exports: All goods | 216 | 231 | 253 | 311 | 396 | 483 | 548 |
| Agriculture | 7 | 4 | 6 | 10 | 11 | 16 | 14 |
| Manufactures | 202 | 220 | 238 | 285 | 372 | 440 | 509 |
| Imports: All goods | 237 | 266 | 266 | 168 | 167 | 261 | 229 |
| Agriculture | 37 | 37 | 29 | 27 | 28 | 62 | 60 |
| Manufactures | 178 | 208 | 215 | 113 | 108 | 177 | 145 |
| Balance: All goods | -21 | -35 | -12 | 143 | 229 | 222 | 319 |
| **Venezuela** | | | | | | | |
| Exports: All goods | 4 656 | 5 444 | 4 590 | 4 039 | 4 640 | 4 749 | 6 602 |
| Agriculture | 315 | 437 | 479 | 393 | 472 | 467 | 566 |
| Manufactures | 4 019 | 4 783 | 3 942 | 3 400 | 3 808 | 3 991 | 5 705 |
| Imports: All goods | 8 179 | 8 181 | 8 140 | 8 371 | 9 764 | 13 173 | 13 477 |
| Agriculture | 36 | 44 | 70 | 72 | 43 | 102 | 64 |
| Manufactures | 531 | 579 | 665 | 1 090 | 1 163 | 1 244 | 1 280 |
| Balance: All goods | -3 522 | -2 737 | -3 550 | -4 332 | -5 124 | -8 424 | -6 876 |
| **Bermuda** | | | | | | | |
| Exports: All goods | 232 | 242 | 265 | 300 | 299 | 282 | 338 |
| Agriculture | 65 | 62 | 61 | 62 | 64 | 68 | 65 |
| Manufactures | 150 | 165 | 185 | 222 | 220 | 192 | 241 |
| Imports: All goods | 8 | 7 | 15 | 9 | 10 | 12 | 30 |
| Agriculture | 0 | 0 | 0 | 0 | 1 | 0 | 0 |
| Manufactures | 7 | 6 | 13 | 8 | 9 | 10 | 29 |
| Balance: All goods | 224 | 236 | 250 | 291 | 288 | 270 | 308 |
| **Cuba** | | | | | | | |
| Exports: All goods | 1 | 1 | 2 | 5 | 6 | 6 | 10 |
| Agriculture | 0 | 0 | 0 | 0 | 0 | 0 | 0 |
| Manufactures | 1 | 1 | 3 | 4 | 6 | 5 | 9 |
| Imports: All goods | 0 | 0 | 0 | 0 | 0 | 0 | 0 |
| Agriculture | 0 | 0 | 0 | 0 | 0 | 0 | 0 |
| Manufactures | 0 | 0 | 0 | 0 | 0 | 0 | 0 |
| Balance: All goods | 1 | 1 | 2 | 5 | 6 | 6 | 10 |
| **French Guiana** | | | | | | | |
| Exports: All goods | 150 | 82 | 323 | 196 | 442 | 301 | 494 |
| Agriculture | 1 | 1 | 1 | 1 | 1 | 1 | 1 |
| Manufactures | 148 | 78 | 322 | 194 | 441 | 300 | 492 |
| Imports: All goods | 1 | 3 | 3 | 3 | 5 | 5 | 2 |
| Agriculture | 0 | 0 | 0 | 0 | 0 | 0 | 0 |
| Manufactures | 1 | 3 | 3 | 3 | 5 | 5 | 2 |
| Balance: All goods | 149 | 79 | 320 | 192 | 436 | 296 | 491 |
| **French West Indies** | | | | | | | |
| Exports: All goods | 119 | 93 | 81 | 82 | 108 | 101 | 92 |
| Agriculture | 11 | 11 | 9 | 9 | 9 | 8 | 8 |
| Manufactures | 101 | 74 | 66 | 65 | 91 | 84 | 74 |
| Imports: All goods | 2 | 2 | 6 | 5 | 3 | 2 | 6 |
| Agriculture | 0 | 0 | 1 | 0 | 0 | 0 | 0 |
| Manufactures | 2 | 1 | 5 | 5 | 3 | 2 | 5 |
| Balance: All goods | 117 | 91 | 75 | 77 | 104 | 99 | 86 |

**Table C-5.   U.S. Trade in Goods by Country or Region, 1991–1997** —*Continued*

(Millions of dollars.)

| Country or region | 1991 | 1992 | 1993 | 1994 | 1995 | 1996 | 1997 |
|---|---|---|---|---|---|---|---|
| **EUROPE** | | | | | | | |
| Exports: All goods ................................................ | 123 469 | 122 617 | 119 785 | 123 479 | 140 564 | 148 810 | 163 273 |
| Agriculture ................................................ | 10 203 | 10 525 | 9 660 | 8 774 | 10 767 | 11 912 | 11 446 |
| Manufactures ................................................ | 102 223 | 101 770 | 102 337 | 105 710 | 118 591 | 126 467 | 141 712 |
| Imports: All goods ................................................ | 104 062 | 112 707 | 119 082 | 136 562 | 152 376 | 164 587 | 181 440 |
| Agriculture ................................................ | 5 127 | 5 168 | 5 088 | 5 574 | 6 233 | 7 077 | 7 398 |
| Manufactures ................................................ | 92 665 | 100 138 | 106 055 | 121 421 | 137 558 | 147 152 | 164 164 |
| Balance: All goods ................................................ | 19 407 | 9 911 | 702 | -13 084 | -11 812 | -15 778 | -18 167 |
| **WESTERN EUROPE** | | | | | | | |
| Exports: All goods ................................................ | 118 682 | 117 100 | 113 681 | 118 177 | 134 863 | 141 543 | 155 384 |
| Agriculture ................................................ | 7 614 | 8 068 | 7 604 | 7 576 | 9 223 | 9 816 | 9 759 |
| Manufactures ................................................ | 100 341 | 99 186 | 98 572 | 102 011 | 114 823 | 122 086 | 136 386 |
| Imports: All goods ................................................ | 102 262 | 110 727 | 115 557 | 130 730 | 145 356 | 157 601 | 172 957 |
| Agriculture ................................................ | 4 904 | 4 970 | 4 876 | 5 384 | 6 033 | 6 744 | 7 209 |
| Manufactures ................................................ | 91 359 | 98 610 | 103 209 | 116 266 | 131 202 | 141 175 | 156 672 |
| Balance: All goods ................................................ | 16 420 | 6 374 | -1 876 | -12 553 | -10 493 | -16 058 | -17 573 |
| **European Union** | | | | | | | |
| Exports: All goods ................................................ | 108 417 | 107 844 | 101 501 | 107 777 | 123 671 | 127 711 | 140 774 |
| Agriculture ................................................ | 7 003 | 7 339 | 6 881 | 6 872 | 8 272 | 8 723 | 8 570 |
| Manufactures ................................................ | 91 668 | 91 446 | 87 768 | 92 894 | 105 387 | 110 025 | 123 656 |
| Imports: All goods ................................................ | 93 030 | 101 201 | 105 493 | 119 467 | 131 871 | 142 947 | 157 528 |
| Agriculture ................................................ | 4 266 | 4 474 | 4 402 | 4 881 | 5 481 | 6 107 | 6 565 |
| Manufactures ................................................ | 83 777 | 90 885 | 95 067 | 107 202 | 120 380 | 129 993 | 144 498 |
| Balance: All goods ................................................ | 15 387 | 6 643 | -3 993 | -11 690 | -8 200 | -15 236 | -16 755 |
| **Austria** | | | | | | | |
| Exports: All goods ................................................ | 1 056 | 1 256 | 1 326 | 1 372 | 2 017 | 2 010 | 2 075 |
| Agriculture ................................................ | 35 | 35 | 30 | 41 | 22 | 28 | 26 |
| Manufactures ................................................ | 995 | 1 196 | 1 267 | 1 300 | 1 964 | 1 945 | 2 012 |
| Imports: All goods ................................................ | 1 264 | 1 307 | 1 411 | 1 750 | 1 963 | 2 200 | 2 368 |
| Agriculture ................................................ | 66 | 49 | 51 | 61 | 27 | 36 | 39 |
| Manufactures ................................................ | 1 184 | 1 232 | 1 308 | 1 645 | 1 903 | 2 138 | 2 277 |
| Balance: All goods ................................................ | -208 | -50 | -85 | -378 | 54 | -191 | -294 |
| **Belgium and Luxembourg** | | | | | | | |
| Exports: All goods ................................................ | 10 789 | 10 047 | 9 439 | 11 168 | 12 840 | 12 774 | 14 132 |
| Agriculture ................................................ | 452 | 449 | 452 | 470 | 602 | 675 | 612 |
| Manufactures ................................................ | 7 991 | 7 451 | 7 210 | 8 055 | 9 590 | 9 784 | 11 421 |
| Imports: All goods ................................................ | 4 117 | 4 703 | 5 402 | 6 642 | 6 288 | 6 980 | 8 151 |
| Agriculture ................................................ | 97 | 111 | 113 | 128 | 136 | 137 | 162 |
| Manufactures ................................................ | 3 832 | 4 285 | 5 122 | 6 220 | 5 947 | 6 573 | 7 649 |
| Balance: All goods ................................................ | 6 671 | 5 344 | 4 037 | 4 526 | 6 552 | 5 795 | 5 982 |
| **Denmark** | | | | | | | |
| Exports: All goods ................................................ | 1 574 | 1 473 | 1 092 | 1 215 | 1 518 | 1 731 | 1 757 |
| Agriculture ................................................ | 117 | 126 | 144 | 141 | 173 | 188 | 226 |
| Manufactures ................................................ | 1 256 | 1 175 | 904 | 1 027 | 1 251 | 1 468 | 1 484 |
| Imports: All goods ................................................ | 1 661 | 1 667 | 1 664 | 2 122 | 1 945 | 2 142 | 2 138 |
| Agriculture ................................................ | 443 | 356 | 390 | 430 | 430 | 416 | 417 |
| Manufactures ................................................ | 1 126 | 1 223 | 1 234 | 1 637 | 1 551 | 1 733 | 1 752 |
| Balance: All goods ................................................ | -87 | -194 | -572 | -907 | -427 | -411 | -381 |
| **Finland** | | | | | | | |
| Exports: All goods ................................................ | 952 | 785 | 848 | 1 068 | 1 250 | 2 439 | 1 741 |
| Agriculture ................................................ | 46 | 47 | 44 | 72 | 74 | 126 | 125 |
| Manufactures ................................................ | 777 | 621 | 677 | 821 | 968 | 2 128 | 1 484 |
| Imports: All goods ................................................ | 1 085 | 1 185 | 1 608 | 1 801 | 2 270 | 2 389 | 2 392 |
| Agriculture ................................................ | 77 | 50 | 68 | 83 | 48 | 55 | 65 |
| Manufactures ................................................ | 991 | 1 108 | 1 474 | 1 645 | 2 118 | 2 100 | 2 190 |
| Balance: All goods ................................................ | -133 | -400 | -761 | -732 | -1 020 | 50 | -650 |

### Table C-5.   U.S. Trade in Goods by Country or Region, 1991–1997 —*Continued*

(Millions of dollars.)

| Country or region | 1991 | 1992 | 1993 | 1994 | 1995 | 1996 | 1997 |
|---|---|---|---|---|---|---|---|
| **France** | | | | | | | |
| Exports: All goods | 15 345 | 14 593 | 13 267 | 13 619 | 14 245 | 14 456 | 15 965 |
| Agriculture | 566 | 588 | 568 | 431 | 522 | 490 | 535 |
| Manufactures | 13 685 | 13 109 | 12 099 | 12 639 | 12 983 | 13 199 | 14 769 |
| Imports: All goods | 13 333 | 14 797 | 15 279 | 16 699 | 17 209 | 18 646 | 20 636 |
| Agriculture | 637 | 735 | 692 | 765 | 881 | 958 | 1 131 |
| Manufactures | 11 950 | 13 272 | 13 875 | 15 125 | 15 611 | 16 861 | 18 683 |
| Balance: All goods | 2 012 | -205 | -2 013 | -3 080 | -2 964 | -4 190 | -4 672 |
| **Germany** | | | | | | | |
| Exports: All goods | 21 302 | 21 249 | 18 932 | 19 229 | 22 394 | 23 495 | 24 458 |
| Agriculture | 1 052 | 1 121 | 1 057 | 1 052 | 1 208 | 1 439 | 1 294 |
| Manufactures | 19 442 | 19 217 | 17 193 | 17 417 | 20 166 | 21 177 | 22 201 |
| Imports: All goods | 26 137 | 28 820 | 28 562 | 31 744 | 36 844 | 38 945 | 43 122 |
| Agriculture | 537 | 560 | 524 | 532 | 659 | 712 | 728 |
| Manufactures | 25 489 | 27 954 | 27 734 | 30 909 | 35 915 | 37 901 | 41 995 |
| Balance: All goods | -4 834 | -7 572 | -9 630 | -12 515 | -14 450 | -15 450 | -18 663 |
| **Greece** | | | | | | | |
| Exports: All goods | 1 039 | 901 | 880 | 829 | 1 519 | 825 | 949 |
| Agriculture | 110 | 111 | 104 | 113 | 129 | 139 | 148 |
| Manufactures | 841 | 728 | 729 | 665 | 1 330 | 618 | 750 |
| Imports: All goods | 429 | 370 | 348 | 455 | 397 | 506 | 453 |
| Agriculture | 154 | 152 | 132 | 133 | 104 | 159 | 135 |
| Manufactures | 192 | 159 | 193 | 231 | 268 | 276 | 296 |
| Balance: All goods | 609 | 531 | 533 | 374 | 1 121 | 319 | 496 |
| **Ireland** | | | | | | | |
| Exports: All goods | 2 681 | 2 862 | 2 728 | 3 419 | 4 109 | 3 669 | 4 642 |
| Agriculture | 188 | 192 | 190 | 196 | 235 | 211 | 227 |
| Manufactures | 2 398 | 2 568 | 2 468 | 3 136 | 3 796 | 3 377 | 4 334 |
| Imports: All goods | 1 948 | 2 262 | 2 519 | 2 894 | 4 079 | 4 804 | 5 867 |
| Agriculture | 59 | 77 | 83 | 94 | 97 | 140 | 142 |
| Manufactures | 1 736 | 2 015 | 2 252 | 2 607 | 3 816 | 4 463 | 5 505 |
| Balance: All goods | 733 | 600 | 209 | 525 | 30 | -1 135 | -1 224 |
| **Italy** | | | | | | | |
| Exports: All goods | 8 570 | 8 721 | 6 464 | 7 183 | 8 862 | 8 797 | 8 995 |
| Agriculture | 673 | 669 | 597 | 541 | 695 | 787 | 750 |
| Manufactures | 6 375 | 6 705 | 4 972 | 5 607 | 6 752 | 6 820 | 7 108 |
| Imports: All goods | 11 764 | 12 314 | 13 216 | 14 802 | 16 348 | 18 325 | 19 408 |
| Agriculture | 752 | 852 | 777 | 898 | 1 067 | 1 303 | 1 370 |
| Manufactures | 10 458 | 10 839 | 11 973 | 13 460 | 15 212 | 16 680 | 17 730 |
| Balance: All goods | -3 194 | -3 593 | -6 752 | -7 620 | -7 487 | -9 528 | -10 413 |
| **Netherlands** | | | | | | | |
| Exports: All goods | 13 511 | 13 752 | 12 839 | 13 582 | 16 558 | 16 663 | 19 827 |
| Agriculture | 1 676 | 1 833 | 1 658 | 1 675 | 2 033 | 2 015 | 1 891 |
| Manufactures | 10 331 | 10 602 | 10 256 | 11 066 | 13 145 | 13 415 | 16 763 |
| Imports: All goods | 4 811 | 5 300 | 5 443 | 6 007 | 6 405 | 6 583 | 7 293 |
| Agriculture | 710 | 752 | 849 | 943 | 1 096 | 1 149 | 1 230 |
| Manufactures | 3 775 | 4 230 | 4 447 | 4 749 | 5 066 | 5 238 | 5 665 |
| Balance: All goods | 8 699 | 8 451 | 7 395 | 7 575 | 10 153 | 10 079 | 12 534 |
| **Portugal** | | | | | | | |
| Exports: All goods | 792 | 1 025 | 727 | 1 054 | 898 | 961 | 954 |
| Agriculture | 228 | 238 | 216 | 231 | 269 | 290 | 249 |
| Manufactures | 449 | 675 | 425 | 757 | 527 | 561 | 606 |
| Imports: All goods | 695 | 664 | 785 | 899 | 1 057 | 1 017 | 1 138 |
| Agriculture | 44 | 41 | 43 | 43 | 47 | 62 | 70 |
| Manufactures | 552 | 557 | 665 | 747 | 841 | 835 | 907 |
| Balance: All goods | 96 | 361 | -59 | 156 | -158 | -56 | -184 |

## Table C-5.   U.S. Trade in Goods by Country or Region, 1991–1997 —*Continued*

(Millions of dollars.)

| Country or region | 1991 | 1992 | 1993 | 1994 | 1995 | 1996 | 1997 |
|---|---|---|---|---|---|---|---|
| **Spain** | | | | | | | |
| Exports: All goods ......................................................... | 5 474 | 5 537 | 4 168 | 4 622 | 5 526 | 5 500 | 5 539 |
| Agriculture ............................................................. | 928 | 916 | 775 | 850 | 1 168 | 1 060 | 1 137 |
| Manufactures ........................................................ | 3 795 | 3 866 | 2 827 | 3 119 | 3 637 | 3 737 | 3 700 |
| Imports: All goods ......................................................... | 2 848 | 3 002 | 2 992 | 3 555 | 3 880 | 4 280 | 4 606 |
| Agriculture ............................................................. | 373 | 426 | 353 | 411 | 458 | 507 | 546 |
| Manufactures ........................................................ | 2 081 | 2 254 | 2 281 | 2 812 | 3 186 | 3 451 | 3 753 |
| Balance: All goods ......................................................... | 2 626 | 2 535 | 1 176 | 1 067 | 1 647 | 1 220 | 933 |
| **Sweden** | | | | | | | |
| Exports: All goods ......................................................... | 3 287 | 2 845 | 2 354 | 2 518 | 3 080 | 3 431 | 3 314 |
| Agriculture ............................................................. | 138 | 145 | 152 | 160 | 124 | 128 | 125 |
| Manufactures ........................................................ | 3 006 | 2 533 | 2 074 | 2 208 | 2 772 | 3 137 | 3 025 |
| Imports: All goods ......................................................... | 4 524 | 4 716 | 4 534 | 5 041 | 6 256 | 7 153 | 7 299 |
| Agriculture ............................................................. | 108 | 91 | 88 | 87 | 81 | 75 | 105 |
| Manufactures ........................................................ | 4 234 | 4 426 | 4 281 | 4 752 | 5 971 | 6 880 | 6 890 |
| Balance: All goods ......................................................... | -1 238 | -1 871 | -2 180 | -2 522 | -3 177 | -3 722 | -3 985 |
| **United Kingdom** | | | | | | | |
| Exports: All goods ......................................................... | 22 046 | 22 800 | 26 438 | 26 900 | 28 857 | 30 963 | 36 425 |
| Agriculture ............................................................. | 794 | 868 | 895 | 899 | 1 019 | 1 148 | 1 223 |
| Manufactures ........................................................ | 20 327 | 21 000 | 24 665 | 25 078 | 26 506 | 28 658 | 33 997 |
| Imports: All goods ......................................................... | 18 413 | 20 093 | 21 730 | 25 058 | 26 930 | 28 979 | 32 659 |
| Agriculture ............................................................. | 209 | 224 | 238 | 273 | 349 | 399 | 427 |
| Manufactures ........................................................ | 16 175 | 17 331 | 18 228 | 20 662 | 22 975 | 24 862 | 29 207 |
| Balance: All goods ......................................................... | 3 633 | 2 707 | 4 708 | 1 842 | 1 927 | 1 984 | 3 766 |
| **Western Europe, except European Union** | | | | | | | |
| Exports: All goods ......................................................... | 10 265 | 9 256 | 12 180 | 10 401 | 11 192 | 13 833 | 14 611 |
| Agriculture ............................................................. | 612 | 729 | 724 | 704 | 952 | 1 093 | 1 188 |
| Manufactures ........................................................ | 8 673 | 7 740 | 10 804 | 9 116 | 9 437 | 12 061 | 12 730 |
| Imports: All goods ......................................................... | 9 232 | 9 526 | 10 063 | 11 264 | 13 486 | 14 654 | 15 429 |
| Agriculture ............................................................. | 638 | 496 | 474 | 503 | 552 | 637 | 644 |
| Manufactures ........................................................ | 7 582 | 7 725 | 8 142 | 9 065 | 10 821 | 11 182 | 12 174 |
| Balance: All goods ......................................................... | 1 033 | -270 | 2 117 | -863 | -2 294 | -822 | -818 |
| **Cyprus** | | | | | | | |
| Exports: All goods ......................................................... | 119 | 166 | 138 | 209 | 258 | 257 | 245 |
| Agriculture ............................................................. | 31 | 42 | 43 | 31 | 44 | 37 | 37 |
| Manufactures ........................................................ | 63 | 72 | 59 | 58 | 67 | 73 | 75 |
| Imports: All goods ......................................................... | 12 | 11 | 16 | 18 | 13 | 17 | 16 |
| Agriculture ............................................................. | 1 | 1 | 1 | 1 | 1 | 1 | 1 |
| Manufactures ........................................................ | 10 | 9 | 12 | 15 | 10 | 15 | 13 |
| Balance: All goods ......................................................... | 107 | 155 | 122 | 191 | 245 | 240 | 228 |
| **Iceland** | | | | | | | |
| Exports: All goods ......................................................... | 156 | 119 | 147 | 112 | 171 | 257 | 179 |
| Agriculture ............................................................. | 10 | 11 | 11 | 12 | 15 | 18 | 16 |
| Manufactures ........................................................ | 132 | 96 | 127 | 86 | 137 | 218 | 149 |
| Imports: All goods ......................................................... | 209 | 165 | 233 | 249 | 233 | 236 | 231 |
| Agriculture ............................................................. | 1 | 2 | 0 | 1 | 2 | 3 | 1 |
| Manufactures ........................................................ | 21 | 17 | 24 | 28 | 44 | 45 | 37 |
| Balance: All goods ......................................................... | -53 | -45 | -86 | -137 | -62 | 21 | -52 |
| **Malta and Gozo** | | | | | | | |
| Exports: All goods ......................................................... | 57 | 58 | 172 | 88 | 107 | 125 | 121 |
| Agriculture ............................................................. | 11 | 11 | 4 | 6 | 10 | 20 | 8 |
| Manufactures ........................................................ | 41 | 45 | 166 | 79 | 93 | 103 | 109 |
| Imports: All goods ......................................................... | 65 | 91 | 104 | 96 | 132 | 209 | 224 |
| Agriculture ............................................................. | 0 | 0 | 0 | 0 | 0 | 0 | 0 |
| Manufactures ........................................................ | 63 | 89 | 96 | 96 | 132 | 208 | 222 |
| Balance: All goods ......................................................... | -9 | -33 | 68 | -8 | -26 | -84 | -103 |

## Table C-5.  U.S. Trade in Goods by Country or Region, 1991–1997 —*Continued*

(Millions of dollars.)

| Country or region | 1991 | 1992 | 1993 | 1994 | 1995 | 1996 | 1997 |
|---|---|---|---|---|---|---|---|
| **Norway** | | | | | | | |
| Exports: All goods | 1 489 | 1 279 | 1 212 | 1 267 | 1 293 | 1 559 | 1 721 |
| Agriculture | 98 | 93 | 88 | 124 | 110 | 128 | 81 |
| Manufactures | 1 309 | 1 142 | 1 095 | 1 109 | 1 124 | 1 362 | 1 576 |
| Imports: All goods | 1 624 | 1 969 | 1 958 | 2 353 | 3 087 | 3 993 | 3 752 |
| Agriculture | 29 | 35 | 28 | 25 | 27 | 26 | 29 |
| Manufactures | 929 | 879 | 865 | 961 | 1 241 | 1 436 | 1 451 |
| Balance: All goods | -135 | -690 | -745 | -1 086 | -1 794 | -2 434 | -2 031 |
| **Switzerland** | | | | | | | |
| Exports: All goods | 5 557 | 4 540 | 6 806 | 5 624 | 6 227 | 8 373 | 8 307 |
| Agriculture | 204 | 157 | 147 | 165 | 179 | 180 | 204 |
| Manufactures | 5 317 | 4 346 | 6 615 | 5 406 | 6 019 | 8 155 | 8 062 |
| Imports: All goods | 5 576 | 5 645 | 5 973 | 6 373 | 7 594 | 7 793 | 8 405 |
| Agriculture | 86 | 99 | 92 | 108 | 137 | 132 | 147 |
| Manufactures | 5 427 | 5 525 | 5 845 | 6 219 | 7 411 | 7 636 | 8 195 |
| Balance: All goods | -19 | -1 105 | 834 | -749 | -1 366 | 581 | -98 |
| **Turkey** | | | | | | | |
| Exports: All goods | 2 467 | 2 735 | 3 429 | 2 752 | 2 768 | 2 847 | 3 540 |
| Agriculture | 214 | 378 | 379 | 268 | 516 | 615 | 742 |
| Manufactures | 1 539 | 1 777 | 2 552 | 2 152 | 1 730 | 1 850 | 2 381 |
| Imports: All goods | 1 006 | 1 110 | 1 198 | 1 575 | 1 798 | 1 778 | 2 121 |
| Agriculture | 420 | 300 | 294 | 326 | 343 | 419 | 422 |
| Manufactures | 529 | 750 | 784 | 1 203 | 1 401 | 1 286 | 1 635 |
| Balance: All goods | 1 462 | 1 625 | 2 231 | 1 178 | 970 | 1 068 | 1 419 |
| **Yugoslavia (former)** | | | | | | | |
| Exports: All goods | 371 | 310 | 234 | 297 | 301 | 356 | 437 |
| Agriculture | 42 | 36 | 50 | 98 | 74 | 82 | 95 |
| Manufactures | 242 | 230 | 165 | 193 | 220 | 265 | 330 |
| Imports: All goods | 674 | 463 | 454 | 467 | 475 | 504 | 525 |
| Agriculture | 101 | 54 | 57 | 42 | 41 | 54 | 43 |
| Manufactures | 570 | 406 | 395 | 421 | 433 | 449 | 481 |
| Balance: All goods | -303 | -153 | -220 | -170 | -174 | -148 | -88 |
| **Bosnia-Herzegovina** | | | | | | | |
| Exports: All goods | ..... | 5 | 25 | 39 | 28 | 59 | 103 |
| Agriculture | ..... | 0 | 8 | 36 | 22 | 30 | 31 |
| Manufactures | ..... | 5 | 7 | 3 | 7 | 28 | 70 |
| Imports: All goods | ..... | 10 | 7 | 4 | 3 | 10 | 8 |
| Agriculture | ..... | 1 | 0 | 1 | 0 | 0 | 0 |
| Manufactures | ..... | 9 | 7 | 3 | 3 | 10 | 8 |
| Balance: All goods | ..... | -4 | 18 | 35 | 25 | 49 | 94 |
| **Croatia** | | | | | | | |
| Exports: All goods | ..... | 91 | 103 | 147 | 140 | 106 | 139 |
| Agriculture | ..... | 9 | 15 | 48 | 33 | 18 | 27 |
| Manufactures | ..... | 68 | 84 | 96 | 102 | 84 | 107 |
| Imports: All goods | ..... | 43 | 106 | 115 | 94 | 71 | 83 |
| Agriculture | ..... | 7 | 17 | 16 | 15 | 13 | 10 |
| Manufactures | ..... | 35 | 88 | 95 | 78 | 57 | 71 |
| Balance: All goods | ..... | 48 | -3 | 32 | 46 | 35 | 56 |
| **Macedonia** | | | | | | | |
| Exports: All goods | ..... | 4 | 11 | 14 | 21 | 14 | 34 |
| Agriculture | ..... | 0 | 3 | 3 | 6 | 3 | 8 |
| Manufactures | ..... | 4 | 8 | 11 | 15 | 11 | 25 |
| Imports: All goods | ..... | 47 | 111 | 82 | 89 | 125 | 147 |
| Agriculture | ..... | 11 | 34 | 19 | 17 | 26 | 23 |
| Manufactures | ..... | 35 | 77 | 63 | 72 | 99 | 124 |
| Balance: All goods | ..... | -42 | -100 | -68 | -68 | -111 | -113 |

**Table C-5.  U.S. Trade in Goods by Country or Region, 1991–1997** —*Continued*

(Millions of dollars.)

| Country or region | 1991 | 1992 | 1993 | 1994 | 1995 | 1996 | 1997 |
|---|---|---|---|---|---|---|---|
| **Serbia and Montenegro** | | | | | | | |
| Exports: All goods ........................ | ..... | 6 | 2 | 1 | 2 | 46 | 49 |
| Agriculture ........................ | ..... | 1 | 0 | 0 | 0 | 13 | 1 |
| Manufactures ........................ | ..... | 4 | 1 | 1 | 2 | 32 | 47 |
| Imports: All goods ........................ | ..... | 39 | 0 | 0 | 0 | 8 | 10 |
| Agriculture ........................ | ..... | 4 | 0 | 0 | 0 | 2 | 1 |
| Manufactures ........................ | ..... | 36 | 0 | 0 | 0 | 6 | 9 |
| Balance: All goods ........................ | ..... | -33 | 2 | 1 | 2 | 38 | 39 |
| **Slovenia** | | | | | | | |
| Exports: All goods ........................ | ..... | 38 | 92 | 96 | 110 | 131 | 113 |
| Agriculture ........................ | ..... | 7 | 24 | 11 | 13 | 17 | 28 |
| Manufactures ........................ | ..... | 28 | 65 | 83 | 95 | 110 | 82 |
| Imports: All goods ........................ | ..... | 101 | 229 | 266 | 289 | 289 | 277 |
| Agriculture ........................ | ..... | 3 | 6 | 6 | 9 | 14 | 9 |
| Manufactures ........................ | ..... | 95 | 224 | 259 | 279 | 276 | 268 |
| Balance: All goods ........................ | ..... | -63 | -137 | -169 | -180 | -158 | -164 |
| **EASTERN EUROPE AND FORMER SOVIET REPUBLICS** | | | | | | | |
| Exports: All goods ........................ | 4 787 | 5 517 | 6 104 | 5 301 | 5 701 | 7 267 | 7 889 |
| Agriculture ........................ | 2 588 | 2 456 | 2 056 | 1 197 | 1 544 | 2 096 | 1 688 |
| Manufactures ........................ | 1 882 | 2 584 | 3 765 | 3 699 | 3 768 | 4 381 | 5 326 |
| Imports: All goods ........................ | 1 800 | 1 980 | 3 526 | 5 832 | 7 020 | 6 986 | 8 483 |
| Agriculture ........................ | 223 | 197 | 212 | 190 | 200 | 333 | 189 |
| Manufactures ........................ | 1 306 | 1 528 | 2 846 | 5 154 | 6 356 | 5 977 | 7 492 |
| Balance: All goods ........................ | 2 987 | 3 537 | 2 578 | -531 | -1 319 | 280 | -594 |
| **Albania** | | | | | | | |
| Exports: All goods ........................ | 18 | 36 | 34 | 16 | 14 | 12 | 3 |
| Agriculture ........................ | 9 | 25 | 29 | 14 | 7 | 8 | 2 |
| Manufactures ........................ | 2 | 9 | 5 | 2 | 7 | 4 | 1 |
| Imports: All goods ........................ | 3 | 5 | 8 | 6 | 9 | 10 | 12 |
| Agriculture ........................ | 3 | 4 | 4 | 2 | 4 | 4 | 7 |
| Manufactures ........................ | 0 | 1 | 3 | 4 | 6 | 7 | 4 |
| Balance: All goods ........................ | 15 | 31 | 27 | 10 | 4 | 2 | -9 |
| **Bulgaria** | | | | | | | |
| Exports: All goods ........................ | 142 | 85 | 115 | 110 | 132 | 138 | 110 |
| Agriculture ........................ | 35 | 6 | 26 | 6 | 10 | 30 | 6 |
| Manufactures ........................ | 51 | 41 | 48 | 52 | 63 | 46 | 45 |
| Imports: All goods ........................ | 56 | 79 | 159 | 216 | 188 | 127 | 171 |
| Agriculture ........................ | 36 | 36 | 54 | 16 | 35 | 19 | 18 |
| Manufactures ........................ | 20 | 43 | 104 | 184 | 148 | 107 | 154 |
| Balance: All goods ........................ | 86 | 6 | -44 | -106 | -57 | 11 | -62 |
| **Czechoslovakia (former)** | | | | | | | |
| Exports: All goods ........................ | 123 | 413 | 301 | 340 | 424 | 475 | 672 |
| Agriculture ........................ | 21 | 20 | 16 | 16 | 20 | 14 | 17 |
| Manufactures ........................ | 97 | 383 | 280 | 317 | 376 | 437 | 623 |
| Imports: All goods ........................ | 145 | 241 | 342 | 447 | 493 | 607 | 775 |
| Agriculture ........................ | 17 | 19 | 18 | 18 | 21 | 13 | 13 |
| Manufactures ........................ | 127 | 222 | 321 | 425 | 472 | 591 | 762 |
| Balance: All goods ........................ | -22 | 171 | -41 | -107 | -69 | -132 | -104 |
| **Czech Republic** | | | | | | | |
| Exports: All goods ........................ | ..... | ..... | 267 | 297 | 363 | 412 | 590 |
| Agriculture ........................ | ..... | ..... | 15 | 16 | 18 | 13 | 16 |
| Manufactures ........................ | ..... | ..... | 247 | 275 | 317 | 376 | 543 |
| Imports: All goods ........................ | ..... | ..... | 277 | 316 | 363 | 482 | 610 |
| Agriculture ........................ | ..... | ..... | 14 | 14 | 17 | 10 | 11 |
| Manufactures ........................ | ..... | ..... | 262 | 301 | 346 | 471 | 598 |
| Balance: All goods ........................ | ..... | ..... | -10 | -19 | -1 | -70 | -20 |

**Table C-5.  U.S. Trade in Goods by Country or Region, 1991–1997** —*Continued*

(Millions of dollars.)

| Country or region | 1991 | 1992 | 1993 | 1994 | 1995 | 1996 | 1997 |
|---|---|---|---|---|---|---|---|
| **Slovakia** | | | | | | | |
| Exports: All goods | ..... | ..... | 34 | 43 | 61 | 63 | 82 |
| Agriculture | ..... | ..... | 0 | 1 | 1 | 1 | 2 |
| Manufactures | ..... | ..... | 34 | 42 | 59 | 61 | 80 |
| Imports: All goods | ..... | ..... | 65 | 131 | 129 | 125 | 166 |
| Agriculture | ..... | ..... | 4 | 4 | 3 | 3 | 2 |
| Manufactures | ..... | ..... | 60 | 124 | 126 | 120 | 164 |
| Balance: All goods | ..... | ..... | -31 | -88 | -69 | -62 | -84 |
| **Hungary** | | | | | | | |
| Exports: All goods | 256 | 295 | 435 | 309 | 295 | 331 | 486 |
| Agriculture | 13 | 12 | 11 | 11 | 14 | 9 | 25 |
| Manufactures | 241 | 277 | 421 | 296 | 280 | 320 | 458 |
| Imports: All goods | 367 | 347 | 401 | 470 | 547 | 676 | 1 079 |
| Agriculture | 92 | 61 | 55 | 56 | 54 | 66 | 56 |
| Manufactures | 273 | 287 | 343 | 411 | 491 | 608 | 1 021 |
| Balance: All goods | -111 | -52 | 34 | -161 | -252 | -346 | -594 |
| **Poland** | | | | | | | |
| Exports: All goods | 459 | 641 | 912 | 625 | 776 | 968 | 1 170 |
| Agriculture | 36 | 83 | 178 | 87 | 112 | 218 | 111 |
| Manufactures | 399 | 528 | 719 | 522 | 643 | 711 | 1 002 |
| Imports: All goods | 357 | 375 | 454 | 651 | 664 | 628 | 696 |
| Agriculture | 67 | 63 | 65 | 67 | 58 | 61 | 63 |
| Manufactures | 271 | 301 | 378 | 553 | 599 | 559 | 614 |
| Balance: All goods | 102 | 266 | 458 | -26 | 112 | 340 | 474 |
| **Romania** | | | | | | | |
| Exports: All goods | 209 | 248 | 324 | 340 | 253 | 266 | 258 |
| Agriculture | 74 | 95 | 102 | 67 | 49 | 46 | 15 |
| Manufactures | 66 | 96 | 172 | 208 | 114 | 131 | 124 |
| Imports: All goods | 69 | 87 | 69 | 195 | 222 | 249 | 400 |
| Agriculture | 2 | 2 | 4 | 4 | 1 | 1 | 1 |
| Manufactures | 66 | 54 | 64 | 153 | 220 | 206 | 329 |
| Balance: All goods | 140 | 161 | 254 | 145 | 31 | 17 | -142 |
| **Former Soviet Republics** | | | | | | | |
| Exports: All goods | 3 579 | 3 799 | 3 984 | 3 562 | 3 807 | 5 078 | 5 191 |
| Agriculture | 2 400 | 2 216 | 1 694 | 996 | 1 333 | 1 771 | 1 512 |
| Manufactures | 1 026 | 1 250 | 2 119 | 2 302 | 2 285 | 2 733 | 3 072 |
| Imports: All goods | 802 | 845 | 2 094 | 3 848 | 4 895 | 4 690 | 5 350 |
| Agriculture | 6 | 12 | 11 | 27 | 27 | 169 | 31 |
| Manufactures | 548 | 621 | 1 633 | 3 425 | 4 421 | 3 899 | 4 608 |
| Balance: All goods | 2 777 | 2 953 | 1 890 | -286 | -1 088 | 388 | -159 |
| **Armenia** | | | | | | | |
| Exports: All goods | ..... | 25 | 78 | 74 | 70 | 57 | 62 |
| Agriculture | ..... | 20 | 49 | 50 | 42 | 42 | 22 |
| Manufactures | ..... | 5 | 29 | 24 | 29 | 16 | 39 |
| Imports: All goods | ..... | 1 | 1 | 1 | 16 | 2 | 6 |
| Agriculture | ..... | 0 | 0 | 0 | 0 | 0 | 1 |
| Manufactures | ..... | 1 | 1 | 1 | 1 | 1 | 5 |
| Balance: All goods | ..... | 23 | 77 | 73 | 54 | 56 | 56 |
| **Azerbaijan** | | | | | | | |
| Exports: All goods | ..... | 0 | 37 | 27 | 36 | 54 | 62 |
| Agriculture | ..... | 0 | 0 | 14 | 12 | 6 | 6 |
| Manufactures | ..... | 0 | 37 | 13 | 23 | 48 | 48 |
| Imports: All goods | ..... | 0 | 0 | 0 | 1 | 5 | 6 |
| Agriculture | ..... | 0 | 0 | 0 | 0 | 1 | 1 |
| Manufactures | ..... | 0 | 0 | 0 | 1 | 3 | 4 |
| Balance: All goods | ..... | 0 | 36 | 27 | 35 | 50 | 57 |

**Table C-5.   U.S. Trade in Goods by Country or Region, 1991–1997** *—Continued*

(Millions of dollars.)

| Country or region | 1991 | 1992 | 1993 | 1994 | 1995 | 1996 | 1997 |
|---|---|---|---|---|---|---|---|
| **Belarus** | | | | | | | |
| Exports: All goods | ..... | 25 | 92 | 46 | 48 | 53 | 41 |
| Agriculture | ..... | 16 | 70 | 21 | 15 | 11 | 1 |
| Manufactures | ..... | 9 | 22 | 25 | 33 | 37 | 34 |
| Imports: All goods | ..... | 25 | 34 | 54 | 45 | 52 | 66 |
| Agriculture | ..... | 0 | 0 | 0 | 0 | 0 | 0 |
| Manufactures | ..... | 25 | 33 | 53 | 44 | 51 | 65 |
| Balance: All goods | ..... | 0 | 58 | -7 | 3 | 1 | -25 |
| **Estonia** | | | | | | | |
| Exports: All goods | ..... | 59 | 54 | 33 | 139 | 84 | 47 |
| Agriculture | ..... | 32 | 30 | 8 | 74 | 27 | 25 |
| Manufactures | ..... | 26 | 23 | 23 | 59 | 54 | 21 |
| Imports: All goods | ..... | 12 | 20 | 29 | 62 | 55 | 77 |
| Agriculture | ..... | 1 | 0 | 0 | 0 | 0 | 0 |
| Manufactures | ..... | 8 | 10 | 25 | 56 | 49 | 56 |
| Balance: All goods | ..... | 46 | 34 | 4 | 77 | 29 | -29 |
| **Georgia** | | | | | | | |
| Exports: All goods | ..... | 16 | 48 | 78 | 95 | 83 | 141 |
| Agriculture | ..... | 14 | 32 | 59 | 55 | 48 | 30 |
| Manufactures | ..... | 2 | 16 | 20 | 40 | 35 | 110 |
| Imports: All goods | ..... | 7 | 21 | 1 | 11 | 8 | 7 |
| Agriculture | ..... | 0 | 0 | 0 | 0 | 0 | 0 |
| Manufactures | ..... | 0 | 0 | 1 | 10 | 7 | 6 |
| Balance: All goods | ..... | 9 | 27 | 77 | 85 | 75 | 134 |
| **Kazakhstan** | | | | | | | |
| Exports: All goods | ..... | 15 | 68 | 130 | 81 | 138 | 346 |
| Agriculture | ..... | 9 | 2 | 3 | 1 | 1 | 0 |
| Manufactures | ..... | 5 | 63 | 127 | 77 | 128 | 253 |
| Imports: All goods | ..... | 21 | 41 | 62 | 123 | 121 | 129 |
| Agriculture | ..... | 0 | 1 | 0 | 0 | 0 | 0 |
| Manufactures | ..... | 21 | 37 | 58 | 122 | 112 | 114 |
| Balance: All goods | ..... | -6 | 27 | 68 | -42 | 17 | 217 |
| **Kyrgyzstan** | | | | | | | |
| Exports: All goods | ..... | 2 | 18 | 6 | 25 | 47 | 28 |
| Agriculture | ..... | 0 | 16 | 3 | 14 | 17 | 11 |
| Manufactures | ..... | 2 | 3 | 3 | 11 | 30 | 16 |
| Imports: All goods | ..... | 1 | 2 | 8 | 8 | 5 | 2 |
| Agriculture | ..... | 0 | 0 | 0 | 0 | 0 | 0 |
| Manufactures | ..... | 1 | 2 | 4 | 7 | 5 | 2 |
| Balance: All goods | ..... | 1 | 16 | -2 | 16 | 42 | 26 |
| **Latvia** | | | | | | | |
| Exports: All goods | ..... | 55 | 90 | 101 | 89 | 167 | 218 |
| Agriculture | ..... | 26 | 12 | 5 | 10 | 91 | 119 |
| Manufactures | ..... | 23 | 71 | 87 | 78 | 71 | 98 |
| Imports: All goods | ..... | 11 | 22 | 41 | 82 | 103 | 145 |
| Agriculture | ..... | 0 | 0 | 0 | 0 | 0 | 0 |
| Manufactures | ..... | 8 | 15 | 49 | 60 | 18 | 46 |
| Balance: All goods | ..... | 44 | 67 | 60 | 8 | 64 | 73 |
| **Lithuania** | | | | | | | |
| Exports: All goods | ..... | 44 | 57 | 41 | 52 | 63 | 87 |
| Agriculture | ..... | 25 | 18 | 19 | 12 | 15 | 15 |
| Manufactures | ..... | 17 | 38 | 22 | 39 | 48 | 64 |
| Imports: All goods | ..... | 5 | 16 | 15 | 26 | 34 | 80 |
| Agriculture | ..... | 1 | 1 | 6 | 7 | 11 | 10 |
| Manufactures | ..... | 4 | 5 | 10 | 19 | 23 | 33 |
| Balance: All goods | ..... | 39 | 41 | 26 | 26 | 29 | 8 |

**Table C-5.  U.S. Trade in Goods by Country or Region, 1991–1997** —*Continued*

(Millions of dollars.)

| Country or region | 1991 | 1992 | 1993 | 1994 | 1995 | 1996 | 1997 |
|---|---|---|---|---|---|---|---|
| **Moldova** | | | | | | | |
| Exports: All goods | ..... | 9 | 31 | 23 | 10 | 22 | 20 |
| Agriculture | ..... | 8 | 28 | 20 | 5 | 12 | 4 |
| Manufactures | ..... | 1 | 3 | 4 | 5 | 9 | 16 |
| Imports: All goods | ..... | 0 | 0 | 3 | 25 | 30 | 54 |
| Agriculture | ..... | 0 | 0 | 1 | 1 | 4 | 3 |
| Manufactures | ..... | 0 | 0 | 2 | 24 | 26 | 48 |
| Balance: All goods | ..... | 9 | 31 | 20 | -15 | -8 | -34 |
| **Russia** | | | | | | | |
| Exports: All goods | ..... | 2 112 | 2 970 | 2 578 | 2 823 | 3 346 | 3 365 |
| Agriculture | ..... | 1 108 | 1 221 | 637 | 1 032 | 1 352 | 1 234 |
| Manufactures | ..... | 745 | 1 593 | 1 691 | 1 620 | 1 550 | 1 744 |
| Imports: All goods | ..... | 481 | 1 743 | 3 245 | 4 030 | 3 577 | 4 319 |
| Agriculture | ..... | 5 | 7 | 11 | 8 | 12 | 10 |
| Manufactures | ..... | 361 | 1 356 | 2 847 | 3 631 | 3 057 | 3 814 |
| Balance: All goods | ..... | 1 631 | 1 227 | -667 | -1 207 | -231 | -954 |
| **Tajikistan** | | | | | | | |
| Exports: All goods | ..... | 9 | 12 | 15 | 18 | 17 | 19 |
| Agriculture | ..... | 8 | 10 | 10 | 14 | 12 | 16 |
| Manufactures | ..... | 1 | 2 | 5 | 4 | 5 | 3 |
| Imports: All goods | ..... | 2 | 18 | 60 | 41 | 33 | 9 |
| Agriculture | ..... | 0 | 0 | 2 | 6 | 3 | 0 |
| Manufactures | ..... | 1 | 18 | 58 | 35 | 29 | 8 |
| Balance: All goods | ..... | 7 | -6 | -44 | -23 | -16 | 10 |
| **Turkmenistan** | | | | | | | |
| Exports: All goods | ..... | 35 | 46 | 137 | 34 | 201 | 118 |
| Agriculture | ..... | 0 | 15 | 22 | 11 | 12 | 0 |
| Manufactures | ..... | 35 | 30 | 115 | 24 | 188 | 117 |
| Imports: All goods | ..... | 1 | 2 | 2 | 1 | 1 | 2 |
| Agriculture | ..... | 0 | 1 | 1 | 1 | 0 | 2 |
| Manufactures | ..... | 1 | 1 | 1 | 0 | 0 | 0 |
| Balance: All goods | ..... | 34 | 44 | 136 | 33 | 200 | 116 |
| **Ukraine** | | | | | | | |
| Exports: All goods | ..... | 307 | 310 | 180 | 223 | 395 | 403 |
| Agriculture | ..... | 164 | 137 | 62 | 38 | 44 | 29 |
| Manufactures | ..... | 119 | 171 | 116 | 181 | 244 | 278 |
| Imports: All goods | ..... | 89 | 165 | 323 | 406 | 507 | 410 |
| Agriculture | ..... | 0 | 0 | 6 | 3 | 2 | 1 |
| Manufactures | ..... | 45 | 146 | 315 | 394 | 492 | 369 |
| Balance: All goods | ..... | 218 | 145 | -143 | -182 | -112 | -7 |
| **Uzbekistan** | | | | | | | |
| Exports: All goods | ..... | 51 | 73 | 90 | 63 | 352 | 234 |
| Agriculture | ..... | 49 | 55 | 62 | 0 | 81 | 0 |
| Manufactures | ..... | 2 | 17 | 26 | 63 | 269 | 232 |
| Imports: All goods | ..... | 1 | 7 | 3 | 19 | 159 | 39 |
| Agriculture | ..... | 0 | 0 | 0 | 0 | 134 | 2 |
| Manufactures | ..... | 1 | 7 | 3 | 16 | 24 | 37 |
| Balance: All goods | ..... | 50 | 66 | 87 | 45 | 193 | 195 |
| **ASIA, INCLUDING MIDDLE EAST** | | | | | | | |
| Exports: All goods | 130 629 | 138 262 | 146 726 | 160 995 | 197 402 | 207 328 | 213 547 |
| Agriculture | 16 104 | 17 393 | 17 576 | 20 121 | 27 360 | 27 641 | 24 694 |
| Manufactures | 98 462 | 104 949 | 113 551 | 125 095 | 151 612 | 162 859 | 174 465 |
| Imports: All goods | 210 207 | 233 130 | 256 424 | 291 318 | 321 647 | 326 611 | 354 997 |
| Agriculture | 3 212 | 3 710 | 3 647 | 4 065 | 5 103 | 5 392 | 5 635 |
| Manufactures | 191 633 | 213 227 | 238 203 | 272 402 | 302 014 | 304 103 | 332 063 |
| Balance: All goods | -79 578 | -94 868 | -109 698 | -130 322 | -124 245 | -119 282 | -141 450 |

**Table C-5.   U.S. Trade in Goods by Country or Region, 1991–1997** —*Continued*

(Millions of dollars.)

| Country or region | 1991 | 1992 | 1993 | 1994 | 1995 | 1996 | 1997 |
|---|---|---|---|---|---|---|---|
| **Afghanistan** | | | | | | | |
| Exports: All goods | 3 | 4 | 9 | 5 | 4 | 17 | 12 |
| Agriculture | 0 | 0 | 7 | 0 | 0 | 8 | 2 |
| Manufactures | 1 | 3 | 2 | 4 | 3 | 8 | 7 |
| Imports: All goods | 4 | 2 | 3 | 6 | 5 | 16 | 10 |
| Agriculture | 3 | 1 | 2 | 5 | 5 | 5 | 7 |
| Manufactures | 1 | 1 | 1 | 1 | 1 | 1 | 3 |
| Balance: All goods | -2 | 2 | 7 | -1 | -1 | 1 | 2 |
| **Bangladesh** | | | | | | | |
| Exports: All goods | 179 | 188 | 254 | 232 | 325 | 210 | 259 |
| Agriculture | 94 | 118 | 56 | 159 | 217 | 88 | 120 |
| Manufactures | 84 | 61 | 175 | 61 | 95 | 110 | 133 |
| Imports: All goods | 524 | 831 | 886 | 1 080 | 1 257 | 1 343 | 1 679 |
| Agriculture | 7 | 4 | 2 | 1 | 2 | 1 | 1 |
| Manufactures | 479 | 759 | 804 | 979 | 1 188 | 1 231 | 1 544 |
| Balance: All goods | -345 | -643 | -632 | -848 | -932 | -1 133 | -1 420 |
| **Brunei** | | | | | | | |
| Exports: All goods | 162 | 453 | 473 | 376 | 190 | 375 | 178 |
| Agriculture | 0 | 2 | 2 | 4 | 1 | 1 | 2 |
| Manufactures | 159 | 448 | 473 | 367 | 187 | 371 | 175 |
| Imports: All goods | 26 | 30 | 30 | 46 | 38 | 48 | 56 |
| Agriculture | 0 | 0 | 0 | 0 | 0 | 0 | 0 |
| Manufactures | 13 | 30 | 27 | 46 | 38 | 49 | 56 |
| Balance: All goods | 136 | 424 | 442 | 330 | 152 | 326 | 122 |
| **Burma** | | | | | | | |
| Exports: All goods | 23 | 4 | 12 | 11 | 16 | 32 | 20 |
| Agriculture | 1 | 0 | 0 | 1 | 1 | 2 | 1 |
| Manufactures | 23 | 4 | 12 | 10 | 15 | 30 | 19 |
| Imports: All goods | 27 | 39 | 46 | 67 | 81 | 108 | 115 |
| Agriculture | 2 | 1 | 3 | 6 | 6 | 9 | 6 |
| Manufactures | 15 | 30 | 37 | 51 | 69 | 89 | 98 |
| Balance: All goods | -4 | -34 | -34 | -56 | -65 | -76 | -95 |
| **Cambodia** | | | | | | | |
| Exports: All goods | 0 | 16 | 16 | 8 | 27 | 22 | 19 |
| Agriculture | 0 | 0 | 0 | 1 | 4 | 1 | 2 |
| Manufactures | 0 | 16 | 15 | 7 | 21 | 18 | 15 |
| Imports: All goods | 0 | 0 | 1 | 1 | 5 | 4 | 103 |
| Agriculture | 0 | 0 | 0 | 0 | 4 | 1 | 1 |
| Manufactures | 0 | 0 | 1 | 1 | 1 | 3 | 102 |
| Balance: All goods | 0 | 16 | 15 | 6 | 22 | 17 | -84 |
| **China** | | | | | | | |
| Exports: All goods | 6 278 | 7 418 | 8 763 | 9 282 | 11 754 | 11 993 | 12 862 |
| Agriculture | 724 | 545 | 370 | 1 082 | 2 634 | 2 080 | 1 592 |
| Manufactures | 5 000 | 6 251 | 7 725 | 7 655 | 8 330 | 9 131 | 10 357 |
| Imports: All goods | 18 969 | 25 728 | 31 540 | 38 787 | 45 543 | 51 513 | 62 558 |
| Agriculture | 311 | 357 | 420 | 412 | 463 | 568 | 654 |
| Manufactures | 17 705 | 24 354 | 30 486 | 37 623 | 44 154 | 49 928 | 60 708 |
| Balance: All goods | -12 691 | -18 309 | -22 777 | -29 505 | -33 790 | -39 520 | -49 695 |
| **Hong Kong** | | | | | | | |
| Exports: All goods | 8 137 | 9 077 | 9 874 | 11 441 | 14 231 | 13 966 | 15 117 |
| Agriculture | 769 | 863 | 874 | 1 225 | 1 480 | 1 471 | 1 689 |
| Manufactures | 6 734 | 7 585 | 8 530 | 9 706 | 12 011 | 11 781 | 12 817 |
| Imports: All goods | 9 279 | 9 793 | 9 554 | 9 696 | 10 291 | 9 865 | 10 288 |
| Agriculture | 103 | 114 | 102 | 108 | 90 | 92 | 83 |
| Manufactures | 9 148 | 9 650 | 9 423 | 9 557 | 10 170 | 9 742 | 10 172 |
| Balance: All goods | -1 141 | -716 | 319 | 1 745 | 3 940 | 4 102 | 4 829 |

### Table C-5.   U.S. Trade in Goods by Country or Region, 1991–1997 —*Continued*

(Millions of dollars.)

| Country or region | 1991 | 1992 | 1993 | 1994 | 1995 | 1996 | 1997 |
|---|---|---|---|---|---|---|---|
| **India** | | | | | | | |
| Exports: All goods | 1 999 | 1 917 | 2 778 | 2 294 | 3 296 | 3 328 | 3 608 |
| Agriculture | 103 | 145 | 204 | 120 | 195 | 112 | 153 |
| Manufactures | 1 480 | 1 457 | 2 354 | 1 948 | 2 727 | 2 928 | 3 243 |
| Imports: All goods | 3 192 | 3 780 | 4 554 | 5 310 | 5 726 | 6 170 | 7 322 |
| Agriculture | 253 | 273 | 328 | 423 | 425 | 484 | 571 |
| Manufactures | 2 659 | 3 251 | 4 021 | 4 606 | 5 058 | 5 395 | 6 475 |
| Balance: All goods | -1 193 | -1 863 | -1 776 | -3 016 | -2 430 | -2 841 | -3 715 |
| **Indonesia** | | | | | | | |
| Exports: All goods | 1 891 | 2 779 | 2 770 | 2 809 | 3 360 | 3 977 | 4 522 |
| Agriculture | 298 | 342 | 342 | 480 | 811 | 847 | 770 |
| Manufactures | 1 364 | 2 159 | 2 169 | 2 045 | 2 251 | 2 856 | 3 461 |
| Imports: All goods | 3 241 | 4 529 | 5 435 | 6 547 | 7 435 | 8 250 | 9 188 |
| Agriculture | 680 | 829 | 810 | 1 003 | 1 411 | 1 529 | 1 531 |
| Manufactures | 1 891 | 2 942 | 3 838 | 4 508 | 5 146 | 5 831 | 6 813 |
| Balance: All goods | -1 349 | -1 750 | -2 665 | -3 738 | -4 076 | -4 273 | -4 666 |
| **Japan** | | | | | | | |
| Exports: All goods | 48 125 | 47 813 | 47 891 | 53 488 | 64 343 | 67 607 | 65 549 |
| Agriculture | 7 718 | 8 413 | 8 752 | 9 346 | 11 015 | 11 620 | 10 485 |
| Manufactures | 31 386 | 30 260 | 30 266 | 35 309 | 43 598 | 46 969 | 47 621 |
| Imports: All goods | 91 511 | 97 414 | 107 246 | 119 156 | 123 479 | 115 187 | 121 663 |
| Agriculture | 200 | 198 | 207 | 230 | 272 | 255 | 267 |
| Manufactures | 91 757 | 96 483 | 106 563 | 118 377 | 122 786 | 114 503 | 120 461 |
| Balance: All goods | -43 385 | -49 601 | -59 355 | -65 668 | -59 137 | -47 580 | -56 115 |
| **Macao** | | | | | | | |
| Exports: All goods | 10 | 20 | 27 | 21 | 30 | 30 | 65 |
| Agriculture | 1 | 1 | 1 | 1 | 1 | 0 | 1 |
| Manufactures | 10 | 18 | 27 | 20 | 29 | 29 | 65 |
| Imports: All goods | 581 | 721 | 668 | 791 | 895 | 858 | 1 021 |
| Agriculture | 3 | 1 | 0 | 0 | 0 | 0 | 0 |
| Manufactures | 575 | 715 | 663 | 786 | 892 | 855 | 1 019 |
| Balance: All goods | -570 | -702 | -641 | -770 | -865 | -828 | -956 |
| **Malaysia** | | | | | | | |
| Exports: All goods | 3 900 | 4 363 | 6 064 | 6 969 | 8 816 | 8 546 | 10 780 |
| Agriculture | 153 | 165 | 195 | 229 | 534 | 610 | 477 |
| Manufactures | 3 673 | 4 166 | 5 732 | 6 625 | 8 161 | 7 747 | 10 210 |
| Imports: All goods | 6 101 | 8 294 | 10 563 | 13 982 | 17 455 | 17 829 | 18 027 |
| Agriculture | 307 | 359 | 311 | 336 | 395 | 370 | 394 |
| Manufactures | 5 611 | 7 766 | 10 125 | 13 482 | 16 912 | 17 265 | 17 302 |
| Balance: All goods | -2 202 | -3 931 | -4 499 | -7 013 | -8 639 | -9 283 | -7 247 |
| **Mongolia** | | | | | | | |
| Exports: All goods | 12 | 2 | 17 | 6 | 14 | 4 | 34 |
| Agriculture | 4 | 0 | 14 | 3 | 0 | 0 | 2 |
| Manufactures | 9 | 2 | 2 | 3 | 14 | 4 | 32 |
| Imports: All goods | 1 | 7 | 34 | 27 | 23 | 31 | 42 |
| Agriculture | 1 | 2 | 5 | 2 | 0 | 2 | 2 |
| Manufactures | 0 | 4 | 28 | 22 | 22 | 26 | 35 |
| Balance: All goods | 11 | -4 | -17 | -20 | -9 | -27 | -8 |
| **Nepal** | | | | | | | |
| Exports: All goods | 6 | 5 | 6 | 7 | 10 | 9 | 27 |
| Agriculture | 1 | 0 | 0 | 0 | 0 | 1 | 0 |
| Manufactures | 5 | 4 | 5 | 7 | 9 | 8 | 26 |
| Imports: All goods | 55 | 73 | 91 | 117 | 96 | 117 | 114 |
| Agriculture | 2 | 2 | 4 | 2 | 2 | 8 | 3 |
| Manufactures | 47 | 71 | 87 | 115 | 94 | 109 | 110 |
| Balance: All goods | -49 | -68 | -85 | -109 | -86 | -108 | -87 |

## Table C-5. U.S. Trade in Goods by Country or Region, 1991–1997 —*Continued*

(Millions of dollars.)

| Country or region | 1991 | 1992 | 1993 | 1994 | 1995 | 1996 | 1997 |
|---|---|---|---|---|---|---|---|
| **Pakistan** | | | | | | | |
| Exports: All goods | 950 | 881 | 811 | 718 | 941 | 1 271 | 1 240 |
| Agriculture | 150 | 267 | 186 | 245 | 453 | 352 | 441 |
| Manufactures | 662 | 545 | 542 | 452 | 448 | 890 | 771 |
| Imports: All goods | 662 | 866 | 897 | 1 012 | 1 197 | 1 266 | 1 442 |
| Agriculture | 23 | 27 | 16 | 21 | 17 | 32 | 20 |
| Manufactures | 611 | 817 | 856 | 955 | 1 155 | 1 203 | 1 401 |
| Balance: All goods | 288 | 15 | -86 | -293 | -256 | 6 | -202 |
| **Philippines** | | | | | | | |
| Exports: All goods | 2 265 | 2 759 | 3 529 | 3 886 | 5 295 | 6 142 | 7 417 |
| Agriculture | 368 | 510 | 476 | 564 | 752 | 877 | 851 |
| Manufactures | 1 795 | 2 100 | 2 872 | 3 134 | 4 286 | 5 001 | 6 447 |
| Imports: All goods | 3 471 | 4 355 | 4 894 | 5 719 | 7 007 | 8 161 | 10 445 |
| Agriculture | 418 | 553 | 436 | 434 | 565 | 593 | 627 |
| Manufactures | 2 929 | 3 672 | 4 345 | 5 168 | 6 309 | 7 436 | 9 638 |
| Balance: All goods | -1 206 | -1 596 | -1 364 | -1 833 | -1 712 | -2 019 | -3 028 |
| **Singapore** | | | | | | | |
| Exports: All goods | 8 804 | 9 626 | 11 678 | 13 020 | 15 333 | 16 720 | 17 696 |
| Agriculture | 191 | 206 | 227 | 265 | 292 | 281 | 276 |
| Manufactures | 8 283 | 9 047 | 10 961 | 12 110 | 14 526 | 15 955 | 17 089 |
| Imports: All goods | 9 957 | 11 313 | 12 798 | 15 358 | 18 561 | 20 343 | 20 075 |
| Agriculture | 52 | 53 | 45 | 57 | 65 | 47 | 58 |
| Manufactures | 9 761 | 11 062 | 12 513 | 15 071 | 18 290 | 20 093 | 19 780 |
| Balance: All goods | -1 153 | -1 687 | -1 120 | -2 338 | -3 227 | -3 623 | -2 378 |
| **South Korea** | | | | | | | |
| Exports: All goods | 15 505 | 14 639 | 14 782 | 18 025 | 25 380 | 26 621 | 25 046 |
| Agriculture | 2 091 | 2 213 | 1 912 | 2 311 | 3 736 | 3 828 | 2 833 |
| Manufactures | 11 131 | 10 240 | 10 723 | 13 641 | 18 980 | 20 413 | 19 959 |
| Imports: All goods | 17 018 | 16 682 | 17 118 | 19 629 | 24 184 | 22 655 | 23 173 |
| Agriculture | 54 | 58 | 63 | 67 | 69 | 84 | 79 |
| Manufactures | 16 747 | 16 325 | 16 730 | 19 226 | 23 717 | 22 275 | 22 710 |
| Balance: All goods | -1 514 | -2 043 | -2 336 | -1 604 | 1 196 | 3 966 | 1 873 |
| **Sri Lanka** | | | | | | | |
| Exports: All goods | 121 | 178 | 203 | 198 | 279 | 211 | 155 |
| Agriculture | 61 | 95 | 110 | 92 | 156 | 92 | 40 |
| Manufactures | 59 | 81 | 90 | 103 | 120 | 117 | 113 |
| Imports: All goods | 604 | 789 | 1 002 | 1 093 | 1 260 | 1 393 | 1 620 |
| Agriculture | 19 | 20 | 21 | 25 | 30 | 29 | 32 |
| Manufactures | 583 | 767 | 977 | 1 063 | 1 225 | 1 355 | 1 584 |
| Balance: All goods | -483 | -612 | -798 | -895 | -981 | -1 182 | -1 465 |
| **Taiwan** | | | | | | | |
| Exports: All goods | 13 182 | 15 250 | 16 168 | 17 109 | 19 290 | 18 460 | 20 366 |
| Agriculture | 1 892 | 1 892 | 2 035 | 2 136 | 2 581 | 2 953 | 2 598 |
| Manufactures | 10 031 | 12 213 | 13 125 | 13 853 | 15 613 | 14 404 | 16 830 |
| Imports: All goods | 23 023 | 24 596 | 25 101 | 26 706 | 28 972 | 29 907 | 32 629 |
| Agriculture | 172 | 121 | 108 | 113 | 136 | 155 | 168 |
| Manufactures | 22 638 | 24 231 | 24 708 | 26 316 | 28 566 | 29 517 | 32 192 |
| Balance: All goods | -9 841 | -9 346 | -8 934 | -9 597 | -9 682 | -11 447 | -12 263 |
| **Thailand** | | | | | | | |
| Exports: All goods | 3 753 | 3 989 | 3 766 | 4 865 | 6 665 | 7 198 | 7 349 |
| Agriculture | 283 | 306 | 301 | 382 | 586 | 569 | 530 |
| Manufactures | 3 328 | 3 514 | 3 289 | 4 259 | 5 466 | 6 379 | 6 619 |
| Imports: All goods | 6 122 | 7 529 | 8 542 | 10 306 | 11 348 | 11 336 | 12 602 |
| Agriculture | 521 | 653 | 670 | 701 | 891 | 875 | 844 |
| Manufactures | 4 636 | 5 927 | 6 809 | 8 199 | 9 194 | 9 318 | 10 545 |
| Balance: All goods | -2 369 | -3 540 | -4 775 | -5 441 | -4 683 | -4 139 | -5 252 |

## Table C-5.  U.S. Trade in Goods by Country or Region, 1991–1997 *—Continued*

(Millions of dollars.)

| Country or region | 1991 | 1992 | 1993 | 1994 | 1995 | 1996 | 1997 |
|---|---|---|---|---|---|---|---|
| **Vietnam** | | | | | | | |
| Exports: All goods | 3 | 4 | 7 | 173 | 253 | 616 | 287 |
| Agriculture | 0 | 0 | 0 | 17 | 24 | 33 | 40 |
| Manufactures | 4 | 4 | 7 | 149 | 223 | 573 | 228 |
| Imports: All goods | 0 | 0 | 0 | 51 | 199 | 332 | 389 |
| Agriculture | 0 | 0 | 0 | 38 | 152 | 132 | 158 |
| Manufactures | 0 | 0 | 0 | 5 | 28 | 72 | 136 |
| Balance: All goods | 3 | 4 | 7 | 122 | 54 | 285 | -102 |
| **MIDDLE EAST** | | | | | | | |
| Exports: All goods | 15 315 | 16 873 | 16 821 | 16 045 | 17 537 | 19 967 | 20 928 |
| Agriculture | 1 204 | 1 307 | 1 512 | 1 458 | 1 882 | 1 815 | 1 785 |
| Manufactures | 13 241 | 14 767 | 14 446 | 13 618 | 14 496 | 17 132 | 18 221 |
| Imports: All goods | 15 813 | 15 726 | 15 387 | 15 812 | 16 567 | 19 852 | 20 403 |
| Agriculture | 79 | 85 | 92 | 78 | 103 | 122 | 126 |
| Manufactures | 3 803 | 4 335 | 5 129 | 6 226 | 6 980 | 7 781 | 9 146 |
| Balance: All goods | -497 | 1 147 | 1 434 | 234 | 970 | 115 | 526 |
| **Bahrain** | | | | | | | |
| Exports: All goods | 500 | 489 | 636 | 444 | 255 | 244 | 406 |
| Agriculture | 16 | 14 | 23 | 21 | 23 | 19 | 9 |
| Manufactures | 465 | 455 | 605 | 396 | 199 | 188 | 364 |
| Imports: All goods | 87 | 61 | 97 | 148 | 134 | 116 | 116 |
| Agriculture | 0 | 0 | 0 | 0 | 0 | 0 | 0 |
| Manufactures | 47 | 59 | 93 | 154 | 128 | 105 | 117 |
| Balance: All goods | 413 | 428 | 539 | 296 | 121 | 128 | 290 |
| **Iran** | | | | | | | |
| Exports: All goods | 527 | 747 | 616 | 329 | 277 | 0 | 1 |
| Agriculture | 13 | 51 | 115 | 86 | 136 | 0 | 0 |
| Manufactures | 478 | 680 | 488 | 233 | 136 | 0 | 1 |
| Imports: All goods | 231 | 1 | 0 | 1 | 0 | 0 | 0 |
| Agriculture | 0 | 0 | 0 | 0 | 0 | 0 | 0 |
| Manufactures | 4 | 1 | 0 | 1 | 0 | 0 | 0 |
| Balance: All goods | 297 | 747 | 616 | 328 | 277 | 0 | 1 |
| **Iraq** | | | | | | | |
| Exports: All goods | 0 | 0 | 4 | 1 | 0 | 3 | 82 |
| Agriculture | 0 | 0 | 3 | 0 | 0 | 3 | 82 |
| Manufactures | 0 | 0 | 1 | 0 | 0 | 0 | 0 |
| Imports: All goods | 6 | 0 | 0 | 0 | 0 | 0 | 312 |
| Agriculture | 0 | 0 | 0 | 0 | 0 | 0 | 0 |
| Manufactures | 0 | 0 | 0 | 0 | 0 | 0 | 0 |
| Balance: All goods | -6 | 0 | 4 | 1 | 0 | 3 | -230 |
| **Israel** | | | | | | | |
| Exports: All goods | 3 911 | 4 077 | 4 429 | 4 994 | 5 621 | 6 012 | 5 995 |
| Agriculture | 299 | 363 | 331 | 383 | 477 | 608 | 528 |
| Manufactures | 3 406 | 3 561 | 3 909 | 4 403 | 4 861 | 5 167 | 5 266 |
| Imports: All goods | 3 484 | 3 815 | 4 420 | 5 229 | 5 709 | 6 434 | 7 326 |
| Agriculture | 70 | 70 | 77 | 66 | 81 | 88 | 98 |
| Manufactures | 3 389 | 3 703 | 4 299 | 5 122 | 5 622 | 6 320 | 7 205 |
| Balance: All goods | 428 | 262 | 9 | -232 | -88 | -422 | -1 331 |
| **Jordan** | | | | | | | |
| Exports: All goods | 219 | 258 | 361 | 287 | 335 | 345 | 403 |
| Agriculture | 128 | 103 | 173 | 127 | 163 | 151 | 143 |
| Manufactures | 85 | 138 | 179 | 151 | 159 | 172 | 240 |
| Imports: All goods | 6 | 18 | 19 | 29 | 29 | 25 | 25 |
| Agriculture | 0 | 0 | 0 | 0 | 0 | 1 | 1 |
| Manufactures | 6 | 18 | 19 | 28 | 28 | 23 | 24 |
| Balance: All goods | 213 | 240 | 342 | 258 | 306 | 320 | 377 |

**Table C-5.  U.S. Trade in Goods by Country or Region, 1991–1997** *—Continued*

(Millions of dollars.)

| Country or region | 1991 | 1992 | 1993 | 1994 | 1995 | 1996 | 1997 |
|---|---|---|---|---|---|---|---|
| **Kuwait** | | | | | | | |
| Exports: All goods ........................................ | 1 228 | 1 337 | 999 | 1 176 | 1 437 | 1 984 | 1 390 |
| Agriculture ............................................. | 15 | 31 | 43 | 51 | 66 | 42 | 46 |
| Manufactures ......................................... | 1 190 | 1 256 | 921 | 1 071 | 1 302 | 1 888 | 1 298 |
| Imports: All goods ........................................ | 36 | 281 | 1 818 | 1 458 | 1 335 | 1 651 | 1 816 |
| Agriculture ............................................. | 0 | 0 | 0 | 0 | 0 | 0 | 0 |
| Manufactures ......................................... | 1 | 10 | 51 | 32 | 51 | 28 | 17 |
| Balance: All goods ....................................... | 1 192 | 1 055 | -819 | -282 | 102 | 332 | -426 |
| **Lebanon** | | | | | | | |
| Exports: All goods ........................................ | 165 | 311 | 377 | 442 | 592 | 627 | 552 |
| Agriculture ............................................. | 39 | 50 | 84 | 48 | 114 | 134 | 99 |
| Manufactures ......................................... | 102 | 137 | 191 | 219 | 271 | 286 | 258 |
| Imports: All goods ........................................ | 27 | 28 | 27 | 25 | 35 | 42 | 78 |
| Agriculture ............................................. | 5 | 6 | 6 | 5 | 15 | 23 | 19 |
| Manufactures ......................................... | 22 | 21 | 20 | 20 | 20 | 15 | 52 |
| Balance: All goods ....................................... | 138 | 283 | 350 | 417 | 557 | 586 | 474 |
| **Oman** | | | | | | | |
| Exports: All goods ........................................ | 202 | 257 | 251 | 219 | 222 | 217 | 341 |
| Agriculture ............................................. | 11 | 11 | 10 | 12 | 14 | 14 | 12 |
| Manufactures ......................................... | 184 | 223 | 215 | 199 | 195 | 193 | 317 |
| Imports: All goods ........................................ | 115 | 186 | 277 | 458 | 295 | 414 | 242 |
| Agriculture ............................................. | 0 | 0 | 0 | 0 | 0 | 0 | 0 |
| Manufactures ......................................... | 48 | 86 | 84 | 113 | 138 | 129 | 161 |
| Balance: All goods ....................................... | 87 | 72 | -26 | -239 | -73 | -198 | 98 |
| **Qatar** | | | | | | | |
| Exports: All goods ........................................ | 147 | 189 | 166 | 162 | 226 | 208 | 379 |
| Agriculture ............................................. | 5 | 6 | 7 | 6 | 9 | 6 | 7 |
| Manufactures ......................................... | 136 | 177 | 154 | 145 | 208 | 194 | 344 |
| Imports: All goods ........................................ | 30 | 70 | 65 | 81 | 91 | 157 | 157 |
| Agriculture ............................................. | 0 | 0 | 0 | 0 | 0 | 0 | 0 |
| Manufactures ......................................... | 30 | 66 | 62 | 76 | 77 | 157 | 130 |
| Balance: All goods ....................................... | 118 | 119 | 101 | 81 | 135 | 51 | 222 |
| **Saudi Arabia** | | | | | | | |
| Exports: All goods ........................................ | 6 557 | 7 167 | 6 661 | 6 013 | 6 155 | 7 311 | 8 438 |
| Agriculture ............................................. | 500 | 459 | 446 | 458 | 519 | 551 | 619 |
| Manufactures ......................................... | 5 689 | 6 457 | 5 932 | 5 279 | 5 288 | 6 468 | 7 555 |
| Imports: All goods ........................................ | 10 900 | 10 371 | 7 708 | 7 688 | 8 377 | 10 467 | 9 365 |
| Agriculture ............................................. | 0 | 1 | 1 | 0 | 1 | 1 | 1 |
| Manufactures ......................................... | 122 | 160 | 235 | 374 | 493 | 538 | 534 |
| Balance: All goods ....................................... | -4 343 | -3 205 | -1 047 | -1 675 | -2 222 | -3 156 | -927 |
| **Syria** | | | | | | | |
| Exports: All goods ........................................ | 209 | 165 | 186 | 198 | 223 | 226 | 180 |
| Agriculture ............................................. | 38 | 29 | 23 | 22 | 69 | 50 | 63 |
| Manufactures ......................................... | 162 | 137 | 145 | 134 | 131 | 153 | 104 |
| Imports: All goods ........................................ | 25 | 42 | 130 | 64 | 61 | 15 | 28 |
| Agriculture ............................................. | 2 | 5 | 4 | 3 | 4 | 5 | 4 |
| Manufactures ......................................... | 4 | 7 | 10 | 8 | 11 | 10 | 11 |
| Balance: All goods ....................................... | 184 | 123 | 56 | 134 | 162 | 211 | 153 |
| **United Arab Emirates** | | | | | | | |
| Exports: All goods ........................................ | 1 455 | 1 553 | 1 811 | 1 599 | 2 006 | 2 533 | 2 607 |
| Agriculture ............................................. | 71 | 71 | 95 | 112 | 158 | 123 | 112 |
| Manufactures ......................................... | 1 220 | 1 344 | 1 549 | 1 343 | 1 693 | 2 288 | 2 384 |
| Imports: All goods ........................................ | 713 | 812 | 727 | 449 | 459 | 499 | 920 |
| Agriculture ............................................. | 0 | 1 | 1 | 0 | 1 | 1 | 1 |
| Manufactures ......................................... | 130 | 204 | 255 | 290 | 410 | 454 | 894 |
| Balance: All goods ....................................... | 742 | 741 | 1 084 | 1 150 | 1 547 | 2 034 | 1 687 |

**Table C-5.  U.S. Trade in Goods by Country or Region, 1991–1997** *—Continued*

(Millions of dollars.)

| Country or region | 1991 | 1992 | 1993 | 1994 | 1995 | 1996 | 1997 |
|---|---|---|---|---|---|---|---|
| **Yemen Arab Republic** | | | | | | | |
| Exports: All goods | 191 | 322 | 322 | 178 | 186 | 256 | 153 |
| Agriculture | 67 | 119 | 160 | 132 | 133 | 114 | 65 |
| Manufactures | 123 | 202 | 157 | 44 | 51 | 133 | 87 |
| Imports: All goods | 152 | 41 | 98 | 183 | 42 | 31 | 16 |
| Agriculture | 1 | 2 | 2 | 3 | 2 | 3 | 3 |
| Manufactures | 0 | 1 | 2 | 6 | 3 | 0 | 0 |
| Balance: All goods | 40 | 281 | 224 | -5 | 144 | 225 | 137 |
| **AUSTRALIA AND OCEANIA** | | | | | | | |
| Exports: All goods | 9 797 | 10 682 | 9 938 | 11 687 | 12 794 | 14 087 | 14 450 |
| Agriculture | 379 | 378 | 455 | 522 | 485 | 463 | 525 |
| Manufactures | 8 960 | 9 904 | 9 074 | 10 812 | 11 920 | 13 170 | 13 474 |
| Imports: All goods | 5 337 | 5 097 | 4 752 | 4 914 | 5 085 | 5 601 | 6 465 |
| Agriculture | 1 902 | 1 895 | 1 724 | 1 559 | 1 528 | 1 511 | 1 718 |
| Manufactures | 2 032 | 1 939 | 1 848 | 2 322 | 2 410 | 2 771 | 3 257 |
| Balance: All goods | 4 460 | 5 585 | 5 186 | 6 773 | 7 709 | 8 485 | 7 986 |
| **Australia** | | | | | | | |
| Exports: All goods | 8 404 | 8 876 | 8 276 | 9 781 | 10 789 | 12 008 | 12 063 |
| Agriculture | 270 | 254 | 313 | 387 | 323 | 301 | 331 |
| Manufactures | 7 772 | 8 327 | 7 620 | 9 104 | 10 157 | 11 347 | 11 380 |
| Imports: All goods | 3 988 | 3 688 | 3 297 | 3 202 | 3 323 | 3 869 | 4 602 |
| Agriculture | 1 159 | 1 130 | 1 026 | 896 | 798 | 794 | 917 |
| Manufactures | 1 609 | 1 510 | 1 417 | 1 615 | 1 638 | 2 035 | 2 437 |
| Balance: All goods | 4 416 | 5 188 | 4 979 | 6 579 | 7 466 | 8 140 | 7 461 |
| **French Pacific Islands** | | | | | | | |
| Exports: All goods | 124 | 118 | 125 | 99 | 105 | 118 | 140 |
| Agriculture | 24 | 26 | 26 | 26 | 28 | 35 | 37 |
| Manufactures | 61 | 63 | 82 | 54 | 60 | 65 | 80 |
| Imports: All goods | 33 | 26 | 33 | 37 | 54 | 72 | 87 |
| Agriculture | 0 | 0 | 0 | 2 | 1 | 0 | 5 |
| Manufactures | 32 | 23 | 29 | 26 | 36 | 45 | 48 |
| Balance: All goods | 91 | 92 | 92 | 62 | 51 | 46 | 52 |
| **New Zealand** | | | | | | | |
| Exports: All goods | 1 007 | 1 307 | 1 249 | 1 508 | 1 691 | 1 729 | 1 962 |
| Agriculture | 50 | 60 | 77 | 73 | 96 | 88 | 112 |
| Manufactures | 914 | 1 185 | 1 129 | 1 399 | 1 543 | 1 573 | 1 782 |
| Imports: All goods | 1 209 | 1 218 | 1 208 | 1 421 | 1 452 | 1 463 | 1 579 |
| Agriculture | 708 | 720 | 654 | 623 | 690 | 676 | 755 |
| Manufactures | 338 | 329 | 315 | 569 | 554 | 604 | 658 |
| Balance: All goods | -202 | 89 | 41 | 87 | 240 | 265 | 383 |
| **New Zealand Island Dependencies** | | | | | | | |
| Exports: All goods | 4 | 3 | 3 | 2 | 33 | 32 | 39 |
| Agriculture | 0 | 1 | 0 | 0 | 0 | 0 | 0 |
| Manufactures | 4 | 3 | 3 | 2 | 32 | 32 | 38 |
| Imports: All goods | 4 | 1 | 6 | 6 | 7 | 3 | 4 |
| Agriculture | 1 | 0 | 4 | 0 | 1 | 0 | 0 |
| Manufactures | 3 | 1 | 2 | 3 | 6 | 4 | 3 |
| Balance: All goods | 1 | 1 | -3 | -4 | 25 | 29 | 35 |
| **Papua New Guinea** | | | | | | | |
| Exports: All goods | 96 | 72 | 50 | 66 | 51 | 69 | 117 |
| Agriculture | 1 | 1 | 2 | 2 | 7 | 4 | 6 |
| Manufactures | 92 | 70 | 49 | 63 | 44 | 65 | 110 |
| Imports: All goods | 34 | 64 | 98 | 115 | 50 | 86 | 65 |
| Agriculture | 23 | 26 | 25 | 26 | 27 | 25 | 26 |
| Manufactures | 11 | 1 | 2 | 1 | 1 | 1 | 8 |
| Balance: All goods | 61 | 8 | -47 | -49 | 1 | -16 | 52 |

**Table C-5.  U.S. Trade in Goods by Country or Region, 1991–1997** —*Continued*

(Millions of dollars.)

| Country or region | 1991 | 1992 | 1993 | 1994 | 1995 | 1996 | 1997 |
|---|---|---|---|---|---|---|---|
| **Southern Pacific Islands** | | | | | | | |
| Exports: All goods | 33 | 90 | 34 | 26 | 9 | 12 | 6 |
| Agriculture | 1 | 2 | 0 | 0 | 0 | 0 | 1 |
| Manufactures | 32 | 88 | 34 | 25 | 6 | 12 | 5 |
| Imports: All goods | 3 | 7 | 9 | 5 | 6 | 3 | 4 |
| Agriculture | 1 | 0 | 0 | 0 | 0 | 1 | 0 |
| Manufactures | 1 | 1 | 3 | 1 | 1 | 2 | 1 |
| Balance: All goods | 30 | 84 | 26 | 20 | 3 | 8 | 1 |
| **Trust Territory (former)** | | | | | | | |
| Exports: All goods | 97 | 76 | 70 | 66 | 63 | 71 | 68 |
| Agriculture | 26 | 28 | 28 | 25 | 21 | 22 | 27 |
| Manufactures | 63 | 40 | 36 | 36 | 36 | 42 | 37 |
| Imports: All goods | 9 | 21 | 27 | 24 | 30 | 24 | 32 |
| Agriculture | 1 | 1 | 1 | 2 | 3 | 2 | 3 |
| Manufactures | 7 | 17 | 22 | 17 | 26 | 22 | 38 |
| Balance: All goods | 88 | 55 | 43 | 42 | 33 | 47 | 36 |
| **Western Samoa** | | | | | | | |
| Exports: All goods | 7 | 73 | 10 | 7 | 8 | 12 | 11 |
| Agriculture | 2 | 3 | 4 | 4 | 3 | 5 | 4 |
| Manufactures | 4 | 69 | 6 | 3 | 4 | 6 | 6 |
| Imports: All goods | 1 | 1 | 1 | 0 | 0 | 1 | 3 |
| Agriculture | 1 | 0 | 1 | 0 | 0 | 0 | 0 |
| Manufactures | 0 | 0 | 0 | 0 | 0 | 0 | 2 |
| Balance: All goods | 6 | 72 | 9 | 7 | 7 | 11 | 9 |
| **Other Pacific Islands** | | | | | | | |
| Exports: All goods | 23 | 65 | 117 | 124 | 40 | 34 | 41 |
| Agriculture | 4 | 4 | 4 | 6 | 6 | 7 | 7 |
| Manufactures | 16 | 56 | 113 | 117 | 32 | 25 | 33 |
| Imports: All goods | 49 | 72 | 73 | 103 | 84 | 79 | 88 |
| Agriculture | 8 | 17 | 12 | 9 | 9 | 13 | 12 |
| Manufactures | 32 | 55 | 58 | 89 | 68 | 58 | 60 |
| Balance: All goods | -26 | -7 | 44 | 21 | -44 | -45 | -46 |
| **AFRICA** | | | | | | | |
| Exports: All goods | 8 820 | 9 907 | 9 428 | 9 219 | 9 904 | 10 615 | 11 390 |
| Agriculture | 1 858 | 2 500 | 2 381 | 2 413 | 2 829 | 2 712 | 2 255 |
| Manufactures | 6 464 | 6 869 | 6 411 | 6 330 | 6 431 | 7 133 | 8 443 |
| Imports: All goods | 14 002 | 14 346 | 14 798 | 14 091 | 15 481 | 18 744 | 19 925 |
| Agriculture | 661 | 589 | 621 | 665 | 694 | 903 | 897 |
| Manufactures | 2 315 | 2 386 | 2 632 | 2 986 | 3 281 | 3 338 | 3 797 |
| Balance: All goods | -5 182 | -4 439 | -5 370 | -4 872 | -5 577 | -8 129 | -8 535 |
| **Algeria** | | | | | | | |
| Exports: All goods | 727 | 688 | 938 | 1 192 | 774 | 635 | 692 |
| Agriculture | 427 | 368 | 479 | 586 | 410 | 294 | 316 |
| Manufactures | 256 | 258 | 372 | 580 | 339 | 321 | 361 |
| Imports: All goods | 2 103 | 1 586 | 1 583 | 1 527 | 1 750 | 2 126 | 2 440 |
| Agriculture | 0 | 0 | 0 | 0 | 0 | 0 | 1 |
| Manufactures | 3 | 1 | 7 | 4 | 6 | 30 | 30 |
| Balance: All goods | -1 376 | -898 | -645 | -335 | -976 | -1 491 | -1 748 |
| **Angola** | | | | | | | |
| Exports: All goods | 186 | 158 | 174 | 197 | 260 | 268 | 281 |
| Agriculture | 16 | 11 | 8 | 37 | 33 | 28 | 28 |
| Manufactures | 169 | 134 | 158 | 155 | 220 | 231 | 242 |
| Imports: All goods | 1 775 | 2 303 | 2 092 | 2 061 | 2 232 | 2 902 | 2 779 |
| Agriculture | 0 | 0 | 0 | 0 | 0 | 0 | 0 |
| Manufactures | 11 | 11 | 8 | 12 | 10 | 9 | 6 |
| Balance: All goods | -1 589 | -2 145 | -1 918 | -1 864 | -1 973 | -2 633 | -2 499 |

### Table C-5.  U.S. Trade in Goods by Country or Region, 1991–1997 —Continued

(Millions of dollars.)

| Country or region | 1991 | 1992 | 1993 | 1994 | 1995 | 1996 | 1997 |
|---|---|---|---|---|---|---|---|
| **Benin** | | | | | | | |
| Exports: All goods | 26 | 27 | 22 | 26 | 34 | 27 | 52 |
| Agriculture | 9 | 13 | 6 | 8 | 10 | 2 | 5 |
| Manufactures | 6 | 6 | 6 | 7 | 17 | 13 | 29 |
| Imports: All goods | 23 | 10 | 16 | 10 | 10 | 14 | 8 |
| Agriculture | 0 | 0 | 0 | 1 | 1 | 1 | 1 |
| Manufactures | 0 | 0 | 1 | 2 | 1 | 5 | 1 |
| Balance: All goods | 4 | 18 | 7 | 16 | 24 | 14 | 44 |
| **Botswana** | | | | | | | |
| Exports: All goods | 31 | 47 | 25 | 23 | 36 | 29 | 43 |
| Agriculture | 0 | 2 | 0 | 1 | 4 | 1 | 3 |
| Manufactures | 31 | 45 | 24 | 22 | 32 | 27 | 40 |
| Imports: All goods | 13 | 12 | 8 | 14 | 21 | 27 | 25 |
| Agriculture | 0 | 0 | 1 | 0 | 0 | 0 | 0 |
| Manufactures | 13 | 12 | 7 | 13 | 21 | 27 | 25 |
| Balance: All goods | 18 | 34 | 17 | 9 | 15 | 2 | 19 |
| **Burkina Faso** | | | | | | | |
| Exports: All goods | 24 | 13 | 18 | 7 | 15 | 10 | 18 |
| Agriculture | 16 | 6 | 8 | 2 | 6 | 3 | 6 |
| Manufactures | 5 | 5 | 8 | 4 | 5 | 5 | 10 |
| Imports: All goods | 1 | 0 | 0 | 0 | 0 | 4 | 1 |
| Agriculture | 0 | 0 | 0 | 0 | 0 | 4 | 0 |
| Manufactures | 1 | 0 | 0 | 0 | 0 | 0 | 1 |
| Balance: All goods | 23 | 13 | 17 | 7 | 14 | 7 | 17 |
| **Burundi** | | | | | | | |
| Exports: All goods | 2 | 10 | 2 | 18 | 3 | 2 | 1 |
| Agriculture | 0 | 0 | 0 | 15 | 0 | 0 | 0 |
| Manufactures | 2 | 9 | 2 | 2 | 2 | 1 | 1 |
| Imports: All goods | 8 | 8 | 3 | 8 | 21 | 2 | 14 |
| Agriculture | 8 | 6 | 1 | 3 | 18 | 1 | 14 |
| Manufactures | 0 | 0 | 0 | 2 | 0 | 0 | 0 |
| Balance: All goods | -6 | 1 | 0 | 10 | -18 | 0 | -13 |
| **Cameroon** | | | | | | | |
| Exports: All goods | 45 | 57 | 49 | 54 | 46 | 71 | 121 |
| Agriculture | 13 | 22 | 21 | 11 | 3 | 3 | 12 |
| Manufactures | 27 | 31 | 23 | 39 | 37 | 59 | 105 |
| Imports: All goods | 127 | 84 | 101 | 55 | 57 | 65 | 57 |
| Agriculture | 8 | 7 | 8 | 9 | 19 | 21 | 20 |
| Manufactures | 3 | 2 | 2 | 5 | 5 | 7 | 9 |
| Balance: All goods | -81 | -27 | -53 | -1 | -12 | 7 | 64 |
| **Central African Republic** | | | | | | | |
| Exports: All goods | 1 | 1 | 5 | 3 | 6 | 4 | 4 |
| Agriculture | 0 | 0 | 1 | 0 | 0 | 0 | 1 |
| Manufactures | 1 | 1 | 4 | 2 | 6 | 3 | 3 |
| Imports: All goods | 1 | 1 | 1 | 0 | 0 | 0 | 1 |
| Agriculture | 1 | 1 | 1 | 0 | 0 | 0 | 1 |
| Manufactures | 0 | 0 | 0 | 0 | 0 | 0 | 0 |
| Balance: All goods | 0 | 0 | 4 | 2 | 6 | 4 | 2 |
| **Chad** | | | | | | | |
| Exports: All goods | 14 | 5 | 8 | 8 | 11 | 3 | 3 |
| Agriculture | 5 | 0 | 1 | 1 | 1 | 2 | 2 |
| Manufactures | 8 | 5 | 7 | 7 | 10 | 1 | 1 |
| Imports: All goods | 0 | 0 | 0 | 1 | 3 | 7 | 3 |
| Agriculture | 0 | 0 | 0 | 1 | 0 | 0 | 0 |
| Manufactures | 0 | 0 | 0 | 0 | 0 | 2 | 0 |
| Balance: All goods | 14 | 5 | 8 | 6 | 8 | -4 | 0 |

**Table C-5. U.S. Trade in Goods by Country or Region, 1991–1997** —*Continued*

(Millions of dollars.)

| Country or region | 1991 | 1992 | 1993 | 1994 | 1995 | 1996 | 1997 |
|---|---|---|---|---|---|---|---|
| **Congo** | | | | | | | |
| Exports: All goods | 43 | 59 | 27 | 38 | 55 | 63 | 75 |
| Agriculture | 2 | 6 | 0 | 6 | 6 | 7 | 5 |
| Manufactures | 41 | 53 | 27 | 31 | 48 | 55 | 65 |
| Imports: All goods | 410 | 511 | 500 | 403 | 207 | 315 | 472 |
| Agriculture | 0 | 3 | 3 | 0 | 0 | 3 | 7 |
| Manufactures | 6 | 3 | 4 | 15 | 19 | 24 | 18 |
| Balance: All goods | -366 | -452 | -473 | -365 | -152 | -252 | -397 |
| **Democratic Republic of the Congo** | | | | | | | |
| Exports: All goods | 62 | 33 | 35 | 40 | 77 | 73 | 38 |
| Agriculture | 15 | 8 | 10 | 10 | 31 | 24 | 14 |
| Manufactures | 40 | 19 | 18 | 22 | 34 | 39 | 18 |
| Imports: All goods | 294 | 250 | 238 | 180 | 267 | 259 | 282 |
| Agriculture | 3 | 5 | 2 | 1 | 5 | 3 | 2 |
| Manufactures | 117 | 123 | 97 | 70 | 121 | 116 | 125 |
| Balance: All goods | -232 | -218 | -203 | -140 | -190 | -185 | -244 |
| **Djibouti** | | | | | | | |
| Exports: All goods | 10 | 11 | 13 | 7 | 8 | 8 | 7 |
| Agriculture | 2 | 2 | 2 | 2 | 3 | 2 | 2 |
| Manufactures | 4 | 4 | 4 | 3 | 2 | 2 | 2 |
| Imports: All goods | 0 | 0 | 0 | 0 | 0 | ..... | 0 |
| Agriculture | 0 | 0 | 0 | 0 | 0 | 0 | 0 |
| Manufactures | 0 | 0 | 0 | 0 | 0 | 0 | 0 |
| Balance: All goods | 10 | 11 | 13 | 7 | 8 | 8 | 7 |
| **Egypt** | | | | | | | |
| Exports: All goods | 2 720 | 3 088 | 2 768 | 2 855 | 2 985 | 3 153 | 3 835 |
| Agriculture | 701 | 763 | 646 | 850 | 1 309 | 1 255 | 964 |
| Manufactures | 1 901 | 2 201 | 2 011 | 1 882 | 1 523 | 1 723 | 2 710 |
| Imports: All goods | 206 | 434 | 613 | 549 | 606 | 681 | 658 |
| Agriculture | 10 | 11 | 10 | 15 | 15 | 25 | 13 |
| Manufactures | 153 | 198 | 240 | 325 | 415 | 411 | 545 |
| Balance: All goods | 2 515 | 2 654 | 2 155 | 2 306 | 2 379 | 2 473 | 3 178 |
| **Equatorial Guinea** | | | | | | | |
| Exports: All goods | 13 | 11 | 3 | 2 | 5 | 17 | 47 |
| Agriculture | 2 | 2 | 0 | 0 | 0 | 0 | 0 |
| Manufactures | 10 | 8 | 3 | 2 | 5 | 17 | 47 |
| Imports: All goods | 0 | 0 | 0 | 0 | 31 | 76 | 30 |
| Agriculture | 0 | 0 | 0 | 0 | 0 | 0 | 0 |
| Manufactures | 0 | 0 | 0 | 0 | 3 | 1 | 2 |
| Balance: All goods | 12 | 11 | 3 | 2 | -26 | -59 | 17 |
| **Ethiopia and Eritrea** | | | | | | | |
| Exports: All goods | 210 | 250 | 140 | 152 | 164 | 162 | 138 |
| Agriculture | 59 | 66 | 69 | 91 | 65 | 43 | 21 |
| Manufactures | 151 | 183 | 67 | 59 | 97 | 116 | 114 |
| Imports: All goods | 15 | 9 | 22 | 34 | 33 | 36 | 71 |
| Agriculture | 9 | 7 | 20 | 32 | 31 | 24 | 66 |
| Manufactures | 6 | 1 | 2 | 2 | 2 | 9 | 3 |
| Balance: All goods | 196 | 241 | 118 | 118 | 131 | 126 | 67 |
| **Gabon** | | | | | | | |
| Exports: All goods | 85 | 55 | 48 | 40 | 54 | 56 | 85 |
| Agriculture | 1 | 1 | 1 | 1 | 1 | 0 | 1 |
| Manufactures | 83 | 53 | 46 | 37 | 53 | 54 | 81 |
| Imports: All goods | 712 | 921 | 961 | 1 134 | 1 464 | 1 984 | 2 202 |
| Agriculture | 4 | 3 | 1 | 1 | 1 | 1 | 0 |
| Manufactures | 3 | 2 | 1 | 2 | 2 | 4 | 6 |
| Balance: All goods | -627 | -866 | -913 | -1 094 | -1 410 | -1 928 | -2 118 |

## Table C-5.   U.S. Trade in Goods by Country or Region, 1991–1997 —*Continued*

(Millions of dollars.)

| Country or region | 1991 | 1992 | 1993 | 1994 | 1995 | 1996 | 1997 |
|---|---|---|---|---|---|---|---|
| **Gambia** | | | | | | | |
| Exports: All goods | 11 | 10 | 10 | 4 | 6 | 9 | 10 |
| Agriculture | 2 | 2 | 2 | 1 | 2 | 2 | 2 |
| Manufactures | 6 | 6 | 5 | 2 | 3 | 5 | 6 |
| Imports: All goods | 2 | 1 | 2 | 2 | 2 | 2 | 3 |
| Agriculture | 0 | 0 | 6 | 0 | 0 | 0 | 0 |
| Manufactures | 2 | 1 | 2 | 2 | 2 | 2 | 3 |
| Balance: All goods | 9 | 9 | 8 | 2 | 4 | 7 | 7 |
| **Ghana** | | | | | | | |
| Exports: All goods | 141 | 124 | 215 | 125 | 167 | 296 | 315 |
| Agriculture | 15 | 26 | 43 | 36 | 45 | 64 | 51 |
| Manufactures | 85 | 77 | 160 | 79 | 104 | 206 | 233 |
| Imports: All goods | 152 | 96 | 216 | 199 | 196 | 171 | 155 |
| Agriculture | 67 | 30 | 48 | 13 | 55 | 32 | 13 |
| Manufactures | 59 | 38 | 133 | 153 | 129 | 114 | 118 |
| Balance: All goods | -11 | 27 | 0 | -74 | -29 | 124 | 160 |
| **Guinea** | | | | | | | |
| Exports: All goods | 88 | 60 | 59 | 50 | 67 | 87 | 83 |
| Agriculture | 11 | 13 | 14 | 12 | 15 | 12 | 10 |
| Manufactures | 48 | 31 | 29 | 30 | 34 | 59 | 61 |
| Imports: All goods | 138 | 102 | 117 | 92 | 99 | 117 | 128 |
| Agriculture | 0 | 1 | 1 | 0 | 0 | 2 | 6 |
| Manufactures | 7 | 8 | 7 | 4 | 5 | 6 | 12 |
| Balance: All goods | -50 | -42 | -58 | -42 | -32 | -29 | -45 |
| **Ivory Coast** | | | | | | | |
| Exports: All goods | 81 | 87 | 89 | 111 | 173 | 141 | 151 |
| Agriculture | 27 | 26 | 25 | 23 | 37 | 20 | 18 |
| Manufactures | 45 | 57 | 58 | 84 | 127 | 110 | 124 |
| Imports: All goods | 223 | 187 | 178 | 185 | 214 | 397 | 289 |
| Agriculture | 172 | 143 | 137 | 150 | 180 | 310 | 238 |
| Manufactures | 30 | 22 | 18 | 28 | 28 | 32 | 16 |
| Balance: All goods | -141 | -100 | -90 | -74 | -41 | -256 | -138 |
| **Kenya** | | | | | | | |
| Exports: All goods | 91 | 124 | 131 | 170 | 114 | 105 | 225 |
| Agriculture | 8 | 48 | 29 | 58 | 34 | 10 | 31 |
| Manufactures | 81 | 75 | 84 | 108 | 76 | 89 | 188 |
| Imports: All goods | 69 | 73 | 92 | 109 | 101 | 107 | 114 |
| Agriculture | 42 | 37 | 42 | 51 | 46 | 55 | 56 |
| Manufactures | 22 | 28 | 41 | 56 | 54 | 46 | 57 |
| Balance: All goods | 22 | 51 | 39 | 61 | 13 | -2 | 111 |
| **Lesotho** | | | | | | | |
| Exports: All goods | 3 | 3 | 7 | 3 | 2 | 3 | 2 |
| Agriculture | 2 | 2 | 2 | 3 | 1 | 2 | 1 |
| Manufactures | 2 | 1 | 1 | 1 | 0 | 1 | 1 |
| Imports: All goods | 27 | 53 | 56 | 63 | 62 | 65 | 87 |
| Agriculture | 0 | 0 | 0 | 0 | 0 | 0 | 0 |
| Manufactures | 27 | 53 | 56 | 63 | 62 | 65 | 86 |
| Balance: All goods | -24 | -50 | -48 | -60 | -60 | -63 | -84 |
| **Liberia** | | | | | | | |
| Exports: All goods | 47 | 31 | 39 | 46 | 42 | 50 | 43 |
| Agriculture | 37 | 14 | 13 | 36 | 30 | 35 | 18 |
| Manufactures | 9 | 14 | 5 | 9 | 8 | 13 | 20 |
| Imports: All goods | 9 | 12 | 3 | 4 | 10 | 27 | 5 |
| Agriculture | 6 | 9 | 1 | 1 | 0 | 0 | 2 |
| Manufactures | 3 | 2 | 2 | 2 | 10 | 27 | 3 |
| Balance: All goods | 38 | 18 | 36 | 43 | 32 | 23 | 38 |

### Table C-5.  U.S. Trade in Goods by Country or Region, 1991–1997 —*Continued*

(Millions of dollars.)

| Country or region | 1991 | 1992 | 1993 | 1994 | 1995 | 1996 | 1997 |
|---|---|---|---|---|---|---|---|
| **Madagascar** | | | | | | | |
| Exports: All goods | 14 | 6 | 11 | 48 | 10 | 12 | 12 |
|     Agriculture | 8 | 2 | 4 | 2 | 3 | 2 | 5 |
|     Manufactures | 7 | 4 | 7 | 46 | 7 | 10 | 7 |
| Imports: All goods | 47 | 53 | 43 | 57 | 57 | 46 | 63 |
|     Agriculture | 42 | 48 | 36 | 47 | 39 | 26 | 40 |
|     Manufactures | 2 | 2 | 4 | 7 | 14 | 15 | 19 |
| Balance: All goods | -33 | -47 | -32 | -9 | -47 | -34 | -51 |
| **Malawi** | | | | | | | |
| Exports: All goods | 55 | 14 | 26 | 19 | 18 | 13 | 18 |
|     Agriculture | 9 | 2 | 6 | 4 | 8 | 0 | 0 |
|     Manufactures | 46 | 12 | 10 | 15 | 10 | 10 | 15 |
| Imports: All goods | 72 | 60 | 58 | 57 | 41 | 73 | 83 |
|     Agriculture | 66 | 49 | 51 | 53 | 38 | 71 | 82 |
|     Manufactures | 6 | 9 | 8 | 4 | 3 | 2 | 0 |
| Balance: All goods | -18 | -46 | -32 | -38 | -23 | -59 | -65 |
| **Mali** | | | | | | | |
| Exports: All goods | 18 | 11 | 33 | 19 | 23 | 18 | 26 |
|     Agriculture | 9 | 2 | 0 | 1 | 0 | 0 | 3 |
|     Manufactures | 6 | 4 | 29 | 17 | 19 | 16 | 18 |
| Imports: All goods | 2 | 1 | 1 | 6 | 4 | 5 | 4 |
|     Agriculture | 0 | 0 | 0 | 0 | 0 | 1 | 0 |
|     Manufactures | 1 | 1 | 1 | 4 | 5 | 4 | 4 |
| Balance: All goods | 17 | 10 | 31 | 13 | 20 | 14 | 22 |
| **Mauritania** | | | | | | | |
| Exports: All goods | 22 | 59 | 20 | 14 | 43 | 15 | 21 |
|     Agriculture | 4 | 3 | 4 | 1 | 1 | 1 | 3 |
|     Manufactures | 15 | 51 | 15 | 8 | 16 | 10 | 9 |
| Imports: All goods | 11 | 9 | 6 | 4 | 6 | 5 | 0 |
|     Agriculture | 0 | 0 | 0 | 0 | 0 | 0 | 0 |
|     Manufactures | 1 | 2 | 1 | 0 | 0 | 0 | 0 |
| Balance: All goods | 10 | 51 | 13 | 11 | 38 | 10 | 21 |
| **Mauritius** | | | | | | | |
| Exports: All goods | 15 | 22 | 18 | 24 | 25 | 25 | 31 |
|     Agriculture | 0 | 0 | 1 | 0 | 0 | 0 | 0 |
|     Manufactures | 14 | 21 | 17 | 22 | 24 | 25 | 31 |
| Imports: All goods | 132 | 136 | 198 | 217 | 230 | 217 | 238 |
|     Agriculture | 16 | 2 | 14 | 11 | 8 | 14 | 16 |
|     Manufactures | 113 | 134 | 182 | 207 | 219 | 193 | 208 |
| Balance: All goods | -117 | -113 | -180 | -193 | -205 | -192 | -207 |
| **Morocco** | | | | | | | |
| Exports: All goods | 404 | 496 | 600 | 409 | 517 | 476 | 435 |
|     Agriculture | 132 | 164 | 307 | 136 | 156 | 233 | 162 |
|     Manufactures | 195 | 269 | 231 | 205 | 262 | 136 | 211 |
| Imports: All goods | 154 | 178 | 185 | 192 | 239 | 247 | 296 |
|     Agriculture | 40 | 36 | 33 | 25 | 40 | 46 | 49 |
|     Manufactures | 62 | 72 | 93 | 90 | 110 | 129 | 166 |
| Balance: All goods | 250 | 318 | 415 | 217 | 278 | 229 | 139 |
| **Mozambique** | | | | | | | |
| Exports: All goods | 101 | 150 | 59 | 39 | 49 | 23 | 46 |
|     Agriculture | 22 | 70 | 25 | 19 | 28 | 10 | 26 |
|     Manufactures | 77 | 79 | 11 | 18 | 17 | 10 | 13 |
| Imports: All goods | 23 | 19 | 9 | 15 | 28 | 27 | 31 |
|     Agriculture | 21 | 19 | 7 | 14 | 24 | 25 | 28 |
|     Manufactures | 1 | 1 | 2 | 1 | 1 | 1 | 2 |
| Balance: All goods | 78 | 130 | 50 | 24 | 22 | -4 | 15 |

## Table C-5.  U.S. Trade in Goods by Country or Region, 1991–1997 —*Continued*

(Millions of dollars.)

| Country or region | 1991 | 1992 | 1993 | 1994 | 1995 | 1996 | 1997 |
|---|---|---|---|---|---|---|---|
| **Namibia** | | | | | | | |
| Exports: All goods | 33 | 34 | 22 | 16 | 26 | 23 | 25 |
| Agriculture | 0 | 2 | 9 | 1 | 5 | 5 | 1 |
| Manufactures | 32 | 32 | 10 | 15 | 22 | 17 | 25 |
| Imports: All goods | 35 | 23 | 22 | 28 | 11 | 27 | 63 |
| Agriculture | 1 | 4 | 6 | 3 | 1 | 0 | 0 |
| Manufactures | 25 | 16 | 12 | 20 | 8 | 14 | 32 |
| Balance: All goods | -3 | 11 | -1 | -11 | 15 | -5 | -38 |
| **Niger** | | | | | | | |
| Exports: All goods | 10 | 13 | 16 | 12 | 40 | 27 | 25 |
| Agriculture | 4 | 3 | 2 | 1 | 2 | 1 | 2 |
| Manufactures | 5 | 8 | 12 | 5 | 28 | 7 | 8 |
| Imports: All goods | 5 | 3 | 3 | 2 | 2 | 1 | 30 |
| Agriculture | 0 | 0 | 0 | 0 | 0 | 0 | 0 |
| Manufactures | 3 | 3 | 3 | 2 | 1 | 1 | 41 |
| Balance: All goods | 5 | 10 | 13 | 10 | 38 | 27 | -5 |
| **Nigeria** | | | | | | | |
| Exports: All goods | 831 | 1 001 | 895 | 509 | 603 | 818 | 813 |
| Agriculture | 36 | 71 | 140 | 68 | 117 | 177 | 115 |
| Manufactures | 787 | 911 | 713 | 436 | 460 | 617 | 653 |
| Imports: All goods | 5 168 | 5 103 | 5 301 | 4 430 | 4 930 | 5 978 | 6 349 |
| Agriculture | 37 | 30 | 46 | 43 | 38 | 34 | 24 |
| Manufactures | 10 | 7 | 26 | 18 | 20 | 13 | 8 |
| Balance: All goods | -4 337 | -4 101 | -4 407 | -3 921 | -4 328 | -5 160 | -5 536 |
| **Rwanda** | | | | | | | |
| Exports: All goods | 2 | 3 | 9 | 35 | 38 | 37 | 35 |
| Agriculture | 0 | 0 | 5 | 30 | 32 | 33 | 27 |
| Manufactures | 2 | 1 | 1 | 4 | 6 | 3 | 7 |
| Imports: All goods | 7 | 5 | 4 | 2 | 2 | 9 | 4 |
| Agriculture | 6 | 2 | 1 | 0 | 1 | 7 | 3 |
| Manufactures | 1 | 0 | 0 | 0 | 0 | 0 | 0 |
| Balance: All goods | -5 | -2 | 5 | 33 | 37 | 29 | 31 |
| **Senegal** | | | | | | | |
| Exports: All goods | 76 | 80 | 70 | 42 | 68 | 56 | 52 |
| Agriculture | 24 | 24 | 37 | 12 | 12 | 7 | 7 |
| Manufactures | 37 | 40 | 23 | 18 | 40 | 33 | 31 |
| Imports: All goods | 10 | 10 | 8 | 11 | 5 | 6 | 7 |
| Agriculture | 3 | 1 | 0 | 0 | 0 | 0 | 0 |
| Manufactures | 6 | 5 | 4 | 7 | 5 | 5 | 6 |
| Balance: All goods | 66 | 70 | 63 | 31 | 63 | 50 | 45 |
| **Seychelles** | | | | | | | |
| Exports: All goods | 2 | 2 | 65 | 6 | 7 | 103 | 6 |
| Agriculture | 0 | 0 | 0 | 0 | 0 | 1 | 1 |
| Manufactures | 2 | 2 | 64 | 6 | 7 | 102 | 5 |
| Imports: All goods | 1 | 1 | 4 | 3 | 2 | 3 | 2 |
| Agriculture | 0 | 0 | 0 | 0 | 0 | 0 | 0 |
| Manufactures | 1 | 1 | 4 | 3 | 2 | 2 | 2 |
| Balance: All goods | 1 | 1 | 60 | 3 | 5 | 100 | 4 |
| **Sierra Leone** | | | | | | | |
| Exports: All goods | 25 | 28 | 22 | 24 | 18 | 28 | 16 |
| Agriculture | 7 | 14 | 6 | 10 | 10 | 15 | 9 |
| Manufactures | 15 | 11 | 10 | 11 | 5 | 9 | 4 |
| Imports: All goods | 48 | 61 | 47 | 51 | 29 | 22 | 18 |
| Agriculture | 0 | 1 | 0 | 0 | 2 | 0 | 0 |
| Manufactures | 13 | 23 | 21 | 28 | 21 | 20 | 18 |
| Balance: All goods | -23 | -33 | -25 | -27 | -11 | 6 | -3 |

## Table C-5.   U.S. Trade in Goods by Country or Region, 1991–1997 —*Continued*

(Millions of dollars.)

| Country or region | 1991 | 1992 | 1993 | 1994 | 1995 | 1996 | 1997 |
|---|---|---|---|---|---|---|---|
| **Somalia** | | | | | | | |
| Exports: All goods | 7 | 21 | 46 | 30 | 8 | 4 | 3 |
| Agriculture | 4 | 20 | 11 | 16 | 6 | 3 | 1 |
| Manufactures | 4 | 1 | 20 | 14 | 2 | 1 | 1 |
| Imports: All goods | 3 | 2 | 0 | 0 | 0 | 0 | 0 |
| Agriculture | 0 | 0 | 0 | 0 | 0 | 0 | 0 |
| Manufactures | 0 | 0 | 0 | 0 | 0 | 0 | 0 |
| Balance: All goods | 5 | 18 | 46 | 30 | 8 | 4 | 2 |
| **South Africa** | | | | | | | |
| Exports: All goods | 2 113 | 2 434 | 2 188 | 2 172 | 2 751 | 3 112 | 2 997 |
| Agriculture | 80 | 465 | 238 | 141 | 258 | 288 | 211 |
| Manufactures | 1 958 | 1 864 | 1 856 | 1 895 | 2 342 | 2 597 | 2 598 |
| Imports: All goods | 1 728 | 1 727 | 1 845 | 2 031 | 2 208 | 2 323 | 2 510 |
| Agriculture | 5 | 48 | 57 | 67 | 78 | 107 | 101 |
| Manufactures | 1 475 | 1 422 | 1 490 | 1 646 | 1 763 | 1 789 | 1 985 |
| Balance: All goods | 385 | 707 | 344 | 142 | 543 | 789 | 487 |
| **Sudan** | | | | | | | |
| Exports: All goods | 92 | 52 | 59 | 55 | 43 | 51 | 36 |
| Agriculture | 53 | 14 | 24 | 38 | 11 | 16 | 11 |
| Manufactures | 39 | 39 | 29 | 16 | 33 | 34 | 26 |
| Imports: All goods | 16 | 11 | 12 | 35 | 23 | 19 | 12 |
| Agriculture | 2 | 3 | 5 | 10 | 5 | 7 | 4 |
| Manufactures | 1 | 0 | 1 | 2 | 4 | 2 | 2 |
| Balance: All goods | 77 | 41 | 47 | 19 | 21 | 33 | 24 |
| **Swaziland** | | | | | | | |
| Exports: All goods | 5 | 4 | 3 | 5 | 3 | 2 | 5 |
| Agriculture | 0 | 0 | 0 | 2 | 2 | 0 | 1 |
| Manufactures | 4 | 3 | 2 | 4 | 1 | 2 | 4 |
| Imports: All goods | 28 | 23 | 21 | 38 | 32 | 30 | 44 |
| Agriculture | 18 | 7 | 6 | 17 | 9 | 8 | 23 |
| Manufactures | 8 | 14 | 13 | 19 | 17 | 19 | 20 |
| Balance: All goods | -23 | -20 | -18 | -32 | -29 | -28 | -39 |
| **Tanzania** | | | | | | | |
| Exports: All goods | 34 | 34 | 33 | 49 | 66 | 50 | 65 |
| Agriculture | 4 | 5 | 4 | 16 | 13 | 5 | 13 |
| Manufactures | 23 | 20 | 21 | 26 | 47 | 34 | 42 |
| Imports: All goods | 15 | 11 | 11 | 15 | 22 | 19 | 27 |
| Agriculture | 10 | 6 | 6 | 4 | 7 | 4 | 5 |
| Manufactures | 5 | 4 | 5 | 10 | 13 | 12 | 17 |
| Balance: All goods | 20 | 23 | 21 | 34 | 44 | 31 | 38 |
| **Togo** | | | | | | | |
| Exports: All goods | 24 | 20 | 13 | 12 | 19 | 20 | 26 |
| Agriculture | 8 | 8 | 6 | 3 | 4 | 5 | 3 |
| Manufactures | 12 | 9 | 5 | 8 | 11 | 13 | 10 |
| Imports: All goods | 3 | 6 | 3 | 4 | 3 | 4 | 9 |
| Agriculture | 2 | 2 | 1 | 1 | 1 | 1 | 1 |
| Manufactures | 1 | 1 | 2 | 3 | 2 | 2 | 1 |
| Balance: All goods | 21 | 13 | 9 | 8 | 15 | 16 | 16 |
| **Tunisia** | | | | | | | |
| Exports: All goods | 172 | 232 | 232 | 327 | 215 | 189 | 252 |
| Agriculture | 73 | 92 | 121 | 106 | 89 | 90 | 118 |
| Manufactures | 84 | 122 | 102 | 213 | 114 | 84 | 119 |
| Imports: All goods | 25 | 48 | 41 | 54 | 70 | 76 | 63 |
| Agriculture | 6 | 5 | 4 | 4 | 5 | 0 | 3 |
| Manufactures | 16 | 24 | 25 | 38 | 59 | 34 | 47 |
| Balance: All goods | 146 | 184 | 192 | 273 | 145 | 113 | 189 |

## Table C-5.  U.S. Trade in Goods by Country or Region, 1991–1997 —*Continued*

(Millions of dollars.)

| Country or region | 1991 | 1992 | 1993 | 1994 | 1995 | 1996 | 1997 |
|---|---:|---:|---:|---:|---:|---:|---:|
| **Uganda** | | | | | | | |
| Exports: All goods ............................................... | 13 | 15 | 21 | 28 | 22 | 17 | 35 |
|     Agriculture ............................................... | 5 | 5 | 9 | 7 | 5 | 4 | 17 |
|     Manufactures ........................................... | 6 | 7 | 9 | 18 | 14 | 12 | 17 |
| Imports: All goods ............................................... | 18 | 12 | 10 | 35 | 13 | 16 | 38 |
|     Agriculture ............................................... | 18 | 12 | 10 | 34 | 13 | 16 | 37 |
|     Manufactures ........................................... | 0 | 0 | 0 | 0 | 0 | 0 | 1 |
| Balance: All goods ............................................. | -5 | 3 | 11 | -7 | 9 | 1 | -3 |
| **Zambia** | | | | | | | |
| Exports: All goods ............................................... | 23 | 68 | 42 | 33 | 49 | 46 | 29 |
|     Agriculture ............................................... | 0 | 44 | 11 | 2 | 3 | 0 | 0 |
|     Manufactures ........................................... | 22 | 21 | 23 | 26 | 43 | 43 | 26 |
| Imports: All goods ............................................... | 42 | 70 | 41 | 64 | 33 | 64 | 56 |
|     Agriculture ............................................... | 1 | 0 | 1 | 1 | 0 | 0 | 0 |
|     Manufactures ........................................... | 41 | 70 | 40 | 63 | 32 | 64 | 55 |
| Balance: All goods ............................................. | -19 | -2 | 2 | -31 | 16 | -18 | -27 |
| **Zimbabwe** | | | | | | | |
| Exports: All goods ............................................... | 53 | 144 | 84 | 93 | 122 | 91 | 82 |
|     Agriculture ............................................... | 1 | 88 | 25 | 3 | 9 | 1 | 0 |
|     Manufactures ........................................... | 52 | 55 | 58 | 89 | 112 | 89 | 79 |
| Imports: All goods ............................................... | 90 | 106 | 110 | 102 | 98 | 133 | 140 |
|     Agriculture ............................................... | 30 | 39 | 47 | 46 | 11 | 49 | 40 |
|     Manufactures ........................................... | 57 | 66 | 61 | 51 | 80 | 77 | 94 |
| Balance: All goods ............................................. | -37 | 38 | -25 | -10 | 24 | -42 | -58 |
| **ASEAN (9 countries)** | | | | | | | |
| Exports: All goods ............................................... | 20 802 | 23 979 | 28 301 | 32 114 | 39 929 | 43 610 | 48 253 |
|     Agriculture ............................................... | 1 293 | 1 532 | 1 542 | 1 941 | 3 000 | 3 218 | 2 946 |
|     Manufactures ........................................... | 18 629 | 21 443 | 25 521 | 28 704 | 35 116 | 38 915 | 44 251 |
| Imports: All goods ............................................... | 28 947 | 36 094 | 42 317 | 52 083 | 62 134 | 66 424 | 70 910 |
|     Agriculture ............................................... | 1 978 | 2 447 | 2 273 | 2 570 | 3 479 | 3 545 | 3 612 |
|     Manufactures ........................................... | 24 857 | 31 434 | 37 701 | 46 536 | 55 996 | 60 168 | 64 383 |
| Balance: All goods ............................................. | -8 145 | -12 115 | -14 016 | -19 970 | -22 205 | -22 814 | -22 657 |
| **APEC (17 countries)** | | | | | | | |
| Exports: All goods ............................................... | 241 775 | 262 073 | 279 958 | 320 679 | 364 320 | 390 552 | 428 548 |
|     Agriculture ............................................... | 22 952 | 25 031 | 25 371 | 29 257 | 34 949 | 37 887 | 35 341 |
|     Manufactures ........................................... | 197 633 | 214 799 | 232 988 | 269 095 | 302 347 | 326 489 | 367 569 |
| Imports: All goods ............................................... | 317 445 | 350 460 | 390 021 | 450 388 | 507 539 | 532 964 | 583 380 |
|     Agriculture ............................................... | 10 956 | 12 083 | 12 608 | 13 612 | 15 745 | 17 258 | 18 540 |
|     Manufactures ........................................... | 278 108 | 307 142 | 343 811 | 400 716 | 452 632 | 470 891 | 515 673 |
| Balance: All goods ............................................. | -75 670 | -88 388 | -110 063 | -129 709 | -143 219 | -142 412 | -154 832 |
| **Caribbean Basin Initiative Countries** | | | | | | | |
| Exports: All goods ............................................... | 10 448 | 11 744 | 12 749 | 13 800 | 15 671 | 16 351 | 18 961 |
|     Agriculture ............................................... | 1 494 | 1 532 | 1 736 | 1 760 | 2 155 | 2 426 | 2 565 |
|     Manufactures ........................................... | 7 740 | 9 025 | 9 849 | 10 950 | 12 329 | 12 617 | 14 978 |
| Imports: All goods ............................................... | 8 493 | 9 701 | 10 456 | 11 597 | 12 890 | 14 796 | 16 977 |
|     Agriculture ............................................... | 1 755 | 1 855 | 1 913 | 1 986 | 2 204 | 2 410 | 2 771 |
|     Manufactures ........................................... | 4 507 | 5 485 | 6 311 | 7 361 | 8 576 | 9 486 | 11 218 |
| Balance: All goods ............................................. | 1 955 | 2 043 | 2 293 | 2 204 | 2 781 | 1 555 | 1 984 |

# PART D.   State Exports of Goods

## U.S. Exports of Goods by State, 1997
### (billions of dollars)

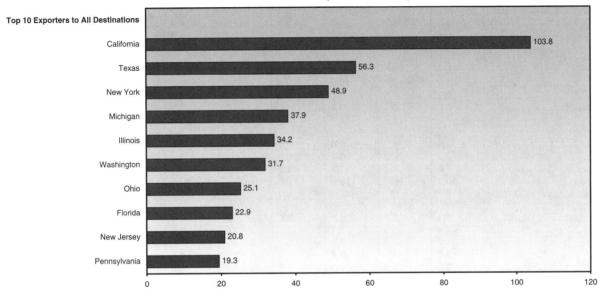

**Top 10 Exporters to All Destinations**

|  |  |
|---|---|
| California | 103.8 |
| Texas | 56.3 |
| New York | 48.9 |
| Michigan | 37.9 |
| Illinois | 34.2 |
| Washington | 31.7 |
| Ohio | 25.1 |
| Florida | 22.9 |
| New Jersey | 20.8 |
| Pennsylvania | 19.3 |

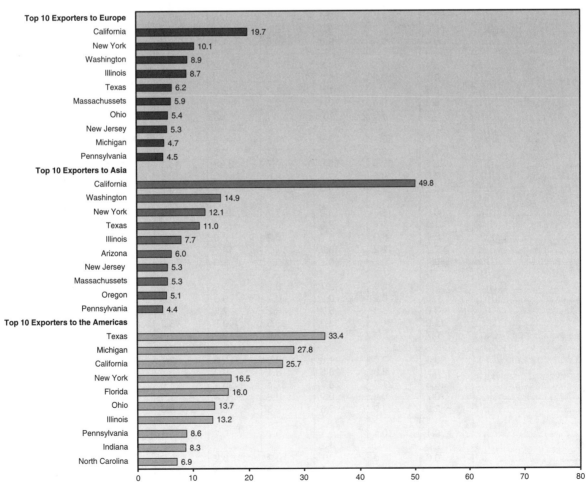

**Top 10 Exporters to Europe**

|  |  |
|---|---|
| California | 19.7 |
| New York | 10.1 |
| Washington | 8.9 |
| Illinois | 8.7 |
| Texas | 6.2 |
| Massachussets | 5.9 |
| Ohio | 5.4 |
| New Jersey | 5.3 |
| Michigan | 4.7 |
| Pennsylvania | 4.5 |

**Top 10 Exporters to Asia**

|  |  |
|---|---|
| California | 49.8 |
| Washington | 14.9 |
| New York | 12.1 |
| Texas | 11.0 |
| Illinois | 7.7 |
| Arizona | 6.0 |
| New Jersey | 5.3 |
| Massachussets | 5.3 |
| Oregon | 5.1 |
| Pennsylvania | 4.4 |

**Top 10 Exporters to the Americas**

|  |  |
|---|---|
| Texas | 33.4 |
| Michigan | 27.8 |
| California | 25.7 |
| New York | 16.5 |
| Florida | 16.0 |
| Ohio | 13.7 |
| Illinois | 13.2 |
| Pennsylvania | 8.6 |
| Indiana | 8.3 |
| North Carolina | 6.9 |

## Table D-1.  State Exports of Goods, 1987 and 1991–1998

(Billions of dollars.)

| State | 1987 | 1991 | 1992 | 1993 | 1994 | 1995 | 1996 | 1997 | 1998 |
|---|---|---|---|---|---|---|---|---|---|
| **All States** | 244.4 | 420.0 | 447.5 | 464.9 | 512.4 | 583.0 | 622.8 | 687.6 | 683.0 |
| Alabama | 1.5 | 2.4 | 2.7 | 2.5 | 3.1 | 3.6 | 3.7 | 4.5 | 4.6 |
| Alaska | 0.5 | 1.1 | 1.1 | 0.8 | 0.9 | 0.9 | 0.9 | 1.0 | 0.8 |
| Arizona | 2.5 | 4.5 | 5.0 | 5.8 | 7.0 | 8.4 | 9.9 | 13.6 | 10.8 |
| Arkansas | 0.4 | 0.8 | 1.1 | 1.1 | 1.5 | 1.8 | 2.0 | 2.2 | 1.9 |
| California | 32.9 | 59.0 | 66.7 | 68.1 | 78.2 | 92.0 | 98.6 | 103.8 | 98.8 |
| Colorado | 4.8 | 6.1 | 6.0 | 6.2 | 7.8 | 9.7 | 10.1 | 11.3 | 10.7 |
| Connecticut | 4.7 | 6.7 | 10.5 | 10.2 | 10.3 | 12.9 | 13.1 | 12.9 | 12.1 |
| Delaware | 2.7 | 3.5 | 3.7 | 3.5 | 3.8 | 4.4 | 4.6 | 5.1 | 5.0 |
| District of Columbia | 0.4 | 0.4 | 0.4 | 4.7 | 5.2 | 5.3 | 5.1 | 4.9 | 4.4 |
| Florida | 7.8 | 12.6 | 14.4 | 14.7 | 16.6 | 18.6 | 19.6 | 22.9 | 23.2 |
| Georgia | 2.4 | 5.2 | 6.0 | 6.1 | 7.1 | 8.6 | 8.6 | 9.8 | 11.2 |
| Hawaii | 0.2 | 0.2 | 0.1 | 0.2 | 0.2 | 0.3 | 0.3 | 0.3 | 0.2 |
| Idaho | 0.4 | 1.0 | 1.1 | 1.2 | 1.5 | 1.9 | 1.6 | 1.7 | 1.5 |
| Illinois | 10.2 | 16.4 | 19.0 | 20.3 | 24.5 | 30.5 | 32.2 | 34.2 | 33.8 |
| Indiana | 3.7 | 6.7 | 7.3 | 8.4 | 9.5 | 11.1 | 12.1 | 13.1 | 13.9 |
| Iowa | 1.1 | 1.4 | 1.5 | 2.0 | 2.3 | 2.6 | 2.7 | 3.1 | 3.4 |
| Kansas | 1.9 | 2.9 | 3.1 | 3.1 | 3.5 | 4.5 | 5.0 | 5.1 | 4.4 |
| Kentucky | 1.7 | 3.3 | 3.8 | 3.3 | 4.2 | 5.0 | 5.8 | 6.9 | 7.4 |
| Louisiana | 3.0 | 3.1 | 3.4 | 3.2 | 3.6 | 4.6 | 4.7 | 4.4 | 4.4 |
| Maine | 0.5 | 1.0 | 1.0 | 1.1 | 1.1 | 1.3 | 1.2 | 1.6 | 1.7 |
| Maryland | 1.5 | 2.7 | 2.7 | 2.7 | 2.8 | 3.4 | 3.5 | 3.9 | 4.0 |
| Massachusetts | 8.3 | 11.2 | 11.6 | 11.6 | 12.6 | 14.4 | 15.4 | 17.4 | 16.5 |
| Michigan | 19.5 | 18.8 | 22.0 | 25.3 | 36.8 | 37.1 | 38.1 | 37.9 | 39.3 |
| Minnesota | 5.6 | 7.9 | 9.0 | 10.0 | 10.0 | 12.4 | 13.9 | 13.8 | 13.5 |
| Mississippi | 0.4 | 0.8 | 0.8 | 0.8 | 1.1 | 1.4 | 1.2 | 1.4 | 1.4 |
| Missouri | 3.4 | 4.3 | 4.3 | 4.7 | 5.2 | 5.7 | 6.6 | 7.0 | 6.8 |
| Montana | 0.1 | 0.2 | 0.2 | 0.2 | 0.3 | 0.3 | 0.3 | 0.4 | 0.4 |
| Nebraska | 0.3 | 0.7 | 1.5 | 1.7 | 2.0 | 2.3 | 2.5 | 2.5 | 2.5 |
| Nevada | 0.3 | 0.4 | 0.4 | 0.5 | 0.5 | 0.7 | 0.7 | 0.8 | 0.8 |
| New Hampshire | 0.7 | 0.9 | 1.0 | 1.1 | 1.2 | 1.5 | 1.7 | 1.9 | 2.0 |
| New Jersey | 7.6 | 13.7 | 13.9 | 14.5 | 16.8 | 18.4 | 18.5 | 20.8 | 20.0 |
| New Mexico | 0.1 | 0.2 | 0.2 | 0.4 | 0.5 | 0.4 | 0.9 | 1.8 | 1.9 |
| New York | 29.6 | 37.5 | 36.8 | 40.7 | 37.3 | 44.1 | 45.0 | 48.9 | 45.6 |
| North Carolina | 3.5 | 6.2 | 7.4 | 8.0 | 9.0 | 10.6 | 11.6 | 13.1 | 12.9 |
| North Dakota | 0.2 | 0.3 | 0.3 | 0.3 | 0.4 | 0.5 | 0.6 | 0.6 | 0.7 |
| Ohio | 6.5 | 13.6 | 15.2 | 17.7 | 19.5 | 20.9 | 22.6 | 25.1 | 24.8 |
| Oklahoma | 1.0 | 2.4 | 2.6 | 2.3 | 2.2 | 2.5 | 2.5 | 2.7 | 2.6 |
| Oregon | 3.1 | 5.0 | 5.7 | 6.2 | 7.0 | 9.9 | 8.5 | 8.4 | 8.1 |
| Pennsylvania | 7.2 | 12.2 | 13.2 | 13.2 | 14.7 | 17.7 | 17.4 | 19.3 | 19.1 |
| Rhode Island | 0.4 | 0.7 | 0.7 | 0.9 | 1.0 | 1.0 | 1.0 | 1.1 | 1.1 |
| South Carolina | 1.0 | 2.0 | 2.7 | 3.2 | 3.5 | 4.5 | 4.9 | 5.7 | 5.9 |
| South Dakota | 0.0 | 0.2 | 0.2 | 0.2 | 0.3 | 0.3 | 0.4 | 0.4 | 0.4 |
| Tennessee | 3.0 | 5.0 | 5.7 | 6.2 | 7.5 | 9.5 | 9.3 | 9.9 | 9.9 |
| Texas | 18.0 | 31.9 | 33.9 | 35.6 | 40.5 | 45.2 | 48.3 | 56.3 | 59.0 |
| Utah | 0.7 | 1.7 | 2.2 | 2.0 | 2.2 | 2.3 | 2.8 | 3.3 | 3.1 |
| Vermont | 0.3 | 2.0 | 1.8 | 2.3 | 2.3 | 2.7 | 2.6 | 2.6 | 2.8 |
| Virginia | 3.1 | 8.8 | 8.5 | 8.1 | 9.9 | 10.4 | 10.9 | 11.5 | 11.5 |
| Washington | 10.3 | 27.3 | 28.7 | 27.4 | 25.1 | 22.0 | 25.5 | 31.7 | 38.0 |
| West Virginia | 0.7 | 0.9 | 0.9 | 0.8 | 0.9 | 1.1 | 1.2 | 1.3 | 1.2 |
| Wisconsin | 2.9 | 4.9 | 5.8 | 5.8 | 6.9 | 8.0 | 8.4 | 9.8 | 9.2 |
| Wyoming | 0.1 | 0.1 | 0.1 | 0.1 | 0.1 | 0.1 | 0.1 | 0.2 | 0.2 |
| Puerto Rico | 2.0 | 3.8 | 4.2 | 4.4 | 4.6 | 4.7 | 5.2 | 5.5 | 6.1 |
| Virgin Islands | 0.0 | 0.0 | 0.1 | 0.2 | 0.2 | 0.2 | 0.2 | 0.2 | 0.1 |
| Unallocated | 19.6 | 53.1 | 45.2 | 39.1 | 35.8 | 39.0 | 48.7 | 57.8 | 57.2 |

## Table D-2.   State Exports of Goods by Destination, 1993–1997

(State of origin by country of destination, millions of dollars.)

| Destination | Alabama | | | | | Alaska | | | | |
|---|---|---|---|---|---|---|---|---|---|---|
| | 1993 | 1994 | 1995 | 1996 | 1997 | 1993 | 1994 | 1995 | 1996 | 1997 |
| All destinations | 2 504.3 | 3 115.4 | 3 587.1 | 3 702.4 | 4 537.2 | 817.9 | 887.7 | 891.5 | 850.4 | 969.0 |
| Canada | 621.7 | 789.0 | 988.5 | 1 177.4 | 1 251.1 | 84.1 | 120.6 | 195.7 | 181.2 | 305.4 |
| Mexico | 185.3 | 222.6 | 193.1 | 324.9 | 813.7 | 0.6 | 1.3 | 0.9 | 1.5 | 1.9 |
| Central and South America and Caribbean | 187.1 | 374.0 | 308.4 | 304.4 | 407.8 | 4.7 | 3.3 | 12.0 | 9.3 | 4.2 |
| Argentina | 21.8 | 22.9 | 21.4 | 26.6 | 25.5 | 0.3 | 0.2 | 5.0 | 0.6 | 0.7 |
| Brazil | 19.9 | 21.6 | 53.0 | 51.1 | 77.5 | 2.1 | 0.1 | 1.4 | 1.0 | 0.5 |
| Chile | 6.8 | 13.9 | 10.2 | 9.8 | 15.1 | 0.2 | 0.2 | 1.9 | 4.7 | 0.7 |
| Colombia | 12.7 | 23.3 | 24.0 | 18.1 | 39.7 | 0.3 | 0.9 | 0.3 | 0.7 | 0.2 |
| Dominican Republic | 15.3 | 20.6 | 27.7 | 22.9 | 30.7 | 0.4 | 0.2 | 0.1 | ..... | 0.2 |
| Venezuela | 11.6 | 7.3 | 9.1 | 10.5 | 13.0 | 0.1 | 0.2 | 0.8 | 1.2 | 0.6 |
| European Union | 631.3 | 723.4 | 883.0 | 820.1 | 864.6 | 95.0 | 121.2 | 113.0 | 134.5 | 237.6 |
| Belgium | 51.9 | 52.7 | 62.1 | 78.4 | 74.4 | 31.7 | 44.5 | 37.9 | 49.7 | 92.4 |
| France | 47.7 | 108.1 | 96.4 | 71.7 | 79.9 | 3.3 | 6.9 | 11.9 | 2.4 | 2.0 |
| Germany | 141.9 | 112.5 | 119.2 | 100.0 | 124.2 | 26.4 | 27.1 | 33.3 | 18.2 | 30.7 |
| Ireland | 15.8 | 32.2 | 6.1 | 8.9 | 11.3 | 0.1 | 0.1 | 0.1 | 0.1 | ..... |
| Italy | 84.9 | 95.2 | 147.9 | 116.3 | 98.5 | 4.5 | 0.6 | 2.8 | 7.6 | 7.0 |
| Luxembourg | 0.4 | 0.2 | 0.3 | 1.6 | 9.0 | ..... | ..... | ..... | ..... | ..... |
| Netherlands | 123.0 | 87.3 | 127.3 | 165.5 | 151.1 | 0.6 | 1.6 | 15.3 | 35.5 | 44.9 |
| Spain | 37.5 | 69.0 | 48.4 | 46.4 | 41.5 | 9.4 | 29.4 | 0.6 | 11.3 | 3.1 |
| United Kingdom | 107.3 | 127.8 | 187.2 | 198.6 | 247.6 | 16.9 | 9.4 | 6.6 | 7.3 | 55.4 |
| Switzerland | 37.3 | 72.2 | 36.5 | 36.3 | 12.5 | 0.8 | 16.3 | 8.5 | 0.8 | 0.8 |
| Asian 10 | 663.3 | 615.0 | 878.8 | 761.1 | 867.4 | 617.6 | 558.0 | 521.6 | 492.3 | 392.6 |
| China | 89.1 | 30.9 | 57.1 | 54.3 | 58.0 | 9.4 | 28.9 | 20.5 | 38.3 | 11.6 |
| Hong Kong | 43.1 | 31.7 | 52.9 | 42.3 | 51.3 | 2.4 | 1.8 | 1.8 | 1.3 | 2.1 |
| Indonesia | 4.9 | 8.3 | 11.3 | 11.5 | 24.2 | 1.4 | ..... | 1.9 | 1.2 | 0.2 |
| Japan | 338.1 | 342.2 | 491.6 | 382.5 | 322.8 | 474.9 | 412.6 | 327.5 | 270.0 | 259.2 |
| Malaysia | 5.8 | 8.5 | 8.9 | 17.3 | 20.9 | ..... | 0.3 | 0.6 | 1.6 | 0.8 |
| Philippines | 2.3 | 2.7 | 4.3 | 7.4 | 5.1 | ..... | 0.2 | 4.1 | 0.2 | 0.1 |
| Singapore | 31.5 | 26.3 | 62.4 | 57.4 | 62.5 | 2.3 | 1.1 | 5.1 | 6.1 | 0.9 |
| South Korea | 104.9 | 125.2 | 140.9 | 129.8 | 268.8 | 92.8 | 75.6 | 93.7 | 127.6 | 97.4 |
| Taiwan | 31.6 | 28.3 | 37.2 | 38.9 | 34.0 | 32.3 | 34.5 | 61.4 | 40.7 | 18.4 |
| Thailand | 12.0 | 10.9 | 12.3 | 19.5 | 19.9 | 2.0 | 2.9 | 5.0 | 5.4 | 2.0 |
| Australia | 28.6 | 124.1 | 60.6 | 56.8 | 71.0 | 1.2 | 0.7 | 3.7 | 1.0 | 1.4 |
| India | 2.0 | 5.2 | 15.4 | 20.3 | 10.1 | ..... | 0.2 | 0.8 | 0.4 | 2.8 |
| Israel | 18.8 | 18.0 | 29.1 | 22.4 | 19.6 | ..... | ..... | 0.5 | 0.8 | 1.3 |
| Pakistan | 0.8 | 1.0 | 16.9 | 1.0 | 6.6 | ..... | ..... | ..... | 0.1 | ..... |
| Saudi Arabia | 33.8 | 21.0 | 24.8 | 21.6 | 28.5 | 0.2 | ..... | 2.1 | 1.0 | 1.8 |
| African 8 | 19.0 | 11.9 | 16.0 | 22.2 | 19.6 | 0.1 | 0.4 | 0.2 | 4.6 | 1.1 |
| Developing Countries | 815.6 | 990.5 | 1 085.4 | 1 169.4 | 1 965.9 | 159.1 | 214.5 | 237.2 | 261.1 | 161.0 |

| Destination | Arizona | | | | | Arkansas | | | | |
|---|---|---|---|---|---|---|---|---|---|---|
| | 1993 | 1994 | 1995 | 1996 | 1997 | 1993 | 1994 | 1995 | 1996 | 1997 |
| All destinations | 5 785.1 | 6 970.6 | 8 402.8 | 9 937.8 | 13 556.7 | 1 109.8 | 1 470.9 | 1 794.4 | 1 997.2 | 2 211.6 |
| Canada | 533.1 | 644.2 | 839.0 | 970.2 | 1 072.2 | 421.1 | 521.1 | 574.1 | 614.9 | 820.4 |
| Mexico | 1 087.4 | 1 206.5 | 1 265.6 | 1 622.2 | 1 963.1 | 68.8 | 94.2 | 59.8 | 102.2 | 140.8 |
| Central and South America and Caribbean | 64.2 | 92.6 | 111.8 | 154.7 | 218.9 | 38.6 | 41.6 | 80.1 | 75.7 | 84.6 |
| Argentina | 8.2 | 13.5 | 10.9 | 12.6 | 19.7 | 4.0 | 4.9 | 12.1 | 9.4 | 9.6 |
| Brazil | 17.5 | 29.7 | 46.1 | 68.4 | 124.3 | 7.0 | 6.2 | 25.4 | 21.2 | 23.0 |
| Chile | 10.7 | 23.2 | 26.4 | 31.3 | 18.1 | 2.9 | 2.5 | 3.0 | 5.1 | 5.6 |
| Colombia | 2.7 | 3.9 | 7.0 | 3.3 | 5.5 | 2.3 | 2.7 | 7.3 | 5.3 | 4.2 |
| Dominican Republic | 1.3 | 1.4 | 0.5 | 1.8 | 1.3 | 0.6 | 1.1 | 1.2 | 0.8 | 4.6 |
| Venezuela | 7.6 | 4.9 | 3.3 | 7.0 | 6.4 | 2.2 | 1.1 | 1.7 | 2.5 | 5.1 |
| European Union | 1 590.1 | 1 879.5 | 2 443.8 | 2 448.6 | 3 686.4 | 182.6 | 185.8 | 258.3 | 268.6 | 302.9 |
| Belgium | 56.8 | 57.6 | 71.9 | 76.3 | 81.6 | 28.1 | 24.1 | 40.5 | 42.8 | 41.4 |
| France | 194.5 | 206.7 | 285.7 | 324.9 | 382.2 | 19.8 | 13.0 | 20.3 | 30.8 | 45.8 |
| Germany | 278.3 | 349.8 | 410.8 | 392.9 | 413.7 | 21.8 | 24.4 | 34.0 | 43.3 | 45.4 |
| Ireland | 41.8 | 90.1 | 132.3 | 105.0 | 96.7 | 9.3 | 7.6 | 5.8 | 6.5 | 8.6 |
| Italy | 46.8 | 58.4 | 78.7 | 79.8 | 94.0 | 5.9 | 4.8 | 19.9 | 20.7 | 27.7 |
| Luxembourg | 0.5 | 0.5 | 0.5 | 0.3 | 0.7 | ..... | 0.9 | 1.0 | 1.3 | 1.3 |
| Netherlands | 99.1 | 134.1 | 291.1 | 558.5 | 1 454.6 | 11.6 | 23.0 | 27.6 | 28.0 | 31.8 |
| Spain | 14.3 | 13.9 | 21.6 | 19.8 | 23.3 | 4.6 | 5.9 | 14.6 | 6.2 | 4.8 |
| United Kingdom | 807.3 | 906.0 | 1 085.1 | 827.1 | 1 061.5 | 65.6 | 64.4 | 76.2 | 74.5 | 84.8 |
| Switzerland | 22.3 | 24.2 | 30.9 | 32.7 | 108.5 | 16.3 | 16.0 | 21.9 | 25.0 | 14.0 |
| Asian 10 | 2 265.1 | 2 859.9 | 3 437.2 | 4 451.6 | 5 975.8 | 257.2 | 361.1 | 381.8 | 391.0 | 417.2 |
| China | 66.7 | 63.5 | 92.5 | 121.2 | 123.7 | 5.2 | 5.6 | 13.7 | 30.2 | 21.4 |
| Hong Kong | 248.2 | 279.3 | 387.0 | 392.7 | 503.5 | 36.4 | 66.0 | 98.0 | 109.2 | 146.9 |
| Indonesia | 7.5 | 14.6 | 22.2 | 16.5 | 53.4 | 1.8 | 2.8 | 3.7 | 6.7 | 5.1 |
| Japan | 666.7 | 808.3 | 1 125.5 | 1 356.2 | 1 806.4 | 111.5 | 157.1 | 139.4 | 126.9 | 117.2 |
| Malaysia | 301.5 | 374.5 | 427.3 | 709.5 | 1 233.9 | 5.6 | 7.4 | 6.3 | 5.2 | 10.0 |
| Philippines | 46.3 | 94.4 | 101.8 | 140.3 | 310.8 | 16.1 | 24.6 | 16.7 | 17.1 | 25.9 |
| Singapore | 248.9 | 351.4 | 302.8 | 364.6 | 473.2 | 17.8 | 25.7 | 25.4 | 22.0 | 20.5 |
| South Korea | 177.5 | 206.2 | 230.2 | 287.8 | 296.9 | 31.7 | 33.8 | 37.2 | 41.4 | 33.1 |
| Taiwan | 477.1 | 604.3 | 648.2 | 895.4 | 1 062.8 | 26.4 | 32.4 | 32.8 | 24.2 | 30.3 |
| Thailand | 24.6 | 63.2 | 99.5 | 167.5 | 111.3 | 4.6 | 5.7 | 8.5 | 7.9 | 6.9 |
| Australia | 79.4 | 108.0 | 80.3 | 82.7 | 94.2 | 14.6 | 15.6 | 16.4 | 13.8 | 24.1 |
| India | 14.6 | 21.8 | 26.7 | 15.9 | 35.1 | 1.4 | 1.4 | 2.3 | 2.1 | 2.4 |
| Israel | 29.0 | 29.4 | 33.6 | 45.7 | 38.6 | 2.0 | 2.9 | 1.8 | 1.9 | 3.5 |
| Pakistan | 0.2 | 1.2 | 1.9 | 1.2 | 2.5 | 0.4 | 4.1 | 0.2 | 0.7 | 0.2 |
| Saudi Arabia | 18.2 | 13.0 | 17.2 | 14.9 | 28.3 | 28.6 | 30.5 | 19.2 | 25.9 | 32.6 |
| African 8 | 5.7 | 12.8 | 39.8 | 15.9 | 30.0 | 13.6 | 11.7 | 8.0 | 7.4 | 6.5 |
| Developing Countries | 2 848.7 | 3 461.7 | 3 818.2 | 4 995.4 | 6 695.9 | 350.3 | 557.7 | 746.7 | 934.1 | 921.8 |

## Table D-2.  State Exports of Goods by Destination, 1993–1997 —*Continued*

(State of origin by country of destination, millions of dollars.)

| Destination | California | | | | | Colorado | | | | |
|---|---|---|---|---|---|---|---|---|---|---|
| | 1993 | 1994 | 1995 | 1996 | 1997 | 1993 | 1994 | 1995 | 1996 | 1997 |
| All destinations | 68 066.3 | 78 190.4 | 92 038.4 | 98 634.0 | 103 802.4 | 6 214.8 | 7 802.1 | 9 688.8 | 10 064.9 | 11 329.2 |
| Canada | 7 157.3 | 8 054.5 | 9 537.7 | 10 577.1 | 11 492.4 | 595.3 | 524.2 | 602.8 | 609.7 | 671.6 |
| Mexico | 5 116.6 | 5 957.0 | 6 171.6 | 7 787.3 | 9 941.9 | 604.4 | 636.8 | 692.7 | 902.5 | 1 418.0 |
| Central and South America and Caribbean | 2 427.8 | 2 662.7 | 2 952.3 | 3 357.8 | 4 307.1 | 521.6 | 521.3 | 518.4 | 519.1 | 516.7 |
| Argentina | 390.6 | 399.9 | 340.8 | 390.3 | 616.3 | 93.0 | 100.3 | 70.7 | 60.5 | 73.4 |
| Brazil | 653.8 | 866.1 | 1 031.5 | 1 260.8 | 1 395.6 | 256.8 | 263.0 | 261.2 | 276.7 | 244.2 |
| Chile | 343.2 | 274.2 | 332.9 | 352.2 | 488.6 | 27.2 | 24.3 | 30.7 | 34.6 | 33.8 |
| Colombia | 130.7 | 172.2 | 170.3 | 193.1 | 228.8 | 28.4 | 27.2 | 30.4 | 31.0 | 35.0 |
| Dominican Republic | 97.8 | 113.6 | 98.8 | 116.3 | 161.7 | 1.9 | 3.8 | 6.4 | 2.7 | 2.7 |
| Venezuela | 195.0 | 140.3 | 146.9 | 187.3 | 264.6 | 34.4 | 22.7 | 27.9 | 33.3 | 34.7 |
| European Union | 14 976.3 | 17 147.1 | 18 897.0 | 18 687.0 | 19 709.4 | 2 259.4 | 3 263.6 | 3 741.7 | 3 674.0 | 3 693.1 |
| Belgium | 778.4 | 887.1 | 958.8 | 1 060.8 | 1 027.9 | 116.6 | 131.3 | 102.0 | 118.7 | 109.4 |
| France | 2 069.3 | 2 387.9 | 2 443.8 | 2 552.3 | 2 422.7 | 350.7 | 512.6 | 715.6 | 624.2 | 521.9 |
| Germany | 3 393.5 | 3 406.8 | 3 752.9 | 3 798.6 | 3 761.4 | 502.5 | 769.9 | 900.5 | 735.0 | 669.4 |
| Ireland | 480.4 | 637.3 | 702.1 | 647.8 | 735.2 | 30.7 | 51.8 | 108.2 | 84.2 | 191.4 |
| Italy | 1 058.1 | 1 302.1 | 1 377.5 | 1 079.5 | 1 140.6 | 280.4 | 364.7 | 380.2 | 557.0 | 694.2 |
| Luxembourg | 37.4 | 51.0 | 49.3 | 41.9 | 107.7 | 0.1 | 0.1 | 1.4 | 0.3 | 1.6 |
| Netherlands | 1 978.5 | 2 624.3 | 2 914.3 | 2 138.1 | 3 096.0 | 259.8 | 363.0 | 428.8 | 548.5 | 500.2 |
| Spain | 521.1 | 593.3 | 777.7 | 769.0 | 716.0 | 88.4 | 144.3 | 138.5 | 181.8 | 166.6 |
| United Kingdom | 3 334.0 | 3 835.4 | 4 507.1 | 4 779.0 | 5 109.8 | 495.8 | 780.3 | 811.4 | 671.6 | 689.3 |
| Switzerland | 637.9 | 787.0 | 812.2 | 881.0 | 1 205.5 | 37.1 | 50.1 | 71.9 | 84.8 | 82.5 |
| Asian 10 | 32 210.1 | 37 949.6 | 47 427.4 | 51 192.1 | 49 784.3 | 1 719.1 | 2 299.4 | 3 400.4 | 3 574.9 | 4 098.4 |
| China | 1 655.1 | 1 507.6 | 1 349.3 | 1 933.0 | 2 274.3 | 13.0 | 22.8 | 29.4 | 52.2 | 74.3 |
| Hong Kong | 2 905.0 | 3 019.9 | 3 541.3 | 3 481.6 | 3 926.2 | 138.3 | 273.5 | 388.5 | 325.7 | 403.5 |
| Indonesia | 645.7 | 404.6 | 499.6 | 771.5 | 801.8 | 13.3 | 14.3 | 33.7 | 36.1 | 55.0 |
| Japan | 11 431.6 | 14 536.6 | 18 288.8 | 19 704.6 | 17 927.4 | 1 017.1 | 1 158.7 | 1 555.6 | 1 590.1 | 1 691.4 |
| Malaysia | 1 510.3 | 2 342.9 | 3 816.2 | 3 252.5 | 3 025.7 | 29.1 | 91.0 | 96.7 | 95.5 | 104.1 |
| Philippines | 1 021.9 | 1 213.1 | 1 616.0 | 1 800.8 | 1 739.2 | 23.1 | 32.5 | 33.2 | 53.5 | 112.7 |
| Singapore | 3 877.8 | 3 993.9 | 4 647.7 | 5 559.7 | 5 336.7 | 193.2 | 308.6 | 591.7 | 638.9 | 622.5 |
| South Korea | 3 749.3 | 4 557.5 | 6 406.6 | 7 398.8 | 6 494.2 | 154.2 | 174.8 | 250.4 | 342.2 | 609.0 |
| Taiwan | 4 451.4 | 4 923.9 | 5 503.5 | 5 396.5 | 6 184.8 | 86.5 | 130.4 | 205.7 | 197.2 | 214.2 |
| Thailand | 962.0 | 1 449.7 | 1 758.4 | 1 893.0 | 2 074.0 | 51.3 | 92.8 | 215.6 | 243.5 | 211.8 |
| Australia | 1 523.0 | 1 970.8 | 1 895.3 | 1 910.4 | 2 045.2 | 278.9 | 310.1 | 396.4 | 390.9 | 330.7 |
| India | 325.0 | 253.5 | 393.0 | 405.8 | 397.5 | 12.0 | 12.6 | 19.5 | 36.9 | 31.2 |
| Israel | 358.8 | 385.2 | 499.8 | 587.3 | 609.9 | 19.1 | 19.7 | 38.7 | 35.4 | 24.5 |
| Pakistan | 37.3 | 45.8 | 43.8 | 46.9 | 35.0 | 1.9 | 1.2 | 1.1 | 1.1 | 1.3 |
| Saudi Arabia | 343.9 | 265.4 | 304.6 | 281.7 | 721.6 | 23.4 | 17.5 | 14.7 | 25.2 | 14.4 |
| African 8 | 413.1 | 323.9 | 264.9 | 306.7 | 329.0 | 40.3 | 26.5 | 31.8 | 21.6 | 27.7 |
| Developing Countries | 31 425.0 | 34 802.4 | 41 604.0 | 45 686.3 | 49 771.3 | 1 955.0 | 2 436.9 | 3 241.8 | 3 630.8 | 4 768.5 |

| Destination | Connecticut | | | | | Delaware | | | | |
|---|---|---|---|---|---|---|---|---|---|---|
| | 1993 | 1994 | 1995 | 1996 | 1997 | 1993 | 1994 | 1995 | 1996 | 1997 |
| All destinations | 10 201.0 | 10 272.0 | 12 942.1 | 13 052.5 | 12 897.1 | 3 454.5 | 3 758.1 | 4 396.8 | 4 584.5 | 5 103.9 |
| Canada | 1 407.3 | 1 481.1 | 1 660.2 | 1 603.9 | 1 847.7 | 628.4 | 692.5 | 717.5 | 739.7 | 788.3 |
| Mexico | 335.5 | 441.4 | 321.9 | 521.5 | 529.5 | 159.3 | 212.6 | 183.1 | 286.1 | 308.2 |
| Central and South America and Caribbean | 945.6 | 1 122.0 | 1 421.8 | 1 333.6 | 1 410.1 | 401.7 | 414.8 | 505.9 | 516.0 | 611.5 |
| Argentina | 74.2 | 105.9 | 94.1 | 84.3 | 108.4 | 51.7 | 59.9 | 83.8 | 102.8 | 119.8 |
| Brazil | 202.2 | 269.3 | 380.6 | 359.9 | 276.5 | 164.4 | 167.0 | 214.7 | 230.2 | 277.8 |
| Chile | 90.7 | 82.6 | 75.3 | 96.0 | 83.9 | 38.2 | 35.9 | 50.2 | 52.2 | 60.8 |
| Colombia | 91.6 | 92.1 | 147.5 | 145.2 | 124.7 | 42.4 | 43.3 | 48.4 | 50.9 | 53.0 |
| Dominican Republic | 67.4 | 67.4 | 84.5 | 94.7 | 152.4 | 2.5 | 4.6 | 6.8 | 1.4 | 2.4 |
| Venezuela | 109.0 | 97.8 | 111.6 | 95.9 | 84.6 | 29.2 | 25.1 | 34.8 | 24.1 | 32.2 |
| European Union | 2 678.7 | 2 584.7 | 3 413.6 | 3 416.0 | 3 636.7 | 997.8 | 1 154.7 | 1 465.6 | 1 455.8 | 1 536.6 |
| Belgium | 314.0 | 342.6 | 405.7 | 453.2 | 482.2 | 467.6 | 484.6 | 695.9 | 662.1 | 656.7 |
| France | 447.3 | 252.7 | 297.6 | 298.5 | 314.6 | 58.5 | 99.7 | 112.6 | 89.9 | 99.9 |
| Germany | 432.3 | 477.8 | 583.3 | 658.4 | 721.9 | 147.0 | 170.0 | 156.9 | 178.3 | 166.2 |
| Ireland | 60.2 | 127.0 | 178.2 | 122.0 | 107.0 | 10.9 | 9.4 | 28.2 | 30.9 | 31.7 |
| Italy | 216.6 | 224.0 | 242.5 | 242.1 | 199.6 | 18.0 | 25.0 | 44.8 | 36.1 | 39.9 |
| Luxembourg | 5.0 | 2.4 | 0.6 | 0.3 | 4.7 | 22.2 | 22.9 | 23.0 | 23.3 | 18.7 |
| Netherlands | 288.9 | 291.1 | 378.0 | 449.8 | 466.9 | 111.2 | 165.0 | 200.9 | 210.7 | 269.9 |
| Spain | 147.7 | 188.9 | 304.5 | 220.1 | 230.0 | 9.1 | 16.1 | 17.3 | 36.2 | 26.1 |
| United Kingdom | 589.8 | 500.4 | 604.1 | 693.7 | 813.0 | 131.2 | 140.4 | 160.1 | 166.5 | 195.6 |
| Switzerland | 118.3 | 142.2 | 142.6 | 204.4 | 139.5 | 7.5 | 7.1 | 10.5 | 11.5 | 15.7 |
| Asian 10 | 2 973.4 | 3 077.2 | 4 034.5 | 4 004.2 | 3 740.2 | 939.4 | 1 004.5 | 1 173.7 | 1 263.7 | 1 514.1 |
| China | 442.0 | 261.9 | 475.8 | 416.5 | 291.2 | 58.9 | 54.2 | 64.2 | 68.4 | 73.6 |
| Hong Kong | 174.8 | 179.1 | 240.3 | 233.9 | 207.5 | 47.7 | 64.9 | 79.4 | 99.7 | 87.3 |
| Indonesia | 106.5 | 98.9 | 139.7 | 227.4 | 240.5 | 48.6 | 50.5 | 68.1 | 69.0 | 79.2 |
| Japan | 919.7 | 1 050.2 | 1 222.5 | 1 178.6 | 1 189.8 | 333.8 | 370.2 | 433.0 | 441.5 | 556.0 |
| Malaysia | 82.9 | 101.5 | 132.4 | 160.6 | 144.9 | 22.8 | 24.2 | 29.6 | 31.2 | 90.5 |
| Philippines | 46.6 | 49.1 | 93.4 | 104.9 | 74.6 | 7.6 | 9.2 | 9.1 | 9.2 | 11.2 |
| Singapore | 183.9 | 349.9 | 357.3 | 287.3 | 270.2 | 96.8 | 74.6 | 88.8 | 105.1 | 147.5 |
| South Korea | 678.5 | 577.5 | 763.3 | 879.2 | 812.9 | 136.9 | 155.9 | 172.5 | 208.0 | 190.2 |
| Taiwan | 286.7 | 333.6 | 429.2 | 331.2 | 364.4 | 140.2 | 149.0 | 170.4 | 167.9 | 205.1 |
| Thailand | 52.0 | 75.5 | 180.6 | 184.6 | 144.2 | 46.2 | 51.8 | 58.6 | 63.7 | 73.4 |
| Australia | 127.3 | 155.4 | 154.3 | 147.2 | 133.0 | 93.3 | 97.5 | 100.4 | 84.0 | 82.8 |
| India | 59.1 | 64.7 | 153.6 | 71.0 | 228.7 | 21.3 | 23.4 | 40.5 | 39.6 | 45.4 |
| Israel | 73.8 | 80.9 | 94.6 | 123.6 | 87.9 | 10.1 | 14.2 | 21.0 | 19.4 | 24.0 |
| Pakistan | 35.4 | 11.4 | 19.7 | 29.0 | 36.4 | 2.5 | 2.5 | 6.5 | 8.4 | 2.0 |
| Saudi Arabia | 54.7 | 42.0 | 59.9 | 89.5 | 62.6 | 28.4 | 18.6 | 21.7 | 14.6 | 24.6 |
| African 8 | 127.8 | 110.3 | 189.0 | 205.3 | 219.0 | 32.2 | 32.8 | 44.6 | 46.1 | 45.9 |
| Developing Countries | 4 286.6 | 4 402.3 | 5 727.1 | 5 748.0 | 5 393.3 | 1 312.1 | 1 368.3 | 1 580.0 | 1 779.7 | 2 056.1 |

## Table D-2. State Exports of Goods by Destination, 1993–1997 —*Continued*

(State of origin by country of destination, millions of dollars.)

| Destination | District of Columbia | | | | | Florida | | | | |
|---|---|---|---|---|---|---|---|---|---|---|
| | 1993 | 1994 | 1995 | 1996 | 1997 | 1993 | 1994 | 1995 | 1996 | 1997 |
| All destinations | 4 702.1 | 5 150.7 | 5 323.5 | 5 084.8 | 4 881.0 | 14 695.8 | 16 559.2 | 18 564.4 | 19 618.2 | 22 888.6 |
| Canada | 36.2 | 120.9 | 81.8 | 102.1 | 142.1 | 1 571.8 | 1 504.8 | 1 608.2 | 1 631.6 | 1 928.4 |
| Mexico | 17.3 | 30.0 | 12.3 | 8.9 | 17.1 | 769.6 | 993.6 | 536.2 | 737.0 | 1 220.8 |
| Central and South America and Caribbean | 145.3 | 209.6 | 96.2 | 141.2 | 168.5 | 7 908.5 | 9 041.1 | 10 070.1 | 10 742.6 | 12 819.2 |
| Argentina | 12.8 | 14.5 | 4.3 | 3.3 | 12.1 | 747.9 | 865.3 | 695.9 | 794.6 | 889.5 |
| Brazil | 49.8 | 47.5 | 54.1 | 95.7 | 111.4 | 728.4 | 1 115.9 | 1 687.6 | 2 092.2 | 2 586.5 |
| Chile | 5.9 | 5.5 | 10.6 | 10.0 | 13.7 | 343.5 | 423.9 | 437.5 | 483.5 | 462.3 |
| Colombia | 35.5 | 115.1 | 1.7 | 10.1 | 1.8 | 878.6 | 1 072.6 | 1 202.7 | 1 185.0 | 1 321.5 |
| Dominican Republic | 1.4 | 1.0 | 3.1 | 2.7 | 1.5 | 531.0 | 684.4 | 724.5 | 768.2 | 989.2 |
| Venezuela | 1.6 | 3.5 | 0.5 | 2.0 | 1.5 | 1 002.1 | 786.0 | 887.0 | 903.0 | 1 339.4 |
| European Union | 812.7 | 937.8 | 1 288.2 | 929.3 | 1 177.8 | 2 014.5 | 2 033.6 | 2 612.9 | 2 909.9 | 2 772.9 |
| Belgium | 2.0 | 1.6 | 2.9 | 4.3 | 7.5 | 135.9 | 116.6 | 125.0 | 106.3 | 147.4 |
| France | 130.2 | 44.7 | 89.8 | 43.5 | 46.9 | 309.0 | 311.1 | 395.4 | 494.2 | 397.5 |
| Germany | 40.6 | 130.9 | 98.6 | 96.8 | 187.2 | 375.9 | 309.9 | 399.4 | 408.1 | 383.4 |
| Ireland | 1.6 | 1.5 | 2.5 | 1.7 | 2.0 | 43.3 | 50.0 | 77.5 | 67.1 | 88.4 |
| Italy | 41.8 | 34.9 | 55.7 | 35.3 | 36.2 | 124.5 | 138.6 | 191.8 | 317.2 | 207.6 |
| Luxembourg | 0.1 | 1.9 | 0.1 | 0.3 | 0.2 | 4.2 | 2.4 | 2.3 | 2.2 | 3.2 |
| Netherlands | 14.6 | 14.6 | 22.8 | 18.7 | 11.3 | 207.4 | 247.9 | 332.6 | 378.7 | 399.6 |
| Spain | 104.3 | 44.6 | 30.8 | 15.5 | 32.1 | 166.3 | 128.9 | 259.5 | 245.7 | 193.8 |
| United Kingdom | 308.4 | 513.6 | 390.5 | 546.3 | 500.1 | 473.2 | 489.9 | 560.1 | 601.3 | 687.1 |
| Switzerland | 35.4 | 39.7 | 75.4 | 404.4 | 214.4 | 74.8 | 75.8 | 104.2 | 105.3 | 94.4 |
| Asian 10 | 1 138.2 | 1 037.1 | 1 144.6 | 873.0 | 1 194.8 | 1 294.0 | 1 862.9 | 2 288.8 | 2 082.8 | 2 474.2 |
| China | 12.7 | 4.8 | 4.0 | 6.0 | 9.0 | 200.8 | 533.4 | 565.9 | 358.6 | 640.1 |
| Hong Kong | 9.6 | 5.3 | 17.3 | 16.3 | 11.8 | 117.7 | 173.3 | 228.7 | 188.5 | 193.0 |
| Indonesia | 10.9 | 6.4 | 19.7 | 18.5 | 29.0 | 42.4 | 27.8 | 36.3 | 52.9 | 26.6 |
| Japan | 148.4 | 127.9 | 213.9 | 86.7 | 116.4 | 350.8 | 487.4 | 584.1 | 554.2 | 588.2 |
| Malaysia | 8.8 | 24.1 | 20.4 | 32.6 | 64.3 | 79.9 | 88.9 | 75.3 | 108.4 | 114.1 |
| Philippines | 41.7 | 27.2 | 57.2 | 39.2 | 19.3 | 23.8 | 36.9 | 26.8 | 52.7 | 67.4 |
| Singapore | 89.3 | 29.9 | 35.6 | 34.6 | 41.4 | 153.2 | 140.1 | 218.5 | 236.9 | 319.9 |
| South Korea | 47.8 | 39.9 | 19.2 | 34.8 | 37.1 | 182.3 | 179.2 | 357.8 | 351.6 | 341.3 |
| Taiwan | 706.4 | 676.2 | 649.7 | 491.3 | 602.8 | 102.5 | 153.4 | 155.3 | 122.2 | 131.2 |
| Thailand | 62.5 | 95.4 | 107.5 | 113.0 | 263.7 | 40.7 | 42.6 | 40.1 | 56.7 | 52.4 |
| Australia | 178.6 | 215.9 | 253.9 | 187.0 | 260.7 | 179.6 | 227.2 | 238.6 | 332.9 | 304.3 |
| India | 110.4 | 77.7 | 121.7 | 88.8 | 77.4 | 94.1 | 56.0 | 152.1 | 66.6 | 163.5 |
| Israel | 65.4 | 47.3 | 3.8 | 6.1 | 5.5 | 52.0 | 96.7 | 120.8 | 153.5 | 112.8 |
| Pakistan | 4.1 | 2.3 | 1.6 | 123.7 | 48.4 | 33.7 | 55.6 | 37.7 | 89.7 | 68.8 |
| Saudi Arabia | 693.5 | 1 318.0 | 1 271.0 | 904.1 | 514.7 | 115.3 | 100.2 | 95.8 | 92.9 | 173.4 |
| African 8 | 31.4 | 35.0 | 67.5 | 94.4 | 28.3 | 101.9 | 122.3 | 139.1 | 116.1 | 128.1 |
| Developing Countries | 3 234.9 | 3 659.8 | 3 329.5 | 3 252.9 | 2 879.0 | 10 309.9 | 12 083.4 | 13 236.7 | 13 901.0 | 16 944.6 |

| Destination | Georgia | | | | | Hawaii | | | | |
|---|---|---|---|---|---|---|---|---|---|---|
| | 1993 | 1994 | 1995 | 1996 | 1997 | 1993 | 1994 | 1995 | 1996 | 1997 |
| All destinations | 6 050.1 | 7 108.1 | 8 626.8 | 8 618.0 | 9 810.0 | 216.8 | 237.4 | 255.7 | 295.2 | 303.2 |
| Canada | 1 468.9 | 1 646.3 | 1 820.7 | 1 896.9 | 1 999.7 | 13.6 | 13.4 | 53.1 | 69.8 | 33.3 |
| Mexico | 324.2 | 469.5 | 403.8 | 516.9 | 685.7 | 0.3 | 6.0 | 0.3 | 0.7 | 1.0 |
| Central and South America and Caribbean | 857.4 | 1 203.2 | 1 490.0 | 1 418.1 | 1 575.5 | 0.7 | 0.7 | 0.7 | 1.3 | 1.1 |
| Argentina | 112.4 | 198.3 | 152.0 | 130.2 | 152.9 | ..... | ..... | ..... | ..... | ..... |
| Brazil | 61.4 | 130.0 | 316.9 | 277.0 | 339.8 | ..... | ..... | 0.1 | 0.1 | 0.2 |
| Chile | 61.3 | 69.7 | 95.2 | 123.6 | 73.1 | 0.1 | ..... | ..... | ..... | 0.1 |
| Colombia | 83.3 | 82.9 | 96.3 | 97.8 | 122.0 | ..... | ..... | ..... | ..... | 0.1 |
| Dominican Republic | 86.3 | 124.7 | 112.2 | 102.5 | 130.8 | ..... | ..... | ..... | 0.5 | ..... |
| Venezuela | 46.1 | 61.8 | 75.3 | 58.9 | 78.5 | 0.1 | ..... | ..... | ..... | ..... |
| European Union | 1 374.4 | 1 578.2 | 2 010.8 | 1 818.5 | 2 351.4 | 8.3 | 6.5 | 7.8 | 9.4 | 7.1 |
| Belgium | 109.4 | 122.1 | 136.4 | 115.7 | 241.0 | ..... | ..... | ..... | 0.1 | 0.1 |
| France | 183.0 | 172.8 | 243.4 | 246.2 | 279.6 | 1.2 | 1.6 | 1.9 | 1.5 | 1.3 |
| Germany | 274.7 | 259.3 | 298.9 | 311.5 | 340.0 | 2.4 | 2.3 | 2.4 | 2.5 | 1.4 |
| Ireland | 31.5 | 24.3 | 32.0 | 38.3 | 92.5 | ..... | ..... | ..... | ..... | 0.2 |
| Italy | 105.4 | 130.3 | 211.1 | 137.3 | 226.8 | 0.2 | 0.2 | 0.1 | 0.3 | 0.7 |
| Luxembourg | 8.4 | 8.1 | 5.8 | 2.9 | 1.4 | ..... | ..... | ..... | ..... | ..... |
| Netherlands | 172.9 | 241.1 | 282.2 | 259.5 | 380.2 | 0.7 | 0.8 | 1.1 | 1.5 | 0.4 |
| Spain | 60.3 | 78.0 | 96.1 | 96.3 | 106.6 | 0.1 | 0.2 | 0.1 | 0.1 | 0.1 |
| United Kingdom | 291.6 | 385.8 | 459.8 | 426.6 | 489.3 | 3.3 | 0.9 | 1.1 | 2.9 | 2.0 |
| Switzerland | 59.2 | 61.7 | 55.4 | 55.6 | 57.5 | 0.3 | 1.0 | 1.3 | 1.0 | 1.2 |
| Asian 10 | 1 186.6 | 1 287.8 | 1 874.8 | 1 732.9 | 1 976.8 | 169.6 | 180.0 | 170.8 | 190.8 | 217.2 |
| China | 112.1 | 105.6 | 136.1 | 136.5 | 186.9 | 1.9 | 4.9 | 0.6 | 0.8 | 6.2 |
| Hong Kong | 138.2 | 176.4 | 242.4 | 267.5 | 301.5 | 8.9 | 13.2 | 5.4 | 4.5 | 8.1 |
| Indonesia | 82.5 | 71.5 | 41.2 | 78.3 | 79.9 | 0.1 | 0.5 | 0.4 | 0.6 | 3.9 |
| Japan | 419.0 | 401.8 | 589.8 | 567.6 | 622.3 | 97.3 | 120.1 | 126.7 | 161.2 | 173.0 |
| Malaysia | 27.4 | 53.1 | 42.2 | 49.5 | 58.3 | 0.4 | 0.2 | 0.7 | 0.6 | 0.3 |
| Philippines | 25.7 | 29.8 | 36.6 | 52.5 | 48.2 | 31.9 | 2.3 | 1.8 | 3.9 | 1.4 |
| Singapore | 92.2 | 92.8 | 134.3 | 158.2 | 213.3 | 3.5 | 2.1 | 5.6 | 5.1 | 11.9 |
| South Korea | 105.5 | 174.1 | 429.1 | 236.5 | 253.5 | 19.0 | 26.2 | 24.8 | 9.3 | 9.7 |
| Taiwan | 143.9 | 138.9 | 138.8 | 120.9 | 136.4 | 3.1 | 9.6 | 3.8 | 4.2 | 2.1 |
| Thailand | 40.1 | 43.8 | 84.3 | 65.4 | 76.4 | 3.5 | 0.9 | 1.0 | 0.6 | 0.6 |
| Australia | 123.0 | 101.8 | 142.4 | 176.4 | 225.3 | 8.0 | 14.0 | 5.4 | 5.1 | 3.3 |
| India | 26.7 | 63.7 | 92.6 | 84.4 | 103.0 | 0.2 | ..... | ..... | ..... | 0.1 |
| Israel | 25.5 | 26.8 | 41.7 | 36.0 | 51.1 | 0.1 | 0.1 | 0.5 | 0.1 | 0.3 |
| Pakistan | 21.0 | 4.0 | 11.8 | 24.0 | 7.8 | ..... | ..... | ..... | 0.3 | ..... |
| Saudi Arabia | 154.9 | 129.0 | 114.8 | 108.8 | 101.6 | ..... | 0.1 | ..... | 0.1 | 0.3 |
| African 8 | 80.9 | 94.5 | 97.1 | 127.3 | 127.7 | 0.1 | 0.6 | 0.1 | 0.1 | 0.2 |
| Developing Countries | 2 504.1 | 3 210.2 | 3 836.4 | 3 906.4 | 4 347.4 | 86.1 | 78.5 | 57.1 | 43.2 | 63.7 |

## Table D-2.    State Exports of Goods by Destination, 1993–1997 —*Continued*

(State of origin by country of destination, millions of dollars.)

| Destination | Idaho | | | | | Illinois | | | | |
|---|---|---|---|---|---|---|---|---|---|---|
| | 1993 | 1994 | 1995 | 1996 | 1997 | 1993 | 1994 | 1995 | 1996 | 1997 |
| All destinations | 1 235.9 | 1 530.5 | 1 892.5 | 1 610.1 | 1 716.1 | 20 347.2 | 24 534.2 | 30 478.2 | 32 224.9 | 34 225.0 |
| Canada | 156.7 | 208.7 | 292.3 | 276.5 | 277.9 | 4 859.7 | 5 763.1 | 6 452.6 | 6 767.3 | 8 044.2 |
| Mexico | 36.3 | 33.7 | 29.1 | 37.4 | 44.2 | 1 364.2 | 1 825.4 | 1 366.1 | 1 844.7 | 2 189.7 |
| Central and South America and Caribbean | 9.4 | 18.7 | 24.3 | 18.7 | 27.1 | 1 475.1 | 2 044.3 | 2 186.9 | 2 368.8 | 3 012.3 |
| Argentina | 1.5 | 6.3 | 3.5 | 3.4 | 6.1 | 230.3 | 265.3 | 259.2 | 293.5 | 459.1 |
| Brazil | 1.6 | 2.9 | 2.5 | 2.2 | 2.3 | 295.4 | 654.5 | 690.2 | 763.5 | 1 070.5 |
| Chile | 0.8 | 0.8 | 1.2 | 3.9 | 3.7 | 201.2 | 219.2 | 256.5 | 297.8 | 235.1 |
| Colombia | 1.0 | 1.0 | 0.6 | 0.7 | 1.1 | 131.3 | 195.1 | 195.4 | 196.9 | 239.0 |
| Dominican Republic | ..... | 0.1 | 0.1 | 0.1 | 0.7 | 55.5 | 76.8 | 94.5 | 101.5 | 106.2 |
| Venezuela | 1.0 | 0.6 | 0.5 | 0.6 | 1.8 | 203.1 | 182.5 | 157.9 | 181.4 | 335.5 |
| European Union | 380.4 | 428.5 | 528.8 | 384.9 | 460.9 | 5 025.2 | 5 970.4 | 7 419.0 | 8 062.6 | 8 713.5 |
| Belgium | 10.4 | 12.2 | 5.8 | 3.2 | 2.1 | 730.8 | 928.7 | 1 077.1 | 1 150.4 | 1 260.6 |
| France | 39.1 | 49.2 | 66.7 | 26.2 | 17.4 | 514.2 | 646.1 | 791.7 | 811.8 | 916.1 |
| Germany | 78.8 | 82.4 | 83.0 | 92.0 | 132.2 | 1 090.7 | 1 224.9 | 1 491.2 | 1 597.7 | 1 643.5 |
| Ireland | 8.2 | 21.2 | 47.3 | 14.7 | 13.9 | 74.4 | 84.0 | 120.6 | 136.6 | 275.9 |
| Italy | 24.9 | 26.7 | 38.9 | 37.8 | 23.4 | 364.7 | 334.6 | 501.2 | 539.3 | 524.3 |
| Luxembourg | ..... | ..... | ..... | 0.1 | ..... | 2.0 | 1.4 | 1.4 | 1.6 | 2.7 |
| Netherlands | 54.0 | 16.0 | 57.1 | 71.5 | 73.1 | 631.0 | 788.6 | 915.8 | 1 171.3 | 1 369.3 |
| Spain | 6.0 | 5.6 | 6.6 | 6.0 | 7.6 | 193.9 | 270.3 | 479.8 | 513.6 | 399.4 |
| United Kingdom | 142.2 | 186.6 | 192.4 | 116.4 | 169.8 | 1 044.2 | 1 276.0 | 1 572.1 | 1 641.8 | 1 830.8 |
| Switzerland | 6.3 | 5.8 | 6.3 | 5.9 | 23.5 | 154.4 | 105.7 | 119.6 | 134.4 | 119.2 |
| Asian 10 | 591.7 | 768.1 | 922.6 | 805.5 | 796.5 | 4 762.3 | 5 894.1 | 8 803.2 | 8 626.1 | 7 714.3 |
| China | 2.3 | 5.9 | 22.3 | 16.0 | 17.4 | 728.3 | 1 001.6 | 1 219.9 | 1 040.4 | 1 005.0 |
| Hong Kong | 27.5 | 29.6 | 41.3 | 35.8 | 72.5 | 296.1 | 378.5 | 763.0 | 629.9 | 985.4 |
| Indonesia | 7.5 | 6.8 | 5.3 | 23.8 | 10.8 | 94.1 | 127.3 | 258.1 | 339.4 | 317.7 |
| Japan | 290.4 | 352.8 | 348.0 | 309.4 | 317.1 | 1 916.8 | 2 121.5 | 2 940.1 | 3 024.6 | 2 437.4 |
| Malaysia | 9.4 | 17.8 | 40.7 | 41.7 | 51.9 | 147.5 | 152.3 | 365.0 | 334.2 | 261.8 |
| Philippines | 60.1 | 57.8 | 75.9 | 120.3 | 73.7 | 103.5 | 139.7 | 335.8 | 297.7 | 324.9 |
| Singapore | 86.1 | 149.5 | 208.6 | 154.8 | 120.2 | 309.8 | 356.3 | 649.7 | 744.7 | 720.6 |
| South Korea | 26.6 | 29.2 | 35.5 | 36.8 | 32.5 | 533.2 | 698.1 | 1 266.2 | 1 301.0 | 892.6 |
| Taiwan | 77.4 | 110.6 | 132.0 | 60.4 | 97.2 | 481.2 | 637.8 | 592.1 | 512.2 | 496.1 |
| Thailand | 4.5 | 8.0 | 13.1 | 6.7 | 3.1 | 151.9 | 281.1 | 413.4 | 401.9 | 272.8 |
| Australia | 25.3 | 17.8 | 18.9 | 11.0 | 20.1 | 679.3 | 786.3 | 1 131.2 | 1 243.1 | 1 196.2 |
| India | 0.2 | 0.7 | 2.0 | 1.1 | 0.6 | 115.5 | 142.8 | 222.8 | 166.8 | 184.0 |
| Israel | 8.0 | 13.3 | 14.8 | 13.5 | 8.5 | 155.4 | 220.9 | 371.0 | 436.1 | 372.4 |
| Pakistan | ..... | 0.2 | 0.1 | 0.2 | 0.1 | 95.2 | 74.8 | 110.1 | 96.5 | 105.3 |
| Saudi Arabia | 1.2 | 0.5 | 1.5 | 5.8 | 3.9 | 190.4 | 213.2 | 200.7 | 251.4 | 349.1 |
| African 8 | 2.2 | 4.4 | 6.7 | 2.8 | 3.9 | 192.9 | 263.8 | 386.7 | 506.1 | 498.5 |
| Developing Countries | 363.6 | 496.6 | 678.4 | 611.1 | 603.4 | 7 297.0 | 9 338.7 | 11 678.1 | 12 072.5 | 12 915.7 |

| Destination | Indiana | | | | | Iowa | | | | |
|---|---|---|---|---|---|---|---|---|---|---|
| | 1993 | 1994 | 1995 | 1996 | 1997 | 1993 | 1994 | 1995 | 1996 | 1997 |
| All destinations | 8 445.2 | 9 534.0 | 11 052.0 | 12 119.0 | 13 097.3 | 1 955.7 | 2 331.4 | 2 577.8 | 2 695.1 | 3 116.7 |
| Canada | 4 264.6 | 4 593.6 | 4 594.8 | 4 630.3 | 5 060.3 | 918.5 | 1 152.8 | 1 220.5 | 1 277.2 | 1 569.1 |
| Mexico | 1 167.7 | 1 492.6 | 1 955.7 | 2 529.3 | 2 573.3 | 78.2 | 99.2 | 81.9 | 110.3 | 167.7 |
| Central and South America and Caribbean | 250.5 | 316.0 | 486.2 | 511.1 | 716.0 | 91.3 | 83.3 | 108.0 | 140.5 | 182.7 |
| Argentina | 31.1 | 45.2 | 59.5 | 65.4 | 133.1 | 14.3 | 14.1 | 17.8 | 24.9 | 37.6 |
| Brazil | 69.5 | 103.5 | 188.8 | 227.0 | 353.0 | 16.3 | 14.7 | 25.4 | 31.5 | 46.3 |
| Chile | 16.6 | 18.5 | 36.7 | 38.1 | 41.0 | 16.9 | 15.0 | 16.3 | 23.5 | 27.7 |
| Colombia | 21.6 | 27.2 | 63.8 | 50.2 | 55.7 | 5.3 | 5.9 | 7.9 | 14.0 | 16.7 |
| Dominican Republic | 6.2 | 11.0 | 5.6 | 6.1 | 7.3 | 1.9 | 1.9 | 2.5 | 2.8 | 3.4 |
| Venezuela | 49.7 | 39.5 | 33.9 | 36.6 | 28.5 | 8.4 | 6.1 | 8.0 | 7.9 | 11.3 |
| European Union | 1 353.3 | 1 555.7 | 1 901.8 | 2 149.5 | 2 377.7 | 396.0 | 430.0 | 483.4 | 507.3 | 524.9 |
| Belgium | 68.7 | 84.8 | 116.5 | 96.1 | 77.1 | 17.8 | 24.5 | 24.5 | 21.7 | 17.6 |
| France | 146.5 | 170.1 | 191.2 | 298.8 | 389.2 | 59.8 | 54.7 | 46.6 | 63.1 | 81.0 |
| Germany | 219.5 | 294.1 | 290.3 | 288.9 | 337.3 | 51.1 | 52.6 | 71.4 | 84.1 | 86.2 |
| Ireland | 67.4 | 46.7 | 54.9 | 71.9 | 109.7 | 7.4 | 12.2 | 10.4 | 10.3 | 9.3 |
| Italy | 94.9 | 103.8 | 116.8 | 147.2 | 132.1 | 51.9 | 56.6 | 64.9 | 73.7 | 59.0 |
| Luxembourg | 3.4 | 2.9 | 2.2 | 2.1 | 3.0 | 1.5 | 0.4 | 0.9 | 0.8 | 0.2 |
| Netherlands | 160.8 | 175.2 | 250.4 | 301.9 | 364.8 | 83.7 | 82.8 | 108.0 | 92.0 | 84.5 |
| Spain | 51.9 | 46.8 | 62.6 | 56.7 | 49.8 | 13.3 | 17.7 | 27.4 | 18.4 | 21.2 |
| United Kingdom | 427.9 | 495.7 | 627.5 | 644.0 | 704.8 | 84.3 | 85.0 | 87.9 | 93.2 | 114.1 |
| Switzerland | 23.9 | 28.3 | 35.8 | 46.6 | 42.5 | 3.7 | 5.1 | 14.7 | 6.2 | 7.4 |
| Asian 10 | 979.8 | 1 182.1 | 1 528.6 | 1 691.4 | 1 757.0 | 314.6 | 394.7 | 486.5 | 465.6 | 464.2 |
| China | 31.7 | 40.6 | 81.4 | 154.6 | 132.1 | 23.6 | 18.4 | 27.3 | 22.6 | 25.1 |
| Hong Kong | 60.1 | 81.8 | 100.9 | 105.4 | 131.6 | 19.6 | 22.4 | 31.3 | 33.5 | 27.3 |
| Indonesia | 7.6 | 8.9 | 14.5 | 14.9 | 18.0 | 5.7 | 12.6 | 12.5 | 10.7 | 12.9 |
| Japan | 491.8 | 571.0 | 733.6 | 747.2 | 729.9 | 86.5 | 111.1 | 145.1 | 159.3 | 161.5 |
| Malaysia | 22.8 | 46.5 | 40.5 | 45.5 | 63.3 | 9.7 | 12.2 | 17.2 | 15.4 | 19.7 |
| Philippines | 12.7 | 29.9 | 66.4 | 33.7 | 50.3 | 7.0 | 9.1 | 16.2 | 16.4 | 15.1 |
| Singapore | 104.7 | 126.5 | 149.8 | 188.1 | 185.2 | 38.9 | 50.1 | 65.8 | 61.6 | 55.0 |
| South Korea | 116.1 | 158.7 | 183.0 | 199.3 | 227.1 | 56.7 | 83.0 | 87.3 | 82.8 | 90.8 |
| Taiwan | 100.4 | 79.0 | 116.1 | 140.9 | 134.4 | 53.3 | 56.9 | 61.3 | 41.3 | 35.1 |
| Thailand | 31.8 | 39.3 | 42.5 | 61.7 | 85.2 | 13.7 | 19.0 | 22.5 | 22.0 | 21.7 |
| Australia | 128.5 | 152.2 | 168.3 | 201.1 | 201.0 | 37.6 | 44.0 | 60.1 | 54.3 | 65.2 |
| India | 13.9 | 18.7 | 35.6 | 46.7 | 50.7 | 1.1 | 2.1 | 12.8 | 5.5 | 7.4 |
| Israel | 14.7 | 22.6 | 31.1 | 35.6 | 33.0 | 13.2 | 10.5 | 10.4 | 12.8 | 9.5 |
| Pakistan | 3.6 | 4.8 | 4.2 | 5.3 | 2.6 | 1.7 | 1.0 | 2.6 | 2.2 | 2.9 |
| Saudi Arabia | 45.7 | 33.7 | 35.1 | 32.9 | 41.0 | 10.3 | 9.5 | 8.3 | 11.6 | 10.9 |
| African 8 | 27.8 | 23.4 | 33.0 | 33.3 | 41.6 | 9.4 | 14.4 | 16.3 | 14.0 | 18.4 |
| Developing Countries | 2 110.8 | 2 569.4 | 3 509.4 | 4 238.0 | 4 548.4 | 489.7 | 561.1 | 615.6 | 652.7 | 744.3 |

## Table D-2.  State Exports of Goods by Destination, 1993–1997 —*Continued*

(State of origin by country of destination, millions of dollars.)

| Destination | Kansas | | | | | Kentucky | | | | |
|---|---|---|---|---|---|---|---|---|---|---|
| | 1993 | 1994 | 1995 | 1996 | 1997 | 1993 | 1994 | 1995 | 1996 | 1997 |
| **All destinations** | 3 109.4 | 3 498.3 | 4 461.5 | 4 971.3 | 5 133.2 | 3 325.9 | 4 188.2 | 5 030.1 | 5 824.2 | 6 904.1 |
| Canada | 473.1 | 571.2 | 687.0 | 696.0 | 834.4 | 1 058.3 | 1 571.1 | 1 804.7 | 1 905.3 | 2 368.9 |
| Mexico | 186.9 | 366.0 | 348.8 | 643.1 | 449.2 | 189.9 | 232.1 | 188.0 | 280.1 | 345.1 |
| Central and South America and Caribbean | 326.1 | 407.3 | 580.5 | 699.7 | 931.2 | 130.9 | 156.5 | 304.0 | 446.6 | 572.9 |
| Argentina | 25.0 | 33.3 | 45.5 | 39.2 | 97.3 | 12.0 | 26.2 | 24.1 | 29.5 | 35.2 |
| Brazil | 12.8 | 40.8 | 50.5 | 58.0 | 126.1 | 30.5 | 15.8 | 39.7 | 46.6 | 69.2 |
| Chile | 22.4 | 18.5 | 68.3 | 47.0 | 17.9 | 11.3 | 12.4 | 17.4 | 23.3 | 24.1 |
| Colombia | 39.7 | 78.6 | 106.7 | 147.3 | 167.7 | 8.8 | 12.1 | 20.7 | 19.3 | 29.1 |
| Dominican Republic | 58.3 | 42.4 | 57.3 | 79.5 | 67.8 | 1.4 | 6.2 | 35.1 | 68.0 | 92.8 |
| Venezuela | 83.5 | 71.4 | 104.7 | 120.7 | 216.0 | 9.0 | 8.7 | 21.4 | 12.5 | 27.3 |
| European Union | 456.1 | 488.4 | 483.8 | 636.9 | 744.6 | 613.6 | 718.4 | 790.2 | 1 099.0 | 1 202.7 |
| Belgium | 40.1 | 57.5 | 64.5 | 63.5 | 75.6 | 138.5 | 123.0 | 58.4 | 56.2 | 51.2 |
| France | 88.4 | 52.3 | 64.3 | 108.1 | 98.2 | 62.5 | 166.8 | 151.6 | 258.9 | 366.5 |
| Germany | 91.5 | 121.5 | 98.0 | 94.9 | 114.8 | 135.0 | 136.6 | 228.6 | 229.6 | 232.7 |
| Ireland | 3.7 | 2.6 | 12.9 | 11.5 | 13.7 | 8.6 | 22.1 | 17.6 | 23.1 | 25.6 |
| Italy | 32.5 | 42.4 | 35.2 | 44.7 | 38.3 | 36.9 | 36.8 | 34.4 | 39.9 | 41.7 |
| Luxembourg | 0.2 | 0.2 | 0.5 | 6.1 | 1.7 | 0.1 | ..... | 0.1 | 0.1 | ..... |
| Netherlands | 51.2 | 36.1 | 32.6 | 73.1 | 102.0 | 53.4 | 56.7 | 60.3 | 114.3 | 132.6 |
| Spain | 18.4 | 27.4 | 37.4 | 23.1 | 33.0 | 38.2 | 33.9 | 35.9 | 51.3 | 53.3 |
| United Kingdom | 88.5 | 92.7 | 90.5 | 129.6 | 173.4 | 95.6 | 114.7 | 167.2 | 283.9 | 255.2 |
| Switzerland | 37.3 | 27.4 | 38.4 | 34.6 | 49.6 | 6.4 | 8.8 | 9.7 | 7.2 | 18.6 |
| Asian 10 | 1 063.9 | 1 125.3 | 1 827.4 | 1 761.2 | 1 501.7 | 1 065.1 | 1 109.8 | 1 478.6 | 1 605.4 | 1 816.8 |
| China | 44.7 | 45.7 | 49.6 | 30.7 | 62.6 | 5.5 | 14.6 | 17.7 | 30.2 | 36.4 |
| Hong Kong | 12.3 | 15.5 | 26.6 | 70.6 | 29.3 | 95.7 | 64.6 | 64.1 | 66.6 | 41.8 |
| Indonesia | 3.2 | 15.4 | 9.6 | 16.0 | 20.0 | 2.7 | 4.7 | 11.1 | 9.4 | 14.3 |
| Japan | 684.5 | 697.4 | 1 057.3 | 1 075.0 | 921.8 | 769.6 | 752.3 | 1 041.8 | 1 143.0 | 1 385.0 |
| Malaysia | 12.3 | 41.2 | 72.9 | 57.8 | 28.2 | 11.0 | 12.3 | 20.4 | 23.2 | 43.1 |
| Philippines | 7.1 | 6.3 | 15.7 | 18.3 | 35.7 | 3.2 | 46.9 | 49.6 | 33.0 | 22.8 |
| Singapore | 38.9 | 25.3 | 24.0 | 51.2 | 33.5 | 74.2 | 90.3 | 88.6 | 96.0 | 91.6 |
| South Korea | 67.3 | 107.7 | 341.5 | 239.3 | 179.1 | 50.8 | 72.2 | 107.0 | 116.1 | 99.6 |
| Taiwan | 183.1 | 159.5 | 216.3 | 171.6 | 153.3 | 38.8 | 38.6 | 53.6 | 66.5 | 58.2 |
| Thailand | 10.6 | 11.4 | 14.1 | 30.7 | 38.1 | 13.6 | 13.2 | 24.7 | 21.4 | 24.1 |
| Australia | 50.8 | 61.6 | 63.5 | 170.4 | 98.7 | 46.8 | 78.1 | 90.8 | 117.9 | 140.0 |
| India | 11.9 | 24.1 | 45.8 | 14.5 | 46.6 | 2.8 | 3.8 | 9.8 | 12.1 | 22.1 |
| Israel | 6.9 | 8.5 | 7.5 | 24.5 | 9.1 | 24.3 | 31.1 | 38.7 | 36.7 | 33.0 |
| Pakistan | 11.4 | 7.7 | 0.9 | 1.7 | 1.6 | 1.1 | 0.6 | 1.0 | 2.0 | 0.9 |
| Saudi Arabia | 23.8 | 20.3 | 18.1 | 14.5 | 64.8 | 38.3 | 48.7 | 40.0 | 29.0 | 40.1 |
| African 8 | 49.9 | 70.7 | 70.0 | 102.1 | 85.9 | 10.0 | 13.9 | 16.6 | 16.3 | 20.4 |
| Developing Countries | 1 166.4 | 1 516.4 | 2 007.7 | 2 199.4 | 2 296.3 | 786.2 | 956.3 | 1 162.0 | 1 405.3 | 1 594.2 |

| Destination | Louisiana | | | | | Maine | | | | |
|---|---|---|---|---|---|---|---|---|---|---|
| | 1993 | 1994 | 1995 | 1996 | 1997 | 1993 | 1994 | 1995 | 1996 | 1997 |
| **All destinations** | 3 220.3 | 3 576.9 | 4 580.7 | 4 730.8 | 4 373.5 | 1 065.3 | 1 138.9 | 1 318.2 | 1 248.8 | 1 590.2 |
| Canada | 372.3 | 449.1 | 557.4 | 542.9 | 663.1 | 362.1 | 406.2 | 469.8 | 489.0 | 557.4 |
| Mexico | 61.1 | 108.9 | 79.8 | 145.5 | 132.6 | 28.7 | 36.0 | 10.7 | 12.3 | 18.4 |
| Central and South America and Caribbean | 417.8 | 391.8 | 537.4 | 517.6 | 597.1 | 42.3 | 39.2 | 36.7 | 40.6 | 52.1 |
| Argentina | 26.7 | 28.6 | 21.3 | 17.6 | 34.4 | 1.3 | 1.5 | 1.3 | 1.2 | 7.6 |
| Brazil | 23.0 | 30.8 | 54.5 | 56.1 | 70.2 | 5.5 | 3.5 | 6.1 | 6.0 | 5.5 |
| Chile | 19.0 | 12.9 | 17.3 | 41.1 | 41.6 | 4.6 | 3.1 | 1.4 | 3.0 | 1.7 |
| Colombia | 31.8 | 24.8 | 59.8 | 37.9 | 37.9 | 1.8 | 2.3 | 1.0 | 1.3 | 2.8 |
| Dominican Republic | 13.0 | 16.6 | 15.5 | 11.9 | 18.9 | 17.8 | 15.6 | 11.3 | 13.1 | 13.3 |
| Venezuela | 66.4 | 70.0 | 62.9 | 72.6 | 87.0 | 4.0 | 2.0 | 3.0 | 1.8 | 5.7 |
| European Union | 639.1 | 785.6 | 1 072.2 | 976.6 | 841.6 | 187.1 | 204.5 | 228.3 | 208.0 | 220.8 |
| Belgium | 159.2 | 206.8 | 241.0 | 237.1 | 187.6 | 29.7 | 30.5 | 10.4 | 8.4 | 8.7 |
| France | 101.4 | 82.4 | 110.9 | 60.2 | 65.1 | 36.3 | 36.9 | 56.5 | 61.3 | 46.1 |
| Germany | 44.1 | 70.4 | 63.6 | 122.1 | 90.1 | 35.7 | 27.6 | 30.9 | 34.0 | 28.4 |
| Ireland | 15.5 | 24.6 | 24.9 | 16.3 | 6.9 | 1.2 | 0.9 | 1.2 | 2.4 | 7.7 |
| Italy | 31.6 | 31.2 | 52.5 | 40.3 | 53.3 | 15.0 | 15.1 | 13.5 | 18.1 | 12.6 |
| Luxembourg | ..... | ..... | 0.5 | 0.3 | 0.2 | ..... | ..... | ..... | ..... | 0.2 |
| Netherlands | 142.2 | 155.8 | 288.6 | 226.8 | 180.0 | 15.2 | 19.1 | 16.7 | 11.8 | 11.2 |
| Spain | 45.2 | 86.8 | 111.6 | 126.0 | 105.6 | 5.2 | 5.5 | 5.9 | 8.3 | 17.7 |
| United Kingdom | 54.0 | 73.0 | 113.6 | 97.2 | 97.9 | 29.0 | 43.8 | 62.4 | 44.5 | 59.1 |
| Switzerland | 10.7 | 10.8 | 9.4 | 9.4 | 3.6 | 2.5 | 1.8 | 3.6 | 3.4 | 5.2 |
| Asian 10 | 1 192.5 | 1 272.7 | 1 701.7 | 1 978.3 | 1 568.4 | 371.5 | 364.7 | 489.8 | 400.5 | 668.6 |
| China | 26.9 | 51.4 | 236.2 | 131.6 | 92.3 | 8.1 | 3.0 | 7.8 | 6.2 | 17.2 |
| Hong Kong | 19.2 | 21.0 | 31.0 | 26.4 | 27.7 | 47.6 | 50.1 | 48.6 | 43.7 | 44.4 |
| Indonesia | 151.4 | 213.5 | 92.3 | 68.6 | 39.7 | 3.0 | 6.5 | 7.4 | 4.1 | 4.5 |
| Japan | 781.5 | 800.5 | 879.8 | 1 111.3 | 974.2 | 68.5 | 109.1 | 102.1 | 99.6 | 88.2 |
| Malaysia | 5.9 | 9.7 | 42.1 | 92.4 | 55.9 | 155.6 | 102.0 | 176.5 | 95.2 | 242.2 |
| Philippines | 10.1 | 6.5 | 6.4 | 9.2 | 10.6 | 2.5 | 1.2 | 3.2 | 3.5 | 5.4 |
| Singapore | 53.2 | 47.9 | 37.8 | 51.8 | 45.6 | 34.8 | 36.5 | 46.3 | 47.9 | 166.1 |
| South Korea | 57.3 | 61.1 | 98.9 | 144.8 | 127.0 | 18.1 | 18.2 | 49.2 | 69.2 | 65.6 |
| Taiwan | 77.1 | 50.2 | 247.3 | 324.3 | 173.4 | 25.9 | 28.9 | 37.5 | 19.6 | 21.3 |
| Thailand | 9.9 | 10.9 | 30.0 | 17.8 | 21.9 | 7.3 | 9.3 | 11.3 | 11.6 | 13.7 |
| Australia | 43.8 | 55.4 | 57.9 | 69.5 | 72.8 | 16.5 | 18.2 | 15.1 | 15.8 | 6.5 |
| India | 5.3 | 10.0 | 25.0 | 21.8 | 20.0 | 2.1 | 1.6 | 3.0 | 2.9 | 2.3 |
| Israel | 15.1 | 46.6 | 60.3 | 38.0 | 25.6 | 6.9 | 22.2 | 26.6 | 39.7 | 9.6 |
| Pakistan | 3.5 | 2.4 | 23.6 | 2.9 | 1.9 | 0.1 | ..... | 0.2 | 0.2 | 0.1 |
| Saudi Arabia | 96.8 | 73.6 | 91.1 | 115.7 | 138.2 | 19.7 | 17.7 | 7.9 | 7.3 | 4.5 |
| African 8 | 158.0 | 86.3 | 68.1 | 96.6 | 83.1 | 3.5 | 2.6 | 3.9 | 7.4 | 16.5 |
| Developing Countries | 1 319.0 | 1 407.9 | 1 900.8 | 1 915.0 | 1 733.5 | 418.9 | 391.6 | 485.8 | 420.2 | 694.9 |

## Table D-2.  State Exports of Goods by Destination, 1993–1997 —*Continued*

(State of origin by country of destination, millions of dollars.)

| Destination | Maryland | | | | | Massachussetts | | | | |
|---|---|---|---|---|---|---|---|---|---|---|
| | 1993 | 1994 | 1995 | 1996 | 1997 | 1993 | 1994 | 1995 | 1996 | 1997 |
| All destinations | 2 713.7 | 2 848.5 | 3 439.0 | 3 509.9 | 3 861.0 | 11 594.0 | 12 586.0 | 14 396.4 | 15 368.4 | 17 368.1 |
| Canada | 601.8 | 621.4 | 551.9 | 553.3 | 653.2 | 2 540.6 | 2 860.4 | 3 339.9 | 3 486.8 | 3 677.5 |
| Mexico | 96.2 | 100.4 | 94.5 | 174.9 | 199.2 | 374.4 | 535.1 | 316.7 | 388.8 | 467.6 |
| Central and South America and Caribbean | 183.4 | 250.7 | 288.8 | 262.3 | 270.2 | 428.9 | 464.7 | 542.7 | 582.8 | 677.4 |
| Argentina | 36.9 | 42.4 | 43.3 | 33.7 | 36.3 | 65.7 | 73.6 | 56.5 | 52.8 | 68.9 |
| Brazil | 28.2 | 33.4 | 73.2 | 62.3 | 51.3 | 108.2 | 134.6 | 181.6 | 219.6 | 264.1 |
| Chile | 12.4 | 29.9 | 47.5 | 54.4 | 48.4 | 37.0 | 44.6 | 50.2 | 43.9 | 50.2 |
| Colombia | 15.9 | 23.0 | 24.3 | 25.1 | 35.5 | 38.9 | 41.9 | 44.3 | 42.0 | 55.0 |
| Dominican Republic | 7.6 | 35.8 | 4.2 | 7.5 | 8.0 | 18.8 | 20.1 | 15.1 | 35.0 | 34.1 |
| Venezuela | 20.9 | 25.8 | 9.2 | 7.7 | 9.9 | 39.0 | 32.5 | 39.9 | 35.8 | 46.0 |
| European Union | 849.3 | 886.9 | 1 167.7 | 1 076.3 | 1 077.5 | 4 398.5 | 4 629.8 | 5 288.6 | 5 353.1 | 5 889.3 |
| Belgium | 169.9 | 196.6 | 166.4 | 167.1 | 197.7 | 188.8 | 245.2 | 326.6 | 492.1 | 417.7 |
| France | 69.8 | 89.4 | 107.8 | 84.2 | 108.8 | 549.2 | 542.0 | 528.2 | 562.8 | 626.7 |
| Germany | 94.5 | 87.9 | 121.7 | 138.5 | 165.3 | 920.4 | 851.8 | 1 040.5 | 1 098.8 | 1 019.4 |
| Ireland | 12.1 | 14.0 | 16.5 | 15.8 | 11.0 | 311.3 | 379.1 | 368.8 | 316.4 | 330.4 |
| Italy | 52.8 | 58.4 | 64.8 | 71.6 | 76.6 | 262.0 | 275.2 | 298.9 | 309.9 | 360.4 |
| Luxembourg | 4.0 | 2.6 | 1.8 | 0.2 | 1.9 | 3.6 | 5.1 | 12.0 | 5.4 | 2.8 |
| Netherlands | 211.4 | 167.9 | 226.6 | 201.8 | 128.3 | 761.9 | 710.1 | 763.4 | 692.3 | 928.9 |
| Spain | 23.2 | 30.3 | 68.4 | 31.2 | 29.4 | 119.7 | 108.6 | 150.8 | 154.2 | 137.1 |
| United Kingdom | 163.6 | 189.9 | 329.9 | 308.6 | 286.7 | 1 028.0 | 1 245.0 | 1 479.0 | 1 415.2 | 1 706.4 |
| Switzerland | 13.0 | 11.2 | 14.8 | 12.3 | 9.0 | 157.8 | 133.2 | 149.5 | 153.4 | 161.6 |
| Asian 10 | 448.1 | 448.6 | 608.8 | 663.8 | 766.2 | 2 768.3 | 3 023.8 | 3 713.9 | 4 316.5 | 5 323.4 |
| China | 49.1 | 39.6 | 68.1 | 99.6 | 84.9 | 117.1 | 130.9 | 144.8 | 162.7 | 159.8 |
| Hong Kong | 51.6 | 50.4 | 56.6 | 54.1 | 73.0 | 372.5 | 378.0 | 464.4 | 432.4 | 536.6 |
| Indonesia | 7.0 | 8.8 | 63.7 | 75.1 | 80.2 | 43.2 | 35.3 | 47.6 | 74.1 | 85.6 |
| Japan | 163.1 | 134.3 | 153.1 | 171.1 | 158.6 | 1 046.5 | 1 155.1 | 1 396.4 | 1 680.5 | 1 969.0 |
| Malaysia | 13.7 | 28.9 | 16.9 | 14.7 | 24.7 | 60.1 | 78.2 | 154.8 | 131.9 | 205.6 |
| Philippines | 9.0 | 25.4 | 38.8 | 23.7 | 40.4 | 116.7 | 72.3 | 126.1 | 198.6 | 331.2 |
| Singapore | 29.5 | 31.6 | 64.5 | 72.5 | 51.4 | 356.3 | 329.0 | 352.4 | 409.0 | 544.8 |
| South Korea | 44.2 | 48.1 | 60.8 | 74.6 | 95.4 | 320.0 | 348.4 | 432.5 | 530.7 | 616.5 |
| Taiwan | 68.3 | 67.2 | 66.0 | 57.4 | 64.7 | 281.8 | 427.6 | 489.6 | 592.2 | 789.0 |
| Thailand | 12.7 | 14.3 | 20.4 | 21.0 | 92.8 | 54.1 | 69.1 | 105.3 | 104.2 | 85.4 |
| Australia | 52.5 | 47.7 | 68.3 | 73.6 | 83.5 | 285.7 | 282.9 | 316.6 | 326.6 | 314.8 |
| India | 16.9 | 15.6 | 28.1 | 23.2 | 59.0 | 47.0 | 55.8 | 60.6 | 54.7 | 61.6 |
| Israel | 17.4 | 34.4 | 35.4 | 27.6 | 23.4 | 143.4 | 139.8 | 134.8 | 159.3 | 176.5 |
| Pakistan | 3.4 | 3.5 | 5.0 | 5.1 | 10.2 | 6.2 | 3.9 | 4.8 | 5.1 | 6.4 |
| Saudi Arabia | 97.9 | 98.8 | 115.9 | 62.6 | 94.1 | 71.2 | 56.4 | 52.3 | 61.6 | 69.4 |
| African 8 | 50.7 | 85.6 | 71.3 | 90.8 | 85.0 | 65.0 | 72.2 | 90.9 | 93.3 | 92.4 |
| Developing Countries | 951.0 | 1 053.1 | 1 370.3 | 1 493.8 | 1 758.0 | 2 989.2 | 3 340.2 | 3 695.6 | 4 153.6 | 5 121.1 |

| Destination | Michigan | | | | | Minnesota | | | | |
|---|---|---|---|---|---|---|---|---|---|---|
| | 1993 | 1994 | 1995 | 1996 | 1997 | 1993 | 1994 | 1995 | 1996 | 1997 |
| All destinations | 25 322.5 | 36 812.1 | 37 102.3 | 38 128.2 | 37 920.1 | 9 974.4 | 10 011.1 | 12 404.3 | 13 884.1 | 13 793.3 |
| Canada | 11 434.1 | 20 809.1 | 21 935.9 | 21 949.6 | 19 760.2 | 1 950.4 | 2 108.5 | 2 442.2 | 2 860.6 | 3 190.2 |
| Mexico | 5 630.5 | 7 088.5 | 5 002.8 | 4 686.8 | 6 458.0 | 228.6 | 329.8 | 505.7 | 846.3 | 822.8 |
| Central and South America and Caribbean | 665.1 | 752.5 | 1 028.8 | 1 209.6 | 1 613.8 | 457.6 | 450.7 | 686.6 | 762.0 | 780.8 |
| Argentina | 44.7 | 77.0 | 68.6 | 137.1 | 219.2 | 32.1 | 44.1 | 33.3 | 40.9 | 89.2 |
| Brazil | 187.4 | 299.7 | 471.4 | 491.8 | 550.5 | 38.6 | 88.8 | 81.2 | 143.3 | 118.3 |
| Chile | 62.4 | 81.9 | 148.3 | 152.2 | 167.3 | 34.3 | 29.4 | 69.2 | 54.5 | 54.9 |
| Colombia | 35.8 | 36.0 | 35.2 | 26.1 | 40.9 | 23.4 | 33.5 | 65.7 | 88.0 | 58.9 |
| Dominican Republic | 20.4 | 20.0 | 18.1 | 12.2 | 6.5 | 33.4 | 14.7 | 22.9 | 10.7 | 36.3 |
| Venezuela | 199.1 | 110.0 | 112.8 | 214.9 | 446.3 | 62.4 | 34.0 | 95.2 | 84.4 | 98.4 |
| European Union | 3 139.9 | 3 553.2 | 4 193.2 | 4 155.6 | 4 745.7 | 3 362.2 | 3 393.6 | 4 049.7 | 4 075.7 | 4 025.2 |
| Belgium | 404.6 | 541.4 | 608.8 | 581.4 | 1 081.1 | 151.6 | 163.7 | 245.7 | 239.7 | 173.4 |
| France | 361.7 | 392.3 | 345.9 | 283.7 | 297.6 | 283.7 | 236.7 | 265.4 | 280.2 | 362.9 |
| Germany | 911.8 | 893.6 | 1 054.5 | 999.4 | 1 057.0 | 530.9 | 473.8 | 514.0 | 658.7 | 593.4 |
| Ireland | 15.7 | 20.8 | 27.6 | 20.0 | 31.8 | 175.8 | 177.6 | 216.9 | 244.1 | 265.6 |
| Italy | 125.5 | 124.8 | 158.8 | 154.3 | 143.0 | 177.8 | 229.8 | 322.6 | 288.2 | 236.3 |
| Luxembourg | 12.7 | 10.7 | 13.2 | 35.1 | 23.2 | 1.4 | 1.2 | 1.8 | 0.8 | 0.7 |
| Netherlands | 120.3 | 155.3 | 175.6 | 205.8 | 238.7 | 947.2 | 968.5 | 1 072.5 | 989.1 | 846.2 |
| Spain | 165.9 | 150.5 | 156.7 | 140.3 | 138.7 | 300.7 | 376.8 | 451.1 | 323.5 | 432.9 |
| United Kingdom | 473.6 | 688.7 | 588.6 | 633.8 | 742.8 | 476.2 | 448.3 | 540.9 | 599.3 | 703.8 |
| Switzerland | 79.4 | 96.0 | 93.1 | 73.2 | 66.7 | 59.2 | 59.4 | 66.4 | 58.6 | 71.3 |
| Asian 10 | 2 271.9 | 2 471.6 | 2 822.0 | 3 300.4 | 3 083.8 | 2 186.7 | 2 292.4 | 2 935.4 | 3 126.2 | 3 027.7 |
| China | 211.3 | 148.8 | 143.2 | 216.3 | 365.5 | 119.0 | 92.5 | 400.5 | 176.7 | 233.8 |
| Hong Kong | 179.1 | 149.7 | 179.7 | 192.6 | 216.4 | 140.4 | 185.0 | 273.7 | 259.8 | 255.4 |
| Indonesia | 10.5 | 28.2 | 29.4 | 36.4 | 37.2 | 37.4 | 71.3 | 68.5 | 94.5 | 146.5 |
| Japan | 1 064.2 | 1 223.4 | 1 451.8 | 1 789.5 | 1 444.3 | 858.8 | 761.6 | 863.6 | 1 047.8 | 1 089.8 |
| Malaysia | 35.8 | 38.4 | 54.5 | 69.8 | 77.2 | 224.9 | 208.6 | 148.3 | 114.1 | 82.5 |
| Philippines | 74.2 | 63.0 | 44.3 | 47.7 | 44.6 | 29.9 | 55.3 | 101.6 | 105.8 | 222.1 |
| Singapore | 81.5 | 84.0 | 119.0 | 110.5 | 117.5 | 142.7 | 190.0 | 230.2 | 259.2 | 245.4 |
| South Korea | 175.9 | 243.0 | 367.2 | 435.7 | 369.3 | 188.6 | 261.2 | 435.4 | 488.3 | 268.4 |
| Taiwan | 337.8 | 359.6 | 293.3 | 198.8 | 207.6 | 265.8 | 262.9 | 255.8 | 449.9 | 257.1 |
| Thailand | 101.6 | 133.4 | 139.7 | 203.0 | 204.2 | 179.3 | 204.1 | 157.9 | 129.9 | 226.8 |
| Australia | 280.6 | 329.7 | 405.5 | 567.4 | 543.9 | 155.6 | 160.5 | 176.4 | 189.7 | 203.3 |
| India | 26.7 | 22.8 | 56.9 | 60.2 | 58.0 | 48.4 | 17.2 | 40.7 | 33.6 | 31.3 |
| Israel | 129.4 | 194.1 | 236.3 | 211.1 | 129.5 | 169.1 | 171.3 | 158.9 | 204.5 | 155.8 |
| Pakistan | 5.5 | 5.9 | 4.2 | 5.7 | 2.9 | 46.8 | 8.2 | 8.3 | 32.3 | 42.0 |
| Saudi Arabia | 976.6 | 675.5 | 477.6 | 793.1 | 618.0 | 80.3 | 65.5 | 78.4 | 64.3 | 67.5 |
| African 8 | 50.8 | 40.6 | 47.2 | 52.7 | 48.4 | 144.6 | 100.9 | 140.5 | 134.6 | 99.5 |
| Developing Countries | 9 200.2 | 10 624.6 | 8 842.2 | 9 391.6 | 11 191.5 | 3 283.1 | 3 279.2 | 4 321.9 | 5 119.6 | 4 743.6 |

## Table D-2.   State Exports of Goods by Destination, 1993–1997 —Continued

(State of origin by country of destination, millions of dollars.)

| Destination | Mississippi | | | | | Missouri | | | | |
|---|---|---|---|---|---|---|---|---|---|---|
| | 1993 | 1994 | 1995 | 1996 | 1997 | 1993 | 1994 | 1995 | 1996 | 1997 |
| All destinations | 803.3 | 1 099.9 | 1 368.7 | 1 221.7 | 1 421.3 | 4 733.3 | 5 234.8 | 5 689.9 | 6 590.5 | 7 043.0 |
| Canada | 305.9 | 352.1 | 372.7 | 387.8 | 430.4 | 1 112.9 | 1 347.9 | 1 369.7 | 1 288.1 | 1 490.1 |
| Mexico | 25.3 | 65.7 | 87.9 | 91.3 | 127.4 | 540.4 | 773.4 | 699.0 | 1 089.0 | 1 042.4 |
| Central and South America and Caribbean | 151.0 | 208.5 | 245.2 | 254.1 | 232.5 | 534.5 | 498.5 | 660.2 | 788.2 | 797.1 |
| Argentina | 10.1 | 6.6 | 2.8 | 5.9 | 5.5 | 55.6 | 78.1 | 88.3 | 125.0 | 115.3 |
| Brazil | 1.8 | 3.0 | 6.9 | 7.7 | 12.5 | 109.5 | 103.1 | 170.7 | 194.7 | 199.7 |
| Chile | 5.2 | 12.3 | 11.9 | 6.6 | 8.4 | 20.0 | 19.5 | 30.5 | 39.8 | 39.8 |
| Colombia | 2.4 | 4.5 | 4.6 | 8.0 | 9.1 | 47.4 | 42.8 | 69.2 | 84.8 | 60.8 |
| Dominican Republic | 19.1 | 14.4 | 21.7 | 20.1 | 19.7 | 7.6 | 11.7 | 18.6 | 18.7 | 20.5 |
| Venezuela | 12.1 | 3.2 | 6.0 | 8.6 | 7.2 | 120.5 | 64.3 | 88.2 | 81.2 | 67.0 |
| European Union | 166.4 | 169.8 | 223.3 | 208.1 | 266.9 | 976.4 | 1 123.4 | 1 330.8 | 1 493.0 | 1 701.7 |
| Belgium | 9.0 | 6.5 | 10.0 | 19.3 | 47.0 | 287.2 | 291.8 | 373.4 | 376.5 | 386.8 |
| France | 12.3 | 17.7 | 24.0 | 17.5 | 12.0 | 74.8 | 77.6 | 91.6 | 72.1 | 81.2 |
| Germany | 27.7 | 20.2 | 20.2 | 17.3 | 17.4 | 121.6 | 117.3 | 156.4 | 171.6 | 202.7 |
| Ireland | 0.6 | 0.5 | 0.6 | 1.6 | 12.0 | 18.9 | 40.9 | 39.8 | 60.3 | 69.0 |
| Italy | 20.2 | 20.4 | 32.0 | 30.8 | 40.3 | 44.2 | 92.1 | 106.9 | 148.8 | 103.2 |
| Luxembourg | 0.1 | 0.2 | ..... | 0.1 | 0.1 | 0.6 | 0.4 | 0.5 | 1.2 | 1.2 |
| Netherlands | 19.7 | 22.1 | 32.8 | 26.3 | 26.1 | 103.8 | 122.7 | 117.3 | 137.7 | 129.7 |
| Spain | 5.2 | 4.6 | 3.3 | 6.2 | 5.0 | 39.8 | 72.9 | 127.3 | 149.9 | 237.0 |
| United Kingdom | 63.8 | 68.5 | 91.3 | 75.2 | 80.9 | 245.0 | 262.5 | 195.6 | 193.6 | 235.8 |
| Switzerland | 1.3 | 1.9 | 1.5 | 2.8 | 2.4 | 16.1 | 14.7 | 24.5 | 30.9 | 24.2 |
| Asian 10 | 78.0 | 78.4 | 177.8 | 127.9 | 139.8 | 807.0 | 945.5 | 986.8 | 1 152.2 | 1 205.3 |
| China | 4.9 | 4.5 | 28.1 | 14.8 | 17.3 | 63.8 | 48.7 | 80.3 | 162.6 | 167.4 |
| Hong Kong | 9.4 | 14.7 | 28.7 | 15.8 | 15.2 | 57.6 | 75.5 | 112.5 | 102.3 | 81.7 |
| Indonesia | 3.5 | 0.4 | 6.1 | 3.1 | 2.6 | 25.3 | 23.4 | 39.2 | 64.3 | 79.4 |
| Japan | 28.4 | 17.9 | 26.5 | 39.0 | 49.2 | 266.8 | 259.4 | 282.0 | 275.5 | 307.6 |
| Malaysia | 2.2 | 1.5 | 1.2 | 0.4 | 0.9 | 49.0 | 51.6 | 49.5 | 54.1 | 58.1 |
| Philippines | 1.4 | 1.3 | 12.7 | 9.2 | 23.4 | 29.6 | 107.5 | 33.4 | 36.7 | 63.0 |
| Singapore | 7.3 | 12.1 | 10.6 | 12.1 | 9.2 | 89.9 | 81.5 | 103.9 | 104.2 | 102.1 |
| South Korea | 13.8 | 16.0 | 29.3 | 19.7 | 11.2 | 93.1 | 104.9 | 131.0 | 152.1 | 151.7 |
| Taiwan | 6.2 | 8.1 | 19.9 | 8.8 | 7.0 | 88.6 | 137.1 | 106.7 | 163.4 | 166.4 |
| Thailand | 1.0 | 2.0 | 14.6 | 5.0 | 3.6 | 43.4 | 55.9 | 48.2 | 37.0 | 27.9 |
| Australia | 7.3 | 7.8 | 14.3 | 13.6 | 14.2 | 88.5 | 111.2 | 123.9 | 162.2 | 165.5 |
| India | 0.4 | 0.7 | 0.6 | 4.0 | 5.4 | 13.1 | 22.1 | 19.2 | 26.4 | 25.5 |
| Israel | 3.0 | 149.1 | 149.6 | 5.1 | 6.0 | 52.1 | 107.6 | 125.6 | 129.4 | 126.8 |
| Pakistan | 0.1 | 0.1 | 0.9 | 0.1 | 1.2 | 17.7 | 3.9 | 15.7 | 3.4 | 23.7 |
| Saudi Arabia | 9.1 | 5.8 | 9.5 | 7.0 | 7.6 | 31.6 | 35.3 | 32.2 | 32.8 | 34.4 |
| African 8 | 7.2 | 9.4 | 3.8 | 7.0 | 8.0 | 41.7 | 21.8 | 56.5 | 57.6 | 48.0 |
| Developing Countries | 281.4 | 539.7 | 715.0 | 559.3 | 639.9 | 2 208.7 | 2 317.0 | 2 460.8 | 3 262.7 | 3 216.2 |

| Destination | Montana | | | | | Nebraska | | | | |
|---|---|---|---|---|---|---|---|---|---|---|
| | 1993 | 1994 | 1995 | 1996 | 1997 | 1993 | 1994 | 1995 | 1996 | 1997 |
| All destinations | 243.3 | 260.0 | 279.2 | 340.9 | 429.8 | 1 740.7 | 1 957.9 | 2 255.3 | 2 452.8 | 2 493.7 |
| Canada | 144.7 | 140.1 | 140.2 | 160.6 | 236.5 | 295.7 | 327.1 | 352.3 | 418.7 | 529.0 |
| Mexico | 1.2 | 5.1 | 8.1 | 46.2 | 20.6 | 60.8 | 108.8 | 80.0 | 168.0 | 142.0 |
| Central and South America and Caribbean | 5.5 | 4.3 | 5.7 | 3.8 | 3.5 | 24.9 | 66.5 | 74.8 | 123.1 | 176.4 |
| Argentina | ..... | 0.2 | 0.3 | 0.2 | 0.2 | 1.7 | 3.3 | 3.0 | 14.8 | 15.3 |
| Brazil | 0.1 | 0.3 | 1.7 | 1.3 | 1.4 | 1.4 | 2.0 | 3.2 | 12.2 | 21.2 |
| Chile | 0.1 | 0.1 | 0.1 | 0.1 | 0.2 | 1.4 | 1.7 | 1.8 | 2.3 | 3.2 |
| Colombia | | | 0.9 | 0.3 | 0.3 | 1.1 | 0.6 | 0.8 | 1.8 | 3.4 |
| Dominican Republic | | | | | 0.1 | 0.1 | 0.1 | 2.9 | 4.4 | 11.5 |
| Venezuela | 2.1 | 1.0 | 0.9 | 1.2 | 0.2 | 9.2 | 45.2 | 49.7 | 76.4 | 110.8 |
| European Union | 64.8 | 84.1 | 88.0 | 82.5 | 106.9 | 202.1 | 221.8 | 213.1 | 237.8 | 285.7 |
| Belgium | 47.6 | 53.1 | 47.3 | 43.6 | 73.5 | 30.2 | 22.6 | 16.9 | 37.6 | 47.1 |
| France | 4.4 | 3.4 | 3.8 | 8.0 | 9.6 | 16.0 | 18.3 | 16.2 | 20.5 | 22.2 |
| Germany | 4.0 | 7.0 | 16.5 | 13.0 | 8.0 | 24.8 | 30.8 | 29.0 | 35.8 | 39.0 |
| Ireland | 0.3 | 0.4 | 1.0 | 1.0 | 0.4 | 7.6 | 10.2 | 11.0 | 8.2 | 13.3 |
| Italy | 1.4 | 2.7 | 1.4 | 0.7 | 1.1 | 19.7 | 27.5 | 23.6 | 29.6 | 23.6 |
| Luxembourg | ..... | ..... | ..... | ..... | ..... | ..... | ..... | ..... | ..... | ..... |
| Netherlands | 1.3 | 1.7 | 5.7 | 3.6 | 2.4 | 57.6 | 62.3 | 73.6 | 58.7 | 60.4 |
| Spain | 0.6 | 0.1 | 0.5 | 0.3 | 0.5 | 4.3 | 6.3 | 5.2 | 6.1 | 6.5 |
| United Kingdom | 4.5 | 14.3 | 11.1 | 8.3 | 9.1 | 33.1 | 30.5 | 27.9 | 30.2 | 40.7 |
| Switzerland | 1.8 | 0.4 | 2.4 | 4.6 | 1.2 | 2.9 | 1.9 | 1.7 | 2.8 | 11.6 |
| Asian 10 | 18.5 | 17.3 | 26.5 | 32.8 | 54.5 | 1 075.2 | 1 137.3 | 1 426.7 | 1 366.0 | 1 206.4 |
| China | 0.5 | 0.1 | 0.2 | 1.6 | 14.2 | 2.6 | 4.1 | 8.6 | 16.4 | 9.8 |
| Hong Kong | 0.5 | 0.6 | 1.3 | 1.5 | 1.6 | 12.2 | 16.8 | 15.0 | 8.2 | 14.3 |
| Indonesia | ..... | ..... | 0.1 | 0.1 | 0.2 | 7.0 | 12.1 | 19.7 | 26.7 | 32.6 |
| Japan | 9.0 | 10.9 | 16.8 | 20.5 | 23.1 | 915.3 | 912.8 | 1 162.7 | 1 103.1 | 870.8 |
| Malaysia | 0.1 | 0.1 | 0.2 | 0.6 | 0.6 | 3.1 | 2.1 | 3.6 | 6.5 | 17.1 |
| Philippines | 3.7 | 0.1 | 0.8 | 0.3 | 0.8 | 1.1 | 1.3 | 2.1 | 7.4 | 9.2 |
| Singapore | 0.2 | 0.4 | 0.9 | 1.9 | 4.0 | 10.8 | 16.7 | 23.8 | 23.8 | 29.0 |
| South Korea | 3.0 | 3.9 | 4.7 | 4.5 | 4.3 | 105.0 | 146.1 | 160.8 | 134.3 | 184.7 |
| Taiwan | 1.3 | 1.2 | 1.2 | 1.1 | 5.3 | 8.9 | 10.8 | 13.2 | 16.7 | 24.9 |
| Thailand | 0.2 | 0.1 | 0.4 | 0.5 | 0.4 | 9.1 | 14.5 | 17.3 | 22.9 | 14.0 |
| Australia | 1.8 | 2.9 | 2.0 | 2.7 | 2.4 | 17.5 | 27.1 | 28.1 | 48.1 | 58.5 |
| India | ..... | 0.1 | 0.1 | 0.1 | 0.1 | 0.9 | 1.4 | 2.9 | 1.3 | 2.5 |
| Israel | 1.3 | 0.3 | 0.3 | 0.7 | 1.3 | 9.1 | 12.5 | 13.2 | 14.3 | 7.3 |
| Pakistan | ..... | ..... | 0.2 | ..... | ..... | 0.2 | ..... | 0.1 | 0.8 | 0.2 |
| Saudi Arabia | 0.6 | 0.7 | 1.1 | 1.2 | 0.4 | 14.5 | 4.8 | 1.6 | 3.1 | 6.3 |
| African 8 | 0.2 | 0.2 | 1.0 | 0.9 | 0.2 | 4.1 | 9.4 | 7.4 | 10.7 | 12.8 |
| Developing Countries | 19.7 | 18.3 | 26.4 | 66.2 | 58.7 | 295.9 | 454.5 | 467.1 | 610.3 | 706.9 |

## Table D-2.  State Exports of Goods by Destination, 1993–1997 —*Continued*

(State of origin by country of destination, millions of dollars.)

| Destination | Nevada | | | | | New Hampshire | | | | |
|---|---|---|---|---|---|---|---|---|---|---|
| | 1993 | 1994 | 1995 | 1996 | 1997 | 1993 | 1994 | 1995 | 1996 | 1997 |
| All destinations | 503.9 | 458.5 | 711.1 | 691.6 | 807.1 | 1 134.9 | 1 247.9 | 1 478.6 | 1 744.9 | 1 931.0 |
| Canada | 123.4 | 148.9 | 211.8 | 265.6 | 272.1 | 377.2 | 422.4 | 494.4 | 642.4 | 672.2 |
| Mexico | 13.1 | 14.5 | 12.8 | 9.2 | 59.9 | 39.6 | 43.4 | 45.2 | 63.6 | 73.8 |
| Central and South America and Caribbean | 15.2 | 22.5 | 34.7 | 44.7 | 34.3 | 87.0 | 92.3 | 97.3 | 92.7 | 117.1 |
| Argentina | 1.4 | 1.0 | 5.3 | 4.6 | 4.6 | 12.3 | 6.6 | 4.8 | 3.5 | 5.8 |
| Brazil | 0.8 | 2.4 | 3.7 | 6.4 | 6.1 | 11.5 | 21.7 | 38.6 | 28.1 | 30.7 |
| Chile | 1.7 | 1.4 | 4.0 | 3.1 | 3.0 | 4.1 | 2.6 | 2.0 | 3.0 | 4.5 |
| Colombia | 1.4 | 1.5 | 2.2 | 1.5 | 3.1 | 1.9 | 2.8 | 4.1 | 3.0 | 3.4 |
| Dominican Republic | ..... | ..... | 0.3 | 1.1 | 0.2 | 41.5 | 48.2 | 34.2 | 31.8 | 39.9 |
| Venezuela | 0.7 | 0.4 | 0.8 | 1.4 | 2.4 | 6.0 | 3.1 | 3.0 | 7.8 | 7.1 |
| European Union | 71.8 | 97.3 | 103.6 | 114.2 | 181.5 | 315.1 | 349.8 | 459.5 | 500.3 | 580.1 |
| Belgium | 1.9 | 2.6 | 2.1 | 3.1 | 10.6 | 15.4 | 13.5 | 15.1 | 10.6 | 15.2 |
| France | 14.1 | 14.7 | 12.1 | 18.0 | 24.1 | 32.1 | 36.9 | 38.1 | 48.3 | 50.0 |
| Germany | 9.9 | 12.6 | 19.7 | 22.1 | 20.2 | 50.9 | 60.4 | 95.3 | 93.5 | 144.9 |
| Ireland | 0.5 | 2.1 | 2.3 | 2.0 | 3.2 | 16.1 | 43.7 | 88.3 | 119.0 | 94.5 |
| Italy | 11.0 | 4.0 | 12.7 | 5.8 | 8.7 | 19.6 | 19.8 | 22.3 | 24.3 | 26.8 |
| Luxembourg | ..... | 0.1 | 0.6 | ..... | 7.3 | 0.1 | 0.3 | 0.1 | ..... | 0.1 |
| Netherlands | 7.6 | 10.3 | 9.1 | 13.4 | 17.2 | 42.8 | 46.2 | 50.2 | 58.4 | 62.5 |
| Spain | 1.7 | 0.7 | 1.2 | 2.3 | 3.2 | 8.9 | 10.5 | 9.5 | 11.3 | 19.2 |
| United Kingdom | 20.6 | 45.2 | 28.1 | 32.6 | 64.5 | 111.5 | 95.7 | 104.7 | 102.7 | 132.5 |
| Switzerland | 158.2 | 4.3 | 13.8 | 5.8 | 5.7 | 10.0 | 7.7 | 9.5 | 9.4 | 11.6 |
| Asian 10 | 82.5 | 109.7 | 269.3 | 176.6 | 197.0 | 182.0 | 242.8 | 289.3 | 344.9 | 360.2 |
| China | 7.4 | 10.9 | 7.5 | 9.1 | 4.6 | 11.7 | 10.6 | 15.0 | 9.0 | 18.0 |
| Hong Kong | 7.1 | 7.1 | 10.4 | 12.4 | 14.5 | 14.6 | 15.7 | 24.9 | 43.5 | 49.7 |
| Indonesia | 1.0 | 0.7 | 2.6 | 5.3 | 1.5 | 3.8 | 4.1 | 4.3 | 6.0 | 8.6 |
| Japan | 26.6 | 34.6 | 82.6 | 77.7 | 82.9 | 57.7 | 60.4 | 59.0 | 81.8 | 109.0 |
| Malaysia | 0.8 | 1.4 | 4.0 | 10.9 | 14.8 | 3.0 | 3.7 | 5.5 | 5.0 | 13.2 |
| Philippines | 18.6 | 29.1 | 131.4 | 12.3 | 33.3 | 2.2 | 5.6 | 5.4 | 7.1 | 5.6 |
| Singapore | 5.2 | 5.9 | 7.0 | 7.4 | 10.6 | 39.5 | 60.5 | 76.1 | 50.3 | 56.7 |
| South Korea | 7.4 | 11.0 | 13.3 | 24.7 | 21.8 | 24.7 | 40.7 | 52.5 | 48.3 | 31.7 |
| Taiwan | 5.8 | 7.6 | 8.5 | 13.6 | 10.6 | 20.6 | 34.8 | 36.0 | 57.4 | 49.5 |
| Thailand | 2.6 | 1.5 | 2.0 | 3.2 | 2.5 | 4.3 | 6.7 | 10.5 | 36.4 | 18.2 |
| Australia | 10.5 | 13.6 | 17.4 | 17.9 | 19.5 | 60.6 | 25.8 | 23.0 | 22.5 | 28.8 |
| India | 1.5 | 1.7 | 4.5 | 3.8 | 2.9 | 5.7 | 5.4 | 9.1 | 6.5 | 6.3 |
| Israel | 3.8 | 6.2 | 4.8 | 4.3 | 2.5 | 9.8 | 10.4 | 10.7 | 18.4 | 18.1 |
| Pakistan | 2.5 | 1.8 | 1.1 | 1.3 | 0.9 | 0.9 | 7.0 | 1.6 | 1.5 | 0.9 |
| Saudi Arabia | 1.1 | 1.4 | 2.3 | 2.9 | 1.7 | 5.4 | 2.7 | 1.4 | 1.9 | 2.9 |
| African 8 | 3.9 | 6.4 | 8.2 | 7.9 | 6.8 | 6.0 | 3.8 | 6.0 | 4.2 | 5.8 |
| Developing Countries | 102.0 | 137.2 | 266.2 | 184.8 | 230.6 | 301.7 | 366.0 | 417.8 | 476.5 | 512.8 |

| Destination | New Jersey | | | | | New Mexico | | | | |
|---|---|---|---|---|---|---|---|---|---|---|
| | 1993 | 1994 | 1995 | 1996 | 1997 | 1993 | 1994 | 1995 | 1996 | 1997 |
| All destinations | 14 540.6 | 16 760.8 | 18 368.6 | 18 458.4 | 20 815.4 | 400.0 | 488.5 | 426.6 | 917.4 | 1 779.9 |
| Canada | 2 539.0 | 2 943.7 | 3 167.2 | 3 379.1 | 3 836.8 | 46.6 | 47.5 | 41.7 | 51.2 | 55.6 |
| Mexico | 788.9 | 1 068.1 | 583.8 | 679.2 | 883.8 | 105.8 | 93.9 | 77.1 | 100.0 | 86.6 |
| Central and South America and Caribbean | 1 287.0 | 1 433.6 | 1 808.6 | 1 932.9 | 2 107.7 | 9.8 | 7.2 | 10.6 | 8.9 | 13.8 |
| Argentina | 137.4 | 177.9 | 139.1 | 148.4 | 202.4 | 4.7 | 0.8 | 1.2 | 1.0 | 1.2 |
| Brazil | 221.6 | 282.6 | 439.5 | 496.1 | 627.2 | 1.7 | 2.2 | 1.3 | 2.1 | 1.5 |
| Chile | 123.7 | 128.7 | 141.8 | 145.4 | 185.6 | 0.3 | 0.3 | 0.5 | 1.0 | 0.8 |
| Colombia | 86.3 | 118.6 | 159.0 | 140.0 | 139.3 | 0.2 | 0.7 | 1.2 | 0.3 | 0.2 |
| Dominican Republic | 108.3 | 124.2 | 194.1 | 144.9 | 182.0 | ..... | ..... | 1.8 | ..... | 0.1 |
| Venezuela | 196.7 | 123.9 | 156.5 | 167.8 | 167.4 | 0.2 | 0.4 | 0.3 | 0.4 | 0.4 |
| European Union | 3 971.9 | 4 350.9 | 4 792.2 | 4 499.6 | 5 269.0 | 77.5 | 114.3 | 112.6 | 103.2 | 153.8 |
| Belgium | 375.5 | 415.8 | 510.6 | 412.9 | 473.5 | 2.2 | 2.2 | 5.0 | 6.5 | 24.0 |
| France | 492.5 | 488.6 | 525.3 | 493.0 | 577.6 | 5.4 | 12.1 | 20.8 | 27.6 | 32.3 |
| Germany | 765.1 | 798.3 | 920.8 | 871.5 | 912.4 | 19.2 | 32.9 | 26.1 | 19.1 | 18.8 |
| Ireland | 238.4 | 265.6 | 306.0 | 233.9 | 435.9 | 2.4 | 1.6 | 5.3 | 19.6 | 24.6 |
| Italy | 325.2 | 295.5 | 351.0 | 280.9 | 350.1 | 4.1 | 8.1 | 5.9 | 4.9 | 5.6 |
| Luxembourg | 4.7 | 1.7 | 3.0 | 1.8 | 2.2 | 0.3 | 0.7 | 0.8 | 0.5 | 0.9 |
| Netherlands | 486.0 | 566.0 | 648.1 | 747.2 | 1 016.1 | 2.0 | 4.4 | 16.3 | 4.9 | 21.3 |
| Spain | 157.8 | 184.4 | 206.3 | 193.6 | 193.5 | 1.2 | 1.2 | 1.1 | 2.0 | 1.6 |
| United Kingdom | 819.1 | 999.0 | 955.7 | 854.9 | 901.1 | 36.5 | 46.4 | 26.7 | 10.7 | 13.4 |
| Switzerland | 244.3 | 263.3 | 321.9 | 252.8 | 310.7 | 4.3 | 9.9 | 4.2 | 1.9 | 15.5 |
| Asian 10 | 3 590.2 | 4 410.9 | 5 154.1 | 4 862.1 | 5 264.4 | 135.7 | 186.5 | 165.9 | 630.8 | 1 426.6 |
| China | 300.9 | 283.1 | 606.8 | 405.0 | 348.9 | 0.4 | 2.0 | 8.2 | 10.3 | 28.5 |
| Hong Kong | 273.1 | 326.8 | 424.5 | 407.6 | 420.6 | 9.6 | 19.5 | 14.1 | 10.1 | 13.6 |
| Indonesia | 63.8 | 65.2 | 122.2 | 138.0 | 301.9 | ..... | 0.1 | 0.6 | 0.5 | 8.7 |
| Japan | 1 138.5 | 1 357.7 | 1 470.2 | 1 577.5 | 1 648.2 | 34.3 | 44.2 | 21.2 | 45.7 | 60.1 |
| Malaysia | 47.0 | 78.1 | 100.8 | 89.5 | 103.8 | 0.3 | 1.4 | 4.1 | 79.8 | 271.0 |
| Philippines | 115.6 | 146.8 | 139.3 | 165.2 | 150.8 | 0.6 | 5.8 | 4.8 | 203.4 | 688.3 |
| Singapore | 210.7 | 262.1 | 249.6 | 231.4 | 304.0 | 5.3 | 2.8 | 8.1 | 5.4 | 2.6 |
| South Korea | 918.2 | 1 260.9 | 1 359.6 | 1 279.5 | 1 356.7 | 56.1 | 68.7 | 59.1 | 184.4 | 197.2 |
| Taiwan | 407.7 | 517.6 | 519.0 | 440.3 | 484.7 | 8.1 | 6.9 | 13.6 | 53.4 | 115.7 |
| Thailand | 114.7 | 112.5 | 162.1 | 128.2 | 144.7 | 21.1 | 35.3 | 32.2 | 37.9 | 40.8 |
| Australia | 272.9 | 275.8 | 321.7 | 319.0 | 333.6 | 2.2 | 3.1 | 3.3 | 5.0 | 10.9 |
| India | 71.8 | 93.2 | 135.2 | 142.5 | 90.0 | 0.1 | 0.4 | 0.3 | 0.6 | 1.8 |
| Israel | 498.4 | 660.4 | 708.7 | 745.9 | 863.5 | 2.6 | 2.1 | 3.8 | 5.7 | 3.1 |
| Pakistan | 24.3 | 21.1 | 25.9 | 32.6 | 16.0 | ..... | ..... | 0.3 | 0.2 | ..... |
| Saudi Arabia | 244.8 | 196.7 | 243.1 | 198.8 | 264.6 | 1.0 | 0.5 | 0.6 | 0.4 | 2.3 |
| African 8 | 88.3 | 102.1 | 143.9 | 133.4 | 139.3 | 0.4 | 0.5 | 0.4 | 1.4 | 1.4 |
| Developing Countries | 6 057.5 | 7 067.2 | 7 775.3 | 7 841.2 | 8 898.2 | 232.2 | 267.8 | 241.4 | 708.5 | 1 481.8 |

## Table D-2.  State Exports of Goods by Destination, 1993–1997 —Continued

(State of origin by country of destination, millions of dollars.)

| Destination | New York | | | | | North Carolina | | | | |
|---|---|---|---|---|---|---|---|---|---|---|
| | 1993 | 1994 | 1995 | 1996 | 1997 | 1993 | 1994 | 1995 | 1996 | 1997 |
| All destinations | 40 702.3 | 37 259.7 | 44 080.1 | 44 964.7 | 48 885.3 | 7 976.4 | 8 968.8 | 10 567.4 | 11 586.6 | 13 102.1 |
| Canada | 6 580.8 | 7 487.2 | 9 243.7 | 8 956.7 | 10 616.0 | 2 289.1 | 2 782.8 | 3 168.5 | 3 520.4 | 3 748.2 |
| Mexico | 1 171.0 | 1 323.9 | 994.0 | 1 303.1 | 1 804.9 | 365.1 | 493.1 | 653.8 | 922.2 | 1 320.5 |
| Central and South America and Caribbean | 2 809.9 | 3 054.5 | 3 401.8 | 3 536.8 | 4 088.7 | 930.4 | 1 072.2 | 1 490.6 | 1 589.0 | 1 814.7 |
| Argentina | 341.3 | 304.3 | 242.4 | 260.5 | 358.5 | 80.0 | 84.2 | 79.1 | 98.4 | 121.2 |
| Brazil | 559.4 | 803.0 | 970.6 | 964.1 | 1 171.2 | 87.0 | 142.4 | 242.4 | 243.8 | 343.2 |
| Chile | 215.3 | 239.5 | 219.9 | 247.0 | 245.5 | 43.3 | 44.8 | 65.0 | 71.8 | 72.2 |
| Colombia | 189.4 | 219.7 | 345.7 | 368.1 | 392.7 | 80.6 | 90.6 | 105.6 | 94.1 | 89.1 |
| Dominican Republic | 296.0 | 350.5 | 260.3 | 289.1 | 365.6 | 67.9 | 63.6 | 104.7 | 119.0 | 144.1 |
| Venezuela | 311.7 | 175.2 | 225.9 | 187.4 | 255.9 | 42.3 | 32.2 | 48.1 | 52.7 | 59.3 |
| European Union | 11 383.2 | 8 152.9 | 9 474.6 | 9 958.1 | 10 108.2 | 1 884.9 | 1 994.4 | 2 300.0 | 2 533.0 | 2 870.7 |
| Belgium | 828.3 | 875.0 | 1 011.5 | 909.5 | 923.6 | 537.3 | 417.0 | 474.9 | 441.5 | 378.2 |
| France | 1 084.2 | 826.0 | 929.9 | 1 057.9 | 1 270.4 | 122.9 | 131.1 | 165.4 | 191.9 | 298.3 |
| Germany | 1 228.8 | 1 212.8 | 1 577.1 | 1 503.8 | 1 684.7 | 352.6 | 396.0 | 476.5 | 482.9 | 550.1 |
| Ireland | 187.7 | 211.9 | 244.0 | 165.8 | 265.7 | 67.0 | 75.2 | 72.2 | 82.3 | 79.9 |
| Italy | 744.6 | 651.8 | 841.5 | 814.8 | 795.7 | 85.4 | 101.9 | 132.6 | 145.5 | 146.7 |
| Luxembourg | 5.8 | 7.7 | 21.7 | 37.4 | 42.0 | 0.4 | 0.6 | 0.2 | 0.5 | 1.4 |
| Netherlands | 1 058.8 | 846.6 | 1 090.9 | 906.5 | 874.9 | 236.0 | 215.5 | 225.7 | 237.6 | 291.5 |
| Spain | 471.4 | 287.1 | 383.2 | 362.9 | 376.9 | 60.5 | 97.6 | 105.6 | 130.8 | 152.1 |
| United Kingdom | 5 297.4 | 2 703.6 | 2 744.8 | 3 593.4 | 3 140.1 | 313.0 | 391.4 | 446.8 | 552.8 | 716.5 |
| Switzerland | 2 627.2 | 1 237.2 | 2 205.3 | 3 126.0 | 3 413.4 | 67.3 | 79.2 | 90.8 | 73.6 | 143.8 |
| Asian 10 | 10 396.1 | 10 724.2 | 13 013.6 | 12 191.5 | 12 122.7 | 1 569.6 | 1 652.3 | 1 904.2 | 1 984.5 | 2 175.2 |
| China | 659.0 | 588.9 | 636.5 | 807.0 | 766.2 | 153.2 | 135.5 | 175.1 | 185.7 | 230.4 |
| Hong Kong | 1 209.2 | 1 498.1 | 1 631.9 | 1 461.2 | 1 646.6 | 158.8 | 180.5 | 234.7 | 197.9 | 270.8 |
| Indonesia | 180.3 | 209.4 | 332.0 | 198.0 | 211.3 | 54.7 | 60.0 | 82.3 | 69.8 | 73.3 |
| Japan | 4 452.6 | 4 634.8 | 5 463.9 | 5 422.1 | 5 369.3 | 720.4 | 743.4 | 760.7 | 824.0 | 811.0 |
| Malaysia | 242.0 | 272.1 | 287.3 | 351.3 | 413.8 | 57.9 | 59.7 | 72.3 | 91.5 | 105.2 |
| Philippines | 224.9 | 215.0 | 277.4 | 278.3 | 396.0 | 30.3 | 38.5 | 52.4 | 67.5 | 79.7 |
| Singapore | 665.4 | 613.1 | 628.0 | 563.1 | 609.1 | 80.4 | 91.4 | 96.2 | 119.3 | 111.9 |
| South Korea | 1 228.6 | 1 344.7 | 1 954.8 | 1 793.1 | 1 423.3 | 114.6 | 132.2 | 183.2 | 201.9 | 202.8 |
| Taiwan | 1 198.5 | 1 082.3 | 1 442.7 | 956.0 | 944.7 | 114.5 | 120.7 | 126.8 | 115.1 | 166.1 |
| Thailand | 335.6 | 265.7 | 359.2 | 361.4 | 342.5 | 84.9 | 90.3 | 120.5 | 111.9 | 124.1 |
| Australia | 336.2 | 503.1 | 625.7 | 711.0 | 744.6 | 141.0 | 152.8 | 180.0 | 192.6 | 177.3 |
| India | 453.5 | 406.8 | 525.2 | 498.5 | 543.5 | 38.1 | 18.0 | 24.2 | 31.6 | 35.0 |
| Israel | 931.1 | 1 007.0 | 1 141.8 | 1 295.0 | 1 499.4 | 36.0 | 58.7 | 60.8 | 67.6 | 63.4 |
| Pakistan | 126.7 | 84.1 | 80.6 | 115.5 | 180.9 | 8.7 | 8.7 | 5.8 | 11.2 | 13.8 |
| Saudi Arabia | 864.9 | 648.9 | 642.3 | 805.2 | 1 075.8 | 92.9 | 81.4 | 86.1 | 71.3 | 75.5 |
| African 8 | 407.3 | 326.2 | 448.4 | 439.0 | 474.0 | 41.7 | 53.1 | 67.7 | 73.8 | 79.0 |
| Developing Countries | 14 646.4 | 14 521.1 | 16 373.7 | 16 127.1 | 17 935.7 | 2 632.6 | 2 955.8 | 3 795.2 | 4 131.9 | 4 990.5 |

| Destination | North Dakota | | | | | Ohio | | | | |
|---|---|---|---|---|---|---|---|---|---|---|
| | 1993 | 1994 | 1995 | 1996 | 1997 | 1993 | 1994 | 1995 | 1996 | 1997 |
| All destinations | 343.7 | 388.9 | 488.6 | 576.2 | 623.1 | 17 651.4 | 19 478.2 | 20 926.5 | 22 555.2 | 25 106.5 |
| Canada | 227.3 | 250.6 | 315.3 | 378.8 | 427.6 | 7 671.9 | 8 501.4 | 8 881.3 | 9 580.4 | 10 471.6 |
| Mexico | 2.9 | 1.8 | 16.8 | 11.5 | 17.6 | 926.6 | 1 423.2 | 1 362.2 | 1 345.1 | 1 583.7 |
| Central and South America and Caribbean | 6.8 | 10.7 | 15.0 | 10.3 | 14.7 | 876.9 | 1 003.1 | 1 249.0 | 1 226.7 | 1 624.6 |
| Argentina | 2.2 | 3.0 | 3.4 | 2.5 | 5.0 | 93.9 | 123.8 | 122.5 | 158.5 | 160.8 |
| Brazil | 0.4 | 1.3 | 3.5 | 2.0 | 2.0 | 164.3 | 225.1 | 339.8 | 348.3 | 615.7 |
| Chile | 1.4 | 0.6 | 1.1 | 1.7 | 1.5 | 71.3 | 71.0 | 91.4 | 101.0 | 127.8 |
| Colombia | 0.8 | 2.4 | 2.0 | 1.3 | 2.1 | 75.5 | 119.8 | 131.7 | 126.7 | 131.7 |
| Dominican Republic | ..... | 0.4 | 1.7 | ..... | 0.4 | 39.6 | 34.7 | 41.1 | 54.9 | 68.2 |
| Venezuela | 0.3 | 0.4 | 0.6 | ..... | 0.2 | 150.8 | 126.6 | 150.2 | 116.1 | 159.7 |
| European Union | 88.3 | 98.1 | 106.1 | 127.7 | 110.7 | 4 210.0 | 4 369.4 | 4 472.4 | 4 725.6 | 5 380.7 |
| Belgium | 52.9 | 68.1 | 68.9 | 72.2 | 56.4 | 301.4 | 330.1 | 371.0 | 425.9 | 444.4 |
| France | 0.4 | 1.6 | 1.3 | 2.8 | 5.0 | 1 906.4 | 1 794.2 | 1 344.3 | 1 331.9 | 1 757.2 |
| Germany | 14.9 | 12.7 | 14.7 | 17.9 | 20.7 | 508.8 | 604.5 | 727.9 | 725.6 | 737.9 |
| Ireland | 0.1 | 0.3 | 0.2 | 0.1 | 0.3 | 97.3 | 107.6 | 126.7 | 101.8 | 146.1 |
| Italy | 0.7 | 1.0 | 0.9 | 1.1 | 2.0 | 191.7 | 212.7 | 275.7 | 279.8 | 287.3 |
| Luxembourg | ..... | ..... | ..... | ..... | ..... | 11.0 | 19.6 | 16.3 | 17.2 | 26.0 |
| Netherlands | 3.6 | 1.7 | 2.8 | 11.9 | 4.2 | 210.5 | 208.4 | 247.3 | 290.3 | 330.6 |
| Spain | 6.4 | 6.6 | 7.5 | 11.0 | 7.7 | 115.3 | 140.0 | 123.2 | 150.7 | 157.7 |
| United Kingdom | 7.2 | 4.2 | 7.2 | 8.7 | 12.6 | 684.7 | 730.7 | 942.2 | 1 089.5 | 1 173.5 |
| Switzerland | ..... | 0.6 | 0.3 | 0.1 | 0.3 | 135.2 | 134.2 | 142.0 | 139.1 | 102.6 |
| Asian 10 | 12.8 | 22.2 | 20.4 | 26.8 | 30.1 | 2 386.5 | 2 723.4 | 3 326.4 | 3 927.3 | 4 233.4 |
| China | 0.7 | 0.7 | 1.7 | 1.9 | 3.6 | 173.3 | 197.3 | 211.4 | 269.5 | 477.4 |
| Hong Kong | 0.2 | 0.2 | 0.8 | 2.5 | 2.0 | 143.3 | 171.2 | 229.1 | 287.8 | 361.3 |
| Indonesia | ..... | 0.5 | 0.6 | 0.8 | 0.8 | 42.9 | 53.9 | 87.0 | 93.8 | 79.3 |
| Japan | 4.8 | 7.4 | 5.3 | 6.1 | 9.7 | 859.4 | 1 033.0 | 1 124.0 | 1 254.0 | 1 190.9 |
| Malaysia | ..... | 0.5 | 2.0 | 0.9 | 1.4 | 108.8 | 139.1 | 150.4 | 172.5 | 214.6 |
| Philippines | 0.1 | 0.9 | 1.1 | 2.4 | 0.8 | 45.2 | 34.4 | 70.3 | 91.3 | 102.4 |
| Singapore | 0.2 | 0.6 | 1.9 | 1.4 | 1.8 | 326.4 | 329.3 | 395.5 | 454.4 | 488.6 |
| South Korea | 0.5 | 1.1 | 2.9 | 7.5 | 4.5 | 315.3 | 374.2 | 538.0 | 773.0 | 804.9 |
| Taiwan | 6.2 | 10.2 | 2.9 | 2.4 | 4.4 | 289.2 | 294.7 | 379.3 | 384.6 | 368.9 |
| Thailand | 0.1 | 0.1 | 1.3 | 0.8 | 1.0 | 82.6 | 96.2 | 141.6 | 146.3 | 145.2 |
| Australia | 1.2 | 2.0 | 8.6 | 10.6 | 14.7 | 365.6 | 347.5 | 362.7 | 382.7 | 397.8 |
| India | ..... | ..... | ..... | 1.0 | 0.5 | 152.1 | 71.0 | 109.1 | 99.7 | 176.5 |
| Israel | 0.1 | 0.2 | 0.5 | 0.6 | 0.7 | 81.7 | 93.7 | 112.6 | 135.6 | 148.2 |
| Pakistan | ..... | ..... | ..... | ..... | ..... | 9.9 | 7.5 | 12.5 | 9.8 | 13.9 |
| Saudi Arabia | 1.0 | 0.2 | 0.4 | 0.1 | 0.2 | 111.9 | 125.1 | 114.5 | 109.6 | 142.0 |
| African 8 | 0.1 | 0.3 | 0.4 | 0.4 | 0.1 | 109.8 | 138.3 | 154.9 | 180.8 | 143.2 |
| Developing Countries | 20.7 | 29.0 | 49.9 | 49.3 | 57.0 | 4 001.0 | 4 673.1 | 5 467.8 | 5 956.8 | 7 092.1 |

## Table D-2.  State Exports of Goods by Destination, 1993–1997 —*Continued*

(State of origin by country of destination, millions of dollars.)

| Destination | Oklahoma | | | | | Oregon | | | | |
|---|---|---|---|---|---|---|---|---|---|---|
| | 1993 | 1994 | 1995 | 1996 | 1997 | 1993 | 1994 | 1995 | 1996 | 1997 |
| All destinations | 2 334.6 | 2 172.0 | 2 467.3 | 2 537.6 | 2 721.6 | 6 204.7 | 6 987.4 | 9 902.1 | 8 481.3 | 8 358.6 |
| Canada | 426.2 | 497.1 | 492.3 | 570.9 | 669.9 | 870.7 | 1 020.9 | 1 097.5 | 890.2 | 1 081.7 |
| Mexico | 157.8 | 139.3 | 120.3 | 178.7 | 239.6 | 109.0 | 120.6 | 86.1 | 52.8 | 88.8 |
| Central and South America and Caribbean | 367.8 | 360.3 | 498.6 | 433.3 | 453.2 | 137.7 | 123.9 | 196.2 | 121.9 | 193.3 |
| Argentina | 37.5 | 57.7 | 55.4 | 78.7 | 55.3 | 10.5 | 13.2 | 11.4 | 10.5 | 12.1 |
| Brazil | 45.7 | 49.8 | 58.6 | 62.2 | 60.9 | 17.6 | 19.0 | 29.2 | 14.9 | 30.6 |
| Chile | 11.3 | 10.6 | 18.3 | 20.4 | 15.2 | 58.1 | 43.4 | 85.4 | 37.7 | 41.7 |
| Colombia | 38.4 | 44.3 | 81.3 | 44.9 | 34.0 | 13.7 | 11.2 | 11.5 | 9.1 | 10.5 |
| Dominican Republic | 0.6 | 0.5 | 0.9 | 8.0 | 1.1 | 0.7 | 0.6 | 1.6 | 6.9 | 6.1 |
| Venezuela | 43.6 | 89.7 | 147.2 | 92.2 | 171.7 | 4.6 | 3.5 | 3.4 | 4.1 | 41.8 |
| European Union | 459.9 | 477.2 | 540.1 | 500.1 | 535.7 | 1 085.7 | 1 164.3 | 1 725.3 | 952.9 | 1 061.8 |
| Belgium | 18.8 | 36.8 | 47.2 | 37.2 | 42.0 | 47.9 | 50.4 | 75.8 | 43.4 | 49.3 |
| France | 36.9 | 42.0 | 49.1 | 58.0 | 80.6 | 92.4 | 115.5 | 242.6 | 117.5 | 81.2 |
| Germany | 54.2 | 63.2 | 80.1 | 64.2 | 60.0 | 367.2 | 305.7 | 414.2 | 306.1 | 213.0 |
| Ireland | 2.8 | 2.9 | 5.0 | 2.5 | 5.1 | 37.9 | 76.7 | 225.3 | 119.3 | 145.9 |
| Italy | 27.4 | 52.3 | 65.0 | 76.8 | 56.1 | 78.7 | 91.8 | 96.7 | 56.8 | 68.4 |
| Luxembourg | 0.4 | 0.9 | 1.3 | 0.7 | 0.9 | 0.1 | 0.9 | 1.1 | 0.1 | ..... |
| Netherlands | 170.9 | 161.0 | 145.9 | 130.7 | 151.6 | 95.2 | 106.9 | 178.9 | 46.1 | 198.3 |
| Spain | 28.1 | 11.8 | 8.9 | 7.3 | 16.0 | 22.0 | 30.7 | 33.7 | 19.3 | 20.0 |
| United Kingdom | 91.4 | 86.1 | 109.9 | 98.1 | 100.7 | 250.2 | 304.9 | 352.4 | 161.6 | 191.0 |
| Switzerland | 5.9 | 4.2 | 13.5 | 9.9 | 9.7 | 20.9 | 17.9 | 24.8 | 20.4 | 28.6 |
| Asian 10 | 377.3 | 399.3 | 458.9 | 473.7 | 446.4 | 3 283.2 | 3 654.0 | 5 675.0 | 5 419.7 | 5 147.9 |
| China | 57.6 | 60.3 | 80.7 | 53.9 | 50.3 | 55.6 | 33.7 | 75.2 | 96.2 | 107.0 |
| Hong Kong | 6.8 | 18.7 | 23.0 | 17.8 | 15.7 | 126.2 | 148.2 | 276.8 | 451.7 | 225.3 |
| Indonesia | 25.4 | 8.3 | 18.2 | 30.3 | 24.9 | 51.2 | 42.4 | 142.0 | 123.2 | 77.9 |
| Japan | 119.0 | 129.6 | 133.6 | 194.9 | 178.7 | 1 257.1 | 1 389.1 | 1 778.7 | 1 487.2 | 1 271.8 |
| Malaysia | 5.4 | 25.6 | 5.0 | 6.5 | 12.9 | 93.7 | 166.5 | 431.6 | 207.3 | 261.2 |
| Philippines | 7.1 | 22.0 | 16.8 | 11.6 | 14.0 | 225.4 | 283.2 | 302.3 | 371.2 | 520.3 |
| Singapore | 84.2 | 55.2 | 56.7 | 56.3 | 70.4 | 228.6 | 252.0 | 507.3 | 560.8 | 449.8 |
| South Korea | 30.2 | 45.8 | 66.8 | 66.0 | 45.3 | 428.5 | 550.9 | 936.5 | 905.5 | 1 037.8 |
| Taiwan | 35.3 | 20.1 | 27.7 | 16.4 | 15.6 | 742.2 | 688.4 | 1 057.7 | 1 047.0 | 1 063.4 |
| Thailand | 6.3 | 13.7 | 30.1 | 20.1 | 18.6 | 74.6 | 99.5 | 167.0 | 169.5 | 133.5 |
| Australia | 37.1 | 38.8 | 48.6 | 67.3 | 60.9 | 162.9 | 205.5 | 302.8 | 253.2 | 168.1 |
| India | 23.7 | 20.0 | 17.6 | 10.7 | 32.6 | 9.5 | 9.3 | 19.2 | 23.7 | 26.2 |
| Israel | 37.2 | 4.9 | 12.5 | 7.5 | 5.9 | 17.5 | 26.5 | 27.8 | 48.0 | 38.6 |
| Pakistan | 9.5 | 4.2 | 4.0 | 3.8 | 18.4 | 102.3 | 177.0 | 238.6 | 224.6 | 261.0 |
| Saudi Arabia | 35.8 | 23.2 | 22.8 | 34.6 | 34.0 | 9.3 | 9.6 | 45.5 | 11.5 | 40.3 |
| African 8 | 28.0 | 16.3 | 19.1 | 39.8 | 38.3 | 33.8 | 48.1 | 46.4 | 39.4 | 39.8 |
| Developing Countries | 1 252.3 | 988.4 | 1 197.6 | 1 156.5 | 1 224.5 | 2 738.1 | 3 134.4 | 4 879.1 | 4 769.0 | 4 678.6 |

| Destination | Pennsylvania | | | | | Puerto Rico | | | | |
|---|---|---|---|---|---|---|---|---|---|---|
| | 1993 | 1994 | 1995 | 1996 | 1997 | 1993 | 1994 | 1995 | 1996 | 1997 |
| All destinations | 13 189.6 | 14 698.6 | 17 680.2 | 17 445.6 | 19 298.4 | 4 365.1 | 4 618.9 | 4 704.5 | 5 188.4 | 5 528.1 |
| Canada | 3 730.3 | 4 066.5 | 4 671.8 | 4 773.7 | 5 615.7 | 387.4 | 671.3 | 535.9 | 575.8 | 689.5 |
| Mexico | 627.3 | 866.4 | 741.2 | 879.0 | 1 140.3 | 129.5 | 137.0 | 205.5 | 226.9 | 216.8 |
| Central and South America and Caribbean | 1 220.5 | 1 363.6 | 1 689.7 | 1 550.3 | 1 820.8 | 876.7 | 852.6 | 950.0 | 981.8 | 1 097.1 |
| Argentina | 166.7 | 201.8 | 161.8 | 127.0 | 154.0 | 60.7 | 51.4 | 32.9 | 39.1 | 38.6 |
| Brazil | 408.5 | 491.1 | 679.1 | 603.6 | 744.7 | 103.4 | 106.2 | 115.3 | 116.7 | 129.8 |
| Chile | 79.0 | 70.9 | 130.6 | 129.3 | 173.4 | 20.5 | 8.4 | 6.2 | 8.8 | 5.3 |
| Colombia | 104.4 | 119.2 | 128.9 | 116.8 | 103.6 | 23.4 | 27.4 | 22.8 | 28.0 | 29.6 |
| Dominican Republic | 44.4 | 50.8 | 70.5 | 97.2 | 115.2 | 331.3 | 393.5 | 455.0 | 473.5 | 549.1 |
| Venezuela | 151.6 | 138.4 | 150.9 | 118.5 | 131.5 | 44.2 | 34.0 | 42.8 | 26.3 | 37.3 |
| European Union | 3 103.1 | 3 277.5 | 4 365.0 | 4 373.1 | 4 487.9 | 1 872.5 | 1 787.3 | 2 042.1 | 2 277.3 | 2 115.0 |
| Belgium | 253.5 | 263.3 | 409.9 | 376.4 | 369.1 | 165.2 | 202.3 | 194.6 | 214.6 | 185.8 |
| France | 282.7 | 278.0 | 388.4 | 411.8 | 446.8 | 211.5 | 209.9 | 309.9 | 309.8 | 318.2 |
| Germany | 573.3 | 583.8 | 692.1 | 631.1 | 652.4 | 597.0 | 652.5 | 781.6 | 935.6 | 532.8 |
| Ireland | 87.2 | 107.6 | 120.1 | 97.4 | 108.6 | 153.4 | 92.2 | 72.8 | 87.5 | 69.4 |
| Italy | 333.3 | 281.1 | 338.4 | 343.3 | 336.2 | 162.8 | 127.0 | 156.5 | 254.6 | 350.7 |
| Luxembourg | 5.0 | 2.9 | 4.5 | 3.7 | 3.1 | ..... | 0.1 | ..... | 5.7 | ..... |
| Netherlands | 465.9 | 500.7 | 725.6 | 647.8 | 664.7 | 165.5 | 164.9 | 206.8 | 235.5 | 415.6 |
| Spain | 146.4 | 140.6 | 174.2 | 193.8 | 184.8 | 59.7 | 38.4 | 37.8 | 42.4 | 32.1 |
| United Kingdom | 711.9 | 812.3 | 1 146.9 | 1 369.9 | 1 436.3 | 319.4 | 249.9 | 238.3 | 148.4 | 179.4 |
| Switzerland | 73.7 | 88.2 | 82.3 | 97.2 | 86.9 | 157.8 | 267.2 | 75.1 | 92.2 | 359.1 |
| Asian 10 | 3 118.2 | 3 676.7 | 4 416.3 | 4 030.3 | 4 429.7 | 624.9 | 611.0 | 697.5 | 841.5 | 797.8 |
| China | 140.3 | 255.8 | 314.8 | 242.5 | 245.2 | 6.7 | 5.6 | 11.8 | 13.7 | 17.5 |
| Hong Kong | 212.2 | 274.6 | 347.3 | 360.4 | 376.6 | 19.9 | 17.5 | 22.9 | 19.1 | 28.5 |
| Indonesia | 46.9 | 62.1 | 124.9 | 121.9 | 167.9 | 13.3 | 14.2 | 8.2 | 11.5 | 17.7 |
| Japan | 853.1 | 861.7 | 1 098.6 | 1 119.4 | 1 162.0 | 429.3 | 397.3 | 400.5 | 413.1 | 448.7 |
| Malaysia | 158.7 | 194.3 | 173.2 | 137.9 | 171.9 | 8.3 | 23.1 | 16.9 | 41.1 | 34.4 |
| Philippines | 93.7 | 89.6 | 136.0 | 154.3 | 142.6 | 7.7 | 5.6 | 8.4 | 6.2 | 6.8 |
| Singapore | 420.7 | 486.8 | 592.9 | 627.8 | 675.0 | 43.4 | 71.4 | 140.9 | 244.8 | 149.8 |
| South Korea | 482.4 | 641.1 | 694.9 | 593.3 | 593.8 | 49.5 | 43.1 | 61.7 | 51.5 | 35.0 |
| Taiwan | 504.0 | 565.3 | 727.6 | 428.1 | 521.3 | 42.5 | 29.5 | 23.0 | 37.7 | 56.4 |
| Thailand | 206.2 | 245.4 | 206.0 | 244.6 | 373.4 | 4.1 | 3.8 | 3.1 | 2.8 | 3.0 |
| Australia | 279.1 | 317.6 | 457.7 | 426.3 | 417.3 | 176.6 | 181.3 | 96.0 | 86.2 | 92.2 |
| India | 123.4 | 99.0 | 133.5 | 135.1 | 161.2 | 8.2 | 10.5 | 10.0 | 5.2 | 11.5 |
| Israel | 115.7 | 113.2 | 137.6 | 155.8 | 128.2 | 5.4 | 3.8 | 6.1 | 8.2 | 7.5 |
| Pakistan | 22.6 | 15.6 | 25.7 | 46.4 | 25.5 | 14.6 | 9.4 | 12.9 | 9.1 | 10.8 |
| Saudi Arabia | 163.5 | 163.6 | 196.3 | 181.3 | 154.6 | 7.0 | 2.3 | 0.4 | 1.4 | 3.5 |
| African 8 | 109.0 | 129.2 | 173.8 | 152.2 | 135.7 | 22.1 | 15.5 | 9.9 | 11.0 | 12.9 |
| Developing Countries | 4 901.6 | 5 854.9 | 6 699.6 | 6 357.2 | 7 233.0 | 1 292.6 | 1 271.3 | 1 523.4 | 1 704.2 | 1 741.7 |

## Table D-2. State Exports of Goods by Destination, 1993–1997 —*Continued*

(State of origin by country of destination, millions of dollars.)

| Destination | Rhode Island | | | | | South Carolina | | | | |
|---|---|---|---|---|---|---|---|---|---|---|
| | 1993 | 1994 | 1995 | 1996 | 1997 | 1993 | 1994 | 1995 | 1996 | 1997 |
| All destinations | 938.4 | 1 011.5 | 956.8 | 954.8 | 1 126.5 | 3 219.5 | 3 510.1 | 4 497.9 | 4 924.9 | 5 673.8 |
| Canada | 286.3 | 268.8 | 294.3 | 322.6 | 329.6 | 1 009.3 | 1 252.7 | 1 538.5 | 1 478.2 | 1 620.7 |
| Mexico | 41.6 | 27.6 | 15.4 | 23.2 | 77.3 | 293.2 | 450.0 | 641.4 | 661.8 | 935.9 |
| Central and South America and Caribbean | 38.1 | 53.1 | 42.7 | 28.7 | 64.8 | 222.2 | 237.7 | 337.9 | 309.2 | 439.7 |
| Argentina | 10.2 | 10.6 | 3.9 | 2.8 | 6.1 | 27.0 | 13.7 | 21.3 | 23.3 | 38.1 |
| Brazil | 3.9 | 8.4 | 9.3 | 6.7 | 32.3 | 15.5 | 26.3 | 75.1 | 63.8 | 87.7 |
| Chile | 3.7 | 10.2 | 7.4 | 3.8 | 3.7 | 18.7 | 30.6 | 23.0 | 27.9 | 26.6 |
| Colombia | 1.8 | 3.1 | 3.1 | 1.3 | 2.6 | 16.1 | 20.9 | 20.6 | 18.6 | 26.9 |
| Dominican Republic | 1.1 | 1.0 | 1.4 | 0.8 | 2.7 | 21.3 | 23.1 | 31.4 | 32.9 | 50.2 |
| Venezuela | 4.0 | 2.0 | 4.0 | 2.2 | 4.1 | 15.9 | 6.3 | 15.3 | 19.8 | 41.4 |
| European Union | 339.2 | 387.9 | 324.8 | 296.6 | 342.1 | 888.3 | 786.2 | 926.8 | 1 452.0 | 1 592.9 |
| Belgium | 34.5 | 40.7 | 25.3 | 24.3 | 39.4 | 69.3 | 70.2 | 91.5 | 102.0 | 110.8 |
| France | 17.6 | 19.2 | 18.3 | 16.4 | 18.3 | 102.3 | 73.0 | 86.0 | 92.8 | 108.0 |
| Germany | 39.0 | 25.2 | 30.1 | 38.6 | 41.2 | 225.5 | 214.8 | 233.6 | 727.4 | 854.7 |
| Ireland | 11.4 | 31.3 | 16.4 | 30.8 | 35.0 | 13.0 | 42.7 | 34.7 | 25.3 | 23.6 |
| Italy | 16.2 | 14.7 | 23.0 | 14.2 | 17.7 | 56.3 | 51.9 | 77.4 | 89.9 | 99.1 |
| Luxembourg | 1.7 | 1.5 | 1.5 | 3.1 | 2.6 | 0.4 | 0.4 | 0.5 | 0.5 | 0.6 |
| Netherlands | 74.1 | 48.4 | 29.1 | 24.7 | 20.8 | 111.8 | 88.6 | 102.4 | 121.9 | 96.7 |
| Spain | 22.5 | 17.4 | 13.5 | 12.8 | 25.3 | 26.0 | 24.3 | 28.6 | 30.0 | 35.4 |
| United Kingdom | 76.0 | 147.0 | 84.0 | 64.1 | 91.7 | 227.9 | 177.3 | 225.5 | 210.0 | 212.9 |
| Switzerland | 15.6 | 25.9 | 19.0 | 17.1 | 26.3 | 22.3 | 15.4 | 17.1 | 17.8 | 23.4 |
| Asian 10 | 154.0 | 191.6 | 209.9 | 216.9 | 236.1 | 562.6 | 585.5 | 760.5 | 712.9 | 773.0 |
| China | 8.0 | 17.7 | 6.1 | 8.1 | 6.9 | 36.4 | 28.9 | 54.0 | 55.9 | 45.9 |
| Hong Kong | 30.1 | 33.7 | 30.3 | 34.9 | 34.5 | 85.5 | 96.6 | 144.6 | 92.6 | 103.0 |
| Indonesia | 0.4 | 0.8 | 0.6 | 1.5 | 1.0 | 10.6 | 11.4 | 12.0 | 12.0 | 35.3 |
| Japan | 42.9 | 46.7 | 65.8 | 61.8 | 89.4 | 153.2 | 180.5 | 181.5 | 201.6 | 273.1 |
| Malaysia | 14.7 | 18.2 | 23.3 | 28.5 | 24.9 | 19.1 | 9.5 | 21.2 | 30.5 | 16.4 |
| Philippines | 8.5 | 9.5 | 10.8 | 16.0 | 15.2 | 11.5 | 5.4 | 11.0 | 13.5 | 9.3 |
| Singapore | 17.3 | 22.1 | 23.9 | 19.7 | 18.4 | 59.5 | 55.5 | 50.6 | 49.8 | 44.7 |
| South Korea | 14.9 | 24.8 | 28.6 | 26.8 | 20.2 | 115.5 | 112.4 | 115.2 | 69.9 | 67.5 |
| Taiwan | 10.9 | 13.3 | 14.3 | 12.4 | 20.0 | 51.9 | 71.0 | 154.1 | 165.8 | 160.3 |
| Thailand | 6.3 | 4.9 | 6.2 | 7.2 | 5.5 | 19.4 | 14.2 | 16.4 | 21.3 | 17.3 |
| Australia | 12.8 | 11.0 | 13.2 | 14.7 | 9.7 | 40.0 | 50.5 | 70.2 | 68.6 | 83.9 |
| India | 2.9 | 4.9 | 4.6 | 2.5 | 2.1 | 10.1 | 11.0 | 32.8 | 24.8 | 29.3 |
| Israel | 6.5 | 5.4 | 6.5 | 5.5 | 4.3 | 14.3 | 11.5 | 24.6 | 22.4 | 20.4 |
| Pakistan | 0.3 | 0.2 | 0.2 | 0.1 | 0.3 | 5.9 | 7.1 | 5.7 | 5.2 | 21.9 |
| Saudi Arabia | 2.8 | 1.9 | 2.0 | 1.9 | 0.9 | 33.2 | 22.3 | 34.1 | 44.6 | 25.9 |
| African 8 | 3.2 | 3.5 | 2.9 | 2.6 | 2.4 | 13.1 | 13.8 | 18.0 | 22.3 | 18.2 |
| Developing Countries | 233.4 | 260.6 | 232.3 | 234.0 | 314.3 | 1 064.5 | 1 193.0 | 1 723.8 | 1 650.7 | 2 027.8 |

| Destination | South Dakota | | | | | Tennessee | | | | |
|---|---|---|---|---|---|---|---|---|---|---|
| | 1993 | 1994 | 1995 | 1996 | 1997 | 1993 | 1994 | 1995 | 1996 | 1997 |
| All destinations | 213.8 | 263.9 | 348.6 | 397.3 | 435.3 | 6 151.1 | 7 506.2 | 9 460.5 | 9 328.3 | 9 916.9 |
| Canada | 107.5 | 130.8 | 142.1 | 164.1 | 167.3 | 1 679.1 | 1 976.2 | 2 101.0 | 2 199.9 | 2 389.4 |
| Mexico | 4.1 | 5.5 | 5.3 | 7.8 | 11.5 | 649.9 | 752.4 | 839.4 | 913.6 | 1 188.1 |
| Central and South America and Caribbean | 4.5 | 5.7 | 11.8 | 17.5 | 14.8 | 436.8 | 492.1 | 707.9 | 771.9 | 894.1 |
| Argentina | 1.1 | 0.3 | 0.2 | 0.2 | 0.5 | 48.1 | 53.7 | 59.8 | 71.3 | 75.0 |
| Brazil | 1.5 | 1.0 | 2.5 | 1.6 | 4.2 | 109.9 | 137.2 | 206.3 | 267.9 | 251.8 |
| Chile | 0.1 | 0.5 | 0.3 | 2.7 | 1.1 | 26.7 | 21.9 | 45.4 | 27.1 | 52.7 |
| Colombia | 0.2 | 0.4 | 1.0 | 0.6 | 0.8 | 32.1 | 44.4 | 53.9 | 48.1 | 88.3 |
| Dominican Republic | ..... | 0.1 | 0.1 | 0.2 | 0.2 | 44.4 | 49.1 | 70.7 | 61.8 | 72.8 |
| Venezuela | 0.3 | 0.4 | 0.5 | 0.6 | 1.7 | 37.2 | 31.1 | 29.3 | 30.7 | 34.4 |
| European Union | 66.4 | 69.5 | 111.2 | 105.8 | 121.7 | 1 553.9 | 1 708.0 | 1 898.3 | 1 869.1 | 2 132.4 |
| Belgium | 1.0 | 0.9 | 0.9 | 1.6 | 2.4 | 78.9 | 90.9 | 145.7 | 147.2 | 156.5 |
| France | 13.4 | 4.2 | 6.7 | 7.2 | 7.4 | 178.6 | 209.7 | 202.3 | 240.5 | 283.6 |
| Germany | 9.9 | 8.3 | 10.6 | 17.1 | 18.2 | 302.0 | 334.7 | 323.5 | 371.8 | 403.1 |
| Ireland | 9.8 | 17.3 | 24.1 | 11.8 | 21.6 | 14.1 | 26.2 | 41.3 | 40.4 | 34.8 |
| Italy | 0.9 | 1.1 | 2.7 | 2.2 | 3.1 | 113.3 | 134.2 | 162.2 | 133.5 | 133.3 |
| Luxembourg | ..... | 0.3 | 1.1 | 0.7 | ..... | 0.4 | 0.9 | 1.0 | 1.0 | 4.8 |
| Netherlands | 23.5 | 25.7 | 26.6 | 31.7 | 29.6 | 380.2 | 372.8 | 413.1 | 343.1 | 385.7 |
| Spain | ..... | 0.1 | 0.6 | 0.9 | 0.5 | 56.6 | 51.6 | 73.7 | 72.7 | 87.3 |
| United Kingdom | 5.2 | 8.7 | 35.5 | 29.6 | 35.7 | 340.1 | 378.4 | 422.9 | 395.5 | 531.7 |
| Switzerland | 0.7 | 1.0 | 1.1 | 0.6 | 0.9 | 13.6 | 14.7 | 16.3 | 23.2 | 25.4 |
| Asian 10 | 19.2 | 38.2 | 58.4 | 81.9 | 104.5 | 1 155.9 | 1 949.4 | 2 984.1 | 2 693.9 | 2 247.4 |
| China | 1.4 | 0.4 | 0.6 | 0.3 | 3.8 | 57.6 | 384.0 | 1 100.6 | 872.5 | 433.2 |
| Hong Kong | 0.9 | 3.1 | 4.8 | 15.0 | 15.6 | 85.0 | 214.6 | 256.8 | 208.5 | 217.7 |
| Indonesia | ..... | 0.1 | 0.1 | 0.2 | 0.7 | 62.1 | 70.7 | 150.4 | 114.7 | 65.5 |
| Japan | 10.3 | 22.1 | 38.6 | 28.0 | 22.0 | 388.8 | 563.3 | 674.3 | 727.7 | 692.8 |
| Malaysia | 0.2 | 0.5 | 1.0 | 12.9 | 17.0 | 15.3 | 36.3 | 46.2 | 43.4 | 37.0 |
| Philippines | 0.3 | 0.5 | 0.4 | 1.2 | 0.7 | 36.4 | 48.7 | 80.8 | 73.0 | 65.6 |
| Singapore | 2.8 | 3.9 | 3.9 | 2.9 | 4.7 | 83.5 | 87.0 | 85.1 | 83.2 | 165.7 |
| South Korea | 1.5 | 2.6 | 1.0 | 3.2 | 4.7 | 181.8 | 230.4 | 284.4 | 320.6 | 279.2 |
| Taiwan | 1.2 | 4.2 | 6.2 | 14.0 | 32.0 | 205.5 | 249.4 | 213.1 | 176.6 | 226.2 |
| Thailand | 0.5 | 0.7 | 1.8 | 4.2 | 3.3 | 39.9 | 65.0 | 92.5 | 73.6 | 64.5 |
| Australia | 4.0 | 2.6 | 5.9 | 5.2 | 5.2 | 132.3 | 129.6 | 158.7 | 162.7 | 206.3 |
| India | 0.3 | 0.4 | 0.3 | 0.6 | 0.3 | 27.4 | 25.3 | 44.4 | 26.3 | 31.9 |
| Israel | 1.6 | 0.8 | 1.7 | 2.8 | 1.1 | 24.8 | 28.4 | 29.7 | 34.7 | 40.2 |
| Pakistan | ..... | ..... | 0.1 | 0.1 | 0.1 | 5.2 | 17.4 | 65.6 | 5.1 | 13.4 |
| Saudi Arabia | 1.4 | 2.0 | 1.0 | 0.2 | 1.1 | 60.2 | 50.7 | 58.7 | 56.4 | 60.6 |
| African 8 | 0.3 | 1.4 | 1.6 | 0.7 | 0.6 | 92.3 | 58.0 | 68.3 | 69.7 | 96.5 |
| Developing Countries | 23.8 | 36.0 | 48.5 | 87.0 | 114.9 | 2 177.2 | 2 960.1 | 4 388.2 | 4 118.2 | 4 198.2 |

## Table D-2.  State Exports of Goods by Destination, 1993–1997 —*Continued*

(State of origin by country of destination, millions of dollars.)

| Destination | Texas | | | | | Utah | | | | |
|---|---|---|---|---|---|---|---|---|---|---|
| | 1993 | 1994 | 1995 | 1996 | 1997 | 1993 | 1994 | 1995 | 1996 | 1997 |
| All destinations | 35 622.5 | 40 489.0 | 45 192.6 | 48 252.1 | 56 292.9 | 2 045.0 | 2 233.1 | 2 313.4 | 2 768.5 | 3 293.3 |
| Canada | 3 811.3 | 4 830.4 | 6 142.0 | 6 616.4 | 8 117.6 | 343.1 | 342.9 | 413.1 | 443.3 | 514.5 |
| Mexico | 12 860.8 | 14 364.9 | 12 589.0 | 15 586.7 | 18 864.1 | 30.5 | 82.7 | 66.7 | 76.4 | 73.0 |
| Central and South America and Caribbean | 3 150.1 | 3 976.2 | 5 073.2 | 5 180.2 | 6 402.8 | 45.1 | 50.2 | 86.3 | 96.4 | 109.8 |
| Argentina | 277.9 | 366.3 | 529.1 | 475.7 | 504.9 | 2.1 | 3.3 | 3.4 | 3.6 | 6.4 |
| Brazil | 402.9 | 492.0 | 878.1 | 1 023.6 | 1 230.5 | 7.9 | 8.0 | 6.9 | 20.7 | 29.8 |
| Chile | 137.8 | 169.7 | 272.7 | 259.6 | 378.2 | 14.7 | 15.1 | 37.7 | 28.3 | 28.5 |
| Colombia | 365.9 | 530.5 | 620.3 | 696.7 | 782.3 | 3.4 | 5.0 | 10.6 | 5.3 | 10.6 |
| Dominican Republic | 79.9 | 122.4 | 108.1 | 120.5 | 156.9 | 1.2 | 2.6 | 7.4 | 11.2 | 3.3 |
| Venezuela | 779.5 | 1 027.0 | 1 136.4 | 1 175.8 | 1 375.5 | 3.0 | 3.3 | 4.2 | 8.3 | 9.3 |
| European Union | 4 598.4 | 4 957.7 | 5 803.7 | 5 419.8 | 6 162.9 | 475.1 | 522.5 | 619.2 | 895.1 | 1 257.1 |
| Belgium | 305.9 | 445.3 | 557.0 | 434.0 | 561.9 | 37.4 | 83.7 | 129.7 | 64.3 | 81.6 |
| France | 490.4 | 539.8 | 557.1 | 570.8 | 584.5 | 18.3 | 16.1 | 26.8 | 42.2 | 41.1 |
| Germany | 626.0 | 563.2 | 722.2 | 719.0 | 882.7 | 159.2 | 187.9 | 196.7 | 210.2 | 146.5 |
| Ireland | 69.2 | 148.3 | 153.8 | 136.8 | 143.1 | 16.0 | 20.8 | 24.5 | 21.6 | 43.4 |
| Italy | 260.9 | 245.7 | 331.3 | 265.6 | 297.9 | 12.4 | 13.0 | 17.7 | 26.3 | 48.6 |
| Luxembourg | 4.4 | 3.3 | 1.7 | 2.5 | 8.0 | 0.2 | 0.4 | 0.6 | 1.6 | 0.1 |
| Netherlands | 972.1 | 934.3 | 1 128.6 | 1 105.2 | 1 161.0 | 140.1 | 117.6 | 90.9 | 116.1 | 118.1 |
| Spain | 161.4 | 174.3 | 194.4 | 168.1 | 181.3 | 6.0 | 5.1 | 7.3 | 19.0 | 14.0 |
| United Kingdom | 1 451.8 | 1 674.6 | 1 915.5 | 1 717.1 | 1 979.3 | 70.1 | 60.8 | 108.8 | 365.9 | 735.1 |
| Switzerland | 106.1 | 112.3 | 127.3 | 104.0 | 106.2 | 182.8 | 78.7 | 4.5 | 6.0 | 17.6 |
| Asian 10 | 6 815.1 | 8 159.0 | 10 826.5 | 9 981.2 | 11 006.0 | 885.4 | 1 086.8 | 1 021.0 | 1 116.0 | 1 204.5 |
| China | 398.7 | 482.4 | 715.0 | 605.4 | 651.8 | 5.6 | 13.8 | 16.4 | 28.1 | 11.7 |
| Hong Kong | 533.4 | 633.0 | 1 070.3 | 906.3 | 974.4 | 169.7 | 384.2 | 59.0 | 36.1 | 39.1 |
| Indonesia | 319.6 | 257.8 | 302.2 | 413.0 | 344.1 | 4.1 | 7.8 | 7.9 | 11.8 | 8.4 |
| Japan | 1 445.8 | 1 558.4 | 2 181.0 | 2 073.9 | 2 218.4 | 244.0 | 296.1 | 404.8 | 468.9 | 516.8 |
| Malaysia | 649.3 | 836.6 | 1 023.3 | 837.4 | 972.8 | 66.2 | 14.9 | 9.7 | 45.9 | 171.6 |
| Philippines | 380.1 | 490.7 | 598.3 | 754.1 | 882.1 | 25.4 | 32.6 | 65.7 | 52.1 | 97.0 |
| Singapore | 1 192.0 | 1 529.3 | 1 755.5 | 1 528.7 | 2 015.8 | 47.4 | 24.1 | 82.5 | 131.9 | 64.6 |
| South Korea | 750.2 | 923.6 | 1 474.0 | 1 354.2 | 1 352.6 | 59.5 | 89.6 | 159.4 | 140.7 | 107.1 |
| Taiwan | 1 000.1 | 1 200.4 | 1 371.4 | 1 179.0 | 1 348.3 | 194.7 | 172.6 | 144.9 | 138.8 | 112.7 |
| Thailand | 146.0 | 246.9 | 335.7 | 329.2 | 245.6 | 68.7 | 51.2 | 70.6 | 61.8 | 75.4 |
| Australia | 422.7 | 472.7 | 634.6 | 723.4 | 636.7 | 29.8 | 27.9 | 35.0 | 34.5 | 36.9 |
| India | 136.8 | 158.9 | 281.6 | 253.5 | 242.7 | 3.4 | 1.7 | 4.5 | 4.1 | 4.6 |
| Israel | 123.9 | 120.7 | 227.5 | 262.6 | 271.5 | 7.3 | 6.1 | 12.6 | 9.7 | 14.6 |
| Pakistan | 85.7 | 43.5 | 54.4 | 69.7 | 88.8 | 0.3 | 0.1 | 0.1 | 0.3 | 0.2 |
| Saudi Arabia | 847.9 | 576.6 | 594.0 | 668.8 | 814.7 | 2.9 | 3.1 | 2.9 | 22.5 | 3.7 |
| African 8 | 424.5 | 388.7 | 618.9 | 765.6 | 835.4 | 5.1 | 3.7 | 5.5 | 11.4 | 8.0 |
| Developing Countries | 24 567.9 | 27 651.6 | 29 511.6 | 32 488.4 | 38 088.2 | 752.3 | 947.8 | 818.0 | 896.7 | 922.3 |

| Destination | Vermont | | | | | Virgin Islands | | | | |
|---|---|---|---|---|---|---|---|---|---|---|
| | 1993 | 1994 | 1995 | 1996 | 1997 | 1993 | 1994 | 1995 | 1996 | 1997 |
| All destinations | 2 276.0 | 2 304.3 | 2 683.6 | 2 610.8 | 2 592.1 | 162.1 | 158.0 | 228.6 | 192.4 | 242.7 |
| Canada | 2 075.2 | 2 064.5 | 2 509.9 | 2 377.6 | 2 310.3 | 10.1 | 7.5 | 12.4 | 7.4 | 4.3 |
| Mexico | 12.2 | 15.9 | 10.4 | 8.5 | 8.7 | 0.2 | 3.8 | 5.6 | 11.7 | 3.9 |
| Central and South America and Caribbean | 8.5 | 8.1 | 10.0 | 16.8 | 22.8 | 83.4 | 71.7 | 134.6 | 123.6 | 114.8 |
| Argentina | 0.7 | 0.6 | 0.9 | 0.9 | 1.0 | 0.9 | 0.2 | 0.6 | 6.4 | 0.2 |
| Brazil | 1.5 | 1.8 | 3.4 | 3.6 | 2.8 | 7.3 | 6.8 | 23.3 | 8.4 | 1.3 |
| Chile | 0.7 | 0.4 | 0.7 | 0.6 | 1.1 | 0.3 | 0.4 | ..... | 0.2 | ..... |
| Colombia | 0.9 | 0.9 | 0.9 | 1.1 | 3.6 | 3.4 | 0.6 | 0.7 | 7.3 | 1.1 |
| Dominican Republic | ..... | 0.2 | 0.1 | 1.3 | 0.1 | 4.1 | 6.4 | 13.2 | 9.2 | 9.6 |
| Venezuela | 2.1 | 1.0 | 1.4 | 0.7 | 1.0 | 0.2 | ..... | 0.7 | 0.2 | 0.2 |
| European Union | 75.6 | 123.7 | 73.9 | 96.6 | 136.6 | 38.7 | 32.4 | 14.3 | 24.4 | 83.2 |
| Belgium | 2.5 | 1.9 | 2.2 | 3.3 | 3.7 | 0.1 | 0.1 | ..... | ..... | 0.3 |
| France | 4.1 | 8.4 | 7.1 | 11.3 | 19.7 | 0.1 | 0.3 | 0.1 | 0.1 | 1.8 |
| Germany | 20.6 | 16.4 | 12.0 | 13.5 | 27.8 | 1.7 | 0.3 | 0.6 | 0.1 | 5.8 |
| Ireland | 1.3 | 30.4 | 3.3 | 1.5 | 2.5 | ..... | ..... | ..... | ..... | ..... |
| Italy | 7.7 | 5.2 | 5.9 | 7.6 | 9.3 | 12.9 | 12.8 | 9.6 | 13.6 | 16.7 |
| Luxembourg | 0.1 | ..... | ..... | 0.9 | 0.6 | ..... | ..... | ..... | ..... | ..... |
| Netherlands | 2.9 | 20.4 | 3.1 | 15.4 | 6.0 | 17.6 | 16.4 | 2.5 | 8.4 | 57.5 |
| Spain | 1.0 | 2.9 | 1.6 | 1.9 | 3.1 | 0.3 | 0.3 | 0.1 | 0.1 | ..... |
| United Kingdom | 28.0 | 29.5 | 29.7 | 32.8 | 49.1 | 2.3 | 1.0 | 0.7 | 1.0 | 0.4 |
| Switzerland | 5.1 | 4.2 | 4.4 | 4.3 | 5.8 | 1.1 | 0.3 | 0.2 | 0.1 | 0.3 |
| Asian 10 | 61.7 | 65.8 | 54.3 | 78.7 | 80.3 | 25.1 | 38.4 | 45.6 | 14.7 | 19.2 |
| China | 9.0 | 4.9 | 3.4 | 5.2 | 2.9 | 2.5 | 2.6 | 3.0 | 1.8 | ..... |
| Hong Kong | 5.1 | 2.4 | 3.2 | 4.5 | 4.1 | 0.7 | 0.2 | 0.9 | ..... | 0.1 |
| Indonesia | 0.4 | 0.6 | 1.1 | 1.1 | 4.2 | ..... | 0.3 | ..... | ..... | ..... |
| Japan | 12.3 | 18.0 | 26.0 | 33.5 | 31.3 | 1.7 | 1.9 | 16.1 | 6.4 | 0.1 |
| Malaysia | 0.1 | 0.3 | 1.1 | 1.1 | 0.6 | ..... | 0.7 | ..... | ..... | 0.4 |
| Philippines | 0.6 | 1.2 | 0.9 | 1.9 | 1.4 | ..... | 0.1 | ..... | ..... | 0.1 |
| Singapore | 11.1 | 13.2 | 8.5 | 8.1 | 10.5 | 8.3 | 8.5 | 0.8 | 0.1 | 0.1 |
| South Korea | 14.5 | 5.4 | 5.7 | 9.3 | 17.6 | 0.4 | 18.3 | 17.3 | 6.3 | 18.4 |
| Taiwan | 7.7 | 17.0 | 3.4 | 12.1 | 6.3 | 0.1 | 6.0 | 7.4 | 0.1 | 0.1 |
| Thailand | 0.9 | 2.6 | 1.0 | 1.7 | 1.4 | 11.3 | ..... | ..... | ..... | ..... |
| Australia | 3.6 | 5.9 | 4.9 | 5.1 | 6.8 | 0.2 | 0.2 | 0.2 | ..... | ..... |
| India | 3.7 | 0.4 | 0.7 | 1.2 | 2.2 | 0.1 | ..... | 4.1 | 0.1 | 2.3 |
| Israel | 1.4 | 1.5 | 1.0 | 1.6 | 4.5 | ..... | 0.1 | 0.2 | ..... | ..... |
| Pakistan | 0.1 | ..... | 2.9 | 0.1 | 0.3 | ..... | ..... | ..... | ..... | ..... |
| Saudi Arabia | 2.2 | 3.4 | 2.6 | 9.9 | 1.2 | ..... | ..... | 0.9 | 0.1 | ..... |
| African 8 | 0.7 | 0.6 | 1.1 | 1.2 | 1.6 | 0.6 | 0.1 | 1.2 | 7.6 | 0.3 |
| Developing Countries | 101.5 | 84.0 | 60.5 | 89.2 | 95.2 | 109.1 | 114.8 | 179.1 | 146.3 | 154.5 |

## Table D-2.  State Exports of Goods by Destination, 1993–1997 —*Continued*

(State of origin by country of destination, millions of dollars.)

| Destination | Virginia | | | | | Washington | | | | |
|---|---|---|---|---|---|---|---|---|---|---|
| | 1993 | 1994 | 1995 | 1996 | 1997 | 1993 | 1994 | 1995 | 1996 | 1997 |
| **All destinations** | 8 118.4 | 9 947.3 | 10 425.2 | 10 926.0 | 11 512.4 | 27 397.7 | 25 062.3 | 22 032.0 | 25 498.0 | 31 745.6 |
| Canada | 1 052.3 | 1 220.5 | 1 465.8 | 1 356.7 | 1 535.8 | 1 723.1 | 1 856.4 | 2 288.6 | 2 437.4 | 2 457.5 |
| Mexico | 302.3 | 365.8 | 320.8 | 342.1 | 430.2 | 207.8 | 411.2 | 188.1 | 254.9 | 272.4 |
| Central and South America and Caribbean | 531.8 | 619.5 | 694.4 | 750.2 | 903.6 | 542.1 | 410.4 | 482.4 | 651.0 | 952.1 |
| Argentina | 40.7 | 49.6 | 68.8 | 45.2 | 84.8 | 26.7 | 36.5 | 97.5 | 44.3 | 60.4 |
| Brazil | 118.8 | 171.2 | 256.4 | 273.4 | 407.3 | 239.2 | 98.9 | 105.5 | 106.7 | 414.2 |
| Chile | 24.6 | 29.6 | 47.8 | 76.4 | 58.5 | 26.8 | 27.6 | 140.5 | 338.8 | 291.8 |
| Colombia | 17.6 | 21.7 | 34.8 | 58.8 | 46.8 | 49.8 | 94.7 | 33.2 | 32.0 | 48.3 |
| Dominican Republic | 8.4 | 25.2 | 13.4 | 12.4 | 19.4 | 0.6 | 1.8 | 1.5 | 2.4 | 3.1 |
| Venezuela | 36.9 | 47.2 | 42.7 | 40.7 | 48.1 | 23.8 | 13.8 | 16.4 | 26.4 | 44.1 |
| European Union | 2 209.0 | 3 077.9 | 3 244.3 | 3 414.4 | 3 326.2 | 5 983.0 | 5 114.5 | 4 469.0 | 4 869.4 | 8 889.1 |
| Belgium | 575.0 | 1 406.8 | 1 379.6 | 1 303.3 | 1 164.5 | 86.7 | 166.7 | 148.6 | 219.2 | 299.9 |
| France | 117.0 | 153.8 | 154.0 | 194.7 | 210.5 | 814.7 | 415.7 | 297.5 | 218.9 | 342.5 |
| Germany | 429.4 | 480.4 | 531.0 | 672.5 | 670.7 | 1 236.9 | 829.1 | 896.6 | 923.4 | 1 518.4 |
| Ireland | 7.0 | 7.1 | 16.3 | 15.8 | 22.1 | 108.0 | 45.1 | 57.0 | 39.7 | 52.9 |
| Italy | 127.8 | 162.0 | 197.1 | 233.5 | 268.3 | 81.2 | 282.6 | 431.4 | 432.0 | 285.5 |
| Luxembourg | 12.0 | 14.4 | 14.7 | 22.5 | 31.3 | 360.0 | 1.8 | 162.5 | 2.1 | 326.5 |
| Netherlands | 134.2 | 185.2 | 261.9 | 202.6 | 211.0 | 574.2 | 448.4 | 713.7 | 904.2 | 877.1 |
| Spain | 175.0 | 178.9 | 141.1 | 192.6 | 184.3 | 228.5 | 388.6 | 152.6 | 141.9 | 192.2 |
| United Kingdom | 423.9 | 286.0 | 315.7 | 338.2 | 323.3 | 2 252.9 | 2 297.4 | 1 272.3 | 1 688.5 | 4 488.1 |
| Switzerland | 39.2 | 37.7 | 43.3 | 59.9 | 69.2 | 24.2 | 59.2 | 24.0 | 61.7 | 68.8 |
| Asian 10 | 2 400.3 | 2 907.6 | 3 008.5 | 2 899.7 | 3 094.5 | 15 482.2 | 14 039.7 | 13 043.6 | 13 920.2 | 14 870.6 |
| China | 79.3 | 65.1 | 119.9 | 107.2 | 134.2 | 1 941.6 | 1 887.1 | 1 088.4 | 1 463.9 | 1 805.6 |
| Hong Kong | 161.2 | 153.7 | 176.3 | 198.4 | 262.3 | 606.1 | 465.0 | 553.7 | 828.4 | 297.0 |
| Indonesia | 28.2 | 28.2 | 31.2 | 35.2 | 48.4 | 342.1 | 383.5 | 78.0 | 81.2 | 253.3 |
| Japan | 1 228.0 | 1 401.9 | 1 256.2 | 1 385.5 | 1 434.2 | 6 662.5 | 6 372.5 | 6 703.0 | 6 316.4 | 6 561.6 |
| Malaysia | 28.4 | 33.6 | 59.5 | 60.8 | 64.0 | 1 458.6 | 853.2 | 206.3 | 260.6 | 977.6 |
| Philippines | 23.1 | 15.9 | 25.9 | 41.4 | 50.6 | 333.8 | 57.8 | 191.3 | 237.8 | 109.1 |
| Singapore | 82.7 | 96.3 | 126.3 | 107.7 | 133.4 | 982.6 | 1 295.0 | 1 037.4 | 966.3 | 1 276.1 |
| South Korea | 524.5 | 856.4 | 971.6 | 737.6 | 751.7 | 1 389.5 | 1 408.3 | 1 851.6 | 2 023.9 | 1 889.2 |
| Taiwan | 197.4 | 202.2 | 181.5 | 156.1 | 152.8 | 1 468.8 | 993.8 | 933.0 | 893.6 | 797.0 |
| Thailand | 47.4 | 54.5 | 60.3 | 69.7 | 62.9 | 296.4 | 323.5 | 400.7 | 848.0 | 904.0 |
| Australia | 89.6 | 95.5 | 113.4 | 113.5 | 101.5 | 358.5 | 469.5 | 241.0 | 610.0 | 479.1 |
| India | 38.1 | 29.7 | 21.4 | 34.1 | 30.5 | 455.1 | 169.2 | 37.6 | 414.6 | 205.2 |
| Israel | 70.1 | 90.3 | 107.7 | 124.6 | 140.8 | 149.3 | 343.6 | 211.6 | 54.8 | 101.6 |
| Pakistan | 9.8 | 6.6 | 8.7 | 8.0 | 16.3 | 5.3 | 1.9 | 4.8 | 6.4 | 16.8 |
| Saudi Arabia | 324.8 | 321.7 | 234.9 | 251.5 | 276.5 | 30.9 | 27.2 | 31.7 | 135.4 | 955.4 |
| African 8 | 113.4 | 140.2 | 81.4 | 63.7 | 39.1 | 294.4 | 65.7 | 104.1 | 107.8 | 146.0 |
| Developing Countries | 3 179.0 | 3 930.6 | 4 079.2 | 4 359.7 | 4 826.2 | 11 607.8 | 10 517.3 | 7 899.8 | 10 879.4 | 12 844.7 |

| Destination | West Virginia | | | | | Wisconsin | | | | |
|---|---|---|---|---|---|---|---|---|---|---|
| | 1993 | 1994 | 1995 | 1996 | 1997 | 1993 | 1994 | 1995 | 1996 | 1997 |
| **All destinations** | 754.1 | 940.6 | 1 097.9 | 1 217.9 | 1 298.8 | 5 810.4 | 6 927.9 | 8 004.5 | 8 409.7 | 9 791.5 |
| Canada | 285.0 | 334.6 | 334.2 | 377.5 | 478.5 | 1 947.1 | 2 438.4 | 2 808.6 | 2 685.6 | 3 096.3 |
| Mexico | 21.0 | 16.7 | 16.4 | 19.3 | 34.4 | 287.7 | 411.9 | 311.0 | 350.5 | 427.3 |
| Central and South America and Caribbean | 45.2 | 66.1 | 91.1 | 101.7 | 65.5 | 431.9 | 464.1 | 577.5 | 664.0 | 785.1 |
| Argentina | 3.0 | 4.1 | 2.5 | 4.8 | 2.7 | 46.8 | 74.9 | 60.9 | 85.3 | 102.2 |
| Brazil | 7.7 | 45.1 | 78.0 | 81.6 | 46.1 | 88.7 | 109.1 | 176.6 | 187.2 | 243.9 |
| Chile | 2.9 | 1.0 | 1.2 | 2.5 | 2.8 | 78.7 | 70.5 | 94.3 | 139.6 | 129.3 |
| Colombia | 14.7 | 5.7 | 2.7 | 3.7 | 3.6 | 32.1 | 43.9 | 45.0 | 41.0 | 42.6 |
| Dominican Republic | 0.9 | 0.9 | 0.4 | 2.0 | 3.4 | 17.3 | 15.1 | 22.8 | 21.4 | 28.8 |
| Venezuela | 8.6 | 1.5 | 0.9 | 1.4 | 1.2 | 50.2 | 23.6 | 29.8 | 27.2 | 52.9 |
| European Union | 190.4 | 291.5 | 412.9 | 419.6 | 403.3 | 1 557.3 | 1 725.6 | 1 915.6 | 2 097.3 | 2 492.9 |
| Belgium | 4.0 | 10.0 | 25.5 | 53.8 | 47.4 | 107.8 | 124.8 | 147.3 | 178.4 | 205.3 |
| France | 14.5 | 20.9 | 23.3 | 24.0 | 34.0 | 277.8 | 317.4 | 358.2 | 319.4 | 454.0 |
| Germany | 15.7 | 24.1 | 29.3 | 19.4 | 28.0 | 307.4 | 325.0 | 387.1 | 441.4 | 462.2 |
| Ireland | 0.6 | 0.5 | 1.6 | 2.5 | 4.8 | 17.0 | 22.4 | 28.6 | 40.6 | 47.8 |
| Italy | 43.2 | 63.3 | 104.5 | 102.3 | 50.1 | 96.2 | 120.2 | 133.7 | 146.9 | 160.2 |
| Luxembourg | ..... | ..... | ..... | ..... | 0.1 | 0.7 | 1.0 | 1.2 | 1.9 | 1.7 |
| Netherlands | 45.8 | 71.3 | 73.0 | 57.2 | 64.4 | 179.7 | 179.4 | 238.9 | 254.8 | 238.9 |
| Spain | 13.3 | 13.4 | 19.5 | 34.8 | 25.0 | 44.9 | 48.2 | 60.9 | 78.2 | 75.4 |
| United Kingdom | 34.0 | 57.7 | 100.6 | 100.0 | 127.2 | 400.2 | 447.2 | 400.3 | 441.9 | 612.6 |
| Switzerland | 1.3 | 1.0 | 0.3 | 1.7 | 2.1 | 43.7 | 64.5 | 71.0 | 57.9 | 51.5 |
| Asian 10 | 189.6 | 200.1 | 193.4 | 231.1 | 218.3 | 961.2 | 1 172.6 | 1 557.6 | 1 696.5 | 1 830.6 |
| China | 19.3 | 22.1 | 20.5 | 12.6 | 9.0 | 78.3 | 89.0 | 102.6 | 110.1 | 146.2 |
| Hong Kong | 28.1 | 35.3 | 19.4 | 22.2 | 14.8 | 160.9 | 158.7 | 184.1 | 186.6 | 186.9 |
| Indonesia | 0.6 | 0.7 | 0.9 | 1.6 | 3.0 | 12.1 | 11.1 | 26.6 | 42.6 | 92.0 |
| Japan | 49.5 | 58.7 | 94.7 | 112.0 | 105.5 | 295.7 | 463.9 | 581.6 | 677.9 | 693.7 |
| Malaysia | 3.6 | 10.1 | 2.4 | 2.2 | 4.7 | 21.6 | 24.5 | 47.0 | 62.4 | 69.8 |
| Philippines | 0.6 | 0.9 | 1.2 | 1.4 | 2.1 | 28.0 | 23.5 | 33.9 | 59.4 | 71.9 |
| Singapore | 39.3 | 30.5 | 18.9 | 28.0 | 21.0 | 99.9 | 112.8 | 124.5 | 137.3 | 149.3 |
| South Korea | 18.1 | 16.7 | 21.2 | 24.5 | 29.8 | 106.5 | 123.4 | 167.4 | 172.1 | 187.9 |
| Taiwan | 21.0 | 15.2 | 10.1 | 17.1 | 13.2 | 120.1 | 119.1 | 214.2 | 164.6 | 160.3 |
| Thailand | 9.5 | 10.0 | 4.2 | 9.6 | 15.2 | 38.0 | 46.6 | 75.6 | 83.6 | 72.8 |
| Australia | 10.3 | 11.4 | 16.3 | 21.8 | 24.8 | 207.4 | 258.1 | 239.1 | 290.0 | 380.5 |
| India | 0.4 | 1.1 | 4.2 | 4.6 | 3.3 | 11.8 | 20.6 | 41.2 | 37.6 | 34.9 |
| Israel | 1.3 | 1.3 | 7.1 | 12.1 | 3.9 | 20.5 | 26.4 | 48.7 | 35.0 | 31.2 |
| Pakistan | ..... | ..... | 0.1 | ..... | ..... | 6.6 | 1.6 | 3.3 | 6.3 | 3.7 |
| Saudi Arabia | 1.2 | 2.6 | 3.5 | 2.3 | 10.8 | 92.8 | 56.5 | 75.7 | 67.2 | 73.0 |
| African 8 | 2.4 | 4.6 | 7.7 | 5.0 | 15.9 | 56.8 | 60.9 | 73.8 | 108.7 | 98.5 |
| Developing Countries | 212.6 | 233.1 | 231.3 | 268.8 | 257.0 | 1 646.6 | 1 852.0 | 2 233.4 | 2 382.4 | 2 874.6 |

**Table D-2.   State Exports of Goods by Destination,
1993–1997**—*Continued*

(State of origin by country of destination, millions of dollars.)

| Destination | Wyoming | | | | |
|---|---|---|---|---|---|
| | 1993 | 1994 | 1995 | 1996 | 1997 |
| **All destinations** | 88.5 | 95.4 | 101.2 | 123.7 | 175.9 |
| Canada | 37.8 | 48.6 | 50.7 | 69.4 | 88.3 |
| Mexico | 4.4 | 4.1 | 4.1 | 3.5 | 4.9 |
| Central and South America and Caribbean | 6.2 | 3.5 | 4.2 | 4.2 | 11.6 |
| Argentina | 0.4 | 0.5 | 0.4 | 0.1 | 1.4 |
| Brazil | 0.6 | 0.4 | 0.2 | 0.7 | 2.4 |
| Chile | 0.2 | 0.2 | 0.3 | 0.4 | 0.3 |
| Colombia | 0.4 | 0.4 | 0.3 | 0.1 | 0.5 |
| Dominican Republic | 0.1 | 0.3 | 0.1 | 0.5 | 0.7 |
| Venezuela | 1.5 | 0.2 | 0.3 | 1.7 | 2.2 |
| European Union | 13.8 | 16.5 | 17.4 | 17.8 | 39.5 |
| Belgium | 0.2 | 0.1 | 0.2 | 3.1 | 9.8 |
| France | 1.4 | 1.2 | 1.5 | 0.6 | 1.3 |
| Germany | 2.8 | 4.0 | 2.7 | 1.9 | 1.7 |
| Ireland | ..... | 0.3 | ..... | 0.3 | 1.0 |
| Italy | 0.8 | 0.5 | 0.5 | 0.2 | 1.7 |
| Luxembourg | ..... | ..... | ..... | ..... | ..... |
| Netherlands | 1.0 | 0.5 | 1.1 | 0.9 | 15.0 |
| Spain | 1.1 | 0.6 | 2.9 | 3.6 | 0.9 |
| United Kingdom | 5.6 | 8.6 | 7.6 | 6.8 | 6.9 |
| Switzerland | 0.6 | 0.5 | 0.6 | 0.6 | 0.3 |
| Asian 10 | 13.8 | 13.3 | 17.2 | 24.0 | 22.8 |
| China | 1.2 | ..... | 0.4 | 0.4 | 2.6 |
| Hong Kong | 0.8 | 1.4 | 1.2 | 0.5 | 2.4 |
| Indonesia | 1.0 | ..... | 1.0 | 0.3 | 0.4 |
| Japan | 4.7 | 6.9 | 9.6 | 18.4 | 11.1 |
| Malaysia | 0.5 | 0.4 | 0.4 | 0.1 | 0.2 |
| Philippines | 0.9 | 0.4 | 0.4 | 1.8 | 0.2 |
| Singapore | 2.0 | 1.0 | 1.1 | 0.6 | 1.3 |
| South Korea | 1.1 | 1.1 | 0.9 | 1.2 | 3.3 |
| Taiwan | 1.5 | 2.0 | 1.8 | 0.7 | 1.1 |
| Thailand | 0.1 | 0.1 | 0.5 | 0.1 | 0.2 |
| Australia | 1.0 | 1.8 | 1.4 | 1.3 | 2.1 |
| India | 0.3 | ..... | 0.1 | 0.2 | 0.5 |
| Israel | 0.3 | 0.3 | 0.7 | 0.2 | 0.2 |
| Pakistan | 0.2 | ..... | ..... | 0.1 | ..... |
| Saudi Arabia | 0.6 | 0.2 | ..... | 0.2 | 0.7 |
| African 8 | 0.2 | 1.0 | 0.2 | 0.2 | 0.5 |
| Developing Countries | 29.8 | 20.5 | 20.0 | 15.7 | 33.2 |

## ALABAMA: Exports of Goods, 1997

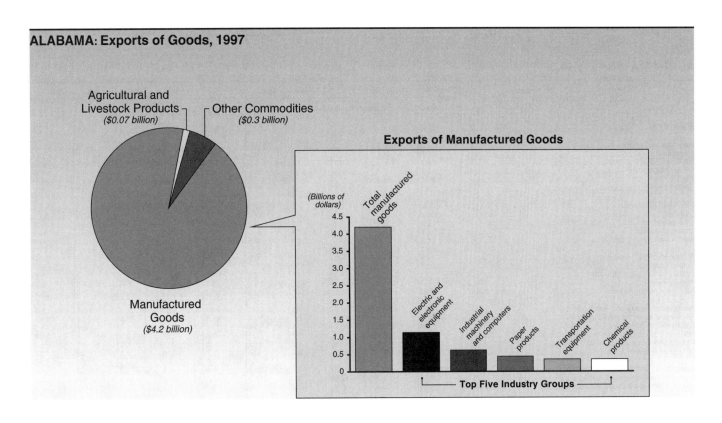

## Table D-3.  State Exports of Goods by Destination and Industry, 1993–1997

**ALABAMA** (Millions of dollars.)

| Industry | 1993 | 1994 | 1995 | 1996 | 1997 | 1993 | 1994 | 1995 | 1996 | 1997 |
|---|---|---|---|---|---|---|---|---|---|---|
| | All destinations | | | | | Canada | | | | |
| **ALL GOODS** | 2 504.3 | 3 115.4 | 3 587.1 | 3 702.4 | 4 537.2 | 621.7 | 789.0 | 988.5 | 1 177.4 | 1 251.1 |
| **Manufactured goods** | 2 173.1 | 2 796.6 | 3 167.0 | 3 359.9 | 4 207.7 | 591.4 | 745.6 | 939.9 | 1 118.6 | 1 199.4 |
| Food products | 33.5 | 32.4 | 49.6 | 40.9 | 52.1 | 27.7 | 26.6 | 41.3 | 31.0 | 37.8 |
| Tobacco products | 1.1 | 1.1 | 0.7 | 2.4 | 1.5 | ..... | ..... | ..... | ..... | ..... |
| Textile mill products | 49.4 | 66.0 | 83.9 | 86.0 | 122.4 | 23.8 | 35.9 | 34.6 | 25.1 | 32.2 |
| Apparel | 72.7 | 79.4 | 94.8 | 129.6 | 168.4 | 12.4 | 11.3 | 12.9 | 13.5 | 18.1 |
| Lumber and wood products | 126.3 | 129.9 | 143.1 | 140.2 | 143.6 | 5.0 | 6.9 | 5.4 | 7.3 | 20.9 |
| Furniture and fixtures | 28.0 | 32.2 | 25.6 | 21.9 | 27.5 | 19.7 | 22.0 | 21.0 | 15.3 | 20.5 |
| Paper products | 264.8 | 333.0 | 500.5 | 440.1 | 442.6 | 27.6 | 35.1 | 56.6 | 81.5 | 89.6 |
| Printing and publishing | 3.6 | 4.9 | 4.3 | 3.2 | 5.6 | 2.2 | 2.8 | 2.7 | 0.9 | 0.8 |
| Chemical products | 194.2 | 219.6 | 292.7 | 335.2 | 356.8 | 47.6 | 51.6 | 57.0 | 56.4 | 69.8 |
| Refined petroleum products | 0.2 | 0.8 | 1.5 | 9.4 | 3.1 | ..... | 0.2 | 0.2 | 8.1 | 1.4 |
| Rubber and plastic products | 56.4 | 61.3 | 56.6 | 64.8 | 82.5 | 31.2 | 31.4 | 24.1 | 24.3 | 42.5 |
| Leather products | 1.0 | 0.5 | 0.7 | 1.7 | 1.3 | 0.3 | 0.1 | 0.4 | 0.4 | 0.1 |
| Stone, clay and glass products | 39.9 | 42.3 | 49.5 | 46.2 | 47.8 | 8.7 | 9.6 | 10.2 | 12.1 | 13.4 |
| Primary metals | 114.7 | 140.5 | 187.9 | 146.5 | 199.0 | 32.8 | 40.0 | 50.0 | 48.0 | 82.8 |
| Fabricated metal products | 114.8 | 79.9 | 90.7 | 110.0 | 165.0 | 46.7 | 26.6 | 31.3 | 33.6 | 28.7 |
| Industrial machinery and computers | 358.6 | 393.9 | 457.6 | 457.0 | 625.6 | 79.8 | 92.6 | 106.6 | 109.0 | 111.6 |
| Electric and electronic equipment | 407.0 | 487.9 | 610.0 | 819.6 | 1 140.0 | 170.0 | 211.7 | 239.9 | 358.2 | 210.5 |
| Transportation equipment | 214.4 | 591.6 | 418.8 | 400.5 | 357.8 | 30.7 | 101.7 | 207.1 | 250.2 | 232.6 |
| Scientific and measuring instruments | 59.5 | 62.1 | 64.0 | 63.8 | 220.0 | 13.0 | 24.1 | 26.3 | 28.1 | 172.5 |
| Miscellaneous manufactures | 23.3 | 27.0 | 24.1 | 31.1 | 32.8 | 10.9 | 14.0 | 10.2 | 13.7 | 10.1 |
| Unidentified manufactures | 9.7 | 10.2 | 10.2 | 9.6 | 12.1 | 1.2 | 1.6 | 2.0 | 1.9 | 3.4 |
| **Agricultural and livestock products** | 36.6 | 69.2 | 125.4 | 64.7 | 69.5 | 16.4 | 21.3 | 25.8 | 30.7 | 22.3 |
| Agricultural products | 32.7 | 65.5 | 121.3 | 58.3 | 62.4 | 15.1 | 19.2 | 24.1 | 27.3 | 17.9 |
| Livestock and livestock products | 3.9 | 3.8 | 4.1 | 6.5 | 7.1 | 1.3 | 2.1 | 1.6 | 3.5 | 4.3 |
| **Other commodities** | 294.6 | 249.5 | 294.7 | 277.8 | 259.9 | 13.9 | 22.1 | 22.9 | 28.1 | 29.4 |
| Forestry products | 0.3 | 0.3 | 0.6 | 0.4 | 0.3 | 0.1 | 0.1 | 0.2 | 0.1 | 0.1 |
| Fish and other marine products | 8.8 | 11.6 | 13.7 | 9.2 | 4.6 | 4.5 | 6.3 | 4.2 | 2.9 | 3.4 |
| Metallic ores and concentrates | 1.2 | 1.0 | 1.8 | 2.2 | 2.0 | 1.0 | 1.0 | 1.2 | 1.4 | 2.0 |
| Bituminous coal and lignite | 247.1 | 199.5 | 235.1 | 218.7 | 204.9 | ..... | 0.8 | ..... | 0.7 | ..... |
| Crude petroleum and natural gas | ..... | ..... | ..... | 2.6 | ..... | ..... | ..... | ..... | 2.6 | ..... |
| Nonmetallic minerals | 3.6 | 3.5 | 4.5 | 4.7 | 6.9 | 1.1 | 1.0 | 2.7 | 3.6 | 5.9 |
| Scrap and waste | 3.1 | 2.7 | 8.0 | 5.8 | 5.6 | 0.5 | 0.6 | 3.1 | 1.9 | 2.7 |
| Used merchandise | 6.8 | 6.4 | 7.6 | 7.7 | 7.4 | 0.8 | 1.2 | 1.1 | 1.1 | 1.6 |
| Goods imported and returned unchanged | 4.8 | 8.7 | 7.9 | 11.9 | 12.7 | 4.8 | 8.7 | 7.9 | 11.9 | 12.7 |
| Special classification provisions | 18.9 | 15.7 | 15.6 | 14.6 | 15.6 | 1.0 | 2.4 | 2.5 | 2.0 | 1.2 |

## Table D-3.  State Exports of Goods by Destination and Industry, 1993–1997 —*Continued*

**ALABAMA** (Millions of dollars.)

| Industry | South and Central America and Caribbean | | | | | Mexico | | | | |
|---|---|---|---|---|---|---|---|---|---|---|
| | 1993 | 1994 | 1995 | 1996 | 1997 | 1993 | 1994 | 1995 | 1996 | 1997 |
| **ALL GOODS** | 187.1 | 374.0 | 308.4 | 304.4 | 407.8 | 185.3 | 222.6 | 193.1 | 324.9 | 813.7 |
| **Manufactured goods** | 157.3 | 338.9 | 253.1 | 259.9 | 345.0 | 180.3 | 218.8 | 190.6 | 323.1 | 809.0 |
| Food products | 2.0 | 1.5 | 1.7 | 1.8 | 4.3 | 0.3 | 0.6 | 0.3 | 1.0 | 0.9 |
| Tobacco products | 0.1 | 0.1 | 0.1 | 1.1 | 0.3 | ..... | ..... | ..... | 0.1 | 0.2 |
| Textile mill products | 3.0 | 5.4 | 15.3 | 24.5 | 46.6 | 4.7 | 2.2 | 3.8 | 5.7 | 11.5 |
| Apparel | 39.2 | 42.7 | 42.5 | 56.1 | 92.8 | 6.4 | 12.2 | 26.1 | 43.7 | 42.0 |
| Lumber and wood products | 4.7 | 6.8 | 8.0 | 12.8 | 14.4 | 2.0 | 3.5 | 2.0 | 0.6 | 0.4 |
| Furniture and fixtures | 3.0 | 1.3 | 1.7 | 2.5 | 1.8 | 1.0 | 4.0 | 0.7 | 0.5 | 0.8 |
| Paper products | 18.2 | 7.1 | 14.1 | 20.6 | 19.9 | 11.8 | 11.2 | 11.3 | 8.1 | 10.2 |
| Printing and publishing | 0.1 | 0.3 | 0.1 | 0.2 | 0.2 | 0.2 | 0.4 | 0.4 | 0.6 | 2.9 |
| Chemical products | 10.6 | 9.3 | 19.8 | 22.4 | 28.1 | 14.0 | 13.8 | 12.4 | 15.2 | 19.8 |
| Refined petroleum products | 0.1 | 0.1 | 0.3 | 0.4 | 0.5 | ..... | 0.1 | ..... | 0.2 | 0.1 |
| Rubber and plastic products | 2.9 | 6.1 | 8.3 | 8.5 | 9.3 | 3.8 | 5.8 | 3.8 | 6.5 | 4.9 |
| Leather products | 0.3 | 0.1 | ..... | 0.3 | ..... | ..... | ..... | ..... | ..... | ..... |
| Stone, clay and glass products | 1.1 | 1.9 | 1.8 | 1.8 | 2.0 | 1.9 | 2.0 | 2.3 | 3.2 | 3.2 |
| Primary metals | 8.1 | 11.4 | 16.3 | 17.1 | 13.2 | 29.8 | 49.7 | 26.6 | 23.6 | 28.2 |
| Fabricated metal products | 10.3 | 10.4 | 15.2 | 14.3 | 16.9 | 1.9 | 2.8 | 5.8 | 7.3 | 15.7 |
| Industrial machinery and computers | 22.5 | 26.8 | 32.2 | 38.2 | 54.9 | 11.1 | 19.5 | 12.4 | 20.4 | 33.8 |
| Electric and electronic equipment | 10.0 | 11.6 | 21.7 | 10.2 | 13.5 | 81.3 | 82.7 | 75.6 | 176.8 | 618.1 |
| Transportation equipment | 13.4 | 192.0 | 48.2 | 23.8 | 18.5 | 1.0 | 1.6 | 1.3 | 2.7 | 4.5 |
| Scientific and measuring instruments | 5.8 | 1.7 | 2.3 | 1.3 | 6.0 | 8.4 | 5.9 | 3.8 | 2.3 | 3.6 |
| Miscellaneous manufactures | 1.4 | 1.4 | 2.8 | 1.8 | 1.5 | 0.3 | 0.3 | 0.2 | 4.1 | 7.7 |
| Unidentified manufactures | 0.5 | 0.8 | 0.7 | 0.3 | 0.4 | 0.4 | 0.6 | 1.8 | 0.3 | 0.4 |
| **Agricultural and livestock products** | 3.8 | 13.7 | 13.5 | 7.1 | 13.4 | 0.9 | 0.3 | 1.3 | 1.3 | 4.0 |
| Agricultural products | 2.7 | 12.9 | 12.6 | 6.0 | 11.8 | 0.1 | 0.2 | 0.9 | 0.9 | 3.3 |
| Livestock and livestock products | 1.1 | 0.8 | 0.9 | 1.2 | 1.6 | 0.8 | 0.1 | 0.5 | 0.4 | 0.7 |
| **Other commodities** | 26.0 | 21.4 | 41.8 | 37.4 | 49.2 | 4.1 | 3.5 | 1.2 | 0.5 | 0.8 |
| Forestry products | ..... | ..... | ..... | 0.1 | 0.1 | ..... | 0.1 | 0.1 | ..... | ..... |
| Fish and other marine products | ..... | ..... | ..... | ..... | ..... | ..... | ..... | ..... | ..... | ..... |
| Metallic ores and concentrates | ..... | ..... | ..... | ..... | ..... | ..... | ..... | ..... | ..... | ..... |
| Bituminous coal and lignite | 23.1 | 19.9 | 39.8 | 35.5 | 46.9 | 2.2 | 2.1 | ..... | ..... | ..... |
| Crude petroleum and natural gas | ..... | ..... | ..... | ..... | ..... | ..... | ..... | ..... | ..... | ..... |
| Nonmetallic minerals | 2.0 | 1.1 | 0.8 | 0.3 | 0.4 | 0.5 | 0.9 | 0.5 | 0.1 | 0.2 |
| Scrap and waste | 0.1 | ..... | 0.2 | 0.1 | 0.3 | 0.1 | 0.4 | 0.5 | 0.3 | 0.3 |
| Used merchandise | 0.8 | 0.2 | 0.7 | 0.6 | 1.4 | 0.7 | ..... | 0.1 | 0.1 | 0.1 |
| Goods imported and returned unchanged | ..... | ..... | ..... | ..... | ..... | ..... | ..... | ..... | ..... | ..... |
| Special classification provisions | ..... | 0.2 | 0.2 | 0.8 | 0.1 | 0.7 | ..... | ..... | ..... | 0.1 |

| Industry | European Union | | | | | United Kingdom | | | | |
|---|---|---|---|---|---|---|---|---|---|---|
| | 1993 | 1994 | 1995 | 1996 | 1997 | 1993 | 1994 | 1995 | 1996 | 1997 |
| **ALL GOODS** | 631.3 | 723.4 | 883.0 | 820.1 | 864.6 | 107.3 | 127.8 | 187.2 | 198.6 | 247.6 |
| **Manufactured goods** | 520.4 | 632.1 | 749.9 | 697.1 | 748.3 | 87.6 | 109.9 | 169.2 | 179.9 | 221.5 |
| Food products | 1.6 | 1.4 | 1.0 | 2.5 | 2.9 | 0.4 | 0.3 | 0.4 | 1.1 | 1.1 |
| Tobacco products | 0.2 | 0.1 | 0.2 | 0.3 | 0.3 | ..... | ..... | ..... | 0.2 | ..... |
| Textile mill products | 9.6 | 10.5 | 11.5 | 13.0 | 13.2 | 3.1 | 4.3 | 4.0 | 5.3 | 6.5 |
| Apparel | 7.7 | 8.5 | 4.6 | 3.9 | 7.3 | 3.9 | 5.4 | 1.5 | 2.5 | 1.1 |
| Lumber and wood products | 62.3 | 71.8 | 73.7 | 74.2 | 65.2 | 9.7 | 8.9 | 8.2 | 6.8 | 8.1 |
| Furniture and fixtures | 1.8 | 1.1 | 0.6 | 1.2 | 2.5 | ..... | ..... | ..... | 0.1 | 0.6 |
| Paper products | 63.3 | 88.1 | 138.6 | 119.6 | 123.7 | 18.0 | 24.7 | 37.0 | 29.6 | 23.3 |
| Printing and publishing | 0.6 | 0.9 | 0.8 | 0.7 | 1.0 | 0.3 | 0.1 | ..... | 0.2 | 0.2 |
| Chemical products | 22.9 | 28.2 | 46.3 | 60.8 | 81.5 | 1.3 | 8.1 | 27.2 | 30.1 | 51.1 |
| Refined petroleum products | 0.1 | 0.1 | 0.2 | 0.3 | 0.4 | ..... | ..... | ..... | 0.1 | 0.1 |
| Rubber and plastic products | 11.5 | 10.6 | 12.1 | 16.4 | 18.1 | 1.8 | 1.0 | 1.4 | 6.7 | 5.1 |
| Leather products | 0.3 | 0.2 | 0.2 | 1.0 | 1.0 | 0.1 | 0.1 | ..... | ..... | ..... |
| Stone, clay and glass products | 17.7 | 17.7 | 23.6 | 17.7 | 15.1 | 0.7 | 1.2 | 2.1 | 3.0 | 1.8 |
| Primary metals | 10.5 | 12.8 | 22.1 | 9.6 | 17.3 | 2.7 | 3.0 | 3.1 | 2.0 | 2.5 |
| Fabricated metal products | 13.6 | 15.9 | 11.9 | 15.8 | 15.1 | 4.9 | 5.5 | 5.9 | 7.7 | 5.6 |
| Industrial machinery and computers | 127.8 | 142.4 | 167.4 | 157.9 | 175.4 | 5.5 | 16.1 | 36.1 | 36.3 | 59.1 |
| Electric and electronic equipment | 68.0 | 86.6 | 121.4 | 122.0 | 127.7 | 19.3 | 17.2 | 30.6 | 36.7 | 43.2 |
| Transportation equipment | 83.5 | 117.0 | 94.7 | 59.8 | 55.2 | 8.8 | 7.9 | 6.6 | 7.8 | 5.2 |
| Scientific and measuring instruments | 10.8 | 12.2 | 12.0 | 12.8 | 17.0 | 4.1 | 3.7 | 3.0 | 2.0 | 5.4 |
| Miscellaneous manufactures | 4.5 | 3.3 | 3.9 | 3.3 | 3.2 | 2.5 | 1.8 | 1.6 | 1.6 | 1.2 |
| Unidentified manufactures | 2.1 | 2.6 | 3.4 | 4.3 | 5.3 | 0.3 | 0.5 | 0.4 | 0.2 | 0.3 |
| **Agricultural and livestock products** | 6.3 | 4.3 | 12.1 | 5.8 | 7.1 | 2.7 | 3.3 | 3.3 | 1.8 | 2.0 |
| Agricultural products | 5.7 | 3.8 | 11.8 | 5.1 | 6.9 | 2.7 | 3.3 | 3.2 | 1.6 | 2.0 |
| Livestock and livestock products | 0.6 | 0.5 | 0.3 | 0.6 | 0.2 | ..... | ..... | 0.1 | 0.2 | ..... |
| **Other commodities** | 104.6 | 87.0 | 121.0 | 117.2 | 109.3 | 16.9 | 14.6 | 14.6 | 16.8 | 24.1 |
| Forestry products | 0.1 | 0.1 | 0.1 | 0.1 | 0.1 | ..... | ..... | 0.1 | 0.1 | ..... |
| Fish and other marine products | ..... | ..... | 0.4 | 0.3 | 0.1 | ..... | ..... | ..... | ..... | ..... |
| Metallic ores and concentrates | 0.2 | ..... | 0.6 | 0.6 | ..... | ..... | ..... | 0.6 | 0.6 | ..... |
| Bituminous coal and lignite | 86.2 | 77.0 | 105.9 | 106.3 | 96.4 | 14.7 | 9.5 | 9.5 | 12.3 | 18.9 |
| Crude petroleum and natural gas | ..... | ..... | ..... | ..... | ..... | ..... | ..... | ..... | ..... | ..... |
| Nonmetallic minerals | ..... | 0.3 | 0.3 | 0.6 | 0.2 | ..... | ..... | ..... | 0.2 | 0.1 |
| Scrap and waste | 0.8 | 0.4 | 1.2 | 1.1 | 0.8 | 0.7 | 0.2 | ..... | 0.5 | 0.4 |
| Used merchandise | 2.7 | 3.6 | 3.6 | 3.4 | 2.0 | 0.7 | 1.4 | 0.8 | 0.7 | 0.4 |
| Goods imported and returned unchanged | ..... | ..... | ..... | ..... | ..... | ..... | ..... | ..... | ..... | ..... |
| Special classification provisions | 14.6 | 5.7 | 8.8 | 4.9 | 9.7 | 0.7 | 3.4 | 3.5 | 2.6 | 4.3 |

## Table D-3.  State Exports of Goods by Destination and Industry, 1993–1997 —*Continued*

**ALABAMA** (Millions of dollars.)

| Industry | 1993 | 1994 | 1995 | 1996 | 1997 | 1993 | 1994 | 1995 | 1996 | 1997 |
|---|---|---|---|---|---|---|---|---|---|---|
| | Germany | | | | | France | | | | |
| **ALL GOODS** | 141.9 | 112.5 | 119.2 | 100.0 | 124.2 | 47.7 | 108.1 | 96.4 | 71.7 | 79.9 |
| **Manufactured goods** | 127.8 | 110.8 | 115.2 | 97.8 | 120.2 | 46.7 | 106.5 | 92.7 | 70.6 | 76.8 |
| Food products | 0.2 | 0.1 | 0.2 | 0.4 | 0.6 | 0.2 | 0.1 | 0.2 | ..... | 0.1 |
| Tobacco products | ..... | ..... | 0.1 | | | ..... | ..... | ..... | 0.1 | ..... |
| Textile mill products | 0.4 | 0.4 | 1.2 | 1.6 | 0.7 | 0.3 | 0.3 | 0.4 | 1.0 | 0.5 |
| Apparel | 1.8 | 1.1 | 1.1 | 0.6 | 0.2 | ..... | 0.2 | ..... | 0.2 | ..... |
| Lumber and wood products | 7.1 | 7.8 | 8.0 | 6.9 | 6.3 | 1.6 | 2.2 | 1.7 | 2.5 | 2.4 |
| Furniture and fixtures | 1.1 | ..... | 0.2 | 0.1 | 0.4 | ..... | ..... | ..... | 0.1 | 0.7 |
| Paper products | 8.7 | 12.1 | 17.0 | 26.1 | 37.7 | 12.1 | 17.9 | 30.4 | 20.9 | 19.7 |
| Printing and publishing | ..... | 0.1 | ..... | 0.1 | | ..... | 0.1 | 0.1 | 0.1 | 0.1 |
| Chemical products | 2.5 | 1.9 | 2.7 | 9.8 | 14.2 | 1.1 | 0.9 | 0.8 | 0.5 | 1.1 |
| Refined petroleum products | ..... | ..... | 0.2 | 0.2 | | ..... | ..... | ..... | ..... | 0.1 |
| Rubber and plastic products | 0.7 | 1.8 | 2.8 | 1.2 | 3.2 | 2.3 | 2.7 | 2.4 | 3.2 | 4.5 |
| Leather products | 0.1 | ..... | ..... | 0.9 | 0.4 | ..... | 0.1 | 0.1 | ..... | 0.1 |
| Stone, clay and glass products | 8.7 | 8.4 | 10.4 | 6.1 | 4.6 | 1.7 | 2.1 | 1.8 | 2.3 | 3.4 |
| Primary metals | 3.7 | 6.1 | 7.2 | 3.8 | 8.2 | 0.9 | 2.0 | 3.4 | 1.1 | 3.7 |
| Fabricated metal products | 3.5 | 3.6 | 2.7 | 4.0 | 4.4 | 0.5 | 1.4 | 0.5 | 0.6 | 1.3 |
| Industrial machinery and computers | 17.5 | 32.8 | 21.4 | 12.6 | 10.5 | 3.9 | 19.8 | 20.6 | 7.9 | 9.4 |
| Electric and electronic equipment | 12.1 | 16.3 | 19.7 | 11.1 | 12.1 | 6.3 | 15.3 | 13.0 | 3.5 | 3.9 |
| Transportation equipment | 57.1 | 15.8 | 16.2 | 9.2 | 13.9 | 13.9 | 38.4 | 13.9 | 22.2 | 20.5 |
| Scientific and measuring instruments | 1.6 | 2.0 | 2.0 | 2.1 | 2.3 | 1.7 | 2.6 | 3.3 | 4.0 | 5.2 |
| Miscellaneous manufactures | 0.8 | 0.3 | 1.3 | 0.7 | 0.3 | ..... | 0.1 | 0.2 | 0.3 | 0.1 |
| Unidentified manufactures | 0.3 | 0.3 | 0.8 | 0.2 | 0.1 | 0.2 | 0.1 | 0.1 | 0.1 | 0.1 |
| **Agricultural and livestock products** | 0.3 | 0.1 | 0.6 | 0.4 | 1.3 | 0.3 | 0.2 | 0.1 | 0.1 | 0.1 |
| Agricultural products | 0.3 | ..... | 0.6 | 0.4 | 1.2 | ..... | 0.1 | ..... | ..... | 0.1 |
| Livestock and livestock products | ..... | ..... | ..... | ..... | 0.1 | 0.3 | 0.1 | 0.1 | 0.1 | ..... |
| **Other commodities** | 13.8 | 1.6 | 3.4 | 1.9 | 2.8 | 0.7 | 1.4 | 3.5 | 1.0 | 3.0 |
| Forestry products | ..... | ..... | ..... | ..... | | ..... | ..... | ..... | ..... | |
| Fish and other marine products | ..... | ..... | 0.3 | 0.3 | 0.1 | ..... | ..... | ..... | ..... | |
| Metallic ores and concentrates | 0.2 | ..... | ..... | ..... | | ..... | ..... | ..... | ..... | |
| Bituminous coal and lignite | ..... | ..... | ..... | ..... | | ..... | ..... | ..... | ..... | |
| Crude petroleum and natural gas | ..... | ..... | ..... | ..... | | ..... | ..... | ..... | ..... | |
| Nonmetallic minerals | ..... | 0.2 | 0.3 | ..... | 0.1 | ..... | ..... | ..... | ..... | |
| Scrap and waste | 0.1 | 0.1 | 0.5 | 0.3 | ..... | ..... | ..... | ..... | ..... | |
| Used merchandise | 0.8 | 1.2 | 2.0 | 1.2 | 1.3 | 0.4 | 0.3 | 0.4 | 0.6 | 0.1 |
| Goods imported and returned unchanged | ..... | ..... | ..... | ..... | | ..... | ..... | ..... | | |
| Special classification provisions | 12.7 | ..... | 0.2 | 0.1 | 1.3 | 0.3 | 1.0 | 3.1 | 0.4 | 2.9 |
| | The Netherlands | | | | | Asian 10 | | | | |
| **ALL GOODS** | 123.0 | 87.3 | 127.3 | 165.5 | 151.1 | 663.3 | 615.0 | 878.8 | 761.1 | 867.4 |
| **Manufactured goods** | 122.4 | 86.0 | 124.1 | 164.6 | 148.4 | 520.5 | 482.3 | 742.0 | 687.9 | 825.6 |
| Food products | 0.2 | ..... | ..... | 0.3 | 0.2 | 1.4 | 0.8 | 1.2 | 2.1 | 4.4 |
| Tobacco products | ..... | ..... | ..... | ..... | | ..... | ..... | ..... | 0.1 | 0.1 |
| Textile mill products | 1.7 | 1.6 | 1.2 | 1.3 | 1.2 | 2.0 | 2.1 | 2.7 | 3.7 | 3.9 |
| Apparel | 0.4 | 0.4 | 0.4 | 0.1 | 0.1 | 5.7 | 3.4 | 7.8 | 11.0 | 6.3 |
| Lumber and wood products | 2.4 | 2.1 | 2.2 | 3.6 | 4.8 | 38.9 | 32.9 | 45.7 | 38.7 | 36.6 |
| Furniture and fixtures | 0.6 | 0.2 | 0.1 | 0.1 | 0.1 | 0.3 | 0.2 | 0.5 | 1.1 | 0.7 |
| Paper products | 2.2 | 1.3 | 1.9 | 4.5 | 8.0 | 140.4 | 181.1 | 262.9 | 178.9 | 190.8 |
| Printing and publishing | 0.2 | 0.1 | 0.1 | ..... | 0.1 | 0.3 | 0.4 | 0.2 | 0.2 | 0.5 |
| Chemical products | 6.6 | 4.6 | 3.4 | 0.7 | 0.6 | 66.0 | 69.0 | 109.0 | 137.4 | 135.8 |
| Refined petroleum products | ..... | ..... | ..... | ..... | | ..... | 0.2 | 0.1 | 0.1 | 0.1 |
| Rubber and plastic products | 1.8 | 1.5 | 0.7 | ..... | 0.1 | 4.0 | 3.8 | 4.8 | 4.5 | 3.1 |
| Leather products | ..... | ..... | ..... | ..... | 0.4 | 0.1 | ..... | 0.1 | 0.1 | ..... |
| Stone, clay and glass products | 2.0 | 2.7 | 4.2 | 1.9 | 2.4 | 7.5 | 6.7 | 7.1 | 6.3 | 9.0 |
| Primary metals | 2.5 | 0.2 | 1.0 | 0.5 | 0.2 | 11.2 | 14.3 | 25.8 | 12.4 | 15.2 |
| Fabricated metal products | 2.0 | 1.2 | 0.5 | 1.0 | 0.4 | 27.2 | 13.4 | 17.3 | 27.7 | 76.7 |
| Industrial machinery and computers | 82.8 | 45.8 | 65.1 | 81.8 | 69.0 | 76.2 | 60.2 | 87.0 | 91.9 | 178.8 |
| Electric and electronic equipment | 13.8 | 22.2 | 34.8 | 58.6 | 54.1 | 63.0 | 64.1 | 112.8 | 120.7 | 132.9 |
| Transportation equipment | 0.8 | 0.7 | 7.4 | 9.5 | 5.9 | 61.7 | 16.5 | 42.2 | 33.0 | 10.5 |
| Scientific and measuring instruments | 1.6 | 0.9 | 0.5 | 0.5 | 0.4 | 10.7 | 7.9 | 10.2 | 10.7 | 12.5 |
| Miscellaneous manufactures | 0.7 | 0.2 | 0.3 | 0.1 | 0.3 | 3.2 | 3.8 | 3.2 | 5.1 | 6.5 |
| Unidentified manufactures | 0.1 | 0.1 | 0.2 | 0.1 | 0.2 | 0.8 | 1.6 | 1.4 | 2.3 | 1.2 |
| **Agricultural and livestock products** | 0.4 | 0.4 | 0.1 | 0.3 | 0.2 | 7.4 | 27.6 | 47.8 | 17.1 | 15.9 |
| Agricultural products | 0.1 | 0.1 | 0.1 | 0.1 | 0.1 | 7.4 | 27.5 | 47.3 | 16.5 | 15.8 |
| Livestock and livestock products | 0.3 | 0.3 | ..... | 0.2 | 0.1 | 0.1 | 0.2 | 0.5 | 0.6 | 0.1 |
| **Other commodities** | 0.2 | 0.9 | 3.0 | 0.6 | 2.5 | 135.4 | 105.1 | 89.0 | 56.0 | 25.9 |
| Forestry products | ..... | ..... | ..... | ..... | | 0.1 | ..... | 0.1 | 0.1 | ..... |
| Fish and other marine products | ..... | ..... | ..... | ..... | | 4.3 | 5.3 | 9.1 | 5.9 | 1.1 |
| Metallic ores and concentrates | ..... | ..... | ..... | ..... | | ..... | ..... | ..... | 0.2 | ..... |
| Bituminous coal and lignite | ..... | ..... | 2.7 | ..... | 2.3 | 129.8 | 94.9 | 77.5 | 45.2 | 20.4 |
| Crude petroleum and natural gas | ..... | ..... | ..... | ..... | | ..... | ..... | ..... | ..... | ..... |
| Nonmetallic minerals | ..... | ..... | ..... | 0.3 | | ..... | 0.1 | 0.1 | 0.1 | 0.1 |
| Scrap and waste | ..... | ..... | 0.1 | ..... | | 0.5 | 0.1 | 0.1 | 0.4 | 0.1 |
| Used merchandise | ..... | 0.1 | ..... | ..... | | 0.2 | 0.2 | 0.6 | 1.2 | 0.2 |
| Goods imported and returned unchanged | ..... | ..... | ..... | ..... | | ..... | ..... | ..... | | ..... |
| Special classification provisions | 0.2 | 0.8 | 0.2 | 0.2 | 0.1 | 0.5 | 4.4 | 1.5 | 2.8 | 3.9 |

## Table D-3. State Exports of Goods by Destination and Industry, 1993–1997 —*Continued*

### ALABAMA (Millions of dollars.)

| Industry | 1993 | 1994 | 1995 | 1996 | 1997 | 1993 | 1994 | 1995 | 1996 | 1997 |
|---|---|---|---|---|---|---|---|---|---|---|
| | Japan | | | | | South Korea | | | | |
| **ALL GOODS** | 338.1 | 342.2 | 491.6 | 382.5 | 322.8 | 104.9 | 125.2 | 140.9 | 129.8 | 268.8 |
| **Manufactured goods** | 204.1 | 234.5 | 393.1 | 323.2 | 297.6 | 102.5 | 119.1 | 133.7 | 126.6 | 265.4 |
| Food products | 0.9 | 0.5 | ..... | 0.5 | 0.8 | 0.3 | 0.3 | 1.0 | 1.3 | 3.0 |
| Tobacco products | ..... | ..... | ..... | ..... | ..... | ..... | ..... | ..... | ..... | ..... |
| Textile mill products | 0.3 | 0.2 | 0.3 | 0.7 | 0.4 | 0.2 | 0.2 | 0.4 | 0.4 | 0.2 |
| Apparel | 5.4 | 2.9 | 6.9 | 10.2 | 5.0 | ..... | ..... | ..... | 0.1 | 0.1 |
| Lumber and wood products | 28.9 | 29.9 | 40.2 | 34.4 | 33.4 | 6.8 | 0.4 | 0.4 | 0.3 | 0.1 |
| Furniture and fixtures | 0.2 | 0.1 | 0.3 | 0.4 | 0.3 | ..... | ..... | 0.1 | ..... | ..... |
| Paper products | 90.6 | 112.9 | 182.2 | 111.0 | 118.3 | 41.4 | 68.0 | 79.8 | 63.7 | 53.6 |
| Printing and publishing | 0.1 | 0.1 | 0.1 | 0.1 | 0.1 | ..... | 0.1 | ..... | 0.1 | 0.2 |
| Chemical products | 29.1 | 33.7 | 39.8 | 57.6 | 39.5 | 8.0 | 8.9 | 16.1 | 25.9 | 21.8 |
| Refined petroleum products | ..... | ..... | ..... | ..... | ..... | ..... | ..... | ..... | ..... | 0.1 |
| Rubber and plastic products | 0.2 | 0.1 | 0.1 | 1.1 | 0.4 | 3.0 | 2.7 | 3.7 | 2.5 | 1.0 |
| Leather products | ..... | ..... | ..... | ..... | ..... | ..... | ..... | ..... | ..... | ..... |
| Stone, clay and glass products | 5.4 | 3.4 | 3.0 | 1.4 | 2.3 | 0.3 | 0.2 | 0.2 | 0.6 | 0.7 |
| Primary metals | 2.5 | 0.6 | 5.4 | 0.5 | 2.9 | 1.5 | 0.4 | 1.2 | 1.6 | 2.1 |
| Fabricated metal products | 13.2 | 3.6 | 0.9 | 0.9 | 1.1 | 5.6 | 3.5 | 5.1 | 5.0 | 59.6 |
| Industrial machinery and computers | 12.5 | 20.0 | 24.3 | 27.7 | 25.5 | 10.3 | 11.8 | 12.5 | 11.3 | 103.6 |
| Electric and electronic equipment | 10.8 | 16.9 | 50.0 | 56.4 | 59.6 | 21.9 | 19.8 | 9.7 | 6.1 | 12.0 |
| Transportation equipment | 1.5 | 6.7 | 33.5 | 15.0 | 2.8 | 0.1 | 0.5 | 2.0 | 4.5 | 1.2 |
| Scientific and measuring instruments | 1.4 | 1.7 | 5.2 | 3.3 | 3.8 | 2.7 | 1.2 | 0.9 | 2.6 | 5.3 |
| Miscellaneous manufactures | 0.9 | 0.7 | 0.7 | 1.8 | 1.4 | 0.4 | 1.0 | 0.5 | 0.5 | 0.6 |
| Unidentified manufactures | 0.3 | 0.4 | 0.2 | 0.1 | 0.1 | ..... | 0.1 | 0.1 | ..... | 0.3 |
| **Agricultural and livestock products** | 1.1 | 7.2 | 11.3 | 6.9 | 3.5 | 2.1 | 6.1 | 6.7 | 3.0 | 3.4 |
| Agricultural products | 1.1 | 7.1 | 11.1 | 6.3 | 3.5 | 2.1 | 6.1 | 6.5 | 3.0 | 3.4 |
| Livestock and livestock products | ..... | 0.1 | 0.1 | 0.6 | 0.1 | ..... | ..... | 0.3 | ..... | ..... |
| **Other commodities** | 132.8 | 100.6 | 87.3 | 52.4 | 21.7 | 0.3 | ..... | 0.5 | 0.2 | ..... |
| Forestry products | ..... | ..... | ..... | ..... | ..... | ..... | ..... | ..... | ..... | ..... |
| Fish and other marine products | 4.3 | 5.3 | 9.1 | 5.7 | 1.0 | ..... | ..... | ..... | ..... | ..... |
| Metallic ores and concentrates | ..... | ..... | ..... | 0.2 | ..... | ..... | ..... | ..... | ..... | ..... |
| Bituminous coal and lignite | 127.9 | 94.9 | 77.5 | 45.2 | 20.4 | ..... | ..... | ..... | ..... | ..... |
| Crude petroleum and natural gas | ..... | ..... | ..... | ..... | ..... | ..... | ..... | ..... | ..... | ..... |
| Nonmetallic minerals | ..... | 0.1 | 0.1 | ..... | ..... | ..... | ..... | ..... | ..... | ..... |
| Scrap and waste | 0.5 | ..... | ..... | ..... | ..... | ..... | ..... | ..... | ..... | ..... |
| Used merchandise | 0.1 | 0.1 | 0.5 | 1.0 | 0.1 | ..... | ..... | ..... | 0.1 | ..... |
| Goods imported and returned unchanged | ..... | ..... | ..... | ..... | ..... | ..... | ..... | ..... | ..... | ..... |
| Special classification provisions | ..... | ..... | 0.1 | 0.2 | 0.1 | 0.3 | ..... | 0.5 | 0.1 | ..... |
| | Taiwan | | | | | Singapore | | | | |
| **ALL GOODS** | 31.6 | 28.3 | 37.2 | 38.9 | 34.0 | 31.5 | 26.3 | 62.4 | 57.4 | 62.5 |
| **Manufactured goods** | 28.2 | 24.0 | 31.1 | 37.8 | 31.6 | 31.3 | 26.1 | 61.7 | 56.0 | 59.5 |
| Food products | 0.1 | ..... | ..... | 0.1 | 0.2 | ..... | ..... | ..... | ..... | ..... |
| Tobacco products | ..... | ..... | ..... | ..... | ..... | ..... | ..... | ..... | ..... | ..... |
| Textile mill products | ..... | 0.2 | 0.1 | 0.1 | 0.2 | 0.5 | 0.8 | 0.7 | 1.0 | 0.9 |
| Apparel | ..... | 0.3 | 0.6 | 0.3 | 0.8 | ..... | 0.1 | 0.2 | 0.1 | 0.1 |
| Lumber and wood products | 1.9 | 1.9 | 3.6 | 1.5 | 0.9 | ..... | ..... | 0.1 | ..... | 0.2 |
| Furniture and fixtures | 0.1 | ..... | ..... | ..... | ..... | ..... | ..... | ..... | ..... | ..... |
| Paper products | 0.4 | ..... | 0.2 | ..... | 0.9 | 0.2 | ..... | ..... | ..... | 0.1 |
| Printing and publishing | ..... | 0.2 | 0.1 | ..... | ..... | ..... | ..... | ..... | ..... | ..... |
| Chemical products | 4.7 | 5.0 | 8.0 | 9.5 | 8.7 | 8.8 | 9.2 | 21.9 | 20.8 | 29.0 |
| Refined petroleum products | ..... | 0.1 | ..... | 0.1 | ..... | ..... | ..... | ..... | ..... | ..... |
| Rubber and plastic products | 0.1 | 0.1 | 0.2 | 0.2 | 0.1 | ..... | ..... | ..... | 0.1 | 0.2 |
| Leather products | ..... | ..... | ..... | 0.1 | ..... | ..... | ..... | ..... | ..... | ..... |
| Stone, clay and glass products | 0.3 | 0.8 | 0.9 | 1.1 | 1.5 | 0.3 | 0.4 | 0.8 | 1.0 | 1.5 |
| Primary metals | 3.1 | 0.9 | 2.1 | 1.2 | 1.5 | 0.8 | 2.1 | 10.6 | 0.4 | 0.7 |
| Fabricated metal products | 2.5 | 1.1 | 2.1 | 3.5 | 2.5 | 1.4 | 1.3 | 3.1 | 2.8 | 2.4 |
| Industrial machinery and computers | 6.0 | 4.3 | 3.7 | 3.3 | 8.1 | 9.0 | 5.2 | 4.2 | 9.6 | 8.4 |
| Electric and electronic equipment | 3.7 | 6.2 | 7.4 | 7.8 | 3.9 | 7.7 | 5.0 | 16.0 | 15.2 | 12.9 |
| Transportation equipment | 3.2 | 1.5 | 0.6 | 8.0 | 0.4 | 0.4 | 0.8 | 3.1 | 3.4 | 1.7 |
| Scientific and measuring instruments | 1.8 | 0.7 | 1.1 | 0.7 | 1.5 | 1.4 | 0.6 | 0.2 | 0.3 | 0.5 |
| Miscellaneous manufactures | 0.1 | 0.4 | 0.2 | 0.3 | 0.3 | 0.4 | 0.3 | 0.3 | 1.0 | 0.8 |
| Unidentified manufactures | 0.1 | 0.2 | 0.1 | ..... | 0.1 | 0.1 | 0.3 | 0.2 | ..... | 0.1 |
| **Agricultural and livestock products** | 1.4 | 4.1 | 6.2 | 0.5 | 2.3 | ..... | 0.1 | ..... | ..... | ..... |
| Agricultural products | 1.4 | 4.1 | 6.2 | 0.5 | 2.3 | ..... | 0.1 | ..... | ..... | ..... |
| Livestock and livestock products | ..... | ..... | ..... | ..... | ..... | ..... | ..... | ..... | ..... | ..... |
| **Other commodities** | 2.0 | 0.1 | ..... | 0.6 | 0.1 | 0.2 | 0.2 | 0.7 | 1.4 | 3.0 |
| Forestry products | ..... | ..... | ..... | ..... | ..... | ..... | ..... | ..... | ..... | ..... |
| Fish and other marine products | ..... | ..... | ..... | ..... | ..... | ..... | ..... | ..... | ..... | ..... |
| Metallic ores and concentrates | ..... | ..... | ..... | ..... | ..... | ..... | ..... | ..... | ..... | ..... |
| Bituminous coal and lignite | 1.9 | ..... | ..... | ..... | ..... | ..... | ..... | ..... | ..... | ..... |
| Crude petroleum and natural gas | ..... | ..... | ..... | ..... | ..... | ..... | ..... | ..... | ..... | ..... |
| Nonmetallic minerals | ..... | ..... | ..... | ..... | 0.1 | ..... | ..... | ..... | ..... | ..... |
| Scrap and waste | ..... | 0.1 | ..... | ..... | ..... | ..... | ..... | ..... | ..... | ..... |
| Used merchandise | ..... | ..... | ..... | ..... | ..... | 0.1 | 0.1 | 0.1 | 0.1 | 0.1 |
| Goods imported and returned unchanged | ..... | ..... | ..... | ..... | ..... | ..... | ..... | ..... | ..... | ..... |
| Special classification provisions | 0.1 | ..... | ..... | 0.6 | ..... | ..... | 0.1 | 0.6 | 1.3 | 3.0 |

## ALASKA: Exports of Goods, 1997

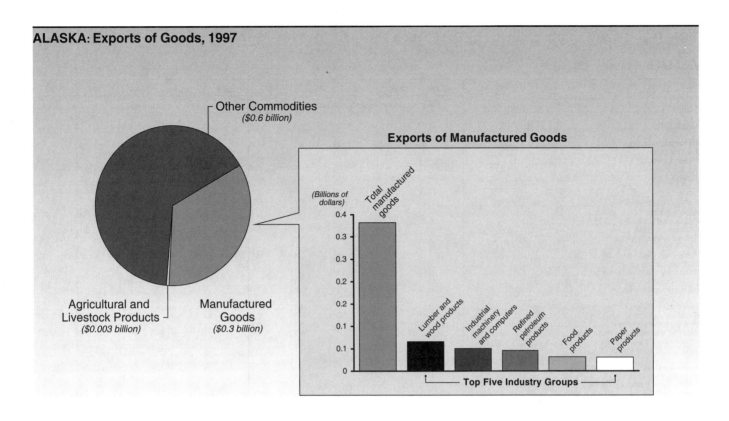

---

## Table D-3.   State Exports of Goods by Destination and Industry, 1993–1997 —Continued

### ALASKA (Millions of dollars.)

| Industry | 1993 | 1994 | 1995 | 1996 | 1997 | 1993 | 1994 | 1995 | 1996 | 1997 |
|---|---|---|---|---|---|---|---|---|---|---|
| | All destinations | | | | | Canada | | | | |
| **ALL GOODS** | 817.9 | 887.7 | 891.5 | 850.4 | 969.0 | 84.1 | 120.6 | 195.7 | 181.2 | 305.4 |
| **Manufactured goods** | 387.9 | 486.2 | 406.3 | 345.2 | 332.3 | 44.8 | 67.5 | 85.4 | 102.6 | 118.7 |
| Food products | 19.3 | 22.5 | 34.8 | 44.0 | 31.8 | 2.7 | 7.5 | 10.7 | 30.6 | 23.0 |
| Tobacco products | ..... | ..... | ..... | ..... | ..... | ..... | ..... | ..... | ..... | ..... |
| Textile mill products | 0.5 | 0.3 | 0.7 | 0.5 | 1.2 | 0.1 | 0.1 | 0.2 | 0.1 | 0.4 |
| Apparel | 0.9 | 0.4 | 0.7 | 0.8 | 1.2 | 0.1 | 0.1 | 0.1 | ..... | 0.2 |
| Lumber and wood products | 165.7 | 153.9 | 79.2 | 44.1 | 65.7 | 1.6 | 3.5 | 19.4 | 6.0 | 21.9 |
| Furniture and fixtures | 0.1 | 0.5 | 0.3 | 0.2 | 0.7 | 0.1 | 0.1 | 0.1 | 0.1 | 0.2 |
| Paper products | 104.4 | 84.0 | 108.6 | 79.3 | 31.0 | 0.4 | 0.8 | 2.0 | 2.3 | 2.2 |
| Printing and publishing | 0.8 | 1.2 | 1.2 | 0.5 | 0.6 | 0.2 | 0.9 | 1.0 | 0.3 | 0.4 |
| Chemical products | 2.6 | 20.1 | 16.2 | 12.3 | 11.1 | 1.4 | 0.8 | 3.3 | 3.4 | 5.8 |
| Refined petroleum products | 33.6 | 58.4 | 46.6 | 60.1 | 45.9 | 12.1 | 10.4 | 12.0 | 21.1 | 26.9 |
| Rubber and plastic products | 1.2 | 1.6 | 8.3 | 4.7 | 5.3 | 1.0 | 1.0 | 1.8 | 0.9 | 0.8 |
| Leather products | 0.1 | 0.1 | 0.2 | ..... | 0.2 | ..... | 0.1 | 0.1 | ..... | ..... |
| Stone, clay and glass products | 0.3 | 0.5 | 0.7 | 0.9 | 1.3 | 0.1 | 0.2 | 0.3 | 0.3 | 0.3 |
| Primary metals | 1.4 | 3.6 | 4.5 | 2.1 | 7.7 | 0.9 | 1.8 | 2.5 | 1.6 | 5.7 |
| Fabricated metal products | 1.9 | 19.5 | 7.1 | 3.2 | 5.1 | 1.2 | 17.9 | 1.0 | 0.4 | 1.3 |
| Industrial machinery and computers | 15.7 | 16.3 | 24.0 | 28.7 | 50.3 | 8.4 | 6.6 | 6.1 | 9.4 | 10.2 |
| Electric and electronic equipment | 6.6 | 9.4 | 14.9 | 19.9 | 27.7 | 1.4 | 1.1 | 3.1 | 11.7 | 2.9 |
| Transportation equipment | 21.3 | 76.3 | 43.4 | 29.5 | 26.8 | 8.1 | 5.1 | 17.7 | 8.6 | 8.9 |
| Scientific and measuring instruments | 8.4 | 13.1 | 9.7 | 11.5 | 15.9 | 3.3 | 6.7 | 2.5 | 4.9 | 6.3 |
| Miscellaneous manufactures | 1.6 | 1.5 | 2.3 | 1.4 | 1.0 | 0.4 | 0.8 | 0.7 | 0.1 | 0.4 |
| Unidentified manufactures | 1.6 | 2.7 | 3.0 | 1.6 | 1.9 | 1.3 | 2.1 | 0.9 | 0.9 | 0.8 |
| **Agricultural and livestock products** | 1.6 | 4.1 | 4.7 | 2.3 | 2.9 | 1.2 | 1.2 | 2.9 | 0.9 | 2.0 |
| Agricultural products | 1.1 | 3.2 | 4.1 | 1.9 | 2.2 | 0.8 | 0.4 | 2.2 | 0.6 | 1.2 |
| Livestock and livestock products | 0.5 | 0.9 | 0.6 | 0.4 | 0.8 | 0.4 | 0.7 | 0.6 | 0.3 | 0.8 |
| **Other commodities** | 428.4 | 397.3 | 480.5 | 502.9 | 633.8 | 38.0 | 51.9 | 107.4 | 77.8 | 184.7 |
| Forestry products | ..... | ..... | ..... | ..... | ..... | ..... | ..... | ..... | ..... | ..... |
| Fish and other marine products | 131.8 | 121.6 | 94.9 | 101.0 | 68.8 | 16.0 | 17.2 | 26.2 | 34.4 | 24.9 |
| Metallic ores and concentrates | 126.6 | 97.8 | 194.8 | 215.5 | 362.5 | 4.2 | 21.4 | 66.7 | 30.8 | 126.5 |
| Bituminous coal and lignite | 25.2 | 22.9 | 29.5 | 26.7 | 42.8 | ..... | ..... | ..... | ..... | 17.4 |
| Crude petroleum and natural gas | 126.2 | 140.0 | 144.7 | 144.9 | 141.0 | ..... | ..... | ..... | ..... | ..... |
| Nonmetallic minerals | ..... | 0.1 | 0.9 | 0.4 | 0.1 | ..... | ..... | ..... | 0.2 | ..... |
| Scrap and waste | 2.3 | 5.0 | 3.5 | 2.1 | 2.1 | 2.3 | 4.9 | 3.1 | 1.8 | 2.1 |
| Used merchandise | 1.1 | 2.5 | 1.4 | 1.9 | 1.5 | 0.6 | 1.1 | 0.6 | 0.4 | 1.1 |
| Goods imported and returned unchanged | 14.5 | 7.0 | 10.5 | 10.0 | 12.2 | 14.5 | 7.0 | 10.5 | 10.0 | 12.2 |
| Special classification provisions | 0.6 | 0.4 | 0.2 | 0.5 | 2.7 | 0.4 | 0.1 | 0.1 | 0.1 | 0.3 |

## Table D-3.  State Exports of Goods by Destination and Industry, 1993–1997 —*Continued*

### ALASKA (Millions of dollars.)

| Industry | 1993 | 1994 | 1995 | 1996 | 1997 | 1993 | 1994 | 1995 | 1996 | 1997 |
|---|---|---|---|---|---|---|---|---|---|---|
| | South and Central America and Caribbean | | | | | Mexico | | | | |
| **ALL GOODS** | 4.7 | 3.3 | 12.0 | 9.3 | 4.2 | 0.6 | 1.3 | 0.9 | 1.5 | 1.9 |
| **Manufactured goods** | 4.5 | 3.1 | 11.9 | 9.1 | 4.2 | 0.6 | 1.3 | 0.9 | 1.5 | 1.9 |
| Food products | 0.2 | 0.1 | 0.2 | ..... | 0.1 | ..... | 0.1 | ..... | ..... | ..... |
| Tobacco products | ..... | ..... | ..... | ..... | ..... | ..... | ..... | ..... | ..... | ..... |
| Textile mill products | 0.1 | 0.1 | ..... | ..... | ..... | ..... | ..... | ..... | 0.2 | ..... |
| Apparel | ..... | ..... | 0.1 | 0.1 | 0.6 | ..... | 0.1 | ..... | 0.1 | ..... |
| Lumber and wood products | ..... | ..... | ..... | ..... | ..... | ..... | ..... | ..... | ..... | ..... |
| Furniture and fixtures | ..... | ..... | 0.1 | ..... | ..... | ..... | ..... | ..... | ..... | ..... |
| Paper products | ..... | 0.5 | 1.3 | 0.8 | 0.1 | 0.1 | 0.1 | 0.1 | 0.1 | 0.1 |
| Printing and publishing | 0.3 | ..... | ..... | ..... | ..... | ..... | ..... | ..... | ..... | ..... |
| Chemical products | 0.2 | 0.1 | 1.0 | 0.3 | 0.4 | ..... | 0.5 | ..... | 0.1 | 0.1 |
| Refined petroleum products | ..... | ..... | ..... | ..... | ..... | ..... | ..... | ..... | ..... | ..... |
| Rubber and plastic products | ..... | ..... | 0.6 | 0.4 | 0.2 | ..... | ..... | ..... | ..... | 0.2 |
| Leather products | ..... | ..... | ..... | ..... | 0.1 | ..... | ..... | ..... | ..... | ..... |
| Stone, clay and glass products | 0.1 | ..... | 0.1 | 0.1 | ..... | ..... | 0.1 | ..... | ..... | ..... |
| Primary metals | ..... | ..... | 0.5 | 0.1 | ..... | 0.1 | 0.1 | 0.1 | ..... | ..... |
| Fabricated metal products | 0.1 | 0.2 | 0.1 | 0.8 | ..... | ..... | ..... | ..... | ..... | ..... |
| Industrial machinery and computers | 0.5 | 0.7 | 1.6 | 4.7 | 1.3 | 0.2 | 0.1 | 0.3 | 0.5 | 0.3 |
| Electric and electronic equipment | 0.4 | 0.4 | 5.7 | 0.8 | 0.5 | ..... | 0.1 | 0.2 | 0.3 | 0.5 |
| Transportation equipment | 2.5 | 1.1 | 0.5 | 0.1 | 0.5 | ..... | ..... | ..... | ..... | ..... |
| Scientific and measuring instruments | ..... | ..... | 0.2 | 0.3 | 0.2 | ..... | ..... | ..... | 0.3 | 0.7 |
| Miscellaneous manufactures | ..... | ..... | ..... | 0.5 | 0.1 | ..... | ..... | ..... | ..... | ..... |
| Unidentified manufactures | ..... | ..... | ..... | ..... | ..... | ..... | ..... | ..... | ..... | ..... |
| **Agricultural and livestock products** | 0.1 | 0.2 | ..... | 0.1 | ..... | ..... | ..... | 0.1 | ..... | ..... |
| Agricultural products | 0.1 | 0.2 | ..... | 0.1 | ..... | ..... | ..... | 0.1 | ..... | ..... |
| Livestock and livestock products | ..... | ..... | ..... | ..... | ..... | ..... | ..... | ..... | ..... | ..... |
| **Other commodities** | ..... | ..... | ..... | 0.1 | ..... | ..... | ..... | ..... | ..... | ..... |
| Forestry products | ..... | ..... | ..... | ..... | ..... | ..... | ..... | ..... | ..... | ..... |
| Fish and other marine products | ..... | ..... | ..... | ..... | ..... | ..... | ..... | ..... | ..... | ..... |
| Metallic ores and concentrates | ..... | ..... | ..... | ..... | ..... | ..... | ..... | ..... | ..... | ..... |
| Bituminous coal and lignite | ..... | ..... | ..... | ..... | ..... | ..... | ..... | ..... | ..... | ..... |
| Crude petroleum and natural gas | ..... | ..... | ..... | ..... | ..... | ..... | ..... | ..... | ..... | ..... |
| Nonmetallic minerals | ..... | ..... | ..... | 0.1 | ..... | ..... | ..... | ..... | ..... | ..... |
| Scrap and waste | ..... | ..... | ..... | ..... | ..... | ..... | ..... | ..... | ..... | ..... |
| Used merchandise | ..... | ..... | ..... | ..... | ..... | ..... | ..... | ..... | ..... | ..... |
| Goods imported and returned unchanged | ..... | ..... | ..... | ..... | ..... | ..... | ..... | ..... | ..... | ..... |
| Special classification provisions | ..... | ..... | ..... | ..... | ..... | ..... | ..... | ..... | ..... | ..... |
| | European Union | | | | | United Kingdom | | | | |
| **ALL GOODS** | 95.0 | 121.2 | 113.0 | 134.5 | 237.6 | 16.9 | 9.4 | 6.6 | 7.3 | 55.4 |
| **Manufactured goods** | 23.1 | 59.0 | 40.0 | 27.6 | 69.3 | 5.5 | 6.3 | 5.1 | 2.5 | 34.9 |
| Food products | 0.9 | 1.1 | 3.2 | 1.3 | 0.8 | 0.1 | 0.4 | 0.4 | 0.4 | 0.3 |
| Tobacco products | ..... | ..... | ..... | ..... | ..... | ..... | ..... | ..... | ..... | ..... |
| Textile mill products | 0.1 | ..... | 0.2 | 0.1 | 0.5 | ..... | ..... | ..... | ..... | 0.1 |
| Apparel | 0.5 | ..... | ..... | 0.1 | 0.1 | ..... | ..... | ..... | ..... | ..... |
| Lumber and wood products | ..... | 0.1 | 0.2 | 0.1 | 0.1 | ..... | ..... | ..... | ..... | ..... |
| Furniture and fixtures | ..... | ..... | ..... | 0.1 | ..... | ..... | ..... | ..... | ..... | ..... |
| Paper products | 12.3 | 14.0 | 15.2 | 11.0 | 3.5 | ..... | ..... | ..... | ..... | ..... |
| Printing and publishing | 0.1 | ..... | ..... | ..... | ..... | 0.1 | ..... | ..... | ..... | ..... |
| Chemical products | 0.3 | 1.0 | 1.3 | 2.4 | 1.5 | 0.1 | 0.8 | 0.3 | 0.2 | 0.5 |
| Refined petroleum products | ..... | ..... | ..... | ..... | ..... | ..... | ..... | ..... | ..... | ..... |
| Rubber and plastic products | ..... | 0.1 | 0.5 | 1.6 | 3.2 | ..... | 0.1 | 0.2 | 0.4 | 0.3 |
| Leather products | ..... | ..... | ..... | ..... | 0.1 | ..... | ..... | ..... | ..... | ..... |
| Stone, clay and glass products | ..... | ..... | ..... | 0.2 | 0.2 | ..... | ..... | ..... | ..... | ..... |
| Primary metals | 0.1 | 0.3 | 0.2 | 0.2 | 0.8 | 0.1 | ..... | ..... | ..... | 0.2 |
| Fabricated metal products | 0.1 | 0.7 | 3.9 | 1.1 | 3.2 | 0.1 | 0.4 | 2.4 | ..... | 3.0 |
| Industrial machinery and computers | 3.0 | 3.9 | 3.5 | 4.7 | 29.1 | 2.3 | 2.9 | 0.7 | 0.4 | 25.9 |
| Electric and electronic equipment | 1.8 | 1.8 | 0.7 | 1.3 | 17.6 | 1.5 | 1.1 | 0.2 | 0.1 | 1.8 |
| Transportation equipment | 2.6 | 35.2 | 9.2 | 1.9 | 2.7 | 1.0 | 0.5 | 0.2 | 0.8 | 1.6 |
| Scientific and measuring instruments | 1.2 | 0.5 | 1.5 | 1.4 | 5.6 | ..... | ..... | 0.5 | 0.1 | 1.3 |
| Miscellaneous manufactures | ..... | 0.1 | 0.1 | 0.1 | 0.1 | ..... | 0.1 | 0.1 | ..... | ..... |
| Unidentified manufactures | 0.1 | ..... | 0.1 | ..... | 0.3 | ..... | ..... | ..... | ..... | ..... |
| **Agricultural and livestock products** | 0.1 | 2.0 | 1.5 | 0.3 | 0.1 | ..... | 1.5 | 0.7 | ..... | ..... |
| Agricultural products | 0.1 | 1.9 | 1.5 | 0.3 | 0.1 | ..... | 1.5 | 0.7 | ..... | ..... |
| Livestock and livestock products | ..... | ..... | ..... | ..... | ..... | ..... | ..... | ..... | ..... | ..... |
| **Other commodities** | 71.7 | 60.2 | 71.5 | 106.6 | 168.2 | 11.4 | 1.6 | 0.8 | 4.8 | 20.5 |
| Forestry products | ..... | ..... | ..... | ..... | ..... | ..... | ..... | ..... | ..... | ..... |
| Fish and other marine products | 4.6 | 5.2 | 5.0 | 4.8 | 3.6 | 1.0 | 0.6 | 0.6 | 0.4 | 0.5 |
| Metallic ores and concentrates | 66.8 | 53.9 | 66.2 | 101.7 | 164.4 | 10.4 | ..... | 0.1 | 4.4 | 19.8 |
| Bituminous coal and lignite | ..... | ..... | ..... | ..... | ..... | ..... | ..... | ..... | ..... | ..... |
| Crude petroleum and natural gas | ..... | ..... | ..... | ..... | ..... | ..... | ..... | ..... | ..... | ..... |
| Nonmetallic minerals | ..... | ..... | ..... | ..... | ..... | ..... | ..... | ..... | ..... | ..... |
| Scrap and waste | ..... | ..... | 0.2 | ..... | ..... | ..... | ..... | 0.1 | ..... | ..... |
| Used merchandise | 0.2 | 1.0 | ..... | ..... | 0.1 | ..... | 1.0 | ..... | ..... | 0.1 |
| Goods imported and returned unchanged | ..... | ..... | ..... | ..... | ..... | ..... | ..... | ..... | ..... | ..... |
| Special classification provisions | 0.1 | 0.1 | ..... | ..... | 0.1 | 0.1 | ..... | ..... | ..... | 0.1 |

## Table D-3. State Exports of Goods by Destination and Industry, 1993–1997 —*Continued*

**ALASKA** (Millions of dollars.)

| Industry | 1993 | 1994 | 1995 | 1996 | 1997 | 1993 | 1994 | 1995 | 1996 | 1997 |
|---|---|---|---|---|---|---|---|---|---|---|
| | Germany | | | | | France | | | | |
| **ALL GOODS** | 26.4 | 27.1 | 33.3 | 18.2 | 30.7 | 3.3 | 6.9 | 11.9 | 2.4 | 2.0 |
| **Manufactured goods** | 12.1 | 14.0 | 18.7 | 13.2 | 5.2 | 0.7 | 4.5 | 9.0 | 1.1 | 1.5 |
| Food products | 0.1 | 0.1 | 0.2 | 0.4 | 0.1 | ..... | ..... | ..... | ..... | 0.2 |
| Tobacco products | ..... | ..... | ..... | ..... | ..... | ..... | ..... | ..... | ..... | ..... |
| Textile mill products | ..... | ..... | 0.2 | ..... | ..... | ..... | ..... | ..... | ..... | ..... |
| Apparel | ..... | ..... | ..... | ..... | 0.1 | ..... | ..... | ..... | ..... | ..... |
| Lumber and wood products | ..... | ..... | 0.1 | ..... | ..... | ..... | ..... | ..... | ..... | ..... |
| Furniture and fixtures | ..... | ..... | ..... | 0.1 | ..... | ..... | ..... | ..... | ..... | ..... |
| Paper products | 9.4 | 12.0 | 15.1 | 9.5 | 3.1 | ..... | ..... | ..... | 0.1 | ..... |
| Printing and publishing | 0.1 | ..... | ..... | ..... | ..... | ..... | ..... | ..... | ..... | ..... |
| Chemical products | ..... | ..... | ..... | 0.1 | 0.1 | ..... | ..... | 0.2 | 0.7 | 0.1 |
| Refined petroleum products | ..... | ..... | ..... | ..... | ..... | ..... | ..... | ..... | ..... | ..... |
| Rubber and plastic products | ..... | 0.1 | 0.1 | 0.1 | ..... | ..... | ..... | ..... | ..... | 0.1 |
| Leather products | ..... | ..... | ..... | ..... | ..... | ..... | ..... | ..... | ..... | ..... |
| Stone, clay and glass products | ..... | ..... | ..... | 0.2 | 0.1 | ..... | ..... | ..... | ..... | ..... |
| Primary metals | ..... | ..... | ..... | ..... | ..... | ..... | ..... | 0.2 | ..... | 0.2 |
| Fabricated metal products | ..... | 0.3 | 1.3 | 1.1 | ..... | ..... | ..... | ..... | ..... | ..... |
| Industrial machinery and computers | 0.4 | 0.1 | 0.1 | 0.1 | 0.3 | ..... | 0.1 | 0.5 | ..... | 0.2 |
| Electric and electronic equipment | 0.1 | 0.2 | 0.2 | 0.2 | 0.4 | ..... | 0.1 | ..... | ..... | 0.1 |
| Transportation equipment | 0.9 | 0.7 | 0.4 | 0.9 | 0.7 | 0.4 | 4.3 | 8.0 | 0.1 | 0.1 |
| Scientific and measuring instruments | 1.0 | 0.4 | 0.9 | 0.4 | 0.2 | 0.1 | ..... | ..... | 0.2 | 0.5 |
| Miscellaneous manufactures | ..... | ..... | ..... | 0.1 | ..... | ..... | ..... | ..... | ..... | ..... |
| Unidentified manufactures | 0.1 | ..... | ..... | ..... | ..... | ..... | ..... | ..... | ..... | ..... |
| **Agricultural and livestock products** | ..... | 0.1 | ..... | ..... | ..... | 0.1 | 0.2 | 0.2 | ..... | ..... |
| Agricultural products | ..... | 0.1 | ..... | ..... | ..... | 0.1 | 0.2 | 0.2 | ..... | ..... |
| Livestock and livestock products | ..... | ..... | ..... | ..... | ..... | ..... | ..... | ..... | ..... | ..... |
| **Other commodities** | 14.3 | 13.1 | 14.6 | 4.9 | 25.5 | 2.5 | 2.1 | 2.8 | 1.3 | 0.5 |
| Forestry products | ..... | ..... | ..... | ..... | ..... | ..... | ..... | ..... | ..... | ..... |
| Fish and other marine products | 0.4 | 0.4 | 0.1 | 0.6 | 0.5 | 1.5 | 2.1 | 2.8 | 1.3 | 0.5 |
| Metallic ores and concentrates | 13.9 | 12.6 | 14.4 | 4.4 | 25.0 | 1.0 | ..... | ..... | ..... | ..... |
| Bituminous coal and lignite | ..... | ..... | ..... | ..... | ..... | ..... | ..... | ..... | ..... | ..... |
| Crude petroleum and natural gas | ..... | ..... | ..... | ..... | ..... | ..... | ..... | ..... | ..... | ..... |
| Nonmetallic minerals | ..... | ..... | ..... | ..... | ..... | ..... | ..... | ..... | ..... | ..... |
| Scrap and waste | ..... | ..... | ..... | ..... | ..... | ..... | ..... | ..... | ..... | ..... |
| Used merchandise | ..... | ..... | ..... | ..... | ..... | 0.1 | ..... | ..... | ..... | ..... |
| Goods imported and returned unchanged | ..... | ..... | ..... | ..... | ..... | ..... | ..... | ..... | ..... | ..... |
| Special classification provisions | ..... | 0.1 | ..... | ..... | ..... | ..... | ..... | ..... | ..... | ..... |
| | The Netherlands | | | | | Asian 10 | | | | |
| **ALL GOODS** | 0.6 | 1.6 | 15.3 | 35.5 | 44.9 | 617.6 | 558.0 | 521.6 | 492.3 | 392.6 |
| **Manufactured goods** | 0.5 | 1.2 | 0.9 | 5.4 | 23.2 | 299.1 | 273.4 | 222.0 | 176.6 | 114.0 |
| Food products | ..... | ..... | 0.2 | 0.2 | 0.1 | 11.0 | 5.0 | 13.4 | 5.0 | 5.0 |
| Tobacco products | ..... | ..... | ..... | ..... | ..... | ..... | ..... | ..... | ..... | ..... |
| Textile mill products | ..... | ..... | ..... | ..... | 0.5 | 0.2 | ..... | 0.1 | ..... | 0.1 |
| Apparel | ..... | ..... | ..... | ..... | ..... | 0.2 | 0.1 | 0.5 | 0.4 | 0.2 |
| Lumber and wood products | ..... | ..... | ..... | ..... | ..... | 164.0 | 150.1 | 59.5 | 37.9 | 41.0 |
| Furniture and fixtures | ..... | ..... | ..... | ..... | ..... | ..... | ..... | ..... | ..... | ..... |
| Paper products | 0.1 | ..... | ..... | ..... | 0.2 | 89.0 | 65.7 | 83.9 | 63.6 | 25.0 |
| Printing and publishing | ..... | ..... | ..... | ..... | ..... | 0.1 | 0.1 | ..... | ..... | 0.1 |
| Chemical products | ..... | ..... | 0.3 | ..... | ..... | ..... | 1.6 | 1.5 | 5.2 | 2.3 |
| Refined petroleum products | ..... | ..... | ..... | ..... | ..... | 21.5 | 26.4 | 34.4 | 36.0 | 18.9 |
| Rubber and plastic products | ..... | ..... | 0.1 | 0.3 | 1.5 | ..... | 0.1 | 4.8 | 1.0 | 0.5 |
| Leather products | ..... | ..... | ..... | ..... | ..... | ..... | ..... | ..... | ..... | ..... |
| Stone, clay and glass products | ..... | ..... | ..... | ..... | ..... | ..... | 0.2 | 0.1 | 0.1 | 0.7 |
| Primary metals | ..... | ..... | ..... | 0.1 | 0.2 | 0.2 | 0.2 | 0.4 | 0.1 | 0.1 |
| Fabricated metal products | ..... | ..... | ..... | 0.1 | ..... | 0.2 | 0.2 | 0.6 | 0.4 | 0.4 |
| Industrial machinery and computers | 0.1 | 0.1 | 0.2 | 3.3 | 2.6 | 1.6 | 2.1 | 1.3 | 1.7 | 1.7 |
| Electric and electronic equipment | ..... | 0.4 | ..... | 0.9 | 15.2 | 1.3 | 1.1 | 1.4 | 3.5 | 2.2 |
| Transportation equipment | 0.2 | 0.6 | 0.1 | ..... | 0.2 | 5.2 | 17.6 | 14.5 | 17.5 | 12.8 |
| Scientific and measuring instruments | 0.1 | ..... | ..... | 0.5 | 2.4 | 3.3 | 2.1 | 4.1 | 3.5 | 2.4 |
| Miscellaneous manufactures | ..... | ..... | ..... | 0.1 | ..... | 1.0 | 0.5 | 1.2 | 0.4 | 0.4 |
| Unidentified manufactures | ..... | ..... | ..... | ..... | 0.2 | 0.2 | 0.2 | 0.2 | 0.2 | 0.1 |
| **Agricultural and livestock products** | ..... | 0.1 | 0.3 | 0.1 | ..... | 0.1 | 0.2 | 0.1 | 0.4 | 0.3 |
| Agricultural products | ..... | 0.1 | 0.3 | 0.1 | ..... | ..... | 0.1 | 0.1 | 0.4 | 0.3 |
| Livestock and livestock products | ..... | ..... | ..... | ..... | ..... | 0.1 | 0.1 | ..... | 0.1 | ..... |
| **Other commodities** | 0.1 | 0.3 | 14.1 | 30.0 | 21.7 | 318.4 | 284.4 | 299.5 | 315.3 | 278.4 |
| Forestry products | ..... | ..... | ..... | ..... | ..... | ..... | ..... | ..... | ..... | ..... |
| Fish and other marine products | ..... | 0.3 | 0.1 | 0.3 | ..... | 111.1 | 98.8 | 63.2 | 60.9 | 38.8 |
| Metallic ores and concentrates | ..... | ..... | 14.1 | 29.7 | 21.7 | 55.5 | 22.5 | 61.2 | 82.3 | 71.1 |
| Bituminous coal and lignite | ..... | ..... | ..... | ..... | ..... | 25.2 | 22.9 | 29.5 | 26.7 | 25.3 |
| Crude petroleum and natural gas | ..... | ..... | ..... | ..... | ..... | 126.2 | 140.0 | 144.7 | 144.9 | 141.0 |
| Nonmetallic minerals | ..... | ..... | ..... | ..... | ..... | ..... | 0.1 | 0.9 | ..... | ..... |
| Scrap and waste | ..... | ..... | ..... | ..... | ..... | ..... | ..... | ..... | ..... | ..... |
| Used merchandise | ..... | ..... | ..... | ..... | ..... | 0.1 | ..... | ..... | 0.1 | ..... |
| Goods imported and returned unchanged | ..... | ..... | ..... | ..... | ..... | ..... | ..... | ..... | ..... | ..... |
| Special classification provisions | ..... | ..... | ..... | ..... | ..... | 0.2 | 0.1 | ..... | 0.4 | 2.1 |

## Table D-3. State Exports of Goods by Destination and Industry, 1993–1997 —*Continued*

**ALASKA** (Millions of dollars.)

| Industry | 1993 | 1994 | 1995 | 1996 | 1997 | 1993 | 1994 | 1995 | 1996 | 1997 |
|---|---|---|---|---|---|---|---|---|---|---|
| | Japan | | | | | South Korea | | | | |
| **ALL GOODS** | 474.9 | 412.6 | 327.5 | 270.0 | 259.2 | 92.8 | 75.6 | 93.7 | 127.6 | 97.4 |
| **Manufactured goods** | 220.3 | 167.2 | 109.4 | 67.3 | 47.8 | 29.9 | 36.8 | 21.6 | 34.2 | 32.3 |
| Food products | 10.6 | 4.9 | 7.2 | 4.1 | 3.2 | 0.3 | 0.1 | 5.4 | 0.1 | 0.1 |
| Tobacco products | ..... | ..... | ..... | ..... | ..... | ..... | ..... | ..... | ..... | ..... |
| Textile mill products | ..... | ..... | 0.1 | ..... | ..... | ..... | ..... | ..... | ..... | ..... |
| Apparel | 0.1 | ..... | 0.1 | 0.3 | ..... | ..... | ..... | ..... | ..... | ..... |
| Lumber and wood products | 131.9 | 121.7 | 44.4 | 26.6 | 27.6 | 20.1 | 21.6 | 13.2 | 7.8 | 8.1 |
| Furniture and fixtures | ..... | ..... | ..... | ..... | ..... | ..... | ..... | ..... | ..... | ..... |
| Paper products | 57.6 | 14.2 | 20.3 | 11.2 | 6.7 | 0.1 | 0.5 | 0.1 | ..... | ..... |
| Printing and publishing | ..... | 0.1 | ..... | ..... | ..... | ..... | ..... | ..... | ..... | ..... |
| Chemical products | ..... | 1.4 | 0.7 | 4.0 | 1.1 | ..... | ..... | 0.5 | 0.8 | 0.4 |
| Refined petroleum products | 15.2 | 20.0 | 25.7 | 12.1 | 2.0 | 4.8 | 6.4 | ..... | 14.6 | 15.3 |
| Rubber and plastic products | ..... | 0.1 | 4.6 | 0.6 | ..... | ..... | ..... | ..... | ..... | ..... |
| Leather products | ..... | ..... | ..... | ..... | ..... | ..... | ..... | ..... | ..... | ..... |
| Stone, clay and glass products | ..... | 0.2 | 0.1 | 0.1 | 0.7 | ..... | ..... | ..... | ..... | ..... |
| Primary metals | ..... | ..... | ..... | ..... | ..... | ..... | ..... | ..... | ..... | ..... |
| Fabricated metal products | 0.1 | 0.1 | ..... | ..... | 0.2 | ..... | ..... | ..... | ..... | 0.1 |
| Industrial machinery and computers | 0.2 | 0.2 | 0.4 | 0.5 | 0.7 | ..... | ..... | 0.1 | 0.7 | ..... |
| Electric and electronic equipment | 0.5 | 0.2 | 0.2 | 0.3 | 1.3 | 0.1 | 0.2 | 0.7 | 1.1 | 0.1 |
| Transportation equipment | 0.9 | 2.3 | 1.2 | 4.0 | 2.3 | 4.2 | 7.8 | 1.3 | 9.0 | 8.0 |
| Scientific and measuring instruments | 2.9 | 1.7 | 3.9 | 3.2 | 1.7 | 0.2 | ..... | ..... | ..... | ..... |
| Miscellaneous manufactures | ..... | 0.1 | 0.3 | ..... | 0.1 | ..... | ..... | 0.1 | ..... | ..... |
| Unidentified manufactures | 0.1 | 0.1 | ..... | 0.1 | 0.1 | ..... | ..... | 0.1 | 0.1 | ..... |
| **Agricultural and livestock products** | 0.1 | 0.1 | 0.1 | 0.2 | 0.1 | ..... | ..... | ..... | 0.1 | 0.1 |
| Agricultural products | ..... | ..... | 0.1 | 0.1 | 0.1 | ..... | ..... | ..... | ..... | 0.1 |
| Livestock and livestock products | 0.1 | 0.1 | ..... | ..... | ..... | ..... | ..... | ..... | ..... | ..... |
| **Other commodities** | 254.6 | 245.2 | 218.0 | 202.5 | 211.3 | 63.0 | 38.8 | 72.1 | 93.4 | 65.0 |
| Forestry products | ..... | ..... | ..... | ..... | ..... | ..... | ..... | ..... | ..... | ..... |
| Fish and other marine products | 90.5 | 87.5 | 46.1 | 39.9 | 22.0 | 19.9 | 10.9 | 16.4 | 20.7 | 15.5 |
| Metallic ores and concentrates | 37.8 | 17.6 | 26.2 | 17.4 | 46.8 | 17.7 | 4.9 | 26.1 | 46.0 | 24.1 |
| Bituminous coal and lignite | ..... | ..... | ..... | ..... | ..... | 25.2 | 22.9 | 29.5 | 26.7 | 25.3 |
| Crude petroleum and natural gas | 126.2 | 140.0 | 144.7 | 144.9 | 141.0 | ..... | ..... | ..... | ..... | ..... |
| Nonmetallic minerals | ..... | 0.1 | 0.9 | ..... | ..... | ..... | ..... | ..... | ..... | ..... |
| Scrap and waste | ..... | ..... | ..... | ..... | ..... | ..... | ..... | ..... | ..... | ..... |
| Used merchandise | ..... | ..... | ..... | ..... | ..... | ..... | ..... | ..... | ..... | ..... |
| Goods imported and returned unchanged | ..... | ..... | ..... | ..... | ..... | ..... | ..... | ..... | ..... | ..... |
| Special classification provisions | ..... | ..... | ..... | 0.3 | 1.4 | 0.1 | 0.1 | ..... | ..... | 0.1 |
| | Taiwan | | | | | Singapore | | | | |
| **ALL GOODS** | 32.3 | 34.5 | 61.4 | 40.7 | 18.4 | 2.3 | 1.1 | 5.1 | 6.1 | 0.9 |
| **Manufactured goods** | 32.2 | 34.4 | 61.1 | 40.7 | 18.3 | 2.3 | 1.0 | 5.1 | 5.9 | 0.9 |
| Food products | 0.1 | ..... | 0.3 | 0.4 | 1.3 | ..... | ..... | ..... | ..... | ..... |
| Tobacco products | ..... | ..... | ..... | ..... | ..... | ..... | ..... | ..... | ..... | ..... |
| Textile mill products | ..... | ..... | ..... | ..... | ..... | ..... | ..... | ..... | ..... | ..... |
| Apparel | ..... | ..... | ..... | ..... | ..... | ..... | ..... | ..... | ..... | ..... |
| Lumber and wood products | 7.6 | 6.8 | 1.8 | 1.5 | 4.0 | ..... | ..... | ..... | ..... | ..... |
| Furniture and fixtures | ..... | ..... | ..... | ..... | ..... | ..... | ..... | ..... | ..... | ..... |
| Paper products | 23.4 | 26.8 | 46.5 | 37.3 | 10.3 | ..... | ..... | ..... | ..... | ..... |
| Printing and publishing | ..... | ..... | ..... | ..... | ..... | ..... | ..... | ..... | ..... | ..... |
| Chemical products | ..... | ..... | 0.1 | 0.3 | 0.5 | ..... | 0.2 | ..... | ..... | 0.1 |
| Refined petroleum products | ..... | ..... | ..... | ..... | ..... | 1.6 | ..... | 4.8 | 5.6 | ..... |
| Rubber and plastic products | ..... | ..... | 0.2 | 0.3 | 0.4 | ..... | ..... | ..... | ..... | ..... |
| Leather products | ..... | ..... | ..... | ..... | ..... | ..... | ..... | ..... | ..... | ..... |
| Stone, clay and glass products | ..... | ..... | ..... | ..... | ..... | ..... | ..... | ..... | ..... | ..... |
| Primary metals | ..... | 0.1 | ..... | ..... | ..... | ..... | ..... | ..... | ..... | ..... |
| Fabricated metal products | ..... | ..... | ..... | ..... | ..... | 0.1 | ..... | ..... | ..... | ..... |
| Industrial machinery and computers | 0.2 | 0.3 | 0.3 | 0.2 | 0.1 | 0.5 | 0.5 | 0.2 | ..... | ..... |
| Electric and electronic equipment | 0.1 | 0.1 | 0.2 | 0.1 | 0.1 | 0.1 | 0.1 | ..... | ..... | ..... |
| Transportation equipment | ..... | ..... | 11.7 | 0.2 | 1.5 | ..... | 0.1 | 0.1 | 0.1 | 0.2 |
| Scientific and measuring instruments | ..... | 0.1 | ..... | 0.2 | ..... | ..... | ..... | ..... | ..... | 0.5 |
| Miscellaneous manufactures | 0.8 | 0.1 | ..... | 0.1 | 0.1 | ..... | ..... | ..... | ..... | ..... |
| Unidentified manufactures | ..... | ..... | ..... | ..... | ..... | ..... | ..... | ..... | ..... | ..... |
| **Agricultural and livestock products** | ..... | ..... | ..... | ..... | ..... | ..... | 0.1 | ..... | 0.1 | ..... |
| Agricultural products | ..... | ..... | ..... | ..... | ..... | ..... | 0.1 | ..... | 0.1 | ..... |
| Livestock and livestock products | ..... | ..... | ..... | ..... | ..... | ..... | ..... | ..... | ..... | ..... |
| **Other commodities** | ..... | 0.2 | 0.4 | ..... | ..... | 0.1 | ..... | ..... | 0.1 | 0.1 |
| Forestry products | ..... | ..... | ..... | ..... | ..... | ..... | ..... | ..... | ..... | ..... |
| Fish and other marine products | ..... | 0.2 | 0.4 | ..... | ..... | ..... | ..... | ..... | 0.1 | ..... |
| Metallic ores and concentrates | ..... | ..... | ..... | ..... | ..... | ..... | ..... | ..... | ..... | ..... |
| Bituminous coal and lignite | ..... | ..... | ..... | ..... | ..... | ..... | ..... | ..... | ..... | ..... |
| Crude petroleum and natural gas | ..... | ..... | ..... | ..... | ..... | ..... | ..... | ..... | ..... | ..... |
| Nonmetallic minerals | ..... | ..... | ..... | ..... | ..... | ..... | ..... | ..... | ..... | ..... |
| Scrap and waste | ..... | ..... | ..... | ..... | ..... | ..... | ..... | ..... | ..... | ..... |
| Used merchandise | ..... | ..... | ..... | ..... | ..... | 0.1 | ..... | ..... | ..... | ..... |
| Goods imported and returned unchanged | ..... | ..... | ..... | ..... | ..... | ..... | ..... | ..... | ..... | ..... |
| Special classification provisions | ..... | ..... | ..... | ..... | ..... | ..... | ..... | ..... | ..... | ..... |

## ARIZONA: Exports of Goods, 1997

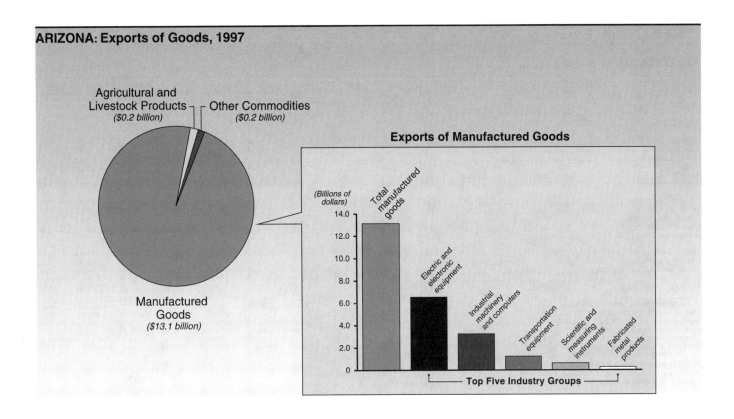

Agricultural and Livestock Products ($0.2 billion)

Other Commodities ($0.2 billion)

Manufactured Goods ($13.1 billion)

**Exports of Manufactured Goods**

(Billions of dollars)

Top Five Industry Groups

---

## Table D-3.  State Exports of Goods by Destination and Industry, 1993–1997 —Continued

### ARIZONA (Millions of dollars.)

| Industry | 1993 | 1994 | 1995 | 1996 | 1997 | 1993 | 1994 | 1995 | 1996 | 1997 |
|---|---|---|---|---|---|---|---|---|---|---|
| | All destinations | | | | | Canada | | | | |
| **ALL GOODS** | 5 785.1 | 6 970.6 | 8 402.8 | 9 937.8 | 13 556.7 | 533.1 | 644.2 | 839.0 | 970.2 | 1 072.2 |
| **Manufactured goods** | 5 477.4 | 6 632.5 | 7 910.1 | 9 561.0 | 13 138.7 | 460.2 | 561.8 | 736.2 | 858.9 | 960.8 |
| Food products | 74.6 | 89.1 | 57.3 | 63.1 | 105.9 | 20.3 | 17.4 | 16.3 | 14.7 | 16.0 |
| Tobacco products | 0.3 | 0.6 | 0.8 | 1.5 | 1.9 | ..... | ..... | ..... | ..... | ..... |
| Textile mill products | 22.0 | 16.6 | 21.2 | 24.4 | 32.2 | 0.1 | 0.5 | 0.2 | 0.2 | 0.4 |
| Apparel | 110.6 | 87.7 | 55.3 | 111.4 | 114.1 | 22.0 | 21.6 | 20.9 | 20.2 | 20.6 |
| Lumber and wood products | 7.1 | 6.1 | 6.5 | 6.4 | 7.1 | 0.3 | 0.2 | 0.3 | 0.8 | 0.7 |
| Furniture and fixtures | 43.7 | 24.0 | 18.7 | 38.3 | 27.7 | 1.5 | 2.9 | 2.1 | 4.0 | 7.3 |
| Paper products | 72.4 | 76.7 | 106.5 | 113.3 | 128.2 | 1.9 | 1.7 | 1.7 | 1.9 | 1.3 |
| Printing and publishing | 14.1 | 12.8 | 22.8 | 25.8 | 13.1 | 5.2 | 3.2 | 3.0 | 2.8 | 2.0 |
| Chemical products | 88.6 | 122.4 | 201.8 | 185.3 | 161.0 | 18.0 | 17.9 | 21.0 | 21.8 | 23.6 |
| Refined petroleum products | 3.1 | 2.4 | 2.9 | 3.9 | 65.8 | 0.2 | 0.2 | 0.2 | 1.0 | 19.5 |
| Rubber and plastic products | 101.3 | 119.1 | 117.4 | 150.3 | 177.9 | 5.5 | 4.5 | 4.6 | 5.5 | 8.0 |
| Leather products | 5.7 | 6.2 | 5.1 | 5.1 | 8.0 | 0.5 | 0.4 | 0.6 | 0.6 | 0.9 |
| Stone, clay and glass products | 10.3 | 13.9 | 20.1 | 21.1 | 25.4 | 0.5 | 0.8 | 1.0 | 1.7 | 1.5 |
| Primary metals | 256.6 | 245.0 | 368.7 | 420.1 | 248.6 | 17.0 | 16.7 | 48.3 | 34.7 | 43.3 |
| Fabricated metal products | 97.3 | 163.7 | 162.6 | 239.1 | 277.5 | 10.6 | 25.6 | 49.5 | 75.5 | 80.4 |
| Industrial machinery and computers | 763.5 | 826.5 | 883.9 | 1 098.3 | 3 237.6 | 62.9 | 71.6 | 89.8 | 117.5 | 155.1 |
| Electric and electronic equipment | 2 833.9 | 3 636.5 | 4 503.3 | 5 428.8 | 6 539.5 | 164.7 | 220.6 | 293.5 | 339.6 | 350.7 |
| Transportation equipment | 501.7 | 655.0 | 718.2 | 942.8 | 1 228.8 | 75.3 | 86.9 | 106.7 | 138.1 | 145.5 |
| Scientific and measuring instruments | 383.1 | 431.9 | 522.2 | 559.3 | 622.5 | 39.4 | 47.1 | 56.2 | 57.9 | 64.8 |
| Miscellaneous manufactures | 69.0 | 75.8 | 94.2 | 101.1 | 90.6 | 9.4 | 15.6 | 12.2 | 12.5 | 9.8 |
| Unidentified manufactures | 18.7 | 20.5 | 20.6 | 21.6 | 25.1 | 4.7 | 6.5 | 8.1 | 7.9 | 9.4 |
| **Agricultural and livestock products** | 141.8 | 156.4 | 181.5 | 176.9 | 216.6 | 56.2 | 49.9 | 66.7 | 70.7 | 66.5 |
| Agricultural products | 135.5 | 145.9 | 178.5 | 168.6 | 196.4 | 55.7 | 49.8 | 66.4 | 70.5 | 66.4 |
| Livestock and livestock products | 6.3 | 10.5 | 3.0 | 8.3 | 20.1 | 0.5 | 0.1 | 0.4 | 0.1 | 0.1 |
| **Other commodities** | 165.9 | 181.7 | 311.2 | 199.8 | 201.5 | 16.7 | 32.4 | 36.1 | 40.6 | 44.9 |
| Forestry products | 0.7 | 0.4 | 0.5 | 0.8 | 0.8 | 0.2 | ..... | 0.2 | 0.1 | 0.2 |
| Fish and other marine products | 0.5 | 0.8 | 0.8 | 1.0 | 0.4 | 0.1 | 0.2 | 0.8 | 0.4 | ..... |
| Metallic ores and concentrates | 59.8 | 66.6 | 206.1 | 80.1 | 62.5 | 2.2 | 2.7 | 1.5 | 2.4 | 1.4 |
| Bituminous coal and lignite | ..... | ..... | ..... | ..... | ..... | ..... | ..... | ..... | ..... | ..... |
| Crude petroleum and natural gas | ..... | ..... | 0.3 | ..... | 0.2 | ..... | ..... | 0.1 | ..... | 0.1 |
| Nonmetallic minerals | 1.9 | 5.2 | 6.0 | 4.9 | 2.9 | 0.3 | 0.4 | 0.2 | 0.2 | 0.2 |
| Scrap and waste | 1.9 | 7.8 | 28.4 | 13.1 | 28.4 | 0.2 | 3.1 | 16.1 | 4.1 | 9.3 |
| Used merchandise | 11.8 | 9.9 | 8.0 | 15.4 | 18.4 | 1.0 | 1.6 | 1.2 | 6.9 | 4.2 |
| Goods imported and returned unchanged | 8.8 | 14.4 | 10.9 | 20.7 | 23.9 | 8.8 | 14.4 | 10.9 | 20.7 | 23.9 |
| Special classification provisions | 80.4 | 76.7 | 50.1 | 64.0 | 63.9 | 3.9 | 10.0 | 5.2 | 5.9 | 5.7 |

## Table D-3. State Exports of Goods by Destination and Industry, 1993–1997 —*Continued*

**ARIZONA** (Millions of dollars.)

| Industry | 1993 | 1994 | 1995 | 1996 | 1997 | 1993 | 1994 | 1995 | 1996 | 1997 |
|---|---|---|---|---|---|---|---|---|---|---|
| | South and Central America and Caribbean | | | | | Mexico | | | | |
| **ALL GOODS** | 64.2 | 92.6 | 111.8 | 154.7 | 218.9 | 1 087.4 | 1 206.5 | 1 265.6 | 1 622.2 | 1 963.1 |
| **Manufactured goods** | 59.4 | 80.3 | 101.3 | 142.0 | 213.3 | 1 024.6 | 1 153.5 | 1 234.5 | 1 580.8 | 1 897.6 |
| Food products | 1.3 | 1.6 | 2.8 | 2.2 | 2.8 | 39.8 | 49.6 | 22.4 | 30.7 | 55.2 |
| Tobacco products | ..... | ..... | ..... | ..... | ..... | 0.3 | 0.6 | 0.8 | 1.5 | 1.9 |
| Textile mill products | 0.6 | 0.6 | ..... | 0.1 | 0.1 | 20.2 | 13.7 | 18.1 | 22.2 | 22.6 |
| Apparel | ..... | 0.2 | 0.1 | 0.1 | 0.3 | 82.3 | 60.7 | 25.8 | 82.9 | 85.9 |
| Lumber and wood products | 0.3 | 0.2 | 0.1 | 0.2 | 0.1 | 6.1 | 5.1 | 4.9 | 3.6 | 4.8 |
| Furniture and fixtures | 0.2 | 0.3 | 0.4 | 0.6 | 0.3 | 40.0 | 18.2 | 13.7 | 29.0 | 16.7 |
| Paper products | 0.1 | 0.2 | 0.2 | 1.4 | 1.7 | 68.5 | 72.1 | 101.6 | 106.7 | 120.8 |
| Printing and publishing | 0.1 | 0.2 | 0.5 | 0.2 | 0.3 | 2.5 | 2.9 | 3.5 | 5.5 | 5.0 |
| Chemical products | 4.4 | 5.3 | 3.9 | 7.4 | 5.3 | 25.5 | 34.9 | 36.3 | 43.1 | 52.2 |
| Refined petroleum products | ..... | 0.1 | 0.1 | ..... | 8.0 | 2.2 | 1.7 | 2.3 | 2.5 | 25.4 |
| Rubber and plastic products | 0.2 | 0.8 | 2.7 | 1.9 | 2.8 | 70.0 | 79.6 | 83.9 | 111.2 | 133.6 |
| Leather products | ..... | ..... | ..... | ..... | 0.1 | 2.1 | 3.0 | 1.8 | 1.9 | 4.4 |
| Stone, clay and glass products | 0.3 | 0.2 | 0.2 | 0.2 | 0.2 | 4.5 | 5.2 | 4.2 | 8.9 | 9.4 |
| Primary metals | 0.2 | 1.7 | 1.7 | 2.9 | 1.9 | 36.9 | 41.4 | 52.1 | 92.9 | 103.8 |
| Fabricated metal products | 1.1 | 1.3 | 0.6 | 4.3 | 2.1 | 58.5 | 86.3 | 60.6 | 78.8 | 117.1 |
| Industrial machinery and computers | 11.5 | 16.6 | 21.8 | 37.0 | 31.8 | 229.2 | 242.6 | 227.3 | 303.4 | 348.7 |
| Electric and electronic equipment | 20.8 | 30.3 | 43.7 | 57.4 | 70.0 | 262.5 | 334.9 | 495.2 | 528.8 | 630.0 |
| Transportation equipment | 12.7 | 15.3 | 13.0 | 16.2 | 72.2 | 33.1 | 41.9 | 23.1 | 70.1 | 74.5 |
| Scientific and measuring instruments | 3.0 | 4.2 | 7.4 | 8.2 | 10.5 | 23.9 | 36.5 | 29.3 | 29.0 | 51.0 |
| Miscellaneous manufactures | 1.1 | 0.7 | 1.4 | 1.2 | 2.3 | 11.6 | 17.3 | 24.2 | 21.0 | 27.5 |
| Unidentified manufactures | 0.9 | 0.4 | 0.2 | 0.3 | 0.6 | 5.1 | 5.2 | 3.5 | 7.2 | 7.2 |
| **Agricultural and livestock products** | 1.5 | 5.5 | 0.9 | 2.7 | 3.9 | 30.2 | 30.3 | 14.8 | 26.7 | 49.7 |
| Agricultural products | 1.6 | 5.4 | 0.9 | 2.6 | 3.9 | 24.4 | 20.0 | 12.9 | 19.3 | 29.9 |
| Livestock and livestock products | ..... | 0.1 | ..... | ..... | 0.2 | 5.7 | 10.3 | 1.9 | 7.4 | 19.7 |
| **Other commodities** | 3.2 | 6.9 | 9.7 | 10.1 | 1.6 | 32.7 | 22.6 | 16.3 | 14.6 | 15.8 |
| Forestry products | ..... | ..... | ..... | ..... | ..... | 0.3 | 0.2 | 0.2 | 0.2 | 0.4 |
| Fish and other marine products | ..... | ..... | ..... | ..... | ..... | 0.1 | 0.1 | 0.1 | 0.2 | 0.1 |
| Metallic ores and concentrates | 2.8 | 4.7 | 8.2 | 2.5 | 0.7 | ..... | 1.3 | 6.1 | 1.8 | ..... |
| Bituminous coal and lignite | ..... | ..... | ..... | ..... | ..... | ..... | ..... | ..... | ..... | ..... |
| Crude petroleum and natural gas | ..... | ..... | ..... | ..... | ..... | ..... | ..... | 0.2 | ..... | ..... |
| Nonmetallic minerals | ..... | 0.3 | 0.4 | 0.3 | 0.2 | 0.5 | 0.4 | 0.4 | 0.5 | 0.6 |
| Scrap and waste | ..... | ..... | 0.1 | 0.1 | 0.1 | 0.1 | 2.0 | 1.5 | 1.0 | 1.1 |
| Used merchandise | 0.2 | 0.2 | 0.5 | 0.5 | ..... | 3.8 | 3.9 | 1.8 | 4.9 | 6.0 |
| Goods imported and returned unchanged | ..... | ..... | ..... | ..... | ..... | ..... | ..... | ..... | ..... | ..... |
| Special classification provisions | 0.3 | 1.9 | 0.5 | 6.7 | 0.6 | 27.8 | 14.5 | 6.1 | 5.9 | 7.6 |
| | European Union | | | | | United Kingdom | | | | |
| **ALL GOODS** | 1 590.1 | 1 879.5 | 2 443.8 | 2 448.6 | 3 686.4 | 807.3 | 906.0 | 1 085.1 | 827.1 | 1 061.5 |
| **Manufactured goods** | 1 509.8 | 1 787.3 | 2 238.8 | 2 346.4 | 3 548.7 | 791.2 | 872.9 | 1 014.4 | 792.6 | 1 038.1 |
| Food products | 5.8 | 5.2 | 6.4 | 5.8 | 7.2 | 2.9 | 1.8 | 2.0 | 2.0 | 2.9 |
| Tobacco products | ..... | ..... | ..... | ..... | ..... | ..... | ..... | ..... | ..... | ..... |
| Textile mill products | 0.3 | 0.4 | 0.3 | 0.3 | 0.8 | ..... | ..... | 0.1 | 0.1 | 0.4 |
| Apparel | 1.1 | 0.5 | 1.3 | 2.9 | 1.9 | 0.1 | 0.1 | 0.2 | 0.3 | 0.3 |
| Lumber and wood products | 0.1 | 0.1 | 0.1 | 0.7 | 0.2 | ..... | ..... | 0.1 | 0.2 | 0.1 |
| Furniture and fixtures | 1.0 | 2.1 | 0.8 | 1.9 | 1.5 | 0.1 | 0.2 | 0.1 | 0.6 | 0.6 |
| Paper products | 0.4 | 1.2 | 1.2 | 1.6 | 1.0 | 0.2 | 0.5 | 0.4 | 0.5 | 0.1 |
| Printing and publishing | 4.5 | 3.6 | 3.6 | 3.9 | 2.8 | 1.8 | 1.8 | 1.3 | 1.7 | 0.9 |
| Chemical products | 11.6 | 14.4 | 48.6 | 21.1 | 21.3 | 1.0 | 1.5 | 1.7 | 3.7 | 5.8 |
| Refined petroleum products | 0.2 | ..... | 0.1 | ..... | ..... | *i* | ..... | ..... | ..... | ..... |
| Rubber and plastic products | 8.9 | 10.8 | 11.0 | 11.3 | 15.9 | 1.0 | 2.0 | 1.5 | 2.7 | 3.9 |
| Leather products | 1.1 | 0.7 | 0.8 | 0.8 | 0.6 | 0.7 | 0.4 | 0.4 | 0.4 | 0.2 |
| Stone, clay and glass products | 1.1 | 1.2 | 9.6 | 1.8 | 9.0 | 0.2 | 0.2 | 0.3 | 0.3 | 0.7 |
| Primary metals | 6.1 | 7.3 | 11.8 | 18.8 | 11.1 | 0.9 | 0.9 | 1.5 | 3.5 | 1.6 |
| Fabricated metal products | 7.0 | 16.3 | 36.7 | 51.2 | 38.9 | 1.0 | 2.1 | 2.9 | 6.4 | 8.8 |
| Industrial machinery and computers | 242.1 | 249.1 | 244.5 | 243.8 | 1 432.4 | 45.9 | 49.3 | 40.4 | 36.7 | 492.5 |
| Electric and electronic equipment | 778.6 | 913.4 | 1 177.5 | 1 177.1 | 1 141.3 | 609.1 | 661.4 | 819.3 | 555.2 | 339.6 |
| Transportation equipment | 232.7 | 322.5 | 365.0 | 464.6 | 556.2 | 83.5 | 110.9 | 90.3 | 123.0 | 127.2 |
| Scientific and measuring instruments | 193.2 | 222.2 | 301.2 | 319.6 | 289.6 | 36.6 | 32.1 | 43.0 | 45.9 | 46.1 |
| Miscellaneous manufactures | 11.0 | 13.0 | 13.9 | 16.9 | 14.5 | 5.5 | 6.9 | 7.9 | 9.0 | 5.9 |
| Unidentified manufactures | 2.9 | 3.3 | 4.3 | 2.3 | 2.4 | 0.7 | 0.7 | 1.0 | 0.4 | 0.4 |
| **Agricultural and livestock products** | 15.2 | 16.3 | 22.3 | 28.7 | 39.2 | 0.3 | 0.6 | 1.0 | 1.6 | 1.6 |
| Agricultural products | 15.1 | 16.3 | 22.3 | 28.7 | 39.2 | 0.3 | 0.6 | 1.0 | 1.5 | 1.6 |
| Livestock and livestock products | ..... | ..... | ..... | 0.1 | 0.1 | ..... | ..... | ..... | ..... | ..... |
| **Other commodities** | 65.1 | 75.9 | 182.7 | 73.5 | 98.5 | 15.8 | 32.5 | 69.6 | 33.0 | 21.9 |
| Forestry products | ..... | ..... | 0.1 | 0.3 | 0.3 | ..... | ..... | ..... | ..... | 0.1 |
| Fish and other marine products | ..... | ..... | ..... | 0.1 | ..... | ..... | ..... | ..... | ..... | ..... |
| Metallic ores and concentrates | 18.8 | 38.0 | 145.9 | 38.2 | 51.7 | 1.3 | 16.9 | 58.9 | 25.0 | 12.1 |
| Bituminous coal and lignite | ..... | ..... | ..... | ..... | ..... | ..... | ..... | ..... | ..... | ..... |
| Crude petroleum and natural gas | ..... | ..... | ..... | ..... | ..... | ..... | ..... | ..... | ..... | ..... |
| Nonmetallic minerals | 0.4 | 1.4 | 0.3 | 0.2 | 0.1 | 0.1 | 1.2 | ..... | 0.1 | ..... |
| Scrap and waste | ..... | ..... | 7.3 | 5.1 | 12.3 | ..... | ..... | 0.2 | ..... | ..... |
| Used merchandise | 3.8 | 2.7 | 2.6 | 1.1 | 4.2 | 1.7 | 0.2 | 0.3 | 0.2 | 1.9 |
| Goods imported and returned unchanged | ..... | ..... | ..... | ..... | ..... | ..... | ..... | ..... | ..... | ..... |
| Special classification provisions | 42.1 | 33.7 | 26.7 | 28.4 | 30.0 | 12.8 | 14.1 | 10.3 | 7.7 | 7.8 |

## Table D-3.  State Exports of Goods by Destination and Industry, 1993–1997 —*Continued*

**ARIZONA** (Millions of dollars.)

| Industry | 1993 | 1994 | 1995 | 1996 | 1997 | 1993 | 1994 | 1995 | 1996 | 1997 |
|---|---|---|---|---|---|---|---|---|---|---|
| | Germany | | | | | France | | | | |
| **ALL GOODS** | 278.3 | 349.8 | 410.8 | 392.9 | 413.7 | 194.5 | 206.7 | 285.7 | 324.9 | 382.2 |
| **Manufactured goods** | 253.1 | 336.1 | 381.7 | 380.9 | 393.8 | 190.5 | 201.6 | 280.7 | 313.5 | 373.0 |
| Food products | 1.3 | 1.6 | 1.6 | 1.0 | 0.4 | 1.2 | 0.5 | 0.4 | 0.5 | 0.5 |
| Tobacco products | ..... | ..... | ..... | ..... | ..... | ..... | ..... | ..... | ..... | ..... |
| Textile mill products | 0.1 | 0.3 | 0.2 | ..... | ..... | ..... | 0.1 | ..... | ..... | ..... |
| Apparel | 0.2 | 0.1 | 0.6 | 0.4 | 0.6 | 0.5 | ..... | 0.1 | 0.1 | 0.1 |
| Lumber and wood products | ..... | ..... | ..... | 0.2 | ..... | ..... | ..... | ..... | ..... | ..... |
| Furniture and fixtures | 0.2 | 1.0 | 0.5 | 0.2 | 0.2 | ..... | 0.2 | 0.1 | 0.4 | 0.3 |
| Paper products | 0.1 | 0.3 | 0.1 | 0.1 | 0.1 | ..... | 0.2 | 0.1 | ..... | ..... |
| Printing and publishing | 0.3 | 0.4 | 0.8 | 0.6 | 1.0 | 0.7 | 0.1 | 0.3 | 0.2 | 0.3 |
| Chemical products | 4.4 | 1.5 | 2.8 | 3.1 | 2.0 | 0.8 | 0.4 | 0.6 | 3.0 | 1.7 |
| Refined petroleum products | ..... | ..... | ..... | ..... | ..... | ..... | ..... | ..... | ..... | ..... |
| Rubber and plastic products | 4.1 | 6.0 | 4.6 | 1.9 | 1.3 | 0.9 | 0.3 | 1.6 | 3.0 | 6.5 |
| Leather products | 0.3 | 0.2 | 0.3 | 0.2 | 0.3 | ..... | ..... | ..... | 0.2 | ..... |
| Stone, clay and glass products | 0.3 | 0.5 | 0.7 | 1.1 | 1.7 | 0.1 | 0.2 | 8.2 | 0.1 | 0.1 |
| Primary metals | 2.8 | 4.0 | 4.0 | 7.5 | 1.9 | 0.1 | 0.1 | 0.3 | 0.7 | 0.2 |
| Fabricated metal products | 2.6 | 5.8 | 20.6 | 35.2 | 14.2 | 1.6 | 3.3 | 6.1 | 4.9 | 8.0 |
| Industrial machinery and computers | 50.4 | 51.0 | 52.9 | 47.9 | 40.6 | 40.7 | 32.1 | 39.2 | 37.7 | 41.8 |
| Electric and electronic equipment | 45.3 | 51.9 | 82.2 | 86.9 | 92.3 | 65.6 | 82.9 | 101.4 | 82.6 | 109.0 |
| Transportation equipment | 98.9 | 163.0 | 144.0 | 143.2 | 194.9 | 27.8 | 24.9 | 56.2 | 107.1 | 127.4 |
| Scientific and measuring instruments | 38.1 | 44.6 | 62.4 | 47.8 | 39.0 | 49.7 | 55.3 | 65.1 | 71.6 | 75.8 |
| Miscellaneous manufactures | 2.9 | 3.3 | 2.8 | 3.0 | 2.6 | 0.4 | 0.4 | 0.3 | 0.8 | 0.8 |
| Unidentified manufactures | 0.9 | 0.7 | 0.7 | 0.5 | 0.5 | 0.3 | 0.5 | 0.6 | 0.4 | 0.5 |
| **Agricultural and livestock products** | 1.1 | 0.6 | 1.9 | 0.8 | 0.7 | 0.2 | 0.4 | 0.1 | 0.2 | 0.1 |
| Agricultural products | 1.1 | 0.6 | 1.9 | 0.8 | 0.7 | 0.2 | 0.4 | 0.1 | 0.2 | 0.1 |
| Livestock and livestock products | ..... | ..... | ..... | ..... | ..... | ..... | ..... | ..... | ..... | ..... |
| **Other commodities** | 24.1 | 13.0 | 27.2 | 11.1 | 19.3 | 3.8 | 4.7 | 4.9 | 11.2 | 9.1 |
| Forestry products | ..... | ..... | ..... | ..... | ..... | ..... | ..... | ..... | ..... | ..... |
| Fish and other marine products | ..... | ..... | ..... | ..... | ..... | ..... | ..... | ..... | 0.1 | ..... |
| Metallic ores and concentrates | 3.6 | 2.3 | 12.1 | 1.9 | ..... | ..... | ..... | ..... | ..... | ..... |
| Bituminous coal and lignite | ..... | ..... | ..... | ..... | ..... | ..... | ..... | ..... | ..... | ..... |
| Crude petroleum and natural gas | ..... | ..... | ..... | ..... | ..... | ..... | ..... | ..... | ..... | ..... |
| Nonmetallic minerals | 0.1 | 0.1 | 0.3 | ..... | ..... | ..... | ..... | ..... | ..... | ..... |
| Scrap and waste | ..... | ..... | 7.1 | 5.1 | 12.2 | ..... | ..... | ..... | ..... | ..... |
| Used merchandise | 0.7 | 1.9 | 1.6 | 0.3 | 0.8 | 1.1 | 0.3 | 0.2 | 0.1 | 1.1 |
| Goods imported and returned unchanged | ..... | ..... | ..... | ..... | ..... | ..... | ..... | ..... | ..... | ..... |
| Special classification provisions | 19.7 | 8.8 | 6.2 | 3.8 | 6.3 | 2.7 | 4.5 | 4.8 | 10.9 | 7.9 |
| | The Netherlands | | | | | Asian 10 | | | | |
| **ALL GOODS** | 99.1 | 134.1 | 291.1 | 558.5 | 1 454.6 | 2 265.1 | 2 859.9 | 3 437.2 | 4 451.6 | 5 975.8 |
| **Manufactured goods** | 90.2 | 114.8 | 212.8 | 541.8 | 1 407.0 | 2 184.8 | 2 774.7 | 3 312.4 | 4 352.3 | 5 895.7 |
| Food products | 0.2 | 1.0 | 1.2 | 1.7 | 1.8 | 3.4 | 4.2 | 6.3 | 7.9 | 13.7 |
| Tobacco products | ..... | ..... | ..... | ..... | ..... | ..... | ..... | ..... | ..... | ..... |
| Textile mill products | ..... | ..... | ..... | ..... | 0.3 | 0.4 | 1.3 | 2.5 | 1.4 | 8.0 |
| Apparel | ..... | ..... | 0.1 | 0.2 | 0.3 | 4.5 | 4.0 | 7.0 | 4.3 | 4.4 |
| Lumber and wood products | ..... | ..... | ..... | 0.1 | ..... | 0.1 | 0.1 | 0.3 | 0.8 | 1.1 |
| Furniture and fixtures | ..... | ..... | ..... | 0.4 | ..... | 0.4 | 0.2 | 1.0 | 1.3 | 0.8 |
| Paper products | 0.1 | 0.1 | 0.2 | 0.2 | 0.3 | 0.5 | 0.8 | 1.3 | 1.3 | 2.6 |
| Printing and publishing | 0.1 | 0.1 | 0.1 | 0.2 | 0.1 | 1.2 | 2.0 | 11.5 | 11.6 | 2.0 |
| Chemical products | 0.9 | 6.4 | 40.4 | 4.7 | 3.6 | 20.9 | 42.5 | 83.1 | 85.3 | 43.9 |
| Refined petroleum products | 0.1 | ..... | ..... | ..... | ..... | 0.1 | 0.1 | 0.2 | 0.2 | 12.8 |
| Rubber and plastic products | 0.1 | 0.2 | 0.2 | 0.9 | 0.3 | 12.9 | 19.8 | 12.7 | 18.6 | 13.9 |
| Leather products | ..... | ..... | ..... | ..... | ..... | 1.7 | 2.0 | 1.6 | 1.5 | 1.6 |
| Stone, clay and glass products | 0.1 | ..... | 0.2 | 0.1 | 5.8 | 3.6 | 5.8 | 4.2 | 8.3 | 5.0 |
| Primary metals | 0.5 | 0.9 | 1.8 | 0.8 | 0.3 | 195.4 | 177.0 | 253.5 | 263.8 | 85.3 |
| Fabricated metal products | 0.4 | 0.6 | 1.9 | 1.1 | 4.6 | 15.4 | 29.1 | 9.1 | 21.8 | 19.2 |
| Industrial machinery and computers | 26.1 | 22.6 | 24.3 | 23.8 | 733.9 | 148.0 | 169.6 | 230.7 | 317.6 | 1 162.4 |
| Electric and electronic equipment | 7.3 | 9.0 | 29.4 | 374.8 | 542.3 | 1 549.3 | 2 048.6 | 2 403.9 | 3 246.5 | 4 102.5 |
| Transportation equipment | 4.4 | 3.8 | 7.3 | 4.6 | 7.3 | 108.3 | 159.7 | 148.5 | 210.6 | 243.5 |
| Scientific and measuring instruments | 49.2 | 69.3 | 104.3 | 126.0 | 103.4 | 84.7 | 80.1 | 96.3 | 108.8 | 142.3 |
| Miscellaneous manufactures | 0.3 | 0.5 | 0.8 | 2.0 | 2.5 | 31.9 | 24.9 | 36.3 | 38.5 | 28.3 |
| Unidentified manufactures | 0.2 | 0.3 | 0.5 | 0.3 | 0.1 | 1.9 | 3.0 | 2.5 | 2.1 | 2.4 |
| **Agricultural and livestock products** | 0.3 | 0.7 | 2.3 | 4.6 | 7.5 | 36.6 | 52.2 | 65.0 | 43.7 | 49.9 |
| Agricultural products | 0.3 | 0.7 | 2.3 | 4.6 | 7.5 | 36.5 | 52.2 | 64.3 | 43.1 | 49.8 |
| Livestock and livestock products | ..... | ..... | ..... | ..... | ..... | ..... | ..... | 0.7 | 0.6 | 0.1 |
| **Other commodities** | 8.5 | 18.6 | 76.0 | 12.2 | 40.2 | 43.7 | 33.0 | 59.7 | 55.6 | 30.2 |
| Forestry products | ..... | ..... | ..... | ..... | ..... | 0.2 | 0.1 | ..... | 0.1 | ..... |
| Fish and other marine products | ..... | ..... | ..... | ..... | ..... | 0.4 | 0.4 | ..... | 0.2 | 0.2 |
| Metallic ores and concentrates | 8.3 | 18.2 | 74.8 | 11.3 | 39.0 | 35.7 | 19.2 | 44.4 | 35.1 | 8.6 |
| Bituminous coal and lignite | ..... | ..... | ..... | ..... | ..... | ..... | ..... | ..... | ..... | ..... |
| Crude petroleum and natural gas | ..... | ..... | ..... | ..... | ..... | ..... | ..... | ..... | ..... | ..... |
| Nonmetallic minerals | ..... | ..... | ..... | ..... | ..... | 0.4 | 2.6 | 4.6 | 3.6 | 1.8 |
| Scrap and waste | ..... | ..... | ..... | ..... | ..... | 1.5 | 2.7 | 3.5 | 2.8 | 5.7 |
| Used merchandise | ..... | ..... | ..... | 0.3 | 0.1 | 2.5 | 0.8 | 0.8 | 1.5 | 2.8 |
| Goods imported and returned unchanged | ..... | ..... | ..... | ..... | ..... | ..... | ..... | ..... | ..... | ..... |
| Special classification provisions | 0.2 | 0.3 | 1.1 | 0.6 | 1.1 | 2.9 | 7.1 | 6.4 | 12.4 | 11.0 |

## Table D-3.   State Exports of Goods by Destination and Industry, 1993–1997 —*Continued*

**ARIZONA** (Millions of dollars.)

| Industry | 1993 | 1994 | 1995 | 1996 | 1997 | 1993 | 1994 | 1995 | 1996 | 1997 |
|---|---|---|---|---|---|---|---|---|---|---|
| | Japan | | | | | South Korea | | | | |
| **ALL GOODS** | 666.7 | 808.3 | 1 125.5 | 1 356.2 | 1 806.4 | 177.5 | 206.2 | 230.2 | 287.8 | 296.9 |
| **Manufactured goods** | 618.2 | 777.0 | 1 069.4 | 1 326.9 | 1 785.4 | 157.4 | 185.5 | 202.8 | 268.0 | 282.5 |
| Food products | 0.7 | 1.0 | 2.2 | 2.1 | 5.8 | 1.2 | 1.0 | 1.4 | 2.5 | 2.1 |
| Tobacco products | ..... | ..... | ..... | ..... | ..... | ..... | ..... | ..... | ..... | ..... |
| Textile mill products | ..... | 0.5 | 0.3 | 0.5 | 2.1 | ..... | ..... | 0.1 | 0.2 | 0.2 |
| Apparel | 4.0 | 3.2 | 4.5 | 3.6 | 3.6 | ..... | 0.4 | 2.1 | 0.1 | 0.1 |
| Lumber and wood products | ..... | 0.1 | 0.2 | 0.6 | 0.7 | ..... | ..... | ..... | 0.1 | ..... |
| Furniture and fixtures | ..... | 0.1 | 0.7 | 1.1 | 0.2 | 0.2 | 0.1 | 0.1 | 0.1 | 0.1 |
| Paper products | ..... | 0.1 | 0.2 | 0.2 | 0.3 | 0.1 | 0.1 | 0.2 | 0.2 | 0.3 |
| Printing and publishing | 0.3 | 0.8 | 0.8 | 0.6 | 0.6 | 0.1 | 0.1 | 0.1 | 0.1 | 0.1 |
| Chemical products | 13.7 | 36.2 | 73.4 | 72.0 | 23.7 | 1.0 | 1.3 | 3.5 | 3.2 | 2.8 |
| Refined petroleum products | ..... | ..... | ..... | ..... | 0.8 | ..... | ..... | ..... | ..... | 1.0 |
| Rubber and plastic products | 1.4 | 1.0 | 1.4 | 2.3 | 1.9 | 0.8 | 3.7 | 6.2 | 12.1 | 3.4 |
| Leather products | 1.4 | 1.6 | 1.3 | 0.6 | 0.5 | ..... | ..... | ..... | 0.6 | 0.6 |
| Stone, clay and glass products | 1.9 | 1.7 | 2.1 | 1.6 | 2.3 | 0.1 | ..... | 0.5 | 0.3 | 0.2 |
| Primary metals | 74.0 | 74.8 | 101.4 | 74.1 | 12.4 | 8.6 | 2.5 | 13.3 | 10.1 | 15.5 |
| Fabricated metal products | 0.6 | 0.9 | 2.0 | 11.7 | 4.4 | 0.3 | 0.5 | 0.3 | 0.3 | 0.4 |
| Industrial machinery and computers | 47.3 | 48.5 | 78.0 | 92.6 | 423.9 | 13.2 | 16.7 | 27.4 | 33.5 | 73.5 |
| Electric and electronic equipment | 424.1 | 555.8 | 745.7 | 987.0 | 1 225.9 | 118.2 | 140.8 | 126.9 | 172.8 | 147.6 |
| Transportation equipment | 4.4 | 12.6 | 13.9 | 17.5 | 17.2 | 4.3 | 7.9 | 4.2 | 14.7 | 15.8 |
| Scientific and measuring instruments | 20.1 | 20.2 | 23.3 | 31.3 | 38.2 | 8.2 | 8.5 | 12.4 | 13.9 | 17.0 |
| Miscellaneous manufactures | 23.6 | 17.2 | 17.5 | 26.7 | 20.5 | 0.9 | 1.7 | 3.9 | 3.0 | 1.6 |
| Unidentified manufactures | 0.6 | 0.7 | 0.6 | 0.6 | 0.4 | 0.2 | 0.1 | 0.3 | 0.2 | 0.3 |
| **Agricultural and livestock products** | 10.2 | 7.7 | 5.4 | 4.7 | 4.9 | 18.9 | 18.1 | 24.7 | 17.8 | 9.3 |
| Agricultural products | 10.2 | 7.6 | 5.4 | 4.2 | 4.8 | 18.9 | 18.1 | 24.7 | 17.8 | 9.3 |
| Livestock and livestock products | ..... | ..... | ..... | 0.5 | 0.1 | ..... | ..... | ..... | ..... | ..... |
| **Other commodities** | 38.3 | 23.6 | 50.7 | 24.6 | 16.1 | 1.2 | 2.6 | 2.7 | 2.0 | 5.0 |
| Forestry products | ..... | ..... | ..... | ..... | ..... | 0.1 | 0.1 | ..... | ..... | ..... |
| Fish and other marine products | 0.4 | 0.4 | ..... | ..... | 0.1 | ..... | ..... | ..... | ..... | ..... |
| Metallic ores and concentrates | 35.7 | 19.2 | 44.4 | 18.6 | 8.6 | ..... | ..... | ..... | ..... | ..... |
| Bituminous coal and lignite | ..... | ..... | ..... | ..... | ..... | ..... | ..... | ..... | ..... | ..... |
| Crude petroleum and natural gas | ..... | ..... | ..... | ..... | ..... | ..... | ..... | ..... | ..... | ..... |
| Nonmetallic minerals | 0.3 | 2.5 | 4.4 | 3.1 | 1.4 | ..... | 0.1 | 0.1 | 0.1 | ..... |
| Scrap and waste | 0.3 | ..... | ..... | 0.3 | 0.8 | 1.0 | 2.3 | 2.4 | 1.7 | 4.2 |
| Used merchandise | 1.4 | 0.5 | 0.6 | 0.6 | 1.7 | ..... | ..... | ..... | ..... | ..... |
| Goods imported and returned unchanged | ..... | ..... | ..... | ..... | ..... | ..... | ..... | ..... | ..... | ..... |
| Special classification provisions | 0.3 | 0.9 | 1.3 | 1.9 | 3.7 | 0.1 | 0.1 | 0.1 | 0.3 | 0.8 |

| Industry | 1993 | 1994 | 1995 | 1996 | 1997 | 1993 | 1994 | 1995 | 1996 | 1997 |
|---|---|---|---|---|---|---|---|---|---|---|
| | Taiwan | | | | | Singapore | | | | |
| **ALL GOODS** | 477.1 | 604.3 | 648.2 | 895.4 | 1 062.8 | 248.9 | 351.4 | 302.8 | 364.6 | 473.2 |
| **Manufactured goods** | 474.4 | 598.4 | 639.9 | 888.0 | 1 054.8 | 247.3 | 348.8 | 300.8 | 359.9 | 470.1 |
| Food products | ..... | 0.1 | 0.4 | 0.9 | 1.6 | 1.0 | 1.5 | 1.4 | 1.1 | 1.1 |
| Tobacco products | ..... | ..... | ..... | ..... | ..... | ..... | ..... | ..... | ..... | ..... |
| Textile mill products | ..... | ..... | 0.1 | ..... | ..... | ..... | ..... | 0.2 | 0.1 | 0.1 |
| Apparel | ..... | 0.1 | ..... | ..... | ..... | ..... | ..... | ..... | 0.1 | 0.2 |
| Lumber and wood products | ..... | ..... | 0.1 | ..... | 0.1 | 0.1 | ..... | ..... | 0.1 | ..... |
| Furniture and fixtures | ..... | ..... | ..... | ..... | ..... | 0.1 | ..... | 0.2 | ..... | ..... |
| Paper products | ..... | 0.1 | 0.1 | 0.1 | 0.1 | ..... | 0.1 | 0.2 | 0.1 | 0.3 |
| Printing and publishing | ..... | 0.1 | 0.1 | 0.2 | 0.1 | 0.1 | 0.1 | 0.2 | 0.9 | 0.1 |
| Chemical products | 1.5 | 1.5 | 1.7 | 1.1 | 2.0 | 1.4 | 1.2 | 2.3 | 4.3 | 6.0 |
| Refined petroleum products | ..... | ..... | ..... | 0.1 | ..... | ..... | ..... | ..... | 0.1 | 8.0 |
| Rubber and plastic products | 0.3 | 0.3 | 0.7 | 0.3 | 0.5 | 2.6 | 2.1 | 2.2 | 1.6 | 1.5 |
| Leather products | ..... | ..... | ..... | ..... | 0.1 | 0.1 | 0.1 | ..... | 0.1 | 0.2 |
| Stone, clay and glass products | 0.3 | 1.6 | 0.7 | 5.2 | ..... | 0.1 | 1.9 | 0.5 | 0.3 | 0.2 |
| Primary metals | 75.1 | 63.0 | 72.5 | 95.1 | 32.3 | 2.5 | 1.1 | 28.4 | 8.1 | 6.7 |
| Fabricated metal products | 11.3 | 24.3 | 1.0 | 1.0 | 6.6 | 0.8 | 2.1 | 2.9 | 3.0 | 2.3 |
| Industrial machinery and computers | 20.3 | 24.6 | 24.6 | 26.6 | 151.1 | 13.6 | 12.8 | 17.7 | 24.0 | 126.5 |
| Electric and electronic equipment | 310.1 | 396.0 | 463.6 | 663.5 | 761.7 | 183.8 | 278.9 | 190.4 | 236.2 | 218.0 |
| Transportation equipment | 42.1 | 71.7 | 62.2 | 85.1 | 85.4 | 33.6 | 39.4 | 45.5 | 67.2 | 83.3 |
| Scientific and measuring instruments | 12.7 | 14.3 | 10.9 | 8.2 | 11.8 | 5.9 | 5.4 | 7.0 | 10.3 | 14.4 |
| Miscellaneous manufactures | 0.2 | 0.3 | 0.8 | 0.3 | 0.8 | 1.4 | 1.4 | 1.3 | 2.1 | 1.2 |
| Unidentified manufactures | 0.4 | 0.4 | 0.3 | 0.3 | 0.2 | 0.2 | 0.7 | 0.5 | 0.2 | 0.2 |
| **Agricultural and livestock products** | 2.1 | 3.4 | 5.7 | 5.1 | 5.2 | 0.1 | 0.1 | ..... | ..... | ..... |
| Agricultural products | 2.1 | 3.4 | 5.7 | 5.1 | 5.2 | 0.1 | 0.1 | ..... | ..... | ..... |
| Livestock and livestock products | ..... | ..... | ..... | ..... | ..... | ..... | ..... | ..... | ..... | ..... |
| **Other commodities** | 0.6 | 2.5 | 2.7 | 2.2 | 2.8 | 1.5 | 2.5 | 2.0 | 4.7 | 3.1 |
| Forestry products | ..... | ..... | ..... | ..... | ..... | 0.1 | ..... | ..... | ..... | ..... |
| Fish and other marine products | ..... | ..... | ..... | ..... | ..... | ..... | ..... | ..... | ..... | ..... |
| Metallic ores and concentrates | ..... | ..... | ..... | ..... | ..... | ..... | ..... | ..... | ..... | ..... |
| Bituminous coal and lignite | ..... | ..... | ..... | ..... | ..... | ..... | ..... | ..... | ..... | ..... |
| Crude petroleum and natural gas | ..... | ..... | ..... | ..... | ..... | ..... | ..... | ..... | ..... | ..... |
| Nonmetallic minerals | 0.1 | ..... | ..... | 0.3 | 0.3 | ..... | ..... | ..... | ..... | ..... |
| Scrap and waste | ..... | ..... | 0.1 | 0.4 | ..... | ..... | ..... | ..... | ..... | ..... |
| Used merchandise | ..... | 0.1 | ..... | 0.2 | 0.5 | 0.1 | ..... | ..... | 0.4 | 0.3 |
| Goods imported and returned unchanged | ..... | ..... | ..... | ..... | ..... | ..... | ..... | ..... | ..... | ..... |
| Special classification provisions | 0.5 | 2.4 | 2.5 | 1.3 | 1.9 | 1.3 | 2.5 | 2.0 | 4.3 | 2.8 |

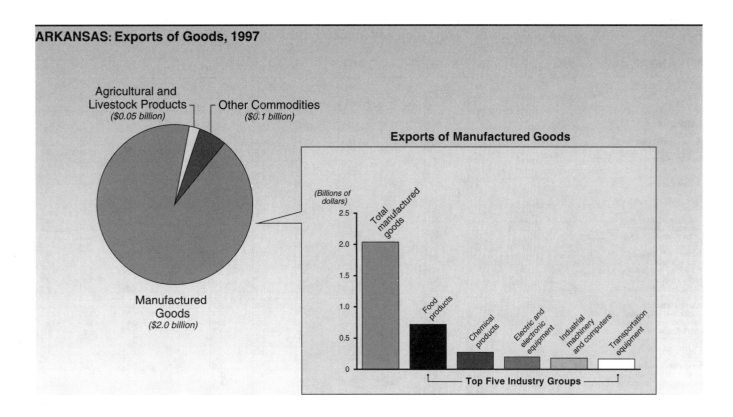

**ARKANSAS: Exports of Goods, 1997**

Agricultural and Livestock Products ($0.05 billion)

Other Commodities ($0.1 billion)

Manufactured Goods ($2.0 billion)

Exports of Manufactured Goods

(Billions of dollars)

Top Five Industry Groups

## Table D-3.   State Exports of Goods by Destination and Industry, 1993–1997 —*Continued*

**ARKANSAS** (Millions of dollars.)

| Industry | 1993 | 1994 | 1995 | 1996 | 1997 | 1993 | 1994 | 1995 | 1996 | 1997 |
|---|---|---|---|---|---|---|---|---|---|---|
| | All destinations | | | | | Canada | | | | |
| **ALL GOODS** | 1 109.8 | 1 470.9 | 1 794.4 | 1 997.2 | 2 211.6 | 421.1 | 521.1 | 574.1 | 614.9 | 820.4 |
| **Manufactured goods** | 1 052.6 | 1 409.9 | 1 715.5 | 1 903.3 | 2 036.5 | 392.5 | 497.1 | 554.0 | 591.6 | 710.4 |
| Food products | 304.6 | 486.8 | 673.6 | 811.9 | 718.3 | 55.6 | 44.9 | 51.9 | 53.1 | 58.4 |
| Tobacco products | ..... | ..... | ..... | ..... | ..... | | | | | |
| Textile mill products | 6.6 | 9.8 | 9.6 | 11.0 | 8.7 | 5.4 | 7.1 | 7.3 | 8.9 | 5.3 |
| Apparel | 3.7 | 3.8 | 6.1 | 4.9 | 2.1 | 2.0 | 2.1 | 1.8 | 1.0 | 0.7 |
| Lumber and wood products | 9.4 | 6.2 | 7.5 | 8.7 | 11.6 | 6.8 | 4.0 | 5.4 | 6.5 | 8.8 |
| Furniture and fixtures | 16.3 | 31.6 | 19.9 | 19.5 | 22.2 | 12.4 | 28.6 | 12.8 | 14.9 | 14.4 |
| Paper products | 22.0 | 32.4 | 43.3 | 40.0 | 32.4 | 15.0 | 20.1 | 18.1 | 24.1 | 20.5 |
| Printing and publishing | 5.7 | 8.7 | 43.0 | 43.3 | 40.8 | 4.0 | 6.6 | 40.8 | 41.2 | 38.6 |
| Chemical products | 185.0 | 202.3 | 247.7 | 228.4 | 273.7 | 33.7 | 33.9 | 52.3 | 39.1 | 37.0 |
| Refined petroleum products | 2.4 | 3.1 | 2.7 | 2.9 | 3.3 | 2.1 | 1.8 | 2.3 | 2.4 | 2.6 |
| Rubber and plastic products | 23.5 | 32.7 | 33.1 | 33.9 | 44.3 | 16.5 | 21.5 | 24.4 | 25.2 | 28.0 |
| Leather products | 2.8 | 3.3 | 7.1 | 9.7 | 13.5 | 1.3 | 1.2 | 1.3 | 0.5 | 0.9 |
| Stone, clay and glass products | 8.2 | 7.7 | 9.9 | 10.4 | 9.6 | 2.0 | 1.5 | 1.8 | 1.8 | 1.5 |
| Primary metals | 20.1 | 63.4 | 61.1 | 98.1 | 164.6 | 17.0 | 54.1 | 36.1 | 70.1 | 136.8 |
| Fabricated metal products | 55.0 | 63.5 | 69.6 | 69.2 | 78.2 | 34.2 | 39.7 | 35.1 | 41.1 | 47.3 |
| Industrial machinery and computers | 122.2 | 152.4 | 172.5 | 168.1 | 181.6 | 49.3 | 72.7 | 77.7 | 78.5 | 83.1 |
| Electric and electronic equipment | 110.4 | 137.2 | 155.4 | 168.0 | 199.7 | 85.3 | 93.8 | 105.7 | 96.6 | 107.7 |
| Transportation equipment | 104.3 | 100.5 | 101.9 | 123.9 | 168.6 | 36.9 | 49.8 | 64.8 | 73.1 | 102.1 |
| Scientific and measuring instruments | 33.7 | 47.9 | 31.8 | 34.9 | 44.7 | 6.6 | 7.5 | 7.4 | 7.4 | 9.4 |
| Miscellaneous manufactures | 14.4 | 13.8 | 15.6 | 13.4 | 14.4 | 5.4 | 5.2 | 5.4 | 5.1 | 6.2 |
| Unidentified manufactures | 2.2 | 2.9 | 4.3 | 3.1 | 4.2 | 0.7 | 1.1 | 1.4 | 1.0 | 1.4 |
| **Agricultural and livestock products** | 31.3 | 42.3 | 39.1 | 42.2 | 45.7 | 13.8 | 17.4 | 10.9 | 14.8 | 17.6 |
| Agricultural products | 7.8 | 16.1 | 7.8 | 6.4 | 3.8 | 2.3 | 2.4 | 1.3 | 1.8 | 1.3 |
| Livestock and livestock products | 23.5 | 26.3 | 31.3 | 35.8 | 41.9 | 11.4 | 15.0 | 9.6 | 13.0 | 16.3 |
| **Other commodities** | 25.8 | 18.6 | 39.9 | 51.7 | 129.4 | 14.9 | 6.6 | 9.3 | 8.4 | 92.5 |
| Forestry products | ..... | ..... | ..... | ..... | ..... | ..... | ..... | ..... | ..... | |
| Fish and other marine products | 3.0 | 5.6 | 16.2 | 33.1 | 24.3 | 1.3 | 1.4 | 0.9 | 0.3 | 0.1 |
| Metallic ores and concentrates | 0.9 | 0.3 | 0.2 | 0.3 | 0.1 | 0.4 | ..... | ..... | 0.1 | ..... |
| Bituminous coal and lignite | 6.8 | 5.0 | 4.4 | 3.3 | 2.9 | ..... | ..... | ..... | ..... | ..... |
| Crude petroleum and natural gas | 0.2 | ..... | ..... | 0.2 | 79.5 | ..... | ..... | ..... | ..... | 79.5 |
| Nonmetallic minerals | 1.5 | 1.6 | 2.2 | 1.6 | 2.2 | 0.8 | 0.9 | 0.4 | 0.2 | 0.2 |
| Scrap and waste | 1.3 | 1.6 | 2.4 | 1.7 | 1.8 | 0.8 | 1.0 | 1.4 | 0.6 | 1.2 |
| Used merchandise | 0.4 | 0.8 | 0.8 | 0.7 | 0.7 | 0.1 | 0.1 | 0.3 | 0.2 | 0.2 |
| Goods imported and returned unchanged | 11.2 | 2.7 | 5.8 | 6.0 | 8.9 | 11.2 | 2.7 | 5.8 | 6.0 | 8.9 |
| Special classification provisions | 0.5 | 0.9 | 7.9 | 4.8 | 8.9 | 0.3 | 0.4 | 0.4 | 1.0 | 2.3 |

## Table D-3.  State Exports of Goods by Destination and Industry, 1993–1997 —*Continued*

**ARKANSAS** (Millions of dollars.)

| Industry | 1993 | 1994 | 1995 | 1996 | 1997 | 1993 | 1994 | 1995 | 1996 | 1997 |
|---|---|---|---|---|---|---|---|---|---|---|
| | South and Central America and Caribbean | | | | | Mexico | | | | |
| **ALL GOODS** | 38.6 | 41.6 | 80.1 | 75.7 | 84.6 | 68.8 | 94.2 | 59.8 | 102.2 | 140.8 |
| **Manufactured goods** | 33.9 | 37.8 | 71.1 | 67.8 | 76.5 | 63.8 | 85.4 | 46.4 | 90.5 | 121.9 |
| Food products | 9.8 | 11.7 | 15.5 | 13.8 | 15.0 | 6.0 | 6.4 | 5.3 | 10.3 | 10.5 |
| Tobacco products | ..... | ..... | ..... | ..... | ..... | ..... | ..... | ..... | ..... | ..... |
| Textile mill products | 0.1 | 1.5 | 1.4 | 0.5 | 0.2 | 0.6 | 0.4 | 0.3 | 0.7 | 1.6 |
| Apparel | 0.1 | 0.5 | 2.0 | 1.0 | 0.5 | 0.4 | 0.2 | 0.8 | 1.7 | 0.1 |
| Lumber and wood products | ..... | 0.1 | 0.1 | 0.4 | 0.2 | 0.3 | 0.3 | 0.1 | 0.1 | 0.3 |
| Furniture and fixtures | 0.3 | 0.3 | 3.2 | 2.2 | 3.3 | 0.8 | 0.5 | 0.2 | 0.2 | 0.6 |
| Paper products | 0.3 | 0.6 | 0.6 | 1.2 | 0.3 | 2.1 | 5.9 | 3.7 | 6.2 | 5.1 |
| Printing and publishing | 0.1 | 0.1 | 0.2 | 0.1 | 0.2 | 0.4 | 0.5 | 0.1 | 0.2 | 0.3 |
| Chemical products | 4.9 | 6.3 | 7.1 | 9.4 | 12.5 | 2.1 | 6.1 | 5.2 | 5.3 | 10.8 |
| Refined petroleum products | 0.1 | ..... | 0.1 | ..... | 0.1 | 0.1 | 0.1 | ..... | 0.2 | 0.4 |
| Rubber and plastic products | 0.6 | 0.6 | 1.4 | 1.5 | 5.1 | 1.3 | 2.4 | 0.9 | 1.1 | 1.6 |
| Leather products | ..... | ..... | 0.3 | 0.1 | 0.1 | 0.9 | 1.2 | 4.9 | 7.8 | 11.0 |
| Stone, clay and glass products | 0.1 | ..... | 0.2 | 0.7 | 0.6 | 0.2 | 0.6 | 0.3 | 0.4 | 1.2 |
| Primary metals | 0.3 | 0.6 | 2.7 | 8.4 | 8.3 | 1.8 | 4.2 | 7.1 | 7.4 | 9.8 |
| Fabricated metal products | 2.2 | 2.2 | 3.2 | 2.9 | 2.4 | 1.6 | 3.7 | 2.2 | 2.4 | 2.9 |
| Industrial machinery and computers | 7.4 | 5.2 | 15.4 | 11.4 | 11.5 | 9.7 | 16.6 | 4.2 | 5.9 | 10.0 |
| Electric and electronic equipment | 3.1 | 3.9 | 10.8 | 9.2 | 8.3 | 4.7 | 9.3 | 5.0 | 27.7 | 40.1 |
| Transportation equipment | 2.2 | 1.3 | 1.0 | 0.7 | 3.5 | 26.6 | 21.8 | 2.5 | 10.6 | 12.6 |
| Scientific and measuring instruments | 0.9 | 1.3 | 2.2 | 1.6 | 1.9 | 1.9 | 3.2 | 1.5 | 0.5 | 1.2 |
| Miscellaneous manufactures | 1.2 | 1.1 | 2.6 | 1.4 | 1.4 | 2.0 | 1.8 | 2.0 | 1.6 | 1.6 |
| Unidentified manufactures | 0.1 | 0.3 | 1.3 | 1.1 | 1.3 | 0.2 | 0.3 | 0.1 | 0.2 | 0.2 |
| **Agricultural and livestock products** | 4.4 | 3.9 | 8.9 | 7.7 | 7.8 | 4.8 | 8.1 | 6.1 | 7.9 | 12.4 |
| Agricultural products | 0.1 | ..... | ..... | ..... | 0.2 | 2.4 | 5.9 | 1.3 | 0.7 | 0.3 |
| Livestock and livestock products | 4.3 | 3.9 | 8.9 | 7.7 | 7.5 | 2.4 | 2.2 | 4.8 | 7.2 | 12.2 |
| **Other commodities** | 0.3 | 0.1 | 0.1 | 0.1 | 0.3 | 0.2 | 0.6 | 7.3 | 3.9 | 6.5 |
| Forestry products | ..... | ..... | ..... | ..... | ..... | ..... | ..... | ..... | ..... | ..... |
| Fish and other marine products | ..... | ..... | ..... | ..... | ..... | ..... | ..... | ..... | ..... | ..... |
| Metallic ores and concentrates | ..... | ..... | ..... | ..... | ..... | 0.1 | 0.2 | ..... | ..... | ..... |
| Bituminous coal and lignite | ..... | ..... | ..... | ..... | ..... | ..... | ..... | ..... | ..... | ..... |
| Crude petroleum and natural gas | 0.2 | ..... | ..... | ..... | ..... | ..... | ..... | ..... | ..... | ..... |
| Nonmetallic minerals | 0.1 | ..... | ..... | ..... | ..... | ..... | 0.1 | 0.1 | 0.1 | 0.1 |
| Scrap and waste | ..... | ..... | ..... | ..... | ..... | ..... | ..... | ..... | 0.3 | ..... |
| Used merchandise | ..... | ..... | ..... | ..... | 0.3 | 0.1 | ..... | 0.1 | ..... | ..... |
| Goods imported and returned unchanged | ..... | ..... | ..... | ..... | ..... | ..... | ..... | ..... | ..... | ..... |
| Special classification provisions | ..... | ..... | ..... | ..... | ..... | ..... | 0.4 | 7.2 | 3.5 | 6.3 |
| | European Union | | | | | United Kingdom | | | | |
| **ALL GOODS** | 182.6 | 185.8 | 258.3 | 268.6 | 302.9 | 65.6 | 64.4 | 76.2 | 74.5 | 84.8 |
| **Manufactured goods** | 172.6 | 178.5 | 249.0 | 260.3 | 297.2 | 60.9 | 60.4 | 71.5 | 71.6 | 82.0 |
| Food products | 42.5 | 58.3 | 42.4 | 70.1 | 68.8 | 19.1 | 19.1 | 15.6 | 27.0 | 27.0 |
| Tobacco products | ..... | ..... | ..... | ..... | ..... | ..... | ..... | ..... | ..... | ..... |
| Textile mill products | 0.3 | 0.4 | 0.3 | 0.2 | 1.2 | ..... | 0.1 | ..... | 0.1 | ..... |
| Apparel | 0.6 | 0.3 | 0.5 | 0.3 | 0.3 | 0.1 | 0.1 | 0.1 | ..... | ..... |
| Lumber and wood products | 0.9 | 1.1 | 0.9 | 1.0 | 1.5 | 0.3 | 0.2 | 0.4 | 0.2 | 0.2 |
| Furniture and fixtures | 0.9 | 0.7 | 1.9 | 1.0 | 1.2 | 0.3 | 0.3 | 0.5 | 0.5 | 0.8 |
| Paper products | 1.9 | 4.0 | 19.9 | 7.2 | 5.9 | 0.6 | 1.3 | 2.5 | 0.3 | 0.8 |
| Printing and publishing | 0.6 | 0.5 | 0.7 | 0.6 | 0.9 | 0.3 | 0.3 | 0.5 | 0.4 | 0.5 |
| Chemical products | 40.8 | 41.3 | 77.7 | 74.0 | 88.3 | 9.7 | 11.8 | 23.7 | 16.4 | 20.6 |
| Refined petroleum products | ..... | 0.4 | 0.2 | 0.3 | 0.1 | ..... | ..... | 0.1 | 0.1 | ..... |
| Rubber and plastic products | 1.5 | 1.7 | 3.5 | 2.8 | 4.7 | 1.2 | 0.6 | 1.1 | 0.5 | 1.2 |
| Leather products | ..... | 0.1 | 0.2 | 0.8 | 1.3 | ..... | ..... | ..... | ..... | ..... |
| Stone, clay and glass products | 4.3 | 3.6 | 5.1 | 5.0 | 4.7 | 0.9 | 0.4 | 0.7 | 0.9 | 1.1 |
| Primary metals | 0.6 | 2.4 | 9.6 | 4.0 | 5.2 | 0.4 | 1.3 | 2.8 | 1.4 | 1.5 |
| Fabricated metal products | 7.5 | 8.7 | 18.0 | 14.3 | 16.2 | 3.0 | 4.1 | 5.0 | 5.6 | 5.4 |
| Industrial machinery and computers | 27.3 | 23.5 | 32.4 | 29.8 | 31.4 | 6.4 | 7.2 | 9.5 | 9.5 | 9.6 |
| Electric and electronic equipment | 5.2 | 9.8 | 13.1 | 18.0 | 24.2 | 1.9 | 3.2 | 3.0 | 3.2 | 7.4 |
| Transportation equipment | 28.7 | 15.7 | 16.8 | 23.8 | 32.9 | 15.2 | 8.8 | 5.0 | 3.6 | 3.0 |
| Scientific and measuring instruments | 6.1 | 3.3 | 3.2 | 4.9 | 6.3 | 0.7 | 0.9 | 0.5 | 1.1 | 1.9 |
| Miscellaneous manufactures | 2.5 | 2.4 | 2.0 | 2.0 | 2.0 | 0.6 | 0.5 | 0.4 | 0.4 | 0.6 |
| Unidentified manufactures | 0.4 | 0.5 | 0.6 | 0.4 | 0.4 | 0.2 | 0.2 | 0.2 | 0.1 | 0.2 |
| **Agricultural and livestock products** | 2.2 | 1.3 | 2.9 | 2.3 | 0.6 | ..... | 0.1 | 0.2 | 0.1 | 0.2 |
| Agricultural products | 0.1 | 0.2 | 2.2 | 1.6 | 0.2 | ..... | 0.1 | 0.2 | ..... | ..... |
| Livestock and livestock products | 2.1 | 1.1 | 0.7 | 0.7 | 0.5 | ..... | ..... | ..... | 0.1 | 0.2 |
| **Other commodities** | 7.8 | 6.0 | 6.5 | 5.9 | 5.1 | 4.6 | 3.9 | 4.5 | 2.8 | 2.6 |
| Forestry products | ..... | ..... | ..... | ..... | ..... | ..... | ..... | ..... | ..... | ..... |
| Fish and other marine products | ..... | ..... | ..... | 0.4 | 0.1 | ..... | ..... | ..... | ..... | ..... |
| Metallic ores and concentrates | 0.2 | 0.2 | 0.1 | 0.1 | ..... | ..... | ..... | ..... | ..... | ..... |
| Bituminous coal and lignite | 6.8 | 5.0 | 4.4 | 3.3 | 2.9 | 4.6 | 3.9 | 4.4 | 1.8 | 1.1 |
| Crude petroleum and natural gas | ..... | ..... | ..... | 0.2 | ..... | ..... | ..... | ..... | ..... | ..... |
| Nonmetallic minerals | 0.2 | 0.1 | 0.7 | 0.9 | 1.5 | ..... | ..... | ..... | 0.7 | 1.4 |
| Scrap and waste | 0.4 | 0.6 | 0.7 | 0.8 | 0.4 | ..... | ..... | ..... | ..... | ..... |
| Used merchandise | ..... | 0.1 | 0.4 | 0.1 | 0.1 | ..... | ..... | ..... | 0.1 | 0.1 |
| Goods imported and returned unchanged | ..... | ..... | ..... | ..... | ..... | ..... | ..... | ..... | ..... | ..... |
| Special classification provisions | 0.1 | ..... | 0.1 | 0.2 | ..... | ..... | ..... | ..... | 0.2 | ..... |

## Table D-3. State Exports of Goods by Destination and Industry, 1993–1997 —Continued

**ARKANSAS** (Millions of dollars.)

| Industry | 1993 | 1994 | 1995 | 1996 | 1997 | 1993 | 1994 | 1995 | 1996 | 1997 |
|---|---|---|---|---|---|---|---|---|---|---|
| | Germany | | | | | France | | | | |
| **ALL GOODS** | 21.8 | 24.4 | 34.0 | 43.3 | 45.4 | 19.8 | 13.0 | 20.3 | 30.8 | 45.8 |
| **Manufactured goods** | 21.6 | 24.2 | 33.7 | 41.4 | 45.2 | 19.3 | 12.3 | 19.5 | 30.0 | 45.3 |
| Food products | 8.5 | 10.2 | 6.4 | 14.3 | 20.8 | 1.8 | 1.9 | 2.1 | 3.5 | 6.5 |
| Tobacco products | ..... | ..... | ..... | ..... | ..... | ..... | ..... | ..... | ..... | ..... |
| Textile mill products | 0.1 | ..... | ..... | ..... | ..... | ..... | ..... | 0.2 | ..... | 0.1 |
| Apparel | 0.2 | 0.1 | 0.1 | ..... | 0.1 | ..... | ..... | 0.1 | ..... | ..... |
| Lumber and wood products | 0.2 | 0.3 | 0.3 | 0.4 | 1.0 | 0.3 | 0.2 | 0.2 | 0.2 | 0.2 |
| Furniture and fixtures | 0.2 | 0.2 | ..... | 0.1 | ..... | 0.1 | 0.1 | 0.1 | 0.2 | 0.2 |
| Paper products | 0.1 | ..... | ..... | ..... | ..... | 0.3 | ..... | 1.7 | 2.7 | 3.0 |
| Printing and publishing | ..... | 0.1 | ..... | 0.1 | ..... | ..... | 0.1 | 0.1 | ..... | ..... |
| Chemical products | 2.3 | 1.7 | 2.6 | 0.9 | 1.7 | 1.2 | 0.7 | 0.7 | 0.8 | 1.6 |
| Refined petroleum products | ..... | ..... | ..... | ..... | ..... | ..... | 0.2 | 0.1 | ..... | ..... |
| Rubber and plastic products | 0.1 | 0.1 | 0.2 | 0.1 | 0.3 | 0.1 | 0.6 | 0.5 | 0.4 | 0.4 |
| Leather products | ..... | 0.1 | ..... | ..... | ..... | ..... | ..... | ..... | ..... | ..... |
| Stone, clay and glass products | 1.8 | 0.9 | 1.7 | 0.5 | 0.8 | 0.2 | 0.3 | 0.3 | 0.5 | 0.5 |
| Primary metals | 0.2 | 0.6 | 5.7 | 1.2 | 2.6 | ..... | ..... | ..... | 0.1 | ..... |
| Fabricated metal products | 2.9 | 1.6 | 4.2 | 1.5 | 1.7 | 0.3 | 0.7 | 3.6 | 3.0 | 6.9 |
| Industrial machinery and computers | 1.9 | 3.6 | 3.9 | 7.3 | 4.4 | 2.1 | 1.0 | 3.3 | 2.2 | 2.6 |
| Electric and electronic equipment | 0.8 | 3.3 | 6.3 | 11.9 | 6.4 | 0.4 | 0.6 | 0.4 | 0.8 | 2.5 |
| Transportation equipment | 0.3 | 0.4 | 1.0 | 2.2 | 4.7 | 12.0 | 5.4 | 5.5 | 14.2 | 18.5 |
| Scientific and measuring instruments | 1.7 | 1.0 | 0.3 | 0.6 | 0.3 | 0.5 | 0.3 | 0.7 | 1.2 | 2.0 |
| Miscellaneous manufactures | 0.2 | 0.1 | 0.8 | 0.2 | 0.3 | 0.1 | 0.2 | 0.1 | ..... | 0.2 |
| Unidentified manufactures | 0.1 | 0.1 | 0.1 | 0.1 | 0.1 | ..... | ..... | ..... | ..... | ..... |
| **Agricultural and livestock products** | ..... | 0.1 | 0.2 | 1.5 | ..... | ..... | ..... | 0.1 | ..... | 0.1 |
| Agricultural products | ..... | 0.1 | 0.2 | 1.4 | ..... | ..... | ..... | 0.1 | ..... | ..... |
| Livestock and livestock products | ..... | ..... | ..... | 0.1 | ..... | ..... | ..... | ..... | ..... | 0.1 |
| **Other commodities** | 0.2 | 0.1 | 0.1 | 0.4 | 0.2 | 0.5 | 0.6 | 0.8 | 0.8 | 0.4 |
| Forestry products | ..... | ..... | ..... | ..... | ..... | ..... | ..... | ..... | ..... | ..... |
| Fish and other marine products | ..... | ..... | ..... | 0.3 | 0.1 | ..... | ..... | ..... | ..... | ..... |
| Metallic ores and concentrates | ..... | ..... | ..... | ..... | ..... | ..... | 0.1 | ..... | ..... | ..... |
| Bituminous coal and lignite | ..... | ..... | ..... | ..... | ..... | ..... | ..... | ..... | ..... | ..... |
| Crude petroleum and natural gas | ..... | ..... | ..... | ..... | ..... | ..... | ..... | ..... | ..... | ..... |
| Nonmetallic minerals | 0.1 | 0.1 | 0.1 | 0.1 | 0.1 | ..... | ..... | 0.1 | ..... | ..... |
| Scrap and waste | ..... | ..... | ..... | ..... | ..... | 0.4 | 0.6 | 0.7 | 0.8 | 0.4 |
| Used merchandise | ..... | ..... | ..... | ..... | ..... | ..... | ..... | ..... | ..... | ..... |
| Goods imported and returned unchanged | ..... | ..... | ..... | ..... | ..... | ..... | ..... | ..... | ..... | ..... |
| Special classification provisions | ..... | ..... | ..... | ..... | ..... | ..... | ..... | ..... | ..... | ..... |

| Industry | 1993 | 1994 | 1995 | 1996 | 1997 | 1993 | 1994 | 1995 | 1996 | 1997 |
|---|---|---|---|---|---|---|---|---|---|---|
| | The Netherlands | | | | | Asian 10 | | | | |
| **ALL GOODS** | 11.6 | 23.0 | 27.6 | 28.0 | 31.8 | 257.2 | 361.1 | 381.8 | 391.0 | 417.2 |
| **Manufactured goods** | 11.4 | 23.0 | 27.0 | 27.9 | 31.8 | 249.4 | 349.8 | 359.1 | 349.9 | 388.1 |
| Food products | 5.4 | 14.3 | 13.1 | 11.9 | 7.7 | 98.5 | 164.7 | 170.7 | 167.0 | 195.6 |
| Tobacco products | ..... | ..... | ..... | ..... | ..... | ..... | ..... | ..... | ..... | ..... |
| Textile mill products | 0.2 | ..... | ..... | ..... | 1.0 | 0.2 | 0.2 | 0.3 | 0.4 | 0.4 |
| Apparel | ..... | ..... | ..... | ..... | ..... | 0.6 | 0.5 | 0.8 | 0.9 | 0.4 |
| Lumber and wood products | 0.1 | ..... | ..... | 0.1 | 0.1 | 1.3 | 0.7 | 0.9 | 0.6 | 0.8 |
| Furniture and fixtures | ..... | ..... | 1.1 | ..... | ..... | 1.3 | 1.2 | 1.3 | 0.7 | 0.7 |
| Paper products | 0.4 | 0.8 | ..... | ..... | ..... | 2.3 | 1.5 | 0.6 | 0.6 | 0.2 |
| Printing and publishing | ..... | ..... | ..... | ..... | ..... | 0.2 | 0.3 | 0.5 | 0.4 | 0.2 |
| Chemical products | 3.3 | 3.8 | 6.4 | 11.4 | 9.4 | 93.5 | 100.8 | 96.4 | 91.4 | 97.9 |
| Refined petroleum products | ..... | ..... | ..... | ..... | ..... | ..... | 0.7 | ..... | ..... | 0.1 |
| Rubber and plastic products | ..... | ..... | ..... | 0.1 | ..... | 1.4 | 4.8 | 2.1 | 2.4 | 2.4 |
| Leather products | ..... | ..... | ..... | ..... | ..... | 0.2 | 0.7 | 0.3 | 0.6 | 0.1 |
| Stone, clay and glass products | 0.1 | 0.9 | 1.1 | 0.9 | 0.3 | 0.4 | 1.4 | 1.9 | 1.4 | 1.0 |
| Primary metals | ..... | ..... | 0.5 | 0.5 | 0.9 | 0.2 | 0.5 | 2.0 | 4.4 | 3.8 |
| Fabricated metal products | 0.1 | 0.1 | 0.2 | 0.2 | 0.2 | 4.6 | 3.0 | 8.1 | 4.9 | 4.3 |
| Industrial machinery and computers | 0.7 | 1.0 | 2.4 | 1.5 | 4.0 | 17.2 | 22.1 | 31.6 | 31.5 | 30.5 |
| Electric and electronic equipment | 0.3 | 1.4 | 1.5 | 0.4 | 6.0 | 8.2 | 14.0 | 14.1 | 11.5 | 14.4 |
| Transportation equipment | 0.3 | 0.1 | 0.1 | ..... | 1.5 | 1.2 | 2.1 | 9.4 | 10.9 | 9.1 |
| Scientific and measuring instruments | 0.4 | 0.3 | 0.5 | 0.7 | 0.5 | 16.3 | 27.4 | 14.9 | 17.9 | 23.6 |
| Miscellaneous manufactures | ..... | 0.1 | ..... | 0.1 | ..... | 1.5 | 2.5 | 2.7 | 2.3 | 2.3 |
| Unidentified manufactures | 0.1 | ..... | 0.1 | ..... | 0.1 | 0.2 | 0.5 | 0.5 | 0.3 | 0.4 |
| **Agricultural and livestock products** | ..... | ..... | ..... | 0.1 | ..... | 5.7 | 7.5 | 7.2 | 9.1 | 5.5 |
| Agricultural products | ..... | ..... | ..... | ..... | ..... | 2.9 | 4.0 | 1.4 | 2.1 | 0.5 |
| Livestock and livestock products | ..... | ..... | ..... | 0.1 | ..... | 2.9 | 3.5 | 5.8 | 6.9 | 5.0 |
| **Other commodities** | 0.2 | 0.1 | 0.6 | ..... | ..... | 2.1 | 3.9 | 15.5 | 32.0 | 23.5 |
| Forestry products | ..... | ..... | ..... | ..... | ..... | ..... | ..... | ..... | ..... | ..... |
| Fish and other marine products | ..... | ..... | ..... | ..... | ..... | 1.4 | 3.3 | 14.2 | 31.3 | 22.9 |
| Metallic ores and concentrates | 0.1 | ..... | 0.1 | ..... | ..... | 0.1 | ..... | ..... | ..... | ..... |
| Bituminous coal and lignite | ..... | ..... | ..... | ..... | ..... | ..... | ..... | ..... | ..... | ..... |
| Crude petroleum and natural gas | ..... | ..... | ..... | ..... | ..... | ..... | ..... | ..... | ..... | ..... |
| Nonmetallic minerals | ..... | ..... | 0.4 | ..... | ..... | 0.4 | 0.3 | 1.0 | 0.4 | 0.4 |
| Scrap and waste | ..... | ..... | ..... | ..... | ..... | 0.1 | ..... | 0.1 | ..... | ..... |
| Used merchandise | ..... | ..... | ..... | ..... | ..... | 0.1 | 0.1 | ..... | 0.2 | ..... |
| Goods imported and returned unchanged | ..... | ..... | ..... | ..... | ..... | ..... | ..... | ..... | ..... | ..... |
| Special classification provisions | ..... | ..... | 0.1 | ..... | ..... | ..... | ..... | 0.1 | 0.1 | 0.2 |

## Table D-3.  State Exports of Goods by Destination and Industry, 1993–1997 —*Continued*

### ARKANSAS (Millions of dollars.)

| Industry | 1993 | 1994 | 1995 | 1996 | 1997 | 1993 | 1994 | 1995 | 1996 | 1997 |
|---|---|---|---|---|---|---|---|---|---|---|
| | Japan | | | | | South Korea | | | | |
| **ALL GOODS** | 111.5 | 157.1 | 139.4 | 126.9 | 117.2 | 31.7 | 33.8 | 37.2 | 41.4 | 33.1 |
| **Manufactured goods** | 110.1 | 153.7 | 130.1 | 98.8 | 96.3 | 28.6 | 30.0 | 32.2 | 38.1 | 33.0 |
| Food products | 56.7 | 90.5 | 65.7 | 41.3 | 41.2 | 0.1 | 0.8 | 3.0 | 2.8 | 1.8 |
| Tobacco products | ..... | ..... | ..... | ..... | ..... | ..... | ..... | ..... | ..... | ..... |
| Textile mill products | ..... | ..... | 0.1 | 0.2 | 0.2 | ..... | ..... | 0.1 | 0.1 | 0.1 |
| Apparel | 0.4 | 0.1 | 0.6 | 0.2 | ..... | ..... | ..... | ..... | 0.3 | ..... |
| Lumber and wood products | 1.1 | 0.5 | 0.6 | 0.3 | 0.4 | ..... | ..... | ..... | 0.1 | 0.1 |
| Furniture and fixtures | 0.5 | 0.4 | 0.9 | 0.2 | 0.5 | ..... | ..... | ..... | 0.1 | ..... |
| Paper products | 0.1 | 0.2 | ..... | ..... | ..... | 0.5 | 0.1 | ..... | 0.1 | ..... |
| Printing and publishing | ..... | 0.1 | 0.3 | ..... | ..... | ..... | ..... | ..... | 0.1 | ..... |
| Chemical products | 37.5 | 38.2 | 37.9 | 36.4 | 37.2 | 24.0 | 24.1 | 20.7 | 23.4 | 22.0 |
| Refined petroleum products | ..... | ..... | ..... | ..... | ..... | ..... | ..... | ..... | ..... | ..... |
| Rubber and plastic products | 0.8 | 3.0 | 1.1 | 1.2 | 0.7 | 0.1 | ..... | 0.1 | 0.5 | 0.1 |
| Leather products | ..... | ..... | 0.1 | 0.1 | ..... | ..... | ..... | ..... | 0.2 | ..... |
| Stone, clay and glass products | 0.3 | 0.6 | 1.2 | 0.3 | ..... | ..... | 0.1 | 0.1 | 0.2 | 0.4 |
| Primary metals | ..... | 0.1 | 0.1 | 0.6 | 0.6 | ..... | 0.4 | 0.2 | 0.1 | 0.2 |
| Fabricated metal products | 2.1 | 0.5 | 1.9 | 0.8 | 0.1 | 0.3 | 0.3 | 1.9 | 0.4 | 0.3 |
| Industrial machinery and computers | 6.6 | 8.3 | 12.0 | 9.8 | 7.7 | 1.9 | 3.3 | 2.9 | 3.9 | 5.7 |
| Electric and electronic equipment | 1.6 | 6.8 | 3.3 | 1.7 | 2.8 | 1.4 | 0.4 | 1.5 | 1.6 | 1.0 |
| Transportation equipment | 0.3 | 0.7 | 2.2 | 3.0 | 2.8 | ..... | ..... | 1.1 | 3.3 | 0.5 |
| Scientific and measuring instruments | 1.1 | 2.5 | 0.9 | 1.9 | 1.0 | 0.1 | 0.1 | 0.1 | 0.2 | 0.6 |
| Miscellaneous manufactures | 0.9 | 1.0 | 1.2 | 0.7 | 0.8 | 0.1 | 0.1 | 0.1 | 0.5 | 0.1 |
| Unidentified manufactures | 0.1 | 0.1 | 0.1 | 0.1 | 0.1 | 0.1 | 0.1 | 0.2 | ..... | ..... |
| **Agricultural and livestock products** | 0.1 | 0.6 | 0.8 | 0.6 | 0.8 | 3.1 | 3.5 | 1.0 | 2.3 | 0.1 |
| Agricultural products | 0.1 | 0.6 | 0.8 | 0.5 | 0.4 | 2.7 | 3.1 | 0.5 | 1.6 | 0.1 |
| Livestock and livestock products | ..... | ..... | ..... | ..... | 0.4 | 0.4 | 0.4 | 0.5 | 0.7 | ..... |
| **Other commodities** | 1.3 | 2.8 | 8.5 | 27.6 | 20.1 | ..... | 0.3 | 4.0 | 1.1 | ..... |
| Forestry products | ..... | ..... | ..... | ..... | ..... | ..... | ..... | ..... | ..... | ..... |
| Fish and other marine products | 1.1 | 2.6 | 8.3 | 27.5 | 20.1 | ..... | 0.3 | 4.0 | 1.1 | ..... |
| Metallic ores and concentrates | 0.1 | ..... | ..... | ..... | ..... | ..... | ..... | ..... | ..... | ..... |
| Bituminous coal and lignite | ..... | ..... | ..... | ..... | ..... | ..... | ..... | ..... | ..... | ..... |
| Crude petroleum and natural gas | ..... | ..... | ..... | ..... | ..... | ..... | ..... | ..... | ..... | ..... |
| Nonmetallic minerals | 0.1 | 0.1 | 0.1 | ..... | ..... | ..... | ..... | ..... | ..... | ..... |
| Scrap and waste | ..... | ..... | 0.1 | ..... | ..... | ..... | ..... | ..... | ..... | ..... |
| Used merchandise | ..... | 0.1 | ..... | ..... | ..... | ..... | ..... | ..... | ..... | ..... |
| Goods imported and returned unchanged | ..... | ..... | ..... | ..... | ..... | ..... | ..... | ..... | ..... | ..... |
| Special classification provisions | ..... | ..... | ..... | 0.1 | ..... | ..... | ..... | ..... | ..... | ..... |

| Industry | 1993 | 1994 | 1995 | 1996 | 1997 | 1993 | 1994 | 1995 | 1996 | 1997 |
|---|---|---|---|---|---|---|---|---|---|---|
| | Taiwan | | | | | Singapore | | | | |
| **ALL GOODS** | 26.4 | 32.4 | 32.8 | 24.2 | 30.3 | 17.8 | 25.7 | 25.4 | 22.0 | 20.5 |
| **Manufactured goods** | 26.0 | 31.8 | 31.5 | 23.4 | 29.9 | 17.6 | 25.5 | 25.1 | 21.9 | 20.3 |
| Food products | 0.3 | 0.1 | 0.1 | 0.5 | 0.3 | 7.9 | 12.2 | 7.0 | 6.3 | 5.0 |
| Tobacco products | ..... | ..... | ..... | ..... | ..... | ..... | ..... | ..... | ..... | ..... |
| Textile mill products | ..... | ..... | ..... | ..... | ..... | 0.1 | ..... | ..... | ..... | ..... |
| Apparel | ..... | ..... | ..... | ..... | ..... | 0.1 | 0.1 | 0.1 | 0.1 | 0.1 |
| Lumber and wood products | 0.2 | 0.1 | 0.2 | 0.2 | 0.3 | ..... | ..... | ..... | ..... | ..... |
| Furniture and fixtures | 0.4 | 0.1 | ..... | ..... | ..... | 0.1 | 0.1 | ..... | 0.1 | ..... |
| Paper products | 1.6 | 0.3 | ..... | ..... | ..... | 0.1 | 0.2 | 0.2 | 0.3 | ..... |
| Printing and publishing | ..... | ..... | ..... | ..... | ..... | 0.1 | 0.1 | 0.1 | 0.1 | 0.1 |
| Chemical products | 20.2 | 25.5 | 22.1 | 15.8 | 19.7 | 4.4 | 5.4 | 7.9 | 7.3 | 5.9 |
| Refined petroleum products | ..... | ..... | ..... | ..... | ..... | ..... | 0.6 | ..... | ..... | ..... |
| Rubber and plastic products | 0.1 | ..... | ..... | 0.1 | 0.1 | 0.3 | 0.7 | 0.6 | 0.3 | 1.0 |
| Leather products | ..... | ..... | ..... | ..... | ..... | 0.1 | 0.1 | 0.1 | ..... | ..... |
| Stone, clay and glass products | ..... | 0.3 | 0.1 | ..... | ..... | ..... | 0.4 | 0.5 | 0.6 | 0.5 |
| Primary metals | ..... | ..... | 0.1 | 0.1 | ..... | 0.1 | ..... | 0.9 | 0.5 | 0.6 |
| Fabricated metal products | 0.1 | 0.1 | 0.1 | 0.1 | 0.5 | 1.6 | 1.0 | 1.9 | 1.3 | 0.7 |
| Industrial machinery and computers | 1.1 | 2.4 | 4.0 | 3.9 | 4.0 | 0.8 | 1.3 | 1.7 | 1.5 | 1.8 |
| Electric and electronic equipment | 1.2 | 1.6 | 3.3 | 1.9 | 4.1 | 1.7 | 2.7 | 2.4 | 2.0 | 2.5 |
| Transportation equipment | 0.1 | ..... | 0.1 | ..... | 0.2 | ..... | ..... | 0.2 | 1.5 | 1.8 |
| Scientific and measuring instruments | 0.6 | 0.7 | 1.1 | 0.5 | 0.4 | ..... | ..... | 0.1 | 0.1 | 0.2 |
| Miscellaneous manufactures | 0.1 | 0.4 | 0.2 | 0.3 | 0.2 | 0.2 | 0.3 | 0.2 | 0.2 | 0.1 |
| Unidentified manufactures | ..... | ..... | ..... | ..... | 0.1 | ..... | ..... | ..... | ..... | ..... |
| **Agricultural and livestock products** | 0.1 | 0.1 | 0.7 | 0.7 | 0.3 | ..... | ..... | ..... | ..... | ..... |
| Agricultural products | ..... | ..... | ..... | ..... | ..... | ..... | ..... | ..... | ..... | ..... |
| Livestock and livestock products | 0.1 | 0.1 | 0.7 | 0.7 | 0.3 | ..... | ..... | ..... | ..... | ..... |
| **Other commodities** | 0.4 | 0.5 | 0.7 | 0.1 | 0.1 | 0.2 | 0.1 | 0.3 | 0.1 | 0.3 |
| Forestry products | ..... | ..... | ..... | ..... | ..... | ..... | ..... | ..... | ..... | ..... |
| Fish and other marine products | 0.3 | 0.3 | 0.2 | ..... | ..... | ..... | 0.1 | 0.1 | ..... | ..... |
| Metallic ores and concentrates | ..... | ..... | ..... | ..... | ..... | ..... | ..... | ..... | ..... | ..... |
| Bituminous coal and lignite | ..... | ..... | ..... | ..... | ..... | ..... | ..... | ..... | ..... | ..... |
| Crude petroleum and natural gas | ..... | ..... | ..... | ..... | ..... | ..... | ..... | ..... | ..... | ..... |
| Nonmetallic minerals | 0.1 | 0.2 | 0.5 | ..... | 0.1 | 0.2 | ..... | 0.2 | 0.1 | 0.2 |
| Scrap and waste | ..... | ..... | ..... | ..... | ..... | ..... | ..... | ..... | ..... | ..... |
| Used merchandise | ..... | ..... | ..... | ..... | ..... | ..... | ..... | ..... | ..... | ..... |
| Goods imported and returned unchanged | ..... | ..... | ..... | ..... | ..... | ..... | ..... | ..... | ..... | ..... |
| Special classification provisions | ..... | ..... | ..... | ..... | ..... | ..... | ..... | ..... | ..... | ..... |

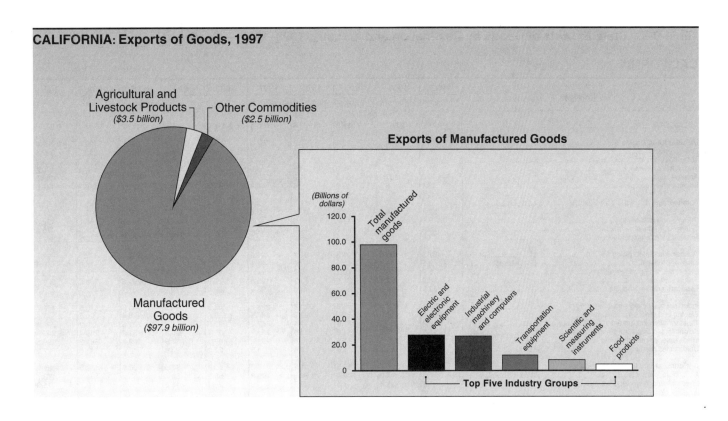

## CALIFORNIA: Exports of Goods, 1997

Agricultural and Livestock Products ($3.5 billion)

Other Commodities ($2.5 billion)

Manufactured Goods ($97.9 billion)

### Exports of Manufactured Goods

(Billions of dollars)

Total manufactured goods

Electric and electronic equipment

Industrial machinery and computers

Transportation equipment

Scientific and measuring instruments

Food products

Top Five Industry Groups

---

### Table D-3.   State Exports of Goods by Destination and Industry, 1993–1997 —Continued

**CALIFORNIA** (Millions of dollars.)

| Industry | 1993 | 1994 | 1995 | 1996 | 1997 | 1993 | 1994 | 1995 | 1996 | 1997 |
|---|---|---|---|---|---|---|---|---|---|---|
| | All destinations | | | | | Canada | | | | |
| **ALL GOODS** | 68 066.3 | 78 190.4 | 92 038.4 | 98 634.0 | 103 802.4 | 7 157.3 | 8 054.5 | 9 537.7 | 10 577.1 | 11 492.4 |
| **Manufactured goods** | 63 319.9 | 72 794.8 | 85 881.4 | 92 687.2 | 97 881.1 | 6 283.7 | 7 205.3 | 8 600.0 | 9 610.2 | 10 485.7 |
| Food products | 4 083.1 | 4 531.5 | 4 953.0 | 5 246.5 | 5 096.7 | 515.9 | 518.6 | 526.1 | 591.2 | 620.8 |
| Tobacco products | 2.1 | 1.9 | 11.6 | 2.3 | 2.2 | ..... | ..... | ..... | ..... | 0.1 |
| Textile mill products | 286.1 | 352.2 | 377.0 | 444.2 | 473.6 | 21.5 | 21.8 | 22.8 | 32.1 | 40.4 |
| Apparel | 1 127.1 | 1 164.4 | 1 339.0 | 1 505.8 | 1 584.8 | 51.9 | 49.0 | 65.7 | 73.0 | 102.6 |
| Lumber and wood products | 508.4 | 473.4 | 425.8 | 448.6 | 470.9 | 62.3 | 64.7 | 59.5 | 50.8 | 60.6 |
| Furniture and fixtures | 216.2 | 246.8 | 241.6 | 267.0 | 316.4 | 39.9 | 47.1 | 60.0 | 57.8 | 64.8 |
| Paper products | 603.9 | 818.7 | 1 030.2 | 1 112.5 | 1 197.2 | 38.2 | 45.7 | 58.7 | 66.2 | 63.7 |
| Printing and publishing | 424.6 | 458.8 | 487.7 | 519.9 | 573.9 | 105.1 | 94.3 | 94.4 | 87.4 | 100.1 |
| Chemical products | 2 364.9 | 2 733.0 | 3 087.4 | 3 262.0 | 3 732.8 | 230.6 | 239.1 | 269.4 | 272.8 | 305.4 |
| Refined petroleum products | 1 733.8 | 1 275.5 | 937.2 | 1 165.6 | 1 039.0 | 73.8 | 74.0 | 70.7 | 69.2 | 95.6 |
| Rubber and plastic products | 828.2 | 975.4 | 1 065.4 | 1 280.2 | 1 408.2 | 97.5 | 103.3 | 124.0 | 125.9 | 133.5 |
| Leather products | 193.9 | 214.7 | 224.6 | 233.4 | 210.6 | 15.4 | 19.1 | 26.2 | 22.2 | 22.9 |
| Stone, clay and glass products | 282.1 | 309.5 | 543.0 | 521.4 | 690.4 | 45.2 | 44.3 | 57.8 | 60.6 | 69.1 |
| Primary metals | 1 227.7 | 1 470.9 | 1 694.5 | 1 494.3 | 1 671.5 | 138.4 | 121.9 | 112.5 | 194.3 | 135.1 |
| Fabricated metal products | 1 413.2 | 1 341.8 | 1 615.5 | 1 900.7 | 1 907.3 | 182.1 | 190.0 | 207.6 | 232.1 | 278.0 |
| Industrial machinery and computers | 15 904.9 | 17 651.4 | 21 216.0 | 25 491.7 | 26 899.7 | 2 003.1 | 2 382.2 | 2 765.8 | 3 048.7 | 3 240.5 |
| Electric and electronic equipment | 15 590.1 | 19 800.7 | 25 932.3 | 27 198.5 | 27 715.3 | 1 424.2 | 1 734.0 | 2 280.3 | 2 776.9 | 2 909.9 |
| Transportation equipment | 10 103.5 | 11 806.7 | 12 420.0 | 10 981.8 | 12 055.7 | 623.5 | 716.2 | 1 021.9 | 1 008.6 | 1 273.3 |
| Scientific and measuring instruments | 4 902.7 | 5 399.1 | 6 247.2 | 7 457.5 | 8 469.9 | 415.0 | 473.7 | 498.5 | 565.2 | 613.8 |
| Miscellaneous manufactures | 1 183.7 | 1 413.9 | 1 691.7 | 1 806.9 | 1 968.4 | 156.3 | 202.3 | 205.0 | 198.6 | 264.3 |
| Unidentified manufactures | 339.6 | 354.5 | 340.6 | 346.4 | 396.5 | 43.9 | 63.9 | 73.0 | 76.8 | 90.9 |
| **Agricultural and livestock products** | 2 620.8 | 3 215.5 | 3 320.9 | 3 242.6 | 3 458.1 | 668.6 | 635.7 | 707.2 | 682.6 | 743.7 |
| Agricultural products | 2 478.8 | 3 099.1 | 3 194.2 | 3 109.7 | 3 325.6 | 664.8 | 630.4 | 701.9 | 677.0 | 739.0 |
| Livestock and livestock products | 142.0 | 116.4 | 126.8 | 132.9 | 132.5 | 3.8 | 5.3 | 5.3 | 5.7 | 4.7 |
| **Other commodities** | 2 125.7 | 2 180.0 | 2 836.1 | 2 704.2 | 2 463.3 | 205.0 | 213.5 | 230.5 | 284.3 | 263.0 |
| Forestry products | 23.0 | 29.7 | 32.1 | 26.1 | 37.2 | 1.7 | 2.2 | 2.8 | 3.7 | 4.6 |
| Fish and other marine products | 168.9 | 200.7 | 238.7 | 231.9 | 224.1 | 25.9 | 23.9 | 25.8 | 24.7 | 22.6 |
| Metallic ores and concentrates | 0.6 | 0.8 | 3.8 | 6.4 | 16.4 | ..... | 0.1 | 2.4 | 1.4 | 1.9 |
| Bituminous coal and lignite | 4.7 | 2.7 | 0.9 | 4.0 | 3.3 | ..... | ..... | ..... | 4.0 | ..... |
| Crude petroleum and natural gas | 8.4 | 5.4 | 15.0 | 30.1 | 34.9 | 1.0 | 1.1 | 2.0 | 1.6 | 0.7 |
| Nonmetallic minerals | 87.2 | 82.6 | 77.3 | 82.7 | 87.7 | 7.9 | 5.6 | 4.0 | 4.2 | 5.4 |
| Scrap and waste | 652.9 | 862.3 | 1 467.6 | 1 143.4 | 861.8 | 27.2 | 35.9 | 39.2 | 35.2 | 26.4 |
| Used merchandise | 342.7 | 260.0 | 264.3 | 292.3 | 251.3 | 9.6 | 11.8 | 7.1 | 9.7 | 6.3 |
| Goods imported and returned unchanged | 89.8 | 89.2 | 102.8 | 128.3 | 151.0 | 89.8 | 89.2 | 102.8 | 128.3 | 151.0 |
| Special classification provisions | 747.5 | 646.7 | 633.6 | 759.0 | 795.5 | 41.7 | 43.7 | 44.5 | 71.6 | 44.0 |

## Table D-3.　State Exports of Goods by Destination and Industry, 1993–1997 —*Continued*

**CALIFORNIA** (Millions of dollars.)

| Industry | 1993 | 1994 | 1995 | 1996 | 1997 | 1993 | 1994 | 1995 | 1996 | 1997 |
|---|---|---|---|---|---|---|---|---|---|---|
| | South and Central America and Caribbean | | | | | Mexico | | | | |
| **ALL GOODS** | 2 427.8 | 2 662.7 | 2 952.3 | 3 357.8 | 4 307.1 | 5 116.6 | 5 957.0 | 6 171.6 | 7 787.3 | 9 941.9 |
| **Manufactured goods** | 2 344.8 | 2 564.6 | 2 838.6 | 3 220.7 | 4 157.3 | 4 906.6 | 5 736.2 | 5 952.6 | 7 496.0 | 9 582.4 |
| Food products | 70.9 | 87.6 | 80.2 | 100.2 | 142.4 | 200.6 | 252.3 | 188.8 | 292.2 | 332.5 |
| Tobacco products | ..... | ..... | ..... | ..... | 0.2 | ..... | ..... | 1.5 | 1.3 | 0.2 |
| Textile mill products | 45.3 | 47.6 | 30.5 | 34.5 | 49.8 | 47.3 | 80.6 | 110.8 | 118.4 | 120.8 |
| Apparel | 146.6 | 157.1 | 180.2 | 201.0 | 317.0 | 217.2 | 212.9 | 203.1 | 309.6 | 433.2 |
| Lumber and wood products | 8.4 | 8.6 | 10.8 | 11.6 | 10.9 | 244.3 | 195.7 | 121.7 | 139.1 | 156.5 |
| Furniture and fixtures | 6.7 | 9.1 | 9.5 | 12.1 | 23.4 | 47.6 | 58.3 | 31.4 | 45.7 | 57.0 |
| Paper products | 52.2 | 59.7 | 103.5 | 100.2 | 122.6 | 168.1 | 212.2 | 234.5 | 295.9 | 337.2 |
| Printing and publishing | 9.1 | 9.9 | 13.2 | 19.0 | 17.8 | 36.7 | 47.6 | 48.2 | 58.5 | 72.5 |
| Chemical products | 125.4 | 153.8 | 143.2 | 158.9 | 206.2 | 228.9 | 277.0 | 264.5 | 368.4 | 476.4 |
| Refined petroleum products | 173.0 | 168.5 | 68.9 | 155.0 | 114.7 | 226.1 | 273.4 | 208.6 | 230.2 | 267.3 |
| Rubber and plastic products | 37.3 | 35.5 | 31.3 | 51.7 | 91.9 | 243.7 | 333.7 | 345.1 | 472.0 | 492.2 |
| Leather products | 8.5 | 16.6 | 20.5 | 17.0 | 11.9 | 20.1 | 15.2 | 12.3 | 16.9 | 18.4 |
| Stone, clay and glass products | 6.7 | 10.0 | 10.2 | 10.7 | 14.0 | 41.5 | 44.7 | 39.0 | 49.3 | 70.0 |
| Primary metals | 36.9 | 27.5 | 31.9 | 43.7 | 135.6 | 227.9 | 235.5 | 291.8 | 309.0 | 386.7 |
| Fabricated metal products | 42.3 | 35.3 | 41.3 | 44.0 | 58.4 | 269.4 | 272.9 | 302.3 | 417.3 | 423.0 |
| Industrial machinery and computers | 590.3 | 629.8 | 753.6 | 907.8 | 1 293.8 | 762.3 | 899.5 | 786.8 | 1 119.5 | 1 451.3 |
| Electric and electronic equipment | 306.4 | 480.5 | 530.5 | 499.2 | 667.5 | 1 225.6 | 1 585.0 | 2 128.4 | 2 500.5 | 3 378.6 |
| Transportation equipment | 487.8 | 369.1 | 471.4 | 511.1 | 447.2 | 252.5 | 257.6 | 231.5 | 228.2 | 396.3 |
| Scientific and measuring instruments | 111.9 | 133.2 | 184.0 | 214.5 | 289.2 | 234.1 | 220.3 | 181.9 | 239.4 | 295.5 |
| Miscellaneous manufactures | 66.9 | 109.3 | 111.9 | 116.8 | 128.1 | 187.4 | 237.9 | 202.9 | 261.8 | 389.8 |
| Unidentified manufactures | 12.3 | 15.7 | 11.8 | 11.5 | 14.9 | 25.2 | 23.9 | 17.8 | 23.0 | 27.0 |
| **Agricultural and livestock products** | 55.9 | 69.7 | 83.5 | 101.5 | 112.0 | 80.9 | 97.5 | 90.2 | 159.8 | 189.6 |
| Agricultural products | 54.5 | 68.0 | 80.4 | 98.8 | 106.8 | 56.9 | 86.2 | 85.4 | 154.1 | 173.7 |
| Livestock and livestock products | 1.4 | 1.8 | 3.1 | 2.7 | 5.2 | 24.0 | 11.3 | 4.8 | 5.7 | 15.9 |
| **Other commodities** | 27.1 | 28.3 | 30.3 | 35.5 | 37.7 | 129.1 | 123.3 | 128.7 | 131.6 | 169.9 |
| Forestry products | 0.1 | 3.0 | 0.3 | 0.3 | 0.3 | 1.0 | 3.4 | 6.5 | 3.8 | 6.5 |
| Fish and other marine products | 0.9 | 1.7 | 1.3 | 1.9 | 1.5 | 7.6 | 11.9 | 3.4 | 4.8 | 6.7 |
| Metallic ores and concentrates | ..... | ..... | ..... | 0.9 | 6.6 | ..... | ..... | 0.1 | 0.1 | 0.1 |
| Bituminous coal and lignite | ..... | ..... | ..... | ..... | ..... | ..... | ..... | 0.1 | ..... | 0.1 |
| Crude petroleum and natural gas | 0.1 | 0.1 | ..... | 0.1 | 0.1 | 6.6 | 3.1 | 12.4 | 26.4 | 32.1 |
| Nonmetallic minerals | 5.6 | 3.8 | 3.6 | 3.7 | 10.6 | 2.5 | 2.3 | 3.3 | 4.4 | 7.6 |
| Scrap and waste | 1.8 | 2.0 | 9.2 | 10.7 | 2.6 | 9.2 | 14.4 | 34.6 | 37.8 | 37.2 |
| Used merchandise | 9.0 | 9.1 | 7.9 | 9.4 | 8.9 | 66.1 | 52.4 | 21.3 | 19.9 | 19.5 |
| Goods imported and returned unchanged | ..... | ..... | ..... | ..... | ..... | ..... | ..... | ..... | ..... | ..... |
| Special classification provisions | 9.8 | 8.9 | 8.0 | 8.6 | 7.0 | 36.0 | 35.6 | 47.0 | 34.4 | 60.2 |
| | European Union | | | | | United Kingdom | | | | |
| **ALL GOODS** | 14 976.3 | 17 147.1 | 18 897.0 | 18 687.0 | 19 709.4 | 3 334.0 | 3 835.4 | 4 507.1 | 4 779.0 | 5 109.8 |
| **Manufactured goods** | 14 335.1 | 16 532.8 | 18 106.4 | 17 716.5 | 18 987.3 | 3 154.1 | 3 647.2 | 4 313.5 | 4 606.4 | 4 950.0 |
| Food products | 858.1 | 951.9 | 939.4 | 1 151.7 | 999.1 | 161.4 | 161.7 | 181.2 | 223.4 | 228.4 |
| Tobacco products | 0.1 | 0.2 | 9.0 | ..... | 0.1 | ..... | ..... | ..... | ..... | ..... |
| Textile mill products | 74.0 | 89.7 | 82.5 | 106.8 | 110.8 | 22.5 | 25.0 | 21.0 | 35.8 | 30.5 |
| Apparel | 177.4 | 147.8 | 204.9 | 220.8 | 210.6 | 25.4 | 21.9 | 22.3 | 31.2 | 44.3 |
| Lumber and wood products | 38.1 | 41.7 | 45.0 | 34.4 | 49.7 | 5.0 | 5.0 | 5.7 | 4.0 | 5.4 |
| Furniture and fixtures | 25.2 | 31.8 | 26.7 | 30.5 | 38.6 | 7.5 | 8.0 | 9.8 | 11.1 | 15.7 |
| Paper products | 45.7 | 35.9 | 38.1 | 48.1 | 54.7 | 14.9 | 11.8 | 9.2 | 8.8 | 11.8 |
| Printing and publishing | 110.0 | 92.8 | 89.6 | 104.9 | 108.1 | 44.2 | 26.6 | 25.4 | 39.4 | 33.8 |
| Chemical products | 657.1 | 732.4 | 785.2 | 703.9 | 804.4 | 125.5 | 129.6 | 98.7 | 108.3 | 153.6 |
| Refined petroleum products | 56.3 | 32.0 | 26.2 | 30.5 | 37.5 | 1.6 | 0.9 | 0.9 | 0.8 | 1.9 |
| Rubber and plastic products | 109.6 | 102.9 | 112.0 | 118.5 | 141.8 | 28.5 | 23.9 | 28.6 | 37.7 | 34.8 |
| Leather products | 21.7 | 25.7 | 27.8 | 25.7 | 23.8 | 5.9 | 7.1 | 3.8 | 2.5 | 5.2 |
| Stone, clay and glass products | 34.2 | 38.5 | 44.7 | 55.4 | 80.9 | 8.3 | 10.4 | 19.5 | 23.6 | 31.9 |
| Primary metals | 405.6 | 520.9 | 568.3 | 234.7 | 308.3 | 53.9 | 40.5 | 180.3 | 97.2 | 136.4 |
| Fabricated metal products | 193.6 | 179.8 | 187.6 | 197.5 | 217.4 | 46.0 | 45.3 | 55.0 | 62.4 | 71.5 |
| Industrial machinery and computers | 4 607.4 | 4 836.0 | 5 802.7 | 6 485.6 | 6 949.8 | 1 090.0 | 1 297.4 | 1 453.8 | 1 693.9 | 1 818.3 |
| Electric and electronic equipment | 2 954.5 | 3 388.4 | 4 078.7 | 3 659.8 | 4 036.3 | 843.8 | 1 021.0 | 1 303.5 | 1 198.9 | 1 249.9 |
| Transportation equipment | 2 113.4 | 3 297.9 | 2 801.2 | 2 044.0 | 1 919.1 | 287.1 | 396.2 | 431.7 | 506.1 | 492.1 |
| Scientific and measuring instruments | 1 561.2 | 1 675.1 | 1 885.0 | 2 090.0 | 2 488.4 | 303.3 | 318.5 | 359.5 | 394.6 | 449.3 |
| Miscellaneous manufactures | 210.1 | 233.0 | 287.6 | 322.8 | 358.1 | 62.3 | 76.3 | 84.6 | 110.3 | 119.8 |
| Unidentified manufactures | 81.7 | 78.3 | 64.3 | 51.0 | 50.0 | 16.9 | 20.0 | 18.9 | 16.5 | 15.3 |
| **Agricultural and livestock products** | 290.6 | 235.8 | 262.0 | 290.3 | 291.1 | 65.5 | 48.3 | 44.6 | 51.7 | 61.0 |
| Agricultural products | 238.5 | 208.7 | 236.8 | 257.7 | 258.9 | 44.1 | 42.1 | 38.2 | 39.9 | 49.8 |
| Livestock and livestock products | 52.1 | 27.2 | 25.2 | 32.6 | 32.2 | 21.4 | 6.2 | 6.5 | 11.8 | 11.2 |
| **Other commodities** | 350.5 | 378.5 | 528.6 | 680.2 | 431.0 | 114.4 | 139.9 | 149.0 | 120.8 | 98.7 |
| Forestry products | 1.7 | 3.4 | 2.4 | 3.4 | 5.1 | 0.7 | 1.0 | 1.0 | 1.1 | 1.1 |
| Fish and other marine products | 6.8 | 14.3 | 13.1 | 10.1 | 23.0 | 1.0 | 1.3 | 0.9 | 1.1 | 1.5 |
| Metallic ores and concentrates | 0.1 | 0.4 | 0.3 | 0.5 | 2.8 | ..... | ..... | 0.3 | 0.4 | 0.2 |
| Bituminous coal and lignite | 0.2 | ..... | ..... | ..... | ..... | ..... | ..... | ..... | ..... | ..... |
| Crude petroleum and natural gas | 0.1 | 0.1 | ..... | 0.3 | 0.1 | ..... | ..... | ..... | ..... | ..... |
| Nonmetallic minerals | 21.8 | 24.6 | 26.5 | 23.8 | 22.0 | 3.1 | 4.3 | 6.1 | 5.0 | 6.8 |
| Scrap and waste | 88.0 | 155.2 | 303.4 | 421.5 | 182.6 | 25.6 | 68.8 | 63.6 | 10.2 | 7.3 |
| Used merchandise | 94.4 | 56.0 | 67.5 | 99.3 | 79.0 | 41.5 | 19.1 | 27.7 | 59.3 | 44.0 |
| Goods imported and returned unchanged | ..... | ..... | ..... | ..... | ..... | ..... | ..... | ..... | ..... | ..... |
| Special classification provisions | 137.5 | 124.6 | 115.4 | 121.4 | 116.5 | 42.5 | 45.4 | 49.6 | 43.7 | 38.0 |

## Table D-3. State Exports of Goods by Destination and Industry, 1993–1997 —*Continued*

**CALIFORNIA** (Millions of dollars.)

| Industry | 1993 | 1994 | 1995 | 1996 | 1997 | 1993 | 1994 | 1995 | 1996 | 1997 |
|---|---|---|---|---|---|---|---|---|---|---|
| | Germany | | | | | France | | | | |
| **ALL GOODS** | 3 393.5 | 3 406.8 | 3 752.9 | 3 798.6 | 3 761.4 | 2 069.3 | 2 387.9 | 2 443.8 | 2 552.3 | 2 422.7 |
| **Manufactured goods** | 3 291.2 | 3 312.3 | 3 658.7 | 3 710.0 | 3 689.8 | 1 964.9 | 2 286.4 | 2 211.3 | 2 131.7 | 2 223.9 |
| Food products | 235.5 | 246.7 | 264.7 | 326.5 | 260.5 | 101.3 | 75.6 | 62.7 | 86.3 | 89.2 |
| Tobacco products | ..... | ..... | ..... | ..... | ..... | ..... | ..... | ..... | ..... | ..... |
| Textile mill products | 4.7 | 6.4 | 4.2 | 5.2 | 4.1 | 2.8 | 4.4 | 4.2 | 2.5 | 6.6 |
| Apparel | 24.5 | 19.9 | 29.6 | 27.2 | 18.7 | 33.4 | 17.4 | 29.5 | 24.0 | 59.2 |
| Lumber and wood products | 17.6 | 17.8 | 14.2 | 12.5 | 13.1 | 1.8 | 2.3 | 2.7 | 2.2 | 3.0 |
| Furniture and fixtures | 3.4 | 4.6 | 5.2 | 7.3 | 8.5 | 6.7 | 7.9 | 4.8 | 2.1 | 5.5 |
| Paper products | 4.2 | 4.2 | 5.6 | 5.6 | 9.7 | 3.3 | 2.7 | 2.9 | 3.1 | 2.1 |
| Printing and publishing | 28.4 | 19.1 | 18.4 | 18.7 | 20.0 | 9.9 | 8.5 | 10.0 | 12.7 | 10.2 |
| Chemical products | 116.8 | 124.4 | 125.0 | 145.4 | 163.6 | 52.8 | 53.4 | 50.0 | 51.6 | 59.1 |
| Refined petroleum products | 0.5 | 0.5 | 1.9 | 0.4 | 0.4 | 0.2 | 0.1 | 0.1 | 0.2 | 0.4 |
| Rubber and plastic products | 14.7 | 15.2 | 21.5 | 20.3 | 29.4 | 11.1 | 11.4 | 17.6 | 14.0 | 14.3 |
| Leather products | 5.4 | 7.5 | 7.7 | 7.4 | 7.6 | 1.9 | 3.3 | 2.9 | 3.1 | 3.2 |
| Stone, clay and glass products | 12.4 | 14.1 | 8.7 | 15.9 | 30.8 | 3.0 | 2.7 | 4.5 | 4.6 | 6.2 |
| Primary metals | 18.9 | 20.9 | 32.7 | 37.4 | 38.7 | 275.0 | 397.6 | 280.4 | 17.3 | 26.5 |
| Fabricated metal products | 58.8 | 50.7 | 47.4 | 37.2 | 38.4 | 18.5 | 14.9 | 17.0 | 20.5 | 27.3 |
| Industrial machinery and computers | 949.0 | 916.0 | 1 301.1 | 1 409.6 | 1 329.6 | 605.8 | 632.5 | 742.3 | 903.7 | 782.0 |
| Electric and electronic equipment | 776.4 | 797.9 | 863.0 | 705.2 | 749.2 | 375.5 | 395.2 | 503.8 | 373.3 | 480.9 |
| Transportation equipment | 534.9 | 545.1 | 321.2 | 343.9 | 301.6 | 192.4 | 359.0 | 163.3 | 243.1 | 234.4 |
| Scientific and measuring instruments | 416.3 | 434.6 | 513.4 | 503.8 | 581.9 | 231.0 | 265.7 | 271.3 | 332.6 | 372.8 |
| Miscellaneous manufactures | 40.5 | 48.6 | 58.9 | 70.1 | 75.1 | 30.2 | 24.1 | 34.3 | 30.1 | 36.1 |
| Unidentified manufactures | 28.4 | 18.0 | 14.2 | 10.5 | 8.8 | 8.4 | 7.7 | 7.3 | 4.8 | 5.0 |
| **Agricultural and livestock products** | 45.3 | 44.7 | 48.0 | 47.1 | 37.3 | 32.2 | 12.8 | 15.7 | 13.3 | 16.0 |
| Agricultural products | 41.6 | 40.0 | 44.9 | 45.4 | 35.6 | 16.9 | 10.0 | 13.9 | 10.3 | 14.8 |
| Livestock and livestock products | 3.6 | 4.6 | 3.1 | 1.7 | 1.7 | 15.3 | 2.8 | 1.8 | 3.1 | 1.2 |
| **Other commodities** | 57.0 | 49.9 | 46.3 | 41.5 | 34.3 | 72.2 | 88.6 | 216.7 | 407.3 | 182.8 |
| Forestry products | 0.2 | 0.3 | 0.3 | 0.6 | 0.9 | ..... | ..... | 0.1 | 0.1 | 0.2 |
| Fish and other marine products | 0.9 | 1.3 | 0.8 | 0.9 | 1.4 | 1.5 | 1.8 | 3.1 | 2.4 | 2.2 |
| Metallic ores and concentrates | ..... | ..... | ..... | ..... | 1.5 | ..... | ..... | ..... | ..... | ..... |
| Bituminous coal and lignite | ..... | ..... | ..... | ..... | ..... | ..... | ..... | ..... | ..... | ..... |
| Crude petroleum and natural gas | ..... | ..... | ..... | ..... | ..... | ..... | ..... | ..... | ..... | ..... |
| Nonmetallic minerals | 4.4 | 6.2 | 5.2 | 7.1 | 4.5 | 1.6 | 2.0 | 1.4 | 0.7 | 0.5 |
| Scrap and waste | 6.6 | 2.5 | 0.8 | 0.6 | 0.4 | 35.8 | 64.2 | 194.6 | 382.0 | 152.9 |
| Used merchandise | 22.5 | 13.0 | 14.3 | 15.3 | 9.7 | 8.4 | 9.3 | 6.3 | 8.4 | 7.9 |
| Goods imported and returned unchanged | ..... | ..... | ..... | ..... | ..... | ..... | ..... | ..... | ..... | ..... |
| Special classification provisions | 22.4 | 26.6 | 24.9 | 16.9 | 15.9 | 25.0 | 11.3 | 11.3 | 13.6 | 19.2 |
| | The Netherlands | | | | | Asian 10 | | | | |
| **ALL GOODS** | 1 978.5 | 2 624.3 | 2 914.3 | 2 138.1 | 3 096.0 | 32 210.1 | 37 949.6 | 47 427.4 | 51 192.1 | 49 784.3 |
| **Manufactured goods** | 1 919.9 | 2 574.1 | 2 857.8 | 2 078.6 | 3 032.8 | 29 633.9 | 34 673.4 | 43 733.4 | 47 953.9 | 46 520.6 |
| Food products | 106.3 | 114.3 | 103.9 | 114.6 | 99.7 | 2 137.6 | 2 371.4 | 2 788.3 | 2 666.3 | 2 540.5 |
| Tobacco products | 0.1 | 0.2 | ..... | ..... | ..... | 1.2 | 0.9 | 0.2 | 0.3 | 1.3 |
| Textile mill products | 2.0 | 1.9 | 1.4 | 1.3 | 2.1 | 72.4 | 88.1 | 101.8 | 124.2 | 117.5 |
| Apparel | 6.4 | 7.6 | 26.1 | 24.7 | 11.3 | 500.1 | 560.2 | 635.8 | 641.0 | 450.9 |
| Lumber and wood products | 3.7 | 2.6 | 4.1 | 2.8 | 9.5 | 137.6 | 143.7 | 167.5 | 186.0 | 164.1 |
| Furniture and fixtures | 2.4 | 5.2 | 2.5 | 3.0 | 1.9 | 70.5 | 73.1 | 79.8 | 93.5 | 105.4 |
| Paper products | 4.8 | 4.7 | 2.7 | 4.1 | 4.0 | 256.7 | 407.4 | 506.5 | 514.0 | 528.8 |
| Printing and publishing | 10.1 | 21.9 | 12.3 | 11.1 | 13.6 | 118.5 | 145.4 | 163.6 | 169.7 | 167.4 |
| Chemical products | 139.7 | 175.5 | 248.3 | 174.1 | 175.1 | 869.8 | 1 066.2 | 1 375.8 | 1 452.2 | 1 647.0 |
| Refined petroleum products | 26.4 | 15.4 | 15.3 | 17.8 | 22.0 | 1 086.2 | 654.7 | 460.4 | 509.4 | 390.0 |
| Rubber and plastic products | 19.9 | 21.5 | 11.8 | 13.6 | 23.4 | 247.2 | 304.2 | 369.7 | 420.7 | 459.5 |
| Leather products | 1.4 | 2.7 | 6.8 | 5.3 | 2.0 | 115.3 | 125.0 | 126.1 | 137.8 | 120.5 |
| Stone, clay and glass products | 2.1 | 3.6 | 2.4 | 3.1 | 2.1 | 133.7 | 149.8 | 357.1 | 316.7 | 423.3 |
| Primary metals | 5.0 | 5.7 | 6.7 | 6.3 | 10.3 | 371.8 | 484.6 | 622.5 | 648.2 | 636.6 |
| Fabricated metal products | 9.2 | 10.5 | 9.3 | 25.0 | 24.6 | 549.7 | 529.0 | 734.3 | 875.0 | 791.3 |
| Industrial machinery and computers | 913.8 | 773.4 | 847.5 | 929.1 | 1 466.1 | 6 108.6 | 6 972.9 | 9 154.1 | 11 774.7 | 11 748.8 |
| Electric and electronic equipment | 220.9 | 277.3 | 348.8 | 361.2 | 471.4 | 8 613.8 | 11 413.7 | 15 367.1 | 16 678.6 | 15 449.0 |
| Transportation equipment | 251.6 | 930.1 | 985.2 | 104.3 | 301.1 | 5 623.9 | 6 192.4 | 6 949.6 | 6 125.5 | 5 983.1 |
| Scientific and measuring instruments | 170.8 | 176.9 | 195.2 | 257.0 | 364.3 | 2 031.0 | 2 345.2 | 2 885.2 | 3 687.3 | 3 986.9 |
| Miscellaneous manufactures | 16.7 | 18.2 | 21.6 | 15.4 | 21.9 | 475.9 | 536.3 | 766.0 | 794.0 | 676.9 |
| Unidentified manufactures | 6.4 | 4.9 | 5.5 | 4.8 | 6.4 | 112.5 | 109.2 | 121.9 | 138.8 | 131.7 |
| **Agricultural and livestock products** | 35.4 | 26.5 | 24.9 | 32.9 | 36.7 | 1 352.7 | 1 978.4 | 1 909.9 | 1 813.4 | 1 871.3 |
| Agricultural products | 34.1 | 25.2 | 23.3 | 31.0 | 32.2 | 1 307.3 | 1 932.2 | 1 838.7 | 1 749.9 | 1 809.6 |
| Livestock and livestock products | 1.3 | 1.3 | 1.6 | 1.9 | 4.5 | 45.5 | 46.2 | 71.2 | 63.5 | 61.7 |
| **Other commodities** | 23.2 | 23.8 | 31.6 | 26.6 | 26.6 | 1 223.5 | 1 297.8 | 1 784.1 | 1 424.8 | 1 392.5 |
| Forestry products | 0.3 | 1.6 | 0.6 | 0.9 | 1.7 | 17.1 | 16.3 | 18.0 | 13.5 | 18.4 |
| Fish and other marine products | 0.6 | 0.9 | 1.0 | 1.4 | 2.8 | 123.6 | 143.7 | 190.4 | 184.2 | 160.5 |
| Metallic ores and concentrates | ..... | 0.1 | ..... | ..... | 0.8 | 0.4 | 0.2 | 0.9 | 3.5 | 4.5 |
| Bituminous coal and lignite | ..... | ..... | ..... | ..... | ..... | 4.5 | 2.6 | 0.8 | ..... | 3.2 |
| Crude petroleum and natural gas | ..... | ..... | ..... | ..... | ..... | 0.4 | 0.6 | 0.5 | 1.3 | 1.1 |
| Nonmetallic minerals | 2.2 | 1.7 | 5.0 | 3.8 | 3.7 | 37.6 | 36.1 | 34.8 | 40.1 | 31.2 |
| Scrap and waste | 1.7 | 5.2 | 18.0 | 4.1 | 2.0 | 519.0 | 642.4 | 1 061.7 | 619.9 | 592.8 |
| Used merchandise | 4.6 | 3.5 | 2.7 | 5.3 | 3.6 | 78.5 | 90.6 | 132.5 | 114.9 | 96.4 |
| Goods imported and returned unchanged | ..... | ..... | ..... | ..... | ..... | ..... | ..... | ..... | ..... | ..... |
| Special classification provisions | 13.9 | 10.7 | 4.3 | 11.2 | 11.9 | 442.5 | 365.4 | 344.5 | 447.3 | 484.4 |

## Table D-3.  State Exports of Goods by Destination and Industry, 1993–1997 —*Continued*

### CALIFORNIA (Millions of dollars.)

| Industry | 1993 | 1994 | 1995 | 1996 | 1997 | 1993 | 1994 | 1995 | 1996 | 1997 |
|---|---|---|---|---|---|---|---|---|---|---|
| | Japan | | | | | South Korea | | | | |
| **ALL GOODS** | 11 431.6 | 14 536.6 | 18 288.8 | 19 704.6 | 17 927.4 | 3 749.3 | 4 557.5 | 6 406.6 | 7 398.8 | 6 494.2 |
| **Manufactured goods** | 10 265.2 | 13 124.2 | 16 667.8 | 18 234.2 | 16 587.7 | 3 346.1 | 4 117.7 | 5 840.8 | 6 961.8 | 6 037.8 |
| Food products | 1 321.5 | 1 473.8 | 1 680.8 | 1 580.6 | 1 445.8 | 329.8 | 311.0 | 438.8 | 347.8 | 304.2 |
| Tobacco products | 0.1 | 0.8 | 0.1 | ..... | 1.2 | 0.6 | 0.1 | 0.1 | 0.2 | 0.1 |
| Textile mill products | 30.5 | 36.3 | 34.7 | 42.2 | 36.7 | 5.1 | 9.5 | 16.7 | 18.2 | 17.7 |
| Apparel | 445.6 | 489.8 | 556.4 | 554.1 | 370.9 | 9.2 | 15.6 | 21.9 | 30.2 | 24.3 |
| Lumber and wood products | 65.2 | 81.0 | 107.8 | 121.8 | 102.4 | 21.1 | 27.3 | 32.0 | 29.2 | 22.0 |
| Furniture and fixtures | 41.0 | 36.4 | 37.2 | 45.8 | 54.9 | 3.3 | 7.0 | 10.8 | 8.6 | 12.1 |
| Paper products | 103.3 | 132.7 | 172.0 | 151.6 | 120.7 | 23.8 | 37.5 | 59.1 | 58.4 | 58.0 |
| Printing and publishing | 61.2 | 80.7 | 90.7 | 80.6 | 76.5 | 6.3 | 9.8 | 15.8 | 20.3 | 22.8 |
| Chemical products | 328.9 | 405.8 | 532.6 | 517.1 | 629.5 | 138.3 | 157.3 | 231.4 | 245.9 | 267.0 |
| Refined petroleum products | 233.1 | 98.4 | 89.0 | 116.7 | 97.2 | 243.8 | 191.4 | 115.1 | 114.5 | 60.1 |
| Rubber and plastic products | 98.0 | 111.5 | 120.8 | 151.1 | 180.9 | 25.6 | 29.9 | 41.2 | 44.3 | 53.8 |
| Leather products | 82.2 | 83.3 | 91.6 | 90.1 | 72.2 | 5.3 | 6.4 | 5.6 | 15.7 | 20.3 |
| Stone, clay and glass products | 39.6 | 50.2 | 58.2 | 59.5 | 63.9 | 19.3 | 19.6 | 39.3 | 39.1 | 35.0 |
| Primary metals | 128.7 | 138.6 | 190.9 | 231.5 | 167.7 | 49.9 | 54.6 | 112.2 | 102.3 | 98.6 |
| Fabricated metal products | 264.9 | 298.1 | 358.2 | 381.9 | 221.4 | 61.9 | 51.1 | 70.7 | 91.2 | 74.0 |
| Industrial machinery and computers | 2 033.5 | 2 367.1 | 3 155.7 | 4 224.6 | 3 832.2 | 827.0 | 1 143.9 | 1 942.1 | 2 430.5 | 1 824.4 |
| Electric and electronic equipment | 1 646.7 | 2 261.2 | 3 070.2 | 3 696.6 | 3 624.4 | 1 050.1 | 1 445.5 | 1 973.9 | 2 237.6 | 2 190.7 |
| Transportation equipment | 1 993.0 | 3 376.3 | 4 253.6 | 3 767.0 | 3 241.1 | 217.8 | 210.9 | 252.3 | 432.4 | 256.1 |
| Scientific and measuring instruments | 1 004.2 | 1 228.7 | 1 546.1 | 1 894.4 | 1 780.5 | 268.3 | 352.0 | 396.2 | 586.6 | 635.6 |
| Miscellaneous manufactures | 292.5 | 334.4 | 461.8 | 447.8 | 400.4 | 29.2 | 26.9 | 55.7 | 97.1 | 50.7 |
| Unidentified manufactures | 51.2 | 39.1 | 59.3 | 79.1 | 67.3 | 10.3 | 10.6 | 10.0 | 11.7 | 10.4 |
| **Agricultural and livestock products** | 713.6 | 912.1 | 1 053.4 | 933.3 | 832.2 | 190.4 | 205.1 | 203.8 | 190.1 | 185.0 |
| Agricultural products | 683.9 | 881.2 | 1 002.5 | 887.6 | 785.6 | 185.3 | 199.6 | 197.2 | 185.1 | 181.3 |
| Livestock and livestock products | 29.7 | 30.9 | 51.0 | 45.7 | 46.6 | 5.1 | 5.5 | 6.6 | 5.0 | 3.8 |
| **Other commodities** | 452.8 | 500.3 | 567.5 | 537.1 | 507.4 | 212.7 | 234.7 | 361.9 | 246.8 | 271.5 |
| Forestry products | 0.8 | 1.4 | 1.7 | 2.3 | 5.5 | 1.9 | 1.8 | 1.6 | 1.6 | 1.3 |
| Fish and other marine products | 94.2 | 106.1 | 122.1 | 106.2 | 86.0 | 8.6 | 5.1 | 7.2 | 10.5 | 7.3 |
| Metallic ores and concentrates | 0.2 | 0.1 | 0.3 | 1.8 | 2.4 | ..... | ..... | ..... | ..... | 0.1 |
| Bituminous coal and lignite | 4.4 | 2.6 | ..... | ..... | 3.1 | ..... | ..... | 0.1 | ..... | ..... |
| Crude petroleum and natural gas | 0.1 | ..... | ..... | 0.2 | 0.8 | 0.1 | 0.2 | 0.1 | 0.1 | 0.1 |
| Nonmetallic minerals | 16.2 | 21.0 | 21.1 | 27.6 | 17.8 | 4.3 | 2.1 | 2.0 | 3.4 | 2.6 |
| Scrap and waste | 136.5 | 149.2 | 213.0 | 110.2 | 82.1 | 160.8 | 173.1 | 276.8 | 145.3 | 179.6 |
| Used merchandise | 54.2 | 49.7 | 78.2 | 76.8 | 58.0 | 2.5 | 16.0 | 26.6 | 6.4 | 6.4 |
| Goods imported and returned unchanged | ..... | ..... | ..... | ..... | ..... | ..... | ..... | ..... | ..... | ..... |
| Special classification provisions | 146.1 | 170.2 | 131.0 | 212.0 | 251.7 | 34.5 | 36.5 | 47.5 | 79.5 | 74.0 |
| | Taiwan | | | | | Singapore | | | | |
| **ALL GOODS** | 4 451.4 | 4 923.9 | 5 503.5 | 5 396.5 | 6 184.8 | 3 877.8 | 3 993.9 | 4 647.7 | 5 559.7 | 5 336.7 |
| **Manufactured goods** | 4 205.9 | 4 577.7 | 5 162.5 | 5 100.8 | 5 869.2 | 3 705.2 | 3 918.8 | 4 592.9 | 5 495.3 | 5 279.5 |
| Food products | 142.6 | 165.0 | 182.9 | 170.3 | 175.8 | 59.4 | 67.9 | 63.7 | 62.9 | 61.0 |
| Tobacco products | ..... | ..... | ..... | ..... | ..... | ..... | ..... | ..... | ..... | ..... |
| Textile mill products | 7.7 | 8.1 | 10.0 | 10.2 | 7.8 | 4.3 | 3.5 | 4.7 | 7.4 | 5.9 |
| Apparel | 4.2 | 4.8 | 6.2 | 6.1 | 8.8 | 6.5 | 11.0 | 12.4 | 23.8 | 17.6 |
| Lumber and wood products | 13.6 | 14.7 | 10.4 | 9.4 | 9.5 | 4.7 | 2.6 | 1.6 | 1.7 | 2.2 |
| Furniture and fixtures | 8.1 | 5.9 | 8.6 | 7.3 | 7.4 | 2.3 | 6.0 | 6.7 | 7.2 | 5.6 |
| Paper products | 27.4 | 47.3 | 69.2 | 56.3 | 52.1 | 15.6 | 21.3 | 30.4 | 38.3 | 35.4 |
| Printing and publishing | 10.5 | 10.3 | 13.9 | 12.1 | 11.8 | 8.5 | 8.5 | 9.6 | 11.7 | 11.3 |
| Chemical products | 118.2 | 138.6 | 138.4 | 162.6 | 222.2 | 63.4 | 88.9 | 92.4 | 88.4 | 79.2 |
| Refined petroleum products | 206.6 | 131.2 | 108.8 | 125.4 | 34.2 | 160.8 | 146.5 | 103.7 | 107.0 | 112.6 |
| Rubber and plastic products | 27.1 | 28.5 | 35.4 | 30.9 | 39.8 | 24.2 | 32.0 | 41.9 | 54.8 | 50.9 |
| Leather products | 3.4 | 3.1 | 3.7 | 1.6 | 3.0 | 1.5 | 2.2 | 2.1 | 4.3 | 4.7 |
| Stone, clay and glass products | 29.4 | 29.1 | 31.6 | 35.6 | 31.6 | 10.3 | 9.5 | 21.3 | 20.1 | 21.0 |
| Primary metals | 55.0 | 52.2 | 78.9 | 57.1 | 52.6 | 19.9 | 16.1 | 18.2 | 26.3 | 27.8 |
| Fabricated metal products | 45.8 | 43.0 | 49.6 | 58.1 | 52.6 | 30.6 | 32.0 | 36.9 | 55.1 | 146.9 |
| Industrial machinery and computers | 564.5 | 653.6 | 935.2 | 1 313.5 | 1 819.3 | 1 229.2 | 1 249.7 | 1 273.7 | 1 494.3 | 1 642.1 |
| Electric and electronic equipment | 1 295.9 | 1 451.2 | 1 755.1 | 1 888.2 | 1 886.9 | 1 593.0 | 1 779.7 | 2 360.5 | 2 891.6 | 2 382.5 |
| Transportation equipment | 1 400.5 | 1 533.4 | 1 426.2 | 780.9 | 980.9 | 279.6 | 221.3 | 243.0 | 256.2 | 284.3 |
| Scientific and measuring instruments | 201.7 | 208.6 | 232.4 | 333.3 | 432.7 | 139.7 | 157.4 | 209.1 | 281.8 | 323.7 |
| Miscellaneous manufactures | 32.7 | 39.3 | 53.1 | 31.3 | 29.2 | 36.7 | 44.8 | 50.8 | 53.0 | 56.7 |
| Unidentified manufactures | 10.9 | 9.8 | 13.1 | 10.7 | 10.8 | 15.3 | 18.0 | 10.1 | 9.4 | 8.0 |
| **Agricultural and livestock products** | 115.4 | 184.0 | 129.4 | 129.7 | 147.7 | 25.1 | 31.5 | 33.4 | 25.7 | 28.8 |
| Agricultural products | 113.5 | 181.4 | 125.7 | 126.9 | 145.1 | 25.0 | 31.4 | 33.3 | 25.4 | 28.2 |
| Livestock and livestock products | 1.8 | 2.6 | 3.7 | 2.8 | 2.5 | 0.1 | 0.1 | 0.1 | 0.3 | 0.6 |
| **Other commodities** | 130.1 | 162.2 | 211.6 | 166.0 | 168.0 | 147.5 | 43.5 | 21.3 | 38.7 | 28.4 |
| Forestry products | 2.0 | 1.9 | 1.6 | 0.9 | 1.6 | 0.4 | 0.2 | 0.2 | 0.4 | 0.2 |
| Fish and other marine products | 11.1 | 17.9 | 26.2 | 28.5 | 27.1 | 1.0 | 1.4 | 1.0 | 1.0 | 1.9 |
| Metallic ores and concentrates | 0.1 | ..... | 0.1 | 0.3 | 1.1 | ..... | ..... | ..... | ..... | ..... |
| Bituminous coal and lignite | ..... | ..... | 0.7 | ..... | ..... | ..... | ..... | ..... | ..... | ..... |
| Crude petroleum and natural gas | ..... | 0.2 | ..... | 0.4 | ..... | ..... | ..... | ..... | ..... | ..... |
| Nonmetallic minerals | 5.7 | 3.9 | 4.1 | 3.6 | 4.7 | 3.0 | 0.8 | 0.7 | 0.5 | 0.8 |
| Scrap and waste | 73.7 | 96.4 | 133.8 | 98.6 | 97.0 | 2.9 | 2.4 | 2.6 | 1.9 | 0.8 |
| Used merchandise | 2.7 | 2.4 | 2.9 | 1.8 | 1.6 | 5.1 | 3.0 | 5.1 | 5.3 | 4.5 |
| Goods imported and returned unchanged | ..... | ..... | ..... | ..... | ..... | ..... | ..... | ..... | ..... | ..... |
| Special classification provisions | 34.8 | 39.4 | 42.2 | 32.0 | 34.8 | 135.0 | 35.7 | 11.8 | 29.5 | 20.2 |

## COLORADO: Exports of Goods, 1997

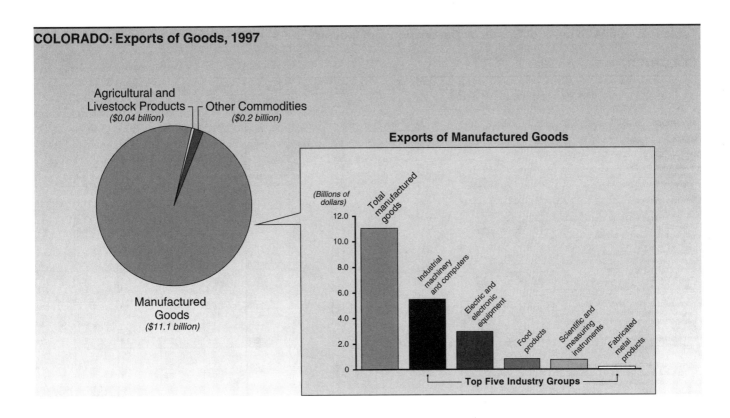

Agricultural and Livestock Products ($0.04 billion)

Other Commodities ($0.2 billion)

Manufactured Goods ($11.1 billion)

### Exports of Manufactured Goods

(Billions of dollars)

Top Five Industry Groups

## Table D-3.   State Exports of Goods by Destination and Industry, 1993–1997 —*Continued*

### COLORADO (Millions of dollars.)

| Industry | 1993 | 1994 | 1995 | 1996 | 1997 | 1993 | 1994 | 1995 | 1996 | 1997 |
|---|---|---|---|---|---|---|---|---|---|---|
| | All destinations | | | | | Canada | | | | |
| **ALL GOODS** | 6 214.8 | 7 802.1 | 9 688.8 | 10 064.9 | 11 329.2 | 595.3 | 524.2 | 602.8 | 609.7 | 671.6 |
| **Manufactured goods** | 6 071.1 | 7 641.5 | 9 423.0 | 9 824.4 | 11 056.6 | 563.8 | 490.1 | 561.7 | 559.3 | 614.1 |
| Food products | 282.4 | 449.6 | 539.5 | 612.2 | 829.9 | 108.0 | 118.9 | 107.3 | 105.4 | 114.5 |
| Tobacco products | 0.1 | 0.2 | 0.2 | ..... | ..... | ..... | ..... | ..... | ..... | ..... |
| Textile mill products | 6.4 | 7.0 | 9.9 | 11.5 | 11.6 | 2.6 | 1.6 | 1.9 | 1.3 | 1.4 |
| Apparel | 19.6 | 21.6 | 23.8 | 23.5 | 27.0 | 5.9 | 6.6 | 6.7 | 7.4 | 9.9 |
| Lumber and wood products | 4.5 | 5.5 | 4.0 | 12.0 | 6.5 | 0.3 | 0.5 | 0.2 | 0.8 | 1.5 |
| Furniture and fixtures | 14.5 | 16.8 | 12.4 | 13.1 | 15.0 | 3.1 | 2.7 | 3.9 | 3.9 | 4.7 |
| Paper products | 11.5 | 10.0 | 13.2 | 14.9 | 12.9 | 2.0 | 2.5 | 2.7 | 3.6 | 2.7 |
| Printing and publishing | 64.0 | 74.8 | 69.8 | 92.3 | 75.5 | 5.5 | 5.4 | 5.5 | 5.3 | 6.9 |
| Chemical products | 51.5 | 71.7 | 109.5 | 111.8 | 131.3 | 8.7 | 12.8 | 28.9 | 27.2 | 20.8 |
| Refined petroleum products | 2.0 | 7.3 | 4.9 | 2.8 | 3.4 | 0.4 | 2.7 | 1.5 | 1.2 | 1.0 |
| Rubber and plastic products | 61.8 | 86.4 | 101.3 | 91.7 | 97.4 | 6.3 | 8.4 | 10.1 | 9.1 | 10.4 |
| Leather products | 21.9 | 20.6 | 17.1 | 20.1 | 22.8 | 0.5 | 0.6 | 1.7 | 3.1 | 3.9 |
| Stone, clay and glass products | 60.5 | 82.8 | 86.8 | 76.0 | 87.0 | 5.4 | 3.8 | 4.4 | 3.9 | 4.3 |
| Primary metals | 65.3 | 76.6 | 156.1 | 121.8 | 122.2 | 6.0 | 6.3 | 13.3 | 48.1 | 28.4 |
| Fabricated metal products | 57.4 | 91.9 | 105.6 | 167.7 | 200.1 | 19.6 | 19.5 | 18.4 | 51.4 | 51.8 |
| Industrial machinery and computers | 3 441.3 | 4 621.9 | 5 650.5 | 5 574.2 | 5 491.7 | 209.6 | 146.2 | 162.7 | 123.0 | 130.4 |
| Electric and electronic equipment | 1 213.4 | 1 292.8 | 1 743.4 | 2 031.1 | 2 964.6 | 46.9 | 56.2 | 89.4 | 64.9 | 109.6 |
| Transportation equipment | 103.6 | 76.5 | 91.0 | 96.6 | 134.6 | 78.9 | 29.8 | 28.6 | 25.7 | 39.9 |
| Scientific and measuring instruments | 529.1 | 574.5 | 622.8 | 691.0 | 760.0 | 44.6 | 52.1 | 58.1 | 60.5 | 55.6 |
| Miscellaneous manufactures | 46.7 | 38.5 | 41.4 | 47.3 | 50.4 | 5.8 | 9.3 | 10.9 | 8.7 | 12.0 |
| Unidentified manufactures | 13.5 | 14.5 | 19.8 | 12.7 | 12.7 | 3.7 | 4.3 | 5.5 | 5.0 | 4.4 |
| **Agricultural and livestock products** | 19.0 | 33.5 | 35.4 | 32.0 | 41.6 | 5.9 | 5.2 | 8.5 | 7.0 | 7.1 |
| Agricultural products | 16.8 | 29.5 | 27.4 | 22.6 | 25.8 | 5.6 | 4.8 | 8.4 | 6.4 | 6.0 |
| Livestock and livestock products | 2.3 | 3.9 | 8.0 | 9.5 | 15.8 | 0.3 | 0.5 | 0.1 | 0.5 | 1.2 |
| **Other commodities** | 124.6 | 127.2 | 230.3 | 208.5 | 231.0 | 25.7 | 28.9 | 32.6 | 43.4 | 50.4 |
| Forestry products | 0.3 | 0.9 | 1.0 | 1.8 | 2.1 | 0.1 | 0.1 | 0.5 | 0.8 | 0.6 |
| Fish and other marine products | 0.9 | 0.3 | 0.6 | 0.2 | 1.7 | 0.2 | ..... | 0.3 | 0.1 | ..... |
| Metallic ores and concentrates | 0.2 | 22.2 | 81.5 | 47.5 | 64.6 | ..... | 0.4 | 1.0 | 0.6 | 1.4 |
| Bituminous coal and lignite | 52.1 | 32.8 | 62.4 | 57.1 | 59.9 | ..... | ..... | ..... | ..... | ..... |
| Crude petroleum and natural gas | 12.1 | 9.5 | 16.8 | 24.8 | 17.5 | ..... | 0.5 | ..... | 4.9 | 1.6 |
| Nonmetallic minerals | 11.4 | 18.1 | 20.5 | 24.3 | 25.0 | 2.7 | 3.4 | 5.1 | 6.8 | 7.4 |
| Scrap and waste | 1.7 | 2.1 | 11.8 | 2.9 | 4.2 | 0.8 | 0.7 | 2.9 | 1.9 | 2.0 |
| Used merchandise | 7.0 | 11.4 | 9.8 | 13.4 | 12.7 | 2.4 | 4.8 | 4.2 | 5.9 | 8.7 |
| Goods imported and returned unchanged | 16.0 | 15.6 | 15.1 | 17.6 | 24.3 | 16.0 | 15.6 | 15.1 | 17.6 | 24.3 |
| Special classification provisions | 22.8 | 14.3 | 10.9 | 18.9 | 19.1 | 3.5 | 3.5 | 3.5 | 4.8 | 4.5 |

## Table D-3.  State Exports of Goods by Destination and Industry, 1993–1997 —*Continued*

### COLORADO (Millions of dollars.)

| Industry | 1993 | 1994 | 1995 | 1996 | 1997 | 1993 | 1994 | 1995 | 1996 | 1997 |
|---|---|---|---|---|---|---|---|---|---|---|
| | South and Central America and Caribbean | | | | | Mexico | | | | |
| ALL GOODS | 521.6 | 521.3 | 518.4 | 519.1 | 516.7 | 604.4 | 636.8 | 692.7 | 902.5 | 1 418.0 |
| Manufactured goods | 517.5 | 514.5 | 510.5 | 511.5 | 510.5 | 580.7 | 622.4 | 660.3 | 851.5 | 1 359.2 |
| Food products | 1.3 | 1.7 | 2.1 | 3.0 | 7.6 | 18.9 | 52.6 | 15.7 | 17.2 | 42.1 |
| Tobacco products | ..... | 0.1 | 0.2 | ..... | ..... | ..... | ..... | ..... | ..... | ..... |
| Textile mill products | 0.4 | 1.2 | 2.2 | 2.7 | 2.2 | 0.9 | 1.7 | 1.6 | 2.8 | 3.2 |
| Apparel | 0.7 | 0.7 | 3.2 | 2.5 | 0.7 | 0.7 | 0.3 | 0.2 | 0.8 | 1.2 |
| Lumber and wood products | 0.2 | 1.3 | 0.1 | 0.2 | 0.1 | 0.2 | 0.3 | 0.1 | 0.3 | 0.3 |
| Furniture and fixtures | 0.2 | 2.7 | 0.5 | 0.4 | 0.6 | 1.2 | 1.1 | 0.5 | 1.1 | 0.9 |
| Paper products | 0.7 | 1.1 | 0.7 | 1.3 | 0.9 | 2.5 | 1.3 | 2.3 | 3.2 | 1.4 |
| Printing and publishing | 0.9 | 1.7 | 1.0 | 1.7 | 3.3 | 9.1 | 4.1 | 3.5 | 17.0 | 9.9 |
| Chemical products | 11.5 | 8.0 | 22.9 | 17.0 | 17.0 | 9.3 | 22.6 | 30.3 | 16.6 | 26.7 |
| Refined petroleum products | 0.2 | 0.1 | 0.2 | 0.1 | ..... | 0.1 | 2.8 | 0.4 | 0.2 | 0.3 |
| Rubber and plastic products | 6.6 | 9.9 | 15.3 | 10.3 | 8.6 | 5.9 | 6.7 | 17.7 | 9.4 | 7.3 |
| Leather products | 3.0 | 2.5 | 2.7 | 1.5 | 1.7 | 0.2 | 0.2 | 0.3 | 0.4 | 2.5 |
| Stone, clay and glass products | 1.7 | 1.6 | 1.5 | 1.4 | 1.4 | 1.5 | 0.9 | 0.7 | 0.8 | 0.8 |
| Primary metals | 7.4 | 7.0 | 5.2 | 5.6 | 10.0 | 10.9 | 4.6 | 5.7 | 4.5 | 10.7 |
| Fabricated metal products | 4.6 | 4.9 | 5.9 | 17.7 | 5.9 | 3.4 | 3.9 | 2.4 | 2.0 | 7.5 |
| Industrial machinery and computers | 401.7 | 391.2 | 371.2 | 381.6 | 371.4 | 376.3 | 454.8 | 519.8 | 722.4 | 1 083.8 |
| Electric and electronic equipment | 56.3 | 58.9 | 52.7 | 34.2 | 42.3 | 116.9 | 43.2 | 49.7 | 38.8 | 139.1 |
| Transportation equipment | 2.3 | 3.7 | 3.4 | 6.7 | 5.0 | 1.5 | 2.4 | 0.9 | 0.6 | 3.7 |
| Scientific and measuring instruments | 13.2 | 14.9 | 16.2 | 20.9 | 27.4 | 15.4 | 15.7 | 5.9 | 10.8 | 13.2 |
| Miscellaneous manufactures | 2.9 | 0.9 | 1.0 | 1.5 | 2.3 | 5.2 | 2.3 | 2.2 | 2.1 | 3.0 |
| Unidentified manufactures | 1.6 | 0.8 | 2.3 | 1.1 | 2.1 | 0.5 | 0.7 | 0.3 | 0.4 | 1.4 |
| Agricultural and livestock products | 2.2 | 1.7 | 2.6 | 1.9 | 2.1 | 1.3 | 2.7 | 1.1 | 4.1 | 3.4 |
| Agricultural products | 2.2 | 1.7 | 2.6 | 1.9 | 2.0 | 0.9 | 2.2 | 1.1 | 4.0 | 3.2 |
| Livestock and livestock products | ..... | ..... | ..... | 0.1 | ..... | 0.4 | 0.4 | ..... | ..... | 0.3 |
| Other commodities | 2.0 | 5.1 | 5.3 | 5.7 | 4.1 | 22.3 | 11.7 | 31.3 | 46.9 | 55.4 |
| Forestry products | ..... | ..... | ..... | ..... | ..... | ..... | 0.3 | 0.2 | 0.2 | 0.1 |
| Fish and other marine products | ..... | ..... | ..... | ..... | ..... | ..... | ..... | ..... | ..... | ..... |
| Metallic ores and concentrates | ..... | 2.2 | 0.1 | 0.1 | 0.2 | ..... | ..... | ..... | 0.1 | ..... |
| Bituminous coal and lignite | ..... | ..... | ..... | ..... | ..... | ..... | ..... | 13.3 | 25.3 | 38.0 |
| Crude petroleum and natural gas | ..... | ..... | ..... | ..... | ..... | 12.1 | 9.0 | 16.7 | 19.7 | 15.9 |
| Nonmetallic minerals | 0.9 | 1.9 | 4.6 | 4.9 | 3.4 | 0.6 | 0.5 | 0.5 | 0.5 | 0.5 |
| Scrap and waste | ..... | 0.3 | 0.3 | ..... | ..... | 0.3 | 0.4 | 0.4 | 0.2 | 0.4 |
| Used merchandise | 0.1 | 0.3 | 0.2 | 0.3 | 0.4 | 1.5 | 0.8 | 0.1 | 0.4 | 0.2 |
| Goods imported and returned unchanged | ..... | ..... | ..... | ..... | ..... | ..... | ..... | ..... | ..... | ..... |
| Special classification provisions | 0.9 | 0.3 | 0.2 | 0.5 | 0.2 | 8.0 | 0.8 | ..... | 0.5 | 0.1 |
| | European Union | | | | | United Kingdom | | | | |
| ALL GOODS | 2 259.4 | 3 263.6 | 3 741.7 | 3 674.0 | 3 693.1 | 495.8 | 780.3 | 811.4 | 671.6 | 689.3 |
| Manufactured goods | 2 234.4 | 3 225.6 | 3 669.8 | 3 631.9 | 3 634.4 | 492.9 | 774.7 | 802.8 | 662.0 | 678.6 |
| Food products | 8.8 | 16.5 | 22.6 | 22.2 | 35.5 | 2.9 | 6.1 | 4.0 | 3.8 | 6.4 |
| Tobacco products | ..... | ..... | ..... | ..... | ..... | ..... | ..... | ..... | ..... | ..... |
| Textile mill products | 0.6 | 0.8 | 1.2 | 2.4 | 2.4 | 0.1 | ..... | 0.1 | 0.5 | 0.2 |
| Apparel | 6.3 | 7.3 | 8.2 | 6.2 | 8.2 | 1.1 | 1.6 | 2.0 | 1.6 | 2.1 |
| Lumber and wood products | 1.8 | 0.7 | 0.1 | 0.8 | 0.3 | 0.1 | ..... | ..... | 0.2 | ..... |
| Furniture and fixtures | 7.0 | 7.4 | 5.3 | 5.4 | 6.6 | 3.6 | 3.3 | 2.0 | 1.8 | 2.6 |
| Paper products | 3.6 | 2.4 | 4.8 | 2.6 | 2.5 | 0.5 | 0.8 | 3.3 | 0.6 | 0.6 |
| Printing and publishing | 32.9 | 43.7 | 39.9 | 39.9 | 26.4 | 3.8 | 5.6 | 5.2 | 5.8 | 5.0 |
| Chemical products | 13.7 | 14.2 | 15.7 | 21.3 | 25.6 | 5.1 | 2.2 | 1.7 | 2.3 | 4.7 |
| Refined petroleum products | ..... | 0.8 | 1.3 | 0.5 | 0.8 | ..... | ..... | 0.5 | ..... | 0.4 |
| Rubber and plastic products | 22.1 | 30.3 | 30.0 | 28.9 | 27.0 | 3.9 | 4.0 | 6.6 | 7.5 | 7.0 |
| Leather products | 1.1 | 1.7 | 2.0 | 2.1 | 2.6 | 0.5 | 1.0 | 0.5 | 0.4 | 0.2 |
| Stone, clay and glass products | 32.3 | 41.5 | 36.7 | 38.3 | 40.4 | 9.2 | 18.7 | 14.4 | 13.5 | 10.8 |
| Primary metals | 20.1 | 35.3 | 59.8 | 26.0 | 21.0 | 5.1 | 9.1 | 7.9 | 6.1 | 2.8 |
| Fabricated metal products | 17.4 | 49.1 | 58.0 | 69.9 | 72.5 | 3.9 | 6.2 | 6.5 | 6.7 | 7.7 |
| Industrial machinery and computers | 1 269.2 | 2 115.2 | 2 416.9 | 2 233.0 | 1 990.4 | 283.6 | 500.5 | 555.1 | 430.6 | 383.2 |
| Electric and electronic equipment | 495.2 | 547.3 | 658.7 | 798.8 | 1 013.8 | 132.5 | 172.1 | 152.9 | 136.6 | 198.6 |
| Transportation equipment | 10.1 | 21.3 | 25.2 | 19.8 | 21.8 | 1.5 | 12.0 | 9.1 | 6.8 | 4.3 |
| Scientific and measuring instruments | 270.3 | 273.1 | 266.4 | 297.0 | 325.4 | 33.6 | 28.5 | 28.4 | 35.4 | 40.4 |
| Miscellaneous manufactures | 18.8 | 13.4 | 12.5 | 14.9 | 9.7 | 1.3 | 2.2 | 1.7 | 1.6 | 1.1 |
| Unidentified manufactures | 3.0 | 3.6 | 4.4 | 2.0 | 1.4 | 0.6 | 0.6 | 0.8 | 0.4 | 0.3 |
| Agricultural and livestock products | 6.4 | 9.9 | 10.2 | 6.5 | 8.4 | 1.6 | 2.6 | 2.5 | 1.2 | 1.7 |
| Agricultural products | 6.3 | 8.8 | 9.0 | 5.9 | 6.1 | 1.5 | 2.6 | 2.5 | 1.0 | 1.2 |
| Livestock and livestock products | 0.1 | 1.1 | 1.2 | 0.6 | 2.3 | ..... | ..... | ..... | 0.2 | 0.5 |
| Other commodities | 18.7 | 28.0 | 61.6 | 35.5 | 50.3 | 1.3 | 2.9 | 6.1 | 8.4 | 9.0 |
| Forestry products | 0.1 | ..... | 0.1 | 0.1 | 1.0 | ..... | ..... | ..... | ..... | ..... |
| Fish and other marine products | ..... | 0.1 | 0.1 | 0.1 | 1.4 | ..... | ..... | ..... | ..... | ..... |
| Metallic ores and concentrates | 0.2 | 13.8 | 39.0 | 16.6 | 25.6 | ..... | 0.3 | 2.5 | 1.7 | 3.0 |
| Bituminous coal and lignite | 8.0 | 6.6 | 13.2 | 3.3 | 8.0 | ..... | ..... | ..... | ..... | 2.8 |
| Crude petroleum and natural gas | ..... | ..... | ..... | ..... | ..... | ..... | ..... | ..... | ..... | ..... |
| Nonmetallic minerals | 3.6 | 2.6 | 3.3 | 4.6 | 4.8 | ..... | 0.3 | 1.4 | 1.4 | 0.9 |
| Scrap and waste | 0.1 | 0.1 | 0.1 | ..... | 0.4 | ..... | ..... | 0.1 | ..... | 0.1 |
| Used merchandise | 1.3 | 1.0 | 2.7 | 4.4 | 1.3 | 0.2 | 0.4 | 1.0 | 3.2 | 0.3 |
| Goods imported and returned unchanged | ..... | ..... | ..... | ..... | ..... | ..... | ..... | ..... | ..... | ..... |
| Special classification provisions | 5.3 | 3.9 | 3.1 | 6.4 | 7.7 | 1.0 | 1.8 | 1.0 | 2.0 | 2.1 |

## Table D-3.  State Exports of Goods by Destination and Industry, 1993–1997 —Continued

**COLORADO** (Millions of dollars.)

| Industry | 1993 | 1994 | 1995 | 1996 | 1997 | 1993 | 1994 | 1995 | 1996 | 1997 |
|---|---|---|---|---|---|---|---|---|---|---|
| | Germany | | | | | France | | | | |
| **ALL GOODS** | 502.5 | 769.9 | 900.5 | 735.0 | 669.4 | 350.7 | 512.6 | 715.6 | 624.2 | 521.9 |
| **Manufactured goods** | 500.5 | 767.1 | 898.0 | 731.7 | 664.3 | 349.5 | 510.9 | 713.5 | 622.3 | 519.4 |
| Food products | 1.7 | 1.7 | 11.1 | 6.7 | 1.3 | 1.1 | 0.9 | 0.6 | 0.5 | 0.7 |
| Tobacco products | ..... | ..... | ..... | ..... | ..... | ..... | ..... | ..... | ..... | ..... |
| Textile mill products | 0.1 | ..... | ..... | 0.1 | 0.5 | ..... | ..... | ..... | 0.2 | 0.2 |
| Apparel | 1.8 | 2.3 | 1.6 | 1.6 | 1.7 | 0.8 | 0.6 | 0.4 | 0.1 | 0.6 |
| Lumber and wood products | ..... | ..... | ..... | ..... | ..... | ..... | 0.1 | ..... | 0.1 | ..... |
| Furniture and fixtures | 0.6 | 0.9 | 0.8 | 0.6 | 0.6 | 0.8 | 1.9 | 1.3 | 1.8 | 2.6 |
| Paper products | 2.3 | 0.9 | 0.8 | 1.3 | 1.1 | 0.2 | 0.3 | 0.2 | 0.2 | 0.1 |
| Printing and publishing | 4.2 | 6.7 | 8.5 | 4.5 | 2.7 | 3.0 | 5.0 | 3.9 | 4.2 | 2.4 |
| Chemical products | 1.4 | 1.4 | 1.3 | 2.1 | 3.6 | 2.2 | 1.4 | 2.0 | 5.9 | 5.3 |
| Refined petroleum products | ..... | ..... | ..... | ..... | ..... | ..... | ..... | ..... | ..... | ..... |
| Rubber and plastic products | 5.1 | 9.6 | 7.7 | 8.5 | 9.0 | 5.5 | 4.1 | 3.3 | 1.0 | 1.3 |
| Leather products | 0.2 | 0.3 | 0.1 | 0.2 | 0.1 | 0.1 | ..... | ..... | 0.1 | 0.2 |
| Stone, clay and glass products | 11.9 | 10.3 | 7.9 | 6.2 | 8.2 | 0.9 | 1.5 | 1.5 | 2.0 | 5.2 |
| Primary metals | 2.4 | 5.4 | 19.7 | 2.5 | 2.2 | 4.3 | 8.2 | 20.4 | 6.7 | 5.6 |
| Fabricated metal products | 9.8 | 35.6 | 47.3 | 59.1 | 57.5 | 0.7 | 0.9 | 1.1 | 0.6 | 1.6 |
| Industrial machinery and computers | 302.5 | 529.1 | 578.5 | 433.8 | 389.8 | 196.1 | 384.9 | 559.6 | 459.2 | 342.1 |
| Electric and electronic equipment | 99.2 | 106.8 | 141.8 | 134.5 | 110.5 | 87.5 | 66.8 | 86.6 | 98.9 | 109.3 |
| Transportation equipment | 2.5 | 3.5 | 4.5 | 2.6 | 4.3 | 1.5 | 2.0 | 2.4 | 5.8 | 8.0 |
| Scientific and measuring instruments | 50.9 | 49.5 | 61.9 | 64.4 | 69.0 | 33.9 | 29.5 | 28.5 | 33.6 | 33.1 |
| Miscellaneous manufactures | 3.2 | 2.1 | 3.2 | 2.8 | 1.9 | 10.4 | 2.4 | 1.1 | 1.0 | 0.8 |
| Unidentified manufactures | 0.7 | 1.0 | 1.1 | 0.4 | 0.2 | 0.3 | 0.4 | 0.6 | 0.2 | 0.2 |
| **Agricultural and livestock products** | 0.2 | 0.7 | 0.9 | 0.9 | 0.8 | 0.5 | 1.2 | 0.6 | 0.9 | 0.6 |
| Agricultural products | 0.2 | 0.4 | 0.9 | 0.9 | 0.6 | 0.5 | 1.2 | 0.6 | 0.9 | 0.6 |
| Livestock and livestock products | ..... | 0.3 | ..... | ..... | 0.2 | ..... | ..... | ..... | ..... | ..... |
| **Other commodities** | 1.8 | 2.1 | 1.6 | 2.4 | 4.3 | 0.7 | 0.5 | 1.5 | 1.0 | 1.8 |
| Forestry products | ..... | ..... | ..... | ..... | 0.9 | ..... | ..... | ..... | ..... | ..... |
| Fish and other marine products | ..... | ..... | ..... | ..... | 0.1 | ..... | ..... | 0.1 | 0.1 | ..... |
| Metallic ores and concentrates | ..... | 1.2 | 0.4 | ..... | ..... | ..... | ..... | ..... | ..... | ..... |
| Bituminous coal and lignite | ..... | ..... | ..... | ..... | ..... | ..... | ..... | ..... | ..... | ..... |
| Crude petroleum and natural gas | ..... | ..... | ..... | ..... | ..... | ..... | ..... | ..... | ..... | ..... |
| Nonmetallic minerals | ..... | 0.1 | ..... | ..... | 0.1 | ..... | ..... | ..... | 0.1 | ..... |
| Scrap and waste | ..... | ..... | ..... | ..... | ..... | ..... | 0.1 | ..... | ..... | ..... |
| Used merchandise | 0.8 | 0.2 | 0.6 | 0.5 | 0.3 | 0.1 | 0.2 | 0.8 | 0.2 | 0.3 |
| Goods imported and returned unchanged | ..... | ..... | ..... | ..... | ..... | ..... | ..... | ..... | ..... | ..... |
| Special classification provisions | 1.0 | 0.6 | 0.7 | 1.9 | 2.8 | 0.4 | 0.3 | 0.6 | 0.7 | 1.5 |
| | The Netherlands | | | | | Asian 10 | | | | |
| **ALL GOODS** | 259.8 | 363.0 | 428.8 | 548.5 | 500.2 | 1 719.1 | 2 299.4 | 3 400.4 | 3 574.9 | 4 098.4 |
| **Manufactured goods** | 257.2 | 351.7 | 407.2 | 541.3 | 488.3 | 1 665.1 | 2 248.6 | 3 305.7 | 3 497.6 | 4 024.1 |
| Food products | 0.8 | 0.8 | 1.9 | 1.2 | 1.1 | 140.5 | 252.3 | 379.7 | 441.2 | 520.9 |
| Tobacco products | ..... | ..... | ..... | ..... | ..... | ..... | ..... | ..... | ..... | ..... |
| Textile mill products | 0.1 | 0.2 | 0.4 | 0.5 | 0.7 | 1.4 | 0.8 | 1.7 | 1.4 | 1.4 |
| Apparel | 0.2 | 0.3 | 3.3 | 1.6 | 1.5 | 3.5 | 3.9 | 3.4 | 5.0 | 3.8 |
| Lumber and wood products | ..... | 0.1 | ..... | 0.2 | ..... | 0.4 | 1.1 | 1.8 | 8.5 | 3.4 |
| Furniture and fixtures | 1.1 | 0.6 | 0.7 | 0.7 | 0.3 | 2.1 | 2.1 | 1.1 | 1.5 | 1.1 |
| Paper products | 0.1 | 0.1 | 0.1 | 0.2 | 0.2 | 1.5 | 2.0 | 1.5 | 3.0 | 4.0 |
| Printing and publishing | 1.0 | 2.0 | 1.9 | 3.1 | 1.0 | 10.3 | 13.0 | 14.4 | 21.6 | 22.3 |
| Chemical products | 0.2 | 2.4 | 1.7 | 2.6 | 4.1 | 4.2 | 10.2 | 8.0 | 19.8 | 12.5 |
| Refined petroleum products | ..... | ..... | ..... | ..... | ..... | 1.1 | 0.9 | 1.4 | 0.6 | 0.5 |
| Rubber and plastic products | 0.6 | 1.1 | 2.6 | 2.0 | 1.7 | 14.1 | 21.3 | 20.6 | 24.4 | 32.2 |
| Leather products | 0.2 | 0.1 | 0.1 | 0.1 | 0.1 | 8.8 | 10.3 | 7.2 | 8.3 | 9.9 |
| Stone, clay and glass products | 2.3 | 3.0 | 2.3 | 3.6 | 2.6 | 16.3 | 30.9 | 37.7 | 26.0 | 34.2 |
| Primary metals | 1.2 | 2.3 | 2.5 | 3.5 | 2.8 | 15.7 | 17.7 | 66.2 | 20.0 | 38.3 |
| Fabricated metal products | 0.9 | 1.0 | 1.4 | 1.6 | 2.4 | 6.9 | 11.4 | 17.5 | 20.3 | 50.1 |
| Industrial machinery and computers | 200.2 | 277.8 | 293.5 | 397.9 | 325.9 | 887.7 | 1 175.5 | 1 744.5 | 1 697.9 | 1 460.2 |
| Electric and electronic equipment | 18.1 | 19.4 | 45.0 | 70.7 | 91.5 | 406.4 | 510.0 | 748.5 | 913.4 | 1 493.2 |
| Transportation equipment | 1.1 | 1.5 | 5.9 | 2.2 | 3.0 | 6.3 | 15.5 | 23.3 | 36.1 | 46.4 |
| Scientific and measuring instruments | 27.7 | 36.6 | 40.8 | 43.1 | 48.3 | 125.6 | 158.7 | 211.3 | 230.5 | 268.2 |
| Miscellaneous manufactures | 1.2 | 1.8 | 2.8 | 6.2 | 1.0 | 9.7 | 8.8 | 11.8 | 15.7 | 19.6 |
| Unidentified manufactures | 0.2 | 0.4 | 0.4 | 0.4 | 0.2 | 2.6 | 2.4 | 4.1 | 2.4 | 2.0 |
| **Agricultural and livestock products** | 0.5 | 0.5 | 0.4 | 0.3 | 0.4 | 1.0 | 3.0 | 5.7 | 8.2 | 9.2 |
| Agricultural products | 0.5 | 0.5 | 0.4 | 0.3 | 0.4 | 0.6 | 1.7 | 1.9 | 2.0 | 2.6 |
| Livestock and livestock products | ..... | ..... | ..... | ..... | ..... | 0.4 | 1.3 | 3.8 | 6.2 | 6.6 |
| **Other commodities** | 2.1 | 10.8 | 21.2 | 7.0 | 11.5 | 53.1 | 47.8 | 89.0 | 69.1 | 65.1 |
| Forestry products | ..... | ..... | ..... | ..... | ..... | ..... | 0.5 | ..... | 0.7 | 0.4 |
| Fish and other marine products | ..... | ..... | ..... | ..... | ..... | 0.6 | 0.1 | 0.1 | ..... | 0.2 |
| Metallic ores and concentrates | ..... | 10.4 | 20.2 | 5.7 | 9.0 | ..... | 5.5 | 41.2 | 29.2 | 36.7 |
| Bituminous coal and lignite | ..... | ..... | ..... | ..... | ..... | 44.1 | 26.2 | 35.9 | 26.4 | 13.8 |
| Crude petroleum and natural gas | ..... | ..... | ..... | ..... | ..... | ..... | ..... | ..... | 0.1 | ..... |
| Nonmetallic minerals | 0.5 | ..... | 0.8 | 0.7 | 2.1 | 3.3 | 8.5 | 6.7 | 5.7 | 8.0 |
| Scrap and waste | ..... | ..... | ..... | ..... | ..... | 0.5 | 0.5 | 0.5 | 0.7 | 0.4 |
| Used merchandise | ..... | ..... | ..... | 0.1 | ..... | 0.7 | 1.3 | 1.5 | 1.8 | 1.0 |
| Goods imported and returned unchanged | ..... | ..... | ..... | ..... | ..... | ..... | ..... | ..... | ..... | ..... |
| Special classification provisions | 1.5 | 0.4 | 0.2 | 0.5 | 0.4 | 3.9 | 5.1 | 3.1 | 4.5 | 4.6 |

## Table D-3.  State Exports of Goods by Destination and Industry, 1993–1997 —*Continued*

### COLORADO (Millions of dollars.)

| Industry | 1993 | 1994 | 1995 | 1996 | 1997 | 1993 | 1994 | 1995 | 1996 | 1997 |
|---|---|---|---|---|---|---|---|---|---|---|
| | Japan | | | | | South Korea | | | | |
| **ALL GOODS** | 1 017.1 | 1 158.7 | 1 555.6 | 1 590.1 | 1 691.4 | 154.2 | 174.8 | 250.4 | 342.2 | 609.0 |
| **Manufactured goods** | 983.5 | 1 137.2 | 1 490.7 | 1 538.7 | 1 637.5 | 147.2 | 164.4 | 238.4 | 329.8 | 606.6 |
| Food products | 125.6 | 226.6 | 337.4 | 324.6 | 342.0 | 5.0 | 7.0 | 13.3 | 33.6 | 82.4 |
| Tobacco products | ..... | ..... | ..... | ..... | ..... | ..... | ..... | ..... | ..... | ..... |
| Textile mill products | 0.7 | 0.4 | 0.4 | 0.3 | 0.4 | 0.1 | 0.1 | 0.8 | 0.2 | 0.4 |
| Apparel | 2.9 | 3.3 | 2.9 | 3.6 | 2.8 | 0.1 | ..... | ..... | 0.1 | 0.1 |
| Lumber and wood products | 0.3 | 0.6 | 1.2 | 7.6 | 0.3 | ..... | 0.3 | 0.3 | 0.3 | 1.9 |
| Furniture and fixtures | 1.1 | 0.3 | 0.2 | 0.8 | 0.3 | ..... | ..... | ..... | 0.3 | ..... |
| Paper products | 0.6 | 0.3 | 0.2 | 0.9 | 0.8 | 0.1 | ..... | 0.2 | 0.1 | 0.2 |
| Printing and publishing | 7.2 | 8.8 | 9.9 | 16.7 | 13.7 | 0.3 | 0.4 | 1.5 | 1.6 | 3.3 |
| Chemical products | 1.0 | 1.4 | 3.9 | 6.3 | 4.1 | 1.2 | 0.7 | 0.8 | 2.2 | 3.1 |
| Refined petroleum products | 0.4 | 0.1 | 0.4 | 0.4 | 0.3 | 0.7 | 0.6 | 0.7 | 0.2 | ..... |
| Rubber and plastic products | 4.1 | 4.6 | 7.2 | 7.7 | 8.6 | 3.4 | 7.0 | 3.8 | 3.6 | 5.2 |
| Leather products | 0.7 | 0.6 | 1.3 | 0.8 | 1.1 | 1.6 | 2.4 | 2.3 | 4.2 | 2.1 |
| Stone, clay and glass products | 1.2 | 2.9 | 6.7 | 4.9 | 8.8 | 3.2 | 3.1 | 2.6 | 2.9 | 1.8 |
| Primary metals | 11.3 | 10.6 | 8.2 | 9.2 | 9.2 | 0.4 | 0.7 | 0.6 | 0.5 | 2.2 |
| Fabricated metal products | 2.8 | 3.6 | 11.5 | 15.1 | 43.1 | 0.5 | 1.0 | 0.6 | 0.3 | 0.6 |
| Industrial machinery and computers | 562.9 | 629.2 | 791.1 | 802.3 | 640.9 | 61.5 | 64.4 | 105.4 | 116.9 | 95.9 |
| Electric and electronic equipment | 180.9 | 146.1 | 180.7 | 168.1 | 357.4 | 55.6 | 62.7 | 84.1 | 139.9 | 385.2 |
| Transportation equipment | 1.6 | 1.1 | 4.4 | 21.5 | 33.8 | 2.0 | 0.2 | 2.6 | 2.0 | 1.3 |
| Scientific and measuring instruments | 74.2 | 91.5 | 116.1 | 140.8 | 163.4 | 10.0 | 12.8 | 16.4 | 18.4 | 17.0 |
| Miscellaneous manufactures | 3.5 | 4.5 | 5.9 | 6.6 | 5.8 | 1.2 | 0.6 | 1.3 | 1.8 | 3.4 |
| Unidentified manufactures | 0.5 | 0.7 | 1.1 | 0.4 | 0.5 | 0.4 | 0.3 | 1.3 | 0.6 | 0.6 |
| **Agricultural and livestock products** | 0.5 | 1.1 | 1.3 | 0.8 | 1.1 | 0.2 | 0.3 | 0.4 | 0.3 | 0.4 |
| Agricultural products | 0.5 | 1.1 | 1.3 | 0.8 | 1.0 | ..... | 0.1 | 0.1 | 0.3 | 0.4 |
| Livestock and livestock products | ..... | ..... | ..... | ..... | 0.1 | 0.1 | 0.1 | 0.4 | ..... | ..... |
| **Other commodities** | 33.1 | 20.4 | 63.6 | 50.6 | 52.8 | 6.8 | 10.1 | 11.5 | 12.1 | 2.0 |
| Forestry products | ..... | 0.1 | ..... | ..... | ..... | ..... | ..... | ..... | 0.6 | 0.4 |
| Fish and other marine products | 0.6 | 0.1 | ..... | ..... | ..... | ..... | ..... | 0.1 | ..... | 0.2 |
| Metallic ores and concentrates | ..... | 5.2 | 41.2 | 29.1 | 36.6 | ..... | 0.3 | ..... | ..... | ..... |
| Bituminous coal and lignite | 29.5 | 11.4 | 19.9 | 16.8 | 13.8 | 6.4 | 8.2 | 10.3 | 9.7 | ..... |
| Crude petroleum and natural gas | ..... | ..... | ..... | 0.1 | ..... | ..... | ..... | ..... | ..... | ..... |
| Nonmetallic minerals | 0.7 | ..... | ..... | ..... | ..... | 0.3 | 0.8 | 0.8 | 1.4 | 1.3 |
| Scrap and waste | ..... | ..... | 0.1 | 0.4 | 0.2 | 0.1 | 0.1 | 0.1 | ..... | ..... |
| Used merchandise | 0.4 | 0.9 | 0.6 | 1.3 | 0.4 | ..... | ..... | ..... | ..... | ..... |
| Goods imported and returned unchanged | ..... | ..... | ..... | ..... | ..... | ..... | ..... | ..... | ..... | ..... |
| Special classification provisions | 1.9 | 2.7 | 1.8 | 2.8 | 1.8 | 0.1 | 0.8 | 0.2 | 0.4 | 0.2 |

| Industry | 1993 | 1994 | 1995 | 1996 | 1997 | 1993 | 1994 | 1995 | 1996 | 1997 |
|---|---|---|---|---|---|---|---|---|---|---|
| | Taiwan | | | | | Singapore | | | | |
| **ALL GOODS** | 86.5 | 130.4 | 205.7 | 197.2 | 214.2 | 193.2 | 308.6 | 591.7 | 638.9 | 622.5 |
| **Manufactured goods** | 76.1 | 117.2 | 198.4 | 195.3 | 212.4 | 191.7 | 306.8 | 586.9 | 638.0 | 619.8 |
| Food products | 3.6 | 3.2 | 6.9 | 14.5 | 19.4 | 0.2 | 0.3 | 0.7 | 2.2 | 1.7 |
| Tobacco products | ..... | ..... | ..... | ..... | ..... | ..... | ..... | ..... | ..... | ..... |
| Textile mill products | 0.1 | 0.1 | ..... | 0.2 | 0.2 | 0.1 | ..... | 0.3 | 0.4 | 0.2 |
| Apparel | 0.1 | 0.1 | 0.1 | 0.3 | 0.3 | ..... | 0.2 | ..... | 0.4 | 0.1 |
| Lumber and wood products | 0.1 | ..... | 0.2 | 0.3 | 0.1 | ..... | ..... | ..... | 0.1 | 0.1 |
| Furniture and fixtures | 0.7 | 0.2 | ..... | ..... | ..... | 0.1 | 1.3 | 0.5 | 0.2 | 0.1 |
| Paper products | 0.1 | ..... | 0.1 | 0.2 | 0.3 | 0.5 | 1.0 | 0.7 | 0.7 | 2.2 |
| Printing and publishing | 0.8 | 0.7 | 0.5 | 0.5 | 0.6 | 1.3 | 1.2 | 1.1 | 1.1 | 2.1 |
| Chemical products | 0.3 | 0.3 | 0.7 | 1.1 | 0.9 | 0.7 | 1.0 | 0.6 | 2.6 | 0.6 |
| Refined petroleum products | ..... | 0.1 | 0.1 | ..... | 0.2 | ..... | ..... | ..... | ..... | ..... |
| Rubber and plastic products | 1.5 | 2.4 | 0.7 | 3.0 | 4.1 | 4.1 | 5.3 | 6.3 | 6.9 | 8.6 |
| Leather products | 0.8 | 0.9 | 0.4 | 0.3 | 2.4 | 2.3 | 2.6 | 1.2 | 1.3 | 2.0 |
| Stone, clay and glass products | 4.7 | 7.7 | 7.1 | 6.6 | 6.9 | 1.8 | 2.4 | 3.4 | 1.9 | 0.5 |
| Primary metals | 0.3 | 0.9 | 1.2 | 1.4 | 4.9 | 2.5 | 3.3 | 24.6 | 3.9 | 17.0 |
| Fabricated metal products | 0.3 | 0.9 | 0.5 | 0.4 | 1.1 | 2.4 | 2.7 | 2.0 | 1.2 | 2.0 |
| Industrial machinery and computers | 36.1 | 41.7 | 74.9 | 46.2 | 54.2 | 88.0 | 159.4 | 375.9 | 374.6 | 304.8 |
| Electric and electronic equipment | 18.2 | 45.7 | 92.3 | 100.8 | 96.4 | 64.9 | 104.2 | 132.6 | 211.1 | 252.0 |
| Transportation equipment | 0.2 | 0.2 | 0.1 | 0.8 | 0.3 | 1.0 | 1.2 | 1.7 | 2.0 | 1.6 |
| Scientific and measuring instruments | 7.3 | 10.6 | 11.7 | 14.8 | 17.5 | 19.0 | 19.8 | 33.5 | 26.0 | 23.7 |
| Miscellaneous manufactures | 0.5 | 1.3 | 0.8 | 3.7 | 2.3 | 2.4 | 0.4 | 1.2 | 1.3 | 0.5 |
| Unidentified manufactures | 0.5 | 0.2 | 0.3 | 0.3 | 0.2 | 0.6 | 0.5 | 0.6 | 0.3 | 0.1 |
| **Agricultural and livestock products** | ..... | ..... | ..... | 0.2 | 0.1 | ..... | ..... | ..... | ..... | ..... |
| Agricultural products | ..... | ..... | ..... | 0.2 | 0.1 | ..... | ..... | ..... | ..... | ..... |
| Livestock and livestock products | ..... | ..... | ..... | ..... | ..... | ..... | ..... | ..... | ..... | ..... |
| **Other commodities** | 10.4 | 13.2 | 7.3 | 1.8 | 1.8 | 1.5 | 1.8 | 4.8 | 0.9 | 2.6 |
| Forestry products | ..... | ..... | ..... | ..... | ..... | ..... | ..... | ..... | ..... | ..... |
| Fish and other marine products | ..... | ..... | ..... | ..... | ..... | ..... | ..... | ..... | ..... | ..... |
| Metallic ores and concentrates | ..... | ..... | ..... | ..... | ..... | ..... | ..... | ..... | ..... | ..... |
| Bituminous coal and lignite | 8.2 | 6.7 | 5.7 | ..... | ..... | ..... | ..... | ..... | ..... | ..... |
| Crude petroleum and natural gas | ..... | ..... | ..... | ..... | ..... | ..... | ..... | ..... | ..... | ..... |
| Nonmetallic minerals | 1.7 | 6.3 | 1.0 | 1.5 | 1.7 | 0.1 | 0.6 | 4.3 | 0.6 | 1.0 |
| Scrap and waste | ..... | 0.1 | ..... | 0.1 | ..... | ..... | ..... | ..... | ..... | ..... |
| Used merchandise | ..... | ..... | 0.4 | ..... | ..... | 0.1 | 0.1 | ..... | ..... | ..... |
| Goods imported and returned unchanged | ..... | ..... | ..... | ..... | ..... | ..... | ..... | ..... | ..... | ..... |
| Special classification provisions | 0.4 | ..... | 0.1 | 0.1 | 0.1 | 1.3 | 1.1 | 0.5 | 0.3 | 1.5 |

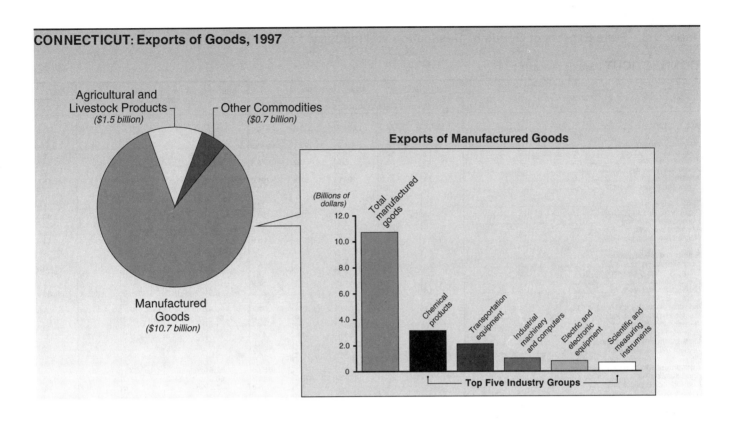

**CONNECTICUT: Exports of Goods, 1997**

Agricultural and Livestock Products ($1.5 billion)

Other Commodities ($0.7 billion)

Manufactured Goods ($10.7 billion)

**Exports of Manufactured Goods**

(Billions of dollars)

Top Five Industry Groups

## Table D-3. State Exports of Goods by Destination and Industry, 1993–1997 —*Continued*

**CONNECTICUT** (Millions of dollars.)

| Industry | 1993 | 1994 | 1995 | 1996 | 1997 | 1993 | 1994 | 1995 | 1996 | 1997 |
|---|---|---|---|---|---|---|---|---|---|---|
| | All destinations | | | | | Canada | | | | |
| **ALL GOODS** | 10 201.0 | 10 272.0 | 12 942.1 | 13 052.5 | 12 897.1 | 1 407.3 | 1 481.1 | 1 660.2 | 1 603.9 | 1 847.7 |
| **Manufactured goods** | 7 990.9 | 8 257.5 | 9 985.7 | 9 705.0 | 10 730.2 | 1 275.1 | 1 344.3 | 1 500.1 | 1 478.0 | 1 715.3 |
| Food products | 220.0 | 313.4 | 433.6 | 414.0 | 404.3 | 11.0 | 19.2 | 23.8 | 28.6 | 29.4 |
| Tobacco products | 0.6 | 0.4 | 0.6 | 3.8 | 2.2 | 0.1 | 0.1 | 0.2 | 0.2 | 0.3 |
| Textile mill products | 66.5 | 61.8 | 58.2 | 60.7 | 77.8 | 23.5 | 22.7 | 23.5 | 26.9 | 40.5 |
| Apparel | 42.9 | 61.0 | 99.9 | 115.8 | 231.5 | 3.6 | 4.8 | 6.1 | 5.4 | 5.9 |
| Lumber and wood products | 34.1 | 31.7 | 39.0 | 27.3 | 30.4 | 4.5 | 6.2 | 7.8 | 7.6 | 9.1 |
| Furniture and fixtures | 14.8 | 17.7 | 20.4 | 37.4 | 43.6 | 5.1 | 6.7 | 9.9 | 12.9 | 14.6 |
| Paper products | 459.7 | 497.6 | 656.8 | 641.7 | 619.2 | 46.0 | 52.0 | 55.5 | 53.2 | 73.2 |
| Printing and publishing | 87.9 | 127.1 | 112.0 | 115.3 | 105.2 | 31.4 | 55.8 | 72.9 | 70.0 | 72.2 |
| Chemical products | 2 104.2 | 2 326.8 | 2 845.7 | 2 933.5 | 3 146.1 | 350.5 | 361.0 | 302.0 | 346.8 | 383.6 |
| Refined petroleum products | 377.1 | 460.8 | 570.1 | 522.8 | 452.8 | 37.6 | 34.1 | 40.3 | 50.5 | 34.5 |
| Rubber and plastic products | 89.9 | 96.8 | 108.8 | 113.2 | 134.9 | 30.6 | 27.0 | 29.4 | 32.2 | 30.8 |
| Leather products | 6.5 | 9.3 | 7.8 | 9.6 | 6.5 | 1.1 | 1.4 | 1.5 | 0.9 | 1.3 |
| Stone, clay and glass products | 21.8 | 23.5 | 27.2 | 36.1 | 30.8 | 7.1 | 9.2 | 9.2 | 9.3 | 9.0 |
| Primary metals | 277.1 | 308.5 | 485.8 | 351.3 | 273.4 | 62.8 | 73.7 | 103.4 | 59.8 | 87.9 |
| Fabricated metal products | 372.1 | 264.7 | 277.4 | 329.4 | 414.6 | 65.2 | 70.9 | 78.7 | 79.0 | 91.3 |
| Industrial machinery and computers | 752.8 | 725.6 | 867.5 | 865.4 | 1 019.9 | 150.2 | 152.7 | 177.2 | 175.5 | 233.9 |
| Electric and electronic equipment | 615.5 | 664.0 | 721.3 | 770.3 | 802.0 | 128.0 | 147.8 | 153.4 | 159.4 | 181.7 |
| Transportation equipment | 1 598.4 | 1 447.9 | 1 729.3 | 1 652.3 | 2 119.7 | 181.4 | 161.3 | 158.6 | 224.0 | 261.1 |
| Scientific and measuring instruments | 709.8 | 683.9 | 686.0 | 576.1 | 677.8 | 98.0 | 99.4 | 98.1 | 79.9 | 97.4 |
| Miscellaneous manufactures | 83.3 | 76.0 | 88.2 | 93.5 | 101.3 | 32.2 | 30.2 | 39.6 | 46.5 | 47.7 |
| Unidentified manufactures | 55.8 | 58.9 | 150.1 | 35.6 | 36.4 | 5.3 | 8.1 | 108.8 | 9.4 | 10.0 |
| **Agricultural and livestock products** | 1 147.9 | 1 044.6 | 1 728.4 | 2 330.8 | 1 501.0 | 16.3 | 11.1 | 27.0 | 31.6 | 19.7 |
| Agricultural products | 1 119.4 | 1 018.5 | 1 702.6 | 2 317.8 | 1 483.0 | 11.9 | 6.7 | 22.4 | 30.0 | 19.2 |
| Livestock and livestock products | 28.5 | 26.0 | 25.8 | 13.0 | 18.0 | 4.4 | 4.3 | 4.6 | 1.6 | 0.5 |
| **Other commodities** | 1 062.2 | 969.9 | 1 228.0 | 1 016.7 | 666.0 | 115.9 | 125.7 | 133.2 | 94.3 | 112.7 |
| Forestry products | 3.3 | 5.4 | 3.7 | 4.0 | 4.1 | 1.1 | 2.6 | 1.7 | 1.4 | 1.8 |
| Fish and other marine products | 7.4 | 7.9 | 6.6 | 6.8 | 9.3 | 2.4 | 1.8 | 1.2 | 1.7 | 2.3 |
| Metallic ores and concentrates | 58.1 | 42.0 | 70.4 | 25.6 | 28.5 | 30.1 | 35.5 | 20.6 | 14.5 | 27.9 |
| Bituminous coal and lignite | 612.3 | 530.2 | 658.2 | 580.4 | 309.5 | 23.3 | 15.9 | 18.8 | 11.6 | 11.7 |
| Crude petroleum and natural gas | 5.0 | 0.2 | 8.7 | 10.4 | 4.3 | ..... | ..... | 0.1 | ..... | ..... |
| Nonmetallic minerals | 29.9 | 48.0 | 54.6 | 67.7 | 58.0 | 0.9 | 1.2 | 0.8 | 1.0 | 1.0 |
| Scrap and waste | 246.8 | 236.3 | 316.1 | 227.6 | 160.4 | 18.6 | 20.3 | 56.0 | 21.7 | 26.2 |
| Used merchandise | 14.3 | 15.0 | 6.3 | 7.3 | 8.3 | 1.3 | 0.6 | 0.4 | 1.5 | 1.8 |
| Goods imported and returned unchanged | 20.8 | 30.6 | 21.1 | 28.1 | 29.8 | 20.8 | 30.6 | 21.1 | 28.1 | 29.8 |
| Special classification provisions | 64.1 | 54.3 | 82.4 | 58.7 | 53.7 | 17.4 | 17.2 | 12.5 | 12.7 | 10.3 |

**Table D-3. State Exports of Goods by Destination and Industry, 1993–1997** —*Continued*

**CONNECTICUT** (Millions of dollars.)

| Industry | 1993 | 1994 | 1995 | 1996 | 1997 | 1993 | 1994 | 1995 | 1996 | 1997 |
|---|---|---|---|---|---|---|---|---|---|---|
| | South and Central America and Caribbean | | | | | Mexico | | | | |
| **ALL GOODS** | 945.6 | 1 122.0 | 1 421.8 | 1 333.6 | 1 410.1 | 335.5 | 441.4 | 321.9 | 521.5 | 529.5 |
| **Manufactured goods** | 797.9 | 965.9 | 1 224.0 | 1 190.1 | 1 248.6 | 273.5 | 368.6 | 275.1 | 396.7 | 464.9 |
| Food products | 57.2 | 62.8 | 98.6 | 78.4 | 77.2 | 6.5 | 3.7 | 1.4 | 6.2 | 5.1 |
| Tobacco products | 0.1 | 0.1 | 0.2 | 0.2 | 0.3 | 0.1 | ..... | ..... | ..... | 0.2 |
| Textile mill products | 20.5 | 15.7 | 2.3 | 3.1 | 3.4 | 1.3 | 0.9 | 0.9 | 1.0 | 2.7 |
| Apparel | 23.1 | 34.8 | 69.0 | 80.6 | 191.5 | 8.1 | 10.1 | 10.7 | 13.6 | 15.3 |
| Lumber and wood products | 0.3 | 0.2 | 0.4 | 0.6 | 0.5 | 0.1 | 0.1 | 0.5 | ..... | 1.7 |
| Furniture and fixtures | 1.6 | 1.0 | 1.5 | 1.3 | 3.8 | 0.1 | 0.4 | 0.3 | 0.3 | 0.3 |
| Paper products | 58.6 | 58.0 | 80.7 | 91.3 | 90.9 | 39.8 | 49.6 | 58.5 | 54.8 | 49.3 |
| Printing and publishing | 8.3 | 8.8 | 4.2 | 2.2 | 1.3 | 0.3 | 0.8 | 0.3 | 0.5 | 1.5 |
| Chemical products | 327.7 | 407.3 | 553.0 | 510.3 | 491.2 | 63.6 | 92.8 | 79.0 | 109.6 | 154.6 |
| Refined petroleum products | 113.3 | 172.3 | 185.2 | 137.9 | 98.8 | 7.3 | 4.6 | 5.5 | 38.5 | 34.6 |
| Rubber and plastic products | 5.1 | 7.6 | 8.4 | 6.4 | 9.8 | 4.4 | 8.0 | 7.5 | 7.4 | 11.3 |
| Leather products | 0.3 | 0.4 | 0.5 | 0.1 | 0.7 | 0.4 | ..... | ..... | ..... | 0.3 |
| Stone, clay and glass products | 1.0 | 1.1 | 2.2 | 1.8 | 1.7 | 1.0 | 0.8 | 1.3 | 0.5 | 1.3 |
| Primary metals | 5.9 | 10.0 | 11.8 | 5.5 | 17.9 | 23.9 | 15.0 | 14.9 | 29.5 | 22.4 |
| Fabricated metal products | 9.6 | 16.6 | 16.2 | 14.0 | 24.5 | 8.6 | 16.3 | 10.9 | 16.1 | 26.0 |
| Industrial machinery and computers | 57.7 | 50.4 | 64.6 | 85.1 | 79.4 | 20.9 | 36.9 | 17.7 | 23.4 | 29.5 |
| Electric and electronic equipment | 54.8 | 54.7 | 61.0 | 74.0 | 86.6 | 65.3 | 74.7 | 53.0 | 59.9 | 75.2 |
| Transportation equipment | 18.3 | 25.1 | 30.6 | 54.2 | 18.2 | 1.8 | 44.1 | 1.6 | 19.1 | 3.9 |
| Scientific and measuring instruments | 20.4 | 24.6 | 24.6 | 34.6 | 43.9 | 14.1 | 7.4 | 7.3 | 13.0 | 20.6 |
| Miscellaneous manufactures | 5.7 | 6.1 | 3.8 | 3.1 | 3.0 | 5.2 | 1.6 | 3.0 | 2.6 | 8.1 |
| Unidentified manufactures | 8.5 | 8.3 | 5.4 | 5.4 | 4.4 | 0.8 | 0.7 | 0.7 | 0.7 | 0.9 |
| **Agricultural and livestock products** | 86.5 | 97.4 | 123.8 | 109.1 | 153.8 | 57.6 | 61.3 | 38.9 | 117.4 | 61.0 |
| Agricultural products | 81.4 | 92.3 | 120.3 | 107.5 | 150.8 | 56.0 | 59.6 | 37.0 | 117.2 | 60.2 |
| Livestock and livestock products | 5.2 | 5.1 | 3.5 | 1.7 | 3.0 | 1.5 | 1.7 | 1.9 | 0.2 | 0.8 |
| **Other commodities** | 61.2 | 58.6 | 74.0 | 34.3 | 7.8 | 4.5 | 11.6 | 7.9 | 7.4 | 3.6 |
| Forestry products | 0.3 | 0.1 | 0.2 | 0.1 | 0.1 | 0.1 | 1.8 | 0.1 | 0.1 | 0.1 |
| Fish and other marine products | ..... | ..... | ..... | ..... | ..... | 0.2 | 0.1 | ..... | ..... | 0.2 |
| Metallic ores and concentrates | ..... | ..... | ..... | ..... | ..... | ..... | ..... | ..... | ..... | ..... |
| Bituminous coal and lignite | 48.4 | 41.2 | 23.6 | 11.1 | ..... | ..... | ..... | 2.4 | 3.3 | ..... |
| Crude petroleum and natural gas | 1.9 | ..... | 5.7 | ..... | 4.1 | ..... | ..... | ..... | ..... | ..... |
| Nonmetallic minerals | 2.3 | 2.7 | 3.2 | 10.3 | 1.9 | 1.2 | 2.2 | 0.7 | 3.5 | 0.8 |
| Scrap and waste | 5.3 | 9.3 | 14.8 | 12.3 | 0.4 | 2.4 | 6.3 | 4.6 | 0.2 | 0.9 |
| Used merchandise | 0.6 | 0.9 | 0.8 | 0.3 | 0.5 | ..... | ..... | ..... | ..... | 0.1 |
| Goods imported and returned unchanged | ..... | ..... | ..... | ..... | ..... | ..... | ..... | ..... | ..... | ..... |
| Special classification provisions | 2.4 | 4.5 | 25.8 | 0.4 | 0.5 | 0.5 | 1.1 | 0.1 | 0.1 | 1.6 |
| | European Union | | | | | United Kingdom | | | | |
| **ALL GOODS** | 2 678.7 | 2 584.7 | 3 413.6 | 3 416.0 | 3 636.7 | 589.8 | 500.4 | 604.1 | 693.7 | 813.0 |
| **Manufactured goods** | 2 222.2 | 2 096.9 | 2 710.2 | 2 661.0 | 3 045.7 | 533.1 | 431.2 | 533.5 | 581.8 | 733.8 |
| Food products | 39.7 | 36.3 | 29.7 | 151.4 | 216.5 | 2.6 | 5.8 | 3.8 | 14.8 | 28.8 |
| Tobacco products | 0.1 | ..... | ..... | 0.2 | 0.2 | ..... | ..... | ..... | ..... | ..... |
| Textile mill products | 12.4 | 13.7 | 23.1 | 20.2 | 17.0 | 1.6 | 1.4 | 2.5 | 3.1 | 2.6 |
| Apparel | 3.3 | 5.9 | 6.5 | 6.2 | 7.1 | 0.6 | 1.6 | 1.6 | 1.0 | 1.8 |
| Lumber and wood products | 15.5 | 18.2 | 21.9 | 14.4 | 13.7 | 1.3 | 2.4 | 2.0 | 1.8 | 1.7 |
| Furniture and fixtures | 4.9 | 5.1 | 3.9 | 5.3 | 8.0 | 1.9 | 1.4 | 1.5 | 1.9 | 3.0 |
| Paper products | 130.5 | 134.1 | 165.0 | 175.7 | 192.4 | 18.2 | 20.5 | 27.4 | 32.2 | 48.9 |
| Printing and publishing | 15.6 | 14.9 | 13.0 | 21.6 | 13.8 | 6.5 | 8.9 | 7.9 | 16.5 | 9.6 |
| Chemical products | 430.9 | 468.4 | 572.5 | 620.9 | 670.5 | 24.7 | 28.2 | 29.9 | 31.7 | 38.4 |
| Refined petroleum products | 65.1 | 95.5 | 114.1 | 113.7 | 104.4 | 2.0 | 1.2 | 2.8 | 2.4 | 7.7 |
| Rubber and plastic products | 24.6 | 27.0 | 33.2 | 31.5 | 45.3 | 6.9 | 8.5 | 11.9 | 10.7 | 13.6 |
| Leather products | 0.8 | 1.7 | 1.3 | 3.8 | 1.6 | 0.2 | 0.2 | 0.3 | 0.9 | 0.7 |
| Stone, clay and glass products | 6.5 | 6.0 | 6.8 | 10.0 | 9.7 | 1.4 | 1.6 | 2.3 | 2.6 | 1.7 |
| Primary metals | 37.5 | 36.6 | 77.1 | 96.7 | 41.6 | 4.7 | 7.8 | 45.2 | 29.3 | 19.0 |
| Fabricated metal products | 47.2 | 48.1 | 63.9 | 70.8 | 76.0 | 14.0 | 13.4 | 15.3 | 26.7 | 19.7 |
| Industrial machinery and computers | 223.8 | 234.3 | 311.5 | 304.3 | 337.1 | 72.6 | 80.1 | 103.8 | 106.1 | 117.6 |
| Electric and electronic equipment | 156.1 | 144.4 | 181.1 | 158.9 | 172.3 | 52.9 | 55.5 | 72.7 | 53.7 | 59.2 |
| Transportation equipment | 620.9 | 481.5 | 748.5 | 643.5 | 885.2 | 264.4 | 144.3 | 150.7 | 183.7 | 303.9 |
| Scientific and measuring instruments | 358.4 | 295.0 | 307.5 | 183.4 | 201.0 | 47.1 | 38.7 | 39.8 | 52.4 | 44.0 |
| Miscellaneous manufactures | 19.8 | 17.2 | 16.0 | 17.0 | 20.0 | 7.0 | 6.2 | 5.5 | 5.8 | 6.6 |
| Unidentified manufactures | 8.7 | 13.2 | 13.7 | 11.5 | 12.4 | 2.6 | 3.7 | 6.4 | 4.6 | 5.2 |
| **Agricultural and livestock products** | 115.2 | 168.9 | 268.3 | 368.0 | 324.9 | 0.4 | 5.7 | 0.3 | 1.5 | 0.9 |
| Agricultural products | 113.1 | 166.7 | 264.9 | 365.2 | 321.6 | 0.2 | 5.5 | 0.1 | 1.5 | 0.9 |
| Livestock and livestock products | 2.1 | 2.1 | 3.4 | 2.8 | 3.4 | 0.1 | 0.2 | 0.2 | ..... | 0.1 |
| **Other commodities** | 341.3 | 318.9 | 435.1 | 387.0 | 266.0 | 56.3 | 63.5 | 70.3 | 110.5 | 78.2 |
| Forestry products | 0.6 | 0.3 | 1.2 | 1.5 | 0.8 | 0.6 | 0.3 | 0.4 | 0.5 | 0.3 |
| Fish and other marine products | 4.8 | 5.6 | 5.1 | 5.0 | 6.8 | ..... | ..... | ..... | ..... | ..... |
| Metallic ores and concentrates | 20.9 | 2.7 | 32.4 | 2.8 | 0.5 | 1.5 | 0.1 | 1.7 | 2.1 | ..... |
| Bituminous coal and lignite | 268.7 | 219.1 | 308.4 | 288.3 | 141.7 | 37.1 | 35.9 | 51.1 | 85.8 | 62.6 |
| Crude petroleum and natural gas | ..... | ..... | 2.1 | 0.1 | ..... | ..... | ..... | ..... | ..... | ..... |
| Nonmetallic minerals | 16.0 | 27.3 | 25.9 | 24.8 | 26.3 | 1.1 | 1.5 | 1.1 | 1.5 | 1.3 |
| Scrap and waste | 6.8 | 39.4 | 41.0 | 42.1 | 64.1 | 2.3 | 11.7 | 6.0 | 6.7 | 2.9 |
| Used merchandise | 6.8 | 7.8 | 3.2 | 3.3 | 3.7 | 4.8 | 5.4 | 1.3 | 2.8 | 2.4 |
| Goods imported and returned unchanged | ..... | ..... | ..... | ..... | ..... | ..... | ..... | ..... | ..... | ..... |
| Special classification provisions | 16.8 | 16.7 | 15.8 | 19.2 | 22.1 | 8.8 | 8.7 | 8.6 | 11.1 | 8.7 |

## Table D-3. State Exports of Goods by Destination and Industry, 1993–1997 —Continued

## CONNECTICUT (Millions of dollars.)

| Industry | 1993 | 1994 | 1995 | 1996 | 1997 | 1993 | 1994 | 1995 | 1996 | 1997 |
|---|---|---|---|---|---|---|---|---|---|---|
| | Germany | | | | | France | | | | |
| **ALL GOODS** | 432.3 | 477.8 | 583.3 | 658.4 | 721.9 | 447.3 | 252.7 | 297.6 | 298.5 | 314.6 |
| **Manufactured goods** | 391.4 | 425.8 | 488.2 | 537.4 | 597.1 | 379.3 | 221.5 | 219.2 | 240.8 | 269.0 |
| Food products | 9.5 | 6.1 | 3.0 | 6.4 | 3.9 | 7.3 | 4.5 | 3.0 | 17.8 | 36.7 |
| Tobacco products | ..... | ..... | ..... | ..... | 0.1 | ..... | ..... | ..... | ..... | ..... |
| Textile mill products | 3.3 | 4.9 | 14.5 | 11.7 | 9.7 | 1.0 | 0.7 | 0.5 | 0.5 | 0.8 |
| Apparel | 0.5 | 1.6 | 1.4 | 2.0 | 2.2 | 0.7 | 0.4 | 0.8 | 0.6 | 0.3 |
| Lumber and wood products | 2.6 | 2.7 | 3.4 | 1.5 | 1.1 | 2.6 | 1.8 | 3.3 | 2.3 | 2.3 |
| Furniture and fixtures | 1.7 | 0.4 | 0.5 | 0.9 | 2.5 | 0.9 | 2.7 | 0.5 | 1.6 | 2.0 |
| Paper products | 53.5 | 56.5 | 59.3 | 75.8 | 83.6 | 16.0 | 15.1 | 19.5 | 16.8 | 8.7 |
| Printing and publishing | 1.2 | 0.7 | 0.6 | 0.5 | 0.9 | 0.7 | 0.3 | 0.9 | 2.3 | 0.9 |
| Chemical products | 59.5 | 75.0 | 99.2 | 143.3 | 165.8 | 10.4 | 10.5 | 15.3 | 25.7 | 17.1 |
| Refined petroleum products | 4.6 | 4.2 | 7.3 | 2.7 | 6.0 | 5.2 | 6.9 | 8.2 | 14.0 | 9.9 |
| Rubber and plastic products | 3.4 | 5.0 | 7.6 | 6.1 | 11.4 | 4.4 | 3.6 | 3.5 | 3.4 | 3.9 |
| Leather products | 0.1 | 0.4 | 0.1 | 0.3 | 0.2 | 0.2 | 0.2 | 0.6 | 1.9 | 0.2 |
| Stone, clay and glass products | 2.4 | 1.8 | 1.6 | 2.5 | 3.6 | 0.9 | 0.7 | 1.0 | 3.3 | 1.4 |
| Primary metals | 5.4 | 8.2 | 10.4 | 11.1 | 8.5 | 6.0 | 4.2 | 3.0 | 2.7 | 2.2 |
| Fabricated metal products | 9.7 | 8.9 | 9.2 | 10.8 | 11.7 | 7.3 | 8.2 | 6.5 | 5.0 | 6.9 |
| Industrial machinery and computers | 57.0 | 61.3 | 68.6 | 77.9 | 86.7 | 22.1 | 25.9 | 34.1 | 32.5 | 46.2 |
| Electric and electronic equipment | 23.1 | 24.1 | 27.2 | 20.9 | 25.9 | 16.6 | 11.3 | 18.6 | 12.2 | 9.2 |
| Transportation equipment | 69.6 | 94.4 | 109.3 | 120.4 | 132.4 | 189.8 | 54.4 | 19.0 | 81.0 | 95.4 |
| Scientific and measuring instruments | 78.8 | 59.2 | 59.2 | 38.1 | 36.2 | 83.8 | 67.3 | 77.3 | 14.6 | 19.8 |
| Miscellaneous manufactures | 3.4 | 4.6 | 3.8 | 2.6 | 3.0 | 2.6 | 2.1 | 3.2 | 2.0 | 4.5 |
| Unidentified manufactures | 2.0 | 5.7 | 2.0 | 2.1 | 1.8 | 0.7 | 0.7 | 0.6 | 0.5 | 0.7 |
| **Agricultural and livestock products** | 31.5 | 17.1 | 39.7 | 83.8 | 66.2 | 0.1 | 0.1 | 27.5 | 11.6 | 15.2 |
| Agricultural products | 31.5 | 17.1 | 39.0 | 83.7 | 66.2 | ..... | 0.1 | 27.5 | 11.6 | 15.2 |
| Livestock and livestock products | ..... | ..... | 0.6 | 0.2 | ..... | ..... | ..... | ..... | ..... | ..... |
| **Other commodities** | 9.4 | 34.9 | 55.4 | 37.2 | 58.6 | 67.9 | 31.1 | 50.9 | 46.0 | 30.4 |
| Forestry products | ..... | ..... | 0.4 | 0.6 | 0.1 | ..... | ..... | 0.1 | ..... | 0.2 |
| Fish and other marine products | 0.3 | 0.1 | 0.1 | ..... | 0.2 | 3.0 | 3.7 | 3.5 | 2.7 | 1.2 |
| Metallic ores and concentrates | ..... | ..... | ..... | ..... | 0.4 | ..... | ..... | 0.1 | 0.1 | ..... |
| Bituminous coal and lignite | ..... | ..... | 28.7 | 9.7 | 2.4 | 60.5 | 21.8 | 44.1 | 38.9 | 21.7 |
| Crude petroleum and natural gas | ..... | ..... | ..... | ..... | ..... | ..... | ..... | ..... | ..... | ..... |
| Nonmetallic minerals | 4.6 | 14.5 | 9.8 | 9.3 | 10.3 | 2.2 | 3.4 | 2.3 | 3.9 | 4.5 |
| Scrap and waste | 1.8 | 15.8 | 14.6 | 15.1 | 39.2 | 0.5 | 0.4 | 0.2 | 0.1 | ..... |
| Used merchandise | 0.5 | 0.7 | 0.4 | 0.2 | 0.1 | 0.2 | 1.3 | 0.1 | ..... | 0.6 |
| Goods imported and returned unchanged | ..... | ..... | ..... | ..... | ..... | ..... | ..... | ..... | ..... | ..... |
| Special classification provisions | 2.3 | 3.9 | 1.4 | 1.9 | 6.2 | 1.3 | 0.3 | 0.4 | 0.3 | 2.1 |
| | The Netherlands | | | | | Asian 10 | | | | |
| **ALL GOODS** | 288.9 | 291.1 | 378.0 | 449.8 | 466.9 | 2 973.4 | 3 077.2 | 4 034.5 | 4 004.2 | 3 740.2 |
| **Manufactured goods** | 191.4 | 208.3 | 234.1 | 277.1 | 335.8 | 2 252.8 | 2 432.0 | 3 049.6 | 2 730.9 | 3 007.0 |
| Food products | 7.2 | 4.4 | 6.0 | 57.2 | 72.3 | 20.5 | 73.5 | 127.4 | 83.8 | 39.1 |
| Tobacco products | ..... | ..... | ..... | 0.1 | ..... | ..... | ..... | ..... | 0.4 | 0.8 |
| Textile mill products | 1.2 | 1.6 | 1.4 | 0.8 | 1.6 | 4.9 | 4.0 | 4.6 | 4.6 | 7.6 |
| Apparel | 0.2 | 0.8 | 1.8 | 1.5 | 1.4 | 2.4 | 2.2 | 5.5 | 7.1 | 8.4 |
| Lumber and wood products | 1.2 | 2.0 | 2.1 | 1.1 | 1.1 | 12.7 | 5.4 | 6.8 | 3.1 | 3.6 |
| Furniture and fixtures | 0.2 | 0.2 | 0.6 | ..... | ..... | 2.1 | 2.2 | 3.9 | 15.8 | 14.0 |
| Paper products | 12.0 | 12.4 | 22.0 | 20.3 | 18.5 | 164.5 | 183.8 | 262.5 | 214.9 | 181.6 |
| Printing and publishing | 4.8 | 1.5 | 0.7 | 0.9 | 0.7 | 22.2 | 24.0 | 16.7 | 15.7 | 12.1 |
| Chemical products | 48.0 | 60.4 | 58.1 | 73.1 | 49.3 | 727.6 | 761.7 | 974.3 | 1 027.8 | 991.7 |
| Refined petroleum products | 23.8 | 47.7 | 45.2 | 41.4 | 30.3 | 100.0 | 111.3 | 131.4 | 100.9 | 74.6 |
| Rubber and plastic products | 1.4 | 1.3 | 1.9 | 1.3 | 1.4 | 14.2 | 18.6 | 19.4 | 23.1 | 26.8 |
| Leather products | ..... | ..... | 0.1 | 0.1 | 0.1 | 3.4 | 5.5 | 3.9 | 3.8 | 2.1 |
| Stone, clay and glass products | 0.1 | 0.4 | 0.7 | 0.2 | 1.5 | 4.0 | 3.7 | 4.9 | 10.0 | 6.7 |
| Primary metals | 5.7 | 5.4 | 2.5 | 1.9 | 2.3 | 119.0 | 148.3 | 244.7 | 67.3 | 79.4 |
| Fabricated metal products | 3.2 | 4.3 | 4.6 | 9.8 | 11.7 | 207.4 | 76.3 | 69.8 | 115.0 | 157.0 |
| Industrial machinery and computers | 19.0 | 14.9 | 18.0 | 18.4 | 23.1 | 218.7 | 172.5 | 192.0 | 182.1 | 248.0 |
| Electric and electronic equipment | 11.7 | 11.9 | 8.7 | 12.8 | 14.5 | 150.1 | 183.2 | 207.8 | 252.2 | 219.4 |
| Transportation equipment | 10.5 | 6.0 | 27.3 | 13.0 | 48.8 | 320.7 | 480.3 | 585.9 | 405.0 | 710.5 |
| Scientific and measuring instruments | 38.0 | 31.3 | 31.4 | 21.3 | 54.9 | 141.9 | 155.8 | 161.5 | 178.8 | 205.2 |
| Miscellaneous manufactures | 2.8 | 1.3 | 0.6 | 1.2 | 1.5 | 13.1 | 14.5 | 18.3 | 16.4 | 14.4 |
| Unidentified manufactures | 0.5 | 0.6 | 0.4 | 0.6 | 0.6 | 3.4 | 5.3 | 8.4 | 3.1 | 4.1 |
| **Agricultural and livestock products** | 31.3 | 33.6 | 52.4 | 108.8 | 110.3 | 359.4 | 317.8 | 611.7 | 990.5 | 549.1 |
| Agricultural products | 30.1 | 33.4 | 50.7 | 107.5 | 109.0 | 347.6 | 307.6 | 601.1 | 985.4 | 541.3 |
| Livestock and livestock products | 1.3 | 0.2 | 1.8 | 1.3 | 1.3 | 11.9 | 10.2 | 10.6 | 5.1 | 7.7 |
| **Other commodities** | 66.2 | 49.2 | 91.5 | 63.9 | 20.8 | 361.2 | 327.5 | 373.2 | 282.8 | 184.1 |
| Forestry products | 0.1 | ..... | 0.1 | 0.3 | ..... | 0.8 | 0.2 | ..... | 0.5 | 0.6 |
| Fish and other marine products | 0.4 | 0.2 | 0.1 | ..... | ..... | ..... | ..... | 0.2 | ..... | ..... |
| Metallic ores and concentrates | 19.3 | 2.6 | 30.6 | 0.2 | 0.2 | 7.2 | 3.7 | 15.1 | 8.3 | ..... |
| Bituminous coal and lignite | 39.7 | 40.1 | 50.8 | 52.9 | 9.1 | 184.7 | 179.7 | 193.3 | 118.7 | 91.2 |
| Crude petroleum and natural gas | ..... | ..... | ..... | ..... | ..... | 2.8 | 0.1 | 0.8 | 10.4 | 0.1 |
| Nonmetallic minerals | 5.9 | 5.5 | 7.7 | 7.4 | 8.5 | 8.7 | 9.1 | 11.3 | 18.8 | 18.1 |
| Scrap and waste | 0.1 | 0.2 | 0.4 | 0.1 | 0.1 | 135.0 | 117.5 | 127.4 | 103.5 | 57.5 |
| Used merchandise | 0.5 | 0.2 | 0.1 | ..... | 0.1 | 4.7 | 5.1 | 1.7 | 1.2 | 2.2 |
| Goods imported and returned unchanged | ..... | ..... | ..... | ..... | ..... | ..... | ..... | ..... | ..... | ..... |
| Special classification provisions | 0.3 | 0.5 | 1.7 | 3.0 | 2.8 | 17.3 | 11.8 | 23.3 | 21.4 | 14.4 |

## Table D-3.  State Exports of Goods by Destination and Industry, 1993–1997 —*Continued*

**CONNECTICUT** (Millions of dollars.)

| Industry | 1993 | 1994 | 1995 | 1996 | 1997 | 1993 | 1994 | 1995 | 1996 | 1997 |
|---|---|---|---|---|---|---|---|---|---|---|
| | Japan | | | | | South Korea | | | | |
| **ALL GOODS** | 919.7 | 1 050.2 | 1 222.5 | 1 178.6 | 1 189.8 | 678.5 | 577.5 | 763.3 | 879.2 | 812.9 |
| **Manufactured goods** | 608.9 | 771.9 | 878.7 | 798.4 | 855.3 | 446.7 | 361.9 | 493.1 | 489.2 | 616.2 |
| Food products | 15.9 | 22.3 | 20.6 | 11.3 | 14.0 | 0.5 | 0.8 | 4.5 | 1.3 | 1.3 |
| Tobacco products | ..... | ..... | ..... | ..... | ..... | ..... | ..... | ..... | 0.3 | 0.1 |
| Textile mill products | 1.5 | 0.8 | 0.9 | 1.1 | 2.2 | 0.4 | 0.5 | 0.4 | 0.2 | 0.3 |
| Apparel | 1.1 | 1.1 | 4.1 | 5.7 | 2.9 | 0.2 | 0.4 | 0.1 | 0.1 | 0.2 |
| Lumber and wood products | 3.1 | 2.1 | 1.7 | 0.9 | 1.9 | 1.3 | 0.7 | 3.6 | 1.2 | 0.9 |
| Furniture and fixtures | 0.9 | 0.7 | 1.1 | 10.1 | 5.7 | 0.1 | 0.8 | 1.0 | 1.6 | 1.3 |
| Paper products | 93.9 | 81.7 | 105.2 | 89.9 | 78.5 | 14.8 | 16.9 | 17.4 | 13.1 | 10.4 |
| Printing and publishing | 4.7 | 4.6 | 2.5 | 2.1 | 1.8 | 0.4 | 0.5 | 0.6 | 0.1 | 0.6 |
| Chemical products | 210.8 | 199.3 | 238.6 | 238.0 | 237.6 | 115.2 | 119.3 | 145.7 | 146.5 | 135.7 |
| Refined petroleum products | 34.9 | 43.8 | 65.7 | 57.7 | 43.8 | 21.1 | 23.4 | 13.2 | 15.7 | 20.9 |
| Rubber and plastic products | 4.5 | 7.7 | 7.7 | 9.8 | 9.0 | 0.6 | 1.6 | 1.2 | 0.6 | 3.2 |
| Leather products | 2.0 | 2.2 | 1.9 | 1.1 | 1.0 | 0.6 | 1.3 | 0.4 | 0.1 | 0.1 |
| Stone, clay and glass products | 0.9 | 1.4 | 2.3 | 5.4 | 3.7 | 1.5 | 0.8 | 0.8 | 0.9 | 0.8 |
| Primary metals | 55.6 | 93.4 | 70.5 | 27.0 | 24.5 | 11.5 | 28.0 | 59.4 | 22.9 | 32.9 |
| Fabricated metal products | 2.5 | 3.9 | 7.6 | 16.9 | 29.7 | 56.3 | 21.6 | 20.7 | 61.9 | 19.4 |
| Industrial machinery and computers | 32.6 | 38.0 | 58.7 | 48.0 | 53.5 | 31.2 | 23.5 | 23.8 | 32.4 | 38.0 |
| Electric and electronic equipment | 35.8 | 61.4 | 79.4 | 66.9 | 26.0 | 11.5 | 12.0 | 14.0 | 46.7 | 63.0 |
| Transportation equipment | 20.1 | 102.2 | 121.2 | 97.3 | 201.2 | 164.3 | 92.8 | 159.9 | 117.4 | 251.2 |
| Scientific and measuring instruments | 78.0 | 95.0 | 75.9 | 100.4 | 109.5 | 13.3 | 14.6 | 23.9 | 23.0 | 32.2 |
| Miscellaneous manufactures | 9.2 | 9.5 | 8.5 | 8.1 | 8.2 | 1.6 | 2.2 | 2.1 | 2.4 | 2.8 |
| Unidentified manufactures | 0.7 | 1.0 | 4.8 | 0.8 | 0.6 | 0.4 | 0.3 | 0.6 | 0.6 | 0.6 |
| **Agricultural and livestock products** | 149.6 | 109.3 | 163.2 | 279.8 | 277.5 | 90.3 | 92.1 | 137.4 | 273.1 | 109.8 |
| Agricultural products | 148.2 | 108.4 | 162.3 | 279.4 | 277.0 | 89.1 | 91.7 | 136.5 | 273.1 | 109.8 |
| Livestock and livestock products | 1.4 | 0.9 | 0.9 | 0.4 | 0.5 | 1.2 | 0.4 | 0.9 | ..... | ..... |
| **Other commodities** | 161.2 | 168.9 | 180.6 | 100.4 | 57.0 | 141.5 | 123.5 | 132.7 | 116.8 | 86.8 |
| Forestry products | ..... | ..... | ..... | 0.1 | ..... | ..... | ..... | ..... | 0.3 | 0.6 |
| Fish and other marine products | ..... | 0.1 | 0.1 | ..... | ..... | ..... | ..... | ..... | ..... | ..... |
| Metallic ores and concentrates | 1.3 | 3.7 | 2.5 | ..... | ..... | ..... | ..... | ..... | ..... | ..... |
| Bituminous coal and lignite | 122.3 | 108.0 | 127.2 | 55.6 | 16.1 | 62.4 | 70.9 | 66.1 | 62.3 | 65.9 |
| Crude petroleum and natural gas | ..... | 0.1 | ..... | 3.1 | 0.1 | 2.8 | ..... | 0.6 | ..... | ..... |
| Nonmetallic minerals | 6.6 | 6.1 | 7.0 | 12.1 | 15.1 | 0.5 | 0.5 | 1.0 | 0.5 | 0.4 |
| Scrap and waste | 24.7 | 45.6 | 40.4 | 26.8 | 21.4 | 75.1 | 52.0 | 64.6 | 53.1 | 19.6 |
| Used merchandise | 4.6 | 3.7 | 0.6 | 0.5 | 1.7 | ..... | ..... | ..... | ..... | ..... |
| Goods imported and returned unchanged | ..... | ..... | ..... | ..... | ..... | ..... | ..... | ..... | ..... | ..... |
| Special classification provisions | 1.7 | 1.6 | 2.8 | 2.3 | 2.5 | 0.6 | 0.1 | 0.3 | 0.6 | 0.3 |
| | Taiwan | | | | | Singapore | | | | |
| **ALL GOODS** | 286.7 | 333.6 | 429.2 | 331.2 | 364.4 | 183.9 | 349.9 | 357.3 | 287.3 | 270.2 |
| **Manufactured goods** | 264.0 | 271.4 | 379.4 | 281.9 | 283.0 | 178.6 | 347.4 | 355.6 | 285.1 | 263.0 |
| Food products | 0.6 | 1.8 | 1.5 | 1.7 | 2.7 | 0.7 | 0.7 | 0.5 | 0.7 | 0.9 |
| Tobacco products | ..... | ..... | ..... | ..... | ..... | ..... | ..... | ..... | ..... | 0.3 |
| Textile mill products | 0.4 | 0.3 | 0.3 | 0.3 | 0.6 | 0.3 | 0.7 | 1.0 | 0.3 | 0.6 |
| Apparel | ..... | 0.2 | 0.4 | 0.3 | 0.7 | ..... | 0.1 | 0.1 | 0.1 | 0.4 |
| Lumber and wood products | 2.6 | 1.9 | 1.0 | 0.3 | 0.4 | 0.1 | 0.1 | 0.1 | ..... | ..... |
| Furniture and fixtures | 0.6 | ..... | 1.1 | 1.4 | 2.7 | 0.1 | 0.4 | 0.1 | 1.8 | 3.5 |
| Paper products | 19.8 | 18.4 | 28.3 | 26.2 | 18.2 | 2.6 | 3.0 | 3.9 | 5.3 | 7.0 |
| Printing and publishing | 2.5 | 3.3 | 1.4 | 0.8 | 0.8 | 2.7 | 3.6 | 1.4 | 1.0 | 0.6 |
| Chemical products | 140.6 | 136.4 | 187.6 | 155.1 | 150.4 | 59.6 | 44.5 | 64.8 | 71.4 | 45.7 |
| Refined petroleum products | 6.0 | 4.3 | 1.2 | 1.3 | 1.2 | 6.5 | 22.1 | 28.4 | 4.7 | 1.5 |
| Rubber and plastic products | 2.5 | 2.9 | 4.5 | 3.6 | 2.6 | 2.0 | 2.8 | 2.5 | 3.2 | 5.2 |
| Leather products | ..... | ..... | ..... | ..... | ..... | 0.2 | 0.1 | ..... | ..... | ..... |
| Stone, clay and glass products | 0.6 | 0.3 | 0.3 | 1.1 | 0.3 | 0.1 | 0.1 | 0.2 | 0.3 | 0.4 |
| Primary metals | 23.8 | 13.2 | 42.7 | 3.1 | 3.3 | 11.0 | 3.1 | 2.1 | 1.3 | 9.2 |
| Fabricated metal products | 3.6 | 3.7 | 2.8 | 1.7 | 2.4 | 2.8 | 7.5 | 6.5 | 6.7 | 8.3 |
| Industrial machinery and computers | 14.4 | 13.2 | 16.6 | 10.2 | 11.6 | 15.5 | 22.6 | 22.9 | 24.1 | 20.4 |
| Electric and electronic equipment | 14.3 | 7.4 | 12.5 | 16.0 | 14.9 | 24.4 | 25.5 | 36.5 | 47.6 | 19.8 |
| Transportation equipment | 19.7 | 53.4 | 62.8 | 44.2 | 58.5 | 40.0 | 198.9 | 164.1 | 105.1 | 117.7 |
| Scientific and measuring instruments | 11.4 | 9.5 | 10.4 | 12.2 | 10.5 | 8.8 | 10.1 | 19.2 | 10.2 | 20.3 |
| Miscellaneous manufactures | 0.4 | 0.6 | 3.4 | 2.0 | 0.6 | 0.5 | 0.9 | 1.0 | 0.8 | 1.0 |
| Unidentified manufactures | 0.2 | 0.7 | 0.5 | 0.3 | 0.4 | 0.5 | 0.6 | 0.4 | 0.3 | 0.3 |
| **Agricultural and livestock products** | 0.7 | 58.8 | 42.6 | 30.2 | 56.6 | 0.1 | ..... | 0.1 | 0.1 | 0.1 |
| Agricultural products | ..... | 58.2 | 42.0 | 30.0 | 56.2 | ..... | ..... | ..... | ..... | ..... |
| Livestock and livestock products | 0.7 | 0.6 | 0.5 | 0.2 | 0.4 | 0.1 | ..... | ..... | 0.1 | 0.1 |
| **Other commodities** | 22.0 | 3.4 | 7.2 | 19.1 | 24.8 | 5.2 | 2.5 | 1.6 | 2.1 | 7.1 |
| Forestry products | ..... | ..... | ..... | ..... | ..... | 0.4 | 0.1 | ..... | ..... | ..... |
| Fish and other marine products | ..... | ..... | ..... | ..... | ..... | ..... | ..... | ..... | ..... | ..... |
| Metallic ores and concentrates | ..... | ..... | ..... | ..... | ..... | ..... | ..... | ..... | ..... | ..... |
| Bituminous coal and lignite | ..... | 0.9 | ..... | 0.8 | 9.1 | ..... | ..... | ..... | ..... | ..... |
| Crude petroleum and natural gas | ..... | ..... | ..... | ..... | ..... | ..... | ..... | ..... | 0.1 | ..... |
| Nonmetallic minerals | 0.6 | 1.1 | 1.1 | 1.4 | 0.3 | 0.2 | 0.3 | 0.7 | 1.6 | 0.4 |
| Scrap and waste | 21.0 | 0.9 | 1.9 | 13.3 | 13.0 | ..... | 0.1 | 0.3 | 0.2 | ..... |
| Used merchandise | ..... | ..... | 0.5 | 0.2 | ..... | ..... | 0.1 | ..... | 0.1 | ..... |
| Goods imported and returned unchanged | ..... | ..... | ..... | ..... | ..... | ..... | ..... | ..... | ..... | ..... |
| Special classification provisions | 0.4 | 0.5 | 3.7 | 3.4 | 2.2 | 4.6 | 1.8 | 0.7 | 0.2 | 6.6 |

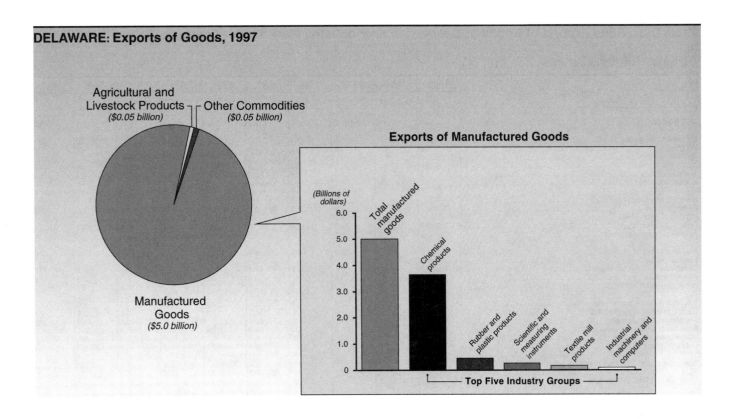

**DELAWARE: Exports of Goods, 1997**

Agricultural and Livestock Products ($0.05 billion) — Other Commodities ($0.05 billion)

Manufactured Goods ($5.0 billion)

**Exports of Manufactured Goods**

(Billions of dollars)

Top Five Industry Groups

Total manufactured goods / Chemical products / Rubber and plastic products / Scientific and measuring instruments / Textile mill products / Industrial machinery and computers

## Table D-3.  State Exports of Goods by Destination and Industry, 1993–1997 —*Continued*

**DELAWARE** (Millions of dollars.)

| Industry | 1993 | 1994 | 1995 | 1996 | 1997 | 1993 | 1994 | 1995 | 1996 | 1997 |
|---|---|---|---|---|---|---|---|---|---|---|
| | All destinations | | | | | Canada | | | | |
| **ALL GOODS** | 3 454.5 | 3 758.1 | 4 396.8 | 4 584.5 | 5 103.9 | 628.4 | 692.5 | 717.5 | 739.7 | 788.3 |
| **Manufactured goods** | 3 361.5 | 3 666.9 | 4 282.6 | 4 474.2 | 5 004.4 | 569.6 | 640.2 | 652.2 | 681.2 | 741.2 |
| Food products | 18.6 | 21.0 | 24.4 | 37.0 | 46.7 | 12.9 | 13.1 | 11.6 | 8.2 | 21.5 |
| Tobacco products | ..... | ..... | ..... | ..... | ..... | ..... | ..... | ..... | ..... | ..... |
| Textile mill products | 106.9 | 125.9 | 133.5 | 128.7 | 175.4 | 2.8 | 1.3 | 1.5 | 1.2 | 5.4 |
| Apparel | 9.1 | 10.2 | 8.4 | 3.4 | 4.5 | 5.5 | 6.1 | 4.7 | 0.5 | 0.7 |
| Lumber and wood products | 1.8 | 1.1 | 1.8 | 1.5 | 1.7 | 0.9 | 0.2 | 0.3 | 0.3 | 0.2 |
| Furniture and fixtures | 4.8 | 3.2 | 2.0 | 2.4 | 3.7 | 4.3 | 2.8 | 1.7 | 1.5 | 2.1 |
| Paper products | 24.4 | 34.8 | 45.7 | 53.7 | 60.4 | 0.6 | 1.1 | 2.2 | 6.9 | 7.3 |
| Printing and publishing | 2.4 | 2.0 | 1.9 | 2.3 | 2.3 | 1.4 | 0.6 | 0.6 | 1.3 | 0.8 |
| Chemical products | 2 310.8 | 2 614.1 | 3 124.5 | 3 251.7 | 3 649.6 | 406.5 | 455.9 | 488.8 | 504.5 | 539.0 |
| Refined petroleum products | 2.2 | 1.8 | 1.3 | 2.2 | 1.7 | 1.4 | 1.0 | 0.8 | 0.3 | 0.4 |
| Rubber and plastic products | 330.0 | 305.3 | 359.6 | 378.9 | 454.5 | 54.6 | 65.1 | 65.6 | 74.7 | 72.1 |
| Leather products | 1.6 | 0.9 | 0.5 | 0.4 | 0.8 | 0.3 | 0.5 | 0.2 | 0.2 | 0.2 |
| Stone, clay and glass products | 21.2 | 32.2 | 56.8 | 48.3 | 56.1 | 1.0 | 0.9 | 1.0 | 1.0 | 0.8 |
| Primary metals | 19.8 | 28.2 | 36.1 | 43.6 | 29.5 | 14.8 | 23.1 | 6.6 | 3.5 | 20.6 |
| Fabricated metal products | 33.1 | 34.8 | 31.5 | 25.0 | 14.5 | 9.2 | 10.6 | 9.0 | 6.5 | 2.4 |
| Industrial machinery and computers | 122.5 | 71.1 | 71.5 | 76.1 | 96.6 | 11.5 | 10.1 | 11.4 | 11.2 | 14.3 |
| Electric and electronic equipment | 29.1 | 33.6 | 37.4 | 33.8 | 26.2 | 5.8 | 9.6 | 13.3 | 14.6 | 10.0 |
| Transportation equipment | 51.9 | 58.7 | 42.0 | 77.9 | 89.8 | 4.3 | 13.4 | 5.8 | 5.8 | 3.4 |
| Scientific and measuring instruments | 262.9 | 273.5 | 291.1 | 288.4 | 269.9 | 30.7 | 23.0 | 26.1 | 37.7 | 39.1 |
| Miscellaneous manufactures | 6.2 | 11.8 | 11.0 | 16.3 | 18.9 | 0.5 | 0.7 | 0.2 | 0.5 | 0.2 |
| Unidentified manufactures | 2.2 | 2.7 | 1.5 | 2.6 | 1.6 | 0.6 | 1.1 | 0.7 | 0.7 | 0.8 |
| **Agricultural and livestock products** | 66.7 | 57.7 | 68.3 | 58.5 | 49.6 | 52.8 | 44.6 | 50.9 | 44.5 | 32.5 |
| Agricultural products | 66.6 | 57.4 | 68.0 | 58.5 | 49.3 | 52.8 | 44.6 | 50.8 | 44.5 | 32.5 |
| Livestock and livestock products | 0.1 | 0.3 | 0.2 | 0.1 | 0.3 | 0.1 | ..... | 0.1 | ..... | ..... |
| **Other commodities** | 26.3 | 33.5 | 45.9 | 51.8 | 49.9 | 6.0 | 7.7 | 14.4 | 14.0 | 14.6 |
| Forestry products | 0.8 | 0.1 | 0.1 | ..... | 0.1 | 0.7 | ..... | ..... | ..... | 0.1 |
| Fish and other marine products | 1.3 | 1.0 | 1.0 | 0.3 | 0.3 | 1.3 | 0.9 | 1.0 | 0.2 | 0.3 |
| Metallic ores and concentrates | 3.3 | 3.6 | 6.3 | 7.5 | 9.4 | 1.1 | 1.5 | 2.8 | 3.6 | 2.9 |
| Bituminous coal and lignite | ..... | ..... | ..... | ..... | ..... | ..... | ..... | ..... | ..... | ..... |
| Crude petroleum and natural gas | ..... | ..... | ..... | 0.3 | 0.6 | ..... | ..... | ..... | ..... | ..... |
| Nonmetallic minerals | 4.2 | 5.0 | 5.0 | 7.5 | 11.3 | 0.1 | 0.1 | 0.3 | 0.2 | 0.4 |
| Scrap and waste | 10.0 | 14.3 | 21.7 | 21.0 | 15.2 | 0.4 | 0.7 | 3.9 | 0.3 | 3.2 |
| Used merchandise | 0.6 | 0.4 | 0.3 | 0.8 | 1.0 | 0.2 | 0.2 | 0.1 | ..... | ..... |
| Goods imported and returned unchanged | 2.1 | 4.2 | 6.0 | 9.5 | 7.6 | 2.1 | 4.2 | 6.0 | 9.5 | 7.6 |
| Special classification provisions | 3.9 | 5.0 | 5.5 | 4.8 | 4.4 | 0.1 | 0.1 | 0.2 | 0.1 | 0.1 |

## Table D-3.  State Exports of Goods by Destination and Industry, 1993–1997 —*Continued*

**DELAWARE** (Millions of dollars.)

| Industry | 1993 | 1994 | 1995 | 1996 | 1997 | 1993 | 1994 | 1995 | 1996 | 1997 |
|---|---|---|---|---|---|---|---|---|---|---|
| | South and Central America and Caribbean | | | | | Mexico | | | | |
| **ALL GOODS** | 401.7 | 414.8 | 505.9 | 516.0 | 611.5 | 159.3 | 212.6 | 183.1 | 286.1 | 308.2 |
| **Manufactured goods** | 400.1 | 411.9 | 501.0 | 513.9 | 607.2 | 155.9 | 204.2 | 178.0 | 273.2 | 290.2 |
| Food products | 0.8 | 0.4 | 0.5 | 1.4 | 1.0 | 0.4 | 0.4 | 0.3 | 0.4 | 1.0 |
| Tobacco products | ..... | ..... | ..... | ..... | ..... | ..... | ..... | ..... | ..... | ..... |
| Textile mill products | 5.8 | 9.8 | 11.8 | 7.0 | 13.9 | 2.2 | 4.2 | 2.0 | 4.6 | 7.5 |
| Apparel | 0.3 | 0.1 | 1.1 | 0.8 | 0.3 | ..... | 0.6 | 0.7 | 0.4 | 1.3 |
| Lumber and wood products | ..... | ..... | 0.1 | ..... | ..... | ..... | ..... | ..... | ..... | ..... |
| Furniture and fixtures | ..... | ..... | ..... | 0.1 | 0.1 | ..... | ..... | ..... | ..... | ..... |
| Paper products | 0.6 | 1.2 | 2.0 | 2.2 | 3.2 | 0.5 | 0.6 | 1.5 | 1.5 | 1.3 |
| Printing and publishing | ..... | 0.1 | 0.2 | 0.2 | 0.7 | ..... | 0.1 | ..... | ..... | ..... |
| Chemical products | 309.8 | 320.9 | 403.5 | 418.8 | 480.4 | 122.1 | 158.3 | 139.8 | 185.0 | 230.4 |
| Refined petroleum products | 0.1 | 0.1 | 0.1 | ..... | 0.1 | ..... | 0.1 | ..... | 1.4 | ..... |
| Rubber and plastic products | 22.5 | 17.3 | 21.9 | 19.8 | 29.6 | 11.2 | 10.6 | 11.9 | 14.0 | 27.0 |
| Leather products | 0.5 | ..... | ..... | ..... | 0.1 | 0.7 | 0.2 | ..... | ..... | ..... |
| Stone, clay and glass products | 0.7 | 0.3 | 7.4 | 9.7 | 14.4 | 0.3 | 0.2 | 0.4 | 0.3 | 0.2 |
| Primary metals | 0.2 | 0.3 | 0.3 | 0.3 | 0.4 | 0.2 | 0.3 | 0.2 | 0.5 | 0.7 |
| Fabricated metal products | 1.1 | 0.6 | 1.3 | 1.3 | 1.1 | 1.4 | 1.5 | 0.3 | 1.0 | 0.7 |
| Industrial machinery and computers | 6.2 | 3.9 | 3.6 | 3.8 | 15.4 | 2.2 | 2.9 | 3.0 | 6.0 | 1.7 |
| Electric and electronic equipment | 0.6 | 0.7 | 1.2 | 1.6 | 4.1 | 5.1 | 2.6 | 0.2 | 0.8 | 0.4 |
| Transportation equipment | 26.0 | 26.5 | 13.2 | 6.2 | 10.7 | ..... | 0.6 | 0.1 | 41.2 | 0.2 |
| Scientific and measuring instruments | 23.5 | 26.4 | 29.0 | 33.3 | 26.2 | 5.6 | 14.2 | 11.3 | 9.1 | 5.5 |
| Miscellaneous manufactures | 1.4 | 2.8 | 3.6 | 7.2 | 5.4 | 3.7 | 6.7 | 6.2 | 6.9 | 12.1 |
| Unidentified manufactures | 0.1 | 0.3 | 0.2 | 0.1 | 0.1 | 0.1 | 0.2 | 0.1 | 0.1 | 0.1 |
| **Agricultural and livestock products** | 0.1 | ..... | 0.2 | ..... | 0.2 | 0.1 | 2.9 | 1.1 | ..... | ..... |
| Agricultural products | 0.1 | ..... | 0.2 | ..... | 0.2 | 0.1 | 2.9 | 1.1 | ..... | ..... |
| Livestock and livestock products | ..... | ..... | ..... | ..... | ..... | ..... | ..... | ..... | ..... | ..... |
| **Other commodities** | 1.5 | 2.9 | 4.5 | 2.1 | 4.1 | 3.3 | 5.5 | 4.1 | 12.9 | 18.0 |
| Forestry products | ..... | ..... | ..... | ..... | ..... | 0.1 | ..... | ..... | ..... | ..... |
| Fish and other marine products | ..... | ..... | ..... | ..... | ..... | ..... | ..... | ..... | ..... | ..... |
| Metallic ores and concentrates | 0.1 | 0.1 | 0.9 | 0.3 | 1.7 | 0.3 | 0.4 | 0.4 | 0.4 | 1.2 |
| Bituminous coal and lignite | ..... | ..... | ..... | ..... | ..... | ..... | ..... | ..... | ..... | ..... |
| Crude petroleum and natural gas | ..... | ..... | ..... | ..... | ..... | ..... | ..... | ..... | ..... | 0.2 |
| Nonmetallic minerals | 0.4 | 0.3 | 0.4 | ..... | 0.3 | 1.7 | 2.2 | 1.6 | 2.2 | 2.9 |
| Scrap and waste | 0.5 | 0.5 | 0.2 | ..... | ..... | ..... | ..... | 0.1 | 8.1 | 11.6 |
| Used merchandise | ..... | ..... | ..... | ..... | 0.3 | ..... | ..... | ..... | ..... | ..... |
| Goods imported and returned unchanged | ..... | ..... | ..... | ..... | ..... | ..... | ..... | ..... | ..... | ..... |
| Special classification provisions | 0.5 | 1.9 | 3.0 | 1.7 | 1.8 | 1.2 | 2.9 | 2.0 | 2.2 | 2.1 |
| | European Union | | | | | United Kingdom | | | | |
| **ALL GOODS** | 997.8 | 1 154.7 | 1 465.6 | 1 455.8 | 1 536.6 | 131.2 | 140.4 | 160.1 | 166.5 | 195.6 |
| **Manufactured goods** | 986.8 | 1 142.6 | 1 439.7 | 1 429.8 | 1 515.3 | 130.2 | 139.6 | 159.6 | 165.9 | 193.0 |
| Food products | 0.7 | 0.7 | 0.5 | 0.3 | 0.7 | 0.2 | 0.1 | ..... | ..... | ..... |
| Tobacco products | ..... | ..... | ..... | ..... | ..... | ..... | ..... | ..... | ..... | ..... |
| Textile mill products | 58.1 | 67.6 | 71.2 | 61.8 | 78.6 | 1.3 | 0.7 | 0.9 | 0.9 | 3.7 |
| Apparel | 2.1 | 2.4 | 1.0 | 0.6 | 0.5 | 1.1 | 1.2 | 0.5 | 0.4 | 0.1 |
| Lumber and wood products | 0.1 | 0.9 | 1.3 | 1.0 | 1.1 | ..... | 0.1 | 0.2 | 0.2 | 0.1 |
| Furniture and fixtures | 0.2 | 0.1 | 0.1 | 0.4 | 0.1 | 0.2 | ..... | ..... | ..... | ..... |
| Paper products | 7.9 | 8.5 | 14.2 | 12.1 | 17.1 | 0.4 | 0.6 | 2.0 | 1.4 | 1.8 |
| Printing and publishing | 0.4 | 0.4 | 0.6 | 0.3 | 0.2 | ..... | ..... | 0.2 | ..... | ..... |
| Chemical products | 615.6 | 742.2 | 975.5 | 1 013.4 | 1 076.7 | 92.7 | 102.8 | 103.3 | 122.7 | 154.5 |
| Refined petroleum products | 0.3 | 0.2 | 0.2 | 0.1 | 0.5 | ..... | ..... | ..... | ..... | 0.2 |
| Rubber and plastic products | 127.4 | 108.9 | 144.2 | 132.9 | 154.3 | 17.6 | 16.4 | 21.6 | 17.5 | 14.2 |
| Leather products | 0.1 | 0.1 | 0.1 | 0.1 | ..... | ..... | ..... | ..... | ..... | ..... |
| Stone, clay and glass products | 16.2 | 29.3 | 45.2 | 32.2 | 38.8 | ..... | 0.5 | 0.5 | 0.2 | 0.4 |
| Primary metals | 0.5 | 2.7 | 2.4 | 2.0 | 3.5 | 0.2 | 1.4 | 2.0 | 1.0 | 1.7 |
| Fabricated metal products | 9.0 | 13.3 | 12.7 | 7.3 | 2.2 | 1.2 | 1.3 | 2.8 | 1.5 | 0.8 |
| Industrial machinery and computers | 28.8 | 28.3 | 22.6 | 25.8 | 26.0 | 6.4 | 3.2 | 7.8 | 8.6 | 7.5 |
| Electric and electronic equipment | 8.1 | 12.2 | 10.7 | 7.3 | 3.5 | 1.1 | 3.1 | 3.6 | 2.3 | 1.5 |
| Transportation equipment | 3.2 | 3.5 | 3.1 | 3.2 | 10.9 | 0.7 | 1.1 | 1.2 | 0.4 | 2.7 |
| Scientific and measuring instruments | 106.8 | 119.5 | 133.2 | 126.8 | 100.0 | 6.8 | 6.9 | 12.8 | 7.7 | 3.5 |
| Miscellaneous manufactures | 0.4 | 1.2 | 0.7 | 0.8 | 0.3 | 0.1 | ..... | 0.2 | ..... | 0.1 |
| Unidentified manufactures | 0.9 | 0.6 | 0.3 | 1.3 | 0.2 | 0.3 | 0.2 | 0.1 | 1.1 | 0.1 |
| **Agricultural and livestock products** | ..... | 0.3 | 11.3 | 13.7 | 16.4 | ..... | ..... | ..... | ..... | ..... |
| Agricultural products | ..... | ..... | 11.2 | 13.7 | 16.4 | ..... | ..... | ..... | ..... | ..... |
| Livestock and livestock products | ..... | 0.3 | 0.2 | ..... | ..... | ..... | ..... | ..... | ..... | ..... |
| **Other commodities** | 11.0 | 11.8 | 14.6 | 12.3 | 4.9 | 0.9 | 0.8 | 0.5 | 0.6 | 2.6 |
| Forestry products | ..... | ..... | ..... | ..... | ..... | ..... | ..... | ..... | ..... | ..... |
| Fish and other marine products | ..... | ..... | ..... | ..... | ..... | ..... | ..... | ..... | ..... | ..... |
| Metallic ores and concentrates | 1.6 | 1.3 | 2.1 | 2.9 | 3.2 | ..... | ..... | 0.2 | 0.1 | 2.2 |
| Bituminous coal and lignite | ..... | ..... | ..... | ..... | ..... | ..... | ..... | ..... | ..... | ..... |
| Crude petroleum and natural gas | ..... | ..... | ..... | 0.3 | 0.4 | ..... | ..... | ..... | ..... | ..... |
| Nonmetallic minerals | 0.8 | 1.0 | 0.9 | 1.1 | 0.5 | 0.5 | 0.6 | 0.3 | 0.4 | 0.2 |
| Scrap and waste | 8.1 | 9.3 | 11.5 | 7.7 | ..... | ..... | ..... | ..... | ..... | ..... |
| Used merchandise | 0.4 | 0.2 | ..... | 0.1 | 0.6 | 0.3 | 0.2 | ..... | ..... | 0.1 |
| Goods imported and returned unchanged | ..... | ..... | ..... | ..... | ..... | ..... | ..... | ..... | ..... | ..... |
| Special classification provisions | 0.1 | 0.1 | 0.2 | 0.1 | 0.2 | ..... | ..... | ..... | ..... | ..... |

## Table D-3.  State Exports of Goods by Destination and Industry, 1993–1997 —Continued

### DELAWARE (Millions of dollars.)

| Industry | 1993 | 1994 | 1995 | 1996 | 1997 | 1993 | 1994 | 1995 | 1996 | 1997 |
|---|---|---|---|---|---|---|---|---|---|---|
| | Germany | | | | | France | | | | |
| **ALL GOODS** | 147.0 | 170.0 | 156.9 | 178.3 | 166.2 | 58.5 | 99.7 | 112.6 | 89.9 | 99.9 |
| **Manufactured goods** | 139.0 | 160.6 | 143.8 | 168.1 | 165.7 | 58.5 | 99.4 | 112.4 | 89.9 | 99.7 |
| Food products | 0.1 | ..... | ..... | ..... | 0.2 | ..... | ..... | 0.1 | 0.1 | 0.2 |
| Tobacco products | ..... | ..... | ..... | ..... | ..... | ..... | ..... | ..... | ..... | ..... |
| Textile mill products | 5.1 | 5.6 | 5.0 | 2.4 | 2.2 | 1.4 | 1.6 | 1.9 | 3.0 | 3.0 |
| Apparel | 0.1 | 0.9 | 0.3 | ..... | 0.3 | 0.3 | ..... | ..... | ..... | 0.1 |
| Lumber and wood products | ..... | 0.3 | 0.3 | 0.2 | 0.2 | ..... | ..... | ..... | ..... | ..... |
| Furniture and fixtures | ..... | ..... | ..... | ..... | ..... | ..... | ..... | ..... | ..... | ..... |
| Paper products | 0.7 | 0.6 | 0.9 | 1.4 | 1.8 | 0.7 | 0.2 | 0.3 | 0.7 | 0.2 |
| Printing and publishing | 0.3 | 0.2 | 0.1 | ..... | ..... | ..... | ..... | ..... | ..... | ..... |
| Chemical products | 31.8 | 36.1 | 30.5 | 35.7 | 62.3 | 28.7 | 50.6 | 50.3 | 43.4 | 46.2 |
| Refined petroleum products | ..... | 0.1 | 0.1 | 0.1 | 0.1 | ..... | ..... | ..... | ..... | ..... |
| Rubber and plastic products | 21.2 | 17.4 | 18.0 | 24.4 | 49.1 | 2.8 | 2.9 | 3.4 | 2.4 | 2.6 |
| Leather products | ..... | ..... | ..... | ..... | ..... | ..... | ..... | ..... | ..... | ..... |
| Stone, clay and glass products | 0.7 | 0.1 | ..... | 0.4 | 0.3 | 14.5 | 26.5 | 42.9 | 30.0 | 37.4 |
| Primary metals | 0.2 | 0.2 | 0.1 | 0.1 | 0.2 | ..... | ..... | ..... | 0.6 | 1.0 |
| Fabricated metal products | 2.9 | 1.9 | 2.0 | 1.9 | 0.6 | 2.2 | 5.3 | 4.7 | 1.2 | 0.1 |
| Industrial machinery and computers | 2.4 | 3.3 | 3.1 | 1.1 | 1.4 | 2.6 | 5.6 | 3.0 | 3.9 | 6.5 |
| Electric and electronic equipment | 1.6 | 1.9 | 1.2 | 1.5 | 0.5 | 0.7 | 2.8 | 2.2 | 0.9 | 0.3 |
| Transportation equipment | 0.8 | 1.6 | 0.5 | 0.8 | 0.4 | 0.2 | 0.1 | 0.2 | 1.8 | 0.1 |
| Scientific and measuring instruments | 71.0 | 90.1 | 81.4 | 97.5 | 46.0 | 4.3 | 3.5 | 3.2 | 1.7 | 2.1 |
| Miscellaneous manufactures | ..... | 0.3 | 0.4 | 0.7 | ..... | ..... | ..... | ..... | ..... | ..... |
| Unidentified manufactures | 0.1 | ..... | ..... | ..... | 0.1 | ..... | 0.1 | ..... | ..... | ..... |
| **Agricultural and livestock products** | ..... | ..... | 0.1 | ..... | ..... | ..... | 0.3 | 0.1 | ..... | ..... |
| Agricultural products | ..... | ..... | ..... | ..... | ..... | ..... | ..... | ..... | ..... | ..... |
| Livestock and livestock products | ..... | ..... | ..... | ..... | ..... | ..... | 0.3 | 0.1 | ..... | ..... |
| **Other commodities** | 7.9 | 9.4 | 13.0 | 10.2 | 0.5 | ..... | ..... | ..... | ..... | 0.1 |
| Forestry products | ..... | ..... | ..... | ..... | ..... | ..... | ..... | ..... | ..... | ..... |
| Fish and other marine products | ..... | ..... | ..... | ..... | ..... | ..... | ..... | ..... | ..... | ..... |
| Metallic ores and concentrates | 1.6 | 0.5 | 1.7 | 2.6 | ..... | ..... | ..... | ..... | ..... | ..... |
| Bituminous coal and lignite | ..... | ..... | ..... | ..... | ..... | ..... | ..... | ..... | ..... | ..... |
| Crude petroleum and natural gas | ..... | ..... | ..... | ..... | ..... | ..... | ..... | ..... | ..... | ..... |
| Nonmetallic minerals | ..... | 0.1 | ..... | ..... | ..... | ..... | ..... | ..... | ..... | 0.1 |
| Scrap and waste | 6.2 | 8.8 | 11.3 | 7.6 | ..... | ..... | ..... | ..... | ..... | ..... |
| Used merchandise | ..... | ..... | ..... | ..... | 0.5 | ..... | ..... | ..... | ..... | ..... |
| Goods imported and returned unchanged | ..... | ..... | ..... | ..... | ..... | ..... | ..... | ..... | ..... | ..... |
| Special classification provisions | ..... | ..... | ..... | ..... | ..... | ..... | ..... | ..... | ..... | ..... |
| | The Netherlands | | | | | Asian 10 | | | | |
| **ALL GOODS** | 111.2 | 165.0 | 200.9 | 210.7 | 269.9 | 939.4 | 1 004.5 | 1 173.7 | 1 263.7 | 1 514.1 |
| **Manufactured goods** | 111.2 | 164.8 | 200.9 | 210.7 | 269.3 | 936.3 | 999.1 | 1 165.8 | 1 253.6 | 1 505.9 |
| Food products | ..... | 0.1 | 0.1 | 0.1 | ..... | 3.2 | 5.1 | 6.6 | 9.6 | 6.5 |
| Tobacco products | ..... | ..... | ..... | ..... | ..... | ..... | ..... | ..... | ..... | ..... |
| Textile mill products | 0.5 | 0.2 | 0.2 | 0.3 | 0.2 | 32.2 | 39.3 | 43.0 | 50.0 | 64.7 |
| Apparel | ..... | ..... | ..... | ..... | ..... | 0.8 | 0.8 | 0.4 | 0.5 | 0.4 |
| Lumber and wood products | 0.1 | 0.2 | 0.2 | 0.1 | ..... | ..... | ..... | 0.1 | 0.1 | 0.3 |
| Furniture and fixtures | ..... | 0.1 | ..... | ..... | ..... | 0.2 | 0.2 | ..... | 0.1 | 0.1 |
| Paper products | 0.4 | 0.4 | 0.8 | 0.9 | 1.0 | 13.7 | 22.0 | 25.0 | 30.4 | 30.9 |
| Printing and publishing | ..... | ..... | ..... | ..... | ..... | 0.4 | 0.1 | 0.1 | 0.2 | 0.2 |
| Chemical products | 92.0 | 127.2 | 148.8 | 174.4 | 225.2 | 686.8 | 764.4 | 887.0 | 935.7 | 1 116.1 |
| Refined petroleum products | ..... | ..... | ..... | ..... | 0.1 | 0.4 | 0.4 | 0.3 | 0.3 | 0.3 |
| Rubber and plastic products | 6.9 | 25.8 | 45.0 | 29.3 | 40.0 | 85.2 | 77.1 | 83.3 | 105.8 | 130.3 |
| Leather products | ..... | ..... | ..... | ..... | ..... | ..... | ..... | 0.1 | 0.1 | 0.3 |
| Stone, clay and glass products | ..... | 0.7 | ..... | ..... | ..... | 2.5 | 1.1 | 1.3 | 1.1 | 0.6 |
| Primary metals | ..... | ..... | 0.1 | ..... | ..... | 3.8 | 1.7 | 26.2 | 35.1 | 3.6 |
| Fabricated metal products | 0.6 | 2.5 | 0.2 | 0.4 | 0.5 | 9.3 | 6.3 | 4.1 | 5.7 | 6.8 |
| Industrial machinery and computers | 6.8 | 5.0 | 3.0 | 3.8 | 1.0 | 29.2 | 14.3 | 14.2 | 11.7 | 20.2 |
| Electric and electronic equipment | 1.3 | 0.3 | 0.1 | 0.3 | 0.3 | 4.1 | 5.9 | 6.7 | 5.5 | 4.9 |
| Transportation equipment | 0.8 | 0.2 | 0.5 | 0.1 | ..... | 0.5 | 0.3 | 0.2 | 0.3 | 46.8 |
| Scientific and measuring instruments | 1.7 | 1.9 | 2.0 | 1.2 | 1.1 | 63.7 | 59.7 | 67.0 | 60.4 | 72.1 |
| Miscellaneous manufactures | ..... | 0.1 | ..... | ..... | ..... | 0.2 | 0.2 | 0.1 | 0.8 | 0.7 |
| Unidentified manufactures | ..... | ..... | ..... | ..... | ..... | 0.1 | 0.2 | 0.1 | 0.2 | 0.2 |
| **Agricultural and livestock products** | ..... | ..... | ..... | ..... | ..... | ..... | ..... | ..... | ..... | 0.5 |
| Agricultural products | ..... | ..... | ..... | ..... | ..... | ..... | ..... | ..... | ..... | 0.2 |
| Livestock and livestock products | ..... | ..... | ..... | ..... | ..... | ..... | ..... | ..... | ..... | 0.3 |
| **Other commodities** | ..... | 0.2 | ..... | ..... | 0.6 | 3.1 | 5.5 | 7.9 | 10.2 | 7.7 |
| Forestry products | ..... | ..... | ..... | ..... | ..... | ..... | ..... | ..... | ..... | ..... |
| Fish and other marine products | ..... | ..... | ..... | ..... | ..... | ..... | ..... | ..... | ..... | ..... |
| Metallic ores and concentrates | ..... | 0.2 | ..... | ..... | 0.6 | 0.1 | 0.2 | 0.1 | 0.3 | 0.3 |
| Bituminous coal and lignite | ..... | ..... | ..... | ..... | ..... | ..... | ..... | ..... | ..... | ..... |
| Crude petroleum and natural gas | ..... | ..... | ..... | ..... | ..... | ..... | ..... | ..... | ..... | ..... |
| Nonmetallic minerals | ..... | ..... | ..... | ..... | ..... | 1.3 | 1.4 | 1.9 | 3.9 | 7.2 |
| Scrap and waste | ..... | ..... | ..... | ..... | ..... | 1.0 | 3.8 | 5.9 | 4.8 | 0.2 |
| Used merchandise | ..... | ..... | ..... | ..... | ..... | 0.1 | ..... | ..... | 0.5 | ..... |
| Goods imported and returned unchanged | ..... | ..... | ..... | ..... | ..... | ..... | ..... | ..... | ..... | ..... |
| Special classification provisions | ..... | ..... | ..... | ..... | ..... | 0.7 | ..... | 0.1 | 0.6 | ..... |

## Table D-3.  State Exports of Goods by Destination and Industry, 1993–1997 —*Continued*

**DELAWARE** (Millions of dollars.)

| Industry | Japan 1993 | 1994 | 1995 | 1996 | 1997 | South Korea 1993 | 1994 | 1995 | 1996 | 1997 |
|---|---|---|---|---|---|---|---|---|---|---|
| **ALL GOODS** | 333.8 | 370.2 | 433.0 | 441.5 | 556.0 | 136.9 | 155.9 | 172.5 | 208.0 | 190.2 |
| **Manufactured goods** | 332.0 | 368.6 | 431.4 | 437.6 | 550.1 | 135.9 | 152.1 | 166.3 | 202.6 | 189.1 |
| Food products | ..... | 0.1 | 0.6 | 1.2 | 0.4 | 0.2 | 0.4 | 2.1 | 1.4 | 0.5 |
| Tobacco products | ..... | ..... | ..... | ..... | ..... | ..... | ..... | ..... | ..... | ..... |
| Textile mill products | 28.3 | 31.7 | 30.6 | 34.2 | 41.4 | 1.6 | 3.5 | 4.1 | 6.1 | 7.1 |
| Apparel | 0.3 | 0.3 | 0.1 | 0.2 | 0.4 | ..... | 0.1 | ..... | ..... | ..... |
| Lumber and wood products | ..... | ..... | 0.1 | ..... | 0.2 | ..... | ..... | ..... | ..... | ..... |
| Furniture and fixtures | 0.1 | 0.2 | ..... | ..... | ..... | ..... | ..... | ..... | ..... | ..... |
| Paper products | 9.4 | 13.2 | 10.4 | 14.2 | 11.1 | 0.1 | 0.1 | 0.6 | 1.3 | 1.6 |
| Printing and publishing | 0.3 | ..... | ..... | ..... | ..... | ..... | ..... | ..... | ..... | ..... |
| Chemical products | 229.5 | 265.7 | 323.2 | 322.7 | 348.9 | 105.7 | 118.9 | 121.4 | 124.7 | 137.6 |
| Refined petroleum products | ..... | ..... | 0.1 | ..... | ..... | ..... | ..... | ..... | ..... | ..... |
| Rubber and plastic products | 37.2 | 30.5 | 27.8 | 44.3 | 64.5 | 19.0 | 16.6 | 21.2 | 20.2 | 27.1 |
| Leather products | ..... | ..... | ..... | ..... | ..... | ..... | ..... | ..... | ..... | ..... |
| Stone, clay and glass products | 0.5 | 0.4 | 0.2 | 0.2 | 0.2 | 0.2 | 0.3 | 0.1 | ..... | 0.2 |
| Primary metals | 0.1 | 0.1 | 12.4 | 0.1 | 0.1 | ..... | 0.1 | 0.1 | 33.7 | 1.6 |
| Fabricated metal products | 2.6 | 4.2 | 2.8 | 2.9 | 2.1 | 0.4 | 0.2 | 0.2 | 0.5 | 0.5 |
| Industrial machinery and computers | 4.6 | 1.8 | 1.7 | 1.8 | 5.4 | 1.7 | 3.2 | 4.4 | 1.2 | 1.7 |
| Electric and electronic equipment | 0.8 | 1.8 | 1.9 | 0.8 | 2.1 | 0.5 | 0.7 | 2.0 | 1.9 | 0.5 |
| Transportation equipment | ..... | ..... | ..... | 0.1 | 45.6 | ..... | ..... | ..... | ..... | ..... |
| Scientific and measuring instruments | 18.0 | 18.6 | 19.2 | 14.7 | 27.5 | 6.3 | 7.8 | 10.2 | 11.3 | 10.3 |
| Miscellaneous manufactures | 0.1 | 0.1 | 0.1 | 0.1 | 0.1 | ..... | 0.1 | ..... | 0.3 | 0.4 |
| Unidentified manufactures | ..... | ..... | ..... | ..... | 0.1 | ..... | 0.1 | ..... | ..... | ..... |
| **Agricultural and livestock products** | ..... | ..... | ..... | ..... | ..... | ..... | ..... | ..... | ..... | ..... |
| Agricultural products | ..... | ..... | ..... | ..... | ..... | ..... | ..... | ..... | ..... | ..... |
| Livestock and livestock products | ..... | ..... | ..... | ..... | ..... | ..... | ..... | ..... | ..... | ..... |
| **Other commodities** | 1.8 | 1.6 | 1.6 | 3.9 | 5.9 | 1.0 | 3.8 | 6.2 | 5.5 | 1.1 |
| Forestry products | ..... | ..... | ..... | ..... | ..... | ..... | ..... | ..... | ..... | ..... |
| Fish and other marine products | ..... | ..... | ..... | ..... | ..... | ..... | ..... | ..... | ..... | ..... |
| Metallic ores and concentrates | 0.1 | 0.2 | 0.1 | 0.1 | 0.3 | ..... | ..... | ..... | 0.2 | ..... |
| Bituminous coal and lignite | ..... | ..... | ..... | ..... | ..... | ..... | ..... | ..... | ..... | ..... |
| Crude petroleum and natural gas | ..... | ..... | ..... | ..... | ..... | ..... | ..... | ..... | ..... | ..... |
| Nonmetallic minerals | 1.2 | 1.3 | 1.5 | 3.3 | 5.6 | ..... | ..... | 0.4 | 0.5 | 1.1 |
| Scrap and waste | ..... | ..... | ..... | ..... | ..... | 1.0 | 3.8 | 5.8 | 4.7 | ..... |
| Used merchandise | ..... | ..... | ..... | 0.5 | ..... | ..... | ..... | ..... | ..... | ..... |
| Goods imported and returned unchanged | ..... | ..... | ..... | ..... | ..... | ..... | ..... | ..... | ..... | ..... |
| Special classification provisions | 0.6 | ..... | 0.1 | ..... | ..... | ..... | ..... | ..... | ..... | ..... |

| Industry | Taiwan 1993 | 1994 | 1995 | 1996 | 1997 | Singapore 1993 | 1994 | 1995 | 1996 | 1997 |
|---|---|---|---|---|---|---|---|---|---|---|
| **ALL GOODS** | 140.2 | 149.0 | 170.4 | 167.9 | 205.1 | 96.8 | 74.6 | 88.8 | 105.1 | 147.5 |
| **Manufactured goods** | 140.1 | 148.9 | 170.3 | 167.2 | 204.9 | 96.8 | 74.6 | 88.7 | 105.0 | 147.0 |
| Food products | ..... | ..... | ..... | 0.1 | 0.3 | ..... | ..... | ..... | 0.2 | ..... |
| Tobacco products | ..... | ..... | ..... | ..... | ..... | ..... | ..... | ..... | ..... | ..... |
| Textile mill products | 0.9 | 1.0 | 2.4 | 1.9 | 3.5 | 0.3 | 0.6 | 1.7 | 3.2 | 3.4 |
| Apparel | ..... | ..... | ..... | 0.1 | ..... | ..... | ..... | ..... | ..... | ..... |
| Lumber and wood products | ..... | ..... | ..... | 0.1 | ..... | ..... | ..... | ..... | ..... | ..... |
| Furniture and fixtures | ..... | ..... | ..... | ..... | 0.1 | ..... | ..... | ..... | ..... | ..... |
| Paper products | ..... | 0.9 | 1.1 | 1.2 | 4.8 | 0.1 | 0.1 | 0.3 | 0.2 | 0.4 |
| Printing and publishing | ..... | ..... | ..... | ..... | ..... | ..... | ..... | ..... | 0.1 | 0.1 |
| Chemical products | 109.4 | 121.5 | 122.7 | 137.4 | 165.4 | 56.8 | 58.5 | 71.3 | 86.1 | 125.4 |
| Refined petroleum products | 0.1 | 0.1 | ..... | 0.2 | 0.1 | 0.2 | 0.2 | 0.2 | 0.1 | 0.1 |
| Rubber and plastic products | 5.1 | 5.6 | 8.2 | 8.6 | 11.0 | 7.2 | 6.2 | 7.5 | 7.9 | 9.0 |
| Leather products | ..... | ..... | ..... | ..... | ..... | ..... | ..... | ..... | ..... | ..... |
| Stone, clay and glass products | 0.2 | 0.1 | 0.2 | 0.3 | 0.2 | 1.5 | 0.1 | 0.1 | 0.1 | 0.1 |
| Primary metals | 0.4 | 0.4 | 13.4 | 1.0 | 1.6 | 3.1 | 0.9 | 0.3 | 0.2 | 0.1 |
| Fabricated metal products | 1.0 | 0.4 | 0.2 | 0.3 | 1.6 | 4.6 | 0.4 | 0.4 | 1.4 | 2.2 |
| Industrial machinery and computers | 2.8 | 2.6 | 2.5 | 1.7 | 2.8 | 15.5 | 2.3 | 3.5 | 2.2 | 2.7 |
| Electric and electronic equipment | 1.0 | 0.8 | 0.7 | 0.3 | 0.4 | 1.1 | 1.0 | 0.5 | 0.2 | 0.3 |
| Transportation equipment | 0.1 | 0.1 | ..... | 0.1 | 0.1 | 0.3 | ..... | 0.1 | ..... | 0.1 |
| Scientific and measuring instruments | 19.1 | 15.5 | 18.8 | 13.9 | 12.9 | 6.0 | 4.3 | 2.8 | 2.8 | 3.0 |
| Miscellaneous manufactures | ..... | ..... | ..... | ..... | ..... | ..... | ..... | ..... | 0.1 | 0.1 |
| Unidentified manufactures | ..... | ..... | ..... | ..... | ..... | ..... | ..... | ..... | ..... | ..... |
| **Agricultural and livestock products** | ..... | ..... | ..... | ..... | 0.1 | ..... | ..... | ..... | ..... | ..... |
| Agricultural products | ..... | ..... | ..... | ..... | 0.1 | ..... | ..... | ..... | ..... | ..... |
| Livestock and livestock products | ..... | ..... | ..... | ..... | ..... | ..... | ..... | ..... | ..... | ..... |
| **Other commodities** | 0.1 | ..... | ..... | 0.7 | 0.1 | ..... | ..... | ..... | 0.1 | 0.5 |
| Forestry products | ..... | ..... | ..... | ..... | ..... | ..... | ..... | ..... | ..... | ..... |
| Fish and other marine products | ..... | ..... | ..... | ..... | ..... | ..... | ..... | ..... | ..... | ..... |
| Metallic ores and concentrates | 0.1 | ..... | ..... | ..... | ..... | ..... | ..... | ..... | ..... | ..... |
| Bituminous coal and lignite | ..... | ..... | ..... | ..... | ..... | ..... | ..... | ..... | ..... | ..... |
| Crude petroleum and natural gas | ..... | ..... | ..... | ..... | ..... | ..... | ..... | ..... | ..... | ..... |
| Nonmetallic minerals | 0.1 | ..... | ..... | 0.1 | 0.1 | ..... | ..... | ..... | ..... | 0.4 |
| Scrap and waste | ..... | ..... | ..... | ..... | ..... | ..... | ..... | ..... | ..... | 0.1 |
| Used merchandise | ..... | ..... | ..... | ..... | ..... | ..... | ..... | ..... | ..... | ..... |
| Goods imported and returned unchanged | ..... | ..... | ..... | ..... | ..... | ..... | ..... | ..... | ..... | ..... |
| Special classification provisions | ..... | ..... | ..... | 0.6 | ..... | ..... | ..... | ..... | ..... | ..... |

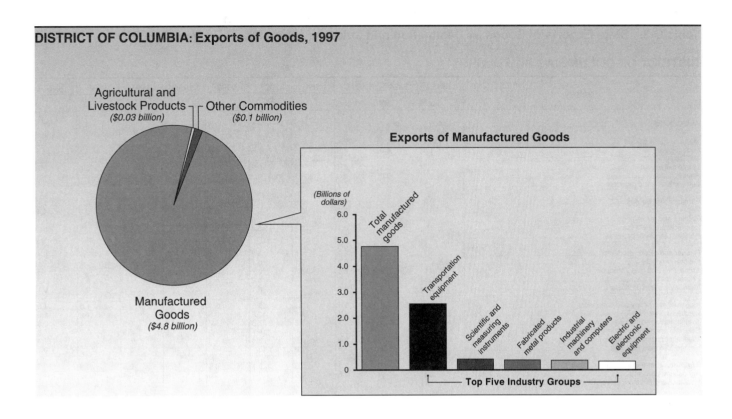

## DISTRICT OF COLUMBIA: Exports of Goods, 1997

Agricultural and
Livestock Products
($0.03 billion)

Other Commodities
($0.1 billion)

Manufactured
Goods
($4.8 billion)

### Exports of Manufactured Goods

(Billions of dollars)

Total manufactured goods

Transportation equipment

Scientific and measuring instruments

Fabricated metal products

Industrial machinery and computers

Electric and electronic equipment

Top Five Industry Groups

## Table D-3.   State Exports of Goods by Destination and Industry, 1993–1997 —*Continued*

### DISTRICT OF COLUMBIA (Millions of dollars.)

| Industry | 1993 | 1994 | 1995 | 1996 | 1997 | 1993 | 1994 | 1995 | 1996 | 1997 |
|---|---|---|---|---|---|---|---|---|---|---|
| | All destinations | | | | | Canada | | | | |
| **ALL GOODS** | 4 702.1 | 5 150.7 | 5 323.5 | 5 084.8 | 4 881.0 | 36.2 | 120.9 | 81.8 | 102.1 | 142.1 |
| **Manufactured goods** | 4 325.3 | 5 003.8 | 5 126.8 | 4 897.2 | 4 766.2 | 23.9 | 110.3 | 66.9 | 82.9 | 124.7 |
| Food products | 126.6 | 63.6 | 47.2 | 47.2 | 43.8 | 1.8 | 3.5 | 3.6 | 6.4 | 10.8 |
| Tobacco products | ..... | ..... | ..... | ..... | ..... | | | | | |
| Textile mill products | 2.1 | 2.4 | 4.4 | 7.2 | 3.3 | 0.1 | 0.2 | 0.4 | 0.6 | 0.5 |
| Apparel | 14.4 | 7.8 | 11.5 | 15.6 | 14.7 | ..... | ..... | 0.2 | 0.1 | 0.2 |
| Lumber and wood products | 3.2 | 0.7 | 0.7 | 0.7 | 0.5 | 0.1 | ..... | ..... | 0.1 | 0.1 |
| Furniture and fixtures | 2.6 | 7.8 | 6.5 | 11.1 | 11.3 | 0.1 | 0.2 | 0.1 | 0.4 | 0.2 |
| Paper products | 2.7 | 9.8 | 7.8 | 2.0 | 4.5 | 1.0 | 9.1 | 5.7 | 0.3 | 2.2 |
| Printing and publishing | 8.4 | 12.2 | 10.6 | 9.5 | 15.8 | 1.1 | 1.0 | 0.7 | 0.9 | 4.4 |
| Chemical products | 229.1 | 192.9 | 299.0 | 213.6 | 166.5 | 5.4 | 20.8 | 7.4 | 3.5 | 5.3 |
| Refined petroleum products | 1.0 | 5.3 | 2.3 | 2.7 | 0.9 | ..... | 2.1 | 0.7 | 0.8 | ..... |
| Rubber and plastic products | 33.1 | 29.0 | 32.1 | 70.5 | 74.8 | 0.3 | 0.1 | 0.1 | 37.0 | 45.9 |
| Leather products | 0.2 | 0.1 | 0.5 | 0.3 | 0.4 | ..... | ..... | 0.1 | ..... | ..... |
| Stone, clay and glass products | 4.6 | 1.1 | 2.1 | 2.8 | 3.3 | 0.1 | 0.1 | 0.2 | 0.7 | 0.3 |
| Primary metals | 17.5 | 15.5 | 11.5 | 8.5 | 37.4 | 0.5 | 0.3 | 1.5 | 0.2 | 5.7 |
| Fabricated metal products | 478.8 | 693.0 | 901.6 | 344.2 | 386.5 | 0.5 | 1.7 | 0.5 | 0.5 | 1.3 |
| Industrial machinery and computers | 311.2 | 275.8 | 283.0 | 245.0 | 371.7 | 2.0 | 2.2 | 2.0 | 5.0 | 8.1 |
| Electric and electronic equipment | 196.3 | 250.7 | 337.6 | 216.8 | 336.2 | 1.2 | 2.3 | 4.2 | 8.2 | 13.1 |
| Transportation equipment | 2 295.1 | 2 766.4 | 2 520.4 | 3 283.7 | 2 549.3 | 7.8 | 60.3 | 34.3 | 12.3 | 17.3 |
| Scientific and measuring instruments | 193.5 | 162.1 | 180.4 | 80.7 | 420.4 | 1.2 | 5.9 | 4.7 | 5.5 | 8.7 |
| Miscellaneous manufactures | 2.9 | 3.8 | 11.2 | 3.4 | 5.8 | 0.2 | 0.1 | 0.1 | 0.2 | 0.2 |
| Unidentified manufactures | 401.8 | 503.6 | 456.4 | 331.7 | 319.1 | 0.3 | 0.3 | 0.4 | 0.4 | 0.5 |
| **Agricultural and livestock products** | 214.6 | 60.2 | 127.0 | 116.4 | 33.2 | 6.1 | 7.3 | 7.4 | 8.9 | 9.9 |
| Agricultural products | 214.5 | 60.0 | 125.5 | 115.1 | 32.7 | 6.0 | 7.3 | 7.4 | 8.9 | 9.9 |
| Livestock and livestock products | 0.1 | 0.2 | 1.6 | 1.4 | 0.5 | 0.1 | ..... | ..... | ..... | ..... |
| **Other commodities** | 162.2 | 86.7 | 69.7 | 71.2 | 81.5 | 6.2 | 3.4 | 7.5 | 10.2 | 7.5 |
| Forestry products | ..... | ..... | ..... | ..... | 0.1 | ..... | ..... | ..... | ..... | ..... |
| Fish and other marine products | ..... | ..... | 0.3 | 0.1 | 0.9 | ..... | ..... | ..... | ..... | ..... |
| Metallic ores and concentrates | ..... | 1.5 | 1.0 | 0.2 | 0.1 | ..... | ..... | 1.0 | ..... | ..... |
| Bituminous coal and lignite | ..... | ..... | ..... | ..... | ..... | ..... | ..... | ..... | ..... | ..... |
| Crude petroleum and natural gas | 1.7 | 0.2 | ..... | ..... | ..... | 1.7 | 0.1 | ..... | ..... | ..... |
| Nonmetallic minerals | 0.2 | ..... | 0.2 | 0.1 | 0.4 | ..... | ..... | ..... | ..... | 0.2 |
| Scrap and waste | 0.1 | 0.9 | 0.7 | 0.5 | 0.3 | 0.1 | 0.1 | 0.1 | 0.2 | 0.1 |
| Used merchandise | 136.1 | 58.0 | 45.5 | 36.1 | 30.8 | 0.1 | ..... | 0.3 | 0.1 | 0.3 |
| Goods imported and returned unchanged | 3.5 | 1.9 | 4.5 | 6.5 | 5.2 | 3.5 | 1.9 | 4.5 | 6.5 | 5.2 |
| Special classification provisions | 20.5 | 24.1 | 17.6 | 27.7 | 43.7 | 0.8 | 1.3 | 1.5 | 3.4 | 1.6 |

## Table D-3.  State Exports of Goods by Destination and Industry, 1993–1997 —Continued

### DISTRICT OF COLUMBIA (Millions of dollars.)

| Industry | 1993 | 1994 | 1995 | 1996 | 1997 | 1993 | 1994 | 1995 | 1996 | 1997 |
|---|---|---|---|---|---|---|---|---|---|---|
| | South and Central America and Caribbean | | | | | Mexico | | | | |
| **ALL GOODS** | 145.3 | 209.6 | 96.2 | 141.2 | 168.5 | 17.3 | 30.0 | 12.3 | 8.9 | 17.1 |
| **Manufactured goods** | 138.1 | 205.2 | 92.4 | 135.5 | 164.0 | 16.7 | 28.6 | 11.2 | 4.7 | 16.8 |
| Food products | 1.5 | 4.3 | 4.8 | 1.8 | 2.5 | 6.3 | 19.3 | 7.7 | 0.3 | 8.7 |
| Tobacco products | ..... | ..... | ..... | ..... | ..... | ..... | ..... | ..... | ..... | ..... |
| Textile mill products | 0.3 | 0.5 | 0.1 | 1.4 | 0.5 | ..... | ..... | ..... | 0.3 | 0.1 |
| Apparel | 1.4 | 0.8 | 0.9 | 1.1 | 3.2 | ..... | 0.1 | 0.1 | ..... | ..... |
| Lumber and wood products | 0.1 | 0.1 | 0.1 | 0.1 | ..... | ..... | ..... | ..... | ..... | ..... |
| Furniture and fixtures | 0.3 | 2.6 | 4.9 | 7.6 | 7.5 | ..... | ..... | ..... | 0.1 | ..... |
| Paper products | 0.1 | ..... | 0.1 | 0.3 | 0.2 | 0.2 | 0.2 | 0.7 | 0.2 | 1.4 |
| Printing and publishing | 1.0 | 1.4 | 0.8 | 1.3 | 0.8 | 0.2 | 0.2 | 0.1 | 0.1 | 0.1 |
| Chemical products | 2.7 | 3.4 | 3.1 | 3.8 | 5.8 | 0.1 | 0.7 | 0.1 | 0.5 | 0.1 |
| Refined petroleum products | 0.1 | ..... | 0.1 | 0.9 | ..... | ..... | ..... | ..... | ..... | ..... |
| Rubber and plastic products | 3.7 | 3.4 | 5.2 | 4.6 | 5.3 | 0.1 | 0.9 | ..... | ..... | 0.1 |
| Leather products | 0.1 | ..... | 0.2 | 0.1 | 0.1 | ..... | ..... | ..... | ..... | ..... |
| Stone, clay and glass products | 0.1 | 0.2 | 0.1 | 0.5 | 0.2 | ..... | ..... | ..... | ..... | ..... |
| Primary metals | 0.8 | 2.9 | ..... | 0.1 | 0.2 | ..... | 0.1 | ..... | 0.1 | 0.2 |
| Fabricated metal products | 1.2 | 1.5 | 0.8 | 0.2 | 6.1 | 0.1 | ..... | ..... | 0.1 | 0.1 |
| Industrial machinery and computers | 40.0 | 8.6 | 8.1 | 16.1 | 10.5 | 1.1 | 1.4 | 0.5 | 1.0 | 1.6 |
| Electric and electronic equipment | 10.4 | 18.8 | 25.1 | 13.6 | 47.8 | 0.6 | 3.2 | 1.1 | 1.2 | 1.0 |
| Transportation equipment | 37.8 | 125.4 | 13.1 | 47.8 | 52.8 | 5.7 | 0.9 | 0.3 | 0.4 | 0.3 |
| Scientific and measuring instruments | 6.7 | 5.7 | 6.9 | 5.1 | 4.7 | 2.0 | 1.5 | 0.3 | 0.7 | 1.5 |
| Miscellaneous manufactures | 0.2 | 0.3 | 0.3 | 0.9 | 0.7 | ..... | ..... | ..... | ..... | 1.4 |
| Unidentified manufactures | 29.9 | 25.4 | 17.9 | 27.8 | 15.1 | ..... | 0.1 | 0.1 | ..... | 0.1 |
| **Agricultural and livestock products** | 2.4 | 1.9 | 2.5 | 0.3 | 0.1 | 0.5 | 0.9 | 0.4 | 0.3 | ..... |
| Agricultural products | 2.4 | 1.9 | 2.5 | 0.3 | 0.1 | 0.5 | 0.9 | 0.4 | 0.3 | ..... |
| Livestock and livestock products | ..... | ..... | ..... | ..... | ..... | ..... | ..... | ..... | ..... | ..... |
| **Other commodities** | 4.8 | 2.5 | 1.3 | 5.4 | 4.4 | 0.1 | 0.5 | 0.7 | 3.9 | 0.3 |
| Forestry products | ..... | ..... | ..... | ..... | ..... | ..... | ..... | ..... | ..... | ..... |
| Fish and other marine products | ..... | ..... | ..... | ..... | ..... | ..... | ..... | ..... | ..... | ..... |
| Metallic ores and concentrates | ..... | ..... | ..... | ..... | ..... | ..... | ..... | ..... | ..... | ..... |
| Bituminous coal and lignite | ..... | ..... | ..... | ..... | ..... | ..... | ..... | ..... | ..... | ..... |
| Crude petroleum and natural gas | ..... | ..... | ..... | ..... | ..... | ..... | ..... | ..... | ..... | ..... |
| Nonmetallic minerals | ..... | ..... | ..... | ..... | ..... | ..... | ..... | ..... | ..... | ..... |
| Scrap and waste | ..... | 0.7 | 0.1 | 0.1 | 0.1 | ..... | ..... | 0.3 | ..... | ..... |
| Used merchandise | 3.0 | 0.4 | 0.2 | 1.0 | 2.4 | ..... | 0.2 | ..... | 3.7 | 0.1 |
| Goods imported and returned unchanged | ..... | ..... | ..... | ..... | ..... | ..... | ..... | ..... | ..... | ..... |
| Special classification provisions | 1.7 | 1.5 | 1.1 | 4.3 | 1.9 | 0.1 | 0.2 | 0.3 | 0.2 | 0.1 |
| | European Union | | | | | United Kingdom | | | | |
| **ALL GOODS** | 812.7 | 937.8 | 1 288.2 | 929.3 | 1 177.8 | 308.4 | 513.6 | 390.5 | 546.3 | 500.1 |
| **Manufactured goods** | 693.8 | 917.9 | 1 257.5 | 907.6 | 1 127.4 | 264.3 | 505.6 | 384.2 | 540.1 | 467.1 |
| Food products | 7.0 | 9.8 | 4.3 | 6.0 | 2.1 | 0.2 | 1.0 | 0.1 | 0.3 | 0.3 |
| Tobacco products | ..... | ..... | ..... | ..... | ..... | ..... | ..... | ..... | ..... | ..... |
| Textile mill products | 0.5 | 0.5 | 0.5 | 0.3 | 0.2 | 0.1 | 0.2 | 0.1 | 0.1 | 0.1 |
| Apparel | 2.5 | 2.9 | 2.8 | 4.3 | 1.8 | 0.8 | 1.9 | 1.6 | 1.8 | 1.3 |
| Lumber and wood products | 0.1 | 0.1 | ..... | 0.2 | 0.1 | ..... | ..... | ..... | ..... | ..... |
| Furniture and fixtures | 0.4 | 0.4 | 0.3 | 0.4 | 1.1 | 0.1 | 0.3 | 0.1 | 0.1 | 0.1 |
| Paper products | 0.2 | 0.1 | 0.4 | 0.4 | 0.2 | 0.2 | ..... | 0.1 | ..... | 0.1 |
| Printing and publishing | 2.6 | 5.1 | 2.3 | 1.7 | 3.5 | 1.5 | 1.6 | 0.9 | 1.1 | 1.0 |
| Chemical products | 17.5 | 20.6 | 50.0 | 26.4 | 27.9 | 10.2 | 13.6 | 8.5 | 15.8 | 16.0 |
| Refined petroleum products | 0.1 | 1.8 | 0.8 | 0.1 | 0.1 | ..... | ..... | ..... | ..... | ..... |
| Rubber and plastic products | 3.2 | 1.4 | 0.8 | 1.4 | 2.1 | ..... | 0.6 | 0.5 | 0.1 | 0.2 |
| Leather products | ..... | ..... | ..... | ..... | 0.2 | ..... | ..... | ..... | ..... | 0.1 |
| Stone, clay and glass products | 0.4 | 0.3 | 0.6 | 0.8 | 0.3 | 0.2 | 0.2 | 0.4 | 0.4 | 0.1 |
| Primary metals | 2.9 | 1.5 | 2.4 | 1.9 | 1.2 | 1.8 | 1.2 | 0.2 | 0.5 | 0.4 |
| Fabricated metal products | 112.5 | 151.3 | 223.5 | 85.1 | 117.5 | 11.4 | 19.8 | 56.2 | 65.9 | 31.3 |
| Industrial machinery and computers | 57.5 | 70.1 | 72.6 | 40.7 | 86.5 | 9.0 | 23.5 | 19.0 | 14.7 | 30.4 |
| Electric and electronic equipment | 61.1 | 57.1 | 87.8 | 54.8 | 78.6 | 13.0 | 18.2 | 45.3 | 20.5 | 24.7 |
| Transportation equipment | 382.2 | 534.7 | 766.2 | 621.0 | 742.5 | 192.9 | 388.4 | 232.9 | 376.4 | 329.6 |
| Scientific and measuring instruments | 18.5 | 27.2 | 28.9 | 34.1 | 27.9 | 7.0 | 16.4 | 16.3 | 19.0 | 9.8 |
| Miscellaneous manufactures | 1.4 | 0.8 | 1.7 | 0.8 | 1.6 | 0.1 | 0.2 | 0.4 | 0.2 | 0.2 |
| Unidentified manufactures | 23.3 | 32.1 | 11.6 | 27.1 | 32.1 | 15.7 | 18.6 | 1.6 | 23.3 | 21.2 |
| **Agricultural and livestock products** | 4.9 | 3.5 | 0.6 | 1.9 | 1.6 | 1.6 | 2.3 | 0.5 | 0.6 | 0.3 |
| Agricultural products | 4.9 | 3.5 | 0.6 | 1.4 | 1.6 | 1.6 | 2.3 | 0.5 | 0.6 | 0.3 |
| Livestock and livestock products | ..... | ..... | ..... | 0.5 | ..... | ..... | ..... | ..... | ..... | ..... |
| **Other commodities** | 114.1 | 16.4 | 30.1 | 19.8 | 48.8 | 42.5 | 5.7 | 5.7 | 5.6 | 32.6 |
| Forestry products | ..... | ..... | ..... | ..... | ..... | ..... | ..... | ..... | ..... | ..... |
| Fish and other marine products | ..... | ..... | ..... | ..... | 0.8 | ..... | ..... | ..... | ..... | ..... |
| Metallic ores and concentrates | ..... | 1.5 | ..... | 0.2 | ..... | ..... | 1.5 | ..... | ..... | ..... |
| Bituminous coal and lignite | ..... | ..... | ..... | ..... | ..... | ..... | ..... | ..... | ..... | ..... |
| Crude petroleum and natural gas | ..... | 0.1 | ..... | ..... | ..... | ..... | ..... | ..... | ..... | ..... |
| Nonmetallic minerals | ..... | ..... | ..... | ..... | ..... | ..... | ..... | ..... | ..... | ..... |
| Scrap and waste | ..... | ..... | 0.1 | ..... | 0.1 | ..... | ..... | ..... | ..... | ..... |
| Used merchandise | 111.5 | 12.7 | 27.9 | 18.0 | 21.8 | 42.3 | 3.5 | 4.5 | 4.5 | 7.2 |
| Goods imported and returned unchanged | ..... | ..... | ..... | ..... | ..... | ..... | ..... | ..... | ..... | ..... |
| Special classification provisions | 2.5 | 2.1 | 2.2 | 1.6 | 26.2 | 0.2 | 0.6 | 1.3 | 1.1 | 25.4 |

## Table D-3. State Exports of Goods by Destination and Industry, 1993–1997 —Continued

## DISTRICT OF COLUMBIA (Millions of dollars.)

| Industry | 1993 | 1994 | 1995 | 1996 | 1997 | 1993 | 1994 | 1995 | 1996 | 1997 |
|---|---|---|---|---|---|---|---|---|---|---|
| | Germany | | | | | France | | | | |
| **ALL GOODS** | 40.6 | 130.9 | 98.6 | 96.8 | 187.2 | 130.2 | 44.7 | 89.8 | 43.5 | 46.9 |
| **Manufactured goods** | 32.2 | 125.5 | 90.0 | 92.1 | 181.5 | 77.2 | 44.0 | 87.8 | 38.0 | 44.0 |
| Food products | 2.5 | 1.4 | 0.4 | ..... | ..... | ..... | ..... | 0.1 | 0.5 | 0.4 |
| Tobacco products | ..... | ..... | ..... | ..... | ..... | ..... | ..... | ..... | ..... | ..... |
| Textile mill products | ..... | ..... | 0.3 | 0.2 | ..... | 0.2 | 0.1 | ..... | ..... | ..... |
| Apparel | 0.8 | ..... | 0.1 | 0.3 | 0.2 | 0.4 | ..... | ..... | ..... | ..... |
| Lumber and wood products | ..... | ..... | ..... | ..... | ..... | ..... | ..... | ..... | ..... | ..... |
| Furniture and fixtures | 0.2 | 0.1 | 0.1 | 0.3 | 0.6 | ..... | ..... | 0.1 | ..... | ..... |
| Paper products | ..... | 0.1 | 0.1 | 0.2 | ..... | ..... | ..... | ..... | ..... | ..... |
| Printing and publishing | 0.3 | 0.2 | 0.3 | 0.1 | 1.4 | 0.5 | 2.9 | 1.0 | 0.2 | 0.6 |
| Chemical products | 0.1 | 1.5 | 0.1 | 0.3 | 1.2 | 0.2 | 0.2 | 8.9 | 0.4 | 1.2 |
| Refined petroleum products | ..... | ..... | ..... | ..... | ..... | ..... | ..... | ..... | ..... | ..... |
| Rubber and plastic products | 0.4 | ..... | ..... | 0.1 | ..... | ..... | ..... | ..... | ..... | 0.2 |
| Leather products | ..... | ..... | ..... | ..... | ..... | ..... | ..... | ..... | ..... | 0.1 |
| Stone, clay and glass products | ..... | ..... | 0.1 | ..... | ..... | ..... | ..... | ..... | ..... | 0.1 |
| Primary metals | ..... | 0.1 | 0.3 | 0.3 | 0.3 | 0.7 | 0.1 | ..... | ..... | 0.1 |
| Fabricated metal products | 1.3 | 97.3 | 57.3 | 0.8 | 2.4 | 2.1 | 2.3 | 19.8 | 2.3 | 0.5 |
| Industrial machinery and computers | 3.5 | 6.0 | 4.5 | 4.7 | 18.0 | 4.1 | 3.7 | 2.8 | 5.2 | 4.9 |
| Electric and electronic equipment | 9.8 | 5.6 | 6.3 | 4.4 | 6.9 | 7.2 | 3.7 | 3.3 | 2.6 | 8.7 |
| Transportation equipment | 12.1 | 12.1 | 19.0 | 79.0 | 141.5 | 57.5 | 27.7 | 49.4 | 24.7 | 24.5 |
| Scientific and measuring instruments | 0.7 | 0.5 | 0.3 | 0.9 | 1.9 | 3.3 | 2.9 | 1.7 | 2.1 | 2.5 |
| Miscellaneous manufactures | 0.2 | 0.2 | 0.7 | 0.4 | 0.8 | 0.8 | 0.2 | 0.5 | 0.1 | 0.2 |
| Unidentified manufactures | 0.2 | 0.4 | 0.1 | ..... | 6.3 | 0.1 | 0.1 | 0.1 | 0.1 | 0.1 |
| **Agricultural and livestock products** | 2.7 | 1.0 | ..... | ..... | ..... | ..... | ..... | ..... | ..... | ..... |
| Agricultural products | 2.7 | 1.0 | ..... | ..... | ..... | ..... | ..... | ..... | ..... | ..... |
| Livestock and livestock products | ..... | ..... | ..... | ..... | ..... | ..... | ..... | ..... | ..... | ..... |
| **Other commodities** | 5.7 | 4.4 | 8.5 | 4.7 | 5.6 | 53.1 | 0.7 | 2.0 | 5.5 | 2.9 |
| Forestry products | ..... | ..... | ..... | ..... | ..... | ..... | ..... | ..... | ..... | ..... |
| Fish and other marine products | ..... | ..... | ..... | ..... | ..... | ..... | ..... | ..... | ..... | ..... |
| Metallic ores and concentrates | ..... | ..... | ..... | ..... | ..... | ..... | ..... | ..... | ..... | ..... |
| Bituminous coal and lignite | ..... | ..... | ..... | ..... | ..... | ..... | ..... | ..... | ..... | ..... |
| Crude petroleum and natural gas | ..... | ..... | ..... | ..... | ..... | ..... | ..... | ..... | ..... | ..... |
| Nonmetallic minerals | ..... | ..... | ..... | ..... | ..... | ..... | ..... | ..... | ..... | ..... |
| Scrap and waste | ..... | ..... | ..... | ..... | ..... | ..... | ..... | ..... | ..... | ..... |
| Used merchandise | 5.5 | 4.3 | 8.1 | 4.5 | 5.4 | 52.9 | 0.5 | 1.9 | 5.4 | 2.9 |
| Goods imported and returned unchanged | ..... | ..... | ..... | ..... | ..... | ..... | ..... | ..... | ..... | ..... |
| Special classification provisions | 0.2 | 0.1 | 0.4 | 0.2 | 0.2 | 0.2 | 0.2 | 0.1 | ..... | 0.1 |
| | The Netherlands | | | | | Asian 10 | | | | |
| **ALL GOODS** | 14.6 | 14.6 | 22.8 | 18.7 | 11.3 | 1 138.2 | 1 037.1 | 1 144.6 | 873.0 | 1 194.8 |
| **Manufactured goods** | 11.7 | 12.5 | 19.8 | 17.4 | 9.8 | 1 123.3 | 992.4 | 1 122.3 | 851.6 | 1 182.2 |
| Food products | 2.9 | 3.9 | 2.0 | 3.9 | 1.2 | 2.4 | 3.9 | 8.5 | 11.6 | 3.4 |
| Tobacco products | ..... | ..... | ..... | ..... | ..... | ..... | ..... | ..... | ..... | ..... |
| Textile mill products | ..... | ..... | ..... | ..... | ..... | 0.3 | 0.8 | 0.3 | 0.2 | 0.3 |
| Apparel | ..... | ..... | ..... | 0.1 | ..... | 0.7 | 0.8 | 1.7 | 1.5 | 2.3 |
| Lumber and wood products | ..... | ..... | ..... | ..... | ..... | ..... | 0.3 | 0.3 | ..... | 0.1 |
| Furniture and fixtures | ..... | ..... | ..... | ..... | ..... | 0.7 | 3.0 | 0.3 | 0.2 | 0.3 |
| Paper products | ..... | ..... | ..... | ..... | ..... | ..... | 0.1 | 0.3 | 0.5 | 0.1 |
| Printing and publishing | 0.3 | 0.1 | ..... | ..... | 0.1 | 1.7 | 1.4 | 1.6 | 1.8 | 2.1 |
| Chemical products | 3.4 | 4.3 | 14.8 | 0.1 | 0.1 | 162.2 | 121.8 | 211.6 | 100.4 | 90.0 |
| Refined petroleum products | ..... | ..... | ..... | ..... | ..... | 0.2 | 0.1 | ..... | ..... | 0.2 |
| Rubber and plastic products | 2.4 | 0.7 | ..... | ..... | 0.6 | 6.8 | 3.8 | 2.1 | 3.0 | 1.4 |
| Leather products | ..... | ..... | ..... | ..... | ..... | ..... | ..... | 0.1 | 0.2 | 0.1 |
| Stone, clay and glass products | ..... | ..... | ..... | ..... | ..... | 0.1 | ..... | 0.5 | 0.1 | 1.9 |
| Primary metals | ..... | ..... | ..... | ..... | ..... | 5.1 | 7.2 | 4.3 | 1.8 | 8.4 |
| Fabricated metal products | ..... | ..... | 0.1 | ..... | ..... | 201.0 | 187.2 | 185.6 | 56.2 | 35.0 |
| Industrial machinery and computers | 1.7 | 1.8 | 0.9 | 2.0 | 2.8 | 72.2 | 63.7 | 86.8 | 80.7 | 77.1 |
| Electric and electronic equipment | 0.4 | 0.9 | 1.2 | 1.6 | 2.2 | 71.0 | 56.9 | 81.1 | 49.1 | 93.4 |
| Transportation equipment | 0.3 | 0.3 | 0.6 | 9.4 | 2.2 | 498.8 | 416.5 | 405.8 | 420.3 | 721.3 |
| Scientific and measuring instruments | 0.3 | 0.2 | 0.1 | 0.2 | 0.3 | 46.0 | 11.8 | 14.5 | 14.3 | 108.8 |
| Miscellaneous manufactures | ..... | 0.1 | ..... | ..... | 0.1 | 0.3 | 1.5 | 0.3 | 0.4 | 0.5 |
| Unidentified manufactures | ..... | 0.2 | ..... | ..... | 0.3 | 53.7 | 111.4 | 116.8 | 109.4 | 35.5 |
| **Agricultural and livestock products** | 0.5 | ..... | ..... | 0.5 | 0.5 | 0.4 | 0.3 | 0.9 | 2.1 | 2.0 |
| Agricultural products | 0.5 | ..... | ..... | ..... | 0.5 | 0.4 | 0.2 | 0.7 | 1.8 | 2.0 |
| Livestock and livestock products | ..... | ..... | ..... | 0.5 | ..... | ..... | 0.1 | 0.2 | 0.3 | 0.1 |
| **Other commodities** | 2.4 | 2.1 | 2.9 | 0.8 | 1.0 | 14.4 | 44.4 | 21.5 | 19.3 | 10.6 |
| Forestry products | ..... | ..... | ..... | ..... | ..... | ..... | ..... | ..... | ..... | ..... |
| Fish and other marine products | ..... | ..... | ..... | ..... | ..... | ..... | ..... | 0.2 | 0.1 | 0.1 |
| Metallic ores and concentrates | ..... | ..... | ..... | ..... | ..... | ..... | ..... | ..... | ..... | 0.1 |
| Bituminous coal and lignite | ..... | ..... | ..... | ..... | ..... | ..... | ..... | ..... | ..... | ..... |
| Crude petroleum and natural gas | ..... | ..... | ..... | ..... | ..... | ..... | ..... | ..... | ..... | ..... |
| Nonmetallic minerals | ..... | ..... | ..... | ..... | ..... | 0.1 | ..... | 0.1 | 0.1 | 0.1 |
| Scrap and waste | ..... | ..... | ..... | ..... | ..... | ..... | ..... | 0.1 | 0.3 | ..... |
| Used merchandise | 2.3 | 2.1 | 2.9 | 0.8 | 0.9 | 4.4 | 28.2 | 13.3 | 7.5 | 2.0 |
| Goods imported and returned unchanged | ..... | ..... | ..... | ..... | ..... | ..... | ..... | ..... | ..... | ..... |
| Special classification provisions | 0.1 | ..... | ..... | 0.1 | 0.1 | 9.9 | 16.1 | 7.7 | 11.3 | 8.3 |

## Table D-3.  State Exports of Goods by Destination and Industry, 1993–1997 —*Continued*

### DISTRICT OF COLUMBIA (Millions of dollars.)

| Industry | 1993 | 1994 | 1995 | 1996 | 1997 | 1993 | 1994 | 1995 | 1996 | 1997 |
|---|---|---|---|---|---|---|---|---|---|---|
| | Japan | | | | | South Korea | | | | |
| **ALL GOODS** | 148.4 | 127.9 | 213.9 | 86.7 | 116.4 | 47.8 | 39.9 | 19.2 | 34.8 | 37.1 |
| **Manufactured goods** | 146.6 | 105.6 | 205.2 | 82.7 | 115.6 | 47.8 | 34.4 | 18.0 | 32.7 | 37.0 |
| Food products | 0.1 | ..... | ..... | ..... | ..... | 1.3 | 2.6 | ..... | ..... | 0.1 |
| Tobacco products | ..... | ..... | ..... | ..... | ..... | ..... | ..... | ..... | ..... | ..... |
| Textile mill products | 0.2 | 0.1 | 0.1 | 0.1 | 0.1 | ..... | ..... | ..... | ..... | ..... |
| Apparel | 0.4 | 0.3 | 1.3 | 0.9 | 1.3 | ..... | ..... | 0.1 | ..... | ..... |
| Lumber and wood products | ..... | ..... | ..... | ..... | ..... | ..... | ..... | ..... | ..... | ..... |
| Furniture and fixtures | 0.3 | 2.9 | 0.2 | 0.1 | 0.1 | ..... | ..... | ..... | ..... | ..... |
| Paper products | ..... | ..... | ..... | 0.2 | | ..... | ..... | ..... | ..... | ..... |
| Printing and publishing | 0.6 | 0.5 | 0.6 | 0.8 | 0.9 | 0.1 | 0.2 | 0.2 | 0.4 | 0.3 |
| Chemical products | 131.7 | 93.8 | 195.9 | 68.3 | 80.2 | 24.6 | 23.3 | 12.0 | 27.3 | 6.8 |
| Refined petroleum products | ..... | ..... | ..... | ..... | ..... | ..... | ..... | ..... | ..... | ..... |
| Rubber and plastic products | 3.5 | ..... | 0.2 | 0.2 | 0.4 | ..... | ..... | ..... | 0.1 | 0.1 |
| Leather products | ..... | ..... | 0.1 | 0.1 | 0.1 | ..... | ..... | ..... | ..... | ..... |
| Stone, clay and glass products | ..... | ..... | ..... | 0.1 | ..... | ..... | ..... | ..... | ..... | 0.1 |
| Primary metals | 0.6 | 0.3 | ..... | 0.1 | 7.9 | ..... | ..... | ..... | ..... | 0.1 |
| Fabricated metal products | 0.1 | ..... | 0.1 | 0.2 | 0.2 | 0.1 | 0.1 | ..... | ..... | 0.1 |
| Industrial machinery and computers | 5.4 | 3.8 | 3.1 | 6.1 | 16.2 | 0.4 | 1.4 | 1.7 | 2.2 | 6.1 |
| Electric and electronic equipment | 1.4 | 1.4 | 1.9 | 2.2 | 4.6 | 6.3 | 6.5 | 2.1 | 1.9 | 21.5 |
| Transportation equipment | 0.7 | 0.5 | 1.1 | 1.9 | 0.8 | 8.2 | 0.2 | 1.5 | 0.3 | 0.3 |
| Scientific and measuring instruments | 1.3 | 0.5 | 0.4 | 1.0 | 2.7 | 6.6 | 0.1 | 0.3 | 0.2 | 1.1 |
| Miscellaneous manufactures | 0.1 | 1.4 | 0.2 | 0.1 | 0.1 | ..... | ..... | ..... | ..... | 0.2 |
| Unidentified manufactures | ..... | 0.1 | 0.1 | 0.3 | 0.1 | ..... | 0.1 | ..... | 0.1 | 0.1 |
| **Agricultural and livestock products** | 0.4 | ..... | ..... | ..... | ..... | ..... | ..... | ..... | ..... | ..... |
| Agricultural products | 0.4 | ..... | ..... | ..... | ..... | ..... | ..... | ..... | ..... | ..... |
| Livestock and livestock products | ..... | ..... | ..... | ..... | ..... | ..... | ..... | ..... | ..... | ..... |
| **Other commodities** | 1.4 | 22.3 | 8.7 | 4.0 | 0.8 | ..... | 5.5 | 1.2 | 2.1 | 0.2 |
| Forestry products | ..... | ..... | ..... | ..... | ..... | ..... | ..... | ..... | ..... | ..... |
| Fish and other marine products | ..... | ..... | ..... | ..... | ..... | ..... | ..... | ..... | ..... | ..... |
| Metallic ores and concentrates | ..... | ..... | ..... | ..... | 0.1 | ..... | ..... | ..... | ..... | ..... |
| Bituminous coal and lignite | ..... | ..... | ..... | ..... | ..... | ..... | ..... | ..... | ..... | ..... |
| Crude petroleum and natural gas | ..... | ..... | ..... | ..... | ..... | ..... | ..... | ..... | ..... | ..... |
| Nonmetallic minerals | ..... | ..... | ..... | ..... | ..... | ..... | ..... | ..... | 0.1 | 0.1 |
| Scrap and waste | ..... | ..... | ..... | ..... | ..... | ..... | ..... | ..... | ..... | ..... |
| Used merchandise | 1.4 | 22.1 | 8.5 | 2.7 | 0.6 | ..... | 5.4 | 1.2 | 2.0 | ..... |
| Goods imported and returned unchanged | ..... | ..... | ..... | ..... | ..... | ..... | ..... | ..... | ..... | ..... |
| Special classification provisions | ..... | 0.1 | 0.1 | 1.2 | ..... | ..... | ..... | ..... | 0.1 | ..... |
| | Taiwan | | | | | Singapore | | | | |
| **ALL GOODS** | 706.4 | 676.2 | 649.7 | 491.3 | 602.8 | 89.3 | 29.9 | 35.6 | 34.6 | 41.4 |
| **Manufactured goods** | 698.4 | 660.9 | 645.3 | 485.1 | 600.3 | 89.1 | 29.8 | 35.0 | 34.0 | 41.3 |
| Food products | ..... | ..... | ..... | ..... | ..... | ..... | 0.2 | 0.3 | 0.6 | 0.3 |
| Tobacco products | ..... | ..... | ..... | ..... | ..... | ..... | ..... | ..... | ..... | ..... |
| Textile mill products | 0.1 | ..... | 0.1 | ..... | 0.1 | ..... | ..... | ..... | ..... | ..... |
| Apparel | ..... | ..... | ..... | ..... | 0.1 | ..... | ..... | ..... | ..... | 0.1 |
| Lumber and wood products | ..... | ..... | ..... | ..... | ..... | ..... | ..... | ..... | ..... | ..... |
| Furniture and fixtures | 0.4 | ..... | ..... | 0.1 | ..... | ..... | ..... | ..... | ..... | ..... |
| Paper products | ..... | 0.1 | 0.2 | 0.2 | ..... | ..... | ..... | ..... | ..... | ..... |
| Printing and publishing | 0.1 | 0.3 | 0.1 | 0.2 | 0.1 | 0.2 | 0.1 | 0.1 | ..... | 0.3 |
| Chemical products | 1.6 | 1.0 | 0.8 | 1.2 | 0.8 | ..... | 0.1 | ..... | ..... | ..... |
| Refined petroleum products | 0.1 | 0.1 | ..... | ..... | 0.2 | ..... | ..... | ..... | ..... | ..... |
| Rubber and plastic products | 1.5 | 0.8 | 1.1 | 0.2 | 0.1 | ..... | ..... | ..... | ..... | ..... |
| Leather products | ..... | ..... | ..... | ..... | ..... | ..... | ..... | ..... | ..... | ..... |
| Stone, clay and glass products | 0.1 | ..... | ..... | ..... | ..... | ..... | ..... | ..... | ..... | ..... |
| Primary metals | 4.4 | 6.9 | 4.1 | 0.9 | ..... | ..... | 0.1 | ..... | ..... | ..... |
| Fabricated metal products | 161.3 | 148.2 | 145.9 | 47.3 | 27.5 | 25.5 | 0.3 | 0.4 | 0.7 | 0.1 |
| Industrial machinery and computers | 56.7 | 50.9 | 69.2 | 64.1 | 45.6 | 0.9 | 1.8 | 0.4 | 1.3 | 1.2 |
| Electric and electronic equipment | 37.0 | 17.1 | 28.4 | 14.4 | 19.9 | 4.0 | 2.4 | 10.4 | 5.0 | 4.9 |
| Transportation equipment | 349.3 | 316.2 | 271.4 | 240.2 | 390.8 | 57.6 | 24.5 | 23.0 | 25.7 | 33.7 |
| Scientific and measuring instruments | 33.4 | 8.5 | 8.0 | 9.4 | 85.6 | 0.7 | 0.3 | 0.3 | 0.3 | 0.7 |
| Miscellaneous manufactures | 0.1 | ..... | ..... | ..... | 0.1 | ..... | ..... | ..... | 0.1 | ..... |
| Unidentified manufactures | 52.3 | 110.7 | 116.0 | 106.9 | 29.5 | ..... | ..... | ..... | ..... | ..... |
| **Agricultural and livestock products** | ..... | ..... | ..... | ..... | ..... | ..... | ..... | ..... | ..... | ..... |
| Agricultural products | ..... | ..... | ..... | ..... | ..... | ..... | ..... | ..... | ..... | ..... |
| Livestock and livestock products | ..... | ..... | ..... | ..... | ..... | ..... | ..... | ..... | ..... | ..... |
| **Other commodities** | 8.0 | 15.3 | 4.4 | 6.2 | 2.5 | 0.3 | 0.2 | 0.7 | 0.6 | ..... |
| Forestry products | ..... | ..... | ..... | ..... | ..... | ..... | ..... | ..... | ..... | ..... |
| Fish and other marine products | ..... | ..... | ..... | ..... | ..... | ..... | ..... | ..... | ..... | ..... |
| Metallic ores and concentrates | ..... | ..... | ..... | ..... | ..... | ..... | ..... | ..... | ..... | ..... |
| Bituminous coal and lignite | ..... | ..... | ..... | ..... | ..... | ..... | ..... | ..... | ..... | ..... |
| Crude petroleum and natural gas | ..... | ..... | ..... | ..... | ..... | ..... | ..... | ..... | ..... | ..... |
| Nonmetallic minerals | 0.1 | ..... | ..... | ..... | ..... | ..... | ..... | ..... | ..... | ..... |
| Scrap and waste | ..... | ..... | ..... | ..... | ..... | ..... | ..... | ..... | ..... | ..... |
| Used merchandise | 0.1 | 0.4 | 0.3 | 0.9 | ..... | 0.3 | 0.1 | 0.3 | 0.3 | ..... |
| Goods imported and returned unchanged | ..... | ..... | ..... | ..... | ..... | ..... | ..... | ..... | ..... | ..... |
| Special classification provisions | 7.9 | 14.9 | 4.1 | 5.3 | 2.5 | ..... | 0.1 | 0.3 | 0.3 | ..... |

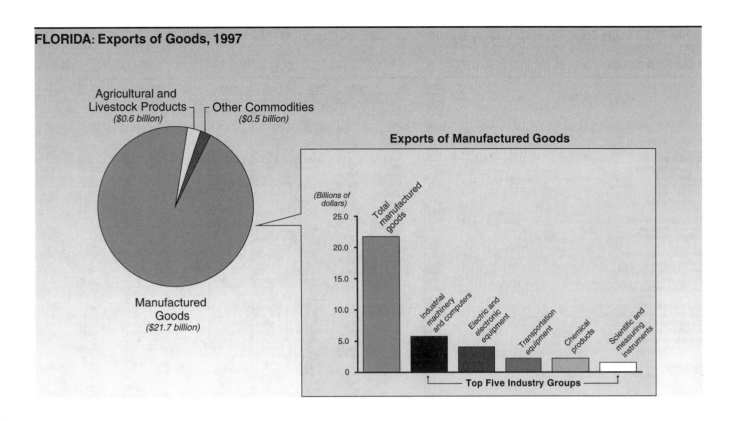

## FLORIDA: Exports of Goods, 1997

Agricultural and Livestock Products ($0.6 billion)

Other Commodities ($0.5 billion)

Manufactured Goods ($21.7 billion)

**Exports of Manufactured Goods**

Top Five Industry Groups

## Table D-3.   State Exports of Goods by Destination and Industry, 1993–1997 —*Continued*

**FLORIDA** (Millions of dollars.)

| Industry | 1993 | 1994 | 1995 | 1996 | 1997 | 1993 | 1994 | 1995 | 1996 | 1997 |
|---|---|---|---|---|---|---|---|---|---|---|
| | All destinations | | | | | Canada | | | | |
| **ALL GOODS** | 14 695.8 | 16 559.2 | 18 564.4 | 19 618.2 | 22 888.6 | 1 571.8 | 1 504.8 | 1 608.2 | 1 631.6 | 1 928.4 |
| **Manufactured goods** | 13 494.2 | 15 235.3 | 17 495.1 | 18 467.7 | 21 715.1 | 1 225.8 | 1 169.1 | 1 251.9 | 1 285.1 | 1 531.3 |
| Food products | 753.9 | 835.2 | 882.0 | 877.2 | 960.9 | 125.5 | 125.3 | 131.1 | 133.5 | 138.8 |
| Tobacco products | 13.9 | 9.6 | 18.9 | 23.9 | 28.0 | 0.1 | 0.2 | 0.3 | 0.5 | 0.7 |
| Textile mill products | 153.0 | 157.9 | 192.3 | 247.4 | 355.8 | 4.6 | 6.1 | 8.8 | 8.1 | 11.2 |
| Apparel | 483.2 | 541.5 | 558.8 | 582.3 | 713.6 | 5.5 | 6.3 | 11.1 | 12.0 | 15.8 |
| Lumber and wood products | 158.7 | 171.1 | 193.8 | 186.8 | 229.1 | 5.2 | 5.4 | 5.3 | 4.6 | 4.6 |
| Furniture and fixtures | 99.8 | 110.5 | 113.0 | 136.4 | 165.3 | 6.5 | 7.4 | 6.7 | 7.7 | 8.2 |
| Paper products | 369.8 | 381.6 | 589.3 | 522.1 | 544.6 | 13.1 | 16.2 | 20.1 | 15.1 | 24.5 |
| Printing and publishing | 152.7 | 191.7 | 206.3 | 171.5 | 194.4 | 83.1 | 100.7 | 100.6 | 79.6 | 87.2 |
| Chemical products | 1 265.7 | 1 706.0 | 2 007.9 | 1 890.4 | 2 239.3 | 90.3 | 92.9 | 130.7 | 129.2 | 151.1 |
| Refined petroleum products | 200.4 | 121.8 | 99.5 | 121.3 | 130.4 | 9.9 | 3.5 | 0.9 | 1.2 | 3.0 |
| Rubber and plastic products | 330.4 | 385.4 | 472.4 | 480.8 | 582.7 | 31.0 | 33.1 | 30.6 | 29.4 | 32.6 |
| Leather products | 52.3 | 53.1 | 63.6 | 73.7 | 80.2 | 1.9 | 2.2 | 3.5 | 3.8 | 4.6 |
| Stone, clay and glass products | 147.0 | 144.7 | 155.8 | 157.6 | 168.7 | 11.4 | 9.5 | 10.8 | 15.1 | 17.2 |
| Primary metals | 362.6 | 435.4 | 517.3 | 409.0 | 510.2 | 85.2 | 108.7 | 122.9 | 80.1 | 89.2 |
| Fabricated metal products | 434.6 | 385.4 | 424.1 | 451.1 | 558.3 | 101.4 | 40.3 | 31.8 | 36.8 | 38.3 |
| Industrial machinery and computers | 2 884.2 | 3 409.4 | 4 097.0 | 4 743.8 | 5 769.7 | 196.9 | 151.4 | 144.5 | 206.8 | 263.5 |
| Electric and electronic equipment | 2 193.7 | 2 595.1 | 2 956.4 | 3 282.0 | 4 058.5 | 181.5 | 186.6 | 187.1 | 186.9 | 210.9 |
| Transportation equipment | 1 998.3 | 2 011.6 | 2 144.0 | 2 185.8 | 2 245.1 | 143.7 | 141.2 | 148.5 | 154.8 | 231.8 |
| Scientific and measuring instruments | 1 051.2 | 1 164.8 | 1 341.1 | 1 453.2 | 1 571.5 | 107.8 | 105.9 | 126.9 | 151.5 | 161.6 |
| Miscellaneous manufactures | 247.3 | 280.5 | 328.0 | 329.7 | 427.3 | 11.3 | 14.0 | 15.9 | 13.9 | 20.2 |
| Unidentified manufactures | 141.5 | 143.1 | 133.5 | 141.8 | 181.4 | 10.0 | 12.1 | 13.7 | 14.3 | 16.2 |
| **Agricultural and livestock products** | 806.4 | 910.6 | 579.8 | 651.9 | 640.3 | 276.2 | 248.0 | 260.4 | 250.4 | 267.5 |
| Agricultural products | 780.5 | 885.6 | 553.6 | 624.4 | 615.5 | 272.4 | 245.8 | 257.1 | 245.5 | 262.8 |
| Livestock and livestock products | 25.9 | 25.0 | 26.2 | 27.5 | 24.8 | 3.8 | 2.2 | 3.4 | 4.9 | 4.7 |
| **Other commodities** | 395.2 | 413.3 | 489.5 | 498.7 | 533.2 | 69.8 | 87.8 | 95.8 | 96.1 | 129.6 |
| Forestry products | 48.4 | 33.3 | 32.9 | 34.9 | 35.1 | 1.2 | 1.4 | 1.7 | 1.2 | 1.2 |
| Fish and other marine products | 64.9 | 67.8 | 87.7 | 78.8 | 81.3 | 21.0 | 21.0 | 24.8 | 26.2 | 28.9 |
| Metallic ores and concentrates | 1.9 | 2.2 | 3.5 | 3.4 | 3.2 | ..... | ..... | 1.5 | 0.2 | 1.1 |
| Bituminous coal and lignite | ..... | 12.1 | 7.7 | 4.2 | 3.2 | ..... | ..... | ..... | ..... | ..... |
| Crude petroleum and natural gas | 0.5 | 0.6 | 0.8 | 1.6 | 1.6 | ..... | ..... | ..... | ..... | ..... |
| Nonmetallic minerals | 14.6 | 25.6 | 12.7 | 15.2 | 29.1 | 0.9 | 6.1 | 0.8 | 1.4 | 12.2 |
| Scrap and waste | 33.2 | 46.8 | 124.8 | 72.9 | 64.5 | 1.4 | 2.9 | 14.4 | 4.1 | 2.5 |
| Used merchandise | 107.1 | 87.6 | 78.7 | 100.3 | 123.6 | 3.2 | 3.5 | 2.4 | 5.7 | 5.6 |
| Goods imported and returned unchanged | 33.6 | 47.0 | 44.2 | 48.3 | 69.7 | 33.6 | 47.0 | 44.2 | 48.3 | 69.7 |
| Special classification provisions | 90.8 | 90.3 | 96.5 | 139.2 | 121.8 | 8.5 | 5.9 | 6.1 | 9.1 | 8.4 |

## Table D-3.  State Exports of Goods by Destination and Industry, 1993–1997 —*Continued*

**FLORIDA** (Millions of dollars.)

| Industry | 1993 | 1994 | 1995 | 1996 | 1997 | 1993 | 1994 | 1995 | 1996 | 1997 |
|---|---|---|---|---|---|---|---|---|---|---|
| | South and Central America and Caribbean | | | | | Mexico | | | | |
| **ALL GOODS** | 7 908.5 | 9 041.1 | 10 070.1 | 10 742.6 | 12 819.2 | 769.6 | 993.6 | 536.2 | 737.0 | 1 220.8 |
| **Manufactured goods** | 7 560.0 | 8 632.6 | 9 783.0 | 10 466.3 | 12 514.2 | 646.9 | 786.4 | 520.2 | 726.2 | 1 188.3 |
| Food products | 398.1 | 422.7 | 475.7 | 479.8 | 536.0 | 17.0 | 22.5 | 6.7 | 8.8 | 12.0 |
| Tobacco products | 4.3 | 3.4 | 6.7 | 12.2 | 15.3 | ..... | ..... | ..... | 0.1 | 0.4 |
| Textile mill products | 123.6 | 126.8 | 150.1 | 198.8 | 295.6 | 3.3 | 2.3 | 4.8 | 16.4 | 28.9 |
| Apparel | 431.9 | 480.1 | 511.6 | 521.8 | 636.2 | 19.3 | 7.1 | 4.6 | 8.3 | 25.6 |
| Lumber and wood products | 122.2 | 136.3 | 156.9 | 151.4 | 197.3 | 3.2 | 1.5 | 1.0 | 1.0 | 1.4 |
| Furniture and fixtures | 69.1 | 78.2 | 88.2 | 102.8 | 117.2 | 6.7 | 5.7 | 1.9 | 2.6 | 3.6 |
| Paper products | 215.5 | 224.5 | 343.1 | 339.8 | 358.0 | 47.2 | 54.3 | 52.1 | 49.5 | 49.0 |
| Printing and publishing | 42.8 | 46.4 | 59.2 | 55.6 | 69.6 | 10.3 | 21.0 | 12.2 | 7.1 | 6.3 |
| Chemical products | 470.7 | 528.6 | 613.3 | 665.2 | 718.1 | 60.7 | 74.6 | 62.3 | 139.2 | 298.0 |
| Refined petroleum products | 150.5 | 70.2 | 64.0 | 38.6 | 46.6 | 2.6 | 6.6 | 1.0 | 17.4 | 14.8 |
| Rubber and plastic products | 218.1 | 251.7 | 325.1 | 307.8 | 382.2 | 18.6 | 29.8 | 18.1 | 19.0 | 22.9 |
| Leather products | 39.5 | 41.0 | 43.3 | 46.3 | 58.4 | 1.7 | 1.2 | 1.1 | 0.5 | 1.4 |
| Stone, clay and glass products | 96.8 | 90.8 | 99.3 | 100.0 | 107.3 | 7.4 | 5.6 | 2.1 | 3.0 | 3.7 |
| Primary metals | 145.4 | 159.0 | 175.2 | 219.7 | 259.0 | 106.9 | 130.3 | 51.1 | 25.7 | 65.5 |
| Fabricated metal products | 242.0 | 240.6 | 270.4 | 275.6 | 367.2 | 32.9 | 48.0 | 30.4 | 28.6 | 31.4 |
| Industrial machinery and computers | 1 861.9 | 2 293.1 | 2 759.7 | 3 218.0 | 3 852.3 | 115.3 | 150.5 | 118.7 | 198.1 | 263.8 |
| Electric and electronic equipment | 1 185.4 | 1 466.8 | 1 737.8 | 1 909.8 | 2 474.9 | 100.2 | 115.3 | 87.6 | 117.8 | 248.8 |
| Transportation equipment | 1 157.1 | 1 269.7 | 1 166.5 | 1 027.6 | 1 055.1 | 31.2 | 39.9 | 22.5 | 25.5 | 46.1 |
| Scientific and measuring instruments | 347.8 | 434.3 | 429.5 | 497.4 | 562.6 | 48.5 | 43.3 | 29.9 | 42.2 | 51.3 |
| Miscellaneous manufactures | 158.0 | 175.4 | 218.2 | 207.8 | 287.9 | 11.8 | 23.7 | 10.6 | 12.7 | 11.1 |
| Unidentified manufactures | 79.4 | 93.2 | 89.4 | 90.3 | 117.1 | 2.0 | 3.0 | 1.5 | 2.6 | 2.5 |
| **Agricultural and livestock products** | 184.5 | 250.9 | 90.2 | 98.7 | 97.4 | 112.8 | 196.2 | 7.8 | 3.2 | 9.8 |
| Agricultural products | 173.9 | 241.2 | 77.7 | 87.1 | 86.3 | 112.1 | 194.9 | 7.1 | 2.5 | 9.0 |
| Livestock and livestock products | 10.7 | 9.7 | 12.5 | 11.6 | 11.2 | 0.6 | 1.3 | 0.6 | 0.7 | 0.7 |
| **Other commodities** | 164.0 | 157.6 | 196.8 | 177.7 | 207.7 | 9.9 | 11.0 | 8.3 | 7.5 | 22.7 |
| Forestry products | 2.6 | 2.0 | 2.2 | 3.3 | 2.9 | ..... | ..... | ..... | 0.1 | 0.2 |
| Fish and other marine products | 17.6 | 13.2 | 14.1 | 14.7 | 15.6 | 0.6 | 0.6 | 0.8 | 0.5 | 1.8 |
| Metallic ores and concentrates | 0.1 | 0.1 | 0.3 | 0.6 | 0.1 | ..... | ..... | ..... | ..... | ..... |
| Bituminous coal and lignite | ..... | ..... | 0.2 | 2.3 | 1.4 | ..... | ..... | ..... | ..... | ..... |
| Crude petroleum and natural gas | 0.3 | 0.4 | 0.7 | 1.3 | 1.5 | ..... | ..... | ..... | ..... | ..... |
| Nonmetallic minerals | 7.6 | 9.1 | 8.7 | 10.4 | 12.5 | 0.3 | 0.5 | 0.4 | 0.8 | 0.8 |
| Scrap and waste | 22.6 | 30.7 | 72.9 | 39.4 | 39.6 | 0.5 | 1.6 | 3.8 | 1.6 | 6.0 |
| Used merchandise | 65.7 | 57.1 | 54.0 | 58.7 | 77.5 | 4.4 | 5.5 | 0.6 | 2.1 | 8.8 |
| Goods imported and returned unchanged | ..... | ..... | ..... | ..... | ..... | ..... | ..... | ..... | ..... | ..... |
| Special classification provisions | 47.6 | 45.1 | 43.8 | 47.1 | 56.6 | 4.0 | 2.7 | 2.7 | 2.4 | 5.1 |
| | European Union | | | | | United Kingdom | | | | |
| **ALL GOODS** | 2 014.5 | 2 033.6 | 2 612.9 | 2 909.9 | 2 772.9 | 473.2 | 489.9 | 560.1 | 601.3 | 687.1 |
| **Manufactured goods** | 1 859.4 | 1 899.4 | 2 469.0 | 2 750.3 | 2 608.5 | 447.1 | 471.8 | 539.4 | 574.2 | 649.2 |
| Food products | 131.6 | 144.5 | 156.6 | 156.6 | 158.1 | 21.6 | 28.2 | 28.2 | 25.5 | 18.3 |
| Tobacco products | 2.0 | 3.5 | 8.3 | 7.5 | 5.1 | ..... | 0.5 | 1.1 | 0.6 | 1.1 |
| Textile mill products | 8.1 | 9.2 | 11.9 | 7.5 | 7.2 | 1.9 | 2.8 | 3.0 | 2.1 | 2.2 |
| Apparel | 13.1 | 32.0 | 14.2 | 17.0 | 17.6 | 0.8 | 1.7 | 3.2 | 6.1 | 7.4 |
| Lumber and wood products | 16.6 | 12.9 | 12.0 | 10.3 | 9.9 | 4.6 | 3.3 | 4.4 | 4.1 | 3.5 |
| Furniture and fixtures | 7.7 | 5.7 | 5.9 | 9.9 | 10.1 | 1.0 | 1.3 | 1.1 | 2.6 | 3.2 |
| Paper products | 34.0 | 32.3 | 84.4 | 49.1 | 50.2 | 6.8 | 4.5 | 9.8 | 8.5 | 7.6 |
| Printing and publishing | 7.0 | 8.1 | 12.3 | 8.7 | 14.0 | 3.3 | 2.4 | 6.1 | 4.1 | 5.5 |
| Chemical products | 192.3 | 209.1 | 250.1 | 236.0 | 204.8 | 51.8 | 54.1 | 50.8 | 41.9 | 59.7 |
| Refined petroleum products | 12.6 | 22.1 | 18.2 | 27.3 | 34.7 | 1.4 | 0.1 | 0.5 | 5.3 | 1.7 |
| Rubber and plastic products | 30.4 | 38.3 | 52.4 | 72.5 | 66.6 | 8.6 | 10.5 | 16.1 | 43.9 | 26.8 |
| Leather products | 2.7 | 3.3 | 5.9 | 7.2 | 5.7 | 0.5 | 0.9 | 0.8 | 0.8 | 1.0 |
| Stone, clay and glass products | 9.7 | 12.8 | 16.0 | 13.2 | 13.3 | 2.5 | 4.3 | 5.4 | 3.5 | 3.5 |
| Primary metals | 11.9 | 15.5 | 20.6 | 21.0 | 28.5 | 3.2 | 5.0 | 7.1 | 5.6 | 8.5 |
| Fabricated metal products | 25.5 | 20.0 | 29.0 | 31.3 | 38.0 | 7.2 | 8.2 | 8.8 | 9.9 | 8.7 |
| Industrial machinery and computers | 375.1 | 384.7 | 501.7 | 522.3 | 576.1 | 96.0 | 97.2 | 95.0 | 103.4 | 111.7 |
| Electric and electronic equipment | 255.6 | 275.0 | 346.2 | 429.8 | 359.8 | 72.0 | 102.0 | 107.4 | 97.4 | 122.5 |
| Transportation equipment | 353.0 | 296.3 | 491.8 | 627.6 | 515.3 | 84.7 | 64.0 | 100.7 | 98.7 | 127.4 |
| Scientific and measuring instruments | 310.4 | 333.3 | 383.0 | 435.3 | 430.4 | 66.2 | 69.0 | 79.9 | 98.6 | 102.8 |
| Miscellaneous manufactures | 33.4 | 27.1 | 34.3 | 37.0 | 44.0 | 8.8 | 6.8 | 7.0 | 9.2 | 13.0 |
| Unidentified manufactures | 26.7 | 13.5 | 14.4 | 23.3 | 19.4 | 3.9 | 4.8 | 3.0 | 2.5 | 13.2 |
| **Agricultural and livestock products** | 71.3 | 66.3 | 69.3 | 73.1 | 77.4 | 8.8 | 9.1 | 7.2 | 8.6 | 11.2 |
| Agricultural products | 67.1 | 62.1 | 66.5 | 68.5 | 74.8 | 7.9 | 8.6 | 6.7 | 7.3 | 10.8 |
| Livestock and livestock products | 4.2 | 4.2 | 2.9 | 4.6 | 2.6 | 0.9 | 0.6 | 0.6 | 1.3 | 0.4 |
| **Other commodities** | 83.8 | 67.9 | 74.6 | 86.5 | 87.0 | 17.3 | 8.9 | 13.4 | 18.5 | 26.7 |
| Forestry products | 41.1 | 27.2 | 25.9 | 27.2 | 28.2 | 1.5 | 1.2 | 1.6 | 2.2 | 2.6 |
| Fish and other marine products | 8.7 | 4.8 | 9.7 | 9.4 | 4.8 | 0.9 | 0.7 | 0.5 | 0.5 | 0.5 |
| Metallic ores and concentrates | 0.3 | 0.8 | 0.1 | 0.7 | 0.8 | ..... | ..... | ..... | ..... | ..... |
| Bituminous coal and lignite | ..... | ..... | 0.8 | 0.8 | 0.8 | ..... | ..... | ..... | ..... | 0.3 |
| Crude petroleum and natural gas | ..... | 0.1 | 0.1 | 0.1 | ..... | ..... | ..... | ..... | ..... | ..... |
| Nonmetallic minerals | 0.5 | 7.0 | 1.9 | 0.9 | 1.1 | 0.1 | 0.1 | 0.1 | 0.2 | 0.7 |
| Scrap and waste | 1.8 | 3.9 | 6.4 | 5.6 | 3.7 | 0.1 | 0.1 | 0.8 | 1.0 | 0.7 |
| Used merchandise | 13.3 | 10.4 | 11.6 | 13.7 | 23.9 | 7.0 | 2.8 | 4.7 | 6.1 | 13.0 |
| Goods imported and returned unchanged | ..... | ..... | ..... | ..... | ..... | ..... | ..... | ..... | ..... | ..... |
| Special classification provisions | 18.0 | 13.7 | 18.0 | 28.1 | 23.6 | 7.7 | 4.0 | 5.7 | 8.5 | 8.9 |

## Table D-3.  State Exports of Goods by Destination and Industry, 1993–1997 —Continued

**FLORIDA** (Millions of dollars.)

| Industry | 1993 | 1994 | 1995 | 1996 | 1997 | 1993 | 1994 | 1995 | 1996 | 1997 |
|---|---|---|---|---|---|---|---|---|---|---|
| | Germany | | | | | France | | | | |
| **ALL GOODS** | 375.9 | 309.9 | 399.4 | 408.1 | 383.4 | 309.0 | 311.1 | 395.4 | 494.2 | 397.5 |
| **Manufactured goods** | 345.6 | 287.1 | 377.3 | 385.7 | 362.6 | 277.6 | 285.1 | 369.7 | 463.6 | 365.3 |
| Food products | 7.1 | 10.7 | 14.0 | 17.8 | 11.5 | 30.2 | 26.4 | 26.2 | 36.3 | 33.1 |
| Tobacco products | ..... | ..... | ..... | 0.2 | 0.3 | ..... | ..... | ..... | 0.1 | ..... |
| Textile mill products | 2.4 | 2.0 | 2.6 | 1.3 | 0.7 | 1.2 | 1.5 | 2.9 | 0.5 | 0.6 |
| Apparel | 3.8 | 1.4 | 2.3 | 2.6 | 3.6 | 2.8 | 9.9 | 4.3 | 1.5 | 1.3 |
| Lumber and wood products | 4.4 | 3.7 | 2.0 | 2.0 | 0.9 | 0.2 | 0.7 | 0.2 | 0.2 | 0.2 |
| Furniture and fixtures | 0.9 | 0.5 | 1.4 | 1.4 | 0.9 | 1.5 | 0.7 | 1.0 | 1.7 | 1.7 |
| Paper products | 4.7 | 0.7 | 1.1 | 1.5 | 0.6 | 8.2 | 9.6 | 35.9 | 14.9 | 19.0 |
| Printing and publishing | 1.3 | 1.2 | 1.1 | 0.9 | 2.5 | 0.5 | 0.8 | 1.9 | 0.7 | 0.9 |
| Chemical products | 33.3 | 42.6 | 40.3 | 39.4 | 27.1 | 15.6 | 23.5 | 45.6 | 38.2 | 24.0 |
| Refined petroleum products | 0.3 | 0.1 | 0.3 | 0.4 | 3.8 | 0.1 | 2.9 | ..... | 2.1 | 5.3 |
| Rubber and plastic products | 4.9 | 6.2 | 7.3 | 7.4 | 7.9 | 5.4 | 7.0 | 7.0 | 2.0 | 4.4 |
| Leather products | 0.3 | 0.5 | 1.0 | 2.5 | 1.9 | 0.3 | 0.6 | 3.1 | 2.4 | 1.2 |
| Stone, clay and glass products | 0.6 | 1.1 | 1.4 | 2.1 | 1.6 | 2.1 | 2.5 | 2.4 | 1.6 | 1.1 |
| Primary metals | 1.6 | 1.9 | 2.4 | 4.2 | 5.3 | 1.1 | 2.6 | 1.5 | 1.9 | 5.6 |
| Fabricated metal products | 7.0 | 3.7 | 6.3 | 4.0 | 4.4 | 1.3 | 1.1 | 2.7 | 2.9 | 8.1 |
| Industrial machinery and computers | 69.5 | 43.2 | 67.3 | 62.9 | 85.2 | 27.7 | 31.3 | 38.4 | 40.0 | 41.9 |
| Electric and electronic equipment | 41.2 | 41.2 | 48.8 | 43.1 | 50.5 | 29.7 | 29.1 | 39.7 | 156.5 | 36.2 |
| Transportation equipment | 92.0 | 71.3 | 114.5 | 116.8 | 89.3 | 69.4 | 56.6 | 73.2 | 91.6 | 107.8 |
| Scientific and measuring instruments | 49.2 | 47.6 | 50.6 | 66.6 | 56.4 | 72.5 | 72.8 | 76.8 | 63.7 | 64.8 |
| Miscellaneous manufactures | 6.2 | 5.1 | 7.0 | 6.3 | 6.5 | 5.0 | 4.1 | 5.9 | 3.8 | 6.7 |
| Unidentified manufactures | 14.7 | 2.4 | 5.4 | 2.3 | 1.5 | 3.0 | 1.5 | 1.2 | 1.1 | 1.4 |
| **Agricultural and livestock products** | 6.2 | 6.0 | 8.7 | 8.8 | 6.8 | 24.8 | 21.2 | 19.2 | 19.9 | 22.4 |
| Agricultural products | 5.8 | 5.5 | 8.3 | 8.1 | 6.5 | 24.4 | 20.4 | 18.8 | 19.4 | 22.0 |
| Livestock and livestock products | 0.4 | 0.5 | 0.4 | 0.7 | 0.4 | 0.4 | 0.8 | 0.4 | 0.5 | 0.4 |
| **Other commodities** | 24.1 | 16.8 | 13.4 | 13.6 | 14.0 | 6.5 | 4.8 | 6.6 | 10.7 | 9.9 |
| Forestry products | 15.9 | 10.7 | 9.3 | 9.2 | 9.2 | 0.3 | 0.2 | 0.1 | 0.2 | 0.5 |
| Fish and other marine products | 0.7 | 0.3 | 0.5 | 0.3 | 0.4 | 2.8 | 1.4 | 2.5 | 4.5 | 2.1 |
| Metallic ores and concentrates | 0.3 | 0.2 | 0.1 | 0.4 | 0.7 | ..... | ..... | ..... | 0.1 | ..... |
| Bituminous coal and lignite | ..... | ..... | ..... | ..... | ..... | ..... | ..... | ..... | ..... | ..... |
| Crude petroleum and natural gas | ..... | ..... | ..... | 0.1 | ..... | ..... | ..... | ..... | ..... | ..... |
| Nonmetallic minerals | 0.2 | 0.2 | ..... | 0.1 | 0.1 | ..... | ..... | ..... | ..... | ..... |
| Scrap and waste | ..... | 0.2 | 0.3 | 0.3 | 0.1 | 0.1 | 0.2 | ..... | 0.2 | 0.1 |
| Used merchandise | 1.9 | 1.4 | 1.1 | 1.2 | 2.0 | 2.0 | 1.9 | 1.8 | 1.8 | 3.0 |
| Goods imported and returned unchanged | ..... | ..... | ..... | ..... | ..... | ..... | ..... | ..... | ..... | ..... |
| Special classification provisions | 5.1 | 4.0 | 2.1 | 2.0 | 1.6 | 1.3 | 1.1 | 2.1 | 3.9 | 4.2 |
| | The Netherlands | | | | | Asian 10 | | | | |
| **ALL GOODS** | 207.4 | 247.9 | 332.6 | 378.7 | 399.6 | 1 294.0 | 1 862.9 | 2 288.8 | 2 082.8 | 2 474.2 |
| **Manufactured goods** | 167.9 | 214.0 | 293.7 | 335.5 | 360.6 | 1 118.4 | 1 669.9 | 2 065.1 | 1 808.1 | 2 229.2 |
| Food products | 23.5 | 38.7 | 60.3 | 53.2 | 64.5 | 50.8 | 90.0 | 57.9 | 67.1 | 59.6 |
| Tobacco products | 1.1 | 2.6 | 4.9 | 2.1 | 2.0 | 0.6 | 0.3 | 1.8 | 1.6 | 2.5 |
| Textile mill products | 1.2 | 1.1 | 0.5 | 0.4 | 0.4 | 3.9 | 6.0 | 5.8 | 6.4 | 5.9 |
| Apparel | 1.1 | 0.8 | 1.3 | 1.5 | 1.3 | 9.0 | 10.1 | 10.7 | 15.6 | 12.3 |
| Lumber and wood products | 0.7 | 0.3 | 1.1 | 0.6 | 0.3 | 2.4 | 4.0 | 4.7 | 4.8 | 5.0 |
| Furniture and fixtures | 1.3 | 0.5 | 0.2 | 0.9 | 1.7 | 1.6 | 5.0 | 4.1 | 5.1 | 4.8 |
| Paper products | 3.0 | 1.0 | 0.5 | 0.5 | 0.4 | 36.5 | 38.2 | 55.5 | 40.2 | 37.1 |
| Printing and publishing | 0.6 | 0.8 | 1.0 | 0.7 | 0.3 | 4.7 | 11.3 | 18.0 | 16.5 | 12.8 |
| Chemical products | 19.9 | 24.0 | 31.6 | 46.8 | 27.3 | 214.1 | 538.5 | 582.6 | 324.7 | 433.1 |
| Refined petroleum products | 0.7 | 1.3 | 0.2 | 0.4 | 0.1 | 22.0 | 14.7 | 6.7 | 17.8 | 5.8 |
| Rubber and plastic products | 2.9 | 3.6 | 6.5 | 4.6 | 5.4 | 15.8 | 18.5 | 27.3 | 27.4 | 27.4 |
| Leather products | ..... | 0.4 | 0.1 | 0.1 | 0.3 | 4.2 | 3.6 | 8.1 | 13.1 | 7.6 |
| Stone, clay and glass products | 0.9 | 0.5 | 0.7 | 0.7 | 0.8 | 14.1 | 18.0 | 19.6 | 18.7 | 20.0 |
| Primary metals | 0.4 | 0.3 | 0.9 | 0.6 | 0.7 | 7.6 | 13.8 | 130.4 | 40.9 | 37.9 |
| Fabricated metal products | 1.7 | 1.5 | 1.5 | 2.3 | 1.7 | 13.3 | 17.7 | 29.8 | 54.6 | 48.9 |
| Industrial machinery and computers | 18.4 | 36.2 | 38.8 | 57.7 | 125.0 | 155.7 | 211.4 | 329.5 | 359.0 | 491.2 |
| Electric and electronic equipment | 14.8 | 12.0 | 16.4 | 17.1 | 13.0 | 283.3 | 393.5 | 385.9 | 413.7 | 584.2 |
| Transportation equipment | 28.1 | 25.2 | 62.3 | 42.6 | 27.9 | 90.2 | 77.1 | 93.2 | 126.3 | 115.6 |
| Scientific and measuring instruments | 44.3 | 60.0 | 62.3 | 85.8 | 84.8 | 163.4 | 171.3 | 265.8 | 219.2 | 264.0 |
| Miscellaneous manufactures | 2.1 | 2.2 | 1.7 | 2.7 | 2.4 | 17.6 | 22.0 | 22.5 | 31.4 | 37.3 |
| Unidentified manufactures | 1.2 | 1.0 | 0.8 | 14.2 | 0.5 | 7.7 | 4.8 | 5.0 | 4.1 | 16.1 |
| **Agricultural and livestock products** | 16.2 | 16.2 | 18.5 | 20.6 | 20.6 | 123.0 | 132.0 | 132.0 | 173.0 | 182.3 |
| Agricultural products | 15.3 | 15.7 | 18.0 | 20.0 | 20.1 | 117.0 | 124.8 | 125.6 | 167.7 | 177.0 |
| Livestock and livestock products | 0.8 | 0.5 | 0.5 | 0.6 | 0.4 | 6.0 | 7.2 | 6.3 | 5.4 | 5.3 |
| **Other commodities** | 23.3 | 17.6 | 20.4 | 22.6 | 18.5 | 52.5 | 60.9 | 91.7 | 101.7 | 62.7 |
| Forestry products | 20.4 | 14.4 | 14.4 | 14.9 | 15.3 | 2.1 | 1.4 | 1.6 | 1.8 | 1.1 |
| Fish and other marine products | 1.3 | 0.7 | 2.7 | 2.4 | 0.5 | 15.2 | 25.9 | 35.9 | 24.4 | 25.4 |
| Metallic ores and concentrates | ..... | 0.4 | ..... | ..... | ..... | 1.5 | 1.3 | 1.7 | 1.8 | 1.3 |
| Bituminous coal and lignite | ..... | ..... | 0.8 | ..... | ..... | ..... | ..... | 0.9 | 0.3 | 0.9 |
| Crude petroleum and natural gas | ..... | ..... | ..... | ..... | ..... | ..... | ..... | ..... | 0.1 | ..... |
| Nonmetallic minerals | 0.1 | 0.1 | 0.1 | 0.3 | 0.1 | 2.2 | 1.7 | 0.3 | 0.6 | 0.5 |
| Scrap and waste | 0.2 | 0.3 | 0.6 | 1.2 | 0.2 | 6.7 | 6.9 | 24.7 | 19.7 | 9.4 |
| Used merchandise | 0.3 | 0.5 | 0.7 | 0.6 | 0.7 | 16.2 | 5.5 | 4.3 | 4.9 | 2.3 |
| Goods imported and returned unchanged | ..... | ..... | ..... | ..... | ..... | ..... | ..... | ..... | ..... | ..... |
| Special classification provisions | 1.0 | 1.2 | 1.0 | 3.3 | 1.6 | 8.6 | 18.2 | 22.3 | 48.0 | 21.8 |

## Table D-3.  State Exports of Goods by Destination and Industry, 1993–1997 —*Continued*

**FLORIDA** (Millions of dollars.)

| Industry | 1993 | 1994 | 1995 | 1996 | 1997 | 1993 | 1994 | 1995 | 1996 | 1997 |
|---|---|---|---|---|---|---|---|---|---|---|
| | Japan | | | | | South Korea | | | | |
| **ALL GOODS** | 350.8 | 487.4 | 584.1 | 554.2 | 588.2 | 182.3 | 179.2 | 357.8 | 351.6 | 341.3 |
| **Manufactured goods** | 283.8 | 398.6 | 493.6 | 470.5 | 504.5 | 116.0 | 112.6 | 268.2 | 244.4 | 220.0 |
| Food products | 35.1 | 68.0 | 37.3 | 48.0 | 40.3 | 5.6 | 10.5 | 8.0 | 4.9 | 5.1 |
| Tobacco products | 0.3 | 0.3 | 1.1 | 0.3 | 0.5 | 0.3 | ..... | ..... | 0.2 | ..... |
| Textile mill products | 1.5 | 2.0 | 1.0 | 2.7 | 2.1 | 0.6 | 0.3 | 1.2 | 0.5 | 0.3 |
| Apparel | 6.6 | 5.4 | 7.3 | 8.2 | 5.2 | 0.1 | 0.6 | 0.6 | 0.3 | 0.2 |
| Lumber and wood products | 0.4 | 1.1 | 3.3 | 3.4 | 3.0 | 0.2 | 0.5 | 0.3 | 0.5 | 0.3 |
| Furniture and fixtures | 0.3 | 0.7 | 0.9 | 1.6 | 2.5 | 0.2 | 2.3 | 0.6 | 0.4 | 0.3 |
| Paper products | 13.8 | 13.4 | 26.5 | 14.4 | 8.6 | 15.3 | 12.2 | 25.0 | 16.9 | 18.7 |
| Printing and publishing | 1.1 | 6.7 | 10.6 | 7.9 | 3.7 | 0.1 | 0.1 | 0.4 | 0.3 | 1.4 |
| Chemical products | 35.6 | 30.6 | 42.6 | 31.9 | 38.3 | 12.7 | 11.0 | 23.3 | 25.8 | 23.9 |
| Refined petroleum products | 2.7 | 2.7 | 5.3 | 6.1 | 4.5 | 4.0 | 0.2 | ..... | ..... | 0.1 |
| Rubber and plastic products | 4.0 | 5.0 | 7.1 | 7.9 | 8.7 | 1.2 | 1.7 | 2.8 | 2.0 | 2.9 |
| Leather products | 0.3 | 0.9 | 3.4 | 5.4 | 4.5 | ..... | ..... | ..... | 0.4 | 0.1 |
| Stone, clay and glass products | 2.0 | 2.2 | 2.4 | 3.2 | 2.7 | 1.0 | 3.0 | 1.7 | 1.7 | 1.3 |
| Primary metals | 0.3 | 0.4 | 1.0 | 2.2 | 2.0 | 1.4 | 2.3 | 35.7 | 12.5 | 13.5 |
| Fabricated metal products | 1.7 | 3.0 | 4.1 | 6.9 | 15.8 | 1.7 | 1.5 | 5.6 | 7.3 | 8.5 |
| Industrial machinery and computers | 41.9 | 43.2 | 51.4 | 71.7 | 86.2 | 18.2 | 22.6 | 97.8 | 86.8 | 47.3 |
| Electric and electronic equipment | 40.3 | 98.3 | 87.5 | 85.4 | 85.0 | 23.8 | 24.9 | 27.3 | 38.9 | 44.9 |
| Transportation equipment | 9.6 | 10.2 | 18.3 | 16.9 | 14.9 | 6.2 | 7.0 | 14.1 | 21.7 | 19.1 |
| Scientific and measuring instruments | 74.5 | 94.6 | 173.2 | 134.1 | 163.0 | 21.9 | 10.6 | 20.5 | 17.7 | 21.7 |
| Miscellaneous manufactures | 10.8 | 8.2 | 7.8 | 11.1 | 11.7 | 1.2 | 0.9 | 2.7 | 4.9 | 9.7 |
| Unidentified manufactures | 1.2 | 1.6 | 1.7 | 1.1 | 1.4 | 0.4 | 0.5 | 0.5 | 0.8 | 0.7 |
| **Agricultural and livestock products** | 45.2 | 60.5 | 50.7 | 53.0 | 63.2 | 59.7 | 61.4 | 75.9 | 99.4 | 114.0 |
| Agricultural products | 41.9 | 56.6 | 46.9 | 48.8 | 59.4 | 59.7 | 61.4 | 75.9 | 99.3 | 114.0 |
| Livestock and livestock products | 3.3 | 3.9 | 3.8 | 4.1 | 3.8 | ..... | ..... | ..... | 0.1 | ..... |
| **Other commodities** | 21.8 | 28.2 | 39.8 | 30.8 | 20.5 | 6.6 | 5.1 | 13.6 | 7.7 | 7.3 |
| Forestry products | 1.0 | 0.9 | 0.9 | 0.8 | 0.7 | 1.0 | 0.4 | 0.6 | 0.1 | 0.2 |
| Fish and other marine products | 5.5 | 16.5 | 23.8 | 15.0 | 12.1 | ..... | 0.2 | 0.4 | ..... | 0.1 |
| Metallic ores and concentrates | ..... | ..... | ..... | ..... | ..... | ..... | ..... | ..... | ..... | ..... |
| Bituminous coal and lignite | ..... | ..... | 0.9 | 0.3 | 0.9 | ..... | ..... | ..... | ..... | ..... |
| Crude petroleum and natural gas | ..... | ..... | ..... | ..... | ..... | ..... | ..... | ..... | ..... | ..... |
| Nonmetallic minerals | ..... | 0.1 | ..... | ..... | ..... | 1.6 | 0.9 | ..... | 0.1 | ..... |
| Scrap and waste | 0.3 | 1.0 | 3.4 | 2.1 | 1.7 | 3.5 | 3.5 | 12.1 | 6.1 | 3.9 |
| Used merchandise | 14.4 | 2.1 | 0.7 | 0.6 | 0.4 | ..... | ..... | ..... | 0.6 | 0.6 |
| Goods imported and returned unchanged | ..... | ..... | ..... | ..... | ..... | ..... | ..... | ..... | ..... | ..... |
| Special classification provisions | 0.6 | 7.6 | 10.1 | 11.9 | 4.7 | 0.3 | 0.1 | 0.5 | 0.8 | 2.5 |
| | Taiwan | | | | | Singapore | | | | |
| **ALL GOODS** | 102.5 | 153.4 | 155.3 | 122.2 | 131.2 | 153.2 | 140.1 | 218.5 | 236.9 | 319.9 |
| **Manufactured goods** | 89.8 | 138.8 | 138.0 | 104.1 | 113.7 | 149.2 | 136.4 | 215.4 | 232.1 | 315.7 |
| Food products | 1.8 | 3.7 | 2.9 | 3.6 | 3.2 | 2.1 | 2.0 | 2.8 | 1.8 | 1.4 |
| Tobacco products | ..... | ..... | 0.2 | 0.2 | ..... | ..... | ..... | 0.1 | ..... | 0.4 |
| Textile mill products | 0.3 | 0.6 | 1.3 | 0.8 | 0.2 | 0.5 | 1.1 | 0.2 | 0.4 | 0.8 |
| Apparel | 0.4 | 0.4 | 0.3 | 1.3 | 1.0 | 1.4 | 1.0 | 0.4 | 1.8 | 1.1 |
| Lumber and wood products | 0.8 | 0.5 | 0.7 | 0.4 | 0.5 | ..... | 0.1 | ..... | 0.1 | 0.1 |
| Furniture and fixtures | 0.4 | 0.5 | 0.5 | 0.1 | 0.4 | 0.2 | 1.0 | 0.3 | 0.3 | 0.2 |
| Paper products | 0.2 | 2.9 | 1.3 | 0.3 | 0.6 | 0.5 | 0.2 | 0.5 | 0.2 | 0.2 |
| Printing and publishing | 0.8 | 1.2 | 5.2 | 6.3 | 6.3 | 1.0 | 0.8 | 0.7 | 0.4 | 0.4 |
| Chemical products | 10.2 | 11.6 | 12.7 | 10.3 | 13.3 | 10.7 | 13.0 | 11.7 | 9.5 | 17.4 |
| Refined petroleum products | 1.2 | 0.5 | 0.3 | 1.4 | 0.3 | ..... | 0.1 | ..... | 0.1 | 0.3 |
| Rubber and plastic products | 1.8 | 2.9 | 3.7 | 3.1 | 2.3 | 4.2 | 3.9 | 6.9 | 8.8 | 5.2 |
| Leather products | 0.1 | ..... | 0.3 | 0.3 | 0.9 | ..... | 0.1 | 2.3 | 3.9 | 0.9 |
| Stone, clay and glass products | 2.5 | 1.1 | 2.3 | 0.7 | 0.5 | 0.6 | 1.2 | 0.8 | 0.6 | 1.2 |
| Primary metals | 0.5 | 4.1 | 52.4 | 7.5 | 4.1 | 2.0 | 1.6 | 0.5 | 0.8 | 0.9 |
| Fabricated metal products | 2.7 | 6.2 | 3.3 | 2.4 | 2.1 | 1.7 | 1.4 | 1.6 | 1.3 | 1.4 |
| Industrial machinery and computers | 15.3 | 15.5 | 20.9 | 24.2 | 29.6 | 32.8 | 24.8 | 38.9 | 27.3 | 25.6 |
| Electric and electronic equipment | 21.2 | 65.5 | 15.2 | 18.5 | 30.1 | 70.9 | 60.2 | 113.9 | 135.4 | 202.9 |
| Transportation equipment | 10.7 | 6.7 | 4.7 | 11.3 | 4.4 | 12.1 | 14.1 | 18.7 | 22.1 | 25.6 |
| Scientific and measuring instruments | 13.5 | 12.7 | 8.6 | 9.8 | 12.5 | 6.9 | 8.1 | 11.7 | 13.6 | 17.7 |
| Miscellaneous manufactures | 1.3 | 1.7 | 0.7 | 1.3 | 1.2 | 0.6 | 1.0 | 2.9 | 3.0 | 2.0 |
| Unidentified manufactures | 4.2 | 0.5 | 0.5 | 0.3 | 0.2 | 0.8 | 0.7 | 0.6 | 0.7 | 9.9 |
| **Agricultural and livestock products** | 2.1 | 2.5 | 2.7 | 2.5 | 2.9 | 0.6 | 1.0 | 0.8 | 0.5 | 0.5 |
| Agricultural products | 0.7 | 0.9 | 1.5 | 2.1 | 2.4 | 0.3 | 0.2 | 0.4 | 0.4 | 0.4 |
| Livestock and livestock products | 1.5 | 1.5 | 1.2 | 0.5 | 0.5 | 0.4 | 0.7 | 0.4 | 0.1 | ..... |
| **Other commodities** | 10.6 | 12.1 | 14.6 | 15.5 | 14.7 | 3.3 | 2.8 | 2.3 | 4.4 | 3.7 |
| Forestry products | ..... | ..... | 0.1 | ..... | ..... | ..... | ..... | ..... | ..... | ..... |
| Fish and other marine products | 9.5 | 7.9 | 10.4 | 7.8 | 11.2 | 0.1 | 0.1 | 0.1 | ..... | 0.2 |
| Metallic ores and concentrates | ..... | ..... | ..... | ..... | ..... | ..... | ..... | ..... | ..... | ..... |
| Bituminous coal and lignite | ..... | ..... | ..... | ..... | ..... | ..... | ..... | ..... | ..... | ..... |
| Crude petroleum and natural gas | ..... | ..... | ..... | 0.1 | ..... | ..... | ..... | ..... | ..... | ..... |
| Nonmetallic minerals | 0.1 | 0.7 | 0.2 | 0.1 | 0.2 | ..... | ..... | ..... | ..... | ..... |
| Scrap and waste | 0.4 | 0.9 | 0.9 | 1.7 | 1.3 | 0.9 | 0.1 | 0.1 | 0.1 | 0.1 |
| Used merchandise | 0.3 | ..... | 0.3 | 0.1 | 0.2 | 0.4 | 0.3 | 0.7 | 0.4 | 0.4 |
| Goods imported and returned unchanged | ..... | ..... | ..... | ..... | ..... | ..... | ..... | ..... | ..... | ..... |
| Special classification provisions | 0.2 | 2.6 | 2.8 | 5.8 | 1.8 | 1.9 | 2.2 | 1.4 | 3.8 | 3.0 |

# GEORGIA: Exports of Goods, 1997

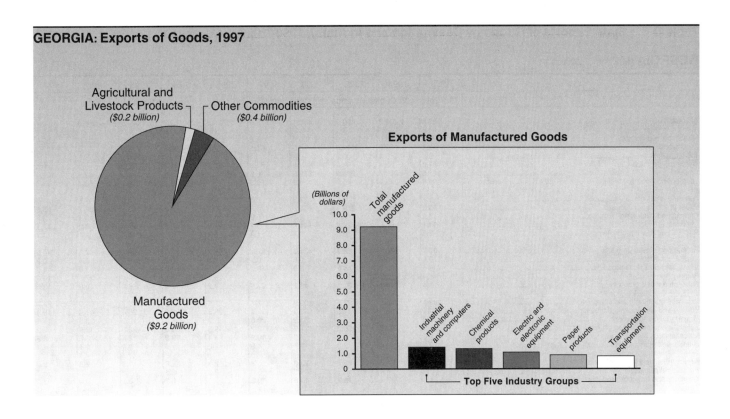

## Table D-3.   State Exports of Goods by Destination and Industry, 1993–1997 —*Continued*

### GEORGIA (Millions of dollars.)

| Industry | 1993 | 1994 | 1995 | 1996 | 1997 | 1993 | 1994 | 1995 | 1996 | 1997 |
|---|---|---|---|---|---|---|---|---|---|---|
| | All destinations | | | | | Canada | | | | |
| **ALL GOODS** | 6 050.1 | 7 108.1 | 8 626.8 | 8 618.0 | 9 810.0 | 1 468.9 | 1 646.3 | 1 820.7 | 1 896.9 | 1 999.7 |
| **Manufactured goods** | 5 567.0 | 6 567.7 | 8 063.9 | 8 062.1 | 9 214.9 | 1 309.0 | 1 499.9 | 1 678.6 | 1 738.5 | 1 835.4 |
| Food products | 315.1 | 506.4 | 695.5 | 836.7 | 632.2 | 87.1 | 81.0 | 71.6 | 86.5 | 66.9 |
| Tobacco products | 2.8 | 2.8 | 4.1 | 3.6 | 5.5 | 0.4 | 0.8 | 0.8 | 0.9 | 1.1 |
| Textile mill products | 614.2 | 618.6 | 579.9 | 652.0 | 708.0 | 205.8 | 199.6 | 202.3 | 228.7 | 274.3 |
| Apparel | 235.4 | 288.8 | 332.2 | 397.6 | 445.6 | 18.1 | 23.3 | 22.3 | 24.5 | 27.6 |
| Lumber and wood products | 238.0 | 250.8 | 230.1 | 198.9 | 258.2 | 9.7 | 13.8 | 11.4 | 15.8 | 21.6 |
| Furniture and fixtures | 33.1 | 36.1 | 35.0 | 40.9 | 54.7 | 12.9 | 12.7 | 10.1 | 10.2 | 11.6 |
| Paper products | 487.1 | 684.3 | 1 092.7 | 915.6 | 904.7 | 104.5 | 111.3 | 137.9 | 153.5 | 162.3 |
| Printing and publishing | 31.3 | 44.6 | 56.3 | 51.6 | 52.4 | 12.8 | 10.7 | 8.9 | 9.4 | 8.7 |
| Chemical products | 468.3 | 584.5 | 683.0 | 811.7 | 1 312.6 | 152.8 | 172.5 | 158.5 | 171.7 | 241.5 |
| Refined petroleum products | 51.9 | 63.1 | 82.7 | 78.0 | 82.6 | 5.5 | 8.4 | 7.8 | 1.3 | 1.5 |
| Rubber and plastic products | 194.6 | 232.5 | 230.2 | 221.7 | 226.7 | 48.2 | 64.2 | 62.9 | 65.9 | 77.1 |
| Leather products | 5.2 | 5.3 | 8.3 | 6.9 | 5.9 | 1.1 | 0.8 | 1.0 | 1.8 | 1.0 |
| Stone, clay and glass products | 39.1 | 45.2 | 40.3 | 42.1 | 50.4 | 12.1 | 11.5 | 10.6 | 13.0 | 15.7 |
| Primary metals | 208.5 | 191.8 | 229.1 | 282.2 | 306.7 | 31.8 | 47.2 | 59.5 | 57.7 | 58.6 |
| Fabricated metal products | 130.8 | 121.7 | 133.0 | 158.9 | 177.2 | 64.6 | 51.2 | 40.3 | 42.9 | 51.7 |
| Industrial machinery and computers | 811.2 | 1 021.1 | 1 241.5 | 1 271.4 | 1 407.6 | 180.9 | 263.0 | 287.6 | 281.9 | 308.1 |
| Electric and electronic equipment | 554.9 | 746.1 | 789.3 | 852.1 | 1 079.3 | 152.8 | 205.8 | 232.5 | 259.2 | 241.2 |
| Transportation equipment | 721.3 | 653.2 | 1 028.5 | 673.0 | 828.2 | 132.8 | 139.9 | 258.1 | 212.4 | 153.8 |
| Scientific and measuring instruments | 351.7 | 389.7 | 480.4 | 475.5 | 568.9 | 59.3 | 62.9 | 71.4 | 72.4 | 83.4 |
| Miscellaneous manufactures | 51.1 | 57.6 | 67.4 | 68.9 | 81.8 | 10.2 | 11.7 | 13.5 | 20.4 | 18.1 |
| Unidentified manufactures | 21.3 | 23.4 | 24.7 | 22.6 | 25.6 | 5.6 | 7.6 | 9.5 | 8.3 | 9.6 |
| **Agricultural and livestock products** | 122.3 | 132.0 | 164.0 | 137.1 | 182.5 | 59.7 | 32.6 | 38.5 | 37.5 | 42.8 |
| Agricultural products | 100.9 | 106.0 | 135.1 | 108.5 | 150.0 | 57.1 | 28.7 | 35.7 | 31.5 | 36.9 |
| Livestock and livestock products | 21.4 | 26.0 | 28.9 | 28.6 | 32.6 | 2.6 | 3.9 | 2.8 | 6.0 | 5.8 |
| **Other commodities** | 360.8 | 408.4 | 398.9 | 418.9 | 412.6 | 100.2 | 113.8 | 103.7 | 120.9 | 121.5 |
| Forestry products | 1.4 | 3.2 | 3.0 | 2.2 | 1.8 | 0.1 | 0.1 | ..... | 0.1 | 0.2 |
| Fish and other marine products | 3.0 | 2.4 | 4.1 | 2.1 | 5.2 | 1.7 | 0.7 | 0.5 | 0.3 | 0.1 |
| Metallic ores and concentrates | 5.1 | 6.0 | 5.7 | 4.4 | 3.6 | 5.1 | 6.0 | 5.2 | 4.1 | 2.4 |
| Bituminous coal and lignite | 0.8 | ..... | ..... | ..... | ..... | 0.8 | ..... | ..... | ..... | ..... |
| Crude petroleum and natural gas | 0.1 | 0.4 | 0.2 | ..... | 0.4 | 0.1 | 0.4 | 0.2 | ..... | ..... |
| Nonmetallic minerals | 234.3 | 259.4 | 265.4 | 278.9 | 287.7 | 50.7 | 52.4 | 56.7 | 60.6 | 61.5 |
| Scrap and waste | 30.4 | 43.6 | 56.5 | 40.7 | 35.8 | 2.7 | 4.7 | 5.2 | 11.6 | 10.6 |
| Used merchandise | 13.7 | 12.5 | 15.5 | 19.5 | 20.0 | 0.5 | 2.0 | 2.2 | 1.9 | 2.2 |
| Goods imported and returned unchanged | 36.3 | 45.0 | 30.5 | 36.9 | 41.7 | 36.3 | 45.0 | 30.5 | 36.9 | 41.7 |
| Special classification provisions | 35.8 | 35.8 | 18.0 | 34.2 | 16.5 | 2.2 | 2.5 | 3.1 | 5.4 | 3.0 |

## Table D-3.   State Exports of Goods by Destination and Industry, 1993–1997 —*Continued*

**GEORGIA** (Millions of dollars.)

| Industry | 1993 | 1994 | 1995 | 1996 | 1997 | 1993 | 1994 | 1995 | 1996 | 1997 |
|---|---|---|---|---|---|---|---|---|---|---|
| | South and Central America and Caribbean | | | | | Mexico | | | | |
| **ALL GOODS** | 857.4 | 1 203.2 | 1 490.0 | 1 418.1 | 1 575.5 | 324.2 | 469.5 | 403.8 | 516.9 | 685.7 |
| **Manufactured goods** | 825.8 | 1 153.6 | 1 435.9 | 1 380.9 | 1 532.3 | 309.4 | 451.7 | 392.9 | 503.2 | 665.0 |
| Food products | 48.4 | 73.7 | 117.4 | 98.5 | 101.5 | 12.5 | 36.1 | 15.4 | 18.8 | 23.9 |
| Tobacco products | 0.8 | 0.4 | 0.3 | 0.2 | 0.1 | ..... | ..... | ..... | ..... | ..... |
| Textile mill products | 37.8 | 53.2 | 61.2 | 67.3 | 77.3 | 20.4 | 24.9 | 26.3 | 55.1 | 46.5 |
| Apparel | 161.0 | 206.7 | 224.9 | 279.8 | 286.3 | 7.2 | 23.0 | 50.2 | 60.8 | 100.5 |
| Lumber and wood products | 45.6 | 49.1 | 45.0 | 36.3 | 58.6 | 7.8 | 3.9 | 0.6 | 0.7 | 1.8 |
| Furniture and fixtures | 1.7 | 1.8 | 4.1 | 3.3 | 6.6 | 0.9 | 1.4 | 0.5 | 1.5 | 1.6 |
| Paper products | 68.3 | 108.4 | 219.1 | 174.3 | 174.3 | 19.1 | 79.1 | 60.3 | 52.7 | 53.8 |
| Printing and publishing | 3.0 | 3.2 | 5.2 | 2.3 | 5.9 | 4.2 | 9.7 | 7.3 | 3.4 | 3.8 |
| Chemical products | 54.1 | 84.9 | 125.4 | 144.0 | 215.1 | 27.0 | 40.6 | 37.0 | 59.2 | 75.1 |
| Refined petroleum products | 3.8 | 7.7 | 9.5 | 7.9 | 11.4 | 0.4 | 1.8 | 0.9 | 1.1 | 1.7 |
| Rubber and plastic products | 37.0 | 36.4 | 52.4 | 31.3 | 22.3 | 33.7 | 63.0 | 48.5 | 40.9 | 44.5 |
| Leather products | 0.2 | 0.7 | 0.9 | 0.6 | 0.7 | 0.3 | 0.2 | 0.2 | 0.4 | 0.2 |
| Stone, clay and glass products | 6.6 | 3.7 | 4.5 | 5.8 | 6.7 | 1.1 | 2.4 | 1.1 | 1.6 | 4.6 |
| Primary metals | 14.4 | 12.6 | 18.0 | 21.2 | 30.0 | 26.0 | 22.1 | 20.0 | 27.6 | 14.6 |
| Fabricated metal products | 13.4 | 14.6 | 21.1 | 43.7 | 27.9 | 7.2 | 7.8 | 6.6 | 9.0 | 13.5 |
| Industrial machinery and computers | 109.1 | 155.5 | 192.4 | 206.9 | 217.7 | 31.5 | 51.9 | 45.7 | 54.0 | 82.1 |
| Electric and electronic equipment | 82.5 | 202.5 | 141.5 | 100.8 | 131.4 | 23.3 | 33.2 | 25.4 | 41.8 | 118.4 |
| Transportation equipment | 56.8 | 33.1 | 26.2 | 33.3 | 29.6 | 30.7 | 6.4 | 10.2 | 23.5 | 11.6 |
| Scientific and measuring instruments | 75.0 | 98.0 | 156.3 | 111.9 | 113.2 | 49.3 | 33.0 | 23.6 | 43.9 | 60.3 |
| Miscellaneous manufactures | 3.6 | 5.0 | 7.1 | 7.9 | 10.8 | 5.4 | 9.8 | 12.5 | 5.6 | 5.2 |
| Unidentified manufactures | 2.9 | 2.7 | 2.9 | 3.7 | 4.9 | 1.2 | 1.4 | 0.9 | 1.4 | 1.4 |
| **Agricultural and livestock products** | 16.0 | 32.8 | 32.2 | 23.0 | 25.3 | 2.3 | 2.8 | 1.3 | 2.9 | 8.6 |
| Agricultural products | 1.9 | 14.9 | 13.5 | 7.5 | 5.8 | 2.3 | 2.5 | 1.2 | 2.5 | 5.7 |
| Livestock and livestock products | 14.1 | 17.9 | 18.7 | 15.5 | 19.3 | ..... | 0.3 | 0.1 | 0.4 | 3.0 |
| **Other commodities** | 15.6 | 16.6 | 22.0 | 14.1 | 17.9 | 12.5 | 15.1 | 9.6 | 10.8 | 12.1 |
| Forestry products | 0.5 | 0.4 | 1.3 | 0.2 | 0.5 | 0.4 | 0.3 | 0.1 | 0.3 | 0.3 |
| Fish and other marine products | 0.5 | 0.7 | 0.6 | 0.4 | 0.4 | 0.2 | 0.3 | ..... | ..... | 0.3 |
| Metallic ores and concentrates | ..... | ..... | ..... | 0.1 | 0.7 | ..... | ..... | ..... | ..... | 0.4 |
| Bituminous coal and lignite | ..... | ..... | ..... | ..... | ..... | ..... | ..... | ..... | ..... | ..... |
| Crude petroleum and natural gas | ..... | ..... | ..... | ..... | 0.3 | ..... | ..... | ..... | ..... | ..... |
| Nonmetallic minerals | 7.8 | 7.4 | 10.8 | 9.3 | 11.1 | 4.6 | 6.5 | 3.8 | 4.7 | 5.0 |
| Scrap and waste | 1.5 | 2.2 | 3.0 | 0.7 | 1.7 | 1.1 | 2.8 | 3.9 | 4.5 | 4.6 |
| Used merchandise | 4.2 | 4.4 | 4.2 | 2.5 | 2.5 | 0.2 | 0.6 | 0.2 | 0.1 | 0.6 |
| Goods imported and returned unchanged | ..... | ..... | ..... | ..... | ..... | ..... | ..... | ..... | ..... | ..... |
| Special classification provisions | 1.1 | 1.7 | 2.0 | 0.9 | 0.7 | 6.1 | 4.5 | 1.6 | 1.2 | 0.9 |

| Industry | 1993 | 1994 | 1995 | 1996 | 1997 | 1993 | 1994 | 1995 | 1996 | 1997 |
|---|---|---|---|---|---|---|---|---|---|---|
| | European Union | | | | | United Kingdom | | | | |
| **ALL GOODS** | 1 374.4 | 1 578.2 | 2 010.8 | 1 818.5 | 2 351.4 | 291.6 | 385.8 | 459.8 | 426.6 | 489.3 |
| **Manufactured goods** | 1 220.3 | 1 409.8 | 1 814.4 | 1 643.5 | 2 170.2 | 266.3 | 364.6 | 443.9 | 414.5 | 472.7 |
| Food products | 26.3 | 27.7 | 42.0 | 51.6 | 29.5 | 3.1 | 6.3 | 4.4 | 3.0 | 2.2 |
| Tobacco products | 0.8 | 1.2 | 1.7 | 1.9 | 2.9 | 0.2 | 0.4 | 0.2 | 0.2 | ..... |
| Textile mill products | 64.7 | 58.7 | 65.3 | 75.3 | 78.1 | 27.0 | 26.3 | 32.6 | 38.7 | 40.6 |
| Apparel | 15.5 | 12.5 | 10.3 | 8.1 | 7.0 | 1.4 | 2.4 | 1.1 | 1.0 | 1.6 |
| Lumber and wood products | 105.9 | 120.5 | 111.8 | 79.9 | 125.5 | 21.2 | 23.9 | 23.5 | 16.0 | 27.9 |
| Furniture and fixtures | 4.7 | 6.0 | 6.2 | 6.9 | 7.5 | 2.7 | 2.8 | 2.9 | 2.8 | 3.8 |
| Paper products | 146.8 | 166.1 | 296.8 | 221.1 | 273.9 | 22.1 | 25.5 | 31.4 | 27.4 | 34.8 |
| Printing and publishing | 5.8 | 13.8 | 27.5 | 24.0 | 17.9 | 2.1 | 2.0 | 18.0 | 6.9 | 10.2 |
| Chemical products | 68.6 | 88.8 | 111.8 | 120.6 | 270.4 | 20.8 | 30.3 | 41.1 | 44.3 | 45.4 |
| Refined petroleum products | 26.0 | 29.2 | 47.9 | 38.0 | 31.7 | 2.3 | 0.8 | 3.7 | ..... | 0.6 |
| Rubber and plastic products | 34.4 | 35.9 | 28.7 | 28.5 | 22.1 | 10.2 | 11.0 | 5.5 | 6.3 | 5.1 |
| Leather products | 1.0 | 1.9 | 2.3 | 1.6 | 1.7 | 0.1 | ..... | 0.2 | 0.9 | 1.0 |
| Stone, clay and glass products | 10.7 | 16.9 | 13.3 | 10.3 | 12.6 | 1.2 | 6.3 | 1.6 | 2.0 | 2.9 |
| Primary metals | 16.2 | 20.7 | 17.5 | 29.3 | 61.5 | 4.1 | 6.2 | 3.9 | 6.2 | 12.1 |
| Fabricated metal products | 20.1 | 16.0 | 18.3 | 28.4 | 41.5 | 6.7 | 3.4 | 6.3 | 6.7 | 10.3 |
| Industrial machinery and computers | 267.1 | 300.7 | 405.7 | 410.4 | 430.6 | 38.9 | 55.7 | 59.3 | 60.6 | 73.0 |
| Electric and electronic equipment | 110.7 | 148.4 | 169.5 | 148.8 | 241.2 | 40.8 | 68.5 | 80.4 | 79.5 | 57.2 |
| Transportation equipment | 184.5 | 213.0 | 277.5 | 217.4 | 352.3 | 29.4 | 43.1 | 59.8 | 70.8 | 107.4 |
| Scientific and measuring instruments | 96.7 | 112.8 | 142.6 | 126.3 | 141.0 | 26.9 | 44.5 | 62.7 | 37.7 | 32.8 |
| Miscellaneous manufactures | 8.5 | 12.8 | 12.6 | 11.9 | 17.9 | 3.4 | 2.6 | 3.1 | 2.6 | 2.7 |
| Unidentified manufactures | 5.4 | 6.1 | 5.2 | 3.3 | 3.3 | 1.8 | 2.4 | 2.1 | 1.1 | 1.2 |
| **Agricultural and livestock products** | 30.5 | 30.1 | 65.5 | 33.6 | 48.5 | 4.5 | 5.0 | 9.3 | 4.3 | 6.4 |
| Agricultural products | 29.1 | 28.3 | 64.8 | 31.4 | 45.7 | 4.5 | 5.0 | 9.1 | 4.2 | 6.4 |
| Livestock and livestock products | 1.4 | 1.8 | 0.7 | 2.3 | 2.8 | ..... | ..... | 0.1 | 0.1 | ..... |
| **Other commodities** | 123.7 | 138.4 | 130.9 | 141.4 | 132.7 | 20.8 | 16.2 | 6.6 | 7.8 | 10.2 |
| Forestry products | 0.3 | 0.8 | 0.1 | 0.4 | 0.1 | 0.1 | ..... | ..... | 0.1 | ..... |
| Fish and other marine products | ..... | ..... | 0.3 | 0.1 | ..... | ..... | ..... | ..... | 0.1 | ..... |
| Metallic ores and concentrates | ..... | ..... | 0.5 | 0.1 | 0.1 | ..... | ..... | ..... | ..... | ..... |
| Bituminous coal and lignite | ..... | ..... | ..... | ..... | ..... | ..... | ..... | ..... | ..... | ..... |
| Crude petroleum and natural gas | ..... | ..... | ..... | ..... | ..... | ..... | ..... | ..... | ..... | ..... |
| Nonmetallic minerals | 95.9 | 109.9 | 108.0 | 112.5 | 116.5 | 14.4 | 13.4 | 1.6 | 4.9 | 6.4 |
| Scrap and waste | 13.7 | 11.6 | 14.1 | 9.7 | 4.4 | 1.5 | 1.1 | 1.1 | 0.2 | 0.7 |
| Used merchandise | 2.6 | 1.5 | 5.7 | 5.3 | 4.3 | 0.7 | 0.5 | 3.4 | 1.1 | 1.5 |
| Goods imported and returned unchanged | ..... | ..... | ..... | ..... | ..... | ..... | ..... | ..... | ..... | ..... |
| Special classification provisions | 11.1 | 14.6 | 2.1 | 13.4 | 7.2 | 4.0 | 1.3 | 0.5 | 1.5 | 1.6 |

## Table D-3.  State Exports of Goods by Destination and Industry, 1993–1997 —*Continued*

### GEORGIA (Millions of dollars.)

| Industry | 1993 | 1994 | 1995 | 1996 | 1997 | 1993 | 1994 | 1995 | 1996 | 1997 |
|---|---|---|---|---|---|---|---|---|---|---|
| | Germany | | | | | France | | | | |
| **ALL GOODS** | 274.7 | 259.3 | 298.9 | 311.5 | 340.0 | 183.0 | 172.8 | 243.4 | 246.2 | 279.6 |
| **Manufactured goods** | 258.7 | 235.2 | 282.1 | 289.4 | 318.6 | 179.0 | 169.4 | 239.4 | 244.2 | 276.9 |
| Food products | 3.3 | 2.5 | 2.6 | 5.9 | 3.1 | 2.1 | 2.7 | 2.5 | 2.0 | 1.8 |
| Tobacco products | ..... | ..... | 0.5 | 0.6 | 0.3 | ..... | ..... | ..... | ..... | 0.7 |
| Textile mill products | 10.4 | 8.2 | 10.4 | 12.6 | 10.6 | 4.5 | 2.8 | 2.2 | 2.2 | 2.0 |
| Apparel | 6.1 | 3.1 | 2.1 | 1.5 | 1.5 | 1.8 | 0.5 | 0.5 | 0.2 | 0.3 |
| Lumber and wood products | 16.2 | 22.5 | 17.6 | 17.9 | 32.9 | 1.1 | 2.0 | 1.2 | 0.7 | 2.1 |
| Furniture and fixtures | 0.8 | 2.1 | 0.5 | 0.4 | 1.2 | 0.2 | 0.1 | 0.3 | 0.3 | 0.3 |
| Paper products | 15.4 | 15.2 | 19.8 | 14.9 | 15.9 | 31.5 | 28.2 | 58.1 | 51.4 | 60.3 |
| Printing and publishing | 0.4 | 0.4 | 0.9 | 4.5 | 0.7 | 0.2 | 0.4 | 0.8 | 0.8 | 0.5 |
| Chemical products | 8.3 | 8.0 | 10.0 | 11.5 | 16.0 | 2.6 | 4.8 | 6.4 | 10.0 | 15.8 |
| Refined petroleum products | 0.7 | ..... | ..... | 0.1 | ..... | 10.8 | 11.8 | 18.1 | 15.9 | 10.0 |
| Rubber and plastic products | 7.8 | 5.4 | 5.3 | 5.0 | 6.2 | 1.7 | 3.1 | 2.5 | 1.8 | 1.3 |
| Leather products | 0.4 | 0.7 | 0.6 | 0.2 | ..... | 0.1 | 0.3 | 0.2 | 0.1 | 0.1 |
| Stone, clay and glass products | 0.9 | 1.0 | 1.1 | 0.9 | 1.6 | 0.5 | 0.2 | 0.6 | 0.8 | 5.4 |
| Primary metals | 9.1 | 0.9 | 4.3 | 12.5 | 9.6 | 0.8 | 1.0 | 1.0 | 3.2 | 1.1 |
| Fabricated metal products | 5.2 | 4.8 | 3.0 | 4.1 | 6.7 | 3.4 | 1.5 | 1.8 | 2.2 | 4.9 |
| Industrial machinery and computers | 68.5 | 60.9 | 80.2 | 74.1 | 68.6 | 48.0 | 67.9 | 105.3 | 110.5 | 111.8 |
| Electric and electronic equipment | 13.4 | 9.0 | 21.3 | 17.7 | 43.7 | 9.9 | 19.4 | 15.1 | 7.6 | 6.9 |
| Transportation equipment | 61.6 | 49.1 | 61.8 | 62.0 | 58.0 | 51.7 | 15.6 | 12.7 | 25.0 | 41.9 |
| Scientific and measuring instruments | 26.7 | 36.5 | 36.7 | 40.3 | 37.6 | 6.6 | 5.7 | 9.2 | 8.3 | 8.4 |
| Miscellaneous manufactures | 2.1 | 3.7 | 2.6 | 2.2 | 3.7 | 0.9 | 0.8 | 0.5 | 1.1 | 1.2 |
| Unidentified manufactures | 1.4 | 1.1 | 0.7 | 0.6 | 0.5 | 0.6 | 0.7 | 0.4 | 0.3 | 0.2 |
| **Agricultural and livestock products** | 3.5 | 3.7 | 5.1 | 2.7 | 1.8 | 2.4 | 2.4 | 2.2 | 0.3 | 0.9 |
| Agricultural products | 3.4 | 3.3 | 5.0 | 2.3 | 1.6 | 1.2 | 1.2 | 1.7 | 0.3 | 0.8 |
| Livestock and livestock products | 0.1 | 0.4 | 0.1 | 0.4 | 0.2 | 1.2 | 1.2 | 0.5 | ..... | 0.1 |
| **Other commodities** | 12.5 | 20.4 | 11.7 | 19.4 | 19.5 | 1.6 | 1.0 | 1.8 | 1.7 | 1.8 |
| Forestry products | ..... | ..... | ..... | ..... | ..... | ..... | ..... | ..... | ..... | ..... |
| Fish and other marine products | ..... | ..... | 0.3 | ..... | ..... | ..... | ..... | ..... | ..... | ..... |
| Metallic ores and concentrates | ..... | ..... | ..... | ..... | ..... | ..... | ..... | ..... | ..... | ..... |
| Bituminous coal and lignite | ..... | ..... | ..... | ..... | ..... | ..... | ..... | ..... | ..... | ..... |
| Crude petroleum and natural gas | ..... | ..... | ..... | ..... | ..... | ..... | ..... | ..... | ..... | ..... |
| Nonmetallic minerals | 8.7 | 8.1 | 10.6 | 8.5 | 17.3 | 0.8 | 0.7 | 0.3 | 0.6 | 0.5 |
| Scrap and waste | 0.3 | 0.3 | 0.2 | 0.1 | ..... | ..... | ..... | ..... | ..... | 0.1 |
| Used merchandise | 0.9 | 0.2 | 0.2 | 1.6 | 1.0 | 0.5 | 0.1 | 1.4 | 0.8 | 0.5 |
| Goods imported and returned unchanged | ..... | ..... | ..... | ..... | ..... | ..... | ..... | ..... | ..... | ..... |
| Special classification provisions | 2.5 | 11.8 | 0.5 | 9.2 | 1.2 | 0.3 | 0.2 | 0.1 | 0.1 | 0.6 |
| | The Netherlands | | | | | Asian 10 | | | | |
| **ALL GOODS** | 172.9 | 241.1 | 282.2 | 259.5 | 380.2 | 1 186.6 | 1 287.8 | 1 874.8 | 1 732.9 | 1 976.8 |
| **Manufactured goods** | 143.3 | 216.2 | 229.5 | 220.0 | 321.0 | 1 101.4 | 1 187.0 | 1 756.2 | 1 613.4 | 1 845.8 |
| Food products | 4.0 | 7.0 | 14.4 | 26.7 | 9.9 | 82.2 | 126.4 | 201.6 | 221.8 | 171.2 |
| Tobacco products | 0.4 | 0.7 | 0.9 | 1.1 | 1.5 | 0.6 | 0.3 | 0.4 | 0.4 | 0.3 |
| Textile mill products | 8.5 | 6.6 | 4.9 | 8.2 | 7.5 | 109.8 | 114.6 | 103.5 | 103.1 | 106.8 |
| Apparel | 0.2 | 1.3 | 1.1 | 1.3 | 0.6 | 23.7 | 14.7 | 16.2 | 17.3 | 13.9 |
| Lumber and wood products | 14.9 | 22.9 | 22.7 | 11.9 | 18.4 | 44.6 | 52.0 | 49.6 | 51.5 | 39.9 |
| Furniture and fixtures | 0.1 | 0.1 | 0.8 | 0.2 | 0.8 | 4.3 | 3.6 | 4.6 | 5.2 | 6.9 |
| Paper products | 37.6 | 45.7 | 79.5 | 59.1 | 73.0 | 105.0 | 178.7 | 316.4 | 228.7 | 171.1 |
| Printing and publishing | 0.6 | 3.6 | 1.2 | 4.5 | 3.2 | 1.6 | 2.6 | 2.8 | 8.2 | 8.9 |
| Chemical products | 10.9 | 8.5 | 13.4 | 12.0 | 70.3 | 103.9 | 130.4 | 139.6 | 181.3 | 381.3 |
| Refined petroleum products | 1.5 | 1.6 | 1.9 | 1.4 | 1.7 | 11.3 | 9.8 | 11.9 | 22.3 | 27.7 |
| Rubber and plastic products | 6.6 | 7.8 | 6.1 | 5.0 | 1.9 | 23.2 | 15.8 | 22.5 | 32.8 | 42.3 |
| Leather products | ..... | 0.5 | 0.6 | 0.1 | 0.2 | 2.4 | 1.3 | 2.6 | 1.6 | 1.6 |
| Stone, clay and glass products | 1.1 | 2.0 | 2.8 | 2.3 | 0.6 | 6.1 | 8.5 | 5.8 | 6.8 | 7.1 |
| Primary metals | 0.5 | 1.0 | 0.4 | 0.6 | 3.3 | 107.9 | 82.7 | 106.8 | 133.7 | 125.8 |
| Fabricated metal products | 0.5 | 1.5 | 0.7 | 1.0 | 1.1 | 17.9 | 22.1 | 38.4 | 24.1 | 25.5 |
| Industrial machinery and computers | 28.1 | 27.3 | 37.3 | 45.7 | 58.6 | 133.7 | 158.8 | 179.0 | 166.1 | 187.3 |
| Electric and electronic equipment | 8.0 | 6.2 | 13.1 | 6.0 | 13.9 | 99.2 | 104.7 | 144.6 | 216.5 | 262.3 |
| Transportation equipment | 15.3 | 61.9 | 23.4 | 28.7 | 41.4 | 170.0 | 103.7 | 347.2 | 93.6 | 127.2 |
| Scientific and measuring instruments | 3.6 | 8.4 | 2.9 | 2.8 | 10.5 | 32.3 | 39.8 | 45.8 | 78.9 | 117.8 |
| Miscellaneous manufactures | 0.5 | 1.2 | 0.8 | 0.9 | 2.3 | 19.3 | 13.8 | 14.0 | 17.0 | 18.2 |
| Unidentified manufactures | 0.5 | 0.3 | 0.5 | 0.3 | 0.2 | 2.5 | 2.6 | 2.8 | 2.5 | 2.8 |
| **Agricultural and livestock products** | 16.7 | 13.4 | 29.9 | 12.9 | 31.9 | 4.2 | 6.4 | 13.6 | 14.6 | 25.0 |
| Agricultural products | 16.7 | 13.4 | 29.9 | 11.7 | 29.5 | 1.9 | 5.9 | 10.2 | 12.3 | 24.0 |
| Livestock and livestock products | ..... | ..... | ..... | 1.1 | 2.4 | 2.2 | 0.5 | 3.5 | 2.3 | 1.0 |
| **Other commodities** | 12.8 | 11.5 | 22.8 | 26.6 | 27.3 | 81.1 | 94.4 | 105.0 | 104.9 | 106.0 |
| Forestry products | ..... | ..... | ..... | ..... | ..... | 0.1 | 0.6 | 0.7 | 0.8 | 0.4 |
| Fish and other marine products | ..... | ..... | ..... | ..... | ..... | 0.4 | 0.7 | 2.4 | 0.5 | 1.6 |
| Metallic ores and concentrates | ..... | ..... | 0.5 | 0.1 | 0.1 | ..... | ..... | ..... | ..... | ..... |
| Bituminous coal and lignite | ..... | ..... | ..... | ..... | ..... | ..... | ..... | ..... | ..... | ..... |
| Crude petroleum and natural gas | ..... | ..... | ..... | ..... | ..... | ..... | ..... | ..... | ..... | ..... |
| Nonmetallic minerals | 11.9 | 10.2 | 18.3 | 23.7 | 25.1 | 71.6 | 75.6 | 81.0 | 86.7 | 87.4 |
| Scrap and waste | 0.4 | 0.8 | 3.4 | 2.6 | 1.4 | 5.8 | 15.6 | 19.2 | 9.4 | 10.7 |
| Used merchandise | 0.1 | 0.1 | 0.4 | 0.1 | 0.4 | 0.3 | 1.0 | 0.5 | 1.6 | 2.9 |
| Goods imported and returned unchanged | ..... | ..... | ..... | ..... | ..... | ..... | ..... | ..... | ..... | ..... |
| Special classification provisions | 0.4 | 0.4 | 0.2 | 0.1 | 0.3 | 2.8 | 0.9 | 1.2 | 5.8 | 3.0 |

## Table D-3.  State Exports of Goods by Destination and Industry, 1993–1997 —*Continued*

**GEORGIA** (Millions of dollars.)

| Industry | 1993 | 1994 | 1995 | 1996 | 1997 | 1993 | 1994 | 1995 | 1996 | 1997 |
|---|---|---|---|---|---|---|---|---|---|---|
| | Japan | | | | | South Korea | | | | |
| **ALL GOODS** | 419.0 | 401.8 | 589.8 | 567.6 | 622.3 | 105.5 | 174.1 | 429.1 | 236.5 | 253.5 |
| **Manufactured goods** | 376.4 | 358.2 | 540.4 | 512.7 | 558.5 | 90.3 | 155.4 | 410.0 | 217.8 | 235.0 |
| Food products | 28.4 | 25.2 | 46.9 | 44.7 | 20.8 | 0.6 | 2.5 | 4.5 | 4.8 | 3.0 |
| Tobacco products | ..... | 0.1 | 0.2 | 0.2 | 0.2 | ..... | ..... | ..... | ..... | ..... |
| Textile mill products | 20.1 | 18.5 | 20.7 | 16.3 | 15.4 | 15.7 | 17.2 | 7.5 | 5.7 | 4.4 |
| Apparel | 10.6 | 5.7 | 9.8 | 7.3 | 6.4 | 0.1 | 0.1 | 0.6 | 0.6 | 0.5 |
| Lumber and wood products | 17.9 | 25.7 | 26.8 | 29.9 | 17.9 | 3.8 | 2.8 | 1.3 | 0.6 | 3.1 |
| Furniture and fixtures | 1.0 | 1.0 | 2.1 | 2.1 | 3.5 | 0.1 | 0.5 | 0.1 | 0.4 | 0.6 |
| Paper products | 29.8 | 65.8 | 131.8 | 83.2 | 63.3 | 15.1 | 48.1 | 89.4 | 53.7 | 32.9 |
| Printing and publishing | 0.7 | 1.0 | 1.1 | 4.6 | 5.1 | ..... | ..... | 0.1 | 0.1 | 0.1 |
| Chemical products | 15.9 | 16.5 | 18.4 | 16.3 | 103.3 | 17.7 | 13.4 | 22.9 | 75.4 | 115.1 |
| Refined petroleum products | 0.3 | 0.1 | 0.2 | 0.2 | 0.1 | ..... | ..... | ..... | 0.1 | |
| Rubber and plastic products | 15.9 | 9.6 | 16.2 | 21.2 | 29.4 | 2.3 | 0.2 | 1.0 | 0.6 | 2.7 |
| Leather products | 1.5 | 0.5 | 0.2 | 0.5 | 0.7 | 0.1 | 0.3 | 1.9 | 0.1 | 0.1 |
| Stone, clay and glass products | 0.9 | 1.5 | 1.4 | 1.5 | 2.4 | 0.4 | 1.4 | 0.6 | 0.7 | 0.6 |
| Primary metals | 82.5 | 77.8 | 91.3 | 109.0 | 90.5 | 0.3 | 0.5 | 1.0 | 9.2 | 9.2 |
| Fabricated metal products | 9.5 | 15.6 | 14.2 | 7.7 | 7.6 | 1.4 | 0.8 | 2.6 | 1.2 | 1.7 |
| Industrial machinery and computers | 41.9 | 41.1 | 39.0 | 38.9 | 45.0 | 10.1 | 9.3 | 20.8 | 29.1 | 18.7 |
| Electric and electronic equipment | 31.2 | 19.8 | 36.1 | 69.7 | 52.4 | 5.2 | 23.1 | 20.3 | 12.7 | 13.8 |
| Transportation equipment | 46.5 | 13.9 | 62.7 | 31.4 | 54.6 | 4.8 | 22.5 | 226.4 | 5.5 | 9.7 |
| Scientific and measuring instruments | 7.5 | 9.1 | 12.7 | 20.2 | 31.8 | 9.2 | 9.8 | 6.4 | 12.1 | 16.0 |
| Miscellaneous manufactures | 13.1 | 8.8 | 7.3 | 7.0 | 7.7 | 3.0 | 2.2 | 2.4 | 4.8 | 2.7 |
| Unidentified manufactures | 0.9 | 1.1 | 1.1 | 0.6 | 0.6 | 0.4 | 0.3 | 0.2 | 0.3 | 0.3 |
| **Agricultural and livestock products** | 1.3 | 0.9 | 2.3 | 5.4 | 15.4 | ..... | 0.1 | 0.3 | 0.1 | 0.2 |
| Agricultural products | 1.3 | 0.9 | 2.3 | 5.3 | 15.1 | ..... | 0.1 | 0.3 | 0.1 | 0.2 |
| Livestock and livestock products | ..... | ..... | ..... | 0.1 | 0.3 | ..... | | | | |
| **Other commodities** | 41.3 | 42.7 | 47.2 | 49.5 | 48.4 | 15.2 | 18.5 | 18.7 | 18.6 | 18.4 |
| Forestry products | ..... | 0.1 | 0.5 | 0.3 | 0.1 | ..... | ..... | ..... | ..... | ..... |
| Fish and other marine products | 0.4 | 0.3 | 0.9 | 0.1 | 0.3 | ..... | ..... | ..... | 0.2 | 0.2 |
| Metallic ores and concentrates | ..... | ..... | ..... | ..... | ..... | ..... | ..... | ..... | ..... | ..... |
| Bituminous coal and lignite | ..... | ..... | ..... | ..... | ..... | ..... | ..... | ..... | ..... | ..... |
| Crude petroleum and natural gas | ..... | ..... | ..... | ..... | ..... | ..... | ..... | ..... | ..... | ..... |
| Nonmetallic minerals | 39.3 | 39.9 | 45.1 | 47.7 | 46.8 | 13.7 | 15.7 | 15.1 | 13.7 | 15.4 |
| Scrap and waste | 1.2 | 1.8 | 0.2 | 0.9 | ..... | 1.1 | 2.7 | 3.4 | 1.3 | 1.2 |
| Used merchandise | 0.1 | 0.5 | 0.2 | 0.2 | 0.7 | ..... | 0.1 | ..... | ..... | 0.4 |
| Goods imported and returned unchanged | ..... | ..... | ..... | ..... | ..... | ..... | ..... | ..... | ..... | ..... |
| Special classification provisions | 0.2 | 0.1 | 0.1 | 0.3 | 0.3 | 0.3 | ..... | 0.1 | 3.4 | 1.1 |
| | Taiwan | | | | | Singapore | | | | |
| **ALL GOODS** | 143.9 | 138.9 | 138.8 | 120.9 | 136.4 | 92.2 | 92.8 | 134.3 | 158.2 | 213.3 |
| **Manufactured goods** | 129.7 | 118.3 | 119.1 | 106.1 | 116.7 | 91.4 | 92.4 | 133.8 | 157.6 | 212.5 |
| Food products | 1.0 | 1.8 | 1.4 | 2.8 | 1.6 | 8.0 | 10.8 | 13.6 | 10.0 | 7.5 |
| Tobacco products | ..... | ..... | ..... | ..... | ..... | 0.3 | 0.1 | ..... | ..... | ..... |
| Textile mill products | 8.7 | 11.8 | 3.8 | 4.0 | 4.5 | 25.5 | 25.6 | 26.6 | 24.8 | 24.9 |
| Apparel | 0.2 | 0.4 | 0.4 | 0.1 | 0.3 | 0.6 | 0.6 | 0.8 | 1.1 | 1.1 |
| Lumber and wood products | 18.2 | 16.4 | 10.8 | 6.5 | 6.7 | 0.1 | 0.2 | ..... | ..... | ..... |
| Furniture and fixtures | 2.2 | 0.9 | 0.4 | 0.3 | 0.1 | 0.1 | 0.2 | 0.8 | 1.3 | 1.9 |
| Paper products | 7.5 | 15.5 | 28.5 | 16.5 | 17.5 | 1.1 | 1.1 | 5.1 | 5.6 | 4.8 |
| Printing and publishing | 0.1 | 0.2 | 0.7 | 1.0 | 0.6 | 0.5 | 0.4 | 0.4 | 1.2 | 1.4 |
| Chemical products | 20.9 | 14.9 | 20.2 | 29.0 | 41.7 | 3.2 | 2.4 | 4.7 | 5.6 | 8.6 |
| Refined petroleum products | 0.1 | ..... | 0.1 | ..... | 0.1 | 1.5 | ..... | 1.1 | 5.7 | 0.4 |
| Rubber and plastic products | 0.7 | 0.4 | 0.7 | 1.4 | 0.9 | 1.0 | 0.9 | 1.2 | 2.8 | 4.7 |
| Leather products | ..... | ..... | ..... | 0.1 | ..... | ..... | ..... | 0.1 | ..... | 0.1 |
| Stone, clay and glass products | 1.0 | 0.8 | 0.4 | 1.4 | 0.6 | 1.3 | 0.2 | 0.4 | 0.1 | 0.5 |
| Primary metals | 19.0 | 0.8 | 1.6 | 1.2 | 3.3 | 0.6 | 0.5 | 1.8 | 1.5 | 1.7 |
| Fabricated metal products | 0.8 | 1.8 | 1.4 | 1.6 | 1.5 | 2.3 | 1.9 | 0.8 | 2.1 | 3.8 |
| Industrial machinery and computers | 31.1 | 32.8 | 24.4 | 18.3 | 15.4 | 18.4 | 12.1 | 17.6 | 15.0 | 26.5 |
| Electric and electronic equipment | 10.7 | 11.6 | 17.3 | 10.7 | 14.7 | 10.8 | 10.9 | 10.0 | 21.0 | 27.1 |
| Transportation equipment | 2.0 | 2.3 | 1.5 | 5.8 | 1.3 | 11.1 | 18.7 | 38.1 | 30.8 | 46.8 |
| Scientific and measuring instruments | 4.5 | 4.5 | 3.5 | 4.5 | 5.1 | 3.7 | 4.9 | 10.0 | 27.9 | 49.7 |
| Miscellaneous manufactures | 0.7 | 0.9 | 1.6 | 0.8 | 0.6 | 0.7 | 0.7 | 0.5 | 0.5 | 0.5 |
| Unidentified manufactures | 0.3 | 0.4 | 0.4 | 0.2 | 0.2 | 0.3 | 0.3 | 0.3 | 0.3 | 0.3 |
| **Agricultural and livestock products** | 0.1 | 0.1 | 0.1 | 1.1 | 1.9 | 0.1 | 0.1 | ..... | ..... | 0.1 |
| Agricultural products | 0.1 | 0.1 | 0.1 | 1.1 | 1.9 | 0.1 | 0.1 | ..... | ..... | 0.1 |
| Livestock and livestock products | ..... | ..... | ..... | ..... | ..... | ..... | ..... | ..... | ..... | ..... |
| **Other commodities** | 14.1 | 20.5 | 19.6 | 13.7 | 17.8 | 0.7 | 0.3 | 0.5 | 0.6 | 0.7 |
| Forestry products | ..... | ..... | ..... | 0.1 | ..... | ..... | ..... | ..... | 0.1 | ..... |
| Fish and other marine products | ..... | ..... | ..... | ..... | 0.1 | ..... | 0.2 | 0.2 | 0.1 | 0.2 |
| Metallic ores and concentrates | ..... | ..... | ..... | ..... | ..... | ..... | ..... | ..... | ..... | ..... |
| Bituminous coal and lignite | ..... | ..... | ..... | ..... | ..... | ..... | ..... | ..... | ..... | ..... |
| Crude petroleum and natural gas | ..... | ..... | ..... | ..... | ..... | ..... | ..... | ..... | ..... | ..... |
| Nonmetallic minerals | 11.0 | 10.8 | 11.3 | 8.4 | 11.7 | 0.4 | ..... | ..... | ..... | 0.3 |
| Scrap and waste | 2.9 | 9.5 | 8.2 | 4.7 | 5.1 | ..... | ..... | ..... | ..... | ..... |
| Used merchandise | ..... | 0.1 | ..... | ..... | ..... | ..... | ..... | ..... | 0.1 | 0.1 |
| Goods imported and returned unchanged | ..... | ..... | ..... | ..... | ..... | ..... | ..... | ..... | ..... | ..... |
| Special classification provisions | 0.1 | ..... | ..... | 0.5 | 0.9 | 0.3 | 0.1 | 0.2 | 0.3 | 0.1 |

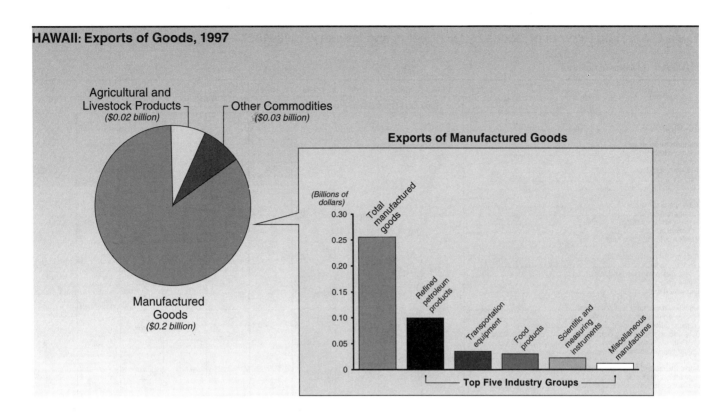

HAWAII: Exports of Goods, 1997

Agricultural and Livestock Products ($0.02 billion)

Other Commodities ($0.03 billion)

Manufactured Goods ($0.2 billion)

Exports of Manufactured Goods

Top Five Industry Groups

## Table D-3.   State Exports of Goods by Destination and Industry, 1993–1997 —*Continued*

**HAWAII** (Millions of dollars.)

| Industry | 1993 | 1994 | 1995 | 1996 | 1997 | 1993 | 1994 | 1995 | 1996 | 1997 |
|---|---|---|---|---|---|---|---|---|---|---|
| | All destinations | | | | | Canada | | | | |
| **ALL GOODS** | 216.8 | 237.4 | 255.7 | 295.2 | 303.2 | 13.6 | 13.4 | 53.1 | 69.8 | 33.3 |
| **Manufactured goods** | 171.7 | 183.0 | 210.6 | 247.3 | 255.8 | 5.4 | 4.2 | 43.6 | 59.2 | 22.5 |
| Food products | 46.0 | 44.1 | 35.7 | 35.6 | 30.5 | 1.8 | 1.6 | 5.4 | 8.0 | 3.4 |
| Tobacco products | 0.1 | ..... | ..... | 0.1 | | | | | 0.1 | ..... |
| Textile mill products | 1.0 | 0.4 | 1.0 | 1.3 | 1.3 | ..... | ..... | 0.1 | 0.3 | ..... |
| Apparel | 10.1 | 8.0 | 13.3 | 11.8 | 9.2 | ..... | ..... | 0.2 | 0.1 | ..... |
| Lumber and wood products | 1.7 | 0.4 | 3.7 | 4.1 | 2.5 | ..... | ..... | 2.9 | 3.8 | 1.5 |
| Furniture and fixtures | 2.6 | 3.4 | 1.7 | 2.4 | 0.8 | ..... | ..... | 0.2 | 0.6 | 0.1 |
| Paper products | 0.7 | 0.4 | 3.7 | 4.5 | 1.6 | ..... | ..... | 2.3 | 3.5 | 1.0 |
| Printing and publishing | 9.5 | 12.2 | 4.4 | 4.5 | 3.0 | ..... | ..... | 0.3 | 0.5 | ..... |
| Chemical products | 3.6 | 5.1 | 6.0 | 15.1 | 6.5 | 0.1 | 0.1 | 2.9 | 8.7 | 2.3 |
| Refined petroleum products | 18.7 | 49.7 | 50.4 | 70.8 | 99.5 | ..... | ..... | 0.4 | 0.9 | 0.2 |
| Rubber and plastic products | 0.4 | 0.4 | 1.1 | 2.1 | 1.3 | ..... | ..... | 0.5 | 1.6 | 0.7 |
| Leather products | 1.9 | 4.9 | 4.0 | 3.4 | 2.8 | ..... | ..... | ..... | 0.2 | ..... |
| Stone, clay and glass products | 0.6 | 0.6 | 1.9 | 1.3 | 0.8 | ..... | ..... | 0.4 | 0.7 | 0.3 |
| Primary metals | 1.4 | 0.8 | 3.1 | 6.5 | 1.8 | ..... | ..... | 2.6 | 5.7 | 1.4 |
| Fabricated metal products | 0.7 | 1.5 | 2.5 | 2.1 | 1.2 | ..... | ..... | 1.3 | 1.3 | 0.2 |
| Industrial machinery and computers | 8.4 | 9.2 | 10.3 | 13.7 | 11.0 | 0.4 | 0.2 | 5.4 | 7.4 | 2.6 |
| Electric and electronic equipment | 5.8 | 5.7 | 14.7 | 13.3 | 9.4 | 0.1 | 0.3 | 7.9 | 4.2 | 1.1 |
| Transportation equipment | 40.5 | 14.9 | 19.5 | 20.7 | 35.2 | 2.1 | 0.8 | 8.5 | 8.7 | 5.1 |
| Scientific and measuring instruments | 8.5 | 10.9 | 16.9 | 17.8 | 22.9 | 0.3 | 0.5 | 1.3 | 2.0 | 1.7 |
| Miscellaneous manufactures | 7.4 | 7.7 | 13.9 | 14.1 | 12.3 | ..... | 0.1 | 0.4 | 0.2 | 0.1 |
| Unidentified manufactures | 2.2 | 2.7 | 3.0 | 2.2 | 2.4 | 0.3 | 0.5 | 0.6 | 0.7 | 0.8 |
| **Agricultural and livestock products** | 18.8 | 21.6 | 27.6 | 25.9 | 22.2 | 6.2 | 5.8 | 4.8 | 2.3 | 2.0 |
| Agricultural products | 15.9 | 18.2 | 23.8 | 24.0 | 21.1 | 3.6 | 2.7 | 1.8 | 1.8 | 1.7 |
| Livestock and livestock products | 2.9 | 3.5 | 3.7 | 1.9 | 1.1 | 2.6 | 3.1 | 3.0 | 0.6 | 0.3 |
| **Other commodities** | 26.3 | 32.7 | 17.5 | 22.0 | 25.2 | 1.9 | 3.4 | 4.6 | 8.2 | 8.8 |
| Forestry products | 0.2 | 0.1 | 0.1 | 0.1 | 0.1 | ..... | ..... | ..... | ..... | ..... |
| Fish and other marine products | 5.7 | 7.4 | 7.2 | 5.3 | 4.1 | ..... | 0.5 | 1.2 | 2.4 | 1.4 |
| Metallic ores and concentrates | ..... | ..... | ..... | ..... | ..... | ..... | ..... | ..... | ..... | ..... |
| Bituminous coal and lignite | ..... | ..... | ..... | ..... | ..... | ..... | ..... | ..... | ..... | ..... |
| Crude petroleum and natural gas | ..... | ..... | ..... | ..... | | | | | | |
| Nonmetallic minerals | ..... | 0.1 | 0.1 | 0.1 | 0.1 | ..... | ..... | 0.1 | 0.1 | 0.1 |
| Scrap and waste | 2.3 | 1.6 | 0.7 | 2.8 | 0.4 | ..... | ..... | 0.1 | 0.3 | ..... |
| Used merchandise | 16.3 | 21.0 | 6.6 | 8.3 | 14.1 | 0.4 | 0.7 | 0.6 | 0.5 | 1.3 |
| Goods imported and returned unchanged | 1.4 | 2.2 | 2.3 | 4.6 | 5.9 | 1.4 | 2.2 | 2.3 | 4.6 | 5.9 |
| Special classification provisions | 0.3 | 0.4 | 0.4 | 0.8 | 0.4 | ..... | ..... | 0.2 | 0.4 | 0.1 |

## Table D-3.    State Exports of Goods by Destination and Industry, 1993–1997 —*Continued*

**HAWAII** (Millions of dollars.)

| Industry | 1993 | 1994 | 1995 | 1996 | 1997 | 1993 | 1994 | 1995 | 1996 | 1997 |
|---|---|---|---|---|---|---|---|---|---|---|
| | South and Central America and Caribbean | | | | | Mexico | | | | |
| **ALL GOODS** | 0.7 | 0.7 | 0.7 | 1.3 | 1 1 | 0.3 | 6.0 | 0.3 | 0.7 | 1.0 |
| **Manufactured goods** | 0.6 | 0.5 | 0.6 | 1.2 | 1.1 | 0.3 | 5.9 | 0.2 | 0.5 | 0.8 |
| Food products | ..... | ..... | ..... | ..... | 0.1 | ..... | ..... | ..... | ..... | ..... |
| Tobacco products | ..... | ..... | ..... | ..... | ..... | ..... | ..... | ..... | ..... | ..... |
| Textile mill products | ..... | ..... | ..... | ..... | ..... | ..... | ..... | ..... | 0.3 | 0.2 |
| Apparel | 0.1 | 0.2 | 0.1 | 0.1 | 0.1 | ..... | ..... | ..... | ..... | 0.1 |
| Lumber and wood products | ..... | ..... | ..... | ..... | ..... | ..... | ..... | ..... | ..... | ..... |
| Furniture and fixtures | ..... | ..... | ..... | ..... | ..... | ..... | ..... | ..... | ..... | ..... |
| Paper products | ..... | ..... | ..... | 0.1 | 0.1 | ..... | ..... | ..... | ..... | ..... |
| Printing and publishing | ..... | ..... | ..... | ..... | ..... | ..... | ..... | ..... | ..... | ..... |
| Chemical products | ..... | 0.1 | ..... | ..... | ..... | ..... | ..... | ..... | ..... | ..... |
| Refined petroleum products | ..... | ..... | ..... | ..... | ..... | ..... | ..... | ..... | ..... | ..... |
| Rubber and plastic products | ..... | ..... | ..... | 0.1 | 0.1 | ..... | ..... | ..... | ..... | ..... |
| Leather products | ..... | ..... | ..... | ..... | 0.1 | ..... | ..... | ..... | ..... | ..... |
| Stone, clay and glass products | ..... | ..... | ..... | ..... | ..... | ..... | ..... | ..... | ..... | ..... |
| Primary metals | ..... | ..... | ..... | 0.2 | ..... | ..... | ..... | ..... | ..... | ..... |
| Fabricated metal products | ..... | ..... | 0.1 | ..... | ..... | ..... | ..... | 0.1 | ..... | ..... |
| Industrial machinery and computers | ..... | 0.1 | ..... | ..... | 0.1 | 0.2 | 0.3 | ..... | 0.1 | 0.1 |
| Electric and electronic equipment | ..... | ..... | ..... | ..... | ..... | ..... | 0.1 | ..... | ..... | ..... |
| Transportation equipment | 0.1 | ..... | ..... | 0.5 | 0.1 | ..... | 5.4 | ..... | ..... | ..... |
| Scientific and measuring instruments | ..... | ..... | ..... | ..... | ..... | ..... | ..... | ..... | ..... | 0.3 |
| Miscellaneous manufactures | 0.3 | 0.2 | 0.2 | 0.2 | 0.3 | ..... | ..... | ..... | ..... | 0.1 |
| Unidentified manufactures | ..... | ..... | ..... | ..... | ..... | ..... | ..... | ..... | ..... | ..... |
| **Agricultural and livestock products** | ..... | ..... | 0.1 | ..... | ..... | ..... | ..... | ..... | 0.2 | ..... |
| Agricultural products | ..... | ..... | ..... | ..... | ..... | ..... | ..... | ..... | 0.2 | ..... |
| Livestock and livestock products | ..... | ..... | ..... | ..... | ..... | ..... | ..... | ..... | ..... | ..... |
| **Other commodities** | 0.1 | 0.1 | 0.2 | ..... | ..... | ..... | 0.1 | ..... | ..... | 0.2 |
| Forestry products | ..... | ..... | ..... | ..... | ..... | ..... | ..... | ..... | ..... | ..... |
| Fish and other marine products | ..... | 0.1 | 0.2 | ..... | 0.1 | ..... | ..... | ..... | ..... | 0.1 |
| Metallic ores and concentrates | ..... | ..... | ..... | ..... | ..... | ..... | ..... | ..... | ..... | ..... |
| Bituminous coal and lignite | ..... | ..... | ..... | ..... | ..... | ..... | ..... | ..... | ..... | ..... |
| Crude petroleum and natural gas | ..... | ..... | ..... | ..... | ..... | ..... | ..... | ..... | ..... | ..... |
| Nonmetallic minerals | ..... | ..... | ..... | ..... | ..... | ..... | ..... | ..... | ..... | ..... |
| Scrap and waste | ..... | ..... | ..... | ..... | ..... | ..... | ..... | ..... | ..... | ..... |
| Used merchandise | ..... | 0.1 | ..... | ..... | ..... | ..... | ..... | ..... | ..... | ..... |
| Goods imported and returned unchanged | ..... | ..... | ..... | ..... | ..... | ..... | ..... | ..... | ..... | ..... |
| Special classification provisions | ..... | ..... | ..... | ..... | ..... | ..... | ..... | ..... | ..... | ..... |
| | European Union | | | | | United Kingdom | | | | |
| **ALL GOODS** | 8.3 | 6.5 | 7.8 | 9.4 | 7.1 | 3.3 | 0.9 | 1.1 | 2.9 | 2.0 |
| **Manufactured goods** | 6.4 | 3.9 | 5.3 | 6.0 | 5.6 | 3.2 | 0.5 | 0.9 | 1.2 | 1.8 |
| Food products | 0.4 | 0.1 | 0.1 | 0.5 | 0.1 | 0.1 | ..... | ..... | ..... | ..... |
| Tobacco products | ..... | ..... | ..... | ..... | ..... | ..... | ..... | ..... | ..... | ..... |
| Textile mill products | ..... | ..... | ..... | ..... | ..... | ..... | ..... | ..... | ..... | ..... |
| Apparel | 0.3 | 0.3 | 0.4 | 0.4 | 0.2 | ..... | ..... | 0.1 | ..... | ..... |
| Lumber and wood products | ..... | ..... | ..... | ..... | ..... | ..... | ..... | ..... | ..... | ..... |
| Furniture and fixtures | ..... | ..... | ..... | ..... | ..... | ..... | ..... | ..... | ..... | ..... |
| Paper products | ..... | ..... | 0.1 | ..... | ..... | ..... | ..... | ..... | ..... | ..... |
| Printing and publishing | ..... | ..... | 0.1 | ..... | 0.3 | ..... | ..... | ..... | ..... | ..... |
| Chemical products | 0.2 | 0.1 | 0.1 | 0.4 | 0.1 | ..... | ..... | 0.1 | 0.3 | ..... |
| Refined petroleum products | ..... | ..... | ..... | ..... | ..... | ..... | ..... | ..... | ..... | ..... |
| Rubber and plastic products | ..... | ..... | ..... | ..... | ..... | ..... | ..... | ..... | ..... | ..... |
| Leather products | 0.2 | 0.2 | 0.1 | 0.1 | 0.5 | ..... | ..... | ..... | ..... | ..... |
| Stone, clay and glass products | ..... | ..... | 0.4 | ..... | 0.1 | ..... | ..... | ..... | ..... | ..... |
| Primary metals | ..... | ..... | ..... | ..... | ..... | ..... | ..... | ..... | ..... | ..... |
| Fabricated metal products | ..... | ..... | ..... | 0.1 | 0.1 | ..... | ..... | ..... | ..... | 0.1 |
| Industrial machinery and computers | 0.2 | 0.3 | 0.3 | 0.6 | 0.3 | 0.1 | ..... | 0.3 | ..... | 0.3 |
| Electric and electronic equipment | 0.1 | 0.2 | 0.5 | 0.7 | 1.3 | 0.1 | 0.1 | 0.1 | 0.1 | 0.5 |
| Transportation equipment | 3.3 | 1.4 | 1.5 | 0.6 | 0.2 | 2.4 | ..... | ..... | ..... | 0.1 |
| Scientific and measuring instruments | 1.0 | 0.7 | 1.2 | 1.9 | 1.6 | 0.3 | 0.2 | 0.2 | 0.5 | 0.7 |
| Miscellaneous manufactures | 0.3 | 0.4 | 0.4 | 0.3 | 0.6 | ..... | 0.1 | 0.1 | 0.1 | 0.1 |
| Unidentified manufactures | 0.2 | 0.1 | 0.1 | 0.1 | 0.1 | ..... | ..... | ..... | ..... | ..... |
| **Agricultural and livestock products** | 1.3 | 1.6 | 1.8 | 1.5 | 0.8 | 0.1 | 0.1 | 0.1 | 0.1 | 0.1 |
| Agricultural products | 1.2 | 1.5 | 1.6 | 1.2 | 0.6 | ..... | ..... | ..... | 0.1 | ..... |
| Livestock and livestock products | 0.1 | 0.1 | 0.2 | 0.2 | 0.2 | 0.1 | 0.1 | 0.1 | 0.1 | ..... |
| **Other commodities** | 0.6 | 1.0 | 0.7 | 1.9 | 0.7 | 0.1 | 0.4 | 0.2 | 1.5 | 0.2 |
| Forestry products | ..... | ..... | ..... | ..... | ..... | ..... | ..... | ..... | ..... | ..... |
| Fish and other marine products | 0.1 | 0.4 | 0.4 | 0.2 | 0.2 | ..... | ..... | ..... | 0.1 | 0.1 |
| Metallic ores and concentrates | ..... | ..... | ..... | ..... | ..... | ..... | ..... | ..... | ..... | ..... |
| Bituminous coal and lignite | ..... | ..... | ..... | ..... | ..... | ..... | ..... | ..... | ..... | ..... |
| Crude petroleum and natural gas | ..... | ..... | ..... | ..... | ..... | ..... | ..... | ..... | ..... | ..... |
| Nonmetallic minerals | ..... | ..... | ..... | ..... | ..... | ..... | ..... | ..... | ..... | ..... |
| Scrap and waste | ..... | ..... | ..... | ..... | ..... | ..... | ..... | ..... | ..... | ..... |
| Used merchandise | 0.5 | 0.6 | 0.3 | 1.7 | 0.4 | 0.1 | 0.4 | 0.1 | 1.5 | 0.1 |
| Goods imported and returned unchanged | ..... | ..... | ..... | ..... | ..... | ..... | ..... | ..... | ..... | ..... |
| Special classification provisions | ..... | ..... | ..... | ..... | 0.1 | ..... | ..... | ..... | ..... | ..... |

## Table D-3.  State Exports of Goods by Destination and Industry, 1993–1997 —*Continued*

### HAWAII (Millions of dollars.)

| Industry | 1993 | 1994 | 1995 | 1996 | 1997 | 1993 | 1994 | 1995 | 1996 | 1997 |
|---|---|---|---|---|---|---|---|---|---|---|
| | Germany | | | | | France | | | | |
| **ALL GOODS** | 2.4 | 2.3 | 2.4 | 2.5 | 1.4 | 1.2 | 1.6 | 1.9 | 1.5 | 1.3 |
| **Manufactured goods** | 1.2 | 1.2 | 1.3 | 1.5 | 0.7 | 1.1 | 1.5 | 1.9 | 1.5 | 1.1 |
| Food products | ..... | ..... | ..... | 0.4 | 0.1 | 0.1 | ..... | 0.1 | 0.1 | ..... |
| Tobacco products | ..... | ..... | ..... | ..... | ..... | ..... | ..... | ..... | ..... | ..... |
| Textile mill products | ..... | ..... | ..... | ..... | ..... | ..... | ..... | ..... | ..... | ..... |
| Apparel | ..... | ..... | 0.1 | 0.1 | ..... | ..... | ..... | 0.1 | 0.1 | ..... |
| Lumber and wood products | ..... | ..... | ..... | ..... | ..... | ..... | ..... | ..... | ..... | ..... |
| Furniture and fixtures | ..... | ..... | ..... | ..... | ..... | ..... | ..... | ..... | ..... | ..... |
| Paper products | ..... | ..... | ..... | ..... | ..... | ..... | ..... | ..... | ..... | ..... |
| Printing and publishing | ..... | ..... | ..... | ..... | ..... | ..... | ..... | ..... | ..... | 0.2 |
| Chemical products | ..... | ..... | ..... | ..... | ..... | 0.1 | 0.1 | ..... | 0.1 | ..... |
| Refined petroleum products | ..... | ..... | ..... | ..... | ..... | ..... | ..... | ..... | ..... | ..... |
| Rubber and plastic products | ..... | ..... | ..... | ..... | ..... | ..... | ..... | ..... | ..... | ..... |
| Leather products | ..... | ..... | ..... | ..... | ..... | 0.2 | 0.2 | ..... | 0.1 | 0.1 |
| Stone, clay and glass products | ..... | ..... | ..... | ..... | ..... | ..... | ..... | ..... | ..... | ..... |
| Primary metals | ..... | ..... | ..... | ..... | ..... | ..... | ..... | ..... | ..... | ..... |
| Fabricated metal products | ..... | ..... | ..... | ..... | ..... | ..... | ..... | ..... | ..... | ..... |
| Industrial machinery and computers | ..... | 0.2 | ..... | 0.6 | ..... | 0.1 | ..... | ..... | ..... | ..... |
| Electric and electronic equipment | ..... | 0.1 | 0.3 | 0.1 | 0.1 | ..... | ..... | 0.1 | 0.2 | 0.3 |
| Transportation equipment | 0.8 | 0.7 | 0.5 | ..... | ..... | ..... | 0.6 | 0.8 | ..... | ..... |
| Scientific and measuring instruments | ..... | 0.1 | ..... | 0.1 | 0.3 | 0.5 | 0.3 | 0.7 | 0.7 | 0.2 |
| Miscellaneous manufactures | 0.1 | ..... | 0.1 | 0.1 | 0.1 | ..... | 0.2 | 0.1 | ..... | 0.1 |
| Unidentified manufactures | 0.1 | ..... | ..... | ..... | ..... | ..... | ..... | ..... | ..... | ..... |
| **Agricultural and livestock products** | 1.0 | 0.9 | 1.0 | 0.9 | 0.6 | ..... | 0.1 | ..... | ..... | 0.1 |
| Agricultural products | 1.0 | 0.9 | 0.9 | 0.8 | 0.5 | ..... | 0.1 | ..... | ..... | ..... |
| Livestock and livestock products | ..... | ..... | 0.1 | ..... | ..... | ..... | ..... | ..... | ..... | ..... |
| **Other commodities** | 0.3 | 0.2 | 0.2 | 0.2 | 0.1 | ..... | ..... | ..... | ..... | 0.1 |
| Forestry products | ..... | ..... | ..... | ..... | ..... | ..... | ..... | ..... | ..... | ..... |
| Fish and other marine products | ..... | ..... | ..... | ..... | ..... | ..... | ..... | ..... | ..... | ..... |
| Metallic ores and concentrates | ..... | ..... | ..... | ..... | ..... | ..... | ..... | ..... | ..... | ..... |
| Bituminous coal and lignite | ..... | ..... | ..... | ..... | ..... | ..... | ..... | ..... | ..... | ..... |
| Crude petroleum and natural gas | ..... | ..... | ..... | ..... | ..... | ..... | ..... | ..... | ..... | ..... |
| Nonmetallic minerals | ..... | ..... | ..... | ..... | ..... | ..... | ..... | ..... | ..... | ..... |
| Scrap and waste | ..... | ..... | ..... | ..... | ..... | ..... | ..... | ..... | ..... | ..... |
| Used merchandise | 0.2 | 0.1 | 0.2 | 0.2 | 0.1 | ..... | ..... | ..... | ..... | 0.1 |
| Goods imported and returned unchanged | ..... | ..... | ..... | ..... | ..... | ..... | ..... | ..... | ..... | ..... |
| Special classification provisions | ..... | ..... | ..... | ..... | ..... | ..... | ..... | ..... | ..... | ..... |

| Industry | 1993 | 1994 | 1995 | 1996 | 1997 | 1993 | 1994 | 1995 | 1996 | 1997 |
|---|---|---|---|---|---|---|---|---|---|---|
| | The Netherlands | | | | | Asian 10 | | | | |
| **ALL GOODS** | 0.7 | 0.8 | 1.1 | 1.5 | 0.4 | 169.6 | 180.0 | 170.8 | 190.8 | 217.2 |
| **Manufactured goods** | 0.3 | 0.2 | 0.3 | 1.1 | 0.2 | 135.4 | 138.9 | 139.5 | 158.3 | 183.6 |
| Food products | 0.2 | ..... | ..... | ..... | ..... | 40.5 | 39.6 | 27.7 | 25.5 | 25.7 |
| Tobacco products | ..... | ..... | ..... | ..... | ..... | ..... | ..... | ..... | ..... | ..... |
| Textile mill products | ..... | ..... | ..... | ..... | ..... | 0.6 | 0.4 | 0.6 | 0.6 | 0.6 |
| Apparel | ..... | ..... | ..... | ..... | ..... | 9.4 | 7.3 | 12.4 | 10.4 | 8.5 |
| Lumber and wood products | ..... | ..... | ..... | ..... | ..... | 1.5 | 0.3 | 0.7 | 0.2 | 0.5 |
| Furniture and fixtures | ..... | ..... | ..... | ..... | ..... | 2.4 | 3.3 | 1.4 | 1.4 | 0.6 |
| Paper products | ..... | ..... | ..... | ..... | ..... | 0.7 | 0.3 | 1.3 | 0.8 | 0.5 |
| Printing and publishing | ..... | ..... | ..... | ..... | ..... | 6.4 | 6.2 | 1.9 | 2.5 | 2.4 |
| Chemical products | ..... | ..... | ..... | ..... | ..... | 2.3 | 4.0 | 1.9 | 4.9 | 3.1 |
| Refined petroleum products | ..... | ..... | ..... | ..... | ..... | 11.5 | 38.8 | 45.5 | 65.0 | 92.1 |
| Rubber and plastic products | ..... | ..... | ..... | ..... | ..... | 0.1 | 0.2 | 0.5 | 0.3 | 0.3 |
| Leather products | ..... | ..... | ..... | ..... | ..... | 1.7 | 4.6 | 3.9 | 3.0 | 2.1 |
| Stone, clay and glass products | ..... | ..... | ..... | ..... | ..... | 0.5 | 0.4 | 0.7 | 0.5 | 0.4 |
| Primary metals | ..... | ..... | ..... | ..... | ..... | 0.7 | 0.7 | 0.5 | 0.6 | 0.2 |
| Fabricated metal products | ..... | ..... | ..... | 0.1 | ..... | 0.4 | 1.2 | 0.6 | 0.5 | 0.7 |
| Industrial machinery and computers | 0.1 | ..... | ..... | ..... | ..... | 5.7 | 6.5 | 2.3 | 3.7 | 6.7 |
| Electric and electronic equipment | ..... | ..... | 0.1 | 0.2 | ..... | 4.3 | 4.2 | 5.6 | 6.7 | 6.1 |
| Transportation equipment | ..... | ..... | 0.1 | 0.1 | 0.5 | 33.3 | 4.7 | 5.4 | 5.3 | 4.0 |
| Scientific and measuring instruments | ..... | ..... | ..... | 0.2 | ..... | 6.2 | 7.9 | 13.0 | 13.2 | 18.1 |
| Miscellaneous manufactures | ..... | ..... | ..... | ..... | ..... | 6.2 | 6.5 | 11.8 | 12.5 | 10.1 |
| Unidentified manufactures | ..... | ..... | ..... | ..... | ..... | 1.3 | 1.6 | 1.7 | 0.9 | 1.1 |
| **Agricultural and livestock products** | 0.2 | 0.3 | 0.4 | 0.3 | 0.1 | 11.0 | 13.6 | 20.4 | 21.2 | 19.0 |
| Agricultural products | 0.1 | 0.2 | 0.3 | 0.2 | 0.1 | 10.8 | 13.3 | 19.9 | 20.2 | 18.4 |
| Livestock and livestock products | 0.1 | 0.1 | 0.1 | 0.1 | ..... | 0.1 | 0.3 | 0.5 | 1.0 | 0.5 |
| **Other commodities** | 0.2 | 0.4 | 0.4 | 0.1 | 0.1 | 23.2 | 27.6 | 10.9 | 11.2 | 14.7 |
| Forestry products | ..... | ..... | ..... | ..... | ..... | 0.1 | 0.1 | ..... | 0.1 | ..... |
| Fish and other marine products | ..... | 0.4 | 0.4 | 0.1 | 0.1 | 5.5 | 6.3 | 5.4 | 2.8 | 2.3 |
| Metallic ores and concentrates | ..... | ..... | ..... | ..... | ..... | ..... | ..... | ..... | ..... | ..... |
| Bituminous coal and lignite | ..... | ..... | ..... | ..... | ..... | ..... | ..... | ..... | ..... | ..... |
| Crude petroleum and natural gas | ..... | ..... | ..... | ..... | ..... | ..... | ..... | ..... | ..... | ..... |
| Nonmetallic minerals | ..... | ..... | ..... | ..... | ..... | ..... | 0.1 | ..... | ..... | ..... |
| Scrap and waste | ..... | ..... | ..... | ..... | ..... | 2.3 | 1.6 | 0.6 | 2.5 | 0.4 |
| Used merchandise | 0.2 | ..... | ..... | ..... | 0.1 | 15.0 | 19.1 | 4.7 | 5.5 | 11.8 |
| Goods imported and returned unchanged | ..... | ..... | ..... | ..... | ..... | ..... | ..... | ..... | ..... | ..... |
| Special classification provisions | ..... | ..... | ..... | ..... | ..... | 0.3 | 0.4 | 0.2 | 0.4 | 0.2 |

## Table D-3.  State Exports of Goods by Destination and Industry, 1993–1997 —*Continued*

**HAWAII** (Millions of dollars.)

| Industry | 1993 | 1994 | 1995 | 1996 | 1997 | 1993 | 1994 | 1995 | 1996 | 1997 |
|---|---|---|---|---|---|---|---|---|---|---|
| | Japan | | | | | South Korea | | | | |
| **ALL GOODS** | 97.3 | 120.1 | 126.7 | 161.2 | 173.0 | 19.0 | 26.2 | 24.8 | 9.3 | 9.7 |
| **Manufactured goods** | 65.2 | 80.6 | 97.4 | 133.4 | 146.1 | 18.0 | 25.6 | 24.5 | 8.9 | 9.6 |
| Food products | 27.5 | 22.8 | 19.4 | 17.5 | 17.1 | 4.6 | 4.7 | 4.5 | 4.3 | 3.8 |
| Tobacco products | ..... | ..... | ..... | ..... | ..... | ..... | ..... | ..... | ..... | ..... |
| Textile mill products | 0.1 | 0.2 | 0.3 | 0.6 | 0.6 | ..... | ..... | ..... | ..... | ..... |
| Apparel | 9.3 | 7.0 | 12.1 | 10.0 | 7.9 | ..... | 0.1 | 0.2 | 0.1 | ..... |
| Lumber and wood products | 0.4 | 0.1 | 0.7 | 0.2 | 0.4 | ..... | ..... | ..... | ..... | ..... |
| Furniture and fixtures | 1.1 | 1.3 | 1.1 | 1.2 | 0.5 | ..... | 1.9 | ..... | ..... | ..... |
| Paper products | 0.6 | 0.3 | 0.9 | 0.6 | 0.4 | ..... | ..... | ..... | ..... | ..... |
| Printing and publishing | 6.1 | 6.0 | 1.7 | 2.3 | 2.0 | ..... | ..... | ..... | ..... | ..... |
| Chemical products | 1.3 | 2.2 | 1.1 | 4.4 | 2.0 | ..... | ..... | ..... | 0.1 | 0.1 |
| Refined petroleum products | ..... | 13.0 | 21.7 | 60.2 | 83.2 | 11.5 | 17.9 | 17.8 | ..... | ..... |
| Rubber and plastic products | 0.1 | 0.2 | 0.5 | 0.2 | 0.3 | ..... | ..... | ..... | ..... | ..... |
| Leather products | 1.6 | 4.4 | 3.8 | 2.8 | 2.1 | ..... | ..... | ..... | ..... | ..... |
| Stone, clay and glass products | 0.4 | 0.4 | 0.5 | 0.4 | 0.3 | ..... | ..... | ..... | ..... | ..... |
| Primary metals | 0.1 | ..... | 0.1 | 0.1 | 0.1 | ..... | ..... | ..... | ..... | ..... |
| Fabricated metal products | 0.1 | 1.1 | 0.5 | 0.4 | 0.4 | ..... | ..... | ..... | ..... | ..... |
| Industrial machinery and computers | 0.7 | 2.8 | 1.2 | 1.4 | 2.5 | 0.1 | ..... | 0.2 | 0.6 | 0.4 |
| Electric and electronic equipment | 2.1 | 3.3 | 3.7 | 5.7 | 3.7 | 0.4 | 0.4 | 0.3 | 0.6 | 2.2 |
| Transportation equipment | 2.7 | 1.8 | 4.0 | 2.7 | 1.7 | 0.8 | 0.5 | 0.9 | 1.8 | 0.4 |
| Scientific and measuring instruments | 5.3 | 7.5 | 12.3 | 11.6 | 12.3 | 0.4 | ..... | 0.5 | 0.9 | 2.1 |
| Miscellaneous manufactures | 5.0 | 5.4 | 10.5 | 10.7 | 7.8 | 0.1 | ..... | 0.1 | 0.3 | 0.4 |
| Unidentified manufactures | 0.9 | 0.9 | 1.3 | 0.6 | 1.0 | 0.1 | ..... | ..... | ..... | ..... |
| **Agricultural and livestock products** | 10.6 | 13.3 | 19.6 | 20.1 | 18.4 | 0.1 | 0.1 | 0.2 | ..... | 0.1 |
| Agricultural products | 10.5 | 13.1 | 19.2 | 19.5 | 18.0 | 0.1 | 0.1 | 0.2 | ..... | 0.1 |
| Livestock and livestock products | 0.1 | 0.2 | 0.4 | 0.6 | 0.4 | ..... | ..... | ..... | ..... | ..... |
| **Other commodities** | 21.5 | 26.2 | 9.7 | 7.7 | 8.5 | 0.8 | 0.4 | ..... | 0.3 | 0.1 |
| Forestry products | 0.1 | 0.1 | ..... | ..... | ..... | ..... | ..... | ..... | ..... | ..... |
| Fish and other marine products | 5.5 | 6.2 | 4.8 | 2.7 | 1.9 | ..... | ..... | ..... | 0.1 | ..... |
| Metallic ores and concentrates | ..... | ..... | ..... | ..... | ..... | ..... | ..... | ..... | ..... | ..... |
| Bituminous coal and lignite | ..... | ..... | ..... | ..... | ..... | ..... | ..... | ..... | ..... | ..... |
| Crude petroleum and natural gas | ..... | ..... | ..... | ..... | ..... | ..... | ..... | ..... | ..... | ..... |
| Nonmetallic minerals | ..... | 0.1 | ..... | ..... | ..... | ..... | ..... | ..... | ..... | ..... |
| Scrap and waste | 1.0 | 0.7 | 0.4 | 0.2 | 0.2 | 0.8 | 0.4 | ..... | ..... | ..... |
| Used merchandise | 14.6 | 18.8 | 4.3 | 4.7 | 6.3 | ..... | ..... | ..... | ..... | ..... |
| Goods imported and returned unchanged | ..... | ..... | ..... | ..... | ..... | ..... | ..... | ..... | ..... | ..... |
| Special classification provisions | 0.3 | 0.3 | 0.2 | 0.1 | 0.1 | ..... | ..... | ..... | 0.2 | ..... |
| | Taiwan | | | | | Singapore | | | | |
| **ALL GOODS** | 3.1 | 9.6 | 3.8 | 4.2 | 2.1 | 3.5 | 2.1 | 5.6 | 5.1 | 11.9 |
| **Manufactured goods** | 2.5 | 9.3 | 3.6 | 1.7 | 1.6 | 3.5 | 2.1 | 5.6 | 4.5 | 6.6 |
| Food products | 0.5 | 0.6 | 0.4 | 0.2 | 0.3 | 0.9 | 1.2 | 1.1 | 1.1 | 1.3 |
| Tobacco products | ..... | ..... | ..... | ..... | ..... | ..... | ..... | ..... | ..... | ..... |
| Textile mill products | 0.4 | ..... | 0.1 | ..... | ..... | ..... | ..... | ..... | ..... | ..... |
| Apparel | ..... | ..... | ..... | ..... | 0.1 | ..... | ..... | ..... | 0.1 | 0.4 |
| Lumber and wood products | 0.2 | ..... | ..... | ..... | ..... | ..... | ..... | ..... | ..... | ..... |
| Furniture and fixtures | 0.1 | ..... | 0.3 | ..... | ..... | ..... | ..... | ..... | ..... | ..... |
| Paper products | ..... | ..... | ..... | ..... | ..... | ..... | ..... | ..... | 0.1 | ..... |
| Printing and publishing | ..... | ..... | ..... | ..... | 0.1 | ..... | ..... | ..... | ..... | ..... |
| Chemical products | 0.1 | 0.1 | 0.1 | 0.1 | 0.1 | 0.2 | 0.1 | ..... | 0.1 | 0.2 |
| Refined petroleum products | ..... | 7.9 | 1.9 | ..... | 0.1 | ..... | ..... | 4.2 | 2.3 | ..... |
| Rubber and plastic products | ..... | ..... | ..... | ..... | ..... | ..... | ..... | ..... | ..... | ..... |
| Leather products | ..... | ..... | ..... | 0.1 | ..... | ..... | 0.1 | ..... | ..... | ..... |
| Stone, clay and glass products | 0.1 | 0.1 | 0.2 | ..... | 0.1 | ..... | ..... | ..... | ..... | ..... |
| Primary metals | ..... | ..... | ..... | ..... | ..... | ..... | ..... | ..... | ..... | ..... |
| Fabricated metal products | ..... | ..... | ..... | ..... | 0.2 | ..... | ..... | ..... | ..... | ..... |
| Industrial machinery and computers | 0.4 | 0.1 | 0.1 | 0.7 | 0.1 | 0.5 | 0.1 | ..... | 0.1 | ..... |
| Electric and electronic equipment | 0.2 | ..... | 0.1 | ..... | ..... | 1.2 | 0.3 | 0.1 | 0.1 | ..... |
| Transportation equipment | 0.2 | 0.2 | 0.2 | 0.2 | ..... | 0.2 | 0.1 | ..... | 0.1 | 1.7 |
| Scientific and measuring instruments | 0.1 | 0.2 | 0.1 | 0.1 | 0.1 | 0.2 | 0.1 | 0.1 | 0.4 | 2.9 |
| Miscellaneous manufactures | 0.1 | 0.1 | 0.1 | 0.1 | 0.3 | 0.1 | 0.1 | 0.1 | 0.1 | ..... |
| Unidentified manufactures | 0.1 | ..... | ..... | ..... | ..... | 0.1 | ..... | ..... | ..... | ..... |
| **Agricultural and livestock products** | 0.1 | ..... | 0.1 | 0.2 | 0.1 | ..... | ..... | ..... | ..... | 0.1 |
| Agricultural products | 0.1 | ..... | ..... | ..... | ..... | ..... | ..... | ..... | ..... | 0.1 |
| Livestock and livestock products | ..... | ..... | ..... | 0.1 | 0.1 | ..... | ..... | ..... | ..... | ..... |
| **Other commodities** | 0.5 | 0.3 | 0.1 | 2.3 | 0.3 | 0.1 | 0.1 | ..... | 0.6 | 5.2 |
| Forestry products | ..... | ..... | ..... | ..... | ..... | ..... | ..... | ..... | ..... | ..... |
| Fish and other marine products | ..... | ..... | ..... | ..... | 0.2 | ..... | ..... | ..... | ..... | ..... |
| Metallic ores and concentrates | ..... | ..... | ..... | ..... | ..... | ..... | ..... | ..... | ..... | ..... |
| Bituminous coal and lignite | ..... | ..... | ..... | ..... | ..... | ..... | ..... | ..... | ..... | ..... |
| Crude petroleum and natural gas | ..... | ..... | ..... | ..... | ..... | ..... | ..... | ..... | ..... | ..... |
| Nonmetallic minerals | ..... | ..... | ..... | ..... | ..... | ..... | ..... | ..... | ..... | ..... |
| Scrap and waste | 0.4 | 0.2 | ..... | 2.3 | ..... | ..... | ..... | ..... | ..... | ..... |
| Used merchandise | ..... | ..... | 0.1 | ..... | 0.1 | 0.1 | ..... | ..... | 0.6 | 5.2 |
| Goods imported and returned unchanged | ..... | ..... | ..... | ..... | ..... | ..... | ..... | ..... | ..... | ..... |
| Special classification provisions | ..... | ..... | ..... | ..... | ..... | ..... | ..... | ..... | ..... | ..... |

## IDAHO: Exports of Goods, 1997

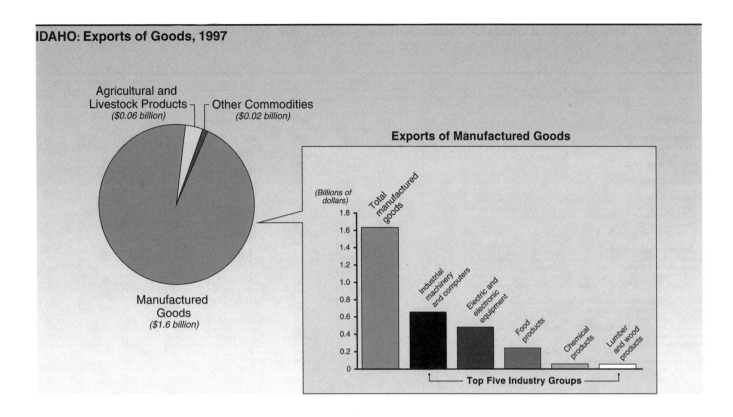

Agricultural and Livestock Products ($0.06 billion)

Other Commodities ($0.02 billion)

Manufactured Goods ($1.6 billion)

**Exports of Manufactured Goods**

(Billions of dollars)

Top Five Industry Groups

## Table D-3.   State Exports of Goods by Destination and Industry, 1993–1997 —*Continued*

### IDAHO (Millions of dollars.)

| Industry | 1993 | 1994 | 1995 | 1996 | 1997 | 1993 | 1994 | 1995 | 1996 | 1997 |
|---|---|---|---|---|---|---|---|---|---|---|
| | All destinations | | | | | Canada | | | | |
| **ALL GOODS** | 1 235.9 | 1 530.5 | 1 892.5 | 1 610.1 | 1 716.1 | 156.7 | 208.7 | 292.3 | 276.5 | 277.9 |
| **Manufactured goods** | 1 182.3 | 1 468.9 | 1 831.0 | 1 539.3 | 1 634.4 | 135.2 | 182.8 | 267.3 | 245.5 | 241.5 |
| Food products | 129.3 | 154.5 | 213.0 | 225.5 | 242.8 | 21.2 | 27.6 | 29.0 | 27.2 | 27.1 |
| Tobacco products | ..... | ..... | ..... | ..... | ..... | | | | | |
| Textile mill products | 0.3 | 0.3 | 2.8 | 0.9 | 0.3 | 0.1 | 0.1 | 0.1 | ..... | ..... |
| Apparel | 1.4 | 2.8 | 6.1 | 1.9 | 1.0 | 0.2 | 0.3 | 0.3 | 0.4 | 0.5 |
| Lumber and wood products | 49.3 | 49.6 | 47.7 | 46.4 | 54.6 | 13.6 | 13.2 | 9.5 | 10.7 | 16.8 |
| Furniture and fixtures | 3.2 | 2.6 | 2.6 | 5.1 | 9.8 | 0.1 | 0.1 | 0.3 | 0.3 | 0.5 |
| Paper products | 40.4 | 50.9 | 69.3 | 35.1 | 32.6 | 10.2 | 10.0 | 13.1 | 12.7 | 18.5 |
| Printing and publishing | 1.3 | 2.9 | 4.4 | 4.9 | 3.1 | 0.9 | 2.1 | 3.3 | 2.9 | 1.0 |
| Chemical products | 45.1 | 49.9 | 52.4 | 57.3 | 57.5 | 34.7 | 40.7 | 46.3 | 49.4 | 48.6 |
| Refined petroleum products | 0.2 | 0.3 | 0.2 | 0.2 | 0.2 | ..... | ..... | ..... | ..... | ..... |
| Rubber and plastic products | 1.6 | 5.6 | 4.4 | 13.7 | 4.2 | 0.7 | 0.7 | 0.8 | 1.0 | 1.3 |
| Leather products | 1.6 | 1.2 | 1.6 | 3.4 | 4.9 | 0.1 | 0.1 | 0.2 | 0.7 | 1.8 |
| Stone, clay and glass products | 0.3 | 0.7 | 0.7 | 1.0 | 1.5 | 0.1 | 0.4 | 0.1 | 0.5 | 1.1 |
| Primary metals | 1.9 | 2.8 | 6.1 | 1.9 | 2.6 | 0.8 | 1.4 | 0.5 | 0.5 | 0.9 |
| Fabricated metal products | 14.5 | 17.5 | 22.9 | 21.1 | 19.6 | 3.3 | 5.8 | 3.8 | 2.9 | 3.8 |
| Industrial machinery and computers | 515.3 | 571.0 | 676.1 | 626.5 | 656.2 | 24.7 | 22.8 | 28.1 | 37.3 | 39.1 |
| Electric and electronic equipment | 339.5 | 517.8 | 648.7 | 438.2 | 483.8 | 13.9 | 45.6 | 94.7 | 79.6 | 61.5 |
| Transportation equipment | 20.3 | 16.7 | 45.2 | 25.9 | 20.5 | 7.4 | 7.7 | 32.6 | 14.4 | 14.5 |
| Scientific and measuring instruments | 12.7 | 16.3 | 19.6 | 20.5 | 31.4 | 1.5 | 2.2 | 2.3 | 1.8 | 1.6 |
| Miscellaneous manufactures | 2.8 | 3.3 | 3.7 | 5.2 | 3.6 | 1.2 | 0.8 | 0.7 | 0.7 | 0.6 |
| Unidentified manufactures | 1.3 | 2.2 | 3.2 | 4.7 | 4.2 | 0.4 | 1.3 | 1.7 | 2.6 | 2.1 |
| **Agricultural and livestock products** | 42.7 | 51.2 | 49.5 | 54.5 | 62.8 | 12.8 | 18.0 | 16.6 | 17.8 | 22.5 |
| Agricultural products | 40.2 | 46.7 | 45.7 | 51.8 | 59.9 | 10.6 | 13.5 | 13.2 | 15.4 | 19.5 |
| Livestock and livestock products | 2.5 | 4.5 | 3.8 | 2.7 | 3.0 | 2.2 | 4.5 | 3.4 | 2.4 | 2.9 |
| **Other commodities** | 10.9 | 10.4 | 12.1 | 16.3 | 18.9 | 8.7 | 7.9 | 8.4 | 13.2 | 13.9 |
| Forestry products | 0.2 | 0.3 | 0.2 | 0.2 | 0.4 | 0.1 | 0.1 | 0.1 | 0.1 | 0.2 |
| Fish and other marine products | 2.5 | 2.0 | 1.9 | 1.8 | 2.0 | 2.4 | 2.0 | 1.7 | 1.8 | 1.9 |
| Metallic ores and concentrates | 3.7 | 1.8 | 0.5 | 5.8 | 6.2 | 3.7 | 1.8 | 0.5 | 5.8 | 6.0 |
| Bituminous coal and lignite | ..... | ..... | ..... | ..... | ..... | ..... | ..... | ..... | ..... | ..... |
| Crude petroleum and natural gas | ..... | ..... | 0.1 | ..... | ..... | ..... | ..... | ..... | ..... | ..... |
| Nonmetallic minerals | 1.8 | 2.1 | 2.2 | 2.0 | 3.3 | 0.6 | 0.8 | 0.9 | 0.9 | 1.1 |
| Scrap and waste | 0.1 | 0.3 | 0.6 | ..... | 0.1 | ..... | 0.3 | 0.6 | ..... | 0.1 |
| Used merchandise | 0.4 | 1.0 | 0.8 | 1.8 | 1.3 | ..... | 0.6 | 0.5 | 1.2 | 0.3 |
| Goods imported and returned unchanged | 1.6 | 2.1 | 3.9 | 3.2 | 3.9 | 1.6 | 2.1 | 3.9 | 3.2 | 3.9 |
| Special classification provisions | 0.6 | 0.8 | 1.8 | 1.6 | 1.8 | 0.2 | 0.2 | 0.2 | 0.3 | 0.3 |

## Table D-3.  State Exports of Goods by Destination and Industry, 1993–1997 —*Continued*

**IDAHO** (Millions of dollars.)

| Industry | 1993 | 1994 | 1995 | 1996 | 1997 | 1993 | 1994 | 1995 | 1996 | 1997 |
|---|---|---|---|---|---|---|---|---|---|---|
| | South and Central America and Caribbean | | | | | Mexico | | | | |
| **ALL GOODS** | 9.4 | 18.7 | 24.3 | 18.7 | 27.1 | 36.3 | 33.7 | 29.1 | 37.4 | 44.2 |
| **Manufactured goods** | 7.0 | 12.4 | 18.8 | 13.8 | 17.8 | 33.7 | 31.4 | 26.8 | 34.8 | 42.9 |
| Food products | 2.1 | 1.7 | 3.2 | 3.9 | 3.4 | 7.3 | 8.0 | 10.2 | 13.6 | 19.4 |
| Tobacco products | ..... | ..... | ..... | ..... | ..... | ..... | ..... | ..... | ..... | ..... |
| Textile mill products | ..... | 0.1 | 2.4 | 0.6 | ..... | ..... | ..... | ..... | ..... | ..... |
| Apparel | ..... | 1.5 | 4.6 | 0.5 | ..... | 0.2 | 0.2 | ..... | ..... | ..... |
| Lumber and wood products | ..... | ..... | 0.1 | ..... | 0.6 | 1.2 | 0.7 | 0.2 | 0.2 | 1.2 |
| Furniture and fixtures | ..... | ..... | ..... | ..... | ..... | 0.1 | ..... | ..... | ..... | ..... |
| Paper products | ..... | ..... | ..... | ..... | ..... | 0.6 | 2.4 | 1.0 | 1.6 | 2.3 |
| Printing and publishing | 0.1 | ..... | ..... | ..... | ..... | ..... | 0.2 | 0.1 | 0.1 | 0.1 |
| Chemical products | ..... | 0.2 | 0.3 | 0.3 | 0.3 | 8.2 | 6.8 | 3.6 | 6.0 | 5.7 |
| Refined petroleum products | ..... | ..... | ..... | ..... | ..... | ..... | ..... | ..... | ..... | ..... |
| Rubber and plastic products | ..... | 2.4 | 0.1 | ..... | ..... | 0.4 | 0.4 | 1.4 | 1.4 | 0.4 |
| Leather products | ..... | ..... | ..... | ..... | 0.1 | ..... | ..... | ..... | ..... | 0.1 |
| Stone, clay and glass products | ..... | ..... | ..... | ..... | ..... | ..... | ..... | ..... | ..... | ..... |
| Primary metals | ..... | ..... | 0.1 | ..... | 0.2 | 0.1 | 0.1 | 0.1 | 0.1 | 0.1 |
| Fabricated metal products | 1.0 | 1.0 | 2.7 | 1.7 | 1.5 | 0.1 | 0.2 | 0.4 | 0.3 | 0.2 |
| Industrial machinery and computers | 2.7 | 4.3 | 3.9 | 4.6 | 9.5 | 8.8 | 8.8 | 8.0 | 9.4 | 11.3 |
| Electric and electronic equipment | 0.3 | 0.7 | 0.6 | 0.8 | 0.6 | 2.0 | 1.1 | 1.0 | 0.6 | 1.2 |
| Transportation equipment | 0.4 | 0.2 | 0.2 | 1.0 | 0.8 | 4.7 | 1.7 | 0.5 | 1.1 | 0.9 |
| Scientific and measuring instruments | ..... | 0.1 | 0.1 | 0.1 | 0.2 | 0.1 | ..... | 0.2 | ..... | ..... |
| Miscellaneous manufactures | ..... | 0.1 | 0.5 | 0.1 | 0.1 | ..... | 0.5 | ..... | 0.3 | 0.1 |
| Unidentified manufactures | ..... | 0.1 | ..... | ..... | 0.2 | 0.1 | ..... | 0.1 | 0.1 | 0.1 |
| **Agricultural and livestock products** | 2.3 | 6.1 | 5.4 | 4.6 | 9.0 | 2.6 | 2.0 | 2.0 | 2.5 | 1.0 |
| Agricultural products | 2.3 | 6.2 | 5.3 | 4.7 | 9.1 | 2.3 | 1.9 | 1.9 | 2.4 | 0.9 |
| Livestock and livestock products | ..... | ..... | ..... | ..... | ..... | 0.3 | 0.1 | 0.2 | ..... | ..... |
| **Other commodities** | ..... | 0.1 | 0.1 | 0.3 | 0.2 | 0.1 | 0.3 | 0.3 | 0.1 | 0.4 |
| Forestry products | ..... | ..... | ..... | ..... | ..... | ..... | 0.1 | 0.2 | 0.1 | 0.1 |
| Fish and other marine products | ..... | ..... | ..... | ..... | 0.1 | ..... | ..... | ..... | ..... | ..... |
| Metallic ores and concentrates | ..... | ..... | ..... | ..... | ..... | ..... | ..... | ..... | ..... | 0.1 |
| Bituminous coal and lignite | ..... | ..... | ..... | ..... | ..... | ..... | ..... | ..... | ..... | ..... |
| Crude petroleum and natural gas | ..... | ..... | ..... | ..... | ..... | ..... | ..... | ..... | ..... | ..... |
| Nonmetallic minerals | ..... | 0.1 | ..... | 0.2 | 0.1 | ..... | 0.1 | 0.1 | ..... | ..... |
| Scrap and waste | ..... | ..... | ..... | ..... | ..... | 0.1 | 0.1 | 0.1 | ..... | 0.2 |
| Used merchandise | ..... | ..... | ..... | 0.1 | ..... | ..... | ..... | ..... | ..... | ..... |
| Goods imported and returned unchanged | ..... | ..... | ..... | ..... | ..... | ..... | ..... | ..... | ..... | ..... |
| Special classification provisions | ..... | ..... | ..... | ..... | ..... | ..... | ..... | ..... | ..... | ..... |
| | European Union | | | | | United Kingdom | | | | |
| **ALL GOODS** | 380.4 | 428.5 | 528.8 | 384.9 | 460.9 | 142.2 | 186.6 | 192.4 | 116.4 | 169.8 |
| **Manufactured goods** | 367.3 | 412.1 | 512.9 | 367.3 | 441.8 | 140.1 | 183.9 | 190.8 | 114.0 | 168.8 |
| Food products | 1.0 | 1.0 | 6.1 | 6.7 | 4.9 | 0.3 | 0.5 | 2.3 | 1.3 | 2.0 |
| Tobacco products | ..... | ..... | ..... | ..... | ..... | ..... | ..... | ..... | ..... | ..... |
| Textile mill products | 0.1 | ..... | 0.1 | 0.1 | ..... | ..... | ..... | ..... | ..... | ..... |
| Apparel | 0.7 | 0.6 | 0.8 | 0.9 | 0.3 | ..... | ..... | ..... | ..... | 0.1 |
| Lumber and wood products | 26.1 | 26.9 | 25.2 | 19.1 | 10.7 | 10.4 | 10.7 | 7.1 | 4.4 | 1.3 |
| Furniture and fixtures | 2.7 | 2.5 | 2.2 | 4.2 | 7.4 | 2.7 | 2.4 | 2.0 | 0.1 | ..... |
| Paper products | 1.8 | 5.3 | 9.7 | 1.2 | 2.3 | 0.1 | 0.2 | 0.1 | ..... | ..... |
| Printing and publishing | 0.2 | 0.3 | 0.5 | 0.8 | 1.0 | 0.2 | 0.2 | 0.3 | 0.2 | 0.4 |
| Chemical products | 0.6 | 0.4 | 0.8 | 0.4 | 1.3 | 0.1 | 0.2 | 0.2 | 0.2 | 0.5 |
| Refined petroleum products | ..... | ..... | ..... | ..... | ..... | ..... | ..... | ..... | ..... | ..... |
| Rubber and plastic products | 0.2 | 0.2 | 0.6 | 0.2 | 0.2 | ..... | ..... | ..... | ..... | 0.1 |
| Leather products | 0.3 | 0.1 | 0.2 | 0.6 | 0.9 | ..... | ..... | 0.1 | ..... | ..... |
| Stone, clay and glass products | ..... | ..... | 0.4 | 0.2 | 0.2 | ..... | ..... | 0.3 | 0.2 | ..... |
| Primary metals | 0.9 | 1.0 | 0.8 | 0.4 | 0.7 | 0.8 | 0.8 | 0.3 | 0.1 | 0.2 |
| Fabricated metal products | 5.7 | 5.5 | 8.4 | 6.4 | 4.8 | 0.4 | 0.6 | 0.9 | 0.6 | 0.6 |
| Industrial machinery and computers | 233.3 | 232.2 | 289.2 | 255.2 | 330.5 | 91.4 | 114.6 | 121.6 | 87.0 | 131.7 |
| Electric and electronic equipment | 82.7 | 126.4 | 155.3 | 60.9 | 67.6 | 31.4 | 52.2 | 51.0 | 16.4 | 29.1 |
| Transportation equipment | 3.1 | 1.6 | 2.4 | 2.7 | 2.0 | 0.3 | 0.2 | 0.4 | 0.3 | 0.3 |
| Scientific and measuring instruments | 6.7 | 7.0 | 8.7 | 4.6 | 5.7 | 1.8 | 0.9 | 3.9 | 1.7 | 2.3 |
| Miscellaneous manufactures | 0.6 | 0.7 | 1.2 | 1.5 | 0.9 | 0.3 | 0.1 | 0.2 | 0.1 | 0.1 |
| Unidentified manufactures | 0.3 | 0.4 | 0.4 | 1.4 | 0.3 | 0.1 | 0.1 | 0.1 | 1.2 | ..... |
| **Agricultural and livestock products** | 13.0 | 15.7 | 14.9 | 16.5 | 17.2 | 2.1 | 2.7 | 1.3 | 1.8 | 0.6 |
| Agricultural products | 12.9 | 15.7 | 14.9 | 16.5 | 17.2 | 2.1 | 2.7 | 1.3 | 1.8 | 0.6 |
| Livestock and livestock products | ..... | ..... | ..... | ..... | ..... | ..... | ..... | ..... | ..... | ..... |
| **Other commodities** | 0.2 | 0.7 | 1.0 | 1.1 | 1.9 | ..... | ..... | 0.3 | 0.6 | 0.4 |
| Forestry products | ..... | ..... | ..... | ..... | ..... | ..... | ..... | ..... | ..... | ..... |
| Fish and other marine products | ..... | ..... | ..... | ..... | ..... | ..... | ..... | ..... | ..... | ..... |
| Metallic ores and concentrates | ..... | ..... | ..... | ..... | ..... | ..... | ..... | ..... | ..... | ..... |
| Bituminous coal and lignite | ..... | ..... | ..... | ..... | ..... | ..... | ..... | ..... | ..... | ..... |
| Crude petroleum and natural gas | ..... | ..... | ..... | ..... | ..... | ..... | ..... | ..... | ..... | ..... |
| Nonmetallic minerals | 0.2 | 0.7 | 0.4 | 0.3 | 1.5 | ..... | ..... | ..... | ..... | 0.4 |
| Scrap and waste | ..... | ..... | ..... | ..... | ..... | ..... | ..... | ..... | ..... | ..... |
| Used merchandise | ..... | ..... | 0.2 | 0.1 | 0.1 | ..... | ..... | ..... | ..... | ..... |
| Goods imported and returned unchanged | ..... | ..... | ..... | ..... | ..... | ..... | ..... | ..... | ..... | ..... |
| Special classification provisions | ..... | ..... | 0.3 | 0.7 | 0.2 | ..... | ..... | 0.3 | 0.6 | ..... |

## Table D-3.  State Exports of Goods by Destination and Industry, 1993–1997 —Continued

**IDAHO** (Millions of dollars.)

| Industry | 1993 | 1994 | 1995 | 1996 | 1997 | 1993 | 1994 | 1995 | 1996 | 1997 |
|---|---|---|---|---|---|---|---|---|---|---|
| | Germany | | | | | France | | | | |
| **ALL GOODS** | 78.8 | 82.4 | 83.0 | 92.0 | 132.2 | 39.1 | 49.2 | 66.7 | 26.2 | 17.4 |
| **Manufactured goods** | 78.5 | 81.7 | 82.7 | 91.7 | 131.1 | 35.7 | 47.4 | 64.4 | 21.2 | 12.6 |
| Food products | 0.3 | 0.1 | 0.2 | 0.2 | 0.1 | ..... | ..... | 0.7 | ..... | ..... |
| Tobacco products | ..... | ..... | ..... | ..... | ..... | ..... | ..... | ..... | ..... | ..... |
| Textile mill products | ..... | ..... | ..... | ..... | ..... | ..... | ..... | ..... | ..... | ..... |
| Apparel | 0.1 | ..... | ..... | 0.2 | ..... | ..... | ..... | ..... | ..... | ..... |
| Lumber and wood products | 6.4 | 7.7 | 10.9 | 10.7 | 5.5 | 0.1 | 0.2 | ..... | 0.1 | ..... |
| Furniture and fixtures | 0.1 | ..... | 0.2 | 4.0 | 7.4 | ..... | ..... | ..... | ..... | ..... |
| Paper products | ..... | ..... | ..... | ..... | ..... | ..... | 1.3 | 2.6 | ..... | 0.6 |
| Printing and publishing | ..... | 0.1 | 0.1 | 0.3 | 0.2 | ..... | ..... | 0.1 | 0.1 | 0.1 |
| Chemical products | 0.3 | 0.1 | 0.2 | 0.1 | 0.3 | ..... | ..... | 0.2 | ..... | 0.1 |
| Refined petroleum products | ..... | ..... | ..... | ..... | ..... | ..... | ..... | ..... | ..... | ..... |
| Rubber and plastic products | ..... | 0.1 | 0.4 | 0.1 | 0.1 | 0.1 | ..... | ..... | ..... | ..... |
| Leather products | ..... | ..... | ..... | 0.1 | ..... | ..... | ..... | ..... | ..... | 0.2 |
| Stone, clay and glass products | ..... | ..... | 0.1 | ..... | ..... | ..... | ..... | ..... | ..... | ..... |
| Primary metals | ..... | 0.1 | 0.2 | 0.2 | 0.1 | 0.1 | ..... | 0.1 | ..... | ..... |
| Fabricated metal products | 0.8 | 1.9 | 2.7 | 2.6 | 1.1 | 0.8 | 1.2 | 2.0 | 1.0 | 1.1 |
| Industrial machinery and computers | 55.7 | 53.9 | 48.7 | 65.2 | 104.0 | 20.6 | 23.6 | 28.5 | 16.6 | 8.4 |
| Electric and electronic equipment | 13.4 | 16.4 | 17.9 | 6.4 | 10.9 | 13.4 | 18.6 | 29.2 | 2.9 | 1.7 |
| Transportation equipment | 0.6 | 0.4 | 0.4 | 1.0 | 0.4 | 0.5 | 0.5 | 0.3 | 0.3 | 0.3 |
| Scientific and measuring instruments | 0.5 | 0.6 | 0.2 | 0.5 | 0.9 | 0.2 | 1.9 | 0.6 | 0.1 | 0.1 |
| Miscellaneous manufactures | ..... | ..... | 0.1 | 0.1 | ..... | ..... | 0.1 | ..... | 0.1 | ..... |
| Unidentified manufactures | 0.1 | 0.1 | 0.1 | ..... | 0.1 | ..... | ..... | ..... | ..... | ..... |
| **Agricultural and livestock products** | 0.3 | 0.2 | 0.1 | 0.3 | 0.1 | 3.4 | 1.8 | 2.2 | 4.9 | 4.8 |
| Agricultural products | 0.3 | 0.2 | 0.1 | 0.3 | 0.1 | 3.4 | 1.8 | 2.2 | 4.9 | 4.8 |
| Livestock and livestock products | ..... | ..... | ..... | ..... | ..... | ..... | ..... | ..... | ..... | ..... |
| **Other commodities** | ..... | 0.6 | 0.2 | 0.1 | 0.9 | ..... | ..... | ..... | 0.1 | ..... |
| Forestry products | ..... | ..... | ..... | ..... | ..... | ..... | ..... | ..... | ..... | ..... |
| Fish and other marine products | ..... | ..... | ..... | ..... | ..... | ..... | ..... | ..... | ..... | ..... |
| Metallic ores and concentrates | ..... | ..... | ..... | ..... | ..... | ..... | ..... | ..... | ..... | ..... |
| Bituminous coal and lignite | ..... | ..... | ..... | ..... | ..... | ..... | ..... | ..... | ..... | ..... |
| Crude petroleum and natural gas | ..... | ..... | ..... | ..... | ..... | ..... | ..... | ..... | ..... | ..... |
| Nonmetallic minerals | ..... | 0.6 | 0.2 | 0.1 | 0.8 | ..... | ..... | ..... | ..... | ..... |
| Scrap and waste | ..... | ..... | ..... | ..... | ..... | ..... | ..... | ..... | ..... | ..... |
| Used merchandise | ..... | ..... | ..... | ..... | 0.1 | ..... | ..... | ..... | ..... | ..... |
| Goods imported and returned unchanged | ..... | ..... | ..... | ..... | ..... | ..... | ..... | ..... | ..... | ..... |
| Special classification provisions | ..... | ..... | ..... | ..... | 0.1 | ..... | ..... | ..... | 0.1 | ..... |
| | The Netherlands | | | | | Asian 10 | | | | |
| **ALL GOODS** | 54.0 | 16.0 | 57.1 | 71.5 | 73.1 | 591.7 | 768.1 | 922.6 | 805.5 | 796.5 |
| **Manufactured goods** | 49.0 | 10.4 | 51.5 | 67.4 | 67.1 | 580.9 | 759.8 | 913.3 | 794.6 | 785.4 |
| Food products | 0.1 | 0.1 | 1.5 | 0.7 | 1.1 | 94.9 | 111.5 | 159.0 | 166.2 | 180.1 |
| Tobacco products | ..... | ..... | ..... | ..... | ..... | ..... | ..... | ..... | ..... | ..... |
| Textile mill products | ..... | ..... | ..... | 0.1 | ..... | 0.1 | 0.1 | 0.1 | 0.1 | 0.2 |
| Apparel | 0.7 | 0.4 | 0.6 | 0.6 | 0.1 | 0.2 | 0.1 | 0.4 | 0.2 | 0.1 |
| Lumber and wood products | 4.3 | 3.5 | 3.8 | 1.9 | 0.5 | 8.5 | 8.6 | 11.9 | 15.1 | 21.6 |
| Furniture and fixtures | ..... | ..... | ..... | ..... | ..... | ..... | ..... | 0.1 | 0.6 | 1.5 |
| Paper products | ..... | ..... | ..... | ..... | 0.1 | 27.5 | 31.5 | 44.8 | 19.1 | 9.0 |
| Printing and publishing | ..... | ..... | ..... | 0.1 | 0.2 | 0.1 | 0.1 | 0.4 | 0.6 | 0.2 |
| Chemical products | ..... | ..... | 0.1 | 0.1 | 0.2 | 0.7 | 0.2 | 0.2 | 0.5 | 0.8 |
| Refined petroleum products | ..... | ..... | ..... | ..... | ..... | 0.2 | 0.2 | 0.1 | 0.1 | 0.1 |
| Rubber and plastic products | ..... | ..... | ..... | ..... | ..... | 0.2 | 0.8 | 0.4 | 0.7 | 0.3 |
| Leather products | 0.3 | 0.1 | 0.1 | 0.1 | ..... | 1.1 | 1.0 | 1.2 | 2.1 | 1.8 |
| Stone, clay and glass products | ..... | ..... | ..... | ..... | 0.2 | 0.1 | 0.2 | ..... | 0.1 | 0.1 |
| Primary metals | ..... | ..... | ..... | ..... | 0.1 | 0.1 | 0.2 | 0.6 | 0.4 | 0.4 |
| Fabricated metal products | 0.1 | 0.3 | 0.3 | 0.2 | 0.4 | 3.8 | 3.0 | 3.2 | 6.5 | 7.2 |
| Industrial machinery and computers | 42.3 | 4.9 | 43.7 | 62.6 | 62.7 | 214.5 | 275.4 | 314.7 | 289.7 | 236.7 |
| Electric and electronic equipment | 1.1 | 0.5 | 0.4 | 0.4 | 0.5 | 224.5 | 319.3 | 367.0 | 278.8 | 318.8 |
| Transportation equipment | ..... | 0.1 | 0.7 | 0.1 | 0.3 | 1.2 | 0.9 | 0.6 | 2.5 | 0.5 |
| Scientific and measuring instruments | 0.1 | 0.1 | 0.2 | 0.4 | 0.4 | 2.5 | 5.7 | 7.1 | 8.8 | 3.8 |
| Miscellaneous manufactures | ..... | ..... | ..... | ..... | ..... | 0.8 | 0.9 | 0.9 | 1.9 | 1.4 |
| Unidentified manufactures | ..... | ..... | ..... | 0.1 | 0.1 | 0.3 | 0.2 | 0.6 | 0.3 | 0.6 |
| **Agricultural and livestock products** | 4.8 | 5.5 | 5.2 | 3.8 | 5.8 | 9.2 | 7.2 | 7.0 | 9.8 | 9.4 |
| Agricultural products | 4.8 | 5.5 | 5.2 | 3.8 | 5.8 | 9.2 | 7.2 | 7.0 | 9.8 | 9.4 |
| Livestock and livestock products | ..... | ..... | ..... | ..... | ..... | ..... | ..... | ..... | ..... | ..... |
| **Other commodities** | 0.1 | 0.1 | 0.4 | 0.2 | 0.2 | 1.7 | 1.2 | 2.2 | 1.1 | 1.7 |
| Forestry products | ..... | ..... | ..... | ..... | ..... | ..... | ..... | ..... | ..... | ..... |
| Fish and other marine products | ..... | ..... | ..... | ..... | ..... | 0.1 | ..... | 0.2 | ..... | ..... |
| Metallic ores and concentrates | ..... | ..... | ..... | ..... | ..... | ..... | ..... | ..... | ..... | ..... |
| Bituminous coal and lignite | ..... | ..... | ..... | ..... | ..... | ..... | ..... | ..... | ..... | ..... |
| Crude petroleum and natural gas | ..... | ..... | ..... | ..... | ..... | ..... | ..... | ..... | ..... | ..... |
| Nonmetallic minerals | 0.1 | 0.1 | 0.2 | 0.2 | 0.1 | 1.0 | 0.5 | 0.7 | 0.6 | 0.5 |
| Scrap and waste | ..... | ..... | ..... | ..... | ..... | 0.1 | ..... | ..... | ..... | ..... |
| Used merchandise | ..... | ..... | 0.2 | ..... | ..... | 0.1 | 0.1 | ..... | 0.1 | 0.2 |
| Goods imported and returned unchanged | ..... | ..... | ..... | ..... | ..... | ..... | ..... | ..... | ..... | ..... |
| Special classification provisions | ..... | ..... | ..... | ..... | 0.1 | 0.4 | 0.6 | 1.3 | 0.4 | 1.0 |

## Table D-3.  State Exports of Goods by Destination and Industry, 1993–1997 —*Continued*

**IDAHO** (Millions of dollars.)

| Industry | 1993 | 1994 | 1995 | 1996 | 1997 | 1993 | 1994 | 1995 | 1996 | 1997 |
|---|---|---|---|---|---|---|---|---|---|---|
| | Japan | | | | | South Korea | | | | |
| **ALL GOODS** | 290.4 | 352.8 | 348.0 | 309.4 | 317.1 | 26.6 | 29.2 | 35.5 | 36.8 | 32.5 |
| **Manufactured goods** | 281.7 | 346.7 | 341.7 | 302.0 | 310.5 | 26.1 | 28.6 | 34.2 | 36.4 | 31.6 |
| Food products | 70.7 | 80.4 | 95.2 | 105.1 | 125.6 | 12.0 | 12.5 | 25.9 | 27.1 | 21.9 |
| Tobacco products | ..... | ..... | ..... | ..... | ..... | ..... | ..... | ..... | ..... | ..... |
| Textile mill products | ..... | ..... | 0.1 | 0.1 | 0.2 | ..... | ..... | ..... | ..... | ..... |
| Apparel | 0.1 | 0.1 | 0.3 | 0.2 | 0.1 | ..... | ..... | ..... | ..... | ..... |
| Lumber and wood products | 5.6 | 6.3 | 9.3 | 13.2 | 19.3 | 0.8 | 0.5 | 0.8 | 0.3 | 0.6 |
| Furniture and fixtures | ..... | ..... | ..... | 0.5 | 1.5 | ..... | ..... | ..... | ..... | ..... |
| Paper products | 1.4 | 2.8 | 7.5 | 5.0 | 2.9 | 1.2 | 0.8 | 0.3 | 1.0 | 0.4 |
| Printing and publishing | ..... | ..... | ..... | 0.1 | ..... | ..... | ..... | ..... | ..... | ..... |
| Chemical products | 0.2 | 0.1 | 0.2 | 0.4 | 0.2 | 0.4 | ..... | ..... | ..... | ..... |
| Refined petroleum products | ..... | ..... | ..... | ..... | ..... | ..... | ..... | ..... | 0.1 | ..... |
| Rubber and plastic products | 0.2 | 0.2 | 0.3 | 0.4 | ..... | ..... | 0.2 | ..... | ..... | 0.1 |
| Leather products | ..... | 0.2 | 0.1 | 0.1 | 0.1 | ..... | 0.2 | 0.3 | 0.2 | 0.5 |
| Stone, clay and glass products | 0.1 | 0.1 | ..... | 0.1 | 0.1 | ..... | ..... | ..... | ..... | ..... |
| Primary metals | ..... | 0.1 | 0.1 | 0.1 | 0.2 | ..... | ..... | ..... | ..... | ..... |
| Fabricated metal products | 0.7 | 0.2 | 0.2 | 0.4 | 1.1 | 0.9 | 0.9 | 1.1 | 1.8 | 2.3 |
| Industrial machinery and computers | 172.7 | 225.3 | 184.1 | 142.7 | 131.8 | 2.1 | 3.0 | 2.1 | 4.1 | 3.1 |
| Electric and electronic equipment | 27.0 | 29.1 | 41.4 | 29.9 | 24.2 | 7.9 | 10.1 | 3.2 | 1.4 | 2.5 |
| Transportation equipment | 0.4 | 0.3 | 0.3 | 0.3 | 0.3 | 0.1 | 0.1 | 0.2 | 0.2 | ..... |
| Scientific and measuring instruments | 1.6 | 1.0 | 1.7 | 2.1 | 2.4 | 0.3 | 0.1 | ..... | 0.1 | 0.2 |
| Miscellaneous manufactures | 0.6 | 0.5 | 0.7 | 1.5 | 0.2 | 0.1 | 0.2 | 0.1 | 0.1 | 0.1 |
| Unidentified manufactures | 0.2 | 0.1 | 0.2 | ..... | 0.2 | ..... | ..... | 0.2 | ..... | ..... |
| **Agricultural and livestock products** | 7.7 | 5.7 | 5.6 | 7.0 | 5.9 | ..... | 0.2 | ..... | ..... | 0.3 |
| Agricultural products | 7.7 | 5.7 | 5.6 | 7.0 | 5.9 | ..... | 0.2 | ..... | ..... | 0.3 |
| Livestock and livestock products | ..... | ..... | ..... | ..... | ..... | ..... | ..... | ..... | ..... | ..... |
| **Other commodities** | 1.0 | 0.4 | 0.7 | 0.5 | 0.6 | 0.5 | 0.4 | 1.2 | 0.4 | 0.7 |
| Forestry products | ..... | ..... | ..... | ..... | ..... | ..... | ..... | ..... | ..... | ..... |
| Fish and other marine products | ..... | ..... | 0.2 | ..... | ..... | 0.1 | ..... | ..... | ..... | ..... |
| Metallic ores and concentrates | ..... | ..... | ..... | ..... | ..... | ..... | ..... | ..... | ..... | ..... |
| Bituminous coal and lignite | ..... | ..... | ..... | ..... | ..... | ..... | ..... | ..... | ..... | ..... |
| Crude petroleum and natural gas | ..... | ..... | ..... | ..... | ..... | ..... | ..... | ..... | ..... | ..... |
| Nonmetallic minerals | 1.0 | 0.4 | 0.5 | 0.3 | 0.3 | ..... | ..... | 0.1 | ..... | ..... |
| Scrap and waste | ..... | ..... | ..... | ..... | ..... | 0.1 | ..... | ..... | ..... | ..... |
| Used merchandise | ..... | ..... | ..... | ..... | ..... | ..... | ..... | ..... | ..... | ..... |
| Goods imported and returned unchanged | ..... | ..... | ..... | ..... | ..... | ..... | ..... | ..... | ..... | ..... |
| Special classification provisions | ..... | ..... | ..... | 0.1 | 0.2 | 0.4 | 0.4 | 1.1 | 0.3 | 0.7 |
| | Taiwan | | | | | Singapore | | | | |
| **ALL GOODS** | 77.4 | 110.6 | 132.0 | 60.4 | 97.2 | 86.1 | 149.5 | 208.6 | 154.8 | 120.2 |
| **Manufactured goods** | 76.5 | 109.6 | 131.2 | 59.7 | 96.2 | 85.9 | 149.5 | 208.6 | 154.7 | 120.2 |
| Food products | 7.1 | 10.8 | 15.6 | 14.5 | 11.3 | 0.5 | 0.5 | 2.3 | 0.4 | 0.3 |
| Tobacco products | ..... | ..... | ..... | ..... | ..... | ..... | ..... | ..... | ..... | ..... |
| Textile mill products | ..... | ..... | ..... | ..... | ..... | ..... | ..... | ..... | ..... | ..... |
| Apparel | ..... | ..... | ..... | ..... | ..... | ..... | ..... | ..... | ..... | ..... |
| Lumber and wood products | 1.9 | 1.6 | 1.3 | 1.4 | 1.0 | 0.1 | ..... | ..... | ..... | ..... |
| Furniture and fixtures | ..... | ..... | ..... | ..... | ..... | ..... | ..... | ..... | ..... | ..... |
| Paper products | 8.4 | 11.2 | 15.2 | 2.8 | 1.8 | 1.2 | 0.8 | 0.1 | 0.1 | ..... |
| Printing and publishing | 0.1 | ..... | ..... | ..... | ..... | ..... | 0.1 | ..... | ..... | 0.1 |
| Chemical products | ..... | ..... | ..... | 0.1 | 0.3 | ..... | ..... | ..... | ..... | ..... |
| Refined petroleum products | 0.2 | 0.2 | 0.1 | ..... | 0.1 | ..... | ..... | ..... | ..... | ..... |
| Rubber and plastic products | ..... | ..... | ..... | ..... | ..... | ..... | 0.3 | ..... | ..... | ..... |
| Leather products | 0.8 | 0.1 | 0.2 | 1.5 | 0.3 | ..... | ..... | ..... | ..... | ..... |
| Stone, clay and glass products | ..... | 0.1 | ..... | ..... | ..... | ..... | ..... | ..... | ..... | ..... |
| Primary metals | ..... | ..... | ..... | ..... | ..... | ..... | ..... | ..... | ..... | ..... |
| Fabricated metal products | 0.2 | 0.4 | 0.4 | 0.5 | 0.4 | 0.6 | 0.5 | 0.5 | 0.2 | 1.1 |
| Industrial machinery and computers | 5.8 | 5.6 | 22.8 | 6.9 | 5.1 | 20.1 | 22.0 | 75.9 | 97.1 | 84.1 |
| Electric and electronic equipment | 51.5 | 79.5 | 75.5 | 28.5 | 75.7 | 63.1 | 124.9 | 129.7 | 55.2 | 34.3 |
| Transportation equipment | 0.5 | 0.1 | ..... | 0.3 | ..... | 0.2 | 0.1 | ..... | 1.5 | ..... |
| Scientific and measuring instruments | ..... | ..... | 0.1 | 3.1 | 0.1 | 0.1 | 0.1 | 0.1 | ..... | ..... |
| Miscellaneous manufactures | ..... | ..... | 0.1 | ..... | 0.1 | ..... | 0.1 | ..... | ..... | 0.1 |
| Unidentified manufactures | ..... | ..... | ..... | ..... | 0.1 | ..... | ..... | ..... | ..... | 0.1 |
| **Agricultural and livestock products** | 0.8 | 0.9 | 0.6 | 0.6 | 0.7 | 0.2 | ..... | ..... | ..... | ..... |
| Agricultural products | 0.8 | 0.9 | 0.6 | 0.6 | 0.7 | 0.2 | ..... | ..... | ..... | ..... |
| Livestock and livestock products | ..... | ..... | ..... | ..... | ..... | ..... | ..... | ..... | ..... | ..... |
| **Other commodities** | 0.1 | 0.1 | 0.1 | 0.1 | 0.2 | ..... | ..... | ..... | 0.1 | ..... |
| Forestry products | ..... | ..... | ..... | ..... | ..... | ..... | ..... | ..... | ..... | ..... |
| Fish and other marine products | ..... | ..... | ..... | ..... | ..... | ..... | ..... | ..... | ..... | ..... |
| Metallic ores and concentrates | ..... | ..... | ..... | ..... | ..... | ..... | ..... | ..... | ..... | ..... |
| Bituminous coal and lignite | ..... | ..... | ..... | ..... | ..... | ..... | ..... | ..... | ..... | ..... |
| Crude petroleum and natural gas | ..... | ..... | ..... | ..... | ..... | ..... | ..... | ..... | ..... | ..... |
| Nonmetallic minerals | ..... | ..... | 0.1 | 0.1 | 0.1 | ..... | ..... | ..... | 0.1 | ..... |
| Scrap and waste | ..... | ..... | ..... | ..... | ..... | ..... | ..... | ..... | ..... | ..... |
| Used merchandise | 0.1 | 0.1 | ..... | ..... | 0.1 | ..... | ..... | ..... | ..... | ..... |
| Goods imported and returned unchanged | ..... | ..... | ..... | ..... | ..... | ..... | ..... | ..... | ..... | ..... |
| Special classification provisions | ..... | ..... | ..... | ..... | ..... | ..... | ..... | ..... | ..... | ..... |

## ILLINOIS: Exports of Goods, 1997

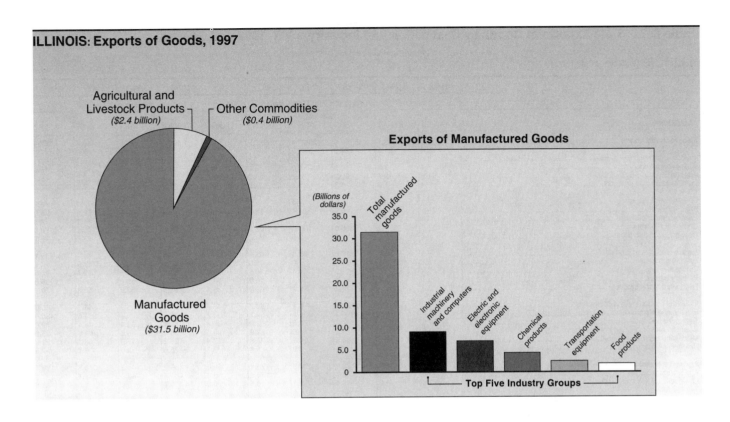

## Table D-3.   State Exports of Goods by Destination and Industry, 1993–1997 —Continued

**ILLINOIS** (Millions of dollars.)

| Industry | 1993 | 1994 | 1995 | 1996 | 1997 | 1993 | 1994 | 1995 | 1996 | 1997 |
|---|---|---|---|---|---|---|---|---|---|---|
| | All destinations | | | | | Canada | | | | |
| **ALL GOODS** | 20 347.2 | 24 534.2 | 30 478.2 | 32 224.9 | 34 225.0 | 4 859.7 | 5 763.1 | 6 452.6 | 6 767.3 | 8 044.2 |
| **Manufactured goods** | 18 762.1 | 22 464.2 | 27 660.6 | 28 747.9 | 31 454.4 | 4 686.3 | 5 556.5 | 6 224.4 | 6 493.3 | 7 777.1 |
| Food products | 1 178.5 | 1 279.4 | 1 677.9 | 1 629.1 | 1 919.2 | 253.5 | 259.3 | 286.6 | 305.9 | 324.7 |
| Tobacco products | 0.4 | 0.7 | 7.8 | 8.3 | 8.5 | 0.1 | ..... | 2.1 | 7.9 | 8.2 |
| Textile mill products | 44.0 | 51.1 | 74.4 | 84.7 | 97.0 | 13.6 | 14.0 | 17.3 | 19.4 | 22.2 |
| Apparel | 77.4 | 63.3 | 69.8 | 86.5 | 98.0 | 8.3 | 7.2 | 10.1 | 10.7 | 11.6 |
| Lumber and wood products | 48.5 | 45.7 | 54.6 | 52.4 | 91.9 | 11.3 | 12.4 | 14.5 | 11.2 | 31.1 |
| Furniture and fixtures | 78.3 | 89.0 | 100.5 | 110.9 | 117.6 | 41.5 | 50.6 | 59.7 | 57.6 | 60.4 |
| Paper products | 267.7 | 404.6 | 549.0 | 565.0 | 672.9 | 72.2 | 95.0 | 117.0 | 127.1 | 132.1 |
| Printing and publishing | 291.7 | 294.4 | 322.1 | 314.4 | 324.6 | 165.8 | 168.6 | 170.6 | 155.0 | 177.8 |
| Chemical products | 2 917.7 | 3 484.7 | 4 152.9 | 4 156.2 | 4 337.6 | 465.4 | 525.7 | 614.9 | 640.7 | 731.1 |
| Refined petroleum products | 57.5 | 70.2 | 82.8 | 179.3 | 169.4 | 27.1 | 38.3 | 32.9 | 31.9 | 31.9 |
| Rubber and plastic products | 396.3 | 507.6 | 627.7 | 735.5 | 843.0 | 159.3 | 174.3 | 196.5 | 216.0 | 251.5 |
| Leather products | 49.5 | 46.6 | 50.3 | 55.9 | 56.9 | 7.8 | 8.7 | 10.0 | 10.1 | 10.6 |
| Stone, clay and glass products | 152.8 | 168.5 | 179.0 | 200.2 | 237.1 | 59.1 | 64.2 | 59.4 | 65.8 | 70.7 |
| Primary metals | 413.8 | 467.1 | 644.6 | 630.3 | 833.9 | 180.4 | 226.8 | 275.1 | 285.2 | 383.8 |
| Fabricated metal products | 567.7 | 658.4 | 778.4 | 917.9 | 922.6 | 236.4 | 268.7 | 314.1 | 421.5 | 336.2 |
| Industrial machinery and computers | 5 513.0 | 6 641.5 | 7 663.1 | 8 153.1 | 9 065.8 | 1 651.8 | 2 017.3 | 2 125.8 | 2 081.9 | 2 711.6 |
| Electric and electronic equipment | 3 837.6 | 4 830.9 | 6 822.4 | 6 560.9 | 7 006.5 | 664.1 | 798.2 | 1 068.8 | 1 054.9 | 1 269.2 |
| Transportation equipment | 1 385.1 | 1 725.6 | 2 023.0 | 2 289.1 | 2 470.2 | 439.3 | 537.3 | 567.3 | 674.6 | 805.7 |
| Scientific and measuring instruments | 933.4 | 1 112.6 | 1 274.1 | 1 467.9 | 1 593.5 | 129.1 | 170.2 | 171.9 | 209.2 | 275.3 |
| Miscellaneous manufactures | 429.9 | 425.7 | 423.9 | 448.7 | 479.9 | 84.2 | 97.9 | 86.6 | 83.3 | 102.1 |
| Unidentified manufactures | 121.5 | 96.5 | 82.5 | 101.6 | 108.3 | 16.1 | 21.7 | 23.3 | 23.4 | 29.2 |
| **Agricultural and livestock products** | 1 191.8 | 1 605.9 | 2 295.8 | 2 993.9 | 2 357.1 | 17.9 | 22.7 | 21.6 | 56.0 | 43.2 |
| Agricultural products | 1 172.2 | 1 588.6 | 2 275.8 | 2 964.1 | 2 314.3 | 13.5 | 18.4 | 17.2 | 50.0 | 35.9 |
| Livestock and livestock products | 19.7 | 17.3 | 20.1 | 29.9 | 42.8 | 4.4 | 4.3 | 4.3 | 6.0 | 7.3 |
| **Other commodities** | 393.2 | 464.1 | 521.8 | 483.0 | 413.5 | 155.4 | 183.9 | 206.6 | 218.0 | 223.9 |
| Forestry products | 2.3 | 2.2 | 2.2 | 3.2 | 3.6 | 0.7 | 0.7 | 0.6 | 0.7 | 1.1 |
| Fish and other marine products | 3.6 | 2.2 | 3.3 | 3.4 | 5.5 | 2.9 | 1.2 | 1.6 | 1.2 | 0.8 |
| Metallic ores and concentrates | 3.2 | 3.5 | 23.7 | 15.0 | 2.7 | 0.5 | 0.7 | 1.2 | 0.7 | 0.6 |
| Bituminous coal and lignite | 58.0 | 55.2 | 76.8 | 50.5 | 2.8 | ..... | ..... | 0.5 | 0.6 | ..... |
| Crude petroleum and natural gas | 70.7 | 49.9 | 43.4 | 46.5 | 56.5 | 51.0 | 39.1 | 40.3 | 44.0 | 50.4 |
| Nonmetallic minerals | 53.0 | 117.6 | 70.2 | 62.9 | 66.6 | 17.2 | 23.3 | 25.2 | 19.0 | 22.2 |
| Scrap and waste | 60.2 | 89.6 | 131.8 | 79.4 | 76.5 | 19.7 | 31.6 | 48.1 | 32.5 | 30.4 |
| Used merchandise | 58.0 | 36.6 | 50.2 | 58.5 | 45.4 | 2.2 | 6.7 | 3.9 | 4.8 | 7.0 |
| Goods imported and returned unchanged | 43.7 | 64.4 | 68.1 | 76.4 | 93.7 | 43.7 | 64.4 | 68.1 | 76.4 | 93.7 |
| Special classification provisions | 40.6 | 42.9 | 52.2 | 87.2 | 60.2 | 17.5 | 16.2 | 17.2 | 38.1 | 17.8 |

## Table D-3.  State Exports of Goods by Destination and Industry, 1993–1997 —Continued

**ILLINOIS** (Millions of dollars.)

| Industry | 1993 | 1994 | 1995 | 1996 | 1997 | 1993 | 1994 | 1995 | 1996 | 1997 |
|---|---|---|---|---|---|---|---|---|---|---|
| | South and Central America and Caribbean | | | | | Mexico | | | | |
| **ALL GOODS** | 1 475.1 | 2 044.3 | 2 186.9 | 2 368.8 | 3 012.3 | 1 364.2 | 1 825.4 | 1 366.1 | 1 844.7 | 2 189.7 |
| **Manufactured goods** | 1 449.1 | 1 909.4 | 2 154.9 | 2 261.4 | 2 825.6 | 1 279.9 | 1 609.2 | 1 197.2 | 1 448.7 | 1 967.9 |
| Food products | 68.0 | 81.5 | 124.2 | 98.2 | 137.1 | 113.4 | 177.7 | 146.9 | 165.9 | 171.7 |
| Tobacco products | 0.1 | ..... | ..... | ..... | ..... | ..... | ..... | ..... | ..... | ..... |
| Textile mill products | 5.1 | 7.6 | 9.3 | 9.2 | 9.1 | 6.5 | 4.9 | 5.7 | 11.0 | 15.4 |
| Apparel | 17.3 | 19.4 | 20.6 | 38.3 | 40.0 | 27.9 | 3.7 | 2.5 | 3.0 | 8.2 |
| Lumber and wood products | 1.4 | 1.9 | 1.3 | 4.9 | 4.8 | 2.0 | 1.9 | 2.9 | 7.8 | 10.2 |
| Furniture and fixtures | 4.1 | 4.9 | 6.5 | 4.4 | 5.7 | 3.6 | 4.0 | 1.7 | 2.0 | 2.9 |
| Paper products | 15.1 | 29.4 | 48.3 | 61.4 | 75.5 | 34.1 | 59.9 | 43.1 | 52.0 | 78.0 |
| Printing and publishing | 8.4 | 4.0 | 14.9 | 21.3 | 19.5 | 9.6 | 13.6 | 14.8 | 14.1 | 9.3 |
| Chemical products | 223.5 | 371.4 | 366.0 | 390.6 | 408.9 | 77.7 | 104.6 | 91.3 | 140.5 | 178.6 |
| Refined petroleum products | 2.4 | 2.2 | 3.7 | 3.6 | 23.2 | 3.9 | 3.1 | 4.1 | 43.7 | 26.1 |
| Rubber and plastic products | 18.3 | 25.9 | 46.5 | 55.0 | 63.5 | 31.3 | 63.5 | 50.4 | 74.9 | 109.1 |
| Leather products | 3.8 | 3.1 | 4.8 | 1.9 | 3.5 | 9.5 | 10.5 | 8.0 | 7.9 | 7.7 |
| Stone, clay and glass products | 7.9 | 9.6 | 14.5 | 14.4 | 19.8 | 12.0 | 17.5 | 11.5 | 17.7 | 22.3 |
| Primary metals | 15.1 | 12.2 | 21.6 | 19.8 | 18.8 | 63.2 | 67.0 | 65.6 | 100.8 | 138.0 |
| Fabricated metal products | 35.2 | 46.1 | 72.2 | 55.7 | 62.9 | 39.1 | 69.3 | 53.9 | 59.3 | 110.3 |
| Industrial machinery and computers | 529.1 | 705.5 | 722.9 | 779.1 | 858.7 | 348.4 | 497.9 | 298.1 | 334.7 | 460.8 |
| Electric and electronic equipment | 265.0 | 319.0 | 394.1 | 420.9 | 739.7 | 391.2 | 372.3 | 303.4 | 284.6 | 435.0 |
| Transportation equipment | 162.3 | 168.9 | 147.8 | 108.6 | 142.0 | 36.6 | 52.1 | 32.4 | 44.1 | 89.8 |
| Scientific and measuring instruments | 54.6 | 81.8 | 115.2 | 134.6 | 161.9 | 48.6 | 56.1 | 40.6 | 61.6 | 65.2 |
| Miscellaneous manufactures | 9.4 | 11.9 | 16.8 | 36.5 | 27.8 | 17.4 | 24.2 | 17.0 | 18.1 | 21.5 |
| Unidentified manufactures | 3.4 | 2.9 | 3.9 | 3.0 | 3.4 | 3.7 | 5.5 | 3.0 | 5.1 | 7.5 |
| **Agricultural and livestock products** | 12.5 | 125.0 | 23.8 | 98.3 | 174.6 | 51.6 | 186.2 | 144.3 | 378.5 | 198.7 |
| Agricultural products | 11.4 | 124.1 | 22.7 | 97.2 | 174.0 | 50.8 | 185.4 | 143.9 | 378.1 | 197.9 |
| Livestock and livestock products | 1.2 | 1.0 | 1.1 | 1.1 | 0.6 | 0.8 | 0.7 | 0.4 | 0.4 | 0.8 |
| **Other commodities** | 13.3 | 9.9 | 8.4 | 9.1 | 12.0 | 32.8 | 30.0 | 24.5 | 17.5 | 23.1 |
| Forestry products | 0.2 | 0.2 | 0.8 | 0.5 | 0.2 | 0.2 | 0.3 | ..... | 0.2 | 0.2 |
| Fish and other marine products | ..... | 0.1 | 0.5 | 0.8 | 0.4 | ..... | 0.1 | ..... | ..... | 0.2 |
| Metallic ores and concentrates | ..... | ..... | 0.1 | 0.1 | ..... | 0.1 | 2.1 | 1.0 | 0.1 | 0.3 |
| Bituminous coal and lignite | 3.5 | 3.3 | 0.2 | ..... | ..... | 0.2 | ..... | ..... | 0.1 | 0.1 |
| Crude petroleum and natural gas | 0.4 | 0.4 | 0.3 | 0.1 | 0.7 | 19.0 | 10.1 | 2.5 | 2.0 | 4.8 |
| Nonmetallic minerals | 5.1 | 2.7 | 2.4 | 3.8 | 6.4 | 1.4 | 1.5 | 0.8 | 1.7 | 1.7 |
| Scrap and waste | 0.8 | 1.5 | 2.2 | 0.9 | 1.3 | 8.8 | 13.8 | 17.1 | 10.1 | 13.3 |
| Used merchandise | 2.5 | 0.7 | 1.5 | 1.7 | 0.7 | 2.0 | 1.4 | 2.3 | 2.5 | 1.3 |
| Goods imported and returned unchanged | ..... | ..... | ..... | ..... | ..... | ..... | ..... | ..... | ..... | ..... |
| Special classification provisions | 0.7 | 0.9 | 0.5 | 1.3 | 2.3 | 1.2 | 0.8 | 0.7 | 0.7 | 1.2 |
| | European Union | | | | | United Kingdom | | | | |
| **ALL GOODS** | 5 025.2 | 5 970.4 | 7 419.0 | 8 062.6 | 8 713.5 | 1 044.2 | 1 276.0 | 1 572.1 | 1 641.8 | 1 830.8 |
| **Manufactured goods** | 4 715.1 | 5 535.4 | 6 699.1 | 7 345.2 | 8 075.6 | 1 008.0 | 1 244.3 | 1 527.5 | 1 612.9 | 1 802.8 |
| Food products | 110.7 | 114.7 | 147.8 | 251.5 | 294.9 | 24.5 | 21.2 | 13.0 | 21.1 | 18.9 |
| Tobacco products | 0.1 | 0.3 | 0.1 | ..... | 0.1 | ..... | ..... | ..... | ..... | ..... |
| Textile mill products | 7.1 | 10.4 | 22.4 | 23.9 | 27.7 | 2.5 | 3.1 | 5.6 | 5.3 | 5.6 |
| Apparel | 7.7 | 18.1 | 20.0 | 15.6 | 18.4 | 1.9 | 2.8 | 3.1 | 3.7 | 7.8 |
| Lumber and wood products | 14.5 | 12.6 | 17.6 | 12.9 | 27.4 | 8.0 | 4.5 | 7.1 | 4.5 | 19.3 |
| Furniture and fixtures | 14.5 | 17.1 | 13.8 | 20.9 | 18.8 | 6.7 | 10.5 | 7.0 | 7.5 | 7.7 |
| Paper products | 100.0 | 146.2 | 222.2 | 190.4 | 245.2 | 18.7 | 24.2 | 40.5 | 44.8 | 49.2 |
| Printing and publishing | 47.6 | 41.6 | 57.2 | 59.4 | 53.0 | 24.9 | 20.0 | 26.9 | 28.9 | 19.1 |
| Chemical products | 886.7 | 982.0 | 1 128.3 | 1 292.4 | 1 443.9 | 112.4 | 136.8 | 232.5 | 216.4 | 217.1 |
| Refined petroleum products | 6.8 | 10.8 | 16.0 | 56.7 | 42.4 | 1.5 | 1.1 | 0.8 | 0.9 | 6.8 |
| Rubber and plastic products | 103.4 | 144.2 | 181.0 | 186.2 | 211.0 | 35.9 | 40.1 | 39.9 | 37.5 | 39.1 |
| Leather products | 5.2 | 4.3 | 5.3 | 5.2 | 4.9 | 1.6 | 1.3 | 2.3 | 1.3 | 1.3 |
| Stone, clay and glass products | 28.2 | 26.3 | 37.5 | 34.8 | 47.2 | 13.1 | 8.8 | 10.2 | 9.0 | 12.5 |
| Primary metals | 49.1 | 49.6 | 104.8 | 73.2 | 93.7 | 14.4 | 16.4 | 44.1 | 24.6 | 35.0 |
| Fabricated metal products | 105.8 | 114.9 | 142.7 | 157.3 | 182.9 | 43.6 | 48.5 | 54.3 | 52.2 | 54.7 |
| Industrial machinery and computers | 1 517.3 | 1 733.7 | 2 062.0 | 2 180.8 | 2 365.1 | 297.2 | 334.1 | 406.0 | 448.0 | 489.0 |
| Electric and electronic equipment | 778.2 | 996.3 | 1 239.9 | 1 279.3 | 1 425.5 | 227.9 | 354.6 | 405.3 | 414.7 | 547.6 |
| Transportation equipment | 365.7 | 535.4 | 630.3 | 828.0 | 863.9 | 54.2 | 106.2 | 111.5 | 179.8 | 149.4 |
| Scientific and measuring instruments | 342.2 | 378.3 | 452.3 | 503.2 | 527.4 | 68.1 | 64.7 | 76.4 | 67.8 | 75.3 |
| Miscellaneous manufactures | 207.8 | 181.8 | 179.4 | 158.0 | 168.2 | 44.9 | 37.3 | 34.7 | 40.3 | 43.6 |
| Unidentified manufactures | 16.3 | 17.1 | 18.4 | 15.4 | 14.0 | 5.7 | 8.1 | 6.5 | 4.3 | 3.8 |
| **Agricultural and livestock products** | 215.6 | 335.6 | 576.8 | 594.1 | 578.9 | 2.1 | 6.6 | 14.5 | 9.7 | 5.4 |
| Agricultural products | 213.4 | 333.5 | 573.5 | 591.1 | 571.3 | 1.9 | 6.5 | 13.7 | 9.3 | 2.4 |
| Livestock and livestock products | 2.3 | 2.1 | 3.3 | 3.0 | 7.6 | 0.2 | 0.1 | 0.8 | 0.4 | 3.0 |
| **Other commodities** | 94.5 | 99.5 | 143.1 | 123.3 | 59.0 | 34.2 | 25.1 | 30.2 | 19.2 | 22.5 |
| Forestry products | 0.6 | 0.3 | 0.6 | 1.5 | 1.8 | 0.4 | ..... | ..... | 0.4 | 0.5 |
| Fish and other marine products | 0.2 | 0.2 | 0.1 | 0.2 | 0.6 | ..... | 0.2 | ..... | ..... | ..... |
| Metallic ores and concentrates | 0.5 | ..... | 20.5 | 12.1 | 1.1 | 0.5 | ..... | 0.2 | ..... | ..... |
| Bituminous coal and lignite | 45.2 | 34.6 | 60.9 | 42.1 | 2.3 | 17.7 | 8.9 | 3.6 | ..... | ..... |
| Crude petroleum and natural gas | ..... | ..... | 0.2 | 0.2 | 0.4 | ..... | ..... | 0.2 | 0.2 | 0.4 |
| Nonmetallic minerals | 10.2 | 23.6 | 11.2 | 13.9 | 12.5 | 2.4 | 3.0 | 3.8 | 5.2 | 5.2 |
| Scrap and waste | 6.4 | 9.5 | 7.8 | 7.7 | 7.2 | 0.6 | 0.4 | 1.4 | 0.6 | 0.7 |
| Used merchandise | 18.4 | 17.2 | 24.7 | 29.3 | 19.0 | 8.4 | 7.6 | 11.8 | 5.0 | 8.4 |
| Goods imported and returned unchanged | ..... | ..... | ..... | ..... | ..... | ..... | ..... | ..... | ..... | ..... |
| Special classification provisions | 13.1 | 13.9 | 17.1 | 16.2 | 14.2 | 4.0 | 5.0 | 9.1 | 7.8 | 7.2 |

## Table D-3.  State Exports of Goods by Destination and Industry, 1993–1997 —*Continued*

**ILLINOIS** (Millions of dollars.)

| Industry | 1993 | 1994 | 1995 | 1996 | 1997 | 1993 | 1994 | 1995 | 1996 | 1997 |
|---|---|---|---|---|---|---|---|---|---|---|
| | Germany | | | | | France | | | | |
| **ALL GOODS** | 1 090.7 | 1 224.9 | 1 491.2 | 1 597.7 | 1 643.5 | 514.2 | 646.1 | 791.7 | 811.8 | 916.1 |
| **Manufactured goods** | 1 078.3 | 1 177.4 | 1 368.9 | 1 497.7 | 1 551.0 | 503.8 | 638.2 | 780.3 | 803.4 | 902.5 |
| Food products | 18.0 | 19.0 | 28.8 | 31.7 | 32.0 | 8.8 | 7.4 | 10.8 | 9.8 | 10.2 |
| Tobacco products | ..... | 0.3 | ..... | ..... | 0.1 | ..... | ..... | ..... | ..... | ..... |
| Textile mill products | 1.9 | 2.4 | 4.9 | 4.4 | 6.0 | 0.6 | 1.8 | 5.3 | 3.9 | 6.0 |
| Apparel | 1.4 | 3.5 | 3.1 | 3.1 | 0.9 | 0.4 | 3.9 | 3.5 | 3.4 | 2.2 |
| Lumber and wood products | 3.3 | 3.7 | 3.7 | 3.6 | 3.1 | 0.4 | 0.1 | 0.7 | 0.5 | 0.6 |
| Furniture and fixtures | 2.2 | 2.2 | 1.9 | 6.2 | 3.5 | 2.3 | 1.3 | 2.4 | 4.5 | 3.6 |
| Paper products | 25.3 | 38.6 | 66.0 | 44.5 | 47.5 | 13.0 | 22.5 | 20.3 | 12.0 | 20.7 |
| Printing and publishing | 8.3 | 6.4 | 11.2 | 10.6 | 9.7 | 2.9 | 2.5 | 5.4 | 2.9 | 4.5 |
| Chemical products | 280.8 | 284.4 | 270.1 | 359.2 | 356.9 | 70.7 | 84.1 | 107.4 | 121.1 | 104.3 |
| Refined petroleum products | 0.5 | 0.4 | 0.3 | 0.3 | 0.4 | 0.6 | 0.8 | 0.3 | 5.2 | 0.2 |
| Rubber and plastic products | 23.0 | 38.3 | 53.9 | 40.4 | 35.4 | 5.7 | 6.9 | 12.5 | 14.9 | 16.8 |
| Leather products | 0.6 | 0.4 | 0.6 | 0.6 | 0.6 | 0.1 | 0.4 | 0.4 | 0.3 | 0.3 |
| Stone, clay and glass products | 5.4 | 5.5 | 8.0 | 7.7 | 14.3 | 2.2 | 2.1 | 3.6 | 2.8 | 5.2 |
| Primary metals | 12.5 | 7.5 | 9.7 | 15.3 | 17.4 | 5.9 | 5.3 | 7.3 | 6.8 | 12.7 |
| Fabricated metal products | 20.8 | 22.2 | 24.5 | 27.6 | 35.3 | 9.9 | 10.6 | 14.3 | 13.1 | 16.9 |
| Industrial machinery and computers | 277.4 | 272.1 | 365.9 | 387.0 | 434.3 | 184.5 | 237.6 | 311.1 | 277.1 | 285.7 |
| Electric and electronic equipment | 100.4 | 160.7 | 157.0 | 137.1 | 186.1 | 83.2 | 96.5 | 109.5 | 192.6 | 274.5 |
| Transportation equipment | 103.6 | 106.7 | 120.4 | 180.7 | 145.2 | 46.6 | 78.4 | 93.1 | 56.1 | 64.8 |
| Scientific and measuring instruments | 111.6 | 123.9 | 162.5 | 181.2 | 166.5 | 43.6 | 51.3 | 50.7 | 60.0 | 54.7 |
| Miscellaneous manufactures | 77.7 | 76.3 | 73.5 | 54.6 | 54.0 | 21.2 | 23.4 | 20.4 | 15.8 | 17.3 |
| Unidentified manufactures | 3.7 | 2.8 | 2.8 | 2.0 | 1.8 | 1.4 | 1.1 | 1.3 | 0.9 | 1.1 |
| **Agricultural and livestock products** | 3.2 | 31.1 | 109.3 | 78.5 | 78.3 | 4.7 | 3.5 | 4.9 | 3.1 | 7.1 |
| Agricultural products | 1.7 | 30.1 | 108.2 | 77.2 | 77.2 | 4.6 | 3.3 | 4.6 | 3.1 | 5.2 |
| Livestock and livestock products | 1.4 | 1.0 | 1.2 | 1.3 | 1.1 | 0.1 | 0.2 | 0.3 | ..... | 1.8 |
| **Other commodities** | 9.2 | 16.4 | 13.0 | 21.5 | 14.2 | 5.8 | 4.5 | 6.5 | 5.2 | 6.5 |
| Forestry products | ..... | 0.2 | 0.3 | 0.2 | 0.1 | ..... | ..... | ..... | 0.6 | 1.1 |
| Fish and other marine products | ..... | 0.1 | ..... | ..... | 0.2 | ..... | 0.2 | ..... | 0.2 | ..... |
| Metallic ores and concentrates | ..... | ..... | ..... | ..... | ..... | ..... | ..... | ..... | 0.1 | ..... |
| Bituminous coal and lignite | ..... | ..... | ..... | ..... | 1.7 | ..... | ..... | ..... | ..... | ..... |
| Crude petroleum and natural gas | ..... | ..... | ..... | ..... | ..... | ..... | ..... | ..... | ..... | ..... |
| Nonmetallic minerals | 1.5 | 5.9 | 1.4 | 1.7 | 1.5 | 0.4 | 1.0 | 0.3 | 0.3 | 0.3 |
| Scrap and waste | 3.7 | 3.7 | 2.4 | 1.7 | 1.4 | ..... | ..... | 0.2 | 0.7 | 1.4 |
| Used merchandise | 2.4 | 3.9 | 4.9 | 15.0 | 6.3 | 3.0 | 1.0 | 3.4 | 2.1 | 1.6 |
| Goods imported and returned unchanged | ..... | ..... | ..... | ..... | ..... | ..... | ..... | ..... | ..... | ..... |
| Special classification provisions | 1.5 | 2.6 | 3.9 | 2.8 | 3.1 | 2.3 | 2.5 | 2.6 | 1.3 | 2.1 |
| | The Netherlands | | | | | Asian 10 | | | | |
| **ALL GOODS** | 631.0 | 788.6 | 915.8 | 1 171.3 | 1 369.3 | 4 762.3 | 5 894.1 | 8 803.2 | 8 626.1 | 7 714.3 |
| **Manufactured goods** | 422.7 | 489.8 | 590.2 | 796.3 | 957.0 | 4 089.4 | 5 123.7 | 7 888.1 | 7 420.6 | 6 827.9 |
| Food products | 26.0 | 24.5 | 44.4 | 90.1 | 93.1 | 405.7 | 356.1 | 710.0 | 541.1 | 612.3 |
| Tobacco products | ..... | ..... | ..... | ..... | ..... | 0.2 | 0.2 | 0.2 | 0.2 | ..... |
| Textile mill products | 0.3 | 0.5 | 1.5 | 3.8 | 2.6 | 5.2 | 6.1 | 8.4 | 10.2 | 10.1 |
| Apparel | 1.3 | 4.5 | 7.2 | 1.8 | 1.1 | 10.3 | 10.2 | 10.5 | 12.5 | 8.8 |
| Lumber and wood products | 0.5 | 0.5 | 0.4 | 0.3 | 0.3 | 16.6 | 13.2 | 14.3 | 12.6 | 13.7 |
| Furniture and fixtures | 0.6 | 1.9 | 0.5 | 0.5 | 1.3 | 8.4 | 7.4 | 11.3 | 18.8 | 19.0 |
| Paper products | 6.0 | 6.2 | 14.7 | 29.4 | 54.5 | 32.3 | 51.5 | 76.4 | 83.7 | 90.9 |
| Printing and publishing | 3.3 | 4.0 | 3.7 | 4.9 | 6.9 | 24.0 | 27.2 | 32.6 | 31.6 | 31.4 |
| Chemical products | 135.7 | 148.1 | 157.4 | 172.6 | 260.3 | 899.9 | 1 148.9 | 1 462.0 | 1 253.7 | 1 092.6 |
| Refined petroleum products | 1.5 | 3.0 | 2.8 | 36.4 | 29.2 | 14.2 | 13.9 | 22.6 | 37.2 | 23.1 |
| Rubber and plastic products | 15.1 | 20.6 | 25.5 | 31.6 | 40.6 | 44.8 | 57.6 | 97.3 | 124.3 | 133.7 |
| Leather products | 0.1 | 0.2 | 0.1 | 0.4 | 0.6 | 9.4 | 7.7 | 9.0 | 14.1 | 15.8 |
| Stone, clay and glass products | 1.2 | 2.2 | 6.3 | 7.0 | 7.1 | 27.4 | 32.3 | 35.8 | 47.2 | 55.4 |
| Primary metals | 1.2 | 4.0 | 3.4 | 2.1 | 4.7 | 71.0 | 80.2 | 141.4 | 113.8 | 158.0 |
| Fabricated metal products | 10.6 | 8.1 | 12.3 | 14.6 | 11.6 | 88.2 | 106.6 | 136.7 | 153.8 | 164.6 |
| Industrial machinery and computers | 120.1 | 119.3 | 114.3 | 113.9 | 125.9 | 629.7 | 802.1 | 1 260.9 | 1 345.5 | 1 180.5 |
| Electric and electronic equipment | 54.4 | 58.4 | 77.3 | 72.7 | 82.0 | 1 302.4 | 1 820.1 | 3 138.1 | 2 823.0 | 2 427.7 |
| Transportation equipment | 14.0 | 52.7 | 73.7 | 159.7 | 174.3 | 171.7 | 189.7 | 266.1 | 259.0 | 256.3 |
| Scientific and measuring instruments | 15.0 | 19.9 | 35.6 | 40.0 | 45.5 | 242.0 | 304.7 | 353.6 | 409.6 | 408.6 |
| Miscellaneous manufactures | 15.0 | 10.1 | 7.6 | 12.9 | 14.5 | 76.9 | 76.4 | 89.4 | 115.4 | 114.3 |
| Unidentified manufactures | 0.9 | 1.2 | 1.4 | 1.4 | 0.8 | 9.2 | 11.7 | 11.5 | 13.4 | 11.0 |
| **Agricultural and livestock products** | 185.6 | 264.4 | 291.6 | 346.1 | 408.0 | 610.8 | 651.6 | 792.0 | 1 113.4 | 805.2 |
| Agricultural products | 185.4 | 264.0 | 291.2 | 345.8 | 407.7 | 601.3 | 643.2 | 784.3 | 1 103.2 | 797.8 |
| Livestock and livestock products | 0.2 | 0.4 | 0.4 | 0.3 | 0.3 | 9.5 | 8.4 | 7.7 | 10.2 | 7.4 |
| **Other commodities** | 22.8 | 34.4 | 34.0 | 28.9 | 4.3 | 62.1 | 118.8 | 123.1 | 92.1 | 81.2 |
| Forestry products | ..... | ..... | ..... | ..... | ..... | 0.7 | 0.4 | 0.1 | 0.2 | 0.2 |
| Fish and other marine products | ..... | ..... | ..... | ..... | 0.3 | 0.3 | 0.4 | 1.0 | 1.0 | 3.4 |
| Metallic ores and concentrates | ..... | ..... | 20.2 | 11.8 | 0.9 | 2.0 | 0.6 | 0.9 | 2.0 | 0.6 |
| Bituminous coal and lignite | 17.9 | 20.3 | 10.1 | 12.8 | ..... | 9.1 | 17.3 | 15.2 | 7.4 | 0.1 |
| Crude petroleum and natural gas | ..... | ..... | ..... | ..... | ..... | 0.1 | 0.2 | 0.1 | 0.1 | 0.1 |
| Nonmetallic minerals | 2.3 | 10.3 | 2.2 | 1.3 | 2.3 | 17.3 | 51.6 | 24.3 | 22.6 | 21.1 |
| Scrap and waste | 0.4 | 0.1 | 0.1 | 0.3 | ..... | 23.6 | 31.8 | 53.5 | 24.6 | 22.1 |
| Used merchandise | 2.0 | 0.6 | 1.0 | 2.3 | 0.6 | 3.8 | 7.3 | 13.5 | 14.4 | 14.2 |
| Goods imported and returned unchanged | ..... | ..... | ..... | ..... | ..... | ..... | ..... | ..... | ..... | ..... |
| Special classification provisions | 0.1 | 3.1 | 0.2 | 0.5 | 0.2 | 5.2 | 9.3 | 14.5 | 19.8 | 19.4 |

## Table D-3.  State Exports of Goods by Destination and Industry, 1993–1997 —Continued

**ILLINOIS** (Millions of dollars.)

| Industry | Japan 1993 | Japan 1994 | Japan 1995 | Japan 1996 | Japan 1997 | South Korea 1993 | South Korea 1994 | South Korea 1995 | South Korea 1996 | South Korea 1997 |
|---|---|---|---|---|---|---|---|---|---|---|
| ALL GOODS | 1 916.8 | 2 121.5 | 2 940.1 | 3 024.6 | 2 437.4 | 533.2 | 698.1 | 1 266.2 | 1 301.0 | 892.6 |
| Manufactured goods | 1 351.7 | 1 671.5 | 2 599.1 | 2 554.6 | 2 031.4 | 495.2 | 614.2 | 1 026.5 | 1 024.4 | 785.2 |
| Food products | 264.4 | 187.7 | 256.6 | 254.3 | 184.2 | 29.2 | 24.8 | 48.6 | 34.0 | 38.1 |
| Tobacco products | ..... | ..... | ..... | ..... | ..... | 0.1 | 0.1 | 0.2 | ..... | ..... |
| Textile mill products | 0.7 | 1.3 | 1.5 | 4.4 | 2.4 | 0.2 | 0.8 | 1.1 | 1.3 | 1.4 |
| Apparel | 8.2 | 7.4 | 7.3 | 8.0 | 5.5 | 0.2 | 0.1 | 0.4 | 1.5 | 0.7 |
| Lumber and wood products | 11.8 | 8.6 | 9.8 | 7.7 | 8.7 | 3.2 | 2.5 | 1.9 | 2.1 | 2.7 |
| Furniture and fixtures | 4.1 | 3.6 | 5.5 | 10.2 | 4.3 | 0.2 | 0.4 | 0.5 | 1.1 | 1.7 |
| Paper products | 7.4 | 9.3 | 9.9 | 13.7 | 13.3 | 6.8 | 8.9 | 5.9 | 5.4 | 4.0 |
| Printing and publishing | 6.5 | 7.3 | 7.9 | 8.1 | 7.6 | 1.1 | 1.3 | 1.9 | 2.6 | 2.1 |
| Chemical products | 240.5 | 249.9 | 370.4 | 338.2 | 353.2 | 106.1 | 72.5 | 166.4 | 138.5 | 108.9 |
| Refined petroleum products | 4.0 | 5.2 | 6.4 | 8.1 | 7.4 | 3.1 | 2.8 | 3.5 | 5.5 | 5.8 |
| Rubber and plastic products | 21.1 | 26.4 | 48.8 | 59.7 | 64.1 | 4.5 | 7.3 | 10.5 | 10.9 | 9.7 |
| Leather products | 1.1 | 1.0 | 1.1 | 3.2 | 1.6 | 0.5 | 0.3 | 0.1 | 1.1 | 0.5 |
| Stone, clay and glass products | 9.6 | 9.5 | 6.4 | 5.2 | 9.5 | 3.8 | 3.6 | 7.2 | 16.3 | 15.7 |
| Primary metals | 22.8 | 26.0 | 50.9 | 31.9 | 43.9 | 5.0 | 7.3 | 10.7 | 14.8 | 36.2 |
| Fabricated metal products | 36.7 | 42.3 | 40.4 | 48.2 | 50.8 | 12.5 | 13.2 | 21.0 | 22.0 | 22.5 |
| Industrial machinery and computers | 220.7 | 263.5 | 366.6 | 386.5 | 386.7 | 100.8 | 118.8 | 202.7 | 230.6 | 145.4 |
| Electric and electronic equipment | 270.5 | 562.3 | 1 058.7 | 994.1 | 569.8 | 151.3 | 246.8 | 409.3 | 408.9 | 251.8 |
| Transportation equipment | 51.0 | 73.9 | 119.1 | 88.3 | 76.0 | 34.4 | 52.6 | 68.1 | 67.1 | 82.8 |
| Scientific and measuring instruments | 126.7 | 145.4 | 182.7 | 224.7 | 185.2 | 27.4 | 40.4 | 52.7 | 44.4 | 45.8 |
| Miscellaneous manufactures | 41.7 | 37.8 | 45.1 | 56.6 | 54.4 | 3.9 | 8.4 | 12.4 | 14.4 | 8.3 |
| Unidentified manufactures | 2.3 | 3.1 | 3.8 | 3.4 | 2.8 | 1.0 | 1.4 | 1.6 | 1.7 | 1.2 |
| Agricultural and livestock products | 539.3 | 405.2 | 294.1 | 443.1 | 374.4 | 27.9 | 42.2 | 218.4 | 262.1 | 100.4 |
| Agricultural products | 534.8 | 401.0 | 289.7 | 437.6 | 371.2 | 27.8 | 41.7 | 217.7 | 261.3 | 98.6 |
| Livestock and livestock products | 4.5 | 4.2 | 4.4 | 5.6 | 3.2 | 0.2 | 0.6 | 0.7 | 0.9 | 1.8 |
| Other commodities | 25.8 | 44.7 | 47.0 | 26.8 | 31.5 | 10.0 | 41.7 | 21.2 | 14.5 | 7.0 |
| Forestry products | ..... | ..... | ..... | 0.1 | 0.1 | 0.3 | ..... | ..... | 0.1 | ..... |
| Fish and other marine products | 0.1 | 0.3 | 0.5 | 0.6 | 2.1 | ..... | 0.1 | 0.1 | 0.1 | ..... |
| Metallic ores and concentrates | 0.5 | 0.2 | ..... | ..... | 0.2 | ..... | ..... | ..... | ..... | ..... |
| Bituminous coal and lignite | 4.0 | 12.7 | 7.6 | 4.0 | ..... | 5.0 | 4.6 | 7.6 | 3.0 | ..... |
| Crude petroleum and natural gas | ..... | ..... | ..... | ..... | ..... | ..... | 0.1 | 0.1 | ..... | ..... |
| Nonmetallic minerals | 5.1 | 7.2 | 7.5 | 4.3 | 5.8 | 3.2 | 33.0 | 7.7 | 4.0 | 4.0 |
| Scrap and waste | 12.0 | 15.3 | 13.8 | 3.1 | 4.4 | 1.1 | 3.3 | 4.4 | 5.1 | 1.6 |
| Used merchandise | 2.6 | 6.2 | 11.6 | 12.5 | 12.8 | ..... | 0.2 | 0.4 | 0.5 | 0.4 |
| Goods imported and returned unchanged | ..... | ..... | ..... | ..... | ..... | ..... | ..... | ..... | ..... | ..... |
| Special classification provisions | 1.3 | 2.9 | 6.0 | 2.2 | 6.0 | 0.2 | 0.3 | 1.0 | 1.7 | 1.0 |

| Industry | Taiwan 1993 | Taiwan 1994 | Taiwan 1995 | Taiwan 1996 | Taiwan 1997 | Singapore 1993 | Singapore 1994 | Singapore 1995 | Singapore 1996 | Singapore 1997 |
|---|---|---|---|---|---|---|---|---|---|---|
| ALL GOODS | 481.2 | 637.8 | 592.1 | 512.2 | 496.1 | 309.8 | 356.3 | 649.7 | 744.7 | 720.6 |
| Manufactured goods | 467.6 | 562.6 | 571.2 | 454.0 | 462.1 | 307.8 | 354.1 | 646.1 | 740.4 | 710.2 |
| Food products | 19.8 | 22.3 | 28.0 | 29.2 | 44.0 | 19.7 | 22.7 | 30.3 | 29.3 | 41.1 |
| Tobacco products | ..... | ..... | ..... | 0.2 | ..... | ..... | ..... | ..... | ..... | ..... |
| Textile mill products | 0.6 | 0.5 | 0.6 | 0.4 | 0.3 | 0.8 | 1.2 | 1.5 | 1.0 | 1.0 |
| Apparel | 0.4 | 0.3 | 0.5 | 0.5 | 0.3 | 0.3 | 0.4 | 0.6 | 0.6 | 0.7 |
| Lumber and wood products | 0.3 | 0.6 | 0.7 | 0.7 | 0.3 | 0.1 | 0.2 | 0.4 | 0.3 | 0.2 |
| Furniture and fixtures | 1.2 | 0.9 | 1.8 | 1.4 | 0.9 | 0.4 | 0.8 | 1.0 | 1.5 | 0.8 |
| Paper products | 9.3 | 14.4 | 21.6 | 19.5 | 22.6 | 1.3 | 3.1 | 6.3 | 6.8 | 5.3 |
| Printing and publishing | 0.9 | 1.2 | 1.6 | 2.1 | 2.4 | 4.7 | 3.5 | 2.4 | 3.8 | 5.6 |
| Chemical products | 175.6 | 250.3 | 248.9 | 139.9 | 75.4 | 37.9 | 39.9 | 60.0 | 80.2 | 42.4 |
| Refined petroleum products | 1.1 | 1.5 | 1.6 | 2.0 | 1.8 | 0.3 | 0.3 | 6.0 | 14.2 | 1.2 |
| Rubber and plastic products | 3.5 | 4.7 | 5.4 | 4.9 | 6.8 | 4.7 | 7.6 | 10.3 | 21.9 | 18.8 |
| Leather products | 1.8 | 0.7 | 0.5 | 0.5 | 0.2 | 0.1 | 0.1 | 0.3 | 0.3 | 1.5 |
| Stone, clay and glass products | 4.3 | 4.4 | 5.1 | 4.0 | 3.8 | 1.9 | 3.2 | 4.3 | 6.1 | 7.7 |
| Primary metals | 6.9 | 7.0 | 9.3 | 9.1 | 15.7 | 7.4 | 5.2 | 7.2 | 5.2 | 8.3 |
| Fabricated metal products | 13.3 | 11.4 | 22.5 | 15.2 | 27.0 | 6.3 | 7.2 | 13.3 | 18.2 | 19.7 |
| Industrial machinery and computers | 66.1 | 68.9 | 68.7 | 68.4 | 67.6 | 38.0 | 64.1 | 234.7 | 216.2 | 165.0 |
| Electric and electronic equipment | 90.6 | 102.6 | 84.8 | 91.9 | 126.7 | 145.4 | 146.9 | 206.9 | 232.7 | 278.9 |
| Transportation equipment | 41.1 | 37.7 | 31.0 | 19.8 | 15.4 | 6.1 | 7.4 | 20.3 | 47.4 | 45.0 |
| Scientific and measuring instruments | 18.1 | 19.2 | 23.6 | 25.8 | 27.6 | 25.0 | 32.8 | 33.8 | 47.2 | 60.0 |
| Miscellaneous manufactures | 11.5 | 11.7 | 14.0 | 17.6 | 22.1 | 6.0 | 6.5 | 5.3 | 6.3 | 5.7 |
| Unidentified manufactures | 1.3 | 2.3 | 1.0 | 1.2 | 1.0 | 1.3 | 1.1 | 1.1 | 1.2 | 1.0 |
| Agricultural and livestock products | 8.2 | 67.5 | 10.2 | 53.9 | 26.7 | 0.6 | 0.2 | 0.3 | 0.2 | 7.1 |
| Agricultural products | 7.6 | 67.0 | 9.4 | 52.6 | 26.7 | 0.6 | 0.2 | 0.3 | 0.1 | 7.1 |
| Livestock and livestock products | 0.6 | 0.6 | 0.8 | 1.3 | 0.1 | ..... | ..... | ..... | ..... | ..... |
| Other commodities | 5.4 | 7.6 | 10.6 | 4.4 | 7.3 | 1.4 | 2.0 | 3.3 | 4.1 | 3.3 |
| Forestry products | ..... | 0.1 | ..... | ..... | ..... | 0.1 | ..... | ..... | 0.1 | ..... |
| Fish and other marine products | ..... | ..... | ..... | ..... | ..... | ..... | 0.1 | 0.1 | ..... | ..... |
| Metallic ores and concentrates | ..... | ..... | ..... | ..... | ..... | ..... | ..... | ..... | ..... | ..... |
| Bituminous coal and lignite | ..... | ..... | ..... | ..... | ..... | ..... | ..... | ..... | ..... | ..... |
| Crude petroleum and natural gas | ..... | ..... | ..... | ..... | ..... | ..... | ..... | ..... | ..... | ..... |
| Nonmetallic minerals | 3.0 | 3.0 | 2.5 | 2.5 | 3.6 | 0.7 | 1.2 | 0.8 | 0.9 | 0.8 |
| Scrap and waste | 1.8 | 4.3 | 7.8 | 1.5 | 3.2 | 0.1 | 0.1 | 1.6 | 1.9 | 0.6 |
| Used merchandise | 0.2 | 0.1 | 0.1 | ..... | 0.1 | 0.1 | 0.2 | 0.3 | 0.5 | 0.2 |
| Goods imported and returned unchanged | ..... | ..... | ..... | ..... | ..... | ..... | ..... | ..... | ..... | ..... |
| Special classification provisions | 0.3 | 0.1 | 0.3 | 0.4 | 0.4 | 0.5 | 0.4 | 0.5 | 0.7 | 1.7 |

## INDIANA: Exports of Goods, 1997

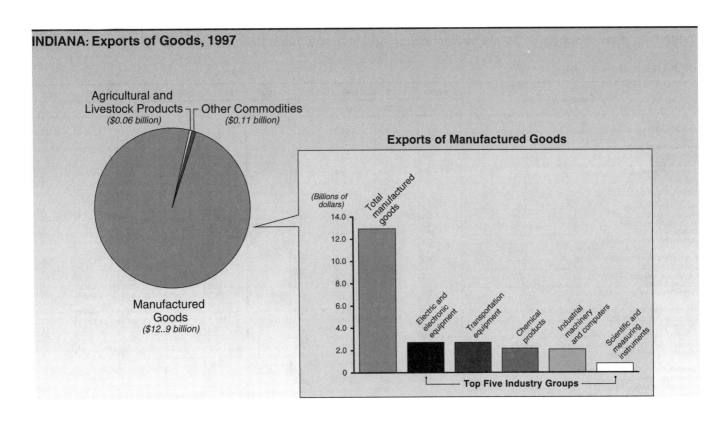

## Table D-3.   State Exports of Goods by Destination and Industry, 1993–1997 —Continued

### INDIANA (Millions of dollars.)

| Industry | 1993 | 1994 | 1995 | 1996 | 1997 | 1993 | 1994 | 1995 | 1996 | 1997 |
|---|---|---|---|---|---|---|---|---|---|---|
| | All destinations | | | | | Canada | | | | |
| **ALL GOODS** | 8 445.2 | 9 534.0 | 11 052.0 | 12 119.0 | 13 097.3 | 4 264.6 | 4 593.6 | 4 594.8 | 4 630.3 | 5 060.3 |
| **Manufactured goods** | 8 311.6 | 9 384.0 | 10 898.3 | 11 950.8 | 12 930.8 | 4 198.4 | 4 515.2 | 4 514.4 | 4 538.8 | 4 957.4 |
| Food products | 153.7 | 182.0 | 224.7 | 243.7 | 248.7 | 58.6 | 49.4 | 52.8 | 70.9 | 60.7 |
| Tobacco products | ..... | ..... | 7.8 | ..... | ..... | ..... | ..... | ..... | ..... | ..... |
| Textile mill products | 16.9 | 19.6 | 32.4 | 27.1 | 33.6 | 11.5 | 13.2 | 22.2 | 20.2 | 20.2 |
| Apparel | 11.7 | 12.5 | 21.6 | 20.9 | 23.7 | 4.3 | 6.0 | 6.1 | 5.1 | 6.5 |
| Lumber and wood products | 112.5 | 125.6 | 116.7 | 116.9 | 130.5 | 28.7 | 29.6 | 29.2 | 31.2 | 39.8 |
| Furniture and fixtures | 96.1 | 134.9 | 92.8 | 90.1 | 101.4 | 69.5 | 105.2 | 59.9 | 47.0 | 49.2 |
| Paper products | 48.2 | 60.8 | 110.5 | 121.0 | 103.1 | 23.6 | 22.7 | 29.7 | 34.2 | 35.8 |
| Printing and publishing | 59.3 | 70.4 | 103.9 | 97.0 | 122.2 | 25.9 | 24.5 | 31.9 | 37.1 | 62.1 |
| Chemical products | 1 198.6 | 1 314.4 | 1 681.8 | 1 971.2 | 2 162.3 | 183.8 | 212.2 | 281.2 | 254.7 | 261.3 |
| Refined petroleum products | 19.2 | 24.4 | 22.2 | 24.7 | 23.7 | 9.4 | 11.4 | 10.7 | 11.0 | 12.6 |
| Rubber and plastic products | 188.6 | 252.9 | 310.1 | 401.1 | 449.3 | 109.1 | 136.3 | 142.5 | 146.6 | 162.7 |
| Leather products | 4.4 | 10.0 | 11.1 | 9.5 | 10.4 | 1.0 | 1.0 | 1.1 | 1.0 | 1.2 |
| Stone, clay and glass products | 83.9 | 81.2 | 104.8 | 85.0 | 112.3 | 68.0 | 63.0 | 64.5 | 52.0 | 49.1 |
| Primary metals | 229.8 | 307.7 | 445.3 | 450.1 | 516.0 | 131.7 | 156.5 | 212.6 | 205.9 | 277.4 |
| Fabricated metal products | 394.9 | 345.7 | 371.6 | 451.8 | 516.9 | 292.1 | 203.1 | 192.3 | 190.9 | 206.4 |
| Industrial machinery and computers | 1 284.3 | 1 509.6 | 1 700.0 | 1 866.8 | 2 082.4 | 517.9 | 576.0 | 665.3 | 678.9 | 783.4 |
| Electric and electronic equipment | 1 577.4 | 1 799.5 | 2 104.6 | 2 582.5 | 2 704.4 | 861.1 | 889.0 | 602.3 | 508.5 | 615.1 |
| Transportation equipment | 1 797.6 | 1 918.4 | 2 364.8 | 2 504.2 | 2 692.5 | 1 456.0 | 1 583.8 | 1 787.7 | 1 940.3 | 2 020.8 |
| Scientific and measuring instruments | 957.2 | 1 130.6 | 993.1 | 804.6 | 813.4 | 318.7 | 402.8 | 303.4 | 282.4 | 265.7 |
| Miscellaneous manufactures | 59.4 | 54.1 | 51.4 | 55.4 | 60.5 | 22.5 | 14.6 | 10.3 | 10.9 | 15.5 |
| Unidentified manufactures | 17.8 | 29.5 | 27.1 | 27.3 | 23.3 | 4.7 | 15.1 | 8.7 | 9.9 | 11.8 |
| **Agricultural and livestock products** | 58.5 | 53.0 | 52.9 | 55.8 | 60.0 | 15.5 | 10.2 | 9.1 | 8.6 | 22.4 |
| Agricultural products | 54.7 | 47.5 | 48.6 | 50.9 | 55.9 | 12.4 | 5.4 | 5.6 | 4.9 | 19.6 |
| Livestock and livestock products | 3.8 | 5.5 | 4.2 | 4.9 | 4.1 | 3.0 | 4.9 | 3.4 | 3.6 | 2.9 |
| **Other commodities** | 75.1 | 97.1 | 100.8 | 112.4 | 106.4 | 50.8 | 68.1 | 71.3 | 83.0 | 80.5 |
| Forestry products | 0.9 | 1.0 | 1.1 | 1.0 | 1.2 | ..... | 0.1 | ..... | 0.1 | 0.1 |
| Fish and other marine products | 2.6 | 1.4 | 1.7 | 0.7 | 1.7 | 1.6 | 1.0 | 1.0 | 0.3 | ..... |
| Metallic ores and concentrates | 0.2 | 0.3 | 0.5 | 0.8 | 1.1 | ..... | ..... | ..... | 0.1 | ..... |
| Bituminous coal and lignite | 0.9 | 0.9 | 3.2 | 3.6 | 1.6 | ..... | 0.8 | ..... | 1.3 | ..... |
| Crude petroleum and natural gas | ..... | ..... | 0.2 | 2.0 | 0.1 | ..... | ..... | 0.1 | 2.0 | ..... |
| Nonmetallic minerals | 2.7 | 2.1 | 3.2 | 3.2 | 4.0 | 2.3 | 1.9 | 2.3 | 3.0 | 2.9 |
| Scrap and waste | 12.4 | 25.3 | 37.0 | 35.2 | 37.2 | 12.1 | 24.2 | 30.9 | 33.4 | 35.6 |
| Used merchandise | 10.8 | 12.0 | 9.3 | 10.3 | 5.3 | 0.8 | 1.5 | 0.4 | 0.6 | 1.2 |
| Goods imported and returned unchanged | 27.6 | 31.0 | 31.7 | 36.5 | 35.7 | 27.6 | 31.0 | 31.7 | 36.5 | 35.7 |
| Special classification provisions | 16.8 | 22.9 | 12.8 | 19.0 | 18.6 | 6.3 | 7.7 | 5.0 | 5.6 | 5.0 |

## Table D-3.  State Exports of Goods by Destination and Industry, 1993–1997 —*Continued*

**INDIANA** (Millions of dollars.)

| Industry | South and Central America and Caribbean | | | | | Mexico | | | | |
|---|---|---|---|---|---|---|---|---|---|---|
| | 1993 | 1994 | 1995 | 1996 | 1997 | 1993 | 1994 | 1995 | 1996 | 1997 |
| **ALL GOODS** | 250.5 | 316.0 | 486.2 | 511.1 | 716.0 | 1 167.7 | 1 492.6 | 1 955.7 | 2 529.3 | 2 573.3 |
| **Manufactured goods** | 248.5 | 308.4 | 478.6 | 501.7 | 709.2 | 1 156.9 | 1 480.8 | 1 952.3 | 2 524.5 | 2 567.7 |
| Food products | 12.5 | 11.3 | 23.5 | 16.8 | 8.5 | 4.9 | 10.8 | 3.0 | 3.2 | 21.3 |
| Tobacco products | ..... | ..... | ..... | ..... | ..... | ..... | ..... | ..... | ..... | ..... |
| Textile mill products | 0.3 | 0.5 | 0.7 | 0.4 | 3.3 | 0.3 | 0.3 | 0.7 | 1.1 | 3.9 |
| Apparel | 1.3 | 0.3 | 0.6 | 0.7 | 0.9 | 0.2 | 0.5 | 9.7 | 9.2 | 11.4 |
| Lumber and wood products | 1.0 | 0.6 | 1.5 | 1.8 | 1.1 | 1.0 | 2.8 | 2.8 | 2.7 | 2.6 |
| Furniture and fixtures | 3.8 | 3.2 | 5.1 | 6.6 | 6.3 | 2.7 | 4.6 | 2.2 | 2.1 | 5.6 |
| Paper products | 3.1 | 6.2 | 22.6 | 22.4 | 10.3 | 5.6 | 15.7 | 40.1 | 43.0 | 34.7 |
| Printing and publishing | 4.2 | 7.6 | 10.6 | 12.8 | 18.8 | 2.0 | 6.0 | 6.4 | 6.7 | 7.3 |
| Chemical products | 63.0 | 80.4 | 173.2 | 180.1 | 229.3 | 37.7 | 28.0 | 46.9 | 75.2 | 82.6 |
| Refined petroleum products | 0.2 | 0.4 | 0.7 | 1.3 | 1.1 | 0.8 | 0.6 | 0.5 | 1.1 | 1.2 |
| Rubber and plastic products | 8.2 | 7.4 | 12.5 | 9.9 | 15.0 | 21.1 | 48.9 | 80.3 | 136.2 | 135.1 |
| Leather products | 0.2 | 0.5 | 0.9 | 0.5 | 0.5 | 0.1 | 1.7 | 0.9 | 0.3 | 0.2 |
| Stone, clay and glass products | 0.6 | 1.0 | 1.2 | 0.9 | 15.4 | 2.9 | 4.4 | 22.8 | 18.1 | 30.0 |
| Primary metals | 5.9 | 4.1 | 14.6 | 11.6 | 13.5 | 18.5 | 47.8 | 76.2 | 101.0 | 98.0 |
| Fabricated metal products | 5.9 | 6.5 | 9.3 | 10.4 | 13.8 | 30.0 | 67.8 | 81.2 | 138.7 | 145.3 |
| Industrial machinery and computers | 78.0 | 111.2 | 93.0 | 98.7 | 103.2 | 144.0 | 157.5 | 159.3 | 164.8 | 231.1 |
| Electric and electronic equipment | 16.8 | 27.8 | 46.9 | 48.1 | 64.9 | 500.6 | 662.3 | 1 144.5 | 1 711.9 | 1 643.3 |
| Transportation equipment | 30.9 | 22.7 | 38.2 | 60.8 | 178.6 | 25.5 | 33.0 | 29.3 | 44.3 | 47.4 |
| Scientific and measuring instruments | 9.8 | 13.8 | 19.5 | 15.4 | 22.2 | 356.2 | 383.8 | 242.5 | 61.4 | 63.9 |
| Miscellaneous manufactures | 1.8 | 2.1 | 3.0 | 2.0 | 1.3 | 1.0 | 1.6 | 1.0 | 1.0 | 0.9 |
| Unidentified manufactures | 0.9 | 0.7 | 1.1 | 0.8 | 1.2 | 1.7 | 2.9 | 2.1 | 2.4 | 1.9 |
| **Agricultural and livestock products** | 1.9 | 6.8 | 4.0 | 4.2 | 1.7 | 1.7 | 0.4 | 0.7 | 1.3 | 1.2 |
| Agricultural products | 1.9 | 6.8 | 4.0 | 4.3 | 1.6 | 1.5 | 0.4 | 0.7 | 1.2 | 1.0 |
| Livestock and livestock products | ..... | 0.1 | ..... | ..... | ..... | 0.2 | ..... | ..... | 0.1 | 0.2 |
| **Other commodities** | 0.2 | 0.6 | 3.6 | 5.1 | 5.1 | 9.0 | 11.5 | 2.6 | 3.5 | 4.4 |
| Forestry products | ..... | ..... | ..... | ..... | 0.1 | 0.6 | 0.6 | 0.8 | 0.8 | 0.7 |
| Fish and other marine products | ..... | ..... | ..... | ..... | ..... | ..... | ..... | ..... | ..... | 1.4 |
| Metallic ores and concentrates | ..... | ..... | ..... | ..... | ..... | ..... | ..... | ..... | ..... | 0.1 |
| Bituminous coal and lignite | ..... | ..... | 3.2 | 2.3 | 1.6 | ..... | ..... | ..... | ..... | ..... |
| Crude petroleum and natural gas | ..... | ..... | ..... | ..... | ..... | ..... | ..... | ..... | ..... | ..... |
| Nonmetallic minerals | 0.1 | ..... | 0.1 | ..... | 0.4 | ..... | ..... | ..... | ..... | 0.1 |
| Scrap and waste | ..... | 0.3 | 0.2 | ..... | ..... | 0.1 | 0.1 | 0.2 | 0.6 | 0.6 |
| Used merchandise | 0.1 | 0.2 | 0.1 | 0.3 | ..... | 0.1 | 0.1 | ..... | ..... | ..... |
| Goods imported and returned unchanged | ..... | ..... | ..... | ..... | ..... | ..... | ..... | ..... | ..... | ..... |
| Special classification provisions | ..... | ..... | 0.1 | 2.5 | 3.0 | 8.2 | 10.7 | 1.6 | 2.1 | 1.5 |

| Industry | European Union | | | | | United Kingdom | | | | |
|---|---|---|---|---|---|---|---|---|---|---|
| | 1993 | 1994 | 1995 | 1996 | 1997 | 1993 | 1994 | 1995 | 1996 | 1997 |
| **ALL GOODS** | 1 353.3 | 1 555.7 | 1 901.8 | 2 149.5 | 2 377.7 | 427.9 | 495.7 | 627.5 | 644.0 | 704.8 |
| **Manufactured goods** | 1 312.9 | 1 515.0 | 1 859.1 | 2 099.2 | 2 341.2 | 420.2 | 486.0 | 617.7 | 633.5 | 699.5 |
| Food products | 24.2 | 33.8 | 37.2 | 37.9 | 31.9 | 13.0 | 18.7 | 19.8 | 14.9 | 9.8 |
| Tobacco products | ..... | ..... | 7.7 | ..... | ..... | ..... | ..... | ..... | ..... | ..... |
| Textile mill products | 1.4 | 3.6 | 3.7 | 2.4 | 3.7 | 0.6 | 0.6 | 1.0 | 0.8 | 0.7 |
| Apparel | 3.1 | 4.0 | 3.0 | 2.1 | 2.4 | 0.9 | 2.0 | 1.2 | 0.7 | 0.5 |
| Lumber and wood products | 52.7 | 59.9 | 51.2 | 49.3 | 53.2 | 5.7 | 8.1 | 8.2 | 7.5 | 6.0 |
| Furniture and fixtures | 5.5 | 3.8 | 5.2 | 6.5 | 8.4 | 1.1 | 0.9 | 1.0 | 1.3 | 1.9 |
| Paper products | 4.6 | 4.3 | 3.8 | 5.2 | 8.9 | 1.3 | 1.3 | 0.8 | 1.3 | 2.3 |
| Printing and publishing | 16.2 | 19.5 | 33.5 | 18.5 | 16.5 | 9.3 | 8.8 | 15.3 | 12.5 | 11.4 |
| Chemical products | 470.4 | 537.7 | 640.8 | 870.2 | 999.7 | 98.3 | 108.4 | 177.7 | 184.6 | 191.6 |
| Refined petroleum products | 1.6 | 2.4 | 2.6 | 2.0 | 1.8 | 0.4 | 0.5 | 1.2 | 0.6 | 0.7 |
| Rubber and plastic products | 33.9 | 33.5 | 40.6 | 59.5 | 75.5 | 10.0 | 10.3 | 13.0 | 24.9 | 22.4 |
| Leather products | 1.8 | 2.6 | 2.6 | 3.3 | 3.9 | 0.7 | 1.5 | 1.8 | 2.1 | 2.4 |
| Stone, clay and glass products | 7.1 | 7.2 | 9.0 | 7.0 | 9.5 | 2.1 | 1.7 | 2.7 | 2.4 | 3.3 |
| Primary metals | 49.1 | 63.9 | 76.7 | 62.5 | 66.5 | 14.1 | 18.2 | 26.4 | 21.5 | 25.6 |
| Fabricated metal products | 22.3 | 21.7 | 32.9 | 38.5 | 49.6 | 6.1 | 7.8 | 9.6 | 10.9 | 11.4 |
| Industrial machinery and computers | 253.7 | 309.6 | 349.1 | 343.2 | 364.4 | 152.0 | 181.7 | 206.7 | 203.4 | 214.8 |
| Electric and electronic equipment | 90.0 | 93.3 | 115.6 | 113.2 | 133.6 | 25.2 | 26.2 | 31.5 | 35.0 | 39.4 |
| Transportation equipment | 149.6 | 159.2 | 260.0 | 253.7 | 267.6 | 54.3 | 56.1 | 63.1 | 62.2 | 66.0 |
| Scientific and measuring instruments | 106.9 | 134.8 | 163.2 | 200.4 | 224.1 | 18.9 | 26.2 | 30.6 | 38.2 | 83.7 |
| Miscellaneous manufactures | 13.5 | 14.3 | 13.2 | 18.0 | 16.8 | 5.0 | 4.9 | 3.9 | 7.5 | 4.5 |
| Unidentified manufactures | 5.3 | 5.8 | 7.7 | 5.8 | 3.2 | 1.6 | 2.0 | 2.2 | 1.2 | 1.2 |
| **Agricultural and livestock products** | 30.3 | 28.6 | 27.8 | 35.6 | 27.7 | 1.3 | 1.7 | 1.0 | 1.7 | 2.2 |
| Agricultural products | 30.1 | 28.3 | 27.4 | 35.1 | 27.3 | 1.3 | 1.5 | 1.0 | 1.7 | 2.2 |
| Livestock and livestock products | 0.3 | 0.4 | 0.4 | 0.5 | 0.4 | ..... | 0.2 | ..... | ..... | ..... |
| **Other commodities** | 10.1 | 12.1 | 14.9 | 14.7 | 8.9 | 6.4 | 8.0 | 8.8 | 8.8 | 3.1 |
| Forestry products | 0.2 | 0.2 | 0.1 | ..... | 0.1 | ..... | ..... | ..... | ..... | ..... |
| Fish and other marine products | 0.3 | 0.2 | 0.4 | 0.3 | 0.2 | ..... | ..... | ..... | ..... | ..... |
| Metallic ores and concentrates | 0.1 | 0.2 | 0.5 | 0.7 | 1.0 | 0.1 | 0.1 | 0.3 | 0.5 | 0.6 |
| Bituminous coal and lignite | 0.9 | ..... | ..... | ..... | ..... | ..... | ..... | ..... | ..... | ..... |
| Crude petroleum and natural gas | ..... | ..... | 0.1 | ..... | ..... | ..... | ..... | ..... | ..... | ..... |
| Nonmetallic minerals | 0.1 | ..... | 0.7 | 0.1 | 0.2 | ..... | ..... | 0.2 | ..... | ..... |
| Scrap and waste | 0.1 | 0.6 | 2.7 | 0.5 | 0.2 | 0.1 | 0.1 | 1.9 | 0.2 | 0.1 |
| Used merchandise | 7.2 | 7.9 | 8.2 | 8.4 | 2.1 | 5.8 | 6.9 | 5.9 | 7.0 | 0.1 |
| Goods imported and returned unchanged | ..... | ..... | ..... | ..... | ..... | ..... | ..... | ..... | ..... | ..... |
| Special classification provisions | 1.2 | 2.8 | 2.1 | 4.8 | 5.2 | 0.4 | 0.9 | 0.4 | 1.2 | 2.3 |

## Table D-3. State Exports of Goods by Destination and Industry, 1993–1997 —*Continued*

**INDIANA** (Millions of dollars.)

| Industry | 1993 | 1994 | 1995 | 1996 | 1997 | 1993 | 1994 | 1995 | 1996 | 1997 |
|---|---|---|---|---|---|---|---|---|---|---|
| | Germany | | | | | France | | | | |
| **ALL GOODS** | 219.5 | 294.1 | 290.3 | 288.9 | 337.3 | 146.5 | 170.1 | 191.2 | 298.8 | 389.2 |
| **Manufactured goods** | 216.1 | 291.2 | 286.9 | 285.5 | 333.1 | 145.2 | 169.3 | 189.0 | 295.4 | 386.7 |
| Food products | 1.3 | 1.9 | 1.9 | 2.6 | 3.0 | 0.5 | 0.5 | 0.6 | 1.0 | 0.7 |
| Tobacco products | ..... | ..... | ..... | ..... | | | | | | |
| Textile mill products | 0.5 | 2.5 | 0.8 | 0.4 | 0.6 | 0.1 | 0.2 | 0.1 | 0.4 | 0.4 |
| Apparel | 0.9 | 1.3 | 0.8 | 0.3 | 0.7 | 0.1 | 0.1 | 0.1 | 0.3 | 0.3 |
| Lumber and wood products | 26.8 | 32.4 | 23.6 | 20.1 | 23.3 | 3.3 | 0.7 | 0.4 | 0.7 | 0.8 |
| Furniture and fixtures | 1.3 | 0.4 | 0.6 | 0.6 | 0.6 | 1.0 | 1.5 | 2.0 | 3.2 | 3.0 |
| Paper products | 0.3 | 0.1 | 0.2 | 0.3 | 1.1 | 0.3 | 0.4 | 0.2 | 1.1 | 2.1 |
| Printing and publishing | 0.7 | 1.8 | 7.3 | 1.6 | 1.8 | 0.7 | 0.8 | 2.3 | 0.5 | 0.2 |
| Chemical products | 55.3 | 117.0 | 108.1 | 120.1 | 145.7 | 74.8 | 73.6 | 76.1 | 185.6 | 261.6 |
| Refined petroleum products | ..... | ..... | ..... | ..... | 0.1 | 0.2 | 0.6 | 0.5 | 0.5 | 0.7 |
| Rubber and plastic products | 6.4 | 7.6 | 3.6 | 4.4 | 5.5 | 1.2 | 0.7 | 3.7 | 3.2 | 5.0 |
| Leather products | 0.5 | 0.6 | 0.4 | 0.7 | 0.9 | 0.1 | 0.1 | ..... | ..... | 0.1 |
| Stone, clay and glass products | 2.9 | 3.7 | 3.8 | 2.5 | 2.5 | 0.3 | 0.5 | 1.3 | 1.1 | 2.0 |
| Primary metals | 17.9 | 27.4 | 24.6 | 8.2 | 11.6 | 7.0 | 6.4 | 8.6 | 7.7 | 6.6 |
| Fabricated metal products | 4.9 | 3.4 | 5.7 | 8.5 | 7.2 | 2.7 | 1.9 | 2.7 | 6.0 | 13.0 |
| Industrial machinery and computers | 25.7 | 27.7 | 31.9 | 33.6 | 38.9 | 17.5 | 29.5 | 26.9 | 22.1 | 21.0 |
| Electric and electronic equipment | 24.2 | 21.2 | 30.2 | 19.2 | 26.6 | 9.5 | 9.7 | 17.8 | 17.1 | 21.5 |
| Transportation equipment | 28.1 | 19.4 | 20.3 | 22.8 | 27.7 | 10.9 | 16.1 | 20.3 | 21.0 | 21.9 |
| Scientific and measuring instruments | 13.3 | 18.0 | 18.9 | 35.3 | 29.3 | 13.6 | 24.5 | 23.9 | 22.2 | 24.1 |
| Miscellaneous manufactures | 4.0 | 4.3 | 3.4 | 3.7 | 5.7 | 1.4 | 1.2 | 1.1 | 1.4 | 1.3 |
| Unidentified manufactures | 1.0 | 0.7 | 0.8 | 0.7 | 0.5 | 0.3 | 0.4 | 0.4 | 0.4 | 0.3 |
| **Agricultural and livestock products** | 3.1 | 2.4 | 2.0 | 1.8 | 2.2 | 0.4 | 0.4 | 1.4 | 2.8 | 0.4 |
| Agricultural products | 3.0 | 2.4 | 1.8 | 1.6 | 2.0 | 0.4 | 0.4 | 1.4 | 2.8 | 0.3 |
| Livestock and livestock products | ..... | ..... | 0.1 | 0.1 | 0.2 | ..... | ..... | ..... | ..... | ..... |
| **Other commodities** | 0.3 | 0.6 | 1.4 | 1.6 | 2.0 | 0.9 | 0.3 | 0.8 | 0.6 | 2.1 |
| Forestry products | 0.1 | 0.2 | 0.1 | ..... | 0.1 | ..... | ..... | ..... | ..... | ..... |
| Fish and other marine products | ..... | 0.1 | ..... | ..... | ..... | ..... | ..... | ..... | 0.1 | ..... |
| Metallic ores and concentrates | ..... | ..... | ..... | ..... | ..... | 0.1 | 0.1 | 0.2 | 0.2 | 0.4 |
| Bituminous coal and lignite | ..... | ..... | ..... | ..... | ..... | ..... | ..... | ..... | ..... | ..... |
| Crude petroleum and natural gas | ..... | ..... | ..... | ..... | ..... | ..... | ..... | ..... | ..... | ..... |
| Nonmetallic minerals | ..... | ..... | 0.1 | ..... | 0.1 | ..... | ..... | ..... | ..... | ..... |
| Scrap and waste | ..... | ..... | 0.1 | 0.2 | ..... | ..... | 0.1 | 0.5 | 0.1 | 0.1 |
| Used merchandise | 0.2 | 0.2 | 0.8 | 0.9 | 1.6 | 0.8 | 0.1 | 0.1 | ..... | 0.1 |
| Goods imported and returned unchanged | ..... | ..... | ..... | ..... | ..... | ..... | ..... | ..... | ..... | ..... |
| Special classification provisions | ..... | 0.1 | 0.2 | 0.4 | 0.3 | ..... | ..... | ..... | 0.2 | 1.5 |
| | The Netherlands | | | | | Asian 10 | | | | |
| **ALL GOODS** | 160.8 | 175.2 | 250.4 | 301.9 | 364.8 | 979.8 | 1 182.1 | 1 528.6 | 1 691.4 | 1 757.0 |
| **Manufactured goods** | 160.5 | 174.7 | 249.2 | 300.2 | 363.4 | 974.4 | 1 177.2 | 1 520.1 | 1 686.1 | 1 749.9 |
| Food products | 6.8 | 9.2 | 5.8 | 8.8 | 10.6 | 48.2 | 71.8 | 97.1 | 103.5 | 117.4 |
| Tobacco products | ..... | ..... | ..... | ..... | ..... | | | | | |
| Textile mill products | 0.1 | 0.2 | 0.9 | 0.1 | 0.3 | 3.0 | 1.5 | 2.4 | 2.6 | 1.6 |
| Apparel | 0.1 | ..... | 0.5 | 0.4 | 0.1 | 1.0 | 0.7 | 1.4 | 1.9 | 1.0 |
| Lumber and wood products | 1.2 | 1.5 | 2.6 | 1.2 | 0.7 | 21.3 | 25.4 | 23.2 | 23.6 | 25.1 |
| Furniture and fixtures | 1.6 | 0.4 | 0.7 | 0.4 | 1.6 | 4.2 | 5.3 | 6.9 | 8.5 | 11.0 |
| Paper products | 0.3 | 0.2 | 0.5 | 0.1 | 1.1 | 5.1 | 5.1 | 7.8 | 11.8 | 9.5 |
| Printing and publishing | 1.4 | 3.1 | 2.8 | 1.8 | 1.3 | 6.2 | 6.2 | 9.6 | 11.7 | 9.8 |
| Chemical products | 69.8 | 71.4 | 75.1 | 118.7 | 150.2 | 351.0 | 376.3 | 448.0 | 458.1 | 424.8 |
| Refined petroleum products | ..... | ..... | 0.4 | 0.6 | ..... | 5.0 | 7.6 | 5.8 | 6.9 | 5.5 |
| Rubber and plastic products | 10.4 | 9.9 | 13.7 | 16.4 | 30.6 | 8.7 | 18.3 | 21.3 | 32.7 | 44.6 |
| Leather products | ..... | ..... | ..... | 0.1 | 0.2 | 1.1 | 4.0 | 5.0 | 3.7 | 4.0 |
| Stone, clay and glass products | 0.1 | 0.1 | 0.3 | 0.1 | 0.2 | 4.0 | 4.3 | 4.8 | 5.2 | 6.9 |
| Primary metals | 0.7 | 1.4 | 6.2 | 12.1 | 11.6 | 15.5 | 23.1 | 49.9 | 51.8 | 46.9 |
| Fabricated metal products | 1.7 | 1.1 | 2.4 | 3.4 | 5.1 | 34.3 | 35.2 | 42.7 | 55.7 | 80.9 |
| Industrial machinery and computers | 11.6 | 22.5 | 26.5 | 24.5 | 35.1 | 194.3 | 238.7 | 296.6 | 425.0 | 440.0 |
| Electric and electronic equipment | 15.9 | 15.8 | 9.2 | 6.5 | 7.3 | 80.6 | 99.4 | 142.6 | 155.7 | 211.8 |
| Transportation equipment | 31.6 | 29.8 | 72.2 | 64.1 | 77.3 | 54.5 | 83.4 | 123.2 | 116.6 | 106.8 |
| Scientific and measuring instruments | 5.5 | 5.9 | 26.5 | 38.5 | 27.8 | 120.0 | 153.2 | 214.7 | 190.5 | 181.0 |
| Miscellaneous manufactures | 0.5 | 0.9 | 0.9 | 0.8 | 1.9 | 13.7 | 14.7 | 13.8 | 16.8 | 18.0 |
| Unidentified manufactures | 1.2 | 1.2 | 2.0 | 1.8 | 0.4 | 2.6 | 2.9 | 3.1 | 3.8 | 3.2 |
| **Agricultural and livestock products** | 0.3 | 0.5 | 0.6 | 0.6 | 0.3 | 1.5 | 1.7 | 2.8 | 2.7 | 3.6 |
| Agricultural products | 0.2 | 0.3 | 0.3 | 0.3 | 0.2 | 1.5 | 1.7 | 2.7 | 2.0 | 2.9 |
| Livestock and livestock products | 0.1 | 0.2 | 0.3 | 0.3 | 0.1 | ..... | ..... | 0.2 | 0.6 | 0.7 |
| **Other commodities** | 0.1 | 0.1 | 0.7 | 1.1 | 1.1 | 4.0 | 3.2 | 5.8 | 2.6 | 3.5 |
| Forestry products | ..... | ..... | ..... | ..... | ..... | 0.1 | ..... | 0.1 | ..... | ..... |
| Fish and other marine products | ..... | ..... | ..... | ..... | ..... | 0.7 | 0.1 | 0.2 | ..... | ..... |
| Metallic ores and concentrates | ..... | ..... | ..... | ..... | ..... | 0.1 | ..... | ..... | ..... | ..... |
| Bituminous coal and lignite | ..... | ..... | ..... | ..... | ..... | ..... | ..... | ..... | ..... | ..... |
| Crude petroleum and natural gas | ..... | ..... | ..... | ..... | ..... | ..... | ..... | ..... | ..... | ..... |
| Nonmetallic minerals | ..... | ..... | ..... | 0.1 | ..... | 0.1 | ..... | 0.1 | 0.1 | 0.1 | 0.4 |
| Scrap and waste | ..... | ..... | 0.1 | ..... | ..... | 0.1 | 0.1 | 2.7 | 0.5 | 0.8 |
| Used merchandise | ..... | ..... | 0.3 | 0.4 | 0.2 | 2.5 | 2.0 | 0.5 | 0.1 | 0.1 |
| Goods imported and returned unchanged | ..... | ..... | ..... | ..... | ..... | ..... | ..... | ..... | ..... | ..... |
| Special classification provisions | ..... | 0.1 | 0.2 | 0.7 | 0.8 | 0.5 | 0.9 | 2.2 | 1.9 | 2.1 |

## Table D-3.  State Exports of Goods by Destination and Industry, 1993–1997 —*Continued*

**INDIANA** (Millions of dollars.)

| Industry | 1993 | 1994 | 1995 | 1996 | 1997 | 1993 | 1994 | 1995 | 1996 | 1997 |
|---|---|---|---|---|---|---|---|---|---|---|
| | Japan | | | | | South Korea | | | | |
| **ALL GOODS** | 491.8 | 571.0 | 733.6 | 747.2 | 729.9 | 116.1 | 158.7 | 183.0 | 199.3 | 227.1 |
| **Manufactured goods** | 489.6 | 569.5 | 732.8 | 745.2 | 725.7 | 116.1 | 158.6 | 180.3 | 198.2 | 226.0 |
| Food products | 40.9 | 63.9 | 86.8 | 88.0 | 102.0 | 1.3 | 1.6 | 1.4 | 3.5 | 3.1 |
| Tobacco products | ..... | ..... | ..... | ..... | ..... | ..... | ..... | ..... | ..... | ..... |
| Textile mill products | 0.2 | 0.3 | 0.1 | 1.4 | 0.4 | 1.9 | 0.2 | 0.4 | 0.1 | 0.1 |
| Apparel | 0.5 | 0.3 | 0.5 | 0.8 | 0.5 | ..... | ..... | 0.1 | 0.1 | 0.1 |
| Lumber and wood products | 8.7 | 12.8 | 11.1 | 10.6 | 11.4 | 2.0 | 3.5 | 3.5 | 1.8 | 0.3 |
| Furniture and fixtures | 1.4 | 1.2 | 3.4 | 4.5 | 5.4 | 0.4 | 0.2 | 0.4 | 0.7 | 0.6 |
| Paper products | 0.4 | 0.3 | 0.9 | 3.6 | 3.7 | 0.6 | 0.8 | 0.2 | 0.6 | 0.4 |
| Printing and publishing | 1.0 | 1.1 | 2.2 | 2.2 | 1.8 | 0.5 | 1.1 | 1.5 | 1.6 | 1.1 |
| Chemical products | 250.2 | 252.0 | 296.3 | 294.8 | 240.1 | 26.4 | 31.8 | 32.7 | 30.8 | 33.1 |
| Refined petroleum products | 2.3 | 2.7 | 2.7 | 2.3 | 2.0 | 0.6 | 1.9 | 0.7 | 1.1 | 0.2 |
| Rubber and plastic products | 2.1 | 3.9 | 4.0 | 10.8 | 7.2 | 1.4 | 1.8 | 2.0 | 2.8 | 8.3 |
| Leather products | 0.1 | 0.7 | 0.3 | 0.4 | 0.4 | 0.2 | 0.4 | 0.3 | 0.2 | 0.2 |
| Stone, clay and glass products | 1.4 | 1.1 | 1.6 | 1.8 | 2.7 | 0.4 | 0.2 | 1.0 | 0.5 | 0.6 |
| Primary metals | 2.3 | 3.8 | 8.5 | 12.7 | 6.6 | 1.8 | 3.0 | 4.3 | 3.9 | 3.0 |
| Fabricated metal products | 9.4 | 8.8 | 12.0 | 17.6 | 31.0 | 1.2 | 1.7 | 3.3 | 3.1 | 3.9 |
| Industrial machinery and computers | 32.1 | 36.2 | 45.1 | 62.8 | 69.5 | 23.8 | 42.8 | 54.3 | 77.9 | 109.2 |
| Electric and electronic equipment | 14.5 | 32.1 | 32.3 | 40.7 | 55.8 | 25.8 | 12.1 | 10.9 | 9.5 | 15.8 |
| Transportation equipment | 19.6 | 28.4 | 45.7 | 46.1 | 57.7 | 18.1 | 38.4 | 45.6 | 35.4 | 20.7 |
| Scientific and measuring instruments | 93.1 | 111.5 | 171.8 | 134.7 | 115.6 | 7.5 | 13.5 | 13.3 | 20.1 | 21.1 |
| Miscellaneous manufactures | 8.3 | 7.9 | 6.4 | 8.4 | 10.8 | 1.7 | 3.3 | 4.2 | 3.7 | 3.9 |
| Unidentified manufactures | 1.0 | 0.7 | 0.9 | 1.1 | 1.2 | 0.4 | 0.3 | 0.6 | 0.9 | 0.4 |
| **Agricultural and livestock products** | 1.1 | 0.8 | 0.5 | 1.0 | 2.3 | ..... | ..... | 0.2 | 0.9 | 1.0 |
| Agricultural products | 1.1 | 0.8 | 0.4 | 0.8 | 1.8 | ..... | ..... | 0.1 | 0.8 | 1.0 |
| Livestock and livestock products | ..... | ..... | 0.1 | 0.2 | 0.6 | ..... | ..... | ..... | 0.1 | ..... |
| **Other commodities** | 1.1 | 0.6 | 0.3 | 1.0 | 1.9 | ..... | ..... | 2.5 | 0.3 | 0.1 |
| Forestry products | 0.1 | ..... | ..... | ..... | ..... | ..... | ..... | ..... | ..... | ..... |
| Fish and other marine products | 0.6 | ..... | 0.1 | ..... | ..... | ..... | ..... | ..... | ..... | ..... |
| Metallic ores and concentrates | ..... | ..... | ..... | ..... | ..... | ..... | ..... | ..... | ..... | ..... |
| Bituminous coal and lignite | ..... | ..... | ..... | ..... | ..... | ..... | ..... | ..... | ..... | ..... |
| Crude petroleum and natural gas | ..... | ..... | ..... | ..... | ..... | ..... | ..... | ..... | ..... | ..... |
| Nonmetallic minerals | ..... | 0.1 | ..... | ..... | 0.2 | ..... | ..... | ..... | ..... | ..... |
| Scrap and waste | ..... | ..... | ..... | 0.3 | 0.2 | ..... | ..... | 2.3 | ..... | ..... |
| Used merchandise | 0.3 | 0.2 | ..... | ..... | ..... | ..... | ..... | ..... | ..... | ..... |
| Goods imported and returned unchanged | ..... | ..... | ..... | ..... | ..... | ..... | ..... | ..... | ..... | ..... |
| Special classification provisions | 0.1 | 0.3 | 0.1 | 0.7 | 1.4 | ..... | ..... | 0.2 | 0.2 | ..... |

| Industry | 1993 | 1994 | 1995 | 1996 | 1997 | 1993 | 1994 | 1995 | 1996 | 1997 |
|---|---|---|---|---|---|---|---|---|---|---|
| | Taiwan | | | | | Singapore | | | | |
| **ALL GOODS** | 100.4 | 79.0 | 116.1 | 140.9 | 134.4 | 104.7 | 126.5 | 149.8 | 188.1 | 185.2 |
| **Manufactured goods** | 100.2 | 78.4 | 115.4 | 140.5 | 133.8 | 104.3 | 126.4 | 148.0 | 188.0 | 185.2 |
| Food products | 1.5 | 1.7 | 2.0 | 2.4 | 3.3 | 1.7 | 2.2 | 1.9 | 2.5 | 2.0 |
| Tobacco products | ..... | ..... | ..... | ..... | ..... | ..... | ..... | ..... | ..... | ..... |
| Textile mill products | 0.4 | 0.4 | 0.5 | 0.3 | 0.5 | 0.1 | 0.1 | 0.5 | 0.3 | 0.1 |
| Apparel | 0.1 | 0.1 | 0.1 | ..... | 0.1 | ..... | ..... | 0.4 | 0.3 | 0.1 |
| Lumber and wood products | 6.4 | 4.5 | 3.4 | 2.6 | 1.3 | 1.4 | 1.0 | 0.9 | 1.5 | 1.7 |
| Furniture and fixtures | 0.7 | 1.0 | 0.5 | 0.1 | 0.3 | 0.6 | 0.7 | 0.7 | 0.6 | 1.1 |
| Paper products | ..... | 0.2 | 0.9 | 2.2 | 1.5 | 1.1 | 0.5 | 0.6 | 1.2 | 0.3 |
| Printing and publishing | 0.7 | 1.0 | 1.4 | 1.5 | 1.6 | 2.3 | 1.6 | 2.5 | 4.4 | 2.7 |
| Chemical products | 14.6 | 20.5 | 22.0 | 19.9 | 23.4 | 12.7 | 16.3 | 33.5 | 35.7 | 34.3 |
| Refined petroleum products | 1.3 | 2.1 | 1.6 | 1.9 | 1.6 | 0.1 | 0.1 | 0.2 | 0.1 | 0.2 |
| Rubber and plastic products | 0.4 | 0.3 | 2.1 | 4.8 | 13.9 | 2.6 | 3.6 | 3.4 | 4.6 | 5.8 |
| Leather products | ..... | 0.3 | 1.3 | 0.9 | 1.1 | ..... | 0.1 | ..... | ..... | ..... |
| Stone, clay and glass products | 0.6 | 0.3 | 0.3 | 0.4 | 0.2 | 0.1 | 0.1 | 0.2 | 0.2 | 0.3 |
| Primary metals | 1.9 | 2.4 | 8.3 | 18.8 | 12.0 | 3.9 | 3.6 | 3.1 | 7.7 | 13.5 |
| Fabricated metal products | 2.2 | 1.2 | 1.3 | 1.8 | 2.2 | 17.3 | 18.9 | 17.5 | 22.1 | 25.3 |
| Industrial machinery and computers | 35.4 | 17.4 | 23.3 | 23.5 | 30.3 | 38.4 | 46.5 | 44.0 | 55.8 | 43.9 |
| Electric and electronic equipment | 14.9 | 14.0 | 32.9 | 44.4 | 28.2 | 9.9 | 13.7 | 16.6 | 22.7 | 23.3 |
| Transportation equipment | 12.5 | 3.2 | 7.9 | 7.2 | 3.0 | 1.5 | 3.6 | 9.9 | 12.2 | 13.2 |
| Scientific and measuring instruments | 4.8 | 6.6 | 4.6 | 6.7 | 8.4 | 10.0 | 12.4 | 10.7 | 13.7 | 16.4 |
| Miscellaneous manufactures | 1.4 | 1.0 | 0.9 | 1.0 | 0.7 | 0.4 | 0.6 | 0.8 | 2.3 | 0.8 |
| Unidentified manufactures | 0.3 | 0.2 | 0.2 | 0.3 | 0.4 | 0.3 | 0.7 | 0.5 | 0.2 | 0.2 |
| **Agricultural and livestock products** | 0.1 | 0.2 | ..... | ..... | ..... | ..... | ..... | ..... | ..... | ..... |
| Agricultural products | 0.1 | 0.2 | ..... | ..... | ..... | ..... | ..... | ..... | ..... | ..... |
| Livestock and livestock products | ..... | ..... | ..... | ..... | ..... | ..... | ..... | ..... | ..... | ..... |
| **Other commodities** | 0.2 | 0.5 | 0.7 | 0.4 | 0.6 | 0.4 | 0.1 | 1.8 | 0.1 | ..... |
| Forestry products | ..... | ..... | 0.1 | ..... | ..... | ..... | ..... | ..... | ..... | ..... |
| Fish and other marine products | ..... | 0.1 | ..... | ..... | ..... | 0.1 | ..... | 0.1 | ..... | ..... |
| Metallic ores and concentrates | 0.1 | ..... | ..... | ..... | ..... | ..... | ..... | ..... | ..... | ..... |
| Bituminous coal and lignite | ..... | ..... | ..... | ..... | ..... | ..... | ..... | ..... | ..... | ..... |
| Crude petroleum and natural gas | ..... | ..... | ..... | ..... | ..... | ..... | ..... | ..... | ..... | ..... |
| Nonmetallic minerals | ..... | ..... | ..... | ..... | ..... | ..... | ..... | ..... | ..... | ..... |
| Scrap and waste | ..... | ..... | 0.2 | 0.1 | ..... | ..... | ..... | ..... | ..... | ..... |
| Used merchandise | ..... | ..... | ..... | ..... | ..... | ..... | 0.1 | 0.4 | ..... | ..... |
| Goods imported and returned unchanged | ..... | ..... | ..... | ..... | ..... | ..... | ..... | ..... | ..... | ..... |
| Special classification provisions | ..... | 0.3 | 0.4 | 0.2 | 0.5 | 0.3 | ..... | 1.3 | ..... | ..... |

## IOWA: Exports of Goods, 1997

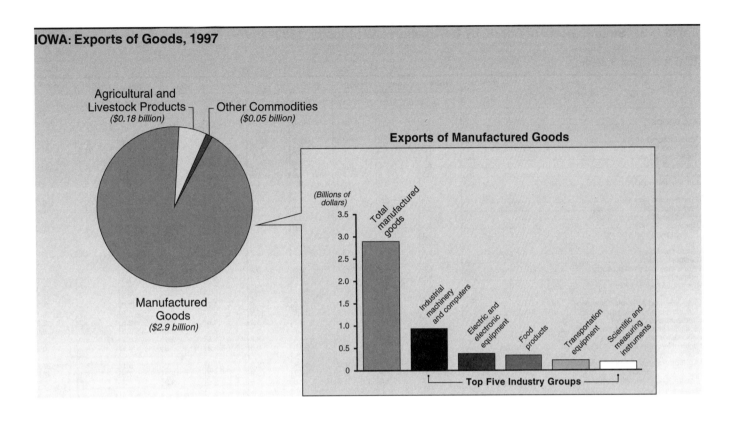

Agricultural and Livestock Products ($0.18 billion)

Other Commodities ($0.05 billion)

Manufactured Goods ($2.9 billion)

**Exports of Manufactured Goods**

(Billions of dollars)

Top Five Industry Groups

## Table D-3.   State Exports of Goods by Destination and Industry, 1993–1997 —Continued

**IOWA** (Millions of dollars.)

| Industry | 1993 | 1994 | 1995 | 1996 | 1997 | 1993 | 1994 | 1995 | 1996 | 1997 |
|---|---|---|---|---|---|---|---|---|---|---|
| | All destinations | | | | | Canada | | | | |
| ALL GOODS | 1 955.7 | 2 331.4 | 2 577.8 | 2 695.1 | 3 116.7 | 918.5 | 1 152.8 | 1 220.5 | 1 277.2 | 1 569.1 |
| Manufactured goods | 1 791.8 | 2 137.3 | 2 387.9 | 2 484.8 | 2 892.1 | 882.5 | 1 117.4 | 1 178.9 | 1 247.2 | 1 532.5 |
| Food products | 205.7 | 235.3 | 295.9 | 296.3 | 337.8 | 92.5 | 111.0 | 119.9 | 135.8 | 166.7 |
| Tobacco products | ..... | ..... | ..... | 0.2 | ..... | ..... | ..... | ..... | 0.2 | ..... |
| Textile mill products | 5.3 | 4.8 | 4.4 | 5.2 | 5.7 | 2.0 | 2.4 | 1.7 | 1.6 | 1.9 |
| Apparel | 7.3 | 6.2 | 8.5 | 10.1 | 10.8 | 3.0 | 2.4 | 1.9 | 0.7 | 1.6 |
| Lumber and wood products | 27.7 | 28.1 | 23.6 | 19.2 | 24.2 | 20.7 | 21.6 | 17.9 | 13.6 | 17.9 |
| Furniture and fixtures | 39.3 | 43.2 | 46.9 | 56.8 | 63.1 | 34.5 | 36.6 | 39.5 | 48.1 | 52.1 |
| Paper products | 19.3 | 20.7 | 29.8 | 34.9 | 36.5 | 4.2 | 4.1 | 6.0 | 6.7 | 5.7 |
| Printing and publishing | 31.1 | 37.3 | 39.6 | 33.5 | 34.9 | 25.0 | 28.7 | 23.6 | 25.3 | 29.5 |
| Chemical products | 109.2 | 119.4 | 136.4 | 160.6 | 174.3 | 34.3 | 38.0 | 44.7 | 57.6 | 67.5 |
| Refined petroleum products | 0.5 | 0.5 | 0.6 | 8.9 | 1.3 | 0.2 | 0.2 | 0.2 | 8.2 | 0.5 |
| Rubber and plastic products | 116.1 | 121.9 | 121.9 | 135.6 | 151.5 | 69.9 | 63.0 | 61.4 | 57.2 | 60.8 |
| Leather products | 17.4 | 14.0 | 13.0 | 8.1 | 6.8 | 0.3 | 0.5 | 0.9 | 1.3 | 0.8 |
| Stone, clay and glass products | 8.7 | 6.6 | 6.1 | 13.4 | 14.1 | 1.3 | 1.7 | 2.3 | 5.0 | 7.8 |
| Primary metals | 16.8 | 51.1 | 57.7 | 65.6 | 103.0 | 6.6 | 13.8 | 13.3 | 16.4 | 53.7 |
| Fabricated metal products | 101.6 | 123.3 | 114.1 | 114.9 | 121.6 | 49.5 | 56.1 | 40.4 | 38.7 | 48.9 |
| Industrial machinery and computers | 448.6 | 635.5 | 744.8 | 745.7 | 934.4 | 246.5 | 398.6 | 456.0 | 437.1 | 572.3 |
| Electric and electronic equipment | 292.8 | 320.5 | 311.4 | 297.0 | 375.1 | 150.7 | 162.2 | 148.9 | 153.2 | 193.7 |
| Transportation equipment | 127.7 | 144.2 | 189.9 | 187.1 | 227.0 | 106.7 | 122.2 | 143.7 | 151.4 | 194.6 |
| Scientific and measuring instruments | 156.0 | 153.8 | 163.1 | 208.7 | 193.2 | 16.8 | 29.8 | 31.6 | 64.6 | 32.6 |
| Miscellaneous manufactures | 54.8 | 63.0 | 73.3 | 77.2 | 68.7 | 15.0 | 21.6 | 22.1 | 21.5 | 20.4 |
| Unidentified manufactures | 5.9 | 7.9 | 6.8 | 6.0 | 8.0 | 2.6 | 2.9 | 3.0 | 3.2 | 3.4 |
| Agricultural and livestock products | 122.9 | 145.4 | 145.1 | 165.0 | 178.2 | 15.3 | 8.1 | 13.7 | 8.7 | 14.8 |
| Agricultural products | 108.5 | 129.8 | 129.4 | 147.0 | 158.7 | 14.4 | 6.5 | 10.6 | 6.6 | 12.2 |
| Livestock and livestock products | 14.4 | 15.6 | 15.7 | 18.0 | 19.4 | 0.9 | 1.6 | 3.1 | 2.0 | 2.6 |
| Other commodities | 41.1 | 48.6 | 44.8 | 45.2 | 46.4 | 20.7 | 27.3 | 27.9 | 21.3 | 21.8 |
| Forestry products | 0.2 | 0.3 | 0.5 | 0.2 | 0.4 | 0.1 | 0.2 | 0.4 | 0.2 | 0.3 |
| Fish and other marine products | 4.6 | 4.6 | 7.1 | 6.3 | 8.1 | 0.1 | ..... | 0.3 | 0.3 | 0.5 |
| Metallic ores and concentrates | 2.2 | 2.9 | 1.1 | ..... | 1.0 | ..... | ..... | 1.0 | ..... | 0.3 |
| Bituminous coal and lignite | ..... | ..... | 0.1 | 2.7 | 0.7 | ..... | ..... | ..... | 1.8 | 0.1 |
| Crude petroleum and natural gas | ..... | 0.1 | ..... | ..... | 0.1 | ..... | 0.1 | ..... | ..... | ..... |
| Nonmetallic minerals | 0.2 | 0.2 | 0.3 | 1.2 | 0.7 | 0.1 | ..... | 0.1 | 0.6 | 0.2 |
| Scrap and waste | 15.4 | 18.7 | 12.9 | 7.2 | 7.8 | 14.0 | 13.7 | 11.2 | 6.8 | 6.8 |
| Used merchandise | 2.7 | 1.8 | 1.7 | 7.6 | 8.3 | 0.1 | 0.1 | 0.4 | 0.5 | 0.6 |
| Goods imported and returned unchanged | 5.7 | 12.5 | 12.9 | 7.9 | 11.5 | 5.7 | 12.5 | 12.9 | 7.9 | 11.5 |
| Special classification provisions | 10.1 | 7.5 | 8.2 | 12.2 | 7.8 | 0.6 | 0.7 | 1.5 | 3.2 | 1.4 |

## Table D-3. State Exports of Goods by Destination and Industry, 1993–1997 —*Continued*

**IOWA** (Millions of dollars.)

| Industry | 1993 | 1994 | 1995 | 1996 | 1997 | 1993 | 1994 | 1995 | 1996 | 1997 |
|---|---|---|---|---|---|---|---|---|---|---|
| | South and Central America and Caribbean | | | | | Mexico | | | | |
| **ALL GOODS** | 91.3 | 83.3 | 108.0 | 140.5 | 182.7 | 78.2 | 99.2 | 81.9 | 110.3 | 167.7 |
| **Manufactured goods** | 78.2 | 72.8 | 101.3 | 125.6 | 163.2 | 74.1 | 82.5 | 72.6 | 90.8 | 140.0 |
| Food products | 3.5 | 4.5 | 7.1 | 7.8 | 11.1 | 28.9 | 12.0 | 11.5 | 21.4 | 41.6 |
| Tobacco products | | | | | | | | | | |
| Textile mill products | 0.1 | | 0.4 | 0.2 | 0.2 | | 0.1 | | 0.1 | 0.2 |
| Apparel | 0.1 | 0.5 | 1.0 | 0.9 | 0.5 | 0.3 | 0.2 | 0.2 | 0.6 | 0.1 |
| Lumber and wood products | | 0.2 | 0.1 | 0.1 | 0.4 | 0.1 | 0.1 | 0.2 | 0.3 | 0.4 |
| Furniture and fixtures | 0.4 | 0.9 | 1.1 | 1.9 | 1.6 | 1.5 | 1.7 | 0.8 | 0.6 | 1.0 |
| Paper products | 0.4 | 0.8 | 1.3 | 2.5 | 3.3 | 3.2 | 4.0 | 3.4 | 5.8 | 6.0 |
| Printing and publishing | 0.1 | | 0.4 | 0.1 | 0.2 | 0.7 | 1.0 | 0.9 | 1.8 | 2.0 |
| Chemical products | 8.4 | 10.9 | 12.1 | 13.6 | 11.7 | 6.9 | 8.2 | 6.3 | 8.4 | 10.3 |
| Refined petroleum products | 0.1 | | | | | | | | 0.1 | |
| Rubber and plastic products | 11.8 | 13.1 | 13.0 | 16.2 | 19.7 | 5.6 | 6.1 | 6.0 | 4.8 | 6.9 |
| Leather products | | 0.1 | 0.1 | | | 0.3 | 0.3 | 0.8 | 0.4 | 0.7 |
| Stone, clay and glass products | 0.2 | 0.3 | 0.2 | 0.3 | 0.2 | 0.9 | 0.5 | 0.4 | 1.0 | 0.6 |
| Primary metals | 1.3 | 1.9 | 3.7 | 5.3 | 6.1 | 1.5 | 2.3 | 1.5 | 2.2 | 4.2 |
| Fabricated metal products | 4.6 | 3.6 | 5.2 | 6.1 | 11.3 | 2.2 | 4.0 | 2.6 | 3.6 | 5.4 |
| Industrial machinery and computers | 24.6 | 23.2 | 33.8 | 40.8 | 51.9 | 12.3 | 25.0 | 12.0 | 22.3 | 24.5 |
| Electric and electronic equipment | 6.1 | 4.6 | 11.2 | 16.8 | 32.1 | 4.4 | 8.9 | 5.3 | 6.1 | 19.1 |
| Transportation equipment | 1.7 | 1.7 | 2.0 | 2.3 | 4.1 | 0.8 | 3.2 | 12.5 | 3.7 | 3.2 |
| Scientific and measuring instruments | 12.3 | 3.1 | 4.4 | 5.7 | 5.7 | 2.4 | 2.6 | 7.5 | 5.5 | 8.0 |
| Miscellaneous manufactures | 2.4 | 2.8 | 3.8 | 4.4 | 2.8 | 1.8 | 2.1 | 0.7 | 2.0 | 5.2 |
| Unidentified manufactures | 0.2 | 0.3 | 0.4 | 0.3 | 0.5 | 0.2 | 0.3 | 0.1 | 0.2 | 0.5 |
| **Agricultural and livestock products** | 12.2 | 9.8 | 6.2 | 12.7 | 18.8 | 3.9 | 16.0 | 9.1 | 18.9 | 27.2 |
| Agricultural products | 10.6 | 7.9 | 4.2 | 10.7 | 15.8 | 1.2 | 12.3 | 7.8 | 16.1 | 23.9 |
| Livestock and livestock products | 1.7 | 1.8 | 1.9 | 2.0 | 3.0 | 2.6 | 3.8 | 1.3 | 2.8 | 3.3 |
| **Other commodities** | 0.8 | 0.7 | 0.5 | 2.3 | 0.8 | 0.3 | 0.7 | 0.2 | 0.6 | 0.5 |
| Forestry products | | 0.1 | | | | | | | | |
| Fish and other marine products | 0.3 | 0.1 | 0.4 | 0.6 | 0.3 | | | | | |
| Metallic ores and concentrates | | | | | | | | | | |
| Bituminous coal and lignite | | | | 0.9 | | | | | | |
| Crude petroleum and natural gas | | | | | | | | | | |
| Nonmetallic minerals | | | | 0.3 | | | | | | 0.1 |
| Scrap and waste | | | | | | | | | | |
| Used merchandise | 0.2 | | | 0.4 | 0.4 | | 0.5 | | | 0.1 |
| Goods imported and returned unchanged | | | | | | | | | | |
| Special classification provisions | 0.4 | 0.5 | 0.1 | 0.1 | 0.1 | 0.2 | 0.1 | 0.1 | 0.6 | 0.3 |
| | European Union | | | | | United Kingdom | | | | |
| **ALL GOODS** | 396.0 | 430.0 | 483.4 | 507.3 | 524.9 | 84.3 | 85.0 | 87.9 | 93.2 | 114.1 |
| **Manufactured goods** | 324.1 | 345.3 | 390.9 | 404.8 | 438.7 | 78.6 | 80.7 | 85.5 | 87.4 | 109.8 |
| Food products | 11.7 | 12.7 | 18.3 | 11.9 | 18.2 | 4.4 | 3.4 | 8.1 | 5.0 | 7.7 |
| Tobacco products | | | | | | | | | | |
| Textile mill products | 0.9 | 1.1 | 1.0 | 1.4 | 1.5 | 0.2 | 0.1 | 0.1 | 0.2 | 0.2 |
| Apparel | 1.4 | 2.1 | 2.8 | 3.4 | 3.9 | | 0.1 | 0.2 | 0.1 | |
| Lumber and wood products | 1.8 | 2.2 | 2.2 | 2.5 | 3.2 | | | 0.1 | 0.1 | 0.2 |
| Furniture and fixtures | 2.1 | 3.4 | 4.4 | 5.1 | 5.5 | 0.7 | 1.8 | 3.1 | 3.3 | 3.8 |
| Paper products | 7.8 | 8.8 | 14.4 | 15.2 | 15.1 | 0.2 | 0.6 | 0.6 | 0.5 | 0.8 |
| Printing and publishing | 2.2 | 4.2 | 4.0 | 2.0 | 1.3 | 1.7 | 3.2 | 3.2 | 1.0 | 0.9 |
| Chemical products | 29.3 | 23.9 | 32.2 | 37.7 | 32.7 | 5.1 | 4.0 | 3.8 | 7.6 | 9.3 |
| Refined petroleum products | | | | | | | | | | |
| Rubber and plastic products | 11.7 | 18.5 | 16.2 | 24.7 | 28.2 | 3.7 | 4.6 | 3.4 | 0.6 | 1.1 |
| Leather products | 0.5 | 1.6 | 0.5 | 0.7 | 0.7 | | | 0.1 | 0.1 | 0.2 |
| Stone, clay and glass products | 4.0 | 2.7 | 2.5 | 6.0 | 4.0 | 0.7 | 0.4 | 0.6 | 1.0 | 0.6 |
| Primary metals | 2.2 | 2.1 | 2.8 | 5.1 | 7.0 | 1.4 | 0.4 | 1.0 | 1.1 | 1.7 |
| Fabricated metal products | 15.8 | 16.1 | 13.9 | 13.2 | 12.6 | 7.0 | 7.2 | 6.5 | 4.9 | 5.7 |
| Industrial machinery and computers | 79.6 | 93.0 | 103.1 | 101.5 | 114.1 | 11.0 | 14.9 | 16.7 | 16.8 | 22.7 |
| Electric and electronic equipment | 58.0 | 66.0 | 66.1 | 60.7 | 75.2 | 21.5 | 19.9 | 16.3 | 15.1 | 23.0 |
| Transportation equipment | 10.3 | 8.2 | 12.8 | 18.4 | 14.3 | 1.8 | 1.4 | 1.5 | 4.1 | 3.6 |
| Scientific and measuring instruments | 67.7 | 59.9 | 71.3 | 73.8 | 79.9 | 13.2 | 10.5 | 10.3 | 15.9 | 18.7 |
| Miscellaneous manufactures | 15.7 | 16.2 | 20.5 | 20.5 | 19.7 | 5.4 | 7.5 | 9.6 | 9.5 | 9.0 |
| Unidentified manufactures | 1.4 | 2.7 | 1.8 | 1.1 | 1.6 | 0.5 | 0.5 | 0.5 | 0.6 | 0.7 |
| **Agricultural and livestock products** | 62.7 | 78.3 | 88.3 | 92.0 | 78.7 | 0.1 | 0.2 | 0.2 | 1.0 | 1.0 |
| Agricultural products | 60.4 | 77.0 | 86.7 | 90.8 | 77.2 | | | | 0.9 | 0.9 |
| Livestock and livestock products | 2.3 | 1.3 | 1.7 | 1.2 | 1.5 | 0.1 | 0.2 | 0.2 | 0.1 | 0.2 |
| **Other commodities** | 9.2 | 6.3 | 4.3 | 10.5 | 7.4 | 5.6 | 4.1 | 2.2 | 4.7 | 3.3 |
| Forestry products | | | | | 0.1 | | | | | |
| Fish and other marine products | 0.3 | 0.1 | 0.6 | 0.5 | | | | 0.1 | | |
| Metallic ores and concentrates | 2.2 | 2.9 | | | 0.7 | 2.2 | 2.9 | | | |
| Bituminous coal and lignite | | | | | | | | | | |
| Crude petroleum and natural gas | | | | | | | | | | |
| Nonmetallic minerals | | | | 0.1 | | | | | | |
| Scrap and waste | 0.9 | | 0.5 | 0.1 | 0.6 | | | 0.4 | | |
| Used merchandise | 0.1 | 0.3 | 0.2 | 5.7 | 3.5 | | | 0.1 | 1.4 | 1.7 |
| Goods imported and returned unchanged | | | | | | | | | | |
| Special classification provisions | 5.8 | 3.0 | 2.9 | 4.2 | 2.6 | 3.5 | 1.2 | 1.5 | 3.4 | 1.6 |

# Table D-3. State Exports of Goods by Destination and Industry, 1993–1997 —*Continued*

**IOWA** (Millions of dollars.)

| Industry | 1993 | 1994 | 1995 | 1996 | 1997 | 1993 | 1994 | 1995 | 1996 | 1997 |
|---|---|---|---|---|---|---|---|---|---|---|
| | Germany | | | | | France | | | | |
| **ALL GOODS** | 51.1 | 52.6 | 71.4 | 84.1 | 86.2 | 59.8 | 54.7 | 46.6 | 63.1 | 81.0 |
| **Manufactured goods** | 47.8 | 49.6 | 67.3 | 82.0 | 83.8 | 42.3 | 38.5 | 28.4 | 48.9 | 74.5 |
| Food products | 2.1 | 1.3 | 1.9 | 2.7 | 3.9 | 0.5 | 0.5 | 0.5 | 0.2 | 0.9 |
| Tobacco products | ..... | ..... | ..... | ..... | ..... | ..... | ..... | ..... | ..... | ..... |
| Textile mill products | ..... | 0.1 | 0.2 | 0.6 | 0.8 | 0.1 | ..... | ..... | ..... | ..... |
| Apparel | 0.3 | 0.1 | 0.2 | 0.3 | 0.1 | 0.2 | 0.3 | 0.3 | ..... | ..... |
| Lumber and wood products | ..... | ..... | 0.1 | 0.1 | 0.1 | ..... | 0.1 | 0.1 | ..... | ..... |
| Furniture and fixtures | 0.4 | 0.2 | 0.2 | 0.3 | 0.5 | ..... | ..... | ..... | ..... | ..... |
| Paper products | 2.2 | 1.5 | 2.0 | 4.3 | 3.9 | ..... | 0.2 | 0.5 | 0.4 | 5.5 |
| Printing and publishing | 0.2 | 0.2 | 0.1 | 0.1 | 0.1 | 0.1 | 0.3 | ..... | 0.1 | 0.1 |
| Chemical products | 7.4 | 3.9 | 9.9 | 8.0 | 3.7 | 3.4 | 1.8 | 2.1 | 1.5 | 2.4 |
| Refined petroleum products | ..... | ..... | ..... | ..... | ..... | ..... | ..... | ..... | ..... | ..... |
| Rubber and plastic products | 0.3 | 0.7 | 1.7 | 4.8 | 9.7 | 1.1 | 1.0 | 0.4 | 0.2 | 4.7 |
| Leather products | 0.1 | ..... | ..... | 0.1 | ..... | 0.1 | 0.1 | ..... | ..... | ..... |
| Stone, clay and glass products | 1.3 | 0.9 | 0.5 | 0.5 | 0.9 | 0.2 | ..... | 0.1 | ..... | ..... |
| Primary metals | ..... | ..... | ..... | 1.4 | 2.9 | ..... | 0.6 | ..... | 0.1 | 0.3 |
| Fabricated metal products | 0.9 | 2.2 | 1.2 | 1.1 | 1.2 | 2.3 | 2.0 | 1.0 | 1.0 | 1.4 |
| Industrial machinery and computers | 18.2 | 22.5 | 30.8 | 25.3 | 29.2 | 9.7 | 7.2 | 8.0 | 10.0 | 8.6 |
| Electric and electronic equipment | 5.9 | 7.6 | 9.6 | 7.8 | 7.6 | 8.8 | 9.8 | 4.9 | 11.4 | 15.5 |
| Transportation equipment | 4.5 | 3.6 | 3.2 | 8.6 | 7.4 | 2.3 | 1.0 | 0.8 | 0.6 | 0.9 |
| Scientific and measuring instruments | 1.6 | 2.0 | 3.2 | 12.4 | 8.3 | 11.0 | 12.0 | 7.7 | 21.3 | 32.1 |
| Miscellaneous manufactures | 2.2 | 2.2 | 2.4 | 3.2 | 3.1 | 2.0 | 1.5 | 1.6 | 1.9 | 2.0 |
| Unidentified manufactures | 0.2 | 0.4 | 0.2 | 0.2 | 0.3 | 0.2 | 0.2 | 0.1 | 0.1 | 0.1 |
| **Agricultural and livestock products** | 2.9 | 2.6 | 3.5 | 1.0 | 0.4 | 15.9 | 14.9 | 17.9 | 13.8 | 6.0 |
| Agricultural products | 2.7 | 2.5 | 3.2 | 0.9 | 0.3 | 15.9 | 14.9 | 17.9 | 13.8 | 6.0 |
| Livestock and livestock products | 0.1 | 0.1 | 0.3 | 0.1 | ..... | ..... | ..... | ..... | ..... | ..... |
| **Other commodities** | 0.4 | 0.5 | 0.6 | 1.2 | 2.0 | 1.6 | 1.3 | 0.4 | 0.3 | 0.5 |
| Forestry products | ..... | ..... | ..... | ..... | 0.1 | ..... | ..... | ..... | ..... | ..... |
| Fish and other marine products | ..... | ..... | ..... | ..... | ..... | 0.1 | ..... | 0.2 | 0.2 | ..... |
| Metallic ores and concentrates | ..... | ..... | ..... | ..... | 0.7 | ..... | ..... | ..... | ..... | ..... |
| Bituminous coal and lignite | ..... | ..... | ..... | ..... | ..... | ..... | ..... | ..... | ..... | ..... |
| Crude petroleum and natural gas | ..... | ..... | ..... | ..... | ..... | ..... | ..... | ..... | ..... | ..... |
| Nonmetallic minerals | ..... | ..... | ..... | ..... | ..... | ..... | ..... | ..... | ..... | ..... |
| Scrap and waste | ..... | ..... | ..... | ..... | ..... | ..... | ..... | ..... | ..... | ..... |
| Used merchandise | 0.1 | 0.2 | 0.1 | 0.7 | 1.0 | ..... | ..... | ..... | ..... | ..... |
| Goods imported and returned unchanged | ..... | ..... | ..... | ..... | ..... | ..... | ..... | ..... | ..... | ..... |
| Special classification provisions | 0.3 | 0.2 | 0.5 | 0.5 | 0.3 | 1.5 | 1.3 | 0.2 | 0.1 | 0.5 |
| | The Netherlands | | | | | Asian 10 | | | | |
| **ALL GOODS** | 83.7 | 82.8 | 108.0 | 92.0 | 84.5 | 314.6 | 394.7 | 486.5 | 465.6 | 464.2 |
| **Manufactured goods** | 81.2 | 82.2 | 107.8 | 91.7 | 83.8 | 291.5 | 370.7 | 460.4 | 438.4 | 437.3 |
| Food products | 0.5 | 0.7 | 0.6 | 1.1 | 2.1 | 59.3 | 86.4 | 129.6 | 110.8 | 91.2 |
| Tobacco products | ..... | ..... | ..... | ..... | ..... | ..... | ..... | ..... | ..... | ..... |
| Textile mill products | 0.6 | 0.8 | 0.5 | 0.6 | 0.4 | 1.7 | 0.7 | 1.2 | 1.9 | 1.7 |
| Apparel | 0.6 | 1.3 | 2.0 | 2.9 | 3.4 | 2.4 | 0.9 | 2.4 | 4.1 | 4.1 |
| Lumber and wood products | 0.2 | 0.1 | 0.1 | 0.2 | 0.7 | 4.9 | 3.5 | 3.0 | 2.6 | 2.3 |
| Furniture and fixtures | ..... | 0.2 | 0.1 | 0.1 | 0.2 | 0.1 | 0.1 | 0.5 | 0.4 | 1.1 |
| Paper products | 4.9 | 6.1 | 7.5 | 8.1 | 4.5 | 1.9 | 1.9 | 2.8 | 3.5 | 5.2 |
| Printing and publishing | ..... | 0.2 | 0.1 | ..... | 0.1 | 0.7 | 2.3 | 8.7 | 2.2 | 1.2 |
| Chemical products | 4.5 | 6.3 | 8.2 | 14.0 | 9.8 | 22.6 | 30.2 | 30.8 | 33.3 | 43.2 |
| Refined petroleum products | ..... | ..... | ..... | ..... | ..... | 0.1 | 0.3 | 0.3 | 0.4 | 0.6 |
| Rubber and plastic products | 1.8 | 3.1 | 2.8 | 7.8 | 10.9 | 12.7 | 16.5 | 15.7 | 21.5 | 24.2 |
| Leather products | 0.1 | 0.1 | 0.1 | 0.1 | 0.1 | 16.2 | 11.6 | 10.7 | 5.6 | 4.3 |
| Stone, clay and glass products | 1.0 | 1.0 | 1.1 | 2.5 | 2.3 | 1.6 | 1.2 | 0.4 | 0.7 | 1.2 |
| Primary metals | 0.5 | 0.3 | 0.4 | 0.7 | 1.8 | 4.8 | 30.7 | 35.0 | 35.6 | 31.3 |
| Fabricated metal products | 2.5 | 2.1 | 2.6 | 3.3 | 2.2 | 24.3 | 36.4 | 46.3 | 45.7 | 35.8 |
| Industrial machinery and computers | 18.3 | 22.2 | 23.7 | 26.3 | 26.1 | 53.0 | 58.2 | 75.4 | 81.3 | 94.8 |
| Electric and electronic equipment | 6.7 | 5.6 | 6.1 | 2.6 | 2.3 | 41.7 | 43.4 | 46.9 | 35.5 | 29.5 |
| Transportation equipment | 0.4 | 0.5 | 4.9 | 0.9 | 0.1 | 6.1 | 3.6 | 6.1 | 3.5 | 5.9 |
| Scientific and measuring instruments | 35.2 | 30.1 | 45.8 | 19.9 | 16.1 | 24.8 | 29.6 | 29.1 | 31.7 | 45.3 |
| Miscellaneous manufactures | 3.1 | 1.5 | 1.1 | 0.7 | 0.6 | 11.7 | 12.3 | 14.6 | 17.2 | 13.2 |
| Unidentified manufactures | 0.1 | 0.1 | 0.1 | ..... | 0.1 | 0.8 | 1.0 | 0.9 | 0.7 | 1.0 |
| **Agricultural and livestock products** | 1.6 | 0.4 | 0.1 | ..... | ..... | 15.7 | 11.9 | 16.7 | 18.6 | 18.8 |
| Agricultural products | 1.4 | 0.3 | ..... | ..... | ..... | 11.9 | 7.9 | 13.3 | 14.9 | 14.6 |
| Livestock and livestock products | 0.2 | 0.1 | 0.1 | ..... | ..... | 3.7 | 3.9 | 3.5 | 3.8 | 4.2 |
| **Other commodities** | 0.9 | 0.2 | 0.1 | 0.3 | 0.7 | 7.4 | 12.1 | 9.3 | 8.6 | 8.1 |
| Forestry products | ..... | ..... | ..... | ..... | ..... | 0.1 | ..... | ..... | ..... | ..... |
| Fish and other marine products | ..... | ..... | ..... | ..... | ..... | 3.9 | 4.2 | 5.4 | 4.6 | 5.3 |
| Metallic ores and concentrates | ..... | ..... | ..... | ..... | ..... | ..... | ..... | 0.2 | ..... | ..... |
| Bituminous coal and lignite | ..... | ..... | ..... | ..... | ..... | ..... | ..... | ..... | ..... | 0.5 |
| Crude petroleum and natural gas | ..... | ..... | ..... | ..... | ..... | ..... | ..... | ..... | ..... | ..... |
| Nonmetallic minerals | ..... | ..... | ..... | 0.1 | ..... | ..... | 0.1 | 0.2 | 0.2 | 0.3 |
| Scrap and waste | 0.9 | ..... | ..... | 0.1 | 0.6 | 0.5 | 4.4 | 0.2 | 0.1 | 0.1 |
| Used merchandise | ..... | ..... | ..... | 0.1 | 0.1 | 0.9 | 0.6 | 0.8 | 0.2 | 1.2 |
| Goods imported and returned unchanged | ..... | 0.1 | 0.1 | ..... | ..... | ..... | ..... | ..... | ..... | ..... |
| Special classification provisions | ..... | ..... | ..... | ..... | ..... | 2.0 | 2.7 | 2.7 | 3.5 | 0.6 |

## Table D-3.   State Exports of Goods by Destination and Industry, 1993–1997 —*Continued*

**IOWA** (Millions of dollars.)

| Industry | 1993 | 1994 | 1995 | 1996 | 1997 | 1993 | 1994 | 1995 | 1996 | 1997 |
|---|---|---|---|---|---|---|---|---|---|---|
| | Japan | | | | | South Korea | | | | |
| **ALL GOODS** | 86.5 | 111.1 | 145.1 | 159.3 | 161.5 | 56.7 | 83.0 | 87.3 | 82.8 | 90.8 |
| **Manufactured goods** | 72.7 | 100.3 | 130.0 | 142.1 | 146.9 | 52.2 | 75.9 | 82.9 | 79.7 | 88.2 |
| Food products | 16.2 | 24.3 | 53.2 | 57.3 | 50.1 | 13.6 | 19.0 | 16.6 | 13.1 | 12.9 |
| Tobacco products | ..... | ..... | ..... | ..... | ..... | ..... | ..... | ..... | ..... | ..... |
| Textile mill products | 0.5 | 0.5 | 0.7 | 1.6 | 1.5 | 0.1 | ..... | 0.2 | 0.1 | 0.1 |
| Apparel | 2.1 | 0.7 | 2.3 | 3.9 | 3.6 | 0.1 | ..... | ..... | ..... | 0.1 |
| Lumber and wood products | 0.6 | 0.9 | 0.7 | 0.6 | 0.4 | 3.9 | 2.1 | 1.8 | 1.4 | 1.2 |
| Furniture and fixtures | ..... | 0.1 | 0.3 | 0.3 | 0.6 | ..... | ..... | 0.1 | 0.1 | 0.4 |
| Paper products | 0.4 | 0.1 | 0.2 | 0.7 | 0.6 | 0.4 | 0.7 | 0.8 | 1.0 | 0.6 |
| Printing and publishing | 0.4 | 0.5 | 0.6 | 0.5 | 0.3 | ..... | 0.7 | 0.8 | 0.4 | 0.1 |
| Chemical products | 10.8 | 16.0 | 13.2 | 14.1 | 22.9 | 2.8 | 3.8 | 3.8 | 5.0 | 5.5 |
| Refined petroleum products | ..... | 0.1 | 0.1 | 0.1 | 0.2 | ..... | 0.1 | 0.1 | ..... | 0.1 |
| Rubber and plastic products | 3.6 | 5.7 | 5.1 | 5.9 | 6.2 | 0.1 | 0.8 | 1.2 | 2.3 | 3.0 |
| Leather products | ..... | ..... | 0.1 | 0.1 | 0.1 | 3.6 | 4.6 | 6.6 | 3.9 | 4.0 |
| Stone, clay and glass products | 0.4 | 0.3 | ..... | 0.1 | 0.1 | 0.9 | 0.3 | 0.1 | 0.2 | 0.2 |
| Primary metals | 0.4 | 1.0 | 0.2 | 1.6 | 2.6 | 0.2 | 24.6 | 24.6 | 23.7 | 22.9 |
| Fabricated metal products | 5.4 | 5.3 | 5.4 | 6.5 | 6.2 | 1.2 | 1.2 | 4.1 | 3.4 | 2.5 |
| Industrial machinery and computers | 15.0 | 22.1 | 18.5 | 20.1 | 20.0 | 10.6 | 8.9 | 13.5 | 17.8 | 17.8 |
| Electric and electronic equipment | 7.5 | 11.5 | 10.6 | 10.6 | 6.1 | 9.6 | 4.6 | 3.2 | 2.2 | 4.6 |
| Transportation equipment | 1.4 | 1.8 | 2.6 | 1.4 | 2.8 | 0.4 | 0.5 | 0.7 | 0.2 | 0.4 |
| Scientific and measuring instruments | 4.7 | 6.2 | 12.5 | 13.2 | 19.9 | 3.8 | 3.2 | 3.5 | 3.7 | 9.2 |
| Miscellaneous manufactures | 2.9 | 2.9 | 3.5 | 3.4 | 2.5 | 0.7 | 0.7 | 1.2 | 1.0 | 2.4 |
| Unidentified manufactures | 0.4 | 0.2 | 0.4 | 0.2 | 0.2 | 0.1 | 0.1 | 0.1 | 0.1 | 0.1 |
| **Agricultural and livestock products** | 10.0 | 7.7 | 11.2 | 12.1 | 11.6 | 2.3 | 1.2 | 2.7 | 1.5 | 1.2 |
| Agricultural products | 9.1 | 7.1 | 10.3 | 11.1 | 10.7 | 1.9 | 0.6 | 2.2 | 0.8 | 0.4 |
| Livestock and livestock products | 0.9 | 0.6 | 0.8 | 1.0 | 0.9 | 0.3 | 0.6 | 0.5 | 0.7 | 0.8 |
| **Other commodities** | 3.8 | 3.2 | 4.0 | 5.1 | 3.0 | 2.2 | 5.9 | 1.7 | 1.6 | 1.5 |
| Forestry products | ..... | ..... | ..... | ..... | ..... | ..... | ..... | ..... | ..... | ..... |
| Fish and other marine products | 1.8 | 2.1 | 2.5 | 2.7 | 2.3 | 1.9 | 1.8 | 1.3 | 1.6 | 1.3 |
| Metallic ores and concentrates | ..... | ..... | ..... | ..... | ..... | ..... | ..... | ..... | ..... | ..... |
| Bituminous coal and lignite | ..... | ..... | ..... | ..... | ..... | ..... | ..... | ..... | ..... | ..... |
| Crude petroleum and natural gas | ..... | ..... | ..... | ..... | ..... | ..... | ..... | ..... | ..... | ..... |
| Nonmetallic minerals | ..... | ..... | ..... | ..... | ..... | ..... | ..... | ..... | ..... | 0.1 |
| Scrap and waste | 0.3 | 0.1 | ..... | ..... | ..... | ..... | 4.0 | 0.1 | ..... | ..... |
| Used merchandise | 0.7 | 0.2 | 0.1 | 0.1 | 0.5 | ..... | ..... | ..... | ..... | ..... |
| Goods imported and returned unchanged | ..... | ..... | ..... | ..... | ..... | ..... | ..... | ..... | ..... | ..... |
| Special classification provisions | 1.0 | 0.7 | 1.4 | 2.4 | 0.2 | 0.3 | 0.1 | 0.2 | ..... | ..... |
| | Taiwan | | | | | Singapore | | | | |
| **ALL GOODS** | 53.3 | 56.9 | 61.3 | 41.3 | 35.1 | 38.9 | 50.1 | 65.8 | 61.6 | 55.0 |
| **Manufactured goods** | 52.7 | 56.0 | 60.9 | 40.5 | 34.3 | 38.1 | 48.6 | 64.2 | 60.5 | 53.6 |
| Food products | 15.1 | 26.7 | 32.5 | 21.1 | 13.0 | 2.5 | 2.4 | 3.3 | 1.9 | 1.5 |
| Tobacco products | ..... | ..... | ..... | ..... | ..... | ..... | ..... | ..... | ..... | ..... |
| Textile mill products | 0.1 | ..... | 0.1 | ..... | ..... | ..... | ..... | ..... | ..... | ..... |
| Apparel | ..... | 0.1 | 0.1 | ..... | ..... | 0.1 | ..... | ..... | ..... | ..... |
| Lumber and wood products | 0.3 | 0.4 | 0.4 | 0.6 | 0.7 | ..... | ..... | ..... | ..... | ..... |
| Furniture and fixtures | ..... | ..... | ..... | ..... | ..... | 0.1 | ..... | ..... | ..... | ..... |
| Paper products | 0.1 | 0.1 | 0.3 | 0.3 | 0.8 | 0.6 | 0.7 | 0.7 | 0.8 | 1.0 |
| Printing and publishing | ..... | 0.7 | 1.3 | 0.3 | 0.1 | 0.1 | 0.2 | 4.6 | 0.3 | 0.5 |
| Chemical products | 2.8 | 2.2 | 2.6 | 3.1 | 3.1 | 0.4 | 0.2 | 0.4 | 0.7 | 1.2 |
| Refined petroleum products | ..... | ..... | 0.2 | 0.2 | 0.2 | ..... | ..... | ..... | ..... | ..... |
| Rubber and plastic products | 1.1 | 2.0 | 0.7 | 0.7 | 1.2 | 0.6 | 0.3 | 0.8 | 0.8 | 0.9 |
| Leather products | 12.3 | 6.3 | 4.0 | 1.2 | 0.1 | ..... | ..... | ..... | ..... | ..... |
| Stone, clay and glass products | ..... | 0.4 | ..... | ..... | ..... | ..... | 0.1 | ..... | ..... | ..... |
| Primary metals | 0.8 | 0.9 | 1.6 | 1.0 | ..... | 0.1 | 0.2 | 0.1 | 0.4 | 0.4 |
| Fabricated metal products | 1.1 | 2.4 | 1.8 | 1.0 | 0.5 | 14.8 | 20.1 | 26.8 | 30.2 | 22.1 |
| Industrial machinery and computers | 5.2 | 5.8 | 8.9 | 5.5 | 7.8 | 5.8 | 6.1 | 8.2 | 9.2 | 14.8 |
| Electric and electronic equipment | 4.6 | 4.5 | 3.7 | 2.1 | 2.4 | 10.1 | 10.6 | 13.4 | 8.2 | 4.3 |
| Transportation equipment | 1.8 | ..... | 0.2 | 0.1 | 1.4 | 0.3 | 0.3 | 0.2 | 0.4 | 0.2 |
| Scientific and measuring instruments | 5.2 | 2.1 | 1.4 | 1.7 | 1.3 | 0.7 | 4.7 | 3.6 | 5.1 | 5.4 |
| Miscellaneous manufactures | 1.9 | 1.0 | 1.2 | 1.4 | 1.5 | 1.6 | 2.4 | 1.8 | 2.2 | 0.9 |
| Unidentified manufactures | 0.1 | 0.2 | 0.1 | 0.1 | 0.2 | 0.1 | 0.2 | 0.1 | 0.1 | 0.1 |
| **Agricultural and livestock products** | 0.1 | 0.1 | 0.2 | 0.6 | 0.5 | 0.2 | ..... | ..... | 0.3 | 0.3 |
| Agricultural products | ..... | ..... | ..... | ..... | ..... | 0.2 | ..... | ..... | 0.3 | 0.3 |
| Livestock and livestock products | 0.1 | ..... | 0.1 | 0.6 | 0.4 | ..... | ..... | ..... | ..... | ..... |
| **Other commodities** | 0.5 | 0.8 | 0.3 | 0.2 | 0.3 | 0.6 | 1.4 | 1.6 | 0.8 | 1.1 |
| Forestry products | 0.1 | ..... | ..... | ..... | ..... | ..... | ..... | ..... | ..... | ..... |
| Fish and other marine products | 0.1 | 0.1 | 0.2 | 0.1 | 0.3 | ..... | ..... | 0.1 | ..... | ..... |
| Metallic ores and concentrates | ..... | ..... | ..... | ..... | ..... | ..... | ..... | ..... | ..... | ..... |
| Bituminous coal and lignite | ..... | ..... | ..... | ..... | ..... | ..... | ..... | ..... | ..... | 0.5 |
| Crude petroleum and natural gas | ..... | ..... | ..... | ..... | ..... | ..... | ..... | ..... | ..... | ..... |
| Nonmetallic minerals | ..... | 0.1 | 0.1 | ..... | ..... | ..... | ..... | ..... | ..... | ..... |
| Scrap and waste | 0.1 | 0.3 | ..... | 0.1 | ..... | ..... | ..... | ..... | ..... | ..... |
| Used merchandise | ..... | ..... | ..... | ..... | ..... | 0.2 | 0.2 | 0.5 | 0.2 | 0.4 |
| Goods imported and returned unchanged | ..... | ..... | ..... | ..... | ..... | ..... | ..... | ..... | ..... | ..... |
| Special classification provisions | 0.2 | 0.3 | ..... | ..... | ..... | 0.4 | 1.2 | 1.0 | 0.6 | 0.1 |

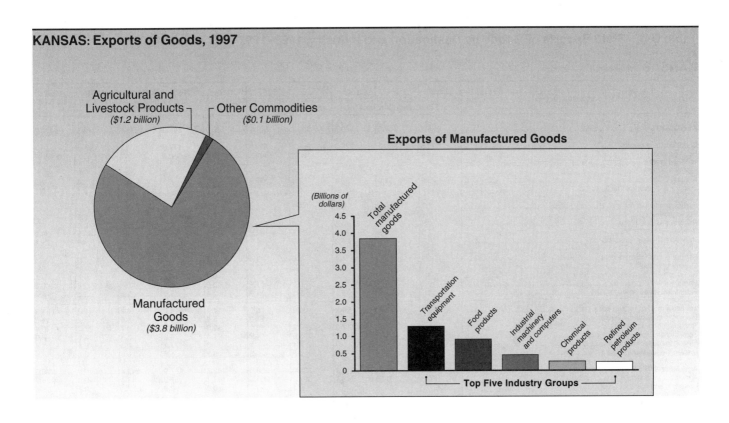

## KANSAS: Exports of Goods, 1997

Agricultural and Livestock Products ($1.2 billion)

Other Commodities ($0.1 billion)

Manufactured Goods ($3.8 billion)

**Exports of Manufactured Goods**

(Billions of dollars)

Top Five Industry Groups

Total manufactured goods / Transportation equipment / Food products / Industrial machinery and computers / Chemical products / Refined petroleum products

---

## Table D-3.  State Exports of Goods by Destination and Industry, 1993–1997 —*Continued*

**KANSAS** (Millions of dollars.)

| Industry | 1993 | 1994 | 1995 | 1996 | 1997 | 1993 | 1994 | 1995 | 1996 | 1997 |
|---|---|---|---|---|---|---|---|---|---|---|
| | All destinations | | | | | Canada | | | | |
| **ALL GOODS** | 3 109.4 | 3 498.3 | 4 461.5 | 4 971.3 | 5 133.2 | 473.1 | 571.2 | 687.0 | 696.0 | 834.4 |
| **Manufactured goods** | 2 180.9 | 2 450.3 | 2 803.6 | 3 192.7 | 3 846.1 | 444.9 | 541.8 | 667.8 | 651.5 | 795.7 |
| Food products | 656.6 | 681.5 | 854.8 | 887.3 | 912.6 | 93.4 | 97.3 | 102.5 | 90.8 | 113.0 |
| Tobacco products | ..... | ..... | ..... | ..... | ..... | ..... | ..... | ..... | ..... | ..... |
| Textile mill products | 3.5 | 2.3 | 2.9 | 10.1 | 25.8 | 2.5 | 0.8 | 1.0 | 0.7 | 0.8 |
| Apparel | 28.7 | 36.6 | 49.6 | 65.3 | 84.1 | 0.4 | 0.4 | 0.7 | 0.7 | 1.7 |
| Lumber and wood products | 4.7 | 6.7 | 5.7 | 4.0 | 3.7 | 1.4 | 1.4 | 2.5 | 1.2 | 0.9 |
| Furniture and fixtures | 4.3 | 7.9 | 7.8 | 9.0 | 7.5 | 1.1 | 1.5 | 1.4 | 1.6 | 1.8 |
| Paper products | 10.1 | 13.4 | 17.6 | 16.9 | 13.9 | 3.6 | 4.4 | 5.7 | 5.1 | 4.4 |
| Printing and publishing | 15.7 | 18.8 | 15.5 | 16.4 | 11.2 | 11.6 | 13.0 | 9.6 | 9.2 | 8.5 |
| Chemical products | 115.0 | 141.7 | 166.1 | 253.0 | 269.7 | 30.5 | 28.2 | 32.7 | 34.5 | 34.4 |
| Refined petroleum products | 71.7 | 87.5 | 101.3 | 157.5 | 250.5 | 1.1 | 3.5 | 2.8 | 4.6 | 5.2 |
| Rubber and plastic products | 50.3 | 64.5 | 64.4 | 52.2 | 51.1 | 23.1 | 26.7 | 29.4 | 31.1 | 34.4 |
| Leather products | 1.0 | 2.2 | 1.3 | 1.1 | 1.6 | 0.1 | 0.3 | 0.3 | 0.3 | 0.3 |
| Stone, clay and glass products | 9.1 | 14.7 | 16.8 | 25.1 | 15.6 | 5.7 | 5.6 | 6.0 | 7.4 | 6.9 |
| Primary metals | 30.0 | 18.6 | 20.0 | 14.4 | 22.1 | 4.2 | 5.9 | 9.4 | 9.4 | 14.7 |
| Fabricated metal products | 43.2 | 54.7 | 70.2 | 61.5 | 67.2 | 15.0 | 17.0 | 28.3 | 19.3 | 25.3 |
| Industrial machinery and computers | 266.0 | 309.1 | 348.5 | 398.5 | 457.5 | 102.7 | 136.4 | 144.3 | 144.6 | 168.2 |
| Electric and electronic equipment | 131.9 | 141.3 | 156.5 | 140.4 | 148.4 | 44.0 | 52.2 | 58.5 | 55.3 | 56.9 |
| Transportation equipment | 585.3 | 688.1 | 735.9 | 883.8 | 1 287.9 | 73.3 | 114.9 | 195.3 | 192.8 | 274.6 |
| Scientific and measuring instruments | 137.0 | 128.5 | 145.3 | 158.8 | 183.6 | 25.6 | 26.2 | 30.4 | 34.5 | 35.1 |
| Miscellaneous manufactures | 10.5 | 11.3 | 10.4 | 17.4 | 16.5 | 2.6 | 2.2 | 2.9 | 3.4 | 3.9 |
| Unidentified manufactures | 6.4 | 21.0 | 12.9 | 20.0 | 15.6 | 2.8 | 4.0 | 4.0 | 4.8 | 4.8 |
| **Agricultural and livestock products** | 849.8 | 945.9 | 1 565.2 | 1 639.4 | 1 203.4 | 3.5 | 1.0 | 1.1 | 3.0 | 2.7 |
| Agricultural products | 849.1 | 944.9 | 1 564.6 | 1 637.4 | 1 202.3 | 3.2 | 0.7 | 0.7 | 2.1 | 2.1 |
| Livestock and livestock products | 0.7 | 1.0 | 0.6 | 1.9 | 1.1 | 0.4 | 0.3 | 0.4 | 0.9 | 0.6 |
| **Other commodities** | 78.8 | 102.1 | 92.7 | 139.2 | 83.6 | 24.7 | 28.4 | 18.1 | 41.5 | 36.0 |
| Forestry products | 0.4 | 0.1 | 0.1 | 0.2 | 0.2 | ..... | ..... | 0.1 | 0.2 | 0.2 |
| Fish and other marine products | ..... | 2.2 | 0.7 | 1.9 | 5.3 | ..... | ..... | ..... | ..... | ..... |
| Metallic ores and concentrates | ..... | ..... | ..... | ..... | 0.2 | ..... | ..... | ..... | ..... | ..... |
| Bituminous coal and lignite | 0.1 | ..... | 3.0 | 0.3 | 2.3 | 0.1 | ..... | ..... | 0.3 | 2.3 |
| Crude petroleum and natural gas | 2.1 | 3.6 | 3.1 | 4.8 | 3.8 | 2.1 | 3.6 | 3.0 | 4.8 | 3.6 |
| Nonmetallic minerals | 2.2 | 3.9 | 4.5 | 2.0 | 2.4 | 0.3 | 1.4 | 1.1 | 1.4 | 1.4 |
| Scrap and waste | 0.2 | 2.0 | 1.3 | 0.6 | 1.0 | 0.1 | 0.6 | 0.9 | 0.3 | 0.6 |
| Used merchandise | 0.7 | 1.8 | 4.4 | 7.2 | 2.4 | 0.3 | 0.1 | 0.1 | 0.4 | 0.3 |
| Goods imported and returned unchanged | 19.2 | 18.0 | 6.9 | 22.7 | 21.4 | 19.2 | 18.0 | 6.9 | 22.7 | 21.4 |
| Special classification provisions | 53.8 | 70.5 | 68.7 | 99.6 | 44.6 | 2.5 | 4.7 | 5.9 | 11.5 | 6.2 |

## Table D-3.  State Exports of Goods by Destination and Industry, 1993–1997 —*Continued*

**KANSAS** (Millions of dollars.)

| Industry | 1993 | 1994 | 1995 | 1996 | 1997 | 1993 | 1994 | 1995 | 1996 | 1997 |
|---|---|---|---|---|---|---|---|---|---|---|
| | South and Central America and Caribbean | | | | | Mexico | | | | |
| **ALL GOODS** | 326.1 | 407.3 | 580.5 | 699.7 | 931.2 | 186.9 | 366.0 | 348.8 | 643.1 | 449.2 |
| **Manufactured goods** | 178.5 | 265.1 | 329.9 | 388.7 | 620.3 | 84.0 | 177.0 | 106.2 | 201.5 | 240.7 |
| Food products | 54.8 | 68.9 | 73.1 | 120.8 | 112.3 | 16.3 | 30.4 | 25.4 | 30.1 | 28.7 |
| Tobacco products | ..... | ..... | ..... | ..... | ..... | ..... | ..... | ..... | ..... | ..... |
| Textile mill products | 0.2 | 0.6 | 0.3 | 0.2 | 0.2 | 0.3 | 0.2 | 0.6 | 7.0 | 24.1 |
| Apparel | 23.8 | 31.0 | 39.9 | 57.4 | 72.3 | 0.1 | 0.3 | 1.5 | 0.4 | 7.3 |
| Lumber and wood products | ..... | ..... | ..... | 0.1 | ..... | 0.1 | ..... | 0.1 | 0.1 | 0.1 |
| Furniture and fixtures | 0.7 | 0.5 | 0.1 | 0.1 | 0.9 | 0.4 | 1.3 | 0.5 | 0.2 | 0.7 |
| Paper products | 1.1 | 1.4 | 1.1 | 1.1 | 1.2 | 1.2 | 3.2 | 4.1 | 5.4 | 3.3 |
| Printing and publishing | 0.3 | 0.2 | 0.5 | 1.6 | 0.3 | 0.4 | 0.8 | 1.5 | 2.6 | 0.8 |
| Chemical products | 7.3 | 8.3 | 12.5 | 28.4 | 24.6 | 5.0 | 28.6 | 14.5 | 40.2 | 28.2 |
| Refined petroleum products | 0.1 | 5.6 | 24.2 | 14.5 | 54.6 | ..... | ..... | 17.3 | 59.6 | 71.4 |
| Rubber and plastic products | 4.4 | 12.7 | 7.4 | 1.5 | 1.4 | 4.1 | 5.2 | 4.3 | 4.6 | 4.9 |
| Leather products | ..... | 0.1 | 0.1 | 0.2 | 0.2 | ..... | 0.2 | 0.1 | ..... | 0.2 |
| Stone, clay and glass products | 0.1 | 4.5 | 7.3 | 14.1 | 4.4 | 0.7 | 1.4 | 0.2 | 0.2 | 0.1 |
| Primary metals | 3.2 | 2.5 | 2.8 | 0.8 | 1.5 | 0.6 | 0.6 | 0.1 | 0.6 | 0.5 |
| Fabricated metal products | 1.9 | 2.9 | 3.7 | 8.1 | 11.2 | 2.4 | 3.0 | 1.6 | 2.2 | 4.2 |
| Industrial machinery and computers | 20.6 | 25.9 | 24.2 | 35.2 | 75.2 | 11.2 | 14.7 | 16.9 | 14.3 | 21.3 |
| Electric and electronic equipment | 8.7 | 6.0 | 8.7 | 10.1 | 27.0 | 5.4 | 6.7 | 5.6 | 3.7 | 11.8 |
| Transportation equipment | 45.7 | 88.3 | 117.9 | 87.2 | 226.1 | 30.9 | 72.3 | 8.7 | 27.3 | 28.4 |
| Scientific and measuring instruments | 4.7 | 4.7 | 4.7 | 5.0 | 4.7 | 4.4 | 6.3 | 2.6 | 2.3 | 3.0 |
| Miscellaneous manufactures | 0.3 | 0.6 | 0.9 | 2.1 | 1.7 | 0.3 | 1.1 | 0.3 | 0.4 | 1.1 |
| Unidentified manufactures | 0.4 | 0.3 | 0.4 | 0.2 | 0.3 | 0.3 | 0.6 | 0.4 | 0.4 | 0.6 |
| **Agricultural and livestock products** | 146.2 | 141.2 | 249.9 | 308.0 | 308.6 | 102.7 | 187.9 | 242.4 | 440.9 | 206.9 |
| Agricultural products | 146.2 | 141.2 | 249.9 | 307.9 | 308.5 | 102.4 | 187.3 | 242.4 | 440.8 | 206.9 |
| Livestock and livestock products | ..... | ..... | ..... | 0.1 | 0.1 | 0.3 | 0.6 | ..... | 0.1 | ..... |
| **Other commodities** | 1.5 | 1.0 | 0.7 | 3.0 | 2.2 | 0.2 | 1.1 | 0.2 | 0.7 | 1.7 |
| Forestry products | ..... | ..... | ..... | ..... | ..... | ..... | ..... | ..... | ..... | ..... |
| Fish and other marine products | ..... | 0.1 | ..... | ..... | 0.9 | ..... | ..... | ..... | ..... | ..... |
| Metallic ores and concentrates | ..... | ..... | ..... | ..... | ..... | ..... | ..... | ..... | ..... | ..... |
| Bituminous coal and lignite | ..... | ..... | ..... | ..... | ..... | ..... | ..... | ..... | ..... | ..... |
| Crude petroleum and natural gas | ..... | ..... | ..... | ..... | ..... | ..... | ..... | ..... | ..... | ..... |
| Nonmetallic minerals | ..... | ..... | ..... | ..... | ..... | ..... | ..... | 0.1 | ..... | ..... |
| Scrap and waste | ..... | ..... | ..... | ..... | ..... | ..... | 0.7 | ..... | ..... | ..... |
| Used merchandise | ..... | ..... | ..... | 0.1 | 0.1 | 0.1 | 0.2 | 0.1 | ..... | 0.2 |
| Goods imported and returned unchanged | ..... | ..... | ..... | ..... | ..... | ..... | ..... | ..... | ..... | ..... |
| Special classification provisions | 1.4 | 0.9 | 0.6 | 2.9 | 1.3 | 0.1 | 0.2 | 0.1 | 0.6 | 1.4 |
| | European Union | | | | | United Kingdom | | | | |
| **ALL GOODS** | 456.1 | 488.4 | 483.8 | 636.9 | 744.6 | 88.5 | 92.7 | 90.5 | 129.6 | 173.4 |
| **Manufactured goods** | 411.9 | 449.8 | 442.4 | 597.0 | 710.0 | 87.3 | 92.0 | 87.0 | 128.4 | 169.0 |
| Food products | 49.7 | 55.8 | 50.8 | 63.5 | 37.1 | 14.4 | 18.2 | 13.8 | 15.7 | 6.9 |
| Tobacco products | ..... | ..... | ..... | ..... | ..... | ..... | ..... | ..... | ..... | ..... |
| Textile mill products | 0.3 | 0.2 | 0.4 | 0.3 | 0.2 | 0.1 | ..... | 0.2 | 0.1 | 0.2 |
| Apparel | 0.5 | 0.9 | 1.3 | 1.2 | 1.0 | 0.2 | 0.3 | 0.7 | 0.8 | 0.5 |
| Lumber and wood products | 1.6 | 2.5 | 2.1 | 1.7 | 1.5 | ..... | ..... | 0.1 | 0.3 | ..... |
| Furniture and fixtures | 0.3 | 0.6 | 0.4 | 0.6 | 0.7 | 0.1 | 0.4 | 0.3 | 0.3 | 0.3 |
| Paper products | 2.2 | 2.5 | 5.0 | 3.0 | 2.4 | 0.7 | 0.6 | 0.5 | 0.6 | 0.6 |
| Printing and publishing | 1.1 | 1.2 | 1.0 | 0.8 | 0.6 | 0.6 | 0.9 | 0.5 | 0.5 | 0.4 |
| Chemical products | 41.0 | 45.6 | 52.1 | 72.8 | 115.7 | 4.9 | 1.8 | 4.2 | 10.4 | 16.2 |
| Refined petroleum products | 30.7 | 30.7 | 29.5 | 51.2 | 61.9 | 0.7 | 0.9 | 0.4 | 1.0 | 0.7 |
| Rubber and plastic products | 4.4 | 5.7 | 7.8 | 6.1 | 3.7 | 1.9 | 1.4 | 1.3 | 1.7 | 0.9 |
| Leather products | 0.2 | 0.3 | 0.2 | 0.2 | 0.1 | ..... | ..... | ..... | ..... | ..... |
| Stone, clay and glass products | 1.1 | 0.8 | 1.5 | 1.9 | 2.2 | 0.1 | 0.1 | 0.4 | 0.9 | 1.2 |
| Primary metals | 4.0 | 2.9 | 2.8 | 1.5 | 1.5 | 1.4 | 1.5 | 0.6 | 0.4 | 0.6 |
| Fabricated metal products | 5.4 | 7.0 | 9.4 | 5.6 | 8.9 | 2.2 | 2.2 | 2.2 | 3.3 | 5.7 |
| Industrial machinery and computers | 42.2 | 45.1 | 58.3 | 64.0 | 80.3 | 13.6 | 13.9 | 11.9 | 17.1 | 22.9 |
| Electric and electronic equipment | 17.7 | 15.7 | 18.9 | 19.3 | 21.8 | 4.9 | 4.8 | 4.7 | 6.9 | 6.6 |
| Transportation equipment | 159.2 | 185.1 | 145.2 | 234.8 | 299.8 | 25.6 | 33.6 | 33.4 | 37.7 | 80.3 |
| Scientific and measuring instruments | 46.4 | 43.9 | 51.9 | 50.9 | 65.9 | 14.0 | 9.8 | 10.6 | 14.6 | 21.9 |
| Miscellaneous manufactures | 2.9 | 2.0 | 2.5 | 4.8 | 3.7 | 1.4 | 1.2 | 0.9 | 3.9 | 2.6 |
| Unidentified manufactures | 1.2 | 1.2 | 1.2 | 12.7 | 0.9 | 0.4 | 0.3 | 0.3 | 12.2 | 0.5 |
| **Agricultural and livestock products** | 12.8 | 32.4 | 30.9 | 34.2 | 24.0 | ..... | 0.1 | ..... | ..... | ..... |
| Agricultural products | 12.8 | 32.4 | 30.9 | 34.1 | 24.0 | ..... | 0.1 | ..... | ..... | ..... |
| Livestock and livestock products | 0.1 | ..... | ..... | ..... | ..... | ..... | ..... | ..... | ..... | ..... |
| **Other commodities** | 31.4 | 6.2 | 10.4 | 5.8 | 10.6 | 1.1 | 0.7 | 3.4 | 1.2 | 4.4 |
| Forestry products | ..... | ..... | ..... | ..... | ..... | ..... | ..... | ..... | ..... | ..... |
| Fish and other marine products | ..... | 1.9 | 0.3 | 0.4 | 0.4 | ..... | ..... | ..... | ..... | ..... |
| Metallic ores and concentrates | ..... | ..... | ..... | ..... | ..... | ..... | ..... | ..... | ..... | ..... |
| Bituminous coal and lignite | ..... | ..... | 2.2 | ..... | ..... | ..... | ..... | 1.9 | ..... | ..... |
| Crude petroleum and natural gas | ..... | ..... | ..... | ..... | ..... | ..... | ..... | ..... | ..... | ..... |
| Nonmetallic minerals | ..... | ..... | 0.5 | 0.1 | ..... | ..... | ..... | ..... | ..... | ..... |
| Scrap and waste | ..... | ..... | 0.1 | 0.1 | 0.1 | ..... | ..... | ..... | ..... | ..... |
| Used merchandise | 0.1 | 1.2 | 3.7 | 2.6 | 1.1 | 0.1 | 0.1 | 0.1 | ..... | 0.3 |
| Goods imported and returned unchanged | ..... | ..... | ..... | ..... | ..... | ..... | ..... | ..... | ..... | ..... |
| Special classification provisions | 31.2 | 3.1 | 3.7 | 2.8 | 9.0 | 1.0 | 0.6 | 1.4 | 1.2 | 4.1 |

## Table D-3.   State Exports of Goods by Destination and Industry, 1993–1997 —*Continued*

**KANSAS** (Millions of dollars.)

| Industry | 1993 | 1994 | 1995 | 1996 | 1997 | 1993 | 1994 | 1995 | 1996 | 1997 |
|---|---|---|---|---|---|---|---|---|---|---|
| | Germany | | | | | France | | | | |
| **ALL GOODS** | 91.5 | 121.5 | 98.0 | 94.9 | 114.8 | 88.4 | 52.3 | 64.3 | 108.1 | 98.2 |
| **Manufactured goods** | 89.2 | 120.7 | 97.1 | 94.4 | 111.1 | 59.9 | 51.2 | 63.7 | 107.3 | 97.3 |
| Food products | 4.9 | 5.6 | 7.0 | 7.5 | 3.0 | 8.1 | 8.2 | 8.7 | 6.3 | ..... |
| Tobacco products | ..... | ..... | ..... | ..... | ..... | ..... | ..... | ..... | ..... | ..... |
| Textile mill products | ..... | ..... | ..... | ..... | ..... | ..... | ..... | 0.1 | ..... | ..... |
| Apparel | ..... | 0.1 | 0.1 | ..... | 0.1 | ..... | ..... | 0.1 | ..... | ..... |
| Lumber and wood products | 0.2 | 0.8 | 0.3 | ..... | ..... | ..... | ..... | ..... | ..... | ..... |
| Furniture and fixtures | 0.1 | 0.1 | 0.1 | 0.2 | 0.1 | ..... | 0.1 | ..... | ..... | ..... |
| Paper products | 0.1 | ..... | 0.1 | 0.1 | 0.3 | 1.2 | 1.4 | 4.1 | 1.7 | 1.3 |
| Printing and publishing | 0.1 | 0.1 | ..... | ..... | 0.1 | 0.3 | 0.1 | 0.2 | ..... | ..... |
| Chemical products | 6.8 | 9.2 | 8.1 | 9.6 | 5.7 | 1.2 | 1.0 | 4.3 | 1.7 | 2.4 |
| Refined petroleum products | 2.9 | 2.8 | ..... | 1.5 | 5.1 | ..... | 0.1 | 0.8 | 0.2 | ..... |
| Rubber and plastic products | 0.5 | 0.4 | 1.0 | 0.5 | 0.3 | 0.2 | 0.3 | 0.6 | 0.5 | 0.5 |
| Leather products | ..... | 0.1 | 0.1 | ..... | ..... | ..... | ..... | ..... | ..... | ..... |
| Stone, clay and glass products | 0.2 | 0.4 | 0.1 | 0.1 | 0.2 | 0.1 | 0.1 | 0.2 | 0.3 | 0.5 |
| Primary metals | 0.1 | 0.3 | 0.3 | 0.1 | 0.1 | 0.1 | 0.2 | 0.1 | ..... | 0.2 |
| Fabricated metal products | 1.6 | 0.3 | 0.5 | 0.4 | 0.6 | 0.5 | 0.7 | 2.9 | 0.7 | 0.2 |
| Industrial machinery and computers | 7.1 | 9.4 | 10.6 | 9.5 | 7.6 | 5.5 | 2.6 | 4.0 | 3.8 | 7.6 |
| Electric and electronic equipment | 2.5 | 2.8 | 2.3 | 3.3 | 2.0 | 3.1 | 2.8 | 2.7 | 2.4 | 4.0 |
| Transportation equipment | 46.2 | 73.4 | 51.7 | 49.6 | 71.8 | 32.0 | 25.6 | 21.7 | 79.7 | 62.6 |
| Scientific and measuring instruments | 15.0 | 14.3 | 14.4 | 11.5 | 13.6 | 6.8 | 7.6 | 12.2 | 9.3 | 17.2 |
| Miscellaneous manufactures | 0.7 | 0.3 | 0.1 | 0.2 | 0.2 | 0.4 | 0.1 | 1.0 | 0.3 | 0.5 |
| Unidentified manufactures | 0.2 | 0.3 | 0.4 | 0.1 | 0.2 | 0.2 | 0.2 | 0.1 | 0.1 | 0.1 |
| **Agricultural and livestock products** | 1.0 | 0.1 | ..... | 0.1 | ..... | 0.5 | 0.3 | ..... | ..... | ..... |
| Agricultural products | 1.0 | 0.1 | ..... | ..... | ..... | 0.5 | 0.3 | ..... | ..... | ..... |
| Livestock and livestock products | ..... | ..... | ..... | ..... | ..... | ..... | ..... | ..... | ..... | ..... |
| **Other commodities** | 1.3 | 0.7 | 0.9 | 0.5 | 3.6 | 27.9 | 0.8 | 0.6 | 0.7 | 0.8 |
| Forestry products | ..... | ..... | ..... | ..... | ..... | ..... | ..... | ..... | ..... | ..... |
| Fish and other marine products | ..... | ..... | ..... | ..... | ..... | ..... | ..... | ..... | ..... | ..... |
| Metallic ores and concentrates | ..... | ..... | ..... | ..... | ..... | ..... | ..... | ..... | ..... | ..... |
| Bituminous coal and lignite | ..... | ..... | ..... | ..... | ..... | ..... | ..... | ..... | ..... | ..... |
| Crude petroleum and natural gas | ..... | ..... | ..... | ..... | ..... | ..... | ..... | ..... | ..... | ..... |
| Nonmetallic minerals | ..... | ..... | ..... | ..... | ..... | ..... | ..... | ..... | ..... | ..... |
| Scrap and waste | ..... | ..... | 0.1 | ..... | 0.1 | ..... | ..... | ..... | ..... | ..... |
| Used merchandise | ..... | 0.1 | ..... | ..... | ..... | 0.1 | 0.1 | 0.1 | 0.3 | ..... |
| Goods imported and returned unchanged | ..... | ..... | ..... | ..... | ..... | ..... | ..... | ..... | ..... | ..... |
| Special classification provisions | 1.3 | 0.6 | 0.8 | 0.4 | 3.4 | 27.8 | 0.7 | 0.5 | 0.5 | 0.8 |
| | The Netherlands | | | | | Asian 10 | | | | |
| **ALL GOODS** | 51.2 | 36.1 | 32.6 | 73.1 | 102.0 | 1 063.9 | 1 125.3 | 1 827.4 | 1 761.2 | 1 501.7 |
| **Manufactured goods** | 46.2 | 34.2 | 32.3 | 72.8 | 101.8 | 637.7 | 645.9 | 877.1 | 923.3 | 971.3 |
| Food products | 6.3 | 5.5 | 4.6 | 2.5 | 0.7 | 362.1 | 357.1 | 540.6 | 567.0 | 594.9 |
| Tobacco products | ..... | ..... | ..... | ..... | ..... | ..... | ..... | ..... | ..... | ..... |
| Textile mill products | ..... | ..... | ..... | ..... | ..... | 0.1 | 0.2 | 0.3 | 1.3 | 0.2 |
| Apparel | 0.1 | 0.2 | 0.1 | ..... | 0.1 | 2.8 | 3.5 | 5.6 | 4.9 | 1.0 |
| Lumber and wood products | ..... | ..... | ..... | 0.1 | 0.1 | 1.5 | 2.5 | 0.9 | 0.7 | 0.9 |
| Furniture and fixtures | ..... | ..... | ..... | ..... | ..... | 1.5 | 3.3 | 2.7 | 2.8 | 2.4 |
| Paper products | ..... | ..... | ..... | 0.1 | 0.1 | 0.2 | 0.2 | 0.3 | 1.1 | 1.1 |
| Printing and publishing | ..... | ..... | ..... | 0.2 | 0.1 | 1.6 | 2.5 | 2.2 | 1.3 | 0.5 |
| Chemical products | 11.0 | 11.8 | 10.0 | 31.9 | 57.0 | 17.7 | 19.6 | 45.3 | 59.1 | 42.8 |
| Refined petroleum products | 6.2 | ..... | 0.5 | 17.7 | 15.6 | 30.1 | 37.5 | 20.8 | 21.1 | 52.8 |
| Rubber and plastic products | 0.3 | 0.6 | 0.6 | 0.2 | 0.4 | 6.4 | 7.0 | 10.2 | 6.3 | 5.1 |
| Leather products | ..... | 0.1 | ..... | ..... | ..... | 0.6 | 1.0 | 0.7 | 0.4 | 0.6 |
| Stone, clay and glass products | 0.4 | 0.1 | 0.1 | 0.2 | 0.1 | 0.8 | 1.4 | 0.8 | 1.0 | 1.2 |
| Primary metals | 0.3 | 0.3 | 0.1 | 0.1 | 0.2 | 3.5 | 1.5 | 1.2 | 1.6 | 2.7 |
| Fabricated metal products | 0.3 | 0.2 | 0.8 | 0.5 | 0.2 | 13.7 | 16.5 | 18.1 | 18.6 | 13.7 |
| Industrial machinery and computers | 4.2 | 5.8 | 7.4 | 7.3 | 11.8 | 45.2 | 42.9 | 56.7 | 70.1 | 61.8 |
| Electric and electronic equipment | 1.2 | 1.0 | 2.8 | 2.3 | 3.3 | 44.1 | 49.0 | 55.8 | 36.8 | 24.7 |
| Transportation equipment | 13.6 | 6.1 | 1.7 | 5.4 | 7.4 | 77.4 | 69.7 | 87.0 | 92.2 | 113.3 |
| Scientific and measuring instruments | 2.1 | 2.3 | 3.4 | 4.0 | 4.8 | 24.5 | 25.9 | 23.9 | 31.7 | 39.5 |
| Miscellaneous manufactures | ..... | 0.1 | 0.1 | ..... | ..... | 2.9 | 3.7 | 2.4 | 4.7 | 4.0 |
| Unidentified manufactures | 0.1 | 0.1 | 0.1 | 0.1 | ..... | 0.8 | 1.0 | 1.5 | 0.8 | 8.1 |
| **Agricultural and livestock products** | 4.9 | ..... | ..... | 0.1 | 0.1 | 407.0 | 417.9 | 890.7 | 753.6 | 521.9 |
| Agricultural products | 4.8 | ..... | ..... | 0.1 | 0.1 | 407.0 | 417.8 | 890.7 | 753.2 | 521.9 |
| Livestock and livestock products | ..... | ..... | ..... | ..... | ..... | ..... | ..... | ..... | 0.4 | ..... |
| **Other commodities** | 0.1 | 1.9 | 0.3 | 0.2 | 0.1 | 19.3 | 61.6 | 59.6 | 84.4 | 8.4 |
| Forestry products | ..... | ..... | ..... | ..... | ..... | 0.4 | 0.1 | ..... | ..... | ..... |
| Fish and other marine products | ..... | 1.9 | 0.2 | 0.1 | ..... | ..... | 0.3 | 0.3 | 0.9 | 4.0 |
| Metallic ores and concentrates | ..... | ..... | ..... | ..... | ..... | ..... | ..... | ..... | ..... | 0.2 |
| Bituminous coal and lignite | ..... | ..... | ..... | ..... | ..... | ..... | ..... | ..... | ..... | ..... |
| Crude petroleum and natural gas | ..... | ..... | ..... | ..... | ..... | ..... | ..... | ..... | ..... | 0.2 |
| Nonmetallic minerals | ..... | ..... | ..... | ..... | ..... | 1.8 | 2.4 | 2.6 | 0.4 | 0.9 |
| Scrap and waste | ..... | ..... | ..... | ..... | ..... | 0.1 | 0.6 | 0.2 | 0.2 | 0.2 |
| Used merchandise | ..... | ..... | ..... | ..... | ..... | ..... | 0.2 | 0.3 | 3.7 | 0.2 |
| Goods imported and returned unchanged | ..... | ..... | ..... | ..... | ..... | ..... | ..... | ..... | ..... | ..... |
| Special classification provisions | 0.1 | ..... | ..... | 0.1 | 0.1 | 17.0 | 57.9 | 56.2 | 79.1 | 2.8 |

## Table D-3.   State Exports of Goods by Destination and Industry, 1993–1997 —*Continued*

**KANSAS** (Millions of dollars.)

| Industry | 1993 | 1994 | 1995 | 1996 | 1997 | 1993 | 1994 | 1995 | 1996 | 1997 |
|---|---|---|---|---|---|---|---|---|---|---|
| | Japan | | | | | South Korea | | | | |
| **ALL GOODS** | 684.5 | 697.4 | 1 057.3 | 1 075.0 | 921.8 | 67.3 | 107.7 | 341.5 | 239.3 | 179.1 |
| **Manufactured goods** | 410.5 | 386.4 | 510.6 | 542.0 | 573.2 | 42.6 | 56.6 | 145.8 | 132.8 | 127.5 |
| Food products | 312.3 | 280.0 | 408.3 | 427.5 | 432.6 | 24.2 | 31.5 | 77.9 | 78.3 | 101.3 |
| Tobacco products | ..... | ..... | ..... | ..... | ..... | ..... | ..... | ..... | ..... | ..... |
| Textile mill products | ..... | 0.1 | 0.2 | 0.7 | 0.2 | ..... | ..... | ..... | 0.1 | ..... |
| Apparel | 2.4 | 3.3 | 4.8 | 4.8 | 0.9 | 0.3 | ..... | 0.4 | ..... | ..... |
| Lumber and wood products | 0.7 | 1.1 | 0.6 | 0.6 | 0.7 | 0.6 | 1.1 | 0.2 | ..... | ..... |
| Furniture and fixtures | 1.3 | 3.0 | 2.4 | 2.1 | 1.2 | 0.1 | ..... | ..... | ..... | 0.3 |
| Paper products | 0.1 | 0.1 | 0.1 | ..... | 0.2 | ..... | ..... | ..... | 0.3 | ..... |
| Printing and publishing | 0.1 | 0.1 | 0.1 | 0.4 | 0.2 | ..... | 0.1 | ..... | ..... | ..... |
| Chemical products | 10.4 | 11.4 | 14.0 | 18.3 | 25.9 | 2.5 | 1.8 | 21.9 | 30.7 | 2.5 |
| Refined petroleum products | 29.8 | 29.2 | 20.3 | 20.1 | 44.6 | ..... | 1.9 | 0.2 | 0.2 | 7.6 |
| Rubber and plastic products | 2.7 | 1.8 | 4.3 | 2.5 | 1.5 | 1.4 | 2.0 | 2.8 | 2.8 | 1.9 |
| Leather products | ..... | ..... | 0.1 | 0.2 | 0.1 | ..... | ..... | ..... | ..... | 0.3 |
| Stone, clay and glass products | ..... | 0.2 | 0.2 | 0.3 | 0.1 | 0.5 | 0.6 | 0.1 | 0.3 | 0.1 |
| Primary metals | ..... | 0.1 | 0.7 | 0.6 | 0.2 | ..... | 0.1 | ..... | 0.5 | 0.2 |
| Fabricated metal products | 4.1 | 5.2 | 7.7 | 7.1 | 6.6 | 2.2 | 1.3 | 1.8 | 2.6 | 0.2 |
| Industrial machinery and computers | 6.7 | 7.4 | 14.9 | 16.3 | 17.3 | 3.8 | 4.9 | 7.5 | 6.1 | 5.5 |
| Electric and electronic equipment | 18.3 | 21.3 | 24.2 | 18.3 | 6.1 | 1.4 | 2.6 | 2.9 | 2.8 | 1.5 |
| Transportation equipment | 17.1 | 15.3 | 2.4 | 14.5 | 25.8 | 1.7 | 2.1 | 23.3 | 0.6 | 0.7 |
| Scientific and measuring instruments | 2.9 | 4.9 | 3.0 | 5.1 | 6.2 | 3.2 | 6.2 | 6.3 | 6.7 | 3.1 |
| Miscellaneous manufactures | 1.5 | 1.7 | 1.6 | 2.2 | 2.6 | 0.2 | 0.2 | 0.3 | 0.6 | 0.8 |
| Unidentified manufactures | 0.1 | 0.3 | 0.4 | 0.2 | 0.2 | 0.1 | 0.1 | 0.1 | 0.1 | 1.4 |
| **Agricultural and livestock products** | 272.6 | 262.0 | 511.1 | 528.5 | 347.7 | 24.2 | 50.8 | 195.6 | 106.5 | 51.6 |
| Agricultural products | 272.6 | 262.0 | 511.1 | 528.5 | 347.7 | 24.2 | 50.8 | 195.6 | 106.5 | 51.6 |
| Livestock and livestock products | ..... | ..... | ..... | ..... | ..... | ..... | ..... | ..... | ..... | ..... |
| **Other commodities** | 1.4 | 49.0 | 35.7 | 4.5 | 0.8 | 0.6 | 0.3 | 0.1 | ..... | 0.1 |
| Forestry products | 0.2 | 0.1 | ..... | ..... | ..... | 0.2 | ..... | ..... | ..... | ..... |
| Fish and other marine products | ..... | 0.1 | ..... | ..... | ..... | ..... | ..... | ..... | ..... | ..... |
| Metallic ores and concentrates | ..... | ..... | ..... | ..... | 0.2 | ..... | ..... | ..... | ..... | ..... |
| Bituminous coal and lignite | ..... | ..... | ..... | ..... | ..... | ..... | ..... | ..... | ..... | ..... |
| Crude petroleum and natural gas | ..... | ..... | ..... | ..... | ..... | ..... | ..... | ..... | ..... | ..... |
| Nonmetallic minerals | 0.9 | 1.1 | 1.0 | 0.1 | 0.1 | 0.2 | 0.1 | ..... | ..... | ..... |
| Scrap and waste | ..... | ..... | ..... | ..... | ..... | ..... | ..... | ..... | ..... | ..... |
| Used merchandise | ..... | 0.1 | 0.2 | 3.7 | 0.1 | ..... | 0.1 | 0.1 | ..... | ..... |
| Goods imported and returned unchanged | ..... | ..... | ..... | ..... | ..... | ..... | ..... | ..... | ..... | ..... |
| Special classification provisions | 0.3 | 47.7 | 34.3 | 0.6 | 0.4 | 0.2 | 0.1 | ..... | ..... | ..... |

| Industry | 1993 | 1994 | 1995 | 1996 | 1997 | 1993 | 1994 | 1995 | 1996 | 1997 |
|---|---|---|---|---|---|---|---|---|---|---|
| | Taiwan | | | | | Singapore | | | | |
| **ALL GOODS** | 183.1 | 159.5 | 216.3 | 171.6 | 153.3 | 38.9 | 25.3 | 24.0 | 51.2 | 33.5 |
| **Manufactured goods** | 57.2 | 53.5 | 75.4 | 71.8 | 59.0 | 38.1 | 25.1 | 23.6 | 50.7 | 32.8 |
| Food products | 17.1 | 24.9 | 43.0 | 43.2 | 34.9 | 0.5 | 0.6 | 0.4 | 0.7 | 0.5 |
| Tobacco products | ..... | ..... | ..... | ..... | ..... | ..... | ..... | ..... | ..... | ..... |
| Textile mill products | ..... | ..... | ..... | ..... | ..... | ..... | ..... | ..... | ..... | ..... |
| Apparel | ..... | 0.1 | ..... | ..... | ..... | ..... | ..... | ..... | ..... | ..... |
| Lumber and wood products | 0.1 | 0.1 | ..... | ..... | 0.1 | ..... | ..... | ..... | ..... | ..... |
| Furniture and fixtures | ..... | 0.1 | 0.1 | ..... | 0.1 | ..... | ..... | 0.1 | 0.2 | 0.1 |
| Paper products | ..... | ..... | ..... | 0.1 | 0.1 | ..... | ..... | ..... | ..... | ..... |
| Printing and publishing | 0.2 | 0.5 | ..... | 0.5 | ..... | 0.3 | 0.5 | 0.2 | 0.1 | ..... |
| Chemical products | 0.5 | 0.9 | 4.8 | 0.3 | 5.8 | 0.8 | 0.1 | 1.0 | 1.2 | 0.8 |
| Refined petroleum products | ..... | 0.1 | 0.2 | 0.3 | 0.1 | ..... | ..... | ..... | 0.2 | 0.1 |
| Rubber and plastic products | 0.5 | 0.4 | 1.0 | 0.3 | 0.8 | 0.8 | 0.7 | 0.5 | 0.3 | 0.3 |
| Leather products | ..... | ..... | ..... | ..... | ..... | ..... | ..... | ..... | ..... | ..... |
| Stone, clay and glass products | 0.2 | 0.4 | 0.2 | 0.1 | 0.1 | 0.1 | 0.1 | 0.1 | 0.1 | 0.1 |
| Primary metals | 2.7 | 0.9 | 0.1 | ..... | 0.1 | ..... | 0.1 | ..... | 0.1 | 0.1 |
| Fabricated metal products | 1.1 | 4.0 | 4.5 | 3.1 | 1.2 | 0.8 | 0.8 | 0.5 | 1.7 | 1.1 |
| Industrial machinery and computers | 5.6 | 5.3 | 6.4 | 9.3 | 4.4 | 7.7 | 5.6 | 3.8 | 9.4 | 11.5 |
| Electric and electronic equipment | 12.8 | 7.9 | 8.3 | 3.9 | 6.4 | 7.1 | 7.7 | 6.1 | 7.1 | 4.3 |
| Transportation equipment | 9.7 | 1.6 | 3.7 | 6.0 | 1.5 | 14.6 | 2.5 | 4.5 | 20.3 | 6.1 |
| Scientific and measuring instruments | 5.8 | 4.7 | 2.9 | 4.3 | 3.2 | 5.1 | 6.0 | 5.9 | 8.5 | 7.4 |
| Miscellaneous manufactures | 0.5 | 1.4 | 0.1 | 0.4 | 0.1 | 0.1 | 0.1 | 0.1 | 0.7 | 0.1 |
| Unidentified manufactures | 0.3 | 0.1 | 0.1 | ..... | 0.1 | 0.1 | 0.3 | 0.4 | 0.1 | 0.2 |
| **Agricultural and livestock products** | 109.6 | 104.6 | 122.3 | 99.0 | 93.5 | 0.5 | 0.1 | ..... | 0.1 | 0.1 |
| Agricultural products | 109.6 | 104.6 | 122.3 | 99.0 | 93.5 | 0.5 | 0.1 | ..... | 0.1 | 0.1 |
| Livestock and livestock products | ..... | ..... | ..... | ..... | ..... | ..... | ..... | ..... | ..... | ..... |
| **Other commodities** | 16.3 | 1.3 | 18.7 | 0.7 | 0.8 | 0.3 | 0.1 | 0.4 | 0.4 | 0.6 |
| Forestry products | ..... | ..... | ..... | ..... | ..... | ..... | ..... | ..... | ..... | ..... |
| Fish and other marine products | ..... | ..... | ..... | ..... | ..... | ..... | ..... | ..... | ..... | ..... |
| Metallic ores and concentrates | ..... | ..... | ..... | ..... | ..... | ..... | ..... | ..... | ..... | ..... |
| Bituminous coal and lignite | ..... | ..... | ..... | ..... | ..... | ..... | ..... | ..... | ..... | ..... |
| Crude petroleum and natural gas | ..... | ..... | ..... | ..... | ..... | ..... | ..... | ..... | ..... | 0.1 |
| Nonmetallic minerals | 0.6 | 1.2 | 1.5 | 0.3 | 0.8 | 0.2 | ..... | ..... | ..... | ..... |
| Scrap and waste | ..... | ..... | * ..... | 0.1 | ..... | ..... | ..... | ..... | ..... | ..... |
| Used merchandise | ..... | ..... | ..... | ..... | ..... | ..... | ..... | ..... | ..... | ..... |
| Goods imported and returned unchanged | ..... | ..... | ..... | ..... | ..... | ..... | ..... | ..... | ..... | ..... |
| Special classification provisions | 15.7 | 0.1 | 17.1 | 0.3 | 0.1 | 0.1 | 0.1 | 0.4 | 0.4 | 0.4 |

## KENTUCKY: Exports of Goods, 1997

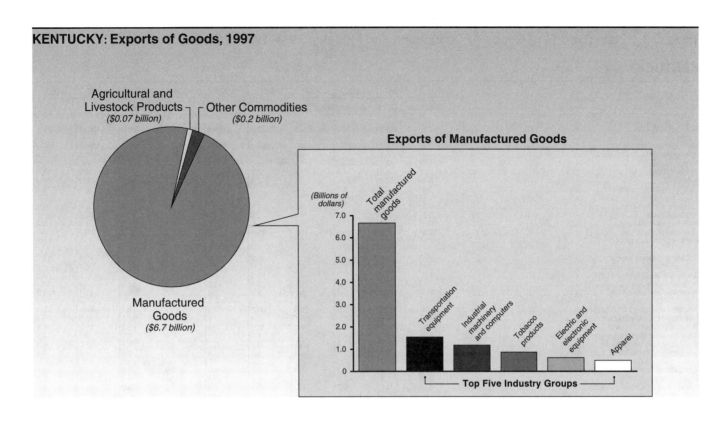

## Table D-3. State Exports of Goods by Destination and Industry, 1993–1997 —*Continued*

### KENTUCKY (Millions of dollars.)

| Industry | 1993 | 1994 | 1995 | 1996 | 1997 | 1993 | 1994 | 1995 | 1996 | 1997 |
|---|---|---|---|---|---|---|---|---|---|---|
| | All destinations | | | | | Canada | | | | |
| **ALL GOODS** | 3 325.9 | 4 188.2 | 5 030.1 | 5 824.2 | 6 904.1 | 1 058.3 | 1 571.1 | 1 804.7 | 1 905.3 | 2 368.9 |
| **Manufactured goods** | 3 101.6 | 4 051.8 | 4 810.5 | 5 581.7 | 6 664.3 | 1 020.0 | 1 528.9 | 1 751.9 | 1 846.2 | 2 309.7 |
| Food products | 193.1 | 222.2 | 305.6 | 305.5 | 312.2 | 39.0 | 50.1 | 57.1 | 54.7 | 38.7 |
| Tobacco products | 721.2 | 809.2 | 967.5 | 862.1 | 868.9 | 0.9 | 1.6 | 1.4 | 1.8 | 1.2 |
| Textile mill products | 32.1 | 46.7 | 52.9 | 59.7 | 57.3 | 22.2 | 26.5 | 34.5 | 33.3 | 30.6 |
| Apparel | 34.0 | 61.0 | 169.8 | 311.8 | 495.6 | 13.0 | 18.2 | 29.5 | 20.8 | 24.4 |
| Lumber and wood products | 38.4 | 33.9 | 35.0 | 37.8 | 53.1 | 5.1 | 5.1 | 5.0 | 6.4 | 9.3 |
| Furniture and fixtures | 35.4 | 44.5 | 48.0 | 58.6 | 62.4 | 29.8 | 38.3 | 40.1 | 45.0 | 51.8 |
| Paper products | 45.5 | 53.6 | 66.0 | 91.1 | 81.9 | 24.7 | 25.7 | 35.2 | 44.3 | 47.0 |
| Printing and publishing | 54.2 | 51.0 | 78.4 | 77.2 | 97.3 | 33.5 | 27.3 | 60.1 | 58.8 | 77.8 |
| Chemical products | 180.8 | 176.8 | 260.7 | 333.0 | 365.7 | 82.1 | 99.5 | 134.0 | 136.5 | 154.0 |
| Refined petroleum products | 22.1 | 13.0 | 14.4 | 14.4 | 10.5 | 17.2 | 7.5 | 8.9 | 8.8 | 6.8 |
| Rubber and plastic products | 61.9 | 86.5 | 104.2 | 120.0 | 148.0 | 44.3 | 54.9 | 60.5 | 63.9 | 84.3 |
| Leather products | 4.6 | 8.5 | 11.6 | 14.7 | 9.6 | 0.4 | 3.0 | 4.3 | 3.2 | 2.3 |
| Stone, clay and glass products | 67.5 | 72.7 | 63.3 | 80.6 | 118.1 | 22.2 | 23.2 | 15.1 | 16.5 | 19.8 |
| Primary metals | 244.8 | 240.7 | 240.4 | 280.1 | 296.7 | 96.0 | 162.3 | 111.8 | 114.2 | 194.2 |
| Fabricated metal products | 66.8 | 68.2 | 87.4 | 96.3 | 128.5 | 27.6 | 32.5 | 42.8 | 51.1 | 69.6 |
| Industrial machinery and computers | 356.1 | 609.2 | 690.4 | 950.6 | 1 182.1 | 159.2 | 221.7 | 264.7 | 274.5 | 366.6 |
| Electric and electronic equipment | 380.3 | 428.5 | 479.1 | 545.8 | 620.0 | 117.2 | 121.3 | 138.0 | 168.9 | 187.1 |
| Transportation equipment | 487.8 | 879.3 | 958.8 | 1 133.8 | 1 544.3 | 254.2 | 576.4 | 664.8 | 696.4 | 892.4 |
| Scientific and measuring instruments | 35.1 | 77.0 | 105.0 | 128.3 | 136.1 | 15.9 | 17.1 | 21.3 | 23.5 | 25.7 |
| Miscellaneous manufactures | 33.9 | 61.5 | 64.1 | 65.7 | 65.9 | 12.6 | 13.4 | 19.3 | 20.0 | 21.3 |
| Unidentified manufactures | 6.1 | 7.9 | 7.9 | 14.5 | 10.2 | 2.7 | 3.4 | 3.7 | 3.6 | 4.8 |
| **Agricultural and livestock products** | 37.8 | 50.8 | 74.3 | 45.8 | 67.9 | 6.5 | 10.5 | 7.9 | 8.1 | 7.6 |
| Agricultural products | 23.8 | 31.2 | 27.7 | 31.9 | 51.4 | 3.0 | 2.7 | 1.9 | 3.6 | 3.4 |
| Livestock and livestock products | 14.0 | 19.6 | 46.6 | 13.8 | 16.5 | 3.6 | 7.8 | 5.9 | 4.4 | 4.3 |
| **Other commodities** | 186.4 | 85.7 | 145.3 | 196.8 | 171.9 | 31.8 | 31.7 | 44.9 | 51.1 | 51.6 |
| Forestry products | 0.2 | 0.1 | 0.4 | 0.2 | 0.3 | ..... | ..... | 0.1 | 0.1 | ..... |
| Fish and other marine products | 0.1 | 0.1 | 1.7 | 1.4 | 1.7 | 0.1 | ..... | 0.2 | 0.4 | 0.2 |
| Metallic ores and concentrates | 0.4 | 0.4 | 4.8 | 0.1 | 0.1 | 0.4 | 0.4 | 4.7 | ..... | 0.1 |
| Bituminous coal and lignite | 153.0 | 52.2 | 84.5 | 136.3 | 105.1 | 12.0 | 9.0 | 6.0 | 8.6 | 6.4 |
| Crude petroleum and natural gas | 0.3 | 0.7 | 0.3 | 0.5 | 0.3 | 0.1 | 0.4 | 0.1 | ..... | ..... |
| Nonmetallic minerals | 6.7 | 7.0 | 8.1 | 11.5 | 13.3 | 0.5 | 0.7 | 1.4 | 2.1 | 1.8 |
| Scrap and waste | 7.5 | 7.1 | 12.8 | 8.7 | 8.9 | 3.4 | 5.7 | 8.8 | 7.8 | 6.8 |
| Used merchandise | 2.6 | 2.8 | 2.1 | 3.7 | 4.6 | 0.7 | 1.2 | 0.2 | 0.9 | 0.8 |
| Goods imported and returned unchanged | 12.3 | 13.6 | 21.8 | 30.3 | 35.1 | 12.3 | 13.6 | 21.8 | 30.3 | 35.1 |
| Special classification provisions | 3.3 | 1.7 | 8.7 | 4.1 | 2.4 | 2.3 | 0.6 | 1.6 | 0.9 | 0.3 |

## Table D-3.  State Exports of Goods by Destination and Industry, 1993–1997 —*Continued*

**KENTUCKY** (Millions of dollars.)

| Industry | 1993 | 1994 | 1995 | 1996 | 1997 | 1993 | 1994 | 1995 | 1996 | 1997 |
|---|---|---|---|---|---|---|---|---|---|---|
| | South and Central America and Caribbean | | | | | Mexico | | | | |
| **ALL GOODS** | 130.9 | 156.5 | 304.0 | 446.6 | 572.9 | 189.9 | 232.1 | 188.0 | 280.1 | 345.1 |
| **Manufactured goods** | 112.4 | 152.9 | 296.2 | 438.1 | 566.5 | 184.7 | 224.6 | 179.2 | 274.0 | 337.9 |
| Food products | 4.4 | 5.7 | 6.1 | 6.7 | 9.7 | 3.3 | 6.3 | 9.0 | 11.2 | 7.4 |
| Tobacco products | 28.0 | 22.3 | 19.0 | 13.4 | 13.5 | 0.1 | 1.3 | 0.7 | 0.2 | 0.2 |
| Textile mill products | 0.7 | 4.5 | 4.9 | 11.3 | 2.7 | 0.3 | 0.8 | 1.5 | 2.9 | 10.3 |
| Apparel | 5.1 | 21.2 | 120.4 | 236.2 | 317.1 | 0.1 | 0.2 | 0.2 | 9.2 | 31.4 |
| Lumber and wood products | 0.3 | 0.5 | 1.2 | 0.2 | 1.1 | 0.8 | 0.5 | 0.3 | 0.4 | 0.8 |
| Furniture and fixtures | 0.5 | 0.2 | 1.7 | 1.3 | 1.6 | 0.3 | 0.6 | 0.3 | 0.3 | 0.2 |
| Paper products | 0.8 | 0.8 | 2.5 | 4.0 | 2.4 | 14.0 | 15.5 | 17.7 | 23.5 | 17.2 |
| Printing and publishing | 0.6 | 0.7 | 0.8 | 1.5 | 1.9 | 8.1 | 10.8 | 1.2 | 1.4 | 0.9 |
| Chemical products | 12.3 | 7.2 | 16.3 | 19.2 | 21.5 | 4.2 | 6.7 | 6.3 | 6.4 | 9.7 |
| Refined petroleum products | 2.4 | 2.7 | 2.1 | 2.7 | 1.3 | ..... | 0.1 | 0.1 | ..... | 0.1 |
| Rubber and plastic products | 1.1 | 2.4 | 4.2 | 4.3 | 10.2 | 2.3 | 14.3 | 16.9 | 18.9 | 18.9 |
| Leather products | 0.4 | 0.4 | 0.4 | 0.5 | 0.4 | ..... | ..... | ..... | 0.2 | 1.3 |
| Stone, clay and glass products | 1.9 | 2.3 | 4.2 | 4.9 | 7.1 | 1.4 | 5.9 | 4.6 | 4.2 | 4.2 |
| Primary metals | 2.3 | 2.2 | 7.5 | 10.5 | 8.4 | 44.2 | 30.6 | 15.8 | 36.8 | 37.1 |
| Fabricated metal products | 3.3 | 3.2 | 3.4 | 5.5 | 8.0 | 3.0 | 4.6 | 6.0 | 11.1 | 14.7 |
| Industrial machinery and computers | 21.6 | 38.4 | 49.1 | 73.4 | 88.1 | 23.9 | 31.7 | 20.7 | 44.7 | 78.5 |
| Electric and electronic equipment | 19.7 | 24.6 | 35.5 | 24.8 | 42.2 | 68.1 | 73.8 | 52.3 | 76.1 | 78.9 |
| Transportation equipment | 4.2 | 4.3 | 5.6 | 6.9 | 16.2 | 6.4 | 10.6 | 12.3 | 16.2 | 16.6 |
| Scientific and measuring instruments | 0.8 | 3.6 | 4.8 | 4.9 | 8.6 | 1.5 | 2.8 | 4.0 | 3.5 | 4.5 |
| Miscellaneous manufactures | 2.0 | 5.2 | 5.8 | 5.5 | 3.6 | 2.2 | 6.9 | 9.1 | 6.0 | 4.3 |
| Unidentified manufactures | 0.2 | 0.4 | 0.4 | 0.4 | 1.1 | 0.4 | 0.7 | 0.4 | 0.6 | 0.8 |
| **Agricultural and livestock products** | 0.9 | 2.6 | 2.4 | 1.3 | 2.7 | 3.0 | 3.8 | 0.6 | 0.8 | 2.4 |
| Agricultural products | 0.6 | 1.0 | 1.8 | 0.4 | 1.6 | 1.4 | 1.5 | 0.4 | 0.8 | 0.9 |
| Livestock and livestock products | 0.3 | 1.5 | 0.7 | 0.9 | 1.1 | 1.6 | 2.3 | 0.2 | ..... | 1.5 |
| **Other commodities** | 17.5 | 1.1 | 5.4 | 7.2 | 3.7 | 2.2 | 3.7 | 8.2 | 5.3 | 4.8 |
| Forestry products | ..... | 0.1 | 0.1 | ..... | 0.1 | ..... | ..... | ..... | ..... | ..... |
| Fish and other marine products | ..... | ..... | 1.5 | 0.8 | 0.1 | ..... | ..... | ..... | ..... | ..... |
| Metallic ores and concentrates | ..... | ..... | 0.1 | ..... | ..... | ..... | ..... | ..... | ..... | ..... |
| Bituminous coal and lignite | 16.0 | ..... | 1.5 | 4.6 | ..... | ..... | ..... | ..... | ..... | ..... |
| Crude petroleum and natural gas | ..... | ..... | 0.1 | 0.3 | 0.1 | ..... | ..... | ..... | ..... | 0.1 |
| Nonmetallic minerals | 1.2 | 0.9 | 1.9 | 1.2 | 2.7 | 2.0 | 3.2 | 2.1 | 3.5 | 4.4 |
| Scrap and waste | ..... | ..... | ..... | ..... | ..... | ..... | ..... | ..... | ..... | 0.2 |
| Used merchandise | 0.3 | 0.1 | 0.2 | 0.3 | 0.6 | 0.1 | 0.4 | 0.2 | ..... | ..... |
| Goods imported and returned unchanged | ..... | ..... | ..... | ..... | ..... | ..... | ..... | ..... | ..... | ..... |
| Special classification provisions | ..... | ..... | ..... | ..... | ..... | ..... | 0.1 | 5.9 | 1.8 | 0.1 |
| | European Union | | | | | United Kingdom | | | | |
| **ALL GOODS** | 613.6 | 718.4 | 790.2 | 1 099.0 | 1 202.7 | 95.6 | 114.7 | 167.2 | 283.9 | 255.2 |
| **Manufactured goods** | 503.4 | 672.6 | 719.5 | 998.9 | 1 092.4 | 88.2 | 99.7 | 136.5 | 249.2 | 210.3 |
| Food products | 88.0 | 84.7 | 98.6 | 106.0 | 114.4 | 13.5 | 17.2 | 21.0 | 28.7 | 27.9 |
| Tobacco products | 92.7 | 92.7 | 70.1 | 35.4 | 45.2 | ..... | ..... | ..... | ..... | ..... |
| Textile mill products | 4.1 | 8.3 | 6.6 | 10.9 | 7.1 | 1.7 | 0.9 | 0.3 | 1.2 | 0.4 |
| Apparel | 4.5 | 6.6 | 3.3 | 3.0 | 2.2 | 1.2 | 0.6 | 0.1 | 0.2 | 0.3 |
| Lumber and wood products | 21.7 | 21.8 | 21.8 | 23.5 | 37.5 | 7.8 | 5.3 | 6.0 | 10.9 | 16.2 |
| Furniture and fixtures | 2.8 | 4.0 | 4.6 | 5.4 | 3.7 | 1.4 | 1.6 | 1.4 | 1.8 | 2.2 |
| Paper products | 1.1 | 2.4 | 4.3 | 8.0 | 5.2 | 0.5 | 0.7 | 1.1 | 1.8 | 1.3 |
| Printing and publishing | 6.0 | 6.4 | 8.5 | 9.2 | 9.7 | 5.4 | 5.7 | 7.5 | 7.1 | 7.7 |
| Chemical products | 49.7 | 19.2 | 41.4 | 91.0 | 114.0 | 4.5 | 4.8 | 6.9 | 24.4 | 29.1 |
| Refined petroleum products | 0.3 | 0.4 | 0.3 | 0.5 | 0.6 | ..... | ..... | ..... | ..... | ..... |
| Rubber and plastic products | 9.6 | 6.7 | 13.7 | 17.6 | 14.3 | 2.6 | 2.0 | 6.0 | 9.9 | 7.7 |
| Leather products | 2.8 | 2.7 | 1.7 | 2.7 | 1.6 | 0.3 | 0.2 | 0.4 | 1.4 | 1.1 |
| Stone, clay and glass products | 11.2 | 7.1 | 6.8 | 5.2 | 4.2 | 6.2 | 3.3 | 1.6 | 1.4 | 1.1 |
| Primary metals | 2.3 | 6.0 | 12.6 | 12.6 | 15.1 | 0.3 | 1.2 | 2.1 | 4.0 | 6.0 |
| Fabricated metal products | 12.4 | 12.1 | 11.3 | 11.1 | 13.1 | 5.4 | 5.5 | 3.6 | 4.5 | 5.2 |
| Industrial machinery and computers | 50.6 | 162.8 | 188.2 | 341.1 | 388.9 | 16.9 | 22.2 | 42.3 | 97.0 | 53.8 |
| Electric and electronic equipment | 69.3 | 74.9 | 74.9 | 85.5 | 85.0 | 12.3 | 15.2 | 19.2 | 24.4 | 13.4 |
| Transportation equipment | 55.4 | 100.0 | 86.4 | 144.3 | 146.7 | 4.3 | 9.0 | 11.9 | 24.1 | 30.9 |
| Scientific and measuring instruments | 8.8 | 32.6 | 46.5 | 66.8 | 64.3 | 1.8 | 2.3 | 3.3 | 4.2 | 3.6 |
| Miscellaneous manufactures | 8.7 | 19.9 | 16.2 | 17.3 | 17.8 | 1.5 | 1.6 | 1.3 | 1.9 | 2.1 |
| Unidentified manufactures | 1.4 | 1.5 | 1.7 | 1.8 | 1.6 | 0.7 | 0.4 | 0.4 | 0.4 | 0.4 |
| **Agricultural and livestock products** | 12.6 | 12.3 | 16.2 | 11.3 | 15.6 | 3.4 | 0.4 | 6.0 | 0.2 | 1.0 |
| Agricultural products | 9.0 | 10.3 | 10.0 | 10.7 | 15.5 | 0.1 | 0.1 | 0.1 | 0.2 | 1.0 |
| Livestock and livestock products | 3.6 | 2.0 | 6.2 | 0.6 | ..... | 3.2 | 0.3 | 5.9 | ..... | ..... |
| **Other commodities** | 97.6 | 33.4 | 54.6 | 88.8 | 94.7 | 4.0 | 14.6 | 24.6 | 34.5 | 43.9 |
| Forestry products | 0.1 | ..... | ..... | ..... | ..... | ..... | ..... | ..... | ..... | ..... |
| Fish and other marine products | ..... | ..... | ..... | ..... | 0.5 | ..... | ..... | ..... | ..... | ..... |
| Metallic ores and concentrates | ..... | ..... | ..... | ..... | ..... | ..... | ..... | ..... | ..... | ..... |
| Bituminous coal and lignite | 96.1 | 31.7 | 51.3 | 84.0 | 89.7 | 3.0 | 14.1 | 24.2 | 34.3 | 42.9 |
| Crude petroleum and natural gas | ..... | ..... | ..... | 0.1 | ..... | ..... | ..... | ..... | ..... | ..... |
| Nonmetallic minerals | 0.2 | 0.1 | 0.7 | 1.8 | 1.0 | ..... | ..... | ..... | ..... | ..... |
| Scrap and waste | ..... | 1.0 | 1.3 | 0.2 | 1.1 | ..... | ..... | ..... | ..... | ..... |
| Used merchandise | 0.4 | 0.4 | 0.9 | 1.7 | 1.6 | 0.3 | 0.2 | 0.3 | ..... | 0.8 |
| Goods imported and returned unchanged | ..... | ..... | ..... | ..... | ..... | ..... | ..... | ..... | ..... | ..... |
| Special classification provisions | 0.8 | 0.3 | 0.3 | 1.1 | 0.7 | 0.7 | 0.2 | ..... | 0.1 | 0.1 |

## Table D-3.   State Exports of Goods by Destination and Industry, 1993–1997 —*Continued*

**KENTUCKY** (Millions of dollars.)

| Industry | Germany | | | | | France | | | | |
|---|---|---|---|---|---|---|---|---|---|---|
| | 1993 | 1994 | 1995 | 1996 | 1997 | 1993 | 1994 | 1995 | 1996 | 1997 |
| **ALL GOODS** | 135.0 | 136.6 | 228.6 | 229.6 | 232.7 | 62.5 | 166.8 | 151.6 | 258.9 | 366.5 |
| **Manufactured goods** | 134.8 | 135.2 | 213.0 | 215.0 | 231.0 | 42.1 | 161.8 | 144.9 | 247.5 | 355.0 |
| Food products | 33.0 | 27.9 | 27.8 | 25.7 | 28.3 | 10.0 | 7.9 | 11.5 | 15.8 | 14.2 |
| Tobacco products | ..... | 4.3 | 54.8 | 25.4 | 32.4 | ..... | ..... | 0.2 | 0.1 | 0.1 |
| Textile mill products | 0.2 | 0.2 | 0.4 | 0.7 | 0.1 | ..... | ..... | 0.2 | 0.6 | 0.1 |
| Apparel | 1.4 | 1.0 | 1.1 | 1.6 | 1.1 | 0.3 | 0.2 | 0.4 | 0.1 | 0.1 |
| Lumber and wood products | 5.1 | 5.9 | 5.2 | 3.5 | 11.2 | 0.1 | 0.2 | 0.2 | 0.8 | 1.5 |
| Furniture and fixtures | 1.0 | 0.7 | 1.3 | 0.9 | 0.6 | ..... | 0.1 | 0.1 | 0.8 | 0.2 |
| Paper products | 0.5 | 0.2 | 0.2 | 0.4 | 0.3 | ..... | 1.3 | 2.7 | 5.0 | 2.8 |
| Printing and publishing | 0.1 | 0.2 | 0.3 | 0.3 | 0.3 | ..... | 0.2 | 0.1 | 1.0 | 1.0 |
| Chemical products | 28.8 | 3.9 | 13.4 | 19.6 | 20.6 | 2.1 | 3.2 | 3.7 | 10.8 | 21.1 |
| Refined petroleum products | ..... | ..... | ..... | ..... | 0.1 | ..... | ..... | ..... | ..... | ..... |
| Rubber and plastic products | 2.6 | 1.7 | 1.9 | 1.1 | 1.7 | 0.3 | 1.0 | 0.5 | 0.9 | 1.1 |
| Leather products | 0.7 | 1.3 | 0.2 | 0.3 | ..... | 0.2 | ..... | 0.2 | 0.2 | ..... |
| Stone, clay and glass products | 1.7 | 1.8 | 3.3 | 1.5 | 1.5 | 0.7 | 0.7 | 0.3 | 0.8 | 0.6 |
| Primary metals | 1.5 | 1.0 | 0.5 | 0.8 | 2.4 | 0.1 | 0.4 | 0.4 | 0.6 | 0.4 |
| Fabricated metal products | 1.8 | 1.9 | 1.5 | 2.1 | 3.2 | 1.6 | 1.6 | 1.4 | 1.1 | 1.9 |
| Industrial machinery and computers | 10.7 | 9.5 | 25.3 | 26.4 | 41.0 | 6.9 | 84.1 | 75.9 | 157.5 | 251.9 |
| Electric and electronic equipment | 9.7 | 12.5 | 5.4 | 4.4 | 8.1 | 11.5 | 18.7 | 15.0 | 17.4 | 16.3 |
| Transportation equipment | 34.4 | 57.9 | 58.9 | 87.0 | 71.7 | 3.2 | 7.0 | 1.2 | 3.8 | 10.2 |
| Scientific and measuring instruments | 0.8 | 2.6 | 10.9 | 10.6 | 3.0 | 0.3 | 18.0 | 17.6 | 18.2 | 19.4 |
| Miscellaneous manufactures | 0.5 | 0.4 | 0.2 | 2.4 | 2.7 | 4.7 | 17.1 | 13.2 | 11.6 | 11.9 |
| Unidentified manufactures | 0.4 | 0.3 | 0.4 | 0.2 | 0.5 | 0.1 | 0.1 | 0.2 | 0.3 | 0.1 |
| **Agricultural and livestock products** | 0.1 | ..... | 0.1 | ..... | 0.1 | 0.6 | 1.0 | 0.2 | 0.6 | 0.1 |
| Agricultural products | 0.1 | ..... | 0.1 | ..... | 0.1 | 0.5 | 0.8 | 0.1 | 0.1 | 0.1 |
| Livestock and livestock products | ..... | ..... | ..... | ..... | ..... | 0.1 | 0.2 | 0.1 | 0.5 | ..... |
| **Other commodities** | ..... | 1.4 | 15.5 | 14.6 | 1.6 | 19.8 | 4.0 | 6.5 | 10.8 | 11.3 |
| Forestry products | ..... | ..... | ..... | ..... | ..... | ..... | ..... | ..... | ..... | ..... |
| Fish and other marine products | ..... | ..... | ..... | ..... | ..... | ..... | ..... | ..... | ..... | ..... |
| Metallic ores and concentrates | ..... | ..... | ..... | ..... | ..... | ..... | ..... | ..... | ..... | ..... |
| Bituminous coal and lignite | ..... | 0.3 | 13.8 | 14.1 | 0.4 | 19.7 | 4.0 | 6.5 | 10.8 | 10.6 |
| Crude petroleum and natural gas | ..... | ..... | ..... | ..... | ..... | ..... | ..... | ..... | ..... | ..... |
| Nonmetallic minerals | ..... | ..... | ..... | ..... | ..... | ..... | ..... | ..... | ..... | ..... |
| Scrap and waste | ..... | 0.9 | 1.2 | 0.2 | 1.0 | ..... | ..... | ..... | ..... | ..... |
| Used merchandise | ..... | 0.1 | 0.3 | ..... | ..... | ..... | ..... | ..... | ..... | 0.7 |
| Goods imported and returned unchanged | ..... | ..... | ..... | ..... | ..... | ..... | ..... | ..... | ..... | ..... |
| Special classification provisions | ..... | ..... | 0.2 | 0.2 | 0.1 | ..... | ..... | ..... | ..... | ..... |

| Industry | The Netherlands | | | | | Asian 10 | | | | |
|---|---|---|---|---|---|---|---|---|---|---|
| | 1993 | 1994 | 1995 | 1996 | 1997 | 1993 | 1994 | 1995 | 1996 | 1997 |
| **ALL GOODS** | 53.4 | 56.7 | 60.3 | 114.3 | 132.6 | 1 065.1 | 1 109.8 | 1 478.6 | 1 605.4 | 1 816.8 |
| **Manufactured goods** | 32.6 | 54.3 | 51.4 | 96.5 | 101.0 | 1 022.0 | 1 089.1 | 1 416.3 | 1 552.5 | 1 791.6 |
| Food products | 3.5 | 2.4 | 3.7 | 1.4 | 2.6 | 34.6 | 38.7 | 84.4 | 81.3 | 93.6 |
| Tobacco products | ..... | ..... | ..... | 0.5 | ..... | 509.3 | 546.6 | 708.1 | 654.9 | 638.9 |
| Textile mill products | 0.1 | 0.1 | 0.1 | ..... | ..... | 4.2 | 6.4 | 5.2 | 0.8 | 5.2 |
| Apparel | 0.4 | 0.9 | 0.4 | 0.3 | 0.1 | 9.7 | 11.3 | 13.5 | 40.6 | 118.2 |
| Lumber and wood products | 1.4 | 1.9 | 1.5 | 1.3 | 1.2 | 9.7 | 5.0 | 5.6 | 5.2 | 3.2 |
| Furniture and fixtures | ..... | ..... | 0.1 | ..... | 0.1 | 1.7 | 0.8 | 0.5 | 3.1 | 4.5 |
| Paper products | ..... | ..... | 0.1 | 0.1 | 0.1 | 4.4 | 8.2 | 5.3 | 9.2 | 8.4 |
| Printing and publishing | 0.1 | 0.1 | 0.2 | 0.4 | 0.3 | 4.1 | 4.7 | 5.6 | 4.7 | 5.2 |
| Chemical products | 6.1 | 2.5 | 4.6 | 18.0 | 22.9 | 18.0 | 22.3 | 44.1 | 67.1 | 44.8 |
| Refined petroleum products | 0.1 | 0.2 | 0.1 | 0.4 | 0.4 | 0.7 | 1.4 | 1.3 | 1.3 | 0.3 |
| Rubber and plastic products | 2.2 | 0.5 | 0.8 | 1.6 | 1.4 | 3.2 | 5.3 | 6.2 | 9.5 | 16.6 |
| Leather products | 1.2 | 0.1 | ..... | 0.2 | ..... | 0.7 | 1.3 | 3.0 | 6.4 | 3.0 |
| Stone, clay and glass products | 1.1 | 0.6 | 0.4 | 0.3 | 0.2 | 29.3 | 32.8 | 30.1 | 47.9 | 73.1 |
| Primary metals | 0.1 | 0.4 | 1.5 | 0.8 | 1.4 | 98.0 | 37.4 | 90.7 | 102.5 | 37.7 |
| Fabricated metal products | 0.6 | 0.6 | 0.6 | 0.4 | 0.6 | 15.4 | 10.1 | 13.8 | 9.1 | 12.2 |
| Industrial machinery and computers | 5.6 | 30.0 | 22.5 | 33.4 | 24.6 | 63.9 | 81.2 | 104.5 | 138.1 | 156.5 |
| Electric and electronic equipment | 6.6 | 5.6 | 6.6 | 7.4 | 7.1 | 58.4 | 83.1 | 114.2 | 115.5 | 147.0 |
| Transportation equipment | 2.5 | 6.9 | 6.5 | 10.2 | 13.8 | 142.7 | 163.3 | 154.6 | 221.9 | 384.3 |
| Scientific and measuring instruments | 0.8 | 1.1 | 0.9 | 18.9 | 23.8 | 5.8 | 14.9 | 13.9 | 18.6 | 22.5 |
| Miscellaneous manufactures | 0.2 | 0.3 | 0.6 | 0.5 | 0.4 | 7.3 | 13.3 | 10.6 | 13.6 | 15.5 |
| Unidentified manufactures | 0.1 | 0.1 | 0.2 | 0.3 | 0.3 | 0.8 | 1.2 | 1.1 | 1.1 | 1.2 |
| **Agricultural and livestock products** | 0.1 | 1.2 | 2.6 | ..... | ..... | 7.0 | 6.0 | 35.5 | 10.3 | 11.9 |
| Agricultural products | 0.1 | 1.2 | 2.6 | ..... | ..... | 2.2 | 0.7 | 2.0 | 2.4 | 2.4 |
| Livestock and livestock products | ..... | ..... | ..... | ..... | ..... | 4.8 | 5.3 | 33.5 | 7.8 | 9.5 |
| **Other commodities** | 20.7 | 1.3 | 6.3 | 17.8 | 31.6 | 36.1 | 14.6 | 26.8 | 42.7 | 13.2 |
| Forestry products | ..... | ..... | ..... | ..... | ..... | ..... | ..... | 0.3 | ..... | 0.1 |
| Fish and other marine products | ..... | ..... | ..... | ..... | ..... | ..... | ..... | ..... | ..... | 0.6 |
| Metallic ores and concentrates | ..... | ..... | ..... | ..... | ..... | ..... | ..... | ..... | ..... | ..... |
| Bituminous coal and lignite | 20.6 | 1.2 | 6.3 | 17.8 | 31.6 | 28.9 | 11.6 | 22.0 | 39.1 | 8.7 |
| Crude petroleum and natural gas | ..... | ..... | ..... | ..... | ..... | 0.2 | 0.2 | ..... | 0.1 | ..... |
| Nonmetallic minerals | ..... | 0.1 | ..... | ..... | ..... | 2.8 | 2.1 | 2.0 | 2.6 | 2.3 |
| Scrap and waste | ..... | ..... | ..... | ..... | ..... | 4.0 | 0.3 | 2.3 | 0.6 | 0.7 |
| Used merchandise | ..... | ..... | ..... | ..... | ..... | 0.1 | 0.1 | 0.1 | 0.1 | ..... |
| Goods imported and returned unchanged | ..... | ..... | ..... | ..... | ..... | ..... | ..... | ..... | ..... | ..... |
| Special classification provisions | ..... | ..... | ..... | ..... | ..... | 0.1 | 0.3 | 0.3 | 0.2 | 0.8 |

## Table D-3. State Exports of Goods by Destination and Industry, 1993–1997 —*Continued*

**KENTUCKY** (Millions of dollars.)

| Industry | 1993 | 1994 | 1995 | 1996 | 1997 | 1993 | 1994 | 1995 | 1996 | 1997 |
|---|---|---|---|---|---|---|---|---|---|---|
| | Japan | | | | | South Korea | | | | |
| **ALL GOODS** | 769.6 | 752.3 | 1 041.8 | 1 143.0 | 1 385.0 | 50.8 | 72.2 | 107.0 | 116.1 | 99.6 |
| **Manufactured goods** | 738.7 | 736.7 | 985.8 | 1 105.0 | 1 368.7 | 46.1 | 70.5 | 106.8 | 116.0 | 98.7 |
| Food products | 25.8 | 24.8 | 30.8 | 25.1 | 33.2 | 2.3 | 4.2 | 11.8 | 19.5 | 17.9 |
| Tobacco products | 360.4 | 383.7 | 563.7 | 529.2 | 537.8 | 12.1 | 11.5 | 21.4 | 19.3 | 19.5 |
| Textile mill products | 2.8 | 5.2 | 4.5 | 0.4 | 4.9 | ..... | 0.1 | 0.1 | 0.1 | 0.1 |
| Apparel | 9.3 | 10.6 | 12.7 | 40.0 | 117.5 | ..... | ..... | 0.1 | ..... | 0.2 |
| Lumber and wood products | 2.9 | 2.7 | 3.8 | 2.4 | 0.6 | 0.2 | 0.3 | 0.2 | 0.3 | 0.6 |
| Furniture and fixtures | 1.7 | 0.4 | 0.2 | 2.9 | 4.1 | ..... | ..... | ..... | ..... | ..... |
| Paper products | 3.5 | 6.5 | 3.8 | 7.0 | 6.9 | ..... | 0.1 | 0.1 | 0.3 | 0.2 |
| Printing and publishing | 0.8 | 1.3 | 0.9 | 0.8 | 1.1 | 0.7 | 0.7 | 1.2 | 0.8 | 1.0 |
| Chemical products | 7.9 | 13.1 | 20.4 | 25.2 | 27.7 | 1.1 | 1.5 | 2.2 | 6.0 | 3.9 |
| Refined petroleum products | 0.5 | 0.7 | 0.8 | 0.6 | 0.1 | ..... | 0.1 | ..... | ..... | ..... |
| Rubber and plastic products | 2.1 | 3.0 | 3.5 | 6.3 | 8.6 | 0.2 | 0.5 | 0.9 | 1.0 | 4.2 |
| Leather products | ..... | 0.1 | 0.8 | 2.3 | 0.9 | 0.2 | 0.3 | 0.4 | 0.1 | ..... |
| Stone, clay and glass products | 27.5 | 31.5 | 28.3 | 43.0 | 70.8 | 0.9 | 0.6 | 0.6 | 2.1 | 0.7 |
| Primary metals | 86.6 | 26.9 | 64.0 | 88.9 | 12.3 | 4.4 | 2.2 | 14.0 | 2.3 | 6.6 |
| Fabricated metal products | 1.4 | 2.2 | 7.5 | 4.3 | 6.0 | 0.3 | 0.8 | 2.1 | 1.1 | 1.6 |
| Industrial machinery and computers | 42.1 | 37.8 | 49.4 | 58.0 | 56.0 | 5.0 | 12.2 | 18.5 | 31.0 | 25.8 |
| Electric and electronic equipment | 25.1 | 26.9 | 42.9 | 43.3 | 94.2 | 8.0 | 23.8 | 25.5 | 21.1 | 5.5 |
| Transportation equipment | 133.1 | 148.5 | 138.6 | 209.4 | 366.1 | 7.3 | 6.3 | 3.5 | 6.3 | 5.5 |
| Scientific and measuring instruments | 2.7 | 7.8 | 6.3 | 10.9 | 13.3 | 0.4 | 1.8 | 2.8 | 1.9 | 2.3 |
| Miscellaneous manufactures | 2.1 | 2.5 | 2.2 | 4.5 | 6.0 | 2.7 | 3.3 | 1.3 | 2.6 | 3.1 |
| Unidentified manufactures | 0.4 | 0.5 | 0.6 | 0.4 | 0.6 | 0.2 | 0.3 | 0.1 | 0.1 | 0.2 |
| **Agricultural and livestock products** | 4.8 | 3.7 | 33.6 | 8.7 | 10.9 | 0.1 | 1.3 | 0.1 | ..... | ..... |
| Agricultural products | 0.2 | ..... | 0.2 | 0.9 | 1.5 | 0.1 | ..... | ..... | ..... | ..... |
| Livestock and livestock products | 4.6 | 3.7 | 33.4 | 7.8 | 9.4 | ..... | 1.2 | 0.1 | ..... | ..... |
| **Other commodities** | 26.1 | 11.9 | 22.5 | 29.3 | 5.4 | 4.6 | 0.4 | ..... | 0.1 | 0.8 |
| Forestry products | ..... | ..... | ..... | ..... | ..... | ..... | ..... | ..... | ..... | ..... |
| Fish and other marine products | ..... | ..... | ..... | ..... | 0.3 | ..... | ..... | ..... | ..... | 0.3 |
| Metallic ores and concentrates | ..... | ..... | ..... | ..... | ..... | ..... | ..... | ..... | ..... | ..... |
| Bituminous coal and lignite | 25.0 | 11.6 | 22.0 | 28.7 | 4.4 | 1.7 | ..... | ..... | ..... | ..... |
| Crude petroleum and natural gas | 0.1 | 0.1 | ..... | ..... | ..... | 0.1 | 0.1 | ..... | ..... | ..... |
| Nonmetallic minerals | 0.4 | ..... | 0.1 | 0.3 | 0.4 | ..... | ..... | ..... | 0.1 | 0.1 |
| Scrap and waste | 0.5 | 0.1 | 0.1 | ..... | ..... | 2.8 | ..... | ..... | ..... | 0.4 |
| Used merchandise | ..... | 0.1 | ..... | ..... | ..... | ..... | ..... | ..... | ..... | ..... |
| Goods imported and returned unchanged | ..... | ..... | ..... | ..... | ..... | ..... | ..... | ..... | ..... | ..... |
| Special classification provisions | 0.1 | ..... | 0.2 | 0.2 | 0.2 | ..... | 0.3 | ..... | ..... | ..... |
| | Taiwan | | | | | Singapore | | | | |
| **ALL GOODS** | 38.8 | 38.6 | 53.6 | 66.5 | 58.2 | 74.2 | 90.3 | 88.6 | 96.0 | 91.6 |
| **Manufactured goods** | 31.8 | 36.3 | 50.0 | 52.6 | 55.7 | 74.1 | 90.3 | 88.6 | 96.0 | 91.5 |
| Food products | 2.1 | 3.8 | 23.4 | 15.3 | 20.0 | 1.1 | 1.0 | 1.7 | 2.2 | 1.4 |
| Tobacco products | 2.6 | 2.3 | 0.9 | 1.8 | 1.0 | 54.3 | 64.5 | 56.6 | 59.4 | 38.4 |
| Textile mill products | ..... | ..... | ..... | ..... | ..... | 0.1 | ..... | ..... | ..... | ..... |
| Apparel | 0.1 | 0.1 | ..... | ..... | ..... | ..... | 0.2 | ..... | 0.1 | 0.1 |
| Lumber and wood products | 0.1 | 0.1 | 0.4 | 0.7 | 1.1 | ..... | ..... | ..... | ..... | ..... |
| Furniture and fixtures | ..... | ..... | ..... | ..... | ..... | ..... | ..... | 0.2 | 0.1 | 0.2 |
| Paper products | ..... | 0.1 | 0.1 | 0.1 | ..... | 0.2 | 0.3 | 0.5 | 0.2 | 0.3 |
| Printing and publishing | 1.1 | 1.0 | 0.6 | 0.5 | 0.5 | 1.1 | 1.0 | 2.2 | 1.5 | 1.6 |
| Chemical products | 1.9 | 3.6 | 4.2 | 3.8 | 4.5 | 1.2 | 1.5 | 3.3 | 4.3 | 3.9 |
| Refined petroleum products | ..... | ..... | ..... | 0.1 | ..... | ..... | ..... | ..... | ..... | ..... |
| Rubber and plastic products | 0.1 | 0.2 | 0.1 | 0.3 | 0.3 | 0.1 | 0.8 | 0.7 | 0.5 | 0.3 |
| Leather products | ..... | ..... | 0.3 | 1.1 | 0.1 | ..... | 0.1 | 0.4 | 0.5 | 0.3 |
| Stone, clay and glass products | 0.1 | 0.1 | 0.1 | 0.3 | 0.3 | ..... | ..... | ..... | 0.2 | ..... |
| Primary metals | 4.4 | 3.4 | 5.6 | 3.4 | 6.5 | 0.6 | 0.4 | 0.4 | 0.3 | 5.2 |
| Fabricated metal products | 1.0 | 0.4 | 0.3 | 0.6 | 0.5 | 5.6 | 1.1 | 0.7 | 1.1 | 0.8 |
| Industrial machinery and computers | 4.2 | 1.9 | 5.1 | 10.1 | 10.0 | 4.3 | 8.3 | 8.7 | 11.4 | 20.2 |
| Electric and electronic equipment | 11.1 | 12.0 | 6.0 | 10.5 | 8.8 | 4.1 | 5.8 | 6.0 | 7.1 | 8.6 |
| Transportation equipment | ..... | 3.3 | 0.8 | 1.3 | 0.7 | 0.2 | 0.8 | 2.4 | 2.9 | 4.1 |
| Scientific and measuring instruments | 1.3 | 0.8 | 0.4 | 1.3 | 0.6 | 0.8 | 1.9 | 2.2 | 2.0 | 3.1 |
| Miscellaneous manufactures | 1.6 | 3.1 | 1.6 | 1.3 | 0.6 | 0.3 | 2.4 | 2.3 | 2.2 | 2.7 |
| Unidentified manufactures | ..... | 0.1 | 0.1 | ..... | 0.1 | ..... | 0.1 | 0.1 | 0.1 | 0.1 |
| **Agricultural and livestock products** | 1.9 | ..... | 1.7 | 1.4 | 0.7 | ..... | ..... | ..... | ..... | ..... |
| Agricultural products | 1.9 | ..... | 1.7 | 1.4 | 0.7 | ..... | ..... | ..... | ..... | ..... |
| Livestock and livestock products | ..... | ..... | ..... | ..... | ..... | ..... | ..... | ..... | ..... | ..... |
| **Other commodities** | 5.2 | 2.2 | 1.9 | 12.6 | 1.8 | ..... | ..... | ..... | ..... | ..... |
| Forestry products | ..... | ..... | ..... | ..... | 0.1 | ..... | ..... | ..... | ..... | ..... |
| Fish and other marine products | ..... | ..... | ..... | ..... | ..... | ..... | ..... | ..... | ..... | ..... |
| Metallic ores and concentrates | ..... | ..... | ..... | ..... | ..... | ..... | ..... | ..... | ..... | ..... |
| Bituminous coal and lignite | 2.2 | ..... | ..... | 10.4 | ..... | ..... | ..... | ..... | ..... | ..... |
| Crude petroleum and natural gas | ..... | ..... | ..... | ..... | ..... | ..... | ..... | ..... | ..... | ..... |
| Nonmetallic minerals | 2.3 | 2.0 | 1.8 | 2.1 | 1.6 | ..... | ..... | ..... | ..... | ..... |
| Scrap and waste | 0.7 | 0.2 | 0.1 | ..... | ..... | ..... | ..... | ..... | ..... | ..... |
| Used merchandise | ..... | ..... | ..... | ..... | ..... | ..... | ..... | ..... | ..... | ..... |
| Goods imported and returned unchanged | ..... | ..... | ..... | ..... | ..... | ..... | ..... | ..... | ..... | ..... |
| Special classification provisions | ..... | ..... | ..... | ..... | ..... | ..... | ..... | ..... | ..... | ..... |

## LOUISIANA: Exports of Goods, 1997

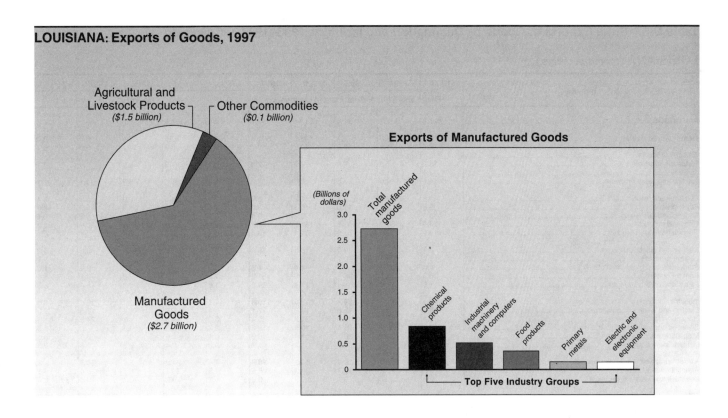

Agricultural and Livestock Products ($1.5 billion)

Other Commodities ($0.1 billion)

Manufactured Goods ($2.7 billion)

**Exports of Manufactured Goods**

(Billions of dollars)

Total manufactured goods

Chemical products

Industrial machinery and computers

Food products

Primary metals

Electric and electronic equipment

Top Five Industry Groups

## Table D-3.   State Exports of Goods by Destination and Industry, 1993–1997 —*Continued*

### LOUISIANA (Millions of dollars.)

| Industry | 1993 | 1994 | 1995 | 1996 | 1997 | 1993 | 1994 | 1995 | 1996 | 1997 |
|---|---|---|---|---|---|---|---|---|---|---|
| | All destinations | | | | | Canada | | | | |
| **ALL GOODS** | 3 220.3 | 3 576.9 | 4 580.7 | 4 730.8 | 4 373.5 | 372.3 | 449.1 | 557.4 | 542.9 | 663.1 |
| **Manufactured goods** | 2 173.0 | 2 464.6 | 2 953.5 | 2 613.6 | 2 730.5 | 350.5 | 419.9 | 518.1 | 512.3 | 601.7 |
| Food products | 334.0 | 459.2 | 559.3 | 344.9 | 361.2 | 13.2 | 15.4 | 26.9 | 25.4 | 36.1 |
| Tobacco products | ..... | ..... | 10.5 | ..... | ..... | ..... | ..... | ..... | ..... | ..... |
| Textile mill products | 23.8 | 22.0 | 20.7 | 20.8 | 24.9 | 5.1 | 7.8 | 6.2 | 6.6 | 7.3 |
| Apparel | 3.6 | 3.9 | 4.9 | 11.7 | 17.2 | 1.0 | 0.4 | 0.5 | 0.2 | 1.3 |
| Lumber and wood products | 43.9 | 46.0 | 37.4 | 40.4 | 30.7 | 4.4 | 4.6 | 3.5 | 5.2 | 5.0 |
| Furniture and fixtures | 5.3 | 9.3 | 4.7 | 4.2 | 6.2 | 0.4 | 0.2 | 0.5 | 0.7 | 1.0 |
| Paper products | 115.8 | 120.9 | 186.2 | 141.8 | 100.9 | 18.6 | 21.8 | 26.8 | 22.2 | 24.6 |
| Printing and publishing | 1.4 | 1.5 | 6.1 | 2.1 | 2.3 | 0.2 | 0.4 | 0.9 | 0.5 | 0.7 |
| Chemical products | 672.5 | 642.6 | 827.4 | 813.2 | 839.1 | 187.2 | 227.9 | 254.8 | 265.5 | 305.4 |
| Refined petroleum products | 68.0 | 92.6 | 146.6 | 158.6 | 133.4 | 17.7 | 8.6 | 15.9 | 17.9 | 23.9 |
| Rubber and plastic products | 36.1 | 40.7 | 35.6 | 39.7 | 50.9 | 7.5 | 6.1 | 7.7 | 9.5 | 10.0 |
| Leather products | 2.4 | 3.4 | 1.6 | 1.0 | 4.5 | 0.1 | 0.1 | 0.1 | 0.1 | 0.2 |
| Stone, clay and glass products | 18.9 | 13.8 | 17.9 | 20.1 | 12.5 | 0.5 | 0.6 | 1.0 | 2.3 | 1.1 |
| Primary metals | 72.3 | 73.0 | 180.9 | 88.4 | 152.2 | 9.5 | 18.2 | 30.0 | 26.5 | 35.5 |
| Fabricated metal products | 61.9 | 67.6 | 57.7 | 78.2 | 89.5 | 11.7 | 12.4 | 16.9 | 13.7 | 18.0 |
| Industrial machinery and computers | 385.2 | 498.7 | 466.8 | 480.0 | 520.1 | 39.7 | 47.6 | 52.1 | 46.8 | 57.8 |
| Electric and electronic equipment | 100.5 | 118.0 | 128.1 | 131.9 | 145.9 | 11.2 | 18.0 | 43.8 | 40.6 | 40.0 |
| Transportation equipment | 122.4 | 140.5 | 137.2 | 106.9 | 105.4 | 3.9 | 6.1 | 9.4 | 4.6 | 8.2 |
| Scientific and measuring instruments | 90.5 | 95.2 | 103.7 | 116.7 | 113.7 | 17.4 | 21.0 | 18.9 | 21.7 | 23.5 |
| Miscellaneous manufactures | 10.8 | 10.7 | 13.2 | 8.1 | 15.2 | 0.7 | 1.7 | 1.1 | 0.8 | 1.0 |
| Unidentified manufactures | 3.8 | 5.1 | 6.9 | 4.6 | 4.7 | 0.6 | 1.0 | 1.2 | 1.4 | 1.4 |
| **Agricultural and livestock products** | 975.2 | 1 027.6 | 1 508.6 | 2 002.6 | 1 510.8 | 3.8 | 7.0 | 5.8 | 5.6 | 7.4 |
| Agricultural products | 970.8 | 1 023.3 | 1 501.3 | 1 992.8 | 1 497.4 | 3.8 | 6.9 | 5.7 | 5.4 | 6.9 |
| Livestock and livestock products | 4.4 | 4.3 | 7.3 | 9.8 | 13.4 | ..... | 0.1 | 0.1 | 0.2 | 0.5 |
| **Other commodities** | 72.1 | 84.7 | 118.7 | 114.6 | 132.1 | 18.0 | 22.2 | 33.4 | 25.0 | 53.9 |
| Forestry products | 0.1 | ..... | 0.1 | 0.1 | 0.5 | 0.1 | ..... | 0.1 | ..... | ..... |
| Fish and other marine products | 27.3 | 26.0 | 24.9 | 20.2 | 26.2 | 8.2 | 6.7 | 9.3 | 8.4 | 10.2 |
| Metallic ores and concentrates | 0.7 | 2.0 | 0.6 | 0.7 | ..... | 0.6 | 2.0 | 0.2 | 0.6 | ..... |
| Bituminous coal and lignite | 7.4 | 22.2 | 34.8 | 35.9 | 37.3 | ..... | ..... | ..... | ..... | ..... |
| Crude petroleum and natural gas | 0.9 | 3.8 | 0.6 | 2.5 | 21.7 | ..... | ..... | ..... | 2.0 | 20.6 |
| Nonmetallic minerals | 4.9 | 4.4 | 10.5 | 9.0 | 12.0 | 1.2 | 1.9 | 1.2 | 0.7 | 1.4 |
| Scrap and waste | 10.5 | 8.6 | 17.7 | 10.0 | 5.8 | 0.6 | 3.0 | 0.7 | 0.4 | 1.3 |
| Used merchandise | 12.5 | 8.6 | 8.3 | 21.7 | 7.4 | 0.2 | 1.1 | 2.1 | 1.1 | 1.6 |
| Goods imported and returned unchanged | 5.7 | 7.3 | 19.0 | 10.8 | 18.4 | 5.7 | 7.3 | 19.0 | 10.8 | 18.4 |
| Special classification provisions | 2.0 | 1.7 | 2.1 | 3.7 | 2.8 | 1.4 | 0.2 | 0.7 | 1.0 | 0.4 |

## Table D-3.  State Exports of Goods by Destination and Industry, 1993–1997 —*Continued*

**LOUISIANA** (Millions of dollars.)

| Industry | 1993 | 1994 | 1995 | 1996 | 1997 | 1993 | 1994 | 1995 | 1996 | 1997 |
|---|---|---|---|---|---|---|---|---|---|---|
| | South and Central America and Caribbean | | | | | Mexico | | | | |
| **ALL GOODS** | 417.8 | 391.8 | 537.4 | 517.6 | 597.1 | 61.1 | 108.9 | 79.8 | 145.5 | 132.6 |
| **Manufactured goods** | 410.5 | 374.9 | 522.7 | 468.5 | 562.3 | 52.8 | 82.4 | 69.9 | 116.9 | 128.7 |
| Food products | 30.5 | 31.9 | 50.9 | 40.2 | 52.7 | 4.2 | 6.6 | 12.8 | 5.0 | 10.7 |
| Tobacco products | ..... | ..... | | | | | | | | |
| Textile mill products | 13.9 | 7.2 | 7.4 | 7.2 | 7.8 | 0.1 | 1.2 | 0.7 | 2.9 | 3.1 |
| Apparel | 1.1 | 1.6 | 1.7 | 1.4 | 2.9 | 0.3 | 0.7 | 0.4 | 5.1 | 11.9 |
| Lumber and wood products | 4.6 | 4.0 | 3.5 | 5.5 | 7.1 | 1.5 | 1.5 | 0.2 | 0.1 | 1.1 |
| Furniture and fixtures | 1.6 | 4.0 | 2.1 | 1.6 | 3.0 | 2.6 | 4.3 | 0.6 | 0.1 | 0.4 |
| Paper products | 9.3 | 8.2 | 17.0 | 10.3 | 8.0 | 2.6 | 8.2 | 5.8 | 10.0 | 8.9 |
| Printing and publishing | 0.4 | 0.3 | 0.4 | 0.7 | 0.4 | 0.1 | 0.1 | 0.1 | 0.2 | 0.1 |
| Chemical products | 125.9 | 68.8 | 131.6 | 131.7 | 119.1 | 12.0 | 13.4 | 13.5 | 20.9 | 32.2 |
| Refined petroleum products | 19.9 | 19.0 | 31.0 | 34.1 | 16.3 | 0.1 | 0.5 | 0.4 | 0.4 | 0.5 |
| Rubber and plastic products | 8.5 | 7.3 | 9.0 | 10.5 | 10.3 | 1.5 | 2.9 | 2.7 | 3.6 | 5.4 |
| Leather products | 0.2 | 0.1 | 0.1 | 0.1 | 0.1 | | | | | 0.1 |
| Stone, clay and glass products | 4.6 | 3.4 | 5.2 | 4.4 | 4.9 | 3.3 | 4.0 | 1.0 | 2.6 | 1.8 |
| Primary metals | 30.0 | 16.5 | 48.1 | 15.9 | 81.9 | 1.8 | 1.7 | 2.8 | 4.1 | 6.8 |
| Fabricated metal products | 11.8 | 11.6 | 14.4 | 17.4 | 24.6 | 1.6 | 3.2 | 2.0 | 3.8 | 3.3 |
| Industrial machinery and computers | 89.9 | 116.0 | 124.7 | 119.6 | 150.8 | 11.1 | 20.2 | 14.1 | 19.6 | 16.0 |
| Electric and electronic equipment | 18.8 | 15.3 | 12.8 | 18.2 | 17.1 | 3.4 | 4.5 | 4.7 | 6.5 | 8.0 |
| Transportation equipment | 23.4 | 40.7 | 42.8 | 31.2 | 35.4 | 3.2 | 4.5 | 3.2 | 24.2 | 4.9 |
| Scientific and measuring instruments | 13.3 | 16.2 | 16.4 | 15.5 | 18.2 | 2.7 | 3.9 | 4.5 | 7.3 | 12.3 |
| Miscellaneous manufactures | 1.6 | 1.2 | 0.7 | 1.4 | 0.9 | 0.4 | 0.6 | 0.1 | 0.2 | 0.5 |
| Unidentified manufactures | 1.2 | 1.6 | 2.8 | 1.7 | 1.2 | 0.2 | 0.4 | 0.3 | 0.3 | 0.5 |
| **Agricultural and livestock products** | 3.7 | 12.6 | 10.9 | 30.2 | 28.8 | 4.6 | 24.3 | 5.7 | 20.7 | 1.3 |
| Agricultural products | 3.6 | 12.5 | 10.7 | 30.2 | 28.5 | 4.3 | 24.1 | 5.7 | 20.4 | 0.5 |
| Livestock and livestock products | 0.1 | ..... | 0.1 | ..... | 0.2 | 0.2 | 0.2 | 0.1 | 0.3 | 0.8 |
| **Other commodities** | 3.6 | 4.3 | 3.8 | 18.9 | 6.1 | 3.7 | 2.2 | 4.2 | 7.9 | 2.5 |
| Forestry products | ..... | ..... | ..... | ..... | ..... | ..... | ..... | ..... | ..... | ..... |
| Fish and other marine products | 0.2 | ..... | | 0.2 | | ..... | ..... | ..... | 0.1 | 0.1 |
| Metallic ores and concentrates | ..... | ..... | ..... | ..... | ..... | ..... | ..... | ..... | 0.1 | ..... |
| Bituminous coal and lignite | ..... | ..... | ..... | ..... | ..... | ..... | ..... | ..... | ..... | ..... |
| Crude petroleum and natural gas | 0.6 | 2.6 | 0.5 | 0.4 | 0.2 | ..... | 1.2 | ..... | ..... | 0.8 |
| Nonmetallic minerals | 1.1 | 0.9 | 1.9 | 3.8 | 3.2 | 0.9 | ..... | ..... | ..... | 0.2 |
| Scrap and waste | 0.2 | 0.2 | 0.3 | 0.4 | 0.9 | 2.0 | 0.6 | 3.9 | 7.6 | 1.4 |
| Used merchandise | 1.1 | 0.2 | 0.9 | 13.7 | 1.6 | 0.7 | 0.4 | 0.1 | ..... | ..... |
| Goods imported and returned unchanged | ..... | ..... | ..... | ..... | ..... | ..... | ..... | ..... | ..... | ..... |
| Special classification provisions | 0.5 | 0.4 | 0.3 | 0.3 | 0.2 | ..... | ..... | ..... | ..... | ..... |
| | European Union | | | | | United Kingdom | | | | |
| **ALL GOODS** | 639.1 | 785.6 | 1 072.2 | 976.6 | 841.6 | 54.0 | 73.0 | 113.6 | 97.2 | 97.9 |
| **Manufactured goods** | 483.5 | 589.8 | 811.8 | 621.0 | 551.6 | 53.4 | 72.5 | 112.9 | 96.0 | 96.3 |
| Food products | 191.6 | 216.1 | 277.6 | 112.9 | 73.4 | 7.0 | 12.5 | 12.8 | 4.8 | 4.7 |
| Tobacco products | ..... | ..... | 10.5 | ..... | ..... | ..... | ..... | ..... | ..... | ..... |
| Textile mill products | 0.7 | 0.7 | 1.2 | 1.0 | 2.7 | 0.3 | 0.4 | 0.5 | 0.3 | 1.3 |
| Apparel | 0.3 | 0.4 | 0.7 | 0.3 | 0.5 | ..... | ..... | 0.1 | ..... | 0.3 |
| Lumber and wood products | 6.1 | 8.1 | 8.8 | 9.3 | 10.7 | 0.1 | 0.2 | 0.3 | 0.3 | 0.3 |
| Furniture and fixtures | 0.1 | 0.1 | 0.8 | 1.2 | 0.7 | ..... | ..... | 0.1 | ..... | 0.1 |
| Paper products | 34.3 | 43.2 | 72.3 | 56.1 | 37.1 | 12.5 | 14.6 | 15.0 | 16.1 | 8.3 |
| Printing and publishing | 0.2 | 0.5 | 3.6 | 0.2 | 0.6 | 0.1 | 0.2 | 1.9 | 0.1 | 0.2 |
| Chemical products | 95.8 | 160.9 | 196.9 | 214.4 | 186.6 | 7.1 | 13.5 | 23.5 | 20.4 | 24.8 |
| Refined petroleum products | 4.9 | 16.6 | 28.0 | 27.7 | 22.4 | ..... | 3.0 | 10.2 | 9.2 | 4.3 |
| Rubber and plastic products | 6.5 | 6.2 | 7.7 | 8.1 | 17.5 | 1.4 | 0.9 | 2.1 | 1.6 | 2.9 |
| Leather products | 1.9 | 2.6 | 0.9 | 0.6 | 3.9 | ..... | ..... | ..... | ..... | ..... |
| Stone, clay and glass products | 2.9 | 2.2 | 5.2 | 4.2 | 0.1 | ..... | ..... | 0.4 | 0.1 | ..... |
| Primary metals | 6.9 | 5.7 | 22.4 | 17.0 | 5.6 | 1.5 | 1.2 | 1.2 | 1.8 | 2.9 |
| Fabricated metal products | 8.3 | 7.9 | 6.4 | 6.6 | 8.6 | 2.2 | 3.0 | 2.3 | 2.1 | 4.1 |
| Industrial machinery and computers | 54.2 | 63.7 | 105.1 | 98.3 | 102.8 | 10.6 | 13.0 | 25.0 | 23.6 | 24.0 |
| Electric and electronic equipment | 32.9 | 25.6 | 21.4 | 26.7 | 26.8 | 4.0 | 2.5 | 4.0 | 3.4 | 5.9 |
| Transportation equipment | 11.4 | 4.5 | 8.1 | 5.9 | 17.5 | 3.3 | 1.9 | 4.3 | 1.7 | 3.5 |
| Scientific and measuring instruments | 22.1 | 21.9 | 27.6 | 28.4 | 24.3 | 3.1 | 5.4 | 8.2 | 10.3 | 8.4 |
| Miscellaneous manufactures | 2.1 | 2.2 | 5.9 | 1.8 | 9.6 | 0.1 | ..... | 0.9 | 0.1 | 0.1 |
| Unidentified manufactures | 0.4 | 0.4 | 0.6 | 0.2 | 0.3 | 0.1 | 0.1 | 0.2 | 0.1 | 0.1 |
| **Agricultural and livestock products** | 126.7 | 150.8 | 198.1 | 307.2 | 234.8 | 0.1 | 0.2 | 0.1 | 0.3 | ..... |
| Agricultural products | 125.3 | 149.8 | 195.6 | 305.4 | 232.9 | 0.1 | 0.1 | 0.1 | 0.2 | ..... |
| Livestock and livestock products | 1.4 | 1.0 | 2.5 | 1.8 | 1.9 | ..... | 0.1 | 0.1 | ..... | ..... |
| **Other commodities** | 28.9 | 45.0 | 62.3 | 48.4 | 55.2 | 0.4 | 0.3 | 0.6 | 0.9 | 1.6 |
| Forestry products | ..... | ..... | ..... | ..... | 0.5 | ..... | ..... | ..... | ..... | ..... |
| Fish and other marine products | 16.3 | 14.7 | 9.6 | 5.5 | 10.6 | ..... | ..... | ..... | ..... | ..... |
| Metallic ores and concentrates | 0.1 | ..... | 0.3 | ..... | ..... | 0.1 | ..... | ..... | ..... | ..... |
| Bituminous coal and lignite | 7.4 | 22.2 | 33.1 | 35.8 | 37.3 | ..... | ..... | ..... | ..... | ..... |
| Crude petroleum and natural gas | ..... | ..... | ..... | ..... | ..... | ..... | ..... | ..... | ..... | ..... |
| Nonmetallic minerals | 0.4 | 0.9 | 4.5 | 2.1 | 2.2 | 0.1 | ..... | 0.1 | ..... | 0.1 |
| Scrap and waste | 0.6 | 4.8 | 12.4 | 1.2 | 2.1 | ..... | ..... | 0.1 | ..... | 0.6 |
| Used merchandise | 4.1 | 2.3 | 2.2 | 2.6 | 2.3 | 0.3 | 0.2 | 0.2 | 0.8 | 0.6 |
| Goods imported and returned unchanged | ..... | ..... | ..... | ..... | ..... | ..... | ..... | ..... | ..... | ..... |
| Special classification provisions | 0.1 | 0.1 | 0.3 | 1.2 | 0.3 | ..... | 0.1 | 0.2 | 0.1 | 0.2 |

## Table D-3.  State Exports of Goods by Destination and Industry, 1993–1997 —*Continued*

**LOUISIANA** (Millions of dollars.)

| Industry | Germany 1993 | 1994 | 1995 | 1996 | 1997 | France 1993 | 1994 | 1995 | 1996 | 1997 |
|---|---|---|---|---|---|---|---|---|---|---|
| **ALL GOODS** | 44.1 | 70.4 | 63.6 | 122.1 | 90.1 | 101.4 | 82.4 | 110.9 | 60.2 | 65.1 |
| **Manufactured goods** | 42.6 | 37.8 | 49.9 | 52.1 | 58.4 | 85.9 | 68.7 | 92.1 | 58.5 | 46.2 |
| Food products | 6.4 | 2.7 | 2.9 | 2.5 | 2.0 | 56.1 | 44.7 | 54.0 | 24.1 | 8.0 |
| Tobacco products | ..... | ..... | ..... | ..... | ..... | ..... | ..... | ..... | ..... | ..... |
| Textile mill products | ..... | ..... | ..... | ..... | ..... | ..... | ..... | ..... | 0.1 | 0.4 |
| Apparel | 0.1 | ..... | ..... | 0.1 | 0.1 | 0.1 | 0.1 | 0.1 | ..... | ..... |
| Lumber and wood products | 1.3 | 1.4 | 1.4 | 1.7 | 1.2 | 0.3 | 0.9 | 1.0 | 0.6 | 0.4 |
| Furniture and fixtures | ..... | ..... | ..... | 0.9 | 0.3 | ..... | ..... | 0.5 | ..... | 0.1 |
| Paper products | 5.2 | 4.7 | 6.6 | 8.4 | 7.5 | 4.5 | 0.8 | 1.1 | 1.9 | 4.3 |
| Printing and publishing | ..... | 0.1 | 0.2 | ..... | ..... | ..... | ..... | 1.3 | 0.1 | 0.2 |
| Chemical products | 1.7 | 2.3 | 7.9 | 4.5 | 11.3 | 6.3 | 4.5 | 9.6 | 9.8 | 4.7 |
| Refined petroleum products | 0.2 | 0.1 | 1.9 | 3.2 | 3.3 | 0.1 | 1.5 | ..... | 3.4 | 1.3 |
| Rubber and plastic products | 0.3 | 0.1 | 0.1 | 0.1 | 0.1 | 0.4 | 0.1 | 0.1 | 0.1 | 0.4 |
| Leather products | ..... | ..... | ..... | ..... | ..... | 1.6 | 1.3 | 0.9 | 0.1 | 2.9 |
| Stone, clay and glass products | ..... | ..... | 0.1 | ..... | ..... | 0.1 | ..... | 0.1 | ..... | ..... |
| Primary metals | 0.4 | 1.0 | 2.1 | 0.8 | 0.6 | 0.2 | 0.4 | 0.6 | 1.9 | 0.4 |
| Fabricated metal products | 3.3 | 0.8 | 0.8 | 0.8 | 0.8 | 0.2 | 0.1 | 0.2 | 0.7 | 0.2 |
| Industrial machinery and computers | 16.1 | 17.5 | 20.2 | 23.2 | 23.4 | 5.4 | 8.3 | 11.3 | 8.4 | 8.8 |
| Electric and electronic equipment | 5.0 | 4.2 | 2.8 | 3.5 | 1.4 | 7.6 | 4.0 | 6.2 | 4.1 | 3.8 |
| Transportation equipment | 1.0 | 0.6 | 1.2 | 1.2 | 5.3 | 1.7 | 0.8 | 0.8 | 0.9 | 0.5 |
| Scientific and measuring instruments | 1.3 | 1.8 | 1.0 | 0.6 | 0.9 | 0.7 | 0.5 | 1.0 | 1.6 | 0.9 |
| Miscellaneous manufactures | 0.2 | 0.2 | 0.5 | 0.5 | 0.2 | 0.6 | 0.8 | 3.2 | 0.4 | 8.8 |
| Unidentified manufactures | 0.1 | 0.1 | 0.1 | ..... | 0.1 | ..... | ..... | 0.1 | 0.1 | 0.1 |
| **Agricultural and livestock products** | 0.1 | 31.4 | 13.5 | 69.8 | 31.4 | 14.5 | 12.9 | 18.3 | 1.4 | 18.7 |
| Agricultural products | ..... | 31.3 | 12.5 | 69.7 | 31.1 | 14.1 | 12.8 | 18.2 | 1.3 | 18.5 |
| Livestock and livestock products | ..... | 0.1 | 1.1 | 0.1 | 0.3 | 0.3 | 0.1 | 0.2 | 0.2 | 0.2 |
| **Other commodities** | 1.5 | 1.2 | 0.2 | 0.2 | 0.3 | 1.1 | 0.7 | 0.5 | 0.3 | 0.1 |
| Forestry products | ..... | ..... | ..... | ..... | ..... | ..... | ..... | ..... | ..... | ..... |
| Fish and other marine products | 0.1 | ..... | ..... | ..... | ..... | ..... | 0.1 | 0.1 | ..... | ..... |
| Metallic ores and concentrates | ..... | ..... | ..... | ..... | ..... | ..... | ..... | ..... | ..... | ..... |
| Bituminous coal and lignite | ..... | ..... | ..... | ..... | ..... | ..... | ..... | ..... | ..... | ..... |
| Crude petroleum and natural gas | ..... | ..... | ..... | ..... | ..... | ..... | ..... | ..... | ..... | ..... |
| Nonmetallic minerals | ..... | 0.8 | ..... | ..... | ..... | ..... | ..... | ..... | ..... | ..... |
| Scrap and waste | ..... | ..... | ..... | ..... | ..... | ..... | ..... | ..... | ..... | ..... |
| Used merchandise | 1.3 | 0.4 | 0.2 | 0.2 | 0.2 | 1.1 | 0.7 | 0.3 | 0.3 | 0.1 |
| Goods imported and returned unchanged | ..... | ..... | ..... | ..... | ..... | ..... | ..... | ..... | ..... | ..... |
| Special classification provisions | 0.1 | ..... | ..... | 0.1 | 0.1 | ..... | ..... | ..... | ..... | ..... |

| Industry | The Netherlands 1993 | 1994 | 1995 | 1996 | 1997 | Asian 10 1993 | 1994 | 1995 | 1996 | 1997 |
|---|---|---|---|---|---|---|---|---|---|---|
| **ALL GOODS** | 142.2 | 155.8 | 288.6 | 226.8 | 180.0 | 1 192.5 | 1 272.7 | 1 701.7 | 1 978.3 | 1 568.4 |
| **Manufactured goods** | 133.5 | 153.4 | 247.5 | 199.2 | 150.3 | 433.6 | 530.2 | 565.4 | 426.0 | 405.9 |
| Food products | 77.5 | 75.5 | 108.9 | 48.3 | 45.3 | 20.9 | 64.6 | 86.6 | 52.1 | 61.7 |
| Tobacco products | ..... | ..... | ..... | ..... | ..... | ..... | ..... | ..... | ..... | ..... |
| Textile mill products | 0.1 | ..... | ..... | ..... | 0.3 | 1.7 | 3.7 | 3.7 | 1.7 | 2.1 |
| Apparel | ..... | ..... | 0.2 | 0.1 | 0.1 | 0.8 | 0.4 | 1.1 | 4.3 | 0.2 |
| Lumber and wood products | 0.4 | 0.4 | 0.8 | 1.5 | 1.4 | 16.8 | 24.4 | 20.2 | 19.1 | 5.4 |
| Furniture and fixtures | ..... | ..... | 0.1 | 0.1 | ..... | 0.2 | 0.2 | 0.2 | 0.2 | 0.4 |
| Paper products | 4.1 | 8.2 | 26.9 | 19.1 | 5.8 | 31.0 | 17.7 | 26.9 | 27.4 | 11.6 |
| Printing and publishing | ..... | ..... | 0.2 | ..... | ..... | 0.2 | 0.2 | 0.8 | 0.3 | 0.4 |
| Chemical products | 16.0 | 39.6 | 53.7 | 87.0 | 55.1 | 177.1 | 126.8 | 174.2 | 126.3 | 147.2 |
| Refined petroleum products | 0.1 | 2.1 | 2.6 | 3.9 | 4.2 | 9.0 | 14.0 | 17.9 | 7.2 | 2.6 |
| Rubber and plastic products | 3.3 | 4.5 | 4.5 | 5.5 | 12.2 | 5.8 | 15.3 | 5.5 | 4.4 | 4.0 |
| Leather products | ..... | ..... | ..... | ..... | ..... | 0.2 | 0.5 | ..... | ..... | 0.1 |
| Stone, clay and glass products | 2.6 | 2.0 | 4.1 | 0.1 | ..... | 1.0 | 1.3 | 0.6 | 2.6 | 2.6 |
| Primary metals | 0.1 | 0.5 | 2.1 | 0.9 | 1.0 | 12.8 | 22.3 | 65.7 | 16.2 | 11.8 |
| Fabricated metal products | 1.4 | 0.9 | 0.9 | 0.5 | 0.7 | 10.5 | 21.5 | 9.1 | 24.5 | 18.5 |
| Industrial machinery and computers | 7.0 | 6.2 | 25.0 | 15.5 | 8.8 | 79.6 | 128.6 | 84.3 | 73.5 | 74.1 |
| Electric and electronic equipment | 6.3 | 1.5 | 2.4 | 3.1 | 5.6 | 18.4 | 43.8 | 33.9 | 23.1 | 30.3 |
| Transportation equipment | 1.8 | 0.3 | 1.1 | 0.3 | 0.3 | 28.9 | 22.7 | 12.9 | 14.8 | 11.0 |
| Scientific and measuring instruments | 12.8 | 11.7 | 13.7 | 13.1 | 9.6 | 15.7 | 18.1 | 16.8 | 25.4 | 19.7 |
| Miscellaneous manufactures | ..... | 0.1 | 0.3 | 0.1 | 0.1 | 2.7 | 3.5 | 4.3 | 2.5 | 2.0 |
| Unidentified manufactures | 0.1 | ..... | ..... | ..... | ..... | 0.4 | 0.6 | 0.6 | 0.4 | 0.4 |
| **Agricultural and livestock products** | 8.0 | 1.6 | 24.9 | 24.6 | 25.8 | 743.4 | 733.8 | 1 127.7 | 1 543.4 | 1 155.3 |
| Agricultural products | 8.0 | 1.6 | 24.9 | 24.5 | 25.7 | 741.9 | 731.6 | 1 124.2 | 1 537.5 | 1 147.0 |
| Livestock and livestock products | 0.1 | 0.1 | ..... | 0.1 | 0.1 | 1.5 | 2.2 | 3.5 | 5.9 | 8.2 |
| **Other commodities** | 0.6 | 0.7 | 16.2 | 2.9 | 3.8 | 15.6 | 8.7 | 8.6 | 9.0 | 7.3 |
| Forestry products | ..... | ..... | ..... | ..... | 0.4 | ..... | ..... | ..... | ..... | ..... |
| Fish and other marine products | ..... | ..... | ..... | ..... | ..... | 2.6 | 4.6 | 5.9 | 6.0 | 5.3 |
| Metallic ores and concentrates | ..... | ..... | 0.3 | ..... | ..... | ..... | ..... | ..... | ..... | ..... |
| Bituminous coal and lignite | ..... | ..... | ..... | ..... | ..... | ..... | ..... | ..... | ..... | ..... |
| Crude petroleum and natural gas | ..... | ..... | ..... | ..... | ..... | ..... | ..... | ..... | ..... | 0.1 |
| Nonmetallic minerals | 0.1 | ..... | 4.0 | 1.7 | 2.1 | ..... | ..... | 0.3 | 0.2 | 0.2 |
| Scrap and waste | 0.5 | 0.6 | 11.9 | 1.1 | 0.9 | 7.1 | ..... | 0.4 | 0.1 | 0.1 |
| Used merchandise | ..... | 0.1 | 0.1 | 0.2 | 0.4 | 5.8 | 3.5 | 1.5 | 2.1 | 1.0 |
| Goods imported and returned unchanged | ..... | ..... | ..... | ..... | ..... | ..... | ..... | 0.5 | 0.5 | 0.4 |
| Special classification provisions | ..... | ..... | ..... | ..... | ..... | ..... | ..... | 0.5 | 0.4 | 0.5 |

## Table D-3.   State Exports of Goods by Destination and Industry, 1993–1997 —*Continued*

**LOUISIANA** (Millions of dollars.)

| Industry | 1993 | 1994 | 1995 | 1996 | 1997 | 1993 | 1994 | 1995 | 1996 | 1997 |
|---|---|---|---|---|---|---|---|---|---|---|
| | Japan | | | | | South Korea | | | | |
| **ALL GOODS** | 781.5 | 800.5 | 879.8 | 1 111.3 | 974.2 | 57.3 | 61.1 | 98.9 | 144.8 | 127.0 |
| **Manufactured goods** | 87.1 | 90.4 | 110.7 | 111.1 | 127.7 | 45.9 | 49.5 | 84.3 | 54.1 | 56.7 |
| Food products | 8.3 | 12.6 | 13.7 | 33.8 | 43.4 | 1.8 | 2.1 | 2.0 | 3.3 | 3.8 |
| Tobacco products | ..... | ..... | ..... | ..... | ..... | ..... | ..... | ..... | ..... | ..... |
| Textile mill products | 0.4 | 0.7 | 0.4 | 0.9 | 0.5 | ..... | ..... | 0.1 | ..... | 0.1 |
| Apparel | 0.3 | 0.1 | 0.7 | 4.1 | 0.1 | 0.3 | 0.2 | 0.1 | ..... | ..... |
| Lumber and wood products | 4.4 | 2.0 | 2.1 | 3.3 | 3.5 | 11.8 | 18.9 | 16.5 | 7.3 | 0.4 |
| Furniture and fixtures | ..... | ..... | ..... | ..... | 0.1 | ..... | ..... | ..... | ..... | ..... |
| Paper products | 11.0 | 2.3 | 6.6 | 5.7 | 3.1 | 4.4 | 0.1 | ..... | 0.6 | 0.6 |
| Printing and publishing | 0.1 | ..... | 0.1 | ..... | 0.1 | ..... | ..... | ..... | ..... | ..... |
| Chemical products | 46.0 | 52.4 | 63.5 | 48.2 | 44.7 | 24.4 | 18.9 | 32.6 | 26.7 | 39.5 |
| Refined petroleum products | 2.0 | 1.5 | 0.1 | 0.2 | ..... | ..... | 2.6 | 2.8 | 1.3 | 0.1 |
| Rubber and plastic products | 0.7 | 0.7 | 0.8 | 1.2 | 2.3 | 0.4 | 0.3 | 0.7 | 0.7 | 0.6 |
| Leather products | 0.2 | 0.1 | ..... | ..... | ..... | ..... | 0.1 | ..... | ..... | ..... |
| Stone, clay and glass products | 0.1 | 0.6 | ..... | 0.1 | 0.3 | ..... | 0.1 | ..... | ..... | ..... |
| Primary metals | 3.7 | 3.1 | 4.1 | ..... | 4.9 | 0.1 | 0.2 | 19.8 | 0.2 | 0.4 |
| Fabricated metal products | 0.3 | 0.7 | 0.8 | 0.9 | 3.1 | 0.2 | 0.2 | 1.0 | 2.0 | 1.8 |
| Industrial machinery and computers | 2.1 | 4.8 | 3.8 | 3.2 | 11.0 | 1.4 | 2.5 | 2.5 | 4.8 | 2.9 |
| Electric and electronic equipment | 0.6 | 1.4 | 4.5 | 4.3 | 2.9 | 0.2 | 2.2 | 4.4 | 1.1 | 2.8 |
| Transportation equipment | 0.2 | 0.9 | 2.5 | 0.7 | 1.1 | ..... | 0.2 | 0.6 | 0.1 | 1.5 |
| Scientific and measuring instruments | 5.5 | 5.9 | 6.0 | 3.4 | 6.1 | 0.7 | 0.8 | 1.0 | 5.5 | 1.2 |
| Miscellaneous manufactures | 1.1 | 0.3 | 0.6 | 0.9 | 0.5 | ..... | ..... | ..... | 0.6 | 0.7 |
| Unidentified manufactures | 0.1 | 0.2 | 0.1 | 0.1 | 0.1 | ..... | 0.1 | 0.2 | ..... | ..... |
| **Agricultural and livestock products** | 693.8 | 708.3 | 767.9 | 997.6 | 845.0 | 4.3 | 11.4 | 14.4 | 90.7 | 70.3 |
| Agricultural products | 693.4 | 707.9 | 767.4 | 997.1 | 844.4 | 3.8 | 10.8 | 13.1 | 89.7 | 69.6 |
| Livestock and livestock products | 0.4 | 0.4 | 0.6 | 0.5 | 0.6 | 0.6 | 0.6 | 1.3 | 0.9 | 0.6 |
| **Other commodities** | 0.6 | 1.8 | 1.2 | 2.7 | 1.5 | 7.0 | 0.1 | 0.2 | 0.1 | ..... |
| Forestry products | ..... | ..... | ..... | ..... | ..... | ..... | ..... | ..... | ..... | ..... |
| Fish and other marine products | 0.4 | 1.1 | 0.6 | 0.4 | 0.7 | ..... | ..... | ..... | ..... | ..... |
| Metallic ores and concentrates | ..... | ..... | ..... | ..... | ..... | ..... | ..... | ..... | ..... | ..... |
| Bituminous coal and lignite | ..... | ..... | ..... | ..... | ..... | ..... | ..... | ..... | ..... | ..... |
| Crude petroleum and natural gas | ..... | ..... | ..... | ..... | ..... | ..... | ..... | ..... | ..... | ..... |
| Nonmetallic minerals | ..... | ..... | ..... | 0.2 | 0.2 | ..... | ..... | ..... | ..... | ..... |
| Scrap and waste | ..... | ..... | 0.1 | ..... | ..... | 7.0 | ..... | 0.2 | ..... | ..... |
| Used merchandise | 0.2 | 0.4 | 0.3 | 2.0 | 0.6 | ..... | ..... | ..... | ..... | ..... |
| Goods imported and returned unchanged | ..... | ..... | ..... | ..... | ..... | ..... | ..... | ..... | ..... | ..... |
| Special classification provisions | ..... | 0.3 | 0.1 | ..... | 0.1 | ..... | 0.1 | ..... | 0.1 | ..... |
| | Taiwan | | | | | Singapore | | | | |
| **ALL GOODS** | 77.1 | 50.2 | 247.3 | 324.3 | 173.4 | 53.2 | 47.9 | 37.8 | 51.8 | 45.6 |
| **Manufactured goods** | 37.3 | 34.3 | 63.7 | 46.4 | 43.3 | 52.8 | 47.5 | 37.2 | 51.0 | 44.6 |
| Food products | 0.3 | 0.6 | 4.8 | 0.7 | 5.4 | 4.3 | 3.5 | 1.9 | 4.6 | 2.6 |
| Tobacco products | ..... | ..... | ..... | ..... | ..... | ..... | ..... | ..... | ..... | ..... |
| Textile mill products | 0.2 | 0.1 | ..... | 0.1 | ..... | 0.4 | 0.1 | 0.1 | ..... | 0.1 |
| Apparel | ..... | ..... | 0.2 | ..... | ..... | ..... | ..... | ..... | 0.1 | ..... |
| Lumber and wood products | 0.1 | 0.4 | 0.7 | 7.5 | 1.2 | 0.1 | 0.5 | 0.3 | 0.2 | ..... |
| Furniture and fixtures | ..... | ..... | ..... | ..... | ..... | ..... | ..... | ..... | ..... | ..... |
| Paper products | 1.1 | ..... | 0.8 | 2.0 | 0.1 | 1.3 | 0.3 | 0.5 | 0.5 | 0.8 |
| Printing and publishing | ..... | ..... | 0.2 | 0.1 | 0.2 | ..... | ..... | ..... | ..... | ..... |
| Chemical products | 20.5 | 20.9 | 40.2 | 20.3 | 22.8 | 23.4 | 12.1 | 12.7 | 9.4 | 8.3 |
| Refined petroleum products | 3.9 | 2.4 | 2.7 | 1.8 | 0.2 | 0.3 | ..... | 0.5 | ..... | 0.2 |
| Rubber and plastic products | 1.1 | 0.3 | 0.3 | 0.2 | 0.3 | 0.3 | 7.3 | 0.2 | 0.3 | 0.2 |
| Leather products | ..... | ..... | ..... | ..... | ..... | ..... | 0.2 | ..... | ..... | ..... |
| Stone, clay and glass products | 0.2 | 0.1 | 0.2 | ..... | ..... | 0.2 | 0.1 | 0.2 | 0.4 | 0.1 |
| Primary metals | 2.0 | 1.0 | 2.0 | 0.1 | 0.1 | 0.4 | 0.9 | 0.9 | 0.8 | 2.8 |
| Fabricated metal products | 1.2 | 0.6 | 0.7 | 2.0 | 0.4 | 0.8 | 1.1 | 0.8 | 2.0 | 2.3 |
| Industrial machinery and computers | 1.3 | 1.7 | 2.1 | 3.2 | 3.7 | 10.7 | 11.1 | 11.5 | 15.3 | 17.8 |
| Electric and electronic equipment | 2.5 | 0.8 | 1.3 | 1.3 | 1.1 | 4.0 | 4.4 | 4.1 | 6.1 | 5.3 |
| Transportation equipment | 0.2 | 2.1 | 3.5 | 3.0 | 3.0 | 4.6 | 4.1 | 1.2 | 2.4 | 0.3 |
| Scientific and measuring instruments | 2.8 | 3.1 | 3.8 | 4.0 | 4.6 | 1.8 | 1.6 | 1.9 | 8.7 | 3.8 |
| Miscellaneous manufactures | ..... | ..... | ..... | ..... | ..... | ..... | 0.2 | 0.1 | 0.1 | 0.1 |
| Unidentified manufactures | ..... | 0.1 | 0.1 | ..... | 0.1 | 0.1 | ..... | 0.1 | 0.1 | ..... |
| **Agricultural and livestock products** | 37.5 | 12.5 | 177.7 | 272.3 | 125.4 | 0.3 | 0.3 | 0.4 | 0.6 | 0.4 |
| Agricultural products | 37.5 | 12.5 | 177.4 | 271.8 | 125.1 | ..... | ..... | ..... | ..... | ..... |
| Livestock and livestock products | ..... | ..... | 0.3 | 0.5 | 0.3 | 0.3 | 0.3 | 0.4 | 0.6 | 0.4 |
| **Other commodities** | 2.2 | 3.4 | 5.9 | 5.6 | 4.7 | 0.1 | 0.1 | 0.2 | 0.2 | 0.6 |
| Forestry products | ..... | ..... | ..... | ..... | ..... | ..... | ..... | ..... | ..... | ..... |
| Fish and other marine products | 2.2 | 3.4 | 5.2 | 5.5 | 4.6 | ..... | 0.1 | ..... | ..... | ..... |
| Metallic ores and concentrates | ..... | ..... | ..... | ..... | ..... | ..... | ..... | ..... | ..... | ..... |
| Bituminous coal and lignite | ..... | ..... | ..... | ..... | ..... | ..... | ..... | ..... | ..... | ..... |
| Crude petroleum and natural gas | ..... | ..... | ..... | ..... | ..... | ..... | ..... | ..... | ..... | ..... |
| Nonmetallic minerals | ..... | ..... | 0.2 | ..... | 0.1 | ..... | ..... | ..... | ..... | ..... |
| Scrap and waste | ..... | ..... | 0.1 | 0.1 | ..... | ..... | ..... | ..... | ..... | ..... |
| Used merchandise | ..... | ..... | 0.4 | ..... | ..... | 0.1 | ..... | ..... | ..... | 0.3 |
| Goods imported and returned unchanged | ..... | ..... | ..... | ..... | ..... | ..... | ..... | ..... | ..... | ..... |
| Special classification provisions | ..... | ..... | 0.1 | ..... | ..... | ..... | ..... | 0.1 | 0.2 | 0.3 |

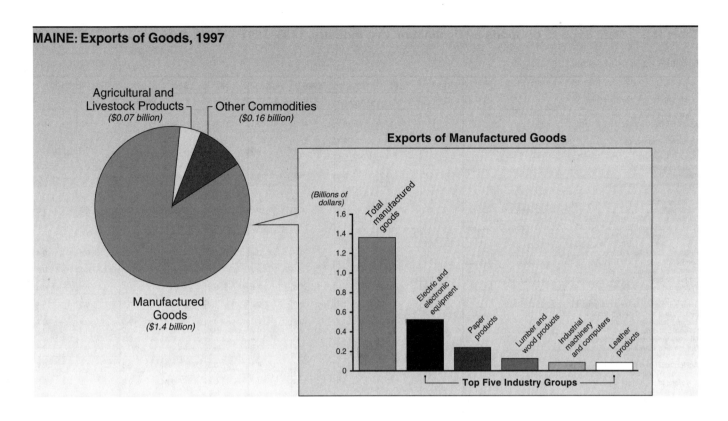

**MAINE: Exports of Goods, 1997**

Agricultural and Livestock Products ($0.07 billion)

Other Commodities ($0.16 billion)

Manufactured Goods ($1.4 billion)

Exports of Manufactured Goods

(Billions of dollars)

Top Five Industry Groups

Total manufactured goods / Electric and electronic equipment / Paper products / Lumber and wood products / Industrial machinery and computers / Leather products

### Table D-3. State Exports of Goods by Destination and Industry, 1993–1997 —Continued

**MAINE** (Millions of dollars.)

| Industry | 1993 | 1994 | 1995 | 1996 | 1997 | 1993 | 1994 | 1995 | 1996 | 1997 |
|---|---|---|---|---|---|---|---|---|---|---|
| | All destinations | | | | | Canada | | | | |
| **ALL GOODS** | 1 065.3 | 1 138.9 | 1 318.2 | 1 248.8 | 1 590.2 | 362.1 | 406.2 | 469.8 | 489.0 | 557.4 |
| **Manufactured goods** | 940.0 | 983.6 | 1 138.5 | 1 051.6 | 1 361.0 | 306.8 | 327.2 | 369.3 | 376.5 | 415.1 |
| Food products | 39.3 | 38.8 | 43.2 | 44.7 | 50.8 | 21.2 | 21.6 | 27.0 | 28.2 | 33.5 |
| Tobacco products | 0.2 | ..... | ..... | ..... | ..... | ..... | ..... | ..... | ..... | ..... |
| Textile mill products | 6.1 | 6.0 | 7.8 | 7.9 | 7.6 | 2.0 | 2.8 | 3.8 | 3.7 | 4.2 |
| Apparel | 6.4 | 7.3 | 8.8 | 9.7 | 10.7 | 1.4 | 1.4 | 1.7 | 2.7 | 3.3 |
| Lumber and wood products | 110.6 | 114.0 | 121.2 | 112.8 | 126.6 | 104.1 | 107.8 | 115.7 | 105.4 | 118.3 |
| Furniture and fixtures | 6.4 | 6.2 | 6.3 | 4.0 | 5.1 | 2.7 | 2.1 | 3.2 | 2.1 | 3.2 |
| Paper products | 155.6 | 179.1 | 245.6 | 258.3 | 239.1 | 68.7 | 62.4 | 64.1 | 67.1 | 71.8 |
| Printing and publishing | 6.5 | 3.4 | 4.0 | 5.3 | 3.8 | 2.1 | 2.2 | 2.4 | 2.1 | 2.9 |
| Chemical products | 21.0 | 29.3 | 25.9 | 39.3 | 38.8 | 6.8 | 7.5 | 9.4 | 11.5 | 11.2 |
| Refined petroleum products | 6.8 | 3.3 | 7.0 | 2.2 | 14.9 | 3.6 | 3.2 | 6.9 | 2.2 | 14.2 |
| Rubber and plastic products | 15.6 | 18.1 | 22.6 | 25.0 | 23.9 | 9.1 | 13.3 | 14.5 | 16.4 | 14.1 |
| Leather products | 144.8 | 160.2 | 124.4 | 62.7 | 84.8 | 11.3 | 10.4 | 8.6 | 5.4 | 7.1 |
| Stone, clay and glass products | 2.2 | 5.3 | 3.1 | 4.4 | 3.7 | 1.2 | 3.5 | 2.0 | 1.9 | 1.4 |
| Primary metals | 11.4 | 12.4 | 18.1 | 20.2 | 13.6 | 5.3 | 5.0 | 8.6 | 6.4 | 4.3 |
| Fabricated metal products | 35.4 | 38.6 | 33.6 | 16.3 | 25.8 | 6.0 | 6.1 | 6.7 | 8.8 | 7.7 |
| Industrial machinery and computers | 56.7 | 57.6 | 68.4 | 78.0 | 86.1 | 20.3 | 25.3 | 29.3 | 36.2 | 36.0 |
| Electric and electronic equipment | 268.1 | 241.3 | 316.9 | 259.8 | 522.7 | 23.6 | 29.5 | 32.4 | 33.6 | 33.9 |
| Transportation equipment | 25.6 | 29.4 | 37.5 | 55.5 | 68.9 | 12.5 | 14.7 | 23.2 | 30.6 | 37.8 |
| Scientific and measuring instruments | 13.8 | 23.4 | 31.4 | 36.2 | 22.3 | 2.4 | 4.8 | 6.0 | 9.0 | 6.9 |
| Miscellaneous manufactures | 4.6 | 5.5 | 8.5 | 5.7 | 8.2 | 1.4 | 2.2 | 2.0 | 1.7 | 2.0 |
| Unidentified manufactures | 2.8 | 4.4 | 4.1 | 3.4 | 3.4 | 1.3 | 1.5 | 1.8 | 1.5 | 1.2 |
| **Agricultural and livestock products** | 51.7 | 45.1 | 50.6 | 55.8 | 70.1 | 23.5 | 14.8 | 18.1 | 24.4 | 32.7 |
| Agricultural products | 7.7 | 5.4 | 4.9 | 6.8 | 31.0 | 6.8 | 4.6 | 3.8 | 5.0 | 12.7 |
| Livestock and livestock products | 44.0 | 39.8 | 45.7 | 48.9 | 39.1 | 16.7 | 10.2 | 14.3 | 19.3 | 20.0 |
| **Other commodities** | 73.5 | 110.2 | 129.1 | 141.4 | 159.1 | 31.8 | 64.3 | 82.4 | 88.2 | 109.6 |
| Forestry products | 0.5 | 4.2 | 0.2 | 1.8 | 0.7 | ..... | 3.7 | ..... | 0.3 | 0.2 |
| Fish and other marine products | 54.4 | 88.7 | 95.5 | 107.1 | 125.1 | 17.1 | 44.2 | 51.3 | 61.4 | 79.6 |
| Metallic ores and concentrates | ..... | ..... | ..... | ..... | 0.2 | ..... | ..... | ..... | ..... | ..... |
| Bituminous coal and lignite | ..... | ..... | ..... | ..... | 0.8 | ..... | ..... | ..... | ..... | 0.8 |
| Crude petroleum and natural gas | 0.1 | ..... | ..... | ..... | 1.4 | 0.1 | ..... | ..... | ..... | 1.4 |
| Nonmetallic minerals | 2.7 | 0.6 | 0.2 | 0.6 | 0.5 | 0.1 | 0.5 | 0.2 | 0.4 | 0.3 |
| Scrap and waste | 3.3 | 6.3 | 19.6 | 7.8 | 5.6 | 2.7 | 5.9 | 19.0 | 3.2 | 5.3 |
| Used merchandise | 0.7 | 0.9 | 2.0 | 0.9 | 3.7 | 0.5 | 0.5 | 0.5 | 0.3 | 0.9 |
| Goods imported and returned unchanged | 10.9 | 8.8 | 11.2 | 21.6 | 20.9 | 10.9 | 8.8 | 11.2 | 21.6 | 20.9 |
| Special classification provisions | 1.0 | 0.7 | 0.3 | 1.3 | 0.3 | 0.3 | 0.6 | 0.2 | 1.0 | 0.2 |

## Table D-3.  State Exports of Goods by Destination and Industry, 1993–1997 —*Continued*

**MAINE** (Millions of dollars.)

| Industry | 1993 | 1994 | 1995 | 1996 | 1997 | 1993 | 1994 | 1995 | 1996 | 1997 |
|---|---|---|---|---|---|---|---|---|---|---|
| | South and Central America and Caribbean | | | | | Mexico | | | | |
| **ALL GOODS** | 42.3 | 39.2 | 36.7 | 40.6 | 52.1 | 28.7 | 36.0 | 10.7 | 12.3 | 18.4 |
| **Manufactured goods** | 39.4 | 36.0 | 32.7 | 37.1 | 47.5 | 28.1 | 35.3 | 9.5 | 10.0 | 17.3 |
| Food products | 1.3 | 1.1 | 1.2 | 1.5 | 2.1 | 0.6 | 0.1 | 0.2 | 0.3 | ..... |
| Tobacco products | ..... | ..... | ..... | ..... | ..... | ..... | ..... | ..... | ..... | ..... |
| Textile mill products | 0.9 | 0.5 | 0.2 | 0.4 | 0.3 | ..... | 0.6 | 0.8 | 0.2 | 0.1 |
| Apparel | 2.6 | 4.3 | 5.2 | 5.2 | 5.7 | ..... | ..... | ..... | ..... | ..... |
| Lumber and wood products | 0.1 | 0.1 | ..... | 0.1 | ..... | 0.1 | 0.1 | 0.1 | ..... | 0.1 |
| Furniture and fixtures | 0.1 | 0.5 | 0.4 | 0.2 | 0.1 | ..... | 0.2 | ..... | ..... | ..... |
| Paper products | 2.5 | 3.0 | 1.9 | 4.4 | 9.1 | 0.1 | 0.9 | 0.8 | 0.9 | 1.2 |
| Printing and publishing | ..... | ..... | ..... | ..... | ..... | ..... | 0.1 | 0.1 | 0.1 | 0.1 |
| Chemical products | 1.6 | 0.8 | 1.1 | 1.9 | 1.7 | 0.7 | 0.9 | 0.6 | 1.5 | 1.8 |
| Refined petroleum products | ..... | ..... | ..... | ..... | ..... | ..... | 0.1 | ..... | ..... | ..... |
| Rubber and plastic products | 1.2 | 0.5 | 1.4 | 0.8 | 0.3 | 0.1 | 0.1 | 0.1 | 0.4 | 0.4 |
| Leather products | 11.7 | 11.9 | 10.2 | 4.2 | 5.2 | 11.1 | 13.0 | 4.6 | 0.7 | 1.1 |
| Stone, clay and glass products | ..... | 0.2 | 0.1 | 0.4 | 0.7 | 0.3 | 0.6 | ..... | 0.3 | 0.9 |
| Primary metals | 0.2 | 0.1 | 0.2 | ..... | 0.3 | ..... | 0.1 | ..... | 0.6 | 0.9 |
| Fabricated metal products | 0.5 | 0.2 | 0.3 | 1.6 | 1.8 | 9.4 | 13.5 | 0.2 | 0.1 | 0.4 |
| Industrial machinery and computers | 3.5 | 1.7 | 1.4 | 2.0 | 2.6 | 1.7 | 1.3 | 0.3 | 0.9 | 3.4 |
| Electric and electronic equipment | 12.6 | 10.4 | 8.2 | 12.5 | 16.1 | 3.4 | 2.9 | 1.0 | 3.2 | 6.1 |
| Transportation equipment | 0.1 | 0.2 | 0.2 | 0.2 | 0.1 | 0.1 | 0.4 | 0.5 | 0.4 | 0.2 |
| Scientific and measuring instruments | 0.1 | 0.3 | 0.3 | 0.7 | 0.7 | 0.4 | 0.1 | 0.2 | 0.4 | 0.3 |
| Miscellaneous manufactures | 0.4 | 0.4 | 0.1 | 0.3 | 0.4 | ..... | 0.1 | 0.1 | ..... | ..... |
| Unidentified manufactures | ..... | 0.2 | 0.2 | 0.4 | 0.3 | 0.1 | ..... | ..... | 0.1 | 0.1 |
| **Agricultural and livestock products** | 2.5 | 2.8 | 3.4 | 3.2 | 4.1 | 0.5 | 0.6 | 0.8 | 1.8 | 0.8 |
| Agricultural products | 0.1 | 0.1 | 0.7 | 0.3 | ..... | 0.1 | ..... | ..... | 0.6 | ..... |
| Livestock and livestock products | 2.4 | 2.7 | 2.8 | 2.9 | 4.1 | 0.4 | 0.6 | 0.8 | 1.2 | 0.8 |
| **Other commodities** | 0.5 | 0.5 | 0.5 | 0.3 | 0.4 | 0.1 | 0.1 | 0.4 | 0.5 | 0.3 |
| Forestry products | ..... | ..... | 0.1 | ..... | ..... | ..... | ..... | ..... | ..... | ..... |
| Fish and other marine products | 0.3 | 0.2 | 0.3 | 0.2 | 0.4 | ..... | ..... | ..... | 0.1 | ..... |
| Metallic ores and concentrates | ..... | ..... | ..... | ..... | ..... | ..... | ..... | ..... | ..... | ..... |
| Bituminous coal and lignite | ..... | ..... | ..... | ..... | ..... | ..... | ..... | ..... | ..... | ..... |
| Crude petroleum and natural gas | ..... | ..... | ..... | ..... | ..... | ..... | ..... | ..... | ..... | ..... |
| Nonmetallic minerals | ..... | ..... | ..... | ..... | ..... | ..... | ..... | ..... | ..... | ..... |
| Scrap and waste | 0.2 | 0.1 | ..... | 0.1 | ..... | ..... | 0.1 | 0.4 | 0.4 | 0.3 |
| Used merchandise | ..... | 0.1 | 0.1 | ..... | 0.1 | ..... | ..... | ..... | ..... | ..... |
| Goods imported and returned unchanged | ..... | ..... | ..... | ..... | ..... | ..... | ..... | ..... | ..... | ..... |
| Special classification provisions | ..... | ..... | ..... | ..... | ..... | 0.1 | ..... | ..... | ..... | ..... |
| | European Union | | | | | United Kingdom | | | | |
| **ALL GOODS** | 187.1 | 204.5 | 228.3 | 208.0 | 220.8 | 29.0 | 43.8 | 62.4 | 44.5 | 59.1 |
| **Manufactured goods** | 173.2 | 196.8 | 219.6 | 197.7 | 197.9 | 28.2 | 43.3 | 60.1 | 43.0 | 58.2 |
| Food products | 11.2 | 8.7 | 11.6 | 11.3 | 10.3 | 0.7 | 0.7 | 1.3 | 1.5 | 0.7 |
| Tobacco products | ..... | ..... | ..... | ..... | ..... | ..... | ..... | ..... | ..... | ..... |
| Textile mill products | 1.1 | 0.5 | 0.8 | 0.6 | 0.6 | 0.4 | 0.2 | 0.3 | 0.2 | 0.2 |
| Apparel | 0.5 | 0.5 | 0.8 | 1.0 | 1.0 | 0.2 | ..... | 0.2 | 0.2 | 0.3 |
| Lumber and wood products | 3.3 | 2.6 | 2.4 | 3.1 | 3.8 | 1.2 | 0.4 | 0.5 | 0.8 | 0.8 |
| Furniture and fixtures | 0.7 | 0.3 | 0.8 | 0.4 | 0.4 | 0.5 | 0.2 | 0.3 | 0.4 | 0.4 |
| Paper products | 46.5 | 48.3 | 65.9 | 59.5 | 57.3 | 8.6 | 15.2 | 36.5 | 23.3 | 28.0 |
| Printing and publishing | 0.6 | 0.7 | 0.7 | 2.4 | 0.4 | 0.1 | 0.4 | 0.3 | 0.2 | 0.1 |
| Chemical products | 6.1 | 6.0 | 7.4 | 16.9 | 13.0 | 0.8 | 0.3 | 0.3 | 0.4 | 1.3 |
| Refined petroleum products | ..... | ..... | ..... | ..... | ..... | ..... | ..... | ..... | ..... | ..... |
| Rubber and plastic products | 1.3 | 1.5 | 2.8 | 2.5 | 2.9 | 0.2 | 0.5 | 0.9 | 0.5 | 0.3 |
| Leather products | 42.1 | 51.6 | 35.8 | 17.1 | 21.5 | 6.1 | 11.9 | 4.2 | 3.1 | 6.9 |
| Stone, clay and glass products | 0.1 | 0.3 | 0.4 | 0.9 | 0.3 | ..... | ..... | 0.2 | 0.2 | 0.1 |
| Primary metals | 3.8 | 4.9 | 6.8 | 4.1 | 4.6 | 0.1 | 0.2 | 0.3 | 1.5 | 0.5 |
| Fabricated metal products | 2.4 | 4.5 | 4.0 | 3.2 | 3.5 | 1.2 | 1.5 | 2.4 | 1.3 | 2.0 |
| Industrial machinery and computers | 18.6 | 17.5 | 20.8 | 17.6 | 22.3 | 1.1 | 2.8 | 3.6 | 2.7 | 6.4 |
| Electric and electronic equipment | 15.9 | 21.6 | 26.7 | 21.9 | 29.4 | 5.3 | 7.0 | 7.1 | 4.9 | 7.4 |
| Transportation equipment | 9.7 | 11.4 | 10.8 | 17.6 | 20.4 | 0.4 | 0.3 | 0.5 | 0.6 | 1.8 |
| Scientific and measuring instruments | 7.6 | 13.2 | 18.3 | 15.5 | 3.8 | 0.7 | 0.2 | 0.3 | 0.3 | 0.4 |
| Miscellaneous manufactures | 1.0 | 1.1 | 1.8 | 1.3 | 1.5 | 0.3 | 0.4 | 0.2 | 0.4 | 0.4 |
| Unidentified manufactures | 0.5 | 1.7 | 1.2 | 0.7 | 0.8 | 0.2 | 1.1 | 0.7 | 0.3 | 0.2 |
| **Agricultural and livestock products** | 5.0 | 4.9 | 3.8 | 3.2 | 19.4 | ..... | 0.2 | 0.3 | 0.4 | 0.3 |
| Agricultural products | 0.4 | 0.6 | 0.3 | 0.7 | 18.0 | ..... | 0.1 | 0.3 | 0.4 | 0.3 |
| Livestock and livestock products | 4.6 | 4.3 | 3.5 | 2.5 | 1.4 | ..... | ..... | ..... | ..... | ..... |
| **Other commodities** | 9.0 | 2.7 | 4.9 | 7.1 | 3.5 | 0.9 | 0.3 | 2.1 | 1.1 | 0.6 |
| Forestry products | 0.5 | 0.3 | 0.1 | 1.6 | 0.5 | ..... | ..... | ..... | 0.3 | 0.2 |
| Fish and other marine products | 5.2 | 2.1 | 3.3 | 4.7 | 2.4 | 0.4 | 0.1 | 0.8 | 0.6 | 0.4 |
| Metallic ores and concentrates | ..... | ..... | ..... | ..... | ..... | ..... | ..... | ..... | ..... | ..... |
| Bituminous coal and lignite | ..... | ..... | ..... | ..... | ..... | ..... | ..... | ..... | ..... | ..... |
| Crude petroleum and natural gas | ..... | ..... | ..... | ..... | ..... | ..... | ..... | ..... | ..... | ..... |
| Nonmetallic minerals | 2.6 | ..... | ..... | 0.2 | 0.1 | ..... | ..... | ..... | 0.1 | ..... |
| Scrap and waste | 0.2 | ..... | 0.2 | ..... | ..... | ..... | ..... | 0.2 | ..... | ..... |
| Used merchandise | 0.1 | 0.3 | 1.2 | 0.4 | 0.4 | 0.1 | 0.2 | 1.1 | 0.1 | 0.1 |
| Goods imported and returned unchanged | ..... | ..... | ..... | ..... | ..... | ..... | ..... | ..... | ..... | ..... |
| Special classification provisions | 0.4 | 0.1 | 0.1 | 0.2 | ..... | 0.4 | ..... | ..... | ..... | ..... |

## Table D-3. State Exports of Goods by Destination and Industry, 1993–1997 —Continued

**MAINE** (Millions of dollars.)

| Industry | 1993 | 1994 | 1995 | 1996 | 1997 | 1993 | 1994 | 1995 | 1996 | 1997 |
|---|---|---|---|---|---|---|---|---|---|---|
| | Germany | | | | | France | | | | |
| **ALL GOODS** | 35.7 | 27.6 | 30.9 | 34.0 | 28.4 | 36.3 | 36.9 | 56.5 | 61.3 | 46.1 |
| **Manufactured goods** | 34.6 | 27.0 | 30.2 | 32.8 | 28.2 | 34.9 | 36.5 | 56.2 | 61.1 | 45.6 |
| Food products | 7.0 | 2.7 | 5.5 | 5.0 | 2.3 | 1.0 | 0.3 | 0.2 | 0.9 | 0.9 |
| Tobacco products | ..... | ..... | ..... | ..... | ..... | ..... | ..... | ..... | ..... | ..... |
| Textile mill products | ..... | 0.1 | 0.1 | ..... | ..... | 0.3 | 0.1 | 0.3 | 0.2 | 0.1 |
| Apparel | 0.1 | 0.1 | 0.2 | 0.1 | 0.2 | 0.1 | 0.1 | 0.1 | 0.2 | 0.2 |
| Lumber and wood products | 0.5 | ..... | 0.3 | 0.2 | 1.3 | 0.1 | 0.1 | ..... | ..... | 0.1 |
| Furniture and fixtures | ..... | ..... | ..... | ..... | ..... | 0.1 | ..... | ..... | ..... | ..... |
| Paper products | 1.5 | 2.3 | 4.9 | 2.3 | 0.1 | 6.4 | 2.0 | 11.3 | 15.0 | 21.6 |
| Printing and publishing | 0.1 | 0.1 | 0.1 | ..... | 0.1 | 0.1 | 0.2 | 0.2 | 0.1 | ..... |
| Chemical products | 0.6 | 0.3 | 0.4 | 0.6 | 1.3 | 3.1 | 3.7 | 5.0 | 12.0 | 7.9 |
| Refined petroleum products | ..... | ..... | ..... | ..... | ..... | ..... | ..... | ..... | ..... | ..... |
| Rubber and plastic products | 0.2 | 0.1 | 0.4 | 0.1 | 0.3 | 0.5 | 0.5 | 1.0 | 1.3 | 1.5 |
| Leather products | 8.9 | 5.6 | 1.4 | 0.1 | 0.2 | 9.0 | 9.8 | 8.9 | 5.9 | 5.4 |
| Stone, clay and glass products | ..... | 0.1 | ..... | ..... | ..... | ..... | ..... | ..... | ..... | ..... |
| Primary metals | 0.1 | 0.4 | 0.3 | 0.2 | 0.5 | 0.1 | 0.2 | 0.2 | 0.2 | 0.1 |
| Fabricated metal products | 0.3 | 0.6 | 0.9 | 0.8 | 0.6 | 0.5 | 0.5 | 0.1 | 0.1 | ..... |
| Industrial machinery and computers | 8.3 | 5.3 | 4.6 | 5.8 | 3.0 | 3.7 | 3.6 | 4.6 | 3.3 | 2.1 |
| Electric and electronic equipment | 1.2 | 1.6 | 2.3 | 2.5 | 4.4 | 3.1 | 3.4 | 7.8 | 7.2 | 4.3 |
| Transportation equipment | 5.1 | 6.0 | 8.2 | 14.0 | 13.0 | 1.5 | 0.9 | 0.2 | 0.4 | 0.1 |
| Scientific and measuring instruments | 0.4 | 1.1 | 0.4 | 0.4 | 0.2 | 5.1 | 11.0 | 16.3 | 14.2 | 1.1 |
| Miscellaneous manufactures | 0.2 | 0.5 | 0.2 | 0.3 | 0.3 | 0.1 | ..... | ..... | 0.1 | 0.1 |
| Unidentified manufactures | ..... | 0.1 | 0.1 | 0.1 | 0.3 | ..... | 0.1 | ..... | ..... | ..... |
| **Agricultural and livestock products** | 0.2 | 0.3 | 0.1 | 0.2 | 0.1 | 0.1 | 0.2 | ..... | ..... | 0.1 |
| Agricultural products | 0.2 | 0.3 | ..... | 0.2 | 0.1 | ..... | ..... | ..... | ..... | ..... |
| Livestock and livestock products | ..... | ..... | ..... | ..... | ..... | 0.1 | 0.1 | ..... | ..... | 0.1 |
| **Other commodities** | 0.9 | 0.3 | 0.7 | 1.1 | 0.1 | 1.4 | 0.2 | 0.4 | 0.3 | 0.4 |
| Forestry products | 0.5 | 0.1 | ..... | 1.0 | ..... | ..... | ..... | ..... | ..... | ..... |
| Fish and other marine products | 0.4 | 0.1 | 0.6 | ..... | ..... | 1.4 | 0.2 | 0.3 | 0.2 | 0.4 |
| Metallic ores and concentrates | ..... | ..... | ..... | ..... | ..... | ..... | ..... | ..... | ..... | ..... |
| Bituminous coal and lignite | ..... | ..... | ..... | ..... | ..... | ..... | ..... | ..... | ..... | ..... |
| Crude petroleum and natural gas | ..... | ..... | ..... | ..... | ..... | ..... | ..... | ..... | ..... | ..... |
| Nonmetallic minerals | ..... | ..... | ..... | ..... | ..... | ..... | ..... | ..... | ..... | ..... |
| Scrap and waste | ..... | ..... | ..... | ..... | ..... | ..... | ..... | ..... | ..... | ..... |
| Used merchandise | ..... | ..... | ..... | ..... | ..... | ..... | ..... | ..... | ..... | ..... |
| Goods imported and returned unchanged | ..... | ..... | ..... | ..... | ..... | ..... | ..... | ..... | ..... | ..... |
| Special classification provisions | ..... | ..... | 0.1 | ..... | ..... | ..... | ..... | ..... | ..... | ..... |
| | The Netherlands | | | | | Asian 10 | | | | |
| **ALL GOODS** | 15.2 | 19.1 | 16.7 | 11.8 | 11.2 | 371.5 | 364.7 | 489.8 | 400.5 | 668.6 |
| **Manufactured goods** | 12.5 | 16.2 | 14.9 | 9.2 | 9.5 | 327.0 | 308.0 | 432.7 | 339.2 | 616.0 |
| Food products | 0.9 | 1.0 | 1.4 | 0.6 | 0.5 | 3.8 | 5.7 | 1.8 | 2.4 | 3.5 |
| Tobacco products | ..... | ..... | ..... | ..... | ..... | ..... | ..... | ..... | ..... | ..... |
| Textile mill products | ..... | ..... | ..... | ..... | ..... | 1.8 | 1.2 | 1.8 | 2.7 | 1.8 |
| Apparel | ..... | ..... | ..... | 0.1 | ..... | 1.8 | 1.0 | 0.9 | 0.6 | 0.6 |
| Lumber and wood products | 0.7 | 0.4 | 0.5 | 0.7 | 0.1 | 2.5 | 3.2 | 2.4 | 4.2 | 3.9 |
| Furniture and fixtures | ..... | ..... | ..... | ..... | ..... | 2.7 | 2.6 | 1.1 | 0.8 | 1.0 |
| Paper products | 2.8 | 2.3 | 3.0 | 0.9 | ..... | 26.6 | 44.6 | 92.7 | 102.8 | 87.3 |
| Printing and publishing | ..... | ..... | ..... | 2.0 | ..... | 0.3 | 0.1 | 0.3 | 0.3 | 0.2 |
| Chemical products | 0.3 | 0.1 | 0.3 | 0.9 | 0.8 | 4.1 | 12.4 | 5.1 | 4.6 | 7.6 |
| Refined petroleum products | ..... | ..... | ..... | ..... | ..... | 3.2 | ..... | ..... | ..... | 0.4 |
| Rubber and plastic products | 0.1 | 0.1 | 0.1 | ..... | 0.1 | 2.2 | 1.6 | -2.3 | 3.0 | 4.6 |
| Leather products | 0.6 | 2.2 | 1.1 | 0.1 | 0.2 | 56.9 | 62.5 | 57.0 | 28.6 | 39.8 |
| Stone, clay and glass products | ..... | ..... | ..... | ..... | ..... | 0.3 | 0.6 | 0.2 | 0.4 | 0.1 |
| Primary metals | 3.4 | 3.9 | 5.1 | 1.6 | 3.3 | 1.8 | 1.5 | 0.9 | 1.2 | 3.0 |
| Fabricated metal products | 0.3 | 0.3 | 0.3 | 0.3 | 0.3 | 1.2 | 1.2 | 19.3 | 1.8 | 10.9 |
| Industrial machinery and computers | 0.9 | 1.4 | 0.8 | 0.8 | 1.0 | 6.3 | 5.9 | 11.5 | 9.2 | 11.0 |
| Electric and electronic equipment | 0.2 | 0.4 | 0.3 | 0.4 | 1.2 | 205.4 | 158.8 | 227.7 | 165.0 | 427.9 |
| Transportation equipment | 2.1 | 3.7 | 1.4 | 0.5 | 1.4 | 1.9 | 1.0 | 1.3 | 2.2 | 0.9 |
| Scientific and measuring instruments | 0.1 | 0.2 | 0.5 | ..... | 0.4 | 2.4 | 2.3 | 4.2 | 7.0 | 8.1 |
| Miscellaneous manufactures | ..... | ..... | ..... | 0.1 | 0.2 | 1.3 | 1.2 | 2.1 | 2.1 | 3.1 |
| Unidentified manufactures | ..... | 0.1 | 0.1 | ..... | 0.1 | 0.5 | 0.5 | 0.4 | 0.3 | 0.4 |
| **Agricultural and livestock products** | 2.2 | 2.4 | 1.5 | 1.5 | 1.1 | 15.3 | 16.7 | 19.5 | 19.6 | 11.1 |
| Agricultural products | 0.2 | ..... | ..... | 0.1 | ..... | 0.3 | 0.1 | ..... | 0.1 | 0.2 |
| Livestock and livestock products | 2.1 | 2.4 | 1.5 | 1.5 | 1.1 | 15.0 | 16.6 | 19.4 | 19.6 | 10.9 |
| **Other commodities** | 0.5 | 0.5 | 0.2 | 1.1 | 0.5 | 29.2 | 40.1 | 37.6 | 41.6 | 41.5 |
| Forestry products | ..... | 0.2 | ..... | 0.2 | 0.3 | ..... | 0.1 | ..... | ..... | ..... |
| Fish and other marine products | 0.4 | 0.3 | 0.2 | 0.6 | 0.1 | 28.8 | 39.7 | 37.3 | 37.4 | 39.7 |
| Metallic ores and concentrates | ..... | ..... | ..... | ..... | ..... | ..... | ..... | ..... | ..... | ..... |
| Bituminous coal and lignite | ..... | ..... | ..... | ..... | ..... | ..... | ..... | ..... | ..... | ..... |
| Crude petroleum and natural gas | ..... | ..... | ..... | ..... | ..... | ..... | ..... | ..... | ..... | ..... |
| Nonmetallic minerals | 0.1 | ..... | ..... | 0.1 | 0.1 | ..... | ..... | ..... | ..... | ..... |
| Scrap and waste | ..... | ..... | ..... | ..... | ..... | ..... | 0.1 | 0.1 | 4.1 | ..... |
| Used merchandise | ..... | ..... | ..... | ..... | 0.1 | 0.1 | 0.1 | 0.1 | ..... | 1.8 |
| Goods imported and returned unchanged | ..... | ..... | ..... | ..... | ..... | ..... | ..... | ..... | ..... | ..... |
| Special classification provisions | ..... | ..... | ..... | 0.2 | ..... | 0.3 | 0.1 | ..... | ..... | ..... |

## Table D-3.   State Exports of Goods by Destination and Industry, 1993–1997 —Continued

**MAINE** (Millions of dollars.)

| Industry | 1993 | 1994 | 1995 | 1996 | 1997 | 1993 | 1994 | 1995 | 1996 | 1997 |
|---|---|---|---|---|---|---|---|---|---|---|
| | Japan | | | | | South Korea | | | | |
| **ALL GOODS** | 68.5 | 109.1 | 102.1 | 99.6 | 88.2 | 18.1 | 18.2 | 49.2 | 69.2 | 65.6 |
| **Manufactured goods** | 40.6 | 71.1 | 68.9 | 65.8 | 53.6 | 16.4 | 16.6 | 46.4 | 67.6 | 64.9 |
| Food products | 2.0 | 4.6 | 1.4 | 1.8 | 2.4 | ..... | 0.1 | 0.2 | 0.1 | 0.2 |
| Tobacco products | ..... | ..... | ..... | ..... | ..... | ..... | ..... | ..... | ..... | ..... |
| Textile mill products | 0.2 | 0.7 | 0.2 | 0.1 | ..... | ..... | ..... | 0.5 | 0.7 | 0.1 |
| Apparel | 1.6 | 0.7 | 0.5 | 0.4 | 0.2 | ..... | ..... | ..... | ..... | 0.1 |
| Lumber and wood products | 1.7 | 1.5 | 0.6 | 2.3 | 1.7 | 0.4 | 0.2 | 0.1 | 0.1 | 0.1 |
| Furniture and fixtures | 1.3 | 1.9 | 0.3 | 0.3 | 0.1 | ..... | ..... | ..... | 0.1 | 0.1 |
| Paper products | 17.8 | 30.4 | 43.6 | 34.5 | 29.7 | 4.7 | 7.7 | 38.3 | 57.6 | 48.2 |
| Printing and publishing | ..... | ..... | ..... | 0.1 | ..... | ..... | ..... | ..... | 0.1 | ..... |
| Chemical products | 2.8 | 10.5 | 3.0 | 2.9 | 4.0 | 0.1 | ..... | ..... | 0.3 | 1.0 |
| Refined petroleum products | ..... | ..... | ..... | ..... | ..... | ..... | ..... | ..... | ..... | ..... |
| Rubber and plastic products | 0.3 | 0.3 | 0.8 | 0.6 | 0.7 | 0.5 | ..... | 0.1 | ..... | ..... |
| Leather products | 3.0 | 1.9 | 1.1 | 1.1 | 0.8 | 8.1 | 4.5 | 2.3 | 1.2 | 1.5 |
| Stone, clay and glass products | 0.1 | 0.2 | 0.1 | 0.1 | 0.1 | ..... | 0.1 | ..... | ..... | ..... |
| Primary metals | 1.0 | 0.7 | 0.1 | 0.2 | 1.4 | ..... | ..... | 0.1 | 0.3 | 0.2 |
| Fabricated metal products | 0.3 | 0.7 | 0.9 | 0.7 | 0.8 | ..... | ..... | ..... | 0.4 | ..... |
| Industrial machinery and computers | 3.0 | 3.3 | 6.8 | 4.5 | 1.9 | 0.1 | 0.6 | 0.6 | 0.8 | 2.7 |
| Electric and electronic equipment | 2.6 | 12.0 | 7.3 | 11.6 | 5.9 | 2.2 | 2.0 | 4.1 | 4.4 | 6.3 |
| Transportation equipment | 1.2 | 0.4 | 0.3 | 1.0 | 0.5 | 0.1 | 0.1 | ..... | ..... | 0.1 |
| Scientific and measuring instruments | 0.4 | 0.3 | 0.6 | 2.0 | 1.6 | ..... | 1.2 | ..... | 1.3 | 3.5 |
| Miscellaneous manufactures | 1.1 | 0.9 | 1.1 | 1.5 | 1.5 | ..... | 0.1 | ..... | 0.1 | 0.7 |
| Unidentified manufactures | 0.2 | 0.1 | 0.2 | 0.1 | 0.1 | ..... | ..... | ..... | ..... | ..... |
| **Agricultural and livestock products** | 0.6 | 0.2 | 0.1 | 0.1 | 1.3 | 0.3 | 0.3 | 0.6 | 0.6 | 0.3 |
| Agricultural products | 0.3 | 0.1 | ..... | 0.1 | 0.1 | ..... | ..... | ..... | ..... | ..... |
| Livestock and livestock products | 0.2 | 0.1 | ..... | 0.1 | 1.2 | 0.3 | 0.3 | 0.6 | 0.6 | 0.3 |
| **Other commodities** | 27.4 | 37.8 | 33.1 | 33.8 | 33.3 | 1.5 | 1.4 | 2.2 | 0.9 | 0.3 |
| Forestry products | ..... | 0.1 | ..... | ..... | ..... | ..... | ..... | ..... | ..... | ..... |
| Fish and other marine products | 27.1 | 37.7 | 33.0 | 32.5 | 33.0 | 1.5 | 1.3 | 2.1 | 0.5 | 0.3 |
| Metallic ores and concentrates | ..... | ..... | ..... | ..... | ..... | ..... | ..... | ..... | ..... | ..... |
| Bituminous coal and lignite | ..... | ..... | ..... | ..... | ..... | ..... | ..... | ..... | ..... | ..... |
| Crude petroleum and natural gas | ..... | ..... | ..... | ..... | ..... | ..... | ..... | ..... | ..... | ..... |
| Nonmetallic minerals | ..... | ..... | ..... | ..... | ..... | ..... | ..... | ..... | ..... | ..... |
| Scrap and waste | ..... | ..... | ..... | 1.3 | ..... | ..... | ..... | ..... | 0.4 | ..... |
| Used merchandise | ..... | ..... | 0.1 | ..... | 0.3 | ..... | ..... | ..... | ..... | ..... |
| Goods imported and returned unchanged | ..... | ..... | ..... | ..... | ..... | ..... | ..... | ..... | ..... | ..... |
| Special classification provisions | 0.3 | ..... | ..... | ..... | ..... | ..... | ..... | ..... | ..... | ..... |
| | Taiwan | | | | | Singapore | | | | |
| **ALL GOODS** | 25.9 | 28.9 | 37.5 | 19.6 | 21.3 | 34.8 | 36.5 | 46.3 | 47.9 | 166.1 |
| **Manufactured goods** | 25.5 | 28.4 | 34.4 | 18.0 | 20.6 | 34.8 | 36.5 | 46.2 | 47.8 | 164.6 |
| Food products | 1.2 | 0.2 | ..... | 0.1 | 0.1 | 0.1 | 0.1 | ..... | ..... | ..... |
| Tobacco products | ..... | ..... | ..... | ..... | ..... | ..... | ..... | ..... | ..... | ..... |
| Textile mill products | 0.1 | ..... | 0.1 | 0.1 | 0.1 | 0.2 | 0.1 | ..... | ..... | ..... |
| Apparel | ..... | ..... | 0.1 | ..... | ..... | ..... | ..... | 0.1 | ..... | ..... |
| Lumber and wood products | 0.4 | 1.1 | 1.4 | 0.6 | 0.4 | ..... | ..... | 0.1 | 0.1 | ..... |
| Furniture and fixtures | 1.2 | ..... | 0.4 | 0.1 | 0.3 | 0.1 | 0.1 | ..... | ..... | ..... |
| Paper products | 0.8 | 0.2 | 0.7 | 3.5 | 1.3 | 0.4 | 4.0 | 3.4 | 0.6 | 0.2 |
| Printing and publishing | ..... | ..... | ..... | ..... | ..... | 0.2 | ..... | ..... | ..... | ..... |
| Chemical products | 0.2 | 0.7 | 0.6 | 0.5 | 0.4 | ..... | ..... | 0.1 | 0.1 | 0.4 |
| Refined petroleum products | ..... | ..... | ..... | ..... | ..... | ..... | ..... | ..... | ..... | 0.1 |
| Rubber and plastic products* | 0.2 | 0.1 | 0.6 | 0.3 | 0.4 | 1.1 | 1.0 | 0.5 | 1.7 | 2.8 |
| Leather products | 11.5 | 15.3 | 9.4 | 0.3 | 0.3 | 1.1 | 0.2 | 0.1 | 0.3 | 0.1 |
| Stone, clay and glass products | 0.2 | ..... | ..... | 0.1 | ..... | ..... | ..... | ..... | 0.1 | ..... |
| Primary metals | 0.4 | 0.2 | 0.3 | 0.2 | 0.4 | 0.1 | 0.1 | 0.1 | 0.1 | 0.2 |
| Fabricated metal products | 0.4 | ..... | 9.0 | ..... | 4.1 | 0.3 | 0.1 | 0.2 | 0.1 | ..... |
| Industrial machinery and computers | 0.7 | 0.5 | 0.4 | 0.7 | 1.9 | 0.8 | 0.2 | 0.5 | 1.2 | 0.7 |
| Electric and electronic equipment | 7.7 | 9.3 | 10.7 | 9.3 | 9.4 | 29.1 | 30.2 | 37.6 | 42.0 | 159.6 |
| Transportation equipment | 0.4 | 0.4 | 0.3 | 0.2 | ..... | ..... | ..... | 0.1 | 0.6 | 0.2 |
| Scientific and measuring instruments | 0.1 | 0.2 | 0.3 | 2.0 | 1.4 | 1.0 | 0.1 | 2.5 | 0.6 | 0.1 |
| Miscellaneous manufactures | ..... | ..... | ..... | ..... | ..... | 0.1 | 0.1 | 0.9 | ..... | 0.1 |
| Unidentified manufactures | ..... | 0.1 | ..... | 0.1 | ..... | 0.1 | 0.1 | 0.1 | 0.1 | 0.1 |
| **Agricultural and livestock products** | 0.4 | 0.4 | 1.7 | 1.4 | 0.7 | ..... | ..... | ..... | ..... | ..... |
| Agricultural products | ..... | ..... | ..... | ..... | 0.1 | ..... | ..... | ..... | ..... | ..... |
| Livestock and livestock products | 0.4 | 0.4 | 1.7 | 1.4 | 0.5 | ..... | ..... | ..... | ..... | ..... |
| **Other commodities** | ..... | 0.1 | 1.4 | 0.2 | ..... | ..... | ..... | 0.1 | 0.1 | 1.5 |
| Forestry products | ..... | ..... | 1.4 | 0.2 | ..... | ..... | ..... | ..... | ..... | ..... |
| Fish and other marine products | ..... | ..... | ..... | ..... | ..... | ..... | ..... | 0.1 | 0.1 | ..... |
| Metallic ores and concentrates | ..... | ..... | ..... | ..... | ..... | ..... | ..... | ..... | ..... | ..... |
| Bituminous coal and lignite | ..... | ..... | ..... | ..... | ..... | ..... | ..... | ..... | ..... | ..... |
| Crude petroleum and natural gas | ..... | ..... | ..... | ..... | ..... | ..... | ..... | ..... | ..... | ..... |
| Nonmetallic minerals | ..... | ..... | ..... | ..... | ..... | ..... | ..... | ..... | ..... | ..... |
| Scrap and waste | ..... | 0.1 | ..... | ..... | ..... | ..... | ..... | ..... | ..... | ..... |
| Used merchandise | ..... | ..... | ..... | ..... | ..... | ..... | ..... | ..... | ..... | 1.5 |
| Goods imported and returned unchanged | ..... | ..... | ..... | ..... | ..... | ..... | ..... | ..... | ..... | ..... |
| Special classification provisions | ..... | ..... | ..... | ..... | ..... | ..... | ..... | ..... | ..... | ..... |

## MARYLAND: Exports of Goods, 1997

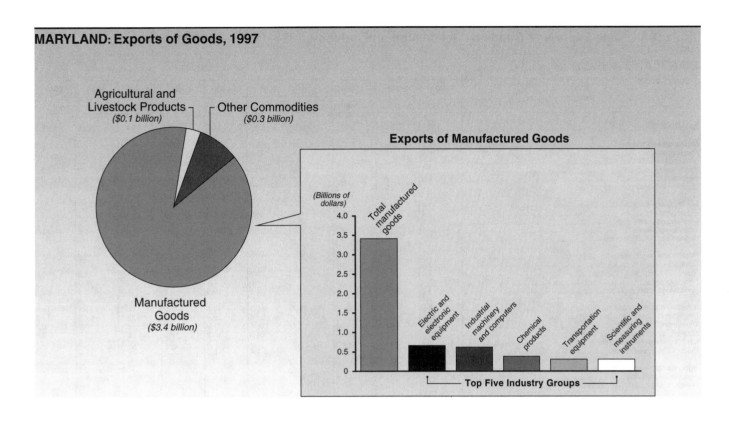

## Table D-3.   State Exports of Goods by Destination and Industry, 1993–1997 —*Continued*

**MARYLAND** (Millions of dollars.)

| Industry | 1993 | 1994 | 1995 | 1996 | 1997 | 1993 | 1994 | 1995 | 1996 | 1997 |
|---|---|---|---|---|---|---|---|---|---|---|
| | All destinations | | | | | Canada | | | | |
| **ALL GOODS** | 2 713.7 | 2 848.5 | 3 439.0 | 3 509.9 | 3 861.0 | 601.8 | 621.4 | 551.9 | 553.3 | 653.2 |
| **Manufactured goods** | 2 359.1 | 2 575.6 | 2 976.7 | 3 054.9 | 3 412.3 | 557.5 | 570.7 | 495.8 | 492.2 | 584.5 |
| Food products | 117.5 | 131.6 | 147.2 | 193.8 | 246.6 | 24.6 | 26.7 | 20.4 | 12.0 | 21.4 |
| Tobacco products | 0.1 | ..... | 5.8 | 0.2 | 0.3 | ..... | ..... | ..... | ..... | ..... |
| Textile mill products | 48.7 | 58.0 | 52.4 | 61.7 | 108.8 | 10.7 | 14.9 | 11.8 | 12.8 | 14.3 |
| Apparel | 18.0 | 22.2 | 25.2 | 30.0 | 32.1 | 4.7 | 5.6 | 6.9 | 7.7 | 6.1 |
| Lumber and wood products | 20.4 | 27.1 | 32.1 | 37.4 | 37.3 | 3.5 | 3.2 | 3.2 | 4.2 | 4.9 |
| Furniture and fixtures | 9.7 | 13.0 | 10.0 | 20.1 | 13.1 | 3.1 | 6.0 | 1.2 | 2.2 | 3.4 |
| Paper products | 33.4 | 34.5 | 37.2 | 40.2 | 34.2 | 25.6 | 26.5 | 20.7 | 20.1 | 21.0 |
| Printing and publishing | 71.3 | 131.9 | 133.4 | 129.6 | 135.9 | 15.6 | 24.6 | 29.5 | 29.1 | 27.6 |
| Chemical products | 307.2 | 316.0 | 379.8 | 393.9 | 384.3 | 93.8 | 91.1 | 77.4 | 68.4 | 84.4 |
| Refined petroleum products | 19.8 | 28.9 | 20.4 | 31.7 | 37.3 | 1.8 | 3.8 | 1.9 | 4.6 | 2.2 |
| Rubber and plastic products | 56.5 | 73.3 | 79.9 | 79.8 | 95.7 | 13.0 | 17.1 | 15.0 | 14.8 | 16.1 |
| Leather products | 13.4 | 4.4 | 5.3 | 7.2 | 5.2 | 2.6 | 2.3 | 2.7 | 1.6 | 1.1 |
| Stone, clay and glass products | 24.5 | 27.6 | 40.0 | 35.9 | 33.6 | 10.9 | 10.7 | 12.9 | 12.4 | 15.0 |
| Primary metals | 52.3 | 50.4 | 66.5 | 106.4 | 111.0 | 16.1 | 19.8 | 22.0 | 35.8 | 49.6 |
| Fabricated metal products | 180.3 | 182.0 | 168.5 | 189.1 | 162.8 | 23.1 | 22.7 | 24.4 | 18.9 | 26.2 |
| Industrial machinery and computers | 440.0 | 455.1 | 568.2 | 618.2 | 619.9 | 140.4 | 135.7 | 119.4 | 128.6 | 158.5 |
| Electric and electronic equipment | 318.4 | 345.7 | 498.6 | 485.6 | 662.8 | 58.9 | 58.5 | 56.3 | 52.2 | 57.6 |
| Transportation equipment | 322.0 | 360.8 | 312.0 | 268.2 | 310.8 | 40.3 | 48.9 | 26.6 | 27.1 | 34.2 |
| Scientific and measuring instruments | 233.4 | 254.7 | 310.6 | 255.3 | 309.8 | 48.0 | 41.6 | 33.6 | 30.4 | 28.4 |
| Miscellaneous manufactures | 27.7 | 23.6 | 33.5 | 31.3 | 33.8 | 9.7 | 8.5 | 6.6 | 6.3 | 8.6 |
| Unidentified manufactures | 44.3 | 34.8 | 50.0 | 39.2 | 37.1 | 11.1 | 2.6 | 3.1 | 3.0 | 3.8 |
| **Agricultural and livestock products** | 104.6 | 76.4 | 149.8 | 151.9 | 119.5 | 5.8 | 8.1 | 5.9 | 3.5 | 5.1 |
| Agricultural products | 103.6 | 74.9 | 149.0 | 150.3 | 115.9 | 5.3 | 7.0 | 5.8 | 3.2 | 3.8 |
| Livestock and livestock products | 1.0 | 1.5 | 0.9 | 1.6 | 3.5 | 0.5 | 1.1 | 0.1 | 0.4 | 1.3 |
| **Other commodities** | 250.1 | 196.4 | 312.4 | 303.1 | 329.2 | 38.5 | 42.6 | 50.2 | 57.5 | 63.5 |
| Forestry products | 1.9 | 2.4 | 3.4 | 2.5 | 2.5 | 1.0 | 0.8 | 0.6 | 0.9 | 0.4 |
| Fish and other marine products | 5.0 | 5.0 | 4.2 | 3.8 | 8.7 | 2.9 | 2.2 | 2.3 | 1.9 | 5.6 |
| Metallic ores and concentrates | 0.4 | 0.6 | 3.7 | 6.8 | 12.7 | ..... | ..... | ..... | ..... | 0.1 |
| Bituminous coal and lignite | 93.3 | 94.6 | 143.5 | 176.3 | 178.2 | ..... | 3.8 | 5.1 | 3.2 | 5.3 |
| Crude petroleum and natural gas | ..... | 0.5 | ..... | 1.6 | 1.4 | ..... | 0.5 | ..... | 1.5 | 1.4 |
| Nonmetallic minerals | 36.3 | 25.6 | 33.4 | 26.1 | 40.3 | 0.7 | 1.0 | 2.4 | 2.1 | 2.0 |
| Scrap and waste | 26.2 | 26.7 | 34.4 | 26.3 | 27.0 | 14.0 | 16.3 | 22.9 | 18.5 | 19.9 |
| Used merchandise | 43.1 | 13.9 | 12.3 | 15.1 | 17.4 | 0.4 | 3.4 | 0.6 | 2.3 | 5.7 |
| Goods imported and returned unchanged | 16.8 | 13.7 | 14.7 | 25.5 | 21.4 | 16.8 | 13.7 | 14.7 | 25.5 | 21.4 |
| Special classification provisions | 27.0 | 13.5 | 62.8 | 19.1 | 19.6 | 2.8 | 1.0 | 1.6 | 1.4 | 1.7 |

## Table D-3.  State Exports of Goods by Destination and Industry, 1993–1997 —*Continued*

**MARYLAND** (Millions of dollars.)

| Industry | 1993 | 1994 | 1995 | 1996 | 1997 | 1993 | 1994 | 1995 | 1996 | 1997 |
|---|---|---|---|---|---|---|---|---|---|---|
| | South and Central America and Caribbean | | | | | Mexico | | | | |
| **ALL GOODS** | 183.4 | 250.7 | 288.8 | 262.3 | 270.2 | 96.2 | 100.4 | 94.5 | 174.9 | 199.2 |
| **Manufactured goods** | 178.2 | 243.8 | 280.7 | 252.1 | 262.6 | 95.8 | 100.1 | 93.1 | 174.0 | 198.0 |
| Food products | 16.9 | 16.2 | 17.3 | 13.5 | 15.6 | 17.1 | 14.3 | 8.4 | 13.2 | 12.9 |
| Tobacco products | ..... | ..... | ..... | ..... | ..... | | | | | |
| Textile mill products | 1.3 | 2.7 | 2.3 | 2.3 | 3.9 | 2.0 | 2.1 | 2.2 | 2.2 | 2.7 |
| Apparel | 6.8 | 6.2 | 5.7 | 5.1 | 11.0 | 0.4 | 0.7 | 0.5 | 1.2 | 0.9 |
| Lumber and wood products | ..... | 0.2 | 0.3 | 0.5 | 0.6 | 0.1 | 0.1 | 0.1 | 0.4 | 0.2 |
| Furniture and fixtures | 1.4 | 0.5 | 0.8 | 0.8 | 1.0 | ..... | 0.1 | 2.8 | 12.1 | 3.7 |
| Paper products | 1.2 | 1.7 | 5.4 | 6.0 | 5.9 | 1.3 | 1.1 | 1.6 | 7.7 | 1.1 |
| Printing and publishing | 1.3 | 0.9 | 1.1 | 0.5 | 0.6 | 0.5 | 0.6 | 0.4 | 0.5 | 0.2 |
| Chemical products | 26.0 | 23.4 | 33.7 | 35.9 | 36.3 | 11.7 | 16.4 | 9.5 | 13.9 | 11.4 |
| Refined petroleum products | ..... | 0.2 | 0.2 | 0.1 | 0.1 | ..... | ..... | ..... | ..... | ..... |
| Rubber and plastic products | 2.4 | 6.8 | 9.7 | 6.2 | 6.8 | 3.6 | 4.5 | 5.9 | 10.0 | 6.5 |
| Leather products | 0.3 | 0.2 | 0.1 | 1.0 | 0.4 | ..... | ..... | ..... | ..... | 0.5 |
| Stone, clay and glass products | 3.4 | 2.4 | 2.3 | 1.0 | 3.8 | 0.6 | 0.5 | 1.0 | 3.2 | 0.9 |
| Primary metals | 13.7 | 7.3 | 2.4 | 5.1 | 7.0 | 1.7 | 2.0 | 4.0 | 6.9 | 5.9 |
| Fabricated metal products | 6.2 | 4.5 | 7.7 | 13.3 | 6.8 | 2.5 | 2.5 | 4.9 | 8.1 | 12.8 |
| Industrial machinery and computers | 36.7 | 56.2 | 98.8 | 85.3 | 82.1 | 17.6 | 25.0 | 16.2 | 16.6 | 14.8 |
| Electric and electronic equipment | 21.1 | 46.7 | 34.8 | 28.3 | 31.4 | 8.3 | 9.1 | 23.3 | 64.9 | 112.7 |
| Transportation equipment | 18.0 | 42.6 | 26.1 | 21.7 | 18.1 | 11.9 | 2.7 | 1.3 | 1.0 | 0.7 |
| Scientific and measuring instruments | 17.4 | 21.9 | 21.4 | 13.4 | 24.3 | 15.7 | 17.5 | 9.7 | 11.6 | 9.8 |
| Miscellaneous manufactures | 0.7 | 0.7 | 4.6 | 4.5 | 5.4 | 0.5 | 0.2 | 0.9 | 0.3 | 0.1 |
| Unidentified manufactures | 3.5 | 2.8 | 5.8 | 7.7 | 1.4 | 0.2 | 0.5 | 0.5 | 0.2 | 0.3 |
| **Agricultural and livestock products** | 1.8 | 1.9 | 2.0 | 3.1 | 2.0 | ..... | ..... | 1.1 | 0.1 | 0.2 |
| Agricultural products | 1.7 | 1.8 | 1.8 | 3.0 | 1.8 | ..... | ..... | 1.1 | 0.1 | 0.2 |
| Livestock and livestock products | ..... | 0.1 | 0.2 | 0.1 | 0.2 | ..... | ..... | ..... | ..... | ..... |
| **Other commodities** | 3.4 | 5.1 | 6.2 | 7.1 | 5.6 | 0.4 | 0.3 | 0.2 | 0.8 | 1.0 |
| Forestry products | 0.1 | 0.1 | 0.2 | 0.2 | 0.2 | 0.1 | 0.1 | 0.1 | 0.3 | 0.8 |
| Fish and other marine products | ..... | 0.4 | ..... | ..... | ..... | ..... | ..... | ..... | ..... | 0.1 |
| Metallic ores and concentrates | ..... | 0.1 | 0.3 | 0.8 | 1.3 | ..... | ..... | ..... | ..... | ..... |
| Bituminous coal and lignite | ..... | 1.3 | 1.5 | 3.2 | ..... | ..... | ..... | ..... | ..... | ..... |
| Crude petroleum and natural gas | ..... | ..... | ..... | ..... | ..... | ..... | ..... | ..... | 0.1 | ..... |
| Nonmetallic minerals | 1.0 | 0.9 | 1.9 | 1.5 | 1.2 | ..... | ..... | ..... | ..... | ..... |
| Scrap and waste | 0.4 | 0.9 | 0.6 | 0.3 | 0.5 | ..... | ..... | 0.1 | ..... | ..... |
| Used merchandise | 1.5 | 1.3 | 1.1 | 0.9 | 1.9 | 0.2 | ..... | ..... | ..... | 0.1 |
| Goods imported and returned unchanged | ..... | ..... | ..... | ..... | ..... | ..... | ..... | ..... | ..... | ..... |
| Special classification provisions | 0.5 | 0.2 | 0.7 | 0.3 | 0.4 | ..... | 0.1 | ..... | 0.3 | 0.1 |
| | European Union | | | | | United Kingdom | | | | |
| **ALL GOODS** | 849.3 | 886.9 | 1 167.7 | 1 076.3 | 1 077.5 | 163.6 | 189.9 | 329.9 | 308.6 | 286.7 |
| **Manufactured goods** | 725.3 | 804.9 | 969.7 | 963.8 | 962.3 | 142.1 | 180.7 | 318.3 | 295.0 | 278.2 |
| Food products | 6.1 | 8.4 | 8.3 | 10.2 | 12.8 | 1.0 | 0.9 | 2.0 | 1.7 | 4.4 |
| Tobacco products | ..... | ..... | 5.7 | | | ..... | ..... | ..... | | ..... |
| Textile mill products | 20.7 | 21.4 | 20.4 | 26.5 | 38.9 | 3.6 | 6.0 | 9.2 | 12.1 | 16.3 |
| Apparel | 2.9 | 3.6 | 4.5 | 6.1 | 5.1 | 0.6 | 1.1 | 0.8 | 0.7 | 1.7 |
| Lumber and wood products | 13.5 | 16.7 | 21.3 | 21.5 | 21.2 | 2.2 | 1.9 | 3.2 | 3.4 | 2.0 |
| Furniture and fixtures | 1.9 | 1.7 | 2.5 | 2.0 | 2.2 | 0.3 | 0.3 | 0.2 | 0.4 | 0.5 |
| Paper products | 1.3 | 1.0 | 1.6 | 1.6 | 1.8 | 0.4 | 0.3 | 0.8 | 0.6 | 0.9 |
| Printing and publishing | 43.6 | 97.5 | 87.4 | 75.7 | 89.0 | 23.2 | 54.7 | 71.5 | 68.2 | 71.4 |
| Chemical products | 99.2 | 106.6 | 161.0 | 167.2 | 130.3 | 15.8 | 21.0 | 45.0 | 54.0 | 28.2 |
| Refined petroleum products | 10.7 | 16.9 | 11.4 | 18.4 | 21.9 | 2.8 | 2.4 | 2.0 | 4.0 | 5.5 |
| Rubber and plastic products | 17.1 | 18.8 | 16.6 | 18.1 | 24.9 | 4.5 | 6.3 | 6.0 | 4.7 | 5.1 |
| Leather products | 0.9 | 0.8 | 1.7 | 4.0 | 2.4 | ..... | 0.2 | 0.1 | ..... | ..... |
| Stone, clay and glass products | 2.8 | 4.2 | 5.7 | 5.8 | 6.5 | 0.9 | 1.0 | 1.4 | 1.9 | 2.8 |
| Primary metals | 9.7 | 7.3 | 13.1 | 36.9 | 26.2 | 2.4 | 2.0 | 2.8 | 10.5 | 7.4 |
| Fabricated metal products | 97.4 | 86.3 | 70.9 | 90.6 | 28.6 | 4.3 | 4.0 | 5.2 | 3.3 | 6.1 |
| Industrial machinery and computers | 78.0 | 83.9 | 146.8 | 132.9 | 115.6 | 16.6 | 22.8 | 46.1 | 44.8 | 28.5 |
| Electric and electronic equipment | 83.2 | 84.2 | 119.6 | 116.5 | 145.8 | 23.0 | 25.5 | 56.5 | 51.8 | 65.5 |
| Transportation equipment | 155.1 | 164.1 | 131.7 | 129.8 | 189.9 | 26.8 | 13.3 | 9.3 | 10.3 | 11.4 |
| Scientific and measuring instruments | 67.0 | 71.5 | 121.1 | 87.2 | 88.5 | 11.2 | 14.6 | 53.4 | 17.0 | 16.2 |
| Miscellaneous manufactures | 7.0 | 5.4 | 8.4 | 8.6 | 7.7 | 1.7 | 1.5 | 2.2 | 5.3 | 3.8 |
| Unidentified manufactures | 7.2 | 4.5 | 10.0 | 4.1 | 3.0 | 0.8 | 0.7 | 0.7 | 0.4 | 0.5 |
| **Agricultural and livestock products** | 7.9 | 7.2 | 41.8 | 5.8 | 0.5 | 0.3 | 0.2 | 0.2 | 0.2 | 0.1 |
| Agricultural products | 7.7 | 6.8 | 41.5 | 5.6 | 0.4 | 0.1 | ..... | 0.1 | 0.1 | ..... |
| Livestock and livestock products | 0.2 | 0.3 | 0.3 | 0.2 | 0.1 | 0.1 | 0.2 | 0.1 | 0.1 | 0.1 |
| **Other commodities** | 116.1 | 74.8 | 156.1 | 106.8 | 114.7 | 21.2 | 9.1 | 11.4 | 13.4 | 8.4 |
| Forestry products | 0.1 | 0.7 | 1.6 | 0.2 | 0.2 | 0.1 | 0.5 | 1.6 | 0.1 | 0.2 |
| Fish and other marine products | 1.0 | 0.5 | 0.3 | 0.2 | 0.4 | 0.2 | 0.3 | 0.3 | 0.2 | 0.3 |
| Metallic ores and concentrates | 0.4 | 0.5 | 3.3 | 3.5 | 8.9 | ..... | ..... | 0.1 | 1.7 | 2.8 |
| Bituminous coal and lignite | 65.9 | 59.3 | 87.2 | 85.7 | 87.3 | 11.0 | 6.8 | 7.5 | 9.6 | 2.6 |
| Crude petroleum and natural gas | ..... | ..... | ..... | ..... | ..... | | | | | |
| Nonmetallic minerals | 1.0 | 1.1 | 1.6 | 2.9 | 5.2 | 0.1 | 0.2 | 0.2 | 0.1 | 0.1 |
| Scrap and waste | 0.5 | 1.1 | 1.3 | 0.7 | 0.2 | 0.3 | 0.3 | 0.1 | ..... | ..... |
| Used merchandise | 28.4 | 3.0 | 3.0 | 4.9 | 3.7 | 8.7 | 0.7 | 0.9 | 0.7 | 1.4 |
| Goods imported and returned unchanged | ..... | ..... | ..... | ..... | ..... | | | | | |
| Special classification provisions | 18.7 | 8.7 | 57.9 | 8.8 | 9.0 | 0.9 | 0.3 | 0.6 | 1.0 | 1.1 |

## Table D-3. State Exports of Goods by Destination and Industry, 1993–1997 —*Continued*

**MARYLAND** (Millions of dollars.)

| Industry | 1993 | 1994 | 1995 | 1996 | 1997 | 1993 | 1994 | 1995 | 1996 | 1997 |
|---|---|---|---|---|---|---|---|---|---|---|
| | Germany | | | | | France | | | | |
| **ALL GOODS** | 94.5 | 87.9 | 121.7 | 138.5 | 165.3 | 69.8 | 89.4 | 107.8 | 84.2 | 108.8 |
| **Manufactured goods** | 92.1 | 86.9 | 119.9 | 135.7 | 155.8 | 52.9 | 85.5 | 104.2 | 75.4 | 98.1 |
| Food products | 1.7 | 2.0 | 1.2 | 1.1 | 1.5 | ..... | ..... | ..... | 0.2 | ..... |
| Tobacco products | ..... | ..... | ..... | ..... | ..... | ..... | ..... | ..... | ..... | ..... |
| Textile mill products | 5.0 | 3.1 | 1.6 | 6.1 | 12.3 | 2.0 | 1.5 | 1.4 | 1.6 | 1.4 |
| Apparel | 0.2 | 0.4 | 1.1 | 1.6 | 0.7 | 0.3 | 0.3 | 0.3 | 0.4 | 0.4 |
| Lumber and wood products | 3.3 | 3.1 | 4.5 | 3.2 | 4.5 | 0.3 | 0.4 | 0.1 | 0.4 | 0.1 |
| Furniture and fixtures | 0.2 | 0.3 | 1.4 | 1.0 | 0.8 | 0.4 | 0.3 | 0.2 | 0.1 | 0.1 |
| Paper products | 0.4 | 0.2 | 0.1 | 0.3 | 0.3 | 0.1 | 0.1 | 0.1 | ..... | ..... |
| Printing and publishing | 5.7 | 9.2 | 3.0 | 1.6 | 7.4 | 4.1 | 14.6 | 6.3 | 3.8 | 7.6 |
| Chemical products | 14.2 | 18.7 | 34.5 | 38.5 | 33.6 | 10.7 | 5.6 | 13.7 | 8.6 | 6.2 |
| Refined petroleum products | ..... | ..... | ..... | 0.1 | 0.1 | 1.1 | ..... | ..... | ..... | ..... |
| Rubber and plastic products | 4.4 | 5.5 | 3.3 | 5.1 | 5.6 | 2.0 | 1.6 | 1.4 | 2.4 | 1.6 |
| Leather products | ..... | ..... | 0.4 | 0.8 | 1.1 | 0.3 | 0.1 | 0.4 | 2.4 | 0.1 |
| Stone, clay and glass products | 0.3 | 0.3 | 0.7 | 0.6 | 0.6 | 0.4 | 1.6 | 2.7 | 2.4 | 0.7 |
| Primary metals | 1.2 | 0.6 | 0.4 | 5.2 | 5.2 | 0.5 | 0.2 | 0.4 | 0.4 | 0.3 |
| Fabricated metal products | 1.1 | 0.9 | 0.5 | 4.2 | 1.0 | 0.5 | 0.2 | 1.1 | 0.3 | 0.4 |
| Industrial machinery and computers | 16.3 | 13.6 | 26.3 | 27.3 | 37.6 | 6.1 | 8.7 | 15.1 | 14.4 | 15.6 |
| Electric and electronic equipment | 19.9 | 14.8 | 19.1 | 15.8 | 13.1 | 8.8 | 11.3 | 15.0 | 15.1 | 9.4 |
| Transportation equipment | 7.0 | 4.1 | 8.9 | 8.5 | 17.3 | 4.7 | 31.1 | 37.3 | 13.1 | 35.6 |
| Scientific and measuring instruments | 8.7 | 7.8 | 10.5 | 11.8 | 11.4 | 9.4 | 7.1 | 7.5 | 9.0 | 17.9 |
| Miscellaneous manufactures | 1.3 | 1.7 | 1.7 | 1.1 | 1.3 | 0.9 | 0.4 | 1.0 | 0.4 | 0.4 |
| Unidentified manufactures | 1.2 | 0.6 | 0.6 | 1.8 | 0.3 | 0.4 | 0.4 | 0.3 | 0.2 | 0.2 |
| **Agricultural and livestock products** | 0.1 | 0.1 | 0.3 | 0.3 | 0.1 | ..... | ..... | 0.1 | ..... | ..... |
| Agricultural products | ..... | ..... | 0.3 | 0.2 | 0.1 | ..... | ..... | ..... | ..... | ..... |
| Livestock and livestock products | ..... | 0.1 | ..... | ..... | ..... | ..... | ..... | 0.1 | ..... | ..... |
| **Other commodities** | 2.3 | 0.9 | 1.5 | 2.6 | 9.4 | 16.9 | 3.9 | 3.5 | 8.7 | 10.7 |
| Forestry products | ..... | 0.1 | ..... | ..... | ..... | ..... | ..... | ..... | ..... | ..... |
| Fish and other marine products | ..... | ..... | ..... | ..... | ..... | ..... | ..... | ..... | ..... | ..... |
| Metallic ores and concentrates | ..... | ..... | ..... | ..... | 2.9 | ..... | 0.1 | ..... | 0.2 | 0.1 |
| Bituminous coal and lignite | ..... | ..... | 0.5 | ..... | 4.0 | 3.9 | 2.2 | 2.0 | 6.6 | 8.8 |
| Crude petroleum and natural gas | ..... | ..... | ..... | ..... | ..... | ..... | ..... | ..... | ..... | ..... |
| Nonmetallic minerals | 0.1 | 0.1 | 0.1 | 0.2 | 1.5 | ..... | ..... | ..... | ..... | 0.1 |
| Scrap and waste | ..... | ..... | 0.3 | 0.3 | ..... | 0.1 | ..... | 0.3 | ..... | ..... |
| Used merchandise | 2.0 | 0.6 | 0.4 | 1.7 | 0.9 | 12.6 | 0.5 | 0.4 | 0.2 | 0.9 |
| Goods imported and returned unchanged | ..... | ..... | ..... | ..... | ..... | ..... | ..... | ..... | ..... | ..... |
| Special classification provisions | 0.2 | 0.2 | 0.3 | 0.3 | 0.2 | 0.2 | 1.0 | 0.8 | 1.6 | 0.9 |
| | The Netherlands | | | | | Asian 10 | | | | |
| **ALL GOODS** | 211.4 | 167.9 | 226.6 | 201.8 | 128.3 | 448.1 | 448.6 | 608.8 | 663.8 | 766.2 |
| **Manufactured goods** | 181.0 | 152.9 | 162.1 | 185.3 | 101.7 | 384.6 | 411.8 | 564.1 | 628.7 | 723.1 |
| Food products | 0.7 | 0.3 | 0.9 | 1.4 | 2.2 | 20.0 | 30.9 | 35.0 | 37.3 | 36.2 |
| Tobacco products | ..... | ..... | ..... | ..... | ..... | ..... | ..... | ..... | 0.2 | 0.2 |
| Textile mill products | 0.8 | 0.7 | 0.3 | 0.4 | 1.5 | 8.2 | 11.1 | 8.5 | 11.8 | 37.1 |
| Apparel | 0.2 | 0.6 | 0.2 | 0.5 | 0.7 | 1.0 | 3.5 | 5.7 | 7.4 | 6.0 |
| Lumber and wood products | 0.9 | 1.3 | 1.3 | 2.4 | 1.5 | 2.6 | 5.3 | 4.4 | 8.7 | 8.5 |
| Furniture and fixtures | 0.1 | 0.2 | 0.2 | 0.2 | ..... | 0.3 | 1.3 | 0.7 | 0.8 | 0.9 |
| Paper products | 0.2 | 0.1 | 0.1 | 0.2 | ..... | 3.4 | 3.2 | 3.1 | 2.9 | 2.1 |
| Printing and publishing | 9.1 | 18.0 | 5.5 | 0.9 | 0.5 | 3.6 | 3.9 | 7.6 | 9.3 | 3.3 |
| Chemical products | 23.1 | 15.9 | 16.4 | 14.5 | 8.1 | 55.0 | 50.3 | 64.4 | 74.6 | 85.1 |
| Refined petroleum products | 0.6 | 1.8 | 1.8 | 3.7 | 9.1 | 0.2 | 0.2 | 0.6 | 2.0 | 2.0 |
| Rubber and plastic products | 1.2 | 0.5 | 0.9 | 1.5 | 1.5 | 10.3 | 12.1 | 13.8 | 9.6 | 16.4 |
| Leather products | 0.1 | 0.2 | 0.3 | 0.3 | 0.6 | 9.1 | 0.4 | 0.5 | 0.3 | 0.5 |
| Stone, clay and glass products | 0.8 | 1.0 | 0.6 | 0.5 | 0.8 | 4.6 | 7.3 | 14.7 | 11.4 | 5.4 |
| Primary metals | 0.8 | 1.4 | 5.3 | 10.0 | 2.7 | 8.2 | 10.2 | 16.2 | 12.6 | 10.4 |
| Fabricated metal products | 55.0 | 44.4 | 45.1 | 75.8 | 12.0 | 9.8 | 27.4 | 22.5 | 40.4 | 38.0 |
| Industrial machinery and computers | 20.0 | 16.4 | 19.7 | 14.1 | 7.0 | 84.8 | 83.9 | 110.9 | 165.2 | 132.1 |
| Electric and electronic equipment | 4.2 | 3.3 | 6.4 | 8.6 | 22.2 | 81.6 | 76.9 | 167.1 | 135.1 | 189.3 |
| Transportation equipment | 59.5 | 43.5 | 49.3 | 41.4 | 26.5 | 23.0 | 20.9 | 21.7 | 19.3 | 17.9 |
| Scientific and measuring instruments | 2.1 | 2.5 | 5.1 | 7.8 | 4.0 | 43.9 | 54.6 | 54.7 | 67.6 | 116.6 |
| Miscellaneous manufactures | 1.5 | 0.6 | 2.0 | 1.0 | 0.5 | 7.1 | 5.9 | 8.0 | 9.4 | 8.4 |
| Unidentified manufactures | 0.2 | 0.2 | 0.5 | 0.1 | 0.1 | 8.1 | 2.5 | 3.7 | 3.0 | 6.7 |
| **Agricultural and livestock products** | ..... | ..... | 0.1 | ..... | 0.2 | 9.3 | 1.3 | 3.7 | 1.1 | 2.1 |
| Agricultural products | ..... | ..... | 0.1 | ..... | 0.2 | 9.3 | 1.3 | 3.6 | 0.2 | 0.4 |
| Livestock and livestock products | ..... | ..... | ..... | ..... | ..... | ..... | ..... | 0.1 | 0.9 | 1.8 |
| **Other commodities** | 30.4 | 14.9 | 64.4 | 16.4 | 26.4 | 54.1 | 35.6 | 41.1 | 34.0 | 40.9 |
| Forestry products | ..... | ..... | ..... | ..... | ..... | 0.5 | 0.6 | 0.6 | 0.7 | 0.6 |
| Fish and other marine products | 0.8 | ..... | ..... | ..... | 0.1 | 1.0 | 1.8 | 1.6 | 1.3 | 1.8 |
| Metallic ores and concentrates | 0.3 | 0.2 | 2.9 | 1.3 | 1.3 | ..... | ..... | 0.1 | 2.2 | 1.1 |
| Bituminous coal and lignite | 8.7 | 7.3 | 5.5 | 7.7 | 17.8 | 7.4 | 1.1 | 0.6 | 1.0 | ..... |
| Crude petroleum and natural gas | ..... | ..... | ..... | ..... | ..... | ..... | ..... | ..... | ..... | ..... |
| Nonmetallic minerals | ..... | ..... | 0.1 | 0.4 | 0.6 | 33.3 | 22.3 | 26.6 | 18.7 | 31.6 |
| Scrap and waste | ..... | 0.3 | 0.1 | 0.1 | ..... | 8.1 | 6.0 | 6.3 | 2.4 | 1.5 |
| Used merchandise | 4.1 | 0.3 | ..... | 1.7 | 0.2 | 1.8 | 2.2 | 3.8 | 1.9 | 0.5 |
| Goods imported and returned unchanged | ..... | ..... | ..... | ..... | ..... | ..... | ..... | ..... | ..... | ..... |
| Special classification provisions | 16.5 | 6.9 | 55.8 | 5.2 | 6.4 | 2.0 | 1.4 | 1.4 | 5.8 | 3.9 |

## Table D-3.  State Exports of Goods by Destination and Industry, 1993–1997 —*Continued*

**MARYLAND** (Millions of dollars.)

| Industry | 1993 | 1994 | 1995 | 1996 | 1997 | 1993 | 1994 | 1995 | 1996 | 1997 |
|---|---|---|---|---|---|---|---|---|---|---|
| | Japan | | | | | South Korea | | | | |
| **ALL GOODS** | 163.1 | 134.3 | 153.1 | 171.1 | 158.6 | 44.2 | 48.1 | 60.8 | 74.6 | 95.4 |
| **Manufactured goods** | 127.9 | 122.7 | 138.8 | 160.0 | 148.4 | 35.2 | 41.9 | 53.9 | 70.5 | 88.0 |
| Food products | 8.3 | 10.7 | 13.2 | 15.6 | 6.8 | 0.8 | 1.5 | 2.2 | 3.5 | 4.1 |
| Tobacco products | ..... | ..... | ..... | 0.2 | ..... | ..... | ..... | ..... | ..... | 0.2 |
| Textile mill products | 1.7 | 2.4 | 2.8 | 3.2 | 3.0 | 1.6 | 1.5 | 1.2 | 1.6 | 4.2 |
| Apparel | 0.5 | 2.9 | 4.9 | 6.2 | 3.0 | 0.1 | 0.1 | ..... | 0.4 | 1.2 |
| Lumber and wood products | 1.5 | 3.1 | 2.2 | 1.2 | 2.0 | 0.1 | 0.1 | 0.2 | 1.1 | 0.9 |
| Furniture and fixtures | 0.2 | 0.6 | 0.1 | 0.3 | 0.3 | ..... | ..... | ..... | 0.2 | 0.1 |
| Paper products | 0.5 | 0.3 | 0.9 | 0.5 | 0.5 | ..... | ..... | 0.1 | 0.2 | 0.1 |
| Printing and publishing | 2.0 | 1.7 | 3.4 | 1.9 | 0.9 | 0.4 | 0.6 | 0.7 | 1.5 | 0.7 |
| Chemical products | 37.5 | 30.5 | 28.7 | 32.9 | 37.8 | 2.9 | 3.9 | 7.2 | 10.6 | 12.3 |
| Refined petroleum products | ..... | ..... | ..... | 0.1 | 0.2 | ..... | ..... | 0.1 | 0.2 | 0.2 |
| Rubber and plastic products | 4.5 | 6.2 | 7.5 | 1.6 | 4.3 | 2.3 | 2.2 | 2.0 | 1.9 | 1.5 |
| Leather products | 8.5 | 0.2 | 0.2 | 0.2 | 0.1 | 0.2 | ..... | ..... | ..... | 0.1 |
| Stone, clay and glass products | 0.2 | 0.1 | 0.8 | 0.6 | 0.4 | 0.6 | 0.8 | 1.2 | 1.2 | 1.2 |
| Primary metals | 3.9 | 4.1 | 2.1 | 4.8 | 2.5 | ..... | 0.1 | 1.7 | 0.7 | 0.4 |
| Fabricated metal products | 1.2 | 3.8 | 1.9 | 20.2 | 3.7 | 1.4 | 2.2 | 2.8 | 3.1 | 3.9 |
| Industrial machinery and computers | 8.9 | 8.2 | 10.2 | 16.4 | 20.6 | 6.6 | 12.8 | 12.8 | 18.1 | 22.7 |
| Electric and electronic equipment | 11.8 | 23.0 | 22.2 | 26.4 | 25.1 | 9.9 | 8.6 | 12.7 | 10.3 | 18.6 |
| Transportation equipment | 8.7 | 3.6 | 16.7 | 6.8 | 3.3 | 1.8 | 0.3 | 0.5 | 4.8 | 0.9 |
| Scientific and measuring instruments | 18.4 | 18.5 | 15.4 | 15.8 | 27.5 | 6.1 | 6.6 | 7.0 | 10.0 | 13.2 |
| Miscellaneous manufactures | 3.5 | 2.2 | 3.1 | 3.1 | 1.5 | 0.5 | 0.4 | 1.1 | 1.0 | 0.9 |
| Unidentified manufactures | 6.1 | 0.5 | 2.4 | 1.9 | 5.0 | 0.1 | 0.2 | 0.2 | 0.2 | 0.6 |
| **Agricultural and livestock products** | 7.8 | ..... | 1.2 | 0.3 | 0.2 | ..... | 0.1 | ..... | ..... | 1.1 |
| Agricultural products | 7.8 | ..... | 1.1 | 0.2 | 0.2 | ..... | 0.1 | ..... | ..... | ..... |
| Livestock and livestock products | ..... | ..... | 0.1 | 0.1 | ..... | ..... | ..... | ..... | ..... | 1.1 |
| **Other commodities** | 27.4 | 11.5 | 13.1 | 10.8 | 10.0 | 9.0 | 6.1 | 6.9 | 4.0 | 6.3 |
| Forestry products | 0.5 | 0.2 | 0.1 | 0.2 | 0.3 | ..... | 0.3 | 0.5 | 0.2 | 0.1 |
| Fish and other marine products | 1.0 | 1.4 | 1.5 | 1.3 | 1.6 | ..... | 0.4 | ..... | ..... | 0.1 |
| Metallic ores and concentrates | ..... | ..... | 0.1 | 1.3 | 0.2 | ..... | ..... | ..... | 0.6 | 0.2 |
| Bituminous coal and lignite | 3.8 | 1.1 | 0.6 | 1.0 | ..... | 3.6 | ..... | ..... | ..... | ..... |
| Crude petroleum and natural gas | ..... | ..... | ..... | ..... | ..... | ..... | ..... | ..... | ..... | ..... |
| Nonmetallic minerals | 20.0 | 6.6 | 7.1 | 5.1 | 7.0 | 4.8 | 5.2 | 6.1 | 3.0 | 5.6 |
| Scrap and waste | ..... | ..... | 0.1 | ..... | 0.1 | ..... | ..... | ..... | ..... | ..... |
| Used merchandise | 1.5 | 1.8 | 3.2 | 1.2 | 0.3 | ..... | ..... | ..... | ..... | ..... |
| Goods imported and returned unchanged | ..... | ..... | ..... | ..... | ..... | ..... | ..... | ..... | ..... | ..... |
| Special classification provisions | 0.6 | 0.4 | 0.5 | 0.7 | 0.6 | 0.6 | 0.1 | 0.3 | 0.1 | 0.3 |
| | Taiwan | | | | | Singapore | | | | |
| **ALL GOODS** | 68.3 | 67.2 | 66.0 | 57.4 | 64.7 | 29.5 | 31.6 | 64.5 | 72.5 | 51.4 |
| **Manufactured goods** | 57.0 | 54.2 | 52.4 | 47.8 | 48.9 | 28.7 | 30.7 | 63.1 | 71.7 | 51.1 |
| Food products | 0.6 | 0.4 | 0.2 | 0.4 | 0.2 | 0.6 | 1.1 | 0.7 | 0.6 | 1.4 |
| Tobacco products | ..... | ..... | ..... | ..... | ..... | ..... | ..... | ..... | ..... | ..... |
| Textile mill products | 0.4 | 0.5 | 0.3 | 0.7 | 2.1 | 1.5 | 2.7 | 1.2 | 1.0 | 1.0 |
| Apparel | ..... | ..... | 0.2 | 0.2 | 0.6 | ..... | ..... | 0.3 | 0.1 | ..... |
| Lumber and wood products | 0.7 | 1.1 | 0.7 | 2.9 | 0.3 | 0.1 | 0.1 | 0.1 | ..... | 0.1 |
| Furniture and fixtures | ..... | ..... | 0.4 | ..... | ..... | ..... | ..... | ..... | 0.1 | 0.2 |
| Paper products | 0.5 | ..... | 0.2 | ..... | ..... | 0.1 | 0.1 | 0.1 | 0.1 | 0.1 |
| Printing and publishing | 0.5 | ..... | 0.1 | 0.2 | 0.3 | 0.1 | ..... | 0.1 | 0.4 | 0.4 |
| Chemical products | 2.5 | 3.0 | 4.4 | 5.3 | 5.1 | 5.2 | 7.3 | 15.2 | 15.8 | 14.5 |
| Refined petroleum products | ..... | ..... | ..... | 0.1 | 0.1 | ..... | ..... | ..... | 0.6 | 0.6 |
| Rubber and plastic products | 1.0 | 1.3 | 0.9 | 0.5 | 0.7 | 0.6 | 0.3 | 1.1 | 0.7 | 0.9 |
| Leather products | ..... | 0.1 | ..... | ..... | ..... | ..... | ..... | ..... | ..... | ..... |
| Stone, clay and glass products | 0.9 | 3.5 | 3.0 | 0.2 | 0.3 | 0.1 | ..... | 0.1 | 1.1 | 0.5 |
| Primary metals | 0.4 | 2.4 | 6.5 | 0.3 | 0.3 | 0.5 | 0.1 | 0.5 | 0.1 | 0.3 |
| Fabricated metal products | 2.0 | 14.6 | 4.2 | 6.0 | 5.3 | 1.9 | 1.6 | 3.2 | 2.0 | 1.6 |
| Industrial machinery and computers | 23.4 | 7.2 | 15.5 | 18.3 | 12.8 | 7.5 | 8.3 | 22.1 | 39.4 | 18.0 |
| Electric and electronic equipment | 13.0 | 10.6 | 8.9 | 6.4 | 12.1 | 4.8 | 2.4 | 6.1 | 3.9 | 5.5 |
| Transportation equipment | 0.7 | 1.5 | 1.1 | 2.2 | 2.8 | 0.6 | 1.4 | 0.6 | 0.7 | 0.5 |
| Scientific and measuring instruments | 9.2 | 6.8 | 5.4 | 3.8 | 5.2 | 4.5 | 4.7 | 11.6 | 4.4 | 3.6 |
| Miscellaneous manufactures | 0.3 | 0.5 | 0.2 | 0.1 | 0.3 | 0.6 | 0.6 | 0.2 | 0.6 | 1.8 |
| Unidentified manufactures | 1.0 | 0.6 | 0.2 | 0.1 | 0.2 | 0.1 | 0.2 | 0.1 | 0.2 | 0.1 |
| **Agricultural and livestock products** | ..... | ..... | 0.1 | ..... | ..... | ..... | ..... | ..... | ..... | ..... |
| Agricultural products | ..... | ..... | 0.1 | ..... | ..... | ..... | ..... | ..... | ..... | ..... |
| Livestock and livestock products | ..... | ..... | ..... | ..... | ..... | ..... | ..... | ..... | ..... | ..... |
| **Other commodities** | 11.2 | 13.1 | 13.6 | 9.6 | 15.8 | 0.8 | 0.9 | 1.4 | 0.8 | 0.3 |
| Forestry products | ..... | ..... | ..... | 0.1 | ..... | ..... | ..... | ..... | ..... | ..... |
| Fish and other marine products | ..... | ..... | ..... | ..... | ..... | ..... | ..... | ..... | ..... | ..... |
| Metallic ores and concentrates | ..... | ..... | ..... | 0.1 | 0.1 | ..... | ..... | ..... | ..... | ..... |
| Bituminous coal and lignite | ..... | ..... | ..... | ..... | ..... | ..... | ..... | ..... | ..... | ..... |
| Crude petroleum and natural gas | ..... | ..... | ..... | ..... | ..... | ..... | ..... | ..... | ..... | ..... |
| Nonmetallic minerals | 6.7 | 7.7 | 9.3 | 8.6 | 15.4 | 0.1 | 0.4 | 1.2 | 0.4 | 0.2 |
| Scrap and waste | 4.3 | 4.9 | 3.7 | 0.8 | ..... | ..... | ..... | ..... | 0.3 | ..... |
| Used merchandise | ..... | ..... | 0.4 | ..... | 0.1 | 0.1 | 0.3 | 0.1 | 0.1 | ..... |
| Goods imported and returned unchanged | ..... | ..... | ..... | ..... | ..... | ..... | ..... | ..... | ..... | ..... |
| Special classification provisions | 0.1 | 0.4 | 0.1 | 0.1 | 0.2 | 0.5 | 0.1 | 0.1 | 0.1 | 0.1 |

## MASSACHUSSETTS: Exports of Goods, 1997

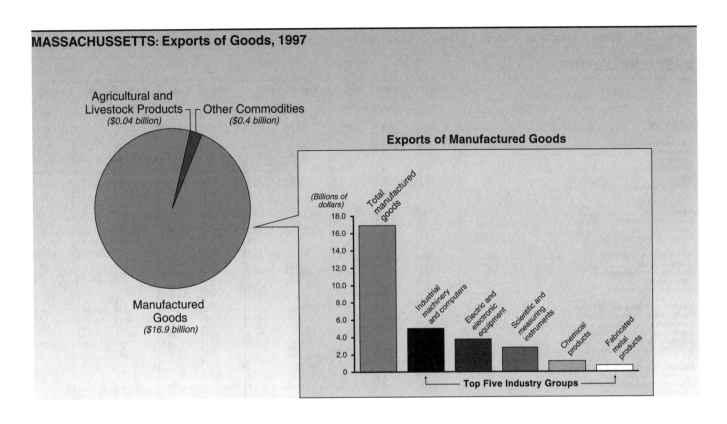

## Table D-3.   State Exports of Goods by Destination and Industry, 1993–1997 —*Continued*

### MASSACHUSSETTS (Millions of dollars.)

| Industry | 1993 | 1994 | 1995 | 1996 | 1997 | 1993 | 1994 | 1995 | 1996 | 1997 |
|---|---|---|---|---|---|---|---|---|---|---|
| | All destinations | | | | | Canada | | | | |
| **ALL GOODS** | 11 594.0 | 12 586.0 | 14 396.4 | 15 368.4 | 17 368.1 | 2 540.6 | 2 860.4 | 3 339.9 | 3 486.8 | 3 677.5 |
| **Manufactured goods** | 11 134.2 | 12 132.8 | 13 930.7 | 14 864.6 | 16 918.9 | 2 381.9 | 2 696.4 | 3 140.3 | 3 294.5 | 3 507.6 |
| Food products | 125.3 | 162.0 | 199.8 | 276.1 | 300.8 | 34.5 | 35.4 | 44.4 | 46.6 | 70.0 |
| Tobacco products | 0.1 | 0.1 | ..... | ..... | 0.1 | 0.1 | ..... | ..... | ..... | 0.1 |
| Textile mill products | 220.2 | 216.5 | 227.5 | 215.8 | 263.9 | 59.0 | 58.7 | 75.4 | 96.7 | 114.9 |
| Apparel | 84.5 | 77.0 | 106.1 | 100.9 | 88.6 | 32.6 | 30.6 | 54.5 | 46.4 | 36.2 |
| Lumber and wood products | 78.5 | 79.2 | 92.1 | 100.7 | 129.9 | 7.9 | 7.8 | 9.2 | 12.5 | 17.2 |
| Furniture and fixtures | 21.8 | 22.3 | 23.6 | 23.9 | 31.5 | 7.7 | 9.6 | 13.3 | 10.3 | 11.2 |
| Paper products | 236.6 | 271.4 | 359.2 | 398.3 | 431.1 | 94.9 | 104.4 | 123.9 | 141.8 | 148.4 |
| Printing and publishing | 173.4 | 148.1 | 167.3 | 178.7 | 201.9 | 38.7 | 59.5 | 66.6 | 75.2 | 86.7 |
| Chemical products | 558.7 | 716.7 | 896.2 | 1 023.9 | 1 225.1 | 141.7 | 180.1 | 183.2 | 227.2 | 226.4 |
| Refined petroleum products | 97.7 | 25.9 | 45.1 | 60.6 | 32.5 | 33.3 | 3.2 | 13.1 | 19.4 | 19.1 |
| Rubber and plastic products | 426.2 | 470.2 | 466.0 | 404.4 | 453.2 | 68.2 | 71.1 | 87.1 | 84.1 | 83.3 |
| Leather products | 126.8 | 123.4 | 111.6 | 99.4 | 118.3 | 19.4 | 19.8 | 21.3 | 19.1 | 18.2 |
| Stone, clay and glass products | 76.1 | 77.7 | 91.1 | 90.9 | 100.2 | 20.8 | 23.7 | 26.1 | 25.4 | 23.5 |
| Primary metals | 177.4 | 193.6 | 219.9 | 252.9 | 345.0 | 45.6 | 51.5 | 58.3 | 56.6 | 86.9 |
| Fabricated metal products | 451.0 | 448.6 | 476.2 | 476.2 | 550.4 | 106.4 | 125.3 | 143.3 | 160.1 | 150.8 |
| Industrial machinery and computers | 3 645.3 | 3 908.0 | 4 318.7 | 4 599.4 | 5 017.7 | 830.9 | 900.5 | 941.9 | 998.7 | 1 012.9 |
| Electric and electronic equipment | 2 128.6 | 2 688.4 | 3 262.7 | 3 214.1 | 3 779.6 | 431.7 | 584.3 | 759.2 | 672.0 | 708.6 |
| Transportation equipment | 352.2 | 308.2 | 393.6 | 498.3 | 553.4 | 178.8 | 191.7 | 262.4 | 351.5 | 420.9 |
| Scientific and measuring instruments | 1 877.8 | 1 909.6 | 2 159.2 | 2 470.6 | 2 809.0 | 159.3 | 164.8 | 174.0 | 165.0 | 179.4 |
| Miscellaneous manufactures | 195.3 | 201.8 | 233.8 | 237.0 | 264.6 | 58.4 | 56.8 | 63.0 | 66.0 | 69.3 |
| Unidentified manufactures | 80.8 | 84.1 | 81.1 | 68.1 | 66.8 | 11.9 | 17.5 | 20.0 | 19.6 | 23.7 |
| **Agricultural and livestock products** | 46.3 | 50.3 | 46.3 | 42.3 | 37.7 | 37.7 | 33.3 | 29.9 | 25.2 | 23.9 |
| Agricultural products | 43.0 | 42.9 | 39.1 | 36.6 | 30.4 | 35.9 | 32.3 | 28.1 | 22.2 | 20.5 |
| Livestock and livestock products | 3.3 | 7.4 | 7.2 | 5.6 | 7.3 | 1.7 | 1.0 | 1.8 | 2.9 | 3.4 |
| **Other commodities** | 413.5 | 402.9 | 419.3 | 461.6 | 411.5 | 121.1 | 130.7 | 169.7 | 167.1 | 146.0 |
| Forestry products | 12.4 | 9.0 | 5.5 | 3.4 | 3.0 | 0.8 | 0.4 | 0.4 | 0.7 | 0.8 |
| Fish and other marine products | 149.9 | 171.2 | 180.6 | 186.0 | 162.1 | 42.0 | 45.0 | 52.0 | 54.4 | 42.2 |
| Metallic ores and concentrates | 0.3 | 0.6 | 2.8 | 0.7 | 1.0 | 0.2 | 0.2 | 2.6 | 0.3 | ..... |
| Bituminous coal and lignite | 5.2 | 1.8 | ..... | 0.6 | 1.9 | ..... | ..... | ..... | 0.6 | ..... |
| Crude petroleum and natural gas | 2.2 | 0.3 | 0.3 | 1.0 | 1.4 | 2.0 | 0.1 | ..... | 0.8 | 1.0 |
| Nonmetallic minerals | 8.4 | 7.4 | 8.9 | 6.9 | 7.9 | 0.9 | 1.2 | 1.9 | 1.5 | 1.9 |
| Scrap and waste | 85.3 | 86.7 | 95.3 | 66.2 | 71.5 | 24.2 | 29.6 | 51.2 | 29.8 | 34.1 |
| Used merchandise | 33.3 | 17.3 | 18.7 | 28.0 | 30.1 | 6.3 | 4.1 | 3.6 | 5.7 | 3.9 |
| Goods imported and returned unchanged | 39.3 | 43.9 | 40.9 | 57.1 | 54.5 | 39.3 | 43.9 | 40.9 | 57.1 | 54.5 |
| Special classification provisions | 77.2 | 64.6 | 66.3 | 111.7 | 78.0 | 5.2 | 6.3 | 17.0 | 16.3 | 7.7 |

## Table D-3.  State Exports of Goods by Destination and Industry, 1993–1997 —*Continued*

### MASSACHUSSETTS (Millions of dollars.)

| Industry | 1993 | 1994 | 1995 | 1996 | 1997 | 1993 | 1994 | 1995 | 1996 | 1997 |
|---|---|---|---|---|---|---|---|---|---|---|
| | South and Central America and Caribbean | | | | | Mexico | | | | |
| **ALL GOODS** | 428.9 | 464.7 | 542.7 | 582.8 | 677.4 | 374.4 | 535.1 | 316.7 | 388.8 | 467.6 |
| **Manufactured goods** | 421.4 | 455.5 | 538.0 | 573.5 | 668.9 | 361.3 | 522.0 | 308.9 | 383.3 | 465.0 |
| Food products | 13.5 | 17.7 | 24.5 | 25.8 | 27.7 | 6.0 | 4.8 | 3.6 | 5.6 | 8.3 |
| Tobacco products | ..... | ..... | ..... | ..... | ..... | ..... | ..... | ..... | ..... | |
| Textile mill products | 7.0 | 9.1 | 5.8 | 6.1 | 9.3 | 10.9 | 9.1 | 4.2 | 5.9 | 9.4 |
| Apparel | 9.5 | 13.7 | 12.7 | 12.5 | 10.2 | 3.9 | 1.3 | 0.8 | 2.0 | 1.9 |
| Lumber and wood products | 0.8 | 0.3 | 0.4 | 0.3 | 1.1 | 0.7 | 0.3 | 0.1 | 0.1 | 1.3 |
| Furniture and fixtures | 0.9 | 1.4 | 1.3 | 1.0 | 1.5 | 2.1 | 0.8 | 0.5 | 0.7 | 0.6 |
| Paper products | 17.5 | 18.9 | 35.5 | 30.7 | 24.7 | 8.7 | 14.6 | 15.3 | 9.5 | 13.3 |
| Printing and publishing | 5.4 | 4.2 | 6.8 | 3.6 | 5.9 | 2.1 | 2.6 | 1.9 | 3.1 | 2.2 |
| Chemical products | 30.7 | 40.7 | 79.6 | 79.2 | 98.4 | 12.1 | 38.4 | 41.7 | 49.3 | 75.1 |
| Refined petroleum products | 6.1 | 0.8 | 0.3 | 0.2 | 0.4 | 0.1 | 0.2 | 0.4 | 0.4 | 0.7 |
| Rubber and plastic products | 14.0 | 15.8 | 18.6 | 25.3 | 25.6 | 9.5 | 9.9 | 8.5 | 11.8 | 14.7 |
| Leather products | 12.7 | 12.3 | 11.6 | 13.0 | 8.9 | 13.5 | 10.9 | 6.4 | 8.3 | 11.5 |
| Stone, clay and glass products | 4.9 | 3.1 | 4.4 | 3.6 | 5.1 | 4.7 | 2.6 | 3.9 | 2.9 | 3.0 |
| Primary metals | 4.1 | 3.5 | 3.8 | 4.0 | 3.9 | 2.5 | 24.0 | 13.8 | 5.3 | 3.6 |
| Fabricated metal products | 33.4 | 39.9 | 52.2 | 44.8 | 34.5 | 19.8 | 25.2 | 21.6 | 22.8 | 29.1 |
| Industrial machinery and computers | 142.4 | 152.6 | 141.8 | 166.0 | 215.2 | 119.6 | 143.8 | 83.1 | 123.3 | 144.9 |
| Electric and electronic equipment | 43.1 | 55.0 | 69.1 | 76.0 | 95.0 | 79.9 | 183.7 | 62.0 | 82.6 | 96.2 |
| Transportation equipment | 7.7 | 6.7 | 7.3 | 8.0 | 10.1 | 2.3 | 3.6 | 0.2 | 2.2 | 1.7 |
| Scientific and measuring instruments | 54.6 | 47.0 | 51.8 | 60.6 | 78.2 | 54.9 | 39.5 | 36.7 | 43.0 | 41.2 |
| Miscellaneous manufactures | 9.6 | 10.0 | 7.0 | 10.1 | 10.9 | 7.0 | 6.0 | 3.7 | 3.5 | 5.4 |
| Unidentified manufactures | 3.4 | 2.4 | 3.1 | 2.7 | 2.3 | 1.0 | 1.0 | 0.8 | 1.0 | 1.0 |
| **Agricultural and livestock products** | 0.9 | 0.8 | 1.4 | 4.3 | 4.4 | ..... | 0.1 | ..... | ..... | 0.1 |
| Agricultural products | 0.7 | 0.5 | 0.8 | 3.0 | 2.5 | ..... | ..... | ..... | ..... | 0.1 |
| Livestock and livestock products | 0.2 | 0.3 | 0.7 | 1.3 | 1.9 | ..... | 0.1 | ..... | ..... | ..... |
| **Other commodities** | 6.6 | 8.4 | 3.3 | 5.1 | 4.1 | 13.1 | 13.0 | 7.8 | 5.5 | 2.5 |
| Forestry products | 3.0 | 1.9 | 0.8 | 0.3 | 0.1 | ..... | 0.1 | ..... | 0.1 | ..... |
| Fish and other marine products | 0.3 | 0.5 | 0.2 | 0.3 | 0.6 | 0.1 | 0.3 | 0.1 | 0.1 | 0.1 |
| Metallic ores and concentrates | ..... | ..... | ..... | ..... | ..... | ..... | ..... | ..... | ..... | ..... |
| Bituminous coal and lignite | ..... | ..... | ..... | ..... | ..... | ..... | ..... | ..... | ..... | ..... |
| Crude petroleum and natural gas | ..... | ..... | ..... | ..... | ..... | ..... | ..... | ..... | ..... | ..... |
| Nonmetallic minerals | 0.5 | 0.4 | 0.1 | 0.1 | 0.2 | 0.1 | 1.5 | 0.2 | 0.3 | 0.1 |
| Scrap and waste | 0.3 | 4.9 | 0.6 | 0.3 | 0.4 | ..... | 0.1 | 3.0 | 3.0 | 1.2 |
| Used merchandise | 2.3 | 0.5 | 1.3 | 0.9 | 0.7 | 0.2 | 0.1 | ..... | ..... | 0.1 |
| Goods imported and returned unchanged | ..... | ..... | ..... | ..... | ..... | ..... | ..... | ..... | ..... | ..... |
| Special classification provisions | 0.3 | 0.2 | 0.2 | 3.1 | 2.2 | 12.6 | 10.8 | 4.5 | 2.1 | 0.9 |

| Industry | 1993 | 1994 | 1995 | 1996 | 1997 | 1993 | 1994 | 1995 | 1996 | 1997 |
|---|---|---|---|---|---|---|---|---|---|---|
| | European Union | | | | | United Kingdom | | | | |
| **ALL GOODS** | 4 398.5 | 4 629.8 | 5 288.6 | 5 353.1 | 5 889.3 | 1 028.0 | 1 245.0 | 1 479.0 | 1 415.2 | 1 706.4 |
| **Manufactured goods** | 4 220.3 | 4 457.0 | 5 126.0 | 5 154.8 | 5 733.9 | 991.5 | 1 210.0 | 1 453.1 | 1 383.1 | 1 680.2 |
| Food products | 32.2 | 51.3 | 64.2 | 79.7 | 65.3 | 3.0 | 4.5 | 6.4 | 10.2 | 13.5 |
| Tobacco products | ..... | ..... | ..... | ..... | ..... | ..... | ..... | ..... | ..... | ..... |
| Textile mill products | 78.5 | 77.9 | 75.3 | 49.9 | 69.8 | 18.6 | 20.2 | 18.7 | 14.7 | 17.1 |
| Apparel | 20.4 | 15.9 | 11.3 | 12.5 | 14.6 | 8.0 | 6.3 | 5.5 | 5.1 | 9.6 |
| Lumber and wood products | 34.0 | 37.3 | 37.0 | 50.3 | 68.2 | 4.8 | 4.4 | 3.6 | 6.5 | 9.6 |
| Furniture and fixtures | 6.0 | 5.4 | 5.1 | 5.9 | 8.8 | 1.8 | 2.4 | 1.9 | 1.3 | 1.8 |
| Paper products | 43.0 | 52.9 | 91.5 | 104.3 | 121.9 | 12.2 | 16.1 | 18.0 | 13.6 | 19.4 |
| Printing and publishing | 92.4 | 43.1 | 57.9 | 49.5 | 50.8 | 21.7 | 12.6 | 21.9 | 15.2 | 15.1 |
| Chemical products | 189.6 | 233.1 | 328.5 | 359.5 | 466.9 | 34.7 | 72.0 | 113.4 | 132.6 | 140.5 |
| Refined petroleum products | 20.4 | 6.4 | 1.1 | 25.4 | 2.7 | ..... | 1.6 | 0.2 | 1.2 | 2.3 |
| Rubber and plastic products | 228.1 | 250.9 | 208.5 | 163.7 | 177.6 | 46.1 | 49.4 | 49.3 | 44.9 | 51.2 |
| Leather products | 33.8 | 24.5 | 24.6 | 19.9 | 23.6 | 9.3 | 4.9 | 6.1 | 3.2 | 3.0 |
| Stone, clay and glass products | 23.2 | 27.4 | 29.0 | 31.7 | 36.4 | 4.0 | 6.9 | 7.5 | 7.4 | 7.0 |
| Primary metals | 61.9 | 65.2 | 87.4 | 99.3 | 130.6 | 15.7 | 18.8 | 31.4 | 31.0 | 56.7 |
| Fabricated metal products | 196.8 | 152.8 | 141.1 | 146.9 | 153.0 | 22.4 | 27.8 | 21.2 | 24.8 | 25.1 |
| Industrial machinery and computers | 1 360.8 | 1 470.2 | 1 619.4 | 1 509.8 | 1 696.8 | 265.6 | 312.2 | 363.6 | 406.4 | 566.8 |
| Electric and electronic equipment | 714.9 | 859.4 | 1 138.7 | 1 116.7 | 1 230.2 | 254.3 | 368.9 | 481.5 | 339.8 | 392.9 |
| Transportation equipment | 63.1 | 45.4 | 64.3 | 60.3 | 53.9 | 6.8 | 6.2 | 7.1 | 8.3 | 11.9 |
| Scientific and measuring instruments | 937.0 | 952.1 | 1 042.3 | 1 175.8 | 1 263.1 | 233.4 | 243.6 | 252.4 | 279.4 | 306.2 |
| Miscellaneous manufactures | 60.2 | 59.9 | 77.2 | 77.9 | 86.3 | 22.7 | 22.7 | 36.7 | 32.6 | 26.5 |
| Unidentified manufactures | 24.0 | 25.9 | 21.9 | 16.0 | 13.3 | 6.4 | 8.4 | 6.7 | 5.2 | 4.0 |
| **Agricultural and livestock products** | 5.8 | 9.9 | 10.6 | 10.1 | 6.6 | 2.4 | 4.8 | 3.0 | 2.9 | 2.7 |
| Agricultural products | 5.3 | 8.0 | 8.4 | 9.4 | 5.7 | 2.2 | 3.8 | 2.3 | 2.7 | 2.7 |
| Livestock and livestock products | 0.5 | 1.8 | 2.2 | 0.8 | 0.9 | 0.2 | 1.0 | 0.7 | 0.2 | ..... |
| **Other commodities** | 172.4 | 162.9 | 152.0 | 188.2 | 148.8 | 34.1 | 30.1 | 22.9 | 29.2 | 23.5 |
| Forestry products | 5.8 | 4.4 | 2.4 | 0.9 | 0.8 | 0.2 | 0.2 | 0.3 | 0.3 | 0.2 |
| Fish and other marine products | 74.2 | 74.3 | 76.8 | 83.7 | 66.4 | 2.9 | 2.4 | 3.3 | 3.2 | 4.9 |
| Metallic ores and concentrates | ..... | 0.4 | 0.1 | 0.3 | 0.9 | ..... | 0.2 | ..... | ..... | 0.8 |
| Bituminous coal and lignite | 5.2 | 1.8 | ..... | ..... | 1.9 | ..... | ..... | ..... | ..... | 1.9 |
| Crude petroleum and natural gas | 0.1 | 0.1 | ..... | 0.1 | 0.2 | ..... | ..... | ..... | ..... | 0.1 |
| Nonmetallic minerals | 4.2 | 3.1 | 3.5 | 3.5 | 4.3 | 0.6 | 1.6 | 2.4 | 2.2 | 1.8 |
| Scrap and waste | 27.9 | 39.1 | 27.8 | 24.0 | 27.4 | 11.2 | 6.8 | 4.9 | 3.1 | 2.0 |
| Used merchandise | 14.2 | 9.3 | 10.6 | 15.9 | 13.9 | 2.0 | 3.0 | 4.5 | 7.8 | 5.1 |
| Goods imported and returned unchanged | ..... | ..... | ..... | ..... | ..... | ..... | ..... | ..... | ..... | ..... |
| Special classification provisions | 40.8 | 30.5 | 30.6 | 59.7 | 32.9 | 17.2 | 15.9 | 7.5 | 12.6 | 6.7 |

## Table D-3. State Exports of Goods by Destination and Industry, 1993–1997 —*Continued*

**MASSACHUSSETTS** (Millions of dollars.)

| Industry | 1993 | 1994 | 1995 | 1996 | 1997 | 1993 | 1994 | 1995 | 1996 | 1997 |
|---|---|---|---|---|---|---|---|---|---|---|
| | Germany | | | | | France | | | | |
| **ALL GOODS** | 920.4 | 851.8 | 1 040.5 | 1 098.8 | 1 019.4 | 549.2 | 542.0 | 528.2 | 562.8 | 626.7 |
| **Manufactured goods** | 898.1 | 829.1 | 1 014.4 | 1 068.7 | 998.6 | 501.6 | 505.8 | 491.9 | 514.4 | 587.5 |
| Food products | 1.1 | 1.2 | 1.8 | 1.7 | 3.1 | 2.4 | 1.3 | 1.4 | 2.4 | 2.2 |
| Tobacco products | ..... | ..... | ..... | ..... | ..... | | | | | |
| Textile mill products | 20.5 | 22.1 | 21.6 | 6.1 | 20.3 | 10.4 | 8.6 | 6.0 | 3.8 | 5.4 |
| Apparel | 2.7 | 2.8 | 1.3 | 3.1 | 0.5 | 1.2 | 0.8 | 0.7 | 0.6 | 0.6 |
| Lumber and wood products | 8.8 | 11.6 | 11.5 | 9.6 | 10.1 | 2.6 | 5.0 | 1.5 | 2.8 | 2.2 |
| Furniture and fixtures | 2.1 | 1.2 | 1.3 | 1.2 | 1.2 | 0.3 | 0.1 | ..... | 0.4 | 0.4 |
| Paper products | 5.2 | 5.4 | 6.9 | 16.6 | 11.4 | 2.3 | 3.3 | 2.3 | 2.5 | 2.0 |
| Printing and publishing | 40.6 | 11.6 | 12.5 | 14.5 | 12.7 | 7.0 | 2.1 | 3.7 | 2.5 | 3.0 |
| Chemical products | 44.5 | 46.4 | 70.2 | 69.2 | 72.6 | 23.6 | 24.9 | 32.1 | 36.6 | 51.0 |
| Refined petroleum products | | | | | | 16.1 | | | 15.9 | |
| Rubber and plastic products | 32.4 | 27.9 | 21.5 | 19.7 | 28.7 | 21.2 | 18.1 | 16.1 | 8.1 | 12.8 |
| Leather products | 9.3 | 5.8 | 5.6 | 5.7 | 7.2 | 4.0 | 3.4 | 2.1 | 1.0 | 2.7 |
| Stone, clay and glass products | 7.8 | 7.5 | 6.2 | 7.7 | 6.1 | 2.9 | 4.3 | 4.8 | 4.5 | 6.2 |
| Primary metals | 21.4 | 19.9 | 28.9 | 33.2 | 24.5 | 5.8 | 9.8 | 8.3 | 8.7 | 12.3 |
| Fabricated metal products | 145.3 | 90.7 | 76.1 | 73.5 | 54.7 | 5.3 | 8.2 | 8.3 | 7.1 | 19.5 |
| Industrial machinery and computers | 235.0 | 234.4 | 273.2 | 240.6 | 239.6 | 203.3 | 190.7 | 184.1 | 187.9 | 212.9 |
| Electric and electronic equipment | 119.7 | 137.0 | 221.8 | 266.3 | 240.5 | 77.7 | 77.9 | 81.4 | 97.7 | 127.1 |
| Transportation equipment | 8.6 | 6.7 | 8.3 | 9.7 | 8.5 | 3.4 | 3.6 | 6.8 | 5.3 | 4.7 |
| Scientific and measuring instruments | 178.7 | 180.9 | 231.5 | 273.2 | 238.8 | 106.0 | 138.9 | 126.5 | 120.6 | 114.0 |
| Miscellaneous manufactures | 7.9 | 10.2 | 9.8 | 13.9 | 14.7 | 3.9 | 2.4 | 3.8 | 4.7 | 7.3 |
| Unidentified manufactures | 6.5 | 5.8 | 4.4 | 3.4 | 3.3 | 2.3 | 2.3 | 2.0 | 1.3 | 1.1 |
| **Agricultural and livestock products** | 0.6 | 0.7 | 1.1 | 1.3 | 0.5 | 0.6 | 1.0 | 0.9 | 1.1 | 0.8 |
| Agricultural products | 0.6 | 0.7 | 1.1 | 1.2 | 0.4 | 0.5 | 0.5 | 0.9 | 0.7 | 0.4 |
| Livestock and livestock products | ..... | ..... | 0.1 | ..... | 0.1 | 0.1 | 0.5 | ..... | 0.4 | 0.3 |
| **Other commodities** | 21.8 | 22.0 | 24.9 | 28.9 | 20.3 | 47.0 | 35.2 | 35.4 | 47.3 | 38.4 |
| Forestry products | 0.8 | 0.6 | 0.2 | 0.1 | 0.2 | 0.1 | 0.2 | | | |
| Fish and other marine products | 3.5 | 4.5 | 10.0 | 10.6 | 4.3 | 35.9 | 29.7 | 32.6 | 37.7 | 29.9 |
| Metallic ores and concentrates | ..... | 0.1 | 0.1 | ..... | ..... | | 0.1 | ..... | 0.1 | ..... |
| Bituminous coal and lignite | ..... | ..... | ..... | ..... | ..... | 2.1 | 0.6 | ..... | ..... | ..... |
| Crude petroleum and natural gas | ..... | ..... | ..... | ..... | ..... | ..... | ..... | ..... | ..... | ..... |
| Nonmetallic minerals | 2.4 | 0.8 | 0.4 | 0.5 | 0.9 | 0.6 | 0.2 | 0.2 | 0.1 | 0.4 |
| Scrap and waste | 5.1 | 9.6 | 8.4 | 7.9 | 7.2 | 0.2 | ..... | 0.1 | ..... | ..... |
| Used merchandise | 2.3 | 2.9 | 3.3 | 2.3 | 1.6 | 2.6 | 1.0 | 0.6 | 2.3 | 3.6 |
| Goods imported and returned unchanged | ..... | ..... | ..... | ..... | ..... | ..... | ..... | ..... | ..... | ..... |
| Special classification provisions | 7.7 | 3.4 | 2.5 | 7.5 | 6.1 | 5.6 | 3.3 | 1.9 | 7.0 | 4.5 |
| | The Netherlands | | | | | Asian 10 | | | | |
| **ALL GOODS** | 761.9 | 710.1 | 763.4 | 692.3 | 928.9 | 2 768.3 | 3 023.8 | 3 713.9 | 4 316.5 | 5 323.4 |
| **Manufactured goods** | 753.7 | 703.0 | 744.5 | 664.7 | 914.9 | 2 708.5 | 2 949.5 | 3 636.7 | 4 237.4 | 5 233.6 |
| Food products | 0.2 | 0.6 | 0.8 | 1.4 | 1.2 | 31.8 | 46.1 | 50.7 | 100.7 | 107.0 |
| Tobacco products | ..... | ..... | ..... | ..... | ..... | | | | | |
| Textile mill products | 4.9 | 3.1 | 3.6 | 1.1 | 3.7 | 37.8 | 36.8 | 43.4 | 39.8 | 39.8 |
| Apparel | 3.7 | 1.7 | 0.4 | 0.4 | 1.2 | 8.0 | 7.4 | 16.6 | 18.7 | 18.9 |
| Lumber and wood products | 2.4 | 1.7 | 2.3 | 3.1 | 5.6 | 32.7 | 31.8 | 36.9 | 34.5 | 37.0 |
| Furniture and fixtures | 0.2 | 0.2 | 0.2 | 1.0 | 2.4 | 0.9 | 1.9 | 2.0 | 2.8 | 2.7 |
| Paper products | 12.4 | 10.9 | 24.3 | 20.4 | 29.6 | 52.3 | 63.4 | 63.5 | 80.3 | 98.8 |
| Printing and publishing | 5.6 | 4.0 | 4.8 | 5.3 | 7.1 | 18.6 | 21.0 | 23.5 | 36.1 | 43.0 |
| Chemical products | 32.7 | 26.9 | 39.6 | 35.8 | 120.1 | 137.1 | 158.1 | 186.8 | 225.5 | 255.8 |
| Refined petroleum products | 4.1 | 3.6 | 0.6 | 7.9 | ..... | 30.1 | 4.9 | 15.1 | 5.5 | 5.0 |
| Rubber and plastic products | 101.3 | 122.8 | 86.2 | 54.2 | 51.3 | 67.1 | 86.6 | 92.4 | 77.8 | 97.1 |
| Leather products | 1.3 | 1.7 | 2.0 | 2.6 | 1.8 | 34.4 | 47.3 | 41.8 | 35.3 | 50.4 |
| Stone, clay and glass products | 2.2 | 1.7 | 4.3 | 4.5 | 5.1 | 16.4 | 16.5 | 21.5 | 20.5 | 22.5 |
| Primary metals | 5.4 | 3.1 | 1.9 | 3.3 | 8.1 | 45.7 | 36.6 | 43.2 | 50.1 | 70.5 |
| Fabricated metal products | 5.1 | 4.1 | 3.7 | 12.4 | 19.5 | 60.8 | 70.2 | 85.8 | 140.2 | 282.6 |
| Industrial machinery and computers | 289.6 | 253.1 | 264.2 | 249.0 | 264.3 | 812.9 | 864.0 | 1 125.4 | 1 397.1 | 1 542.7 |
| Electric and electronic equipment | 63.4 | 74.3 | 93.4 | 93.3 | 133.6 | 683.2 | 824.7 | 1 032.5 | 1 066.1 | 1 424.9 |
| Transportation equipment | 7.4 | 3.8 | 11.3 | 6.8 | 4.1 | 72.4 | 39.1 | 23.6 | 27.7 | 42.1 |
| Scientific and measuring instruments | 202.3 | 175.8 | 189.9 | 151.0 | 243.4 | 508.2 | 531.7 | 658.9 | 809.3 | 1 014.4 |
| Miscellaneous manufactures | 8.0 | 8.3 | 9.6 | 10.1 | 12.2 | 47.1 | 52.7 | 64.7 | 62.2 | 72.0 |
| Unidentified manufactures | 1.5 | 1.5 | 1.4 | 1.0 | 0.8 | 11.0 | 8.8 | 8.7 | 7.2 | 6.3 |
| **Agricultural and livestock products** | 0.4 | 0.9 | 0.7 | 2.6 | 0.6 | 0.8 | 1.7 | 1.1 | 1.6 | 1.2 |
| Agricultural products | 0.4 | 0.9 | 0.6 | 2.6 | 0.6 | 0.4 | 0.8 | 0.4 | 1.3 | 0.8 |
| Livestock and livestock products | ..... | ..... | ..... | ..... | ..... | 0.4 | 0.9 | 0.8 | 0.3 | 0.4 |
| **Other commodities** | 7.8 | 6.2 | 18.2 | 25.0 | 13.4 | 58.9 | 72.6 | 76.1 | 77.5 | 88.6 |
| Forestry products | ..... | ..... | ..... | ..... | ..... | 1.3 | 1.2 | 1.2 | 1.3 | 0.9 |
| Fish and other marine products | 1.1 | 1.3 | 1.6 | 2.0 | 0.7 | 30.5 | 47.1 | 48.3 | 43.9 | 49.8 |
| Metallic ores and concentrates | ..... | ..... | ..... | 0.2 | ..... | ..... | ..... | ..... | ..... | ..... |
| Bituminous coal and lignite | 1.1 | ..... | ..... | ..... | ..... | ..... | ..... | ..... | ..... | ..... |
| Crude petroleum and natural gas | ..... | ..... | ..... | ..... | ..... | ..... | ..... | 0.1 | ..... | 0.1 |
| Nonmetallic minerals | 0.1 | 0.1 | ..... | ..... | 0.6 | 2.4 | 0.8 | 2.2 | 0.9 | 0.9 |
| Scrap and waste | 0.6 | 0.8 | 0.7 | 0.3 | 0.5 | 6.8 | 9.5 | 11.5 | 8.2 | 8.2 |
| Used merchandise | 3.1 | 0.4 | 0.2 | 1.1 | 0.4 | 5.6 | 2.5 | 1.5 | 3.9 | 2.1 |
| Goods imported and returned unchanged | ..... | ..... | ..... | ..... | ..... | ..... | ..... | ..... | ..... | ..... |
| Special classification provisions | 1.7 | 3.6 | 15.7 | 21.3 | 11.2 | 12.2 | 11.4 | 11.1 | 19.2 | 26.6 |

## Table D-3.   State Exports of Goods by Destination and Industry, 1993–1997 —*Continued*

**MASSACHUSSETTS** (Millions of dollars.)

| Industry | 1993 | 1994 | 1995 | 1996 | 1997 | 1993 | 1994 | 1995 | 1996 | 1997 |
|---|---|---|---|---|---|---|---|---|---|---|
| | Japan | | | | | South Korea | | | | |
| **ALL GOODS** | 1 046.5 | 1 155.1 | 1 396.4 | 1 680.5 | 1 969.0 | 320.0 | 348.4 | 432.5 | 530.7 | 616.5 |
| **Manufactured goods** | 1 007.2 | 1 109.7 | 1 349.7 | 1 633.9 | 1 917.0 | 318.2 | 340.3 | 425.6 | 520.8 | 607.1 |
| Food products | 2.1 | 3.7 | 6.1 | 30.2 | 25.8 | 14.2 | 26.9 | 25.1 | 32.3 | 48.0 |
| Tobacco products | ..... | ..... | ..... | ..... | ..... | ..... | ..... | ..... | ..... | ..... |
| Textile mill products | 3.7 | 4.0 | 6.0 | 6.1 | 6.0 | 2.2 | 4.5 | 5.3 | 3.0 | 4.9 |
| Apparel | 4.0 | 4.1 | 10.6 | 12.4 | 11.2 | 0.1 | 0.2 | 0.7 | 0.2 | 0.4 |
| Lumber and wood products | 9.8 | 7.8 | 10.5 | 10.5 | 8.3 | 7.2 | 5.6 | 5.6 | 7.6 | 10.3 |
| Furniture and fixtures | 0.8 | 0.4 | 1.1 | 1.1 | 1.6 | ..... | 0.1 | 0.2 | 0.5 | 0.2 |
| Paper products | 7.9 | 8.4 | 13.3 | 12.2 | 11.1 | 4.1 | 3.9 | 4.5 | 5.0 | 6.4 |
| Printing and publishing | 6.9 | 7.6 | 10.3 | 14.6 | 24.2 | 2.6 | 3.1 | 4.2 | 6.3 | 3.5 |
| Chemical products | 63.0 | 54.3 | 58.0 | 72.4 | 110.8 | 17.9 | 23.0 | 35.9 | 31.5 | 27.5 |
| Refined petroleum products | 0.6 | 3.2 | 3.1 | 3.4 | 2.3 | 28.9 | 0.3 | 3.0 | 0.5 | 0.7 |
| Rubber and plastic products | 32.9 | 54.0 | 62.7 | 55.3 | 56.8 | 8.7 | 6.8 | 5.9 | 3.7 | 4.2 |
| Leather products | 5.7 | 12.5 | 9.4 | 9.3 | 14.9 | 3.6 | 2.7 | 3.8 | 3.7 | 8.9 |
| Stone, clay and glass products | 7.0 | 7.5 | 7.3 | 9.0 | 7.3 | 2.9 | 3.7 | 4.1 | 3.4 | 3.0 |
| Primary metals | 17.0 | 19.8 | 21.5 | 18.9 | 15.6 | 5.6 | 2.4 | 6.6 | 4.7 | 14.3 |
| Fabricated metal products | 20.0 | 26.3 | 19.1 | 22.0 | 24.0 | 6.2 | 7.1 | 16.1 | 13.4 | 8.6 |
| Industrial machinery and computers | 340.7 | 389.6 | 499.5 | 653.7 | 697.0 | 71.3 | 91.7 | 105.7 | 155.4 | 175.8 |
| Electric and electronic equipment | 188.9 | 223.1 | 309.0 | 303.7 | 375.4 | 48.4 | 67.5 | 91.2 | 128.1 | 198.4 |
| Transportation equipment | 3.5 | 4.1 | 2.2 | 2.4 | 3.6 | 35.9 | 26.8 | 12.8 | 10.0 | 8.0 |
| Scientific and measuring instruments | 263.7 | 249.0 | 264.1 | 365.1 | 476.4 | 55.5 | 60.0 | 89.4 | 106.0 | 79.1 |
| Miscellaneous manufactures | 23.1 | 27.5 | 33.1 | 30.0 | 42.4 | 2.0 | 2.9 | 4.8 | 4.7 | 4.2 |
| Unidentified manufactures | 5.8 | 2.8 | 2.7 | 1.6 | 2.1 | 0.8 | 1.0 | 0.8 | 0.7 | 0.7 |
| **Agricultural and livestock products** | 0.2 | 0.4 | 0.2 | 1.3 | 0.6 | 0.1 | 0.2 | 0.1 | ..... | ..... |
| Agricultural products | 0.2 | 0.3 | 0.2 | 1.1 | 0.4 | 0.1 | 0.1 | 0.1 | ..... | ..... |
| Livestock and livestock products | ..... | 0.1 | ..... | 0.2 | 0.1 | ..... | 0.1 | ..... | ..... | ..... |
| **Other commodities** | 39.0 | 45.1 | 46.5 | 45.3 | 51.4 | 1.7 | 7.8 | 6.7 | 9.8 | 9.4 |
| Forestry products | ..... | ..... | ..... | 0.1 | ..... | ..... | ..... | ..... | 0.1 | ..... |
| Fish and other marine products | 27.3 | 35.7 | 39.2 | 33.6 | 36.5 | 1.0 | 7.0 | 5.4 | 6.5 | 6.6 |
| Metallic ores and concentrates | ..... | ..... | ..... | ..... | ..... | ..... | ..... | ..... | ..... | ..... |
| Bituminous coal and lignite | ..... | ..... | ..... | ..... | ..... | ..... | ..... | ..... | ..... | ..... |
| Crude petroleum and natural gas | ..... | ..... | ..... | ..... | ..... | ..... | ..... | ..... | ..... | ..... |
| Nonmetallic minerals | 2.3 | 0.6 | 1.8 | 0.4 | 0.4 | ..... | 0.1 | 0.1 | ..... | ..... |
| Scrap and waste | 0.5 | 0.4 | 0.4 | 0.2 | 0.1 | ..... | ..... | ..... | 0.1 | 1.5 |
| Used merchandise | 2.5 | 2.2 | 0.5 | 1.8 | 0.9 | 0.1 | ..... | 0.6 | 1.6 | 0.3 |
| Goods imported and returned unchanged | ..... | ..... | ..... | ..... | ..... | ..... | ..... | ..... | ..... | ..... |
| Special classification provisions | 6.5 | 6.1 | 4.5 | 9.2 | 13.5 | 0.5 | 0.6 | 0.7 | 1.5 | 0.9 |
| | Taiwan | | | | | Singapore | | | | |
| **ALL GOODS** | 281.8 | 427.6 | 489.6 | 592.2 | 789.0 | 356.3 | 329.0 | 352.4 | 409.0 | 544.8 |
| **Manufactured goods** | 280.4 | 425.2 | 488.3 | 590.1 | 782.6 | 352.2 | 324.8 | 346.4 | 402.9 | 537.9 |
| Food products | 11.7 | 8.3 | 12.3 | 24.7 | 21.7 | ..... | 0.1 | ..... | 0.2 | 0.6 |
| Tobacco products | ..... | ..... | ..... | ..... | ..... | ..... | ..... | ..... | ..... | ..... |
| Textile mill products | 5.1 | 5.3 | 3.1 | 3.5 | 3.3 | 2.3 | 2.3 | 2.5 | 1.9 | 2.4 |
| Apparel | 0.4 | 0.2 | 0.4 | 1.3 | 1.5 | 1.4 | 1.3 | 1.6 | 0.8 | 0.6 |
| Lumber and wood products | 10.2 | 10.4 | 7.8 | 4.6 | 4.5 | 0.2 | 0.5 | 0.8 | 0.5 | 0.4 |
| Furniture and fixtures | ..... | 0.1 | 0.1 | 0.1 | ..... | ..... | 0.2 | 0.1 | 0.2 | 0.1 |
| Paper products | 5.9 | 5.7 | 5.2 | 5.1 | 6.0 | 4.6 | 8.6 | 6.8 | 7.0 | 7.0 |
| Printing and publishing | 3.0 | 4.0 | 2.4 | 5.2 | 4.0 | 3.3 | 2.4 | 2.9 | 2.9 | 2.5 |
| Chemical products | 10.9 | 11.6 | 12.3 | 18.9 | 19.9 | 11.9 | 17.3 | 18.2 | 27.3 | 22.9 |
| Refined petroleum products | 0.2 | 0.3 | 0.2 | 0.3 | 0.4 | 0.1 | 0.2 | 0.3 | 0.3 | 0.3 |
| Rubber and plastic products | 5.0 | 6.7 | 4.8 | 3.9 | 4.8 | 5.8 | 5.1 | 3.0 | 2.6 | 4.6 |
| Leather products | 2.2 | 3.6 | 1.9 | 1.7 | 3.6 | 1.4 | 1.5 | 0.9 | 0.8 | 0.9 |
| Stone, clay and glass products | 1.3 | 1.2 | 3.2 | 2.5 | 3.8 | 1.5 | 0.4 | 1.7 | 1.2 | 1.7 |
| Primary metals | 5.4 | 2.6 | 2.6 | 6.5 | 6.3 | 2.5 | 2.9 | 3.1 | 3.8 | 12.0 |
| Fabricated metal products | 7.7 | 10.3 | 4.7 | 58.7 | 161.3 | 6.3 | 9.0 | 12.5 | 13.2 | 15.0 |
| Industrial machinery and computers | 63.4 | 70.2 | 108.4 | 145.5 | 168.2 | 109.0 | 67.7 | 88.3 | 131.2 | 179.3 |
| Electric and electronic equipment | 97.3 | 228.2 | 235.8 | 172.2 | 224.6 | 137.5 | 129.6 | 113.5 | 108.9 | 134.4 |
| Transportation equipment | 2.1 | 1.3 | 0.4 | 6.2 | 5.8 | 1.5 | 0.6 | 0.5 | 1.0 | 19.4 |
| Scientific and measuring instruments | 46.0 | 52.0 | 78.0 | 123.7 | 138.5 | 57.0 | 68.6 | 83.4 | 93.9 | 127.3 |
| Miscellaneous manufactures | 1.8 | 1.9 | 3.7 | 3.7 | 3.2 | 4.9 | 5.4 | 5.3 | 4.2 | 6.0 |
| Unidentified manufactures | 1.0 | 1.1 | 1.0 | 1.9 | 1.0 | 0.9 | 0.9 | 1.1 | 0.7 | 0.6 |
| **Agricultural and livestock products** | 0.2 | 0.1 | 0.2 | 0.1 | 0.1 | 0.1 | 0.1 | ..... | 0.1 | ..... |
| Agricultural products | ..... | 0.1 | ..... | 0.1 | 0.1 | 0.1 | 0.1 | ..... | ..... | ..... |
| Livestock and livestock products | 0.1 | ..... | 0.2 | ..... | ..... | ..... | ..... | ..... | 0.1 | ..... |
| **Other commodities** | 1.2 | 2.3 | 1.0 | 2.1 | 6.3 | 4.0 | 4.1 | 6.0 | 6.0 | 6.9 |
| Forestry products | ..... | ..... | ..... | ..... | 0.1 | 0.3 | 0.3 | 0.3 | 0.2 | 0.1 |
| Fish and other marine products | 0.4 | 0.8 | 0.2 | 0.1 | ..... | 0.1 | 0.1 | 0.2 | 0.2 | 1.3 |
| Metallic ores and concentrates | ..... | ..... | ..... | ..... | ..... | ..... | ..... | ..... | ..... | ..... |
| Bituminous coal and lignite | ..... | ..... | ..... | ..... | ..... | ..... | ..... | ..... | ..... | ..... |
| Crude petroleum and natural gas | ..... | ..... | ..... | ..... | ..... | ..... | ..... | ..... | ..... | ..... |
| Nonmetallic minerals | ..... | ..... | 0.1 | 0.3 | 0.1 | ..... | ..... | 0.1 | 0.1 | 0.1 |
| Scrap and waste | 0.2 | 1.0 | ..... | 0.1 | 0.3 | 0.2 | 0.9 | 1.1 | 0.6 | 0.2 |
| Used merchandise | 0.3 | ..... | ..... | 0.1 | ..... | 0.1 | ..... | 0.3 | 0.1 | 0.2 |
| Goods imported and returned unchanged | ..... | ..... | ..... | ..... | ..... | ..... | ..... | ..... | ..... | ..... |
| Special classification provisions | 0.3 | 0.4 | 0.6 | 1.3 | 5.7 | 3.3 | 2.8 | 4.1 | 4.9 | 5.0 |

## MICHIGAN: Exports of Goods, 1997

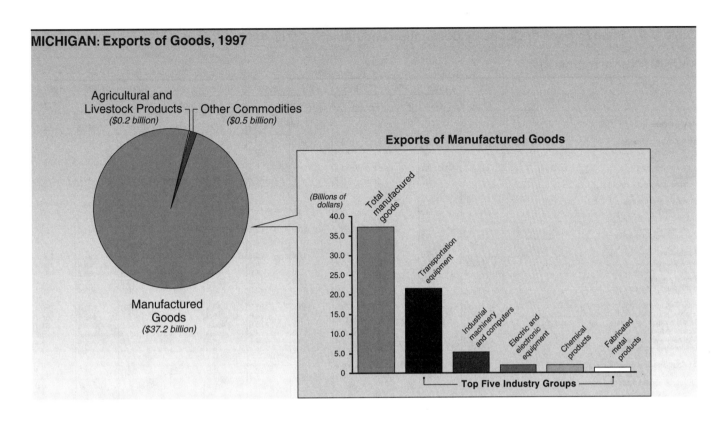

## Table D-3.   State Exports of Goods by Destination and Industry, 1993–1997 —*Continued*

**MICHIGAN** (Millions of dollars.)

| Industry | 1993 | 1994 | 1995 | 1996 | 1997 | 1993 | 1994 | 1995 | 1996 | 1997 |
|---|---|---|---|---|---|---|---|---|---|---|
| | All destinations | | | | | Canada | | | | |
| **ALL GOODS** | 25 322.5 | 36 812.1 | 37 102.3 | 38 128.2 | 37 920.1 | 11 434.1 | 20 809.1 | 21 935.9 | 21 949.6 | 19 760.2 |
| **Manufactured goods** | 24 775.7 | 36 196.2 | 36 392.8 | 37 498.5 | 37 240.6 | 11 019.7 | 20 329.5 | 21 369.5 | 21 465.3 | 19 228.9 |
| Food products | 293.9 | 346.1 | 396.7 | 463.0 | 468.6 | 124.9 | 154.2 | 157.5 | 163.7 | 173.1 |
| Tobacco products | 1.7 | 0.3 | 2.3 | ..... | ..... | ..... | ..... | 0.1 | ..... | ..... |
| Textile mill products | 84.4 | 89.2 | 96.1 | 57.0 | 72.7 | 17.3 | 18.0 | 22.1 | 22.7 | 28.3 |
| Apparel | 66.6 | 121.3 | 155.9 | 187.9 | 176.5 | 21.9 | 28.8 | 95.8 | 101.2 | 94.1 |
| Lumber and wood products | 74.4 | 90.6 | 88.1 | 80.7 | 82.4 | 48.1 | 55.7 | 46.5 | 50.4 | 49.6 |
| Furniture and fixtures | 755.5 | 700.1 | 793.5 | 695.4 | 735.3 | 284.9 | 291.7 | 368.6 | 435.4 | 449.4 |
| Paper products | 127.4 | 146.3 | 168.9 | 184.9 | 181.4 | 71.9 | 86.3 | 103.7 | 121.9 | 104.7 |
| Printing and publishing | 78.8 | 92.9 | 93.6 | 81.3 | 87.8 | 55.1 | 66.9 | 67.3 | 59.9 | 53.7 |
| Chemical products | 990.1 | 1 156.7 | 1 315.2 | 1 669.3 | 1 930.1 | 192.9 | 257.6 | 352.7 | 617.7 | 717.8 |
| Refined petroleum products | 59.1 | 56.9 | 53.8 | 80.6 | 78.1 | 44.9 | 42.7 | 39.1 | 66.8 | 58.1 |
| Rubber and plastic products | 504.9 | 573.8 | 576.5 | 629.1 | 705.8 | 116.4 | 156.8 | 184.3 | 235.5 | 266.1 |
| Leather products | 147.1 | 79.5 | 116.2 | 133.0 | 172.4 | 1.8 | 2.4 | 2.8 | 3.5 | 5.2 |
| Stone, clay and glass products | 322.5 | 381.7 | 405.3 | 470.8 | 481.4 | 180.4 | 227.9 | 257.7 | 296.9 | 301.7 |
| Primary metals | 611.3 | 719.5 | 811.7 | 735.4 | 801.6 | 318.7 | 423.6 | 486.2 | 427.0 | 461.6 |
| Fabricated metal products | 2 049.0 | 1 367.5 | 1 158.1 | 1 299.7 | 1 251.6 | 1 197.8 | 419.3 | 502.1 | 504.1 | 553.5 |
| Industrial machinery and computers | 2 885.8 | 3 991.2 | 4 169.3 | 4 281.4 | 5 332.6 | 1 401.6 | 2 297.3 | 2 144.4 | 2 270.0 | 2 988.0 |
| Electric and electronic equipment | 1 672.8 | 1 870.3 | 1 777.9 | 1 805.3 | 1 961.7 | 567.5 | 573.1 | 690.6 | 746.4 | 728.8 |
| Transportation equipment | 13 400.0 | 23 546.7 | 23 241.0 | 23 688.9 | 21 588.0 | 6 246.9 | 15 000.7 | 15 532.6 | 15 030.2 | 11 777.4 |
| Scientific and measuring instruments | 480.6 | 635.1 | 736.7 | 743.4 | 909.1 | 94.4 | 182.3 | 275.2 | 274.4 | 378.7 |
| Miscellaneous manufactures | 127.3 | 179.9 | 187.2 | 175.6 | 185.3 | 23.3 | 27.8 | 25.1 | 22.2 | 24.5 |
| Unidentified manufactures | 42.6 | 50.6 | 48.9 | 35.8 | 38.1 | 9.1 | 16.2 | 15.0 | 15.3 | 14.4 |
| **Agricultural and livestock products** | 169.1 | 171.4 | 181.4 | 173.8 | 197.8 | 86.7 | 72.7 | 70.3 | 70.2 | 96.8 |
| Agricultural products | 148.3 | 152.2 | 168.6 | 164.3 | 190.3 | 67.4 | 55.1 | 58.5 | 62.7 | 90.8 |
| Livestock and livestock products | 20.8 | 19.3 | 12.8 | 9.5 | 7.5 | 19.3 | 17.6 | 11.8 | 7.5 | 5.9 |
| **Other commodities** | 377.8 | 444.5 | 528.1 | 455.9 | 481.7 | 327.7 | 406.9 | 496.1 | 414.1 | 434.5 |
| Forestry products | 0.4 | 0.4 | 1.5 | 1.6 | 1.5 | 0.3 | 0.2 | 0.3 | 0.4 | 1.4 |
| Fish and other marine products | 4.9 | 3.1 | 3.6 | 2.9 | 3.4 | 4.9 | 2.9 | 3.1 | 2.7 | 2.8 |
| Metallic ores and concentrates | 0.8 | 4.9 | 78.8 | 8.1 | 0.4 | ..... | 4.6 | 78.8 | 7.8 | 0.3 |
| Bituminous coal and lignite | 3.1 | 1.4 | 1.1 | 0.8 | ..... | ..... | 1.4 | 1.1 | 0.8 | ..... |
| Crude petroleum and natural gas | 24.9 | 33.5 | 51.3 | 36.8 | 27.2 | 24.9 | 33.3 | 51.2 | 36.8 | 27.2 |
| Nonmetallic minerals | 17.2 | 19.5 | 21.4 | 21.0 | 19.4 | 16.8 | 18.7 | 20.5 | 19.9 | 18.3 |
| Scrap and waste | 53.1 | 81.8 | 107.4 | 97.5 | 107.2 | 45.4 | 72.2 | 90.0 | 75.1 | 83.3 |
| Used merchandise | 11.4 | 10.3 | 10.3 | 11.3 | 12.8 | 3.9 | 4.0 | 5.6 | 4.8 | 5.3 |
| Goods imported and returned unchanged | 212.6 | 248.8 | 216.7 | 235.1 | 277.0 | 212.6 | 248.8 | 216.7 | 235.1 | 277.0 |
| Special classification provisions | 49.2 | 40.9 | 36.0 | 41.0 | 32.7 | 18.9 | 20.8 | 28.8 | 30.9 | 18.8 |

## Table D-3.   State Exports of Goods by Destination and Industry, 1993–1997 —*Continued*

### MICHIGAN (Millions of dollars.)

| Industry | 1993 | 1994 | 1995 | 1996 | 1997 | 1993 | 1994 | 1995 | 1996 | 1997 |
|---|---|---|---|---|---|---|---|---|---|---|
| | South and Central America and Caribbean | | | | | Mexico | | | | |
| **ALL GOODS** | 665.1 | 752.5 | 1 028.8 | 1 209.6 | 1 613.8 | 5 630.5 | 7 088.5 | 5 002.8 | 4 686.8 | 6 458.0 |
| **Manufactured goods** | 658.1 | 744.9 | 1 019.2 | 1 195.0 | 1 609.7 | 5 624.9 | 7 082.3 | 4 994.8 | 4 664.4 | 6 424.9 |
| Food products | 11.7 | 18.4 | 27.1 | 33.5 | 18.2 | 10.6 | 14.6 | 5.1 | 6.7 | 10.7 |
| Tobacco products | ..... | ..... | ..... | ..... | ..... | ..... | 0.3 | ..... | ..... | ..... |
| Textile mill products | 3.1 | 3.6 | 14.0 | 2.1 | 2.6 | 56.3 | 59.7 | 50.9 | 24.6 | 26.6 |
| Apparel | 7.9 | 0.9 | 0.5 | 0.8 | 2.4 | 25.5 | 52.2 | 31.7 | 40.6 | 51.9 |
| Lumber and wood products | 0.1 | 0.7 | 0.4 | 3.1 | 0.9 | 1.6 | 7.4 | 9.9 | 1.0 | 0.7 |
| Furniture and fixtures | 8.6 | 6.2 | 17.7 | 28.6 | 43.4 | 350.9 | 302.1 | 285.2 | 95.6 | 79.9 |
| Paper products | 3.2 | 3.7 | 3.5 | 4.6 | 2.5 | 24.6 | 26.1 | 24.5 | 18.8 | 29.5 |
| Printing and publishing | 1.2 | 1.3 | 1.5 | 1.2 | 2.7 | 1.4 | 1.4 | 1.4 | 1.2 | 2.1 |
| Chemical products | 36.6 | 58.6 | 56.5 | 53.3 | 62.5 | 133.5 | 128.1 | 89.4 | 108.9 | 163.1 |
| Refined petroleum products | 0.2 | 0.3 | 0.4 | 0.6 | 1.8 | 7.6 | 7.1 | 7.4 | 7.2 | 10.8 |
| Rubber and plastic products | 6.0 | 11.4 | 10.9 | 17.6 | 28.8 | 320.5 | 335.2 | 302.4 | 287.5 | 298.4 |
| Leather products | 14.3 | 14.5 | 10.2 | 4.9 | 5.1 | 41.7 | 48.8 | 94.2 | 110.9 | 138.1 |
| Stone, clay and glass products | 3.7 | 4.1 | 3.1 | 3.2 | 4.6 | 64.8 | 76.2 | 74.8 | 69.7 | 60.7 |
| Primary metals | 2.7 | 2.7 | 4.2 | 10.9 | 12.1 | 205.4 | 205.9 | 122.8 | 126.0 | 118.4 |
| Fabricated metal products | 6.7 | 9.8 | 10.2 | 27.2 | 17.8 | 680.4 | 732.1 | 410.7 | 495.1 | 449.1 |
| Industrial machinery and computers | 73.1 | 148.4 | 179.8 | 146.2 | 183.2 | 312.9 | 449.8 | 555.0 | 590.4 | 736.4 |
| Electric and electronic equipment | 8.4 | 11.6 | 23.7 | 30.1 | 24.6 | 756.3 | 495.6 | 449.5 | 449.5 | 656.7 |
| Transportation equipment | 451.9 | 435.2 | 639.7 | 810.9 | 1 176.8 | 2 460.6 | 3 624.6 | 2 265.0 | 2 058.0 | 3 351.1 |
| Scientific and measuring instruments | 10.0 | 8.0 | 9.7 | 11.0 | 13.2 | 153.9 | 211.5 | 198.5 | 166.3 | 223.2 |
| Miscellaneous manufactures | 6.7 | 3.8 | 4.4 | 3.9 | 4.9 | 13.5 | 9.0 | 2.5 | 1.9 | 13.4 |
| Unidentified manufactures | 2.1 | 1.6 | 1.5 | 1.2 | 1.4 | 3.0 | 4.7 | 3.9 | 4.3 | 4.2 |
| **Agricultural and livestock products** | 6.7 | 6.6 | 9.4 | 12.2 | 3.3 | 1.5 | 3.6 | 4.1 | 12.8 | 13.8 |
| Agricultural products | 6.6 | 6.7 | 9.4 | 12.2 | 3.3 | 1.3 | 3.1 | 4.1 | 12.8 | 13.5 |
| Livestock and livestock products | ..... | 0.1 | ..... | ..... | ..... | 0.2 | 0.4 | ..... | ..... | 0.3 |
| **Other commodities** | 0.5 | 0.9 | 0.2 | 2.4 | 0.9 | 4.0 | 2.6 | 3.9 | 9.6 | 19.3 |
| Forestry products | ..... | 0.1 | ..... | ..... | ..... | ..... | ..... | ..... | ..... | ..... |
| Fish and other marine products | ..... | ..... | ..... | ..... | ..... | ..... | ..... | ..... | ..... | ..... |
| Metallic ores and concentrates | ..... | ..... | ..... | ..... | ..... | ..... | ..... | ..... | ..... | ..... |
| Bituminous coal and lignite | ..... | ..... | ..... | ..... | ..... | ..... | ..... | ..... | ..... | ..... |
| Crude petroleum and natural gas | ..... | ..... | ..... | ..... | ..... | ..... | 0.2 | ..... | ..... | ..... |
| Nonmetallic minerals | 0.1 | ..... | ..... | ..... | ..... | 0.1 | 0.4 | 0.2 | 0.5 | 0.6 |
| Scrap and waste | ..... | 0.2 | 0.1 | 2.0 | 0.2 | 0.3 | 1.2 | 3.4 | 8.4 | 16.7 |
| Used merchandise | 0.2 | 0.3 | 0.1 | ..... | 0.3 | 0.1 | 0.1 | ..... | 0.2 | 1.0 |
| Goods imported and returned unchanged | ..... | ..... | ..... | ..... | ..... | ..... | ..... | ..... | ..... | ..... |
| Special classification provisions | 0.2 | 0.3 | ..... | 0.3 | 0.3 | 3.4 | 0.7 | 0.2 | 0.6 | 1.0 |
| | European Union | | | | | United Kingdom | | | | |
| **ALL GOODS** | 3 139.9 | 3 553.2 | 4 193.2 | 4 155.6 | 4 745.7 | 473.6 | 688.7 | 588.6 | 633.8 | 742.8 |
| **Manufactured goods** | 3 049.0 | 3 473.9 | 4 111.7 | 4 071.1 | 4 658.7 | 434.9 | 652.6 | 551.1 | 592.6 | 699.8 |
| Food products | 32.2 | 31.1 | 39.4 | 44.3 | 61.2 | 10.8 | 7.9 | 6.8 | 8.2 | 27.1 |
| Tobacco products | ..... | ..... | 0.4 | ..... | ..... | ..... | ..... | ..... | ..... | ..... |
| Textile mill products | 2.0 | 1.9 | 3.1 | 3.6 | 4.5 | 0.5 | 0.5 | 0.9 | 0.8 | 1.1 |
| Apparel | 3.2 | 3.8 | 4.7 | 12.6 | 11.1 | 0.6 | 0.6 | 0.4 | 0.3 | 0.4 |
| Lumber and wood products | 15.3 | 19.3 | 19.6 | 13.9 | 17.8 | 3.1 | 1.8 | 1.4 | 0.7 | 0.7 |
| Furniture and fixtures | 26.5 | 27.5 | 34.2 | 49.1 | 49.6 | 15.1 | 14.6 | 11.8 | 20.8 | 22.0 |
| Paper products | 15.6 | 17.5 | 21.0 | 24.9 | 31.0 | 6.8 | 7.2 | 8.0 | 7.8 | 9.5 |
| Printing and publishing | 8.9 | 11.3 | 7.7 | 7.2 | 15.3 | 3.2 | 3.4 | 2.5 | 2.6 | 7.5 |
| Chemical products | 318.0 | 375.2 | 370.6 | 352.0 | 402.3 | 44.1 | 60.7 | 70.6 | 65.0 | 76.5 |
| Refined petroleum products | 0.9 | 1.1 | 0.9 | 1.3 | 1.7 | 0.1 | 0.3 | 0.2 | 0.3 | 0.4 |
| Rubber and plastic products | 23.8 | 26.6 | 27.2 | 29.8 | 34.9 | 8.7 | 8.2 | 7.0 | 8.7 | 9.4 |
| Leather products | 3.4 | 1.8 | 1.8 | 1.9 | 4.6 | 1.4 | 0.6 | 0.7 | 1.0 | 2.7 |
| Stone, clay and glass products | 14.2 | 20.8 | 22.3 | 55.8 | 59.3 | 1.9 | 1.8 | 1.6 | 1.3 | 1.5 |
| Primary metals | 21.5 | 29.4 | 86.5 | 73.5 | 87.2 | 6.7 | 10.0 | 18.0 | 16.0 | 17.1 |
| Fabricated metal products | 51.1 | 96.2 | 105.9 | 110.6 | 125.6 | 13.4 | 17.6 | 24.1 | 26.9 | 32.3 |
| Industrial machinery and computers | 501.4 | 435.6 | 547.2 | 525.1 | 655.4 | 104.9 | 92.6 | 126.7 | 130.7 | 151.1 |
| Electric and electronic equipment | 135.6 | 194.0 | 250.6 | 194.0 | 192.3 | 23.7 | 26.0 | 37.6 | 32.7 | 39.2 |
| Transportation equipment | 1 730.6 | 2 033.4 | 2 403.4 | 2 398.4 | 2 703.9 | 166.6 | 369.9 | 200.2 | 234.2 | 261.2 |
| Scientific and measuring instruments | 109.9 | 101.4 | 117.5 | 137.3 | 159.0 | 13.8 | 17.4 | 22.8 | 26.2 | 28.5 |
| Miscellaneous manufactures | 26.6 | 35.5 | 36.7 | 29.8 | 35.3 | 6.0 | 6.5 | 5.2 | 5.4 | 7.8 |
| Unidentified manufactures | 8.3 | 10.6 | 10.9 | 6.3 | 6.9 | 3.6 | 4.9 | 4.5 | 2.7 | 3.9 |
| **Agricultural and livestock products** | 63.7 | 63.7 | 74.7 | 69.0 | 75.3 | 34.1 | 30.9 | 35.2 | 37.1 | 39.2 |
| Agricultural products | 63.3 | 63.5 | 74.5 | 68.6 | 74.7 | 34.0 | 30.9 | 35.2 | 37.1 | 39.2 |
| Livestock and livestock products | 0.4 | 0.2 | 0.2 | 0.4 | 0.6 | 0.1 | ..... | ..... | ..... | ..... |
| **Other commodities** | 27.2 | 15.6 | 6.7 | 15.4 | 11.7 | 4.5 | 5.3 | 2.3 | 4.1 | 3.8 |
| Forestry products | 0.1 | 0.1 | 0.6 | 0.3 | ..... | ..... | ..... | 0.1 | 0.2 | ..... |
| Fish and other marine products | ..... | 0.1 | ..... | 0.1 | ..... | ..... | ..... | ..... | 0.1 | ..... |
| Metallic ores and concentrates | ..... | ..... | ..... | 0.3 | 0.1 | ..... | ..... | ..... | 0.1 | ..... |
| Bituminous coal and lignite | ..... | ..... | ..... | ..... | ..... | ..... | ..... | ..... | ..... | ..... |
| Crude petroleum and natural gas | ..... | ..... | 0.1 | ..... | ..... | ..... | ..... | ..... | ..... | ..... |
| Nonmetallic minerals | 0.2 | 0.3 | 0.4 | 0.3 | ..... | ..... | ..... | ..... | ..... | ..... |
| Scrap and waste | 1.4 | 1.1 | 1.9 | 6.7 | 1.7 | 0.9 | 0.9 | 1.3 | 0.5 | 1.4 |
| Used merchandise | 4.2 | 3.0 | 1.5 | 3.7 | 3.3 | 1.7 | 1.2 | 0.1 | 2.0 | 0.6 |
| Goods imported and returned unchanged | ..... | ..... | ..... | ..... | ..... | ..... | ..... | ..... | ..... | ..... |
| Special classification provisions | 21.4 | 11.0 | 2.2 | 4.1 | 6.5 | 1.9 | 3.2 | 0.7 | 1.4 | 1.8 |

## Table D-3. State Exports of Goods by Destination and Industry, 1993–1997 —Continued

**MICHIGAN** (Millions of dollars.)

| Industry | 1993 | 1994 | 1995 | 1996 | 1997 | 1993 | 1994 | 1995 | 1996 | 1997 |
|---|---|---|---|---|---|---|---|---|---|---|
| | Germany | | | | | France | | | | |
| **ALL GOODS** | 911.8 | 893.6 | 1 054.5 | 999.4 | 1 057.0 | 361.7 | 392.3 | 345.9 | 283.7 | 297.6 |
| **Manufactured goods** | 907.5 | 886.7 | 1 047.0 | 990.5 | 1 052.0 | 358.6 | 386.0 | 341.7 | 280.1 | 292.4 |
| Food products | 11.2 | 12.7 | 15.6 | 19.9 | 19.0 | 2.4 | 0.8 | 1.2 | 0.8 | 1.6 |
| Tobacco products | ..... | ..... | ..... | ..... | ..... | ..... | ..... | ..... | ..... | ..... |
| Textile mill products | 0.7 | 0.8 | 1.3 | 1.2 | 1.0 | 0.2 | 0.1 | 0.4 | 0.4 | 0.3 |
| Apparel | 1.1 | 1.9 | 3.3 | 10.6 | 2.5 | 0.7 | 0.9 | 0.2 | 0.1 | 0.1 |
| Lumber and wood products | 7.6 | 10.0 | 11.3 | 7.1 | 8.8 | 0.5 | 0.3 | 0.6 | 0.3 | 0.4 |
| Furniture and fixtures | 2.2 | 1.1 | 1.9 | 2.2 | 2.9 | 4.8 | 5.5 | 5.1 | 4.1 | 8.4 |
| Paper products | 1.8 | 1.6 | 2.6 | 2.8 | 2.4 | 2.2 | 2.2 | 3.8 | 2.7 | 3.4 |
| Printing and publishing | 1.6 | 2.6 | 1.5 | 1.2 | 1.9 | 0.7 | 0.5 | 0.6 | 0.4 | 1.0 |
| Chemical products | 26.9 | 29.1 | 27.7 | 24.7 | 30.1 | 34.1 | 99.7 | 36.5 | 31.3 | 22.1 |
| Refined petroleum products | 0.2 | 0.2 | 0.2 | 0.3 | 0.3 | 0.1 | ..... | ..... | ..... | 0.1 |
| Rubber and plastic products | 5.2 | 3.1 | 4.1 | 5.4 | 5.3 | 1.7 | 1.4 | 3.4 | 5.6 | 5.8 |
| Leather products | 1.4 | 0.3 | 0.1 | 0.1 | 0.2 | 0.1 | 0.3 | 0.3 | 0.2 | 0.5 |
| Stone, clay and glass products | 4.2 | 8.6 | 14.0 | 26.1 | 39.7 | 0.5 | 3.6 | 0.6 | 1.1 | 0.5 |
| Primary metals | 2.2 | 3.3 | 26.8 | 6.6 | 11.8 | 4.8 | 6.5 | 10.2 | 8.7 | 15.3 |
| Fabricated metal products | 17.6 | 44.3 | 43.6 | 42.1 | 37.5 | 4.5 | 9.2 | 8.2 | 9.4 | 13.7 |
| Industrial machinery and computers | 99.8 | 108.0 | 139.0 | 115.8 | 147.6 | 151.7 | 99.3 | 108.4 | 63.1 | 89.0 |
| Electric and electronic equipment | 34.1 | 34.1 | 37.6 | 24.2 | 25.0 | 7.3 | 23.2 | 34.0 | 16.5 | 17.6 |
| Transportation equipment | 648.8 | 591.7 | 674.8 | 648.3 | 633.9 | 127.9 | 121.1 | 113.0 | 122.0 | 100.5 |
| Scientific and measuring instruments | 33.5 | 24.2 | 29.2 | 41.8 | 66.4 | 11.4 | 7.8 | 11.3 | 11.1 | 9.6 |
| Miscellaneous manufactures | 5.8 | 6.9 | 10.1 | 9.0 | 14.7 | 2.5 | 2.9 | 2.6 | 1.5 | 2.1 |
| Unidentified manufactures | 1.8 | 2.4 | 2.3 | 1.1 | 0.9 | 0.6 | 0.8 | 1.4 | 0.7 | 0.5 |
| **Agricultural and livestock products** | 3.4 | 3.4 | 6.2 | 6.7 | 4.2 | 2.0 | 2.9 | 3.5 | 2.6 | 3.2 |
| Agricultural products | 3.4 | 3.4 | 6.1 | 6.6 | 4.0 | 1.9 | 2.8 | 3.5 | 2.5 | 3.0 |
| Livestock and livestock products | 0.1 | ..... | ..... | 0.1 | 0.2 | 0.1 | 0.1 | ..... | 0.1 | 0.2 |
| **Other commodities** | 0.9 | 3.4 | 1.4 | 2.2 | 0.8 | 1.1 | 3.3 | 0.7 | 1.0 | 2.0 |
| Forestry products | ..... | ..... | ..... | ..... | ..... | ..... | ..... | ..... | ..... | ..... |
| Fish and other marine products | ..... | ..... | ..... | ..... | ..... | ..... | ..... | ..... | ..... | ..... |
| Metallic ores and concentrates | ..... | ..... | ..... | ..... | ..... | ..... | ..... | ..... | 0.1 | ..... |
| Bituminous coal and lignite | ..... | ..... | ..... | ..... | ..... | ..... | ..... | ..... | ..... | ..... |
| Crude petroleum and natural gas | ..... | ..... | ..... | ..... | ..... | ..... | ..... | ..... | ..... | ..... |
| Nonmetallic minerals | ..... | ..... | 0.1 | 0.2 | 0.1 | ..... | 0.1 | 0.2 | 0.3 | ..... |
| Scrap and waste | ..... | 0.1 | 0.2 | 0.1 | ..... | ..... | 0.1 | 0.1 | ..... | 0.1 |
| Used merchandise | 0.6 | 0.1 | 0.2 | 0.7 | ..... | 0.7 | 0.9 | 0.2 | 0.4 | 1.7 |
| Goods imported and returned unchanged | ..... | ..... | ..... | ..... | ..... | ..... | ..... | ..... | ..... | ..... |
| Special classification provisions | 0.2 | 3.2 | 0.9 | 1.4 | 0.8 | 0.4 | 2.2 | 0.1 | 0.2 | 0.1 |
| | The Netherlands | | | | | Asian 10 | | | | |
| **ALL GOODS** | 120.3 | 155.3 | 175.6 | 205.8 | 238.7 | 2 271.9 | 2 471.6 | 2 822.0 | 3 300.4 | 3 083.8 |
| **Manufactured goods** | 117.8 | 153.6 | 170.3 | 201.7 | 235.0 | 2 259.8 | 2 445.8 | 2 804.1 | 3 290.2 | 3 074.0 |
| Food products | 2.3 | 3.4 | 5.1 | 3.8 | 5.3 | 95.5 | 113.4 | 144.2 | 188.6 | 161.2 |
| Tobacco products | ..... | ..... | ..... | ..... | ..... | 1.7 | ..... | ..... | ..... | ..... |
| Textile mill products | 0.1 | ..... | 0.2 | 0.1 | 0.1 | 3.3 | 4.1 | 2.8 | 2.0 | 8.3 |
| Apparel | 0.1 | 0.1 | 0.1 | 0.2 | 0.1 | 6.9 | 34.6 | 21.6 | 28.6 | 15.3 |
| Lumber and wood products | 0.2 | 0.1 | 0.3 | 0.1 | 0.3 | 8.0 | 5.5 | 7.5 | 8.1 | 10.5 |
| Furniture and fixtures | 0.4 | 2.2 | 1.1 | 0.6 | 0.2 | 52.0 | 48.5 | 69.1 | 62.5 | 71.2 |
| Paper products | 0.5 | 1.4 | 1.5 | 5.7 | 10.4 | 4.7 | 5.7 | 5.9 | 5.9 | 5.3 |
| Printing and publishing | 0.8 | 1.0 | 0.4 | 0.8 | 0.9 | 5.9 | 5.2 | 8.6 | 6.1 | 8.2 |
| Chemical products | 12.4 | 18.5 | 14.3 | 26.6 | 32.4 | 240.7 | 276.0 | 372.1 | 448.7 | 488.5 |
| Refined petroleum products | 0.2 | 0.1 | 0.2 | 0.1 | 0.2 | 4.4 | 4.6 | 4.5 | 3.6 | 4.0 |
| Rubber and plastic products | 3.9 | 4.2 | 5.6 | 4.6 | 5.9 | 25.8 | 30.5 | 38.9 | 43.0 | 56.7 |
| Leather products | 0.1 | 0.2 | 0.1 | ..... | 0.2 | 83.4 | 8.7 | 5.2 | 10.3 | 16.9 |
| Stone, clay and glass products | 1.0 | 1.2 | 1.6 | 1.1 | 1.6 | 38.8 | 30.9 | 28.0 | 31.5 | 39.9 |
| Primary metals | 0.6 | 1.2 | 1.2 | 1.4 | 1.4 | 54.8 | 48.3 | 97.2 | 82.0 | 110.3 |
| Fabricated metal products | 1.7 | 2.1 | 4.0 | 4.9 | 7.2 | 90.0 | 91.4 | 105.1 | 135.1 | 80.5 |
| Industrial machinery and computers | 35.5 | 36.4 | 43.7 | 72.7 | 82.1 | 407.2 | 435.4 | 522.8 | 519.6 | 515.3 |
| Electric and electronic equipment | 3.7 | 5.2 | 7.0 | 10.0 | 17.5 | 123.3 | 219.6 | 238.0 | 264.7 | 260.0 |
| Transportation equipment | 42.8 | 63.5 | 60.9 | 44.0 | 39.9 | 874.0 | 880.2 | 917.8 | 1 229.8 | 1 021.6 |
| Scientific and measuring instruments | 10.3 | 11.3 | 20.5 | 23.4 | 26.0 | 81.2 | 98.2 | 96.6 | 109.5 | 94.7 |
| Miscellaneous manufactures | 0.9 | 1.3 | 1.9 | 1.2 | 2.9 | 52.0 | 96.2 | 109.7 | 107.8 | 99.5 |
| Unidentified manufactures | 0.4 | 0.5 | 0.7 | 0.4 | 0.4 | 6.1 | 8.6 | 8.5 | 2.7 | 6.0 |
| **Agricultural and livestock products** | 1.8 | 1.4 | 4.3 | 3.4 | 2.6 | 3.1 | 15.7 | 5.0 | 3.6 | 3.0 |
| Agricultural products | 1.7 | 1.4 | 4.2 | 3.2 | 2.5 | 2.3 | 14.7 | 4.5 | 2.1 | 2.6 |
| Livestock and livestock products | ..... | ..... | 0.1 | 0.2 | 0.1 | 0.8 | 0.9 | 0.5 | 1.4 | 0.5 |
| **Other commodities** | 0.7 | 0.3 | 1.1 | 0.7 | 1.1 | 8.9 | 10.2 | 13.0 | 6.6 | 6.8 |
| Forestry products | ..... | ..... | 0.2 | ..... | ..... | ..... | ..... | ..... | 0.2 | ..... |
| Fish and other marine products | ..... | ..... | ..... | ..... | ..... | ..... | ..... | 0.5 | ..... | 0.3 |
| Metallic ores and concentrates | ..... | ..... | ..... | ..... | ..... | 0.8 | 0.3 | 0.1 | ..... | ..... |
| Bituminous coal and lignite | ..... | ..... | ..... | ..... | ..... | ..... | ..... | ..... | ..... | ..... |
| Crude petroleum and natural gas | ..... | ..... | ..... | ..... | ..... | ..... | ..... | ..... | ..... | ..... |
| Nonmetallic minerals | 0.1 | 0.1 | ..... | ..... | ..... | 0.1 | 0.1 | 0.1 | 0.2 | 0.4 |
| Scrap and waste | ..... | ..... | 0.1 | 0.2 | 0.1 | 3.0 | 3.6 | 7.5 | 2.1 | 1.2 |
| Used merchandise | 0.1 | 0.1 | 0.6 | 0.4 | 0.8 | 1.5 | 2.1 | 1.2 | 1.3 | 1.2 |
| Goods imported and returned unchanged | ..... | ..... | ..... | ..... | ..... | ..... | ..... | ..... | ..... | ..... |
| Special classification provisions | 0.5 | 0.1 | ..... | 0.2 | 0.3 | 3.6 | 4.0 | 3.6 | 2.8 | 3.8 |

## Table D-3.  State Exports of Goods by Destination and Industry, 1993–1997 —*Continued*

**MICHIGAN** (Millions of dollars.)

| Industry | 1993 | 1994 | 1995 | 1996 | 1997 | 1993 | 1994 | 1995 | 1996 | 1997 |
|---|---|---|---|---|---|---|---|---|---|---|
| | Japan | | | | | South Korea | | | | |
| **ALL GOODS** | 1 064.2 | 1 223.4 | 1 451.8 | 1 789.5 | 1 444.3 | 175.9 | 243.0 | 367.2 | 435.7 | 369.3 |
| **Manufactured goods** | 1 059.5 | 1 218.6 | 1 443.3 | 1 784.2 | 1 440.0 | 174.6 | 242.1 | 366.0 | 434.5 | 368.2 |
| Food products | 60.3 | 63.6 | 83.3 | 93.0 | 80.1 | 8.7 | 8.9 | 24.4 | 45.4 | 27.0 |
| Tobacco products | ..... | ..... | ..... | ..... | ..... | 0.1 | ..... | ..... | ..... | ..... |
| Textile mill products | 2.7 | 3.3 | 1.1 | 1.0 | 7.1 | ..... | 0.2 | 0.3 | 0.4 | 0.1 |
| Apparel | 6.2 | 33.9 | 17.8 | 23.2 | 11.6 | 0.1 | 0.2 | 3.0 | 4.2 | 3.3 |
| Lumber and wood products | 5.1 | 3.3 | 4.7 | 5.1 | 6.2 | 0.7 | 0.6 | 0.4 | 0.7 | 0.4 |
| Furniture and fixtures | 18.4 | 17.8 | 19.1 | 20.6 | 21.5 | 2.5 | 1.2 | 5.2 | 2.9 | 2.5 |
| Paper products | 1.2 | 2.5 | 1.3 | 2.7 | 1.0 | 1.3 | 1.3 | 2.7 | 1.4 | 1.5 |
| Printing and publishing | 3.2 | 2.2 | 5.7 | 1.1 | 2.0 | 0.3 | 0.4 | 0.5 | 0.7 | 0.7 |
| Chemical products | 131.5 | 136.8 | 184.1 | 213.4 | 267.5 | 14.7 | 22.9 | 69.7 | 100.6 | 62.9 |
| Refined petroleum products | 0.4 | 0.4 | 0.4 | 0.6 | 0.6 | 0.3 | 0.5 | 0.8 | 0.3 | 0.4 |
| Rubber and plastic products | 17.9 | 17.1 | 29.3 | 24.9 | 31.2 | 1.1 | 3.6 | 3.1 | 8.4 | 14.1 |
| Leather products | 80.9 | 5.9 | 2.3 | 2.3 | 2.5 | 0.5 | 0.7 | 0.3 | 0.1 | 0.1 |
| Stone, clay and glass products | 10.1 | 16.4 | 11.9 | 17.6 | 27.5 | 6.2 | 7.6 | 6.5 | 5.2 | 7.2 |
| Primary metals | 34.9 | 28.9 | 45.9 | 39.8 | 71.0 | 3.5 | 2.9 | 26.4 | 22.9 | 21.1 |
| Fabricated metal products | 46.7 | 46.8 | 62.2 | 72.4 | 49.0 | 2.5 | 4.1 | 10.0 | 26.0 | 6.0 |
| Industrial machinery and computers | 126.2 | 147.1 | 156.9 | 174.8 | 160.5 | 52.5 | 49.7 | 70.3 | 47.7 | 69.1 |
| Electric and electronic equipment | 32.7 | 40.5 | 66.1 | 67.1 | 70.7 | 11.3 | 17.7 | 15.4 | 23.7 | 24.8 |
| Transportation equipment | 435.4 | 601.4 | 690.6 | 950.8 | 566.5 | 42.5 | 70.1 | 88.6 | 115.2 | 96.1 |
| Scientific and measuring instruments | 38.1 | 43.3 | 48.3 | 61.2 | 39.6 | 12.0 | 20.8 | 17.6 | 19.4 | 25.3 |
| Miscellaneous manufactures | 6.2 | 6.0 | 10.6 | 11.7 | 22.5 | 13.2 | 27.8 | 20.1 | 8.8 | 5.2 |
| Unidentified manufactures | 1.3 | 1.3 | 1.4 | 1.0 | 1.4 | 0.5 | 0.8 | 0.8 | 0.4 | 0.4 |
| **Agricultural and livestock products** | 1.4 | 1.6 | 2.0 | 1.9 | 2.4 | 0.2 | 0.1 | 0.3 | 0.3 | 0.2 |
| Agricultural products | 1.2 | 1.5 | 1.7 | 1.1 | 2.4 | 0.1 | ..... | 0.1 | 0.2 | ..... |
| Livestock and livestock products | 0.2 | 0.1 | 0.3 | 0.8 | ..... | 0.1 | ..... | 0.2 | 0.2 | 0.1 |
| **Other commodities** | 3.3 | 3.2 | 6.5 | 3.5 | 1.8 | 1.1 | 0.9 | 1.0 | 0.9 | 0.9 |
| Forestry products | ..... | ..... | ..... | 0.2 | ..... | ..... | ..... | ..... | ..... | ..... |
| Fish and other marine products | ..... | ..... | 0.4 | ..... | ..... | ..... | ..... | ..... | ..... | ..... |
| Metallic ores and concentrates | 0.8 | 0.2 | ..... | ..... | ..... | ..... | ..... | 0.1 | ..... | ..... |
| Bituminous coal and lignite | ..... | ..... | ..... | ..... | ..... | ..... | ..... | ..... | ..... | ..... |
| Crude petroleum and natural gas | ..... | ..... | ..... | ..... | ..... | ..... | ..... | ..... | ..... | ..... |
| Nonmetallic minerals | ..... | ..... | ..... | 0.1 | 0.1 | ..... | ..... | ..... | ..... | ..... |
| Scrap and waste | 0.9 | 0.2 | 4.9 | 0.7 | 0.3 | ..... | ..... | ..... | ..... | ..... |
| Used merchandise | 0.4 | 1.6 | 0.2 | 1.1 | 0.6 | 1.0 | 0.3 | 0.1 | ..... | ..... |
| Goods imported and returned unchanged | ..... | ..... | ..... | ..... | ..... | ..... | ..... | ..... | ..... | ..... |
| Special classification provisions | 1.2 | 1.1 | 1.0 | 1.3 | 0.8 | 0.1 | 0.5 | 0.7 | 0.8 | 0.9 |
| | Taiwan | | | | | Singapore | | | | |
| **ALL GOODS** | 337.8 | 359.6 | 293.3 | 198.8 | 207.6 | 81.5 | 84.0 | 119.0 | 110.5 | 117.5 |
| **Manufactured goods** | 335.6 | 357.9 | 291.7 | 197.9 | 205.2 | 81.1 | 83.5 | 118.8 | 110.3 | 117.1 |
| Food products | 11.9 | 20.6 | 12.8 | 12.8 | 16.2 | 0.4 | 0.5 | 1.0 | 0.9 | 0.7 |
| Tobacco products | ..... | ..... | ..... | ..... | ..... | 0.8 | ..... | ..... | ..... | ..... |
| Textile mill products | 0.1 | 0.2 | 0.2 | ..... | 0.3 | 0.2 | 0.1 | 0.2 | 0.2 | 0.2 |
| Apparel | 0.1 | 0.1 | 0.1 | ..... | ..... | 0.1 | 0.1 | 0.3 | ..... | ..... |
| Lumber and wood products | 1.7 | 1.2 | 1.4 | 1.2 | 1.2 | 0.1 | 0.2 | 0.3 | 0.5 | 0.6 |
| Furniture and fixtures | 1.9 | 2.1 | 1.7 | 1.7 | 2.8 | 11.2 | 9.3 | 13.9 | 14.7 | 12.5 |
| Paper products | 0.4 | 0.6 | 0.5 | 0.4 | 0.9 | 0.2 | 0.2 | 0.2 | 0.2 | 0.5 |
| Printing and publishing | 0.7 | 0.6 | 0.6 | 0.8 | 0.6 | 0.7 | 0.4 | 0.6 | 2.4 | 3.6 |
| Chemical products | 30.1 | 43.8 | 37.7 | 33.2 | 35.1 | 6.0 | 8.0 | 9.1 | 7.2 | 19.0 |
| Refined petroleum products | 1.8 | 1.5 | 1.0 | 0.8 | 0.7 | 0.4 | 0.4 | 0.1 | 0.3 | 0.1 |
| Rubber and plastic products | 1.7 | 2.9 | 1.2 | 1.0 | 1.7 | 0.5 | 1.1 | 1.7 | 3.0 | 2.5 |
| Leather products | 0.8 | 0.4 | 0.1 | 0.2 | 0.1 | ..... | ..... | ..... | 0.1 | ..... |
| Stone, clay and glass products | 2.1 | 1.0 | 1.3 | 1.4 | 0.8 | 0.9 | 1.0 | 2.1 | 0.5 | 0.9 |
| Primary metals | 5.0 | 5.3 | 14.9 | 5.8 | 7.8 | 0.5 | 1.1 | 1.0 | 0.8 | 1.3 |
| Fabricated metal products | 17.3 | 15.0 | 13.6 | 13.4 | 8.2 | 5.2 | 6.8 | 4.3 | 2.6 | 2.3 |
| Industrial machinery and computers | 31.3 | 40.9 | 48.7 | 35.9 | 36.8 | 40.7 | 33.8 | 61.2 | 45.4 | 50.7 |
| Electric and electronic equipment | 28.2 | 37.4 | 37.3 | 35.7 | 25.8 | 3.5 | 8.3 | 11.8 | 15.5 | 11.0 |
| Transportation equipment | 165.1 | 123.6 | 78.0 | 43.6 | 55.8 | 5.7 | 8.5 | 7.6 | 11.7 | 7.1 |
| Scientific and measuring instruments | 9.6 | 8.0 | 5.5 | 5.8 | 6.3 | 2.5 | 2.0 | 1.6 | 2.8 | 2.8 |
| Miscellaneous manufactures | 24.1 | 50.2 | 31.7 | 3.9 | 1.8 | 1.2 | 1.2 | 1.3 | 1.2 | 1.1 |
| Unidentified manufactures | 1.5 | 2.7 | 3.3 | 0.3 | 2.3 | 0.2 | 0.3 | 0.3 | 0.3 | 0.1 |
| **Agricultural and livestock products** | 0.5 | 0.9 | 0.4 | 0.5 | 0.4 | 0.2 | 0.1 | ..... | 0.1 | ..... |
| Agricultural products | 0.1 | 0.1 | 0.4 | 0.4 | 0.1 | ..... | 0.1 | ..... | 0.1 | ..... |
| Livestock and livestock products | 0.3 | 0.8 | ..... | 0.1 | 0.3 | 0.2 | ..... | ..... | ..... | ..... |
| **Other commodities** | 1.7 | 0.9 | 1.2 | 0.3 | 2.1 | 0.2 | 0.5 | 0.2 | 0.1 | 0.4 |
| Forestry products | ..... | ..... | ..... | ..... | ..... | ..... | ..... | ..... | ..... | ..... |
| Fish and other marine products | ..... | ..... | ..... | ..... | ..... | ..... | ..... | ..... | ..... | ..... |
| Metallic ores and concentrates | ..... | 0.1 | ..... | ..... | ..... | ..... | ..... | ..... | ..... | ..... |
| Bituminous coal and lignite | ..... | ..... | ..... | ..... | ..... | ..... | ..... | ..... | ..... | ..... |
| Crude petroleum and natural gas | ..... | ..... | ..... | ..... | ..... | ..... | ..... | ..... | ..... | ..... |
| Nonmetallic minerals | ..... | ..... | ..... | ..... | 0.1 | ..... | ..... | ..... | ..... | ..... |
| Scrap and waste | ..... | ..... | 0.1 | ..... | 0.2 | ..... | ..... | ..... | ..... | ..... |
| Used merchandise | ..... | 0.1 | 0.5 | 0.1 | 0.5 | ..... | ..... | ..... | ..... | ..... |
| Goods imported and returned unchanged | ..... | ..... | ..... | ..... | ..... | ..... | ..... | ..... | ..... | ..... |
| Special classification provisions | 1.7 | 0.6 | 0.5 | 0.2 | 1.3 | 0.1 | 0.4 | 0.1 | 0.1 | 0.4 |

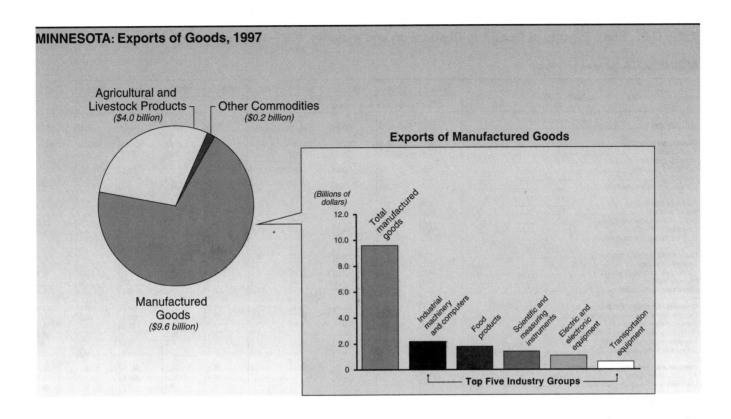

## MINNESOTA: Exports of Goods, 1997

Agricultural and Livestock Products ($4.0 billion)

Other Commodities ($0.2 billion)

Manufactured Goods ($9.6 billion)

**Exports of Manufactured Goods**

Top Five Industry Groups

---

### Table D-3.  State Exports of Goods by Destination and Industry, 1993–1997 —Continued

**MINNESOTA** (Millions of dollars.)

| Industry | 1993 | 1994 | 1995 | 1996 | 1997 | 1993 | 1994 | 1995 | 1996 | 1997 |
|---|---|---|---|---|---|---|---|---|---|---|
| | All destinations | | | | | Canada | | | | |
| **ALL GOODS** | 9 974.4 | 10 011.1 | 12 404.3 | 13 884.1 | 13 793.3 | 1 950.4 | 2 108.5 | 2 442.2 | 2 860.6 | 3 190.2 |
| **Manufactured goods** | 7 073.2 | 7 201.1 | 8 115.4 | 8 811.6 | 9 590.0 | 1 835.8 | 1 971.1 | 2 331.6 | 2 715.7 | 2 936.4 |
| Food products | 1 605.5 | 1 508.1 | 1 718.4 | 1 714.5 | 1 801.4 | 167.5 | 208.3 | 230.8 | 251.5 | 314.0 |
| Tobacco products | ..... | ..... | ..... | 0.3 | ..... | ..... | ..... | ..... | ..... | ..... |
| Textile mill products | 33.5 | 19.9 | 24.0 | 24.2 | 26.9 | 10.6 | 7.2 | 8.1 | 8.4 | 12.0 |
| Apparel | 29.1 | 24.6 | 17.5 | 19.7 | 24.0 | 9.3 | 8.9 | 10.5 | 10.6 | 11.8 |
| Lumber and wood products | 38.9 | 42.8 | 53.5 | 56.2 | 56.1 | 19.5 | 21.4 | 22.0 | 25.3 | 24.6 |
| Furniture and fixtures | 19.9 | 24.1 | 24.7 | 26.9 | 35.0 | 9.3 | 10.2 | 11.1 | 13.1 | 15.4 |
| Paper products | 204.7 | 153.6 | 154.7 | 170.1 | 194.7 | 64.3 | 72.9 | 91.3 | 97.9 | 113.0 |
| Printing and publishing | 54.7 | 54.2 | 67.2 | 68.5 | 71.7 | 25.3 | 23.7 | 24.6 | 25.1 | 27.9 |
| Chemical products | 245.9 | 206.5 | 223.7 | 266.7 | 332.6 | 55.1 | 65.1 | 67.5 | 78.1 | 96.1 |
| Refined petroleum products | 6.6 | 6.5 | 10.7 | 18.4 | 28.2 | 4.8 | 4.7 | 9.3 | 17.0 | 9.7 |
| Rubber and plastic products | 169.1 | 194.3 | 188.5 | 208.6 | 237.6 | 32.6 | 37.9 | 43.2 | 51.0 | 58.2 |
| Leather products | 24.1 | 32.8 | 31.5 | 32.9 | 40.3 | 1.7 | 1.4 | 2.0 | 2.6 | 4.0 |
| Stone, clay and glass products | 136.2 | 175.1 | 107.6 | 100.0 | 116.4 | 33.7 | 35.3 | 40.7 | 34.2 | 35.5 |
| Primary metals | 65.7 | 64.4 | 93.3 | 74.9 | 91.8 | 24.6 | 23.6 | 27.5 | 28.1 | 28.9 |
| Fabricated metal products | 218.7 | 234.7 | 208.6 | 233.3 | 269.8 | 95.9 | 85.2 | 90.8 | 122.2 | 119.0 |
| Industrial machinery and computers | 1 515.7 | 1 562.5 | 1 787.1 | 1 974.7 | 2 181.5 | 293.0 | 309.9 | 350.5 | 413.6 | 473.2 |
| Electric and electronic equipment | 776.0 | 891.6 | 988.3 | 1 008.1 | 1 089.6 | 153.1 | 164.9 | 168.0 | 200.6 | 209.0 |
| Transportation equipment | 372.9 | 424.8 | 485.8 | 517.5 | 577.3 | 211.3 | 277.7 | 345.5 | 361.5 | 340.2 |
| Scientific and measuring instruments | 967.9 | 1 021.3 | 1 166.9 | 1 354.0 | 1 415.7 | 104.4 | 108.8 | 100.1 | 109.5 | 121.0 |
| Miscellaneous manufactures | 72.2 | 82.4 | 119.6 | 114.4 | 114.7 | 30.2 | 38.7 | 57.9 | 50.1 | 51.1 |
| Unidentified manufactures | 515.8 | 477.0 | 643.8 | 827.7 | 884.7 | 489.7 | 465.2 | 630.2 | 815.1 | 871.9 |
| **Agricultural and livestock products** | 2 788.9 | 2 672.5 | 4 177.6 | 4 949.9 | 3 981.6 | 35.8 | 37.2 | 39.7 | 54.6 | 63.8 |
| Agricultural products | 2 778.4 | 2 662.8 | 4 171.1 | 4 942.9 | 3 973.8 | 28.4 | 31.7 | 34.7 | 49.3 | 57.2 |
| Livestock and livestock products | 10.5 | 9.7 | 6.5 | 7.0 | 7.8 | 7.4 | 5.5 | 5.0 | 5.2 | 6.6 |
| **Other commodities** | 112.3 | 137.4 | 111.3 | 122.6 | 221.6 | 78.8 | 100.3 | 71.0 | 90.3 | 189.9 |
| Forestry products | 1.4 | 0.9 | 1.4 | 1.9 | 0.9 | 0.8 | 0.6 | 1.1 | 0.8 | 0.3 |
| Fish and other marine products | 5.2 | 7.7 | 5.7 | 5.1 | 4.3 | 3.6 | 6.0 | 3.7 | 2.6 | 2.7 |
| Metallic ores and concentrates | 17.5 | 21.7 | 2.3 | 23.2 | 112.7 | 17.4 | 19.3 | 0.2 | 21.5 | 111.2 |
| Bituminous coal and lignite | ..... | ..... | 0.3 | 0.8 | ..... | ..... | ..... | ..... | 0.8 | ..... |
| Crude petroleum and natural gas | 0.1 | 2.0 | 1.1 | 0.1 | ..... | 0.1 | 2.0 | 1.1 | ..... | ..... |
| Nonmetallic minerals | 22.4 | 18.2 | 10.8 | 7.5 | 14.9 | 5.4 | 4.5 | 3.7 | 4.6 | 8.7 |
| Scrap and waste | 19.2 | 29.3 | 28.6 | 18.8 | 20.1 | 18.7 | 28.9 | 27.2 | 17.8 | 17.8 |
| Used merchandise | 6.6 | 10.3 | 9.5 | 8.2 | 10.8 | 1.2 | 1.4 | 1.8 | 1.8 | 2.6 |
| Goods imported and returned unchanged | 25.4 | 31.3 | 26.6 | 35.0 | 42.4 | 25.4 | 31.3 | 26.6 | 35.0 | 42.4 |
| Special classification provisions | 14.4 | 15.8 | 25.2 | 21.9 | 15.5 | 6.1 | 6.3 | 5.6 | 5.4 | 4.3 |

## Table D-3.  State Exports of Goods by Destination and Industry, 1993–1997 —*Continued*

**MINNESOTA** (Millions of dollars.)

| Industry | 1993 | 1994 | 1995 | 1996 | 1997 | 1993 | 1994 | 1995 | 1996 | 1997 |
|---|---|---|---|---|---|---|---|---|---|---|
| | South and Central America and Caribbean | | | | | Mexico | | | | |
| **ALL GOODS** | 457.6 | 450.7 | 686.6 | 762.0 | 780.8 | 228.6 | 329.8 | 505.7 | 846.3 | 822.8 |
| **Manufactured goods** | 265.2 | 278.8 | 327.4 | 354.2 | 433.9 | 198.8 | 274.5 | 243.2 | 292.7 | 352.0 |
| Food products | 73.4 | 65.1 | 116.9 | 116.4 | 154.5 | 59.9 | 69.2 | 66.8 | 60.2 | 61.0 |
| Tobacco products | ..... | ..... | ..... | ..... | ..... | ..... | ..... | ..... | ..... | ..... |
| Textile mill products | 1.6 | 1.8 | 0.6 | 1.6 | 0.9 | 0.5 | 0.6 | 0.2 | 0.4 | 1.7 |
| Apparel | 4.3 | 4.2 | 2.1 | 2.5 | 1.3 | 0.8 | 0.9 | 0.5 | 0.4 | 2.2 |
| Lumber and wood products | 0.5 | 0.6 | 1.0 | 1.0 | 0.9 | 0.6 | 1.1 | 0.4 | 0.2 | 0.3 |
| Furniture and fixtures | 0.9 | 1.1 | 1.3 | 1.3 | 1.4 | 1.1 | 2.0 | 0.7 | 1.2 | 3.1 |
| Paper products | 14.6 | 14.3 | 7.0 | 5.6 | 6.3 | 3.7 | 7.0 | 8.8 | 10.0 | 12.2 |
| Printing and publishing | 1.4 | 1.2 | 2.0 | 1.3 | 1.6 | 2.7 | 7.4 | 10.0 | 17.3 | 20.8 |
| Chemical products | 16.9 | 19.5 | 14.2 | 18.7 | 17.0 | 3.0 | 4.0 | 3.8 | 4.8 | 5.3 |
| Refined petroleum products | 0.2 | ..... | ..... | ..... | 0.1 | 0.1 | 0.1 | 0.2 | 0.1 | ..... |
| Rubber and plastic products | 6.3 | 7.8 | 6.5 | 7.2 | 8.9 | 2.3 | 4.0 | 4.5 | 5.2 | 6.9 |
| Leather products | 5.7 | 7.2 | 3.9 | 2.4 | 1.9 | ..... | 0.3 | ..... | ..... | 0.1 |
| Stone, clay and glass products | 4.7 | 3.9 | 3.5 | 2.8 | 5.3 | 0.7 | 1.5 | 1.0 | 2.3 | 3.5 |
| Primary metals | 1.0 | 0.3 | 1.8 | 1.9 | 1.9 | 0.8 | 2.7 | 7.7 | 11.3 | 5.0 |
| Fabricated metal products | 8.9 | 6.3 | 6.7 | 8.5 | 10.8 | 6.1 | 7.3 | 9.5 | 8.0 | 9.0 |
| Industrial machinery and computers | 44.4 | 57.6 | 68.5 | 89.4 | 102.0 | 51.6 | 65.1 | 36.4 | 50.9 | 54.8 |
| Electric and electronic equipment | 41.0 | 46.1 | 48.9 | 40.2 | 46.6 | 29.3 | 58.7 | 52.3 | 78.5 | 110.7 |
| Transportation equipment | 3.2 | 3.4 | 3.5 | 5.6 | 13.3 | 4.0 | 4.3 | 2.5 | 3.2 | 4.2 |
| Scientific and measuring instruments | 34.0 | 34.9 | 34.3 | 43.1 | 54.9 | 29.4 | 35.3 | 31.4 | 36.7 | 48.0 |
| Miscellaneous manufactures | 1.0 | 2.7 | 4.1 | 4.4 | 3.7 | 1.5 | 2.5 | 6.0 | 1.2 | 1.8 |
| Unidentified manufactures | 1.3 | 0.5 | 0.6 | 0.6 | 0.8 | 0.5 | 0.6 | 0.4 | 0.7 | 1.3 |
| **Agricultural and livestock products** | 191.8 | 171.1 | 358.0 | 407.4 | 345.7 | 26.5 | 53.5 | 261.1 | 552.2 | 468.6 |
| Agricultural products | 191.7 | 171.2 | 357.6 | 407.3 | 345.7 | 24.9 | 50.1 | 260.6 | 551.6 | 468.1 |
| Livestock and livestock products | 0.1 | ..... | 0.4 | 0.1 | ..... | 1.7 | 3.4 | 0.5 | 0.6 | 0.5 |
| **Other commodities** | 0.6 | 0.8 | 1.2 | 0.4 | 1.2 | 3.2 | 1.8 | 1.5 | 1.4 | 2.2 |
| Forestry products | ..... | ..... | ..... | 0.1 | ..... | ..... | ..... | ..... | 0.6 | ..... |
| Fish and other marine products | ..... | ..... | ..... | ..... | ..... | 0.1 | 0.1 | 0.1 | ..... | 0.2 |
| Metallic ores and concentrates | ..... | ..... | ..... | ..... | ..... | ..... | ..... | ..... | ..... | ..... |
| Bituminous coal and lignite | ..... | ..... | 0.3 | ..... | ..... | ..... | ..... | ..... | ..... | ..... |
| Crude petroleum and natural gas | ..... | ..... | ..... | ..... | ..... | ..... | ..... | ..... | ..... | ..... |
| Nonmetallic minerals | 0.1 | 0.1 | ..... | ..... | 0.2 | 2.5 | 1.3 | 0.8 | 0.2 | 0.2 |
| Scrap and waste | ..... | ..... | ..... | ..... | ..... | 0.4 | 0.1 | ..... | 0.3 | 1.6 |
| Used merchandise | 0.4 | 0.4 | 0.5 | 0.2 | 0.7 | 0.2 | 0.2 | 0.5 | 0.1 | 0.1 |
| Goods imported and returned unchanged | ..... | ..... | ..... | ..... | ..... | ..... | ..... | ..... | ..... | ..... |
| Special classification provisions | ..... | 0.1 | 0.4 | 0.1 | 0.2 | 0.1 | 0.2 | 0.1 | 0.2 | 0.1 |
| | European Union | | | | | United Kingdom | | | | |
| **ALL GOODS** | 3 362.2 | 3 393.6 | 4 049.7 | 4 075.7 | 4 025.2 | 476.2 | 448.3 | 540.9 | 599.3 | 703.8 |
| **Manufactured goods** | 2 480.1 | 2 378.2 | 2 661.6 | 2 814.4 | 2 910.1 | 401.9 | 410.6 | 465.8 | 499.4 | 550.8 |
| Food products | 880.0 | 764.6 | 844.8 | 832.8 | 793.4 | 108.0 | 94.0 | 105.1 | 126.2 | 129.9 |
| Tobacco products | ..... | ..... | ..... | ..... | ..... | ..... | ..... | ..... | ..... | ..... |
| Textile mill products | 10.1 | 6.8 | 7.8 | 8.5 | 6.0 | 2.8 | 1.9 | 1.0 | 2.0 | 1.4 |
| Apparel | 8.9 | 7.8 | 1.5 | 2.5 | 4.6 | 1.5 | 1.4 | 0.1 | 0.5 | 0.6 |
| Lumber and wood products | 5.0 | 4.4 | 5.5 | 5.2 | 6.7 | 1.8 | 1.5 | 3.1 | 3.2 | 3.8 |
| Furniture and fixtures | 4.3 | 3.9 | 5.3 | 5.6 | 6.4 | 1.4 | 1.2 | 1.5 | 1.2 | 2.4 |
| Paper products | 65.0 | 38.5 | 26.4 | 32.2 | 30.6 | 9.6 | 5.8 | 5.2 | 7.8 | 7.2 |
| Printing and publishing | 16.9 | 14.1 | 20.3 | 14.9 | 12.9 | 3.6 | 5.9 | 9.4 | 5.6 | 6.0 |
| Chemical products | 64.4 | 64.2 | 60.8 | 78.5 | 88.9 | 18.2 | 15.9 | 13.8 | 20.7 | 29.7 |
| Refined petroleum products | 0.3 | 0.4 | 0.4 | 0.4 | 16.9 | 0.2 | 0.2 | ..... | ..... | ..... |
| Rubber and plastic products | 56.0 | 55.9 | 51.8 | 55.4 | 63.8 | 9.5 | 11.8 | 8.9 | 8.7 | 12.5 |
| Leather products | 3.2 | 6.1 | 9.4 | 9.3 | 8.1 | 0.2 | 0.5 | 1.0 | 1.4 | 1.6 |
| Stone, clay and glass products | 22.8 | 23.2 | 15.1 | 18.4 | 22.2 | 4.2 | 8.4 | 2.0 | 2.3 | 2.7 |
| Primary metals | 7.7 | 14.2 | 32.0 | 11.0 | 14.3 | 1.4 | 2.0 | 1.6 | 1.6 | 3.5 |
| Fabricated metal products | 25.9 | 39.2 | 43.8 | 46.3 | 47.5 | 11.3 | 15.0 | 14.5 | 12.9 | 15.8 |
| Industrial machinery and computers | 511.9 | 513.0 | 572.4 | 645.9 | 729.1 | 110.4 | 98.5 | 114.5 | 112.7 | 135.6 |
| Electric and electronic equipment | 223.2 | 239.8 | 287.5 | 263.3 | 252.7 | 46.1 | 73.1 | 88.7 | 74.3 | 62.3 |
| Transportation equipment | 115.3 | 91.5 | 80.1 | 77.0 | 116.4 | 9.6 | 11.3 | 18.4 | 10.3 | 14.9 |
| Scientific and measuring instruments | 430.8 | 466.1 | 567.4 | 669.3 | 655.4 | 54.6 | 54.0 | 69.0 | 97.2 | 108.9 |
| Miscellaneous manufactures | 21.9 | 18.8 | 23.4 | 32.9 | 30.2 | 5.8 | 6.6 | 6.4 | 9.6 | 10.6 |
| Unidentified manufactures | 6.5 | 5.7 | 5.7 | 5.2 | 4.1 | 1.7 | 1.8 | 1.5 | 1.3 | 1.4 |
| **Agricultural and livestock products** | 868.9 | 998.6 | 1 373.3 | 1 244.3 | 1 099.4 | 71.2 | 33.4 | 72.7 | 95.0 | 148.6 |
| Agricultural products | 868.1 | 998.3 | 1 373.2 | 1 243.8 | 1 099.0 | 71.2 | 33.3 | 72.7 | 94.9 | 148.6 |
| Livestock and livestock products | 0.8 | 0.3 | 0.1 | 0.5 | 0.3 | ..... | ..... | ..... | 0.1 | ..... |
| **Other commodities** | 13.2 | 16.9 | 14.7 | 17.0 | 15.8 | 3.1 | 4.3 | 2.4 | 4.8 | 4.3 |
| Forestry products | 0.1 | 0.2 | 0.2 | 0.4 | 0.3 | ..... | ..... | 0.1 | ..... | ..... |
| Fish and other marine products | 1.3 | 1.1 | 1.6 | 2.3 | 1.3 | ..... | ..... | ..... | ..... | ..... |
| Metallic ores and concentrates | ..... | ..... | ..... | ..... | ..... | ..... | ..... | ..... | ..... | ..... |
| Bituminous coal and lignite | ..... | ..... | ..... | ..... | ..... | ..... | ..... | ..... | ..... | ..... |
| Crude petroleum and natural gas | ..... | ..... | ..... | ..... | ..... | ..... | ..... | ..... | ..... | ..... |
| Nonmetallic minerals | 4.2 | 3.9 | 3.6 | 1.2 | 0.8 | ..... | ..... | ..... | ..... | ..... |
| Scrap and waste | ..... | 0.1 | ..... | 0.2 | 0.3 | ..... | ..... | ..... | ..... | ..... |
| Used merchandise | 2.1 | 5.6 | 1.5 | 2.9 | 5.6 | 0.1 | 1.2 | 0.5 | 1.0 | 2.3 |
| Goods imported and returned unchanged | ..... | ..... | ..... | ..... | ..... | ..... | ..... | ..... | ..... | ..... |
| Special classification provisions | 5.4 | 5.9 | 7.7 | 10.1 | 7.4 | 3.0 | 3.0 | 1.9 | 3.8 | 1.9 |

## Table D-3. State Exports of Goods by Destination and Industry, 1993–1997 —Continued

**MINNESOTA** (Millions of dollars.)

| Industry | 1993 | 1994 | 1995 | 1996 | 1997 | 1993 | 1994 | 1995 | 1996 | 1997 |
|---|---|---|---|---|---|---|---|---|---|---|
| | Germany | | | | | France | | | | |
| **ALL GOODS** | 530.9 | 473.8 | 514.0 | 658.7 | 593.4 | 283.7 | 236.7 | 265.4 | 280.2 | 362.9 |
| **Manufactured goods** | 375.8 | 349.4 | 402.0 | 470.3 | 422.9 | 227.7 | 205.2 | 212.3 | 224.7 | 308.2 |
| Food products | 71.4 | 55.9 | 62.6 | 66.3 | 54.4 | 50.1 | 20.8 | 13.9 | 18.8 | 42.2 |
| Tobacco products | ..... | ..... | ..... | ..... | ..... | ..... | ..... | ..... | ..... | ..... |
| Textile mill products | 2.8 | 1.5 | 4.6 | 3.4 | 1.3 | 1.3 | 1.4 | 0.7 | 0.8 | 0.9 |
| Apparel | 0.9 | 0.8 | 0.5 | 0.4 | 1.9 | 0.3 | 0.4 | 0.3 | 0.3 | 0.5 |
| Lumber and wood products | 2.0 | 1.1 | 1.4 | 0.9 | 2.2 | 0.1 | 0.4 | 0.1 | 0.2 | 0.1 |
| Furniture and fixtures | 1.5 | 0.9 | 1.3 | 1.0 | 1.3 | 0.3 | 0.3 | 0.5 | 0.3 | 0.1 |
| Paper products | 15.5 | 9.9 | 5.7 | 6.8 | 4.1 | 10.1 | 8.5 | 6.0 | 6.6 | 5.8 |
| Printing and publishing | 8.1 | 4.0 | 5.1 | 3.4 | 1.6 | 1.7 | 1.7 | 1.7 | 1.2 | 0.9 |
| Chemical products | 12.7 | 11.4 | 10.0 | 11.2 | 10.9 | 9.2 | 11.4 | 12.6 | 16.4 | 18.4 |
| Refined petroleum products | ..... | ..... | 0.1 | 0.1 | 0.1 | | | | | |
| Rubber and plastic products | 17.4 | 16.6 | 17.3 | 21.6 | 20.3 | 4.7 | 5.7 | 5.6 | 5.7 | 7.9 |
| Leather products | 0.8 | 0.6 | 0.9 | 3.2 | 0.4 | 0.1 | ..... | ..... | 0.1 | 0.1 |
| Stone, clay and glass products | 7.0 | 7.0 | 7.5 | 9.7 | 13.9 | 1.5 | 2.0 | 1.4 | 1.8 | 2.5 |
| Primary metals | 1.7 | 2.6 | 3.6 | 4.4 | 5.5 | 0.3 | 0.8 | 2.6 | 1.1 | 0.7 |
| Fabricated metal products | 5.8 | 8.5 | 10.6 | 10.0 | 11.9 | 1.6 | 2.1 | 2.4 | 3.3 | 3.1 |
| Industrial machinery and computers | 81.3 | 77.3 | 84.5 | 113.1 | 98.0 | 68.7 | 66.9 | 59.1 | 63.3 | 75.5 |
| Electric and electronic equipment | 22.3 | 24.2 | 35.5 | 43.3 | 40.4 | 18.3 | 15.5 | 21.4 | 21.6 | 32.9 |
| Transportation equipment | 17.0 | 9.7 | 13.5 | 12.9 | 6.5 | 2.2 | 6.5 | 3.4 | 3.3 | 34.3 |
| Scientific and measuring instruments | 102.8 | 113.2 | 131.3 | 153.2 | 143.9 | 54.9 | 59.0 | 78.7 | 77.6 | 80.1 |
| Miscellaneous manufactures | 3.6 | 3.2 | 4.8 | 4.5 | 3.6 | 1.7 | 1.4 | 1.4 | 1.9 | 1.8 |
| Unidentified manufactures | 1.0 | 1.0 | 1.3 | 1.0 | 0.7 | 0.5 | 0.5 | 0.4 | 0.4 | 0.4 |
| **Agricultural and livestock products** | 153.4 | 122.2 | 110.1 | 186.4 | 168.2 | 54.7 | 28.6 | 52.1 | 54.1 | 52.8 |
| Agricultural products | 152.7 | 122.1 | 110.0 | 186.0 | 168.1 | 54.7 | 28.6 | 52.1 | 54.1 | 52.8 |
| Livestock and livestock products | 0.7 | 0.1 | 0.1 | 0.4 | 0.1 | ..... | ..... | ..... | ..... | ..... |
| **Other commodities** | 1.6 | 2.2 | 1.9 | 2.0 | 2.3 | 1.3 | 3.0 | 1.0 | 1.5 | 1.8 |
| Forestry products | ..... | ..... | 0.1 | ..... | 0.1 | ..... | ..... | ..... | 0.1 | 0.1 |
| Fish and other marine products | 0.1 | 0.2 | ..... | 0.1 | 0.1 | ..... | ..... | ..... | ..... | ..... |
| Metallic ores and concentrates | ..... | ..... | ..... | ..... | ..... | ..... | ..... | ..... | ..... | ..... |
| Bituminous coal and lignite | ..... | ..... | ..... | ..... | ..... | ..... | ..... | ..... | ..... | ..... |
| Crude petroleum and natural gas | ..... | ..... | ..... | ..... | ..... | ..... | ..... | ..... | ..... | ..... |
| Nonmetallic minerals | 0.3 | 0.3 | 0.4 | 0.1 | 0.1 | ..... | ..... | ..... | 0.1 | ..... |
| Scrap and waste | ..... | ..... | ..... | ..... | ..... | ..... | ..... | ..... | ..... | ..... |
| Used merchandise | 0.6 | 1.1 | 0.2 | 1.1 | 0.9 | 0.3 | 2.2 | 0.2 | ..... | 1.0 |
| Goods imported and returned unchanged | ..... | ..... | ..... | ..... | ..... | ..... | ..... | ..... | ..... | ..... |
| Special classification provisions | 0.6 | 0.6 | 1.2 | 0.7 | 1.2 | 0.9 | 0.7 | 0.8 | 1.2 | 0.7 |
| | The Netherlands | | | | | Asian 10 | | | | |
| **ALL GOODS** | 947.2 | 968.5 | 1 072.8 | 989.1 | 846.2 | 2 186.7 | 2 292.4 | 2 935.4 | 3 126.2 | 3 027.7 |
| **Manufactured goods** | 707.2 | 635.6 | 582.2 | 609.9 | 574.6 | 1 530.9 | 1 606.0 | 1 779.9 | 1 844.3 | 2 109.5 |
| Food products | 283.6 | 279.2 | 281.8 | 277.0 | 211.1 | 109.4 | 145.3 | 198.3 | 205.1 | 182.9 |
| Tobacco products | ..... | ..... | ..... | ..... | ..... | ..... | ..... | ..... | ..... | ..... |
| Textile mill products | 1.1 | 0.7 | 0.1 | 0.2 | 0.2 | 9.0 | 2.2 | 6.3 | 4.4 | 4.7 |
| Apparel | 5.8 | 4.1 | 0.2 | 0.5 | 0.5 | 4.0 | 1.7 | 2.1 | 2.7 | 3.1 |
| Lumber and wood products | ..... | 0.2 | ..... | 0.1 | 0.1 | 12.7 | 15.0 | 23.9 | 23.7 | 22.6 |
| Furniture and fixtures | 0.3 | 0.6 | 0.8 | 1.7 | 1.3 | 1.9 | 3.3 | 3.4 | 3.1 | 5.7 |
| Paper products | 18.6 | 6.0 | 3.1 | 5.6 | 6.6 | 42.2 | 10.9 | 15.1 | 16.3 | 22.7 |
| Printing and publishing | 1.1 | 0.7 | 2.1 | 2.8 | 1.8 | 3.3 | 3.4 | 4.9 | 5.8 | 4.7 |
| Chemical products | 6.6 | 6.3 | 6.4 | 9.7 | 6.2 | 82.3 | 41.4 | 47.2 | 66.4 | 94.9 |
| Refined petroleum products | ..... | ..... | 0.1 | ..... | 16.6 | 0.9 | 1.0 | 0.7 | 0.7 | 0.9 |
| Rubber and plastic products | 14.9 | 10.3 | 5.9 | 6.1 | 8.5 | 64.8 | 81.2 | 76.0 | 81.7 | 88.1 |
| Leather products | 1.1 | 0.8 | 0.6 | 0.4 | 1.5 | 9.0 | 13.0 | 12.3 | 14.5 | 21.4 |
| Stone, clay and glass products | 5.0 | 2.9 | 0.8 | 1.4 | 1.0 | 68.3 | 105.6 | 40.6 | 35.4 | 39.5 |
| Primary metals | 3.1 | 6.5 | 3.4 | 1.6 | 1.0 | 28.7 | 20.9 | 18.7 | 18.0 | 35.4 |
| Fabricated metal products | 2.3 | 1.8 | 2.1 | 10.3 | 2.9 | 67.9 | 86.8 | 35.5 | 39.6 | 50.5 |
| Industrial machinery and computers | 91.3 | 70.9 | 63.8 | 58.9 | 68.4 | 440.7 | 422.1 | 558.0 | 570.6 | 628.3 |
| Electric and electronic equipment | 97.3 | 83.3 | 68.4 | 45.0 | 21.9 | 273.9 | 323.1 | 354.4 | 328.7 | 401.4 |
| Transportation equipment | 61.9 | 41.3 | 22.9 | 24.0 | 19.9 | 18.6 | 29.8 | 24.6 | 26.7 | 51.3 |
| Scientific and measuring instruments | 109.9 | 116.9 | 116.2 | 160.5 | 202.5 | 278.8 | 282.3 | 333.8 | 381.0 | 432.4 |
| Miscellaneous manufactures | 2.7 | 2.3 | 2.7 | 3.3 | 2.3 | 11.2 | 14.0 | 19.3 | 16.2 | 15.3 |
| Unidentified manufactures | 0.6 | 0.7 | 0.6 | 0.7 | 0.4 | 3.4 | 2.8 | 4.7 | 3.8 | 3.5 |
| **Agricultural and livestock products** | 239.2 | 331.7 | 487.3 | 375.9 | 268.4 | 642.7 | 673.2 | 1 138.7 | 1 273.6 | 910.4 |
| Agricultural products | 239.2 | 331.7 | 487.3 | 375.9 | 268.4 | 642.3 | 672.7 | 1 138.2 | 1 273.0 | 910.1 |
| Livestock and livestock products | ..... | ..... | ..... | ..... | ..... | 0.4 | 0.5 | 0.5 | 0.6 | 0.4 |
| **Other commodities** | 0.8 | 1.1 | 3.3 | 3.3 | 3.2 | 13.1 | 13.2 | 16.8 | 8.3 | 7.8 |
| Forestry products | ..... | ..... | ..... | ..... | ..... | 0.4 | ..... | ..... | ..... | 0.1 |
| Fish and other marine products | ..... | 0.3 | 0.1 | 0.1 | 0.2 | 0.2 | 0.1 | 0.1 | 0.1 | ..... |
| Metallic ores and concentrates | ..... | ..... | ..... | ..... | ..... | ..... | ..... | 0.1 | 0.1 | ..... |
| Bituminous coal and lignite | ..... | ..... | ..... | ..... | ..... | ..... | ..... | ..... | ..... | ..... |
| Crude petroleum and natural gas | ..... | ..... | ..... | ..... | ..... | ..... | ..... | ..... | 0.1 | ..... |
| Nonmetallic minerals | ..... | ..... | ..... | 0.1 | ..... | 10.1 | 8.0 | 2.5 | 1.4 | 4.4 |
| Scrap and waste | ..... | ..... | ..... | ..... | ..... | 0.1 | 0.3 | 1.2 | 0.4 | 0.3 |
| Used merchandise | 0.4 | ..... | 0.3 | 0.2 | ..... | 0.9 | 2.3 | 2.9 | 1.8 | 0.8 |
| Goods imported and returned unchanged | ..... | ..... | ..... | ..... | ..... | ..... | ..... | ..... | ..... | ..... |
| Special classification provisions | 0.4 | 0.8 | 3.0 | 2.9 | 2.9 | 1.5 | 2.4 | 9.9 | 4.3 | 2.2 |

## Table D-3.  State Exports of Goods by Destination and Industry, 1993–1997 —Continued

**MINNESOTA** (Millions of dollars.)

| Industry | 1993 | 1994 | 1995 | 1996 | 1997 | 1993 | 1994 | 1995 | 1996 | 1997 |
|---|---|---|---|---|---|---|---|---|---|---|
| | Japan | | | | | South Korea | | | | |
| **ALL GOODS** | 858.8 | 761.6 | 863.6 | 1 047.8 | 1 089.8 | 188.6 | 261.2 | 435.4 | 488.3 | 268.4 |
| **Manufactured goods** | 441.4 | 390.4 | 464.2 | 574.3 | 636.2 | 178.3 | 187.1 | 261.0 | 207.8 | 200.5 |
| Food products | 42.6 | 33.4 | 35.8 | 46.6 | 38.5 | 25.0 | 30.3 | 33.2 | 31.0 | 40.8 |
| Tobacco products | ..... | ..... | ..... | ..... | ..... | ..... | ..... | ..... | ..... | ..... |
| Textile mill products | 4.6 | 0.8 | 0.7 | 1.1 | 0.5 | 1.1 | ..... | 1.0 | 0.4 | 0.9 |
| Apparel | 2.3 | 1.1 | 1.4 | 1.4 | 0.9 | 0.7 | 0.1 | 0.1 | 0.2 | 0.1 |
| Lumber and wood products | 10.3 | 13.0 | 21.2 | 20.3 | 19.0 | 0.8 | 0.8 | 0.7 | 1.7 | 0.8 |
| Furniture and fixtures | 0.7 | 0.8 | 1.4 | 1.5 | 2.1 | 0.3 | 0.2 | 0.6 | 0.6 | 0.6 |
| Paper products | 13.9 | 3.8 | 5.1 | 5.6 | 6.1 | 7.8 | 2.0 | 3.5 | 2.5 | 1.9 |
| Printing and publishing | 1.0 | 1.2 | 1.7 | 1.8 | 1.5 | 0.2 | 0.3 | 0.6 | 0.5 | 0.4 |
| Chemical products | 45.4 | 11.0 | 15.9 | 30.2 | 35.1 | 4.9 | 4.6 | 11.1 | 9.3 | 11.7 |
| Refined petroleum products | ..... | ..... | ..... | ..... | ..... | 0.6 | 0.9 | 0.6 | 0.3 | 0.5 |
| Rubber and plastic products | 18.8 | 32.2 | 25.4 | 23.0 | 24.1 | 5.6 | 4.3 | 4.2 | 3.6 | 3.9 |
| Leather products | 3.5 | 4.4 | 5.9 | 7.1 | 9.3 | ..... | 0.3 | 0.4 | 0.2 | 0.2 |
| Stone, clay and glass products | 9.1 | 5.8 | 6.8 | 6.0 | 7.2 | 2.2 | 1.7 | 3.8 | 7.8 | 3.8 |
| Primary metals | 4.1 | 1.2 | 1.2 | 2.5 | 3.0 | 1.8 | 0.7 | 0.7 | 0.5 | 0.9 |
| Fabricated metal products | 4.4 | 7.2 | 7.0 | 11.1 | 10.9 | 4.0 | 6.5 | 4.7 | 6.1 | 10.1 |
| Industrial machinery and computers | 101.4 | 87.9 | 133.8 | 131.3 | 138.3 | 74.3 | 81.4 | 119.5 | 85.1 | 63.1 |
| Electric and electronic equipment | 27.7 | 42.1 | 37.0 | 43.0 | 41.2 | 23.5 | 22.6 | 43.2 | 23.3 | 23.3 |
| Transportation equipment | 4.2 | 7.8 | 8.0 | 6.8 | 7.2 | 2.6 | 2.3 | 1.7 | 3.1 | 2.0 |
| Scientific and measuring instruments | 139.6 | 130.6 | 146.6 | 228.0 | 287.3 | 21.9 | 26.6 | 28.8 | 29.7 | 34.1 |
| Miscellaneous manufactures | 7.2 | 5.3 | 7.7 | 5.6 | 2.6 | 0.6 | 1.0 | 1.9 | 1.8 | 1.0 |
| Unidentified manufactures | 0.6 | 0.8 | 1.6 | 1.3 | 1.2 | 0.4 | 0.4 | 0.5 | 0.3 | 0.3 |
| **Agricultural and livestock products** | 413.0 | 368.6 | 397.8 | 470.9 | 451.8 | 8.4 | 71.7 | 173.3 | 280.2 | 67.5 |
| Agricultural products | 412.7 | 368.2 | 397.5 | 470.8 | 451.5 | 8.4 | 71.7 | 173.3 | 279.8 | 67.5 |
| Livestock and livestock products | 0.3 | 0.4 | 0.3 | 0.1 | 0.2 | ..... | ..... | ..... | 0.4 | ..... |
| **Other commodities** | 4.4 | 2.6 | 1.6 | 2.7 | 1.8 | 1.8 | 2.3 | 1.1 | 0.3 | 0.4 |
| Forestry products | ..... | ..... | ..... | ..... | ..... | 0.2 | ..... | ..... | ..... | ..... |
| Fish and other marine products | 0.2 | ..... | ..... | ..... | ..... | ..... | ..... | ..... | ..... | ..... |
| Metallic ores and concentrates | ..... | ..... | ..... | ..... | ..... | ..... | ..... | ..... | ..... | ..... |
| Bituminous coal and lignite | ..... | ..... | ..... | ..... | ..... | ..... | ..... | ..... | ..... | ..... |
| Crude petroleum and natural gas | ..... | ..... | ..... | ..... | ..... | ..... | ..... | ..... | ..... | ..... |
| Nonmetallic minerals | 3.3 | 1.5 | 0.2 | 0.1 | 0.2 | 1.3 | 2.1 | ..... | ..... | 0.2 |
| Scrap and waste | ..... | ..... | ..... | ..... | ..... | 0.1 | 0.2 | 0.3 | 0.1 | ..... |
| Used merchandise | 0.4 | 0.8 | 0.5 | 1.0 | 0.4 | ..... | ..... | 0.8 | 0.1 | ..... |
| Goods imported and returned unchanged | ..... | ..... | ..... | ..... | ..... | ..... | ..... | ..... | ..... | ..... |
| Special classification provisions | 0.6 | 0.3 | 0.9 | 1.6 | 1.3 | 0.3 | ..... | 0.1 | 0.1 | 0.1 |

| Industry | 1993 | 1994 | 1995 | 1996 | 1997 | 1993 | 1994 | 1995 | 1996 | 1997 |
|---|---|---|---|---|---|---|---|---|---|---|
| | Taiwan | | | | | Singapore | | | | |
| **ALL GOODS** | 265.8 | 262.9 | 255.8 | 449.9 | 257.1 | 142.7 | 190.0 | 230.2 | 259.2 | 245.4 |
| **Manufactured goods** | 135.5 | 134.1 | 147.5 | 134.2 | 147.6 | 142.0 | 189.1 | 228.8 | 257.9 | 244.7 |
| Food products | 13.1 | 18.7 | 24.4 | 19.6 | 12.6 | 3.8 | 5.0 | 6.9 | 4.5 | 3.6 |
| Tobacco products | ..... | ..... | ..... | ..... | ..... | ..... | ..... | ..... | ..... | ..... |
| Textile mill products | 0.5 | 0.1 | 0.1 | ..... | ..... | 0.4 | 0.4 | 4.0 | 1.3 | 0.9 |
| Apparel | 0.2 | ..... | 0.1 | 0.1 | 0.1 | ..... | 0.1 | 0.1 | 0.1 | 0.3 |
| Lumber and wood products | 1.0 | 0.9 | 0.5 | 0.9 | 0.5 | 0.3 | ..... | 0.1 | 0.2 | ..... |
| Furniture and fixtures | 0.1 | 0.4 | 0.2 | 0.1 | 0.2 | 0.3 | 0.4 | 0.3 | 0.5 | 0.8 |
| Paper products | 5.0 | 1.0 | 1.4 | 1.1 | 3.0 | 0.9 | 0.8 | 2.1 | 3.6 | 4.9 |
| Printing and publishing | 0.4 | 0.3 | 0.3 | 1.4 | 0.4 | 0.3 | 0.9 | 1.0 | 0.7 | 0.8 |
| Chemical products | 5.3 | 3.4 | 5.1 | 4.2 | 6.1 | 1.7 | 1.6 | 2.3 | 3.1 | 6.6 |
| Refined petroleum products | ..... | ..... | ..... | ..... | 0.1 | ..... | ..... | ..... | 0.1 | ..... |
| Rubber and plastic products | 10.7 | 10.4 | 13.1 | 10.9 | 15.4 | 16.8 | 19.6 | 20.5 | 31.1 | 21.4 |
| Leather products | 2.5 | 1.6 | 1.0 | 1.2 | 0.6 | 0.6 | 0.5 | 1.3 | 1.0 | 1.6 |
| Stone, clay and glass products | 3.3 | 2.2 | 2.6 | 3.2 | 1.7 | 2.1 | 3.0 | 2.6 | 1.5 | 4.0 |
| Primary metals | 0.8 | 0.4 | 0.4 | 0.4 | 0.5 | 1.9 | 2.3 | 2.8 | 2.8 | 3.0 |
| Fabricated metal products | 1.8 | 5.2 | 2.8 | 5.4 | 6.5 | 4.1 | 5.8 | 5.4 | 5.5 | 5.3 |
| Industrial machinery and computers | 40.3 | 30.6 | 34.9 | 28.0 | 39.7 | 39.1 | 36.7 | 48.2 | 88.4 | 91.2 |
| Electric and electronic equipment | 26.4 | 31.5 | 32.4 | 28.9 | 28.9 | 47.0 | 73.5 | 78.6 | 57.9 | 29.5 |
| Transportation equipment | 2.0 | 1.4 | 2.3 | 2.1 | 3.8 | 2.5 | 9.7 | 7.0 | 8.2 | 31.4 |
| Scientific and measuring instruments | 20.8 | 23.9 | 23.3 | 24.1 | 25.3 | 18.0 | 25.5 | 40.3 | 44.3 | 36.0 |
| Miscellaneous manufactures | 0.9 | 1.8 | 1.6 | 2.2 | 2.0 | 1.0 | 2.9 | 4.7 | 2.7 | 2.6 |
| Unidentified manufactures | 0.2 | 0.3 | 0.9 | 0.4 | 0.3 | 1.1 | 0.4 | 0.6 | 0.7 | 0.7 |
| **Agricultural and livestock products** | 125.9 | 124.9 | 106.2 | 314.4 | 106.1 | ..... | ..... | 0.8 | 0.7 | 0.2 |
| Agricultural products | 125.9 | 124.9 | 106.2 | 314.4 | 106.0 | ..... | ..... | 0.8 | 0.7 | 0.2 |
| Livestock and livestock products | ..... | 0.1 | ..... | ..... | ..... | ..... | ..... | ..... | ..... | ..... |
| **Other commodities** | 4.4 | 3.8 | 2.1 | 1.3 | 3.4 | 0.7 | 0.8 | 0.6 | 0.6 | 0.5 |
| Forestry products | ..... | ..... | ..... | ..... | ..... | ..... | ..... | ..... | ..... | ..... |
| Fish and other marine products | ..... | ..... | ..... | ..... | ..... | ..... | ..... | ..... | ..... | ..... |
| Metallic ores and concentrates | ..... | ..... | ..... | ..... | ..... | ..... | ..... | ..... | ..... | ..... |
| Bituminous coal and lignite | ..... | ..... | ..... | ..... | ..... | ..... | ..... | ..... | ..... | ..... |
| Crude petroleum and natural gas | ..... | ..... | ..... | ..... | ..... | ..... | ..... | ..... | ..... | ..... |
| Nonmetallic minerals | 4.3 | 3.7 | 2.1 | 1.2 | 3.2 | 0.1 | ..... | ..... | ..... | ..... |
| Scrap and waste | ..... | ..... | ..... | ..... | ..... | ..... | ..... | ..... | ..... | ..... |
| Used merchandise | ..... | ..... | ..... | ..... | ..... | 0.1 | ..... | ..... | ..... | 0.1 |
| Goods imported and returned unchanged | ..... | 0.1 | ..... | ..... | ..... | ..... | ..... | ..... | ..... | ..... |
| Special classification provisions | ..... | ..... | ..... | ..... | 0.1 | 0.6 | 0.8 | 0.6 | 0.5 | 0.4 |

## MISSISSIPPI: Exports of Goods, 1997

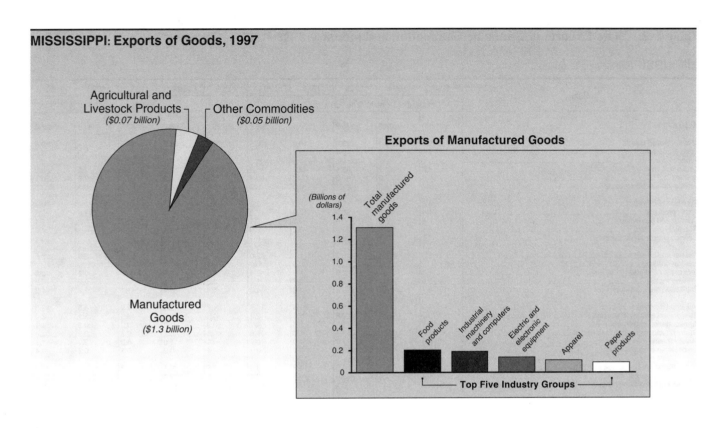

## Table D-3.   State Exports of Goods by Destination and Industry, 1993–1997 —*Continued*

**MISSISSIPPI** (Millions of dollars.)

| Industry | 1993 | 1994 | 1995 | 1996 | 1997 | 1993 | 1994 | 1995 | 1996 | 1997 |
|---|---|---|---|---|---|---|---|---|---|---|
| | All destinations | | | | | Canada | | | | |
| **ALL GOODS** | 803.3 | 1 099.9 | 1 368.7 | 1 221.7 | 1 421.3 | 305.9 | 352.1 | 372.7 | 387.8 | 430.4 |
| **Manufactured goods** | 770.4 | 1 055.1 | 1 261.1 | 1 145.5 | 1 307.5 | 298.9 | 342.9 | 354.4 | 366.8 | 408.9 |
| Food products | 46.2 | 76.7 | 138.5 | 159.6 | 203.5 | 15.1 | 18.1 | 21.5 | 18.7 | 12.5 |
| Tobacco products | 0.1 | 0.1 | 0.1 | 0.2 | 0.1 | ..... | ..... | ..... | ..... | ..... |
| Textile mill products | 29.2 | 50.6 | 59.9 | 76.6 | 81.9 | 7.7 | 21.7 | 22.9 | 28.3 | 24.6 |
| Apparel | 30.8 | 28.3 | 54.5 | 89.7 | 111.1 | 4.9 | 4.8 | 6.7 | 8.5 | 5.6 |
| Lumber and wood products | 21.7 | 26.4 | 30.5 | 34.8 | 54.2 | 4.8 | 5.9 | 4.8 | 9.8 | 11.2 |
| Furniture and fixtures | 65.6 | 56.7 | 47.6 | 45.7 | 66.4 | 52.5 | 41.7 | 29.5 | 25.9 | 38.2 |
| Paper products | 108.1 | 122.3 | 169.4 | 119.0 | 91.2 | 13.0 | 15.7 | 23.3 | 18.0 | 28.8 |
| Printing and publishing | 16.6 | 20.1 | 18.8 | 15.5 | 17.0 | 6.4 | 8.6 | 5.9 | 5.2 | 4.5 |
| Chemical products | 61.7 | 62.9 | 70.7 | 79.5 | 71.9 | 28.0 | 28.3 | 23.4 | 27.6 | 38.1 |
| Refined petroleum products | 7.1 | 6.1 | 13.3 | 9.4 | 10.9 | 0.7 | 1.0 | 1.1 | 1.0 | 1.1 |
| Rubber and plastic products | 29.9 | 33.8 | 37.2 | 36.3 | 43.3 | 13.6 | 12.7 | 17.3 | 20.3 | 29.5 |
| Leather products | 1.0 | 0.7 | 0.6 | 1.2 | 0.8 | 0.2 | 0.1 | 0.4 | 0.2 | ..... |
| Stone, clay and glass products | 13.8 | 14.3 | 14.6 | 16.7 | 20.1 | 8.8 | 7.7 | 7.4 | 7.2 | 7.0 |
| Primary metals | 22.1 | 25.9 | 27.4 | 18.6 | 33.8 | 8.5 | 12.3 | 10.1 | 8.5 | 8.7 |
| Fabricated metal products | 22.6 | 28.0 | 35.1 | 51.1 | 62.4 | 9.5 | 10.4 | 11.7 | 16.5 | 20.2 |
| Industrial machinery and computers | 77.1 | 105.2 | 106.8 | 131.7 | 190.3 | 31.9 | 53.7 | 58.9 | 63.2 | 71.7 |
| Electric and electronic equipment | 115.3 | 160.5 | 178.7 | 162.8 | 139.1 | 49.0 | 59.0 | 68.4 | 71.7 | 76.1 |
| Transportation equipment | 76.3 | 208.8 | 216.8 | 70.0 | 52.9 | 38.0 | 32.6 | 29.6 | 29.3 | 16.9 |
| Scientific and measuring instruments | 11.5 | 10.0 | 13.5 | 13.1 | 35.4 | 2.3 | 2.6 | 3.0 | 2.3 | 6.0 |
| Miscellaneous manufactures | 12.0 | 15.7 | 24.8 | 11.7 | 15.4 | 3.7 | 5.4 | 7.8 | 4.0 | 5.9 |
| Unidentified manufactures | 1.5 | 2.1 | 2.2 | 2.3 | 5.7 | 0.4 | 0.6 | 0.8 | 0.6 | 2.3 |
| **Agricultural and livestock products** | 22.2 | 28.5 | 81.1 | 52.5 | 65.0 | 0.9 | 1.1 | 1.8 | 3.4 | 1.6 |
| Agricultural products | 21.9 | 27.5 | 80.4 | 51.2 | 63.0 | 0.8 | 0.4 | 1.7 | 3.2 | 0.7 |
| Livestock and livestock products | 0.3 | 1.0 | 0.7 | 1.3 | 2.1 | 0.1 | 0.7 | 0.1 | 0.2 | 0.9 |
| **Other commodities** | 10.7 | 16.3 | 26.5 | 23.7 | 48.8 | 6.1 | 8.1 | 16.5 | 17.6 | 19.9 |
| Forestry products | | | | | 0.1 | ..... | ..... | ..... | ..... | ..... |
| Fish and other marine products | 3.3 | 3.6 | 6.0 | 6.3 | 4.5 | 2.2 | 3.1 | 4.7 | 4.4 | 3.4 |
| Metallic ores and concentrates | ..... | ..... | ..... | ..... | 0.8 | ..... | ..... | ..... | ..... | ..... |
| Bituminous coal and lignite | ..... | ..... | ..... | ..... | ..... | ..... | ..... | ..... | ..... | ..... |
| Crude petroleum and natural gas | ..... | 2.8 | 3.0 | ..... | 0.4 | ..... | 0.1 | ..... | ..... | ..... |
| Nonmetallic minerals | 1.0 | 2.3 | 2.6 | 4.0 | 2.1 | 0.2 | 0.5 | 1.7 | 2.4 | 1.3 |
| Scrap and waste | 1.3 | 1.6 | 6.9 | 5.0 | 8.4 | 0.4 | 0.6 | 5.5 | 4.8 | 8.1 |
| Used merchandise | 1.6 | 1.1 | 1.8 | 1.4 | 0.7 | 0.4 | 0.2 | 1.0 | 0.3 | 0.1 |
| Goods imported and returned unchanged | 2.9 | 3.5 | 3.5 | 5.5 | 6.9 | 2.9 | 3.5 | 3.5 | 5.5 | 6.9 |
| Special classification provisions | 0.5 | 1.2 | 2.7 | 1.5 | 25.0 | ..... | 0.1 | 0.2 | 0.1 | 0.1 |

## Table D-3.  State Exports of Goods by Destination and Industry, 1993–1997 —*Continued*

**MISSISSIPPI** (Millions of dollars.)

| Industry | 1993 | 1994 | 1995 | 1996 | 1997 | 1993 | 1994 | 1995 | 1996 | 1997 |
|---|---|---|---|---|---|---|---|---|---|---|
| | South and Central America and Caribbean | | | | | Mexico | | | | |
| **ALL GOODS** | 151.0 | 208.5 | 245.2 | 254.1 | 232.5 | 25.3 | 65.7 | 87.9 | 91.3 | 127.4 |
| **Manufactured goods** | 148.7 | 204.4 | 238.3 | 248.8 | 228.5 | 24.2 | 59.2 | 79.5 | 87.1 | 80.4 |
| Food products | 4.4 | 2.5 | 12.4 | 9.0 | 4.7 | 1.7 | 14.0 | 7.2 | 6.3 | 4.6 |
| Tobacco products | ..... | ..... | ..... | ..... | ..... | ..... | ..... | ..... | ..... | ..... |
| Textile mill products | 18.2 | 26.7 | 33.4 | 42.6 | 46.9 | 0.1 | 0.3 | 0.7 | 2.8 | 6.6 |
| Apparel | 24.4 | 22.3 | 42.3 | 65.0 | 81.4 | 0.6 | 0.2 | 3.5 | 13.5 | 20.1 |
| Lumber and wood products | 3.3 | 4.0 | 5.4 | 4.0 | 3.3 | 0.4 | 0.8 | 0.4 | 0.3 | 2.6 |
| Furniture and fixtures | 0.8 | 0.8 | 1.5 | 2.0 | 2.9 | 2.2 | 3.1 | 0.9 | 0.2 | 0.9 |
| Paper products | 21.4 | 58.8 | 58.9 | 47.9 | 17.8 | 1.0 | 1.8 | 1.8 | 1.6 | 1.8 |
| Printing and publishing | 0.1 | 0.4 | 0.5 | 0.2 | 0.1 | 0.3 | 0.2 | 0.3 | 0.3 | 1.4 |
| Chemical products | 16.1 | 22.2 | 22.9 | 23.2 | 15.9 | 1.3 | 2.4 | 2.7 | 4.8 | 4.0 |
| Refined petroleum products | 0.5 | 0.7 | 0.7 | 0.6 | 0.3 | ..... | ..... | ..... | ..... | 0.1 |
| Rubber and plastic products | 3.5 | 7.4 | 5.3 | 4.4 | 2.0 | 5.0 | 5.2 | 0.6 | 2.3 | 3.5 |
| Leather products | ..... | ..... | ..... | 0.3 | 0.1 | 0.1 | ..... | ..... | ..... | ..... |
| Stone, clay and glass products | 1.1 | 1.2 | 2.0 | 1.8 | 2.4 | 0.1 | 0.9 | 0.2 | 0.1 | 0.3 |
| Primary metals | 5.9 | 5.3 | 5.7 | 3.3 | 1.7 | 2.3 | 3.1 | 2.5 | 2.2 | 10.2 |
| Fabricated metal products | 5.1 | 3.0 | 3.2 | 4.3 | 4.2 | 1.4 | 5.4 | 1.1 | 2.2 | 4.2 |
| Industrial machinery and computers | 14.9 | 13.5 | 16.5 | 17.9 | 14.1 | 1.7 | 2.8 | 1.9 | 4.5 | 13.3 |
| Electric and electronic equipment | 10.9 | 25.9 | 9.8 | 8.6 | 12.2 | 4.8 | 16.6 | 48.5 | 43.1 | 3.4 |
| Transportation equipment | 15.8 | 6.9 | 12.5 | 6.6 | 9.7 | 0.9 | 1.0 | 0.3 | 0.5 | 1.1 |
| Scientific and measuring instruments | 1.7 | 0.8 | 3.7 | 5.8 | 7.0 | 0.1 | 0.2 | 0.3 | 0.2 | 0.4 |
| Miscellaneous manufactures | 0.6 | 1.4 | 1.2 | 1.0 | 0.9 | 0.1 | 1.0 | 6.3 | 2.1 | 1.7 |
| Unidentified manufactures | 0.2 | 0.5 | 0.5 | 0.5 | 0.7 | 0.1 | 0.2 | 0.1 | 0.2 | 0.4 |
| **Agricultural and livestock products** | 1.2 | 2.7 | 4.9 | 4.5 | 3.4 | 0.9 | 2.1 | 3.2 | 3.7 | 21.3 |
| Agricultural products | 1.1 | 2.6 | 4.9 | 4.4 | 3.4 | 0.9 | 2.1 | 3.2 | 3.7 | 21.1 |
| Livestock and livestock products | ..... | ..... | 0.1 | 0.1 | ..... | ..... | ..... | ..... | ..... | 0.2 |
| **Other commodities** | 1.3 | 1.5 | 1.9 | 0.7 | 0.7 | 0.1 | 4.3 | 5.2 | 0.5 | 25.6 |
| Forestry products | ..... | ..... | ..... | ..... | ..... | ..... | ..... | ..... | ..... | ..... |
| Fish and other marine products | ..... | ..... | ..... | ..... | ..... | ..... | ..... | ..... | ..... | ..... |
| Metallic ores and concentrates | ..... | ..... | ..... | ..... | 0.2 | ..... | ..... | ..... | ..... | 0.6 |
| Bituminous coal and lignite | ..... | ..... | ..... | ..... | ..... | ..... | ..... | ..... | ..... | ..... |
| Crude petroleum and natural gas | ..... | ..... | ..... | ..... | ..... | ..... | 2.8 | 3.0 | ..... | 0.4 |
| Nonmetallic minerals | 0.2 | 0.4 | 0.1 | 0.4 | 0.2 | ..... | 0.6 | ..... | ..... | ..... |
| Scrap and waste | 0.6 | 0.7 | 1.2 | ..... | ..... | ..... | ..... | ..... | ..... | ..... |
| Used merchandise | 0.4 | 0.3 | 0.6 | 0.2 | 0.2 | 0.1 | 0.2 | ..... | ..... | 0.1 |
| Goods imported and returned unchanged | ..... | ..... | ..... | ..... | ..... | ..... | ..... | ..... | ..... | ..... |
| Special classification provisions | 0.1 | 0.1 | ..... | 0.1 | ..... | ..... | 0.8 | 2.2 | 0.5 | 24.5 |
| | European Union | | | | | United Kingdom | | | | |
| **ALL GOODS** | 166.4 | 169.8 | 223.3 | 208.1 | 266.9 | 63.8 | 68.5 | 91.3 | 75.2 | 80.9 |
| **Manufactured goods** | 147.8 | 151.0 | 201.3 | 184.0 | 240.3 | 49.6 | 52.7 | 71.5 | 56.8 | 68.0 |
| Food products | 4.3 | 9.6 | 7.1 | 16.3 | 7.5 | ..... | ..... | 0.4 | 0.6 | 2.4 |
| Tobacco products | ..... | 0.1 | 0.1 | 0.1 | 0.1 | ..... | 0.1 | 0.1 | 0.1 | 0.1 |
| Textile mill products | 1.9 | 0.8 | 1.0 | 1.2 | 2.6 | 1.4 | 0.3 | 0.3 | 0.4 | 0.9 |
| Apparel | 0.5 | 0.4 | 1.4 | 1.2 | 1.5 | 0.2 | 0.1 | 0.5 | 0.5 | 0.4 |
| Lumber and wood products | 5.6 | 8.3 | 9.4 | 12.1 | 21.9 | 0.1 | 0.5 | 0.4 | 1.4 | 3.4 |
| Furniture and fixtures | 5.8 | 6.4 | 8.1 | 8.7 | 15.2 | 0.5 | 0.5 | 1.1 | 0.9 | 3.5 |
| Paper products | 51.9 | 43.9 | 84.0 | 50.2 | 41.5 | 14.2 | 10.1 | 29.8 | 13.0 | 9.2 |
| Printing and publishing | 5.6 | 7.2 | 8.4 | 6.9 | 8.2 | 2.5 | 4.2 | 3.7 | 3.2 | 3.4 |
| Chemical products | 3.2 | 4.0 | 8.7 | 12.3 | 4.7 | 1.2 | 1.1 | 1.4 | 2.3 | 1.1 |
| Refined petroleum products | 1.8 | 2.3 | 7.4 | 1.1 | 3.5 | 0.6 | 0.7 | 1.8 | 0.5 | 1.4 |
| Rubber and plastic products | 2.4 | 4.1 | 5.7 | 5.4 | 2.7 | 0.5 | 0.9 | 2.4 | 2.6 | 0.6 |
| Leather products | 0.4 | 0.5 | ..... | ..... | 0.3 | 0.2 | 0.2 | ..... | ..... | ..... |
| Stone, clay and glass products | 1.4 | 2.4 | 2.0 | 2.6 | 3.2 | 0.1 | 0.9 | 0.1 | 0.2 | 0.2 |
| Primary metals | 0.6 | 0.4 | 2.0 | 1.6 | 1.2 | 0.1 | ..... | 0.4 | 0.3 | 1.0 |
| Fabricated metal products | 1.9 | 1.8 | 3.0 | 7.0 | 16.4 | 0.5 | 0.9 | 1.5 | 4.9 | 12.9 |
| Industrial machinery and computers | 16.1 | 15.6 | 16.9 | 27.0 | 62.0 | 3.9 | 4.0 | 5.0 | 9.0 | 9.2 |
| Electric and electronic equipment | 24.7 | 25.4 | 18.7 | 13.9 | 14.0 | 11.6 | 17.4 | 11.3 | 6.8 | 7.0 |
| Transportation equipment | 11.5 | 10.1 | 10.8 | 11.4 | 15.1 | 8.0 | 7.3 | 7.7 | 8.8 | 10.1 |
| Scientific and measuring instruments | 4.5 | 3.9 | 3.4 | 2.3 | 15.8 | 1.2 | 1.5 | 1.8 | 0.8 | 0.8 |
| Miscellaneous manufactures | 3.4 | 3.5 | 2.9 | 2.0 | 2.3 | 2.8 | 2.1 | 1.8 | 0.2 | 0.4 |
| Unidentified manufactures | 0.3 | 0.3 | 0.3 | 0.7 | 0.7 | 0.1 | 0.1 | 0.2 | 0.3 | 0.2 |
| **Agricultural and livestock products** | 17.1 | 17.8 | 20.6 | 21.7 | 25.0 | 13.6 | 15.5 | 19.6 | 18.2 | 12.6 |
| Agricultural products | 17.1 | 17.8 | 20.6 | 21.6 | 24.8 | 13.6 | 15.5 | 19.6 | 18.1 | 12.6 |
| Livestock and livestock products | ..... | ..... | ..... | 0.1 | 0.2 | ..... | ..... | ..... | 0.1 | ..... |
| **Other commodities** | 1.5 | 1.0 | 1.4 | 2.4 | 1.5 | 0.7 | 0.3 | 0.1 | 0.2 | 0.3 |
| Forestry products | ..... | ..... | ..... | ..... | ..... | ..... | ..... | ..... | ..... | ..... |
| Fish and other marine products | 0.7 | 0.4 | 0.8 | 1.6 | 0.8 | 0.4 | ..... | ..... | ..... | ..... |
| Metallic ores and concentrates | ..... | ..... | ..... | ..... | ..... | ..... | ..... | ..... | ..... | ..... |
| Bituminous coal and lignite | ..... | ..... | ..... | ..... | ..... | ..... | ..... | ..... | ..... | ..... |
| Crude petroleum and natural gas | ..... | ..... | ..... | ..... | ..... | ..... | ..... | ..... | ..... | ..... |
| Nonmetallic minerals | 0.1 | ..... | ..... | 0.1 | 0.2 | ..... | ..... | ..... | ..... | ..... |
| Scrap and waste | 0.2 | 0.4 | 0.2 | ..... | 0.2 | 0.1 | 0.1 | ..... | ..... | 0.1 |
| Used merchandise | 0.1 | 0.1 | 0.2 | 0.3 | 0.1 | 0.1 | 0.1 | 0.1 | 0.1 | 0.1 |
| Goods imported and returned unchanged | ..... | ..... | ..... | ..... | ..... | ..... | ..... | ..... | ..... | ..... |
| Special classification provisions | 0.4 | 0.1 | 0.1 | 0.5 | 0.2 | 0.1 | 0.1 | ..... | ..... | 0.1 |

## Table D-3.  State Exports of Goods by Destination and Industry, 1993–1997 —*Continued*

**MISSISSIPPI** (Millions of dollars.)

| Industry | 1993 | 1994 | 1995 | 1996 | 1997 | 1993 | 1994 | 1995 | 1996 | 1997 |
|---|---|---|---|---|---|---|---|---|---|---|
| | Germany | | | | | France | | | | |
| **ALL GOODS** | 27.7 | 20.2 | 20.2 | 17.3 | 17.4 | 12.3 | 17.7 | 24.0 | 17.5 | 12.0 |
| **Manufactured goods** | 27.3 | 19.8 | 19.2 | 15.5 | 16.5 | 12.0 | 17.6 | 23.9 | 17.2 | 11.9 |
| Food products | ..... | 0.1 | ..... | 2.2 | 0.4 | 0.1 | ..... | ..... | 0.2 | ..... |
| Tobacco products | ..... | ..... | ..... | ..... | ..... | ..... | ..... | ..... | ..... | ..... |
| Textile mill products | 0.1 | ..... | ..... | 0.1 | 0.1 | ..... | 0.2 | 0.2 | 0.1 | ..... |
| Apparel | 0.1 | 0.1 | 0.1 | 0.2 | 0.2 | ..... | 0.1 | 0.6 | ..... | 0.1 |
| Lumber and wood products | 1.1 | 1.0 | 0.9 | 0.8 | 0.9 | 0.1 | 0.4 | 0.3 | 0.8 | 0.7 |
| Furniture and fixtures | 1.7 | 2.4 | 1.0 | 0.6 | 0.5 | 0.4 | 0.5 | 0.6 | 0.9 | 1.3 |
| Paper products | 8.0 | 3.1 | 1.3 | 1.3 | 1.4 | 5.3 | 8.8 | 15.3 | 4.0 | 2.6 |
| Printing and publishing | 0.1 | ..... | ..... | ..... | 0.1 | ..... | ..... | ..... | ..... | ..... |
| Chemical products | 0.4 | 1.2 | 3.1 | 0.3 | 1.1 | 0.2 | ..... | ..... | 1.8 | 0.1 |
| Refined petroleum products | ..... | ..... | ..... | ..... | ..... | ..... | ..... | ..... | ..... | 0.4 |
| Rubber and plastic products | 0.7 | 1.6 | 1.3 | 0.6 | 0.6 | 0.3 | 0.5 | 0.9 | 1.0 | 0.2 |
| Leather products | ..... | ..... | ..... | ..... | ..... | ..... | ..... | ..... | ..... | ..... |
| Stone, clay and glass products | ..... | ..... | ..... | ..... | 0.2 | 0.2 | 0.4 | 0.4 | 0.8 | 1.0 |
| Primary metals | ..... | ..... | 1.3 | 0.2 | ..... | 0.1 | ..... | 0.2 | ..... | ..... |
| Fabricated metal products | 0.5 | 0.3 | 0.3 | 0.6 | 0.6 | 0.3 | 0.1 | 0.1 | 0.2 | 0.1 |
| Industrial machinery and computers | 7.4 | 4.4 | 4.9 | 5.4 | 7.0 | 3.1 | 4.9 | 4.4 | 6.3 | 3.5 |
| Electric and electronic equipment | 3.2 | 2.7 | 1.9 | 1.2 | 1.0 | 1.2 | 0.2 | 0.2 | 0.4 | 0.6 |
| Transportation equipment | 2.2 | 2.1 | 2.3 | 1.7 | 1.7 | 0.2 | 0.2 | 0.2 | 0.3 | 0.6 |
| Scientific and measuring instruments | 1.6 | 0.4 | 0.3 | 0.2 | 0.3 | 0.4 | 0.5 | 0.4 | 0.1 | 0.3 |
| Miscellaneous manufactures | ..... | 0.1 | 0.4 | 0.2 | 0.4 | 0.1 | 0.6 | 0.1 | 0.2 | 0.3 |
| Unidentified manufactures | ..... | ..... | ..... | 0.1 | 0.1 | ..... | ..... | ..... | ..... | 0.1 |
| **Agricultural and livestock products** | 0.1 | ..... | ..... | ..... | ..... | ..... | ..... | ..... | ..... | ..... |
| Agricultural products | 0.1 | ..... | ..... | ..... | ..... | ..... | ..... | ..... | ..... | ..... |
| Livestock and livestock products | ..... | ..... | ..... | ..... | ..... | ..... | ..... | ..... | ..... | ..... |
| **Other commodities** | 0.3 | 0.4 | 1.0 | 1.8 | 0.9 | 0.2 | 0.1 | 0.1 | 0.3 | 0.1 |
| Forestry products | ..... | ..... | ..... | ..... | ..... | ..... | ..... | ..... | ..... | ..... |
| Fish and other marine products | 0.3 | 0.4 | 0.8 | 1.6 | 0.8 | ..... | ..... | ..... | ..... | ..... |
| Metallic ores and concentrates | ..... | ..... | ..... | ..... | ..... | ..... | ..... | ..... | ..... | ..... |
| Bituminous coal and lignite | ..... | ..... | ..... | ..... | ..... | ..... | ..... | ..... | ..... | ..... |
| Crude petroleum and natural gas | ..... | ..... | ..... | ..... | ..... | ..... | ..... | ..... | ..... | ..... |
| Nonmetallic minerals | ..... | ..... | ..... | ..... | ..... | ..... | ..... | ..... | ..... | ..... |
| Scrap and waste | ..... | ..... | 0.1 | ..... | 0.1 | 0.1 | 0.1 | 0.1 | ..... | ..... |
| Used merchandise | ..... | ..... | 0.1 | 0.1 | ..... | ..... | ..... | ..... | ..... | ..... |
| Goods imported and returned unchanged | ..... | ..... | ..... | ..... | ..... | ..... | ..... | ..... | ..... | ..... |
| Special classification provisions | ..... | ..... | ..... | 0.1 | ..... | 0.2 | ..... | ..... | 0.3 | 0.1 |
| | The Netherlands | | | | | Asian 10 | | | | |
| **ALL GOODS** | 19.7 | 22.1 | 32.8 | 26.3 | 26.1 | 78.0 | 78.4 | 177.8 | 127.9 | 139.8 |
| **Manufactured goods** | 19.4 | 21.9 | 32.7 | 26.2 | 25.7 | 75.8 | 74.6 | 126.9 | 107.5 | 129.4 |
| Food products | 3.1 | 7.9 | 5.0 | 6.9 | 3.0 | 2.1 | 7.4 | 24.7 | 19.2 | 17.6 |
| Tobacco products | ..... | ..... | ..... | ..... | ..... | ..... | ..... | ..... | ..... | ..... |
| Textile mill products | 0.3 | 0.1 | 0.3 | 0.5 | 1.3 | 0.9 | 0.4 | 1.0 | 0.7 | 0.6 |
| Apparel | 0.1 | ..... | 0.1 | 0.3 | 0.2 | 0.2 | 0.3 | 0.5 | 0.9 | 2.0 |
| Lumber and wood products | ..... | 0.2 | 0.1 | 0.1 | 0.3 | 4.8 | 6.0 | 7.4 | 6.4 | 8.9 |
| Furniture and fixtures | 0.9 | 0.2 | 0.7 | 1.0 | 1.2 | 0.2 | 0.9 | 2.4 | 1.6 | 1.9 |
| Paper products | 3.1 | 6.0 | 11.2 | 6.9 | 4.0 | 19.1 | 1.3 | 1.3 | 1.2 | 1.1 |
| Printing and publishing | 2.8 | 2.8 | 4.6 | 3.6 | 4.7 | 1.3 | 1.4 | 1.2 | 0.5 | 0.5 |
| Chemical products | 0.9 | 0.7 | 3.7 | 1.6 | 1.5 | 2.3 | 2.2 | 10.5 | 7.8 | 6.4 |
| Refined petroleum products | ..... | 1.6 | 4.6 | 0.3 | 0.3 | 3.5 | 1.9 | 3.8 | 6.5 | 5.5 |
| Rubber and plastic products | 0.1 | ..... | 0.1 | 0.2 | 0.2 | 1.0 | 1.5 | 1.4 | 0.9 | 1.9 |
| Leather products | ..... | ..... | ..... | ..... | ..... | 0.3 | ..... | 0.1 | 0.6 | 0.4 |
| Stone, clay and glass products | 0.7 | 0.8 | 0.8 | 1.1 | 1.4 | 0.7 | 1.2 | 2.0 | 3.3 | 5.9 |
| Primary metals | 0.3 | ..... | ..... | 0.5 | 0.1 | 4.5 | 4.0 | 4.7 | 1.3 | 7.6 |
| Fabricated metal products | 0.2 | ..... | 0.1 | 0.1 | 0.1 | 3.3 | 4.9 | 14.7 | 15.8 | 13.1 |
| Industrial machinery and computers | 0.5 | 0.2 | 0.4 | 1.2 | 0.8 | 5.7 | 6.0 | 9.8 | 13.5 | 19.0 |
| Electric and electronic equipment | 5.7 | 0.7 | 0.6 | 1.1 | 1.4 | 17.7 | 23.6 | 21.8 | 14.8 | 24.6 |
| Transportation equipment | 0.3 | 0.1 | 0.2 | 0.3 | 2.4 | 3.0 | 6.3 | 12.0 | 9.7 | 5.6 |
| Scientific and measuring instruments | 0.1 | 0.4 | 0.2 | 0.3 | 2.4 | 1.5 | 1.2 | 1.7 | 1.2 | 3.8 |
| Miscellaneous manufactures | 0.2 | 0.1 | ..... | 0.1 | 0.3 | 3.6 | 3.8 | 5.8 | 1.5 | 2.7 |
| Unidentified manufactures | ..... | 0.1 | ..... | 0.1 | 0.1 | 0.2 | 0.2 | 0.2 | 0.3 | 0.4 |
| **Agricultural and livestock products** | ..... | ..... | ..... | ..... | 0.3 | 1.1 | 2.9 | 49.6 | 18.7 | 9.4 |
| Agricultural products | ..... | ..... | ..... | ..... | 0.1 | 1.0 | 2.5 | 49.1 | 17.8 | 9.0 |
| Livestock and livestock products | ..... | ..... | ..... | ..... | 0.2 | 0.1 | 0.4 | 0.5 | 0.8 | 0.4 |
| **Other commodities** | 0.2 | 0.2 | 0.1 | ..... | 0.1 | 1.1 | 0.9 | 1.3 | 1.7 | 1.0 |
| Forestry products | ..... | ..... | ..... | ..... | ..... | ..... | ..... | ..... | ..... | ..... |
| Fish and other marine products | ..... | ..... | ..... | ..... | ..... | 0.4 | 0.1 | 0.5 | 0.2 | 0.3 |
| Metallic ores and concentrates | ..... | ..... | ..... | ..... | ..... | ..... | ..... | ..... | ..... | ..... |
| Bituminous coal and lignite | ..... | ..... | ..... | ..... | ..... | ..... | ..... | ..... | ..... | ..... |
| Crude petroleum and natural gas | ..... | ..... | ..... | ..... | ..... | ..... | ..... | ..... | ..... | ..... |
| Nonmetallic minerals | 0.1 | ..... | ..... | ..... | 0.1 | 0.3 | 0.7 | 0.6 | 0.6 | 0.4 |
| Scrap and waste | 0.1 | 0.2 | ..... | ..... | ..... | ..... | ..... | ..... | ..... | ..... |
| Used merchandise | ..... | ..... | ..... | ..... | ..... | 0.3 | 0.1 | ..... | 0.5 | 0.1 |
| Goods imported and returned unchanged | ..... | ..... | ..... | ..... | ..... | ..... | ..... | ..... | ..... | ..... |
| Special classification provisions | ..... | ..... | 0.1 | ..... | ..... | ..... | ..... | 0.1 | 0.2 | 0.2 |

## Table D-3.  State Exports of Goods by Destination and Industry, 1993–1997 —Continued

**MISSISSIPPI** (Millions of dollars.)

| Industry | Japan 1993 | 1994 | 1995 | 1996 | 1997 | South Korea 1993 | 1994 | 1995 | 1996 | 1997 |
|---|---|---|---|---|---|---|---|---|---|---|
| **ALL GOODS** | 28.4 | 17.9 | 26.5 | 39.0 | 49.2 | 13.8 | 16.0 | 29.3 | 19.7 | 11.2 |
| **Manufactured goods** | 27.2 | 16.6 | 20.0 | 30.2 | 43.9 | 13.5 | 15.6 | 28.4 | 19.2 | 10.5 |
| Food products | 0.6 | 1.5 | 3.3 | 10.3 | 11.4 | 0.1 | ..... | 0.1 | 0.1 | 0.3 |
| Tobacco products | ..... | ..... | ..... | ..... | ..... | ..... | ..... | ..... | ..... | ..... |
| Textile mill products | 0.5 | 0.2 | 0.4 | 0.2 | 0.1 | ..... | ..... | 0.1 | ..... | ..... |
| Apparel | 0.1 | 0.2 | 0.4 | 0.8 | 1.6 | 0.1 | ..... | ..... | 0.1 | 0.4 |
| Lumber and wood products | 0.7 | 1.6 | 1.3 | 0.3 | 3.8 | 2.0 | 2.9 | 4.2 | 3.4 | 3.3 |
| Furniture and fixtures | ..... | 0.3 | 0.4 | 0.6 | 1.3 | ..... | 0.2 | 0.1 | 0.5 | 0.1 |
| Paper products | 13.7 | 0.9 | 1.0 | 0.7 | 0.2 | 2.4 | 0.3 | 0.3 | 0.1 | 0.1 |
| Printing and publishing | ..... | ..... | ..... | 0.1 | 0.1 | 0.3 | 0.1 | 0.1 | ..... | ..... |
| Chemical products | 1.4 | 1.7 | 1.9 | 0.3 | 0.2 | 0.2 | 0.1 | 6.4 | 0.2 | 0.4 |
| Refined petroleum products | 3.0 | 1.8 | 2.6 | 4.4 | 3.6 | 0.4 | 0.1 | 0.5 | 1.2 | 0.8 |
| Rubber and plastic products | 0.2 | 0.4 | 0.4 | 0.1 | 0.2 | 0.2 | 0.2 | 0.8 | 0.4 | 0.2 |
| Leather products | ..... | ..... | ..... | ..... | 0.1 | ..... | ..... | ..... | ..... | ..... |
| Stone, clay and glass products | 0.2 | 0.3 | 1.2 | 1.3 | 1.6 | 0.1 | 0.5 | 0.1 | 0.1 | 0.2 |
| Primary metals | 0.1 | 0.3 | 0.1 | 0.1 | ..... | ..... | 0.8 | 0.6 | 0.3 | 0.1 |
| Fabricated metal products | 0.2 | 0.6 | 1.1 | 0.8 | 1.4 | 2.0 | 2.1 | 5.6 | 5.4 | 0.8 |
| Industrial machinery and computers | 2.1 | 2.2 | 2.7 | 2.7 | 5.9 | 0.7 | 0.6 | 0.9 | 2.0 | 0.5 |
| Electric and electronic equipment | 2.7 | 2.2 | 1.8 | 1.0 | 5.4 | 0.2 | 2.1 | 1.2 | 2.3 | 2.2 |
| Transportation equipment | 0.7 | 1.4 | 0.2 | 5.8 | 3.4 | 1.7 | 2.0 | 2.0 | 1.8 | 0.2 |
| Scientific and measuring instruments | 0.3 | 0.5 | 0.8 | 0.4 | 2.4 | 0.1 | 0.1 | 0.2 | 0.4 | 0.1 |
| Miscellaneous manufactures | 0.5 | 0.4 | 0.3 | 0.4 | 1.3 | 2.9 | 3.2 | 5.1 | 0.9 | 0.9 |
| Unidentified manufactures | 0.1 | 0.1 | ..... | 0.1 | ..... | ..... | ..... | ..... | ..... | 0.1 |
| **Agricultural and livestock products** | 0.5 | 0.7 | 5.9 | 7.7 | 4.8 | 0.3 | 0.1 | 0.4 | 0.5 | 0.6 |
| Agricultural products | 0.4 | 0.7 | 5.9 | 7.6 | 4.7 | 0.2 | ..... | 0.4 | 0.5 | 0.6 |
| Livestock and livestock products | ..... | ..... | 0.1 | 0.1 | 0.2 | 0.1 | 0.1 | ..... | ..... | ..... |
| **Other commodities** | 0.8 | 0.6 | 0.6 | 1.1 | 0.4 | 0.1 | 0.2 | 0.5 | 0.1 | 0.1 |
| Forestry products | ..... | ..... | ..... | ..... | ..... | ..... | ..... | ..... | ..... | ..... |
| Fish and other marine products | 0.3 | 0.1 | 0.4 | 0.2 | 0.1 | ..... | ..... | ..... | ..... | ..... |
| Metallic ores and concentrates | ..... | ..... | ..... | ..... | ..... | ..... | ..... | ..... | ..... | ..... |
| Bituminous coal and lignite | ..... | ..... | ..... | ..... | ..... | ..... | ..... | ..... | ..... | ..... |
| Crude petroleum and natural gas | ..... | ..... | ..... | ..... | ..... | ..... | ..... | ..... | ..... | ..... |
| Nonmetallic minerals | 0.2 | 0.5 | 0.3 | 0.4 | 0.3 | 0.1 | 0.1 | 0.3 | 0.1 | 0.1 |
| Scrap and waste | ..... | ..... | ..... | ..... | ..... | ..... | ..... | ..... | ..... | ..... |
| Used merchandise | 0.3 | ..... | ..... | 0.5 | ..... | ..... | 0.1 | ..... | ..... | ..... |
| Goods imported and returned unchanged | ..... | ..... | ..... | ..... | ..... | ..... | ..... | ..... | ..... | ..... |
| Special classification provisions | ..... | ..... | ..... | ..... | ..... | ..... | ..... | 0.1 | ..... | ..... |

| Industry | Taiwan 1993 | 1994 | 1995 | 1996 | 1997 | Singapore 1993 | 1994 | 1995 | 1996 | 1997 |
|---|---|---|---|---|---|---|---|---|---|---|
| **ALL GOODS** | 6.2 | 8.1 | 19.9 | 8.8 | 7.0 | 7.3 | 12.1 | 10.6 | 12.1 | 9.2 |
| **Manufactured goods** | 6.2 | 6.8 | 11.3 | 5.8 | 6.6 | 7.1 | 12.1 | 10.5 | 11.9 | 9.1 |
| Food products | 0.1 | ..... | 0.2 | 0.7 | 0.9 | ..... | ..... | ..... | ..... | 0.2 |
| Tobacco products | ..... | ..... | ..... | ..... | ..... | ..... | ..... | ..... | ..... | ..... |
| Textile mill products | ..... | ..... | ..... | ..... | ..... | 0.1 | ..... | 0.1 | 0.1 | ..... |
| Apparel | ..... | ..... | ..... | ..... | ..... | ..... | ..... | ..... | ..... | ..... |
| Lumber and wood products | 1.7 | 1.1 | 0.8 | 1.2 | 0.1 | ..... | 0.1 | 0.2 | 0.2 | 0.1 |
| Furniture and fixtures | ..... | 0.3 | 1.5 | 0.4 | 0.2 | 0.1 | ..... | 0.3 | ..... | ..... |
| Paper products | 1.2 | 0.1 | ..... | 0.1 | 0.3 | ..... | ..... | 0.1 | ..... | ..... |
| Printing and publishing | ..... | ..... | ..... | ..... | ..... | ..... | ..... | 0.1 | 0.3 | 0.4 |
| Chemical products | 0.1 | 0.1 | 0.1 | 0.1 | 0.3 | 0.1 | ..... | 1.6 | 5.5 | 3.1 |
| Refined petroleum products | ..... | ..... | 0.6 | 0.9 | 1.1 | ..... | ..... | ..... | ..... | ..... |
| Rubber and plastic products | 0.1 | 0.2 | ..... | ..... | 0.2 | 0.2 | ..... | ..... | 0.1 | ..... |
| Leather products | ..... | ..... | ..... | ..... | ..... | 0.3 | ..... | ..... | ..... | ..... |
| Stone, clay and glass products | ..... | ..... | ..... | ..... | ..... | ..... | 0.1 | 0.2 | 1.0 | 0.3 |
| Primary metals | 0.7 | 1.3 | 2.2 | 0.1 | 0.2 | ..... | 0.1 | ..... | 0.1 | 0.1 |
| Fabricated metal products | 0.3 | 0.1 | 0.1 | 0.1 | 0.2 | ..... | 0.1 | 0.1 | 0.1 | 0.3 |
| Industrial machinery and computers | 0.7 | 2.0 | 0.9 | 0.2 | 0.8 | 0.3 | 0.2 | 0.8 | 1.4 | 1.3 |
| Electric and electronic equipment | 0.7 | 0.7 | 1.9 | 0.9 | 1.1 | 5.4 | 9.4 | 6.8 | 2.8 | 2.2 |
| Transportation equipment | 0.3 | 0.5 | 2.5 | 0.8 | 0.2 | 0.2 | 1.9 | ..... | 0.2 | 0.3 |
| Scientific and measuring instruments | 0.2 | 0.3 | 0.2 | ..... | 0.8 | ..... | ..... | 0.1 | 0.1 | 0.4 |
| Miscellaneous manufactures | 0.1 | ..... | 0.2 | 0.1 | 0.2 | ..... | ..... | ..... | 0.1 | ..... |
| Unidentified manufactures | ..... | ..... | ..... | ..... | 0.1 | ..... | ..... | ..... | ..... | ..... |
| **Agricultural and livestock products** | ..... | 1.2 | 8.6 | 3.0 | 0.2 | ..... | ..... | ..... | 0.1 | ..... |
| Agricultural products | ..... | 1.1 | 8.6 | 2.5 | ..... | ..... | ..... | ..... | ..... | ..... |
| Livestock and livestock products | ..... | 0.2 | 0.1 | 0.5 | 0.2 | ..... | ..... | ..... | 0.1 | ..... |
| **Other commodities** | ..... | ..... | ..... | ..... | 0.2 | 0.2 | ..... | ..... | 0.1 | 0.1 |
| Forestry products | ..... | ..... | ..... | ..... | ..... | ..... | ..... | ..... | ..... | ..... |
| Fish and other marine products | ..... | ..... | ..... | ..... | 0.2 | 0.1 | ..... | ..... | ..... | ..... |
| Metallic ores and concentrates | ..... | ..... | ..... | ..... | ..... | ..... | ..... | ..... | ..... | ..... |
| Bituminous coal and lignite | ..... | ..... | ..... | ..... | ..... | ..... | ..... | ..... | ..... | ..... |
| Crude petroleum and natural gas | ..... | ..... | ..... | ..... | ..... | ..... | ..... | ..... | ..... | ..... |
| Nonmetallic minerals | ..... | ..... | ..... | ..... | ..... | ..... | ..... | ..... | 0.1 | ..... |
| Scrap and waste | ..... | ..... | ..... | ..... | ..... | ..... | ..... | ..... | ..... | ..... |
| Used merchandise | ..... | ..... | ..... | ..... | ..... | ..... | ..... | ..... | ..... | ..... |
| Goods imported and returned unchanged | ..... | ..... | ..... | ..... | ..... | ..... | ..... | ..... | ..... | ..... |
| Special classification provisions | ..... | ..... | ..... | ..... | ..... | ..... | ..... | ..... | ..... | ..... |

## MISSOURI: Exports of Goods, 1997

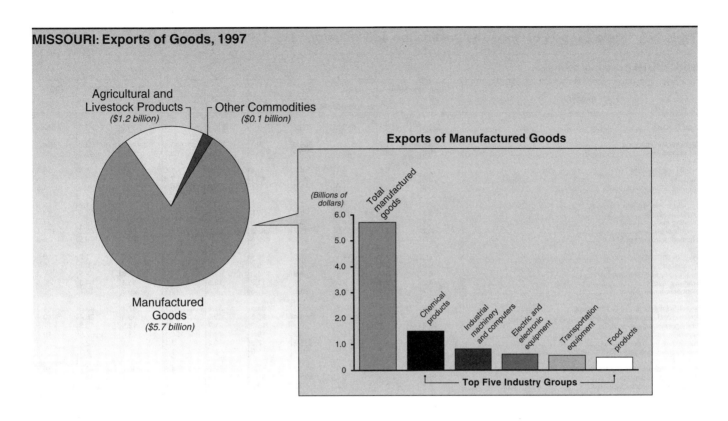

## Table D-3.   State Exports of Goods by Destination and Industry, 1993–1997 —Continued

**MISSOURI** (Millions of dollars.)

| Industry | 1993 | 1994 | 1995 | 1996 | 1997 | 1993 | 1994 | 1995 | 1996 | 1997 |
|---|---|---|---|---|---|---|---|---|---|---|
| | All destinations | | | | | . Canada | | | | |
| **ALL GOODS** | 4 733.3 | 5 234.8 | 5 689.9 | 6 590.5 | 7 043.0 | 1 112.9 | 1 347.9 | 1 369.7 | 1 288.1 | 1 490.1 |
| **Manufactured goods** | 3 910.2 | 4 392.8 | 4 857.7 | 5 122.3 | 5 711.9 | 1 074.4 | 1 305.0 | 1 319.3 | 1 237.2 | 1 432.7 |
| Food products | 379.3 | 287.7 | 391.7 | 369.5 | 493.2 | 45.9 | 60.9 | 78.2 | 57.3 | 73.4 |
| Tobacco products | ..... | ..... | ..... | ..... | ..... | ..... | ..... | ..... | ..... | ..... |
| Textile mill products | 12.5 | 12.2 | 21.8 | 24.3 | 21.8 | 3.4 | 4.1 | 7.5 | 8.4 | 7.0 |
| Apparel | 35.6 | 40.8 | 49.8 | 58.4 | 58.8 | 2.2 | 2.8 | 4.6 | 3.9 | 3.9 |
| Lumber and wood products | 39.7 | 45.0 | 45.3 | 47.0 | 56.1 | 11.0 | 11.9 | 11.4 | 13.5 | 15.7 |
| Furniture and fixtures | 29.2 | 44.5 | 37.0 | 40.9 | 47.0 | 18.2 | 33.2 | 25.1 | 21.8 | 27.8 |
| Paper products | 32.1 | 44.5 | 49.7 | 47.7 | 50.3 | 11.8 | 20.7 | 16.5 | 12.8 | 19.9 |
| Printing and publishing | 79.1 | 84.7 | 103.3 | 99.1 | 132.0 | 31.1 | 36.6 | 46.1 | 45.6 | 63.9 |
| Chemical products | 1 307.5 | 1 389.3 | 1 524.8 | 1 593.7 | 1 529.7 | 258.2 | 293.2 | 325.2 | 293.6 | 285.8 |
| Refined petroleum products | 68.6 | 73.7 | 71.4 | 108.8 | 154.4 | 10.6 | 10.3 | 7.0 | 3.7 | 11.0 |
| Rubber and plastic products | 122.8 | 129.4 | 143.1 | 144.7 | 207.3 | 52.3 | 53.5 | 49.2 | 41.2 | 57.0 |
| Leather products | 5.4 | 8.6 | 9.3 | 12.6 | 20.9 | 2.4 | 3.2 | 3.0 | 6.4 | 13.9 |
| Stone, clay and glass products | 43.6 | 49.4 | 56.7 | 49.1 | 41.8 | 20.2 | 19.1 | 14.8 | 13.9 | 16.8 |
| Primary metals | 93.6 | 119.5 | 159.6 | 179.3 | 266.9 | 39.2 | 42.9 | 46.7 | 44.7 | 75.7 |
| Fabricated metal products | 169.3 | 275.8 | 249.8 | 229.7 | 302.9 | 84.5 | 148.6 | 90.3 | 81.6 | 80.9 |
| Industrial machinery and computers | 488.3 | 543.4 | 616.2 | 666.4 | 825.0 | 163.3 | 197.0 | 214.6 | 209.1 | 266.2 |
| Electric and electronic equipment | 380.8 | 522.7 | 490.1 | 583.9 | 618.5 | 105.6 | 126.2 | 126.9 | 143.4 | 157.1 |
| Transportation equipment | 404.3 | 469.5 | 569.1 | 564.3 | 570.3 | 183.6 | 199.6 | 207.9 | 180.5 | 199.0 |
| Scientific and measuring instruments | 171.3 | 203.3 | 218.9 | 250.1 | 257.6 | 20.5 | 29.2 | 28.3 | 38.4 | 38.6 |
| Miscellaneous manufactures | 36.0 | 34.1 | 35.2 | 39.1 | 43.4 | 6.9 | 7.5 | 9.8 | 11.8 | 15.1 |
| Unidentified manufactures | 11.4 | 14.7 | 14.8 | 13.7 | 14.2 | 3.5 | 4.5 | 6.0 | 5.6 | 4.3 |
| **Agricultural and livestock products** | 721.1 | 738.1 | 697.3 | 1 354.9 | 1 182.1 | 5.7 | 4.0 | 4.4 | 5.5 | 7.1 |
| Agricultural products | 717.1 | 734.8 | 694.4 | 1 351.4 | 1 178.9 | 2.6 | 2.4 | 2.9 | 3.6 | 5.4 |
| Livestock and livestock products | 3.9 | 3.3 | 3.0 | 3.5 | 3.2 | 3.1 | 1.5 | 1.4 | 2.0 | 1.7 |
| **Other commodities** | 102.0 | 104.0 | 134.9 | 113.2 | 149.0 | 32.8 | 39.0 | 46.1 | 45.4 | 50.3 |
| Forestry products | 4.1 | 5.2 | 4.6 | 4.0 | 3.6 | 0.1 | 0.1 | ..... | 0.1 | 0.1 |
| Fish and other marine products | 0.9 | 0.6 | 1.0 | 0.6 | 0.8 | 0.8 | 0.3 | 0.3 | 0.3 | 0.5 |
| Metallic ores and concentrates | 10.7 | 11.9 | 16.9 | 14.3 | 11.7 | 7.8 | 11.9 | 16.4 | 13.7 | 10.8 |
| Bituminous coal and lignite | 34.3 | 19.1 | 8.8 | 5.2 | 42.6 | ..... | 1.1 | ..... | 0.7 | ..... |
| Crude petroleum and natural gas | 0.1 | ..... | 0.1 | 0.1 | 0.1 | 0.1 | ..... | ..... | ..... | ..... |
| Nonmetallic minerals | 5.3 | 4.5 | 5.3 | 4.9 | 5.3 | 2.6 | 2.7 | 2.8 | 2.3 | 2.8 |
| Scrap and waste | 6.2 | 19.1 | 45.2 | 32.5 | 37.4 | 2.1 | 3.3 | 7.0 | 3.8 | 10.1 |
| Used merchandise | 5.8 | 8.5 | 4.9 | 5.5 | 14.2 | 0.8 | 1.9 | 1.6 | 1.4 | 4.1 |
| Goods imported and returned unchanged | 14.8 | 14.0 | 16.0 | 20.9 | 20.1 | 14.8 | 14.0 | 16.0 | 20.9 | 20.1 |
| Special classification provisions | 19.6 | 21.1 | 32.1 | 25.2 | 13.1 | 3.7 | 3.5 | 1.8 | 2.3 | 1.9 |

## Table D-3.  State Exports of Goods by Destination and Industry, 1993–1997 —*Continued*

**MISSOURI** (Millions of dollars.)

| Industry | 1993 | 1994 | 1995 | 1996 | 1997 | 1993 | 1994 | 1995 | 1996 | 1997 |
|---|---|---|---|---|---|---|---|---|---|---|
| | South and Central America and Caribbean | | | | | Mexico | | | | |
| **ALL GOODS** | 534.5 | 498.5 | 660.2 | 788.2 | 797.1 | 540.4 | 773.4 | 699.0 | 1 089.0 | 1 042.4 |
| **Manufactured goods** | 398.6 | 434.7 | 576.8 | 666.9 | 739.1 | 343.6 | 480.4 | 448.7 | 533.8 | 594.2 |
| Food products | 38.0 | 39.2 | 48.9 | 60.3 | 78.4 | 27.6 | 30.3 | 41.0 | 47.3 | 32.7 |
| Tobacco products | ..... | ..... | ..... | ..... | ..... | ..... | ..... | ..... | ..... | ..... |
| Textile mill products | 2.7 | 2.8 | 4.1 | 4.8 | 3.6 | 1.4 | 1.5 | 2.6 | 1.5 | 2.0 |
| Apparel | 15.6 | 19.2 | 27.1 | 35.8 | 42.1 | 6.1 | 7.8 | 7.6 | 3.6 | 3.4 |
| Lumber and wood products | 0.6 | 0.6 | 1.0 | 1.6 | 2.1 | 0.5 | 0.3 | 0.8 | 0.7 | 1.5 |
| Furniture and fixtures | 2.1 | 1.5 | 1.4 | 1.6 | 2.3 | 2.2 | 2.5 | 0.7 | 1.7 | 3.3 |
| Paper products | 1.7 | 1.3 | 2.5 | 2.8 | 5.0 | 6.3 | 11.9 | 13.3 | 21.6 | 14.1 |
| Printing and publishing | 2.7 | 3.2 | 4.3 | 3.0 | 4.0 | 13.8 | 18.2 | 17.3 | 19.6 | 21.0 |
| Chemical products | 182.2 | 208.6 | 263.0 | 305.2 | 265.5 | 87.9 | 128.8 | 89.2 | 86.2 | 101.1 |
| Refined petroleum products | 39.6 | 43.1 | 50.3 | 89.2 | 129.8 | 0.4 | 0.4 | 0.5 | 0.5 | 0.5 |
| Rubber and plastic products | 7.7 | 7.1 | 14.5 | 18.3 | 18.4 | 10.1 | 17.5 | 12.0 | 11.2 | 16.4 |
| Leather products | 0.3 | 0.6 | 2.9 | 2.4 | 0.9 | 0.3 | 0.6 | 0.3 | 0.1 | 0.7 |
| Stone, clay and glass products | 4.4 | 3.3 | 6.3 | 4.9 | 4.8 | 1.5 | 1.7 | 1.6 | 2.0 | 2.4 |
| Primary metals | 4.2 | 2.9 | 5.3 | 6.1 | 11.2 | 12.5 | 30.6 | 49.4 | 64.3 | 85.4 |
| Fabricated metal products | 7.7 | 10.4 | 23.7 | 21.9 | 21.5 | 8.4 | 17.7 | 20.0 | 18.1 | 37.4 |
| Industrial machinery and computers | 41.5 | 44.8 | 64.7 | 60.7 | 84.4 | 34.4 | 46.1 | 47.1 | 49.5 | 54.3 |
| Electric and electronic equipment | 18.1 | 18.7 | 22.6 | 18.4 | 25.5 | 62.6 | 86.7 | 86.4 | 126.4 | 140.4 |
| Transportation equipment | 9.9 | 6.5 | 12.2 | 9.2 | 15.8 | 21.7 | 22.8 | 12.8 | 18.5 | 22.5 |
| Scientific and measuring instruments | 11.8 | 15.4 | 18.6 | 18.9 | 19.1 | 43.2 | 50.1 | 43.4 | 57.3 | 49.7 |
| Miscellaneous manufactures | 6.7 | 4.7 | 2.2 | 1.2 | 2.6 | 2.2 | 3.1 | 2.1 | 2.4 | 4.0 |
| Unidentified manufactures | 1.0 | 0.7 | 0.9 | 0.7 | 1.6 | 0.7 | 1.7 | 0.7 | 1.3 | 1.7 |
| **Agricultural and livestock products** | 113.6 | 46.3 | 76.8 | 120.3 | 57.4 | 186.2 | 284.5 | 234.7 | 542.7 | 438.9 |
| Agricultural products | 113.5 | 46.0 | 76.4 | 120.1 | 57.2 | 185.9 | 283.8 | 234.7 | 542.7 | 438.3 |
| Livestock and livestock products | 0.1 | 0.3 | 0.4 | 0.2 | 0.2 | 0.3 | 0.8 | ..... | ..... | 0.6 |
| **Other commodities** | 22.2 | 17.5 | 6.6 | 0.9 | 0.6 | 10.6 | 8.5 | 15.6 | 12.5 | 9.3 |
| Forestry products | ..... | ..... | ..... | ..... | 0.1 | ..... | ..... | ..... | ..... | ..... |
| Fish and other marine products | ..... | ..... | ..... | ..... | ..... | ..... | 0.1 | ..... | ..... | ..... |
| Metallic ores and concentrates | ..... | ..... | ..... | ..... | ..... | ..... | ..... | ..... | ..... | ..... |
| Bituminous coal and lignite | 20.9 | 16.8 | 6.0 | ..... | ..... | ..... | ..... | ..... | ..... | ..... |
| Crude petroleum and natural gas | ..... | ..... | ..... | ..... | ..... | ..... | ..... | ..... | ..... | ..... |
| Nonmetallic minerals | 0.6 | 0.2 | 0.3 | 0.2 | 0.1 | 0.6 | 0.2 | 0.9 | 1.0 | 1.0 |
| Scrap and waste | 0.5 | 0.1 | 0.1 | ..... | ..... | 0.3 | 0.4 | 0.4 | 0.8 | 4.6 |
| Used merchandise | 0.2 | 0.3 | ..... | 0.1 | 0.1 | 0.1 | 0.3 | 0.1 | ..... | 0.1 |
| Goods imported and returned unchanged | ..... | ..... | ..... | ..... | ..... | ..... | ..... | ..... | ..... | ..... |
| Special classification provisions | 0.1 | ..... | 0.2 | 0.7 | 0.3 | 9.5 | 7.5 | 14.1 | 10.6 | 3.6 |
| | European Union | | | | | United Kingdom | | | | |
| **ALL GOODS** | 976.4 | 1 123.4 | 1 330.8 | 1 493.0 | 1 701.7 | 245.0 | 262.5 | 195.6 | 193.6 | 235.8 |
| **Manufactured goods** | 888.8 | 977.5 | 1 195.4 | 1 262.0 | 1 316.9 | 243.3 | 256.5 | 189.8 | 182.7 | 225.6 |
| Food products | 48.4 | 34.0 | 52.5 | 47.3 | 64.1 | 9.1 | 5.2 | 9.5 | 5.7 | 6.1 |
| Tobacco products | ..... | ..... | ..... | ..... | ..... | ..... | ..... | ..... | ..... | ..... |
| Textile mill products | 1.9 | 1.5 | 3.3 | 3.5 | 4.2 | 0.7 | 0.5 | 0.9 | 1.0 | 1.7 |
| Apparel | 7.7 | 6.8 | 6.7 | 8.4 | 4.4 | 2.1 | 1.2 | 1.7 | 3.5 | 1.5 |
| Lumber and wood products | 21.5 | 23.7 | 22.9 | 22.9 | 27.3 | 6.1 | 7.2 | 6.2 | 7.9 | 9.7 |
| Furniture and fixtures | 3.8 | 3.8 | 4.9 | 7.9 | 8.4 | 1.1 | 1.3 | 1.9 | 3.4 | 3.9 |
| Paper products | 5.9 | 4.0 | 8.0 | 5.5 | 7.1 | 1.7 | 0.4 | 0.9 | 0.5 | 0.7 |
| Printing and publishing | 15.0 | 11.7 | 15.7 | 11.2 | 20.3 | 9.0 | 7.5 | 10.2 | 6.7 | 12.3 |
| Chemical products | 391.8 | 364.8 | 451.6 | 482.0 | 511.6 | 52.3 | 56.8 | 37.4 | 40.9 | 48.9 |
| Refined petroleum products | 7.4 | 17.7 | 10.1 | 7.2 | 5.2 | 1.3 | 1.9 | 1.9 | 2.6 | 1.5 |
| Rubber and plastic products | 26.9 | 32.1 | 38.2 | 42.1 | 56.5 | 5.8 | 6.0 | 6.1 | 6.8 | 12.7 |
| Leather products | 1.0 | 0.9 | 0.8 | 0.5 | 0.8 | 0.3 | 0.3 | 0.2 | 0.2 | 0.3 |
| Stone, clay and glass products | 8.2 | 19.0 | 23.0 | 19.5 | 9.9 | 2.7 | 3.1 | 3.7 | 3.3 | 4.0 |
| Primary metals | 4.5 | 10.0 | 12.5 | 23.8 | 26.4 | 1.0 | 1.1 | 2.1 | 9.2 | 8.6 |
| Fabricated metal products | 22.1 | 22.2 | 27.9 | 24.3 | 26.5 | 7.6 | 6.4 | 5.6 | 6.6 | 4.8 |
| Industrial machinery and computers | 95.7 | 97.7 | 106.9 | 126.8 | 142.3 | 28.0 | 32.9 | 32.6 | 37.5 | 51.1 |
| Electric and electronic equipment | 60.1 | 87.6 | 79.6 | 96.1 | 83.5 | 20.0 | 21.2 | 18.0 | 17.0 | 18.6 |
| Transportation equipment | 104.8 | 174.6 | 254.6 | 257.1 | 236.8 | 82.6 | 95.2 | 40.8 | 17.1 | 24.8 |
| Scientific and measuring instruments | 51.8 | 55.1 | 65.0 | 65.0 | 72.8 | 6.9 | 5.0 | 6.8 | 9.5 | 11.5 |
| Miscellaneous manufactures | 8.3 | 7.5 | 8.5 | 8.6 | 6.9 | 4.2 | 2.3 | 2.4 | 2.5 | 2.2 |
| Unidentified manufactures | 2.1 | 2.7 | 2.7 | 2.3 | 1.9 | 0.7 | 0.7 | 0.9 | 0.9 | 0.6 |
| **Agricultural and livestock products** | 72.2 | 137.2 | 126.7 | 218.0 | 341.1 | 0.1 | 3.9 | 3.1 | 7.5 | 5.7 |
| Agricultural products | 71.9 | 136.5 | 126.1 | 216.9 | 340.9 | 0.1 | 3.9 | 3.0 | 7.5 | 5.7 |
| Livestock and livestock products | 0.2 | 0.7 | 0.6 | 1.1 | 0.2 | ..... | ..... | ..... | 0.1 | 0.1 |
| **Other commodities** | 15.5 | 8.7 | 8.7 | 13.1 | 43.7 | 1.6 | 2.1 | 2.7 | 3.4 | 4.4 |
| Forestry products | ..... | ..... | ..... | ..... | 0.2 | ..... | ..... | ..... | ..... | ..... |
| Fish and other marine products | 0.1 | 0.1 | 0.3 | 0.2 | 0.1 | ..... | ..... | ..... | ..... | ..... |
| Metallic ores and concentrates | 2.8 | ..... | 0.4 | 0.3 | 0.7 | ..... | ..... | 0.4 | 0.3 | 0.3 |
| Bituminous coal and lignite | 5.9 | 1.2 | 2.8 | 4.5 | 30.5 | ..... | ..... | ..... | ..... | ..... |
| Crude petroleum and natural gas | ..... | ..... | ..... | ..... | ..... | ..... | ..... | ..... | ..... | ..... |
| Nonmetallic minerals | 1.0 | 0.7 | 0.6 | 0.6 | 0.7 | 0.2 | 0.3 | 0.2 | 0.2 | 0.2 |
| Scrap and waste | 0.4 | ..... | 0.1 | 0.2 | 0.1 | 0.2 | ..... | 0.1 | 0.1 | ..... |
| Used merchandise | 2.6 | 3.2 | 0.9 | 2.6 | 7.1 | 0.2 | 0.1 | 0.2 | 1.3 | 3.3 |
| Goods imported and returned unchanged | ..... | ..... | ..... | ..... | ..... | ..... | ..... | ..... | ..... | ..... |
| Special classification provisions | 2.8 | 3.4 | 3.6 | 4.6 | 4.3 | 1.0 | 1.7 | 1.8 | 1.5 | 0.6 |

## Table D-3.  State Exports of Goods by Destination and Industry, 1993–1997 —*Continued*

### MISSOURI (Millions of dollars.)

| Industry | 1993 | 1994 | 1995 | 1996 | 1997 | 1993 | 1994 | 1995 | 1996 | 1997 |
|---|---|---|---|---|---|---|---|---|---|---|
| | Germany | | | | | France | | | | |
| **ALL GOODS** | 121.6 | 117.3 | 156.4 | 171.6 | 202.7 | 74.8 | 77.6 | 91.6 | 72.1 | 81.2 |
| **Manufactured goods** | 119.2 | 114.7 | 148.4 | 170.1 | 198.7 | 69.5 | 75.4 | 83.8 | 66.7 | 70.7 |
| Food products | 1.8 | 2.0 | 1.7 | 1.6 | 1.4 | 3.3 | 1.8 | 2.2 | 0.6 | 0.6 |
| Tobacco products | ..... | ..... | ..... | ..... | ..... | ..... | ..... | ..... | ..... | ..... |
| Textile mill products | 0.2 | 0.3 | 1.5 | 1.3 | 1.0 | 0.4 | 0.2 | 0.2 | 0.3 | 0.3 |
| Apparel | 2.6 | 2.2 | 1.8 | 1.5 | 1.0 | 0.3 | 0.3 | 1.1 | 1.3 | 0.1 |
| Lumber and wood products | 2.8 | 2.9 | 6.0 | 1.7 | 1.7 | 2.3 | 1.2 | 2.4 | 3.2 | 4.4 |
| Furniture and fixtures | 0.4 | 0.6 | 0.4 | 0.3 | 0.2 | 1.3 | 0.9 | 0.9 | 1.7 | 2.0 |
| Paper products | 1.4 | 0.9 | 1.5 | 1.4 | 2.0 | 0.2 | 0.1 | 0.1 | 0.1 | 0.2 |
| Printing and publishing | 2.1 | 1.7 | 1.9 | 1.4 | 4.5 | 1.3 | 0.9 | 1.3 | 0.8 | 0.8 |
| Chemical products | 49.5 | 41.7 | 53.4 | 55.5 | 91.3 | 23.9 | 21.2 | 27.3 | 16.8 | 19.1 |
| Refined petroleum products | 0.2 | 0.2 | 0.2 | 0.1 | 0.3 | 0.1 | 0.1 | 0.2 | 0.1 | ..... |
| Rubber and plastic products | 2.6 | 2.6 | 2.7 | 1.5 | 4.3 | 1.1 | 1.2 | 2.1 | 2.0 | 1.6 |
| Leather products | 0.3 | 0.4 | 0.3 | 0.1 | 0.3 | 0.1 | 0.1 | ..... | ..... | ..... |
| Stone, clay and glass products | 2.7 | 3.3 | 4.4 | 2.0 | 2.1 | 0.4 | 0.4 | 0.5 | 0.6 | 0.8 |
| Primary metals | 0.8 | 1.2 | 1.6 | 1.5 | 1.2 | 0.5 | 0.4 | 0.6 | 0.3 | 0.6 |
| Fabricated metal products | 1.7 | 1.6 | 1.6 | 1.9 | 5.3 | 0.8 | 0.7 | 0.7 | 1.5 | 1.2 |
| Industrial machinery and computers | 19.6 | 18.2 | 20.4 | 28.7 | 31.4 | 12.1 | 7.4 | 11.8 | 13.3 | 10.5 |
| Electric and electronic equipment | 9.1 | 14.9 | 20.6 | 49.5 | 27.0 | 9.9 | 19.7 | 11.7 | 6.5 | 8.4 |
| Transportation equipment | 11.7 | 5.6 | 8.7 | 4.5 | 5.5 | 2.7 | 4.8 | 6.6 | 5.6 | 5.6 |
| Scientific and measuring instruments | 8.4 | 12.6 | 18.6 | 14.0 | 16.9 | 7.8 | 13.4 | 11.9 | 11.1 | 13.5 |
| Miscellaneous manufactures | 0.8 | 1.1 | 0.7 | 1.0 | 0.9 | 0.7 | 0.3 | 1.9 | 0.9 | 0.9 |
| Unidentified manufactures | 0.3 | 0.6 | 0.5 | 0.6 | 0.3 | 0.2 | 0.3 | 0.3 | 0.2 | 0.1 |
| **Agricultural and livestock products** | 0.7 | 0.7 | 7.7 | 0.2 | 0.3 | 0.2 | ..... | 4.3 | ..... | 0.1 |
| Agricultural products | 0.7 | 0.7 | 7.6 | 0.2 | 0.3 | 0.2 | ..... | 4.3 | ..... | 0.1 |
| Livestock and livestock products | ..... | ..... | 0.2 | ..... | ..... | ..... | ..... | ..... | ..... | ..... |
| **Other commodities** | 1.7 | 1.8 | 0.3 | 1.2 | 3.6 | 5.1 | 2.1 | 3.5 | 5.4 | 10.3 |
| Forestry products | ..... | ..... | ..... | ..... | ..... | ..... | ..... | ..... | ..... | ..... |
| Fish and other marine products | ..... | ..... | ..... | ..... | ..... | 0.1 | 0.1 | 0.3 | 0.2 | 0.1 |
| Metallic ores and concentrates | ..... | ..... | ..... | ..... | ..... | ..... | ..... | ..... | ..... | ..... |
| Bituminous coal and lignite | ..... | ..... | ..... | ..... | ..... | 4.1 | 1.2 | 2.8 | 4.5 | 9.4 |
| Crude petroleum and natural gas | ..... | ..... | ..... | ..... | ..... | ..... | ..... | ..... | ..... | ..... |
| Nonmetallic minerals | 0.5 | 0.2 | 0.1 | 0.1 | 0.2 | 0.1 | 0.1 | 0.1 | 0.1 | 0.2 |
| Scrap and waste | 0.1 | ..... | ..... | ..... | ..... | 0.1 | ..... | ..... | ..... | ..... |
| Used merchandise | 1.0 | 1.6 | 0.1 | 0.5 | 2.4 | 0.6 | 0.7 | 0.3 | 0.5 | 0.5 |
| Goods imported and returned unchanged | ..... | ..... | ..... | ..... | ..... | ..... | ..... | ..... | ..... | ..... |
| Special classification provisions | 0.1 | ..... | 0.1 | 0.6 | 1.0 | ..... | ..... | ..... | ..... | 0.1 |
| | The Netherlands | | | | | Asian 10 | | | | |
| **ALL GOODS** | 103.8 | 122.7 | 117.3 | 137.7 | 129.7 | 807.0 | 945.5 | 986.8 | 1 152.2 | 1 205.3 |
| **Manufactured goods** | 47.3 | 50.7 | 64.2 | 61.1 | 50.8 | 762.8 | 858.5 | 915.8 | 990.6 | 1 072.3 |
| Food products | 5.0 | 9.4 | 23.0 | 17.6 | 15.5 | 75.9 | 81.0 | 105.9 | 138.3 | 202.1 |
| Tobacco products | ..... | ..... | ..... | ..... | ..... | ..... | ..... | ..... | ..... | ..... |
| Textile mill products | 0.1 | 0.1 | 0.3 | 0.3 | 0.1 | 1.6 | 1.4 | 2.2 | 4.7 | 2.8 |
| Apparel | 1.3 | 1.3 | 0.5 | 0.5 | 0.3 | 2.9 | 2.3 | 2.4 | 4.9 | 2.1 |
| Lumber and wood products | 2.6 | 3.2 | 0.1 | 0.4 | 0.1 | 5.1 | 7.2 | 7.1 | 6.1 | 5.7 |
| Furniture and fixtures | 0.5 | 0.6 | 0.5 | 0.3 | 0.3 | 1.6 | 1.7 | 2.8 | 4.6 | 3.3 |
| Paper products | 0.8 | 0.8 | 0.2 | 0.4 | 0.6 | 3.8 | 5.1 | 7.2 | 2.9 | 2.7 |
| Printing and publishing | 0.2 | 0.2 | 0.1 | 0.3 | 0.6 | 9.7 | 10.8 | 13.9 | 12.4 | 13.9 |
| Chemical products | 9.7 | 11.9 | 9.5 | 10.0 | 8.2 | 275.9 | 287.0 | 278.8 | 270.3 | 232.9 |
| Refined petroleum products | ..... | ..... | 0.1 | 0.1 | 0.1 | 7.4 | 1.6 | 2.8 | 3.5 | 2.3 |
| Rubber and plastic products | 2.3 | 1.1 | 1.0 | 2.2 | 1.9 | 15.7 | 9.9 | 19.0 | 24.3 | 47.4 |
| Leather products | 0.2 | ..... | 0.1 | ..... | ..... | 1.2 | 2.8 | 1.9 | 2.6 | 2.9 |
| Stone, clay and glass products | 0.1 | 0.2 | 0.3 | 0.2 | 0.4 | 4.6 | 3.8 | 7.2 | 6.2 | 4.5 |
| Primary metals | 0.3 | 0.2 | 1.0 | 2.4 | 0.5 | 24.3 | 24.4 | 39.7 | 33.9 | 49.3 |
| Fabricated metal products | 4.2 | 3.6 | 4.9 | 2.7 | 2.9 | 32.9 | 62.9 | 64.4 | 65.1 | 78.2 |
| Industrial machinery and computers | 6.5 | 9.0 | 8.1 | 15.4 | 12.7 | 93.7 | 80.2 | 105.2 | 115.3 | 124.2 |
| Electric and electronic equipment | 5.0 | 5.7 | 8.4 | 4.9 | 2.1 | 111.4 | 181.2 | 146.4 | 166.6 | 172.6 |
| Transportation equipment | 0.8 | 0.5 | 1.4 | 0.8 | 1.6 | 55.2 | 44.6 | 50.5 | 70.6 | 60.2 |
| Scientific and measuring instruments | 6.8 | 1.9 | 3.2 | 1.6 | 2.2 | 30.8 | 38.6 | 47.3 | 46.2 | 55.1 |
| Miscellaneous manufactures | 0.8 | 0.7 | 1.4 | 0.9 | 0.4 | 7.6 | 6.1 | 9.2 | 10.5 | 8.7 |
| Unidentified manufactures | 0.1 | 0.2 | 0.2 | 0.1 | 0.1 | 1.5 | 2.0 | 1.8 | 1.7 | 1.6 |
| **Agricultural and livestock products** | 56.0 | 71.3 | 52.7 | 76.2 | 73.4 | 24.9 | 58.2 | 14.5 | 122.3 | 91.9 |
| Agricultural products | 56.0 | 71.3 | 52.7 | 76.2 | 73.4 | 24.8 | 58.1 | 14.1 | 122.0 | 91.4 |
| Livestock and livestock products | ..... | ..... | ..... | ..... | ..... | 0.1 | 0.1 | 0.5 | 0.3 | 0.4 |
| **Other commodities** | 0.5 | 0.7 | 0.4 | 0.4 | 5.4 | 19.3 | 28.9 | 56.5 | 39.4 | 41.1 |
| Forestry products | ..... | ..... | ..... | ..... | 0.1 | 4.0 | 5.1 | 4.4 | 3.9 | 3.3 |
| Fish and other marine products | ..... | ..... | ..... | ..... | ..... | 0.1 | ..... | 0.4 | 0.1 | 0.3 |
| Metallic ores and concentrates | 0.1 | ..... | ..... | ..... | ..... | 0.1 | ..... | ..... | 0.2 | 0.2 |
| Bituminous coal and lignite | ..... | ..... | ..... | ..... | 5.3 | 7.4 | ..... | ..... | ..... | 9.8 |
| Crude petroleum and natural gas | ..... | ..... | ..... | ..... | ..... | ..... | ..... | 0.1 | ..... | 0.1 |
| Nonmetallic minerals | ..... | ..... | ..... | 0.1 | ..... | 0.4 | 0.4 | 0.5 | 0.5 | 0.5 |
| Scrap and waste | ..... | ..... | ..... | ..... | ..... | 3.0 | 15.2 | 37.1 | 27.4 | 22.5 |
| Used merchandise | ..... | 0.4 | 0.1 | ..... | ..... | 0.8 | 1.9 | 1.9 | 1.1 | 1.7 |
| Goods imported and returned unchanged | ..... | ..... | ..... | ..... | ..... | ..... | ..... | ..... | ..... | ..... |
| Special classification provisions | 0.4 | 0.2 | 0.4 | 0.3 | ..... | 3.5 | 6.4 | 12.1 | 6.0 | 2.7 |

## Table D-3.   State Exports of Goods by Destination and Industry, 1993–1997 —Continued

**MISSOURI** (Millions of dollars.)

| Industry | 1993 | 1994 | 1995 | 1996 | 1997 | 1993 | 1994 | 1995 | 1996 | 1997 |
|---|---|---|---|---|---|---|---|---|---|---|
| | Japan | | | | | South Korea | | | | |
| **ALL GOODS** | 266.8 | 259.4 | 282.0 | 275.5 | 307.6 | 93.1 | 104.9 | 131.0 | 152.1 | 151.7 |
| **Manufactured goods** | 255.5 | 245.9 | 253.7 | 260.3 | 269.2 | 92.5 | 102.7 | 119.0 | 134.9 | 136.8 |
| Food products | 45.4 | 48.1 | 57.0 | 42.6 | 40.7 | 3.8 | 5.3 | 6.6 | 6.8 | 24.7 |
| Tobacco products | ..... | ..... | ..... | ..... | ..... | ..... | ..... | ..... | ..... | ..... |
| Textile mill products | 1.2 | 0.6 | 1.3 | 2.7 | 1.6 | 0.1 | 0.4 | 0.4 | 0.3 | 0.1 |
| Apparel | 1.9 | 1.6 | 1.7 | 4.3 | 1.2 | 0.3 | 0.2 | 0.1 | 0.1 | 0.1 |
| Lumber and wood products | 3.0 | 4.3 | 3.8 | 3.6 | 3.6 | 1.9 | 2.8 | 2.9 | 2.1 | 1.5 |
| Furniture and fixtures | 0.6 | 0.4 | 0.9 | 1.3 | 1.0 | ..... | 0.1 | 0.4 | 0.4 | 0.1 |
| Paper products | 0.4 | 0.5 | 0.1 | 0.2 | 0.4 | 1.8 | 3.1 | 3.9 | 0.9 | 0.7 |
| Printing and publishing | 3.8 | 2.8 | 3.1 | 3.9 | 2.4 | 0.9 | 2.1 | 2.7 | 2.4 | 2.8 |
| Chemical products | 77.8 | 78.2 | 55.8 | 44.1 | 46.7 | 19.1 | 24.6 | 26.9 | 31.9 | 20.5 |
| Refined petroleum products | 0.1 | 0.2 | 0.5 | 0.8 | 0.5 | 0.3 | 0.1 | 0.2 | 0.2 | 0.1 |
| Rubber and plastic products | 3.5 | 2.7 | 4.1 | 4.5 | 5.7 | 6.2 | 2.7 | 4.8 | 7.6 | 6.8 |
| Leather products | 0.1 | 0.3 | 0.3 | 0.3 | 0.3 | 0.2 | 1.4 | ..... | 0.2 | 0.6 |
| Stone, clay and glass products | 0.3 | 0.8 | 2.2 | 0.6 | 0.4 | 0.4 | 0.8 | 1.7 | 0.6 | 0.9 |
| Primary metals | 7.0 | 2.8 | 12.2 | 6.4 | 5.8 | 2.2 | 1.4 | 6.8 | 7.1 | 2.2 |
| Fabricated metal products | 4.0 | 3.9 | 7.5 | 3.8 | 5.0 | 2.9 | 5.5 | 10.1 | 11.7 | 11.9 |
| Industrial machinery and computers | 21.2 | 21.9 | 21.1 | 21.2 | 28.7 | 16.5 | 15.1 | 19.3 | 16.5 | 19.7 |
| Electric and electronic equipment | 22.8 | 23.8 | 20.5 | 36.2 | 42.8 | 27.9 | 25.2 | 23.6 | 33.7 | 34.5 |
| Transportation equipment | 47.6 | 35.7 | 42.9 | 59.8 | 48.8 | 0.5 | 1.5 | 1.3 | 3.3 | 2.6 |
| Scientific and measuring instruments | 10.6 | 13.8 | 14.3 | 20.2 | 30.1 | 6.9 | 9.9 | 6.5 | 7.8 | 5.9 |
| Miscellaneous manufactures | 3.4 | 2.7 | 3.6 | 3.2 | 3.1 | 0.3 | 0.2 | 0.5 | 1.1 | 0.7 |
| Unidentified manufactures | 0.6 | 0.8 | 0.6 | 0.5 | 0.3 | 0.3 | 0.3 | 0.3 | 0.3 | 0.2 |
| **Agricultural and livestock products** | 0.2 | 2.6 | 5.7 | 0.5 | 16.6 | 0.1 | 0.6 | 8.0 | 12.2 | 8.7 |
| Agricultural products | 0.2 | 2.5 | 5.6 | 0.5 | 16.5 | ..... | 0.6 | 7.6 | 12.1 | 8.6 |
| Livestock and livestock products | ..... | 0.1 | ..... | ..... | 0.1 | 0.1 | ..... | 0.3 | 0.1 | 0.1 |
| **Other commodities** | 11.1 | 10.9 | 22.6 | 14.7 | 21.8 | 0.5 | 1.6 | 4.1 | 5.0 | 6.2 |
| Forestry products | 0.1 | 0.1 | 0.1 | ..... | ..... | ..... | ..... | ..... | ..... | ..... |
| Fish and other marine products | 0.1 | ..... | 0.3 | 0.1 | 0.3 | ..... | ..... | 0.1 | ..... | ..... |
| Metallic ores and concentrates | 0.1 | ..... | ..... | 0.2 | 0.2 | ..... | ..... | ..... | ..... | ..... |
| Bituminous coal and lignite | 7.4 | ..... | ..... | ..... | 9.8 | ..... | ..... | ..... | ..... | ..... |
| Crude petroleum and natural gas | ..... | ..... | ..... | ..... | ..... | ..... | ..... | ..... | ..... | 0.1 |
| Nonmetallic minerals | 0.1 | 0.1 | 0.1 | 0.1 | 0.1 | ..... | ..... | ..... | ..... | 0.1 |
| Scrap and waste | 2.0 | 7.6 | 14.7 | 12.8 | 9.6 | 0.4 | 1.2 | 3.8 | 2.8 | 5.9 |
| Used merchandise | 0.7 | 1.5 | 1.7 | 1.1 | 1.6 | ..... | ..... | ..... | ..... | 0.1 |
| Goods imported and returned unchanged | ..... | ..... | ..... | ..... | ..... | ..... | ..... | ..... | ..... | ..... |
| Special classification provisions | 0.7 | 1.5 | 5.7 | 0.4 | 0.3 | 0.1 | 0.4 | 0.1 | 2.2 | 0.1 |

| Industry | 1993 | 1994 | 1995 | 1996 | 1997 | 1993 | 1994 | 1995 | 1996 | 1997 |
|---|---|---|---|---|---|---|---|---|---|---|
| | Taiwan | | | | | Singapore | | | | |
| **ALL GOODS** | 88.6 | 137.1 | 106.7 | 163.4 | 166.4 | 89.9 | 81.5 | 103.9 | 104.2 | 102.1 |
| **Manufactured goods** | 88.0 | 92.1 | 101.5 | 91.0 | 97.8 | 86.3 | 76.5 | 97.3 | 101.7 | 99.5 |
| Food products | 12.9 | 14.1 | 14.9 | 8.5 | 16.6 | 0.6 | 1.1 | 0.4 | 0.4 | 0.8 |
| Tobacco products | ..... | ..... | ..... | ..... | ..... | ..... | ..... | ..... | ..... | ..... |
| Textile mill products | 0.1 | ..... | 0.1 | 0.3 | 0.1 | ..... | ..... | ..... | 0.2 | ..... |
| Apparel | 0.1 | ..... | 0.1 | 0.1 | 0.2 | 0.1 | 0.1 | ..... | 0.1 | 0.2 |
| Lumber and wood products | 0.1 | ..... | 0.2 | ..... | 0.3 | ..... | ..... | ..... | 0.1 | 0.1 |
| Furniture and fixtures | 0.1 | 0.1 | 0.1 | ..... | 0.2 | ..... | 0.3 | 0.1 | 0.3 | 0.3 |
| Paper products | 0.8 | 0.5 | 1.0 | ..... | 0.1 | 0.2 | 0.2 | 0.7 | 0.6 | 0.2 |
| Printing and publishing | 0.3 | 0.8 | 0.7 | 0.8 | 0.9 | 1.2 | 1.3 | 2.1 | 1.7 | 3.7 |
| Chemical products | 28.0 | 33.2 | 36.8 | 29.6 | 25.1 | 50.6 | 40.1 | 46.6 | 51.8 | 43.2 |
| Refined petroleum products | 0.3 | 0.2 | 0.2 | 0.3 | 0.1 | 0.6 | 0.6 | 0.8 | 1.1 | 0.7 |
| Rubber and plastic products | 0.5 | 0.5 | 0.9 | 0.9 | 1.3 | 0.3 | 0.2 | 0.4 | 0.7 | 1.8 |
| Leather products | 0.1 | ..... | 0.1 | ..... | ..... | ..... | 0.1 | ..... | ..... | ..... |
| Stone, clay and glass products | 0.5 | 0.5 | 0.4 | 2.7 | 0.8 | 0.4 | 0.2 | 0.3 | 0.2 | 0.2 |
| Primary metals | 1.1 | 2.1 | 1.3 | 1.8 | 0.5 | 0.3 | 0.5 | 1.1 | 1.4 | 2.3 |
| Fabricated metal products | 2.6 | 5.3 | 5.9 | 3.8 | 4.3 | 3.2 | 4.4 | 4.3 | 4.4 | 8.8 |
| Industrial machinery and computers | 13.6 | 7.4 | 10.3 | 10.7 | 9.6 | 6.6 | 7.3 | 10.0 | 13.0 | 12.7 |
| Electric and electronic equipment | 22.7 | 22.3 | 24.9 | 27.5 | 33.2 | 15.5 | 16.2 | 23.5 | 18.5 | 17.9 |
| Transportation equipment | 0.4 | 0.5 | 0.5 | 0.8 | 0.5 | 4.2 | 0.9 | 2.4 | 2.8 | 4.0 |
| Scientific and measuring instruments | 3.0 | 3.6 | 2.4 | 2.1 | 3.5 | 1.5 | 2.1 | 3.2 | 2.7 | 2.0 |
| Miscellaneous manufactures | 0.6 | 0.7 | 0.5 | 0.8 | 0.4 | 0.7 | 0.6 | 1.0 | 1.6 | 0.5 |
| Unidentified manufactures | 0.2 | 0.2 | 0.2 | 0.2 | 0.3 | 0.2 | 0.3 | 0.3 | 0.2 | 0.2 |
| **Agricultural and livestock products** | 0.2 | 42.2 | 0.3 | 69.1 | 66.2 | ..... | ..... | 0.1 | 0.1 | 0.1 |
| Agricultural products | 0.2 | 42.2 | 0.2 | 69.0 | 66.2 | ..... | ..... | 0.1 | 0.1 | ..... |
| Livestock and livestock products | ..... | ..... | 0.1 | ..... | ..... | ..... | ..... | ..... | ..... | 0.1 |
| **Other commodities** | 0.4 | 2.8 | 4.9 | 3.3 | 2.4 | 3.5 | 5.0 | 6.5 | 2.5 | 2.5 |
| Forestry products | 0.3 | 0.1 | ..... | 0.2 | ..... | 1.8 | 1.7 | 1.4 | 1.0 | 0.9 |
| Fish and other marine products | ..... | ..... | ..... | ..... | ..... | ..... | ..... | ..... | ..... | ..... |
| Metallic ores and concentrates | ..... | ..... | ..... | ..... | ..... | ..... | ..... | ..... | ..... | ..... |
| Bituminous coal and lignite | ..... | ..... | ..... | ..... | ..... | ..... | ..... | ..... | ..... | ..... |
| Crude petroleum and natural gas | ..... | ..... | ..... | ..... | ..... | ..... | ..... | ..... | ..... | ..... |
| Nonmetallic minerals | 0.1 | 0.1 | 0.1 | 0.4 | 0.2 | ..... | ..... | ..... | ..... | ..... |
| Scrap and waste | ..... | 2.6 | 4.6 | 2.6 | 2.1 | ..... | ..... | 0.2 | ..... | ..... |
| Used merchandise | ..... | ..... | ..... | ..... | ..... | 0.1 | 0.1 | 0.1 | ..... | ..... |
| Goods imported and returned unchanged | ..... | ..... | ..... | ..... | ..... | ..... | ..... | ..... | ..... | ..... |
| Special classification provisions | ..... | ..... | 0.1 | 0.1 | 0.1 | 1.6 | 3.1 | 4.8 | 1.5 | 1.6 |

## MONTANA: Exports of Goods, 1997

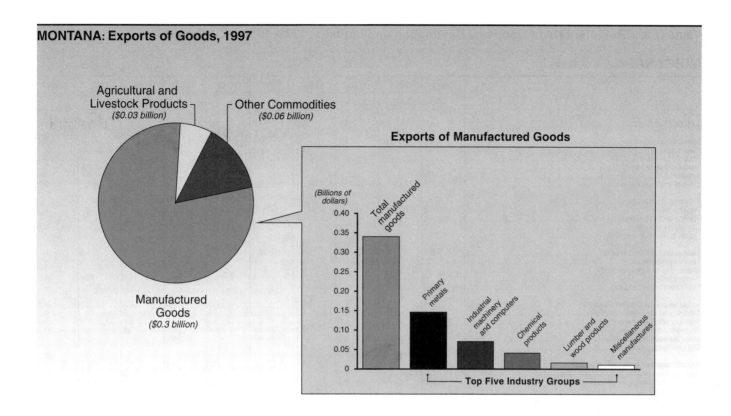

Agricultural and Livestock Products ($0.03 billion)

Other Commodities ($0.06 billion)

Manufactured Goods ($0.3 billion)

### Exports of Manufactured Goods

Top Five Industry Groups

## Table D-3.   State Exports of Goods by Destination and Industry, 1993–1997 —*Continued*

**MONTANA** (Millions of dollars.)

| Industry | 1993 | 1994 | 1995 | 1996 | 1997 | 1993 | 1994 | 1995 | 1996 | 1997 |
|---|---|---|---|---|---|---|---|---|---|---|
| | All destinations | | | | | Canada | | | | |
| **ALL GOODS** | 243.3 | 260.0 | 279.2 | 340.9 | 429.8 | 144.7 | 140.1 | 140.2 | 160.6 | 236.5 |
| **Manufactured goods** | 182.8 | 192.0 | 206.0 | 263.7 | 339.9 | 90.7 | 80.0 | 78.4 | 100.5 | 165.5 |
| Food products | 4.2 | 4.7 | 6.6 | 6.3 | 4.6 | 1.9 | 2.1 | 3.5 | 4.2 | 3.6 |
| Tobacco products | ..... | ..... | ..... | ..... | ..... | ..... | ..... | ..... | ..... | ..... |
| Textile mill products | 0.4 | 0.4 | 0.1 | 0.6 | 0.9 | ..... | 0.2 | 0.1 | 0.1 | 0.2 |
| Apparel | 0.4 | 0.4 | 1.0 | 1.2 | 0.8 | 0.2 | 0.1 | 0.2 | 0.2 | 0.1 |
| Lumber and wood products | 12.0 | 13.7 | 15.9 | 13.6 | 16.5 | 10.1 | 11.3 | 14.0 | 12.5 | 15.3 |
| Furniture and fixtures | 0.2 | 0.3 | 0.3 | 0.2 | 0.4 | 0.1 | 0.2 | 0.2 | 0.2 | 0.2 |
| Paper products | 5.7 | 6.2 | 4.1 | 4.3 | 4.4 | 5.2 | 6.1 | 3.9 | 4.3 | 4.3 |
| Printing and publishing | 2.6 | 2.1 | 1.0 | 0.8 | 0.6 | 1.2 | 0.8 | 0.7 | 0.8 | 0.5 |
| Chemical products | 17.0 | 13.0 | 17.5 | 16.3 | 41.4 | 16.3 | 11.4 | 12.3 | 12.3 | 37.6 |
| Refined petroleum products | 2.4 | 1.5 | 1.2 | 1.7 | 1.4 | 1.7 | 1.4 | 1.1 | 1.6 | 1.3 |
| Rubber and plastic products | 2.7 | 2.8 | 3.2 | 4.6 | 4.1 | 2.2 | 2.3 | 2.6 | 2.8 | 3.5 |
| Leather products | 0.8 | 0.8 | 1.0 | 2.1 | 2.0 | 0.6 | 0.5 | 0.7 | 1.1 | 1.3 |
| Stone, clay and glass products | 4.7 | 4.2 | 4.0 | 3.7 | 5.7 | 4.7 | 4.0 | 4.0 | 3.0 | 5.5 |
| Primary metals | 49.2 | 54.0 | 49.7 | 97.1 | 146.0 | 1.6 | 1.5 | 1.3 | 26.6 | 62.6 |
| Fabricated metal products | 1.3 | 1.7 | 1.6 | 1.5 | 2.1 | 1.0 | 1.1 | 1.1 | 1.0 | 0.9 |
| Industrial machinery and computers | 42.7 | 41.5 | 70.1 | 72.5 | 71.1 | 16.5 | 14.9 | 20.2 | 18.8 | 17.7 |
| Electric and electronic equipment | 2.5 | 3.4 | 6.5 | 7.3 | 9.6 | 1.1 | 1.0 | 3.5 | 2.0 | 1.9 |
| Transportation equipment | 12.2 | 8.8 | 5.3 | 5.5 | 7.6 | 10.5 | 7.2 | 3.7 | 3.0 | 3.2 |
| Scientific and measuring instruments | 5.1 | 4.7 | 6.1 | 10.8 | 9.2 | 1.4 | 0.6 | 0.8 | 1.2 | 1.6 |
| Miscellaneous manufactures | 15.6 | 26.5 | 9.4 | 12.8 | 10.6 | 13.7 | 12.7 | 3.7 | 4.4 | 3.7 |
| Unidentified manufactures | 1.2 | 1.2 | 1.4 | 0.8 | 0.8 | 0.7 | 0.6 | 0.7 | 0.5 | 0.5 |
| **Agricultural and livestock products** | 11.5 | 22.1 | 28.2 | 33.4 | 28.8 | 10.5 | 18.1 | 21.3 | 20.2 | 23.6 |
| Agricultural products | 3.2 | 7.1 | 13.1 | 24.2 | 19.2 | 2.6 | 3.6 | 6.5 | 11.8 | 14.7 |
| Livestock and livestock products | 8.3 | 15.0 | 15.1 | 9.2 | 9.5 | 7.9 | 14.5 | 14.8 | 8.4 | 9.0 |
| **Other commodities** | 49.0 | 45.8 | 45.0 | 43.8 | 61.2 | 43.5 | 42.1 | 40.5 | 39.8 | 47.3 |
| Forestry products | 0.2 | 0.3 | 0.1 | 0.2 | 0.1 | 0.2 | 0.2 | 0.1 | 0.1 | 0.1 |
| Fish and other marine products | ..... | ..... | 0.1 | 0.4 | | | | | | |
| Metallic ores and concentrates | 27.0 | 14.3 | 12.2 | 7.8 | 22.6 | 24.7 | 14.3 | 11.9 | 7.8 | 11.3 |
| Bituminous coal and lignite | 0.2 | 0.2 | 0.7 | 0.1 | 1.5 | 0.1 | 0.2 | 0.7 | 0.1 | 1.5 |
| Crude petroleum and natural gas | 0.8 | 0.2 | 1.4 | ..... | | 0.8 | 0.2 | 1.4 | | |
| Nonmetallic minerals | 7.7 | 9.8 | 9.2 | 9.3 | 8.5 | 5.6 | 6.9 | 6.3 | 6.6 | 7.0 |
| Scrap and waste | 6.4 | 10.4 | 9.9 | 7.8 | 7.7 | 6.4 | 10.0 | 9.9 | 7.8 | 7.7 |
| Used merchandise | 1.6 | 2.8 | 2.4 | 3.5 | 2.3 | 1.3 | 2.7 | 2.2 | 3.0 | 2.2 |
| Goods imported and returned unchanged | 4.4 | 7.5 | 7.9 | 14.3 | 17.5 | 4.4 | 7.5 | 7.9 | 14.3 | 17.5 |
| Special classification provisions | 0.6 | 0.4 | 1.2 | 0.4 | 0.9 | ..... | 0.1 | 0.2 | 0.1 | 0.1 |

## Table D-3. State Exports of Goods by Destination and Industry, 1993–1997 —Continued

**MONTANA** (Millions of dollars.)

| Industry | 1993 | 1994 | 1995 | 1996 | 1997 | 1993 | 1994 | 1995 | 1996 | 1997 |
|---|---|---|---|---|---|---|---|---|---|---|
| | South and Central America and Caribbean | | | | | Mexico | | | | |
| **ALL GOODS** | 5.5 | 4.3 | 5.7 | 3.8 | 3.5 | 1.2 | 5.1 | 8.1 | 46.2 | 20.6 |
| **Manufactured goods** | 5.1 | 3.0 | 4.8 | 3.0 | 3.2 | 0.8 | 1.7 | 1.7 | 34.1 | 16.4 |
| Food products | ..... | 0.6 | 1.1 | 0.4 | 0.3 | ..... | ..... | 0.1 | ..... | ..... |
| Tobacco products | ..... | ..... | ..... | ..... | ..... | ..... | ..... | ..... | ..... | ..... |
| Textile mill products | ..... | ..... | ..... | ..... | ..... | ..... | ..... | ..... | 0.2 | 0.1 |
| Apparel | ..... | ..... | ..... | ..... | ..... | ..... | ..... | ..... | 0.1 | ..... |
| Lumber and wood products | ..... | ..... | ..... | ..... | 0.3 | 0.1 | 0.1 | ..... | ..... | 0.5 |
| Furniture and fixtures | ..... | ..... | ..... | ..... | ..... | ..... | ..... | ..... | ..... | ..... |
| Paper products | 0.2 | ..... | ..... | ..... | ..... | ..... | ..... | ..... | ..... | ..... |
| Printing and publishing | ..... | ..... | ..... | ..... | ..... | ..... | ..... | ..... | ..... | ..... |
| Chemical products | 0.1 | 0.2 | 1.8 | 1.1 | 0.1 | ..... | ..... | ..... | ..... | 0.1 |
| Refined petroleum products | ..... | ..... | ..... | ..... | ..... | ..... | ..... | ..... | ..... | ..... |
| Rubber and plastic products | 0.1 | 0.1 | 0.1 | ..... | 0.1 | 0.2 | 0.1 | ..... | 1.0 | 0.1 |
| Leather products | ..... | ..... | ..... | 0.1 | ..... | ..... | ..... | ..... | ..... | ..... |
| Stone, clay and glass products | ..... | ..... | ..... | ..... | 0.1 | ..... | ..... | ..... | ..... | ..... |
| Primary metals | ..... | ..... | ..... | ..... | 0.1 | ..... | 0.1 | 1.0 | 27.8 | 11.2 |
| Fabricated metal products | ..... | 0.1 | 0.1 | ..... | ..... | ..... | ..... | ..... | ..... | 0.1 |
| Industrial machinery and computers | 3.8 | 1.5 | 1.3 | 1.0 | 1.1 | 0.3 | 1.0 | 0.3 | 3.7 | 3.1 |
| Electric and electronic equipment | 0.1 | ..... | 0.1 | 0.2 | 0.5 | ..... | 0.1 | ..... | ..... | 0.1 |
| Transportation equipment | 0.7 | 0.1 | ..... | ..... | 0.1 | ..... | 0.2 | 0.1 | 1.0 | 1.0 |
| Scientific and measuring instruments | 0.1 | ..... | 0.1 | 0.1 | 0.4 | 0.1 | 0.1 | 0.1 | 0.1 | 0.2 |
| Miscellaneous manufactures | 0.1 | 0.2 | 0.2 | 0.1 | 0.2 | ..... | ..... | ..... | 0.1 | ..... |
| Unidentified manufactures | ..... | ..... | ..... | 0.1 | ..... | ..... | ..... | ..... | ..... | ..... |
| **Agricultural and livestock products** | 0.1 | 0.3 | 0.2 | 0.1 | 0.2 | 0.4 | 3.4 | 6.4 | 12.1 | 4.2 |
| Agricultural products | ..... | ..... | 0.1 | ..... | ..... | 0.2 | 3.2 | 6.3 | 12.1 | 4.2 |
| Livestock and livestock products | 0.1 | 0.3 | 0.2 | 0.1 | 0.2 | 0.2 | 0.1 | ..... | ..... | ..... |
| **Other commodities** | 0.3 | 1.0 | 0.7 | 0.7 | 0.1 | ..... | ..... | ..... | ..... | ..... |
| Forestry products | ..... | ..... | ..... | ..... | ..... | ..... | ..... | ..... | ..... | ..... |
| Fish and other marine products | ..... | ..... | ..... | ..... | ..... | ..... | ..... | ..... | ..... | ..... |
| Metallic ores and concentrates | ..... | ..... | ..... | ..... | ..... | ..... | ..... | ..... | ..... | ..... |
| Bituminous coal and lignite | ..... | ..... | ..... | ..... | ..... | ..... | ..... | ..... | ..... | ..... |
| Crude petroleum and natural gas | ..... | ..... | ..... | ..... | ..... | ..... | ..... | ..... | ..... | ..... |
| Nonmetallic minerals | 0.2 | 0.9 | 0.7 | 0.7 | ..... | ..... | ..... | ..... | ..... | ..... |
| Scrap and waste | ..... | ..... | ..... | ..... | ..... | ..... | ..... | ..... | ..... | ..... |
| Used merchandise | ..... | ..... | ..... | ..... | 0.1 | ..... | ..... | ..... | ..... | ..... |
| Goods imported and returned unchanged | ..... | ..... | ..... | ..... | ..... | ..... | ..... | ..... | ..... | ..... |
| Special classification provisions | ..... | ..... | ..... | ..... | ..... | ..... | ..... | ..... | ..... | ..... |
| | European Union | | | | | United Kingdom | | | | |
| **ALL GOODS** | 64.8 | 84.1 | 88.0 | 82.5 | 106.9 | 4.5 | 14.3 | 11.1 | 8.3 | 9.1 |
| **Manufactured goods** | 64.7 | 83.6 | 87.4 | 81.9 | 106.3 | 4.5 | 14.2 | 11.0 | 8.1 | 8.8 |
| Food products | ..... | 0.2 | 0.1 | ..... | 0.3 | ..... | 0.2 | 0.1 | ..... | 0.2 |
| Tobacco products | ..... | ....., | ..... | ..... | ..... | ..... | ..... | ..... | ..... | ..... |
| Textile mill products | ..... | ..... | ..... | ..... | ..... | ..... | ..... | ..... | ..... | ..... |
| Apparel | 0.1 | ..... | 0.2 | 0.6 | 0.5 | ..... | ..... | 0.1 | 0.3 | 0.2 |
| Lumber and wood products | 0.2 | ..... | ..... | 0.1 | ..... | 0.1 | ..... | ..... | ..... | ..... |
| Furniture and fixtures | ..... | ..... | 0.1 | ..... | ..... | ..... | ..... | 0.1 | ..... | ..... |
| Paper products | ..... | ..... | ..... | ..... | ..... | ..... | ..... | ..... | ..... | ..... |
| Printing and publishing | 0.1 | 0.1 | 0.1 | ..... | ..... | ..... | ..... | ..... | ..... | ..... |
| Chemical products | 0.3 | 0.9 | 1.0 | 1.7 | 2.4 | ..... | 0.2 | 0.1 | 0.3 | 0.1 |
| Refined petroleum products | 0.1 | ..... | ..... | ..... | 0.1 | 0.1 | ..... | ..... | ..... | 0.1 |
| Rubber and plastic products | ..... | 0.1 | 0.2 | 0.1 | 0.2 | ..... | ..... | 0.1 | 0.1 | 0.1 |
| Leather products | ..... | 0.1 | 0.1 | 0.4 | 0.5 | ..... | 0.1 | ..... | 0.4 | 0.4 |
| Stone, clay and glass products | ..... | ..... | 0.1 | 0.1 | 0.1 | ..... | ..... | ..... | ..... | ..... |
| Primary metals | 47.4 | 52.4 | 47.1 | 42.4 | 71.5 | ..... | 0.1 | 0.1 | 0.1 | 0.8 |
| Fabricated metal products | 0.1 | 0.2 | 0.2 | 0.2 | 0.4 | ..... | ..... | ..... | ..... | 0.1 |
| Industrial machinery and computers | 12.4 | 15.5 | 31.1 | 26.0 | 18.6 | 3.1 | 2.9 | 8.8 | 5.0 | 4.3 |
| Electric and electronic equipment | 0.3 | 1.5 | 1.8 | 2.7 | 4.8 | 0.1 | 0.5 | 0.5 | 0.9 | 0.7 |
| Transportation equipment | 0.5 | 0.5 | 0.8 | 0.7 | 1.9 | 0.2 | 0.4 | 0.5 | 0.2 | 0.8 |
| Scientific and measuring instruments | 2.1 | 2.1 | 2.7 | 5.7 | 3.1 | 0.3 | 0.6 | 0.2 | 0.3 | 0.4 |
| Miscellaneous manufactures | 0.7 | 9.6 | 1.7 | 0.9 | 1.8 | 0.5 | 9.2 | 0.4 | 0.4 | 0.5 |
| Unidentified manufactures | 0.2 | 0.3 | 0.3 | 0.1 | 0.1 | 0.1 | 0.1 | 0.1 | ..... | ..... |
| **Agricultural and livestock products** | 0.1 | 0.1 | 0.1 | 0.1 | 0.4 | ..... | ..... | ..... | 0.1 | 0.3 |
| Agricultural products | 0.1 | ..... | 0.1 | 0.1 | 0.2 | ..... | ..... | ..... | ..... | 0.1 |
| Livestock and livestock products | ..... | 0.1 | ..... | 0.1 | 0.2 | ..... | ..... | ..... | 0.1 | 0.2 |
| **Other commodities** | ..... | 0.3 | 0.4 | 0.5 | 0.1 | ..... | ..... | 0.1 | 0.1 | ..... |
| Forestry products | ..... | ..... | 0.1 | 0.1 | ..... | ..... | ..... | ..... | ..... | ..... |
| Fish and other marine products | ..... | ..... | ..... | ..... | ..... | ..... | ..... | ..... | ..... | ..... |
| Metallic ores and concentrates | ..... | ..... | 0.3 | ..... | ..... | ..... | ..... | ..... | ..... | ..... |
| Bituminous coal and lignite | ..... | ..... | ..... | ..... | ..... | ..... | ..... | ..... | ..... | ..... |
| Crude petroleum and natural gas | ..... | ..... | ..... | ..... | ..... | ..... | ..... | ..... | ..... | ..... |
| Nonmetallic minerals | ..... | ..... | ..... | ..... | ..... | ..... | ..... | ..... | ..... | ..... |
| Scrap and waste | ..... | 0.3 | ..... | ..... | ..... | ..... | ..... | ..... | ..... | ..... |
| Used merchandise | ..... | ..... | 0.1 | 0.4 | ..... | ..... | ..... | 0.1 | 0.1 | ..... |
| Goods imported and returned unchanged | ..... | ..... | ..... | ..... | ..... | ..... | ..... | ..... | ..... | ..... |
| Special classification provisions | ..... | ..... | ..... | 0.1 | 0.1 | ..... | ..... | ..... | ..... | ..... |

## Table D-3.  State Exports of Goods by Destination and Industry, 1993–1997 —Continued

**MONTANA** (Millions of dollars.)

| Industry | 1993 | 1994 | 1995 | 1996 | 1997 | 1993 | 1994 | 1995 | 1996 | 1997 |
|---|---|---|---|---|---|---|---|---|---|---|
| | Germany | | | | | France | | | | |
| **ALL GOODS** | 4.0 | 7.0 | 16.5 | 13.0 | 8.0 | 4.4 | 3.4 | 3.8 | 8.0 | 9.6 |
| **Manufactured goods** | 3.9 | 6.8 | 16.1 | 12.9 | 7.9 | 4.4 | 3.4 | 3.8 | 7.9 | 9.6 |
| Food products | ..... | ..... | ..... | ..... | ..... | ..... | ..... | ..... | ..... | ..... |
| Tobacco products | ..... | ..... | ..... | ..... | ..... | ..... | ..... | ..... | ..... | ..... |
| Textile mill products | ..... | ..... | ..... | ..... | ..... | ..... | ..... | ..... | ..... | ..... |
| Apparel | ..... | ..... | ..... | 0.2 | 0.1 | ..... | ..... | ..... | 0.1 | 0.1 |
| Lumber and wood products | ..... | ..... | ..... | ..... | ..... | ..... | ..... | ..... | ..... | ..... |
| Furniture and fixtures | ..... | ..... | ..... | ..... | ..... | ..... | ..... | ..... | ..... | ..... |
| Paper products | ..... | ..... | ..... | ..... | ..... | ..... | ..... | ..... | ..... | ..... |
| Printing and publishing | ..... | ..... | 0.1 | ..... | ..... | ..... | ..... | ..... | ..... | ..... |
| Chemical products | 0.1 | 0.2 | 0.4 | 0.1 | 0.3 | ..... | 0.3 | 0.2 | 0.1 | ..... |
| Refined petroleum products | ..... | ..... | ..... | ..... | ..... | ..... | ..... | ..... | ..... | ..... |
| Rubber and plastic products | ..... | ..... | ..... | 0.1 | 0.1 | ..... | 0.1 | ..... | ..... | ..... |
| Leather products | ..... | ..... | 0.1 | ..... | ..... | ..... | ..... | ..... | ..... | ..... |
| Stone, clay and glass products | ..... | ..... | ..... | ..... | ..... | ..... | ..... | ..... | ..... | ..... |
| Primary metals | ..... | ..... | ..... | ..... | ..... | ..... | ..... | ..... | ..... | ..... |
| Fabricated metal products | ..... | 0.1 | 0.1 | 0.1 | 0.2 | ..... | ..... | ..... | ..... | ..... |
| Industrial machinery and computers | 2.6 | 5.7 | 13.7 | 8.6 | 5.2 | 3.8 | 2.2 | 2.6 | 6.7 | 6.2 |
| Electric and electronic equipment | 0.1 | 0.1 | 0.1 | 1.1 | 1.0 | ..... | 0.1 | 0.1 | 0.2 | 1.9 |
| Transportation equipment | 0.2 | ..... | 0.1 | 0.1 | ..... | ..... | ..... | ..... | 0.4 | 0.5 |
| Scientific and measuring instruments | 0.7 | 0.6 | 0.7 | 2.7 | 0.8 | 0.4 | 0.4 | 0.7 | 0.3 | 0.4 |
| Miscellaneous manufactures | 0.1 | ..... | 0.6 | 0.1 | 0.2 | ..... | ..... | 0.1 | ..... | 0.4 |
| Unidentified manufactures | ..... | 0.1 | 0.1 | ..... | ..... | ..... | 0.1 | ..... | ..... | ..... |
| **Agricultural and livestock products** | 0.1 | 0.1 | 0.1 | ..... | 0.1 | ..... | ..... | ..... | ..... | ..... |
| Agricultural products | ..... | ..... | 0.1 | ..... | 0.1 | ..... | ..... | ..... | ..... | ..... |
| Livestock and livestock products | ..... | 0.1 | ..... | ..... | ..... | ..... | ..... | ..... | ..... | ..... |
| **Other commodities** | ..... | ..... | 0.3 | 0.1 | ..... | ..... | ..... | 0.1 | 0.1 | 0.1 |
| Forestry products | ..... | ..... | ..... | ..... | ..... | ..... | ..... | 0.1 | 0.1 | ..... |
| Fish and other marine products | ..... | ..... | ..... | ..... | ..... | ..... | ..... | ..... | ..... | ..... |
| Metallic ores and concentrates | ..... | ..... | 0.3 | ..... | ..... | ..... | ..... | ..... | ..... | ..... |
| Bituminous coal and lignite | ..... | ..... | ..... | ..... | ..... | ..... | ..... | ..... | ..... | ..... |
| Crude petroleum and natural gas | ..... | ..... | ..... | ..... | ..... | ..... | ..... | ..... | ..... | ..... |
| Nonmetallic minerals | ..... | ..... | ..... | ..... | ..... | ..... | ..... | ..... | ..... | ..... |
| Scrap and waste | ..... | ..... | ..... | ..... | ..... | ..... | ..... | ..... | ..... | ..... |
| Used merchandise | ..... | ..... | ..... | 0.1 | ..... | ..... | ..... | ..... | ..... | ..... |
| Goods imported and returned unchanged | ..... | ..... | ..... | ..... | ..... | ..... | ..... | ..... | ..... | ..... |
| Special classification provisions | ..... | ..... | ..... | ..... | ..... | ..... | ..... | ..... | ..... | 0.1 |

| Industry | 1993 | 1994 | 1995 | 1996 | 1997 | 1993 | 1994 | 1995 | 1996 | 1997 |
|---|---|---|---|---|---|---|---|---|---|---|
| | The Netherlands | | | | | Asian 10 | | | | |
| **ALL GOODS** | 1.3 | 1.7 | 5.7 | 3.6 | 2.4 | 18.5 | 17.3 | 26.5 | 32.8 | 54.5 |
| **Manufactured goods** | 1.3 | 1.7 | 5.6 | 3.6 | 2.3 | 13.9 | 14.9 | 23.6 | 30.4 | 40.9 |
| Food products | ..... | ..... | ..... | ..... | ..... | 1.9 | 1.6 | 1.5 | 1.2 | 0.3 |
| Tobacco products | ..... | ..... | ..... | ..... | ..... | ..... | ..... | ..... | ..... | ..... |
| Textile mill products | ..... | ..... | ..... | ..... | ..... | 0.4 | 0.1 | ..... | 0.3 | 0.6 |
| Apparel | ..... | ..... | ..... | ..... | ..... | 0.1 | 0.2 | 0.6 | 0.2 | 0.1 |
| Lumber and wood products | ..... | ..... | ..... | ..... | ..... | 1.4 | 2.2 | 1.8 | 0.9 | 0.4 |
| Furniture and fixtures | ..... | ..... | ..... | ..... | ..... | ..... | ..... | ..... | ..... | 0.1 |
| Paper products | ..... | ..... | ..... | ..... | ..... | ..... | ..... | 0.1 | ..... | ..... |
| Printing and publishing | ..... | ..... | ..... | ..... | ..... | ..... | ..... | ..... | ..... | ..... |
| Chemical products | ..... | ..... | ..... | 0.1 | 0.1 | 0.2 | 0.3 | 1.2 | 0.8 | 0.7 |
| Refined petroleum products | ..... | ..... | ..... | ..... | ..... | 0.5 | 0.1 | ..... | ..... | ..... |
| Rubber and plastic products | ..... | ..... | ..... | ..... | ..... | 0.1 | ..... | 0.1 | 0.5 | 0.2 |
| Leather products | ..... | ..... | ..... | ..... | ..... | 0.1 | 0.2 | 0.2 | 0.5 | 0.1 |
| Stone, clay and glass products | ..... | ..... | ..... | ..... | ..... | ..... | 0.1 | ..... | 0.4 | 0.1 |
| Primary metals | ..... | ..... | ..... | ..... | ..... | 0.1 | ..... | 0.3 | 0.3 | 0.4 |
| Fabricated metal products | ..... | ..... | ..... | ..... | ..... | ..... | ..... | 0.1 | 0.2 | 0.5 |
| Industrial machinery and computers | 1.0 | 1.1 | 4.1 | 1.4 | 1.2 | 6.7 | 7.0 | 11.9 | 17.5 | 28.5 |
| Electric and electronic equipment | ..... | 0.1 | 0.2 | 0.2 | 0.5 | 0.5 | 0.5 | 0.8 | 1.2 | 1.7 |
| Transportation equipment | ..... | 0.1 | 0.1 | ..... | ..... | 0.3 | 0.5 | 0.3 | 0.1 | 0.4 |
| Scientific and measuring instruments | 0.1 | 0.2 | 0.6 | 1.7 | 0.3 | 0.9 | 1.2 | 1.8 | 3.0 | 3.1 |
| Miscellaneous manufactures | ..... | 0.2 | 0.5 | 0.1 | 0.1 | 0.4 | 0.6 | 2.6 | 3.2 | 3.7 |
| Unidentified manufactures | ..... | ..... | ..... | ..... | ..... | 0.1 | 0.2 | 0.2 | 0.1 | 0.1 |
| **Agricultural and livestock products** | ..... | ..... | ..... | ..... | ..... | 0.2 | 0.2 | 0.1 | 0.7 | 0.1 |
| Agricultural products | ..... | ..... | ..... | ..... | ..... | 0.2 | 0.2 | 0.1 | 0.2 | 0.1 |
| Livestock and livestock products | ..... | ..... | ..... | ..... | ..... | ..... | ..... | ..... | 0.5 | ..... |
| **Other commodities** | ..... | ..... | ..... | ..... | ..... | 4.4 | 2.2 | 2.8 | 1.7 | 13.5 |
| Forestry products | ..... | ..... | ..... | ..... | ..... | ..... | 0.2 | ..... | ..... | ..... |
| Fish and other marine products | ..... | ..... | ..... | ..... | ..... | ..... | ..... | 0.1 | ..... | ..... |
| Metallic ores and concentrates | ..... | ..... | ..... | ..... | ..... | 2.4 | ..... | ..... | ..... | 11.4 |
| Bituminous coal and lignite | ..... | ..... | ..... | ..... | ..... | 0.2 | ..... | ..... | ..... | ..... |
| Crude petroleum and natural gas | ..... | ..... | ..... | ..... | ..... | ..... | ..... | ..... | ..... | ..... |
| Nonmetallic minerals | ..... | ..... | ..... | ..... | ..... | 1.2 | 1.7 | 1.7 | 1.4 | 1.4 |
| Scrap and waste | ..... | ..... | ..... | ..... | ..... | ..... | ..... | ..... | ..... | ..... |
| Used merchandise | ..... | ..... | ..... | ..... | ..... | 0.1 | ..... | 0.1 | 0.1 | ..... |
| Goods imported and returned unchanged | ..... | ..... | ..... | ..... | ..... | ..... | ..... | ..... | ..... | ..... |
| Special classification provisions | ..... | ..... | ..... | ..... | ..... | 0.6 | 0.3 | 0.9 | 0.2 | 0.7 |

## Table D-3.   State Exports of Goods by Destination and Industry, 1993–1997 —*Continued*

**MONTANA** (Millions of dollars.)

| Industry | 1993 | 1994 | 1995 | 1996 | 1997 | 1993 | 1994 | 1995 | 1996 | 1997 |
|---|---|---|---|---|---|---|---|---|---|---|
| | Japan | | | | | South Korea | | | | |
| **ALL GOODS** | 9.0 | 10.9 | 16.8 | 20.5 | 23.1 | 3.0 | 3.9 | 4.7 | 4.5 | 4.3 |
| **Manufactured goods** | 5.8 | 10.0 | 16.0 | 19.7 | 22.5 | 2.4 | 3.1 | 3.4 | 3.8 | 3.4 |
| Food products | 0.2 | 0.1 | 0.1 | 0.3 | 0.1 | 1.5 | 1.5 | 1.3 | 0.6 | ..... |
| Tobacco products | ..... | ..... | ..... | ..... | ..... | ..... | ..... | ..... | ..... | ..... |
| Textile mill products | ..... | ..... | ..... | ..... | ..... | ..... | ..... | ..... | ..... | ..... |
| Apparel | 0.1 | 0.2 | 0.5 | 0.1 | 0.1 | ..... | ..... | ..... | ..... | ..... |
| Lumber and wood products | 1.4 | 2.0 | 1.6 | 0.7 | 0.3 | ..... | 0.1 | 0.2 | 0.2 | 0.1 |
| Furniture and fixtures | ..... | ..... | ..... | ..... | ..... | ..... | ..... | ..... | ..... | ..... |
| Paper products | ..... | ..... | ..... | ..... | ..... | ..... | ..... | ..... | ..... | ..... |
| Printing and publishing | ..... | ..... | ..... | ..... | ..... | ..... | ..... | ..... | ..... | ..... |
| Chemical products | 0.1 | 0.1 | 0.2 | 0.1 | 0.2 | ..... | ..... | ..... | ..... | 0.1 |
| Refined petroleum products | 0.5 | 0.1 | ..... | ..... | ..... | ..... | ..... | ..... | ..... | ..... |
| Rubber and plastic products | ..... | ..... | 0.1 | 0.1 | 0.1 | ..... | ..... | ..... | 0.1 | 0.1 |
| Leather products | 0.1 | 0.2 | 0.2 | 0.3 | 0.1 | ..... | ..... | ..... | ..... | ..... |
| Stone, clay and glass products | ..... | ..... | ..... | ..... | 0.1 | ..... | ..... | ..... | ..... | ..... |
| Primary metals | ..... | ..... | ..... | ..... | ..... | ..... | ..... | ..... | ..... | ..... |
| Fabricated metal products | ..... | ..... | ..... | 0.1 | ..... | ..... | ..... | ..... | ..... | ..... |
| Industrial machinery and computers | 2.2 | 5.3 | 9.0 | 13.0 | 16.4 | 0.6 | 1.1 | 1.4 | 2.0 | 2.8 |
| Electric and electronic equipment | 0.1 | 0.2 | 0.2 | 0.6 | 1.3 | ..... | 0.1 | 0.1 | 0.1 | ..... |
| Transportation equipment | ..... | ..... | 0.2 | 0.1 | 0.1 | 0.1 | 0.1 | ..... | ..... | ..... |
| Scientific and measuring instruments | 0.6 | 0.9 | 1.4 | 1.8 | 2.0 | 0.1 | 0.1 | 0.1 | 0.7 | 0.2 |
| Miscellaneous manufactures | 0.3 | 0.5 | 2.3 | 2.4 | 1.8 | ..... | ..... | 0.2 | ..... | 0.1 |
| Unidentified manufactures | 0.1 | 0.2 | 0.1 | ..... | ..... | ..... | ..... | ..... | ..... | ..... |
| **Agricultural and livestock products** | ..... | 0.1 | ..... | 0.5 | 0.1 | 0.1 | 0.1 | 0.1 | 0.2 | ..... |
| Agricultural products | ..... | 0.1 | ..... | 0.1 | ..... | ..... | 0.1 | 0.1 | 0.1 | ..... |
| Livestock and livestock products | ..... | ..... | ..... | 0.4 | ..... | ..... | ..... | ..... | 0.1 | ..... |
| **Other commodities** | 3.2 | 0.8 | 0.8 | 0.3 | 0.5 | 0.6 | 0.7 | 1.2 | 0.5 | 0.9 |
| Forestry products | ..... | ..... | ..... | ..... | ..... | ..... | 0.2 | ..... | ..... | ..... |
| Fish and other marine products | ..... | ..... | 0.1 | ..... | ..... | ..... | ..... | ..... | ..... | ..... |
| Metallic ores and concentrates | 2.4 | ..... | ..... | ..... | ..... | ..... | ..... | ..... | ..... | ..... |
| Bituminous coal and lignite | 0.2 | ..... | ..... | ..... | ..... | ..... | ..... | ..... | ..... | ..... |
| Crude petroleum and natural gas | ..... | ..... | ..... | ..... | ..... | ..... | ..... | ..... | ..... | ..... |
| Nonmetallic minerals | 0.6 | 0.8 | 0.6 | 0.3 | 0.4 | ..... | 0.2 | 0.3 | 0.3 | 0.3 |
| Scrap and waste | ..... | ..... | ..... | ..... | ..... | ..... | ..... | ..... | ..... | ..... |
| Used merchandise | 0.1 | ..... | 0.1 | 0.1 | ..... | ..... | ..... | ..... | ..... | ..... |
| Goods imported and returned unchanged | ..... | ..... | ..... | ..... | ..... | ..... | ..... | ..... | ..... | ..... |
| Special classification provisions | ..... | ..... | ..... | ..... | 0.1 | 0.6 | 0.3 | 0.9 | 0.2 | 0.6 |
| | Taiwan | | | | | Singapore | | | | |
| **ALL GOODS** | 1.3 | 1.2 | 1.2 | 1.1 | 5.3 | 0.2 | 0.4 | 0.9 | 1.9 | 4.0 |
| **Manufactured goods** | 0.8 | 0.7 | 0.7 | 0.8 | 4.9 | 0.2 | 0.3 | 0.8 | 1.9 | 3.9 |
| Food products | ..... | ..... | ..... | ..... | ..... | ..... | ..... | ..... | ..... | ..... |
| Tobacco products | ..... | ..... | ..... | ..... | ..... | ..... | ..... | ..... | ..... | ..... |
| Textile mill products | 0.3 | 0.1 | ..... | ..... | 0.1 | ..... | ..... | ..... | ..... | ..... |
| Apparel | ..... | ..... | ..... | ..... | ..... | ..... | ..... | ..... | ..... | ..... |
| Lumber and wood products | ..... | ..... | ..... | ..... | ..... | ..... | ..... | ..... | ..... | ..... |
| Furniture and fixtures | ..... | ..... | ..... | ..... | ..... | ..... | ..... | ..... | ..... | ..... |
| Paper products | ..... | ..... | ..... | ..... | ..... | ..... | ..... | ..... | ..... | ..... |
| Printing and publishing | ..... | ..... | ..... | ..... | ..... | ..... | ..... | ..... | ..... | ..... |
| Chemical products | 0.1 | ..... | 0.3 | 0.1 | 0.2 | ..... | ..... | ..... | 0.3 | 0.2 |
| Refined petroleum products | ..... | ..... | ..... | ..... | ..... | ..... | ..... | ..... | ..... | ..... |
| Rubber and plastic products | ..... | ..... | ..... | ..... | ..... | ..... | ..... | ..... | 0.2 | ..... |
| Leather products | ..... | ..... | ..... | ..... | ..... | ..... | ..... | ..... | ..... | ..... |
| Stone, clay and glass products | ..... | ..... | ..... | ..... | ..... | ..... | 0.1 | ..... | ..... | ..... |
| Primary metals | ..... | ..... | ..... | ..... | ..... | ..... | ..... | ..... | 0.1 | 0.3 |
| Fabricated metal products | ..... | ..... | ..... | ..... | ..... | ..... | ..... | ..... | ..... | ..... |
| Industrial machinery and computers | 0.1 | 0.4 | 0.3 | 0.4 | 4.2 | ..... | 0.1 | 0.5 | 0.9 | 3.1 |
| Electric and electronic equipment | 0.1 | ..... | ..... | 0.1 | 0.1 | ..... | 0.1 | 0.1 | 0.3 | 0.2 |
| Transportation equipment | ..... | ..... | ..... | ..... | 0.2 | ..... | ..... | ..... | ..... | ..... |
| Scientific and measuring instruments | 0.1 | 0.1 | 0.1 | 0.1 | 0.1 | ..... | ..... | 0.1 | ..... | 0.1 |
| Miscellaneous manufactures | ..... | ..... | ..... | ..... | ..... | ..... | ..... | ..... | ..... | 0.1 |
| Unidentified manufactures | ..... | ..... | ..... | ..... | ..... | ..... | ..... | ..... | ..... | ..... |
| **Agricultural and livestock products** | ..... | ..... | ..... | ..... | ..... | ..... | ..... | ..... | ..... | ..... |
| Agricultural products | ..... | ..... | ..... | ..... | ..... | ..... | ..... | ..... | ..... | ..... |
| Livestock and livestock products | ..... | ..... | ..... | ..... | ..... | ..... | ..... | ..... | ..... | ..... |
| **Other commodities** | 0.5 | 0.5 | 0.5 | 0.3 | 0.4 | 0.1 | 0.1 | 0.1 | ..... | ..... |
| Forestry products | ..... | ..... | ..... | ..... | ..... | ..... | ..... | ..... | ..... | ..... |
| Fish and other marine products | ..... | ..... | ..... | ..... | ..... | ..... | ..... | ..... | ..... | ..... |
| Metallic ores and concentrates | ..... | ..... | ..... | ..... | ..... | ..... | ..... | ..... | ..... | ..... |
| Bituminous coal and lignite | ..... | ..... | ..... | ..... | ..... | ..... | ..... | ..... | ..... | ..... |
| Crude petroleum and natural gas | ..... | ..... | ..... | ..... | ..... | ..... | ..... | ..... | ..... | ..... |
| Nonmetallic minerals | 0.5 | 0.5 | 0.5 | 0.3 | 0.4 | 0.1 | 0.1 | 0.1 | ..... | ..... |
| Scrap and waste | ..... | ..... | ..... | ..... | ..... | ..... | ..... | ..... | ..... | ..... |
| Used merchandise | ..... | ..... | ..... | ..... | ..... | ..... | ..... | ..... | ..... | ..... |
| Goods imported and returned unchanged | ..... | ..... | ..... | ..... | ..... | ..... | ..... | ..... | ..... | ..... |
| Special classification provisions | ..... | ..... | ..... | ..... | ..... | ..... | ..... | ..... | ..... | ..... |

## NEBRASKA: Exports of Goods, 1997

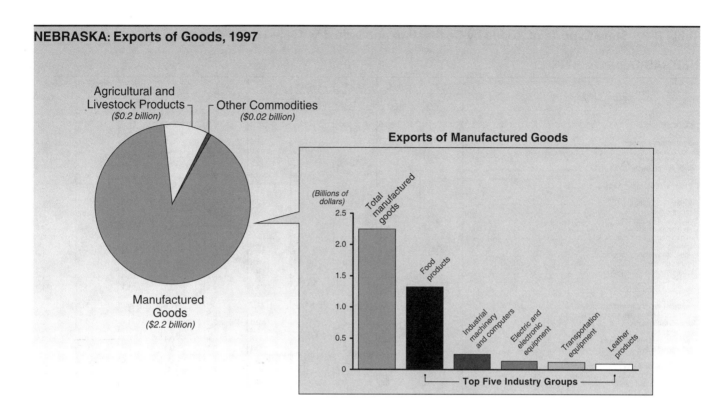

## Table D-3.   State Exports of Goods by Destination and Industry, 1993–1997 —*Continued*

### NEBRASKA (Millions of dollars.)

| Industry | 1993 | 1994 | 1995 | 1996 | 1997 | 1993 | 1994 | 1995 | 1996 | 1997 |
|---|---|---|---|---|---|---|---|---|---|---|
| | All destinations | | | | | Canada | | | | |
| **ALL GOODS** | 1 740.7 | 1 957.9 | 2 255.3 | 2 452.8 | 2 493.7 | 295.7 | 327.1 | 352.3 | 418.7 | 529.0 |
| **Manufactured goods** | 1 678.0 | 1 860.3 | 2 148.8 | 2 201.1 | 2 247.5 | 288.2 | 315.3 | 340.7 | 397.4 | 504.6 |
| Food products | 1 108.1 | 1 209.6 | 1 477.4 | 1 427.0 | 1 324.8 | 101.5 | 105.5 | 111.4 | 134.1 | 151.7 |
| Tobacco products | ..... | 0.1 | 0.1 | ..... | ..... | ..... | ..... | ..... | ..... | ..... |
| Textile mill products | 1.7 | 0.8 | 1.8 | 1.6 | 1.8 | 1.2 | 0.1 | 0.1 | 0.4 | 0.1 |
| Apparel | 4.6 | 5.0 | 6.1 | 8.5 | 8.3 | 0.3 | 0.2 | 0.1 | 0.3 | 0.3 |
| Lumber and wood products | 1.8 | 0.6 | 1.5 | 2.6 | 3.0 | 0.8 | 0.4 | 0.1 | 0.4 | 0.5 |
| Furniture and fixtures | 3.9 | 6.6 | 8.0 | 10.4 | 23.3 | 3.5 | 4.2 | 5.9 | 6.3 | 19.6 |
| Paper products | 3.3 | 3.8 | 3.5 | 3.2 | 4.5 | 1.6 | 1.4 | 2.0 | 1.9 | 2.7 |
| Printing and publishing | 5.2 | 5.4 | 4.9 | 4.6 | 5.6 | 4.4 | 3.8 | 4.0 | 4.1 | 4.7 |
| Chemical products | 32.1 | 36.7 | 40.9 | 46.8 | 68.7 | 14.7 | 14.6 | 19.4 | 18.2 | 24.7 |
| Refined petroleum products | 0.6 | 0.6 | 0.5 | 1.2 | 0.7 | 0.5 | 0.5 | 0.3 | 0.6 | 0.3 |
| Rubber and plastic products | 13.5 | 16.3 | 19.3 | 24.1 | 21.7 | 8.9 | 11.7 | 11.8 | 10.1 | 10.4 |
| Leather products | 53.6 | 69.2 | 69.6 | 81.0 | 92.6 | 1.6 | 1.5 | 0.6 | ..... | 0.1 |
| Stone, clay and glass products | 2.2 | 3.2 | 3.6 | 2.7 | 2.5 | 0.6 | 0.4 | 0.8 | 0.7 | 0.8 |
| Primary metals | 43.7 | 44.5 | 43.3 | 39.2 | 64.3 | 12.5 | 13.2 | 13.9 | 21.9 | 31.5 |
| Fabricated metal products | 32.9 | 38.4 | 39.1 | 40.2 | 41.2 | 15.9 | 17.2 | 18.1 | 15.5 | 16.3 |
| Industrial machinery and computers | 115.4 | 137.0 | 140.1 | 192.7 | 245.6 | 44.7 | 63.0 | 66.4 | 90.7 | 124.1 |
| Electric and electronic equipment | 86.2 | 117.3 | 122.6 | 130.8 | 138.1 | 12.9 | 17.6 | 17.2 | 19.0 | 27.3 |
| Transportation equipment | 128.6 | 122.0 | 110.5 | 119.3 | 121.9 | 52.0 | 48.2 | 55.8 | 58.9 | 70.3 |
| Scientific and measuring instruments | 34.1 | 35.8 | 48.8 | 58.0 | 69.1 | 8.3 | 8.5 | 10.0 | 11.6 | 15.8 |
| Miscellaneous manufactures | 4.2 | 5.1 | 4.8 | 4.5 | 6.4 | 1.6 | 2.5 | 1.8 | 1.3 | 2.1 |
| Unidentified manufactures | 2.2 | 2.4 | 2.5 | 2.6 | 3.3 | 0.7 | 0.9 | 1.1 | 1.4 | 1.6 |
| **Agricultural and livestock products** | 53.1 | 85.3 | 94.3 | 228.9 | 222.5 | 3.0 | 1.7 | 1.6 | 1.9 | 3.1 |
| Agricultural products | 51.6 | 81.4 | 93.2 | 227.4 | 219.5 | 2.8 | 0.9 | 1.2 | 1.6 | 2.1 |
| Livestock and livestock products | 1.5 | 3.9 | 1.1 | 1.4 | 3.0 | 0.3 | 0.7 | 0.4 | 0.2 | 1.0 |
| **Other commodities** | 9.6 | 12.3 | 12.2 | 22.8 | 23.7 | 4.5 | 10.0 | 10.0 | 19.5 | 21.3 |
| Forestry products | ..... | 0.1 | 0.2 | 0.2 | 0.2 | ..... | 0.1 | ..... | ..... | ..... |
| Fish and other marine products | 0.5 | 0.4 | ..... | 1.3 | 0.6 | ..... | 0.3 | ..... | 0.2 | 0.6 |
| Metallic ores and concentrates | 0.1 | 0.2 | ..... | ..... | ..... | ..... | ..... | ..... | ..... | ..... |
| Bituminous coal and lignite | ..... | ..... | ..... | 0.6 | 0.4 | ..... | ..... | ..... | ..... | ..... |
| Crude petroleum and natural gas | 0.1 | 0.6 | 0.8 | 10.1 | 8.5 | 0.1 | 0.6 | 0.8 | 10.1 | 8.5 |
| Nonmetallic minerals | 0.4 | 0.6 | 0.6 | 0.6 | 0.4 | 0.4 | 0.5 | 0.5 | 0.3 | 0.3 |
| Scrap and waste | 4.8 | 7.5 | 6.3 | 3.7 | 3.5 | 1.6 | 6.0 | 5.6 | 3.7 | 3.3 |
| Used merchandise | 1.9 | 0.6 | 1.7 | 2.5 | 3.1 | 0.9 | 0.3 | 1.1 | 1.7 | 2.0 |
| Goods imported and returned unchanged | 1.1 | 1.5 | 1.7 | 3.3 | 6.4 | 1.1 | 1.5 | 1.7 | 3.3 | 6.4 |
| Special classification provisions | 0.6 | 0.8 | 0.7 | 0.5 | 0.6 | 0.4 | 0.8 | 0.2 | 0.1 | 0.3 |

## Table D-3.  State Exports of Goods by Destination and Industry, 1993–1997 —*Continued*

**NEBRASKA** (Millions of dollars.)

| Industry | 1993 | 1994 | 1995 | 1996 | 1997 | 1993 | 1994 | 1995 | 1996 | 1997 |
|---|---|---|---|---|---|---|---|---|---|---|
| | South and Central America and Caribbean | | | | | Mexico | | | | |
| **ALL GOODS** | 24.9 | 66.5 | 74.8 | 123.1 | 176.4 | 60.8 | 108.8 | 80.0 | 168.0 | 142.0 |
| **Manufactured goods** | 18.4 | 32.7 | 27.1 | 53.7 | 102.9 | 38.6 | 78.9 | 57.3 | 61.7 | 80.1 |
| Food products | 5.9 | 20.3 | 7.4 | 19.6 | 54.0 | 10.2 | 34.1 | 27.3 | 32.0 | 35.7 |
| Tobacco products | ..... | ..... | ..... | ..... | ..... | ..... | 0.1 | 0.1 | ..... | 0.3 |
| Textile mill products | ..... | ..... | 0.1 | 0.1 | 0.1 | ..... | ..... | 0.1 | ..... | ..... |
| Apparel | ..... | ..... | ..... | ..... | 0.4 | 0.1 | ..... | 0.2 | 0.2 | ..... |
| Lumber and wood products | 0.1 | ..... | 0.3 | ..... | 0.1 | ..... | ..... | ..... | ..... | ..... |
| Furniture and fixtures | 0.1 | 0.2 | 0.4 | 0.1 | 0.6 | 0.2 | 1.7 | 0.1 | 0.1 | ..... |
| Paper products | 0.1 | 0.4 | 0.1 | 0.4 | 0.5 | 1.4 | 0.7 | 0.4 | 0.3 | 0.6 |
| Printing and publishing | ..... | ..... | ..... | 0.1 | ..... | 0.1 | 0.4 | 0.5 | ..... | 0.1 |
| Chemical products | 2.8 | 3.1 | 3.1 | 4.5 | 6.9 | 2.4 | 5.4 | 5.5 | 4.3 | 4.9 |
| Refined petroleum products | ..... | 0.1 | ..... | 0.1 | ..... | ..... | ..... | ..... | ..... | ..... |
| Rubber and plastic products | 0.3 | 0.3 | 2.1 | 0.7 | 0.4 | 0.6 | 0.9 | 0.4 | 1.7 | 1.9 |
| Leather products | ..... | ..... | 3.1 | 4.1 | 6.4 | 0.1 | ..... | ..... | ..... | ..... |
| Stone, clay and glass products | 0.6 | 0.1 | ..... | 0.1 | 0.1 | 0.1 | 0.8 | ..... | ..... | 0.1 |
| Primary metals | ..... | 0.3 | 0.3 | 0.7 | 0.3 | 0.6 | 4.5 | 0.7 | 1.2 | 1.5 |
| Fabricated metal products | 0.9 | 0.9 | 0.7 | 1.1 | 2.7 | 1.9 | 3.1 | 1.2 | 1.5 | 1.4 |
| Industrial machinery and computers | 4.3 | 3.4 | 6.0 | 18.7 | 21.7 | 5.9 | 10.3 | 5.0 | 5.7 | 13.3 |
| Electric and electronic equipment | 1.5 | 1.8 | 1.4 | 0.6 | 4.4 | 10.6 | 11.0 | 11.9 | 11.0 | 13.4 |
| Transportation equipment | 0.1 | 0.7 | 0.5 | 0.5 | 2.1 | 2.1 | 1.7 | 1.4 | 1.7 | 1.7 |
| Scientific and measuring instruments | 1.2 | 0.8 | 1.2 | 1.4 | 1.4 | 1.7 | 3.8 | 2.3 | 1.8 | 4.7 |
| Miscellaneous manufactures | 0.5 | 0.2 | 0.3 | 0.7 | 0.6 | 0.4 | 0.1 | 0.1 | 0.1 | 0.2 |
| Unidentified manufactures | 0.1 | 0.1 | 0.1 | 0.1 | 0.1 | 0.1 | 0.1 | 0.1 | 0.2 | 0.4 |
| **Agricultural and livestock products** | 6.1 | 33.7 | 47.4 | 69.2 | 73.4 | 22.1 | 29.6 | 22.6 | 105.3 | 61.0 |
| Agricultural products | 5.8 | 33.3 | 47.0 | 68.6 | 72.8 | 21.1 | 27.2 | 22.4 | 105.1 | 59.6 |
| Livestock and livestock products | 0.2 | 0.3 | 0.3 | 0.5 | 0.6 | 1.0 | 2.5 | 0.2 | 0.3 | 1.4 |
| **Other commodities** | 0.4 | 0.2 | 0.3 | 0.2 | 0.1 | 0.1 | 0.2 | 0.1 | 0.9 | 0.9 |
| Forestry products | ..... | ..... | ..... | ..... | ..... | ..... | ..... | ..... | 0.1 | ..... |
| Fish and other marine products | ..... | ..... | ..... | ..... | ..... | ..... | ..... | ..... | ..... | ..... |
| Metallic ores and concentrates | ..... | ..... | ..... | ..... | ..... | ..... | 0.2 | ..... | ..... | ..... |
| Bituminous coal and lignite | ..... | ..... | ..... | ..... | ..... | ..... | ..... | ..... | 0.6 | ..... |
| Crude petroleum and natural gas | ..... | ..... | ..... | ..... | ..... | ..... | ..... | ..... | ..... | ..... |
| Nonmetallic minerals | ..... | ..... | ..... | ..... | ..... | ..... | ..... | ..... | 0.2 | ..... |
| Scrap and waste | ..... | ..... | ..... | ..... | ..... | ..... | ..... | ..... | ..... | 0.1 |
| Used merchandise | 0.4 | 0.2 | 0.1 | 0.2 | 0.1 | 0.1 | ..... | ..... | ..... | 0.7 |
| Goods imported and returned unchanged | ..... | ..... | ..... | ..... | ..... | ..... | ..... | ..... | ..... | ..... |
| Special classification provisions | ..... | ..... | 0.3 | ..... | ..... | ..... | ..... | ..... | ..... | ..... |
| | European Union | | | | | United Kingdom | | | | |
| **ALL GOODS** | 202.1 | 221.8 | 213.1 | 237.8 | 285.7 | 33.1 | 30.5 | 27.9 | 30.2 | 40.7 |
| **Manufactured goods** | 181.0 | 204.3 | 200.0 | 207.4 | 220.1 | 32.8 | 30.4 | 27.6 | 26.7 | 39.4 |
| Food products | 28.0 | 21.3 | 31.0 | 25.7 | 29.5 | 1.6 | 2.5 | 2.9 | 0.5 | 0.3 |
| Tobacco products | ..... | ..... | ..... | ..... | ..... | ..... | ..... | ..... | ..... | ..... |
| Textile mill products | ..... | 0.1 | 0.2 | 0.6 | 0.7 | ..... | ..... | ..... | ..... | ..... |
| Apparel | 0.2 | 0.2 | 0.3 | 1.3 | 1.0 | ..... | ..... | 0.1 | 0.2 | 0.1 |
| Lumber and wood products | ..... | ..... | 0.3 | 0.2 | ..... | ..... | ..... | ..... | 0.2 | ..... |
| Furniture and fixtures | 0.1 | 0.3 | 0.3 | 1.7 | 1.4 | ..... | 0.3 | 0.1 | 0.5 | 0.3 |
| Paper products | 0.1 | 0.1 | 0.3 | 0.1 | 0.1 | 0.1 | ..... | 0.1 | 0.1 | ..... |
| Printing and publishing | 0.3 | 0.4 | 0.1 | 0.1 | 0.1 | 0.2 | 0.1 | ..... | ..... | ..... |
| Chemical products | 3.6 | 3.4 | 4.3 | 9.0 | 17.8 | 0.4 | 0.3 | 0.3 | 0.4 | 4.7 |
| Refined petroleum products | ..... | 0.1 | 0.1 | 0.1 | ..... | ..... | ..... | ..... | ..... | ..... |
| Rubber and plastic products | 1.7 | 1.0 | 2.7 | 4.1 | 2.6 | 1.1 | 0.4 | 0.2 | 0.3 | 0.3 |
| Leather products | 19.2 | 27.1 | 20.6 | 25.4 | 12.8 | ..... | ..... | ..... | ..... | ..... |
| Stone, clay and glass products | 0.2 | 0.2 | 0.4 | 0.5 | 0.5 | ..... | ..... | 0.3 | 0.2 | ..... |
| Primary metals | 25.4 | 19.2 | 18.8 | 6.9 | 17.2 | 0.1 | 0.2 | 0.1 | 0.5 | 0.4 |
| Fabricated metal products | 4.5 | 6.1 | 7.7 | 6.1 | 6.7 | 0.3 | 0.4 | 1.1 | 0.5 | 0.3 |
| Industrial machinery and computers | 15.7 | 23.9 | 21.5 | 25.0 | 29.4 | 6.7 | 11.3 | 10.6 | 11.0 | 15.8 |
| Electric and electronic equipment | 24.9 | 43.7 | 48.0 | 52.6 | 48.3 | 2.7 | 4.0 | 3.2 | 3.9 | 4.5 |
| Transportation equipment | 41.4 | 44.0 | 22.1 | 22.5 | 23.9 | 17.8 | 9.0 | 6.1 | 4.8 | 7.2 |
| Scientific and measuring instruments | 13.9 | 11.5 | 19.3 | 24.3 | 26.4 | 1.4 | 1.7 | 2.1 | 3.1 | 4.8 |
| Miscellaneous manufactures | 1.1 | 1.3 | 1.5 | 0.7 | 1.4 | 0.2 | 0.1 | 0.3 | 0.2 | 0.4 |
| Unidentified manufactures | 0.5 | 0.5 | 0.5 | 0.4 | 0.4 | 0.2 | 0.1 | 0.1 | 0.2 | 0.2 |
| **Agricultural and livestock products** | 20.3 | 17.5 | 12.7 | 30.0 | 65.2 | 0.1 | ..... | 0.2 | 3.2 | 1.2 |
| Agricultural products | 20.3 | 17.5 | 12.7 | 30.0 | 65.2 | 0.1 | ..... | 0.2 | 3.2 | 1.2 |
| Livestock and livestock products | ..... | ..... | ..... | ..... | ..... | ..... | ..... | ..... | ..... | ..... |
| **Other commodities** | 0.7 | 0.1 | 0.4 | 0.3 | 0.3 | 0.2 | ..... | 0.2 | 0.2 | 0.1 |
| Forestry products | ..... | ..... | ..... | ..... | 0.1 | ..... | ..... | ..... | ..... | ..... |
| Fish and other marine products | ..... | ..... | ..... | ..... | ..... | ..... | ..... | ..... | ..... | ..... |
| Metallic ores and concentrates | ..... | ..... | ..... | ..... | ..... | ..... | ..... | ..... | ..... | ..... |
| Bituminous coal and lignite | ..... | ..... | ..... | ..... | ..... | ..... | ..... | ..... | ..... | ..... |
| Crude petroleum and natural gas | ..... | ..... | ..... | ..... | ..... | ..... | ..... | ..... | ..... | ..... |
| Nonmetallic minerals | ..... | ..... | ..... | ..... | ..... | ..... | ..... | ..... | ..... | ..... |
| Scrap and waste | ..... | ..... | 0.1 | ..... | ..... | ..... | ..... | 0.1 | ..... | ..... |
| Used merchandise | 0.6 | ..... | 0.3 | 0.1 | ..... | 0.1 | ..... | 0.1 | 0.1 | ..... |
| Goods imported and returned unchanged | ..... | ..... | ..... | ..... | ..... | ..... | ..... | ..... | ..... | ..... |
| Special classification provisions | ..... | ..... | ..... | 0.2 | 0.2 | ..... | ..... | ..... | 0.1 | 0.1 |

## Table D-3.   State Exports of Goods by Destination and Industry, 1993–1997 —*Continued*

**NEBRASKA** (Millions of dollars.)

| Industry | 1993 | 1994 | 1995 | 1996 | 1997 | 1993 | 1994 | 1995 | 1996 | 1997 |
|---|---|---|---|---|---|---|---|---|---|---|
| | Germany | | | | | France | | | | |
| **ALL GOODS** | 24.8 | 30.8 | 29.0 | 35.8 | 39.0 | 16.0 | 18.3 | 16.2 | 20.5 | 22.2 |
| **Manufactured goods** | 23.9 | 30.2 | 27.4 | 34.3 | 37.7 | 15.6 | 18.1 | 15.7 | 20.0 | 15.9 |
| Food products | 7.3 | 7.3 | 7.5 | 10.0 | 10.0 | 9.3 | 6.4 | 5.3 | 4.1 | 2.6 |
| Tobacco products | ..... | ..... | ..... | ..... | ..... | ..... | ..... | ..... | ..... | ..... |
| Textile mill products | ..... | ..... | ..... | ..... | ..... | ..... | ..... | 0.1 | ..... | ..... |
| Apparel | 0.1 | 0.1 | 0.1 | 0.1 | 0.1 | ..... | ..... | ..... | ..... | ..... |
| Lumber and wood products | ..... | ..... | 0.1 | ..... | ..... | ..... | ..... | ..... | ..... | ..... |
| Furniture and fixtures | ..... | ..... | ..... | ..... | ..... | ..... | ..... | ..... | 0.3 | ..... |
| Paper products | ..... | ..... | ..... | ..... | ..... | ..... | ..... | 0.1 | ..... | ..... |
| Printing and publishing | 0.1 | 0.1 | ..... | ..... | ..... | ..... | ..... | ..... | 0.1 | ..... |
| Chemical products | 0.6 | 0.9 | 0.9 | 1.5 | 1.6 | 0.1 | ..... | 0.1 | 0.4 | 0.4 |
| Refined petroleum products | ..... | ..... | ..... | ..... | ..... | ..... | ..... | ..... | ..... | ..... |
| Rubber and plastic products | ..... | 0.1 | 1.0 | 0.3 | 0.1 | ..... | 0.1 | 0.7 | 2.4 | 1.1 |
| Leather products | 0.1 | ..... | ..... | 0.2 | ..... | 0.3 | ..... | ..... | 0.1 | 0.1 |
| Stone, clay and glass products | 0.1 | ..... | ..... | 0.2 | ..... | ..... | ..... | ..... | 0.1 | 0.1 |
| Primary metals | 0.1 | 0.1 | 0.2 | 0.3 | 0.1 | ..... | ..... | ..... | ..... | 0.1 |
| Fabricated metal products | 0.7 | 0.9 | 2.3 | 3.4 | 3.5 | 0.4 | 0.5 | 0.1 | 0.1 | 0.3 |
| Industrial machinery and computers | 1.9 | 2.8 | 1.5 | 3.4 | 1.5 | 1.3 | 1.5 | 1.5 | 3.6 | 3.8 |
| Electric and electronic equipment | 2.6 | 3.1 | 4.8 | 3.8 | 9.4 | 0.8 | 1.2 | 1.8 | 1.4 | 1.8 |
| Transportation equipment | 5.5 | 10.8 | 2.6 | 5.0 | 3.9 | 1.0 | 6.1 | 1.4 | 1.2 | 1.4 |
| Scientific and measuring instruments | 4.1 | 2.8 | 5.5 | 5.7 | 7.0 | 2.1 | 1.9 | 4.2 | 6.0 | 4.1 |
| Miscellaneous manufactures | 0.4 | 0.9 | 0.6 | 0.3 | 0.4 | 0.3 | 0.3 | 0.3 | 0.1 | 0.2 |
| Unidentified manufactures | 0.2 | 0.1 | 0.1 | ..... | ..... | ..... | ..... | 0.1 | 0.1 | ..... |
| **Agricultural and livestock products** | 0.5 | 0.6 | 1.3 | 1.5 | 1.0 | 0.4 | 0.1 | 0.5 | 0.5 | 6.3 |
| Agricultural products | 0.5 | 0.6 | 1.3 | 1.5 | 1.0 | 0.4 | 0.1 | 0.5 | 0.5 | 6.3 |
| Livestock and livestock products | ..... | ..... | ..... | ..... | ..... | ..... | ..... | ..... | ..... | ..... |
| **Other commodities** | 0.4 | ..... | 0.3 | 0.1 | 0.2 | ..... | ..... | ..... | ..... | ..... |
| Forestry products | ..... | ..... | ..... | ..... | 0.1 | ..... | ..... | ..... | ..... | ..... |
| Fish and other marine products | ..... | ..... | ..... | ..... | ..... | ..... | ..... | ..... | ..... | ..... |
| Metallic ores and concentrates | ..... | ..... | ..... | ..... | ..... | ..... | ..... | ..... | ..... | ..... |
| Bituminous coal and lignite | ..... | ..... | ..... | ..... | ..... | ..... | ..... | ..... | ..... | ..... |
| Crude petroleum and natural gas | ..... | ..... | ..... | ..... | ..... | ..... | ..... | ..... | ..... | ..... |
| Nonmetallic minerals | ..... | ..... | ..... | ..... | ..... | ..... | ..... | ..... | ..... | ..... |
| Scrap and waste | ..... | ..... | ..... | ..... | ..... | ..... | ..... | ..... | ..... | ..... |
| Used merchandise | 0.4 | ..... | 0.2 | ..... | ..... | ..... | ..... | ..... | ..... | ..... |
| Goods imported and returned unchanged | ..... | ..... | ..... | ..... | ..... | ..... | ..... | ..... | ..... | ..... |
| Special classification provisions | ..... | ..... | ..... | ..... | ..... | ..... | ..... | ..... | ..... | ..... |
| | The Netherlands | | | | | Asian 10 | | | | |
| **ALL GOODS** | 57.6 | 62.3 | 73.6 | 58.7 | 60.4 | 1 075.2 | 1 137.3 | 1 426.7 | 1 366.0 | 1 206.4 |
| **Manufactured goods** | 57.3 | 62.0 | 73.3 | 58.5 | 57.6 | 1 070.2 | 1 133.3 | 1 422.6 | 1 360.7 | 1 195.1 |
| Food products | 3.6 | 2.8 | 11.9 | 2.2 | 5.0 | 949.2 | 996.5 | 1 259.3 | 1 168.0 | 990.1 |
| Tobacco products | ..... | ..... | ..... | ..... | ..... | ..... | ..... | ..... | ..... | ..... |
| Textile mill products | ..... | ..... | 0.1 | 0.5 | 0.6 | 0.4 | 0.5 | 0.9 | 0.4 | 0.5 |
| Apparel | ..... | ..... | 0.1 | 0.9 | 0.7 | 3.9 | 4.6 | 5.0 | 6.5 | 6.4 |
| Lumber and wood products | ..... | ..... | ..... | ..... | ..... | 0.1 | 0.2 | 0.5 | 1.8 | 1.3 |
| Furniture and fixtures | ..... | ..... | ..... | ..... | ..... | ..... | 0.1 | 1.1 | 1.9 | 1.6 |
| Paper products | ..... | ..... | ..... | ..... | ..... | 0.1 | 1.2 | 0.4 | 0.1 | 0.3 |
| Printing and publishing | ..... | ..... | ..... | ..... | ..... | 0.1 | 0.7 | 0.2 | 0.2 | 0.6 |
| Chemical products | 0.2 | 0.1 | ..... | 0.3 | 0.5 | 6.1 | 5.6 | 4.6 | 7.5 | 9.6 |
| Refined petroleum products | ..... | 0.1 | ..... | ..... | ..... | ..... | ..... | ..... | 0.5 | 0.3 |
| Rubber and plastic products | 0.1 | 0.1 | 0.3 | 0.1 | ..... | 1.6 | 1.4 | 1.9 | 6.0 | 3.4 |
| Leather products | ..... | ..... | ..... | ..... | ..... | 32.6 | 40.6 | 45.2 | 51.5 | 73.3 |
| Stone, clay and glass products | ..... | ..... | ..... | ..... | ..... | 0.6 | 1.7 | 2.1 | 1.2 | 1.0 |
| Primary metals | 23.8 | 18.5 | 18.3 | 5.5 | 15.5 | 4.9 | 7.0 | 9.2 | 7.6 | 13.6 |
| Fabricated metal products | 2.1 | 3.4 | 3.1 | 0.7 | 0.9 | 5.8 | 8.0 | 8.2 | 12.6 | 7.7 |
| Industrial machinery and computers | 0.7 | 0.6 | 1.2 | 1.9 | 0.8 | 13.3 | 13.7 | 18.7 | 24.1 | 18.9 |
| Electric and electronic equipment | 12.8 | 20.5 | 27.6 | 36.5 | 21.9 | 26.0 | 29.9 | 32.8 | 36.4 | 37.8 |
| Transportation equipment | 13.2 | 15.2 | 9.3 | 7.7 | 9.3 | 19.4 | 13.3 | 20.0 | 19.0 | 11.7 |
| Scientific and measuring instruments | 0.6 | 0.6 | 1.2 | 2.1 | 2.4 | 5.4 | 7.5 | 11.5 | 13.7 | 15.1 |
| Miscellaneous manufactures | ..... | ..... | ..... | ..... | ..... | 0.3 | 0.6 | 0.6 | 1.4 | 1.7 |
| Unidentified manufactures | ..... | 0.1 | ..... | ..... | ..... | 0.3 | 0.3 | 0.3 | 0.3 | 0.4 |
| **Agricultural and livestock products** | 0.3 | 0.3 | 0.2 | 0.2 | 2.7 | 1.3 | 2.2 | 3.7 | 4.0 | 10.9 |
| Agricultural products | 0.3 | 0.3 | 0.2 | 0.2 | 2.7 | 1.3 | 2.1 | 3.6 | 3.7 | 10.9 |
| Livestock and livestock products | ..... | ..... | ..... | ..... | ..... | ..... | 0.2 | 0.1 | 0.3 | ..... |
| **Other commodities** | ..... | ..... | ..... | ..... | ..... | 3.7 | 1.7 | 0.4 | 1.3 | 0.4 |
| Forestry products | ..... | ..... | ..... | ..... | ..... | ..... | ..... | ..... | ..... | 0.1 |
| Fish and other marine products | ..... | ..... | ..... | ..... | ..... | 0.3 | 0.1 | ..... | 0.9 | ..... |
| Metallic ores and concentrates | ..... | ..... | ..... | ..... | ..... | ..... | ..... | ..... | ..... | ..... |
| Bituminous coal and lignite | ..... | ..... | ..... | ..... | ..... | ..... | ..... | ..... | ..... | ..... |
| Crude petroleum and natural gas | ..... | ..... | ..... | ..... | ..... | ..... | ..... | ..... | ..... | ..... |
| Nonmetallic minerals | ..... | ..... | ..... | ..... | ..... | ..... | ..... | ..... | 0.1 | ..... |
| Scrap and waste | ..... | ..... | ..... | ..... | ..... | 3.2 | 1.6 | 0.1 | ..... | 0.2 |
| Used merchandise | ..... | ..... | ..... | ..... | ..... | ..... | ..... | 0.1 | 0.2 | ..... |
| Goods imported and returned unchanged | ..... | ..... | ..... | ..... | ..... | ..... | ..... | ..... | ..... | ..... |
| Special classification provisions | ..... | ..... | ..... | ..... | ..... | 0.1 | ..... | 0.2 | 0.2 | 0.1 |

## Table D-3.  State Exports of Goods by Destination and Industry, 1993–1997 —Continued

**NEBRASKA** (Millions of dollars.)

| Industry | 1993 | 1994 | 1995 | 1996 | 1997 | 1993 | 1994 | 1995 | 1996 | 1997 |
|---|---|---|---|---|---|---|---|---|---|---|
| | Japan | | | | | South Korea | | | | |
| **ALL GOODS** | 915.3 | 912.8 | 1 162.7 | 1 103.1 | 870.8 | 105.0 | 146.1 | 160.8 | 134.3 | 184.7 |
| **Manufactured goods** | 914.7 | 911.7 | 1 160.2 | 1 098.7 | 866.5 | 103.0 | 144.3 | 160.7 | 134.1 | 184.5 |
| Food products | 878.4 | 874.4 | 1 114.8 | 1 041.3 | 820.3 | 64.7 | 111.3 | 124.7 | 97.0 | 121.0 |
| Tobacco products | ..... | ..... | ..... | ..... | ..... | ..... | ..... | ..... | ..... | ..... |
| Textile mill products | ..... | ..... | ..... | ..... | 0.1 | 0.1 | 0.3 | 0.5 | 0.4 | 0.3 |
| Apparel | 3.8 | 4.4 | 4.3 | 6.1 | 4.8 | ..... | 0.1 | 0.7 | 0.2 | 0.4 |
| Lumber and wood products | ..... | ..... | ..... | 0.1 | 0.2 | ..... | ..... | ..... | ..... | 0.4 |
| Furniture and fixtures | ..... | ..... | 0.1 | 0.1 | 0.2 | ..... | ..... | ..... | ..... | 0.4 |
| Paper products | ..... | 1.1 | ..... | ..... | ..... | ..... | ..... | ..... | ..... | ..... |
| Printing and publishing | 0.1 | 0.6 | 0.1 | 0.1 | 0.1 | ..... | ..... | ..... | ..... | 0.1 |
| Chemical products | 3.9 | 3.0 | 2.1 | 2.5 | 4.7 | 0.5 | 0.7 | 0.5 | 1.3 | 1.7 |
| Refined petroleum products | ..... | ..... | ..... | ..... | ..... | ..... | ..... | ..... | ..... | ..... |
| Rubber and plastic products | 0.5 | 0.9 | 1.0 | 2.6 | 2.7 | 0.6 | 0.1 | 0.2 | ..... | 0.2 |
| Leather products | 0.8 | 1.8 | 1.6 | 2.3 | 4.2 | 26.0 | 23.8 | 22.4 | 23.0 | 47.5 |
| Stone, clay and glass products | 0.3 | 0.5 | 1.3 | 0.7 | 0.7 | 0.3 | 0.8 | 0.5 | 0.5 | 0.3 |
| Primary metals | ..... | ..... | ..... | ..... | 0.1 | 0.1 | ..... | ..... | 0.9 | 0.8 |
| Fabricated metal products | 0.7 | 2.2 | 0.6 | 0.7 | 0.5 | 2.1 | 2.1 | 2.8 | 2.8 | 2.0 |
| Industrial machinery and computers | 6.5 | 5.6 | 5.3 | 10.0 | 4.6 | 1.1 | 2.2 | 5.1 | 2.4 | 1.8 |
| Electric and electronic equipment | 0.8 | 1.9 | 5.7 | 8.6 | 5.4 | 6.6 | 1.0 | 1.1 | 2.7 | 3.8 |
| Transportation equipment | 15.9 | 11.5 | 17.5 | 14.3 | 9.4 | 0.4 | 0.3 | 0.3 | 0.7 | 0.6 |
| Scientific and measuring instruments | 2.8 | 3.5 | 5.2 | 9.0 | 8.3 | 0.5 | 1.6 | 1.8 | 1.8 | 3.1 |
| Miscellaneous manufactures | 0.1 | 0.3 | 0.4 | 0.3 | 0.3 | ..... | ..... | ..... | 0.1 | 0.1 |
| Unidentified manufactures | 0.1 | 0.1 | 0.2 | 0.1 | 0.1 | 0.1 | 0.1 | ..... | ..... | 0.1 |
| **Agricultural and livestock products** | 0.4 | 1.0 | 2.4 | 3.1 | 4.2 | 0.2 | 0.2 | 0.1 | 0.2 | 0.2 |
| Agricultural products | 0.4 | 1.0 | 2.4 | 3.0 | 4.2 | 0.2 | 0.2 | 0.1 | 0.2 | 0.2 |
| Livestock and livestock products | ..... | ..... | ..... | 0.1 | ..... | ..... | ..... | ..... | ..... | ..... |
| **Other commodities** | 0.3 | ..... | ..... | 1.3 | 0.2 | 1.8 | 1.5 | ..... | ..... | ..... |
| Forestry products | ..... | ..... | ..... | ..... | ..... | ..... | ..... | ..... | ..... | ..... |
| Fish and other marine products | 0.2 | ..... | ..... | 0.9 | ..... | 0.1 | 0.1 | ..... | ..... | ..... |
| Metallic ores and concentrates | ..... | ..... | ..... | ..... | ..... | ..... | ..... | ..... | ..... | ..... |
| Bituminous coal and lignite | ..... | ..... | ..... | ..... | ..... | ..... | ..... | ..... | ..... | ..... |
| Crude petroleum and natural gas | ..... | ..... | ..... | ..... | ..... | ..... | ..... | ..... | ..... | ..... |
| Nonmetallic minerals | ..... | ..... | ..... | ..... | ..... | ..... | ..... | ..... | ..... | ..... |
| Scrap and waste | ..... | ..... | ..... | ..... | ..... | 1.6 | 1.5 | ..... | ..... | ..... |
| Used merchandise | ..... | ..... | ..... | 0.1 | ..... | ..... | ..... | ..... | ..... | ..... |
| Goods imported and returned unchanged | ..... | ..... | ..... | ..... | ..... | ..... | ..... | ..... | ..... | ..... |
| Special classification provisions | ..... | ..... | ..... | 0.2 | 0.1 | 0.1 | ..... | ..... | ..... | ..... |

| Industry | 1993 | 1994 | 1995 | 1996 | 1997 | 1993 | 1994 | 1995 | 1996 | 1997 |
|---|---|---|---|---|---|---|---|---|---|---|
| | Taiwan | | | | | Singapore | | | | |
| **ALL GOODS** | 8.9 | 10.8 | 13.2 | 16.7 | 24.9 | 10.8 | 16.7 | 23.8 | 23.8 | 29.0 |
| **Manufactured goods** | 8.8 | 10.6 | 13.1 | 16.4 | 24.0 | 10.7 | 16.6 | 23.8 | 23.8 | 29.0 |
| Food products | 2.7 | 5.5 | 7.5 | 7.7 | 12.7 | 0.2 | 0.2 | 0.4 | 0.5 | 0.4 |
| Tobacco products | ..... | ..... | ..... | ..... | ..... | ..... | ..... | ..... | ..... | ..... |
| Textile mill products | ..... | ..... | ..... | ..... | ..... | ..... | 0.1 | 0.1 | ..... | ..... |
| Apparel | ..... | ..... | ..... | 0.1 | 0.2 | ..... | ..... | ..... | ..... | 0.1 |
| Lumber and wood products | ..... | 0.1 | ..... | ..... | ..... | ..... | ..... | ..... | ..... | ..... |
| Furniture and fixtures | ..... | ..... | ..... | ..... | 0.2 | ..... | 0.1 | ..... | ..... | ..... |
| Paper products | ..... | 0.1 | ..... | 0.1 | ..... | ..... | ..... | ..... | ..... | ..... |
| Printing and publishing | ..... | ..... | ..... | ..... | ..... | ..... | ..... | 0.1 | 0.1 | ..... |
| Chemical products | 0.4 | 0.5 | 0.6 | 1.6 | 1.0 | 0.2 | ..... | 0.1 | 0.1 | ..... |
| Refined petroleum products | ..... | ..... | ..... | ..... | 0.3 | ..... | ..... | ..... | ..... | ..... |
| Rubber and plastic products | 0.1 | ..... | 0.2 | 0.8 | 0.1 | ..... | ..... | 0.1 | 0.1 | ..... |
| Leather products | ..... | ..... | ..... | ..... | 0.1 | ..... | ..... | ..... | ..... | ..... |
| Stone, clay and glass products | ..... | ..... | ..... | ..... | ..... | ..... | 0.1 | 0.1 | ..... | ..... |
| Primary metals | 1.2 | 0.2 | 0.5 | 0.4 | 0.6 | 3.4 | 6.5 | 8.2 | 5.7 | 11.3 |
| Fabricated metal products | 0.1 | 0.1 | 0.7 | 0.2 | 0.1 | 0.4 | 0.1 | 0.3 | 0.1 | 0.2 |
| Industrial machinery and computers | 1.9 | 1.4 | 0.5 | 0.8 | 1.5 | 0.3 | 0.6 | 0.7 | 1.6 | 2.4 |
| Electric and electronic equipment | 1.3 | 1.5 | 1.8 | 2.8 | 4.0 | 5.6 | 7.9 | 12.3 | 14.4 | 13.4 |
| Transportation equipment | 0.1 | ..... | 0.1 | 1.0 | 0.9 | 0.2 | 0.6 | 0.4 | 0.5 | 0.4 |
| Scientific and measuring instruments | 0.8 | 1.0 | 0.9 | 0.7 | 1.4 | 0.2 | 0.3 | 0.9 | 0.8 | 0.7 |
| Miscellaneous manufactures | ..... | 0.1 | ..... | ..... | 1.0 | ..... | ..... | ..... | ..... | 0.1 |
| Unidentified manufactures | ..... | ..... | ..... | ..... | 0.1 | ..... | ..... | ..... | ..... | ..... |
| **Agricultural and livestock products** | 0.1 | 0.1 | 0.1 | 0.4 | 0.9 | ..... | ..... | ..... | ..... | 0.1 |
| Agricultural products | 0.1 | 0.1 | 0.1 | 0.4 | 0.9 | ..... | ..... | ..... | ..... | 0.1 |
| Livestock and livestock products | ..... | ..... | ..... | ..... | ..... | ..... | ..... | ..... | ..... | ..... |
| **Other commodities** | ..... | 0.1 | ..... | ..... | ..... | ..... | ..... | 0.1 | ..... | ..... |
| Forestry products | ..... | ..... | ..... | ..... | ..... | ..... | ..... | ..... | ..... | ..... |
| Fish and other marine products | ..... | ..... | ..... | ..... | ..... | ..... | ..... | ..... | ..... | ..... |
| Metallic ores and concentrates | ..... | ..... | ..... | ..... | ..... | ..... | ..... | ..... | ..... | ..... |
| Bituminous coal and lignite | ..... | ..... | ..... | ..... | ..... | ..... | ..... | ..... | ..... | ..... |
| Crude petroleum and natural gas | ..... | ..... | ..... | ..... | ..... | ..... | ..... | ..... | ..... | ..... |
| Nonmetallic minerals | ..... | ..... | ..... | ..... | ..... | ..... | ..... | ..... | ..... | ..... |
| Scrap and waste | ..... | 0.1 | ..... | ..... | ..... | ..... | ..... | ..... | ..... | ..... |
| Used merchandise | ..... | ..... | ..... | ..... | ..... | ..... | ..... | ..... | ..... | ..... |
| Goods imported and returned unchanged | ..... | ..... | ..... | ..... | ..... | ..... | ..... | ..... | ..... | ..... |
| Special classification provisions | ..... | ..... | ..... | ..... | ..... | ..... | ..... | ..... | ..... | ..... |

## NEVADA: Exports of Goods, 1997

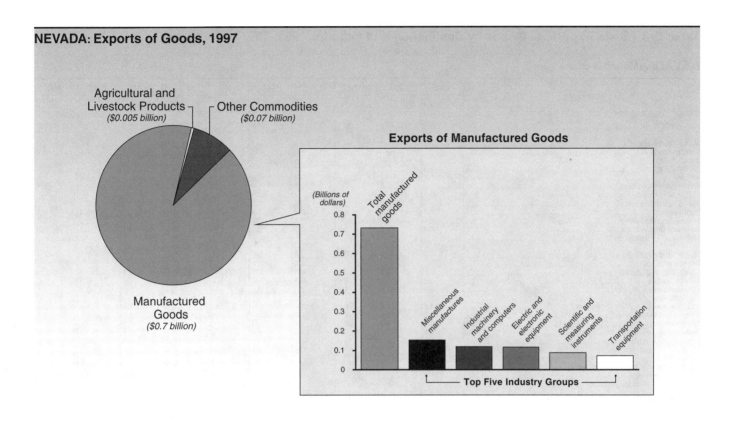

## Table D-3. State Exports of Goods by Destination and Industry, 1993–1997 —Continued

**NEVADA** (Millions of dollars.)

| Industry | 1993 | 1994 | 1995 | 1996 | 1997 | 1993 | 1994 | 1995 | 1996 | 1997 |
|---|---|---|---|---|---|---|---|---|---|---|
| | All destinations | | | | | Canada | | | | |
| **ALL GOODS** | 503.9 | 458.5 | 711.1 | 691.6 | 807.1 | 123.4 | 148.9 | 211.8 | 265.6 | 272.1 |
| **Manufactured goods** | 471.0 | 420.4 | 659.4 | 631.7 | 732.3 | 108.6 | 131.0 | 190.1 | 240.7 | 243.6 |
| Food products | 8.1 | 7.2 | 15.0 | 15.2 | 6.4 | 3.9 | 2.1 | 3.3 | 2.0 | 2.6 |
| Tobacco products | ..... | ..... | ..... | ..... | ..... | ..... | ..... | ..... | ..... | ..... |
| Textile mill products | 0.8 | 1.2 | 3.1 | 1.4 | 1.9 | 0.1 | 0.1 | 0.3 | 0.3 | 0.4 |
| Apparel | 10.8 | 6.4 | 13.6 | 14.4 | 12.8 | 5.9 | 3.3 | 3.5 | 3.0 | 1.2 |
| Lumber and wood products | 2.4 | 4.8 | 3.2 | 2.0 | 3.8 | 1.1 | 2.3 | 1.6 | 1.4 | 2.6 |
| Furniture and fixtures | 1.5 | 1.5 | 2.0 | 3.6 | 1.8 | 0.5 | 0.5 | 0.3 | 0.8 | 0.3 |
| Paper products | 2.4 | 2.4 | 3.0 | 5.0 | 5.5 | 1.4 | 0.8 | 1.0 | 2.7 | 2.6 |
| Printing and publishing | 9.7 | 7.4 | 7.4 | 8.2 | 10.8 | 7.0 | 4.5 | 3.7 | 5.7 | 7.5 |
| Chemical products | 7.0 | 10.6 | 21.7 | 22.8 | 19.3 | 3.9 | 5.8 | 7.0 | 7.4 | 10.8 |
| Refined petroleum products | 0.3 | 0.8 | 0.5 | 0.5 | 0.4 | 0.1 | 0.6 | 0.4 | 0.4 | 0.2 |
| Rubber and plastic products | 7.7 | 9.7 | 11.0 | 17.4 | 27.0 | 2.6 | 3.0 | 3.5 | 7.1 | 9.7 |
| Leather products | 0.4 | 1.0 | 4.2 | 4.8 | 2.8 | 0.1 | 0.2 | 1.2 | 0.4 | 0.4 |
| Stone, clay and glass products | 4.9 | 6.8 | 6.2 | 5.7 | 5.8 | 2.0 | 3.1 | 2.9 | 2.1 | 1.5 |
| Primary metals | 165.3 | 50.7 | 47.2 | 23.8 | 33.8 | 3.2 | 17.7 | 18.8 | 11.3 | 4.1 |
| Fabricated metal products | 12.9 | 28.8 | 69.1 | 22.7 | 44.2 | 5.5 | 7.3 | 11.9 | 11.2 | 21.3 |
| Industrial machinery and computers | 55.7 | 68.8 | 130.8 | 94.7 | 119.3 | 12.7 | 16.0 | 17.7 | 22.3 | 34.0 |
| Electric and electronic equipment | 45.1 | 55.4 | 92.7 | 102.0 | 117.3 | 25.9 | 28.2 | 40.4 | 58.0 | 62.3 |
| Transportation equipment | 15.5 | 14.7 | 50.4 | 54.7 | 72.7 | 3.3 | 3.7 | 38.3 | 27.4 | 33.5 |
| Scientific and measuring instruments | 55.1 | 67.0 | 81.0 | 70.6 | 88.2 | 11.4 | 10.9 | 13.2 | 11.9 | 12.3 |
| Miscellaneous manufactures | 61.9 | 70.3 | 94.0 | 158.3 | 153.6 | 17.3 | 19.5 | 19.3 | 63.5 | 34.0 |
| Unidentified manufactures | 3.5 | 4.8 | 3.4 | 3.9 | 5.0 | 0.9 | 1.6 | 1.6 | 2.0 | 2.4 |
| **Agricultural and livestock products** | 2.8 | 6.8 | 4.5 | 6.0 | 4.9 | 1.9 | 2.9 | 2.7 | 3.9 | 3.6 |
| Agricultural products | 0.9 | 6.1 | 3.3 | 5.2 | 3.4 | 0.8 | 2.7 | 2.4 | 3.3 | 2.9 |
| Livestock and livestock products | 1.9 | 0.7 | 1.3 | 0.8 | 1.5 | 1.1 | 0.2 | 0.4 | 0.6 | 0.7 |
| **Other commodities** | 30.1 | 31.3 | 47.1 | 53.9 | 70.0 | 12.9 | 15.0 | 19.0 | 21.0 | 24.9 |
| Forestry products | ..... | 0.2 | 0.1 | 0.1 | 0.1 | ..... | 0.1 | ..... | ..... | ..... |
| Fish and other marine products | 0.6 | 0.6 | 0.1 | 0.4 | ..... | 0.3 | 0.4 | 0.1 | ..... | ..... |
| Metallic ores and concentrates | 0.4 | ..... | ..... | ..... | 1.0 | 0.3 | ..... | ..... | ..... | 1.0 |
| Bituminous coal and lignite | ..... | ..... | ..... | ..... | ..... | ..... | ..... | ..... | ..... | ..... |
| Crude petroleum and natural gas | ..... | ..... | ..... | 0.4 | ..... | ..... | ..... | ..... | ..... | ..... |
| Nonmetallic minerals | 12.4 | 12.9 | 14.5 | 15.3 | 15.7 | 2.4 | 2.8 | 2.5 | 2.7 | 2.7 |
| Scrap and waste | 5.7 | 1.3 | 1.1 | 1.2 | 1.0 | 3.9 | 1.0 | 0.2 | 0.4 | 0.3 |
| Used merchandise | 5.3 | 6.1 | 16.0 | 20.5 | 30.8 | 0.2 | 0.6 | 1.3 | 2.4 | 1.2 |
| Goods imported and returned unchanged | 5.6 | 10.0 | 13.9 | 14.6 | 19.5 | 5.6 | 10.0 | 13.9 | 14.6 | 19.5 |
| Special classification provisions | 0.1 | 0.2 | 1.4 | 1.4 | 1.8 | 0.1 | 0.1 | 0.9 | 0.7 | 0.1 |

## Table D-3.   State Exports of Goods by Destination and Industry, 1993–1997 —Continued

**NEVADA** (Millions of dollars.)

| Industry | 1993 | 1994 | 1995 | 1996 | 1997 | 1993 | 1994 | 1995 | 1996 | 1997 |
|---|---|---|---|---|---|---|---|---|---|---|
| | South and Central America and Caribbean | | | | | Mexico | | | | |
| **ALL GOODS** | 15.2 | 22.5 | 34.7 | 44.7 | 34.3 | 13.1 | 14.5 | 12.8 | 9.2 | 59.9 |
| **Manufactured goods** | 14.9 | 21.8 | 34.0 | 43.1 | 33.7 | 12.8 | 12.8 | 12.6 | 9.0 | 59.7 |
| Food products | ..... | 0.4 | 0.4 | 1.9 | 0.1 | 0.9 | 1.8 | 0.8 | 0.4 | 0.2 |
| Tobacco products | ..... | * | ..... | ..... | ..... | ..... | ..... | ..... | ..... | ..... |
| Textile mill products | 0.1 | ..... | 0.1 | 0.2 | ..... | 0.1 | 0.3 | 1.8 | 0.1 | 0.2 |
| Apparel | 0.1 | 0.1 | ..... | 0.1 | 0.2 | 3.8 | 0.6 | 0.2 | 0.1 | 0.1 |
| Lumber and wood products | ..... | 1.3 | 0.1 | 0.1 | 0.2 | 0.4 | 0.2 | 0.4 | ..... | 0.2 |
| Furniture and fixtures | ..... | 0.1 | 0.1 | 0.2 | 0.5 | 0.1 | ..... | ..... | ..... | ..... |
| Paper products | 0.1 | 0.5 | 0.8 | 0.8 | 1.4 | 0.2 | 0.3 | 0.7 | 0.3 | 0.4 |
| Printing and publishing | 0.1 | 0.2 | ..... | 0.1 | 0.1 | 0.4 | 0.6 | 0.9 | 0.2 | 0.2 |
| Chemical products | 0.1 | 0.3 | 0.5 | 0.8 | 0.7 | 0.6 | 0.6 | 0.7 | 1.2 | 1.8 |
| Refined petroleum products | ..... | ..... | ..... | ..... | ..... | ..... | ..... | ..... | ..... | ..... |
| Rubber and plastic products | 0.4 | 0.4 | 0.5 | 0.8 | 0.6 | 0.5 | 0.9 | 0.7 | 1.2 | 0.8 |
| Leather products | ..... | ..... | ..... | 0.4 | 0.1 | 0.2 | ..... | ..... | ..... | ..... |
| Stone, clay and glass products | 0.2 | 0.3 | 0.3 | 0.4 | 0.4 | ..... | ..... | 0.1 | ..... | 0.1 |
| Primary metals | 3.2 | 2.0 | 2.5 | 0.8 | 0.6 | 0.2 | 0.3 | 0.6 | 0.3 | 2.6 |
| Fabricated metal products | 0.6 | 1.4 | 1.8 | 1.6 | 2.3 | 0.4 | 0.1 | 0.2 | 0.1 | 3.1 |
| Industrial machinery and computers | 4.2 | 4.4 | 8.5 | 7.2 | 5.6 | 1.8 | 2.3 | 2.4 | 1.4 | 2.9 |
| Electric and electronic equipment | 0.9 | 1.1 | 1.8 | 2.7 | 2.1 | 0.9 | 2.0 | 1.8 | 1.7 | 2.9 |
| Transportation equipment | 0.9 | 0.4 | 0.3 | 1.1 | 1.4 | 0.2 | 0.4 | 0.2 | 0.3 | 0.7 |
| Scientific and measuring instruments | 1.5 | 1.7 | 2.3 | 2.5 | 3.6 | 1.0 | 1.3 | 0.4 | 1.0 | 2.1 |
| Miscellaneous manufactures | 2.2 | 7.1 | 13.9 | 21.4 | 13.5 | 0.3 | 0.4 | 0.5 | 0.5 | 41.4 |
| Unidentified manufactures | 0.2 | 0.3 | 0.1 | 0.1 | 0.1 | 1.0 | 0.4 | 0.1 | 0.2 | 0.2 |
| **Agricultural and livestock products** | ..... | ..... | ..... | 0.6 | ..... | ..... | 1.4 | 0.2 | 0.1 | 0.1 |
| Agricultural products | ..... | ..... | ..... | 0.5 | ..... | ..... | 1.4 | 0.2 | 0.1 | 0.1 |
| Livestock and livestock products | ..... | ..... | ..... | ..... | ..... | ..... | ..... | ..... | ..... | ..... |
| **Other commodities** | 0.4 | 0.6 | 0.6 | 1.1 | 0.5 | 0.2 | 0.3 | 0.1 | 0.1 | 0.1 |
| Forestry products | ..... | ..... | ..... | ..... | ..... | ..... | ..... | ..... | ..... | ..... |
| Fish and other marine products | ..... | ..... | ..... | ..... | ..... | ..... | ..... | ..... | ..... | ..... |
| Metallic ores and concentrates | ..... | ..... | ..... | ..... | ..... | ..... | ..... | ..... | ..... | ..... |
| Bituminous coal and lignite | ..... | ..... | ..... | ..... | ..... | ..... | ..... | ..... | ..... | ..... |
| Crude petroleum and natural gas | ..... | ..... | ..... | 0.4 | ..... | ..... | ..... | ..... | ..... | ..... |
| Nonmetallic minerals | 0.3 | 0.6 | 0.5 | 0.5 | 0.5 | 0.2 | 0.2 | ..... | 0.1 | ..... |
| Scrap and waste | ..... | ..... | ..... | ..... | ..... | ..... | ..... | ..... | ..... | ..... |
| Used merchandise | 0.1 | ..... | 0.1 | ..... | ..... | ..... | 0.1 | ..... | 0.1 | ..... |
| Goods imported and returned unchanged | ..... | ..... | ..... | ..... | ..... | ..... | ..... | ..... | ..... | ..... |
| Special classification provisions | ..... | ..... | ..... | 0.1 | 0.1 | ..... | ..... | ..... | ..... | ..... |
| | European Union | | | | | United Kingdom | | | | |
| **ALL GOODS** | 71.8 | 97.3 | 103.6 | 114.2 | 181.5 | 20.6 | 45.2 | 28.1 | 32.6 | 64.5 |
| **Manufactured goods** | 64.0 | 91.6 | 94.5 | 105.7 | 153.3 | 17.9 | 44.1 | 25.5 | 30.2 | 43.3 |
| Food products | 0.3 | 0.1 | 0.1 | 1.1 | 0.8 | ..... | ..... | ..... | ..... | ..... |
| Tobacco products | ..... | ..... | ..... | ..... | ..... | ..... | ..... | ..... | ..... | ..... |
| Textile mill products | ..... | 0.1 | 0.3 | 0.2 | 0.1 | ..... | ..... | 0.1 | 0.1 | ..... |
| Apparel | 0.3 | 0.5 | 0.6 | 2.0 | 3.4 | ..... | 0.1 | 0.2 | 0.2 | 0.9 |
| Lumber and wood products | 0.1 | ..... | 0.1 | 0.1 | 0.1 | ..... | ..... | ..... | ..... | ..... |
| Furniture and fixtures | 0.3 | 0.2 | 0.2 | 0.2 | 0.5 | ..... | ..... | ..... | 0.1 | 0.1 |
| Paper products | 0.1 | 0.2 | 0.1 | 0.2 | 0.1 | ..... | 0.1 | 0.1 | 0.1 | ..... |
| Printing and publishing | 0.2 | 0.3 | 0.5 | 0.8 | 1.0 | 0.1 | 0.1 | 0.1 | 0.6 | 0.6 |
| Chemical products | 0.6 | 0.5 | 0.8 | 1.4 | 2.5 | 0.1 | ..... | 0.2 | 0.3 | 0.3 |
| Refined petroleum products | ..... | ..... | ..... | ..... | ..... | ..... | ..... | ..... | ..... | ..... |
| Rubber and plastic products | 0.7 | 1.4 | 1.2 | 1.3 | 1.4 | 0.2 | 0.4 | 0.5 | 0.8 | 0.4 |
| Leather products | ..... | 0.1 | 0.2 | 0.1 | 0.5 | ..... | ..... | ..... | ..... | 0.1 |
| Stone, clay and glass products | 0.7 | 0.8 | 0.9 | 0.9 | 0.9 | 0.1 | 0.2 | ..... | ..... | 0.2 |
| Primary metals | 1.6 | 21.3 | 2.4 | 3.0 | 15.9 | 0.1 | 20.2 | 0.8 | 1.0 | 10.3 |
| Fabricated metal products | 1.0 | 1.7 | 1.6 | 3.0 | 3.4 | ..... | 0.1 | 0.4 | 1.7 | 1.4 |
| Industrial machinery and computers | 7.8 | 13.8 | 15.1 | 19.4 | 20.7 | 3.5 | 4.3 | 5.7 | 5.9 | 6.9 |
| Electric and electronic equipment | 4.4 | 9.5 | 10.9 | 11.2 | 14.0 | 0.8 | 3.4 | 3.1 | 2.7 | 3.4 |
| Transportation equipment | 5.9 | 5.0 | 5.5 | 10.0 | 23.4 | 3.9 | 3.3 | 2.5 | 3.1 | 4.4 |
| Scientific and measuring instruments | 23.2 | 18.0 | 35.2 | 23.1 | 30.1 | 7.3 | 9.3 | 10.1 | 11.3 | 11.0 |
| Miscellaneous manufactures | 16.3 | 17.6 | 18.0 | 26.9 | 33.4 | 1.4 | 2.5 | 1.5 | 2.2 | 2.0 |
| Unidentified manufactures | 0.6 | 0.5 | 0.7 | 0.6 | 1.3 | 0.2 | 0.1 | 0.3 | 0.1 | 1.1 |
| **Agricultural and livestock products** | ..... | ..... | 0.2 | 0.1 | ..... | ..... | ..... | ..... | 0.1 | ..... |
| Agricultural products | ..... | ..... | 0.2 | ..... | ..... | ..... | ..... | ..... | ..... | ..... |
| Livestock and livestock products | ..... | ..... | ..... | 0.1 | ..... | ..... | ..... | ..... | 0.1 | ..... |
| **Other commodities** | 7.8 | 5.7 | 8.8 | 8.4 | 28.2 | 2.6 | 1.1 | 2.5 | 2.3 | 21.2 |
| Forestry products | ..... | ..... | ..... | ..... | ..... | ..... | ..... | ..... | ..... | ..... |
| Fish and other marine products | ..... | ..... | ..... | ..... | ..... | ..... | ..... | ..... | ..... | ..... |
| Metallic ores and concentrates | ..... | ..... | ..... | ..... | ..... | ..... | ..... | ..... | ..... | ..... |
| Bituminous coal and lignite | ..... | ..... | ..... | ..... | ..... | ..... | ..... | ..... | ..... | ..... |
| Crude petroleum and natural gas | ..... | ..... | ..... | ..... | ..... | ..... | ..... | ..... | ..... | ..... |
| Nonmetallic minerals | 5.7 | 5.4 | 6.7 | 6.4 | 6.8 | 0.8 | 1.0 | 1.2 | 0.9 | 0.8 |
| Scrap and waste | 0.1 | ..... | ..... | ..... | ..... | ..... | ..... | ..... | ..... | ..... |
| Used merchandise | 1.9 | 0.2 | 2.1 | 1.7 | 20.6 | 1.8 | 0.1 | 1.3 | 1.3 | 20.3 |
| Goods imported and returned unchanged | ..... | ..... | ..... | ..... | ..... | ..... | ..... | ..... | ..... | ..... |
| Special classification provisions | ..... | 0.1 | 0.1 | 0.3 | 0.7 | ..... | ..... | ..... | 0.2 | 0.1 |

## Table D-3.   State Exports of Goods by Destination and Industry, 1993–1997 —*Continued*

**NEVADA** (Millions of dollars.)

| Industry | 1993 | 1994 | 1995 | 1996 | 1997 | 1993 | 1994 | 1995 | 1996 | 1997 |
|---|---|---|---|---|---|---|---|---|---|---|
| | Germany | | | | | France | | | | |
| **ALL GOODS** | 9.9 | 12.6 | 19.7 | 22.1 | 20.2 | 14.1 | 14.7 | 12.1 | 18.0 | 24.1 |
| **Manufactured goods** | 8.0 | 11.0 | 16.0 | 19.7 | 18.2 | 11.4 | 12.5 | 9.9 | 15.7 | 23.8 |
| Food products | 0.2 | 0.1 | ..... | ..... | 0.4 | 0.2 | ..... | ..... | ..... | ..... |
| Tobacco products | ..... | ..... | ..... | ..... | ..... | ..... | ..... | ..... | ..... | ..... |
| Textile mill products | ..... | ..... | ..... | ..... | ..... | ..... | ..... | ..... | ..... | ..... |
| Apparel | 0.1 | 0.2 | 0.1 | 0.2 | 0.1 | ..... | 0.1 | 0.1 | 0.3 | 0.1 |
| Lumber and wood products | ..... | ..... | ..... | ..... | ..... | ..... | ..... | ..... | ..... | ..... |
| Furniture and fixtures | 0.1 | 0.1 | ..... | ..... | ..... | ..... | 0.1 | 0.1 | ..... | 0.2 |
| Paper products | ..... | ..... | ..... | ..... | ..... | ..... | ..... | ..... | ..... | ..... |
| Printing and publishing | ..... | 0.1 | 0.3 | 0.1 | 0.2 | ..... | ..... | ..... | ..... | ..... |
| Chemical products | 0.1 | ..... | ..... | 0.1 | 0.1 | 0.4 | 0.3 | 0.4 | 0.4 | 0.4 |
| Refined petroleum products | ..... | ..... | ..... | ..... | ..... | ..... | ..... | ..... | ..... | ..... |
| Rubber and plastic products | ..... | ..... | 0.1 | 0.2 | 0.3 | ..... | ..... | ..... | 0.1 | 0.1 |
| Leather products | ..... | ..... | ..... | ..... | ..... | ..... | ..... | ..... | ..... | ..... |
| Stone, clay and glass products | 0.1 | 0.2 | 0.2 | 0.3 | 0.5 | 0.2 | 0.2 | 0.1 | 0.1 | 0.1 |
| Primary metals | 0.4 | 0.1 | 0.2 | 0.4 | 1.4 | 0.1 | 0.3 | 0.4 | 0.7 | 0.3 |
| Fabricated metal products | 0.2 | 0.2 | 0.2 | 0.6 | 0.6 | ..... | 0.4 | 0.2 | 0.1 | 0.2 |
| Industrial machinery and computers | 1.3 | 1.9 | 4.6 | 1.6 | 1.9 | 0.8 | 4.0 | 1.0 | 2.9 | 1.5 |
| Electric and electronic equipment | 0.9 | 1.1 | 2.0 | 2.3 | 1.6 | 1.2 | 0.8 | 0.8 | 1.3 | 0.9 |
| Transportation equipment | 0.6 | 0.9 | 0.7 | 0.7 | 1.2 | 1.1 | 0.5 | 1.6 | 5.6 | 7.9 |
| Scientific and measuring instruments | 2.0 | 3.0 | 4.4 | 4.1 | 5.2 | 1.4 | 1.0 | 1.3 | 1.5 | 3.5 |
| Miscellaneous manufactures | 1.8 | 2.8 | 3.0 | 8.4 | 4.8 | 6.2 | 4.8 | 3.8 | 2.7 | 8.5 |
| Unidentified manufactures | 0.1 | 0.1 | 0.1 | 0.1 | 0.1 | ..... | 0.1 | 0.1 | 0.1 | ..... |
| **Agricultural and livestock products** | ..... | ..... | ..... | ..... | ..... | ..... | ..... | ..... | ..... | ..... |
| Agricultural products | ..... | ..... | ..... | ..... | ..... | ..... | ..... | ..... | ..... | ..... |
| Livestock and livestock products | ..... | ..... | ..... | ..... | ..... | ..... | ..... | ..... | ..... | ..... |
| **Other commodities** | 1.9 | 1.6 | 3.7 | 2.5 | 2.0 | 2.6 | 2.2 | 2.2 | 2.3 | 0.3 |
| Forestry products | ..... | ..... | ..... | ..... | ..... | ..... | ..... | ..... | ..... | ..... |
| Fish and other marine products | ..... | ..... | ..... | ..... | ..... | ..... | ..... | ..... | ..... | ..... |
| Metallic ores and concentrates | ..... | ..... | ..... | ..... | ..... | ..... | ..... | ..... | ..... | ..... |
| Bituminous coal and lignite | ..... | ..... | ..... | ..... | ..... | ..... | ..... | ..... | ..... | ..... |
| Crude petroleum and natural gas | ..... | ..... | ..... | ..... | ..... | ..... | ..... | ..... | ..... | ..... |
| Nonmetallic minerals | 1.7 | 1.5 | 2.9 | 2.3 | 1.8 | 2.6 | 2.2 | 2.2 | 2.3 | 0.1 |
| Scrap and waste | 0.1 | ..... | ..... | ..... | ..... | ..... | ..... | ..... | ..... | ..... |
| Used merchandise | 0.1 | 0.1 | 0.8 | 0.1 | ..... | ..... | ..... | ..... | ..... | ..... |
| Goods imported and returned unchanged | ..... | ..... | ..... | ..... | ..... | ..... | ..... | ..... | ..... | ..... |
| Special classification provisions | ..... | ..... | ..... | 0.1 | 0.1 | ..... | ..... | ..... | 0.1 | 0.2 |

| Industry | 1993 | 1994 | 1995 | 1996 | 1997 | 1993 | 1994 | 1995 | 1996 | 1997 |
|---|---|---|---|---|---|---|---|---|---|---|
| | The Netherlands | | | | | Asian 10 | | | | |
| **ALL GOODS** | 7.6 | 10.3 | 9.1 | 13.4 | 17.2 | 82.5 | 109.7 | 269.3 | 176.6 | 197.0 |
| **Manufactured goods** | 7.6 | 10.3 | 9.0 | 13.1 | 16.6 | 76.1 | 99.9 | 251.8 | 156.6 | 182.8 |
| Food products | ..... | ..... | ..... | ..... | 0.2 | 0.4 | 0.9 | 6.4 | 8.9 | 1.9 |
| Tobacco products | ..... | ..... | ..... | ..... | ..... | ..... | ..... | ..... | ..... | ..... |
| Textile mill products | ..... | 0.1 | 0.1 | 0.1 | ..... | 0.2 | 0.5 | 0.5 | 0.5 | 0.7 |
| Apparel | ..... | ..... | ..... | ..... | ..... | 0.5 | 1.7 | 8.4 | 7.5 | 6.7 |
| Lumber and wood products | ..... | ..... | ..... | ..... | ..... | 0.1 | 0.1 | ..... | 0.3 | 0.5 |
| Furniture and fixtures | 0.1 | ..... | ..... | ..... | ..... | 0.3 | 0.1 | 0.7 | 1.3 | 0.1 |
| Paper products | ..... | 0.1 | ..... | ..... | ..... | 0.5 | 0.5 | 0.3 | 0.7 | 0.9 |
| Printing and publishing | ..... | 0.1 | ..... | 0.1 | ..... | 1.4 | 1.1 | 1.9 | 1.0 | 1.5 |
| Chemical products | 0.1 | 0.1 | 0.1 | 0.1 | 0.1 | 1.1 | 2.7 | 12.2 | 11.3 | 2.6 |
| Refined petroleum products | ..... | ..... | ..... | ..... | ..... | 0.2 | 0.1 | 0.1 | 0.1 | 0.2 |
| Rubber and plastic products | 0.2 | 0.8 | 0.1 | 0.1 | 0.1 | 2.6 | 2.5 | 3.3 | 5.3 | 13.5 |
| Leather products | ..... | ..... | ..... | ..... | 0.1 | 0.1 | 0.4 | 2.5 | 3.7 | 1.7 |
| Stone, clay and glass products | ..... | 0.1 | 0.3 | 0.3 | ..... | 1.1 | 1.6 | 0.9 | 1.7 | 2.5 |
| Primary metals | ..... | ..... | 0.1 | 0.1 | ..... | 3.5 | 4.1 | 9.3 | 5.1 | 7.2 |
| Fabricated metal products | 0.6 | 0.7 | 0.2 | 0.3 | 0.1 | 3.7 | 16.1 | 51.8 | 4.2 | 11.5 |
| Industrial machinery and computers | 0.3 | 1.8 | 0.4 | 0.3 | 1.3 | 19.2 | 22.3 | 70.2 | 31.1 | 46.3 |
| Electric and electronic equipment | 0.4 | 0.6 | 1.3 | 1.2 | 2.3 | 10.4 | 10.5 | 30.5 | 21.3 | 28.2 |
| Transportation equipment | ..... | 0.2 | 0.3 | 0.3 | 0.8 | 2.4 | 3.1 | 3.8 | 5.7 | 9.1 |
| Scientific and measuring instruments | 1.3 | 1.4 | 1.7 | 1.7 | 3.2 | 12.9 | 14.5 | 19.8 | 21.7 | 27.8 |
| Miscellaneous manufactures | 4.5 | 4.4 | 4.3 | 8.4 | 8.2 | 14.7 | 16.8 | 28.8 | 24.7 | 19.6 |
| Unidentified manufactures | ..... | 0.1 | ..... | ..... | ..... | 0.5 | 0.3 | 0.4 | 0.6 | 0.4 |
| **Agricultural and livestock products** | ..... | ..... | 0.1 | ..... | ..... | 0.8 | 1.8 | 1.4 | 0.8 | 1.0 |
| Agricultural products | ..... | ..... | 0.1 | ..... | ..... | 0.1 | 1.4 | 0.5 | 0.8 | 0.3 |
| Livestock and livestock products | ..... | ..... | ..... | ..... | ..... | 0.8 | 0.4 | 0.9 | ..... | 0.7 |
| **Other commodities** | ..... | ..... | ..... | 0.3 | 0.5 | 5.7 | 8.0 | 16.1 | 19.2 | 13.1 |
| Forestry products | ..... | ..... | ..... | ..... | ..... | ..... | 0.1 | 0.1 | ..... | 0.1 |
| Fish and other marine products | ..... | ..... | ..... | ..... | ..... | 0.2 | 0.1 | ..... | 0.4 | ..... |
| Metallic ores and concentrates | ..... | ..... | ..... | ..... | ..... | ..... | ..... | ..... | ..... | ..... |
| Bituminous coal and lignite | ..... | ..... | ..... | ..... | ..... | ..... | ..... | ..... | ..... | ..... |
| Crude petroleum and natural gas | ..... | ..... | ..... | ..... | ..... | ..... | ..... | ..... | ..... | ..... |
| Nonmetallic minerals | ..... | ..... | ..... | ..... | 0.1 | 2.4 | 2.6 | 2.9 | 3.5 | 3.7 |
| Scrap and waste | ..... | ..... | ..... | ..... | ..... | 0.2 | 0.3 | 0.8 | 0.7 | 0.4 |
| Used merchandise | ..... | ..... | ..... | ..... | 0.3 | 2.8 | 4.8 | 11.9 | 14.5 | 8.4 |
| Goods imported and returned unchanged | ..... | ..... | ..... | ..... | ..... | ..... | ..... | ..... | ..... | ..... |
| Special classification provisions | ..... | ..... | ..... | ..... | 0.1 | ..... | ..... | 0.4 | 0.2 | 0.6 |

## Table D-3.  State Exports of Goods by Destination and Industry, 1993–1997 —Continued

**NEVADA** (Millions of dollars.)

| Industry | 1993 | 1994 | 1995 | 1996 | 1997 | 1993 | 1994 | 1995 | 1996 | 1997 |
|---|---|---|---|---|---|---|---|---|---|---|
| | Japan | | | | | South Korea | | | | |
| **ALL GOODS** | 26.6 | 34.6 | 82.6 | 77.7 | 82.9 | 7.4 | 11.0 | 13.3 | 24.7 | 21.8 |
| **Manufactured goods** | 23.5 | 28.4 | 69.8 | 62.4 | 72.8 | 6.0 | 10.3 | 12.0 | 24.3 | 21.4 |
| Food products | 0.3 | 0.7 | 0.2 | 0.6 | 0.2 | ..... | 0.1 | 0.3 | 0.8 | ..... |
| Tobacco products | ..... | ..... | ..... | ..... | ..... | ..... | ..... | ..... | ..... | ..... |
| Textile mill products | ..... | 0.1 | 0.4 | 0.3 | 0.4 | ..... | ..... | ..... | ..... | 0.1 |
| Apparel | 0.4 | 1.5 | 7.6 | 7.1 | 5.9 | ..... | ..... | 0.1 | 0.2 | 0.3 |
| Lumber and wood products | 0.1 | ..... | ..... | 0.2 | 0.4 | ..... | ..... | ..... | 0.1 | ..... |
| Furniture and fixtures | ..... | 0.1 | 0.6 | 0.2 | ..... | 0.2 | ..... | ..... | ..... | ..... |
| Paper products | 0.1 | 0.3 | 0.1 | 0.2 | 0.1 | 0.1 | ..... | 0.1 | 0.1 | 0.7 |
| Printing and publishing | 1.2 | 0.7 | 1.5 | 0.6 | 0.4 | ..... | 0.1 | ..... | ..... | ..... |
| Chemical products | 0.2 | 0.3 | 8.3 | 5.7 | 0.9 | 0.1 | 0.5 | 0.3 | 0.4 | 0.4 |
| Refined petroleum products | ..... | ..... | ..... | ..... | ..... | ..... | ..... | ..... | ..... | ..... |
| Rubber and plastic products | 0.6 | 0.9 | 0.8 | 0.2 | 1.3 | 0.4 | 0.2 | 0.2 | 0.2 | 0.2 |
| Leather products | 0.1 | 0.3 | 2.3 | 3.4 | 1.5 | ..... | ..... | 0.1 | 0.1 | ..... |
| Stone, clay and glass products | 0.8 | 0.7 | 0.6 | 1.0 | 1.9 | 0.1 | 0.1 | ..... | 0.1 | 0.3 |
| Primary metals | 0.1 | 0.2 | 1.0 | 1.7 | 1.1 | 0.2 | 0.2 | 0.3 | 0.9 | 3.0 |
| Fabricated metal products | 0.7 | 0.7 | 0.8 | 0.8 | 3.3 | 0.2 | 0.2 | 0.3 | 0.2 | 0.8 |
| Industrial machinery and computers | 1.7 | 4.7 | 5.9 | 8.9 | 20.1 | 1.6 | 3.7 | 3.1 | 8.8 | 4.8 |
| Electric and electronic equipment | 1.1 | 2.5 | 5.3 | 5.5 | 4.5 | 0.3 | 0.2 | 1.3 | 6.3 | 5.0 |
| Transportation equipment | 1.8 | 2.2 | 3.1 | 3.6 | 8.0 | ..... | 0.1 | ..... | 0.6 | 0.1 |
| Scientific and measuring instruments | 2.4 | 4.0 | 7.6 | 5.4 | 8.9 | 2.1 | 2.7 | 4.2 | 3.7 | 5.0 |
| Miscellaneous manufactures | 11.7 | 8.5 | 23.4 | 16.8 | 13.7 | 0.6 | 2.1 | 1.5 | 1.7 | 0.6 |
| Unidentified manufactures | 0.2 | 0.1 | 0.2 | 0.2 | 0.2 | ..... | ..... | 0.1 | 0.1 | 0.1 |
| **Agricultural and livestock products** | ..... | 1.3 | 0.3 | ..... | 0.7 | 0.8 | 0.4 | 0.9 | 0.3 | 0.3 |
| Agricultural products | ..... | 1.3 | 0.3 | ..... | 0.3 | ..... | ..... | 0.1 | 0.3 | ..... |
| Livestock and livestock products | ..... | ..... | ..... | ..... | 0.4 | 0.8 | 0.4 | 0.9 | ..... | 0.3 |
| **Other commodities** | 3.1 | 4.9 | 12.6 | 15.2 | 9.4 | 0.6 | 0.3 | 0.3 | 0.2 | 0.1 |
| Forestry products | ..... | ..... | ..... | ..... | ..... | ..... | 0.1 | 0.1 | ..... | ..... |
| Fish and other marine products | ..... | 0.1 | ..... | 0.1 | ..... | ..... | ..... | ..... | ..... | ..... |
| Metallic ores and concentrates | ..... | ..... | ..... | ..... | ..... | ..... | ..... | ..... | ..... | ..... |
| Bituminous coal and lignite | ..... | ..... | ..... | ..... | ..... | ..... | ..... | ..... | ..... | ..... |
| Crude petroleum and natural gas | ..... | ..... | ..... | ..... | ..... | ..... | ..... | ..... | ..... | ..... |
| Nonmetallic minerals | 0.8 | 1.0 | 1.1 | 1.3 | 1.4 | 0.2 | 0.3 | 0.2 | 0.1 | ..... |
| Scrap and waste | ..... | ..... | 0.2 | ..... | ..... | ..... | ..... | ..... | ..... | ..... |
| Used merchandise | 2.2 | 3.7 | 10.9 | 13.7 | 7.5 | 0.4 | ..... | ..... | ..... | ..... |
| Goods imported and returned unchanged | ..... | ..... | ..... | ..... | ..... | ..... | ..... | ..... | ..... | ..... |
| Special classification provisions | ..... | ..... | 0.3 | 0.1 | 0.5 | ..... | ..... | ..... | ..... | 0.1 |
| | Taiwan | | | | | Singapore | | | | |
| **ALL GOODS** | 5.8 | 7.6 | 8.5 | 13.6 | 10.6 | 5.2 | 5.9 | 7.0 | 7.4 | 10.6 |
| **Manufactured goods** | 5.1 | 7.0 | 8.0 | 12.5 | 9.8 | 5.1 | 5.6 | 6.6 | 7.1 | 10.0 |
| Food products | ..... | ..... | 0.7 | 2.7 | ..... | ..... | ..... | 1.8 | ..... | ..... |
| Tobacco products | ..... | ..... | ..... | ..... | ..... | ..... | ..... | ..... | ..... | ..... |
| Textile mill products | ..... | ..... | ..... | ..... | ..... | ..... | ..... | ..... | ..... | ..... |
| Apparel | ..... | ..... | ..... | ..... | ..... | 0.1 | ..... | ..... | 0.1 | 0.3 |
| Lumber and wood products | ..... | ..... | ..... | ..... | ..... | ..... | ..... | ..... | ..... | ..... |
| Furniture and fixtures | ..... | ..... | ..... | ..... | ..... | ..... | ..... | ..... | ..... | ..... |
| Paper products | ..... | ..... | ..... | ..... | ..... | 0.2 | 0.1 | ..... | 0.1 | ..... |
| Printing and publishing | ..... | ..... | ..... | 0.1 | ..... | 0.1 | ..... | 0.1 | ..... | 0.7 |
| Chemical products | 0.1 | 0.9 | 0.4 | 0.3 | 0.1 | 0.4 | 0.2 | 0.5 | 0.3 | 0.2 |
| Refined petroleum products | 0.1 | ..... | ..... | ..... | ..... | ..... | ..... | ..... | ..... | ..... |
| Rubber and plastic products | 0.3 | ..... | ..... | 0.1 | ..... | 0.3 | 0.1 | 0.1 | 0.2 | ..... |
| Leather products | ..... | ..... | ..... | ..... | ..... | ..... | ..... | 0.1 | ..... | 0.1 |
| Stone, clay and glass products | 0.1 | ..... | 0.2 | 0.1 | ..... | ..... | ..... | ..... | ..... | 0.1 |
| Primary metals | 0.8 | 1.1 | 1.0 | 1.0 | 1.6 | 0.4 | 0.4 | 0.1 | 0.5 | 0.4 |
| Fabricated metal products | ..... | 0.4 | 0.6 | 0.3 | 0.2 | 0.3 | 0.6 | 0.3 | 0.6 | 0.4 |
| Industrial machinery and computers | 0.6 | 1.4 | 1.7 | 4.6 | 1.1 | 1.1 | 1.3 | 0.8 | 1.6 | 2.1 |
| Electric and electronic equipment | 0.6 | 0.7 | 0.6 | 0.3 | 0.9 | 0.5 | 0.9 | 0.7 | 0.6 | 1.9 |
| Transportation equipment | ..... | 0.1 | ..... | 0.1 | 0.1 | ..... | 0.2 | 0.3 | 0.3 | 0.2 |
| Scientific and measuring instruments | 1.8 | 1.0 | 1.6 | 2.1 | 5.0 | 0.9 | 0.7 | 1.1 | 1.2 | 1.7 |
| Miscellaneous manufactures | 0.4 | 1.3 | 1.0 | 0.5 | 0.6 | 0.6 | 0.9 | 0.7 | 1.5 | 1.8 |
| Unidentified manufactures | ..... | ..... | ..... | ..... | ..... | 0.2 | 0.1 | ..... | ..... | ..... |
| **Agricultural and livestock products** | ..... | ..... | ..... | 0.1 | ..... | ..... | ..... | ..... | ..... | ..... |
| Agricultural products | ..... | ..... | ..... | 0.1 | ..... | ..... | ..... | ..... | ..... | ..... |
| Livestock and livestock products | ..... | ..... | ..... | ..... | ..... | ..... | ..... | ..... | ..... | ..... |
| **Other commodities** | 0.7 | 0.6 | 0.5 | 1.0 | 0.7 | 0.1 | 0.3 | 0.5 | 0.4 | 0.6 |
| Forestry products | ..... | ..... | ..... | ..... | ..... | ..... | ..... | ..... | ..... | ..... |
| Fish and other marine products | 0.2 | ..... | ..... | 0.3 | ..... | ..... | ..... | ..... | ..... | ..... |
| Metallic ores and concentrates | ..... | ..... | ..... | ..... | ..... | ..... | ..... | ..... | ..... | ..... |
| Bituminous coal and lignite | ..... | ..... | ..... | ..... | ..... | ..... | ..... | ..... | ..... | ..... |
| Crude petroleum and natural gas | ..... | ..... | ..... | ..... | ..... | ..... | ..... | ..... | ..... | ..... |
| Nonmetallic minerals | 0.5 | 0.4 | 0.4 | 0.7 | 0.4 | ..... | 0.1 | 0.1 | 0.1 | ..... |
| Scrap and waste | ..... | 0.1 | ..... | ..... | 0.2 | ..... | ..... | ..... | 0.1 | 0.1 |
| Used merchandise | ..... | ..... | ..... | 0.1 | 0.1 | 0.1 | 0.1 | 0.3 | 0.3 | 0.4 |
| Goods imported and returned unchanged | ..... | ..... | ..... | ..... | ..... | ..... | ..... | ..... | ..... | ..... |
| Special classification provisions | ..... | ..... | ..... | ..... | ..... | ..... | ..... | ..... | ..... | ..... |

## NEW HAMPSHIRE: Exports of Goods, 1997

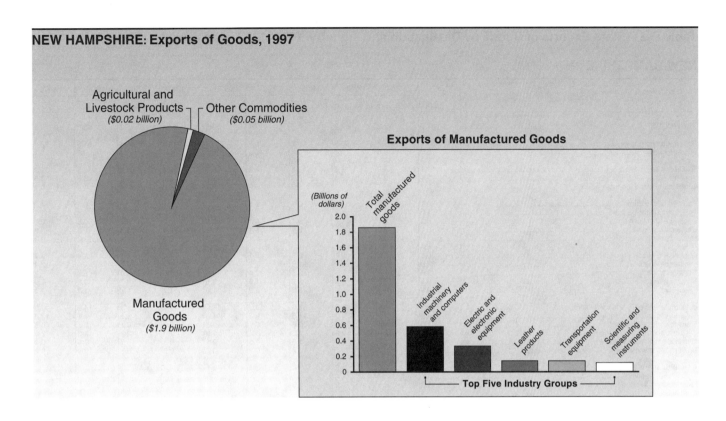

## Table D-3. State Exports of Goods by Destination and Industry, 1993–1997 —Continued

### NEW HAMPSHIRE (Millions of dollars.)

| Industry | 1993 | 1994 | 1995 | 1996 | 1997 | 1993 | 1994 | 1995 | 1996 | 1997 |
|---|---|---|---|---|---|---|---|---|---|---|
| | All destinations | | | | | Canada | | | | |
| **ALL GOODS** | 1 134.9 | 1 247.9 | 1 478.6 | 1 744.9 | 1 931.0 | 377.2 | 422.4 | 494.4 | 642.4 | 672.2 |
| **Manufactured goods** | 1 094.2 | 1 198.3 | 1 419.7 | 1 674.4 | 1 859.3 | 358.7 | 399.4 | 465.8 | 609.1 | 639.9 |
| Food products | 7.1 | 5.9 | 7.9 | 18.5 | 33.9 | 5.0 | 3.6 | 4.5 | 3.5 | 15.2 |
| Tobacco products | ..... | 0.1 | ..... | ..... | ..... | ..... | 0.1 | ..... | ..... | ..... |
| Textile mill products | 14.1 | 20.7 | 26.3 | 28.1 | 29.4 | 7.8 | 8.2 | 9.5 | 9.2 | 11.8 |
| Apparel | 16.7 | 16.8 | 15.3 | 12.8 | 13.8 | 2.8 | 2.0 | 2.3 | 2.4 | 3.4 |
| Lumber and wood products | 44.3 | 43.5 | 49.2 | 45.5 | 64.6 | 24.7 | 21.3 | 24.3 | 26.3 | 32.1 |
| Furniture and fixtures | 1.0 | 2.2 | 6.4 | 3.3 | 5.2 | 0.5 | 1.3 | 5.0 | 1.3 | 2.9 |
| Paper products | 20.6 | 27.5 | 40.2 | 28.3 | 38.2 | 14.4 | 19.5 | 29.8 | 22.6 | 25.1 |
| Printing and publishing | 9.5 | 7.2 | 10.3 | 11.9 | 16.1 | 2.1 | 1.9 | 2.8 | 4.7 | 8.3 |
| Chemical products | 51.6 | 86.8 | 60.4 | 49.1 | 89.5 | 28.2 | 30.1 | 22.0 | 13.4 | 48.5 |
| Refined petroleum products | 3.4 | 4.6 | 2.1 | 2.0 | 3.2 | 2.7 | 3.9 | 1.1 | 1.3 | 1.5 |
| Rubber and plastic products | 27.8 | 45.7 | 57.0 | 63.6 | 65.4 | 13.3 | 19.6 | 26.0 | 29.7 | 34.7 |
| Leather products | 65.0 | 64.4 | 69.5 | 145.0 | 143.6 | 6.9 | 5.5 | 6.5 | 8.1 | 10.6 |
| Stone, clay and glass products | 29.3 | 31.2 | 34.2 | 45.6 | 50.0 | 3.1 | 3.6 | 3.6 | 4.0 | 4.7 |
| Primary metals | 15.2 | 22.6 | 22.7 | 31.0 | 24.6 | 9.3 | 12.6 | 11.2 | 10.4 | 9.9 |
| Fabricated metal products | 49.0 | 43.0 | 50.0 | 60.8 | 72.3 | 18.9 | 13.3 | 14.3 | 16.2 | 20.9 |
| Industrial machinery and computers | 457.9 | 424.5 | 493.0 | 550.0 | 583.5 | 148.3 | 119.8 | 88.0 | 144.7 | 116.5 |
| Electric and electronic equipment | 120.9 | 160.7 | 232.3 | 265.2 | 332.7 | 30.1 | 53.3 | 87.3 | 139.2 | 136.9 |
| Transportation equipment | 32.6 | 70.7 | 110.1 | 156.5 | 142.1 | 17.7 | 56.2 | 98.6 | 143.2 | 126.7 |
| Scientific and measuring instruments | 98.7 | 93.9 | 100.1 | 131.6 | 117.7 | 14.5 | 15.4 | 18.8 | 19.6 | 20.1 |
| Miscellaneous manufactures | 12.2 | 11.2 | 17.4 | 13.4 | 14.2 | 6.1 | 4.8 | 6.3 | 5.6 | 5.6 |
| Unidentified manufactures | 17.2 | 15.1 | 15.4 | 12.2 | 19.0 | 2.4 | 3.2 | 3.8 | 3.7 | 4.2 |
| **Agricultural and livestock products** | 12.3 | 16.8 | 19.8 | 21.3 | 23.0 | 1.3 | 1.2 | 1.8 | 2.8 | 2.7 |
| Agricultural products | 1.0 | 0.5 | 1.2 | 1.7 | 1.0 | 0.6 | 0.5 | 0.8 | 1.2 | 0.9 |
| Livestock and livestock products | 11.3 | 16.3 | 18.6 | 19.6 | 22.0 | 0.7 | 0.7 | 1.0 | 1.6 | 1.8 |
| **Other commodities** | 28.3 | 32.9 | 39.1 | 49.2 | 48.7 | 17.1 | 21.8 | 26.8 | 30.6 | 29.7 |
| Forestry products | 0.1 | ..... | ..... | 0.1 | 0.1 | ..... | ..... | ..... | ..... | ..... |
| Fish and other marine products | 7.3 | 12.9 | 16.4 | 19.1 | 17.9 | 1.3 | 4.8 | 8.1 | 4.0 | 4.7 |
| Metallic ores and concentrates | ..... | ..... | ..... | 0.1 | 0.2 | ..... | ..... | ..... | ..... | ..... |
| Bituminous coal and lignite | ..... | ..... | ..... | ..... | ..... | ..... | ..... | ..... | ..... | ..... |
| Crude petroleum and natural gas | 0.2 | ..... | 0.1 | ..... | ..... | 0.2 | ..... | 0.1 | ..... | ..... |
| Nonmetallic minerals | 0.8 | 0.8 | 1.0 | 0.9 | 1.7 | 0.1 | 0.4 | 0.3 | 0.1 | 0.4 |
| Scrap and waste | 6.4 | 8.2 | 6.5 | 4.0 | 4.7 | 4.2 | 6.5 | 6.1 | 3.7 | 4.7 |
| Used merchandise | 1.7 | 0.6 | 1.4 | 1.4 | 4.4 | 1.0 | 0.3 | 0.8 | 0.9 | 2.0 |
| Goods imported and returned unchanged | 9.5 | 9.0 | 9.7 | 19.5 | 16.8 | 9.5 | 9.0 | 9.7 | 19.5 | 16.8 |
| Special classification provisions | 2.3 | 1.3 | 4.0 | 4.2 | 2.9 | 0.8 | 0.8 | 1.7 | 2.3 | 1.1 |

## Table D-3.　State Exports of Goods by Destination and Industry, 1993–1997 —Continued

**NEW HAMPSHIRE** (Millions of dollars.)

| Industry | 1993 | 1994 | 1995 | 1996 | 1997 | 1993 | 1994 | 1995 | 1996 | 1997 |
|---|---|---|---|---|---|---|---|---|---|---|
| | South and Central America and Caribbean | | | | | Mexico | | | | |
| **ALL GOODS** | 87.0 | 92.3 | 97.3 | 92.7 | 117.1 | 39.6 | 43.4 | 45.2 | 63.6 | 73.8 |
| **Manufactured goods** | 81.1 | 85.8 | 90.3 | 86.2 | 108.3 | 38.1 | 42.4 | 44.3 | 61.9 | 72.1 |
| Food products | 0.7 | 0.6 | 0.4 | 0.3 | 2.6 | 0.1 | 0.1 | ..... | 9.7 | 5.7 |
| Tobacco products | ..... | ..... | ..... | ..... | ..... | ..... | ..... | ..... | ..... | ..... |
| Textile mill products | 1.1 | 5.9 | 3.3 | 3.5 | 3.6 | 0.9 | 0.8 | 1.5 | 3.2 | 3.6 |
| Apparel | 2.1 | 2.7 | 3.4 | 2.3 | 1.9 | 3.8 | 3.5 | 3.6 | 3.8 | 3.6 |
| Lumber and wood products | 0.1 | ..... | 0.1 | 0.3 | 0.7 | 0.1 | ..... | ..... | ..... | 0.1 |
| Furniture and fixtures | 0.1 | 0.2 | ..... | 0.3 | 0.1 | ..... | ..... | ..... | 0.1 | ..... |
| Paper products | 1.0 | 2.7 | 1.8 | 0.6 | 1.9 | 1.0 | 0.8 | 2.1 | 1.5 | 1.8 |
| Printing and publishing | 0.2 | 0.1 | 1.0 | 0.1 | 0.4 | 0.6 | 0.3 | 0.5 | 0.6 | 0.6 |
| Chemical products | 0.6 | 2.0 | 2.0 | 3.6 | 4.1 | 4.5 | 6.5 | 6.3 | 4.9 | 5.9 |
| Refined petroleum products | ..... | 0.1 | ..... | ..... | 0.1 | 0.5 | 0.3 | 0.6 | 0.2 | 0.3 |
| Rubber and plastic products | 0.8 | 2.3 | 2.1 | 2.8 | 5.1 | 1.1 | 1.4 | 1.7 | 2.6 | 3.4 |
| Leather products | 33.9 | 30.1 | 20.9 | 21.8 | 27.7 | 0.2 | 0.1 | 0.2 | 2.0 | 2.9 |
| Stone, clay and glass products | 2.6 | 2.2 | 2.6 | 2.6 | 2.4 | 2.9 | 3.5 | 2.4 | 5.3 | 8.2 |
| Primary metals | 0.6 | 0.2 | 0.4 | 2.2 | 1.6 | 0.5 | 1.3 | 0.7 | 0.8 | 1.0 |
| Fabricated metal products | 2.3 | 0.9 | 1.0 | 0.5 | 1.9 | 1.0 | 1.7 | 1.7 | 1.1 | 2.1 |
| Industrial machinery and computers | 22.8 | 23.0 | 38.3 | 26.6 | 30.5 | 14.5 | 14.2 | 12.3 | 14.2 | 16.9 |
| Electric and electronic equipment | 6.5 | 7.9 | 7.0 | 14.5 | 18.3 | 4.6 | 6.2 | 8.1 | 7.7 | 12.2 |
| Transportation equipment | 2.5 | 0.4 | 0.3 | 0.6 | 0.9 | 0.5 | 0.2 | 0.1 | 0.3 | 0.3 |
| Scientific and measuring instruments | 2.5 | 2.9 | 2.8 | 2.3 | 3.1 | 1.0 | 1.0 | 2.2 | 3.0 | 2.8 |
| Miscellaneous manufactures | 0.2 | 1.2 | 2.7 | 1.3 | 1.0 | 0.1 | 0.1 | 0.2 | 0.6 | 0.4 |
| Unidentified manufactures | 0.3 | 0.3 | 0.2 | 0.2 | 0.2 | 0.2 | 0.3 | 0.1 | 0.4 | 0.3 |
| **Agricultural and livestock products** | 5.8 | 6.5 | 7.0 | 6.4 | 8.1 | 0.1 | ..... | ..... | ..... | ..... |
| Agricultural products | ..... | ..... | ..... | ..... | ..... | ..... | ..... | ..... | ..... | ..... |
| Livestock and livestock products | 5.8 | 6.5 | 7.0 | 6.3 | 8.1 | ..... | ..... | ..... | ..... | ..... |
| **Other commodities** | ..... | 0.1 | 0.1 | 0.1 | 0.8 | 1.5 | 0.9 | 0.9 | 1.7 | 1.6 |
| Forestry products | ..... | ..... | ..... | ..... | ..... | ..... | ..... | ..... | ..... | ..... |
| Fish and other marine products | ..... | ..... | ..... | ..... | ..... | 0.6 | 0.5 | 0.2 | 0.5 | 0.3 |
| Metallic ores and concentrates | ..... | ..... | ..... | ..... | ..... | ..... | ..... | ..... | ..... | ..... |
| Bituminous coal and lignite | ..... | ..... | ..... | ..... | ..... | ..... | ..... | ..... | ..... | ..... |
| Crude petroleum and natural gas | ..... | ..... | ..... | ..... | ..... | ..... | ..... | ..... | ..... | ..... |
| Nonmetallic minerals | ..... | ..... | ..... | ..... | ..... | 0.7 | 0.4 | 0.6 | 0.6 | 1.2 |
| Scrap and waste | ..... | ..... | ..... | ..... | ..... | 0.1 | ..... | ..... | ..... | ..... |
| Used merchandise | ..... | ..... | 0.1 | 0.1 | 0.4 | 0.1 | ..... | ..... | ..... | 0.1 |
| Goods imported and returned unchanged | ..... | ..... | ..... | ..... | ..... | ..... | ..... | ..... | ..... | ..... |
| Special classification provisions | ..... | 0.1 | ..... | 0.1 | 0.4 | 0.1 | ..... | ..... | 0.5 | 0.1 |

| Industry | 1993 | 1994 | 1995 | 1996 | 1997 | 1993 | 1994 | 1995 | 1996 | 1997 |
|---|---|---|---|---|---|---|---|---|---|---|
| | European Union | | | | | United Kingdom | | | | |
| **ALL GOODS** | 315.1 | 349.8 | 459.5 | 500.3 | 580.1 | 111.5 | 95.7 | 104.7 | 102.7 | 132.5 |
| **Manufactured goods** | 306.9 | 339.7 | 448.1 | 485.3 | 562.9 | 109.7 | 94.0 | 102.9 | 100.6 | 129.4 |
| Food products | 0.5 | 0.2 | 0.5 | 0.8 | 0.8 | 0.3 | 0.1 | 0.1 | 0.4 | 0.1 |
| Tobacco products | ..... | ..... | ..... | ..... | ..... | ..... | ..... | ..... | ..... | ..... |
| Textile mill products | 2.3 | 4.2 | 6.4 | 6.3 | 5.5 | 0.7 | 1.2 | 2.3 | 2.4 | 1.6 |
| Apparel | 5.9 | 5.5 | 3.9 | 2.8 | 2.6 | 1.0 | 0.6 | 0.6 | 0.2 | 0.3 |
| Lumber and wood products | 9.9 | 11.5 | 10.6 | 7.6 | 15.4 | 5.2 | 6.0 | 5.1 | 4.1 | 9.6 |
| Furniture and fixtures | 0.2 | 0.4 | 0.7 | 0.7 | 1.8 | ..... | 0.1 | 0.1 | 0.2 | 0.4 |
| Paper products | 2.0 | 3.1 | 4.8 | 2.3 | 7.6 | 0.4 | 1.2 | 2.8 | 0.6 | 4.3 |
| Printing and publishing | 1.4 | 1.5 | 2.2 | 2.9 | 2.2 | 0.7 | 0.4 | 0.9 | 1.1 | 0.6 |
| Chemical products | 7.9 | 10.2 | 12.3 | 12.2 | 14.4 | 1.4 | 1.7 | 2.2 | 2.4 | 3.7 |
| Refined petroleum products | 0.2 | 0.1 | 0.1 | ..... | 0.2 | ..... | ..... | ..... | ..... | ..... |
| Rubber and plastic products | 5.4 | 10.8 | 11.0 | 12.6 | 11.0 | 2.3 | 2.9 | 5.1 | 5.4 | 3.6 |
| Leather products | 19.6 | 18.4 | 18.0 | 35.0 | 27.3 | 3.1 | 2.4 | 5.1 | 10.8 | 7.4 |
| Stone, clay and glass products | 9.7 | 10.0 | 12.8 | 18.2 | 18.5 | 1.8 | 1.3 | 2.4 | 4.8 | 3.8 |
| Primary metals | 3.0 | 5.6 | 5.1 | 6.7 | 7.5 | 0.7 | 1.8 | 1.9 | 3.1 | 3.4 |
| Fabricated metal products | 14.3 | 15.4 | 17.9 | 28.5 | 26.7 | 3.0 | 3.4 | 3.2 | 5.1 | 4.9 |
| Industrial machinery and computers | 136.6 | 150.7 | 219.8 | 234.6 | 282.8 | 69.7 | 48.4 | 42.0 | 34.2 | 42.5 |
| Electric and electronic equipment | 40.6 | 39.2 | 56.4 | 57.9 | 78.9 | 9.7 | 11.2 | 12.9 | 16.8 | 27.3 |
| Transportation equipment | 8.2 | 7.0 | 8.6 | 8.7 | 8.6 | 0.7 | 1.1 | 3.0 | 1.4 | 1.5 |
| Scientific and measuring instruments | 28.6 | 36.6 | 43.6 | 39.6 | 44.3 | 7.4 | 8.3 | 11.6 | 6.8 | 13.2 |
| Miscellaneous manufactures | 4.2 | 3.0 | 6.7 | 2.8 | 2.8 | 0.5 | 0.6 | 0.3 | 0.2 | 0.2 |
| Unidentified manufactures | 6.4 | 6.3 | 6.6 | 5.2 | 4.2 | 1.1 | 1.2 | 1.2 | 0.6 | 0.9 |
| **Agricultural and livestock products** | 1.4 | 2.9 | 2.7 | 2.7 | 3.4 | ..... | ..... | ..... | ..... | ..... |
| Agricultural products | 0.1 | ..... | 0.1 | ..... | ..... | ..... | ..... | ..... | ..... | ..... |
| Livestock and livestock products | 1.3 | 2.9 | 2.7 | 2.7 | 3.4 | ..... | ..... | ..... | ..... | ..... |
| **Other commodities** | 6.8 | 7.2 | 8.7 | 12.2 | 13.8 | 1.8 | 1.7 | 1.8 | 2.1 | 3.1 |
| Forestry products | 0.1 | ..... | ..... | ..... | ..... | ..... | ..... | ..... | ..... | ..... |
| Fish and other marine products | 3.9 | 5.2 | 6.4 | 11.0 | 11.7 | 0.3 | 0.2 | 0.5 | 1.5 | 2.3 |
| Metallic ores and concentrates | ..... | ..... | ..... | 0.1 | ..... | ..... | ..... | ..... | ..... | ..... |
| Bituminous coal and lignite | ..... | ..... | ..... | ..... | ..... | ..... | ..... | ..... | ..... | ..... |
| Crude petroleum and natural gas | ..... | ..... | ..... | ..... | ..... | ..... | ..... | ..... | ..... | ..... |
| Nonmetallic minerals | ..... | ..... | 0.2 | ..... | 0.1 | ..... | ..... | ..... | ..... | ..... |
| Scrap and waste | 2.0 | 1.7 | 0.3 | 0.2 | ..... | 1.1 | 1.2 | ..... | ..... | ..... |
| Used merchandise | 0.4 | 0.2 | 0.3 | 0.3 | 1.2 | 0.2 | 0.2 | 0.1 | 0.3 | 0.3 |
| Goods imported and returned unchanged | ..... | ..... | ..... | ..... | ..... | ..... | ..... | ..... | ..... | ..... |
| Special classification provisions | 0.4 | 0.1 | 1.5 | 0.7 | 0.7 | 0.1 | 0.1 | 1.2 | 0.4 | 0.4 |

## Table D-3.   State Exports of Goods by Destination and Industry, 1993–1997 —*Continued*

**NEW HAMPSHIRE** (Millions of dollars.)

| Industry | 1993 | 1994 | 1995 | 1996 | 1997 | 1993 | 1994 | 1995 | 1996 | 1997 |
|---|---|---|---|---|---|---|---|---|---|---|
| | Germany | | | | | France | | | | |
| **ALL GOODS** | 50.9 | 60.4 | 95.3 | 93.5 | 144.9 | 32.1 | 36.9 | 38.1 | 48.3 | 50.0 |
| **Manufactured goods** | 50.2 | 59.6 | 93.6 | 91.0 | 142.2 | 29.7 | 34.2 | 34.4 | 45.0 | 47.3 |
| Food products | ..... | ..... | ..... | ..... | ..... | 0.1 | ..... | 0.1 | 0.2 | 0.3 |
| Tobacco products | ..... | ..... | ..... | ..... | ..... | ..... | ..... | ..... | ..... | ..... |
| Textile mill products | 0.9 | 1.1 | 2.1 | 1.6 | 1.6 | 0.1 | 0.4 | 0.2 | 0.3 | 0.4 |
| Apparel | 0.4 | 0.4 | 0.4 | ..... | 0.4 | 0.6 | 0.6 | 0.2 | ..... | ..... |
| Lumber and wood products | 0.7 | 0.6 | 0.9 | 0.5 | 1.2 | 0.1 | 0.3 | 0.2 | ..... | 0.1 |
| Furniture and fixtures | ..... | 0.1 | 0.1 | ..... | 0.1 | ..... | ..... | 0.1 | 0.1 | ..... |
| Paper products | 0.3 | 0.2 | 0.4 | 0.2 | 1.0 | 0.5 | 0.3 | 0.5 | 0.4 | 0.3 |
| Printing and publishing | 0.3 | 0.4 | 0.2 | 0.2 | 0.1 | 0.1 | 0.1 | 0.1 | 0.1 | ..... |
| Chemical products | 1.9 | 3.2 | 2.6 | 1.0 | 2.0 | 0.4 | 0.5 | 1.1 | 0.5 | 1.2 |
| Refined petroleum products | ..... | ..... | ..... | ..... | 0.1 | ..... | ..... | ..... | ..... | ..... |
| Rubber and plastic products | 1.6 | 1.7 | 2.6 | 2.9 | 2.7 | 0.5 | 2.9 | 1.5 | 1.4 | 1.3 |
| Leather products | 2.8 | 3.3 | 1.6 | 3.5 | 0.4 | 3.8 | 6.0 | 3.0 | 3.6 | 3.0 |
| Stone, clay and glass products | 2.8 | 2.9 | 3.1 | 3.6 | 6.1 | 1.9 | 1.3 | 2.5 | 3.8 | 2.7 |
| Primary metals | 0.5 | 0.7 | 1.0 | 1.2 | 1.2 | 0.3 | 1.1 | 0.3 | 0.8 | 1.3 |
| Fabricated metal products | 1.6 | 1.1 | 1.4 | 2.4 | 1.9 | 0.3 | 0.7 | 1.0 | 1.4 | 1.0 |
| Industrial machinery and computers | 16.8 | 26.6 | 52.1 | 48.7 | 99.2 | 10.0 | 8.6 | 11.3 | 21.0 | 25.1 |
| Electric and electronic equipment | 7.6 | 5.5 | 7.3 | 8.9 | 8.7 | 3.1 | 3.7 | 5.4 | 5.1 | 5.0 |
| Transportation equipment | 2.5 | 1.7 | 2.4 | 2.1 | 2.5 | 1.1 | 0.5 | 0.5 | 0.3 | 0.7 |
| Scientific and measuring instruments | 7.2 | 8.7 | 9.2 | 12.5 | 11.3 | 5.5 | 6.5 | 5.9 | 5.6 | 4.1 |
| Miscellaneous manufactures | 1.8 | 1.0 | 5.3 | 1.0 | 1.0 | 1.2 | 0.4 | 0.3 | 0.3 | 0.5 |
| Unidentified manufactures | 0.5 | 0.5 | 0.8 | 0.6 | 0.4 | 0.2 | 0.3 | 0.4 | 0.3 | 0.3 |
| **Agricultural and livestock products** | ..... | ..... | ..... | ..... | ..... | ..... | 0.1 | ..... | ..... | ..... |
| Agricultural products | ..... | ..... | ..... | ..... | ..... | ..... | ..... | ..... | ..... | ..... |
| Livestock and livestock products | ..... | ..... | ..... | ..... | ..... | ..... | 0.1 | ..... | ..... | ..... |
| **Other commodities** | 0.7 | 0.8 | 1.7 | 2.5 | 2.7 | 2.4 | 2.7 | 3.6 | 3.4 | 2.7 |
| Forestry products | ..... | ..... | ..... | ..... | ..... | ..... | ..... | ..... | ..... | ..... |
| Fish and other marine products | 0.5 | 0.8 | 1.5 | 2.4 | 1.9 | 2.3 | 2.6 | 3.6 | 3.3 | 2.5 |
| Metallic ores and concentrates | ..... | ..... | ..... | ..... | ..... | ..... | ..... | ..... | ..... | ..... |
| Bituminous coal and lignite | ..... | ..... | ..... | ..... | ..... | ..... | ..... | ..... | ..... | ..... |
| Crude petroleum and natural gas | ..... | ..... | ..... | ..... | ..... | ..... | ..... | ..... | ..... | ..... |
| Nonmetallic minerals | ..... | ..... | 0.2 | ..... | ..... | ..... | ..... | ..... | ..... | ..... |
| Scrap and waste | ..... | ..... | ..... | ..... | ..... | ..... | ..... | ..... | ..... | ..... |
| Used merchandise | 0.1 | ..... | ..... | ..... | 0.7 | ..... | ..... | ..... | ..... | ..... |
| Goods imported and returned unchanged | ..... | ..... | ..... | ..... | ..... | ..... | ..... | ..... | ..... | ..... |
| Special classification provisions | 0.1 | ..... | 0.1 | 0.1 | 0.1 | 0.1 | ..... | ..... | 0.1 | ..... |
| | The Netherlands | | | | | Asian 10 | | | | |
| **ALL GOODS** | 42.8 | 46.2 | 50.2 | 58.4 | 62.5 | 182.0 | 242.8 | 289.3 | 344.9 | 360.2 |
| **Manufactured goods** | 42.0 | 44.0 | 48.5 | 56.8 | 59.4 | 177.4 | 236.2 | 283.7 | 337.3 | 353.6 |
| Food products | 0.1 | ..... | 0.2 | 0.1 | 0.2 | 0.5 | 0.9 | 2.0 | 4.2 | 8.8 |
| Tobacco products | ..... | ..... | ..... | ..... | ..... | ..... | ..... | ..... | ..... | ..... |
| Textile mill products | 0.1 | ..... | 0.2 | ..... | 0.1 | 0.9 | 1.2 | 5.0 | 5.3 | 3.3 |
| Apparel | 1.7 | 2.8 | 1.6 | 2.3 | 1.7 | 1.5 | 1.5 | 1.4 | 1.2 | 2.1 |
| Lumber and wood products | 0.5 | 0.7 | 0.6 | 0.4 | 0.6 | 7.2 | 7.5 | 12.3 | 8.8 | 13.0 |
| Furniture and fixtures | ..... | ..... | 0.3 | 0.1 | 0.1 | 0.2 | 0.2 | 0.1 | 0.5 | 0.2 |
| Paper products | 0.6 | 1.1 | 0.8 | 0.5 | 0.8 | 1.0 | 0.4 | 1.3 | 0.6 | 1.5 |
| Printing and publishing | 0.1 | 0.5 | 0.5 | 0.8 | 0.4 | 1.9 | 3.1 | 3.6 | 3.2 | 4.0 |
| Chemical products | 2.6 | 3.0 | 3.1 | 4.6 | 4.1 | 8.8 | 28.5 | 13.5 | 11.4 | 12.7 |
| Refined petroleum products | ..... | ..... | 0.1 | ..... | ..... | 0.1 | 0.2 | 0.2 | 0.4 | 0.8 |
| Rubber and plastic products | 0.2 | 0.1 | 0.1 | 0.7 | 0.5 | 6.6 | 11.1 | 14.8 | 14.5 | 8.3 |
| Leather products | ..... | 0.5 | 0.1 | 2.3 | 5.3 | 2.2 | 3.6 | 18.8 | 72.5 | 68.4 |
| Stone, clay and glass products | 1.7 | 2.3 | 2.9 | 2.3 | 3.7 | 9.6 | 10.3 | 11.1 | 13.6 | 14.3 |
| Primary metals | 0.5 | 0.8 | 0.2 | 0.1 | 0.1 | 0.9 | 0.9 | 1.9 | 3.4 | 3.2 |
| Fabricated metal products | 6.9 | 3.5 | 9.9 | 14.3 | 13.2 | 10.4 | 8.6 | 10.6 | 10.3 | 14.2 |
| Industrial machinery and computers | 15.1 | 16.3 | 17.1 | 18.3 | 18.5 | 62.6 | 83.5 | 99.8 | 97.6 | 91.8 |
| Electric and electronic equipment | 4.3 | 3.0 | 2.4 | 1.9 | 2.9 | 31.0 | 42.4 | 62.7 | 37.6 | 72.3 |
| Transportation equipment | 2.5 | 1.5 | 1.3 | 0.9 | 0.3 | 2.1 | 2.2 | 0.6 | 1.9 | 2.8 |
| Scientific and measuring instruments | 3.4 | 7.3 | 6.8 | 6.0 | 6.2 | 28.0 | 27.4 | 21.8 | 46.7 | 27.9 |
| Miscellaneous manufactures | 0.2 | 0.2 | 0.1 | 0.6 | 0.2 | 0.7 | 1.4 | 0.7 | 2.4 | 3.0 |
| Unidentified manufactures | 1.5 | 0.5 | 0.4 | 0.5 | 0.6 | 1.1 | 1.3 | 1.5 | 1.0 | 1.1 |
| **Agricultural and livestock products** | 0.6 | 1.9 | 1.7 | 1.5 | 2.1 | 2.2 | 4.0 | 3.8 | 4.1 | 4.6 |
| Agricultural products | ..... | ..... | ..... | ..... | ..... | ..... | ..... | 0.2 | 0.5 | 0.1 |
| Livestock and livestock products | 0.6 | 1.9 | 1.7 | 1.5 | 2.1 | 2.2 | 4.0 | 3.5 | 3.6 | 4.6 |
| **Other commodities** | 0.1 | 0.3 | ..... | 0.1 | 1.1 | 2.4 | 2.6 | 1.8 | 3.5 | 2.0 |
| Forestry products | 0.1 | 0.3 | ..... | ..... | 1.0 | ..... | ..... | ..... | ..... | ..... |
| Fish and other marine products | ..... | ..... | ..... | ..... | ..... | 1.4 | 2.4 | 1.3 | 3.0 | 1.3 |
| Metallic ores and concentrates | ..... | ..... | ..... | ..... | ..... | ..... | ..... | ..... | ..... | 0.1 |
| Bituminous coal and lignite | ..... | ..... | ..... | ..... | ..... | ..... | ..... | ..... | ..... | ..... |
| Crude petroleum and natural gas | ..... | ..... | ..... | ..... | ..... | ..... | ..... | ..... | ..... | ..... |
| Nonmetallic minerals | ..... | ..... | ..... | ..... | 0.1 | ..... | ..... | ..... | ..... | ..... |
| Scrap and waste | ..... | ..... | ..... | ..... | ..... | ..... | ..... | 0.1 | 0.1 | ..... |
| Used merchandise | ..... | ..... | ..... | ..... | ..... | 0.3 | 0.1 | 0.1 | 0.1 | 0.1 |
| Goods imported and returned unchanged | ..... | ..... | ..... | ..... | ..... | ..... | ..... | ..... | ..... | ..... |
| Special classification provisions | ..... | ..... | ..... | ..... | ..... | 0.6 | 0.1 | 0.3 | 0.3 | 0.4 |

## Table D-3.  State Exports of Goods by Destination and Industry, 1993–1997 —*Continued*

**NEW HAMPSHIRE** (Millions of dollars.)

| Industry | 1993 | 1994 | 1995 | 1996 | 1997 | 1993 | 1994 | 1995 | 1996 | 1997 |
|---|---|---|---|---|---|---|---|---|---|---|
| | Japan | | | | | South Korea | | | | |
| **ALL GOODS** | 57.7 | 60.4 | 59.0 | 81.8 | 109.0 | 24.7 | 40.7 | 52.5 | 48.3 | 31.7 |
| **Manufactured goods** | 55.5 | 57.9 | 57.6 | 78.3 | 107.4 | 24.5 | 40.2 | 52.0 | 47.8 | 31.7 |
| Food products | 0.2 | 0.2 | 0.8 | 0.2 | 0.5 | 0.1 | 0.6 | 0.5 | 0.3 | 0.5 |
| Tobacco products | ..... | ..... | ..... | ..... | ..... | ..... | ..... | ..... | ..... | ..... |
| Textile mill products | 0.2 | 0.2 | 0.2 | 0.1 | 0.1 | 0.1 | ..... | 0.4 | ..... | 0.5 |
| Apparel | 0.7 | 0.4 | 0.5 | 0.7 | 0.4 | 0.1 | 0.1 | 0.2 | 0.2 | ..... |
| Lumber and wood products | 3.1 | 2.9 | 5.6 | 3.1 | 3.9 | ..... | ..... | 0.6 | 1.8 | 1.8 |
| Furniture and fixtures | 0.2 | 0.1 | ..... | 0.2 | 0.1 | ..... | ..... | 0.1 | 0.1 | ..... |
| Paper products | 0.1 | 0.1 | 0.2 | 0.2 | 0.4 | ..... | ..... | 0.1 | 0.1 | 0.1 |
| Printing and publishing | 0.3 | 0.2 | 0.2 | 0.2 | 0.6 | 0.1 | 0.2 | 0.2 | 0.1 | 0.3 |
| Chemical products | 1.3 | 1.9 | 1.9 | 1.7 | 2.3 | 2.4 | 6.3 | 2.0 | 1.2 | 1.2 |
| Refined petroleum products | ..... | ..... | ..... | 0.1 | 0.2 | 0.1 | 0.1 | 0.1 | 0.2 | 0.4 |
| Rubber and plastic products | 1.9 | 1.4 | 1.8 | 2.2 | 1.4 | 2.8 | 6.7 | 10.1 | 9.5 | 2.0 |
| Leather products | ..... | 0.3 | 1.8 | 6.1 | 8.5 | 0.2 | 0.2 | 0.7 | 5.8 | 3.0 |
| Stone, clay and glass products | 6.4 | 7.1 | 7.1 | 8.9 | 8.6 | 0.7 | 1.2 | 1.9 | 1.8 | 1.8 |
| Primary metals | 0.2 | 0.5 | 0.7 | 1.8 | 0.4 | 0.1 | 0.1 | 0.3 | 0.3 | 0.2 |
| Fabricated metal products | 3.0 | 1.7 | 1.3 | 1.8 | 2.5 | 2.7 | 4.4 | 5.9 | 5.4 | 5.6 |
| Industrial machinery and computers | 16.3 | 20.0 | 18.5 | 29.0 | 44.3 | 10.0 | 13.2 | 22.5 | 13.7 | 6.6 |
| Electric and electronic equipment | 5.0 | 7.1 | 8.4 | 10.7 | 21.7 | 1.0 | 3.3 | 4.3 | 4.6 | 4.4 |
| Transportation equipment | 0.3 | 0.2 | 0.2 | 0.6 | 0.2 | 0.4 | ..... | ..... | 0.1 | 0.4 |
| Scientific and measuring instruments | 15.5 | 12.6 | 7.8 | 9.2 | 9.6 | 3.5 | 3.6 | 1.9 | 2.5 | 2.8 |
| Miscellaneous manufactures | 0.5 | 0.9 | 0.4 | 1.6 | 1.3 | 0.1 | ..... | ..... | 0.1 | 0.1 |
| Unidentified manufactures | 0.3 | 0.4 | 0.4 | 0.2 | 0.2 | 0.1 | 0.1 | 0.1 | 0.1 | 0.1 |
| **Agricultural and livestock products** | 0.1 | ..... | 0.1 | 0.5 | 0.1 | 0.2 | 0.5 | 0.4 | 0.4 | ..... |
| Agricultural products | ..... | ..... | 0.1 | 0.5 | 0.1 | ..... | ..... | 0.1 | ..... | ..... |
| Livestock and livestock products | ..... | ..... | ..... | ..... | ..... | 0.2 | 0.5 | 0.3 | 0.4 | ..... |
| **Other commodities** | 2.2 | 2.5 | 1.3 | 3.0 | 1.5 | ..... | ..... | 0.1 | 0.1 | ..... |
| Forestry products | ..... | ..... | ..... | ..... | ..... | ..... | ..... | ..... | ..... | ..... |
| Fish and other marine products | 1.4 | 2.4 | 1.1 | 2.8 | 1.1 | ..... | ..... | 0.1 | ..... | ..... |
| Metallic ores and concentrates | ..... | ..... | ..... | ..... | 0.1 | ..... | ..... | ..... | ..... | ..... |
| Bituminous coal and lignite | ..... | ..... | ..... | ..... | ..... | ..... | ..... | ..... | ..... | ..... |
| Crude petroleum and natural gas | ..... | ..... | ..... | ..... | ..... | ..... | ..... | ..... | ..... | ..... |
| Nonmetallic minerals | ..... | ..... | ..... | ..... | ..... | ..... | ..... | ..... | ..... | ..... |
| Scrap and waste | ..... | ..... | ..... | ..... | ..... | ..... | ..... | ..... | ..... | ..... |
| Used merchandise | 0.3 | 0.1 | 0.1 | 0.1 | 0.1 | ..... | ..... | ..... | ..... | ..... |
| Goods imported and returned unchanged | ..... | ..... | ..... | ..... | ..... | ..... | ..... | ..... | ..... | ..... |
| Special classification provisions | 0.5 | 0.1 | 0.1 | 0.1 | 0.1 | ..... | ..... | ..... | 0.1 | ..... |
| | Taiwan | | | | | Singapore | | | | |
| **ALL GOODS** | 20.6 | 34.8 | 36.0 | 57.4 | 49.5 | 39.5 | 60.5 | 76.1 | 50.3 | 56.7 |
| **Manufactured goods** | 20.3 | 34.4 | 35.6 | 56.9 | 49.0 | 39.4 | 60.5 | 75.9 | 50.2 | 56.5 |
| Food products | 0.1 | ..... | 0.4 | 0.5 | 0.3 | ..... | ..... | ..... | ..... | ..... |
| Tobacco products | ..... | ..... | ..... | ..... | ..... | ..... | ..... | ..... | ..... | ..... |
| Textile mill products | ..... | 0.1 | 0.1 | 0.1 | 0.1 | 0.3 | 0.4 | 0.7 | 0.1 | 0.1 |
| Apparel | 0.1 | 0.3 | 0.4 | 0.2 | 0.4 | 0.1 | 0.2 | ..... | ..... | 0.1 |
| Lumber and wood products | 2.8 | 2.8 | 3.7 | 1.3 | 3.1 | ..... | 0.1 | 0.2 | 0.1 | 0.2 |
| Furniture and fixtures | ..... | ..... | ..... | 0.1 | ..... | ..... | 0.1 | ..... | 0.1 | 0.1 |
| Paper products | 0.1 | 0.1 | 0.2 | ..... | 0.3 | 0.1 | 0.1 | 0.2 | ..... | 0.3 |
| Printing and publishing | 0.1 | 0.4 | 0.5 | 0.7 | 0.6 | 0.7 | 0.7 | 0.4 | 0.6 | 0.8 |
| Chemical products | 0.7 | 9.5 | 2.7 | 2.3 | 1.8 | 3.3 | 3.5 | 3.8 | 4.0 | 4.4 |
| Refined petroleum products | ..... | ..... | ..... | 0.1 | 0.1 | ..... | ..... | ..... | 0.1 | 0.1 |
| Rubber and plastic products | 0.5 | 1.5 | 1.9 | 1.3 | 0.6 | 0.7 | 0.4 | 0.3 | 0.7 | 3.1 |
| Leather products | 0.1 | 0.3 | 4.2 | 23.1 | 20.3 | 0.7 | 0.7 | 1.4 | 3.0 | 3.4 |
| Stone, clay and glass products | 0.3 | 0.2 | 0.4 | 0.7 | 0.6 | 0.7 | 0.8 | 0.6 | 0.9 | 1.4 |
| Primary metals | 0.1 | 0.1 | 0.3 | 0.2 | 0.5 | 0.3 | 0.2 | 0.2 | 0.3 | 0.5 |
| Fabricated metal products | 1.7 | 0.4 | 1.3 | 1.3 | 2.7 | 1.4 | 1.3 | 0.7 | 0.5 | 1.6 |
| Industrial machinery and computers | 7.1 | 11.8 | 11.4 | 17.9 | 9.6 | 10.3 | 21.3 | 23.5 | 17.0 | 9.1 |
| Electric and electronic equipment | 2.9 | 3.1 | 6.2 | 4.8 | 6.4 | 18.3 | 26.8 | 38.4 | 13.2 | 23.2 |
| Transportation equipment | 0.8 | 1.1 | 0.3 | 1.0 | 0.4 | 0.1 | 0.1 | 0.1 | 0.1 | 0.1 |
| Scientific and measuring instruments | 2.5 | 2.3 | 1.4 | 1.0 | 1.0 | 2.2 | 3.7 | 5.1 | 9.2 | 8.0 |
| Miscellaneous manufactures | ..... | ..... | ..... | 0.2 | 0.1 | 0.1 | 0.1 | 0.1 | 0.3 | 0.1 |
| Unidentified manufactures | 0.5 | 0.3 | 0.2 | 0.2 | 0.1 | 0.1 | 0.1 | 0.1 | 0.1 | 0.3 |
| **Agricultural and livestock products** | 0.2 | 0.3 | 0.4 | 0.4 | 0.5 | ..... | ..... | ..... | ..... | 0.1 |
| Agricultural products | ..... | ..... | ..... | ..... | ..... | ..... | ..... | ..... | ..... | ..... |
| Livestock and livestock products | 0.2 | 0.3 | 0.4 | 0.4 | 0.5 | ..... | ..... | ..... | ..... | 0.1 |
| **Other commodities** | ..... | ..... | ..... | 0.1 | 0.1 | ..... | ..... | 0.2 | 0.1 | 0.1 |
| Forestry products | ..... | ..... | ..... | ..... | ..... | ..... | ..... | ..... | ..... | ..... |
| Fish and other marine products | ..... | ..... | ..... | ..... | 0.1 | ..... | ..... | ..... | ..... | ..... |
| Metallic ores and concentrates | ..... | ..... | ..... | ..... | ..... | ..... | ..... | ..... | ..... | ..... |
| Bituminous coal and lignite | ..... | ..... | ..... | ..... | ..... | ..... | ..... | ..... | ..... | ..... |
| Crude petroleum and natural gas | ..... | ..... | ..... | ..... | ..... | ..... | ..... | ..... | ..... | ..... |
| Nonmetallic minerals | ..... | ..... | ..... | ..... | ..... | ..... | ..... | ..... | ..... | ..... |
| Scrap and waste | ..... | ..... | ..... | ..... | ..... | ..... | ..... | 0.1 | ..... | ..... |
| Used merchandise | ..... | ..... | ..... | ..... | ..... | ..... | ..... | ..... | 0.1 | ..... |
| Goods imported and returned unchanged | ..... | ..... | ..... | ..... | ..... | ..... | ..... | ..... | ..... | ..... |
| Special classification provisions | ..... | ..... | ..... | 0.1 | ..... | ..... | ..... | 0.1 | 0.1 | 0.1 |

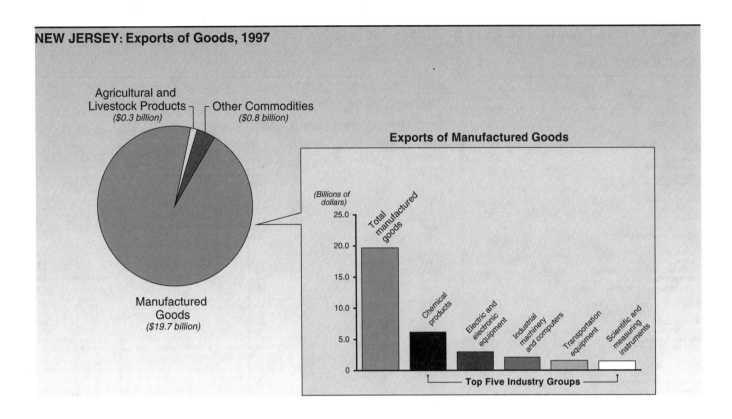

**NEW JERSEY: Exports of Goods, 1997**

Agricultural and Livestock Products ($0.3 billion)

Other Commodities ($0.8 billion)

Manufactured Goods ($19.7 billion)

Exports of Manufactured Goods

(Billions of dollars)

Top Five Industry Groups

## Table D-3.   State Exports of Goods by Destination and Industry, 1993–1997 —*Continued*

**NEW JERSEY** (Millions of dollars.)

| Industry | 1993 | 1994 | 1995 | 1996 | 1997 | 1993 | 1994 | 1995 | 1996 | 1997 |
|---|---|---|---|---|---|---|---|---|---|---|
| | All destinations | | | | | Canada | | | | |
| **ALL GOODS** | 14 540.6 | 16 760.8 | 18 368.6 | 18 458.4 | 20 815.4 | 2 539.0 | 2 943.7 | 3 167.2 | 3 379.1 | 3 836.8 |
| **Manufactured goods** | 13 633.3 | 15 646.3 | 17 119.1 | 17 283.0 | 19 688.6 | 2 378.5 | 2 741.2 | 2 940.3 | 3 144.0 | 3 569.9 |
| Food products | 873.7 | 1 146.1 | 1 114.0 | 1 120.7 | 1 134.9 | 218.5 | 256.5 | 277.3 | 304.3 | 301.7 |
| Tobacco products | 2.6 | 1.7 | 14.1 | 4.8 | 1.9 | 0.8 | 1.2 | 1.1 | 0.8 | 0.8 |
| Textile mill products | 209.6 | 163.6 | 165.4 | 173.9 | 227.5 | 28.0 | 24.5 | 31.3 | 37.6 | 42.1 |
| Apparel | 188.7 | 191.0 | 216.1 | 249.2 | 266.1 | 18.9 | 19.7 | 15.3 | 22.5 | 35.1 |
| Lumber and wood products | 23.2 | 27.4 | 30.2 | 56.2 | 49.9 | 4.1 | 5.2 | 5.5 | 6.6 | 8.7 |
| Furniture and fixtures | 75.2 | 91.7 | 85.6 | 79.5 | 148.6 | 25.3 | 26.2 | 37.8 | 28.5 | 96.2 |
| Paper products | 457.6 | 523.0 | 826.4 | 642.3 | 545.8 | 75.4 | 84.7 | 105.2 | 86.4 | 97.0 |
| Printing and publishing | 437.5 | 412.7 | 455.7 | 495.7 | 532.7 | 218.2 | 199.6 | 199.6 | 204.8 | 200.2 |
| Chemical products | 3 563.1 | 3 974.9 | 4 642.6 | 4 858.5 | 6 160.8 | 700.3 | 807.1 | 930.3 | 1 003.1 | 1 179.7 |
| Refined petroleum products | 66.4 | 150.8 | 180.4 | 149.5 | 108.6 | 9.1 | 18.6 | 10.2 | 18.6 | 16.4 |
| Rubber and plastic products | 287.9 | 326.0 | 338.0 | 343.0 | 414.7 | 100.2 | 110.9 | 116.0 | 122.6 | 148.0 |
| Leather products | 49.8 | 52.6 | 57.3 | 47.4 | 59.9 | 5.1 | 6.6 | 7.0 | 11.2 | 13.1 |
| Stone, clay and glass products | 146.5 | 143.7 | 153.9 | 192.7 | 211.9 | 28.3 | 27.6 | 29.4 | 38.4 | 47.3 |
| Primary metals | 576.2 | 690.8 | 753.5 | 674.5 | 790.2 | 127.5 | 161.0 | 196.7 | 182.9 | 189.7 |
| Fabricated metal products | 411.5 | 388.6 | 561.4 | 590.4 | 591.6 | 59.9 | 71.5 | 70.7 | 75.5 | 79.4 |
| Industrial machinery and computers | 1 646.3 | 1 901.0 | 2 002.4 | 1 824.1 | 2 101.3 | 222.5 | 308.7 | 303.8 | 302.4 | 333.7 |
| Electric and electronic equipment | 2 207.5 | 2 693.4 | 2 678.9 | 2 622.7 | 2 991.6 | 204.7 | 203.6 | 224.6 | 220.6 | 292.3 |
| Transportation equipment | 879.4 | 1 259.8 | 1 312.1 | 1 509.8 | 1 551.0 | 76.9 | 142.9 | 133.1 | 219.7 | 227.9 |
| Scientific and measuring instruments | 1 233.4 | 1 229.3 | 1 249.0 | 1 349.4 | 1 463.5 | 181.5 | 187.6 | 163.3 | 179.4 | 172.0 |
| Miscellaneous manufactures | 182.6 | 172.4 | 198.7 | 191.8 | 223.3 | 64.1 | 64.8 | 67.7 | 63.7 | 72.5 |
| Unidentified manufactures | 114.5 | 105.6 | 83.6 | 106.7 | 112.8 | 9.0 | 12.7 | 14.4 | 14.5 | 15.9 |
| **Agricultural and livestock products** | 221.8 | 269.2 | 308.3 | 395.0 | 343.7 | 66.8 | 94.8 | 84.6 | 87.8 | 108.0 |
| Agricultural products | 205.1 | 248.3 | 283.6 | 368.5 | 307.1 | 54.6 | 82.4 | 71.6 | 71.3 | 81.8 |
| Livestock and livestock products | 16.7 | 20.9 | 24.7 | 26.5 | 36.6 | 12.2 | 12.4 | 13.0 | 16.4 | 26.2 |
| **Other commodities** | 685.4 | 845.3 | 941.1 | 780.4 | 783.1 | 93.8 | 107.7 | 142.4 | 147.3 | 158.8 |
| Forestry products | 9.5 | 11.1 | 11.3 | 18.0 | 17.4 | 1.2 | 1.9 | 2.1 | 2.1 | 3.9 |
| Fish and other marine products | 23.3 | 30.7 | 43.8 | 46.1 | 31.0 | 7.4 | 7.4 | 13.1 | 15.6 | 13.6 |
| Metallic ores and concentrates | 3.0 | 13.2 | 4.6 | 4.5 | 3.8 | 0.8 | 0.6 | 1.2 | 1.6 | 2.1 |
| Bituminous coal and lignite | 18.4 | 24.4 | 20.2 | 37.7 | 33.0 | ..... | ..... | ..... | ..... | 0.4 |
| Crude petroleum and natural gas | 0.7 | 1.6 | 2.8 | 1.8 | 2.5 | 0.1 | 0.6 | 1.3 | ..... | 0.1 |
| Nonmetallic minerals | 203.1 | 223.8 | 256.7 | 262.0 | 285.9 | 13.5 | 15.1 | 17.4 | 17.8 | 17.6 |
| Scrap and waste | 329.9 | 446.9 | 474.5 | 290.8 | 283.2 | 25.2 | 36.3 | 53.7 | 57.1 | 62.6 |
| Used merchandise | 31.4 | 31.2 | 54.4 | 30.6 | 38.5 | 1.7 | 1.4 | 1.4 | 1.9 | 4.6 |
| Goods imported and returned unchanged | 36.7 | 37.4 | 44.3 | 43.2 | 44.6 | 36.7 | 37.4 | 44.3 | 43.2 | 44.6 |
| Special classification provisions | 29.5 | 25.1 | 28.7 | 45.7 | 43.3 | 7.0 | 6.8 | 7.8 | 7.9 | 9.3 |

## Table D-3. State Exports of Goods by Destination and Industry, 1993–1997 —*Continued*

**NEW JERSEY** (Millions of dollars.)

| Industry | 1993 | 1994 | 1995 | 1996 | 1997 | 1993 | 1994 | 1995 | 1996 | 1997 |
|---|---|---|---|---|---|---|---|---|---|---|
| | South and Central America and Caribbean | | | | | Mexico | | | | |
| **ALL GOODS** | 1 287.0 | 1 433.6 | 1 808.6 | 1 932.9 | 2 107.7 | 788.9 | 1 068.1 | 583.8 | 679.2 | 883.8 |
| **Manufactured goods** | 1 165.3 | 1 294.8 | 1 627.0 | 1 675.4 | 1 920.9 | 775.6 | 1 052.5 | 569.0 | 663.4 | 865.0 |
| Food products | 76.0 | 98.7 | 142.0 | 146.7 | 159.1 | 29.8 | 57.8 | 23.2 | 28.8 | 19.1 |
| Tobacco products | 0.2 | ..... | 1.0 | 0.4 | 0.9 | ..... | ..... | ..... | ..... | ..... |
| Textile mill products | 38.0 | 38.3 | 41.1 | 42.0 | 53.0 | 21.0 | 20.8 | 8.1 | 11.7 | 20.5 |
| Apparel | 68.8 | 69.5 | 61.8 | 76.8 | 87.2 | 11.9 | 12.9 | 20.5 | 19.3 | 17.4 |
| Lumber and wood products | 1.0 | 0.8 | 1.9 | 4.1 | 6.2 | 1.7 | 4.8 | 0.8 | 0.2 | 0.4 |
| Furniture and fixtures | 2.7 | 2.7 | 4.0 | 6.9 | 7.0 | 12.8 | 12.4 | 4.6 | 6.4 | 11.9 |
| Paper products | 35.1 | 53.3 | 80.0 | 73.9 | 66.4 | 13.8 | 16.1 | 21.6 | 16.5 | 17.5 |
| Printing and publishing | 14.2 | 12.9 | 23.3 | 30.0 | 25.6 | 19.4 | 20.8 | 12.6 | 17.4 | 14.6 |
| Chemical products | 364.6 | 434.1 | 599.5 | 667.7 | 831.0 | 136.1 | 172.8 | 171.4 | 215.6 | 283.1 |
| Refined petroleum products | 9.2 | 25.0 | 14.0 | 10.4 | 7.0 | 1.1 | 0.8 | 1.4 | 1.5 | 3.1 |
| Rubber and plastic products | 16.1 | 19.7 | 30.0 | 28.4 | 37.7 | 35.0 | 51.1 | 24.9 | 15.7 | 28.3 |
| Leather products | 4.5 | 4.3 | 7.1 | 4.6 | 10.9 | 1.0 | 1.2 | 0.4 | 0.3 | 0.5 |
| Stone, clay and glass products | 20.4 | 17.9 | 17.0 | 15.6 | 18.7 | 5.8 | 4.1 | 1.9 | 7.6 | 8.1 |
| Primary metals | 63.8 | 38.9 | 32.9 | 23.1 | 22.9 | 35.8 | 38.2 | 24.2 | 71.8 | 35.0 |
| Fabricated metal products | 12.4 | 16.8 | 22.9 | 23.1 | 24.1 | 22.7 | 20.9 | 17.0 | 21.1 | 24.5 |
| Industrial machinery and computers | 145.8 | 173.6 | 224.8 | 175.9 | 244.8 | 42.9 | 97.4 | 47.8 | 46.5 | 114.0 |
| Electric and electronic equipment | 159.4 | 172.5 | 133.4 | 158.4 | 136.6 | 312.4 | 452.0 | 153.9 | 140.0 | 162.6 |
| Transportation equipment | 29.3 | 24.0 | 64.4 | 77.1 | 53.0 | 2.4 | 9.9 | 3.5 | 2.9 | 2.2 |
| Scientific and measuring instruments | 71.9 | 65.2 | 95.3 | 82.4 | 98.5 | 57.7 | 45.2 | 25.0 | 33.0 | 90.3 |
| Miscellaneous manufactures | 20.9 | 17.4 | 22.6 | 19.5 | 20.7 | 10.0 | 10.2 | 5.0 | 5.6 | 8.2 |
| Unidentified manufactures | 11.2 | 9.1 | 8.3 | 8.5 | 9.2 | 2.2 | 3.1 | 1.0 | 1.4 | 3.9 |
| **Agricultural and livestock products** | 100.9 | 111.9 | 156.1 | 228.9 | 164.1 | 7.9 | 7.2 | 5.6 | 2.3 | 8.6 |
| Agricultural products | 100.8 | 111.7 | 153.4 | 228.8 | 163.7 | 7.9 | 6.5 | 5.5 | 2.3 | 8.6 |
| Livestock and livestock products | 0.1 | 0.2 | 2.8 | 0.1 | 0.3 | ..... | 0.7 | ..... | ..... | ..... |
| **Other commodities** | 20.9 | 26.9 | 25.5 | 28.7 | 22.9 | 5.3 | 8.4 | 9.2 | 13.4 | 10.1 |
| Forestry products | 1.2 | 1.5 | 2.0 | 2.4 | 2.5 | 0.6 | 0.6 | 1.1 | 1.1 | 1.4 |
| Fish and other marine products | 1.3 | 1.3 | 1.2 | 1.9 | 0.4 | ..... | 0.1 | 0.1 | 0.1 | 1.8 |
| Metallic ores and concentrates | 0.1 | 0.2 | 0.2 | 0.1 | ..... | 0.1 | ..... | ..... | ..... | 0.1 |
| Bituminous coal and lignite | 0.2 | 3.1 | 0.2 | 1.8 | 1.1 | ..... | ..... | ..... | 0.1 | 0.1 |
| Crude petroleum and natural gas | ..... | 0.1 | 0.1 | ..... | ..... | ..... | ..... | ..... | ..... | ..... |
| Nonmetallic minerals | 7.3 | 4.6 | 5.8 | 12.0 | 10.3 | 2.1 | 1.9 | 1.5 | 1.6 | 1.5 |
| Scrap and waste | 3.2 | 10.4 | 7.0 | 4.7 | 2.8 | 0.7 | 3.8 | 2.5 | 6.7 | 0.7 |
| Used merchandise | 6.5 | 5.2 | 7.9 | 4.5 | 3.3 | 0.3 | 0.1 | 0.4 | ..... | 0.1 |
| Goods imported and returned unchanged | ..... | ..... | ..... | ..... | ..... | ..... | ..... | ..... | ..... | ..... |
| Special classification provisions | 1.1 | 0.6 | 1.0 | 1.2 | 2.5 | 1.4 | 1.8 | 3.7 | 3.9 | 4.3 |
| | European Union | | | | | United Kingdom | | | | |
| **ALL GOODS** | 3 971.9 | 4 350.9 | 4 792.2 | 4 499.6 | 5 269.0 | 819.4 | 999.0 | 955.7 | 854.9 | 901.1 |
| **Manufactured goods** | 3 631.2 | 3 898.1 | 4 388.2 | 4 184.7 | 5 000.3 | 701.2 | 807.6 | 829.3 | 774.2 | 861.7 |
| Food products | 92.4 | 100.7 | 98.4 | 91.7 | 100.8 | 19.1 | 16.3 | 16.5 | 15.6 | 14.9 |
| Tobacco products | 1.1 | 0.3 | 9.6 | 0.7 | 0.1 | 0.3 | ..... | 0.5 | 0.4 | ..... |
| Textile mill products | 29.0 | 14.9 | 21.2 | 17.6 | 23.1 | 6.5 | 4.0 | 7.8 | 4.1 | 5.7 |
| Apparel | 24.3 | 26.6 | 32.8 | 33.6 | 36.4 | 2.2 | 4.2 | 5.8 | 5.3 | 7.5 |
| Lumber and wood products | 3.8 | 4.8 | 6.6 | 7.0 | 7.6 | 1.0 | 1.7 | 2.3 | 1.7 | 4.1 |
| Furniture and fixtures | 6.3 | 4.2 | 7.0 | 6.2 | 9.1 | 1.7 | 1.6 | 2.2 | 1.6 | 2.1 |
| Paper products | 169.2 | 194.6 | 332.6 | 224.5 | 157.1 | 40.6 | 55.4 | 93.1 | 57.7 | 43.0 |
| Printing and publishing | 104.1 | 95.8 | 118.9 | 132.6 | 179.5 | 76.4 | 60.1 | 57.1 | 65.9 | 108.5 |
| Chemical products | 1 253.0 | 1 320.5 | 1 463.9 | 1 502.4 | 2 164.8 | 167.4 | 181.1 | 167.2 | 202.3 | 220.3 |
| Refined petroleum products | 15.5 | 38.3 | 63.3 | 36.0 | 18.3 | 3.4 | 4.1 | 34.1 | 2.9 | 3.5 |
| Rubber and plastic products | 72.2 | 65.3 | 68.1 | 67.9 | 88.2 | 17.1 | 21.0 | 16.2 | 13.6 | 19.1 |
| Leather products | 8.4 | 9.6 | 7.8 | 7.1 | 10.9 | 3.0 | 3.9 | 2.4 | 1.6 | 2.7 |
| Stone, clay and glass products | 41.0 | 39.2 | 47.9 | 55.8 | 54.0 | 12.6 | 11.8 | 14.0 | 17.4 | 13.7 |
| Primary metals | 88.2 | 176.5 | 145.7 | 137.8 | 216.8 | 15.2 | 77.1 | 45.6 | 56.2 | 52.0 |
| Fabricated metal products | 86.8 | 86.9 | 88.0 | 80.5 | 88.3 | 30.4 | 20.8 | 20.6 | 17.1 | 20.7 |
| Industrial machinery and computers | 434.5 | 445.3 | 448.2 | 396.8 | 457.3 | 94.4 | 116.1 | 113.6 | 96.8 | 107.0 |
| Electric and electronic equipment | 410.8 | 437.3 | 540.2 | 445.2 | 501.6 | 83.4 | 72.0 | 88.2 | 93.4 | 112.6 |
| Transportation equipment | 265.8 | 310.5 | 332.6 | 414.3 | 332.1 | 29.9 | 42.2 | 30.8 | 35.9 | 40.9 |
| Scientific and measuring instruments | 472.6 | 476.6 | 501.8 | 468.5 | 491.6 | 82.5 | 100.6 | 98.2 | 70.5 | 64.9 |
| Miscellaneous manufactures | 34.4 | 32.7 | 34.6 | 33.5 | 41.5 | 9.2 | 8.7 | 8.8 | 9.3 | 14.9 |
| Unidentified manufactures | 17.8 | 17.5 | 18.9 | 24.9 | 21.1 | 4.8 | 4.5 | 4.0 | 4.8 | 3.6 |
| **Agricultural and livestock products** | 20.5 | 32.6 | 31.6 | 50.1 | 23.4 | 0.7 | 0.8 | 2.6 | 29.6 | 8.4 |
| Agricultural products | 18.0 | 29.0 | 26.3 | 44.5 | 20.2 | 0.6 | 0.8 | 2.5 | 28.8 | 7.8 |
| Livestock and livestock products | 2.5 | 3.6 | 5.3 | 5.6 | 3.2 | 0.1 | 0.1 | 0.1 | 0.7 | 0.6 |
| **Other commodities** | 320.2 | 420.1 | 372.4 | 264.8 | 245.3 | 117.5 | 190.6 | 123.9 | 51.1 | 31.0 |
| Forestry products | 2.8 | 3.5 | 2.3 | 4.4 | 5.7 | 0.5 | 1.6 | 0.2 | 0.9 | 1.4 |
| Fish and other marine products | 8.3 | 13.5 | 12.3 | 13.1 | 7.1 | ..... | 0.1 | ..... | 0.6 | 0.4 |
| Metallic ores and concentrates | 1.9 | 10.8 | 3.1 | 2.1 | 0.6 | 0.4 | 5.4 | 0.7 | 0.6 | 0.4 |
| Bituminous coal and lignite | 18.1 | 21.2 | 19.9 | 24.5 | 13.4 | ..... | 0.8 | 3.3 | 2.5 | 0.9 |
| Crude petroleum and natural gas | 0.2 | 0.1 | 0.4 | 0.6 | 0.9 | ..... | ..... | 0.1 | 0.4 | 0.6 |
| Nonmetallic minerals | 82.1 | 78.6 | 93.0 | 78.7 | 94.2 | 5.5 | 5.9 | 8.4 | 6.0 | 11.6 |
| Scrap and waste | 186.0 | 269.8 | 208.3 | 115.0 | 103.8 | 105.4 | 166.7 | 96.6 | 30.2 | 9.1 |
| Used merchandise | 14.1 | 14.2 | 25.9 | 8.6 | 10.1 | 4.2 | 8.6 | 13.0 | 4.5 | 4.0 |
| Goods imported and returned unchanged | ..... | ..... | ..... | ..... | ..... | | | | | |
| Special classification provisions | 6.6 | 8.5 | 7.3 | 17.6 | 9.3 | 1.4 | 1.5 | 1.6 | 5.6 | 2.6 |

## Table D-3.  State Exports of Goods by Destination and Industry, 1993–1997 —*Continued*

**NEW JERSEY** (Millions of dollars.)

| Industry | 1993 | 1994 | 1995 | 1996 | 1997 | 1993 | 1994 | 1995 | 1996 | 1997 |
|---|---|---|---|---|---|---|---|---|---|---|
| | Germany | | | | | France | | | | |
| **ALL GOODS** | 765.1 | 798.3 | 920.8 | 871.5 | 912.4 | 492.5 | 488.6 | 525.3 | 493.0 | 577.6 |
| **Manufactured goods** | 686.2 | 716.1 | 834.6 | 800.3 | 841.7 | 487.1 | 477.7 | 515.8 | 478.4 | 560.9 |
| Food products | 14.9 | 14.0 | 7.5 | 15.7 | 18.4 | 16.9 | 19.4 | 12.6 | 10.8 | 4.5 |
| Tobacco products | 0.5 | ..... | ..... | ..... | ..... | 0.1 | 0.2 | 0.2 | 0.1 | ..... |
| Textile mill products | 4.2 | 1.7 | 2.0 | 2.0 | 4.1 | 3.8 | 2.0 | 1.2 | 2.4 | 1.6 |
| Apparel | 4.3 | 4.8 | 6.9 | 6.2 | 4.1 | 2.3 | 2.9 | 3.0 | 5.3 | 4.8 |
| Lumber and wood products | 0.3 | 1.2 | 1.6 | 2.2 | 0.5 | 0.9 | 0.8 | 1.0 | 0.8 | 0.8 |
| Furniture and fixtures | 2.6 | 1.2 | 1.1 | 1.1 | 1.0 | 0.3 | 0.3 | 1.0 | 0.7 | 0.7 |
| Paper products | 30.6 | 22.2 | 43.1 | 30.3 | 20.4 | 10.0 | 10.6 | 19.0 | 13.9 | 4.9 |
| Printing and publishing | 7.1 | 10.9 | 14.7 | 21.9 | 15.4 | 3.8 | 6.5 | 5.4 | 6.6 | 12.0 |
| Chemical products | 182.1 | 198.1 | 216.4 | 227.3 | 274.9 | 150.4 | 154.9 | 159.4 | 109.7 | 244.6 |
| Refined petroleum products | 2.8 | 2.9 | 2.9 | 2.1 | 2.1 | 1.0 | 1.2 | 1.5 | 7.8 | 2.6 |
| Rubber and plastic products | 7.8 | 5.5 | 9.0 | 7.4 | 9.9 | 8.8 | 7.0 | 7.5 | 6.7 | 8.8 |
| Leather products | 2.6 | 0.7 | 1.1 | 2.6 | 3.1 | 0.9 | 1.2 | 1.1 | 1.1 | 2.5 |
| Stone, clay and glass products | 3.1 | 5.5 | 7.9 | 4.3 | 4.8 | 2.5 | 3.7 | 5.9 | 5.9 | 6.3 |
| Primary metals | 30.7 | 46.6 | 22.8 | 15.7 | 12.2 | 6.6 | 4.5 | 13.8 | 5.5 | 9.7 |
| Fabricated metal products | 18.3 | 26.9 | 28.3 | 33.2 | 31.1 | 5.2 | 5.5 | 7.0 | 6.6 | 6.5 |
| Industrial machinery and computers | 104.9 | 92.7 | 108.7 | 95.7 | 105.7 | 47.8 | 44.1 | 50.5 | 43.2 | 49.5 |
| Electric and electronic equipment | 82.7 | 76.1 | 113.9 | 88.4 | 96.0 | 41.8 | 39.4 | 43.2 | 40.9 | 42.9 |
| Transportation equipment | 33.4 | 59.1 | 77.0 | 61.4 | 52.0 | 106.2 | 104.2 | 109.1 | 146.3 | 91.9 |
| Scientific and measuring instruments | 143.8 | 134.6 | 159.1 | 172.8 | 174.6 | 69.3 | 62.8 | 67.5 | 56.6 | 60.7 |
| Miscellaneous manufactures | 5.2 | 6.1 | 6.5 | 5.2 | 8.0 | 6.4 | 4.9 | 4.5 | 6.6 | 4.9 |
| Unidentified manufactures | 4.2 | 5.5 | 4.2 | 4.9 | 3.3 | 1.9 | 1.7 | 1.5 | 1.0 | 0.9 |
| **Agricultural and livestock products** | 3.8 | 0.4 | 1.6 | 0.5 | 1.9 | 0.2 | 7.8 | 0.6 | 3.4 | 2.6 |
| Agricultural products | 2.4 | 0.2 | 0.3 | 0.1 | 1.7 | 0.2 | 7.8 | 0.6 | 3.4 | 2.6 |
| Livestock and livestock products | 1.4 | 0.3 | 1.3 | 0.4 | 0.3 | 0.1 | ..... | ..... | ..... | ..... |
| **Other commodities** | 75.1 | 81.7 | 84.5 | 70.7 | 68.8 | 5.3 | 3.0 | 8.9 | 11.2 | 14.1 |
| Forestry products | 0.7 | 0.8 | 0.6 | 0.4 | 1.6 | 0.9 | 0.4 | 0.5 | 0.4 | 0.3 |
| Fish and other marine products | 0.2 | 0.1 | ..... | ..... | ..... | 0.8 | 0.1 | 0.5 | 1.3 | ..... |
| Metallic ores and concentrates | 0.3 | 0.3 | 0.4 | 0.8 | ..... | ..... | ..... | ..... | ..... | 0.1 |
| Bituminous coal and lignite | ..... | ..... | ..... | ..... | ..... | ..... | 0.3 | 3.5 | 4.9 | 8.6 |
| Crude petroleum and natural gas | ..... | ..... | ..... | 0.1 | ..... | 0.1 | ..... | ..... | ..... | ..... |
| Nonmetallic minerals | 4.0 | 5.1 | 6.4 | 5.8 | 5.9 | 1.3 | 0.6 | 0.5 | 1.7 | 1.4 |
| Scrap and waste | 62.8 | 72.2 | 74.8 | 61.9 | 59.9 | 0.3 | 0.6 | 0.7 | 0.5 | 0.2 |
| Used merchandise | 6.3 | 1.8 | 1.6 | 0.5 | 0.8 | 1.2 | 0.2 | 2.3 | 1.3 | 2.4 |
| Goods imported and returned unchanged | ..... | ..... | ..... | ..... | ..... | ..... | ..... | ..... | ..... | ..... |
| Special classification provisions | 0.8 | 1.3 | 0.8 | 1.3 | 0.4 | 0.8 | 0.9 | 0.8 | 0.9 | 0.9 |
| | The Netherlands | | | | | Asian 10 | | | | |
| **ALL GOODS** | 486.0 | 566.0 | 648.1 | 747.2 | 1 016.1 | 3 590.2 | 4 410.9 | 5 154.1 | 4 862.1 | 5 264.4 |
| **Manufactured goods** | 462.1 | 542.6 | 620.6 | 711.5 | 992.4 | 3 387.0 | 4 208.3 | 4 880.8 | 4 619.9 | 4 992.1 |
| Food products | 5.8 | 6.7 | 15.2 | 12.5 | 19.8 | 256.8 | 498.4 | 435.9 | 416.0 | 417.7 |
| Tobacco products | 0.1 | ..... | 0.4 | 0.2 | 0.1 | ..... | ..... | 1.6 | 0.4 | ..... |
| Textile mill products | 4.9 | 3.6 | 2.2 | 2.0 | 1.9 | 35.9 | 31.0 | 37.0 | 36.4 | 49.8 |
| Apparel | 3.4 | 5.3 | 7.5 | 9.0 | 9.7 | 37.4 | 36.2 | 59.6 | 63.8 | 61.5 |
| Lumber and wood products | 0.3 | 0.1 | 0.1 | 0.5 | 0.2 | 8.6 | 6.8 | 7.2 | 26.2 | 10.7 |
| Furniture and fixtures | 0.3 | 0.3 | 0.5 | 0.4 | 0.3 | 2.5 | 14.6 | 6.2 | 11.0 | 8.9 |
| Paper products | 21.8 | 32.6 | 38.7 | 31.6 | 19.5 | 115.8 | 125.8 | 197.7 | 178.4 | 145.7 |
| Printing and publishing | 3.4 | 2.8 | 22.2 | 20.0 | 27.6 | 32.9 | 38.9 | 59.7 | 60.6 | 64.2 |
| Chemical products | 136.6 | 165.2 | 226.2 | 373.9 | 627.5 | 667.8 | 772.4 | 916.4 | 943.9 | 1 106.0 |
| Refined petroleum products | 4.1 | 4.4 | 6.5 | 19.8 | 3.5 | 17.0 | 8.6 | 12.6 | 10.1 | 9.5 |
| Rubber and plastic products | 9.0 | 4.9 | 9.4 | 7.2 | 6.6 | 39.7 | 50.3 | 60.5 | 67.8 | 65.9 |
| Leather products | 0.2 | 0.6 | 0.4 | 0.5 | 0.8 | 25.8 | 25.3 | 29.0 | 17.9 | 20.1 |
| Stone, clay and glass products | 10.2 | 3.4 | 3.2 | 7.3 | 12.5 | 31.4 | 35.2 | 35.2 | 40.7 | 55.7 |
| Primary metals | 19.9 | 25.7 | 11.2 | 17.5 | 18.9 | 198.0 | 205.4 | 269.6 | 178.3 | 202.3 |
| Fabricated metal products | 8.2 | 11.7 | 7.8 | 7.0 | 5.1 | 82.2 | 86.4 | 198.4 | 151.7 | 140.3 |
| Industrial machinery and computers | 73.4 | 75.6 | 66.8 | 50.0 | 81.2 | 456.9 | 549.9 | 621.2 | 593.8 | 585.9 |
| Electric and electronic equipment | 103.4 | 142.3 | 145.6 | 85.4 | 71.6 | 870.6 | 1 167.0 | 1 298.0 | 1 103.3 | 1 233.2 |
| Transportation equipment | 21.4 | 31.5 | 21.5 | 21.5 | 20.6 | 198.5 | 218.6 | 290.3 | 251.8 | 315.1 |
| Scientific and measuring instruments | 30.4 | 19.8 | 29.4 | 40.7 | 62.0 | 263.8 | 298.1 | 287.3 | 411.7 | 436.8 |
| Miscellaneous manufactures | 4.0 | 4.4 | 3.9 | 3.0 | 2.1 | 30.8 | 27.3 | 43.2 | 43.9 | 49.8 |
| Unidentified manufactures | 1.6 | 1.5 | 1.9 | 1.3 | 0.9 | 14.4 | 12.0 | 14.2 | 12.3 | 12.7 |
| **Agricultural and livestock products** | 0.5 | 3.2 | 5.3 | 4.5 | 1.5 | 12.9 | 6.1 | 7.7 | 6.3 | 14.1 |
| Agricultural products | 0.2 | 1.1 | 2.2 | 1.9 | 0.4 | 11.9 | 3.7 | 5.2 | 2.7 | 8.6 |
| Livestock and livestock products | 0.3 | 2.1 | 3.0 | 2.6 | 1.1 | 1.0 | 2.3 | 2.5 | 3.6 | 5.6 |
| **Other commodities** | 23.4 | 20.2 | 22.2 | 31.2 | 22.2 | 190.3 | 196.5 | 265.5 | 235.8 | 258.1 |
| Forestry products | 0.6 | 0.1 | 0.3 | 0.4 | 0.1 | 3.4 | 3.3 | 3.2 | 6.9 | 3.1 |
| Fish and other marine products | ..... | 0.1 | ..... | 0.2 | 0.5 | 4.1 | 6.4 | 14.6 | 12.6 | 6.2 |
| Metallic ores and concentrates | 0.3 | 4.9 | 1.6 | 0.5 | ..... | 0.1 | 0.5 | ..... | 0.5 | 0.8 |
| Bituminous coal and lignite | 9.0 | 0.7 | ..... | 9.7 | ..... | ..... | ..... | ..... | ..... | ..... |
| Crude petroleum and natural gas | ..... | ..... | ..... | ..... | ..... | 0.2 | 0.8 | 1.0 | 1.1 | 1.2 |
| Nonmetallic minerals | 11.6 | 12.3 | 10.5 | 17.7 | 19.9 | 86.4 | 108.8 | 118.8 | 133.7 | 142.7 |
| Scrap and waste | 0.4 | 0.3 | 1.2 | 1.3 | 0.3 | 84.9 | 70.4 | 117.7 | 69.4 | 91.0 |
| Used merchandise | 0.6 | 0.5 | 8.2 | 0.9 | 1.1 | 2.9 | 2.8 | 4.3 | 4.1 | 4.0 |
| Goods imported and returned unchanged | ..... | ..... | ..... | ..... | ..... | ..... | ..... | ..... | ..... | ..... |
| Special classification provisions | 1.0 | 1.3 | 0.3 | 0.5 | 0.3 | 8.3 | 3.6 | 5.8 | 7.6 | 8.9 |

## Table D-3.  State Exports of Goods by Destination and Industry, 1993–1997 —*Continued*

### NEW JERSEY (Millions of dollars.)

| Industry | Japan 1993 | 1994 | 1995 | 1996 | 1997 | South Korea 1993 | 1994 | 1995 | 1996 | 1997 |
|---|---|---|---|---|---|---|---|---|---|---|
| ALL GOODS | 1 138.5 | 1 357.7 | 1 470.2 | 1 577.5 | 1 648.2 | 918.2 | 1 260.9 | 1 359.6 | 1 279.5 | 1 356.7 |
| Manufactured goods | 1 051.5 | 1 253.0 | 1 372.9 | 1 462.2 | 1 529.5 | 848.7 | 1 220.5 | 1 278.0 | 1 238.8 | 1 295.6 |
| Food products | 68.0 | 238.0 | 123.5 | 152.9 | 146.7 | 138.0 | 177.6 | 213.2 | 166.9 | 155.3 |
| Tobacco products | ..... | ..... | ..... | 0.4 | ..... | ..... | ..... | ..... | ..... | ..... |
| Textile mill products | 4.9 | 5.1 | 4.7 | 5.0 | 8.2 | 6.7 | 5.7 | 7.7 | 6.4 | 6.5 |
| Apparel | 24.1 | 21.7 | 40.2 | 44.8 | 35.0 | 2.0 | 2.5 | 6.9 | 6.2 | 7.5 |
| Lumber and wood products | 4.2 | 4.7 | 4.8 | 4.4 | 3.8 | 2.9 | 1.2 | 1.0 | 4.6 | 3.5 |
| Furniture and fixtures | 0.5 | 0.4 | 1.0 | 2.4 | 1.2 | 0.5 | 0.6 | 2.0 | 6.3 | 1.4 |
| Paper products | 33.4 | 39.8 | 64.1 | 38.9 | 14.2 | 4.6 | 5.8 | 4.8 | 5.8 | 5.6 |
| Printing and publishing | 13.1 | 13.5 | 17.2 | 16.7 | 18.4 | 1.6 | 2.8 | 3.6 | 6.0 | 3.4 |
| Chemical products | 254.7 | 256.0 | 288.9 | 316.9 | 412.7 | 81.5 | 109.1 | 117.6 | 137.6 | 143.9 |
| Refined petroleum products | 0.4 | 0.9 | 1.2 | 1.0 | 1.6 | 2.3 | 1.7 | 3.1 | 2.8 | 2.5 |
| Rubber and plastic products | 14.8 | 18.8 | 20.6 | 17.8 | 15.7 | 9.1 | 11.3 | 12.9 | 13.5 | 10.8 |
| Leather products | 4.7 | 6.6 | 8.0 | 6.5 | 6.2 | 9.8 | 7.1 | 4.9 | 3.4 | 4.2 |
| Stone, clay and glass products | 13.5 | 13.3 | 15.1 | 16.4 | 12.7 | 5.9 | 5.6 | 6.2 | 8.2 | 8.9 |
| Primary metals | 100.0 | 86.1 | 110.7 | 85.5 | 96.4 | 28.2 | 31.1 | 47.1 | 34.0 | 31.6 |
| Fabricated metal products | 12.6 | 11.6 | 9.7 | 12.5 | 13.5 | 21.9 | 24.2 | 21.3 | 23.8 | 27.8 |
| Industrial machinery and computers | 84.0 | 94.6 | 110.1 | 116.1 | 167.2 | 137.1 | 232.5 | 271.4 | 217.5 | 192.7 |
| Electric and electronic equipment | 245.5 | 245.2 | 356.9 | 378.9 | 282.1 | 229.3 | 381.8 | 283.4 | 302.9 | 358.9 |
| Transportation equipment | 7.2 | 8.8 | 12.4 | 10.0 | 15.6 | 130.3 | 157.6 | 209.2 | 187.9 | 247.0 |
| Scientific and measuring instruments | 149.6 | 172.8 | 160.6 | 219.0 | 262.1 | 27.5 | 56.8 | 50.1 | 92.8 | 71.5 |
| Miscellaneous manufactures | 12.4 | 11.7 | 19.1 | 12.6 | 11.6 | 4.7 | 3.4 | 9.9 | 10.5 | 10.2 |
| Unidentified manufactures | 3.8 | 3.4 | 4.3 | 3.5 | 4.5 | 4.9 | 2.3 | 1.7 | 1.9 | 2.4 |
| Agricultural and livestock products | 0.4 | 0.6 | 0.5 | 1.0 | 0.6 | 9.7 | 1.7 | 1.3 | 1.0 | 4.1 |
| Agricultural products | 0.4 | 0.4 | 0.4 | 0.8 | 0.4 | 9.1 | 0.4 | 0.1 | 0.1 | 0.4 |
| Livestock and livestock products | ..... | ..... | 0.2 | 0.1 | 0.2 | 0.6 | 1.3 | 1.2 | 0.8 | 3.7 |
| Other commodities | 86.5 | 104.0 | 96.7 | 114.4 | 118.2 | 59.8 | 38.7 | 80.2 | 39.7 | 57.0 |
| Forestry products | 2.0 | 1.5 | 1.6 | 2.7 | 2.1 | 0.5 | ..... | 0.1 | 0.1 | 0.2 |
| Fish and other marine products | 3.5 | 4.2 | 4.0 | 3.8 | 4.5 | 0.5 | 1.0 | 7.6 | 4.1 | 0.9 |
| Metallic ores and concentrates | ..... | 0.5 | ..... | 0.2 | 0.7 | ..... | ..... | ..... | ..... | ..... |
| Bituminous coal and lignite | ..... | ..... | ..... | ..... | ..... | ..... | ..... | ..... | ..... | ..... |
| Crude petroleum and natural gas | 0.1 | 0.6 | 0.7 | 0.5 | 0.6 | 0.1 | 0.1 | 0.1 | 0.1 | 0.1 |
| Nonmetallic minerals | 63.9 | 80.9 | 80.7 | 97.7 | 99.8 | 12.2 | 13.4 | 14.7 | 12.0 | 12.8 |
| Scrap and waste | 13.9 | 12.9 | 7.1 | 6.7 | 6.1 | 41.8 | 23.4 | 55.7 | 20.0 | 41.2 |
| Used merchandise | 1.5 | 1.8 | 0.9 | 1.3 | 2.2 | 0.2 | 0.3 | 0.8 | 0.7 | 0.6 |
| Goods imported and returned unchanged | ..... | ..... | ..... | ..... | ..... | ..... | ..... | ..... | ..... | ..... |
| Special classification provisions | 1.6 | 1.7 | 1.7 | 1.5 | 2.2 | 4.5 | 0.5 | 1.2 | 2.7 | 1.3 |

| Industry | Taiwan 1993 | 1994 | 1995 | 1996 | 1997 | Singapore 1993 | 1994 | 1995 | 1996 | 1997 |
|---|---|---|---|---|---|---|---|---|---|---|
| ALL GOODS | 407.7 | 517.6 | 519.0 | 440.3 | 484.7 | 210.7 | 262.1 | 249.6 | 231.4 | 304.0 |
| Manufactured goods | 398.1 | 507.0 | 502.8 | 425.4 | 463.5 | 209.1 | 260.0 | 246.3 | 228.7 | 301.0 |
| Food products | 13.2 | 13.2 | 16.7 | 16.4 | 22.5 | 6.3 | 7.0 | 8.1 | 6.4 | 5.9 |
| Tobacco products | ..... | ..... | ..... | ..... | ..... | ..... | ..... | ..... | ..... | ..... |
| Textile mill products | 3.5 | 1.1 | 2.1 | 0.7 | 0.8 | 2.6 | 3.5 | 3.3 | 2.3 | 6.3 |
| Apparel | 0.8 | 0.8 | 1.2 | 0.5 | 0.8 | 1.4 | 1.7 | 1.9 | 2.5 | 2.7 |
| Lumber and wood products | 0.3 | 0.4 | 0.7 | 0.9 | 0.6 | ..... | ..... | 0.1 | 7.3 | 0.2 |
| Furniture and fixtures | 0.3 | 0.1 | 0.1 | 0.4 | 0.8 | 0.2 | 12.0 | 1.4 | 0.7 | 1.6 |
| Paper products | 4.7 | 7.3 | 10.2 | 10.9 | 11.1 | 9.7 | 13.6 | 14.8 | 11.7 | 11.3 |
| Printing and publishing | 2.5 | 3.8 | 8.0 | 10.2 | 9.7 | 6.3 | 9.1 | 8.6 | 8.6 | 7.7 |
| Chemical products | 90.3 | 142.1 | 197.6 | 174.3 | 162.9 | 82.1 | 81.8 | 93.2 | 83.5 | 125.9 |
| Refined petroleum products | 4.4 | 2.8 | 3.0 | 2.1 | 2.0 | 1.6 | 1.3 | 1.5 | 0.9 | 1.1 |
| Rubber and plastic products | 3.8 | 3.6 | 2.7 | 5.5 | 5.4 | 2.4 | 4.1 | 3.3 | 3.3 | 3.7 |
| Leather products | 0.6 | 0.2 | 0.2 | 0.2 | 0.3 | 2.0 | 4.8 | 2.2 | 0.3 | 1.4 |
| Stone, clay and glass products | 3.1 | 2.1 | 2.6 | 2.8 | 3.1 | 3.3 | 3.3 | 1.8 | 2.1 | 1.8 |
| Primary metals | 26.1 | 32.3 | 33.0 | 13.9 | 23.2 | 8.4 | 15.4 | 4.2 | 4.1 | 7.4 |
| Fabricated metal products | 8.5 | 9.0 | 6.5 | 4.4 | 8.5 | 2.0 | 3.4 | 3.6 | 5.7 | 27.4 |
| Industrial machinery and computers | 50.9 | 57.9 | 37.4 | 37.2 | 48.1 | 26.3 | 29.4 | 42.1 | 33.4 | 30.4 |
| Electric and electronic equipment | 138.2 | 192.7 | 129.8 | 96.2 | 124.1 | 30.2 | 48.5 | 32.9 | 22.3 | 27.2 |
| Transportation equipment | 16.0 | 18.6 | 25.0 | 21.1 | 11.4 | 3.1 | 3.6 | 5.1 | 9.8 | 12.7 |
| Scientific and measuring instruments | 24.4 | 15.3 | 22.6 | 24.5 | 24.8 | 18.0 | 14.7 | 16.0 | 19.3 | 22.8 |
| Miscellaneous manufactures | 5.0 | 2.3 | 2.0 | 2.1 | 2.2 | 1.8 | 1.7 | 1.3 | 3.7 | 2.9 |
| Unidentified manufactures | 1.5 | 1.3 | 1.6 | 1.1 | 1.1 | 1.6 | 1.0 | 0.7 | 0.7 | 0.7 |
| Agricultural and livestock products | 0.8 | 0.6 | 1.0 | 0.4 | 1.1 | 0.3 | 0.7 | 0.6 | 0.5 | 0.6 |
| Agricultural products | 0.7 | 0.6 | 0.9 | 0.2 | 1.0 | 0.3 | 0.5 | 0.4 | 0.1 | 0.2 |
| Livestock and livestock products | ..... | ..... | 0.1 | 0.1 | 0.1 | ..... | 0.2 | 0.1 | 0.4 | 0.4 |
| Other commodities | 8.9 | 10.0 | 15.1 | 14.5 | 20.1 | 1.2 | 1.3 | 2.8 | 2.2 | 2.5 |
| Forestry products | 0.1 | 0.1 | 0.1 | 0.1 | 0.2 | 0.1 | 0.1 | 0.1 | ..... | ..... |
| Fish and other marine products | 0.1 | 0.1 | ..... | 0.2 | 0.1 | ..... | ..... | ..... | 0.9 | ..... |
| Metallic ores and concentrates | ..... | ..... | ..... | ..... | ..... | ..... | ..... | ..... | ..... | ..... |
| Bituminous coal and lignite | ..... | ..... | ..... | ..... | ..... | ..... | ..... | ..... | ..... | ..... |
| Crude petroleum and natural gas | ..... | ..... | 0.2 | 0.4 | 0.5 | ..... | ..... | ..... | 0.1 | 0.1 |
| Nonmetallic minerals | 5.3 | 6.9 | 5.6 | 6.3 | 5.3 | 0.4 | 0.4 | 0.7 | 0.7 | 1.2 |
| Scrap and waste | 1.6 | 2.0 | 8.2 | 6.5 | 11.9 | ..... | 0.2 | ..... | ..... | 0.5 |
| Used merchandise | 0.6 | ..... | 0.1 | ..... | 0.1 | 0.3 | 0.4 | 0.6 | 0.1 | 0.1 |
| Goods imported and returned unchanged | ..... | ..... | ..... | ..... | ..... | ..... | ..... | ..... | ..... | ..... |
| Special classification provisions | 1.1 | 0.7 | 0.9 | 1.0 | 2.1 | 0.4 | 0.2 | 1.4 | 0.5 | 0.6 |

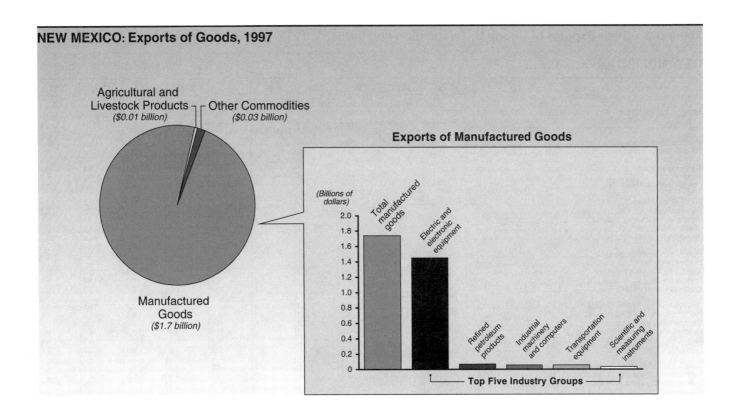

**NEW MEXICO: Exports of Goods, 1997**

Agricultural and Livestock Products ($0.01 billion)

Other Commodities ($0.03 billion)

Manufactured Goods ($1.7 billion)

**Exports of Manufactured Goods**

(Billions of dollars)

Total manufactured goods

Electric and electronic equipment

Refined petroleum products

Industrial machinery and computers

Transportation equipment

Scientific and measuring instruments

Top Five Industry Groups

## Table D-3.   State Exports of Goods by Destination and Industry, 1993–1997 —*Continued*

### NEW MEXICO (Millions of dollars.)

| Industry | 1993 | 1994 | 1995 | 1996 | 1997 | 1993 | 1994 | 1995 | 1996 | 1997 |
|---|---|---|---|---|---|---|---|---|---|---|
| | All destinations | | | | | Canada | | | | |
| **ALL GOODS** | 400.0 | 488.5 | 426.6 | 917.4 | 1 779.9 | 46.6 | 47.5 | 41.7 | 51.2 | 55.6 |
| **Manufactured goods** | 377.2 | 450.7 | 385.4 | 892.6 | 1 739.3 | 35.0 | 35.7 | 30.4 | 40.6 | 43.6 |
| Food products | 4.0 | 5.2 | 2.0 | 4.5 | 8.9 | 2.1 | 1.4 | 0.5 | 2.4 | 2.2 |
| Tobacco products | ..... | ..... | ..... | ..... | 0.1 | ..... | ..... | ..... | ..... | ..... |
| Textile mill products | 0.3 | 0.5 | 1.0 | 3.7 | 4.0 | 0.1 | ..... | 0.1 | ..... | 0.2 |
| Apparel | 0.6 | 7.6 | 9.2 | 1.8 | 2.8 | 0.1 | 0.1 | 0.3 | 0.3 | 0.1 |
| Lumber and wood products | 5.3 | 6.9 | 2.5 | 5.3 | 4.0 | 0.4 | 0.9 | 0.8 | 1.2 | 2.3 |
| Furniture and fixtures | 3.2 | 2.2 | 0.8 | 0.6 | 0.9 | 0.6 | 0.3 | 0.3 | 0.1 | 0.2 |
| Paper products | 0.8 | 0.8 | 0.9 | 1.8 | 1.5 | 0.1 | 0.1 | 0.2 | 0.3 | 0.5 |
| Printing and publishing | 0.9 | 3.8 | 1.0 | 1.4 | 1.6 | 0.1 | 0.3 | 0.3 | 0.3 | 0.3 |
| Chemical products | 13.1 | 15.2 | 15.0 | 11.3 | 16.8 | 6.6 | 5.0 | 5.9 | 3.6 | 5.2 |
| Refined petroleum products | 67.8 | 50.2 | 37.9 | 54.2 | 68.3 | ..... | 0.8 | ..... | ..... | ..... |
| Rubber and plastic products | 4.0 | 5.0 | 4.4 | 4.3 | 5.3 | 0.4 | 0.7 | 0.6 | 0.5 | 0.3 |
| Leather products | 0.3 | 0.2 | 0.2 | 0.3 | 0.2 | ..... | ..... | ..... | ..... | ..... |
| Stone, clay and glass products | 32.4 | 21.0 | 4.5 | 2.5 | 2.5 | 0.2 | 0.2 | 0.3 | 0.4 | 0.4 |
| Primary metals | 2.1 | 2.7 | 3.3 | 3.8 | 5.3 | 0.6 | 1.0 | 1.2 | 1.1 | 1.9 |
| Fabricated metal products | 1.8 | 1.1 | 2.6 | 1.6 | 3.5 | 0.4 | 0.3 | 0.5 | 0.4 | 0.7 |
| Industrial machinery and computers | 70.3 | 69.2 | 37.9 | 39.8 | 55.2 | 8.2 | 9.7 | 5.3 | 7.9 | 12.7 |
| Electric and electronic equipment | 125.3 | 203.0 | 214.7 | 686.5 | 1 450.3 | 8.2 | 8.3 | 8.5 | 7.2 | 8.1 |
| Transportation equipment | 9.3 | 25.7 | 13.0 | 29.5 | 55.0 | 2.3 | 3.5 | 3.1 | 11.6 | 5.4 |
| Scientific and measuring instruments | 18.3 | 17.2 | 21.4 | 27.4 | 33.3 | 2.7 | 1.8 | 1.4 | 1.7 | 1.7 |
| Miscellaneous manufactures | 15.5 | 10.7 | 11.0 | 10.4 | 16.7 | 1.7 | 0.9 | 0.8 | 0.8 | 0.6 |
| Unidentified manufactures | 1.7 | 2.5 | 2.2 | 1.9 | 3.3 | 0.4 | 0.6 | 0.6 | 0.6 | 0.6 |
| **Agricultural and livestock products** | 11.7 | 16.0 | 20.9 | 12.0 | 10.3 | 5.5 | 4.4 | 4.7 | 2.9 | 2.3 |
| Agricultural products | 9.0 | 15.6 | 20.1 | 11.4 | 9.8 | 3.4 | 4.3 | 4.7 | 2.8 | 2.2 |
| Livestock and livestock products | 2.7 | 0.4 | 0.7 | 0.6 | 0.5 | 2.1 | 0.1 | ..... | 0.2 | ..... |
| **Other commodities** | 11.1 | 21.8 | 20.3 | 12.9 | 30.2 | 6.2 | 7.4 | 6.5 | 7.7 | 9.8 |
| Forestry products | 0.1 | 0.1 | ..... | 0.1 | 0.1 | 0.1 | ..... | ..... | 0.1 | 0.1 |
| Fish and other marine products | 0.5 | 0.3 | 0.5 | 0.1 | 0.5 | ..... | 0.1 | 0.3 | 0.1 | ..... |
| Metallic ores and concentrates | 0.1 | ..... | 0.1 | 0.8 | 3.0 | ..... | ..... | ..... | ..... | ..... |
| Bituminous coal and lignite | ..... | ..... | ..... | ..... | ..... | ..... | ..... | ..... | ..... | ..... |
| Crude petroleum and natural gas | 0.7 | ..... | 3.1 | ..... | ..... | 0.6 | ..... | ..... | ..... | ..... |
| Nonmetallic minerals | 2.5 | 4.9 | 4.9 | 4.0 | 4.2 | 1.8 | 2.3 | 2.4 | 2.6 | 2.8 |
| Scrap and waste | 0.5 | 0.9 | 2.9 | 0.5 | 0.6 | ..... | 0.1 | 0.1 | 0.2 | 0.2 |
| Used merchandise | 3.2 | 10.5 | 4.8 | 2.4 | 14.4 | 0.2 | 0.3 | 0.3 | 0.8 | 0.1 |
| Goods imported and returned unchanged | 3.3 | 4.6 | 3.4 | 3.3 | 6.3 | 3.3 | 4.6 | 3.4 | 3.3 | 6.3 |
| Special classification provisions | 0.2 | 0.5 | 0.7 | 1.5 | 1.1 | 0.1 | ..... | 0.1 | 0.6 | 0.2 |

## Table D-3.  State Exports of Goods by Destination and Industry, 1993–1997 —*Continued*

**NEW MEXICO** (Millions of dollars.)

| Industry | 1993 | 1994 | 1995 | 1996 | 1997 | 1993 | 1994 | 1995 | 1996 | 1997 |
|---|---|---|---|---|---|---|---|---|---|---|
| | South and Central America and Caribbean | | | | | Mexico | | | | |
| **ALL GOODS** | 9.8 | 7.2 | 10.6 | 8.9 | 13.8 | 105.8 | 93.9 | 77.1 | 100.0 | 86.6 |
| **Manufactured goods** | 8.9 | 5.6 | 9.8 | 6.8 | 13.4 | 103.3 | 87.6 | 64.9 | 96.1 | 80.5 |
| Food products | 0.1 | 0.2 | ..... | 0.1 | 0.1 | 1.5 | 2.7 | 0.8 | 0.5 | 1.2 |
| Tobacco products | ..... | ..... | ..... | ..... | ..... | ..... | ..... | ..... | ..... | ..... |
| Textile mill products | ..... | ..... | ..... | ..... | 0.1 | 0.1 | 0.1 | 0.5 | 3.4 | 3.0 |
| Apparel | ..... | ..... | ..... | 0.1 | 0.1 | 0.1 | 6.6 | 7.8 | 0.3 | 1.2 |
| Lumber and wood products | ..... | ..... | 0.1 | ..... | ..... | 1.8 | 1.6 | 0.4 | 0.5 | 0.2 |
| Furniture and fixtures | 0.1 | 0.2 | ..... | ..... | ..... | 0.1 | 0.1 | 0.2 | 0.2 | 0.2 |
| Paper products | 0.3 | ..... | 0.1 | 0.1 | ..... | 0.4 | 0.3 | 0.4 | 0.3 | 0.5 |
| Printing and publishing | ..... | 0.1 | 0.1 | 0.2 | 0.2 | 0.1 | 0.1 | ..... | ..... | ..... |
| Chemical products | 0.1 | 0.5 | 0.3 | 0.2 | 0.3 | 1.5 | 0.6 | 1.2 | 3.9 | 2.7 |
| Refined petroleum products | ..... | ..... | ..... | ..... | ..... | 67.8 | 49.3 | 37.8 | 54.0 | 56.6 |
| Rubber and plastic products | 0.2 | 0.1 | 0.2 | 0.1 | 0.2 | 0.3 | 0.7 | 0.9 | 0.7 | 1.3 |
| Leather products | 0.1 | 0.1 | ..... | 0.1 | ..... | ..... | ..... | 0.1 | ..... | ..... |
| Stone, clay and glass products | 0.1 | ..... | 0.2 | 0.1 | 0.2 | 0.1 | 0.4 | 0.3 | 0.3 | 0.4 |
| Primary metals | 0.2 | 0.1 | 0.1 | ..... | 0.2 | 0.2 | 0.4 | 0.4 | 1.6 | 1.9 |
| Fabricated metal products | 0.1 | ..... | ..... | 0.1 | 0.4 | 0.4 | 0.3 | 0.5 | 0.3 | 0.6 |
| Industrial machinery and computers | 4.5 | 1.2 | 5.3 | 3.3 | 2.8 | 11.9 | 9.0 | 2.4 | 4.2 | 4.2 |
| Electric and electronic equipment | 1.5 | 0.7 | 1.2 | 0.5 | 5.4 | 16.0 | 13.5 | 9.5 | 23.7 | 1.6 |
| Transportation equipment | 0.4 | 0.7 | 0.2 | 0.1 | 0.5 | 0.3 | 0.1 | 0.4 | 0.4 | 2.1 |
| Scientific and measuring instruments | 0.7 | 0.6 | 0.8 | 0.8 | 1.0 | 0.3 | 1.0 | 0.9 | 1.0 | 2.3 |
| Miscellaneous manufactures | 0.4 | 0.8 | 0.9 | 0.9 | 2.1 | 0.3 | 0.2 | 0.1 | 0.1 | 0.1 |
| Unidentified manufactures | 0.1 | 0.1 | 0.2 | ..... | ..... | 0.2 | 0.6 | 0.4 | 0.7 | 0.5 |
| **Agricultural and livestock products** | 0.7 | 1.5 | 0.8 | 1.8 | 0.3 | 1.8 | 4.2 | 5.5 | 2.8 | 3.3 |
| Agricultural products | 0.7 | 1.6 | 0.9 | 1.9 | 0.2 | 1.2 | 4.0 | 5.4 | 2.4 | 2.9 |
| Livestock and livestock products | ..... | ..... | ..... | ..... | ..... | 0.6 | 0.1 | ..... | 0.3 | 0.5 |
| **Other commodities** | 0.1 | 0.1 | ..... | 0.3 | 0.1 | 0.8 | 2.1 | 6.7 | 1.1 | 2.8 |
| Forestry products | ..... | ..... | ..... | ..... | ..... | ..... | ..... | ..... | ..... | ..... |
| Fish and other marine products | ..... | ..... | ..... | ..... | ..... | ..... | ..... | ..... | ..... | ..... |
| Metallic ores and concentrates | ..... | ..... | ..... | ..... | ..... | ..... | ..... | ..... | 0.5 | 2.2 |
| Bituminous coal and lignite | ..... | ..... | ..... | ..... | ..... | ..... | ..... | ..... | ..... | ..... |
| Crude petroleum and natural gas | ..... | ..... | ..... | ..... | ..... | ..... | ..... | 3.1 | ..... | ..... |
| Nonmetallic minerals | 0.1 | 0.1 | 0.1 | ..... | ..... | 0.2 | 1.1 | 1.0 | 0.1 | 0.1 |
| Scrap and waste | ..... | ..... | ..... | ..... | ..... | 0.4 | 0.7 | 2.5 | 0.3 | 0.3 |
| Used merchandise | 0.1 | 0.1 | 0.1 | 0.2 | 0.2 | 0.1 | 0.2 | ..... | 0.1 | 0.1 |
| Goods imported and returned unchanged | ..... | ..... | ..... | ..... | ..... | ..... | ..... | ..... | ..... | ..... |
| Special classification provisions | ..... | ..... | ..... | ..... | ..... | ..... | ..... | ..... | 0.1 | ..... |
| | European Union | | | | | United Kingdom | | | | |
| **ALL GOODS** | 77.5 | 114.3 | 112.6 | 103.2 | 153.8 | 36.5 | 46.4 | 26.7 | 10.7 | 13.4 |
| **Manufactured goods** | 75.2 | 110.9 | 105.1 | 99.5 | 148.8 | 36.2 | 46.0 | 25.9 | 9.9 | 12.8 |
| Food products | 0.2 | 0.3 | 0.1 | 0.2 | 2.3 | 0.2 | 0.1 | 0.1 | ..... | 1.8 |
| Tobacco products | ..... | ..... | ..... | ..... | ..... | ..... | ..... | ..... | ..... | ..... |
| Textile mill products | ..... | 0.1 | 0.1 | ..... | 0.1 | ..... | ..... | ..... | ..... | ..... |
| Apparel | 0.2 | 0.2 | 0.6 | 0.1 | 0.2 | ..... | ..... | 0.3 | ..... | ..... |
| Lumber and wood products | 2.2 | 1.8 | 0.5 | 1.1 | 0.2 | ..... | ..... | ..... | ..... | ..... |
| Furniture and fixtures | 0.1 | 0.1 | 0.1 | ..... | 0.3 | ..... | ..... | ..... | ..... | ..... |
| Paper products | ..... | ..... | ..... | ..... | ..... | ..... | ..... | ..... | ..... | ..... |
| Printing and publishing | 0.4 | 3.1 | 0.2 | 0.6 | 0.5 | 0.1 | 0.5 | 0.1 | 0.4 | 0.4 |
| Chemical products | 3.7 | 7.5 | 6.2 | 1.4 | 6.6 | 0.1 | 0.5 | 0.2 | 0.3 | 0.4 |
| Refined petroleum products | ..... | ..... | ..... | ..... | 0.1 | ..... | ..... | ..... | ..... | ..... |
| Rubber and plastic products | 1.4 | 1.0 | 0.8 | 1.4 | 1.2 | 0.6 | 0.2 | 0.2 | 0.8 | 0.7 |
| Leather products | 0.1 | 0.1 | 0.1 | ..... | 0.1 | ..... | ..... | ..... | ..... | ..... |
| Stone, clay and glass products | 25.7 | 13.0 | 1.0 | 0.8 | 0.5 | 15.9 | 9.0 | 0.4 | 0.1 | 0.1 |
| Primary metals | 0.3 | 0.5 | 0.4 | 0.5 | 0.4 | 0.2 | 0.2 | ..... | 0.1 | 0.1 |
| Fabricated metal products | 0.6 | 0.2 | 0.7 | 0.3 | 1.0 | 0.1 | ..... | ..... | 0.2 | 0.4 |
| Industrial machinery and computers | 18.3 | 20.5 | 15.6 | 10.9 | 9.0 | 15.0 | 15.2 | 0.5 | 1.3 | 2.1 |
| Electric and electronic equipment | 7.0 | 49.4 | 60.4 | 55.3 | 71.3 | 1.7 | 18.9 | 20.7 | 4.0 | 3.3 |
| Transportation equipment | 1.9 | 2.0 | 5.2 | 12.3 | 42.0 | 0.2 | 0.1 | 0.4 | 0.2 | 0.6 |
| Scientific and measuring instruments | 5.4 | 5.2 | 8.1 | 7.9 | 8.6 | 1.5 | 0.8 | 2.1 | 1.7 | 2.4 |
| Miscellaneous manufactures | 7.0 | 5.2 | 4.4 | 6.4 | 4.2 | 0.3 | 0.2 | 0.7 | 0.6 | 0.3 |
| Unidentified manufactures | 0.7 | 0.7 | 0.6 | 0.1 | 0.3 | 0.2 | 0.2 | 0.1 | ..... | ..... |
| **Agricultural and livestock products** | 0.5 | 1.0 | 2.8 | 1.6 | 2.9 | ..... | 0.2 | 0.4 | ..... | ..... |
| Agricultural products | 0.5 | 0.8 | 2.5 | 1.6 | 2.9 | ..... | ..... | 0.1 | ..... | ..... |
| Livestock and livestock products | ..... | 0.2 | 0.3 | ..... | ..... | ..... | 0.2 | 0.3 | ..... | ..... |
| **Other commodities** | 1.7 | 2.4 | 4.7 | 2.0 | 2.1 | 0.3 | 0.2 | 0.4 | 0.8 | 0.7 |
| Forestry products | ..... | ..... | ..... | ..... | ..... | ..... | ..... | ..... | ..... | ..... |
| Fish and other marine products | ..... | ..... | ..... | ..... | 0.1 | ..... | ..... | ..... | ..... | ..... |
| Metallic ores and concentrates | ..... | ..... | ..... | 0.3 | 0.8 | ..... | ..... | ..... | 0.3 | ..... |
| Bituminous coal and lignite | ..... | ..... | ..... | ..... | ..... | ..... | ..... | ..... | ..... | ..... |
| Crude petroleum and natural gas | ..... | ..... | ..... | ..... | ..... | ..... | ..... | ..... | ..... | ..... |
| Nonmetallic minerals | 0.1 | 0.2 | 0.6 | 0.5 | 0.1 | 0.1 | 0.1 | 0.1 | ..... | ..... |
| Scrap and waste | ..... | ..... | 0.1 | ..... | ..... | ..... | ..... | ..... | ..... | ..... |
| Used merchandise | 1.5 | 2.1 | 3.8 | 0.8 | 0.5 | 0.2 | 0.1 | 0.2 | 0.3 | 0.2 |
| Goods imported and returned unchanged | ..... | ..... | ..... | ..... | ..... | ..... | ..... | ..... | ..... | ..... |
| Special classification provisions | ..... | 0.1 | 0.2 | 0.4 | 0.6 | ..... | ..... | 0.1 | 0.1 | 0.4 |

## Table D-3.  State Exports of Goods by Destination and Industry, 1993–1997 —*Continued*

### NEW MEXICO (Millions of dollars.)

| Industry | 1993 | 1994 | 1995 | 1996 | 1997 | 1993 | 1994 | 1995 | 1996 | 1997 |
|---|---|---|---|---|---|---|---|---|---|---|
| | Germany | | | | | France | | | | |
| **ALL GOODS** | 19.2 | 32.9 | 26.1 | 19.1 | 18.8 | 5.4 | 12.1 | 20.8 | 27.6 | 32.3 |
| **Manufactured goods** | 18.8 | 32.4 | 22.2 | 18.5 | 18.2 | 4.1 | 10.4 | 20.2 | 27.0 | 32.1 |
| Food products | ..... | ..... | ..... | ..... | 0.1 | ..... | ..... | ..... | ..... | ..... |
| Tobacco products | ..... | ..... | ..... | ..... | ..... | ..... | ..... | ..... | ..... | ..... |
| Textile mill products | ..... | ..... | ..... | ..... | ..... | ..... | ..... | ..... | ..... | ..... |
| Apparel | 0.1 | 0.1 | 0.1 | ..... | ..... | ..... | ..... | ..... | ..... | ..... |
| Lumber and wood products | 0.6 | 0.5 | 0.2 | 0.8 | ..... | 0.1 | 0.3 | 0.2 | 0.2 | ..... |
| Furniture and fixtures | ..... | ..... | ..... | ..... | ..... | ..... | ..... | ..... | ..... | ..... |
| Paper products | ..... | ..... | ..... | ..... | ..... | ..... | ..... | ..... | ..... | ..... |
| Printing and publishing | 0.3 | 2.5 | ..... | ..... | ..... | ..... | ..... | ..... | ..... | 0.1 |
| Chemical products | ..... | 0.1 | 0.4 | 0.4 | 1.0 | 0.1 | 0.4 | 0.7 | ..... | 0.9 |
| Refined petroleum products | ..... | ..... | ..... | ..... | ..... | ..... | ..... | ..... | ..... | 0.1 |
| Rubber and plastic products | 0.4 | 0.3 | 0.5 | 0.4 | 0.2 | ..... | ..... | ..... | ..... | 0.1 |
| Leather products | ..... | ..... | ..... | ..... | 0.1 | ..... | ..... | ..... | ..... | ..... |
| Stone, clay and glass products | 9.8 | 3.9 | 0.3 | 0.2 | 0.1 | ..... | ..... | 0.1 | ..... | 0.1 |
| Primary metals | ..... | 0.1 | 0.2 | ..... | ..... | ..... | ..... | ..... | ..... | ..... |
| Fabricated metal products | 0.1 | 0.1 | 0.1 | ..... | 0.1 | 0.1 | ..... | 0.5 | ..... | ..... |
| Industrial machinery and computers | 0.4 | 0.8 | 2.0 | 2.1 | 1.0 | 0.4 | 2.9 | 4.3 | 2.4 | 1.2 |
| Electric and electronic equipment | 1.4 | 19.7 | 9.7 | 7.3 | 9.7 | 0.9 | 5.0 | 11.9 | 21.5 | 28.0 |
| Transportation equipment | 0.9 | 0.2 | 3.4 | 0.7 | 1.8 | 0.1 | 0.4 | 0.1 | 0.7 | ..... |
| Scientific and measuring instruments | 1.3 | 0.8 | 2.5 | 1.9 | 1.2 | 1.2 | 0.5 | 1.7 | 1.7 | 1.3 |
| Miscellaneous manufactures | 3.2 | 2.9 | 2.6 | 4.5 | 2.5 | 0.9 | 0.7 | 0.4 | 0.3 | 0.3 |
| Unidentified manufactures | 0.2 | 0.2 | 0.2 | ..... | 0.2 | 0.2 | 0.1 | 0.1 | ..... | ..... |
| **Agricultural and livestock products** | 0.3 | 0.3 | 1.5 | 0.2 | 0.4 | ..... | ..... | ..... | ..... | ..... |
| Agricultural products | 0.3 | 0.3 | 1.5 | 0.2 | 0.4 | ..... | ..... | ..... | ..... | ..... |
| Livestock and livestock products | ..... | ..... | ..... | ..... | ..... | ..... | ..... | ..... | ..... | ..... |
| **Other commodities** | 0.2 | 0.2 | 2.4 | 0.4 | 0.2 | 1.2 | 1.8 | 0.7 | 0.6 | 0.1 |
| Forestry products | ..... | ..... | ..... | ..... | ..... | ..... | ..... | ..... | ..... | ..... |
| Fish and other marine products | ..... | ..... | ..... | ..... | 0.1 | ..... | ..... | ..... | ..... | ..... |
| Metallic ores and concentrates | ..... | ..... | ..... | ..... | ..... | ..... | ..... | ..... | ..... | ..... |
| Bituminous coal and lignite | ..... | ..... | ..... | ..... | ..... | ..... | ..... | ..... | ..... | ..... |
| Crude petroleum and natural gas | ..... | ..... | ..... | ..... | ..... | ..... | ..... | ..... | ..... | ..... |
| Nonmetallic minerals | ..... | 0.1 | ..... | ..... | ..... | ..... | ..... | 0.5 | 0.4 | 0.1 |
| Scrap and waste | ..... | ..... | ..... | ..... | ..... | ..... | ..... | ..... | ..... | ..... |
| Used merchandise | 0.1 | 0.1 | 2.4 | 0.3 | 0.1 | 1.2 | 1.8 | 0.1 | ..... | ..... |
| Goods imported and returned unchanged | ..... | ..... | ..... | ..... | ..... | ..... | ..... | ..... | ..... | ..... |
| Special classification provisions | ..... | 0.1 | ..... | 0.1 | ..... | ..... | ..... | 0.1 | 0.1 | ..... |
| | The Netherlands | | | | | Asian 10 | | | | |
| **ALL GOODS** | 2.0 | 4.4 | 16.3 | 4.9 | 21.3 | 135.7 | 186.5 | 165.9 | 630.8 | 1 426.6 |
| **Manufactured goods** | 1.9 | 4.2 | 15.9 | 4.7 | 20.4 | 133.7 | 181.5 | 160.5 | 628.0 | 1 424.1 |
| Food products | ..... | 0.1 | ..... | ..... | 0.1 | 0.1 | 0.3 | 0.4 | 0.4 | 0.7 |
| Tobacco products | ..... | ..... | ..... | ..... | ..... | ..... | ..... | ..... | 0.1 | ..... |
| Textile mill products | ..... | ..... | ..... | ..... | 0.1 | 0.1 | 0.2 | 0.1 | 0.2 | 0.5 |
| Apparel | ..... | ..... | ..... | ..... | ..... | 0.2 | 0.7 | 0.5 | 1.0 | 1.0 |
| Lumber and wood products | 0.3 | ..... | ..... | ..... | ..... | 0.6 | 2.2 | 0.5 | 2.0 | 1.3 |
| Furniture and fixtures | ..... | 0.1 | ..... | ..... | ..... | ..... | 0.1 | 0.1 | 0.2 | 0.2 |
| Paper products | ..... | ..... | ..... | ..... | ..... | ..... | 0.4 | 0.1 | 0.8 | 0.4 |
| Printing and publishing | ..... | ..... | ..... | ..... | ..... | 0.2 | 0.1 | 0.2 | 0.2 | 0.5 |
| Chemical products | 0.3 | ..... | 0.2 | 0.1 | 0.2 | 0.4 | 0.6 | 0.6 | 1.2 | 0.7 |
| Refined petroleum products | ..... | ..... | ..... | ..... | ..... | ..... | 0.1 | ..... | ..... | 11.6 |
| Rubber and plastic products | ..... | 0.2 | ..... | ..... | ..... | 1.2 | 2.1 | 1.2 | 0.9 | 0.8 |
| Leather products | ..... | ..... | ..... | ..... | ..... | ..... | 0.1 | 0.1 | 0.1 | ..... |
| Stone, clay and glass products | ..... | ..... | ..... | 0.1 | 0.1 | 5.4 | 6.8 | 2.0 | 0.7 | 0.8 |
| Primary metals | ..... | 0.1 | 0.1 | 0.2 | 0.1 | 0.1 | 0.3 | 1.1 | 0.4 | 0.7 |
| Fabricated metal products | ..... | ..... | ..... | ..... | 0.3 | 0.1 | 0.1 | 0.6 | 0.3 | 0.4 |
| Industrial machinery and computers | 0.7 | 0.6 | 0.6 | 0.7 | 0.4 | 24.4 | 25.3 | 7.2 | 9.7 | 20.4 |
| Electric and electronic equipment | 0.1 | 2.7 | 14.6 | 3.4 | 4.0 | 88.5 | 128.5 | 130.3 | 593.9 | 1 360.1 |
| Transportation equipment | ..... | ..... | 0.1 | ..... | 14.1 | 2.8 | 5.9 | 3.9 | 3.6 | 4.3 |
| Scientific and measuring instruments | 0.1 | 0.1 | 0.2 | 0.2 | 1.1 | 3.8 | 4.7 | 7.3 | 10.4 | 11.7 |
| Miscellaneous manufactures | 0.2 | ..... | ..... | ..... | ..... | 5.6 | 2.9 | 4.1 | 1.7 | 8.1 |
| Unidentified manufactures | ..... | ..... | ..... | ..... | ..... | 0.2 | 0.3 | 0.3 | 0.3 | 0.2 |
| **Agricultural and livestock products** | 0.1 | 0.1 | 0.3 | 0.2 | 0.3 | 0.7 | 2.4 | 3.7 | 1.6 | 0.8 |
| Agricultural products | 0.1 | 0.1 | 0.3 | 0.2 | 0.3 | 0.7 | 2.4 | 3.4 | 1.5 | 0.7 |
| Livestock and livestock products | ..... | ..... | ..... | ..... | ..... | ..... | ..... | 0.3 | 0.1 | 0.1 |
| **Other commodities** | ..... | 0.1 | ..... | ..... | 0.5 | 1.4 | 2.6 | 1.6 | 1.2 | 1.7 |
| Forestry products | ..... | ..... | ..... | ..... | ..... | ..... | 0.1 | ..... | ..... | ..... |
| Fish and other marine products | ..... | ..... | ..... | ..... | ..... | 0.5 | 0.2 | 0.2 | ..... | 0.3 |
| Metallic ores and concentrates | ..... | ..... | ..... | ..... | 0.5 | 0.1 | ..... | ..... | ..... | ..... |
| Bituminous coal and lignite | ..... | ..... | ..... | ..... | ..... | ..... | ..... | ..... | ..... | ..... |
| Crude petroleum and natural gas | ..... | ..... | ..... | ..... | ..... | ..... | ..... | ..... | ..... | ..... |
| Nonmetallic minerals | ..... | ..... | ..... | ..... | ..... | 0.3 | 1.2 | 0.8 | 0.8 | 1.2 |
| Scrap and waste | ..... | ..... | ..... | ..... | ..... | ..... | ..... | ..... | ..... | 0.1 |
| Used merchandise | ..... | 0.1 | ..... | ..... | ..... | 0.5 | 1.0 | 0.4 | 0.3 | 0.1 |
| Goods imported and returned unchanged | ..... | ..... | ..... | ..... | ..... | ..... | ..... | ..... | ..... | ..... |
| Special classification provisions | ..... | ..... | ..... | ..... | ..... | ..... | ..... | 0.1 | 0.1 | 0.1 |

## Table D-3. State Exports of Goods by Destination and Industry, 1993–1997 —Continued

### NEW MEXICO (Millions of dollars.)

| Industry | 1993 | 1994 | 1995 | 1996 | 1997 | 1993 | 1994 | 1995 | 1996 | 1997 |
|---|---|---|---|---|---|---|---|---|---|---|
| | Japan | | | | | South Korea | | | | |
| **ALL GOODS** | 34.3 | 44.2 | 21.2 | 45.7 | 60.1 | 56.1 | 68.7 | 59.1 | 184.4 | 197.2 |
| **Manufactured goods** | 32.6 | 40.6 | 18.9 | 43.6 | 58.5 | 56.1 | 67.8 | 57.1 | 184.2 | 196.8 |
| Food products | 0.1 | 0.3 | 0.1 | ..... | 0.3 | ..... | ..... | ..... | 0.1 | 0.1 |
| Tobacco products | ..... | ..... | ..... | 0.1 | ..... | ..... | ..... | ..... | ..... | ..... |
| Textile mill products | 0.1 | 0.2 | 0.1 | 0.1 | 0.3 | ..... | ..... | ..... | ..... | ..... |
| Apparel | 0.1 | 0.7 | 0.4 | 0.7 | 0.9 | ..... | ..... | ..... | ..... | ..... |
| Lumber and wood products | 0.4 | 2.2 | 0.4 | 2.0 | 1.0 | ..... | ..... | ..... | ..... | 0.1 |
| Furniture and fixtures | ..... | ..... | 0.1 | ..... | ..... | ..... | ..... | ..... | ..... | 0.1 |
| Paper products | ..... | 0.3 | ..... | 0.2 | 0.2 | ..... | ..... | ..... | ..... | ..... |
| Printing and publishing | ..... | 0.1 | 0.1 | 0.1 | 0.1 | 0.1 | ..... | ..... | ..... | ..... |
| Chemical products | 0.3 | 0.3 | 0.3 | 0.5 | 0.4 | ..... | ..... | ..... | ..... | ..... |
| Refined petroleum products | ..... | ..... | ..... | ..... | ..... | ..... | ..... | ..... | ..... | ..... |
| Rubber and plastic products | ..... | 0.2 | 0.2 | 0.4 | 0.4 | 0.1 | 0.1 | 0.1 | 0.1 | ..... |
| Leather products | ..... | ..... | 0.1 | ..... | ..... | ..... | ..... | ..... | ..... | ..... |
| Stone, clay and glass products | ..... | 0.2 | 0.1 | 0.1 | 0.1 | ..... | 0.1 | 0.1 | 0.2 | 0.2 |
| Primary metals | 0.1 | 0.1 | 1.0 | 0.1 | 0.1 | ..... | ..... | ..... | ..... | ..... |
| Fabricated metal products | ..... | ..... | 0.2 | 0.2 | 0.3 | ..... | ..... | ..... | ..... | ..... |
| Industrial machinery and computers | 20.5 | 20.6 | 0.7 | 2.1 | 3.7 | 0.3 | 0.2 | 0.3 | 0.6 | 0.4 |
| Electric and electronic equipment | 2.6 | 7.1 | 6.5 | 28.3 | 38.6 | 54.7 | 65.0 | 55.4 | 181.4 | 194.8 |
| Transportation equipment | 2.0 | 4.1 | 3.4 | 3.0 | 3.9 | 0.3 | 1.4 | 0.4 | 0.4 | 0.1 |
| Scientific and measuring instruments | 1.4 | 2.0 | 3.9 | 4.4 | 4.7 | 0.4 | 0.5 | 0.5 | 1.3 | 0.8 |
| Miscellaneous manufactures | 4.9 | 2.1 | 1.3 | 1.1 | 3.4 | 0.1 | 0.3 | 0.2 | ..... | 0.1 |
| Unidentified manufactures | 0.1 | 0.1 | 0.1 | ..... | ..... | ..... | ..... | ..... | ..... | ..... |
| **Agricultural and livestock products** | 0.7 | 1.5 | 1.1 | 1.3 | 0.7 | ..... | 0.9 | 2.0 | 0.1 | ..... |
| Agricultural products | 0.7 | 1.5 | 1.0 | 1.3 | 0.7 | ..... | 0.9 | 1.8 | ..... | ..... |
| Livestock and livestock products | ..... | ..... | 0.1 | ..... | ..... | ..... | ..... | 0.2 | 0.1 | ..... |
| **Other commodities** | 1.1 | 2.2 | 1.2 | 0.7 | 1.0 | ..... | ..... | 0.1 | 0.1 | 0.4 |
| Forestry products | ..... | ..... | ..... | ..... | ..... | ..... | ..... | ..... | ..... | ..... |
| Fish and other marine products | 0.5 | ..... | 0.2 | ..... | ..... | ..... | ..... | ..... | ..... | 0.3 |
| Metallic ores and concentrates | 0.1 | ..... | ..... | ..... | ..... | ..... | ..... | ..... | ..... | ..... |
| Bituminous coal and lignite | ..... | ..... | ..... | ..... | ..... | ..... | ..... | ..... | ..... | ..... |
| Crude petroleum and natural gas | ..... | ..... | ..... | ..... | ..... | ..... | ..... | ..... | ..... | ..... |
| Nonmetallic minerals | 0.1 | 1.1 | 0.6 | 0.5 | 0.7 | ..... | ..... | 0.1 | 0.1 | ..... |
| Scrap and waste | ..... | ..... | ..... | ..... | 0.1 | ..... | ..... | ..... | ..... | ..... |
| Used merchandise | 0.4 | 1.0 | 0.3 | 0.1 | 0.1 | ..... | ..... | ..... | 0.1 | ..... |
| Goods imported and returned unchanged | ..... | ..... | ..... | ..... | ..... | ..... | ..... | ..... | ..... | ..... |
| Special classification provisions | ..... | ..... | 0.1 | 0.1 | 0.1 | ..... | ..... | ..... | ..... | ..... |

| Industry | 1993 | 1994 | 1995 | 1996 | 1997 | 1993 | 1994 | 1995 | 1996 | 1997 |
|---|---|---|---|---|---|---|---|---|---|---|
| | Taiwan | | | | | Singapore | | | | |
| **ALL GOODS** | 8.1 | 6.9 | 13.6 | 53.4 | 115.7 | 5.3 | 2.8 | 8.1 | 5.4 | 2.6 |
| **Manufactured goods** | 7.9 | 6.7 | 13.4 | 53.4 | 115.6 | 5.2 | 2.7 | 8.0 | 5.4 | 2.5 |
| Food products | ..... | ..... | 0.1 | 0.1 | 0.1 | ..... | ..... | 0.2 | 0.1 | 0.1 |
| Tobacco products | ..... | ..... | ..... | ..... | ..... | ..... | ..... | ..... | ..... | ..... |
| Textile mill products | ..... | ..... | ..... | ..... | 0.1 | ..... | ..... | ..... | ..... | 0.1 |
| Apparel | ..... | ..... | ..... | 0.1 | ..... | ..... | ..... | ..... | ..... | 0.1 |
| Lumber and wood products | ..... | ..... | ..... | ..... | 0.1 | ..... | ..... | ..... | ..... | ..... |
| Furniture and fixtures | ..... | ..... | ..... | ..... | ..... | ..... | ..... | ..... | ..... | 0.1 |
| Paper products | ..... | ..... | ..... | 0.1 | ..... | ..... | ..... | ..... | ..... | ..... |
| Printing and publishing | ..... | ..... | 0.1 | ..... | 0.4 | ..... | ..... | 0.1 | ..... | ..... |
| Chemical products | ..... | 0.1 | 0.1 | 0.1 | 0.2 | ..... | ..... | 0.1 | 0.2 | ..... |
| Refined petroleum products | ..... | ..... | ..... | ..... | 11.5 | ..... | ..... | ..... | ..... | ..... |
| Rubber and plastic products | ..... | ..... | ..... | ..... | ..... | 0.3 | 0.1 | 0.1 | 0.1 | 0.2 |
| Leather products | ..... | ..... | ..... | ..... | ..... | ..... | ..... | ..... | ..... | ..... |
| Stone, clay and glass products | 0.4 | 0.1 | 0.9 | 0.3 | 0.3 | 2.3 | 0.3 | 0.2 | ..... | ..... |
| Primary metals | 0.1 | 0.1 | ..... | ..... | 0.1 | ..... | ..... | 0.1 | 0.1 | ..... |
| Fabricated metal products | ..... | ..... | ..... | ..... | ..... | ..... | ..... | ..... | 0.1 | 0.1 |
| Industrial machinery and computers | 0.8 | 0.7 | 0.4 | 0.2 | 2.1 | 1.2 | 1.4 | 3.5 | 4.1 | 1.3 |
| Electric and electronic equipment | 6.2 | 5.2 | 11.4 | 51.5 | 99.0 | 0.7 | 0.6 | 1.0 | 0.2 | 0.3 |
| Transportation equipment | ..... | 0.1 | ..... | ..... | ..... | 0.3 | ..... | ..... | ..... | ..... |
| Scientific and measuring instruments | 0.2 | 0.2 | 0.3 | 0.5 | 1.6 | 0.3 | 0.1 | 0.7 | 0.2 | 0.1 |
| Miscellaneous manufactures | ..... | 0.1 | 0.1 | 0.2 | 0.1 | 0.1 | 0.2 | 2.0 | 0.1 | 0.1 |
| Unidentified manufactures | ..... | ..... | ..... | 0.2 | 0.1 | ..... | ..... | ..... | ..... | ..... |
| **Agricultural and livestock products** | ..... | ..... | ..... | ..... | ..... | ..... | ..... | ..... | ..... | ..... |
| Agricultural products | ..... | ..... | ..... | ..... | ..... | ..... | ..... | ..... | ..... | ..... |
| Livestock and livestock products | ..... | ..... | ..... | ..... | ..... | ..... | ..... | ..... | ..... | ..... |
| **Other commodities** | 0.2 | 0.1 | 0.2 | 0.1 | 0.1 | ..... | 0.1 | 0.1 | ..... | 0.1 |
| Forestry products | ..... | 0.1 | ..... | ..... | ..... | ..... | ..... | ..... | ..... | ..... |
| Fish and other marine products | ..... | ..... | ..... | ..... | ..... | ..... | ..... | ..... | ..... | ..... |
| Metallic ores and concentrates | ..... | ..... | ..... | ..... | ..... | ..... | ..... | ..... | ..... | ..... |
| Bituminous coal and lignite | ..... | ..... | ..... | ..... | ..... | ..... | ..... | ..... | ..... | ..... |
| Crude petroleum and natural gas | ..... | ..... | ..... | ..... | ..... | ..... | ..... | ..... | ..... | ..... |
| Nonmetallic minerals | 0.2 | 0.1 | 0.1 | 0.1 | 0.1 | ..... | 0.1 | ..... | ..... | 0.1 |
| Scrap and waste | ..... | ..... | ..... | ..... | ..... | ..... | ..... | ..... | ..... | ..... |
| Used merchandise | ..... | ..... | ..... | ..... | ..... | ..... | ..... | ..... | ..... | ..... |
| Goods imported and returned unchanged | ..... | ..... | ..... | ..... | ..... | ..... | ..... | ..... | ..... | ..... |
| Special classification provisions | ..... | ..... | ..... | ..... | ..... | ..... | ..... | ..... | ..... | ..... |

## NEW YORK: Exports of Goods, 1997

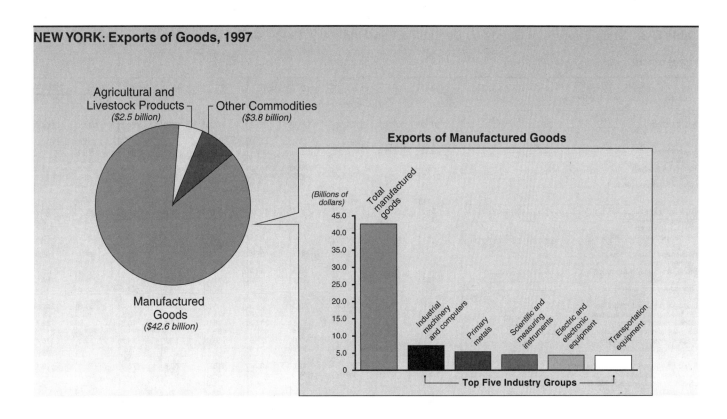

Agricultural and Livestock Products ($2.5 billion)

Other Commodities ($3.8 billion)

Manufactured Goods ($42.6 billion)

### Exports of Manufactured Goods

(Billions of dollars)

Top Five Industry Groups

---

## Table D-3.   State Exports of Goods by Destination and Industry, 1993–1997 —*Continued*

### NEW YORK (Millions of dollars.)

| Industry | 1993 | 1994 | 1995 | 1996 | 1997 | 1993 | 1994 | 1995 | 1996 | 1997 |
|---|---|---|---|---|---|---|---|---|---|---|
| | All destinations | | | | | Canada | | | | |
| **ALL GOODS** | 40 702.3 | 37 259.7 | 44 080.1 | 44 964.7 | 48 885.3 | 6 580.8 | 7 487.2 | 9 243.7 | 8 956.7 | 10 616.0 |
| **Manufactured goods** | 34 951.6 | 32 145.7 | 38 094.9 | 38 794.8 | 42 577.2 | 5 824.0 | 6 580.3 | 8 337.9 | 8 003.9 | 9 363.9 |
| Food products | 1 816.3 | 1 917.3 | 2 186.1 | 2 264.2 | 2 685.6 | 248.6 | 242.8 | 225.9 | 254.8 | 283.8 |
| Tobacco products | 160.8 | 248.8 | 196.2 | 70.7 | 73.4 | 0.1 | 0.1 | ..... | 0.1 | 0.1 |
| Textile mill products | 703.9 | 705.5 | 748.1 | 741.1 | 775.2 | 145.6 | 150.2 | 161.0 | 174.1 | 183.3 |
| Apparel | 643.2 | 620.8 | 607.1 | 597.8 | 669.0 | 60.1 | 65.1 | 73.1 | 89.3 | 112.1 |
| Lumber and wood products | 323.8 | 352.1 | 375.8 | 354.5 | 413.9 | 114.1 | 148.7 | 183.1 | 164.1 | 225.9 |
| Furniture and fixtures | 106.3 | 98.3 | 113.5 | 96.0 | 106.6 | 28.1 | 29.3 | 47.7 | 35.4 | 28.0 |
| Paper products | 1 165.2 | 1 273.9 | 1 783.4 | 1 547.1 | 1 589.8 | 236.6 | 236.8 | 300.1 | 314.6 | 341.1 |
| Printing and publishing | 811.7 | 729.6 | 769.1 | 700.2 | 697.1 | 339.3 | 356.7 | 373.6 | 386.8 | 393.1 |
| Chemical products | 2 977.6 | 3 335.8 | 3 544.1 | 3 459.0 | 3 443.2 | 476.5 | 484.9 | 528.4 | 680.4 | 653.7 |
| Refined petroleum products | 432.2 | 292.0 | 317.1 | 373.0 | 410.9 | 58.0 | 38.1 | 66.2 | 81.2 | 99.1 |
| Rubber and plastic products | 502.9 | 554.2 | 664.9 | 675.7 | 818.9 | 151.5 | 172.6 | 198.7 | 210.5 | 201.9 |
| Leather products | 141.3 | 147.4 | 147.9 | 154.3 | 153.7 | 22.0 | 24.5 | 26.4 | 31.6 | 36.1 |
| Stone, clay and glass products | 359.6 | 375.5 | 408.4 | 428.8 | 518.1 | 80.9 | 83.5 | 86.5 | 89.6 | 92.1 |
| Primary metals | 7 342.2 | 3 047.9 | 4 671.2 | 6 013.9 | 5 426.5 | 871.8 | 690.7 | 940.5 | 887.2 | 1 264.5 |
| Fabricated metal products | 541.9 | 499.9 | 604.4 | 655.1 | 753.7 | 102.4 | 131.9 | 150.0 | 165.8 | 178.9 |
| Industrial machinery and computers | 4 630.7 | 5 234.6 | 6 255.7 | 5 777.6 | 7 217.5 | 780.0 | 876.6 | 1 193.4 | 1 104.8 | 1 380.5 |
| Electric and electronic equipment | 3 112.6 | 3 567.8 | 4 058.0 | 3 587.4 | 4 387.1 | 1 091.9 | 1 433.3 | 1 715.5 | 1 233.6 | 1 574.0 |
| Transportation equipment | 3 316.6 | 2 969.6 | 3 887.4 | 3 808.1 | 4 345.9 | 250.4 | 529.1 | 1 087.2 | 1 050.8 | 1 226.8 |
| Scientific and measuring instruments | 3 293.8 | 3 311.7 | 3 706.5 | 4 203.3 | 4 535.5 | 578.3 | 629.0 | 709.3 | 739.2 | 754.3 |
| Miscellaneous manufactures | 2 336.7 | 2 530.6 | 2 815.4 | 3 045.7 | 3 240.5 | 120.8 | 147.5 | 158.5 | 173.2 | 196.2 |
| Unidentified manufactures | 232.4 | 332.4 | 234.7 | 241.4 | 315.1 | 67.2 | 109.0 | 112.7 | 136.8 | 138.5 |
| **Agricultural and livestock products** | 2 707.2 | 1 784.1 | 2 520.3 | 2 921.3 | 2 477.1 | 137.3 | 173.8 | 163.6 | 170.3 | 173.2 |
| Agricultural products | 2 566.0 | 1 620.9 | 2 328.6 | 2 733.1 | 2 277.3 | 122.5 | 157.4 | 149.3 | 145.7 | 151.0 |
| Livestock and livestock products | 141.2 | 163.2 | 191.7 | 188.1 | 199.8 | 14.8 | 16.3 | 14.3 | 24.6 | 22.2 |
| **Other commodities** | 3 043.4 | 3 329.9 | 3 464.9 | 3 248.6 | 3 831.0 | 619.6 | 733.1 | 742.2 | 782.5 | 1 078.9 |
| Forestry products | 32.8 | 33.5 | 31.2 | 21.4 | 13.3 | 4.2 | 5.9 | 5.7 | 3.8 | 3.6 |
| Fish and other marine products | 64.4 | 62.7 | 61.5 | 59.3 | 55.8 | 15.9 | 11.6 | 10.7 | 13.3 | 15.0 |
| Metallic ores and concentrates | 15.0 | 34.6 | 49.3 | 48.6 | 54.8 | 3.6 | 19.0 | 22.7 | 9.9 | 37.1 |
| Bituminous coal and lignite | 186.6 | 215.5 | 285.2 | 264.4 | 282.0 | 5.2 | 18.2 | 43.9 | 49.5 | 83.6 |
| Crude petroleum and natural gas | 5.8 | 34.2 | 14.3 | 107.5 | 364.7 | 4.1 | 32.7 | 1.7 | 78.2 | 334.0 |
| Nonmetallic minerals | 68.0 | 107.2 | 92.6 | 77.2 | 75.0 | 7.1 | 7.7 | 9.4 | 15.7 | 8.6 |
| Scrap and waste | 864.9 | 950.3 | 1 326.7 | 994.1 | 895.4 | 384.7 | 368.4 | 427.3 | 320.1 | 275.5 |
| Used merchandise | 1 352.2 | 1 382.6 | 1 191.7 | 1 150.9 | 1 558.1 | 18.0 | 17.2 | 16.7 | 23.9 | 27.4 |
| Goods imported and returned unchanged | 153.9 | 179.7 | 187.9 | 237.7 | 272.7 | 153.9 | 179.7 | 187.9 | 237.7 | 272.7 |
| Special classification provisions | 299.6 | 329.7 | 224.5 | 287.6 | 259.3 | 22.7 | 72.7 | 16.4 | 30.4 | 21.5 |

## Table D-3.  State Exports of Goods by Destination and Industry, 1993–1997 —Continued

**NEW YORK**  (Millions of dollars.)

| Industry | 1993 | 1994 | 1995 | 1996 | 1997 | 1993 | 1994 | 1995 | 1996 | 1997 |
|---|---|---|---|---|---|---|---|---|---|---|
| | South and Central America and Caribbean | | | | | Mexico | | | | |
| **ALL GOODS** | 2 809.9 | 3 054.5 | 3 401.8 | 3 536.8 | 4 088.7 | 1 171.0 | 1 323.9 | 994.0 | 1 303.1 | 1 804.9 |
| **Manufactured goods** | 2 586.3 | 2 835.7 | 3 015.8 | 2 913.6 | 3 496.2 | 1 036.0 | 1 226.3 | 877.5 | 1 103.3 | 1 633.5 |
| Food products | 225.8 | 236.6 | 231.9 | 274.9 | 388.9 | 129.3 | 91.4 | 109.2 | 91.4 | 139.5 |
| Tobacco products | 13.3 | 46.1 | 60.1 | 50.4 | 28.8 | ..... | ..... | ..... | ..... | ..... |
| Textile mill products | 128.3 | 131.0 | 141.9 | 130.1 | 141.5 | 29.7 | 32.9 | 14.3 | 29.2 | 43.3 |
| Apparel | 274.9 | 294.8 | 252.4 | 240.7 | 300.3 | 18.1 | 24.9 | 15.9 | 23.8 | 29.2 |
| Lumber and wood products | 10.3 | 5.2 | 6.3 | 6.6 | 9.4 | 1.3 | 1.7 | 2.9 | 4.0 | 5.1 |
| Furniture and fixtures | 9.6 | 10.0 | 12.8 | 11.5 | 16.8 | 2.1 | 2.9 | 2.7 | 2.0 | 3.0 |
| Paper products | 154.8 | 152.5 | 248.4 | 229.7 | 262.8 | 59.5 | 75.5 | 84.8 | 83.9 | 92.7 |
| Printing and publishing | 32.7 | 22.2 | 16.5 | 15.3 | 19.8 | 8.7 | 11.8 | 8.8 | 14.1 | 8.7 |
| Chemical products | 247.4 | 295.2 | 358.4 | 304.8 | 292.6 | 82.4 | 99.2 | 77.8 | 144.6 | 141.4 |
| Refined petroleum products | 64.5 | 62.5 | 58.2 | 76.3 | 42.1 | 6.2 | 12.8 | 5.4 | 16.9 | 45.4 |
| Rubber and plastic products | 60.7 | 55.3 | 86.9 | 80.3 | 87.4 | 41.5 | 71.2 | 65.5 | 54.4 | 68.5 |
| Leather products | 10.7 | 9.4 | 14.7 | 12.5 | 12.5 | 3.4 | 1.9 | 1.2 | 0.8 | 1.4 |
| Stone, clay and glass products | 36.2 | 28.5 | 32.5 | 30.4 | 40.8 | 9.1 | 11.4 | 10.8 | 14.4 | 12.8 |
| Primary metals | 100.5 | 74.9 | 112.0 | 62.4 | 76.2 | 111.8 | 136.6 | 70.2 | 96.4 | 129.0 |
| Fabricated metal products | 42.3 | 34.9 | 40.3 | 41.0 | 56.3 | 32.5 | 23.0 | 20.7 | 33.8 | 47.9 |
| Industrial machinery and computers | 383.8 | 442.4 | 387.6 | 466.3 | 604.3 | 105.8 | 113.0 | 70.3 | 91.3 | 242.6 |
| Electric and electronic equipment | 233.5 | 262.7 | 252.3 | 226.0 | 295.0 | 171.1 | 220.2 | 98.8 | 140.3 | 233.6 |
| Transportation equipment | 223.2 | 273.0 | 222.4 | 157.5 | 303.2 | 25.0 | 61.3 | 10.8 | 7.8 | 37.5 |
| Scientific and measuring instruments | 243.7 | 296.8 | 379.9 | 383.4 | 401.9 | 163.1 | 202.3 | 191.4 | 237.3 | 318.6 |
| Miscellaneous manufactures | 70.3 | 73.2 | 84.5 | 97.0 | 91.8 | 33.0 | 25.2 | 14.2 | 12.0 | 16.4 |
| Unidentified manufactures | 20.1 | 28.9 | 15.6 | 16.4 | 23.8 | 2.2 | 7.0 | 1.8 | 5.0 | 17.0 |
| **Agricultural and livestock products** | 136.9 | 132.8 | 283.3 | 512.6 | 469.4 | 110.6 | 68.6 | 75.4 | 136.3 | 118.1 |
| Agricultural products | 135.7 | 131.1 | 281.7 | 504.0 | 461.2 | 109.5 | 67.7 | 75.1 | 136.2 | 117.8 |
| Livestock and livestock products | 1.4 | 1.8 | 1.6 | 8.5 | 8.2 | 1.0 | 0.9 | 0.3 | 0.2 | 0.3 |
| **Other commodities** | 86.7 | 85.9 | 102.6 | 110.6 | 123.1 | 24.4 | 29.0 | 41.2 | 63.5 | 53.3 |
| Forestry products | 2.5 | 2.9 | 4.1 | 3.1 | 0.9 | 1.6 | 3.2 | 0.5 | 0.8 | 1.0 |
| Fish and other marine products | 0.5 | 0.9 | 0.7 | 0.8 | 1.2 | 0.4 | 0.1 | ..... | 0.1 | 0.1 |
| Metallic ores and concentrates | 0.3 | 0.6 | 1.8 | 1.8 | 0.8 | 0.1 | 0.7 | 0.1 | 0.5 | ..... |
| Bituminous coal and lignite | 26.4 | 38.9 | 53.4 | 68.9 | 75.4 | 6.4 | 7.4 | 12.8 | 14.0 | 9.3 |
| Crude petroleum and natural gas | 0.2 | 0.3 | 0.1 | ..... | 0.3 | ..... | ..... | 11.6 | 29.1 | 8.3 |
| Nonmetallic minerals | 6.6 | 5.6 | 6.7 | 2.8 | 2.4 | 2.3 | 1.8 | 1.9 | 2.4 | 1.5 |
| Scrap and waste | 18.9 | 15.5 | 18.8 | 12.0 | 13.2 | 0.8 | 5.8 | 10.4 | 6.2 | 16.6 |
| Used merchandise | 19.7 | 11.7 | 12.2 | 15.8 | 24.1 | 9.2 | 8.4 | 1.5 | 8.7 | 13.5 |
| Goods imported and returned unchanged | ..... | ..... | ..... | ..... | ..... | ..... | ..... | ..... | ..... | ..... |
| Special classification provisions | 11.7 | 9.5 | 4.9 | 5.3 | 4.9 | 3.4 | 1.6 | 2.3 | 1.8 | 3.0 |
| | European Union | | | | | United Kingdom | | | | |
| **ALL GOODS** | 11 383.2 | 8 152.9 | 9 474.6 | 9 958.1 | 10 108.2 | 5 297.4 | 2 703.6 | 2 744.8 | 3 593.4 | 3 140.1 |
| **Manufactured goods** | 9 847.3 | 6 984.5 | 8 133.0 | 8 912.3 | 8 853.1 | 4 946.3 | 2 323.1 | 2 397.6 | 3 295.5 | 2 609.8 |
| Food products | 161.3 | 147.5 | 143.5 | 158.9 | 262.0 | 34.4 | 39.8 | 37.0 | 31.5 | 33.8 |
| Tobacco products | 68.8 | 125.3 | 86.2 | 0.1 | 6.6 | 0.1 | ..... | ..... | ..... | ..... |
| Textile mill products | 126.6 | 129.2 | 153.5 | 136.8 | 131.4 | 29.7 | 29.4 | 41.3 | 36.3 | 38.9 |
| Apparel | 60.3 | 48.4 | 58.4 | 55.9 | 55.4 | 6.8 | 8.9 | 9.6 | 10.1 | 16.8 |
| Lumber and wood products | 52.4 | 49.0 | 64.5 | 54.1 | 55.2 | 9.3 | 7.9 | 11.0 | 8.2 | 10.0 |
| Furniture and fixtures | 29.3 | 25.5 | 19.4 | 14.4 | 20.2 | 8.9 | 8.8 | 6.2 | 5.6 | 9.6 |
| Paper products | 216.2 | 253.4 | 395.3 | 302.4 | 319.8 | 57.7 | 42.0 | 58.2 | 57.2 | 75.8 |
| Printing and publishing | 106.5 | 107.7 | 143.2 | 92.0 | 106.7 | 47.6 | 53.6 | 79.3 | 49.1 | 56.3 |
| Chemical products | 458.2 | 606.7 | 735.7 | 591.7 | 704.2 | 69.3 | 81.2 | 84.8 | 96.5 | 137.9 |
| Refined petroleum products | 73.7 | 69.6 | 82.4 | 94.1 | 142.1 | 3.7 | 4.3 | 4.6 | 6.1 | 6.1 |
| Rubber and plastic products | 105.1 | 96.6 | 144.6 | 130.5 | 207.6 | 21.4 | 19.7 | 25.2 | 28.0 | 40.8 |
| Leather products | 17.2 | 21.7 | 20.5 | 16.3 | 18.7 | 1.6 | 2.8 | 3.0 | 1.9 | 2.5 |
| Stone, clay and glass products | 64.0 | 71.0 | 69.1 | 65.9 | 84.5 | 12.9 | 14.7 | 16.7 | 16.3 | 16.2 |
| Primary metals | 3 818.6 | 1 029.5 | 1 112.6 | 2 050.9 | 952.8 | 3 689.4 | 915.5 | 902.0 | 1 858.4 | 798.4 |
| Fabricated metal products | 92.6 | 90.5 | 84.2 | 105.3 | 140.3 | 27.8 | 29.0 | 23.0 | 27.8 | 43.4 |
| Industrial machinery and computers | 944.9 | 1 211.0 | 1 308.2 | 1 203.8 | 1 446.1 | 306.3 | 501.6 | 412.3 | 320.2 | 475.8 |
| Electric and electronic equipment | 593.2 | 566.5 | 665.5 | 718.4 | 808.3 | 175.7 | 149.6 | 173.8 | 198.4 | 243.9 |
| Transportation equipment | 1 147.3 | 799.3 | 972.0 | 924.3 | 956.2 | 84.0 | 112.6 | 103.9 | 97.5 | 107.2 |
| Scientific and measuring instruments | 1 068.3 | 821.4 | 1 123.4 | 1 401.9 | 1 521.0 | 267.0 | 194.2 | 275.6 | 330.5 | 331.8 |
| Miscellaneous manufactures | 609.9 | 686.9 | 715.3 | 773.5 | 886.2 | 85.4 | 99.8 | 114.2 | 109.2 | 155.8 |
| Unidentified manufactures | 33.1 | 28.0 | 35.8 | 21.2 | 27.9 | 7.5 | 7.6 | 15.8 | 6.6 | 8.7 |
| **Agricultural and livestock products** | 754.9 | 348.6 | 474.2 | 302.6 | 272.1 | 48.1 | 68.9 | 65.9 | 46.2 | 58.8 |
| Agricultural products | 671.0 | 245.6 | 353.0 | 214.1 | 161.7 | 9.3 | 11.8 | 9.4 | 7.5 | 7.1 |
| Livestock and livestock products | 83.9 | 103.0 | 121.2 | 88.5 | 110.4 | 38.7 | 57.1 | 56.4 | 38.7 | 51.7 |
| **Other commodities** | 781.0 | 819.8 | 867.4 | 743.2 | 983.0 | 303.0 | 311.6 | 281.3 | 251.6 | 471.5 |
| Forestry products | 0.4 | 0.6 | 0.6 | 0.6 | 1.0 | ..... | ..... | ..... | 0.2 | 0.2 |
| Fish and other marine products | 5.0 | 4.2 | 5.8 | 9.0 | 6.1 | 1.7 | 1.5 | 1.0 | 0.8 | 0.8 |
| Metallic ores and concentrates | 7.1 | 4.3 | 7.8 | 8.9 | 4.8 | 0.2 | 0.4 | 1.1 | 1.8 | 2.4 |
| Bituminous coal and lignite | 79.7 | 51.4 | 51.9 | 64.4 | 58.6 | ..... | ..... | ..... | 10.3 | 12.5 |
| Crude petroleum and natural gas | ..... | 0.9 | 0.7 | ..... | ..... | ..... | ..... | ..... | ..... | ..... |
| Nonmetallic minerals | 12.7 | 11.7 | 10.2 | 9.4 | 13.9 | 1.6 | 1.8 | 1.9 | 1.3 | 1.5 |
| Scrap and waste | 39.7 | 88.2 | 202.1 | 93.3 | 39.4 | 6.0 | 7.0 | 10.1 | 4.9 | 3.1 |
| Used merchandise | 577.6 | 609.0 | 535.5 | 475.9 | 806.6 | 278.8 | 296.4 | 256.0 | 199.9 | 442.2 |
| Goods imported and returned unchanged | ..... | ..... | ..... | ..... | ..... | ..... | ..... | ..... | ..... | ..... |
| Special classification provisions | 58.7 | 49.6 | 52.7 | 81.8 | 52.6 | 14.8 | 4.4 | 11.0 | 32.4 | 8.8 |

## Table D-3.  State Exports of Goods by Destination and Industry, 1993–1997 —*Continued*

**NEW YORK** (Millions of dollars.)

| Industry | 1993 | 1994 | 1995 | 1996 | 1997 | 1993 | 1994 | 1995 | 1996 | 1997 |
|---|---|---|---|---|---|---|---|---|---|---|
| | Germany | | | | | France | | | | |
| **ALL GOODS** | 1 228.8 | 1 212.8 | 1 577.1 | 1 503.8 | 1 684.7 | 1 084.2 | 826.0 | 929.9 | 1 057.9 | 1 270.4 |
| **Manufactured goods** | 1 014.5 | 1 002.4 | 1 307.1 | 1 310.5 | 1 451.8 | 918.1 | 684.0 | 769.6 | 928.1 | 1 115.7 |
| Food products | 18.3 | 10.8 | 17.5 | 24.0 | 28.3 | 18.9 | 7.7 | 9.0 | 11.9 | 10.1 |
| Tobacco products | ..... | 0.5 | 0.3 | ..... | 0.7 | ..... | ..... | ..... | ..... | ..... |
| Textile mill products | 26.0 | 35.7 | 44.6 | 27.8 | 27.3 | 10.4 | 13.0 | 11.0 | 9.3 | 6.9 |
| Apparel | 10.9 | 9.8 | 14.2 | 12.1 | 7.8 | 8.7 | 5.2 | 6.7 | 3.9 | 4.1 |
| Lumber and wood products | 10.0 | 5.1 | 7.5 | 6.7 | 8.4 | 3.8 | 2.8 | 3.6 | 4.3 | 3.6 |
| Furniture and fixtures | 5.9 | 5.2 | 3.9 | 2.2 | 3.1 | 3.2 | 5.6 | 3.5 | 1.8 | 1.6 |
| Paper products | 53.4 | 57.6 | 71.5 | 70.8 | 53.3 | 11.8 | 27.1 | 28.1 | 26.4 | 23.6 |
| Printing and publishing | 24.6 | 25.9 | 19.1 | 17.7 | 22.9 | 7.6 | 6.4 | 10.0 | 6.5 | 5.4 |
| Chemical products | 51.0 | 51.7 | 82.4 | 53.0 | 79.2 | 48.4 | 102.0 | 83.7 | 123.1 | 111.7 |
| Refined petroleum products | 5.5 | 4.2 | 4.4 | 5.2 | 27.8 | 11.7 | 9.0 | 9.7 | 3.4 | 3.5 |
| Rubber and plastic products | 16.2 | 13.2 | 19.6 | 13.6 | 39.4 | 40.7 | 30.3 | 47.7 | 38.6 | 54.0 |
| Leather products | 3.6 | 5.1 | 1.6 | 1.7 | 2.8 | 1.1 | 1.5 | 3.6 | 2.0 | 2.8 |
| Stone, clay and glass products | 11.1 | 12.8 | 17.7 | 15.7 | 27.9 | 20.5 | 22.4 | 18.9 | 16.1 | 18.6 |
| Primary metals | 10.1 | 38.4 | 50.9 | 59.4 | 71.1 | 11.1 | 11.5 | 30.8 | 22.3 | 29.3 |
| Fabricated metal products | 17.0 | 18.4 | 13.3 | 20.3 | 28.8 | 5.3 | 6.4 | 7.1 | 8.7 | 18.0 |
| Industrial machinery and computers | 163.4 | 189.1 | 241.8 | 222.8 | 245.1 | 119.4 | 124.6 | 143.8 | 153.1 | 146.2 |
| Electric and electronic equipment | 82.5 | 94.8 | 117.1 | 143.2 | 154.6 | 71.3 | 69.9 | 74.7 | 72.0 | 90.9 |
| Transportation equipment | 269.7 | 215.0 | 290.6 | 271.4 | 265.5 | 207.2 | 45.7 | 50.3 | 53.7 | 95.2 |
| Scientific and measuring instruments | 191.5 | 173.7 | 250.2 | 295.0 | 320.0 | 262.7 | 136.1 | 160.3 | 303.2 | 424.7 |
| Miscellaneous manufactures | 38.0 | 29.9 | 33.7 | 43.3 | 34.4 | 51.3 | 53.2 | 64.3 | 66.0 | 64.1 |
| Unidentified manufactures | 5.8 | 5.4 | 5.1 | 4.5 | 3.4 | 3.0 | 3.3 | 2.9 | 1.8 | 1.3 |
| **Agricultural and livestock products** | 101.3 | 93.3 | 147.4 | 77.6 | 77.0 | 22.6 | 21.0 | 39.1 | 28.4 | 18.1 |
| Agricultural products | 98.7 | 88.5 | 139.0 | 74.3 | 73.9 | 4.6 | 6.2 | 10.3 | 12.6 | 0.5 |
| Livestock and livestock products | 2.6 | 4.9 | 8.4 | 3.3 | 3.2 | 17.9 | 14.7 | 28.8 | 15.7 | 17.5 |
| **Other commodities** | 113.1 | 117.1 | 122.6 | 115.7 | 155.8 | 143.6 | 121.0 | 121.2 | 101.4 | 136.6 |
| Forestry products | ..... | 0.2 | 0.1 | 0.2 | 0.2 | ..... | ..... | 0.2 | ..... | 0.4 |
| Fish and other marine products | 1.1 | 0.5 | 0.7 | ..... | 0.1 | 0.8 | 0.1 | 0.7 | 1.8 | 0.3 |
| Metallic ores and concentrates | 1.2 | 0.2 | 0.1 | 0.1 | 1.1 | 0.1 | 0.2 | 0.1 | 0.4 | 0.4 |
| Bituminous coal and lignite | 9.4 | 2.0 | 6.1 | 4.0 | 22.3 | 19.5 | 17.6 | 5.6 | 1.4 | 1.4 |
| Crude petroleum and natural gas | ..... | ..... | ..... | ..... | ..... | ..... | ..... | ..... | ..... | ..... |
| Nonmetallic minerals | 3.6 | 4.2 | 3.9 | 4.0 | 3.7 | 0.7 | 0.7 | 0.7 | 0.9 | 1.4 |
| Scrap and waste | 2.9 | 2.9 | 10.3 | 4.4 | 4.2 | 0.9 | 1.6 | 4.5 | 2.0 | 1.4 |
| Used merchandise | 85.2 | 94.9 | 81.2 | 81.6 | 99.1 | 111.5 | 99.0 | 106.0 | 89.9 | 128.4 |
| Goods imported and returned unchanged | ..... | ..... | ..... | ..... | ..... | ..... | ..... | ..... | ..... | ..... |
| Special classification provisions | 9.8 | 12.1 | 20.0 | 21.3 | 25.1 | 10.0 | 1.8 | 3.4 | 4.9 | 3.0 |
| | The Netherlands | | | | | Asian 10 | | | | |
| **ALL GOODS** | 1 058.8 | 846.6 | 1 090.9 | 906.5 | 874.9 | 10 396.1 | 10 724.2 | 13 013.6 | 12 191.5 | 12 122.7 |
| **Manufactured goods** | 811.2 | 702.5 | 933.6 | 753.9 | 774.8 | 8 698.9 | 9 073.6 | 10 853.6 | 9 822.1 | 10 086.9 |
| Food products | 13.5 | 12.4 | 16.9 | 12.7 | 21.5 | 473.3 | 628.6 | 819.8 | 928.5 | 1 022.5 |
| Tobacco products | ..... | 0.2 | 31.7 | ..... | 0.1 | 18.2 | 23.7 | 24.7 | 10.8 | 20.8 |
| Textile mill products | 11.8 | 8.2 | 7.2 | 8.1 | 6.6 | 124.3 | 119.7 | 118.8 | 110.1 | 105.2 |
| Apparel | 3.5 | 2.3 | 4.0 | 1.9 | 1.8 | 122.1 | 105.7 | 143.3 | 131.0 | 114.7 |
| Lumber and wood products | 3.7 | 2.9 | 3.6 | 2.0 | 3.2 | 120.9 | 121.0 | 96.3 | 100.8 | 90.4 |
| Furniture and fixtures | 3.4 | 0.1 | 0.6 | 0.8 | 0.5 | 10.2 | 13.3 | 15.5 | 17.9 | 17.6 |
| Paper products | 46.0 | 46.4 | 91.0 | 63.2 | 80.7 | 336.7 | 381.9 | 493.1 | 391.5 | 367.1 |
| Printing and publishing | 7.9 | 6.8 | 6.9 | 4.9 | 3.5 | 202.9 | 125.2 | 90.1 | 81.3 | 97.7 |
| Chemical products | 88.8 | 106.5 | 91.1 | 78.4 | 110.1 | 1 457.4 | 1 562.8 | 1 512.2 | 1 415.8 | 1 329.3 |
| Refined petroleum products | 18.6 | 21.2 | 24.3 | 21.7 | 11.1 | 163.8 | 64.6 | 30.3 | 48.3 | 46.3 |
| Rubber and plastic products | 8.1 | 11.6 | 13.3 | 18.4 | 27.3 | 69.4 | 89.6 | 100.1 | 127.5 | 161.5 |
| Leather products | 1.1 | 1.0 | 0.6 | 0.7 | 0.6 | 70.9 | 79.1 | 73.2 | 82.5 | 77.1 |
| Stone, clay and glass products | 4.9 | 3.3 | 1.6 | 1.0 | 2.2 | 128.9 | 133.6 | 164.9 | 184.6 | 234.7 |
| Primary metals | 78.4 | 7.7 | 12.3 | 9.4 | 11.1 | 683.6 | 723.3 | 1 048.7 | 696.6 | 507.3 |
| Fabricated metal products | 6.9 | 9.3 | 6.6 | 7.2 | 13.8 | 185.7 | 168.5 | 250.9 | 259.6 | 256.6 |
| Industrial machinery and computers | 86.0 | 120.4 | 192.1 | 150.1 | 138.9 | 1 497.5 | 1 753.8 | 2 470.8 | 2 038.5 | 2 256.2 |
| Electric and electronic equipment | 75.9 | 59.8 | 71.7 | 65.4 | 50.6 | 576.4 | 603.8 | 727.0 | 750.2 | 916.6 |
| Transportation equipment | 146.4 | 133.2 | 161.7 | 93.8 | 116.0 | 721.1 | 541.7 | 525.7 | 768.9 | 606.2 |
| Scientific and measuring instruments | 192.3 | 136.3 | 182.8 | 204.8 | 165.8 | 865.5 | 912.6 | 944.1 | 1 021.3 | 1 020.7 |
| Miscellaneous manufactures | 12.1 | 11.1 | 10.7 | 8.3 | 8.6 | 823.3 | 820.9 | 937.1 | 869.6 | 818.4 |
| Unidentified manufactures | 1.8 | 1.7 | 2.7 | 1.2 | 1.1 | 46.7 | 116.0 | 23.7 | 16.4 | 19.8 |
| **Agricultural and livestock products** | 179.1 | 74.8 | 90.1 | 90.8 | 26.4 | 912.4 | 798.3 | 1 226.4 | 1 536.2 | 1 203.8 |
| Agricultural products | 178.2 | 73.4 | 89.7 | 90.0 | 26.2 | 892.1 | 774.4 | 1 189.3 | 1 481.8 | 1 149.7 |
| Livestock and livestock products | 0.9 | 1.4 | 0.4 | 0.8 | 0.2 | 20.3 | 23.9 | 37.1 | 54.4 | 54.1 |
| **Other commodities** | 68.5 | 69.4 | 67.2 | 61.7 | 73.7 | 784.8 | 852.3 | 933.6 | 833.2 | 832.0 |
| Forestry products | ..... | ..... | ..... | ..... | ..... | 23.4 | 20.5 | 19.5 | 12.7 | 6.3 |
| Fish and other marine products | 0.1 | 0.1 | 0.1 | 0.1 | 0.1 | 40.0 | 42.7 | 41.0 | 29.9 | 29.6 |
| Metallic ores and concentrates | 0.1 | 0.2 | 0.7 | 0.6 | 0.6 | 1.8 | 3.2 | 16.6 | 25.8 | 12.0 |
| Bituminous coal and lignite | 29.5 | 7.2 | 20.1 | 28.1 | 13.1 | 3.1 | 2.3 | 2.6 | 4.5 | 3.8 |
| Crude petroleum and natural gas | ..... | 0.1 | 0.6 | ..... | ..... | 1.2 | 0.2 | 0.2 | ..... | 22.0 |
| Nonmetallic minerals | 1.2 | 0.5 | 0.8 | 0.5 | 0.9 | 30.0 | 70.1 | 57.5 | 40.3 | 45.3 |
| Scrap and waste | 4.8 | 11.6 | 21.5 | 4.0 | 2.0 | 316.8 | 329.4 | 493.2 | 433.5 | 454.1 |
| Used merchandise | 28.6 | 39.7 | 14.2 | 16.4 | 47.6 | 211.8 | 241.8 | 201.2 | 158.2 | 135.9 |
| Goods imported and returned unchanged | ..... | ..... | ..... | ..... | ..... | ..... | ..... | ..... | ..... | ..... |
| Special classification provisions | 4.0 | 10.0 | 9.3 | 12.0 | 9.4 | 156.6 | 142.2 | 101.8 | 128.2 | 123.2 |

## Table D-3.  State Exports of Goods by Destination and Industry, 1993–1997 —*Continued*

**NEW YORK** (Millions of dollars.)

| Industry | 1993 | 1994 | 1995 | 1996 | 1997 | 1993 | 1994 | 1995 | 1996 | 1997 |
|---|---|---|---|---|---|---|---|---|---|---|
| | Japan | | | | | South Korea | | | | |
| **ALL GOODS** | 4 452.6 | 4 634.8 | 5 463.9 | 5 422.1 | 5 369.3 | 1 228.6 | 1 344.7 | 1 954.8 | 1 793.1 | 1 423.3 |
| **Manufactured goods** | 3 557.8 | 3 696.1 | 4 260.7 | 4 061.0 | 4 195.2 | 920.4 | 1 033.5 | 1 486.5 | 1 299.3 | 1 079.6 |
| Food products | 157.4 | 156.8 | 209.5 | 241.1 | 255.8 | 94.9 | 150.6 | 198.2 | 174.6 | 168.5 |
| Tobacco products | 2.2 | 0.2 | 0.1 | ..... | 0.1 | 0.1 | 0.3 | 0.1 | 1.0 | 0.1 |
| Textile mill products | 25.1 | 24.0 | 30.8 | 31.0 | 24.2 | 9.1 | 10.0 | 8.2 | 12.9 | 6.9 |
| Apparel | 89.3 | 77.2 | 99.2 | 95.4 | 85.0 | 1.8 | 2.1 | 7.8 | 8.1 | 3.2 |
| Lumber and wood products | 76.4 | 64.6 | 34.4 | 34.9 | 26.6 | 13.4 | 21.3 | 25.2 | 21.3 | 21.9 |
| Furniture and fixtures | 6.6 | 8.9 | 10.0 | 9.8 | 9.6 | 0.2 | 0.6 | 1.2 | 2.6 | 1.7 |
| Paper products | 88.0 | 82.4 | 126.0 | 88.3 | 117.4 | 88.8 | 104.7 | 139.4 | 75.8 | 66.8 |
| Printing and publishing | 137.4 | 42.1 | 45.0 | 46.1 | 57.7 | 3.7 | 3.0 | 5.0 | 4.2 | 4.0 |
| Chemical products | 988.3 | 1 011.7 | 836.1 | 855.0 | 825.4 | 134.1 | 125.5 | 158.5 | 104.6 | 86.9 |
| Refined petroleum products | 25.1 | 14.1 | 13.8 | 18.4 | 25.8 | 22.8 | 7.4 | 1.2 | 1.5 | 0.5 |
| Rubber and plastic products | 42.6 | 56.9 | 64.8 | 78.4 | 101.7 | 5.6 | 7.1 | 7.2 | 11.6 | 14.4 |
| Leather products | 25.7 | 37.3 | 34.3 | 51.1 | 36.7 | 2.4 | 1.0 | 1.5 | 3.5 | 4.5 |
| Stone, clay and glass products | 53.7 | 49.3 | 52.9 | 81.4 | 113.7 | 31.9 | 31.8 | 37.4 | 26.6 | 23.7 |
| Primary metals | 122.3 | 134.5 | 299.9 | 251.2 | 192.9 | 15.4 | 23.5 | 103.1 | 131.8 | 51.3 |
| Fabricated metal products | 109.7 | 97.6 | 158.9 | 117.8 | 95.1 | 11.5 | 17.4 | 23.9 | 26.9 | 19.0 |
| Industrial machinery and computers | 545.1 | 703.7 | 1 005.9 | 749.8 | 890.2 | 233.3 | 303.5 | 561.1 | 446.9 | 317.7 |
| Electric and electronic equipment | 137.7 | 157.8 | 230.8 | 227.8 | 261.3 | 65.9 | 79.5 | 89.2 | 102.2 | 105.0 |
| Transportation equipment | 196.3 | 272.9 | 276.2 | 284.5 | 353.4 | 118.1 | 72.3 | 37.0 | 43.5 | 72.4 |
| Scientific and measuring instruments | 464.0 | 442.1 | 489.9 | 542.0 | 521.7 | 44.0 | 51.9 | 62.7 | 84.1 | 91.8 |
| Miscellaneous manufactures | 234.0 | 197.6 | 234.1 | 249.7 | 194.7 | 18.4 | 16.1 | 14.9 | 12.9 | 15.7 |
| Unidentified manufactures | 31.1 | 64.5 | 7.9 | 7.2 | 6.3 | 4.8 | 3.7 | 3.8 | 2.6 | 3.8 |
| **Agricultural and livestock products** | 557.5 | 554.1 | 853.1 | 1 054.5 | 892.6 | 101.3 | 119.6 | 229.7 | 290.9 | 114.4 |
| Agricultural products | 553.8 | 545.8 | 830.6 | 1 012.4 | 849.7 | 97.1 | 115.0 | 225.0 | 286.0 | 112.2 |
| Livestock and livestock products | 3.7 | 8.3 | 22.5 | 42.1 | 42.9 | 4.2 | 4.6 | 4.7 | 4.9 | 2.2 |
| **Other commodities** | 337.4 | 384.5 | 350.1 | 306.6 | 281.5 | 206.8 | 191.7 | 238.6 | 203.0 | 229.3 |
| Forestry products | 0.1 | 0.1 | 1.6 | 0.2 | 0.6 | 0.1 | 0.6 | 0.1 | 0.1 | ..... |
| Fish and other marine products | 34.8 | 34.1 | 30.3 | 23.1 | 21.4 | 1.6 | 2.0 | 4.4 | 1.9 | 3.2 |
| Metallic ores and concentrates | 0.6 | 0.1 | 4.2 | 7.3 | 11.0 | 0.3 | 2.1 | 0.1 | 0.1 | 0.5 |
| Bituminous coal and lignite | 3.1 | 2.3 | 1.0 | 1.4 | 0.3 | ..... | ..... | 1.6 | 3.1 | 3.4 |
| Crude petroleum and natural gas | 1.1 | 0.1 | ..... | ..... | ..... | ..... | ..... | 0.2 | ..... | ..... |
| Nonmetallic minerals | 19.9 | 49.0 | 40.4 | 34.5 | 39.9 | 3.0 | 4.3 | 3.1 | 1.7 | 1.2 |
| Scrap and waste | 63.8 | 71.3 | 112.4 | 71.1 | 61.4 | 139.1 | 116.7 | 163.0 | 164.0 | 179.0 |
| Used merchandise | 133.3 | 156.6 | 120.9 | 103.5 | 77.6 | 8.2 | 17.7 | 35.1 | 12.7 | 15.0 |
| Goods imported and returned unchanged | ..... | ..... | ..... | ..... | ..... | ..... | ..... | ..... | ..... | ..... |
| Special classification provisions | 80.7 | 71.0 | 39.3 | 65.4 | 69.2 | 54.5 | 48.2 | 31.0 | 19.4 | 26.8 |
| | Taiwan | | | | | Singapore | | | | |
| **ALL GOODS** | 1 198.5 | 1 082.3 | 1 442.7 | 956.0 | 944.7 | 665.4 | 613.1 | 628.0 | 563.1 | 609.1 |
| **Manufactured goods** | 1 078.7 | 940.5 | 1 333.7 | 823.2 | 778.6 | 623.8 | 574.4 | 610.2 | 552.1 | 596.2 |
| Food products | 39.8 | 80.6 | 94.5 | 80.8 | 84.8 | 15.0 | 17.1 | 20.2 | 25.0 | 22.4 |
| Tobacco products | 0.2 | 0.2 | 0.1 | 0.3 | 14.9 | ..... | ..... | ..... | ..... | 0.1 |
| Textile mill products | 12.6 | 11.2 | 10.8 | 7.6 | 8.9 | 7.0 | 7.1 | 5.6 | 5.7 | 4.7 |
| Apparel | 2.1 | 2.0 | 3.5 | 3.3 | 2.0 | 4.0 | 4.4 | 3.9 | 5.0 | 3.2 |
| Lumber and wood products | 11.4 | 11.4 | 11.6 | 11.5 | 8.9 | 3.9 | 4.4 | 4.4 | 3.4 | 3.6 |
| Furniture and fixtures | 1.0 | 0.2 | 0.8 | 0.7 | 0.5 | 0.6 | 1.0 | 0.7 | 1.5 | 0.6 |
| Paper products | 28.0 | 34.5 | 36.8 | 22.4 | 19.1 | 16.2 | 11.9 | 19.6 | 16.0 | 19.3 |
| Printing and publishing | 29.3 | 46.4 | 4.2 | 2.2 | 2.6 | 12.8 | 14.0 | 12.9 | 10.7 | 12.4 |
| Chemical products | 108.3 | 115.6 | 177.7 | 167.5 | 133.6 | 23.9 | 26.1 | 39.2 | 31.4 | 42.6 |
| Refined petroleum products | 11.4 | 3.9 | 4.5 | 1.4 | 2.4 | 87.1 | 30.5 | 8.1 | 23.1 | 8.1 |
| Rubber and plastic products | 5.2 | 3.1 | 5.5 | 5.7 | 8.4 | 4.4 | 6.0 | 5.6 | 6.2 | 3.7 |
| Leather products | 3.7 | 1.8 | 0.9 | 0.5 | 1.7 | 0.4 | 0.6 | 0.7 | 0.2 | 0.4 |
| Stone, clay and glass products | 7.5 | 14.8 | 15.1 | 13.8 | 14.2 | 7.8 | 9.0 | 12.4 | 10.4 | 12.3 |
| Primary metals | 301.2 | 187.2 | 249.3 | 119.2 | 67.1 | 47.1 | 20.3 | 56.6 | 23.6 | 12.2 |
| Fabricated metal products | 28.6 | 20.0 | 11.5 | 14.5 | 17.1 | 5.1 | 6.0 | 5.6 | 7.7 | 16.6 |
| Industrial machinery and computers | 111.5 | 107.5 | 137.3 | 103.6 | 152.7 | 84.5 | 106.0 | 110.0 | 109.5 | 125.1 |
| Electric and electronic equipment | 82.7 | 94.1 | 129.3 | 137.2 | 149.5 | 65.3 | 53.4 | 51.4 | 75.8 | 103.2 |
| Transportation equipment | 174.6 | 42.1 | 331.4 | 62.8 | 37.4 | 4.9 | 3.9 | 9.1 | 9.7 | 15.5 |
| Scientific and measuring instruments | 88.4 | 102.8 | 91.4 | 56.0 | 42.7 | 167.7 | 203.3 | 165.3 | 124.4 | 128.3 |
| Miscellaneous manufactures | 29.5 | 21.5 | 15.0 | 10.5 | 8.4 | 64.0 | 47.6 | 75.1 | 61.4 | 60.4 |
| Unidentified manufactures | 1.7 | 39.4 | 2.5 | 1.6 | 1.5 | 2.1 | 2.0 | 3.8 | 1.2 | 1.5 |
| **Agricultural and livestock products** | 91.7 | 78.9 | 42.7 | 77.1 | 65.6 | ..... | 3.7 | 5.7 | 1.6 | 0.1 |
| Agricultural products | 91.6 | 78.8 | 42.3 | 76.8 | 65.3 | ..... | 3.7 | 5.6 | 1.5 | 0.1 |
| Livestock and livestock products | ..... | 0.1 | 0.3 | 0.3 | 0.2 | ..... | ..... | 0.1 | ..... | ..... |
| **Other commodities** | 28.1 | 63.0 | 66.4 | 55.8 | 100.5 | 41.6 | 35.0 | 12.1 | 9.4 | 12.8 |
| Forestry products | 0.4 | ..... | ..... | 0.6 | 0.2 | 0.1 | 0.3 | 0.2 | ..... | 0.5 |
| Fish and other marine products | 0.2 | 0.2 | 0.3 | 0.1 | ..... | 0.3 | 0.3 | ..... | ..... | 0.5 |
| Metallic ores and concentrates | 0.7 | ..... | ..... | ..... | ..... | ..... | ..... | 0.1 | ..... | ..... |
| Bituminous coal and lignite | ..... | ..... | ..... | ..... | ..... | ..... | ..... | ..... | ..... | ..... |
| Crude petroleum and natural gas | ..... | ..... | ..... | ..... | 21.9 | ..... | ..... | ..... | ..... | ..... |
| Nonmetallic minerals | 1.2 | 0.6 | 1.1 | 1.1 | 1.5 | 0.1 | 0.4 | 1.1 | 0.1 | 0.1 |
| Scrap and waste | 13.2 | 33.2 | 48.3 | 32.1 | 62.7 | 1.8 | 0.4 | 0.6 | 0.9 | 1.3 |
| Used merchandise | 4.6 | 16.7 | 6.8 | 10.7 | 6.5 | 33.6 | 30.3 | 8.4 | 7.2 | 9.4 |
| Goods imported and returned unchanged | ..... | ..... | ..... | ..... | ..... | ..... | ..... | ..... | ..... | ..... |
| Special classification provisions | 7.8 | 12.3 | 9.8 | 11.3 | 7.7 | 5.6 | 3.2 | 1.8 | 1.2 | 1.0 |

## NORTH CAROLINA: Exports of Goods, 1997

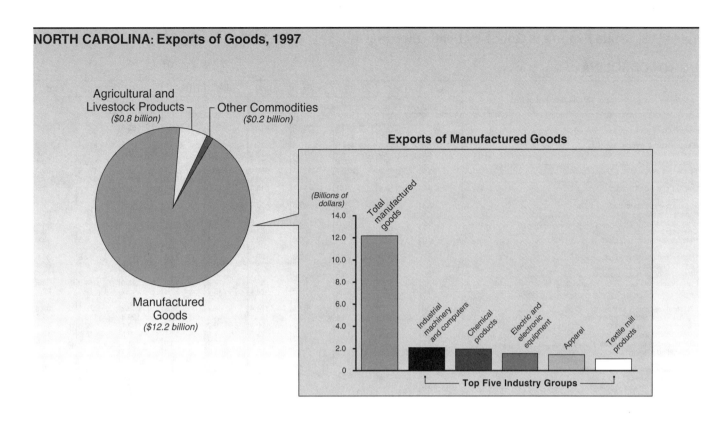

## Table D-3. State Exports of Goods by Destination and Industry, 1993–1997 —Continued

### NORTH CAROLINA (Millions of dollars.)

| Industry | 1993 | 1994 | 1995 | 1996 | 1997 | 1993 | 1994 | 1995 | 1996 | 1997 |
|---|---|---|---|---|---|---|---|---|---|---|
| | All destinations | | | | | Canada | | | | |
| **ALL GOODS** | 7 976.4 | 8 968.8 | 10 567.4 | 11 586.6 | 13 102.1 | 2 289.1 | 2 782.8 | 3 168.5 | 3 520.4 | 3 748.2 |
| **Manufactured goods** | 7 251.4 | 8 224.7 | 9 773.5 | 10 743.7 | 12 169.9 | 2 219.6 | 2 706.4 | 3 090.0 | 3 435.6 | 3 655.1 |
| Food products | 111.8 | 150.8 | 183.8 | 183.6 | 158.8 | 17.8 | 26.5 | 34.8 | 33.2 | 33.1 |
| Tobacco products | 730.6 | 703.1 | 650.4 | 471.2 | 350.3 | 3.9 | 8.2 | 7.5 | 6.8 | 9.8 |
| Textile mill products | 619.3 | 742.7 | 910.4 | 997.5 | 1 074.8 | 164.5 | 220.2 | 274.9 | 299.0 | 350.1 |
| Apparel | 584.3 | 698.1 | 1 097.8 | 1 233.4 | 1 449.1 | 61.7 | 77.8 | 96.1 | 102.9 | 125.1 |
| Lumber and wood products | 154.0 | 171.9 | 187.0 | 189.7 | 199.5 | 15.6 | 14.8 | 16.8 | 20.3 | 28.6 |
| Furniture and fixtures | 150.9 | 170.3 | 166.1 | 174.5 | 196.1 | 72.7 | 75.3 | 64.3 | 58.9 | 73.0 |
| Paper products | 133.2 | 159.1 | 200.1 | 205.7 | 243.7 | 53.6 | 57.5 | 63.8 | 59.0 | 58.3 |
| Printing and publishing | 34.4 | 40.5 | 41.0 | 39.6 | 44.5 | 20.2 | 23.1 | 23.0 | 21.3 | 22.1 |
| Chemical products | 1 001.7 | 1 134.8 | 1 418.9 | 1 610.0 | 1 952.5 | 262.8 | 280.6 | 309.7 | 401.1 | 482.9 |
| Refined petroleum products | 3.0 | 3.8 | 4.7 | 5.4 | 10.3 | 0.5 | 0.6 | 0.6 | 0.3 | 1.1 |
| Rubber and plastic products | 135.4 | 152.3 | 174.7 | 215.7 | 305.5 | 39.1 | 39.0 | 46.8 | 63.4 | 103.3 |
| Leather products | 23.1 | 23.8 | 32.9 | 37.0 | 39.9 | 12.7 | 13.1 | 17.6 | 16.9 | 19.4 |
| Stone, clay and glass products | 51.0 | 69.0 | 78.9 | 67.4 | 107.4 | 25.3 | 35.7 | 37.1 | 35.6 | 40.7 |
| Primary metals | 318.4 | 403.1 | 508.6 | 652.1 | 782.5 | 79.7 | 129.7 | 122.8 | 180.1 | 166.9 |
| Fabricated metal products | 198.9 | 202.3 | 212.8 | 234.8 | 327.8 | 101.9 | 104.8 | 105.2 | 92.0 | 147.9 |
| Industrial machinery and computers | 1 155.0 | 1 451.1 | 1 796.0 | 2 016.0 | 2 089.7 | 514.3 | 708.4 | 877.3 | 918.7 | 922.3 |
| Electric and electronic equipment | 1 029.9 | 1 084.2 | 1 182.3 | 1 385.7 | 1 552.5 | 415.5 | 490.1 | 591.3 | 690.7 | 516.5 |
| Transportation equipment | 473.3 | 473.9 | 489.1 | 524.6 | 692.9 | 280.7 | 328.3 | 323.3 | 340.0 | 459.3 |
| Scientific and measuring instruments | 259.4 | 283.7 | 339.2 | 380.2 | 450.3 | 59.6 | 51.6 | 56.9 | 65.9 | 66.4 |
| Miscellaneous manufactures | 67.4 | 86.3 | 76.2 | 97.7 | 115.7 | 11.6 | 13.5 | 12.4 | 19.4 | 18.4 |
| Unidentified manufactures | 16.3 | 19.9 | 22.5 | 21.8 | 26.2 | 5.8 | 7.7 | 7.8 | 10.1 | 9.9 |
| **Agricultural and livestock products** | 647.5 | 634.6 | 687.7 | 715.0 | 764.5 | 16.7 | 13.1 | 17.6 | 20.8 | 17.3 |
| Agricultural products | 642.4 | 630.5 | 681.4 | 709.5 | 759.8 | 15.9 | 11.8 | 14.6 | 17.9 | 16.3 |
| Livestock and livestock products | 5.0 | 4.1 | 6.4 | 5.5 | 4.7 | 0.8 | 1.3 | 3.0 | 2.8 | 1.1 |
| **Other commodities** | 77.5 | 109.6 | 106.2 | 127.9 | 167.7 | 52.8 | 63.3 | 61.0 | 64.0 | 75.8 |
| Forestry products | 0.7 | 1.6 | 4.3 | 4.8 | 6.5 | 0.1 | 0.1 | 0.8 | 0.1 | 0.2 |
| Fish and other marine products | 9.9 | 10.0 | 12.2 | 13.7 | 38.7 | 8.2 | 5.0 | 6.0 | 3.2 | 4.2 |
| Metallic ores and concentrates | 0.1 | 0.2 | ..... | 0.3 | 0.7 | ..... | ..... | ..... | ..... | ..... |
| Bituminous coal and lignite | ..... | ..... | ..... | ..... | ..... | ..... | ..... | ..... | ..... | ..... |
| Crude petroleum and natural gas | 2.6 | 1.8 | 2.2 | 3.8 | 1.7 | 2.3 | 1.6 | 2.1 | 3.2 | 1.5 |
| Nonmetallic minerals | 8.4 | 29.3 | 15.1 | 18.9 | 13.6 | 0.9 | 6.9 | 1.5 | 1.1 | 1.3 |
| Scrap and waste | 13.4 | 14.6 | 20.5 | 22.5 | 22.8 | 4.4 | 5.7 | 9.3 | 5.1 | 6.1 |
| Used merchandise | 3.0 | 3.2 | 6.5 | 2.5 | 5.8 | 0.2 | 0.6 | 0.8 | 0.2 | 1.0 |
| Goods imported and returned unchanged | 35.2 | 40.9 | 38.4 | 45.6 | 54.3 | 35.2 | 40.9 | 38.4 | 45.6 | 54.3 |
| Special classification provisions | 4.3 | 8.0 | 7.1 | 15.8 | 23.6 | 1.4 | 2.7 | 2.0 | 5.4 | 7.2 |

## Table D-3.  State Exports of Goods by Destination and Industry, 1993–1997 —*Continued*

### NORTH CAROLINA (Millions of dollars.)

| Industry | 1993 | 1994 | 1995 | 1996 | 1997 | 1993 | 1994 | 1995 | 1996 | 1997 |
|---|---|---|---|---|---|---|---|---|---|---|
| | South and Central America and Caribbean | | | | | Mexico | | | | |
| **ALL GOODS** | 930.4 | 1 072.2 | 1 490.6 | 1 589.0 | 1 814.7 | 365.1 | 493.1 | 653.8 | 922.2 | 1 320.5 |
| **Manufactured goods** | 927.3 | 1 064.8 | 1 484.0 | 1 580.4 | 1 805.5 | 363.0 | 490.6 | 650.6 | 919.4 | 1 309.8 |
| Food products | 4.5 | 8.0 | 9.4 | 18.4 | 23.1 | 2.7 | 1.6 | 4.1 | 4.8 | 6.4 |
| Tobacco products | 10.9 | 8.1 | 10.5 | 11.5 | 18.7 | ..... | 0.1 | 0.1 | 0.1 | 0.1 |
| Textile mill products | 148.6 | 152.9 | 220.7 | 174.7 | 150.9 | 35.5 | 51.4 | 48.1 | 118.6 | 150.2 |
| Apparel | 348.3 | 418.6 | 589.6 | 685.5 | 750.4 | 74.0 | 100.9 | 291.8 | 373.4 | 511.2 |
| Lumber and wood products | 8.0 | 9.4 | 10.1 | 14.1 | 15.5 | 3.0 | 3.6 | 0.7 | 1.2 | 1.6 |
| Furniture and fixtures | 3.6 | 4.5 | 6.8 | 7.5 | 10.6 | 6.8 | 7.5 | 3.3 | 2.2 | 2.1 |
| Paper products | 10.6 | 17.0 | 39.1 | 41.2 | 52.6 | 11.4 | 13.2 | 9.0 | 12.1 | 32.8 |
| Printing and publishing | 0.9 | 2.4 | 3.1 | 3.5 | 4.8 | 2.2 | 6.6 | 3.1 | 3.1 | 7.2 |
| Chemical products | 115.8 | 151.9 | 215.8 | 223.0 | 283.4 | 41.1 | 42.6 | 69.7 | 95.7 | 110.9 |
| Refined petroleum products | 0.3 | 0.6 | 1.2 | 0.6 | 0.7 | 0.1 | 0.1 | 0.2 | 0.5 | 3.0 |
| Rubber and plastic products | 16.8 | 16.0 | 21.8 | 17.8 | 28.1 | 13.6 | 22.4 | 16.0 | 12.8 | 36.6 |
| Leather products | 1.1 | 2.4 | 2.1 | 4.7 | 6.9 | 0.1 | 0.2 | 0.2 | 0.1 | 0.4 |
| Stone, clay and glass products | 2.9 | 3.1 | 5.9 | 5.0 | 3.1 | 5.6 | 9.4 | 1.9 | 2.7 | 4.8 |
| Primary metals | 36.8 | 47.9 | 44.7 | 50.1 | 69.1 | 12.8 | 13.5 | 13.6 | 14.3 | 22.5 |
| Fabricated metal products | 16.0 | 13.3 | 16.5 | 23.2 | 28.1 | 15.2 | 22.4 | 15.7 | 19.5 | 22.2 |
| Industrial machinery and computers | 80.8 | 107.0 | 164.8 | 157.4 | 171.4 | 41.7 | 58.9 | 49.7 | 78.1 | 107.3 |
| Electric and electronic equipment | 61.7 | 64.1 | 76.4 | 98.2 | 123.1 | 84.3 | 117.1 | 109.8 | 158.9 | 244.2 |
| Transportation equipment | 45.7 | 21.7 | 24.9 | 14.7 | 20.9 | 2.2 | 3.4 | 2.1 | 2.0 | 11.1 |
| Scientific and measuring instruments | 9.4 | 10.3 | 15.0 | 21.0 | 29.0 | 7.6 | 11.3 | 9.5 | 15.9 | 19.1 |
| Miscellaneous manufactures | 2.6 | 3.9 | 3.8 | 6.6 | 11.9 | 2.1 | 3.0 | 1.1 | 2.5 | 13.9 |
| Unidentified manufactures | 1.7 | 1.8 | 1.5 | 1.8 | 3.3 | 1.1 | 1.4 | 1.1 | 1.0 | 2.1 |
| **Agricultural and livestock products** | 1.5 | 2.3 | 3.0 | 4.1 | 4.8 | 0.9 | 1.0 | 2.8 | 1.9 | 8.8 |
| Agricultural products | 1.1 | 1.8 | 2.5 | 3.1 | 4.4 | 0.8 | 1.0 | 2.6 | 1.9 | 8.6 |
| Livestock and livestock products | 0.4 | 0.5 | 0.5 | 1.0 | 0.4 | 0.1 | ..... | 0.2 | ..... | 0.2 |
| **Other commodities** | 1.7 | 5.1 | 3.6 | 4.6 | 4.3 | 1.2 | 1.5 | 0.4 | 0.9 | 1.9 |
| Forestry products | 0.1 | 0.1 | 0.2 | 0.1 | 0.2 | ..... | ..... | ..... | ..... | 0.1 |
| Fish and other marine products | ..... | ..... | 0.1 | 0.1 | 0.1 | 0.1 | ..... | 0.1 | ..... | ..... |
| Metallic ores and concentrates | ..... | 0.1 | ..... | ..... | ..... | ..... | ..... | ..... | ..... | ..... |
| Bituminous coal and lignite | ..... | ..... | ..... | ..... | ..... | ..... | ..... | ..... | ..... | ..... |
| Crude petroleum and natural gas | ..... | ..... | ..... | ..... | ..... | 0.2 | 0.2 | ..... | ..... | ..... |
| Nonmetallic minerals | 0.6 | 4.2 | 1.8 | 0.4 | 0.6 | ..... | 0.1 | 0.1 | 0.2 | 0.6 |
| Scrap and waste | 0.2 | 0.1 | 0.2 | 0.1 | 0.2 | 0.1 | 0.3 | 0.1 | 0.4 | 0.5 |
| Used merchandise | 0.6 | 0.2 | 0.7 | 0.8 | 0.7 | 0.2 | 0.2 | 0.1 | ..... | ..... |
| Goods imported and returned unchanged | ..... | ..... | ..... | ..... | ..... | ..... | ..... | ..... | ..... | ..... |
| Special classification provisions | 0.3 | 0.4 | 0.4 | 2.9 | 2.5 | 0.6 | 0.7 | 0.1 | 0.3 | 0.7 |
| | European Union | | | | | United Kingdom | | | | |
| **ALL GOODS** | 1 884.9 | 1 994.4 | 2 300.0 | 2 533.0 | 2 870.7 | 313.0 | 391.4 | 446.8 | 552.8 | 716.5 |
| **Manufactured goods** | 1 707.4 | 1 810.7 | 2 091.0 | 2 237.0 | 2 570.1 | 276.0 | 366.0 | 422.4 | 497.5 | 667.9 |
| Food products | 4.0 | 5.8 | 7.4 | 10.0 | 6.8 | 0.8 | 1.8 | 1.1 | 1.5 | 3.1 |
| Tobacco products | 378.1 | 273.9 | 231.9 | 163.3 | 74.4 | 0.1 | ..... | ..... | ..... | ..... |
| Textile mill products | 157.1 | 179.3 | 206.2 | 220.8 | 203.7 | 34.0 | 31.2 | 38.4 | 43.4 | 42.7 |
| Apparel | 37.2 | 28.7 | 29.2 | 17.0 | 18.8 | 3.4 | 4.2 | 6.7 | 7.3 | 7.2 |
| Lumber and wood products | 60.6 | 75.4 | 82.3 | 77.0 | 92.0 | 9.9 | 12.7 | 10.8 | 21.0 | 17.0 |
| Furniture and fixtures | 22.5 | 29.8 | 36.7 | 31.3 | 39.3 | 3.4 | 11.8 | 19.1 | 12.9 | 16.2 |
| Paper products | 29.5 | 34.5 | 45.0 | 46.6 | 47.3 | 8.0 | 8.8 | 13.6 | 10.3 | 11.1 |
| Printing and publishing | 4.3 | 3.9 | 5.3 | 5.6 | 4.7 | 1.3 | 1.1 | 1.9 | 2.2 | 2.0 |
| Chemical products | 221.4 | 325.8 | 363.5 | 430.9 | 555.7 | 37.6 | 96.6 | 62.1 | 73.0 | 102.0 |
| Refined petroleum products | 0.1 | 0.1 | 0.2 | 0.6 | 2.2 | ..... | ..... | 0.1 | 0.1 | 0.3 |
| Rubber and plastic products | 35.2 | 42.1 | 56.3 | 65.9 | 73.6 | 7.3 | 10.6 | 12.3 | 13.8 | 16.6 |
| Leather products | 5.9 | 4.7 | 3.5 | 5.6 | 5.6 | 0.4 | 0.7 | 0.4 | 2.5 | 2.5 |
| Stone, clay and glass products | 7.5 | 9.2 | 20.1 | 11.9 | 39.5 | 0.8 | 1.3 | 1.6 | 1.3 | 22.1 |
| Primary metals | 82.6 | 80.2 | 104.0 | 131.8 | 174.1 | 38.4 | 26.4 | 21.1 | 36.1 | 56.8 |
| Fabricated metal products | 28.3 | 26.2 | 29.2 | 44.5 | 53.3 | 8.5 | 6.6 | 8.8 | 11.4 | 7.8 |
| Industrial machinery and computers | 263.8 | 289.7 | 405.4 | 464.5 | 505.0 | 32.5 | 43.0 | 88.7 | 100.1 | 148.9 |
| Electric and electronic equipment | 148.8 | 166.3 | 192.3 | 198.1 | 304.4 | 29.4 | 37.6 | 62.3 | 63.9 | 88.9 |
| Transportation equipment | 82.2 | 64.5 | 76.1 | 107.9 | 152.4 | 18.2 | 25.4 | 26.6 | 43.0 | 61.6 |
| Scientific and measuring instruments | 108.1 | 128.2 | 159.1 | 157.5 | 174.6 | 24.2 | 26.2 | 31.6 | 37.4 | 45.0 |
| Miscellaneous manufactures | 27.6 | 39.0 | 33.4 | 43.5 | 39.8 | 17.0 | 18.9 | 14.0 | 15.3 | 15.0 |
| Unidentified manufactures | 2.8 | 3.4 | 3.7 | 2.7 | 2.8 | 0.9 | 1.1 | 1.2 | 0.8 | 1.1 |
| **Agricultural and livestock products** | 164.6 | 170.2 | 193.0 | 270.0 | 253.8 | 34.6 | 23.1 | 20.6 | 49.2 | 38.6 |
| Agricultural products | 162.0 | 168.5 | 190.8 | 268.4 | 251.8 | 34.6 | 23.1 | 20.5 | 49.1 | 38.6 |
| Livestock and livestock products | 2.5 | 1.7 | 2.2 | 1.6 | 2.0 | ..... | ..... | ..... | ..... | ..... |
| **Other commodities** | 12.9 | 13.5 | 16.0 | 26.0 | 46.7 | 2.3 | 2.4 | 3.9 | 6.1 | 10.1 |
| Forestry products | 0.1 | 0.3 | 0.3 | 0.6 | 0.6 | ..... | ..... | ..... | ..... | ..... |
| Fish and other marine products | 0.5 | 3.3 | 2.9 | 7.9 | 27.7 | ..... | ..... | ..... | ..... | 0.8 |
| Metallic ores and concentrates | ..... | ..... | ..... | 0.2 | 0.6 | ..... | ..... | ..... | 0.2 | 0.4 |
| Bituminous coal and lignite | ..... | ..... | ..... | ..... | ..... | ..... | ..... | ..... | ..... | ..... |
| Crude petroleum and natural gas | ..... | 0.1 | ..... | 0.4 | ..... | ..... | ..... | ..... | 0.3 | ..... |
| Nonmetallic minerals | 4.6 | 6.1 | 7.0 | 10.8 | 6.3 | 1.6 | 1.9 | 2.4 | 3.2 | 1.9 |
| Scrap and waste | 6.1 | 0.3 | 2.5 | 2.3 | 1.1 | 0.4 | ..... | 0.8 | 0.7 | 0.3 |
| Used merchandise | 0.8 | 0.9 | 0.8 | 0.7 | 2.3 | 0.1 | 0.1 | 0.4 | 0.3 | 1.7 |
| Goods imported and returned unchanged | ..... | ..... | ..... | ..... | ..... | ..... | ..... | ..... | ..... | ..... |
| Special classification provisions | 0.7 | 2.6 | 2.4 | 3.2 | 8.1 | 0.2 | 0.3 | 0.3 | 1.4 | 5.0 |

## Table D-3. State Exports of Goods by Destination and Industry, 1993–1997 —*Continued*

### NORTH CAROLINA (Millions of dollars.)

| Industry | 1993 | 1994 | 1995 | 1996 | 1997 | 1993 | 1994 | 1995 | 1996 | 1997 |
|---|---|---|---|---|---|---|---|---|---|---|
| | Germany | | | | | France | | | | |
| **ALL GOODS** | 352.6 | 396.0 | 476.5 | 482.9 | 550.1 | 122.9 | 131.1 | 165.4 | 191.9 | 298.3 |
| **Manufactured goods** | 304.0 | 334.6 | 428.2 | 430.8 | 488.3 | 111.8 | 124.8 | 152.6 | 182.4 | 263.7 |
| Food products | 0.8 | 0.6 | 0.6 | 0.9 | 0.4 | 0.1 | 0.1 | 0.1 | 0.3 | 0.4 |
| Tobacco products | 20.3 | 12.8 | 6.1 | 1.9 | ..... | | | | | |
| Textile mill products | 46.8 | 49.9 | 50.1 | 47.3 | 41.8 | 11.0 | 13.1 | 15.4 | 15.0 | 13.6 |
| Apparel | 2.3 | 1.7 | 1.9 | 1.1 | 1.8 | 3.0 | 1.1 | 1.2 | 0.9 | 0.4 |
| Lumber and wood products | 16.2 | 18.1 | 21.7 | 14.1 | 13.3 | 1.3 | 2.1 | 1.8 | 2.0 | 2.8 |
| Furniture and fixtures | 6.7 | 6.4 | 8.1 | 6.6 | 9.5 | 2.1 | 1.4 | 1.2 | 2.3 | 0.7 |
| Paper products | 2.9 | 6.8 | 12.0 | 10.7 | 8.3 | 3.5 | 4.4 | 3.7 | 4.7 | 8.7 |
| Printing and publishing | 0.8 | 0.9 | 1.0 | 1.1 | 0.8 | 0.4 | 0.5 | 0.3 | 0.6 | 0.4 |
| Chemical products | 34.8 | 53.6 | 63.0 | 72.0 | 84.9 | 16.2 | 21.1 | 19.2 | 20.9 | 30.9 |
| Refined petroleum products | ..... | ..... | ..... | 0.1 | 0.1 | | | | | 1.2 |
| Rubber and plastic products | 7.6 | 6.2 | 10.1 | 13.4 | 15.6 | 3.5 | 5.4 | 7.9 | 5.7 | 10.1 |
| Leather products | 1.6 | 0.8 | 1.4 | 1.1 | 0.2 | 2.2 | 1.7 | 0.2 | ..... | ..... |
| Stone, clay and glass products | 2.0 | 2.9 | 5.7 | 2.5 | 2.4 | 0.5 | 0.7 | 1.3 | 1.1 | 1.5 |
| Primary metals | 12.1 | 10.3 | 16.3 | 22.3 | 24.6 | 12.9 | 13.1 | 12.0 | 22.0 | 45.6 |
| Fabricated metal products | 4.3 | 5.6 | 7.9 | 10.9 | 15.1 | 2.4 | 2.3 | 2.6 | 2.8 | 3.8 |
| Industrial machinery and computers | 38.7 | 56.2 | 84.7 | 95.7 | 103.2 | 23.6 | 26.3 | 48.8 | 50.8 | 62.6 |
| Electric and electronic equipment | 20.1 | 23.6 | 38.8 | 34.0 | 47.3 | 8.7 | 6.5 | 12.3 | 16.7 | 35.7 |
| Transportation equipment | 39.5 | 16.4 | 21.1 | 21.1 | 44.7 | 5.4 | 7.1 | 8.4 | 13.8 | 22.0 |
| Scientific and measuring instruments | 43.4 | 56.9 | 72.7 | 64.7 | 68.7 | 12.4 | 15.0 | 12.6 | 16.1 | 17.2 |
| Miscellaneous manufactures | 2.5 | 4.2 | 4.4 | 8.5 | 5.0 | 2.5 | 2.5 | 3.2 | 6.3 | 5.9 |
| Unidentified manufactures | 0.7 | 0.8 | 0.6 | 0.6 | 0.6 | 0.3 | 0.3 | 0.4 | 0.2 | 0.2 |
| **Agricultural and livestock products** | 47.9 | 59.7 | 46.0 | 50.3 | 54.7 | 10.1 | 5.7 | 11.9 | 8.5 | 20.7 |
| Agricultural products | 46.6 | 59.6 | 45.1 | 50.0 | 54.0 | 9.8 | 5.3 | 11.9 | 8.5 | 20.7 |
| Livestock and livestock products | 1.3 | 0.1 | 0.9 | 0.2 | 0.7 | 0.3 | 0.4 | ..... | ..... | ..... |
| **Other commodities** | 0.7 | 1.7 | 2.4 | 1.9 | 7.0 | 1.0 | 0.6 | 0.9 | 0.9 | 13.9 |
| Forestry products | ..... | ..... | 0.1 | 0.3 | 0.5 | ..... | ..... | ..... | ..... | ..... |
| Fish and other marine products | ..... | ..... | ..... | ..... | 5.0 | 0.2 | ..... | 0.1 | 0.2 | 13.3 |
| Metallic ores and concentrates | ..... | ..... | ..... | ..... | ..... | ..... | ..... | ..... | ..... | ..... |
| Bituminous coal and lignite | ..... | ..... | ..... | ..... | ..... | ..... | ..... | ..... | ..... | ..... |
| Crude petroleum and natural gas | ..... | ..... | ..... | ..... | ..... | ..... | ..... | ..... | ..... | ..... |
| Nonmetallic minerals | 0.3 | 0.3 | 0.5 | 0.7 | 0.6 | 0.2 | 0.3 | 0.5 | 0.5 | ..... |
| Scrap and waste | ..... | 0.3 | 0.3 | 0.2 | 0.2 | ..... | ..... | 0.1 | ..... | 0.3 |
| Used merchandise | 0.1 | ..... | ..... | ..... | 0.1 | 0.3 | ..... | 0.1 | 0.1 | 0.2 |
| Goods imported and returned unchanged | ..... | ..... | ..... | ..... | ..... | ..... | ..... | ..... | ..... | ..... |
| Special classification provisions | 0.2 | 1.3 | 1.4 | 0.6 | 0.8 | 0.2 | 0.2 | 0.1 | 0.1 | 0.1 |
| | The Netherlands | | | | | Asian 10 | | | | |
| **ALL GOODS** | 236.0 | 215.5 | 225.7 | 237.6 | 291.5 | 1 569.6 | 1 652.3 | 1 904.2 | 1 984.5 | 2 175.2 |
| **Manufactured goods** | 227.1 | 203.3 | 210.1 | 233.0 | 284.8 | 1 235.7 | 1 271.7 | 1 498.5 | 1 621.4 | 1 803.2 |
| Food products | 0.5 | 1.6 | 2.4 | 0.5 | 0.5 | 59.7 | 76.3 | 79.4 | 77.5 | 69.6 |
| Tobacco products | 0.3 | ..... | 0.1 | ..... | ..... | 144.8 | 135.1 | 125.3 | 116.5 | 107.8 |
| Textile mill products | 19.0 | 21.5 | 27.4 | 50.0 | 55.0 | 70.5 | 84.9 | 93.0 | 98.1 | 120.5 |
| Apparel | 0.7 | 0.5 | 0.9 | 0.9 | 1.3 | 40.7 | 53.8 | 68.0 | 29.9 | 17.8 |
| Lumber and wood products | 1.5 | 2.1 | 4.2 | 2.4 | 2.2 | 56.1 | 54.3 | 63.6 | 62.4 | 46.5 |
| Furniture and fixtures | 7.1 | 5.9 | 3.8 | 3.8 | 6.0 | 6.4 | 23.5 | 29.3 | 35.8 | 31.2 |
| Paper products | 7.0 | 6.4 | 5.2 | 8.3 | 10.4 | 15.2 | 21.5 | 24.2 | 29.0 | 31.6 |
| Printing and publishing | 0.5 | 0.3 | 0.3 | 0.3 | 0.2 | 2.0 | 2.7 | 3.5 | 3.5 | 3.5 |
| Chemical products | 20.2 | 16.3 | 28.7 | 24.0 | 56.3 | 214.5 | 199.8 | 292.2 | 289.9 | 273.6 |
| Refined petroleum products | ..... | ..... | ..... | ..... | 0.2 | 0.2 | 0.9 | 1.1 | 0.3 | 0.7 |
| Rubber and plastic products | 11.2 | 10.3 | 13.6 | 16.4 | 16.3 | 20.9 | 24.5 | 26.1 | 41.8 | 50.7 |
| Leather products | 0.3 | 0.3 | 0.1 | 0.2 | ..... | 2.7 | 1.8 | 6.9 | 4.8 | 2.0 |
| Stone, clay and glass products | 2.1 | 1.4 | 5.4 | 2.5 | 10.0 | 6.2 | 6.9 | 7.7 | 7.1 | 9.6 |
| Primary metals | 0.7 | 2.2 | 4.0 | 8.1 | 8.2 | 75.2 | 96.3 | 165.4 | 204.5 | 294.2 |
| Fabricated metal products | 1.3 | 1.7 | 1.7 | 1.6 | 1.5 | 22.8 | 25.3 | 30.5 | 36.9 | 52.8 |
| Industrial machinery and computers | 121.1 | 97.3 | 83.4 | 79.8 | 61.5 | 145.5 | 185.1 | 200.7 | 283.6 | 270.4 |
| Electric and electronic equipment | 16.6 | 16.0 | 12.3 | 18.1 | 42.7 | 271.3 | 191.3 | 167.8 | 175.5 | 275.3 |
| Transportation equipment | 8.8 | 6.4 | 4.6 | 5.9 | 1.9 | 18.9 | 21.1 | 32.0 | 23.8 | 19.8 |
| Scientific and measuring instruments | 7.0 | 7.9 | 8.5 | 8.9 | 9.0 | 45.0 | 48.5 | 61.6 | 78.6 | 100.2 |
| Miscellaneous manufactures | 1.1 | 4.9 | 3.1 | 1.2 | 1.5 | 15.5 | 16.2 | 17.7 | 19.4 | 22.4 |
| Unidentified manufactures | 0.2 | 0.2 | 0.3 | 0.2 | 0.2 | 1.5 | 1.8 | 2.5 | 2.4 | 2.9 |
| **Agricultural and livestock products** | 8.1 | 10.9 | 14.7 | 4.1 | 5.6 | 327.0 | 365.6 | 385.4 | 335.8 | 341.1 |
| Agricultural products | 7.8 | 10.6 | 14.5 | 3.7 | 5.0 | 326.1 | 365.2 | 385.0 | 335.7 | 340.4 |
| Livestock and livestock products | 0.3 | 0.3 | 0.2 | 0.3 | 0.6 | 1.0 | 0.4 | 0.4 | 0.1 | 0.7 |
| **Other commodities** | 0.8 | 1.3 | 0.9 | 0.6 | 1.1 | 6.8 | 15.0 | 20.3 | 27.2 | 31.0 |
| Forestry products | ..... | 0.2 | 0.1 | 0.2 | 0.1 | 0.3 | 0.9 | 2.6 | 3.9 | 5.3 |
| Fish and other marine products | 0.1 | ..... | ..... | ..... | 0.2 | 0.7 | 1.6 | 2.4 | 2.2 | 5.9 |
| Metallic ores and concentrates | ..... | ..... | ..... | ..... | ..... | ..... | ..... | 0.1 | ..... | ..... |
| Bituminous coal and lignite | ..... | ..... | ..... | ..... | ..... | ..... | ..... | ..... | ..... | ..... |
| Crude petroleum and natural gas | ..... | ..... | ..... | ..... | ..... | ..... | ..... | ..... | ..... | ..... |
| Nonmetallic minerals | 0.4 | 0.1 | 0.4 | ..... | 0.4 | 2.0 | 3.4 | 3.5 | 6.1 | 4.5 |
| Scrap and waste | ..... | ..... | ..... | ..... | ..... | 2.3 | 7.4 | 7.9 | 12.0 | 12.4 |
| Used merchandise | 0.3 | 0.3 | ..... | ..... | 0.1 | 0.7 | 0.4 | 2.0 | ..... | 0.2 |
| Goods imported and returned unchanged | ..... | ..... | ..... | ..... | ..... | ..... | ..... | ..... | ..... | ..... |
| Special classification provisions | 0.1 | 0.7 | 0.4 | 0.3 | 0.3 | 0.7 | 1.3 | 1.8 | 3.0 | 2.7 |

### Table D-3.  State Exports of Goods by Destination and Industry, 1993–1997 —*Continued*

## NORTH CAROLINA (Millions of dollars.)

| Industry | 1993 | 1994 | 1995 | 1996 | 1997 | 1993 | 1994 | 1995 | 1996 | 1997 |
|---|---|---|---|---|---|---|---|---|---|---|
| | Japan | | | | | South Korea | | | | |
| **ALL GOODS** | 720.4 | 743.4 | 760.7 | 824.0 | 811.0 | 114.6 | 132.2 | 183.2 | 201.9 | 202.8 |
| **Manufactured goods** | 561.7 | 562.0 | 577.7 | 692.2 | 688.9 | 98.4 | 113.7 | 145.2 | 155.7 | 158.3 |
| Food products | 28.0 | 34.5 | 33.9 | 43.5 | 30.0 | 5.4 | 4.7 | 2.5 | 1.6 | 2.6 |
| Tobacco products | 84.6 | 78.5 | 78.2 | 91.4 | 85.3 | 13.4 | 12.3 | 7.2 | 4.9 | 3.6 |
| Textile mill products | 26.5 | 31.9 | 28.3 | 31.4 | 28.7 | 11.5 | 12.6 | 14.9 | 10.5 | 7.3 |
| Apparel | 31.6 | 43.5 | 52.4 | 19.2 | 8.7 | 0.1 | 0.2 | 0.2 | 0.8 | 0.8 |
| Lumber and wood products | 39.5 | 32.5 | 40.1 | 34.2 | 13.5 | 2.7 | 7.0 | 6.2 | 5.0 | 4.2 |
| Furniture and fixtures | 3.3 | 17.0 | 22.2 | 29.5 | 21.9 | 0.6 | 1.6 | 3.0 | 2.5 | 3.1 |
| Paper products | 5.2 | 7.5 | 7.6 | 7.2 | 9.8 | 0.7 | 0.8 | 2.8 | 2.2 | 4.2 |
| Printing and publishing | 0.7 | 0.7 | 1.0 | 0.7 | 0.7 | 0.2 | 0.3 | 0.2 | 0.2 | 0.1 |
| Chemical products | 31.2 | 34.8 | 54.5 | 55.2 | 44.6 | 25.5 | 25.0 | 31.3 | 49.6 | 43.9 |
| Refined petroleum products | 0.1 | ..... | ..... | 0.1 | 0.2 | 0.2 | 0.6 | 0.9 | ..... | 0.1 |
| Rubber and plastic products | 15.4 | 16.9 | 19.4 | 30.4 | 39.0 | 1.3 | 1.3 | 1.7 | 2.3 | 2.7 |
| Leather products | 0.3 | 0.5 | 0.4 | 1.0 | 0.4 | ..... | ..... | ..... | ..... | ..... |
| Stone, clay and glass products | 0.7 | 1.4 | 2.3 | 3.3 | 3.8 | 1.2 | 1.1 | 1.2 | 0.6 | 1.4 |
| Primary metals | 30.8 | 40.6 | 75.9 | 106.5 | 138.7 | 0.8 | 0.7 | 14.8 | 9.8 | 12.3 |
| Fabricated metal products | 6.7 | 8.5 | 6.9 | 8.0 | 20.4 | 4.6 | 2.8 | 2.5 | 8.1 | 4.1 |
| Industrial machinery and computers | 33.2 | 44.6 | 42.6 | 95.2 | 88.3 | 15.0 | 28.1 | 27.0 | 30.3 | 26.6 |
| Electric and electronic equipment | 181.6 | 115.4 | 50.9 | 64.1 | 69.9 | 5.8 | 5.5 | 6.9 | 7.2 | 25.5 |
| Transportation equipment | 11.2 | 13.7 | 15.2 | 9.6 | 7.1 | 1.6 | 2.8 | 12.2 | 8.6 | 2.8 |
| Scientific and measuring instruments | 18.1 | 28.8 | 35.0 | 50.5 | 62.8 | 7.0 | 4.4 | 6.0 | 7.0 | 9.9 |
| Miscellaneous manufactures | 12.5 | 10.1 | 9.8 | 10.2 | 14.2 | 0.8 | 1.6 | 3.5 | 4.2 | 2.3 |
| Unidentified manufactures | 0.6 | 0.7 | 1.0 | 1.1 | 0.8 | 0.1 | 0.2 | 0.2 | 0.2 | 0.7 |
| **Agricultural and livestock products** | 156.1 | 179.4 | 175.4 | 124.5 | 116.5 | 16.0 | 18.0 | 37.3 | 45.7 | 44.0 |
| Agricultural products | 156.0 | 179.4 | 175.4 | 124.4 | 116.3 | 15.9 | 18.0 | 37.3 | 45.7 | 44.0 |
| Livestock and livestock products | 0.1 | ..... | ..... | 0.1 | 0.1 | 0.1 | ..... | ..... | ..... | ..... |
| **Other commodities** | 2.6 | 2.0 | 7.6 | 7.3 | 5.7 | 0.2 | 0.5 | 0.6 | 0.4 | 0.5 |
| Forestry products | 0.1 | ..... | 0.5 | ..... | ..... | ..... | ..... | ..... | ..... | ..... |
| Fish and other marine products | 0.4 | 0.9 | 2.0 | 1.8 | 4.3 | ..... | ..... | 0.1 | 0.2 | 0.2 |
| Metallic ores and concentrates | ..... | ..... | ..... | ..... | ..... | ..... | ..... | ..... | ..... | ..... |
| Bituminous coal and lignite | ..... | ..... | ..... | ..... | ..... | ..... | ..... | ..... | ..... | ..... |
| Crude petroleum and natural gas | ..... | ..... | ..... | ..... | ..... | ..... | ..... | ..... | ..... | ..... |
| Nonmetallic minerals | 1.4 | 0.7 | 3.2 | 4.8 | 0.5 | 0.1 | 0.2 | 0.2 | 0.2 | 0.1 |
| Scrap and waste | 0.2 | ..... | 0.1 | 0.3 | 0.7 | ..... | ..... | ..... | ..... | ..... |
| Used merchandise | 0.6 | 0.4 | 1.7 | ..... | ..... | ..... | ..... | ..... | ..... | 0.1 |
| Goods imported and returned unchanged | ..... | ..... | ..... | ..... | ..... | ..... | ..... | ..... | ..... | ..... |
| Special classification provisions | ..... | 0.1 | 0.1 | 0.4 | 0.2 | 0.1 | 0.2 | 0.3 | ..... | 0.1 |
| | Taiwan | | | | | Singapore | | | | |
| **ALL GOODS** | 114.5 | 120.7 | 126.8 | 115.1 | 166.1 | 80.4 | 91.4 | 96.2 | 119.3 | 111.9 |
| **Manufactured goods** | 74.5 | 90.4 | 105.0 | 90.6 | 137.6 | 65.5 | 68.1 | 70.2 | 93.5 | 98.6 |
| Food products | 2.8 | 3.3 | 3.4 | 2.0 | 1.5 | 1.1 | 0.9 | 1.8 | 1.1 | 0.6 |
| Tobacco products | 9.6 | 6.0 | 4.9 | 4.1 | 5.2 | 8.5 | 6.8 | 3.3 | 1.3 | 2.6 |
| Textile mill products | 4.8 | 8.2 | 6.2 | 7.8 | 12.8 | 6.3 | 7.5 | 4.7 | 5.1 | 4.8 |
| Apparel | 0.5 | 1.2 | 2.8 | 1.8 | 1.5 | 2.0 | 2.4 | 2.6 | 1.3 | 1.7 |
| Lumber and wood products | 9.4 | 8.5 | 7.0 | 6.0 | 7.4 | 0.1 | 0.1 | 0.3 | 0.4 | 0.4 |
| Furniture and fixtures | 0.6 | 1.2 | 0.7 | 0.4 | 0.5 | 0.1 | 0.3 | 0.4 | 0.7 | 1.1 |
| Paper products | 1.6 | 1.8 | 2.0 | 1.8 | 2.7 | 1.9 | 2.3 | 2.7 | 8.3 | 4.1 |
| Printing and publishing | 0.1 | 0.2 | 0.2 | 0.5 | 0.6 | ..... | 0.2 | 0.7 | 0.1 | 0.1 |
| Chemical products | 9.0 | 11.4 | 20.7 | 14.5 | 22.6 | 5.1 | 2.2 | 4.0 | 6.7 | 7.8 |
| Refined petroleum products | ..... | 0.1 | 0.1 | ..... | 0.1 | ..... | ..... | ..... | 0.1 | 0.1 |
| Rubber and plastic products | 1.0 | 2.4 | 1.6 | 1.5 | 1.8 | 1.2 | 1.1 | 0.7 | 3.8 | 1.6 |
| Leather products | ..... | ..... | 0.1 | ..... | ..... | 0.1 | 0.1 | ..... | ..... | ..... |
| Stone, clay and glass products | 0.4 | 1.8 | 1.2 | 0.8 | 0.8 | 0.4 | 0.3 | 0.1 | 0.1 | 0.2 |
| Primary metals | 9.5 | 9.9 | 14.2 | 11.8 | 9.9 | 0.8 | 1.3 | 1.7 | 1.9 | 2.3 |
| Fabricated metal products | 2.2 | 2.4 | 6.2 | 5.2 | 8.9 | 1.5 | 2.2 | 2.0 | 3.4 | 2.1 |
| Industrial machinery and computers | 11.4 | 18.8 | 18.2 | 17.1 | 21.4 | 15.8 | 15.3 | 20.0 | 34.7 | 29.5 |
| Electric and electronic equipment | 7.2 | 6.2 | 8.1 | 7.7 | 28.3 | 18.1 | 20.4 | 20.3 | 17.7 | 29.6 |
| Transportation equipment | 0.5 | 0.9 | 0.7 | 1.5 | 2.8 | 0.7 | 0.6 | 0.6 | 1.9 | 2.6 |
| Scientific and measuring instruments | 3.2 | 5.1 | 5.4 | 4.8 | 7.6 | 1.4 | 3.1 | 3.7 | 4.0 | 6.3 |
| Miscellaneous manufactures | 0.4 | 1.0 | 1.2 | 1.1 | 0.9 | 0.2 | 0.7 | 0.5 | 0.7 | 0.9 |
| Unidentified manufactures | 0.2 | 0.2 | 0.2 | 0.2 | 0.3 | 0.1 | 0.3 | 0.2 | 0.2 | 0.3 |
| **Agricultural and livestock products** | 39.0 | 29.7 | 21.3 | 22.6 | 25.7 | 14.8 | 23.2 | 25.7 | 25.4 | 12.7 |
| Agricultural products | 39.0 | 29.4 | 21.1 | 22.6 | 25.7 | 14.8 | 23.2 | 25.7 | 25.4 | 12.7 |
| Livestock and livestock products | ..... | 0.3 | 0.3 | ..... | ..... | ..... | ..... | ..... | ..... | ..... |
| **Other commodities** | 1.0 | 0.6 | 0.5 | 1.8 | 2.8 | 0.1 | 0.1 | 0.3 | 0.3 | 0.6 |
| Forestry products | ..... | ..... | ..... | ..... | ..... | ..... | ..... | 0.2 | 0.1 | ..... |
| Fish and other marine products | ..... | 0.2 | 0.1 | ..... | 0.1 | ..... | ..... | ..... | ..... | ..... |
| Metallic ores and concentrates | ..... | ..... | ..... | ..... | ..... | ..... | 0.1 | ..... | ..... | ..... |
| Bituminous coal and lignite | ..... | ..... | ..... | ..... | ..... | ..... | ..... | ..... | ..... | ..... |
| Crude petroleum and natural gas | ..... | ..... | ..... | ..... | ..... | ..... | ..... | ..... | ..... | ..... |
| Nonmetallic minerals | 0.4 | 0.1 | 0.1 | 0.1 | 2.4 | ..... | ..... | ..... | ..... | 0.4 |
| Scrap and waste | 0.1 | ..... | ..... | 1.1 | 0.1 | ..... | ..... | ..... | ..... | ..... |
| Used merchandise | ..... | ..... | ..... | ..... | ..... | ..... | ..... | ..... | ..... | ..... |
| Goods imported and returned unchanged | ..... | ..... | ..... | ..... | ..... | ..... | ..... | ..... | ..... | ..... |
| Special classification provisions | 0.5 | 0.3 | 0.3 | 0.5 | 0.2 | ..... | ..... | ..... | 0.1 | 0.1 |

## NORTH DAKOTA: Exports of Goods, 1997

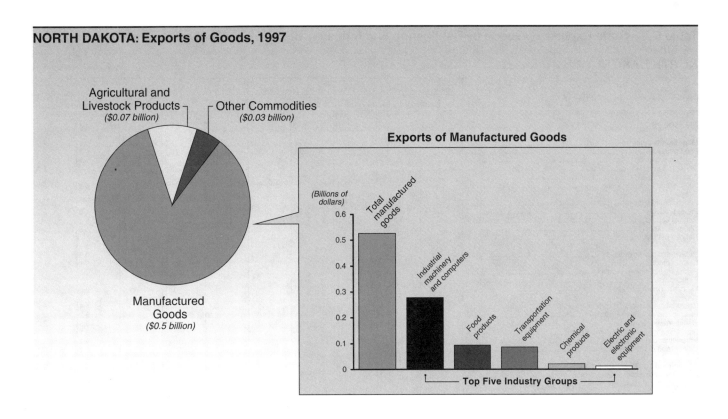

## Table D-3.  State Exports of Goods by Destination and Industry, 1993–1997 —*Continued*

**NORTH DAKOTA** (Millions of dollars.)

| Industry | 1993 | 1994 | 1995 | 1996 | 1997 | 1993 | 1994 | 1995 | 1996 | 1997 |
|---|---|---|---|---|---|---|---|---|---|---|
| | All destinations | | | | | Canada | | | | |
| **ALL GOODS** | 343.7 | 388.9 | 488.6 | 576.2 | 623.1 | 227.3 | 250.6 | 315.3 | 378.8 | 427.6 |
| **Manufactured goods** | 279.4 | 319.5 | 402.1 | 470.1 | 525.6 | 190.9 | 207.6 | 263.5 | 320.6 | 376.0 |
| Food products | 21.3 | 25.3 | 31.8 | 74.0 | 93.8 | 17.9 | 21.3 | 24.8 | 67.2 | 83.7 |
| Tobacco products | ..... | ..... | ..... | ..... | ..... | ..... | ..... | ..... | ..... | ..... |
| Textile mill products | 0.3 | 0.3 | 0.5 | 0.3 | 1.1 | 0.2 | 0.3 | 0.4 | 0.3 | 0.5 |
| Apparel | 0.2 | 0.5 | 0.3 | 0.2 | 0.1 | 0.1 | 0.2 | 0.1 | 0.1 | ..... |
| Lumber and wood products | 2.4 | 1.3 | 0.8 | 0.9 | 1.5 | 2.3 | 0.9 | 0.6 | 0.6 | 0.7 |
| Furniture and fixtures | 11.6 | 11.0 | 6.4 | 1.7 | 1.7 | 11.5 | 10.5 | 6.3 | 1.6 | 1.5 |
| Paper products | 0.5 | 2.3 | 0.4 | 2.0 | 2.9 | 0.5 | 0.3 | 0.3 | 0.4 | 0.3 |
| Printing and publishing | 1.4 | 0.7 | 1.2 | 0.8 | 0.6 | 1.2 | 0.6 | 0.7 | 0.8 | 0.5 |
| Chemical products | 10.5 | 6.4 | 13.7 | 16.3 | 21.1 | 4.7 | 3.0 | 9.7 | 10.8 | 16.3 |
| Refined petroleum products | 1.1 | 1.4 | 0.2 | 0.4 | 3.2 | 1.0 | 1.4 | 0.2 | 0.4 | 3.1 |
| Rubber and plastic products | 5.8 | 7.7 | 7.2 | 4.6 | 7.5 | 4.6 | 5.2 | 4.8 | 4.1 | 6.0 |
| Leather products | 0.3 | 0.4 | 0.5 | 0.3 | 0.1 | 0.2 | 0.2 | 0.4 | 0.1 | 0.1 |
| Stone, clay and glass products | 0.8 | 0.4 | 0.5 | 0.5 | 0.4 | 0.7 | 0.3 | 0.3 | 0.2 | 0.2 |
| Primary metals | 3.1 | 1.9 | 2.4 | 4.8 | 2.2 | 1.9 | 1.7 | 2.2 | 1.3 | 1.7 |
| Fabricated metal products | 3.4 | 4.4 | 5.4 | 5.8 | 7.2 | 3.2 | 3.6 | 3.4 | 3.8 | 5.9 |
| Industrial machinery and computers | 157.6 | 195.3 | 227.2 | 258.9 | 278.1 | 88.3 | 104.0 | 110.2 | 139.8 | 167.5 |
| Electric and electronic equipment | 6.8 | 7.8 | 9.0 | 9.8 | 12.1 | 5.8 | 5.8 | 6.8 | 6.0 | 7.3 |
| Transportation equipment | 49.1 | 48.3 | 90.6 | 83.9 | 86.4 | 45.1 | 46.0 | 89.4 | 80.7 | 77.8 |
| Scientific and measuring instruments | 1.4 | 1.8 | 1.5 | 2.6 | 2.7 | 0.7 | 0.6 | 1.0 | 1.2 | 1.6 |
| Miscellaneous manufactures | 0.9 | 1.2 | 1.6 | 1.4 | 1.9 | 0.4 | 1.0 | 1.1 | 0.7 | 0.8 |
| Unidentified manufactures | 1.0 | 1.0 | 1.0 | 1.0 | 1.0 | 0.7 | 0.7 | 0.7 | 0.7 | 0.4 |
| **Agricultural and livestock products** | 40.3 | 36.6 | 50.6 | 72.5 | 65.3 | 14.1 | 13.7 | 17.9 | 27.1 | 23.7 |
| Agricultural products | 35.5 | 31.7 | 45.5 | 67.0 | 57.7 | 10.0 | 8.9 | 12.9 | 21.9 | 16.3 |
| Livestock and livestock products | 4.7 | 4.9 | 5.2 | 5.5 | 7.6 | 4.1 | 4.8 | 5.0 | 5.2 | 7.3 |
| **Other commodities** | 24.0 | 32.8 | 35.8 | 33.6 | 32.1 | 22.2 | 29.3 | 34.0 | 31.0 | 27.9 |
| Forestry products | ..... | ..... | ..... | ..... | ..... | ..... | ..... | ..... | ..... | ..... |
| Fish and other marine products | 0.1 | 0.1 | 0.3 | 0.1 | 0.1 | 0.1 | 0.1 | 0.3 | 0.1 | 0.1 |
| Metallic ores and concentrates | 0.1 | 2.3 | 5.2 | ..... | ..... | ..... | 2.3 | 5.2 | ..... | ..... |
| Bituminous coal and lignite | 0.3 | 0.1 | ..... | ..... | ..... | ..... | ..... | ..... | ..... | ..... |
| Crude petroleum and natural gas | 4.5 | 5.0 | 3.1 | 2.3 | 2.8 | 4.5 | 5.0 | 3.1 | 2.3 | 2.8 |
| Nonmetallic minerals | 0.1 | 0.1 | 0.1 | 0.6 | 0.4 | 0.1 | 0.1 | 0.1 | 0.6 | 0.4 |
| Scrap and waste | 8.4 | 8.8 | 7.8 | 7.4 | 8.6 | 7.6 | 8.3 | 6.5 | 6.1 | 5.8 |
| Used merchandise | 2.9 | 6.6 | 2.2 | 4.9 | 6.0 | 2.3 | 3.7 | 1.8 | 3.8 | 4.8 |
| Goods imported and returned unchanged | 7.5 | 9.7 | 16.6 | 17.8 | 13.7 | 7.5 | 9.7 | 16.6 | 17.8 | 13.7 |
| Special classification provisions | 0.2 | 0.2 | 0.5 | 0.5 | 0.5 | 0.2 | 0.1 | 0.4 | 0.3 | 0.4 |

## Table D-3.  State Exports of Goods by Destination and Industry, 1993–1997 —*Continued*

### NORTH DAKOTA  (Millions of dollars.)

| Industry | 1993 | 1994 | 1995 | 1996 | 1997 | 1993 | 1994 | 1995 | 1996 | 1997 |
|---|---|---|---|---|---|---|---|---|---|---|
| | South and Central America and Caribbean | | | | | Mexico | | | | |
| **ALL GOODS** | 6.8 | 10.7 | 15.0 | 10.3 | 14.7 | 2.9 | 1.8 | 16.8 | 11.5 | 17.6 |
| **Manufactured goods** | 6.6 | 9.6 | 13.0 | 10.2 | 14.3 | 1.9 | 1.6 | 15.2 | 10.1 | 16.7 |
| Food products | 1.5 | 1.6 | 0.4 | 0.2 | 0.1 | 0.2 | 0.1 | 3.0 | 0.8 | 2.6 |
| Tobacco products | ..... | ..... | ..... | ..... | ..... | ..... | ..... | ..... | ..... | ..... |
| Textile mill products | ..... | ..... | ..... | ..... | ..... | ..... | ..... | ..... | ..... | 0.5 |
| Apparel | ..... | 0.3 | ..... | ..... | ..... | ..... | ..... | ..... | ..... | ..... |
| Lumber and wood products | ..... | 0.1 | 0.1 | ..... | 0.2 | ..... | ..... | ..... | 0.2 | 0.3 |
| Furniture and fixtures | ..... | 0.1 | 0.1 | ..... | ..... | ..... | ..... | ..... | ..... | ..... |
| Paper products | ..... | ..... | 0.1 | ..... | ..... | ..... | ..... | ..... | 1.6 | 2.4 |
| Printing and publishing | ..... | ..... | 0.2 | ..... | ..... | ..... | ..... | ..... | ..... | ..... |
| Chemical products | ..... | ..... | 0.1 | ..... | 0.1 | 0.4 | ..... | 0.1 | 1.6 | 0.4 |
| Refined petroleum products | ..... | ..... | ..... | ..... | ..... | ..... | ..... | ..... | ..... | 0.1 |
| Rubber and plastic products | 0.1 | ..... | ..... | 0.1 | 0.1 | ..... | ..... | 0.1 | 0.2 | 0.2 |
| Leather products | ..... | ..... | ..... | ..... | ..... | ..... | ..... | 0.1 | ..... | ..... |
| Stone, clay and glass products | ..... | ..... | ..... | ..... | ..... | ..... | ..... | ..... | ..... | ..... |
| Primary metals | ..... | ..... | ..... | ..... | ..... | ..... | 0.1 | ..... | ..... | ..... |
| Fabricated metal products | 0.1 | 0.1 | ..... | ..... | ..... | ..... | 0.1 | 1.5 | 0.2 | 0.3 |
| Industrial machinery and computers | 4.8 | 6.9 | 11.7 | 9.0 | 13.2 | 0.7 | 1.1 | 9.9 | 4.4 | 6.8 |
| Electric and electronic equipment | ..... | 0.1 | 0.3 | ..... | 0.3 | 0.3 | ..... | 0.3 | 0.2 | 0.6 |
| Transportation equipment | 0.1 | 0.3 | 0.3 | 0.3 | 0.1 | ..... | 0.1 | ..... | 0.5 | 2.0 |
| Scientific and measuring instruments | 0.1 | ..... | 0.1 | 0.6 | ..... | ..... | ..... | ..... | 0.1 | 0.2 |
| Miscellaneous manufactures | ..... | ..... | ..... | ..... | 0.3 | ..... | ..... | ..... | 0.1 | ..... |
| Unidentified manufactures | ..... | 0.1 | 0.1 | ..... | ..... | ..... | ..... | ..... | 0.1 | 0.1 |
| **Agricultural and livestock products** | 0.2 | 0.1 | 1.9 | ..... | 0.4 | 0.5 | ..... | 1.6 | 0.8 | 0.7 |
| Agricultural products | 0.2 | 0.1 | 1.9 | 0.1 | 0.4 | ..... | ..... | 1.6 | 0.7 | 0.6 |
| Livestock and livestock products | ..... | ..... | ..... | ..... | ..... | 0.5 | ..... | ..... | 0.1 | 0.1 |
| **Other commodities** | 0.1 | 1.2 | 0.1 | 0.1 | 0.1 | 0.4 | 0.1 | ..... | 0.6 | 0.1 |
| Forestry products | ..... | ..... | ..... | ..... | ..... | ..... | ..... | ..... | ..... | ..... |
| Fish and other marine products | ..... | ..... | ..... | ..... | ..... | ..... | ..... | ..... | ..... | ..... |
| Metallic ores and concentrates | ..... | ..... | ..... | ..... | ..... | 0.1 | ..... | ..... | ..... | ..... |
| Bituminous coal and lignite | ..... | ..... | ..... | ..... | ..... | 0.3 | 0.1 | ..... | ..... | ..... |
| Crude petroleum and natural gas | ..... | ..... | ..... | ..... | ..... | ..... | ..... | ..... | ..... | ..... |
| Nonmetallic minerals | ..... | ..... | ..... | ..... | ..... | ..... | ..... | ..... | ..... | ..... |
| Scrap and waste | ..... | ..... | ..... | ..... | ..... | ..... | ..... | ..... | ..... | ..... |
| Used merchandise | 0.1 | 1.1 | 0.1 | 0.1 | 0.1 | ..... | 0.1 | ..... | 0.6 | 0.1 |
| Goods imported and returned unchanged | ..... | ..... | ..... | ..... | ..... | ..... | ..... | ..... | ..... | ..... |
| Special classification provisions | ..... | ..... | ..... | ..... | ..... | ..... | ..... | ..... | ..... | ..... |
| | European Union | | | | | United Kingdom | | | | |
| **ALL GOODS** | 88.3 | 98.1 | 106.1 | 127.7 | 110.7 | 7.2 | 4.2 | 7.2 | 8.7 | 12.6 |
| **Manufactured goods** | 64.7 | 75.9 | 80.2 | 86.3 | 74.7 | 5.7 | 3.3 | 5.7 | 4.9 | 7.6 |
| Food products | 1.4 | 1.5 | 2.1 | 3.5 | 3.8 | 0.4 | 0.3 | 0.6 | 0.6 | 0.6 |
| Tobacco products | ..... | ..... | ..... | ..... | ..... | ..... | ..... | ..... | ..... | ..... |
| Textile mill products | ..... | ..... | ..... | ..... | ..... | ..... | ..... | ..... | ..... | ..... |
| Apparel | 0.1 | ..... | 0.1 | 0.1 | ..... | ..... | ..... | ..... | ..... | ..... |
| Lumber and wood products | ..... | ..... | ..... | 0.1 | 0.1 | ..... | ..... | ..... | ..... | ..... |
| Furniture and fixtures | ..... | 0.4 | ..... | ..... | 0.1 | ..... | 0.4 | ..... | ..... | ..... |
| Paper products | ..... | ..... | ..... | ..... | ..... | ..... | ..... | ..... | ..... | ..... |
| Printing and publishing | ..... | ..... | 0.3 | ..... | ..... | ..... | ..... | 0.2 | ..... | ..... |
| Chemical products | 4.9 | 1.8 | 2.9 | 3.0 | 3.3 | 4.5 | 1.5 | 2.7 | 3.0 | 3.1 |
| Refined petroleum products | ..... | ..... | ..... | ..... | ..... | ..... | ..... | ..... | ..... | ..... |
| Rubber and plastic products | 0.6 | 1.0 | 1.4 | 0.1 | 0.1 | ..... | ..... | 1.3 | ..... | ..... |
| Leather products | 0.1 | 0.2 | ..... | 0.2 | ..... | ..... | ..... | ..... | ..... | ..... |
| Stone, clay and glass products | ..... | ..... | ..... | ..... | ..... | ..... | ..... | ..... | ..... | ..... |
| Primary metals | 0.1 | ..... | 0.1 | ..... | 0.1 | ..... | ..... | 0.1 | ..... | ..... |
| Fabricated metal products | 0.1 | 0.1 | 0.1 | 0.3 | 0.2 | ..... | ..... | ..... | ..... | ..... |
| Industrial machinery and computers | 54.9 | 69.4 | 71.0 | 74.4 | 60.0 | 0.6 | 0.5 | 0.7 | 0.7 | 2.1 |
| Electric and electronic equipment | 0.3 | 0.6 | 1.0 | 2.4 | 2.4 | 0.1 | 0.2 | ..... | 0.3 | 0.3 |
| Transportation equipment | 1.8 | 0.5 | 0.6 | 1.4 | 3.9 | ..... | 0.2 | 0.1 | 0.2 | 1.2 |
| Scientific and measuring instruments | 0.1 | 0.2 | 0.2 | 0.5 | 0.3 | ..... | ..... | ..... | ..... | 0.1 |
| Miscellaneous manufactures | 0.2 | 0.1 | 0.2 | 0.1 | 0.2 | 0.1 | ..... | ..... | ..... | 0.1 |
| Unidentified manufactures | 0.1 | 0.1 | 0.1 | 0.1 | 0.1 | ..... | ..... | ..... | ..... | ..... |
| **Agricultural and livestock products** | 23.6 | 20.9 | 25.5 | 41.1 | 35.4 | 1.5 | 0.9 | 1.5 | 3.7 | 5.0 |
| Agricultural products | 23.6 | 20.9 | 25.5 | 41.1 | 35.4 | 1.5 | 0.9 | 1.5 | 3.7 | 5.0 |
| Livestock and livestock products | ..... | ..... | ..... | ..... | ..... | ..... | ..... | ..... | ..... | ..... |
| **Other commodities** | 0.1 | 1.4 | 0.4 | 0.2 | 0.6 | ..... | ..... | ..... | 0.1 | ..... |
| Forestry products | ..... | ..... | ..... | ..... | ..... | ..... | ..... | ..... | ..... | ..... |
| Fish and other marine products | ..... | ..... | ..... | ..... | ..... | ..... | ..... | ..... | ..... | ..... |
| Metallic ores and concentrates | ..... | ..... | ..... | ..... | ..... | ..... | ..... | ..... | ..... | ..... |
| Bituminous coal and lignite | ..... | ..... | ..... | ..... | ..... | ..... | ..... | ..... | ..... | ..... |
| Crude petroleum and natural gas | ..... | ..... | ..... | ..... | ..... | ..... | ..... | ..... | ..... | ..... |
| Nonmetallic minerals | ..... | ..... | ..... | ..... | ..... | ..... | ..... | ..... | ..... | ..... |
| Scrap and waste | 0.1 | ..... | ..... | ..... | ..... | ..... | ..... | ..... | ..... | ..... |
| Used merchandise | ..... | 1.3 | 0.3 | 0.1 | 0.5 | ..... | ..... | ..... | ..... | ..... |
| Goods imported and returned unchanged | ..... | ..... | ..... | ..... | ..... | ..... | ..... | ..... | ..... | ..... |
| Special classification provisions | ..... | ..... | 0.1 | 0.1 | ..... | ..... | ..... | ..... | 0.1 | ..... |

## Table D-3.  State Exports of Goods by Destination and Industry, 1993–1997 —*Continued*

### NORTH DAKOTA (Millions of dollars.)

| Industry | 1993 | 1994 | 1995 | 1996 | 1997 | 1993 | 1994 | 1995 | 1996 | 1997 |
|---|---|---|---|---|---|---|---|---|---|---|
| | Germany | | | | | France | | | | |
| **ALL GOODS** | 14.9 | 12.7 | 14.7 | 17.9 | 20.7 | 0.4 | 1.6 | 1.3 | 2.8 | 5.0 |
| **Manufactured goods** | 3.5 | 3.1 | 2.8 | 2.7 | 3.7 | 0.4 | 1.6 | 1.2 | 2.8 | 4.9 |
| Food products | 0.8 | 0.7 | 1.0 | 1.2 | 1.6 | ..... | 0.1 | ..... | ..... | ..... |
| Tobacco products | ..... | ..... | ..... | ..... | ..... | ..... | ..... | ..... | ..... | ..... |
| Textile mill products | ..... | ..... | ..... | ..... | ..... | ..... | ..... | ..... | ..... | ..... |
| Apparel | 0.1 | ..... | ..... | ..... | ..... | ..... | ..... | ..... | ..... | ..... |
| Lumber and wood products | ..... | ..... | ..... | ..... | ..... | ..... | ..... | ..... | ..... | ..... |
| Furniture and fixtures | ..... | ..... | ..... | ..... | ..... | ..... | ..... | ..... | ..... | ..... |
| Paper products | ..... | ..... | ..... | ..... | ..... | ..... | ..... | ..... | ..... | ..... |
| Printing and publishing | ..... | ..... | ..... | ..... | ..... | ..... | ..... | ..... | ..... | ..... |
| Chemical products | ..... | ..... | ..... | ..... | ..... | ..... | 0.1 | ..... | ..... | 0.1 |
| Refined petroleum products | ..... | ..... | ..... | ..... | ..... | ..... | ..... | ..... | ..... | ..... |
| Rubber and plastic products | 0.5 | 0.9 | 0.1 | 0.1 | ..... | ..... | ..... | ..... | ..... | ..... |
| Leather products | ..... | ..... | ..... | ..... | ..... | ..... | ..... | ..... | ..... | ..... |
| Stone, clay and glass products | ..... | ..... | ..... | ..... | ..... | ..... | ..... | ..... | ..... | ..... |
| Primary metals | ..... | ..... | ..... | ..... | 0.1 | ..... | ..... | ..... | ..... | ..... |
| Fabricated metal products | ..... | ..... | ..... | 0.1 | 0.1 | ..... | ..... | ..... | 0.1 | ..... |
| Industrial machinery and computers | 1.2 | 0.9 | 1.2 | 0.9 | 1.2 | 0.2 | 1.2 | 0.9 | 1.3 | 1.6 |
| Electric and electronic equipment | ..... | 0.2 | 0.2 | 0.1 | 0.2 | 0.1 | 0.1 | ..... | 0.5 | 1.5 |
| Transportation equipment | 0.6 | 0.2 | 0.2 | 0.2 | 0.5 | ..... | 0.1 | ..... | 0.5 | 1.3 |
| Scientific and measuring instruments | ..... | 0.1 | 0.1 | ..... | ..... | ..... | ..... | 0.1 | 0.4 | 0.1 |
| Miscellaneous manufactures | 0.1 | ..... | ..... | ..... | ..... | ..... | ..... | ..... | ..... | 0.1 |
| Unidentified manufactures | ..... | ..... | ..... | ..... | ..... | ..... | ..... | ..... | ..... | ..... |
| **Agricultural and livestock products** | 11.4 | 9.6 | 11.8 | 15.2 | 17.0 | 0.1 | ..... | ..... | ..... | 0.1 |
| Agricultural products | 11.4 | 9.6 | 11.8 | 15.2 | 17.0 | 0.1 | ..... | ..... | ..... | 0.1 |
| Livestock and livestock products | ..... | ..... | ..... | ..... | ..... | ..... | ..... | ..... | ..... | ..... |
| **Other commodities** | 0.1 | ..... | ..... | ..... | 0.1 | ..... | ..... | 0.1 | ..... | ..... |
| Forestry products | ..... | ..... | ..... | ..... | ..... | ..... | ..... | ..... | ..... | ..... |
| Fish and other marine products | ..... | ..... | ..... | ..... | ..... | ..... | ..... | ..... | ..... | ..... |
| Metallic ores and concentrates | ..... | ..... | ..... | ..... | ..... | ..... | ..... | ..... | ..... | ..... |
| Bituminous coal and lignite | ..... | ..... | ..... | ..... | ..... | ..... | ..... | ..... | ..... | ..... |
| Crude petroleum and natural gas | ..... | ..... | ..... | ..... | ..... | ..... | ..... | ..... | ..... | ..... |
| Nonmetallic minerals | ..... | ..... | ..... | ..... | ..... | ..... | ..... | ..... | ..... | ..... |
| Scrap and waste | 0.1 | ..... | ..... | ..... | ..... | ..... | ..... | ..... | ..... | ..... |
| Used merchandise | ..... | ..... | ..... | ..... | 0.1 | ..... | ..... | ..... | ..... | ..... |
| Goods imported and returned unchanged | ..... | ..... | ..... | ..... | ..... | ..... | ..... | 0.1 | ..... | ..... |
| Special classification provisions | ..... | ..... | ..... | ..... | ..... | ..... | ..... | ..... | ..... | ..... |
| | The Netherlands | | | | | Asian 10 | | | | |
| **ALL GOODS** | 3.6 | 1.7 | 2.8 | 11.9 | 4.2 | 12.8 | 22.2 | 20.4 | 26.8 | 30.1 |
| **Manufactured goods** | 1.4 | 0.6 | 0.7 | 1.9 | 0.6 | 10.9 | 20.5 | 18.0 | 24.5 | 24.2 |
| Food products | 0.1 | ..... | 0.1 | 0.2 | 0.1 | 0.3 | 0.8 | 1.4 | 2.2 | 3.3 |
| Tobacco products | ..... | ..... | ..... | ..... | ..... | ..... | ..... | ..... | ..... | ..... |
| Textile mill products | ..... | ..... | ..... | ..... | ..... | ..... | ..... | ..... | ..... | ..... |
| Apparel | ..... | ..... | ..... | ..... | ..... | ..... | ..... | ..... | 0.1 | ..... |
| Lumber and wood products | ..... | ..... | ..... | 0.1 | ..... | 0.1 | 0.3 | 0.2 | ..... | 0.2 |
| Furniture and fixtures | ..... | ..... | ..... | ..... | ..... | ..... | ..... | ..... | ..... | ..... |
| Paper products | ..... | ..... | ..... | ..... | ..... | ..... | 2.0 | ..... | ..... | ..... |
| Printing and publishing | ..... | ..... | ..... | ..... | ..... | ..... | ..... | ..... | ..... | ..... |
| Chemical products | 0.1 | 0.1 | 0.2 | 0.1 | ..... | 0.3 | 1.4 | 1.0 | 0.9 | 0.9 |
| Refined petroleum products | ..... | ..... | ..... | ..... | ..... | ..... | ..... | ..... | ..... | ..... |
| Rubber and plastic products | ..... | ..... | ..... | ..... | ..... | 0.5 | 1.5 | 0.8 | 0.1 | 0.8 |
| Leather products | 0.1 | 0.2 | ..... | 0.2 | ..... | ..... | ..... | ..... | ..... | ..... |
| Stone, clay and glass products | ..... | ..... | ..... | ..... | ..... | ..... | 0.1 | ..... | 0.2 | ..... |
| Primary metals | 0.1 | ..... | ..... | ..... | 0.1 | 0.6 | 0.1 | ..... | 3.5 | 0.3 |
| Fabricated metal products | ..... | ..... | ..... | ..... | 0.1 | 0.1 | 0.5 | 0.3 | 0.1 | 0.3 |
| Industrial machinery and computers | 0.3 | 0.2 | 0.2 | 0.2 | ..... | 6.6 | 10.8 | 13.5 | 15.3 | 14.5 |
| Electric and electronic equipment | ..... | ..... | ..... | 1.2 | 0.1 | 0.3 | 0.8 | 0.2 | 0.8 | 1.0 |
| Transportation equipment | 0.7 | ..... | ..... | ..... | 0.2 | 1.6 | 1.3 | 0.1 | 0.7 | 1.6 |
| Scientific and measuring instruments | ..... | ..... | ..... | ..... | ..... | 0.2 | 0.8 | 0.1 | 0.1 | 0.1 |
| Miscellaneous manufactures | ..... | ..... | ..... | ..... | ..... | 0.2 | ..... | 0.2 | 0.3 | 0.6 |
| Unidentified manufactures | ..... | ..... | ..... | ..... | ..... | ..... | ..... | ..... | 0.1 | 0.3 |
| **Agricultural and livestock products** | 2.2 | 1.1 | 2.1 | 9.9 | 3.6 | 0.8 | 0.9 | 1.0 | 1.0 | 2.8 |
| Agricultural products | 2.2 | 1.1 | 2.1 | 9.9 | 3.6 | 0.7 | 0.9 | 1.0 | 0.8 | 2.8 |
| Livestock and livestock products | ..... | ..... | ..... | ..... | ..... | ..... | ..... | ..... | 0.2 | ..... |
| **Other commodities** | ..... | ..... | ..... | ..... | ..... | 1.1 | 0.8 | 1.4 | 1.3 | 3.2 |
| Forestry products | ..... | ..... | ..... | ..... | ..... | ..... | ..... | ..... | ..... | ..... |
| Fish and other marine products | ..... | ..... | ..... | ..... | ..... | ..... | ..... | ..... | ..... | ..... |
| Metallic ores and concentrates | ..... | ..... | ..... | ..... | ..... | ..... | ..... | ..... | ..... | ..... |
| Bituminous coal and lignite | ..... | ..... | ..... | ..... | ..... | ..... | ..... | ..... | ..... | ..... |
| Crude petroleum and natural gas | ..... | ..... | ..... | ..... | ..... | ..... | ..... | ..... | ..... | ..... |
| Nonmetallic minerals | ..... | ..... | ..... | ..... | ..... | ..... | ..... | ..... | ..... | ..... |
| Scrap and waste | ..... | ..... | ..... | ..... | ..... | 0.7 | 0.5 | 1.4 | 1.3 | 2.8 |
| Used merchandise | ..... | ..... | ..... | ..... | ..... | 0.4 | 0.3 | ..... | ..... | 0.3 |
| Goods imported and returned unchanged | ..... | ..... | ..... | ..... | ..... | ..... | ..... | ..... | ..... | ..... |
| Special classification provisions | ..... | ..... | ..... | ..... | ..... | ..... | ..... | ..... | ..... | ..... |

## Table D-3.  State Exports of Goods by Destination and Industry, 1993–1997 —*Continued*

**NORTH DAKOTA**  (Millions of dollars.)

| Industry | 1993 | 1994 | 1995 | 1996 | 1997 | 1993 | 1994 | 1995 | 1996 | 1997 |
|---|---|---|---|---|---|---|---|---|---|---|
| | Japan | | | | | South Korea | | | | |
| **ALL GOODS** | 4.8 | 7.4 | 5.3 | 6.1 | 9.7 | 0.5 | 1.1 | 2.9 | 7.5 | 4.5 |
| **Manufactured goods** | 3.8 | 6.3 | 4.6 | 5.6 | 7.1 | 0.4 | 1.0 | 2.7 | 7.1 | 4.2 |
| Food products | | 0.5 | | 0.9 | 2.0 | 0.1 | 0.3 | 1.0 | 0.9 | 0.6 |
| Tobacco products | | | | | | | | | | |
| Textile mill products | | | | | | | | | | |
| Apparel | | | | | | | | | | |
| Lumber and wood products | | 0.2 | 0.2 | | 0.2 | | | | | |
| Furniture and fixtures | | | | | | | | | | |
| Paper products | | | | | | | | | | |
| Printing and publishing | | | | | | | | | | |
| Chemical products | 0.3 | 1.3 | 1.0 | 0.8 | 0.8 | | | 0.1 | | |
| Refined petroleum products | | | | | | | | | | |
| Rubber and plastic products | 0.5 | 1.2 | 0.5 | 0.1 | | | | | | |
| Leather products | | | | | | | | | | |
| Stone, clay and glass products | | | | | | | | | | |
| Primary metals | 0.6 | 0.1 | | | | | | | 1.9 | |
| Fabricated metal products | | | 0.2 | | 0.1 | | | | 0.1 | |
| Industrial machinery and computers | 2.0 | 1.4 | 2.4 | 2.6 | 3.2 | | 0.2 | 1.5 | 4.0 | 3.2 |
| Electric and electronic equipment | 0.1 | 0.1 | | 0.8 | 0.2 | 0.1 | 0.5 | | | |
| Transportation equipment | 0.1 | 0.6 | | 0.2 | 0.4 | | | | | |
| Scientific and measuring instruments | | 0.8 | 0.1 | 0.1 | | 0.1 | | | | 0.1 |
| Miscellaneous manufactures | 0.2 | | 0.2 | | 0.1 | | | | 0.2 | 0.2 |
| Unidentified manufactures | | | | | | | | | | |
| **Agricultural and livestock products** | 0.6 | 0.8 | 0.7 | 0.5 | 2.4 | 0.1 | | 0.1 | 0.4 | 0.2 |
| Agricultural products | 0.6 | 0.8 | 0.7 | 0.5 | 2.4 | 0.1 | | 0.1 | 0.2 | 0.2 |
| Livestock and livestock products | | | | | | | | | 0.2 | |
| **Other commodities** | 0.4 | 0.3 | | | 0.1 | | | | | 0.2 |
| Forestry products | | | | | | | | | | |
| Fish and other marine products | | | | | | | | | | |
| Metallic ores and concentrates | | | | | | | | | | |
| Bituminous coal and lignite | | | | | | | | | | |
| Crude petroleum and natural gas | | | | | | | | | | |
| Nonmetallic minerals | | | | | | | | | | |
| Scrap and waste | | | | | | | | | | |
| Used merchandise | 0.4 | 0.3 | | | 0.1 | | | | | 0.2 |
| Goods imported and returned unchanged | | | | | | | | | | |
| Special classification provisions | | | | | | | | | | |

| Industry | 1993 | 1994 | 1995 | 1996 | 1997 | 1993 | 1994 | 1995 | 1996 | 1997 |
|---|---|---|---|---|---|---|---|---|---|---|
| | Taiwan | | | | | Singapore | | | | |
| **ALL GOODS** | 6.2 | 10.2 | 2.9 | 2.4 | 4.4 | 0.2 | 0.6 | 1.9 | 1.4 | 1.8 |
| **Manufactured goods** | 6.2 | 10.1 | 2.8 | 2.2 | 4.4 | 0.2 | 0.6 | 1.9 | 1.4 | 1.8 |
| Food products | 0.1 | 0.1 | 0.3 | 0.2 | 0.3 | | | | | |
| Tobacco products | | | | | | | | | | |
| Textile mill products | | | | | | | | | | |
| Apparel | | | | | | | | | | |
| Lumber and wood products | | | | | | | | | | |
| Furniture and fixtures | | | | | | | | | | |
| Paper products | | 0.9 | | | | | | | | |
| Printing and publishing | | | | | | | | | | |
| Chemical products | | | | | | | | | | |
| Refined petroleum products | | | | | | | | | | |
| Rubber and plastic products | | | | | 0.5 | | 0.3 | | | |
| Leather products | | | | | | | | | | |
| Stone, clay and glass products | | | | | | | | | | |
| Primary metals | | | | | | | | | | |
| Fabricated metal products | | 0.1 | | | 0.1 | | | | | |
| Industrial machinery and computers | 4.5 | 8.4 | 2.4 | 1.7 | 2.5 | | 0.2 | 1.8 | 1.3 | 1.5 |
| Electric and electronic equipment | | 0.1 | | | 0.1 | 0.1 | 0.1 | | | 0.1 |
| Transportation equipment | 1.5 | 0.6 | | 0.3 | 0.8 | | | | | |
| Scientific and measuring instruments | | | | | | | | | | |
| Miscellaneous manufactures | | | | | 0.1 | | | | | 0.2 |
| Unidentified manufactures | | | | | | | | | | |
| **Agricultural and livestock products** | | 0.1 | 0.1 | 0.2 | | | | | | |
| Agricultural products | | 0.1 | 0.1 | 0.2 | | | | | | |
| Livestock and livestock products | | | | | | | | | | |
| **Other commodities** | | | | | | | | | | |
| Forestry products | | | | | | | | | | |
| Fish and other marine products | | | | | | | | | | |
| Metallic ores and concentrates | | | | | | | | | | |
| Bituminous coal and lignite | | | | | | | | | | |
| Crude petroleum and natural gas | | | | | | | | | | |
| Nonmetallic minerals | | | | | | | | | | |
| Scrap and waste | | | | | | | | | | |
| Used merchandise | | | | | | | | | | |
| Goods imported and returned unchanged | | | | | | | | | | |
| Special classification provisions | | | | | | | | | | |

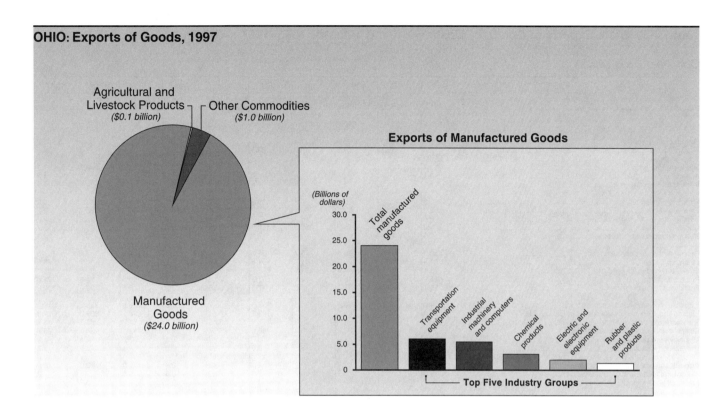

**OHIO: Exports of Goods, 1997**

Agricultural and Livestock Products ($0.1 billion)

Other Commodities ($1.0 billion)

Manufactured Goods ($24.0 billion)

**Exports of Manufactured Goods**

Top Five Industry Groups

## Table D-3.  State Exports of Goods by Destination and Industry, 1993–1997 —Continued

**OHIO** (Millions of dollars.)

| Industry | 1993 | 1994 | 1995 | 1996 | 1997 | 1993 | 1994 | 1995 | 1996 | 1997 |
|---|---|---|---|---|---|---|---|---|---|---|
| | All destinations | | | | | Canada | | | | |
| **ALL GOODS** | 17 651.4 | 19 478.2 | 20 926.5 | 22 555.2 | 25 106.5 | 7 671.9 | 8 501.4 | 8 881.3 | 9 580.4 | 10 471.6 |
| **Manufactured goods** | 16 969.0 | 18 836.5 | 20 241.1 | 21 523.0 | 24 039.5 | 7 226.5 | 8 094.0 | 8 422.9 | 9 036.0 | 10 050.4 |
| Food products | 328.8 | 373.5 | 418.3 | 445.2 | 547.7 | 117.8 | 117.8 | 129.3 | 157.8 | 221.1 |
| Tobacco products | 0.1 | ..... | 0.9 | 0.1 | 0.1 | ..... | ..... | ..... | ..... | ..... |
| Textile mill products | 95.1 | 103.5 | 129.3 | 162.1 | 213.2 | 60.3 | 66.7 | 74.3 | 92.5 | 111.1 |
| Apparel | 22.8 | 29.8 | 31.5 | 43.2 | 62.3 | 7.6 | 11.5 | 8.6 | 21.6 | 39.4 |
| Lumber and wood products | 140.7 | 158.0 | 163.5 | 161.3 | 174.3 | 38.8 | 45.5 | 44.0 | 41.0 | 48.0 |
| Furniture and fixtures | 104.3 | 136.2 | 145.0 | 136.2 | 142.1 | 74.2 | 100.0 | 105.1 | 92.0 | 96.0 |
| Paper products | 242.6 | 277.7 | 394.7 | 455.7 | 457.1 | 96.6 | 107.7 | 177.6 | 217.7 | 220.9 |
| Printing and publishing | 72.0 | 81.6 | 130.3 | 140.6 | 139.6 | 39.0 | 45.7 | 61.0 | 57.8 | 64.3 |
| Chemical products | 2 209.3 | 2 421.0 | 2 861.1 | 2 957.3 | 3 119.2 | 547.9 | 667.7 | 743.4 | 835.9 | 909.2 |
| Refined petroleum products | 59.7 | 87.0 | 75.7 | 109.2 | 82.4 | 29.3 | 32.8 | 35.3 | 32.0 | 33.5 |
| Rubber and plastic products | 929.1 | 1 102.3 | 1 251.2 | 1 227.8 | 1 336.5 | 498.9 | 499.7 | 557.7 | 541.2 | 619.3 |
| Leather products | 36.7 | 33.1 | 41.3 | 70.5 | 76.3 | 7.0 | 8.3 | 10.5 | 13.3 | 12.0 |
| Stone, clay and glass products | 499.0 | 542.4 | 521.4 | 580.6 | 661.6 | 203.6 | 211.7 | 205.7 | 207.2 | 245.2 |
| Primary metals | 619.4 | 787.5 | 886.2 | 920.6 | 1 177.5 | 367.3 | 381.0 | 439.6 | 440.1 | 523.4 |
| Fabricated metal products | 832.6 | 846.9 | 1 033.9 | 1 144.0 | 1 123.9 | 491.7 | 445.2 | 530.8 | 595.8 | 514.1 |
| Industrial machinery and computers | 3 704.3 | 4 208.2 | 4 575.8 | 4 932.8 | 5 460.1 | 1 403.9 | 1 727.4 | 1 638.6 | 1 769.7 | 2 066.8 |
| Electric and electronic equipment | 1 658.1 | 1 938.1 | 1 860.7 | 1 880.0 | 1 977.7 | 675.6 | 701.2 | 550.2 | 635.3 | 675.4 |
| Transportation equipment | 4 503.1 | 4 752.6 | 4 721.1 | 5 089.7 | 6 046.8 | 2 310.3 | 2 621.9 | 2 837.2 | 3 000.8 | 3 279.2 |
| Scientific and measuring instruments | 731.5 | 738.2 | 754.7 | 826.5 | 1 002.8 | 179.9 | 205.9 | 168.1 | 178.1 | 252.9 |
| Miscellaneous manufactures | 135.6 | 163.2 | 188.8 | 188.8 | 193.5 | 66.6 | 77.9 | 88.6 | 88.1 | 101.1 |
| Unidentified manufactures | 44.2 | 55.5 | 55.7 | 50.9 | 45.0 | 10.3 | 18.7 | 17.1 | 18.1 | 17.6 |
| **Agricultural and livestock products** | 194.0 | 181.1 | 137.6 | 124.8 | 97.4 | 94.1 | 76.2 | 97.8 | 80.6 | 72.2 |
| Agricultural products | 183.1 | 170.5 | 124.2 | 113.9 | 82.6 | 84.3 | 66.7 | 85.6 | 70.8 | 63.6 |
| Livestock and livestock products | 10.9 | 10.6 | 13.4 | 10.9 | 14.8 | 9.8 | 9.5 | 12.2 | 9.8 | 8.6 |
| **Other commodities** | 488.4 | 460.6 | 547.8 | 907.4 | 969.5 | 351.3 | 331.2 | 360.6 | 463.8 | 349.1 |
| Forestry products | 4.5 | 6.7 | 11.3 | 15.0 | 12.8 | 3.2 | 1.9 | 1.8 | 2.3 | 3.8 |
| Fish and other marine products | 1.9 | 1.7 | 2.5 | 1.4 | 1.3 | 1.7 | 1.0 | 1.7 | 0.9 | 0.5 |
| Metallic ores and concentrates | 69.2 | 63.1 | 78.0 | 119.4 | 51.2 | 68.8 | 62.7 | 76.8 | 115.8 | 30.3 |
| Bituminous coal and lignite | 201.3 | 150.0 | 133.9 | 132.3 | 81.0 | 156.4 | 114.8 | 87.7 | 130.7 | 79.5 |
| Crude petroleum and natural gas | 5.2 | 3.6 | 2.8 | 266.8 | 428.7 | 4.6 | 3.2 | 1.8 | 3.8 | 0.7 |
| Nonmetallic minerals | 21.5 | 16.2 | 17.1 | 18.8 | 18.8 | 12.2 | 8.6 | 8.3 | 10.5 | 8.1 |
| Scrap and waste | 67.0 | 56.2 | 105.5 | 137.0 | 149.7 | 26.3 | 33.7 | 66.9 | 65.8 | 74.6 |
| Used merchandise | 11.5 | 11.4 | 8.0 | 20.0 | 12.7 | 1.6 | 1.5 | 1.5 | 1.6 | 4.3 |
| Goods imported and returned unchanged | 66.0 | 91.1 | 99.9 | 120.8 | 139.2 | 66.0 | 91.1 | 99.9 | 120.8 | 139.2 |
| Special classification provisions | 40.2 | 60.7 | 88.9 | 75.7 | 75.6 | 10.6 | 12.8 | 14.2 | 11.6 | 7.9 |

## Table D-3.  State Exports of Goods by Destination and Industry, 1993–1997 —*Continued*

**OHIO** (Millions of dollars.)

| Industry | 1993 | 1994 | 1995 | 1996 | 1997 | 1993 | 1994 | 1995 | 1996 | 1997 |
|---|---|---|---|---|---|---|---|---|---|---|
| | South and Central America and Caribbean | | | | | Mexico | | | | |
| **ALL GOODS** | 876.9 | 1 003.1 | 1 249.0 | 1 226.7 | 1 624.6 | 926.6 | 1 423.2 | 1 362.2 | 1 345.1 | 1 583.7 |
| **Manufactured goods** | 859.1 | 988.8 | 1 227.3 | 1 217.4 | 1 611.4 | 914.2 | 1 406.5 | 1 329.2 | 1 289.8 | 1 486.2 |
| Food products | 16.4 | 12.1 | 20.6 | 19.0 | 23.8 | 23.7 | 26.9 | 18.6 | 17.4 | 25.5 |
| Tobacco products | ..... | ..... | ..... | ..... | ..... | ..... | ..... | ..... | ..... | ..... |
| Textile mill products | 10.7 | 14.8 | 28.7 | 20.7 | 28.8 | 2.3 | 2.1 | 3.0 | 6.7 | 11.7 |
| Apparel | 4.1 | 5.8 | 6.3 | 2.8 | 3.3 | 1.4 | 1.8 | 0.5 | 1.3 | 4.2 |
| Lumber and wood products | 3.0 | 1.8 | 2.1 | 1.8 | 4.0 | 2.3 | 4.0 | 3.4 | 2.6 | 3.9 |
| Furniture and fixtures | 2.3 | 5.1 | 8.3 | 8.5 | 9.8 | 8.8 | 11.1 | 4.0 | 3.7 | 9.2 |
| Paper products | 52.0 | 53.2 | 83.4 | 65.1 | 69.7 | 25.9 | 40.6 | 36.7 | 32.4 | 41.2 |
| Printing and publishing | 2.4 | 1.9 | 4.7 | 5.9 | 5.2 | 3.7 | 5.0 | 3.6 | 6.8 | 5.2 |
| Chemical products | 254.3 | 288.0 | 375.8 | 352.0 | 350.6 | 124.2 | 165.8 | 144.1 | 157.5 | 213.7 |
| Refined petroleum products | 2.5 | 19.4 | 9.6 | 7.9 | 7.1 | 13.4 | 15.1 | 17.8 | 6.4 | 3.9 |
| Rubber and plastic products | 53.3 | 51.6 | 68.3 | 73.7 | 81.0 | 69.6 | 177.8 | 174.6 | 147.2 | 161.8 |
| Leather products | 22.9 | 18.5 | 23.9 | 41.7 | 51.8 | 0.6 | 1.1 | 0.4 | 0.7 | 0.6 |
| Stone, clay and glass products | 15.1 | 19.0 | 26.4 | 31.2 | 33.7 | 25.5 | 20.2 | 22.7 | 29.6 | 60.7 |
| Primary metals | 15.9 | 26.1 | 48.2 | 48.7 | 97.3 | 74.4 | 102.2 | 59.6 | 94.8 | 121.8 |
| Fabricated metal products | 22.1 | 27.0 | 31.4 | 31.5 | 47.5 | 36.6 | 93.3 | 106.6 | 99.0 | 109.8 |
| Industrial machinery and computers | 224.9 | 254.9 | 299.3 | 324.6 | 392.6 | 139.7 | 221.3 | 226.0 | 236.2 | 319.1 |
| Electric and electronic equipment | 80.8 | 87.8 | 81.1 | 76.4 | 123.7 | 286.3 | 432.0 | 432.0 | 359.5 | 311.8 |
| Transportation equipment | 42.8 | 59.1 | 64.7 | 46.9 | 178.7 | 32.7 | 54.8 | 51.7 | 57.7 | 45.6 |
| Scientific and measuring instruments | 21.8 | 31.8 | 28.7 | 40.4 | 88.3 | 35.5 | 22.7 | 19.1 | 23.5 | 26.7 |
| Miscellaneous manufactures | 8.9 | 8.1 | 12.6 | 14.8 | 10.7 | 5.6 | 6.8 | 3.5 | 4.4 | 6.7 |
| Unidentified manufactures | 2.9 | 2.9 | 3.3 | 3.5 | 3.6 | 2.1 | 1.8 | 1.4 | 2.5 | 3.2 |
| **Agricultural and livestock products** | 15.1 | 7.6 | 3.7 | 2.7 | 4.4 | 0.9 | 0.8 | 11.0 | 0.6 | 8.5 |
| Agricultural products | 15.0 | 7.5 | 3.6 | 2.7 | 0.6 | 0.9 | 0.6 | 10.9 | 0.4 | 7.2 |
| Livestock and livestock products | 0.1 | 0.2 | 0.2 | ..... | 3.9 | ..... | 0.2 | ..... | 0.2 | 1.3 |
| **Other commodities** | 2.7 | 6.8 | 17.9 | 6.6 | 8.8 | 11.4 | 15.9 | 22.0 | 54.7 | 89.0 |
| Forestry products | 0.2 | 3.3 | 4.9 | 2.8 | 1.6 | 0.2 | 0.4 | 3.7 | 6.3 | 4.4 |
| Fish and other marine products | ..... | 0.4 | 0.3 | ..... | ..... | ..... | ..... | ..... | ..... | ..... |
| Metallic ores and concentrates | 0.1 | ..... | ..... | 0.1 | ..... | ..... | ..... | ..... | 0.7 | 20.0 |
| Bituminous coal and lignite | ..... | ..... | 7.9 | ..... | ..... | 0.1 | ..... | ..... | ..... | ..... |
| Crude petroleum and natural gas | 0.1 | ..... | 0.1 | ..... | 0.1 | 0.5 | 0.4 | 0.2 | 0.3 | 0.1 |
| Nonmetallic minerals | 0.4 | 0.6 | 1.0 | 0.8 | 1.4 | 0.5 | 0.9 | 0.6 | 0.8 | 1.2 |
| Scrap and waste | 0.4 | 0.2 | 0.8 | ..... | 0.3 | 9.3 | 13.2 | 16.8 | 44.0 | 62.8 |
| Used merchandise | 0.9 | 1.0 | 1.0 | 1.4 | 1.2 | ..... | 0.2 | ..... | ..... | 0.1 |
| Goods imported and returned unchanged | ..... | ..... | ..... | ..... | ..... | ..... | ..... | ..... | ..... | ..... |
| Special classification provisions | 0.7 | 1.3 | 1.8 | 1.4 | 4.2 | 0.7 | 0.7 | 0.7 | 2.7 | 0.4 |
| | European Union | | | | | United Kingdom | | | | |
| **ALL GOODS** | 4 210.0 | 4 369.4 | 4 472.4 | 4 725.6 | 5 380.7 | 684.7 | 730.7 | 942.2 | 1 089.5 | 1 173.5 |
| **Manufactured goods** | 4 123.1 | 4 296.7 | 4 400.1 | 4 626.9 | 5 324.4 | 673.3 | 721.2 | 928.7 | 1 052.5 | 1 143.1 |
| Food products | 54.0 | 71.4 | 105.5 | 122.2 | 133.3 | 11.4 | 15.3 | 22.0 | 17.0 | 17.1 |
| Tobacco products | ..... | ..... | 0.6 | ..... | ..... | ..... | ..... | ..... | ..... | ..... |
| Textile mill products | 5.9 | 6.1 | 9.5 | 23.1 | 38.1 | 0.8 | 1.4 | 1.4 | 2.4 | 2.6 |
| Apparel | 5.7 | 7.1 | 7.2 | 7.6 | 6.0 | 1.9 | 2.1 | 1.4 | 1.3 | 0.8 |
| Lumber and wood products | 64.7 | 68.6 | 67.0 | 62.5 | 61.9 | 16.3 | 17.9 | 16.0 | 14.7 | 12.1 |
| Furniture and fixtures | 7.8 | 6.2 | 6.4 | 9.8 | 8.4 | 2.8 | 2.5 | 1.9 | 2.1 | 3.0 |
| Paper products | 33.3 | 18.9 | 29.1 | 32.5 | 35.8 | 7.8 | 6.1 | 9.1 | 10.8 | 11.2 |
| Printing and publishing | 14.1 | 12.9 | 31.5 | 25.0 | 25.8 | 4.4 | 4.6 | 13.8 | 13.1 | 14.9 |
| Chemical products | 546.7 | 567.8 | 611.9 | 642.4 | 672.4 | 109.0 | 108.0 | 127.6 | 119.4 | 126.0 |
| Refined petroleum products | 2.9 | 2.0 | 4.5 | 9.6 | 19.6 | 0.3 | 0.2 | 0.4 | 0.5 | 8.1 |
| Rubber and plastic products | 147.1 | 171.3 | 204.9 | 220.3 | 213.3 | 29.9 | 28.2 | 39.7 | 43.2 | 42.7 |
| Leather products | 2.4 | 1.7 | 2.3 | 3.2 | 3.9 | 1.4 | 0.9 | 1.1 | 1.2 | 0.9 |
| Stone, clay and glass products | 119.8 | 122.1 | 116.7 | 125.8 | 137.6 | 15.9 | 10.1 | 18.2 | 11.1 | 11.5 |
| Primary metals | 79.4 | 148.5 | 175.4 | 156.6 | 189.0 | 28.7 | 40.6 | 56.0 | 57.1 | 66.8 |
| Fabricated metal products | 99.0 | 82.4 | 87.6 | 112.5 | 141.0 | 20.6 | 19.2 | 23.1 | 25.3 | 37.0 |
| Industrial machinery and computers | 788.3 | 880.5 | 1 055.4 | 1 047.7 | 1 072.4 | 202.0 | 224.3 | 244.2 | 251.0 | 282.5 |
| Electric and electronic equipment | 236.1 | 264.0 | 296.8 | 307.3 | 299.8 | 77.9 | 75.6 | 84.6 | 94.7 | 95.2 |
| Transportation equipment | 1 678.2 | 1 612.5 | 1 291.6 | 1 394.9 | 1 923.3 | 92.8 | 107.6 | 205.7 | 319.1 | 344.5 |
| Scientific and measuring instruments | 200.4 | 208.1 | 249.0 | 285.5 | 300.0 | 38.0 | 39.6 | 45.8 | 55.2 | 52.8 |
| Miscellaneous manufactures | 23.4 | 32.2 | 32.5 | 28.9 | 34.8 | 8.1 | 13.4 | 13.1 | 11.1 | 11.7 |
| Unidentified manufactures | 14.0 | 12.4 | 14.7 | 9.6 | 8.1 | 3.3 | 3.6 | 3.5 | 2.1 | 1.7 |
| **Agricultural and livestock products** | 16.4 | 11.5 | 7.3 | 29.9 | 2.6 | 0.2 | 0.6 | 1.9 | 1.2 | 0.8 |
| Agricultural products | 16.2 | 11.2 | 7.2 | 29.4 | 1.8 | 0.2 | 0.6 | 1.9 | 1.2 | 0.8 |
| Livestock and livestock products | 0.2 | 0.3 | 0.1 | 0.4 | 0.7 | ..... | ..... | ..... | ..... | 0.1 |
| **Other commodities** | 70.5 | 61.2 | 65.0 | 68.9 | 53.7 | 11.2 | 8.8 | 11.6 | 35.8 | 29.6 |
| Forestry products | 0.3 | 0.2 | 0.3 | 1.6 | 2.2 | ..... | ..... | ..... | ..... | 0.4 |
| Fish and other marine products | 0.1 | ..... | 0.2 | 0.2 | 0.6 | ..... | ..... | ..... | 0.2 | 0.3 |
| Metallic ores and concentrates | 0.3 | 0.3 | 1.0 | 1.4 | 0.5 | ..... | ..... | ..... | 0.2 | ..... |
| Bituminous coal and lignite | 44.0 | 26.2 | 28.6 | 1.7 | 1.5 | ..... | ..... | ..... | ..... | ..... |
| Crude petroleum and natural gas | ..... | ..... | ..... | ..... | 0.1 | ..... | ..... | ..... | ..... | ..... |
| Nonmetallic minerals | 4.4 | 2.2 | 3.2 | 1.9 | 1.8 | 1.5 | 0.2 | 0.2 | 0.2 | 0.4 |
| Scrap and waste | 2.9 | 3.7 | 6.5 | 18.5 | 6.6 | 1.2 | 1.1 | 4.0 | 17.4 | 5.8 |
| Used merchandise | 5.1 | 5.5 | 3.8 | 14.3 | 3.8 | 1.4 | 1.5 | 0.8 | 3.7 | 1.4 |
| Goods imported and returned unchanged | ..... | ..... | ..... | ..... | ..... | ..... | ..... | ..... | ..... | ..... |
| Special classification provisions | 13.3 | 23.1 | 21.4 | 29.2 | 36.6 | 6.9 | 6.1 | 6.7 | 14.0 | 21.2 |

## Table D-3. State Exports of Goods by Destination and Industry, 1993–1997 —Continued

**OHIO** (Millions of dollars.)

| Industry | 1993 | 1994 | 1995 | 1996 | 1997 | 1993 | 1994 | 1995 | 1996 | 1997 |
|---|---|---|---|---|---|---|---|---|---|---|
| | Germany | | | | | France | | | | |
| **ALL GOODS** | 508.8 | 604.5 | 727.9 | 725.6 | 737.9 | 1 906.4 | 1 794.2 | 1 344.3 | 1 331.9 | 1 757.2 |
| **Manufactured goods** | 503.1 | 595.4 | 721.3 | 714.3 | 731.3 | 1 898.1 | 1 776.4 | 1 328.6 | 1 327.1 | 1 754.9 |
| Food products | 9.8 | 13.6 | 14.9 | 26.4 | 36.6 | 6.3 | 6.6 | 9.9 | 10.7 | 4.8 |
| Tobacco products | ..... | ..... | ..... | ..... | ..... | ..... | ..... | ..... | ..... | ..... |
| Textile mill products | 2.3 | 2.0 | 4.8 | 17.6 | 28.6 | 0.8 | 0.7 | 0.3 | 0.4 | 0.3 |
| Apparel | 0.8 | 1.2 | 1.2 | 1.2 | 1.1 | 0.3 | 0.5 | 1.0 | 1.0 | 0.8 |
| Lumber and wood products | 22.5 | 22.6 | 23.5 | 18.2 | 19.2 | 3.6 | 3.0 | 3.2 | 3.8 | 3.2 |
| Furniture and fixtures | 0.8 | 0.8 | 1.7 | 1.8 | 1.4 | 2.7 | 1.8 | 1.4 | 3.9 | 2.2 |
| Paper products | 2.5 | 1.4 | 2.2 | 2.3 | 3.4 | 5.1 | 1.2 | 1.5 | 1.3 | 1.0 |
| Printing and publishing | 3.5 | 2.6 | 4.4 | 2.6 | 3.4 | 2.0 | 2.0 | 5.2 | 3.1 | 1.2 |
| Chemical products | 47.7 | 58.2 | 64.7 | 60.0 | 56.1 | 125.0 | 104.6 | 130.7 | 114.0 | 106.9 |
| Refined petroleum products | 0.5 | 0.1 | 0.4 | 0.3 | 0.4 | 0.3 | 0.1 | 0.2 | 0.2 | 7.0 |
| Rubber and plastic products | 36.5 | 37.6 | 47.2 | 46.3 | 40.6 | 17.5 | 19.0 | 23.3 | 23.8 | 16.2 |
| Leather products | 0.4 | 0.3 | 0.2 | 0.2 | 1.8 | 0.2 | ..... | 0.6 | 1.2 | 0.1 |
| Stone, clay and glass products | 22.2 | 33.1 | 39.2 | 38.0 | 23.0 | 6.6 | 5.3 | 7.0 | 6.1 | 7.0 |
| Primary metals | 15.0 | 26.2 | 31.5 | 28.3 | 37.7 | 14.6 | 38.7 | 40.0 | 41.3 | 58.1 |
| Fabricated metal products | 15.0 | 18.6 | 18.2 | 14.0 | 17.2 | 26.3 | 12.8 | 12.1 | 25.7 | 27.5 |
| Industrial machinery and computers | 180.3 | 213.6 | 281.6 | 278.4 | 260.3 | 117.7 | 118.4 | 139.9 | 130.3 | 101.9 |
| Electric and electronic equipment | 58.6 | 57.7 | 61.8 | 61.2 | 66.0 | 27.7 | 45.3 | 28.8 | 27.1 | 25.7 |
| Transportation equipment | 23.5 | 36.8 | 53.1 | 42.2 | 70.0 | 1 507.3 | 1 386.8 | 896.3 | 900.3 | 1 360.4 |
| Scientific and measuring instruments | 55.4 | 60.6 | 62.8 | 68.8 | 59.8 | 29.7 | 26.8 | 24.6 | 30.0 | 25.9 |
| Miscellaneous manufactures | 4.0 | 5.9 | 3.8 | 4.1 | 2.3 | 3.2 | 1.8 | 1.8 | 2.4 | 4.2 |
| Unidentified manufactures | 1.9 | 2.6 | 4.1 | 2.4 | 2.3 | 1.2 | 1.1 | 0.8 | 0.6 | 0.6 |
| **Agricultural and livestock products** | 0.9 | 0.7 | 1.2 | 2.5 | 0.5 | 0.1 | ..... | 0.1 | 0.1 | ..... |
| Agricultural products | 0.8 | 0.5 | 1.1 | 2.4 | 0.2 | 0.1 | ..... | 0.1 | 0.1 | ..... |
| Livestock and livestock products | ..... | 0.2 | 0.1 | 0.1 | 0.3 | ..... | ..... | ..... | ..... | ..... |
| **Other commodities** | 4.8 | 8.4 | 5.4 | 8.7 | 6.0 | 8.2 | 17.7 | 15.6 | 4.7 | 2.2 |
| Forestry products | ..... | ..... | ..... | 0.8 | 0.2 | 0.2 | 0.1 | 0.1 | ..... | ..... |
| Fish and other marine products | 0.1 | ..... | ..... | ..... | ..... | ..... | ..... | ..... | ..... | 0.1 |
| Metallic ores and concentrates | 0.1 | 0.2 | ..... | 0.6 | 0.1 | 0.1 | ..... | ..... | ..... | 0.1 |
| Bituminous coal and lignite | ..... | ..... | ..... | ..... | ..... | 4.8 | 12.8 | 11.9 | ..... | ..... |
| Crude petroleum and natural gas | ..... | ..... | ..... | ..... | 0.1 | ..... | ..... | ..... | ..... | ..... |
| Nonmetallic minerals | 1.7 | 1.3 | 2.5 | 1.2 | 1.2 | 0.4 | 0.3 | 0.2 | 0.1 | 0.1 |
| Scrap and waste | 0.8 | 0.3 | 0.1 | 0.2 | 0.2 | 0.1 | 0.1 | ..... | ..... | 0.1 |
| Used merchandise | 0.4 | 0.8 | 0.9 | 2.8 | 1.1 | 1.8 | 0.8 | 0.1 | 1.9 | 0.4 |
| Goods imported and returned unchanged | ..... | ..... | ..... | ..... | ..... | ..... | ..... | ..... | ..... | ..... |
| Special classification provisions | 1.8 | 5.7 | 1.9 | 3.2 | 3.2 | 0.9 | 3.6 | 3.3 | 2.6 | 1.5 |
| | The Netherlands | | | | | Asian 10 | | | | |
| **ALL GOODS** | 210.5 | 208.4 | 247.3 | 290.3 | 330.6 | 2 386.5 | 2 723.4 | 3 326.4 | 3 927.3 | 4 233.4 |
| **Manufactured goods** | 181.7 | 203.8 | 244.2 | 286.5 | 326.7 | 2 339.0 | 2 671.0 | 3 255.7 | 3 631.8 | 3 780.6 |
| Food products | 3.4 | 5.5 | 4.4 | 5.9 | 7.9 | 90.8 | 122.3 | 114.7 | 96.0 | 101.4 |
| Tobacco products | ..... | ..... | ..... | ..... | ..... | ..... | ..... | 0.3 | ..... | ..... |
| Textile mill products | 0.2 | 0.3 | 0.8 | 0.5 | 0.6 | 9.2 | 6.5 | 6.2 | 11.3 | 14.1 |
| Apparel | 0.3 | 0.4 | 0.5 | 0.8 | 0.3 | 2.4 | 1.8 | 5.7 | 6.3 | 6.4 |
| Lumber and wood products | 2.2 | 1.6 | 1.4 | 3.9 | 2.3 | 20.8 | 24.4 | 29.1 | 34.8 | 37.1 |
| Furniture and fixtures | 0.7 | 0.4 | 0.5 | 0.6 | 0.2 | 7.0 | 6.9 | 11.5 | 13.2 | 10.2 |
| Paper products | 5.2 | 5.0 | 5.7 | 8.3 | 8.9 | 19.6 | 47.4 | 56.5 | 69.2 | 70.5 |
| Printing and publishing | 1.9 | 1.4 | 2.5 | 1.9 | 1.1 | 7.2 | 10.2 | 22.1 | 37.9 | 27.6 |
| Chemical products | 48.9 | 42.6 | 40.1 | 60.7 | 56.6 | 513.0 | 460.9 | 679.8 | 684.1 | 678.5 |
| Refined petroleum products | 0.3 | 0.2 | 0.3 | 7.2 | 2.7 | 9.8 | 13.9 | 3.1 | 51.8 | 10.7 |
| Rubber and plastic products | 10.6 | 21.1 | 24.1 | 17.1 | 9.0 | 86.6 | 120.8 | 143.4 | 132.3 | 167.2 |
| Leather products | 0.1 | 0.2 | 0.1 | 0.1 | 0.1 | 3.1 | 2.6 | 3.1 | 6.5 | 3.5 |
| Stone, clay and glass products | 2.0 | 6.5 | 2.3 | 2.4 | 3.1 | 112.1 | 143.2 | 119.7 | 150.0 | 152.9 |
| Primary metals | 3.7 | 7.8 | 8.4 | 8.7 | 9.0 | 57.4 | 89.6 | 128.6 | 128.4 | 165.5 |
| Fabricated metal products | 5.9 | 5.7 | 7.9 | 14.5 | 16.1 | 96.3 | 115.7 | 180.0 | 187.1 | 216.8 |
| Industrial machinery and computers | 57.9 | 58.2 | 67.7 | 81.1 | 129.1 | 622.9 | 704.8 | 884.2 | 992.5 | 978.3 |
| Electric and electronic equipment | 16.5 | 22.2 | 32.4 | 33.2 | 32.5 | 289.7 | 364.9 | 377.4 | 404.3 | 455.2 |
| Transportation equipment | 9.8 | 11.2 | 20.8 | 17.9 | 18.3 | 180.3 | 226.0 | 253.7 | 377.6 | 423.1 |
| Scientific and measuring instruments | 10.8 | 11.3 | 19.8 | 19.6 | 26.1 | 188.2 | 179.5 | 200.8 | 216.2 | 233.4 |
| Miscellaneous manufactures | 0.8 | 0.9 | 1.6 | 1.4 | 1.9 | 17.3 | 21.8 | 29.5 | 26.8 | 22.7 |
| Unidentified manufactures | 0.7 | 1.3 | 2.8 | 0.5 | 0.9 | 5.5 | 8.0 | 6.5 | 5.5 | 5.3 |
| **Agricultural and livestock products** | 0.3 | 0.2 | 0.2 | 1.0 | 0.4 | 9.8 | 17.4 | 1.8 | 0.7 | 1.3 |
| Agricultural products | 0.2 | 0.2 | 0.2 | 0.8 | 0.3 | 9.5 | 17.4 | 1.7 | 0.7 | 1.2 |
| Livestock and livestock products | 0.1 | ..... | ..... | 0.2 | 0.1 | 0.3 | ..... | 0.1 | ..... | 0.1 |
| **Other commodities** | 28.5 | 4.5 | 2.9 | 2.8 | 3.5 | 37.8 | 34.9 | 68.9 | 294.8 | 451.5 |
| Forestry products | ..... | ..... | ..... | ..... | ..... | 0.6 | 0.5 | 0.1 | 1.2 | 0.2 |
| Fish and other marine products | ..... | ..... | ..... | ..... | ..... | ..... | ..... | 0.1 | 0.4 | 0.1 |
| Metallic ores and concentrates | ..... | ..... | 0.6 | 0.1 | ..... | ..... | ..... | 0.1 | 1.4 | 0.3 |
| Bituminous coal and lignite | 25.4 | ..... | ..... | ..... | ..... | 0.8 | 8.9 | 9.8 | ..... | ..... |
| Crude petroleum and natural gas | ..... | ..... | ..... | ..... | ..... | ..... | ..... | 0.7 | 262.7 | 427.7 |
| Nonmetallic minerals | 0.2 | ..... | ..... | 0.2 | 0.1 | 2.8 | 2.5 | 2.5 | 1.7 | 1.5 |
| Scrap and waste | 0.2 | 0.3 | 0.8 | 0.3 | 0.2 | 20.4 | 4.9 | 13.4 | 6.7 | 4.0 |
| Used merchandise | 0.2 | 0.3 | 0.2 | 0.5 | 0.2 | 2.1 | 2.4 | 1.1 | 1.3 | 1.6 |
| Goods imported and returned unchanged | ..... | ..... | ..... | ..... | ..... | ..... | ..... | ..... | ..... | ..... |
| Special classification provisions | 2.6 | 3.8 | 1.3 | 1.7 | 2.9 | 11.1 | 15.5 | 41.2 | 19.5 | 16.1 |

## Table D-3.  State Exports of Goods by Destination and Industry, 1993–1997 —*Continued*

**OHIO** (Millions of dollars.)

| Industry | 1993 | 1994 | 1995 | 1996 | 1997 | 1993 | 1994 | 1995 | 1996 | 1997 |
|---|---|---|---|---|---|---|---|---|---|---|
| | Japan | | | | | South Korea | | | | |
| **ALL GOODS** | 859.4 | 1 033.0 | 1 124.0 | 1 254.0 | 1 190.9 | 315.3 | 374.2 | 538.0 | 773.0 | 804.9 |
| **Manufactured goods** | 835.1 | 1 001.4 | 1 084.2 | 1 227.3 | 1 136.5 | 310.4 | 371.0 | 532.9 | 596.1 | 565.8 |
| Food products | 34.8 | 67.3 | 64.9 | 61.1 | 52.8 | 11.2 | 10.2 | 18.5 | 5.5 | 12.0 |
| Tobacco products | ..... | ..... | ..... | ..... | ..... | ..... | ..... | 0.3 | ..... | ..... |
| Textile mill products | 4.4 | 2.5 | 2.3 | 2.3 | 1.6 | 0.5 | 1.6 | 0.7 | 1.0 | 1.9 |
| Apparel | 0.7 | 0.6 | 2.8 | 1.0 | 3.0 | ..... | 0.2 | 0.7 | 1.4 | 0.8 |
| Lumber and wood products | 10.5 | 8.2 | 11.5 | 11.9 | 14.9 | 2.3 | 2.2 | 3.3 | 4.8 | 1.6 |
| Furniture and fixtures | 4.1 | 3.1 | 5.1 | 6.1 | 3.2 | 0.2 | 0.3 | 1.7 | 1.8 | 1.3 |
| Paper products | 1.7 | 3.1 | 4.6 | 7.7 | 7.2 | 3.6 | 7.6 | 6.9 | 5.9 | 6.3 |
| Printing and publishing | 2.1 | 3.7 | 10.3 | 26.6 | 12.9 | 0.4 | 0.7 | 1.5 | 2.7 | 2.2 |
| Chemical products | 208.2 | 174.5 | 217.9 | 207.0 | 199.7 | 82.6 | 86.7 | 142.1 | 162.9 | 154.7 |
| Refined petroleum products | 0.5 | 5.5 | 0.9 | 25.1 | 0.9 | 8.5 | 3.9 | 0.9 | 0.9 | 7.0 |
| Rubber and plastic products | 54.1 | 85.1 | 90.6 | 78.7 | 101.2 | 6.1 | 8.3 | 17.4 | 12.4 | 13.2 |
| Leather products | 0.3 | 0.5 | 1.0 | 1.7 | 0.7 | 0.5 | 0.1 | 0.4 | 2.5 | 1.2 |
| Stone, clay and glass products | 54.5 | 87.6 | 65.8 | 83.6 | 99.0 | 31.5 | 23.1 | 22.3 | 29.9 | 19.2 |
| Primary metals | 31.4 | 60.3 | 51.8 | 58.5 | 64.9 | 4.9 | 9.3 | 14.0 | 9.4 | 10.1 |
| Fabricated metal products | 44.4 | 56.8 | 90.8 | 75.2 | 25.6 | 9.0 | 12.8 | 19.6 | 19.7 | 42.5 |
| Industrial machinery and computers | 151.5 | 155.1 | 178.7 | 255.2 | 242.4 | 75.3 | 115.9 | 179.0 | 203.2 | 173.1 |
| Electric and electronic equipment | 79.4 | 118.9 | 105.0 | 115.7 | 97.7 | 32.2 | 37.2 | 49.0 | 51.7 | 40.6 |
| Transportation equipment | 55.1 | 66.5 | 67.6 | 105.8 | 108.2 | 14.7 | 20.4 | 17.3 | 38.8 | 35.9 |
| Scientific and measuring instruments | 91.2 | 93.1 | 102.5 | 97.0 | 93.6 | 19.8 | 22.4 | 28.3 | 32.7 | 34.9 |
| Miscellaneous manufactures | 4.2 | 5.8 | 7.3 | 5.2 | 5.0 | 6.1 | 6.0 | 8.1 | 7.8 | 6.2 |
| Unidentified manufactures | 2.0 | 3.2 | 2.8 | 1.9 | 1.9 | 1.1 | 2.2 | 0.9 | 0.9 | 0.8 |
| **Agricultural and livestock products** | 9.1 | 16.8 | 0.3 | 0.1 | 0.6 | ..... | ..... | ..... | ..... | 0.2 |
| Agricultural products | 9.1 | 16.8 | 0.3 | 0.1 | 0.5 | ..... | ..... | ..... | ..... | 0.2 |
| Livestock and livestock products | ..... | ..... | ..... | ..... | 0.1 | ..... | ..... | ..... | ..... | ..... |
| **Other commodities** | 15.2 | 14.8 | 39.5 | 26.6 | 53.8 | 5.0 | 3.2 | 5.1 | 176.9 | 239.0 |
| Forestry products | 0.5 | 0.2 | ..... | 0.8 | ..... | ..... | ..... | ..... | ..... | ..... |
| Fish and other marine products | ..... | 0.1 | 0.1 | 0.2 | 0.1 | ..... | ..... | ..... | 0.1 | ..... |
| Metallic ores and concentrates | ..... | ..... | ..... | ..... | ..... | ..... | ..... | ..... | ..... | ..... |
| Bituminous coal and lignite | 0.8 | 8.9 | 9.8 | ..... | ..... | ..... | ..... | ..... | ..... | ..... |
| Crude petroleum and natural gas | ..... | ..... | ..... | 16.1 | 45.0 | ..... | ..... | 0.1 | 173.2 | 237.5 |
| Nonmetallic minerals | 1.4 | 1.2 | 1.1 | 0.7 | 0.2 | 0.2 | 0.2 | 0.3 | 0.3 | 0.5 |
| Scrap and waste | 6.2 | 1.6 | 3.8 | 3.2 | 2.4 | 2.7 | 0.5 | 0.9 | 0.6 | 0.5 |
| Used merchandise | 1.6 | 1.7 | 0.1 | 0.5 | 0.9 | 0.3 | 0.3 | 0.3 | ..... | 0.1 |
| Goods imported and returned unchanged | ..... | ..... | ..... | ..... | ..... | ..... | ..... | ..... | ..... | ..... |
| Special classification provisions | 4.6 | 1.2 | 24.6 | 5.0 | 5.2 | 1.7 | 2.2 | 3.5 | 2.5 | 0.4 |
| | Taiwan | | | | | Singapore | | | | |
| **ALL GOODS** | 289.2 | 294.7 | 379.3 | 384.6 | 368.9 | 326.4 | 329.3 | 395.5 | 454.4 | 488.6 |
| **Manufactured goods** | 286.6 | 293.3 | 373.4 | 324.0 | 341.2 | 324.6 | 327.9 | 393.8 | 453.3 | 487.0 |
| Food products | 20.5 | 19.4 | 14.7 | 11.7 | 13.7 | 6.1 | 3.9 | 2.0 | 1.8 | 1.8 |
| Tobacco products | ..... | ..... | ..... | ..... | ..... | ..... | ..... | ..... | ..... | ..... |
| Textile mill products | 0.8 | 0.2 | 0.2 | 0.1 | 0.7 | 1.0 | 0.5 | 0.5 | 2.2 | 2.9 |
| Apparel | ..... | 0.1 | 0.2 | 0.5 | 0.1 | 0.1 | 0.1 | 0.1 | 0.3 | 0.5 |
| Lumber and wood products | 3.1 | 6.8 | 5.1 | 6.0 | 5.3 | 0.9 | 0.7 | 1.0 | 0.9 | 0.9 |
| Furniture and fixtures | 0.7 | 0.7 | 0.9 | 0.7 | 0.8 | 1.3 | 0.9 | 1.0 | 1.6 | 1.6 |
| Paper products | 5.6 | 22.1 | 19.4 | 23.1 | 30.3 | 0.9 | 1.1 | 1.8 | 4.4 | 8.5 |
| Printing and publishing | 0.7 | 0.7 | 0.6 | 0.6 | 0.9 | 2.1 | 2.7 | 3.5 | 5.1 | 7.8 |
| Chemical products | 59.9 | 58.9 | 96.1 | 81.8 | 89.8 | 89.4 | 71.9 | 112.1 | 99.6 | 118.0 |
| Refined petroleum products | 0.2 | 0.5 | 0.4 | 24.2 | 0.4 | 0.3 | 0.1 | 0.2 | 0.2 | 0.5 |
| Rubber and plastic products | 9.5 | 9.6 | 8.9 | 5.9 | 6.1 | 7.1 | 7.2 | 8.9 | 11.6 | 10.1 |
| Leather products | 0.7 | 1.1 | 0.4 | 0.1 | 0.1 | 0.1 | 0.1 | ..... | 0.2 | 0.2 |
| Stone, clay and glass products | 6.2 | 8.9 | 7.4 | 6.5 | 8.3 | 5.9 | 5.0 | 4.2 | 4.9 | 5.0 |
| Primary metals | 10.5 | 6.0 | 7.6 | 11.9 | 15.7 | 3.2 | 5.0 | 12.6 | 16.2 | 18.3 |
| Fabricated metal products | 9.6 | 11.1 | 21.4 | 10.9 | 14.3 | 16.1 | 15.8 | 15.8 | 17.7 | 10.0 |
| Industrial machinery and computers | 81.9 | 74.9 | 119.0 | 84.4 | 91.6 | 56.3 | 52.1 | 70.6 | 74.0 | 61.8 |
| Electric and electronic equipment | 29.8 | 27.5 | 25.7 | 19.6 | 23.9 | 47.4 | 51.4 | 38.9 | 37.8 | 43.6 |
| Transportation equipment | 30.5 | 27.3 | 25.5 | 16.9 | 6.5 | 74.5 | 96.3 | 110.6 | 158.5 | 179.9 |
| Scientific and measuring instruments | 14.3 | 14.4 | 15.9 | 17.4 | 29.7 | 10.1 | 10.7 | 8.0 | 14.8 | 14.4 |
| Miscellaneous manufactures | 1.2 | 2.4 | 3.3 | 1.2 | 2.0 | 1.2 | 1.7 | 1.2 | 0.9 | 0.9 |
| Unidentified manufactures | 0.7 | 0.6 | 0.7 | 0.6 | 0.8 | 0.6 | 0.6 | 0.7 | 0.5 | 0.4 |
| **Agricultural and livestock products** | ..... | ..... | ..... | ..... | ..... | ..... | ..... | 0.1 | ..... | ..... |
| Agricultural products | ..... | ..... | ..... | ..... | ..... | ..... | ..... | 0.1 | ..... | ..... |
| Livestock and livestock products | ..... | ..... | ..... | ..... | ..... | ..... | ..... | ..... | ..... | ..... |
| **Other commodities** | 2.7 | 1.4 | 5.8 | 60.6 | 27.7 | 1.8 | 1.4 | 1.6 | 1.1 | 1.6 |
| Forestry products | ..... | 0.2 | ..... | 0.1 | 0.1 | ..... | ..... | ..... | ..... | ..... |
| Fish and other marine products | ..... | ..... | ..... | ..... | ..... | ..... | ..... | ..... | ..... | ..... |
| Metallic ores and concentrates | ..... | ..... | ..... | ..... | 0.1 | ..... | ..... | ..... | ..... | ..... |
| Bituminous coal and lignite | ..... | ..... | ..... | ..... | ..... | ..... | ..... | ..... | ..... | ..... |
| Crude petroleum and natural gas | ..... | ..... | 0.6 | 57.0 | 26.4 | ..... | ..... | ..... | ..... | ..... |
| Nonmetallic minerals | 0.4 | 0.2 | 0.3 | 0.3 | 0.3 | ..... | 0.1 | 0.1 | ..... | ..... |
| Scrap and waste | 0.8 | 0.4 | 1.5 | 1.4 | 0.1 | 0.2 | 0.1 | ..... | 0.1 | 0.3 |
| Used merchandise | ..... | ..... | ..... | 0.3 | 0.3 | 0.1 | 0.3 | 0.5 | 0.4 | 0.1 |
| Goods imported and returned unchanged | ..... | ..... | ..... | ..... | ..... | ..... | ..... | ..... | ..... | ..... |
| Special classification provisions | 1.4 | 0.6 | 3.3 | 1.6 | 0.5 | 1.5 | 1.0 | 1.0 | 0.6 | 1.2 |

## OKLAHOMA: Exports of Goods, 1997

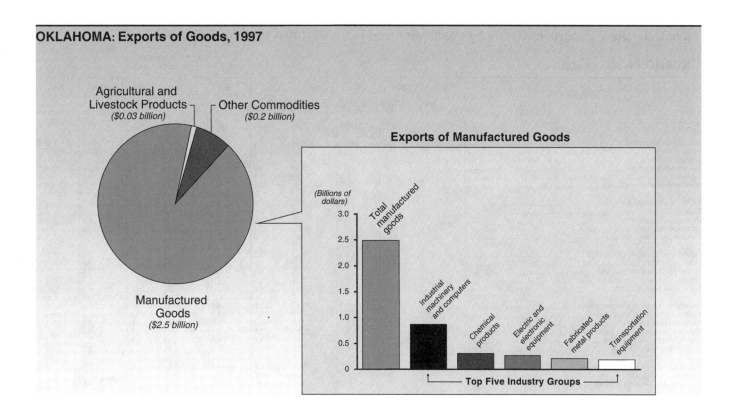

Agricultural and Livestock Products ($0.03 billion)

Other Commodities ($0.2 billion)

Manufactured Goods ($2.5 billion)

### Exports of Manufactured Goods

(Billions of dollars)

Top Five Industry Groups

## Table D-3.   State Exports of Goods by Destination and Industry, 1993–1997 —Continued

**OKLAHOMA** (Millions of dollars.)

| Industry | 1993 | 1994 | 1995 | 1996 | 1997 | 1993 | 1994 | 1995 | 1996 | 1997 |
|---|---|---|---|---|---|---|---|---|---|---|
| | All destinations | | | | | Canada | | | | |
| **ALL GOODS** | 2 334.6 | 2 172.0 | 2 467.3 | 2 537.6 | 2 721.6 | 426.2 | 497.1 | 492.3 | 570.9 | 669.9 |
| **Manufactured goods** | 1 974.1 | 1 990.3 | 2 178.3 | 2 285.0 | 2 489.1 | 406.6 | 476.8 | 468.2 | 538.3 | 629.1 |
| Food products | 56.7 | 59.5 | 59.4 | 56.6 | 71.6 | 6.6 | 5.4 | 5.3 | 6.0 | 9.1 |
| Tobacco products | ..... | 0.3 | 6.1 | ..... | ..... | ..... | ..... | ..... | ..... | ..... |
| Textile mill products | 7.0 | 5.3 | 6.6 | 4.1 | 8.0 | 0.9 | 1.0 | 1.3 | 1.6 | 0.4 |
| Apparel | 15.7 | 22.8 | 16.8 | 19.1 | 16.8 | 1.1 | 1.6 | 0.9 | 3.0 | 2.9 |
| Lumber and wood products | 1.0 | 0.5 | 3.2 | 1.5 | 3.1 | 0.2 | 0.1 | 0.2 | 0.4 | 0.2 |
| Furniture and fixtures | 2.9 | 2.4 | 2.8 | 5.0 | 6.3 | 1.1 | 1.1 | 1.2 | 1.3 | 1.7 |
| Paper products | 8.0 | 8.0 | 9.3 | 6.9 | 9.4 | 2.3 | 2.6 | 2.5 | 2.5 | 2.2 |
| Printing and publishing | 8.1 | 4.9 | 4.7 | 4.6 | 8.9 | 1.1 | 1.1 | 1.1 | 1.2 | 1.6 |
| Chemical products | 138.7 | 239.4 | 280.1 | 309.3 | 309.7 | 28.8 | 51.1 | 40.2 | 41.7 | 40.8 |
| Refined petroleum products | 145.7 | 91.9 | 49.3 | 117.8 | 129.4 | 6.5 | 7.5 | 6.2 | 4.4 | 7.8 |
| Rubber and plastic products | 65.8 | 57.0 | 59.2 | 61.1 | 71.7 | 43.7 | 44.0 | 43.2 | 42.7 | 47.3 |
| Leather products | 1.1 | 1.3 | 1.4 | 1.1 | 0.8 | 0.2 | 0.3 | 0.3 | 0.3 | 0.2 |
| Stone, clay and glass products | 37.5 | 30.0 | 47.3 | 34.7 | 36.3 | 19.5 | 14.4 | 14.9 | 14.9 | 14.7 |
| Primary metals | 70.5 | 92.9 | 125.1 | 90.6 | 94.2 | 18.9 | 30.8 | 26.0 | 30.2 | 35.2 |
| Fabricated metal products | 129.5 | 151.0 | 148.8 | 164.6 | 212.6 | 52.8 | 74.4 | 56.9 | 68.0 | 102.1 |
| Industrial machinery and computers | 741.8 | 689.1 | 816.8 | 820.8 | 869.5 | 122.6 | 144.4 | 144.6 | 176.4 | 208.9 |
| Electric and electronic equipment | 257.4 | 258.6 | 216.5 | 213.8 | 271.9 | 36.6 | 27.3 | 37.0 | 35.7 | 52.8 |
| Transportation equipment | 175.7 | 152.7 | 158.3 | 234.9 | 189.8 | 36.9 | 35.9 | 52.7 | 73.4 | 65.4 |
| Scientific and measuring instruments | 96.0 | 106.5 | 131.9 | 114.4 | 154.4 | 19.7 | 26.6 | 24.2 | 26.6 | 28.4 |
| Miscellaneous manufactures | 8.5 | 9.0 | 13.2 | 14.4 | 16.0 | 4.9 | 4.2 | 6.3 | 4.9 | 4.6 |
| Unidentified manufactures | 6.4 | 7.1 | 21.5 | 9.8 | 8.8 | 2.3 | 2.9 | 3.3 | 3.3 | 2.9 |
| **Agricultural and livestock products** | 185.3 | 37.3 | 30.5 | 19.7 | 27.1 | 7.8 | 7.5 | 10.4 | 8.2 | 10.6 |
| Agricultural products | 183.5 | 36.4 | 29.3 | 18.5 | 26.3 | 6.5 | 6.9 | 9.8 | 7.8 | 10.2 |
| Livestock and livestock products | 1.8 | 0.9 | 1.2 | 1.2 | 0.8 | 1.3 | 0.6 | 0.6 | 0.5 | 0.4 |
| **Other commodities** | 175.2 | 144.4 | 258.5 | 232.9 | 205.4 | 11.8 | 12.9 | 13.7 | 24.5 | 30.3 |
| Forestry products | 0.4 | 0.2 | 0.5 | 0.5 | 0.3 | ..... | ..... | ..... | ..... | ..... |
| Fish and other marine products | 0.1 | 0.6 | 0.2 | 0.2 | ..... | 0.1 | ..... | ..... | 0.2 | ..... |
| Metallic ores and concentrates | 5.7 | 5.8 | 8.1 | 3.2 | 8.3 | 1.7 | 0.9 | 0.3 | ..... | 0.2 |
| Bituminous coal and lignite | 105.5 | 95.8 | 168.9 | 133.5 | 99.7 | ..... | ..... | ..... | ..... | ..... |
| Crude petroleum and natural gas | 43.7 | 20.1 | 54.6 | 56.0 | 47.2 | 0.1 | ..... | 1.1 | 6.5 | 5.8 |
| Nonmetallic minerals | 3.3 | 3.2 | 3.2 | 5.2 | 4.4 | 0.1 | 0.3 | 0.2 | 0.3 | 0.2 |
| Scrap and waste | 1.2 | 0.8 | 0.7 | 1.8 | 1.4 | 0.2 | 0.4 | 0.3 | 0.8 | 0.5 |
| Used merchandise | 3.1 | 4.4 | 3.9 | 4.9 | 14.0 | 0.6 | 1.2 | 0.9 | 1.5 | 3.4 |
| Goods imported and returned unchanged | 7.7 | 8.4 | 7.9 | 13.4 | 18.2 | 7.7 | 8.4 | 7.9 | 13.4 | 18.2 |
| Special classification provisions | 4.4 | 5.3 | 10.5 | 14.3 | 12.0 | 1.3 | 1.7 | 2.9 | 1.8 | 2.0 |

## Table D-3.  State Exports of Goods by Destination and Industry, 1993–1997 —*Continued*

**OKLAHOMA** (Millions of dollars.)

| Industry | 1993 | 1994 | 1995 | 1996 | 1997 | 1993 | 1994 | 1995 | 1996 | 1997 |
|---|---|---|---|---|---|---|---|---|---|---|
| | South and Central America and Caribbean | | | | | Mexico | | | | |
| **ALL GOODS** | 367.8 | 360.3 | 498.6 | 433.3 | 453.2 | 157.8 | 139.3 | 120.3 | 178.7 | 239.6 |
| **Manufactured goods** | 314.3 | 330.5 | 444.7 | 377.8 | 406.6 | 103.9 | 118.9 | 110.7 | 170.3 | 232.8 |
| Food products | 1.8 | 1.8 | 1.3 | 1.1 | 2.2 | 5.5 | 1.9 | 1.0 | 0.8 | 1.8 |
| Tobacco products | ..... | ..... | ..... | ..... | ..... | ..... | ..... | ..... | ..... | ..... |
| Textile mill products | 1.1 | 0.6 | 0.4 | 0.5 | 1.4 | 0.6 | 1.6 | 0.4 | 0.2 | 4.4 |
| Apparel | 11.3 | 10.7 | 7.4 | 12.1 | 12.1 | 1.1 | 1.9 | 2.2 | 0.8 | 0.4 |
| Lumber and wood products | ..... | ..... | 0.3 | ..... | 0.2 | 0.1 | 0.2 | 0.1 | 0.1 | 0.2 |
| Furniture and fixtures | ..... | 0.2 | 0.2 | 0.4 | 0.2 | 0.1 | 0.1 | 0.5 | 1.8 | 3.6 |
| Paper products | 0.2 | 0.1 | 0.4 | 0.3 | 0.6 | 1.9 | 2.2 | 1.2 | 1.1 | 2.0 |
| Printing and publishing | ..... | ..... | 0.1 | 0.1 | 0.9 | 3.1 | 0.2 | 0.1 | 0.2 | 0.8 |
| Chemical products | 19.9 | 28.0 | 51.4 | 59.5 | 38.4 | 9.4 | 36.8 | 52.6 | 71.3 | 45.3 |
| Refined petroleum products | 42.7 | 41.5 | 20.8 | 21.3 | 10.5 | 12.9 | 6.4 | 0.3 | 0.3 | 1.5 |
| Rubber and plastic products | 2.4 | 2.4 | 3.3 | 3.0 | 3.2 | 11.1 | 3.2 | 2.4 | 2.8 | 8.4 |
| Leather products | ..... | 0.1 | 0.1 | ..... | ..... | ..... | 0.1 | ..... | 0.1 | ..... |
| Stone, clay and glass products | 0.7 | 0.7 | 2.9 | 1.3 | 1.2 | 14.2 | 10.8 | 7.8 | 9.9 | 16.8 |
| Primary metals | 7.8 | 5.4 | 17.3 | 12.0 | 16.5 | 9.4 | 11.3 | 10.7 | 14.7 | 20.3 |
| Fabricated metal products | 13.3 | 7.3 | 9.1 | 12.9 | 23.4 | 3.1 | 3.9 | 2.8 | 5.8 | 6.6 |
| Industrial machinery and computers | 189.9 | 207.3 | 306.9 | 226.4 | 247.2 | 14.6 | 18.5 | 10.3 | 20.0 | 30.1 |
| Electric and electronic equipment | 9.4 | 11.2 | 5.3 | 7.1 | 25.1 | 11.0 | 12.8 | 14.5 | 25.9 | 46.7 |
| Transportation equipment | 8.3 | 7.9 | 7.3 | 12.1 | 14.4 | 1.9 | 2.8 | 1.4 | 2.0 | 5.6 |
| Scientific and measuring instruments | 4.0 | 3.4 | 7.5 | 5.5 | 5.9 | 3.1 | 3.4 | 1.6 | 8.1 | 35.6 |
| Miscellaneous manufactures | 0.3 | 0.6 | 1.3 | 1.4 | 1.6 | 0.1 | 0.4 | 0.4 | 0.6 | 0.7 |
| Unidentified manufactures | 0.9 | 1.2 | 1.5 | 0.8 | 1.6 | 0.9 | 0.4 | 0.3 | 3.7 | 2.2 |
| **Agricultural and livestock products** | 0.3 | 0.1 | 0.2 | 0.3 | 0.5 | 44.5 | 18.2 | 6.4 | 0.8 | 3.6 |
| Agricultural products | 0.1 | 0.2 | 0.2 | 0.2 | 0.5 | 44.3 | 18.0 | 6.3 | 0.7 | 3.5 |
| Livestock and livestock products | 0.2 | ..... | ..... | ..... | ..... | 0.2 | 0.1 | 0.1 | 0.2 | 0.1 |
| **Other commodities** | 53.2 | 29.6 | 53.6 | 55.2 | 46.0 | 9.4 | 2.3 | 3.3 | 7.5 | 3.3 |
| Forestry products | 0.1 | ..... | 0.1 | 0.1 | ..... | ..... | ..... | ..... | 0.1 | 0.1 |
| Fish and other marine products | ..... | ..... | ..... | ..... | ..... | ..... | ..... | ..... | ..... | ..... |
| Metallic ores and concentrates | 0.1 | ..... | 0.1 | 0.3 | 0.3 | ..... | ..... | ..... | ..... | 0.1 |
| Bituminous coal and lignite | 24.6 | 18.3 | 29.3 | 35.1 | 28.7 | ..... | ..... | ..... | ..... | ..... |
| Crude petroleum and natural gas | 25.5 | 8.6 | 22.4 | 17.4 | 7.4 | 8.2 | 0.3 | 2.3 | 5.8 | ..... |
| Nonmetallic minerals | 1.6 | 2.1 | 1.5 | 1.9 | 1.2 | 0.1 | 0.3 | 0.2 | 0.8 | 1.7 |
| Scrap and waste | ..... | ..... | ..... | ..... | ..... | 0.5 | 0.3 | 0.2 | 0.8 | 0.4 |
| Used merchandise | 0.6 | 0.6 | 0.3 | 0.3 | 8.2 | 0.5 | 0.7 | 0.2 | ..... | 0.4 |
| Goods imported and returned unchanged | ..... | ..... | ..... | ..... | ..... | ..... | ..... | ..... | ..... | ..... |
| Special classification provisions | 0.8 | 0.1 | 0.2 | 0.1 | 0.2 | 0.1 | 0.7 | 0.3 | ..... | 0.5 |
| | European Union | | | | | United Kingdom | | | | |
| **ALL GOODS** | 459.9 | 477.2 | 540.1 | 500.1 | 535.7 | 91.4 | 86.1 | 109.9 | 98.1 | 100.7 |
| **Manufactured goods** | 408.8 | 415.2 | 433.6 | 414.1 | 471.3 | 84.6 | 77.6 | 95.0 | 84.7 | 83.5 |
| Food products | 1.1 | 2.2 | 5.3 | 3.9 | 5.1 | 0.1 | 0.3 | 0.8 | 1.1 | 0.7 |
| Tobacco products | ..... | ..... | 6.1 | ..... | ..... | ..... | ..... | ..... | ..... | ..... |
| Textile mill products | 0.9 | 0.8 | 3.5 | 0.7 | 0.7 | 0.1 | 0.1 | 1.2 | 0.7 | 0.3 |
| Apparel | 1.7 | 6.8 | 5.0 | 1.8 | 0.6 | 0.2 | 0.3 | 0.4 | 0.6 | 0.3 |
| Lumber and wood products | 0.3 | 0.1 | 2.1 | 0.2 | 0.4 | ..... | ..... | 0.6 | ..... | ..... |
| Furniture and fixtures | 0.1 | 0.3 | 0.3 | 0.7 | 0.1 | ..... | 0.1 | 0.2 | 0.3 | ..... |
| Paper products | 1.3 | 1.4 | 3.3 | 1.8 | 3.5 | 0.1 | 0.1 | 0.3 | 0.1 | 0.3 |
| Printing and publishing | 0.9 | 0.6 | 0.7 | 1.2 | 2.2 | 0.7 | 0.5 | 0.5 | 0.7 | 1.8 |
| Chemical products | 25.1 | 49.0 | 52.3 | 77.3 | 104.1 | 1.8 | 2.2 | 4.0 | 5.2 | 4.4 |
| Refined petroleum products | 49.2 | 21.4 | 8.1 | 31.2 | 36.6 | 0.6 | 0.8 | 0.5 | 0.4 | 0.5 |
| Rubber and plastic products | 2.4 | 2.8 | 3.6 | 2.3 | 2.1 | 0.8 | 1.0 | 1.3 | 0.7 | 0.7 |
| Leather products | 0.5 | 0.4 | 0.6 | 0.4 | 0.2 | ..... | ..... | 0.1 | 0.2 | 0.1 |
| Stone, clay and glass products | 0.7 | 3.1 | 5.2 | 2.8 | 1.9 | 0.2 | 0.2 | 1.4 | 0.8 | 0.8 |
| Primary metals | 3.7 | 3.8 | 5.7 | 5.8 | 6.5 | 0.7 | 1.3 | 1.6 | 3.3 | 2.5 |
| Fabricated metal products | 14.2 | 15.5 | 18.6 | 18.8 | 20.1 | 2.2 | 2.2 | 2.6 | 4.5 | 4.6 |
| Industrial machinery and computers | 86.0 | 73.5 | 108.3 | 93.2 | 92.4 | 28.6 | 25.4 | 33.6 | 29.7 | 29.1 |
| Electric and electronic equipment | 137.6 | 157.5 | 113.8 | 89.3 | 98.0 | 3.7 | 14.8 | 12.4 | 11.5 | 10.3 |
| Transportation equipment | 51.7 | 43.9 | 36.3 | 46.4 | 47.6 | 36.5 | 20.1 | 10.3 | 14.2 | 14.2 |
| Scientific and measuring instruments | 29.3 | 28.9 | 38.4 | 33.4 | 45.6 | 7.9 | 7.7 | 10.3 | 10.4 | 12.4 |
| Miscellaneous manufactures | 1.2 | 2.2 | 3.0 | 2.4 | 2.9 | 0.1 | 0.2 | 0.3 | 0.1 | 0.5 |
| Unidentified manufactures | 0.8 | 0.9 | 13.3 | 0.6 | 0.7 | 0.3 | 0.3 | 12.6 | 0.2 | 0.1 |
| **Agricultural and livestock products** | 9.0 | 10.0 | 11.6 | 8.7 | 10.0 | 0.9 | 2.1 | 4.2 | 3.0 | 1.7 |
| Agricultural products | 9.0 | 9.9 | 11.3 | 8.4 | 9.9 | 0.9 | 2.1 | 4.0 | 3.0 | 1.7 |
| Livestock and livestock products | ..... | 0.1 | 0.3 | 0.3 | 0.1 | ..... | ..... | 0.1 | ..... | ..... |
| **Other commodities** | 42.1 | 52.0 | 94.9 | 77.4 | 54.4 | 5.9 | 6.4 | 10.6 | 10.4 | 15.5 |
| Forestry products | 0.1 | ..... | 0.3 | 0.2 | 0.1 | 0.1 | ..... | 0.1 | 0.1 | ..... |
| Fish and other marine products | ..... | ..... | ..... | ..... | ..... | ..... | ..... | ..... | ..... | ..... |
| Metallic ores and concentrates | ..... | 4.7 | 4.0 | 0.4 | ..... | ..... | ..... | ..... | ..... | ..... |
| Bituminous coal and lignite | 39.1 | 43.9 | 87.0 | 73.4 | 49.5 | 4.6 | 5.4 | 8.8 | 8.9 | 14.3 |
| Crude petroleum and natural gas | 0.6 | 1.4 | ..... | ..... | ..... | 0.4 | ..... | ..... | ..... | ..... |
| Nonmetallic minerals | 0.1 | ..... | 0.1 | 0.4 | 0.4 | 0.1 | ..... | ..... | 0.1 | 0.1 |
| Scrap and waste | 0.2 | 0.1 | 0.1 | 0.1 | 0.1 | ..... | ..... | 0.1 | ..... | ..... |
| Used merchandise | 0.7 | 0.7 | 0.5 | 0.3 | 1.1 | 0.1 | ..... | 0.1 | 0.1 | ..... |
| Goods imported and returned unchanged | ..... | ..... | ..... | ..... | ..... | ..... | ..... | ..... | ..... | ..... |
| Special classification provisions | 1.4 | 1.3 | 2.7 | 2.5 | 3.0 | 0.7 | 0.9 | 1.5 | 1.3 | 1.0 |

## Table D-3. State Exports of Goods by Destination and Industry, 1993–1997 —*Continued*

**OKLAHOMA** (Millions of dollars.)

| Industry | 1993 | 1994 | 1995 | 1996 | 1997 | 1993 | 1994 | 1995 | 1996 | 1997 |
|---|---|---|---|---|---|---|---|---|---|---|
| | Germany | | | | | France | | | | |
| **ALL GOODS** | 54.2 | 63.2 | 80.1 | 64.2 | 60.0 | 36.9 | 42.0 | 49.1 | 58.0 | 80.6 |
| **Manufactured goods** | 51.1 | 60.0 | 73.2 | 61.9 | 56.9 | 35.4 | 40.0 | 45.3 | 56.2 | 79.1 |
| Food products | ..... | 0.1 | 0.6 | 0.3 | 0.4 | 0.3 | 0.8 | 2.6 | 1.5 | 2.8 |
| Tobacco products | ..... | | | | | | | | | |
| Textile mill products | 0.4 | 0.5 | 0.1 | ..... | 0.1 | 0.1 | | | | |
| Apparel | 0.1 | 0.9 | 1.0 | 0.5 | 0.1 | 0.9 | 2.5 | 0.4 | ..... | ..... |
| Lumber and wood products | ..... | ..... | 0.4 | ..... | | | | 0.1 | | |
| Furniture and fixtures | ..... | ..... | 0.1 | ..... | ..... | | | ..... | ..... | ..... |
| Paper products | | 0.2 | | | 0.1 | 0.1 | | 0.2 | 0.1 | 0.1 |
| Printing and publishing | ..... | ..... | ..... | 0.1 | 0.1 | | | | | 0.2 |
| Chemical products | 6.8 | 7.1 | 6.9 | 10.2 | 13.4 | 5.6 | 9.0 | 8.6 | 15.6 | 41.2 |
| Refined petroleum products | 3.4 | 3.8 | 2.8 | 1.5 | 1.6 | 4.1 | 8.4 | 2.4 | 3.3 | 3.0 |
| Rubber and plastic products | 0.4 | 1.0 | 0.2 | 0.4 | 0.4 | 0.1 | 0.1 | 0.2 | 0.1 | ..... |
| Leather products | 0.2 | 0.2 | 0.2 | 0.1 | ..... | ..... | 0.1 | 0.2 | ..... | ..... |
| Stone, clay and glass products | 0.4 | 1.7 | 1.4 | 0.9 | 0.9 | 0.1 | 0.3 | 1.3 | 0.1 | ..... |
| Primary metals | 0.4 | 0.4 | 2.2 | 0.8 | 0.8 | 0.1 | 0.4 | 1.1 | 0.6 | 1.0 |
| Fabricated metal products | 3.2 | 2.8 | 2.5 | 2.8 | 1.7 | 0.3 | 0.7 | 1.2 | 0.5 | 1.3 |
| Industrial machinery and computers | 10.9 | 11.5 | 16.6 | 16.0 | 14.5 | 7.2 | 5.1 | 7.9 | 9.8 | 7.4 |
| Electric and electronic equipment | 7.7 | 12.5 | 19.9 | 8.5 | 4.5 | 11.5 | 6.1 | 12.2 | 8.2 | 9.8 |
| Transportation equipment | 8.2 | 10.8 | 11.9 | 12.4 | 10.7 | 2.0 | 2.4 | 2.8 | 11.0 | 7.7 |
| Scientific and measuring instruments | 8.6 | 6.1 | 6.0 | 6.5 | 7.2 | 2.9 | 3.5 | 3.1 | 4.5 | 4.0 |
| Miscellaneous manufactures | 0.2 | 0.4 | 0.4 | 0.7 | 0.3 | 0.1 | 0.3 | 0.7 | 0.7 | 0.5 |
| Unidentified manufactures | 0.1 | 0.2 | 0.2 | 0.1 | 0.1 | 0.1 | 0.2 | 0.1 | 0.1 | 0.1 |
| **Agricultural and livestock products** | 2.3 | 2.9 | 2.5 | 2.0 | 2.1 | 0.2 | 0.4 | 0.6 | 0.4 | 1.1 |
| Agricultural products | 2.3 | 2.9 | 2.5 | 2.0 | 2.1 | 0.2 | 0.4 | 0.6 | 0.4 | 1.1 |
| Livestock and livestock products | ..... | ..... | ..... | ..... | ..... | ..... | ..... | ..... | ..... | ..... |
| **Other commodities** | 0.7 | 0.4 | 4.4 | 0.3 | 1.0 | 1.3 | 1.6 | 3.2 | 1.4 | 0.4 |
| Forestry products | ..... | ..... | ..... | ..... | ..... | ..... | ..... | ..... | ..... | ..... |
| Fish and other marine products | ..... | ..... | ..... | ..... | ..... | ..... | ..... | ..... | ..... | ..... |
| Metallic ores and concentrates | ..... | ..... | ..... | ..... | ..... | ..... | ..... | ..... | ..... | ..... |
| Bituminous coal and lignite | ..... | ..... | 3.7 | ..... | ..... | 1.1 | 1.4 | 2.9 | 0.9 | ..... |
| Crude petroleum and natural gas | 0.1 | ..... | ..... | ..... | ..... | ..... | ..... | ..... | ..... | ..... |
| Nonmetallic minerals | 0.1 | ..... | ..... | ..... | 0.3 | ..... | ..... | ..... | 0.3 | 0.1 |
| Scrap and waste | ..... | ..... | ..... | 0.1 | ..... | ..... | ..... | ..... | ..... | ..... |
| Used merchandise | 0.4 | 0.3 | 0.1 | ..... | ..... | 0.2 | 0.2 | 0.2 | 0.1 | 0.3 |
| Goods imported and returned unchanged | ..... | ..... | ..... | ..... | ..... | ..... | ..... | ..... | ..... | ..... |
| Special classification provisions | 0.2 | 0.1 | 0.7 | 0.2 | 0.6 | 0.1 | ..... | 0.1 | 0.1 | ..... |
| | The Netherlands | | | | | Asian 10 | | | | |
| **ALL GOODS** | 170.9 | 161.0 | 145.9 | 130.7 | 151.6 | 377.3 | 399.3 | 458.9 | 473.7 | 446.4 |
| **Manufactured goods** | 147.1 | 146.6 | 111.5 | 123.0 | 150.1 | 352.6 | 372.2 | 413.3 | 428.8 | 391.0 |
| Food products | 0.4 | 0.8 | 0.5 | 0.5 | 0.4 | 39.9 | 45.9 | 42.1 | 43.8 | 49.5 |
| Tobacco products | ..... | ..... | ..... | ..... | ..... | | | | | |
| Textile mill products | ..... | ..... | 0.4 | ..... | ..... | 0.5 | 0.5 | 0.5 | 0.6 | 0.4 |
| Apparel | 0.2 | 0.8 | 2.8 | 0.6 | ..... | 0.1 | 0.9 | 0.5 | 0.5 | 0.3 |
| Lumber and wood products | ..... | ..... | ..... | ..... | ..... | 0.3 | 0.1 | 0.4 | 0.7 | 0.3 |
| Furniture and fixtures | | | | | | 0.1 | 0.4 | ..... | 0.7 | 0.3 |
| Paper products | 0.8 | 1.1 | 2.5 | 1.4 | 2.9 | 1.8 | 1.2 | 0.9 | 1.0 | 0.5 |
| Printing and publishing | ..... | ..... | 0.1 | 0.2 | ..... | 2.8 | 2.6 | 2.2 | 1.5 | 2.8 |
| Chemical products | 2.3 | 4.8 | 12.4 | 20.5 | 20.2 | 40.3 | 53.8 | 63.0 | 39.3 | 33.9 |
| Refined petroleum products | 38.6 | 6.1 | 0.8 | 24.7 | 29.9 | 27.4 | 12.8 | 11.6 | 53.3 | 71.1 |
| Rubber and plastic products | 0.3 | 0.4 | 1.6 | 0.4 | 0.3 | 3.0 | 2.1 | 3.7 | 6.0 | 7.1 |
| Leather products | ..... | ..... | ..... | ..... | 0.1 | 0.4 | 0.3 | 0.3 | 0.3 | 0.1 |
| Stone, clay and glass products | ..... | ..... | 0.2 | 0.7 | ..... | 1.3 | 0.8 | 12.5 | 3.4 | 1.4 |
| Primary metals | 0.6 | 1.0 | 0.2 | 0.5 | 0.2 | 5.9 | 8.2 | 14.7 | 7.0 | 4.4 |
| Fabricated metal products | 0.5 | 0.5 | 1.6 | 1.5 | 0.8 | 29.3 | 36.2 | 48.3 | 40.4 | 39.7 |
| Industrial machinery and computers | 18.9 | 12.5 | 15.9 | 11.6 | 14.3 | 93.5 | 118.7 | 107.1 | 109.1 | 106.7 |
| Electric and electronic equipment | 80.0 | 113.9 | 64.2 | 56.1 | 65.4 | 42.8 | 36.8 | 26.7 | 44.3 | 27.7 |
| Transportation equipment | 0.8 | 0.5 | 1.5 | 0.7 | 0.6 | 38.9 | 28.9 | 36.4 | 54.3 | 22.8 |
| Scientific and measuring instruments | 3.4 | 3.6 | 5.9 | 2.9 | 14.5 | 22.4 | 20.2 | 40.0 | 18.5 | 16.5 |
| Miscellaneous manufactures | 0.1 | 0.6 | 0.9 | 0.1 | 0.4 | 1.6 | 1.3 | 1.6 | 3.6 | 5.0 |
| Unidentified manufactures | 0.1 | ..... | 0.2 | 0.1 | ..... | 0.5 | 0.6 | 0.9 | 0.4 | 0.4 |
| **Agricultural and livestock products** | 0.7 | 0.1 | 0.4 | 0.5 | 0.7 | 0.4 | 0.3 | 0.1 | 0.4 | 0.9 |
| Agricultural products | 0.7 | 0.1 | 0.3 | 0.3 | 0.6 | 0.4 | 0.2 | ..... | 0.2 | 0.8 |
| Livestock and livestock products | ..... | ..... | 0.1 | 0.3 | 0.1 | ..... | ..... | 0.1 | 0.2 | 0.1 |
| **Other commodities** | 23.1 | 14.3 | 34.0 | 7.2 | 0.8 | 24.3 | 26.9 | 45.4 | 44.6 | 54.4 |
| Forestry products | ..... | ..... | 0.2 | 0.1 | ..... | 0.2 | 0.1 | ..... | ..... | 0.1 |
| Fish and other marine products | ..... | ..... | ..... | ..... | ..... | ..... | 0.6 | 0.2 | ..... | ..... |
| Metallic ores and concentrates | ..... | 4.7 | 4.0 | ..... | ..... | ..... | 0.2 | 3.7 | 2.4 | 7.5 |
| Bituminous coal and lignite | 23.0 | 9.4 | 29.5 | 7.0 | 0.4 | 12.8 | 15.0 | 8.6 | 7.4 | 6.3 |
| Crude petroleum and natural gas | ..... | ..... | ..... | ..... | ..... | 9.3 | 9.9 | 28.7 | 26.3 | 33.9 |
| Nonmetallic minerals | ..... | ..... | ..... | ..... | ..... | 1.1 | 0.3 | 0.8 | 1.1 | 0.7 |
| Scrap and waste | ..... | ..... | ..... | ..... | 0.1 | 0.2 | 0.1 | ..... | 0.1 | 0.3 |
| Used merchandise | ..... | ..... | ..... | ..... | ..... | 0.2 | 0.2 | 0.4 | 0.3 | 0.5 |
| Goods imported and returned unchanged | ..... | ..... | ..... | ..... | ..... | ..... | ..... | ..... | ..... | ..... |
| Special classification provisions | 0.1 | 0.2 | 0.2 | 0.1 | 0.2 | 0.5 | 0.7 | 3.1 | 6.9 | 5.1 |

## Table D-3.  State Exports of Goods by Destination and Industry, 1993–1997 —*Continued*

### OKLAHOMA (Millions of dollars.)

| Industry | 1993 | 1994 | 1995 | 1996 | 1997 | 1993 | 1994 | 1995 | 1996 | 1997 |
|---|---|---|---|---|---|---|---|---|---|---|
| | Japan | | | | | South Korea | | | | |
| ALL GOODS | 119.0 | 129.6 | 133.6 | 194.9 | 178.7 | 30.2 | 45.8 | 66.8 | 66.0 | 45.3 |
| **Manufactured goods** | 105.9 | 113.9 | 120.2 | 170.5 | 155.9 | 30.2 | 43.8 | 57.1 | 60.8 | 25.9 |
| Food products | 24.3 | 27.2 | 26.6 | 29.9 | 40.6 | 9.5 | 8.4 | 5.1 | 4.7 | 2.1 |
| Tobacco products | ..... | ..... | ..... | ..... | ..... | ..... | ..... | ..... | ..... | ..... |
| Textile mill products | 0.1 | 0.1 | 0.1 | 0.1 | 0.1 | ..... | ..... | 0.1 | 0.3 | 0.1 |
| Apparel | 0.1 | 0.5 | 0.3 | 0.3 | 0.2 | ..... | ..... | ..... | ..... | ..... |
| Lumber and wood products | 0.1 | ..... | ..... | 0.1 | 0.1 | 0.1 | ..... | ..... | ..... | 0.1 |
| Furniture and fixtures | ..... | 0.1 | ..... | 0.4 | ..... | ..... | ..... | ..... | 0.1 | ..... |
| Paper products | 0.5 | 0.3 | 0.3 | ..... | ..... | ..... | ..... | ..... | 0.1 | ..... |
| Printing and publishing | 2.6 | 2.5 | 1.4 | 0.6 | 2.3 | ..... | ..... | ..... | ..... | ..... |
| Chemical products | 12.3 | 24.9 | 21.1 | 16.9 | 15.2 | 3.3 | 9.1 | 0.7 | 3.1 | 2.2 |
| Refined petroleum products | 11.6 | 7.5 | 6.0 | 49.0 | 55.3 | 0.9 | 1.0 | 0.3 | 0.6 | 0.6 |
| Rubber and plastic products | 0.2 | 0.6 | 0.3 | 0.7 | 0.4 | 2.0 | 0.5 | 0.7 | 3.4 | 2.5 |
| Leather products | 0.3 | 0.3 | 0.2 | 0.3 | 0.1 | ..... | ..... | ..... | ..... | ..... |
| Stone, clay and glass products | 0.4 | 0.1 | 0.3 | 0.3 | 0.3 | 0.2 | 0.1 | 9.9 | 2.7 | 0.1 |
| Primary metals | 0.5 | 0.9 | 1.4 | 1.7 | 1.5 | ..... | 3.8 | 1.8 | 0.4 | 0.2 |
| Fabricated metal products | 2.2 | 2.8 | 4.5 | 4.8 | 5.9 | 1.7 | 6.8 | 16.3 | 13.4 | 5.3 |
| Industrial machinery and computers | 16.1 | 20.7 | 21.6 | 21.6 | 13.3 | 3.6 | 6.6 | 10.8 | 14.7 | 5.1 |
| Electric and electronic equipment | 3.1 | 3.5 | 6.8 | 6.7 | 6.9 | 6.7 | 2.5 | 3.4 | 2.5 | 3.7 |
| Transportation equipment | 28.2 | 16.2 | 18.5 | 31.2 | 6.7 | 1.4 | 3.0 | 4.5 | 9.2 | 1.3 |
| Scientific and measuring instruments | 2.7 | 4.7 | 9.1 | 3.4 | 4.0 | 0.6 | 1.7 | 3.1 | 5.1 | 2.0 |
| Miscellaneous manufactures | 0.6 | 0.9 | 1.3 | 2.5 | 2.9 | 0.2 | 0.1 | 0.1 | 0.4 | 0.5 |
| Unidentified manufactures | 0.1 | 0.2 | 0.3 | 0.1 | 0.1 | 0.1 | 0.1 | 0.1 | ..... | ..... |
| **Agricultural and livestock products** | 0.1 | ..... | ..... | 0.2 | 0.2 | ..... | ..... | ..... | 0.2 | 0.1 |
| Agricultural products | ..... | ..... | ..... | ..... | 0.2 | ..... | ..... | ..... | 0.2 | 0.1 |
| Livestock and livestock products | ..... | ..... | ..... | 0.1 | ..... | ..... | ..... | ..... | ..... | ..... |
| **Other commodities** | 13.1 | 15.7 | 13.4 | 24.2 | 22.6 | ..... | 2.0 | 9.8 | 5.1 | 19.3 |
| Forestry products | 0.2 | ..... | ..... | ..... | ..... | ..... | 0.1 | ..... | ..... | ..... |
| Fish and other marine products | ..... | 0.6 | 0.1 | ..... | ..... | ..... | ..... | ..... | ..... | ..... |
| Metallic ores and concentrates | ..... | ..... | 0.1 | 2.4 | 7.5 | ..... | ..... | ..... | ..... | ..... |
| Bituminous coal and lignite | 12.8 | 15.0 | 8.6 | 7.4 | 6.3 | ..... | ..... | ..... | ..... | ..... |
| Crude petroleum and natural gas | ..... | ..... | 4.6 | 13.2 | 8.6 | ..... | 1.9 | 9.5 | 5.1 | 18.9 |
| Nonmetallic minerals | ..... | ..... | ..... | ..... | ..... | ..... | ..... | 0.1 | ..... | ..... |
| Scrap and waste | ..... | ..... | ..... | ..... | ..... | ..... | ..... | ..... | ..... | ..... |
| Used merchandise | ..... | ..... | 0.1 | 0.3 | ..... | ..... | ..... | ..... | ..... | ..... |
| Goods imported and returned unchanged | ..... | ..... | ..... | ..... | ..... | ..... | ..... | ..... | ..... | ..... |
| Special classification provisions | ..... | ..... | ..... | 1.0 | 0.1 | ..... | ..... | 0.1 | ..... | 0.4 |
| | Taiwan | | | | | Singapore | | | | |
| ALL GOODS | 35.3 | 20.1 | 27.7 | 16.4 | 15.6 | 84.2 | 55.2 | 56.7 | 56.3 | 70.4 |
| **Manufactured goods** | 25.9 | 17.1 | 18.9 | 14.8 | 15.5 | 83.5 | 54.8 | 53.7 | 52.8 | 68.4 |
| Food products | 1.7 | 1.4 | 1.2 | 1.9 | 1.8 | 0.1 | 0.1 | 0.4 | 0.1 | 0.1 |
| Tobacco products | ..... | ..... | ..... | ..... | ..... | ..... | ..... | ..... | ..... | ..... |
| Textile mill products | 0.1 | 0.1 | ..... | ..... | ..... | 0.1 | 0.1 | ..... | 0.1 | ..... |
| Apparel | ..... | ..... | 0.1 | ..... | ..... | ..... | 0.2 | 0.1 | 0.1 | ..... |
| Lumber and wood products | ..... | ..... | | 0.2 | ..... | ..... | ..... | 0.1 | ..... | ..... |
| Furniture and fixtures | 0.1 | ..... | ..... | ..... | ..... | ..... | ..... | ..... | ..... | ..... |
| Paper products | ..... | ..... | ..... | 0.1 | ..... | 0.9 | 0.7 | 0.5 | 0.6 | 0.3 |
| Printing and publishing | ..... | 0.1 | ..... | ..... | ..... | ..... | ..... | ..... | 0.3 | 0.4 |
| Chemical products | 8.8 | 4.0 | 5.1 | 2.4 | 0.2 | 9.0 | 10.9 | 10.1 | 8.9 | 9.2 |
| Refined petroleum products | 0.8 | 0.8 | 0.5 | 0.7 | 0.9 | 6.0 | 1.3 | 0.6 | 0.5 | 0.5 |
| Rubber and plastic products | 0.2 | 0.3 | 0.8 | 0.2 | 0.4 | 0.3 | 0.2 | 0.2 | 0.3 | 0.2 |
| Leather products | ..... | ..... | ..... | ..... | ..... | ..... | ..... | ..... | ..... | ..... |
| Stone, clay and glass products | 0.1 | 0.1 | 0.2 | 0.2 | 0.6 | 0.1 | 0.1 | 0.5 | 0.1 | 0.2 |
| Primary metals | 0.3 | 0.6 | 0.6 | 0.4 | 0.4 | 1.2 | 1.5 | 2.6 | 2.2 | 0.9 |
| Fabricated metal products | 2.6 | 3.0 | 2.2 | 1.0 | 2.4 | 1.8 | 5.0 | 4.4 | 4.1 | 7.7 |
| Industrial machinery and computers | 2.4 | 2.2 | 3.5 | 2.9 | 4.4 | 35.1 | 20.8 | 20.6 | 28.1 | 40.2 |
| Electric and electronic equipment | 7.8 | 3.7 | 3.4 | 3.6 | 1.9 | 20.5 | 6.9 | 6.2 | 2.0 | 3.0 |
| Transportation equipment | 0.2 | 0.1 | 0.2 | 0.1 | 0.2 | 4.0 | 2.7 | 3.0 | 1.8 | 2.9 |
| Scientific and measuring instruments | 0.7 | 0.8 | 0.9 | 1.0 | 2.3 | 4.2 | 3.9 | 3.9 | 3.2 | 2.4 |
| Miscellaneous manufactures | ..... | ..... | 0.1 | 0.1 | ..... | 0.1 | 0.1 | 0.1 | 0.5 | 0.3 |
| Unidentified manufactures | ..... | ..... | 0.1 | ..... | ..... | 0.1 | 0.2 | 0.2 | 0.1 | 0.1 |
| **Agricultural and livestock products** | ..... | ..... | ..... | ..... | ..... | ..... | ..... | ..... | ..... | ..... |
| Agricultural products | ..... | ..... | ..... | ..... | ..... | ..... | ..... | ..... | ..... | ..... |
| Livestock and livestock products | ..... | ..... | ..... | ..... | ..... | ..... | ..... | ..... | ..... | ..... |
| **Other commodities** | 9.4 | 3.0 | 8.8 | 1.5 | 0.1 | 0.6 | 0.4 | 3.0 | 3.5 | 2.0 |
| Forestry products | ..... | ..... | ..... | ..... | ..... | ..... | ..... | ..... | ..... | ..... |
| Fish and other marine products | ..... | ..... | 0.1 | ..... | ..... | ..... | ..... | ..... | ..... | ..... |
| Metallic ores and concentrates | ..... | ..... | 3.6 | ..... | ..... | ..... | ..... | ..... | ..... | ..... |
| Bituminous coal and lignite | ..... | ..... | ..... | ..... | ..... | ..... | ..... | ..... | ..... | ..... |
| Crude petroleum and natural gas | 9.3 | 2.8 | 5.1 | 1.3 | ..... | ..... | ..... | ..... | ..... | ..... |
| Nonmetallic minerals | ..... | ..... | ..... | ..... | 0.1 | ..... | 0.1 | 0.1 | 0.2 | 0.1 |
| Scrap and waste | ..... | ..... | ..... | ..... | ..... | 0.2 | ..... | ..... | 0.1 | 0.2 |
| Used merchandise | ..... | ..... | ..... | ..... | ..... | 0.1 | 0.1 | 0.2 | ..... | ..... |
| Goods imported and returned unchanged | ..... | ..... | ..... | ..... | ..... | ..... | ..... | ..... | ..... | ..... |
| Special classification provisions | 0.1 | 0.2 | ..... | 0.2 | ..... | 0.3 | 0.1 | 2.7 | 3.2 | 1.6 |

## OREGON: Exports of Goods, 1997

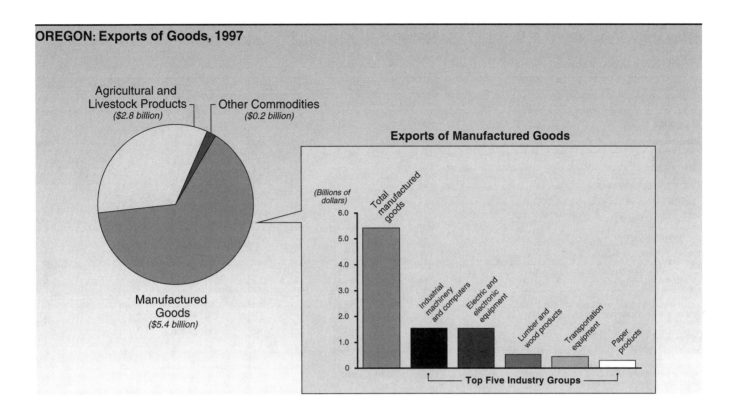

## Table D-3.   State Exports of Goods by Destination and Industry, 1993–1997 —*Continued*

**OREGON** (Millions of dollars.)

| Industry | 1993 | 1994 | 1995 | 1996 | 1997 | 1993 | 1994 | 1995 | 1996 | 1997 |
|---|---|---|---|---|---|---|---|---|---|---|
| | All destinations | | | | | Canada | | | | |
| **ALL GOODS** | 6 204.7 | 6 987.4 | 9 902.1 | 8 481.3 | 8 358.6 | 870.7 | 1 020.9 | 1 097.5 | 890.2 | 1 081.7 |
| **Manufactured goods** | 3 967.9 | 4 552.3 | 6 410.1 | 5 005.4 | 5 419.9 | 797.6 | 951.8 | 1 022.7 | 831.0 | 1 012.5 |
| Food products | 154.3 | 187.7 | 209.9 | 190.0 | 212.2 | 42.4 | 42.3 | 47.0 | 37.5 | 38.3 |
| Tobacco products | ..... | 0.1 | 0.1 | 0.2 | 0.5 | ..... | ..... | 0.1 | 0.2 | 0.1 |
| Textile mill products | 10.5 | 7.3 | 9.8 | 8.3 | 7.3 | 1.4 | 1.5 | 2.2 | 0.8 | 1.0 |
| Apparel | 18.9 | 17.3 | 27.2 | 14.8 | 18.7 | 2.4 | 4.7 | 8.0 | 3.7 | 6.7 |
| Lumber and wood products | 840.4 | 762.0 | 735.2 | 506.5 | 534.9 | 155.3 | 133.0 | 120.9 | 117.4 | 135.7 |
| Furniture and fixtures | 16.4 | 14.8 | 13.5 | 11.8 | 12.9 | 11.7 | 10.2 | 6.4 | 6.0 | 6.7 |
| Paper products | 103.3 | 185.7 | 287.1 | 286.7 | 294.4 | 26.3 | 35.3 | 34.2 | 26.6 | 35.1 |
| Printing and publishing | 26.7 | 32.0 | 26.9 | 26.5 | 27.9 | 7.2 | 6.4 | 7.6 | 7.9 | 11.0 |
| Chemical products | 48.7 | 62.3 | 82.2 | 64.0 | 75.9 | 30.3 | 41.0 | 46.2 | 41.0 | 40.2 |
| Refined petroleum products | 17.3 | 22.1 | 22.9 | 21.8 | 17.8 | 16.2 | 21.4 | 20.5 | 19.5 | 15.8 |
| Rubber and plastic products | 47.2 | 48.2 | 67.8 | 51.1 | 47.7 | 17.4 | 19.7 | 20.4 | 16.6 | 16.2 |
| Leather products | 35.7 | 49.5 | 73.0 | 23.4 | 30.2 | 1.6 | 1.8 | 2.0 | 1.3 | 1.5 |
| Stone, clay and glass products | 23.5 | 25.9 | 24.5 | 31.3 | 35.2 | 10.2 | 9.8 | 9.8 | 9.8 | 9.9 |
| Primary metals | 86.9 | 124.0 | 162.0 | 120.9 | 194.9 | 38.1 | 58.9 | 43.6 | 38.1 | 46.8 |
| Fabricated metal products | 70.5 | 84.3 | 101.7 | 103.1 | 131.6 | 30.3 | 35.6 | 41.7 | 33.0 | 39.1 |
| Industrial machinery and computers | 1 030.0 | 1 162.1 | 2 001.1 | 1 335.7 | 1 542.9 | 151.5 | 190.3 | 217.6 | 146.7 | 146.6 |
| Electric and electronic equipment | 635.7 | 858.6 | 1 506.9 | 1 627.5 | 1 540.3 | 57.2 | 66.0 | 82.5 | 66.8 | 102.2 |
| Transportation equipment | 344.5 | 411.9 | 437.9 | 357.3 | 453.9 | 143.8 | 213.6 | 246.0 | 223.4 | 317.2 |
| Scientific and measuring instruments | 395.2 | 425.9 | 538.4 | 163.5 | 179.0 | 37.9 | 41.4 | 46.0 | 19.8 | 25.7 |
| Miscellaneous manufactures | 50.3 | 53.7 | 67.3 | 42.9 | 40.1 | 12.7 | 11.0 | 14.3 | 11.3 | 13.0 |
| Unidentified manufactures | 12.0 | 16.9 | 14.5 | 18.2 | 21.6 | 3.7 | 8.0 | 5.4 | 3.7 | 3.6 |
| **Agricultural and livestock products** | 2 116.1 | 2 265.3 | 3 253.3 | 3 308.8 | 2 768.6 | 45.2 | 42.5 | 46.0 | 33.1 | 42.0 |
| Agricultural products | 2 115.1 | 2 264.0 | 3 251.9 | 3 306.6 | 2 765.5 | 44.4 | 41.5 | 45.0 | 31.0 | 39.3 |
| Livestock and livestock products | 1.1 | 1.4 | 1.4 | 2.2 | 3.1 | 0.8 | 1.0 | 1.0 | 2.1 | 2.7 |
| **Other commodities** | 120.7 | 169.7 | 238.6 | 167.1 | 170.1 | 27.9 | 26.6 | 28.8 | 26.1 | 27.2 |
| Forestry products | 3.5 | 2.8 | 2.9 | 2.1 | 2.3 | 1.4 | 2.0 | 2.0 | 1.3 | 0.9 |
| Fish and other marine products | 18.3 | 18.9 | 20.4 | 10.8 | 14.6 | 6.1 | 2.9 | 3.6 | 4.6 | 4.6 |
| Metallic ores and concentrates | 0.1 | 0.2 | 0.2 | 0.1 | 0.1 | ..... | 0.2 | 0.2 | ..... | ..... |
| Bituminous coal and lignite | ..... | ..... | 1.0 | ..... | ..... | ..... | ..... | ..... | ..... | ..... |
| Crude petroleum and natural gas | 2.6 | ..... | ..... | ..... | ..... | ..... | ..... | ..... | ..... | ..... |
| Nonmetallic minerals | 1.7 | 2.1 | 2.9 | 1.1 | 0.8 | 0.9 | 0.7 | 0.7 | 0.4 | 0.5 |
| Scrap and waste | 67.9 | 107.7 | 175.4 | 126.9 | 126.1 | 2.5 | 3.0 | 6.4 | 1.5 | 1.9 |
| Used merchandise | 5.7 | 13.1 | 6.4 | 6.7 | 5.7 | 2.7 | 5.4 | 2.2 | 2.3 | 3.2 |
| Goods imported and returned unchanged | 10.9 | 10.2 | 10.8 | 14.0 | 14.9 | 10.9 | 10.2 | 10.8 | 14.0 | 14.9 |
| Special classification provisions | 10.0 | 14.8 | 18.7 | 5.5 | 5.5 | 3.3 | 2.2 | 2.9 | 2.0 | 1.3 |

## Table D-3.  State Exports of Goods by Destination and Industry, 1993–1997 —Continued

**OREGON** (Millions of dollars.)

| Industry | 1993 | 1994 | 1995 | 1996 | 1997 | 1993 | 1994 | 1995 | 1996 | 1997 |
|---|---|---|---|---|---|---|---|---|---|---|
| | South and Central America and Caribbean | | | | | Mexico | | | | |
| **ALL GOODS** | 137.7 | 123.9 | 196.2 | 121.9 | 193.3 | 109.0 | 120.6 | 86.1 | 52.8 | 88.8 |
| **Manufactured goods** | 117.8 | 115.6 | 164.7 | 108.6 | 179.6 | 102.8 | 117.9 | 84.4 | 50.7 | 84.8 |
| Food products | 1.0 | 1.0 | 4.4 | 3.2 | 3.8 | 1.5 | 1.5 | 1.7 | 1.7 | 4.4 |
| Tobacco products | ..... | ..... | ..... | ..... | ..... | ..... | ..... | ..... | ..... | ..... |
| Textile mill products | 5.0 | 2.6 | 2.9 | 4.5 | 2.5 | 0.2 | 0.3 | 0.6 | 0.6 | 1.8 |
| Apparel | 0.7 | 0.6 | 1.6 | 1.3 | 2.5 | 0.8 | 0.4 | 1.3 | 1.2 | 1.7 |
| Lumber and wood products | 1.0 | 2.4 | 4.7 | 9.7 | 9.5 | 3.3 | 2.7 | 1.1 | 2.8 | 6.9 |
| Furniture and fixtures | 0.2 | 0.2 | 0.3 | 0.1 | 0.2 | 0.5 | 0.2 | 0.1 | ..... | ..... |
| Paper products | 4.7 | 7.7 | 11.5 | 5.4 | 10.5 | 5.1 | 11.2 | 9.6 | 3.9 | 5.8 |
| Printing and publishing | 0.2 | 0.1 | 0.1 | ..... | 0.3 | 3.4 | 6.5 | 0.1 | 1.0 | 0.2 |
| Chemical products | 0.9 | 0.8 | 1.1 | 1.6 | 1.7 | 0.2 | 1.4 | 6.1 | 0.5 | 0.8 |
| Refined petroleum products | 0.1 | ..... | 0.1 | 0.1 | 0.1 | 0.1 | 0.1 | 0.2 | ..... | ..... |
| Rubber and plastic products | 0.3 | 1.5 | 1.2 | 0.3 | 0.8 | 4.0 | 3.9 | 4.3 | 1.4 | 3.3 |
| Leather products | 1.7 | 1.9 | 2.1 | 0.3 | 0.4 | 0.1 | 0.1 | ..... | ..... | 0.1 |
| Stone, clay and glass products | ..... | 0.2 | 0.6 | 0.2 | 0.1 | 1.2 | 0.1 | 0.1 | 0.1 | 0.4 |
| Primary metals | 2.6 | 2.9 | 2.6 | 1.0 | 23.6 | 0.7 | 0.3 | 0.2 | 0.1 | 0.2 |
| Fabricated metal products | 2.4 | 3.1 | 4.3 | 2.9 | 5.4 | 0.9 | 1.3 | 1.9 | 1.3 | 2.9 |
| Industrial machinery and computers | 44.0 | 45.2 | 43.2 | 37.5 | 59.1 | 22.3 | 28.9 | 48.0 | 25.6 | 35.1 |
| Electric and electronic equipment | 2.6 | 3.2 | 9.1 | 2.9 | 7.8 | 2.4 | 2.3 | 1.6 | 2.7 | 15.7 |
| Transportation equipment | 42.4 | 31.3 | 61.7 | 33.9 | 46.0 | 48.5 | 48.5 | 3.5 | 4.8 | 1.5 |
| Scientific and measuring instruments | 5.8 | 8.0 | 11.2 | 2.6 | 3.0 | 6.8 | 6.6 | 2.7 | 2.4 | 2.5 |
| Miscellaneous manufactures | 1.6 | 2.6 | 1.9 | 0.8 | 0.9 | 0.2 | 1.2 | 1.0 | 0.4 | 1.1 |
| Unidentified manufactures | 0.4 | 0.3 | 0.3 | 0.4 | 1.5 | 0.8 | 0.3 | 0.2 | 0.2 | 0.3 |
| **Agricultural and livestock products** | 17.2 | 8.0 | 31.3 | 13.2 | 13.2 | 4.7 | 1.8 | 1.2 | 0.7 | 2.6 |
| Agricultural products | 17.2 | 8.0 | 31.2 | 13.3 | 13.2 | 4.7 | 1.8 | 1.2 | 0.6 | 2.5 |
| Livestock and livestock products | ..... | ..... | 0.1 | ..... | ..... | ..... | ..... | ..... | ..... | 0.1 |
| **Other commodities** | 2.8 | 0.4 | 0.2 | ..... | 0.6 | 1.4 | 0.8 | 0.5 | 1.5 | 1.3 |
| Forestry products | ..... | ..... | ..... | ..... | ..... | 1.2 | 0.5 | 0.3 | 0.5 | 1.0 |
| Fish and other marine products | ..... | ..... | ..... | ..... | ..... | ..... | ..... | ..... | ..... | 0.2 |
| Metallic ores and concentrates | ..... | ..... | ..... | ..... | ..... | ..... | ..... | ..... | ..... | ..... |
| Bituminous coal and lignite | ..... | ..... | ..... | ..... | ..... | ..... | ..... | ..... | ..... | ..... |
| Crude petroleum and natural gas | 2.6 | ..... | ..... | ..... | ..... | ..... | ..... | ..... | ..... | ..... |
| Nonmetallic minerals | ..... | ..... | ..... | ..... | ..... | ..... | ..... | ..... | ..... | ..... |
| Scrap and waste | 0.1 | 0.3 | 0.2 | ..... | 0.1 | ..... | 0.1 | ..... | ..... | ..... |
| Used merchandise | ..... | ..... | ..... | 0.1 | 0.2 | 0.2 | 0.2 | 0.1 | ..... | 0.1 |
| Goods imported and returned unchanged | ..... | ..... | ..... | ..... | ..... | ..... | ..... | ..... | ..... | ..... |
| Special classification provisions | ..... | 0.1 | 0.1 | ..... | 0.2 | 0.1 | ..... | ..... | 1.0 | 0.1 |
| | European Union | | | | | United Kingdom | | | | |
| **ALL GOODS** | 1 085.7 | 1 164.3 | 1 725.3 | 952.9 | 1 061.8 | 250.2 | 304.9 | 352.4 | 161.6 | 191.0 |
| **Manufactured goods** | 1 056.5 | 1 124.6 | 1 683.6 | 922.8 | 1 031.1 | 246.7 | 294.0 | 344.5 | 155.2 | 186.7 |
| Food products | 5.6 | 8.1 | 15.4 | 11.3 | 9.5 | 1.4 | 1.5 | 3.5 | 1.3 | 1.4 |
| Tobacco products | ..... | ..... | ..... | ..... | 0.5 | ..... | ..... | ..... | ..... | ..... |
| Textile mill products | 2.0 | 0.4 | 0.5 | 0.4 | 0.5 | 0.8 | 0.2 | 0.2 | ..... | 0.1 |
| Apparel | 6.8 | 2.9 | 2.3 | 0.9 | 1.3 | 1.1 | 0.2 | 0.4 | 0.2 | 0.3 |
| Lumber and wood products | 156.9 | 153.1 | 99.3 | 70.0 | 102.1 | 18.7 | 14.4 | 9.3 | 8.5 | 24.4 |
| Furniture and fixtures | 1.7 | 1.3 | 1.2 | 0.9 | 0.9 | 0.4 | 0.4 | 0.4 | 0.5 | 0.5 |
| Paper products | 6.1 | 31.0 | 65.2 | 7.8 | 11.9 | 1.8 | 1.0 | 0.9 | 0.4 | 1.1 |
| Printing and publishing | 5.3 | 5.1 | 5.8 | 2.6 | 3.7 | 2.9 | 2.4 | 2.9 | 1.0 | 1.3 |
| Chemical products | 6.9 | 8.2 | 10.5 | 7.4 | 11.3 | 1.9 | 3.2 | 2.5 | 2.5 | 4.6 |
| Refined petroleum products | 0.4 | 0.1 | 0.1 | 0.4 | 0.5 | ..... | ..... | ..... | ..... | ..... |
| Rubber and plastic products | 7.4 | 5.4 | 10.6 | 3.1 | 10.9 | 1.1 | 0.4 | 0.6 | 0.6 | 4.2 |
| Leather products | 2.0 | 2.0 | 2.1 | 1.0 | 0.5 | 0.6 | 0.6 | 0.4 | 0.5 | 0.1 |
| Stone, clay and glass products | 4.6 | 8.0 | 4.9 | 7.3 | 10.4 | 1.7 | 2.3 | 1.9 | 3.4 | 4.7 |
| Primary metals | 29.5 | 30.9 | 55.8 | 28.6 | 46.8 | 4.7 | 3.7 | 4.0 | 4.0 | 5.9 |
| Fabricated metal products | 10.3 | 13.9 | 17.1 | 22.2 | 27.4 | 1.4 | 1.4 | 2.8 | 3.8 | 3.0 |
| Industrial machinery and computers | 454.8 | 436.8 | 831.8 | 515.0 | 518.3 | 125.7 | 157.9 | 172.0 | 56.6 | 62.9 |
| Electric and electronic equipment | 130.8 | 223.7 | 305.5 | 168.1 | 178.7 | 33.7 | 57.1 | 92.3 | 53.5 | 50.3 |
| Transportation equipment | 36.9 | 18.4 | 28.8 | 21.0 | 19.6 | 17.2 | 9.4 | 13.2 | 6.9 | 7.3 |
| Scientific and measuring instruments | 173.9 | 159.8 | 209.7 | 46.3 | 70.1 | 29.1 | 35.2 | 34.5 | 10.1 | 13.2 |
| Miscellaneous manufactures | 12.0 | 12.6 | 13.9 | 6.9 | 4.5 | 2.1 | 2.0 | 2.1 | 0.9 | 0.9 |
| Unidentified manufactures | 2.7 | 2.8 | 3.2 | 1.7 | 1.5 | 0.5 | 0.6 | 0.6 | 0.2 | 0.4 |
| **Agricultural and livestock products** | 23.7 | 27.1 | 28.9 | 23.9 | 27.2 | 2.2 | 3.5 | 3.2 | 3.8 | 3.3 |
| Agricultural products | 23.7 | 27.1 | 28.8 | 23.9 | 27.2 | 2.2 | 3.5 | 3.2 | 3.8 | 3.3 |
| Livestock and livestock products | ..... | ..... | 0.1 | ..... | ..... | ..... | ..... | ..... | ..... | ..... |
| **Other commodities** | 5.4 | 12.6 | 12.7 | 6.2 | 3.5 | 1.2 | 7.5 | 4.8 | 2.7 | 1.0 |
| Forestry products | ..... | ..... | 0.4 | 0.1 | 0.1 | ..... | ..... | 0.3 | 0.1 | ..... |
| Fish and other marine products | 1.2 | 2.5 | 0.7 | 0.7 | 0.6 | 0.1 | 0.2 | ..... | 0.1 | 0.2 |
| Metallic ores and concentrates | ..... | ..... | ..... | 0.1 | 0.1 | ..... | ..... | ..... | ..... | ..... |
| Bituminous coal and lignite | ..... | ..... | ..... | ..... | ..... | ..... | ..... | ..... | ..... | ..... |
| Crude petroleum and natural gas | ..... | ..... | ..... | ..... | ..... | ..... | ..... | ..... | ..... | ..... |
| Nonmetallic minerals | ..... | ..... | ..... | 0.3 | ..... | ..... | ..... | ..... | ..... | ..... |
| Scrap and waste | 0.5 | 0.5 | 4.6 | 1.5 | 1.6 | ..... | 0.2 | ..... | ..... | 0.4 |
| Used merchandise | 0.2 | 1.1 | 0.5 | 2.5 | 0.2 | 0.1 | 0.5 | 0.1 | 2.3 | 0.1 |
| Goods imported and returned unchanged | ..... | ..... | ..... | ..... | ..... | ..... | ..... | ..... | ..... | ..... |
| Special classification provisions | 3.4 | 8.5 | 6.5 | 1.0 | 0.9 | 1.0 | 6.5 | 4.3 | 0.2 | 0.3 |

## Table D-3. State Exports of Goods by Destination and Industry, 1993–1997 —*Continued*

**OREGON** (Millions of dollars.)

| Industry | 1993 | 1994 | 1995 | 1996 | 1997 | 1993 | 1994 | 1995 | 1996 | 1997 |
|---|---|---|---|---|---|---|---|---|---|---|
| | Germany | | | | | France | | | | |
| **ALL GOODS** | 367.2 | 305.7 | 414.2 | 306.1 | 213.0 | 92.4 | 115.5 | 242.6 | 117.5 | 81.2 |
| **Manufactured goods** | 362.9 | 298.0 | 406.8 | 300.5 | 208.6 | 90.7 | 112.6 | 239.5 | 115.1 | 78.8 |
| Food products | 0.5 | 0.7 | 1.3 | 0.8 | 1.2 | 0.4 | 0.4 | 1.2 | 0.3 | 0.1 |
| Tobacco products | ..... | ..... | ..... | ..... | ..... | ..... | ..... | ..... | ..... | ..... |
| Textile mill products | 0.1 | 0.1 | ..... | 0.1 | 0.1 | 0.8 | ..... | ..... | ..... | ..... |
| Apparel | 2.1 | 1.3 | 0.7 | 0.2 | 0.2 | 1.3 | 0.6 | 0.2 | ..... | 0.1 |
| Lumber and wood products | 59.5 | 51.8 | 41.2 | 20.8 | 29.3 | 3.1 | 3.4 | 2.1 | 1.2 | 2.3 |
| Furniture and fixtures | 0.7 | 0.2 | 0.2 | 0.1 | 0.1 | 0.1 | 0.3 | 0.1 | ..... | 0.1 |
| Paper products | 2.0 | 13.2 | 15.1 | 4.2 | 1.0 | ..... | 1.1 | 0.1 | ..... | 1.1 |
| Printing and publishing | 1.1 | 1.1 | 0.4 | 0.1 | 0.8 | 0.2 | 0.3 | 1.1 | 0.1 | 0.2 |
| Chemical products | 0.8 | 0.6 | 1.1 | 1.2 | 1.4 | 1.6 | 1.4 | 0.6 | 0.3 | 0.6 |
| Refined petroleum products | 0.3 | ..... | ..... | ..... | ..... | ..... | 0.1 | 0.1 | 0.4 | 0.4 |
| Rubber and plastic products | 0.9 | 1.1 | 0.7 | 0.5 | 0.3 | 1.0 | 1.2 | 0.4 | 0.1 | 0.1 |
| Leather products | 0.5 | 0.4 | 0.4 | 0.3 | 0.1 | 0.1 | 0.1 | 0.1 | ..... | ..... |
| Stone, clay and glass products | 0.6 | 0.6 | 0.6 | 1.2 | 3.9 | 1.1 | 4.4 | 1.7 | 1.9 | 0.8 |
| Primary metals | 14.5 | 13.6 | 31.3 | 3.8 | 8.6 | 2.6 | 5.0 | 7.0 | 5.6 | 14.1 |
| Fabricated metal products | 1.1 | 2.0 | 3.4 | 5.5 | 7.3 | 0.3 | 1.3 | 1.2 | 0.8 | 2.3 |
| Industrial machinery and computers | 199.2 | 126.3 | 204.9 | 221.1 | 114.4 | 35.2 | 43.0 | 136.1 | 80.0 | 26.9 |
| Electric and electronic equipment | 27.3 | 33.8 | 33.7 | 26.7 | 25.4 | 19.3 | 25.0 | 54.5 | 16.1 | 20.8 |
| Transportation equipment | 3.2 | 4.1 | 3.6 | 5.3 | 4.3 | 0.5 | 0.7 | 3.6 | 2.8 | 3.1 |
| Scientific and measuring instruments | 46.3 | 45.3 | 65.8 | 6.9 | 9.3 | 22.6 | 23.3 | 28.3 | 4.4 | 5.3 |
| Miscellaneous manufactures | 1.6 | 1.2 | 1.7 | 1.2 | 0.6 | 0.3 | 0.4 | 0.9 | 0.9 | 0.2 |
| Unidentified manufactures | 0.5 | 0.5 | 0.8 | 0.4 | 0.2 | 0.1 | 0.6 | 0.4 | 0.2 | 0.2 |
| **Agricultural and livestock products** | 4.0 | 6.8 | 6.4 | 4.8 | 4.2 | 1.3 | 1.7 | 2.7 | 1.8 | 2.2 |
| Agricultural products | 4.0 | 6.8 | 6.4 | 4.8 | 4.2 | 1.3 | 1.7 | 2.7 | 1.8 | 2.2 |
| Livestock and livestock products | ..... | ..... | ..... | ..... | ..... | ..... | ..... | ..... | ..... | ..... |
| **Other commodities** | 0.3 | 0.8 | 1.0 | 0.7 | 0.3 | 0.4 | 1.2 | 0.4 | 0.5 | 0.1 |
| Forestry products | ..... | ..... | ..... | 0.1 | ..... | ..... | ..... | ..... | ..... | ..... |
| Fish and other marine products | 0.1 | ..... | ..... | 0.1 | 0.1 | ..... | 0.1 | ..... | ..... | ..... |
| Metallic ores and concentrates | ..... | ..... | ..... | ..... | ..... | ..... | ..... | ..... | 0.1 | ..... |
| Bituminous coal and lignite | ..... | ..... | ..... | ..... | ..... | ..... | ..... | ..... | ..... | ..... |
| Crude petroleum and natural gas | ..... | ..... | ..... | ..... | ..... | ..... | ..... | ..... | ..... | ..... |
| Nonmetallic minerals | ..... | ..... | ..... | ..... | ..... | ..... | ..... | ..... | 0.3 | ..... |
| Scrap and waste | ..... | ..... | 0.4 | 0.1 | 0.1 | 0.1 | 0.1 | ..... | ..... | ..... |
| Used merchandise | 0.1 | 0.1 | 0.1 | 0.1 | 0.1 | ..... | 0.4 | 0.2 | 0.1 | ..... |
| Goods imported and returned unchanged | ..... | ..... | ..... | ..... | ..... | ..... | ..... | ..... | ..... | ..... |
| Special classification provisions | 0.1 | 0.6 | 0.4 | 0.3 | ..... | 0.2 | 0.7 | 0.2 | ..... | 0.1 |
| | The Netherlands | | | | | Asian 10 | | | | |
| **ALL GOODS** | 95.2 | 106.9 | 178.9 | 46.1 | 198.3 | 3 283.2 | 3 654.0 | 5 675.0 | 5 419.7 | 5 147.9 |
| **Manufactured goods** | 87.2 | 100.6 | 171.6 | 41.4 | 192.5 | 1 556.2 | 1 848.7 | 2 919.9 | 2 603.6 | 2 713.1 |
| Food products | 0.2 | 2.3 | 3.3 | 0.3 | 0.2 | 95.4 | 112.9 | 127.2 | 124.1 | 144.6 |
| Tobacco products | ..... | ..... | ..... | ..... | 0.5 | ..... | 0.1 | ..... | ..... | ..... |
| Textile mill products | 0.1 | ..... | 0.1 | 0.1 | 0.1 | 1.3 | 1.4 | 1.9 | 1.2 | 1.0 |
| Apparel | 0.4 | 0.2 | 0.2 | 0.3 | 0.3 | 6.5 | 8.1 | 9.8 | 7.2 | 5.6 |
| Lumber and wood products | 6.5 | 6.9 | 3.7 | 3.2 | 2.8 | 436.0 | 414.3 | 450.6 | 276.0 | 243.2 |
| Furniture and fixtures | 0.2 | 0.1 | 0.1 | ..... | 0.1 | 1.5 | 2.5 | 4.6 | 4.5 | 3.8 |
| Paper products | 0.2 | 1.0 | 4.8 | 1.2 | 1.4 | 57.0 | 96.8 | 159.1 | 234.5 | 223.3 |
| Printing and publishing | 0.7 | 0.6 | 1.1 | 0.2 | 0.2 | 5.6 | 9.7 | 9.3 | 10.4 | 8.1 |
| Chemical products | 0.7 | 1.0 | 4.8 | 0.2 | 0.3 | 7.9 | 8.1 | 14.5 | 9.8 | 16.5 |
| Refined petroleum products | ..... | ..... | ..... | ..... | ..... | 0.2 | 0.2 | 1.7 | 1.2 | 1.2 |
| Rubber and plastic products | 1.6 | 1.1 | 7.1 | 0.1 | 0.2 | 16.8 | 15.3 | 28.2 | 28.5 | 14.5 |
| Leather products | ..... | ..... | 0.2 | ..... | ..... | 29.6 | 42.7 | 65.0 | 17.0 | 25.3 |
| Stone, clay and glass products | ..... | ..... | ..... | 0.1 | ..... | 5.6 | 5.3 | 7.6 | 12.6 | 13.0 |
| Primary metals | 0.4 | 0.8 | 0.2 | 0.3 | 0.3 | 12.8 | 27.4 | 53.6 | 33.7 | 51.9 |
| Fabricated metal products | 0.6 | 0.5 | 0.5 | 0.5 | 0.8 | 20.3 | 25.3 | 29.7 | 33.3 | 43.7 |
| Industrial machinery and computers | 34.6 | 39.7 | 89.5 | 22.0 | 155.2 | 246.4 | 340.2 | 702.2 | 505.7 | 626.2 |
| Electric and electronic equipment | 13.1 | 23.9 | 25.2 | 6.9 | 22.5 | 417.0 | 512.9 | 974.9 | 1 192.9 | 1 196.6 |
| Transportation equipment | 1.3 | 2.1 | 1.8 | 0.6 | 1.0 | 42.0 | 35.8 | 28.6 | 19.9 | 26.9 |
| Scientific and measuring instruments | 24.1 | 13.8 | 21.7 | 4.9 | 5.9 | 133.6 | 167.2 | 217.7 | 71.5 | 49.0 |
| Miscellaneous manufactures | 2.4 | 6.2 | 6.8 | 0.3 | 0.4 | 19.1 | 20.4 | 30.7 | 18.1 | 16.3 |
| Unidentified manufactures | 0.3 | 0.4 | 0.4 | 0.2 | 0.1 | 1.6 | 2.0 | 3.0 | 1.6 | 2.2 |
| **Agricultural and livestock products** | 6.1 | 5.7 | 6.1 | 4.4 | 5.5 | 1 647.1 | 1 686.3 | 2 571.5 | 2 685.2 | 2 300.0 |
| Agricultural products | 6.1 | 5.7 | 6.1 | 4.4 | 5.5 | 1 646.8 | 1 686.0 | 2 571.3 | 2 685.1 | 2 299.8 |
| Livestock and livestock products | ..... | ..... | ..... | ..... | ..... | 0.3 | 0.2 | 0.1 | ..... | 0.2 |
| **Other commodities** | 2.0 | 0.5 | 1.2 | 0.3 | 0.3 | 79.9 | 119.0 | 183.7 | 130.9 | 134.7 |
| Forestry products | ..... | ..... | 0.1 | ..... | ..... | 0.9 | 0.2 | 0.2 | 0.1 | 0.1 |
| Fish and other marine products | ..... | ..... | ..... | 0.2 | 0.1 | 10.3 | 13.1 | 14.9 | 5.4 | 9.1 |
| Metallic ores and concentrates | ..... | ..... | ..... | ..... | ..... | ..... | ..... | ..... | ..... | ..... |
| Bituminous coal and lignite | ..... | ..... | ..... | ..... | ..... | ..... | ..... | ..... | ..... | ..... |
| Crude petroleum and natural gas | ..... | ..... | ..... | ..... | ..... | ..... | ..... | ..... | ..... | ..... |
| Nonmetallic minerals | ..... | ..... | ..... | ..... | ..... | 0.7 | 1.3 | 2.1 | 0.3 | 0.3 |
| Scrap and waste | ..... | ..... | 0.2 | ..... | 0.1 | 64.2 | 99.7 | 157.1 | 122.6 | 121.2 |
| Used merchandise | ..... | ..... | ..... | ..... | ..... | 1.5 | 1.9 | 1.6 | 1.0 | 1.3 |
| Goods imported and returned unchanged | ..... | ..... | ..... | ..... | ..... | ..... | ..... | ..... | ..... | ..... |
| Special classification provisions | 1.9 | 0.5 | 1.0 | ..... | 0.1 | 2.4 | 2.9 | 7.9 | 1.4 | 2.7 |

## Table D-3.  State Exports of Goods by Destination and Industry, 1993–1997 —Continued

**OREGON** (Millions of dollars.)

| Industry | 1993 | 1994 | 1995 | 1996 | 1997 | 1993 | 1994 | 1995 | 1996 | 1997 |
|---|---|---|---|---|---|---|---|---|---|---|
| | Japan | | | | | South Korea | | | | |
| ALL GOODS | 1 257.1 | 1 389.1 | 1 778.7 | 1 487.2 | 1 271.8 | 428.5 | 550.9 | 936.5 | 905.5 | 1 037.8 |
| **Manufactured goods** | 722.8 | 792.6 | 1 058.9 | 751.5 | 633.2 | 197.2 | 249.2 | 355.6 | 355.1 | 609.8 |
| Food products | 62.0 | 68.5 | 78.0 | 75.7 | 89.9 | 8.8 | 11.1 | 10.1 | 8.0 | 9.3 |
| Tobacco products | ..... | ..... | ..... | ..... | ..... | ..... | ..... | ..... | ..... | ..... |
| Textile mill products | 0.3 | 0.4 | 1.5 | 0.8 | 0.6 | 0.3 | ..... | 0.1 | 0.1 | 0.1 |
| Apparel | 5.0 | 6.9 | 9.3 | 4.8 | 5.0 | 0.1 | 0.3 | 0.1 | 2.2 | 0.3 |
| Lumber and wood products | 340.2 | 337.4 | 379.9 | 232.1 | 182.3 | 38.7 | 29.9 | 22.4 | 9.3 | 13.8 |
| Furniture and fixtures | 1.4 | 2.3 | 3.7 | 4.2 | 3.0 | ..... | 0.1 | 0.7 | ..... | ..... |
| Paper products | 22.6 | 5.3 | 6.0 | 19.3 | 9.4 | 8.7 | 27.2 | 32.8 | 32.4 | 29.4 |
| Printing and publishing | 0.9 | 3.8 | 4.0 | 2.9 | 1.5 | 0.3 | 0.2 | 1.4 | 1.1 | 0.8 |
| Chemical products | 2.5 | 2.8 | 6.9 | 5.2 | 7.1 | 1.4 | 1.4 | 2.5 | 0.9 | 2.0 |
| Refined petroleum products | 0.1 | 0.2 | 1.6 | 1.1 | 1.1 | ..... | ..... | ..... | ..... | ..... |
| Rubber and plastic products | 4.8 | 8.7 | 21.5 | 17.0 | 7.8 | 0.5 | 0.8 | 1.8 | 1.1 | 0.5 |
| Leather products | 1.0 | 1.9 | 1.5 | 1.3 | 1.8 | 13.2 | 13.8 | 22.4 | 12.3 | 9.8 |
| Stone, clay and glass products | 3.1 | 3.2 | 3.7 | 5.6 | 8.0 | 0.8 | 1.4 | 2.6 | 4.5 | 2.7 |
| Primary metals | 6.6 | 21.4 | 13.0 | 7.9 | 21.3 | 1.7 | 1.1 | 8.9 | 0.7 | 1.0 |
| Fabricated metal products | 7.9 | 10.4 | 9.8 | 10.8 | 15.1 | 1.0 | 2.4 | 1.0 | 1.3 | 2.4 |
| Industrial machinery and computers | 91.0 | 122.7 | 257.2 | 194.6 | 161.9 | 18.8 | 31.1 | 52.8 | 24.3 | 47.8 |
| Electric and electronic equipment | 86.7 | 94.5 | 127.8 | 101.9 | 88.1 | 87.0 | 100.3 | 163.9 | 247.5 | 466.8 |
| Transportation equipment | 10.1 | 10.8 | 9.4 | 8.0 | 4.1 | 0.5 | 1.7 | 3.3 | 2.3 | 11.8 |
| Scientific and measuring instruments | 65.0 | 77.0 | 99.3 | 44.4 | 12.5 | 12.5 | 24.2 | 26.4 | 5.0 | 9.8 |
| Miscellaneous manufactures | 11.1 | 13.6 | 23.2 | 13.2 | 11.6 | 2.8 | 1.8 | 2.0 | 2.0 | 1.5 |
| Unidentified manufactures | 0.7 | 0.8 | 1.5 | 0.8 | 1.0 | 0.2 | 0.3 | 0.3 | 0.2 | 0.1 |
| **Agricultural and livestock products** | 507.4 | 559.5 | 669.7 | 711.2 | 612.3 | 204.1 | 255.1 | 506.0 | 482.2 | 354.5 |
| Agricultural products | 507.4 | 559.5 | 669.7 | 711.2 | 612.2 | 204.1 | 255.1 | 506.0 | 482.1 | 354.5 |
| Livestock and livestock products | ..... | ..... | ..... | ..... | 0.1 | ..... | ..... | ..... | ..... | ..... |
| **Other commodities** | 26.9 | 37.0 | 50.0 | 24.6 | 26.3 | 27.2 | 46.7 | 74.8 | 68.2 | 73.5 |
| Forestry products | 0.7 | 0.1 | 0.1 | 0.1 | 0.1 | 0.2 | ..... | ..... | ..... | ..... |
| Fish and other marine products | 8.8 | 10.7 | 10.9 | 3.5 | 5.8 | 0.3 | 0.7 | 2.5 | 0.7 | 1.2 |
| Metallic ores and concentrates | ..... | ..... | ..... | ..... | ..... | ..... | ..... | ..... | ..... | ..... |
| Bituminous coal and lignite | ..... | ..... | ..... | ..... | ..... | ..... | ..... | ..... | ..... | ..... |
| Crude petroleum and natural gas | ..... | ..... | ..... | ..... | ..... | ..... | ..... | ..... | ..... | ..... |
| Nonmetallic minerals | ..... | 0.2 | 0.2 | 0.3 | 0.3 | ..... | ..... | ..... | ..... | ..... |
| Scrap and waste | 15.1 | 23.5 | 36.4 | 19.5 | 17.9 | 26.6 | 45.4 | 71.1 | 67.5 | 72.2 |
| Used merchandise | 1.2 | 1.9 | 1.2 | 0.8 | 1.2 | 0.1 | ..... | ..... | ..... | ..... |
| Goods imported and returned unchanged | ..... | ..... | ..... | ..... | ..... | ..... | ..... | ..... | ..... | ..... |
| Special classification provisions | 1.2 | 0.7 | 1.3 | 0.5 | 1.0 | ..... | 0.5 | 1.2 | 0.1 | ..... |
| | Taiwan | | | | | Singapore | | | | |
| ALL GOODS | 742.2 | 688.4 | 1 057.7 | 1 047.0 | 1 063.4 | 228.6 | 252.0 | 507.3 | 560.8 | 449.8 |
| **Manufactured goods** | 144.0 | 147.3 | 202.7 | 159.3 | 206.9 | 223.4 | 249.0 | 499.6 | 550.9 | 444.4 |
| Food products | 5.7 | 8.0 | 10.1 | 6.7 | 7.3 | 2.4 | 3.1 | 5.5 | 3.3 | 2.9 |
| Tobacco products | ..... | ..... | ..... | ..... | ..... | ..... | ..... | ..... | ..... | ..... |
| Textile mill products | 0.2 | 0.2 | ..... | 0.1 | ..... | 0.1 | ..... | ..... | 0.1 | ..... |
| Apparel | 0.2 | 0.5 | ..... | ..... | ..... | 0.8 | 0.1 | 0.1 | 0.1 | ..... |
| Lumber and wood products | 26.3 | 27.1 | 20.9 | 13.4 | 18.6 | 0.5 | 1.0 | 1.7 | 0.8 | 0.9 |
| Furniture and fixtures | ..... | ..... | ..... | ..... | 0.1 | ..... | ..... | 0.1 | ..... | 0.1 |
| Paper products | 7.1 | 9.8 | 24.7 | 15.2 | 21.4 | 1.2 | 4.0 | 15.3 | 15.1 | 14.3 |
| Printing and publishing | 0.9 | 0.6 | 0.5 | 0.6 | 0.4 | 0.8 | 1.9 | 0.6 | 1.4 | 1.7 |
| Chemical products | 2.0 | 1.5 | 1.5 | 0.5 | 0.3 | 0.5 | 0.6 | 0.7 | 0.5 | 2.1 |
| Refined petroleum products | 0.1 | ..... | ..... | ..... | ..... | ..... | ..... | ..... | ..... | ..... |
| Rubber and plastic products | 8.7 | 0.2 | 0.7 | 0.6 | 0.5 | 2.0 | 3.6 | 2.8 | 4.0 | 2.3 |
| Leather products | 7.4 | 9.3 | 8.2 | 0.1 | 0.1 | ..... | 0.1 | ..... | ..... | 0.1 |
| Stone, clay and glass products | 0.4 | 0.4 | 0.3 | 0.6 | 0.6 | 1.0 | 0.1 | 0.2 | 1.2 | 0.3 |
| Primary metals | 0.8 | 1.7 | 2.8 | 19.8 | 26.6 | 0.3 | 1.4 | 25.8 | 1.1 | 0.5 |
| Fabricated metal products | 3.0 | 1.0 | 0.6 | 1.2 | 1.2 | 5.2 | 4.5 | 9.2 | 2.3 | 2.9 |
| Industrial machinery and computers | 14.1 | 20.0 | 36.7 | 30.7 | 84.2 | 74.3 | 86.4 | 155.7 | 164.3 | 190.0 |
| Electric and electronic equipment | 46.9 | 44.9 | 69.1 | 63.0 | 39.6 | 127.8 | 130.8 | 260.2 | 350.3 | 217.1 |
| Transportation equipment | 4.1 | 2.8 | 1.5 | 0.4 | 0.4 | 0.4 | 0.4 | 0.4 | 1.0 | 0.8 |
| Scientific and measuring instruments | 14.7 | 16.9 | 22.4 | 5.6 | 4.9 | 4.7 | 10.2 | 20.5 | 4.8 | 7.8 |
| Miscellaneous manufactures | 1.2 | 1.9 | 2.3 | 0.8 | 0.4 | 1.5 | 0.8 | 0.6 | 0.3 | 0.4 |
| Unidentified manufactures | 0.2 | 0.3 | 0.3 | 0.1 | 0.1 | 0.1 | 0.2 | 0.2 | 0.2 | 0.2 |
| **Agricultural and livestock products** | 593.7 | 532.3 | 839.5 | 878.8 | 846.2 | 4.9 | 2.0 | 5.4 | 9.3 | 4.4 |
| Agricultural products | 593.7 | 532.3 | 839.5 | 878.8 | 846.2 | 4.9 | 2.0 | 5.4 | 9.3 | 4.4 |
| Livestock and livestock products | ..... | ..... | ..... | ..... | ..... | ..... | ..... | ..... | ..... | ..... |
| **Other commodities** | 4.5 | 8.8 | 15.5 | 8.9 | 10.4 | 0.3 | 1.0 | 2.3 | 0.6 | 1.1 |
| Forestry products | ..... | ..... | ..... | ..... | ..... | ..... | ..... | ..... | ..... | ..... |
| Fish and other marine products | 0.1 | 0.1 | 0.1 | 0.3 | 0.4 | ..... | ..... | ..... | 0.1 | 0.1 |
| Metallic ores and concentrates | ..... | ..... | ..... | ..... | ..... | ..... | ..... | ..... | ..... | ..... |
| Bituminous coal and lignite | ..... | ..... | ..... | ..... | ..... | ..... | ..... | ..... | ..... | ..... |
| Crude petroleum and natural gas | ..... | ..... | ..... | ..... | ..... | ..... | ..... | ..... | ..... | ..... |
| Nonmetallic minerals | ..... | ..... | ..... | ..... | ..... | ..... | ..... | ..... | 0.1 | ..... |
| Scrap and waste | 4.2 | 8.2 | 14.3 | 8.6 | 9.4 | ..... | 0.3 | 0.4 | 0.1 | ..... |
| Used merchandise | 0.1 | ..... | ..... | ..... | ..... | ..... | ..... | 0.1 | ..... | ..... |
| Goods imported and returned unchanged | ..... | ..... | ..... | ..... | ..... | ..... | ..... | ..... | ..... | ..... |
| Special classification provisions | 0.1 | 0.4 | 1.1 | 0.1 | 0.5 | 0.3 | 0.6 | 1.6 | 0.4 | 0.9 |

## PENNSYLVANIA: Exports of Goods, 1997

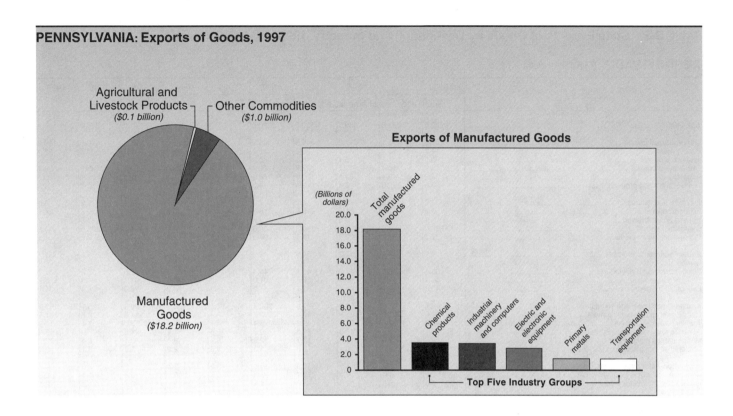

Agricultural and Livestock Products ($0.1 billion)

Other Commodities ($1.0 billion)

Manufactured Goods ($18.2 billion)

**Exports of Manufactured Goods**

(Billions of dollars)

Total manufactured goods

Top Five Industry Groups

Chemical products | Industrial machinery and computers | Electric and electronic equipment | Primary metals | Transportation equipment

## Table D-3.   State Exports of Goods by Destination and Industry, 1993–1997 —*Continued*

**PENNSYLVANIA** (Millions of dollars.)

| Industry | 1993 | 1994 | 1995 | 1996 | 1997 | 1993 | 1994 | 1995 | 1996 | 1997 |
|---|---|---|---|---|---|---|---|---|---|---|
| | All destinations | | | | | Canada | | | | |
| **ALL GOODS** | 13 189.6 | 14 698.6 | 17 680.2 | 17 445.6 | 19 298.4 | 3 730.3 | 4 066.5 | 4 671.8 | 4 773.7 | 5 615.7 |
| **Manufactured goods** | 12 285.8 | 13 755.6 | 16 551.0 | 16 400.2 | 18 172.0 | 3 516.5 | 3 838.7 | 4 387.9 | 4 494.8 | 5 303.9 |
| Food products | 435.4 | 425.9 | 378.9 | 512.7 | 516.5 | 119.3 | 122.3 | 126.9 | 152.8 | 160.2 |
| Tobacco products | 0.5 | 0.3 | 9.7 | 5.9 | 1.1 | 0.2 | 0.1 | ..... | 0.1 | 0.5 |
| Textile mill products | 126.0 | 164.1 | 185.5 | 232.5 | 220.6 | 27.9 | 43.7 | 50.0 | 65.6 | 70.5 |
| Apparel | 93.2 | 153.9 | 236.8 | 251.3 | 221.8 | 23.0 | 17.7 | 56.5 | 55.8 | 48.3 |
| Lumber and wood products | 258.8 | 281.3 | 288.8 | 285.6 | 325.3 | 106.2 | 116.9 | 105.4 | 111.2 | 126.1 |
| Furniture and fixtures | 62.5 | 74.7 | 75.0 | 71.6 | 87.7 | 36.0 | 42.8 | 45.0 | 40.6 | 49.4 |
| Paper products | 156.5 | 182.3 | 289.2 | 250.1 | 308.6 | 84.0 | 111.8 | 179.2 | 143.8 | 179.2 |
| Printing and publishing | 257.6 | 183.9 | 204.8 | 225.4 | 230.4 | 120.3 | 126.9 | 148.5 | 159.5 | 175.2 |
| Chemical products | 2 465.5 | 2 731.0 | 3 570.6 | 3 335.7 | 3 537.2 | 495.2 | 533.8 | 602.9 | 670.6 | 771.3 |
| Refined petroleum products | 152.0 | 143.1 | 151.7 | 156.1 | 192.4 | 64.9 | 72.9 | 77.8 | 84.2 | 92.6 |
| Rubber and plastic products | 354.5 | 438.7 | 501.4 | 565.5 | 601.8 | 102.2 | 122.6 | 140.3 | 159.4 | 177.6 |
| Leather products | 76.4 | 59.3 | 31.8 | 45.9 | 56.9 | 10.4 | 23.7 | 8.6 | 11.2 | 10.4 |
| Stone, clay and glass products | 471.7 | 483.4 | 553.3 | 556.5 | 606.3 | 215.2 | 235.9 | 251.5 | 251.5 | 250.5 |
| Primary metals | 865.7 | 921.2 | 1 741.4 | 1 459.6 | 1 500.8 | 354.0 | 360.7 | 485.8 | 497.3 | 644.9 |
| Fabricated metal products | 430.0 | 533.6 | 618.2 | 581.9 | 663.0 | 159.2 | 154.8 | 179.4 | 202.1 | 255.0 |
| Industrial machinery and computers | 2 208.9 | 2 519.9 | 2 941.6 | 3 079.8 | 3 443.6 | 533.6 | 584.4 | 585.1 | 652.7 | 748.4 |
| Electric and electronic equipment | 1 861.3 | 2 337.5 | 2 455.1 | 2 424.0 | 2 841.1 | 318.2 | 394.3 | 438.3 | 425.4 | 419.2 |
| Transportation equipment | 1 025.5 | 1 030.2 | 1 201.1 | 1 131.7 | 1 480.4 | 493.7 | 461.0 | 579.3 | 467.3 | 749.9 |
| Scientific and measuring instruments | 690.6 | 747.9 | 772.4 | 839.5 | 924.1 | 150.4 | 189.0 | 206.5 | 217.9 | 245.2 |
| Miscellaneous manufactures | 238.1 | 277.0 | 295.4 | 340.8 | 356.9 | 92.7 | 110.1 | 105.6 | 110.0 | 113.8 |
| Unidentified manufactures | 55.1 | 66.3 | 48.4 | 48.4 | 55.5 | 9.9 | 13.5 | 15.2 | 15.6 | 15.8 |
| **Agricultural and livestock products** | 87.8 | 86.4 | 78.7 | 93.4 | 120.2 | 67.6 | 58.4 | 55.5 | 60.6 | 71.5 |
| Agricultural products | 67.0 | 59.2 | 59.4 | 74.4 | 99.0 | 58.8 | 47.6 | 46.8 | 50.9 | 59.4 |
| Livestock and livestock products | 20.9 | 27.2 | 19.3 | 19.1 | 21.2 | 8.8 | 10.8 | 8.8 | 9.7 | 12.1 |
| **Other commodities** | 816.0 | 856.7 | 1 050.5 | 951.9 | 1 006.2 | 146.2 | 169.4 | 228.3 | 218.4 | 240.3 |
| Forestry products | 26.2 | 30.0 | 34.7 | 28.3 | 30.4 | 0.6 | 0.4 | 0.5 | 0.9 | 0.8 |
| Fish and other marine products | 14.6 | 10.7 | 11.1 | 10.8 | 13.5 | 3.4 | 3.9 | 2.0 | 5.0 | 1.9 |
| Metallic ores and concentrates | 11.9 | 21.7 | 27.7 | 26.0 | 24.8 | 3.6 | 6.8 | 8.4 | 7.6 | 7.4 |
| Bituminous coal and lignite | 522.5 | 388.5 | 437.6 | 423.5 | 428.7 | 32.6 | 47.6 | 45.8 | 52.6 | 71.8 |
| Crude petroleum and natural gas | 18.0 | 9.8 | 16.7 | 19.3 | 21.5 | 15.4 | 6.0 | 11.2 | 6.1 | 9.4 |
| Nonmetallic minerals | 32.3 | 34.9 | 44.5 | 42.2 | 37.8 | 3.1 | 2.7 | 4.1 | 4.9 | 3.8 |
| Scrap and waste | 59.5 | 68.5 | 241.4 | 264.3 | 314.8 | 42.8 | 48.4 | 88.3 | 53.6 | 57.4 |
| Used merchandise | 21.3 | 73.2 | 49.7 | 44.1 | 38.6 | 2.9 | 3.1 | 2.9 | 6.0 | 5.3 |
| Goods imported and returned unchanged | 34.0 | 40.9 | 51.9 | 71.4 | 72.3 | 34.0 | 40.9 | 51.9 | 71.4 | 72.3 |
| Special classification provisions | 75.8 | 178.4 | 135.2 | 22.0 | 23.7 | 7.7 | 9.6 | 13.2 | 10.4 | 10.0 |

## Table D-3.  State Exports of Goods by Destination and Industry, 1993–1997 —*Continued*

### PENNSYLVANIA  (Millions of dollars.)

| Industry | 1993 | 1994 | 1995 | 1996 | 1997 | 1993 | 1994 | 1995 | 1996 | 1997 |
|---|---|---|---|---|---|---|---|---|---|---|
| | South and Central America and Caribbean | | | | | Mexico | | | | |
| **ALL GOODS** | 1 220.5 | 1 363.6 | 1 689.7 | 1 550.3 | 1 820.8 | 627.3 | 866.4 | 741.2 | 879.0 | 1 140.3 |
| **Manufactured goods** | 1 157.8 | 1 298.1 | 1 611.3 | 1 446.3 | 1 696.6 | 621.3 | 835.9 | 734.4 | 870.7 | 1 116.9 |
| Food products | 14.2 | 16.2 | 20.2 | 36.0 | 45.2 | 51.4 | 23.9 | 16.1 | 31.2 | 22.4 |
| Tobacco products | 0.1 | ..... | 0.1 | 0.4 | 0.2 | ..... | ..... | ..... | ..... | ..... |
| Textile mill products | 14.8 | 10.1 | 12.1 | 27.7 | 38.9 | 26.4 | 36.5 | 34.8 | 35.9 | 28.7 |
| Apparel | 33.2 | 48.4 | 81.1 | 100.7 | 88.5 | 5.9 | 7.0 | 13.1 | 21.9 | 20.7 |
| Lumber and wood products | 3.0 | 2.8 | 2.4 | 3.4 | 4.3 | 4.8 | 5.3 | 1.2 | 2.3 | 3.6 |
| Furniture and fixtures | 3.2 | 2.6 | 3.2 | 4.2 | 4.9 | 1.9 | 3.7 | 3.5 | 2.2 | 4.4 |
| Paper products | 9.2 | 7.6 | 11.9 | 16.8 | 16.7 | 10.5 | 16.5 | 30.3 | 19.5 | 24.8 |
| Printing and publishing | 5.7 | 5.7 | 3.8 | 2.0 | 2.5 | 1.1 | 2.0 | 2.2 | 2.5 | 4.2 |
| Chemical products | 288.6 | 323.7 | 436.9 | 355.2 | 349.6 | 155.1 | 217.6 | 207.0 | 225.9 | 319.2 |
| Refined petroleum products | 27.3 | 25.1 | 22.3 | 16.1 | 24.8 | 1.2 | 2.6 | 1.9 | 0.9 | 1.0 |
| Rubber and plastic products | 14.7 | 16.4 | 37.2 | 34.5 | 42.3 | 13.4 | 36.6 | 30.4 | 29.2 | 31.2 |
| Leather products | 12.2 | 10.3 | 1.9 | 2.6 | 3.4 | 0.5 | 0.5 | 0.1 | ..... | 0.3 |
| Stone, clay and glass products | 35.4 | 40.5 | 48.2 | 40.8 | 45.4 | 17.2 | 34.7 | 22.5 | 26.2 | 31.4 |
| Primary metals | 62.4 | 67.5 | 76.9 | 67.6 | 101.0 | 55.8 | 79.6 | 93.2 | 91.3 | 113.2 |
| Fabricated metal products | 40.8 | 62.7 | 85.6 | 39.7 | 51.9 | 14.8 | 34.9 | 26.0 | 24.4 | 31.1 |
| Industrial machinery and computers | 266.6 | 276.4 | 269.0 | 241.0 | 332.9 | 97.5 | 156.6 | 96.0 | 125.1 | 183.2 |
| Electric and electronic equipment | 237.6 | 294.8 | 375.9 | 349.5 | 390.4 | 112.4 | 118.5 | 114.5 | 178.8 | 231.1 |
| Transportation equipment | 46.0 | 32.8 | 58.6 | 49.0 | 76.4 | 14.1 | 14.8 | 12.0 | 7.1 | 11.3 |
| Scientific and measuring instruments | 32.1 | 41.6 | 48.0 | 41.6 | 60.0 | 29.5 | 34.1 | 24.6 | 37.0 | 45.6 |
| Miscellaneous manufactures | 6.6 | 8.9 | 12.9 | 13.7 | 12.9 | 6.3 | 8.4 | 3.1 | 6.4 | 7.1 |
| Unidentified manufactures | 3.8 | 3.8 | 3.1 | 3.6 | 4.2 | 1.6 | 2.2 | 2.0 | 3.1 | 2.5 |
| **Agricultural and livestock products** | 5.1 | 7.6 | 4.9 | 15.3 | 29.0 | 3.2 | 3.4 | 1.2 | 2.3 | 4.7 |
| Agricultural products | 2.1 | 4.0 | 2.0 | 12.7 | 27.6 | 0.5 | 0.9 | 0.6 | 1.1 | 2.3 |
| Livestock and livestock products | 3.0 | 3.6 | 2.8 | 2.6 | 1.4 | 2.7 | 2.5 | 0.7 | 1.2 | 2.4 |
| **Other commodities** | 57.5 | 57.8 | 73.5 | 88.8 | 95.3 | 2.9 | 27.1 | 5.6 | 5.9 | 18.7 |
| Forestry products | 3.0 | 3.5 | 3.2 | 3.9 | 3.3 | ..... | ..... | 0.2 | 0.1 | 0.1 |
| Fish and other marine products | 2.7 | 1.1 | 2.3 | 1.4 | 0.6 | ..... | ..... | ..... | 0.2 | 0.1 |
| Metallic ores and concentrates | 2.8 | 3.5 | 4.0 | 5.1 | 3.7 | 0.1 | 1.8 | 2.9 | 2.2 | 2.0 |
| Bituminous coal and lignite | 46.7 | 45.1 | 58.5 | 65.9 | 70.4 | 0.5 | 0.6 | 0.1 | 0.1 | 12.4 |
| Crude petroleum and natural gas | ..... | 0.9 | 1.3 | 6.8 | 5.6 | ..... | ..... | ..... | ..... | ..... |
| Nonmetallic minerals | 1.1 | 1.5 | 2.5 | 2.5 | 4.7 | 0.9 | 1.4 | 1.0 | 1.3 | 1.6 |
| Scrap and waste | 0.3 | 0.9 | 0.7 | 1.4 | 3.7 | 0.2 | 0.5 | 1.2 | 1.4 | 1.7 |
| Used merchandise | 0.5 | 1.0 | 0.5 | 0.5 | 2.3 | 1.0 | 22.7 | 0.1 | 0.2 | 0.1 |
| Goods imported and returned unchanged | ..... | ..... | ..... | ..... | ..... | ..... | ..... | ..... | ..... | ..... |
| Special classification provisions | 0.4 | 0.3 | 0.2 | 1.2 | 1.1 | 0.1 | 0.1 | 0.2 | 0.4 | 0.5 |
| | European Union | | | | | United Kingdom | | | | |
| **ALL GOODS** | 3 103.1 | 3 277.5 | 4 365.0 | 4 373.1 | 4 487.9 | 711.9 | 812.3 | 1 146.9 | 1 369.9 | 1 436.3 |
| **Manufactured goods** | 2 681.8 | 2 816.5 | 3 780.7 | 3 879.9 | 3 952.0 | 622.9 | 663.4 | 888.2 | 1 132.3 | 1 150.3 |
| Food products | 24.7 | 29.5 | 50.5 | 50.7 | 39.9 | 7.0 | 4.5 | 7.7 | 9.0 | 4.6 |
| Tobacco products | ..... | 0.1 | 2.6 | 0.3 | 0.2 | ..... | ..... | ..... | 0.2 | 0.1 |
| Textile mill products | 16.9 | 17.2 | 19.3 | 20.8 | 18.4 | 5.2 | 5.9 | 6.6 | 7.0 | 5.6 |
| Apparel | 19.2 | 25.0 | 27.6 | 24.9 | 22.8 | 5.0 | 6.5 | 6.8 | 5.8 | 6.4 |
| Lumber and wood products | 81.5 | 93.4 | 111.4 | 103.1 | 119.8 | 20.4 | 31.9 | 38.9 | 39.4 | 28.1 |
| Furniture and fixtures | 10.7 | 9.1 | 7.7 | 10.9 | 11.9 | 1.1 | 1.1 | 1.0 | 3.7 | 2.3 |
| Paper products | 29.9 | 22.1 | 28.6 | 34.0 | 36.7 | 10.7 | 9.4 | 11.8 | 14.5 | 16.9 |
| Printing and publishing | 61.3 | 18.9 | 25.0 | 21.1 | 23.8 | 32.5 | 8.4 | 8.2 | 7.3 | 10.4 |
| Chemical products | 630.8 | 716.9 | 967.7 | 993.3 | 992.9 | 99.9 | 92.8 | 162.1 | 295.0 | 255.7 |
| Refined petroleum products | 32.3 | 15.2 | 22.1 | 19.6 | 15.0 | 2.2 | 1.0 | 0.7 | 3.5 | 1.2 |
| Rubber and plastic products | 89.9 | 116.9 | 142.2 | 156.8 | 167.2 | 26.5 | 29.7 | 29.4 | 44.6 | 50.8 |
| Leather products | 12.5 | 12.6 | 12.6 | 18.1 | 11.6 | 2.0 | 2.7 | 2.0 | 1.6 | 1.2 |
| Stone, clay and glass products | 95.1 | 79.3 | 110.7 | 113.3 | 125.1 | 15.3 | 15.1 | 19.3 | 19.6 | 15.1 |
| Primary metals | 180.2 | 154.3 | 367.4 | 370.0 | 316.3 | 62.4 | 47.7 | 90.1 | 100.3 | 100.0 |
| Fabricated metal products | 69.2 | 75.2 | 100.4 | 123.2 | 131.0 | 19.1 | 22.0 | 32.4 | 48.0 | 54.8 |
| Industrial machinery and computers | 405.7 | 425.6 | 696.7 | 749.0 | 747.3 | 136.8 | 141.3 | 196.7 | 206.3 | 246.0 |
| Electric and electronic equipment | 368.5 | 460.8 | 501.9 | 394.5 | 446.8 | 78.1 | 132.6 | 144.4 | 167.5 | 193.1 |
| Transportation equipment | 244.3 | 257.2 | 290.4 | 327.6 | 343.4 | 35.4 | 44.2 | 50.0 | 53.8 | 53.4 |
| Scientific and measuring instruments | 238.1 | 209.0 | 209.4 | 241.2 | 263.2 | 45.5 | 42.9 | 50.5 | 67.0 | 60.9 |
| Miscellaneous manufactures | 60.0 | 65.7 | 75.2 | 99.0 | 111.8 | 14.0 | 19.4 | 25.9 | 35.4 | 40.7 |
| Unidentified manufactures | 10.7 | 12.4 | 11.2 | 8.5 | 7.1 | 3.7 | 4.3 | 3.7 | 2.8 | 3.0 |
| **Agricultural and livestock products** | 4.4 | 7.4 | 10.2 | 9.0 | 8.3 | 0.5 | 0.9 | 3.2 | 3.2 | 3.5 |
| Agricultural products | 1.0 | 2.2 | 4.5 | 4.9 | 4.0 | 0.2 | 0.3 | 2.2 | 2.4 | 2.7 |
| Livestock and livestock products | 3.4 | 5.2 | 5.7 | 4.1 | 4.3 | 0.3 | 0.6 | 1.0 | 0.7 | 0.8 |
| **Other commodities** | 416.9 | 453.5 | 574.1 | 484.2 | 527.6 | 88.5 | 148.0 | 255.5 | 234.4 | 282.5 |
| Forestry products | 8.8 | 10.1 | 12.9 | 10.6 | 13.3 | 0.1 | ..... | 0.1 | ..... | 0.5 |
| Fish and other marine products | 2.9 | 0.8 | 0.2 | 0.6 | 8.8 | 0.1 | ..... | ..... | ..... | 0.5 |
| Metallic ores and concentrates | 3.4 | 6.9 | 8.2 | 6.5 | 6.8 | 0.8 | 0.9 | 2.3 | 1.8 | 2.0 |
| Bituminous coal and lignite | 315.3 | 215.3 | 239.9 | 217.0 | 213.6 | 53.2 | 41.7 | 42.7 | 33.8 | 39.0 |
| Crude petroleum and natural gas | 2.3 | 2.7 | 4.0 | 6.1 | 6.1 | ..... | 2.7 | 3.9 | 5.9 | 6.1 |
| Nonmetallic minerals | 10.1 | 12.1 | 13.3 | 15.5 | 13.8 | 1.1 | 0.2 | 0.3 | 0.7 | 0.4 |
| Scrap and waste | 8.0 | 10.9 | 140.9 | 201.2 | 242.3 | 5.8 | 3.7 | 122.5 | 186.2 | 223.5 |
| Used merchandise | 12.5 | 30.0 | 36.8 | 22.3 | 19.4 | 4.7 | 6.1 | 18.8 | 3.6 | 8.3 |
| Goods imported and returned unchanged | ..... | ..... | ..... | ..... | ..... | ..... | ..... | ..... | ..... | ..... |
| Special classification provisions | 53.5 | 164.7 | 117.9 | 4.3 | 3.5 | 22.6 | 92.7 | 64.8 | 2.4 | 2.2 |

## Table D-3.  State Exports of Goods by Destination and Industry, 1993–1997 —*Continued*

### PENNSYLVANIA  (Millions of dollars.)

| Industry | 1993 | 1994 | 1995 | 1996 | 1997 | 1993 | 1994 | 1995 | 1996 | 1997 |
|---|---|---|---|---|---|---|---|---|---|---|
| | Germany | | | | | France | | | | |
| **ALL GOODS** | 573.3 | 583.8 | 692.1 | 631.1 | 652.4 | 282.7 | 278.0 | 388.4 | 411.8 | 446.8 |
| **Manufactured goods** | 551.7 | 567.7 | 666.7 | 604.8 | 630.1 | 261.4 | 255.3 | 354.8 | 392.3 | 417.6 |
| Food products | 0.7 | 5.4 | 6.0 | 5.7 | 5.3 | 1.5 | 1.4 | 2.0 | 1.9 | 1.3 |
| Tobacco products | ..... | ..... | ..... | ..... | ..... | ..... | ..... | ..... | ..... | ..... |
| Textile mill products | 3.8 | 2.7 | 4.6 | 6.6 | 4.0 | 0.8 | 0.9 | 1.1 | 0.7 | 0.8 |
| Apparel | 3.7 | 5.6 | 5.3 | 5.0 | 3.2 | 1.6 | 2.0 | 2.3 | 2.1 | 2.8 |
| Lumber and wood products | 12.2 | 13.8 | 23.9 | 20.4 | 24.2 | 12.7 | 12.4 | 10.0 | 6.8 | 9.1 |
| Furniture and fixtures | 3.8 | 3.4 | 2.8 | 1.5 | 3.0 | 1.4 | 1.4 | 0.4 | 1.0 | 1.6 |
| Paper products | 2.8 | 3.9 | 6.0 | 7.3 | 7.0 | 2.6 | 1.6 | 3.3 | 5.8 | 6.2 |
| Printing and publishing | 3.9 | 2.4 | 3.4 | 1.7 | 2.2 | 7.8 | 2.0 | 5.7 | 4.1 | 3.2 |
| Chemical products | 83.3 | 89.9 | 86.4 | 81.8 | 111.7 | 40.0 | 49.1 | 58.3 | 70.2 | 68.7 |
| Refined petroleum products | 2.7 | 1.0 | 1.2 | 1.1 | 0.8 | 0.5 | 0.2 | 0.1 | 0.4 | 0.3 |
| Rubber and plastic products | 19.1 | 39.7 | 46.3 | 43.4 | 40.1 | 8.5 | 8.8 | 23.5 | 24.1 | 29.6 |
| Leather products | 3.4 | 1.2 | 1.5 | 4.3 | 0.7 | 1.2 | 0.9 | 1.7 | 3.0 | 0.6 |
| Stone, clay and glass products | 18.1 | 17.3 | 28.4 | 27.0 | 24.4 | 13.7 | 17.7 | 20.1 | 17.4 | 25.9 |
| Primary metals | 27.3 | 20.1 | 30.3 | 19.7 | 31.9 | 28.6 | 21.2 | 25.3 | 30.1 | 33.1 |
| Fabricated metal products | 14.9 | 10.4 | 15.8 | 16.6 | 21.8 | 3.9 | 5.6 | 6.6 | 8.9 | 7.2 |
| Industrial machinery and computers | 78.1 | 76.7 | 135.8 | 137.3 | 112.5 | 41.2 | 47.2 | 111.0 | 128.1 | 113.0 |
| Electric and electronic equipment | 110.4 | 111.3 | 121.5 | 60.7 | 70.5 | 33.3 | 38.9 | 42.2 | 36.0 | 37.9 |
| Transportation equipment | 72.2 | 76.7 | 78.5 | 74.5 | 67.5 | 16.0 | 9.9 | 9.4 | 16.3 | 36.1 |
| Scientific and measuring instruments | 70.6 | 68.9 | 53.5 | 65.2 | 70.6 | 37.5 | 23.5 | 21.5 | 22.9 | 21.6 |
| Miscellaneous manufactures | 19.0 | 15.7 | 13.3 | 23.2 | 27.9 | 7.4 | 9.4 | 9.3 | 11.9 | 18.1 |
| Unidentified manufactures | 1.6 | 1.6 | 2.2 | 1.8 | 1.0 | 1.1 | 1.1 | 1.0 | 0.6 | 0.6 |
| **Agricultural and livestock products** | 0.3 | 0.1 | 0.4 | 0.8 | 0.4 | 0.3 | 1.1 | 0.9 | 0.9 | 0.7 |
| Agricultural products | ..... | ..... | 0.3 | 0.7 | ..... | ..... | 0.3 | 0.3 | 0.4 | 0.3 |
| Livestock and livestock products | 0.3 | 0.1 | 0.1 | 0.1 | 0.4 | 0.2 | 0.8 | 0.6 | 0.4 | 0.4 |
| **Other commodities** | 21.2 | 15.9 | 25.0 | 25.5 | 21.9 | 21.0 | 21.7 | 32.7 | 18.6 | 28.5 |
| Forestry products | 6.6 | 7.3 | 8.4 | 6.8 | 8.8 | ..... | ..... | 1.3 | ..... | 0.2 |
| Fish and other marine products | 0.1 | 0.3 | 0.1 | 0.3 | 0.1 | ..... | ..... | 0.1 | 0.1 | ..... |
| Metallic ores and concentrates | 1.6 | 1.3 | 2.6 | 4.2 | 4.1 | 0.1 | 0.7 | 0.5 | ..... | ..... |
| Bituminous coal and lignite | 6.8 | 0.8 | 4.7 | 2.5 | 2.5 | 18.7 | 4.2 | 18.4 | 12.3 | 21.6 |
| Crude petroleum and natural gas | ..... | ..... | ..... | ..... | ..... | ..... | ..... | ..... | ..... | ..... |
| Nonmetallic minerals | 0.5 | 0.7 | 1.0 | 0.7 | 0.8 | 0.4 | 0.1 | 0.2 | 0.8 | 0.2 |
| Scrap and waste | 0.4 | 1.6 | 3.6 | 1.0 | 0.9 | 0.3 | 0.1 | ..... | 0.3 | 3.2 |
| Used merchandise | 1.2 | 3.3 | 3.6 | 9.1 | 4.3 | 1.5 | 16.4 | 11.5 | 4.9 | 3.2 |
| Goods imported and returned unchanged | ..... | ..... | ..... | ..... | ..... | ..... | ..... | ..... | ..... | ..... |
| Special classification provisions | 4.0 | 0.6 | 1.0 | 0.8 | 0.4 | 0.1 | 0.2 | 0.7 | 0.1 | 0.2 |

| Industry | 1993 | 1994 | 1995 | 1996 | 1997 | 1993 | 1994 | 1995 | 1996 | 1997 |
|---|---|---|---|---|---|---|---|---|---|---|
| | The Netherlands | | | | | Asian 10 | | | | |
| **ALL GOODS** | 465.9 | 500.7 | 725.6 | 647.8 | 664.7 | 3 118.2 | 3 676.7 | 4 416.3 | 4 030.3 | 4 429.7 |
| **Manufactured goods** | 445.0 | 473.8 | 679.2 | 594.5 | 624.3 | 2 978.7 | 3 582.2 | 4 309.2 | 3 945.4 | 4 361.6 |
| Food products | 6.8 | 11.0 | 21.1 | 9.7 | 10.7 | 194.9 | 200.2 | 126.9 | 144.0 | 176.8 |
| Tobacco products | ..... | ..... | ..... | ..... | ..... | 0.1 | 0.1 | 0.1 | 1.1 | 0.1 |
| Textile mill products | 2.1 | 2.6 | 2.6 | 2.3 | 2.2 | 31.5 | 46.8 | 52.4 | 57.2 | 37.1 |
| Apparel | 3.8 | 2.2 | 4.0 | 2.3 | 4.0 | 7.2 | 44.2 | 47.1 | 34.5 | 34.6 |
| Lumber and wood products | 5.0 | 2.0 | 1.2 | 2.1 | 2.7 | 42.0 | 42.3 | 48.7 | 46.9 | 49.9 |
| Furniture and fixtures | 0.8 | 0.2 | 0.4 | 0.3 | 0.5 | 5.2 | 10.2 | 10.6 | 8.3 | 10.0 |
| Paper products | 1.9 | 1.3 | 1.5 | 1.7 | 2.4 | 11.1 | 12.1 | 20.6 | 22.4 | 26.2 |
| Printing and publishing | 14.7 | 2.9 | 3.1 | 4.5 | 5.0 | 50.9 | 13.1 | 12.3 | 28.5 | 9.4 |
| Chemical products | 214.5 | 236.5 | 360.2 | 276.4 | 284.9 | 697.4 | 746.0 | 1 067.2 | 832.3 | 817.8 |
| Refined petroleum products | 14.2 | 4.9 | 8.2 | 5.4 | 1.5 | 18.9 | 19.3 | 19.4 | 25.4 | 40.8 |
| Rubber and plastic products | 14.0 | 18.0 | 19.5 | 15.4 | 15.1 | 96.7 | 106.9 | 104.0 | 130.2 | 134.4 |
| Leather products | 0.8 | 2.7 | 2.5 | 5.6 | 4.2 | 34.7 | 10.7 | 5.4 | 11.0 | 27.0 |
| Stone, clay and glass products | 5.7 | 6.4 | 5.4 | 9.1 | 8.6 | 70.3 | 57.2 | 75.0 | 88.2 | 111.6 |
| Primary metals | 11.4 | 8.6 | 32.9 | 34.2 | 27.0 | 135.2 | 166.4 | 551.6 | 304.7 | 244.2 |
| Fabricated metal products | 10.2 | 9.2 | 9.2 | 9.0 | 9.7 | 111.1 | 147.4 | 186.1 | 145.1 | 118.6 |
| Industrial machinery and computers | 33.5 | 32.5 | 61.5 | 75.2 | 82.3 | 484.9 | 710.9 | 802.6 | 778.8 | 918.2 |
| Electric and electronic equipment | 51.8 | 73.5 | 74.8 | 37.9 | 65.4 | 658.0 | 883.1 | 822.7 | 862.1 | 1 138.1 |
| Transportation equipment | 22.0 | 34.5 | 43.0 | 69.0 | 56.2 | 106.8 | 102.6 | 110.0 | 153.4 | 174.1 |
| Scientific and measuring instruments | 25.1 | 15.3 | 18.8 | 25.1 | 33.6 | 156.8 | 181.1 | 170.3 | 183.8 | 200.0 |
| Miscellaneous manufactures | 5.9 | 8.5 | 8.3 | 8.7 | 7.8 | 53.7 | 59.8 | 69.4 | 80.9 | 79.6 |
| Unidentified manufactures | 0.8 | 0.9 | 1.0 | 0.8 | 0.6 | 11.2 | 21.9 | 6.8 | 6.6 | 13.3 |
| **Agricultural and livestock products** | 1.4 | 2.5 | 1.7 | 1.4 | 1.4 | 5.2 | 7.1 | 4.0 | 3.4 | 3.6 |
| Agricultural products | 0.5 | 1.4 | 0.1 | 0.3 | 0.2 | 2.9 | 2.8 | 3.4 | 2.1 | 3.0 |
| Livestock and livestock products | 0.9 | 1.2 | 1.6 | 1.1 | 1.2 | 2.3 | 4.3 | 0.5 | 1.2 | 0.6 |
| **Other commodities** | 19.5 | 24.3 | 44.7 | 51.9 | 39.0 | 134.4 | 87.4 | 103.1 | 81.6 | 64.6 |
| Forestry products | 0.9 | 1.3 | 1.4 | 1.9 | 1.7 | 13.1 | 15.5 | 17.1 | 11.4 | 12.0 |
| Fish and other marine products | ..... | ..... | ..... | 0.1 | 0.3 | 3.9 | 3.6 | 4.0 | 1.4 | 0.3 |
| Metallic ores and concentrates | 0.1 | 1.9 | 0.2 | 0.1 | 0.1 | 1.8 | 1.6 | 3.3 | 3.7 | 4.4 |
| Bituminous coal and lignite | 5.6 | 7.8 | 22.6 | 37.0 | 24.6 | 84.3 | 42.7 | 48.8 | 39.0 | 24.5 |
| Crude petroleum and natural gas | 2.3 | ..... | 0.1 | 0.2 | ..... | 0.2 | 0.2 | 0.2 | 0.3 | 0.1 |
| Nonmetallic minerals | 7.3 | 9.8 | 9.8 | 11.9 | 10.5 | 14.1 | 14.2 | 18.6 | 13.5 | 12.4 |
| Scrap and waste | 0.1 | 0.5 | 0.6 | 0.2 | 0.8 | 6.7 | 5.6 | 6.9 | 4.7 | 5.1 |
| Used merchandise | 3.2 | 2.8 | 0.7 | 0.3 | 0.9 | 1.0 | 1.7 | 1.7 | 3.7 | 1.6 |
| Goods imported and returned unchanged | ..... | ..... | ..... | ..... | ..... | ..... | ..... | ..... | ..... | ..... |
| Special classification provisions | 0.1 | 0.2 | 9.4 | 0.1 | 0.2 | 9.4 | 2.3 | 2.5 | 3.9 | 4.2 |

## Table D-3.  State Exports of Goods by Destination and Industry, 1993–1997 —Continued

**PENNSYLVANIA** (Millions of dollars.)

| Industry | 1993 | 1994 | 1995 | 1996 | 1997 | 1993 | 1994 | 1995 | 1996 | 1997 |
|---|---|---|---|---|---|---|---|---|---|---|
| | Japan | | | | | South Korea | | | | |
| **ALL GOODS** | 853.1 | 861.7 | 1 098.6 | 1 119.4 | 1 162.0 | 482.4 | 641.1 | 694.9 | 593.3 | 593.8 |
| **Manufactured goods** | 773.9 | 812.6 | 1 044.0 | 1 078.7 | 1 128.9 | 458.0 | 627.7 | 680.6 | 580.2 | 584.5 |
| Food products | 37.4 | 35.3 | 34.9 | 36.7 | 33.3 | 46.9 | 40.3 | 17.4 | 17.3 | 16.3 |
| Tobacco products | 0.1 | ..... | 0.1 | 1.0 | ..... | | | | | |
| Textile mill products | 2.7 | 3.4 | 5.8 | 5.5 | 5.8 | 1.8 | 3.8 | 3.9 | 4.2 | 3.2 |
| Apparel | 4.0 | 35.0 | 40.1 | 24.5 | 25.1 | 0.6 | 0.7 | 0.7 | 1.1 | 4.0 |
| Lumber and wood products | 8.1 | 8.6 | 13.4 | 14.4 | 15.0 | 10.7 | 10.5 | 9.9 | 10.7 | 8.8 |
| Furniture and fixtures | 1.4 | 4.3 | 4.0 | 2.4 | 2.2 | 0.4 | 0.5 | 0.7 | 0.3 | 0.6 |
| Paper products | 2.7 | 2.4 | 3.5 | 5.0 | 6.8 | 2.1 | 2.6 | 4.2 | 3.3 | 2.7 |
| Printing and publishing | 10.4 | 5.7 | 6.2 | 22.6 | 2.3 | 0.3 | 0.8 | 1.5 | 0.9 | 1.2 |
| Chemical products | 213.6 | 181.3 | 229.3 | 275.6 | 272.8 | 106.3 | 124.8 | 146.8 | 122.0 | 115.5 |
| Refined petroleum products | 8.6 | 7.6 | 8.9 | 12.0 | 11.9 | 2.0 | 2.3 | 1.6 | 1.7 | 4.6 |
| Rubber and plastic products | 68.4 | 76.0 | 69.7 | 84.7 | 83.4 | 10.4 | 7.4 | 4.3 | 11.5 | 9.3 |
| Leather products | 33.7 | 8.7 | 1.1 | 7.9 | 23.5 | 0.2 | 0.7 | 1.9 | 0.6 | 0.2 |
| Stone, clay and glass products | 16.9 | 14.3 | 28.5 | 35.5 | 52.1 | 17.3 | 16.3 | 10.5 | 13.3 | 11.1 |
| Primary metals | 77.8 | 70.7 | 162.8 | 133.5 | 99.2 | 13.5 | 14.3 | 112.8 | 39.0 | 35.3 |
| Fabricated metal products | 11.7 | 28.0 | 44.7 | 31.3 | 25.7 | 24.3 | 62.8 | 79.7 | 48.0 | 22.8 |
| Industrial machinery and computers | 82.5 | 90.8 | 105.5 | 98.5 | 115.2 | 70.0 | 197.9 | 151.8 | 144.1 | 174.4 |
| Electric and electronic equipment | 73.1 | 106.8 | 147.9 | 132.9 | 160.8 | 64.0 | 65.3 | 59.2 | 73.8 | 99.1 |
| Transportation equipment | 36.6 | 30.5 | 46.7 | 57.1 | 85.6 | 54.0 | 30.3 | 25.2 | 30.1 | 24.5 |
| Scientific and measuring instruments | 52.5 | 65.7 | 51.4 | 53.1 | 65.9 | 22.0 | 33.1 | 35.0 | 41.9 | 37.2 |
| Miscellaneous manufactures | 30.8 | 36.4 | 38.2 | 43.5 | 40.5 | 7.4 | 7.9 | 11.3 | 15.1 | 12.7 |
| Unidentified manufactures | 0.9 | 1.1 | 1.3 | 1.1 | 1.7 | 4.0 | 5.4 | 2.1 | 1.5 | 0.7 |
| **Agricultural and livestock products** | 0.3 | 0.7 | 0.8 | 0.5 | 0.5 | ..... | ..... | ..... | ..... | 2.0 |
| Agricultural products | ..... | 0.5 | 0.4 | 0.1 | 0.1 | ..... | ..... | ..... | ..... | 2.0 |
| Livestock and livestock products | 0.3 | 0.2 | 0.4 | 0.4 | 0.5 | ..... | ..... | ..... | ..... | ..... |
| **Other commodities** | 78.9 | 48.4 | 53.7 | 40.2 | 32.6 | 24.4 | 13.3 | 14.3 | 13.1 | 7.3 |
| Forestry products | 6.5 | 6.9 | 5.8 | 5.7 | 5.4 | ..... | ..... | 0.2 | 0.1 | 0.4 |
| Fish and other marine products | 0.1 | 0.1 | ..... | 0.1 | ..... | ..... | 0.1 | 0.1 | 0.1 | ..... |
| Metallic ores and concentrates | 0.1 | ..... | ..... | 0.1 | 0.1 | 0.3 | 0.2 | 0.2 | 0.3 | 0.1 |
| Bituminous coal and lignite | 62.0 | 28.8 | 33.3 | 24.4 | 19.4 | 12.7 | 9.1 | 9.8 | 8.4 | 3.5 |
| Crude petroleum and natural gas | ..... | ..... | ..... | ..... | ..... | 0.1 | 0.1 | 0.1 | 0.3 | ..... |
| Nonmetallic minerals | 6.5 | 6.2 | 9.1 | 4.8 | 3.8 | 3.4 | 3.3 | 3.3 | 3.0 | 1.2 |
| Scrap and waste | 2.5 | 4.5 | 3.9 | 2.0 | 2.1 | 3.1 | 0.2 | 0.3 | 0.4 | ..... |
| Used merchandise | 0.6 | 1.2 | 0.9 | 2.2 | 1.3 | 0.1 | 0.1 | 0.2 | 0.5 | 0.1 |
| Goods imported and returned unchanged | ..... | ..... | ..... | ..... | ..... | ..... | ..... | ..... | ..... | ..... |
| Special classification provisions | 0.5 | 0.8 | 0.7 | 0.9 | 0.4 | 4.7 | 0.2 | 0.1 | 0.1 | 1.9 |
| | Taiwan | | | | | Singapore | | | | |
| **ALL GOODS** | 504.0 | 565.3 | 727.6 | 428.1 | 521.3 | 420.7 | 486.8 | 592.9 | 627.8 | 675.0 |
| **Manufactured goods** | 488.1 | 553.4 | 714.2 | 416.8 | 514.5 | 415.7 | 483.9 | 588.9 | 623.7 | 671.0 |
| Food products | 58.0 | 64.1 | 40.8 | 41.2 | 55.2 | 1.7 | 1.5 | 2.1 | 3.7 | 5.4 |
| Tobacco products | ..... | ..... | ..... | 0.1 | ..... | ..... | ..... | ..... | ..... | ..... |
| Textile mill products | 1.8 | 3.9 | 3.1 | 3.8 | 2.1 | 0.6 | 0.7 | 0.9 | 0.7 | 0.8 |
| Apparel | 0.4 | 0.3 | 0.3 | 1.3 | 1.6 | 0.2 | 0.3 | 0.5 | 1.0 | 1.1 |
| Lumber and wood products | 13.0 | 12.2 | 11.3 | 7.2 | 9.3 | 0.7 | 0.9 | 1.4 | 0.8 | 0.6 |
| Furniture and fixtures | 0.5 | 0.9 | 0.8 | 0.8 | 0.5 | 0.9 | 1.3 | 1.7 | 2.3 | 2.6 |
| Paper products | 1.5 | 2.2 | 2.8 | 3.4 | 5.7 | 0.8 | 0.7 | 1.3 | 2.2 | 3.0 |
| Printing and publishing | 31.7 | 0.4 | 0.8 | 0.4 | 0.5 | 5.7 | 0.5 | 0.6 | 0.9 | 1.0 |
| Chemical products | 164.6 | 197.6 | 286.7 | 96.3 | 94.0 | 94.3 | 89.4 | 138.9 | 109.6 | 117.6 |
| Refined petroleum products | 4.8 | 6.0 | 5.8 | 3.0 | 3.5 | 0.5 | 0.2 | 0.4 | 0.7 | 0.7 |
| Rubber and plastic products | 7.9 | 8.1 | 6.0 | 5.8 | 8.4 | 3.0 | 4.5 | 5.9 | 6.3 | 10.7 |
| Leather products | 0.2 | 0.1 | 0.1 | 0.2 | 0.1 | 0.1 | 0.1 | 0.1 | 0.4 | 0.2 |
| Stone, clay and glass products | 13.9 | 9.4 | 8.0 | 13.6 | 15.2 | 5.9 | 4.5 | 4.5 | 5.6 | 8.7 |
| Primary metals | 11.6 | 22.0 | 114.3 | 50.4 | 27.8 | 10.1 | 12.0 | 41.4 | 15.5 | 9.5 |
| Fabricated metal products | 34.9 | 17.9 | 15.4 | 15.2 | 15.4 | 8.2 | 10.0 | 11.0 | 14.8 | 19.4 |
| Industrial machinery and computers | 62.2 | 79.7 | 140.8 | 107.3 | 169.6 | 40.3 | 54.0 | 59.0 | 76.3 | 72.8 |
| Electric and electronic equipment | 49.8 | 62.5 | 46.7 | 42.2 | 67.8 | 215.2 | 281.5 | 294.4 | 340.9 | 383.8 |
| Transportation equipment | 1.0 | 27.2 | 6.6 | 3.6 | 3.7 | 4.2 | 2.9 | 4.0 | 18.8 | 12.8 |
| Scientific and measuring instruments | 24.9 | 25.4 | 20.0 | 18.0 | 22.3 | 16.1 | 13.6 | 14.5 | 16.1 | 14.6 |
| Miscellaneous manufactures | 3.5 | 2.9 | 3.5 | 2.5 | 3.7 | 5.5 | 4.4 | 5.1 | 6.1 | 5.3 |
| Unidentified manufactures | 1.8 | 10.7 | 0.5 | 0.6 | 8.1 | 1.6 | 1.0 | 1.2 | 1.0 | 0.6 |
| **Agricultural and livestock products** | 3.0 | 1.8 | 0.9 | 0.7 | 0.1 | ..... | ..... | ..... | ..... | ..... |
| Agricultural products | 2.8 | 1.7 | 0.9 | 0.6 | 0.1 | ..... | ..... | ..... | ..... | ..... |
| Livestock and livestock products | 0.2 | 0.2 | ..... | 0.1 | ..... | ..... | ..... | ..... | ..... | ..... |
| **Other commodities** | 13.0 | 10.1 | 12.5 | 10.5 | 6.8 | 4.9 | 2.9 | 4.1 | 4.0 | 4.1 |
| Forestry products | 0.2 | 0.3 | 0.4 | 0.8 | 0.1 | 2.2 | 1.0 | 0.9 | 1.0 | 1.3 |
| Fish and other marine products | 1.1 | 0.9 | 1.0 | 0.3 | ..... | 0.2 | 0.1 | 0.4 | 0.1 | ..... |
| Metallic ores and concentrates | 0.4 | 0.3 | 0.2 | 0.2 | 0.1 | 0.3 | 0.3 | 0.1 | 0.3 | ..... |
| Bituminous coal and lignite | 8.6 | 4.8 | 5.8 | 6.0 | 1.5 | ..... | ..... | ..... | ..... | ..... |
| Crude petroleum and natural gas | ..... | 0.1 | ..... | ..... | ..... | 0.2 | 0.1 | ..... | ..... | 0.1 |
| Nonmetallic minerals | 2.0 | 3.3 | 3.5 | 2.9 | 3.9 | 1.8 | 1.1 | 2.3 | 2.0 | 2.4 |
| Scrap and waste | ..... | 0.3 | 0.7 | 0.1 | 0.9 | ..... | 0.1 | 0.1 | 0.1 | 0.1 |
| Used merchandise | ..... | ..... | 0.2 | 0.3 | ..... | 0.1 | 0.2 | 0.1 | 0.2 | ..... |
| Goods imported and returned unchanged | ..... | ..... | ..... | ..... | ..... | ..... | ..... | ..... | ..... | ..... |
| Special classification provisions | 0.7 | 0.2 | 0.7 | 0.1 | 0.3 | 0.1 | 0.1 | 0.1 | 0.4 | 0.1 |

## PUERTO RICO: Exports of Goods, 1997

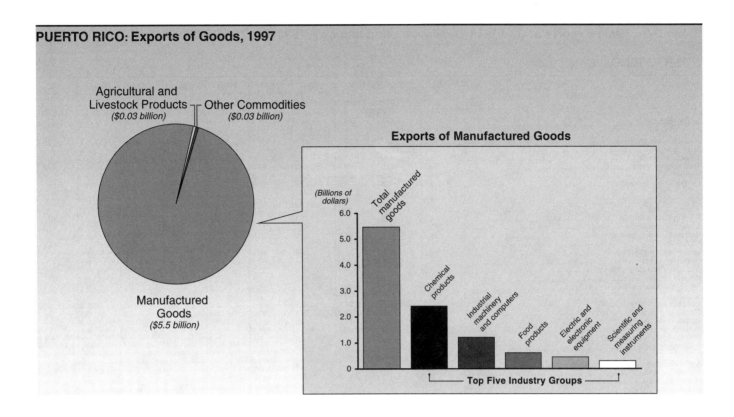

Agricultural and Livestock Products ($0.03 billion)

Other Commodities ($0.03 billion)

Manufactured Goods ($5.5 billion)

### Exports of Manufactured Goods

(Billions of dollars)

Top Five Industry Groups

## Table D-3.   State Exports of Goods by Destination and Industry, 1993–1997 —*Continued*

### PUERTO RICO (Millions of dollars.)

| Industry | 1993 | 1994 | 1995 | 1996 | 1997 | 1993 | 1994 | 1995 | 1996 | 1997 |
|---|---|---|---|---|---|---|---|---|---|---|
| | All destinations | | | | | Canada | | | | |
| **ALL GOODS** | 4 365.1 | 4 618.9 | 4 704.5 | 5 188.4 | 5 528.1 | 387.4 | 671.3 | 535.9 | 575.8 | 689.5 |
| **Manufactured goods** | 4 315.6 | 4 557.2 | 4 648.6 | 5 141.4 | 5 470.7 | 385.0 | 665.8 | 533.7 | 573.5 | 686.5 |
| Food products | 359.3 | 475.2 | 262.4 | 287.1 | 616.1 | 41.5 | 175.9 | 30.2 | 31.1 | 47.7 |
| Tobacco products | 31.2 | 42.8 | 88.5 | 86.7 | 73.6 | ..... | ..... | ..... | ..... | ..... |
| Textile mill products | 37.0 | 44.1 | 66.7 | 73.6 | 64.0 | 0.4 | 0.1 | 0.2 | ..... | 0.2 |
| Apparel | 46.3 | 46.3 | 77.9 | 73.7 | 93.4 | 8.2 | 8.6 | 12.7 | 7.5 | 4.6 |
| Lumber and wood products | 4.6 | 4.8 | 5.3 | 4.2 | 4.3 | 0.2 | 0.1 | 0.1 | 0.3 | 0.2 |
| Furniture and fixtures | 3.4 | 2.3 | 2.4 | 5.3 | 4.1 | 0.3 | 0.3 | 0.1 | 0.9 | 0.6 |
| Paper products | 12.9 | 14.3 | 12.4 | 13.9 | 8.6 | 0.4 | 0.7 | 0.4 | 0.5 | 0.5 |
| Printing and publishing | 7.5 | 3.2 | 2.7 | 3.5 | 2.6 | 1.1 | 0.6 | 0.4 | 0.1 | 0.4 |
| Chemical products | 2 452.9 | 2 390.3 | 2 070.9 | 2 049.5 | 2 411.8 | 248.5 | 369.9 | 375.5 | 407.0 | 491.0 |
| Refined petroleum products | 37.1 | 47.9 | 32.4 | 34.5 | 31.8 | ..... | 0.1 | 0.2 | 0.5 | 1.0 |
| Rubber and plastic products | 20.1 | 22.6 | 21.6 | 21.4 | 24.8 | 3.7 | 4.2 | 4.4 | 3.9 | 5.2 |
| Leather products | 26.1 | 36.3 | 23.0 | 20.8 | 45.7 | ..... | ..... | ..... | ..... | 0.2 |
| Stone, clay and glass products | 11.1 | 5.9 | 6.2 | 11.2 | 31.6 | 7.7 | 3.4 | 0.4 | 0.5 | 0.4 |
| Primary metals | 10.5 | 11.5 | 12.2 | 12.7 | 31.7 | 0.7 | 2.1 | 5.7 | 1.6 | 1.8 |
| Fabricated metal products | 16.5 | 19.5 | 20.0 | 18.0 | 18.5 | 0.6 | 1.2 | 0.7 | 1.0 | 1.0 |
| Industrial machinery and computers | 644.1 | 667.7 | 1 161.6 | 1 685.3 | 1 212.9 | 16.0 | 22.3 | 30.2 | 45.9 | 48.3 |
| Electric and electronic equipment | 287.4 | 398.6 | 403.7 | 350.5 | 454.6 | 34.2 | 56.2 | 43.6 | 45.8 | 66.3 |
| Transportation equipment | 11.8 | 22.3 | 17.4 | 13.3 | 16.1 | 0.4 | 0.8 | 0.5 | 0.7 | 1.0 |
| Scientific and measuring instruments | 272.8 | 271.9 | 344.0 | 361.8 | 310.1 | 19.8 | 17.8 | 26.4 | 23.9 | 13.9 |
| Miscellaneous manufactures | 18.2 | 24.0 | 12.5 | 9.9 | 9.8 | 0.5 | 0.6 | 1.1 | 1.1 | 1.0 |
| Unidentified manufactures | 4.9 | 5.8 | 4.8 | 4.5 | 4.7 | 0.7 | 1.1 | 1.0 | 1.1 | 1.3 |
| **Agricultural and livestock products** | 10.0 | 12.4 | 12.5 | 20.8 | 30.2 | 0.3 | 0.4 | 0.4 | 0.2 | 0.2 |
| Agricultural products | 9.2 | 12.4 | 12.3 | 20.7 | 30.1 | 0.3 | 0.4 | 0.2 | 0.2 | 0.2 |
| Livestock and livestock products | 0.8 | 0.1 | 0.2 | ..... | 0.1 | ..... | ..... | 0.2 | ..... | ..... |
| **Other commodities** | 39.5 | 49.3 | 43.4 | 26.2 | 27.2 | 2.1 | 5.1 | 1.8 | 2.1 | 2.8 |
| Forestry products | 0.4 | 0.5 | 1.2 | 3.6 | 1.5 | ..... | ..... | ..... | ..... | ..... |
| Fish and other marine products | 2.5 | 0.7 | 1.8 | 3.0 | 1.0 | ..... | ..... | ..... | 0.1 | ..... |
| Metallic ores and concentrates | ..... | ..... | ..... | ..... | ..... | ..... | ..... | ..... | ..... | ..... |
| Bituminous coal and lignite | ..... | ..... | ..... | ..... | ..... | ..... | ..... | ..... | ..... | ..... |
| Crude petroleum and natural gas | 4.3 | 1.4 | 0.2 | 0.1 | 1.6 | ..... | ..... | ..... | ..... | ..... |
| Nonmetallic minerals | 0.2 | 0.2 | 0.2 | 0.2 | 0.3 | ..... | 0.1 | ..... | ..... | ..... |
| Scrap and waste | 16.1 | 19.9 | 26.9 | 15.6 | 17.6 | 0.1 | ..... | 0.1 | 0.1 | 0.3 |
| Used merchandise | 2.2 | 1.7 | 2.3 | 0.5 | 0.2 | 0.1 | 0.2 | 0.1 | ..... | ..... |
| Goods imported and returned unchanged | 1.8 | 4.8 | 1.7 | 1.7 | 2.5 | 1.8 | 4.8 | 1.7 | 1.7 | 2.5 |
| Special classification provisions | 12.0 | 20.1 | 9.0 | 1.6 | 2.5 | ..... | ..... | ..... | 0.1 | ..... |

## Table D-3.  State Exports of Goods by Destination and Industry, 1993–1997 —Continued

### PUERTO RICO (Millions of dollars.)

| Industry | 1993 | 1994 | 1995 | 1996 | 1997 | 1993 | 1994 | 1995 | 1996 | 1997 |
|---|---|---|---|---|---|---|---|---|---|---|
| | South and Central America and Caribbean | | | | | Mexico | | | | |
| **ALL GOODS** | 876.7 | 852.6 | 950.0 | 981.8 | 1 097.1 | 129.5 | 137.0 | 205.5 | 226.9 | 216.8 |
| **Manufactured goods** | 843.9 | 809.7 | 913.3 | 961.1 | 1 077.2 | 128.8 | 136.6 | 205.2 | 226.7 | 216.7 |
| Food products | 160.7 | 117.3 | 121.7 | 119.1 | 145.6 | 18.3 | 6.5 | 2.7 | 17.4 | 9.5 |
| Tobacco products | 31.0 | 0.2 | 7.9 | 4.7 | 1.8 | ..... | ..... | ..... | ..... | ..... |
| Textile mill products | 36.5 | 43.5 | 65.6 | 72.8 | 62.3 | 0.1 | 0.1 | ..... | 0.2 | 0.8 |
| Apparel | 33.1 | 34.5 | 61.3 | 62.2 | 86.3 | 2.1 | 0.9 | 0.7 | 0.4 | 0.2 |
| Lumber and wood products | 3.6 | 4.4 | 4.6 | 3.2 | 3.4 | ..... | ..... | 0.1 | ..... | ..... |
| Furniture and fixtures | 1.9 | 1.7 | 1.8 | 1.9 | 1.0 | 0.1 | ..... | ..... | 0.1 | ..... |
| Paper products | 10.1 | 12.5 | 10.5 | 11.7 | 7.3 | 0.5 | 0.7 | 0.7 | 1.0 | 0.4 |
| Printing and publishing | 4.9 | 1.9 | 1.2 | 1.1 | 1.4 | 0.6 | ..... | 0.1 | 0.1 | 0.1 |
| Chemical products | 243.1 | 226.7 | 234.1 | 256.2 | 284.2 | 95.8 | 100.9 | 116.3 | 89.2 | 98.9 |
| Refined petroleum products | 26.1 | 36.6 | 24.5 | 24.2 | 18.8 | 0.8 | 0.8 | 0.4 | 0.3 | 0.2 |
| Rubber and plastic products | 11.2 | 12.6 | 11.2 | 9.8 | 13.8 | 0.3 | 0.9 | 0.8 | 1.6 | 0.6 |
| Leather products | 9.2 | 8.9 | 11.8 | 14.3 | 22.1 | ..... | ..... | ..... | 0.1 | ..... |
| Stone, clay and glass products | 2.0 | 1.5 | 3.7 | 10.3 | 30.3 | 0.5 | 0.2 | ..... | ..... | 0.2 |
| Primary metals | 3.1 | 2.9 | 4.4 | 3.0 | 6.1 | 0.1 | 0.1 | ..... | ..... | ..... |
| Fabricated metal products | 14.2 | 12.8 | 13.2 | 14.5 | 15.4 | 0.2 | 0.4 | 0.4 | 0.1 | 0.2 |
| Industrial machinery and computers | 23.1 | 29.2 | 37.7 | 42.7 | 44.9 | 4.7 | 6.2 | 67.2 | 103.5 | 60.9 |
| Electric and electronic equipment | 104.5 | 129.0 | 133.3 | 156.4 | 183.2 | 1.1 | 11.4 | 10.3 | 5.6 | 31.5 |
| Transportation equipment | 7.8 | 19.4 | 14.1 | 9.0 | 14.2 | ..... | 0.1 | 0.5 | 0.2 | ..... |
| Scientific and measuring instruments | 109.6 | 105.2 | 143.4 | 136.1 | 126.5 | 2.6 | 5.8 | 4.6 | 6.9 | 12.9 |
| Miscellaneous manufactures | 5.9 | 6.0 | 4.6 | 5.5 | 6.5 | 0.9 | 1.5 | 0.3 | 0.1 | 0.2 |
| Unidentified manufactures | 2.3 | 2.7 | 2.6 | 2.1 | 2.1 | 0.2 | 0.2 | ..... | 0.1 | 0.2 |
| **Agricultural and livestock products** | 1.1 | 1.1 | 0.7 | 0.4 | 1.0 | ..... | ..... | ..... | 0.2 | 0.1 |
| Agricultural products | 0.9 | 1.0 | 0.7 | 0.4 | 1.0 | ..... | ..... | ..... | 0.2 | ..... |
| Livestock and livestock products | 0.2 | 0.1 | ..... | ..... | 0.1 | ..... | ..... | ..... | ..... | ..... |
| **Other commodities** | 31.7 | 41.8 | 36.2 | 20.2 | 18.9 | 0.7 | 0.4 | 0.2 | 0.1 | ..... |
| Forestry products | 0.4 | 0.5 | 1.2 | 3.5 | 1.5 | ..... | ..... | ..... | 0.1 | ..... |
| Fish and other marine products | 0.1 | 0.6 | 0.7 | 1.7 | 0.4 | ..... | ..... | ..... | ..... | ..... |
| Metallic ores and concentrates | ..... | ..... | ..... | ..... | ..... | ..... | ..... | ..... | ..... | ..... |
| Bituminous coal and lignite | ..... | ..... | ..... | ..... | ..... | ..... | ..... | ..... | ..... | ..... |
| Crude petroleum and natural gas | 4.2 | 1.4 | 0.2 | 0.1 | 0.1 | ..... | ..... | ..... | ..... | ..... |
| Nonmetallic minerals | 0.1 | 0.1 | 0.2 | 0.1 | 0.2 | ..... | ..... | ..... | ..... | ..... |
| Scrap and waste | 14.5 | 19.0 | 25.8 | 13.8 | 16.2 | ..... | 0.1 | 0.2 | ..... | ..... |
| Used merchandise | 1.5 | 0.6 | 0.5 | 0.4 | 0.2 | 0.6 | 0.3 | ..... | ..... | ..... |
| Goods imported and returned unchanged | ..... | ..... | ..... | ..... | ..... | ..... | ..... | ..... | ..... | ..... |
| Special classification provisions | 11.1 | 19.7 | 7.6 | 0.5 | 0.3 | ..... | ..... | ..... | ..... | ..... |

| Industry | 1993 | 1994 | 1995 | 1996 | 1997 | 1993 | 1994 | 1995 | 1996 | 1997 |
|---|---|---|---|---|---|---|---|---|---|---|
| | European Union | | | | | United Kingdom | | | | |
| **ALL GOODS** | 1 872.5 | 1 787.3 | 2 042.1 | 2 277.3 | 2 115.0 | 319.4 | 249.9 | 238.3 | 148.4 | 179.4 |
| **Manufactured goods** | 1 864.1 | 1 775.0 | 2 027.8 | 2 255.4 | 2 083.5 | 317.0 | 245.2 | 235.3 | 146.6 | 175.0 |
| Food products | 5.5 | 4.1 | 4.5 | 3.7 | 6.1 | ..... | ..... | ..... | ..... | 0.1 |
| Tobacco products | 0.1 | 36.3 | 78.2 | 66.4 | 35.1 | ..... | ..... | ..... | ..... | ..... |
| Textile mill products | ..... | 0.1 | 0.6 | 0.3 | 0.4 | ..... | ..... | ..... | 0.3 | 0.1 |
| Apparel | 0.6 | 0.4 | 1.0 | 0.4 | 0.1 | 0.3 | ..... | ..... | ..... | ..... |
| Lumber and wood products | 0.4 | ..... | ..... | 0.1 | 0.1 | 0.1 | ..... | ..... | ..... | ..... |
| Furniture and fixtures | 1.0 | 0.2 | 0.5 | 2.0 | 2.4 | ..... | ..... | 0.2 | 0.2 | 0.3 |
| Paper products | 1.3 | 0.1 | 0.6 | 0.4 | 0.2 | 0.1 | ..... | ..... | ..... | ..... |
| Printing and publishing | 0.8 | 0.2 | 0.6 | 0.6 | 0.1 | 0.2 | ..... | ..... | 0.1 | ..... |
| Chemical products | 1 130.3 | 972.6 | 895.6 | 925.7 | 1 093.3 | 104.7 | 87.1 | 77.9 | 56.0 | 93.3 |
| Refined petroleum products | 9.8 | 10.2 | 7.1 | 8.4 | 10.4 | ..... | ..... | ..... | ..... | ..... |
| Rubber and plastic products | 3.4 | 4.3 | 4.8 | 4.8 | 4.3 | 2.4 | 3.6 | 2.8 | 3.1 | 2.9 |
| Leather products | 13.8 | 20.4 | 7.8 | 4.8 | 19.7 | 2.8 | 3.2 | 0.8 | 0.2 | 0.6 |
| Stone, clay and glass products | 0.5 | 0.4 | 1.9 | 0.2 | 0.5 | ..... | 0.1 | 0.1 | 0.1 | 0.1 |
| Primary metals | 4.9 | 3.1 | 0.5 | 3.5 | 4.4 | 4.9 | 2.9 | 0.3 | 2.4 | 2.1 |
| Fabricated metal products | 0.6 | 2.5 | 2.2 | 1.1 | 1.0 | 0.2 | 1.7 | 1.5 | 0.6 | 0.4 |
| Industrial machinery and computers | 474.8 | 459.3 | 790.2 | 1 051.2 | 712.0 | 148.8 | 81.9 | 93.0 | 50.6 | 44.2 |
| Electric and electronic equipment | 122.7 | 159.2 | 134.9 | 91.9 | 113.4 | 25.9 | 27.4 | 35.0 | 11.5 | 14.4 |
| Transportation equipment | 3.1 | 1.4 | 1.2 | 2.5 | 0.4 | ..... | ..... | 0.2 | 2.0 | 0.1 |
| Scientific and measuring instruments | 80.1 | 83.6 | 88.7 | 84.2 | 77.3 | 17.0 | 22.4 | 18.0 | 16.9 | 14.8 |
| Miscellaneous manufactures | 9.5 | 15.3 | 6.2 | 2.6 | 1.8 | 9.3 | 14.6 | 5.1 | 2.5 | 1.5 |
| Unidentified manufactures | 1.1 | 1.1 | 0.8 | 0.5 | 0.5 | 0.4 | 0.3 | 0.3 | 0.1 | 0.1 |
| **Agricultural and livestock products** | 7.9 | 11.0 | 11.4 | 19.8 | 28.7 | 2.3 | 4.5 | 3.0 | 1.7 | 4.3 |
| Agricultural products | 7.9 | 11.0 | 11.4 | 19.8 | 28.7 | 2.3 | 4.5 | 3.0 | 1.7 | 4.3 |
| Livestock and livestock products | ..... | ..... | ..... | ..... | ..... | ..... | ..... | ..... | ..... | ..... |
| **Other commodities** | 0.5 | 1.3 | 2.9 | 2.1 | 2.8 | 0.1 | 0.2 | ..... | ..... | 0.1 |
| Forestry products | ..... | ..... | ..... | ..... | ..... | ..... | ..... | ..... | ..... | ..... |
| Fish and other marine products | ..... | 0.1 | 0.2 | 0.6 | 0.2 | ..... | ..... | ..... | ..... | ..... |
| Metallic ores and concentrates | ..... | ..... | ..... | ..... | ..... | ..... | ..... | ..... | ..... | ..... |
| Bituminous coal and lignite | ..... | ..... | ..... | ..... | ..... | ..... | ..... | ..... | ..... | ..... |
| Crude petroleum and natural gas | ..... | ..... | ..... | ..... | 1.6 | ..... | ..... | ..... | ..... | ..... |
| Nonmetallic minerals | ..... | ..... | ..... | ..... | ..... | ..... | ..... | ..... | ..... | ..... |
| Scrap and waste | 0.2 | 0.4 | 0.8 | 1.2 | 0.8 | ..... | 0.1 | ..... | ..... | ..... |
| Used merchandise | ..... | 0.6 | 1.7 | ..... | ..... | ..... | ..... | ..... | ..... | ..... |
| Goods imported and returned unchanged | ..... | ..... | ..... | ..... | ..... | ..... | ..... | ..... | ..... | ..... |
| Special classification provisions | 0.2 | 0.3 | 0.2 | 0.2 | 0.2 | 0.1 | 0.1 | ..... | ..... | ..... |

## Table D-3.   State Exports of Goods by Destination and Industry, 1993–1997 —Continued

**PUERTO RICO** (Millions of dollars.)

| Industry | 1993 | 1994 | 1995 | 1996 | 1997 | 1993 | 1994 | 1995 | 1996 | 1997 |
|---|---|---|---|---|---|---|---|---|---|---|
| | Germany | | | | | France | | | | |
| **ALL GOODS** | 597.0 | 652.5 | 781.6 | 935.6 | 532.8 | 211.5 | 209.9 | 309.9 | 309.8 | 318.2 |
| **Manufactured goods** | 596.8 | 652.0 | 780.7 | 935.2 | 530.3 | 211.4 | 209.4 | 309.8 | 309.3 | 318.0 |
| Food products | 1.4 | 1.5 | 1.8 | 1.1 | 0.7 | 0.9 | 0.4 | 0.3 | 0.3 | 0.3 |
| Tobacco products | ..... | ..... | ..... | ..... | ..... | ..... | ..... | ..... | ..... | ..... |
| Textile mill products | ..... | ..... | 0.6 | ..... | ..... | ..... | ..... | ..... | ..... | ..... |
| Apparel | 0.1 | 0.1 | 0.2 | 0.1 | ..... | ..... | ..... | ..... | ..... | ..... |
| Lumber and wood products | ..... | ..... | ..... | ..... | ..... | ..... | ..... | ..... | ..... | ..... |
| Furniture and fixtures | ..... | ..... | ..... | ..... | ..... | ..... | ..... | ..... | ..... | ..... |
| Paper products | 1.2 | ..... | 0.5 | 0.1 | ..... | ..... | ..... | ..... | ..... | ..... |
| Printing and publishing | 0.3 | ..... | ..... | ..... | 0.1 | ..... | ..... | ..... | ..... | ..... |
| Chemical products | 287.3 | 277.9 | 222.7 | 221.7 | 171.0 | 155.7 | 146.6 | 150.1 | 137.9 | 162.5 |
| Refined petroleum products | 9.8 | 8.3 | 7.1 | 8.4 | 9.4 | ..... | ..... | ..... | ..... | ..... |
| Rubber and plastic products | 0.3 | 0.1 | 0.3 | 0.2 | 0.1 | 0.1 | 0.1 | 0.2 | 0.1 | 0.1 |
| Leather products | 3.5 | 7.6 | 2.3 | 1.8 | 9.3 | 3.0 | 5.5 | 1.5 | 0.9 | 0.4 |
| Stone, clay and glass products | ..... | 0.2 | ..... | ..... | ..... | 0.3 | 0.1 | 0.1 | ..... | 0.2 |
| Primary metals | ..... | 0.2 | ..... | ..... | ..... | ..... | ..... | ..... | ..... | ..... |
| Fabricated metal products | 0.1 | 0.2 | 0.1 | 0.1 | ..... | 0.1 | ..... | ..... | ..... | 0.1 |
| Industrial machinery and computers | 250.3 | 295.8 | 520.6 | 683.7 | 320.6 | 34.0 | 43.9 | 145.2 | 151.3 | 118.6 |
| Electric and electronic equipment | 19.7 | 49.4 | 13.6 | 8.2 | 6.7 | 15.6 | 9.6 | 9.2 | 16.2 | 31.6 |
| Transportation equipment | 1.3 | 0.3 | 0.8 | 0.1 | 0.2 | ..... | 0.5 | ..... | ..... | ..... |
| Scientific and measuring instruments | 21.3 | 9.8 | 9.0 | 9.6 | 11.9 | 1.4 | 2.5 | 3.0 | 2.5 | 3.9 |
| Miscellaneous manufactures | 0.1 | 0.5 | 1.0 | ..... | 0.1 | ..... | ..... | ..... | ..... | ..... |
| Unidentified manufactures | 0.1 | 0.1 | 0.1 | 0.1 | ..... | 0.1 | 0.1 | 0.1 | ..... | ..... |
| **Agricultural and livestock products** | 0.1 | 0.3 | 0.3 | ..... | 0.4 | 0.1 | 0.3 | ..... | ..... | 0.1 |
| Agricultural products | 0.1 | 0.3 | 0.3 | ..... | 0.4 | 0.1 | 0.3 | ..... | ..... | 0.1 |
| Livestock and livestock products | ..... | ..... | ..... | ..... | ..... | ..... | ..... | ..... | ..... | ..... |
| **Other commodities** | 0.1 | 0.2 | 0.7 | 0.4 | 2.2 | ..... | 0.2 | 0.1 | 0.5 | 0.1 |
| Forestry products | ..... | ..... | ..... | ..... | ..... | ..... | ..... | ..... | ..... | ..... |
| Fish and other marine products | ..... | ..... | ..... | ..... | ..... | ..... | ..... | ..... | 0.5 | ..... |
| Metallic ores and concentrates | ..... | ..... | ..... | ..... | ..... | ..... | ..... | ..... | ..... | ..... |
| Bituminous coal and lignite | ..... | ..... | ..... | ..... | ..... | ..... | ..... | ..... | ..... | ..... |
| Crude petroleum and natural gas | ..... | ..... | ..... | ..... | 1.6 | ..... | ..... | ..... | ..... | ..... |
| Nonmetallic minerals | ..... | ..... | ..... | ..... | ..... | ..... | ..... | ..... | ..... | ..... |
| Scrap and waste | ..... | 0.1 | 0.6 | 0.3 | 0.5 | ..... | ..... | ..... | ..... | ..... |
| Used merchandise | ..... | ..... | ..... | ..... | ..... | ..... | 0.2 | ..... | ..... | ..... |
| Goods imported and returned unchanged | ..... | ..... | ..... | ..... | ..... | ..... | ..... | ..... | ..... | ..... |
| Special classification provisions | 0.1 | 0.1 | 0.1 | 0.1 | ..... | ..... | ..... | 0.1 | ..... | 0.1 |
| | The Netherlands | | | | | Asian 10 | | | | |
| **ALL GOODS** | 165.5 | 164.9 | 206.8 | 235.5 | 415.6 | 624.9 | 611.0 | 697.5 | 841.5 | 797.8 |
| **Manufactured goods** | 159.9 | 159.1 | 205.8 | 233.7 | 413.6 | 622.6 | 610.6 | 695.5 | 840.6 | 796.8 |
| Food products | 2.4 | 2.0 | 2.0 | 1.9 | 1.6 | 30.3 | 35.0 | 19.6 | 46.4 | 56.0 |
| Tobacco products | ..... | 5.7 | ..... | 0.2 | ..... | 0.1 | 2.8 | 0.2 | 0.1 | 0.4 |
| Textile mill products | ..... | ..... | ..... | ..... | 0.1 | ..... | 0.1 | 0.1 | 0.2 | 0.3 |
| Apparel | ..... | 0.1 | ..... | ..... | ..... | 0.1 | 0.1 | 0.3 | 0.2 | 0.3 |
| Lumber and wood products | ..... | ..... | ..... | ..... | ..... | ..... | ..... | ..... | ..... | 0.1 |
| Furniture and fixtures | 0.1 | ..... | ..... | 1.7 | 2.0 | ..... | 0.1 | ..... | 0.1 | 0.1 |
| Paper products | ..... | ..... | ..... | 0.2 | 0.1 | 0.3 | 0.2 | 0.1 | 0.3 | ..... |
| Printing and publishing | ..... | ..... | ..... | 0.1 | ..... | ..... | 0.1 | 0.4 | 1.1 | 0.5 |
| Chemical products | 118.4 | 96.5 | 143.0 | 77.3 | 164.2 | 416.6 | 348.4 | 317.1 | 231.8 | 274.9 |
| Refined petroleum products | ..... | 1.9 | ..... | ..... | 0.4 | ..... | ..... | ..... | ..... | 0.4 |
| Rubber and plastic products | ..... | 0.2 | 0.8 | 0.1 | 0.3 | 1.5 | 0.4 | 0.3 | 0.7 | 0.5 |
| Leather products | ..... | 0.1 | 0.2 | 0.7 | 5.3 | 1.5 | 1.7 | 2.0 | 0.3 | 1.8 |
| Stone, clay and glass products | ..... | ..... | 1.4 | ..... | ..... | 0.1 | ..... | ..... | 0.1 | 0.2 |
| Primary metals | ..... | ..... | ..... | ..... | ..... | 0.3 | 1.2 | 0.1 | 3.5 | 17.9 |
| Fabricated metal products | ..... | 0.4 | ..... | ..... | 0.1 | 0.1 | 2.2 | 3.3 | 1.0 | 0.2 |
| Industrial machinery and computers | 6.4 | 7.9 | 7.4 | 106.1 | 199.0 | 105.2 | 131.4 | 216.9 | 420.1 | 324.4 |
| Electric and electronic equipment | 0.9 | 1.5 | 3.9 | 5.1 | 1.5 | 17.7 | 35.5 | 66.1 | 41.5 | 50.6 |
| Transportation equipment | 0.5 | 0.5 | 0.1 | ..... | ..... | 0.2 | 0.2 | 0.2 | 0.7 | 0.3 |
| Scientific and measuring instruments | 31.0 | 42.2 | 46.8 | 40.1 | 39.0 | 47.2 | 50.4 | 68.0 | 91.8 | 67.8 |
| Miscellaneous manufactures | ..... | ..... | ..... | ..... | ..... | 1.1 | 0.5 | 0.4 | 0.2 | 0.1 |
| Unidentified manufactures | 0.1 | 0.1 | ..... | ..... | 0.1 | 0.3 | 0.3 | 0.1 | 0.5 | 0.2 |
| **Agricultural and livestock products** | 5.3 | 5.6 | 0.8 | 0.9 | 1.7 | 0.6 | ..... | ..... | 0.2 | 0.2 |
| Agricultural products | 5.3 | 5.6 | 0.8 | 0.9 | 1.7 | ..... | ..... | ..... | 0.2 | 0.2 |
| Livestock and livestock products | ..... | ..... | ..... | ..... | ..... | 0.6 | ..... | ..... | ..... | ..... |
| **Other commodities** | 0.3 | 0.2 | 0.2 | 0.9 | 0.2 | 1.7 | 0.4 | 2.0 | 0.7 | 0.8 |
| Forestry products | ..... | ..... | ..... | ..... | ..... | ..... | ..... | ..... | ..... | ..... |
| Fish and other marine products | ..... | ..... | ..... | ..... | ..... | 0.1 | ..... | 0.9 | 0.1 | 0.4 |
| Metallic ores and concentrates | ..... | ..... | ..... | ..... | ..... | ..... | ..... | ..... | ..... | ..... |
| Bituminous coal and lignite | ..... | ..... | ..... | ..... | ..... | ..... | ..... | ..... | ..... | ..... |
| Crude petroleum and natural gas | ..... | ..... | ..... | ..... | ..... | ..... | ..... | ..... | ..... | ..... |
| Nonmetallic minerals | ..... | ..... | ..... | ..... | ..... | ..... | ..... | ..... | ..... | ..... |
| Scrap and waste | 0.2 | 0.2 | 0.2 | 0.9 | 0.2 | 1.2 | 0.3 | 0.1 | 0.5 | 0.2 |
| Used merchandise | ..... | ..... | ..... | ..... | ..... | ..... | ..... | ..... | ..... | ..... |
| Goods imported and returned unchanged | ..... | ..... | ..... | ..... | ..... | 0.4 | 0.1 | 1.0 | 0.2 | 0.2 |
| Special classification provisions | ..... | ..... | ..... | ..... | ..... | ..... | ..... | ..... | ..... | ..... |

## Table D-3.  State Exports of Goods by Destination and Industry, 1993–1997 —*Continued*

**PUERTO RICO** (Millions of dollars.)

| Industry | 1993 | 1994 | 1995 | 1996 | 1997 | 1993 | 1994 | 1995 | 1996 | 1997 |
|---|---|---|---|---|---|---|---|---|---|---|
| | Japan | | | | | South Korea | | | | |
| **ALL GOODS** | 429.3 | 397.3 | 400.5 | 413.1 | 448.7 | 49.5 | 43.1 | 61.7 | 51.5 | 35.0 |
| **Manufactured goods** | 429.0 | 397.2 | 399.5 | 412.8 | 448.5 | 48.2 | 43.0 | 61.7 | 51.5 | 35.0 |
| Food products | 2.0 | 0.5 | 0.2 | 0.5 | 0.3 | 0.4 | 0.1 | ..... | ..... | 0.3 |
| Tobacco products | ..... | ..... | ..... | ..... | ..... | 0.1 | ..... | ..... | ..... | ..... |
| Textile mill products | ..... | ..... | ..... | ..... | 0.1 | ..... | ..... | ..... | ..... | ..... |
| Apparel | 0.1 | 0.1 | 0.3 | 0.2 | 0.2 | ..... | ..... | ..... | ..... | ..... |
| Lumber and wood products | ..... | ..... | ..... | ..... | ..... | ..... | ..... | ..... | ..... | ..... |
| Furniture and fixtures | ..... | 0.1 | ..... | ..... | 0.1 | ..... | ..... | ..... | ..... | ..... |
| Paper products | 0.1 | ..... | ..... | 0.2 | ..... | ..... | ..... | 0.1 | ..... | ..... |
| Printing and publishing | ..... | 0.1 | ..... | 1.1 | 0.3 | ..... | ..... | ..... | ..... | 0.1 |
| Chemical products | 311.6 | 269.7 | 221.5 | 150.7 | 194.1 | 41.5 | 33.3 | 51.5 | 38.0 | 21.9 |
| Refined petroleum products | ..... | ..... | ..... | ..... | 0.3 | ..... | ..... | ..... | ..... | ..... |
| Rubber and plastic products | 1.3 | 0.3 | 0.2 | 0.3 | 0.3 | ..... | ..... | ..... | ..... | ..... |
| Leather products | 0.1 | 0.3 | 0.2 | 0.2 | ..... | 0.1 | 0.1 | ..... | 0.1 | 1.8 |
| Stone, clay and glass products | ..... | ..... | ..... | ..... | 0.1 | ..... | ..... | ..... | ..... | ..... |
| Primary metals | ..... | 1.2 | 0.1 | 0.1 | 0.7 | ..... | ..... | ..... | ..... | ..... |
| Fabricated metal products | 0.1 | 2.0 | 2.9 | 0.9 | 0.1 | ..... | ..... | ..... | ..... | ..... |
| Industrial machinery and computers | 63.0 | 65.2 | 92.9 | 168.5 | 184.3 | 2.1 | 6.1 | 7.2 | 8.2 | 8.7 |
| Electric and electronic equipment | 9.8 | 12.7 | 18.7 | 7.6 | 5.8 | 0.8 | 0.8 | 0.6 | 1.2 | 0.9 |
| Transportation equipment | 0.1 | 0.1 | 0.2 | 0.3 | 0.3 | ..... | ..... | ..... | 0.3 | ..... |
| Scientific and measuring instruments | 40.6 | 44.8 | 62.2 | 82.1 | 61.5 | 2.3 | 2.5 | 2.2 | 3.5 | 1.0 |
| Miscellaneous manufactures | ..... | 0.2 | ..... | ..... | ..... | 1.0 | ..... | ..... | ..... | 0.1 |
| Unidentified manufactures | 0.1 | 0.1 | ..... | ..... | ..... | ..... | ..... | ..... | ..... | 0.1 |
| **Agricultural and livestock products** | ..... | ..... | ..... | 0.2 | 0.2 | ..... | ..... | ..... | ..... | ..... |
| Agricultural products | ..... | ..... | ..... | 0.2 | 0.2 | ..... | ..... | ..... | ..... | ..... |
| Livestock and livestock products | ..... | ..... | ..... | ..... | ..... | ..... | ..... | ..... | ..... | ..... |
| **Other commodities** | 0.3 | 0.1 | 1.0 | 0.1 | 0.1 | 1.3 | 0.1 | ..... | ..... | ..... |
| Forestry products | ..... | ..... | ..... | ..... | ..... | ..... | ..... | ..... | ..... | ..... |
| Fish and other marine products | ..... | ..... | 0.9 | 0.1 | ..... | 0.1 | ..... | ..... | ..... | ..... |
| Metallic ores and concentrates | ..... | ..... | ..... | ..... | ..... | ..... | ..... | ..... | ..... | ..... |
| Bituminous coal and lignite | ..... | ..... | ..... | ..... | ..... | ..... | ..... | ..... | ..... | ..... |
| Crude petroleum and natural gas | ..... | ..... | ..... | ..... | ..... | ..... | ..... | ..... | ..... | ..... |
| Nonmetallic minerals | ..... | ..... | ..... | ..... | ..... | ..... | ..... | ..... | ..... | ..... |
| Scrap and waste | ..... | 0.1 | ..... | ..... | ..... | 1.2 | 0.1 | ..... | ..... | ..... |
| Used merchandise | ..... | ..... | ..... | ..... | ..... | ..... | ..... | ..... | ..... | ..... |
| Goods imported and returned unchanged | ..... | ..... | ..... | ..... | ..... | ..... | ..... | ..... | ..... | ..... |
| Special classification provisions | 0.3 | ..... | 0.1 | ..... | 0.1 | ..... | ..... | ..... | ..... | ..... |
| | Taiwan | | | | | Singapore | | | | |
| **ALL GOODS** | 42.5 | 29.5 | 23.0 | 37.7 | 56.4 | 43.4 | 71.4 | 140.9 | 244.8 | 149.8 |
| **Manufactured goods** | 42.5 | 29.5 | 23.0 | 37.6 | 56.4 | 43.4 | 71.3 | 140.8 | 244.5 | 149.7 |
| Food products | 6.0 | 6.5 | 4.8 | 9.6 | 9.2 | 5.6 | 6.8 | 3.3 | 6.5 | 10.5 |
| Tobacco products | ..... | ..... | ..... | ..... | ..... | ..... | 2.8 | 0.2 | 0.1 | 0.4 |
| Textile mill products | ..... | ..... | ..... | ..... | ..... | ..... | ..... | ..... | 0.1 | ..... |
| Apparel | ..... | ..... | ..... | ..... | ..... | ..... | ..... | ..... | ..... | ..... |
| Lumber and wood products | ..... | ..... | ..... | ..... | ..... | ..... | ..... | ..... | ..... | ..... |
| Furniture and fixtures | ..... | ..... | ..... | ..... | ..... | ..... | ..... | ..... | 0.1 | ..... |
| Paper products | ..... | ..... | ..... | ..... | ..... | ..... | ..... | ..... | ..... | ..... |
| Printing and publishing | ..... | ..... | ..... | ..... | ..... | ..... | ..... | ..... | ..... | ..... |
| Chemical products | 30.6 | 17.6 | 14.4 | 20.2 | 21.7 | 4.2 | 6.6 | 4.5 | 2.5 | 10.3 |
| Refined petroleum products | ..... | ..... | ..... | ..... | ..... | ..... | ..... | ..... | ..... | ..... |
| Rubber and plastic products | ..... | ..... | ..... | ..... | ..... | ..... | ..... | ..... | 0.1 | ..... |
| Leather products | 0.1 | ..... | ..... | ..... | ..... | 0.2 | 0.2 | ..... | ..... | ..... |
| Stone, clay and glass products | ..... | ..... | ..... | ..... | ..... | ..... | ..... | ..... | ..... | ..... |
| Primary metals | 0.3 | ..... | ..... | 3.3 | 15.0 | ..... | ..... | ..... | ..... | 0.3 |
| Fabricated metal products | ..... | ..... | ..... | ..... | ..... | ..... | 0.1 | 0.1 | ..... | 0.1 |
| Industrial machinery and computers | 4.3 | 4.5 | 1.8 | 1.7 | 4.6 | 27.7 | 45.6 | 103.9 | 219.0 | 105.3 |
| Electric and electronic equipment | 1.0 | 0.8 | 1.8 | 1.3 | 5.1 | 4.7 | 8.3 | 28.5 | 15.5 | 22.1 |
| Transportation equipment | ..... | ..... | ..... | ..... | ..... | ..... | ..... | ..... | ..... | ..... |
| Scientific and measuring instruments | 0.1 | ..... | 0.2 | 1.5 | 0.7 | 0.9 | 0.9 | 0.4 | 0.5 | 0.5 |
| Miscellaneous manufactures | ..... | ..... | ..... | ..... | ..... | ..... | ..... | ..... | ..... | ..... |
| Unidentified manufactures | 0.1 | ..... | ..... | ..... | ..... | 0.1 | 0.1 | ..... | 0.1 | ..... |
| **Agricultural and livestock products** | ..... | ..... | ..... | ..... | ..... | ..... | ..... | ..... | ..... | ..... |
| Agricultural products | ..... | ..... | ..... | ..... | ..... | ..... | ..... | ..... | ..... | ..... |
| Livestock and livestock products | ..... | ..... | ..... | ..... | ..... | ..... | ..... | ..... | ..... | ..... |
| **Other commodities** | 0.1 | ..... | ..... | ..... | ..... | ..... | 0.1 | 0.1 | 0.3 | 0.1 |
| Forestry products | ..... | ..... | ..... | ..... | ..... | ..... | ..... | ..... | ..... | ..... |
| Fish and other marine products | ..... | ..... | ..... | ..... | ..... | ..... | ..... | ..... | ..... | ..... |
| Metallic ores and concentrates | ..... | ..... | ..... | ..... | ..... | ..... | ..... | ..... | ..... | ..... |
| Bituminous coal and lignite | ..... | ..... | ..... | ..... | ..... | ..... | ..... | ..... | ..... | ..... |
| Crude petroleum and natural gas | ..... | ..... | ..... | ..... | ..... | ..... | ..... | ..... | ..... | ..... |
| Nonmetallic minerals | ..... | ..... | ..... | ..... | ..... | ..... | ..... | ..... | ..... | ..... |
| Scrap and waste | ..... | ..... | ..... | ..... | ..... | ..... | ..... | ..... | 0.3 | ..... |
| Used merchandise | ..... | ..... | ..... | ..... | ..... | ..... | ..... | ..... | ..... | ..... |
| Goods imported and returned unchanged | ..... | ..... | ..... | ..... | ..... | ..... | ..... | ..... | ..... | ..... |
| Special classification provisions | 0.1 | ..... | ..... | ..... | ..... | ..... | 0.1 | 0.1 | ..... | 0.1 |

## RHODE ISLAND: Exports of Goods, 1997

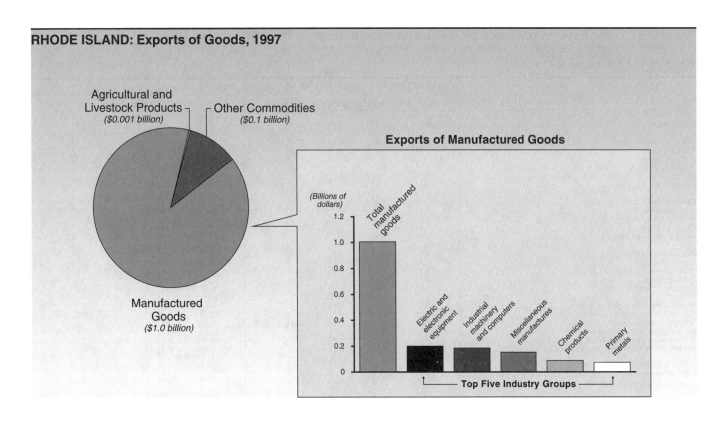

## Table D-3.   State Exports of Goods by Destination and Industry, 1993–1997 —*Continued*

**RHODE ISLAND** (Millions of dollars.)

| Industry | 1993 | 1994 | 1995 | 1996 | 1997 | 1993 | 1994 | 1995 | 1996 | 1997 |
|---|---|---|---|---|---|---|---|---|---|---|
| | All destinations | | | | | Canada | | | | |
| **ALL GOODS** | 938.4 | 1 011.5 | 956.8 | 954.8 | 1 126.5 | 286.3 | 268.8 | 294.3 | 322.6 | 329.6 |
| **Manufactured goods** | 823.8 | 884.6 | 793.7 | 811.7 | 1 005.8 | 239.9 | 216.1 | 234.8 | 260.2 | 275.1 |
| Food products | 6.3 | 6.3 | 8.9 | 11.0 | 5.8 | 5.1 | 4.8 | 7.0 | 5.8 | 3.4 |
| Tobacco products | ..... | ..... | ..... | ..... | 0.1 | ..... | ..... | ..... | 0.1 | ..... |
| Textile mill products | 26.0 | 26.3 | 31.8 | 34.8 | 36.2 | 14.1 | 13.6 | 14.8 | 14.6 | 18.1 |
| Apparel | 2.0 | 2.1 | 2.5 | 1.8 | 2.8 | 1.0 | 0.9 | 1.0 | 0.7 | 1.4 |
| Lumber and wood products | 1.5 | 1.2 | 1.4 | 1.6 | 1.9 | 0.7 | 0.5 | 0.8 | 1.1 | 1.3 |
| Furniture and fixtures | 2.7 | 2.4 | 2.5 | 1.8 | 2.6 | 0.4 | 0.7 | 0.7 | 0.8 | 0.9 |
| Paper products | 9.7 | 7.9 | 10.3 | 10.4 | 18.8 | 4.2 | 3.7 | 5.2 | 5.7 | 4.9 |
| Printing and publishing | 4.9 | 4.3 | 5.8 | 5.9 | 3.9 | 1.2 | 1.0 | 1.1 | 1.7 | 0.8 |
| Chemical products | 77.6 | 51.5 | 51.4 | 38.7 | 88.6 | 24.2 | 19.1 | 17.7 | 15.5 | 17.1 |
| Refined petroleum products | 0.4 | 0.7 | 0.8 | 0.6 | 0.5 | ..... | 0.1 | 0.2 | ..... | 0.1 |
| Rubber and plastic products | 48.7 | 50.4 | 53.0 | 53.6 | 61.0 | 15.5 | 16.2 | 17.3 | 23.8 | 21.7 |
| Leather products | 2.1 | 1.0 | 1.8 | 3.0 | 2.1 | 0.6 | 0.5 | 0.7 | 1.1 | 1.1 |
| Stone, clay and glass products | 7.7 | 6.8 | 7.8 | 6.7 | 6.3 | 6.3 | 5.3 | 4.8 | 3.9 | 4.5 |
| Primary metals | 75.8 | 72.3 | 61.4 | 59.0 | 73.3 | 32.3 | 30.5 | 33.0 | 35.6 | 40.3 |
| Fabricated metal products | 32.5 | 32.3 | 35.6 | 37.8 | 46.5 | 7.8 | 10.3 | 12.4 | 12.9 | 15.5 |
| Industrial machinery and computers | 188.2 | 229.9 | 142.6 | 169.0 | 185.7 | 47.5 | 26.2 | 29.8 | 38.5 | 34.6 |
| Electric and electronic equipment | 112.8 | 153.6 | 146.9 | 156.6 | 200.7 | 19.1 | 24.2 | 31.4 | 41.4 | 52.8 |
| Transportation equipment | 34.8 | 32.7 | 34.9 | 35.3 | 40.6 | 16.4 | 16.5 | 20.1 | 21.0 | 20.4 |
| Scientific and measuring instruments | 52.5 | 55.2 | 57.7 | 63.3 | 70.2 | 13.5 | 14.3 | 15.9 | 18.4 | 12.5 |
| Miscellaneous manufactures | 132.9 | 142.1 | 130.8 | 115.5 | 153.0 | 28.8 | 26.0 | 19.1 | 15.5 | 21.4 |
| Unidentified manufactures | 4.7 | 5.5 | 6.0 | 5.3 | 5.6 | 1.3 | 1.8 | 1.9 | 2.1 | 2.3 |
| **Agricultural and livestock products** | 0.8 | 0.7 | 1.5 | 1.2 | 1.4 | 0.1 | 0.1 | 0.1 | 0.3 | 0.4 |
| Agricultural products | 0.4 | 0.2 | 0.2 | 0.4 | 0.4 | 0.1 | ..... | 0.1 | 0.3 | 0.3 |
| Livestock and livestock products | 0.4 | 0.5 | 1.3 | 0.9 | 1.1 | ..... | ..... | ..... | ..... | 0.1 |
| **Other commodities** | 113.9 | 126.2 | 161.6 | 141.8 | 119.3 | 46.3 | 52.6 | 59.4 | 62.1 | 54.0 |
| Forestry products | ..... | 0.1 | ..... | 0.1 | 0.1 | ..... | 0.1 | ..... | 0.1 | 0.1 |
| Fish and other marine products | 25.7 | 26.6 | 36.3 | 33.3 | 24.5 | 5.0 | 6.8 | 10.8 | 11.2 | 7.3 |
| Metallic ores and concentrates | 0.5 | ..... | 0.1 | 0.1 | 0.1 | 0.1 | ..... | 0.1 | 0.1 | ..... |
| Bituminous coal and lignite | ..... | ..... | ..... | ..... | ..... | ..... | ..... | ..... | ..... | ..... |
| Crude petroleum and natural gas | ..... | ..... | ..... | ..... | ..... | ..... | ..... | ..... | ..... | ..... |
| Nonmetallic minerals | 1.1 | 1.0 | 1.1 | 0.9 | 0.2 | 0.1 | 0.2 | 0.2 | 0.1 | 0.1 |
| Scrap and waste | 81.7 | 93.4 | 117.1 | 95.7 | 82.1 | 37.8 | 42.0 | 43.3 | 44.7 | 40.8 |
| Used merchandise | 0.7 | 1.0 | 1.4 | 4.3 | 5.7 | ..... | ..... | 0.1 | 0.5 | 0.3 |
| Goods imported and returned unchanged | 3.1 | 3.4 | 4.7 | 4.9 | 5.0 | 3.1 | 3.4 | 4.7 | 4.9 | 5.0 |
| Special classification provisions | 1.0 | 0.6 | 0.8 | 2.7 | 1.6 | 0.1 | 0.1 | 0.1 | 0.5 | 0.4 |

## Table D-3.  State Exports of Goods by Destination and Industry, 1993–1997 —*Continued*

### RHODE ISLAND (Millions of dollars.)

| Industry | 1993 | 1994 | 1995 | 1996 | 1997 | 1993 | 1994 | 1995 | 1996 | 1997 |
|---|---|---|---|---|---|---|---|---|---|---|
| | South and Central America and Caribbean | | | | | Mexico | | | | |
| **ALL GOODS** | 38.1 | 53.1 | 42.7 | 28.7 | 64.8 | 41.6 | 27.6 | 15.4 | 23.2 | 77.3 |
| **Manufactured goods** | 37.3 | 52.4 | 42.0 | 27.8 | 63.5 | 41.6 | 27.6 | 15.4 | 23.1 | 77.2 |
| Food products | 0.2 | 0.2 | 0.1 | 0.1 | 0.1 | ..... | ..... | ..... | ..... | ..... |
| Tobacco products | ..... | ..... | ..... | ..... | ..... | ..... | ..... | ..... | ..... | ..... |
| Textile mill products | 0.6 | 0.3 | 0.5 | 0.7 | 1.0 | 0.5 | 0.2 | 0.5 | 0.7 | 0.9 |
| Apparel | ..... | 0.1 | 0.2 | 0.2 | 0.2 | 0.2 | 0.2 | 0.1 | ..... | ..... |
| Lumber and wood products | 0.1 | ..... | ..... | ..... | 0.1 | 0.1 | ..... | ..... | ..... | ..... |
| Furniture and fixtures | ..... | 0.1 | 0.2 | 0.3 | 0.5 | 0.3 | 0.1 | ..... | ..... | 0.1 |
| Paper products | 0.4 | 0.4 | 0.2 | 0.1 | 0.1 | 1.0 | 0.3 | ..... | 0.1 | 6.3 |
| Printing and publishing | 0.3 | 0.4 | 0.7 | 0.2 | 0.2 | 0.6 | 0.2 | 0.2 | 0.2 | 0.3 |
| Chemical products | 2.5 | 3.5 | 4.8 | 2.1 | 4.2 | 5.7 | 1.9 | 0.7 | 1.5 | 2.4 |
| Refined petroleum products | 0.1 | 0.1 | 0.1 | ..... | ..... | ..... | ..... | ..... | ..... | 0.1 |
| Rubber and plastic products | 2.8 | 2.1 | 2.2 | 2.3 | 3.2 | 0.6 | 1.3 | 2.5 | 0.7 | 2.0 |
| Leather products | 0.1 | 0.1 | ..... | 0.1 | ..... | ..... | ..... | ..... | ..... | 0.1 |
| Stone, clay and glass products | 0.3 | 0.4 | 0.1 | 0.1 | 0.2 | 0.1 | 0.1 | 0.2 | 0.9 | 0.2 |
| Primary metals | 0.7 | 1.0 | 0.6 | 1.2 | 1.0 | 10.3 | 6.6 | 1.0 | 3.3 | 17.2 |
| Fabricated metal products | 0.6 | 0.9 | 2.1 | 1.3 | 2.4 | 2.9 | 0.8 | 1.5 | 2.9 | 6.8 |
| Industrial machinery and computers | 10.0 | 14.7 | 5.1 | 3.2 | 24.3 | 4.3 | 4.2 | 2.5 | 4.0 | 12.1 |
| Electric and electronic equipment | 5.2 | 11.7 | 8.1 | 3.1 | 4.7 | 8.2 | 2.8 | 1.9 | 3.0 | 5.5 |
| Transportation equipment | 8.5 | 8.2 | 7.0 | 5.5 | 8.6 | 0.4 | 0.9 | 0.6 | 1.3 | 1.5 |
| Scientific and measuring instruments | 1.5 | 1.8 | 1.3 | 1.9 | 4.2 | 1.2 | 1.1 | 0.6 | 1.4 | 1.2 |
| Miscellaneous manufactures | 3.3 | 6.1 | 8.2 | 5.4 | 8.3 | 4.7 | 6.7 | 2.9 | 2.9 | 20.2 |
| Unidentified manufactures | 0.2 | 0.3 | 0.5 | 0.2 | 0.3 | 0.3 | 0.1 | 0.1 | 0.1 | 0.2 |
| **Agricultural and livestock products** | ..... | ..... | ..... | ..... | ..... | ..... | ..... | ..... | ..... | ..... |
| Agricultural products | ..... | ..... | ..... | ..... | ..... | ..... | ..... | ..... | ..... | ..... |
| Livestock and livestock products | ..... | ..... | ..... | ..... | ..... | ..... | ..... | ..... | ..... | ..... |
| **Other commodities** | 0.8 | 0.6 | 0.7 | 0.9 | 1.3 | ..... | 0.1 | ..... | 0.1 | 0.1 |
| Forestry products | ..... | ..... | ..... | ..... | ..... | ..... | ..... | ..... | ..... | ..... |
| Fish and other marine products | 0.5 | 0.5 | 0.6 | 0.8 | 1.3 | ..... | ..... | ..... | ..... | ..... |
| Metallic ores and concentrates | ..... | ..... | ..... | ..... | ..... | ..... | ..... | ..... | ..... | ..... |
| Bituminous coal and lignite | ..... | ..... | ..... | ..... | ..... | ..... | ..... | ..... | ..... | ..... |
| Crude petroleum and natural gas | ..... | ..... | ..... | ..... | ..... | ..... | ..... | ..... | ..... | ..... |
| Nonmetallic minerals | 0.3 | ..... | ..... | ..... | ..... | ..... | ..... | ..... | ..... | ..... |
| Scrap and waste | ..... | ..... | ..... | 0.1 | ..... | ..... | ..... | ..... | ..... | ..... |
| Used merchandise | ..... | 0.1 | ..... | ..... | 0.1 | ..... | ..... | ..... | ..... | ..... |
| Goods imported and returned unchanged | ..... | ..... | ..... | ..... | ..... | ..... | ..... | ..... | ..... | ..... |
| Special classification provisions | ..... | ..... | ..... | ..... | ..... | ..... | ..... | ..... | 0.1 | ..... |
| | European Union | | | | | United Kingdom | | | | |
| **ALL GOODS** | 339.2 | 387.9 | 324.8 | 296.6 | 342.1 | 76.0 | 147.0 | 84.0 | 64.1 | 91.7 |
| **Manufactured goods** | 281.8 | 327.7 | 240.3 | 234.8 | 292.5 | 70.0 | 144.4 | 80.1 | 58.7 | 84.6 |
| Food products | 0.3 | 0.6 | 0.3 | 0.2 | 0.2 | 0.1 | 0.2 | 0.1 | 0.2 | 0.1 |
| Tobacco products | ..... | ..... | ..... | ..... | ..... | ..... | ..... | ..... | ..... | ..... |
| Textile mill products | 6.0 | 7.9 | 9.3 | 12.2 | 9.9 | 2.8 | 3.0 | 3.8 | 4.9 | 4.1 |
| Apparel | 0.4 | 0.3 | 0.4 | 0.3 | 0.4 | 0.1 | ..... | 0.1 | 0.2 | 0.2 |
| Lumber and wood products | 0.1 | ..... | 0.1 | 0.2 | 0.2 | ..... | ..... | ..... | ..... | 0.2 |
| Furniture and fixtures | 0.8 | 0.9 | 0.5 | 0.4 | 0.7 | 0.7 | 0.7 | 0.4 | 0.3 | 0.4 |
| Paper products | 1.3 | 1.7 | 2.4 | 1.4 | 3.0 | 0.4 | 0.3 | 0.5 | 0.1 | 1.0 |
| Printing and publishing | 0.9 | 1.1 | 2.3 | 2.5 | 1.7 | 0.6 | 0.6 | 1.8 | 1.3 | 1.4 |
| Chemical products | 39.4 | 21.8 | 18.8 | 9.7 | 52.7 | 33.7 | 16.3 | 13.2 | 4.6 | 34.4 |
| Refined petroleum products | 0.1 | 0.4 | 0.3 | 0.1 | 0.1 | ..... | ..... | ..... | ..... | ..... |
| Rubber and plastic products | 20.3 | 20.2 | 17.7 | 13.8 | 15.7 | 2.1 | 2.1 | 3.0 | 2.8 | 4.7 |
| Leather products | 0.2 | 0.1 | 0.3 | 0.4 | 0.3 | ..... | ..... | 0.1 | 0.2 | 0.2 |
| Stone, clay and glass products | 0.4 | 0.4 | 1.6 | 0.6 | 0.4 | 0.1 | 0.1 | 0.1 | 0.1 | 0.1 |
| Primary metals | 25.8 | 28.6 | 20.5 | 12.3 | 7.9 | 2.5 | 4.8 | 6.2 | 3.7 | 1.3 |
| Fabricated metal products | 15.6 | 11.6 | 13.4 | 13.5 | 14.3 | 3.9 | 2.4 | 5.7 | 5.9 | 6.1 |
| Industrial machinery and computers | 84.6 | 134.2 | 69.3 | 80.7 | 75.9 | 3.2 | 91.0 | 23.4 | 12.9 | 7.3 |
| Electric and electronic equipment | 29.2 | 45.2 | 30.0 | 31.4 | 39.8 | 4.1 | 10.2 | 8.0 | 4.9 | 4.9 |
| Transportation equipment | 3.5 | 2.5 | 2.5 | 3.7 | 5.9 | 0.4 | 0.8 | 0.7 | 1.8 | 2.0 |
| Scientific and measuring instruments | 17.5 | 18.5 | 17.3 | 20.8 | 31.5 | 3.6 | 3.6 | 3.4 | 3.7 | 4.6 |
| Miscellaneous manufactures | 33.8 | 29.8 | 31.0 | 28.9 | 30.4 | 11.3 | 7.8 | 9.0 | 10.4 | 11.1 |
| Unidentified manufactures | 1.7 | 2.0 | 2.3 | 1.9 | 1.6 | 0.4 | 0.5 | 0.6 | 0.6 | 0.6 |
| **Agricultural and livestock products** | 0.3 | 0.5 | 0.7 | 0.7 | 0.9 | 0.1 | 0.1 | ..... | 0.1 | 0.5 |
| Agricultural products | ..... | ..... | ..... | ..... | ..... | ..... | ..... | ..... | ..... | ..... |
| Livestock and livestock products | 0.2 | 0.5 | 0.7 | 0.7 | 0.9 | 0.1 | 0.1 | ..... | 0.1 | 0.5 |
| **Other commodities** | 57.2 | 59.6 | 83.9 | 61.0 | 48.7 | 5.9 | 2.5 | 3.9 | 5.3 | 6.6 |
| Forestry products | ..... | 0.1 | ..... | ..... | ..... | ..... | ..... | ..... | ..... | ..... |
| Fish and other marine products | 13.6 | 9.6 | 9.1 | 5.7 | 2.1 | 1.6 | 1.3 | 0.3 | 0.1 | 0.1 |
| Metallic ores and concentrates | 0.3 | ..... | ..... | ..... | 0.1 | 0.3 | ..... | ..... | ..... | ..... |
| Bituminous coal and lignite | ..... | ..... | ..... | ..... | ..... | ..... | ..... | ..... | ..... | ..... |
| Crude petroleum and natural gas | ..... | ..... | ..... | ..... | ..... | ..... | ..... | ..... | ..... | ..... |
| Nonmetallic minerals | ..... | 0.3 | 0.6 | 0.1 | ..... | ..... | 0.1 | ..... | ..... | ..... |
| Scrap and waste | 42.5 | 48.8 | 72.9 | 50.4 | 40.8 | 3.7 | 0.5 | 3.4 | 1.2 | 1.7 |
| Used merchandise | 0.7 | 0.8 | 1.0 | 3.8 | 5.3 | 0.4 | 0.6 | 0.1 | 3.5 | 4.7 |
| Goods imported and returned unchanged | ..... | ..... | ..... | ..... | ..... | ..... | ..... | ..... | ..... | ..... |
| Special classification provisions | 0.1 | 0.1 | 0.3 | 1.0 | 0.4 | ..... | ..... | ..... | 0.4 | 0.1 |

## Table D-3.   State Exports of Goods by Destination and Industry, 1993–1997 —*Continued*

**RHODE ISLAND** (Millions of dollars.)

| Industry | 1993 | 1994 | 1995 | 1996 | 1997 | 1993 | 1994 | 1995 | 1996 | 1997 |
|---|---|---|---|---|---|---|---|---|---|---|
| | Germany | | | | | France | | | | |
| **ALL GOODS** | 39.0 | 25.2 | 30.1 | 38.6 | 41.2 | 17.6 | 19.2 | 18.3 | 16.4 | 18.3 |
| **Manufactured goods** | 38.7 | 24.9 | 29.9 | 38.3 | 40.5 | 12.9 | 16.9 | 16.3 | 14.9 | 17.6 |
| Food products | 0.1 | 0.1 | ..... | ..... | ..... | ..... | ..... | ..... | ..... | ..... |
| Tobacco products | ..... | ..... | ..... | ..... | ..... | ..... | ..... | ..... | ..... | ..... |
| Textile mill products | 1.4 | 1.4 | 2.6 | 3.5 | 2.4 | 0.2 | ..... | ..... | 0.1 | 0.1 |
| Apparel | ..... | 0.1 | 0.2 | ..... | ..... | ..... | ..... | ..... | ..... | ..... |
| Lumber and wood products | ..... | ..... | ..... | ..... | ..... | 0.1 | ..... | ..... | ..... | ..... |
| Furniture and fixtures | ..... | ..... | ..... | ..... | ..... | ..... | ..... | ..... | 0.1 | 0.1 |
| Paper products | 0.2 | 0.4 | 0.3 | 0.2 | 0.8 | 0.2 | 0.3 | ..... | 0.2 | 0.4 |
| Printing and publishing | 0.1 | 0.3 | 0.1 | 0.2 | 0.1 | ..... | 0.1 | ..... | ..... | ..... |
| Chemical products | 1.9 | 1.1 | 1.5 | 1.3 | 10.6 | 0.8 | 0.2 | 0.2 | 0.2 | 0.4 |
| Refined petroleum products | ..... | ..... | ..... | 0.1 | ..... | ..... | ..... | ..... | ..... | ..... |
| Rubber and plastic products | 1.1 | 1.7 | 2.1 | 2.1 | 0.8 | 0.9 | 0.4 | 0.3 | 0.2 | 0.3 |
| Leather products | ..... | 0.1 | ..... | ..... | ..... | ..... | ..... | 0.1 | 0.1 | ..... |
| Stone, clay and glass products | ..... | ..... | 0.5 | ..... | ..... | 0.1 | ..... | ..... | ..... | 0.1 |
| Primary metals | 0.4 | 0.3 | 1.3 | 1.0 | 1.8 | 0.2 | 0.3 | 0.5 | 0.5 | 1.3 |
| Fabricated metal products | 0.8 | 0.9 | 0.8 | 0.6 | 0.7 | 0.9 | 1.8 | 1.9 | 2.2 | 3.4 |
| Industrial machinery and computers | 20.6 | 8.1 | 11.4 | 16.9 | 10.8 | 1.9 | 3.7 | 4.8 | 4.6 | 5.9 |
| Electric and electronic equipment | 2.8 | 2.1 | 2.4 | 3.8 | 3.8 | 1.6 | 2.7 | 1.9 | 2.4 | 1.5 |
| Transportation equipment | 0.3 | 0.5 | 0.2 | 0.3 | 0.5 | 0.7 | 0.2 | 0.2 | 0.1 | 0.4 |
| Scientific and measuring instruments | 4.5 | 5.2 | 3.9 | 5.2 | 6.6 | 1.9 | 2.5 | 2.1 | 1.7 | 2.3 |
| Miscellaneous manufactures | 4.3 | 2.5 | 2.4 | 3.0 | 1.3 | 3.3 | 4.5 | 3.7 | 2.4 | 1.1 |
| Unidentified manufactures | 0.1 | 0.2 | 0.2 | 0.1 | 0.1 | 0.2 | 0.2 | 0.4 | 0.1 | 0.2 |
| **Agricultural and livestock products** | ..... | ..... | ..... | ..... | ..... | ..... | ..... | ..... | ..... | ..... |
| Agricultural products | ..... | ..... | ..... | ..... | ..... | ..... | ..... | ..... | ..... | ..... |
| Livestock and livestock products | ..... | ..... | ..... | ..... | ..... | ..... | ..... | ..... | ..... | ..... |
| **Other commodities** | 0.3 | 0.3 | 0.2 | 0.3 | 0.7 | 4.6 | 2.3 | 2.0 | 1.4 | 0.7 |
| Forestry products | ..... | ..... | ..... | ..... | ..... | ..... | ..... | ..... | ..... | ..... |
| Fish and other marine products | 0.3 | 0.2 | 0.2 | 0.1 | ..... | 4.3 | 2.1 | 1.3 | 1.1 | 0.6 |
| Metallic ores and concentrates | ..... | ..... | ..... | ..... | ..... | ..... | ..... | ..... | ..... | ..... |
| Bituminous coal and lignite | ..... | ..... | ..... | ..... | ..... | ..... | ..... | ..... | ..... | ..... |
| Crude petroleum and natural gas | ..... | ..... | ..... | ..... | ..... | ..... | ..... | ..... | ..... | ..... |
| Nonmetallic minerals | ..... | ..... | ..... | ..... | ..... | ..... | ..... | ..... | ..... | ..... |
| Scrap and waste | ..... | ..... | ..... | 0.1 | 0.5 | ..... | ..... | ..... | ..... | 0.1 |
| Used merchandise | ..... | ..... | ..... | ..... | ..... | 0.3 | 0.2 | 0.7 | 0.2 | 0.1 |
| Goods imported and returned unchanged | ..... | ..... | ..... | ..... | ..... | ..... | ..... | ..... | ..... | ..... |
| Special classification provisions | ..... | ..... | ..... | 0.2 | 0.2 | ..... | ..... | ..... | 0.2 | ..... |
| | The Netherlands | | | | | Asian 10 | | | | |
| **ALL GOODS** | 74.1 | 48.4 | 29.1 | 24.7 | 20.8 | 154.0 | 191.6 | 209.9 | 216.9 | 236.1 |
| **Manufactured goods** | 73.9 | 48.2 | 28.8 | 24.1 | 20.6 | 146.1 | 180.9 | 193.4 | 200.1 | 222.6 |
| Food products | ..... | 0.1 | ..... | ..... | ..... | 0.5 | 0.4 | 0.8 | 3.0 | 0.5 |
| Tobacco products | ..... | ..... | ..... | ..... | ..... | ..... | ..... | ..... | ..... | ..... |
| Textile mill products | ..... | 0.1 | 0.4 | 1.8 | 1.2 | 3.7 | 2.9 | 5.0 | 4.4 | 4.5 |
| Apparel | 0.1 | 0.1 | ..... | ..... | ..... | 0.3 | 0.6 | 0.6 | 0.6 | 0.6 |
| Lumber and wood products | ..... | ..... | ..... | ..... | ..... | 0.4 | 0.4 | 0.4 | 0.3 | 0.3 |
| Furniture and fixtures | ..... | ..... | ..... | ..... | ..... | 0.1 | 0.2 | 0.7 | 0.1 | 0.1 |
| Paper products | 0.3 | 0.5 | 0.7 | 0.4 | 0.7 | 1.0 | 1.3 | 2.3 | 2.6 | 4.1 |
| Printing and publishing | ..... | ..... | ..... | ..... | ..... | 1.2 | 1.1 | 1.0 | 0.7 | 0.6 |
| Chemical products | 0.2 | ..... | 0.1 | 0.2 | 0.6 | 3.4 | 3.5 | 5.8 | 6.1 | 8.6 |
| Refined petroleum products | ..... | ..... | ..... | ..... | ..... | 0.2 | 0.1 | 0.2 | 0.5 | 0.2 |
| Rubber and plastic products | 11.9 | 12.4 | 9.0 | 4.7 | 3.6 | 6.9 | 8.3 | 11.0 | 10.9 | 15.8 |
| Leather products | ..... | ..... | ..... | ..... | ..... | 0.3 | 0.3 | 0.2 | ..... | 0.5 |
| Stone, clay and glass products | 0.1 | 0.1 | ..... | ..... | 0.2 | 0.4 | 0.5 | 1.0 | 1.0 | 0.6 |
| Primary metals | 20.6 | 19.2 | 7.5 | 2.8 | 0.1 | 2.3 | 3.9 | 4.6 | 4.6 | 4.6 |
| Fabricated metal products | 0.2 | 0.1 | 0.4 | 1.7 | 0.9 | 2.9 | 6.0 | 4.2 | 5.4 | 5.3 |
| Industrial machinery and computers | 15.6 | 6.1 | 1.8 | 2.9 | 4.4 | 21.8 | 28.9 | 21.3 | 24.6 | 19.2 |
| Electric and electronic equipment | 18.9 | 7.0 | 6.0 | 7.6 | 5.9 | 43.6 | 61.7 | 67.0 | 71.6 | 92.3 |
| Transportation equipment | 0.8 | 0.5 | 0.3 | 0.3 | 0.7 | 1.2 | 1.4 | 1.1 | 1.4 | 1.7 |
| Scientific and measuring instruments | 3.4 | 1.0 | 0.8 | 1.0 | 1.5 | 13.5 | 14.7 | 16.6 | 15.4 | 15.5 |
| Miscellaneous manufactures | 1.8 | 0.9 | 1.6 | 0.7 | 0.7 | 41.9 | 43.8 | 48.8 | 46.1 | 47.0 |
| Unidentified manufactures | 0.1 | 0.1 | 0.1 | ..... | ..... | 0.7 | 0.9 | 0.7 | 0.7 | 0.8 |
| **Agricultural and livestock products** | ..... | ..... | ..... | ..... | ..... | 0.1 | ..... | 0.6 | 0.2 | ..... |
| Agricultural products | ..... | ..... | ..... | ..... | ..... | ..... | ..... | ..... | ..... | ..... |
| Livestock and livestock products | ..... | ..... | ..... | ..... | ..... | 0.1 | ..... | 0.6 | 0.2 | ..... |
| **Other commodities** | 0.1 | 0.2 | 0.3 | 0.6 | 0.2 | 7.8 | 10.7 | 16.0 | 16.6 | 13.4 |
| Forestry products | ..... | ..... | ..... | ..... | ..... | ..... | ..... | ..... | ..... | ..... |
| Fish and other marine products | 0.1 | 0.2 | 0.1 | 0.5 | 0.2 | 5.9 | 9.0 | 15.0 | 14.8 | 12.2 |
| Metallic ores and concentrates | ..... | ..... | ..... | ..... | ..... | ..... | ..... | ..... | ..... | ..... |
| Bituminous coal and lignite | ..... | ..... | ..... | ..... | ..... | ..... | ..... | ..... | ..... | ..... |
| Crude petroleum and natural gas | ..... | ..... | ..... | ..... | ..... | ..... | ..... | ..... | ..... | ..... |
| Nonmetallic minerals | ..... | ..... | ..... | ..... | ..... | 0.4 | 0.3 | 0.3 | 0.7 | 0.1 |
| Scrap and waste | ..... | ..... | ..... | ..... | ..... | 0.8 | 1.0 | 0.3 | 0.4 | 0.4 |
| Used merchandise | ..... | ..... | ..... | ..... | ..... | ..... | ..... | 0.1 | 0.1 | ..... |
| Goods imported and returned unchanged | ..... | ..... | ..... | ..... | ..... | ..... | ..... | ..... | ..... | ..... |
| Special classification provisions | ..... | ..... | 0.2 | 0.1 | ..... | 0.7 | 0.3 | 0.3 | 0.7 | 0.7 |

## Table D-3.   State Exports of Goods by Destination and Industry, 1993–1997 —*Continued*

## RHODE ISLAND (Millions of dollars.)

| Industry | 1993 | 1994 | 1995 | 1996 | 1997 | 1993 | 1994 | 1995 | 1996 | 1997 |
|---|---|---|---|---|---|---|---|---|---|---|
| | Japan | | | | | South Korea | | | | |
| **ALL GOODS** | 42.9 | 46.7 | 65.8 | 61.8 | 89.4 | 14.9 | 24.8 | 28.6 | 26.8 | 20.2 |
| **Manufactured goods** | 36.6 | 40.0 | 59.3 | 57.1 | 86.5 | 14.7 | 22.2 | 19.7 | 18.8 | 15.6 |
| Food products | 0.5 | 0.3 | ..... | 0.1 | 0.2 | ..... | ..... | 0.2 | ..... | ..... |
| Tobacco products | ..... | ..... | ..... | ..... | ..... | ..... | ..... | ..... | ..... | ..... |
| Textile mill products | 0.2 | 0.4 | 0.2 | 0.2 | 0.2 | ..... | ..... | 0.5 | 1.0 | 1.1 |
| Apparel | ..... | 0.1 | 0.1 | 0.2 | 0.3 | ..... | ..... | 0.1 | 0.1 | ..... |
| Lumber and wood products | ..... | ..... | 0.3 | 0.2 | 0.2 | ..... | ..... | ..... | ..... | ..... |
| Furniture and fixtures | ..... | 0.1 | ..... | ..... | ..... | ..... | ..... | ..... | ..... | ..... |
| Paper products | 0.2 | 0.2 | 0.1 | 0.1 | 0.2 | ..... | ..... | 0.1 | 0.1 | 0.1 |
| Printing and publishing | 0.1 | 0.1 | 0.2 | 0.2 | 0.2 | ..... | ..... | ..... | ..... | ..... |
| Chemical products | 0.5 | 0.5 | 0.9 | 1.0 | 1.5 | 1.0 | 0.7 | 0.5 | 0.8 | 0.4 |
| Refined petroleum products | 0.1 | 0.1 | 0.2 | 0.1 | 0.2 | ..... | ..... | ..... | ..... | ..... |
| Rubber and plastic products | 3.9 | 3.8 | 4.1 | 4.2 | 7.6 | 0.4 | 1.1 | 1.7 | 1.8 | 1.7 |
| Leather products | 0.1 | ..... | 0.1 | ..... | 0.1 | ..... | ..... | 0.1 | ..... | ..... |
| Stone, clay and glass products | 0.2 | 0.2 | 0.7 | 0.5 | 0.1 | 0.1 | ..... | ..... | 0.2 | 0.1 |
| Primary metals | 0.6 | 1.0 | 0.8 | 1.8 | 0.9 | 0.1 | 0.1 | 0.2 | 0.1 | 0.1 |
| Fabricated metal products | 0.4 | 0.9 | 0.4 | 0.5 | 1.4 | 0.5 | 0.7 | 0.7 | 0.7 | 0.6 |
| Industrial machinery and computers | 1.6 | 1.2 | 3.7 | 4.8 | 5.5 | 1.3 | 2.3 | 2.8 | 2.7 | 1.2 |
| Electric and electronic equipment | 1.9 | 6.1 | 17.0 | 20.5 | 36.5 | 5.9 | 10.0 | 7.6 | 4.8 | 4.3 |
| Transportation equipment | 0.2 | 0.3 | 0.2 | 0.4 | 0.7 | 0.4 | 0.4 | 0.2 | 0.6 | 0.1 |
| Scientific and measuring instruments | 5.3 | 6.8 | 8.6 | 6.7 | 6.7 | 1.1 | 1.9 | 1.6 | 1.1 | 1.2 |
| Miscellaneous manufactures | 20.5 | 17.7 | 21.6 | 15.4 | 24.0 | 3.5 | 4.8 | 3.4 | 4.7 | 4.5 |
| Unidentified manufactures | 0.2 | 0.4 | 0.2 | 0.1 | 0.1 | 0.1 | 0.1 | 0.1 | 0.1 | 0.1 |
| **Agricultural and livestock products** | 0.1 | ..... | 0.6 | 0.2 | ..... | ..... | ..... | ..... | ..... | ..... |
| Agricultural products | ..... | ..... | ..... | ..... | ..... | ..... | ..... | ..... | ..... | ..... |
| Livestock and livestock products | 0.1 | ..... | 0.6 | 0.2 | ..... | ..... | ..... | ..... | ..... | ..... |
| **Other commodities** | 6.3 | 6.6 | 5.9 | 4.5 | 2.9 | 0.2 | 2.6 | 8.9 | 8.0 | 4.6 |
| Forestry products | ..... | ..... | ..... | ..... | ..... | ..... | ..... | ..... | ..... | ..... |
| Fish and other marine products | 5.0 | 5.4 | 5.7 | 3.8 | 2.3 | ..... | 2.5 | 8.8 | 8.0 | 4.5 |
| Metallic ores and concentrates | ..... | ..... | ..... | ..... | ..... | ..... | ..... | ..... | ..... | ..... |
| Bituminous coal and lignite | ..... | ..... | ..... | ..... | ..... | ..... | ..... | ..... | ..... | ..... |
| Crude petroleum and natural gas | ..... | ..... | ..... | ..... | ..... | ..... | ..... | ..... | ..... | ..... |
| Nonmetallic minerals | 0.2 | 0.2 | 0.2 | ..... | 0.1 | 0.2 | ..... | ..... | ..... | ..... |
| Scrap and waste | 0.8 | 1.0 | ..... | 0.3 | 0.4 | ..... | ..... | ..... | ..... | ..... |
| Used merchandise | ..... | 0.1 | ..... | ..... | ..... | ..... | ..... | ..... | ..... | ..... |
| Goods imported and returned unchanged | ..... | ..... | ..... | ..... | ..... | ..... | ..... | ..... | ..... | ..... |
| Special classification provisions | 0.3 | ..... | ..... | 0.4 | 0.1 | ..... | ..... | ..... | ..... | 0.1 |
| | Taiwan | | | | | Singapore | | | | |
| **ALL GOODS** | 10.9 | 13.3 | 14.3 | 12.4 | 20.0 | 17.3 | 22.1 | 23.9 | 19.7 | 18.4 |
| **Manufactured goods** | 10.9 | 13.2 | 14.3 | 12.4 | 19.4 | 17.1 | 22.1 | 23.9 | 19.6 | 18.4 |
| Food products | ..... | ..... | ..... | ..... | ..... | ..... | ..... | ..... | ..... | ..... |
| Tobacco products | ..... | ..... | ..... | ..... | ..... | ..... | ..... | ..... | ..... | ..... |
| Textile mill products | 0.1 | 0.2 | 0.2 | 0.1 | 0.6 | 0.1 | 0.4 | 0.5 | 0.1 | ..... |
| Apparel | ..... | ..... | ..... | 0.1 | 0.1 | 0.1 | 0.1 | ..... | 0.1 | ..... |
| Lumber and wood products | ..... | ..... | ..... | ..... | ..... | ..... | ..... | ..... | ..... | ..... |
| Furniture and fixtures | ..... | ..... | ..... | ..... | ..... | ..... | ..... | ..... | ..... | ..... |
| Paper products | ..... | 0.1 | ..... | 0.1 | 0.2 | 0.4 | 0.8 | 1.3 | 0.1 | 0.2 |
| Printing and publishing | 0.2 | 0.1 | ..... | ..... | ..... | ..... | 0.1 | 0.1 | 0.1 | 0.1 |
| Chemical products | 0.4 | 0.8 | 0.6 | 0.3 | 0.8 | 0.5 | 0.6 | 1.0 | 1.1 | 2.7 |
| Refined petroleum products | ..... | ..... | ..... | ..... | ..... | ..... | ..... | ..... | 0.3 | ..... |
| Rubber and plastic products | 0.7 | 0.3 | 0.9 | 1.1 | 1.1 | 0.5 | 1.3 | 1.3 | 1.2 | 1.9 |
| Leather products | ..... | ..... | ..... | ..... | 0.1 | ..... | ..... | ..... | ..... | ..... |
| Stone, clay and glass products | 0.1 | ..... | ..... | 0.1 | ..... | ..... | ..... | ..... | ..... | ..... |
| Primary metals | 0.2 | 0.8 | 1.0 | 0.5 | 1.1 | 0.3 | 0.5 | 0.8 | 0.4 | 0.6 |
| Fabricated metal products | 0.7 | 0.9 | 0.9 | 1.3 | 0.9 | 0.5 | 0.4 | 0.8 | 1.0 | 0.8 |
| Industrial machinery and computers | 1.4 | 2.2 | 2.4 | 2.9 | 3.2 | 4.7 | 7.3 | 4.6 | 5.3 | 3.3 |
| Electric and electronic equipment | 2.2 | 1.8 | 3.5 | 1.8 | 6.2 | 4.8 | 5.9 | 6.3 | 3.2 | 2.6 |
| Transportation equipment | 0.1 | 0.3 | 0.5 | 0.4 | 0.1 | 0.4 | ..... | ..... | 0.1 | 0.7 |
| Scientific and measuring instruments | 0.9 | 1.4 | 1.4 | 1.1 | 1.5 | 2.1 | 1.2 | 1.4 | 1.7 | 2.0 |
| Miscellaneous manufactures | 3.8 | 4.2 | 2.8 | 2.8 | 3.1 | 2.8 | 3.3 | 5.5 | 4.7 | 3.2 |
| Unidentified manufactures | 0.1 | 0.1 | 0.1 | 0.1 | 0.2 | 0.1 | 0.1 | 0.1 | 0.1 | 0.1 |
| **Agricultural and livestock products** | ..... | ..... | ..... | ..... | ..... | ..... | ..... | ..... | ..... | ..... |
| Agricultural products | ..... | ..... | ..... | ..... | ..... | ..... | ..... | ..... | ..... | ..... |
| Livestock and livestock products | ..... | ..... | ..... | ..... | ..... | ..... | ..... | ..... | ..... | ..... |
| **Other commodities** | ..... | 0.1 | ..... | ..... | 0.7 | 0.1 | ..... | 0.1 | 0.1 | 0.1 |
| Forestry products | ..... | ..... | ..... | ..... | ..... | ..... | ..... | ..... | ..... | ..... |
| Fish and other marine products | ..... | 0.1 | ..... | ..... | 0.4 | ..... | ..... | ..... | ..... | ..... |
| Metallic ores and concentrates | ..... | ..... | ..... | ..... | ..... | ..... | ..... | ..... | ..... | ..... |
| Bituminous coal and lignite | ..... | ..... | ..... | ..... | ..... | ..... | ..... | ..... | ..... | ..... |
| Crude petroleum and natural gas | ..... | ..... | ..... | ..... | ..... | ..... | ..... | ..... | ..... | ..... |
| Nonmetallic minerals | ..... | ..... | ..... | ..... | ..... | ..... | ..... | ..... | ..... | ..... |
| Scrap and waste | ..... | ..... | ..... | ..... | ..... | ..... | ..... | 0.1 | ..... | ..... |
| Used merchandise | ..... | ..... | ..... | ..... | ..... | ..... | ..... | ..... | ..... | ..... |
| Goods imported and returned unchanged | ..... | ..... | ..... | ..... | ..... | ..... | ..... | ..... | ..... | ..... |
| Special classification provisions | ..... | ..... | ..... | ..... | 0.2 | 0.1 | ..... | ..... | 0.1 | ..... |

## SOUTH CAROLINA: Exports of Goods, 1997

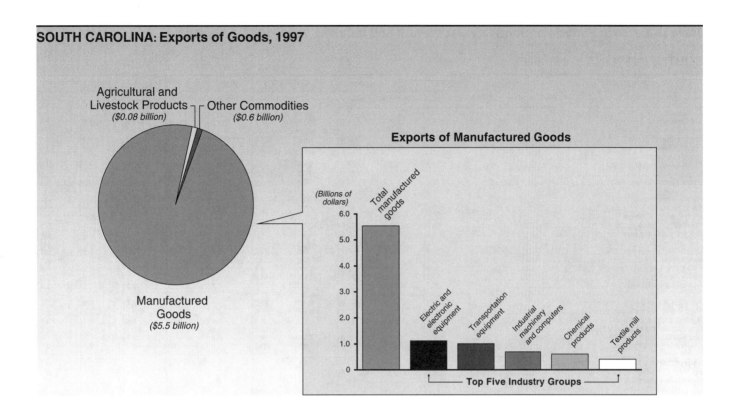

### Table D-3.   State Exports of Goods by Destination and Industry, 1993–1997 —Continued

#### SOUTH CAROLINA (Millions of dollars.)

| Industry | 1993 | 1994 | 1995 | 1996 | 1997 | 1993 | 1994 | 1995 | 1996 | 1997 |
|---|---|---|---|---|---|---|---|---|---|---|
| | All destinations | | | | | Canada | | | | |
| **ALL GOODS** | 3 219.5 | 3 510.1 | 4 497.9 | 4 924.9 | 5 673.8 | 1 009.3 | 1 252.7 | 1 538.5 | 1 478.2 | 1 620.7 |
| **Manufactured goods** | 3 131.5 | 3 398.3 | 4 353.5 | 4 799.2 | 5 540.9 | 961.7 | 1 190.1 | 1 450.2 | 1 384.9 | 1 521.1 |
| Food products | 36.9 | 47.2 | 42.3 | 47.0 | 56.9 | 15.9 | 21.7 | 17.9 | 21.4 | 25.5 |
| Tobacco products | 0.4 | 0.3 | 0.1 | ..... | ..... | ..... | ..... | ..... | ..... | ..... |
| Textile mill products | 279.1 | 308.1 | 377.2 | 374.2 | 402.9 | 130.1 | 140.4 | 169.0 | 182.4 | 192.8 |
| Apparel | 104.6 | 111.5 | 140.9 | 166.6 | 215.5 | 22.1 | 23.6 | 32.9 | 38.4 | 47.6 |
| Lumber and wood products | 16.4 | 19.0 | 20.3 | 29.2 | 54.5 | 5.2 | 5.5 | 6.1 | 7.2 | 8.0 |
| Furniture and fixtures | 13.2 | 15.4 | 13.5 | 14.3 | 16.2 | 5.3 | 7.5 | 4.9 | 3.3 | 3.7 |
| Paper products | 242.1 | 191.4 | 282.7 | 299.6 | 319.0 | 33.3 | 29.1 | 51.8 | 57.1 | 48.6 |
| Printing and publishing | 4.1 | 4.5 | 8.9 | 7.7 | 10.7 | 1.6 | 2.3 | 3.5 | 4.0 | 4.4 |
| Chemical products | 352.2 | 442.8 | 608.2 | 583.0 | 606.9 | 144.7 | 161.2 | 182.8 | 162.1 | 181.6 |
| Refined petroleum products | 1.3 | 1.1 | 8.1 | 15.2 | 13.0 | 0.5 | 0.2 | 0.3 | 0.3 | 1.1 |
| Rubber and plastic products | 212.3 | 278.7 | 373.7 | 339.1 | 341.8 | 151.7 | 220.1 | 307.0 | 234.7 | 225.2 |
| Leather products | 4.7 | 3.0 | 3.0 | 1.9 | 1.4 | 0.6 | 0.1 | 0.2 | 0.2 | 0.2 |
| Stone, clay and glass products | 52.7 | 40.1 | 57.3 | 49.4 | 65.2 | 17.8 | 22.9 | 24.3 | 27.4 | 35.0 |
| Primary metals | 73.9 | 92.3 | 113.2 | 119.0 | 166.7 | 31.9 | 43.7 | 46.9 | 48.5 | 53.9 |
| Fabricated metal products | 105.0 | 130.5 | 152.6 | 138.2 | 182.5 | 62.5 | 84.9 | 95.7 | 70.8 | 115.3 |
| Industrial machinery and computers | 687.5 | 596.8 | 755.6 | 710.6 | 695.0 | 134.2 | 147.5 | 170.2 | 184.7 | 195.8 |
| Electric and electronic equipment | 603.1 | 754.9 | 954.9 | 904.4 | 1 119.6 | 89.8 | 120.2 | 140.6 | 140.5 | 146.2 |
| Transportation equipment | 240.6 | 227.3 | 314.3 | 828.7 | 1 005.7 | 87.7 | 121.5 | 151.3 | 149.1 | 166.7 |
| Scientific and measuring instruments | 66.0 | 94.5 | 93.8 | 131.2 | 226.0 | 19.0 | 27.6 | 34.7 | 41.5 | 56.3 |
| Miscellaneous manufactures | 28.5 | 30.7 | 25.0 | 31.4 | 31.8 | 5.3 | 6.9 | 7.1 | 7.6 | 9.1 |
| Unidentified manufactures | 7.1 | 8.2 | 7.9 | 8.2 | 9.3 | 2.7 | 3.2 | 3.3 | 3.8 | 4.2 |
| **Agricultural and livestock products** | 42.7 | 54.6 | 69.9 | 64.0 | 76.6 | 21.1 | 34.2 | 49.5 | 52.5 | 70.0 |
| Agricultural products | 41.6 | 51.3 | 63.1 | 59.1 | 74.2 | 20.7 | 33.9 | 47.4 | 50.2 | 69.5 |
| Livestock and livestock products | 1.1 | 3.4 | 6.8 | 5.0 | 2.5 | 0.4 | 0.3 | 2.1 | 2.4 | 0.5 |
| **Other commodities** | 45.4 | 57.2 | 74.5 | 61.7 | 56.3 | 26.4 | 28.4 | 38.8 | 40.8 | 29.6 |
| Forestry products | 0.3 | 0.7 | 2.4 | 1.0 | 3.1 | 0.3 | 0.6 | 2.1 | 0.8 | 2.6 |
| Fish and other marine products | 1.9 | 5.9 | 6.7 | 3.9 | 3.5 | 1.9 | 5.5 | 5.6 | 3.5 | 2.1 |
| Metallic ores and concentrates | 1.8 | 0.1 | 0.1 | 0.3 | 0.1 | ..... | ..... | ..... | ..... | ..... |
| Bituminous coal and lignite | ..... | ..... | ..... | 0.1 | | ..... | ..... | ..... | ..... | ..... |
| Crude petroleum and natural gas | 0.3 | 0.4 | 0.6 | 0.3 | 0.4 | ..... | ..... | ..... | ..... | ..... |
| Nonmetallic minerals | 10.3 | 10.5 | 11.7 | 8.1 | 5.3 | 7.5 | 7.5 | 7.8 | 5.2 | 2.5 |
| Scrap and waste | 7.1 | 13.0 | 13.0 | 8.6 | 4.6 | 1.5 | 2.3 | 6.6 | 3.8 | 1.3 |
| Used merchandise | 0.9 | 2.8 | 6.8 | 3.8 | 3.0 | 0.1 | 0.8 | 0.1 | 0.2 | 1.0 |
| Goods imported and returned unchanged | 8.6 | 8.2 | 12.7 | 22.2 | 17.8 | 8.6 | 8.2 | 12.7 | 22.2 | 17.8 |
| Special classification provisions | 14.2 | 15.6 | 20.5 | 13.4 | 18.4 | 6.6 | 3.5 | 3.8 | 5.3 | 2.3 |

## Table D-3.  State Exports of Goods by Destination and Industry, 1993–1997 —*Continued*

### SOUTH CAROLINA (Millions of dollars.)

| Industry | 1993 | 1994 | 1995 | 1996 | 1997 | 1993 | 1994 | 1995 | 1996 | 1997 |
|---|---|---|---|---|---|---|---|---|---|---|
| | South and Central America and Caribbean | | | | | Mexico | | | | |
| **ALL GOODS** | 222.2 | 237.7 | 337.9 | 309.2 | 439.7 | 293.2 | 450.0 | 641.4 | 661.8 | 935.9 |
| **Manufactured goods** | 221.6 | 236.7 | 334.4 | 305.9 | 437.6 | 292.5 | 444.3 | 631.8 | 658.1 | 929.4 |
| Food products | 0.5 | 0.8 | 1.8 | 1.8 | 5.3 | 0.4 | 0.2 | 0.1 | 0.8 | 0.3 |
| Tobacco products | ..... | ..... | ..... | ..... | ..... | ..... | ..... | ..... | ..... | ..... |
| Textile mill products | 28.2 | 28.7 | 57.4 | 45.5 | 43.3 | 9.4 | 18.6 | 23.0 | 27.7 | 53.5 |
| Apparel | 48.3 | 61.6 | 71.2 | 71.4 | 111.2 | 14.0 | 10.0 | 18.3 | 33.7 | 33.1 |
| Lumber and wood products | 0.2 | 1.4 | 0.6 | 0.7 | 0.8 | 0.2 | 0.5 | ..... | 0.2 | 0.1 |
| Furniture and fixtures | 0.2 | 0.7 | 0.7 | 0.7 | 1.7 | 0.2 | 0.3 | 0.2 | 0.9 | 0.4 |
| Paper products | 15.3 | 14.7 | 17.5 | 18.3 | 22.7 | 4.7 | 9.1 | 12.0 | 9.9 | 21.9 |
| Printing and publishing | 0.1 | 0.3 | 0.3 | 0.5 | 1.2 | 0.1 | 0.2 | 3.0 | 0.3 | 0.5 |
| Chemical products | 16.0 | 20.5 | 43.0 | 37.6 | 50.2 | 10.1 | 12.6 | 17.0 | 19.5 | 20.0 |
| Refined petroleum products | 0.2 | 0.1 | 0.9 | 1.6 | 1.2 | ..... | 0.1 | ..... | 0.2 | 0.1 |
| Rubber and plastic products | 16.4 | 9.4 | 11.0 | 18.5 | 22.2 | 5.7 | 8.4 | 14.0 | 19.6 | 25.1 |
| Leather products | 0.1 | ..... | 0.3 | 0.2 | 0.1 | ..... | ..... | ..... | 0.1 | 0.1 |
| Stone, clay and glass products | 8.5 | 2.9 | 2.3 | 1.6 | 2.9 | 0.9 | 1.7 | 1.9 | 2.7 | 0.8 |
| Primary metals | 14.2 | 6.8 | 23.5 | 11.9 | 44.8 | 3.1 | 8.2 | 13.7 | 12.5 | 15.5 |
| Fabricated metal products | 9.0 | 11.3 | 8.0 | 8.2 | 9.5 | 2.7 | 8.0 | 12.7 | 7.3 | 7.4 |
| Industrial machinery and computers | 34.7 | 43.0 | 62.0 | 54.3 | 76.5 | 25.1 | 50.9 | 65.6 | 58.0 | 61.7 |
| Electric and electronic equipment | 18.0 | 17.6 | 17.1 | 12.7 | 21.0 | 188.7 | 294.9 | 433.6 | 432.3 | 635.2 |
| Transportation equipment | 7.6 | 10.4 | 10.5 | 11.2 | 6.1 | 16.9 | 10.4 | 4.8 | 9.1 | 18.5 |
| Scientific and measuring instruments | 0.9 | 3.5 | 3.5 | 5.7 | 12.2 | 8.9 | 8.8 | 10.3 | 21.3 | 32.8 |
| Miscellaneous manufactures | 2.7 | 2.3 | 2.3 | 3.1 | 4.1 | 0.7 | 0.9 | 1.2 | 1.3 | 1.8 |
| Unidentified manufactures | 0.7 | 0.6 | 0.5 | 0.5 | 0.5 | 0.6 | 0.6 | 0.4 | 0.7 | 0.7 |
| **Agricultural and livestock products** | 0.1 | ..... | 0.6 | 1.1 | 0.3 | 0.2 | 0.9 | 2.0 | 0.1 | 0.1 |
| Agricultural products | 0.1 | 0.1 | 0.4 | ..... | 0.3 | 0.1 | ..... | 0.4 | 0.1 | 0.1 |
| Livestock and livestock products | ..... | ..... | 0.1 | 1.1 | ..... | 0.1 | 0.8 | 1.6 | ..... | ..... |
| **Other commodities** | 0.5 | 1.0 | 2.9 | 2.2 | 1.8 | 0.5 | 4.8 | 7.6 | 3.6 | 6.4 |
| Forestry products | ..... | ..... | 0.1 | 0.1 | 0.2 | ..... | ..... | 0.1 | ..... | ..... |
| Fish and other marine products | ..... | ..... | ..... | ..... | ..... | ..... | ..... | ..... | ..... | ..... |
| Metallic ores and concentrates | ..... | ..... | ..... | ..... | ..... | ..... | ..... | ..... | 0.1 | ..... |
| Bituminous coal and lignite | ..... | ..... | ..... | 0.1 | ..... | ..... | ..... | ..... | ..... | ..... |
| Crude petroleum and natural gas | 0.3 | 0.4 | 0.5 | 0.3 | 0.4 | ..... | ..... | ..... | ..... | ..... |
| Nonmetallic minerals | 0.1 | ..... | 0.1 | 0.1 | 0.1 | ..... | 0.1 | ..... | 0.1 | ..... |
| Scrap and waste | ..... | ..... | 0.4 | 0.5 | 0.3 | 0.1 | 0.1 | 0.4 | 0.1 | 0.9 |
| Used merchandise | 0.1 | 0.4 | 1.2 | 0.4 | 0.4 | 0.1 | 0.1 | ..... | ..... | ..... |
| Goods imported and returned unchanged | ..... | ..... | ..... | ..... | ..... | ..... | ..... | ..... | ..... | ..... |
| Special classification provisions | ..... | 0.1 | 0.7 | 0.7 | 0.3 | 0.3 | 4.6 | 7.0 | 3.3 | 5.4 |
| | European Union | | | | | United Kingdom | | | | |
| **ALL GOODS** | 888.3 | 786.2 | 926.8 | 1 452.0 | 1 592.9 | 227.9 | 177.3 | 225.5 | 210.0 | 212.9 |
| **Manufactured goods** | 866.8 | 764.7 | 909.6 | 1 439.5 | 1 576.6 | 224.5 | 173.6 | 223.1 | 207.2 | 210.5 |
| Food products | 14.1 | 14.3 | 16.7 | 15.3 | 16.5 | 3.1 | 3.2 | 3.0 | 4.3 | 5.3 |
| Tobacco products | 0.4 | 0.3 | 0.1 | ..... | ..... | ..... | ..... | ..... | ..... | ..... |
| Textile mill products | 54.0 | 55.2 | 46.8 | 49.4 | 50.9 | 29.9 | 29.1 | 24.0 | 28.2 | 23.6 |
| Apparel | 9.1 | 5.2 | 5.3 | 3.2 | 5.0 | 1.7 | 1.5 | 3.1 | 2.0 | 2.0 |
| Lumber and wood products | 5.8 | 6.6 | 7.3 | 9.3 | 7.7 | 0.3 | 0.6 | 0.4 | 1.1 | 0.6 |
| Furniture and fixtures | 1.0 | 1.5 | 2.4 | 2.8 | 3.6 | 0.2 | 0.2 | 0.4 | 0.4 | 0.5 |
| Paper products | 84.0 | 75.9 | 143.9 | 137.8 | 123.6 | 14.4 | 8.1 | 16.1 | 11.2 | 10.8 |
| Printing and publishing | 1.6 | 1.2 | 1.0 | 2.2 | 3.6 | 0.2 | 0.3 | 0.4 | 0.2 | 0.3 |
| Chemical products | 103.6 | 136.8 | 134.2 | 165.5 | 152.5 | 20.0 | 20.7 | 35.9 | 37.9 | 35.5 |
| Refined petroleum products | 0.2 | 0.1 | 3.5 | 6.4 | 5.6 | 0.1 | ..... | 0.3 | 0.1 | 0.2 |
| Rubber and plastic products | 26.8 | 25.2 | 25.4 | 32.8 | 45.9 | 10.4 | 12.5 | 13.9 | 13.9 | 15.6 |
| Leather products | 0.7 | 2.2 | 0.9 | 0.4 | 0.5 | 0.2 | 1.0 | 0.2 | ..... | 0.1 |
| Stone, clay and glass products | 7.1 | 6.1 | 15.7 | 5.9 | 8.3 | 0.7 | 0.6 | 0.5 | 0.7 | 0.9 |
| Primary metals | 10.7 | 22.9 | 13.4 | 15.4 | 23.4 | 1.6 | 8.9 | 7.7 | 5.9 | 2.0 |
| Fabricated metal products | 20.1 | 15.9 | 17.4 | 27.4 | 29.7 | 3.1 | 5.4 | 4.0 | 9.3 | 10.4 |
| Industrial machinery and computers | 288.3 | 187.0 | 202.5 | 165.0 | 162.9 | 83.3 | 27.9 | 45.4 | 31.8 | 40.7 |
| Electric and electronic equipment | 106.9 | 109.0 | 133.5 | 128.5 | 130.1 | 25.7 | 25.0 | 32.9 | 29.0 | 25.2 |
| Transportation equipment | 97.8 | 51.2 | 107.5 | 619.9 | 704.2 | 22.3 | 20.6 | 28.1 | 22.7 | 26.7 |
| Scientific and measuring instruments | 24.2 | 36.3 | 25.5 | 41.6 | 94.2 | 3.9 | 3.5 | 4.6 | 5.2 | 6.4 |
| Miscellaneous manufactures | 8.6 | 10.0 | 4.8 | 8.9 | 6.6 | 2.8 | 4.0 | 1.4 | 2.6 | 3.0 |
| Unidentified manufactures | 1.7 | 1.8 | 2.0 | 1.8 | 1.7 | 0.6 | 0.5 | 0.6 | 0.5 | 0.6 |
| **Agricultural and livestock products** | 8.1 | 6.0 | 3.7 | 5.2 | 4.0 | 0.2 | 0.2 | 0.8 | 0.6 | 0.3 |
| Agricultural products | 8.1 | 6.0 | 3.4 | 5.0 | 3.7 | 0.2 | 0.1 | 0.5 | 0.5 | 0.3 |
| Livestock and livestock products | ..... | ..... | 0.2 | 0.2 | 0.3 | ..... | ..... | 0.2 | 0.1 | ..... |
| **Other commodities** | 13.5 | 15.4 | 13.5 | 7.3 | 12.3 | 3.2 | 3.6 | 1.6 | 2.1 | 2.1 |
| Forestry products | ..... | ..... | ..... | 0.1 | 0.1 | ..... | ..... | ..... | ..... | ..... |
| Fish and other marine products | ..... | ..... | 0.4 | ..... | 1.4 | ..... | ..... | ..... | ..... | 1.2 |
| Metallic ores and concentrates | 1.8 | 0.1 | 0.1 | 0.2 | 0.1 | ..... | 0.1 | ..... | ..... | 0.1 |
| Bituminous coal and lignite | ..... | ..... | ..... | ..... | ..... | ..... | ..... | ..... | ..... | ..... |
| Crude petroleum and natural gas | ..... | ..... | ..... | ..... | ..... | ..... | ..... | ..... | ..... | ..... |
| Nonmetallic minerals | 2.2 | 2.3 | 2.8 | 2.2 | 2.3 | ..... | ..... | 0.2 | ..... | ..... |
| Scrap and waste | 5.1 | 9.4 | 4.8 | 2.2 | 1.1 | 2.9 | 3.3 | 1.3 | 1.9 | 0.5 |
| Used merchandise | 0.5 | 0.3 | 0.3 | 0.5 | 0.5 | 0.2 | 0.1 | 0.1 | ..... | 0.1 |
| Goods imported and returned unchanged | ..... | ..... | ..... | ..... | ..... | ..... | ..... | ..... | ..... | ..... |
| Special classification provisions | 3.9 | 3.3 | 5.0 | 2.1 | 6.8 | ..... | ..... | 0.1 | 0.2 | 0.3 |

## Table D-3.   State Exports of Goods by Destination and Industry, 1993–1997 —*Continued*

**SOUTH CAROLINA** (Millions of dollars.)

| Industry | 1993 | 1994 | 1995 | 1996 | 1997 | 1993 | 1994 | 1995 | 1996 | 1997 |
|---|---|---|---|---|---|---|---|---|---|---|
| | Germany | | | | | France | | | | |
| **ALL GOODS** | 225.5 | 214.8 | 233.6 | 727.4 | 854.7 | 102.3 | 73.0 | 86.0 | 92.8 | 108.0 |
| **Manufactured goods** | 222.7 | 209.8 | 229.7 | 724.9 | 852.8 | 102.3 | 72.9 | 85.5 | 92.1 | 101.4 |
| Food products | 5.5 | 6.4 | 6.1 | 3.7 | 4.2 | 1.2 | 0.7 | 1.8 | 1.2 | 0.7 |
| Tobacco products | 0.1 | ..... | ..... | ..... | ..... | | | | | |
| Textile mill products | 6.6 | 8.3 | 5.4 | 5.3 | 7.4 | 2.0 | 2.3 | 2.0 | 1.5 | 4.3 |
| Apparel | 1.8 | 1.3 | 0.5 | 0.3 | 0.4 | 0.1 | 0.8 | 0.2 | 0.1 | 0.1 |
| Lumber and wood products | 1.9 | 2.5 | 3.0 | 1.9 | 1.9 | 0.1 | 0.1 | 0.2 | 0.2 | 0.1 |
| Furniture and fixtures | 0.2 | 0.8 | 1.0 | 1.5 | 0.9 | 0.1 | 0.4 | 0.4 | 0.2 | 0.1 |
| Paper products | 5.9 | 5.7 | 12.7 | 8.0 | 9.1 | 15.3 | 12.8 | 24.2 | 21.4 | 18.3 |
| Printing and publishing | 0.5 | 0.1 | 0.1 | 0.3 | 0.2 | 0.2 | 0.3 | 0.1 | ..... | ..... |
| Chemical products | 23.7 | 56.0 | 17.8 | 27.9 | 15.7 | 7.1 | 6.4 | 9.4 | 12.2 | 12.2 |
| Refined petroleum products | ..... | ..... | 1.0 | 2.3 | 2.2 | ..... | ..... | 0.9 | 1.3 | 1.4 |
| Rubber and plastic products | 5.0 | 3.9 | 4.1 | 4.5 | 3.6 | 3.8 | 1.8 | 2.2 | 2.2 | 2.1 |
| Leather products | 0.3 | 1.0 | 0.5 | 0.3 | 0.2 | 0.1 | ..... | 0.1 | 0.1 | ..... |
| Stone, clay and glass products | 3.0 | 1.4 | 2.1 | 3.4 | 4.0 | 0.4 | 0.3 | 0.2 | 1.1 | 0.3 |
| Primary metals | 4.0 | 2.5 | 1.5 | 1.8 | 18.5 | 0.5 | 0.7 | 1.7 | 1.2 | 1.2 |
| Fabricated metal products | 8.1 | 2.9 | 8.2 | 8.8 | 9.0 | 2.8 | 1.4 | 1.2 | 2.6 | 2.0 |
| Industrial machinery and computers | 52.6 | 38.5 | 45.5 | 28.2 | 31.6 | 55.0 | 27.3 | 22.1 | 23.5 | 20.4 |
| Electric and electronic equipment | 37.7 | 38.8 | 48.2 | 42.4 | 38.7 | 7.2 | 10.9 | 12.6 | 17.4 | 17.1 |
| Transportation equipment | 50.2 | 11.0 | 56.1 | 571.7 | 655.5 | 2.9 | 4.1 | 3.6 | 2.9 | 6.0 |
| Scientific and measuring instruments | 13.2 | 27.4 | 15.3 | 11.4 | 48.0 | 2.4 | 1.9 | 1.9 | 2.6 | 14.4 |
| Miscellaneous manufactures | 1.8 | 0.9 | 0.3 | 0.9 | 0.9 | 1.0 | 0.5 | 0.5 | 0.2 | 0.4 |
| Unidentified manufactures | 0.5 | 0.5 | 0.5 | 0.5 | 0.8 | 0.1 | 0.2 | 0.2 | 0.2 | 0.1 |
| **Agricultural and livestock products** | 1.7 | 1.2 | 0.9 | 1.0 | 0.6 | ..... | ..... | ..... | 0.1 | 0.2 |
| Agricultural products | 1.7 | 1.2 | 0.9 | 1.0 | 0.5 | ..... | ..... | ..... | 0.1 | 0.1 |
| Livestock and livestock products | ..... | ..... | ..... | ..... | 0.2 | ..... | ..... | ..... | ..... | ..... |
| **Other commodities** | 1.1 | 3.8 | 2.9 | 1.5 | 1.3 | ..... | 0.1 | 0.5 | 0.6 | 6.5 |
| Forestry products | ..... | ..... | ..... | ..... | ..... | ..... | ..... | ..... | ..... | ..... |
| Fish and other marine products | ..... | ..... | ..... | ..... | ..... | ..... | ..... | 0.4 | ..... | ..... |
| Metallic ores and concentrates | ..... | ..... | ..... | ..... | ..... | ..... | ..... | ..... | ..... | ..... |
| Bituminous coal and lignite | ..... | ..... | ..... | ..... | ..... | ..... | ..... | ..... | ..... | ..... |
| Crude petroleum and natural gas | ..... | ..... | ..... | ..... | ..... | ..... | ..... | ..... | ..... | ..... |
| Nonmetallic minerals | ..... | 0.2 | ..... | 0.7 | 0.8 | ..... | ..... | ..... | ..... | ..... |
| Scrap and waste | 0.7 | 3.5 | 2.0 | 0.1 | 0.4 | ..... | ..... | 0.1 | ..... | ..... |
| Used merchandise | 0.1 | ..... | ..... | 0.1 | ..... | ..... | 0.1 | ..... | 0.4 | 0.3 |
| Goods imported and returned unchanged | ..... | ..... | ..... | ..... | ..... | ..... | ..... | ..... | ..... | ..... |
| Special classification provisions | 0.3 | 0.1 | 0.8 | 0.6 | 0.1 | ..... | ..... | ..... | 0.1 | 6.2 |
| | The Netherlands | | | | | Asian 10 | | | | |
| **ALL GOODS** | 111.8 | 88.6 | 102.4 | 121.9 | 96.7 | 562.6 | 585.5 | 760.5 | 712.9 | 773.0 |
| **Manufactured goods** | 110.7 | 88.2 | 101.8 | 121.5 | 95.8 | 554.7 | 570.3 | 738.2 | 702.3 | 768.9 |
| Food products | 2.9 | 2.7 | 4.7 | 4.4 | 2.7 | 3.4 | 7.3 | 3.5 | 1.9 | 6.9 |
| Tobacco products | 0.2 | 0.2 | 0.1 | ..... | ..... | | | | | |
| Textile mill products | 3.4 | 2.3 | 1.6 | 1.0 | 1.1 | 43.1 | 49.7 | 57.7 | 42.4 | 36.6 |
| Apparel | 0.6 | 0.2 | 0.6 | 0.1 | 1.3 | 8.2 | 7.2 | 9.8 | 17.8 | 15.3 |
| Lumber and wood products | 0.4 | 0.4 | 0.3 | 1.3 | 0.7 | 4.8 | 4.9 | 5.7 | 11.3 | 36.9 |
| Furniture and fixtures | 0.4 | ..... | 0.3 | 0.2 | 0.3 | 0.5 | 0.2 | 0.4 | 0.6 | 0.7 |
| Paper products | 15.7 | 19.4 | 31.4 | 31.6 | 14.0 | 84.1 | 52.2 | 38.8 | 49.4 | 78.7 |
| Printing and publishing | 0.5 | 0.1 | 0.1 | ..... | 0.1 | 0.5 | 0.4 | 0.8 | 0.3 | 0.3 |
| Chemical products | 25.6 | 14.3 | 17.3 | 21.9 | 28.3 | 46.8 | 79.2 | 185.1 | 161.1 | 166.9 |
| Refined petroleum products | 0.1 | ..... | 0.2 | 0.5 | 0.4 | ..... | 0.1 | 2.1 | 3.5 | 3.3 |
| Rubber and plastic products | 1.3 | 1.2 | 0.9 | 6.8 | 11.5 | 6.5 | 8.4 | 7.6 | 23.7 | 16.8 |
| Leather products | ..... | ..... | ..... | ..... | ..... | 3.2 | 0.5 | 1.1 | 0.6 | 0.2 |
| Stone, clay and glass products | 1.8 | 1.7 | 0.1 | 0.3 | 0.6 | 15.5 | 5.0 | 9.7 | 7.5 | 14.8 |
| Primary metals | 1.2 | 2.5 | 0.1 | 1.6 | 0.3 | 10.4 | 8.4 | 11.1 | 17.4 | 21.5 |
| Fabricated metal products | 1.5 | 1.5 | 0.9 | 1.4 | 1.8 | 6.1 | 7.0 | 11.6 | 16.8 | 13.2 |
| Industrial machinery and computers | 30.8 | 24.7 | 24.6 | 15.8 | 7.1 | 110.8 | 107.5 | 152.1 | 137.4 | 99.5 |
| Electric and electronic equipment | 14.2 | 7.1 | 6.2 | 4.4 | 4.4 | 185.9 | 201.9 | 215.0 | 176.5 | 172.6 |
| Transportation equipment | 6.1 | 5.1 | 8.0 | 5.9 | 3.3 | 8.5 | 10.1 | 8.2 | 12.5 | 56.4 |
| Scientific and measuring instruments | 2.2 | 1.3 | 2.1 | 20.1 | 16.6 | 5.5 | 9.2 | 9.4 | 11.8 | 19.3 |
| Miscellaneous manufactures | 1.7 | 3.0 | 2.1 | 4.1 | 1.3 | 10.1 | 9.8 | 7.7 | 9.1 | 8.3 |
| Unidentified manufactures | 0.2 | 0.3 | 0.1 | 0.2 | 0.1 | 0.7 | 1.0 | 0.9 | 0.8 | 0.6 |
| **Agricultural and livestock products** | 0.9 | ..... | 0.1 | 0.3 | 0.4 | 4.9 | 10.3 | 12.6 | 4.4 | 1.7 |
| Agricultural products | 0.9 | ..... | 0.1 | 0.3 | 0.4 | 4.5 | 8.2 | 9.8 | 3.1 | ..... |
| Livestock and livestock products | ..... | ..... | ..... | ..... | ..... | 0.5 | 2.0 | 2.8 | 1.3 | 1.7 |
| **Other commodities** | 0.2 | 0.4 | 0.4 | 0.1 | 0.4 | 3.0 | 4.9 | 9.6 | 6.2 | 2.4 |
| Forestry products | ..... | ..... | ..... | ..... | ..... | ..... | ..... | ..... | ..... | ..... |
| Fish and other marine products | ..... | ..... | ..... | ..... | 0.2 | ..... | 0.4 | 0.7 | 0.4 | ..... |
| Metallic ores and concentrates | ..... | ..... | ..... | ..... | ..... | ..... | ..... | ..... | ..... | ..... |
| Bituminous coal and lignite | ..... | ..... | ..... | ..... | ..... | ..... | ..... | ..... | ..... | ..... |
| Crude petroleum and natural gas | ..... | ..... | ..... | ..... | ..... | ..... | ..... | ..... | ..... | ..... |
| Nonmetallic minerals | 0.1 | 0.3 | ..... | ..... | ..... | 0.5 | 0.5 | 0.9 | 0.1 | 0.2 |
| Scrap and waste | ..... | 0.1 | 0.3 | ..... | 0.2 | 0.1 | 0.7 | 0.3 | 1.6 | 0.3 |
| Used merchandise | ..... | ..... | ..... | ..... | ..... | ..... | 1.1 | 4.9 | 2.5 | 0.4 |
| Goods imported and returned unchanged | ..... | ..... | ..... | ..... | ..... | ..... | ..... | ..... | ..... | ..... |
| Special classification provisions | 0.1 | 0.1 | 0.1 | 0.1 | ..... | 2.3 | 2.1 | 2.9 | 1.6 | 1.5 |

## Table D-3.   State Exports of Goods by Destination and Industry, 1993–1997 —*Continued*

## SOUTH CAROLINA (Millions of dollars.)

| Industry | 1993 | 1994 | 1995 | 1996 | 1997 | 1993 | 1994 | 1995 | 1996 | 1997 |
|---|---|---|---|---|---|---|---|---|---|---|
| | Japan | | | | | South Korea | | | | |
| **ALL GOODS** | 153.2 | 180.5 | 181.5 | 201.6 | 273.1 | 115.5 | 112.4 | 115.2 | 69.9 | 67.5 |
| **Manufactured goods** | 152.8 | 179.4 | 178.7 | 200.5 | 272.8 | 114.8 | 110.8 | 110.2 | 66.2 | 67.0 |
| Food products | 0.3 | 0.8 | 0.4 | 0.7 | 1.4 | ..... | ..... | ..... | 0.3 | 0.1 |
| Tobacco products | ..... | ..... | ..... | ..... | ..... | ..... | ..... | ..... | ..... | ..... |
| Textile mill products | 7.7 | 2.5 | 4.6 | 1.6 | 5.3 | 12.0 | 25.4 | 24.1 | 11.5 | 12.5 |
| Apparel | 6.0 | 5.8 | 8.2 | 16.0 | 13.1 | ..... | ..... | 0.1 | 0.2 | ..... |
| Lumber and wood products | 2.3 | 2.9 | 2.9 | 10.0 | 35.9 | ..... | 0.1 | 0.9 | 0.4 | 0.6 |
| Furniture and fixtures | ..... | 0.1 | 0.2 | 0.5 | 0.5 | ..... | ..... | 0.1 | ..... | ..... |
| Paper products | 28.2 | 23.4 | 8.4 | 11.4 | 18.0 | 3.7 | 1.9 | 7.5 | 8.1 | 9.2 |
| Printing and publishing | 0.1 | 0.2 | 0.4 | ..... | ..... | ..... | ..... | ..... | ..... | ..... |
| Chemical products | 10.2 | 15.3 | 21.9 | 24.2 | 21.5 | 6.6 | 6.2 | 10.6 | 8.0 | 10.2 |
| Refined petroleum products | ..... | ..... | 1.5 | 2.9 | 2.3 | ..... | ..... | 0.3 | 0.4 | 0.4 |
| Rubber and plastic products | 3.0 | 3.8 | 4.4 | 11.4 | 9.4 | 0.9 | 2.6 | 0.8 | 3.0 | 1.9 |
| Leather products | ..... | 0.1 | ..... | 0.1 | 0.1 | ..... | ..... | ..... | 0.2 | ..... |
| Stone, clay and glass products | 1.5 | 0.8 | 1.3 | 1.2 | 5.4 | 9.9 | 0.1 | 0.9 | 1.3 | 2.9 |
| Primary metals | 3.4 | 4.6 | 6.1 | 10.2 | 15.0 | 1.1 | 1.9 | 0.7 | 0.9 | 0.4 |
| Fabricated metal products | 2.1 | 2.0 | 2.9 | 3.4 | 4.4 | 0.7 | 1.2 | 0.8 | 0.6 | 3.2 |
| Industrial machinery and computers | 26.4 | 26.5 | 31.5 | 35.0 | 25.9 | 27.5 | 29.9 | 30.5 | 17.7 | 15.8 |
| Electric and electronic equipment | 50.2 | 77.3 | 73.0 | 62.6 | 51.7 | 49.6 | 37.4 | 30.6 | 11.3 | 7.9 |
| Transportation equipment | 3.4 | 3.8 | 3.2 | 2.0 | 50.9 | 1.3 | 2.3 | 0.6 | 0.7 | 0.8 |
| Scientific and measuring instruments | 2.3 | 4.2 | 3.8 | 4.4 | 10.5 | 0.8 | 1.4 | 1.5 | 0.9 | 0.6 |
| Miscellaneous manufactures | 5.3 | 5.2 | 3.5 | 2.8 | 1.4 | 0.3 | 0.1 | 0.1 | 0.7 | 0.2 |
| Unidentified manufactures | 0.2 | 0.2 | 0.4 | 0.3 | 0.2 | 0.1 | 0.3 | 0.1 | 0.2 | 0.1 |
| **Agricultural and livestock products** | 0.3 | 0.6 | 1.8 | 1.0 | 0.1 | ..... | ..... | 0.1 | ..... | ..... |
| Agricultural products | 0.3 | 0.6 | 1.7 | 1.0 | ..... | ..... | ..... | ..... | ..... | ..... |
| Livestock and livestock products | ..... | ..... | 0.2 | ..... | 0.1 | ..... | ..... | 0.1 | ..... | ..... |
| **Other commodities** | 0.1 | 0.5 | 0.9 | 0.1 | 0.3 | 0.7 | 1.6 | 5.0 | 3.7 | 0.5 |
| Forestry products | ..... | ..... | ..... | ..... | ..... | ..... | ..... | ..... | ..... | ..... |
| Fish and other marine products | ..... | 0.4 | 0.5 | ..... | ..... | ..... | ..... | ..... | ..... | ..... |
| Metallic ores and concentrates | ..... | ..... | ..... | ..... | ..... | ..... | ..... | ..... | ..... | ..... |
| Bituminous coal and lignite | ..... | ..... | ..... | ..... | ..... | ..... | ..... | ..... | ..... | ..... |
| Crude petroleum and natural gas | ..... | ..... | ..... | ..... | ..... | ..... | ..... | ..... | ..... | ..... |
| Nonmetallic minerals | 0.1 | 0.1 | 0.3 | ..... | 0.2 | 0.1 | ..... | ..... | ..... | ..... |
| Scrap and waste | ..... | ..... | ..... | ..... | ..... | ..... | 0.1 | ..... | 0.8 | ..... |
| Used merchandise | ..... | ..... | ..... | ..... | ..... | ..... | 1.1 | 4.4 | 2.5 | 0.4 |
| Goods imported and returned unchanged | ..... | ..... | ..... | ..... | ..... | ..... | ..... | ..... | ..... | ..... |
| Special classification provisions | 0.1 | ..... | 0.1 | 0.1 | 0.1 | 0.6 | 0.4 | 0.5 | 0.3 | 0.1 |
| | Taiwan | | | | | Singapore | | | | |
| **ALL GOODS** | 51.9 | 71.0 | 154.1 | 165.8 | 160.3 | 59.5 | 55.5 | 50.6 | 49.8 | 44.7 |
| **Manufactured goods** | 49.3 | 66.0 | 146.2 | 162.9 | 159.7 | 59.5 | 55.4 | 50.5 | 49.7 | 44.7 |
| Food products | 0.2 | 0.1 | 0.1 | 0.1 | 0.3 | 0.1 | ..... | ..... | 0.2 | 0.5 |
| Tobacco products | ..... | ..... | ..... | ..... | ..... | ..... | ..... | ..... | ..... | ..... |
| Textile mill products | 1.4 | 2.2 | 3.2 | 3.5 | 1.5 | 1.1 | 1.9 | 1.0 | 0.7 | 2.1 |
| Apparel | 0.1 | ..... | 0.1 | 0.1 | 0.3 | 0.3 | 0.4 | 0.2 | 0.3 | 0.3 |
| Lumber and wood products | 1.1 | 0.8 | 0.8 | 0.1 | 0.1 | ..... | 0.1 | 0.1 | ..... | 0.1 |
| Furniture and fixtures | 0.3 | 0.1 | ..... | ..... | 0.1 | ..... | ..... | ..... | ..... | ..... |
| Paper products | 10.7 | 9.8 | 9.6 | 11.6 | 14.9 | 6.3 | 1.1 | 3.3 | 0.9 | 2.4 |
| Printing and publishing | 0.2 | ..... | 0.2 | ..... | ..... | 0.1 | 0.1 | ..... | 0.1 | 0.1 |
| Chemical products | 10.1 | 21.4 | 83.8 | 102.2 | 110.0 | 3.7 | 1.4 | 0.6 | 2.1 | 1.5 |
| Refined petroleum products | ..... | ..... | ..... | ..... | 0.1 | ..... | ..... | ..... | ..... | 0.1 |
| Rubber and plastic products | 0.5 | 0.5 | 0.6 | 3.0 | 0.8 | 0.5 | 0.6 | 0.3 | 1.4 | 0.6 |
| Leather products | ..... | ..... | 0.1 | ..... | 0.1 | 0.1 | 0.1 | 0.1 | ..... | ..... |
| Stone, clay and glass products | 1.6 | 0.5 | 0.6 | 0.7 | 2.0 | 0.6 | 0.5 | 2.1 | 0.8 | 0.7 |
| Primary metals | 0.7 | 0.3 | 0.7 | 0.9 | 1.2 | 0.1 | 0.4 | 0.2 | 0.2 | 0.1 |
| Fabricated metal products | 1.4 | 0.2 | 0.4 | 3.9 | 0.8 | 0.3 | 2.2 | 0.8 | 1.5 | 1.0 |
| Industrial machinery and computers | 12.4 | 16.3 | 28.3 | 15.0 | 5.4 | 3.3 | 5.9 | 7.8 | 7.4 | 4.9 |
| Electric and electronic equipment | 7.2 | 11.4 | 15.7 | 16.6 | 18.7 | 41.3 | 39.1 | 32.7 | 33.0 | 28.5 |
| Transportation equipment | 0.6 | 0.9 | 0.8 | 2.7 | 0.7 | 1.2 | 0.8 | 0.7 | 0.2 | 0.7 |
| Scientific and measuring instruments | 0.4 | 1.1 | 0.9 | 2.0 | 2.5 | 0.2 | 0.3 | 0.4 | 0.6 | 0.5 |
| Miscellaneous manufactures | 0.4 | 0.1 | 0.2 | 0.1 | 0.3 | 0.4 | 0.4 | 0.2 | 0.2 | 0.5 |
| Unidentified manufactures | 0.1 | 0.1 | 0.1 | 0.1 | 0.1 | ..... | 0.1 | 0.1 | 0.1 | ..... |
| **Agricultural and livestock products** | 1.1 | 4.1 | 6.1 | 1.7 | 0.5 | ..... | ..... | ..... | ..... | ..... |
| Agricultural products | 1.0 | 3.3 | 4.0 | 1.0 | ..... | ..... | ..... | ..... | ..... | ..... |
| Livestock and livestock products | 0.1 | 0.8 | 2.0 | 0.7 | 0.5 | ..... | ..... | ..... | ..... | ..... |
| **Other commodities** | 1.5 | 0.9 | 1.8 | 1.3 | 0.2 | ..... | 0.1 | ..... | 0.1 | ..... |
| Forestry products | ..... | ..... | ..... | 0.1 | ..... | ..... | ..... | ..... | ..... | ..... |
| Fish and other marine products | ..... | ..... | ..... | ..... | ..... | ..... | ..... | ..... | ..... | ..... |
| Metallic ores and concentrates | ..... | ..... | ..... | ..... | ..... | ..... | ..... | ..... | ..... | ..... |
| Bituminous coal and lignite | ..... | ..... | ..... | ..... | ..... | ..... | ..... | ..... | ..... | ..... |
| Crude petroleum and natural gas | ..... | ..... | ..... | ..... | ..... | ..... | ..... | ..... | ..... | ..... |
| Nonmetallic minerals | 0.1 | ..... | 0.1 | ..... | ..... | ..... | 0.1 | ..... | ..... | ..... |
| Scrap and waste | 0.1 | ..... | ..... | 0.6 | 0.1 | ..... | ..... | ..... | ..... | ..... |
| Used merchandise | ..... | ..... | ..... | ..... | ..... | ..... | ..... | ..... | ..... | ..... |
| Goods imported and returned unchanged | ..... | ..... | ..... | ..... | ..... | ..... | ..... | ..... | ..... | ..... |
| Special classification provisions | 1.3 | 0.9 | 1.7 | 0.6 | ..... | ..... | ..... | ..... | 0.1 | ..... |

## SOUTH DAKOTA: Exports of Goods, 1997

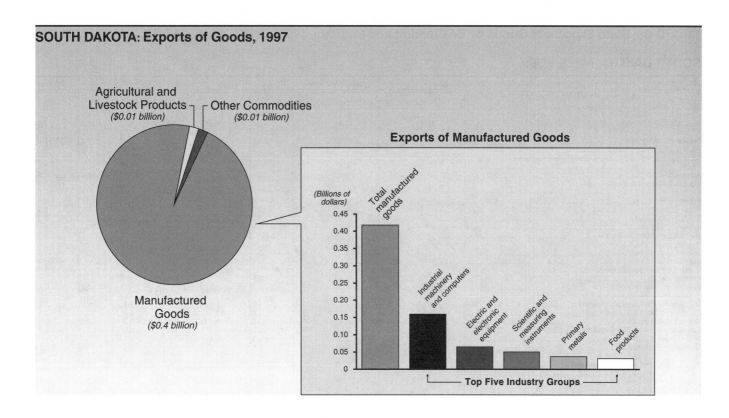

## Table D-3.   State Exports of Goods by Destination and Industry, 1993–1997 —*Continued*

**SOUTH DAKOTA** (Millions of dollars.)

| Industry | 1993 | 1994 | 1995 | 1996 | 1997 | 1993 | 1994 | 1995 | 1996 | 1997 |
|---|---|---|---|---|---|---|---|---|---|---|
| | All destinations | | | | | Canada | | | | |
| **ALL GOODS** | 213.8 | 263.9 | 348.6 | 397.3 | 435.3 | 107.5 | 130.8 | 142.1 | 164.1 | 167.3 |
| **Manufactured goods** | 200.9 | 252.4 | 334.1 | 382.5 | 418.1 | 97.9 | 122.9 | 131.5 | 151.2 | 152.6 |
| Food products | 7.2 | 5.7 | 9.3 | 15.3 | 31.5 | 5.6 | 4.3 | 7.0 | 11.1 | 28.1 |
| Tobacco products | ..... | ..... | ..... | ..... | ..... | ..... | ..... | ..... | ..... | ..... |
| Textile mill products | 0.8 | 1.4 | 2.8 | 4.9 | 4.4 | 0.7 | 0.3 | 0.1 | 0.2 | 0.2 |
| Apparel | 2.9 | 2.7 | 3.0 | 5.8 | 5.1 | 0.4 | 0.2 | 0.2 | 0.4 | 0.4 |
| Lumber and wood products | 0.4 | 0.3 | 0.2 | 0.6 | 0.5 | 0.3 | 0.2 | 0.1 | 0.4 | 0.4 |
| Furniture and fixtures | 0.3 | 0.3 | 0.3 | 0.4 | 0.7 | 0.3 | 0.2 | 0.2 | 0.2 | 0.3 |
| Paper products | 3.0 | 3.0 | 4.4 | 8.2 | 10.4 | 1.5 | 1.2 | 2.0 | 4.4 | 5.4 |
| Printing and publishing | 1.4 | 2.1 | 2.8 | 3.5 | 7.2 | 1.3 | 2.0 | 2.2 | 2.1 | 2.9 |
| Chemical products | 5.3 | 2.2 | 2.9 | 3.9 | 4.3 | 2.8 | 1.4 | 1.5 | 1.3 | 0.9 |
| Refined petroleum products | 0.2 | 0.4 | 0.5 | 0.6 | 1.2 | 0.2 | 0.4 | 0.5 | 0.6 | 1.2 |
| Rubber and plastic products | 3.8 | 3.0 | 4.0 | 4.5 | 5.9 | 1.5 | 1.4 | 2.5 | 1.6 | 2.0 |
| Leather products | 0.3 | 0.2 | 0.2 | 0.2 | 0.4 | 0.2 | 0.1 | 0.2 | 0.1 | 0.1 |
| Stone, clay and glass products | 0.4 | 0.4 | 0.3 | 0.2 | 0.5 | 0.3 | 0.3 | 0.2 | 0.1 | 0.3 |
| Primary metals | 38.1 | 43.2 | 36.1 | 56.1 | 37.3 | 37.9 | 42.8 | 35.9 | 55.9 | 37.0 |
| Fabricated metal products | 2.5 | 2.7 | 3.5 | 4.9 | 6.6 | 1.0 | 1.7 | 2.7 | 2.6 | 4.5 |
| Industrial machinery and computers | 62.9 | 95.8 | 161.5 | 144.6 | 159.6 | 21.9 | 38.0 | 42.9 | 38.1 | 38.6 |
| Electric and electronic equipment | 20.1 | 24.5 | 31.0 | 41.8 | 65.1 | 8.6 | 10.7 | 12.0 | 10.4 | 9.9 |
| Transportation equipment | 11.8 | 16.2 | 18.3 | 23.6 | 22.1 | 8.7 | 13.2 | 15.9 | 13.3 | 15.6 |
| Scientific and measuring instruments | 35.2 | 43.3 | 44.4 | 52.7 | 50.8 | 2.0 | 1.6 | 1.4 | 2.0 | 2.2 |
| Miscellaneous manufactures | 2.4 | 2.4 | 4.9 | 8.0 | 2.2 | 1.1 | 0.9 | 0.9 | 3.8 | 0.9 |
| Unidentified manufactures | 2.2 | 2.7 | 3.7 | 2.9 | 2.6 | 1.7 | 2.1 | 3.2 | 2.7 | 2.1 |
| **Agricultural and livestock products** | 5.9 | 4.4 | 7.3 | 9.9 | 8.5 | 4.5 | 3.4 | 4.6 | 8.9 | 7.9 |
| Agricultural products | 3.9 | 2.7 | 5.2 | 7.6 | 5.8 | 2.8 | 2.3 | 3.3 | 7.3 | 5.7 |
| Livestock and livestock products | 2.0 | 1.6 | 2.1 | 2.3 | 2.7 | 1.7 | 1.1 | 1.3 | 1.5 | 2.3 |
| **Other commodities** | 7.0 | 7.2 | 7.2 | 4.9 | 8.7 | 5.1 | 4.4 | 5.9 | 4.0 | 6.7 |
| Forestry products | 0.4 | 1.2 | 0.4 | ..... | ..... | ..... | ..... | ..... | ..... | ..... |
| Fish and other marine products | 0.1 | ..... | ..... | 0.1 | ..... | ..... | ..... | ..... | 0.1 | ..... |
| Metallic ores and concentrates | ..... | ..... | ..... | ..... | ..... | ..... | ..... | ..... | ..... | ..... |
| Bituminous coal and lignite | 0.9 | ..... | ..... | ..... | ..... | 0.9 | ..... | ..... | ..... | ..... |
| Crude petroleum and natural gas | ..... | 0.2 | ..... | ..... | ..... | ..... | 0.2 | ..... | ..... | ..... |
| Nonmetallic minerals | 1.0 | 0.9 | 1.2 | 1.3 | 2.3 | 0.3 | 0.5 | 0.6 | 0.8 | 0.7 |
| Scrap and waste | 0.6 | 0.8 | 1.0 | 0.5 | 0.2 | 0.6 | 0.7 | 1.0 | 0.4 | 0.2 |
| Used merchandise | 0.7 | 2.1 | 0.7 | 0.4 | 0.7 | 0.1 | 1.5 | 0.4 | 0.2 | 0.6 |
| Goods imported and returned unchanged | 3.2 | 1.5 | 3.6 | 2.3 | 5.1 | 3.2 | 1.5 | 3.6 | 2.3 | 5.1 |
| Special classification provisions | ..... | 0.5 | 0.4 | 0.4 | 0.2 | ..... | ..... | 0.4 | 0.3 | 0.2 |

## Table D-3. State Exports of Goods by Destination and Industry, 1993–1997 —Continued

**SOUTH DAKOTA** (Millions of dollars.)

| Industry | 1993 | 1994 | 1995 | 1996 | 1997 | 1993 | 1994 | 1995 | 1996 | 1997 |
|---|---|---|---|---|---|---|---|---|---|---|
| | South and Central America and Caribbean | | | | | Mexico | | | | |
| **ALL GOODS** | 4.5 | 5.7 | 11.8 | 17.5 | 14.8 | 4.1 | 5.5 | 5.3 | 7.8 | 11.5 |
| **Manufactured goods** | 4.4 | 5.7 | 11.7 | 17.5 | 14.8 | 4.1 | 5.1 | 4.9 | 7.1 | 11.0 |
| Food products | ..... | ..... | ..... | ..... | 0.1 | 0.1 | 0.4 | 1.8 | 3.0 | 2.0 |
| Tobacco products | ..... | ..... | ..... | ..... | ..... | ..... | ..... | ..... | ..... | ..... |
| Textile mill products | ..... | ..... | 0.6 | 0.6 | 0.9 | 0.1 | 0.1 | 0.2 | 0.2 | 0.1 |
| Apparel | 0.1 | 0.2 | 0.5 | 1.0 | 0.6 | 0.1 | 0.1 | 0.3 | 0.4 | 0.5 |
| Lumber and wood products | ..... | ..... | ..... | ..... | ..... | ..... | ..... | ..... | ..... | ..... |
| Furniture and fixtures | ..... | ..... | ..... | ..... | ..... | ..... | ..... | ..... | ..... | 0.1 |
| Paper products | ..... | ..... | ..... | 0.1 | 0.6 | ..... | 0.1 | 0.2 | 0.1 | 0.4 |
| Printing and publishing | ..... | ..... | 0.1 | ..... | 0.1 | ..... | ..... | ..... | 0.1 | 0.3 |
| Chemical products | 0.1 | 0.2 | 0.2 | 0.1 | 0.4 | 0.1 | 0.1 | 0.1 | 0.1 | 0.1 |
| Refined petroleum products | ..... | ..... | ..... | ..... | ..... | ..... | ..... | ..... | ..... | ..... |
| Rubber and plastic products | ..... | ..... | 0.2 | 0.2 | 0.5 | 0.1 | 0.1 | ..... | 0.1 | 1.0 |
| Leather products | ..... | ..... | ..... | ..... | ..... | ..... | ..... | ..... | ..... | 0.1 |
| Stone, clay and glass products | ..... | ..... | ..... | ..... | ..... | ..... | ..... | ..... | ..... | ..... |
| Primary metals | ..... | ..... | ..... | ..... | 0.1 | ..... | 0.1 | ..... | ..... | ..... |
| Fabricated metal products | 0.1 | 0.1 | 0.2 | 0.1 | ..... | 0.6 | ..... | ..... | 0.2 | 0.1 |
| Industrial machinery and computers | 2.2 | 3.7 | 6.2 | 9.8 | 8.6 | 1.0 | 2.3 | 1.1 | 1.7 | 3.8 |
| Electric and electronic equipment | 0.7 | 0.3 | 0.8 | 1.1 | 2.2 | 0.4 | 0.3 | 0.2 | 0.3 | 1.3 |
| Transportation equipment | 0.1 | 0.2 | 0.1 | 0.6 | 0.3 | 1.1 | 1.3 | 0.3 | 0.3 | 0.6 |
| Scientific and measuring instruments | 0.9 | 0.9 | 0.1 | 0.2 | 0.2 | 0.5 | 0.1 | 0.5 | 0.7 | 0.4 |
| Miscellaneous manufactures | ..... | 0.1 | 2.8 | 3.3 | 0.3 | 0.1 | ..... | ..... | ..... | ..... |
| Unidentified manufactures | 0.1 | 0.1 | ..... | ..... | 0.1 | ..... | 0.1 | 0.1 | ..... | ..... |
| **Agricultural and livestock products** | ..... | ..... | ..... | ..... | ..... | 0.1 | 0.4 | 0.4 | 0.6 | 0.3 |
| Agricultural products | ..... | ..... | 0.1 | ..... | ..... | ..... | 0.1 | ..... | ..... | ..... |
| Livestock and livestock products | ..... | ..... | ..... | ..... | ..... | 0.1 | 0.3 | 0.4 | 0.6 | 0.3 |
| **Other commodities** | ..... | ..... | ..... | ..... | ..... | ..... | ..... | ..... | 0.1 | 0.2 |
| Forestry products | ..... | ..... | ..... | ..... | ..... | ..... | ..... | ..... | ..... | ..... |
| Fish and other marine products | ..... | ..... | ..... | ..... | ..... | ..... | ..... | ..... | ..... | ..... |
| Metallic ores and concentrates | ..... | ..... | ..... | ..... | ..... | ..... | ..... | ..... | ..... | ..... |
| Bituminous coal and lignite | ..... | ..... | ..... | ..... | ..... | ..... | ..... | ..... | ..... | ..... |
| Crude petroleum and natural gas | ..... | ..... | ..... | ..... | ..... | ..... | ..... | ..... | ..... | ..... |
| Nonmetallic minerals | ..... | ..... | ..... | ..... | ..... | ..... | ..... | ..... | 0.1 | 0.1 |
| Scrap and waste | ..... | ..... | ..... | ..... | ..... | ..... | ..... | ..... | ..... | ..... |
| Used merchandise | ..... | ..... | ..... | ..... | ..... | ..... | ..... | ..... | ..... | ..... |
| Goods imported and returned unchanged | ..... | ..... | ..... | ..... | ..... | ..... | ..... | ..... | ..... | ..... |
| Special classification provisions | ..... | ..... | ..... | ..... | ..... | ..... | ..... | ..... | ..... | ..... |
| | European Union | | | | | United Kingdom | | | | |
| **ALL GOODS** | 66.4 | 69.5 | 111.2 | 105.8 | 121.7 | 5.2 | 8.7 | 35.5 | 29.6 | 35.7 |
| **Manufactured goods** | 64.7 | 68.9 | 108.8 | 105.3 | 120.9 | 4.9 | 8.6 | 35.2 | 29.4 | 35.4 |
| Food products | 0.2 | 0.3 | 0.1 | 0.1 | ..... | ..... | ..... | ..... | ..... | ..... |
| Tobacco products | ..... | ..... | ..... | ..... | ..... | ..... | ..... | ..... | ..... | ..... |
| Textile mill products | ..... | 0.7 | 1.8 | 3.3 | 2.9 | ..... | ..... | 0.3 | ..... | 0.2 |
| Apparel | 1.8 | 1.6 | 1.7 | 2.7 | 2.0 | ..... | 0.1 | 0.1 | 1.3 | 0.9 |
| Lumber and wood products | ..... | ..... | 0.1 | ..... | ..... | ..... | ..... | ..... | ..... | ..... |
| Furniture and fixtures | ..... | ..... | 0.1 | ..... | ..... | ..... | ..... | ..... | ..... | ..... |
| Paper products | 1.4 | 1.2 | 1.9 | 3.0 | 3.4 | 0.1 | 0.3 | 0.1 | 0.1 | ..... |
| Printing and publishing | 0.1 | ..... | 0.3 | 1.2 | 3.4 | ..... | ..... | ..... | 0.1 | 0.2 |
| Chemical products | 0.4 | 0.3 | 0.6 | 1.0 | 1.4 | ..... | ..... | 0.2 | 0.2 | 0.3 |
| Refined petroleum products | ..... | ..... | ..... | ..... | ..... | ..... | ..... | ..... | ..... | ..... |
| Rubber and plastic products | 1.6 | 0.8 | 0.7 | 1.6 | 1.7 | 0.1 | ..... | 0.1 | 0.7 | 0.7 |
| Leather products | ..... | ..... | ..... | ..... | 0.1 | ..... | ..... | ..... | ..... | ..... |
| Stone, clay and glass products | ..... | ..... | ..... | ..... | ..... | ..... | ..... | ..... | ..... | ..... |
| Primary metals | 0.2 | 0.1 | ..... | ..... | 0.2 | 0.1 | 0.1 | ..... | ..... | ..... |
| Fabricated metal products | 0.3 | 0.2 | 0.3 | 0.6 | 0.5 | ..... | ..... | 0.1 | 0.3 | 0.1 |
| Industrial machinery and computers | 27.4 | 31.3 | 66.2 | 46.3 | 51.3 | 1.3 | 4.9 | 33.4 | 23.7 | 31.2 |
| Electric and electronic equipment | 3.8 | 2.9 | 4.4 | 7.4 | 19.3 | 1.6 | 1.0 | 0.6 | 0.8 | 1.0 |
| Transportation equipment | 0.5 | 0.5 | 1.4 | 3.5 | 1.4 | 0.1 | 0.1 | ..... | 1.6 | 0.2 |
| Scientific and measuring instruments | 26.6 | 28.1 | 28.7 | 33.8 | 32.4 | 1.2 | 1.6 | 0.1 | 0.3 | 0.1 |
| Miscellaneous manufactures | 0.4 | 0.6 | 0.5 | 0.5 | 0.5 | 0.3 | 0.4 | 0.3 | 0.3 | 0.3 |
| Unidentified manufactures | 0.2 | 0.1 | 0.1 | 0.1 | 0.2 | 0.1 | ..... | 0.1 | ..... | ..... |
| **Agricultural and livestock products** | 1.1 | 0.5 | 1.9 | 0.2 | 0.1 | ..... | ..... | 0.1 | ..... | ..... |
| Agricultural products | 1.0 | 0.3 | 1.8 | 0.2 | 0.1 | ..... | ..... | ..... | ..... | ..... |
| Livestock and livestock products | 0.1 | 0.1 | 0.1 | ..... | ..... | ..... | ..... | 0.1 | ..... | ..... |
| **Other commodities** | 0.7 | 0.1 | 0.5 | 0.3 | 0.8 | 0.3 | 0.1 | 0.2 | 0.2 | 0.3 |
| Forestry products | 0.3 | ..... | ..... | ..... | ..... | ..... | ..... | ..... | ..... | ..... |
| Fish and other marine products | ..... | ..... | ..... | ..... | ..... | ..... | ..... | ..... | ..... | ..... |
| Metallic ores and concentrates | ..... | ..... | ..... | ..... | ..... | ..... | ..... | ..... | ..... | ..... |
| Bituminous coal and lignite | ..... | ..... | ..... | ..... | ..... | ..... | ..... | ..... | ..... | ..... |
| Crude petroleum and natural gas | ..... | ..... | ..... | ..... | ..... | ..... | ..... | ..... | ..... | ..... |
| Nonmetallic minerals | ..... | 0.1 | 0.4 | 0.3 | 0.6 | ..... | 0.1 | 0.2 | 0.2 | 0.2 |
| Scrap and waste | ..... | ..... | ..... | ..... | ..... | ..... | ..... | ..... | ..... | ..... |
| Used merchandise | 0.3 | 0.1 | 0.1 | ..... | 0.1 | 0.3 | ..... | ..... | ..... | ..... |
| Goods imported and returned unchanged | ..... | ..... | ..... | ..... | ..... | ..... | ..... | ..... | ..... | ..... |
| Special classification provisions | ..... | ..... | ..... | ..... | 0.1 | ..... | ..... | ..... | ..... | ..... |

## Table D-3.  State Exports of Goods by Destination and Industry, 1993–1997 —Continued

### SOUTH DAKOTA (Millions of dollars.)

| Industry | 1993 | 1994 | 1995 | 1996 | 1997 | 1993 | 1994 | 1995 | 1996 | 1997 |
|---|---|---|---|---|---|---|---|---|---|---|
| | Germany | | | | | France | | | | |
| **ALL GOODS** | 9.9 | 8.3 | 10.6 | 17.1 | 18.2 | 13.4 | 4.2 | 6.7 | 7.2 | 7.4 |
| **Manufactured goods** | 9.8 | 8.3 | 10.6 | 17.1 | 18.1 | 13.4 | 4.2 | 6.6 | 7.2 | 7.4 |
| Food products | 0.1 | 0.2 | ..... | ..... | 0.1 | ..... | ..... | ..... | ..... | ..... |
| Tobacco products | ..... | ..... | ..... | ..... | ..... | ..... | ..... | ..... | ..... | ..... |
| Textile mill products | ..... | 0.3 | 0.1 | 1.6 | 1.5 | ..... | 0.1 | ..... | ..... | ..... |
| Apparel | 0.5 | 0.3 | 0.1 | 0.1 | 0.2 | ..... | ..... | ..... | ..... | ..... |
| Lumber and wood products | ..... | ..... | ..... | ..... | ..... | ..... | ..... | ..... | ..... | ..... |
| Furniture and fixtures | ..... | ..... | ..... | ..... | ..... | ..... | ..... | ..... | ..... | ..... |
| Paper products | ..... | ..... | 0.2 | 1.3 | 1.3 | ..... | ..... | ..... | ..... | ..... |
| Printing and publishing | ..... | ..... | ..... | 0.8 | 2.9 | ..... | ..... | ..... | 0.2 | 0.2 |
| Chemical products | 0.2 | 0.2 | 0.1 | ..... | 0.2 | 0.1 | ..... | 0.2 | 0.2 | 0.2 |
| Refined petroleum products | ..... | ..... | ..... | ..... | ..... | ..... | ..... | ..... | ..... | ..... |
| Rubber and plastic products | 0.6 | ..... | ..... | 0.2 | 0.3 | ..... | ..... | ..... | 0.1 | 0.1 |
| Leather products | ..... | ..... | ..... | ..... | ..... | ..... | ..... | ..... | ..... | ..... |
| Stone, clay and glass products | ..... | ..... | ..... | ..... | ..... | ..... | ..... | ..... | ..... | ..... |
| Primary metals | ..... | ..... | ..... | ..... | ..... | ..... | ..... | ..... | ..... | ..... |
| Fabricated metal products | 0.2 | 0.1 | ..... | ..... | ..... | ..... | ..... | ..... | 0.1 | 0.1 |
| Industrial machinery and computers | 7.3 | 5.5 | 6.8 | 7.7 | 6.1 | 8.7 | 0.6 | 0.7 | 0.8 | 0.7 |
| Electric and electronic equipment | 0.1 | 0.2 | 0.3 | 0.5 | 1.0 | 0.1 | 0.1 | 1.2 | 2.3 | 2.3 |
| Transportation equipment | ..... | ..... | 0.1 | 0.9 | 1.5 | 0.9 | 0.2 | 0.1 | ..... | 0.1 |
| Scientific and measuring instruments | 0.7 | 1.2 | 1.8 | 3.3 | 3.6 | 4.2 | 3.2 | 4.2 | 3.4 | 3.5 |
| Miscellaneous manufactures | ..... | 0.1 | ..... | ..... | ..... | ..... | ..... | ..... | ..... | ..... |
| Unidentified manufactures | ..... | ..... | ..... | ..... | ..... | ..... | ..... | ..... | ..... | 0.1 |
| **Agricultural and livestock products** | ..... | ..... | ..... | ..... | 0.1 | ..... | ..... | ..... | ..... | ..... |
| Agricultural products | ..... | ..... | ..... | ..... | 0.1 | ..... | ..... | ..... | ..... | ..... |
| Livestock and livestock products | ..... | ..... | ..... | ..... | ..... | ..... | ..... | ..... | ..... | ..... |
| **Other commodities** | ..... | ..... | ..... | ..... | ..... | ..... | ..... | 0.1 | ..... | ..... |
| Forestry products | ..... | ..... | ..... | ..... | ..... | ..... | ..... | ..... | ..... | ..... |
| Fish and other marine products | ..... | ..... | ..... | ..... | ..... | ..... | ..... | ..... | ..... | ..... |
| Metallic ores and concentrates | ..... | ..... | ..... | ..... | ..... | ..... | ..... | ..... | ..... | ..... |
| Bituminous coal and lignite | ..... | ..... | ..... | ..... | ..... | ..... | ..... | ..... | ..... | ..... |
| Crude petroleum and natural gas | ..... | ..... | ..... | ..... | ..... | ..... | ..... | ..... | ..... | ..... |
| Nonmetallic minerals | ..... | ..... | ..... | ..... | ..... | ..... | ..... | ..... | ..... | ..... |
| Scrap and waste | ..... | ..... | ..... | ..... | ..... | ..... | ..... | ..... | ..... | ..... |
| Used merchandise | ..... | ..... | ..... | ..... | ..... | ..... | ..... | 0.1 | ..... | ..... |
| Goods imported and returned unchanged | ..... | ..... | ..... | ..... | ..... | ..... | ..... | ..... | ..... | ..... |
| Special classification provisions | ..... | ..... | ..... | ..... | ..... | ..... | ..... | ..... | ..... | ..... |
| | The Netherlands | | | | | Asian 10 | | | | |
| **ALL GOODS** | 23.5 | 25.7 | 26.6 | 31.7 | 29.6 | 19.2 | 38.2 | 58.4 | 81.9 | 104.5 |
| **Manufactured goods** | 23.4 | 25.6 | 26.6 | 31.7 | 29.6 | 18.1 | 36.4 | 57.4 | 81.3 | 103.5 |
| Food products | 0.1 | ..... | ..... | ..... | ..... | 0.6 | 0.3 | 0.1 | 0.6 | 0.9 |
| Tobacco products | ..... | ..... | ..... | ..... | ..... | ..... | ..... | ..... | ..... | ..... |
| Textile mill products | ..... | ..... | 0.1 | ..... | ..... | ..... | 0.3 | 0.1 | 0.5 | 0.3 |
| Apparel | 1.3 | 1.2 | 1.4 | 1.3 | 0.9 | 0.3 | 0.7 | 0.3 | 1.0 | 1.6 |
| Lumber and wood products | ..... | ..... | 0.1 | ..... | ..... | ..... | ..... | ..... | 0.1 | ..... |
| Furniture and fixtures | ..... | ..... | ..... | ..... | ..... | ..... | ..... | ..... | 0.1 | 0.2 |
| Paper products | 1.2 | 0.8 | 0.9 | 1.1 | 0.9 | 0.1 | 0.2 | 0.3 | 0.6 | 0.6 |
| Printing and publishing | ..... | ..... | 0.2 | ..... | ..... | ..... | ..... | 0.1 | 0.1 | 0.1 |
| Chemical products | ..... | ..... | ..... | 0.1 | ..... | 0.2 | 0.2 | 0.3 | 1.2 | 1.2 |
| Refined petroleum products | ..... | ..... | ..... | ..... | ..... | ..... | ..... | ..... | ..... | ..... |
| Rubber and plastic products | 0.4 | 0.5 | 0.4 | 0.6 | 0.6 | 0.1 | 0.7 | 0.6 | 0.9 | 0.5 |
| Leather products | ..... | ..... | ..... | ..... | ..... | 0.1 | ..... | ..... | ..... | 0.1 |
| Stone, clay and glass products | ..... | ..... | ..... | ..... | ..... | 0.1 | ..... | ..... | ..... | 0.1 |
| Primary metals | ..... | ..... | ..... | ..... | ..... | 0.1 | 0.1 | 0.1 | 0.1 | 0.1 |
| Fabricated metal products | ..... | ..... | ..... | 0.1 | 0.2 | 0.2 | 0.3 | 0.2 | 1.1 | 1.1 |
| Industrial machinery and computers | 1.0 | 1.8 | 0.6 | 0.8 | 0.7 | 6.6 | 12.6 | 30.5 | 39.2 | 51.4 |
| Electric and electronic equipment | ..... | 0.5 | 1.2 | 1.6 | 1.9 | 4.9 | 8.8 | 11.3 | 19.5 | 30.0 |
| Transportation equipment | ..... | 0.1 | 0.1 | ..... | ..... | 0.4 | 0.3 | 0.1 | 0.3 | 0.5 |
| Scientific and measuring instruments | 19.2 | 20.7 | 21.6 | 26.0 | 24.3 | 3.6 | 11.1 | 12.8 | 15.6 | 14.8 |
| Miscellaneous manufactures | ..... | 0.1 | 0.1 | 0.1 | 0.1 | 0.7 | 0.7 | 0.6 | 0.2 | ..... |
| Unidentified manufactures | ..... | ..... | ..... | ..... | ..... | 0.2 | 0.2 | 0.1 | 0.1 | 0.1 |
| **Agricultural and livestock products** | 0.1 | ..... | ..... | ..... | ..... | 0.2 | ..... | 0.3 | 0.2 | ..... |
| Agricultural products | ..... | ..... | ..... | ..... | ..... | ..... | ..... | ..... | ..... | ..... |
| Livestock and livestock products | 0.1 | ..... | ..... | ..... | ..... | 0.2 | ..... | 0.3 | 0.1 | ..... |
| **Other commodities** | ..... | ..... | ..... | ..... | ..... | 0.9 | 1.8 | 0.7 | 0.4 | 1.0 |
| Forestry products | ..... | ..... | ..... | ..... | ..... | ..... | 1.2 | 0.4 | ..... | ..... |
| Fish and other marine products | ..... | ..... | ..... | ..... | ..... | ..... | 0.1 | ..... | ..... | ..... |
| Metallic ores and concentrates | ..... | ..... | ..... | ..... | ..... | ..... | ..... | ..... | ..... | ..... |
| Bituminous coal and lignite | ..... | ..... | ..... | ..... | ..... | ..... | ..... | ..... | ..... | ..... |
| Crude petroleum and natural gas | ..... | ..... | ..... | ..... | ..... | ..... | ..... | ..... | ..... | ..... |
| Nonmetallic minerals | ..... | ..... | ..... | ..... | ..... | 0.7 | 0.3 | 0.1 | 0.1 | 0.9 |
| Scrap and waste | ..... | ..... | ..... | ..... | ..... | ..... | 0.1 | ..... | 0.1 | ..... |
| Used merchandise | ..... | ..... | ..... | ..... | ..... | 0.1 | 0.1 | 0.2 | 0.2 | 0.1 |
| Goods imported and returned unchanged | ..... | ..... | ..... | ..... | ..... | ..... | 0.1 | ..... | ..... | ..... |
| Special classification provisions | ..... | ..... | ..... | ..... | ..... | ..... | ..... | ..... | ..... | ..... |

## Table D-3.  State Exports of Goods by Destination and Industry, 1993–1997 —Continued

**SOUTH DAKOTA**  (Millions of dollars.)

| Industry | 1993 | 1994 | 1995 | 1996 | 1997 | 1993 | 1994 | 1995 | 1996 | 1997 |
|---|---|---|---|---|---|---|---|---|---|---|
| | Japan | | | | | South Korea | | | | |
| **ALL GOODS** | 10.3 | 22.1 | 38.6 | 28.0 | 22.0 | 1.5 | 2.6 | 1.0 | 3.2 | 4.7 |
| **Manufactured goods** | 9.6 | 20.8 | 37.9 | 27.7 | 21.2 | 1.5 | 2.5 | 1.0 | 3.2 | 4.7 |
| Food products | 0.6 | 0.2 | ..... | ..... | 0.6 | ..... | ..... | 0.1 | ..... | ..... |
| Tobacco products | ..... | ..... | ..... | ..... | ..... | ..... | ..... | ..... | ..... | ..... |
| Textile mill products | ..... | ..... | ..... | ..... | ..... | ..... | 0.3 | 0.1 | ..... | 0.1 |
| Apparel | 0.2 | 0.7 | 0.2 | 0.2 | 0.1 | ..... | ..... | ..... | 0.8 | 1.3 |
| Lumber and wood products | ..... | ..... | ..... | 0.1 | ..... | ..... | ..... | ..... | ..... | ..... |
| Furniture and fixtures | ..... | ..... | ..... | 0.1 | ..... | ..... | ..... | ..... | ..... | ..... |
| Paper products | ..... | 0.2 | 0.2 | 0.2 | 0.4 | ..... | ..... | ..... | 0.1 | 0.1 |
| Printing and publishing | ..... | ..... | ..... | ..... | ..... | ..... | ..... | ..... | ..... | ..... |
| Chemical products | 0.2 | 0.1 | 0.1 | 0.9 | 0.2 | ..... | ..... | ..... | 0.1 | 0.1 |
| Refined petroleum products | ..... | ..... | ..... | ..... | ..... | ..... | ..... | ..... | ..... | ..... |
| Rubber and plastic products | ..... | 0.2 | 0.3 | 0.3 | 0.3 | ..... | 0.2 | 0.1 | ..... | ..... |
| Leather products | 0.1 | ..... | ..... | ..... | 0.1 | ..... | ..... | ..... | ..... | ..... |
| Stone, clay and glass products | ..... | ..... | ..... | ..... | ..... | ..... | ..... | ..... | ..... | ..... |
| Primary metals | ..... | ..... | ..... | ..... | ..... | ..... | ..... | ..... | ..... | ..... |
| Fabricated metal products | ..... | ..... | 0.1 | ..... | 0.2 | ..... | 0.2 | ..... | 1.0 | 0.8 |
| Industrial machinery and computers | 3.4 | 6.8 | 21.7 | 7.8 | 2.3 | 1.0 | 1.3 | 0.6 | 0.9 | 1.5 |
| Electric and electronic equipment | 1.2 | 1.0 | 2.6 | 2.1 | 2.1 | 0.4 | 0.4 | ..... | 0.1 | 0.3 |
| Transportation equipment | 0.1 | 0.2 | 0.1 | 0.2 | 0.3 | 0.1 | ..... | ..... | ..... | ..... |
| Scientific and measuring instruments | 3.1 | 10.8 | 12.0 | 14.8 | 14.4 | ..... | ..... | 0.1 | 0.2 | 0.2 |
| Miscellaneous manufactures | 0.5 | 0.5 | 0.4 | 0.1 | ..... | 0.1 | ..... | ..... | ..... | ..... |
| Unidentified manufactures | 0.1 | 0.1 | 0.1 | ..... | ..... | ..... | ..... | ..... | ..... | ..... |
| **Agricultural and livestock products** | ..... | ..... | 0.1 | ..... | ..... | ..... | ..... | ..... | ..... | ..... |
| Agricultural products | ..... | ..... | ..... | ..... | ..... | ..... | ..... | ..... | ..... | ..... |
| Livestock and livestock products | ..... | ..... | ..... | ..... | ..... | ..... | ..... | ..... | ..... | ..... |
| **Other commodities** | 0.7 | 1.4 | 0.6 | 0.3 | 0.8 | ..... | 0.1 | ..... | 0.1 | ..... |
| Forestry products | ..... | 1.1 | 0.4 | ..... | ..... | ..... | 0.1 | ..... | ..... | ..... |
| Fish and other marine products | 0.1 | ..... | ..... | ..... | ..... | ..... | ..... | ..... | ..... | ..... |
| Metallic ores and concentrates | ..... | ..... | ..... | ..... | ..... | ..... | ..... | ..... | ..... | ..... |
| Bituminous coal and lignite | ..... | ..... | ..... | ..... | ..... | ..... | ..... | ..... | ..... | ..... |
| Crude petroleum and natural gas | ..... | ..... | ..... | ..... | ..... | ..... | ..... | ..... | ..... | ..... |
| Nonmetallic minerals | 0.6 | 0.1 | ..... | ..... | 0.7 | ..... | ..... | ..... | ..... | ..... |
| Scrap and waste | ..... | ..... | ..... | ..... | ..... | ..... | 0.1 | ..... | 0.1 | ..... |
| Used merchandise | 0.1 | 0.1 | 0.2 | 0.2 | 0.1 | ..... | ..... | ..... | ..... | ..... |
| Goods imported and returned unchanged | ..... | ..... | ..... | ..... | ..... | ..... | ..... | ..... | ..... | ..... |
| Special classification provisions | ..... | ..... | ..... | ..... | ..... | ..... | ..... | ..... | ..... | ..... |
| | Taiwan | | | | | Singapore | | | | |
| **ALL GOODS** | 1.2 | 4.2 | 6.2 | 14.0 | 32.0 | 2.8 | 3.9 | 3.9 | 2.9 | 4.7 |
| **Manufactured goods** | 1.1 | 3.9 | 6.1 | 14.0 | 31.9 | 2.8 | 3.9 | 3.9 | 2.9 | 4.7 |
| Food products | ..... | 0.1 | ..... | ..... | ..... | ..... | ..... | ..... | ..... | ..... |
| Tobacco products | ..... | ..... | ..... | ..... | ..... | ..... | ..... | ..... | ..... | ..... |
| Textile mill products | ..... | ..... | ..... | ..... | ..... | ..... | ..... | ..... | ..... | 0.2 |
| Apparel | ..... | ..... | ..... | 0.1 | ..... | ..... | ..... | ..... | ..... | ..... |
| Lumber and wood products | ..... | ..... | ..... | ..... | ..... | ..... | ..... | ..... | ..... | ..... |
| Furniture and fixtures | ..... | ..... | ..... | ..... | 0.1 | ..... | ..... | ..... | ..... | ..... |
| Paper products | ..... | ..... | ..... | 0.3 | ..... | ..... | ..... | ..... | ..... | ..... |
| Printing and publishing | ..... | ..... | ..... | ..... | ..... | ..... | ..... | ..... | ..... | ..... |
| Chemical products | ..... | ..... | ..... | ..... | 0.3 | ..... | ..... | 0.2 | ..... | 0.3 |
| Refined petroleum products | ..... | ..... | ..... | ..... | ..... | ..... | ..... | ..... | ..... | ..... |
| Rubber and plastic products | ..... | 0.1 | 0.1 | 0.1 | ..... | ..... | 0.1 | ..... | ..... | 0.1 |
| Leather products | ..... | ..... | ..... | ..... | ..... | ..... | ..... | ..... | ..... | ..... |
| Stone, clay and glass products | ..... | ..... | ..... | ..... | ..... | ..... | ..... | ..... | ..... | ..... |
| Primary metals | ..... | ..... | ..... | 0.1 | ..... | ..... | ..... | ..... | ..... | ..... |
| Fabricated metal products | ..... | 0.1 | ..... | ..... | ..... | ..... | ..... | ..... | ..... | ..... |
| Industrial machinery and computers | 0.3 | 0.2 | 0.8 | 6.1 | 19.7 | 0.4 | 0.8 | 2.0 | 1.6 | 1.6 |
| Electric and electronic equipment | 0.6 | 3.5 | 4.9 | 7.3 | 11.5 | 2.3 | 2.9 | 1.6 | 1.2 | 2.4 |
| Transportation equipment | ..... | ..... | ..... | ..... | 0.1 | ..... | ..... | ..... | ..... | ..... |
| Scientific and measuring instruments | ..... | ..... | 0.2 | ..... | ..... | ..... | ..... | ..... | ..... | ..... |
| Miscellaneous manufactures | ..... | ..... | 0.1 | ..... | ..... | ..... | ..... | ..... | ..... | ..... |
| Unidentified manufactures | ..... | ..... | ..... | ..... | ..... | ..... | ..... | ..... | ..... | ..... |
| **Agricultural and livestock products** | ..... | ..... | ..... | ..... | ..... | ..... | ..... | ..... | ..... | ..... |
| Agricultural products | ..... | ..... | ..... | ..... | ..... | ..... | ..... | ..... | ..... | ..... |
| Livestock and livestock products | ..... | ..... | ..... | ..... | ..... | ..... | ..... | ..... | ..... | ..... |
| **Other commodities** | 0.1 | 0.2 | ..... | ..... | 0.1 | ..... | ..... | ..... | ..... | ..... |
| Forestry products | ..... | ..... | ..... | ..... | ..... | ..... | ..... | ..... | ..... | ..... |
| Fish and other marine products | ..... | ..... | ..... | ..... | ..... | ..... | ..... | ..... | ..... | ..... |
| Metallic ores and concentrates | ..... | ..... | ..... | ..... | ..... | ..... | ..... | ..... | ..... | ..... |
| Bituminous coal and lignite | ..... | ..... | ..... | ..... | ..... | ..... | ..... | ..... | ..... | ..... |
| Crude petroleum and natural gas | ..... | ..... | ..... | ..... | ..... | ..... | ..... | ..... | ..... | ..... |
| Nonmetallic minerals | 0.1 | 0.2 | ..... | ..... | 0.1 | ..... | ..... | ..... | ..... | ..... |
| Scrap and waste | ..... | ..... | ..... | ..... | ..... | ..... | ..... | ..... | ..... | ..... |
| Used merchandise | ..... | ..... | ..... | ..... | ..... | ..... | ..... | ..... | ..... | ..... |
| Goods imported and returned unchanged | ..... | ..... | ..... | ..... | ..... | ..... | ..... | ..... | ..... | ..... |
| Special classification provisions | ..... | 0.1 | ..... | ..... | ..... | ..... | ..... | ..... | ..... | ..... |

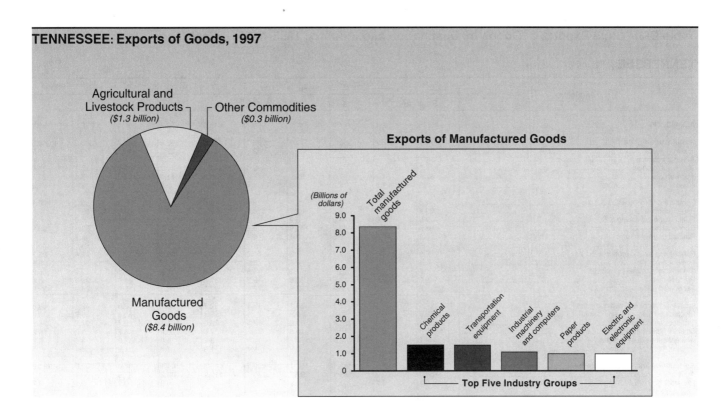

# TENNESSEE: Exports of Goods, 1997

## Table D-3.  State Exports of Goods by Destination and Industry, 1993–1997 —*Continued*

**TENNESSEE** (Millions of dollars.)

| Industry | 1993 | 1994 | 1995 | 1996 | 1997 | 1993 | 1994 | 1995 | 1996 | 1997 |
|---|---|---|---|---|---|---|---|---|---|---|
| | All destinations | | | | | Canada | | | | |
| **ALL GOODS** | 6 151.1 | 7 506.2 | 9 460.5 | 9 328.3 | 9 916.9 | 1 679.1 | 1 976.2 | 2 101.0 | 2 199.9 | 2 389.4 |
| **Manufactured goods** | 5 222.1 | 6 103.7 | 6 974.4 | 7 298.0 | 8 357.7 | 1 638.3 | 1 913.4 | 1 992.7 | 2 081.1 | 2 268.6 |
| Food products | 100.8 | 113.9 | 159.7 | 197.3 | 156.0 | 27.9 | 34.7 | 44.0 | 44.6 | 61.0 |
| Tobacco products | 3.9 | 6.8 | 6.2 | 0.4 | 0.3 | 3.9 | 6.7 | 5.4 | 0.2 | 0.2 |
| Textile mill products | 75.1 | 118.6 | 125.2 | 139.6 | 197.0 | 28.6 | 42.9 | 39.8 | 40.0 | 51.2 |
| Apparel | 92.7 | 121.5 | 130.6 | 159.8 | 196.2 | 8.6 | 12.4 | 8.4 | 15.3 | 19.2 |
| Lumber and wood products | 76.6 | 87.4 | 94.5 | 86.7 | 74.6 | 13.2 | 12.5 | 13.2 | 17.9 | 21.4 |
| Furniture and fixtures | 101.2 | 113.9 | 111.3 | 118.9 | 139.2 | 82.5 | 96.0 | 93.8 | 100.9 | 109.1 |
| Paper products | 636.9 | 760.2 | 971.2 | 897.5 | 995.0 | 59.6 | 71.3 | 92.4 | 95.7 | 101.5 |
| Printing and publishing | 63.5 | 58.8 | 72.8 | 74.2 | 80.2 | 37.3 | 37.6 | 40.8 | 43.9 | 38.7 |
| Chemical products | 1 079.7 | 1 317.6 | 1 453.1 | 1 362.7 | 1 502.5 | 197.6 | 231.1 | 248.9 | 251.9 | 268.0 |
| Refined petroleum products | 1.9 | 4.9 | 8.8 | 3.6 | 5.5 | 0.7 | 1.2 | 1.8 | 0.7 | 1.3 |
| Rubber and plastic products | 171.9 | 205.9 | 239.7 | 256.6 | 359.5 | 92.1 | 98.6 | 117.4 | 119.2 | 138.8 |
| Leather products | 24.9 | 22.6 | 16.7 | 15.6 | 15.1 | 11.9 | 9.0 | 7.1 | 6.6 | 5.5 |
| Stone, clay and glass products | 60.0 | 78.9 | 101.7 | 118.8 | 125.3 | 42.8 | 54.5 | 69.5 | 75.1 | 76.7 |
| Primary metals | 96.1 | 98.1 | 141.5 | 117.7 | 175.1 | 28.1 | 25.5 | 36.1 | 34.7 | 63.5 |
| Fabricated metal products | 206.0 | 222.9 | 247.8 | 186.9 | 218.6 | 72.7 | 68.8 | 68.7 | 76.8 | 96.9 |
| Industrial machinery and computers | 666.3 | 724.1 | 878.7 | 992.2 | 1 095.0 | 235.9 | 272.0 | 307.0 | 335.3 | 372.4 |
| Electric and electronic equipment | 512.2 | 558.0 | 649.6 | 817.5 | 986.7 | 207.6 | 258.8 | 237.1 | 245.8 | 275.7 |
| Transportation equipment | 885.2 | 1 110.3 | 1 175.0 | 1 296.4 | 1 493.5 | 362.4 | 468.5 | 471.1 | 454.7 | 448.4 |
| Scientific and measuring instruments | 259.4 | 254.3 | 257.2 | 323.0 | 378.2 | 93.6 | 73.3 | 50.0 | 75.9 | 68.3 |
| Miscellaneous manufactures | 96.3 | 110.4 | 119.3 | 116.7 | 143.9 | 27.0 | 31.2 | 33.5 | 38.9 | 43.8 |
| Unidentified manufactures | 11.5 | 14.6 | 13.6 | 16.0 | 20.0 | 4.4 | 6.8 | 6.5 | 6.9 | 7.1 |
| **Agricultural and livestock products** | 731.8 | 1 226.8 | 2 314.4 | 1 852.2 | 1 293.9 | 19.2 | 38.9 | 56.2 | 56.3 | 54.3 |
| Agricultural products | 729.8 | 1 225.3 | 2 313.8 | 1 850.1 | 1 292.7 | 19.1 | 38.8 | 55.9 | 55.9 | 54.1 |
| Livestock and livestock products | 2.0 | 1.5 | 0.6 | 2.0 | 1.2 | 0.1 | 0.1 | 0.3 | 0.4 | 0.3 |
| **Other commodities** | 197.2 | 175.8 | 171.7 | 178.2 | 265.3 | 21.6 | 23.9 | 52.1 | 62.6 | 66.4 |
| Forestry products | 0.4 | 1.5 | 0.6 | 1.7 | 0.7 | 0.1 | 0.2 | 0.1 | 0.2 | 0.1 |
| Fish and other marine products | 20.7 | 21.5 | 29.1 | 25.5 | 10.9 | 0.3 | 0.3 | 0.5 | 0.4 | 0.7 |
| Metallic ores and concentrates | ..... | 0.2 | 4.1 | 15.5 | 15.4 | ..... | ..... | 0.1 | 0.1 | 0.1 |
| Bituminous coal and lignite | 87.9 | 94.7 | 54.6 | 47.9 | 72.3 | 0.9 | 0.8 | 1.0 | 1.2 | 0.9 |
| Crude petroleum and natural gas | ..... | ..... | ..... | 0.3 | ..... | ..... | ..... | ..... | ..... | ..... |
| Nonmetallic minerals | 8.4 | 8.4 | 9.2 | 10.3 | 9.8 | 0.3 | 0.2 | 0.1 | 0.3 | 0.4 |
| Scrap and waste | 2.5 | 8.8 | 13.5 | 8.0 | 11.3 | 0.7 | 1.9 | 6.4 | 3.8 | 3.5 |
| Used merchandise | 45.7 | 18.1 | 7.5 | 2.4 | 52.9 | 0.1 | 0.9 | 0.5 | 0.5 | 0.7 |
| Goods imported and returned unchanged | 16.6 | 16.4 | 39.5 | 45.5 | 54.5 | 16.6 | 16.4 | 39.5 | 45.5 | 54.5 |
| Special classification provisions | 14.9 | 6.3 | 13.6 | 21.0 | 37.5 | 2.5 | 3.3 | 3.9 | 10.6 | 5.5 |

## Table D-3.    State Exports of Goods by Destination and Industry, 1993–1997 —*Continued*

**TENNESSEE** (Millions of dollars.)

| Industry | 1993 | 1994 | 1995 | 1996 | 1997 | 1993 | 1994 | 1995 | 1996 | 1997 |
|---|---|---|---|---|---|---|---|---|---|---|
| | South and Central America and Caribbean | | | | | Mexico | | | | |
| **ALL GOODS** | 436.8 | 492.1 | 707.9 | 771.9 | 894.1 | 649.9 | 752.4 | 839.4 | 913.6 | 1 188.1 |
| **Manufactured goods** | 299.4 | 360.2 | 516.7 | 571.1 | 708.1 | 523.8 | 645.2 | 748.7 | 808.6 | 1 048.5 |
| Food products | 10.9 | 12.9 | 15.4 | 22.5 | 22.1 | 31.4 | 27.6 | 10.4 | 23.4 | 11.3 |
| Tobacco products | ..... | ..... | 0.8 | ..... | ..... | ..... | ..... | ..... | ..... | ..... |
| Textile mill products | 4.6 | 6.7 | 8.4 | 12.1 | 20.0 | 1.1 | 7.7 | 12.7 | 13.7 | 23.5 |
| Apparel | 52.9 | 54.2 | 77.3 | 94.8 | 122.2 | 3.8 | 11.1 | 12.0 | 18.4 | 25.4 |
| Lumber and wood products | 0.9 | 1.8 | 3.3 | 0.8 | 1.1 | 2.2 | 2.5 | 3.1 | 3.4 | 3.9 |
| Furniture and fixtures | 1.3 | 1.7 | 1.7 | 2.4 | 2.5 | 2.9 | 3.2 | 3.2 | 3.2 | 6.1 |
| Paper products | 39.4 | 55.6 | 72.3 | 83.3 | 118.9 | 35.4 | 49.4 | 64.5 | 42.9 | 37.5 |
| Printing and publishing | 1.5 | 1.8 | 4.8 | 6.2 | 7.8 | 3.2 | 2.1 | 4.1 | 4.9 | 6.0 |
| Chemical products | 88.5 | 106.7 | 140.2 | 141.9 | 139.6 | 45.6 | 72.6 | 84.6 | 88.8 | 98.8 |
| Refined petroleum products | 0.3 | 0.2 | 0.3 | 0.1 | 0.2 | 0.3 | 3.0 | 5.8 | 2.2 | 1.2 |
| Rubber and plastic products | 5.0 | 6.0 | 12.1 | 17.8 | 41.0 | 25.9 | 23.5 | 22.3 | 25.4 | 85.7 |
| Leather products | 2.4 | 5.1 | 1.6 | 0.4 | 0.9 | 1.3 | 0.7 | 0.3 | 0.4 | 0.5 |
| Stone, clay and glass products | 1.8 | 2.5 | 3.1 | 5.2 | 4.8 | 1.6 | 7.8 | 2.1 | 10.1 | 5.2 |
| Primary metals | 9.0 | 7.9 | 12.7 | 13.0 | 15.3 | 37.8 | 44.3 | 51.0 | 20.0 | 38.4 |
| Fabricated metal products | 5.8 | 6.0 | 9.2 | 7.8 | 10.1 | 87.8 | 106.8 | 116.9 | 25.9 | 33.3 |
| Industrial machinery and computers | 27.4 | 39.4 | 49.1 | 38.1 | 49.4 | 32.7 | 59.1 | 62.6 | 42.4 | 68.6 |
| Electric and electronic equipment | 8.9 | 10.4 | 20.0 | 39.8 | 74.1 | 128.1 | 108.5 | 162.4 | 269.7 | 339.5 |
| Transportation equipment | 20.3 | 21.2 | 53.4 | 60.8 | 52.4 | 76.0 | 101.1 | 116.7 | 197.2 | 234.5 |
| Scientific and measuring instruments | 8.6 | 9.2 | 16.4 | 10.8 | 11.5 | 2.6 | 6.9 | 8.7 | 9.2 | 15.2 |
| Miscellaneous manufactures | 9.1 | 10.2 | 13.7 | 12.2 | 12.8 | 3.2 | 5.8 | 3.2 | 3.1 | 8.2 |
| Unidentified manufactures | 0.6 | 0.7 | 1.1 | 0.9 | 1.4 | 1.0 | 1.4 | 1.9 | 4.4 | 5.5 |
| **Agricultural and livestock products** | 134.7 | 127.5 | 186.1 | 197.7 | 180.1 | 113.3 | 104.1 | 88.0 | 100.6 | 131.0 |
| Agricultural products | 134.0 | 127.3 | 186.1 | 197.7 | 180.1 | 112.2 | 103.2 | 87.9 | 100.4 | 130.3 |
| Livestock and livestock products | 0.7 | 0.2 | ..... | 0.1 | 0.1 | 1.1 | 0.9 | 0.2 | 0.1 | 0.7 |
| **Other commodities** | 2.8 | 4.5 | 5.2 | 3.1 | 5.9 | 12.8 | 3.1 | 2.6 | 4.4 | 8.6 |
| Forestry products | ..... | ..... | ..... | ..... | 0.1 | ..... | ..... | ..... | ..... | 0.1 |
| Fish and other marine products | ..... | ..... | ..... | ..... | 0.1 | ..... | ..... | ..... | ..... | ..... |
| Metallic ores and concentrates | ..... | ..... | ..... | ..... | 0.2 | ..... | ..... | ..... | ..... | ..... |
| Bituminous coal and lignite | 0.8 | 0.9 | 2.6 | 0.3 | 1.3 | ..... | ..... | ..... | ..... | ..... |
| Crude petroleum and natural gas | ..... | ..... | ..... | ..... | ..... | ..... | ..... | ..... | ..... | ..... |
| Nonmetallic minerals | 1.9 | 1.9 | 2.0 | 1.9 | 1.5 | 1.9 | 2.6 | 2.3 | 4.2 | 3.8 |
| Scrap and waste | ..... | 0.1 | 0.1 | 0.1 | 1.1 | ..... | 0.3 | 0.1 | ..... | 0.1 |
| Used merchandise | ..... | 0.2 | 0.1 | 0.2 | 0.3 | 0.1 | 0.1 | ..... | ..... | ..... |
| Goods imported and returned unchanged | ..... | ..... | ..... | ..... | ..... | ..... | ..... | ..... | ..... | ..... |
| Special classification provisions | ..... | 1.3 | 0.4 | 0.7 | 1.5 | 10.8 | 0.1 | 0.1 | 0.1 | 4.5 |

| Industry | 1993 | 1994 | 1995 | 1996 | 1997 | 1993 | 1994 | 1995 | 1996 | 1997 |
|---|---|---|---|---|---|---|---|---|---|---|
| | European Union | | | | | United Kingdom | | | | |
| **ALL GOODS** | 1 553.9 | 1 708.0 | 1 898.8 | 1 869.1 | 2 132.4 | 340.1 | 378.4 | 422.9 | 395.5 | 531.7 |
| **Manufactured goods** | 1 488.6 | 1 612.0 | 1 780.4 | 1 772.4 | 2 015.0 | 336.2 | 373.4 | 408.1 | 384.7 | 502.9 |
| Food products | 13.5 | 15.0 | 45.5 | 52.3 | 20.7 | 0.7 | 0.7 | 0.7 | 2.0 | 1.3 |
| Tobacco products | ..... | ..... | ..... | ..... | ..... | ..... | ..... | ..... | ..... | ..... |
| Textile mill products | 28.1 | 43.9 | 37.5 | 45.2 | 68.6 | 20.2 | 25.7 | 22.7 | 32.1 | 53.3 |
| Apparel | 4.4 | 8.4 | 12.3 | 13.6 | 11.8 | 0.5 | 0.7 | 1.7 | 1.8 | 2.0 |
| Lumber and wood products | 40.9 | 43.2 | 45.7 | 41.1 | 29.4 | 7.6 | 7.0 | 8.5 | 8.0 | 6.3 |
| Furniture and fixtures | 6.0 | 4.6 | 4.0 | 5.3 | 9.2 | 2.7 | 1.5 | 1.2 | 2.9 | 4.6 |
| Paper products | 236.0 | 256.0 | 307.6 | 324.6 | 370.1 | 31.2 | 45.4 | 56.8 | 74.0 | 88.8 |
| Printing and publishing | 14.0 | 11.3 | 14.6 | 12.6 | 16.3 | 7.9 | 7.8 | 9.2 | 8.7 | 10.7 |
| Chemical products | 382.2 | 425.1 | 462.2 | 388.8 | 465.0 | 45.5 | 67.4 | 71.0 | 36.3 | 70.9 |
| Refined petroleum products | 0.2 | 0.3 | 0.1 | 0.1 | 1.7 | ..... | ..... | ..... | ..... | 0.1 |
| Rubber and plastic products | 14.3 | 21.4 | 22.4 | 18.6 | 23.7 | 8.9 | 13.4 | 13.4 | 8.8 | 11.5 |
| Leather products | 5.2 | 3.8 | 4.3 | 3.8 | 2.8 | 0.8 | 0.6 | 0.3 | 0.4 | 0.2 |
| Stone, clay and glass products | 6.6 | 6.4 | 10.7 | 12.3 | 16.0 | 4.3 | 3.6 | 4.3 | 6.5 | 8.9 |
| Primary metals | 8.5 | 8.1 | 13.2 | 13.0 | 25.6 | 1.6 | 2.0 | 2.3 | 3.2 | 5.1 |
| Fabricated metal products | 12.5 | 16.5 | 14.2 | 21.1 | 25.4 | 2.4 | 3.8 | 6.3 | 6.6 | 8.2 |
| Industrial machinery and computers | 208.0 | 180.6 | 229.5 | 233.7 | 240.8 | 61.8 | 25.6 | 41.1 | 48.9 | 55.7 |
| Electric and electronic equipment | 92.2 | 101.4 | 114.9 | 118.8 | 120.2 | 16.9 | 19.4 | 25.1 | 23.8 | 27.0 |
| Transportation equipment | 289.1 | 339.8 | 302.4 | 316.3 | 381.8 | 93.9 | 117.7 | 113.7 | 92.9 | 111.1 |
| Scientific and measuring instruments | 92.2 | 91.0 | 98.6 | 118.6 | 146.3 | 19.1 | 18.7 | 14.5 | 16.8 | 17.7 |
| Miscellaneous manufactures | 32.6 | 33.6 | 38.9 | 31.5 | 37.3 | 9.5 | 11.8 | 14.8 | 10.7 | 18.7 |
| Unidentified manufactures | 2.3 | 1.6 | 1.6 | 1.4 | 2.1 | 0.7 | 0.5 | 0.4 | 0.3 | 0.8 |
| **Agricultural and livestock products** | 58.4 | 67.1 | 95.8 | 61.3 | 51.5 | 2.0 | 3.6 | 12.6 | 6.7 | 3.4 |
| Agricultural products | 58.3 | 67.0 | 95.6 | 61.1 | 51.3 | 2.0 | 3.6 | 12.5 | 6.6 | 3.3 |
| Livestock and livestock products | ..... | 0.1 | 0.2 | 0.2 | 0.2 | ..... | 0.1 | 0.1 | 0.1 | 0.1 |
| **Other commodities** | 6.9 | 28.9 | 22.6 | 35.3 | 66.0 | 1.9 | 1.5 | 2.2 | 4.1 | 25.5 |
| Forestry products | ..... | 1.1 | 0.4 | 0.4 | ..... | ..... | ..... | ..... | ..... | ..... |
| Fish and other marine products | ..... | 0.1 | 0.1 | 0.1 | ..... | ..... | ..... | 0.1 | ..... | ..... |
| Metallic ores and concentrates | ..... | 0.1 | 3.9 | 15.2 | 15.1 | ..... | ..... | ..... | 0.2 | 0.1 |
| Bituminous coal and lignite | 2.8 | 2.2 | ..... | 6.7 | 23.3 | ..... | ..... | ..... | ..... | 17.8 |
| Crude petroleum and natural gas | ..... | ..... | ..... | ..... | 0.3 | ..... | ..... | ..... | 0.3 | ..... |
| Nonmetallic minerals | 1.3 | 1.9 | 1.5 | 1.6 | 1.8 | 0.6 | 0.9 | 0.8 | 0.8 | 0.7 |
| Scrap and waste | 1.0 | 5.9 | 5.8 | 3.1 | 4.8 | 0.5 | 0.1 | 0.2 | 0.3 | 0.4 |
| Used merchandise | 0.5 | 16.4 | 2.6 | 1.2 | 1.1 | 0.4 | 0.2 | 0.6 | 0.4 | 0.3 |
| Goods imported and returned unchanged | ..... | ..... | ..... | ..... | ..... | ..... | ..... | ..... | ..... | ..... |
| Special classification provisions | 1.2 | 1.3 | 8.3 | 6.7 | 19.8 | 0.3 | 0.3 | 0.5 | 2.0 | 6.2 |

## Table D-3. State Exports of Goods by Destination and Industry, 1993–1997 —*Continued*

**TENNESSEE** (Millions of dollars.)

| Industry | 1993 | 1994 | 1995 | 1996 | 1997 | 1993 | 1994 | 1995 | 1996 | 1997 |
|---|---|---|---|---|---|---|---|---|---|---|
| | Germany | | | | | France | | | | |
| **ALL GOODS** | 302.0 | 334.7 | 323.5 | 371.8 | 403.1 | 178.6 | 209.7 | 202.3 | 240.5 | 283.6 |
| **Manufactured goods** | 295.6 | 328.3 | 315.1 | 365.9 | 396.0 | 175.6 | 204.4 | 198.6 | 236.1 | 280.3 |
| Food products | 0.6 | 0.3 | 0.4 | 0.2 | 0.2 | 2.9 | 1.6 | 0.8 | 0.1 | 0.1 |
| Tobacco products | ..... | ..... | ..... | ..... | ..... | ..... | ..... | ..... | ..... | ..... |
| Textile mill products | 1.6 | 1.7 | 1.7 | 2.7 | 2.4 | 1.5 | 1.2 | 1.3 | 5.0 | 4.1 |
| Apparel | 0.5 | 2.6 | 3.6 | 4.2 | 3.7 | 0.9 | 1.0 | 0.4 | 0.2 | 0.8 |
| Lumber and wood products | 6.7 | 9.2 | 10.6 | 6.5 | 5.8 | 4.8 | 3.5 | 3.9 | 5.1 | 2.4 |
| Furniture and fixtures | 1.0 | 0.8 | 0.7 | 0.8 | 0.7 | 0.2 | 0.1 | 0.1 | ..... | 0.2 |
| Paper products | 28.3 | 34.8 | 31.7 | 43.8 | 51.3 | 10.2 | 17.3 | 18.6 | 36.5 | 55.8 |
| Printing and publishing | 1.5 | 1.0 | 0.9 | 1.5 | 1.6 | 1.4 | 1.1 | 1.3 | 0.9 | 1.7 |
| Chemical products | 45.5 | 58.9 | 68.3 | 65.7 | 82.2 | 14.7 | 18.1 | 19.7 | 22.1 | 22.8 |
| Refined petroleum products | ..... | 0.1 | ..... | ..... | ..... | ..... | ..... | ..... | ..... | 0.9 |
| Rubber and plastic products | 2.6 | 4.3 | 3.3 | 2.4 | 4.1 | 0.5 | 0.7 | 0.9 | 1.7 | 1.7 |
| Leather products | 1.6 | 1.9 | 1.5 | 1.7 | 1.6 | 0.9 | 0.3 | 1.0 | 0.7 | 0.1 |
| Stone, clay and glass products | 0.8 | 1.1 | 2.3 | 2.4 | 3.0 | 0.4 | 0.2 | 1.3 | 0.7 | 0.5 |
| Primary metals | 2.8 | 3.5 | 6.0 | 6.4 | 9.4 | 0.4 | 0.3 | 0.2 | 0.2 | 0.5 |
| Fabricated metal products | 3.8 | 4.9 | 1.0 | 4.1 | 2.4 | 0.4 | 0.6 | 1.5 | 1.8 | 2.2 |
| Industrial machinery and computers | 39.6 | 37.3 | 50.7 | 52.5 | 63.4 | 50.1 | 48.9 | 50.4 | 42.7 | 30.8 |
| Electric and electronic equipment | 26.6 | 29.2 | 35.2 | 31.0 | 32.8 | 14.8 | 19.9 | 15.3 | 17.8 | 12.4 |
| Transportation equipment | 107.0 | 113.3 | 79.1 | 124.1 | 115.6 | 45.5 | 65.3 | 48.2 | 43.0 | 80.8 |
| Scientific and measuring instruments | 14.3 | 16.6 | 11.5 | 11.0 | 11.1 | 22.5 | 20.5 | 30.6 | 52.3 | 58.5 |
| Miscellaneous manufactures | 10.3 | 6.7 | 6.1 | 4.6 | 4.0 | 3.3 | 3.6 | 3.1 | 5.1 | 3.9 |
| Unidentified manufactures | 0.5 | 0.3 | 0.4 | 0.3 | 0.4 | 0.1 | 0.2 | 0.1 | 0.2 | 0.3 |
| **Agricultural and livestock products** | 6.2 | 4.8 | 5.9 | 4.3 | 1.6 | 2.2 | 2.4 | 2.8 | 3.1 | 1.2 |
| Agricultural products | 6.2 | 4.8 | 5.8 | 4.2 | 1.5 | 2.2 | 2.4 | 2.8 | 3.1 | 1.2 |
| Livestock and livestock products | ..... | ..... | 0.1 | 0.1 | 0.1 | ..... | ..... | ..... | ..... | ..... |
| **Other commodities** | 0.2 | 1.6 | 2.5 | 1.7 | 5.6 | 0.7 | 2.9 | 0.9 | 1.3 | 2.1 |
| Forestry products | ..... | 1.1 | 0.2 | ..... | ..... | ..... | ..... | ..... | ..... | ..... |
| Fish and other marine products | ..... | ..... | ..... | ..... | ..... | ..... | ..... | ..... | ..... | ..... |
| Metallic ores and concentrates | ..... | ..... | ..... | 0.5 | 1.1 | ..... | ..... | ..... | ..... | ..... |
| Bituminous coal and lignite | ..... | ..... | ..... | ..... | ..... | ..... | ..... | 2.2 | ..... | ..... |
| Crude petroleum and natural gas | ..... | ..... | ..... | ..... | ..... | ..... | ..... | ..... | ..... | ..... |
| Nonmetallic minerals | 0.1 | 0.3 | 0.2 | 0.3 | 0.3 | ..... | ..... | ..... | 0.1 | 0.1 |
| Scrap and waste | ..... | ..... | ..... | ..... | ..... | ..... | ..... | ..... | 0.2 | ..... |
| Used merchandise | ..... | 0.1 | 0.5 | ..... | 0.1 | ..... | ..... | ..... | ..... | ..... |
| Goods imported and returned unchanged | ..... | ..... | ..... | ..... | ..... | ..... | ..... | ..... | ..... | ..... |
| Special classification provisions | ..... | 0.1 | 1.5 | 0.8 | 4.0 | 0.7 | 0.7 | 0.9 | 1.0 | 2.0 |

| Industry | 1993 | 1994 | 1995 | 1996 | 1997 | 1993 | 1994 | 1995 | 1996 | 1997 |
|---|---|---|---|---|---|---|---|---|---|---|
| | The Netherlands | | | | | Asian 10 | | | | |
| **ALL GOODS** | 380.2 | 372.8 | 413.1 | 343.1 | 385.7 | 1 155.9 | 1 949.4 | 2 984.1 | 2 693.9 | 2 247.4 |
| **Manufactured goods** | 355.7 | 352.9 | 397.6 | 326.1 | 361.9 | 817.5 | 1 114.0 | 1 367.0 | 1 465.4 | 1 577.3 |
| Food products | 2.7 | 2.6 | 1.2 | 1.6 | 3.4 | 13.2 | 17.8 | 37.5 | 46.5 | 35.7 |
| Tobacco products | ..... | ..... | ..... | ..... | ..... | ..... | ..... | ..... | ..... | ..... |
| Textile mill products | 2.4 | 2.5 | 3.3 | 2.1 | 2.0 | 7.4 | 10.3 | 16.5 | 18.3 | 19.0 |
| Apparel | 0.5 | 0.6 | 1.7 | 2.1 | 2.2 | 13.4 | 30.1 | 15.9 | 14.6 | 13.3 |
| Lumber and wood products | 2.6 | 2.8 | 2.2 | 1.9 | 1.3 | 15.6 | 22.9 | 23.8 | 18.4 | 13.9 |
| Furniture and fixtures | 0.5 | 0.7 | 0.6 | 0.7 | 0.4 | 4.8 | 3.5 | 5.3 | 3.4 | 4.0 |
| Paper products | 64.3 | 63.7 | 87.6 | 60.4 | 56.5 | 151.6 | 217.6 | 278.1 | 214.7 | 234.7 |
| Printing and publishing | 0.5 | 0.6 | 0.9 | 0.1 | 0.3 | 2.3 | 1.5 | 3.4 | 2.5 | 5.3 |
| Chemical products | 228.8 | 221.0 | 228.3 | 205.2 | 222.0 | 263.5 | 392.9 | 409.0 | 380.2 | 426.5 |
| Refined petroleum products | ..... | ..... | ..... | ..... | 0.1 | 0.1 | 0.1 | 0.6 | 0.1 | 0.1 |
| Rubber and plastic products | 0.3 | 0.6 | 1.0 | 0.7 | 1.0 | 29.9 | 48.4 | 53.5 | 64.3 | 55.5 |
| Leather products | 0.2 | 0.1 | 0.1 | 0.2 | 0.2 | 3.3 | 3.4 | 2.7 | 3.6 | 3.6 |
| Stone, clay and glass products | 0.1 | 0.4 | 0.1 | 0.2 | 0.2 | 5.1 | 5.9 | 11.8 | 10.3 | 19.0 |
| Primary metals | 0.1 | ..... | 0.5 | 0.5 | 0.8 | 5.3 | 5.4 | 13.8 | 15.6 | 17.4 |
| Fabricated metal products | 1.0 | 1.1 | 0.7 | 1.0 | 4.3 | 20.0 | 17.8 | 26.9 | 37.9 | 35.6 |
| Industrial machinery and computers | 9.6 | 15.0 | 13.8 | 13.4 | 16.1 | 101.5 | 107.7 | 166.8 | 262.2 | 176.6 |
| Electric and electronic equipment | 5.4 | 6.8 | 7.6 | 9.1 | 12.4 | 49.9 | 51.1 | 78.8 | 105.7 | 129.6 |
| Transportation equipment | 15.7 | 11.6 | 12.8 | 6.2 | 5.2 | 75.1 | 108.1 | 145.7 | 171.2 | 270.5 |
| Scientific and measuring instruments | 19.2 | 19.4 | 26.5 | 17.3 | 32.1 | 39.0 | 48.7 | 55.5 | 75.3 | 91.3 |
| Miscellaneous manufactures | 1.6 | 3.3 | 8.6 | 3.2 | 1.3 | 15.1 | 19.3 | 20.5 | 19.3 | 24.7 |
| Unidentified manufactures | 0.2 | 0.1 | 0.2 | 0.2 | 0.2 | 1.2 | 1.2 | 1.0 | 1.1 | 0.9 |
| **Agricultural and livestock products** | 24.5 | 19.9 | 15.0 | 15.9 | 20.9 | 229.1 | 720.8 | 1 529.6 | 1 162.4 | 560.6 |
| Agricultural products | 24.5 | 19.9 | 15.0 | 15.9 | 20.9 | 229.1 | 720.8 | 1 529.6 | 1 161.1 | 560.6 |
| Livestock and livestock products | ..... | ..... | ..... | ..... | ..... | ..... | ..... | ..... | 1.2 | ..... |
| **Other commodities** | 0.1 | ..... | 0.4 | 1.2 | 2.9 | 109.3 | 114.6 | 87.6 | 66.2 | 109.5 |
| Forestry products | ..... | ..... | 0.1 | ..... | ..... | 0.3 | 0.2 | 0.1 | 1.2 | 0.3 |
| Fish and other marine products | ..... | ..... | ..... | ..... | ..... | 20.4 | 21.1 | 28.4 | 24.6 | 9.8 |
| Metallic ores and concentrates | ..... | ..... | ..... | ..... | ..... | ..... | ..... | 0.1 | ..... | ..... |
| Bituminous coal and lignite | ..... | ..... | ..... | ..... | ..... | 83.3 | 90.8 | 51.0 | 35.9 | 44.0 |
| Crude petroleum and natural gas | ..... | ..... | ..... | ..... | ..... | ..... | ..... | ..... | ..... | ..... |
| Nonmetallic minerals | ..... | ..... | ..... | ..... | ..... | 2.7 | 1.8 | 2.8 | 2.0 | 1.7 |
| Scrap and waste | ..... | ..... | ..... | ..... | ..... | ..... | 0.3 | 1.0 | 0.9 | 1.8 |
| Used merchandise | 0.1 | ..... | ..... | 0.1 | ..... | 2.3 | 0.4 | 3.9 | 0.1 | 50.4 |
| Goods imported and returned unchanged | ..... | ..... | ..... | ..... | ..... | ..... | ..... | ..... | ..... | ..... |
| Special classification provisions | ..... | ..... | 0.2 | 1.1 | 2.9 | 0.3 | 0.1 | 0.2 | 1.5 | 1.4 |

## Table D-3.  State Exports of Goods by Destination and Industry, 1993–1997 —*Continued*

**TENNESSEE** (Millions of dollars.)

| Industry | 1993 | 1994 | 1995 | 1996 | 1997 | 1993 | 1994 | 1995 | 1996 | 1997 |
|---|---|---|---|---|---|---|---|---|---|---|
| | Japan | | | | | South Korea | | | | |
| **ALL GOODS** | 388.8 | 563.3 | 674.3 | 727.7 | 692.8 | 181.8 | 230.4 | 284.4 | 320.6 | 279.2 |
| **Manufactured goods** | 315.6 | 478.2 | 566.4 | 645.0 | 625.2 | 131.2 | 175.9 | 206.2 | 199.5 | 236.5 |
| Food products | 9.5 | 11.6 | 18.1 | 18.0 | 16.7 | 0.7 | 0.6 | 3.6 | 3.4 | 2.7 |
| Tobacco products | ..... | ..... | ..... | ..... | ..... | ..... | ..... | ..... | ..... | ..... |
| Textile mill products | 1.9 | 3.5 | 7.9 | 4.3 | 2.0 | 1.1 | 2.2 | 2.1 | 4.0 | 5.6 |
| Apparel | 11.5 | 29.3 | 14.4 | 12.1 | 11.2 | 1.0 | ..... | 0.1 | 0.7 | 0.8 |
| Lumber and wood products | 7.2 | 9.7 | 12.7 | 10.5 | 8.4 | 5.6 | 8.0 | 5.4 | 3.2 | 2.3 |
| Furniture and fixtures | 2.2 | 1.2 | 1.0 | 1.3 | 1.5 | 0.4 | 0.3 | 0.6 | 0.4 | 0.4 |
| Paper products | 88.5 | 112.9 | 184.0 | 118.4 | 119.6 | 16.1 | 39.5 | 40.8 | 43.5 | 53.9 |
| Printing and publishing | 0.6 | 0.2 | 0.3 | 0.3 | 0.7 | 0.2 | 0.1 | 0.3 | 0.1 | 0.4 |
| Chemical products | 56.1 | 118.5 | 77.7 | 83.8 | 75.9 | 61.8 | 65.9 | 54.5 | 28.4 | 68.9 |
| Refined petroleum products | ..... | 0.1 | 0.5 | 0.1 | ..... | ..... | ..... | ..... | ..... | 0.1 |
| Rubber and plastic products | 25.4 | 44.0 | 44.2 | 55.7 | 44.8 | 0.9 | 1.2 | 2.2 | 3.8 | 4.7 |
| Leather products | 0.9 | 0.7 | 0.7 | 0.7 | 0.5 | ..... | 0.2 | 0.1 | ..... | ..... |
| Stone, clay and glass products | 2.7 | 5.1 | 5.6 | 4.9 | 16.4 | 0.1 | 0.2 | 4.3 | 4.0 | 0.4 |
| Primary metals | 0.7 | 0.8 | 3.5 | 5.6 | 5.2 | 0.9 | 1.2 | 1.0 | 1.2 | 1.8 |
| Fabricated metal products | 11.6 | 7.8 | 8.1 | 6.7 | 6.8 | 0.9 | 0.9 | 3.6 | 4.1 | 3.1 |
| Industrial machinery and computers | 29.5 | 53.7 | 80.9 | 167.0 | 80.1 | 23.3 | 10.9 | 13.5 | 31.4 | 31.2 |
| Electric and electronic equipment | 7.8 | 13.9 | 24.2 | 24.6 | 21.5 | 1.1 | 1.6 | 4.6 | 18.9 | 16.8 |
| Transportation equipment | 26.2 | 22.4 | 30.8 | 70.8 | 139.9 | 12.9 | 36.2 | 62.4 | 41.7 | 32.4 |
| Scientific and measuring instruments | 22.6 | 28.7 | 36.8 | 48.0 | 56.9 | 3.9 | 6.3 | 6.6 | 9.8 | 10.4 |
| Miscellaneous manufactures | 10.1 | 13.4 | 14.6 | 11.7 | 16.6 | 0.2 | 0.7 | 0.6 | 0.7 | 0.7 |
| Unidentified manufactures | 0.6 | 0.5 | 0.4 | 0.6 | 0.4 | 0.1 | 0.1 | 0.1 | 0.1 | 0.1 |
| **Agricultural and livestock products** | 49.6 | 62.4 | 75.3 | 56.8 | 52.6 | 50.2 | 53.9 | 77.6 | 120.7 | 42.6 |
| Agricultural products | 49.5 | 62.3 | 75.3 | 56.7 | 52.5 | 50.2 | 53.9 | 77.6 | 119.6 | 42.6 |
| Livestock and livestock products | ..... | ..... | ..... | 0.2 | ..... | ..... | ..... | ..... | 1.0 | ..... |
| **Other commodities** | 23.6 | 22.7 | 32.5 | 26.0 | 15.0 | 0.4 | 0.5 | 0.6 | 0.4 | 0.2 |
| Forestry products | ..... | ..... | ..... | 0.1 | ..... | ..... | ..... | ..... | ..... | ..... |
| Fish and other marine products | 20.3 | 20.6 | 27.8 | 24.1 | 9.6 | ..... | 0.2 | 0.1 | ..... | ..... |
| Metallic ores and concentrates | ..... | ..... | 0.1 | ..... | ..... | ..... | ..... | ..... | ..... | ..... |
| Bituminous coal and lignite | 1.1 | 1.1 | ..... | 0.5 | 3.8 | ..... | ..... | ..... | ..... | ..... |
| Crude petroleum and natural gas | ..... | ..... | ..... | ..... | ..... | ..... | ..... | ..... | ..... | ..... |
| Nonmetallic minerals | 0.3 | 0.4 | 0.5 | 0.3 | 0.1 | 0.4 | 0.3 | 0.5 | 0.3 | 0.1 |
| Scrap and waste | ..... | 0.3 | 0.2 | 0.5 | 0.9 | ..... | ..... | ..... | ..... | ..... |
| Used merchandise | 1.9 | 0.3 | 3.8 | 0.1 | 0.1 | ..... | ..... | ..... | ..... | ..... |
| Goods imported and returned unchanged | ..... | ..... | ..... | ..... | ..... | ..... | ..... | ..... | ..... | ..... |
| Special classification provisions | ..... | ..... | 0.1 | 0.4 | 0.6 | ..... | ..... | ..... | 0.1 | ..... |
| | Taiwan | | | | | Singapore | | | | |
| **ALL GOODS** | 205.5 | 249.4 | 213.1 | 176.6 | 226.2 | 83.5 | 87.0 | 85.1 | 83.2 | 165.7 |
| **Manufactured goods** | 82.5 | 119.4 | 111.6 | 108.8 | 123.6 | 81.6 | 86.0 | 82.7 | 81.6 | 164.2 |
| Food products | 0.4 | 1.3 | 1.9 | 1.1 | 0.6 | 0.1 | 0.1 | 0.3 | 0.3 | 0.7 |
| Tobacco products | ..... | ..... | ..... | ..... | ..... | ..... | ..... | ..... | ..... | ..... |
| Textile mill products | 1.4 | 2.1 | 2.7 | 5.5 | 4.4 | 0.3 | 0.2 | 0.6 | 1.2 | 1.1 |
| Apparel | 0.1 | 0.1 | 0.4 | 0.2 | 0.2 | 0.3 | 0.4 | 0.5 | 0.8 | 0.3 |
| Lumber and wood products | 1.3 | 1.4 | 0.5 | 0.5 | 0.2 | 0.2 | 0.2 | 0.8 | 0.6 | 0.5 |
| Furniture and fixtures | 0.2 | 0.3 | ..... | ..... | 0.2 | 0.5 | 0.5 | 1.9 | 0.4 | 0.5 |
| Paper products | 10.2 | 19.0 | 17.0 | 11.4 | 20.5 | 3.5 | 3.4 | 2.7 | 2.5 | 2.8 |
| Printing and publishing | 0.1 | 0.2 | 0.5 | 0.5 | 1.3 | 0.3 | 0.4 | 1.5 | 0.9 | 0.6 |
| Chemical products | 24.2 | 37.3 | 31.1 | 30.1 | 28.6 | 25.1 | 34.5 | 26.5 | 14.2 | 57.4 |
| Refined petroleum products | ..... | ..... | ..... | ..... | ..... | ..... | ..... | ..... | ..... | ..... |
| Rubber and plastic products | 0.9 | 0.4 | 0.3 | 0.2 | 0.4 | 1.0 | 1.1 | 1.2 | 1.5 | 1.8 |
| Leather products | 0.2 | 0.1 | ..... | 0.1 | 0.4 | 0.2 | 0.2 | 0.3 | 0.1 | 0.2 |
| Stone, clay and glass products | 0.3 | 0.2 | 0.4 | 0.3 | 1.3 | 0.9 | ..... | 0.2 | 0.2 | 0.1 |
| Primary metals | 0.9 | 2.1 | 2.2 | 1.2 | 1.2 | 0.4 | 0.5 | 0.9 | 0.8 | 0.6 |
| Fabricated metal products | 1.6 | 0.5 | 2.2 | 8.0 | 8.6 | 1.8 | 1.2 | 1.8 | 2.1 | 2.5 |
| Industrial machinery and computers | 5.6 | 8.2 | 9.2 | 11.9 | 13.2 | 12.3 | 11.5 | 12.4 | 15.0 | 12.7 |
| Electric and electronic equipment | 6.6 | 6.8 | 11.0 | 16.8 | 24.0 | 23.1 | 15.7 | 14.2 | 15.0 | 19.5 |
| Transportation equipment | 23.6 | 33.5 | 27.7 | 14.0 | 9.3 | 7.8 | 10.6 | 11.5 | 21.1 | 57.6 |
| Scientific and measuring instruments | 3.5 | 4.2 | 3.9 | 5.7 | 7.5 | 3.1 | 4.2 | 3.2 | 3.6 | 4.4 |
| Miscellaneous manufactures | 1.4 | 1.6 | 0.4 | 1.2 | 1.5 | 0.8 | 1.2 | 2.0 | 1.3 | 0.7 |
| Unidentified manufactures | 0.1 | 0.2 | 0.1 | 0.1 | 0.1 | 0.2 | 0.2 | 0.1 | 0.2 | 0.1 |
| **Agricultural and livestock products** | 40.6 | 40.0 | 50.0 | 31.7 | 62.0 | 0.2 | 0.2 | 0.8 | 0.2 | ..... |
| Agricultural products | 40.6 | 40.0 | 50.0 | 31.7 | 62.0 | 0.2 | 0.2 | 0.8 | 0.2 | ..... |
| Livestock and livestock products | ..... | ..... | ..... | ..... | ..... | ..... | ..... | ..... | ..... | ..... |
| **Other commodities** | 82.5 | 90.0 | 51.5 | 36.0 | 40.6 | 1.7 | 0.9 | 1.6 | 1.4 | 1.5 |
| Forestry products | ..... | ..... | 0.1 | 0.1 | 0.1 | ..... | ..... | ..... | ..... | ..... |
| Fish and other marine products | ..... | ..... | ..... | ..... | ..... | ..... | ..... | ..... | ..... | ..... |
| Metallic ores and concentrates | ..... | ..... | ..... | ..... | ..... | ..... | ..... | ..... | ..... | ..... |
| Bituminous coal and lignite | 82.2 | 89.7 | 51.0 | 35.4 | 40.1 | ..... | ..... | ..... | ..... | ..... |
| Crude petroleum and natural gas | ..... | ..... | ..... | ..... | ..... | ..... | ..... | ..... | ..... | ..... |
| Nonmetallic minerals | 0.2 | 0.2 | 0.3 | 0.3 | 0.3 | 1.5 | 0.8 | 1.5 | 1.1 | 1.2 |
| Scrap and waste | ..... | ..... | ..... | ..... | ..... | ..... | ..... | ..... | ..... | ..... |
| Used merchandise | ..... | ..... | ..... | ..... | ..... | 0.1 | ..... | ..... | ..... | ..... |
| Goods imported and returned unchanged | ..... | ..... | ..... | ..... | ..... | ..... | ..... | ..... | ..... | ..... |
| Special classification provisions | ..... | ..... | ..... | 0.2 | 0.1 | ..... | ..... | 0.1 | 0.3 | 0.3 |

## TEXAS: Exports of Goods, 1997

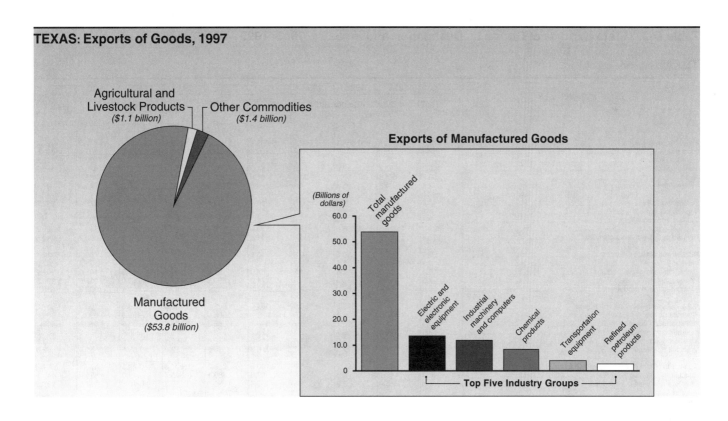

## Table D-3.   State Exports of Goods by Destination and Industry, 1993–1997 —*Continued*

**TEXAS** (Millions of dollars.)

| Industry | 1993 | 1994 | 1995 | 1996 | 1997 | 1993 | 1994 | 1995 | 1996 | 1997 |
|---|---|---|---|---|---|---|---|---|---|---|
| | All destinations | | | | | Canada | | | | |
| **ALL GOODS** | 35 622.5 | 40 489.0 | 45 192.6 | 48 252.1 | 56 292.9 | 3 811.3 | 4 830.4 | 6 142.0 | 6 616.4 | 8 117.6 |
| **Manufactured goods** | 33 901.3 | 38 295.3 | 42 779.2 | 45 988.3 | 53 805.8 | 3 570.2 | 4 563.3 | 5 849.2 | 6 250.4 | 7 705.2 |
| Food products | 1 361.7 | 1 466.8 | 1 257.3 | 1 396.0 | 1 518.9 | 76.3 | 83.5 | 93.1 | 90.8 | 91.4 |
| Tobacco products | 20.2 | 36.6 | 19.4 | 33.1 | 19.6 | ..... | ..... | ..... | ..... | ..... |
| Textile mill products | 339.2 | 409.9 | 433.2 | 487.5 | 537.5 | 6.9 | 8.2 | 7.5 | 9.0 | 13.4 |
| Apparel | 744.5 | 1 005.1 | 957.5 | 1 009.1 | 1 075.2 | 52.9 | 75.7 | 98.9 | 85.5 | 106.4 |
| Lumber and wood products | 260.3 | 223.3 | 165.5 | 153.8 | 181.1 | 9.1 | 8.6 | 8.1 | 7.8 | 9.3 |
| Furniture and fixtures | 228.9 | 308.8 | 278.8 | 391.9 | 524.8 | 31.7 | 103.7 | 106.8 | 66.5 | 100.8 |
| Paper products | 647.5 | 713.6 | 724.7 | 695.8 | 824.7 | 39.3 | 33.6 | 49.8 | 54.1 | 75.0 |
| Printing and publishing | 110.8 | 129.2 | 126.2 | 142.6 | 145.1 | 30.8 | 25.7 | 33.0 | 32.0 | 30.8 |
| Chemical products | 6 001.2 | 7 105.3 | 8 993.6 | 7 916.3 | 8 390.0 | 871.7 | 971.5 | 1 029.9 | 1 114.3 | 1 279.7 |
| Refined petroleum products | 1 820.7 | 1 677.1 | 2 052.3 | 2 364.9 | 2 683.8 | 116.4 | 125.1 | 151.6 | 181.9 | 226.7 |
| Rubber and plastic products | 656.1 | 811.2 | 769.6 | 1 084.9 | 1 480.4 | 57.8 | 71.6 | 84.2 | 104.6 | 151.5 |
| Leather products | 103.3 | 93.5 | 103.9 | 105.1 | 141.7 | 7.4 | 8.3 | 7.9 | 11.0 | 15.9 |
| Stone, clay and glass products | 229.3 | 288.8 | 304.2 | 315.4 | 340.7 | 48.9 | 50.7 | 56.4 | 58.4 | 61.2 |
| Primary metals | 1 040.2 | 1 118.3 | 1 476.5 | 1 811.6 | 2 067.4 | 144.1 | 163.2 | 191.9 | 201.9 | 270.0 |
| Fabricated metal products | 975.7 | 1 194.1 | 1 180.4 | 1 745.7 | 1 686.0 | 181.0 | 218.4 | 225.3 | 276.1 | 339.8 |
| Industrial machinery and computers | 7 902.5 | 8 631.6 | 9 287.7 | 10 194.4 | 11 882.9 | 740.0 | 1 034.7 | 1 354.1 | 1 522.5 | 1 835.7 |
| Electric and electronic equipment | 6 374.6 | 7 888.8 | 10 036.1 | 10 661.3 | 13 566.2 | 535.9 | 845.2 | 1 470.7 | 1 543.9 | 2 055.0 |
| Transportation equipment | 3 174.3 | 3 186.7 | 2 510.4 | 3 039.5 | 3 918.0 | 395.0 | 425.0 | 443.0 | 509.3 | 585.5 |
| Scientific and measuring instruments | 1 571.3 | 1 594.1 | 1 742.5 | 2 026.2 | 2 396.4 | 181.5 | 252.1 | 364.4 | 310.7 | 374.4 |
| Miscellaneous manufactures | 250.6 | 300.7 | 248.5 | 311.0 | 309.8 | 28.8 | 37.5 | 50.2 | 44.9 | 53.0 |
| Unidentified manufactures | 88.2 | 111.4 | 110.8 | 102.1 | 115.8 | 14.7 | 21.0 | 22.7 | 25.3 | 29.8 |
| **Agricultural and livestock products** | 746.1 | 1 015.0 | 1 143.0 | 1 025.8 | 1 123.0 | 58.2 | 52.0 | 72.1 | 68.8 | 78.3 |
| Agricultural products | 688.7 | 923.2 | 1 106.6 | 956.9 | 969.6 | 55.7 | 50.4 | 68.1 | 66.4 | 76.6 |
| Livestock and livestock products | 57.4 | 91.8 | 36.4 | 68.9 | 153.4 | 2.5 | 1.6 | 4.0 | 2.4 | 1.7 |
| **Other commodities** | 975.1 | 1 178.7 | 1 270.5 | 1 238.0 | 1 364.2 | 182.8 | 215.1 | 220.7 | 297.2 | 334.1 |
| Forestry products | 33.6 | 21.1 | 26.0 | 26.9 | 26.8 | 1.0 | 0.6 | 0.6 | 0.8 | 1.4 |
| Fish and other marine products | 32.8 | 33.6 | 27.3 | 27.4 | 25.7 | 0.3 | 1.2 | 0.4 | 0.9 | 0.7 |
| Metallic ores and concentrates | 91.4 | 92.0 | 104.2 | 105.9 | 75.4 | 76.0 | 81.3 | 86.3 | 97.8 | 68.2 |
| Bituminous coal and lignite | 2.2 | 0.9 | 6.2 | 5.1 | 18.0 | ..... | ..... | ..... | 0.6 | ..... |
| Crude petroleum and natural gas | 205.0 | 171.7 | 291.0 | 271.5 | 323.0 | 3.3 | 12.1 | 6.7 | 45.6 | 89.5 |
| Nonmetallic minerals | 50.4 | 69.7 | 86.7 | 73.1 | 82.8 | 4.5 | 4.9 | 4.7 | 4.1 | 3.7 |
| Scrap and waste | 179.0 | 238.3 | 365.1 | 238.2 | 306.4 | 3.0 | 8.0 | 9.2 | 10.1 | 14.0 |
| Used merchandise | 117.0 | 127.6 | 87.3 | 87.0 | 109.5 | 3.8 | 9.4 | 8.3 | 10.9 | 11.3 |
| Goods imported and returned unchanged | 70.7 | 77.0 | 82.9 | 104.7 | 129.5 | 70.7 | 77.0 | 82.9 | 104.7 | 129.5 |
| Special classification provisions | 193.0 | 346.7 | 193.8 | 298.2 | 267.2 | 20.1 | 20.5 | 21.6 | 21.5 | 15.8 |

## Table D-3.  State Exports of Goods by Destination and Industry, 1993–1997 —*Continued*

**TEXAS** (Millions of dollars.)

| Industry | 1993 | 1994 | 1995 | 1996 | 1997 | 1993 | 1994 | 1995 | 1996 | 1997 |
|---|---|---|---|---|---|---|---|---|---|---|
| | South and Central America and Caribbean | | | | | Mexico | | | | |
| **ALL GOODS** | 3 150.1 | 3 976.2 | 5 073.2 | 5 180.2 | 6 402.8 | 12 860.8 | 14 364.9 | 12 589.0 | 15 586.7 | 18 864.1 |
| **Manufactured goods** | 3 071.1 | 3 862.4 | 4 884.1 | 5 032.1 | 6 223.2 | 11 901.0 | 13 275.9 | 11 563.2 | 14 547.8 | 17 727.9 |
| Food products | 62.0 | 78.7 | 131.7 | 125.4 | 100.4 | 783.4 | 861.1 | 566.0 | 701.4 | 899.6 |
| Tobacco products | ..... | ..... | ..... | 0.2 | 0.1 | 20.2 | 36.6 | 19.3 | 32.7 | 18.8 |
| Textile mill products | 9.3 | 7.2 | 12.6 | 10.2 | 14.3 | 296.7 | 360.4 | 368.6 | 420.9 | 465.3 |
| Apparel | 98.4 | 124.8 | 97.8 | 80.6 | 91.0 | 558.1 | 766.6 | 717.0 | 786.8 | 814.1 |
| Lumber and wood products | 2.6 | 4.5 | 3.4 | 4.1 | 8.6 | 141.9 | 120.9 | 48.2 | 41.8 | 50.4 |
| Furniture and fixtures | 6.8 | 6.1 | 7.4 | 8.3 | 10.0 | 158.4 | 166.7 | 133.7 | 276.4 | 372.3 |
| Paper products | 4.6 | 6.8 | 7.4 | 10.1 | 16.4 | 570.7 | 619.2 | 617.2 | 602.8 | 701.8 |
| Printing and publishing | 2.7 | 4.1 | 5.6 | 8.0 | 6.3 | 55.0 | 69.8 | 48.1 | 57.2 | 62.4 |
| Chemical products | 829.4 | 1 025.6 | 1 326.4 | 1 172.2 | 1 239.6 | 1 092.0 | 1 276.5 | 1 377.0 | 1 511.1 | 1 739.7 |
| Refined petroleum products | 323.8 | 363.8 | 466.0 | 635.1 | 841.8 | 404.4 | 371.1 | 489.8 | 590.2 | 942.8 |
| Rubber and plastic products | 25.0 | 28.9 | 50.6 | 40.3 | 46.5 | 444.8 | 566.4 | 491.7 | 785.9 | 1 119.1 |
| Leather products | 0.9 | 2.0 | 5.1 | 4.7 | 2.7 | 74.1 | 68.1 | 69.6 | 69.3 | 97.9 |
| Stone, clay and glass products | 16.1 | 31.0 | 41.6 | 54.3 | 53.0 | 94.6 | 131.1 | 111.3 | 108.4 | 109.2 |
| Primary metals | 93.5 | 112.8 | 137.3 | 135.4 | 171.2 | 559.3 | 632.7 | 763.0 | 1 067.5 | 1 229.5 |
| Fabricated metal products | 90.8 | 96.0 | 89.9 | 89.9 | 184.3 | 422.2 | 582.1 | 509.1 | 898.7 | 646.8 |
| Industrial machinery and computers | 1 083.5 | 1 413.7 | 1 906.3 | 1 960.0 | 2 304.0 | 1 505.2 | 1 735.3 | 1 035.5 | 1 303.9 | 1 867.3 |
| Electric and electronic equipment | 110.7 | 170.8 | 304.9 | 394.9 | 639.9 | 2 608.0 | 3 038.2 | 3 158.8 | 3 699.2 | 4 508.2 |
| Transportation equipment | 240.3 | 295.5 | 167.7 | 166.7 | 338.3 | 1 562.3 | 1 308.3 | 663.9 | 1 085.6 | 1 413.1 |
| Scientific and measuring instruments | 52.0 | 70.4 | 92.1 | 112.4 | 128.2 | 372.1 | 350.4 | 245.1 | 352.8 | 482.9 |
| Miscellaneous manufactures | 10.9 | 8.4 | 11.0 | 11.5 | 18.2 | 139.6 | 162.1 | 90.6 | 120.3 | 133.9 |
| Unidentified manufactures | 7.9 | 11.6 | 19.0 | 7.7 | 8.3 | 38.0 | 52.0 | 39.8 | 35.0 | 52.8 |
| **Agricultural and livestock products** | 20.5 | 46.6 | 81.2 | 55.0 | 100.8 | 515.2 | 607.6 | 429.5 | 576.4 | 584.3 |
| Agricultural products | 16.3 | 42.7 | 78.3 | 52.6 | 97.5 | 480.1 | 548.3 | 419.0 | 524.9 | 447.1 |
| Livestock and livestock products | 4.3 | 3.9 | 2.9 | 2.4 | 3.4 | 35.1 | 59.3 | 10.5 | 51.5 | 137.2 |
| **Other commodities** | 58.5 | 67.2 | 107.8 | 93.2 | 78.8 | 444.6 | 481.4 | 596.3 | 462.4 | 551.9 |
| Forestry products | 0.5 | 1.4 | 0.7 | 2.3 | 2.8 | 7.3 | 11.3 | 16.3 | 18.2 | 17.5 |
| Fish and other marine products | 0.3 | 0.2 | 0.1 | ..... | 0.3 | 30.4 | 31.2 | 24.0 | 24.2 | 22.1 |
| Metallic ores and concentrates | 0.1 | 0.1 | 0.2 | 0.2 | 0.6 | 6.1 | 6.1 | 5.1 | 5.0 | 5.4 |
| Bituminous coal and lignite | 0.4 | 0.1 | 0.3 | 1.1 | 11.7 | 1.7 | 0.6 | 5.8 | 2.7 | 3.0 |
| Crude petroleum and natural gas | 36.7 | 26.4 | 60.2 | 25.8 | 18.9 | 154.8 | 120.7 | 216.5 | 185.8 | 177.2 |
| Nonmetallic minerals | 7.9 | 12.1 | 23.2 | 18.4 | 21.5 | 19.3 | 27.2 | 30.8 | 27.2 | 27.0 |
| Scrap and waste | 3.0 | 4.2 | 12.7 | 25.8 | 3.8 | 135.4 | 167.5 | 240.8 | 133.4 | 223.6 |
| Used merchandise | 8.2 | 7.1 | 8.4 | 12.9 | 15.0 | 43.5 | 56.5 | 19.2 | 20.8 | 27.8 |
| Goods imported and returned unchanged | ..... | ..... | ..... | ..... | ..... | ..... | ..... | ..... | ..... | ..... |
| Special classification provisions | 1.4 | 15.5 | 2.0 | 6.4 | 4.1 | 46.0 | 60.3 | 37.8 | 45.3 | 48.3 |
| | European Union | | | | | United Kingdom | | | | |
| **ALL GOODS** | 4 598.4 | 4 957.7 | 5 803.7 | 5 419.8 | 6 162.9 | 1 451.8 | 1 674.6 | 1 915.5 | 1 717.1 | 1 979.3 |
| **Manufactured goods** | 4 503.2 | 4 833.7 | 5 662.6 | 5 285.9 | 6 033.2 | 1 419.8 | 1 623.2 | 1 876.8 | 1 683.8 | 1 954.0 |
| Food products | 137.7 | 128.0 | 124.6 | 123.0 | 97.1 | 10.9 | 10.6 | 8.8 | 16.5 | 14.9 |
| Tobacco products | ..... | ..... | ..... | ..... | ..... | ..... | ..... | ..... | ..... | ..... |
| Textile mill products | 7.5 | 8.3 | 9.7 | 8.2 | 9.1 | 2.9 | 2.6 | 2.0 | 2.3 | 2.1 |
| Apparel | 14.7 | 15.2 | 19.7 | 27.1 | 32.3 | 3.2 | 3.6 | 2.9 | 4.3 | 4.2 |
| Lumber and wood products | 81.0 | 63.2 | 73.6 | 54.0 | 72.0 | 25.1 | 18.5 | 15.6 | 19.4 | 18.7 |
| Furniture and fixtures | 9.9 | 11.2 | 8.0 | 14.6 | 15.3 | 3.1 | 4.5 | 3.3 | 8.4 | 1.9 |
| Paper products | 13.2 | 24.8 | 19.3 | 9.9 | 9.8 | 1.3 | 1.3 | 1.1 | 0.9 | 1.4 |
| Printing and publishing | 7.7 | 10.4 | 14.4 | 20.6 | 17.2 | 3.6 | 5.0 | 4.8 | 7.0 | 7.5 |
| Chemical products | 894.8 | 1 093.0 | 1 427.1 | 989.8 | 1 076.2 | 127.8 | 143.3 | 182.7 | 114.9 | 138.0 |
| Refined petroleum products | 366.7 | 222.6 | 242.9 | 329.7 | 301.7 | 11.3 | 17.4 | 11.9 | 10.4 | 18.0 |
| Rubber and plastic products | 42.3 | 51.4 | 57.6 | 43.2 | 54.8 | 5.7 | 6.0 | 9.6 | 11.1 | 18.9 |
| Leather products | 9.0 | 6.6 | 9.7 | 8.0 | 10.6 | 1.0 | 0.9 | 1.5 | 1.2 | 3.5 |
| Stone, clay and glass products | 18.3 | 22.5 | 23.8 | 24.2 | 27.2 | 3.4 | 4.1 | 3.4 | 5.0 | 5.0 |
| Primary metals | 70.0 | 64.4 | 98.4 | 83.3 | 102.2 | 12.1 | 11.0 | 19.9 | 24.7 | 31.8 |
| Fabricated metal products | 54.4 | 56.4 | 97.1 | 102.5 | 124.8 | 21.2 | 17.6 | 48.4 | 55.8 | 64.2 |
| Industrial machinery and computers | 1 414.2 | 1 486.7 | 1 730.9 | 1 606.8 | 1 816.1 | 696.6 | 680.5 | 927.7 | 806.2 | 889.9 |
| Electric and electronic equipment | 697.1 | 931.1 | 986.2 | 910.3 | 1 166.7 | 347.8 | 515.0 | 441.5 | 373.8 | 452.4 |
| Transportation equipment | 298.1 | 308.3 | 326.0 | 405.1 | 532.6 | 59.2 | 75.8 | 66.7 | 77.1 | 136.2 |
| Scientific and measuring instruments | 334.7 | 292.1 | 352.4 | 478.5 | 517.2 | 75.8 | 95.2 | 110.4 | 130.1 | 129.0 |
| Miscellaneous manufactures | 20.9 | 27.7 | 29.8 | 38.6 | 43.5 | 4.9 | 7.3 | 11.0 | 11.8 | 14.5 |
| Unidentified manufactures | 11.2 | 10.0 | 11.6 | 8.5 | 6.8 | 3.0 | 2.8 | 3.5 | 3.0 | 1.9 |
| **Agricultural and livestock products** | 30.4 | 48.8 | 57.1 | 45.4 | 35.5 | 8.2 | 19.7 | 13.1 | 7.0 | 4.8 |
| Agricultural products | 22.7 | 27.7 | 42.1 | 39.6 | 30.3 | 2.1 | 1.9 | 2.4 | 3.2 | 1.3 |
| Livestock and livestock products | 7.7 | 21.0 | 15.0 | 5.8 | 5.2 | 6.1 | 17.7 | 10.7 | 3.7 | 3.4 |
| **Other commodities** | 64.8 | 75.2 | 84.0 | 88.4 | 94.2 | 23.7 | 31.7 | 25.7 | 26.3 | 20.6 |
| Forestry products | 4.9 | 3.8 | 3.9 | 3.2 | 2.2 | 0.4 | 0.4 | 0.5 | 0.5 | 1.6 |
| Fish and other marine products | 0.5 | 0.2 | 0.1 | 0.1 | 0.3 | ..... | ..... | ..... | ..... | ..... |
| Metallic ores and concentrates | 0.5 | 3.7 | 9.7 | 1.7 | 0.8 | ..... | 0.4 | 0.5 | 0.1 | 0.2 |
| Bituminous coal and lignite | ..... | ..... | ..... | 0.4 | 1.3 | ..... | ..... | ..... | ..... | ..... |
| Crude petroleum and natural gas | 3.1 | 6.5 | 4.9 | 0.1 | 10.2 | 2.7 | 6.4 | ..... | ..... | 0.1 |
| Nonmetallic minerals | 6.2 | 7.7 | 8.0 | 7.4 | 8.3 | 2.2 | 2.9 | 3.4 | 3.9 | 4.3 |
| Scrap and waste | 4.8 | 12.8 | 21.8 | 23.7 | 23.7 | 0.3 | 0.9 | 2.3 | 3.5 | 1.8 |
| Used merchandise | 31.0 | 24.7 | 25.6 | 16.1 | 17.9 | 12.0 | 11.6 | 14.6 | 7.8 | 4.0 |
| Goods imported and returned unchanged | ..... | ..... | ..... | ..... | ..... | ..... | ..... | ..... | ..... | ..... |
| Special classification provisions | 13.7 | 15.8 | 10.1 | 35.7 | 29.5 | 6.1 | 9.1 | 4.4 | 10.5 | 8.5 |

## Table D-3. State Exports of Goods by Destination and Industry, 1993–1997 —*Continued*

**TEXAS** (Millions of dollars.)

| Industry | 1993 | 1994 | 1995 | 1996 | 1997 | 1993 | 1994 | 1995 | 1996 | 1997 |
|---|---|---|---|---|---|---|---|---|---|---|
| | Germany | | | | | France | | | | |
| **ALL GOODS** | 626.0 | 563.2 | 722.2 | 719.0 | 882.7 | 490.4 | 539.8 | 557.1 | 570.8 | 584.5 |
| **Manufactured goods** | 604.8 | 545.0 | 707.7 | 701.8 | 864.4 | 483.3 | 531.7 | 541.8 | 558.1 | 576.4 |
| Food products | 9.1 | 12.6 | 11.3 | 10.7 | 11.0 | 20.0 | 17.2 | 21.9 | 25.6 | 24.8 |
| Tobacco products | ..... | ..... | ..... | ..... | ..... | ..... | ..... | ..... | ..... | ..... |
| Textile mill products | 1.0 | 0.8 | 1.4 | 2.3 | 1.1 | 0.8 | 0.5 | 0.8 | 0.4 | 0.3 |
| Apparel | 2.2 | 3.0 | 2.8 | 4.1 | 10.0 | 1.5 | 1.1 | 1.6 | 3.7 | 5.6 |
| Lumber and wood products | 11.6 | 10.1 | 7.5 | 6.7 | 13.8 | 1.4 | 1.2 | 1.7 | 1.6 | 1.5 |
| Furniture and fixtures | 2.2 | 3.3 | 1.2 | 1.6 | 8.2 | 0.7 | 1.3 | 1.9 | 2.2 | 3.4 |
| Paper products | 3.1 | 5.8 | 5.6 | 3.2 | 2.7 | 2.2 | 2.6 | 0.6 | 1.7 | 1.8 |
| Printing and publishing | 0.8 | 1.8 | 2.4 | 2.5 | 3.1 | 0.9 | 1.1 | 1.0 | 1.3 | 1.5 |
| Chemical products | 58.0 | 73.4 | 90.2 | 76.8 | 75.8 | 96.2 | 111.6 | 128.2 | 122.0 | 126.7 |
| Refined petroleum products | 6.2 | 9.8 | 8.1 | 12.1 | 13.5 | 59.3 | 64.5 | 72.2 | 96.6 | 63.0 |
| Rubber and plastic products | 2.8 | 5.9 | 6.3 | 6.1 | 5.7 | 1.3 | 2.0 | 2.8 | 3.2 | 2.8 |
| Leather products | 2.9 | 2.3 | 2.9 | 2.0 | 1.9 | 1.3 | 0.9 | 2.3 | 0.9 | 0.8 |
| Stone, clay and glass products | 8.7 | 9.4 | 11.8 | 12.7 | 12.0 | 1.7 | 5.6 | 1.3 | 1.5 | 1.1 |
| Primary metals | 10.1 | 3.2 | 2.4 | 2.2 | 2.6 | 3.8 | 2.2 | 2.7 | 2.8 | 4.1 |
| Fabricated metal products | 6.5 | 6.9 | 8.4 | 13.9 | 20.8 | 3.8 | 13.7 | 16.0 | 8.5 | 7.9 |
| Industrial machinery and computers | 175.7 | 134.6 | 179.3 | 150.0 | 217.5 | 111.8 | 135.3 | 93.0 | 91.4 | 117.1 |
| Electric and electronic equipment | 92.2 | 106.2 | 155.8 | 159.3 | 223.5 | 85.1 | 80.6 | 96.9 | 74.8 | 94.8 |
| Transportation equipment | 58.5 | 44.9 | 65.7 | 41.8 | 61.9 | 60.3 | 46.7 | 60.9 | 59.4 | 50.1 |
| Scientific and measuring instruments | 141.9 | 99.2 | 133.2 | 179.4 | 164.5 | 27.1 | 40.2 | 32.2 | 56.2 | 65.4 |
| Miscellaneous manufactures | 7.8 | 9.1 | 9.0 | 13.3 | 13.8 | 2.1 | 2.4 | 2.5 | 3.4 | 3.2 |
| Unidentified manufactures | 3.4 | 2.6 | 2.3 | 1.1 | 1.0 | 1.7 | 0.9 | 1.4 | 0.8 | 0.8 |
| **Agricultural and livestock products** | 6.3 | 6.4 | 6.1 | 10.0 | 8.0 | 0.5 | 2.8 | 6.2 | 0.6 | 1.5 |
| Agricultural products | 6.0 | 5.8 | 4.5 | 8.8 | 7.0 | 0.2 | 1.7 | 5.2 | 0.6 | 1.5 |
| Livestock and livestock products | 0.2 | 0.6 | 1.6 | 1.2 | 1.0 | 0.2 | 1.0 | 1.0 | ..... | ..... |
| **Other commodities** | 15.0 | 11.8 | 8.4 | 7.2 | 10.4 | 6.7 | 5.3 | 9.0 | 12.2 | 6.7 |
| Forestry products | 3.4 | 2.0 | 1.9 | 0.6 | 0.2 | ..... | 0.1 | 0.3 | 0.7 | 0.1 |
| Fish and other marine products | ..... | ..... | ..... | ..... | ..... | 0.1 | 0.1 | ..... | ..... | ..... |
| Metallic ores and concentrates | ..... | ..... | ..... | ..... | ..... | 0.2 | 1.9 | ..... | ..... | ..... |
| Bituminous coal and lignite | ..... | ..... | ..... | ..... | ..... | ..... | ..... | ..... | 0.4 | ..... |
| Crude petroleum and natural gas | ..... | ..... | ..... | ..... | ..... | ..... | ..... | 2.4 | ..... | 2.2 |
| Nonmetallic minerals | 2.0 | 1.0 | 0.7 | 0.4 | 0.8 | 0.5 | 0.6 | 0.6 | 0.4 | 0.7 |
| Scrap and waste | 0.5 | 0.6 | 1.8 | 0.8 | 0.7 | 1.1 | 0.2 | 0.5 | 0.3 | 0.1 |
| Used merchandise | 6.8 | 6.8 | 2.3 | 1.6 | 3.8 | 3.8 | 1.3 | 4.5 | 3.7 | 0.9 |
| Goods imported and returned unchanged | ..... | ..... | ..... | ..... | ..... | ..... | ..... | ..... | ..... | ..... |
| Special classification provisions | 2.3 | 1.3 | 1.7 | 3.8 | 4.8 | 0.9 | 1.1 | 0.6 | 6.6 | 2.7 |

| Industry | 1993 | 1994 | 1995 | 1996 | 1997 | 1993 | 1994 | 1995 | 1996 | 1997 |
|---|---|---|---|---|---|---|---|---|---|---|
| | The Netherlands | | | | | Asian 10 | | | | |
| **ALL GOODS** | 972.1 | 934.3 | 1 128.6 | 1 105.2 | 1 161.0 | 6 815.1 | 8 159.0 | 10 826.5 | 9 981.2 | 11 006.0 |
| **Manufactured goods** | 963.6 | 922.4 | 1 112.0 | 1 087.4 | 1 147.0 | 6 639.7 | 7 866.9 | 10 307.9 | 9 680.2 | 10 677.6 |
| Food products | 27.0 | 16.9 | 19.5 | 13.4 | 10.8 | 74.4 | 108.4 | 88.2 | 99.6 | 123.4 |
| Tobacco products | ..... | ..... | ..... | ..... | ..... | ..... | ..... | ..... | ..... | 0.2 |
| Textile mill products | 0.5 | 0.6 | 0.9 | 0.6 | 0.6 | 8.4 | 10.4 | 12.2 | 12.8 | 15.5 |
| Apparel | 1.0 | 0.7 | 1.9 | 3.2 | 4.3 | 6.8 | 11.1 | 11.4 | 12.4 | 15.1 |
| Lumber and wood products | 19.4 | 12.9 | 23.0 | 10.8 | 14.4 | 13.0 | 19.8 | 23.3 | 39.4 | 32.1 |
| Furniture and fixtures | 2.7 | 0.9 | 0.4 | 0.4 | 0.2 | 4.7 | 4.3 | 5.9 | 9.1 | 9.5 |
| Paper products | 2.5 | 7.5 | 6.5 | 0.6 | 0.4 | 14.1 | 21.4 | 21.3 | 13.7 | 13.3 |
| Printing and publishing | 0.8 | 0.8 | 2.0 | 1.8 | 1.9 | 4.7 | 5.3 | 10.8 | 11.6 | 11.0 |
| Chemical products | 358.2 | 383.9 | 521.9 | 330.8 | 379.9 | 1 874.6 | 2 238.7 | 3 003.2 | 2 433.3 | 2 329.4 |
| Refined petroleum products | 154.1 | 29.6 | 35.0 | 129.8 | 117.2 | 478.9 | 538.6 | 592.9 | 456.4 | 192.4 |
| Rubber and plastic products | 6.2 | 5.3 | 6.4 | 7.1 | 13.9 | 53.9 | 51.2 | 50.9 | 64.4 | 61.0 |
| Leather products | 1.0 | 1.0 | 1.3 | 1.3 | 0.8 | 9.1 | 6.7 | 8.5 | 8.8 | 10.7 |
| Stone, clay and glass products | 1.6 | 1.4 | 2.3 | 2.3 | 2.3 | 20.0 | 28.9 | 43.5 | 33.7 | 43.7 |
| Primary metals | 27.5 | 7.7 | 12.3 | 23.3 | 41.6 | 68.8 | 70.4 | 130.6 | 137.9 | 115.9 |
| Fabricated metal products | 9.7 | 8.1 | 6.2 | 8.6 | 6.6 | 76.7 | 151.0 | 161.7 | 210.2 | 174.1 |
| Industrial machinery and computers | 204.8 | 252.8 | 271.3 | 252.1 | 300.8 | 1 159.6 | 1 327.2 | 1 600.4 | 1 507.3 | 1 711.4 |
| Electric and electronic equipment | 50.1 | 81.0 | 101.0 | 132.4 | 135.6 | 2 169.6 | 2 645.7 | 3 756.8 | 3 691.2 | 4 801.9 |
| Transportation equipment | 78.5 | 96.5 | 80.3 | 142.7 | 68.3 | 259.2 | 275.9 | 337.7 | 415.9 | 475.6 |
| Scientific and measuring instruments | 16.2 | 11.0 | 16.4 | 21.2 | 43.5 | 298.8 | 290.3 | 390.7 | 448.0 | 490.3 |
| Miscellaneous manufactures | 1.0 | 2.7 | 2.6 | 4.1 | 3.2 | 37.9 | 53.1 | 49.7 | 56.9 | 43.6 |
| Unidentified manufactures | 0.8 | 0.9 | 0.9 | 0.9 | 0.9 | 6.4 | 8.4 | 8.3 | 17.6 | 7.6 |
| **Agricultural and livestock products** | 3.4 | 3.4 | 5.1 | 7.0 | 3.0 | 94.2 | 218.5 | 407.1 | 213.0 | 219.9 |
| Agricultural products | 3.2 | 3.4 | 5.1 | 6.9 | 3.0 | 90.4 | 215.4 | 404.7 | 208.0 | 216.6 |
| Livestock and livestock products | 0.3 | ..... | ..... | ..... | 0.1 | 3.8 | 3.0 | 2.4 | 5.0 | 3.4 |
| **Other commodities** | 5.0 | 8.5 | 11.6 | 10.8 | 11.0 | 81.2 | 73.7 | 111.5 | 88.0 | 108.4 |
| Forestry products | 0.8 | 0.9 | 0.5 | 0.9 | 0.2 | 19.8 | 4.0 | 4.2 | 2.3 | 1.6 |
| Fish and other marine products | ..... | ..... | ..... | ..... | ..... | 1.2 | 0.8 | 2.5 | 1.8 | 1.9 |
| Metallic ores and concentrates | ..... | ..... | 2.2 | 1.4 | 0.2 | 0.1 | 0.1 | 0.7 | 0.7 | 0.2 |
| Bituminous coal and lignite | ..... | ..... | ..... | ..... | 1.3 | ..... | 0.1 | 0.1 | 0.1 | 0.1 |
| Crude petroleum and natural gas | ..... | 0.1 | ..... | ..... | ..... | 5.7 | 2.9 | 0.5 | 13.1 | 26.8 |
| Nonmetallic minerals | 0.6 | 1.3 | 1.5 | 1.7 | 1.4 | 7.6 | 10.4 | 14.4 | 9.6 | 17.5 |
| Scrap and waste | 0.1 | 3.1 | 3.7 | 1.0 | 0.8 | 23.8 | 32.1 | 62.5 | 30.6 | 24.2 |
| Used merchandise | 2.5 | 0.8 | 1.6 | 1.0 | 1.4 | 13.3 | 10.8 | 6.7 | 12.7 | 13.0 |
| Goods imported and returned unchanged | ..... | ..... | ..... | ..... | ..... | ..... | ..... | ..... | ..... | ..... |
| Special classification provisions | 0.9 | 2.3 | 2.1 | 4.7 | 5.7 | 9.8 | 12.5 | 20.1 | 16.9 | 23.2 |

## Table D-3.  State Exports of Goods by Destination and Industry, 1993–1997 —*Continued*

**TEXAS** (Millions of dollars.)

| Industry | 1993 | 1994 | 1995 | 1996 | 1997 | 1993 | 1994 | 1995 | 1996 | 1997 |
|---|---|---|---|---|---|---|---|---|---|---|
| | Japan | | | | | South Korea | | | | |
| **ALL GOODS** | 1 445.8 | 1 558.4 | 2 181.0 | 2 073.9 | 2 218.4 | 750.2 | 923.6 | 1 474.0 | 1 354.2 | 1 352.6 |
| **Manufactured goods** | 1 410.1 | 1 526.5 | 2 099.5 | 2 025.9 | 2 155.8 | 698.7 | 868.7 | 1 386.6 | 1 297.1 | 1 306.0 |
| Food products | 31.5 | 78.7 | 37.5 | 49.3 | 69.9 | 19.5 | 5.6 | 6.5 | 9.0 | 10.9 |
| Tobacco products | ..... | ..... | ..... | ..... | ..... | ..... | ..... | ..... | ..... | ..... |
| Textile mill products | 1.4 | 3.3 | 3.0 | 4.3 | 4.6 | 2.7 | 1.4 | 1.2 | 3.3 | 1.3 |
| Apparel | 4.8 | 6.5 | 7.4 | 9.6 | 9.8 | 0.7 | 2.8 | 1.4 | 0.6 | 0.6 |
| Lumber and wood products | 10.7 | 13.8 | 20.6 | 26.7 | 17.3 | 0.6 | 0.3 | 0.9 | 7.1 | 10.3 |
| Furniture and fixtures | 0.7 | 1.7 | 2.5 | 3.8 | 5.5 | 0.1 | 0.4 | 1.2 | 1.0 | 0.5 |
| Paper products | 4.5 | 5.2 | 6.5 | 4.1 | 2.0 | 1.4 | 1.8 | 3.1 | 1.7 | 1.6 |
| Printing and publishing | 1.1 | 1.3 | 3.4 | 2.9 | 2.9 | 0.3 | 0.2 | 0.7 | 1.7 | 0.6 |
| Chemical products | 458.9 | 528.2 | 651.4 | 483.8 | 435.7 | 290.3 | 356.0 | 595.1 | 505.0 | 493.3 |
| Refined petroleum products | 134.8 | 45.2 | 78.2 | 104.4 | 54.2 | 111.9 | 124.8 | 258.9 | 132.5 | 28.5 |
| Rubber and plastic products | 6.6 | 12.4 | 12.6 | 12.6 | 11.8 | 9.0 | 4.1 | 5.7 | 9.8 | 8.6 |
| Leather products | 3.0 | 2.5 | 4.1 | 4.8 | 3.1 | 4.2 | 1.5 | 1.0 | 0.5 | 0.3 |
| Stone, clay and glass products | 5.3 | 6.5 | 16.7 | 7.9 | 12.9 | 2.6 | 4.1 | 8.7 | 4.7 | 3.3 |
| Primary metals | 22.1 | 19.8 | 25.2 | 24.9 | 23.2 | 6.3 | 15.9 | 27.2 | 33.5 | 28.1 |
| Fabricated metal products | 9.1 | 47.9 | 29.5 | 37.3 | 40.5 | 6.7 | 26.2 | 60.2 | 73.4 | 44.0 |
| Industrial machinery and computers | 195.8 | 188.0 | 243.9 | 219.2 | 314.3 | 95.5 | 80.0 | 82.9 | 103.6 | 130.6 |
| Electric and electronic equipment | 291.9 | 323.0 | 619.7 | 653.7 | 805.3 | 89.3 | 153.9 | 240.8 | 255.9 | 353.8 |
| Transportation equipment | 105.1 | 113.3 | 174.8 | 184.5 | 149.3 | 14.6 | 28.3 | 36.5 | 93.0 | 133.7 |
| Scientific and measuring instruments | 97.3 | 104.7 | 135.5 | 156.1 | 175.4 | 36.1 | 55.2 | 49.0 | 52.6 | 50.2 |
| Miscellaneous manufactures | 23.3 | 22.6 | 24.9 | 23.5 | 16.4 | 6.5 | 5.3 | 4.9 | 7.4 | 5.2 |
| Unidentified manufactures | 2.1 | 1.7 | 2.0 | 12.6 | 1.7 | 0.5 | 0.9 | 0.8 | 0.9 | 0.8 |
| **Agricultural and livestock products** | 14.0 | 18.5 | 63.3 | 34.7 | 18.6 | 33.7 | 43.4 | 68.5 | 35.4 | 40.7 |
| Agricultural products | 13.9 | 18.4 | 62.9 | 34.1 | 17.5 | 33.4 | 42.5 | 68.5 | 35.3 | 40.4 |
| Livestock and livestock products | 0.1 | 0.1 | 0.4 | 0.5 | 1.1 | 0.4 | 0.9 | ..... | 0.1 | 0.2 |
| **Other commodities** | 21.7 | 13.5 | 18.2 | 13.3 | 44.0 | 17.8 | 11.5 | 18.8 | 21.7 | 5.9 |
| Forestry products | 11.1 | 1.0 | 0.9 | 0.2 | 0.3 | 7.9 | 2.2 | 2.5 | 1.2 | 0.4 |
| Fish and other marine products | 0.9 | 0.2 | 1.4 | 1.0 | 0.3 | ..... | ..... | 0.1 | 0.1 | ..... |
| Metallic ores and concentrates | ..... | 0.1 | 0.7 | 0.6 | ..... | ..... | ..... | ..... | ..... | ..... |
| Bituminous coal and lignite | ..... | ..... | ..... | ..... | ..... | ..... | ..... | ..... | ..... | ..... |
| Crude petroleum and natural gas | ..... | 0.4 | 0.1 | ..... | 26.2 | 5.5 | 2.4 | 0.3 | 12.9 | 0.4 |
| Nonmetallic minerals | 3.3 | 4.5 | 5.0 | 2.2 | 4.7 | 0.7 | 1.3 | 2.7 | 2.1 | 1.9 |
| Scrap and waste | 1.5 | 3.4 | 3.0 | 2.4 | 2.7 | 3.2 | 3.8 | 12.6 | 4.1 | 0.9 |
| Used merchandise | 3.1 | 1.9 | 3.0 | 2.4 | 3.5 | 0.4 | 1.3 | 0.3 | 0.3 | 1.2 |
| Goods imported and returned unchanged | ..... | ..... | ..... | ..... | ..... | ..... | ..... | ..... | ..... | ..... |
| Special classification provisions | 1.7 | 1.9 | 4.2 | 4.4 | 6.3 | 0.1 | 0.5 | 0.3 | 1.1 | 1.1 |
| | Taiwan | | | | | Singapore | | | | |
| **ALL GOODS** | 1 000.1 | 1 200.4 | 1 371.4 | 1 179.0 | 1 348.3 | 1 192.0 | 1 529.3 | 1 755.5 | 1 528.7 | 2 015.8 |
| **Manufactured goods** | 984.2 | 1 181.9 | 1 323.4 | 1 152.9 | 1 305.1 | 1 182.9 | 1 519.6 | 1 742.2 | 1 512.6 | 2 003.0 |
| Food products | 10.7 | 16.9 | 16.7 | 14.0 | 14.3 | 1.7 | 1.8 | 3.8 | 4.0 | 3.0 |
| Tobacco products | ..... | ..... | ..... | ..... | 0.2 | ..... | ..... | ..... | ..... | ..... |
| Textile mill products | 1.6 | 2.6 | 3.2 | 0.6 | 2.0 | 0.3 | 0.3 | 1.5 | 1.3 | 1.1 |
| Apparel | 0.1 | 0.2 | 0.2 | 0.2 | 1.0 | 0.5 | 0.8 | 0.5 | 0.8 | 1.2 |
| Lumber and wood products | 0.6 | 0.8 | 0.2 | 0.1 | 0.7 | 0.4 | 0.4 | 0.3 | 0.4 | 1.2 |
| Furniture and fixtures | 0.6 | 0.7 | 0.8 | 0.5 | 0.4 | 0.4 | 0.3 | 0.2 | 1.1 | 0.4 |
| Paper products | 2.4 | 5.0 | 3.4 | 3.9 | 2.1 | 0.9 | 1.1 | 1.2 | 0.3 | 0.8 |
| Printing and publishing | 1.0 | 0.9 | 1.7 | 1.2 | 0.6 | 0.6 | 0.9 | 0.9 | 1.1 | 1.1 |
| Chemical products | 584.2 | 677.0 | 748.4 | 529.9 | 483.8 | 156.6 | 186.6 | 272.1 | 240.4 | 340.3 |
| Refined petroleum products | 20.9 | 45.2 | 42.7 | 20.3 | 25.4 | 48.0 | 249.9 | 136.4 | 85.9 | 35.7 |
| Rubber and plastic products | 6.9 | 7.3 | 8.7 | 10.1 | 10.1 | 5.0 | 6.1 | 6.8 | 8.1 | 9.5 |
| Leather products | 0.8 | 0.9 | 0.7 | 0.5 | 0.6 | 0.3 | 0.3 | 0.4 | 0.4 | 0.3 |
| Stone, clay and glass products | 1.2 | 2.5 | 1.5 | 1.0 | 2.0 | 4.9 | 4.5 | 6.8 | 6.4 | 6.9 |
| Primary metals | 2.4 | 4.9 | 18.2 | 4.0 | 12.4 | 6.9 | 6.6 | 11.0 | 13.7 | 14.3 |
| Fabricated metal products | 24.1 | 27.8 | 11.7 | 5.2 | 9.0 | 12.7 | 10.4 | 15.6 | 22.4 | 21.8 |
| Industrial machinery and computers | 75.0 | 53.9 | 60.5 | 89.0 | 121.6 | 393.7 | 532.6 | 537.2 | 495.5 | 611.4 |
| Electric and electronic equipment | 225.6 | 283.8 | 356.0 | 381.7 | 551.3 | 459.0 | 430.2 | 627.9 | 514.3 | 772.2 |
| Transportation equipment | 5.1 | 16.0 | 20.0 | 5.1 | 26.1 | 37.3 | 45.8 | 45.1 | 64.2 | 88.5 |
| Scientific and measuring instruments | 17.1 | 18.7 | 21.7 | 78.0 | 36.7 | 51.4 | 38.1 | 72.0 | 48.9 | 84.7 |
| Miscellaneous manufactures | 3.4 | 15.9 | 6.2 | 6.7 | 3.8 | 1.0 | 1.2 | 1.3 | 2.4 | 7.4 |
| Unidentified manufactures | 0.6 | 0.8 | 0.8 | 0.8 | 1.1 | 1.3 | 1.6 | 1.1 | 1.0 | 1.0 |
| **Agricultural and livestock products** | 8.6 | 10.7 | 27.6 | 15.9 | 31.4 | 0.1 | 0.4 | 0.5 | 0.2 | ..... |
| Agricultural products | 8.6 | 10.5 | 26.5 | 15.8 | 31.4 | 0.1 | 0.4 | 0.5 | 0.2 | ..... |
| Livestock and livestock products | ..... | 0.2 | 1.0 | 0.1 | ..... | ..... | ..... | ..... | ..... | ..... |
| **Other commodities** | 7.3 | 7.8 | 20.4 | 10.3 | 11.8 | 9.0 | 9.3 | 12.7 | 15.8 | 12.8 |
| Forestry products | 0.1 | ..... | 0.1 | 0.1 | 0.1 | ..... | ..... | 0.1 | 0.1 | ..... |
| Fish and other marine products | 0.1 | 0.7 | 0.4 | 0.4 | ..... | ..... | ..... | ..... | ..... | ..... |
| Metallic ores and concentrates | ..... | ..... | ..... | ..... | ..... | ..... | ..... | ..... | 0.1 | ..... |
| Bituminous coal and lignite | ..... | ..... | ..... | ..... | ..... | ..... | ..... | 0.1 | ..... | 0.1 |
| Crude petroleum and natural gas | 0.1 | ..... | ..... | ..... | ..... | ..... | ..... | 0.1 | ..... | 0.1 |
| Nonmetallic minerals | 0.5 | 1.0 | 1.8 | 1.6 | 4.0 | 1.7 | 1.7 | 2.8 | 1.5 | 2.7 |
| Scrap and waste | 5.2 | 5.3 | 17.2 | 7.6 | 5.3 | 0.4 | 0.4 | 0.3 | 0.5 | 0.5 |
| Used merchandise | 0.7 | 0.2 | 0.2 | ..... | 0.1 | 1.5 | 1.2 | 0.9 | 5.6 | 2.6 |
| Goods imported and returned unchanged | ..... | ..... | ..... | ..... | ..... | ..... | ..... | ..... | ..... | ..... |
| Special classification provisions | 0.6 | 0.7 | 0.7 | 0.5 | 2.2 | 5.4 | 6.0 | 8.5 | 7.9 | 6.8 |

# UTAH: Exports of Goods, 1997

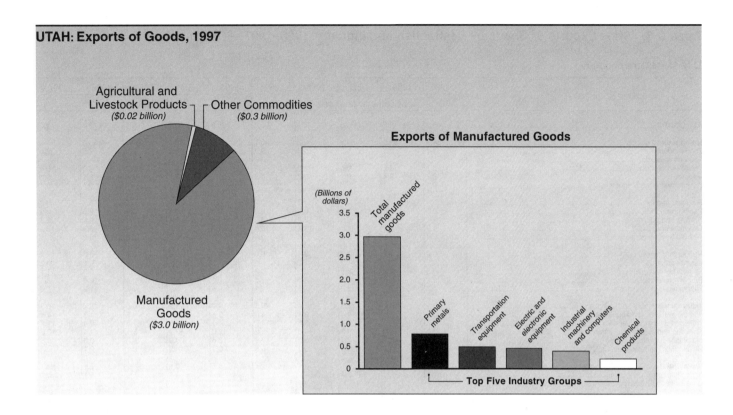

Agricultural and Livestock Products ($0.02 billion)

Other Commodities ($0.3 billion)

Manufactured Goods ($3.0 billion)

**Exports of Manufactured Goods**

(Billions of dollars)

Total manufactured goods

Primary metals

Transportation equipment

Electric and electronic equipment

Industrial machinery and computers

Chemical products

Top Five Industry Groups

## Table D-3.   State Exports of Goods by Destination and Industry, 1993–1997 —*Continued*

**UTAH** (Millions of dollars.)

| Industry | 1993 | 1994 | 1995 | 1996 | 1997 | 1993 | 1994 | 1995 | 1996 | 1997 |
|---|---|---|---|---|---|---|---|---|---|---|
| | All destinations | | | | | Canada | | | | |
| **ALL GOODS** | 2 045.0 | 2 233.1 | 2 313.4 | 2 768.5 | 3 293.3 | 343.1 | 342.9 | 413.1 | 443.3 | 514.5 |
| **Manufactured goods** | 1 734.7 | 1 851.8 | 1 793.3 | 2 379.0 | 2 968.1 | 295.2 | 300.6 | 381.3 | 415.7 | 487.4 |
| Food products | 61.2 | 56.9 | 116.9 | 126.6 | 141.0 | 26.1 | 21.8 | 33.0 | 21.8 | 24.4 |
| Tobacco products | ..... | ..... | ..... | ..... | ..... | ..... | ..... | ..... | ..... | ..... |
| Textile mill products | 2.2 | 2.3 | 3.0 | 2.2 | 3.5 | 0.7 | 1.1 | 1.0 | 0.6 | 0.6 |
| Apparel | 5.7 | 8.7 | 8.5 | 8.8 | 8.2 | 1.0 | 1.0 | 1.5 | 1.1 | 1.4 |
| Lumber and wood products | 1.5 | 0.8 | 2.5 | 1.4 | 1.6 | 0.5 | 0.4 | 0.5 | 0.2 | 0.4 |
| Furniture and fixtures | 3.3 | 3.3 | 3.6 | 3.9 | 5.1 | 2.2 | 1.8 | 1.5 | 1.7 | 2.5 |
| Paper products | 8.3 | 3.3 | 5.0 | 6.9 | 6.1 | 0.4 | 0.4 | 1.4 | 2.3 | 1.1 |
| Printing and publishing | 24.4 | 24.8 | 28.4 | 35.3 | 33.5 | 7.3 | 8.0 | 9.7 | 9.9 | 8.0 |
| Chemical products | 87.6 | 141.4 | 124.7 | 201.6 | 222.1 | 31.4 | 31.0 | 38.7 | 48.5 | 45.1 |
| Refined petroleum products | 0.9 | 0.8 | 1.0 | 1.1 | 0.6 | 0.1 | ..... | 0.2 | 0.1 | 0.1 |
| Rubber and plastic products | 7.5 | 11.3 | 25.7 | 26.1 | 35.7 | 2.2 | 2.0 | 2.1 | 3.3 | 4.3 |
| Leather products | 2.7 | 3.5 | 4.5 | 5.4 | 5.5 | 0.7 | 0.8 | 1.6 | 1.4 | 1.2 |
| Stone, clay and glass products | 5.3 | 4.6 | 5.2 | 6.7 | 8.0 | 1.8 | 1.6 | 1.1 | 1.1 | 1.1 |
| Primary metals | 605.2 | 752.4 | 363.8 | 438.8 | 784.1 | 25.7 | 22.1 | 51.9 | 52.9 | 64.1 |
| Fabricated metal products | 40.4 | 31.3 | 38.0 | 51.2 | 63.2 | 11.6 | 10.6 | 10.9 | 16.3 | 18.6 |
| Industrial machinery and computers | 199.8 | 194.4 | 317.1 | 447.9 | 398.8 | 30.8 | 34.6 | 51.3 | 60.5 | 81.1 |
| Electric and electronic equipment | 320.6 | 222.2 | 319.5 | 362.4 | 462.9 | 65.5 | 53.2 | 48.3 | 42.9 | 48.4 |
| Transportation equipment | 208.4 | 212.6 | 230.8 | 418.8 | 497.1 | 59.2 | 76.8 | 89.8 | 114.1 | 126.4 |
| Scientific and measuring instruments | 99.8 | 109.4 | 118.6 | 146.0 | 177.8 | 16.3 | 15.3 | 17.5 | 17.2 | 26.0 |
| Miscellaneous manufactures | 42.8 | 59.6 | 67.1 | 76.0 | 103.3 | 10.2 | 15.8 | 16.2 | 16.9 | 29.5 |
| Unidentified manufactures | 7.0 | 7.9 | 9.3 | 11.8 | 10.1 | 1.5 | 2.3 | 3.2 | 2.9 | 3.1 |
| **Agricultural and livestock products** | 6.2 | 5.3 | 5.0 | 24.4 | 23.3 | 4.8 | 3.4 | 1.8 | 1.6 | 1.2 |
| Agricultural products | 5.5 | 5.2 | 4.9 | 23.9 | 23.3 | 4.5 | 3.3 | 1.8 | 1.4 | 1.1 |
| Livestock and livestock products | 0.7 | 0.1 | 0.1 | 0.5 | ..... | 0.4 | 0.1 | ..... | 0.2 | ..... |
| **Other commodities** | 304.2 | 376.1 | 515.2 | 365.1 | 302.0 | 43.0 | 38.9 | 30.0 | 26.0 | 25.9 |
| Forestry products | ..... | 0.1 | 0.2 | 0.1 | 0.5 | ..... | ..... | ..... | ..... | 0.1 |
| Fish and other marine products | 1.9 | 1.8 | 3.3 | 6.8 | 6.2 | 0.4 | 0.1 | 0.1 | ..... | ..... |
| Metallic ores and concentrates | 211.6 | 281.4 | 387.8 | 190.3 | 162.8 | 34.1 | 31.6 | 4.8 | 3.2 | ..... |
| Bituminous coal and lignite | 64.3 | 66.2 | 81.9 | 115.1 | 86.1 | ..... | ..... | ..... | ..... | ..... |
| Crude petroleum and natural gas | 0.5 | 0.3 | ..... | ..... | ..... | 0.4 | 0.3 | ..... | ..... | ..... |
| Nonmetallic minerals | 5.3 | 6.7 | 7.3 | 8.1 | 6.5 | 0.3 | 0.5 | 0.6 | 0.9 | 1.0 |
| Scrap and waste | 10.0 | 10.0 | 22.5 | 15.5 | 4.8 | 0.6 | 0.5 | 18.2 | 10.0 | 4.3 |
| Used merchandise | 2.2 | 1.3 | 4.2 | 3.8 | 7.0 | 0.4 | 0.6 | 0.5 | 1.3 | 2.1 |
| Goods imported and returned unchanged | 5.9 | 4.6 | 5.1 | 7.9 | 17.1 | 5.9 | 4.6 | 5.1 | 7.9 | 17.1 |
| Special classification provisions | 2.4 | 3.7 | 2.9 | 17.3 | 10.9 | 0.8 | 0.6 | 0.7 | 2.5 | 1.2 |

## Table D-3.  State Exports of Goods by Destination and Industry, 1993–1997 —*Continued*

**UTAH** (Millions of dollars.)

| Industry | 1993 | 1994 | 1995 | 1996 | 1997 | 1993 | 1994 | 1995 | 1996 | 1997 |
|---|---|---|---|---|---|---|---|---|---|---|
| | South and Central America and Caribbean | | | | | Mexico | | | | |
| **ALL GOODS** | 45.1 | 50.2 | 86.3 | 96.4 | 109.8 | 30.5 | 82.7 | 66.7 | 76.4 | 73.0 |
| **Manufactured goods** | 34.3 | 39.3 | 55.0 | 69.2 | 96.7 | 30.0 | 78.0 | 33.2 | 50.4 | 71.9 |
| Food products | 1.1 | 2.5 | 6.5 | 9.6 | 9.7 | 4.2 | 3.6 | 2.4 | 2.5 | 2.0 |
| Tobacco products | ..... | ..... | ..... | ..... | ..... | ..... | ..... | ..... | ..... | ..... |
| Textile mill products | 0.1 | 0.2 | 0.6 | 0.3 | 1.2 | 0.1 | 0.1 | 0.2 | 0.2 | 0.6 |
| Apparel | 0.2 | 0.4 | 0.2 | 0.2 | 0.3 | ..... | 0.2 | 0.3 | 0.1 | 0.1 |
| Lumber and wood products | 0.1 | ..... | ..... | ..... | ..... | ..... | ..... | ..... | 0.1 | 0.1 |
| Furniture and fixtures | ..... | ..... | 0.2 | 0.3 | 0.2 | 0.2 | 0.2 | 0.1 | 0.1 | 0.2 |
| Paper products | 0.9 | 0.6 | 1.1 | 0.7 | 0.8 | 0.3 | 0.6 | 0.9 | 2.5 | 2.6 |
| Printing and publishing | 1.1 | 1.9 | 0.8 | 2.0 | 3.2 | 0.5 | 2.1 | 1.1 | 0.6 | 2.2 |
| Chemical products | 4.5 | 4.6 | 4.1 | 13.4 | 13.4 | 1.9 | 8.6 | 2.9 | 6.9 | 8.4 |
| Refined petroleum products | 0.4 | 0.1 | 0.2 | 0.4 | 0.5 | 0.1 | 0.6 | 0.6 | 0.2 | ..... |
| Rubber and plastic products | 0.2 | 0.2 | 0.3 | 0.4 | 0.6 | 0.6 | 3.0 | 5.0 | 8.5 | 12.7 |
| Leather products | ..... | ..... | ..... | ..... | ..... | ..... | ..... | 0.1 | 0.1 | 0.2 |
| Stone, clay and glass products | 0.5 | 0.6 | 0.5 | 0.3 | 0.2 | 0.3 | 0.1 | ..... | 0.9 | 1.1 |
| Primary metals | 2.7 | 2.0 | 2.5 | 2.3 | 1.5 | 0.3 | 26.4 | 0.4 | 0.6 | 2.1 |
| Fabricated metal products | 1.1 | 4.7 | 2.2 | 1.8 | 4.1 | 0.8 | 0.7 | 1.3 | 1.2 | 1.8 |
| Industrial machinery and computers | 12.1 | 10.2 | 20.5 | 12.4 | 25.1 | 4.7 | 12.2 | 6.5 | 6.7 | 10.3 |
| Electric and electronic equipment | 3.9 | 2.6 | 4.4 | 2.1 | 4.6 | 3.1 | 4.0 | 4.3 | 4.9 | 4.4 |
| Transportation equipment | 0.7 | 0.2 | 0.4 | 3.8 | 14.7 | ..... | 1.6 | 1.6 | 9.4 | 11.7 |
| Scientific and measuring instruments | 3.3 | 5.7 | 8.1 | 15.2 | 8.2 | 12.0 | 12.9 | 5.1 | 4.4 | 10.8 |
| Miscellaneous manufactures | 1.4 | 2.1 | 2.1 | 3.2 | 7.9 | 0.5 | 0.9 | 0.2 | 0.6 | 0.5 |
| Unidentified manufactures | 0.3 | 0.4 | 0.3 | 0.6 | 0.5 | 0.1 | 0.2 | 0.1 | 0.1 | 0.2 |
| **Agricultural and livestock products** | ..... | ..... | 0.1 | 0.1 | ..... | 0.3 | 0.1 | ..... | 5.1 | 0.1 |
| Agricultural products | ..... | ..... | 0.1 | ..... | ..... | 0.2 | 0.1 | ..... | 5.1 | 0.1 |
| Livestock and livestock products | ..... | ..... | ..... | 0.1 | ..... | 0.1 | ..... | ..... | ..... | ..... |
| **Other commodities** | 10.8 | 11.0 | 31.2 | 27.1 | 13.0 | 0.2 | 4.5 | 33.5 | 20.9 | 1.0 |
| Forestry products | ..... | ..... | ..... | ..... | ..... | ..... | ..... | ..... | ..... | ..... |
| Fish and other marine products | 0.1 | ..... | 0.2 | 0.3 | 0.3 | ..... | ..... | ..... | 0.1 | 0.2 |
| Metallic ores and concentrates | 10.6 | 10.5 | 27.9 | 18.8 | 12.0 | ..... | 2.9 | 33.0 | 19.9 | ..... |
| Bituminous coal and lignite | ..... | ..... | 2.5 | 7.4 | ..... | ..... | ..... | ..... | 0.4 | ..... |
| Crude petroleum and natural gas | ..... | ..... | ..... | ..... | ..... | 0.1 | ..... | ..... | ..... | ..... |
| Nonmetallic minerals | 0.1 | 0.3 | 0.4 | 0.4 | 0.4 | ..... | ..... | 0.1 | 0.1 | ..... |
| Scrap and waste | ..... | ..... | ..... | ..... | ..... | ..... | ..... | ..... | ..... | 0.5 |
| Used merchandise | ..... | ..... | 0.1 | ..... | 0.1 | ..... | ..... | ..... | ..... | ..... |
| Goods imported and returned unchanged | ..... | ..... | ..... | ..... | ..... | ..... | ..... | ..... | ..... | ..... |
| Special classification provisions | ..... | 0.1 | 0.2 | 0.2 | 0.3 | ..... | 1.6 | 0.3 | 0.4 | 0.3 |
| | European Union | | | | | United Kingdom | | | | |
| **ALL GOODS** | 475.1 | 522.5 | 619.2 | 895.1 | 1 257.1 | 70.1 | 60.8 | 108.8 | 365.9 | 735.1 |
| **Manufactured goods** | 439.6 | 432.1 | 499.5 | 829.2 | 1 169.4 | 62.0 | 50.6 | 103.4 | 359.6 | 733.9 |
| Food products | 4.9 | 4.9 | 7.5 | 9.8 | 9.6 | 1.8 | 1.8 | 2.2 | 1.8 | 1.5 |
| Tobacco products | ..... | ..... | ..... | ..... | ..... | ..... | ..... | ..... | ..... | ..... |
| Textile mill products | 0.4 | 0.3 | 0.5 | 0.2 | 0.3 | ..... | 0.1 | 0.1 | 0.1 | 0.1 |
| Apparel | 2.3 | 1.6 | 2.6 | 2.1 | 1.6 | 0.4 | 0.3 | 0.2 | 0.3 | 0.4 |
| Lumber and wood products | 0.7 | ..... | 0.1 | 0.1 | 0.1 | ..... | ..... | 0.1 | ..... | 0.1 |
| Furniture and fixtures | 0.3 | 0.5 | 0.5 | 0.4 | 1.3 | 0.3 | 0.4 | 0.2 | 0.2 | 0.4 |
| Paper products | 2.1 | 0.8 | 0.6 | 0.4 | 0.6 | 0.3 | 0.1 | 0.3 | 0.1 | 0.4 |
| Printing and publishing | 6.5 | 5.0 | 5.5 | 6.9 | 4.3 | 3.2 | 3.2 | 4.4 | 3.0 | 2.9 |
| Chemical products | 8.0 | 10.3 | 12.1 | 13.5 | 28.9 | 1.1 | 0.5 | 2.1 | 0.9 | 3.9 |
| Refined petroleum products | 0.2 | ..... | ..... | ..... | ..... | ..... | ..... | ..... | ..... | ..... |
| Rubber and plastic products | 1.7 | 2.4 | 5.9 | 7.4 | 6.8 | 0.3 | 0.4 | 2.0 | 2.2 | 1.7 |
| Leather products | 0.4 | 0.3 | 0.5 | 0.5 | 0.9 | 0.1 | 0.1 | 0.2 | 0.3 | 0.2 |
| Stone, clay and glass products | 1.2 | 1.1 | 2.1 | 2.2 | 2.5 | 0.2 | 0.1 | 0.1 | 0.2 | 0.4 |
| Primary metals | 107.2 | 130.3 | 114.1 | 290.5 | 652.3 | 9.9 | 5.8 | 37.6 | 280.1 | 646.1 |
| Fabricated metal products | 12.5 | 5.1 | 5.4 | 7.9 | 19.2 | 2.8 | 2.6 | 1.8 | 3.2 | 3.8 |
| Industrial machinery and computers | 108.8 | 83.9 | 100.9 | 139.9 | 94.6 | 21.9 | 14.6 | 18.7 | 16.6 | 17.1 |
| Electric and electronic equipment | 34.5 | 33.7 | 58.1 | 119.9 | 84.0 | 9.6 | 9.5 | 12.6 | 24.6 | 14.8 |
| Transportation equipment | 91.4 | 89.1 | 109.6 | 145.0 | 158.4 | 0.3 | 0.7 | 6.8 | 7.9 | 12.4 |
| Scientific and measuring instruments | 38.6 | 42.9 | 49.5 | 54.6 | 73.0 | 5.8 | 6.4 | 8.6 | 9.5 | 19.5 |
| Miscellaneous manufactures | 16.0 | 18.0 | 22.0 | 26.5 | 29.6 | 3.5 | 3.3 | 5.2 | 8.3 | 8.1 |
| Unidentified manufactures | 1.8 | 1.9 | 2.0 | 1.5 | 1.5 | 0.5 | 0.5 | 0.4 | 0.4 | 0.3 |
| **Agricultural and livestock products** | ..... | 0.3 | 0.3 | 0.2 | 0.2 | ..... | ..... | 0.1 | ..... | 0.1 |
| Agricultural products | ..... | 0.3 | 0.3 | 0.2 | 0.2 | ..... | ..... | 0.1 | ..... | 0.1 |
| Livestock and livestock products | ..... | ..... | 0.1 | ..... | ..... | ..... | ..... | ..... | ..... | ..... |
| **Other commodities** | 35.5 | 90.0 | 119.4 | 65.7 | 87.5 | 8.1 | 10.1 | 5.3 | 6.2 | 1.1 |
| Forestry products | ..... | ..... | ..... | ..... | 0.1 | ..... | ..... | ..... | ..... | ..... |
| Fish and other marine products | 0.1 | 0.2 | 0.2 | 0.4 | 0.2 | ..... | ..... | ..... | ..... | ..... |
| Metallic ores and concentrates | 23.4 | 75.7 | 110.4 | 51.6 | 78.2 | ..... | ..... | 0.6 | ..... | ..... |
| Bituminous coal and lignite | ..... | ..... | ..... | ..... | ..... | ..... | ..... | ..... | ..... | ..... |
| Crude petroleum and natural gas | ..... | ..... | ..... | ..... | ..... | ..... | ..... | ..... | ..... | ..... |
| Nonmetallic minerals | 3.7 | 4.4 | 3.7 | 3.5 | 3.4 | 0.5 | 0.7 | 0.4 | 0.5 | 0.7 |
| Scrap and waste | 7.5 | 9.1 | 4.1 | 5.4 | ..... | 7.5 | 9.1 | 3.9 | 5.4 | ..... |
| Used merchandise | 0.3 | 0.3 | 0.1 | 0.3 | 0.1 | ..... | 0.1 | ..... | ..... | ..... |
| Goods imported and returned unchanged | ..... | ..... | ..... | ..... | ..... | ..... | ..... | ..... | ..... | ..... |
| Special classification provisions | 0.4 | 0.4 | 0.9 | 4.5 | 5.5 | 0.1 | 0.2 | 0.4 | 0.4 | 0.5 |

## Table D-3.  State Exports of Goods by Destination and Industry, 1993–1997 —Continued

**UTAH** (Millions of dollars.)

| Industry | 1993 | 1994 | 1995 | 1996 | 1997 | 1993 | 1994 | 1995 | 1996 | 1997 |
|---|---|---|---|---|---|---|---|---|---|---|
| | Germany | | | | | France | | | | |
| **ALL GOODS** | 159.2 | 187.9 | 196.7 | 210.2 | 146.5 | 18.3 | 16.1 | 26.8 | 42.2 | 41.1 |
| **Manufactured goods** | 156.9 | 186.3 | 195.1 | 207.8 | 127.2 | 16.9 | 15.5 | 26.1 | 40.6 | 40.3 |
| Food products | 0.6 | 0.5 | 0.4 | 0.4 | 0.8 | ..... | 0.2 | 0.5 | 0.5 | 0.6 |
| Tobacco products | ..... | ..... | ..... | ..... | ..... | ..... | ..... | ..... | ..... | ..... |
| Textile mill products | 0.2 | ..... | 0.1 | 0.1 | ..... | ..... | ..... | 0.1 | 0.2 | ..... |
| Apparel | 1.1 | 0.3 | 1.0 | 1.2 | 0.6 | 0.2 | 0.2 | 0.1 | 0.1 | 0.1 |
| Lumber and wood products | ..... | ..... | ..... | ..... | ..... | ..... | ..... | ..... | ..... | ..... |
| Furniture and fixtures | ..... | 0.1 | 0.3 | 0.1 | ..... | ..... | ..... | ..... | ..... | ..... |
| Paper products | 0.3 | ..... | ..... | 0.1 | ..... | 0.1 | ..... | ..... | ..... | ..... |
| Printing and publishing | 0.3 | 0.2 | 0.3 | 1.5 | 0.6 | 0.2 | ..... | 0.1 | 0.3 | 0.1 |
| Chemical products | 2.6 | 1.4 | 1.9 | 1.9 | 4.4 | 1.3 | 1.2 | 0.4 | 0.6 | 3.5 |
| Refined petroleum products | ..... | ..... | ..... | ..... | ..... | ..... | ..... | ..... | ..... | ..... |
| Rubber and plastic products | 0.2 | 0.2 | 1.0 | 0.1 | 0.1 | 0.4 | 0.5 | 0.2 | 1.0 | 0.2 |
| Leather products | 0.1 | ..... | 0.1 | 0.1 | ..... | 0.1 | ..... | ..... | ..... | 0.2 |
| Stone, clay and glass products | 0.7 | 0.6 | 0.2 | 1.1 | 0.8 | 0.1 | 0.1 | 0.3 | 0.4 | 0.5 |
| Primary metals | 92.9 | 117.6 | 61.8 | 1.3 | 0.6 | 0.1 | 0.4 | 0.6 | 0.8 | 0.1 |
| Fabricated metal products | 0.4 | 0.8 | 1.1 | 0.7 | 4.6 | 0.5 | 0.1 | 0.5 | 0.5 | 1.0 |
| Industrial machinery and computers | 31.1 | 25.4 | 39.5 | 65.9 | 15.8 | 3.4 | 2.8 | 7.9 | 13.6 | 7.4 |
| Electric and electronic equipment | 10.3 | 8.0 | 17.2 | 45.2 | 13.3 | 2.2 | 2.5 | 6.4 | 12.0 | 12.3 |
| Transportation equipment | 4.0 | 19.6 | 55.4 | 75.0 | 68.1 | 0.1 | 0.2 | 0.2 | 1.6 | 4.1 |
| Scientific and measuring instruments | 8.8 | 7.5 | 9.6 | 8.7 | 12.5 | 5.3 | 4.8 | 5.5 | 5.7 | 6.1 |
| Miscellaneous manufactures | 3.0 | 3.7 | 4.5 | 4.3 | 4.9 | 2.8 | 2.0 | 3.1 | 3.4 | 4.1 |
| Unidentified manufactures | 0.2 | 0.3 | 0.8 | 0.2 | 0.1 | 0.1 | 0.2 | 0.2 | 0.1 | 0.1 |
| **Agricultural and livestock products** | ..... | 0.2 | 0.1 | ..... | ..... | ..... | ..... | 0.1 | 0.1 | ..... |
| Agricultural products | ..... | 0.2 | ..... | ..... | ..... | ..... | ..... | 0.1 | 0.1 | ..... |
| Livestock and livestock products | ..... | ..... | 0.1 | ..... | ..... | ..... | ..... | ..... | ..... | ..... |
| **Other commodities** | 2.4 | 1.4 | 1.5 | 2.4 | 19.2 | 1.4 | 0.6 | 0.6 | 1.4 | 0.7 |
| Forestry products | ..... | ..... | ..... | ..... | ..... | ..... | ..... | ..... | ..... | ..... |
| Fish and other marine products | ..... | 0.1 | ..... | ..... | 0.1 | ..... | ..... | ..... | ..... | ..... |
| Metallic ores and concentrates | ..... | ..... | ..... | ..... | 17.4 | 1.0 | ..... | ..... | 0.2 | ..... |
| Bituminous coal and lignite | ..... | ..... | ..... | ..... | ..... | ..... | ..... | ..... | ..... | ..... |
| Crude petroleum and natural gas | ..... | ..... | ..... | ..... | ..... | ..... | ..... | ..... | ..... | ..... |
| Nonmetallic minerals | 2.1 | 1.3 | 1.4 | 1.4 | 1.4 | 0.3 | 0.5 | 0.6 | 0.6 | 0.5 |
| Scrap and waste | ..... | ..... | ..... | ..... | ..... | ..... | ..... | ..... | ..... | ..... |
| Used merchandise | 0.1 | ..... | ..... | 0.1 | 0.1 | ..... | 0.1 | ..... | 0.2 | ..... |
| Goods imported and returned unchanged | ..... | ..... | ..... | ..... | ..... | ..... | ..... | ..... | ..... | ..... |
| Special classification provisions | 0.1 | ..... | 0.1 | 0.8 | 0.2 | ..... | ..... | ..... | 0.5 | 0.2 |

| Industry | 1993 | 1994 | 1995 | 1996 | 1997 | 1993 | 1994 | 1995 | 1996 | 1997 |
|---|---|---|---|---|---|---|---|---|---|---|
| | The Netherlands | | | | | Asian 10 | | | | |
| **ALL GOODS** | 140.1 | 117.6 | 90.9 | 116.1 | 118.1 | 885.4 | 1 086.8 | 1 021.0 | 1 116.0 | 1 204.5 |
| **Manufactured goods** | 139.4 | 115.1 | 89.9 | 113.0 | 112.1 | 675.9 | 855.8 | 721.5 | 890.4 | 1 014.5 |
| Food products | 1.0 | 1.6 | 3.0 | 4.8 | 4.5 | 23.6 | 22.7 | 63.3 | 77.3 | 85.1 |
| Tobacco products | ..... | ..... | ..... | ..... | ..... | ..... | ..... | ..... | ..... | ..... |
| Textile mill products | ..... | 0.1 | 0.1 | ..... | ..... | 0.3 | 0.3 | 0.4 | 0.5 | 0.5 |
| Apparel | ..... | 0.1 | 0.8 | 0.2 | 0.3 | 1.5 | 4.7 | 3.0 | 3.7 | 3.5 |
| Lumber and wood products | ..... | ..... | ..... | ..... | ..... | 0.2 | 0.3 | 0.9 | 1.1 | 0.7 |
| Furniture and fixtures | ..... | ..... | ..... | ..... | ..... | 0.3 | 0.3 | 1.2 | 1.0 | 0.6 |
| Paper products | 1.1 | 0.6 | 0.2 | 0.1 | ..... | 4.1 | 0.5 | 0.5 | 0.9 | 0.5 |
| Printing and publishing | 1.8 | 0.9 | 0.5 | 0.6 | 0.3 | 4.8 | 4.7 | 8.2 | 11.7 | 12.7 |
| Chemical products | 0.4 | 2.2 | 3.1 | 6.2 | 9.9 | 27.9 | 76.6 | 55.7 | 108.4 | 114.5 |
| Refined petroleum products | ..... | ..... | ..... | ..... | ..... | ..... | 0.1 | ..... | 0.3 | ..... |
| Rubber and plastic products | 0.4 | 0.8 | 0.7 | 0.2 | 0.4 | 2.0 | 3.0 | 11.7 | 5.5 | 8.3 |
| Leather products | 0.1 | 0.1 | 0.1 | ..... | 0.2 | 1.2 | 2.0 | 2.1 | 3.2 | 2.6 |
| Stone, clay and glass products | ..... | ..... | ..... | ..... | ..... | 1.3 | 1.0 | 1.3 | 2.0 | 2.4 |
| Primary metals | 4.0 | 5.4 | 3.5 | 5.6 | 4.4 | 292.5 | 495.9 | 193.9 | 91.2 | 63.0 |
| Fabricated metal products | 0.1 | 0.1 | 0.6 | 0.6 | 1.2 | 8.1 | 5.9 | 10.4 | 12.4 | 13.3 |
| Industrial machinery and computers | 31.3 | 19.9 | 15.9 | 20.3 | 14.6 | 23.6 | 38.0 | 116.9 | 209.5 | 163.8 |
| Electric and electronic equipment | 4.1 | 4.4 | 6.3 | 14.8 | 15.2 | 203.2 | 121.4 | 192.4 | 181.1 | 306.2 |
| Transportation equipment | 86.3 | 67.8 | 43.9 | 47.7 | 52.7 | 51.7 | 41.9 | 16.7 | 123.8 | 178.5 |
| Scientific and measuring instruments | 6.1 | 7.5 | 8.5 | 9.5 | 5.6 | 16.8 | 18.4 | 21.4 | 34.9 | 33.9 |
| Miscellaneous manufactures | 2.5 | 3.5 | 2.3 | 2.1 | 2.2 | 11.8 | 16.9 | 19.8 | 20.3 | 23.2 |
| Unidentified manufactures | 0.3 | 0.2 | 0.1 | 0.2 | 0.5 | 1.0 | 1.2 | 1.5 | 1.7 | 1.4 |
| **Agricultural and livestock products** | ..... | ..... | ..... | ..... | ..... | 0.2 | 0.6 | 0.6 | 4.7 | 17.0 |
| Agricultural products | ..... | ..... | ..... | ..... | ..... | 0.2 | 0.6 | 0.6 | 4.5 | 17.0 |
| Livestock and livestock products | ..... | ..... | ..... | ..... | ..... | ..... | ..... | ..... | 0.2 | ..... |
| **Other commodities** | 0.6 | 2.4 | 1.0 | 3.1 | 5.9 | 209.3 | 230.4 | 299.0 | 221.0 | 173.1 |
| Forestry products | ..... | ..... | ..... | ..... | ..... | ..... | ..... | 0.2 | ..... | 0.4 |
| Fish and other marine products | ..... | ..... | ..... | ..... | ..... | 1.4 | 1.5 | 2.8 | 6.0 | 5.2 |
| Metallic ores and concentrates | ..... | 1.4 | ..... | 0.5 | 1.9 | 139.3 | 160.4 | 211.7 | 93.5 | 72.7 |
| Bituminous coal and lignite | ..... | ..... | ..... | ..... | ..... | 64.3 | 66.2 | 79.4 | 107.3 | 86.1 |
| Crude petroleum and natural gas | ..... | ..... | ..... | ..... | ..... | ..... | ..... | ..... | ..... | ..... |
| Nonmetallic minerals | 0.4 | 0.9 | 0.9 | 0.4 | 0.3 | 0.9 | 1.1 | 2.2 | 2.8 | 1.4 |
| Scrap and waste | ..... | ..... | ..... | ..... | ..... | 1.8 | ..... | 0.1 | 0.1 | ..... |
| Used merchandise | 0.2 | ..... | ..... | ..... | ..... | 0.8 | 0.3 | 2.1 | 2.1 | 4.4 |
| Goods imported and returned unchanged | ..... | ..... | ..... | ..... | ..... | ..... | ..... | ..... | ..... | ..... |
| Special classification provisions | ..... | 0.1 | ..... | 2.2 | 3.6 | 0.9 | 0.8 | 0.6 | 9.1 | 2.9 |

## Table D-3.  State Exports of Goods by Destination and Industry, 1993–1997 —*Continued*

**UTAH** (Millions of dollars.)

| Industry | 1993 | 1994 | 1995 | 1996 | 1997 | 1993 | 1994 | 1995 | 1996 | 1997 |
|---|---|---|---|---|---|---|---|---|---|---|
| | Japan | | | | | South Korea | | | | |
| **ALL GOODS** | 244.0 | 296.1 | 404.8 | 468.9 | 516.8 | 59.5 | 89.6 | 159.4 | 140.7 | 107.1 |
| **Manufactured goods** | 132.3 | 143.8 | 196.4 | 297.2 | 400.6 | 38.8 | 65.0 | 139.5 | 135.2 | 74.5 |
| Food products | 2.7 | 2.9 | 11.4 | 25.9 | 53.4 | 6.8 | 5.0 | 7.1 | 7.7 | 7.4 |
| Tobacco products | ..... | ..... | ..... | ..... | ..... | ..... | ..... | ..... | ..... | ..... |
| Textile mill products | 0.1 | 0.1 | 0.2 | ..... | 0.1 | ..... | 0.1 | ..... | ..... | 0.1 |
| Apparel | 1.4 | 4.6 | 2.8 | 2.7 | 2.5 | ..... | ..... | 0.1 | 0.6 | 0.6 |
| Lumber and wood products | 0.1 | 0.3 | 0.9 | 0.7 | 0.6 | ..... | ..... | ..... | 0.3 | ..... |
| Furniture and fixtures | 0.2 | 0.2 | 0.5 | 0.4 | 0.1 | ..... | 0.1 | ..... | 0.1 | ..... |
| Paper products | 3.8 | 0.3 | 0.3 | 0.3 | 0.1 | ..... | ..... | 0.1 | ..... | ..... |
| Printing and publishing | 1.7 | 1.7 | 3.7 | 7.2 | 8.3 | 0.3 | 0.2 | 0.9 | 0.1 | 0.4 |
| Chemical products | 14.5 | 42.3 | 26.7 | 37.9 | 67.0 | 0.8 | 0.9 | 1.5 | 36.6 | 13.0 |
| Refined petroleum products | ..... | ..... | ..... | ..... | ..... | ..... | ..... | ..... | ..... | ..... |
| Rubber and plastic products | 1.1 | 1.6 | 1.9 | 2.2 | 3.7 | 0.1 | 0.1 | 0.6 | 0.4 | 0.3 |
| Leather products | 0.9 | 1.3 | 1.6 | 2.2 | 1.4 | ..... | 0.1 | 0.1 | 0.1 | 0.3 |
| Stone, clay and glass products | 0.7 | 0.8 | 0.4 | 0.3 | 0.4 | ..... | ..... | ..... | 0.1 | 0.2 |
| Primary metals | 23.5 | 13.3 | 70.2 | 10.3 | 16.2 | 0.1 | 4.0 | 24.0 | 36.0 | 8.6 |
| Fabricated metal products | 5.9 | 0.5 | 2.1 | 0.7 | 3.0 | 0.4 | 0.3 | 1.2 | 1.8 | 2.0 |
| Industrial machinery and computers | 9.5 | 13.8 | 24.3 | 35.2 | 21.5 | 1.1 | 2.5 | 7.8 | 6.8 | 3.1 |
| Electric and electronic equipment | 4.2 | 7.3 | 19.2 | 30.9 | 37.5 | 23.8 | 45.1 | 87.0 | 29.1 | 14.4 |
| Transportation equipment | 49.7 | 37.4 | 8.3 | 111.4 | 157.7 | ..... | 0.2 | 2.7 | 7.3 | 14.0 |
| Scientific and measuring instruments | 7.4 | 9.1 | 11.8 | 21.0 | 17.2 | 3.5 | 3.1 | 4.3 | 4.0 | 4.2 |
| Miscellaneous manufactures | 4.4 | 6.1 | 9.7 | 7.6 | 9.7 | 1.6 | 3.3 | 1.9 | 3.9 | 5.6 |
| Unidentified manufactures | 0.5 | 0.4 | 0.5 | 0.2 | 0.2 | 0.1 | 0.1 | 0.1 | 0.1 | 0.2 |
| **Agricultural and livestock products** | 0.1 | 0.1 | 0.2 | 0.1 | 0.4 | ..... | 0.1 | 0.1 | 0.7 | ..... |
| Agricultural products | 0.1 | 0.1 | 0.2 | 0.1 | 0.4 | ..... | 0.1 | 0.1 | 0.7 | ..... |
| Livestock and livestock products | ..... | ..... | ..... | ..... | ..... | ..... | ..... | ..... | ..... | ..... |
| **Other commodities** | 111.7 | 152.1 | 208.2 | 171.6 | 115.7 | 20.7 | 24.5 | 19.8 | 4.8 | 32.6 |
| Forestry products | ..... | ..... | 0.1 | ..... | 0.1 | ..... | ..... | ..... | ..... | ..... |
| Fish and other marine products | 0.2 | 0.1 | ..... | 0.2 | 0.7 | ..... | ..... | ..... | 0.6 | 0.2 |
| Metallic ores and concentrates | 78.0 | 106.1 | 143.5 | 83.7 | 49.4 | 20.4 | 24.2 | 19.3 | 3.6 | 23.1 |
| Bituminous coal and lignite | 31.8 | 44.8 | 61.9 | 80.1 | 58.9 | ..... | ..... | ..... | ..... | 8.8 |
| Crude petroleum and natural gas | ..... | ..... | ..... | ..... | ..... | ..... | ..... | ..... | ..... | ..... |
| Nonmetallic minerals | 0.4 | 0.4 | 0.3 | 0.3 | 0.5 | 0.2 | 0.2 | 0.4 | 0.5 | 0.4 |
| Scrap and waste | ..... | ..... | ..... | ..... | ..... | ..... | ..... | ..... | ..... | ..... |
| Used merchandise | 0.8 | 0.3 | 2.0 | 2.0 | 4.4 | ..... | ..... | ..... | ..... | ..... |
| Goods imported and returned unchanged | ..... | ..... | ..... | ..... | ..... | ..... | ..... | ..... | ..... | ..... |
| Special classification provisions | 0.5 | 0.5 | 0.3 | 5.2 | 1.7 | 0.1 | ..... | 0.1 | 0.1 | 0.1 |
| | Taiwan | | | | | Singapore | | | | |
| **ALL GOODS** | 194.7 | 172.6 | 144.9 | 138.8 | 112.7 | 47.4 | 24.1 | 82.5 | 131.9 | 64.6 |
| **Manufactured goods** | 143.3 | 150.5 | 127.1 | 108.8 | 87.8 | 45.4 | 23.7 | 80.8 | 129.4 | 63.8 |
| Food products | 6.9 | 7.8 | 10.8 | 10.8 | 7.8 | 0.3 | 0.4 | 1.7 | 1.6 | 1.3 |
| Tobacco products | ..... | ..... | ..... | ..... | ..... | ..... | ..... | ..... | ..... | ..... |
| Textile mill products | ..... | ..... | ..... | ..... | ..... | ..... | ..... | ..... | ..... | ..... |
| Apparel | ..... | ..... | ..... | 0.1 | ..... | ..... | ..... | ..... | ..... | 0.1 |
| Lumber and wood products | 0.1 | ..... | ..... | ..... | ..... | ..... | ..... | ..... | ..... | ..... |
| Furniture and fixtures | ..... | ..... | ..... | 0.3 | 0.1 | 0.1 | ..... | 0.4 | 0.1 | 0.1 |
| Paper products | 0.1 | ..... | ..... | ..... | ..... | 0.1 | 0.1 | 0.1 | 0.2 | 0.1 |
| Printing and publishing | 0.6 | 1.0 | 2.4 | 1.8 | 1.9 | 0.6 | 0.9 | 0.5 | 0.7 | 0.6 |
| Chemical products | 10.9 | 28.7 | 20.3 | 25.8 | 19.2 | 0.4 | 0.6 | 1.1 | 2.9 | 3.7 |
| Refined petroleum products | ..... | 0.1 | ..... | ..... | ..... | ..... | ..... | ..... | ..... | ..... |
| Rubber and plastic products | 0.3 | 0.7 | 7.4 | 1.6 | 1.9 | 0.2 | 0.2 | 0.8 | ..... | 0.1 |
| Leather products | 0.1 | 0.3 | 0.2 | 0.6 | 0.4 | 0.1 | ..... | ..... | ..... | 0.3 |
| Stone, clay and glass products | ..... | ..... | 0.5 | 1.5 | 0.1 | 0.4 | 0.2 | ..... | ..... | ..... |
| Primary metals | 108.4 | 96.8 | 59.1 | 27.2 | 22.0 | 3.0 | 8.4 | 7.3 | 2.6 | 1.6 |
| Fabricated metal products | 0.4 | 1.1 | 2.9 | 2.2 | 2.1 | 0.3 | 0.8 | 0.2 | 0.4 | 0.9 |
| Industrial machinery and computers | 3.4 | 2.6 | 9.0 | 17.3 | 11.9 | 3.8 | 4.7 | 52.5 | 96.7 | 30.7 |
| Electric and electronic equipment | 8.1 | 5.1 | 7.3 | 15.6 | 15.3 | 32.7 | 4.4 | 12.9 | 21.5 | 20.5 |
| Transportation equipment | 0.5 | 2.7 | 3.7 | 1.1 | 1.8 | ..... | 0.4 | 0.8 | 0.3 | 1.0 |
| Scientific and measuring instruments | 2.2 | 1.7 | 1.5 | 1.4 | 1.6 | 1.3 | 1.2 | 1.1 | 1.0 | 1.5 |
| Miscellaneous manufactures | 1.1 | 1.5 | 1.5 | 1.4 | 1.4 | 2.0 | 1.2 | 1.1 | 1.0 | 1.1 |
| Unidentified manufactures | 0.1 | 0.2 | 0.2 | 0.2 | 0.3 | 0.1 | 0.1 | 0.1 | 0.3 | 0.2 |
| **Agricultural and livestock products** | ..... | 0.3 | ..... | 1.6 | 6.1 | ..... | ..... | ..... | ..... | ..... |
| Agricultural products | ..... | 0.3 | ..... | 1.6 | 6.1 | ..... | ..... | ..... | ..... | ..... |
| Livestock and livestock products | ..... | ..... | ..... | ..... | ..... | ..... | ..... | ..... | ..... | ..... |
| **Other commodities** | 51.4 | 21.8 | 17.8 | 28.4 | 18.9 | 2.0 | 0.4 | 1.7 | 2.5 | 0.8 |
| Forestry products | ..... | ..... | ..... | ..... | ..... | ..... | ..... | ..... | ..... | ..... |
| Fish and other marine products | 0.2 | 0.2 | 0.1 | 0.2 | 0.1 | ..... | ..... | 0.4 | 0.4 | 0.3 |
| Metallic ores and concentrates | 18.6 | ..... | 0.1 | ..... | ..... | ..... | ..... | ..... | ..... | ..... |
| Bituminous coal and lignite | 32.5 | 21.4 | 17.5 | 27.2 | 18.4 | ..... | ..... | ..... | ..... | ..... |
| Crude petroleum and natural gas | ..... | ..... | ..... | ..... | ..... | ..... | ..... | ..... | ..... | ..... |
| Nonmetallic minerals | ..... | ..... | ..... | ..... | ..... | 0.1 | 0.3 | 1.2 | 0.5 | 0.1 |
| Scrap and waste | ..... | ..... | ..... | ..... | ..... | 1.8 | ..... | ..... | ..... | ..... |
| Used merchandise | ..... | ..... | ..... | ..... | ..... | ..... | ..... | ..... | ..... | ..... |
| Goods imported and returned unchanged | ..... | ..... | ..... | ..... | ..... | ..... | ..... | ..... | ..... | ..... |
| Special classification provisions | ..... | 0.1 | 0.1 | 0.9 | 0.4 | ..... | ..... | ..... | 1.6 | 0.3 |

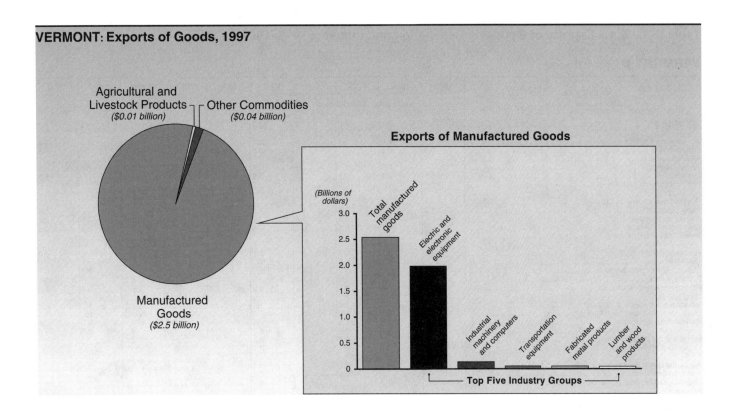

**VERMONT: Exports of Goods, 1997**

Agricultural and Livestock Products ($0.01 billion)

Other Commodities ($0.04 billion)

Manufactured Goods ($2.5 billion)

**Exports of Manufactured Goods**

(Billions of dollars)

Top Five Industry Groups

---

## Table D-3.  State Exports of Goods by Destination and Industry, 1993–1997 —*Continued*

**VERMONT** (Millions of dollars.)

| Industry | 1993 | 1994 | 1995 | 1996 | 1997 | 1993 | 1994 | 1995 | 1996 | 1997 |
|---|---|---|---|---|---|---|---|---|---|---|
| | All destinations | | | | | Canada | | | | |
| **ALL GOODS** | 2 276.0 | 2 304.3 | 2 683.6 | 2 610.8 | 2 592.1 | 2 075.2 | 2 064.5 | 2 509.9 | 2 377.6 | 2 310.3 |
| **Manufactured goods** | 2 171.9 | 2 210.9 | 2 625.7 | 2 534.7 | 2 538.0 | 1 980.0 | 1 983.5 | 2 461.1 | 2 314.0 | 2 266.6 |
| Food products | 9.8 | 12.0 | 11.6 | 14.6 | 24.6 | 7.1 | 8.6 | 7.9 | 10.3 | 19.5 |
| Tobacco products | ..... | ..... | ..... | ..... | ..... | ..... | ..... | ..... | ..... | ..... |
| Textile mill products | 5.5 | 9.4 | 11.7 | 14.2 | 12.5 | 2.0 | 4.1 | 3.1 | 3.2 | 4.2 |
| Apparel | 6.4 | 4.9 | 5.2 | 14.1 | 18.4 | 4.5 | 3.4 | 3.3 | 6.3 | 6.7 |
| Lumber and wood products | 30.7 | 29.7 | 34.8 | 35.8 | 43.9 | 27.9 | 26.4 | 31.5 | 32.9 | 41.1 |
| Furniture and fixtures | 6.3 | 4.4 | 2.5 | 1.3 | 1.4 | 0.9 | 0.7 | 1.0 | 0.6 | 0.9 |
| Paper products | 21.0 | 26.7 | 35.4 | 35.0 | 41.7 | 14.8 | 18.2 | 26.5 | 28.0 | 30.7 |
| Printing and publishing | 9.5 | 6.9 | 7.3 | 8.9 | 7.2 | 5.1 | 4.5 | 5.2 | 5.4 | 4.0 |
| Chemical products | 22.1 | 27.1 | 27.5 | 34.8 | 35.4 | 16.4 | 21.3 | 21.9 | 26.2 | 27.3 |
| Refined petroleum products | 0.2 | 0.2 | 0.2 | 0.9 | 0.1 | 0.1 | 0.2 | 0.2 | 0.9 | 0.1 |
| Rubber and plastic products | 21.5 | 16.7 | 18.3 | 18.1 | 19.7 | 16.5 | 10.6 | 12.7 | 11.0 | 10.5 |
| Leather products | 1.4 | 1.9 | 5.2 | 5.0 | 3.6 | 0.7 | 0.6 | 2.1 | 1.8 | 2.2 |
| Stone, clay and glass products | 4.6 | 4.0 | 4.6 | 5.0 | 4.6 | 3.5 | 3.0 | 3.1 | 2.7 | 3.8 |
| Primary metals | 8.9 | 5.8 | 6.8 | 8.9 | 11.1 | 2.6 | 1.9 | 2.6 | 3.3 | 5.4 |
| Fabricated metal products | 54.5 | 50.5 | 25.8 | 59.0 | 51.2 | 14.5 | 18.0 | 17.9 | 22.9 | 22.8 |
| Industrial machinery and computers | 134.7 | 144.8 | 136.0 | 121.4 | 138.0 | 82.4 | 82.4 | 99.5 | 78.0 | 73.6 |
| Electric and electronic equipment | 1 734.4 | 1 775.2 | 2 202.3 | 2 055.7 | 1 983.1 | 1 718.2 | 1 738.7 | 2 181.1 | 2 037.8 | 1 951.9 |
| Transportation equipment | 42.4 | 28.7 | 27.6 | 37.8 | 54.3 | 36.7 | 19.0 | 20.9 | 22.4 | 38.3 |
| Scientific and measuring instruments | 36.9 | 35.7 | 29.0 | 33.0 | 42.7 | 19.6 | 15.3 | 11.0 | 12.2 | 14.9 |
| Miscellaneous manufactures | 18.5 | 22.4 | 31.1 | 28.6 | 41.8 | 5.6 | 5.7 | 8.5 | 7.0 | 7.6 |
| Unidentified manufactures | 2.8 | 3.9 | 2.7 | 2.6 | 2.6 | 0.9 | 0.8 | 1.1 | 1.1 | 1.2 |
| **Agricultural and livestock products** | 8.6 | 12.7 | 10.5 | 12.3 | 9.4 | 7.4 | 9.2 | 8.6 | 6.5 | 6.2 |
| Agricultural products | 2.0 | 0.9 | 1.0 | 3.3 | 2.2 | 1.8 | 0.4 | 0.6 | 0.6 | 0.6 |
| Livestock and livestock products | 6.6 | 11.8 | 9.5 | 9.1 | 7.2 | 5.6 | 8.8 | 7.9 | 5.9 | 5.7 |
| **Other commodities** | 95.5 | 80.7 | 47.4 | 63.8 | 44.7 | 87.9 | 71.7 | 40.2 | 57.1 | 37.5 |
| Forestry products | 0.3 | 0.3 | 0.2 | 1.2 | 2.5 | 0.1 | ..... | 0.1 | 0.1 | 0.4 |
| Fish and other marine products | 0.3 | 0.7 | 1.0 | 0.8 | 1.1 | 0.2 | 0.7 | 1.0 | 0.8 | 1.1 |
| Metallic ores and concentrates | ..... | ..... | 0.1 | ..... | ..... | ..... | ..... | ..... | ..... | ..... |
| Bituminous coal and lignite | ..... | ..... | ..... | ..... | ..... | ..... | ..... | ..... | ..... | ..... |
| Crude petroleum and natural gas | ..... | ..... | ..... | ..... | ..... | ..... | ..... | ..... | ..... | ..... |
| Nonmetallic minerals | 15.4 | 14.3 | 14.1 | 10.9 | 11.3 | 9.2 | 7.4 | 8.8 | 7.0 | 8.1 |
| Scrap and waste | 2.0 | 2.6 | 5.6 | 2.2 | 2.5 | 1.7 | 2.3 | 5.1 | 2.1 | 2.3 |
| Used merchandise | 1.0 | 1.0 | 2.2 | 1.5 | 1.9 | 0.4 | 0.2 | 1.8 | 0.7 | 1.3 |
| Goods imported and returned unchanged | 75.5 | 60.0 | 22.3 | 44.2 | 22.3 | 75.5 | 60.0 | 22.3 | 44.2 | 22.3 |
| Special classification provisions | 0.9 | 1.8 | 1.8 | 3.0 | 3.1 | 0.8 | 1.1 | 1.2 | 2.3 | 2.0 |

## Table D-3.  State Exports of Goods by Destination and Industry, 1993–1997 —*Continued*

**VERMONT** (Millions of dollars.)

| Industry | 1993 | 1994 | 1995 | 1996 | 1997 | 1993 | 1994 | 1995 | 1996 | 1997 |
|---|---|---|---|---|---|---|---|---|---|---|
| | South and Central America and Caribbean | | | | | Mexico | | | | |
| **ALL GOODS** | 8.5 | 8.1 | 10.0 | 16.8 | 22.8 | 12.2 | 15.9 | 10.4 | 8.5 | 8.7 |
| **Manufactured goods** | 8.2 | 8.0 | 9.7 | 16.5 | 22.4 | 11.9 | 15.1 | 10.3 | 8.3 | 8.6 |
| Food products | 0.8 | 0.2 | ..... | 0.1 | 0.1 | 0.2 | 0.1 | 0.1 | 0.2 | 0.5 |
| Tobacco products | ..... | ..... | ..... | ..... | ..... | ..... | ..... | ..... | ..... | ..... |
| Textile mill products | ..... | 0.6 | ..... | 0.5 | 0.6 | 0.2 | 0.2 | 0.3 | 0.5 | 0.2 |
| Apparel | 0.1 | 0.1 | 0.1 | 5.1 | 9.9 | ..... | ..... | ..... | ..... | 0.1 |
| Lumber and wood products | 0.1 | ..... | 0.1 | ..... | ..... | ..... | ..... | 0.1 | 0.1 | ..... |
| Furniture and fixtures | 0.1 | ..... | ..... | ..... | ..... | ..... | ..... | ..... | ..... | ..... |
| Paper products | 1.2 | 1.7 | 2.4 | 1.5 | 1.8 | 2.2 | 3.0 | 1.8 | 2.0 | 2.4 |
| Printing and publishing | 0.5 | 0.3 | 0.3 | 1.4 | 0.4 | 1.6 | 0.5 | 0.3 | 0.6 | 0.9 |
| Chemical products | 0.2 | 0.4 | 0.2 | 0.7 | 0.5 | 0.3 | 0.3 | 0.2 | 0.3 | 0.5 |
| Refined petroleum products | 0.1 | ..... | ..... | ..... | ..... | ..... | ..... | ..... | ..... | ..... |
| Rubber and plastic products | 0.2 | 0.1 | 0.2 | ..... | 0.3 | 0.2 | 0.4 | 0.4 | 0.2 | 0.2 |
| Leather products | ..... | 0.2 | 0.2 | ..... | ..... | ..... | ..... | ..... | 0.1 | ..... |
| Stone, clay and glass products | 0.1 | 0.1 | ..... | 0.1 | 0.1 | 0.1 | 0.2 | 0.1 | 0.2 | 0.1 |
| Primary metals | 0.5 | 0.4 | 0.8 | 1.1 | 0.8 | 3.1 | 0.9 | 0.2 | 0.6 | 0.5 |
| Fabricated metal products | 0.2 | 0.1 | 0.8 | 0.5 | 3.2 | 0.1 | 0.2 | 0.1 | 0.4 | 0.3 |
| Industrial machinery and computers | 2.5 | 1.0 | 1.4 | 2.5 | 2.6 | 0.5 | 2.6 | 0.9 | 1.1 | 0.9 |
| Electric and electronic equipment | 0.5 | 1.3 | 1.8 | 0.7 | 0.8 | 2.3 | 5.6 | 5.2 | 0.9 | 1.6 |
| Transportation equipment | 0.4 | 0.9 | 0.2 | 1.2 | 0.4 | 0.1 | 0.1 | ..... | 0.7 | 0.1 |
| Scientific and measuring instruments | 0.7 | 0.4 | 0.8 | 0.7 | 0.6 | 0.8 | 1.0 | 0.5 | 0.4 | 0.2 |
| Miscellaneous manufactures | 0.1 | 0.1 | 0.3 | 0.2 | 0.3 | 0.2 | ..... | 0.1 | ..... | ..... |
| Unidentified manufactures | 0.1 | ..... | 0.1 | 0.1 | 0.1 | ..... | 0.1 | ..... | ..... | ..... |
| **Agricultural and livestock products** | ..... | 0.1 | 0.2 | 0.2 | 0.3 | 0.2 | 0.8 | ..... | 0.1 | ..... |
| Agricultural products | ..... | ..... | 0.1 | 0.2 | 0.1 | ..... | ..... | ..... | 0.1 | ..... |
| Livestock and livestock products | ..... | 0.1 | 0.1 | ..... | 0.2 | 0.2 | 0.8 | ..... | ..... | ..... |
| **Other commodities** | 0.3 | ..... | 0.1 | 0.2 | 0.1 | 0.1 | ..... | 0.1 | 0.1 | 0.1 |
| Forestry products | ..... | ..... | ..... | ..... | ..... | ..... | ..... | ..... | ..... | ..... |
| Fish and other marine products | ..... | ..... | ..... | ..... | ..... | 0.1 | ..... | ..... | ..... | ..... |
| Metallic ores and concentrates | ..... | ..... | ..... | ..... | ..... | ..... | ..... | ..... | ..... | ..... |
| Bituminous coal and lignite | ..... | ..... | ..... | ..... | ..... | ..... | ..... | ..... | ..... | ..... |
| Crude petroleum and natural gas | ..... | ..... | ..... | ..... | ..... | ..... | ..... | ..... | ..... | ..... |
| Nonmetallic minerals | ..... | ..... | ..... | 0.2 | ..... | ..... | ..... | ..... | ..... | ..... |
| Scrap and waste | 0.2 | ..... | ..... | ..... | ..... | ..... | ..... | ..... | ..... | ..... |
| Used merchandise | ..... | ..... | ..... | ..... | 0.1 | ..... | ..... | ..... | ..... | ..... |
| Goods imported and returned unchanged | ..... | ..... | ..... | ..... | ..... | ..... | ..... | ..... | ..... | ..... |
| Special classification provisions | ..... | ..... | 0.1 | 0.1 | ..... | ..... | ..... | ..... | ..... | ..... |
| | European Union | | | | | United Kingdom | | | | |
| **ALL GOODS** | 75.6 | 123.7 | 73.9 | 96.6 | 136.6 | 28.0 | 29.5 | 29.7 | 32.8 | 49.1 |
| **Manufactured goods** | 72.5 | 120.5 | 71.2 | 90.9 | 133.3 | 27.9 | 29.3 | 29.3 | 32.5 | 48.8 |
| Food products | 0.1 | 2.0 | 2.4 | 2.8 | 3.4 | 0.1 | 1.8 | 2.1 | 2.2 | 3.0 |
| Tobacco products | ..... | ..... | ..... | ..... | ..... | ..... | ..... | ..... | ..... | ..... |
| Textile mill products | 0.7 | 0.8 | 0.7 | 0.6 | 1.6 | ..... | ..... | 0.1 | 0.1 | 0.1 |
| Apparel | 1.1 | 1.0 | 1.4 | 1.9 | 1.0 | 0.2 | 0.3 | 0.5 | 0.4 | 0.4 |
| Lumber and wood products | 1.5 | 1.8 | 1.7 | 1.4 | 1.8 | 0.8 | 1.2 | 0.9 | 1.2 | 1.4 |
| Furniture and fixtures | 5.3 | 3.6 | 1.3 | 0.1 | 0.2 | 5.2 | 3.5 | 1.3 | 0.1 | 0.2 |
| Paper products | 1.0 | 0.9 | 1.0 | 1.0 | 1.3 | 0.1 | 0.2 | 0.2 | ..... | 0.2 |
| Printing and publishing | 1.1 | 0.6 | 0.5 | 1.0 | 1.4 | 0.8 | 0.4 | 0.4 | 0.6 | 1.0 |
| Chemical products | 3.1 | 3.3 | 3.2 | 4.8 | 5.5 | 2.0 | 2.0 | 2.2 | 2.7 | 2.9 |
| Refined petroleum products | ..... | ..... | ..... | ..... | ..... | ..... | ..... | ..... | ..... | ..... |
| Rubber and plastic products | 2.5 | 2.9 | 3.2 | 5.5 | 7.0 | 0.9 | 1.4 | 1.9 | 3.1 | 4.8 |
| Leather products | 0.4 | 0.5 | 1.9 | 1.9 | 0.8 | 0.1 | 0.1 | 0.5 | 0.3 | 0.3 |
| Stone, clay and glass products | 0.5 | 0.4 | 0.5 | 0.5 | 0.4 | 0.4 | 0.1 | 0.3 | 0.3 | 0.2 |
| Primary metals | 1.1 | 1.2 | 0.5 | 2.3 | 1.6 | 0.4 | 0.5 | 0.5 | 1.6 | 0.9 |
| Fabricated metal products | 6.0 | 19.7 | 3.0 | 14.1 | 9.2 | 0.7 | 0.9 | 1.1 | 3.3 | 5.4 |
| Industrial machinery and computers | 24.2 | 39.8 | 16.8 | 15.7 | 38.6 | 8.2 | 6.6 | 9.5 | 6.0 | 15.0 |
| Electric and electronic equipment | 4.5 | 18.9 | 7.0 | 6.0 | 16.2 | 1.5 | 3.5 | 1.5 | 1.9 | 5.5 |
| Transportation equipment | 3.3 | 2.9 | 3.0 | 6.2 | 7.3 | 2.0 | 0.3 | 0.3 | 1.3 | 1.1 |
| Scientific and measuring instruments | 7.1 | 9.9 | 9.6 | 13.4 | 20.4 | 1.8 | 3.5 | 2.5 | 2.7 | 3.3 |
| Miscellaneous manufactures | 8.3 | 9.5 | 11.7 | 11.2 | 15.0 | 2.4 | 2.5 | 3.2 | 4.3 | 2.8 |
| Unidentified manufactures | 0.7 | 0.8 | 0.8 | 0.5 | 0.4 | 0.2 | 0.3 | 0.3 | 0.3 | 0.2 |
| **Agricultural and livestock products** | 0.2 | 0.1 | 0.1 | 2.1 | 1.4 | ..... | ..... | ..... | ..... | 0.1 |
| Agricultural products | 0.1 | ..... | 0.1 | 2.1 | 1.2 | ..... | ..... | ..... | ..... | 0.1 |
| Livestock and livestock products | ..... | ..... | ..... | 0.1 | 0.2 | ..... | ..... | ..... | ..... | ..... |
| **Other commodities** | 2.9 | 3.1 | 2.5 | 3.6 | 1.9 | 0.1 | 0.2 | 0.4 | 0.3 | 0.2 |
| Forestry products | ..... | ..... | ..... | ..... | ..... | ..... | ..... | ..... | ..... | ..... |
| Fish and other marine products | ..... | ..... | ..... | ..... | ..... | ..... | ..... | ..... | ..... | ..... |
| Metallic ores and concentrates | ..... | ..... | ..... | ..... | ..... | ..... | ..... | ..... | ..... | ..... |
| Bituminous coal and lignite | ..... | ..... | ..... | ..... | ..... | ..... | ..... | ..... | ..... | ..... |
| Crude petroleum and natural gas | ..... | ..... | ..... | ..... | ..... | ..... | ..... | ..... | ..... | ..... |
| Nonmetallic minerals | 2.3 | 2.4 | 1.7 | 2.8 | 1.6 | ..... | ..... | ..... | ..... | 0.1 |
| Scrap and waste | 0.1 | 0.2 | 0.3 | ..... | ..... | 0.1 | 0.1 | 0.1 | ..... | ..... |
| Used merchandise | 0.5 | 0.5 | 0.4 | 0.6 | 0.2 | ..... | 0.1 | 0.3 | 0.3 | 0.1 |
| Goods imported and returned unchanged | ..... | ..... | ..... | ..... | ..... | ..... | ..... | ..... | ..... | ..... |
| Special classification provisions | ..... | 0.1 | 0.1 | 0.2 | 0.1 | ..... | ..... | ..... | ..... | ..... |

# Table D-3. State Exports of Goods by Destination and Industry, 1993–1997 —Continued

## VERMONT (Millions of dollars.)

| Industry | 1993 | 1994 | 1995 | 1996 | 1997 | 1993 | 1994 | 1995 | 1996 | 1997 |
|---|---|---|---|---|---|---|---|---|---|---|
| | Germany | | | | | France | | | | |
| **ALL GOODS** | 20.6 | 16.4 | 12.0 | 13.5 | 27.8 | 4.1 | 8.4 | 7.1 | 11.3 | 19.7 |
| **Manufactured goods** | 20.5 | 16.3 | 11.7 | 13.0 | 27.4 | 4.0 | 8.3 | 7.0 | 11.2 | 19.6 |
| Food products | ..... | ..... | ..... | 0.1 | 0.1 | ..... | ..... | ..... | 0.1 | ..... |
| Tobacco products | ..... | ..... | ..... | ..... | ..... | ..... | ..... | ..... | ..... | ..... |
| Textile mill products | 0.1 | ..... | 0.2 | 0.2 | 0.2 | ..... | ..... | 0.1 | ..... | 0.2 |
| Apparel | 0.3 | 0.1 | 0.2 | 0.5 | 0.1 | ..... | ..... | 0.1 | ..... | ..... |
| Lumber and wood products | 0.2 | 0.1 | 0.2 | 0.1 | 0.1 | ..... | 0.1 | ..... | 0.1 | ..... |
| Furniture and fixtures | ..... | 0.1 | ..... | ..... | ..... | ..... | ..... | 0.1 | ..... | ..... |
| Paper products | 0.1 | 0.1 | 0.1 | 0.1 | 0.1 | 0.1 | 0.3 | 0.1 | 0.2 | 0.1 |
| Printing and publishing | ..... | ..... | ..... | 0.1 | 0.1 | ..... | ..... | ..... | 0.1 | ..... |
| Chemical products | 0.5 | 0.5 | 0.5 | 0.4 | 1.8 | 0.1 | 0.3 | 0.1 | 0.1 | ..... |
| Refined petroleum products | ..... | ..... | ..... | ..... | ..... | ..... | ..... | ..... | ..... | ..... |
| Rubber and plastic products | 0.4 | 0.4 | 0.3 | 0.4 | 0.4 | 0.3 | 0.4 | 0.2 | 0.3 | 0.6 |
| Leather products | 0.1 | 0.1 | 0.2 | 0.1 | 0.1 | 0.1 | 0.1 | 0.1 | 0.1 | 0.1 |
| Stone, clay and glass products | 0.1 | ..... | ..... | ..... | ..... | ..... | ..... | ..... | ..... | ..... |
| Primary metals | 0.4 | 0.3 | 0.4 | 0.2 | 0.3 | ..... | ..... | ..... | 0.1 | ..... |
| Fabricated metal products | 0.2 | 0.5 | 0.8 | 0.1 | 1.6 | 0.2 | 0.3 | 0.1 | 0.2 | 0.1 |
| Industrial machinery and computers | 12.0 | 6.6 | 2.0 | 3.0 | 8.9 | 1.4 | 2.3 | 1.8 | 1.8 | 4.3 |
| Electric and electronic equipment | 1.7 | 2.7 | 1.6 | 1.2 | 2.0 | 0.3 | 1.0 | 0.6 | 0.7 | 5.2 |
| Transportation equipment | 0.9 | 0.5 | 0.3 | 0.4 | 1.4 | 0.1 | 1.0 | 1.7 | 3.8 | 3.5 |
| Scientific and measuring instruments | 2.8 | 2.9 | 3.0 | 5.4 | 8.7 | 0.4 | 1.6 | 1.2 | 1.8 | 4.5 |
| Miscellaneous manufactures | 0.4 | 1.2 | 1.9 | 0.7 | 1.6 | 0.9 | 1.0 | 0.7 | 1.7 | 0.8 |
| Unidentified manufactures | 0.2 | 0.1 | 0.1 | 0.1 | 0.1 | 0.1 | ..... | 0.1 | ..... | ..... |
| **Agricultural and livestock products** | ..... | ..... | ..... | 0.1 | 0.3 | ..... | ..... | ..... | ..... | 0.2 |
| Agricultural products | ..... | ..... | ..... | 0.1 | 0.3 | ..... | ..... | ..... | ..... | 0.2 |
| Livestock and livestock products | ..... | ..... | ..... | ..... | ..... | ..... | ..... | ..... | ..... | ..... |
| **Other commodities** | 0.1 | 0.1 | 0.3 | 0.4 | 0.1 | 0.1 | 0.1 | 0.1 | 0.1 | ..... |
| Forestry products | ..... | ..... | ..... | ..... | ..... | ..... | ..... | ..... | ..... | ..... |
| Fish and other marine products | ..... | ..... | ..... | ..... | ..... | ..... | ..... | ..... | ..... | ..... |
| Metallic ores and concentrates | ..... | ..... | ..... | ..... | ..... | ..... | ..... | ..... | ..... | ..... |
| Bituminous coal and lignite | ..... | ..... | ..... | ..... | ..... | ..... | ..... | ..... | ..... | ..... |
| Crude petroleum and natural gas | ..... | ..... | ..... | ..... | ..... | ..... | ..... | ..... | ..... | ..... |
| Nonmetallic minerals | 0.1 | ..... | ..... | ..... | ..... | ..... | ..... | ..... | ..... | ..... |
| Scrap and waste | ..... | ..... | 0.2 | ..... | ..... | ..... | ..... | ..... | ..... | ..... |
| Used merchandise | ..... | ..... | ..... | 0.3 | ..... | 0.1 | 0.1 | ..... | ..... | ..... |
| Goods imported and returned unchanged | ..... | ..... | ..... | ..... | ..... | ..... | ..... | ..... | ..... | ..... |
| Special classification provisions | ..... | ..... | ..... | 0.1 | ..... | ..... | ..... | ..... | 0.1 | ..... |
| | The Netherlands | | | | | Asian 10 | | | | |
| **ALL GOODS** | 2.9 | 20.4 | 3.1 | 15.4 | 6.0 | 61.7 | 65.8 | 54.3 | 78.7 | 80.3 |
| **Manufactured goods** | 2.5 | 20.0 | 2.9 | 15.4 | 5.8 | 57.4 | 59.8 | 50.2 | 75.1 | 74.9 |
| Food products | ..... | 0.1 | 0.1 | ..... | 0.2 | 0.3 | 0.4 | 0.7 | 1.0 | 1.0 |
| Tobacco products | ..... | ..... | ..... | ..... | ..... | ..... | ..... | ..... | ..... | ..... |
| Textile mill products | ..... | ..... | ..... | ..... | ..... | 1.8 | 3.1 | 6.9 | 8.8 | 5.1 |
| Apparel | ..... | ..... | 0.2 | 0.1 | ..... | 0.4 | 0.4 | 0.2 | 0.5 | 0.5 |
| Lumber and wood products | 0.1 | 0.1 | ..... | ..... | 0.1 | 0.8 | 1.4 | 1.2 | 1.2 | 0.8 |
| Furniture and fixtures | ..... | ..... | ..... | ..... | ..... | ..... | ..... | ..... | 0.4 | 0.2 |
| Paper products | ..... | ..... | ..... | 0.2 | ..... | 1.3 | 1.7 | 2.2 | 1.4 | 2.4 |
| Printing and publishing | 0.1 | ..... | ..... | ..... | ..... | 0.3 | 0.7 | 0.8 | 0.4 | 0.3 |
| Chemical products | 0.3 | 0.1 | 0.1 | ..... | 0.1 | 1.1 | 1.5 | 1.0 | 1.0 | 0.9 |
| Refined petroleum products | ..... | ..... | ..... | ..... | ..... | ..... | ..... | ..... | ..... | ..... |
| Rubber and plastic products | 0.1 | 0.2 | 0.1 | 0.1 | 0.4 | 1.4 | 1.7 | 0.5 | 0.4 | 0.7 |
| Leather products | 0.1 | ..... | 0.1 | 0.1 | 0.1 | 0.2 | 0.4 | 0.7 | 0.8 | 0.4 |
| Stone, clay and glass products | ..... | 0.1 | ..... | ..... | ..... | 0.4 | 0.3 | 0.8 | 1.6 | 0.2 |
| Primary metals | ..... | ..... | 0.1 | 0.1 | 0.1 | 0.4 | 0.4 | 0.4 | 0.9 | 2.3 |
| Fabricated metal products | 0.5 | 16.6 | 0.1 | 9.8 | 0.1 | 15.0 | 12.0 | 3.0 | 10.5 | 12.2 |
| Industrial machinery and computers | 0.4 | 0.5 | 0.6 | 1.8 | 0.8 | 18.3 | 14.8 | 12.5 | 20.0 | 16.1 |
| Electric and electronic equipment | 0.1 | 0.3 | 0.2 | 0.4 | 0.2 | 7.8 | 7.5 | 4.9 | 7.7 | 9.3 |
| Transportation equipment | 0.1 | 1.0 | 0.1 | 0.4 | 0.8 | 0.9 | 1.8 | 1.7 | 5.9 | 4.2 |
| Scientific and measuring instruments | 0.4 | 0.7 | 0.8 | 1.4 | 1.2 | 3.4 | 5.2 | 4.2 | 3.9 | 3.6 |
| Miscellaneous manufactures | 0.3 | 0.3 | 0.4 | 0.7 | 1.7 | 2.9 | 4.8 | 8.1 | 8.3 | 14.0 |
| Unidentified manufactures | ..... | 0.1 | 0.1 | ..... | ..... | 0.6 | 1.9 | 0.4 | 0.6 | 0.7 |
| **Agricultural and livestock products** | ..... | ..... | ..... | ..... | 0.2 | 0.1 | 0.3 | ..... | 1.1 | 0.4 |
| Agricultural products | ..... | ..... | ..... | ..... | 0.2 | ..... | 0.2 | ..... | 0.1 | 0.1 |
| Livestock and livestock products | ..... | ..... | ..... | ..... | ..... | 0.1 | 0.1 | ..... | 1.0 | 0.3 |
| **Other commodities** | 0.4 | 0.3 | 0.1 | ..... | ..... | 4.2 | 5.7 | 4.1 | 2.4 | 5.0 |
| Forestry products | ..... | ..... | ..... | ..... | ..... | 0.2 | 0.3 | 0.2 | 1.0 | 2.0 |
| Fish and other marine products | ..... | ..... | ..... | ..... | ..... | ..... | ..... | ..... | ..... | ..... |
| Metallic ores and concentrates | ..... | ..... | ..... | ..... | ..... | ..... | ..... | 0.1 | ..... | ..... |
| Bituminous coal and lignite | ..... | ..... | ..... | ..... | ..... | ..... | ..... | ..... | ..... | ..... |
| Crude petroleum and natural gas | ..... | ..... | ..... | ..... | ..... | ..... | ..... | ..... | ..... | ..... |
| Nonmetallic minerals | ..... | ..... | ..... | ..... | ..... | 3.9 | 4.5 | 3.3 | 0.9 | 1.5 |
| Scrap and waste | ..... | ..... | ..... | ..... | ..... | ..... | ..... | 0.1 | ..... | 0.2 |
| Used merchandise | 0.4 | 0.3 | ..... | ..... | ..... | ..... | 0.4 | 0.1 | 0.2 | 0.3 |
| Goods imported and returned unchanged | ..... | ..... | ..... | ..... | ..... | ..... | ..... | 0.5 | 0.4 | 0.3 |
| Special classification provisions | ..... | ..... | 0.1 | ..... | ..... | ..... | ..... | 0.4 | 0.3 | 0.9 |

## Table D-3.  State Exports of Goods by Destination and Industry, 1993–1997 —*Continued*

**VERMONT** (Millions of dollars.)

| Industry | Japan | | | | | South Korea | | | | |
|---|---|---|---|---|---|---|---|---|---|---|
| | 1993 | 1994 | 1995 | 1996 | 1997 | 1993 | 1994 | 1995 | 1996 | 1997 |
| **ALL GOODS** | 12.3 | 18.0 | 26.0 | 33.5 | 31.3 | 14.5 | 5.4 | 5.7 | 9.3 | 17.6 |
| **Manufactured goods** | 8.8 | 14.3 | 22.2 | 31.5 | 29.1 | 14.5 | 5.3 | 5.7 | 9.3 | 17.6 |
| Food products | 0.3 | 0.1 | 0.1 | 0.2 | 0.6 | ..... | ..... | ..... | ..... | 0.1 |
| Tobacco products | ..... | ..... | ..... | ..... | ..... | ..... | ..... | ..... | ..... | ..... |
| Textile mill products | 1.5 | 2.2 | 6.7 | 7.7 | 4.3 | ..... | 0.1 | ..... | 0.8 | 0.3 |
| Apparel | 0.3 | 0.3 | 0.2 | 0.3 | 0.3 | ..... | ..... | ..... | 0.1 | 0.1 |
| Lumber and wood products | ..... | ..... | 0.2 | 0.1 | 0.2 | ..... | ..... | ..... | ..... | ..... |
| Furniture and fixtures | ..... | ..... | ..... | 0.1 | 0.1 | ..... | ..... | ..... | 0.2 | ..... |
| Paper products | ..... | 0.1 | 0.4 | 0.1 | 0.1 | 0.3 | 0.7 | 0.7 | 0.5 | 1.0 |
| Printing and publishing | ..... | 0.1 | 0.6 | 0.2 | 0.1 | 0.2 | ..... | ..... | 0.1 | ..... |
| Chemical products | 0.3 | 0.2 | 0.3 | 0.3 | 0.5 | ..... | ..... | 0.1 | 0.2 | 0.1 |
| Refined petroleum products | ..... | ..... | ..... | ..... | ..... | ..... | ..... | ..... | ..... | ..... |
| Rubber and plastic products | 0.7 | 1.5 | 0.3 | 0.2 | 0.2 | ..... | ..... | 0.1 | ..... | 0.1 |
| Leather products | 0.1 | 0.1 | 0.2 | 0.5 | 0.2 | ..... | ..... | 0.1 | ..... | ..... |
| Stone, clay and glass products | 0.2 | 0.1 | 0.5 | 1.4 | 0.1 | ..... | 0.2 | ..... | ..... | ..... |
| Primary metals | 0.1 | 0.1 | 0.1 | 0.1 | 0.1 | ..... | ..... | 0.1 | 0.2 | 1.2 |
| Fabricated metal products | 0.1 | 0.7 | 0.2 | 0.2 | 0.3 | 10.4 | 0.2 | 0.8 | 1.7 | 9.5 |
| Industrial machinery and computers | 0.8 | 0.8 | 1.5 | 3.7 | 4.5 | 1.0 | 1.8 | 1.7 | 2.8 | 2.0 |
| Electric and electronic equipment | 1.0 | 1.5 | 1.9 | 2.1 | 1.3 | 1.8 | 1.6 | 1.0 | 1.1 | 2.0 |
| Transportation equipment | 0.2 | 0.2 | 0.8 | 5.3 | 1.8 | 0.1 | 0.1 | ..... | 0.1 | 0.4 |
| Scientific and measuring instruments | 1.0 | 1.6 | 1.0 | 1.4 | 1.2 | 0.2 | 0.4 | 0.5 | 1.3 | 0.6 |
| Miscellaneous manufactures | 2.3 | 4.4 | 7.1 | 7.6 | 13.4 | 0.3 | 0.1 | 0.6 | 0.1 | 0.2 |
| Unidentified manufactures | 0.1 | 0.1 | 0.1 | ..... | 0.1 | 0.1 | ..... | ..... | ..... | 0.1 |
| **Agricultural and livestock products** | 0.1 | 0.1 | ..... | 1.1 | 0.4 | ..... | ..... | ..... | ..... | ..... |
| Agricultural products | ..... | ..... | ..... | 0.1 | 0.1 | ..... | ..... | ..... | ..... | ..... |
| Livestock and livestock products | 0.1 | 0.1 | ..... | 1.0 | 0.3 | ..... | ..... | ..... | ..... | ..... |
| **Other commodities** | 3.4 | 3.7 | 3.8 | 1.0 | 1.7 | 0.1 | 0.1 | ..... | ..... | ..... |
| Forestry products | ..... | ..... | ..... | ..... | ..... | ..... | ..... | ..... | ..... | ..... |
| Fish and other marine products | ..... | ..... | ..... | ..... | ..... | ..... | ..... | ..... | ..... | ..... |
| Metallic ores and concentrates | ..... | ..... | 0.1 | ..... | ..... | ..... | ..... | ..... | ..... | ..... |
| Bituminous coal and lignite | ..... | ..... | ..... | ..... | ..... | ..... | ..... | ..... | ..... | ..... |
| Crude petroleum and natural gas | ..... | ..... | ..... | ..... | ..... | ..... | ..... | ..... | ..... | ..... |
| Nonmetallic minerals | 3.4 | 3.6 | 3.3 | 0.7 | 1.4 | 0.1 | ..... | ..... | ..... | ..... |
| Scrap and waste | ..... | ..... | ..... | ..... | ..... | ..... | ..... | ..... | ..... | ..... |
| Used merchandise | ..... | ..... | 0.1 | 0.2 | 0.3 | ..... | ..... | ..... | ..... | ..... |
| Goods imported and returned unchanged | ..... | ..... | ..... | ..... | ..... | ..... | ..... | ..... | ..... | ..... |
| Special classification provisions | ..... | ..... | 0.3 | ..... | ..... | ..... | ..... | ..... | ..... | ..... |

| Industry | Taiwan | | | | | Singapore | | | | |
|---|---|---|---|---|---|---|---|---|---|---|
| | 1993 | 1994 | 1995 | 1996 | 1997 | 1993 | 1994 | 1995 | 1996 | 1997 |
| **ALL GOODS** | 7.7 | 17.0 | 3.4 | 12.1 | 6.3 | 11.1 | 13.2 | 8.5 | 8.1 | 10.5 |
| **Manufactured goods** | 7.7 | 17.0 | 3.4 | 12.1 | 6.3 | 10.9 | 12.6 | 8.5 | 7.5 | 9.0 |
| Food products | ..... | ..... | 0.1 | ..... | ..... | ..... | ..... | ..... | 0.1 | ..... |
| Tobacco products | ..... | ..... | ..... | ..... | ..... | ..... | ..... | ..... | ..... | ..... |
| Textile mill products | 0.1 | 0.3 | 0.1 | 0.1 | 0.1 | ..... | ..... | ..... | ..... | 0.1 |
| Apparel | ..... | ..... | ..... | ..... | ..... | ..... | ..... | ..... | ..... | ..... |
| Lumber and wood products | 0.5 | 1.1 | 0.7 | 0.9 | 0.2 | ..... | ..... | ..... | ..... | ..... |
| Furniture and fixtures | ..... | ..... | ..... | ..... | ..... | ..... | ..... | ..... | ..... | ..... |
| Paper products | 0.4 | 0.2 | ..... | 0.1 | 0.1 | 0.3 | 0.4 | 0.6 | 0.4 | 0.6 |
| Printing and publishing | ..... | 0.4 | ..... | ..... | ..... | ..... | 0.1 | ..... | ..... | 0.1 |
| Chemical products | ..... | ..... | ..... | ..... | 0.1 | 0.7 | 0.1 | ..... | ..... | ..... |
| Refined petroleum products | ..... | ..... | ..... | ..... | ..... | ..... | ..... | ..... | ..... | ..... |
| Rubber and plastic products | ..... | ..... | ..... | 0.1 | 0.1 | 0.6 | ..... | ..... | ..... | ..... |
| Leather products | ..... | ..... | ..... | ..... | ..... | ..... | ..... | ..... | ..... | ..... |
| Stone, clay and glass products | 0.1 | ..... | 0.1 | ..... | 0.1 | ..... | ..... | ..... | ..... | ..... |
| Primary metals | 0.2 | 0.2 | 0.1 | 0.1 | 0.4 | ..... | ..... | 0.1 | ..... | 0.2 |
| Fabricated metal products | 3.6 | 10.6 | 0.7 | 7.5 | 1.9 | 0.2 | ..... | ..... | 0.3 | 0.1 |
| Industrial machinery and computers | 0.2 | 0.6 | 0.3 | 1.4 | 0.6 | 5.1 | 9.7 | 6.8 | 5.6 | 2.2 |
| Electric and electronic equipment | 0.9 | 0.9 | 0.6 | 0.8 | 0.2 | 3.7 | 1.5 | 0.4 | 0.5 | 4.9 |
| Transportation equipment | 0.2 | 0.5 | ..... | 0.3 | 1.8 | ..... | 0.1 | 0.1 | ..... | ..... |
| Scientific and measuring instruments | 0.9 | 0.3 | 0.3 | 0.2 | 0.2 | 0.1 | 0.5 | 0.2 | 0.3 | 0.7 |
| Miscellaneous manufactures | ..... | ..... | 0.1 | ..... | ..... | 0.1 | 0.1 | 0.1 | 0.4 | 0.1 |
| Unidentified manufactures | 0.5 | 1.6 | 0.2 | 0.5 | 0.4 | ..... | ..... | ..... | ..... | ..... |
| **Agricultural and livestock products** | ..... | ..... | ..... | ..... | ..... | ..... | ..... | ..... | ..... | ..... |
| Agricultural products | ..... | ..... | ..... | ..... | ..... | ..... | ..... | ..... | ..... | ..... |
| Livestock and livestock products | ..... | ..... | ..... | ..... | ..... | ..... | ..... | ..... | ..... | ..... |
| **Other commodities** | ..... | ..... | ..... | ..... | 0.1 | 0.2 | 0.7 | ..... | 0.6 | 1.5 |
| Forestry products | ..... | ..... | ..... | ..... | ..... | ..... | ..... | ..... | 0.6 | 1.4 |
| Fish and other marine products | ..... | ..... | ..... | ..... | ..... | ..... | ..... | ..... | ..... | ..... |
| Metallic ores and concentrates | ..... | ..... | ..... | ..... | ..... | ..... | ..... | ..... | ..... | ..... |
| Bituminous coal and lignite | ..... | ..... | ..... | ..... | ..... | ..... | ..... | ..... | ..... | ..... |
| Crude petroleum and natural gas | ..... | ..... | ..... | ..... | ..... | ..... | ..... | ..... | ..... | ..... |
| Nonmetallic minerals | ..... | ..... | ..... | ..... | 0.1 | 0.2 | 0.4 | ..... | ..... | ..... |
| Scrap and waste | ..... | ..... | ..... | ..... | ..... | ..... | ..... | ..... | ..... | ..... |
| Used merchandise | ..... | ..... | ..... | ..... | ..... | ..... | 0.3 | ..... | ..... | ..... |
| Goods imported and returned unchanged | ..... | ..... | ..... | ..... | ..... | ..... | ..... | ..... | ..... | ..... |
| Special classification provisions | ..... | ..... | ..... | ..... | ..... | ..... | ..... | ..... | ..... | ..... |

## VIRGIN ISLANDS: Exports of Goods, 1997

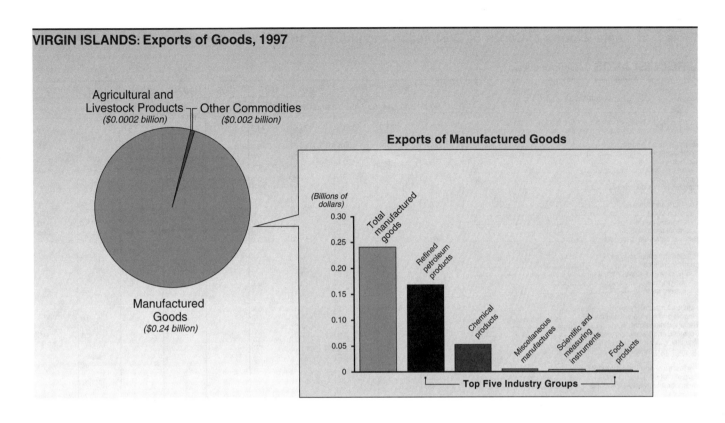

## Table D-3.   State Exports of Goods by Destination and Industry, 1993–1997 —Continued

**VIRGIN ISLANDS** (Millions of dollars.)

| Industry | 1993 | 1994 | 1995 | 1996 | 1997 | 1993 | 1994 | 1995 | 1996 | 1997 |
|---|---|---|---|---|---|---|---|---|---|---|
| | All destinations | | | | | Canada | | | | |
| **ALL GOODS** | 162.1 | 158.0 | 228.6 | 192.4 | 242.7 | 10.1 | 7.5 | 12.4 | 7.4 | 4.3 |
| **Manufactured goods** | 160.5 | 157.6 | 226.9 | 191.1 | 240.8 | 9.7 | 7.3 | 11.9 | 7.1 | 3.2 |
| Food products | 3.9 | 5.6 | 4.2 | 2.0 | 2.4 | 0.7 | 0.5 | 0.3 | 0.3 | 0.3 |
| Tobacco products | 0.3 | 0.4 | 0.6 | ..... | ..... | ..... | ..... | ..... | ..... | ..... |
| Textile mill products | 0.4 | 0.1 | 0.1 | ..... | ..... | ..... | ..... | ..... | ..... | ..... |
| Apparel | 2.6 | 3.5 | 2.3 | 1.3 | 0.3 | ..... | ..... | ..... | ..... | ..... |
| Lumber and wood products | 0.1 | ..... | 0.2 | 0.2 | 0.1 | ..... | ..... | ..... | ..... | ..... |
| Furniture and fixtures | 0.1 | ..... | 0.1 | 0.1 | 0.1 | ..... | ..... | ..... | ..... | 0.1 |
| Paper products | 0.3 | 0.1 | 0.6 | 0.4 | 0.3 | 0.2 | ..... | 0.1 | 0.1 | 0.1 |
| Printing and publishing | 0.9 | 3.8 | 6.4 | 11.7 | 1.6 | ..... | 2.4 | 0.1 | ..... | 0.2 |
| Chemical products | 15.9 | 55.0 | 49.9 | 20.3 | 52.8 | 6.5 | 2.1 | 4.6 | 3.7 | 0.7 |
| Refined petroleum products | 108.0 | 63.9 | 137.1 | 136.5 | 168.1 | ..... | ..... | ..... | 0.2 | ..... |
| Rubber and plastic products | 0.3 | 0.3 | 0.2 | 0.5 | 0.4 | 0.1 | 0.2 | 0.1 | 0.2 | 0.2 |
| Leather products | ..... | 0.4 | 0.1 | 0.1 | 0.1 | ..... | ..... | ..... | ..... | ..... |
| Stone, clay and glass products | 1.0 | 1.3 | 1.1 | 1.0 | 0.8 | ..... | 0.1 | 0.1 | 0.1 | 0.1 |
| Primary metals | 0.4 | 1.5 | 1.3 | 0.4 | 0.6 | ..... | ..... | 0.3 | ..... | ..... |
| Fabricated metal products | 0.6 | 0.3 | 0.4 | 2.0 | 0.1 | ..... | ..... | ..... | ..... | ..... |
| Industrial machinery and computers | 9.6 | 6.5 | 8.0 | 2.5 | 1.9 | 0.4 | 0.8 | 5.3 | 0.6 | 0.5 |
| Electric and electronic equipment | 3.9 | 2.1 | 1.8 | 3.6 | 0.9 | 1.1 | 0.7 | 0.8 | 0.7 | ..... |
| Transportation equipment | 2.1 | 2.0 | 1.1 | 0.7 | 0.9 | 0.3 | 0.3 | 0.1 | ..... | 0.1 |
| Scientific and measuring instruments | 3.2 | 6.5 | 5.2 | 3.5 | 4.1 | 0.1 | 0.1 | ..... | ..... | 0.1 |
| Miscellaneous manufactures | 6.6 | 3.8 | 5.8 | 3.9 | 5.1 | ..... | ..... | ..... | 1.0 | 0.9 |
| Unidentified manufactures | 0.4 | 0.4 | 0.3 | 0.2 | 0.3 | 0.1 | ..... | ..... | 0.1 | ..... |
| **Agricultural and livestock products** | 0.2 | ..... | ..... | ..... | 0.2 | ..... | ..... | ..... | ..... | ..... |
| Agricultural products | ..... | ..... | ..... | ..... | ..... | ..... | ..... | ..... | ..... | ..... |
| Livestock and livestock products | 0.2 | ..... | ..... | ..... | 0.2 | ..... | ..... | ..... | ..... | ..... |
| **Other commodities** | 1.4 | 0.4 | 1.7 | 1.3 | 1.7 | 0.3 | 0.1 | 0.5 | 0.3 | 1.1 |
| Forestry products | ..... | ..... | ..... | ..... | ..... | ..... | ..... | ..... | ..... | ..... |
| Fish and other marine products | ..... | ..... | 0.1 | ..... | 0.1 | ..... | ..... | ..... | ..... | ..... |
| Metallic ores and concentrates | ..... | ..... | ..... | ..... | ..... | ..... | ..... | ..... | ..... | ..... |
| Bituminous coal and lignite | ..... | ..... | ..... | ..... | ..... | ..... | ..... | ..... | ..... | ..... |
| Crude petroleum and natural gas | ..... | ..... | ..... | ..... | ..... | ..... | ..... | ..... | ..... | ..... |
| Nonmetallic minerals | 0.9 | 0.1 | 1.1 | 1.0 | 0.3 | ..... | 0.1 | 0.3 | 0.1 | ..... |
| Scrap and waste | 0.1 | ..... | 0.1 | ..... | ..... | ..... | ..... | ..... | ..... | ..... |
| Used merchandise | 0.2 | 0.2 | 0.2 | 0.1 | 0.1 | 0.1 | ..... | ..... | ..... | ..... |
| Goods imported and returned unchanged | 0.2 | 0.1 | 0.2 | 0.2 | 1.0 | 0.2 | 0.1 | 0.2 | 0.2 | 1.0 |
| Special classification provisions | ..... | ..... | ..... | ..... | 0.1 | ..... | ..... | ..... | ..... | ..... |

## Table D-3.  State Exports of Goods by Destination and Industry, 1993–1997 —Continued

**VIRGIN ISLANDS** (Millions of dollars.)

| Industry | 1993 | 1994 | 1995 | 1996 | 1997 | 1993 | 1994 | 1995 | 1996 | 1997 |
|---|---|---|---|---|---|---|---|---|---|---|
| | South and Central America and Caribbean | | | | | Mexico | | | | |
| **ALL GOODS** | 83.4 | 71.7 | 134.6 | 123.6 | 114.8 | 0.2 | 3.8 | 5.6 | 11.7 | 3.9 |
| **Manufactured goods** | 82.2 | 71.4 | 133.5 | 122.7 | 114.3 | 0.2 | 3.8 | 5.6 | 11.6 | 3.9 |
| Food products | 2.8 | 4.7 | 3.1 | 1.7 | 2.0 | 0.1 | ..... | ..... | ..... | ..... |
| Tobacco products | 0.3 | 0.4 | 0.6 | ..... | ..... | ..... | ..... | ..... | ..... | ..... |
| Textile mill products | ..... | 0.1 | ..... | ..... | ..... | ..... | ..... | ..... | ..... | ..... |
| Apparel | 2.6 | 3.4 | 2.2 | 1.2 | 0.3 | ..... | ..... | ..... | ..... | ..... |
| Lumber and wood products | 0.1 | ..... | 0.1 | 0.1 | 0.1 | ..... | ..... | ..... | ..... | ..... |
| Furniture and fixtures | 0.1 | ..... | ..... | ..... | ..... | ..... | ..... | ..... | ..... | ..... |
| Paper products | 0.1 | 0.1 | 0.5 | 0.1 | ..... | ..... | ..... | ..... | ..... | ..... |
| Printing and publishing | 0.8 | 1.0 | 0.9 | 0.6 | 0.7 | ..... | 0.4 | 5.3 | 11.0 | 0.6 |
| Chemical products | 2.2 | 2.8 | 2.2 | 1.0 | 1.9 | ..... | 3.2 | 0.1 | ..... | 2.5 |
| Refined petroleum products | 61.9 | 46.0 | 112.7 | 110.0 | 100.6 | ..... | ..... | ..... | ..... | ..... |
| Rubber and plastic products | 0.1 | ..... | ..... | 0.2 | ..... | ..... | ..... | ..... | ..... | ..... |
| Leather products | ..... | 0.4 | 0.1 | 0.1 | ..... | ..... | ..... | ..... | ..... | ..... |
| Stone, clay and glass products | 1.0 | 1.2 | 0.9 | 0.8 | 0.7 | ..... | ..... | ..... | ..... | ..... |
| Primary metals | 0.3 | 1.1 | 0.6 | 0.3 | 0.2 | ..... | ..... | 0.1 | ..... | ..... |
| Fabricated metal products | 0.3 | 0.1 | 0.2 | 0.2 | 0.1 | ..... | ..... | ..... | ..... | ..... |
| Industrial machinery and computers | 3.0 | 1.9 | 1.3 | 1.2 | 0.4 | ..... | 0.1 | ..... | ..... | ..... |
| Electric and electronic equipment | 0.7 | 0.5 | 0.1 | 1.1 | 0.2 | ..... | ..... | 0.1 | 0.4 | 0.4 |
| Transportation equipment | 1.5 | 1.4 | 1.1 | 0.6 | 0.7 | ..... | 0.1 | ..... | ..... | ..... |
| Scientific and measuring instruments | 0.4 | 3.4 | 2.9 | 2.0 | 2.8 | ..... | ..... | ..... | 0.1 | 0.3 |
| Miscellaneous manufactures | 3.8 | 2.4 | 3.6 | 1.4 | 3.5 | ..... | ..... | ..... | ..... | ..... |
| Unidentified manufactures | 0.3 | 0.4 | 0.2 | 0.1 | 0.3 | ..... | ..... | ..... | ..... | ..... |
| **Agricultural and livestock products** | 0.2 | ..... | ..... | ..... | ..... | ..... | ..... | ..... | ..... | ..... |
| Agricultural products | ..... | ..... | ..... | ..... | ..... | ..... | ..... | ..... | ..... | ..... |
| Livestock and livestock products | 0.2 | ..... | ..... | ..... | ..... | ..... | ..... | ..... | ..... | ..... |
| **Other commodities** | 1.0 | 0.3 | 1.1 | 0.9 | 0.5 | ..... | ..... | ..... | 0.1 | ..... |
| Forestry products | ..... | ..... | ..... | ..... | ..... | ..... | ..... | ..... | ..... | ..... |
| Fish and other marine products | ..... | ..... | ..... | ..... | ..... | ..... | ..... | ..... | ..... | ..... |
| Metallic ores and concentrates | ..... | ..... | ..... | ..... | ..... | ..... | ..... | ..... | ..... | ..... |
| Bituminous coal and lignite | ..... | ..... | ..... | ..... | ..... | ..... | ..... | ..... | ..... | ..... |
| Crude petroleum and natural gas | ..... | ..... | ..... | ..... | ..... | ..... | ..... | ..... | ..... | ..... |
| Nonmetallic minerals | 0.9 | ..... | 0.8 | 0.8 | 0.2 | ..... | ..... | ..... | 0.1 | ..... |
| Scrap and waste | ..... | ..... | 0.1 | ..... | ..... | ..... | ..... | ..... | ..... | ..... |
| Used merchandise | 0.1 | 0.2 | 0.2 | 0.1 | 0.1 | ..... | ..... | ..... | ..... | ..... |
| Goods imported and returned unchanged | ..... | ..... | ..... | ..... | ..... | ..... | ..... | ..... | ..... | ..... |
| Special classification provisions | ..... | ..... | ..... | ..... | 0.1 | ..... | ..... | ..... | ..... | ..... |

| Industry | 1993 | 1994 | 1995 | 1996 | 1997 | 1993 | 1994 | 1995 | 1996 | 1997 |
|---|---|---|---|---|---|---|---|---|---|---|
| | European Union | | | | | United Kingdom | | | | |
| **ALL GOODS** | 38.7 | 32.4 | 14.3 | 24.4 | 83.2 | 2.3 | 1.0 | 0.7 | 1.0 | 0.4 |
| **Manufactured goods** | 38.6 | 32.4 | 14.3 | 24.4 | 82.9 | 2.3 | 1.0 | 0.7 | 1.0 | 0.2 |
| Food products | 0.1 | ..... | ..... | ..... | ..... | ..... | ..... | ..... | ..... | ..... |
| Tobacco products | ..... | ..... | ..... | ..... | ..... | ..... | ..... | ..... | ..... | ..... |
| Textile mill products | 0.2 | ..... | ..... | ..... | ..... | ..... | ..... | ..... | ..... | ..... |
| Apparel | ..... | ..... | 0.1 | 0.1 | ..... | ..... | ..... | ..... | ..... | ..... |
| Lumber and wood products | ..... | ..... | ..... | ..... | ..... | ..... | ..... | ..... | ..... | ..... |
| Furniture and fixtures | ..... | ..... | ..... | ..... | ..... | ..... | ..... | ..... | ..... | ..... |
| Paper products | ..... | ..... | ..... | ..... | 0.1 | ..... | ..... | ..... | ..... | ..... |
| Printing and publishing | 0.1 | ..... | 0.1 | ..... | ..... | ..... | ..... | ..... | ..... | ..... |
| Chemical products | 4.4 | 19.3 | 9.3 | 5.7 | 26.2 | 1.0 | 0.2 | ..... | ..... | ..... |
| Refined petroleum products | 27.3 | 9.3 | 2.6 | 17.0 | 55.3 | ..... | ..... | ..... | ..... | ..... |
| Rubber and plastic products | ..... | ..... | 0.1 | ..... | ..... | ..... | ..... | 0.1 | ..... | ..... |
| Leather products | ..... | ..... | ..... | ..... | ..... | ..... | ..... | ..... | ..... | ..... |
| Stone, clay and glass products | ..... | ..... | ..... | ..... | ..... | ..... | ..... | ..... | ..... | ..... |
| Primary metals | ..... | ..... | 0.3 | ..... | ..... | ..... | ..... | ..... | ..... | ..... |
| Fabricated metal products | ..... | 0.1 | 0.1 | 0.1 | ..... | ..... | ..... | ..... | ..... | ..... |
| Industrial machinery and computers | 3.5 | 1.7 | 0.8 | 0.3 | 0.9 | 0.3 | 0.2 | 0.2 | ..... | ..... |
| Electric and electronic equipment | 0.9 | 0.3 | 0.5 | 0.2 | 0.1 | 0.6 | 0.2 | ..... | ..... | ..... |
| Transportation equipment | 0.2 | ..... | ..... | ..... | ..... | ..... | ..... | 0.1 | ..... | ..... |
| Scientific and measuring instruments | 0.5 | 1.0 | 0.4 | 0.3 | 0.1 | 0.1 | 0.3 | 0.3 | 0.2 | ..... |
| Miscellaneous manufactures | 1.4 | 0.2 | 0.1 | 0.7 | 0.1 | 0.2 | 0.1 | 0.1 | 0.7 | 0.1 |
| Unidentified manufactures | ..... | ..... | 0.1 | ..... | ..... | ..... | ..... | ..... | ..... | ..... |
| **Agricultural and livestock products** | ..... | ..... | ..... | ..... | 0.2 | ..... | ..... | ..... | ..... | 0.2 |
| Agricultural products | ..... | ..... | ..... | ..... | ..... | ..... | ..... | ..... | ..... | ..... |
| Livestock and livestock products | ..... | ..... | ..... | ..... | 0.2 | ..... | ..... | ..... | ..... | 0.2 |
| **Other commodities** | 0.1 | ..... | ..... | ..... | 0.1 | ..... | ..... | ..... | ..... | ..... |
| Forestry products | ..... | ..... | ..... | ..... | ..... | ..... | ..... | ..... | ..... | ..... |
| Fish and other marine products | ..... | ..... | ..... | ..... | 0.1 | ..... | ..... | ..... | ..... | ..... |
| Metallic ores and concentrates | ..... | ..... | ..... | ..... | ..... | ..... | ..... | ..... | ..... | ..... |
| Bituminous coal and lignite | ..... | ..... | ..... | ..... | ..... | ..... | ..... | ..... | ..... | ..... |
| Crude petroleum and natural gas | ..... | ..... | ..... | ..... | ..... | ..... | ..... | ..... | ..... | ..... |
| Nonmetallic minerals | ..... | ..... | ..... | ..... | ..... | ..... | ..... | ..... | ..... | ..... |
| Scrap and waste | 0.1 | ..... | ..... | ..... | ..... | ..... | ..... | ..... | ..... | ..... |
| Used merchandise | ..... | ..... | ..... | ..... | ..... | ..... | ..... | ..... | ..... | ..... |
| Goods imported and returned unchanged | ..... | ..... | ..... | ..... | ..... | ..... | ..... | ..... | ..... | ..... |
| Special classification provisions | ..... | ..... | ..... | ..... | ..... | ..... | ..... | ..... | ..... | ..... |

## Table D-3.  State Exports of Goods by Destination and Industry, 1993–1997 —*Continued*

### VIRGIN ISLANDS (Millions of dollars.)

| Industry | Germany 1993 | 1994 | 1995 | 1996 | 1997 | France 1993 | 1994 | 1995 | 1996 | 1997 |
|---|---|---|---|---|---|---|---|---|---|---|
| **ALL GOODS** | 1.7 | 0.3 | 0.6 | 0.1 | 5.8 | 0.1 | 0.3 | 0.1 | 0.1 | 1.8 |
| **Manufactured goods** | 1.6 | 0.3 | 0.6 | 0.1 | 5.8 | 0.1 | 0.3 | 0.1 | 0.1 | 1.7 |
| Food products | | | | | | | | | | |
| Tobacco products | | | | | | | | | | |
| Textile mill products | | | | | | | | | | |
| Apparel | | | | | | | | | | |
| Lumber and wood products | | | | | | | | | | |
| Furniture and fixtures | | | | | | | | | | |
| Paper products | | | | | 0.1 | | | | | |
| Printing and publishing | | | | | | | | | | |
| Chemical products | 1.3 | | | | 0.6 | | | | | 1.6 |
| Refined petroleum products | | | | | 5.0 | | | | | |
| Rubber and plastic products | | | | | | | | | | |
| Leather products | | | | | | | | | | |
| Stone, clay and glass products | | | | | | | | | | |
| Primary metals | | | | | | | | | | |
| Fabricated metal products | | | | | | | | | | |
| Industrial machinery and computers | 0.1 | | | | | | | | | |
| Electric and electronic equipment | | | 0.4 | | | 0.1 | 0.1 | | 0.1 | 0.1 |
| Transportation equipment | | | | | | | | | | |
| Scientific and measuring instruments | 0.2 | 0.3 | 0.1 | 0.1 | | | 0.2 | | | |
| Miscellaneous manufactures | | | | | | | | | | |
| Unidentified manufactures | | | | | | | | | | |
| **Agricultural and livestock products** | | | | | | | | | | |
| Agricultural products | | | | | | | | | | |
| Livestock and livestock products | | | | | | | | | | |
| **Other commodities** | 0.1 | | | | | | | | | 0.1 |
| Forestry products | | | | | | | | | | |
| Fish and other marine products | | | | | | | | | | 0.1 |
| Metallic ores and concentrates | | | | | | | | | | |
| Bituminous coal and lignite | | | | | | | | | | |
| Crude petroleum and natural gas | | | | | | | | | | |
| Nonmetallic minerals | | | | | | | | | | |
| Scrap and waste | 0.1 | | | | | | | | | |
| Used merchandise | | | | | | | | | | |
| Goods imported and returned unchanged | | | | | | | | | | |
| Special classification provisions | | | | | | | | | | |

| Industry | The Netherlands 1993 | 1994 | 1995 | 1996 | 1997 | Asian 10 1993 | 1994 | 1995 | 1996 | 1997 |
|---|---|---|---|---|---|---|---|---|---|---|
| **ALL GOODS** | 17.6 | 16.4 | 2.5 | 8.4 | 57.5 | 25.1 | 38.4 | 45.6 | 14.7 | 19.2 |
| **Manufactured goods** | 17.6 | 16.4 | 2.5 | 8.4 | 57.5 | 25.1 | 38.4 | 45.6 | 14.7 | 19.2 |
| Food products | 0.1 | | | | | 0.1 | 0.2 | | | |
| Tobacco products | | | | | | | | | | |
| Textile mill products | | | | | | | | | | |
| Apparel | | | | | | | | | | |
| Lumber and wood products | | | | | | | | 0.1 | 0.1 | |
| Furniture and fixtures | | | | | | | | | | |
| Paper products | | | | | | | | | 0.1 | |
| Printing and publishing | | | | | | | | | | |
| Chemical products | | 6.7 | 2.3 | 0.5 | 15.9 | 2.4 | 27.6 | 28.4 | 8.8 | 18.5 |
| Refined petroleum products | 17.0 | 9.3 | | 7.9 | 41.5 | 18.8 | 8.1 | 15.4 | 2.3 | |
| Rubber and plastic products | | | | | | | | | | 0.1 |
| Leather products | | | | | | | | | | |
| Stone, clay and glass products | | | | | | | | | | 0.1 |
| Primary metals | | | | | | | 0.1 | | | 0.3 |
| Fabricated metal products | | | | | | 0.2 | | | 1.7 | |
| Industrial machinery and computers | 0.4 | 0.4 | | | | 1.3 | 1.1 | 0.5 | 0.2 | 0.1 |
| Electric and electronic equipment | | | | | | 0.7 | 0.2 | 0.2 | 1.2 | 0.1 |
| Transportation equipment | | | | | | | | 0.2 | | |
| Scientific and measuring instruments | | | | | | 0.3 | 0.2 | 0.1 | 0.1 | 0.1 |
| Miscellaneous manufactures | | | | | | 1.2 | 0.8 | 0.9 | | |
| Unidentified manufactures | | | | | | 0.1 | | | | |
| **Agricultural and livestock products** | | | | | | | | | | |
| Agricultural products | | | | | | | | | | |
| Livestock and livestock products | | | | | | | | | | |
| **Other commodities** | | | | | | | | 0.1 | | |
| Forestry products | | | | | | | | | | |
| Fish and other marine products | | | | | | | | 0.1 | | |
| Metallic ores and concentrates | | | | | | | | | | |
| Bituminous coal and lignite | | | | | | | | | | |
| Crude petroleum and natural gas | | | | | | | | | | |
| Nonmetallic minerals | | | | | | | | | | |
| Scrap and waste | | | | | | | | | | |
| Used merchandise | | | | | | | | | | |
| Goods imported and returned unchanged | | | | | | | | | | |
| Special classification provisions | | | | | | | | | | |

## Table D-3.   State Exports of Goods by Destination and Industry, 1993–1997 —Continued

**VIRGIN ISLANDS** (Millions of dollars.)

| Industry | 1993 | 1994 | 1995 | 1996 | 1997 | 1993 | 1994 | 1995 | 1996 | 1997 |
|---|---|---|---|---|---|---|---|---|---|---|
| | Japan | | | | | South Korea | | | | |
| **ALL GOODS** | 1.7 | 1.9 | 16.1 | 6.4 | 0.1 | 0.4 | 18.3 | 17.3 | 6.3 | 18.4 |
| **Manufactured goods** | 1.7 | 1.9 | 16.1 | 6.4 | 0.1 | 0.4 | 18.3 | 17.3 | 6.3 | 18.4 |
| Food products | 0.1 | 0.1 | ..... | ..... | ..... | ..... | ..... | ..... | ..... | ..... |
| Tobacco products | ..... | ..... | ..... | ..... | ..... | ..... | ..... | ..... | ..... | ..... |
| Textile mill products | ..... | ..... | ..... | ..... | ..... | ..... | ..... | ..... | ..... | ..... |
| Apparel | ..... | ..... | ..... | ..... | ..... | ..... | ..... | ..... | ..... | ..... |
| Lumber and wood products | ..... | ..... | ..... | 0.1 | ..... | ..... | ..... | ..... | ..... | ..... |
| Furniture and fixtures | ..... | ..... | ..... | ..... | ..... | ..... | ..... | ..... | ..... | ..... |
| Paper products | ..... | ..... | ..... | 0.1 | ..... | ..... | ..... | ..... | ..... | ..... |
| Printing and publishing | ..... | ..... | ..... | ..... | ..... | ..... | ..... | ..... | ..... | ..... |
| Chemical products | ..... | 0.2 | ..... | 3.6 | ..... | ..... | 18.0 | 17.2 | 5.2 | 18.3 |
| Refined petroleum products | ..... | ..... | 15.4 | 2.3 | ..... | ..... | ..... | ..... | ..... | ..... |
| Rubber and plastic products | ..... | ..... | ..... | ..... | ..... | ..... | ..... | ..... | ..... | ..... |
| Leather products | ..... | ..... | ..... | ..... | ..... | ..... | ..... | ..... | ..... | ..... |
| Stone, clay and glass products | ..... | ..... | ..... | ..... | ..... | ..... | ..... | ..... | ..... | 0.1 |
| Primary metals | ..... | ..... | ..... | ..... | ..... | ..... | ..... | ..... | ..... | ..... |
| Fabricated metal products | ..... | ..... | ..... | ..... | ..... | ..... | ..... | ..... | ..... | ..... |
| Industrial machinery and computers | 0.3 | 0.5 | 0.3 | 0.1 | ..... | 0.3 | 0.2 | ..... | ..... | ..... |
| Electric and electronic equipment | 0.5 | 0.2 | ..... | ..... | ..... | 0.1 | ..... | ..... | 1.1 | 0.1 |
| Transportation equipment | ..... | ..... | 0.1 | ..... | ..... | ..... | ..... | ..... | ..... | ..... |
| Scientific and measuring instruments | 0.1 | 0.1 | 0.1 | ..... | ..... | ..... | 0.1 | ..... | ..... | ..... |
| Miscellaneous manufactures | 0.6 | 0.6 | 0.3 | ..... | ..... | ..... | ..... | ..... | ..... | ..... |
| Unidentified manufactures | ..... | ..... | ..... | ..... | ..... | ..... | ..... | ..... | ..... | ..... |
| **Agricultural and livestock products** | ..... | ..... | ..... | ..... | ..... | ..... | ..... | ..... | ..... | ..... |
| Agricultural products | ..... | ..... | ..... | ..... | ..... | ..... | ..... | ..... | ..... | ..... |
| Livestock and livestock products | ..... | ..... | ..... | ..... | ..... | ..... | ..... | ..... | ..... | ..... |
| **Other commodities** | ..... | ..... | ..... | ..... | ..... | ..... | ..... | 0.1 | ..... | ..... |
| Forestry products | ..... | ..... | ..... | ..... | ..... | ..... | ..... | ..... | ..... | ..... |
| Fish and other marine products | ..... | ..... | ..... | ..... | ..... | ..... | ..... | 0.1 | ..... | ..... |
| Metallic ores and concentrates | ..... | ..... | ..... | ..... | ..... | ..... | ..... | ..... | ..... | ..... |
| Bituminous coal and lignite | ..... | ..... | ..... | ..... | ..... | ..... | ..... | ..... | ..... | ..... |
| Crude petroleum and natural gas | ..... | ..... | ..... | ..... | ..... | ..... | ..... | ..... | ..... | ..... |
| Nonmetallic minerals | ..... | ..... | ..... | ..... | ..... | ..... | ..... | ..... | ..... | ..... |
| Scrap and waste | ..... | ..... | ..... | ..... | ..... | ..... | ..... | ..... | ..... | ..... |
| Used merchandise | ..... | ..... | ..... | ..... | ..... | ..... | ..... | ..... | ..... | ..... |
| Goods imported and returned unchanged | ..... | ..... | ..... | ..... | ..... | ..... | ..... | ..... | ..... | ..... |
| Special classification provisions | ..... | ..... | ..... | ..... | ..... | ..... | ..... | ..... | ..... | ..... |
| | Taiwan | | | | | Singapore | | | | |
| **ALL GOODS** | 0.1 | 6.0 | 7.4 | 0.1 | 0.1 | 8.3 | 8.5 | 0.8 | 0.1 | 0.1 |
| **Manufactured goods** | 0.1 | 6.0 | 7.4 | 0.1 | 0.1 | 8.3 | 8.5 | 0.8 | 0.1 | 0.1 |
| Food products | ..... | 0.1 | ..... | ..... | ..... | ..... | ..... | ..... | ..... | ..... |
| Tobacco products | ..... | ..... | ..... | ..... | ..... | ..... | ..... | ..... | ..... | ..... |
| Textile mill products | ..... | ..... | ..... | ..... | ..... | ..... | ..... | ..... | ..... | ..... |
| Apparel | ..... | ..... | ..... | ..... | ..... | ..... | ..... | ..... | ..... | ..... |
| Lumber and wood products | ..... | ..... | ..... | ..... | ..... | ..... | ..... | ..... | ..... | ..... |
| Furniture and fixtures | ..... | ..... | ..... | ..... | ..... | ..... | ..... | ..... | ..... | ..... |
| Paper products | ..... | ..... | ..... | ..... | ..... | ..... | ..... | ..... | ..... | ..... |
| Printing and publishing | ..... | ..... | ..... | ..... | ..... | ..... | ..... | ..... | ..... | ..... |
| Chemical products | ..... | 5.8 | 7.4 | ..... | 0.1 | ..... | ..... | 0.7 | ..... | ..... |
| Refined petroleum products | ..... | ..... | ..... | ..... | ..... | 7.5 | 8.1 | ..... | ..... | ..... |
| Rubber and plastic products | ..... | ..... | ..... | ..... | ..... | ..... | ..... | ..... | ..... | ..... |
| Leather products | ..... | ..... | ..... | ..... | ..... | ..... | ..... | ..... | ..... | ..... |
| Stone, clay and glass products | ..... | ..... | ..... | ..... | ..... | ..... | ..... | ..... | ..... | ..... |
| Primary metals | ..... | ..... | ..... | ..... | ..... | 0.2 | ..... | ..... | ..... | ..... |
| Fabricated metal products | ..... | ..... | ..... | ..... | ..... | ..... | ..... | ..... | ..... | ..... |
| Industrial machinery and computers | ..... | ..... | 0.1 | ..... | ..... | 0.5 | 0.3 | ..... | ..... | ..... |
| Electric and electronic equipment | ..... | ..... | ..... | ..... | ..... | ..... | ..... | 0.1 | ..... | ..... |
| Transportation equipment | ..... | ..... | ..... | ..... | ..... | ..... | ..... | ..... | ..... | ..... |
| Scientific and measuring instruments | ..... | ..... | ..... | 0.1 | ..... | 0.1 | 0.1 | ..... | ..... | ..... |
| Miscellaneous manufactures | ..... | ..... | ..... | ..... | ..... | ..... | ..... | ..... | ..... | ..... |
| Unidentified manufactures | ..... | ..... | ..... | ..... | ..... | ..... | ..... | ..... | ..... | ..... |
| **Agricultural and livestock products** | ..... | ..... | ..... | ..... | ..... | ..... | ..... | ..... | ..... | ..... |
| Agricultural products | ..... | ..... | ..... | ..... | ..... | ..... | ..... | ..... | ..... | ..... |
| Livestock and livestock products | ..... | ..... | ..... | ..... | ..... | ..... | ..... | ..... | ..... | ..... |
| **Other commodities** | ..... | ..... | ..... | ..... | ..... | ..... | ..... | ..... | ..... | ..... |
| Forestry products | ..... | ..... | ..... | ..... | ..... | ..... | ..... | ..... | ..... | ..... |
| Fish and other marine products | ..... | ..... | ..... | ..... | ..... | ..... | ..... | ..... | ..... | ..... |
| Metallic ores and concentrates | ..... | ..... | ..... | ..... | ..... | ..... | ..... | ..... | ..... | ..... |
| Bituminous coal and lignite | ..... | ..... | ..... | ..... | ..... | ..... | ..... | ..... | ..... | ..... |
| Crude petroleum and natural gas | ..... | ..... | ..... | ..... | ..... | ..... | ..... | ..... | ..... | ..... |
| Nonmetallic minerals | ..... | ..... | ..... | ..... | ..... | ..... | ..... | ..... | ..... | ..... |
| Scrap and waste | ..... | ..... | ..... | ..... | ..... | ..... | ..... | ..... | ..... | ..... |
| Used merchandise | ..... | ..... | ..... | ..... | ..... | ..... | ..... | ..... | ..... | ..... |
| Goods imported and returned unchanged | ..... | ..... | ..... | ..... | ..... | ..... | ..... | ..... | ..... | ..... |
| Special classification provisions | ..... | ..... | ..... | ..... | ..... | ..... | ..... | ..... | ..... | ..... |

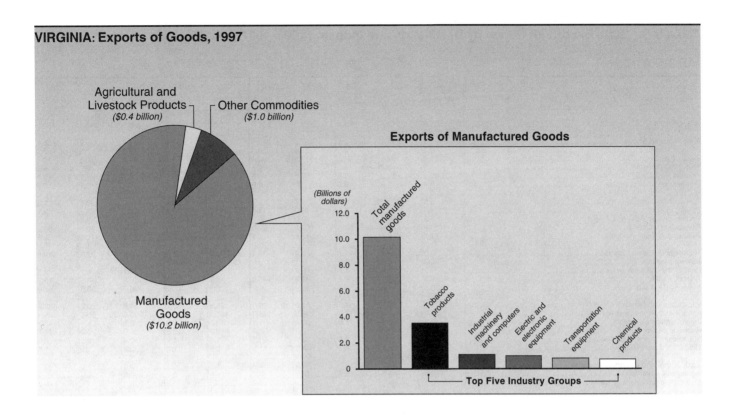

VIRGINIA: Exports of Goods, 1997

Agricultural and Livestock Products ($0.4 billion)

Other Commodities ($1.0 billion)

Manufactured Goods ($10.2 billion)

Exports of Manufactured Goods

(Billions of dollars)

Top Five Industry Groups

Total manufactured goods

Tobacco products

Industrial machinery and computers

Electric and electronic equipment

Transportation equipment

Chemical products

## Table D-3.   State Exports of Goods by Destination and Industry, 1993–1997 —*Continued*

**VIRGINIA** (Millions of dollars.)

| Industry | 1993 | 1994 | 1995 | 1996 | 1997 | 1993 | 1994 | 1995 | 1996 | 1997 |
|---|---|---|---|---|---|---|---|---|---|---|
| | All destinations | | | | | Canada | | | | |
| **ALL GOODS** | 8 118.4 | 9 947.3 | 10 425.2 | 10 926.0 | 11 512.4 | 1 052.3 | 1 220.5 | 1 465.8 | 1 356.7 | 1 535.8 |
| **Manufactured goods** | 7 098.9 | 8 793.6 | 9 294.1 | 9 699.0 | 10 158.5 | 992.6 | 1 154.9 | 1 366.3 | 1 246.6 | 1 413.2 |
| Food products | 201.9 | 201.0 | 175.0 | 234.4 | 235.7 | 20.6 | 16.0 | 16.3 | 21.8 | 31.9 |
| Tobacco products | 2 534.7 | 3 506.1 | 3 185.5 | 3 646.8 | 3 530.3 | 0.1 | 0.1 | 0.1 | 0.1 | 0.1 |
| Textile mill products | 65.9 | 79.1 | 99.6 | 94.4 | 118.5 | 36.8 | 41.1 | 49.2 | 48.1 | 59.6 |
| Apparel | 67.7 | 100.2 | 88.4 | 116.6 | 134.6 | 12.1 | 17.8 | 17.7 | 15.3 | 24.5 |
| Lumber and wood products | 92.1 | 119.4 | 110.7 | 108.5 | 118.7 | 17.5 | 21.8 | 21.0 | 22.4 | 21.2 |
| Furniture and fixtures | 59.9 | 49.6 | 42.4 | 49.5 | 50.6 | 27.2 | 24.4 | 20.7 | 23.4 | 25.0 |
| Paper products | 92.2 | 140.3 | 181.8 | 157.7 | 142.7 | 33.3 | 54.5 | 61.4 | 68.3 | 74.7 |
| Printing and publishing | 29.1 | 26.8 | 35.2 | 41.8 | 39.5 | 14.7 | 14.5 | 12.9 | 19.9 | 17.6 |
| Chemical products | 546.2 | 702.0 | 902.7 | 735.2 | 745.8 | 143.7 | 205.8 | 317.2 | 214.2 | 187.6 |
| Refined petroleum products | 126.4 | 130.1 | 124.5 | 109.2 | 91.1 | 17.8 | 18.4 | 22.5 | 26.8 | 27.1 |
| Rubber and plastic products | 171.0 | 192.7 | 233.5 | 228.6 | 266.7 | 40.9 | 51.7 | 63.9 | 74.7 | 90.9 |
| Leather products | 2.8 | 2.6 | 4.0 | 3.0 | 3.1 | 1.1 | 0.8 | 1.0 | 0.6 | 0.8 |
| Stone, clay and glass products | 40.1 | 64.8 | 76.0 | 89.5 | 82.3 | 19.3 | 27.7 | 27.0 | 23.9 | 30.8 |
| Primary metals | 171.8 | 206.7 | 296.6 | 258.2 | 291.5 | 53.4 | 69.6 | 87.5 | 44.9 | 46.1 |
| Fabricated metal products | 227.6 | 233.8 | 313.6 | 435.3 | 376.8 | 41.3 | 44.9 | 57.4 | 82.1 | 115.6 |
| Industrial machinery and computers | 785.1 | 853.1 | 1 008.0 | 1 044.0 | 1 112.9 | 112.1 | 149.8 | 157.4 | 151.2 | 172.5 |
| Electric and electronic equipment | 553.3 | 566.4 | 652.1 | 726.7 | 1 013.8 | 154.0 | 179.5 | 181.1 | 192.9 | 233.4 |
| Transportation equipment | 834.6 | 980.5 | 988.6 | 868.5 | 821.0 | 198.1 | 157.4 | 195.2 | 165.2 | 191.0 |
| Scientific and measuring instruments | 212.0 | 226.7 | 311.2 | 241.0 | 392.6 | 36.1 | 39.0 | 42.8 | 35.7 | 49.7 |
| Miscellaneous manufactures | 138.5 | 150.0 | 163.6 | 131.6 | 187.1 | 8.8 | 14.8 | 8.8 | 9.6 | 7.8 |
| Unidentified manufactures | 146.0 | 261.9 | 301.1 | 378.5 | 402.3 | 3.7 | 5.0 | 5.1 | 5.6 | 5.4 |
| **Agricultural and livestock products** | 566.1 | 630.5 | 486.2 | 408.8 | 391.3 | 14.5 | 16.4 | 13.0 | 14.4 | 12.9 |
| Agricultural products | 555.2 | 617.3 | 475.6 | 401.0 | 384.6 | 8.3 | 9.1 | 12.5 | 13.8 | 12.5 |
| Livestock and livestock products | 10.9 | 13.2 | 10.6 | 7.9 | 6.7 | 6.2 | 7.3 | 0.5 | 0.6 | 0.4 |
| **Other commodities** | 453.4 | 523.2 | 644.9 | 818.1 | 962.6 | 45.2 | 49.2 | 86.5 | 95.7 | 109.7 |
| Forestry products | 6.0 | 3.5 | 3.3 | 3.9 | 4.2 | 3.9 | 3.3 | 3.2 | 3.8 | 3.6 |
| Fish and other marine products | 10.7 | 15.3 | 16.9 | 19.5 | 27.1 | 3.6 | 4.5 | 4.9 | 5.9 | 10.9 |
| Metallic ores and concentrates | 0.5 | 1.4 | 1.5 | 1.4 | 0.6 | 0.3 | 1.3 | 1.4 | 0.3 | 0.6 |
| Bituminous coal and lignite | 317.2 | 403.9 | 499.8 | 673.6 | 821.0 | 10.0 | 8.4 | 35.6 | 39.4 | 37.8 |
| Crude petroleum and natural gas | 0.1 | ..... | ..... | 0.5 | 2.7 | ..... | ..... | ..... | ..... | ..... |
| Nonmetallic minerals | 6.7 | 7.4 | 7.9 | 10.2 | 8.6 | 1.5 | 1.4 | 1.6 | 1.4 | 1.3 |
| Scrap and waste | 44.5 | 43.7 | 74.7 | 48.7 | 43.7 | 3.7 | 7.7 | 14.7 | 10.7 | 19.4 |
| Used merchandise | 10.6 | 10.2 | 7.5 | 13.1 | 10.1 | 0.5 | 0.8 | 0.6 | 0.9 | 1.4 |
| Goods imported and returned unchanged | 19.6 | 19.6 | 21.9 | 30.8 | 32.9 | 19.6 | 19.6 | 21.9 | 30.8 | 32.9 |
| Special classification provisions | 37.5 | 18.1 | 11.4 | 16.4 | 11.7 | 2.0 | 2.2 | 2.6 | 2.3 | 1.7 |

## Table D-3.   State Exports of Goods by Destination and Industry, 1993–1997 —*Continued*

**VIRGINIA** (Millions of dollars.)

| Industry | 1993 | 1994 | 1995 | 1996 | 1997 | 1993 | 1994 | 1995 | 1996 | 1997 |
|---|---|---|---|---|---|---|---|---|---|---|
| | South and Central America and Caribbean | | | | | Mexico | | | | |
| **ALL GOODS** | 531.8 | 619.5 | 694.4 | 750.2 | 903.6 | 302.3 | 365.8 | 320.8 | 342.1 | 430.2 |
| **Manufactured goods** | 431.2 | 519.1 | 632.1 | 687.0 | 795.5 | 299.5 | 363.3 | 318.4 | 339.2 | 426.1 |
| Food products | 20.6 | 24.3 | 22.5 | 25.6 | 20.7 | 23.6 | 16.2 | 4.3 | 2.9 | 7.1 |
| Tobacco products | 131.3 | 109.1 | 94.6 | 113.9 | 100.8 | 0.3 | 0.1 | 0.3 | 0.3 | 0.6 |
| Textile mill products | 3.5 | 3.2 | 5.2 | 5.1 | 10.5 | 2.5 | 5.2 | 5.2 | 5.7 | 8.5 |
| Apparel | 40.1 | 59.2 | 45.2 | 53.8 | 45.5 | 0.9 | 8.9 | 9.7 | 25.7 | 43.2 |
| Lumber and wood products | 3.4 | 2.9 | 0.9 | 1.7 | 4.6 | 0.5 | 0.8 | 0.1 | 0.1 | 0.2 |
| Furniture and fixtures | 2.5 | 2.4 | 1.7 | 1.7 | 5.0 | 1.7 | 3.1 | 0.9 | 0.4 | 1.2 |
| Paper products | 6.0 | 7.1 | 15.2 | 13.0 | 14.6 | 13.3 | 13.3 | 12.3 | 23.9 | 18.1 |
| Printing and publishing | 0.5 | 0.7 | 1.5 | 0.9 | 0.8 | 1.0 | 1.4 | 1.4 | 2.2 | 1.6 |
| Chemical products | 35.3 | 59.8 | 57.4 | 61.6 | 59.0 | 19.3 | 31.0 | 39.9 | 49.7 | 60.7 |
| Refined petroleum products | 11.0 | 19.6 | 24.4 | 11.6 | 11.4 | 41.2 | 22.9 | 24.7 | 12.2 | 1.3 |
| Rubber and plastic products | 9.0 | 8.9 | 14.7 | 16.9 | 28.6 | 30.4 | 36.9 | 38.2 | 22.9 | 29.8 |
| Leather products | 0.3 | 0.3 | 0.2 | 1.1 | 0.9 | 0.1 | 0.1 | ..... | ..... | ..... |
| Stone, clay and glass products | 1.8 | 2.5 | 1.6 | 6.9 | 9.3 | 1.7 | 10.0 | 7.1 | 3.1 | 3.5 |
| Primary metals | 39.5 | 45.7 | 86.1 | 93.9 | 145.6 | 8.7 | 9.7 | 18.5 | 14.8 | 15.9 |
| Fabricated metal products | 19.6 | 47.6 | 59.4 | 53.2 | 18.2 | 6.8 | 23.2 | 30.7 | 60.6 | 56.9 |
| Industrial machinery and computers | 45.8 | 62.4 | 97.2 | 84.6 | 85.9 | 21.8 | 35.1 | 24.8 | 20.7 | 32.9 |
| Electric and electronic equipment | 37.2 | 37.2 | 61.9 | 101.3 | 135.0 | 101.8 | 75.3 | 90.5 | 80.5 | 126.0 |
| Transportation equipment | 13.3 | 13.1 | 21.9 | 20.9 | 21.2 | 12.2 | 57.0 | 3.8 | 6.7 | 7.2 |
| Scientific and measuring instruments | 6.0 | 7.6 | 9.0 | 10.0 | 62.3 | 10.2 | 10.6 | 5.0 | 4.9 | 7.1 |
| Miscellaneous manufactures | 2.1 | 1.6 | 2.6 | 2.9 | 3.7 | 1.2 | 1.2 | 0.4 | 0.5 | 2.6 |
| Unidentified manufactures | 2.5 | 4.1 | 8.9 | 6.8 | 11.9 | 0.5 | 1.3 | 0.6 | 1.1 | 1.8 |
| **Agricultural and livestock products** | 63.0 | 49.3 | 15.7 | 10.9 | 4.9 | 1.7 | 1.1 | 0.9 | 1.5 | 2.3 |
| Agricultural products | 63.0 | 49.3 | 15.7 | 10.7 | 4.3 | 1.6 | 0.8 | 0.8 | 1.5 | 2.0 |
| Livestock and livestock products | 0.1 | ..... | 0.1 | 0.1 | 0.7 | ..... | 0.3 | 0.1 | ..... | 0.2 |
| **Other commodities** | 37.6 | 51.0 | 46.5 | 52.3 | 103.0 | 1.1 | 1.5 | 1.5 | 1.4 | 1.9 |
| Forestry products | ..... | ..... | ..... | ..... | ..... | 0.1 | ..... | ..... | ..... | 0.1 |
| Fish and other marine products | ..... | 0.1 | 0.1 | ..... | 0.6 | ..... | ..... | 0.8 | ..... | 0.1 |
| Metallic ores and concentrates | ..... | ..... | ..... | ..... | ..... | ..... | ..... | ..... | ..... | ..... |
| Bituminous coal and lignite | 35.7 | 45.8 | 41.0 | 48.5 | 97.4 | ..... | ..... | ..... | ..... | ..... |
| Crude petroleum and natural gas | ..... | ..... | ..... | 0.5 | 2.7 | ..... | ..... | ..... | ..... | ..... |
| Nonmetallic minerals | 0.2 | 0.4 | 0.3 | 0.9 | 0.4 | 1.0 | 0.8 | 0.7 | 1.3 | 1.3 |
| Scrap and waste | 0.3 | 4.2 | 4.0 | 0.2 | 0.3 | ..... | 0.1 | ..... | ..... | 0.4 |
| Used merchandise | 1.2 | 0.4 | 0.6 | 0.7 | 1.2 | ..... | 0.4 | ..... | ..... | ..... |
| Goods imported and returned unchanged | ..... | ..... | ..... | ..... | ..... | ..... | ..... | ..... | ..... | ..... |
| Special classification provisions | 0.1 | 0.1 | 0.4 | 1.5 | 0.3 | ..... | 0.2 | ..... | 0.1 | 0.1 |
| | European Union | | | | | United Kingdom | | | | |
| **ALL GOODS** | 2 209.0 | 3 077.9 | 3 244.3 | 3 414.4 | 3 326.2 | 423.9 | 286.0 | 315.7 | 338.2 | 323.3 |
| **Manufactured goods** | 1 831.8 | 2 613.4 | 2 749.8 | 2 811.5 | 2 668.9 | 370.0 | 254.4 | 284.0 | 300.7 | 275.5 |
| Food products | 26.4 | 28.1 | 16.8 | 25.7 | 18.9 | 4.6 | 5.0 | 6.2 | 4.8 | 5.7 |
| Tobacco products | 590.7 | 1 421.0 | 1 343.8 | 1 282.5 | 1 141.2 | 0.1 | 5.7 | 1.7 | ..... | 0.1 |
| Textile mill products | 8.0 | 12.0 | 21.8 | 15.9 | 17.0 | 2.1 | 1.6 | 4.4 | 4.2 | 5.7 |
| Apparel | 3.8 | 3.8 | 3.2 | 4.3 | 4.9 | 0.6 | 0.6 | 0.6 | 1.5 | 0.7 |
| Lumber and wood products | 42.1 | 47.5 | 52.5 | 49.3 | 50.2 | 3.9 | 4.1 | 5.7 | 6.4 | 7.2 |
| Furniture and fixtures | 7.3 | 4.0 | 6.1 | 9.0 | 6.8 | 1.7 | 0.4 | 0.6 | 5.5 | 2.3 |
| Paper products | 21.4 | 50.2 | 72.3 | 26.8 | 9.3 | 10.4 | 23.7 | 31.7 | 10.7 | 2.6 |
| Printing and publishing | 9.0 | 7.8 | 13.5 | 15.1 | 11.4 | 4.5 | 3.1 | 6.4 | 8.2 | 6.9 |
| Chemical products | 145.1 | 169.1 | 222.6 | 169.5 | 185.8 | 15.5 | 15.7 | 19.5 | 16.6 | 18.4 |
| Refined petroleum products | 9.4 | 4.4 | 12.2 | 4.0 | 11.1 | ..... | 0.1 | 0.1 | ..... | 0.1 |
| Rubber and plastic products | 31.0 | 28.7 | 38.1 | 29.7 | 34.3 | 5.6 | 8.3 | 9.9 | 6.3 | 9.9 |
| Leather products | 0.4 | 0.5 | 1.7 | 0.5 | 0.5 | ..... | 0.1 | 0.4 | ..... | 0.1 |
| Stone, clay and glass products | 6.9 | 7.4 | 11.8 | 16.5 | 12.9 | 0.4 | 0.5 | 3.2 | 2.1 | 5.0 |
| Primary metals | 25.0 | 26.3 | 34.1 | 41.2 | 33.3 | 19.6 | 12.3 | 9.4 | 17.0 | 18.5 |
| Fabricated metal products | 93.7 | 51.9 | 101.6 | 162.3 | 84.6 | 43.1 | 11.5 | 15.4 | 16.2 | 10.2 |
| Industrial machinery and computers | 183.2 | 175.4 | 244.5 | 289.6 | 291.5 | 56.2 | 50.5 | 64.6 | 72.6 | 65.2 |
| Electric and electronic equipment | 109.7 | 120.3 | 124.9 | 140.9 | 170.5 | 37.6 | 34.8 | 36.8 | 32.2 | 39.0 |
| Transportation equipment | 335.8 | 210.8 | 210.9 | 223.2 | 184.6 | 136.2 | 44.7 | 33.8 | 72.7 | 51.0 |
| Scientific and measuring instruments | 69.0 | 74.1 | 83.8 | 73.1 | 86.1 | 16.8 | 20.2 | 20.6 | 16.7 | 16.8 |
| Miscellaneous manufactures | 27.8 | 28.7 | 22.2 | 22.3 | 27.4 | 9.9 | 10.5 | 8.4 | 5.3 | 8.8 |
| Unidentified manufactures | 85.7 | 141.4 | 111.2 | 210.1 | 286.6 | 1.1 | 1.1 | 4.5 | 1.6 | 1.4 |
| **Agricultural and livestock products** | 123.9 | 151.0 | 146.8 | 161.6 | 160.7 | 19.8 | 17.9 | 21.7 | 16.1 | 18.4 |
| Agricultural products | 121.5 | 148.3 | 143.8 | 159.4 | 158.4 | 19.3 | 17.2 | 21.4 | 15.7 | 18.0 |
| Livestock and livestock products | 2.4 | 2.7 | 3.0 | 2.2 | 2.3 | 0.5 | 0.8 | 0.3 | 0.3 | 0.4 |
| **Other commodities** | 253.4 | 313.5 | 347.8 | 441.3 | 496.5 | 34.1 | 13.7 | 10.0 | 21.4 | 29.4 |
| Forestry products | 0.1 | 0.1 | 0.1 | ..... | 0.1 | ..... | ..... | ..... | ..... | ..... |
| Fish and other marine products | 5.1 | 4.7 | 5.0 | 4.3 | 6.4 | 0.1 | 0.2 | 0.1 | 0.1 | 0.1 |
| Metallic ores and concentrates | 0.2 | ..... | ..... | 1.1 | ..... | ..... | ..... | ..... | 1.1 | ..... |
| Bituminous coal and lignite | 209.6 | 289.9 | 328.9 | 417.8 | 475.7 | 28.7 | 9.0 | 5.8 | 14.1 | 25.9 |
| Crude petroleum and natural gas | ..... | ..... | ..... | ..... | ..... | ..... | ..... | ..... | ..... | ..... |
| Nonmetallic minerals | 1.7 | 2.3 | 2.9 | 3.1 | 3.3 | 0.5 | 0.6 | 0.7 | 0.9 | 0.7 |
| Scrap and waste | 0.5 | 1.1 | 0.4 | 0.4 | 0.4 | ..... | 0.3 | 0.1 | 0.1 | ..... |
| Used merchandise | 7.6 | 6.2 | 4.7 | 7.3 | 3.9 | 4.1 | 3.4 | 2.0 | 3.6 | 1.8 |
| Goods imported and returned unchanged | ..... | ..... | ..... | ..... | ..... | ..... | ..... | ..... | ..... | ..... |
| Special classification provisions | 28.6 | 9.1 | 5.8 | 7.2 | 6.7 | 0.7 | 0.1 | 1.3 | 1.6 | 0.9 |

## Table D-3. State Exports of Goods by Destination and Industry, 1993–1997 —Continued

**VIRGINIA** (Millions of dollars.)

| Industry | 1993 | 1994 | 1995 | 1996 | 1997 | 1993 | 1994 | 1995 | 1996 | 1997 |
|---|---|---|---|---|---|---|---|---|---|---|
| | Germany | | | | | France | | | | |
| ALL GOODS | 429.4 | 480.4 | 531.0 | 672.5 | 670.7 | 117.0 | 153.8 | 154.0 | 194.7 | 210.5 |
| Manufactured goods | 369.1 | 407.8 | 480.7 | 585.8 | 588.8 | 82.2 | 105.4 | 111.5 | 132.4 | 144.8 |
| Food products | 0.3 | 0.5 | 0.6 | 8.5 | 1.3 | 3.8 | 0.9 | 0.5 | 0.1 | 0.5 |
| Tobacco products | 9.3 | 22.4 | 18.3 | 18.3 | 14.7 | ..... | ..... | 0.2 | ..... | ..... |
| Textile mill products | 0.8 | 0.9 | 2.4 | 1.6 | 0.9 | 1.6 | 0.8 | 1.0 | 0.9 | 0.4 |
| Apparel | 1.7 | 1.1 | 0.5 | 0.8 | 0.6 | 0.6 | 0.4 | 0.1 | 0.1 | 0.1 |
| Lumber and wood products | 13.4 | 15.6 | 16.2 | 16.0 | 12.0 | 0.5 | 0.5 | 0.2 | 0.1 | 0.1 |
| Furniture and fixtures | 4.3 | 1.3 | 3.1 | 2.2 | 2.8 | 0.3 | 1.2 | 0.8 | 0.1 | 0.3 |
| Paper products | 2.2 | 9.2 | 16.8 | 5.3 | 1.1 | 0.6 | 1.1 | 0.2 | 0.8 | 0.3 |
| Printing and publishing | 1.6 | 2.2 | 2.2 | 1.5 | 1.5 | 0.5 | 0.4 | 1.4 | 0.7 | 0.7 |
| Chemical products | 16.6 | 12.4 | 19.7 | 18.5 | 39.1 | 14.7 | 16.3 | 21.1 | 26.2 | 22.8 |
| Refined petroleum products | 0.1 | 0.2 | 0.7 | 0.1 | ..... | ..... | 0.1 | 1.3 | 1.9 | 2.7 |
| Rubber and plastic products | 13.8 | 10.2 | 8.1 | 7.6 | 6.0 | 4.7 | 4.0 | 8.1 | 2.8 | 1.9 |
| Leather products | 0.1 | 0.1 | 0.4 | 0.2 | 0.1 | 0.1 | ..... | 0.3 | ..... | 0.1 |
| Stone, clay and glass products | 5.0 | 5.4 | 7.5 | 8.1 | 5.9 | 0.6 | 0.2 | 0.1 | 2.6 | 0.4 |
| Primary metals | 0.8 | 0.8 | 11.9 | 4.3 | 5.9 | 0.5 | 1.0 | 0.8 | 2.9 | 1.0 |
| Fabricated metal products | 34.8 | 26.1 | 69.0 | 109.3 | 38.6 | 1.9 | 1.9 | 5.5 | 20.4 | 23.5 |
| Industrial machinery and computers | 48.9 | 51.5 | 70.8 | 80.5 | 90.2 | 19.1 | 23.4 | 32.7 | 39.8 | 34.9 |
| Electric and electronic equipment | 22.9 | 23.5 | 25.6 | 25.5 | 22.8 | 10.2 | 12.0 | 11.8 | 13.4 | 34.5 |
| Transportation equipment | 96.1 | 89.5 | 84.1 | 59.1 | 43.9 | 11.8 | 31.1 | 15.1 | 9.6 | 2.5 |
| Scientific and measuring instruments | 11.8 | 10.5 | 16.3 | 12.7 | 14.1 | 5.5 | 6.0 | 7.2 | 7.2 | 13.8 |
| Miscellaneous manufactures | 5.1 | 5.5 | 2.6 | 7.4 | 7.8 | 4.5 | 2.4 | 2.3 | 1.5 | 3.0 |
| Unidentified manufactures | 79.4 | 118.9 | 103.9 | 198.4 | 279.4 | 0.6 | 1.7 | 0.8 | 1.1 | 1.3 |
| Agricultural and livestock products | 28.6 | 59.0 | 45.3 | 68.2 | 72.1 | 2.7 | 3.6 | 4.7 | 1.6 | 3.1 |
| Agricultural products | 28.4 | 58.9 | 44.6 | 68.1 | 72.0 | 1.5 | 2.5 | 3.5 | 0.8 | 1.9 |
| Livestock and livestock products | 0.1 | 0.1 | 0.6 | 0.1 | 0.1 | 1.3 | 1.1 | 1.2 | 0.8 | 1.2 |
| Other commodities | 31.7 | 13.6 | 5.0 | 18.4 | 9.9 | 32.1 | 44.8 | 37.7 | 60.6 | 62.6 |
| Forestry products | 0.1 | ..... | ..... | ..... | ..... | ..... | ..... | ..... | ..... | ..... |
| Fish and other marine products | 0.3 | 0.9 | 1.0 | 1.0 | 0.6 | 2.3 | 1.4 | 2.5 | 1.3 | 3.9 |
| Metallic ores and concentrates | ..... | ..... | ..... | ..... | ..... | ..... | ..... | ..... | ..... | ..... |
| Bituminous coal and lignite | 3.6 | 3.6 | ..... | 13.0 | 3.3 | 29.2 | 42.9 | 34.6 | 58.3 | 58.0 |
| Crude petroleum and natural gas | ..... | ..... | ..... | ..... | ..... | ..... | ..... | ..... | ..... | ..... |
| Nonmetallic minerals | 0.2 | 0.3 | 0.4 | 0.3 | 0.4 | 0.2 | 0.3 | 0.3 | 0.3 | ..... |
| Scrap and waste | ..... | ..... | ..... | ..... | 0.4 | ..... | ..... | ..... | ..... | ..... |
| Used merchandise | 0.4 | 0.7 | 0.8 | 0.7 | 0.8 | 0.4 | ..... | 0.2 | 0.2 | 0.6 |
| Goods imported and returned unchanged | ..... | ..... | ..... | ..... | ..... | ..... | ..... | ..... | ..... | ..... |
| Special classification provisions | 27.2 | 8.1 | 2.9 | 3.5 | 4.5 | 0.1 | 0.2 | 0.2 | 0.6 | 0.1 |
| | The Netherlands | | | | | Asian 10 | | | | |
| ALL GOODS | 134.2 | 185.2 | 261.9 | 202.6 | 211.0 | 2 400.3 | 2 907.6 | 3 008.5 | 2 899.7 | 3 094.5 |
| Manufactured goods | 116.4 | 129.0 | 186.1 | 142.6 | 140.2 | 2 086.7 | 2 603.0 | 2 698.7 | 2 565.5 | 2 746.9 |
| Food products | 5.0 | 0.8 | 0.6 | 4.4 | 6.3 | 21.3 | 24.5 | 47.4 | 46.4 | 46.7 |
| Tobacco products | 50.1 | 67.2 | 101.2 | 39.3 | 54.9 | 1 104.2 | 1 274.6 | 1 135.8 | 1 217.0 | 1 253.0 |
| Textile mill products | 0.5 | 0.2 | 0.6 | 0.3 | 0.3 | 9.7 | 11.9 | 12.2 | 13.4 | 13.3 |
| Apparel | 0.1 | 0.4 | 0.6 | 0.4 | 0.2 | 7.9 | 8.8 | 10.1 | 16.0 | 14.0 |
| Lumber and wood products | 2.6 | 2.1 | 2.1 | 3.1 | 0.6 | 21.5 | 25.5 | 30.7 | 29.9 | 36.9 |
| Furniture and fixtures | 0.4 | 0.3 | 0.3 | 0.3 | 0.3 | 1.2 | 3.9 | 5.3 | 4.4 | 3.7 |
| Paper products | 4.8 | 10.8 | 15.3 | 6.9 | 0.4 | 13.4 | 10.2 | 12.7 | 17.2 | 18.2 |
| Printing and publishing | 0.4 | 0.5 | 0.9 | 2.1 | 0.8 | 1.6 | 0.9 | 1.9 | 1.6 | 2.9 |
| Chemical products | 10.0 | 9.9 | 17.7 | 18.4 | 13.4 | 136.5 | 154.2 | 173.9 | 144.6 | 176.5 |
| Refined petroleum products | 4.3 | 0.5 | 1.3 | 0.1 | 0.1 | 12.9 | 36.3 | 17.7 | 9.0 | 6.5 |
| Rubber and plastic products | 4.2 | 3.0 | 5.9 | 8.1 | 6.7 | 45.1 | 54.2 | 64.8 | 64.4 | 61.8 |
| Leather products | ..... | ..... | 0.2 | 0.2 | 0.1 | 0.4 | 0.4 | 0.7 | 0.7 | 0.7 |
| Stone, clay and glass products | 0.2 | 0.5 | 0.1 | 0.2 | 0.2 | 6.3 | 13.0 | 22.8 | 33.0 | 18.2 |
| Primary metals | 0.9 | 0.5 | 0.9 | 2.7 | 1.9 | 30.9 | 40.3 | 30.9 | 39.1 | 30.3 |
| Fabricated metal products | 1.3 | 1.9 | 3.9 | 3.1 | 1.8 | 24.6 | 28.1 | 43.1 | 45.4 | 60.9 |
| Industrial machinery and computers | 13.8 | 16.2 | 13.0 | 17.8 | 27.0 | 177.2 | 168.8 | 223.7 | 245.9 | 247.8 |
| Electric and electronic equipment | 2.9 | 3.1 | 5.9 | 11.7 | 9.5 | 90.6 | 86.9 | 106.9 | 113.8 | 165.4 |
| Transportation equipment | 2.1 | 1.5 | 2.9 | 2.1 | 2.9 | 225.0 | 499.3 | 510.2 | 357.8 | 354.7 |
| Scientific and measuring instruments | 10.6 | 7.6 | 9.0 | 11.3 | 9.0 | 57.7 | 55.1 | 120.7 | 69.9 | 95.6 |
| Miscellaneous manufactures | 2.1 | 1.9 | 3.2 | 2.7 | 1.6 | 94.4 | 97.5 | 122.6 | 89.4 | 134.4 |
| Unidentified manufactures | 0.2 | 0.3 | 0.5 | 7.4 | 2.2 | 4.3 | 8.9 | 4.5 | 6.4 | 5.4 |
| Agricultural and livestock products | 6.8 | 4.7 | 4.3 | 2.5 | 1.5 | 222.0 | 227.8 | 168.2 | 152.0 | 168.0 |
| Agricultural products | 6.5 | 4.3 | 3.7 | 1.8 | 1.2 | 220.4 | 226.2 | 166.6 | 150.7 | 167.1 |
| Livestock and livestock products | 0.3 | 0.4 | 0.6 | 0.7 | 0.3 | 1.6 | 1.6 | 1.6 | 1.3 | 0.9 |
| Other commodities | 11.0 | 51.4 | 71.6 | 57.6 | 69.3 | 91.6 | 76.8 | 141.6 | 182.2 | 179.6 |
| Forestry products | ..... | ..... | ..... | ..... | ..... | ..... | 0.1 | ..... | ..... | 0.3 |
| Fish and other marine products | 1.5 | 1.5 | 1.2 | 1.6 | 1.3 | 1.9 | 5.6 | 5.3 | 8.8 | 7.7 |
| Metallic ores and concentrates | 0.1 | ..... | ..... | ..... | ..... | ..... | 0.1 | ..... | ..... | ..... |
| Bituminous coal and lignite | 8.7 | 47.5 | 68.9 | 55.0 | 67.1 | 50.0 | 44.3 | 82.3 | 134.7 | 149.2 |
| Crude petroleum and natural gas | ..... | ..... | ..... | ..... | ..... | ..... | ..... | ..... | ..... | ..... |
| Nonmetallic minerals | 0.2 | 0.4 | 0.1 | 0.1 | 0.3 | 0.5 | 0.6 | 0.5 | 1.2 | 0.9 |
| Scrap and waste | 0.3 | 0.7 | 0.3 | ..... | ..... | 38.5 | 25.3 | 53.2 | 34.0 | 20.5 |
| Used merchandise | 0.1 | 1.3 | 1.0 | 0.8 | 0.1 | 0.5 | 0.5 | 0.2 | 0.4 | 0.3 |
| Goods imported and returned unchanged | ..... | ..... | ..... | ..... | ..... | ..... | ..... | ..... | ..... | ..... |
| Special classification provisions | 0.1 | ..... | 0.2 | 0.1 | 0.4 | 0.3 | 0.4 | 0.2 | 3.0 | 0.8 |

## Table D-3.   State Exports of Goods by Destination and Industry, 1993–1997 —*Continued*

**VIRGINIA** (Millions of dollars.)

| Industry | 1993 | 1994 | 1995 | 1996 | 1997 | 1993 | 1994 | 1995 | 1996 | 1997 |
|---|---|---|---|---|---|---|---|---|---|---|
| | Japan | | | | | South Korea | | | | |
| ALL GOODS | 1 228.0 | 1 401.9 | 1 256.2 | 1 385.5 | 1 434.2 | 524.5 | 856.4 | 971.6 | 737.6 | 751.7 |
| **Manufactured goods** | 1 008.6 | 1 194.2 | 1 095.5 | 1 190.7 | 1 235.0 | 466.7 | 803.6 | 898.8 | 669.7 | 681.9 |
| Food products | 10.9 | 7.9 | 6.2 | 9.3 | 7.7 | 1.2 | 5.2 | 6.2 | 7.8 | 11.9 |
| Tobacco products | 819.4 | 976.5 | 844.9 | 934.6 | 964.4 | 71.3 | 86.6 | 107.7 | 107.8 | 129.5 |
| Textile mill products | 0.6 | 2.4 | 3.1 | 0.9 | 1.1 | 0.5 | 0.4 | 0.4 | 0.9 | 0.9 |
| Apparel | 7.2 | 8.1 | 9.2 | 15.2 | 13.2 | ..... | 0.1 | 0.1 | 0.1 | 0.1 |
| Lumber and wood products | 14.8 | 17.5 | 20.7 | 19.3 | 22.3 | 1.2 | 1.8 | 1.9 | 1.6 | 2.8 |
| Furniture and fixtures | 0.6 | 2.4 | 3.2 | 3.0 | 2.7 | 0.2 | 0.6 | 1.2 | 0.8 | 0.2 |
| Paper products | 4.3 | 1.2 | 1.3 | 1.4 | 1.6 | 2.0 | 1.9 | 1.2 | 1.1 | 1.1 |
| Printing and publishing | 0.2 | 0.4 | 1.0 | 0.4 | 1.5 | 0.3 | 0.1 | 0.1 | ..... | 0.2 |
| Chemical products | 39.6 | 54.7 | 61.5 | 48.1 | 58.9 | 24.6 | 25.7 | 25.3 | 24.6 | 34.4 |
| Refined petroleum products | 1.0 | 2.2 | 0.8 | 2.1 | 0.9 | 1.0 | 2.3 | 2.8 | 1.9 | 0.3 |
| Rubber and plastic products | 30.7 | 32.5 | 29.4 | 24.4 | 24.6 | 4.9 | 8.9 | 14.9 | 16.9 | 9.8 |
| Leather products | ..... | 0.1 | 0.3 | 0.4 | 0.3 | ..... | ..... | ..... | ..... | ..... |
| Stone, clay and glass products | 3.0 | 8.2 | 16.0 | 22.1 | 10.5 | 1.7 | 3.1 | 4.9 | 6.8 | 3.7 |
| Primary metals | 9.4 | 2.3 | 4.9 | 7.2 | 4.5 | 1.5 | 16.1 | 3.3 | 4.6 | 3.7 |
| Fabricated metal products | 2.5 | 4.0 | 3.1 | 6.3 | 8.6 | 12.5 | 15.8 | 29.2 | 12.6 | 21.5 |
| Industrial machinery and computers | 17.3 | 22.7 | 29.6 | 42.5 | 42.4 | 47.9 | 54.6 | 65.1 | 62.2 | 56.1 |
| Electric and electronic equipment | 14.1 | 16.1 | 21.7 | 22.6 | 23.8 | 16.2 | 21.4 | 13.6 | 13.0 | 13.2 |
| Transportation equipment | 3.3 | 4.1 | 3.0 | 4.2 | 6.6 | 189.9 | 474.1 | 484.6 | 342.6 | 331.2 |
| Scientific and measuring instruments | 17.0 | 21.9 | 20.0 | 14.6 | 22.0 | 14.3 | 14.9 | 78.0 | 27.7 | 32.0 |
| Miscellaneous manufactures | 12.3 | 8.5 | 14.9 | 11.6 | 17.1 | 74.7 | 68.8 | 57.7 | 35.9 | 28.6 |
| Unidentified manufactures | 0.5 | 0.5 | 0.8 | 0.5 | 0.6 | 1.0 | 1.4 | 0.6 | 0.6 | 0.7 |
| **Agricultural and livestock products** | 188.2 | 191.1 | 122.3 | 111.9 | 107.1 | ..... | 4.2 | 7.2 | 11.7 | 19.8 |
| Agricultural products | 187.2 | 190.0 | 121.3 | 110.8 | 106.3 | ..... | 4.2 | 6.7 | 11.5 | 19.8 |
| Livestock and livestock products | 1.0 | 1.1 | 1.0 | 1.0 | 0.8 | ..... | ..... | 0.6 | 0.2 | ..... |
| **Other commodities** | 31.2 | 16.6 | 38.4 | 82.9 | 92.2 | 57.8 | 48.6 | 65.5 | 56.2 | 50.0 |
| Forestry products | ..... | ..... | ..... | ..... | ..... | ..... | ..... | ..... | ..... | ..... |
| Fish and other marine products | 1.7 | 3.1 | 2.1 | 1.8 | 1.9 | ..... | 0.7 | ..... | 0.1 | 0.1 |
| Metallic ores and concentrates | ..... | 0.1 | ..... | ..... | ..... | ..... | ..... | ..... | ..... | ..... |
| Bituminous coal and lignite | 29.0 | 12.8 | 34.4 | 78.8 | 89.4 | 20.9 | 24.6 | 37.2 | 45.7 | 46.6 |
| Crude petroleum and natural gas | ..... | ..... | ..... | ..... | ..... | ..... | ..... | ..... | ..... | ..... |
| Nonmetallic minerals | ..... | 0.1 | 0.1 | 0.8 | 0.1 | 0.3 | 0.2 | 0.3 | 0.2 | 0.4 |
| Scrap and waste | ..... | 0.1 | 1.5 | 0.6 | 0.4 | 36.6 | 23.1 | 27.9 | 10.0 | 2.5 |
| Used merchandise | 0.3 | 0.4 | 0.2 | 0.3 | 0.1 | ..... | ..... | ..... | ..... | 0.1 |
| Goods imported and returned unchanged | ..... | ..... | ..... | ..... | ..... | ..... | ..... | ..... | ..... | ..... |
| Special classification provisions | 0.2 | 0.1 | 0.1 | 0.6 | 0.2 | ..... | ..... | ..... | 0.1 | 0.3 |
| | Taiwan | | | | | Singapore | | | | |
| ALL GOODS | 197.4 | 202.2 | 181.5 | 156.1 | 152.8 | 82.7 | 96.3 | 126.3 | 107.7 | 133.4 |
| **Manufactured goods** | 188.9 | 186.9 | 161.9 | 136.7 | 126.5 | 82.0 | 95.4 | 124.8 | 107.0 | 132.7 |
| Food products | 0.1 | 0.1 | 0.8 | 3.5 | 1.6 | 1.0 | 1.9 | 2.4 | 2.5 | 3.3 |
| Tobacco products | 46.4 | 60.9 | 26.2 | 39.1 | 42.5 | 30.6 | 30.6 | 29.2 | 30.8 | 38.5 |
| Textile mill products | 2.0 | 2.0 | 1.3 | 1.3 | 0.5 | 0.5 | 0.2 | 0.1 | 0.1 | 0.2 |
| Apparel | 0.1 | 0.1 | 0.1 | ..... | 0.2 | ..... | ..... | ..... | 0.1 | 0.1 |
| Lumber and wood products | 3.7 | 4.0 | 4.1 | 4.8 | 4.7 | 0.1 | 0.1 | 0.2 | 0.1 | 0.1 |
| Furniture and fixtures | 0.2 | 0.4 | 0.3 | 0.2 | 0.3 | 0.1 | 0.2 | 0.2 | 0.2 | 0.3 |
| Paper products | 2.7 | 2.0 | 1.7 | 2.6 | 2.8 | 0.1 | 0.1 | 0.3 | 0.3 | 0.3 |
| Printing and publishing | 0.2 | ..... | 0.1 | 0.2 | 0.2 | 0.7 | 0.2 | 0.1 | 0.3 | 0.1 |
| Chemical products | 16.8 | 14.8 | 16.5 | 12.9 | 14.1 | 20.3 | 18.0 | 30.6 | 20.9 | 19.8 |
| Refined petroleum products | 8.0 | 18.7 | 1.0 | 2.1 | 1.4 | 0.1 | 10.6 | 10.3 | 0.1 | 0.2 |
| Rubber and plastic products | 1.0 | 1.5 | 1.2 | 1.0 | 1.2 | 4.0 | 3.9 | 4.1 | 4.3 | 3.0 |
| Leather products | ..... | ..... | ..... | 0.2 | ..... | ..... | ..... | ..... | ..... | ..... |
| Stone, clay and glass products | 0.9 | 0.6 | 0.3 | 1.4 | 1.0 | ..... | 0.2 | 0.1 | 0.1 | 0.2 |
| Primary metals | 14.4 | 15.4 | 11.4 | 8.7 | 7.9 | 1.8 | 1.3 | 2.1 | 1.0 | 1.1 |
| Fabricated metal products | 4.3 | 1.8 | 2.5 | 7.7 | 3.2 | 1.8 | 2.2 | 2.0 | 0.3 | 2.8 |
| Industrial machinery and computers | 26.1 | 8.1 | 10.4 | 10.7 | 10.8 | 12.3 | 9.8 | 15.5 | 16.3 | 13.0 |
| Electric and electronic equipment | 29.9 | 17.1 | 35.0 | 26.4 | 20.7 | 5.3 | 10.7 | 14.3 | 23.6 | 35.6 |
| Transportation equipment | 14.9 | 12.7 | 10.4 | 7.2 | 4.3 | 0.4 | 0.8 | 8.4 | 1.2 | 8.3 |
| Scientific and measuring instruments | 13.5 | 5.7 | 4.0 | 3.9 | 6.8 | 1.9 | 3.7 | 4.2 | 3.4 | 3.9 |
| Miscellaneous manufactures | 2.2 | 16.4 | 33.9 | 2.6 | 2.1 | 0.8 | 0.7 | 0.6 | 1.2 | 1.4 |
| Unidentified manufactures | 1.8 | 4.7 | 0.4 | 0.3 | 0.3 | 0.1 | 0.2 | 0.1 | 0.1 | 0.4 |
| **Agricultural and livestock products** | 8.2 | 7.7 | 5.3 | 2.3 | 5.3 | 0.6 | 0.7 | 1.3 | 0.4 | 0.4 |
| Agricultural products | 7.6 | 7.1 | 5.3 | 2.3 | 5.3 | 0.6 | 0.7 | 1.3 | 0.4 | 0.4 |
| Livestock and livestock products | 0.6 | 0.5 | ..... | ..... | ..... | ..... | ..... | ..... | ..... | ..... |
| **Other commodities** | 0.3 | 7.6 | 14.3 | 17.0 | 21.0 | 0.1 | 0.2 | 0.2 | 0.2 | 0.2 |
| Forestry products | ..... | ..... | ..... | ..... | ..... | ..... | ..... | ..... | ..... | ..... |
| Fish and other marine products | ..... | 0.2 | ..... | 0.3 | ..... | ..... | ..... | 0.2 | 0.1 | ..... |
| Metallic ores and concentrates | ..... | ..... | ..... | ..... | ..... | ..... | ..... | ..... | ..... | ..... |
| Bituminous coal and lignite | ..... | 6.9 | 10.7 | 10.2 | 13.2 | ..... | ..... | ..... | ..... | ..... |
| Crude petroleum and natural gas | ..... | ..... | ..... | ..... | ..... | ..... | ..... | ..... | ..... | ..... |
| Nonmetallic minerals | 0.1 | 0.2 | 0.1 | 0.2 | 0.1 | ..... | ..... | ..... | ..... | 0.1 |
| Scrap and waste | 0.2 | ..... | 3.5 | 6.3 | 7.6 | ..... | 0.2 | ..... | ..... | ..... |
| Used merchandise | ..... | ..... | ..... | ..... | ..... | 0.1 | ..... | ..... | ..... | 0.1 |
| Goods imported and returned unchanged | ..... | ..... | ..... | ..... | ..... | ..... | ..... | ..... | ..... | ..... |
| Special classification provisions | ..... | 0.2 | ..... | ..... | 0.1 | ..... | ..... | ..... | 0.2 | ..... |

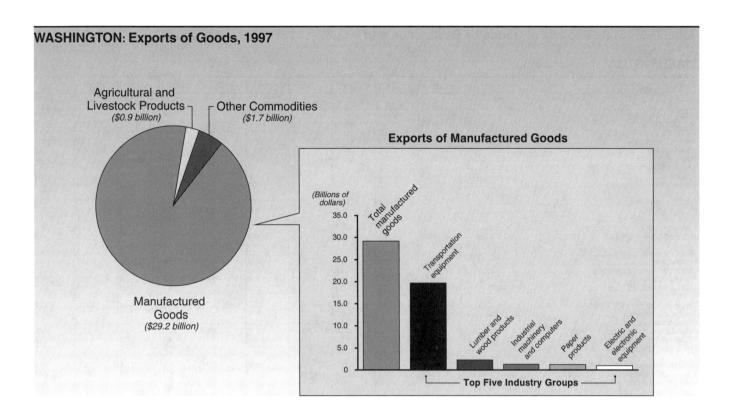

**WASHINGTON: Exports of Goods, 1997**

Agricultural and Livestock Products ($0.9 billion)

Other Commodities ($1.7 billion)

Manufactured Goods ($29.2 billion)

**Exports of Manufactured Goods**

(Billions of dollars)

Top Five Industry Groups

---

### Table D-3.  State Exports of Goods by Destination and Industry, 1993–1997 —Continued

**WASHINGTON** (Millions of dollars.)

| Industry | 1993 | 1994 | 1995 | 1996 | 1997 | 1993 | 1994 | 1995 | 1996 | 1997 |
|---|---|---|---|---|---|---|---|---|---|---|
| | All destinations | | | | | Canada | | | | |
| **ALL GOODS** | 27 397.7 | 25 062.3 | 22 032.0 | 25 498.0 | 31 745.6 | 1 723.1 | 1 856.4 | 2 288.6 | 2 437.4 | 2 457.5 |
| **Manufactured goods** | 24 775.9 | 22 356.4 | 18 945.6 | 22 741.2 | 29 184.9 | 1 426.5 | 1 546.7 | 1 959.2 | 2 074.7 | 2 085.4 |
| Food products | 753.1 | 828.9 | 967.1 | 915.8 | 919.5 | 144.4 | 157.9 | 175.3 | 164.3 | 167.3 |
| Tobacco products | ..... | 0.1 | 0.1 | 0.1 | 0.3 | ..... | 0.1 | ..... | ..... | 0.1 |
| Textile mill products | 16.2 | 24.8 | 33.4 | 33.7 | 31.5 | 4.9 | 4.7 | 6.3 | 7.8 | 9.4 |
| Apparel | 42.1 | 49.3 | 53.0 | 55.5 | 57.9 | 26.4 | 26.8 | 23.7 | 24.2 | 28.6 |
| Lumber and wood products | 2 797.2 | 2 643.0 | 2 870.2 | 2 893.3 | 2 286.8 | 117.9 | 127.6 | 173.4 | 161.8 | 204.5 |
| Furniture and fixtures | 15.5 | 20.7 | 24.4 | 27.5 | 31.4 | 10.6 | 11.1 | 11.2 | 11.0 | 11.4 |
| Paper products | 884.0 | 1 018.9 | 1 600.0 | 1 285.2 | 1 240.6 | 87.6 | 90.9 | 131.6 | 121.8 | 126.8 |
| Printing and publishing | 125.7 | 76.3 | 75.3 | 75.6 | 85.5 | 49.9 | 40.5 | 48.3 | 45.9 | 31.9 |
| Chemical products | 300.8 | 372.4 | 276.0 | 371.7 | 601.0 | 67.0 | 69.0 | 80.6 | 98.6 | 95.4 |
| Refined petroleum products | 59.7 | 72.9 | 94.4 | 177.4 | 147.1 | 46.2 | 59.6 | 81.1 | 131.3 | 138.2 |
| Rubber and plastic products | 66.6 | 75.2 | 94.7 | 97.5 | 113.5 | 45.3 | 44.0 | 45.2 | 48.4 | 61.0 |
| Leather products | 8.7 | 9.7 | 13.2 | 16.9 | 20.8 | 1.8 | 2.6 | 3.5 | 7.1 | 9.9 |
| Stone, clay and glass products | 46.1 | 46.5 | 51.2 | 53.4 | 62.4 | 22.7 | 20.2 | 19.8 | 21.0 | 21.0 |
| Primary metals | 193.2 | 226.1 | 301.8 | 327.7 | 399.1 | 61.5 | 74.9 | 96.7 | 108.8 | 125.6 |
| Fabricated metal products | 101.1 | 129.6 | 142.4 | 126.2 | 195.0 | 59.6 | 55.8 | 80.1 | 67.2 | 95.8 |
| Industrial machinery and computers | 920.0 | 822.4 | 1 055.1 | 1 060.3 | 1 275.8 | 175.7 | 180.7 | 213.7 | 237.4 | 311.6 |
| Electric and electronic equipment | 600.2 | 795.5 | 947.4 | 881.0 | 990.9 | 167.4 | 272.7 | 301.9 | 269.8 | 230.0 |
| Transportation equipment | 17 224.6 | 14 450.4 | 9 581.7 | 13 402.7 | 19 711.3 | 216.1 | 174.3 | 340.2 | 377.9 | 237.4 |
| Scientific and measuring instruments | 476.8 | 532.1 | 583.9 | 672.3 | 785.5 | 59.0 | 68.1 | 67.9 | 74.8 | 90.4 |
| Miscellaneous manufactures | 124.0 | 137.5 | 153.5 | 239.3 | 199.6 | 55.9 | 56.1 | 48.8 | 85.6 | 77.2 |
| Unidentified manufactures | 20.5 | 24.0 | 26.6 | 28.1 | 29.5 | 6.8 | 9.1 | 9.8 | 10.1 | 12.1 |
| **Agricultural and livestock products** | 620.8 | 748.5 | 993.5 | 902.2 | 907.1 | 124.8 | 132.2 | 133.6 | 132.4 | 138.4 |
| Agricultural products | 570.8 | 664.6 | 917.6 | 800.2 | 825.3 | 117.3 | 113.6 | 119.1 | 121.6 | 125.7 |
| Livestock and livestock products | 50.0 | 83.8 | 75.9 | 102.0 | 81.8 | 7.5 | 18.7 | 14.5 | 10.9 | 12.7 |
| **Other commodities** | 2 001.0 | 1 957.5 | 2 092.9 | 1 854.6 | 1 653.6 | 171.7 | 177.5 | 195.8 | 230.2 | 233.7 |
| Forestry products | 20.3 | 19.7 | 21.7 | 22.4 | 27.0 | 0.8 | 1.9 | 2.2 | 2.3 | 2.4 |
| Fish and other marine products | 1 712.5 | 1 691.3 | 1 755.2 | 1 511.8 | 1 298.3 | 89.0 | 90.9 | 102.1 | 109.5 | 98.3 |
| Metallic ores and concentrates | 7.2 | 8.3 | 8.4 | 8.0 | 10.1 | 1.8 | 2.2 | 0.4 | 0.2 | 1.3 |
| Bituminous coal and lignite | 1.7 | 2.9 | 2.2 | 0.7 | 0.6 | ..... | ..... | ..... | ..... | 0.5 |
| Crude petroleum and natural gas | 4.5 | 4.5 | 5.6 | 5.3 | 3.9 | 4.4 | 4.3 | 5.2 | 5.1 | 3.8 |
| Nonmetallic minerals | 9.5 | 9.4 | 10.6 | 16.7 | 19.4 | 8.2 | 8.0 | 8.8 | 9.6 | 9.1 |
| Scrap and waste | 85.2 | 104.4 | 168.1 | 107.2 | 102.5 | 5.8 | 10.0 | 10.2 | 4.2 | 5.8 |
| Used merchandise | 64.5 | 17.7 | 17.3 | 23.3 | 26.6 | 4.0 | 5.3 | 4.6 | 5.9 | 6.6 |
| Goods imported and returned unchanged | 52.6 | 51.6 | 56.8 | 86.8 | 102.8 | 52.6 | 51.6 | 56.8 | 86.8 | 102.8 |
| Special classification provisions | 42.9 | 47.7 | 47.1 | 72.4 | 62.3 | 5.0 | 3.3 | 5.4 | 6.6 | 3.1 |

## Table D-3.  State Exports of Goods by Destination and Industry, 1993–1997 —Continued

**WASHINGTON** (Millions of dollars.)

| Industry | 1993 | 1994 | 1995 | 1996 | 1997 | 1993 | 1994 | 1995 | 1996 | 1997 |
|---|---|---|---|---|---|---|---|---|---|---|
| | South and Central America and Caribbean | | | | | Mexico | | | | |
| **ALL GOODS** | 542.1 | 410.4 | 482.4 | 651.0 | 952.1 | 207.8 | 411.2 | 188.1 | 254.9 | 272.4 |
| **Manufactured goods** | 524.9 | 382.3 | 450.1 | 614.4 | 917.3 | 198.8 | 391.0 | 167.0 | 233.1 | 239.3 |
| Food products | 7.3 | 8.9 | 16.1 | 14.5 | 20.7 | 2.3 | 3.0 | 3.7 | 4.2 | 4.9 |
| Tobacco products | ..... | ..... | ..... | ..... | ..... | ..... | ..... | ..... | ..... | ..... |
| Textile mill products | 0.5 | 0.4 | 2.9 | 3.3 | 1.8 | 1.2 | 2.5 | 2.4 | 2.7 | 2.3 |
| Apparel | 1.1 | 1.5 | 0.6 | 3.6 | 1.5 | 0.2 | 0.9 | 1.5 | 0.4 | 0.7 |
| Lumber and wood products | 0.3 | 0.5 | 0.6 | 1.9 | 2.0 | 0.5 | 0.4 | 16.0 | 1.3 | 1.1 |
| Furniture and fixtures | 0.1 | 0.5 | 1.0 | 0.8 | 0.7 | 0.4 | 0.4 | 0.1 | 0.3 | 0.5 |
| Paper products | 12.9 | 18.9 | 33.2 | 27.6 | 36.8 | 22.3 | 39.8 | 31.8 | 31.4 | 35.3 |
| Printing and publishing | 12.0 | 4.6 | 3.7 | 1.2 | 4.9 | 4.4 | 4.0 | 1.3 | 0.9 | 1.8 |
| Chemical products | 2.8 | 3.0 | 4.7 | 4.5 | 7.8 | 3.5 | 7.9 | 6.5 | 19.1 | 14.9 |
| Refined petroleum products | 0.5 | 1.0 | 0.9 | 0.9 | 0.9 | ..... | 0.3 | 0.6 | 0.6 | 0.9 |
| Rubber and plastic products | 0.5 | 1.0 | 7.1 | 4.4 | 3.4 | 0.6 | 2.0 | 1.5 | 1.7 | 2.6 |
| Leather products | 0.5 | 0.3 | 0.5 | 0.1 | 1.3 | 0.1 | 0.7 | ..... | 0.1 | 0.1 |
| Stone, clay and glass products | 0.5 | 1.5 | 3.2 | 0.5 | 1.0 | 0.6 | 0.5 | 0.9 | 0.5 | 0.5 |
| Primary metals | 0.7 | 0.7 | 1.1 | 1.3 | 3.8 | 1.8 | 2.2 | 2.5 | 6.6 | 26.2 |
| Fabricated metal products | 2.1 | 3.1 | 5.4 | 5.4 | 7.1 | 2.0 | 3.2 | 4.6 | 1.8 | 2.7 |
| Industrial machinery and computers | 32.2 | 28.0 | 42.9 | 42.5 | 81.7 | 14.7 | 67.3 | 64.8 | 106.0 | 76.7 |
| Electric and electronic equipment | 34.2 | 66.8 | 69.1 | 66.0 | 126.6 | 21.5 | 16.9 | 15.3 | 27.1 | 42.4 |
| Transportation equipment | 398.3 | 217.8 | 227.4 | 395.0 | 573.9 | 112.4 | 223.3 | 1.5 | 1.3 | 2.1 |
| Scientific and measuring instruments | 15.7 | 19.3 | 21.5 | 34.4 | 37.7 | 8.8 | 12.3 | 9.9 | 21.0 | 16.2 |
| Miscellaneous manufactures | 1.5 | 3.3 | 7.3 | 4.7 | 2.9 | 1.1 | 3.1 | 1.8 | 5.4 | 5.8 |
| Unidentified manufactures | 1.2 | 1.1 | 0.8 | 1.5 | 0.7 | 0.4 | 0.3 | 0.3 | 0.8 | 1.5 |
| **Agricultural and livestock products** | 13.4 | 25.5 | 30.7 | 33.9 | 31.8 | 7.7 | 15.6 | 11.8 | 16.2 | 26.3 |
| Agricultural products | 12.8 | 25.2 | 30.3 | 33.6 | 31.7 | 7.5 | 15.5 | 11.8 | 16.2 | 26.2 |
| Livestock and livestock products | 0.7 | 0.3 | 0.4 | 0.2 | ..... | 0.2 | 0.1 | ..... | 0.1 | 0.1 |
| **Other commodities** | 3.7 | 2.5 | 1.7 | 2.8 | 3.1 | 1.4 | 4.7 | 9.2 | 5.5 | 6.8 |
| Forestry products | ..... | 0.1 | 0.1 | 0.2 | ..... | 0.4 | 1.1 | 1.8 | 1.5 | 1.6 |
| Fish and other marine products | 1.8 | 0.1 | 0.1 | 0.6 | 0.2 | 0.2 | 0.8 | 1.4 | 0.5 | 0.5 |
| Metallic ores and concentrates | ..... | ..... | ..... | 0.1 | ..... | ..... | ..... | ..... | ..... | ..... |
| Bituminous coal and lignite | ..... | ..... | ..... | ..... | ..... | ..... | ..... | ..... | ..... | ..... |
| Crude petroleum and natural gas | ..... | ..... | ..... | ..... | ..... | ..... | ..... | ..... | ..... | ..... |
| Nonmetallic minerals | ..... | ..... | ..... | ..... | 0.1 | ..... | 0.1 | 0.3 | 0.4 | 0.4 |
| Scrap and waste | 0.4 | 0.2 | 0.2 | 0.1 | ..... | 0.4 | 2.1 | 5.6 | 2.8 | 3.5 |
| Used merchandise | 1.1 | 1.7 | 1.0 | 1.5 | 1.8 | 0.3 | 0.4 | 0.1 | 0.1 | ..... |
| Goods imported and returned unchanged | ..... | ..... | ..... | ..... | ..... | ..... | ..... | ..... | ..... | ..... |
| Special classification provisions | 0.2 | 0.4 | 0.1 | 0.2 | 1.1 | 0.2 | 0.1 | 0.1 | 0.3 | 0.7 |
| | European Union | | | | | United Kingdom | | | | |
| **ALL GOODS** | 5 983.0 | 5 114.5 | 4 469.0 | 4 869.4 | 8 889.1 | 2 252.9 | 2 297.4 | 1 272.3 | 1 688.5 | 4 488.1 |
| **Manufactured goods** | 5 801.2 | 4 984.2 | 4 339.2 | 4 730.9 | 8 730.1 | 2 183.6 | 2 273.7 | 1 247.2 | 1 662.8 | 4 454.5 |
| Food products | 120.1 | 118.2 | 142.3 | 111.8 | 93.3 | 94.2 | 81.7 | 99.7 | 83.0 | 67.7 |
| Tobacco products | ..... | ..... | ..... | ..... | ..... | ..... | ..... | ..... | ..... | ..... |
| Textile mill products | 2.3 | 2.1 | 2.0 | 2.2 | 3.8 | 0.4 | 0.1 | 0.4 | 0.4 | 1.1 |
| Apparel | 2.3 | 2.4 | 2.7 | 3.3 | 9.2 | 0.3 | 0.5 | 1.4 | 1.6 | 6.7 |
| Lumber and wood products | 50.4 | 52.9 | 78.6 | 107.7 | 136.6 | 4.8 | 5.2 | 5.3 | 4.3 | 7.1 |
| Furniture and fixtures | 0.7 | 1.6 | 1.8 | 3.0 | 6.6 | 0.4 | 1.0 | 0.6 | 1.6 | 2.3 |
| Paper products | 171.1 | 220.1 | 406.1 | 253.4 | 264.6 | 13.6 | 36.6 | 68.8 | 39.7 | 28.1 |
| Printing and publishing | 14.3 | 5.6 | 6.9 | 13.3 | 12.2 | 1.5 | 1.3 | 2.2 | 5.1 | 2.8 |
| Chemical products | 135.3 | 152.0 | 75.4 | 100.1 | 171.1 | 9.0 | 5.4 | 6.4 | 43.3 | 10.6 |
| Refined petroleum products | 0.2 | 0.1 | ..... | 0.1 | ..... | ..... | ..... | ..... | ..... | ..... |
| Rubber and plastic products | 3.9 | 3.4 | 5.4 | 6.4 | 7.2 | 0.8 | 0.6 | 1.3 | 1.4 | 2.0 |
| Leather products | 1.6 | 0.9 | 1.3 | 1.7 | 2.2 | 0.4 | 0.1 | 0.5 | 0.4 | 0.8 |
| Stone, clay and glass products | 3.5 | 3.6 | 3.7 | 2.7 | 4.0 | 0.3 | 0.5 | 0.7 | 0.6 | 0.7 |
| Primary metals | 8.9 | 10.8 | 18.4 | 25.6 | 46.4 | 2.7 | 2.7 | 5.6 | 8.3 | 14.3 |
| Fabricated metal products | 9.6 | 11.9 | 11.7 | 15.5 | 22.7 | 3.3 | 5.2 | 4.6 | 7.4 | 12.6 |
| Industrial machinery and computers | 474.2 | 304.4 | 358.8 | 292.1 | 401.8 | 53.9 | 70.2 | 61.1 | 80.5 | 126.2 |
| Electric and electronic equipment | 156.0 | 174.1 | 197.6 | 168.0 | 257.6 | 56.2 | 53.3 | 62.1 | 54.1 | 74.7 |
| Transportation equipment | 4 402.8 | 3 674.6 | 2 758.2 | 3 323.9 | 6 932.8 | 1 903.3 | 1 958.9 | 867.7 | 1 274.8 | 4 024.4 |
| Scientific and measuring instruments | 213.7 | 207.1 | 231.4 | 254.6 | 313.5 | 32.3 | 38.9 | 50.1 | 43.2 | 60.2 |
| Miscellaneous manufactures | 26.4 | 34.8 | 32.0 | 40.0 | 41.4 | 5.1 | 10.4 | 7.3 | 11.0 | 11.6 |
| Unidentified manufactures | 4.0 | 3.4 | 4.8 | 5.5 | 3.1 | 1.2 | 1.1 | 1.3 | 2.1 | 0.7 |
| **Agricultural and livestock products** | 31.7 | 39.9 | 36.5 | 46.6 | 55.2 | 8.4 | 13.8 | 13.3 | 15.2 | 17.3 |
| Agricultural products | 26.4 | 34.0 | 33.6 | 41.1 | 43.2 | 7.6 | 13.0 | 12.6 | 14.5 | 14.8 |
| Livestock and livestock products | 5.4 | 5.9 | 2.9 | 5.4 | 12.0 | 0.7 | 0.8 | 0.6 | 0.7 | 2.5 |
| **Other commodities** | 150.0 | 90.5 | 93.3 | 91.9 | 103.8 | 61.0 | 9.9 | 11.9 | 10.4 | 16.3 |
| Forestry products | 17.9 | 15.4 | 16.8 | 17.7 | 21.9 | ..... | ..... | 0.1 | 0.1 | 0.3 |
| Fish and other marine products | 65.9 | 62.3 | 53.3 | 45.6 | 47.4 | 5.8 | 5.7 | 7.3 | 5.3 | 4.6 |
| Metallic ores and concentrates | ..... | ..... | ..... | ..... | ..... | ..... | ..... | ..... | ..... | ..... |
| Bituminous coal and lignite | ..... | ..... | ..... | ..... | ..... | ..... | ..... | ..... | ..... | ..... |
| Crude petroleum and natural gas | 0.1 | 0.1 | 0.2 | 0.1 | 0.1 | ..... | ..... | ..... | ..... | ..... |
| Nonmetallic minerals | 0.3 | 0.2 | 0.4 | 4.8 | 5.8 | 0.1 | 0.2 | ..... | ..... | 0.1 |
| Scrap and waste | 2.4 | 3.3 | 10.0 | 4.7 | 2.1 | ..... | ..... | 0.2 | 0.1 | 0.2 |
| Used merchandise | 53.5 | 3.3 | 5.2 | 4.9 | 8.9 | 50.6 | 0.8 | 1.8 | 1.2 | 4.9 |
| Goods imported and returned unchanged | ..... | ..... | ..... | ..... | ..... | ..... | ..... | ..... | ..... | ..... |
| Special classification provisions | 9.9 | 5.9 | 7.3 | 13.9 | 17.6 | 4.4 | 3.3 | 2.4 | 3.6 | 6.2 |

## Table D-3.  State Exports of Goods by Destination and Industry, 1993–1997 —Continued

# WASHINGTON (Millions of dollars.)

| Industry | 1993 | 1994 | 1995 | 1996 | 1997 | 1993 | 1994 | 1995 | 1996 | 1997 |
|---|---|---|---|---|---|---|---|---|---|---|
| | Germany | | | | | France | | | | |
| **ALL GOODS** | 1 236.9 | 829.1 | 896.6 | 923.4 | 1 518.4 | 814.7 | 415.7 | 297.5 | 218.9 | 342.5 |
| **Manufactured goods** | 1 210.3 | 803.7 | 878.1 | 893.4 | 1 489.7 | 783.6 | 392.6 | 273.9 | 200.5 | 322.5 |
| Food products | 6.1 | 5.3 | 7.0 | 5.3 | 5.2 | 1.0 | 1.2 | 1.4 | 3.0 | 2.3 |
| Tobacco products | ..... | ..... | ..... | ..... | ..... | | | | | |
| Textile mill products | 0.2 | 0.1 | 0.1 | 0.2 | 0.2 | 0.1 | 0.2 | 0.1 | 0.2 | 0.1 |
| Apparel | 0.3 | 0.4 | 0.7 | 0.3 | 0.4 | 1.0 | 0.5 | 0.1 | 0.1 | 0.2 |
| Lumber and wood products | 22.2 | 22.0 | 41.1 | 51.7 | 68.4 | 0.4 | 0.5 | 1.2 | 1.7 | 3.0 |
| Furniture and fixtures | 0.2 | 0.2 | 0.3 | 0.2 | 0.4 | 0.1 | 0.1 | 0.1 | 0.1 | 1.3 |
| Paper products | 65.6 | 62.0 | 116.7 | 79.8 | 80.2 | 29.7 | 37.8 | 65.4 | 40.9 | 30.2 |
| Printing and publishing | 1.1 | 0.7 | 0.4 | 0.9 | 0.7 | 0.8 | 0.3 | 1.7 | 4.2 | 5.8 |
| Chemical products | 116.3 | 132.4 | 43.8 | 6.8 | 113.6 | 4.1 | 5.9 | 10.4 | 7.3 | 5.7 |
| Refined petroleum products | 0.2 | 0.1 | ..... | ..... | ..... | | | | | |
| Rubber and plastic products | 0.5 | 0.6 | 1.0 | 1.1 | 2.2 | 0.5 | 0.7 | 0.6 | 0.4 | 1.0 |
| Leather products | 0.2 | 0.1 | 0.2 | 0.2 | 0.1 | 0.1 | ..... | ..... | 0.1 | 0.2 |
| Stone, clay and glass products | 1.3 | 2.0 | 1.6 | 1.3 | 1.8 | 0.7 | 0.1 | 0.1 | 0.1 | 0.1 |
| Primary metals | 2.5 | 2.2 | 5.2 | 2.2 | 5.6 | 0.8 | 0.9 | 1.4 | 5.3 | 16.4 |
| Fabricated metal products | 1.9 | 2.7 | 2.5 | 1.6 | 2.5 | 1.0 | 0.6 | 0.4 | 0.8 | 1.0 |
| Industrial machinery and computers | 302.6 | 62.6 | 88.1 | 60.7 | 52.9 | 52.9 | 68.8 | 92.2 | 33.3 | 53.5 |
| Electric and electronic equipment | 23.7 | 28.1 | 30.8 | 28.7 | 43.9 | 23.3 | 32.9 | 41.4 | 34.0 | 72.6 |
| Transportation equipment | 593.2 | 425.5 | 497.5 | 583.1 | 1 030.3 | 631.6 | 216.6 | 35.0 | 47.7 | 104.1 |
| Scientific and measuring instruments | 61.4 | 47.4 | 30.0 | 55.6 | 69.8 | 33.2 | 23.6 | 19.6 | 19.5 | 21.9 |
| Miscellaneous manufactures | 10.1 | 8.5 | 9.8 | 12.9 | 11.2 | 1.7 | 1.5 | 2.3 | 1.3 | 2.5 |
| Unidentified manufactures | 0.7 | 0.7 | 1.2 | 0.8 | 0.5 | 0.4 | 0.4 | 0.4 | 0.8 | 0.5 |
| **Agricultural and livestock products** | 9.1 | 7.7 | 8.7 | 13.5 | 10.0 | 0.8 | 1.5 | 0.7 | 0.7 | 1.4 |
| Agricultural products | 6.5 | 4.3 | 7.7 | 11.9 | 6.4 | 0.6 | 1.4 | 0.6 | 0.7 | 1.2 |
| Livestock and livestock products | 2.6 | 3.4 | 1.0 | 1.5 | 3.6 | 0.2 | 0.1 | ..... | ..... | 0.2 |
| **Other commodities** | 17.5 | 17.7 | 9.8 | 16.5 | 18.6 | 30.3 | 21.6 | 22.9 | 17.7 | 18.6 |
| Forestry products | 3.1 | 5.3 | 2.8 | 3.0 | 4.2 | ..... | ..... | ..... | ..... | 0.2 |
| Fish and other marine products | 10.7 | 10.8 | 3.7 | 5.0 | 4.6 | 27.2 | 18.9 | 19.9 | 13.0 | 14.8 |
| Metallic ores and concentrates | ..... | ..... | ..... | ..... | ..... | | | | | |
| Bituminous coal and lignite | ..... | ..... | ..... | ..... | ..... | | | | | |
| Crude petroleum and natural gas | 0.1 | 0.1 | 0.2 | ..... | ..... | | | | | |
| Nonmetallic minerals | 0.1 | ..... | 0.4 | 4.5 | 5.8 | | | | | |
| Scrap and waste | 0.7 | 0.7 | 1.3 | ..... | ..... | | | | | |
| Used merchandise | 0.2 | 0.2 | 0.3 | 0.3 | 0.1 | 1.9 | 1.9 | 2.0 | 1.3 | 0.7 |
| Goods imported and returned unchanged | ..... | ..... | ..... | ..... | ..... | | | | | |
| Special classification provisions | 2.6 | 0.7 | 1.2 | 3.7 | 4.0 | 1.1 | 0.8 | 0.9 | 3.4 | 3.0 |
| | The Netherlands | | | | | Asian 10 | | | | |
| **ALL GOODS** | 574.2 | 448.4 | 713.7 | 904.2 | 877.1 | 15 482.2 | 14 039.7 | 13 043.6 | 13 920.2 | 14 870.6 |
| **Manufactured goods** | 555.1 | 426.7 | 692.4 | 881.0 | 846.3 | 13 400.7 | 11 880.4 | 10 539.4 | 11 797.6 | 12 999.7 |
| Food products | 11.5 | 21.1 | 22.7 | 13.1 | 10.6 | 450.0 | 487.8 | 541.1 | 522.1 | 509.4 |
| Tobacco products | ..... | ..... | ..... | ..... | ..... | ..... | ..... | ..... | ..... | 0.2 |
| Textile mill products | 0.9 | 0.7 | 0.8 | 0.5 | 0.7 | 6.0 | 10.3 | 14.8 | 13.3 | 9.7 |
| Apparel | 0.2 | 0.1 | 0.1 | 0.1 | 0.4 | 10.0 | 15.2 | 21.8 | 21.5 | 15.4 |
| Lumber and wood products | 0.8 | 1.8 | 2.2 | 2.9 | 5.5 | 2 615.0 | 2 451.9 | 2 589.9 | 2 607.3 | 1 929.2 |
| Furniture and fixtures | ..... | ..... | 0.4 | 0.5 | 0.1 | 2.1 | 4.5 | 8.4 | 10.0 | 9.1 |
| Paper products | 3.0 | 4.1 | 17.4 | 2.9 | 8.0 | 529.2 | 589.5 | 914.8 | 796.8 | 727.1 |
| Printing and publishing | 0.6 | 0.4 | 0.3 | 0.8 | 1.0 | 17.0 | 8.3 | 7.7 | 8.9 | 9.9 |
| Chemical products | 1.8 | 1.9 | 1.9 | 1.6 | 4.5 | 81.4 | 128.5 | 94.9 | 131.3 | 293.5 |
| Refined petroleum products | ..... | ..... | ..... | ..... | ..... | 12.4 | 10.9 | 10.7 | 43.0 | 4.5 |
| Rubber and plastic products | 0.7 | 0.5 | 1.3 | 0.8 | 0.5 | 13.0 | 19.9 | 31.1 | 31.1 | 27.4 |
| Leather products | 0.1 | 0.4 | 0.4 | 0.6 | 0.5 | 3.3 | 3.8 | 6.8 | 6.9 | 6.4 |
| Stone, clay and glass products | 0.3 | 0.2 | 0.1 | ..... | ..... | 17.5 | 19.6 | 22.3 | 26.4 | 33.1 |
| Primary metals | 0.3 | 0.5 | 1.0 | 0.3 | 0.5 | 116.0 | 129.9 | 176.1 | 177.9 | 188.0 |
| Fabricated metal products | 0.8 | 1.0 | 1.1 | 1.1 | 2.0 | 20.6 | 18.7 | 31.2 | 24.9 | 50.3 |
| Industrial machinery and computers | 18.8 | 16.3 | 35.5 | 39.7 | 51.7 | 133.2 | 146.2 | 270.4 | 226.3 | 277.0 |
| Electric and electronic equipment | 8.3 | 11.8 | 13.4 | 12.9 | 14.2 | 149.0 | 140.8 | 231.2 | 218.8 | 248.6 |
| Transportation equipment | 462.2 | 313.5 | 525.9 | 727.3 | 666.6 | 9 072.2 | 7 503.2 | 5 341.9 | 6 646.3 | 8 382.2 |
| Scientific and measuring instruments | 41.1 | 44.7 | 62.1 | 70.4 | 74.6 | 121.0 | 156.8 | 167.9 | 190.3 | 216.0 |
| Miscellaneous manufactures | 3.3 | 7.4 | 5.3 | 5.0 | 4.8 | 27.4 | 29.1 | 48.8 | 88.1 | 55.7 |
| Unidentified manufactures | 0.3 | 0.3 | 0.3 | 0.3 | 0.3 | 4.4 | 5.5 | 7.5 | 6.5 | 6.9 |
| **Agricultural and livestock products** | 5.7 | 5.5 | 4.8 | 5.9 | 10.6 | 417.9 | 492.5 | 731.3 | 622.4 | 594.1 |
| Agricultural products | 5.7 | 5.2 | 4.8 | 5.9 | 10.6 | 383.3 | 435.2 | 674.8 | 538.6 | 539.2 |
| Livestock and livestock products | ..... | 0.3 | ..... | ..... | ..... | 34.6 | 57.3 | 56.4 | 83.9 | 55.0 |
| **Other commodities** | 13.5 | 16.2 | 16.5 | 17.3 | 20.2 | 1 663.6 | 1 666.7 | 1 772.9 | 1 500.2 | 1 276.8 |
| Forestry products | 10.1 | 9.1 | 9.5 | 13.3 | 15.6 | 0.9 | 0.9 | 0.5 | 0.5 | 0.7 |
| Fish and other marine products | 2.1 | 5.4 | 2.7 | 1.6 | 2.2 | 1 550.6 | 1 534.2 | 1 586.6 | 1 345.9 | 1 137.7 |
| Metallic ores and concentrates | ..... | ..... | ..... | ..... | ..... | 5.4 | 6.1 | 8.0 | 7.8 | 8.9 |
| Bituminous coal and lignite | ..... | ..... | ..... | ..... | ..... | 1.7 | 2.9 | 2.2 | 0.6 | 0.1 |
| Crude petroleum and natural gas | ..... | ..... | ..... | ..... | ..... | ..... | 0.1 | 0.1 | ..... | 0.1 |
| Nonmetallic minerals | ..... | ..... | ..... | 0.1 | ..... | 0.9 | 0.9 | 1.0 | 1.6 | 3.7 |
| Scrap and waste | 0.8 | 1.3 | 2.7 | 1.0 | 1.0 | 75.9 | 88.2 | 141.0 | 88.3 | 87.0 |
| Used merchandise | 0.1 | 0.1 | 0.5 | 0.1 | 0.1 | 2.7 | 4.6 | 4.6 | 7.9 | 5.7 |
| Goods imported and returned unchanged | ..... | ..... | ..... | ..... | ..... | ..... | ..... | ..... | ..... | ..... |
| Special classification provisions | 0.3 | 0.3 | 1.1 | 1.2 | 1.2 | 25.5 | 28.9 | 28.9 | 47.6 | 32.9 |

## Table D-3.  State Exports of Goods by Destination and Industry, 1993–1997 —*Continued*

**WASHINGTON** (Millions of dollars.)

| Industry | 1993 | 1994 | 1995 | 1996 | 1997 | 1993 | 1994 | 1995 | 1996 | 1997 |
|---|---|---|---|---|---|---|---|---|---|---|
| | Japan | | | | | South Korea | | | | |
| **ALL GOODS** | 6 662.5 | 6 372.5 | 6 703.0 | 6 316.4 | 6 561.6 | 1 389.5 | 1 408.3 | 1 851.6 | 2 023.9 | 1 889.2 |
| **Manufactured goods** | 5 027.8 | 4 747.3 | 4 968.9 | 4 899.3 | 5 311.1 | 1 258.8 | 1 226.8 | 1 528.1 | 1 766.8 | 1 690.0 |
| Food products | 338.7 | 345.8 | 365.5 | 330.5 | 323.4 | 19.9 | 28.2 | 32.7 | 33.9 | 25.8 |
| Tobacco products | ..... | ..... | ..... | ..... | 0.2 | ..... | ..... | ..... | ..... | ..... |
| Textile mill products | 3.9 | 4.9 | 6.2 | 5.9 | 5.0 | 0.5 | 2.7 | 5.1 | 4.7 | 1.6 |
| Apparel | 8.2 | 13.4 | 16.4 | 17.9 | 10.3 | 0.2 | 0.4 | 3.6 | 1.4 | 1.8 |
| Lumber and wood products | 2 288.8 | 2 247.1 | 2 379.1 | 2 407.3 | 1 721.7 | 217.0 | 133.7 | 156.8 | 147.7 | 150.2 |
| Furniture and fixtures | 1.0 | 2.9 | 6.1 | 5.0 | 4.6 | 0.3 | 0.5 | 0.9 | 2.8 | 1.5 |
| Paper products | 358.2 | 385.4 | 571.6 | 480.1 | 426.9 | 68.1 | 76.9 | 137.6 | 105.2 | 93.5 |
| Printing and publishing | 4.3 | 2.7 | 4.0 | 5.0 | 5.3 | 1.6 | 0.7 | 1.0 | 1.1 | 1.3 |
| Chemical products | 25.3 | 26.3 | 59.6 | 83.6 | 168.5 | 6.1 | 5.4 | 11.1 | 12.5 | 15.3 |
| Refined petroleum products | 4.4 | 1.0 | 7.1 | 1.7 | 1.6 | 2.5 | 2.0 | 2.1 | 21.7 | 1.7 |
| Rubber and plastic products | 7.0 | 10.1 | 21.1 | 20.2 | 15.9 | 2.0 | 2.0 | 5.7 | 4.6 | 5.9 |
| Leather products | 1.0 | 1.5 | 4.6 | 5.5 | 4.7 | 0.1 | 0.4 | 0.5 | 0.7 | 1.2 |
| Stone, clay and glass products | 3.6 | 2.9 | 3.8 | 7.3 | 15.7 | 1.8 | 1.3 | 2.0 | 4.1 | 4.3 |
| Primary metals | 36.9 | 36.6 | 49.3 | 57.4 | 82.2 | 25.4 | 33.4 | 44.0 | 33.4 | 31.2 |
| Fabricated metal products | 10.8 | 7.2 | 14.1 | 10.4 | 8.7 | 0.9 | 0.8 | 4.5 | 2.2 | 3.0 |
| Industrial machinery and computers | 35.3 | 39.3 | 77.0 | 80.2 | 94.1 | 16.5 | 23.9 | 28.9 | 29.2 | 38.3 |
| Electric and electronic equipment | 51.1 | 44.5 | 65.2 | 87.0 | 112.7 | 10.9 | 16.8 | 23.0 | 17.5 | 14.5 |
| Transportation equipment | 1 774.0 | 1 476.6 | 1 198.2 | 1 149.0 | 2 183.8 | 868.4 | 876.5 | 1 036.6 | 1 300.6 | 1 254.7 |
| Scientific and measuring instruments | 54.3 | 74.1 | 78.6 | 78.2 | 86.5 | 14.8 | 18.2 | 25.7 | 33.5 | 36.4 |
| Miscellaneous manufactures | 18.9 | 22.2 | 37.1 | 64.2 | 36.7 | 1.5 | 2.2 | 5.4 | 9.3 | 7.0 |
| Unidentified manufactures | 2.0 | 2.8 | 4.1 | 3.1 | 2.6 | 0.5 | 1.0 | 0.8 | 0.6 | 0.8 |
| **Agricultural and livestock products** | 173.7 | 198.6 | 239.5 | 193.1 | 251.0 | 21.8 | 52.6 | 192.6 | 127.1 | 73.4 |
| Agricultural products | 170.6 | 191.8 | 234.3 | 189.0 | 246.4 | 1.6 | 16.4 | 155.9 | 77.0 | 41.4 |
| Livestock and livestock products | 3.1 | 6.8 | 5.3 | 4.1 | 4.6 | 20.1 | 36.2 | 36.7 | 50.1 | 32.0 |
| **Other commodities** | 1 461.0 | 1 426.6 | 1 494.6 | 1 224.0 | 999.5 | 108.9 | 128.9 | 130.9 | 130.0 | 125.8 |
| Forestry products | 0.6 | 0.5 | 0.3 | 0.3 | 0.3 | ..... | ..... | ..... | ..... | ..... |
| Fish and other marine products | 1 440.0 | 1 401.9 | 1 461.3 | 1 202.6 | 971.9 | 67.1 | 76.9 | 56.4 | 79.8 | 77.8 |
| Metallic ores and concentrates | 5.3 | 6.1 | 8.0 | 7.8 | 8.9 | ..... | ..... | ..... | ..... | ..... |
| Bituminous coal and lignite | ..... | ..... | ..... | ..... | 0.1 | 1.7 | 2.9 | 2.2 | 0.6 | 0.1 |
| Crude petroleum and natural gas | ..... | ..... | 0.1 | ..... | ..... | ..... | ..... | ..... | ..... | ..... |
| Nonmetallic minerals | 0.4 | 0.2 | 0.3 | 0.1 | 0.4 | ..... | ..... | 0.1 | 0.1 | ..... |
| Scrap and waste | 12.8 | 14.1 | 21.4 | 7.9 | 7.6 | 38.0 | 47.6 | 69.8 | 48.1 | 46.6 |
| Used merchandise | 1.1 | 3.4 | 2.7 | 4.5 | 2.4 | 0.2 | ..... | 0.1 | 0.2 | ..... |
| Goods imported and returned unchanged | ..... | ..... | ..... | ..... | ..... | ..... | ..... | ..... | ..... | ..... |
| Special classification provisions | 0.7 | 0.4 | 0.4 | 0.8 | 7.9 | 1.9 | 1.4 | 2.5 | 1.2 | 1.3 |
| | Taiwan | | | | | Singapore | | | | |
| **ALL GOODS** | 1 468.8 | 993.8 | 933.0 | 893.6 | 797.0 | 982.6 | 1 295.0 | 1 037.4 | 966.3 | 1 276.1 |
| **Manufactured goods** | 1 287.1 | 801.9 | 715.9 | 687.0 | 636.4 | 976.1 | 1 289.2 | 1 029.2 | 958.0 | 1 265.5 |
| Food products | 32.3 | 42.7 | 40.3 | 39.3 | 49.3 | 7.6 | 7.7 | 8.9 | 9.5 | 12.3 |
| Tobacco products | ..... | ..... | ..... | ..... | ..... | ..... | ..... | ..... | ..... | ..... |
| Textile mill products | 0.2 | 0.8 | 1.0 | 0.2 | 0.5 | 0.1 | 0.1 | 0.2 | 0.2 | 1.0 |
| Apparel | 0.2 | ..... | ..... | 0.6 | 1.0 | 0.3 | 0.5 | 0.5 | 0.6 | 0.5 |
| Lumber and wood products | 31.0 | 11.5 | 28.1 | 22.6 | 24.2 | 0.4 | 0.2 | 0.3 | 0.6 | 1.1 |
| Furniture and fixtures | 0.3 | 0.4 | 0.4 | 0.8 | 0.7 | 0.1 | 0.2 | 0.2 | 0.3 | 1.2 |
| Paper products | 28.3 | 32.5 | 56.7 | 45.8 | 54.2 | 13.1 | 15.3 | 25.3 | 23.4 | 18.1 |
| Printing and publishing | 2.0 | 0.9 | 0.6 | 0.5 | 0.6 | 2.7 | 0.9 | 0.5 | 0.5 | 0.6 |
| Chemical products | 45.2 | 85.4 | 5.9 | 7.1 | 85.9 | 0.4 | 2.0 | 2.0 | 4.5 | 2.1 |
| Refined petroleum products | 0.5 | 0.7 | 0.4 | 0.3 | 0.2 | 1.1 | 0.5 | ..... | 1.9 | ..... |
| Rubber and plastic products | 0.7 | 0.7 | 0.2 | 0.6 | 0.7 | 0.9 | 0.8 | 1.0 | 1.0 | 1.6 |
| Leather products | 0.7 | 0.4 | 0.3 | 0.1 | 0.1 | ..... | 0.1 | 0.1 | ..... | ..... |
| Stone, clay and glass products | 6.0 | 6.3 | 5.9 | 5.9 | 3.6 | 1.3 | 1.5 | 1.3 | 2.0 | 0.6 |
| Primary metals | 13.5 | 15.1 | 20.0 | 20.4 | 16.0 | 4.9 | 6.6 | 7.5 | 10.3 | 9.2 |
| Fabricated metal products | 1.6 | 3.2 | 0.7 | 2.7 | 2.3 | 1.9 | 2.0 | 0.9 | 2.0 | 2.5 |
| Industrial machinery and computers | 11.9 | 15.4 | 22.8 | 21.2 | 16.9 | 15.3 | 22.4 | 49.7 | 24.4 | 36.4 |
| Electric and electronic equipment | 11.2 | 12.6 | 16.1 | 18.9 | 15.3 | 31.3 | 25.4 | 67.5 | 46.5 | 56.1 |
| Transportation equipment | 1 091.4 | 559.5 | 504.3 | 483.6 | 343.6 | 886.0 | 1 189.1 | 851.0 | 816.0 | 1 105.2 |
| Scientific and measuring instruments | 8.2 | 12.6 | 10.7 | 13.2 | 18.7 | 7.7 | 13.0 | 11.1 | 12.3 | 14.5 |
| Miscellaneous manufactures | 1.5 | 0.8 | 0.9 | 2.5 | 1.7 | 0.7 | 0.6 | 1.0 | 1.6 | 2.0 |
| Unidentified manufactures | 0.4 | 0.3 | 0.3 | 0.7 | 1.0 | 0.4 | 0.3 | 0.4 | 0.3 | 0.4 |
| **Agricultural and livestock products** | 163.3 | 172.0 | 191.6 | 185.9 | 138.6 | 5.5 | 5.1 | 6.8 | 6.0 | 6.3 |
| Agricultural products | 163.2 | 171.8 | 191.5 | 185.5 | 137.9 | 5.5 | 5.1 | 6.8 | 6.0 | 6.3 |
| Livestock and livestock products | 0.1 | 0.2 | ..... | 0.4 | 0.8 | ..... | ..... | ..... | ..... | ..... |
| **Other commodities** | 18.4 | 20.0 | 25.6 | 20.8 | 22.0 | 1.1 | 0.7 | 1.4 | 2.3 | 4.3 |
| Forestry products | 0.1 | ..... | ..... | ..... | 0.1 | ..... | ..... | ..... | ..... | ..... |
| Fish and other marine products | 7.6 | 10.2 | 11.1 | 13.8 | 10.1 | 0.3 | 0.1 | 0.4 | 1.6 | 1.9 |
| Metallic ores and concentrates | ..... | ..... | ..... | ..... | ..... | ..... | ..... | ..... | ..... | ..... |
| Bituminous coal and lignite | ..... | ..... | ..... | ..... | ..... | ..... | ..... | ..... | ..... | ..... |
| Crude petroleum and natural gas | ..... | ..... | ..... | ..... | ..... | ..... | ..... | ..... | ..... | ..... |
| Nonmetallic minerals | 0.4 | 0.4 | 0.1 | 0.2 | 0.3 | ..... | ..... | ..... | ..... | ..... |
| Scrap and waste | 9.5 | 8.2 | 13.9 | 6.3 | 10.9 | ..... | 0.1 | ..... | ..... | 1.1 |
| Used merchandise | ..... | 0.5 | ..... | ..... | 0.1 | 0.2 | 0.2 | 0.5 | 0.4 | 0.1 |
| Goods imported and returned unchanged | ..... | ..... | ..... | ..... | ..... | ..... | ..... | ..... | ..... | ..... |
| Special classification provisions | 0.8 | 0.6 | 0.5 | 0.5 | 0.5 | 0.5 | 0.3 | 0.5 | 0.3 | 1.2 |

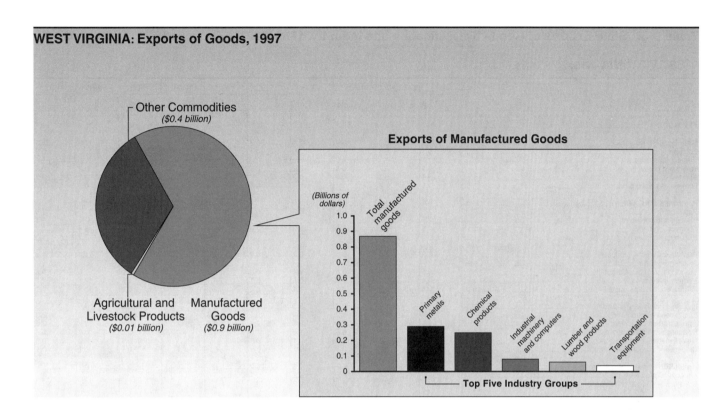

**WEST VIRGINIA: Exports of Goods, 1997**

Other Commodities
($0.4 billion)

Agricultural and
Livestock Products
($0.01 billion)

Manufactured
Goods
($0.9 billion)

**Exports of Manufactured Goods**

(Billions of dollars)

Top Five Industry Groups

## Table D-3.   State Exports of Goods by Destination and Industry, 1993–1997 —*Continued*

**WEST VIRGINIA** (Millions of dollars.)

| Industry | 1993 | 1994 | 1995 | 1996 | 1997 | 1993 | 1994 | 1995 | 1996 | 1997 |
|---|---|---|---|---|---|---|---|---|---|---|
| | All destinations | | | | | Canada | | | | |
| **ALL GOODS** | 754.1 | 940.6 | 1 097.9 | 1 217.9 | 1 298.8 | 285.0 | 334.6 | 334.2 | 377.5 | 478.5 |
| **Manufactured goods** | 550.9 | 637.3 | 708.4 | 820.2 | 867.7 | 210.8 | 245.3 | 255.2 | 292.0 | 313.9 |
| Food products | 1.3 | 2.9 | 14.1 | 5.9 | 5.2 | 1.0 | 2.3 | 2.6 | 2.3 | 2.2 |
| Tobacco products | ..... | ..... | 4.0 | ..... | 0.2 | ..... | ..... | ..... | ..... | ..... |
| Textile mill products | 4.6 | 3.7 | 3.7 | 4.9 | 7.1 | 1.5 | 1.2 | 1.3 | 1.8 | 2.6 |
| Apparel | 0.9 | 0.9 | 1.4 | 1.3 | 4.7 | 0.1 | 0.1 | 0.3 | 0.3 | 0.4 |
| Lumber and wood products | 29.5 | 38.2 | 37.6 | 45.6 | 61.1 | 12.7 | 14.1 | 15.5 | 23.4 | 27.8 |
| Furniture and fixtures | 2.6 | 1.4 | 2.5 | 2.1 | 2.8 | 2.0 | 0.8 | 0.8 | 0.4 | 0.3 |
| Paper products | 3.6 | 3.9 | 5.4 | 6.2 | 7.1 | 3.4 | 3.4 | 4.5 | 4.9 | 4.6 |
| Printing and publishing | 1.5 | 2.1 | 3.2 | 1.0 | 0.7 | 0.5 | 0.5 | 1.2 | 0.9 | 0.3 |
| Chemical products | 238.9 | 280.5 | 232.3 | 289.2 | 249.6 | 76.6 | 98.2 | 80.1 | 85.0 | 83.0 |
| Refined petroleum products | 0.7 | 7.0 | 3.3 | 8.8 | 9.3 | 0.7 | 7.0 | 1.4 | 1.4 | 5.1 |
| Rubber and plastic products | 15.0 | 11.3 | 10.8 | 11.6 | 9.1 | 3.8 | 4.5 | 4.9 | 5.0 | 5.1 |
| Leather products | 0.3 | 0.3 | 0.2 | 3.3 | 1.5 | 0.3 | 0.3 | 0.1 | 0.1 | ..... |
| Stone, clay and glass products | 6.6 | 15.9 | 30.1 | 31.7 | 28.9 | 1.7 | 3.3 | 4.5 | 6.5 | 7.1 |
| Primary metals | 112.7 | 127.9 | 161.6 | 212.6 | 289.8 | 57.9 | 66.0 | 71.6 | 98.8 | 118.3 |
| Fabricated metal products | 11.8 | 13.3 | 18.2 | 18.3 | 16.6 | 6.5 | 8.6 | 11.0 | 12.0 | 10.2 |
| Industrial machinery and computers | 67.4 | 49.9 | 57.0 | 75.5 | 79.6 | 20.7 | 15.5 | 20.0 | 24.5 | 21.3 |
| Electric and electronic equipment | 9.0 | 8.7 | 15.7 | 19.5 | 30.5 | 5.3 | 4.1 | 5.9 | 5.6 | 5.3 |
| Transportation equipment | 19.7 | 45.0 | 81.1 | 58.2 | 38.4 | 10.8 | 11.9 | 24.5 | 15.8 | 15.9 |
| Scientific and measuring instruments | 22.4 | 21.9 | 22.6 | 21.5 | 22.3 | 4.5 | 2.7 | 3.9 | 2.4 | 3.6 |
| Miscellaneous manufactures | 1.1 | 1.2 | 2.1 | 1.8 | 2.2 | 0.4 | 0.4 | 0.6 | 0.5 | 0.5 |
| Unidentified manufactures | 1.3 | 1.3 | 1.4 | 1.1 | 1.2 | 0.4 | 0.5 | 0.6 | 0.5 | 0.3 |
| **Agricultural and livestock products** | 3.6 | 6.1 | 12.3 | 5.9 | 8.0 | 3.0 | 5.8 | 6.3 | 3.7 | 4.3 |
| Agricultural products | 1.4 | 3.8 | 7.4 | 1.5 | 1.7 | 1.3 | 3.7 | 3.1 | 1.2 | 1.4 |
| Livestock and livestock products | 2.2 | 2.3 | 4.9 | 4.5 | 6.3 | 1.7 | 2.1 | 3.2 | 2.5 | 2.9 |
| **Other commodities** | 199.6 | 297.2 | 377.3 | 391.8 | 423.1 | 71.1 | 83.5 | 72.7 | 81.8 | 160.3 |
| Forestry products | 0.6 | 3.5 | 3.6 | 2.6 | 1.4 | ..... | 0.1 | 0.6 | 0.1 | ..... |
| Fish and other marine products | 0.3 | 0.3 | 0.3 | 0.2 | 1.6 | 0.3 | 0.2 | 0.3 | 0.1 | ..... |
| Metallic ores and concentrates | ..... | ..... | 1.3 | 0.1 | 0.1 | ..... | ..... | ..... | 0.1 | 0.1 |
| Bituminous coal and lignite | 189.8 | 277.3 | 360.4 | 367.2 | 394.2 | 63.6 | 67.7 | 61.7 | 61.2 | 136.5 |
| Crude petroleum and natural gas | 0.1 | 0.2 | ..... | ..... | 5.1 | 0.1 | 0.2 | ..... | ..... | 5.1 |
| Nonmetallic minerals | 0.2 | 0.9 | 0.7 | 1.4 | 2.1 | 0.1 | 0.7 | 0.6 | 1.0 | 1.6 |
| Scrap and waste | 3.1 | 2.6 | 4.0 | 2.9 | 3.0 | 2.1 | 2.6 | 3.1 | 2.1 | 2.2 |
| Used merchandise | 0.5 | 0.5 | 0.8 | 0.8 | 2.0 | ..... | 0.2 | 0.3 | 0.6 | 1.3 |
| Goods imported and returned unchanged | 4.6 | 11.6 | 5.9 | 16.3 | 13.3 | 4.6 | 11.6 | 5.9 | 16.3 | 13.3 |
| Special classification provisions | 0.4 | 0.3 | 0.3 | 0.4 | 0.3 | 0.2 | 0.3 | 0.2 | 0.3 | 0.3 |

## Table D-3.  State Exports of Goods by Destination and Industry, 1993–1997 —Continued

### WEST VIRGINIA (Millions of dollars.)

| Industry | 1993 | 1994 | 1995 | 1996 | 1997 | 1993 | 1994 | 1995 | 1996 | 1997 |
|---|---|---|---|---|---|---|---|---|---|---|
| | South and Central America and Caribbean | | | | | Mexico | | | | |
| **ALL GOODS** | 45.2 | 66.1 | 91.1 | 101.7 | 65.5 | 21.0 | 16.7 | 16.4 | 19.3 | 34.4 |
| **Manufactured goods** | 42.5 | 46.6 | 56.4 | 62.4 | 38.8 | 20.9 | 16.6 | 16.4 | 19.0 | 33.5 |
| Food products | 0.1 | 0.1 | 1.6 | 2.0 | 0.5 | ..... | 0.2 | ..... | ..... | 0.2 |
| Tobacco products | ..... | ..... | ..... | ..... | ..... | ..... | ..... | ..... | ..... | ..... |
| Textile mill products | 0.1 | 0.2 | 0.4 | 0.2 | 0.2 | 0.1 | 0.2 | 0.1 | 0.4 | 0.9 |
| Apparel | 0.4 | 0.3 | 0.4 | 0.3 | ..... | 0.2 | ..... | 0.1 | 0.2 | 3.7 |
| Lumber and wood products | 1.5 | 1.4 | ..... | ..... | 0.5 | 0.4 | ..... | ..... | 0.1 | ..... |
| Furniture and fixtures | 0.1 | ..... | ..... | ..... | ..... | ..... | 0.1 | ..... | ..... | ..... |
| Paper products | ..... | ..... | 0.1 | 0.2 | 0.1 | 0.1 | 0.3 | ..... | ..... | 1.5 |
| Printing and publishing | ..... | ..... | ..... | ..... | ..... | 0.1 | ..... | ..... | ..... | 0.1 |
| Chemical products | 12.3 | 15.0 | 12.1 | 15.3 | 17.6 | 10.4 | 7.4 | 6.4 | 6.4 | 7.7 |
| Refined petroleum products | ..... | ..... | ..... | ..... | ..... | ..... | ..... | ..... | 0.2 | 1.0 |
| Rubber and plastic products | 0.2 | 0.3 | 0.2 | 0.2 | 0.2 | 0.1 | 0.3 | 0.2 | 1.4 | 0.6 |
| Leather products | ..... | ..... | ..... | ..... | ..... | ..... | ..... | ..... | ..... | ..... |
| Stone, clay and glass products | 0.1 | 0.8 | 0.6 | 1.4 | 0.6 | ..... | 0.2 | 1.0 | 1.5 | 0.8 |
| Primary metals | 0.4 | 0.5 | 0.2 | 0.6 | 6.1 | 5.1 | 0.6 | 1.9 | 2.7 | 2.7 |
| Fabricated metal products | 0.5 | 0.3 | 0.6 | 1.4 | 0.4 | 0.2 | 0.3 | 2.0 | 0.8 | 1.7 |
| Industrial machinery and computers | 24.6 | 4.1 | 5.7 | 15.3 | 7.7 | 2.0 | 2.7 | 2.3 | 3.6 | 6.0 |
| Electric and electronic equipment | 0.7 | 0.1 | 1.2 | 0.9 | 0.6 | 0.3 | 0.9 | 0.7 | 0.3 | 2.0 |
| Transportation equipment | 1.1 | 22.7 | 32.6 | 22.5 | 2.4 | 0.4 | 0.5 | 0.8 | 0.7 | 3.6 |
| Scientific and measuring instruments | 0.5 | 0.6 | 0.8 | 1.8 | 1.3 | 1.2 | 2.9 | 0.5 | 0.4 | 0.8 |
| Miscellaneous manufactures | 0.1 | 0.2 | ..... | 0.1 | 0.2 | ..... | ..... | 0.1 | 0.2 | 0.3 |
| Unidentified manufactures | 0.1 | 0.2 | 0.1 | 0.1 | ..... | 0.1 | ..... | 0.1 | 0.1 | 0.1 |
| **Agricultural and livestock products** | 0.1 | ..... | 0.2 | 0.3 | 0.2 | ..... | ..... | ..... | 0.1 | ..... |
| Agricultural products | ..... | ..... | 0.2 | 0.2 | 0.1 | ..... | ..... | ..... | ..... | ..... |
| Livestock and livestock products | ..... | ..... | ..... | 0.2 | 0.1 | ..... | ..... | ..... | ..... | ..... |
| **Other commodities** | 2.8 | 19.6 | 34.5 | 39.0 | 26.6 | ..... | ..... | ..... | 0.2 | 0.8 |
| Forestry products | ..... | ..... | ..... | ..... | ..... | ..... | ..... | ..... | ..... | ..... |
| Fish and other marine products | ..... | ..... | ..... | ..... | 1.6 | ..... | ..... | ..... | ..... | ..... |
| Metallic ores and concentrates | ..... | ..... | ..... | ..... | ..... | ..... | ..... | ..... | ..... | ..... |
| Bituminous coal and lignite | 2.5 | 19.3 | 33.8 | 39.0 | 25.0 | ..... | ..... | ..... | ..... | ..... |
| Crude petroleum and natural gas | ..... | ..... | ..... | ..... | ..... | ..... | ..... | ..... | ..... | ..... |
| Nonmetallic minerals | ..... | 0.1 | 0.1 | 0.1 | ..... | ..... | ..... | ..... | 0.2 | 0.5 |
| Scrap and waste | ..... | ..... | 0.3 | ..... | ..... | ..... | ..... | ..... | ..... | ..... |
| Used merchandise | 0.2 | 0.2 | 0.3 | ..... | ..... | ..... | ..... | ..... | ..... | 0.3 |
| Goods imported and returned unchanged | ..... | ..... | ..... | ..... | ..... | ..... | ..... | ..... | ..... | ..... |
| Special classification provisions | ..... | ..... | ..... | ..... | ..... | ..... | ..... | ..... | ..... | ..... |
| | European Union | | | | | United Kingdom | | | | |
| **ALL GOODS** | 190.4 | 291.5 | 412.9 | 419.6 | 403.3 | 34.0 | 57.7 | 100.6 | 100.0 | 127.2 |
| **Manufactured goods** | 84.1 | 126.5 | 191.9 | 217.4 | 230.8 | 19.9 | 42.3 | 70.6 | 71.5 | 91.6 |
| Food products | 0.2 | ..... | 2.5 | 0.1 | 0.7 | ..... | ..... | 1.1 | ..... | 0.6 |
| Tobacco products | ..... | ..... | 4.0 | ..... | ..... | ..... | ..... | ..... | ..... | ..... |
| Textile mill products | 2.0 | 1.3 | 1.1 | 1.3 | 1.7 | 0.3 | 0.3 | 0.3 | 0.4 | 0.5 |
| Apparel | ..... | ..... | 0.2 | 0.1 | 0.2 | ..... | ..... | 0.1 | ..... | 0.1 |
| Lumber and wood products | 11.1 | 20.4 | 19.1 | 17.8 | 24.0 | 0.3 | 0.5 | 1.0 | 1.1 | 1.9 |
| Furniture and fixtures | 0.3 | 0.2 | 0.2 | 0.5 | 0.5 | ..... | ..... | ..... | 0.4 | ..... |
| Paper products | 0.1 | ..... | 0.2 | ..... | 0.1 | ..... | ..... | 0.1 | ..... | ..... |
| Printing and publishing | 0.9 | 1.3 | 1.9 | 0.1 | 0.1 | 0.8 | 1.2 | 0.2 | 0.1 | 0.1 |
| Chemical products | 16.3 | 30.2 | 42.6 | 75.5 | 62.0 | 0.1 | 0.8 | 2.6 | 3.0 | 1.1 |
| Refined petroleum products | ..... | ..... | 1.9 | 7.2 | 2.8 | ..... | ..... | ..... | ..... | ..... |
| Rubber and plastic products | 1.4 | 2.2 | 3.2 | 1.1 | 1.2 | 0.3 | 0.4 | 0.8 | 0.6 | 0.2 |
| Leather products | ..... | ..... | 0.1 | ..... | ..... | ..... | ..... | ..... | ..... | ..... |
| Stone, clay and glass products | 1.6 | 4.9 | 15.6 | 12.0 | 11.7 | 0.3 | 0.7 | 0.7 | 1.0 | 2.1 |
| Primary metals | 25.7 | 36.0 | 56.2 | 68.2 | 84.9 | 9.4 | 24.5 | 42.6 | 51.9 | 72.1 |
| Fabricated metal products | 1.5 | 1.2 | 1.9 | 1.9 | 1.5 | 0.4 | 0.7 | 1.1 | 0.9 | 0.9 |
| Industrial machinery and computers | 8.4 | 13.7 | 15.7 | 12.4 | 12.2 | 3.2 | 8.1 | 6.2 | 5.5 | 3.6 |
| Electric and electronic equipment | 1.3 | 1.1 | 2.0 | 6.3 | 13.0 | 0.2 | 0.4 | 0.6 | 1.4 | 2.1 |
| Transportation equipment | 3.7 | 5.4 | 14.1 | 4.7 | 6.1 | 1.8 | 2.8 | 9.5 | 2.4 | 2.5 |
| Scientific and measuring instruments | 9.1 | 8.2 | 8.4 | 7.7 | 7.2 | 2.5 | 1.9 | 3.1 | 2.6 | 3.5 |
| Miscellaneous manufactures | 0.2 | 0.1 | 0.9 | 0.3 | 0.8 | ..... | ..... | 0.5 | 0.1 | ..... |
| Unidentified manufactures | 0.4 | 0.2 | 0.3 | 0.2 | 0.3 | 0.1 | 0.1 | 0.1 | 0.1 | 0.1 |
| **Agricultural and livestock products** | 0.4 | 0.2 | 5.5 | 1.7 | 2.4 | ..... | ..... | 0.1 | ..... | ..... |
| Agricultural products | ..... | ..... | 3.9 | 0.1 | 0.2 | ..... | ..... | 0.1 | ..... | ..... |
| Livestock and livestock products | 0.4 | 0.2 | 1.6 | 1.6 | 2.2 | ..... | ..... | ..... | ..... | ..... |
| **Other commodities** | 105.9 | 164.7 | 215.5 | 200.5 | 170.1 | 14.1 | 15.3 | 29.9 | 28.5 | 35.6 |
| Forestry products | ..... | 0.1 | 0.1 | 0.1 | ..... | ..... | ..... | ..... | ..... | ..... |
| Fish and other marine products | ..... | ..... | ..... | ..... | ..... | ..... | ..... | ..... | ..... | ..... |
| Metallic ores and concentrates | ..... | ..... | 1.3 | ..... | ..... | ..... | ..... | ..... | ..... | ..... |
| Bituminous coal and lignite | 105.8 | 164.5 | 213.8 | 199.9 | 169.0 | 14.1 | 15.2 | 29.8 | 28.3 | 35.6 |
| Crude petroleum and natural gas | ..... | ..... | ..... | ..... | ..... | ..... | ..... | ..... | ..... | ..... |
| Nonmetallic minerals | ..... | 0.1 | 0.1 | 0.1 | 0.1 | ..... | 0.1 | ..... | ..... | ..... |
| Scrap and waste | ..... | ..... | 0.1 | 0.3 | 0.6 | ..... | ..... | 0.1 | 0.1 | ..... |
| Used merchandise | ..... | ..... | ..... | 0.1 | 0.4 | ..... | ..... | ..... | ..... | ..... |
| Goods imported and returned unchanged | ..... | ..... | ..... | ..... | ..... | ..... | ..... | ..... | ..... | ..... |
| Special classification provisions | ..... | ..... | 0.1 | 0.1 | ..... | ..... | ..... | ..... | ..... | ..... |

## Table D-3. State Exports of Goods by Destination and Industry, 1993–1997 —Continued

### WEST VIRGINIA (Millions of dollars.)

| Industry | 1993 | 1994 | 1995 | 1996 | 1997 | 1993 | 1994 | 1995 | 1996 | 1997 |
|---|---|---|---|---|---|---|---|---|---|---|
| | Germany | | | | | France | | | | |
| ALL GOODS | 15.7 | 24.1 | 29.3 | 19.4 | 28.0 | 14.5 | 20.9 | 23.3 | 24.0 | 34.0 |
| Manufactured goods | 15.4 | 15.7 | 25.5 | 18.7 | 24.1 | 12.0 | 12.8 | 17.5 | 16.3 | 17.6 |
| Food products | ..... | ..... | 0.6 | ..... | 0.1 | ..... | ..... | 0.1 | ..... | ..... |
| Tobacco products | ..... | ..... | ..... | ..... | ..... | ..... | ..... | ..... | ..... | ..... |
| Textile mill products | 1.4 | 0.7 | 0.6 | 0.8 | 1.0 | ..... | ..... | ..... | ..... | ..... |
| Apparel | ..... | ..... | ..... | ..... | ..... | ..... | ..... | ..... | ..... | ..... |
| Lumber and wood products | 4.4 | 6.4 | 5.7 | 4.5 | 7.4 | 0.9 | 1.5 | 0.7 | 0.2 | 0.3 |
| Furniture and fixtures | ..... | ..... | 0.1 | ..... | 0.1 | ..... | ..... | ..... | ..... | ..... |
| Paper products | ..... | ..... | 0.1 | ..... | ..... | ..... | ..... | ..... | ..... | ..... |
| Printing and publishing | ..... | ..... | 0.2 | ..... | ..... | ..... | ..... | 1.1 | ..... | ..... |
| Chemical products | 0.2 | 1.0 | 1.3 | 2.0 | 1.0 | 0.2 | 2.0 | 2.7 | 0.6 | 2.7 |
| Refined petroleum products | ..... | ..... | ..... | ..... | ..... | ..... | ..... | ..... | ..... | ..... |
| Rubber and plastic products | 0.7 | 1.4 | 0.4 | 0.2 | 0.1 | ..... | ..... | 0.5 | 0.1 | 0.1 |
| Leather products | ..... | ..... | ..... | ..... | ..... | ..... | ..... | ..... | ..... | ..... |
| Stone, clay and glass products | 0.2 | 0.2 | 5.2 | 2.1 | 1.0 | 0.4 | 1.0 | 3.4 | 3.8 | 5.1 |
| Primary metals | 3.9 | 2.0 | 5.2 | 4.8 | 4.3 | 6.6 | 4.5 | 3.9 | 5.8 | 2.9 |
| Fabricated metal products | 0.3 | 0.2 | 0.1 | 0.7 | 0.1 | 0.3 | 0.1 | 0.2 | ..... | 0.2 |
| Industrial machinery and computers | 1.2 | 1.1 | 1.4 | 0.8 | 1.5 | 1.1 | 1.5 | 3.4 | 1.4 | 2.4 |
| Electric and electronic equipment | 0.6 | 0.2 | 0.8 | 2.0 | 5.0 | 0.1 | 0.2 | 0.3 | 1.1 | 2.1 |
| Transportation equipment | 1.3 | 1.2 | 2.7 | 0.5 | 1.8 | 0.2 | 0.4 | 0.4 | 1.4 | 0.8 |
| Scientific and measuring instruments | 1.0 | 1.3 | 1.0 | 0.2 | 0.2 | 2.0 | 1.7 | 0.8 | 1.8 | 0.9 |
| Miscellaneous manufactures | ..... | 0.1 | ..... | ..... | 0.6 | ..... | ..... | ..... | 0.1 | 0.1 |
| Unidentified manufactures | 0.1 | ..... | 0.1 | ..... | ..... | 0.1 | ..... | ..... | ..... | ..... |
| Agricultural and livestock products | 0.3 | 0.1 | 3.7 | 0.7 | 1.6 | ..... | ..... | ..... | ..... | 0.1 |
| Agricultural products | ..... | ..... | 3.6 | ..... | ..... | ..... | ..... | ..... | ..... | ..... |
| Livestock and livestock products | 0.3 | 0.1 | 0.1 | 0.7 | 1.5 | ..... | ..... | ..... | ..... | 0.1 |
| Other commodities | ..... | 8.2 | 0.1 | ..... | 2.3 | 2.4 | 8.0 | 5.8 | 7.7 | 16.4 |
| Forestry products | ..... | 0.1 | 0.1 | ..... | ..... | ..... | ..... | ..... | ..... | ..... |
| Fish and other marine products | ..... | ..... | ..... | ..... | ..... | ..... | ..... | ..... | ..... | ..... |
| Metallic ores and concentrates | ..... | ..... | ..... | ..... | ..... | ..... | ..... | ..... | ..... | ..... |
| Bituminous coal and lignite | ..... | 8.2 | ..... | ..... | 2.2 | 2.4 | 8.0 | 5.8 | 7.7 | 16.2 |
| Crude petroleum and natural gas | ..... | ..... | ..... | ..... | ..... | ..... | ..... | ..... | ..... | ..... |
| Nonmetallic minerals | ..... | ..... | ..... | ..... | ..... | ..... | ..... | ..... | ..... | ..... |
| Scrap and waste | ..... | ..... | ..... | ..... | ..... | ..... | ..... | ..... | ..... | 0.1 |
| Used merchandise | ..... | ..... | ..... | ..... | ..... | ..... | ..... | ..... | ..... | ..... |
| Goods imported and returned unchanged | ..... | ..... | ..... | ..... | ..... | ..... | ..... | ..... | ..... | ..... |
| Special classification provisions | ..... | ..... | ..... | ..... | ..... | ..... | ..... | ..... | ..... | ..... |
| | The Netherlands | | | | | Asian 10 | | | | |
| ALL GOODS | 45.8 | 71.3 | 73.0 | 57.2 | 64.4 | 189.6 | 200.1 | 193.4 | 231.1 | 218.3 |
| Manufactured goods | 18.6 | 26.4 | 21.5 | 19.1 | 20.9 | 169.9 | 170.8 | 145.2 | 172.1 | 159.0 |
| Food products | ..... | ..... | 0.4 | 0.1 | ..... | 0.1 | 0.3 | 1.6 | 1.5 | 1.4 |
| Tobacco products | ..... | ..... | ..... | ..... | ..... | ..... | ..... | ..... | ..... | ..... |
| Textile mill products | ..... | ..... | ..... | ..... | ..... | 0.5 | 0.6 | 0.6 | 1.0 | 1.6 |
| Apparel | ..... | ..... | ..... | ..... | ..... | 0.1 | 0.5 | 0.3 | 0.2 | 0.1 |
| Lumber and wood products | 0.1 | 2.8 | 0.1 | 0.3 | 0.3 | 3.7 | 2.2 | 2.7 | 4.1 | 8.0 |
| Furniture and fixtures | 0.1 | 0.1 | 0.1 | 0.1 | 0.3 | 0.1 | ..... | ..... | 0.7 | 1.1 |
| Paper products | ..... | ..... | 0.1 | ..... | ..... | ..... | 0.1 | 0.5 | 1.0 | 0.7 |
| Printing and publishing | ..... | 0.1 | 0.3 | ..... | ..... | ..... | 0.1 | 0.1 | ..... | 0.1 |
| Chemical products | 15.3 | 20.6 | 14.0 | 14.1 | 16.8 | 120.6 | 125.1 | 82.2 | 95.9 | 69.1 |
| Refined petroleum products | ..... | ..... | ..... | ..... | ..... | ..... | ..... | ..... | ..... | ..... |
| Rubber and plastic products | 0.2 | 0.2 | 1.1 | ..... | 0.4 | 8.6 | 3.5 | 1.4 | 3.2 | 1.3 |
| Leather products | ..... | ..... | ..... | ..... | ..... | ..... | ..... | ..... | 3.2 | 1.5 |
| Stone, clay and glass products | ..... | ..... | 0.1 | 0.1 | 0.1 | 2.6 | 2.6 | 6.1 | 7.8 | 7.4 |
| Primary metals | 0.1 | 0.8 | 0.5 | 0.3 | ..... | 18.9 | 15.9 | 24.5 | 23.9 | 37.3 |
| Fabricated metal products | 0.1 | ..... | 0.1 | ..... | ..... | 1.7 | 2.4 | 1.8 | 1.7 | 1.4 |
| Industrial machinery and computers | 1.1 | 0.7 | 1.6 | 2.1 | 1.1 | 5.3 | 8.7 | 7.5 | 9.5 | 7.7 |
| Electric and electronic equipment | 0.2 | 0.1 | ..... | 0.2 | 0.6 | 0.9 | 1.5 | 4.2 | 3.6 | 6.1 |
| Transportation equipment | 0.2 | 0.1 | 0.9 | 0.1 | 0.1 | 1.8 | 1.6 | 4.2 | 8.3 | 6.4 |
| Scientific and measuring instruments | 1.0 | 1.0 | 1.9 | 1.5 | 1.0 | 4.4 | 5.2 | 6.8 | 6.0 | 7.3 |
| Miscellaneous manufactures | 0.1 | ..... | 0.3 | 0.1 | ..... | 0.3 | 0.3 | 0.3 | 0.6 | 0.2 |
| Unidentified manufactures | ..... | ..... | ..... | ..... | ..... | 0.1 | 0.3 | 0.3 | 0.1 | 0.3 |
| Agricultural and livestock products | ..... | 0.1 | 1.5 | 0.8 | 0.1 | 0.1 | ..... | ..... | ..... | ..... |
| Agricultural products | ..... | ..... | ..... | ..... | 0.1 | 0.1 | ..... | ..... | ..... | ..... |
| Livestock and livestock products | ..... | 0.1 | 1.5 | 0.7 | ..... | ..... | ..... | ..... | ..... | ..... |
| Other commodities | 27.2 | 44.8 | 50.0 | 37.3 | 43.4 | 19.6 | 29.2 | 48.2 | 58.9 | 59.3 |
| Forestry products | ..... | ..... | ..... | ..... | ..... | 0.5 | 3.3 | 2.9 | 2.4 | 1.4 |
| Fish and other marine products | ..... | ..... | ..... | ..... | ..... | ..... | ..... | ..... | 0.1 | ..... |
| Metallic ores and concentrates | ..... | ..... | 1.3 | ..... | ..... | ..... | ..... | ..... | ..... | ..... |
| Bituminous coal and lignite | 27.1 | 44.8 | 48.7 | 37.1 | 43.0 | 17.9 | 25.8 | 45.2 | 56.3 | 57.7 |
| Crude petroleum and natural gas | ..... | ..... | ..... | ..... | ..... | ..... | ..... | ..... | ..... | ..... |
| Nonmetallic minerals | ..... | ..... | ..... | ..... | ..... | ..... | ..... | ..... | ..... | ..... |
| Scrap and waste | ..... | ..... | ..... | 0.2 | 0.3 | 1.0 | ..... | ..... | 0.1 | 0.2 |
| Used merchandise | ..... | ..... | ..... | ..... | ..... | ..... | ..... | ..... | ..... | ..... |
| Goods imported and returned unchanged | ..... | ..... | ..... | ..... | ..... | ..... | ..... | ..... | ..... | ..... |
| Special classification provisions | ..... | ..... | ..... | ..... | ..... | 0.1 | ..... | ..... | ..... | ..... |

## Table D-3.  State Exports of Goods by Destination and Industry, 1993–1997 —*Continued*

### WEST VIRGINIA (Millions of dollars.)

| Industry | 1993 | 1994 | 1995 | 1996 | 1997 | 1993 | 1994 | 1995 | 1996 | 1997 |
|---|---|---|---|---|---|---|---|---|---|---|
| | Japan | | | | | South Korea | | | | |
| **ALL GOODS** | 49.5 | 58.7 | 94.7 | 112.0 | 105.5 | 18.1 | 16.7 | 21.2 | 24.5 | 29.8 |
| **Manufactured goods** | 31.5 | 32.8 | 49.4 | 55.6 | 47.8 | 17.1 | 16.7 | 21.1 | 24.4 | 29.8 |
| Food products | 0.1 | 0.1 | 1.1 | 0.7 | 0.6 | ..... | ..... | ..... | 0.4 | 0.1 |
| Tobacco products | ..... | ..... | ..... | ..... | ..... | ..... | ..... | ..... | ..... | ..... |
| Textile mill products | ..... | ..... | 0.1 | 0.2 | 0.1 | ..... | 0.1 | ..... | 0.1 | ..... |
| Apparel | 0.1 | 0.1 | 0.2 | 0.1 | ..... | ..... | ..... | ..... | ..... | 0.1 |
| Lumber and wood products | 1.9 | 1.0 | 0.5 | 0.3 | 1.0 | 0.2 | 0.5 | 0.7 | 0.6 | 1.0 |
| Furniture and fixtures | ..... | ..... | ..... | ..... | 0.1 | ..... | ..... | ..... | 0.5 | 1.0 |
| Paper products | ..... | ..... | ..... | ..... | ..... | ..... | ..... | 0.4 | 0.6 | 0.4 |
| Printing and publishing | ..... | ..... | ..... | ..... | ..... | ..... | ..... | ..... | ..... | 0.1 |
| Chemical products | 11.9 | 14.5 | 16.6 | 24.9 | 16.2 | 12.2 | 11.5 | 13.3 | 15.4 | 14.3 |
| Refined petroleum products | ..... | ..... | ..... | ..... | ..... | ..... | ..... | ..... | ..... | ..... |
| Rubber and plastic products | 1.8 | 1.6 | 0.9 | 0.8 | 0.6 | 1.0 | 0.4 | 0.2 | 0.3 | 0.1 |
| Leather products | ..... | ..... | ..... | ..... | ..... | ..... | ..... | ..... | ..... | ..... |
| Stone, clay and glass products | 1.7 | 1.5 | 4.6 | 1.5 | 4.2 | 0.7 | 0.7 | 0.3 | 0.3 | 0.4 |
| Primary metals | 10.6 | 8.1 | 18.2 | 16.2 | 16.0 | 0.2 | 0.8 | 1.8 | 1.3 | 7.2 |
| Fabricated metal products | 0.7 | 0.9 | 1.2 | 0.4 | 0.3 | 0.1 | 0.1 | ..... | 0.4 | 0.1 |
| Industrial machinery and computers | 0.5 | 0.8 | 1.0 | 2.2 | 1.5 | 1.7 | 1.4 | 3.0 | 3.9 | 1.9 |
| Electric and electronic equipment | 0.3 | 0.6 | 2.1 | 1.9 | 3.0 | 0.2 | 0.4 | 0.3 | 0.1 | 0.3 |
| Transportation equipment | 0.5 | 1.0 | 1.5 | 4.6 | 3.1 | 0.1 | ..... | ..... | ..... | 0.1 |
| Scientific and measuring instruments | 1.0 | 2.3 | 1.3 | 1.5 | 1.0 | 0.6 | 0.8 | 1.0 | 0.6 | 2.6 |
| Miscellaneous manufactures | 0.2 | 0.1 | ..... | 0.4 | ..... | ..... | ..... | ..... | ..... | 0.1 |
| Unidentified manufactures | ..... | 0.1 | 0.1 | ..... | 0.1 | ..... | ..... | ..... | ..... | 0.1 |
| **Agricultural and livestock products** | 0.1 | ..... | ..... | ..... | ..... | ..... | ..... | ..... | ..... | ..... |
| Agricultural products | 0.1 | ..... | ..... | ..... | ..... | ..... | ..... | ..... | ..... | ..... |
| Livestock and livestock products | ..... | ..... | ..... | ..... | ..... | ..... | ..... | ..... | ..... | ..... |
| **Other commodities** | 18.0 | 25.8 | 45.3 | 56.4 | 57.7 | 1.0 | ..... | ..... | ..... | ..... |
| Forestry products | ..... | ..... | ..... | ..... | ..... | ..... | ..... | ..... | ..... | ..... |
| Fish and other marine products | ..... | ..... | ..... | 0.1 | ..... | ..... | ..... | ..... | ..... | ..... |
| Metallic ores and concentrates | ..... | ..... | ..... | ..... | ..... | ..... | ..... | ..... | ..... | ..... |
| Bituminous coal and lignite | 17.9 | 25.8 | 45.2 | 56.3 | 57.7 | ..... | ..... | ..... | ..... | ..... |
| Crude petroleum and natural gas | ..... | ..... | ..... | ..... | ..... | ..... | ..... | ..... | ..... | ..... |
| Nonmetallic minerals | ..... | ..... | ..... | ..... | ..... | ..... | ..... | ..... | ..... | ..... |
| Scrap and waste | ..... | ..... | ..... | ..... | ..... | 1.0 | ..... | ..... | ..... | ..... |
| Used merchandise | ..... | ..... | ..... | ..... | ..... | ..... | ..... | ..... | ..... | ..... |
| Goods imported and returned unchanged | ..... | ..... | ..... | ..... | ..... | ..... | ..... | ..... | ..... | ..... |
| Special classification provisions | ..... | ..... | ..... | ..... | ..... | ..... | ..... | ..... | ..... | ..... |
| | Taiwan | | | | | Singapore | | | | |
| **ALL GOODS** | 21.0 | 15.2 | 10.1 | 17.1 | 13.2 | 39.3 | 30.5 | 18.9 | 28.0 | 21.0 |
| **Manufactured goods** | 21.0 | 15.2 | 10.1 | 17.1 | 13.2 | 39.3 | 30.5 | 18.9 | 28.0 | 21.0 |
| Food products | ..... | ..... | ..... | ..... | ..... | ..... | ..... | 0.2 | 0.2 | 0.1 |
| Tobacco products | ..... | ..... | ..... | ..... | ..... | ..... | ..... | ..... | ..... | ..... |
| Textile mill products | ..... | 0.1 | 0.1 | ..... | ..... | ..... | ..... | ..... | 0.1 | ..... |
| Apparel | ..... | ..... | ..... | ..... | ..... | ..... | ..... | ..... | 0.1 | ..... |
| Lumber and wood products | 1.2 | 0.3 | 0.4 | 1.3 | 1.3 | ..... | ..... | ..... | 0.2 | 0.1 |
| Furniture and fixtures | ..... | ..... | ..... | ..... | ..... | ..... | ..... | ..... | ..... | ..... |
| Paper products | ..... | ..... | ..... | ..... | ..... | ..... | ..... | ..... | ..... | ..... |
| Printing and publishing | ..... | 0.1 | ..... | ..... | ..... | ..... | ..... | ..... | ..... | ..... |
| Chemical products | 13.8 | 10.4 | 7.1 | 7.3 | 6.8 | 31.5 | 25.7 | 10.6 | 18.3 | 13.3 |
| Refined petroleum products | ..... | ..... | ..... | ..... | ..... | ..... | ..... | ..... | ..... | ..... |
| Rubber and plastic products | 0.1 | ..... | 0.1 | ..... | 0.1 | 1.6 | 0.3 | 0.2 | 0.2 | 0.1 |
| Leather products | ..... | ..... | ..... | ..... | ..... | ..... | ..... | ..... | ..... | ..... |
| Stone, clay and glass products | 0.1 | 0.1 | 0.1 | 4.7 | 1.4 | ..... | ..... | ..... | 0.3 | 0.2 |
| Primary metals | 4.8 | 2.4 | 0.9 | 1.0 | 2.1 | 2.9 | 1.7 | 2.3 | 2.3 | 2.1 |
| Fabricated metal products | 0.2 | 0.8 | ..... | 0.4 | 0.4 | 0.2 | 0.4 | 0.4 | ..... | 0.1 |
| Industrial machinery and computers | 0.1 | 0.2 | 0.3 | 0.2 | 0.1 | 0.5 | 0.5 | 0.5 | 1.7 | 0.6 |
| Electric and electronic equipment | ..... | 0.1 | 0.7 | 1.3 | 0.8 | 0.2 | 0.2 | 0.8 | ..... | 0.2 |
| Transportation equipment | 0.2 | ..... | ..... | ..... | ..... | 0.6 | 0.4 | 2.2 | 3.1 | 2.7 |
| Scientific and measuring instruments | 0.3 | 0.5 | 0.3 | 0.8 | 0.1 | 1.9 | 1.2 | 1.6 | 1.5 | 1.5 |
| Miscellaneous manufactures | ..... | 0.2 | 0.1 | 0.1 | ..... | ..... | ..... | ..... | ..... | ..... |
| Unidentified manufactures | ..... | ..... | ..... | ..... | ..... | ..... | ..... | ..... | ..... | ..... |
| **Agricultural and livestock products** | ..... | ..... | ..... | ..... | ..... | ..... | ..... | ..... | ..... | ..... |
| Agricultural products | ..... | ..... | ..... | ..... | ..... | ..... | ..... | ..... | ..... | ..... |
| Livestock and livestock products | ..... | ..... | ..... | ..... | ..... | ..... | ..... | ..... | ..... | ..... |
| **Other commodities** | ..... | ..... | ..... | ..... | ..... | ..... | ..... | ..... | ..... | ..... |
| Forestry products | ..... | ..... | ..... | ..... | ..... | ..... | ..... | ..... | ..... | ..... |
| Fish and other marine products | ..... | ..... | ..... | ..... | ..... | ..... | ..... | ..... | ..... | ..... |
| Metallic ores and concentrates | ..... | ..... | ..... | ..... | ..... | ..... | ..... | ..... | ..... | ..... |
| Bituminous coal and lignite | ..... | ..... | ..... | ..... | ..... | ..... | ..... | ..... | ..... | ..... |
| Crude petroleum and natural gas | ..... | ..... | ..... | ..... | ..... | ..... | ..... | ..... | ..... | ..... |
| Nonmetallic minerals | ..... | ..... | ..... | ..... | ..... | ..... | ..... | ..... | ..... | ..... |
| Scrap and waste | ..... | ..... | ..... | ..... | ..... | ..... | ..... | ..... | ..... | ..... |
| Used merchandise | ..... | ..... | ..... | ..... | ..... | ..... | ..... | ..... | ..... | ..... |
| Goods imported and returned unchanged | ..... | ..... | ..... | ..... | ..... | ..... | ..... | ..... | ..... | ..... |
| Special classification provisions | ..... | ..... | ..... | ..... | ..... | ..... | ..... | ..... | ..... | ..... |

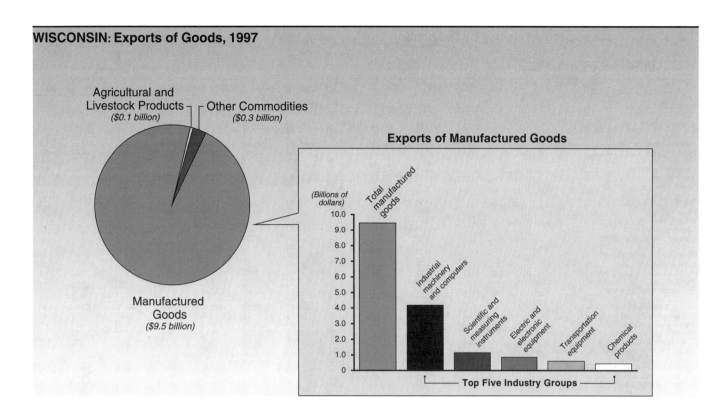

## WISCONSIN: Exports of Goods, 1997

Agricultural and Livestock Products ($0.1 billion)

Other Commodities ($0.3 billion)

Manufactured Goods ($9.5 billion)

### Exports of Manufactured Goods

(Billions of dollars)

Top Five Industry Groups

## Table D-3. State Exports of Goods by Destination and Industry, 1993–1997 —*Continued*

### WISCONSIN (Millions of dollars.)

| Industry | 1993 | 1994 | 1995 | 1996 | 1997 | 1993 | 1994 | 1995 | 1996 | 1997 |
|---|---|---|---|---|---|---|---|---|---|---|
| | All destinations | | | | | Canada | | | | |
| **ALL GOODS** | 5 810.4 | 6 927.9 | 8 004.5 | 8 409.7 | 9 791.5 | 1 947.1 | 2 438.4 | 2 808.6 | 2 685.6 | 3 096.3 |
| **Manufactured goods** | 5 598.6 | 6 636.7 | 7 643.3 | 8 095.1 | 9 455.1 | 1 829.6 | 2 254.6 | 2 549.0 | 2 503.3 | 2 870.6 |
| Food products | 234.5 | 280.3 | 389.4 | 395.8 | 423.3 | 84.1 | 104.6 | 114.7 | 135.6 | 147.1 |
| Tobacco products | ..... | ..... | 1.0 | ..... | ..... | ..... | ..... | ..... | ..... | ..... |
| Textile mill products | 29.4 | 31.1 | 42.6 | 48.8 | 51.5 | 13.6 | 14.6 | 22.7 | 23.6 | 23.2 |
| Apparel | 42.9 | 37.5 | 58.3 | 82.4 | 66.5 | 10.5 | 5.5 | 6.7 | 10.9 | 15.5 |
| Lumber and wood products | 50.8 | 59.9 | 66.9 | 70.5 | 82.7 | 26.1 | 27.1 | 32.0 | 37.4 | 42.8 |
| Furniture and fixtures | 59.6 | 56.6 | 42.6 | 47.9 | 48.7 | 32.5 | 32.1 | 26.4 | 25.2 | 27.6 |
| Paper products | 252.8 | 323.7 | 364.6 | 369.6 | 390.0 | 177.6 | 232.2 | 286.6 | 255.8 | 244.6 |
| Printing and publishing | 41.2 | 40.1 | 45.0 | 51.2 | 59.8 | 26.0 | 22.7 | 29.3 | 30.1 | 33.3 |
| Chemical products | 243.6 | 300.5 | 346.9 | 367.6 | 441.6 | 103.0 | 123.7 | 143.8 | 158.0 | 165.2 |
| Refined petroleum products | 10.2 | 21.9 | 21.4 | 22.5 | 19.6 | 6.7 | 18.8 | 15.6 | 16.3 | 11.5 |
| Rubber and plastic products | 157.9 | 173.5 | 194.9 | 180.6 | 213.5 | 87.8 | 91.8 | 96.7 | 95.3 | 116.0 |
| Leather products | 75.4 | 83.8 | 66.8 | 69.2 | 68.1 | 16.4 | 17.4 | 14.2 | 13.1 | 13.9 |
| Stone, clay and glass products | 37.1 | 52.9 | 59.1 | 68.9 | 62.3 | 13.4 | 13.6 | 13.6 | 15.8 | 19.2 |
| Primary metals | 51.7 | 52.8 | 81.7 | 101.5 | 115.3 | 25.1 | 25.6 | 33.3 | 35.9 | 47.8 |
| Fabricated metal products | 295.2 | 314.4 | 337.5 | 358.6 | 381.0 | 105.8 | 118.3 | 128.4 | 129.9 | 147.3 |
| Industrial machinery and computers | 2 244.0 | 2 719.6 | 3 029.8 | 3 167.4 | 4 178.5 | 643.4 | 845.4 | 961.7 | 908.1 | 1 058.6 |
| Electric and electronic equipment | 515.1 | 590.5 | 725.7 | 769.6 | 859.9 | 134.3 | 155.5 | 187.4 | 187.8 | 226.0 |
| Transportation equipment | 397.1 | 450.5 | 502.7 | 479.7 | 603.4 | 174.5 | 243.1 | 250.2 | 201.8 | 286.4 |
| Scientific and measuring instruments | 696.0 | 855.0 | 1 051.5 | 1 216.2 | 1 145.7 | 80.3 | 87.7 | 109.5 | 144.2 | 166.0 |
| Miscellaneous manufactures | 141.8 | 164.8 | 185.9 | 200.8 | 218.9 | 62.1 | 65.8 | 64.6 | 64.9 | 67.2 |
| Unidentified manufactures | 22.3 | 27.4 | 29.0 | 26.4 | 24.8 | 6.3 | 9.1 | 11.8 | 13.6 | 11.3 |
| **Agricultural and livestock products** | 56.3 | 66.8 | 78.0 | 92.9 | 75.0 | 21.1 | 16.6 | 21.0 | 33.8 | 23.6 |
| Agricultural products | 24.8 | 31.6 | 45.1 | 57.6 | 37.5 | 12.8 | 8.7 | 13.8 | 23.2 | 12.1 |
| Livestock and livestock products | 31.5 | 35.3 | 32.9 | 35.3 | 37.5 | 8.3 | 7.9 | 7.2 | 10.6 | 11.5 |
| **Other commodities** | 155.4 | 224.4 | 283.2 | 221.7 | 261.4 | 96.4 | 167.2 | 238.7 | 148.5 | 202.1 |
| Forestry products | 35.2 | 29.3 | 24.4 | 27.7 | 20.7 | 1.3 | 1.8 | 1.8 | 1.6 | 2.2 |
| Fish and other marine products | 0.7 | 1.1 | 1.1 | 1.2 | 1.1 | 0.6 | 0.9 | 0.5 | 0.5 | 0.4 |
| Metallic ores and concentrates | 50.6 | 111.5 | 130.3 | 82.0 | 62.1 | 50.5 | 111.5 | 130.2 | 81.9 | 62.0 |
| Bituminous coal and lignite | 0.7 | 0.3 | 2.3 | 2.3 | 3.1 | 0.6 | 0.3 | ..... | 2.2 | 3.1 |
| Crude petroleum and natural gas | 0.2 | 0.2 | 0.1 | 2.3 | 1.8 | 0.1 | 0.2 | 0.1 | 2.0 | 1.7 |
| Nonmetallic minerals | 2.3 | 6.5 | 7.3 | 7.6 | 8.3 | 0.7 | 1.6 | 2.3 | 2.6 | 1.8 |
| Scrap and waste | 17.2 | 30.5 | 35.8 | 50.6 | 46.4 | 16.5 | 26.2 | 32.5 | 24.6 | 24.1 |
| Used merchandise | 4.5 | 9.4 | 8.0 | 9.9 | 15.0 | 0.7 | 1.3 | 1.3 | 1.5 | 9.6 |
| Goods imported and returned unchanged | 20.6 | 18.5 | 63.5 | 25.8 | 94.0 | 20.6 | 18.5 | 63.5 | 25.8 | 94.0 |
| Special classification provisions | 23.4 | 17.0 | 10.3 | 12.3 | 8.8 | 4.6 | 5.0 | 6.5 | 5.6 | 3.1 |

## Table D-3.  State Exports of Goods by Destination and Industry, 1993–1997 —*Continued*

**WISCONSIN** (Millions of dollars.)

| Industry | 1993 | 1994 | 1995 | 1996 | 1997 | 1993 | 1994 | 1995 | 1996 | 1997 |
|---|---|---|---|---|---|---|---|---|---|---|
| | South and Central America and Caribbean | | | | | Mexico | | | | |
| **ALL GOODS** | 431.9 | 464.1 | 577.5 | 664.0 | 785.1 | 287.7 | 411.9 | 311.0 | 350.5 | 427.3 |
| **Manufactured goods** | 419.4 | 453.2 | 567.4 | 645.9 | 770.6 | 278.3 | 385.7 | 288.0 | 327.8 | 419.2 |
| Food products | 22.0 | 24.7 | 43.0 | 40.9 | 32.3 | 14.8 | 21.2 | 15.5 | 18.9 | 26.0 |
| Tobacco products | ..... | ..... | ..... | ..... | ..... | ..... | ..... | ..... | ..... | ..... |
| Textile mill products | 3.4 | 2.6 | 3.8 | 5.8 | 8.4 | 0.6 | 0.9 | 1.4 | 1.8 | 2.4 |
| Apparel | 13.6 | 15.5 | 20.2 | 20.9 | 16.2 | 1.3 | 2.3 | 1.4 | 3.0 | 2.7 |
| Lumber and wood products | 0.3 | 0.6 | 0.9 | 1.9 | 1.6 | 1.3 | 1.8 | 2.1 | 2.5 | 1.7 |
| Furniture and fixtures | 1.7 | 1.5 | 1.7 | 3.5 | 3.3 | 2.6 | 3.1 | 0.6 | 0.7 | 1.2 |
| Paper products | 5.5 | 5.4 | 8.4 | 8.9 | 12.6 | 10.8 | 16.8 | 11.9 | 16.9 | 24.5 |
| Printing and publishing | 0.2 | 0.7 | 1.1 | 0.9 | 1.3 | 1.6 | 2.2 | 1.0 | 1.0 | 2.5 |
| Chemical products | 10.8 | 13.3 | 20.3 | 19.4 | 28.3 | 7.6 | 17.7 | 16.7 | 26.9 | 27.4 |
| Refined petroleum products | 0.3 | 0.3 | 0.4 | 0.8 | 1.2 | ..... | 0.1 | 0.1 | 0.2 | 0.2 |
| Rubber and plastic products | 4.6 | 5.5 | 10.2 | 10.5 | 14.7 | 15.2 | 25.9 | 19.5 | 15.0 | 15.0 |
| Leather products | 3.3 | 5.7 | 3.9 | 1.5 | 3.9 | 0.4 | 0.8 | 0.7 | 1.3 | 0.9 |
| Stone, clay and glass products | 1.3 | 4.6 | 1.9 | 1.0 | 2.6 | 0.3 | 1.4 | 1.4 | 1.2 | 1.1 |
| Primary metals | 1.0 | 1.3 | 1.7 | 2.9 | 4.9 | 3.7 | 5.0 | 5.4 | 9.9 | 8.1 |
| Fabricated metal products | 13.5 | 15.1 | 22.2 | 20.0 | 27.0 | 40.1 | 48.6 | 16.1 | 21.3 | 23.8 |
| Industrial machinery and computers | 186.0 | 165.1 | 221.6 | 283.5 | 373.8 | 106.4 | 111.7 | 87.0 | 89.7 | 114.1 |
| Electric and electronic equipment | 27.9 | 34.6 | 45.2 | 48.7 | 63.7 | 43.5 | 66.4 | 62.6 | 69.7 | 91.9 |
| Transportation equipment | 18.7 | 16.9 | 13.6 | 20.8 | 24.7 | 5.4 | 9.1 | 4.9 | 9.7 | 19.2 |
| Scientific and measuring instruments | 87.6 | 121.8 | 121.7 | 126.0 | 112.3 | 16.2 | 34.9 | 29.0 | 30.8 | 48.9 |
| Miscellaneous manufactures | 16.2 | 16.7 | 24.0 | 26.8 | 36.1 | 6.0 | 15.0 | 9.2 | 5.8 | 5.4 |
| Unidentified manufactures | 1.4 | 1.2 | 1.6 | 1.1 | 1.7 | 0.6 | 1.0 | 1.4 | 1.6 | 2.1 |
| **Agricultural and livestock products** | 7.9 | 5.1 | 7.3 | 13.7 | 12.7 | 7.8 | 22.1 | 18.4 | 19.3 | 3.9 |
| Agricultural products | 3.3 | 0.1 | 0.2 | 9.1 | 7.6 | 2.3 | 16.0 | 17.1 | 16.5 | 0.4 |
| Livestock and livestock products | 4.4 | 5.0 | 7.1 | 4.6 | 5.1 | 5.6 | 6.1 | 1.3 | 2.8 | 3.5 |
| **Other commodities** | 4.6 | 5.7 | 2.8 | 4.4 | 1.8 | 1.6 | 4.2 | 4.6 | 3.3 | 4.2 |
| Forestry products | 0.2 | 0.2 | 0.1 | 0.1 | 0.1 | ..... | 0.1 | ..... | ..... | ..... |
| Fish and other marine products | ..... | ..... | ..... | ..... | ..... | ..... | ..... | ..... | 0.2 | 0.2 |
| Metallic ores and concentrates | ..... | ..... | ..... | ..... | ..... | ..... | ..... | ..... | ..... | ..... |
| Bituminous coal and lignite | ..... | ..... | ..... | ..... | ..... | ..... | ..... | ..... | ..... | ..... |
| Crude petroleum and natural gas | ..... | ..... | ..... | ..... | ..... | ..... | ..... | ..... | ..... | ..... |
| Nonmetallic minerals | 0.3 | 1.2 | 0.6 | 0.7 | 0.8 | 0.8 | 3.3 | 3.7 | 3.0 | 3.7 |
| Scrap and waste | ..... | 0.4 | 0.8 | 0.7 | 0.3 | 0.1 | 0.4 | ..... | ..... | ..... |
| Used merchandise | 0.3 | 0.2 | 1.0 | 2.6 | 0.2 | 0.5 | 0.2 | 0.9 | ..... | 0.1 |
| Goods imported and returned unchanged | ..... | ..... | ..... | ..... | ..... | ..... | ..... | ..... | ..... | ..... |
| Special classification provisions | 3.7 | 3.8 | 0.3 | 0.3 | 0.4 | 0.3 | 0.1 | ..... | 0.1 | 0.2 |
| | European Union | | | | | United Kingdom | | | | |
| **ALL GOODS** | 1 557.3 | 1 725.6 | 1 915.6 | 2 097.3 | 2 492.9 | 400.2 | 447.2 | 400.3 | 441.9 | 612.6 |
| **Manufactured goods** | 1 529.3 | 1 698.0 | 1 892.9 | 2 069.1 | 2 472.0 | 384.2 | 441.3 | 397.8 | 438.7 | 609.7 |
| Food products | 49.4 | 53.0 | 71.3 | 66.1 | 74.3 | 13.6 | 12.4 | 15.5 | 13.7 | 20.9 |
| Tobacco products | ..... | ..... | ..... | ..... | ..... | ..... | ..... | ..... | ..... | ..... |
| Textile mill products | 5.9 | 6.0 | 6.0 | 6.8 | 8.5 | 0.7 | 0.4 | 0.3 | 0.6 | 0.7 |
| Apparel | 8.1 | 6.9 | 13.6 | 25.9 | 18.7 | 3.1 | 2.0 | 6.6 | 19.7 | 16.0 |
| Lumber and wood products | 12.3 | 18.1 | 14.3 | 7.8 | 10.8 | 4.7 | 5.8 | 6.5 | 2.2 | 4.8 |
| Furniture and fixtures | 8.2 | 6.9 | 5.8 | 6.8 | 9.2 | 3.3 | 1.9 | 1.6 | 2.4 | 2.2 |
| Paper products | 35.7 | 37.3 | 24.1 | 39.5 | 51.0 | 15.6 | 19.2 | 9.1 | 11.7 | 14.7 |
| Printing and publishing | 9.6 | 10.5 | 8.4 | 13.0 | 15.2 | 4.2 | 4.6 | 4.3 | 6.6 | 7.7 |
| Chemical products | 65.5 | 78.2 | 79.4 | 88.9 | 124.1 | 15.5 | 18.3 | 17.3 | 16.5 | 29.3 |
| Refined petroleum products | 1.0 | 0.8 | 1.3 | 2.1 | 2.1 | 0.1 | 0.1 | ..... | 0.1 | 0.1 |
| Rubber and plastic products | 26.4 | 28.4 | 26.7 | 33.0 | 27.3 | 4.7 | 5.5 | 6.0 | 8.1 | 6.9 |
| Leather products | 9.5 | 11.9 | 10.2 | 12.3 | 14.1 | 1.6 | 3.4 | 1.3 | 3.2 | 3.5 |
| Stone, clay and glass products | 9.9 | 11.8 | 20.3 | 32.3 | 20.3 | 0.8 | 0.8 | 1.1 | 1.4 | 2.0 |
| Primary metals | 14.9 | 11.8 | 27.8 | 38.6 | 36.8 | 2.0 | 1.4 | 2.8 | 4.4 | 6.8 |
| Fabricated metal products | 51.4 | 54.4 | 65.4 | 75.2 | 81.6 | 22.2 | 23.6 | 25.8 | 32.6 | 27.3 |
| Industrial machinery and computers | 697.3 | 790.3 | 778.9 | 861.5 | 1 226.4 | 158.3 | 207.4 | 140.5 | 154.8 | 284.9 |
| Electric and electronic equipment | 128.4 | 141.6 | 185.8 | 210.9 | 200.5 | 50.6 | 55.6 | 67.0 | 62.8 | 70.0 |
| Transportation equipment | 120.9 | 104.2 | 137.3 | 147.8 | 148.3 | 19.4 | 17.6 | 16.8 | 27.1 | 39.4 |
| Scientific and measuring instruments | 243.4 | 294.9 | 379.0 | 356.4 | 359.2 | 53.7 | 52.0 | 64.8 | 57.1 | 56.0 |
| Miscellaneous manufactures | 24.3 | 24.8 | 30.2 | 39.3 | 39.5 | 7.3 | 7.5 | 8.4 | 12.2 | 15.0 |
| Unidentified manufactures | 7.0 | 6.1 | 6.9 | 4.7 | 4.1 | 2.7 | 1.8 | 2.3 | 1.6 | 1.7 |
| **Agricultural and livestock products** | 11.1 | 12.8 | 14.4 | 12.3 | 11.3 | 4.3 | 1.6 | 1.4 | 1.6 | 1.7 |
| Agricultural products | 4.0 | 4.0 | 5.6 | 3.4 | 2.6 | 2.5 | ..... | 0.2 | 0.3 | 0.3 |
| Livestock and livestock products | 7.1 | 8.8 | 8.8 | 8.8 | 8.6 | 1.8 | 1.5 | 1.1 | 1.3 | 1.4 |
| **Other commodities** | 16.9 | 14.8 | 8.4 | 15.9 | 9.7 | 11.7 | 4.3 | 1.1 | 1.5 | 1.1 |
| Forestry products | 0.9 | 0.3 | 0.5 | 0.6 | 0.4 | ..... | ..... | ..... | ..... | ..... |
| Fish and other marine products | ..... | 0.1 | 0.6 | 0.2 | 0.1 | ..... | ..... | ..... | ..... | 0.1 |
| Metallic ores and concentrates | ..... | ..... | 0.1 | ..... | ..... | ..... | ..... | ..... | ..... | ..... |
| Bituminous coal and lignite | ..... | ..... | 2.3 | 0.1 | ..... | ..... | ..... | ..... | ..... | ..... |
| Crude petroleum and natural gas | 0.1 | ..... | ..... | 0.2 | ..... | 0.1 | ..... | ..... | ..... | ..... |
| Nonmetallic minerals | 0.2 | 0.3 | 0.5 | 0.4 | 0.9 | ..... | ..... | ..... | 0.1 | 0.1 |
| Scrap and waste | 0.4 | 2.1 | 0.8 | 9.2 | 3.3 | ..... | 0.8 | 0.1 | ..... | 0.2 |
| Used merchandise | 1.6 | 5.4 | 1.5 | 1.3 | 1.9 | 0.1 | 0.1 | 0.2 | 0.1 | 0.2 |
| Goods imported and returned unchanged | ..... | ..... | ..... | ..... | ..... | ..... | ..... | ..... | ..... | ..... |
| Special classification provisions | 13.7 | 6.6 | 2.1 | 3.8 | 3.0 | 11.5 | 3.4 | 0.8 | 1.3 | 0.5 |

## Table D-3. State Exports of Goods by Destination and Industry, 1993–1997 —*Continued*

### WISCONSIN (Millions of dollars.)

| Industry | 1993 | 1994 | 1995 | 1996 | 1997 | 1993 | 1994 | 1995 | 1996 | 1997 |
|---|---|---|---|---|---|---|---|---|---|---|
| | Germany | | | | | France | | | | |
| ALL GOODS | 307.4 | 325.0 | 387.1 | 441.4 | 462.2 | 277.8 | 317.4 | 358.2 | 319.4 | 454.0 |
| Manufactured goods | 303.0 | 318.7 | 382.1 | 438.5 | 459.6 | 276.5 | 314.2 | 355.8 | 315.6 | 450.6 |
| Food products | 10.6 | 3.1 | 9.7 | 10.1 | 10.5 | 1.3 | 1.7 | 2.0 | 3.5 | 2.6 |
| Tobacco products | ..... | ..... | ..... | ..... | ..... | ..... | ..... | ..... | ..... | ..... |
| Textile mill products | 0.4 | 0.5 | 2.5 | 1.8 | 2.2 | 1.3 | 1.3 | 1.4 | 1.8 | 2.8 |
| Apparel | 2.1 | 2.6 | 1.6 | 1.5 | 0.5 | 0.3 | 0.1 | 0.2 | 0.4 | 0.1 |
| Lumber and wood products | 4.6 | 7.7 | 3.4 | 2.6 | 2.7 | 0.6 | 1.3 | 0.9 | 0.6 | 0.9 |
| Furniture and fixtures | 1.0 | 1.1 | 0.6 | 0.8 | 1.2 | 0.6 | 0.3 | 0.4 | 0.4 | 0.7 |
| Paper products | 4.2 | 4.7 | 2.3 | 4.5 | 9.4 | 1.6 | 2.0 | 0.5 | 1.6 | 1.9 |
| Printing and publishing | 2.5 | 2.7 | 1.8 | 2.4 | 3.0 | 1.7 | 1.5 | 0.5 | 0.8 | 1.4 |
| Chemical products | 14.9 | 13.0 | 11.6 | 14.5 | 24.5 | 5.9 | 6.5 | 8.1 | 10.6 | 15.5 |
| Refined petroleum products | 0.1 | ..... | ..... | 0.1 | 0.1 | 0.1 | 0.1 | 0.1 | 0.1 | 0.1 |
| Rubber and plastic products | 6.1 | 4.0 | 4.4 | 7.7 | 5.6 | 3.2 | 3.3 | 3.0 | 1.7 | 1.9 |
| Leather products | 1.1 | 0.8 | 1.3 | 1.4 | 2.1 | 0.4 | 0.3 | 0.2 | ..... | 0.1 |
| Stone, clay and glass products | 3.2 | 3.4 | 4.6 | 5.3 | 4.7 | 2.5 | 3.1 | 2.7 | 3.9 | 4.3 |
| Primary metals | 3.8 | 2.5 | 6.0 | 9.5 | 7.3 | 2.7 | 0.5 | 0.9 | 1.5 | 3.3 |
| Fabricated metal products | 11.1 | 12.1 | 16.5 | 18.2 | 20.1 | 4.5 | 6.1 | 6.4 | 4.7 | 8.0 |
| Industrial machinery and computers | 138.9 | 155.1 | 178.4 | 195.6 | 222.8 | 142.3 | 145.9 | 143.8 | 142.1 | 255.9 |
| Electric and electronic equipment | 17.9 | 19.8 | 34.9 | 39.2 | 34.0 | 8.2 | 10.0 | 12.5 | 12.9 | 13.5 |
| Transportation equipment | 24.5 | 23.7 | 32.2 | 41.2 | 30.1 | 23.9 | 18.4 | 17.9 | 15.4 | 11.0 |
| Scientific and measuring instruments | 50.2 | 54.4 | 64.7 | 75.4 | 71.0 | 71.3 | 107.1 | 149.3 | 106.9 | 119.6 |
| Miscellaneous manufactures | 4.4 | 6.0 | 3.8 | 5.8 | 7.0 | 3.4 | 3.9 | 4.0 | 6.2 | 6.7 |
| Unidentified manufactures | 1.5 | 1.5 | 1.6 | 1.1 | 0.7 | 0.7 | 0.8 | 0.9 | 0.6 | 0.4 |
| Agricultural and livestock products | 1.1 | 1.9 | 3.2 | 1.3 | 1.0 | 0.8 | 2.9 | 1.6 | 2.2 | 1.9 |
| Agricultural products | 0.2 | 0.3 | 1.9 | ..... | ..... | 0.1 | 1.8 | 0.9 | 1.1 | 0.4 |
| Livestock and livestock products | 0.9 | 1.6 | 1.3 | 1.3 | 1.0 | 0.7 | 1.1 | 0.8 | 1.1 | 1.5 |
| Other commodities | 3.2 | 4.5 | 1.8 | 1.6 | 1.7 | 0.5 | 0.3 | 0.8 | 1.6 | 1.5 |
| Forestry products | 0.2 | 0.1 | 0.3 | 0.3 | 0.2 | ..... | ..... | ..... | 0.1 | ..... |
| Fish and other marine products | ..... | ..... | ..... | ..... | ..... | ..... | ..... | ..... | ..... | ..... |
| Metallic ores and concentrates | ..... | ..... | ..... | ..... | ..... | ..... | ..... | ..... | ..... | ..... |
| Bituminous coal and lignite | ..... | ..... | ..... | ..... | ..... | ..... | ..... | ..... | ..... | ..... |
| Crude petroleum and natural gas | ..... | ..... | ..... | ..... | ..... | ..... | ..... | ..... | ..... | ..... |
| Nonmetallic minerals | 0.1 | ..... | 0.1 | ..... | 0.2 | ..... | ..... | ..... | 0.1 | 0.1 |
| Scrap and waste | 0.2 | 0.1 | 0.5 | 0.5 | ..... | ..... | ..... | 0.2 | 0.6 | 0.4 |
| Used merchandise | 1.4 | 3.4 | 0.3 | ..... | 0.6 | 0.1 | ..... | 0.4 | 0.4 | 0.1 |
| Goods imported and returned unchanged | ..... | ..... | ..... | ..... | ..... | ..... | ..... | ..... | ..... | ..... |
| Special classification provisions | 1.4 | 0.8 | 0.5 | 0.7 | 0.7 | 0.4 | 0.3 | 0.3 | 0.6 | 0.8 |
| | The Netherlands | | | | | Asian 10 | | | | |
| ALL GOODS | 179.7 | 179.4 | 238.9 | 254.8 | 238.9 | 961.2 | 1 172.6 | 1 557.6 | 1 696.5 | 1 830.6 |
| Manufactured goods | 177.1 | 175.2 | 236.0 | 252.5 | 235.6 | 924.8 | 1 139.3 | 1 529.2 | 1 645.6 | 1 775.4 |
| Food products | 12.5 | 15.7 | 22.8 | 16.7 | 17.7 | 47.1 | 65.5 | 115.0 | 99.0 | 107.5 |
| Tobacco products | ..... | ..... | ..... | ..... | ..... | ..... | ..... | 0.9 | ..... | ..... |
| Textile mill products | 2.4 | 2.5 | 0.7 | 1.2 | 1.3 | 2.1 | 3.8 | 5.9 | 7.3 | 6.6 |
| Apparel | 1.3 | 0.8 | 3.4 | 1.8 | 1.6 | 5.5 | 5.0 | 14.5 | 19.3 | 10.6 |
| Lumber and wood products | 0.3 | 1.2 | 1.1 | 0.8 | 0.4 | 8.4 | 10.1 | 13.9 | 16.5 | 21.7 |
| Furniture and fixtures | 1.0 | 0.9 | 0.8 | 1.1 | 0.3 | 4.4 | 2.8 | 3.0 | 3.4 | 3.7 |
| Paper products | 4.3 | 3.9 | 5.3 | 8.6 | 9.8 | 11.6 | 21.7 | 22.7 | 35.9 | 42.6 |
| Printing and publishing | 0.8 | 0.7 | 0.5 | 1.0 | 1.2 | 2.5 | 2.4 | 3.2 | 4.1 | 4.9 |
| Chemical products | 7.0 | 10.5 | 14.2 | 14.1 | 18.3 | 35.5 | 43.5 | 54.8 | 54.0 | 64.3 |
| Refined petroleum products | 0.2 | 0.1 | 0.1 | ..... | ..... | 1.5 | 1.2 | 3.3 | 2.3 | 3.3 |
| Rubber and plastic products | 1.8 | 1.2 | 3.3 | 4.4 | 1.4 | 15.9 | 15.1 | 32.6 | 19.5 | 30.0 |
| Leather products | 0.4 | 1.8 | 3.0 | 3.7 | 2.3 | 42.5 | 45.6 | 36.1 | 36.9 | 32.4 |
| Stone, clay and glass products | 2.5 | 2.3 | 2.7 | 3.5 | 3.1 | 8.9 | 16.6 | 18.0 | 15.8 | 16.1 |
| Primary metals | 3.5 | 4.4 | 6.6 | 5.7 | 5.9 | 4.9 | 6.6 | 9.6 | 8.7 | 12.8 |
| Fabricated metal products | 4.7 | 4.8 | 5.5 | 7.9 | 6.2 | 60.1 | 56.7 | 74.7 | 81.4 | 68.3 |
| Industrial machinery and computers | 62.0 | 69.5 | 85.7 | 96.9 | 112.9 | 301.4 | 440.0 | 598.8 | 563.4 | 730.6 |
| Electric and electronic equipment | 34.3 | 31.7 | 26.3 | 34.6 | 18.5 | 118.6 | 120.8 | 130.9 | 152.3 | 171.6 |
| Transportation equipment | 27.3 | 14.6 | 36.1 | 29.4 | 16.4 | 31.4 | 22.4 | 30.7 | 41.7 | 40.7 |
| Scientific and measuring instruments | 6.9 | 6.5 | 9.7 | 13.0 | 15.9 | 195.6 | 225.1 | 315.2 | 432.8 | 354.5 |
| Miscellaneous manufactures | 3.4 | 1.7 | 7.8 | 7.9 | 2.1 | 23.5 | 29.4 | 41.8 | 48.2 | 50.2 |
| Unidentified manufactures | 0.6 | 0.4 | 0.4 | 0.2 | 0.4 | 3.2 | 4.9 | 3.5 | 3.0 | 3.0 |
| Agricultural and livestock products | 2.5 | 2.3 | 2.2 | 1.7 | 1.9 | 1.7 | 3.2 | 3.1 | 5.4 | 16.1 |
| Agricultural products | 0.5 | 0.3 | 0.6 | 0.6 | 0.5 | 0.3 | 0.8 | 0.8 | 1.5 | 12.7 |
| Livestock and livestock products | 2.0 | 2.0 | 1.6 | 1.1 | 1.5 | 1.4 | 2.4 | 2.4 | 3.9 | 3.4 |
| Other commodities | 0.1 | 1.9 | 0.6 | 0.6 | 1.4 | 34.6 | 30.1 | 25.2 | 45.4 | 39.2 |
| Forestry products | ..... | ..... | ..... | ..... | ..... | 32.8 | 26.9 | 22.0 | 25.4 | 17.9 |
| Fish and other marine products | ..... | ..... | ..... | ..... | ..... | ..... | 0.1 | ..... | 0.1 | ..... |
| Metallic ores and concentrates | ..... | ..... | ..... | ..... | ..... | ..... | ..... | ..... | ..... | ..... |
| Bituminous coal and lignite | ..... | ..... | ..... | ..... | ..... | ..... | ..... | ..... | ..... | ..... |
| Crude petroleum and natural gas | ..... | ..... | ..... | ..... | ..... | ..... | ..... | ..... | ..... | ..... |
| Nonmetallic minerals | ..... | ..... | ..... | ..... | 0.1 | 0.1 | 0.1 | 0.1 | 0.7 | 0.7 |
| Scrap and waste | ..... | 1.0 | ..... | ..... | ..... | 0.2 | 1.4 | 1.6 | 15.8 | 18.7 |
| Used merchandise | ..... | ..... | 0.6 | 0.6 | 0.9 | 0.8 | 1.0 | 0.8 | 2.3 | 0.5 |
| Goods imported and returned unchanged | ..... | ..... | ..... | ..... | ..... | ..... | ..... | ..... | ..... | ..... |
| Special classification provisions | ..... | 0.8 | ..... | 0.1 | 0.3 | 0.6 | 0.6 | 0.6 | 1.1 | 1.3 |

## Table D-3.   State Exports of Goods by Destination and Industry, 1993–1997 —*Continued*

## WISCONSIN (Millions of dollars.)

| Industry | 1993 | 1994 | 1995 | 1996 | 1997 | 1993 | 1994 | 1995 | 1996 | 1997 |
|---|---|---|---|---|---|---|---|---|---|---|
| | Japan | | | | | South Korea | | | | |
| **ALL GOODS** | 295.7 | 463.9 | 581.6 | 677.9 | 693.7 | 106.5 | 123.4 | 167.4 | 172.1 | 187.9 |
| **Manufactured goods** | 293.6 | 461.2 | 578.2 | 658.0 | 671.3 | 106.0 | 121.4 | 165.8 | 170.1 | 186.9 |
| Food products | 21.3 | 34.3 | 52.7 | 51.3 | 49.8 | 13.6 | 11.4 | 14.2 | 12.2 | 12.8 |
| Tobacco products | ..... | ..... | ..... | ..... | ..... | ..... | ..... | ..... | ..... | ..... |
| Textile mill products | 0.3 | 0.4 | 0.6 | 0.8 | 2.1 | 0.2 | 0.7 | 0.5 | 0.3 | 0.6 |
| Apparel | 2.8 | 2.8 | 10.0 | 16.5 | 6.8 | 0.3 | 0.4 | 0.5 | 0.4 | 1.0 |
| Lumber and wood products | 6.6 | 7.3 | 10.1 | 10.8 | 11.1 | 1.1 | 1.9 | 2.5 | 1.8 | 5.9 |
| Furniture and fixtures | 2.0 | 0.9 | 1.0 | 1.0 | 0.6 | 0.4 | 0.4 | 0.6 | 0.4 | 0.5 |
| Paper products | 2.4 | 6.3 | 2.7 | 4.9 | 6.0 | 2.2 | 5.6 | 6.2 | 11.1 | 9.1 |
| Printing and publishing | 1.7 | 1.2 | 1.3 | 1.8 | 2.1 | ..... | 0.1 | 0.2 | 0.3 | 0.3 |
| Chemical products | 15.3 | 18.4 | 21.6 | 19.1 | 26.8 | 3.6 | 7.2 | 9.0 | 10.1 | 11.7 |
| Refined petroleum products | ..... | 0.1 | 0.4 | 0.1 | 0.3 | 0.2 | 0.3 | 0.3 | 0.4 | 0.6 |
| Rubber and plastic products | 4.6 | 5.4 | 18.9 | 4.4 | 6.7 | 1.1 | 1.5 | 1.4 | 1.4 | 1.6 |
| Leather products | 2.1 | 1.6 | 1.5 | 1.6 | 0.6 | 2.0 | 2.2 | 1.3 | 0.6 | 0.7 |
| Stone, clay and glass products | 0.9 | 2.8 | 3.6 | 3.9 | 7.0 | 1.1 | 1.5 | 2.5 | 2.1 | 2.4 |
| Primary metals | 1.0 | 0.8 | 1.4 | 3.0 | 3.0 | 0.3 | 0.3 | 0.8 | 1.3 | 1.2 |
| Fabricated metal products | 12.2 | 14.2 | 17.1 | 24.6 | 24.5 | 3.2 | 7.4 | 7.7 | 7.8 | 4.8 |
| Industrial machinery and computers | 82.8 | 197.7 | 174.4 | 141.8 | 228.6 | 33.8 | 34.4 | 64.1 | 65.9 | 84.4 |
| Electric and electronic equipment | 17.6 | 17.9 | 22.2 | 37.5 | 28.9 | 10.1 | 11.3 | 18.7 | 14.3 | 13.6 |
| Transportation equipment | 3.6 | 5.6 | 9.1 | 8.6 | 10.2 | 1.9 | 3.3 | 2.2 | 3.3 | 5.4 |
| Scientific and measuring instruments | 109.4 | 135.1 | 216.8 | 313.6 | 244.4 | 28.9 | 28.1 | 27.4 | 31.7 | 23.5 |
| Miscellaneous manufactures | 6.0 | 7.4 | 11.3 | 11.8 | 10.8 | 1.6 | 2.8 | 5.3 | 4.4 | 6.3 |
| Unidentified manufactures | 0.7 | 1.0 | 1.5 | 1.1 | 1.1 | 0.3 | 0.4 | 0.5 | 0.5 | 0.5 |
| **Agricultural and livestock products** | 0.9 | 1.7 | 2.2 | 3.1 | 3.1 | 0.4 | 0.7 | 0.5 | 0.5 | 0.3 |
| Agricultural products | 0.2 | 0.3 | 0.5 | 0.5 | 0.7 | ..... | ..... | ..... | 0.1 | 0.1 |
| Livestock and livestock products | 0.7 | 1.4 | 1.7 | 2.6 | 2.4 | 0.4 | 0.7 | 0.5 | 0.4 | 0.2 |
| **Other commodities** | 1.3 | 1.1 | 1.3 | 16.8 | 19.3 | 0.1 | 1.3 | 1.1 | 1.5 | 0.7 |
| Forestry products | ..... | ..... | ..... | ..... | ..... | ..... | ..... | ..... | ..... | 0.3 |
| Fish and other marine products | ..... | ..... | ..... | ..... | ..... | ..... | ..... | ..... | 0.1 | ..... |
| Metallic ores and concentrates | ..... | ..... | ..... | ..... | ..... | ..... | ..... | ..... | ..... | ..... |
| Bituminous coal and lignite | ..... | ..... | ..... | ..... | ..... | ..... | ..... | ..... | ..... | ..... |
| Crude petroleum and natural gas | ..... | ..... | ..... | ..... | ..... | ..... | ..... | ..... | ..... | ..... |
| Nonmetallic minerals | ..... | ..... | 0.1 | 0.4 | 0.3 | ..... | ..... | ..... | ..... | 0.1 |
| Scrap and waste | ..... | ..... | 0.3 | 14.0 | 18.0 | ..... | 1.1 | 1.0 | 1.2 | 0.2 |
| Used merchandise | 0.8 | 0.8 | 0.5 | 1.8 | 0.3 | ..... | ..... | ..... | 0.1 | ..... |
| Goods imported and returned unchanged | ..... | ..... | ..... | ..... | ..... | ..... | ..... | ..... | ..... | ..... |
| Special classification provisions | 0.4 | 0.2 | 0.4 | 0.6 | 0.5 | 0.1 | 0.2 | 0.1 | 0.1 | 0.2 |
| | Taiwan | | | | | Singapore | | | | |
| **ALL GOODS** | 120.1 | 119.1 | 214.2 | 164.6 | 160.3 | 99.9 | 112.8 | 124.5 | 137.3 | 149.3 |
| **Manufactured goods** | 117.9 | 117.3 | 213.1 | 164.1 | 158.9 | 99.7 | 112.2 | 123.9 | 136.8 | 148.9 |
| Food products | 8.6 | 15.0 | 24.3 | 22.2 | 31.9 | 0.9 | 1.2 | 1.3 | 0.8 | 1.5 |
| Tobacco products | ..... | ..... | ..... | ..... | ..... | ..... | ..... | ..... | ..... | ..... |
| Textile mill products | 0.3 | 0.7 | 2.2 | 2.5 | 0.5 | ..... | ..... | 0.3 | 0.2 | 0.2 |
| Apparel | 0.4 | 0.1 | 0.1 | 0.1 | 0.1 | 0.7 | 1.1 | 1.7 | 0.9 | 1.0 |
| Lumber and wood products | 0.4 | 0.4 | 0.5 | 0.7 | 1.9 | 0.1 | ..... | 0.2 | 0.1 | 0.3 |
| Furniture and fixtures | 0.5 | 0.1 | 0.2 | 0.1 | 0.2 | 0.4 | 0.1 | 0.1 | 0.1 | 0.1 |
| Paper products | 0.4 | 0.6 | 1.6 | 4.4 | 4.9 | 1.8 | 1.7 | 3.0 | 3.3 | 4.2 |
| Printing and publishing | 0.2 | 0.1 | 0.4 | 0.4 | 0.1 | 0.2 | 0.2 | 0.3 | 0.2 | 0.3 |
| Chemical products | 5.5 | 5.3 | 9.2 | 6.5 | 6.5 | 2.7 | 2.6 | 3.1 | 6.0 | 3.0 |
| Refined petroleum products | 0.8 | 0.2 | 1.6 | 0.7 | 1.2 | ..... | 0.1 | 0.1 | 0.3 | ..... |
| Rubber and plastic products | 3.0 | 2.6 | 2.8 | 2.0 | 3.2 | 2.3 | 1.6 | 2.3 | 3.7 | 5.2 |
| Leather products | 0.7 | 3.2 | 0.5 | 0.3 | 0.6 | 0.2 | 0.3 | 0.2 | 0.1 | 0.4 |
| Stone, clay and glass products | 0.5 | 0.8 | 1.4 | 0.8 | 0.7 | 0.6 | 1.2 | 1.5 | 1.4 | 0.5 |
| Primary metals | 0.9 | 0.8 | 1.5 | 0.4 | 0.7 | 1.1 | 2.1 | 2.2 | 1.5 | 2.4 |
| Fabricated metal products | 8.8 | 9.2 | 6.6 | 3.6 | 4.4 | 6.7 | 5.8 | 7.1 | 5.3 | 4.1 |
| Industrial machinery and computers | 41.3 | 35.8 | 117.4 | 85.7 | 63.6 | 36.4 | 49.2 | 59.0 | 59.2 | 68.5 |
| Electric and electronic equipment | 20.1 | 24.8 | 28.3 | 15.2 | 14.9 | 20.0 | 24.0 | 16.2 | 24.4 | 28.2 |
| Transportation equipment | 13.7 | 1.1 | 1.7 | 1.1 | 4.9 | 4.0 | 1.8 | 3.3 | 4.5 | 4.4 |
| Scientific and measuring instruments | 9.2 | 12.5 | 11.3 | 15.5 | 15.4 | 12.0 | 10.3 | 11.5 | 14.1 | 12.5 |
| Miscellaneous manufactures | 2.2 | 1.3 | 1.2 | 1.9 | 3.0 | 8.8 | 8.6 | 10.3 | 10.4 | 11.8 |
| Unidentified manufactures | 0.2 | 2.6 | 0.3 | 0.3 | 0.2 | 0.6 | 0.3 | 0.3 | 0.3 | 0.3 |
| **Agricultural and livestock products** | 0.3 | 0.3 | 0.1 | 0.1 | 0.2 | ..... | 0.4 | ..... | 0.1 | ..... |
| Agricultural products | ..... | ..... | ..... | ..... | ..... | ..... | 0.4 | ..... | 0.1 | ..... |
| Livestock and livestock products | 0.3 | 0.3 | 0.1 | 0.1 | 0.1 | ..... | ..... | ..... | ..... | ..... |
| **Other commodities** | 1.9 | 1.5 | 1.0 | 0.3 | 1.2 | 0.2 | 0.2 | 0.6 | 0.4 | 0.4 |
| Forestry products | 1.9 | 1.5 | 1.0 | 0.3 | 0.8 | 0.1 | 0.2 | 0.3 | 0.2 | 0.2 |
| Fish and other marine products | ..... | ..... | ..... | ..... | ..... | ..... | ..... | ..... | ..... | ..... |
| Metallic ores and concentrates | ..... | ..... | ..... | ..... | ..... | ..... | ..... | ..... | ..... | ..... |
| Bituminous coal and lignite | ..... | ..... | ..... | ..... | ..... | ..... | ..... | ..... | ..... | ..... |
| Crude petroleum and natural gas | ..... | ..... | ..... | ..... | ..... | ..... | ..... | ..... | ..... | ..... |
| Nonmetallic minerals | ..... | ..... | ..... | ..... | 0.1 | ..... | ..... | ..... | 0.1 | 0.1 |
| Scrap and waste | ..... | ..... | ..... | ..... | 0.2 | ..... | ..... | 0.1 | ..... | ..... |
| Used merchandise | ..... | ..... | ..... | ..... | 0.1 | ..... | ..... | 0.2 | 0.1 | ..... |
| Goods imported and returned unchanged | ..... | ..... | ..... | ..... | ..... | ..... | ..... | ..... | ..... | ..... |
| Special classification provisions | ..... | ..... | ..... | ..... | ..... | ..... | ..... | ..... | ..... | 0.1 |

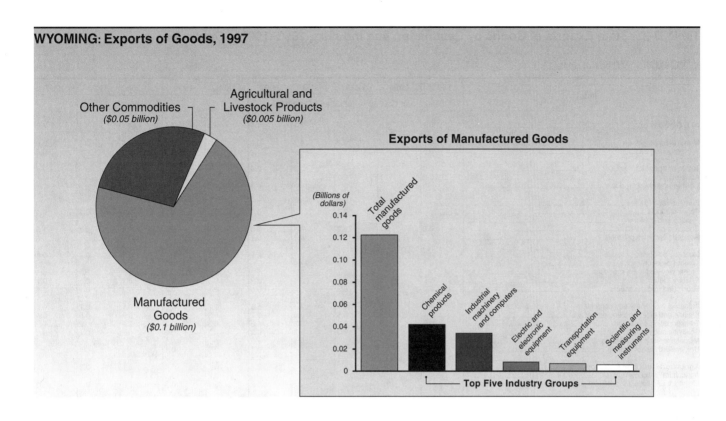

## WYOMING: Exports of Goods, 1997

Other Commodities ($0.05 billion)

Agricultural and Livestock Products ($0.005 billion)

Manufactured Goods ($0.1 billion)

### Exports of Manufactured Goods

(Billions of dollars)

Total manufactured goods

Chemical products

Industrial machinery and computers

Electric and electronic equipment

Transportation equipment

Scientific and measuring instruments

Top Five Industry Groups

## Table D-3. State Exports of Goods by Destination and Industry, 1993–1997 —Continued

### WYOMING (Millions of dollars.)

| Industry | 1993 | 1994 | 1995 | 1996 | 1997 | 1993 | 1994 | 1995 | 1996 | 1997 |
|---|---|---|---|---|---|---|---|---|---|---|
| | All destinations | | | | | Canada | | | | |
| **ALL GOODS** | 88.5 | 95.4 | 101.2 | 123.7 | 175.9 | 37.8 | 48.6 | 50.7 | 69.4 | 88.3 |
| **Manufactured goods** | 75.8 | 80.4 | 83.0 | 100.8 | 122.4 | 31.7 | 39.6 | 39.8 | 55.1 | 69.9 |
| Food products | 3.4 | 3.4 | 8.7 | 14.7 | 5.2 | 1.2 | 1.8 | 0.9 | 1.0 | 2.0 |
| Tobacco products | ..... | ..... | ..... | ..... | ..... | | | | | |
| Textile mill products | 0.5 | 0.2 | 0.1 | 0.5 | 0.8 | ..... | 0.1 | 0.1 | 0.2 | 0.2 |
| Apparel | 0.6 | 1.1 | 0.7 | 0.4 | 0.5 | 0.1 | 0.1 | 0.1 | 0.1 | 0.2 |
| Lumber and wood products | 1.7 | 0.9 | 1.6 | 2.3 | 4.1 | 1.5 | 0.8 | 1.3 | 1.5 | 0.9 |
| Furniture and fixtures | 0.2 | 0.3 | 0.1 | 0.3 | 0.4 | 0.1 | 0.2 | 0.1 | 0.1 | 0.2 |
| Paper products | 0.3 | 0.2 | 0.3 | 0.4 | 3.0 | 0.1 | ..... | 0.1 | 0.1 | 0.3 |
| Printing and publishing | 0.6 | 0.5 | 1.3 | 0.5 | 0.4 | 0.5 | 0.2 | 0.2 | 0.1 | 0.3 |
| Chemical products | 15.3 | 18.4 | 18.5 | 24.6 | 42.0 | 12.6 | 12.1 | 15.4 | 22.3 | 37.1 |
| Refined petroleum products | 0.1 | ..... | ..... | 1.1 | 0.2 | ..... | ..... | ..... | 0.9 | ..... |
| Rubber and plastic products | 1.0 | 0.8 | 1.0 | 1.0 | 1.0 | 0.4 | 0.3 | 0.6 | 0.5 | 0.4 |
| Leather products | 0.2 | 0.2 | ..... | 0.1 | 0.1 | ..... | 0.1 | ..... | ..... | ..... |
| Stone, clay and glass products | 0.4 | 0.4 | 0.6 | 0.4 | 0.5 | 0.1 | 0.1 | 0.1 | 0.2 | 0.3 |
| Primary metals | 3.1 | 2.7 | 2.0 | 3.1 | 2.8 | 1.6 | 2.3 | 1.2 | 0.7 | 1.7 |
| Fabricated metal products | 5.3 | 5.6 | 6.6 | 3.0 | 5.1 | 2.4 | 2.9 | 3.2 | 1.9 | 3.6 |
| Industrial machinery and computers | 23.8 | 27.2 | 19.9 | 24.5 | 34.2 | 7.7 | 15.8 | 10.2 | 12.4 | 13.7 |
| Electric and electronic equipment | 6.8 | 9.1 | 10.3 | 4.7 | 8.1 | 0.9 | 1.1 | 1.5 | 1.7 | 3.0 |
| Transportation equipment | 5.1 | 3.8 | 4.1 | 10.1 | 6.8 | 0.9 | 0.6 | 2.0 | 5.3 | 2.5 |
| Scientific and measuring instruments | 5.3 | 3.2 | 5.2 | 7.5 | 5.8 | 1.2 | 0.8 | 2.4 | 5.5 | 3.1 |
| Miscellaneous manufactures | 1.4 | 1.7 | 1.3 | 1.3 | 0.8 | 0.2 | 0.2 | 0.1 | 0.1 | 0.2 |
| Unidentified manufactures | 0.8 | 0.6 | 0.7 | 0.5 | 0.5 | 0.1 | 0.2 | 0.4 | 0.3 | 0.3 |
| **Agricultural and livestock products** | 3.8 | 1.6 | 1.6 | 2.5 | 5.2 | 1.5 | 1.1 | 1.5 | 1.9 | 3.3 |
| Agricultural products | 3.1 | 0.7 | 0.7 | 1.5 | 2.0 | 1.0 | 0.6 | 0.6 | 1.1 | 1.4 |
| Livestock and livestock products | 0.7 | 0.9 | 0.9 | 1.0 | 3.2 | 0.6 | 0.5 | 0.8 | 0.8 | 1.9 |
| **Other commodities** | 9.0 | 13.4 | 16.6 | 20.3 | 48.3 | 4.6 | 7.9 | 9.5 | 12.3 | 15.1 |
| Forestry products | ..... | 0.2 | 0.1 | ..... | ..... | ..... | 0.1 | ..... | ..... | ..... |
| Fish and other marine products | 0.1 | 0.1 | 0.3 | 0.6 | 10.3 | ..... | ..... | 0.1 | 0.2 | ..... |
| Metallic ores and concentrates | 0.2 | ..... | ..... | ..... | 17.0 | ..... | ..... | ..... | ..... | ..... |
| Bituminous coal and lignite | 1.0 | 2.3 | 2.7 | 6.0 | 4.3 | ..... | ..... | ..... | 0.1 | ..... |
| Crude petroleum and natural gas | ..... | 0.1 | ..... | ..... | 0.8 | ..... | 0.1 | ..... | ..... | 0.8 |
| Nonmetallic minerals | 0.7 | 0.9 | 1.4 | 1.0 | 1.1 | 0.7 | 0.7 | 0.8 | 0.7 | 0.8 |
| Scrap and waste | 0.3 | 1.1 | 1.5 | 1.6 | 0.5 | 0.2 | 1.0 | 1.5 | 1.5 | 0.2 |
| Used merchandise | 2.7 | 3.1 | 4.2 | 1.5 | 1.5 | 0.2 | 0.6 | 0.8 | 0.4 | 0.7 |
| Goods imported and returned unchanged | 3.3 | 5.3 | 6.3 | 9.4 | 12.6 | 3.3 | 5.3 | 6.3 | 9.4 | 12.6 |
| Special classification provisions | 0.7 | 0.3 | 0.1 | 0.2 | 0.2 | 0.1 | 0.1 | 0.1 | 0.1 | ..... |

## Table D-3.  State Exports of Goods by Destination and Industry, 1993–1997 —*Continued*

**WYOMING** (Millions of dollars.)

| Industry | 1993 | 1994 | 1995 | 1996 | 1997 | 1993 | 1994 | 1995 | 1996 | 1997 |
|---|---|---|---|---|---|---|---|---|---|---|
| | South and Central America and Caribbean | | | | | Mexico | | | | |
| **ALL GOODS** | 6.2 | 3.5 | 4.2 | 4.2 | 11.6 | 4.4 | 4.1 | 4.1 | 3.5 | 4.9 |
| **Manufactured goods** | 6.2 | 3.4 | 4.2 | 4.1 | 10.5 | 4.1 | 3.7 | 4.0 | 3.1 | 3.8 |
| Food products | 0.1 | 0.1 | 1.3 | ..... | ..... | 0.6 | 0.2 | 0.1 | 0.5 | 0.4 |
| Tobacco products | ..... | ..... | ..... | ..... | ..... | ..... | ..... | ..... | ..... | ..... |
| Textile mill products | ..... | 0.1 | ..... | 0.3 | 0.4 | 0.4 | ..... | ..... | ..... | ..... |
| Apparel | 0.2 | 0.1 | 0.1 | ..... | ..... | ..... | ..... | ..... | ..... | 0.1 |
| Lumber and wood products | ..... | ..... | 0.1 | ..... | 0.3 | ..... | ..... | ..... | ..... | ..... |
| Furniture and fixtures | ..... | 0.1 | ..... | 0.1 | 0.1 | ..... | ..... | ..... | ..... | ..... |
| Paper products | ..... | ..... | 0.1 | ..... | 0.5 | 0.1 | 0.1 | 0.1 | 0.1 | 0.1 |
| Printing and publishing | ..... | ..... | ..... | ..... | ..... | ..... | ..... | 0.2 | ..... | ..... |
| Chemical products | 0.2 | 0.1 | 0.2 | 0.4 | 0.5 | 0.6 | 0.2 | 1.5 | 0.6 | 1.3 |
| Refined petroleum products | ..... | ..... | ..... | 0.1 | 0.1 | ..... | ..... | ..... | ..... | ..... |
| Rubber and plastic products | ..... | 0.1 | ..... | ..... | 0.2 | 0.2 | 0.1 | 0.1 | 0.1 | 0.2 |
| Leather products | 0.1 | ..... | ..... | ..... | ..... | ..... | ..... | ..... | ..... | ..... |
| Stone, clay and glass products | ..... | ..... | ..... | ..... | ..... | ..... | ..... | ..... | ..... | 0.1 |
| Primary metals | 0.6 | ..... | ..... | 0.1 | 0.2 | 0.1 | 0.1 | 0.1 | 0.1 | 0.1 |
| Fabricated metal products | 2.2 | 1.3 | 0.3 | ..... | 0.6 | 0.1 | 0.2 | 0.2 | 0.1 | 0.1 |
| Industrial machinery and computers | 1.2 | 0.5 | 0.7 | 2.3 | 5.3 | 1.0 | 0.5 | 0.5 | 0.7 | 0.7 |
| Electric and electronic equipment | 0.1 | 0.2 | 0.5 | 0.3 | 0.7 | 0.3 | 1.5 | 0.8 | 0.5 | 0.5 |
| Transportation equipment | 0.9 | 0.5 | 0.3 | 0.2 | 1.2 | 0.3 | 0.2 | 0.2 | 0.2 | ..... |
| Scientific and measuring instruments | 0.4 | 0.3 | 0.3 | 0.3 | 0.2 | 0.2 | 0.2 | 0.2 | 0.1 | 0.2 |
| Miscellaneous manufactures | ..... | 0.1 | ..... | ..... | 0.2 | ..... | 0.1 | ..... | ..... | ..... |
| Unidentified manufactures | ..... | ..... | ..... | ..... | 0.1 | 0.2 | 0.1 | ..... | ..... | ..... |
| **Agricultural and livestock products** | 0.1 | 0.1 | ..... | ..... | 0.1 | 0.2 | 0.4 | 0.1 | 0.3 | 1.1 |
| Agricultural products | ..... | ..... | ..... | ..... | ..... | 0.2 | 0.1 | ..... | 0.2 | 0.1 |
| Livestock and livestock products | ..... | 0.1 | ..... | ..... | 0.2 | 0.1 | 0.3 | ..... | 0.2 | 1.0 |
| **Other commodities** | ..... | ..... | 0.1 | 0.1 | 1.0 | ..... | ..... | ..... | ..... | ..... |
| Forestry products | ..... | ..... | ..... | ..... | ..... | ..... | ..... | ..... | ..... | ..... |
| Fish and other marine products | ..... | ..... | ..... | ..... | 0.9 | ..... | ..... | ..... | ..... | ..... |
| Metallic ores and concentrates | ..... | ..... | ..... | ..... | ..... | ..... | ..... | ..... | ..... | ..... |
| Bituminous coal and lignite | ..... | ..... | ..... | ..... | ..... | ..... | ..... | ..... | ..... | ..... |
| Crude petroleum and natural gas | ..... | ..... | ..... | ..... | ..... | ..... | ..... | ..... | ..... | ..... |
| Nonmetallic minerals | ..... | ..... | ..... | ..... | ..... | ..... | ..... | ..... | ..... | ..... |
| Scrap and waste | ..... | ..... | ..... | ..... | ..... | ..... | ..... | ..... | ..... | ..... |
| Used merchandise | ..... | ..... | ..... | ..... | ..... | ..... | ..... | ..... | ..... | ..... |
| Goods imported and returned unchanged | ..... | ..... | ..... | ..... | 0.1 | ..... | ..... | ..... | ..... | ..... |
| Special classification provisions | ..... | ..... | ..... | 0.1 | ..... | ..... | ..... | ..... | ..... | ..... |
| | European Union | | | | | United Kingdom | | | | |
| **ALL GOODS** | 13.8 | 16.5 | 17.4 | 17.8 | 39.5 | 5.6 | 8.6 | 7.6 | 6.8 | 6.9 |
| **Manufactured goods** | 10.9 | 14.4 | 11.8 | 13.3 | 18.6 | 4.9 | 8.1 | 6.4 | 6.5 | 6.8 |
| Food products | ..... | ..... | 0.1 | 0.1 | 0.2 | ..... | ..... | ..... | 0.1 | ..... |
| Tobacco products | ..... | ..... | ..... | ..... | ..... | ..... | ..... | ..... | ..... | ..... |
| Textile mill products | 0.1 | ..... | ..... | ..... | 0.1 | ..... | ..... | ..... | ..... | 0.1 |
| Apparel | 0.1 | 0.1 | ..... | 0.1 | 0.1 | ..... | ..... | ..... | ..... | ..... |
| Lumber and wood products | ..... | ..... | 0.1 | 0.5 | 2.7 | ..... | ..... | ..... | 0.3 | 2.3 |
| Furniture and fixtures | ..... | 0.1 | ..... | ..... | ..... | ..... | ..... | ..... | ..... | ..... |
| Paper products | ..... | ..... | ..... | ..... | 0.1 | ..... | ..... | ..... | ..... | ..... |
| Printing and publishing | 0.1 | 0.1 | 0.6 | 0.2 | 0.1 | ..... | 0.1 | 0.1 | ..... | ..... |
| Chemical products | 0.8 | 5.5 | 0.9 | 1.0 | 1.0 | 0.6 | 5.3 | 0.7 | 0.8 | 0.7 |
| Refined petroleum products | ..... | ..... | ..... | ..... | ..... | ..... | ..... | ..... | ..... | ..... |
| Rubber and plastic products | 0.1 | 0.1 | 0.1 | ..... | 0.1 | 0.1 | ..... | 0.1 | ..... | ..... |
| Leather products | ..... | ..... | ..... | ..... | ..... | ..... | ..... | ..... | ..... | ..... |
| Stone, clay and glass products | 0.1 | 0.1 | 0.1 | 0.1 | ..... | 0.1 | 0.1 | ..... | 0.1 | ..... |
| Primary metals | ..... | 0.1 | 0.2 | 0.1 | 0.2 | ..... | ..... | 0.2 | ..... | ..... |
| Fabricated metal products | 0.1 | 0.1 | 0.5 | 0.1 | 0.1 | ..... | ..... | ..... | ..... | ..... |
| Industrial machinery and computers | 5.3 | 3.0 | 3.4 | 5.6 | 9.9 | 3.1 | 1.4 | 1.7 | 1.9 | 1.9 |
| Electric and electronic equipment | 1.0 | 2.1 | 3.9 | 0.9 | 1.1 | 0.4 | 0.7 | 3.1 | 0.6 | 0.2 |
| Transportation equipment | 1.3 | 1.2 | 0.7 | 3.4 | 2.2 | 0.3 | 0.2 | 0.1 | 2.6 | 1.4 |
| Scientific and measuring instruments | 1.1 | 0.8 | 0.6 | 0.6 | 0.7 | 0.1 | 0.1 | ..... | 0.1 | 0.1 |
| Miscellaneous manufactures | 0.7 | 0.9 | 0.4 | 0.4 | 0.1 | 0.1 | ..... | 0.4 | ..... | ..... |
| Unidentified manufactures | 0.1 | 0.1 | 0.1 | ..... | ..... | ..... | 0.1 | 0.1 | ..... | ..... |
| **Agricultural and livestock products** | ..... | ..... | ..... | 0.2 | ..... | ..... | ..... | ..... | ..... | ..... |
| Agricultural products | ..... | ..... | ..... | 0.2 | ..... | ..... | ..... | ..... | ..... | ..... |
| Livestock and livestock products | ..... | ..... | ..... | ..... | ..... | ..... | ..... | ..... | ..... | ..... |
| **Other commodities** | 2.8 | 2.1 | 5.6 | 4.4 | 20.9 | 0.8 | 0.5 | 1.2 | 0.3 | 0.2 |
| Forestry products | ..... | ..... | ..... | ..... | ..... | ..... | ..... | ..... | ..... | ..... |
| Fish and other marine products | ..... | 0.1 | ..... | 0.2 | 3.0 | ..... | ..... | ..... | ..... | ..... |
| Metallic ores and concentrates | 0.2 | ..... | ..... | ..... | 16.9 | 0.2 | ..... | ..... | ..... | ..... |
| Bituminous coal and lignite | 1.0 | 0.2 | 2.7 | 3.0 | ..... | ..... | ..... | ..... | ..... | ..... |
| Crude petroleum and natural gas | ..... | ..... | ..... | ..... | ..... | ..... | ..... | ..... | ..... | ..... |
| Nonmetallic minerals | ..... | 0.2 | 0.6 | 0.3 | 0.3 | ..... | ..... | ..... | ..... | 0.1 |
| Scrap and waste | ..... | ..... | ..... | ..... | ..... | ..... | ..... | ..... | ..... | ..... |
| Used merchandise | 1.6 | 1.6 | 2.3 | 0.9 | 0.6 | 0.5 | 0.5 | 1.2 | 0.3 | 0.1 |
| Goods imported and returned unchanged | ..... | ..... | ..... | ..... | ..... | ..... | ..... | ..... | ..... | ..... |
| Special classification provisions | 0.1 | 0.1 | ..... | ..... | 0.1 | ..... | ..... | ..... | ..... | ..... |

# Table D-3.   State Exports of Goods by Destination and Industry, 1993–1997 —*Continued*

## WYOMING (Millions of dollars.)

| Industry | Germany 1993 | 1994 | 1995 | 1996 | 1997 | France 1993 | 1994 | 1995 | 1996 | 1997 |
|---|---|---|---|---|---|---|---|---|---|---|
| **ALL GOODS** | 2.8 | 4.0 | 2.7 | 1.9 | 1.7 | 1.4 | 1.2 | 1.5 | 0.6 | 1.3 |
| **Manufactured goods** | 2.3 | 3.4 | 2.3 | 1.3 | 1.6 | 1.3 | 0.9 | 1.3 | 0.4 | 1.0 |
| Food products | ..... | ..... | ..... | ..... | ..... | ..... | ..... | ..... | ..... | ..... |
| Tobacco products | ..... | ..... | ..... | ..... | ..... | ..... | ..... | ..... | ..... | ..... |
| Textile mill products | ..... | ..... | ..... | ..... | ..... | ..... | ..... | ..... | ..... | ..... |
| Apparel | ..... | ..... | ..... | ..... | ..... | ..... | ..... | ..... | ..... | ..... |
| Lumber and wood products | ..... | ..... | ..... | ..... | ..... | ..... | ..... | 0.1 | ..... | ..... |
| Furniture and fixtures | ..... | ..... | ..... | ..... | ..... | ..... | 0.1 | ..... | ..... | ..... |
| Paper products | ..... | ..... | ..... | ..... | ..... | ..... | ..... | ..... | ..... | ..... |
| Printing and publishing | ..... | ..... | ..... | ..... | 0.1 | ..... | ..... | 0.5 | ..... | ..... |
| Chemical products | 0.1 | ..... | ..... | 0.2 | 0.2 | ..... | ..... | 0.1 | ..... | ..... |
| Refined petroleum products | ..... | ..... | ..... | ..... | ..... | ..... | ..... | ..... | ..... | ..... |
| Rubber and plastic products | ..... | ..... | ..... | ..... | ..... | 0.1 | ..... | ..... | ..... | ..... |
| Leather products | ..... | ..... | ..... | ..... | ..... | ..... | ..... | ..... | ..... | ..... |
| Stone, clay and glass products | ..... | 0.1 | ..... | ..... | ..... | ..... | ..... | ..... | ..... | ..... |
| Primary metals | ..... | ..... | ..... | ..... | ..... | ..... | ..... | ..... | ..... | ..... |
| Fabricated metal products | 0.1 | 0.1 | 0.5 | ..... | 0.1 | ..... | ..... | ..... | ..... | ..... |
| Industrial machinery and computers | 0.6 | 0.9 | 0.8 | 0.3 | 0.2 | 0.6 | 0.1 | 0.3 | 0.3 | 0.5 |
| Electric and electronic equipment | 0.2 | 1.0 | 0.5 | 0.1 | 0.1 | 0.1 | 0.2 | 0.1 | ..... | ..... |
| Transportation equipment | 0.4 | 0.3 | 0.4 | 0.2 | 0.7 | 0.1 | 0.4 | ..... | ..... | 0.1 |
| Scientific and measuring instruments | 0.4 | 0.3 | 0.1 | ..... | 0.2 | 0.4 | ..... | 0.2 | ..... | 0.2 |
| Miscellaneous manufactures | 0.5 | 0.6 | ..... | 0.3 | ..... | ..... | ..... | ..... | ..... | 0.1 |
| Unidentified manufactures | ..... | ..... | 0.1 | ..... | ..... | ..... | ..... | ..... | ..... | ..... |
| **Agricultural and livestock products** | ..... | ..... | ..... | ..... | ..... | ..... | ..... | ..... | 0.1 | ..... |
| Agricultural products | ..... | ..... | ..... | ..... | ..... | ..... | ..... | ..... | 0.1 | ..... |
| Livestock and livestock products | ..... | ..... | ..... | ..... | ..... | ..... | ..... | ..... | ..... | ..... |
| **Other commodities** | 0.5 | 0.6 | 0.4 | 0.5 | 0.1 | 0.1 | 0.3 | 0.2 | 0.1 | 0.2 |
| Forestry products | ..... | ..... | ..... | ..... | ..... | ..... | ..... | ..... | ..... | ..... |
| Fish and other marine products | ..... | ..... | ..... | ..... | ..... | ..... | ..... | ..... | ..... | ..... |
| Metallic ores and concentrates | ..... | ..... | ..... | ..... | ..... | ..... | ..... | ..... | ..... | ..... |
| Bituminous coal and lignite | ..... | ..... | ..... | ..... | ..... | ..... | ..... | ..... | ..... | ..... |
| Crude petroleum and natural gas | ..... | ..... | ..... | ..... | ..... | ..... | ..... | ..... | ..... | ..... |
| Nonmetallic minerals | ..... | ..... | 0.1 | 0.2 | ..... | ..... | ..... | ..... | ..... | ..... |
| Scrap and waste | ..... | ..... | ..... | ..... | ..... | ..... | ..... | ..... | ..... | ..... |
| Used merchandise | 0.5 | 0.6 | 0.3 | 0.3 | 0.1 | 0.1 | 0.3 | 0.2 | 0.1 | 0.2 |
| Goods imported and returned unchanged | ..... | ..... | ..... | ..... | ..... | ..... | ..... | ..... | ..... | ..... |
| Special classification provisions | ..... | ..... | ..... | ..... | ..... | ..... | ..... | ..... | ..... | ..... |

| Industry | The Netherlands 1993 | 1994 | 1995 | 1996 | 1997 | Asian 10 1993 | 1994 | 1995 | 1996 | 1997 |
|---|---|---|---|---|---|---|---|---|---|---|
| **ALL GOODS** | 1.0 | 0.5 | 1.1 | 0.9 | 15.0 | 13.8 | 13.3 | 17.2 | 24.0 | 22.8 |
| **Manufactured goods** | 0.9 | 0.4 | 0.5 | 0.7 | 0.5 | 13.1 | 10.5 | 16.3 | 20.6 | 12.4 |
| Food products | ..... | ..... | ..... | ..... | ..... | 1.4 | 1.2 | 5.4 | 13.0 | 2.5 |
| Tobacco products | ..... | ..... | ..... | ..... | ..... | ..... | ..... | ..... | ..... | ..... |
| Textile mill products | ..... | ..... | ..... | ..... | ..... | ..... | ..... | ..... | ..... | ..... |
| Apparel | ..... | ..... | ..... | ..... | ..... | 0.1 | 0.8 | 0.4 | 0.1 | 0.1 |
| Lumber and wood products | ..... | ..... | ..... | ..... | ..... | 0.1 | 0.1 | 0.1 | 0.2 | 0.2 |
| Furniture and fixtures | ..... | ..... | ..... | ..... | ..... | ..... | ..... | ..... | ..... | 0.1 |
| Paper products | ..... | ..... | ..... | ..... | 0.1 | ..... | ..... | ..... | 0.1 | 1.9 |
| Printing and publishing | ..... | ..... | ..... | 0.1 | ..... | ..... | 0.1 | ..... | ..... | ..... |
| Chemical products | ..... | ..... | ..... | ..... | ..... | 1.1 | 0.4 | 0.3 | 0.2 | 1.1 |
| Refined petroleum products | ..... | ..... | ..... | ..... | ..... | ..... | ..... | ..... | ..... | ..... |
| Rubber and plastic products | ..... | ..... | ..... | ..... | ..... | 0.2 | 0.1 | 0.1 | 0.1 | 0.1 |
| Leather products | ..... | ..... | ..... | ..... | ..... | ..... | ..... | ..... | ..... | ..... |
| Stone, clay and glass products | ..... | ..... | ..... | ..... | ..... | ..... | 0.1 | 0.4 | ..... | 0.1 |
| Primary metals | ..... | ..... | ..... | 0.1 | ..... | 0.8 | 0.2 | ..... | 2.0 | 0.4 |
| Fabricated metal products | ..... | ..... | ..... | ..... | ..... | 0.1 | 0.9 | 2.1 | 0.7 | 0.4 |
| Industrial machinery and computers | 0.8 | 0.1 | 0.2 | 0.1 | 0.4 | 2.9 | 2.1 | 2.2 | 1.5 | 1.6 |
| Electric and electronic equipment | ..... | ..... | 0.1 | 0.1 | ..... | 3.4 | 3.1 | 2.6 | 0.8 | 1.8 |
| Transportation equipment | ..... | 0.1 | 0.1 | ..... | ..... | 1.0 | 0.2 | 0.6 | 0.5 | 0.6 |
| Scientific and measuring instruments | ..... | 0.1 | ..... | 0.2 | ..... | 1.2 | 0.8 | 1.3 | 0.6 | 1.1 |
| Miscellaneous manufactures | ..... | ..... | ..... | ..... | ..... | 0.4 | 0.3 | 0.7 | 0.6 | 0.2 |
| Unidentified manufactures | ..... | ..... | ..... | ..... | ..... | 0.2 | 0.1 | 0.1 | ..... | 0.1 |
| **Agricultural and livestock products** | ..... | ..... | ..... | 0.1 | ..... | 0.2 | ..... | ..... | ..... | 0.4 |
| Agricultural products | ..... | ..... | ..... | 0.1 | ..... | 0.2 | ..... | ..... | ..... | 0.4 |
| Livestock and livestock products | ..... | ..... | ..... | ..... | ..... | ..... | ..... | ..... | ..... | ..... |
| **Other commodities** | 0.1 | ..... | 0.6 | 0.1 | 14.5 | 0.5 | 2.8 | 0.9 | 3.4 | 10.0 |
| Forestry products | ..... | ..... | ..... | ..... | ..... | ..... | 0.1 | 0.1 | ..... | ..... |
| Fish and other marine products | ..... | ..... | ..... | ..... | 0.1 | ..... | ..... | 0.3 | 0.2 | 5.2 |
| Metallic ores and concentrates | ..... | ..... | ..... | ..... | 14.1 | ..... | ..... | ..... | ..... | 0.1 |
| Bituminous coal and lignite | ..... | ..... | ..... | ..... | ..... | ..... | 2.2 | ..... | 3.0 | 4.3 |
| Crude petroleum and natural gas | ..... | ..... | ..... | ..... | ..... | ..... | ..... | ..... | ..... | ..... |
| Nonmetallic minerals | ..... | ..... | 0.5 | 0.1 | 0.2 | ..... | ..... | ..... | ..... | ..... |
| Scrap and waste | ..... | ..... | ..... | ..... | ..... | 0.1 | 0.1 | ..... | 0.1 | 0.3 |
| Used merchandise | 0.1 | ..... | 0.1 | 0.1 | 0.1 | 0.3 | 0.3 | 0.5 | 0.1 | 0.1 |
| Goods imported and returned unchanged | ..... | ..... | ..... | ..... | ..... | ..... | ..... | ..... | ..... | ..... |
| Special classification provisions | ..... | ..... | ..... | ..... | ..... | ..... | 0.1 | ..... | ..... | ..... |

## Table D-3.  State Exports of Goods by Destination and Industry, 1993–1997 —Continued

**WYOMING** (Millions of dollars.)

| Industry | 1993 | 1994 | 1995 | 1996 | 1997 | 1993 | 1994 | 1995 | 1996 | 1997 |
|---|---|---|---|---|---|---|---|---|---|---|
| | Japan | | | | | South Korea | | | | |
| **ALL GOODS** | 4.7 | 6.9 | 9.6 | 18.4 | 11.1 | 1.1 | 1.1 | 0.9 | 1.2 | 3.3 |
| **Manufactured goods** | 4.6 | 4.6 | 9.4 | 15.3 | 5.4 | 1.1 | 1.1 | 0.9 | 1.2 | 1.5 |
| Food products | 1.1 | 0.9 | 5.1 | 12.7 | 2.4 | ..... | ..... | ..... | 0.2 | 0.1 |
| Tobacco products | ..... | ..... | ..... | ..... | ..... | ..... | ..... | ..... | ..... | ..... |
| Textile mill products | ..... | ..... | ..... | ..... | ..... | ..... | ..... | ..... | ..... | ..... |
| Apparel | 0.1 | 0.8 | 0.4 | 0.1 | 0.1 | ..... | ..... | ..... | ..... | ..... |
| Lumber and wood products | ..... | 0.1 | 0.1 | 0.2 | 0.2 | ..... | ..... | ..... | 0.1 | ..... |
| Furniture and fixtures | ..... | ..... | ..... | ..... | ..... | ..... | ..... | ..... | ..... | ..... |
| Paper products | ..... | ..... | ..... | ..... | 0.3 | ..... | ..... | ..... | ..... | ..... |
| Printing and publishing | ..... | ..... | ..... | ..... | ..... | ..... | ..... | ..... | ..... | ..... |
| Chemical products | 0.1 | ..... | 0.3 | 0.1 | 0.3 | ..... | 0.1 | ..... | 0.1 | 0.3 |
| Refined petroleum products | ..... | ..... | ..... | ..... | ..... | ..... | ..... | ..... | ..... | ..... |
| Rubber and plastic products | 0.2 | ..... | ..... | 0.1 | ..... | ..... | ..... | ..... | ..... | ..... |
| Leather products | ..... | ..... | ..... | ..... | ..... | ..... | ..... | ..... | ..... | ..... |
| Stone, clay and glass products | ..... | 0.1 | 0.2 | ..... | 0.1 | ..... | ..... | ..... | ..... | ..... |
| Primary metals | 0.7 | ..... | ..... | 0.1 | 0.3 | ..... | ..... | ..... | 0.2 | ..... |
| Fabricated metal products | ..... | 0.9 | 0.9 | 0.4 | 0.1 | ..... | ..... | ..... | ..... | 0.3 |
| Industrial machinery and computers | 0.4 | 0.1 | 0.1 | 0.2 | 0.2 | 0.1 | 0.6 | 0.3 | 0.2 | 0.1 |
| Electric and electronic equipment | 0.5 | 0.7 | 0.9 | 0.3 | 0.4 | 0.2 | 0.2 | 0.2 | 0.1 | 0.3 |
| Transportation equipment | 0.4 | 0.1 | 0.1 | 0.3 | 0.1 | 0.5 | ..... | ..... | ..... | 0.1 |
| Scientific and measuring instruments | 0.6 | 0.5 | 0.7 | 0.3 | 0.6 | 0.1 | 0.2 | 0.2 | 0.2 | 0.2 |
| Miscellaneous manufactures | 0.3 | 0.2 | 0.3 | 0.5 | 0.2 | ..... | ..... | ..... | ..... | ..... |
| Unidentified manufactures | 0.1 | 0.1 | ..... | ..... | ..... | ..... | ..... | ..... | ..... | ..... |
| **Agricultural and livestock products** | ..... | ..... | ..... | ..... | ..... | ..... | ..... | ..... | ..... | 0.3 |
| Agricultural products | ..... | ..... | ..... | ..... | ..... | ..... | ..... | ..... | ..... | 0.3 |
| Livestock and livestock products | ..... | ..... | ..... | ..... | ..... | ..... | ..... | ..... | ..... | ..... |
| **Other commodities** | 0.1 | 2.4 | 0.2 | 3.1 | 5.7 | ..... | ..... | ..... | ..... | 1.5 |
| Forestry products | ..... | 0.1 | 0.1 | ..... | ..... | ..... | ..... | ..... | ..... | ..... |
| Fish and other marine products | ..... | ..... | 0.1 | ..... | 1.0 | ..... | ..... | ..... | ..... | 1.5 |
| Metallic ores and concentrates | ..... | ..... | ..... | ..... | 0.1 | ..... | ..... | ..... | ..... | ..... |
| Bituminous coal and lignite | ..... | 2.2 | ..... | 3.0 | 4.3 | ..... | ..... | ..... | ..... | ..... |
| Crude petroleum and natural gas | ..... | ..... | ..... | ..... | ..... | ..... | ..... | ..... | ..... | ..... |
| Nonmetallic minerals | ..... | ..... | ..... | ..... | ..... | ..... | ..... | ..... | ..... | ..... |
| Scrap and waste | ..... | ..... | ..... | 0.1 | 0.2 | ..... | ..... | ..... | ..... | ..... |
| Used merchandise | ..... | ..... | ..... | ..... | ..... | ..... | ..... | ..... | ..... | ..... |
| Goods imported and returned unchanged | ..... | ..... | ..... | ..... | ..... | ..... | ..... | ..... | ..... | ..... |
| Special classification provisions | ..... | ..... | ..... | ..... | ..... | ..... | ..... | ..... | ..... | ..... |
| | Taiwan | | | | | Singapore | | | | |
| **ALL GOODS** | 1.5 | 2.0 | 1.8 | 0.7 | 1.1 | 2.0 | 1.0 | 1.1 | 0.6 | 1.3 |
| **Manufactured goods** | 1.4 | 1.9 | 1.8 | 0.6 | 1.1 | 2.0 | 0.9 | 1.0 | 0.6 | 1.3 |
| Food products | 0.2 | ..... | 0.2 | 0.1 | ..... | ..... | 0.1 | ..... | ..... | ..... |
| Tobacco products | ..... | ..... | ..... | ..... | ..... | ..... | ..... | ..... | ..... | ..... |
| Textile mill products | ..... | ..... | ..... | ..... | ..... | ..... | ..... | ..... | ..... | ..... |
| Apparel | ..... | ..... | ..... | ..... | ..... | ..... | ..... | ..... | ..... | ..... |
| Lumber and wood products | ..... | ..... | ..... | ..... | ..... | ..... | ..... | ..... | ..... | ..... |
| Furniture and fixtures | ..... | ..... | ..... | ..... | 0.1 | ..... | ..... | ..... | ..... | ..... |
| Paper products | ..... | ..... | ..... | ..... | ..... | ..... | ..... | ..... | ..... | ..... |
| Printing and publishing | ..... | ..... | ..... | ..... | ..... | ..... | ..... | ..... | ..... | ..... |
| Chemical products | ..... | ..... | ..... | ..... | 0.2 | 0.1 | 0.1 | ..... | ..... | ..... |
| Refined petroleum products | ..... | ..... | ..... | ..... | ..... | ..... | ..... | ..... | ..... | ..... |
| Rubber and plastic products | ..... | ..... | ..... | ..... | 0.1 | ..... | ..... | ..... | ..... | ..... |
| Leather products | ..... | ..... | ..... | ..... | ..... | ..... | ..... | ..... | ..... | ..... |
| Stone, clay and glass products | ..... | ..... | ..... | ..... | ..... | ..... | ..... | ..... | ..... | ..... |
| Primary metals | ..... | 0.1 | ..... | ..... | ..... | ..... | ..... | ..... | 0.1 | ..... |
| Fabricated metal products | ..... | ..... | 1.0 | 0.2 | ..... | ..... | ..... | 0.1 | ..... | ..... |
| Industrial machinery and computers | 0.1 | 0.9 | 0.1 | 0.1 | ..... | 1.5 | 0.2 | 0.3 | 0.4 | 0.9 |
| Electric and electronic equipment | 0.8 | 0.7 | 0.2 | 0.1 | 0.4 | 0.2 | 0.3 | 0.2 | ..... | 0.1 |
| Transportation equipment | ..... | ..... | 0.2 | 0.1 | 0.2 | ..... | 0.1 | ..... | 0.1 | ..... |
| Scientific and measuring instruments | 0.2 | ..... | 0.1 | 0.1 | ..... | 0.2 | 0.1 | 0.1 | ..... | 0.1 |
| Miscellaneous manufactures | ..... | ..... | ..... | ..... | ..... | ..... | ..... | 0.2 | ..... | ..... |
| Unidentified manufactures | ..... | ..... | ..... | ..... | ..... | ..... | ..... | ..... | ..... | ..... |
| **Agricultural and livestock products** | ..... | ..... | ..... | ..... | ..... | ..... | ..... | ..... | ..... | ..... |
| Agricultural products | ..... | ..... | ..... | ..... | ..... | ..... | ..... | ..... | ..... | ..... |
| Livestock and livestock products | ..... | ..... | ..... | ..... | ..... | ..... | ..... | ..... | ..... | ..... |
| **Other commodities** | 0.1 | 0.1 | ..... | ..... | 0.1 | 0.1 | ..... | 0.1 | ..... | ..... |
| Forestry products | ..... | ..... | ..... | ..... | ..... | ..... | ..... | ..... | ..... | ..... |
| Fish and other marine products | ..... | ..... | ..... | ..... | ..... | ..... | ..... | ..... | ..... | ..... |
| Metallic ores and concentrates | ..... | ..... | ..... | ..... | ..... | ..... | ..... | ..... | ..... | ..... |
| Bituminous coal and lignite | ..... | ..... | ..... | ..... | ..... | ..... | ..... | ..... | ..... | ..... |
| Crude petroleum and natural gas | ..... | ..... | ..... | ..... | ..... | ..... | ..... | ..... | ..... | ..... |
| Nonmetallic minerals | ..... | ..... | ..... | ..... | ..... | ..... | ..... | ..... | ..... | ..... |
| Scrap and waste | ..... | ..... | ..... | ..... | 0.1 | ..... | ..... | ..... | ..... | ..... |
| Used merchandise | 0.1 | ..... | ..... | ..... | ..... | ..... | ..... | 0.1 | ..... | ..... |
| Goods imported and returned unchanged | ..... | ..... | ..... | ..... | ..... | ..... | ..... | ..... | ..... | ..... |
| Special classification provisions | ..... | ..... | ..... | ..... | ..... | ..... | ..... | ..... | ..... | ..... |

# PART E.   Metropolitan Area Exports of Goods

## U.S. Exports of Goods by Metropolitan Area, 1997
### (billions of dollars)

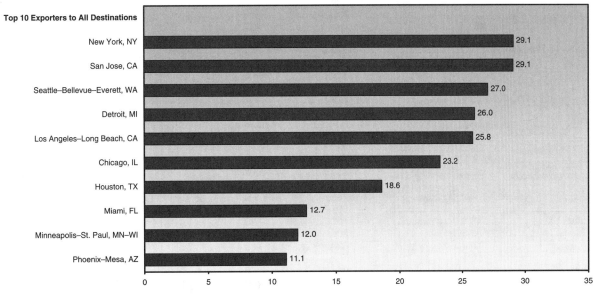

**Top 10 Exporters to All Destinations**

|  |  |
|---|---|
| New York, NY | 29.1 |
| San Jose, CA | 29.1 |
| Seattle–Bellevue–Everett, WA | 27.0 |
| Detroit, MI | 26.0 |
| Los Angeles–Long Beach, CA | 25.8 |
| Chicago, IL | 23.2 |
| Houston, TX | 18.6 |
| Miami, FL | 12.7 |
| Minneapolis–St. Paul, MN–WI | 12.0 |
| Phoenix–Mesa, AZ | 11.1 |

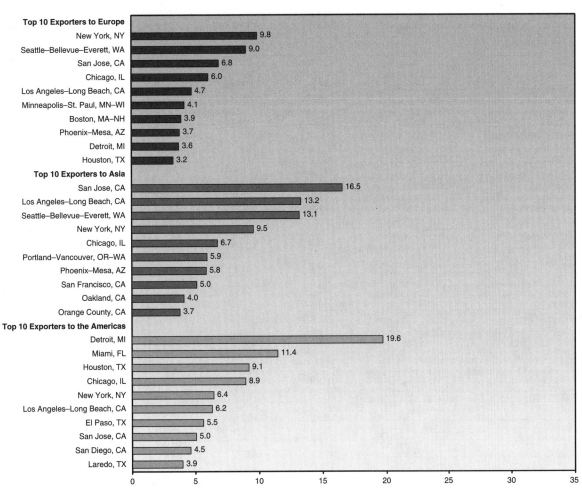

**Top 10 Exporters to Europe**

|  |  |
|---|---|
| New York, NY | 9.8 |
| Seattle–Bellevue–Everett, WA | 9.0 |
| San Jose, CA | 6.8 |
| Chicago, IL | 6.0 |
| Los Angeles–Long Beach, CA | 4.7 |
| Minneapolis–St. Paul, MN–WI | 4.1 |
| Boston, MA–NH | 3.9 |
| Phoenix–Mesa, AZ | 3.7 |
| Detroit, MI | 3.6 |
| Houston, TX | 3.2 |

**Top 10 Exporters to Asia**

|  |  |
|---|---|
| San Jose, CA | 16.5 |
| Los Angeles–Long Beach, CA | 13.2 |
| Seattle–Bellevue–Everett, WA | 13.1 |
| New York, NY | 9.5 |
| Chicago, IL | 6.7 |
| Portland–Vancouver, OR–WA | 5.9 |
| Phoenix–Mesa, AZ | 5.8 |
| San Francisco, CA | 5.0 |
| Oakland, CA | 4.0 |
| Orange County, CA | 3.7 |

**Top 10 Exporters to the Americas**

|  |  |
|---|---|
| Detroit, MI | 19.6 |
| Miami, FL | 11.4 |
| Houston, TX | 9.1 |
| Chicago, IL | 8.9 |
| New York, NY | 6.4 |
| Los Angeles–Long Beach, CA | 6.2 |
| El Paso, TX | 5.5 |
| San Jose, CA | 5.0 |
| San Diego, CA | 4.5 |
| Laredo, TX | 3.9 |

## Table E-1.  Metropolitan Area Exports of Goods, 1993–1997

(Millions of dollars.)

| Metropolitan area | 1993 | 1994 | 1995 | 1996 | 1997 |
|---|---|---|---|---|---|
| Akron, OH | 1 434.9 | 1 606.3 | 1 931.7 | 2 260.3 | 2 353.3 |
| Albany - Schenectady - Troy, NY | 676.2 | 831.4 | 1 061.2 | 1 101.0 | 1 666.2 |
| Albany, GA | 26.4 | 31.8 | 31.5 | 52.5 | 57.3 |
| Albuquerque, NM | 256.7 | 335.5 | 270.1 | 740.3 | 1 564.6 |
| Alexandria, LA | 15.8 | 16.9 | 18.7 | 21.6 | 17.9 |
| Allentown - Bethlehem - Easton, PA | 1 273.9 | 1 371.1 | 1 492.8 | 1 477.2 | 1 808.9 |
| Altoona, PA | 42.6 | 46.4 | 74.2 | 80.2 | 85.9 |
| Anchorage, AK | 128.8 | 198.2 | 150.4 | 109.0 | 213.1 |
| Ann Arbor, MI | 2 218.1 | 2 075.8 | 1 157.9 | 1 311.1 | 1 520.9 |
| Appleton - Oshkosh - Neenah, WI | 529.5 | 507.7 | 593.7 | 608.5 | 647.9 |
| Asheville, NC | 232.3 | 228.6 | 185.2 | 236.7 | 294.2 |
| Atlanta, GA | 3 870.6 | 4 739.1 | 5 811.4 | 5 891.5 | 6 604.6 |
| Augusta - Aiken, GA - SC | 227.4 | 326.3 | 405.2 | 443.9 | 433.8 |
| Austin - San Marcos, TX | 1 721.5 | 2 128.8 | 2 929.2 | 2 743.1 | 3 354.8 |
| Bakersfield, CA | 480.7 | 780.4 | 730.5 | 721.3 | 835.6 |
| Baltimore, MD | 1 783.4 | 1 869.0 | 2 209.2 | 2 110.4 | 2 171.3 |
| Baton Rouge, LA | 564.6 | 458.0 | 569.6 | 552.9 | 577.1 |
| Beaumont - Port Arthur, TX | 87.7 | 97.0 | 118.9 | 115.4 | 133.4 |
| Bellingham, WA | 206.8 | 210.7 | 253.5 | 275.4 | 316.7 |
| Benton Harbor, MI | 338.7 | 368.8 | 369.3 | 317.2 | 260.6 |
| Bergen - Passaic, NJ | 3 924.9 | 4 387.0 | 4 784.0 | 4 499.9 | 4 789.8 |
| Biloxi - Gulfport - Pascagoula, MS | 108.1 | 281.6 | 281.0 | 119.9 | 76.9 |
| Binghamton, NY | 316.2 | 474.9 | 558.1 | 443.3 | 513.3 |
| Birmingham, AL | 533.9 | 453.8 | 550.5 | 625.8 | 941.4 |
| Bloomington, IN | 113.6 | 115.7 | 127.6 | 198.8 | 166.8 |
| Boise City, ID | 1 022.7 | 1 289.8 | 1 635.0 | 1 338.5 | 1 407.3 |
| Boston, MA - NH | 6 472.5 | 7 095.3 | 7 902.7 | 8 715.8 | 9 570.6 |
| Brazoria, TX | 1 475.1 | 1 761.0 | ..... | ..... | ..... |
| Bremerton, WA | 45.0 | 54.6 | 109.8 | 79.9 | 102.4 |
| Bridgeport, CT | 1 125.9 | 918.8 | 952.9 | 788.6 | 981.4 |
| Brockton, MA | 107.0 | 113.1 | 144.0 | 159.7 | 268.7 |
| Brownsville - Harlingen - San Benito, TX | 1 904.4 | 2 113.4 | 2 245.9 | 2 612.6 | 2 697.1 |
| Buffalo - Niagara Falls, NY | 1 135.2 | 1 569.7 | 2 295.8 | 2 262.2 | 2 667.3 |
| Canton - Massillon, OH | 250.2 | 315.9 | 377.2 | 406.0 | 421.6 |
| Cedar Rapids, IA | 342.4 | 363.8 | 402.2 | 391.1 | 429.8 |
| Champaign - Urbana, IL | 87.8 | 89.3 | 103.4 | 214.4 | 423.6 |
| Charleston - North Charleston, SC | 597.3 | 388.5 | 501.6 | 595.1 | 827.6 |
| Charleston, WV | 178.9 | 277.6 | 394.4 | 412.2 | 393.4 |
| Charlotte - Gastonia - Rock Hill, NC - SC | 1 563.7 | 1 782.8 | 2 088.0 | 2 291.3 | 2 588.8 |
| Charlottesville, VA | 113.8 | 123.0 | 157.4 | 140.2 | 195.4 |
| Chattanooga, TN - GA | 218.3 | 237.3 | 301.0 | 273.5 | 331.4 |
| Chicago, IL | 14 446.6 | 17 333.6 | 21 083.4 | 22 030.1 | 23 209.9 |
| Chico - Paradise, CA | 71.0 | 77.2 | 70.1 | 78.1 | 58.1 |
| Cincinnati, OH - KY - IN | 3 898.2 | 4 056.5 | 4 256.7 | 4 784.1 | 5 674.1 |
| Cleveland - Lorain - Elyria, OH | 3 582.8 | 4 093.3 | 4 707.0 | 5 075.2 | 5 511.0 |
| Colorado Springs, CO | 664.3 | 900.7 | 954.7 | 857.0 | 1 006.0 |
| Columbia, MO | 42.9 | 50.2 | 51.1 | 57.9 | 74.9 |
| Columbia, SC | 212.9 | 300.4 | 343.3 | 310.8 | 328.5 |
| Columbus, GA - AL | 183.8 | 172.8 | 245.3 | 253.2 | 282.3 |
| Columbus, OH | 1 167.0 | 1 295.5 | 1 358.2 | 1 497.2 | 1 660.7 |
| Corpus Christi, TX | 186.8 | 153.6 | 162.4 | 241.8 | 387.2 |
| Cumberland, MD - WV | 54.9 | 64.3 | 53.8 | 45.9 | 48.3 |
| Dallas, TX | 4 817.6 | 5 679.7 | 6 870.4 | 7 096.9 | 8 645.9 |
| Danbury, CT | 316.7 | 393.0 | 421.6 | 531.9 | 482.9 |
| Danville, VA | 173.0 | 202.7 | 155.7 | 89.1 | 104.4 |

## Table E-1. Metropolitan Area Exports of Goods, 1993–1997—*Continued*

(Millions of dollars.)

| Metropolitan area | 1993 | 1994 | 1995 | 1996 | 1997 |
|---|---|---|---|---|---|
| Davenport - Moline - Rock Island, IA - IL ............................... | 1 102.6 | 1 098.9 | 1 291.0 | 1 576.1 | 1 933.9 |
| Dayton - Springfield, OH ........................................................ | 2 479.9 | 2 671.3 | 2 404.8 | 2 201.5 | 2 271.5 |
| Daytona Beach, FL .................................................................. | 140.5 | 110.3 | 85.9 | 111.7 | 137.5 |
| Decatur, AL .............................................................................. | 42.3 | 54.5 | 65.6 | 91.6 | 109.5 |
| Denver, CO .............................................................................. | 931.0 | 1 089.8 | 1 385.3 | 1 502.9 | 1 738.1 |
| Des Moines, IA ........................................................................ | 337.2 | 348.9 | 378.5 | 426.0 | 450.5 |
| Detroit, MI ................................................................................ | 16 780.9 | 27 469.7 | 27 314.7 | 27 531.2 | 25 967.4 |
| Dubuque, IA ............................................................................. | 93.1 | 177.6 | 180.7 | 183.5 | 181.2 |
| Dutchess County, NY .............................................................. | 796.5 | 980.6 | 0.0 | 0.0 | 0.0 |
| Eau Claire, WI ......................................................................... | 289.7 | 465.7 | 399.9 | 320.6 | 507.3 |
| El Paso, TX .............................................................................. | 2 967.0 | 3 561.3 | 4 120.8 | 5 212.7 | 5 833.9 |
| Elkhart - Goshen, IN ............................................................... | 419.9 | 460.4 | 501.5 | 367.5 | 414.7 |
| Elmira, NY ................................................................................ | 70.2 | 116.8 | 139.5 | 196.9 | 241.8 |
| Erie, PA .................................................................................... | 311.6 | 285.4 | 490.8 | 321.9 | 598.2 |
| Eugene - Springfield, OR ........................................................ | 157.9 | 173.1 | 190.3 | 168.9 | 190.5 |
| Evansville - Henderson, IN - KY ............................................. | 448.5 | 487.4 | 525.1 | 545.1 | 588.0 |
| Fargo - Moorhead, ND - MN .................................................... | 111.8 | 137.3 | 155.0 | 181.9 | 208.5 |
| Fayetteville - Springdale - Rogers, AR ................................... | 250.4 | 433.8 | 669.3 | 801.2 | 732.8 |
| Fayetteville, NC ....................................................................... | 54.3 | 57.9 | 66.6 | 65.4 | 105.3 |
| Flint, MI .................................................................................... | 958.9 | 1 032.1 | 1 451.7 | 1 318.8 | 1 475.3 |
| Florence, AL ............................................................................ | 29.8 | 25.7 | 29.5 | 25.2 | 35.9 |
| Florence, SC ............................................................................ | 66.3 | 117.2 | 249.0 | 121.6 | 75.8 |
| Fort Collins - Loveland, CO .................................................... | 284.3 | 354.5 | 373.9 | 468.1 | 433.3 |
| Fort Lauderdale, FL ................................................................. | 1 321.4 | 1 506.7 | 1 774.7 | 1 864.5 | 2 143.0 |
| Fort Pierce - Port St. Lucie, FL .............................................. | 73.5 | 92.3 | 114.2 | 107.6 | 118.5 |
| Fort Wayne, IN ........................................................................ | 640.6 | 770.9 | 1 029.4 | 991.4 | 1 078.2 |
| Fort Worth - Arlington, TX ....................................................... | 1 600.2 | 2 052.0 | 1 915.0 | 2 372.7 | 3 045.9 |
| Fresno, CA ............................................................................... | 673.1 | 763.4 | 714.4 | 691.8 | 739.8 |
| Gainesville, FL ........................................................................ | 62.6 | 65.7 | 91.6 | 88.3 | 79.6 |
| Gary, IN ................................................................................... | 225.3 | 267.5 | 310.6 | 303.2 | 336.9 |
| Grand Rapids - Muskegon - Holland, MI ............................... | 1 705.0 | 1 993.5 | 2 304.1 | 2 656.5 | 2 933.1 |
| Greeley, CO ............................................................................. | 276.0 | 501.8 | 582.9 | 558.8 | 693.9 |
| Green Bay, WI ......................................................................... | 134.1 | 187.3 | 212.7 | 188.9 | 281.9 |
| Greensboro - Winston-Salem - High Point, NC ..................... | 2 453.1 | 2 773.3 | 3 356.3 | 3 495.6 | 4 050.8 |
| Greenville - Spartanburg - Anderson, SC ............................. | 1 462.1 | 1 745.0 | 2 305.3 | 2 720.4 | 3 076.9 |
| Hamilton - Middletown, OH ..................................................... | 49.3 | 66.3 | 78.3 | 90.1 | 98.2 |
| Harrisburg - Lebanon - Carlisle, PA ...................................... | 339.2 | 535.0 | 601.0 | 775.5 | 964.4 |
| Hartford, CT ............................................................................. | 1 926.1 | 1 967.1 | 2 167.6 | 2 416.0 | 3 219.8 |
| Hickory - Morganton, NC ........................................................ | 335.2 | 397.9 | 476.1 | 464.3 | 501.2 |
| Honolulu, HI ............................................................................. | 187.8 | 215.5 | 228.2 | 265.7 | 269.5 |
| Houma, LA ............................................................................... | 58.3 | 53.8 | 60.0 | 58.0 | 86.4 |
| Houston, TX ............................................................................. | 12 284.6 | 13 388.2 | 16 247.9 | 16 541.5 | 18 595.9 |
| Huntington - Ashland, WV - KY - OH ..................................... | 136.6 | 162.4 | 237.2 | 193.9 | 218.7 |
| Huntsville, AL .......................................................................... | 573.6 | 672.1 | 829.0 | 899.1 | 1 071.8 |
| Indianapolis, IN ....................................................................... | 2 626.6 | 3 003.8 | 3 555.9 | 4 012.8 | 4 301.8 |
| Jackson, MI ............................................................................. | 95.5 | 96.3 | 98.5 | ·128.1 | 135.0 |
| Jackson, MS ............................................................................ | 141.2 | 154.3 | 203.0 | 231.4 | 318.1 |
| Jackson, TN ............................................................................. | 108.0 | 132.5 | 175.3 | 155.2 | 167.8 |
| Jacksonville, FL ....................................................................... | 404.9 | 500.4 | 604.1 | 677.0 | 721.3 |
| Jamestown, NY ....................................................................... | 156.9 | 209.4 | 256.6 | 241.2 | 283.5 |
| Janesville - Beloit, WI ............................................................. | 76.6 | 76.3 | 80.2 | 107.1 | 128.5 |
| Jersey City, NJ ........................................................................ | 986.2 | 1 351.2 | 1 159.9 | 1 140.8 | 1 319.4 |
| Johnson City - Kingsport - Bristol, TN - VA ......................... | 1 356.7 | 1 580.8 | 1 677.5 | 1 566.5 | 1 698.6 |
| Joplin, MO ............................................................................... | 52.1 | 44.6 | 50.3 | 71.4 | 73.5 |
| Kalamazoo - Battle Creek, MI ................................................ | 650.3 | 869.0 | 897.3 | 836.1 | 919.5 |

## Table E-1.  Metropolitan Area Exports of Goods, 1993–1997—*Continued*

(Millions of dollars.)

| Metropolitan area | 1993 | 1994 | 1995 | 1996 | 1997 |
|---|---|---|---|---|---|
| Kankakee, IL | 79.1 | 86.0 | 137.8 | 113.7 | 118.7 |
| Kansas City, MO - KS | 2 225.9 | 2 578.6 | 3 350.2 | 3 985.1 | 3 817.6 |
| Kenosha, WI | 126.9 | 117.7 | 133.9 | 154.3 | 232.1 |
| Knoxville, TN | 580.4 | 689.2 | 633.2 | 764.1 | 884.2 |
| Kokomo, IN | 1 727.5 | 1 858.4 | 1 648.9 | 2 056.4 | 2 213.1 |
| La Crosse, WI - MN | 90.6 | 93.1 | 276.2 | 273.2 | 297.8 |
| Lafayette, IN | 75.2 | 74.9 | 116.2 | 133.2 | 172.7 |
| Lafayette, LA | 93.6 | 148.7 | 192.7 | 164.8 | 202.2 |
| Lake Charles, LA | 56.1 | 55.9 | 64.6 | 48.2 | 77.9 |
| Lakeland - Winter Haven, FL | 187.0 | 199.2 | 237.7 | 241.5 | 243.6 |
| Lancaster, PA | 406.1 | 469.3 | 581.5 | 626.2 | 620.3 |
| Lansing - East Lansing, MI | 185.7 | 208.6 | 224.0 | 202.2 | 217.5 |
| Laredo, TX | 4 061.8 | 4 157.4 | 2 897.8 | 3 440.7 | 3 959.1 |
| Las Vegas, NV - AZ | 166.6 | 144.8 | 0.0 | 0.0 | 0.0 |
| Lawrence, KS | 5.2 | 6.2 | 4.1 | 5.7 | 6.5 |
| Lawrence, MA - NH | 822.6 | 806.4 | 841.7 | 1 033.6 | 1 810.2 |
| Lexington, KY | 624.2 | 1 078.6 | 1 235.0 | 1 499.9 | 1 886.8 |
| Lima, OH | 294.1 | 166.2 | 226.0 | 207.3 | 242.0 |
| Lincoln, NE | 188.5 | 207.2 | 208.8 | 225.3 | 264.6 |
| Little Rock - North Little Rock, AR | 200.1 | 219.0 | 193.6 | 210.4 | 349.4 |
| Longview - Marshall, TX | 85.0 | 97.3 | 121.2 | 144.2 | 183.6 |
| Los Angeles - Long Beach, CA | 20 013.6 | 22 224.8 | 24 731.0 | 24 437.9 | 25 816.4 |
| Louisville, KY - IN | 1 673.8 | 1 798.8 | 2 199.8 | 2 327.1 | 2 449.1 |
| Lowell, MA - NH | 867.5 | 890.1 | 1 079.9 | 1 119.9 | 1 396.5 |
| Lubbock, TX | 98.6 | 165.1 | 258.7 | 189.0 | 262.2 |
| Lynchburg, VA | 143.2 | 152.5 | 192.1 | 258.8 | 439.2 |
| Macon, GA | 160.5 | 173.3 | 197.6 | 220.1 | 241.3 |
| Madison, WI | 357.7 | 417.1 | 497.5 | 522.4 | 603.0 |
| Manchester, NH | 107.0 | 115.3 | 146.3 | 198.3 | 237.8 |
| Mansfield, OH | 367.6 | 349.9 | 394.9 | 413.0 | 444.0 |
| McAllen - Edinburg - Mission, TX | 1 510.2 | 1 826.4 | 1 617.1 | 1 579.7 | 1 872.9 |
| Melbourne - Titusville - Palm Bay, FL | 315.2 | 315.9 | 310.1 | 635.0 | 408.8 |
| Memphis, TN - AR - MS | 2 055.1 | 2 729.5 | 4 163.8 | 3 786.1 | 3 636.9 |
| Miami, FL | 8 264.3 | 9 266.7 | 10 200.8 | 10 681.2 | 12 692.3 |
| Middlesex - Somerset - Hunterdon, NJ | 2 840.6 | 3 035.9 | 3 448.1 | 3 628.1 | 4 385.4 |
| Milwaukee - Waukesha, WI | 2 337.3 | 2 913.5 | 3 506.9 | 3 717.2 | 3 837.6 |
| Minneapolis - St. Paul, MN - WI | 9 003.8 | 8 863.5 | 11 071.8 | 12 384.0 | 12 006.7 |
| Mobile, AL | 356.7 | 395.3 | 415.8 | 459.9 | 498.7 |
| Modesto, CA | 201.1 | 236.7 | 279.2 | 359.6 | 387.5 |
| Monmouth - Ocean, NJ | 373.4 | 410.2 | 471.8 | 478.2 | 504.8 |
| Monroe, LA | 77.1 | 107.1 | 167.8 | 134.0 | 101.9 |
| Montgomery, AL | 157.8 | 231.0 | 244.1 | 192.9 | 185.5 |
| Muncie, IN | 64.3 | 107.4 | 158.3 | 137.6 | 157.6 |
| Naples, FL | 55.6 | 56.0 | 75.0 | 76.0 | 35.0 |
| Nashua, NH | 290.2 | 235.4 | 282.2 | 291.3 | 339.8 |
| Nashville, TN | 1 104.1 | 1 310.5 | 1 412.3 | 1 445.5 | 1 767.1 |
| Nassau - Suffolk, NY | 2 803.2 | 2 866.3 | 3 558.6 | 3 680.2 | 4 208.5 |
| New Bedford, MA | 141.6 | 154.5 | 186.8 | 165.8 | 153.4 |
| New Haven - Meriden, CT | 1 035.6 | 1 075.5 | 1 106.3 | 1 012.4 | 1 179.8 |
| New London - Norwich, CT - RI | 136.5 | 141.5 | 178.2 | 157.5 | 192.1 |
| New Orleans, LA | 2 034.2 | 2 326.2 | 3 037.8 | 3 316.8 | 2 770.8 |
| New York, NY | 28 192.8 | 23 543.7 | 27 131.1 | 27 970.5 | 29 082.6 |
| Newark, NJ | 4 287.4 | 5 205.5 | 5 640.0 | 5 044.2 | 5 201.8 |
| Newburgh, NY - PA | 382.3 | 152.8 | 148.9 | 153.3 | 222.1 |
| Norfolk - Virginia Beach - Newport News, VA - NC | 677.2 | 807.7 | 1 005.5 | 1 256.9 | 1 396.9 |

## Table E-1.  Metropolitan Area Exports of Goods, 1993–1997—*Continued*

(Millions of dollars.)

| Metropolitan area | 1993 | 1994 | 1995 | 1996 | 1997 |
|---|---|---|---|---|---|
| Oakland, CA ................................................ | 4 181.5 | 5 113.2 | 6 372.5 | 7 309.2 | 6 920.4 |
| Odessa - Midland, TX ................................... | 50.0 | 68.3 | 118.2 | 92.1 | 99.7 |
| Oklahoma City, OK ...................................... | 478.9 | 488.6 | 485.8 | 483.9 | 520.0 |
| Omaha, NE - IA ........................................... | 299.8 | 393.3 | 425.9 | 608.3 | 691.4 |
| Orange County, CA ...................................... | 5 653.4 | 6 716.0 | 8 041.1 | 8 309.3 | 8 798.3 |
| Orlando, FL ................................................. | 930.4 | 848.5 | 968.8 | 1 219.0 | 1 662.8 |
| Panama City, FL .......................................... | 90.9 | 121.2 | 216.5 | 174.8 | 221.1 |
| Parkersburg - Marietta, WV - OH ................. | 298.8 | 313.6 | 186.6 | 211.9 | 262.3 |
| Pensacola, FL .............................................. | 38.8 | 34.0 | 32.2 | 36.8 | 59.8 |
| Philadelphia, PA - NJ ................................... | 5 869.1 | 6 545.8 | 7 896.9 | 7 727.9 | 8 027.8 |
| Phoenix - Mesa, AZ ..................................... | 4 498.9 | 5 561.1 | 6 780.4 | 7 912.1 | 11 108.4 |
| Pine Bluff, AR .............................................. | 125.3 | 152.5 | 153.7 | 152.8 | 139.2 |
| Pittsburgh, PA ............................................. | 2 989.7 | 3 150.6 | 3 982.2 | 3 933.7 | 4 352.2 |
| Pittsfield, MA .............................................. | 77.2 | 112.2 | 151.9 | 175.5 | 219.3 |
| Portland - Vancouver, OR - WA .................... | 5 698.5 | 6 448.8 | 8 931.3 | 9 234.3 | 8 926.5 |
| Portland, ME ............................................... | 355.2 | 319.5 | 373.1 | 339.2 | 617.4 |
| Portsmouth - Rochester, NH - ME ................ | 465.0 | 470.2 | 553.6 | 574.8 | 486.0 |
| Providence - Fall River - Warwick, RI - MA ... | 1 141.7 | 1 246.0 | 1 241.0 | 1 296.2 | 1 601.8 |
| Provo - Orem, UT ......................................... | 170.4 | 200.2 | 201.6 | 301.9 | 360.5 |
| Racine, WI .................................................. | 365.1 | 403.2 | 335.1 | 493.2 | 992.0 |
| Raleigh - Durham - Chapel Hill, NC ............. | 1 620.9 | 1 758.7 | 2 093.2 | 2 609.8 | 2 713.1 |
| Reading, PA ................................................ | 300.6 | 271.6 | 293.4 | 326.2 | 429.5 |
| Redding, CA ................................................ | 32.3 | 28.6 | 41.0 | 53.0 | 39.3 |
| Reno, NV .................................................... | 184.1 | 213.7 | 368.2 | 314.6 | 399.7 |
| Richland - Kennewick - Pasco, WA .............. | 220.3 | 271.6 | 146.6 | 228.1 | 457.9 |
| Richmond - Petersburg, VA .......................... | 4 012.2 | 5 260.6 | 5 389.3 | 5 609.4 | 5 571.7 |
| Riverside - San Bernardino, CA ................... | 1 093.8 | 1 458.8 | 1 856.5 | 1 982.1 | 2 067.9 |
| Roanoke, VA ............................................... | 164.0 | 195.9 | 231.3 | 238.3 | 285.2 |
| Rochester, MN ............................................ | 53.0 | 72.7 | 93.9 | 92.9 | 131.8 |
| Rochester, NY ............................................. | 3 091.5 | 3 143.7 | 3 860.5 | 4 307.7 | 4 694.5 |
| Rockford, IL ................................................ | 521.6 | 616.1 | 641.4 | 721.9 | 758.7 |
| Sacramento, CA .......................................... | 1 075.6 | 1 087.9 | 1 448.3 | 1 908.6 | 1 669.5 |
| Saginaw - Bay City - Midland, MI ................. | 855.4 | 776.8 | 1 035.6 | 1 254.5 | 1 654.4 |
| Salem, OR .................................................. | 66.3 | 72.9 | 112.0 | 123.0 | 160.6 |
| Salinas, CA ................................................. | 294.5 | 322.0 | 359.9 | 337.6 | 393.2 |
| Salt Lake City - Ogden, UT .......................... | 1 660.9 | 1 808.7 | 1 838.2 | 2 111.5 | 2 593.6 |
| San Antonio, TX .......................................... | 563.9 | 656.3 | 771.1 | 1 050.0 | 1 342.8 |
| San Diego, CA ............................................ | 4 357.7 | 4 867.3 | 5 860.9 | 6 719.4 | 7 810.0 |
| San Francisco, CA ...................................... | 9 264.9 | 9 303.8 | 8 133.7 | 8 560.4 | 9 978.5 |
| San Jose, CA .............................................. | 16 171.6 | 19 942.7 | 26 822.8 | 29 331.3 | 29 057.2 |
| Santa Barbara - Santa Maria - Lompoc, CA .. | 424.0 | 420.2 | 565.2 | 648.0 | 623.3 |
| Santa Cruz - Watsonville, CA ...................... | 664.3 | 857.4 | 1 408.2 | 1 943.1 | 2 298.5 |
| Santa Rosa, CA .......................................... | 409.1 | 485.2 | 572.9 | 681.8 | 856.3 |
| Sarasota - Bradenton, FL ............................ | 186.9 | 187.4 | 182.8 | 180.2 | 184.8 |
| Savannah, GA ............................................. | 442.5 | 423.3 | 567.5 | 459.4 | 633.4 |
| Scranton - Wilkes-Barre - Hazleton, PA ...... | 266.6 | 328.2 | 431.9 | 392.0 | 442.4 |
| Seattle - Bellevue - Everett, WA ................. | 23 815.6 | 21 753.0 | 17 815.4 | 21 391.1 | 27 005.8 |
| Sharon, PA ................................................. | 44.1 | 40.4 | 60.7 | 56.9 | 83.9 |
| Sheboygan, WI ............................................ | 207.1 | 244.3 | 258.7 | 283.3 | 320.9 |
| Sherman - Denison, TX ............................... | 34.7 | 36.1 | 90.7 | 147.5 | 172.4 |
| Shreveport - Bossier City, LA ...................... | 108.4 | 134.6 | 169.1 | 172.6 | 180.8 |
| South Bend, IN ........................................... | 179.7 | 160.3 | 389.5 | 494.8 | 522.1 |
| Spokane, WA .............................................. | 254.4 | 269.4 | 310.9 | 347.9 | 445.7 |
| Springfield, IL ............................................. | 23.9 | 29.8 | 35.1 | 35.5 | 44.4 |
| Springfield, MA ........................................... | 389.8 | 434.8 | 512.1 | 530.3 | 568.0 |

## Table E-1.  Metropolitan Area Exports of Goods, 1993–1997—*Continued*

(Millions of dollars.)

| Metropolitan area | 1993 | 1994 | 1995 | 1996 | 1997 |
|---|---|---|---|---|---|
| Springfield, MO | 81.1 | 103.8 | 120.2 | 120.3 | 141.4 |
| St. Joseph, MO | 36.9 | 39.2 | 49.6 | 94.4 | 116.4 |
| St. Louis, MO - IL | 3 400.0 | 3 673.3 | 3 997.7 | 4 497.4 | 4 711.5 |
| Stamford - Norwalk, CT | 3 366.6 | 3 452.7 | 4 937.6 | 4 424.3 | 3 387.6 |
| Stockton - Lodi, CA | 287.5 | 320.3 | 355.7 | 357.8 | 341.6 |
| Syracuse, NY | 1 374.1 | 1 600.9 | 1 894.3 | 1 665.5 | 1 846.7 |
| Tacoma, WA | 1 115.3 | 774.9 | 1 098.9 | 1 179.7 | 1 403.8 |
| Tallahassee, FL | 16.1 | 18.7 | 24.2 | 27.2 | 32.7 |
| Tampa - St. Petersburg - Clearwater, FL | 1 295.7 | 1 835.8 | 2 116.1 | 1 921.8 | 2 273.8 |
| Terre Haute, IN | 67.3 | 88.8 | 163.6 | 253.7 | 264.7 |
| Texarkana, TX - Texarkana, AR | 26.7 | 24.6 | 52.2 | 64.1 | 31.4 |
| Toledo, OH | 836.1 | 986.9 | 1 177.7 | 1 207.5 | 1 261.1 |
| Topeka, KS | 121.1 | 125.2 | 133.0 | 130.2 | 140.7 |
| Trenton, NJ | 223.8 | 237.5 | 392.5 | 267.8 | 343.4 |
| Tucson, AZ | 487.1 | 638.1 | 671.7 | 800.1 | 1 060.5 |
| Tulsa, OK | 1 273.0 | 1 241.0 | 1 485.1 | 1 549.6 | 1 626.4 |
| Utica - Rome, NY | 188.3 | 269.3 | 238.0 | 278.0 | 238.8 |
| Vallejo - Fairfield - Napa, CA | 171.7 | 264.0 | 238.1 | 278.0 | 384.9 |
| Ventura, CA | 640.3 | 698.7 | 953.4 | 967.3 | 1 128.9 |
| Visalia - Tulare - Porterville, CA | 119.6 | 107.7 | 120.6 | 143.7 | 160.5 |
| Washington, DC - MD - VA - WV | 7 250.6 | 7 969.3 | 8 350.4 | 8 083.5 | 7 980.7 |
| Waterbury, CT | 187.5 | 179.6 | 207.6 | 221.6 | 252.0 |
| Waterloo - Cedar Falls, IA | 102.7 | 149.7 | 194.6 | 200.9 | 282.8 |
| Wausau, WI | 122.5 | 113.6 | 117.3 | 148.9 | 184.8 |
| West Palm Beach - Boca Raton, FL | 764.8 | 834.3 | 898.0 | 955.8 | 1 156.0 |
| Wheeling, WV - OH | 7.4 | 10.8 | 9.0 | 15.1 | 77.1 |
| Wichita Falls, TX | 49.6 | 65.1 | 80.7 | 77.0 | 91.2 |
| Wichita, KS | 1 444.0 | 1 540.6 | 1 727.7 | 1 916.8 | 2 273.4 |
| Williamsport, PA | 105.2 | 123.3 | 150.4 | 151.0 | 182.5 |
| Wilmington - Newark, DE - MD | 3 423.8 | 3 720.4 | 4 361.1 | 4 551.1 | 5 140.6 |
| Wilmington, NC | 147.1 | 180.7 | 211.7 | 301.7 | 422.9 |
| Worcester, MA - CT | 1 017.9 | 603.8 | 757.6 | 685.7 | 772.1 |
| Yakima, WA | 135.8 | 147.6 | 168.9 | 176.0 | 213.1 |
| York, PA | 751.8 | 952.0 | 973.9 | 945.1 | 1 015.4 |
| Youngstown - Warren, OH | 189.3 | 185.3 | 225.9 | 223.1 | 323.0 |
| Yuba City, CA | 62.8 | 61.5 | 70.5 | 74.0 | 78.5 |
| Other Metropolitan Areas | 17 525.3 | 21 238.2 | 30 744.9 | 30 793.3 | 33 363.5 |
| Non-Metropolitan Areas | 25 932.9 | 29 367.1 | 34 188.8 | 36 892.0 | 41 567.4 |
| Crossovers | 10 146.1 | 11 085.6 | 13 376.1 | 16 339.3 | 19 942.0 |
| Unknown | 38 889.6 | 35 565.6 | 37 062.3 | 44 315.9 | 51 718.5 |

## Table E-2.  Metropolitan Area Exports of Goods by Industry, 1993–1997

(Millions of dollars.)

| Industry | Atlanta, GA | | | | | |
| --- | --- | --- | --- | --- | --- | --- |
| | 1993 | 1994 | 1995 | 1996 | 1997 | |
| **ALL GOODS** | 3 870.6 | 4 739.1 | 5 811.4 | 5 891.5 | 6 604.6 | |
| **Manufactured products** | 3 605.4 | 4 406.7 | 5 475.2 | 5 561.0 | 6 239.0 | |
| Food products | 236.7 | 418.0 | 616.4 | 767.3 | 556.8 | |
| Tobacco products | 2.5 | 2.7 | 3.9 | 3.5 | 5.4 | |
| Textile mill products | 164.0 | 144.4 | 106.2 | 134.0 | 111.6 | |
| Apparel | 141.5 | 138.8 | 173.0 | 227.5 | 295.8 | |
| Lumber and wood products | 195.5 | 210.4 | 197.8 | 157.8 | 202.1 | |
| Furniture and fixtures | 25.8 | 28.4 | 26.9 | 33.5 | 46.7 | |
| Paper products | 259.0 | 444.8 | 687.6 | 673.2 | 641.5 | |
| Printing and publishing | 25.1 | 39.8 | 50.0 | 45.5 | 42.2 | |
| Chemical products | 275.6 | 344.8 | 407.4 | 455.8 | 722.6 | |
| Refined petroleum products | 50.5 | 59.0 | 77.1 | 76.9 | 80.9 | |
| Rubber and plastic products | 139.9 | 170.9 | 166.9 | 151.4 | 162.4 | |
| Leather products | 4.4 | 3.4 | 3.9 | 5.0 | 4.9 | |
| Stone, clay, and glass products | 21.6 | 27.1 | 17.4 | 20.8 | 30.5 | |
| Primary metals | 148.3 | 138.6 | 177.7 | 229.3 | 246.8 | |
| Fabricated metal products | 83.8 | 90.4 | 105.6 | 119.1 | 118.6 | |
| Industrial machinery and computers | 610.6 | 707.1 | 851.8 | 867.2 | 1 016.3 | |
| Electric and electronic equipment | 486.6 | 656.7 | 674.7 | 725.7 | 910.1 | |
| Transportation equipment | 366.0 | 378.7 | 651.3 | 387.8 | 457.1 | |
| Scientific and measuring instruments | 314.0 | 345.9 | 420.3 | 417.8 | 511.2 | |
| Miscellaneous manufactures | 37.6 | 39.3 | 40.5 | 44.3 | 54.9 | |
| Unidentified manufactures | 16.4 | 17.6 | 18.9 | 17.9 | 20.6 | |
| **Nonmanufactured commodities** | 265.2 | 332.4 | 336.2 | 330.4 | 365.6 | |

**Exports of Goods, 1997**
*(Billions of dollars)*

Totals     Manufactures: Top 5 Groups

| Industry | Austin - San Marcos, TX | | | | | |
| --- | --- | --- | --- | --- | --- | --- |
| | 1993 | 1994 | 1995 | 1996 | 1997 | |
| **ALL GOODS** | 1 721.5 | 2 128.8 | 2 929.2 | 2 743.1 | 3 354.8 | |
| **Manufactured products** | 1 710.8 | 2 120.4 | 2 922.0 | 2 735.0 | 3 335.3 | |
| Food products | 1.1 | 2.0 | 2.9 | 10.0 | 4.0 | |
| Tobacco products | 0.0 | 0.0 | 0.0 | 0.0 | 0.0 | |
| Textile mill products | 0.6 | 0.5 | 1.4 | 4.7 | 5.4 | |
| Apparel | 0.8 | 0.7 | 0.6 | 3.5 | 1.1 | |
| Lumber and wood products | 1.3 | 1.1 | 0.8 | 0.6 | 2.4 | |
| Furniture and fixtures | 1.1 | 1.6 | 0.5 | 1.0 | 1.9 | |
| Paper products | 1.1 | 0.6 | 1.7 | 1.2 | 1.1 | |
| Printing and publishing | 2.5 | 4.3 | 9.1 | 12.4 | 16.8 | |
| Chemical and petroleum products | 9.4 | 11.4 | 18.0 | 24.0 | 31.3 | |
| Refined petroleum products | 3.0 | 3.4 | 3.7 | 3.9 | 5.9 | |
| Leather products | 0.2 | 0.2 | 0.5 | 0.4 | 0.5 | |
| Stone, clay, and glass products | 2.4 | 1.6 | 3.2 | 7.5 | 5.2 | |
| Primary metals | 3.2 | 2.2 | 3.4 | 4.6 | 4.0 | |
| Fabricated metal products | 4.5 | 5.8 | 13.8 | 15.5 | 12.9 | |
| Industrial machinery and computers | 339.6 | 435.6 | 600.4 | 574.8 | 819.8 | |
| Electric and electronic equipment | 1 228.0 | 1 515.0 | 2 079.2 | 1 830.7 | 2 182.3 | |
| Transportation equipment | 18.2 | 23.6 | 33.8 | 36.0 | 39.6 | |
| Scientific and measuring instruments | 87.2 | 102.2 | 138.2 | 172.3 | 188.1 | |
| Miscellaneous manufactures | 3.0 | 4.2 | 5.7 | 26.8 | 6.5 | |
| Unidentified manufactures | 3.7 | 4.2 | 5.1 | 5.1 | 6.4 | |
| **Nonmanufactured commodities** | 10.8 | 8.3 | 7.2 | 8.1 | 19.5 | |

**Exports of Goods, 1997**
*(Billions of dollars)*

Totals     Manufactures: Top 5 Groups

## Table E-2.  Metropolitan Area Exports of Goods by Industry, 1993–1997 —*Continued*

(Millions of dollars.)

| Industry | Bergen - Passaic, NJ | | | | |
|---|---|---|---|---|---|
| | 1993 | 1994 | 1995 | 1996 | 1997 |
| ALL GOODS | 3 924.9 | 4 387.0 | 4 784.0 | 4 499.9 | 4 789.8 |
| Manufactured products | 3 834.0 | 4 286.1 | 4 643.5 | 4 398.7 | 4 673.9 |
| Food products | 271.7 | 293.1 | 339.5 | 297.5 | 306.0 |
| Textile mill products | 80.0 | 57.0 | 65.5 | 70.4 | 79.8 |
| Apparel | 55.5 | 58.8 | 76.6 | 119.8 | 114.6 |
| Lumber and wood products | 8.1 | 8.9 | 7.4 | 15.8 | 13.6 |
| Furniture and fixtures | 11.1 | 10.2 | 9.4 | 12.6 | 10.1 |
| Paper and tobacco products | 277.0 | 322.0 | 548.3 | 370.9 | 276.8 |
| Printing and publishing | 76.0 | 69.9 | 87.8 | 112.1 | 116.2 |
| Chemical products | 798.6 | 939.0 | 1 055.9 | 1 045.4 | 1 015.7 |
| Refined petroleum products | 14.9 | 13.1 | 9.7 | 7.6 | 9.1 |
| Rubber and plastic products | 89.1 | 101.7 | 97.6 | 89.1 | 105.9 |
| Leather products | 26.7 | 26.9 | 31.6 | 17.6 | 21.2 |
| Stone, clay, and glass products | 39.2 | 42.0 | 45.6 | 51.1 | 51.0 |
| Primary metals | 93.1 | 66.6 | 107.4 | 88.6 | 78.1 |
| Fabricated metal products | 119.7 | 93.8 | 99.9 | 104.9 | 112.0 |
| Industrial machinery and computers | 474.4 | 584.8 | 675.4 | 548.7 | 663.6 |
| Electric and electronic equipment | 642.6 | 712.1 | 490.1 | 479.7 | 602.0 |
| Transportation equipment | 287.6 | 344.2 | 395.4 | 396.9 | 487.5 |
| Scientific and measuring instruments | 399.6 | 474.0 | 424.7 | 495.9 | 536.1 |
| Miscellaneous manufactures | 49.5 | 48.4 | 57.1 | 57.6 | 57.3 |
| Unidentified manufactures | 19.6 | 19.7 | 18.5 | 16.5 | 17.4 |
| Nonmanufactured commodities | 90.9 | 100.9 | 140.5 | 101.2 | 115.8 |

**Exports of Goods, 1997**
*(Billions of dollars)*

| Industry | Boston, MA - NH | | | | |
|---|---|---|---|---|---|
| | 1993 | 1994 | 1995 | 1996 | 1997 |
| ALL GOODS | 6 472.5 | 7 095.3 | 7 902.7 | 8 715.8 | 9 570.6 |
| Manufactured products | 6 179.2 | 6 802.5 | 7 606.3 | 8 395.6 | 9 280.8 |
| Food products | 85.7 | 118.6 | 146.8 | 217.5 | 215.2 |
| Tobacco products | 0.0 | 0.1 | 0.0 | 0.0 | 0.0 |
| Textile mill products | 48.7 | 60.1 | 61.1 | 60.9 | 77.0 |
| Apparel | 27.2 | 30.4 | 30.8 | 48.4 | 43.6 |
| Lumber and wood products | 66.8 | 72.7 | 80.5 | 89.1 | 113.4 |
| Furniture and fixtures | 14.1 | 12.3 | 11.1 | 11.5 | 13.6 |
| Paper products | 89.8 | 110.2 | 166.4 | 194.4 | 219.6 |
| Printing and publishing | 103.4 | 90.4 | 92.1 | 111.0 | 111.2 |
| Chemical and petroleum products | 439.3 | 436.2 | 531.1 | 642.1 | 799.8 |
| Rubber and plastic products | 327.5 | 368.0 | 338.6 | 271.1 | 297.9 |
| Leather products | 95.1 | 82.9 | 80.1 | 77.8 | 75.5 |
| Stone, clay, and glass products | 19.8 | 22.6 | 24.0 | 26.0 | 35.1 |
| Primary metals | 57.2 | 62.0 | 78.1 | 80.4 | 110.5 |
| Fabricated metal products | 214.5 | 266.3 | 291.2 | 325.2 | 321.0 |
| Industrial machinery and computers | 1 743.1 | 1 911.5 | 2 037.2 | 2 315.2 | 2 400.4 |
| Electric and electronic equipment | 1 140.9 | 1 495.4 | 1 763.3 | 1 927.9 | 2 225.1 |
| Transportation equipment | 164.4 | 91.5 | 109.0 | 121.8 | 101.9 |
| Scientific and measuring instruments | 1 420.7 | 1 449.1 | 1 632.9 | 1 738.0 | 1 965.8 |
| Miscellaneous manufactures | 80.0 | 81.0 | 93.7 | 104.9 | 122.6 |
| Unidentified manufactures | 40.8 | 41.4 | 38.5 | 32.4 | 31.6 |
| Nonmanufactured commodities | 293.3 | 292.8 | 296.4 | 320.2 | 289.8 |

**Exports of Goods, 1997**
*(Billions of dollars)*

## Table E-2. Metropolitan Area Exports of Goods by Industry, 1993–1997 —*Continued*

(Millions of dollars.)

| Industry | Brownsville - Harlingen - San Benito, TX | | | | |
|---|---|---|---|---|---|
| | 1993 | 1994 | 1995 | 1996 | 1997 |
| ALL GOODS ......................................... | 1 904.4 | 2 113.4 | 2 245.9 | 2 612.6 | 2 697.1 |
| Manufactured products ...................... | 1 669.7 | 1 855.1 | 1 999.8 | 2 358.1 | 2 459.9 |
| Food and tobacco products .................. | 79.0 | 100.1 | 59.2 | 73.7 | 80.1 |
| Textiles and apparel ............................. | 61.1 | 81.1 | 126.7 | 193.8 | 130.4 |
| Lumber and wood products ................. | 10.8 | 9.6 | 10.7 | 4.1 | 3.6 |
| Furniture and fixtures ........................... | 17.2 | 7.8 | 6.1 | 8.6 | 5.0 |
| Paper products .................................... | 45.0 | 63.4 | 59.4 | 52.2 | 41.2 |
| Printing and publishing ........................ | 6.7 | 6.1 | 6.3 | 6.6 | 5.5 |
| Chemical products ............................... | 262.2 | 277.5 | 260.0 | 349.8 | 339.6 |
| Refined petroleum products ................. | 123.6 | 115.5 | 70.2 | 171.0 | 165.0 |
| Rubber and plastic products ................ | 53.1 | 73.3 | 58.6 | 62.3 | 74.9 |
| Leather products ................................. | 11.7 | 2.5 | 0.3 | 3.8 | 8.1 |
| Stone, clay, and glass products ............ | 18.5 | 18.1 | 22.6 | 20.4 | 18.5 |
| Primary metals .................................... | 74.8 | 60.8 | 79.4 | 106.5 | 135.8 |
| Fabricated metal products .................... | 74.5 | 90.7 | 107.4 | 121.1 | 106.2 |
| Industrial machinery and computers ..... | 137.0 | 187.9 | 133.1 | 129.3 | 127.6 |
| Electric and electronic equipment ........ | 304.6 | 443.2 | 716.6 | 762.6 | 825.9 |
| Transportation equipment .................... | 284.5 | 220.1 | 150.9 | 189.5 | 279.3 |
| Scientific and measuring instruments .... | 55.0 | 68.1 | 109.8 | 86.7 | 94.8 |
| Miscellaneous manufactures ................ | 44.1 | 22.4 | 14.6 | 11.5 | 12.8 |
| Unidentified manufactures ................... | 6.3 | 6.9 | 8.0 | 4.5 | 5.6 |
| Nonmanufactured commodities ........ | 234.7 | 258.2 | 246.1 | 254.5 | 237.3 |

Exports of Goods, 1997
*(Billions of dollars)*

| Industry | Chicago, IL | | | | |
|---|---|---|---|---|---|
| | 1993 | 1994 | 1995 | 1996 | 1997 |
| ALL GOODS ......................................... | 14 446.6 | 17 333.6 | 21 083.4 | 22 030.1 | 23 209.9 |
| Manufactured products ...................... | 13 328.1 | 15 897.7 | 18 942.6 | 19 525.6 | 21 374.7 |
| Food products ...................................... | 678.6 | 644.9 | 759.6 | 833.4 | 830.7 |
| Tobacco and textile products ............... | 44.8 | 52.4 | 79.7 | 89.4 | 99.0 |
| Apparel ............................................... | 73.1 | 58.8 | 60.0 | 81.2 | 83.9 |
| Lumber and wood products ................. | 29.6 | 23.5 | 30.6 | 32.5 | 68.4 |
| Furniture and fixtures ........................... | 61.7 | 58.7 | 58.6 | 70.4 | 77.3 |
| Paper products .................................... | 255.7 | 388.7 | 528.0 | 538.3 | 637.0 |
| Printing and publishing ........................ | 196.9 | 190.4 | 203.3 | 216.4 | 206.1 |
| Chemical products ............................... | 2 578.1 | 3 079.2 | 3 482.1 | 3 480.0 | 3 585.9 |
| Refined petroleum products ................. | 55.5 | 67.5 | 73.2 | 167.1 | 160.3 |
| Rubber and plastic products ................ | 310.2 | 415.5 | 481.7 | 553.0 | 650.1 |
| Leather products ................................. | 47.8 | 44.9 | 48.4 | 53.3 | 55.1 |
| Stone, clay, and glass products ........... | 104.6 | 126.4 | 137.4 | 150.8 | 186.5 |
| Primary metals .................................... | 363.8 | 419.5 | 577.8 | 556.8 | 750.4 |
| Fabricated metal products .................... | 403.7 | 463.0 | 539.0 | 657.4 | 632.5 |
| Industrial machinery and computers ..... | 2 495.2 | 2 844.1 | 3 000.7 | 3 125.2 | 3 688.6 |
| Electric and electronic equipment ........ | 3 375.5 | 4 357.8 | 5 977.2 | 5 626.0 | 6 016.3 |
| Transportation equipment .................... | 874.9 | 1 154.5 | 1 282.2 | 1 449.1 | 1 676.9 |
| Scientific and measuring instruments .... | 861.7 | 1 028.5 | 1 172.4 | 1 347.8 | 1 433.9 |
| Miscellaneous manufactures ................ | 403.9 | 395.0 | 379.4 | 405.5 | 437.2 |
| Unidentified manufactures ................... | 113.0 | 84.4 | 71.5 | 92.0 | 98.5 |
| Nonmanufactured commodities ........ | 1 118.5 | 1 435.9 | 2 140.8 | 2 504.5 | 1 835.2 |

Exports of Goods, 1997
*(Billions of dollars)*

## Table E-2.  Metropolitan Area Exports of Goods by Industry, 1993–1997 —*Continued*

(Millions of dollars.)

| Industry | Cincinnati, OH - KY - IN | | | | |
| --- | --- | --- | --- | --- | --- |
| | 1993 | 1994 | 1995 | 1996 | 1997 |
| ALL GOODS ........................................ | 3 898.2 | 4 056.5 | 4 256.7 | 4 784.1 | 5 674.1 |
| Manufactured products ..................... | 3 747.5 | 3 883.9 | 4 000.7 | 4 565.2 | 5 441.4 |
| Food products ................................... | 141.1 | 170.6 | 209.9 | 204.4 | 154.3 |
| Tobacco products ............................. | 0.0 | 0.0 | 0.0 | 0.0 | 0.0 |
| Textile mill products ......................... | 7.5 | 8.9 | 7.6 | 19.8 | 35.7 |
| Apparel ............................................. | 8.4 | 9.5 | 9.7 | 31.7 | 112.1 |
| Lumber and wood products ................. | 13.8 | 15.5 | 15.8 | 15.6 | 23.1 |
| Furniture and fixtures ......................... | 4.2 | 5.0 | 5.7 | 5.0 | 5.2 |
| Paper products ................................. | 90.8 | 88.1 | 194.9 | 239.4 | 120.4 |
| Printing and publishing ..................... | 33.7 | 45.1 | 60.2 | 67.7 | 65.5 |
| Chemical products ............................. | 598.7 | 585.2 | 681.1 | 667.8 | 637.8 |
| Refined petroleum products ............... | 3.6 | 4.4 | 5.4 | 5.1 | 5.1 |
| Rubber and plastic products ............... | 47.8 | 52.6 | 52.8 | 57.8 | 71.3 |
| Leather products ............................... | 21.8 | 21.5 | 21.5 | 42.5 | 38.8 |
| Stone, clay, and glass products ........... | 22.7 | 33.2 | 31.4 | 36.8 | 34.3 |
| Primary metals ................................... | 44.6 | 89.7 | 59.0 | 62.9 | 91.7 |
| Fabricated metal products ................... | 84.0 | 62.0 | 75.9 | 121.3 | 121.4 |
| Industrial machinery, computers, and transportation equipment ................ | 2 393.5 | 2 440.3 | 2 228.7 | 2 580.5 | 3 455.0 |
| Electric and electronic equipment ......... | 123.6 | 140.3 | 180.0 | 197.6 | 245.4 |
| Scientific and measuring instruments .... | 86.8 | 91.6 | 132.3 | 178.1 | 204.0 |
| Miscellaneous manufactures ................ | 16.4 | 14.0 | 22.0 | 26.1 | 14.5 |
| Unidentified manufactures ................... | 4.6 | 6.4 | 6.7 | 5.1 | 5.9 |
| Nonmanufactured commodities ........ | 150.6 | 172.6 | 256.0 | 219.0 | 232.8 |

**Exports of Goods, 1997**
*(Billions of dollars)*

Totals    Manufactures: Top 5 Groups

| Industry | Cleveland - Lorain - Elyria, OH | | | | |
| --- | --- | --- | --- | --- | --- |
| | 1993 | 1994 | 1995 | 1996 | 1997 |
| ALL GOODS ........................................ | 3 582.8 | 4 093.3 | 4 707.0 | 5 075.2 | 5 511.0 |
| Manufactured products ..................... | 3 310.9 | 3 882.1 | 4 512.8 | 4 535.6 | 4 898.7 |
| Food products ................................... | 22.9 | 25.3 | 25.4 | 18.8 | 22.5 |
| Tobacco and textile products ............... | 3.3 | 4.3 | 5.9 | 5.2 | 7.5 |
| Apparel ............................................. | 2.6 | 3.5 | 3.7 | 5.4 | 7.6 |
| Lumber and wood products ................. | 31.3 | 31.1 | 32.0 | 30.3 | 36.2 |
| Furniture and fixtures ......................... | 9.7 | 14.6 | 19.0 | 18.7 | 17.7 |
| Paper products ................................. | 37.0 | 53.0 | 62.3 | 69.7 | 99.2 |
| Printing and publishing ..................... | 13.1 | 14.3 | 24.1 | 17.9 | 22.0 |
| Chemical products ............................. | 929.9 | 1 064.4 | 1 226.0 | 1 157.8 | 1 221.3 |
| Refined petroleum products ............... | 39.0 | 63.3 | 39.5 | 80.7 | 46.6 |
| Rubber and plastic products ............... | 52.4 | 96.3 | 100.5 | 96.5 | 98.4 |
| Leather products ............................... | 0.5 | 0.8 | 1.7 | 1.5 | 1.3 |
| Stone, clay, and glass products ........... | 60.1 | 46.1 | 72.2 | 83.7 | 115.7 |
| Primary metals ................................... | 222.9 | 291.2 | 358.4 | 369.1 | 468.3 |
| Fabricated metal products ................... | 264.3 | 313.6 | 392.3 | 374.1 | 294.5 |
| Industrial machinery and computers ..... | 594.1 | 772.9 | 927.3 | 995.4 | 1 114.8 |
| Electric and electronic equipment ......... | 476.5 | 529.2 | 524.8 | 488.7 | 519.0 |
| Transportation equipment ................... | 232.7 | 207.4 | 318.2 | 343.6 | 364.9 |
| Scientific and measuring instruments .... | 291.7 | 315.3 | 343.4 | 342.2 | 398.2 |
| Miscellaneous manufactures ................ | 16.2 | 22.5 | 23.3 | 25.0 | 31.9 |
| Unidentified manufactures ................... | 10.8 | 13.2 | 12.9 | 11.4 | 10.9 |
| Nonmanufactured commodities ........ | 271.9 | 211.2 | 194.2 | 539.6 | 612.3 |

**Exports of Goods, 1997**
*(Billions of dollars)*

Totals    Manufactures: Top 5 Groups

## Table E-2. Metropolitan Area Exports of Goods by Industry, 1993–1997 —*Continued*

(Millions of dollars.)

| Industry | Dallas, TX | | | | | Exports of Goods, 1997 (Billions of dollars) |
|---|---|---|---|---|---|---|
| | 1993 | 1994 | 1995 | 1996 | 1997 | |
| **ALL GOODS** | 4 817.6 | 5 679.7 | 6 870.4 | 7 096.9 | 8 645.9 | |
| **Manufactured products** | 4 586.8 | 5 308.8 | 6 343.8 | 6 757.2 | 8 285.9 | |
| Food products | 126.4 | 158.1 | 155.0 | 167.1 | 199.1 | |
| Tobacco products | 0.0 | 0.0 | 0.0 | 0.0 | 0.0 | |
| Textile mill products | 11.6 | 11.9 | 20.6 | 24.6 | 20.8 | |
| Apparel | 94.1 | 123.4 | 96.2 | 76.8 | 82.1 | |
| Lumber, wood, furniture and fixtures | 62.6 | 67.6 | 69.4 | 73.0 | 75.9 | |
| Paper products | 20.2 | 33.1 | 34.8 | 40.0 | 53.5 | |
| Printing and publishing | 23.5 | 26.0 | 27.2 | 33.2 | 29.7 | |
| Chemical products | 689.7 | 860.5 | 1 242.5 | 1 096.9 | 1 108.3 | |
| Refined petroleum products | 11.7 | 22.4 | 28.2 | 26.7 | 274.9 | |
| Rubber and plastic products | 41.2 | 38.5 | 45.2 | 57.8 | 56.1 | |
| Leather products | 5.0 | 4.6 | 8.6 | 7.5 | 6.4 | |
| Stone, clay, and glass products | 13.9 | 17.9 | 16.4 | 18.9 | 19.9 | |
| Primary metals | 78.9 | 82.6 | 115.0 | 123.4 | 184.0 | |
| Fabricated metal products | 58.5 | 107.8 | 112.2 | 93.5 | 141.6 | |
| Industrial machinery and computers | 779.9 | 808.0 | 928.7 | 1 069.4 | 1 256.0 | |
| Electric and electronic equipment | 1 617.4 | 1 963.8 | 2 413.3 | 2 716.8 | 3 468.4 | |
| Transportation equipment | 487.3 | 545.0 | 501.0 | 554.7 | 676.2 | |
| Scientific and measuring instruments | 417.3 | 375.7 | 471.9 | 509.4 | 553.3 | |
| Miscellaneous manufactures | 32.3 | 41.8 | 42.7 | 52.6 | 62.1 | |
| Unidentified manufactures | 15.0 | 19.8 | 15.0 | 15.0 | 17.7 | |
| **Nonmanufactured commodities** | 230.9 | 370.9 | 526.6 | 339.6 | 360.0 | |

| Industry | Dayton - Springfield, OH | | | | | Exports of Goods, 1997 (Billions of dollars) |
|---|---|---|---|---|---|---|
| | 1993 | 1994 | 1995 | 1996 | 1997 | |
| **ALL GOODS** | 2 479.9 | 2 671.3 | 2 404.8 | 2 201.5 | 2 271.5 | |
| **Manufactured products** | 2 469.1 | 2 659.5 | 2 390.7 | 2 177.2 | 2 246.3 | |
| Food and paper products | 107.1 | 116.3 | 132.5 | 165.5 | 216.4 | |
| Tobacco products | 0.1 | 0.0 | 0.0 | 0.0 | 0.0 | |
| Textile mill products | 0.9 | 1.0 | 2.3 | 1.9 | 1.6 | |
| Apparel | 1.1 | 1.8 | 1.6 | 2.2 | 3.3 | |
| Lumber and wood products | 4.3 | 4.8 | 3.1 | 2.7 | 3.4 | |
| Furniture and fixtures | 11.1 | 14.3 | 17.9 | 15.3 | 15.9 | |
| Printing and publishing | 6.2 | 6.5 | 10.5 | 11.6 | 9.5 | |
| Chemical products | 23.1 | 30.1 | 31.7 | 55.2 | 31.5 | |
| Refined petroleum products | 0.7 | 0.6 | 1.6 | 1.2 | 1.2 | |
| Rubber and plastic products | 37.9 | 45.1 | 44.4 | 39.7 | 38.4 | |
| Leather products | 0.8 | 0.6 | 0.8 | 1.4 | 2.0 | |
| Stone, clay, and glass products | 9.9 | 6.5 | 5.9 | 7.6 | 10.2 | |
| Primary metals | 12.8 | 24.4 | 20.4 | 21.6 | 24.6 | |
| Fabricated metal products | 97.2 | 70.7 | 52.6 | 41.7 | 46.3 | |
| Industrial machinery and computers | 869.5 | 982.3 | 842.9 | 785.0 | 799.2 | |
| Electric and electronic equipment | 254.7 | 241.0 | 214.6 | 239.1 | 170.0 | |
| Transportation equipment | 924.5 | 989.6 | 916.9 | 713.0 | 720.3 | |
| Scientific and measuring instruments | 99.0 | 112.5 | 81.5 | 59.7 | 133.3 | |
| Miscellaneous manufactures | 5.8 | 6.5 | 6.1 | 9.5 | 15.8 | |
| Unidentified manufactures | 2.5 | 4.9 | 3.5 | 3.1 | 3.4 | |
| **Nonmanufactured commodities** | 10.8 | 11.8 | 14.1 | 24.3 | 25.2 | |

## Table E-2.  Metropolitan Area Exports of Goods by Industry, 1993–1997 —*Continued*

(Millions of dollars.)

| Industry | Detroit, MI | | | | |
|---|---|---|---|---|---|
| | 1993 | 1994 | 1995 | 1996 | 1997 |
| ALL GOODS ........................................ | 16 780.9 | 27 469.7 | 27 314.7 | 27 531.2 | 25 967.4 |
| **Manufactured products** ..................... | 16 490.8 | 27 122.0 | 26 982.6 | 27 219.9 | 25 627.0 |
| Food products ..................................... | 88.4 | 99.0 | 127.2 | 114.0 | 126.4 |
| Tobacco and textile products ............... | 69.0 | 70.7 | 70.8 | 35.1 | 35.8 |
| Apparel ............................................... | 48.0 | 83.1 | 118.6 | 152.0 | 133.7 |
| Lumber and wood products .................. | 20.5 | 19.4 | 24.7 | 14.1 | 11.4 |
| Furniture and fixtures ........................... | 440.2 | 324.2 | 380.4 | 260.7 | 264.2 |
| Paper products .................................... | 59.3 | 58.7 | 66.7 | 67.5 | 68.7 |
| Printing and publishing ........................ | 41.1 | 50.0 | 54.2 | 43.6 | 43.1 |
| Chemical products ............................... | 309.2 | 252.2 | 233.3 | 272.5 | 316.8 |
| Refined petroleum products ................. | 49.3 | 44.5 | 44.5 | 52.2 | 48.2 |
| Rubber, plastic, and leather products .... | 443.0 | 451.4 | 437.8 | 419.3 | 428.6 |
| Stone, clay, and glass products ........... | 194.1 | 246.9 | 250.8 | 293.4 | 284.7 |
| Primary metals .................................... | 496.7 | 601.1 | 621.9 | 494.9 | 518.8 |
| Fabricated metal products ................... | 1 216.6 | 1 031.8 | 764.5 | 835.1 | 783.5 |
| Industrial machinery and computers ..... | 1 580.1 | 2 169.5 | 2 256.1 | 2 387.9 | 3 173.9 |
| Electric and electronic equipment ........ | 1 013.3 | 1 161.2 | 965.8 | 967.2 | 1 223.4 |
| Transportation equipment .................... | 10 068.1 | 19 985.6 | 20 113.9 | 20 387.4 | 17 622.4 |
| Scientific and measuring instruments .... | 288.5 | 393.0 | 374.9 | 368.2 | 465.6 |
| Miscellaneous manufactures ................ | 37.6 | 47.3 | 45.1 | 33.9 | 55.4 |
| Unidentified manufactures ................... | 28.0 | 32.3 | 31.4 | 21.0 | 22.3 |
| **Nonmanufactured commodities** ........ | 290.1 | 347.6 | 332.1 | 311.3 | 340.4 |

**Exports of Goods, 1997**
*(Billions of dollars)*

Totals          Manufactures: Top 5 Groups

| Industry | El Paso, TX | | | | |
|---|---|---|---|---|---|
| | 1993 | 1994 | 1995 | 1996 | 1997 |
| ALL GOODS ........................................ | 2 967.0 | 3 561.3 | 4 120.8 | 5 212.7 | 5 833.9 |
| **Manufactured products** ..................... | 2 883.4 | 3 452.0 | 3 983.7 | 5 032.6 | 5 697.4 |
| Food products ..................................... | 99.3 | 108.4 | 75.3 | 113.5 | 131.0 |
| Tobacco products ................................ | 9.5 | 14.5 | 10.3 | 6.8 | 1.8 |
| Textile mill products ............................ | 137.8 | 173.1 | 207.5 | 232.3 | 259.3 |
| Apparel ............................................... | 346.5 | 372.0 | 347.9 | 432.8 | 410.2 |
| Lumber and wood products .................. | 29.5 | 22.6 | 7.8 | 9.7 | 9.4 |
| Furniture and fixtures ........................... | 82.8 | 130.2 | 114.0 | 222.7 | 298.5 |
| Paper products .................................... | 171.0 | 174.7 | 193.9 | 216.3 | 195.0 |
| Printing and publishing ........................ | 4.2 | 5.7 | 7.4 | 9.3 | 12.0 |
| Chemical products ............................... | 28.0 | 53.3 | 67.0 | 73.2 | 74.4 |
| Refined petroleum products ................. | 1.8 | 1.9 | 2.2 | 3.1 | 2.6 |
| Rubber and plastic products ................ | 99.1 | 155.1 | 166.3 | 379.9 | 509.1 |
| Leather products ................................. | 9.7 | 6.8 | 5.7 | 5.5 | 7.2 |
| Stone, clay, and glass products ........... | 23.1 | 36.1 | 31.3 | 18.8 | 16.5 |
| Primary metals .................................... | 142.9 | 170.6 | 270.5 | 359.0 | 388.1 |
| Fabricated metal products ................... | 73.8 | 115.6 | 115.5 | 191.0 | 234.9 |
| Industrial machinery and computers ..... | 201.6 | 191.3 | 160.9 | 199.6 | 256.2 |
| Electric and electronic equipment ........ | 1 291.8 | 1 518.0 | 1 959.9 | 2 245.4 | 2 505.2 |
| Transportation equipment .................... | 33.7 | 68.4 | 64.3 | 49.5 | 135.4 |
| Scientific and measuring instruments .... | 77.3 | 93.0 | 137.5 | 229.8 | 218.2 |
| Miscellaneous manufactures ................ | 13.5 | 30.8 | 25.5 | 24.2 | 21.4 |
| Unidentified manufactures ................... | 6.5 | 9.6 | 13.0 | 10.0 | 10.8 |
| **Nonmanufactured commodities** ........ | 83.6 | 109.3 | 137.0 | 180.1 | 136.6 |

**Exports of Goods, 1997**
*(Billions of dollars)*

Totals          Manufactures: Top 5 Groups

## Table E-2. Metropolitan Area Exports of Goods by Industry, 1993–1997 —*Continued*

(Millions of dollars.)

| Industry | Fort Worth - Arlington, TX | | | | |
| --- | --- | --- | --- | --- | --- |
| | 1993 | 1994 | 1995 | 1996 | 1997 |
| ALL GOODS ........................................ | 1 600.2 | 2 052.0 | 1 915.0 | 2 372.7 | 3 045.9 |
| Manufactured products ...................... | 1 565.5 | 2 018.3 | 1 881.8 | 2 330.7 | 2 995.0 |
| Food products ............................................. | 50.3 | 47.3 | 53.2 | 45.4 | 37.4 |
| Tobacco products ..................................... | 0.0 | 0.0 | 0.0 | 0.0 | 0.0 |
| Textile mill products ............................. | 4.0 | 3.5 | 4.3 | 9.1 | 16.4 |
| Apparel ....................................................... | 61.5 | 69.3 | 69.0 | 62.8 | 80.3 |
| Lumber and wood products ................. | 1.9 | 1.7 | 4.6 | 3.0 | 1.9 |
| Furniture and fixtures ........................... | 2.0 | 1.9 | 3.3 | 4.2 | 5.8 |
| Paper products ......................................... | 5.6 | 7.0 | 5.8 | 6.7 | 6.2 |
| Printing and publishing ........................ | 2.8 | 5.2 | 4.2 | 6.5 | 8.6 |
| Chemical products .................................. | 54.6 | 52.2 | 67.2 | 73.7 | 98.8 |
| Refined petroleum products ................ | 4.1 | 4.6 | 3.6 | 5.6 | 4.3 |
| Rubber and plastic products ................ | 22.3 | 20.4 | 22.3 | 31.1 | 53.1 |
| Leather products ..................................... | 10.8 | 9.0 | 9.8 | 7.4 | 10.6 |
| Stone, clay, and glass products .......... | 6.2 | 6.7 | 7.0 | 7.3 | 6.8 |
| Primary metals ......................................... | 26.7 | 27.6 | 33.4 | 37.3 | 35.3 |
| Fabricated metal products ................... | 31.4 | 36.9 | 51.7 | 79.5 | 65.8 |
| Industrial machinery and computers ..... | 259.9 | 415.0 | 340.7 | 565.6 | 419.2 |
| Electric and electronic equipment ......... | 365.6 | 394.0 | 547.7 | 718.0 | 1 358.1 |
| Transportation equipment ................... | 485.5 | 695.9 | 495.9 | 516.0 | 611.7 |
| Scientific and measuring instruments .... | 146.6 | 195.1 | 132.3 | 124.0 | 145.6 |
| Miscellaneous manufactures ................ | 18.8 | 18.6 | 18.7 | 20.9 | 19.9 |
| Unidentified manufactures .................... | 5.0 | 6.3 | 6.8 | 6.7 | 9.2 |
| Nonmanufactured commodities ........ | 34.7 | 33.7 | 33.2 | 42.0 | 50.9 |

Exports of Goods, 1997
*(Billions of dollars)*

Totals — All Goods, Manufactures
Manufactures: Top 5 Groups — Electric and Electronic Equipment, Transportation Equipment, Industrial Machinery and Computers, Scientific and Measuring Instruments, Chemical Products

| Industry | Greensboro - Winston-Salem - High Point, NC | | | | |
| --- | --- | --- | --- | --- | --- |
| | 1993 | 1994 | 1995 | 1996 | 1997 |
| ALL GOODS ........................................ | 2 453.1 | 2 773.3 | 3 356.3 | 3 495.6 | 4 050.8 |
| Manufactured products ...................... | 2 384.4 | 2 699.8 | 3 276.2 | 3 439.8 | 3 962.2 |
| Food products ............................................. | 19.6 | 27.3 | 28.8 | 29.9 | 33.4 |
| Tobacco and textile products ............... | 1 085.4 | 1 112.3 | 1 152.6 | 1 029.4 | 869.8 |
| Apparel ....................................................... | 381.1 | 479.9 | 821.2 | 951.7 | 1 159.1 |
| Lumber and wood products ................. | 25.2 | 31.8 | 31.3 | 29.7 | 38.5 |
| Furniture and fixtures ........................... | 58.7 | 66.3 | 84.0 | 97.4 | 101.3 |
| Paper products ......................................... | 9.9 | 14.7 | 26.0 | 32.0 | 51.5 |
| Printing and publishing ........................ | 3.1 | 3.6 | 5.1 | 6.2 | 9.3 |
| Chemical products .................................. | 220.3 | 279.6 | 372.6 | 396.0 | 551.5 |
| Refined petroleum products ................ | 0.2 | 0.4 | 0.2 | 0.5 | 1.7 |
| Rubber and plastic products ................ | 13.2 | 19.4 | 25.5 | 32.9 | 38.5 |
| Leather products ..................................... | 4.4 | 4.7 | 5.4 | 6.5 | 9.1 |
| Stone, clay, and glass products .......... | 6.9 | 8.3 | 11.9 | 10.5 | 33.5 |
| Primary metals ......................................... | 18.7 | 19.0 | 17.8 | 20.5 | 22.9 |
| Fabricated metal products ................... | 73.0 | 70.6 | 57.9 | 47.1 | 64.0 |
| Electric and electronic equipment ......... | 93.9 | 107.5 | 144.1 | 202.7 | 350.2 |
| Transportation equipment ................... | 74.8 | 56.6 | 51.8 | 59.2 | 55.0 |
| Scientific and measuring instruments .... | 108.3 | 127.8 | 160.9 | 177.8 | 215.1 |
| Unidentified manufactures .................... | 2.8 | 3.6 | 3.4 | 3.8 | 5.3 |
| Assorted manufactures ......................... | 185.0 | 266.5 | 275.7 | 305.9 | 352.6 |
| Nonmanufactured commodities ........ | 68.7 | 73.5 | 80.1 | 55.9 | 88.6 |

Exports of Goods, 1997
*(Billions of dollars)*

Totals — All Goods, Manufactures
Manufactures: Top 5 Groups — Apparel, Tobacco Products, Chemical Products, Assorted Manufactures, Electric and Electronic Equipment

## Table E-2. Metropolitan Area Exports of Goods by Industry, 1993–1997 —Continued

(Millions of dollars.)

| Industry | Houston, TX | | | | |
|---|---|---|---|---|---|
| | 1993 | 1994 | 1995 | 1996 | 1997 |
| ALL GOODS | 12 284.6 | 13 388.2 | 16 247.9 | 16 541.5 | 18 595.9 |
| Manufactured products | 11 923.0 | 12 957.7 | 15 666.2 | 15 954.6 | 17 951.4 |
| Food products | 410.6 | 438.7 | 464.2 | 465.4 | 378.5 |
| Textile mill products | 9.8 | 12.0 | 14.8 | 13.1 | 14.8 |
| Apparel | 12.8 | 13.0 | 15.6 | 21.9 | 19.1 |
| Lumber and wood products | 72.1 | 56.9 | 62.6 | 69.3 | 78.8 |
| Furniture and fixtures | 16.3 | 16.8 | 12.3 | 14.8 | 20.6 |
| Paper products | 16.5 | 31.7 | 37.3 | 29.7 | 43.1 |
| Printing and publishing | 12.9 | 13.9 | 15.4 | 15.0 | 14.9 |
| Chemical products | 2 993.9 | 3 626.8 | 4 810.9 | 4 107.8 | 4 436.8 |
| Refined petroleum products | 1 603.2 | 1 460.6 | 1 843.3 | 2 045.6 | 2 103.1 |
| Rubber and plastic products | 112.5 | 143.9 | 155.0 | 161.1 | 167.6 |
| Leather products | 4.9 | 5.0 | 5.3 | 5.2 | 8.1 |
| Stone, clay, and glass products | 60.0 | 64.7 | 79.8 | 104.9 | 125.0 |
| Primary metals | 285.0 | 287.9 | 475.0 | 536.0 | 601.8 |
| Fabricated metal products | 389.6 | 371.7 | 380.4 | 494.3 | 642.4 |
| Industrial machinery and computers | 4 666.8 | 4 973.2 | 5 787.3 | 6 264.4 | 7 224.3 |
| Electric and electronic equipment | 351.7 | 549.1 | 641.7 | 563.7 | 762.1 |
| Transportation equipment | 399.4 | 402.3 | 334.2 | 444.2 | 556.5 |
| Scientific and measuring instruments | 442.6 | 408.3 | 453.0 | 526.8 | 685.3 |
| Miscellaneous manufactures | 42.1 | 58.3 | 48.5 | 49.4 | 45.8 |
| Unidentified manufactures | 20.2 | 22.9 | 29.7 | 22.0 | 22.8 |
| Nonmanufactured commodities | 361.6 | 430.5 | 581.7 | 586.8 | 644.5 |

Exports of Goods, 1997
(Billions of dollars)

| Industry | Indianapolis, IN | | | | |
|---|---|---|---|---|---|
| | 1993 | 1994 | 1995 | 1996 | 1997 |
| ALL GOODS | 2 626.6 | 3 003.8 | 3 555.9 | 4 012.8 | 4 301.8 |
| Manufactured products | 2 597.1 | 2 968.8 | 3 523.9 | 3 970.7 | 4 263.2 |
| Food products | 31.5 | 38.3 | 40.7 | 42.8 | 63.6 |
| Tobacco products | 0.0 | 0.0 | 0.0 | 0.0 | 0.0 |
| Textile mill products | 0.8 | 1.0 | 3.9 | 2.6 | 3.4 |
| Apparel | 4.8 | 7.1 | 7.3 | 6.5 | 7.7 |
| Lumber and wood products | 72.2 | 83.8 | 69.0 | 74.9 | 83.2 |
| Furniture and fixtures | 13.7 | 36.9 | 6.9 | 9.5 | 10.6 |
| Paper products | 9.4 | 22.1 | 60.3 | 56.8 | 53.6 |
| Printing and publishing | 29.9 | 35.5 | 48.7 | 55.6 | 78.1 |
| Chemical products | 717.5 | 733.8 | 873.7 | 1 034.7 | 1 168.3 |
| Refined petroleum products | 3.2 | 4.3 | 3.4 | 5.2 | 2.3 |
| Rubber and plastic products | 57.1 | 82.8 | 94.3 | 129.4 | 130.4 |
| Leather products | 1.3 | 1.7 | 2.3 | 2.2 | 3.3 |
| Stone, clay, and glass products | 11.0 | 24.7 | 54.3 | 35.4 | 46.9 |
| Primary metals | 13.9 | 44.1 | 65.5 | 76.7 | 61.5 |
| Fabricated metal products | 214.1 | 144.3 | 116.3 | 135.4 | 128.9 |
| Industrial machinery and computers | 307.2 | 300.5 | 332.7 | 410.1 | 470.0 |
| Electric and electronic equipment | 685.3 | 911.5 | 1 029.5 | 1 096.3 | 1 043.8 |
| Transportation equipment | 302.8 | 369.4 | 585.9 | 626.3 | 765.7 |
| Scientific and measuring instruments | 106.1 | 110.5 | 112.2 | 151.5 | 118.0 |
| Miscellaneous manufactures | 9.6 | 10.1 | 8.2 | 9.7 | 14.8 |
| Unidentified manufactures | 5.6 | 6.5 | 8.9 | 9.1 | 8.9 |
| Nonmanufactured commodities | 29.6 | 35.0 | 32.0 | 42.0 | 38.6 |

Exports of Goods, 1997
(Billions of dollars)

## Table E-2.  Metropolitan Area Exports of Goods by Industry, 1993–1997 —*Continued*

(Millions of dollars.)

| Industry | Kansas City, MO - KS | | | | |
| --- | --- | --- | --- | --- | --- |
| | 1993 | 1994 | 1995 | 1996 | 1997 |
| ALL GOODS ............................... | 2 225.9 | 2 578.6 | 3 350.2 | 3 985.1 | 3 817.6 |
| | | | | | |
| Manufactured products ..................... | 1 091.7 | 1 347.7 | 1 425.3 | 1 503.5 | 1 910.9 |
| Food products ............................. | 238.2 | 266.0 | 272.6 | 263.0 | 322.2 |
| Tobacco products ........................ | 0.0 | 0.0 | 0.0 | 0.0 | 0.0 |
| Textiles and apparel .................... | 32.3 | 38.5 | 55.4 | 79.7 | 111.8 |
| Lumber and wood products ................ | 13.6 | 14.7 | 14.7 | 13.5 | 14.3 |
| | | | | | |
| Furniture and fixtures .................... | 3.3 | 4.1 | 3.8 | 4.5 | 6.7 |
| Paper products .......................... | 11.2 | 15.0 | 21.9 | 19.2 | 23.4 |
| Printing and publishing .................. | 28.4 | 38.9 | 36.6 | 44.4 | 48.5 |
| Chemical products ....................... | 147.4 | 160.0 | 175.1 | 206.0 | 263.6 |
| Refined petroleum products .............. | 2.9 | 2.6 | 2.8 | 2.7 | 3.2 |
| | | | | | |
| Rubber and plastic products .............. | 20.5 | 26.3 | 30.1 | 25.1 | 31.5 |
| Leather products ........................ | 0.3 | 1.4 | 0.9 | 0.8 | 1.3 |
| Stone, clay, and glass products .......... | 13.4 | 28.5 | 22.9 | 22.0 | 14.7 |
| Primary metals .......................... | 9.1 | 18.2 | 12.4 | 15.7 | 52.6 |
| Fabricated metal products ................ | 67.1 | 102.3 | 129.5 | 129.7 | 175.4 |
| | | | | | |
| Industrial machinery and computers ..... | 191.6 | 216.5 | 243.5 | 288.2 | 361.2 |
| Electric and electronic equipment ........ | 95.4 | 175.0 | 128.5 | 111.5 | 157.6 |
| Transportation equipment ................ | 82.2 | 98.8 | 122.0 | 102.3 | 122.4 |
| Scientific and measuring instruments .... | 122.8 | 116.0 | 129.1 | 146.0 | 168.4 |
| Miscellaneous manufactures .............. | 7.4 | 10.2 | 12.4 | 11.9 | 18.6 |
| | | | | | |
| Unidentified manufactures ................ | 4.6 | 14.7 | 10.8 | 17.3 | 13.6 |
| Nonmanufactured commodities ........ | 1 134.2 | 1 230.8 | 1 924.9 | 2 481.6 | 1 906.8 |

Exports of Goods, 1997

*(Billions of dollars)*

Totals        Manufactures: Top 5 Groups

| Industry | Laredo, TX | | | | |
| --- | --- | --- | --- | --- | --- |
| | 1993 | 1994 | 1995 | 1996 | 1997 |
| ALL GOODS ............................... | 4 061.8 | 4 157.4 | 2 897.8 | 3 440.7 | 3 959.1 |
| | | | | | |
| Manufactured products ..................... | 3 896.1 | 3 969.1 | 2 722.0 | 3 298.4 | 3 816.4 |
| Food products ............................. | 416.3 | 392.7 | 273.8 | 275.6 | 311.6 |
| Tobacco products ........................ | 7.7 | 17.8 | 7.5 | 19.4 | 13.2 |
| Textile mill products ..................... | 47.1 | 54.7 | 36.3 | 46.4 | 43.7 |
| Apparel ................................. | 33.3 | 46.5 | 23.9 | 29.2 | 41.5 |
| | | | | | |
| Lumber and wood products ................ | 52.0 | 24.1 | 9.5 | 7.3 | 8.6 |
| Furniture and fixtures .................... | 30.8 | 45.0 | 21.2 | 5.6 | 11.2 |
| Paper products .......................... | 259.5 | 240.4 | 245.2 | 185.9 | 254.8 |
| Printing and publishing .................. | 23.0 | 27.9 | 12.9 | 12.8 | 15.7 |
| Chemical products ....................... | 254.3 | 269.9 | 244.7 | 226.3 | 282.6 |
| | | | | | |
| Refined petroleum products .............. | 8.4 | 5.9 | 4.8 | 15.6 | 23.7 |
| Rubber and plastic products .............. | 174.2 | 202.9 | 150.3 | 144.2 | 228.8 |
| Leather products ........................ | 25.1 | 31.3 | 29.0 | 30.4 | 48.1 |
| Stone, clay, and glass products .......... | 45.5 | 51.0 | 32.6 | 36.6 | 43.0 |
| Primary metals .......................... | 169.8 | 193.4 | 200.4 | 204.6 | 196.6 |
| | | | | | |
| Fabricated metal products ................ | 174.2 | 244.5 | 186.4 | 359.6 | 89.3 |
| Industrial machinery and computers ..... | 622.1 | 704.2 | 327.6 | 333.1 | 486.6 |
| Electric and electronic equipment ........ | 432.7 | 549.0 | 577.5 | 589.2 | 745.6 |
| Transportation equipment ................ | 912.0 | 702.8 | 254.8 | 671.0 | 805.8 |
| Scientific and measuring instruments .... | 151.2 | 102.6 | 49.6 | 56.5 | 113.7 |
| | | | | | |
| Miscellaneous manufactures .............. | 48.7 | 52.2 | 24.8 | 42.1 | 37.9 |
| Unidentified manufactures ................ | 8.1 | 10.1 | 9.1 | 7.1 | 14.3 |
| Nonmanufactured commodities ........ | 165.7 | 188.2 | 175.8 | 142.3 | 142.8 |

Exports of Goods, 1997

*(Billions of dollars)*

Totals        Manufactures: Top 5 Groups

## Table E-2. Metropolitan Area Exports of Goods by Industry, 1993–1997 —*Continued*

(Millions of dollars.)

| Industry | Los Angeles - Long Beach, CA | | | | |
|---|---|---|---|---|---|
| | 1993 | 1994 | 1995 | 1996 | 1997 |
| ALL GOODS ......................................... | 20 013.6 | 22 224.8 | 24 731.0 | 24 437.9 | 25 816.4 |
| Manufactured products ..................... | 18 389.6 | 20 526.0 | 22 603.3 | 22 602.4 | 23 987.6 |
| Food products ..................................... | 1 134.5 | 1 311.1 | 1 536.1 | 1 526.8 | 1 490.5 |
| Tobacco and textile products ............... | 119.9 | 135.2 | 149.0 | 165.8 | 205.7 |
| Apparel ............................................... | 559.6 | 619.4 | 775.6 | 871.9 | 838.3 |
| Lumber and wood products .................. | 79.7 | 93.5 | 115.7 | 118.4 | 114.9 |
| Furniture and fixtures ........................... | 122.1 | 118.3 | 116.0 | 129.9 | 149.3 |
| Paper products ................................... | 123.7 | 149.3 | 172.2 | 220.7 | 218.2 |
| Printing and publishing ........................ | 143.0 | 167.9 | 143.5 | 149.8 | 176.6 |
| Chemical products .............................. | 895.6 | 930.2 | 1 106.4 | 1 066.6 | 1 277.5 |
| Refined petroleum products ................. | 732.5 | 559.6 | 467.0 | 560.5 | 491.5 |
| Rubber and plastic products ................ | 268.8 | 278.8 | 298.1 | 350.8 | 367.7 |
| Leather products ................................. | 116.4 | 126.7 | 133.0 | 122.6 | 109.2 |
| Stone, clay, and glass products ........... | 89.9 | 94.2 | 126.3 | 118.3 | 136.0 |
| Primary metals ................................... | 288.3 | 302.5 | 442.5 | 485.4 | 448.2 |
| Fabricated metal products ................... | 435.0 | 433.3 | 528.5 | 593.0 | 628.9 |
| Industrial machinery and computers ..... | 2 336.0 | 2 553.8 | 2 836.9 | 3 382.3 | 3 350.2 |
| Electric and electronic equipment ........ | 2 289.4 | 2 467.8 | 2 617.9 | 2 548.7 | 2 836.7 |
| Transportation equipment .................... | 6 966.4 | 8 331.8 | 8 885.9 | 7 732.1 | 8 363.4 |
| Scientific and measuring instruments .... | 989.3 | 1 125.8 | 1 243.5 | 1 526.3 | 1 718.3 |
| Miscellaneous manufactures ................ | 558.9 | 596.8 | 779.6 | 823.4 | 903.7 |
| Unidentified manufactures ................... | 140.5 | 130.2 | 129.6 | 109.1 | 162.8 |
| Nonmanufactured commodities ........ | 1 624.0 | 1 698.8 | 2 127.6 | 1 835.6 | 1 828.8 |

**Exports of Goods, 1997**
*(Billions of dollars)*

| Industry | Memphis, TN - AR - MS | | | | |
|---|---|---|---|---|---|
| | 1993 | 1994 | 1995 | 1996 | 1997 |
| ALL GOODS ......................................... | 2 055.1 | 2 729.5 | 4 163.8 | 3 786.1 | 3 636.9 |
| Manufactured products ..................... | 1 317.7 | 1 525.3 | 1 856.0 | 1 949.9 | 2 335.0 |
| Food and tobacco products .................. | 68.5 | 71.8 | 86.8 | 130.1 | 93.4 |
| Textile mill products ............................. | 2.8 | 2.9 | 3.1 | 7.7 | 6.8 |
| Apparel ............................................... | 3.8 | 10.8 | 4.8 | 4.3 | 5.2 |
| Lumber and wood products .................. | 23.4 | 35.2 | 35.2 | 26.3 | 15.1 |
| Furniture and fixtures ........................... | 6.9 | 7.3 | 5.2 | 4.7 | 7.1 |
| Paper products ................................... | 545.7 | 624.9 | 814.4 | 698.5 | 726.5 |
| Printing and publishing ........................ | 12.0 | 12.9 | 13.7 | 9.8 | 11.1 |
| Chemical products .............................. | 97.6 | 95.9 | 129.6 | 132.2 | 147.8 |
| Refined petroleum products ................. | 0.6 | 1.3 | 2.2 | 1.1 | 2.7 |
| Rubber and plastic products ................ | 25.6 | 29.5 | 39.8 | 41.8 | 59.0 |
| Leather products ................................. | 3.2 | 2.0 | 2.4 | 2.9 | 3.2 |
| Stone, clay, and glass products ........... | 4.3 | 3.6 | 3.2 | 3.1 | 4.6 |
| Primary metals ................................... | 5.2 | 10.6 | 12.7 | 13.0 | 32.6 |
| Fabricated metal products ................... | 16.2 | 13.5 | 19.7 | 41.9 | 46.3 |
| Industrial machinery and computers ..... | 163.7 | 215.0 | 247.3 | 270.4 | 439.1 |
| Electric and electronic equipment ........ | 81.1 | 80.2 | 91.7 | 105.8 | 129.1 |
| Transportation equipment .................... | 131.1 | 178.1 | 184.1 | 262.5 | 311.7 |
| Scientific and measuring instruments .... | 106.5 | 107.0 | 138.9 | 168.4 | 258.6 |
| Miscellaneous manufactures ................ | 15.5 | 18.4 | 16.2 | 20.6 | 28.5 |
| Unidentified manufactures ................... | 4.0 | 4.3 | 4.9 | 4.7 | 6.4 |
| Nonmanufactured commodities ........ | 737.4 | 1 204.2 | 2 307.8 | 1 836.2 | 1 302.0 |

**Exports of Goods, 1997**
*(Billions of dollars)*

## Table E-2.  Metropolitan Area Exports of Goods by Industry, 1993–1997 —*Continued*

(Millions of dollars.)

| Industry | Miami, FL | | | | |
| --- | --- | --- | --- | --- | --- |
| | 1993 | 1994 | 1995 | 1996 | 1997 |
| ALL GOODS ...................................... | 8 264.3 | 9 266.7 | 10 200.8 | 10 681.2 | 12 692.3 |
| **Manufactured products** ...................... | 7 722.2 | 8 572.2 | 9 773.2 | 10 266.6 | 12 250.5 |
| Food products ............................... | 351.6 | 380.1 | 392.9 | 390.9 | 430.8 |
| Tobacco products ............................. | 5.5 | 5.6 | 12.9 | 18.6 | 18.5 |
| Textile mill products ........................ | 121.2 | 123.1 | 146.2 | 203.5 | 315.5 |
| Apparel ....................................... | 363.8 | 387.1 | 377.1 | 408.9 | 524.6 |
| Lumber and wood products ................... | 86.3 | 93.7 | 110.7 | 106.3 | 137.7 |
| Furniture and fixtures ......................... | 66.2 | 76.9 | 80.5 | 92.8 | 115.6 |
| Paper products ................................ | 219.2 | 252.7 | 355.4 | 350.1 | 363.9 |
| Printing and publishing ....................... | 51.8 | 66.7 | 71.5 | 59.3 | 73.3 |
| Chemical products ............................ | 472.7 | 456.1 | 552.3 | 641.2 | 780.2 |
| Refined petroleum products ................. | 143.8 | 69.2 | 61.1 | 36.2 | 53.1 |
| Rubber and plastic products ................. | 202.3 | 221.4 | 294.8 | 275.1 | 322.1 |
| Leather products ............................. | 44.8 | 44.2 | 44.8 | 47.2 | 58.1 |
| Stone, clay, and glass products ............ | 88.2 | 80.3 | 86.5 | 85.3 | 88.6 |
| Primary metals .............................. | 296.3 | 358.6 | 421.2 | 284.7 | 354.6 |
| Fabricated metal products ................... | 201.1 | 203.1 | 245.4 | 234.3 | 312.2 |
| Industrial machinery and computers ..... | 1 784.6 | 2 098.2 | 2 679.8 | 3 167.4 | 3 744.5 |
| Electric and electronic equipment ........ | 1 190.1 | 1 461.5 | 1 690.5 | 1 764.5 | 2 263.4 |
| Transportation equipment .................. | 1 225.3 | 1 271.4 | 1 229.2 | 1 123.6 | 1 204.5 |
| Scientific and measuring instruments .... | 585.9 | 659.3 | 627.8 | 709.5 | 767.9 |
| Miscellaneous manufactures ................ | 156.0 | 192.5 | 228.8 | 208.9 | 245.9 |
| Unidentified manufactures ................... | 65.4 | 70.5 | 63.9 | 58.5 | 75.4 |
| **Nonmanufactured commodities** ........ | 542.1 | 694.5 | 427.7 | 414.6 | 441.7 |

**Exports of Goods, 1997**

*(Billions of dollars)*

| Industry | Middlesex - Somerset - Hunterdon, NJ | | | | |
| --- | --- | --- | --- | --- | --- |
| | 1993 | 1994 | 1995 | 1996 | 1997 |
| ALL GOODS ...................................... | 2 840.6 | 3 035.9 | 3 448.1 | 3 628.1 | 4 385.4 |
| **Manufactured products** ...................... | 2 577.0 | 2 653.8 | 3 099.2 | 3 299.6 | 4 039.7 |
| Food and tobacco products ................. | 67.1 | 77.5 | 105.1 | 110.6 | 130.7 |
| Textile mill products ........................... | 22.2 | 7.7 | 7.4 | 10.9 | 18.4 |
| Apparel ....................................... | 35.9 | 35.4 | 27.4 | 18.1 | 22.0 |
| Lumber and wood products ................. | 3.1 | 4.1 | 2.9 | 11.8 | 6.9 |
| Furniture and fixtures ......................... | 3.2 | 3.8 | 3.9 | 4.1 | 6.3 |
| Paper products ................................ | 58.5 | 44.9 | 44.9 | 38.2 | 54.0 |
| Printing and publishing ....................... | 62.9 | 52.7 | 58.8 | 54.7 | 57.6 |
| Chemical products ............................ | 938.4 | 934.4 | 1 077.9 | 1 254.4 | 1 855.4 |
| Refined petroleum products ................. | 19.1 | 21.5 | 18.8 | 13.1 | 12.2 |
| Rubber and plastic products ................. | 48.8 | 46.8 | 45.7 | 48.7 | 70.6 |
| Leather products ............................. | 7.3 | 8.1 | 7.6 | 8.2 | 12.8 |
| Stone, clay, and glass products ........... | 23.5 | 21.8 | 20.5 | 23.4 | 30.2 |
| Primary metals .............................. | 200.6 | 341.4 | 321.7 | 268.9 | 417.0 |
| Fabricated metal products ................... | 50.7 | 59.6 | 203.0 | 185.0 | 109.3 |
| Industrial machinery and computers ..... | 362.7 | 311.5 | 284.4 | 326.4 | 343.2 |
| Electric and electronic equipment ........ | 182.7 | 216.4 | 281.9 | 260.1 | 246.1 |
| Transportation equipment .................. | 78.4 | 122.5 | 181.2 | 235.2 | 241.0 |
| Scientific and measuring instruments .... | 385.8 | 318.7 | 371.7 | 366.1 | 340.5 |
| Miscellaneous manufactures ................ | 16.3 | 16.8 | 18.9 | 21.8 | 34.3 |
| Unidentified manufactures ................... | 9.9 | 8.0 | 15.3 | 40.0 | 31.0 |
| **Nonmanufactured commodities** ........ | 263.5 | 382.1 | 348.9 | 328.5 | 345.7 |

**Exports of Goods, 1997**

*(Billions of dollars)*

## Table E-2.  Metropolitan Area Exports of Goods by Industry, 1993–1997 —*Continued*

(Millions of dollars.)

| Industry | Milwaukee - Waukesha, WI | | | | |
|---|---|---|---|---|---|
| | 1993 | 1994 | 1995 | 1996 | 1997 |
| **ALL GOODS** | 2 337.3 | 2 913.5 | 3 506.9 | 3 717.2 | 3 837.6 |
| **Manufactured products** | 2 299.9 | 2 857.8 | 3 449.3 | 3 618.1 | 3 769.3 |
| Food and tobacco products | 101.4 | 120.9 | 173.7 | 180.8 | 157.5 |
| Textile mill products | 2.5 | 2.8 | 4.5 | 4.9 | 3.9 |
| Apparel | 10.2 | 8.7 | 13.5 | 12.2 | 7.8 |
| Lumber and wood products | 2.7 | 4.5 | 7.1 | 8.5 | 13.3 |
| Furniture and fixtures | 7.4 | 7.2 | 7.2 | 9.5 | 9.2 |
| Paper products | 14.3 | 17.9 | 24.0 | 29.6 | 31.7 |
| Printing and publishing | 15.4 | 18.0 | 17.6 | 22.2 | 26.9 |
| Chemical products | 115.5 | 147.4 | 164.8 | 184.3 | 206.6 |
| Refined petroleum products | 5.5 | 17.4 | 16.7 | 17.6 | 8.4 |
| Rubber and plastic products | 30.2 | 41.0 | 44.4 | 44.5 | 48.1 |
| Leather products | 71.1 | 76.4 | 59.9 | 61.6 | 58.9 |
| Stone, clay, and glass products | 4.7 | 5.8 | 6.0 | 7.2 | 10.7 |
| Primary metals | 25.0 | 25.2 | 35.0 | 39.9 | 48.3 |
| Fabricated metal products | 125.2 | 147.6 | 154.0 | 146.1 | 141.7 |
| Industrial machinery and computers | 819.7 | 1 025.1 | 1 261.2 | 1 230.0 | 1 360.4 |
| Electric and electronic equipment | 245.5 | 311.9 | 400.5 | 421.9 | 469.9 |
| Transportation equipment | 138.6 | 184.0 | 199.7 | 206.6 | 253.4 |
| Scientific and measuring instruments | 532.1 | 648.1 | 810.5 | 950.1 | 870.1 |
| Miscellaneous manufactures | 24.4 | 38.3 | 38.1 | 31.1 | 33.5 |
| Unidentified manufactures | 8.8 | 9.5 | 10.8 | 9.4 | 9.1 |
| **Nonmanufactured commodities** | 37.4 | 55.7 | 57.6 | 99.1 | 68.3 |

Exports of Goods, 1997 (Billions of dollars) — Milwaukee - Waukesha, WI

| Industry | Minneapolis - St. Paul, MN - WI | | | | |
|---|---|---|---|---|---|
| | 1993 | 1994 | 1995 | 1996 | 1997 |
| **ALL GOODS** | 9 003.8 | 8 863.5 | 11 071.8 | 12 384.0 | 12 006.7 |
| **Manufactured products** | 6 201.0 | 6 150.9 | 6 870.3 | 7 395.5 | 7 999.5 |
| Food products | 1 530.8 | 1 414.8 | 1 615.1 | 1 602.6 | 1 652.3 |
| Tobacco products | 0.0 | 0.0 | 0.0 | 0.1 | 0.0 |
| Textile mill products | 29.2 | 19.2 | 22.5 | 22.3 | 24.9 |
| Apparel | 25.9 | 21.5 | 14.4 | 16.2 | 19.7 |
| Lumber and wood products | 11.5 | 10.9 | 15.6 | 16.5 | 17.3 |
| Furniture and fixtures | 13.6 | 17.3 | 17.2 | 18.3 | 23.8 |
| Paper products | 180.3 | 124.0 | 119.5 | 126.2 | 150.0 |
| Printing and publishing | 41.9 | 41.8 | 51.7 | 53.1 | 56.0 |
| Chemical products | 221.4 | 174.4 | 174.3 | 209.3 | 265.5 |
| Refined petroleum products | 5.6 | 6.0 | 9.8 | 10.6 | 25.7 |
| Rubber and plastic products | 163.0 | 184.3 | 175.9 | 195.3 | 218.5 |
| Leather products | 2.5 | 6.9 | 9.7 | 8.5 | 11.8 |
| Stone, clay, and glass products | 107.0 | 140.0 | 63.6 | 60.1 | 59.0 |
| Primary metals | 42.4 | 47.6 | 72.4 | 48.1 | 54.8 |
| Fabricated metal products | 166.3 | 182.7 | 155.3 | 155.3 | 201.3 |
| Industrial machinery and computers | 1 326.6 | 1 323.6 | 1 483.2 | 1 575.1 | 1 657.4 |
| Electric and electronic equipment | 633.6 | 736.7 | 844.3 | 876.0 | 983.4 |
| Transportation equipment | 188.3 | 169.2 | 166.0 | 186.9 | 237.5 |
| Scientific and measuring instruments | 935.5 | 984.6 | 1 121.9 | 1 298.8 | 1 364.1 |
| Miscellaneous and unidentified manufactures | 575.5 | 545.4 | 738.0 | 916.1 | 976.6 |
| **Nonmanufactured commodities** | 2 802.8 | 2 712.7 | 4 201.5 | 4 988.5 | 4 007.2 |

Exports of Goods, 1997 (Billions of dollars) — Minneapolis - St. Paul, MN - WI

## Table E-2. Metropolitan Area Exports of Goods by Industry, 1993–1997 —*Continued*

(Millions of dollars.)

| Industry | Nassau - Suffolk, NY | | | | |
|---|---|---|---|---|---|
| | 1993 | 1994 | 1995 | 1996 | 1997 |
| ALL GOODS | 2 803.2 | 2 866.3 | 3 558.6 | 3 680.2 | 4 208.5 |
| **Manufactured products** | 2 685.7 | 2 730.4 | 3 407.8 | 3 484.8 | 4 035.6 |
| Food products | 50.7 | 52.6 | 47.5 | 56.0 | 71.5 |
| Tobacco products | 0.4 | 0.2 | 0.3 | 1.3 | 2.3 |
| Textile mill products | 24.8 | 42.6 | 45.8 | 42.6 | 41.4 |
| Apparel | 59.5 | 47.2 | 26.7 | 26.5 | 34.0 |
| Lumber and wood products | 10.5 | 8.2 | 8.2 | 16.7 | 14.9 |
| Furniture and fixtures | 13.9 | 11.6 | 10.5 | 8.4 | 12.8 |
| Paper products | 48.8 | 73.6 | 102.2 | 96.1 | 82.4 |
| Printing and publishing | 137.6 | 57.7 | 54.5 | 53.2 | 64.6 |
| Chemical products | 145.8 | 181.3 | 226.6 | 279.7 | 366.1 |
| Refined petroleum products | 5.3 | 6.3 | 5.4 | 12.9 | 5.8 |
| Rubber and plastic products | 42.4 | 53.2 | 57.8 | 70.2 | 96.6 |
| Leather products | 27.9 | 23.8 | 27.5 | 28.1 | 32.8 |
| Stone, clay, and glass products | 10.7 | 13.5 | 13.7 | 15.8 | 17.7 |
| Primary metals | 44.0 | 66.1 | 164.8 | 79.2 | 104.6 |
| Fabricated metal products | 78.9 | 68.9 | 73.1 | 83.8 | 111.7 |
| Industrial machinery and computers | 469.0 | 521.3 | 629.0 | 696.2 | 822.7 |
| Electric and electronic equipment | 683.7 | 802.6 | 917.4 | 998.8 | 1 149.0 |
| Transportation equipment | 399.8 | 247.5 | 542.6 | 296.5 | 227.0 |
| Scientific and measuring instruments | 279.4 | 265.7 | 305.2 | 487.2 | 656.0 |
| Miscellaneous manufactures | 127.1 | 120.0 | 121.8 | 112.0 | 91.1 |
| Unidentified manufactures | 25.6 | 66.7 | 27.1 | 23.8 | 30.8 |
| **Nonmanufactured commodities** | 117.5 | 135.8 | 150.8 | 195.3 | 172.9 |

**Exports of Goods, 1997**
*(Billions of dollars)*

Totals — All Goods, Manufactures

Manufactures: Top 5 Groups — Electric and Electronic Equipment, Industrial Machinery and Computers, Scientific and Measuring Instruments, Chemical Products, Transportation Equipment

| Industry | New Orleans, LA | | | | |
|---|---|---|---|---|---|
| | 1993 | 1994 | 1995 | 1996 | 1997 |
| ALL GOODS | 2 034.2 | 2 326.2 | 3 037.8 | 3 316.8 | 2 770.8 |
| **Manufactured products** | 1 011.4 | 1 255.5 | 1 476.1 | 1 250.3 | 1 201.1 |
| Food and tobacco products | 252.7 | 377.6 | 464.3 | 226.4 | 237.5 |
| Textile mill products | 14.2 | 14.6 | 12.4 | 14.7 | 17.2 |
| Apparel | 2.8 | 3.0 | 3.7 | 6.8 | 4.8 |
| Lumber and wood products | 14.1 | 19.2 | 28.1 | 31.3 | 19.0 |
| Furniture and fixtures | 4.4 | 8.5 | 3.2 | 2.8 | 3.7 |
| Paper products | 28.0 | 27.3 | 34.9 | 13.1 | 11.7 |
| Printing and publishing | 0.9 | 0.8 | 1.8 | 1.0 | 0.9 |
| Chemical products | 165.2 | 191.0 | 272.1 | 278.3 | 276.0 |
| Refined petroleum products | 27.6 | 51.6 | 83.6 | 133.8 | 108.5 |
| Rubber and plastic products | 26.9 | 34.6 | 26.5 | 26.4 | 25.2 |
| Leather products | 2.2 | 3.2 | 1.2 | 0.9 | 4.3 |
| Stone, clay, and glass products | 9.7 | 4.0 | 6.2 | 11.5 | 6.6 |
| Primary metals | 42.7 | 53.6 | 121.1 | 66.9 | 55.1 |
| Fabricated metal products | 30.8 | 37.2 | 28.3 | 39.9 | 36.0 |
| Industrial machinery and computers | 185.4 | 224.3 | 189.2 | 180.5 | 183.1 |
| Electric and electronic equipment | 66.7 | 79.6 | 65.3 | 72.7 | 87.7 |
| Transportation equipment | 60.2 | 46.4 | 46.3 | 58.1 | 34.5 |
| Scientific and measuring instruments | 71.1 | 73.6 | 80.9 | 80.3 | 84.5 |
| Miscellaneous manufactures | 3.3 | 2.0 | 2.6 | 2.4 | 1.9 |
| Unidentified manufactures | 2.5 | 3.5 | 4.5 | 2.6 | 3.0 |
| **Nonmanufactured commodities** | 1 022.8 | 1 070.7 | 1 561.7 | 2 066.4 | 1 569.7 |

**Exports of Goods, 1997**
*(Billions of dollars)*

Totals — All Goods, Manufactures

Manufactures: Top 5 Groups — Chemical Products, Food and Tobacco Products, Industrial Machinery and Computers, Refined Petroleum Products, Electric and Electronic Equipment

## Table E-2.  Metropolitan Area Exports of Goods by Industry, 1993–1997 —*Continued*

(Millions of dollars.)

| Industry | New York, NY | | | | | |
|---|---|---|---|---|---|---|
| | 1993 | 1994 | 1995 | 1996 | 1997 | |
| ALL GOODS ...................................... | 28 192.8 | 23 543.7 | 27 131.1 | 27 970.5 | 29 082.6 | |
| **Manufactured products** ..................... | 23 041.0 | 19 038.3 | 21 769.5 | 22 508.1 | 23 831.0 | |
| Food and tobacco products .................. | 1 748.6 | 1 947.4 | 2 123.9 | 2 025.4 | 2 384.3 | |
| Textile mill products ............................. | 623.2 | 605.7 | 631.7 | 625.3 | 651.7 | |
| Apparel ................................................. | 528.4 | 523.5 | 529.8 | 493.6 | 543.3 | |
| Lumber and wood products .................. | 104.7 | 102.1 | 76.7 | 62.3 | 67.9 | |
| Furniture and fixtures ........................... | 54.1 | 57.0 | 52.9 | 51.1 | 60.7 | |
| Paper products ..................................... | 882.4 | 935.1 | 1 368.7 | 1 107.5 | 1 125.5 | |
| Printing and publishing ........................ | 588.6 | 579.5 | 552.8 | 506.0 | 534.5 | |
| Chemical products ................................ | 2 074.4 | 2 324.3 | 2 396.1 | 2 241.2 | 2 086.9 | |
| Refined petroleum products ................. | 408.2 | 266.2 | 294.8 | 320.8 | 357.8 | |
| Rubber and plastic products ................ | 161.0 | 157.0 | 186.7 | 190.4 | 306.2 | |
| Leather products .................................. | 82.1 | 94.1 | 87.3 | 94.0 | 80.0 | |
| Stone, clay, and glass products ........... | 95.6 | 105.8 | 116.9 | 125.2 | 142.1 | |
| Primary metals ..................................... | 6 602.9 | 2 314.0 | 3 563.0 | 5 081.2 | 4 368.8 | |
| Fabricated metal products .................... | 299.8 | 239.3 | 311.8 | 309.6 | 321.2 | |
| Industrial machinery and computers ..... | 2 391.6 | 2 647.1 | 3 041.9 | 2 619.3 | 3 377.2 | |
| Electric and electronic equipment ......... | 1 119.3 | 1 026.3 | 1 059.3 | 974.3 | 1 189.4 | |
| Transportation equipment .................... | 2 412.6 | 2 017.2 | 2 032.4 | 2 180.5 | 2 559.5 | |
| Scientific and measuring instruments .... | 628.8 | 635.3 | 673.6 | 596.3 | 542.8 | |
| Miscellaneous manufactures ................ | 2 104.8 | 2 306.8 | 2 584.6 | 2 821.0 | 3 018.3 | |
| Unidentified manufactures ................... | 130.1 | 154.3 | 84.6 | 83.0 | 113.1 | |
| **Nonmanufactured commodities** ........ | 5 151.8 | 4 505.5 | 5 361.6 | 5 462.4 | 5 251.6 | |

**Exports of Goods, 1997**
*(Billions of dollars)*

Totals — All Goods, Manufactures

Manufactures: Top 5 Groups — Primary Metals, Industrial Machinery and Computers, Miscellaneous Manufactures, Transportation Equipment, Food and Tobacco Products

| Industry | Newark, NJ | | | | | |
|---|---|---|---|---|---|---|
| | 1993 | 1994 | 1995 | 1996 | 1997 | |
| ALL GOODS ...................................... | 4 287.4 | 5 205.5 | 5 640.0 | 5 044.2 | 5 201.8 | |
| **Manufactured products** ..................... | 4 066.6 | 4 959.0 | 5 320.1 | 4 778.3 | 4 965.7 | |
| Food and tobacco products .................. | 387.3 | 565.9 | 422.0 | 462.8 | 433.0 | |
| Textile mill products ............................. | 30.6 | 31.4 | 26.4 | 24.6 | 34.6 | |
| Apparel ................................................. | 22.9 | 36.1 | 27.6 | 25.8 | 35.1 | |
| Lumber and wood products .................. | 2.7 | 5.3 | 9.1 | 15.1 | 19.0 | |
| Furniture and fixtures ........................... | 31.9 | 36.6 | 30.3 | 24.5 | 26.3 | |
| Paper products ..................................... | 59.5 | 85.7 | 155.8 | 154.5 | 132.1 | |
| Printing and publishing ........................ | 26.8 | 31.6 | 45.2 | 46.2 | 83.1 | |
| Chemical products ................................ | 1 298.1 | 1 493.5 | 1 708.6 | 1 678.7 | 2 169.5 | |
| Refined petroleum products ................. | 17.6 | 44.0 | 66.6 | 23.0 | 21.2 | |
| Rubber and plastic products ................ | 67.7 | 77.9 | 92.6 | 101.7 | 115.1 | |
| Leather products .................................. | 6.0 | 6.2 | 7.5 | 8.3 | 7.4 | |
| Stone, clay, and glass products ........... | 26.6 | 22.7 | 20.4 | 27.3 | 29.3 | |
| Primary metals ..................................... | 154.4 | 173.1 | 183.1 | 153.4 | 127.1 | |
| Fabricated metal products .................... | 107.5 | 115.5 | 126.2 | 145.1 | 167.7 | |
| Industrial machinery and computers ..... | 342.0 | 412.8 | 440.2 | 398.6 | 489.2 | |
| Electric and electronic equipment ......... | 1 018.8 | 1 354.1 | 1 356.8 | 728.9 | 416.9 | |
| Transportation equipment .................... | 207.3 | 188.3 | 307.8 | 421.0 | 264.4 | |
| Scientific and measuring instruments .... | 196.0 | 205.8 | 216.7 | 263.5 | 312.5 | |
| Miscellaneous manufactures ................ | 32.9 | 41.2 | 50.4 | 46.4 | 53.4 | |
| Unidentified manufactures ................... | 30.0 | 31.2 | 26.8 | 28.7 | 29.0 | |
| **Nonmanufactured commodities** ........ | 220.9 | 246.5 | 319.9 | 265.9 | 236.2 | |

**Exports of Goods, 1997**
*(Billions of dollars)*

Totals — All Goods, Manufactures

Manufactures: Top 5 Groups — Chemical Products, Industrial Machinery and Computers, Food and Tobacco Products, Electric and Electronic Equipment, Scientific and Measuring Instruments

## Table E-2.  Metropolitan Area Exports of Goods by Industry, 1993–1997 —Continued

(Millions of dollars.)

| Industry | Oakland, CA | | | | |
| --- | --- | --- | --- | --- | --- |
| | 1993 | 1994 | 1995 | 1996 | 1997 |
| **ALL GOODS** .......................................... | 4 181.5 | 5 113.2 | 6 372.5 | 7 309.2 | 6 920.4 |
| **Manufactured products** ...................... | 3 886.2 | 4 802.6 | 5 995.1 | 6 917.8 | 6 532.3 |
| Food and tobacco products ................... | 294.6 | 373.7 | 512.3 | 551.7 | 544.4 |
| Textile mill products ............................. | 8.5 | 6.7 | 9.7 | 9.8 | 8.8 |
| Apparel ................................................. | 8.9 | 6.6 | 8.3 | 12.5 | 16.9 |
| Lumber and wood products ................... | 39.3 | 25.5 | 21.9 | 21.7 | 22.1 |
| Furniture and fixtures ............................ | 4.6 | 6.4 | 11.5 | 8.7 | 12.2 |
| Paper products ..................................... | 94.8 | 114.5 | 162.1 | 167.6 | 154.2 |
| Printing and publishing ......................... | 19.2 | 17.9 | 23.4 | 29.0 | 31.8 |
| Chemical and petroleum products ........ | 365.6 | 429.9 | 455.2 | 531.4 | 534.1 |
| Rubber and plastic products ................. | 45.8 | 50.3 | 52.8 | 49.1 | 51.0 |
| Leather products .................................. | 3.6 | 2.4 | 2.3 | 3.1 | 4.4 |
| Stone, clay, and glass products ............ | 11.6 | 15.5 | 17.1 | 23.4 | 22.4 |
| Primary metals ...................................... | 84.5 | 73.5 | 152.6 | 246.4 | 266.0 |
| Fabricated metal products .................... | 222.9 | 245.3 | 253.6 | 254.4 | 121.9 |
| Industrial machinery and computers ..... | 968.9 | 1 021.5 | 1 326.4 | 1 758.8 | 1 804.5 |
| Electric and electronic equipment ........ | 1 052.7 | 1 764.7 | 2 306.6 | 2 419.1 | 2 114.5 |
| Transportation equipment ..................... | 259.2 | 169.4 | 168.5 | 162.5 | 215.5 |
| Scientific and measuring instruments .... | 327.3 | 408.2 | 457.1 | 572.6 | 536.4 |
| Miscellaneous manufactures ................. | 38.4 | 52.3 | 36.5 | 36.3 | 36.1 |
| Unidentified manufactures .................... | 35.8 | 18.3 | 17.3 | 59.6 | 35.0 |
| **Nonmanufactured commodities** ........ | 295.3 | 310.6 | 377.3 | 391.4 | 388.1 |

**Exports of Goods, 1997**
*(Billions of dollars)*

Totals    Manufactures: Top 5 Groups

| Industry | Orange County, CA | | | | |
| --- | --- | --- | --- | --- | --- |
| | 1993 | 1994 | 1995 | 1996 | 1997 |
| **ALL GOODS** .......................................... | 5 653.4 | 6 716.0 | 8 041.1 | 8 309.3 | 8 798.3 |
| **Manufactured products** ...................... | 5 434.3 | 6 407.5 | 7 597.6 | 7 852.2 | 8 403.3 |
| Food products ....................................... | 128.2 | 131.8 | 182.1 | 198.4 | 180.1 |
| Tobacco products ................................. | 0.0 | 0.0 | 0.0 | 0.0 | 0.0 |
| Textile mill products ............................. | 17.4 | 17.4 | 34.6 | 39.2 | 37.4 |
| Apparel ................................................. | 90.3 | 98.0 | 91.3 | 105.4 | 139.7 |
| Lumber and wood products ................... | 26.1 | 18.7 | 16.6 | 25.2 | 31.4 |
| Furniture and fixtures ............................ | 15.4 | 21.3 | 20.6 | 20.2 | 32.6 |
| Paper products ..................................... | 32.2 | 44.1 | 56.4 | 66.5 | 67.1 |
| Printing and publishing ......................... | 26.1 | 23.5 | 29.9 | 42.7 | 35.3 |
| Chemical products ................................ | 236.6 | 343.5 | 420.8 | 473.6 | 491.2 |
| Refined petroleum products .................. | 39.5 | 69.0 | 12.8 | 66.1 | 67.0 |
| Rubber and plastic products ................. | 85.0 | 112.7 | 126.9 | 135.8 | 169.0 |
| Leather products .................................. | 16.9 | 14.0 | 17.8 | 29.4 | 35.3 |
| Stone, clay, and glass products ............ | 21.7 | 18.9 | 32.0 | 42.8 | 39.5 |
| Primary metals ...................................... | 340.2 | 450.4 | 346.8 | 73.6 | 83.8 |
| Fabricated metal products .................... | 142.4 | 128.3 | 152.6 | 171.6 | 198.5 |
| Industrial machinery and computers ..... | 1 575.7 | 1 833.7 | 2 325.1 | 2 255.7 | 2 245.0 |
| Electric and electronic equipment ........ | 1 480.0 | 1 728.5 | 2 193.1 | 2 516.1 | 2 888.4 |
| Transportation equipment ..................... | 374.8 | 518.4 | 619.8 | 648.8 | 574.5 |
| Scientific and measuring instruments .... | 564.3 | 589.6 | 676.5 | 720.8 | 861.2 |
| Miscellaneous manufactures ................. | 183.5 | 201.3 | 196.2 | 186.2 | 192.2 |
| Unidentified manufactures .................... | 37.9 | 44.2 | 45.5 | 34.2 | 34.3 |
| **Nonmanufactured commodities** ........ | 219.1 | 308.5 | 443.5 | 457.1 | 395.0 |

**Exports of Goods, 1997**
*(Billions of dollars)*

Totals    Manufactures: Top 5 Groups

## Table E-2.  Metropolitan Area Exports of Goods by Industry, 1993–1997 —*Continued*

(Millions of dollars.)

| Industry | Philadelphia, PA - NJ | | | | |
|---|---|---|---|---|---|
| | 1993 | 1994 | 1995 | 1996 | 1997 |
| **ALL GOODS** ......................................... | 5 869.1 | 6 545.8 | 7 896.9 | 7 727.9 | 8 027.8 |
| **Manufactured products** ...................... | 5 264.6 | 5 843.3 | 7 112.1 | 6 970.6 | 7 286.8 |
| Food and tobacco products ................... | 329.4 | 343.8 | 315.8 | 363.7 | 379.4 |
| Textile mill products ............................. | 53.6 | 72.9 | 95.6 | 113.2 | 84.7 |
| Apparel ................................................. | 38.0 | 57.1 | 89.4 | 112.3 | 87.9 |
| Lumber and wood products ................... | 16.9 | 16.9 | 13.8 | 17.1 | 14.1 |
| Furniture and fixtures ........................... | 15.1 | 18.4 | 20.7 | 26.7 | 23.9 |
| Paper products ..................................... | 98.6 | 107.6 | 166.1 | 153.9 | 166.8 |
| Printing and publishing ......................... | 299.0 | 254.0 | 264.7 | 292.3 | 290.1 |
| Chemical products ................................ | 1 565.2 | 1 815.0 | 2 467.7 | 2 172.3 | 2 224.3 |
| Refined petroleum products ................. | 78.5 | 71.1 | 69.4 | 95.5 | 108.0 |
| Rubber and plastic products ................. | 226.2 | 263.0 | 306.2 | 337.4 | 358.0 |
| Leather products .................................. | 8.0 | 11.0 | 8.1 | 11.7 | 13.6 |
| Stone, clay, and glass products ........... | 57.4 | 50.5 | 52.9 | 62.2 | 76.2 |
| Primary metals ..................................... | 229.9 | 232.1 | 363.1 | 324.2 | 300.4 |
| Fabricated metal products .................... | 160.9 | 180.1 | 191.1 | 181.1 | 212.9 |
| Industrial machinery and computers ..... | 796.3 | 881.4 | 1 216.5 | 1 132.7 | 1 213.6 |
| Electric and electronic equipment ........ | 572.4 | 706.1 | 732.6 | 723.6 | 815.5 |
| Transportation equipment .................... | 195.1 | 196.0 | 219.8 | 293.4 | 298.7 |
| Scientific and measuring instruments .... | 398.4 | 437.3 | 375.7 | 396.8 | 430.3 |
| Miscellaneous manufactures ................ | 99.9 | 105.5 | 122.1 | 141.7 | 162.4 |
| Unidentified manufactures ................... | 25.7 | 23.4 | 20.7 | 18.8 | 25.9 |
| **Nonmanufactured commodities** ........ | 604.6 | 702.5 | 784.8 | 757.4 | 741.0 |

**Exports of Goods, 1997**
*(Billions of dollars)*

Totals — All Goods, Manufactures

Manufactures: Top 5 Groups — Chemical Products, Industrial Machinery and Computers, Electric and Electronic Equipment, Scientific and Measuring Instruments, Food and Tobacco Products

| Industry | Phoenix - Mesa, AZ | | | | |
|---|---|---|---|---|---|
| | 1993 | 1994 | 1995 | 1996 | 1997 |
| **ALL GOODS** ......................................... | 4 498.9 | 5 561.1 | 6 780.4 | 7 912.1 | 11 108.4 |
| **Manufactured products** ...................... | 4 300.8 | 5 316.8 | 6 380.7 | 7 649.8 | 10 836.4 |
| Food products ....................................... | 43.1 | 57.6 | 37.5 | 37.5 | 70.4 |
| Tobacco products ................................. | 0.0 | 0.0 | 0.0 | 0.0 | 0.0 |
| Textile mill products ............................. | 1.8 | 2.3 | 2.9 | 2.3 | 4.3 |
| Apparel ................................................. | 7.1 | 7.6 | 9.4 | 9.4 | 11.5 |
| Lumber and wood products ................... | 1.9 | 1.4 | 1.6 | 2.9 | 2.5 |
| Furniture and fixtures ........................... | 3.1 | 6.0 | 5.4 | 8.7 | 11.3 |
| Paper products ..................................... | 6.3 | 11.5 | 11.0 | 12.0 | 12.8 |
| Printing and publishing ......................... | 10.0 | 8.5 | 7.4 | 8.6 | 6.5 |
| Chemical products ................................ | 62.3 | 90.9 | 162.0 | 133.5 | 107.6 |
| Refined petroleum products ................. | 1.2 | 1.0 | 0.9 | 0.7 | 62.7 |
| Rubber and plastic products ................. | 34.6 | 44.3 | 43.1 | 47.2 | 60.7 |
| Leather products .................................. | 3.9 | 4.2 | 4.2 | 3.3 | 4.0 |
| Stone, clay, and glass products ........... | 4.2 | 7.0 | 5.2 | 10.1 | 11.3 |
| Primary metals ..................................... | 218.8 | 213.0 | 324.3 | 313.9 | 134.0 |
| Fabricated metal products .................... | 34.2 | 54.0 | 40.7 | 73.5 | 89.9 |
| Industrial machinery and computers ..... | 525.8 | 550.3 | 608.0 | 719.9 | 2 770.8 |
| Electric and electronic equipment ........ | 2 521.1 | 3 262.8 | 3 963.6 | 4 877.3 | 5 860.3 |
| Transportation equipment .................... | 452.0 | 592.9 | 667.3 | 860.3 | 1 093.2 |
| Scientific and measuring instruments .... | 307.4 | 341.4 | 417.6 | 456.6 | 460.4 |
| Miscellaneous manufactures ................ | 50.0 | 46.4 | 54.7 | 59.4 | 46.7 |
| Unidentified manufactures ................... | 11.9 | 13.6 | 13.9 | 12.5 | 15.5 |
| **Nonmanufactured commodities** ........ | 198.1 | 244.3 | 399.7 | 262.3 | 272.0 |

**Exports of Goods, 1997**
*(Billions of dollars)*

Totals — All Goods, Manufactures

Manufactures: Top 5 Groups — Electric and Electronic Equipment, Industrial Machinery and Computers, Transportation Equipment, Scientific and Measuring Instruments, Primary Metals

## Table E-2.  Metropolitan Area Exports of Goods by Industry, 1993–1997 —*Continued*

(Millions of dollars.)

| Industry | Pittsburgh, PA | | | | |
|---|---|---|---|---|---|
| | 1993 | 1994 | 1995 | 1996 | 1997 |
| ALL GOODS | 2 989.7 | 3 150.6 | 3 982.2 | 3 933.7 | 4 352.2 |
| **Manufactured products** | 2 592.8 | 2 800.1 | 3 529.7 | 3 491.2 | 3 902.9 |
| Food products | 21.9 | 26.5 | 27.5 | 32.5 | 30.9 |
| Tobacco and textile products | 9.9 | 5.9 | 8.9 | 15.6 | 13.7 |
| Apparel | 5.3 | 8.7 | 11.0 | 13.7 | 11.2 |
| Lumber and wood products | 32.2 | 32.4 | 41.0 | 35.4 | 39.1 |
| Furniture and fixtures | 7.0 | 7.9 | 2.8 | 3.4 | 6.2 |
| Paper products | 9.5 | 10.6 | 11.6 | 16.4 | 25.1 |
| Printing and publishing | 4.0 | 4.8 | 5.6 | 6.3 | 6.6 |
| Chemical products | 533.8 | 567.9 | 734.5 | 777.5 | 965.8 |
| Refined petroleum products | 21.7 | 20.3 | 25.1 | 27.5 | 21.3 |
| Rubber and plastic products | 21.2 | 28.8 | 27.2 | 25.7 | 31.7 |
| Leather products | 0.5 | 0.6 | 0.7 | 1.2 | 1.0 |
| Stone, clay, and glass products | 248.4 | 238.8 | 285.8 | 299.2 | 338.0 |
| Primary metals | 463.2 | 456.6 | 1 036.0 | 744.8 | 731.9 |
| Fabricated metal products | 71.8 | 87.5 | 104.2 | 102.6 | 124.6 |
| Industrial machinery and computers | 543.2 | 658.6 | 572.4 | 704.1 | 803.3 |
| Electric and electronic equipment | 361.8 | 361.6 | 321.0 | 298.4 | 334.1 |
| Transportation equipment | 57.4 | 72.6 | 93.0 | 105.1 | 136.5 |
| Scientific and measuring instruments | 144.5 | 164.4 | 174.8 | 221.1 | 234.4 |
| Miscellaneous manufactures | 22.0 | 33.0 | 38.2 | 51.8 | 39.1 |
| Unidentified manufactures | 13.5 | 12.7 | 8.4 | 9.0 | 8.4 |
| **Nonmanufactured commodities** | 397.0 | 350.5 | 452.4 | 442.5 | 449.3 |

**Exports of Goods, 1997**
*(Billions of dollars)*

Totals — Manufactures: Top 5 Groups

| Industry | Portland - Vancouver, OR - WA | | | | |
|---|---|---|---|---|---|
| | 1993 | 1994 | 1995 | 1996 | 1997 |
| ALL GOODS | 5 698.5 | 6 448.8 | 8 931.3 | 9 234.3 | 8 926.5 |
| **Manufactured products** | 3 550.1 | 4 095.2 | 5 540.9 | 5 800.9 | 6 037.4 |
| Food and tobacco products | 122.5 | 151.9 | 160.3 | 182.8 | 198.7 |
| Textile mill products | 13.9 | 17.1 | 20.4 | 20.5 | 17.5 |
| Apparel | 21.4 | 22.1 | 31.5 | 37.5 | 66.8 |
| Lumber and wood products | 706.3 | 632.6 | 580.2 | 573.5 | 526.1 |
| Furniture and fixtures | 9.1 | 6.8 | 6.4 | 7.4 | 9.2 |
| Paper products | 128.8 | 211.4 | 313.2 | 348.8 | 338.8 |
| Printing and publishing | 23.5 | 27.1 | 22.0 | 24.4 | 25.0 |
| Chemical products | 31.1 | 41.6 | 55.4 | 68.8 | 87.1 |
| Refined petroleum products | 16.1 | 21.2 | 22.4 | 22.3 | 18.4 |
| Rubber, plastic, and leather products | 69.9 | 89.7 | 121.2 | 192.8 | 165.4 |
| Stone, clay, and glass products | 20.9 | 20.1 | 21.9 | 32.3 | 41.2 |
| Primary metals | 106.0 | 152.6 | 193.8 | 161.3 | 181.0 |
| Fabricated metal products | 59.3 | 70.4 | 88.8 | 98.1 | 118.1 |
| Industrial machinery and computers | 1 028.8 | 1 100.2 | 1 703.2 | 1 432.6 | 1 694.0 |
| Electric and electronic equipment | 463.7 | 700.3 | 1 270.3 | 1 685.5 | 1 565.2 |
| Transportation equipment | 304.2 | 366.0 | 389.2 | 317.8 | 407.1 |
| Scientific and measuring instruments | 371.6 | 405.8 | 481.6 | 535.3 | 522.4 |
| Miscellaneous manufactures | 42.1 | 45.0 | 47.6 | 39.7 | 33.1 |
| Unidentified manufactures | 10.9 | 13.3 | 11.7 | 19.6 | 22.2 |
| **Nonmanufactured commodities** | 2 148.4 | 2 353.7 | 3 390.4 | 3 433.4 | 2 889.0 |

**Exports of Goods, 1997**
*(Billions of dollars)*

Totals — Manufactures: Top 5 Groups

## Table E-2.  Metropolitan Area Exports of Goods by Industry, 1993–1997 —*Continued*

(Millions of dollars.)

| Industry | Rochester, NY | | | | |
|---|---|---|---|---|---|
| | 1993 | 1994 | 1995 | 1996 | 1997 |
| ALL GOODS ...................................... | 3 091.5 | 3 143.7 | 3 860.5 | 4 307.7 | 4 694.5 |
| **Manufactured products** ..................... | 3 018.7 | 3 078.9 | 3 789.0 | 4 243.0 | 4 635.1 |
| Food products ...................................... | 20.6 | 21.4 | 30.1 | 33.6 | 61.8 |
| Tobacco products ................................. | 0.0 | 0.0 | 0.0 | 0.0 | 0.0 |
| Textile mill products ............................. | 5.7 | 7.3 | 7.1 | 5.0 | 6.0 |
| Apparel ................................................ | 5.4 | 1.9 | 1.2 | 2.7 | 3.8 |
| Furniture and fixtures .......................... | 4.6 | 3.7 | 2.4 | 2.9 | 4.2 |
| Paper and chemical products ............... | 158.7 | 227.2 | 281.0 | 308.3 | 299.8 |
| Printing, publishing, and lumber ........... | 16.9 | 14.2 | 64.9 | 57.8 | 16.1 |
| Refined petroleum products ................. | 0.3 | 0.4 | 1.1 | 0.5 | 0.8 |
| Rubber, plastic, and leather products .... | 176.4 | 215.1 | 278.8 | 243.6 | 229.4 |
| Stone, clay, and glass products ........... | 20.0 | 30.7 | 25.7 | 25.4 | 25.5 |
| Primary metals ..................................... | 18.5 | 28.6 | 25.7 | 37.8 | 38.0 |
| Fabricated metal products .................... | 34.7 | 30.9 | 27.5 | 41.5 | 46.4 |
| Industrial machinery and computers ..... | 282.0 | 361.0 | 496.8 | 487.1 | 636.9 |
| Electric and electronic equipment, and scientific instruments ...................... | 2 224.9 | 2 062.1 | 2 404.9 | 2 869.0 | 3 106.7 |
| Transportation equipment .................... | 36.2 | 57.7 | 118.2 | 100.5 | 126.0 |
| Miscellaneous manufactures ................ | 10.3 | 11.0 | 17.6 | 22.6 | 29.6 |
| Unidentified manufactures ................... | 3.5 | 5.7 | 5.8 | 4.6 | 4.2 |
| **Nonmanufactured commodities** ........ | 72.8 | 64.7 | 71.5 | 64.7 | 59.4 |

**Exports of Goods, 1997**
*(Billions of dollars)*

| Industry | San Diego, CA | | | | |
|---|---|---|---|---|---|
| | 1993 | 1994 | 1995 | 1996 | 1997 |
| ALL GOODS ...................................... | 4 357.7 | 4 867.3 | 5 860.9 | 6 719.4 | 7 810.0 |
| **Manufactured products** ..................... | 4 261.9 | 4 754.0 | 5 752.9 | 6 583.0 | 7 649.4 |
| Food and tobacco products .................. | 193.3 | 209.0 | 185.6 | 137.1 | 172.1 |
| Textile mill products ............................. | 16.0 | 22.4 | 21.0 | 29.8 | 36.3 |
| Apparel ................................................ | 97.7 | 98.6 | 111.2 | 128.4 | 115.7 |
| Lumber and wood products .................. | 169.5 | 134.9 | 64.5 | 76.9 | 83.8 |
| Furniture and fixtures .......................... | 23.2 | 34.0 | 26.5 | 37.3 | 39.8 |
| Paper products .................................... | 85.0 | 117.3 | 149.1 | 170.8 | 204.5 |
| Printing and publishing ........................ | 64.7 | 65.9 | 57.5 | 55.2 | 65.6 |
| Chemical products ............................... | 182.9 | 209.4 | 255.9 | 302.6 | 349.6 |
| Refined petroleum products ................. | 11.1 | 10.5 | 10.2 | 11.1 | 18.3 |
| Rubber and plastic products ................ | 158.3 | 208.5 | 257.6 | 316.4 | 324.6 |
| Leather products .................................. | 12.0 | 18.5 | 23.3 | 29.2 | 22.0 |
| Stone, clay, and glass products ........... | 29.3 | 29.9 | 33.0 | 31.9 | 41.7 |
| Primary metals ..................................... | 129.9 | 134.4 | 170.9 | 188.5 | 216.1 |
| Fabricated metal products .................... | 162.0 | 141.9 | 167.7 | 222.1 | 187.1 |
| Industrial machinery and computers ..... | 873.9 | 989.8 | 1 066.9 | 1 237.6 | 1 295.9 |
| Electric and electronic equipment ........ | 1 129.1 | 1 432.0 | 2 122.6 | 2 489.7 | 3 078.5 |
| Transportation equipment .................... | 238.7 | 182.2 | 236.8 | 211.9 | 299.5 |
| Scientific and measuring instruments .... | 507.8 | 470.1 | 490.8 | 552.9 | 618.0 |
| Miscellaneous manufactures ................ | 146.8 | 211.4 | 270.9 | 323.4 | 441.5 |
| Unidentified manufactures ................... | 30.6 | 33.3 | 30.8 | 30.2 | 38.8 |
| **Nonmanufactured commodities** ........ | 95.8 | 113.3 | 108.0 | 136.4 | 160.6 |

**Exports of Goods, 1997**
*(Billions of dollars)*

## Table E-2.  Metropolitan Area Exports of Goods by Industry, 1993–1997 —*Continued*

(Millions of dollars.)

| Industry | San Francisco, CA | | | | |
|---|---|---|---|---|---|
| | 1993 | 1994 | 1995 | 1996 | 1997 |
| ALL GOODS ........................................ | 9 264.9 | 9 303.8 | 8 133.7 | 8 560.4 | 9 978.5 |
| **Manufactured products** ...................... | 8 717.1 | 8 781.5 | 7 532.3 | 8 066.6 | 9 508.3 |
| Food and tobacco products .................. | 999.7 | 1 032.4 | 957.5 | 896.9 | 836.5 |
| Textiles, tobacco, and furniture ............ | 123.6 | 153.0 | 134.5 | 152.6 | 134.6 |
| Apparel ................................................. | 312.0 | 266.8 | 279.7 | 298.1 | 345.3 |
| Lumber and wood products .................. | 15.3 | 29.0 | 39.9 | 39.8 | 36.5 |
| Paper products ..................................... | 122.5 | 175.5 | 184.8 | 150.8 | 157.9 |
| Printing and publishing ......................... | 29.8 | 34.0 | 31.1 | 33.1 | 35.1 |
| Chemical and petroleum products ........ | 1 110.1 | 859.5 | 654.0 | 704.5 | 789.5 |
| Rubber and plastic products ................. | 106.0 | 95.6 | 49.0 | 63.1 | 79.3 |
| Leather products .................................. | 12.4 | 16.6 | 14.9 | 15.1 | 10.8 |
| Stone, clay, and glass products ........... | 58.7 | 59.0 | 39.7 | 42.0 | 52.6 |
| Primary metals ..................................... | 176.9 | 171.5 | 179.3 | 223.7 | 283.6 |
| Fabricated metal products .................... | 193.8 | 168.3 | 129.9 | 153.5 | 150.3 |
| Industrial machinery and computers ..... | 1 942.7 | 1 652.0 | 882.8 | 1 309.0 | 1 727.0 |
| Electric and electronic equipment ........ | 1 227.1 | 1 393.3 | 1 491.0 | 1 620.5 | 2 170.1 |
| Transportation equipment .................... | 1 751.1 | 2 086.1 | 1 824.9 | 1 555.2 | 1 725.1 |
| Scientific and measuring instruments .... | 389.8 | 384.1 | 420.8 | 609.6 | 787.0 |
| Miscellaneous manufactures ................ | 126.1 | 178.2 | 198.8 | 180.5 | 167.4 |
| Unidentified manufactures .................... | 19.8 | 26.8 | 19.8 | 18.6 | 19.5 |
| **Nonmanufactured commodities** ........ | 547.7 | 522.3 | 601.3 | 493.8 | 470.3 |

Exports of Goods, 1997
*(Billions of dollars)*

Totals          Manufactures: Top 5 Groups

| Industry | San Jose, CA | | | | |
|---|---|---|---|---|---|
| | 1993 | 1994 | 1995 | 1996 | 1997 |
| ALL GOODS ........................................ | 16 171.6 | 19 942.7 | 26 822.8 | 29 331.3 | 29 057.2 |
| **Manufactured products** ...................... | 15 961.0 | 19 709.1 | 26 597.6 | 29 047.9 | 28 791.1 |
| Food products ....................................... | 123.1 | 114.0 | 122.2 | 136.7 | 138.1 |
| Tobacco products ................................. | 0.0 | 0.0 | 0.0 | 0.0 | 0.0 |
| Textile mill products ............................. | 2.1 | 4.4 | 5.7 | 4.8 | 4.1 |
| Apparel ................................................. | 3.8 | 4.8 | 5.5 | 6.3 | 6.6 |
| Lumber and wood products ................... | 5.5 | 3.9 | 6.6 | 6.8 | 7.8 |
| Furniture and fixtures ........................... | 6.4 | 11.6 | 15.5 | 13.5 | 15.6 |
| Paper products ..................................... | 13.3 | 15.2 | 29.6 | 37.4 | 47.2 |
| Printing and publishing ......................... | 87.2 | 86.1 | 90.0 | 87.5 | 105.0 |
| Chemical products ................................ | 209.7 | 206.0 | 209.2 | 231.5 | 252.2 |
| Refined petroleum products ................. | 1.9 | 4.1 | 1.3 | 0.7 | 1.6 |
| Rubber and plastic products ................. | 38.2 | 62.6 | 83.0 | 101.9 | 99.2 |
| Leather products .................................. | 1.3 | 1.5 | 2.1 | 3.6 | 3.3 |
| Stone, clay, and glass products ........... | 17.8 | 16.9 | 20.6 | 28.2 | 35.0 |
| Primary metals ..................................... | 91.1 | 107.8 | 117.9 | 102.8 | 120.6 |
| Fabricated metal products .................... | 64.1 | 57.1 | 80.7 | 93.0 | 68.5 |
| Industrial machinery and computers ..... | 6 507.8 | 7 659.5 | 10 279.7 | 12 395.2 | 13 044.5 |
| Electric and electronic equipment ........ | 7 137.4 | 9 445.3 | 13 254.6 | 13 210.1 | 11 855.1 |
| Transportation equipment .................... | 119.9 | 123.6 | 160.1 | 149.5 | 211.7 |
| Scientific and measuring instruments .... | 1 437.6 | 1 657.7 | 2 001.6 | 2 325.1 | 2 671.7 |
| Miscellaneous manufactures ................ | 55.0 | 71.9 | 62.9 | 65.3 | 51.7 |
| Unidentified manufactures .................... | 37.9 | 55.3 | 48.5 | 48.1 | 51.5 |
| **Nonmanufactured commodities** ........ | 210.6 | 233.6 | 225.3 | 283.4 | 266.1 |

Exports of Goods, 1997
*(Billions of dollars)*

Totals          Manufactures: Top 5 Groups

## Table E-2.  Metropolitan Area Exports of Goods by Industry, 1993–1997 —*Continued*

(Millions of dollars.)

| Industry | \multicolumn{5}{c}{Seattle - Bellevue - Everett, WA} | |
|---|---|---|---|---|---|---|
| | 1993 | 1994 | 1995 | 1996 | 1997 | |
| ALL GOODS ........................................ | 23 815.6 | 21 753.0 | 17 815.4 | 21 391.1 | 27 005.8 | |
| **Manufactured products** ...................... | 21 810.5 | 19 703.6 | 15 661.9 | 19 430.0 | 25 266.1 | |
| Food products ......................................... | 503.1 | 558.3 | 631.4 | 607.6 | 591.9 | |
| Tobacco products .................................. | 0.0 | 0.0 | 0.1 | 0.1 | 0.3 | |
| Textile mill products ............................. | 8.1 | 10.6 | 12.6 | 13.4 | 15.4 | |
| Apparel ................................................... | 33.2 | 33.3 | 38.2 | 44.4 | 51.8 | |
| Lumber and wood products .................. | 2 139.9 | 2 126.8 | 2 306.6 | 2 313.7 | 1 726.0 | |
| Furniture and fixtures ........................... | 10.2 | 14.9 | 18.8 | 18.1 | 22.7 | |
| Paper, printing, and publishing ............. | 366.0 | 667.0 | 958.1 | 714.1 | 405.7 | |
| Chemical products ................................ | 61.9 | 71.0 | 84.2 | 82.7 | 109.4 | |
| Refined petroleum products ................. | 20.4 | 22.9 | 38.5 | 94.5 | 63.4 | |
| Rubber and plastic products ................. | 47.8 | 49.7 | 67.6 | 67.3 | 74.9 | |
| Leather products ................................... | 7.9 | 9.3 | 11.9 | 14.2 | 17.0 | |
| Stone, clay, and glass products ............ | 36.2 | 36.2 | 39.0 | 37.5 | 39.8 | |
| Primary metals ...................................... | 52.4 | 61.8 | 91.0 | 90.8 | 106.8 | |
| Fabricated metal products .................... | 53.8 | 87.0 | 73.9 | 76.0 | 117.0 | |
| Industrial machinery and computers ..... | 374.4 | 385.3 | 474.3 | 548.7 | 775.6 | |
| Electric and electronic equipment ......... | 476.0 | 655.9 | 724.7 | 609.2 | 692.3 | |
| Transportation equipment ..................... | 17 103.5 | 14 352.9 | 9 472.9 | 13 289.2 | 19 574.7 | |
| Scientific and measuring instruments .... | 392.8 | 424.0 | 468.8 | 579.3 | 683.8 | |
| Miscellaneous manufactures ................ | 109.3 | 120.5 | 131.0 | 211.6 | 177.5 | |
| Unidentified manufactures .................... | 13.6 | 16.3 | 18.3 | 17.8 | 20.3 | |
| **Nonmanufactured commodities** ........ | 2 005.1 | 2 049.4 | 2 153.5 | 1 961.1 | 1 739.8 | |

**Exports of Goods, 1997**
*(Billions of dollars)*

| Industry | \multicolumn{5}{c}{St. Louis, MO - IL} | |
|---|---|---|---|---|---|---|
| | 1993 | 1994 | 1995 | 1996 | 1997 | |
| ALL GOODS ........................................ | 3 400.0 | 3 673.3 | 3 997.7 | 4 497.4 | 4 711.5 | |
| **Manufactured products** ...................... | 3 020.2 | 3 251.5 | 3 598.3 | 3 871.3 | 4 109.2 | |
| Food products ......................................... | 259.4 | 147.7 | 207.5 | 239.4 | 342.4 | |
| Tobacco products .................................. | 0.0 | 0.0 | 0.0 | 0.0 | 0.0 | |
| Textile mill products ............................. | 4.8 | 5.6 | 9.6 | 9.6 | 8.1 | |
| Apparel ................................................... | 32.5 | 35.3 | 41.8 | 43.3 | 40.6 | |
| Lumber and wood products .................. | 7.6 | 12.3 | 13.0 | 11.5 | 8.9 | |
| Furniture and fixtures ........................... | 14.8 | 19.7 | 17.6 | 19.6 | 17.2 | |
| Paper products ...................................... | 15.0 | 15.5 | 26.0 | 32.4 | 27.4 | |
| Printing and publishing ......................... | 30.0 | 31.6 | 46.3 | 43.4 | 61.4 | |
| Chemical products ................................ | 1 185.8 | 1 245.9 | 1 368.8 | 1 404.5 | 1 287.8 | |
| Refined petroleum products ................. | 66.1 | 72.1 | 68.5 | 108.2 | 147.1 | |
| Rubber and plastic products ................. | 92.3 | 102.9 | 113.8 | 116.4 | 174.3 | |
| Leather products ................................... | 3.2 | 5.5 | 6.7 | 9.2 | 16.3 | |
| Stone, clay, and glass products ............ | 19.8 | 18.0 | 15.6 | 14.4 | 15.2 | |
| Primary metals ...................................... | 88.4 | 101.6 | 141.0 | 152.1 | 179.5 | |
| Fabricated metal products .................... | 114.9 | 171.9 | 133.9 | 117.1 | 156.3 | |
| Industrial machinery and computers ..... | 328.9 | 377.8 | 445.2 | 497.0 | 573.7 | |
| Electric and electronic equipment ......... | 295.6 | 337.1 | 355.6 | 403.3 | 416.8 | |
| Transportation equipment ..................... | 280.0 | 340.0 | 366.7 | 407.5 | 393.9 | |
| Scientific and measuring instruments .... | 152.9 | 183.9 | 197.3 | 219.5 | 217.7 | |
| Miscellaneous manufactures ................ | 21.0 | 17.9 | 12.5 | 13.4 | 15.5 | |
| Unidentified manufactures .................... | 7.3 | 9.4 | 10.9 | 9.6 | 9.0 | |
| **Nonmanufactured commodities** ........ | 379.8 | 421.8 | 399.4 | 626.2 | 602.3 | |

**Exports of Goods, 1997**
*(Billions of dollars)*

## Table E-2.  Metropolitan Area Exports of Goods by Industry, 1993–1997 —*Continued*

(Millions of dollars.)

| Industry | Stamford - Norwalk, CT | | | | | |
|---|---|---|---|---|---|---|
| | 1993 | 1994 | 1995 | 1996 | 1997 | |
| **ALL GOODS** | 3 366.6 | 3 452.7 | 4 937.6 | 4 424.3 | 3 387.6 | |
| **Manufactured products** | 2 191.1 | 2 403.4 | 3 576.4 | 3 095.1 | 2 727.2 | |
| Food products | 134.9 | 178.6 | 214.9 | 116.2 | 115.7 | |
| Tobacco products | 0.4 | 0.2 | 0.3 | 0.8 | 1.6 | |
| Textile mill products | 4.0 | 1.9 | 2.7 | 2.2 | 2.4 | |
| Apparel | 2.1 | 2.1 | 1.7 | 2.5 | 4.2 | |
| Lumber and wood products | 4.6 | 1.9 | 5.5 | 1.7 | 2.2 | |
| Furniture and fixtures | 2.4 | 2.0 | 2.1 | 2.1 | 4.9 | |
| Paper, printing, and publishing | 412.5 | 457.6 | 634.6 | 619.5 | 568.6 | |
| Chemical products | 737.4 | 826.9 | 1 188.2 | 1 233.9 | 1 121.8 | |
| Refined petroleum products | 342.0 | 435.2 | 551.4 | 490.3 | 435.3 | |
| Rubber and plastic products | 10.8 | 12.5 | 12.6 | 10.9 | 13.3 | |
| Leather products | 3.0 | 4.3 | 3.0 | 1.8 | 3.1 | |
| Stone, clay, and glass products | 2.9 | 3.9 | 4.1 | 5.1 | 2.9 | |
| Primary metals | 150.6 | 172.0 | 297.1 | 168.6 | 65.2 | |
| Fabricated metal products | 15.7 | 13.0 | 11.9 | 13.2 | 19.0 | |
| Industrial machinery and computers | 124.4 | 102.7 | 133.5 | 119.6 | 135.2 | |
| Electric and electronic equipment | 102.4 | 94.9 | 116.7 | 83.9 | 70.0 | |
| Transportation equipment | 70.4 | 35.6 | 262.2 | 152.9 | 70.1 | |
| Scientific and measuring instruments | 59.6 | 43.5 | 118.3 | 55.0 | 75.5 | |
| Miscellaneous manufactures | 7.6 | 8.9 | 6.1 | 6.6 | 7.2 | |
| Unidentified manufactures | 3.3 | 5.7 | 9.3 | 8.4 | 9.0 | |
| **Nonmanufactured commodities** | 1 175.5 | 1 049.3 | 1 361.1 | 1 329.2 | 660.4 | |

**Exports of Goods, 1997**
*(Billions of dollars)*

Totals — Manufactures: Top 5 Groups

| Industry | Washington, DC - MD - VA - WV | | | | | |
|---|---|---|---|---|---|---|
| | 1993 | 1994 | 1995 | 1996 | 1997 | |
| **ALL GOODS** | 7 250.6 | 7 969.3 | 8 350.4 | 8 083.5 | 7 980.7 | |
| **Manufactured products** | 6 612.4 | 7 558.8 | 7 968.9 | 7 784.0 | 7 791.4 | |
| Food products | 252.7 | 186.2 | 119.6 | 154.6 | 143.5 | |
| Tobacco products | 0.0 | 0.0 | 0.7 | 0.5 | 0.1 | |
| Textile mill products | 7.5 | 6.5 | 9.3 | 11.1 | 8.3 | |
| Apparel | 25.0 | 17.1 | 18.9 | 23.6 | 24.6 | |
| Lumber and wood products | 18.4 | 32.7 | 15.8 | 12.8 | 14.9 | |
| Furniture and fixtures | 16.5 | 18.5 | 13.7 | 17.8 | 20.5 | |
| Paper products | 10.1 | 15.1 | 16.0 | 13.2 | 12.5 | |
| Printing and publishing | 27.9 | 30.7 | 35.9 | 35.3 | 38.3 | |
| Chemical and petroleum products | 439.3 | 409.2 | 540.0 | 429.1 | 306.8 | |
| Rubber and plastic products | 53.3 | 44.2 | 57.4 | 100.6 | 105.8 | |
| Leather products | 2.5 | 1.6 | 2.4 | 1.2 | 1.1 | |
| Stone, clay, and glass products | 16.1 | 18.0 | 20.5 | 15.9 | 14.0 | |
| Primary metals | 40.4 | 29.6 | 40.6 | 32.2 | 66.6 | |
| Fabricated metal products | 616.6 | 781.7 | 1 024.5 | 534.0 | 550.6 | |
| Industrial machinery and computers | 643.4 | 633.8 | 675.9 | 637.2 | 781.9 | |
| Electric and electronic equipment | 540.7 | 619.6 | 843.5 | 733.1 | 983.6 | |
| Transportation equipment | 2 987.2 | 3 620.3 | 3 359.6 | 4 010.9 | 3 265.9 | |
| Scientific and measuring instruments | 389.2 | 371.9 | 422.4 | 280.0 | 726.5 | |
| Miscellaneous manufactures | 17.3 | 17.8 | 40.9 | 40.6 | 44.0 | |
| Unidentified manufactures | 508.2 | 704.3 | 711.3 | 700.3 | 681.9 | |
| **Nonmanufactured commodities** | 638.2 | 410.5 | 381.6 | 299.5 | 189.3 | |

**Exports of Goods, 1997**
*(Billions of dollars)*

Totals — Manufactures: Top 5 Groups

## Table E-2.  Metropolitan Area Exports of Goods by Industry, 1993–1997 —*Continued*

(Millions of dollars.)

| Industry | Wilmington - Newark, DE - MD | | | | |
|---|---|---|---|---|---|
| | 1993 | 1994 | 1995 | 1996 | 1997 |
| **ALL GOODS** ...................................... | 3 423.8 | 3 720.4 | 4 361.1 | 4 551.1 | 5 140.6 |
| **Manufactured products** ...................... | 3 333.4 | 3 631.3 | 4 248.6 | 4 442.1 | 5 043.6 |
| Food products .................................... | 11.4 | 11.1 | 11.0 | 8.4 | 19.9 |
| Textile and paper products ................... | 151.4 | 189.5 | 159.0 | 165.1 | 254.1 |
| Apparel ............................................... | 1.6 | 2.5 | 1.8 | 2.8 | 3.6 |
| Lumber and wood products .................. | 7.1 | 7.9 | 10.7 | 8.4 | 4.0 |
| Furniture and fixtures ........................... | 0.7 | 0.5 | 0.5 | 1.2 | 2.0 |
| Paper and chemical products ............... | 2 278.3 | 2 572.1 | 3 120.1 | 3 257.5 | 3 675.3 |
| Printing and publishing ........................ | 4.6 | 2.1 | 1.9 | 2.3 | 2.3 |
| Refined petroleum products ................. | 2.1 | 1.7 | 1.2 | 2.2 | 1.7 |
| Rubber, plastics, stone, clay, and glass ........................................ | 334.4 | 308.2 | 419.6 | 438.4 | 528.7 |
| Leather products ................................. | 1.2 | 0.6 | 0.3 | 0.2 | 0.5 |
| Fabricated metal products .................... | 32.7 | 34.6 | 31.0 | 24.8 | 13.6 |
| Industrial machinery and computers ..... | 122.8 | 69.8 | 77.6 | 82.9 | 113.9 |
| Electric and electronic equipment, and scientific instruments ...................... | 285.5 | 299.9 | 324.5 | 305.7 | 286.7 |
| Transportation equipment ..................... | 49.4 | 56.4 | 42.3 | 80.3 | 87.9 |
| Unidentified manufactures ................... | 2.3 | 2.8 | 1.6 | 2.7 | 1.6 |
| Assorted manufactures ........................ | 47.8 | 71.7 | 45.5 | 59.3 | 47.8 |
| **Nonmanufactured commodities** ........ | 90.4 | 89.1 | 112.5 | 109.0 | 97.0 |

Exports of Goods, 1997
(Billions of dollars)

## Table E-3.  Metropolitan Area Exports of Goods by Destination, 1993–1997

(Millions of dollars.)

| Destination | 1993 | 1994 | 1995 | 1996 | 1997 | 1993 | 1994 | 1995 | 1996 | 1997 |
|---|---|---|---|---|---|---|---|---|---|---|
| | Akron, OH | | | | | Albany - Schenectady - Troy, NY | | | | |
| ALL DESTINATIONS | 1 434.9 | 1 606.3 | 1 931.7 | 2 260.3 | 2 353.3 | 676.2 | 831.4 | 1 061.2 | 1 101.0 | 1 666.2 |
| North America | 750.2 | 885.2 | 1 006.7 | 1 184.8 | 1 270.9 | 355.7 | 489.2 | 704.6 | 715.0 | 1 140.6 |
| Canada | 686.9 | 778.9 | 895.9 | 1 067.6 | 1 134.3 | 353.1 | 483.9 | 696.9 | 704.3 | 1 123.9 |
| Mexico | 63.2 | 106.3 | 110.7 | 117.2 | 136.6 | 2.7 | 5.3 | 7.7 | 10.6 | 16.8 |
| Caribbean and Central America | 22.5 | 16.6 | 22.5 | 23.1 | 22.5 | 3.4 | 7.9 | 6.2 | 3.9 | 3.9 |
| South America | 85.7 | 96.2 | 156.1 | 193.5 | 212.6 | 21.6 | 21.9 | 27.7 | 27.4 | 27.6 |
| Argentina | 11.7 | 14.0 | 13.5 | 15.3 | 22.3 | 1.8 | 3.3 | 4.3 | 3.2 | 4.6 |
| Brazil | 18.6 | 37.1 | 57.0 | 96.9 | 92.0 | 10.9 | 11.6 | 10.5 | 16.0 | 14.4 |
| Other South America | 55.3 | 45.2 | 85.7 | 81.3 | 98.4 | 8.8 | 7.0 | 13.0 | 8.3 | 8.6 |
| Europe | 282.0 | 305.6 | 400.5 | 458.2 | 435.6 | 152.4 | 171.6 | 124.1 | 124.2 | 166.1 |
| Belgium | 45.8 | 41.7 | 65.4 | 116.5 | 107.1 | 2.1 | 2.1 | 2.1 | 2.2 | 2.5 |
| France | 32.2 | 35.2 | 44.6 | 48.1 | 48.9 | 13.8 | 14.3 | 20.9 | 11.9 | 10.5 |
| Germany | 57.6 | 63.8 | 79.8 | 74.5 | 63.7 | 8.1 | 9.5 | 8.5 | 11.1 | 9.6 |
| Netherlands | 11.6 | 23.2 | 24.4 | 15.4 | 10.1 | 75.1 | 98.6 | 30.8 | 34.5 | 45.1 |
| United Kingdom | 68.7 | 81.1 | 98.6 | 110.8 | 115.9 | 20.0 | 18.7 | 21.0 | 18.2 | 25.5 |
| Turkey | 1.5 | 1.9 | 2.9 | 5.6 | 8.6 | 0.7 | 0.6 | 0.2 | 0.5 | 1.4 |
| Former Soviet Republics | 2.9 | 1.9 | 3.7 | 2.2 | 1.8 | 11.2 | 2.2 | 6.0 | 8.8 | 12.3 |
| Poland | 7.1 | 0.8 | 0.5 | 1.5 | 3.3 | 0.3 | 0.3 | 0.1 | 0.2 | 0.2 |
| Other Eastern Europe | 0.7 | 1.5 | 1.4 | 3.3 | 1.8 | 0.4 | 0.2 | 0.2 | 0.5 | 0.8 |
| Other Europe | 54.0 | 54.5 | 79.3 | 80.2 | 74.4 | 20.8 | 25.1 | 34.3 | 36.1 | 58.3 |
| Asia | 181.1 | 217.0 | 256.7 | 304.3 | 322.0 | 114.8 | 109.4 | 170.2 | 202.0 | 265.1 |
| Japan | 77.9 | 102.2 | 108.3 | 109.4 | 113.5 | 25.4 | 28.5 | 33.1 | 44.2 | 33.0 |
| China | 7.3 | 10.5 | 6.3 | 17.2 | 28.0 | 3.6 | 4.5 | 9.2 | 14.0 | 12.3 |
| Hong Kong | 15.4 | 12.2 | 13.6 | 19.7 | 29.4 | 10.8 | 12.6 | 31.0 | 41.1 | 41.7 |
| Taiwan | 18.3 | 26.6 | 22.0 | 18.9 | 25.6 | 27.1 | 17.1 | 23.2 | 31.8 | 45.5 |
| Singapore | 7.5 | 7.6 | 10.7 | 16.9 | 12.4 | 6.8 | 8.4 | 12.1 | 13.7 | 19.7 |
| South Korea | 22.1 | 22.2 | 41.3 | 44.8 | 35.1 | 16.8 | 19.0 | 36.6 | 29.9 | 30.3 |
| Indonesia | 3.7 | 10.2 | 12.3 | 14.0 | 14.3 | 5.0 | 3.4 | 5.2 | 6.1 | 59.9 |
| India | 3.6 | 3.0 | 9.6 | 13.1 | 10.8 | 1.6 | 3.5 | 1.7 | 3.5 | 3.5 |
| Other Asia | 25.2 | 22.4 | 32.6 | 50.3 | 52.8 | 17.7 | 12.4 | 18.1 | 17.6 | 19.3 |
| Africa | 57.8 | 32.8 | 11.6 | 14.8 | 19.8 | 3.3 | 3.8 | 6.5 | 3.6 | 2.9 |
| North Africa | 46.6 | 21.3 | 3.3 | 3.3 | 4.8 | 0.9 | 0.6 | 3.1 | 0.8 | 1.4 |
| Republic of South Africa | 5.6 | 6.4 | 5.5 | 8.4 | 11.0 | 1.6 | 1.9 | 2.7 | 1.6 | 0.7 |
| Other Subsaharan Africa | 5.5 | 5.0 | 2.8 | 3.1 | 4.0 | 0.8 | 1.3 | 0.7 | 1.1 | 0.7 |
| Middle East | 39.1 | 34.6 | 48.8 | 40.9 | 40.4 | 7.4 | 11.8 | 8.2 | 10.0 | 44.2 |
| Australia | 16.6 | 18.2 | 28.8 | 40.8 | 29.4 | 17.5 | 15.8 | 13.7 | 15.0 | 15.8 |
| Rest of World | ..... | ..... | ..... | ..... | ..... | ..... | ..... | ..... | ..... | ..... |
| | Albuquerque, NM | | | | | Allentown - Bethlehem - Easton, PA | | | | |
| ALL DESTINATIONS | 256.7 | 335.5 | 270.1 | 740.3 | 1 564.6 | 1 273.9 | 1 371.1 | 1 492.8 | 1 477.2 | 1 808.9 |
| North America | 51.7 | 44.9 | 25.5 | 22.0 | 29.6 | 314.7 | 373.8 | 419.5 | 421.4 | 497.0 |
| Canada | 24.3 | 19.7 | 17.2 | 17.8 | 22.5 | 279.4 | 342.4 | 380.4 | 376.2 | 436.6 |
| Mexico | 27.4 | 25.2 | 8.3 | 4.2 | 7.1 | 35.3 | 31.4 | 39.2 | 45.1 | 60.3 |
| Caribbean and Central America | 1.2 | 1.5 | 3.4 | 1.5 | 6.8 | 18.1 | 15.5 | 18.4 | 30.5 | 27.2 |
| South America | 1.5 | 1.3 | 4.4 | 2.1 | 2.7 | 71.1 | 50.1 | 101.9 | 115.1 | 134.7 |
| Argentina | 0.2 | 0.3 | 0.9 | 0.3 | 0.6 | 4.0 | 4.6 | 3.6 | 5.3 | 10.4 |
| Brazil | 1.0 | 0.2 | 0.5 | 0.3 | 0.6 | 12.8 | 16.3 | 21.5 | 33.5 | 24.4 |
| Other South America | 0.2 | 0.8 | 3.0 | 1.4 | 1.5 | 54.2 | 29.3 | 76.8 | 76.3 | 99.9 |
| Europe | 64.3 | 105.8 | 80.2 | 85.4 | 121.3 | 307.2 | 328.7 | 358.6 | 303.8 | 381.1 |
| Belgium | 0.5 | 0.6 | 1.0 | 5.1 | 21.4 | 24.3 | 29.4 | 40.3 | 27.5 | 36.3 |
| France | 2.2 | 6.6 | 14.6 | 26.5 | 31.7 | 27.6 | 16.9 | 25.3 | 46.0 | 61.1 |
| Germany | 14.1 | 28.7 | 13.1 | 13.6 | 12.9 | 87.8 | 76.4 | 77.8 | 27.4 | 48.4 |
| Netherlands | 1.0 | 3.1 | 14.9 | 4.0 | 5.3 | 93.6 | 132.3 | 130.3 | 97.5 | 119.1 |
| United Kingdom | 33.8 | 44.7 | 23.7 | 7.8 | 10.4 | 28.2 | 27.3 | 27.6 | 38.2 | 52.6 |
| Turkey | 0.1 | ..... | ..... | ..... | 0.3 | 2.5 | 0.6 | 1.1 | 2.3 | 1.6 |
| Former Soviet Republics | 3.2 | 14.5 | 0.6 | 0.7 | 1.6 | 2.1 | 2.0 | 1.4 | 9.6 | 4.0 |
| Poland | ..... | ..... | ..... | ..... | 0.1 | 4.2 | 3.6 | 8.8 | 12.1 | 11.3 |
| Other Eastern Europe | 0.2 | 0.2 | 0.1 | 0.4 | ..... | 3.6 | 2.9 | 0.9 | 3.5 | 9.2 |
| Other Europe | 9.1 | 7.4 | 12.1 | 27.3 | 37.7 | 33.4 | 37.1 | 45.0 | 39.7 | 37.4 |
| Asia | 130.6 | 175.1 | 150.6 | 619.5 | 1 390.9 | 458.4 | 542.5 | 496.9 | 528.1 | 678.2 |
| Japan | 30.5 | 36.5 | 14.8 | 40.2 | 52.3 | 64.1 | 58.4 | 74.2 | 55.2 | 83.3 |
| China | 0.2 | 1.6 | 8.0 | 9.7 | 28.3 | 8.7 | 8.9 | 18.4 | 18.9 | 23.6 |
| Hong Kong | 9.0 | 19.1 | 13.3 | 9.7 | 7.7 | 9.0 | 14.8 | 24.9 | 18.0 | 17.2 |
| Taiwan | 7.4 | 6.4 | 13.1 | 53.1 | 103.0 | 15.3 | 16.4 | 24.3 | 28.7 | 38.0 |
| Singapore | 5.0 | 1.9 | 5.4 | 2.7 | 1.6 | 181.3 | 174.4 | 143.3 | 212.9 | 206.0 |
| South Korea | 55.5 | 67.4 | 56.7 | 183.5 | 195.9 | 27.9 | 45.3 | 50.3 | 34.7 | 40.9 |
| Indonesia | ..... | ..... | ..... | ..... | 0.1 | 3.8 | 2.5 | 27.4 | 31.7 | 61.7 |
| India | 0.1 | 0.4 | 0.2 | 0.6 | 1.6 | 13.3 | 7.0 | 3.7 | 6.6 | 5.6 |
| Other Asia | 22.9 | 41.8 | 39.0 | 320.0 | 1 000.5 | 135.1 | 214.9 | 130.4 | 121.2 | 201.9 |
| Africa | 2.8 | 1.5 | 0.3 | 0.7 | 0.9 | 51.4 | 18.0 | 14.2 | 12.4 | 17.2 |
| North Africa | 2.4 | 0.7 | 0.1 | ..... | 0.2 | 36.1 | 3.0 | 3.2 | 3.0 | 6.4 |
| Republic of South Africa | 0.1 | 0.2 | 0.1 | 0.3 | 0.6 | 6.6 | 5.5 | 5.7 | 6.0 | 6.8 |
| Other Subsaharan Africa | 0.2 | 0.6 | 0.1 | 0.4 | 0.1 | 8.7 | 9.5 | 5.3 | 3.5 | 4.0 |
| Middle East | 3.2 | 3.4 | 3.3 | 5.8 | 3.4 | 24.3 | 19.2 | 36.6 | 25.8 | 28.9 |
| Australia | 1.3 | 1.9 | 2.4 | 3.2 | 9.1 | 28.6 | 23.3 | 46.8 | 40.0 | 44.5 |
| Rest of World | 0.1 | ..... | ..... | 0.1 | ..... | ..... | ..... | ..... | 0.2 | ..... |

## Table E-3.  Metropolitan Area Exports of Goods by Destination, 1993–1997—*Continued*

(Millions of dollars.)

| Destination | 1993 | 1994 | 1995 | 1996 | 1997 | 1993 | 1994 | 1995 | 1996 | 1997 |
|---|---|---|---|---|---|---|---|---|---|---|
| | Anchorage, AK | | | | | Appleton - Oshkosh - Neenah, WI | | | | |
| **ALL DESTINATIONS** | 128.8 | 198.2 | 150.4 | 109.0 | 213.1 | 529.5 | 507.7 | 593.7 | 608.5 | 647.9 |
| **North America** | 23.1 | 15.9 | 32.4 | 19.8 | 141.1 | 330.6 | 357.7 | 402.8 | 363.1 | 374.8 |
| Canada | 23.0 | 15.8 | 32.4 | 19.7 | 141.1 | 278.7 | 320.2 | 367.5 | 339.9 | 343.0 |
| Mexico | 0.1 | 0.1 | 0.1 | 0.1 | ..... | 51.9 | 37.5 | 35.3 | 23.2 | 31.8 |
| **Caribbean and Central America** | 0.3 | 0.1 | 0.3 | ..... | 0.1 | 18.6 | 10.9 | 9.2 | 17.0 | 13.4 |
| **South America** | 0.1 | 0.6 | 0.5 | 0.3 | 0.4 | 17.4 | 19.3 | 23.8 | 29.4 | 42.9 |
| Argentina | ..... | ..... | ..... | ..... | ..... | 4.2 | 5.1 | 6.2 | 6.9 | 10.6 |
| Brazil | ..... | ..... | ..... | ..... | 0.1 | 1.5 | 3.9 | 3.2 | 4.8 | 5.1 |
| Other South America | 0.1 | 0.6 | 0.4 | 0.2 | 0.2 | 11.7 | 10.3 | 14.4 | 17.7 | 27.2 |
| **Europe** | 13.6 | 75.6 | 20.9 | 15.1 | 14.7 | 58.4 | 53.5 | 73.5 | 76.8 | 96.2 |
| Belgium | ..... | ..... | ..... | 0.1 | ..... | 1.7 | 1.2 | 2.8 | 1.9 | 4.0 |
| France | 0.2 | 4.1 | ..... | 0.1 | 0.4 | 4.1 | 4.5 | 3.6 | 3.8 | 6.2 |
| Germany | 1.1 | 0.4 | 0.2 | 0.2 | 0.6 | 6.7 | 7.9 | 14.8 | 15.1 | 13.6 |
| Netherlands | 0.2 | 0.1 | 0.2 | 0.2 | 0.2 | 4.5 | 6.9 | 6.6 | 8.4 | 14.8 |
| United Kingdom | 2.4 | 2.4 | 0.6 | 1.3 | 4.0 | 23.4 | 14.2 | 12.2 | 17.5 | 16.9 |
| Turkey | ..... | ..... | ..... | ..... | ..... | 0.3 | ..... | 0.7 | 0.8 | 3.2 |
| Former Soviet Republics | 7.1 | 37.4 | 16.3 | 12.3 | 7.6 | ..... | 0.2 | 0.6 | 0.3 | 0.3 |
| Poland | ..... | ..... | ..... | ..... | ..... | 0.1 | ..... | 0.3 | 0.1 | 0.1 |
| Other Eastern Europe | 2.1 | 0.7 | 0.1 | ..... | ..... | 0.8 | 0.2 | 1.5 | 1.1 | 0.5 |
| Other Europe | 0.5 | 30.4 | 3.5 | 0.9 | 1.9 | 16.9 | 18.4 | 30.3 | 27.8 | 36.4 |
| **Asia** | 91.3 | 102.8 | 96.2 | 73.6 | 56.1 | 51.1 | 40.7 | 39.6 | 79.0 | 72.6 |
| Japan | 46.0 | 54.7 | 38.2 | 21.8 | 11.3 | 4.2 | 3.4 | 3.8 | 7.6 | 7.1 |
| China | ..... | 7.9 | 0.2 | 4.2 | 0.3 | 7.7 | 6.3 | 4.1 | 6.1 | 7.1 |
| Hong Kong | 1.3 | 1.4 | 0.9 | 0.5 | 1.5 | 6.8 | 4.3 | 5.5 | 5.4 | 8.2 |
| Taiwan | 0.1 | 0.8 | 12.6 | 0.3 | 1.9 | 10.6 | 2.7 | 1.0 | 17.0 | 4.6 |
| Singapore | 0.3 | 0.4 | 0.3 | 0.3 | 0.8 | 7.3 | 5.3 | 5.5 | 15.7 | 14.9 |
| South Korea | 43.0 | 37.2 | 39.9 | 45.0 | 39.6 | 5.5 | 10.0 | 6.4 | 10.2 | 5.9 |
| Indonesia | ..... | ..... | ..... | ..... | 0.1 | 0.1 | 1.7 | 1.3 | 1.7 | 4.3 |
| India | ..... | ..... | ..... | ..... | ..... | 0.1 | 0.1 | 0.3 | 0.4 | 1.3 |
| Other Asia | 0.4 | 0.3 | 4.1 | 1.4 | 0.8 | 8.8 | 6.9 | 11.7 | 14.9 | 19.3 |
| **Africa** | 0.1 | 0.2 | ..... | 0.1 | 0.2 | 9.7 | 3.2 | 7.6 | 8.9 | 14.8 |
| North Africa | ..... | ..... | ..... | ..... | 0.1 | 3.2 | 0.4 | 1.5 | 1.7 | 7.4 |
| Republic of South Africa | ..... | 0.1 | ..... | ..... | 0.1 | 5.9 | 2.6 | 5.6 | 6.8 | 6.9 |
| Other Subsaharan Africa | ..... | ..... | ..... | ..... | ..... | 0.5 | 0.2 | 0.5 | 0.5 | 0.5 |
| **Middle East** | 0.1 | 2.9 | ..... | ..... | 0.4 | 31.6 | 9.0 | 19.4 | 19.7 | 14.4 |
| **Australia** | 0.2 | 0.1 | 0.1 | ..... | 0.1 | 12.2 | 13.4 | 17.8 | 14.5 | 18.9 |
| **Rest of World** | ..... | ..... | ..... | ..... | ..... | ..... | ..... | ..... | ..... | ..... |

| Destination | 1993 | 1994 | 1995 | 1996 | 1997 | 1993 | 1994 | 1995 | 1996 | 1997 |
|---|---|---|---|---|---|---|---|---|---|---|
| | Asheville, NC | | | | | Atlanta, GA | | | | |
| **ALL DESTINATIONS** | 232.3 | 228.6 | 185.2 | 236.7 | 294.2 | 3 870.6 | 4 739.1 | 5 811.4 | 5 891.5 | 6 604.6 |
| **North America** | 157.8 | 171.8 | 130.7 | 168.2 | 202.2 | 960.7 | 1 260.3 | 1 300.5 | 1 373.6 | 1 578.5 |
| Canada | 150.0 | 160.5 | 116.5 | 152.3 | 177.2 | 755.9 | 903.3 | 1 004.5 | 1 010.2 | 1 024.2 |
| Mexico | 7.8 | 11.3 | 14.2 | 15.9 | 25.0 | 204.7 | 357.0 | 296.0 | 363.4 | 554.3 |
| **Caribbean and Central America** | 1.5 | 0.8 | 0.9 | 0.6 | 2.6 | 269.2 | 325.0 | 399.5 | 380.6 | 431.4 |
| **South America** | 4.1 | 5.7 | 7.8 | 5.2 | 7.6 | 336.5 | 534.1 | 708.5 | 650.0 | 748.0 |
| Argentina | 0.3 | 0.5 | 0.1 | 0.2 | 1.0 | 101.1 | 182.3 | 134.7 | 105.1 | 126.2 |
| Brazil | 2.2 | 3.1 | 4.8 | 2.3 | 4.1 | 48.8 | 113.3 | 287.3 | 248.8 | 304.8 |
| Other South America | 1.6 | 2.1 | 2.9 | 2.7 | 2.4 | 186.5 | 238.5 | 286.5 | 296.0 | 317.0 |
| **Europe** | 45.0 | 28.9 | 28.3 | 41.7 | 51.5 | 1 122.2 | 1 346.0 | 1 549.9 | 1 678.2 | 1 914.3 |
| Belgium | 0.5 | 0.7 | 1.4 | 2.6 | 2.8 | 89.1 | 100.1 | 83.7 | 78.8 | 202.0 |
| France | 1.5 | 1.0 | 2.8 | 1.9 | 2.5 | 118.0 | 98.4 | 116.6 | 158.1 | 198.7 |
| Germany | 27.8 | 6.6 | 3.7 | 5.2 | 6.3 | 213.7 | 183.3 | 204.4 | 207.0 | 192.2 |
| Netherlands | 6.5 | 7.2 | 5.5 | 9.5 | 8.8 | 126.0 | 192.5 | 217.2 | 212.8 | 262.6 |
| United Kingdom | 3.8 | 6.4 | 8.9 | 14.3 | 16.7 | 203.0 | 284.1 | 347.0 | 305.3 | 358.2 |
| Turkey | ..... | 0.3 | 0.2 | 0.2 | 0.6 | 23.5 | 15.3 | 30.9 | 30.0 | 33.9 |
| Former Soviet Republics | 1.3 | 0.2 | 0.5 | 0.2 | 0.6 | 23.6 | 113.3 | 120.0 | 284.2 | 148.1 |
| Poland | ..... | ..... | 0.2 | 0.2 | 0.1 | 22.4 | 19.4 | 9.9 | 10.3 | 15.0 |
| Other Eastern Europe | 0.3 | ..... | 0.3 | 1.9 | 0.5 | 15.6 | 19.7 | 20.5 | 19.7 | 21.7 |
| Other Europe | 3.4 | 6.4 | 4.7 | 5.8 | 12.7 | 287.4 | 319.7 | 399.7 | 372.0 | 481.8 |
| **Asia** | 20.0 | 18.8 | 15.9 | 17.6 | 23.8 | 850.7 | 993.4 | 1 546.1 | 1 467.7 | 1 553.5 |
| Japan | 2.1 | 2.1 | 2.7 | 4.3 | 5.8 | 276.5 | 278.8 | 394.7 | 419.8 | 420.0 |
| China | 2.2 | 6.7 | 0.2 | 0.7 | 5.0 | 97.2 | 49.3 | 88.5 | 117.4 | 106.5 |
| Hong Kong | 0.3 | 2.1 | 2.9 | 1.1 | 1.6 | 94.0 | 137.0 | 200.5 | 220.3 | 242.1 |
| Taiwan | 0.7 | 0.7 | 0.9 | 0.8 | 1.4 | 110.5 | 114.8 | 119.6 | 99.2 | 109.9 |
| Singapore | 0.1 | 0.5 | 1.0 | 0.7 | 0.7 | 58.7 | 63.6 | 81.4 | 126.0 | 172.9 |
| South Korea | 3.7 | 4.5 | 4.8 | 4.5 | 3.9 | 66.9 | 121.2 | 377.0 | 154.3 | 125.9 |
| Indonesia | 0.1 | 0.8 | 0.5 | 1.8 | 0.1 | 36.4 | 56.6 | 29.7 | 64.9 | 69.3 |
| India | 0.1 | 0.1 | 0.3 | 1.0 | 1.3 | 14.2 | 59.6 | 84.6 | 78.3 | 89.6 |
| Other Asia | 10.6 | 1.3 | 2.7 | 2.6 | 4.0 | 96.2 | 112.5 | 170.1 | 187.7 | 217.1 |
| **Africa** | 0.5 | 0.4 | 0.4 | 1.4 | 1.1 | 93.1 | 90.9 | 104.8 | 115.5 | 118.2 |
| North Africa | 0.1 | 0.1 | 0.1 | 0.4 | 0.3 | 32.0 | 38.5 | 37.4 | 27.2 | 24.0 |
| Republic of South Africa | 0.2 | 0.3 | 0.3 | 0.9 | 0.3 | 26.9 | 35.3 | 57.1 | 64.2 | 61.6 |
| Other Subsaharan Africa | 0.2 | ..... | ..... | 0.1 | 0.5 | 34.3 | 17.1 | 10.2 | 24.1 | 32.6 |
| **Middle East** | 2.2 | 0.7 | 0.5 | 1.1 | 4.4 | 170.5 | 120.6 | 102.8 | 102.4 | 113.8 |
| **Australia** | 1.2 | 1.5 | 0.6 | 0.9 | 0.8 | 67.6 | 68.9 | 99.2 | 123.5 | 146.8 |
| **Rest of World** | ..... | ..... | ..... | ..... | ..... | 0.1 | ..... | ..... | ..... | ..... |

## Table E-3.  Metropolitan Area Exports of Goods by Destination, 1993–1997—*Continued*

(Millions of dollars.)

| Destination | 1993 | 1994 | 1995 | 1996 | 1997 | 1993 | 1994 | 1995 | 1996 | 1997 |
|---|---|---|---|---|---|---|---|---|---|---|
| | Augusta - Aiken, GA - SC | | | | | Austin - San Marcos, TX | | | | |
| **ALL DESTINATIONS** | 227.4 | 326.3 | 405.2 | 443.9 | 433.8 | 1 721.5 | 2 128.8 | 2 929.2 | 2 743.1 | 3 354.8 |
| **North America** | 81.1 | 124.5 | 158.0 | 207.4 | 219.8 | 329.6 | 327.7 | 369.9 | 472.8 | 719.7 |
| Canada | 76.6 | 105.4 | 142.1 | 188.0 | 199.9 | 296.0 | 281.3 | 334.6 | 417.2 | 607.7 |
| Mexico | 4.5 | 19.1 | 15.9 | 19.4 | 19.9 | 33.6 | 46.4 | 35.4 | 55.6 | 112.0 |
| **Caribbean and Central America** | 7.8 | 21.6 | 19.0 | 11.1 | 5.0 | 8.1 | 10.9 | 13.8 | 12.9 | 17.2 |
| **South America** | 14.8 | 11.3 | 34.6 | 19.8 | 13.2 | 19.6 | 21.8 | 31.3 | 30.2 | 34.8 |
| Argentina | 3.7 | 1.2 | 3.4 | 1.6 | 2.1 | 4.2 | 4.5 | 4.4 | 3.1 | 4.8 |
| Brazil | 7.6 | 7.8 | 19.4 | 11.8 | 4.2 | 4.3 | 6.3 | 10.0 | 6.7 | 10.1 |
| Other South America | 3.5 | 2.4 | 11.8 | 6.4 | 6.9 | 11.1 | 11.1 | 17.0 | 20.3 | 19.9 |
| **Europe** | 53.8 | 111.5 | 129.0 | 146.7 | 141.8 | 428.6 | 495.3 | 642.5 | 541.3 | 599.4 |
| Belgium | 5.0 | 8.9 | 20.4 | 14.9 | 6.8 | 8.0 | 14.5 | 29.5 | 10.2 | 8.1 |
| France | 6.7 | 36.2 | 40.2 | 26.8 | 28.5 | 22.6 | 30.8 | 51.6 | 31.9 | 50.6 |
| Germany | 5.8 | 14.2 | 12.1 | 18.6 | 23.5 | 42.1 | 51.4 | 111.9 | 112.5 | 154.3 |
| Netherlands | 7.1 | 6.1 | 6.2 | 5.9 | 11.5 | 14.5 | 18.2 | 19.2 | 24.6 | 28.5 |
| United Kingdom | 8.4 | 15.7 | 17.9 | 35.7 | 22.4 | 254.4 | 291.5 | 315.2 | 261.7 | 256.5 |
| Turkey | 2.2 | 1.1 | 0.3 | 1.1 | 0.7 | 1.4 | 0.5 | 1.0 | 1.6 | 3.2 |
| Former Soviet Republics | ..... | ..... | 0.3 | 0.7 | 0.5 | 1.3 | 1.5 | 0.8 | 1.0 | 1.4 |
| Poland | 0.2 | 0.2 | 0.7 | 1.8 | 1.7 | 0.3 | 1.3 | 0.9 | 0.8 | 0.3 |
| Other Eastern Europe | 0.2 | 0.5 | 0.4 | 1.2 | 1.5 | 2.0 | 2.5 | 1.9 | 3.9 | 2.4 |
| Other Europe | 18.3 | 28.5 | 30.5 | 39.9 | 44.7 | 82.0 | 82.9 | 110.6 | 93.2 | 94.1 |
| **Asia** | 57.7 | 41.7 | 37.2 | 35.9 | 33.4 | 888.7 | 1 204.9 | 1 781.0 | 1 604.3 | 1 909.8 |
| Japan | 7.1 | 12.2 | 16.2 | 14.7 | 9.7 | 117.9 | 150.2 | 303.8 | 343.8 | 372.8 |
| China | 0.5 | 1.6 | 1.8 | 0.6 | 1.1 | 2.2 | 7.0 | 20.8 | 48.7 | 69.9 |
| Hong Kong | 2.1 | 3.0 | 3.3 | 2.5 | 4.1 | 179.6 | 223.7 | 346.2 | 298.2 | 370.0 |
| Taiwan | 19.1 | 9.3 | 2.4 | 3.1 | 3.4 | 32.3 | 66.5 | 86.4 | 124.0 | 174.1 |
| Singapore | 1.0 | 0.6 | 2.0 | 2.8 | 5.5 | 123.0 | 166.4 | 188.7 | 146.9 | 202.7 |
| South Korea | 15.7 | 5.7 | 1.5 | 1.5 | 2.2 | 27.0 | 50.1 | 118.9 | 118.5 | 182.9 |
| Indonesia | 0.6 | 0.2 | 0.5 | 1.0 | 0.5 | 5.9 | 2.7 | 8.3 | 7.0 | 18.1 |
| India | 0.6 | 0.4 | 0.6 | 1.8 | 0.5 | 6.1 | 7.5 | 21.0 | 7.8 | 5.6 |
| Other Asia | 10.9 | 8.6 | 8.7 | 8.1 | 6.5 | 394.6 | 530.7 | 686.9 | 509.5 | 513.9 |
| **Africa** | 1.3 | 1.6 | 3.8 | 3.9 | 4.0 | 8.0 | 7.2 | 12.4 | 13.1 | 6.7 |
| North Africa | 0.1 | 0.2 | 1.0 | 0.9 | 0.5 | 4.0 | 3.4 | 9.3 | 2.2 | 2.2 |
| Republic of South Africa | 1.0 | 1.2 | 2.3 | 2.7 | 3.3 | 3.4 | 2.7 | 2.4 | 2.6 | 3.2 |
| Other Subsaharan Africa | 0.2 | 0.2 | 0.5 | 0.4 | 0.3 | 0.6 | 1.0 | 0.6 | 8.3 | 1.3 |
| **Middle East** | 1.7 | 3.4 | 9.2 | 4.6 | 8.3 | 30.0 | 46.3 | 62.2 | 50.5 | 41.1 |
| **Australia** | 9.1 | 10.7 | 14.4 | 14.4 | 8.3 | 9.0 | 14.7 | 16.1 | 18.1 | 26.2 |
| **Rest of World** | ..... | ..... | ..... | ..... | ..... | ..... | ..... | ..... | ..... | ..... |
| | Bakersfield, CA | | | | | Baltimore, MD | | | | |
| **ALL DESTINATIONS** | 480.7 | 780.4 | 730.5 | 721.3 | 835.6 | 1 783.4 | 1 869.0 | 2 209.2 | 2 110.4 | 2 171.3 |
| **North America** | 72.4 | 68.7 | 77.0 | 82.6 | 98.1 | 451.4 | 492.4 | 430.0 | 453.6 | 478.6 |
| Canada | 66.3 | 62.0 | 71.1 | 75.8 | 90.4 | 404.8 | 429.2 | 376.9 | 378.6 | 429.9 |
| Mexico | 6.1 | 6.7 | 6.0 | 6.8 | 7.7 | 46.6 | 63.2 | 53.1 | 75.0 | 48.7 |
| **Caribbean and Central America** | 1.8 | 1.5 | 2.2 | 2.4 | 2.7 | 30.6 | 52.8 | 38.1 | 38.8 | 34.1 |
| **South America** | 3.7 | 6.3 | 4.5 | 9.8 | 68.5 | 72.7 | 100.4 | 154.3 | 128.7 | 130.0 |
| Argentina | 1.1 | 3.9 | 1.0 | 2.1 | 0.4 | 12.3 | 13.9 | 17.6 | 14.4 | 14.9 |
| Brazil | 0.7 | ..... | 0.3 | 0.6 | 1.5 | 18.9 | 19.0 | 54.6 | 34.4 | 26.8 |
| Other South America | 2.0 | 2.3 | 3.1 | 7.2 | 66.6 | 41.5 | 67.4 | 82.1 | 79.9 | 88.4 |
| **Europe** | 102.9 | 88.7 | 113.3 | 137.7 | 119.0 | 644.7 | 667.1 | 894.7 | 788.7 | 752.4 |
| Belgium | 3.2 | 5.4 | 8.0 | 10.4 | 10.3 | 115.4 | 136.1 | 108.0 | 96.6 | 92.0 |
| France | 4.3 | 4.3 | 5.7 | 2.9 | 3.9 | 46.3 | 64.3 | 58.1 | 53.1 | 72.4 |
| Germany | 28.1 | 20.0 | 31.9 | 40.1 | 33.9 | 45.6 | 41.2 | 62.6 | 68.3 | 89.3 |
| Netherlands | 4.5 | 4.3 | 8.0 | 11.6 | 9.5 | 199.5 | 156.8 | 206.9 | 182.9 | 107.6 |
| United Kingdom | 13.7 | 15.7 | 12.1 | 17.8 | 10.5 | 97.5 | 128.1 | 218.1 | 192.9 | 184.8 |
| Turkey | 9.4 | ..... | ..... | 0.4 | 17.4 | 27.4 | 14.9 | 17.8 | 12.3 | 21.7 |
| Former Soviet Republics | 1.0 | 0.4 | ..... | 0.2 | 2.4 | 15.3 | 14.6 | 6.6 | 14.5 | 10.3 |
| Poland | ..... | 0.1 | 3.3 | 4.0 | ..... | 2.3 | 3.3 | 6.7 | 1.8 | 7.3 |
| Other Eastern Europe | 1.0 | 6.1 | 3.1 | 1.5 | 0.9 | 6.3 | 15.5 | 34.9 | 31.2 | 41.3 |
| Other Europe | 37.7 | 32.5 | 41.3 | 48.7 | 30.2 | 89.0 | 92.3 | 174.9 | 135.1 | 125.7 |
| **Asia** | 264.8 | 587.8 | 432.7 | 453.6 | 526.7 | 280.7 | 262.4 | 308.0 | 355.0 | 370.7 |
| Japan | 105.5 | 162.3 | 164.6 | 141.7 | 125.5 | 112.8 | 66.3 | 83.2 | 78.4 | 80.4 |
| China | 0.6 | 181.4 | 15.2 | 99.8 | 150.5 | 13.2 | 10.8 | 22.5 | 36.4 | 16.9 |
| Hong Kong | 11.8 | 13.8 | 13.8 | 15.6 | 14.0 | 18.7 | 22.8 | 23.4 | 26.6 | 27.6 |
| Taiwan | 19.0 | 37.7 | 25.3 | 21.2 | 25.1 | 45.5 | 45.1 | 36.5 | 42.0 | 39.8 |
| Singapore | 6.3 | 3.8 | 4.4 | 2.8 | 3.5 | 18.4 | 20.8 | 46.6 | 53.6 | 31.0 |
| South Korea | 61.8 | 70.6 | 73.7 | 71.5 | 79.5 | 25.4 | 30.0 | 33.6 | 43.0 | 48.6 |
| Indonesia | 37.2 | 71.4 | 80.7 | 68.2 | 76.8 | 5.9 | 7.3 | 4.8 | 15.7 | 15.2 |
| India | 0.1 | 1.0 | 12.9 | 0.3 | 4.4 | 10.0 | 6.6 | 10.2 | 11.8 | 8.0 |
| Other Asia | 22.6 | 45.6 | 42.0 | 32.6 | 47.4 | 30.7 | 52.8 | 47.1 | 47.5 | 103.3 |
| **Africa** | 29.0 | 20.7 | 92.5 | 25.1 | 6.7 | 128.6 | 115.1 | 137.3 | 207.2 | 206.1 |
| North Africa | 22.1 | 20.0 | 91.6 | 24.9 | 5.8 | 83.5 | 63.1 | 82.7 | 127.0 | 131.6 |
| Republic of South Africa | 0.3 | 0.5 | 0.6 | 0.2 | 0.3 | 31.4 | 40.6 | 42.8 | 67.9 | 58.3 |
| Other Subsaharan Africa | 6.6 | 0.2 | 0.3 | 0.1 | 0.7 | 13.6 | 11.4 | 11.8 | 12.3 | 16.3 |
| **Middle East** | 4.0 | 3.4 | 4.5 | 5.1 | 8.7 | 144.3 | 150.8 | 198.8 | 95.9 | 152.1 |
| **Australia** | 2.1 | 3.4 | 3.8 | 4.9 | 5.2 | 30.4 | 27.8 | 48.0 | 42.5 | 47.2 |
| **Rest of World** | ..... | ..... | ..... | ..... | ..... | ..... | ..... | ..... | ..... | ..... |

## Table E-3.  Metropolitan Area Exports of Goods by Destination, 1993–1997—*Continued*

(Millions of dollars.)

| Destination | 1993 | 1994 | 1995 | 1996 | 1997 | 1993 | 1994 | 1995 | 1996 | 1997 |
|---|---|---|---|---|---|---|---|---|---|---|
| | Bellingham, WA | | | | | Benton Harbor, MI | | | | |
| **ALL DESTINATIONS** | 206.8 | 210.7 | 253.5 | 275.4 | 316.7 | 338.7 | 368.8 | 369.3 | 317.2 | 260.6 |
| **North America** | 116.6 | 120.8 | 159.3 | 184.1 | 212.5 | 115.6 | 126.8 | 88.3 | 108.9 | 88.9 |
| Canada | 115.2 | 117.6 | 155.8 | 179.7 | 210.4 | 60.7 | 66.9 | 79.2 | 80.8 | 79.3 |
| Mexico | 1.3 | 3.2 | 3.4 | 4.5 | 2.1 | 54.9 | 59.9 | 9.1 | 28.1 | 9.5 |
| **Caribbean and Central America** | 0.3 | 0.9 | 0.2 | 0.7 | 0.6 | 2.8 | 1.8 | 3.8 | 0.8 | 0.2 |
| **South America** | 1.5 | 1.9 | 10.6 | 5.9 | 7.0 | 3.5 | 9.5 | 9.8 | 6.1 | 6.6 |
| Argentina | 0.6 | 0.9 | 0.8 | 0.8 | 2.1 | 0.7 | 3.4 | 1.5 | 0.5 | 0.6 |
| Brazil | 0.1 | 0.2 | 4.0 | 2.3 | 1.3 | 1.1 | 4.8 | 6.7 | 4.7 | 3.5 |
| Other South America | 0.7 | 0.7 | 5.8 | 2.8 | 3.6 | 1.6 | 1.3 | 1.6 | 0.9 | 2.5 |
| **Europe** | 28.2 | 23.9 | 18.1 | 14.8 | 25.3 | 130.1 | 123.6 | 129.0 | 70.8 | 64.7 |
| Belgium | 2.9 | 4.0 | 3.7 | 3.0 | 3.7 | 0.7 | 1.4 | 1.9 | 0.7 | 3.4 |
| France | 4.3 | 1.6 | 1.6 | 0.8 | 1.4 | 83.7 | 59.8 | 54.4 | 18.6 | 10.5 |
| Germany | 5.6 | 1.7 | 2.6 | 2.7 | 2.9 | 11.9 | 22.0 | 22.0 | 10.2 | 8.6 |
| Netherlands | 0.7 | 0.3 | 0.8 | 0.3 | 2.6 | 4.3 | 6.4 | 11.0 | 14.5 | 12.9 |
| United Kingdom | 5.2 | 1.8 | 2.3 | 2.3 | 5.1 | 15.1 | 13.8 | 21.3 | 10.8 | 15.5 |
| Turkey | ..... | ..... | ..... | ..... | ..... | 0.8 | 0.1 | 0.5 | 0.5 | 0.9 |
| Former Soviet Republics | 0.4 | 3.3 | 1.0 | 0.6 | ..... | 1.2 | 0.8 | 0.2 | 0.2 | 0.1 |
| Poland | ..... | ..... | ..... | 0.1 | 0.1 | 0.2 | 0.4 | 0.4 | 0.8 | 0.3 |
| Other Eastern Europe | 0.3 | 0.1 | 0.1 | 0.1 | ..... | 0.3 | 5.4 | 0.5 | 0.7 | 0.3 |
| Other Europe | 8.9 | 11.0 | 5.9 | 4.9 | 9.4 | 11.8 | 13.5 | 16.6 | 13.8 | 11.8 |
| **Asia** | 56.0 | 57.3 | 51.0 | 57.8 | 63.4 | 65.7 | 72.4 | 102.4 | 85.7 | 65.9 |
| Japan | 36.4 | 40.3 | 40.8 | 37.2 | 37.8 | 14.4 | 25.0 | 21.4 | 18.1 | 10.0 |
| China | 5.5 | 0.5 | 1.7 | 7.9 | 8.7 | 2.9 | 3.2 | 2.1 | 1.2 | 0.7 |
| Hong Kong | 0.9 | 1.5 | 1.7 | 2.6 | 2.3 | 4.2 | 5.5 | 18.6 | 7.0 | 2.8 |
| Taiwan | 2.3 | 1.4 | 1.2 | 1.3 | 2.6 | 20.3 | 17.6 | 26.9 | 22.0 | 16.1 |
| Singapore | 1.4 | 0.7 | 0.8 | 2.4 | 1.4 | 1.1 | 1.7 | 2.6 | 4.7 | 1.9 |
| South Korea | 5.6 | 3.9 | 1.0 | 2.6 | 2.0 | 16.6 | 16.0 | 18.0 | 24.4 | 24.2 |
| Indonesia | 0.6 | 0.5 | 0.4 | 0.1 | 0.9 | 0.5 | 0.3 | 1.0 | 0.8 | 0.7 |
| India | 0.3 | 0.5 | 1.1 | ..... | ..... | 1.1 | 0.5 | 2.4 | 2.1 | 1.6 |
| Other Asia | 3.0 | 8.0 | 2.2 | 3.8 | 7.5 | 4.5 | 2.7 | 9.4 | 5.4 | 8.0 |
| **Africa** | 0.1 | 0.1 | 0.2 | 0.2 | 0.4 | 3.5 | 6.7 | 6.5 | 7.8 | 5.5 |
| North Africa | 0.1 | ..... | 0.1 | ..... | ..... | 0.5 | 0.6 | 0.6 | 0.5 | 0.4 |
| Republic of South Africa | ..... | 0.1 | ..... | 0.1 | 0.2 | 2.0 | 5.7 | 5.3 | 7.1 | 5.0 |
| Other Subsaharan Africa | ..... | ..... | 0.1 | ..... | 0.2 | 1.0 | 0.4 | 0.6 | 0.3 | 0.1 |
| **Middle East** | 2.1 | 0.9 | 0.9 | 1.0 | 1.0 | 7.9 | 13.8 | 13.0 | 17.3 | 13.2 |
| **Australia** | 1.9 | 4.8 | 13.3 | 10.9 | 6.5 | 9.6 | 14.1 | 16.5 | 19.6 | 15.6 |
| **Rest of World** | ..... | ..... | ..... | ..... | ..... | ..... | ..... | ..... | 0.1 | ..... |
| | Bergen - Passaic, NJ | | | | | Binghamton, NY | | | | |
| **ALL DESTINATIONS** | 3 924.9 | 4 387.0 | 4 784.0 | 4 499.9 | 4 789.8 | 316.2 | 474.9 | 558.1 | 443.3 | 513.3 |
| **North America** | 763.6 | 960.6 | 779.6 | 818.5 | 992.0 | 127.3 | 207.8 | 259.7 | 233.0 | 243.9 |
| Canada | 522.1 | 588.7 | 662.4 | 678.8 | 779.3 | 122.4 | 196.8 | 251.1 | 224.8 | 231.4 |
| Mexico | 241.6 | 371.9 | 117.2 | 139.8 | 212.7 | 4.8 | 11.0 | 8.6 | 8.2 | 12.6 |
| **Caribbean and Central America** | 107.2 | 120.2 | 184.4 | 153.6 | 122.1 | 2.7 | 2.3 | 2.0 | 1.4 | 1.9 |
| **South America** | 236.9 | 262.4 | 308.3 | 316.1 | 360.1 | 13.9 | 18.7 | 15.5 | 16.4 | 17.7 |
| Argentina | 51.0 | 60.7 | 35.0 | 42.7 | 47.5 | 4.1 | 3.3 | 2.6 | 2.4 | 3.0 |
| Brazil | 68.1 | 82.7 | 121.1 | 131.3 | 139.8 | 5.8 | 11.6 | 10.4 | 12.3 | 11.0 |
| Other South America | 117.7 | 119.0 | 152.1 | 142.0 | 172.7 | 3.9 | 3.8 | 2.5 | 1.7 | 3.7 |
| **Europe** | 1 234.1 | 1 343.9 | 1 552.5 | 1 336.2 | 1 347.4 | 75.6 | 106.6 | 129.2 | 96.8 | 126.6 |
| Belgium | 156.0 | 165.8 | 193.3 | 163.3 | 161.0 | 4.3 | 1.0 | 1.3 | 5.7 | 10.5 |
| France | 151.2 | 142.9 | 194.9 | 177.5 | 210.7 | 25.5 | 24.4 | 22.5 | 18.1 | 16.0 |
| Germany | 122.0 | 143.4 | 218.2 | 148.4 | 124.2 | 16.4 | 16.2 | 22.5 | 18.0 | 23.2 |
| Netherlands | 170.7 | 200.0 | 161.4 | 146.6 | 157.4 | 1.8 | 4.0 | 4.8 | 3.4 | 1.7 |
| United Kingdom | 283.0 | 301.3 | 308.7 | 276.0 | 248.2 | 7.4 | 11.2 | 37.0 | 28.9 | 48.7 |
| Turkey | 10.6 | 10.5 | 17.6 | 11.3 | 16.4 | ..... | 8.5 | 13.9 | 0.3 | 0.1 |
| Former Soviet Republics | 25.6 | 26.1 | 32.3 | 28.5 | 37.9 | 0.1 | 0.8 | 0.3 | 0.3 | 0.9 |
| Poland | 5.9 | 3.0 | 8.3 | 7.1 | 3.6 | 2.2 | 0.5 | 0.2 | 1.3 | ..... |
| Other Eastern Europe | 9.0 | 9.7 | 13.2 | 24.1 | 25.5 | ..... | 0.3 | 1.3 | 1.4 | 0.9 |
| Other Europe | 299.9 | 341.2 | 404.5 | 353.4 | 362.5 | 17.8 | 39.8 | 25.4 | 19.4 | 24.7 |
| **Asia** | 1 253.4 | 1 442.2 | 1 688.5 | 1 628.8 | 1 714.2 | 83.2 | 127.1 | 141.5 | 83.3 | 115.6 |
| Japan | 298.3 | 343.5 | 375.5 | 401.4 | 486.2 | 13.6 | 25.3 | 12.4 | 11.0 | 7.3 |
| China | 92.4 | 57.3 | 88.2 | 94.0 | 96.4 | 11.0 | 14.7 | 23.2 | 17.5 | 47.1 |
| Hong Kong | 62.2 | 66.9 | 92.8 | 81.4 | 96.7 | 8.0 | 5.3 | 10.4 | 9.0 | 16.0 |
| Taiwan | 119.7 | 139.8 | 143.4 | 100.3 | 95.7 | 6.1 | 9.8 | 24.3 | 11.9 | 11.9 |
| Singapore | 75.9 | 105.3 | 95.7 | 80.0 | 96.3 | 13.0 | 14.2 | 19.8 | 14.9 | 9.4 |
| South Korea | 493.2 | 627.3 | 745.3 | 713.4 | 718.9 | 23.1 | 29.9 | 16.6 | 5.5 | 5.4 |
| Indonesia | 10.9 | 15.4 | 22.1 | 28.0 | 20.1 | 0.8 | 1.8 | 2.8 | 3.1 | 1.9 |
| India | 21.1 | 21.6 | 30.7 | 25.9 | 16.2 | 0.3 | 3.3 | 3.8 | 0.4 | 3.9 |
| Other Asia | 79.7 | 65.0 | 94.7 | 104.4 | 87.7 | 7.4 | 22.8 | 28.2 | 10.1 | 12.7 |
| **Africa** | 37.8 | 39.1 | 47.9 | 45.8 | 50.6 | 5.0 | 3.4 | 4.1 | 3.5 | 1.9 |
| North Africa | 9.0 | 11.8 | 11.2 | 11.5 | 17.9 | 1.5 | 2.3 | 1.9 | 1.6 | 0.9 |
| Republic of South Africa | 11.4 | 15.6 | 21.5 | 22.4 | 20.3 | 3.2 | 0.9 | 1.5 | 1.8 | 0.9 |
| Other Subsaharan Africa | 17.4 | 11.7 | 15.2 | 11.8 | 12.3 | 0.4 | 0.2 | 0.7 | ..... | ..... |
| **Middle East** | 237.1 | 167.9 | 161.9 | 144.3 | 151.1 | 2.2 | 2.6 | 2.7 | 4.8 | 3.3 |
| **Australia** | 55.0 | 50.7 | 60.9 | 56.4 | 52.3 | 6.3 | 6.4 | 3.4 | 4.1 | 2.4 |
| **Rest of World** | ..... | ..... | ..... | 0.1 | ..... | ..... | ..... | ..... | ..... | ..... |

## Table E-3. Metropolitan Area Exports of Goods by Destination, 1993–1997—*Continued*

(Millions of dollars.)

| Destination | 1993 | 1994 | 1995 | 1996 | 1997 | 1993 | 1994 | 1995 | 1996 | 1997 |
|---|---|---|---|---|---|---|---|---|---|---|
| | Bloomington, IN | | | | | Boston, MA - NH | | | | |
| **ALL DESTINATIONS** | 113.6 | 115.7 | 127.6 | 198.8 | 166.8 | 6 472.5 | 7 095.3 | 7 902.7 | 8 715.8 | 9 570.6 |
| **North America** | 56.7 | 45.9 | 30.9 | 36.9 | 34.3 | 1 320.3 | 1 523.5 | 1 488.8 | 1 640.5 | 1 605.9 |
| Canada | 53.3 | 43.3 | 29.4 | 34.8 | 32.8 | 1 084.9 | 1 189.5 | 1 355.7 | 1 465.4 | 1 408.3 |
| Mexico | 3.4 | 2.6 | 1.5 | 2.1 | 1.5 | 235.4 | 334.1 | 133.1 | 175.1 | 197.6 |
| **Caribbean and Central America** | 0.4 | 0.2 | 0.4 | 0.4 | 0.3 | 91.2 | 86.7 | 94.1 | 101.2 | 98.2 |
| **South America** | 1.5 | 3.0 | 1.7 | 4.0 | 3.2 | 222.1 | 253.2 | 293.9 | 301.2 | 341.6 |
| Argentina | ..... | ..... | ..... | 0.3 | ..... | 42.9 | 53.1 | 42.5 | 36.9 | 43.9 |
| Brazil | 0.7 | 2.4 | 1.4 | 2.1 | 2.0 | 78.4 | 95.2 | 123.7 | 158.5 | 165.0 |
| Other South America | 0.9 | 0.6 | 0.2 | 1.5 | 1.3 | 100.7 | 104.8 | 127.8 | 105.8 | 132.6 |
| **Europe** | 11.6 | 9.8 | 16.2 | 28.1 | 26.2 | 2 804.7 | 3 102.3 | 3 492.1 | 3 728.5 | 3 862.4 |
| Belgium | 1.0 | 0.2 | 0.6 | 0.5 | 0.5 | 92.6 | 133.6 | 196.6 | 349.6 | 298.6 |
| France | 1.0 | 0.4 | 1.9 | 1.1 | 1.4 | 317.5 | 331.0 | 339.5 | 415.7 | 399.3 |
| Germany | 0.6 | 0.8 | 0.8 | 0.3 | 0.4 | 511.4 | 497.6 | 601.7 | 693.3 | 588.7 |
| Netherlands | 0.9 | 1.1 | 2.0 | 0.1 | 0.9 | 517.3 | 486.0 | 481.3 | 418.9 | 663.4 |
| United Kingdom | 1.4 | 0.6 | 1.6 | 0.4 | 0.5 | 578.4 | 698.0 | 808.3 | 863.9 | 893.8 |
| Turkey | 0.1 | ..... | ..... | ..... | ..... | 16.0 | 11.2 | 15.8 | 28.1 | 34.0 |
| Former Soviet Republics | ..... | ..... | ..... | ..... | ..... | 32.8 | 42.8 | 38.9 | 32.2 | 43.5 |
| Poland | ..... | ..... | ..... | ..... | 0.3 | 8.8 | 12.7 | 19.3 | 21.2 | 20.3 |
| Other Eastern Europe | ..... | ..... | ..... | ..... | ..... | 21.9 | 23.1 | 25.7 | 23.6 | 23.0 |
| Other Europe | 6.6 | 6.6 | 9.3 | 25.6 | 22.1 | 708.0 | 866.3 | 964.9 | 882.0 | 897.9 |
| **Asia** | 36.2 | 48.7 | 68.0 | 125.9 | 94.6 | 1 635.2 | 1 764.5 | 2 117.1 | 2 453.3 | 3 171.7 |
| Japan | 8.5 | 11.4 | 10.9 | 15.2 | 9.2 | 656.7 | 718.5 | 806.9 | 907.5 | 1 139.2 |
| China | 7.1 | 11.2 | 33.3 | 88.2 | 54.1 | 66.5 | 73.3 | 80.0 | 95.9 | 90.2 |
| Hong Kong | 4.4 | 11.2 | 6.9 | 11.8 | 17.0 | 173.8 | 182.7 | 233.4 | 234.9 | 341.4 |
| Taiwan | 8.0 | 0.1 | 0.6 | 0.9 | 1.1 | 151.2 | 222.2 | 242.9 | 277.6 | 382.6 |
| Singapore | 3.7 | 6.5 | 2.2 | 3.3 | 2.4 | 187.0 | 208.2 | 206.7 | 292.0 | 394.0 |
| South Korea | 0.9 | 0.9 | 2.9 | 2.4 | 2.2 | 214.3 | 182.5 | 239.6 | 305.5 | 386.5 |
| Indonesia | 0.3 | ..... | 0.1 | ..... | 0.4 | 33.3 | 22.1 | 22.5 | 31.9 | 27.6 |
| India | ..... | ..... | 0.1 | ..... | 0.1 | 36.7 | 36.8 | 39.9 | 33.6 | 42.0 |
| Other Asia | 3.1 | 7.4 | 11.0 | 4.0 | 8.0 | 115.7 | 118.2 | 245.2 | 274.4 | 368.2 |
| **Africa** | 1.4 | 0.2 | 1.4 | 0.2 | 0.4 | 68.3 | 53.9 | 65.9 | 81.1 | 87.4 |
| North Africa | 0.9 | 0.2 | 0.9 | 0.2 | ..... | 24.5 | 15.9 | 15.8 | 11.2 | 15.6 |
| Republic of South Africa | 0.2 | ..... | ..... | ..... | ..... | 36.7 | 32.2 | 41.5 | 47.2 | 56.6 |
| Other Subsaharan Africa | 0.3 | ..... | 0.4 | ..... | 0.3 | 7.1 | 5.8 | 8.6 | 22.7 | 15.1 |
| **Middle East** | 2.3 | 3.8 | 5.3 | 0.9 | 2.6 | 130.1 | 121.6 | 143.1 | 187.0 | 215.0 |
| **Australia** | 3.6 | 4.1 | 3.6 | 2.4 | 5.2 | 200.5 | 189.6 | 207.6 | 223.1 | 188.5 |
| **Rest of World** | ..... | ..... | ..... | ..... | ..... | 0.1 | 0.1 | ..... | ..... | ..... |

| Destination | 1993 | 1994 | 1995 | 1996 | 1997 | 1993 | 1994 | 1995 | 1996 | 1997 |
|---|---|---|---|---|---|---|---|---|---|---|
| | Bridgeport, CT | | | | | Brownsville - Harlingen - San Benito, TX | | | | |
| **ALL DESTINATIONS** | 1 125.9 | 918.8 | 952.9 | 788.6 | 981.4 | 1 904.4 | 2 113.4 | 2 245.9 | 2 612.6 | 2 697.1 |
| **North America** | 157.1 | 188.3 | 170.4 | 194.5 | 237.3 | 1 862.1 | 2 060.9 | 2 178.1 | 2 560.9 | 2 634.0 |
| Canada | 128.0 | 115.2 | 133.9 | 148.3 | 170.9 | 35.6 | 133.9 | 453.1 | 372.9 | 467.8 |
| Mexico | 29.1 | 73.1 | 36.5 | 46.2 | 66.4 | 1 826.5 | 1 927.0 | 1 725.0 | 2 188.0 | 2 166.3 |
| **Caribbean and Central America** | 44.7 | 48.7 | 70.8 | 78.3 | 186.5 | 10.4 | 19.0 | 21.6 | 13.6 | 14.3 |
| **South America** | 31.2 | 49.9 | 40.6 | 20.4 | 22.1 | 2.1 | 2.0 | 2.9 | 1.5 | 6.6 |
| Argentina | 6.4 | 19.1 | 3.4 | 2.1 | 1.1 | 0.7 | 0.1 | 0.2 | 0.2 | 0.4 |
| Brazil | 11.6 | 11.4 | 12.8 | 10.2 | 13.1 | 0.3 | 0.5 | 0.5 | 0.3 | 1.7 |
| Other South America | 13.2 | 19.3 | 24.4 | 8.1 | 7.9 | 1.1 | 1.4 | 2.3 | 1.0 | 4.5 |
| **Europe** | 538.3 | 364.2 | 409.0 | 281.3 | 278.5 | 16.2 | 18.3 | 24.9 | 20.5 | 24.0 |
| Belgium | 9.2 | 16.9 | 6.4 | 4.2 | 4.6 | ..... | ..... | 0.2 | 0.8 | 0.7 |
| France | 18.5 | 9.0 | 13.5 | 15.0 | 9.2 | 0.8 | 1.2 | 3.8 | 1.0 | 1.3 |
| Germany | 26.4 | 47.6 | 51.0 | 25.7 | 37.2 | 0.9 | 2.8 | 3.2 | 5.7 | 7.6 |
| Netherlands | 18.1 | 16.4 | 16.2 | 13.2 | 24.5 | 0.9 | 0.7 | 2.2 | 1.9 | 2.4 |
| United Kingdom | 117.6 | 82.3 | 82.9 | 118.6 | 125.8 | 8.9 | 7.8 | 8.6 | 6.4 | 7.1 |
| Turkey | 265.1 | 74.4 | 15.4 | 16.4 | 9.1 | ..... | ..... | ..... | 0.1 | 0.1 |
| Former Soviet Republics | 1.7 | 1.3 | 2.2 | 2.0 | 1.2 | ..... | ..... | ..... | ..... | ..... |
| Poland | 1.2 | 0.4 | 0.7 | 4.4 | 0.4 | 0.8 | 0.4 | ..... | ..... | 0.1 |
| Other Eastern Europe | 0.9 | 0.8 | 0.6 | 0.5 | 3.0 | ..... | ..... | 0.5 | 0.1 | 0.1 |
| Other Europe | 79.5 | 115.1 | 220.1 | 81.3 | 63.6 | 3.7 | 5.2 | 6.3 | 4.5 | 4.6 |
| **Asia** | 307.7 | 214.3 | 216.6 | 169.3 | 229.8 | 11.8 | 10.3 | 15.8 | 13.1 | 14.3 |
| Japan | 31.2 | 27.9 | 23.6 | 29.1 | 18.0 | 0.7 | 0.6 | 2.2 | 3.1 | 2.4 |
| China | 18.7 | 8.1 | 8.3 | 5.4 | 6.2 | 0.6 | 1.5 | 1.1 | 0.1 | 0.2 |
| Hong Kong | 36.0 | 16.0 | 26.7 | 20.6 | 15.0 | 0.5 | 0.4 | 1.0 | 0.9 | 2.3 |
| Taiwan | 18.6 | 15.3 | 16.9 | 9.3 | 6.8 | 0.7 | 1.0 | 1.8 | 0.4 | 1.0 |
| Singapore | 16.9 | 11.9 | 8.9 | 6.4 | 7.5 | 0.6 | 0.6 | 1.8 | 4.1 | 5.4 |
| South Korea | 158.5 | 107.2 | 104.9 | 80.1 | 108.5 | 7.1 | 4.1 | 3.9 | 2.4 | 2.1 |
| Indonesia | 2.8 | 2.6 | 2.0 | 1.2 | 1.5 | ..... | ..... | ..... | 0.4 | ..... |
| India | 1.9 | 2.9 | 3.1 | 1.7 | 1.6 | ..... | ..... | 0.6 | 0.5 | 0.1 |
| Other Asia | 23.0 | 22.4 | 22.3 | 15.5 | 64.7 | 1.6 | 2.0 | 3.4 | 1.1 | 0.8 |
| **Africa** | 5.9 | 8.6 | 3.6 | 4.3 | 3.2 | 0.7 | 0.2 | 0.7 | 1.0 | 2.5 |
| North Africa | 1.7 | 6.6 | 2.3 | 3.1 | 0.7 | ..... | ..... | ..... | ..... | 0.3 |
| Republic of South Africa | 3.7 | 1.8 | 1.2 | 0.9 | 2.4 | 0.7 | 0.1 | ..... | ..... | 0.3 |
| Other Subsaharan Africa | 0.4 | 0.2 | 0.1 | 0.3 | 0.1 | ..... | 0.1 | 0.7 | 1.0 | 2.0 |
| **Middle East** | 17.2 | 10.5 | 15.9 | 16.4 | 10.7 | 0.7 | 1.4 | 0.9 | 1.1 | 0.7 |
| **Australia** | 23.8 | 34.3 | 26.0 | 24.1 | 13.3 | 0.3 | 1.1 | 1.1 | 0.9 | 0.7 |
| **Rest of World** | ..... | ..... | ..... | ..... | ..... | ..... | ..... | ..... | ..... | ..... |

## Table E-3.  Metropolitan Area Exports of Goods by Destination, 1993–1997—*Continued*

(Millions of dollars.)

| Destination | 1993 | 1994 | 1995 | 1996 | 1997 | 1993 | 1994 | 1995 | 1996 | 1997 |
|---|---|---|---|---|---|---|---|---|---|---|
| | Buffalo - Niagara Falls, NY | | | | | Canton - Massillon, OH | | | | |
| **ALL DESTINATIONS** | 1 135.2 | 1 569.7 | 2 295.8 | 2 262.2 | 2 667.3 | 250.2 | 315.9 | 377.2 | 406.0 | 421.6 |
| **North America** | 678.2 | 1 051.0 | 1 702.5 | 1 638.7 | 1 943.7 | 133.4 | 156.5 | 178.6 | 193.6 | 203.8 |
| Canada | 620.7 | 997.7 | 1 660.3 | 1 599.5 | 1 881.1 | 109.0 | 128.2 | 170.5 | 174.2 | 195.6 |
| Mexico | 57.5 | 53.3 | 42.2 | 39.1 | 62.7 | 24.4 | 28.3 | 8.1 | 19.3 | 8.2 |
| **Caribbean and Central America** | 5.0 | 5.5 | 7.6 | 6.0 | 8.7 | 1.4 | 3.0 | 3.2 | 2.2 | 2.6 |
| **South America** | 28.8 | 32.5 | 80.0 | 63.3 | 77.1 | 19.0 | 32.0 | 22.4 | 33.2 | 41.2 |
| Argentina | 4.2 | 4.8 | 6.4 | 7.1 | 15.8 | 1.6 | 2.7 | 1.3 | 7.3 | 8.5 |
| Brazil | 9.9 | 9.9 | 23.1 | 25.9 | 32.7 | 13.0 | 20.6 | 11.7 | 13.7 | 24.3 |
| Other South America | 14.8 | 17.8 | 50.4 | 30.3 | 28.7 | 4.4 | 8.7 | 9.4 | 12.2 | 8.3 |
| **Europe** | 172.1 | 202.9 | 200.0 | 238.8 | 278.1 | 49.4 | 52.5 | 72.6 | 79.0 | 63.3 |
| Belgium | 12.5 | 12.8 | 18.6 | 27.5 | 19.0 | 1.5 | 0.8 | 1.7 | 1.6 | 1.1 |
| France | 15.5 | 18.7 | 19.2 | 20.4 | 28.1 | 4.3 | 11.8 | 12.8 | 9.8 | 9.3 |
| Germany | 29.0 | 29.5 | 33.3 | 41.7 | 59.6 | 10.1 | 8.0 | 19.4 | 34.7 | 20.2 |
| Netherlands | 8.0 | 7.9 | 9.9 | 8.4 | 7.7 | 4.7 | 7.6 | 9.7 | 7.0 | 5.6 |
| United Kingdom | 46.3 | 38.6 | 38.8 | 54.1 | 65.2 | 14.8 | 13.0 | 16.8 | 14.4 | 14.9 |
| Turkey | 4.5 | 3.2 | 3.3 | 8.4 | 5.0 | 0.1 | 0.2 | 0.9 | 0.6 | 0.3 |
| Former Soviet Republics | 3.9 | 11.2 | 5.2 | 0.6 | 1.8 | ..... | 0.5 | ..... | 0.1 | 0.2 |
| Poland | 0.2 | 0.3 | 0.8 | 5.5 | 2.9 | ..... | ..... | ..... | ..... | ..... |
| Other Eastern Europe | 1.8 | 2.1 | 2.6 | 4.7 | 2.8 | 6.1 | 0.8 | 0.1 | 0.1 | 0.1 |
| Other Europe | 50.5 | 78.6 | 68.2 | 67.6 | 86.2 | 7.9 | 9.8 | 11.0 | 10.7 | 11.5 |
| **Asia** | 203.2 | 228.3 | 267.1 | 267.3 | 308.9 | 30.3 | 43.0 | 71.0 | 70.1 | 81.4 |
| Japan | 67.8 | 77.0 | 93.0 | 86.8 | 95.0 | 2.4 | 2.0 | 2.4 | 4.7 | 3.3 |
| China | 20.9 | 14.6 | 19.2 | 12.5 | 32.5 | 1.7 | 6.2 | 9.9 | 6.0 | 20.6 |
| Hong Kong | 16.8 | 18.8 | 21.0 | 22.2 | 28.0 | 0.9 | 1.7 | 8.4 | 6.4 | 14.1 |
| Taiwan | 27.6 | 30.6 | 22.9 | 24.1 | 23.1 | 4.7 | 2.0 | 3.7 | 2.4 | 0.8 |
| Singapore | 14.4 | 21.6 | 19.3 | 18.3 | 18.7 | 0.8 | 0.8 | 1.2 | 1.4 | 0.6 |
| South Korea | 23.2 | 32.0 | 47.9 | 60.4 | 54.7 | 7.5 | 6.4 | 13.3 | 6.3 | 3.4 |
| Indonesia | 2.6 | 6.5 | 9.4 | 6.4 | 4.0 | 0.1 | 3.4 | 11.1 | 13.2 | 12.6 |
| India | 3.7 | 4.7 | 4.6 | 5.8 | 14.1 | 4.0 | 0.9 | 2.9 | 5.8 | 5.1 |
| Other Asia | 26.2 | 22.6 | 29.8 | 30.9 | 38.9 | 8.2 | 19.7 | 18.2 | 24.0 | 21.1 |
| **Africa** | 13.8 | 14.5 | 10.4 | 13.1 | 14.6 | 5.3 | 10.3 | 10.0 | 10.9 | 13.6 |
| North Africa | 1.0 | 1.8 | 1.5 | 1.7 | 1.5 | 0.8 | 0.2 | 0.3 | 0.2 | 0.5 |
| Republic of South Africa | 11.1 | 11.3 | 8.2 | 10.0 | 11.7 | 4.1 | 9.5 | 9.0 | 10.0 | 12.3 |
| Other Subsaharan Africa | 1.7 | 1.3 | 0.6 | 1.4 | 1.4 | 0.4 | 0.7 | 0.7 | 0.7 | 0.8 |
| **Middle East** | 21.5 | 19.9 | 15.4 | 20.9 | 21.7 | 2.4 | 3.6 | 2.0 | 2.1 | 2.2 |
| **Australia** | 12.5 | 15.1 | 12.9 | 14.1 | 14.3 | 9.1 | 15.1 | 17.5 | 15.0 | 13.4 |
| **Rest of World** | ..... | ..... | ..... | ..... | ..... | ..... | ..... | ..... | ..... | ..... . |
| | Charlotte - Gastonia - Rock Hill, NC - SC | | | | | Charleston - North Charleston, SC | | | | |
| **ALL DESTINATIONS** | 1 563.7 | 1 782.8 | 2 088.0 | 2 291.3 | 2 588.8 | 597.3 | 388.5 | 501.6 | 595.1 | 827.6 |
| **North America** | 532.7 | 714.0 | 806.2 | 838.0 | 997.1 | 77.8 | 106.6 | 140.3 | 122.9 | 197.4 |
| Canada | 430.0 | 559.5 | 682.0 | 683.3 | 819.6 | 53.3 | 71.9 | 96.9 | 99.0 | 169.6 |
| Mexico | 102.7 | 154.5 | 124.3 | 154.7 | 177.5 | 24.5 | 34.7 | 43.4 | 24.0 | 27.8 |
| **Caribbean and Central America** | 21.0 | 26.9 | 50.2 | 55.3 | 71.0 | 10.1 | 4.5 | 12.7 | 6.2 | 15.2 |
| **South America** | 92.5 | 116.2 | 157.5 | 168.6 | 193.9 | 26.4 | 12.0 | 33.7 | 32.5 | 85.0 |
| Argentina | 9.7 | 14.6 | 11.2 | 28.6 | 20.5 | 5.1 | 1.8 | 2.0 | 5.2 | 15.9 |
| Brazil | 31.0 | 43.0 | 65.2 | 65.5 | 90.9 | 2.6 | 1.7 | 14.6 | 9.6 | 40.4 |
| Other South America | 51.8 | 58.6 | 81.1 | 74.5 | 82.4 | 18.8 | 8.5 | 17.2 | 17.7 | 28.7 |
| **Europe** | 433.4 | 453.6 | 495.4 | 579.1 | 686.8 | 292.8 | 148.9 | 150.1 | 190.8 | 251.6 |
| Belgium | 100.2 | 91.7 | 103.3 | 117.1 | 101.1 | 12.2 | 8.7 | 12.4 | 18.7 | 27.5 |
| France | 31.3 | 33.7 | 39.4 | 53.7 | 83.8 | 9.9 | 4.5 | 9.6 | 18.0 | 20.9 |
| Germany | 70.8 | 89.1 | 108.1 | 96.7 | 134.1 | 98.4 | 47.8 | 46.9 | 58.3 | 91.6 |
| Netherlands | 15.9 | 25.4 | 32.3 | 43.0 | 43.7 | 63.5 | 34.8 | 27.1 | 27.3 | 35.5 |
| United Kingdom | 84.5 | 82.7 | 90.1 | 101.2 | 155.9 | 81.8 | 35.5 | 29.6 | 30.9 | 43.2 |
| Turkey | 5.1 | 5.9 | 4.5 | 9.0 | 12.0 | 3.6 | 0.6 | 3.0 | 3.2 | 1.8 |
| Former Soviet Republics | 1.4 | 1.1 | 2.4 | 1.1 | 5.8 | ..... | 0.1 | 0.2 | 0.3 | 3.2 |
| Poland | 1.3 | 0.8 | 0.5 | 2.0 | 4.5 | ..... | 0.1 | 0.1 | ..... | 0.8 |
| Other Eastern Europe | 1.2 | 2.1 | 3.3 | 5.1 | 16.3 | 0.9 | 0.2 | 0.3 | 0.9 | 0.9 |
| Other Europe | 121.7 | 121.1 | 111.5 | 150.2 | 129.7 | 22.4 | 16.7 | 20.9 | 33.1 | 26.2 |
| **Asia** | 372.8 | 362.6 | 471.6 | 543.0 | 510.5 | 122.1 | 89.3 | 119.4 | 185.9 | 238.3 |
| Japan | 77.4 | 90.6 | 110.4 | 147.2 | 114.3 | 20.6 | 11.8 | 16.7 | 21.2 | 29.4 |
| China | 93.9 | 86.1 | 111.2 | 114.5 | 106.6 | 19.2 | 13.7 | 21.4 | 18.3 | 15.1 |
| Hong Kong | 32.7 | 27.3 | 32.8 | 39.3 | 49.6 | 7.7 | 6.6 | 12.9 | 14.7 | 13.2 |
| Taiwan | 17.7 | 23.6 | 21.6 | 25.1 | 38.0 | 18.6 | 8.6 | 10.3 | 82.3 | 112.1 |
| Singapore | 18.8 | 21.6 | 27.7 | 33.4 | 33.0 | 6.1 | 8.9 | 5.9 | 3.0 | 1.7 |
| South Korea | 32.7 | 36.6 | 57.1 | 80.6 | 62.3 | 29.3 | 27.2 | 28.8 | 18.7 | 20.6 |
| Indonesia | 37.1 | 31.4 | 48.2 | 29.8 | 21.5 | 2.4 | 2.9 | 5.1 | 3.0 | 22.5 |
| India | 29.6 | 6.2 | 8.5 | 11.9 | 13.1 | 1.7 | 3.9 | 4.9 | 5.6 | 4.1 |
| Other Asia | 32.9 | 39.4 | 54.2 | 61.2 | 72.1 | 16.6 | 5.7 | 13.4 | 19.0 | 19.6 |
| **Africa** | 10.6 | 26.1 | 18.1 | 17.5 | 31.9 | 4.9 | 6.3 | 6.5 | 17.9 | 10.3 |
| North Africa | 3.2 | 4.2 | 4.7 | 7.0 | 16.1 | 1.0 | 1.5 | 2.3 | 11.9 | 5.3 |
| Republic of South Africa | 5.9 | 8.1 | 9.1 | 7.5 | 9.2 | 2.9 | 3.3 | 4.0 | 5.1 | 4.5 |
| Other Subsaharan Africa | 1.5 | 13.8 | 4.4 | 3.0 | 6.6 | 1.1 | 1.5 | 0.1 | 0.9 | 0.5 |
| **Middle East** | 55.2 | 47.6 | 53.9 | 55.8 | 57.0 | 58.4 | 10.7 | 15.8 | 25.4 | 21.4 |
| **Australia** | 45.6 | 35.8 | 35.0 | 33.9 | 40.6 | 4.6 | 10.1 | 23.1 | 13.5 | 8.4 |
| **Rest of World** | ..... | ..... | ..... | ..... | ..... | ..... | ..... | ..... | ..... | ..... |

## Table E-3. Metropolitan Area Exports of Goods by Destination, 1993–1997—*Continued*

(Millions of dollars.)

| Destination | 1993 | 1994 | 1995 | 1996 | 1997 | 1993 | 1994 | 1995 | 1996 | 1997 |
|---|---|---|---|---|---|---|---|---|---|---|
| | Chattanooga, TN - GA | | | | | Chicago, IL | | | | |
| **ALL DESTINATIONS** | 218.3 | 237.3 | 301.0 | 273.5 | 331.4 | 14 446.6 | 17 333.6 | 21 083.4 | 22 030.1 | 23 209.9 |
| **North America** | 100.5 | 107.5 | 122.6 | 124.7 | 146.7 | 3 999.2 | 4 830.9 | 5 137.8 | 5 701.9 | 6 733.8 |
| Canada | 90.9 | 97.6 | 116.6 | 114.9 | 127.8 | 2 978.1 | 3 582.1 | 4 180.2 | 4 412.7 | 5 203.0 |
| Mexico | 9.6 | 9.9 | 6.0 | 9.9 | 18.9 | 1 021.1 | 1 248.8 | 957.6 | 1 289.2 | 1 530.7 |
| **Caribbean and Central America** | 3.9 | 6.8 | 19.7 | 25.4 | 39.8 | 219.9 | 262.4 | 305.5 | 301.8 | 321.2 |
| **South America** | 8.2 | 8.0 | 11.7 | 9.6 | 15.4 | 784.3 | 1 091.4 | 1 118.0 | 1 294.8 | 1 825.2 |
| Argentina | 0.2 | 0.2 | 1.4 | 1.3 | 2.3 | 172.9 | 172.8 | 187.9 | 186.9 | 322.3 |
| Brazil | 0.4 | 0.5 | 2.0 | 2.8 | 5.5 | 203.4 | 432.7 | 440.7 | 541.5 | 722.2 |
| Other South America | 7.6 | 7.2 | 8.3 | 5.6 | 7.7 | 408.0 | 485.9 | 489.4 | 566.3 | 780.7 |
| **Europe** | 34.3 | 44.5 | 60.1 | 44.1 | 56.9 | 3 938.9 | 4 317.5 | 5 214.7 | 5 659.3 | 6 006.0 |
| Belgium | 4.3 | 8.2 | 9.7 | 5.1 | 5.0 | 380.2 | 481.7 | 500.2 | 561.8 | 665.7 |
| France | 1.4 | 2.7 | 5.0 | 3.2 | 4.4 | 316.1 | 386.7 | 413.9 | 468.4 | 563.9 |
| Germany | 7.0 | 7.8 | 15.3 | 8.6 | 14.4 | 766.8 | 903.6 | 1 040.2 | 1 112.7 | 1 140.4 |
| Netherlands | 1.6 | 5.7 | 9.0 | 5.9 | 6.8 | 309.1 | 352.3 | 463.5 | 594.9 | 703.1 |
| United Kingdom | 10.9 | 12.1 | 11.6 | 12.1 | 9.9 | 794.8 | 1 009.5 | 1 227.3 | 1 218.2 | 1 305.1 |
| Turkey | 0.3 | 0.3 | 0.7 | 0.3 | 2.2 | 76.2 | 25.7 | 55.0 | 86.3 | 106.9 |
| Former Soviet Republics | 0.1 | 0.2 | 0.2 | 0.2 | 0.4 | 173.4 | 90.0 | 84.5 | 73.8 | 104.1 |
| Poland | ..... | 0.1 | 0.7 | 0.3 | 0.3 | 92.6 | 55.9 | 71.3 | 106.4 | 123.8 |
| Other Eastern Europe | 0.1 | 0.1 | 0.4 | 0.5 | 0.9 | 103.2 | 51.6 | 61.0 | 62.7 | 58.6 |
| Other Europe | 8.6 | 7.2 | 7.4 | 8.0 | 12.5 | 926.5 | 960.5 | 1 297.9 | 1 374.1 | 1 234.4 |
| **Asia** | 55.8 | 53.3 | 69.4 | 50.2 | 53.6 | 4 444.9 | 5 508.9 | 7 459.8 | 7 291.7 | 6 653.7 |
| Japan | 7.0 | 11.9 | 14.0 | 16.3 | 9.9 | 1 608.1 | 1 777.8 | 2 343.4 | 2 453.5 | 1 962.0 |
| China | 3.8 | 0.9 | 14.2 | 2.3 | 2.8 | 656.2 | 915.0 | 938.8 | 894.6 | 816.4 |
| Hong Kong | 4.5 | 3.9 | 6.0 | 4.1 | 5.5 | 270.7 | 338.3 | 663.1 | 553.8 | 810.9 |
| Taiwan | 3.9 | 10.6 | 8.0 | 5.8 | 15.0 | 425.1 | 575.5 | 491.8 | 411.5 | 396.2 |
| Singapore | 20.6 | 12.1 | 9.8 | 8.0 | 8.0 | 271.9 | 295.3 | 356.9 | 427.5 | 492.2 |
| South Korea | 2.9 | 2.0 | 1.8 | 3.3 | 2.2 | 488.3 | 652.2 | 1 099.4 | 1 136.7 | 781.6 |
| Indonesia | 0.6 | 0.6 | 0.4 | 0.2 | 0.5 | 76.7 | 111.0 | 169.3 | 238.4 | 253.3 |
| India | 0.2 | 0.7 | 0.8 | 0.2 | 0.9 | 111.0 | 138.5 | 188.1 | 124.1 | 169.7 |
| Other Asia | 12.2 | 10.5 | 14.4 | 9.9 | 8.9 | 537.0 | 705.3 | 1 209.0 | 1 051.6 | 971.3 |
| **Africa** | 1.8 | 3.0 | 1.9 | 4.9 | 2.9 | 242.5 | 340.5 | 579.0 | 558.1 | 459.5 |
| North Africa | 1.3 | 0.9 | 1.2 | 0.6 | 0.3 | 129.0 | 192.6 | 369.7 | 305.2 | 207.5 |
| Republic of South Africa | 0.3 | 0.9 | 0.6 | 3.2 | 2.5 | 73.9 | 104.9 | 163.2 | 183.6 | 176.9 |
| Other Subsaharan Africa | 0.3 | 1.2 | 0.1 | 1.1 | 0.1 | 39.6 | 42.9 | 46.1 | 69.3 | 75.1 |
| **Middle East** | 8.9 | 6.4 | 8.1 | 7.2 | 5.7 | 395.1 | 483.0 | 661.1 | 662.0 | 639.0 |
| **Australia** | 4.9 | 7.7 | 7.6 | 7.2 | 10.3 | 416.5 | 492.1 | 515.2 | 478.1 | 561.8 |
| **Rest of World** | ..... | ..... | ..... | ..... | ..... | 5.2 | 7.0 | 92.3 | 82.5 | 9.9 |
| | Cincinnati, OH - KY - IN | | | | | Cleveland - Lorain - Elyria, OH | | | | |
| **ALL DESTINATIONS** | 3 898.2 | 4 056.5 | 4 256.7 | 4 784.1 | 5 674.1 | 3 582.8 | 4 093.3 | 4 707.0 | 5 075.2 | 5 511.0 |
| **North America** | 730.8 | 904.8 | 1 040.9 | 1 194.8 | 1 153.3 | 1 467.0 | 1 633.7 | 1 822.1 | 1 988.4 | 2 148.3 |
| Canada | 549.2 | 686.3 | 885.1 | 1 010.4 | 914.4 | 1 255.9 | 1 294.3 | 1 445.9 | 1 610.7 | 1 717.9 |
| Mexico | 181.6 | 218.4 | 155.8 | 184.4 | 239.0 | 211.1 | 339.4 | 376.1 | 377.6 | 430.4 |
| **Caribbean and Central America** | 120.9 | 109.1 | 146.6 | 130.8 | 137.6 | 30.6 | 39.9 | 37.7 | 33.1 | 43.1 |
| **South America** | 114.6 | 98.2 | 192.9 | 171.9 | 348.6 | 197.1 | 281.8 | 322.2 | 322.3 | 387.4 |
| Argentina | 8.2 | 10.6 | 16.7 | 19.4 | 20.7 | 44.2 | 58.5 | 54.2 | 79.7 | 65.1 |
| Brazil | 25.9 | 14.8 | 63.8 | 45.8 | 190.6 | 61.1 | 85.9 | 117.7 | 111.2 | 163.8 |
| Other South America | 80.5 | 72.8 | 112.3 | 106.7 | 137.3 | 91.9 | 137.5 | 150.3 | 131.5 | 158.4 |
| **Europe** | 2 279.0 | 2 193.1 | 1 972.2 | 2 157.3 | 2 656.4 | 841.6 | 959.5 | 1 095.0 | 1 067.0 | 1 109.2 |
| Belgium | 67.7 | 94.3 | 99.1 | 91.0 | 85.5 | 65.5 | 66.2 | 57.8 | 58.8 | 55.0 |
| France | 1 575.4 | 1 467.5 | 963.8 | 984.3 | 1 390.2 | 149.5 | 165.0 | 188.0 | 145.4 | 156.4 |
| Germany | 102.5 | 120.6 | 150.9 | 186.2 | 230.1 | 126.3 | 163.8 | 198.9 | 211.5 | 212.3 |
| Netherlands | 77.3 | 54.2 | 55.7 | 60.1 | 75.1 | 51.1 | 55.4 | 62.4 | 75.0 | 113.8 |
| United Kingdom | 154.5 | 181.9 | 313.4 | 436.2 | 446.2 | 181.7 | 181.0 | 194.4 | 207.9 | 223.6 |
| Turkey | 132.9 | 82.0 | 147.6 | 111.1 | 97.8 | 22.6 | 23.6 | 50.1 | 40.3 | 64.6 |
| Former Soviet Republics | 4.7 | 1.3 | 2.4 | 1.5 | 3.0 | 6.5 | 6.1 | 16.2 | 9.9 | 12.4 |
| Poland | 1.0 | 6.4 | 6.5 | 6.7 | 8.5 | 1.2 | 2.1 | 3.3 | 7.5 | 4.9 |
| Other Eastern Europe | 5.1 | 2.1 | 3.2 | 11.3 | 12.7 | 8.5 | 8.6 | 6.0 | 18.3 | 23.5 |
| Other Europe | 157.7 | 182.8 | 229.8 | 268.8 | 307.4 | 228.7 | 287.5 | 317.9 | 292.4 | 242.7 |
| **Asia** | 552.1 | 652.5 | 787.3 | 968.5 | 1 195.8 | 787.9 | 871.2 | 1 132.7 | 1 410.5 | 1 523.2 |
| Japan | 230.6 | 281.1 | 313.6 | 415.1 | 595.0 | 227.7 | 276.7 | 327.2 | 365.4 | 324.1 |
| China | 37.9 | 51.3 | 34.6 | 55.7 | 69.4 | 59.6 | 65.2 | 74.4 | 74.7 | 185.4 |
| Hong Kong | 21.0 | 31.3 | 39.4 | 52.5 | 40.9 | 48.0 | 69.2 | 69.4 | 87.5 | 121.3 |
| Taiwan | 70.0 | 52.5 | 93.3 | 43.7 | 50.4 | 95.1 | 84.2 | 118.5 | 178.7 | 133.2 |
| Singapore | 94.6 | 111.4 | 132.0 | 182.7 | 219.0 | 142.6 | 133.3 | 175.9 | 158.7 | 172.8 |
| South Korea | 36.2 | 47.8 | 45.6 | 73.6 | 55.6 | 106.8 | 123.4 | 195.8 | 391.2 | 444.2 |
| Indonesia | 4.9 | 13.6 | 17.7 | 10.1 | 12.9 | 18.6 | 6.5 | 22.7 | 22.4 | 18.0 |
| India | 3.1 | 4.8 | 7.3 | 14.4 | 21.9 | 24.0 | 38.4 | 49.4 | 27.2 | 32.4 |
| Other Asia | 53.7 | 58.7 | 103.8 | 120.7 | 130.7 | 65.7 | 74.4 | 99.5 | 104.7 | 91.8 |
| **Africa** | 19.2 | 16.7 | 27.6 | 55.4 | 38.3 | 63.6 | 87.6 | 95.3 | 71.5 | 73.5 |
| North Africa | 9.0 | 5.6 | 17.2 | 30.9 | 21.1 | 8.3 | 15.1 | 13.0 | 11.9 | 12.6 |
| Republic of South Africa | 8.1 | 10.4 | 8.3 | 23.1 | 14.4 | 51.3 | 68.4 | 78.2 | 56.3 | 55.1 |
| Other Subsaharan Africa | 2.0 | 0.7 | 2.1 | 1.4 | 2.8 | 4.0 | 4.2 | 4.1 | 3.4 | 5.9 |
| **Middle East** | 40.2 | 49.4 | 44.1 | 43.4 | 66.6 | 76.4 | 89.3 | 85.4 | 80.1 | 117.1 |
| **Australia** | 41.3 | 32.7 | 45.2 | 62.0 | 77.5 | 118.5 | 130.3 | 116.6 | 101.6 | 109.1 |
| **Rest of World** | ..... | ..... | ..... | ..... | ..... | ..... | ..... | ..... | 0.6 | ..... |

## Table E-3.  Metropolitan Area Exports of Goods by Destination, 1993–1997—*Continued*

(Millions of dollars.)

| Destination | 1993 | 1994 | 1995 | 1996 | 1997 | 1993 | 1994 | 1995 | 1996 | 1997 |
|---|---|---|---|---|---|---|---|---|---|---|
| | Colorado Springs, CO | | | | | Columbus, OH | | | | |
| **ALL DESTINATIONS** | 664.3 | 900.7 | 954.7 | 857.0 | 1 006.0 | 1 167.0 | 1 295.5 | 1 358.2 | 1 497.2 | 1 660.7 |
| **North America** | 144.7 | 84.6 | 113.2 | 70.5 | 115.8 | 560.0 | 635.1 | 699.9 | 766.0 | 838.1 |
| Canada | 139.4 | 77.0 | 110.5 | 63.6 | 60.6 | 516.8 | 570.2 | 629.0 | 692.1 | 757.3 |
| Mexico | 5.2 | 7.6 | 2.8 | 6.9 | 55.2 | 43.2 | 64.9 | 71.0 | 74.0 | 80.8 |
| **Caribbean and Central America** | 0.9 | 0.7 | 1.7 | 1.2 | 1.4 | 10.9 | 14.4 | 13.8 | 13.9 | 16.5 |
| **South America** | 2.8 | 3.2 | 5.1 | 7.2 | 6.7 | 58.4 | 48.2 | 47.2 | 38.3 | 57.6 |
| Argentina | 0.2 | 0.6 | 0.9 | 0.4 | 0.3 | 7.1 | 5.1 | 4.8 | 5.5 | 6.3 |
| Brazil | 1.1 | 1.4 | 1.3 | 2.3 | 3.8 | 15.4 | 20.8 | 24.3 | 13.8 | 22.9 |
| Other South America | 1.5 | 1.2 | 2.8 | 4.6 | 2.6 | 35.8 | 22.2 | 18.1 | 19.0 | 28.4 |
| **Europe** | 274.1 | 376.8 | 416.5 | 336.6 | 380.1 | 265.8 | 305.0 | 313.1 | 300.7 | 357.3 |
| Belgium | 3.1 | 2.3 | 3.5 | 4.2 | 2.4 | 14.8 | 12.4 | 12.4 | 19.8 | 32.0 |
| France | 19.2 | 21.6 | 20.5 | 17.7 | 22.0 | 13.5 | 12.9 | 15.0 | 14.0 | 18.4 |
| Germany | 80.6 | 39.0 | 56.4 | 57.3 | 58.6 | 65.1 | 84.0 | 77.5 | 63.8 | 44.6 |
| Netherlands | 50.2 | 115.3 | 100.6 | 76.9 | 41.1 | 12.4 | 11.1 | 16.8 | 36.9 | 37.4 |
| United Kingdom | 66.3 | 121.8 | 138.1 | 70.9 | 75.3 | 52.4 | 52.1 | 67.7 | 61.0 | 70.6 |
| Turkey | 0.2 | ..... | 0.4 | 0.3 | 0.5 | 0.4 | 0.5 | 1.2 | 1.4 | 2.2 |
| Former Soviet Republics | 1.7 | 0.1 | 0.6 | 0.2 | 0.5 | 4.0 | 1.0 | 2.3 | 1.4 | 1.7 |
| Poland | ..... | 0.2 | 0.3 | 1.2 | 0.5 | 0.2 | 0.4 | 1.7 | 0.4 | 1.8 |
| Other Eastern Europe | ..... | 1.3 | 1.6 | 1.1 | 1.3 | 3.2 | 4.2 | 2.5 | 2.4 | 2.4 |
| Other Europe | 52.9 | 75.2 | 94.7 | 106.8 | 177.8 | 99.8 | 126.6 | 116.1 | 99.8 | 146.3 |
| **Asia** | 226.5 | 422.3 | 404.4 | 426.4 | 482.6 | 219.3 | 244.4 | 233.6 | 315.7 | 328.3 |
| Japan | 111.3 | 153.8 | 178.1 | 185.7 | 157.2 | 80.2 | 89.3 | 70.9 | 116.3 | 113.2 |
| China | 0.4 | 0.7 | 1.5 | 6.3 | 13.7 | 5.7 | 9.4 | 18.0 | 10.6 | 10.8 |
| Hong Kong | 30.1 | 89.7 | 59.9 | 47.9 | 75.4 | 18.7 | 11.7 | 18.2 | 21.9 | 21.9 |
| Taiwan | 9.6 | 26.7 | 23.8 | 36.2 | 43.9 | 21.1 | 37.6 | 40.9 | 61.0 | 82.2 |
| Singapore | 21.2 | 61.8 | 50.7 | 36.1 | 34.7 | 18.1 | 9.5 | 11.6 | 22.8 | 18.1 |
| South Korea | 24.9 | 33.6 | 38.9 | 51.2 | 75.2 | 53.4 | 47.7 | 43.4 | 51.7 | 45.2 |
| Indonesia | 0.1 | 0.1 | 11.6 | 0.3 | 0.2 | 0.9 | 7.1 | 0.3 | 1.2 | 3.2 |
| India | 0.1 | 0.2 | 1.0 | 0.9 | 0.4 | 5.9 | 8.8 | 10.0 | 7.4 | 7.2 |
| Other Asia | 28.8 | 55.7 | 39.0 | 61.9 | 81.9 | 15.3 | 23.3 | 20.2 | 22.7 | 26.4 |
| **Africa** | 3.0 | 2.8 | 1.8 | 1.4 | 1.7 | 9.2 | 8.1 | 6.6 | 10.7 | 9.0 |
| North Africa | 0.1 | 0.1 | 0.1 | 0.2 | 0.5 | 1.2 | 2.5 | 1.3 | 4.1 | 2.3 |
| Republic of South Africa | 2.0 | 2.3 | 0.5 | 0.7 | 0.8 | 5.2 | 2.9 | 3.7 | 5.7 | 4.4 |
| Other Subsaharan Africa | 0.9 | 0.4 | 1.2 | 0.5 | 0.4 | 2.8 | 2.7 | 1.6 | 0.9 | 2.3 |
| **Middle East** | 3.3 | 1.6 | 2.9 | 5.4 | 6.3 | 28.8 | 25.6 | 29.4 | 24.6 | 25.2 |
| **Australia** | 9.1 | 8.8 | 9.1 | 8.4 | 11.5 | 14.6 | 14.7 | 14.4 | 27.2 | 28.6 |
| **Rest of World** | ..... | ..... | ..... | ..... | ..... | ..... | ..... | ..... | ..... | ..... |
| | Columbia, SC | | | | | Corpus Christi, TX | | | | |
| **ALL DESTINATIONS** | 212.9 | 300.4 | 343.3 | 310.8 | 328.5 | 186.8 | 153.6 | 162.4 | 241.8 | 387.2 |
| **North America** | 55.0 | 86.6 | 94.4 | 97.7 | 106.6 | 145.9 | 113.0 | 93.1 | 180.0 | 291.3 |
| Canada | 51.5 | 80.6 | 91.7 | 92.1 | 100.2 | 129.1 | 88.6 | 68.7 | 139.6 | 201.6 |
| Mexico | 3.6 | 6.0 | 2.7 | 5.5 | 6.3 | 16.8 | 24.4 | 24.4 | 40.4 | 89.7 |
| **Caribbean and Central America** | 2.4 | 4.9 | 9.4 | 11.7 | 8.7 | 3.5 | 0.9 | 0.8 | 0.7 | 1.0 |
| **South America** | 15.3 | 8.9 | 12.4 | 11.8 | 17.4 | 8.5 | 5.2 | 5.4 | 7.1 | 5.3 |
| Argentina | 12.3 | 1.7 | 4.0 | 1.2 | 1.9 | 0.2 | 3.8 | 0.5 | 1.1 | 0.2 |
| Brazil | 0.9 | 2.9 | 5.4 | 7.4 | 9.8 | 0.1 | ..... | 0.2 | 0.2 | 0.2 |
| Other South America | 2.1 | 4.2 | 3.0 | 3.2 | 5.7 | 8.2 | 1.5 | 4.6 | 5.8 | 4.9 |
| **Europe** | 86.1 | 138.8 | 140.9 | 106.6 | 126.3 | 4.9 | 11.8 | 37.1 | 21.9 | 39.4 |
| Belgium | 8.5 | 15.9 | 16.7 | 12.7 | 9.5 | ..... | 1.3 | 0.5 | 0.1 | ..... |
| France | 14.2 | 14.5 | 22.7 | 20.2 | 27.3 | 0.3 | 1.0 | 1.0 | 1.5 | 0.7 |
| Germany | 12.1 | 42.4 | 17.7 | 14.7 | 22.1 | 1.0 | 1.8 | 2.4 | 1.1 | 3.0 |
| Netherlands | 9.6 | 8.9 | 10.6 | 11.3 | 7.5 | 0.1 | 0.1 | 0.1 | ..... | 1.0 |
| United Kingdom | 18.6 | 10.6 | 23.9 | 14.5 | 13.1 | 1.4 | 3.2 | 3.1 | 2.8 | 3.5 |
| Turkey | 0.5 | 0.3 | 0.8 | 0.2 | 0.4 | ..... | ..... | ..... | ..... | ..... |
| Former Soviet Republics | 0.2 | 0.2 | 0.4 | 2.6 | 0.2 | 1.6 | 4.1 | 29.2 | 14.6 | 20.8 |
| Poland | 0.1 | 0.1 | 0.3 | 0.1 | 0.1 | ..... | ..... | ..... | ..... | |
| Other Eastern Europe | 0.9 | 0.9 | 0.3 | 0.5 | 2.6 | ..... | ..... | 0.2 | 1.2 | ..... |
| Other Europe | 21.4 | 45.0 | 47.5 | 29.9 | 43.6 | 0.4 | 0.5 | 0.5 | 0.5 | 10.2 |
| **Asia** | 42.5 | 51.8 | 71.5 | 66.5 | 57.7 | 10.2 | 10.0 | 21.9 | 29.1 | 42.0 |
| Japan | 10.2 | 11.1 | 16.3 | 26.2 | 20.6 | 1.1 | 1.9 | 3.7 | 2.8 | 10.1 |
| China | 0.4 | 0.9 | 9.2 | 0.4 | 0.6 | 6.0 | 3.7 | 0.3 | 1.0 | 14.5 |
| Hong Kong | 5.4 | 9.9 | 7.1 | 3.7 | 10.2 | 0.1 | 0.3 | 2.3 | 1.1 | 0.4 |
| Taiwan | 1.1 | 2.5 | 6.8 | 16.6 | 6.9 | 0.5 | 0.7 | 4.8 | 7.2 | 2.7 |
| Singapore | 0.7 | 0.4 | 0.8 | 1.4 | 1.3 | 1.1 | 1.7 | 5.8 | 4.6 | 3.7 |
| South Korea | 20.9 | 24.2 | 25.2 | 14.0 | 15.2 | 0.1 | 0.1 | 0.2 | 0.5 | 0.5 |
| Indonesia | 0.6 | 0.3 | 0.1 | 0.1 | 0.1 | 0.6 | ..... | 0.1 | 1.3 | 0.7 |
| India | 1.4 | 0.7 | 3.6 | 2.1 | 1.2 | 0.3 | 0.1 | 0.9 | 0.1 | ..... |
| Other Asia | 2.0 | 1.8 | 2.4 | 2.1 | 1.7 | 0.3 | 1.5 | 3.8 | 10.5 | 9.4 |
| **Africa** | 1.2 | 0.9 | 1.2 | 2.2 | 1.7 | 0.6 | 0.2 | 0.4 | 0.3 | 2.1 |
| North Africa | 0.1 | 0.1 | ..... | ..... | 0.4 | 0.3 | 0.1 | 0.1 | ..... | 0.3 |
| Republic of South Africa | 1.0 | 0.7 | 0.6 | 2.1 | 1.0 | 0.1 | 0.1 | 0.2 | 0.2 | 0.1 |
| Other Subsaharan Africa | 0.1 | 0.1 | 0.6 | 0.1 | 0.3 | 0.1 | ..... | 0.1 | ..... | 1.7 |
| **Middle East** | 6.7 | 6.1 | 9.9 | 10.2 | 6.6 | 12.7 | 11.6 | 3.4 | 1.6 | 2.4 |
| **Australia** | 3.8 | 2.3 | 3.5 | 4.3 | 3.6 | 0.5 | 0.8 | 0.3 | 1.1 | 3.7 |
| **Rest of World** | ..... | ..... | ..... | ..... | ..... | ..... | ..... | ..... | ..... | ..... |

## Table E-3. Metropolitan Area Exports of Goods by Destination, 1993–1997—*Continued*

(Millions of dollars.)

| Destination | 1993 | 1994 | 1995 | 1996 | 1997 | 1993 | 1994 | 1995 | 1996 | 1997 |
|---|---|---|---|---|---|---|---|---|---|---|
| | Dallas, TX | | | | | Danbury, CT | | | | |
| **ALL DESTINATIONS** | 4 817.6 | 5 679.7 | 6 870.4 | 7 096.9 | 8 645.9 | 316.7 | 393.0 | 421.6 | 531.9 | 482.9 |
| **North America** | 1 139.7 | 1 485.9 | 1 559.7 | 1 692.1 | 2 282.9 | 97.1 | 93.6 | 98.6 | 97.2 | 107.6 |
| Canada | 621.3 | 773.0 | 847.9 | 996.6 | 1 309.6 | 92.0 | 85.5 | 94.6 | 94.0 | 102.9 |
| Mexico | 518.4 | 713.0 | 711.7 | 695.5 | 973.3 | 5.0 | 8.1 | 4.0 | 3.3 | 4.7 |
| **Caribbean and Central America** | 118.8 | 150.2 | 147.0 | 139.3 | 293.0 | 3.9 | 3.4 | 3.7 | 5.1 | 5.8 |
| **South America** | 258.8 | 377.4 | 447.0 | 418.8 | 471.4 | 38.5 | 36.8 | 38.4 | 46.1 | 60.5 |
| Argentina | 29.1 | 49.7 | 71.0 | 76.6 | 68.9 | 16.3 | 11.0 | 11.2 | 11.5 | 13.8 |
| Brazil | 44.0 | 69.1 | 117.0 | 130.9 | 142.1 | 3.4 | 5.6 | 10.5 | 11.5 | 18.2 |
| Other South America | 185.7 | 258.6 | 258.9 | 211.3 | 260.4 | 18.8 | 20.2 | 16.7 | 23.1 | 28.6 |
| **Europe** | 1 035.1 | 1 062.0 | 1 227.9 | 1 368.5 | 1 611.3 | 57.7 | 82.2 | 85.1 | 137.1 | 91.6 |
| Belgium | 41.2 | 37.6 | 39.8 | 52.3 | 83.2 | 2.0 | 7.5 | 11.4 | 7.4 | 6.6 |
| France | 119.4 | 114.3 | 105.2 | 114.5 | 137.0 | 5.7 | 6.2 | 6.1 | 13.7 | 7.5 |
| Germany | 250.5 | 209.5 | 257.7 | 257.9 | 283.2 | 12.9 | 11.0 | 17.2 | 23.3 | 17.9 |
| Netherlands | 127.2 | 163.8 | 227.1 | 219.7 | 234.1 | 5.8 | 5.1 | 8.6 | 17.5 | 10.5 |
| United Kingdom | 190.1 | 231.8 | 245.1 | 287.2 | 324.7 | 13.9 | 14.3 | 18.7 | 35.8 | 24.4 |
| Turkey | 34.5 | 52.0 | 59.3 | 69.5 | 103.8 | 0.3 | 0.1 | 0.5 | 1.2 | 1.2 |
| Former Soviet Republics | 27.1 | 11.8 | 12.3 | 29.5 | 29.6 | 0.2 | 0.2 | 1.9 | 3.5 | 2.6 |
| Poland | 4.0 | 2.6 | 6.4 | 8.5 | 7.5 | 0.4 | 1.5 | 1.3 | 1.9 | 1.4 |
| Other Eastern Europe | 6.6 | 9.5 | 13.0 | 14.3 | 21.4 | 0.3 | 0.2 | 0.2 | 0.9 | 0.7 |
| Other Europe | 234.5 | 229.2 | 262.0 | 315.2 | 386.8 | 16.1 | 36.0 | 19.2 | 31.9 | 18.8 |
| **Asia** | 1 863.8 | 2 290.7 | 3 066.6 | 3 019.6 | 3 530.5 | 88.6 | 139.4 | 164.1 | 185.7 | 186.9 |
| Japan | 434.4 | 496.7 | 715.4 | 677.5 | 901.5 | 35.4 | 61.0 | 76.4 | 79.1 | 40.1 |
| China | 43.4 | 109.4 | 163.6 | 123.4 | 100.7 | 6.8 | 3.3 | 4.9 | 3.0 | 12.5 |
| Hong Kong | 83.4 | 100.2 | 145.7 | 179.7 | 159.3 | 25.8 | 36.5 | 30.7 | 33.3 | 40.8 |
| Taiwan | 347.7 | 396.6 | 478.0 | 422.5 | 469.5 | 3.1 | 4.4 | 11.6 | 10.7 | 10.2 |
| Singapore | 249.4 | 246.1 | 381.8 | 309.9 | 437.5 | 4.4 | 13.0 | 12.6 | 10.0 | 7.2 |
| South Korea | 180.1 | 225.5 | 283.8 | 279.6 | 271.7 | 4.3 | 7.0 | 8.8 | 24.0 | 58.8 |
| Indonesia | 49.3 | 59.6 | 85.6 | 85.3 | 65.6 | 4.4 | 5.7 | 7.7 | 8.0 | 5.4 |
| India | 35.6 | 50.7 | 46.1 | 49.9 | 51.0 | 0.9 | 1.3 | 2.0 | 5.3 | 2.7 |
| Other Asia | 440.7 | 605.9 | 766.5 | 891.8 | 1 073.8 | 3.5 | 7.0 | 9.4 | 12.3 | 9.2 |
| **Africa** | 86.6 | 77.1 | 101.7 | 107.0 | 152.5 | 3.4 | 9.2 | 4.1 | 6.8 | 4.8 |
| North Africa | 35.2 | 26.3 | 36.6 | 43.0 | 41.8 | 2.3 | 2.5 | 0.9 | 0.9 | 0.5 |
| Republic of South Africa | 30.4 | 34.4 | 44.6 | 39.4 | 49.8 | 0.4 | 0.6 | 0.8 | 2.4 | 1.4 |
| Other Subsaharan Africa | 21.1 | 16.4 | 20.6 | 24.6 | 61.0 | 0.8 | 6.1 | 2.4 | 3.5 | 2.9 |
| **Middle East** | 222.0 | 149.7 | 161.3 | 206.4 | 192.7 | 15.2 | 11.9 | 11.7 | 40.8 | 9.4 |
| **Australia** | 92.5 | 86.6 | 159.2 | 145.1 | 111.4 | 12.3 | 16.5 | 15.8 | 13.0 | 16.3 |
| **Rest of World** | 0.2 | ..... | ..... | ..... | 0.1 | ..... | ..... | ..... | ..... | ..... |
| | Davenport - Moline - Rock Island, IA-IL | | | | | Daytona Beach, FL | | | | |
| **ALL DESTINATIONS** | 1 102.6 | 1 098.9 | 1 291.0 | 1 576.1 | 1 933.9 | 140.5 | 110.3 | 85.9 | 111.7 | 137.5 |
| **North America** | 440.5 | 332.9 | 328.3 | 455.4 | 609.9 | 39.5 | 26.1 | 17.3 | 24.5 | 36.7 |
| Canada | 390.4 | 270.6 | 299.9 | 393.4 | 511.7 | 20.4 | 15.4 | 15.5 | 23.7 | 33.9 |
| Mexico | 50.1 | 62.3 | 28.4 | 62.0 | 98.2 | 19.1 | 10.7 | 1.8 | 0.8 | 2.9 |
| **Caribbean and Central America** | 19.4 | 23.2 | 23.8 | 24.8 | 27.5 | 4.8 | 6.5 | 6.3 | 7.5 | 10.3 |
| **South America** | 71.7 | 102.3 | 98.4 | 141.2 | 203.4 | 6.5 | 3.4 | 6.9 | 4.8 | 4.9 |
| Argentina | 22.5 | 46.0 | 40.7 | 62.3 | 74.7 | 0.2 | 0.8 | 1.4 | 0.4 | 2.1 |
| Brazil | 3.6 | 12.1 | 15.3 | 15.1 | 46.8 | 4.6 | 0.7 | 2.3 | 2.1 | 0.7 |
| Other South America | 45.6 | 44.1 | 42.5 | 63.9 | 81.9 | 1.6 | 1.9 | 3.3 | 2.3 | 2.1 |
| **Europe** | 353.4 | 397.2 | 523.0 | 598.5 | 663.9 | 44.3 | 47.8 | 34.1 | 43.1 | 46.3 |
| Belgium | 6.7 | 9.1 | 12.9 | 11.9 | 8.9 | 2.7 | 1.1 | 1.3 | 3.5 | 2.1 |
| France | 68.5 | 69.6 | 99.5 | 92.5 | 95.1 | 1.0 | 2.6 | 2.2 | 1.3 | 5.3 |
| Germany | 173.8 | 166.5 | 218.6 | 234.2 | 230.8 | 23.0 | 9.2 | 9.5 | 10.2 | 10.1 |
| Netherlands | 11.0 | 19.5 | 27.0 | 22.7 | 29.0 | 5.7 | 9.3 | 8.3 | 10.0 | 9.2 |
| United Kingdom | 36.9 | 34.6 | 55.3 | 48.9 | 54.5 | 5.3 | 5.1 | 3.9 | 9.2 | 10.4 |
| Turkey | 0.1 | 0.1 | 0.2 | ..... | 1.0 | ..... | ..... | 0.1 | ..... | ..... |
| Former Soviet Republics | 4.8 | 26.7 | 0.9 | 43.8 | 93.1 | 0.3 | 0.1 | 0.4 | 0.5 | 0.1 |
| Poland | ..... | 0.4 | ..... | 0.8 | 3.2 | 0.1 | ..... | ..... | ..... | 0.1 |
| Other Eastern Europe | 4.2 | 12.2 | 25.5 | 30.8 | 34.8 | 0.3 | 0.3 | 0.2 | 0.2 | 0.1 |
| Other Europe | 47.4 | 58.6 | 83.1 | 112.9 | 113.6 | 5.9 | 20.1 | 8.3 | 8.0 | 8.9 |
| **Asia** | 91.7 | 118.1 | 176.3 | 158.6 | 162.0 | 34.3 | 18.9 | 14.3 | 21.7 | 30.4 |
| Japan | 33.1 | 51.4 | 73.6 | 61.8 | 62.3 | 2.2 | 4.7 | 3.2 | 3.2 | 4.7 |
| China | 6.4 | 3.8 | 4.0 | 3.8 | 5.1 | 0.2 | 0.4 | ..... | 0.6 | 0.2 |
| Hong Kong | 6.0 | 6.5 | 5.9 | 6.7 | 7.9 | 0.4 | 0.9 | 0.7 | 1.1 | 2.1 |
| Taiwan | 6.5 | 6.7 | 10.5 | 8.7 | 9.3 | 8.2 | 2.5 | 3.7 | 5.6 | 6.6 |
| Singapore | 6.9 | 7.9 | 8.6 | 7.4 | 9.9 | 19.9 | 1.7 | 0.6 | 1.0 | 1.7 |
| South Korea | 5.9 | 15.0 | 34.7 | 27.1 | 27.3 | 1.7 | 1.8 | 2.1 | 4.2 | 5.9 |
| Indonesia | 2.3 | 3.8 | 3.9 | 3.5 | 5.0 | 0.2 | 0.4 | 0.3 | 0.5 | 3.7 |
| India | 0.7 | 0.6 | 1.7 | 0.8 | 0.7 | 0.4 | 1.4 | 2.0 | 2.1 | 1.8 |
| Other Asia | 23.9 | 22.4 | 33.5 | 38.8 | 34.7 | 1.3 | 5.1 | 1.8 | 3.3 | 3.7 |
| **Africa** | 23.0 | 32.4 | 32.9 | 38.9 | 49.5 | 1.1 | 1.2 | 0.4 | 0.5 | 0.6 |
| North Africa | 1.4 | 2.1 | 2.7 | 4.0 | 2.8 | 0.8 | 0.9 | ..... | 0.1 | ..... |
| Republic of South Africa | 19.7 | 29.4 | 29.8 | 34.2 | 46.2 | 0.3 | 0.3 | 0.3 | 0.3 | 0.3 |
| Other Subsaharan Africa | 1.9 | 0.9 | 0.3 | 0.7 | 0.5 | ..... | ..... | 0.1 | 0.1 | 0.2 |
| **Middle East** | 28.1 | 7.6 | 11.8 | 14.0 | 14.5 | 9.5 | 5.1 | 5.4 | 8.4 | 6.9 |
| **Australia** | 74.8 | 85.1 | 96.4 | 144.7 | 203.2 | 0.4 | 1.3 | 0.9 | 1.2 | 1.4 |
| **Rest of World** | ..... | ..... | ..... | ..... | ..... | ..... | ..... | ..... | ..... | ..... |

## Table E-3.  Metropolitan Area Exports of Goods by Destination, 1993–1997—Continued

(Millions of dollars.)

| Destination | 1993 | 1994 | 1995 | 1996 | 1997 | 1993 | 1994 | 1995 | 1996 | 1997 |
|---|---|---|---|---|---|---|---|---|---|---|
| | Dayton - Springfield, OH | | | | | Denver, CO | | | | |
| ALL DESTINATIONS | 2 479.9 | 2 671.3 | 2 404.8 | 2 201.5 | 2 271.5 | 931.0 | 1 089.8 | 1 385.3 | 1 502.9 | 1 738.1 |
| North America | 1 852.5 | 2 019.7 | 1 594.5 | 1 403.1 | 1 437.6 | 260.5 | 231.0 | 261.5 | 329.9 | 337.6 |
| Canada | 1 633.0 | 1 845.3 | 1 473.8 | 1 272.7 | 1 310.6 | 160.7 | 166.2 | 190.8 | 254.5 | 268.7 |
| Mexico | 219.5 | 174.4 | 120.7 | 130.4 | 127.0 | 99.8 | 64.8 | 70.7 | 75.3 | 68.9 |
| Caribbean and Central America | 8.9 | 7.3 | 7.6 | 6.0 | 10.5 | 11.4 | 13.7 | 14.7 | 12.3 | 12.9 |
| South America | 35.8 | 30.6 | 37.5 | 33.6 | 41.3 | 42.1 | 61.6 | 67.4 | 65.6 | 89.9 |
| Argentina | 3.2 | 3.9 | 4.3 | 6.4 | 6.9 | 9.6 | 11.3 | 8.7 | 9.4 | 9.6 |
| Brazil | 12.1 | 9.5 | 20.5 | 12.4 | 18.4 | 5.9 | 14.1 | 21.9 | 16.0 | 37.6 |
| Other South America | 20.5 | 17.2 | 12.8 | 14.9 | 16.0 | 26.7 | 36.3 | 36.8 | 40.2 | 42.6 |
| Europe | 369.5 | 368.6 | 452.5 | 456.9 | 479.8 | 288.7 | 362.3 | 448.0 | 474.3 | 639.3 |
| Belgium | 12.8 | 11.6 | 17.8 | 19.8 | 19.5 | 80.8 | 92.4 | 60.9 | 68.2 | 68.8 |
| France | 53.9 | 43.7 | 47.6 | 46.4 | 58.3 | 19.7 | 23.1 | 33.1 | 32.2 | 67.2 |
| Germany | 73.7 | 77.5 | 86.3 | 84.5 | 89.5 | 33.2 | 38.2 | 71.1 | 68.6 | 64.3 |
| Netherlands | 27.1 | 26.9 | 31.5 | 26.0 | 26.9 | 16.6 | 28.0 | 58.0 | 57.7 | 96.7 |
| United Kingdom | 95.4 | 86.1 | 102.3 | 105.0 | 111.0 | 41.1 | 60.8 | 78.6 | 73.7 | 73.7 |
| Turkey | 7.6 | 9.4 | 5.7 | 5.3 | 10.1 | 1.4 | 1.9 | 3.2 | 3.1 | 3.6 |
| Former Soviet Republics | 1.1 | 0.7 | 2.2 | 1.1 | 2.6 | 23.7 | 26.9 | 25.1 | 44.2 | 85.5 |
| Poland | 1.4 | 0.4 | 0.8 | 1.0 | 2.5 | 2.2 | 3.6 | 2.7 | 3.0 | 2.8 |
| Other Eastern Europe | 0.7 | 2.0 | 1.8 | 1.6 | 2.3 | 5.8 | 7.3 | 13.9 | 7.2 | 4.7 |
| Other Europe | 95.8 | 110.5 | 156.5 | 166.2 | 157.0 | 64.1 | 80.2 | 101.4 | 116.5 | 172.1 |
| Asia | 141.4 | 163.7 | 218.4 | 228.7 | 229.6 | 247.2 | 329.8 | 483.3 | 505.5 | 572.3 |
| Japan | 63.6 | 65.2 | 87.2 | 110.2 | 99.3 | 113.4 | 136.0 | 240.2 | 266.2 | 304.0 |
| China | 13.0 | 8.7 | 15.5 | 13.7 | 19.3 | 6.1 | 14.5 | 12.6 | 25.5 | 10.9 |
| Hong Kong | 11.7 | 12.7 | 16.5 | 14.2 | 13.2 | 19.5 | 24.2 | 58.7 | 37.0 | 45.9 |
| Taiwan | 13.5 | 22.5 | 20.0 | 12.4 | 16.2 | 21.8 | 32.3 | 22.3 | 17.1 | 22.8 |
| Singapore | 8.8 | 14.2 | 16.1 | 15.0 | 10.4 | 24.6 | 30.1 | 32.5 | 48.6 | 58.9 |
| South Korea | 10.4 | 18.4 | 26.5 | 25.8 | 24.0 | 41.5 | 32.4 | 40.9 | 39.9 | 58.7 |
| Indonesia | 0.4 | 1.0 | 2.1 | 4.0 | 2.6 | 1.4 | 2.3 | 4.4 | 1.7 | 10.8 |
| India | 1.4 | 2.3 | 6.9 | 3.9 | 5.4 | 3.6 | 3.7 | 6.7 | 12.8 | 12.0 |
| Other Asia | 18.5 | 18.7 | 27.7 | 29.5 | 39.2 | 15.2 | 54.3 | 65.0 | 56.9 | 48.3 |
| Africa | 17.5 | 19.1 | 20.2 | 24.5 | 15.6 | 14.5 | 22.9 | 28.2 | 33.9 | 21.8 |
| North Africa | 11.2 | 7.0 | 7.8 | 9.0 | 4.6 | 2.1 | 10.6 | 14.4 | 25.6 | 7.3 |
| Republic of South Africa | 5.0 | 10.9 | 10.6 | 13.2 | 9.7 | 10.4 | 7.8 | 8.0 | 5.9 | 9.8 |
| Other Subsaharan Africa | 1.3 | 1.2 | 1.9 | 2.2 | 1.3 | 1.9 | 4.4 | 5.8 | 2.4 | 4.6 |
| Middle East | 19.8 | 21.0 | 31.5 | 26.8 | 27.4 | 29.5 | 30.4 | 34.7 | 39.4 | 22.3 |
| Australia | 34.6 | 41.3 | 42.5 | 21.9 | 29.7 | 37.1 | 37.8 | 47.5 | 41.9 | 42.0 |
| Rest of World | ..... | ..... | ..... | ..... | ..... | ..... | 0.2 | ..... | ..... | ..... |
| | Detroit, MI | | | | | Elkhart - Goshen, IN | | | | |
| ALL DESTINATIONS | 16 780.9 | 27 469.7 | 27 314.7 | 27 531.2 | 25 967.4 | 419.9 | 460.4 | 501.5 | 367.5 | 414.7 |
| North America | 11 332.8 | 21 734.2 | 20 821.2 | 19 963.9 | 18 434.6 | 203.6 | 239.2 | 234.6 | 225.8 | 269.1 |
| Canada | 6 085.5 | 15 214.8 | 16 351.4 | 15 995.5 | 12 907.4 | 198.6 | 231.0 | 230.6 | 218.3 | 254.5 |
| Mexico | 5 247.3 | 6 519.5 | 4 469.8 | 3 968.4 | 5 527.2 | 5.0 | 8.2 | 4.0 | 7.5 | 14.5 |
| Caribbean and Central America | 50.8 | 63.1 | 87.7 | 83.0 | 85.0 | 3.3 | 2.5 | 3.3 | 3.4 | 4.9 |
| South America | 413.0 | 449.0 | 633.1 | 763.6 | 1 120.7 | 8.6 | 13.6 | 13.2 | 13.3 | 17.3 |
| Argentina | 9.5 | 26.7 | 24.1 | 67.1 | 97.3 | 2.3 | 4.1 | 3.3 | 4.0 | 4.2 |
| Brazil | 125.1 | 218.8 | 330.9 | 317.0 | 394.1 | 0.9 | 1.3 | 3.1 | 3.6 | 6.7 |
| Other South America | 278.5 | 203.5 | 278.0 | 379.5 | 629.3 | 5.4 | 8.3 | 6.8 | 5.7 | 6.4 |
| Europe | 2 342.1 | 2 691.7 | 3 244.7 | 3 229.9 | 3 634.7 | 125.3 | 120.6 | 170.4 | 49.8 | 57.8 |
| Belgium | 296.9 | 413.0 | 438.6 | 431.3 | 893.5 | 4.7 | 3.3 | 19.3 | 0.5 | 0.6 |
| France | 162.0 | 147.3 | 168.7 | 158.3 | 171.5 | 7.8 | 9.0 | 5.1 | 4.7 | 4.6 |
| Germany | 716.8 | 690.6 | 819.8 | 756.4 | 748.5 | 19.7 | 17.1 | 24.4 | 12.6 | 12.1 |
| Netherlands | 73.6 | 85.8 | 96.4 | 103.2 | 112.2 | 4.0 | 4.3 | 8.4 | 3.8 | 6.0 |
| United Kingdom | 236.2 | 436.9 | 282.3 | 331.3 | 365.2 | 44.4 | 59.4 | 92.9 | 12.4 | 12.9 |
| Turkey | 20.3 | 46.0 | 16.0 | 20.9 | 24.4 | 0.6 | 0.6 | 0.7 | 1.7 | 2.4 |
| Former Soviet Republics | 28.0 | 57.8 | 66.3 | 62.6 | 86.0 | 7.3 | 0.1 | 0.4 | 0.5 | 0.5 |
| Poland | 3.0 | 3.8 | 19.7 | 14.8 | 3.4 | 0.1 | 0.7 | 2.6 | 2.4 | 1.8 |
| Other Eastern Europe | 14.5 | 21.5 | 30.7 | 53.2 | 75.4 | 0.2 | 0.7 | 1.0 | 1.7 | 2.1 |
| Other Europe | 790.7 | 789.0 | 1 306.2 | 1 297.7 | 1 154.5 | 36.5 | 25.4 | 15.6 | 9.7 | 14.8 |
| Asia | 1 149.4 | 1 220.2 | 1 309.8 | 1 635.3 | 1 397.4 | 56.4 | 61.0 | 59.0 | 58.3 | 47.6 |
| Japan | 502.9 | 661.4 | 750.6 | 1 031.7 | 599.0 | 30.9 | 31.9 | 23.2 | 19.8 | 15.4 |
| China | 161.6 | 96.2 | 74.4 | 92.2 | 289.1 | 1.2 | 1.6 | 2.7 | 1.2 | 2.0 |
| Hong Kong | 57.9 | 45.9 | 37.2 | 51.7 | 44.2 | 4.1 | 4.7 | 6.9 | 9.6 | 7.0 |
| Taiwan | 172.2 | 132.5 | 110.3 | 67.8 | 78.7 | 6.1 | 5.1 | 3.4 | 2.7 | 2.4 |
| Singapore | 42.9 | 35.6 | 59.1 | 45.4 | 51.4 | 4.0 | 4.7 | 4.2 | 4.8 | 2.9 |
| South Korea | 72.2 | 104.6 | 135.4 | 145.9 | 133.1 | 4.0 | 6.0 | 7.7 | 9.7 | 7.0 |
| Indonesia | 5.5 | 17.8 | 15.1 | 22.7 | 21.4 | 0.4 | 0.5 | 0.4 | 0.7 | 0.7 |
| India | 14.6 | 10.3 | 30.7 | 29.4 | 25.5 | 0.7 | 1.5 | 3.6 | 1.0 | 1.2 |
| Other Asia | 119.5 | 116.0 | 97.0 | 148.5 | 155.0 | 5.1 | 4.9 | 6.8 | 8.8 | 9.0 |
| Africa | 32.4 | 33.5 | 38.4 | 67.2 | 55.8 | 2.6 | 1.5 | 2.5 | 4.5 | 2.5 |
| North Africa | 9.8 | 14.1 | 16.8 | 36.3 | 33.2 | 0.6 | 0.4 | 0.7 | 1.4 | 1.0 |
| Republic of South Africa | 7.3 | 15.2 | 16.6 | 18.4 | 13.5 | 1.8 | 1.0 | 1.5 | 1.7 | 1.1 |
| Other Subsaharan Africa | 15.3 | 4.2 | 4.9 | 12.5 | 9.0 | 0.2 | ..... | 0.3 | 1.4 | 0.4 |
| Middle East | 1 322.9 | 1 124.9 | 950.4 | 1 421.1 | 909.4 | 7.9 | 8.4 | 8.4 | 5.8 | 7.6 |
| Australia | 137.6 | 152.9 | 224.4 | 367.2 | 329.9 | 12.2 | 13.7 | 10.1 | 6.7 | 7.9 |
| Rest of World | ..... | 0.1 | 5.1 | ..... | ..... | ..... | ..... | ..... | ..... | ..... |

## Table E-3. Metropolitan Area Exports of Goods by Destination, 1993–1997—*Continued*

(Millions of dollars.)

| Destination | 1993 | 1994 | 1995 | 1996 | 1997 | 1993 | 1994 | 1995 | 1996 | 1997 |
|---|---|---|---|---|---|---|---|---|---|---|
| | Elmira, NY | | | | | El Paso, TX | | | | |
| **ALL DESTINATIONS** | 70.2 | 116.8 | 139.5 | 196.9 | 241.8 | 2 967.0 | 3 561.3 | 4 120.8 | 5 212.7 | 5 833.9 |
| **North America** | 24.6 | 32.8 | 38.0 | 39.6 | 34.3 | 2 773.6 | 3 307.8 | 3 732.6 | 4 882.1 | 5 435.8 |
| Canada | 23.5 | 27.5 | 37.6 | 38.7 | 32.8 | 201.9 | 396.7 | 558.1 | 509.8 | 663.8 |
| Mexico | 1.1 | 5.4 | 0.4 | 0.9 | 1.5 | 2 571.7 | 2 911.1 | 3 174.5 | 4 372.2 | 4 772.0 |
| **Caribbean and Central America** | 0.4 | 1.1 | 1.0 | 0.8 | 2.7 | 16.2 | 25.1 | 24.7 | 24.7 | 17.8 |
| **South America** | 6.0 | 6.2 | 4.9 | 4.2 | 8.9 | 4.6 | 7.1 | 19.4 | 17.6 | 79.3 |
| Argentina | 1.1 | 1.5 | 0.7 | 0.5 | 1.4 | 0.5 | 2.4 | 2.8 | 5.8 | 5.1 |
| Brazil | 2.6 | 3.0 | 2.8 | 2.2 | 4.3 | 0.8 | 1.6 | 4.8 | 4.5 | 4.9 |
| Other South America | 2.3 | 1.6 | 1.3 | 1.5 | 3.2 | 3.4 | 3.2 | 11.8 | 7.3 | 69.4 |
| **Europe** | 18.7 | 33.2 | 39.5 | 49.7 | 57.4 | 88.2 | 106.8 | 131.0 | 131.5 | 157.0 |
| Belgium | 1.4 | ..... | 1.0 | 1.9 | 4.6 | 2.5 | 5.9 | 7.0 | 4.5 | 6.9 |
| France | 1.9 | 2.6 | 7.4 | 11.5 | 7.9 | 6.9 | 9.3 | 13.3 | 15.7 | 18.1 |
| Germany | 2.3 | 4.1 | 4.5 | 5.9 | 9.9 | 20.4 | 22.0 | 16.1 | 20.6 | 18.5 |
| Netherlands | 0.3 | 1.2 | 2.1 | 3.4 | 3.6 | 10.6 | 13.5 | 27.8 | 26.7 | 30.5 |
| United Kingdom | 5.4 | 9.9 | 11.7 | 9.4 | 19.8 | 27.6 | 36.6 | 39.0 | 24.9 | 37.8 |
| Turkey | ..... | 0.1 | 2.6 | 1.0 | 0.3 | 1.4 | 1.4 | 0.8 | 1.7 | 1.8 |
| Former Soviet Republics | ..... | 0.1 | ..... | 0.4 | 0.2 | ..... | 0.1 | 0.2 | 0.1 | ..... |
| Poland | 0.4 | 0.7 | 0.1 | 0.3 | 0.1 | ..... | 0.1 | ..... | ..... | 0.1 |
| Other Eastern Europe | 0.1 | 0.7 | 0.3 | 1.2 | 0.8 | 0.9 | 0.5 | 1.2 | 1.0 | 1.0 |
| Other Europe | 6.8 | 13.9 | 9.9 | 14.8 | 10.3 | 17.9 | 17.5 | 25.7 | 36.0 | 42.4 |
| **Asia** | 17.0 | 37.8 | 48.4 | 92.4 | 125.1 | 76.3 | 103.5 | 202.3 | 148.9 | 131.0 |
| Japan | 1.8 | 12.7 | 26.6 | 52.7 | 67.1 | 10.7 | 17.4 | 29.8 | 24.2 | 27.2 |
| China | 3.2 | 5.6 | 7.9 | 8.2 | 5.4 | 1.4 | 6.1 | 19.3 | 18.2 | 14.4 |
| Hong Kong | 0.5 | 0.4 | 0.4 | 0.2 | 1.9 | 10.1 | 9.4 | 10.3 | 5.5 | 9.0 |
| Taiwan | 0.3 | 0.6 | 1.0 | 1.9 | 4.8 | 6.8 | 7.0 | 9.1 | 63.1 | 11.8 |
| Singapore | 0.3 | 0.3 | 0.7 | 1.3 | 5.6 | 10.1 | 17.4 | 81.6 | 11.7 | 28.5 |
| South Korea | 2.8 | 2.8 | 4.1 | 20.4 | 26.6 | 2.6 | 6.6 | 9.7 | 2.3 | 3.5 |
| Indonesia | 0.8 | 0.4 | 0.1 | 0.1 | 2.4 | 0.6 | 0.9 | 1.5 | 3.4 | 3.4 |
| India | 2.9 | 4.5 | 3.0 | 4.0 | 3.8 | ..... | 0.1 | 10.8 | 0.1 | 0.2 |
| Other Asia | 4.3 | 10.5 | 4.6 | 3.7 | 7.4 | 34.0 | 38.5 | 30.2 | 20.4 | 32.9 |
| **Africa** | 1.6 | 2.1 | 2.5 | 2.3 | 4.5 | 0.7 | 0.5 | 2.0 | 0.8 | 1.1 |
| North Africa | 0.1 | 0.2 | 0.2 | 0.5 | 2.0 | 0.1 | ..... | 0.6 | ..... | 0.1 |
| Republic of South Africa | 1.5 | 1.9 | 2.0 | 1.7 | 2.3 | 0.5 | 0.5 | 1.4 | 0.5 | 0.6 |
| Other Subsaharan Africa | ..... | ..... | 0.2 | 0.1 | 0.1 | 0.1 | 0.1 | ..... | 0.3 | 0.5 |
| **Middle East** | 1.0 | 0.5 | 0.9 | 0.9 | 2.3 | 1.5 | 1.8 | 2.0 | 2.5 | 4.7 |
| **Australia** | 1.0 | 3.0 | 4.4 | 7.1 | 6.7 | 5.8 | 8.6 | 6.6 | 4.5 | 7.3 |
| **Rest of World** | ..... | ..... | ..... | ..... | ..... | ..... | ..... | ..... | ..... | ..... |
| | Erie, PA | | | | | Eugene - Springfield, OR | | | | |
| **ALL DESTINATIONS** | 311.6 | 285.4 | 490.8 | 321.9 | 598.2 | 157.9 | 173.1 | 190.3 | 168.9 | 190.5 |
| **North America** | 195.2 | 174.4 | 304.5 | 175.0 | 386.4 | 67.3 | 76.9 | 85.2 | 69.3 | 79.1 |
| Canada | 182.1 | 166.3 | 298.4 | 161.9 | 380.7 | 65.6 | 71.1 | 73.0 | 66.9 | 75.8 |
| Mexico | 13.1 | 8.1 | 6.1 | 13.1 | 5.6 | 1.7 | 5.8 | 12.2 | 2.5 | 3.3 |
| **Caribbean and Central America** | 3.4 | 2.6 | 2.7 | 1.8 | 2.4 | 0.8 | 0.8 | 0.5 | 0.6 | 1.1 |
| **South America** | 5.5 | 9.0 | 11.1 | 11.4 | 20.4 | 2.2 | 4.1 | 5.6 | 8.2 | 11.3 |
| Argentina | 0.6 | 0.7 | 1.5 | 1.6 | 2.8 | 0.1 | 0.4 | 1.2 | 1.9 | 1.9 |
| Brazil | 2.5 | 4.5 | 5.3 | 4.2 | 12.1 | 1.3 | 1.4 | 2.1 | 3.4 | 5.2 |
| Other South America | 2.4 | 3.7 | 4.2 | 5.6 | 5.5 | 0.8 | 2.3 | 2.4 | 3.0 | 4.1 |
| **Europe** | 45.0 | 38.7 | 72.7 | 62.4 | 59.8 | 34.0 | 41.1 | 43.0 | 43.0 | 52.5 |
| Belgium | 2.0 | 2.6 | 8.0 | 2.8 | 5.4 | 1.8 | 1.6 | 2.2 | 2.2 | 2.0 |
| France | 3.4 | 2.2 | 5.9 | 5.1 | 6.2 | 6.6 | 9.6 | 8.2 | 10.4 | 12.4 |
| Germany | 11.8 | 6.3 | 8.2 | 10.6 | 13.9 | 10.4 | 10.1 | 8.5 | 8.8 | 11.1 |
| Netherlands | 1.8 | 1.1 | 4.3 | 4.7 | 1.3 | 1.7 | 2.9 | 3.8 | 4.2 | 7.8 |
| United Kingdom | 6.4 | 6.3 | 15.6 | 14.0 | 9.3 | 7.0 | 7.6 | 7.1 | 7.6 | 6.5 |
| Turkey | 0.7 | 0.5 | 1.9 | 2.9 | 1.8 | 0.1 | 0.1 | 0.1 | ..... | ..... |
| Former Soviet Republics | ..... | 0.1 | 0.9 | 3.5 | 1.5 | 0.4 | 2.8 | 3.6 | 0.4 | 0.7 |
| Poland | ..... | 0.1 | 0.4 | 0.6 | 0.6 | ..... | ..... | ..... | 0.2 | 0.3 |
| Other Eastern Europe | 0.4 | 1.0 | 0.5 | 0.3 | 0.5 | 0.1 | 0.2 | 0.3 | 0.6 | 0.7 |
| Other Europe | 18.5 | 18.5 | 27.1 | 18.0 | 19.3 | 5.9 | 6.2 | 9.2 | 8.5 | 11.0 |
| **Asia** | 46.8 | 42.2 | 48.3 | 49.0 | 83.4 | 44.6 | 42.7 | 47.4 | 39.1 | 39.4 |
| Japan | 6.6 | 6.6 | 6.5 | 6.8 | 9.8 | 13.6 | 24.0 | 27.4 | 19.9 | 17.5 |
| China | 3.1 | 2.7 | 3.4 | 1.7 | 4.3 | 10.8 | 0.1 | 0.3 | 1.6 | 1.1 |
| Hong Kong | 2.2 | 2.8 | 3.0 | 4.1 | 6.2 | 3.1 | 2.8 | 2.9 | 3.3 | 3.4 |
| Taiwan | 12.3 | 6.8 | 5.9 | 4.1 | 7.7 | 6.2 | 2.5 | 3.0 | 1.1 | 3.0 |
| Singapore | 2.1 | 1.7 | 2.7 | 3.4 | 2.4 | 0.9 | 1.7 | 3.2 | 3.3 | 3.3 |
| South Korea | 12.1 | 12.2 | 11.4 | 10.6 | 15.3 | 5.4 | 7.6 | 5.7 | 3.9 | 4.7 |
| Indonesia | 0.5 | 0.6 | 1.4 | 2.5 | 7.0 | 0.3 | 0.6 | 0.1 | 0.3 | 0.8 |
| India | 4.0 | 1.8 | 2.5 | 2.7 | 2.0 | 0.2 | ..... | ..... | ..... | 0.1 |
| Other Asia | 3.9 | 7.2 | 11.5 | 13.0 | 28.7 | 4.1 | 3.3 | 4.7 | 5.7 | 5.6 |
| **Africa** | 3.7 | 5.2 | 27.7 | 6.3 | 25.7 | 0.4 | 0.4 | 0.5 | 0.6 | 1.4 |
| North Africa | 0.3 | 0.5 | 1.3 | 1.7 | 15.5 | ..... | ..... | ..... | ..... | ..... |
| Republic of South Africa | 3.0 | 4.4 | 4.5 | 4.2 | 5.6 | 0.4 | 0.4 | 0.4 | 0.5 | 1.3 |
| Other Subsaharan Africa | 0.4 | 0.3 | 21.8 | 0.4 | 4.6 | ..... | ..... | 0.1 | ..... | ..... |
| **Middle East** | 9.4 | 8.4 | 18.7 | 10.2 | 9.7 | 2.0 | 1.1 | 2.2 | 1.0 | 0.4 |
| **Australia** | 2.7 | 4.8 | 5.0 | 5.7 | 10.4 | 6.7 | 6.0 | 5.8 | 7.1 | 5.3 |
| **Rest of World** | ..... | ..... | ..... | ..... | ..... | ..... | ..... | ..... | ..... | ..... |

## Table E-3.  Metropolitan Area Exports of Goods by Destination, 1993–1997—*Continued*

(Millions of dollars.)

| Destination | 1993 | 1994 | 1995 | 1996 | 1997 | 1993 | 1994 | 1995 | 1996 | 1997 |
|---|---|---|---|---|---|---|---|---|---|---|
| | Fargo - Moorhead, ND - MN | | | | | Flint, MI | | | | |
| ALL DESTINATIONS | 111.8 | 137.3 | 155.0 | 181.9 | 208.5 | 958.9 | 1 032.1 | 1 451.7 | 1 318.8 | 1 475.3 |
| North America | 80.9 | 103.5 | 117.7 | 121.3 | 152.9 | 697.3 | 730.5 | 1 095.9 | 974.9 | 1 057.9 |
| Canada | 79.7 | 103.0 | 107.2 | 113.6 | 145.0 | 626.9 | 639.1 | 990.6 | 884.1 | 1 036.2 |
| Mexico | 1.1 | 0.5 | 10.6 | 7.7 | 7.9 | 70.4 | 91.4 | 105.4 | 90.7 | 21.7 |
| Caribbean and Central America | 0.1 | 0.1 | 0.1 | 0.4 | 0.1 | 1.3 | 2.1 | 2.9 | 3.1 | 4.0 |
| South America | 1.9 | 1.4 | 1.1 | 0.4 | 0.8 | 43.8 | 47.7 | 64.9 | 67.2 | 129.4 |
| Argentina | 1.5 | 1.1 | 0.5 | 0.2 | 0.3 | 20.2 | 23.8 | 24.0 | 13.2 | 66.9 |
| Brazil | 0.1 | ..... | 0.2 | ..... | 0.1 | 20.2 | 18.6 | 27.2 | 47.9 | 54.5 |
| Other South America | 0.3 | 0.3 | 0.4 | 0.2 | 0.5 | 3.3 | 5.3 | 13.6 | 6.1 | 8.1 |
| Europe | 27.0 | 24.3 | 31.8 | 50.1 | 45.6 | 25.8 | 28.0 | 30.3 | 34.8 | 48.4 |
| Belgium | 0.9 | 1.2 | 1.7 | 1.3 | 1.1 | 0.5 | 0.2 | 0.1 | 3.3 | 2.1 |
| France | 0.1 | 0.3 | 0.7 | 2.1 | 2.9 | 0.6 | 1.4 | 0.6 | 0.6 | 1.3 |
| Germany | 11.8 | 9.8 | 12.7 | 15.6 | 17.6 | 7.1 | 1.4 | 6.1 | 6.9 | 21.5 |
| Netherlands | 2.1 | 1.1 | 2.1 | 10.3 | 3.9 | 5.9 | 10.4 | 8.6 | 7.4 | 8.4 |
| United Kingdom | 2.0 | 1.4 | 2.0 | 4.2 | 6.8 | 3.3 | 4.7 | 4.3 | 5.1 | 6.3 |
| Turkey | 0.9 | 0.2 | 1.2 | 1.1 | 0.8 | 1.6 | 0.9 | 2.3 | 1.2 | 0.3 |
| Former Soviet Republics | 1.3 | 0.9 | 1.2 | 2.4 | 1.4 | 4.0 | 2.9 | 0.5 | 0.1 | 0.1 |
| Poland | 0.1 | 0.1 | 0.2 | 0.2 | 0.3 | ..... | ..... | ..... | ..... | ..... |
| Other Eastern Europe | ..... | ..... | 0.1 | ..... | 0.2 | ..... | ..... | ..... | ..... | ..... |
| Other Europe | 7.8 | 9.2 | 9.9 | 12.8 | 10.7 | 2.9 | 6.0 | 7.8 | 10.1 | 8.4 |
| Asia | 1.3 | 7.3 | 3.1 | 7.5 | 7.0 | 57.7 | 67.9 | 72.6 | 38.4 | 48.3 |
| Japan | 0.4 | 1.9 | 2.1 | 2.5 | 4.8 | 11.1 | 11.2 | 32.8 | 19.4 | 30.9 |
| China | ..... | ..... | ..... | ..... | 0.5 | 0.6 | 1.7 | 1.6 | 0.2 | 0.2 |
| Hong Kong | 0.1 | 0.1 | ..... | 1.5 | 0.1 | 13.8 | 11.5 | 5.7 | 5.1 | 6.1 |
| Taiwan | 0.3 | 4.1 | 0.2 | 0.1 | 0.4 | 14.1 | 16.4 | 15.5 | 8.7 | 7.7 |
| Singapore | 0.1 | 0.1 | ..... | 0.3 | 0.2 | 2.7 | 6.1 | 3.1 | 0.7 | 0.2 |
| South Korea | 0.2 | 0.6 | 0.2 | 2.4 | 0.4 | 0.4 | 0.3 | 1.0 | 0.6 | 0.8 |
| Indonesia | ..... | ..... | 0.1 | ..... | ..... | ..... | ..... | 0.1 | 0.7 | 0.6 |
| India | ..... | ..... | ..... | ..... | ..... | 0.1 | 1.6 | 3.7 | 1.3 | 0.3 |
| Other Asia | 0.2 | 0.6 | 0.3 | 0.7 | 0.5 | 14.9 | 19.1 | 9.1 | 1.7 | 1.7 |
| Africa | 0.1 | 0.2 | 0.3 | 0.3 | 0.2 | 3.3 | 3.2 | 3.9 | 3.2 | 0.9 |
| North Africa | ..... | ..... | ..... | ..... | ..... | 0.5 | 0.5 | 0.3 | 0.3 | 0.6 |
| Republic of South Africa | 0.1 | 0.2 | 0.3 | 0.3 | 0.1 | 2.7 | 2.7 | 3.4 | 2.5 | 0.2 |
| Other Subsaharan Africa | ..... | ..... | ..... | ..... | 0.1 | 0.1 | ..... | 0.2 | 0.3 | 0.1 |
| Middle East | 0.3 | 0.2 | 0.5 | 0.7 | 0.7 | 89.8 | 85.1 | 115.0 | 125.0 | 129.0 |
| Australia | 0.3 | 0.3 | 0.4 | 1.1 | 1.2 | 39.9 | 67.5 | 66.2 | 72.3 | 57.3 |
| Rest of World | ..... | ..... | ..... | ..... | ..... | ..... | ..... | ..... | ..... | ..... |
| | Florence, SC | | | | | Fresno, CA | | | | |
| ALL DESTINATIONS | 66.3 | 117.2 | 249.0 | 121.6 | 75.8 | 673.1 | 763.4 | 714.4 | 691.8 | 739.8 |
| North America | 23.0 | 17.7 | 28.7 | 35.5 | 41.1 | 186.1 | 177.7 | 176.4 | 185.1 | 198.9 |
| Canada | 22.4 | 16.3 | 27.0 | 32.1 | 36.3 | 163.3 | 152.2 | 164.0 | 173.6 | 182.2 |
| Mexico | 0.6 | 1.4 | 1.7 | 3.4 | 4.9 | 22.8 | 25.5 | 12.4 | 11.5 | 16.7 |
| Caribbean and Central America | 0.8 | 0.5 | 0.4 | 2.0 | 1.8 | 2.7 | 5.7 | 3.0 | 2.8 | 2.5 |
| South America | 3.0 | 2.3 | 15.2 | 4.3 | 4.1 | 10.6 | 20.3 | 21.9 | 27.2 | 26.3 |
| Argentina | 0.3 | 0.2 | 2.5 | 0.2 | 1.0 | 1.5 | 1.8 | 1.5 | 1.3 | 3.0 |
| Brazil | 1.3 | 0.5 | 9.0 | 2.6 | 1.7 | 5.2 | 6.8 | 9.8 | 13.0 | 8.4 |
| Other South America | 1.4 | 1.6 | 3.7 | 1.5 | 1.4 | 3.9 | 11.6 | 10.5 | 12.9 | 14.9 |
| Europe | 23.8 | 24.5 | 30.8 | 31.6 | 20.6 | 150.2 | 141.4 | 136.3 | 132.3 | 162.2 |
| Belgium | ..... | 1.5 | 2.5 | 0.8 | 0.1 | 7.9 | 11.0 | 10.5 | 7.3 | 11.3 |
| France | 1.6 | 1.9 | 2.1 | 1.5 | 1.4 | 6.3 | 6.1 | 5.6 | 8.6 | 7.7 |
| Germany | 1.8 | 2.0 | 3.9 | 3.9 | 1.6 | 42.8 | 28.9 | 32.2 | 22.3 | 24.9 |
| Netherlands | 2.0 | 4.9 | 6.6 | 5.0 | 4.1 | 13.0 | 12.8 | 10.6 | 11.9 | 17.6 |
| United Kingdom | 3.9 | 4.0 | 5.4 | 11.8 | 7.3 | 36.1 | 34.7 | 33.3 | 35.3 | 40.9 |
| Turkey | 8.2 | 2.7 | 0.4 | ..... | 0.1 | 0.3 | 0.1 | 0.5 | 0.4 | 1.0 |
| Former Soviet Republics | ..... | ..... | ..... | ..... | ..... | 0.4 | 2.4 | 2.6 | 0.7 | 0.5 |
| Poland | ..... | ..... | ..... | ..... | ..... | 0.2 | 0.3 | 1.0 | 1.1 | 2.5 |
| Other Eastern Europe | 0.1 | ..... | ..... | ..... | ..... | 2.3 | 0.2 | 0.3 | 0.7 | 0.8 |
| Other Europe | 6.2 | 7.5 | 9.9 | 8.6 | 6.1 | 40.9 | 44.9 | 39.7 | 44.0 | 55.1 |
| Asia | 13.1 | 61.8 | 157.5 | 40.4 | 5.4 | 283.8 | 381.8 | 346.2 | 301.4 | 311.2 |
| Japan | 1.0 | 3.4 | 5.4 | 4.0 | 1.2 | 94.4 | 115.5 | 135.4 | 105.6 | 82.6 |
| China | 1.7 | 7.3 | 6.8 | 3.4 | 0.4 | 0.9 | 63.1 | 27.2 | 13.5 | 35.9 |
| Hong Kong | 2.9 | 15.9 | 47.5 | 0.7 | 0.3 | 14.2 | 15.5 | 13.5 | 17.2 | 19.6 |
| Taiwan | 2.2 | 18.9 | 81.5 | 27.4 | 0.7 | 14.6 | 25.5 | 18.5 | 18.9 | 28.3 |
| Singapore | 0.2 | 0.4 | 0.5 | 1.0 | 0.6 | 7.4 | 7.5 | 7.0 | 4.3 | 10.0 |
| South Korea | 0.8 | 1.8 | 6.1 | 0.8 | 0.8 | 115.2 | 102.6 | 83.1 | 70.8 | 59.6 |
| Indonesia | ..... | 3.5 | 2.3 | 0.8 | 0.1 | 12.0 | 24.6 | 22.8 | 33.6 | 30.8 |
| India | 0.7 | 3.8 | 1.2 | 0.1 | 0.6 | 0.6 | 0.3 | 2.6 | 0.8 | 1.4 |
| Other Asia | 3.5 | 6.8 | 6.2 | 2.3 | 0.7 | 24.5 | 27.2 | 36.2 | 36.8 | 43.0 |
| Africa | 1.6 | 7.7 | 13.4 | 4.0 | 0.8 | 4.8 | 5.9 | 5.3 | 5.2 | 6.5 |
| North Africa | 1.4 | 6.9 | 13.1 | 3.7 | 0.5 | 2.4 | 1.4 | 2.4 | 1.0 | 2.0 |
| Republic of South Africa | 0.1 | 0.8 | 0.3 | 0.3 | 0.3 | 1.4 | 1.8 | 2.6 | 4.0 | 1.8 |
| Other Subsaharan Africa | ..... | 0.1 | ..... | ..... | ..... | 1.0 | 2.7 | 0.4 | 0.1 | 2.6 |
| Middle East | 0.6 | 2.3 | 2.5 | 3.0 | 1.3 | 20.5 | 19.9 | 15.6 | 24.1 | 17.2 |
| Australia | 0.4 | 0.4 | 0.5 | 0.8 | 0.6 | 14.3 | 10.7 | 9.6 | 13.7 | 15.0 |
| Rest of World | ..... | ..... | ..... | ..... | ..... | ..... | ..... | ..... | ..... | ..... |

## Table E-3.  Metropolitan Area Exports of Goods by Destination, 1993–1997—*Continued*

(Millions of dollars.)

| Destination | 1993 | 1994 | 1995 | 1996 | 1997 | 1993 | 1994 | 1995 | 1996 | 1997 |
|---|---|---|---|---|---|---|---|---|---|---|
| | Fort Lauderdale, FL | | | | | Fort Wayne, IN | | | | |
| **ALL DESTINATIONS** | 1 321.4 | 1 506.7 | 1 774.7 | 1 864.5 | 2 143.0 | 640.6 | 770.9 | 1 029.4 | 991.4 | 1 078.2 |
| **North America** | 179.0 | 202.7 | 181.5 | 199.6 | 332.8 | 401.9 | 517.8 | 707.4 | 691.9 | 773.2 |
| Canada | 113.8 | 122.4 | 139.6 | 127.7 | 164.3 | 331.9 | 421.9 | 544.3 | 496.9 | 591.0 |
| Mexico | 65.2 | 80.3 | 41.9 | 71.9 | 168.5 | 70.0 | 95.9 | 163.1 | 195.0 | 182.1 |
| **Caribbean and Central America** | 265.1 | 294.5 | 354.2 | 364.7 | 485.9 | 7.0 | 5.9 | 3.7 | 3.2 | 6.3 |
| **South America** | 363.5 | 430.1 | 544.9 | 590.1 | 632.7 | 23.2 | 22.7 | 35.6 | 25.0 | 30.0 |
| Argentina | 57.7 | 77.4 | 62.6 | 89.4 | 94.2 | 3.0 | 3.5 | 7.8 | 3.6 | 4.1 |
| Brazil | 67.2 | 80.8 | 130.9 | 145.0 | 133.3 | 2.3 | 3.7 | 4.7 | 5.9 | 7.9 |
| Other South America | 238.6 | 271.9 | 351.4 | 355.6 | 405.1 | 17.9 | 15.5 | 23.0 | 15.5 | 18.0 |
| **Europe** | 282.5 | 309.3 | 388.4 | 360.0 | 372.2 | 120.0 | 133.5 | 167.1 | 157.1 | 137.6 |
| Belgium | 10.8 | 10.1 | 15.6 | 18.4 | 16.7 | 5.0 | 4.1 | 12.3 | 5.2 | 8.5 |
| France | 36.6 | 42.1 | 45.7 | 47.1 | 41.4 | 10.8 | 11.2 | 14.3 | 18.4 | 22.0 |
| Germany | 47.5 | 42.6 | 67.0 | 64.2 | 56.5 | 28.2 | 30.5 | 31.7 | 27.2 | 21.8 |
| Netherlands | 19.1 | 14.9 | 24.7 | 23.5 | 20.1 | 7.6 | 12.8 | 9.1 | 11.5 | 4.9 |
| United Kingdom | 65.0 | 99.0 | 81.7 | 70.9 | 80.7 | 23.2 | 21.7 | 29.4 | 29.9 | 23.5 |
| Turkey | 8.3 | 3.2 | 4.9 | 7.3 | 11.3 | 0.5 | 1.9 | 9.7 | 0.9 | 0.9 |
| Former Soviet Republics | 4.0 | 7.2 | 10.5 | 7.1 | 10.5 | 0.8 | 0.1 | 1.6 | 0.3 | 1.6 |
| Poland | 0.5 | 1.2 | 1.2 | 0.8 | 1.7 | 1.3 | 1.5 | 2.7 | 2.2 | 2.5 |
| Other Eastern Europe | 8.7 | 5.4 | 13.2 | 13.6 | 10.0 | 1.2 | 2.1 | 2.4 | 1.3 | 2.3 |
| Other Europe | 82.1 | 83.5 | 123.8 | 107.3 | 123.3 | 41.5 | 47.5 | 53.9 | 60.3 | 49.6 |
| **Asia** | 153.0 | 139.9 | 175.1 | 186.9 | 177.3 | 50.7 | 60.0 | 75.0 | 83.5 | 95.7 |
| Japan | 26.6 | 31.9 | 41.3 | 50.2 | 39.2 | 8.4 | 12.8 | 12.1 | 11.8 | 14.5 |
| China | 8.3 | 10.4 | 12.9 | 9.4 | 6.8 | 3.3 | 1.0 | 2.3 | 3.8 | 2.7 |
| Hong Kong | 13.1 | 12.1 | 21.7 | 18.2 | 21.9 | 2.3 | 2.0 | 1.6 | 2.6 | 2.5 |
| Taiwan | 8.8 | 7.3 | 12.1 | 11.3 | 9.3 | 9.2 | 7.8 | 8.7 | 7.1 | 9.3 |
| Singapore | 50.2 | 32.1 | 38.0 | 40.4 | 39.3 | 6.1 | 9.1 | 11.3 | 13.4 | 12.9 |
| South Korea | 12.8 | 16.6 | 16.6 | 18.5 | 15.9 | 8.4 | 5.5 | 9.7 | 9.3 | 13.3 |
| Indonesia | 2.6 | 3.4 | 4.6 | 5.6 | 2.7 | 0.5 | 1.9 | 1.5 | 0.9 | 0.9 |
| India | 0.7 | 2.6 | 2.9 | 3.5 | 2.4 | 0.9 | 0.8 | 1.9 | 3.0 | 5.6 |
| Other Asia | 29.9 | 23.6 | 24.9 | 29.8 | 39.9 | 11.5 | 18.9 | 26.0 | 31.6 | 34.1 |
| **Africa** | 21.6 | 43.2 | 34.6 | 36.2 | 46.0 | 11.3 | 8.1 | 9.6 | 6.6 | 10.2 |
| North Africa | 2.6 | 3.4 | 13.2 | 17.8 | 15.4 | 4.7 | 1.7 | 3.1 | 1.2 | 3.0 |
| Republic of South Africa | 6.9 | 11.5 | 12.1 | 13.8 | 15.4 | 5.7 | 5.3 | 4.6 | 4.2 | 4.0 |
| Other Subsaharan Africa | 12.0 | 28.4 | 9.3 | 4.7 | 15.1 | 1.0 | 1.1 | 1.9 | 1.2 | 3.2 |
| **Middle East** | 40.3 | 62.2 | 73.7 | 104.2 | 62.0 | 11.1 | 11.0 | 20.1 | 11.8 | 13.8 |
| **Australia** | 16.4 | 24.8 | 22.3 | 22.8 | 34.1 | 15.3 | 11.9 | 11.0 | 12.3 | 11.5 |
| **Rest of World** | ..... | ..... | ..... | ..... | ..... | ..... | ..... | ..... | ..... | ..... |
| | Fort Worth - Arlington, TX | | | | | Gary, IN | | | | |
| **ALL DESTINATIONS** | 1 600.2 | 2 052.0 | 1 915.0 | 2 372.7 | 3 045.9 | 225.3 | 267.5 | 310.6 | 303.2 | 336.9 |
| **North America** | 332.8 | 451.0 | 413.6 | 697.3 | 844.3 | 124.4 | 134.2 | 153.9 | 145.7 | 164.9 |
| Canada | 199.8 | 288.0 | 293.8 | 542.9 | 578.2 | 118.6 | 128.0 | 147.5 | 138.2 | 146.1 |
| Mexico | 133.0 | 163.1 | 119.7 | 154.4 | 266.1 | 5.8 | 6.2 | 6.5 | 7.5 | 18.8 |
| **Caribbean and Central America** | 48.6 | 54.2 | 57.8 | 61.0 | 81.8 | 1.2 | 2.3 | 2.4 | 1.1 | 3.6 |
| **South America** | 73.9 | 127.4 | 148.6 | 193.8 | 355.7 | 6.9 | 11.3 | 14.5 | 11.7 | 18.2 |
| Argentina | 9.0 | 24.5 | 19.2 | 31.2 | 48.5 | 2.6 | 2.7 | 3.2 | 3.4 | 4.7 |
| Brazil | 25.5 | 22.5 | 54.1 | 55.6 | 117.9 | 0.9 | 3.6 | 3.6 | 1.8 | 3.1 |
| Other South America | 39.4 | 80.4 | 75.3 | 107.1 | 189.4 | 3.3 | 5.0 | 7.7 | 6.5 | 10.4 |
| **Europe** | 498.3 | 764.6 | 477.2 | 437.2 | 424.7 | 44.6 | 53.2 | 57.1 | 56.6 | 57.4 |
| Belgium | 38.2 | 23.6 | 20.7 | 22.8 | 36.3 | 0.7 | 2.5 | 2.1 | 2.0 | 1.4 |
| France | 36.7 | 51.2 | 47.3 | 26.8 | 30.3 | 11.5 | 14.2 | 14.6 | 12.7 | 10.4 |
| Germany | 51.7 | 36.8 | 34.2 | 28.9 | 40.1 | 7.9 | 9.6 | 10.3 | 10.8 | 10.2 |
| Netherlands | 75.1 | 88.0 | 81.5 | 105.9 | 72.5 | 3.5 | 4.1 | 4.7 | 6.1 | 6.1 |
| United Kingdom | 69.3 | 65.5 | 55.4 | 85.6 | 110.0 | 12.0 | 13.8 | 12.5 | 13.8 | 16.2 |
| Turkey | 155.8 | 347.3 | 104.3 | 53.0 | 25.6 | 0.2 | 0.1 | 0.3 | 0.4 | 0.8 |
| Former Soviet Republics | 1.9 | 1.4 | 5.1 | 8.6 | 15.4 | ..... | 0.1 | ..... | ..... | ..... |
| Poland | 3.4 | 3.2 | 1.6 | 4.6 | 2.8 | 0.5 | 0.7 | 0.9 | 0.7 | 0.2 |
| Other Eastern Europe | 12.4 | 13.5 | 5.9 | 2.0 | 4.5 | 0.2 | 0.3 | 0.7 | 0.2 | 0.4 |
| Other Europe | 54.0 | 134.0 | 121.4 | 99.0 | 87.3 | 7.9 | 7.9 | 10.9 | 9.9 | 11.9 |
| **Asia** | 512.9 | 493.0 | 615.1 | 730.8 | 1 071.3 | 39.1 | 57.0 | 71.7 | 75.7 | 76.6 |
| Japan | 44.8 | 40.7 | 54.7 | 29.7 | 35.1 | 5.2 | 9.6 | 14.7 | 12.2 | 13.4 |
| China | 23.8 | 19.7 | 45.5 | 51.2 | 66.5 | 0.8 | 3.2 | 7.5 | 6.8 | 5.9 |
| Hong Kong | 23.1 | 70.5 | 104.5 | 92.4 | 125.8 | 1.8 | 2.3 | 2.8 | 1.8 | 2.4 |
| Taiwan | 12.0 | 22.3 | 33.2 | 23.1 | 49.0 | 5.7 | 5.6 | 7.1 | 6.1 | 9.3 |
| Singapore | 219.0 | 166.4 | 180.8 | 219.0 | 388.2 | 17.3 | 19.1 | 19.2 | 23.9 | 27.4 |
| South Korea | 57.9 | 62.8 | 85.1 | 189.5 | 217.6 | 4.5 | 7.2 | 9.5 | 9.8 | 7.2 |
| Indonesia | 35.7 | 13.8 | 10.7 | 21.6 | 16.4 | 0.7 | 1.0 | 2.5 | 1.5 | 2.3 |
| India | 8.8 | 8.9 | 19.9 | 11.1 | 16.1 | 0.2 | 0.8 | 0.8 | 1.5 | 0.5 |
| Other Asia | 87.9 | 88.0 | 80.7 | 93.3 | 156.5 | 3.1 | 8.2 | 7.6 | 12.1 | 8.1 |
| **Africa** | 28.7 | 58.9 | 36.1 | 39.8 | 48.0 | 1.7 | 1.3 | 3.7 | 2.4 | 3.6 |
| North Africa | 18.5 | 28.4 | 10.6 | 15.8 | 22.6 | 0.2 | 0.2 | 0.6 | 0.2 | 0.2 |
| Republic of South Africa | 2.1 | 19.3 | 9.9 | 4.1 | 4.2 | 1.2 | 0.8 | 1.7 | 2.0 | 3.1 |
| Other Subsaharan Africa | 8.1 | 11.2 | 15.7 | 20.0 | 21.2 | 0.2 | 0.2 | 1.4 | 0.2 | 0.3 |
| **Middle East** | 75.6 | 64.0 | 110.0 | 160.0 | 167.9 | 2.0 | 2.0 | 1.5 | 2.8 | 3.7 |
| **Australia** | 29.3 | 38.8 | 56.6 | 52.8 | 52.2 | 5.5 | 6.2 | 5.8 | 7.2 | 8.8 |
| **Rest of World** | ..... | ..... | ..... | ..... | ..... | ..... | ..... | ..... | ..... | ..... |

## Table E-3.  Metropolitan Area Exports of Goods by Destination, 1993–1997—*Continued*

(Millions of dollars.)

| Destination | 1993 | 1994 | 1995 | 1996 | 1997 | 1993 | 1994 | 1995 | 1996 | 1997 |
|---|---|---|---|---|---|---|---|---|---|---|
| | Grand Rapids - Muskegon - Holland, MI | | | | | Greensboro - Winston-Salem - High Point, NC | | | | |
| **ALL DESTINATIONS** | 1 705.0 | 1 993.5 | 2 304.1 | 2 656.5 | 2 933.1 | 2 453.1 | 2 773.3 | 3 356.3 | 3 495.6 | 4 050.8 |
| **North America** | 786.3 | 906.5 | 1 037.1 | 1 179.9 | 1 429.2 | 524.6 | 684.0 | 935.2 | 1 148.0 | 1 588.7 |
| Canada | 695.1 | 779.1 | 907.6 | 1 016.8 | 1 192.5 | 402.1 | 497.8 | 537.2 | 541.3 | 669.8 |
| Mexico | 91.2 | 127.4 | 129.5 | 163.1 | 236.6 | 122.5 | 186.2 | 398.0 | 606.6 | 919.0 |
| **Caribbean and Central America** | 34.8 | 26.2 | 22.1 | 23.9 | 18.8 | 379.2 | 425.1 | 604.3 | 665.6 | 711.0 |
| **South America** | 30.9 | 40.9 | 55.8 | 53.6 | 64.3 | 132.0 | 164.4 | 223.9 | 208.2 | 239.5 |
| Argentina | 3.4 | 6.3 | 8.3 | 7.7 | 16.0 | 22.9 | 28.6 | 34.6 | 35.2 | 50.3 |
| Brazil | 14.4 | 20.5 | 24.9 | 16.8 | 17.8 | 26.7 | 47.4 | 82.8 | 79.9 | 89.5 |
| Other South America | 13.1 | 14.1 | 22.6 | 29.2 | 30.6 | 82.5 | 88.4 | 106.5 | 93.1 | 99.7 |
| **Europe** | 239.8 | 289.3 | 351.9 | 394.0 | 462.4 | 846.6 | 877.5 | 945.9 | 864.2 | 867.1 |
| Belgium | 4.6 | 7.6 | 11.1 | 10.3 | 10.0 | 389.6 | 257.9 | 258.7 | 159.0 | 118.4 |
| France | 18.9 | 18.4 | 27.0 | 24.1 | 38.6 | 30.9 | 32.1 | 36.4 | 35.7 | 45.4 |
| Germany | 54.8 | 60.1 | 73.7 | 99.3 | 132.8 | 136.1 | 149.3 | 131.6 | 110.8 | 94.6 |
| Netherlands | 13.3 | 24.6 | 24.8 | 40.7 | 55.2 | 34.4 | 36.8 | 49.9 | 62.3 | 83.4 |
| United Kingdom | 64.1 | 75.4 | 92.4 | 96.0 | 105.0 | 73.8 | 85.1 | 104.1 | 107.8 | 110.3 |
| Turkey | 1.5 | 2.0 | 2.8 | 3.9 | 6.1 | 14.1 | 16.0 | 6.1 | 8.9 | 30.6 |
| Former Soviet Republics | 1.4 | 1.4 | 1.8 | 1.4 | 1.8 | 7.4 | 2.2 | 12.0 | 18.1 | 12.1 |
| Poland | 12.1 | 7.3 | 11.9 | 15.2 | 9.3 | 1.3 | 4.1 | 5.4 | 10.7 | 12.9 |
| Other Eastern Europe | 10.3 | 7.2 | 6.0 | 7.8 | 8.4 | 0.6 | 2.6 | 3.6 | 11.2 | 9.3 |
| Other Europe | 59.0 | 85.3 | 100.4 | 95.4 | 95.2 | 158.3 | 291.3 | 338.2 | 339.8 | 350.0 |
| **Asia** | 532.8 | 636.1 | 763.9 | 928.4 | 864.7 | 331.7 | 361.4 | 411.1 | 429.7 | 455.7 |
| Japan | 278.0 | 292.9 | 343.4 | 417.1 | 433.8 | 147.7 | 158.0 | 182.9 | 199.3 | 183.4 |
| China | 12.0 | 12.6 | 39.0 | 78.6 | 54.1 | 7.3 | 6.8 | 13.3 | 9.1 | 15.2 |
| Hong Kong | 54.6 | 37.9 | 55.7 | 57.3 | 72.5 | 56.5 | 58.9 | 60.1 | 45.3 | 51.8 |
| Taiwan | 82.1 | 134.3 | 97.0 | 58.9 | 52.8 | 27.1 | 26.7 | 32.8 | 23.7 | 34.3 |
| Singapore | 17.2 | 19.2 | 22.1 | 24.1 | 19.0 | 17.7 | 17.2 | 10.7 | 13.9 | 22.9 |
| South Korea | 35.4 | 55.8 | 112.6 | 159.7 | 101.3 | 31.7 | 36.9 | 34.4 | 22.4 | 35.2 |
| Indonesia | 2.2 | 8.1 | 7.9 | 8.3 | 7.2 | 9.9 | 14.3 | 16.1 | 16.0 | 28.4 |
| India | 1.1 | 2.1 | 5.5 | 6.2 | 4.6 | 2.1 | 1.7 | 3.1 | 7.0 | 6.9 |
| Other Asia | 50.3 | 73.2 | 80.7 | 118.1 | 119.4 | 31.6 | 40.9 | 57.5 | 92.9 | 77.6 |
| **Africa** | 4.0 | 5.3 | 9.3 | 9.0 | 13.5 | 34.2 | 54.9 | 61.4 | 47.1 | 58.7 |
| North Africa | 0.8 | 1.3 | 3.2 | 1.3 | 4.3 | 17.8 | 25.3 | 31.1 | 10.7 | 10.6 |
| Republic of South Africa | 2.6 | 3.5 | 5.6 | 7.1 | 8.4 | 13.3 | 20.2 | 26.0 | 31.8 | 35.4 |
| Other Subsaharan Africa | 0.5 | 0.4 | 0.5 | 0.6 | 0.8 | 3.0 | 9.4 | 4.3 | 4.5 | 12.8 |
| **Middle East** | 37.6 | 48.8 | 27.2 | 32.2 | 31.8 | 170.6 | 164.4 | 135.2 | 82.3 | 77.1 |
| **Australia** | 38.7 | 40.4 | 36.8 | 35.4 | 48.4 | 34.2 | 41.6 | 39.1 | 50.4 | 52.6 |
| **Rest of World** | ..... | ..... | ..... | ..... | ..... | ..... | ..... | 0.2 | 0.2 | 0.3 |
| | Greenville - Spartanburg - Anderson, SC | | | | | Green Bay, WI | | | | |
| **ALL DESTINATIONS** | 1 462.1 | 1 745.0 | 2 305.3 | 2 720.4 | 3 076.9 | 134.1 | 187.3 | 212.7 | 188.9 | 281.9 |
| **North America** | 721.1 | 952.0 | 1 307.1 | 1 247.5 | 1 433.5 | 77.3 | 110.8 | 116.0 | 108.6 | 177.3 |
| Canada | 537.3 | 658.8 | 853.8 | 808.4 | 832.7 | 70.2 | 96.3 | 100.3 | 98.8 | 167.8 |
| Mexico | 183.7 | 293.2 | 453.3 | 439.0 | 600.7 | 7.1 | 14.6 | 15.7 | 9.7 | 9.5 |
| **Caribbean and Central America** | 50.9 | 55.4 | 69.7 | 59.5 | 84.4 | 1.3 | 2.7 | 2.5 | 1.4 | 2.3 |
| **South America** | 42.2 | 67.0 | 58.9 | 73.8 | 84.9 | 4.1 | 3.2 | 6.1 | 4.0 | 5.6 |
| Argentina | 4.6 | 5.1 | 7.7 | 10.7 | 13.3 | 1.0 | 0.2 | 1.2 | 0.8 | 0.1 |
| Brazil | 7.9 | 13.9 | 22.6 | 22.7 | 21.0 | 0.4 | 0.9 | 1.7 | 1.3 | 2.8 |
| Other South America | 29.7 | 47.9 | 28.6 | 40.4 | 50.5 | 2.7 | 2.2 | 3.2 | 1.9 | 2.7 |
| **Europe** | 307.0 | 320.3 | 449.5 | 936.8 | 1 016.9 | 20.9 | 34.4 | 42.2 | 30.7 | 46.2 |
| Belgium | 30.4 | 26.2 | 45.6 | 46.9 | 47.1 | 2.1 | 3.5 | 3.4 | 2.4 | 4.4 |
| France | 32.5 | 26.0 | 35.0 | 36.7 | 35.4 | 2.1 | 2.8 | 3.8 | 1.2 | 8.5 |
| Germany | 77.4 | 82.6 | 129.6 | 620.0 | 699.7 | 2.7 | 3.7 | 2.5 | 4.0 | 6.3 |
| Netherlands | 21.2 | 27.5 | 41.0 | 37.4 | 22.0 | 4.8 | 10.7 | 17.1 | 5.8 | 4.5 |
| United Kingdom | 75.6 | 83.7 | 111.0 | 97.9 | 93.0 | 4.6 | 6.6 | 9.1 | 7.7 | 9.7 |
| Turkey | 1.8 | 2.6 | 3.9 | 3.8 | 5.1 | 0.4 | 0.1 | 1.0 | ..... | 0.4 |
| Former Soviet Republics | 0.7 | 1.5 | 0.2 | 0.4 | 0.6 | 0.1 | ..... | ..... | 0.1 | ..... |
| Poland | 0.7 | 0.1 | 0.4 | 0.8 | 0.6 | ..... | ..... | ..... | 0.2 | ..... |
| Other Eastern Europe | 0.2 | 0.9 | 0.5 | 1.3 | 1.0 | ..... | 0.1 | ..... | 0.9 | ..... |
| Other Europe | 66.6 | 69.2 | 82.4 | 91.6 | 112.4 | 4.2 | 6.8 | 5.2 | 8.4 | 12.5 |
| **Asia** | 285.4 | 296.4 | 351.7 | 315.0 | 363.5 | 25.0 | 29.9 | 37.1 | 35.3 | 42.3 |
| Japan | 107.2 | 136.7 | 107.6 | 87.2 | 131.0 | 10.1 | 17.2 | 17.7 | 15.1 | 18.6 |
| China | 7.7 | 4.4 | 8.1 | 19.1 | 17.8 | 1.0 | 0.6 | 0.1 | 0.1 | 0.7 |
| Hong Kong | 51.6 | 54.9 | 67.5 | 60.3 | 58.5 | 0.5 | 0.6 | 1.1 | 1.1 | 1.0 |
| Taiwan | 15.3 | 25.4 | 45.4 | 30.1 | 29.7 | 1.8 | 0.5 | 1.4 | 3.9 | 5.0 |
| Singapore | 17.0 | 15.0 | 29.3 | 34.4 | 36.5 | 0.7 | 0.5 | 0.9 | 0.4 | 1.3 |
| South Korea | 43.6 | 34.3 | 35.7 | 25.7 | 20.8 | 5.8 | 6.3 | 5.9 | 4.3 | 11.5 |
| Indonesia | 4.3 | 2.3 | 3.6 | 4.8 | 9.9 | ..... | ..... | 0.2 | 0.5 | 1.0 |
| India | 5.8 | 2.3 | 20.7 | 11.6 | 15.0 | 0.5 | 0.6 | 1.6 | 0.2 | 0.1 |
| Other Asia | 32.9 | 21.1 | 33.7 | 41.9 | 44.3 | 4.6 | 3.6 | 8.1 | 9.5 | 3.1 |
| **Africa** | 11.1 | 9.8 | 13.6 | 15.2 | 12.6 | 1.2 | 1.6 | 1.1 | 3.3 | 2.1 |
| North Africa | 3.5 | 1.3 | 2.9 | 2.4 | 2.8 | 0.4 | 0.7 | 0.4 | ..... | 0.5 |
| Republic of South Africa | 3.3 | 4.1 | 7.1 | 9.9 | 6.4 | 0.8 | 0.7 | 0.6 | 3.2 | 1.5 |
| Other Subsaharan Africa | 4.4 | 4.4 | 3.6 | 2.9 | 3.3 | ..... | 0.2 | 0.1 | ..... | ..... |
| **Middle East** | 29.8 | 25.0 | 37.1 | 50.1 | 28.9 | 2.8 | 1.5 | 5.3 | 2.2 | 1.0 |
| **Australia** | 14.7 | 19.1 | 17.8 | 22.5 | 52.2 | 1.5 | 3.2 | 2.4 | 3.4 | 5.1 |
| **Rest of World** | ..... | ..... | ..... | ..... | ..... | ..... | ..... | ..... | ..... | ..... |

# Table E-3.  Metropolitan Area Exports of Goods by Destination, 1993–1997—*Continued*

(Millions of dollars.)

| Destination | 1993 | 1994 | 1995 | 1996 | 1997 | 1993 | 1994 | 1995 | 1996 | 1997 |
|---|---|---|---|---|---|---|---|---|---|---|
| | Harrisburg - Lebanon - Carlisle, PA | | | | | Hartford, CT | | | | |
| ALL DESTINATIONS | 339.2 | 535.0 | 601.0 | 775.5 | 964.4 | 1 926.1 | 1 967.1 | 2 167.6 | 2 416.0 | 3 219.8 |
| North America | 227.3 | 264.8 | 274.6 | 387.6 | 445.9 | 385.2 | 414.3 | 406.6 | 452.4 | 567.5 |
| Canada | 148.0 | 164.9 | 164.2 | 229.8 | 269.6 | 319.3 | 333.1 | 349.7 | 392.3 | 477.9 |
| Mexico | 79.3 | 99.9 | 110.4 | 157.7 | 176.3 | 65.9 | 81.1 | 56.9 | 60.1 | 89.6 |
| Caribbean and Central America | 5.5 | 6.5 | 4.7 | 4.6 | 8.7 | 57.2 | 54.5 | 66.5 | 55.6 | 99.4 |
| South America | 7.1 | 19.3 | 33.7 | 32.8 | 39.7 | 51.9 | 47.7 | 57.3 | 83.6 | 63.1 |
| Argentina | 0.6 | 1.9 | 3.1 | 4.5 | 4.4 | 7.7 | 12.0 | 9.7 | 6.7 | 7.4 |
| Brazil | 2.8 | 7.8 | 12.1 | 8.7 | 11.4 | 7.8 | 11.0 | 15.3 | 18.0 | 22.1 |
| Other South America | 3.7 | 9.5 | 18.5 | 19.6 | 23.9 | 36.4 | 24.8 | 32.2 | 58.9 | 33.5 |
| Europe | 63.9 | 98.4 | 118.3 | 143.7 | 203.1 | 792.4 | 687.7 | 810.9 | 919.6 | 1 222.9 |
| Belgium | 1.4 | 3.3 | 4.1 | 3.1 | 5.1 | 23.0 | 17.5 | 31.2 | 42.0 | 50.3 |
| France | 7.9 | 17.0 | 17.1 | 18.4 | 25.9 | 205.7 | 79.1 | 39.6 | 40.4 | 96.4 |
| Germany | 8.8 | 3.0 | 3.7 | 6.6 | 11.1 | 131.6 | 150.1 | 171.9 | 201.2 | 244.9 |
| Netherlands | 12.5 | 0.7 | 1.1 | 1.4 | 21.3 | 19.8 | 19.2 | 44.8 | 30.4 | 72.0 |
| United Kingdom | 27.5 | 62.9 | 73.7 | 82.9 | 98.5 | 196.6 | 160.9 | 190.3 | 194.5 | 277.6 |
| Turkey | ..... | ..... | 0.1 | 0.5 | 0.5 | 6.9 | 3.5 | 6.8 | 5.5 | 6.5 |
| Former Soviet Republics | 0.6 | | 2.6 | 4.0 | 2.2 | 5.6 | 18.3 | 8.5 | 10.3 | 7.4 | 13.0 |
| Poland | ..... | 0.3 | 0.1 | 0.1 | 0.4 | 3.7 | 4.8 | 4.4 | 6.2 | 3.0 |
| Other Eastern Europe | 0.6 | 0.4 | 0.4 | 1.3 | 2.1 | 7.2 | 3.7 | 4.3 | 3.4 | 7.1 |
| Other Europe | 4.8 | 8.2 | 13.9 | 27.2 | 32.5 | 179.5 | 240.3 | 307.4 | 388.7 | 452.1 |
| Asia | 29.5 | 139.2 | 162.6 | 197.6 | 255.5 | 550.6 | 652.8 | 711.5 | 726.8 | 1 145.1 |
| Japan | 8.5 | 41.9 | 54.1 | 63.1 | 71.0 | 68.0 | 177.6 | 221.5 | 196.9 | 317.5 |
| China | 0.3 | 0.2 | 1.1 | 4.3 | 4.9 | 191.6 | 50.0 | 33.9 | 22.0 | 27.4 |
| Hong Kong | 1.9 | 40.2 | 44.0 | 57.0 | 64.3 | 24.0 | 17.9 | 26.8 | 30.0 | 34.0 |
| Taiwan | 4.4 | 4.3 | 4.9 | 5.3 | 8.8 | 32.2 | 65.0 | 42.9 | 55.2 | 73.5 |
| Singapore | 1.7 | 32.5 | 39.6 | 43.7 | 62.4 | 57.0 | 218.4 | 192.7 | 146.5 | 157.1 |
| South Korea | 5.2 | 7.2 | 9.1 | 10.7 | 12.9 | 105.5 | 51.3 | 110.1 | 167.5 | 206.8 |
| Indonesia | 0.3 | ..... | ..... | 0.1 | 0.3 | 16.8 | 5.6 | 9.3 | 21.2 | 108.9 |
| India | 0.1 | 0.4 | 1.4 | 2.0 | 5.7 | 2.4 | 5.1 | 8.7 | 9.3 | 109.3 |
| Other Asia | 7.2 | 12.5 | 8.3 | 11.3 | 25.2 | 53.1 | 61.8 | 65.6 | 78.2 | 110.6 |
| Africa | 0.4 | 1.2 | 0.9 | 1.9 | 1.1 | 31.5 | 37.2 | 60.6 | 138.1 | 68.1 |
| North Africa | 0.1 | 0.4 | 0.1 | 0.2 | 0.1 | 16.0 | 10.3 | 11.0 | 98.1 | 2.9 |
| Republic of South Africa | 0.2 | 0.6 | 0.7 | 1.5 | 0.6 | 10.9 | 22.1 | 36.3 | 33.6 | 49.3 |
| Other Subsaharan Africa | 0.1 | 0.2 | 0.1 | 0.2 | 0.4 | 4.7 | 4.8 | 13.2 | 6.3 | 15.9 |
| Middle East | 3.1 | 4.1 | 3.5 | 5.4 | 5.3 | 38.9 | 53.0 | 36.8 | 21.8 | 33.1 |
| Australia | 2.4 | 1.5 | 2.6 | 1.9 | 5.1 | 18.3 | 19.9 | 17.4 | 17.6 | 20.5 |
| Rest of World | ..... | ..... | ..... | ..... | ..... | ..... | ..... | ..... | 0.4 | ..... |
| | Hickory - Morganton, NC | | | | | Honolulu, HI | | | | |
| ALL DESTINATIONS | 335.2 | 397.9 | 476.1 | 464.3 | 501.2 | 187.8 | 215.5 | 228.2 | 265.7 | 269.5 |
| North America | 142.9 | 172.8 | 168.2 | 125.3 | 165.2 | 6.9 | 14.5 | 48.4 | 63.9 | 26.5 |
| Canada | 93.6 | 121.2 | 125.9 | 106.7 | 123.4 | 6.5 | 8.6 | 48.1 | 63.7 | 25.8 |
| Mexico | 49.3 | 51.6 | 42.3 | 18.6 | 41.8 | 0.3 | 5.9 | 0.2 | 0.3 | 0.7 |
| Caribbean and Central America | 8.4 | 16.6 | 22.4 | 22.2 | 19.0 | 0.7 | 0.6 | 0.6 | 0.5 | 0.9 |
| South America | 35.1 | 40.8 | 35.6 | 42.1 | 45.4 | 0.2 | 0.1 | 0.1 | 0.2 | 0.3 |
| Argentina | 23.1 | 21.3 | 10.2 | 5.6 | 9.1 | ..... | ..... | ..... | ..... | ..... |
| Brazil | 1.9 | 5.8 | 6.8 | 20.8 | 23.1 | ..... | ..... | ..... | ..... | 0.1 |
| Other South America | 10.1 | 13.6 | 18.7 | 15.7 | 13.2 | 0.2 | 0.1 | ..... | 0.2 | 0.1 |
| Europe | 60.9 | 75.2 | 90.1 | 97.0 | 104.0 | 7.3 | 5.8 | 6.8 | 7.9 | 7.4 |
| Belgium | 3.8 | 2.6 | 1.9 | 1.2 | 4.3 | ..... | ..... | ..... | ..... | ..... |
| France | 5.7 | 4.9 | 4.1 | 2.6 | 2.1 | 0.4 | 1.4 | 1.2 | 0.7 | 1.0 |
| Germany | 10.3 | 11.3 | 18.8 | 20.5 | 36.9 | 2.0 | 1.9 | 2.0 | 2.0 | 1.1 |
| Netherlands | 11.2 | 9.6 | 8.0 | 9.7 | 9.5 | 0.3 | 0.3 | 0.4 | 0.7 | 0.2 |
| United Kingdom | 15.1 | 28.9 | 39.3 | 35.2 | 23.2 | 3.0 | 0.7 | 1.0 | 2.6 | 1.7 |
| Turkey | 0.6 | 0.1 | 0.4 | 2.0 | 1.3 | ..... | ..... | ..... | ..... | ..... |
| Former Soviet Republics | ..... | 0.1 | ..... | 0.4 | 1.8 | 0.7 | ..... | ..... | ..... | 0.2 |
| Poland | ..... | ..... | 0.1 | 0.1 | 1.0 | ..... | ..... | ..... | ..... | ..... |
| Other Eastern Europe | 1.5 | 3.2 | 2.9 | 7.0 | 2.3 | ..... | ..... | ..... | 0.1 | 0.1 |
| Other Europe | 12.6 | 14.5 | 14.5 | 18.4 | 21.6 | 0.8 | 1.5 | 2.2 | 1.7 | 3.0 |
| Asia | 55.1 | 71.8 | 123.5 | 140.9 | 134.3 | 164.9 | 168.0 | 167.3 | 188.0 | 228.6 |
| Japan | 29.8 | 43.4 | 71.6 | 91.0 | 90.2 | 79.9 | 96.0 | 108.6 | 143.4 | 153.7 |
| China | 2.0 | 2.4 | 0.2 | 3.1 | 3.3 | 1.6 | 4.0 | 0.3 | 0.7 | 6.1 |
| Hong Kong | 10.9 | 8.6 | 7.1 | 4.3 | 6.4 | 8.7 | 12.4 | 4.1 | 4.3 | 7.6 |
| Taiwan | 3.2 | 1.7 | 7.5 | 5.7 | 3.7 | 3.0 | 9.5 | 5.3 | 4.1 | 1.8 |
| Singapore | 1.8 | 1.6 | 2.0 | 4.5 | 3.9 | 3.5 | 2.1 | 5.6 | 5.0 | 11.7 |
| South Korea | 0.6 | 1.6 | 19.3 | 11.3 | 7.8 | 18.8 | 26.1 | 24.8 | 9.0 | 9.2 |
| Indonesia | 0.2 | 0.9 | 0.9 | 0.5 | 2.0 | 0.1 | 0.5 | 0.4 | 0.6 | 3.7 |
| India | 0.5 | 1.6 | 4.3 | 3.1 | 3.5 | 0.1 | ..... | ..... | ..... | 0.1 |
| Other Asia | 6.1 | 10.0 | 10.6 | 17.4 | 13.5 | 49.2 | 17.4 | 18.3 | 20.8 | 34.6 |
| Africa | 1.0 | 1.4 | 1.9 | 1.5 | 1.4 | 0.2 | 12.4 | 0.1 | 0.1 | 0.2 |
| North Africa | ..... | ..... | 0.2 | 0.2 | 0.3 | ..... | 11.8 | ..... | ..... | ..... |
| Republic of South Africa | 1.0 | 1.2 | 0.9 | 1.2 | 1.0 | ..... | 0.5 | ..... | ..... | ..... |
| Other Subsaharan Africa | ..... | 0.1 | 0.9 | ..... | 0.2 | 0.2 | 0.1 | ..... | 0.1 | 0.1 |
| Middle East | 28.4 | 15.0 | 7.9 | 7.7 | 20.1 | 0.1 | 0.2 | 0.3 | 0.2 | 3.1 |
| Australia | 3.5 | 4.4 | 26.4 | 27.6 | 11.8 | 7.5 | 13.8 | 4.7 | 4.9 | 2.7 |
| Rest of World | ..... | ..... | ..... | ..... | ..... | ..... | ..... | ..... | ..... | ..... |

## Table E-3.  Metropolitan Area Exports of Goods by Destination, 1993–1997—*Continued*

(Millions of dollars.)

| Destination | 1993 | 1994 | 1995 | 1996 | 1997 | 1993 | 1994 | 1995 | 1996 | 1997 |
|---|---|---|---|---|---|---|---|---|---|---|
| | Houston, TX | | | | | Huntsville, AL | | | | |
| **ALL DESTINATIONS** | 12 284.6 | 13 388.2 | 16 247.9 | 16 541.5 | 18 595.9 | 573.6 | 672.1 | 829.0 | 899.1 | 1 071.8 |
| **North America** | 2 335.2 | 2 839.7 | 3 166.6 | 3 525.5 | 4 728.3 | 247.1 | 350.1 | 427.4 | 531.2 | 678.3 |
| Canada | 1 212.5 | 1 513.6 | 1 726.8 | 1 965.2 | 2 548.4 | 216.8 | 293.5 | 382.7 | 470.5 | 492.8 |
| Mexico | 1 122.8 | 1 326.0 | 1 439.8 | 1 560.3 | 2 179.9 | 30.4 | 56.6 | 44.7 | 60.7 | 185.4 |
| **Caribbean and Central America** | 623.4 | 726.1 | 858.7 | 828.4 | 1 071.6 | 0.7 | 1.2 | 9.9 | 1.9 | 2.6 |
| **South America** | 1 552.2 | 1 908.0 | 2 724.9 | 2 870.0 | 3 320.3 | 11.9 | 11.6 | 14.1 | 12.3 | 18.1 |
| Argentina | 184.8 | 236.4 | 371.8 | 278.1 | 288.8 | 0.5 | 2.8 | 1.1 | 1.4 | 2.7 |
| Brazil | 248.0 | 294.3 | 601.3 | 704.3 | 790.3 | 4.2 | 6.0 | 10.0 | 6.3 | 11.4 |
| Other South America | 1 119.5 | 1 377.3 | 1 751.8 | 1 887.6 | 2 241.1 | 7.2 | 2.8 | 3.0 | 4.6 | 4.0 |
| **Europe** | 2 646.7 | 2 610.7 | 3 023.7 | 2 984.7 | 3 187.9 | 182.8 | 190.4 | 242.8 | 225.3 | 233.0 |
| Belgium | 141.1 | 206.8 | 233.1 | 183.3 | 180.8 | 1.7 | 2.6 | 1.6 | 1.0 | 1.9 |
| France | 236.6 | 268.8 | 250.7 | 301.7 | 272.5 | 5.5 | 22.7 | 25.2 | 9.6 | 14.9 |
| Germany | 161.2 | 126.8 | 151.1 | 171.4 | 220.0 | 79.1 | 59.1 | 55.4 | 33.6 | 37.0 |
| Netherlands | 463.7 | 430.9 | 480.0 | 552.2 | 553.6 | 63.4 | 40.6 | 62.9 | 82.9 | 64.9 |
| United Kingdom | 732.5 | 839.3 | 1 024.3 | 872.5 | 985.8 | 15.5 | 24.2 | 56.4 | 69.7 | 84.3 |
| Turkey | 71.9 | 68.7 | 128.1 | 97.4 | 124.8 | 0.4 | 0.6 | 0.9 | 2.7 | 0.6 |
| Former Soviet Republics | 280.9 | 182.2 | 189.5 | 252.1 | 224.9 | 1.5 | 2.6 | 2.9 | 1.5 | 4.7 |
| Poland | 7.6 | 9.3 | 20.1 | 11.6 | 10.2 | 0.1 | 1.1 | 0.9 | 0.5 | 0.6 |
| Other Eastern Europe | 34.7 | 24.7 | 38.3 | 39.0 | 25.1 | 1.6 | 3.6 | 1.8 | 0.6 | 1.6 |
| Other Europe | 516.6 | 453.3 | 508.5 | 503.4 | 590.3 | 14.0 | 33.4 | 34.7 | 23.2 | 22.5 |
| **Asia** | 3 093.2 | 3 532.6 | 4 412.6 | 3 717.9 | 3 442.8 | 107.2 | 92.2 | 101.4 | 107.5 | 118.3 |
| Japan | 616.1 | 617.4 | 765.9 | 623.2 | 552.3 | 31.0 | 30.5 | 31.5 | 33.0 | 30.1 |
| China | 284.0 | 270.4 | 403.1 | 281.0 | 261.7 | 5.5 | 4.2 | 6.4 | 5.3 | 6.1 |
| Hong Kong | 184.0 | 182.6 | 394.6 | 242.4 | 223.1 | 13.4 | 10.7 | 18.2 | 14.6 | 18.1 |
| Taiwan | 503.3 | 601.7 | 633.1 | 398.9 | 452.8 | 7.2 | 7.1 | 5.6 | 3.9 | 7.6 |
| Singapore | 498.4 | 830.8 | 775.4 | 677.5 | 799.1 | 15.6 | 9.4 | 8.8 | 16.2 | 13.2 |
| South Korea | 388.0 | 405.5 | 768.5 | 585.8 | 473.6 | 27.4 | 24.2 | 17.0 | 14.0 | 21.0 |
| Indonesia | 204.9 | 152.2 | 158.0 | 250.6 | 202.1 | 0.5 | 0.2 | 0.2 | 0.9 | 1.2 |
| India | 76.4 | 76.1 | 146.5 | 158.2 | 140.5 | 1.3 | 1.2 | 4.1 | 6.0 | 3.6 |
| Other Asia | 338.0 | 395.8 | 367.4 | 500.4 | 337.5 | 5.3 | 4.8 | 9.6 | 13.6 | 17.5 |
| **Africa** | 609.5 | 721.9 | 928.5 | 1 101.7 | 1 223.0 | 1.5 | 2.4 | 3.3 | 2.5 | 4.5 |
| North Africa | 224.1 | 364.3 | 326.1 | 274.7 | 360.2 | 0.2 | 1.0 | 0.9 | 0.1 | 0.6 |
| Republic of South Africa | 68.5 | 88.3 | 105.9 | 147.4 | 148.4 | 1.1 | 1.3 | 2.3 | 2.3 | 3.8 |
| Other Subsaharan Africa | 316.9 | 269.3 | 496.5 | 679.5 | 714.4 | 0.2 | 0.1 | 0.1 | 0.1 | 0.1 |
| **Middle East** | 1 252.0 | 845.0 | 906.9 | 1 176.4 | 1 342.8 | 15.7 | 14.4 | 15.6 | 8.4 | 8.6 |
| **Australia** | 172.3 | 204.2 | 226.0 | 336.9 | 279.2 | 6.6 | 9.7 | 14.4 | 10.0 | 8.5 |
| **Rest of World** | ..... | ..... | ..... | ..... | ..... | ..... | ..... | ..... | ..... | ..... |
| | Indianapolis, IN | | | | | Jacksonville, FL | | | | |
| **ALL DESTINATIONS** | 2 626.6 | 3 003.8 | 3 555.9 | 4 012.8 | 4 301.8 | 404.9 | 500.4 | 604.1 | 677.0 | 721.3 |
| **North America** | 1 484.3 | 1 728.4 | 1 974.6 | 2 139.7 | 2 069.3 | 100.0 | 116.4 | 106.5 | 123.0 | 160.7 |
| Canada | 1 080.8 | 1 088.6 | 1 079.1 | 1 099.2 | 1 302.4 | 77.3 | 85.7 | 87.5 | 98.3 | 131.5 |
| Mexico | 403.5 | 639.8 | 895.5 | 1 040.5 | 766.9 | 22.8 | 30.7 | 19.0 | 24.7 | 29.2 |
| **Caribbean and Central America** | 19.6 | 32.4 | 37.0 | 36.4 | 34.6 | 76.6 | 78.9 | 97.2 | 108.1 | 116.0 |
| **South America** | 75.6 | 102.9 | 223.2 | 273.4 | 384.4 | 28.7 | 64.9 | 69.7 | 43.0 | 32.7 |
| Argentina | 14.4 | 21.5 | 26.1 | 40.5 | 62.5 | 3.7 | 2.3 | 2.8 | 3.6 | 4.4 |
| Brazil | 29.8 | 38.1 | 103.1 | 142.1 | 243.4 | 6.0 | 6.0 | 8.0 | 7.7 | 11.7 |
| Other South America | 31.4 | 43.3 | 94.0 | 90.9 | 78.5 | 19.0 | 56.6 | 59.0 | 31.6 | 16.5 |
| **Europe** | 634.8 | 654.6 | 720.0 | 886.8 | 1 071.3 | 132.3 | 136.1 | 166.5 | 183.6 | 204.2 |
| Belgium | 23.9 | 32.7 | 31.1 | 37.7 | 46.5 | 6.8 | 5.6 | 5.9 | 5.6 | 7.5 |
| France | 90.6 | 88.7 | 105.4 | 201.3 | 280.6 | 12.1 | 15.3 | 16.7 | 24.4 | 23.7 |
| Germany | 71.6 | 87.7 | 77.2 | 100.0 | 142.0 | 15.5 | 19.0 | 25.4 | 20.4 | 15.6 |
| Netherlands | 56.2 | 66.4 | 99.2 | 129.2 | 149.1 | 7.9 | 11.3 | 12.9 | 12.7 | 12.5 |
| United Kingdom | 152.9 | 165.8 | 155.9 | 215.6 | 219.8 | 39.9 | 42.2 | 51.0 | 48.8 | 62.4 |
| Turkey | 20.3 | 10.0 | 33.5 | 17.8 | 25.4 | 1.0 | 0.5 | 0.8 | 0.5 | 2.1 |
| Former Soviet Republics | 6.2 | 4.2 | 2.1 | 5.4 | 2.5 | 5.1 | 0.9 | 0.6 | 1.0 | 0.6 |
| Poland | 6.3 | 2.8 | 2.1 | 0.9 | 1.7 | 5.6 | 1.6 | 0.5 | 0.5 | 0.8 |
| Other Eastern Europe | 7.6 | 3.3 | 10.8 | 14.1 | 17.5 | 0.1 | 0.3 | 0.4 | 0.8 | 1.6 |
| Other Europe | 199.2 | 193.0 | 202.6 | 165.0 | 186.3 | 38.2 | 39.4 | 52.2 | 68.8 | 77.4 |
| **Asia** | 358.8 | 413.1 | 505.3 | 565.9 | 633.7 | 51.1 | 86.2 | 143.4 | 190.5 | 176.7 |
| Japan | 253.4 | 265.8 | 312.8 | 326.5 | 282.5 | 19.4 | 44.8 | 79.6 | 108.9 | 105.6 |
| China | 3.1 | 7.9 | 6.1 | 9.3 | 19.9 | 1.4 | 1.2 | 1.6 | 4.3 | 7.0 |
| Hong Kong | 16.3 | 23.9 | 29.4 | 33.7 | 57.3 | 2.1 | 4.9 | 7.5 | 8.9 | 11.3 |
| Taiwan | 21.8 | 31.2 | 28.2 | 31.7 | 34.6 | 7.6 | 8.7 | 12.2 | 16.2 | 19.9 |
| Singapore | 13.5 | 15.6 | 28.5 | 30.2 | 35.0 | 2.7 | 2.8 | 5.5 | 8.9 | 7.4 |
| South Korea | 19.8 | 29.0 | 38.3 | 48.8 | 40.6 | 10.2 | 11.5 | 14.3 | 18.8 | 10.0 |
| Indonesia | 4.0 | 3.4 | 6.6 | 7.9 | 9.2 | 2.1 | 2.2 | 13.1 | 12.2 | 2.8 |
| India | 2.6 | 2.9 | 10.4 | 14.4 | 23.8 | 1.8 | 2.9 | 3.7 | 3.7 | 3.3 |
| Other Asia | 24.2 | 33.5 | 45.1 | 63.5 | 130.8 | 3.8 | 7.3 | 6.0 | 8.6 | 9.3 |
| **Africa** | 13.2 | 14.3 | 18.4 | 20.4 | 26.4 | 4.2 | 5.1 | 6.2 | 7.1 | 7.6 |
| North Africa | 1.8 | 5.4 | 5.9 | 6.2 | 7.2 | 0.4 | 0.4 | 1.2 | 1.3 | 1.5 |
| Republic of South Africa | 7.4 | 8.4 | 10.2 | 12.7 | 17.6 | 3.0 | 3.3 | 4.1 | 4.6 | 3.9 |
| Other Subsaharan Africa | 4.0 | 0.5 | 2.3 | 1.4 | 1.7 | 0.9 | 1.4 | 0.9 | 1.2 | 2.2 |
| **Middle East** | 18.5 | 29.9 | 40.0 | 42.4 | 38.5 | 6.5 | 6.7 | 7.9 | 12.8 | 10.6 |
| **Australia** | 21.8 | 26.8 | 36.7 | 47.7 | 43.5 | 5.4 | 6.1 | 6.6 | 9.0 | 13.0 |
| **Rest of World** | ..... | 1.3 | 0.7 | ..... | ..... | ..... | ..... | ..... | ..... | ..... |

## Table E-3.  Metropolitan Area Exports of Goods by Destination, 1993–1997—*Continued*

(Millions of dollars.)

| Destination | 1993 | 1994 | 1995 | 1996 | 1997 | 1993 | 1994 | 1995 | 1996 | 1997 |
|---|---|---|---|---|---|---|---|---|---|---|
| | Jackson, MS | | | | | Jackson, TN | | | | |
| **ALL DESTINATIONS** | 141.2 | 154.3 | 203.0 | 231.4 | 318.1 | 108.0 | 132.5 | 175.3 | 155.2 | 167.8 |
| **North America** | 43.2 | 45.8 | 48.3 | 50.8 | 65.3 | 51.9 | 68.4 | 86.7 | 83.9 | 119.0 |
| Canada | 34.6 | 37.3 | 44.6 | 42.9 | 53.9 | 51.4 | 66.3 | 83.1 | 79.6 | 108.0 |
| Mexico | 8.6 | 8.4 | 3.7 | 7.9 | 11.4 | 0.5 | 2.1 | 3.5 | 4.3 | 11.0 |
| **Caribbean and Central America** | 8.7 | 9.0 | 11.8 | 11.4 | 6.2 | 0.8 | 1.0 | 1.8 | 1.1 | 2.1 |
| **South America** | 13.4 | 13.6 | 16.6 | 11.4 | 12.2 | 4.1 | 2.3 | 4.9 | 5.0 | 2.7 |
| Argentina | 6.4 | 3.6 | 0.5 | 2.4 | 0.8 | 3.6 | 2.1 | 3.2 | 1.8 | 0.5 |
| Brazil | 1.0 | 1.6 | 1.3 | 1.5 | 2.9 | ..... | ..... | 1.3 | 2.2 | 1.2 |
| Other South America | 6.0 | 8.4 | 14.7 | 7.5 | 8.5 | 0.5 | 0.3 | 0.4 | 0.9 | 1.0 |
| **Europe** | 32.0 | 47.6 | 69.1 | 123.4 | 197.4 | 44.2 | 51.6 | 70.8 | 57.2 | 34.2 |
| Belgium | 1.8 | 0.3 | 1.4 | 4.7 | 1.6 | 3.4 | 4.2 | 33.8 | 34.3 | 9.7 |
| France | 3.4 | 4.3 | 3.2 | 4.8 | 4.3 | 20.5 | 20.8 | 13.5 | 5.8 | 0.6 |
| Germany | 6.5 | 6.0 | 6.3 | 7.5 | 6.9 | 7.5 | 11.6 | 7.3 | 4.4 | 3.5 |
| Netherlands | 2.0 | 2.8 | 6.1 | 2.5 | 6.0 | 4.5 | 5.9 | 5.7 | 4.8 | 3.8 |
| United Kingdom | 4.2 | 3.9 | 5.7 | 8.4 | 8.1 | 2.2 | 2.4 | 4.7 | 2.4 | 8.3 |
| Turkey | 0.9 | 1.1 | 0.7 | 0.7 | 0.5 | ..... | ..... | ..... | ..... | ..... |
| Former Soviet Republics | 7.7 | 21.9 | 37.7 | 82.4 | 147.3 | ..... | ..... | ..... | ..... | ..... |
| Poland | 3.5 | 1.2 | 1.7 | 2.1 | 3.5 | ..... | ..... | 0.1 | ..... | ..... |
| Other Eastern Europe | 0.1 | 1.4 | 1.6 | 3.1 | 1.5 | 0.1 | 1.4 | 1.5 | 0.7 | ..... |
| Other Europe | 1.9 | 4.7 | 4.8 | 7.3 | 17.9 | 6.0 | 5.2 | 4.2 | 4.7 | 8.3 |
| **Asia** | 19.7 | 26.4 | 46.2 | 25.4 | 27.2 | 1.8 | 3.9 | 8.6 | 4.3 | 6.9 |
| Japan | 5.9 | 7.9 | 8.1 | 9.0 | 12.4 | 0.4 | 1.7 | 5.5 | 2.0 | 3.7 |
| China | 1.6 | 0.5 | 4.4 | 1.4 | 0.9 | ..... | ..... | ..... | 0.1 | 0.5 |
| Hong Kong | 4.4 | 7.3 | 15.7 | 4.8 | 1.9 | ..... | 0.1 | ..... | 0.1 | 0.3 |
| Taiwan | 1.4 | 4.2 | 5.6 | 1.7 | 3.5 | 0.1 | 0.1 | 0.2 | 0.3 | 0.3 |
| Singapore | 0.7 | 0.4 | 0.7 | 1.8 | 1.4 | 0.2 | 0.6 | 1.2 | 0.5 | 0.1 |
| South Korea | 2.3 | 4.7 | 10.1 | 4.8 | 2.7 | 0.3 | 0.4 | 0.8 | 0.2 | 0.6 |
| Indonesia | 1.6 | 0.1 | 0.1 | 0.5 | 0.3 | ..... | 0.1 | ..... | ..... | ..... |
| India | 0.2 | 0.1 | 0.1 | 0.1 | 2.8 | 0.1 | ..... | ..... | ..... | 0.2 |
| Other Asia | 1.6 | 1.0 | 1.5 | 1.3 | 1.4 | 0.9 | 0.8 | 0.8 | 1.1 | 1.2 |
| **Africa** | 12.1 | 4.9 | 2.5 | 2.7 | 2.1 | 0.1 | 0.1 | 0.2 | 0.3 | 0.3 |
| North Africa | 6.4 | 2.9 | 0.5 | 0.5 | 0.2 | ..... | ..... | ..... | ..... | 0.1 |
| Republic of South Africa | 4.5 | 1.3 | 1.7 | 1.9 | 1.7 | 0.1 | 0.1 | 0.2 | 0.2 | 0.2 |
| Other Subsaharan Africa | 1.1 | 0.7 | 0.3 | 0.4 | 0.2 | | | | | |
| **Middle East** | 11.1 | 5.4 | 7.1 | 4.3 | 5.4 | 0.2 | 0.3 | 0.5 | 0.5 | 0.2 |
| **Australia** | 1.0 | 1.7 | 1.5 | 1.9 | 2.3 | 4.8 | 4.9 | 1.9 | 2.9 | 2.5 |
| **Rest of World** | ..... | ..... | ..... | ..... | ..... | ..... | ..... | ..... | ..... | ..... |
| | Jamestown, NY | | | | | Jersey City, NJ | | | | |
| **ALL DESTINATIONS** | 156.9 | 209.4 | 256.6 | 241.2 | 283.5 | 986.2 | 1 351.2 | 1 159.9 | 1 140.8 | 1 319.4 |
| **North America** | 125.6 | 168.6 | 178.3 | 162.6 | 195.4 | 132.6 | 135.3 | 152.1 | 197.1 | 206.4 |
| Canada | 107.2 | 159.9 | 175.6 | 154.2 | 177.1 | 76.9 | 92.3 | 111.8 | 153.4 | 153.9 |
| Mexico | 18.4 | 8.7 | 2.8 | 8.4 | 18.4 | 55.7 | 42.9 | 40.3 | 43.8 | 52.5 |
| **Caribbean and Central America** | 1.5 | 0.8 | 0.9 | 1.2 | 1.4 | 52.0 | 39.6 | 47.0 | 39.5 | 48.9 |
| **South America** | 3.0 | 3.8 | 5.4 | 4.7 | 3.6 | 29.1 | 29.9 | 36.1 | 30.7 | 38.7 |
| Argentina | 0.2 | 0.2 | 0.1 | ..... | 1.1 | 4.1 | 3.6 | 2.2 | 3.6 | 2.2 |
| Brazil | 0.5 | 1.8 | 3.6 | 1.6 | 1.5 | 7.9 | 7.5 | 14.6 | 9.5 | 6.9 |
| Other South America | 2.3 | 1.9 | 1.7 | 3.1 | 0.9 | 17.0 | 18.8 | 19.3 | 17.6 | 29.6 |
| **Europe** | 10.8 | 20.7 | 49.5 | 56.4 | 62.0 | 208.5 | 410.9 | 173.7 | 96.5 | 121.0 |
| Belgium | 0.3 | 0.6 | 0.3 | 0.5 | 0.8 | 4.8 | 3.5 | 3.6 | 5.8 | 2.5 |
| France | 1.3 | 3.4 | 3.5 | 1.4 | 3.3 | 7.3 | 7.1 | 6.2 | 7.1 | 12.3 |
| Germany | 1.3 | 0.9 | 1.4 | 0.7 | 1.9 | 21.9 | 46.3 | 24.9 | 16.5 | 21.5 |
| Netherlands | 0.1 | ..... | 1.5 | 1.3 | 0.1 | 18.3 | 5.4 | 6.1 | 4.8 | 8.5 |
| United Kingdom | 5.3 | 13.1 | 37.5 | 46.6 | 51.5 | 15.1 | 23.4 | 23.4 | 15.2 | 14.0 |
| Turkey | ..... | ..... | 0.8 | 0.1 | ..... | 87.1 | 267.9 | 59.1 | 7.9 | 2.3 |
| Former Soviet Republics | 0.5 | 0.6 | 0.4 | 0.5 | 0.5 | 8.2 | 12.1 | 5.5 | 4.5 | 3.6 |
| Poland | ..... | 0.3 | ..... | ..... | ..... | 10.0 | 17.9 | 13.7 | 1.1 | 1.7 |
| Other Eastern Europe | 0.4 | 0.2 | 0.3 | ..... | ..... | 4.7 | 2.7 | 2.3 | 1.7 | 2.4 |
| Other Europe | 1.6 | 1.6 | 3.8 | 5.4 | 3.8 | 31.1 | 24.5 | 28.9 | 31.8 | 52.2 |
| **Asia** | 14.9 | 13.3 | 19.9 | 12.4 | 16.0 | 137.4 | 150.8 | 147.3 | 129.3 | 129.9 |
| Japan | 11.0 | 7.9 | 9.7 | 7.8 | 8.6 | 37.5 | 42.4 | 38.0 | 38.6 | 34.6 |
| China | 0.1 | 0.1 | 0.4 | ..... | 1.1 | 21.4 | 23.3 | 26.3 | 26.3 | 22.9 |
| Hong Kong | 1.9 | 2.5 | 1.9 | 1.9 | 2.1 | 21.9 | 20.9 | 29.2 | 20.2 | 18.2 |
| Taiwan | 0.2 | 0.2 | 0.6 | 0.2 | 0.1 | 4.6 | 3.9 | 3.1 | 2.0 | 2.3 |
| Singapore | 0.1 | 0.3 | 0.1 | 1.0 | 1.7 | 8.8 | 17.9 | 6.5 | 6.2 | 8.1 |
| South Korea | 1.1 | 1.1 | 3.3 | 0.8 | 0.4 | 11.6 | 17.8 | 15.1 | 12.8 | 23.9 |
| Indonesia | ..... | ..... | 2.5 | ..... | 0.1 | 2.4 | 2.1 | 1.0 | 2.1 | 1.8 |
| India | ..... | 0.2 | 0.8 | ..... | 0.6 | 9.9 | 9.8 | 11.0 | 6.2 | 1.9 |
| Other Asia | 0.5 | 1.0 | 0.6 | 0.6 | 1.4 | 19.2 | 12.7 | 17.0 | 14.8 | 16.2 |
| **Africa** | 0.5 | 0.9 | 1.5 | 1.9 | 0.5 | 8.1 | 13.4 | 13.8 | 6.1 | 20.9 |
| North Africa | ..... | ..... | ..... | 0.1 | ..... | 1.3 | 1.6 | 2.7 | 1.9 | 11.7 |
| Republic of South Africa | 0.4 | 0.8 | 1.5 | 1.8 | 0.5 | 6.1 | 10.0 | 7.9 | 2.2 | 5.1 |
| Other Subsaharan Africa | ..... | ..... | ..... | ..... | ..... | 0.8 | 1.8 | 3.3 | 2.0 | 4.1 |
| **Middle East** | 0.2 | 0.8 | 0.5 | 0.5 | 0.5 | 413.4 | 564.6 | 583.9 | 636.8 | 747.9 |
| **Australia** | 0.4 | 0.5 | 0.4 | 1.5 | 4.1 | 5.1 | 6.7 | 5.9 | 4.7 | 5.8 |
| **Rest of World** | ..... | ..... | ..... | ..... | ..... | ..... | ..... | ..... | ..... | ..... |

## Table E-3.  Metropolitan Area Exports of Goods by Destination, 1993–1997—*Continued*

(Millions of dollars.)

| Destination | 1993 | 1994 | 1995 | 1996 | 1997 | 1993 | 1994 | 1995 | 1996 | 1997 |
|---|---|---|---|---|---|---|---|---|---|---|
| | Kalamazoo - Battle Creek, MI | | | | | Kansas City, MO - KS | | | | |
| ALL DESTINATIONS | 650.3 | 869.0 | 897.3 | 836.1 | 919.5 | 2 225.9 | 2 578.6 | 3 350.2 | 3 985.1 | 3 817.6 |
| North America | 246.3 | 361.8 | 386.6 | 358.6 | 420.5 | 618.8 | 847.5 | 876.5 | 1 357.2 | 1 189.8 |
| Canada | 218.9 | 305.4 | 347.3 | 312.4 | 350.5 | 293.9 | 339.1 | 367.1 | 367.9 | 428.5 |
| Mexico | 27.3 | 56.4 | 39.2 | 46.1 | 70.0 | 325.0 | 508.4 | 509.4 | 989.3 | 761.3 |
| Caribbean and Central America | 9.4 | 10.8 | 13.6 | 14.1 | 16.6 | 114.3 | 103.4 | 145.6 | 199.9 | 201.3 |
| South America | 21.6 | 32.4 | 33.8 | 34.2 | 27.3 | 199.5 | 210.1 | 347.1 | 430.4 | 465.8 |
| Argentina | 2.8 | 6.4 | 4.1 | 8.6 | 5.7 | 12.1 | 14.9 | 25.2 | 27.0 | 58.3 |
| Brazil | 7.9 | 12.5 | 15.3 | 10.8 | 10.3 | 26.3 | 20.4 | 35.2 | 53.9 | 32.0 |
| Other South America | 11.0 | 13.5 | 14.4 | 14.8 | 11.3 | 161.2 | 174.8 | 286.7 | 349.5 | 375.5 |
| Europe | 202.5 | 271.6 | 257.3 | 233.4 | 250.0 | 481.7 | 362.0 | 437.1 | 468.4 | 553.0 |
| Belgium | 66.1 | 65.3 | 94.4 | 66.7 | 65.4 | 17.5 | 51.1 | 56.6 | 46.8 | 18.2 |
| France | 40.5 | 103.8 | 44.0 | 31.7 | 28.4 | 21.2 | 21.1 | 33.4 | 21.2 | 43.7 |
| Germany | 9.2 | 13.0 | 12.9 | 11.2 | 12.5 | 64.0 | 55.7 | 63.6 | 57.3 | 92.0 |
| Netherlands | 8.0 | 10.0 | 11.8 | 9.9 | 9.2 | 29.0 | 26.2 | 31.5 | 50.8 | 34.6 |
| United Kingdom | 36.8 | 36.7 | 53.9 | 47.1 | 78.8 | 44.7 | 61.0 | 51.6 | 76.2 | 83.4 |
| Turkey | 2.4 | 1.8 | 1.9 | 1.6 | 2.4 | 11.8 | 1.6 | 4.2 | 19.0 | 78.9 |
| Former Soviet Republics | 0.8 | 0.9 | 1.8 | 2.2 | 0.4 | 184.3 | 38.2 | 51.5 | 53.6 | 37.8 |
| Poland | 0.2 | 0.1 | 0.3 | 0.6 | 0.6 | 4.4 | 1.5 | 2.3 | 10.8 | 8.9 |
| Other Eastern Europe | 0.5 | 0.2 | 0.3 | 0.2 | 1.8 | 49.6 | 26.3 | 11.5 | 21.3 | 19.6 |
| Other Europe | 37.9 | 39.8 | 36.0 | 62.1 | 50.6 | 55.3 | 79.2 | 130.9 | 111.4 | 135.9 |
| Asia | 126.2 | 149.3 | 164.3 | 152.9 | 153.0 | 444.9 | 639.1 | 1 150.3 | 1 120.3 | 997.3 |
| Japan | 60.6 | 62.1 | 72.5 | 59.9 | 63.1 | 174.1 | 253.7 | 537.5 | 641.3 | 506.3 |
| China | 1.6 | 5.5 | 5.5 | 2.8 | 3.2 | 24.4 | 43.3 | 53.8 | 61.3 | 94.9 |
| Hong Kong | 15.0 | 28.7 | 15.9 | 13.4 | 13.4 | 12.6 | 12.0 | 20.1 | 14.2 | 14.1 |
| Taiwan | 8.7 | 12.8 | 11.4 | 9.0 | 6.8 | 129.0 | 96.3 | 147.6 | 131.1 | 134.8 |
| Singapore | 1.9 | 3.7 | 3.3 | 5.1 | 13.2 | 19.2 | 21.8 | 21.6 | 26.8 | 27.5 |
| South Korea | 21.0 | 22.3 | 35.8 | 31.4 | 28.4 | 31.1 | 60.7 | 225.7 | 142.7 | 88.4 |
| Indonesia | 1.3 | 1.2 | 2.7 | 2.0 | 2.1 | 4.5 | 5.5 | 17.6 | 24.3 | 48.5 |
| India | 5.9 | 4.5 | 6.2 | 9.9 | 12.1 | 2.6 | 6.9 | 4.1 | 5.9 | 11.7 |
| Other Asia | 10.2 | 8.6 | 11.1 | 19.3 | 10.8 | 47.4 | 138.9 | 122.3 | 72.7 | 71.0 |
| Africa | 8.0 | 4.9 | 6.1 | 6.0 | 6.2 | 137.2 | 154.5 | 151.0 | 146.6 | 138.9 |
| North Africa | 0.5 | 1.3 | 1.8 | 3.1 | 1.3 | 95.5 | 106.9 | 67.7 | 57.8 | 77.4 |
| Republic of South Africa | 7.4 | 3.3 | 2.6 | 2.7 | 4.8 | 26.4 | 16.5 | 40.1 | 17.3 | 11.6 |
| Other Subsaharan Africa | 0.1 | 0.3 | 1.7 | 0.2 | ..... | 15.3 | 31.1 | 43.3 | 71.6 | 49.9 |
| Middle East | 14.3 | 10.3 | 12.7 | 12.2 | 10.4 | 127.2 | 167.8 | 163.5 | 167.7 | 209.3 |
| Australia | 22.0 | 27.9 | 22.9 | 24.7 | 35.4 | 24.7 | 41.7 | 34.7 | 63.0 | 41.4 |
| Rest of World | ..... | ..... | ..... | ..... | ..... | 77.5 | 52.4 | 44.3 | 31.5 | 20.8 |
| | Kenosha, WI | | | | | Knoxville, TN | | | | |
| ALL DESTINATIONS | 126.9 | 117.7 | 133.9 | 154.3 | 232.1 | 580.4 | 689.2 | 633.2 | 764.1 | 884.2 |
| North America | 50.9 | 45.7 | 47.0 | 57.1 | 93.5 | 238.6 | 273.0 | 195.2 | 263.0 | 265.8 |
| Canada | 45.3 | 40.8 | 44.1 | 54.6 | 86.9 | 228.4 | 259.1 | 169.8 | 215.5 | 187.0 |
| Mexico | 5.6 | 4.9 | 2.8 | 2.4 | 6.5 | 10.2 | 13.9 | 25.4 | 47.5 | 78.8 |
| Caribbean and Central America | 11.6 | 14.3 | 18.6 | 18.1 | 16.9 | 13.1 | 13.7 | 17.3 | 22.3 | 40.4 |
| South America | 1.9 | 2.3 | 3.9 | 2.9 | 4.5 | 11.2 | 31.5 | 35.8 | 41.8 | 51.2 |
| Argentina | 0.2 | 0.3 | 0.2 | 0.2 | 0.6 | 3.3 | 13.5 | 10.8 | 19.6 | 15.9 |
| Brazil | 0.2 | 0.2 | 1.8 | 0.5 | 0.9 | 1.5 | 1.7 | 2.1 | 3.6 | 8.2 |
| Other South America | 1.4 | 1.8 | 1.9 | 2.3 | 2.9 | 6.4 | 16.3 | 22.9 | 18.7 | 27.1 |
| Europe | 29.4 | 26.0 | 31.0 | 43.5 | 51.6 | 173.8 | 163.0 | 194.3 | 230.4 | 291.2 |
| Belgium | 0.3 | 0.6 | 0.6 | 0.4 | 1.9 | 1.6 | 1.8 | 2.3 | 2.9 | 3.1 |
| France | 0.9 | 0.5 | 1.0 | 1.1 | 2.1 | 8.0 | 12.8 | 14.8 | 22.4 | 35.5 |
| Germany | 2.9 | 2.5 | 2.6 | 3.8 | 3.3 | 29.7 | 35.5 | 42.2 | 31.5 | 26.5 |
| Netherlands | 0.8 | 1.8 | 3.9 | 4.1 | 5.8 | 11.7 | 12.7 | 12.6 | 13.5 | 22.9 |
| United Kingdom | 17.4 | 14.3 | 15.7 | 24.4 | 19.1 | 98.8 | 75.4 | 71.4 | 97.9 | 157.0 |
| Turkey | 0.2 | 0.1 | 0.1 | 0.2 | 0.2 | 0.4 | 0.6 | 1.3 | 2.4 | 3.5 |
| Former Soviet Republics | ..... | ..... | 0.1 | ..... | 0.3 | 1.4 | 1.1 | 1.0 | 1.6 | 1.2 |
| Poland | 0.5 | 0.1 | ..... | 0.1 | 0.1 | 0.8 | 0.5 | 1.1 | 1.2 | 0.4 |
| Other Eastern Europe | ..... | 0.3 | 0.4 | 1.1 | 0.6 | 0.5 | 0.7 | 3.8 | 4.0 | 5.6 |
| Other Europe | 6.4 | 5.8 | 6.7 | 8.2 | 18.2 | 20.9 | 21.8 | 43.8 | 53.1 | 35.5 |
| Asia | 19.9 | 23.1 | 23.9 | 26.2 | 57.1 | 115.1 | 180.4 | 156.0 | 168.1 | 183.7 |
| Japan | 13.0 | 13.3 | 15.3 | 17.5 | 39.8 | 42.8 | 112.0 | 53.4 | 60.8 | 67.2 |
| China | 0.4 | 1.3 | 0.8 | 0.5 | 1.8 | 13.4 | 5.4 | 5.0 | 2.9 | 2.4 |
| Hong Kong | 0.8 | 2.5 | 1.4 | 0.9 | 2.4 | 2.9 | 3.9 | 7.4 | 12.1 | 19.2 |
| Taiwan | 2.0 | 1.5 | 1.0 | 2.1 | 3.1 | 6.8 | 7.4 | 7.5 | 11.8 | 12.1 |
| Singapore | 0.9 | 1.0 | 1.0 | 1.1 | 1.9 | 6.6 | 6.6 | 4.1 | 5.3 | 7.7 |
| South Korea | 1.4 | 2.2 | 2.2 | 0.8 | 5.5 | 29.1 | 31.1 | 55.8 | 40.1 | 44.0 |
| Indonesia | 0.2 | 0.2 | 0.5 | 0.7 | 0.7 | 0.4 | 0.8 | 0.1 | 4.9 | 0.3 |
| India | ..... | 0.2 | 0.1 | 0.1 | 0.2 | 1.2 | 0.4 | 1.5 | 3.2 | 4.5 |
| Other Asia | 1.2 | 0.9 | 1.6 | 2.5 | 1.7 | 11.8 | 12.9 | 21.2 | 26.9 | 26.3 |
| Africa | 1.1 | 1.0 | 2.4 | 1.9 | 2.1 | 2.9 | 5.4 | 6.1 | 7.6 | 6.6 |
| North Africa | 0.3 | 0.2 | 0.3 | 0.4 | 0.2 | 1.0 | 1.8 | 1.4 | 2.2 | 1.8 |
| Republic of South Africa | 0.7 | 0.7 | 1.1 | 1.5 | 1.7 | 1.8 | 3.5 | 4.6 | 4.9 | 4.3 |
| Other Subsaharan Africa | 0.1 | 0.1 | 1.0 | 0.1 | 0.2 | 0.1 | 0.1 | 0.1 | 0.5 | 0.5 |
| Middle East | 4.0 | 2.3 | 1.3 | 1.0 | 1.5 | 17.4 | 12.8 | 13.7 | 10.8 | 13.1 |
| Australia | 8.0 | 2.9 | 5.8 | 3.5 | 4.9 | 8.3 | 9.3 | 14.8 | 20.0 | 32.2 |
| Rest of World | ..... | ..... | ..... | ..... | ..... | ..... | ..... | ..... | ..... | ..... |

## Table E-3. Metropolitan Area Exports of Goods by Destination, 1993–1997—Continued

(Millions of dollars.)

| Destination | 1993 | 1994 | 1995 | 1996 | 1997 | 1993 | 1994 | 1995 | 1996 | 1997 |
|---|---|---|---|---|---|---|---|---|---|---|
| | Lafayette, LA | | | | | Lakeland - Winter Haven, FL | | | | |
| **ALL DESTINATIONS** | 93.6 | 148.7 | 192.7 | 164.8 | 202.2 | 187.0 | 199.2 | 237.7 | 241.5 | 243.6 |
| **North America** | 28.1 | 32.7 | 43.4 | 45.2 | 71.2 | 55.9 | 54.0 | 64.6 | 40.6 | 43.5 |
| Canada | 20.9 | 26.4 | 36.4 | 34.9 | 63.6 | 47.5 | 49.4 | 56.8 | 38.7 | 41.8 |
| Mexico | 7.2 | 6.2 | 7.0 | 10.3 | 7.6 | 8.4 | 4.6 | 7.8 | 1.9 | 1.7 |
| **Caribbean and Central America** | 4.8 | 12.1 | 11.9 | 8.2 | 8.7 | 21.3 | 26.0 | 25.7 | 23.8 | 31.0 |
| **South America** | 12.9 | 46.8 | 35.1 | 45.2 | 54.4 | 6.4 | 6.6 | 8.3 | 10.8 | 11.9 |
| Argentina | ..... | 5.3 | 1.1 | 2.4 | 1.2 | 0.2 | 1.0 | 0.5 | 1.8 | 1.5 |
| Brazil | 5.0 | 3.4 | 5.0 | 2.2 | 3.1 | 1.7 | 1.6 | 2.0 | 2.3 | 1.9 |
| Other South America | 7.8 | 38.0 | 29.0 | 40.7 | 50.2 | 4.5 | 4.0 | 5.7 | 6.7 | 8.4 |
| **Europe** | 17.5 | 21.7 | 69.9 | 34.9 | 31.3 | 64.5 | 72.0 | 109.9 | 117.2 | 109.4 |
| Belgium | ..... | 0.1 | 11.9 | 0.3 | 0.6 | 7.5 | 6.7 | 9.1 | 2.3 | 2.4 |
| France | 2.2 | 3.8 | 4.7 | 1.2 | 1.2 | 12.3 | 7.9 | 9.2 | 23.3 | 24.4 |
| Germany | 0.8 | 0.7 | 1.9 | 0.4 | 0.7 | 4.4 | 4.3 | 6.0 | 5.3 | 4.9 |
| Netherlands | 1.6 | 1.0 | 22.7 | 12.3 | 3.6 | 5.4 | 12.6 | 33.8 | 26.9 | 37.3 |
| United Kingdom | 2.9 | 3.6 | 13.4 | 8.2 | 13.6 | 21.8 | 22.1 | 8.7 | 6.3 | 5.0 |
| Turkey | ..... | 0.2 | 0.2 | 0.1 | 0.2 | 0.3 | ..... | 2.6 | 7.8 | 0.4 |
| Former Soviet Republics | 0.1 | 1.5 | 5.2 | 5.4 | ..... | 0.3 | 0.4 | 0.5 | 0.2 | 0.2 |
| Poland | ..... | ..... | 0.1 | ..... | 0.1 | ..... | ..... | 1.2 | 3.1 | 1.7 |
| Other Eastern Europe | 1.6 | 0.1 | 0.2 | 0.2 | 0.5 | 1.1 | 0.2 | 1.7 | 0.4 | 0.2 |
| Other Europe | 8.3 | 10.8 | 9.4 | 6.8 | 10.8 | 11.5 | 17.7 | 37.0 | 41.5 | 32.8 |
| **Asia** | 7.7 | 12.9 | 9.8 | 16.2 | 9.8 | 32.4 | 35.0 | 22.2 | 37.1 | 39.1 |
| Japan | 0.7 | 2.3 | 1.3 | 0.8 | 1.4 | 18.0 | 27.7 | 14.7 | 28.0 | 22.6 |
| China | 0.9 | 0.3 | 0.2 | 1.0 | 1.3 | 6.8 | 3.9 | 1.0 | 2.0 | 2.0 |
| Hong Kong | 1.7 | 2.9 | 2.2 | 0.7 | 0.8 | 0.8 | 0.4 | 0.5 | 1.1 | 0.5 |
| Taiwan | 0.5 | 0.5 | 0.1 | 0.1 | 0.3 | 0.2 | 1.0 | 0.4 | 0.9 | 1.9 |
| Singapore | 2.4 | 3.0 | 2.0 | 1.3 | 1.5 | 1.0 | 0.7 | 0.6 | 1.3 | 0.5 |
| South Korea | 0.3 | ..... | 0.5 | 0.9 | 0.5 | 2.2 | 0.6 | 2.1 | 1.5 | 4.3 |
| Indonesia | 0.2 | 0.4 | 0.7 | 0.5 | 0.2 | ..... | ..... | 1.3 | 0.1 | 2.0 |
| India | 0.1 | 0.1 | 0.2 | 0.9 | 1.0 | 1.5 | ..... | 0.1 | 0.1 | 0.1 |
| Other Asia | 0.9 | 3.4 | 2.8 | 10.1 | 2.8 | 2.0 | 0.7 | 1.6 | 2.0 | 5.1 |
| **Africa** | 14.9 | 19.7 | 11.4 | 11.3 | 13.8 | 2.6 | 3.6 | 2.4 | 3.8 | 3.3 |
| North Africa | 1.1 | 0.7 | 1.0 | 0.3 | 4.8 | 0.1 | ..... | 1.1 | 2.5 | 1.5 |
| Republic of South Africa | 1.1 | 1.0 | 2.5 | ..... | ..... | 1.8 | 2.8 | 1.0 | 0.9 | 1.8 |
| Other Subsaharan Africa | 12.7 | 18.1 | 7.9 | 10.9 | 9.0 | 0.6 | 0.8 | 0.4 | 0.4 | 0.1 |
| **Middle East** | 7.2 | 2.1 | 9.8 | 2.1 | 9.7 | 1.7 | 1.0 | 3.7 | 4.4 | 3.4 |
| **Australia** | 0.6 | 0.7 | 1.5 | 1.8 | 3.2 | 2.3 | 1.0 | 0.9 | 3.8 | 2.0 |
| **Rest of World** | ..... | ..... | ..... | ..... | ..... | ..... | ..... | ..... | ..... | ..... |
| | Lancaster, PA | | | | | Lansing - East Lansing, MI | | | | |
| **ALL DESTINATIONS** | 406.1 | 469.3 | 581.5 | 626.2 | 620.3 | 185.7 | 208.6 | 224.0 | 202.2 | 217.5 |
| **North America** | 185.7 | 219.7 | 197.4 | 218.0 | 215.2 | 143.9 | 157.4 | 165.6 | 146.6 | 168.4 |
| Canada | 165.3 | 163.3 | 171.3 | 181.0 | 186.7 | 138.9 | 155.2 | 162.1 | 138.1 | 161.4 |
| Mexico | 20.4 | 56.4 | 26.1 | 37.0 | 28.4 | 5.1 | 2.3 | 3.5 | 8.5 | 7.0 |
| **Caribbean and Central America** | 10.4 | 19.9 | 23.0 | 34.0 | 40.1 | 1.7 | 2.7 | 1.2 | 1.5 | 1.5 |
| **South America** | 41.2 | 35.3 | 53.1 | 77.4 | 75.7 | 1.0 | 2.0 | 1.7 | 5.0 | 3.8 |
| Argentina | 2.3 | 5.7 | 7.5 | 6.5 | 15.2 | 0.1 | 0.3 | 0.4 | 0.6 | 1.3 |
| Brazil | 34.8 | 21.9 | 37.6 | 63.2 | 52.6 | 0.2 | 0.9 | 0.8 | 2.0 | 1.0 |
| Other South America | 4.2 | 7.7 | 7.9 | 7.7 | 7.9 | 0.7 | 0.8 | 0.5 | 2.5 | 1.5 |
| **Europe** | 112.4 | 113.1 | 159.4 | 132.3 | 129.5 | 15.5 | 19.7 | 20.9 | 22.8 | 24.5 |
| Belgium | 25.3 | 23.7 | 19.6 | 13.3 | 9.9 | 0.1 | 0.4 | 0.6 | 0.1 | 0.6 |
| France | 3.5 | 13.3 | 18.4 | 21.8 | 17.0 | 0.5 | 0.6 | 0.3 | 1.2 | 2.1 |
| Germany | 4.9 | 9.3 | 11.5 | 11.1 | 13.3 | 6.4 | 5.1 | 8.7 | 8.0 | 8.2 |
| Netherlands | 1.4 | 2.7 | 13.7 | 7.9 | 20.2 | 0.4 | 1.6 | 0.4 | 0.9 | 0.9 |
| United Kingdom | 39.4 | 41.9 | 39.4 | 34.8 | 22.4 | 3.4 | 5.2 | 6.7 | 5.9 | 9.9 |
| Turkey | 2.5 | 0.7 | 1.1 | 0.5 | 0.8 | 0.1 | 1.0 | ..... | 0.1 | 0.1 |
| Former Soviet Republics | 1.0 | 0.9 | 4.7 | 1.7 | 12.4 | ..... | ..... | 0.3 | ..... | 0.3 |
| Poland | 1.8 | 0.8 | 0.9 | 0.9 | 0.3 | 0.3 | ..... | ..... | 0.3 | ..... |
| Other Eastern Europe | 2.5 | 1.1 | 1.0 | 1.9 | 1.2 | ..... | 0.1 | ..... | 3.3 | 0.2 |
| Other Europe | 30.2 | 18.8 | 49.1 | 38.4 | 31.9 | 4.2 | 5.8 | 3.7 | 3.0 | 2.2 |
| **Asia** | 35.5 | 48.1 | 97.6 | 120.9 | 132.6 | 16.3 | 19.7 | 21.3 | 16.5 | 9.0 |
| Japan | 11.7 | 11.8 | 25.0 | 24.8 | 22.3 | 9.8 | 13.8 | 11.9 | 8.8 | 3.8 |
| China | 3.2 | 8.2 | 2.2 | 3.9 | 2.5 | 0.9 | 0.8 | 1.1 | 0.4 | ..... |
| Hong Kong | 3.2 | 4.2 | 17.4 | 14.3 | 16.8 | 1.2 | 1.3 | 1.9 | 1.3 | 1.1 |
| Taiwan | 4.6 | 5.9 | 8.9 | 16.0 | 11.9 | 0.6 | 0.4 | 0.4 | 0.4 | 0.1 |
| Singapore | 2.5 | 4.1 | 3.6 | 5.2 | 7.8 | 0.6 | 0.8 | 1.1 | 1.0 | 0.7 |
| South Korea | 5.8 | 6.4 | 18.7 | 39.0 | 54.2 | 2.4 | 1.8 | 2.2 | 2.4 | 1.2 |
| Indonesia | ..... | 0.2 | 0.2 | ..... | ..... | 0.1 | ..... | ..... | ..... | ..... |
| India | 0.5 | 1.1 | 2.4 | 1.0 | 1.2 | ..... | ..... | 0.2 | 0.7 | 0.4 |
| Other Asia | 4.0 | 6.3 | 19.2 | 16.8 | 15.9 | 0.7 | 0.8 | 2.6 | 1.6 | 1.5 |
| **Africa** | 1.8 | 3.3 | 7.3 | 5.5 | 2.8 | 0.7 | 0.8 | 4.0 | 0.6 | 0.5 |
| North Africa | 0.7 | 0.7 | 0.9 | 0.1 | 0.3 | 0.1 | 0.2 | 3.5 | 0.5 | 0.3 |
| Republic of South Africa | 1.1 | 2.0 | 5.2 | 4.8 | 0.9 | 0.5 | 0.5 | 0.4 | 0.1 | 0.1 |
| Other Subsaharan Africa | 0.1 | 0.5 | 1.2 | 0.6 | 1.6 | ..... | 0.1 | 0.1 | ..... | 0.1 |
| **Middle East** | 3.8 | 4.2 | 14.9 | 7.9 | 6.6 | 6.0 | 5.8 | 7.9 | 7.9 | 7.8 |
| **Australia** | 15.3 | 25.8 | 28.8 | 30.3 | 17.8 | 0.7 | 0.4 | 1.3 | 1.3 | 2.0 |
| **Rest of World** | ..... | ..... | ..... | ..... | ..... | ..... | ..... | ..... | ..... | ..... |

## Table E-3. Metropolitan Area Exports of Goods by Destination, 1993–1997—*Continued*

(Millions of dollars.)

| Destination | 1993 | 1994 | 1995 | 1996 | 1997 | 1993 | 1994 | 1995 | 1996 | 1997 |
|---|---|---|---|---|---|---|---|---|---|---|
| | Laredo, TX | | | | | Lawrence, MA - NH | | | | |
| **ALL DESTINATIONS** | 4 061.8 | 4 157.4 | 2 897.8 | 3 440.7 | 3 959.1 | 822.6 | 806.4 | 841.7 | 1 033.6 | 1 810.2 |
| **North America** | 4 055.8 | 4 135.7 | 2 880.4 | 3 420.5 | 3 927.6 | 120.8 | 153.6 | 185.3 | 188.7 | 240.1 |
| Canada | 17.8 | 87.1 | 295.1 | 242.3 | 268.2 | 114.0 | 142.7 | 179.1 | 178.5 | 226.7 |
| Mexico | 4 037.9 | 4 048.6 | 2 585.2 | 3 178.2 | 3 659.5 | 6.8 | 10.9 | 6.3 | 10.2 | 13.4 |
| **Caribbean and Central America** | 0.5 | 4.9 | 3.4 | 2.1 | 1.1 | 5.4 | 3.5 | 3.6 | 5.7 | 6.7 |
| **South America** | 1.2 | 1.6 | 6.1 | 3.3 | 3.8 | 7.8 | 10.2 | 15.5 | 15.2 | 33.3 |
| Argentina | 0.4 | 0.2 | 0.1 | 0.5 | 0.1 | 1.4 | 1.2 | 2.5 | 2.5 | 5.8 |
| Brazil | 0.2 | 0.3 | 0.3 | 0.1 | ..... | 1.3 | 3.9 | 6.3 | 6.4 | 18.1 |
| Other South America | 0.5 | 1.1 | 5.7 | 2.7 | 3.7 | 5.1 | 5.0 | 6.7 | 6.3 | 9.4 |
| **Europe** | 3.1 | 12.1 | 4.0 | 8.0 | 6.9 | 421.8 | 378.3 | 375.9 | 354.1 | 728.0 |
| Belgium | 0.1 | 0.3 | 0.6 | 2.2 | 0.7 | 4.8 | 6.2 | 6.8 | 7.8 | 7.9 |
| France | 0.3 | 1.0 | 0.7 | 1.0 | 0.7 | 75.2 | 79.6 | 43.6 | 30.8 | 49.5 |
| Germany | 0.6 | 0.3 | 0.4 | 0.8 | 0.1 | 174.3 | 119.0 | 118.4 | 133.4 | 139.8 |
| Netherlands | ..... | 7.4 | 0.8 | ..... | 0.6 | 24.9 | 15.2 | 29.9 | 22.2 | 54.4 |
| United Kingdom | 1.3 | 1.8 | 0.6 | 1.8 | 1.2 | 59.2 | 66.0 | 61.3 | 62.0 | 349.1 |
| Turkey | ..... | ..... | 0.1 | ..... | ..... | 0.1 | 0.3 | 0.2 | 0.5 | 0.8 |
| Former Soviet Republics | ..... | ..... | ..... | ..... | ..... | 3.6 | 4.3 | 2.1 | 4.6 | 10.1 |
| Poland | ..... | 0.1 | ..... | ..... | ..... | 2.1 | 1.1 | 3.4 | 0.9 | 3.6 |
| Other Eastern Europe | ..... | ..... | ..... | ..... | ..... | 0.9 | 2.0 | 2.8 | 2.4 | 1.8 |
| Other Europe | 0.8 | 1.3 | 0.7 | 2.2 | 3.6 | 76.7 | 84.6 | 107.3 | 89.5 | 111.1 |
| **Asia** | 0.9 | 2.6 | 3.1 | 5.3 | 18.1 | 221.3 | 216.8 | 219.1 | 433.9 | 735.1 |
| Japan | 0.3 | 0.8 | 1.4 | 0.6 | 4.7 | 136.2 | 112.9 | 111.0 | 192.8 | 325.0 |
| China | ..... | ..... | 0.1 | 0.1 | 5.2 | 11.3 | 10.1 | 11.4 | 16.4 | 24.3 |
| Hong Kong | 0.3 | 0.7 | 0.3 | 0.2 | 2.3 | 18.5 | 17.9 | 20.8 | 23.2 | 38.7 |
| Taiwan | 0.1 | 0.4 | 0.6 | 0.6 | 0.1 | 15.3 | 17.6 | 23.6 | 147.6 | 251.0 |
| Singapore | 0.2 | 0.4 | 0.3 | 2.3 | 3.0 | 16.0 | 18.8 | 16.9 | 12.3 | 22.0 |
| South Korea | ..... | 0.3 | 0.3 | 1.3 | 1.5 | 11.0 | 22.0 | 20.2 | 22.2 | 39.3 |
| Indonesia | ..... | ..... | ..... | ..... | ..... | 0.7 | 0.4 | 0.7 | 0.8 | 1.2 |
| India | ..... | 0.1 | ..... | ..... | 0.4 | 3.3 | 4.0 | 3.1 | 2.8 | 4.4 |
| Other Asia | ..... | ..... | 0.1 | 0.2 | 0.9 | 9.1 | 13.0 | 11.5 | 15.9 | 29.2 |
| **Africa** | 0.1 | ..... | ..... | ..... | ..... | 4.5 | 7.4 | 8.4 | 5.3 | 7.4 |
| North Africa | ..... | ..... | ..... | ..... | ..... | 0.5 | 1.3 | 1.1 | 0.6 | 1.0 |
| Republic of South Africa | ..... | ..... | ..... | ..... | ..... | 3.8 | 6.0 | 7.0 | 4.7 | 6.3 |
| Other Subsaharan Africa | ..... | ..... | ..... | ..... | ..... | 0.1 | 0.1 | 0.3 | ..... | 0.1 |
| **Middle East** | 0.1 | 0.4 | 0.3 | 0.9 | 0.2 | 27.3 | 18.3 | 16.6 | 11.6 | 29.9 |
| **Australia** | 0.1 | 0.1 | 0.5 | 0.5 | 1.4 | 13.6 | 18.4 | 17.4 | 19.1 | 29.7 |
| **Rest of World** | ..... | ..... | ..... | ..... | ..... | ..... | ..... | ..... | ..... | ..... |

| Destination | 1993 | 1994 | 1995 | 1996 | 1997 | 1993 | 1994 | 1995 | 1996 | 1997 |
|---|---|---|---|---|---|---|---|---|---|---|
| | Lexington, KY | | | | | Lima, OH | | | | |
| **ALL DESTINATIONS** | 624.2 | 1 078.6 | 1 235.0 | 1 499.9 | 1 886.8 | 294.1 | 166.2 | 226.0 | 207.3 | 242.0 |
| **North America** | 228.0 | 535.9 | 629.6 | 690.9 | 897.5 | 244.0 | 96.8 | 142.7 | 112.5 | 146.3 |
| Canada | 204.7 | 493.8 | 589.5 | 619.5 | 793.6 | 241.1 | 91.6 | 140.2 | 109.3 | 140.3 |
| Mexico | 23.3 | 42.2 | 40.0 | 71.4 | 103.9 | 2.9 | 5.3 | 2.6 | 3.2 | 6.1 |
| **Caribbean and Central America** | 3.3 | 2.8 | 4.8 | 7.4 | 5.2 | 0.1 | 0.3 | 0.8 | 0.4 | 1.3 |
| **South America** | 24.7 | 29.1 | 36.0 | 45.8 | 64.3 | 3.0 | 6.3 | 6.3 | 12.1 | 13.0 |
| Argentina | 1.1 | 12.9 | 9.1 | 13.5 | 16.6 | 0.1 | 1.0 | 1.4 | 2.4 | 3.8 |
| Brazil | 17.7 | 2.7 | 11.8 | 14.0 | 24.0 | 0.9 | 1.6 | 1.3 | 4.4 | 3.4 |
| Other South America | 5.9 | 13.5 | 15.1 | 18.3 | 23.7 | 2.0 | 3.7 | 3.5 | 5.3 | 5.8 |
| **Europe** | 136.2 | 226.5 | 236.6 | 410.4 | 467.7 | 19.8 | 24.5 | 24.7 | 20.3 | 16.1 |
| Belgium | 28.1 | 8.2 | 2.6 | 4.6 | 4.3 | 3.9 | 3.6 | 2.7 | 2.7 | 2.1 |
| France | 25.6 | 123.3 | 108.4 | 195.7 | 279.8 | 1.8 | 0.9 | 3.3 | 2.7 | 1.1 |
| Germany | 2.7 | 5.7 | 20.5 | 25.1 | 19.1 | 1.1 | 3.2 | 4.5 | 3.4 | 3.0 |
| Netherlands | 23.5 | 32.4 | 27.1 | 47.7 | 56.5 | 0.7 | 0.6 | 0.5 | 1.0 | 0.3 |
| United Kingdom | 18.9 | 31.9 | 61.8 | 113.7 | 64.1 | 8.5 | 10.0 | 6.8 | 2.7 | 4.0 |
| Turkey | 0.6 | 7.3 | 0.4 | 10.0 | 21.2 | 0.3 | 0.2 | ..... | 0.1 | 0.2 |
| Former Soviet Republics | 0.2 | 0.1 | 0.3 | 0.1 | 0.5 | ..... | ..... | 0.1 | 0.1 | 0.4 |
| Poland | ..... | 0.1 | ..... | 0.2 | 0.2 | ..... | 0.2 | ..... | 0.1 | 0.1 |
| Other Eastern Europe | 0.3 | 0.2 | 0.1 | 0.1 | 4.9 | 0.1 | 0.1 | ..... | 1.6 | ..... |
| Other Europe | 36.4 | 17.5 | 15.4 | 13.1 | 17.1 | 3.5 | 5.8 | 6.8 | 5.9 | 4.7 |
| **Asia** | 214.3 | 248.1 | 287.7 | 291.7 | 377.6 | 15.0 | 23.2 | 25.0 | 28.8 | 38.8 |
| Japan | 193.5 | 206.7 | 229.9 | 208.1 | 300.2 | 2.5 | 5.7 | 8.2 | 6.4 | 17.6 |
| China | 0.4 | 1.8 | 2.2 | 5.5 | 2.9 | 4.7 | 4.4 | 5.4 | 3.8 | 5.8 |
| Hong Kong | 2.8 | 5.1 | 7.1 | 6.7 | 10.2 | 0.9 | 0.4 | 0.7 | 0.7 | 0.7 |
| Taiwan | 5.7 | 2.3 | 5.9 | 11.3 | 8.6 | 1.0 | 3.2 | 1.0 | 1.7 | 0.2 |
| Singapore | 2.6 | 8.5 | 8.8 | 9.5 | 13.0 | 1.6 | 1.4 | 2.8 | 4.1 | 4.5 |
| South Korea | 6.0 | 14.6 | 23.3 | 35.0 | 26.0 | 1.2 | 3.6 | 1.3 | 3.1 | 3.8 |
| Indonesia | 0.2 | 0.4 | 1.3 | 1.2 | 7.0 | 0.5 | 0.4 | 1.2 | 0.8 | 0.4 |
| India | 0.4 | 0.9 | 1.6 | 1.6 | 1.4 | ..... | ..... | ..... | ..... | ..... |
| Other Asia | 2.8 | 7.7 | 7.7 | 12.6 | 8.3 | 2.7 | 4.1 | 4.5 | 8.1 | 5.8 |
| **Africa** | 1.6 | 1.6 | 5.5 | 6.7 | 9.1 | 1.3 | 0.6 | 1.8 | 1.6 | 1.4 |
| North Africa | 0.6 | 0.3 | 0.8 | 2.9 | 4.7 | 1.0 | ..... | 0.1 | ..... | 0.3 |
| Republic of South Africa | 0.3 | 0.6 | 3.9 | 3.3 | 3.7 | 0.3 | 0.6 | 1.6 | 1.4 | 0.8 |
| Other Subsaharan Africa | 0.8 | 0.6 | 0.8 | 0.5 | 0.6 | ..... | ..... | 0.1 | 0.1 | 0.2 |
| **Middle East** | 5.7 | 6.3 | 5.4 | 3.7 | 4.0 | 1.1 | 0.7 | 0.5 | 0.9 | 2.0 |
| **Australia** | 10.4 | 28.2 | 29.5 | 43.4 | 61.5 | 9.8 | 13.7 | 24.2 | 30.7 | 23.0 |
| **Rest of World** | ..... | ..... | ..... | ..... | ..... | ..... | ..... | ..... | ..... | ..... |

## Table E-3.  Metropolitan Area Exports of Goods by Destination, 1993–1997—*Continued*

(Millions of dollars.)

| Destination | 1993 | 1994 | 1995 | 1996 | 1997 | 1993 | 1994 | 1995 | 1996 | 1997 |
|---|---|---|---|---|---|---|---|---|---|---|
| | Lincoln, NE | | | | | Little Rock - North Little Rock, AR | | | | |
| ALL DESTINATIONS | 188.5 | 207.2 | 208.8 | 225.3 | 264.6 | 200.1 | 219.0 | 193.6 | 210.4 | 349.4 |
| North America | 54.0 | 51.4 | 58.6 | 68.3 | 94.9 | 100.8 | 107.9 | 85.6 | 93.4 | 194.9 |
| Canada | 38.8 | 42.4 | 53.7 | 64.2 | 89.8 | 69.0 | 76.9 | 77.8 | 82.3 | 162.5 |
| Mexico | 15.2 | 9.0 | 4.9 | 4.1 | 5.1 | 31.8 | 31.0 | 7.8 | 11.1 | 32.5 |
| Caribbean and Central America | 1.7 | 1.3 | 0.6 | 0.4 | 1.2 | 2.8 | 3.9 | 3.1 | 4.2 | 5.0 |
| South America | 3.3 | 3.3 | 4.6 | 6.3 | 9.0 | 4.9 | 4.3 | 5.7 | 6.8 | 12.5 |
| Argentina | 0.8 | 1.2 | 0.9 | 0.7 | 1.0 | 1.6 | 1.1 | 1.0 | 0.8 | 2.4 |
| Brazil | 0.7 | 0.7 | 1.5 | 3.1 | 3.9 | 0.2 | 0.6 | 1.2 | 2.6 | 4.3 |
| Other South America | 1.8 | 1.4 | 2.3 | 2.5 | 4.1 | 3.0 | 2.7 | 3.5 | 3.4 | 5.9 |
| Europe | 50.2 | 70.9 | 57.0 | 55.5 | 79.9 | 44.0 | 40.2 | 41.0 | 46.8 | 57.7 |
| Belgium | 2.7 | 1.3 | 1.5 | 5.6 | 9.5 | 0.3 | 0.3 | 0.6 | 0.9 | 0.8 |
| France | 2.2 | 7.4 | 2.5 | 1.9 | 3.5 | 4.2 | 5.6 | 7.7 | 17.3 | 7.9 |
| Germany | 7.2 | 13.4 | 8.6 | 12.7 | 17.7 | 1.4 | 1.6 | 2.6 | 1.8 | 1.8 |
| Netherlands | 15.9 | 19.3 | 12.8 | 8.5 | 10.5 | 1.1 | 2.4 | 2.2 | 2.8 | 7.9 |
| United Kingdom | 10.7 | 13.5 | 14.0 | 12.9 | 20.1 | 22.0 | 13.5 | 11.4 | 10.8 | 11.1 |
| Turkey | 0.1 | ..... | 0.2 | 0.2 | 0.2 | ..... | ..... | ..... | 0.1 | 0.1 |
| Former Soviet Republics | 0.1 | 0.3 | 0.2 | 0.2 | 1.0 | 3.3 | 9.2 | 6.7 | 4.5 | 12.5 |
| Poland | 0.1 | 0.4 | 0.7 | 0.1 | 0.3 | ..... | ..... | ..... | ..... | 1.7 |
| Other Eastern Europe | 0.7 | 1.3 | 1.0 | 0.4 | 0.5 | 0.4 | ..... | 0.1 | 0.2 | 2.1 |
| Other Europe | 10.5 | 13.9 | 15.5 | 12.9 | 16.6 | 11.2 | 7.4 | 9.7 | 8.6 | 11.8 |
| Asia | 56.2 | 61.6 | 73.1 | 72.9 | 63.5 | 31.3 | 43.2 | 42.0 | 45.4 | 59.2 |
| Japan | 41.7 | 45.4 | 50.9 | 46.2 | 35.4 | 4.4 | 3.4 | 5.5 | 6.7 | 5.7 |
| China | 0.3 | 0.2 | 0.6 | 2.7 | 4.7 | 0.1 | 0.9 | 1.2 | 2.1 | 1.0 |
| Hong Kong | 1.2 | 1.8 | 1.2 | 0.7 | 1.4 | 0.8 | 0.7 | 2.7 | 5.9 | 5.8 |
| Taiwan | 1.6 | 2.0 | 1.7 | 3.8 | 2.7 | 2.6 | 4.0 | 5.3 | 3.2 | 4.0 |
| Singapore | 0.9 | 0.7 | 0.8 | 1.4 | 1.4 | 2.1 | 2.7 | 3.8 | 3.5 | 5.2 |
| South Korea | 2.4 | 3.3 | 7.8 | 4.1 | 3.7 | 1.8 | 2.6 | 5.1 | 3.7 | 4.4 |
| Indonesia | 0.1 | 0.1 | 0.2 | 0.4 | 2.5 | 0.3 | 0.7 | 0.9 | 1.1 | 0.9 |
| India | 0.2 | 0.6 | 0.4 | 0.2 | 0.4 | 0.2 | 0.2 | 0.3 | 0.4 | 0.6 |
| Other Asia | 7.8 | 7.5 | 9.6 | 13.3 | 11.2 | 19.1 | 28.1 | 17.1 | 18.7 | 31.6 |
| Africa | 2.4 | 2.1 | 2.8 | 2.4 | 4.5 | 1.4 | 1.6 | 1.7 | 2.2 | 2.0 |
| North Africa | 1.0 | 0.8 | 1.1 | 0.4 | 1.4 | 0.2 | 0.2 | 0.1 | 0.6 | 0.6 |
| Republic of South Africa | 1.1 | 1.0 | 1.5 | 1.7 | 2.4 | 0.8 | 1.0 | 1.3 | 1.4 | 1.0 |
| Other Subsaharan Africa | 0.2 | 0.2 | 0.2 | 0.4 | 0.7 | 0.4 | 0.3 | 0.2 | 0.1 | 0.4 |
| Middle East | 10.5 | 2.7 | 1.3 | 2.3 | 2.3 | 7.8 | 12.2 | 8.6 | 7.6 | 9.0 |
| Australia | 10.2 | 13.7 | 10.7 | 17.2 | 9.3 | 7.2 | 5.8 | 5.8 | 4.0 | 8.9 |
| Rest of World | ..... | ..... | ..... | ..... | ..... | ..... | ..... | ..... | ..... | ..... |
| | Los Angeles - Long Beach, CA | | | | | Louisville, KY - IN | | | | |
| ALL DESTINATIONS | 20 013.6 | 22 224.8 | 24 731.0 | 24 437.9 | 25 816.4 | 1 673.8 | 1 798.8 | 2 199.8 | 2 327.1 | 2 449.1 |
| North America | 2 932.9 | 3 232.6 | 3 558.2 | 4 044.4 | 4 949.8 | 317.9 | 372.1 | 381.2 | 445.7 | 574.6 |
| Canada | 1 765.8 | 1 894.6 | 2 378.7 | 2 457.5 | 2 831.3 | 223.6 | 279.9 | 357.6 | 411.5 | 534.8 |
| Mexico | 1 167.2 | 1 337.9 | 1 179.5 | 1 586.8 | 2 118.5 | 94.3 | 92.1 | 23.6 | 34.2 | 39.8 |
| Caribbean and Central America | 174.2 | 173.2 | 175.1 | 206.6 | 225.4 | 30.6 | 28.6 | 26.0 | 24.8 | 27.2 |
| South America | 998.8 | 885.5 | 1 155.0 | 992.5 | 1 030.4 | 61.2 | 54.1 | 78.1 | 55.9 | 91.9 |
| Argentina | 212.5 | 122.6 | 112.3 | 122.7 | 142.5 | 7.8 | 8.3 | 16.9 | 5.9 | 30.9 |
| Brazil | 290.2 | 361.2 | 445.2 | 478.2 | 363.8 | 9.8 | 8.5 | 19.3 | 15.9 | 20.6 |
| Other South America | 496.1 | 401.7 | 597.5 | 391.6 | 524.1 | 43.6 | 37.3 | 41.9 | 34.2 | 40.3 |
| Europe | 3 917.6 | 4 987.5 | 4 875.6 | 4 337.3 | 4 681.8 | 377.4 | 432.1 | 471.3 | 591.0 | 699.6 |
| Belgium | 138.4 | 167.4 | 180.1 | 298.5 | 192.6 | 100.2 | 94.8 | 28.6 | 24.1 | 30.7 |
| France | 460.4 | 583.3 | 401.3 | 479.5 | 474.3 | 20.6 | 24.9 | 26.5 | 45.1 | 57.2 |
| Germany | 606.3 | 548.2 | 536.1 | 545.7 | 508.0 | 104.1 | 124.7 | 174.6 | 154.9 | 172.6 |
| Netherlands | 541.1 | 1 178.6 | 1 353.9 | 473.9 | 613.7 | 7.1 | 8.5 | 16.3 | 30.3 | 39.4 |
| United Kingdom | 624.2 | 718.8 | 824.8 | 911.4 | 824.2 | 38.1 | 40.7 | 47.1 | 84.7 | 109.9 |
| Turkey | 88.5 | 23.2 | 27.3 | 38.0 | 321.3 | 5.4 | 3.7 | 9.1 | 33.4 | 60.1 |
| Former Soviet Republics | 93.7 | 89.4 | 124.9 | 167.7 | 120.1 | 9.5 | 3.3 | 7.5 | 10.0 | 26.1 |
| Poland | 17.7 | 15.1 | 14.3 | 14.6 | 15.0 | 0.3 | 0.1 | 0.8 | 0.7 | 1.6 |
| Other Eastern Europe | 25.0 | 34.6 | 39.0 | 42.8 | 50.0 | 1.1 | 1.4 | 3.0 | 4.2 | 7.2 |
| Other Europe | 1 322.0 | 1 629.0 | 1 374.0 | 1 365.1 | 1 562.6 | 91.0 | 130.1 | 157.8 | 203.5 | 194.8 |
| Asia | 11 155.7 | 11 960.7 | 13 759.0 | 13 562.6 | 13 209.1 | 734.9 | 713.2 | 1 020.6 | 1 017.3 | 875.9 |
| Japan | 4 313.2 | 5 806.9 | 7 060.5 | 6 719.4 | 5 907.4 | 501.9 | 453.8 | 712.9 | 709.3 | 601.8 |
| China | 711.8 | 522.7 | 482.3 | 751.1 | 857.1 | 2.3 | 1.4 | 10.4 | 13.6 | 22.9 |
| Hong Kong | 740.8 | 763.0 | 1 010.1 | 893.7 | 952.3 | 86.9 | 53.9 | 40.7 | 30.8 | 17.9 |
| Taiwan | 2 151.2 | 2 140.1 | 1 977.4 | 1 325.7 | 1 532.7 | 21.5 | 24.0 | 37.9 | 47.5 | 43.6 |
| Singapore | 510.6 | 464.8 | 481.8 | 524.6 | 576.5 | 62.9 | 76.8 | 70.4 | 87.2 | 65.9 |
| South Korea | 1 399.5 | 1 395.3 | 1 698.1 | 2 086.3 | 1 835.0 | 39.0 | 42.8 | 73.8 | 67.6 | 59.8 |
| Indonesia | 436.6 | 113.7 | 167.6 | 334.9 | 361.7 | 1.6 | 2.3 | 6.1 | 6.6 | 3.4 |
| India | 156.1 | 35.8 | 66.2 | 70.0 | 61.9 | 0.5 | 0.7 | 2.7 | 7.4 | 6.2 |
| Other Asia | 736.0 | 718.5 | 815.0 | 856.9 | 1 124.3 | 18.4 | 57.5 | 65.8 | 47.3 | 54.5 |
| Africa | 116.1 | 105.1 | 110.2 | 144.9 | 153.4 | 7.5 | 6.8 | 10.4 | 11.9 | 12.7 |
| North Africa | 41.6 | 30.1 | 29.5 | 70.0 | 79.5 | 3.3 | 3.1 | 5.6 | 6.4 | 5.8 |
| Republic of South Africa | 36.8 | 38.3 | 38.6 | 50.1 | 42.5 | 0.4 | 1.5 | 2.6 | 4.1 | 5.5 |
| Other Subsaharan Africa | 37.7 | 36.6 | 42.1 | 24.8 | 31.3 | 3.8 | 2.2 | 2.3 | 1.4 | 1.4 |
| Middle East | 297.8 | 283.4 | 404.8 | 464.1 | 849.5 | 118.8 | 157.6 | 170.3 | 135.9 | 128.4 |
| Australia | 420.4 | 596.8 | 692.9 | 685.5 | 717.0 | 25.6 | 34.3 | 41.6 | 44.5 | 38.9 |
| Rest of World | 0.1 | ..... | ..... | ..... | 0.1 | ..... | ..... | 0.2 | ..... | ..... |

## Table E-3. Metropolitan Area Exports of Goods by Destination, 1993–1997—*Continued*

(Millions of dollars.)

| Destination | 1993 | 1994 | 1995 | 1996 | 1997 | 1993 | 1994 | 1995 | 1996 | 1997 |
|---|---|---|---|---|---|---|---|---|---|---|
| | Lowell, MA - NH | | | | | Lubbock, TX | | | | |
| ALL DESTINATIONS | 867.5 | 890.1 | 1 079.9 | 1 119.9 | 1 396.5 | 98.6 | 165.1 | 258.7 | 189.0 | 262.2 |
| North America | 107.0 | 122.2 | 144.9 | 161.8 | 175.2 | 50.6 | 62.6 | 70.1 | 65.7 | 79.8 |
| Canada | 94.0 | 103.8 | 131.0 | 146.2 | 152.3 | 6.6 | 11.9 | 17.9 | 12.2 | 9.4 |
| Mexico | 13.0 | 18.4 | 13.9 | 15.6 | 22.9 | 44.0 | 50.7 | 52.3 | 53.5 | 70.4 |
| Caribbean and Central America | 3.2 | 4.1 | 3.2 | 3.8 | 7.7 | 0.9 | 1.0 | 0.4 | 0.9 | 1.2 |
| South America | 20.7 | 28.1 | 26.4 | 19.1 | 49.8 | 1.7 | 16.9 | 29.3 | 29.5 | 34.3 |
| Argentina | 4.1 | 3.7 | 3.1 | 3.8 | 6.8 | ..... | 0.1 | 0.2 | 8.3 | 0.8 |
| Brazil | 8.4 | 10.5 | 17.0 | 8.0 | 28.5 | 0.2 | 1.7 | 1.6 | 0.1 | 11.2 |
| Other South America | 8.3 | 13.9 | 6.3 | 7.3 | 14.4 | 1.4 | 15.2 | 27.4 | 21.1 | 22.4 |
| Europe | 443.5 | 442.5 | 501.8 | 482.9 | 623.4 | 18.6 | 13.7 | 20.9 | 14.2 | 33.2 |
| Belgium | 24.2 | 30.4 | 31.7 | 31.4 | 11.6 | 0.1 | 0.1 | 0.1 | 0.3 | 0.8 |
| France | 81.8 | 68.0 | 69.9 | 41.8 | 95.0 | 0.4 | 0.1 | 0.9 | 0.9 | 0.6 |
| Germany | 66.4 | 63.1 | 86.5 | 75.2 | 117.7 | 0.3 | 1.7 | 1.1 | 1.0 | 1.0 |
| Netherlands | 64.9 | 62.1 | 74.3 | 84.3 | 81.9 | 0.3 | 2.1 | 1.4 | 1.3 | 0.2 |
| United Kingdom | 87.3 | 95.2 | 104.9 | 90.8 | 116.4 | 6.1 | 2.4 | 1.0 | 1.0 | 3.1 |
| Turkey | 1.4 | 1.1 | 1.4 | 1.2 | 1.3 | 0.4 | ..... | 1.2 | 0.8 | 19.7 |
| Former Soviet Republics | 0.2 | 0.7 | 10.8 | 2.0 | 7.1 | 2.2 | ..... | ..... | ..... | ..... |
| Poland | 0.3 | 1.1 | 0.7 | 0.5 | 1.0 | ..... | ..... | ..... | ..... | 0.5 |
| Other Eastern Europe | 1.6 | 2.1 | 4.0 | 7.1 | 7.8 | 0.3 | 0.3 | 1.4 | 1.1 | 0.6 |
| Other Europe | 115.3 | 118.9 | 117.5 | 148.7 | 183.5 | 8.5 | 7.1 | 13.8 | 8.0 | 6.7 |
| Asia | 216.5 | 222.6 | 343.0 | 391.4 | 464.8 | 22.4 | 62.6 | 130.2 | 62.3 | 106.0 |
| Japan | 100.6 | 108.3 | 160.7 | 217.2 | 238.5 | 2.8 | 1.1 | 2.2 | 0.8 | 1.0 |
| China | 3.7 | 5.7 | 10.6 | 16.5 | 8.0 | ..... | 16.5 | 15.0 | 15.0 | 28.5 |
| Hong Kong | 34.6 | 27.2 | 43.6 | 27.6 | 26.6 | 1.5 | 2.3 | 7.5 | 1.9 | 2.1 |
| Taiwan | 16.3 | 14.3 | 27.4 | 17.0 | 35.3 | 2.5 | 3.7 | 13.8 | 9.3 | 22.5 |
| Singapore | 23.8 | 22.4 | 29.1 | 23.8 | 37.4 | 0.9 | 0.5 | 0.5 | 0.5 | 0.4 |
| South Korea | 22.5 | 26.8 | 46.9 | 60.0 | 73.2 | 1.6 | 4.7 | 4.2 | 2.2 | 1.1 |
| Indonesia | 1.0 | 1.2 | 1.8 | 5.8 | 6.9 | 1.9 | 7.9 | 12.8 | 3.1 | 5.9 |
| India | 1.7 | 2.7 | 4.6 | 3.8 | 4.1 | ..... | ..... | 15.1 | 1.2 | 0.3 |
| Other Asia | 12.3 | 13.9 | 18.2 | 19.7 | 34.9 | 11.2 | 25.9 | 59.1 | 28.3 | 44.1 |
| Africa | 10.7 | 14.2 | 9.7 | 8.1 | 9.4 | 0.3 | 4.7 | 2.4 | 10.8 | 3.9 |
| North Africa | 0.8 | 1.5 | 0.7 | 0.5 | 1.1 | 0.2 | 4.6 | 2.4 | 10.7 | 1.1 |
| Republic of South Africa | 7.8 | 10.9 | 7.6 | 6.7 | 6.6 | ..... | ..... | ..... | ..... | ..... |
| Other Subsaharan Africa | 2.2 | 1.8 | 1.5 | 0.9 | 1.7 | 0.1 | 0.1 | ..... | 0.1 | 2.7 |
| Middle East | 39.4 | 30.2 | 15.9 | 14.2 | 22.6 | 3.5 | 2.9 | 2.3 | 2.9 | 2.9 |
| Australia | 26.3 | 26.2 | 35.0 | 38.5 | 43.6 | 0.7 | 0.7 | 3.1 | 2.7 | 0.8 |
| Rest of World | ..... | ..... | ..... | ..... | ..... | ..... | ..... | ..... | ..... | ..... |
| | Lynchburg, VA | | | | | Madison, WI | | | | |
| ALL DESTINATIONS | 143.2 | 152.5 | 192.1 | 258.8 | 439.2 | 357.7 | 417.1 | 497.5 | 522.4 | 603.0 |
| North America | 71.3 | 75.6 | 73.6 | 86.3 | 144.1 | 94.6 | 120.5 | 127.2 | 140.1 | 183.6 |
| Canada | 46.0 | 62.0 | 63.0 | 74.2 | 110.7 | 86.9 | 105.0 | 118.4 | 132.4 | 165.7 |
| Mexico | 25.3 | 13.6 | 10.6 | 12.1 | 33.4 | 7.6 | 15.6 | 8.8 | 7.7 | 18.0 |
| Caribbean and Central America | 0.8 | 1.1 | 1.9 | 2.3 | 3.5 | 3.6 | 3.7 | 3.5 | 3.6 | 2.8 |
| South America | 8.6 | 15.2 | 36.1 | 66.5 | 79.2 | 17.5 | 18.3 | 29.3 | 27.1 | 31.5 |
| Argentina | 4.9 | 2.6 | 8.2 | 5.5 | 25.3 | 2.6 | 3.3 | 3.7 | 2.6 | 3.4 |
| Brazil | 1.2 | 7.1 | 15.9 | 34.2 | 24.8 | 6.8 | 7.0 | 16.3 | 13.6 | 12.4 |
| Other South America | 2.4 | 5.4 | 12.0 | 26.8 | 29.1 | 8.0 | 7.9 | 9.4 | 11.0 | 15.7 |
| Europe | 31.8 | 33.9 | 42.3 | 50.9 | 70.9 | 150.3 | 156.7 | 178.8 | 197.4 | 220.3 |
| Belgium | 1.8 | 1.3 | 1.2 | 0.4 | 0.5 | 2.5 | 1.3 | 2.4 | 4.0 | 3.3 |
| France | 5.7 | 5.4 | 1.6 | 2.8 | 3.5 | 18.4 | 20.9 | 20.9 | 20.2 | 36.2 |
| Germany | 5.8 | 5.9 | 8.2 | 12.8 | 9.3 | 38.0 | 34.8 | 40.4 | 51.2 | 47.8 |
| Netherlands | 1.6 | 0.7 | 1.0 | 2.1 | 3.3 | 19.0 | 13.3 | 15.2 | 19.7 | 21.0 |
| United Kingdom | 8.3 | 8.2 | 10.0 | 9.7 | 11.6 | 29.8 | 36.8 | 43.4 | 44.3 | 52.8 |
| Turkey | ..... | 0.2 | 0.7 | 0.1 | 0.1 | 0.5 | 1.4 | 0.5 | 0.9 | 2.0 |
| Former Soviet Republics | 0.4 | 1.7 | 0.8 | 0.3 | 18.0 | 1.3 | 4.6 | 4.1 | 1.6 | 1.7 |
| Poland | ..... | 1.9 | 1.3 | 0.9 | 2.0 | 1.3 | 1.0 | 0.8 | 2.7 | 1.3 |
| Other Eastern Europe | ..... | 0.2 | 0.6 | 0.2 | 1.0 | 1.9 | 3.5 | 3.5 | 5.5 | 4.7 |
| Other Europe | 8.1 | 8.5 | 17.0 | 21.6 | 21.5 | 37.6 | 39.1 | 47.7 | 47.2 | 49.6 |
| Asia | 18.9 | 19.3 | 28.8 | 37.9 | 75.5 | 62.9 | 82.6 | 105.2 | 107.9 | 115.1 |
| Japan | 3.7 | 5.6 | 8.1 | 9.3 | 10.9 | 24.8 | 34.7 | 50.2 | 50.2 | 50.4 |
| China | 1.5 | 2.4 | 3.7 | 3.1 | 3.1 | 9.0 | 5.2 | 5.9 | 5.1 | 6.1 |
| Hong Kong | 1.4 | 1.9 | 2.6 | 6.0 | 34.5 | 5.7 | 8.5 | 5.2 | 6.7 | 7.8 |
| Taiwan | 7.4 | 3.2 | 3.4 | 3.3 | 7.7 | 4.3 | 7.6 | 8.2 | 9.1 | 10.4 |
| Singapore | 1.2 | 1.3 | 3.0 | 3.2 | 3.1 | 4.6 | 8.8 | 8.3 | 7.9 | 10.5 |
| South Korea | 1.4 | 2.0 | 2.1 | 5.7 | 5.0 | 8.4 | 8.9 | 14.9 | 12.5 | 13.4 |
| Indonesia | 0.2 | 0.3 | 0.6 | 1.2 | 1.4 | 0.1 | 0.2 | 0.6 | 0.3 | 1.2 |
| India | ..... | 0.1 | ..... | 0.1 | 1.3 | 1.3 | 3.1 | 3.1 | 2.9 | 3.1 |
| Other Asia | 2.1 | 2.5 | 5.5 | 6.1 | 8.4 | 4.7 | 5.6 | 8.8 | 13.1 | 12.2 |
| Africa | 3.1 | 1.8 | 2.7 | 4.7 | 3.8 | 7.4 | 7.2 | 18.2 | 12.2 | 14.1 |
| North Africa | 0.3 | ..... | ..... | 1.6 | 2.5 | 4.1 | 3.1 | 13.3 | 5.9 | 6.8 |
| Republic of South Africa | 2.7 | 1.7 | 2.7 | 3.1 | 0.5 | 3.0 | 3.1 | 4.3 | 5.8 | 6.4 |
| Other Subsaharan Africa | ..... | 0.1 | ..... | ..... | 0.7 | 0.3 | 1.1 | 0.6 | 0.4 | 0.9 |
| Middle East | 4.4 | 2.8 | 5.4 | 7.5 | 55.2 | 12.4 | 16.9 | 22.5 | 21.1 | 20.3 |
| Australia | 4.3 | 2.9 | 1.3 | 2.7 | 7.1 | 9.0 | 11.1 | 12.7 | 13.0 | 15.1 |
| Rest of World | ..... | ..... | ..... | ..... | ..... | ..... | ..... | ..... | ..... | ..... |

## Table E-3. Metropolitan Area Exports of Goods by Destination, 1993–1997—*Continued*

(Millions of dollars.)

| Destination | 1993 | 1994 | 1995 | 1996 | 1997 | 1993 | 1994 | 1995 | 1996 | 1997 |
|---|---|---|---|---|---|---|---|---|---|---|
| | Manchester, NH | | | | | Mansfield, OH | | | | |
| **ALL DESTINATIONS** | 107.0 | 115.3 | 146.3 | 198.3 | 237.8 | 367.6 | 349.9 | 394.9 | 413.0 | 444.0 |
| **North America** | 46.9 | 67.8 | 72.4 | 115.1 | 134.0 | 199.4 | 219.1 | 251.7 | 279.2 | 313.6 |
| Canada | 33.1 | 51.0 | 57.9 | 96.9 | 114.9 | 179.0 | 194.7 | 235.2 | 259.4 | 269.3 |
| Mexico | 13.8 | 16.8 | 14.6 | 18.2 | 19.1 | 20.4 | 24.4 | 16.5 | 19.7 | 44.3 |
| **Caribbean and Central America** | 5.6 | 4.6 | 6.1 | 5.9 | 7.7 | 7.1 | 2.0 | 2.6 | 2.8 | 2.5 |
| **South America** | 2.1 | 1.9 | 4.1 | 5.7 | 3.1 | 9.1 | 13.2 | 10.8 | 8.0 | 7.8 |
| Argentina | 0.2 | 0.4 | 0.1 | 0.1 | 0.3 | 0.9 | 1.2 | 1.7 | 0.6 | 1.8 |
| Brazil | 0.2 | 0.3 | 2.0 | 1.3 | 1.4 | 2.9 | 3.7 | 2.8 | 1.3 | 0.8 |
| Other South America | 1.8 | 1.2 | 1.9 | 4.3 | 1.4 | 5.4 | 8.2 | 6.4 | 6.1 | 5.2 |
| **Europe** | 34.3 | 24.9 | 39.3 | 44.7 | 53.4 | 49.7 | 51.0 | 73.7 | 70.5 | 71.8 |
| Belgium | 1.7 | 4.8 | 0.3 | 1.4 | 3.2 | 1.5 | 1.0 | 1.0 | 1.4 | 0.7 |
| France | 4.8 | 3.4 | 2.5 | 2.4 | 3.3 | 6.5 | 6.0 | 9.7 | 12.6 | 8.2 |
| Germany | 4.8 | 3.1 | 5.1 | 6.2 | 7.8 | 14.2 | 15.1 | 18.7 | 13.7 | 20.2 |
| Netherlands | 7.7 | 2.3 | 9.0 | 15.9 | 12.1 | 2.3 | 2.8 | 5.1 | 2.3 | 2.1 |
| United Kingdom | 6.6 | 5.7 | 13.1 | 9.7 | 11.8 | 10.5 | 10.2 | 22.9 | 22.9 | 19.7 |
| Turkey | 0.1 | 0.2 | 0.2 | 0.1 | 0.1 | 0.4 | 0.4 | 0.6 | 0.3 | 0.4 |
| Former Soviet Republics | 1.6 | 0.4 | 0.7 | 0.9 | 0.8 | 0.1 | ..... | ..... | 0.1 | 0.3 |
| Poland | ..... | 0.1 | 0.1 | ..... | 0.1 | ..... | ..... | ..... | 0.2 | 0.2 |
| Other Eastern Europe | ..... | ..... | 1.4 | 0.8 | 0.3 | 0.1 | ..... | ..... | ..... | 0.3 |
| Other Europe | 7.0 | 5.0 | 6.9 | 7.3 | 13.9 | 14.1 | 15.6 | 15.7 | 16.9 | 19.9 |
| **Asia** | 10.2 | 11.9 | 18.5 | 23.3 | 28.7 | 49.7 | 37.4 | 31.3 | 26.4 | 29.2 |
| Japan | 2.6 | 2.8 | 2.7 | 4.0 | 5.8 | 18.9 | 15.0 | 6.2 | 5.4 | 6.9 |
| China | 0.9 | 0.6 | 1.6 | 0.5 | 2.0 | 1.5 | 3.4 | 0.9 | 1.2 | 2.1 |
| Hong Kong | 1.1 | 1.3 | 5.1 | 6.8 | 5.3 | 0.2 | 0.3 | 0.6 | 1.3 | 1.9 |
| Taiwan | 0.6 | 1.7 | 1.9 | 3.4 | 4.6 | 3.2 | 2.1 | 2.3 | 2.2 | 3.0 |
| Singapore | 1.1 | 2.0 | 1.4 | 2.1 | 2.5 | 0.8 | 1.3 | 1.5 | 1.0 | 1.7 |
| South Korea | 2.1 | 1.6 | 3.1 | 2.6 | 3.6 | 4.7 | 2.9 | 5.7 | 5.4 | 3.0 |
| Indonesia | 0.1 | ..... | 0.4 | 0.2 | 0.2 | ..... | ..... | ..... | 0.3 | 0.4 |
| India | 0.2 | 0.3 | 0.4 | 0.2 | 0.2 | 17.7 | 6.0 | 10.6 | 6.0 | 4.6 |
| Other Asia | 1.6 | 1.7 | 2.0 | 3.5 | 4.4 | 2.7 | 6.3 | 3.6 | 3.5 | 5.7 |
| **Africa** | 0.2 | 0.7 | 0.9 | 0.6 | 1.5 | 11.1 | 7.3 | 6.3 | 9.4 | 3.7 |
| North Africa | ..... | 0.4 | 0.6 | 0.6 | 0.9 | 6.4 | 0.8 | 0.6 | 2.2 | 1.0 |
| Republic of South Africa | 0.1 | 0.2 | 0.2 | 0.1 | 0.5 | 4.3 | 6.0 | 5.6 | 6.8 | 2.4 |
| Other Subsaharan Africa | 0.1 | 0.1 | 0.1 | ..... | ..... | 0.4 | 0.4 | 0.1 | 0.3 | 0.2 |
| **Middle East** | 0.8 | 0.7 | 1.1 | 1.0 | 5.0 | 1.9 | 4.0 | 2.0 | 2.2 | 2.9 |
| **Australia** | 6.8 | 2.7 | 3.9 | 1.9 | 4.5 | 39.6 | 15.9 | 16.5 | 14.6 | 12.4 |
| **Rest of World** | ..... | ..... | ..... | ..... | ..... | ..... | ..... | ..... | ..... | ..... |
| | McAllen - Edinburg - Mission, TX | | | | | Melbourne - Titusville - Palm Bay, FL | | | | |
| **ALL DESTINATIONS** | 1 510.2 | 1 826.4 | 1 617.1 | 1 579.7 | 1 872.9 | 315.2 | 315.9 | 310.1 | 635.0 | 408.8 |
| **North America** | 1 490.5 | 1 798.3 | 1 576.4 | 1 533.8 | 1 786.0 | 47.8 | 62.5 | 79.6 | 137.4 | 144.4 |
| Canada | 63.0 | 78.3 | 121.8 | 126.8 | 173.8 | 44.7 | 53.7 | 76.2 | 127.4 | 123.5 |
| Mexico | 1 427.5 | 1 720.0 | 1 454.6 | 1 407.0 | 1 612.2 | 3.1 | 8.8 | 3.4 | 10.0 | 20.8 |
| **Caribbean and Central America** | 4.1 | 5.8 | 4.9 | 5.7 | 2.1 | 6.8 | 16.1 | 5.5 | 6.0 | 8.2 |
| **South America** | 0.5 | 0.7 | 5.9 | 2.3 | 4.1 | 15.7 | 11.9 | 10.4 | 12.7 | 32.7 |
| Argentina | 0.1 | 0.4 | 0.4 | 0.6 | 0.4 | 6.1 | 5.3 | 0.9 | 1.3 | 1.0 |
| Brazil | 0.1 | 0.1 | 4.9 | 1.2 | 1.1 | 3.5 | 2.0 | 3.2 | 4.9 | 9.7 |
| Other South America | 0.3 | 0.2 | 0.5 | 0.5 | 2.6 | 6.1 | 4.6 | 6.3 | 6.5 | 22.0 |
| **Europe** | 11.8 | 14.7 | 21.4 | 27.2 | 60.4 | 86.2 | 81.1 | 75.4 | 334.1 | 99.4 |
| Belgium | ..... | ..... | 0.2 | 0.2 | 0.2 | 4.5 | 3.5 | 2.0 | 3.3 | 5.4 |
| France | 3.2 | 1.7 | 1.6 | 1.5 | 1.5 | 12.3 | 12.2 | 13.3 | 129.4 | 11.4 |
| Germany | 1.6 | 1.6 | 2.5 | 5.3 | 15.1 | 27.5 | 11.6 | 14.2 | 20.9 | 13.2 |
| Netherlands | 1.1 | 1.2 | 2.7 | 1.4 | 2.6 | 1.8 | 3.8 | 2.8 | 5.8 | 4.8 |
| United Kingdom | 3.9 | 6.5 | 9.4 | 13.4 | 31.7 | 21.2 | 33.8 | 22.5 | 30.5 | 35.6 |
| Turkey | ..... | ..... | 0.2 | 0.1 | 0.1 | 1.0 | 0.7 | ..... | 1.5 | 1.9 |
| Former Soviet Republics | ..... | ..... | ..... | ..... | ..... | 0.7 | 0.7 | 1.9 | 1.0 | 4.0 |
| Poland | ..... | ..... | ..... | ..... | 0.1 | ..... | ..... | 0.2 | 0.1 | 0.3 |
| Other Eastern Europe | 0.3 | 0.1 | ..... | ..... | 0.1 | 2.0 | 1.5 | 1.8 | 1.6 | 0.6 |
| Other Europe | 1.7 | 3.5 | 4.7 | 5.2 | 9.1 | 15.2 | 13.1 | 16.6 | 139.9 | 22.2 |
| **Asia** | 2.6 | 5.4 | 6.1 | 7.8 | 18.4 | 79.2 | 112.4 | 116.3 | 119.2 | 100.1 |
| Japan | 1.4 | 0.9 | 1.3 | 0.9 | 10.5 | 14.8 | 12.0 | 7.7 | 4.1 | 6.3 |
| China | ..... | 1.4 | ..... | ..... | 0.2 | 8.6 | 22.0 | 2.7 | 1.6 | 2.3 |
| Hong Kong | 0.3 | 0.4 | 2.0 | 1.7 | 0.7 | 3.0 | 11.5 | 7.2 | 6.2 | 6.0 |
| Taiwan | 0.2 | 0.3 | 0.3 | 0.5 | 0.4 | 1.6 | 2.6 | 1.8 | 1.9 | 4.1 |
| Singapore | 0.2 | 0.4 | 0.8 | 1.0 | 3.9 | 11.4 | 17.2 | 62.5 | 77.9 | 12.4 |
| South Korea | 0.1 | 0.1 | 0.3 | 0.4 | 0.4 | 5.4 | 4.2 | 11.5 | 4.8 | 15.2 |
| Indonesia | ..... | ..... | ..... | ..... | 0.1 | 4.5 | 1.6 | 2.6 | 1.5 | 0.3 |
| India | 0.1 | 0.1 | 0.1 | 0.2 | ..... | 0.4 | 1.2 | 1.5 | 2.7 | 1.1 |
| Other Asia | 0.3 | 1.8 | 1.3 | 3.0 | 2.2 | 29.6 | 40.1 | 18.8 | 18.6 | 52.2 |
| **Africa** | 0.1 | 0.1 | 0.6 | 1.0 | 0.4 | 2.6 | 3.8 | 13.0 | 7.7 | 7.1 |
| North Africa | ..... | ..... | ..... | ..... | ..... | 0.4 | 1.4 | 9.3 | 5.7 | 4.5 |
| Republic of South Africa | ..... | ..... | 0.2 | 0.1 | 0.1 | 0.7 | 1.1 | 0.8 | 0.8 | 0.5 |
| Other Subsaharan Africa | 0.1 | 0.1 | 0.4 | 1.0 | 0.3 | 1.5 | 1.2 | 2.8 | 1.2 | 2.1 |
| **Middle East** | 0.5 | 0.5 | 0.8 | 1.1 | 0.9 | 8.2 | 7.3 | 5.6 | 9.6 | 14.2 |
| **Australia** | 0.2 | 1.0 | 1.0 | 0.8 | 0.6 | 2.4 | 18.8 | 4.2 | 6.7 | 2.8 |
| **Rest of World** | ..... | ..... | ..... | ..... | ..... | 66.4 | 1.9 | ..... | 1.7 | ..... |

## Table E-3.  Metropolitan Area Exports of Goods by Destination, 1993–1997—*Continued*

(Millions of dollars.)

| Destination | 1993 | 1994 | 1995 | 1996 | 1997 | 1993 | 1994 | 1995 | 1996 | 1997 |
|---|---|---|---|---|---|---|---|---|---|---|
| | Memphis, TN - AR - MS | | | | | Miami, FL | | | | |
| **ALL DESTINATIONS** | 2 055.1 | 2 729.5 | 4 163.8 | 3 786.1 | 3 636.9 | 8 264.3 | 9 266.7 | 10 200.8 | 10 681.2 | 12 692.3 |
| **North America** | 517.6 | 598.6 | 623.7 | 665.6 | 790.8 | 833.9 | 976.7 | 659.2 | 725.6 | 1 066.8 |
| Canada | 318.9 | 359.7 | 433.3 | 468.4 | 522.9 | 312.2 | 314.5 | 366.2 | 322.2 | 379.2 |
| Mexico | 198.7 | 238.8 | 190.5 | 197.2 | 267.9 | 521.7 | 662.2 | 293.1 | 403.4 | 687.6 |
| **Caribbean and Central America** | 48.5 | 58.1 | 88.2 | 82.0 | 82.4 | 2 528.1 | 2 608.2 | 2 808.0 | 2 907.5 | 3 449.3 |
| **South America** | 155.1 | 152.2 | 253.7 | 287.8 | 263.9 | 3 899.5 | 4 620.1 | 5 241.5 | 5 718.9 | 6 855.4 |
| Argentina | 9.3 | 9.4 | 12.5 | 18.3 | 18.9 | 642.6 | 723.8 | 536.5 | 626.4 | 705.9 |
| Brazil | 78.5 | 84.3 | 137.4 | 171.2 | 130.7 | 555.6 | 868.8 | 1 336.5 | 1 696.5 | 2 128.8 |
| Other South America | 67.3 | 58.6 | 103.8 | 98.4 | 114.2 | 2 701.3 | 3 027.4 | 3 368.4 | 3 396.0 | 4 020.7 |
| **Europe** | 637.0 | 590.0 | 732.0 | 755.6 | 1 013.9 | 624.4 | 629.7 | 847.5 | 836.7 | 829.8 |
| Belgium | 42.0 | 43.9 | 54.6 | 64.7 | 110.2 | 24.7 | 35.8 | 25.3 | 23.3 | 47.1 |
| France | 73.9 | 99.6 | 90.4 | 111.9 | 151.6 | 109.3 | 103.2 | 145.2 | 138.1 | 146.7 |
| Germany | 66.2 | 66.4 | 73.7 | 118.9 | 111.7 | 80.8 | 70.7 | 75.5 | 48.6 | 52.6 |
| Netherlands | 78.0 | 75.2 | 100.7 | 69.4 | 97.5 | 65.6 | 82.9 | 95.7 | 106.8 | 111.8 |
| United Kingdom | 71.4 | 69.3 | 99.2 | 101.5 | 110.3 | 93.3 | 93.1 | 131.9 | 149.9 | 159.9 |
| Turkey | 59.7 | 25.6 | 76.4 | 54.6 | 124.6 | 3.3 | 2.7 | 3.0 | 5.0 | 8.9 |
| Former Soviet Republics | 60.2 | 13.9 | 8.7 | 20.8 | 121.5 | 11.2 | 11.0 | 12.2 | 13.9 | 12.1 |
| Poland | 0.3 | 0.3 | 0.1 | 0.7 | 0.7 | 3.6 | 2.4 | 2.0 | 1.6 | 1.3 |
| Other Eastern Europe | 37.4 | 23.2 | 12.3 | 20.7 | 8.8 | 11.4 | 9.1 | 8.8 | 8.9 | 5.1 |
| Other Europe | 148.1 | 172.6 | 216.0 | 192.4 | 177.0 | 221.1 | 218.8 | 347.8 | 340.4 | 284.4 |
| **Asia** | 501.2 | 1 133.7 | 2 137.5 | 1 654.5 | 1 169.1 | 223.1 | 302.9 | 478.3 | 327.5 | 319.2 |
| Japan | 177.7 | 224.7 | 324.1 | 250.8 | 263.5 | 81.0 | 120.9 | 114.1 | 81.7 | 102.6 |
| China | 18.7 | 350.1 | 1 023.8 | 806.5 | 362.2 | 12.2 | 10.1 | 38.9 | 11.4 | 12.5 |
| Hong Kong | 23.5 | 116.5 | 113.0 | 49.6 | 58.8 | 46.5 | 72.8 | 99.6 | 64.9 | 64.9 |
| Taiwan | 58.7 | 72.1 | 81.4 | 65.3 | 102.9 | 15.6 | 23.4 | 68.5 | 28.5 | 20.3 |
| Singapore | 8.9 | 12.9 | 15.3 | 23.6 | 62.1 | 19.3 | 24.0 | 29.7 | 27.1 | 27.7 |
| South Korea | 77.7 | 112.2 | 137.2 | 196.2 | 113.9 | 8.3 | 18.0 | 62.7 | 29.8 | 16.9 |
| Indonesia | 48.3 | 59.9 | 131.9 | 93.9 | 45.6 | 6.7 | 4.4 | 7.7 | 7.6 | 5.0 |
| India | 17.2 | 12.1 | 30.0 | 8.2 | 10.1 | 16.0 | 5.7 | 5.9 | 7.3 | 7.6 |
| Other Asia | 70.5 | 173.1 | 280.7 | 160.6 | 149.9 | 17.5 | 23.6 | 51.2 | 69.2 | 61.7 |
| **Africa** | 99.4 | 112.2 | 183.6 | 215.1 | 161.7 | 59.0 | 54.0 | 67.4 | 62.7 | 65.5 |
| North Africa | 25.5 | 69.2 | 136.4 | 166.8 | 89.6 | 7.9 | 8.6 | 13.2 | 16.9 | 13.3 |
| Republic of South Africa | 64.7 | 41.5 | 44.2 | 44.3 | 32.7 | 14.6 | 12.8 | 15.2 | 16.8 | 22.8 |
| Other Subsaharan Africa | 9.2 | 1.4 | 3.0 | 4.0 | 39.4 | 36.5 | 32.6 | 39.0 | 29.0 | 29.4 |
| **Middle East** | 56.9 | 49.4 | 94.5 | 72.6 | 74.1 | 67.3 | 50.9 | 69.1 | 73.1 | 74.4 |
| **Australia** | 39.2 | 35.4 | 49.8 | 52.8 | 79.8 | 28.9 | 24.4 | 29.8 | 29.3 | 31.7 |
| **Rest of World** | ..... | ..... | 0.7 | ..... | 1.2 | ..... | ..... | ..... | ..... | 0.2 |
| | Middlesex - Somerset - Hunterdon, NJ | | | | | Milwaukee - Waukesha, WI | | | | |
| **ALL DESTINATIONS** | 2 840.6 | 3 035.9 | 3 448.1 | 3 628.1 | 4 385.4 | 2 337.3 | 2 913.5 | 3 506.9 | 3 717.2 | 3 837.6 |
| **North America** | 565.2 | 710.3 | 747.2 | 807.9 | 875.7 | 756.2 | 961.3 | 1 088.7 | 1 082.0 | 1 242.9 |
| Canada | 474.0 | 624.1 | 679.3 | 714.3 | 742.3 | 631.1 | 764.7 | 946.1 | 918.6 | 1 045.0 |
| Mexico | 91.2 | 86.2 | 68.0 | 93.7 | 133.4 | 125.1 | 196.6 | 142.6 | 163.5 | 197.9 |
| **Caribbean and Central America** | 62.5 | 63.4 | 55.9 | 46.7 | 65.6 | 39.2 | 45.6 | 55.8 | 50.9 | 52.3 |
| **South America** | 122.0 | 139.6 | 149.4 | 177.2 | 241.4 | 182.4 | 222.1 | 275.2 | 333.1 | 309.0 |
| Argentina | 22.2 | 29.4 | 24.9 | 22.4 | 39.2 | 17.3 | 44.2 | 28.7 | 32.0 | 37.8 |
| Brazil | 33.2 | 58.0 | 73.9 | 90.4 | 123.9 | 54.4 | 70.8 | 105.2 | 130.8 | 118.4 |
| Other South America | 66.6 | 52.1 | 50.6 | 64.3 | 78.3 | 110.7 | 107.0 | 141.3 | 170.3 | 152.9 |
| **Europe** | 1 187.2 | 1 273.2 | 1 389.4 | 1 565.3 | 2 051.6 | 668.4 | 848.7 | 1 014.9 | 1 085.0 | 1 131.6 |
| Belgium | 82.8 | 82.8 | 109.5 | 73.6 | 89.3 | 47.6 | 98.5 | 106.9 | 128.8 | 135.2 |
| France | 138.1 | 141.3 | 113.2 | 67.7 | 122.3 | 119.0 | 164.1 | 211.4 | 161.2 | 178.0 |
| Germany | 269.5 | 248.8 | 247.9 | 288.3 | 320.2 | 109.3 | 126.8 | 158.5 | 170.5 | 188.6 |
| Netherlands | 117.2 | 120.9 | 162.1 | 296.1 | 593.9 | 61.5 | 59.6 | 89.9 | 105.1 | 96.5 |
| United Kingdom | 139.5 | 272.0 | 169.6 | 176.1 | 199.8 | 135.8 | 140.8 | 170.2 | 174.0 | 197.0 |
| Turkey | 10.9 | 3.5 | 145.5 | 284.3 | 222.9 | 7.8 | 10.0 | 6.0 | 16.9 | 8.1 |
| Former Soviet Republics | 12.2 | 17.5 | 33.0 | 16.1 | 14.0 | 5.4 | 3.6 | 3.6 | 13.0 | 19.3 |
| Poland | 3.1 | 3.6 | 5.5 | 4.2 | 8.0 | 1.4 | 1.7 | 2.9 | 3.8 | 7.3 |
| Other Eastern Europe | 2.8 | 4.3 | 7.0 | 5.8 | 5.7 | 9.6 | 11.4 | 7.8 | 12.1 | 10.3 |
| Other Europe | 411.2 | 378.7 | 396.2 | 353.1 | 475.5 | 171.0 | 232.2 | 257.8 | 299.5 | 291.4 |
| **Asia** | 648.2 | 639.2 | 907.5 | 805.3 | 884.3 | 500.6 | 591.3 | 821.0 | 904.0 | 829.4 |
| Japan | 324.0 | 321.9 | 388.1 | 391.6 | 438.6 | 161.1 | 196.6 | 279.7 | 386.6 | 316.9 |
| China | 34.6 | 30.8 | 145.8 | 81.9 | 43.1 | 48.7 | 49.7 | 44.3 | 43.6 | 54.8 |
| Hong Kong | 36.8 | 47.7 | 57.3 | 45.6 | 68.5 | 75.0 | 74.8 | 83.0 | 87.2 | 82.5 |
| Taiwan | 62.1 | 61.4 | 67.9 | 53.8 | 64.0 | 54.1 | 64.7 | 131.5 | 62.3 | 65.0 |
| Singapore | 33.3 | 33.5 | 36.1 | 41.5 | 36.8 | 34.5 | 53.3 | 46.7 | 48.5 | 43.7 |
| South Korea | 84.1 | 87.8 | 109.2 | 91.7 | 107.0 | 48.2 | 59.7 | 75.4 | 81.3 | 75.4 |
| Indonesia | 5.8 | 4.2 | 9.9 | 13.8 | 19.7 | 8.6 | 5.6 | 13.2 | 25.0 | 19.7 |
| India | 11.9 | 15.1 | 25.4 | 20.4 | 24.3 | 6.8 | 10.5 | 26.2 | 22.5 | 22.5 |
| Other Asia | 55.3 | 36.7 | 67.7 | 65.0 | 82.4 | 63.6 | 76.3 | 120.9 | 147.0 | 148.9 |
| **Africa** | 83.6 | 54.2 | 50.6 | 47.9 | 58.6 | 46.7 | 63.1 | 59.6 | 70.7 | 70.3 |
| North Africa | 52.6 | 24.1 | 12.8 | 9.6 | 13.4 | 15.3 | 27.0 | 18.9 | 16.0 | 26.5 |
| Republic of South Africa | 25.6 | 25.2 | 35.8 | 35.3 | 41.6 | 27.9 | 32.2 | 38.1 | 50.7 | 39.2 |
| Other Subsaharan Africa | 5.3 | 4.9 | 1.9 | 3.0 | 3.6 | 3.6 | 3.9 | 2.6 | 4.1 | 4.6 |
| **Middle East** | 78.0 | 66.0 | 53.0 | 61.7 | 78.3 | 51.4 | 62.1 | 62.5 | 67.1 | 67.4 |
| **Australia** | 94.0 | 89.9 | 95.2 | 116.1 | 129.8 | 92.3 | 119.3 | 129.2 | 124.3 | 134.8 |
| **Rest of World** | ..... | ..... | ..... | ..... | ..... | ..... | ..... | ..... | ..... | ..... |

## Table E-3. Metropolitan Area Exports of Goods by Destination, 1993–1997—*Continued*

(Millions of dollars.)

| Destination | 1993 | 1994 | 1995 | 1996 | 1997 | 1993 | 1994 | 1995 | 1996 | 1997 |
|---|---|---|---|---|---|---|---|---|---|---|
| | Minneapolis - St. Paul, MN - WI | | | | | Mobile, AL | | | | |
| ALL DESTINATIONS | 9 003.8 | 8 863.5 | 11 071.8 | 12 384.0 | 12 006.7 | 356.7 | 395.3 | 415.8 | 459.9 | 498.7 |
| North America | 1 637.9 | 1 805.4 | 2 213.2 | 2 854.7 | 3 014.3 | 72.4 | 85.5 | 78.8 | 105.1 | 111.3 |
| Canada | 1 425.1 | 1 492.4 | 1 719.2 | 2 025.1 | 2 208.7 | 62.6 | 73.5 | 66.4 | 89.2 | 92.6 |
| Mexico | 212.8 | 313.1 | 494.0 | 829.5 | 805.6 | 9.9 | 11.9 | 12.4 | 15.9 | 18.6 |
| Caribbean and Central America | 230.5 | 180.1 | 246.5 | 270.7 | 276.8 | 11.0 | 13.0 | 19.1 | 31.1 | 29.7 |
| South America | 202.0 | 244.1 | 408.8 | 458.5 | 474.2 | 17.1 | 21.0 | 19.7 | 18.7 | 25.4 |
| Argentina | 30.7 | 42.2 | 30.1 | 36.4 | 83.9 | 0.4 | 1.2 | 1.1 | 1.8 | 3.7 |
| Brazil | 37.2 | 85.5 | 73.7 | 135.3 | 110.2 | 2.7 | 3.5 | 7.8 | 6.5 | 10.1 |
| Other South America | 134.1 | 116.4 | 305.0 | 286.8 | 280.0 | 13.9 | 16.3 | 10.8 | 10.5 | 11.6 |
| Europe | 3 609.4 | 3 479.4 | 4 101.6 | 4 293.2 | 4 111.3 | 166.4 | 186.3 | 177.8 | 167.3 | 146.3 |
| Belgium | 147.2 | 159.0 | 238.9 | 235.1 | 166.5 | 5.7 | 5.3 | 4.9 | 5.7 | 3.2 |
| France | 274.3 | 226.2 | 253.4 | 270.3 | 350.5 | 15.2 | 19.2 | 14.1 | 22.6 | 16.6 |
| Germany | 502.6 | 444.3 | 477.7 | 612.7 | 545.1 | 17.8 | 16.5 | 19.8 | 12.6 | 14.1 |
| Netherlands | 854.5 | 888.4 | 996.9 | 941.6 | 821.6 | 40.5 | 33.0 | 24.8 | 13.4 | 12.9 |
| United Kingdom | 445.2 | 403.5 | 487.9 | 556.8 | 653.3 | 10.9 | 19.3 | 38.1 | 39.1 | 62.9 |
| Turkey | 80.2 | 53.5 | 118.9 | 167.7 | 173.9 | 4.0 | 1.3 | 0.2 | 0.2 | 0.2 |
| Former Soviet Republics | 188.9 | 95.0 | 31.1 | 120.0 | 43.1 | 0.4 | ..... | 0.6 | 0.5 | 0.6 |
| Poland | 28.0 | 12.2 | 13.7 | 54.1 | 14.5 | ..... | 0.2 | 0.6 | 0.2 | ..... |
| Other Eastern Europe | 50.1 | 25.0 | 26.8 | 39.1 | 35.6 | 0.9 | 0.8 | 0.1 | 1.0 | 0.3 |
| Other Europe | 1 038.3 | 1 172.3 | 1 456.3 | 1 295.9 | 1 307.2 | 71.0 | 90.7 | 74.6 | 72.1 | 35.5 |
| Asia | 2 152.5 | 2 141.9 | 2 798.4 | 2 950.3 | 2 771.4 | 75.0 | 68.4 | 103.6 | 115.6 | 163.9 |
| Japan | 816.1 | 709.6 | 817.2 | 993.5 | 1 016.5 | 57.2 | 55.8 | 73.2 | 67.4 | 43.4 |
| China | 114.3 | 89.2 | 393.6 | 160.0 | 208.6 | 0.3 | 0.7 | 3.1 | 1.4 | 6.0 |
| Hong Kong | 105.3 | 133.7 | 207.1 | 193.8 | 164.4 | 0.5 | 0.2 | 1.7 | 2.7 | 4.4 |
| Taiwan | 254.7 | 250.6 | 242.0 | 436.0 | 249.6 | 2.3 | 1.0 | 3.3 | 11.9 | 4.0 |
| Singapore | 133.1 | 177.1 | 213.0 | 230.8 | 213.9 | 0.7 | 0.6 | 3.7 | 5.2 | 3.2 |
| South Korea | 177.6 | 245.1 | 403.8 | 466.6 | 244.6 | 4.9 | 4.0 | 13.7 | 19.6 | 95.8 |
| Indonesia | 27.1 | 69.3 | 64.0 | 87.3 | 143.5 | 1.6 | 1.7 | 0.8 | 1.7 | 0.9 |
| India | 46.6 | 16.2 | 39.5 | 32.2 | 28.3 | 0.2 | 0.4 | 0.3 | ..... | 0.3 |
| Other Asia | 477.8 | 451.1 | 418.2 | 350.0 | 502.0 | 7.2 | 3.9 | 3.8 | 5.7 | 5.9 |
| Africa | 545.6 | 454.6 | 511.1 | 810.2 | 747.1 | 3.0 | 7.7 | 3.9 | 7.2 | 5.9 |
| North Africa | 371.2 | 347.1 | 354.9 | 657.3 | 619.3 | 1.0 | 5.3 | 1.1 | 3.0 | 2.6 |
| Republic of South Africa | 76.7 | 55.9 | 69.5 | 58.6 | 65.0 | 1.2 | 1.8 | 1.3 | 1.6 | 3.0 |
| Other Subsaharan Africa | 97.7 | 51.7 | 86.7 | 94.3 | 62.8 | 0.7 | 0.7 | 1.5 | 2.5 | 0.3 |
| Middle East | 411.7 | 373.9 | 427.5 | 381.4 | 332.4 | 8.6 | 8.5 | 8.6 | 9.1 | 9.2 |
| Australia | 141.0 | 145.2 | 162.2 | 172.4 | 179.4 | 3.0 | 5.0 | 4.2 | 5.7 | 7.0 |
| Rest of World | 73.1 | 38.8 | 202.5 | 192.5 | 99.8 | ..... | ..... | ..... | ..... | ..... |
| | Modesto, CA | | | | | Monmouth - Ocean, NJ | | | | |
| ALL DESTINATIONS | 201.1 | 236.7 | 279.2 | 359.6 | 387.5 | 373.4 | 410.2 | 471.8 | 478.2 | 504.8 |
| North America | 53.6 | 54.3 | 56.1 | 63.0 | 68.9 | 90.4 | 119.7 | 123.7 | 138.7 | 145.1 |
| Canada | 48.3 | 47.2 | 49.7 | 56.0 | 61.0 | 49.5 | 77.5 | 79.2 | 91.7 | 98.6 |
| Mexico | 5.3 | 7.1 | 6.4 | 7.1 | 7.9 | 41.0 | 42.2 | 44.5 | 47.0 | 46.5 |
| Caribbean and Central America | 6.6 | 7.5 | 7.7 | 8.0 | 10.0 | 8.1 | 6.1 | 7.3 | 8.4 | 11.9 |
| South America | 6.1 | 7.6 | 9.7 | 11.3 | 15.1 | 38.9 | 47.9 | 44.8 | 52.8 | 43.6 |
| Argentina | 1.6 | 1.6 | 1.2 | 2.3 | 2.9 | 7.7 | 7.9 | 4.3 | 8.4 | 7.2 |
| Brazil | 1.1 | 1.4 | 3.3 | 3.8 | 5.5 | 11.5 | 10.9 | 14.9 | 14.8 | 13.8 |
| Other South America | 3.4 | 4.6 | 5.2 | 5.1 | 6.6 | 19.7 | 29.1 | 25.6 | 29.6 | 22.6 |
| Europe | 93.0 | 119.3 | 139.8 | 202.3 | 207.9 | 98.8 | 112.8 | 143.5 | 139.6 | 151.6 |
| Belgium | 2.5 | 4.3 | 5.9 | 7.2 | 6.8 | 0.5 | 2.3 | 2.5 | 2.2 | 4.3 |
| France | 7.6 | 11.9 | 7.4 | 6.4 | 12.7 | 12.7 | 15.6 | 14.9 | 14.1 | 16.0 |
| Germany | 33.6 | 40.3 | 46.7 | 69.1 | 61.9 | 15.6 | 13.9 | 14.8 | 16.1 | 12.6 |
| Netherlands | 6.4 | 10.4 | 11.4 | 11.0 | 16.3 | 16.6 | 19.3 | 23.9 | 21.8 | 20.8 |
| United Kingdom | 25.3 | 28.7 | 38.2 | 59.3 | 67.9 | 17.4 | 20.4 | 24.6 | 27.4 | 32.0 |
| Turkey | 0.3 | 0.2 | 0.3 | 0.7 | 0.3 | 1.9 | 1.3 | 1.3 | 1.8 | 1.8 |
| Former Soviet Republics | 0.2 | 0.8 | 2.6 | 0.9 | 0.7 | 2.4 | 6.9 | 8.8 | 4.7 | 2.9 |
| Poland | 0.4 | 0.4 | 0.4 | 0.6 | 0.5 | 0.4 | 0.6 | 1.4 | 1.6 | 3.0 |
| Other Eastern Europe | 0.1 | 0.2 | 0.3 | 0.3 | 0.8 | 2.7 | 3.1 | 3.9 | 1.9 | 5.3 |
| Other Europe | 16.6 | 22.1 | 26.9 | 46.9 | 40.2 | 28.6 | 29.4 | 47.4 | 48.0 | 52.9 |
| Asia | 24.6 | 31.4 | 48.0 | 52.7 | 65.9 | 101.5 | 89.4 | 115.2 | 105.9 | 118.9 |
| Japan | 9.6 | 12.6 | 23.6 | 20.3 | 22.5 | 22.2 | 23.2 | 26.7 | 18.9 | 21.1 |
| China | 0.5 | 0.7 | 0.4 | 0.4 | 1.4 | 6.6 | 6.5 | 5.4 | 14.7 | 13.8 |
| Hong Kong | 2.5 | 5.3 | 5.2 | 5.6 | 9.5 | 18.8 | 19.7 | 24.1 | 19.6 | 15.4 |
| Taiwan | 3.4 | 4.2 | 5.9 | 5.2 | 10.4 | 8.4 | 4.4 | 3.8 | 4.7 | 22.4 |
| Singapore | 2.3 | 1.8 | 2.8 | 2.1 | 2.3 | 5.8 | 5.2 | 6.8 | 6.1 | 6.3 |
| South Korea | 1.9 | 2.5 | 4.2 | 5.8 | 5.6 | 20.2 | 14.3 | 10.3 | 16.3 | 14.5 |
| Indonesia | 0.5 | 0.5 | 0.3 | 0.7 | 0.8 | 9.8 | 5.4 | 5.1 | 5.3 | 6.9 |
| India | ..... | 0.2 | 0.3 | 3.8 | 5.9 | 2.8 | 1.2 | 3.3 | 2.2 | 5.1 |
| Other Asia | 3.7 | 3.6 | 5.4 | 8.6 | 7.5 | 6.8 | 9.6 | 29.6 | 18.0 | 13.3 |
| Africa | 1.6 | 1.7 | 2.4 | 1.9 | 1.4 | 4.8 | 4.8 | 10.6 | 6.8 | 5.5 |
| North Africa | 0.5 | 1.1 | 1.5 | 0.5 | 0.6 | 2.5 | 1.4 | 6.3 | 3.1 | 2.8 |
| Republic of South Africa | 0.8 | 0.5 | 0.8 | 1.1 | 0.6 | 1.6 | 2.7 | 3.9 | 3.0 | 2.3 |
| Other Subsaharan Africa | 0.2 | 0.1 | 0.1 | 0.2 | 0.2 | 0.7 | 0.8 | 0.4 | 0.8 | 0.4 |
| Middle East | 9.0 | 8.4 | 6.5 | 8.9 | 12.2 | 23.1 | 21.3 | 14.7 | 17.3 | 22.4 |
| Australia | 6.5 | 6.7 | 9.0 | 11.5 | 6.1 | 7.8 | 8.1 | 12.0 | 8.6 | 5.7 |
| Rest of World | ..... | ..... | ..... | ..... | ..... | ..... | ..... | ..... | ..... | ..... |

## Table E-3.  Metropolitan Area Exports of Goods by Destination, 1993–1997—*Continued*

(Millions of dollars.)

| Destination | 1993 | 1994 | 1995 | 1996 | 1997 | 1993 | 1994 | 1995 | 1996 | 1997 |
|---|---|---|---|---|---|---|---|---|---|---|
| | Monroe, LA | | | | | Muncie, IN | | | | |
| **ALL DESTINATIONS** | 77.1 | 107.1 | 167.8 | 134.0 | 101.9 | 64.3 | 107.4 | 158.3 | 137.6 | 157.6 |
| **North America** | 18.4 | 26.8 | 39.0 | 31.5 | 39.2 | 37.2 | 54.9 | 98.4 | 84.0 | 101.7 |
| Canada | 16.3 | 24.2 | 36.7 | 28.5 | 33.4 | 35.4 | 51.9 | 95.9 | 82.7 | 95.6 |
| Mexico | 2.0 | 2.5 | 2.3 | 3.0 | 5.8 | 1.8 | 2.9 | 2.4 | 1.3 | 6.1 |
| **Caribbean and Central America** | 1.9 | 0.7 | 1.9 | 0.9 | 0.8 | 0.3 | 0.3 | 0.3 | 0.5 | 0.1 |
| **South America** | 3.1 | 6.0 | 14.6 | 6.8 | 4.8 | 1.0 | 1.1 | 1.4 | 0.9 | 2.3 |
| Argentina | 0.2 | 0.2 | 0.3 | 0.1 | 0.1 | ..... | 0.2 | 0.1 | ..... | 0.1 |
| Brazil | 1.2 | 4.4 | 9.8 | 5.1 | 3.1 | 0.4 | 0.7 | 0.8 | 0.6 | 1.7 |
| Other South America | 1.8 | 1.5 | 4.5 | 1.6 | 1.6 | 0.6 | 0.2 | 0.5 | 0.3 | 0.5 |
| **Europe** | 36.4 | 42.0 | 68.1 | 58.6 | 35.6 | 6.8 | 9.9 | 11.8 | 11.4 | 7.3 |
| Belgium | 4.2 | 3.7 | 0.4 | 0.8 | 1.9 | 1.0 | 1.0 | 1.1 | 1.0 | 1.2 |
| France | 5.2 | 1.8 | 1.9 | 2.1 | 0.9 | ..... | 0.2 | 0.3 | 0.3 | ..... |
| Germany | 5.8 | 4.8 | 7.2 | 8.4 | 12.1 | 0.3 | 0.3 | 0.3 | 0.5 | 0.2 |
| Netherlands | 3.8 | 8.2 | 27.8 | 18.9 | 5.8 | 0.1 | 0.2 | 0.1 | 0.2 | ..... |
| United Kingdom | 13.7 | 16.1 | 20.6 | 18.4 | 8.9 | 4.8 | 7.7 | 8.8 | 8.4 | 4.2 |
| Turkey | 0.1 | 0.1 | ..... | 0.2 | ..... | ..... | ..... | ..... | ..... | ..... |
| Former Soviet Republics | 0.2 | 0.3 | 0.2 | 0.2 | 0.1 | ..... | ..... | ..... | ..... | ..... |
| Poland | ..... | ..... | ..... | ..... | ..... | ..... | ..... | ..... | ..... | ..... |
| Other Eastern Europe | ..... | 0.1 | 0.1 | 0.1 | ..... | ..... | ..... | ..... | ..... | ..... |
| Other Europe | 3.5 | 6.7 | 9.6 | 9.5 | 5.9 | 0.6 | 0.6 | 1.2 | 0.9 | 1.6 |
| **Asia** | 7.1 | 14.2 | 27.7 | 24.1 | 16.0 | 16.3 | 37.4 | 44.2 | 38.5 | 44.5 |
| Japan | 1.2 | 4.3 | 7.9 | 6.4 | 6.3 | 0.6 | 0.2 | 0.2 | 0.6 | 1.2 |
| China | 0.5 | 1.2 | 1.7 | 0.9 | 0.7 | 0.7 | 3.3 | 2.6 | 0.5 | 1.0 |
| Hong Kong | 0.7 | 0.4 | 3.8 | 7.2 | 2.7 | 0.1 | 0.4 | 10.8 | 9.4 | 4.8 |
| Taiwan | ..... | 0.1 | 0.1 | 0.1 | 0.2 | 0.7 | 0.4 | 0.2 | 0.1 | 0.1 |
| Singapore | 1.6 | 0.5 | 0.4 | 0.7 | 1.5 | 1.1 | 1.0 | 0.2 | 0.4 | 0.2 |
| South Korea | ..... | ..... | ..... | 0.3 | 0.1 | 11.3 | 31.7 | 29.5 | 25.5 | 36.4 |
| Indonesia | 0.1 | 0.5 | 2.0 | 1.9 | 0.6 | ..... | ..... | ..... | 1.1 | ..... |
| India | ..... | 0.1 | 0.1 | ..... | ..... | ..... | 0.1 | 0.5 | 0.4 | 0.4 |
| Other Asia | 2.9 | 7.1 | 11.6 | 6.7 | 3.9 | 1.8 | 0.3 | 0.1 | 0.5 | 0.4 |
| **Africa** | 0.2 | 1.2 | 0.7 | 0.6 | 0.1 | 0.1 | 0.2 | 0.4 | 0.1 | 0.1 |
| North Africa | ..... | ..... | 0.1 | 0.1 | ..... | ..... | ..... | ..... | ..... | ..... |
| Republic of South Africa | 0.2 | 0.6 | 0.7 | 0.5 | 0.1 | 0.1 | 0.2 | 0.4 | 0.1 | 0.1 |
| Other Subsaharan Africa | ..... | 0.7 | ..... | ..... | ..... | ..... | ..... | ..... | ..... | ..... |
| **Middle East** | 0.4 | 2.0 | 1.5 | 1.2 | 1.0 | 0.1 | ..... | ..... | 0.2 | 0.1 |
| **Australia** | 9.7 | 14.2 | 14.3 | 10.3 | 4.4 | 2.4 | 3.7 | 1.9 | 2.0 | 1.5 |
| **Rest of World** | ..... | ..... | ..... | ..... | ..... | ..... | ..... | ..... | ..... | ..... |
| | Nashua, NH | | | | | Nashville, TN | | | | |
| **ALL DESTINATIONS** | 290.2 | 235.4 | 282.2 | 291.3 | 339.8 | 1 104.1 | 1 310.5 | 1 412.3 | 1 445.5 | 1 767.1 |
| **North America** | 128.2 | 70.6 | 79.2 | 79.2 | 95.2 | 503.9 | 596.3 | 694.0 | 617.5 | 777.7 |
| Canada | 120.8 | 64.2 | 63.4 | 63.8 | 76.2 | 275.4 | 348.6 | 404.2 | 416.9 | 465.2 |
| Mexico | 7.5 | 6.4 | 15.8 | 15.4 | 18.9 | 228.5 | 247.7 | 289.8 | 200.7 | 312.5 |
| **Caribbean and Central America** | 0.5 | 1.2 | 1.1 | 4.4 | 11.0 | 29.7 | 38.5 | 39.2 | 28.9 | 53.4 |
| **South America** | 6.9 | 8.2 | 5.2 | 4.6 | 6.8 | 18.6 | 21.7 | 28.1 | 38.9 | 84.1 |
| Argentina | 3.1 | 3.1 | 1.4 | 0.4 | 1.7 | 4.4 | 4.4 | 5.1 | 5.6 | 13.3 |
| Brazil | 2.4 | 3.3 | 2.0 | 3.3 | 3.7 | 3.4 | 7.9 | 13.0 | 13.2 | 20.7 |
| Other South America | 1.4 | 1.8 | 1.9 | 0.9 | 1.3 | 10.8 | 9.3 | 10.1 | 20.1 | 50.2 |
| **Europe** | 64.4 | 73.9 | 96.5 | 101.4 | 108.0 | 294.7 | 352.0 | 323.4 | 331.4 | 398.0 |
| Belgium | 3.8 | 2.6 | 3.8 | 2.0 | 3.9 | 9.3 | 9.2 | 9.7 | 7.5 | 20.3 |
| France | 3.4 | 3.5 | 5.6 | 7.2 | 4.9 | 37.2 | 39.3 | 33.7 | 32.3 | 36.3 |
| Germany | 13.8 | 16.4 | 23.6 | 20.0 | 16.1 | 49.7 | 61.7 | 51.6 | 61.8 | 79.1 |
| Netherlands | 10.2 | 11.3 | 11.4 | 12.6 | 11.7 | 29.3 | 27.4 | 29.8 | 24.3 | 25.9 |
| United Kingdom | 9.2 | 11.8 | 14.9 | 14.1 | 25.0 | 106.4 | 138.1 | 130.3 | 126.2 | 144.3 |
| Turkey | 1.2 | 0.2 | 0.7 | ..... | 0.3 | 0.7 | 0.6 | 2.2 | 3.0 | 4.6 |
| Former Soviet Republics | 0.2 | 0.2 | 0.2 | 7.7 | 1.5 | 1.0 | 0.3 | 2.9 | 1.2 | 1.9 |
| Poland | 0.3 | 0.2 | 0.1 | ..... | ..... | 5.2 | 4.1 | 6.1 | 9.2 | 8.8 |
| Other Eastern Europe | 1.2 | 2.4 | 1.8 | 0.7 | 1.4 | 1.2 | 2.3 | 2.6 | 3.1 | 1.2 |
| Other Europe | 21.1 | 25.4 | 34.5 | 37.0 | 43.2 | 54.7 | 69.0 | 54.5 | 62.7 | 75.6 |
| **Asia** | 61.9 | 68.0 | 88.7 | 85.6 | 95.0 | 214.6 | 257.0 | 264.2 | 368.4 | 357.6 |
| Japan | 16.4 | 16.7 | 12.1 | 14.0 | 37.1 | 84.4 | 110.3 | 137.9 | 262.5 | 224.3 |
| China | 4.7 | 2.7 | 1.3 | 1.8 | 3.0 | 0.7 | 1.5 | 2.3 | 3.3 | 6.4 |
| Hong Kong | 3.1 | 2.0 | 4.4 | 6.3 | 8.3 | 4.5 | 4.7 | 6.2 | 5.9 | 14.0 |
| Taiwan | 8.4 | 13.3 | 8.4 | 13.0 | 4.4 | 108.1 | 119.8 | 81.7 | 55.5 | 55.6 |
| Singapore | 17.3 | 21.2 | 35.0 | 16.6 | 24.9 | 4.0 | 4.4 | 9.5 | 9.8 | 11.2 |
| South Korea | 6.5 | 9.4 | 20.5 | 8.3 | 4.0 | 6.9 | 9.3 | 14.0 | 13.8 | 23.2 |
| Indonesia | 0.5 | 0.1 | 0.3 | ..... | 0.3 | 0.9 | 0.4 | 1.6 | 0.9 | 2.6 |
| India | 2.2 | 0.2 | 0.5 | 0.8 | 0.7 | 0.6 | 1.0 | 1.2 | 1.9 | 2.5 |
| Other Asia | 2.9 | 2.4 | 6.1 | 24.8 | 12.3 | 4.6 | 5.7 | 9.8 | 14.8 | 17.7 |
| **Africa** | 18.4 | 5.6 | 3.3 | 3.1 | 10.0 | 3.6 | 4.7 | 7.4 | 6.9 | 10.3 |
| North Africa | 14.3 | 3.3 | 0.2 | 0.9 | 8.1 | 0.5 | 2.0 | 1.3 | 2.3 | 2.4 |
| Republic of South Africa | 3.3 | 2.1 | 2.7 | 2.0 | 1.9 | 2.5 | 2.3 | 3.1 | 3.3 | 5.2 |
| Other Subsaharan Africa | 0.8 | 0.2 | 0.4 | 0.3 | 0.1 | 0.6 | 0.4 | 3.0 | 1.3 | 2.7 |
| **Middle East** | 5.8 | 5.5 | 5.4 | 10.1 | 10.3 | 24.2 | 24.9 | 33.6 | 32.1 | 62.2 |
| **Australia** | 4.0 | 2.3 | 2.9 | 2.9 | 3.6 | 14.9 | 15.2 | 22.4 | 21.3 | 23.8 |
| **Rest of World** | ..... | ..... | ..... | ..... | ..... | ..... | ..... | ..... | ..... | ..... |

## Table E-3. Metropolitan Area Exports of Goods by Destination, 1993–1997—*Continued*

(Millions of dollars.)

| Destination | 1993 | 1994 | 1995 | 1996 | 1997 | 1993 | 1994 | 1995 | 1996 | 1997 |
|---|---|---|---|---|---|---|---|---|---|---|
| | Nassau - Suffolk, NY | | | | | Newark, NJ | | | | |
| **ALL DESTINATIONS** | 2 803.2 | 2 866.3 | 3 558.6 | 3 680.2 | 4 208.5 | 4 287.4 | 5 205.5 | 5 640.0 | 5 044.2 | 5 201.8 |
| **North America** | 534.3 | 640.4 | 692.9 | 787.2 | 889.5 | 985.9 | 1 244.7 | 1 061.0 | 1 052.3 | 1 291.1 |
| Canada | 435.1 | 505.7 | 569.6 | 607.4 | 657.0 | 727.2 | 828.8 | 819.3 | 855.0 | 1 020.9 |
| Mexico | 99.2 | 134.7 | 123.3 | 179.8 | 232.4 | 258.6 | 415.9 | 241.7 | 197.3 | 270.2 |
| **Caribbean and Central America** | 110.7 | 100.2 | 74.0 | 74.7 | 91.1 | 96.0 | 118.9 | 157.3 | 168.3 | 187.7 |
| **South America** | 138.3 | 163.5 | 163.3 | 165.0 | 223.1 | 290.1 | 324.7 | 427.0 | 436.4 | 513.4 |
| Argentina | 16.3 | 22.1 | 19.9 | 20.8 | 28.0 | 30.8 | 46.4 | 46.6 | 48.6 | 76.0 |
| Brazil | 35.8 | 49.9 | 60.7 | 56.1 | 95.8 | 77.9 | 95.0 | 166.3 | 188.3 | 266.3 |
| Other South America | 86.2 | 91.5 | 82.7 | 88.1 | 99.3 | 181.4 | 183.3 | 214.1 | 199.4 | 171.2 |
| **Europe** | 887.2 | 969.1 | 1 107.0 | 1 346.2 | 1 644.4 | 1 401.5 | 1 508.9 | 1 754.1 | 1 587.0 | 1 659.6 |
| Belgium | 22.8 | 23.1 | 29.0 | 57.1 | 87.1 | 84.3 | 108.4 | 129.1 | 89.5 | 124.4 |
| France | 90.9 | 97.9 | 112.3 | 190.1 | 267.8 | 145.5 | 138.3 | 128.0 | 145.6 | 129.4 |
| Germany | 153.2 | 184.0 | 208.0 | 278.0 | 316.9 | 255.3 | 265.0 | 323.2 | 289.5 | 287.1 |
| Netherlands | 98.3 | 73.1 | 72.9 | 82.0 | 102.9 | 109.3 | 168.0 | 225.5 | 157.0 | 117.7 |
| United Kingdom | 215.3 | 258.7 | 278.1 | 278.9 | 372.1 | 161.5 | 184.5 | 224.5 | 207.7 | 235.8 |
| Turkey | 16.1 | 12.7 | 19.7 | 20.9 | 26.9 | 36.0 | 42.8 | 52.3 | 35.0 | 30.9 |
| Former Soviet Republics | 15.6 | 19.4 | 16.3 | 17.7 | 24.6 | 137.8 | 82.7 | 62.1 | 83.1 | 94.3 |
| Poland | 8.7 | 5.2 | 5.8 | 10.3 | 14.8 | 16.3 | 20.5 | 15.7 | 20.6 | 18.1 |
| Other Eastern Europe | 15.5 | 27.8 | 32.8 | 42.4 | 25.0 | 6.2 | 5.9 | 11.4 | 8.3 | 8.6 |
| Other Europe | 250.8 | 267.3 | 332.1 | 368.8 | 406.4 | 449.4 | 492.9 | 582.3 | 550.8 | 613.3 |
| **Asia** | 783.4 | 648.9 | 1 131.3 | 931.4 | 954.5 | 1 228.1 | 1 729.5 | 1 826.4 | 1 490.5 | 1 184.0 |
| Japan | 203.5 | 123.1 | 158.6 | 200.3 | 227.4 | 343.1 | 525.7 | 530.1 | 482.8 | 361.8 |
| China | 67.7 | 45.4 | 38.1 | 56.1 | 60.0 | 116.7 | 139.1 | 171.1 | 100.0 | 59.0 |
| Hong Kong | 86.6 | 96.5 | 126.5 | 101.4 | 126.1 | 101.4 | 132.8 | 164.6 | 184.5 | 135.4 |
| Taiwan | 183.7 | 128.0 | 454.9 | 171.8 | 135.9 | 163.9 | 209.4 | 235.3 | 203.1 | 167.0 |
| Singapore | 42.2 | 47.1 | 49.4 | 72.0 | 93.5 | 58.0 | 67.2 | 71.9 | 64.0 | 97.5 |
| South Korea | 65.6 | 73.8 | 117.1 | 138.9 | 126.3 | 230.5 | 361.5 | 287.3 | 157.8 | 132.7 |
| Indonesia | 13.3 | 8.9 | 11.9 | 18.4 | 14.2 | 25.3 | 29.1 | 72.7 | 40.4 | 56.5 |
| India | 26.3 | 31.4 | 50.0 | 53.9 | 34.6 | 16.4 | 30.9 | 40.8 | 62.3 | 27.2 |
| Other Asia | 94.5 | 94.6 | 124.8 | 118.6 | 136.3 | 172.8 | 233.8 | 252.5 | 195.6 | 147.0 |
| **Africa** | 49.2 | 42.4 | 64.6 | 55.8 | 62.0 | 80.5 | 63.1 | 83.2 | 77.5 | 77.8 |
| North Africa | 15.5 | 10.0 | 9.5 | 10.8 | 15.7 | 37.8 | 25.2 | 21.9 | 25.3 | 24.2 |
| Republic of South Africa | 21.5 | 22.7 | 29.7 | 26.8 | 29.2 | 11.4 | 15.5 | 21.0 | 24.9 | 23.5 |
| Other Subsaharan Africa | 12.2 | 9.6 | 25.4 | 18.2 | 17.2 | 31.3 | 22.4 | 40.4 | 27.3 | 30.1 |
| **Middle East** | 264.4 | 248.0 | 259.8 | 260.3 | 255.3 | 133.1 | 135.9 | 228.1 | 154.8 | 196.5 |
| **Australia** | 35.7 | 53.8 | 65.7 | 59.6 | 88.6 | 71.6 | 78.8 | 102.6 | 76.9 | 91.4 |
| **Rest of World** | ..... | ..... | ..... | ..... | ..... | 0.7 | 1.1 | 0.3 | 0.6 | 0.4 |
| | New Bedford, MA | | | | | Newburgh, NY - PA | | | | |
| **ALL DESTINATIONS** | 141.6 | 154.5 | 186.8 | 165.8 | 153.4 | 382.3 | 152.8 | 148.9 | 153.3 | 222.1 |
| **North America** | 39.8 | 57.6 | 85.7 | 65.3 | 54.7 | 314.8 | 90.2 | 77.2 | 75.5 | 145.3 |
| Canada | 37.0 | 42.5 | 57.8 | 41.0 | 31.4 | 302.2 | 77.5 | 61.4 | 61.8 | 137.9 |
| Mexico | 2.8 | 15.0 | 27.8 | 24.3 | 23.3 | 12.7 | 12.7 | 15.8 | 13.7 | 7.4 |
| **Caribbean and Central America** | 4.0 | 3.8 | 4.3 | 3.0 | 1.2 | 1.3 | 2.4 | 2.7 | 1.5 | 2.0 |
| **South America** | 1.7 | 0.7 | 1.2 | 2.8 | 3.0 | 4.4 | 5.0 | 6.0 | 6.7 | 9.5 |
| Argentina | 0.1 | 0.1 | ..... | 0.3 | 0.5 | 1.4 | 0.4 | 0.3 | 1.9 | 2.6 |
| Brazil | 1.3 | 0.2 | 0.9 | 1.7 | 2.0 | 1.7 | 2.7 | 2.9 | 2.6 | 4.5 |
| Other South America | 0.4 | 0.5 | 0.3 | 0.9 | 0.4 | 1.3 | 1.9 | 2.8 | 2.2 | 2.4 |
| **Europe** | 63.4 | 58.7 | 63.6 | 65.4 | 55.3 | 33.5 | 30.3 | 36.4 | 35.4 | 38.1 |
| Belgium | 2.5 | 2.8 | 2.4 | 6.0 | 3.5 | 1.5 | 1.6 | 2.2 | 4.2 | 2.5 |
| France | 20.8 | 17.9 | 20.6 | 23.9 | 22.3 | 2.7 | 2.5 | 4.4 | 2.2 | 7.4 |
| Germany | 6.4 | 10.1 | 16.4 | 14.4 | 6.9 | 5.6 | 4.5 | 8.6 | 9.2 | 8.1 |
| Netherlands | 3.3 | 1.8 | 1.7 | 0.9 | 1.3 | 2.4 | 3.7 | 2.4 | 2.3 | 3.1 |
| United Kingdom | 23.2 | 19.2 | 14.8 | 14.3 | 14.4 | 8.7 | 10.7 | 9.1 | 9.8 | 8.2 |
| Turkey | 0.2 | 0.1 | 0.3 | 0.2 | 0.5 | 0.5 | 0.2 | 0.1 | ..... | 0.3 |
| Former Soviet Republics | 0.1 | ..... | 0.1 | ..... | ..... | 2.0 | 1.0 | 0.8 | 0.3 | 0.1 |
| Poland | ..... | ..... | ..... | ..... | ..... | 0.5 | 0.2 | 0.2 | 0.1 | 0.1 |
| Other Eastern Europe | 0.2 | 0.2 | ..... | 0.1 | 0.1 | 0.1 | 0.1 | 0.3 | 0.2 | 0.3 |
| Other Europe | 6.7 | 6.5 | 7.3 | 5.5 | 6.3 | 9.6 | 5.7 | 8.3 | 7.0 | 8.0 |
| **Asia** | 29.4 | 29.6 | 27.6 | 25.7 | 35.8 | 22.9 | 21.2 | 23.7 | 31.3 | 24.3 |
| Japan | 16.9 | 16.9 | 9.1 | 10.7 | 16.0 | 4.6 | 3.7 | 5.2 | 5.7 | 5.8 |
| China | ..... | 0.1 | 1.0 | 0.9 | 1.3 | 4.5 | 3.6 | 1.4 | 8.2 | 4.2 |
| Hong Kong | 3.8 | 2.2 | 1.8 | 2.4 | 4.6 | 2.4 | 3.1 | 4.1 | 5.4 | 3.3 |
| Taiwan | 4.4 | 2.8 | 3.8 | 1.8 | 2.3 | 2.0 | 1.2 | 1.6 | 1.5 | 1.3 |
| Singapore | 1.4 | 1.3 | 3.3 | 1.6 | 2.2 | 2.7 | 2.7 | 1.9 | 1.6 | 1.7 |
| South Korea | 1.2 | 4.2 | 7.0 | 6.6 | 6.9 | 2.2 | 2.6 | 3.1 | 2.4 | 1.6 |
| Indonesia | ..... | 0.5 | 0.1 | 0.1 | 0.1 | 0.3 | 0.1 | 0.2 | 0.3 | 0.4 |
| India | 0.2 | ..... | 0.2 | 0.5 | 0.2 | 0.1 | 0.2 | 0.8 | 0.3 | 0.6 |
| Other Asia | 1.5 | 1.5 | 1.3 | 1.0 | 2.1 | 4.3 | 4.0 | 5.5 | 5.8 | 5.4 |
| **Africa** | 0.2 | 0.4 | 0.6 | 1.3 | 0.3 | 1.5 | 0.6 | 0.4 | 0.4 | 0.7 |
| North Africa | ..... | ..... | 0.4 | 1.1 | ..... | ..... | 0.2 | 0.1 | 0.1 | 0.3 |
| Republic of South Africa | 0.1 | 0.2 | 0.1 | 0.1 | 0.2 | 0.9 | 0.3 | 0.2 | 0.2 | 0.2 |
| Other Subsaharan Africa | 0.1 | 0.1 | 0.1 | ..... | ..... | 0.6 | 0.1 | 0.1 | 0.1 | 0.2 |
| **Middle East** | 0.6 | 1.6 | 0.4 | 1.0 | 0.5 | 0.8 | 1.2 | 1.3 | 0.8 | 0.7 |
| **Australia** | 2.5 | 2.2 | 3.3 | 1.3 | 2.6 | 3.0 | 1.9 | 1.2 | 1.6 | 1.5 |
| **Rest of World** | ..... | ..... | ..... | ..... | ..... | ..... | ..... | ..... | ..... | ..... |

## Table E-3.  Metropolitan Area Exports of Goods by Destination, 1993–1997—*Continued*

(Millions of dollars.)

| Destination | 1993 | 1994 | 1995 | 1996 | 1997 | 1993 | 1994 | 1995 | 1996 | 1997 |
|---|---|---|---|---|---|---|---|---|---|---|
| | New Haven - Meriden, CT | | | | | New London - Norwich, CT - RI | | | | |
| ALL DESTINATIONS | 1 035.6 | 1 075.5 | 1 106.3 | 1 012.4 | 1 179.8 | 136.5 | 141.5 | 178.2 | 157.5 | 192.1 |
| North America | 319.4 | 332.6 | 399.7 | 316.7 | 362.1 | 54.9 | 67.0 | 78.9 | 76.4 | 98.0 |
| Canada | 294.5 | 298.9 | 378.0 | 291.1 | 335.9 | 53.0 | 64.3 | 77.9 | 73.7 | 95.0 |
| Mexico | 24.9 | 33.7 | 21.7 | 25.7 | 26.2 | 1.9 | 2.6 | 0.9 | 2.7 | 3.0 |
| Caribbean and Central America | 15.2 | 15.6 | 20.7 | 25.5 | 30.3 | 1.5 | 0.9 | 1.2 | 1.4 | 2.1 |
| South America | 26.6 | 43.4 | 45.5 | 49.7 | 52.2 | 3.9 | 2.7 | 9.0 | 10.4 | 11.7 |
| Argentina | 5.8 | 9.2 | 6.2 | 6.1 | 11.1 | 1.0 | 0.4 | 0.6 | 0.9 | 0.2 |
| Brazil | 6.9 | 18.8 | 15.1 | 19.5 | 19.3 | 0.7 | 1.3 | 6.3 | 4.8 | 6.6 |
| Other South America | 13.9 | 15.4 | 24.2 | 24.2 | 21.8 | 2.3 | 1.0 | 2.2 | 4.7 | 4.8 |
| Europe | 410.7 | 407.7 | 346.3 | 317.5 | 399.5 | 36.1 | 43.4 | 61.9 | 48.6 | 52.5 |
| Belgium | 9.0 | 6.4 | 5.9 | 7.1 | 10.1 | 1.8 | 2.6 | 2.9 | 3.2 | 3.0 |
| France | 78.4 | 70.6 | 48.6 | 12.6 | 18.2 | 12.3 | 10.1 | 10.2 | 9.9 | 7.2 |
| Germany | 110.9 | 116.2 | 115.5 | 155.6 | 193.9 | 6.6 | 9.1 | 24.6 | 16.1 | 14.1 |
| Netherlands | 12.3 | 12.7 | 9.5 | 9.7 | 18.2 | 3.8 | 1.7 | 2.3 | 1.2 | 0.9 |
| United Kingdom | 64.8 | 47.6 | 52.5 | 52.4 | 55.4 | 3.2 | 8.6 | 7.1 | 8.1 | 9.2 |
| Turkey | 5.6 | 2.9 | 5.3 | 5.9 | 8.3 | 0.3 | 0.3 | 0.8 | 0.7 | 0.5 |
| Former Soviet Republics | 6.1 | 21.9 | 3.9 | 2.0 | 5.0 | 0.1 | ..... | 0.9 | 0.3 | 1.2 |
| Poland | 1.7 | 4.7 | 5.8 | 1.1 | 1.8 | 0.1 | 0.6 | 0.7 | 0.5 | 2.3 |
| Other Eastern Europe | 3.9 | 7.7 | 2.4 | 2.1 | 3.5 | ..... | 0.1 | 0.6 | 0.5 | 0.1 |
| Other Europe | 118.0 | 117.0 | 96.9 | 68.9 | 85.1 | 7.8 | 10.5 | 11.8 | 8.2 | 14.0 |
| Asia | 216.3 | 226.1 | 236.8 | 251.7 | 287.7 | 36.6 | 23.6 | 19.2 | 15.7 | 24.3 |
| Japan | 122.4 | 126.6 | 134.1 | 153.7 | 153.4 | 1.5 | 1.5 | 2.1 | 1.6 | 2.6 |
| China | 21.9 | 10.5 | 15.6 | 13.0 | 16.2 | 23.2 | 10.4 | 1.9 | 1.8 | 3.3 |
| Hong Kong | 9.8 | 14.6 | 15.5 | 12.7 | 15.8 | 3.1 | 3.0 | 1.4 | 2.8 | 6.9 |
| Taiwan | 13.9 | 17.5 | 16.1 | 15.9 | 20.4 | 1.5 | 1.5 | 4.4 | 4.6 | 0.8 |
| Singapore | 16.2 | 18.4 | 23.2 | 29.2 | 14.1 | 0.6 | 1.4 | 2.3 | 0.9 | 1.3 |
| South Korea | 13.0 | 13.6 | 12.7 | 9.3 | 28.2 | 4.1 | 1.7 | 1.2 | 1.2 | 1.4 |
| Indonesia | 2.1 | 2.2 | 2.4 | 2.7 | 2.8 | 0.1 | 0.1 | 1.3 | 0.6 | 0.9 |
| India | 1.3 | 2.1 | 1.8 | 1.2 | 3.1 | 0.1 | 0.4 | 1.3 | 0.5 | 2.2 |
| Other Asia | 15.7 | 20.6 | 15.5 | 13.9 | 33.7 | 2.3 | 3.6 | 3.3 | 1.7 | 4.8 |
| Africa | 8.2 | 8.4 | 8.7 | 9.1 | 6.9 | 0.9 | 1.4 | 3.5 | 2.3 | 1.0 |
| North Africa | 1.5 | 4.4 | 3.2 | 4.1 | 2.0 | 0.4 | 0.1 | 2.4 | 1.9 | 0.4 |
| Republic of South Africa | 5.0 | 3.4 | 4.5 | 4.3 | 3.8 | 0.5 | 1.0 | 0.5 | 0.4 | 0.6 |
| Other Subsaharan Africa | 1.8 | 0.6 | 0.9 | 0.8 | 1.1 | ..... | 0.3 | 0.6 | ..... | ..... |
| Middle East | 22.3 | 22.9 | 31.7 | 26.5 | 28.8 | 1.8 | 1.3 | 2.6 | 1.7 | 1.2 |
| Australia | 16.8 | 18.7 | 16.7 | 15.6 | 12.3 | 0.9 | 1.2 | 1.8 | 0.9 | 1.4 |
| Rest of World | ..... | ..... | 0.2 | 0.1 | ..... | ..... | ..... | ..... | ..... | ..... |
| | New Orleans, LA | | | | | New York, NY | | | | |
| ALL DESTINATIONS | 2 034.2 | 2 326.2 | 3 037.8 | 3 316.8 | 2 770.8 | 28 192.8 | 23 543.7 | 27 131.1 | 27 970.5 | 29 082.6 |
| North America | 132.7 | 203.3 | 202.6 | 235.8 | 259.4 | 2 415.7 | 2 493.4 | 2 371.9 | 2 722.6 | 3 412.0 |
| Canada | 109.3 | 139.3 | 157.0 | 158.9 | 204.8 | 1 806.8 | 1 851.1 | 1 916.8 | 2 099.0 | 2 458.9 |
| Mexico | 23.4 | 64.0 | 45.7 | 76.9 | 54.6 | 608.9 | 642.3 | 455.1 | 623.6 | 953.1 |
| Caribbean and Central America | 147.2 | 121.1 | 156.9 | 149.6 | 159.1 | 715.7 | 868.6 | 837.4 | 961.3 | 1 092.5 |
| South America | 95.1 | 117.5 | 192.3 | 209.9 | 181.5 | 1 390.1 | 1 349.2 | 1 601.1 | 1 584.6 | 1 850.4 |
| Argentina | 6.4 | 11.7 | 7.0 | 6.5 | 17.6 | 272.0 | 214.6 | 170.8 | 192.7 | 250.5 |
| Brazil | 7.8 | 13.6 | 24.7 | 24.9 | 39.9 | 319.0 | 465.0 | 485.4 | 425.1 | 579.3 |
| Other South America | 80.8 | 92.2 | 160.7 | 178.6 | 124.0 | 799.1 | 669.6 | 944.9 | 966.9 | 1 020.5 |
| Europe | 459.9 | 554.5 | 700.5 | 713.4 | 535.3 | 12 343.0 | 7 484.5 | 9 175.4 | 10 145.3 | 9 791.1 |
| Belgium | 91.1 | 102.1 | 123.8 | 154.0 | 103.4 | 748.9 | 777.1 | 861.6 | 742.4 | 753.1 |
| France | 81.9 | 61.9 | 81.5 | 34.6 | 34.9 | 557.5 | 412.8 | 421.6 | 440.1 | 455.6 |
| Germany | 17.4 | 42.6 | 27.3 | 84.9 | 45.2 | 722.4 | 706.6 | 940.0 | 772.7 | 859.3 |
| Netherlands | 105.0 | 111.4 | 168.7 | 153.5 | 119.2 | 670.3 | 507.0 | 798.8 | 588.8 | 515.1 |
| United Kingdom | 14.9 | 26.4 | 40.2 | 35.5 | 40.8 | 4 546.9 | 1 912.9 | 1 800.8 | 2 613.9 | 1 943.4 |
| Turkey | 8.4 | 18.6 | 28.7 | 14.1 | 12.6 | 251.5 | 276.0 | 239.4 | 237.9 | 231.3 |
| Former Soviet Republics | 37.2 | 29.7 | 13.0 | 6.5 | 4.1 | 598.3 | 432.0 | 407.2 | 310.2 | 269.6 |
| Poland | 0.1 | 3.1 | 0.2 | 0.2 | 0.6 | 82.2 | 36.8 | 42.7 | 39.4 | 47.9 |
| Other Eastern Europe | 7.4 | 2.5 | 0.3 | 7.9 | 4.2 | 163.0 | 164.8 | 190.7 | 157.5 | 118.7 |
| Other Europe | 96.5 | 156.1 | 216.7 | 222.3 | 170.3 | 4 001.5 | 2 258.4 | 3 472.6 | 4 242.6 | 4 597.0 |
| Asia | 966.8 | 1 080.9 | 1 504.0 | 1 782.4 | 1 389.8 | 8 590.3 | 8 772.7 | 10 355.6 | 9 645.3 | 9 500.4 |
| Japan | 713.8 | 734.3 | 805.7 | 1 053.3 | 916.9 | 3 554.6 | 3 832.3 | 4 538.1 | 4 355.6 | 4 289.3 |
| China | 16.9 | 44.7 | 226.0 | 120.8 | 71.1 | 504.2 | 461.3 | 456.7 | 625.2 | 512.8 |
| Hong Kong | 12.4 | 11.5 | 16.7 | 11.7 | 13.9 | 1 000.6 | 1 280.2 | 1 312.5 | 1 070.1 | 1 211.4 |
| Taiwan | 52.3 | 26.2 | 214.0 | 294.2 | 150.3 | 843.4 | 771.4 | 806.2 | 626.3 | 600.8 |
| Singapore | 16.9 | 24.1 | 14.8 | 20.7 | 24.5 | 373.9 | 249.0 | 272.9 | 238.6 | 242.2 |
| South Korea | 27.9 | 22.1 | 59.1 | 109.2 | 86.2 | 929.7 | 964.1 | 1 457.0 | 1 271.5 | 959.7 |
| Indonesia | 109.6 | 201.0 | 75.3 | 58.5 | 33.0 | 140.9 | 173.9 | 284.7 | 146.5 | 119.3 |
| India | 1.8 | 5.7 | 20.0 | 15.4 | 4.0 | 403.6 | 345.2 | 443.5 | 401.4 | 443.2 |
| Other Asia | 15.1 | 11.3 | 72.5 | 98.7 | 89.9 | 839.6 | 695.5 | 784.2 | 910.2 | 1 121.7 |
| Africa | 126.7 | 47.6 | 62.0 | 62.5 | 74.5 | 854.9 | 746.2 | 835.7 | 793.6 | 888.7 |
| North Africa | 14.1 | 23.6 | 18.2 | 13.8 | 22.8 | 436.9 | 383.9 | 336.1 | 289.2 | 353.8 |
| Republic of South Africa | 8.0 | 5.7 | 9.0 | 9.0 | 9.7 | 121.2 | 130.4 | 168.0 | 136.9 | 150.4 |
| Other Subsaharan Africa | 104.6 | 18.3 | 34.9 | 39.7 | 42.0 | 296.7 | 232.0 | 331.6 | 367.5 | 384.5 |
| Middle East | 91.8 | 175.1 | 197.5 | 131.1 | 129.6 | 1 704.6 | 1 605.7 | 1 736.0 | 1 862.8 | 2 331.4 |
| Australia | 14.1 | 26.2 | 22.0 | 31.9 | 41.6 | 157.3 | 221.1 | 217.9 | 254.9 | 215.3 |
| Rest of World | ..... | ..... | ..... | ..... | ..... | 21.1 | 2.3 | ..... | 0.1 | 0.8 |

# Table E-3. Metropolitan Area Exports of Goods by Destination, 1993–1997—Continued

(Millions of dollars.)

| Destination | 1993 | 1994 | 1995 | 1996 | 1997 | 1993 | 1994 | 1995 | 1996 | 1997 |
|---|---|---|---|---|---|---|---|---|---|---|
| | Norfolk - Virginia Beach - Newport News, VA - NC | | | | | Oakland, CA | | | | |
| ALL DESTINATIONS | 677.2 | 807.7 | 1 005.5 | 1 256.9 | 1 396.9 | 4 181.5 | 5 113.2 | 6 372.5 | 7 309.2 | 6 920.4 |
| North America | 154.9 | 181.5 | 249.5 | 287.0 | 317.1 | 573.7 | 763.7 | 713.7 | 878.9 | 1 022.5 |
| Canada | 142.2 | 157.0 | 219.2 | 205.6 | 230.1 | 461.2 | 586.0 | 598.2 | 747.2 | 855.1 |
| Mexico | 12.7 | 24.5 | 30.3 | 81.4 | 87.1 | 112.5 | 177.7 | 115.5 | 131.7 | 167.4 |
| Caribbean and Central America | 9.7 | 5.2 | 6.6 | 16.3 | 20.2 | 20.6 | 19.4 | 45.8 | 58.5 | 72.1 |
| South America | 34.7 | 54.6 | 78.7 | 90.2 | 98.0 | 92.9 | 76.5 | 67.5 | 120.0 | 161.9 |
| Argentina | 7.1 | 6.5 | 9.3 | 6.6 | 10.6 | 16.0 | 18.1 | 14.3 | 10.0 | 23.8 |
| Brazil | 16.7 | 37.1 | 47.1 | 53.8 | 59.7 | 8.5 | 13.4 | 23.2 | 86.2 | 92.4 |
| Other South America | 10.8 | 11.0 | 22.3 | 29.8 | 27.7 | 68.3 | 45.0 | 30.1 | 23.8 | 45.8 |
| Europe | 329.9 | 402.0 | 455.6 | 574.8 | 610.9 | 757.0 | 1 022.0 | 1 440.5 | 1 382.5 | 1 371.8 |
| Belgium | 10.2 | 36.3 | 52.0 | 56.5 | 66.9 | 36.1 | 48.0 | 53.3 | 39.7 | 29.5 |
| France | 30.7 | 55.3 | 66.5 | 95.8 | 101.4 | 77.0 | 103.0 | 122.7 | 132.7 | 131.0 |
| Germany | 58.8 | 68.4 | 83.3 | 110.1 | 118.8 | 181.4 | 250.5 | 353.9 | 339.5 | 315.1 |
| Netherlands | 13.5 | 31.4 | 58.1 | 49.2 | 46.5 | 74.8 | 117.9 | 169.8 | 150.2 | 143.0 |
| United Kingdom | 29.8 | 23.4 | 28.5 | 37.5 | 43.1 | 173.7 | 209.1 | 341.6 | 346.0 | 370.7 |
| Turkey | 42.5 | 20.9 | 7.9 | 3.3 | 7.2 | 2.1 | 1.5 | 1.3 | 4.7 | 5.3 |
| Former Soviet Republics | 1.8 | 5.4 | 6.3 | 5.0 | 5.2 | 14.1 | 28.5 | 20.7 | 22.4 | 29.5 |
| Poland | 0.2 | 0.2 | 0.6 | 1.0 | 1.3 | 1.5 | 2.9 | 3.8 | 4.9 | 5.2 |
| Other Eastern Europe | 0.9 | 0.4 | 2.5 | 7.0 | 7.3 | 5.3 | 8.8 | 24.6 | 21.8 | 16.0 |
| Other Europe | 141.7 | 160.4 | 149.8 | 209.4 | 213.2 | 190.9 | 251.8 | 348.7 | 320.6 | 326.6 |
| Asia | 113.7 | 118.5 | 167.6 | 207.5 | 253.3 | 2 390.5 | 2 976.8 | 3 903.0 | 4 649.5 | 4 029.3 |
| Japan | 27.2 | 31.4 | 33.0 | 49.2 | 56.8 | 913.2 | 1 043.0 | 1 343.1 | 1 647.0 | 1 262.8 |
| China | 1.9 | 4.8 | 24.2 | 15.4 | 21.5 | 90.9 | 70.6 | 94.5 | 133.9 | 168.5 |
| Hong Kong | 8.9 | 10.1 | 13.0 | 18.5 | 29.4 | 286.4 | 305.2 | 336.9 | 278.8 | 342.5 |
| Taiwan | 5.5 | 9.7 | 14.6 | 22.3 | 23.1 | 351.4 | 460.1 | 610.0 | 746.5 | 699.7 |
| Singapore | 3.3 | 4.2 | 5.0 | 7.9 | 11.9 | 297.9 | 367.3 | 535.3 | 833.5 | 651.4 |
| South Korea | 49.0 | 45.4 | 61.4 | 39.4 | 29.1 | 176.8 | 351.4 | 491.6 | 492.8 | 410.3 |
| Indonesia | 2.4 | 0.7 | 1.5 | 15.9 | 26.7 | 36.1 | 28.6 | 40.3 | 74.1 | 59.7 |
| India | 0.6 | 4.6 | 0.4 | 3.5 | 2.4 | 15.5 | 21.3 | 58.8 | 44.0 | 16.1 |
| Other Asia | 14.9 | 7.7 | 14.5 | 35.5 | 52.3 | 222.1 | 329.3 | 392.5 | 399.0 | 418.3 |
| Africa | 13.7 | 23.2 | 25.3 | 17.9 | 29.9 | 188.9 | 85.5 | 25.6 | 38.8 | 42.8 |
| North Africa | 9.1 | 18.0 | 20.2 | 11.3 | 21.2 | 16.0 | 8.3 | 3.8 | 7.2 | 14.5 |
| Republic of South Africa | 2.5 | 4.0 | 4.0 | 5.2 | 7.9 | 8.1 | 11.5 | 12.9 | 22.8 | 15.7 |
| Other Subsaharan Africa | 2.1 | 1.3 | 1.0 | 1.3 | 0.8 | 164.8 | 65.7 | 8.9 | 8.8 | 12.5 |
| Middle East | 13.3 | 14.6 | 11.0 | 37.8 | 45.2 | 50.8 | 54.8 | 52.5 | 61.4 | 72.6 |
| Australia | 7.2 | 8.0 | 11.3 | 24.9 | 22.3 | 107.1 | 114.6 | 123.8 | 119.7 | 147.4 |
| Rest of World | ..... | ..... | ..... | 0.5 | ..... | ..... | ..... | ..... | ..... | ..... |
| | Omaha, NE - IA | | | | | Orange County, CA | | | | |
| ALL DESTINATIONS | 299.8 | 393.3 | 425.9 | 608.3 | 691.4 | 5 653.4 | 6 716.0 | 8 041.1 | 8 309.3 | 8 798.3 |
| North America | 110.7 | 137.9 | 150.6 | 257.0 | 231.9 | 1 313.1 | 1 585.3 | 1 962.5 | 2 208.3 | 2 442.2 |
| Canada | 92.5 | 94.7 | 103.5 | 127.3 | 153.3 | 722.2 | 833.0 | 1 004.0 | 1 033.3 | 1 024.0 |
| Mexico | 18.2 | 43.2 | 47.2 | 129.7 | 78.6 | 590.9 | 752.3 | 958.5 | 1 175.1 | 1 418.2 |
| Caribbean and Central America | 5.7 | 11.2 | 7.4 | 7.4 | 4.5 | 34.5 | 37.8 | 32.5 | 38.9 | 62.5 |
| South America | 10.2 | 46.5 | 50.0 | 81.0 | 120.6 | 108.3 | 132.1 | 192.8 | 208.9 | 242.8 |
| Argentina | 0.2 | 0.4 | 0.2 | 0.6 | 1.3 | 24.0 | 29.8 | 47.1 | 33.5 | 42.0 |
| Brazil | 0.4 | 0.6 | 0.5 | 3.1 | 6.9 | 40.0 | 50.8 | 90.0 | 120.0 | 131.6 |
| Other South America | 9.6 | 45.5 | 49.3 | 77.4 | 112.3 | 44.3 | 51.6 | 55.7 | 55.4 | 69.2 |
| Europe | 89.8 | 91.1 | 94.3 | 122.5 | 149.2 | 1 746.3 | 2 016.9 | 2 293.4 | 1 918.2 | 2 012.6 |
| Belgium | 17.3 | 16.2 | 10.2 | 22.7 | 32.3 | 37.3 | 38.9 | 56.9 | 55.6 | 58.1 |
| France | 3.2 | 2.7 | 2.8 | 4.8 | 9.1 | 465.4 | 640.4 | 657.2 | 461.1 | 423.5 |
| Germany | 3.3 | 4.3 | 4.0 | 6.8 | 7.2 | 285.8 | 322.8 | 363.3 | 286.9 | 302.3 |
| Netherlands | 37.3 | 38.8 | 48.2 | 46.9 | 43.6 | 134.3 | 141.6 | 176.5 | 219.1 | 221.0 |
| United Kingdom | 18.6 | 11.8 | 6.9 | 13.1 | 16.5 | 384.1 | 400.2 | 443.4 | 359.0 | 454.6 |
| Turkey | 0.3 | 0.2 | 0.2 | 0.4 | 0.1 | 7.5 | 4.6 | 7.9 | 9.2 | 11.9 |
| Former Soviet Republics | 0.3 | 0.5 | 1.2 | 12.6 | 0.7 | 17.1 | 16.0 | 14.5 | 24.7 | 24.8 |
| Poland | ..... | ..... | 0.9 | 0.6 | 0.1 | 3.7 | 2.6 | 6.4 | 8.6 | 8.2 |
| Other Eastern Europe | 0.5 | 1.1 | 4.1 | 1.4 | 0.8 | 12.2 | 17.0 | 17.3 | 20.7 | 24.1 |
| Other Europe | 9.0 | 15.5 | 15.9 | 13.3 | 38.8 | 398.9 | 432.7 | 550.0 | 473.3 | 484.1 |
| Asia | 52.9 | 58.6 | 78.9 | 91.9 | 122.8 | 2 188.3 | 2 651.7 | 3 243.9 | 3 623.9 | 3 706.9 |
| Japan | 12.6 | 14.7 | 20.1 | 29.2 | 26.2 | 897.8 | 1 160.7 | 1 380.1 | 1 531.8 | 1 393.1 |
| China | 1.4 | 2.3 | 3.2 | 5.6 | 1.5 | 62.4 | 65.7 | 147.3 | 133.0 | 87.6 |
| Hong Kong | 6.6 | 12.6 | 10.6 | 2.6 | 2.9 | 220.7 | 226.8 | 257.9 | 243.4 | 313.8 |
| Taiwan | 3.8 | 1.9 | 1.9 | 3.1 | 7.4 | 277.8 | 330.4 | 376.5 | 425.4 | 512.7 |
| Singapore | 7.9 | 10.5 | 16.5 | 15.7 | 26.3 | 339.5 | 297.5 | 325.4 | 358.4 | 299.6 |
| South Korea | 13.2 | 6.5 | 4.6 | 7.3 | 6.7 | 201.9 | 315.0 | 458.4 | 537.9 | 686.8 |
| Indonesia | 0.1 | 1.3 | 3.3 | 2.5 | 9.0 | 7.5 | 12.6 | 10.9 | 56.2 | 50.5 |
| India | 0.5 | 0.4 | 1.6 | 0.5 | 1.2 | 15.3 | 15.7 | 26.6 | 33.7 | 27.7 |
| Other Asia | 6.8 | 8.5 | 17.1 | 25.5 | 41.6 | 165.4 | 227.3 | 260.7 | 304.1 | 335.2 |
| Africa | 10.9 | 16.3 | 10.8 | 15.0 | 17.6 | 34.3 | 40.6 | 50.7 | 43.2 | 48.9 |
| North Africa | 7.9 | 9.6 | 6.3 | 11.3 | 9.5 | 8.3 | 11.6 | 21.4 | 10.2 | 13.9 |
| Republic of South Africa | 1.8 | 2.3 | 2.9 | 3.2 | 2.3 | 21.2 | 25.1 | 26.2 | 27.8 | 26.9 |
| Other Subsaharan Africa | 1.2 | 4.4 | 1.6 | 0.5 | 5.8 | 4.7 | 3.9 | 3.1 | 5.2 | 8.1 |
| Middle East | 15.4 | 24.4 | 23.4 | 14.1 | 12.1 | 94.3 | 88.0 | 97.9 | 101.0 | 125.5 |
| Australia | 4.2 | 7.1 | 10.5 | 19.4 | 32.7 | 134.2 | 163.6 | 167.4 | 166.8 | 156.8 |
| Rest of World | ..... | ..... | ..... | ..... | ..... | 0.1 | ..... | 0.1 | ..... | ..... |

## Table E-3.  Metropolitan Area Exports of Goods by Destination, 1993–1997—*Continued*

(Millions of dollars.)

| Destination | 1993 | 1994 | 1995 | 1996 | 1997 | 1993 | 1994 | 1995 | 1996 | 1997 |
|---|---|---|---|---|---|---|---|---|---|---|
| | Orlando, FL | | | | | Parkersburg - Marietta, WV - OH | | | | |
| **ALL DESTINATIONS** | 930.4 | 848.5 | 968.8 | 1 219.0 | 1 662.8 | 298.8 | 313.6 | 186.6 | 211.9 | 262.3 |
| **North America** | 272.4 | 222.0 | 176.1 | 177.6 | 237.4 | 87.1 | 98.0 | 80.6 | 97.4 | 113.8 |
| Canada | 230.1 | 146.9 | 131.6 | 151.9 | 201.1 | 77.9 | 89.9 | 74.8 | 90.7 | 106.7 |
| Mexico | 42.2 | 75.1 | 44.5 | 25.7 | 36.3 | 9.2 | 8.1 | 5.8 | 6.8 | 7.1 |
| **Caribbean and Central America** | 30.6 | 45.5 | 39.8 | 63.6 | 74.0 | 2.4 | 3.1 | 1.2 | 1.5 | 2.9 |
| **South America** | 105.0 | 122.0 | 114.6 | 100.5 | 134.1 | 10.9 | 9.7 | 3.3 | 4.8 | 5.6 |
| Argentina | 4.2 | 6.8 | 20.8 | 8.2 | 13.0 | 2.5 | 2.2 | 1.4 | 1.4 | 1.4 |
| Brazil | 13.0 | 24.9 | 50.2 | 40.8 | 35.2 | 2.0 | 2.3 | 1.2 | 2.1 | 2.7 |
| Other South America | 87.8 | 90.3 | 43.6 | 51.6 | 85.9 | 6.5 | 5.2 | 0.8 | 1.4 | 1.5 |
| **Europe** | 262.2 | 186.1 | 250.4 | 348.0 | 297.1 | 46.0 | 55.7 | 39.0 | 44.9 | 72.5 |
| Belgium | 29.1 | 8.6 | 19.1 | 16.3 | 13.1 | 19.1 | 19.0 | 17.6 | 17.9 | 30.6 |
| France | 30.2 | 20.9 | 22.1 | 23.7 | 22.9 | 1.2 | 1.9 | 2.1 | 2.5 | 6.6 |
| Germany | 46.1 | 32.2 | 42.8 | 46.4 | 54.4 | 1.2 | 2.7 | 1.6 | 1.8 | 3.5 |
| Netherlands | 14.5 | 16.9 | 25.9 | 39.4 | 25.7 | 16.6 | 21.4 | 4.4 | 4.2 | 7.8 |
| United Kingdom | 73.0 | 32.5 | 47.6 | 61.8 | 83.4 | 3.6 | 5.6 | 8.9 | 13.2 | 15.6 |
| Turkey | 2.3 | 2.8 | 2.5 | 3.7 | 4.7 | 0.4 | ..... | 0.4 | 0.3 | 0.2 |
| Former Soviet Republics | 22.5 | 4.9 | 3.1 | 3.6 | 3.0 | ..... | 0.1 | ..... | ..... | ..... |
| Poland | 1.1 | 0.6 | 11.3 | 49.9 | 10.2 | ..... | ..... | ..... | ..... | ..... |
| Other Eastern Europe | 2.6 | 1.7 | 1.8 | 8.7 | 5.1 | 0.1 | 0.3 | 0.1 | 0.1 | 0.1 |
| Other Europe | 40.6 | 65.1 | 74.2 | 94.5 | 74.6 | 3.7 | 4.5 | 3.9 | 4.9 | 8.1 |
| **Asia** | 171.0 | 179.5 | 295.6 | 433.9 | 741.5 | 146.2 | 139.7 | 57.1 | 55.9 | 58.0 |
| Japan | 18.1 | 23.3 | 29.4 | 49.1 | 45.6 | 23.1 | 20.8 | 13.5 | 8.2 | 23.7 |
| China | 26.7 | 14.8 | 28.0 | 80.4 | 282.6 | 16.5 | 16.6 | 14.8 | 12.2 | 1.1 |
| Hong Kong | 4.5 | 9.8 | 10.8 | 7.5 | 13.4 | 27.3 | 28.1 | 5.2 | 5.5 | 4.0 |
| Taiwan | 14.2 | 7.2 | 9.1 | 10.0 | 13.8 | 15.5 | 11.2 | 1.9 | 1.3 | 1.4 |
| Singapore | 4.9 | 14.5 | 28.3 | 35.0 | 173.0 | 34.6 | 30.4 | 12.2 | 18.1 | 16.5 |
| South Korea | 72.3 | 74.5 | 162.0 | 191.1 | 179.8 | 14.7 | 13.1 | 5.6 | 5.6 | 4.3 |
| Indonesia | 3.0 | 1.2 | 3.4 | 2.7 | 3.5 | 0.7 | 0.6 | 0.5 | 0.3 | 0.6 |
| India | 1.2 | 1.4 | 2.9 | 5.6 | 3.7 | 0.4 | 0.7 | 0.6 | 0.7 | 0.7 |
| Other Asia | 26.1 | 32.9 | 21.5 | 52.4 | 26.2 | 13.4 | 18.2 | 2.9 | 3.8 | 5.9 |
| **Africa** | 12.4 | 20.0 | 24.2 | 16.4 | 14.8 | 0.3 | 0.2 | 0.3 | 0.3 | 1.8 |
| North Africa | 8.3 | 12.8 | 10.1 | 6.5 | 2.7 | 0.1 | 0.2 | ..... | 0.1 | 1.5 |
| Republic of South Africa | 2.9 | 3.7 | 5.1 | 7.2 | 7.5 | 0.1 | ..... | ..... | 0.2 | 0.2 |
| Other Subsaharan Africa | 1.3 | 3.6 | 9.0 | 2.8 | 4.7 | ..... | 0.1 | ..... | ..... | 0.1 |
| **Middle East** | 60.5 | 66.9 | 60.1 | 65.7 | 151.8 | 1.4 | 2.6 | 0.9 | 1.7 | 2.1 |
| **Australia** | 16.3 | 6.4 | 8.0 | 13.3 | 12.1 | 4.5 | 4.7 | 4.1 | 5.4 | 5.5 |
| **Rest of World** | ..... | ..... | ..... | ..... | ..... | ..... | ..... | ..... | ..... | ..... |

| Destination | 1993 | 1994 | 1995 | 1996 | 1997 | 1993 | 1994 | 1995 | 1996 | 1997 |
|---|---|---|---|---|---|---|---|---|---|---|
| | Philadelphia, PA - NJ | | | | | Phoenix - Mesa, AZ | | | | |
| **ALL DESTINATIONS** | 5 869.1 | 6 545.8 | 7 896.9 | 7 727.9 | 8 027.8 | 4 498.9 | 5 561.1 | 6 780.4 | 7 912.1 | 11 108.4 |
| **North America** | 1 500.3 | 1 771.5 | 1 942.3 | 1 994.3 | 2 171.5 | 607.6 | 772.6 | 916.9 | 1 045.0 | 1 253.0 |
| Canada | 1 245.7 | 1 426.5 | 1 641.4 | 1 690.9 | 1 845.7 | 376.5 | 455.6 | 630.7 | 690.2 | 794.8 |
| Mexico | 254.7 | 345.0 | 300.9 | 303.4 | 325.7 | 231.1 | 317.0 | 286.2 | 354.8 | 458.2 |
| **Caribbean and Central America** | 201.4 | 240.4 | 307.3 | 409.2 | 369.2 | 6.6 | 8.4 | 8.3 | 10.5 | 17.4 |
| **South America** | 556.0 | 696.1 | 870.1 | 682.7 | 778.3 | 45.3 | 69.1 | 87.9 | 125.0 | 147.7 |
| Argentina | 79.8 | 124.4 | 106.4 | 75.3 | 81.8 | 7.5 | 12.5 | 9.6 | 10.7 | 13.1 |
| Brazil | 256.2 | 325.8 | 450.1 | 344.9 | 410.3 | 17.3 | 28.4 | 43.7 | 65.9 | 98.2 |
| Other South America | 220.0 | 245.9 | 313.6 | 262.5 | 286.2 | 20.5 | 28.2 | 34.7 | 48.3 | 36.4 |
| **Europe** | 1 655.9 | 1 761.1 | 2 280.4 | 2 386.1 | 2 313.4 | 1 506.4 | 1 766.6 | 2 295.3 | 2 291.4 | 3 744.6 |
| Belgium | 129.2 | 137.3 | 199.1 | 168.0 | 168.8 | 54.2 | 55.7 | 68.6 | 73.2 | 78.6 |
| France | 123.3 | 129.7 | 180.7 | 186.0 | 168.6 | 178.8 | 182.4 | 246.8 | 284.5 | 335.1 |
| Germany | 221.1 | 232.0 | 262.3 | 264.9 | 299.7 | 236.2 | 288.3 | 337.7 | 316.3 | 336.2 |
| Netherlands | 235.8 | 217.4 | 363.7 | 313.3 | 262.6 | 87.1 | 125.0 | 281.5 | 550.6 | 1 421.7 |
| United Kingdom | 389.9 | 464.0 | 691.8 | 800.5 | 793.7 | 779.9 | 877.1 | 1 046.9 | 781.9 | 1 010.6 |
| Turkey | 45.4 | 21.0 | 17.7 | 29.9 | 28.8 | 17.6 | 18.0 | 7.8 | 11.1 | 18.2 |
| Former Soviet Republics | 25.4 | 30.2 | 40.6 | 86.6 | 53.8 | 3.1 | 7.0 | 8.2 | 6.7 | 165.7 |
| Poland | 5.9 | 6.8 | 9.2 | 16.4 | 20.7 | 1.6 | 1.2 | 0.9 | 1.5 | 0.8 |
| Other Eastern Europe | 11.4 | 14.4 | 19.3 | 12.4 | 26.8 | 2.7 | 3.9 | 3.4 | 4.6 | 10.0 |
| Other Europe | 468.5 | 508.3 | 496.0 | 508.0 | 489.8 | 145.1 | 208.1 | 293.5 | 261.1 | 367.9 |
| **Asia** | 1 609.1 | 1 732.1 | 2 041.9 | 1 833.2 | 1 954.3 | 2 201.8 | 2 784.2 | 3 319.4 | 4 292.4 | 5 767.2 |
| Japan | 464.8 | 411.4 | 423.5 | 492.8 | 479.0 | 616.3 | 753.7 | 1 049.3 | 1 275.3 | 1 716.0 |
| China | 52.9 | 92.9 | 123.8 | 111.6 | 119.5 | 65.4 | 61.2 | 90.6 | 119.9 | 120.1 |
| Hong Kong | 123.2 | 140.6 | 167.3 | 186.9 | 183.0 | 241.5 | 269.6 | 375.5 | 381.3 | 477.2 |
| Taiwan | 374.0 | 408.1 | 469.0 | 219.1 | 303.2 | 462.3 | 585.3 | 618.7 | 855.1 | 1 013.2 |
| Singapore | 134.6 | 125.3 | 163.2 | 128.4 | 154.6 | 244.8 | 347.5 | 297.2 | 345.9 | 452.6 |
| South Korea | 211.4 | 270.3 | 306.4 | 259.4 | 273.5 | 174.2 | 202.3 | 227.5 | 279.1 | 289.0 |
| Indonesia | 26.3 | 45.2 | 72.3 | 56.7 | 78.0 | 7.4 | 13.0 | 15.7 | 13.7 | 18.9 |
| India | 24.0 | 43.9 | 60.2 | 67.1 | 82.9 | 13.9 | 19.9 | 25.1 | 14.3 | 33.9 |
| Other Asia | 197.9 | 194.5 | 256.2 | 311.2 | 280.6 | 376.1 | 531.8 | 619.8 | 1 007.8 | 1 646.4 |
| **Africa** | 94.7 | 85.1 | 86.0 | 75.8 | 80.3 | 7.3 | 18.6 | 24.5 | 21.3 | 28.4 |
| North Africa | 43.4 | 34.3 | 28.4 | 19.9 | 30.7 | 2.0 | 10.6 | 6.8 | 6.2 | 8.3 |
| Republic of South Africa | 34.8 | 36.2 | 44.4 | 42.5 | 37.7 | 3.6 | 4.5 | 12.1 | 11.8 | 15.0 |
| Other Subsaharan Africa | 16.5 | 14.5 | 13.1 | 13.5 | 12.0 | 1.7 | 3.5 | 5.6 | 3.2 | 5.1 |
| **Middle East** | 132.7 | 119.8 | 145.0 | 153.7 | 170.9 | 53.8 | 46.9 | 57.7 | 65.4 | 77.8 |
| **Australia** | 118.9 | 139.5 | 224.1 | 192.9 | 189.8 | 70.2 | 94.6 | 70.4 | 61.0 | 72.3 |
| **Rest of World** | ..... | 0.1 | ..... | ..... | ..... | ..... | ..... | ..... | ..... | ..... |

## Table E-3.  Metropolitan Area Exports of Goods by Destination, 1993–1997—*Continued*

(Millions of dollars.)

| Destination | 1993 | 1994 | 1995 | 1996 | 1997 | 1993 | 1994 | 1995 | 1996 | 1997 |
|---|---|---|---|---|---|---|---|---|---|---|
| | Pittsfield, MA | | | | | Pittsburgh, PA | | | | |
| **ALL DESTINATIONS** | 77.2 | 112.2 | 151.9 | 175.5 | 219.3 | 2 989.7 | 3 150.6 | 3 982.2 | 3 933.7 | 4 352.2 |
| **North America** | 29.6 | 51.0 | 58.5 | 75.8 | 95.7 | 922.0 | 955.1 | 1 010.3 | 1 170.4 | 1 564.1 |
| Canada | 23.2 | 33.1 | 36.1 | 52.7 | 55.6 | 741.9 | 731.0 | 823.6 | 948.5 | 1 222.5 |
| Mexico | 6.4 | 17.9 | 22.4 | 23.1 | 40.1 | 180.1 | 224.1 | 186.7 | 221.9 | 341.6 |
| **Caribbean and Central America** | 0.1 | 0.3 | 0.5 | 9.6 | 10.0 | 59.9 | 56.2 | 68.6 | 72.0 | 66.8 |
| **South America** | 8.9 | 3.6 | 3.5 | 13.8 | 14.2 | 274.0 | 288.5 | 281.6 | 266.3 | 374.5 |
| Argentina | 2.4 | 1.0 | 0.4 | 1.7 | 0.8 | 60.2 | 62.3 | 30.7 | 29.2 | 36.9 |
| Brazil | 0.5 | 0.3 | 1.5 | 2.3 | 5.6 | 80.8 | 89.5 | 118.3 | 121.6 | 213.9 |
| Other South America | 6.0 | 2.4 | 1.7 | 9.7 | 7.8 | 133.0 | 136.7 | 132.6 | 115.5 | 123.7 |
| **Europe** | 21.4 | 31.3 | 49.1 | 33.1 | 34.7 | 792.0 | 728.6 | 1 103.0 | 1 077.3 | 1 099.3 |
| Belgium | 0.1 | 0.5 | 2.3 | 0.3 | 0.2 | 67.9 | 55.5 | 141.0 | 143.1 | 149.9 |
| France | 0.7 | 0.5 | 1.5 | 2.2 | 2.1 | 64.9 | 45.6 | 76.5 | 72.7 | 81.5 |
| Germany | 3.8 | 5.8 | 5.5 | 4.6 | 5.2 | 116.8 | 110.2 | 143.3 | 161.3 | 149.9 |
| Netherlands | 10.4 | 14.5 | 23.1 | 19.1 | 18.2 | 71.2 | 74.1 | 116.2 | 139.8 | 120.3 |
| United Kingdom | 2.0 | 2.3 | 6.8 | 3.6 | 4.4 | 186.1 | 166.5 | 184.7 | 190.4 | 230.0 |
| Turkey | ..... | ..... | ..... | ..... | ..... | 17.6 | 8.3 | 35.4 | 15.0 | 26.0 |
| Former Soviet Republics | 0.1 | 0.1 | 2.6 | ..... | 0.1 | 15.2 | 11.8 | 22.3 | 23.8 | 21.3 |
| Poland | 0.5 | 0.8 | ..... | ..... | 0.1 | 6.4 | 6.4 | 6.7 | 5.5 | 7.2 |
| Other Eastern Europe | 0.4 | 0.6 | ..... | ..... | ..... | 11.6 | 16.4 | 19.3 | 26.3 | 47.8 |
| Other Europe | 3.4 | 6.3 | 7.2 | 3.3 | 4.4 | 234.3 | 233.7 | 357.6 | 299.2 | 265.3 |
| **Asia** | 13.0 | 23.8 | 33.3 | 40.0 | 61.1 | 683.8 | 807.7 | 1 156.8 | 964.8 | 944.1 |
| Japan | 5.4 | 6.6 | 8.5 | 10.8 | 8.4 | 189.9 | 205.9 | 350.8 | 309.6 | 295.6 |
| China | 1.1 | 8.2 | 1.4 | 3.3 | 3.9 | 53.9 | 115.1 | 125.5 | 72.7 | 63.3 |
| Hong Kong | 0.7 | 3.3 | 3.4 | 9.0 | 9.7 | 27.2 | 27.9 | 49.6 | 39.5 | 53.9 |
| Taiwan | 1.8 | 3.1 | 3.5 | 3.5 | 2.4 | 54.9 | 63.7 | 158.1 | 116.2 | 97.1 |
| Singapore | 0.6 | 0.4 | 1.1 | 1.8 | 20.8 | 46.1 | 51.5 | 91.3 | 109.4 | 107.5 |
| South Korea | 0.9 | 1.1 | 1.9 | 2.7 | 7.1 | 107.3 | 176.6 | 187.2 | 149.6 | 111.5 |
| Indonesia | 0.5 | 0.1 | 11.6 | 6.4 | 4.6 | 9.4 | 11.2 | 18.7 | 27.9 | 16.1 |
| India | 0.3 | ..... | 0.2 | 0.8 | 0.2 | 76.9 | 33.2 | 41.1 | 37.9 | 48.9 |
| Other Asia | 1.6 | 1.0 | 1.7 | 1.6 | 4.0 | 118.2 | 122.5 | 134.6 | 102.0 | 150.3 |
| **Africa** | 0.3 | 0.2 | 0.5 | 0.3 | 0.2 | 51.5 | 75.7 | 75.5 | 107.7 | 93.5 |
| North Africa | ..... | ..... | ..... | ..... | 0.1 | 21.9 | 22.4 | 13.1 | 42.6 | 36.1 |
| Republic of South Africa | 0.3 | 0.2 | 0.5 | ..... | 0.1 | 24.1 | 48.2 | 56.5 | 58.4 | 49.6 |
| Other Subsaharan Africa | ..... | ..... | ..... | 0.1 | ..... | 5.5 | 5.1 | 6.0 | 6.7 | 7.9 |
| **Middle East** | 0.4 | 1.5 | 1.9 | 0.3 | 2.0 | 146.7 | 178.9 | 206.7 | 192.4 | 127.7 |
| **Australia** | 3.4 | 0.4 | 4.4 | 2.8 | 1.4 | 59.9 | 59.9 | 79.7 | 82.8 | 82.0 |
| **Rest of World** | ..... | ..... | ..... | ..... | ..... | ..... | ..... | ..... | ..... | ..... |
| | Portland, ME | | | | | Portland - Vancouver, OR - WA | | | | |
| **ALL DESTINATIONS** | 355.2 | 319.5 | 373.1 | 339.2 | 617.4 | 5 698.5 | 6 448.8 | 8 931.3 | 9 234.3 | 8 926.5 |
| **North America** | 48.8 | 61.2 | 61.7 | 61.5 | 69.3 | 732.1 | 919.4 | 927.9 | 960.1 | 1 099.8 |
| Canada | 47.3 | 59.0 | 60.6 | 58.3 | 67.0 | 621.2 | 759.7 | 843.9 | 839.1 | 994.1 |
| Mexico | 1.5 | 2.3 | 1.2 | 3.2 | 2.3 | 110.9 | 159.7 | 84.0 | 121.1 | 105.8 |
| **Caribbean and Central America** | 13.7 | 11.5 | 8.1 | 14.4 | 13.2 | 16.4 | 16.7 | 23.5 | 25.9 | 34.8 |
| **South America** | 4.8 | 3.6 | 4.2 | 6.8 | 8.8 | 103.1 | 91.8 | 157.2 | 106.0 | 182.1 |
| Argentina | 0.2 | 0.3 | 0.5 | 0.6 | 0.7 | 6.9 | 7.6 | 6.9 | 7.4 | 15.9 |
| Brazil | 2.0 | 0.9 | 1.6 | 2.5 | 2.9 | 13.7 | 15.7 | 24.8 | 23.6 | 41.8 |
| Other South America | 2.6 | 2.4 | 2.0 | 3.8 | 5.2 | 82.5 | 68.4 | 125.5 | 75.0 | 124.3 |
| **Europe** | 81.0 | 82.9 | 74.3 | 77.7 | 78.4 | 1 170.3 | 1 133.0 | 1 497.0 | 1 248.4 | 1 297.3 |
| Belgium | 26.0 | 24.6 | 2.3 | 2.3 | 3.1 | 43.0 | 43.4 | 69.5 | 43.7 | 49.2 |
| France | 19.3 | 24.3 | 34.1 | 37.9 | 18.7 | 98.6 | 117.3 | 142.5 | 93.7 | 100.3 |
| Germany | 4.4 | 3.9 | 4.3 | 5.6 | 5.1 | 425.4 | 208.1 | 264.1 | 240.1 | 194.5 |
| Netherlands | 2.7 | 1.6 | 2.5 | 3.7 | 2.4 | 89.5 | 96.9 | 169.2 | 185.7 | 280.8 |
| United Kingdom | 6.6 | 6.8 | 8.7 | 6.5 | 7.3 | 235.0 | 295.9 | 328.7 | 299.4 | 332.0 |
| Turkey | 0.8 | 0.7 | 0.5 | 1.5 | 0.8 | 3.5 | 3.3 | 13.7 | 30.7 | 3.2 |
| Former Soviet Republics | 1.3 | 0.9 | 0.1 | 0.7 | 0.2 | 29.7 | 40.3 | 30.6 | 13.9 | 22.7 |
| Poland | 0.2 | ..... | ..... | ..... | ..... | 1.8 | 1.4 | 2.9 | 2.5 | 4.2 |
| Other Eastern Europe | 0.3 | 0.2 | 0.2 | 0.4 | 0.8 | 5.8 | 10.3 | 10.3 | 7.9 | 5.5 |
| Other Europe | 19.4 | 19.8 | 21.5 | 19.2 | 39.9 | 238.1 | 316.1 | 465.5 | 330.8 | 304.8 |
| **Asia** | 198.3 | 149.2 | 213.5 | 167.3 | 437.5 | 3 281.0 | 3 780.5 | 5 800.7 | 6 284.5 | 5 884.7 |
| Japan | 23.5 | 29.8 | 25.6 | 26.4 | 25.0 | 1 196.2 | 1 359.7 | 1 677.9 | 1 804.3 | 1 558.0 |
| China | 3.3 | 0.2 | 1.2 | 1.9 | 2.4 | 43.0 | 37.2 | 71.1 | 109.0 | 120.2 |
| Hong Kong | 3.2 | 5.1 | 1.7 | 2.0 | 1.9 | 119.0 | 139.0 | 260.2 | 521.9 | 291.6 |
| Taiwan | 1.5 | 1.7 | 2.3 | 2.5 | 1.7 | 737.3 | 688.3 | 1 051.1 | 1 078.9 | 1 121.5 |
| Singapore | 11.9 | 12.2 | 17.9 | 31.0 | 155.4 | 100.2 | 123.3 | 311.0 | 331.5 | 221.0 |
| South Korea | 1.2 | 0.9 | 1.5 | 3.0 | 7.2 | 396.0 | 527.3 | 911.4 | 977.0 | 1 099.3 |
| Indonesia | ..... | 0.1 | ..... | 1.3 | 0.9 | 50.7 | 41.3 | 141.0 | 146.7 | 96.7 |
| India | 0.1 | 0.1 | 0.1 | 0.4 | 0.2 | 8.8 | 9.2 | 16.5 | 18.6 | 14.8 |
| Other Asia | 153.6 | 99.1 | 163.1 | 98.8 | 242.9 | 629.9 | 855.0 | 1 360.4 | 1 296.6 | 1 361.6 |
| **Africa** | 0.2 | 1.5 | 1.9 | 3.3 | 3.7 | 156.1 | 234.8 | 112.0 | 125.7 | 97.8 |
| North Africa | ..... | 0.7 | 0.5 | 1.0 | 0.5 | 119.6 | 183.2 | 68.0 | 80.5 | 26.9 |
| Republic of South Africa | 0.2 | 0.6 | 1.2 | 1.7 | 2.6 | 23.2 | 16.7 | 23.8 | 34.8 | 63.9 |
| Other Subsaharan Africa | ..... | 0.2 | 0.2 | 0.7 | 0.5 | 13.4 | 34.9 | 20.2 | 10.4 | 7.0 |
| **Middle East** | 7.3 | 7.8 | 6.2 | 4.2 | 4.7 | 85.8 | 81.1 | 133.4 | 206.8 | 135.1 |
| **Australia** | 1.0 | 1.8 | 3.2 | 3.8 | 2.0 | 153.7 | 191.7 | 279.7 | 276.9 | 194.8 |
| **Rest of World** | ..... | ..... | ..... | ..... | ..... | ..... | ..... | ..... | ..... | 0.2 |

## Table E-3.  Metropolitan Area Exports of Goods by Destination, 1993–1997—*Continued*

(Millions of dollars.)

| Destination | 1993 | 1994 | 1995 | 1996 | 1997 | 1993 | 1994 | 1995 | 1996 | 1997 |
|---|---|---|---|---|---|---|---|---|---|---|
| | Portsmouth - Rochester, NH - ME | | | | | Providence - Fall River - Warwick, RI - MA | | | | |
| **ALL DESTINATIONS** | 465.0 | 470.2 | 553.6 | 574.8 | 486.0 | 1 141.7 | 1 246.0 | 1 241.0 | 1 296.2 | 1 601.8 |
| **North America** | 111.6 | 157.6 | 173.6 | 234.7 | 192.2 | 370.7 | 365.1 | 383.0 | 445.2 | 528.5 |
| Canada | 87.6 | 131.5 | 159.8 | 224.8 | 179.0 | 317.6 | 312.4 | 345.7 | 385.2 | 408.4 |
| Mexico | 24.1 | 26.1 | 13.8 | 9.9 | 13.2 | 53.1 | 52.7 | 37.3 | 60.0 | 120.1 |
| **Caribbean and Central America** | 39.6 | 18.0 | 32.2 | 28.0 | 33.9 | 13.1 | 15.9 | 12.7 | 11.9 | 14.0 |
| **South America** | 20.4 | 18.7 | 33.0 | 23.5 | 21.1 | 31.0 | 43.9 | 37.3 | 24.8 | 59.4 |
| Argentina | 8.3 | 1.3 | 1.5 | 1.7 | 1.6 | 10.3 | 10.9 | 4.2 | 2.7 | 6.0 |
| Brazil | 2.7 | 11.9 | 27.1 | 15.8 | 13.2 | 6.3 | 11.7 | 13.4 | 11.1 | 37.0 |
| Other South America | 9.3 | 5.4 | 4.5 | 6.0 | 6.3 | 14.4 | 21.3 | 19.7 | 11.0 | 16.4 |
| **Europe** | 158.1 | 173.5 | 203.3 | 175.3 | 156.2 | 465.3 | 520.6 | 452.8 | 437.3 | 542.2 |
| Belgium | 5.2 | 2.3 | 7.8 | 3.0 | 4.9 | 36.5 | 53.2 | 29.2 | 33.6 | 48.6 |
| France | 15.9 | 19.5 | 19.2 | 25.1 | 25.0 | 23.8 | 23.7 | 23.9 | 21.2 | 25.4 |
| Germany | 24.7 | 20.1 | 24.8 | 19.9 | 20.4 | 51.6 | 39.9 | 45.8 | 56.1 | 67.5 |
| Netherlands | 8.6 | 11.8 | 10.9 | 9.4 | 17.1 | 77.6 | 55.0 | 38.2 | 30.0 | 33.3 |
| United Kingdom | 65.8 | 47.0 | 35.0 | 27.2 | 20.1 | 88.4 | 161.3 | 118.5 | 94.8 | 134.6 |
| Turkey | 1.1 | 1.4 | 0.6 | 0.6 | 1.5 | 0.9 | 0.6 | 2.4 | 5.4 | 9.8 |
| Former Soviet Republics | 0.1 | .... | 0.8 | 0.1 | 0.3 | 3.0 | 3.0 | 2.8 | 3.3 | 4.4 |
| Poland | 0.1 | 0.6 | .... | .... | 0.1 | 7.9 | 8.4 | 4.0 | 4.1 | 4.3 |
| Other Eastern Europe | 0.9 | 4.2 | 1.0 | 0.6 | 0.5 | 7.5 | 6.0 | 3.2 | 3.8 | 2.8 |
| Other Europe | 35.7 | 66.5 | 103.2 | 89.4 | 66.3 | 168.1 | 169.5 | 184.7 | 185.1 | 211.7 |
| **Asia** | 86.2 | 88.8 | 98.1 | 101.7 | 67.1 | 219.5 | 262.0 | 312.5 | 330.7 | 418.4 |
| Japan | 19.8 | 19.2 | 16.9 | 27.6 | 22.7 | 53.1 | 61.1 | 85.1 | 86.0 | 126.3 |
| China | 1.1 | 2.6 | 7.6 | 2.4 | 1.8 | 8.1 | 17.3 | 7.1 | 10.0 | 6.3 |
| Hong Kong | 22.3 | 18.7 | 22.5 | 11.4 | 8.5 | 48.1 | 46.5 | 47.7 | 55.7 | 52.1 |
| Taiwan | 15.7 | 17.8 | 15.6 | 20.3 | 7.4 | 18.0 | 23.1 | 30.1 | 33.0 | 42.1 |
| Singapore | 6.9 | 7.7 | 11.2 | 13.2 | 13.3 | 19.7 | 26.0 | 28.0 | 25.2 | 34.1 |
| South Korea | 8.7 | 8.4 | 4.5 | 9.7 | 5.5 | 16.9 | 27.6 | 32.7 | 30.9 | 37.3 |
| Indonesia | 2.3 | 3.7 | 3.5 | 3.5 | 1.6 | 0.8 | 1.6 | 0.9 | 2.0 | 1.2 |
| India | 2.9 | 3.1 | 5.9 | 3.4 | 2.6 | 2.9 | 5.3 | 5.7 | 3.6 | 5.0 |
| Other Asia | 6.5 | 7.6 | 10.3 | 10.3 | 3.7 | 51.9 | 53.6 | 75.3 | 84.5 | 114.1 |
| **Africa** | 0.9 | 1.1 | 1.0 | 0.6 | 1.6 | 5.0 | 5.1 | 6.2 | 5.5 | 6.5 |
| North Africa | 0.2 | 0.1 | 0.1 | 0.1 | 1.0 | 1.0 | 0.6 | 2.0 | 0.9 | 1.0 |
| Republic of South Africa | 0.4 | 0.4 | 0.8 | 0.5 | 0.5 | 3.0 | 3.6 | 2.9 | 3.8 | 4.2 |
| Other Subsaharan Africa | 0.2 | 0.6 | .... | 0.1 | .... | 0.9 | 0.8 | 1.3 | 0.8 | 1.3 |
| **Middle East** | 4.2 | 3.5 | 3.6 | 3.5 | 3.5 | 22.0 | 19.7 | 18.8 | 21.5 | 16.0 |
| **Australia** | 44.0 | 8.9 | 8.7 | 7.4 | 10.5 | 15.0 | 13.7 | 17.7 | 19.3 | 16.7 |
| **Rest of World** | .... | .... | .... | .... | .... | .... | .... | .... | .... | .... |
| | Provo - Orem, UT | | | | | Racine, WI | | | | |
| **ALL DESTINATIONS** | 170.4 | 200.2 | 201.6 | 301.9 | 360.5 | 365.1 | 403.2 | 335.1 | 493.2 | 992.0 |
| **North America** | 84.1 | 67.5 | 63.1 | 45.6 | 55.3 | 168.1 | 207.3 | 213.8 | 162.5 | 190.5 |
| Canada | 79.5 | 59.9 | 58.5 | 40.9 | 51.5 | 161.8 | 202.9 | 211.5 | 157.0 | 177.9 |
| Mexico | 4.6 | 7.6 | 4.6 | 4.7 | 3.9 | 6.3 | 4.4 | 2.3 | 5.5 | 12.6 |
| **Caribbean and Central America** | 0.1 | 0.3 | 1.0 | 1.3 | 1.0 | 5.7 | 1.7 | 2.7 | 5.1 | 12.5 |
| **South America** | 3.0 | 4.2 | 5.7 | 7.2 | 8.0 | 11.4 | 7.0 | 8.7 | 41.6 | 122.7 |
| Argentina | 0.2 | 0.1 | 0.1 | 0.1 | 0.8 | 1.3 | 0.3 | 1.7 | 17.6 | 22.5 |
| Brazil | 1.2 | 1.5 | 2.4 | 4.1 | 3.6 | 2.4 | 3.8 | 3.5 | 7.0 | 66.8 |
| Other South America | 1.6 | 2.7 | 3.2 | 2.9 | 3.7 | 7.7 | 2.9 | 3.5 | 16.9 | 33.3 |
| **Europe** | 29.5 | 22.4 | 31.7 | 66.3 | 56.4 | 114.8 | 98.2 | 68.4 | 143.3 | 438.9 |
| Belgium | 1.6 | 1.4 | 1.7 | 4.0 | 4.3 | 4.9 | 2.2 | 0.5 | 3.3 | 3.2 |
| France | 1.5 | 1.4 | 2.3 | 7.8 | 5.8 | 27.7 | 26.1 | 11.7 | 29.1 | 82.9 |
| Germany | 4.0 | 2.7 | 4.3 | 9.7 | 4.5 | 45.9 | 24.6 | 12.7 | 27.4 | 56.6 |
| Netherlands | 7.1 | 4.4 | 6.6 | 10.1 | 8.4 | 4.3 | 8.9 | 23.4 | 21.2 | 3.0 |
| United Kingdom | 5.9 | 4.4 | 5.0 | 11.0 | 10.4 | 17.1 | 17.3 | 5.8 | 15.7 | 60.2 |
| Turkey | 0.2 | 0.1 | 0.1 | 0.1 | 0.1 | 0.9 | 0.1 | 1.1 | 2.4 | 4.4 |
| Former Soviet Republics | 0.1 | 0.6 | 2.6 | 0.9 | 2.8 | 0.4 | 2.5 | 0.3 | 4.7 | 135.6 |
| Poland | 0.2 | 0.1 | 0.1 | 0.1 | .... | 1.3 | 0.6 | 0.1 | 2.9 | 13.3 |
| Other Eastern Europe | 0.4 | 0.2 | 0.1 | 0.2 | 0.3 | 2.1 | 2.9 | 0.1 | 8.2 | 9.6 |
| Other Europe | 8.4 | 7.3 | 9.0 | 22.3 | 19.8 | 10.2 | 12.9 | 12.7 | 28.4 | 70.1 |
| **Asia** | 42.4 | 96.3 | 91.3 | 170.4 | 224.9 | 14.1 | 19.1 | 19.7 | 33.9 | 51.9 |
| Japan | 19.1 | 47.1 | 41.7 | 75.7 | 134.4 | 4.7 | 8.7 | 5.4 | 7.6 | 10.6 |
| China | 1.1 | 1.5 | 0.8 | 1.7 | 1.2 | 0.5 | 0.7 | 0.4 | 2.1 | 1.3 |
| Hong Kong | 1.6 | 4.5 | 4.2 | 4.8 | 8.1 | 1.7 | 0.7 | 1.6 | 1.7 | 2.5 |
| Taiwan | 12.8 | 35.7 | 29.0 | 36.0 | 34.5 | 1.0 | 0.6 | 2.3 | 2.8 | 4.1 |
| Singapore | 1.6 | 1.8 | 2.7 | 3.0 | 3.6 | 0.8 | 0.8 | 1.2 | 1.1 | 2.5 |
| South Korea | 2.2 | 1.4 | 3.3 | 38.8 | 19.8 | 0.7 | 1.5 | 1.3 | 1.0 | 1.5 |
| Indonesia | 0.1 | .... | 0.1 | 0.1 | 0.1 | 0.3 | 0.2 | 0.4 | 1.0 | 2.4 |
| India | 0.1 | 0.1 | 0.2 | 0.9 | 1.5 | 0.6 | 1.8 | 2.8 | 1.2 | 1.0 |
| Other Asia | 3.9 | 4.4 | 9.3 | 9.4 | 21.6 | 3.8 | 4.1 | 4.3 | 15.5 | 26.0 |
| **Africa** | 0.9 | 1.2 | 1.3 | 0.9 | 1.4 | 4.5 | 3.3 | 2.7 | 19.7 | 24.4 |
| North Africa | 0.1 | 0.6 | 0.7 | 0.3 | 0.5 | 1.6 | 0.5 | 0.2 | 2.7 | 3.1 |
| Republic of South Africa | 0.8 | 0.5 | 0.5 | 0.4 | 0.8 | 2.7 | 2.4 | 2.2 | 15.1 | 19.4 |
| Other Subsaharan Africa | .... | 0.2 | 0.1 | 0.3 | 0.2 | 0.2 | 0.4 | 0.3 | 1.8 | 1.9 |
| **Middle East** | 1.6 | 2.2 | 1.4 | 3.4 | 3.4 | 5.1 | 5.5 | 4.5 | 7.4 | 10.3 |
| **Australia** | 8.7 | 5.9 | 6.1 | 6.8 | 10.0 | 41.4 | 61.2 | 14.5 | 79.8 | 140.7 |
| **Rest of World** | .... | .... | .... | .... | .... | .... | .... | .... | .... | .... |

## Table E-3.  Metropolitan Area Exports of Goods by Destination, 1993–1997—*Continued*

(Millions of dollars.)

| Destination | 1993 | 1994 | 1995 | 1996 | 1997 | 1993 | 1994 | 1995 | 1996 | 1997 |
|---|---|---|---|---|---|---|---|---|---|---|
| | Raleigh - Durham - Chapel Hill, NC | | | | | Reading, PA | | | | |
| **ALL DESTINATIONS** | 1 620.9 | 1 758.7 | 2 093.2 | 2 609.8 | 2 713.1 | 300.6 | 271.6 | 293.4 | 326.2 | 429.5 |
| **North America** | 735.7 | 857.4 | 1 055.9 | 1 363.3 | 1 117.0 | 224.1 | 187.1 | 170.8 | 205.3 | 241.3 |
| Canada | 699.8 | 810.0 | 1 005.2 | 1 282.9 | 1 050.4 | 218.8 | 173.4 | 152.6 | 181.5 | 213.1 |
| Mexico | 36.0 | 47.5 | 50.8 | 80.4 | 66.6 | 5.3 | 13.7 | 18.2 | 23.8 | 28.2 |
| **Caribbean and Central America** | 25.0 | 29.6 | 35.3 | 58.3 | 66.1 | 2.8 | 2.0 | 2.0 | 2.3 | 2.8 |
| **South America** | 76.9 | 81.2 | 111.0 | 138.4 | 182.5 | 3.4 | 5.2 | 6.2 | 7.8 | 7.6 |
| Argentina | 19.7 | 14.6 | 15.5 | 23.2 | 31.6 | 0.6 | 0.3 | 0.6 | 0.7 | 0.8 |
| Brazil | 17.5 | 34.0 | 51.0 | 54.4 | 88.7 | 0.8 | 1.0 | 2.5 | 3.3 | 1.7 |
| Other South America | 39.7 | 32.7 | 44.6 | 60.8 | 62.2 | 2.0 | 3.9 | 3.0 | 3.8 | 5.0 |
| **Europe** | 318.9 | 378.0 | 475.7 | 586.4 | 816.4 | 29.3 | 34.1 | 47.6 | 42.8 | 50.8 |
| Belgium | 14.0 | 15.1 | 31.8 | 45.3 | 51.5 | 3.4 | 1.6 | 1.7 | 1.9 | 1.6 |
| France | 32.5 | 37.2 | 46.6 | 66.1 | 101.9 | 1.7 | 1.9 | 2.9 | 2.7 | 6.8 |
| Germany | 34.6 | 49.1 | 101.3 | 104.3 | 131.1 | 7.7 | 5.2 | 7.2 | 6.2 | 9.1 |
| Netherlands | 140.0 | 107.7 | 94.1 | 91.1 | 110.4 | 1.3 | 1.0 | 3.0 | 4.1 | 7.8 |
| United Kingdom | 30.7 | 81.4 | 62.3 | 105.6 | 220.0 | 10.1 | 17.3 | 17.5 | 14.7 | 14.0 |
| Turkey | 2.8 | 0.7 | 4.1 | 13.9 | 21.8 | 0.3 | ..... | 0.4 | 2.2 | 0.4 |
| Former Soviet Republics | 3.1 | 2.9 | 9.6 | 19.2 | 17.5 | 0.1 | 0.2 | 1.7 | 0.3 | ..... |
| Poland | 3.4 | 1.3 | 2.9 | 2.5 | 1.4 | 0.3 | ..... | 0.1 | 0.1 | 0.1 |
| Other Eastern Europe | 3.2 | 3.5 | 4.5 | 1.9 | 2.5 | ..... | ..... | 0.5 | 1.7 | 0.7 |
| Other Europe | 54.6 | 78.9 | 118.5 | 136.4 | 158.4 | 4.4 | 6.9 | 12.6 | 8.9 | 10.3 |
| **Asia** | 393.8 | 321.1 | 313.3 | 359.5 | 449.8 | 26.5 | 31.6 | 47.1 | 50.9 | 112.4 |
| Japan | 231.5 | 180.9 | 122.0 | 159.1 | 178.9 | 15.6 | 15.6 | 19.5 | 17.8 | 18.4 |
| China | 20.7 | 6.2 | 10.7 | 14.4 | 19.1 | 0.2 | 0.8 | 0.7 | 1.7 | 1.0 |
| Hong Kong | 26.9 | 33.3 | 52.0 | 51.0 | 88.4 | 2.6 | 1.5 | 2.8 | 6.2 | 4.0 |
| Taiwan | 13.7 | 18.6 | 19.0 | 19.4 | 47.4 | 0.9 | 1.7 | 4.0 | 4.0 | 3.4 |
| Singapore | 14.9 | 11.9 | 17.8 | 26.3 | 27.0 | 3.8 | 5.1 | 3.7 | 3.1 | 15.8 |
| South Korea | 20.2 | 21.1 | 17.8 | 21.8 | 28.5 | 1.4 | 2.6 | 4.6 | 5.8 | 10.4 |
| Indonesia | 4.0 | 6.5 | 7.1 | 5.6 | 7.4 | ..... | 0.1 | 0.4 | 0.2 | 0.3 |
| India | 4.6 | 7.4 | 5.5 | 7.4 | 6.9 | 0.8 | 0.9 | 1.3 | 1.7 | 1.9 |
| Other Asia | 57.3 | 35.2 | 61.3 | 54.4 | 46.2 | 1.1 | 3.4 | 10.1 | 10.5 | 57.1 |
| **Africa** | 22.2 | 31.7 | 26.1 | 21.1 | 19.8 | 6.3 | 2.7 | 6.7 | 5.0 | 2.0 |
| North Africa | 14.4 | 22.6 | 12.7 | 5.2 | 7.8 | 0.1 | 0.1 | 0.4 | 1.1 | 0.2 |
| Republic of South Africa | 5.9 | 7.0 | 10.4 | 10.5 | 8.8 | 4.6 | 2.0 | 5.9 | 3.4 | 1.6 |
| Other Subsaharan Africa | 1.9 | 2.2 | 3.0 | 5.4 | 3.2 | 1.6 | 0.5 | 0.3 | 0.4 | 0.1 |
| **Middle East** | 20.8 | 22.1 | 26.8 | 35.2 | 24.6 | 3.5 | 3.8 | 7.6 | 7.6 | 7.5 |
| **Australia** | 27.5 | 37.5 | 49.0 | 47.6 | 36.8 | 4.6 | 5.2 | 5.5 | 4.5 | 5.2 |
| **Rest of World** | ..... | ..... | ..... | ..... | ..... | ..... | ..... | ..... | ..... | ..... |
| | Reno, NV | | | | | Richmond - Petersburg, VA | | | | |
| **ALL DESTINATIONS** | 184.1 | 213.7 | 368.2 | 314.6 | 399.7 | 4 012.2 | 5 260.6 | 5 389.3 | 5 609.4 | 5 571.7 |
| **North America** | 76.4 | 76.8 | 100.0 | 157.5 | 198.8 | 415.8 | 537.6 | 697.2 | 543.4 | 514.8 |
| Canada | 73.4 | 73.5 | 98.0 | 155.0 | 148.7 | 299.2 | 390.7 | 521.5 | 417.6 | 374.8 |
| Mexico | 2.9 | 3.3 | 2.0 | 2.5 | 50.2 | 116.6 | 146.9 | 175.7 | 125.7 | 140.0 |
| **Caribbean and Central America** | 0.9 | 1.7 | 3.4 | 5.3 | 2.2 | 96.6 | 81.3 | 60.3 | 73.9 | 57.2 |
| **South America** | 2.6 | 4.0 | 16.0 | 18.5 | 16.6 | 162.7 | 223.9 | 301.5 | 279.7 | 321.0 |
| Argentina | 0.5 | 0.3 | 4.3 | 2.9 | 2.8 | 16.3 | 19.7 | 34.8 | 19.3 | 30.1 |
| Brazil | 0.4 | 1.5 | 2.7 | 2.7 | 3.9 | 72.2 | 103.0 | 158.9 | 143.4 | 180.7 |
| Other South America | 1.7 | 2.3 | 9.1 | 12.9 | 9.9 | 74.2 | 101.2 | 107.8 | 117.0 | 110.2 |
| **Europe** | 43.8 | 51.2 | 58.4 | 62.1 | 80.9 | 1 300.3 | 2 140.6 | 2 128.3 | 2 370.3 | 2 185.4 |
| Belgium | 1.1 | 0.8 | 1.5 | 1.5 | 8.7 | 515.6 | 1 320.0 | 1 268.8 | 1 207.5 | 1 053.3 |
| France | 6.7 | 8.9 | 8.1 | 12.4 | 11.9 | 30.1 | 21.0 | 28.7 | 24.7 | 31.4 |
| Germany | 3.6 | 4.5 | 6.8 | 6.2 | 6.4 | 61.2 | 108.8 | 103.8 | 118.0 | 111.4 |
| Netherlands | 4.7 | 7.0 | 4.7 | 9.0 | 9.1 | 69.8 | 92.1 | 136.3 | 63.1 | 99.8 |
| United Kingdom | 8.7 | 7.5 | 9.7 | 9.5 | 20.0 | 72.4 | 75.4 | 91.1 | 69.5 | 68.5 |
| Turkey | 0.5 | 13.2 | 0.4 | 2.2 | 0.5 | 185.5 | 71.3 | 105.7 | 108.5 | 103.8 |
| Former Soviet Republics | 0.1 | 1.2 | 0.4 | 1.7 | 0.6 | 103.8 | 177.6 | 65.0 | 406.8 | 316.8 |
| Poland | ..... | ..... | 0.1 | 0.1 | 0.1 | 14.0 | 11.6 | 11.8 | 25.3 | 42.8 |
| Other Eastern Europe | 0.2 | 0.2 | 0.3 | 1.7 | 0.3 | 6.9 | 1.9 | 28.2 | 23.8 | 30.5 |
| Other Europe | 18.2 | 7.9 | 26.5 | 17.9 | 23.3 | 240.9 | 260.9 | 289.1 | 323.3 | 327.2 |
| **Asia** | 45.7 | 62.9 | 168.9 | 54.1 | 83.0 | 1 572.1 | 1 755.0 | 1 683.2 | 1 732.4 | 1 844.8 |
| Japan | 12.7 | 14.0 | 16.3 | 21.3 | 22.1 | 1 044.0 | 1 193.1 | 1 066.5 | 1 179.1 | 1 216.6 |
| China | 1.9 | 3.8 | 1.0 | 1.2 | 0.8 | 29.7 | 32.5 | 45.0 | 41.0 | 66.4 |
| Hong Kong | 2.4 | 1.7 | 3.5 | 2.6 | 3.0 | 110.4 | 102.0 | 111.5 | 118.5 | 131.9 |
| Taiwan | 1.4 | 1.8 | 2.0 | 3.3 | 2.4 | 70.7 | 96.5 | 78.3 | 58.9 | 64.9 |
| Singapore | 1.3 | 2.6 | 1.4 | 1.7 | 3.2 | 42.9 | 46.6 | 57.4 | 57.0 | 75.2 |
| South Korea | 3.6 | 5.3 | 4.4 | 4.1 | 4.4 | 186.3 | 193.2 | 221.4 | 177.8 | 202.2 |
| Indonesia | 0.4 | 0.3 | 0.5 | 0.5 | 0.5 | 11.9 | 18.4 | 22.5 | 10.2 | 11.9 |
| India | 0.3 | 0.2 | 1.2 | 1.3 | 0.5 | 9.9 | 9.3 | 7.3 | 12.2 | 10.3 |
| Other Asia | 21.6 | 33.3 | 138.7 | 18.1 | 46.0 | 66.3 | 63.3 | 73.3 | 77.7 | 65.3 |
| **Africa** | 2.9 | 3.7 | 6.2 | 4.8 | 5.1 | 81.4 | 70.6 | 94.3 | 110.1 | 120.7 |
| North Africa | 0.8 | 0.4 | 0.3 | 0.2 | 0.4 | 57.0 | 57.1 | 66.6 | 82.5 | 96.8 |
| Republic of South Africa | 1.8 | 2.1 | 5.3 | 3.6 | 4.1 | 2.0 | 4.9 | 9.3 | 4.1 | 3.7 |
| Other Subsaharan Africa | 0.4 | 1.3 | 0.5 | 1.0 | 0.6 | 22.4 | 8.6 | 18.3 | 23.5 | 20.2 |
| **Middle East** | 5.5 | 6.9 | 5.6 | 4.0 | 3.2 | 349.6 | 417.1 | 398.0 | 466.7 | 502.5 |
| **Australia** | 6.3 | 6.2 | 9.7 | 8.3 | 9.9 | 33.6 | 34.6 | 26.6 | 32.9 | 25.4 |
| **Rest of World** | ..... | ..... | ..... | ..... | ..... | ..... | ..... | ..... | ..... | ..... |

## Table E-3.  Metropolitan Area Exports of Goods by Destination, 1993–1997—*Continued*

(Millions of dollars.)

| Destination | 1993 | 1994 | 1995 | 1996 | 1997 | 1993 | 1994 | 1995 | 1996 | 1997 |
|---|---|---|---|---|---|---|---|---|---|---|
| | Riverside - San Bernardino, CA | | | | | Roanoke, VA | | | | |
| **ALL DESTINATIONS** | 1 093.8 | 1 458.8 | 1 856.5 | 1 982.1 | 2 067.9 | 164.0 | 195.9 | 231.3 | 238.3 | 285.2 |
| **North America** | 301.2 | 344.5 | 352.3 | 379.4 | 496.3 | 40.7 | 46.8 | 53.7 | 55.5 | 95.8 |
| Canada | 154.9 | 176.8 | 213.6 | 219.3 | 260.9 | 38.4 | 42.4 | 49.5 | 51.1 | 63.8 |
| Mexico | 146.4 | 167.6 | 138.7 | 160.1 | 235.4 | 2.3 | 4.4 | 4.3 | 4.4 | 32.0 |
| **Caribbean and Central America** | 8.6 | 9.3 | 10.5 | 8.3 | 13.9 | 7.9 | 8.7 | 10.0 | 7.6 | 10.5 |
| **South America** | 21.0 | 28.4 | 34.0 | 40.7 | 68.9 | 10.4 | 9.0 | 10.5 | 11.6 | 21.7 |
| Argentina | 2.7 | 5.9 | 5.6 | 8.9 | 22.8 | 1.0 | 1.2 | 0.5 | 0.7 | 0.7 |
| Brazil | 6.7 | 9.2 | 14.9 | 14.0 | 15.1 | 2.0 | 1.4 | 3.1 | 4.9 | 7.8 |
| Other South America | 11.5 | 13.2 | 13.6 | 17.9 | 31.0 | 7.4 | 6.3 | 6.8 | 6.0 | 13.2 |
| **Europe** | 228.6 | 251.8 | 490.7 | 505.5 | 407.0 | 31.2 | 39.5 | 51.2 | 73.4 | 84.7 |
| Belgium | 6.0 | 4.6 | 8.6 | 8.8 | 12.1 | 0.2 | 1.0 | 0.5 | 1.7 | 1.8 |
| France | 21.3 | 23.0 | 67.2 | 176.8 | 24.7 | 12.0 | 14.4 | 17.7 | 25.1 | 32.1 |
| Germany | 60.9 | 54.2 | 66.7 | 77.3 | 78.8 | 4.1 | 4.6 | 12.9 | 7.0 | 6.8 |
| Netherlands | 14.8 | 15.7 | 30.3 | 18.9 | 29.8 | 3.8 | 5.3 | 4.0 | 6.7 | 2.3 |
| United Kingdom | 51.5 | 83.8 | 224.8 | 124.8 | 115.1 | 6.2 | 8.0 | 7.1 | 7.9 | 15.2 |
| Turkey | 2.0 | 2.8 | 3.1 | 3.9 | 4.1 | 0.1 | 0.2 | 1.0 | 3.5 | 5.9 |
| Former Soviet Republics | 0.5 | 3.2 | 2.0 | 5.3 | 46.4 | ..... | ..... | 0.2 | 0.2 | 4.9 |
| Poland | 1.0 | 0.4 | 0.9 | 0.9 | 1.4 | 0.6 | 0.1 | 0.1 | 0.2 | 0.1 |
| Other Eastern Europe | 2.5 | 2.4 | 3.3 | 4.4 | 4.9 | 0.7 | 0.2 | 0.3 | 5.4 | 0.3 |
| Other Europe | 68.1 | 61.6 | 83.7 | 84.3 | 89.6 | 3.4 | 5.8 | 7.4 | 15.8 | 15.4 |
| **Asia** | 448.8 | 725.3 | 861.2 | 932.5 | 956.3 | 61.2 | 71.8 | 73.5 | 52.9 | 57.1 |
| Japan | 168.5 | 247.9 | 307.4 | 339.7 | 294.5 | 5.5 | 6.5 | 8.3 | 7.6 | 8.7 |
| China | 35.0 | 50.5 | 41.0 | 45.7 | 60.8 | 3.9 | 4.1 | 5.9 | 2.2 | 1.7 |
| Hong Kong | 33.8 | 58.4 | 83.2 | 101.8 | 138.0 | 7.4 | 8.1 | 6.5 | 5.0 | 4.5 |
| Taiwan | 52.7 | 94.0 | 97.5 | 92.8 | 104.8 | 9.8 | 10.7 | 19.4 | 8.1 | 7.8 |
| Singapore | 49.7 | 58.2 | 72.5 | 82.5 | 73.3 | 4.8 | 10.1 | 10.5 | 6.9 | 10.2 |
| South Korea | 48.8 | 87.9 | 112.8 | 125.0 | 124.6 | 21.5 | 21.0 | 12.4 | 12.5 | 13.2 |
| Indonesia | 5.4 | 8.2 | 18.9 | 13.2 | 13.0 | 0.1 | 0.1 | 0.6 | 0.3 | 0.3 |
| India | 2.5 | 15.8 | 10.8 | 11.1 | 10.4 | 3.1 | 3.3 | 0.6 | 2.1 | 1.0 |
| Other Asia | 52.4 | 104.3 | 117.0 | 120.6 | 137.0 | 5.1 | 7.7 | 9.3 | 8.2 | 9.7 |
| **Africa** | 12.1 | 11.2 | 9.2 | 11.3 | 15.0 | 1.3 | 8.8 | 1.6 | 3.7 | 2.4 |
| North Africa | 5.4 | 4.2 | 2.4 | 4.7 | 3.0 | ..... | 8.1 | 0.4 | 0.7 | 0.5 |
| Republic of South Africa | 3.3 | 4.3 | 4.5 | 5.3 | 10.0 | 0.8 | 0.7 | 0.8 | 1.0 | 1.2 |
| Other Subsaharan Africa | 3.4 | 2.8 | 2.4 | 1.3 | 2.0 | 0.5 | ..... | 0.4 | 2.0 | 0.6 |
| **Middle East** | 24.7 | 23.3 | 32.5 | 21.5 | 30.4 | 3.9 | 2.5 | 21.4 | 23.2 | 3.2 |
| **Australia** | 48.8 | 65.0 | 66.1 | 83.0 | 80.1 | 7.5 | 8.7 | 9.4 | 10.5 | 9.8 |
| **Rest of World** | ..... | ..... | ..... | ..... | ..... | ..... | ..... | ..... | ..... | ..... |
| | Rochester, NY | | | | | Rockford, IL | | | | |
| **ALL DESTINATIONS** | 3 091.5 | 3 143.7 | 3 860.5 | 4 307.7 | 4 694.5 | 521.6 | 616.1 | 641.4 | 721.9 | 758.7 |
| **North America** | 976.4 | 1 198.0 | 1 306.7 | 1 437.9 | 1 612.7 | 253.2 | 321.7 | 341.2 | 363.2 | 372.8 |
| Canada | 727.6 | 862.9 | 1 036.1 | 1 123.5 | 1 224.0 | 244.3 | 306.1 | 332.6 | 340.2 | 339.2 |
| Mexico | 248.7 | 335.1 | 270.6 | 314.3 | 388.7 | 8.9 | 15.5 | 8.6 | 23.0 | 33.5 |
| **Caribbean and Central America** | 31.4 | 17.8 | 19.0 | 17.4 | 23.8 | 2.1 | 3.1 | 2.9 | 2.3 | 3.0 |
| **South America** | 256.1 | 218.7 | 299.2 | 306.1 | 305.0 | 11.7 | 11.5 | 8.9 | 12.0 | 14.3 |
| Argentina | 25.9 | 11.3 | 9.9 | 7.4 | 17.0 | 0.8 | 1.3 | 1.1 | 1.9 | 3.5 |
| Brazil | 149.4 | 149.7 | 237.9 | 260.6 | 244.3 | 6.0 | 2.5 | 2.9 | 3.7 | 4.8 |
| Other South America | 80.8 | 57.8 | 51.4 | 38.0 | 43.7 | 5.0 | 7.7 | 5.0 | 6.4 | 6.0 |
| **Europe** | 1 076.3 | 846.7 | 1 190.0 | 1 361.6 | 1 491.2 | 154.7 | 166.0 | 188.5 | 206.4 | 233.2 |
| Belgium | 11.5 | 34.1 | 75.6 | 39.8 | 22.2 | 12.8 | 5.6 | 2.9 | 4.9 | 3.3 |
| France | 301.5 | 168.4 | 222.3 | 291.1 | 379.5 | 12.4 | 25.0 | 30.8 | 44.2 | 59.1 |
| Germany | 205.4 | 144.1 | 239.0 | 277.3 | 289.9 | 29.5 | 33.8 | 37.4 | 41.9 | 57.6 |
| Netherlands | 170.3 | 115.2 | 121.1 | 146.7 | 158.0 | 16.6 | 16.5 | 15.5 | 7.8 | 6.1 |
| United Kingdom | 296.5 | 262.5 | 343.5 | 364.8 | 369.8 | 42.1 | 43.2 | 50.3 | 53.4 | 60.4 |
| Turkey | 4.7 | 7.2 | 2.5 | 1.4 | 2.7 | 4.1 | 0.7 | 3.6 | 2.9 | 2.4 |
| Former Soviet Republics | 0.6 | 2.0 | 5.1 | 8.8 | 3.4 | 0.3 | 0.1 | 0.1 | 0.4 | 1.0 |
| Poland | 0.5 | 0.4 | 0.5 | 1.2 | 1.2 | 0.2 | 0.2 | 1.3 | 0.9 | 1.0 |
| Other Eastern Europe | 2.1 | 3.5 | 2.3 | 1.8 | 3.1 | 0.5 | 2.1 | 0.6 | 1.6 | 1.0 |
| Other Europe | 83.3 | 109.2 | 178.2 | 228.6 | 261.3 | 36.3 | 38.9 | 45.9 | 48.5 | 41.2 |
| **Asia** | 644.1 | 685.9 | 810.3 | 892.3 | 920.7 | 77.8 | 90.9 | 79.8 | 114.4 | 103.8 |
| Japan | 382.8 | 394.5 | 472.5 | 494.5 | 464.9 | 16.9 | 13.7 | 15.7 | 17.6 | 23.4 |
| China | 6.8 | 9.9 | 13.8 | 8.4 | 16.2 | 11.4 | 19.7 | 10.6 | 18.5 | 14.6 |
| Hong Kong | 29.6 | 36.3 | 47.2 | 116.1 | 142.4 | 6.1 | 7.9 | 3.9 | 7.9 | 5.2 |
| Taiwan | 21.1 | 21.9 | 24.6 | 40.5 | 38.3 | 10.4 | 16.9 | 18.1 | 13.9 | 9.4 |
| Singapore | 165.2 | 172.7 | 180.4 | 125.9 | 123.8 | 6.2 | 12.4 | 9.7 | 16.1 | 19.8 |
| South Korea | 20.1 | 27.6 | 43.1 | 61.7 | 72.4 | 16.7 | 10.6 | 9.1 | 17.6 | 9.6 |
| Indonesia | 2.1 | 7.0 | 3.5 | 4.8 | 3.0 | 2.9 | 3.1 | 3.8 | 1.4 | 4.9 |
| India | 4.2 | 4.7 | 4.8 | 15.2 | 26.9 | 0.6 | 0.6 | 0.5 | 0.6 | 1.8 |
| Other Asia | 12.2 | 11.4 | 20.5 | 25.2 | 32.9 | 6.5 | 6.1 | 8.4 | 20.8 | 15.2 |
| **Africa** | 8.3 | 7.1 | 14.9 | 9.7 | 9.9 | 4.7 | 3.7 | 3.0 | 3.6 | 6.2 |
| North Africa | 1.8 | 1.3 | 9.2 | 3.7 | 3.7 | 1.2 | 0.6 | 0.2 | 0.6 | 2.7 |
| Republic of South Africa | 2.7 | 4.6 | 3.3 | 4.1 | 5.0 | 3.3 | 2.0 | 2.6 | 2.5 | 2.7 |
| Other Subsaharan Africa | 3.7 | 1.2 | 2.5 | 1.9 | 1.3 | 0.2 | 1.1 | 0.2 | 0.5 | 0.8 |
| **Middle East** | 25.9 | 24.2 | 33.0 | 23.9 | 31.2 | 7.5 | 8.3 | 6.9 | 8.8 | 9.0 |
| **Australia** | 73.2 | 145.2 | 187.4 | 258.8 | 300.0 | 10.0 | 11.1 | 10.3 | 11.1 | 16.4 |
| **Rest of World** | ..... | ..... | ..... | ..... | ..... | ..... | ..... | ..... | ..... | ..... |

## Table E-3.  Metropolitan Area Exports of Goods by Destination, 1993–1997—Continued

(Millions of dollars.)

| Destination | 1993 | 1994 | 1995 | 1996 | 1997 | 1993 | 1994 | 1995 | 1996 | 1997 |
|---|---|---|---|---|---|---|---|---|---|---|
| | Sacramento, CA | | | | | Salinas, CA | | | | |
| **ALL DESTINATIONS** | 1 075.6 | 1 087.9 | 1 448.3 | 1 908.6 | 1 669.5 | 294.5 | 322.0 | 359.9 | 337.6 | 393.2 |
| **North America** | 116.5 | 134.7 | 148.2 | 180.2 | 239.4 | 167.4 | 152.4 | 182.6 | 159.5 | 180.4 |
| Canada | 82.0 | 81.5 | 101.3 | 114.7 | 169.5 | 160.3 | 143.8 | 176.8 | 156.6 | 171.4 |
| Mexico | 34.5 | 53.1 | 46.8 | 65.5 | 69.9 | 7.1 | 8.5 | 5.8 | 3.0 | 8.9 |
| **Caribbean and Central America** | 1.9 | 4.1 | 4.4 | 19.8 | 11.2 | 0.7 | 0.5 | 0.4 | 0.2 | 0.6 |
| **South America** | 17.5 | 23.2 | 45.7 | 52.1 | 81.2 | 0.7 | 1.3 | 1.2 | 1.4 | 3.1 |
| Argentina | 4.4 | 5.9 | 9.7 | 11.2 | 14.6 | 0.2 | 0.3 | 0.5 | 0.3 | 0.1 |
| Brazil | 8.5 | 12.9 | 18.3 | 27.5 | 44.0 | 0.1 | 0.2 | 0.1 | 0.1 | 0.6 |
| Other South America | 4.6 | 4.3 | 17.7 | 13.4 | 22.6 | 0.4 | 0.9 | 0.6 | 1.0 | 2.4 |
| **Europe** | 427.1 | 412.1 | 494.1 | 637.0 | 530.7 | 30.5 | 37.7 | 22.5 | 25.9 | 46.8 |
| Belgium | 14.7 | 19.7 | 10.8 | 14.9 | 8.5 | 1.2 | 2.7 | 1.2 | 0.6 | 1.4 |
| France | 150.0 | 105.7 | 129.9 | 193.8 | 138.9 | 1.8 | 2.1 | 1.5 | 1.9 | 3.4 |
| Germany | 127.0 | 127.7 | 131.4 | 189.8 | 180.7 | 2.5 | 1.6 | 1.7 | 3.2 | 3.1 |
| Netherlands | 40.1 | 51.4 | 98.2 | 56.8 | 45.5 | 7.7 | 4.1 | 1.3 | 2.6 | 8.2 |
| United Kingdom | 27.8 | 24.8 | 31.1 | 47.3 | 48.7 | 7.7 | 9.8 | 5.3 | 7.1 | 12.3 |
| Turkey | 0.6 | 0.3 | 0.3 | 0.5 | 0.8 | 0.1 | 0.1 | 0.3 | 0.3 | 0.4 |
| Former Soviet Republics | 5.3 | 3.2 | 3.4 | 2.8 | 4.3 | 0.1 | 0.1 | 0.6 | 0.2 | 0.8 |
| Poland | 0.1 | 3.7 | 0.2 | 0.6 | 0.5 | ..... | ..... | 0.1 | 0.1 | 0.1 |
| Other Eastern Europe | 1.7 | 0.7 | 1.5 | 3.1 | 3.6 | 0.6 | 0.4 | 0.2 | 0.3 | 0.3 |
| Other Europe | 59.8 | 75.0 | 87.1 | 127.3 | 99.2 | 8.7 | 16.7 | 10.3 | 9.8 | 16.7 |
| **Asia** | 421.6 | 435.5 | 656.0 | 909.6 | 712.2 | 91.2 | 126.1 | 148.6 | 146.0 | 154.9 |
| Japan | 206.9 | 204.9 | 310.6 | 470.2 | 360.6 | 51.1 | 74.9 | 80.4 | 66.3 | 66.7 |
| China | 7.8 | 6.6 | 6.6 | 14.5 | 11.7 | 0.5 | 1.3 | 5.8 | 8.4 | 7.9 |
| Hong Kong | 35.9 | 37.2 | 59.8 | 47.3 | 28.6 | 24.1 | 20.9 | 26.8 | 36.1 | 46.2 |
| Taiwan | 19.3 | 19.6 | 34.1 | 45.7 | 35.6 | 5.5 | 12.1 | 10.7 | 12.9 | 14.1 |
| Singapore | 92.1 | 84.6 | 90.8 | 140.3 | 79.7 | 3.6 | 6.2 | 8.1 | 6.9 | 6.0 |
| South Korea | 28.4 | 39.8 | 82.6 | 111.2 | 106.8 | 2.0 | 5.3 | 5.1 | 3.5 | 2.8 |
| Indonesia | 1.6 | 2.3 | 4.4 | 7.6 | 13.3 | 0.2 | 0.5 | 1.6 | 3.1 | 4.1 |
| India | 7.6 | 9.8 | 16.3 | 14.2 | 16.0 | ..... | 0.5 | 2.1 | 0.1 | 0.1 |
| Other Asia | 22.1 | 30.7 | 50.8 | 58.6 | 59.9 | 4.3 | 4.6 | 7.9 | 8.8 | 6.9 |
| **Africa** | 5.1 | 6.7 | 6.5 | 10.9 | 8.3 | 0.7 | 1.0 | 1.1 | 0.8 | 0.8 |
| North Africa | 2.4 | 2.8 | 3.4 | 6.8 | 3.2 | 0.1 | 0.3 | 0.2 | 0.2 | 0.1 |
| Republic of South Africa | 2.6 | 3.5 | 2.8 | 3.0 | 4.7 | 0.2 | 0.4 | 0.7 | 0.2 | 0.5 |
| Other Subsaharan Africa | 0.1 | 0.5 | 0.3 | 1.0 | 0.4 | 0.4 | 0.3 | 0.2 | 0.3 | 0.3 |
| **Middle East** | 19.5 | 17.6 | 15.4 | 22.5 | 21.3 | 2.4 | 2.3 | 2.3 | 1.7 | 3.8 |
| **Australia** | 66.3 | 54.1 | 78.0 | 76.5 | 65.2 | 1.0 | 0.6 | 1.2 | 2.0 | 2.8 |
| **Rest of World** | ..... | ..... | ..... | ..... | ..... | ..... | ..... | ..... | ..... | ..... |
| | Salt Lake City - Ogden, UT | | | | | San Antonio, TX | | | | |
| **ALL DESTINATIONS** | 1 660.9 | 1 808.7 | 1 838.2 | 2 111.5 | 2 593.6 | 563.9 | 656.3 | 771.1 | 1 050.0 | 1 342.8 |
| **North America** | 255.9 | 323.6 | 369.7 | 424.1 | 474.6 | 328.9 | 384.5 | 408.7 | 663.0 | 886.0 |
| Canada | 232.7 | 251.4 | 310.0 | 355.7 | 411.7 | 73.4 | 100.1 | 204.5 | 110.2 | 113.7 |
| Mexico | 23.3 | 72.2 | 59.8 | 68.4 | 62.9 | 255.5 | 284.4 | 204.2 | 552.7 | 772.3 |
| **Caribbean and Central America** | 6.2 | 5.5 | 10.9 | 16.6 | 8.9 | 11.8 | 15.9 | 7.4 | 7.0 | 15.5 |
| **South America** | 31.1 | 35.8 | 62.7 | 62.9 | 76.7 | 12.2 | 13.7 | 23.5 | 30.0 | 35.3 |
| Argentina | 1.6 | 3.0 | 3.1 | 3.2 | 3.8 | 3.3 | 4.6 | 7.4 | 12.7 | 8.5 |
| Brazil | 6.2 | 6.1 | 3.8 | 14.3 | 21.8 | 2.0 | 2.7 | 6.4 | 4.3 | 6.0 |
| Other South America | 23.3 | 26.7 | 55.8 | 45.3 | 51.1 | 6.9 | 6.4 | 9.7 | 13.0 | 20.8 |
| **Europe** | 561.1 | 485.0 | 497.5 | 750.2 | 1 122.0 | 112.9 | 114.9 | 129.0 | 122.0 | 120.0 |
| Belgium | 34.8 | 81.1 | 125.2 | 57.5 | 74.1 | 10.2 | 5.8 | 3.3 | 4.1 | 5.3 |
| France | 15.5 | 12.6 | 22.8 | 32.6 | 33.8 | 8.9 | 11.5 | 10.1 | 9.0 | 6.3 |
| Germany | 152.9 | 166.3 | 141.6 | 155.4 | 97.0 | 24.0 | 21.1 | 22.2 | 16.3 | 21.4 |
| Netherlands | 63.0 | 42.8 | 40.8 | 73.3 | 71.0 | 5.6 | 4.4 | 2.9 | 2.6 | 5.5 |
| United Kingdom | 60.9 | 52.5 | 96.2 | 346.4 | 712.4 | 14.7 | 31.8 | 34.3 | 24.5 | 25.6 |
| Turkey | 2.1 | 2.3 | 1.8 | 1.7 | 4.0 | 10.3 | 6.9 | 7.8 | 3.0 | 0.6 |
| Former Soviet Republics | 5.9 | 2.8 | 8.9 | 4.3 | 4.2 | 5.2 | 0.5 | 9.3 | 9.6 | 16.0 |
| Poland | 0.4 | 0.3 | 0.8 | 1.1 | 2.2 | 0.3 | 0.2 | 0.3 | 0.8 | 1.9 |
| Other Eastern Europe | 2.6 | 1.6 | 1.8 | 3.4 | 3.3 | 2.8 | 1.4 | 2.9 | 1.5 | 0.5 |
| Other Europe | 223.2 | 122.8 | 57.5 | 74.4 | 120.0 | 30.9 | 31.3 | 35.7 | 50.7 | 36.9 |
| **Asia** | 767.3 | 925.6 | 849.3 | 775.7 | 858.9 | 66.8 | 93.4 | 161.5 | 189.8 | 250.8 |
| Japan | 157.6 | 191.9 | 322.9 | 275.1 | 296.1 | 17.0 | 23.9 | 60.3 | 71.5 | 74.4 |
| China | 3.6 | 11.8 | 12.6 | 20.3 | 9.9 | 8.3 | 9.4 | 5.1 | 12.8 | 22.4 |
| Hong Kong | 166.5 | 378.8 | 50.9 | 23.1 | 29.0 | 4.9 | 4.1 | 4.4 | 7.2 | 8.7 |
| Taiwan | 174.0 | 129.1 | 90.2 | 69.8 | 55.9 | 8.0 | 4.5 | 6.7 | 12.4 | 33.2 |
| Singapore | 44.1 | 20.1 | 77.3 | 127.3 | 57.0 | 2.1 | 3.0 | 3.8 | 4.5 | 4.5 |
| South Korea | 51.5 | 84.8 | 150.1 | 94.4 | 70.7 | 10.4 | 18.9 | 14.1 | 23.8 | 36.5 |
| Indonesia | 3.8 | 7.5 | 7.1 | 11.3 | 7.9 | ..... | 0.1 | 3.2 | 1.8 | 0.7 |
| India | 3.1 | 1.5 | 3.9 | 2.5 | 2.7 | 0.2 | 2.0 | 0.8 | 0.6 | 2.0 |
| Other Asia | 163.1 | 100.1 | 134.4 | 151.9 | 329.8 | 15.9 | 27.5 | 63.1 | 55.2 | 68.5 |
| **Africa** | 6.9 | 3.8 | 6.6 | 15.6 | 9.2 | 5.4 | 3.0 | 2.6 | 10.9 | 8.3 |
| North Africa | 2.3 | 0.5 | 1.5 | 5.0 | 2.2 | 1.8 | 0.7 | 0.6 | 8.7 | 5.8 |
| Republic of South Africa | 2.8 | 2.5 | 3.8 | 6.6 | 4.7 | 2.2 | 1.1 | 1.5 | 1.4 | 1.0 |
| Other Subsaharan Africa | 1.9 | 0.8 | 1.3 | 3.9 | 2.3 | 1.3 | 1.3 | 0.5 | 0.8 | 1.5 |
| **Middle East** | 12.1 | 9.2 | 15.9 | 42.9 | 19.5 | 12.5 | 10.1 | 9.6 | 10.9 | 13.9 |
| **Australia** | 20.1 | 20.1 | 25.3 | 23.6 | 23.8 | 13.6 | 20.8 | 28.8 | 16.3 | 13.0 |
| **Rest of World** | ..... | ..... | 0.2 | ..... | ..... | ..... | ..... | ..... | ..... | ..... |

## Table E-3.  Metropolitan Area Exports of Goods by Destination, 1993–1997—*Continued*

(Millions of dollars.)

| Destination | 1993 | 1994 | 1995 | 1996 | 1997 | 1993 | 1994 | 1995 | 1996 | 1997 |
|---|---|---|---|---|---|---|---|---|---|---|
| | Savannah, GA | | | | | Santa Barbara - Santa Maria - Lompoc, CA | | | | |
| **ALL DESTINATIONS** | 442.5 | 423.3 | 567.5 | 459.4 | 633.4 | 424.0 | 420.2 | 565.2 | 648.0 | 623.3 |
| **North America** | 98.4 | 91.8 | 69.7 | 80.0 | 75.7 | 56.2 | 51.2 | 39.0 | 58.0 | 71.8 |
| Canada | 55.9 | 71.3 | 53.4 | 55.4 | 57.0 | 47.1 | 42.9 | 36.0 | 51.9 | 61.3 |
| Mexico | 42.5 | 20.5 | 16.3 | 24.6 | 18.7 | 9.2 | 8.3 | 3.0 | 6.1 | 10.5 |
| **Caribbean and Central America** | 42.9 | 51.8 | 36.6 | 29.4 | 24.4 | 2.7 | 1.5 | 2.0 | 6.5 | 5.5 |
| **South America** | 8.7 | 26.6 | 29.7 | 33.1 | 37.3 | 7.2 | 16.9 | 13.0 | 21.8 | 35.0 |
| Argentina | 0.7 | 1.0 | 3.1 | 6.7 | 4.2 | 0.6 | 0.6 | 1.0 | 1.1 | 0.7 |
| Brazil | 0.1 | 4.1 | 4.2 | 2.9 | 11.1 | 2.4 | 0.7 | 1.3 | 1.0 | 4.5 |
| Other South America | 7.9 | 21.5 | 22.3 | 23.5 | 21.9 | 4.2 | 15.5 | 10.7 | 19.7 | 29.8 |
| **Europe** | 94.1 | 66.1 | 215.6 | 127.8 | 211.8 | 125.2 | 123.3 | 147.5 | 154.6 | 163.1 |
| Belgium | 2.0 | 3.6 | 16.8 | 8.0 | 6.4 | 1.6 | 2.6 | 1.3 | 1.1 | 2.4 |
| France | 30.0 | 5.0 | 25.6 | 15.4 | 12.3 | 8.9 | 9.5 | 9.1 | 8.9 | 11.7 |
| Germany | 4.4 | 4.7 | 14.5 | 23.6 | 29.8 | 46.9 | 52.7 | 55.8 | 61.0 | 50.0 |
| Netherlands | 8.7 | 15.3 | 28.2 | 13.2 | 32.2 | 8.3 | 8.0 | 9.3 | 10.5 | 11.5 |
| United Kingdom | 23.9 | 17.9 | 28.1 | 28.3 | 25.5 | 21.5 | 17.7 | 33.4 | 27.8 | 26.4 |
| Turkey | 3.3 | 2.1 | 7.5 | 5.0 | 8.3 | 5.7 | 4.3 | 1.6 | 1.5 | 1.9 |
| Former Soviet Republics | 1.8 | 0.9 | 3.2 | 2.1 | 1.6 | 7.8 | 0.7 | 2.2 | 1.6 | 1.4 |
| Poland | ..... | ..... | 0.2 | 0.3 | 0.1 | 0.8 | 0.4 | 0.2 | 0.2 | 0.8 |
| Other Eastern Europe | 1.7 | ..... | 0.1 | 0.4 | ..... | 0.7 | 0.4 | 0.8 | 0.9 | 1.4 |
| Other Europe | 18.1 | 16.5 | 91.3 | 31.5 | 95.5 | 23.0 | 27.0 | 33.8 | 41.1 | 55.7 |
| **Asia** | 148.8 | 150.3 | 165.7 | 127.4 | 197.0 | 215.4 | 203.7 | 260.7 | 307.0 | 318.3 |
| Japan | 39.3 | 16.5 | 53.6 | 22.8 | 15.4 | 35.8 | 45.5 | 88.2 | 66.0 | 57.1 |
| China | 6.6 | 49.4 | 31.5 | 6.7 | 49.0 | 2.1 | 2.3 | 3.4 | 3.2 | 3.2 |
| Hong Kong | 2.2 | 0.4 | 1.3 | 3.0 | 4.5 | 4.9 | 4.1 | 6.1 | 7.5 | 5.5 |
| Taiwan | 0.7 | 1.0 | 2.1 | 2.4 | 6.0 | 4.8 | 4.5 | 7.6 | 12.6 | 11.4 |
| Singapore | 3.7 | 1.6 | 20.2 | 3.1 | 4.5 | 12.4 | 5.4 | 5.3 | 11.5 | 10.6 |
| South Korea | 2.7 | 27.2 | 17.3 | 53.5 | 95.2 | 54.1 | 24.5 | 27.6 | 26.2 | 32.0 |
| Indonesia | 42.2 | 9.4 | 1.4 | 6.7 | 1.5 | 12.1 | 3.2 | 1.9 | 0.7 | 1.6 |
| India | 10.7 | 1.6 | 2.1 | 1.8 | 7.6 | 2.7 | 4.0 | 6.2 | 5.0 | 5.8 |
| Other Asia | 40.8 | 43.2 | 36.2 | 27.5 | 13.3 | 86.4 | 110.1 | 114.4 | 174.4 | 191.1 |
| **Africa** | 13.0 | 24.7 | 17.0 | 30.1 | 33.0 | 5.6 | 3.5 | 3.2 | 3.4 | 3.6 |
| North Africa | 4.0 | 6.0 | 4.7 | 2.5 | 4.9 | 0.6 | 0.6 | 0.6 | 0.4 | 1.0 |
| Republic of South Africa | 3.2 | 4.8 | 5.0 | 9.4 | 10.8 | 3.2 | 1.9 | 1.8 | 2.8 | 2.3 |
| Other Subsaharan Africa | 5.7 | 13.8 | 7.3 | 18.2 | 17.3 | 1.8 | 1.0 | 0.8 | 0.2 | 0.4 |
| **Middle East** | 7.1 | 10.3 | 30.4 | 13.1 | 16.6 | 3.6 | 12.3 | 90.6 | 86.9 | 14.3 |
| **Australia** | 29.6 | 1.6 | 2.9 | 18.4 | 37.6 | 8.1 | 7.8 | 9.0 | 9.8 | 11.8 |
| **Rest of World** | ..... | ..... | ..... | ..... | ..... | ..... | ..... | ..... | 0.1 | ..... |
| | South Bend, IN | | | | | Scranton - Wilkes-Barre - Hazleton, PA | | | | |
| **ALL DESTINATIONS** | 179.7 | 160.3 | 389.5 | 494.8 | 522.1 | 266.6 | 328.2 | 431.9 | 392.0 | 442.4 |
| **North America** | 65.9 | 88.1 | 173.7 | 209.1 | 180.5 | 125.7 | 171.4 | 222.0 | 195.4 | 204.3 |
| Canada | 51.2 | 64.9 | 110.6 | 122.9 | 126.7 | 121.7 | 163.0 | 215.9 | 189.4 | 193.6 |
| Mexico | 14.7 | 23.2 | 63.1 | 86.1 | 53.8 | 4.0 | 8.4 | 6.0 | 6.0 | 10.6 |
| **Caribbean and Central America** | 1.5 | 1.6 | 2.8 | 1.5 | 2.2 | 15.7 | 13.1 | 15.3 | 6.5 | 8.0 |
| **South America** | 6.9 | 11.9 | 11.3 | 8.7 | 10.5 | 10.2 | 17.3 | 13.7 | 11.7 | 19.1 |
| Argentina | 0.9 | 1.4 | 1.7 | 3.1 | 4.3 | 1.1 | 1.5 | 0.8 | 0.5 | 2.0 |
| Brazil | 0.7 | 7.5 | 5.9 | 2.2 | 1.6 | 6.9 | 12.0 | 8.4 | 7.2 | 10.6 |
| Other South America | 5.4 | 3.1 | 3.6 | 3.4 | 4.7 | 2.3 | 3.8 | 4.4 | 4.0 | 6.5 |
| **Europe** | 17.4 | 20.8 | 91.0 | 164.9 | 242.8 | 40.2 | 41.0 | 52.1 | 61.4 | 64.8 |
| Belgium | 0.4 | 0.5 | 7.3 | 2.6 | 1.0 | 1.1 | 1.4 | 2.2 | 3.7 | 1.6 |
| France | 1.5 | 3.1 | 4.9 | 7.7 | 7.0 | 3.5 | 5.9 | 6.6 | 9.2 | 12.7 |
| Germany | 3.0 | 4.9 | 13.4 | 23.2 | 19.6 | 7.4 | 6.5 | 10.4 | 11.7 | 10.5 |
| Netherlands | 0.5 | 0.8 | 1.4 | 29.0 | 87.8 | 6.6 | 8.4 | 13.3 | 16.0 | 13.1 |
| United Kingdom | 6.2 | 6.8 | 45.0 | 68.5 | 110.8 | 5.3 | 4.2 | 6.4 | 8.3 | 12.5 |
| Turkey | 0.5 | 0.1 | 1.4 | 0.8 | 1.8 | 0.4 | 0.3 | 0.2 | 0.2 | 0.4 |
| Former Soviet Republics | ..... | 0.5 | 0.9 | 1.9 | 1.4 | 0.8 | 0.3 | 1.3 | 0.6 | 0.6 |
| Poland | ..... | ..... | ..... | ..... | ..... | ..... | 0.4 | 0.1 | 0.1 | 0.1 |
| Other Eastern Europe | 0.9 | 1.4 | 0.6 | 1.0 | 0.5 | 0.1 | 0.7 | 0.4 | 0.4 | 0.4 |
| Other Europe | 4.3 | 2.7 | 16.1 | 30.2 | 13.0 | 14.9 | 13.0 | 11.4 | 10.8 | 12.8 |
| **Asia** | 25.1 | 20.8 | 34.8 | 51.1 | 56.4 | 64.1 | 75.8 | 116.5 | 101.0 | 138.3 |
| Japan | 8.1 | 4.9 | 16.7 | 21.1 | 33.2 | 10.6 | 7.8 | 9.6 | 10.9 | 10.8 |
| China | 0.8 | 0.5 | 0.2 | 1.5 | 0.6 | 1.6 | 1.6 | 2.1 | 3.2 | 5.0 |
| Hong Kong | 3.3 | 3.1 | 3.3 | 3.0 | 4.9 | 4.1 | 5.1 | 6.6 | 5.4 | 5.6 |
| Taiwan | 1.4 | 1.4 | 2.2 | 11.4 | 3.4 | 1.1 | 5.6 | 2.1 | 2.9 | 4.6 |
| Singapore | 3.3 | 2.5 | 2.8 | 4.0 | 3.8 | 5.3 | 43.3 | 85.7 | 69.8 | 102.2 |
| South Korea | 4.4 | 5.2 | 4.7 | 4.1 | 4.0 | 1.5 | 3.6 | 2.9 | 2.9 | 2.6 |
| Indonesia | ..... | 0.2 | 0.3 | 0.2 | 0.3 | 0.1 | 0.1 | 0.2 | 0.5 | 1.3 |
| India | 0.6 | ..... | 1.1 | 1.5 | 1.5 | 0.4 | 0.5 | 1.5 | 1.3 | 1.3 |
| Other Asia | 3.2 | 3.0 | 3.4 | 4.4 | 4.5 | 39.2 | 8.2 | 5.9 | 4.1 | 4.8 |
| **Africa** | 16.1 | 3.2 | 44.9 | 8.6 | 5.2 | 1.9 | 0.9 | 0.9 | 0.9 | 1.3 |
| North Africa | 13.7 | 0.5 | 37.5 | 2.0 | 1.6 | 1.1 | 0.4 | 0.2 | 0.4 | 0.7 |
| Republic of South Africa | 0.2 | 0.6 | 0.7 | 2.6 | 2.1 | 0.7 | 0.3 | 0.3 | 0.4 | 0.5 |
| Other Subsaharan Africa | 2.2 | 2.2 | 6.7 | 4.1 | 1.6 | 0.2 | 0.2 | 0.4 | 0.2 | 0.1 |
| **Middle East** | 45.9 | 13.1 | 28.3 | 39.3 | 14.2 | 5.3 | 3.0 | 3.4 | 9.6 | 3.6 |
| **Australia** | 0.8 | 0.8 | 2.8 | 11.8 | 10.2 | 3.4 | 5.6 | 8.0 | 5.4 | 3.0 |
| **Rest of World** | ..... | 0.1 | ..... | ..... | ..... | ..... | ..... | ..... | ..... | ..... |

## Table E-3.  Metropolitan Area Exports of Goods by Destination, 1993–1997—*Continued*

(Millions of dollars.)

| Destination | 1993 | 1994 | 1995 | 1996 | 1997 | 1993 | 1994 | 1995 | 1996 | 1997 |
|---|---|---|---|---|---|---|---|---|---|---|
| | Santa Cruz - Watsonville, CA | | | | | San Diego, CA | | | | |
| **ALL DESTINATIONS** | 664.3 | 857.4 | 1 408.2 | 1 943.1 | 2 298.5 | 4 357.7 | 4 867.3 | 5 860.9 | 6 719.4 | 7 810.0 |
| **North America** | 80.1 | 95.5 | 78.9 | 108.5 | 178.4 | 2 248.5 | 2 473.5 | 2 981.5 | 3 587.2 | 4 155.7 |
| Canada | 43.5 | 49.8 | 44.5 | 45.9 | 54.3 | 401.1 | 441.3 | 496.8 | 613.2 | 793.2 |
| Mexico | 36.7 | 45.7 | 34.5 | 62.6 | 124.1 | 1 847.5 | 2 032.2 | 2 484.7 | 2 973.9 | 3 362.6 |
| **Caribbean and Central America** | 0.5 | 0.8 | 0.8 | 2.1 | 0.6 | 25.5 | 51.0 | 71.9 | 57.1 | 81.9 |
| **South America** | 12.4 | 17.1 | 8.7 | 7.9 | 12.2 | 76.3 | 149.3 | 195.1 | 197.3 | 281.6 |
| Argentina | 1.2 | 2.8 | 0.4 | 0.4 | 0.7 | 20.9 | 54.6 | 19.8 | 15.5 | 55.6 |
| Brazil | 8.1 | 7.9 | 4.4 | 5.0 | 8.8 | 15.8 | 53.1 | 93.6 | 94.1 | 127.5 |
| Other South America | 3.1 | 6.3 | 4.0 | 2.5 | 2.7 | 39.6 | 41.6 | 81.7 | 87.8 | 98.5 |
| **Europe** | 125.1 | 107.5 | 185.6 | 215.6 | 263.8 | 932.6 | 898.0 | 1 035.3 | 1 152.5 | 1 387.0 |
| Belgium | 1.5 | 0.9 | 0.5 | 0.9 | 0.3 | 26.4 | 32.7 | 37.2 | 44.2 | 53.4 |
| France | 5.0 | 7.0 | 8.0 | 13.9 | 13.7 | 129.0 | 88.7 | 108.7 | 107.9 | 144.5 |
| Germany | 14.1 | 14.0 | 14.0 | 21.7 | 10.5 | 269.5 | 227.7 | 245.4 | 275.1 | 266.8 |
| Netherlands | 28.8 | 34.0 | 69.2 | 53.6 | 87.1 | 87.8 | 92.3 | 117.1 | 136.4 | 202.5 |
| United Kingdom | 34.4 | 30.4 | 39.4 | 80.5 | 112.4 | 150.1 | 179.3 | 230.7 | 277.5 | 329.0 |
| Turkey | 1.4 | 0.1 | 0.3 | 0.1 | 0.1 | 6.1 | 6.2 | 9.2 | 6.1 | 6.2 |
| Former Soviet Republics | 0.2 | 0.5 | 0.8 | 1.3 | 1.0 | 11.0 | 11.0 | 13.4 | 24.7 | 47.4 |
| Poland | 0.3 | 0.2 | 0.2 | 0.2 | 0.1 | 4.9 | 2.7 | 2.1 | 2.9 | 4.3 |
| Other Eastern Europe | 0.3 | 0.3 | 0.3 | 0.7 | 0.6 | 6.8 | 9.5 | 12.9 | 13.4 | 20.0 |
| Other Europe | 39.1 | 20.1 | 53.0 | 42.8 | 38.0 | 240.9 | 247.9 | 258.7 | 264.3 | 312.9 |
| **Asia** | 436.8 | 626.1 | 1 120.6 | 1 591.2 | 1 824.6 | 899.3 | 1 049.5 | 1 311.6 | 1 526.4 | 1 620.9 |
| Japan | 35.4 | 28.8 | 42.3 | 67.7 | 60.4 | 296.8 | 360.2 | 506.2 | 517.5 | 580.4 |
| China | 4.0 | 3.9 | 2.5 | 92.8 | 32.5 | 29.0 | 21.1 | 37.0 | 57.9 | 82.8 |
| Hong Kong | 6.4 | 6.4 | 8.3 | 47.4 | 46.5 | 115.1 | 166.5 | 141.4 | 165.8 | 142.0 |
| Taiwan | 9.4 | 22.0 | 33.1 | 40.7 | 39.6 | 98.6 | 97.4 | 123.2 | 154.8 | 151.9 |
| Singapore | 217.3 | 354.1 | 458.9 | 560.8 | 706.1 | 100.1 | 126.2 | 137.2 | 156.2 | 155.0 |
| South Korea | 11.5 | 19.3 | 35.9 | 55.4 | 30.9 | 87.0 | 85.6 | 111.3 | 181.5 | 164.1 |
| Indonesia | 2.6 | 0.5 | 0.1 | 1.8 | 0.3 | 14.3 | 17.2 | 22.9 | 37.8 | 44.2 |
| India | 1.2 | 0.7 | 0.6 | 2.5 | 0.7 | 5.4 | 10.1 | 15.6 | 19.9 | 15.8 |
| Other Asia | 149.0 | 190.5 | 538.8 | 722.2 | 907.6 | 152.9 | 165.2 | 216.7 | 235.0 | 284.7 |
| **Africa** | 0.8 | 2.1 | 4.1 | 0.8 | 0.9 | 58.7 | 106.2 | 123.9 | 57.5 | 77.2 |
| North Africa | 0.1 | ..... | 0.1 | 0.1 | ..... | 38.3 | 85.7 | 90.4 | 34.0 | 31.7 |
| Republic of South Africa | 0.8 | 2.1 | 3.9 | 0.6 | 0.8 | 11.8 | 16.7 | 21.6 | 19.4 | 26.0 |
| Other Subsaharan Africa | ..... | ..... | 0.1 | ..... | 0.1 | 8.5 | 3.9 | 11.9 | 4.1 | 19.5 |
| **Middle East** | 1.8 | 1.5 | 2.0 | 2.9 | 4.4 | 58.5 | 62.0 | 68.4 | 52.1 | 95.8 |
| **Australia** | 6.7 | 6.8 | 7.5 | 14.2 | 13.6 | 58.3 | 77.7 | 73.2 | 89.3 | 109.9 |
| **Rest of World** | ..... | ..... | ..... | ..... | ..... | ..... | ..... | ..... | ..... | ..... |

| Destination | 1993 | 1994 | 1995 | 1996 | 1997 | 1993 | 1994 | 1995 | 1996 | 1997 |
|---|---|---|---|---|---|---|---|---|---|---|
| | Seattle - Bellevue - Everett, WA | | | | | San Francisco, CA | | | | |
| **ALL DESTINATIONS** | 23 815.6 | 21 753.0 | 17 815.4 | 21 391.1 | 27 005.8 | 9 264.9 | 9 303.8 | 8 133.7 | 8 560.4 | 9 978.5 |
| **North America** | 1 137.2 | 1 344.7 | 1 417.0 | 1 503.0 | 1 400.6 | 798.2 | 788.9 | 740.5 | 697.2 | 826.8 |
| Canada | 979.6 | 1 064.0 | 1 351.8 | 1 450.3 | 1 341.9 | 389.8 | 392.0 | 438.5 | 422.4 | 479.6 |
| Mexico | 157.6 | 280.8 | 65.2 | 52.7 | 58.7 | 408.4 | 396.9 | 302.0 | 274.9 | 347.2 |
| **Caribbean and Central America** | 131.6 | 102.1 | 21.5 | 19.8 | 26.1 | 232.6 | 237.8 | 203.9 | 212.0 | 271.5 |
| **South America** | 340.1 | 245.7 | 369.8 | 535.4 | 796.5 | 486.9 | 486.8 | 429.7 | 307.2 | 452.5 |
| Argentina | 22.5 | 30.9 | 85.2 | 24.9 | 34.1 | 58.4 | 75.0 | 34.9 | 56.1 | 92.7 |
| Brazil | 230.0 | 76.5 | 68.5 | 80.0 | 379.6 | 136.4 | 182.3 | 85.4 | 140.2 | 208.7 |
| Other South America | 87.5 | 138.4 | 216.1 | 430.5 | 382.8 | 292.1 | 229.5 | 309.4 | 111.0 | 151.0 |
| **Europe** | 6 270.3 | 5 568.0 | 4 187.6 | 4 972.9 | 8 956.0 | 2 448.1 | 2 457.1 | 2 085.1 | 2 411.6 | 2 929.4 |
| Belgium | 63.5 | 151.2 | 114.0 | 159.8 | 233.8 | 317.8 | 383.5 | 398.8 | 374.3 | 415.7 |
| France | 739.9 | 322.7 | 146.4 | 134.4 | 252.1 | 172.2 | 172.6 | 174.9 | 124.0 | 138.2 |
| Germany | 736.4 | 569.3 | 634.6 | 720.2 | 1 204.7 | 452.3 | 482.0 | 267.9 | 323.5 | 388.2 |
| Netherlands | 533.2 | 404.4 | 650.8 | 857.2 | 822.5 | 274.2 | 239.5 | 159.4 | 220.1 | 279.9 |
| United Kingdom | 2 175.2 | 2 182.4 | 1 118.3 | 1 503.0 | 4 345.2 | 499.2 | 487.4 | 442.0 | 568.1 | 653.9 |
| Turkey | 418.3 | 320.7 | 129.1 | 13.1 | 20.4 | 29.9 | 26.2 | 17.3 | 56.7 | 132.5 |
| Former Soviet Republics | 28.2 | 431.8 | 266.4 | 547.4 | 263.3 | 71.1 | 57.8 | 73.5 | 72.1 | 74.5 |
| Poland | 155.3 | 78.5 | 88.9 | 49.8 | 272.0 | 4.7 | 4.7 | 1.6 | 7.1 | 9.3 |
| Other Eastern Europe | 233.7 | 151.7 | 17.6 | 19.4 | 182.1 | 10.7 | 11.0 | 9.7 | 9.9 | 10.9 |
| Other Europe | 1 186.7 | 955.3 | 1 021.4 | 968.5 | 1 359.8 | 616.1 | 592.4 | 539.8 | 655.8 | 826.4 |
| **Asia** | 14 651.2 | 13 089.3 | 11 166.6 | 12 940.5 | 13 076.8 | 4 552.5 | 4 516.6 | 4 267.4 | 4 485.3 | 5 031.9 |
| Japan | 5 607.5 | 5 568.6 | 5 730.0 | 5 317.1 | 5 221.4 | 1 674.3 | 1 818.0 | 1 926.6 | 2 049.5 | 2 123.5 |
| China | 1 857.8 | 1 852.8 | 1 026.3 | 1 391.3 | 1 730.1 | 389.4 | 241.4 | 181.8 | 172.1 | 269.3 |
| Hong Kong | 546.9 | 398.2 | 449.0 | 733.0 | 214.7 | 639.8 | 563.8 | 488.7 | 491.4 | 498.9 |
| Taiwan | 1 240.4 | 748.7 | 708.7 | 693.3 | 560.3 | 371.2 | 506.3 | 513.8 | 355.7 | 366.8 |
| Singapore | 931.1 | 1 246.9 | 921.1 | 890.3 | 1 176.4 | 753.0 | 631.0 | 433.2 | 419.6 | 406.9 |
| South Korea | 1 210.9 | 1 203.0 | 1 436.0 | 1 746.5 | 1 624.0 | 201.7 | 223.8 | 234.2 | 295.2 | 288.0 |
| Indonesia | 328.2 | 376.3 | 42.4 | 48.9 | 226.5 | 42.6 | 65.1 | 42.2 | 43.3 | 55.2 |
| India | 453.1 | 163.7 | 31.0 | 405.0 | 197.5 | 33.0 | 34.8 | 27.6 | 17.7 | 21.5 |
| Other Asia | 2 475.4 | 1 531.1 | 822.1 | 1 715.0 | 2 125.9 | 447.5 | 432.5 | 419.4 | 640.8 | 1 001.8 |
| **Africa** | 460.6 | 244.2 | 215.0 | 276.2 | 681.2 | 189.9 | 134.5 | 60.5 | 66.1 | 72.9 |
| North Africa | 117.7 | 155.1 | 120.5 | 18.5 | 487.9 | 150.9 | 95.5 | 45.7 | 32.8 | 26.9 |
| Republic of South Africa | 268.4 | 43.3 | 73.4 | 79.5 | 49.5 | 27.5 | 25.8 | 8.7 | 26.6 | 33.9 |
| Other Subsaharan Africa | 74.4 | 45.8 | 21.1 | 178.2 | 143.9 | 11.5 | 13.2 | 6.1 | 6.7 | 12.1 |
| **Middle East** | 558.4 | 727.8 | 249.4 | 605.0 | 1 644.2 | 291.4 | 273.0 | 191.5 | 210.3 | 228.7 |
| **Australia** | 266.3 | 430.8 | 188.3 | 538.2 | 424.0 | 265.3 | 409.2 | 155.0 | 170.7 | 164.8 |
| **Rest of World** | ..... | 0.3 | 0.2 | 0.2 | 0.5 | ..... | ..... | ..... | ..... | ..... |

## Table E-3.  Metropolitan Area Exports of Goods by Destination, 1993–1997—*Continued*

(Millions of dollars.)

| Destination | 1993 | 1994 | 1995 | 1996 | 1997 | 1993 | 1994 | 1995 | 1996 | 1997 |
|---|---|---|---|---|---|---|---|---|---|---|
| | Sheboygan, WI | | | | | Shreveport - Bossier City, LA | | | | |
| **ALL DESTINATIONS** | 207.1 | 244.3 | 258.7 | 283.3 | 320.9 | 108.4 | 134.6 | 169.1 | 172.6 | 180.8 |
| **North America** | 73.1 | 92.8 | 94.5 | 118.1 | 138.1 | 41.6 | 52.7 | 63.0 | 64.4 | 60.9 |
| Canada | 60.1 | 62.5 | 70.6 | 95.4 | 116.1 | 40.3 | 51.0 | 61.8 | 58.9 | 55.8 |
| Mexico | 13.0 | 30.3 | 23.9 | 22.7 | 22.1 | 1.4 | 1.7 | 1.2 | 5.5 | 5.1 |
| **Caribbean and Central America** | 4.1 | 8.3 | 7.3 | 4.8 | 5.1 | 1.8 | 2.8 | 2.8 | 2.6 | 1.6 |
| **South America** | 23.2 | 15.9 | 16.4 | 8.5 | 15.3 | 4.6 | 3.5 | 4.2 | 3.8 | 5.1 |
| Argentina | 5.6 | 3.3 | 4.7 | 0.9 | 2.3 | 1.4 | 1.8 | 0.9 | 1.5 | 1.8 |
| Brazil | 1.1 | 1.0 | 3.8 | 0.9 | 1.4 | 0.4 | 0.2 | 0.2 | 0.3 | 1.2 |
| Other South America | 16.4 | 11.6 | 7.8 | 6.7 | 11.7 | 2.8 | 1.6 | 3.1 | 2.0 | 2.0 |
| **Europe** | 40.3 | 57.1 | 61.5 | 60.7 | 63.9 | 44.7 | 56.5 | 73.5 | 79.7 | 91.9 |
| Belgium | 1.2 | 2.7 | 3.0 | 1.5 | 1.0 | 0.2 | 0.6 | 0.8 | 0.3 | 0.8 |
| France | 3.2 | 4.6 | 3.2 | 2.6 | 6.2 | 4.8 | 5.5 | 10.0 | 9.0 | 9.0 |
| Germany | 11.2 | 19.6 | 17.3 | 11.0 | 13.2 | 13.4 | 14.0 | 16.1 | 20.0 | 21.0 |
| Netherlands | 4.5 | 7.9 | 2.4 | 1.4 | 1.9 | 1.8 | 1.3 | 2.3 | 2.8 | 4.9 |
| United Kingdom | 9.8 | 11.5 | 14.8 | 13.9 | 13.8 | 4.4 | 6.1 | 10.6 | 6.5 | 7.8 |
| Turkey | 0.3 | 0.1 | 4.3 | 4.5 | 4.8 | 0.1 | 0.6 | 0.2 | ..... | 0.1 |
| Former Soviet Republics | 0.1 | 0.1 | 0.4 | 0.1 | 0.1 | 1.0 | 1.7 | 9.8 | 14.8 | 18.1 |
| Poland | 2.9 | 0.3 | 0.5 | 1.0 | 1.6 | 1.3 | 0.8 | 0.9 | 2.6 | 3.1 |
| Other Eastern Europe | 0.1 | 0.2 | 1.4 | 0.2 | 0.7 | 2.3 | 2.6 | 1.3 | 0.9 | 0.9 |
| Other Europe | 7.1 | 10.0 | 14.2 | 24.4 | 20.6 | 15.4 | 23.4 | 21.6 | 22.8 | 26.2 |
| **Asia** | 47.6 | 52.6 | 57.2 | 72.5 | 74.7 | 7.0 | 10.3 | 14.8 | 12.2 | 10.3 |
| Japan | 2.8 | 4.3 | 4.2 | 6.3 | 10.7 | 0.9 | 2.2 | 4.5 | 2.0 | 1.6 |
| China | 0.5 | 2.1 | 4.1 | 8.5 | 10.8 | ..... | ..... | 0.7 | 0.1 | 0.2 |
| Hong Kong | 16.4 | 16.6 | 14.4 | 8.7 | 10.0 | 0.6 | 0.6 | 0.2 | 0.5 | 2.0 |
| Taiwan | 8.7 | 11.2 | 9.9 | 9.2 | 7.2 | 1.9 | 2.9 | 4.5 | 3.7 | 0.9 |
| Singapore | 6.4 | 8.7 | 8.0 | 10.8 | 10.7 | 1.0 | 1.3 | 0.6 | 0.9 | 2.6 |
| South Korea | 5.3 | 4.1 | 8.4 | 7.1 | 13.6 | 0.7 | 1.6 | 2.1 | 2.3 | 1.7 |
| Indonesia | ..... | ..... | 0.8 | 4.3 | 3.6 | ..... | ..... | 0.1 | ..... | 0.1 |
| India | ..... | ..... | 0.2 | 3.7 | 0.9 | ..... | ..... | ..... | 0.3 | 0.1 |
| Other Asia | 7.5 | 5.6 | 7.3 | 13.9 | 7.2 | 1.7 | 1.7 | 2.1 | 2.5 | 1.2 |
| **Africa** | 7.2 | 2.8 | 3.7 | 5.5 | 7.8 | 1.1 | 0.7 | 0.1 | 0.2 | 1.0 |
| North Africa | 5.0 | 0.6 | 0.8 | 0.1 | 1.5 | 0.2 | 0.3 | ..... | ..... | 0.4 |
| Republic of South Africa | 0.6 | 0.3 | 1.5 | 1.1 | 1.4 | 0.2 | 0.2 | ..... | 0.2 | 0.1 |
| Other Subsaharan Africa | 1.7 | 1.8 | 1.4 | 4.2 | 4.9 | 0.7 | 0.2 | 0.1 | ..... | 0.4 |
| **Middle East** | 8.7 | 10.7 | 13.1 | 6.1 | 9.3 | 1.8 | 5.0 | 3.6 | 2.0 | 3.0 |
| **Australia** | 3.0 | 4.3 | 5.1 | 7.2 | 6.6 | 5.9 | 3.1 | 7.1 | 7.6 | 7.0 |
| **Rest of World** | ..... | ..... | ..... | ..... | ..... | ..... | ..... | ..... | ..... | ..... |

| Destination | 1993 | 1994 | 1995 | 1996 | 1997 | 1993 | 1994 | 1995 | 1996 | 1997 |
|---|---|---|---|---|---|---|---|---|---|---|
| | San Jose, CA | | | | | Spokane, WA | | | | |
| **ALL DESTINATIONS** | 16 171.6 | 19 942.7 | 26 822.8 | 29 331.3 | 29 057.2 | 254.4 | 269.4 | 310.9 | 347.9 | 445.7 |
| **North America** | 2 209.2 | 2 796.5 | 3 273.3 | 3 990.4 | 4 201.4 | 79.4 | 76.8 | 97.9 | 111.0 | 161.3 |
| Canada | 1 919.7 | 2 395.9 | 2 918.4 | 3 532.4 | 3 434.7 | 73.6 | 54.3 | 64.4 | 64.8 | 73.6 |
| Mexico | 289.5 | 400.6 | 354.9 | 457.9 | 766.7 | 5.7 | 22.5 | 33.6 | 46.2 | 87.6 |
| **Caribbean and Central America** | 20.2 | 15.8 | 18.2 | 29.8 | 55.1 | 0.6 | 1.2 | 1.3 | 0.7 | 0.9 |
| **South America** | 237.3 | 270.8 | 388.0 | 511.6 | 708.0 | 12.9 | 6.3 | 8.9 | 18.8 | 24.1 |
| Argentina | 25.8 | 42.6 | 63.2 | 98.7 | 170.1 | 1.7 | 1.2 | 4.8 | 3.2 | 2.0 |
| Brazil | 111.4 | 138.6 | 201.9 | 233.1 | 309.9 | 1.0 | 1.7 | 1.8 | 3.6 | 4.2 |
| Other South America | 100.1 | 89.6 | 123.0 | 179.8 | 227.9 | 10.2 | 3.4 | 2.2 | 11.9 | 18.0 |
| **Europe** | 4 541.7 | 5 136.4 | 6 097.1 | 6 232.6 | 6 818.0 | 71.7 | 74.2 | 90.3 | 90.8 | 123.4 |
| Belgium | 163.6 | 142.7 | 115.5 | 143.5 | 148.1 | 0.5 | 0.4 | 0.1 | 0.4 | 0.3 |
| France | 474.1 | 541.8 | 633.0 | 703.2 | 740.0 | 5.7 | 5.1 | 5.1 | 6.8 | 18.1 |
| Germany | 1 033.8 | 1 017.0 | 1 387.2 | 1 298.6 | 1 265.2 | 19.2 | 17.4 | 20.3 | 32.6 | 39.1 |
| Netherlands | 675.4 | 628.0 | 624.2 | 679.3 | 1 302.0 | 9.2 | 3.7 | 3.8 | 1.8 | 2.2 |
| United Kingdom | 1 086.5 | 1 381.0 | 1 553.2 | 1 632.0 | 1 696.2 | 19.2 | 28.5 | 34.6 | 26.6 | 30.6 |
| Turkey | 23.5 | 28.7 | 14.9 | 16.1 | 25.7 | ..... | 0.6 | 0.1 | 0.6 | 0.5 |
| Former Soviet Republics | 40.3 | 46.1 | 46.5 | 44.1 | 61.6 | 1.2 | 1.0 | 0.6 | 0.4 | 0.2 |
| Poland | 13.3 | 22.7 | 20.6 | 20.5 | 28.4 | 0.3 | 0.1 | 0.1 | 0.1 | ..... |
| Other Eastern Europe | 44.2 | 55.6 | 67.8 | 69.2 | 68.3 | ..... | 0.2 | 0.4 | 0.6 | 0.9 |
| Other Europe | 987.0 | 1 272.8 | 1 634.1 | 1 625.9 | 1 482.5 | 16.4 | 17.2 | 25.3 | 20.8 | 31.4 |
| **Asia** | 8 589.3 | 11 089.3 | 16 341.0 | 17 899.6 | 16 504.3 | 68.2 | 87.1 | 91.7 | 104.2 | 117.3 |
| Japan | 2 097.1 | 2 843.4 | 4 158.4 | 5 122.9 | 4 789.6 | 33.9 | 41.1 | 41.5 | 50.1 | 45.2 |
| China | 247.4 | 228.3 | 253.0 | 338.6 | 415.7 | 0.8 | 0.3 | 0.7 | 1.2 | 2.6 |
| Hong Kong | 665.8 | 709.6 | 930.3 | 965.6 | 1 137.2 | 8.1 | 9.1 | 7.2 | 3.5 | 4.8 |
| Taiwan | 980.8 | 1 074.0 | 1 539.1 | 1 983.3 | 2 474.4 | 5.7 | 3.7 | 11.5 | 9.3 | 14.1 |
| Singapore | 1 403.4 | 1 468.7 | 1 974.0 | 2 333.2 | 2 223.9 | 8.1 | 11.8 | 9.6 | 13.5 | 13.7 |
| South Korea | 1 257.8 | 1 688.0 | 2 792.1 | 3 132.3 | 2 464.8 | 2.9 | 5.0 | 8.3 | 12.1 | 21.0 |
| Indonesia | 27.3 | 39.1 | 73.5 | 85.3 | 74.8 | 0.1 | 0.3 | 0.3 | 1.4 | 0.3 |
| India | 64.5 | 76.7 | 117.7 | 150.2 | 162.9 | 0.1 | 2.3 | 1.4 | 1.4 | 1.8 |
| Other Asia | 1 845.2 | 2 961.5 | 4 502.8 | 3 788.2 | 2 761.0 | 8.6 | 13.5 | 11.3 | 11.6 | 13.7 |
| **Africa** | 86.5 | 111.9 | 103.5 | 108.9 | 105.6 | 2.7 | 9.2 | 1.7 | 3.1 | 2.7 |
| North Africa | 9.7 | 30.7 | 17.3 | 19.2 | 24.7 | 0.5 | 6.9 | 0.6 | 2.1 | 1.9 |
| Republic of South Africa | 68.6 | 68.7 | 79.0 | 84.1 | 73.0 | 2.2 | 1.9 | 0.8 | 1.0 | 0.5 |
| Other Subsaharan Africa | 8.3 | 12.5 | 7.2 | 5.6 | 7.9 | 0.1 | 0.4 | 0.3 | 0.1 | 0.3 |
| **Middle East** | 177.7 | 165.1 | 216.1 | 212.0 | 241.9 | 11.4 | 8.1 | 5.2 | 8.2 | 5.5 |
| **Australia** | 309.5 | 356.7 | 385.7 | 346.3 | 422.1 | 7.4 | 6.5 | 13.9 | 11.1 | 10.6 |
| **Rest of World** | 0.1 | 0.1 | ..... | 0.1 | 0.8 | ..... | ..... | ..... | ..... | ..... |

## Table E-3.  Metropolitan Area Exports of Goods by Destination, 1993–1997—Continued

(Millions of dollars.)

| Destination | 1993 | 1994 | 1995 | 1996 | 1997 | 1993 | 1994 | 1995 | 1996 | 1997 |
|---|---|---|---|---|---|---|---|---|---|---|
| | Springfield, MA | | | | | Springfield, MO | | | | |
| ALL DESTINATIONS | 389.8 | 434.8 | 512.1 | 530.3 | 568.0 | 81.1 | 103.8 | 120.2 | 120.3 | 141.4 |
| North America | 167.7 | 156.9 | 204.6 | 238.5 | 289.5 | 46.1 | 56.9 | 60.2 | 63.7 | 75.7 |
| Canada | 150.2 | 142.0 | 194.2 | 221.2 | 272.3 | 37.8 | 47.3 | 54.0 | 56.5 | 70.6 |
| Mexico | 17.4 | 14.9 | 10.4 | 17.3 | 17.2 | 8.3 | 9.7 | 6.2 | 7.2 | 5.1 |
| Caribbean and Central America | 5.1 | 3.2 | 2.6 | 2.1 | 2.8 | 2.4 | 3.3 | 2.7 | 3.6 | 6.2 |
| South America | 12.8 | 15.2 | 15.2 | 13.8 | 12.8 | 3.2 | 4.6 | 8.8 | 6.6 | 7.5 |
| Argentina | 4.9 | 3.5 | 2.1 | 1.8 | 2.2 | 0.4 | 1.9 | 0.9 | 0.7 | 0.8 |
| Brazil | 1.9 | 4.7 | 5.0 | 5.2 | 3.9 | 0.1 | 1.0 | 1.8 | 1.3 | 2.1 |
| Other South America | 6.0 | 7.0 | 8.2 | 6.8 | 6.7 | 2.7 | 1.7 | 6.1 | 4.5 | 4.6 |
| Europe | 111.5 | 109.4 | 121.0 | 133.1 | 151.6 | 12.7 | 22.9 | 30.8 | 30.8 | 30.8 |
| Belgium | 12.5 | 12.4 | 9.0 | 6.8 | 13.9 | 5.6 | 5.5 | 10.4 | 0.4 | 0.5 |
| France | 8.1 | 7.2 | 8.4 | 11.9 | 9.4 | 0.8 | 1.7 | 2.1 | 5.5 | 2.9 |
| Germany | 16.2 | 17.5 | 20.8 | 22.3 | 12.8 | 1.1 | 0.7 | 2.8 | 1.2 | 0.9 |
| Netherlands | 8.4 | 6.9 | 11.4 | 15.3 | 22.5 | 0.7 | 0.7 | 0.6 | 0.4 | 0.4 |
| United Kingdom | 23.2 | 25.8 | 32.7 | 34.0 | 33.6 | 1.1 | 1.0 | 2.1 | 3.6 | 3.5 |
| Turkey | 1.3 | 1.9 | 2.3 | 6.9 | 8.7 | ..... | ..... | ..... | ..... | 0.2 |
| Former Soviet Republics | 0.3 | 0.6 | 0.4 | 0.2 | 1.3 | ..... | ..... | ..... | 0.3 | 0.9 |
| Poland | 18.8 | 17.6 | 18.2 | 15.4 | 14.6 | ..... | ..... | ..... | ..... | ..... |
| Other Eastern Europe | 0.3 | 0.2 | 1.0 | 0.7 | 0.6 | ..... | ..... | ..... | 0.1 | ..... |
| Other Europe | 22.3 | 19.4 | 16.9 | 19.7 | 34.4 | 3.5 | 13.2 | 12.7 | 19.3 | 21.6 |
| Asia | 68.9 | 108.4 | 126.4 | 108.6 | 90.2 | 13.8 | 13.0 | 14.8 | 13.6 | 17.9 |
| Japan | 14.0 | 31.0 | 35.8 | 30.1 | 21.6 | 5.1 | 4.6 | 3.5 | 4.6 | 4.5 |
| China | 2.4 | 2.2 | 2.9 | 3.1 | 3.3 | 0.5 | 0.5 | 0.3 | 0.7 | 0.5 |
| Hong Kong | 17.6 | 13.6 | 10.9 | 11.6 | 14.4 | 2.2 | 1.2 | 0.7 | 0.7 | 1.4 |
| Taiwan | 4.4 | 10.7 | 3.8 | 4.5 | 5.5 | 1.3 | 0.9 | 3.3 | 0.7 | 1.5 |
| Singapore | 7.8 | 12.4 | 14.1 | 17.6 | 14.6 | 0.8 | 1.0 | 1.3 | 1.4 | 1.6 |
| South Korea | 11.1 | 16.1 | 21.8 | 14.7 | 12.7 | 2.1 | 2.1 | 1.6 | 1.7 | 2.7 |
| Indonesia | 0.8 | 2.3 | 0.4 | 0.5 | 0.2 | ..... | 0.8 | 0.9 | 0.7 | 0.3 |
| India | 0.3 | 1.0 | 0.9 | 0.3 | 0.4 | ..... | ..... | 0.1 | 0.2 | ..... |
| Other Asia | 10.5 | 19.1 | 35.9 | 26.1 | 17.3 | 1.8 | 1.9 | 3.1 | 3.0 | 5.4 |
| Africa | 3.6 | 12.9 | 12.7 | 8.6 | 2.5 | 0.5 | 0.5 | 0.5 | 0.3 | 1.0 |
| North Africa | 1.7 | 0.5 | 0.6 | 0.8 | 0.6 | 0.2 | 0.1 | 0.1 | ..... | 0.4 |
| Republic of South Africa | 1.9 | 8.7 | 9.9 | 6.4 | 1.6 | ..... | 0.1 | 0.2 | 0.1 | 0.4 |
| Other Subsaharan Africa | 0.1 | 3.7 | 2.2 | 1.4 | 0.4 | 0.3 | 0.4 | 0.3 | 0.2 | 0.2 |
| Middle East | 13.0 | 16.4 | 16.1 | 14.0 | 12.4 | 1.6 | 1.0 | 0.7 | 0.8 | 0.6 |
| Australia | 7.2 | 12.4 | 13.3 | 11.5 | 6.3 | 0.9 | 1.6 | 1.6 | 1.0 | 1.6 |
| Rest of World | ..... | ..... | ..... | ..... | ..... | ..... | ..... | ..... | ..... | ..... |
| | Santa Rosa, CA | | | | | Stamford - Norwalk, CT | | | | |
| ALL DESTINATIONS | 409.1 | 485.2 | 572.9 | 681.8 | 856.3 | 3 366.6 | 3 452.7 | 4 937.6 | 4 424.3 | 3 387.6 |
| North America | 68.6 | 78.0 | 86.4 | 101.3 | 148.3 | 392.8 | 464.1 | 478.2 | 533.6 | 553.2 |
| Canada | 55.7 | 61.9 | 69.8 | 76.7 | 111.3 | 272.2 | 316.8 | 342.5 | 306.6 | 327.0 |
| Mexico | 12.8 | 16.2 | 16.5 | 24.6 | 37.1 | 120.7 | 147.3 | 135.7 | 227.0 | 226.2 |
| Caribbean and Central America | 2.0 | 2.5 | 2.7 | 3.1 | 4.1 | 134.0 | 161.2 | 252.9 | 217.6 | 230.3 |
| South America | 9.2 | 7.0 | 8.9 | 13.2 | 19.5 | 362.1 | 457.2 | 570.5 | 519.0 | 382.8 |
| Argentina | 2.0 | 2.7 | 1.6 | 1.2 | 2.0 | 17.3 | 29.9 | 35.4 | 30.8 | 42.8 |
| Brazil | 3.1 | 2.8 | 5.5 | 9.7 | 14.5 | 121.2 | 150.0 | 260.5 | 224.7 | 132.0 |
| Other South America | 4.2 | 1.5 | 1.9 | 2.2 | 3.1 | 223.6 | 277.3 | 274.6 | 263.5 | 208.0 |
| Europe | 163.3 | 180.7 | 216.8 | 223.3 | 297.8 | 991.6 | 857.4 | 1 401.1 | 1 321.3 | 861.8 |
| Belgium | 5.9 | 1.8 | 3.0 | 4.2 | 4.5 | 76.9 | 82.8 | 78.6 | 119.0 | 77.0 |
| France | 18.3 | 20.1 | 18.5 | 22.7 | 27.6 | 108.9 | 58.5 | 129.8 | 157.9 | 81.5 |
| Germany | 30.0 | 29.0 | 32.6 | 34.4 | 54.6 | 90.9 | 93.1 | 121.9 | 138.1 | 106.7 |
| Netherlands | 5.8 | 5.6 | 6.8 | 8.9 | 20.7 | 143.5 | 166.1 | 234.6 | 228.7 | 120.8 |
| United Kingdom | 48.8 | 54.5 | 66.0 | 68.1 | 84.2 | 129.3 | 114.1 | 186.5 | 201.9 | 215.7 |
| Turkey | 0.9 | 0.1 | 0.4 | 0.3 | 1.4 | 173.5 | 79.4 | 109.7 | 128.7 | 70.5 |
| Former Soviet Republics | 0.7 | 2.2 | 0.8 | 0.3 | 0.2 | 30.7 | 18.6 | 15.3 | 18.9 | 9.0 |
| Poland | 0.1 | 0.1 | 0.4 | 0.4 | 0.3 | 0.3 | 1.7 | 0.3 | 3.9 | 1.2 |
| Other Eastern Europe | 0.1 | 0.1 | 0.5 | 0.7 | 1.0 | 13.1 | 4.7 | 19.4 | 39.9 | 27.3 |
| Other Europe | 52.8 | 67.1 | 87.9 | 83.3 | 103.2 | 224.4 | 238.2 | 505.0 | 284.3 | 152.0 |
| Asia | 151.8 | 196.0 | 238.0 | 323.7 | 361.9 | 1 138.0 | 1 166.3 | 1 793.5 | 1 392.6 | 1 073.8 |
| Japan | 95.1 | 122.3 | 147.0 | 188.9 | 208.1 | 405.5 | 441.2 | 484.8 | 309.8 | 265.8 |
| China | 4.2 | 9.9 | 5.7 | 10.8 | 4.8 | 57.9 | 67.0 | 150.2 | 131.0 | 96.4 |
| Hong Kong | 7.9 | 8.6 | 14.4 | 29.4 | 32.2 | 40.6 | 51.3 | 87.6 | 81.2 | 45.0 |
| Taiwan | 12.4 | 13.6 | 17.2 | 23.2 | 18.8 | 133.6 | 99.7 | 207.5 | 120.1 | 98.5 |
| Singapore | 10.1 | 9.8 | 13.6 | 15.5 | 23.1 | 48.3 | 44.6 | 68.7 | 54.7 | 32.1 |
| South Korea | 9.1 | 18.0 | 23.1 | 21.6 | 35.8 | 271.3 | 271.8 | 368.9 | 359.3 | 285.3 |
| Indonesia | 0.2 | 0.6 | 0.5 | 0.2 | 0.5 | 62.1 | 58.9 | 83.6 | 91.0 | 83.4 |
| India | 2.4 | 0.6 | 1.8 | 3.5 | 3.3 | 32.5 | 45.4 | 119.4 | 43.1 | 48.1 |
| Other Asia | 10.4 | 12.7 | 14.6 | 30.6 | 35.2 | 86.3 | 86.5 | 222.8 | 202.4 | 119.0 |
| Africa | 1.8 | 1.3 | 1.5 | 1.3 | 1.5 | 282.4 | 274.0 | 310.0 | 298.1 | 167.5 |
| North Africa | 0.5 | 0.3 | 0.3 | 0.2 | 0.1 | 218.8 | 238.5 | 232.6 | 180.0 | 73.9 |
| Republic of South Africa | 1.2 | 0.7 | 0.9 | 1.1 | 1.3 | 20.3 | 23.8 | 36.5 | 65.4 | 21.4 |
| Other Subsaharan Africa | 0.1 | 0.2 | 0.3 | ..... | 0.1 | 43.3 | 11.7 | 40.9 | 52.8 | 72.2 |
| Middle East | 1.8 | 3.6 | 3.6 | 3.5 | 6.4 | 35.9 | 37.8 | 88.7 | 96.7 | 84.3 |
| Australia | 10.5 | 16.0 | 15.2 | 12.3 | 16.9 | 29.7 | 34.7 | 42.7 | 45.5 | 32.0 |
| Rest of World | ..... | ..... | ..... | ..... | ..... | ..... | ..... | ..... | ..... | 1.9 |

## Table E-3. Metropolitan Area Exports of Goods by Destination, 1993–1997—*Continued*

(Millions of dollars.)

| Destination | 1993 | 1994 | 1995 | 1996 | 1997 | 1993 | 1994 | 1995 | 1996 | 1997 |
|---|---|---|---|---|---|---|---|---|---|---|
| | St. Louis, MO - IL | | | | | Stockton - Lodi, CA | | | | |
| **ALL DESTINATIONS** | 3 400.0 | 3 673.3 | 3 997.7 | 4 497.4 | 4 711.5 | 287.5 | 320.3 | 355.7 | 357.8 | 341.6 |
| **North America** | 997.2 | 1 272.7 | 1 194.2 | 1 265.6 | 1 314.9 | 105.8 | 107.7 | 107.1 | 109.3 | 92.4 |
| Canada | 662.1 | 837.3 | 783.9 | 724.8 | 789.5 | 98.5 | 98.2 | 99.7 | 96.4 | 80.9 |
| Mexico | 335.1 | 435.5 | 410.3 | 540.8 | 525.3 | 7.3 | 9.5 | 7.4 | 13.0 | 11.5 |
| **Caribbean and Central America** | 137.7 | 133.0 | 143.8 | 187.1 | 229.1 | 0.9 | 1.2 | 1.1 | 2.0 | 2.2 |
| **South America** | 329.4 | 319.2 | 398.0 | 487.3 | 458.3 | 5.4 | 6.6 | 11.2 | 8.0 | 22.0 |
| Argentina | 46.5 | 62.7 | 64.1 | 100.1 | 94.3 | 0.3 | 0.4 | 0.4 | 0.4 | 0.6 |
| Brazil | 91.4 | 98.7 | 133.3 | 153.0 | 173.3 | ..... | 0.4 | 0.6 | 0.4 | 11.9 |
| Other South America | 191.5 | 157.8 | 200.6 | 234.2 | 190.6 | 5.1 | 5.8 | 10.2 | 7.2 | 9.6 |
| **Europe** | 984.0 | 1 010.4 | 1 219.9 | 1 347.4 | 1 529.5 | 90.0 | 103.8 | 124.4 | 129.6 | 112.2 |
| Belgium | 271.0 | 251.9 | 328.8 | 342.6 | 376.0 | 1.5 | 2.8 | 5.4 | 1.9 | 2.0 |
| France | 58.2 | 65.7 | 84.1 | 68.0 | 69.5 | 11.3 | 7.8 | 11.8 | 9.3 | 7.2 |
| Germany | 70.5 | 71.0 | 99.0 | 81.8 | 100.5 | 26.0 | 26.3 | 24.5 | 18.0 | 20.9 |
| Netherlands | 115.1 | 137.3 | 120.7 | 131.1 | 129.5 | 5.3 | 6.3 | 9.0 | 11.7 | 9.9 |
| United Kingdom | 242.1 | 222.5 | 155.6 | 148.9 | 187.7 | 17.6 | 10.9 | 15.4 | 13.7 | 18.2 |
| Turkey | 2.7 | 0.7 | 9.1 | 3.9 | 25.5 | 0.5 | 0.4 | 1.5 | 1.2 | 0.7 |
| Former Soviet Republics | 73.6 | 9.9 | 7.2 | 6.1 | 32.7 | 0.4 | 2.4 | 0.1 | 2.0 | 1.3 |
| Poland | 0.6 | 3.2 | 5.0 | 10.0 | 13.6 | 0.1 | ..... | 0.3 | 0.1 | ..... |
| Other Eastern Europe | 6.2 | 5.3 | 13.5 | 18.9 | 8.6 | 0.6 | 1.0 | 0.6 | 2.1 | 0.5 |
| Other Europe | 143.9 | 242.9 | 396.9 | 536.1 | 585.8 | 26.7 | 45.8 | 55.9 | 69.7 | 51.5 |
| **Asia** | 706.9 | 730.1 | 806.6 | 927.0 | 947.4 | 70.8 | 78.4 | 92.5 | 88.6 | 86.4 |
| Japan | 212.1 | 193.1 | 201.8 | 196.8 | 220.0 | 33.8 | 42.5 | 44.5 | 45.8 | 32.4 |
| China | 48.4 | 39.6 | 48.7 | 106.1 | 108.4 | 5.1 | 0.3 | 0.8 | 0.6 | 8.8 |
| Hong Kong | 43.1 | 60.8 | 94.4 | 72.7 | 56.0 | 4.7 | 10.3 | 12.0 | 12.8 | 10.8 |
| Taiwan | 66.6 | 111.1 | 93.4 | 145.3 | 141.6 | 1.9 | 3.8 | 7.8 | 5.1 | 6.1 |
| Singapore | 81.7 | 71.5 | 90.6 | 90.5 | 89.2 | 1.7 | 5.6 | 9.7 | 4.9 | 7.6 |
| South Korea | 84.5 | 85.6 | 103.0 | 124.9 | 121.5 | 6.1 | 5.0 | 6.0 | 7.2 | 6.8 |
| Indonesia | 22.9 | 21.2 | 23.4 | 45.5 | 46.5 | 0.3 | 0.2 | 0.3 | 0.1 | 0.1 |
| India | 12.1 | 18.6 | 17.3 | 21.0 | 19.2 | 1.2 | 2.9 | 1.4 | 1.6 | 6.9 |
| Other Asia | 135.4 | 128.5 | 133.9 | 124.2 | 145.0 | 16.1 | 7.7 | 10.0 | 10.5 | 6.9 |
| **Africa** | 102.9 | 37.1 | 57.6 | 79.2 | 48.0 | 0.7 | 2.5 | 2.0 | 1.9 | 2.7 |
| North Africa | 78.8 | 27.1 | 43.8 | 59.0 | 17.1 | 0.3 | 1.8 | 1.7 | 1.4 | 1.7 |
| Republic of South Africa | 10.9 | 8.4 | 10.4 | 13.3 | 21.0 | 0.3 | 0.4 | 0.2 | 0.1 | 0.4 |
| Other Subsaharan Africa | 13.2 | 1.6 | 3.4 | 6.9 | 9.9 | 0.1 | 0.2 | 0.1 | 0.3 | 0.6 |
| **Middle East** | 57.6 | 74.6 | 67.2 | 68.6 | 61.6 | 11.3 | 15.8 | 12.7 | 12.8 | 17.9 |
| **Australia** | 84.4 | 89.5 | 107.3 | 135.2 | 122.7 | 2.6 | 4.5 | 4.5 | 5.6 | 5.7 |
| **Rest of World** | ..... | 6.7 | 3.1 | ..... | ..... | ..... | ..... | ..... | ..... | ..... |
| | Syracuse, NY | | | | | Tacoma, WA | | | | |
| **ALL DESTINATIONS** | 1 374.1 | 1 600.9 | 1 894.3 | 1 665.5 | 1 846.7 | 1 115.3 | 774.9 | 1 098.9 | 1 179.7 | 1 403.8 |
| **North America** | 704.0 | 781.9 | 943.8 | 859.1 | 908.3 | 103.1 | 128.5 | 142.2 | 172.3 | 202.3 |
| Canada | 648.9 | 711.8 | 912.6 | 822.1 | 866.6 | 92.6 | 114.4 | 125.3 | 149.7 | 176.8 |
| Mexico | 55.2 | 70.1 | 31.2 | 37.1 | 41.7 | 10.5 | 14.0 | 16.9 | 22.6 | 25.5 |
| **Caribbean and Central America** | 5.7 | 7.1 | 9.6 | 8.7 | 8.3 | 3.3 | 2.0 | 3.6 | 5.7 | 2.1 |
| **South America** | 27.0 | 38.0 | 34.5 | 39.4 | 60.2 | 4.2 | 4.5 | 7.7 | 12.8 | 27.4 |
| Argentina | 7.7 | 13.5 | 6.1 | 6.2 | 11.9 | 0.9 | 1.1 | 3.4 | 7.4 | 9.4 |
| Brazil | 11.8 | 10.2 | 17.3 | 21.3 | 34.4 | 0.1 | 0.3 | 1.0 | 1.9 | 10.5 |
| Other South America | 7.5 | 14.3 | 11.2 | 11.9 | 13.8 | 3.2 | 3.1 | 3.3 | 3.5 | 7.5 |
| **Europe** | 261.2 | 352.7 | 384.4 | 257.1 | 345.4 | 129.5 | 127.2 | 303.4 | 304.5 | 316.6 |
| Belgium | 5.2 | 5.1 | 6.8 | 5.5 | 7.7 | 10.1 | 5.6 | 17.4 | 15.6 | 25.9 |
| France | 29.5 | 30.9 | 23.8 | 19.4 | 26.6 | 25.6 | 24.1 | 54.8 | 46.3 | 39.0 |
| Germany | 39.2 | 64.7 | 58.9 | 36.9 | 44.6 | 48.3 | 26.2 | 77.2 | 88.2 | 86.6 |
| Netherlands | 16.2 | 17.8 | 29.3 | 20.7 | 17.6 | 1.6 | 3.4 | 14.8 | 8.0 | 12.3 |
| United Kingdom | 57.6 | 46.1 | 69.6 | 59.3 | 78.1 | 9.8 | 24.7 | 50.7 | 48.5 | 40.0 |
| Turkey | 3.9 | 25.7 | 3.6 | 2.9 | 6.3 | 2.0 | 2.4 | 6.7 | 6.4 | 10.1 |
| Former Soviet Republics | 0.2 | 1.1 | 4.8 | 1.8 | 0.8 | 0.6 | 0.8 | 1.4 | 2.2 | 4.9 |
| Poland | 0.9 | 0.9 | 1.9 | 1.0 | 2.6 | ..... | ..... | 0.5 | 4.0 | 6.7 |
| Other Eastern Europe | 0.7 | 1.0 | 2.2 | 1.7 | 1.6 | 0.1 | 0.2 | 0.3 | 0.5 | 1.2 |
| Other Europe | 107.7 | 159.4 | 183.5 | 107.7 | 159.5 | 31.3 | 39.7 | 79.5 | 84.8 | 89.9 |
| **Asia** | 317.8 | 353.8 | 396.8 | 377.1 | 392.5 | 827.8 | 489.1 | 615.2 | 662.7 | 828.9 |
| Japan | 86.1 | 49.3 | 40.6 | 47.0 | 84.3 | 596.4 | 294.6 | 320.6 | 375.5 | 526.5 |
| China | 21.6 | 19.3 | 32.8 | 29.1 | 47.6 | 46.3 | 17.7 | 40.7 | 47.4 | 47.6 |
| Hong Kong | 30.0 | 25.8 | 51.2 | 67.6 | 47.8 | 10.4 | 10.1 | 22.8 | 27.9 | 20.0 |
| Taiwan | 16.0 | 15.7 | 13.8 | 6.8 | 16.4 | 25.3 | 20.3 | 36.1 | 33.8 | 35.9 |
| Singapore | 27.2 | 77.8 | 47.8 | 52.4 | 63.9 | 8.4 | 5.7 | 7.1 | 8.8 | 23.6 |
| South Korea | 104.0 | 134.6 | 154.9 | 122.5 | 86.6 | 115.1 | 117.2 | 151.0 | 106.7 | 123.5 |
| Indonesia | 4.7 | 3.9 | 7.3 | 2.0 | 2.4 | 1.3 | 2.9 | 6.9 | 11.9 | 14.2 |
| India | 1.9 | 2.5 | 4.6 | 7.3 | 2.4 | 0.8 | 0.8 | 1.3 | 5.1 | 3.8 |
| Other Asia | 26.5 | 24.8 | 43.6 | 42.5 | 41.1 | 23.7 | 19.8 | 28.8 | 45.6 | 33.8 |
| **Africa** | 9.8 | 5.7 | 10.3 | 6.7 | 12.3 | 5.0 | 6.8 | 6.5 | 5.9 | 4.6 |
| North Africa | 7.0 | 1.6 | 1.8 | 1.0 | 6.6 | ..... | 0.2 | 0.2 | 0.6 | 0.2 |
| Republic of South Africa | 2.5 | 3.2 | 6.8 | 4.4 | 4.7 | 3.2 | 4.9 | 5.0 | 4.2 | 3.4 |
| Other Subsaharan Africa | 0.3 | 0.9 | 1.6 | 1.3 | 1.0 | 1.7 | 1.6 | 1.3 | 1.1 | 1.0 |
| **Middle East** | 36.8 | 40.3 | 19.1 | 50.0 | 53.1 | 14.4 | 13.6 | 17.1 | 13.0 | 12.6 |
| **Australia** | 11.9 | 21.5 | 95.7 | 67.2 | 66.6 | 28.0 | 3.3 | 3.3 | 2.9 | 9.4 |
| **Rest of World** | ..... | ..... | ..... | ..... | ..... | ..... | ..... | ..... | ..... | ..... |

## Table E-3. Metropolitan Area Exports of Goods by Destination, 1993–1997—*Continued*

(Millions of dollars.)

| Destination | 1993 | 1994 | 1995 | 1996 | 1997 | 1993 | 1994 | 1995 | 1996 | 1997 |
|---|---|---|---|---|---|---|---|---|---|---|
| | Tampa - St. Petersburg - Clearwater, FL | | | | | Toledo, OH | | | | |
| ALL DESTINATIONS | 1 295.7 | 1 835.8 | 2 116.1 | 1 921.8 | 2 273.8 | 836.1 | 986.9 | 1 177.7 | 1 207.5 | 1 261.1 |
| North America | 298.6 | 345.1 | 344.9 | 391.0 | 452.4 | 457.0 | 586.8 | 785.8 | 729.8 | 891.0 |
| Canada | 262.5 | 284.0 | 271.9 | 279.2 | 325.8 | 411.7 | 536.1 | 742.6 | 693.6 | 803.4 |
| Mexico | 36.1 | 61.1 | 73.0 | 111.8 | 126.7 | 45.3 | 50.7 | 43.1 | 36.2 | 87.7 |
| Caribbean and Central America | 140.3 | 164.4 | 164.8 | 194.4 | 213.6 | 7.3 | 10.7 | 12.7 | 13.1 | 11.8 |
| South America | 112.9 | 160.6 | 176.7 | 187.3 | 215.4 | 38.0 | 53.6 | 63.2 | 67.3 | 61.8 |
| Argentina | 12.0 | 19.2 | 41.4 | 40.7 | 44.7 | 4.3 | 8.7 | 5.2 | 7.0 | 4.2 |
| Brazil | 39.1 | 73.0 | 54.7 | 67.5 | 79.0 | 2.7 | 9.8 | 12.7 | 14.3 | 20.4 |
| Other South America | 61.8 | 68.4 | 80.5 | 79.1 | 91.7 | 31.0 | 35.0 | 45.3 | 46.1 | 37.2 |
| Europe | 265.4 | 279.7 | 343.3 | 328.5 | 471.7 | 112.8 | 128.6 | 151.5 | 183.6 | 133.4 |
| Belgium | 9.5 | 5.7 | 14.8 | 7.3 | 17.7 | 29.7 | 37.3 | 41.1 | 58.8 | 51.3 |
| France | 29.9 | 42.4 | 42.7 | 33.7 | 38.1 | 8.5 | 8.3 | 6.8 | 8.3 | 6.8 |
| Germany | 46.6 | 51.3 | 65.9 | 74.5 | 67.5 | 8.4 | 10.9 | 16.1 | 11.0 | 10.2 |
| Netherlands | 29.0 | 30.8 | 35.8 | 63.1 | 105.1 | 5.5 | 6.2 | 11.3 | 10.4 | 8.8 |
| United Kingdom | 64.9 | 61.5 | 65.2 | 59.6 | 86.6 | 26.7 | 29.3 | 44.6 | 42.8 | 28.2 |
| Turkey | 6.6 | 3.5 | 14.4 | 6.7 | 23.8 | 1.2 | 0.8 | 1.1 | 3.0 | 3.3 |
| Former Soviet Republics | 1.5 | 5.9 | 4.0 | 5.1 | 28.7 | 0.2 | 0.2 | 0.5 | 1.5 | 0.8 |
| Poland | 0.5 | 0.6 | 0.8 | 0.7 | 2.1 | 0.7 | 5.4 | 6.6 | 3.9 | 4.3 |
| Other Eastern Europe | 1.3 | 4.2 | 3.5 | 3.4 | 7.8 | 1.6 | 0.4 | 1.1 | 1.4 | 0.6 |
| Other Europe | .75.6 | 73.8 | 96.2 | 74.4 | 94.1 | 30.4 | 29.8 | 22.2 | 42.6 | 19.0 |
| Asia | 323.2 | 708.1 | 826.5 | 537.2 | 700.1 | 95.8 | 105.7 | 115.6 | 142.7 | 108.6 |
| Japan | 27.2 | 33.7 | 108.2 | 62.2 | 66.8 | 30.5 | 40.2 | 27.8 | 28.4 | 30.8 |
| China | 125.5 | 447.9 | 466.2 | 226.2 | 304.6 | 17.0 | 9.2 | 18.2 | 21.1 | 6.8 |
| Hong Kong | 12.3 | 21.3 | 20.9 | 25.2 | 26.4 | 5.1 | 6.1 | 9.1 | 13.4 | 7.1 |
| Taiwan | 16.8 | 63.6 | 15.3 | 17.7 | 22.2 | 5.9 | 9.5 | 8.3 | 7.3 | 9.2 |
| Singapore | 7.8 | 9.7 | 10.2 | 15.1 | 21.9 | 6.2 | 6.6 | 5.9 | 7.7 | 7.0 |
| South Korea | 8.6 | 6.1 | 13.6 | 13.4 | 21.3 | 17.6 | 22.8 | 22.7 | 36.5 | 22.7 |
| Indonesia | 15.8 | 9.4 | 1.3 | 16.9 | 2.7 | 1.8 | 1.3 | 9.1 | 9.2 | 0.8 |
| India | 66.8 | 36.5 | 119.6 | 36.9 | 135.8 | 1.4 | 1.0 | 3.1 | 7.4 | 13.5 |
| Other Asia | 42.4 | 79.9 | 71.4 | 123.4 | 98.3 | 10.3 | 8.9 | 11.4 | 11.7 | 10.6 |
| Africa | 32.5 | 20.0 | 77.3 | 50.4 | 36.6 | 7.9 | 12.3 | 7.7 | 13.5 | 6.6 |
| North Africa | 23.5 | 12.0 | 62.3 | 36.6 | 23.7 | 4.3 | 7.0 | 1.0 | 0.7 | 0.5 |
| Republic of South Africa | 4.5 | 5.5 | 8.7 | 6.6 | 11.1 | 3.5 | 4.6 | 6.1 | 10.6 | 5.7 |
| Other Subsaharan Africa | 4.5 | 2.5 | 6.3 | 7.3 | 1.9 | 0.1 | 0.7 | 0.5 | 2.2 | 0.3 |
| Middle East | 41.9 | 38.1 | 49.4 | 25.9 | 29.2 | 22.7 | 12.7 | 16.0 | 33.5 | 23.4 |
| Australia | 81.0 | 119.8 | 133.2 | 207.1 | 154.8 | 43.5 | 25.5 | 12.2 | 16.1 | 18.3 |
| Rest of World | ..... | ..... | ..... | ..... | ..... | 51.2 | 51.1 | 13.1 | 7.8 | 6.2 |
| | Topeka, KS | | | | | Trenton, NJ | | | | |
| ALL DESTINATIONS | 121.1 | 125.2 | 133.0 | 130.2 | 140.7 | 223.8 | 237.5 | 392.5 | 267.8 | 343.4 |
| North America | 20.2 | 19.5 | 14.1 | 21.9 | 33.5 | 89.0 | 104.3 | 104.2 | 122.2 | 197.9 |
| Canada | 19.1 | 18.5 | 13.1 | 20.4 | 32.1 | 71.3 | 85.6 | 92.4 | 107.9 | 178.7 |
| Mexico | 1.1 | 1.0 | 1.0 | 1.5 | 1.4 | 17.7 | 18.7 | 11.8 | 14.3 | 19.2 |
| Caribbean and Central America | 0.5 | 0.7 | 0.4 | 0.6 | 0.8 | 3.2 | 3.9 | 3.0 | 1.4 | 1.9 |
| South America | 0.4 | 0.7 | 3.1 | 3.1 | 4.4 | 18.3 | 14.5 | 16.8 | 25.0 | 11.4 |
| Argentina | 0.1 | 0.4 | 0.7 | 1.3 | 0.5 | 1.5 | 2.9 | 1.1 | 0.6 | 0.7 |
| Brazil | ..... | ..... | 0.7 | 0.1 | 0.8 | 7.4 | 7.6 | 11.5 | 13.5 | 5.9 |
| Other South America | 0.3 | 0.3 | 1.8 | 1.7 | 3.1 | 9.4 | 4.0 | 4.2 | 10.9 | 4.8 |
| Europe | 45.2 | 53.6 | 51.0 | 56.4 | 26.5 | 48.5 | 49.6 | 70.6 | 65.5 | 81.3 |
| Belgium | 0.3 | 0.1 | 2.3 | 13.6 | 13.7 | 1.4 | 1.4 | 0.9 | 1.4 | 2.3 |
| France | 8.2 | 8.5 | 8.7 | 6.4 | 0.3 | 6.0 | 5.4 | 7.1 | 11.2 | 14.7 |
| Germany | 3.8 | 4.5 | 5.8 | 5.8 | 0.6 | 11.7 | 12.7 | 13.2 | 13.9 | 10.8 |
| Netherlands | 5.8 | 5.3 | 3.9 | 1.3 | 0.8 | 2.0 | 2.3 | 15.4 | 16.4 | 22.9 |
| United Kingdom | 12.7 | 18.1 | 14.2 | 14.7 | 5.0 | 10.6 | 11.0 | 11.8 | 9.1 | 13.5 |
| Turkey | ..... | ..... | 0.1 | 0.3 | 0.2 | 0.1 | 0.1 | 0.3 | 0.6 | 0.7 |
| Former Soviet Republics | ..... | 0.3 | 0.1 | ..... | ..... | 0.3 | 0.2 | 0.6 | 0.6 | 0.3 |
| Poland | ..... | ..... | 0.1 | 0.1 | ..... | 0.3 | 0.2 | 0.7 | 0.5 | 0.5 |
| Other Eastern Europe | 0.1 | 0.3 | 0.4 | 0.1 | ..... | 0.6 | 0.7 | 1.7 | 1.1 | 1.9 |
| Other Europe | 14.2 | 16.5 | 15.4 | 14.3 | 5.9 | 15.4 | 15.5 | 19.0 | 10.9 | 13.7 |
| Asia | 54.2 | 48.5 | 60.9 | 43.8 | 69.2 | 55.7 | 57.2 | 191.2 | 44.0 | 43.1 |
| Japan | 48.0 | 43.7 | 53.0 | 35.4 | 59.8 | 6.5 | 9.3 | 12.5 | 11.6 | 11.2 |
| China | 0.3 | ..... | ..... | 0.4 | 0.4 | 5.5 | 8.8 | 137.4 | 2.7 | 6.1 |
| Hong Kong | 1.2 | 1.0 | 1.4 | 1.1 | 1.9 | 6.2 | 5.8 | 5.3 | 2.4 | 2.5 |
| Taiwan | 1.8 | 1.1 | 2.2 | 2.5 | 2.1 | 5.0 | 14.6 | 5.0 | 2.8 | 3.2 |
| Singapore | 0.4 | 0.3 | 0.4 | 0.7 | 0.7 | 10.6 | 2.1 | 3.5 | 1.4 | 1.8 |
| South Korea | 0.5 | 0.3 | 0.3 | 0.5 | 0.6 | 4.3 | 4.0 | 5.9 | 4.1 | 3.8 |
| Indonesia | 0.3 | 0.4 | 0.1 | ..... | 0.1 | 2.6 | 2.8 | 3.7 | 4.3 | 1.7 |
| India | ..... | ..... | ..... | 0.1 | 0.3 | 2.0 | 3.3 | 7.8 | 4.0 | 1.7 |
| Other Asia | 1.5 | 1.6 | 3.4 | 3.2 | 3.3 | 13.0 | 6.4 | 10.1 | 10.8 | 11.1 |
| Africa | ..... | 0.2 | 0.4 | 1.5 | 2.7 | 3.1 | 3.7 | 2.1 | 2.7 | 2.0 |
| North Africa | ..... | ..... | ..... | 0.1 | 0.2 | 0.5 | 1.2 | 0.3 | 0.9 | 0.8 |
| Republic of South Africa | ..... | 0.2 | 0.4 | 1.3 | 2.5 | 1.6 | 1.4 | 1.0 | 0.6 | 0.6 |
| Other Subsaharan Africa | ..... | ..... | ..... | ..... | 0.1 | 1.0 | 1.2 | 0.8 | 1.2 | 0.7 |
| Middle East | 0.1 | 0.1 | 0.6 | 1.0 | 0.8 | 3.7 | 3.0 | 2.8 | 3.2 | 3.8 |
| Australia | 0.6 | 2.0 | 2.3 | 1.9 | 2.6 | 2.3 | 1.3 | 1.7 | 3.9 | 2.0 |
| Rest of World | ..... | ..... | ..... | ..... | ..... | ..... | ..... | ..... | ..... | ..... |

## Table E-3. Metropolitan Area Exports of Goods by Destination, 1993–1997—Continued

(Millions of dollars.)

| Destination | 1993 | 1994 | 1995 | 1996 | 1997 | 1993 | 1994 | 1995 | 1996 | 1997 |
|---|---|---|---|---|---|---|---|---|---|---|
| | Tucson, AZ | | | | | Utica - Rome, NY | | | | |
| ALL DESTINATIONS | 487.1 | 638.1 | 671.7 | 800.1 | 1 060.5 | 188.3 | 269.3 | 238.0 | 278.0 | 238.8 |
| North America | 289.2 | 385.1 | 387.4 | 470.5 | 621.2 | 57.5 | 69.0 | 68.8 | 120.9 | 106.4 |
| Canada | 49.5 | 89.5 | 83.6 | 134.1 | 129.8 | 55.4 | 65.2 | 65.9 | 116.8 | 103.6 |
| Mexico | 239.7 | 295.6 | 303.8 | 336.4 | 491.4 | 2.1 | 3.7 | 2.9 | 4.2 | 2.8 |
| Caribbean and Central America | 7.3 | 4.4 | 1.9 | 1.3 | 1.6 | 0.6 | 0.6 | 1.5 | 1.4 | 1.5 |
| South America | 4.5 | 9.9 | 8.4 | 14.2 | 46.3 | 2.0 | 1.9 | 1.6 | 3.4 | 2.5 |
| Argentina | 0.6 | 1.0 | 0.9 | 1.0 | 5.6 | 0.5 | 0.4 | 0.1 | 0.3 | 0.7 |
| Brazil | 0.2 | 0.9 | 1.7 | 2.0 | 25.3 | 0.4 | 0.5 | 0.4 | 2.5 | 0.7 |
| Other South America | 3.7 | 8.0 | 5.8 | 11.1 | 15.4 | 1.1 | 1.0 | 1.1 | 0.6 | 1.0 |
| Europe | 99.6 | 133.4 | 149.4 | 161.9 | 194.1 | 66.2 | 114.1 | 89.1 | 93.1 | 85.7 |
| Belgium | 1.1 | 0.8 | 3.0 | 2.4 | 1.7 | 1.6 | 1.5 | 2.1 | 14.1 | 2.4 |
| France | 9.4 | 16.3 | 30.3 | 23.7 | 27.5 | 7.9 | 9.5 | 25.3 | 11.6 | 14.6 |
| Germany | 29.6 | 46.4 | 50.4 | 57.0 | 48.6 | 3.5 | 5.4 | 7.1 | 5.8 | 5.6 |
| Netherlands | 8.3 | 6.9 | 6.9 | 5.5 | 26.1 | 2.9 | 5.5 | 2.1 | 1.6 | 1.4 |
| United Kingdom | 21.0 | 22.9 | 25.7 | 32.8 | 37.3 | 41.1 | 77.7 | 38.9 | 46.9 | 47.6 |
| Turkey | 0.9 | 0.6 | 0.5 | 0.2 | 0.3 | 0.1 | 0.1 | 0.2 | 0.7 | 0.7 |
| Former Soviet Republics | 1.6 | 0.9 | 0.6 | 0.6 | 0.4 | 0.1 | ..... | 0.9 | 0.4 | 0.1 |
| Poland | 0.2 | 0.1 | 0.6 | 1.1 | 0.5 | ..... | 0.1 | 0.3 | 0.3 | 0.7 |
| Other Eastern Europe | 0.3 | 0.2 | 0.2 | 0.7 | 1.2 | 0.1 | 0.4 | 0.4 | 0.9 | 0.3 |
| Other Europe | 27.2 | 38.3 | 31.0 | 38.0 | 50.6 | 8.9 | 14.0 | 11.9 | 10.9 | 12.3 |
| Asia | 71.6 | 86.6 | 109.8 | 126.8 | 156.8 | 54.3 | 76.5 | 64.5 | 46.4 | 34.4 |
| Japan | 39.1 | 46.8 | 59.1 | 53.4 | 64.0 | 5.4 | 6.0 | 10.1 | 11.2 | 10.2 |
| China | 1.1 | 1.7 | 0.9 | 1.0 | 2.2 | 1.3 | 1.4 | 0.9 | 2.8 | 2.1 |
| Hong Kong | 3.5 | 4.7 | 4.4 | 4.9 | 9.5 | 1.0 | 1.5 | 1.2 | 1.0 | 1.6 |
| Taiwan | 13.6 | 18.7 | 28.3 | 35.8 | 40.8 | 42.9 | 61.1 | 39.2 | 16.6 | 3.1 |
| Singapore | 3.4 | 2.9 | 3.1 | 9.9 | 7.3 | 0.9 | 1.7 | 4.2 | 6.3 | 6.3 |
| South Korea | 2.5 | 2.5 | 2.3 | 6.8 | 5.4 | 1.9 | 3.1 | 4.8 | 3.9 | 5.9 |
| Indonesia | 0.1 | 0.5 | 1.2 | 1.2 | 0.8 | 0.1 | ..... | 0.1 | 0.5 | 0.2 |
| India | 0.7 | 1.8 | 1.1 | 1.3 | 0.7 | 0.1 | 0.2 | 1.0 | 0.8 | 1.2 |
| Other Asia | 7.5 | 6.9 | 9.4 | 12.6 | 26.0 | 0.8 | 1.5 | 3.0 | 3.2 | 3.7 |
| Africa | 1.1 | 2.7 | 3.8 | 1.8 | 16.8 | 1.0 | 0.9 | 1.4 | 1.8 | 0.9 |
| North Africa | 0.2 | 0.3 | 0.2 | 0.1 | 0.5 | 0.6 | 0.1 | 0.2 | 0.5 | 0.5 |
| Republic of South Africa | 0.6 | 1.9 | 2.4 | 1.5 | 10.0 | 0.4 | 0.7 | 1.2 | 1.3 | 0.4 |
| Other Subsaharan Africa | 0.3 | 0.6 | 1.3 | 0.2 | 6.4 | ..... | ..... | ..... | ..... | ..... |
| Middle East | 6.7 | 5.7 | 3.7 | 4.8 | 4.8 | 5.0 | 3.4 | 8.9 | 9.2 | 5.4 |
| Australia | 7.1 | 10.4 | 7.3 | 18.9 | 18.7 | 1.7 | 2.9 | 2.2 | 1.7 | 2.1 |
| Rest of World | ..... | ..... | ..... | ..... | ..... | ..... | ..... | ..... | ..... | ..... |
| | Vallejo - Fairfield - Napa, CA | | | | | Ventura, CA | | | | |
| ALL DESTINATIONS | 171.7 | 264.0 | 238.1 | 278.0 | 384.9 | 640.3 | 698.7 | 953.4 | 967.3 | 1 128.9 |
| North America | 58.0 | 46.1 | 46.5 | 56.1 | 115.4 | 145.6 | 153.1 | 160.9 | 168.7 | 211.0 |
| Canada | 55.2 | 43.7 | 45.3 | 55.0 | 106.0 | 98.4 | 110.8 | 118.7 | 133.2 | 171.7 |
| Mexico | 2.8 | 2.4 | 1.2 | 1.1 | 9.4 | 47.2 | 42.3 | 42.1 | 35.5 | 39.3 |
| Caribbean and Central America | 1.3 | 1.6 | 1.0 | 1.6 | 1.6 | 7.4 | 8.3 | 11.0 | 15.0 | 18.0 |
| South America | 1.6 | 2.3 | 5.8 | 7.3 | 36.3 | 23.1 | 31.0 | 39.6 | 38.0 | 54.5 |
| Argentina | 0.2 | 0.6 | 1.1 | 0.3 | 18.0 | 5.8 | 7.4 | 8.9 | 5.8 | 7.4 |
| Brazil | 0.1 | 0.7 | 2.6 | 3.3 | 4.0 | 8.7 | 11.0 | 16.0 | 14.3 | 27.1 |
| Other South America | 1.3 | 1.0 | 2.1 | 3.7 | 14.4 | 8.6 | 12.7 | 14.7 | 17.9 | 20.0 |
| Europe | 39.4 | 46.9 | 83.4 | 89.0 | 106.5 | 201.1 | 187.7 | 246.7 | 262.3 | 320.5 |
| Belgium | 1.5 | 2.2 | 15.1 | 4.1 | 4.4 | 1.8 | 4.3 | 33.3 | 20.5 | 19.8 |
| France | 5.3 | 4.7 | 6.9 | 4.3 | 6.6 | 18.8 | 19.5 | 24.3 | 42.4 | 46.9 |
| Germany | 9.8 | 6.7 | 10.4 | 10.9 | 11.8 | 47.3 | 47.4 | 43.8 | 54.0 | 58.6 |
| Netherlands | 4.8 | 4.3 | 7.7 | 10.2 | 12.3 | 20.5 | 13.0 | 15.0 | 16.3 | 15.6 |
| United Kingdom | 7.2 | 10.5 | 14.9 | 26.3 | 26.1 | 51.1 | 49.1 | 53.3 | 53.6 | 75.8 |
| Turkey | 0.1 | 0.5 | 0.3 | 0.5 | 0.3 | 2.6 | 1.3 | 2.2 | 3.0 | 5.9 |
| Former Soviet Republics | 0.1 | 2.2 | 0.1 | 0.2 | 0.2 | 2.8 | 7.9 | 14.3 | 4.8 | 3.2 |
| Poland | 0.2 | 0.4 | 0.3 | 0.5 | 1.1 | 0.5 | 0.3 | 0.3 | 0.3 | 0.4 |
| Other Eastern Europe | 0.8 | 1.0 | 2.5 | 0.9 | 2.1 | 1.0 | 1.1 | 1.9 | 2.7 | 2.1 |
| Other Europe | 9.6 | 14.4 | 25.2 | 30.9 | 41.8 | 54.8 | 43.8 | 58.3 | 64.8 | 92.3 |
| Asia | 64.1 | 136.8 | 89.0 | 101.0 | 106.8 | 217.0 | 271.4 | 421.8 | 411.2 | 450.1 |
| Japan | 19.8 | 17.6 | 44.0 | 46.4 | 43.9 | 58.8 | 75.2 | 111.3 | 131.6 | 142.5 |
| China | 28.7 | 2.0 | 8.2 | 4.9 | 9.4 | 6.4 | 5.7 | 7.1 | 8.2 | 11.9 |
| Hong Kong | 1.9 | 1.7 | 2.9 | 5.0 | 7.0 | 18.1 | 21.8 | 34.7 | 36.8 | 56.9 |
| Taiwan | 2.8 | 3.1 | 9.9 | 14.4 | 23.1 | 20.1 | 18.1 | 28.3 | 43.6 | 51.8 |
| Singapore | 2.0 | 11.6 | 3.8 | 6.9 | 5.0 | 30.5 | 50.6 | 42.2 | 38.7 | 46.4 |
| South Korea | 6.4 | 5.3 | 11.9 | 9.8 | 7.7 | 21.7 | 28.2 | 57.2 | 48.7 | 37.7 |
| Indonesia | 0.1 | 2.8 | 1.2 | 1.9 | 2.1 | 1.7 | 5.6 | 3.2 | 2.4 | 4.2 |
| India | 0.1 | 0.9 | 1.0 | 2.0 | 0.9 | 8.8 | 12.8 | 14.9 | 11.1 | 16.0 |
| Other Asia | 2.2 | 91.9 | 6.1 | 9.8 | 7.7 | 51.0 | 53.6 | 122.9 | 90.0 | 82.8 |
| Africa | 1.2 | 25.2 | 1.5 | 2.4 | 2.4 | 6.9 | 7.7 | 12.0 | 10.0 | 13.1 |
| North Africa | ..... | 23.6 | 0.2 | 0.4 | 0.6 | 2.0 | 2.8 | 4.5 | 3.1 | 5.6 |
| Republic of South Africa | 1.2 | 1.6 | 1.0 | 1.8 | 1.4 | 3.7 | 3.8 | 5.5 | 5.7 | 6.1 |
| Other Subsaharan Africa | ..... | 0.1 | 0.2 | 0.2 | 0.4 | 1.2 | 1.0 | 1.9 | 1.3 | 1.4 |
| Middle East | 2.2 | 1.7 | 3.7 | 12.7 | 3.0 | 14.5 | 15.5 | 24.5 | 17.1 | 18.8 |
| Australia | 3.8 | 3.3 | 7.2 | 7.9 | 12.8 | 24.7 | 24.0 | 36.8 | 45.0 | 42.8 |
| Rest of World | ..... | ..... | ..... | ..... | ..... | ..... | ..... | 0.1 | ..... | ..... |

## Table E-3.  Metropolitan Area Exports of Goods by Destination, 1993–1997—*Continued*

(Millions of dollars.)

| Destination | 1993 | 1994 | 1995 | 1996 | 1997 | 1993 | 1994 | 1995 | 1996 | 1997 |
|---|---|---|---|---|---|---|---|---|---|---|
| | Visalia - Tulare - Porterville, CA | | | | | Washington, DC - MD - VA - WV | | | | |
| **ALL DESTINATIONS** | 119.6 | 107.7 | 120.6 | 143.7 | 160.5 | 7 250.6 | 7 969.3 | 8 350.4 | 8 083.5 | 7 980.7 |
| **North America** | 72.8 | 63.6 | 63.5 | 74.0 | 81.8 | 372.2 | 517.6 | 416.2 | 442.3 | 582.4 |
| Canada | 70.9 | 62.1 | 61.4 | 69.5 | 75.2 | 234.2 | 364.5 | 336.8 | 325.3 | 412.9 |
| Mexico | 1.9 | 1.4 | 2.1 | 4.5 | 6.5 | 138.0 | 153.1 | 79.4 | 117.0 | 169.5 |
| **Caribbean and Central America** | 0.4 | 0.4 | 1.1 | 2.6 | 2.0 | 71.7 | 81.3 | 60.6 | 56.9 | 61.0 |
| **South America** | 0.5 | 1.6 | 2.0 | 3.8 | 6.8 | 269.6 | 333.5 | 203.4 | 240.0 | 361.3 |
| Argentina | 0.1 | 1.1 | ..... | 0.2 | 0.1 | 29.5 | 42.5 | 26.0 | 13.2 | 28.8 |
| Brazil | 0.1 | ..... | 0.8 | 1.5 | 1.0 | 76.3 | 70.9 | 86.3 | 136.7 | 201.1 |
| Other South America | 0.3 | 0.5 | 1.1 | 2.1 | 5.7 | 163.8 | 220.1 | 91.1 | 90.0 | 131.4 |
| **Europe** | 6.1 | 6.5 | 11.6 | 12.1 | 15.5 | 2 461.0 | 2 037.5 | 2 617.4 | 2 770.7 | 2 798.3 |
| Belgium | 1.0 | 1.2 | 1.9 | 1.1 | 1.2 | 81.3 | 86.9 | 87.3 | 85.2 | 122.1 |
| France | 0.5 | 0.3 | 0.9 | 1.0 | 1.6 | 173.5 | 107.5 | 145.5 | 98.9 | 103.3 |
| Germany | 1.0 | 0.8 | 1.6 | 1.5 | 1.7 | 322.9 | 406.0 | 400.0 | 504.0 | 590.4 |
| Netherlands | 0.3 | 0.1 | 0.7 | 0.6 | 0.6 | 42.5 | 37.9 | 53.8 | 64.2 | 47.4 |
| United Kingdom | 0.8 | 1.2 | 1.9 | 2.4 | 2.6 | 594.3 | 652.1 | 565.9 | 769.5 | 661.0 |
| Turkey | 0.5 | 0.1 | 0.4 | 0.1 | 0.7 | 218.8 | 24.0 | 27.0 | 23.9 | 28.5 |
| Former Soviet Republics | ..... | ..... | ..... | ..... | 0.1 | 410.0 | 231.2 | 334.6 | 339.6 | 326.8 |
| Poland | ..... | ..... | ..... | ..... | 0.1 | 19.0 | 9.9 | 11.9 | 15.0 | 16.6 |
| Other Eastern Europe | 0.1 | 0.1 | 0.2 | 0.2 | 0.1 | 27.6 | 28.1 | 39.7 | 52.8 | 32.8 |
| Other Europe | 2.0 | 2.7 | 4.1 | 5.3 | 6.9 | 571.1 | 454.0 | 951.6 | 817.7 | 869.5 |
| **Asia** | 36.7 | 30.9 | 39.1 | 45.4 | 48.0 | 1 916.8 | 2 040.8 | 2 385.1 | 1 981.7 | 2 237.5 |
| Japan | 19.3 | 11.2 | 21.9 | 27.7 | 24.6 | 199.0 | 196.7 | 288.5 | 178.3 | 186.6 |
| China | 0.4 | 0.6 | 0.3 | 0.3 | 0.4 | 71.5 | 40.6 | 54.8 | 71.8 | 62.5 |
| Hong Kong | 10.1 | 9.2 | 8.4 | 7.5 | 7.9 | 44.5 | 27.3 | 49.5 | 50.7 | 44.1 |
| Taiwan | 2.0 | 2.9 | 2.5 | 2.8 | 1.9 | 796.0 | 750.9 | 724.8 | 547.8 | 643.9 |
| Singapore | 1.9 | 0.7 | 1.4 | 1.9 | 2.2 | 116.6 | 56.8 | 77.7 | 55.3 | 63.7 |
| South Korea | 1.2 | 3.3 | 1.1 | 1.6 | 2.5 | 303.5 | 584.2 | 655.4 | 495.1 | 484.0 |
| Indonesia | ..... | ..... | ..... | 0.2 | 0.7 | 24.6 | 14.2 | 75.2 | 80.7 | 92.2 |
| India | ..... | 0.2 | 0.3 | 0.2 | 1.2 | 138.5 | 94.4 | 142.5 | 111.9 | 133.7 |
| Other Asia | 1.8 | 2.7 | 3.3 | 3.2 | 6.7 | 222.8 | 275.6 | 316.7 | 390.2 | 526.9 |
| **Africa** | 0.5 | 2.1 | 0.8 | 0.5 | 1.3 | 942.4 | 1 151.4 | 667.5 | 608.6 | 637.4 |
| North Africa | 0.4 | 1.9 | 0.4 | 0.1 | 0.9 | 783.5 | 930.8 | 493.0 | 429.8 | 538.9 |
| Republic of South Africa | 0.1 | 0.1 | 0.3 | 0.4 | 0.3 | 29.2 | 20.9 | 66.2 | 93.0 | 24.2 |
| Other Subsaharan Africa | ..... | 0.1 | 0.1 | ..... | 0.1 | 129.8 | 199.7 | 108.3 | 85.9 | 74.3 |
| **Middle East** | 0.5 | 0.6 | 0.5 | 1.0 | 0.6 | 1 006.9 | 1 563.5 | 1 720.1 | 1 764.1 | 1 014.9 |
| **Australia** | 2.1 | 2.0 | 2.1 | 4.6 | 4.7 | 210.0 | 243.6 | 280.1 | 219.1 | 287.9 |
| **Rest of World** | ..... | ..... | ..... | ..... | ..... | ..... | ..... | ..... | ..... | ..... |
| | Waterbury, CT | | | | | Waterloo - Cedar Falls, IA | | | | |
| **ALL DESTINATIONS** | 187.5 | 179.6 | 207.6 | 221.6 | 252.0 | 102.7 | 149.7 | 194.6 | 200.9 | 282.8 |
| **North America** | 101.5 | 84.3 | 76.3 | 90.4 | 112.3 | 82.2 | 127.4 | 166.7 | 172.2 | 248.5 |
| Canada | 90.3 | 64.3 | 59.0 | 69.5 | 85.4 | 81.0 | 126.1 | 165.9 | 171.1 | 246.3 |
| Mexico | 11.2 | 20.0 | 17.2 | 20.9 | 26.9 | 1.2 | 1.3 | 0.8 | 1.1 | 2.2 |
| **Caribbean and Central America** | 0.6 | 0.6 | 1.8 | 3.6 | 4.5 | 0.3 | 0.1 | 0.5 | 0.4 | 0.2 |
| **South America** | 6.3 | 8.7 | 12.5 | 12.6 | 14.4 | 1.2 | 1.5 | 3.1 | 2.0 | 4.6 |
| Argentina | 1.5 | 3.4 | 5.3 | 3.9 | 4.6 | 0.3 | 0.4 | 0.3 | 0.3 | 2.9 |
| Brazil | 0.5 | 2.0 | 3.7 | 4.3 | 6.0 | 0.1 | 0.3 | 2.2 | 0.8 | 0.5 |
| Other South America | 4.3 | 3.4 | 3.6 | 4.3 | 3.8 | 0.8 | 0.8 | 0.6 | 0.9 | 1.1 |
| **Europe** | 40.3 | 42.1 | 65.0 | 64.1 | 63.6 | 8.0 | 10.9 | 10.6 | 11.4 | 8.4 |
| Belgium | 0.6 | 1.3 | 8.6 | 9.5 | 12.7 | 0.4 | 0.6 | 1.6 | 1.2 | 2.0 |
| France | 4.1 | 5.3 | 8.7 | 5.9 | 4.7 | 0.7 | 1.3 | 0.3 | 1.1 | 0.2 |
| Germany | 7.2 | 6.3 | 9.8 | 9.2 | 9.5 | 0.3 | 0.7 | 0.9 | 0.1 | 0.2 |
| Netherlands | 2.0 | 2.5 | 3.3 | 3.1 | 8.3 | 2.3 | 2.1 | 2.7 | 2.3 | 2.6 |
| United Kingdom | 16.7 | 16.7 | 17.9 | 18.8 | 16.0 | 1.7 | 2.6 | 1.5 | 2.8 | 0.7 |
| Turkey | 0.1 | ..... | 0.2 | 0.1 | 0.1 | ..... | 0.1 | ..... | ..... | ..... |
| Former Soviet Republics | 0.5 | 0.5 | 1.7 | 0.4 | 0.7 | ..... | ..... | ..... | ..... | ..... |
| Poland | ..... | 0.2 | 0.8 | 0.3 | 0.2 | ..... | ..... | 0.1 | ..... | ..... |
| Other Eastern Europe | 1.3 | 0.5 | 0.8 | 1.1 | 0.6 | ..... | ..... | 0.1 | ..... | ..... |
| Other Europe | 7.7 | 8.9 | 13.3 | 15.8 | 10.8 | 2.7 | 3.5 | 3.5 | 3.8 | 2.7 |
| **Asia** | 33.8 | 37.0 | 46.0 | 46.1 | 51.7 | 9.6 | 8.3 | 12.2 | 12.3 | 17.9 |
| Japan | 3.8 | 6.4 | 7.1 | 6.7 | 8.5 | 3.8 | 4.5 | 6.5 | 5.6 | 6.7 |
| China | 0.9 | 0.2 | 1.0 | 1.3 | 2.3 | ..... | ..... | 0.2 | 1.0 | 0.3 |
| Hong Kong | 3.9 | 3.3 | 6.4 | 5.7 | 11.2 | 0.3 | 0.1 | 0.2 | 0.3 | 0.2 |
| Taiwan | 2.2 | 2.3 | 5.5 | 5.6 | 7.3 | 2.5 | 0.6 | 0.8 | 0.7 | 2.5 |
| Singapore | 10.5 | 13.1 | 6.6 | 4.4 | 5.3 | 0.7 | 0.6 | 1.1 | 0.9 | 0.9 |
| South Korea | 3.0 | 2.7 | 3.3 | 3.8 | 3.1 | 1.1 | 1.3 | 1.6 | 1.5 | 1.3 |
| Indonesia | 0.3 | 0.2 | 0.5 | 0.4 | 0.4 | 0.1 | 0.1 | 0.1 | 0.1 | 0.1 |
| India | 0.3 | 0.4 | 2.2 | 1.6 | 1.0 | 0.1 | 0.1 | 0.2 | 0.1 | 0.1 |
| Other Asia | 8.9 | 8.4 | 13.4 | 16.5 | 12.8 | 0.9 | 0.9 | 1.6 | 2.3 | 5.7 |
| **Africa** | 0.8 | 3.9 | 0.7 | 0.4 | 0.4 | 0.6 | 0.6 | 0.6 | 0.8 | 0.5 |
| North Africa | 0.1 | 0.9 | 0.1 | 0.2 | 0.3 | 0.2 | 0.1 | 0.1 | ..... | 0.1 |
| Republic of South Africa | 0.1 | 3.0 | 0.4 | 0.2 | 0.1 | 0.4 | 0.5 | 0.5 | 0.5 | 0.4 |
| Other Subsaharan Africa | 0.5 | ..... | 0.1 | ..... | ..... | ..... | ..... | ..... | 0.3 | ..... |
| **Middle East** | 2.7 | 1.4 | 1.7 | 2.0 | 2.0 | 0.3 | 0.2 | 0.3 | 0.6 | 1.3 |
| **Australia** | 1.5 | 1.5 | 3.6 | 2.4 | 3.0 | 0.5 | 0.7 | 0.7 | 1.2 | 1.5 |
| **Rest of World** | ..... | ..... | ..... | ..... | ..... | ..... | ..... | ..... | ..... | ..... |

## Table E-3.  Metropolitan Area Exports of Goods by Destination, 1993–1997—*Continued*

(Millions of dollars.)

| Destination | 1993 | 1994 | 1995 | 1996 | 1997 | 1993 | 1994 | 1995 | 1996 | 1997 |
|---|---|---|---|---|---|---|---|---|---|---|
| | Wausau, WI | | | | | Williamsport, PA | | | | |
| **ALL DESTINATIONS** | 122.5 | 113.6 | 117.3 | 148.9 | 184.8 | 105.2 | 123.3 | 150.4 | 151.0 | 182.5 |
| **North America** | 58.9 | 59.4 | 59.3 | 65.2 | 79.7 | 57.1 | 69.7 | 79.6 | 71.5 | 92.9 |
| Canada | 52.2 | 50.1 | 52.1 | 56.1 | 67.4 | 54.1 | 65.9 | 76.5 | 68.7 | 90.7 |
| Mexico | 6.7 | 9.3 | 7.2 | 9.1 | 12.3 | 3.0 | 3.8 | 3.1 | 2.8 | 2.1 |
| **Caribbean and Central America** | 1.3 | 0.8 | 0.2 | 0.6 | 1.0 | 0.8 | 0.6 | 1.5 | 4.6 | 12.3 |
| **South America** | 0.4 | 2.0 | 1.4 | 1.9 | 3.4 | 3.7 | 3.4 | 4.6 | 2.2 | 7.6 |
| Argentina | 0.2 | 0.5 | 0.4 | 0.6 | 1.5 | 0.9 | 0.2 | 0.5 | 0.2 | 0.1 |
| Brazil | ..... | 1.3 | 0.3 | 0.1 | 0.1 | 1.8 | 2.0 | 2.8 | 1.1 | 3.0 |
| Other South America | 0.2 | 0.1 | 0.7 | 1.2 | 1.7 | 1.0 | 1.2 | 1.3 | 0.8 | 4.5 |
| **Europe** | 11.7 | 7.1 | 10.8 | 14.8 | 19.5 | 29.1 | 32.7 | 42.5 | 50.1 | 43.4 |
| Belgium | ..... | ..... | ..... | ..... | ..... | 3.6 | 5.0 | 5.4 | 8.2 | 6.8 |
| France | 0.3 | 0.5 | 0.5 | 0.9 | 1.1 | 3.9 | 5.9 | 7.1 | 5.1 | 7.8 |
| Germany | 0.6 | 1.2 | 2.0 | 2.0 | 2.1 | 8.2 | 9.6 | 12.2 | 13.2 | 9.2 |
| Netherlands | 0.6 | 0.3 | 0.5 | 2.5 | 0.8 | 1.6 | 1.1 | 1.1 | 1.3 | 0.8 |
| United Kingdom | 7.2 | 2.3 | 3.8 | 5.3 | 4.6 | 4.7 | 5.4 | 7.6 | 11.5 | 7.8 |
| Turkey | 0.8 | ..... | 0.1 | 2.7 | 2.9 | 1.0 | 0.2 | 0.2 | 0.3 | |
| Former Soviet Republics | ..... | 0.2 | ..... | ..... | ..... | 0.3 | 0.2 | ..... | 0.2 | |
| Poland | ..... | ..... | ..... | ..... | 0.1 | ..... | ..... | ..... | ..... | 0.2 |
| Other Eastern Europe | ..... | ..... | ..... | ..... | 1.2 | 0.5 | 0.6 | 0.3 | 0.6 | 0.2 |
| Other Europe | 2.2 | 2.5 | 3.8 | 1.4 | 6.6 | 5.4 | 4.6 | 8.7 | 9.7 | 10.5 |
| **Asia** | 47.6 | 42.0 | 42.9 | 63.9 | 77.7 | 8.8 | 10.3 | 15.1 | 14.2 | 19.2 |
| Japan | 5.7 | 5.6 | 9.0 | 9.9 | 10.9 | 0.8 | 1.0 | 1.4 | 1.4 | 1.2 |
| China | 1.3 | 0.8 | 1.4 | 4.1 | 4.2 | 0.4 | 0.8 | 0.9 | 0.5 | 1.3 |
| Hong Kong | 29.9 | 24.5 | 20.4 | 24.5 | 26.9 | 0.8 | 0.9 | 1.0 | 1.0 | 2.9 |
| Taiwan | 3.2 | 2.5 | 3.8 | 5.3 | 8.2 | 1.5 | 2.2 | 3.3 | 2.5 | 2.7 |
| Singapore | 5.5 | 4.6 | 1.3 | 5.9 | 10.0 | 0.8 | 1.1 | 4.8 | 4.4 | 0.6 |
| South Korea | 0.9 | 2.9 | 5.0 | 9.0 | 9.0 | 1.2 | 1.1 | 1.0 | 1.3 | 8.0 |
| Indonesia | ..... | ..... | 0.2 | 0.7 | 0.4 | 0.1 | ..... | 0.1 | ..... | 0.1 |
| India | ..... | 0.1 | 0.4 | 0.5 | 0.4 | 0.7 | 1.2 | 0.7 | 0.3 | ..... |
| Other Asia | 1.0 | 1.0 | 1.3 | 4.0 | 7.7 | 2.6 | 2.0 | 2.0 | 2.9 | 2.4 |
| **Africa** | 0.3 | 0.3 | 0.8 | 0.4 | 0.6 | 0.8 | 0.6 | 1.3 | 1.5 | 0.9 |
| North Africa | 0.2 | 0.3 | ..... | 0.3 | 0.2 | ..... | ..... | 0.4 | 0.3 | 0.1 |
| Republic of South Africa | 0.1 | ..... | 0.8 | 0.1 | 0.4 | 0.7 | 0.4 | 0.7 | 1.1 | 0.8 |
| Other Subsaharan Africa | ..... | ..... | ..... | ..... | ..... | 0.2 | 0.2 | 0.1 | 0.1 | 0.1 |
| **Middle East** | 1.8 | 1.7 | 1.4 | 1.6 | 2.2 | 1.1 | 1.5 | 1.7 | 2.0 | 1.7 |
| **Australia** | 0.4 | 0.2 | 0.5 | 0.6 | 0.8 | 3.7 | 4.5 | 4.2 | 4.9 | 4.4 |
| **Rest of World** | ..... | ..... | ..... | ..... | ..... | ..... | ..... | ..... | ..... | ..... |
| | Wilmington - Newark, DE - MD | | | | | Wilmington, NC | | | | |
| **ALL DESTINATIONS** | 3 423.8 | 3 720.4 | 4 361.1 | 4 551.1 | 5 140.6 | 147.1 | 180.7 | 211.7 | 301.7 | 422.9 |
| **North America** | 742.2 | 851.3 | 854.4 | 989.0 | 1 065.6 | 78.5 | 86.8 | 93.9 | 141.8 | 124.9 |
| Canada | 590.3 | 646.8 | 675.7 | 706.6 | 765.3 | 58.3 | 86.3 | 93.5 | 139.1 | 119.9 |
| Mexico | 151.9 | 204.5 | 178.6 | 282.4 | 300.3 | 20.2 | 0.5 | 0.4 | 2.8 | 5.0 |
| **Caribbean and Central America** | 56.1 | 59.9 | 42.9 | 27.8 | 33.1 | 2.1 | 1.4 | 5.8 | 14.0 | 29.3 |
| **South America** | 343.3 | 353.3 | 456.3 | 484.1 | 574.3 | 0.6 | 0.7 | 1.9 | 7.1 | 32.3 |
| Argentina | 51.4 | 59.7 | 83.3 | 102.5 | 119.5 | ..... | ..... | 0.1 | 0.1 | 0.6 |
| Brazil | 163.5 | 165.9 | 213.5 | 228.8 | 276.0 | 0.5 | 0.4 | 1.2 | 6.8 | 28.7 |
| Other South America | 128.4 | 127.7 | 159.5 | 152.9 | 178.8 | 0.1 | 0.3 | 0.6 | 0.3 | 3.0 |
| **Europe** | 1 103.4 | 1 215.7 | 1 538.1 | 1 520.7 | 1 616.0 | 13.8 | 17.8 | 20.2 | 45.1 | 86.0 |
| Belgium | 470.4 | 488.8 | 701.6 | 663.6 | 657.5 | 0.7 | 0.1 | 0.5 | 0.3 | 0.3 |
| France | 59.8 | 100.6 | 114.1 | 90.2 | 99.7 | 0.2 | 0.5 | 0.6 | 0.8 | 12.9 |
| Germany | 153.1 | 171.4 | 163.0 | 190.9 | 191.2 | 1.3 | 1.1 | 4.5 | 19.5 | 20.5 |
| Netherlands | 104.5 | 157.7 | 190.2 | 192.7 | 256.0 | 0.6 | 1.4 | 1.7 | 1.5 | 3.6 |
| United Kingdom | 135.6 | 147.5 | 171.3 | 181.0 | 213.0 | 1.8 | 1.2 | 3.4 | 4.2 | 3.0 |
| Turkey | 29.7 | 19.3 | 35.6 | 28.8 | 23.5 | ..... | ..... | 0.3 | 0.4 | 0.5 |
| Former Soviet Republics | 48.0 | 14.8 | 11.1 | 6.0 | 9.4 | 0.3 | 0.1 | 0.1 | ..... | 1.0 |
| Poland | 0.5 | 0.2 | 0.3 | 0.4 | 1.6 | ..... | ..... | ..... | ..... | ..... |
| Other Eastern Europe | 1.9 | 1.7 | 2.2 | 1.0 | 3.1 | ..... | 0.1 | 0.5 | 0.1 | 0.1 |
| Other Europe | 100.0 | 113.6 | 148.7 | 166.1 | 160.9 | 8.9 | 13.4 | 8.7 | 18.3 | 44.0 |
| **Asia** | 992.7 | 1 060.0 | 1 255.8 | 1 344.6 | 1 649.4 | 25.9 | 40.6 | 52.3 | 62.1 | 124.4 |
| Japan | 336.2 | 374.4 | 439.1 | 447.6 | 572.0 | 1.4 | 8.9 | 6.4 | 13.3 | 15.5 |
| China | 59.2 | 54.8 | 64.7 | 68.5 | 75.7 | 16.7 | 20.1 | 24.2 | 37.2 | 69.9 |
| Hong Kong | 46.2 | 60.7 | 75.6 | 94.9 | 104.2 | 1.1 | 4.3 | 13.6 | 5.0 | 26.3 |
| Taiwan | 140.2 | 149.1 | 170.5 | 167.8 | 208.4 | 1.2 | 0.2 | 3.4 | 2.9 | 6.4 |
| Singapore | 98.2 | 77.3 | 94.3 | 112.3 | 157.1 | 0.8 | 1.2 | 1.0 | 1.1 | 1.3 |
| South Korea | 138.5 | 156.3 | 172.6 | 209.2 | 195.3 | 4.0 | 5.7 | 2.9 | 1.6 | 2.4 |
| Indonesia | 48.1 | 50.0 | 67.5 | 68.2 | 80.3 | ..... | ..... | 0.1 | ..... | ..... |
| India | 21.7 | 25.2 | 41.8 | 39.7 | 45.6 | 0.1 | 0.1 | 0.2 | 0.6 | 1.3 |
| Other Asia | 104.3 | 112.2 | 129.6 | 136.3 | 210.9 | 0.6 | 0.1 | 0.5 | 0.5 | 1.2 |
| **Africa** | 41.9 | 40.0 | 54.2 | 52.0 | 61.9 | 20.2 | 17.6 | 27.5 | 22.7 | 21.5 |
| North Africa | 8.2 | 6.5 | 8.8 | 4.7 | 9.8 | ..... | 0.5 | 12.1 | ..... | 1.5 |
| Republic of South Africa | 25.7 | 24.8 | 30.9 | 23.0 | 25.5 | ..... | ..... | ..... | 0.1 | |
| Other Subsaharan Africa | 8.0 | 8.7 | 14.5 | 24.3 | 26.7 | 20.1 | 17.1 | 15.4 | 22.6 | 20.0 |
| **Middle East** | 49.2 | 41.4 | 59.4 | 49.8 | 56.8 | 5.7 | 15.5 | 9.7 | 8.7 | 4.4 |
| **Australia** | 95.1 | 98.8 | 100.1 | 83.1 | 83.6 | 0.1 | 0.2 | 0.3 | 0.2 | 0.1 |
| **Rest of World** | ..... | ..... | ..... | ..... | ..... | ..... | ..... | ..... | ..... | ..... |

## Table E-3. Metropolitan Area Exports of Goods by Destination, 1993–1997—Continued

(Millions of dollars.)

| Destination | 1993 | 1994 | 1995 | 1996 | 1997 | 1993 | 1994 | 1995 | 1996 | 1997 |
|---|---|---|---|---|---|---|---|---|---|---|
| | Worcester, MA - CT | | | | | West Palm Beach - Boca Raton, FL | | | | |
| ALL DESTINATIONS | 1 017.9 | 603.8 | 757.6 | 685.7 | 772.1 | 764.8 | 834.3 | 898.0 | 955.8 | 1 156.0 |
| North America | 479.2 | 252.7 | 249.6 | 247.8 | 331.7 | 206.2 | 193.7 | 169.0 | 225.0 | 282.7 |
| Canada | 416.2 | 181.9 | 189.5 | 173.2 | 237.6 | 182.7 | 168.3 | 149.7 | 187.5 | 192.9 |
| Mexico | 63.0 | 70.8 | 60.1 | 74.6 | 94.1 | 23.5 | 25.4 | 19.3 | 37.5 | 89.7 |
| Caribbean and Central America | 1.4 | 1.7 | 2.5 | 2.6 | 2.4 | 124.5 | 109.8 | 108.3 | 112.0 | 128.6 |
| South America | 10.4 | 9.4 | 15.8 | 12.4 | 16.4 | 89.4 | 136.9 | 152.7 | 179.9 | 222.9 |
| Argentina | 1.7 | 2.0 | 1.3 | 1.2 | 2.0 | 10.6 | 18.0 | 14.1 | 10.9 | 13.6 |
| Brazil | 3.4 | 2.8 | 6.5 | 4.9 | 7.9 | 26.0 | 37.6 | 65.2 | 103.3 | 125.3 |
| Other South America | 5.4 | 4.6 | 8.1 | 6.3 | 6.6 | 52.8 | 81.4 | 73.3 | 65.7 | 84.0 |
| Europe | 210.7 | 162.7 | 225.1 | 193.8 | 205.1 | 165.5 | 180.9 | 250.6 | 251.5 | 258.1 |
| Belgium | 4.1 | 3.0 | 8.3 | 3.1 | 3.1 | 5.7 | 6.4 | 9.3 | 7.6 | 13.7 |
| France | 21.3 | 17.8 | 17.8 | 14.9 | 20.7 | 18.5 | 22.5 | 24.6 | 17.0 | 22.8 |
| Germany | 49.2 | 48.6 | 76.5 | 62.9 | 56.4 | 33.2 | 26.0 | 35.6 | 53.1 | 47.9 |
| Netherlands | 22.7 | 16.6 | 23.5 | 21.9 | 23.7 | 8.4 | 8.0 | 19.2 | 23.2 | 14.5 |
| United Kingdom | 55.8 | 40.2 | 52.5 | 39.9 | 48.3 | 33.7 | 43.6 | 57.6 | 54.9 | 66.3 |
| Turkey | 1.1 | 0.3 | 0.6 | 0.7 | 0.9 | 2.6 | 1.1 | 2.0 | 3.5 | 7.9 |
| Former Soviet Republics | 0.3 | 0.8 | 0.7 | 1.2 | 0.8 | 2.2 | 2.7 | 24.1 | 2.0 | 4.3 |
| Poland | 0.1 | 0.3 | 0.5 | 0.6 | 0.3 | 1.3 | 4.3 | 1.7 | 2.2 | 2.6 |
| Other Eastern Europe | 2.0 | 0.6 | 0.7 | 1.0 | 0.7 | 1.3 | 1.8 | 2.0 | 3.1 | 3.2 |
| Other Europe | 54.1 | 34.6 | 43.9 | 47.8 | 50.2 | 58.6 | 64.5 | 74.5 | 84.8 | 74.8 |
| Asia | 283.4 | 150.2 | 228.6 | 201.4 | 192.0 | 142.4 | 174.4 | 164.7 | 148.8 | 194.4 |
| Japan | 44.3 | 29.9 | 37.3 | 38.3 | 40.0 | 47.2 | 78.0 | 55.5 | 49.9 | 74.1 |
| China | 15.2 | 12.1 | 17.3 | 4.9 | 7.2 | 4.2 | 18.0 | 7.2 | 9.1 | 10.0 |
| Hong Kong | 22.1 | 9.7 | 18.2 | 35.4 | 29.1 | 10.0 | 10.8 | 23.1 | 22.2 | 23.2 |
| Taiwan | 37.6 | 13.9 | 18.8 | 16.4 | 19.8 | 6.7 | 8.2 | 9.2 | 5.1 | 9.3 |
| Singapore | 76.2 | 11.2 | 22.6 | 36.7 | 19.1 | 22.4 | 21.5 | 26.3 | 10.2 | 16.0 |
| South Korea | 19.4 | 17.1 | 29.1 | 27.2 | 21.4 | 15.2 | 14.8 | 17.7 | 32.1 | 32.6 |
| Indonesia | 1.9 | 1.9 | 2.0 | 2.6 | 6.9 | 0.5 | 0.8 | 0.4 | 2.3 | 0.9 |
| India | 3.6 | 3.3 | 7.5 | 5.2 | 5.9 | 3.2 | 2.8 | 9.1 | 3.2 | 3.2 |
| Other Asia | 63.1 | 51.1 | 75.7 | 34.7 | 42.6 | 33.0 | 19.4 | 16.1 | 14.8 | 25.2 |
| Africa | 5.4 | 3.5 | 13.6 | 5.9 | 3.6 | 10.1 | 14.1 | 28.8 | 19.1 | 25.5 |
| North Africa | 1.5 | 0.7 | 2.3 | 1.6 | 0.3 | 4.4 | 6.2 | 21.0 | 10.9 | 11.1 |
| Republic of South Africa | 3.6 | 2.4 | 10.6 | 3.9 | 2.6 | 3.5 | 4.7 | 3.6 | 5.1 | 7.2 |
| Other Subsaharan Africa | 0.3 | 0.4 | 0.7 | 0.4 | 0.7 | 2.1 | 3.2 | 4.2 | 3.2 | 7.2 |
| Middle East | 11.9 | 8.5 | 7.8 | 9.1 | 8.7 | 13.9 | 13.7 | 14.1 | 14.0 | 24.2 |
| Australia | 15.4 | 15.1 | 14.5 | 12.7 | 12.2 | 12.8 | 10.9 | 9.6 | 5.5 | 19.6 |
| Rest of World | ..... | ..... | ..... | ..... | ..... | ..... | ..... | 0.2 | ..... | ..... |
| | Yakima, WA | | | | | York, PA | | | | |
| ALL DESTINATIONS | 135.8 | 147.6 | 168.9 | 176.0 | 213.1 | 751.8 | 952.0 | 973.9 | 945.1 | 1 015.4 |
| North America | 85.6 | 87.2 | 84.2 | 94.9 | 109.1 | 175.2 | 216.6 | 226.0 | 238.5 | 298.3 |
| Canada | 81.5 | 79.4 | 78.3 | 84.9 | 92.7 | 141.1 | 172.2 | 194.2 | 211.0 | 225.4 |
| Mexico | 4.1 | 7.9 | 5.8 | 10.0 | 16.4 | 34.1 | 44.4 | 31.8 | 27.5 | 72.9 |
| Caribbean and Central America | 2.8 | 2.7 | 3.7 | 3.7 | 4.3 | 9.4 | 9.3 | 16.7 | 14.0 | 9.7 |
| South America | 5.9 | 14.8 | 15.7 | 17.4 | 17.4 | 38.1 | 16.0 | 33.2 | 31.6 | 33.1 |
| Argentina | 0.4 | 0.9 | 0.4 | 3.3 | 1.4 | 22.5 | 4.2 | 7.5 | 6.2 | 3.3 |
| Brazil | 2.1 | 7.7 | 11.4 | 8.6 | 9.4 | 4.1 | 3.2 | 6.2 | 4.9 | 11.9 |
| Other South America | 3.4 | 6.2 | 3.9 | 5.5 | 6.6 | 11.5 | 8.5 | 19.5 | 20.4 | 17.9 |
| Europe | 21.1 | 23.0 | 29.7 | 31.4 | 41.0 | 199.1 | 229.8 | 276.6 | 293.0 | 316.8 |
| Belgium | 0.4 | 1.4 | 0.8 | 0.7 | 0.5 | 2.7 | 4.0 | 3.0 | 4.3 | 5.3 |
| France | 1.6 | 1.7 | 1.1 | 2.3 | 4.1 | 7.5 | 9.6 | 12.3 | 18.2 | 33.6 |
| Germany | 8.3 | 7.7 | 10.6 | 9.5 | 11.1 | 67.6 | 77.8 | 88.0 | 77.8 | 68.8 |
| Netherlands | 1.0 | 0.9 | 0.8 | 1.1 | 2.3 | 29.0 | 38.4 | 50.2 | 50.4 | 57.0 |
| United Kingdom | 7.0 | 6.9 | 12.2 | 13.0 | 9.5 | 40.5 | 44.1 | 52.8 | 61.6 | 63.6 |
| Turkey | ..... | ..... | ..... | ..... | 0.9 | 1.0 | 1.0 | 1.1 | 1.6 | 2.6 |
| Former Soviet Republics | ..... | 0.7 | 0.7 | 0.6 | 1.0 | 0.1 | 0.2 | 0.1 | 0.3 | 2.0 |
| Poland | ..... | ..... | ..... | 0.1 | 0.1 | 1.1 | 1.0 | 0.4 | 0.2 | 0.3 |
| Other Eastern Europe | 0.1 | 0.3 | 0.1 | 0.4 | 0.1 | 0.1 | 0.3 | 1.0 | 0.6 | 0.6 |
| Other Europe | 2.6 | 3.3 | 3.5 | 3.7 | 11.5 | 49.6 | 53.4 | 67.8 | 77.9 | 83.1 |
| Asia | 19.0 | 17.2 | 30.0 | 23.2 | 35.3 | 243.0 | 301.3 | 317.6 | 266.9 | 248.3 |
| Japan | 8.7 | 6.2 | 15.0 | 8.5 | 22.6 | 46.2 | 38.9 | 53.6 | 60.9 | 76.8 |
| China | 0.8 | 0.5 | 1.5 | 1.8 | 0.3 | 14.3 | 23.9 | 32.5 | 16.3 | 20.3 |
| Hong Kong | 1.6 | 2.1 | 1.9 | 2.3 | 1.5 | 20.9 | 23.1 | 20.0 | 15.2 | 16.1 |
| Taiwan | 2.3 | 1.7 | 4.2 | 3.3 | 2.3 | 19.7 | 40.7 | 24.0 | 19.7 | 37.5 |
| Singapore | 0.6 | 0.6 | 0.4 | 0.7 | 0.3 | 25.9 | 40.0 | 42.6 | 29.4 | 18.3 |
| South Korea | 0.6 | 1.8 | 1.6 | 2.7 | 3.6 | 85.4 | 100.3 | 113.6 | 78.6 | 44.9 |
| Indonesia | 0.2 | 0.9 | 2.0 | 0.8 | 0.5 | 1.2 | 1.1 | 2.5 | 1.2 | 1.6 |
| India | 0.2 | ..... | ..... | 0.2 | 0.1 | 2.8 | 7.4 | 7.1 | 2.8 | 2.2 |
| Other Asia | 3.9 | 3.5 | 3.4 | 3.0 | 4.2 | 26.6 | 26.1 | 21.7 | 42.8 | 30.6 |
| Africa | 0.6 | 0.6 | 0.4 | 1.2 | 1.3 | 12.3 | 95.8 | 17.3 | 11.1 | 15.7 |
| North Africa | ..... | 0.3 | ..... | 1.0 | 0.1 | 7.9 | 83.8 | 13.3 | 4.8 | 11.0 |
| Republic of South Africa | 0.5 | 0.3 | 0.4 | 0.2 | 0.9 | 4.1 | 11.5 | 3.9 | 6.0 | 4.0 |
| Other Subsaharan Africa | ..... | ..... | ..... | ..... | 0.2 | 0.3 | 0.5 | 0.1 | 0.3 | 0.7 |
| Middle East | 0.2 | 0.1 | 1.0 | 0.9 | 1.1 | 44.1 | 43.3 | 36.3 | 40.8 | 45.9 |
| Australia | 0.8 | 1.9 | 4.3 | 3.2 | 3.6 | 30.6 | 39.9 | 50.3 | 49.3 | 47.6 |
| Rest of World | ..... | ..... | ..... | ..... | ..... | ..... | ..... | ..... | ..... | ..... |

**Table E-3.  Metropolitan Area Exports of Goods by Destination, 1993–1997**—*Continued*

(Millions of dollars.)

| Destination | 1993 | 1994 | 1995 | 1996 | 1997 |
|---|---|---|---|---|---|
| | Youngstown - Warren, OH | | | | |
| **ALL DESTINATIONS** .......................... | 189.3 | 185.3 | 225.9 | 223.1 | 323.0 |
| **North America** ..................................... | 108.4 | 105.9 | 136.1 | 128.8 | 188.9 |
| Canada ............................................. | 103.5 | 98.3 | 115.0 | 120.9 | 174.4 |
| Mexico .............................................. | 4.9 | 7.5 | 21.1 | 7.9 | 14.5 |
| **Caribbean and Central America** ........ | 7.5 | 3.2 | 4.3 | 2.7 | 5.6 |
| **South America** ................................... | 9.3 | 12.4 | 13.3 | 10.8 | 10.7 |
| Argentina ......................................... | 3.0 | 7.3 | 4.2 | 3.2 | 3.8 |
| Brazil ............................................... | 3.2 | 1.1 | 3.3 | 1.7 | 0.9 |
| Other South America ........................ | 3.0 | 4.0 | 5.8 | 5.9 | 5.9 |
| **Europe** .............................................. | 27.4 | 38.9 | 38.4 | 39.5 | 58.5 |
| Belgium ............................................ | 0.3 | 0.4 | 0.6 | 0.5 | 5.2 |
| France .............................................. | 7.7 | 7.5 | 4.8 | 7.4 | 13.1 |
| Germany ........................................... | 3.2 | 5.5 | 8.5 | 7.2 | 8.7 |
| Netherlands ...................................... | 3.1 | 4.7 | 3.9 | 3.0 | 2.6 |
| United Kingdom ................................ | 6.5 | 7.6 | 10.6 | 12.1 | 21.6 |
| Turkey .............................................. | 0.5 | 3.2 | 2.2 | 0.5 | 0.1 |
| Former Soviet Republics ................... | ..... | ..... | ..... | ..... | ..... |
| Poland .............................................. | 0.1 | ..... | ..... | 0.1 | 0.3 |
| Other Eastern Europe ....................... | 0.1 | 0.2 | 0.1 | 0.1 | 0.1 |
| Other Europe .................................... | 6.1 | 9.9 | 7.7 | 8.6 | 6.7 |
| **Asia** ................................................. | 29.3 | 17.3 | 25.8 | 30.3 | 45.6 |
| Japan ............................................... | 3.4 | 2.0 | 2.2 | 7.4 | 6.6 |
| China ................................................ | 9.3 | 5.9 | 5.4 | 2.1 | 2.6 |
| Hong Kong ........................................ | 0.5 | 0.5 | 0.6 | 0.6 | 0.8 |
| Taiwan .............................................. | 7.0 | 2.8 | 1.9 | 3.1 | 2.5 |
| Singapore ......................................... | 0.5 | 0.4 | 2.6 | 6.0 | 2.6 |
| South Korea ..................................... | 2.9 | 3.9 | 9.3 | 2.2 | 13.1 |
| Indonesia .......................................... | 0.1 | ..... | 0.3 | 2.4 | 0.7 |
| India ................................................. | 0.4 | 1.0 | 1.4 | 1.6 | 1.7 |
| Other Asia ........................................ | 5.3 | 0.7 | 2.2 | 4.8 | 15.1 |
| **Africa** ............................................... | 0.7 | 1.1 | 2.9 | 1.5 | 2.1 |
| North Africa ...................................... | 0.3 | 0.3 | 0.3 | 0.4 | 0.7 |
| Republic of South Africa ................... | 0.3 | 0.5 | 2.6 | 1.0 | 1.1 |
| Other Subsaharan Africa ................... | 0.1 | 0.3 | ..... | 0.1 | 0.3 |
| **Middle East** ...................................... | 3.5 | 3.0 | 1.5 | 7.8 | 7.7 |
| **Australia** ........................................... | 3.0 | 3.5 | 3.7 | 1.7 | 3.7 |
| **Rest of World** ................................... | ..... | ..... | ..... | ..... | ..... |

# NOTES AND DEFINITIONS

The notes are arranged by sections and tables, in the same order as these appear in this volume. Part and table titles are shown in the notes. The notes provide general information about data sources and definitions, as well as additional information specific to individual sections and tables.

## GENERAL NOTES

### Volume Organization
The tables in this book are divided into five main parts.

*Part A. U.S. International Transaction Highlights*, presents an overview of total national foreign trade on a balance of payments basis. It also compares imports and exports with gross domestic product and contains a complete international transactions table showing current account and capital account transactions. Additionally, it shows foreign exchange rates, including trade-weighted indexes against groups of currencies.

*Part B. U.S. Foreign Trade in Services*, shows imports and exports of services. This section shows time series from 1986 to 1997 for total services trade by type of service and by destination. More detailed tables show trade in individual types of services by destination for 1994 to 1997.

*Part C. U.S. Foreign Trade in Goods*, starts with a summary of goods trade for 1970 to 1998. This information is followed by information on trade in goods by end-use and by Standard Industry Classification (SIC) product categories. Additional tables show trade with individual countries and regions, with totals for both manufactured and agricultural goods.

*Part D. State Exports of Goods*, provides comprehensive data on exports by state. First is a table of total exports by state, then exports by destination. The largest part of this section is Table D-3 which shows goods exports to selected destinations by industry group. The table is highlighted with graphs showing total exports of goods and the top export manufacturing industries for each state.

*Part E. Metropolitan Area Exports of Goods*, follows with complete data on metropolitan area exports. One table shows total exports by metropolitan areas. Following this is a table showing exports of goods by industry, with charts highlighting the top exporting manufacturing industries. Finally, there is a table showing metropolitan area exports of goods by destination.

Most of the data in this volume are from federal government sources and may be reproduced freely. A few are from private sources and are used with permission; further use may be subject to copyright restrictions. A list of data sources, including addresses, phone numbers, e-mail addresses, internet addresses, and citations for the relevant government periodicals cited may be found below under "Sources."

### Time Period Covered
Starting dates vary depending on data availability. All tables continue through 1997, and 1998 data available at press time (mid-March 1999) are included.

### Definitions
The following symbols are used for all of the tables in this volume.

..... Data are not available for the item shown.
(**D**)  Data are suppressed to protect confidentiality, that is, to avoid disclosure of data pertaining to an individual business.
(**p**)  Data are preliminary.
(**\***)  The value of this item is less than $500,000.

The following words or phrases are used throughout this volume and apply to all tables.

*f.a.s.* (free alongside ship). The export value including the price of the merchandise, inland freight, insurance, and other costs in placing the goods alongside the carrier at the U.S. port of exportation.

*f.o.b.* (free on board). The export value including the f.a.s. value and the cost of delivery to and placing on board a carrier at the port of exportation.

Values for *exports of goods* in the tables in this book are based on f.a.s. value.

*Imports of goods* are valued based on the U. S. Customs Service appraised value of merchandise. Typically, this is the price paid for merchandise for export to the United States. Import duties, freight, insurance, and other costs of bringing merchandise to the United States are excluded.

*Census basis.* The "census basis" goods data are compiled from the documents collected by the U.S. Customs Service and reflect the movement of goods between foreign countries and the 50 states, the District of Columbia, Puerto Rico, the U.S. Virgin Islands, and U.S. Foreign Trade Zones. They include government and nongovernment shipments of goods and exclude shipments between the United States and its territories and possessions; transactions with U.S. military, diplomatic, and consular installations abroad; U.S. goods returned to the United States by its armed forces; personal and household effects of travelers; and in-transit shipments. The general import values reflect the total arrival of merchandise from foreign countries that immediately enters consumption channels, warehouses, or Foreign Trade Zones.

*Balance of payments (BOP) basis.* Goods export values on a census basis are adjusted by the Bureau of Economic Analysis (BEA) to goods on a BOP basis to make the data consistent with the concepts and definitions used to prepare the international and national accounts. These adjustments are necessary to supplement coverage of the census basis data, to eliminate duplication of transactions recorded elsewhere in the international accounts, and to value transactions according to a standard definition.

The export adjustments include the following: (1) Deduction of U.S. military sales contracts, because the Census Bureau has included these contracts in the goods data, but BEA includes them in the service category "transfers under U.S. military sales contracts." BEA's source material for these contracts is more comprehensive but makes no distinction between goods and services. (2) Addition of private gift parcels mailed to foreigners by individuals through the U.S. Postal Service (only commercial shipments are covered in census goods exports). (3) Addition to nonmonetary gold exports of gold that is purchased by foreign official agencies from private dealers in the United States and held at the Federal Reserve Bank of New York. The census data include only gold that leaves the customs territory. (4) Smaller adjustments including deductions for repairs of goods, exposed motion picture film, and military grant aid, and additions for sales of fish in U.S. territorial waters, exports of electricity to Mexico, and vessels and oil rigs that change ownership for which no export document is filed.

The import adjustments include the following: (1) An addition for inland freight in Canada. Imports of goods from all countries are valued at the foreign port of export, including inland freight charges ("customs value"). In the case of Canada, this value should be the cost of the goods at the U.S. border. However, the customs value for imports for certain Canadian goods is the point of origin in Canada. BEA makes an addition for the inland freight charges of transporting these Canadian goods to the U.S. border to make the value comparable to the customs value as reported by all other countries (the same procedure is used for Mexico as an "other adjustment" but is much smaller). (2) Addition to nonmonetary gold imports for gold sold by foreign official agencies to private purchasers from stock held at the Federal Reserve Bank of New York. The census data include only gold that enters the customs territory. (3) Deduction of U.S. military sales contracts because the Census Bureau has included these contracts in the goods data, but BEA includes them in the service category "direct defense expenditures." BEA's source material is more comprehensive but makes no distinction between goods and services. (4) Smaller adjustments including deductions for repairs of goods and for exposed motion picture film, and additions for imported electricity from Mexico, conversion of vessels for commercial use, and repairs to U.S. vessels abroad.

*National Income and Product Account (NIPA) basis.* The BOP data on trade in goods and services require further adjustment in order to be fully consistent with the concepts and definitions used in the NIPA. The following adjustments are made to BOP-basis trade data to reconcile them with NIPA concepts: (1) Beginning with 1967, BOP gold exports and imports are excluded from the NIPA; imports of gold in the NIPA are the excess of the value of gold in gross domestic purchases over the value of U.S. production of gold. (2) In the NIPA, transfers of goods and services under military grant programs, net, are excluded from exports and included in federal government consumption expenditures. Beginning with 1988, the BOP classify certain items as military grants that the NIPA does not. (3) In the NIPA, Puerto Rico, the Northern Mariana Islands, and the U.S. Territories are included in the rest of the world; in the BOP they are treated as part of the United States. Also, from 1946 to 1959 Alaska and Hawaii are included in the rest of the world. This classification changed in 1960 because they gained statehood in 1959. (4) Some transactions measured on a net basis in the BOP are measured on a gross basis in the NIPA accounts, resulting in higher import and export totals but no change in net exports (exports less imports).

## Sources

Listed below are the agencies from which the data in this book were obtained.

**Board of Governors of the Federal Reserve System**
20th and Constitution Avenue, NW
Washington, DC 20551
Data Inquiries and Publication Sales:
Publications Services
Mail Stop 127
Board of Governors of the Federal Reserve System
Washington, DC 20551
(202) 452-3244
Monthly Publication: *Federal Reserve Bulletin*
Internet Address: http://www.federalreserve.gov

**Bureau of Economic Analysis (BEA),
U.S. Department of Commerce**
Washington, DC 20233
Data Inquiries:
Public Information Office
(202) 606-9900
Monthly Publication: *Survey of Current Business*
Internet Address: http://www.bea.doc.gov

**Bureau of the Census,
U.S. Department of Commerce**
Washington, DC 20233
Data Inquiries:
Foreign Trade Information: (301) 457-3041
Internet Address: http://www.census.gov

**International Monetary Fund**
Publication Sales:
Publication Services, Catalog Orders
700 19th Street, NW
Washington, DC 20431
Telephone: (202) 623-7430
Monthly Publication: *International Financial Statistics*
Internet Address: http://www.imf.org

**Office of Trade and Economic Analysis (OTEA)**
**International Trade Administration,**
**U.S. Department of Commerce**
Washington, DC 20230
Internet Address: http://www.ita.doc.gov/tradestats

# PART A.
# U.S. FOREIGN TRADE HIGHLIGHTS

The data in tables A-1, A-2, and A-3 are from the U.S. economic accounts, a comprehensive and internally consistent set of accounts designed to provide a full picture of the U.S. economy, including its international economic transactions.

## Table A-1.
## U.S. Exports, and Imports, 1946–1998

Source: Bureau of Economic Analysis

### DATA NOTES
The data in this table are excerpted from the National Income and Product Accounts, with percentages calculated by the editors. These data show the relationship of exports and imports to U.S. gross domestic product. Exports are goods and services produced in the United States and are a component of total GDP. Imports are included in the other GDP components—personal consumption expenditures, private investment, and government consumption and gross investment—without being separately identified. Therefore, imports must be subtracted from GDP to avoid overestimating the total. Net exports (exports less imports) show the net contribution of foreign trade to GDP. BEA has adjusted the export and import numbers in this table from a balance of payments basis to a NIPA basis.

### DATA AVAILABILITY
Complete source data (from 1929 to 1998) are available from the BEA web site or can be purchased on diskette. Historical data through 1994, plus definitions and a discussion of methodology and source data, are found in *National Income and Product Accounts of the United States, 1929–1994* (Bureau of Economic Analysis, 1998).

New data normally are released toward the end of each month. The first estimates for each calendar quarter are released in the month after the quarter's end. Revisions for the most recent quarter are released in the second and third months after the quarter's end. In addition, "annual" revisions to the data for the last several years typically occur each July. "Comprehensive" revisions to the data for all time periods typically occur about once every five years. Revisions are published in the *Survey of Current Business*.

## Table A-2.
## U.S. International Trade in Goods and Services, 1960–1998

## Table A-3.
## U.S. International Transactions, 1960–1998

Source: Bureau of Economic Analysis

The U.S. international transactions accounts, or "balance of payments," provide a comprehensive view of economic transactions between the United States and foreign countries. The accounts include estimates of exports and imports of goods and of travel, transportation, and other services; earnings on assets abroad; foreign aid; and private and official capital flows, including direct investment. Data in the accounts have undergone extensive revision in the last few years to incorporate improved data sources and methodology.

The export and import data in Table A-2 are an integral part of the international transactions accounts and are reproduced in a separate table for easy reference. More detailed data on trade in private services are found in Section B of this book. More detailed data on trade in goods are found in Section C.

### DEFINITIONS
*Credits* (+): The following items are treated as credits in the international transactions accounts: exports of goods and services, income received on U.S. assets abroad; unilateral transfers to the United States, capital inflows (i.e., increases in foreign assets in the United States and decreases in U.S. assets abroad), decreases in U.S. official reserve assets, and increases in foreign official assets in the United States.

*Debits* (–): The following items are treated as debits in the international transactions accounts, indicated by minus signs in the data cells: imports of goods and services, income payments on foreign assets in the United States, unilateral transfers to foreigners, capital outflows (i.e., decreases in foreign assets in the United States and increases in U.S. assets abroad), increases in U.S. official reserve assets, and decreases in foreign official assets in the United States.

The balance columns represent the difference between the exports or receipts and the imports or payments. A negative amount indicates an excess of imports or payments over exports or receipts.

In concept, the balance on current account is necessarily offset exactly by the net capital inflow or outflow; for example, a U.S. current account deficit results in more dollars held by foreigners, which must be reflected in additional claims on the United States held by foreigners, whether in the form of U.S. currency, securities, loans, or other forms of obligation. Because of different and incomplete data sources, however, the measured capital account does not exactly offset the current account. The *statistical discrepancy* in the U.S. international accounts—the sum of all credits and debits, with the sign reversed—measures the amount by which measured net capital flow would have to be augmented to offset the current account balance exactly.

### DATA NOTES
*Exports and imports of goods* exclude exports of goods

under U.S. military agency sales contracts identified in Census Bureau export documents and imports of goods under direct defense expenditures identified in import documents. They also reflect various other adjustments (for valuation, coverage, and timing) of Census Bureau statistics to a balance of payments basis.

*Services* include some goods, mainly military equipment (included in transfers under military agency sales contracts); major equipment; other materials, supplies, and petroleum products purchased abroad by U.S. military agencies (included in direct defense expenditures abroad); and fuels purchased by airline and steamship operators (included in other transportation).

*Private remittances and other transfers* include taxes paid by U.S. private residents to foreign governments and taxes paid by private nonresidents to the U.S. government beginning in 1982.

Beginning with the data for 1982, *direct investment income* and the reinvested earnings component of *direct investment* capital are measured on a current-cost (replacement-cost) basis after adjustment to reported depreciation, depletion, and expensed exploration and development costs. For prior years, depreciation is valued in terms of the historical cost of assets and reflects a mix of prices for the various years in which capital investments were made. See *Survey of Current Business*, June 1992, pages 72ff.

*Repayments on U.S. credit and other long-term assets* include sales of foreign obligations to foreigners. The data for 1974 include extraordinary U.S. government transactions with India, described in "Special U.S. Government Transactions," *Survey of Current Business*, June 1974, page 27.

*Foreign official assets in the United States. U.S. Treasury securities* consist of bills, certificates, marketable bonds and notes, and nonmarketable convertible and nonconvertible bonds and notes; *other U.S. government securities* consist of U.S. Treasury and Export-Import Bank obligations, not included elsewhere, and of debt securities of U.S. government corporations and agencies; *other U.S. government liabilities* include, primarily, U.S. government liabilities associated with military agency sales contracts and other transactions arranged with or through foreign official agencies; *other foreign official assets* consist of investments in U.S. corporate stocks and in debt securities of private corporations and state and local governments.

Estimates of *U.S. currency flows abroad* were introduced for the first time as part of the July 1997 revisions. Data for 1974 and subsequent years were affected (see *Survey of Current Business*, July 1997). Beginning with the 1998 revisions, currency flows are published separately from U.S. treasury securities.

For 1978–83, *U.S. Treasury securities* include foreign currency denominated notes sold to private residents abroad.

*Relation of balance on current account to net foreign investment.* Conceptually, "net foreign investment" in the national income and product accounts is equal to the balance on current account plus allocation of special drawing rights. However, the foreign transactions

account in the NIPA includes (1) adjustments to the international transactions accounts for the treatment of gold, (2) adjustments for the different geographical treatment of transactions with U.S. territories and Puerto Rico, and (3) services furnished without payment by financial pension plans except life insurance carriers and private noninsured pension plans. A reconciliation of the balance on goods and services from the international accounts and the NIPA net exports appears periodically in the "Reconciliation and Other Special Tables" section of the *Survey of Current Business*. A reconciliation of the other foreign transactions in the two sets of accounts appears in Table 4.5 of the NIPA.

### DATA AVAILABILITY

Data on exports and imports of goods and services are published monthly in a joint Census-BEA press release (the FT900) available about six weeks after the close of the reference month. The data subsequently are published in the *Survey of Current Business*. The complete balance of payments data are available quarterly. Data first are reported in a BEA press release and are subsequently published in the *Survey of Current Business*. Revisions to historical data are published annually. The most recent historical revisions appear in the July 1998 issue of the *Survey*. Complete historical data may be purchased on diskette from BEA. Historical data are also available on the BEA internet site.

## Table A-4. Exchange Rates, 1992–1997

Sources: *International Financial Statistics*, International Monetary Fund; and Board of Governors of the Federal Reserve System.

### DATA NOTES

The established G-10 index and three newer trade-weighted indexes of the value of the dollar against groups of foreign currency appear at the top of this table. The newer indexes have been developed by the Federal Reserve as a response to two major concerns. One concern is the growing trade between the United States and countries other than the G-10 members. Another concern is the establishment of the European Economic and Monetary Union (EMU), of which five G-10 countries are members. As members, their national currencies are being replaced by the euro. Thus, the G-10 index was discontinued as of the end of 1998, and these new indexes take its place.

These indexes are weighted based on trade flows. The weighting scheme can be summarized as the country's share of U.S. imports, the country's share of U.S. exports, and the country's share of exports that go to another country that is a large importer of U.S. goods.

*The Broad Index* (January 1997=100): Share of U.S. exports determines the selection of a country's currency for the index. Basically, currencies were selected from countries that had a share of U.S. nonoil or nonagricultural exports of at least 0.5 percent. These countries are then divided into the Major Currency and Other Important Trading Partners indexes described below.

The selection of countries is updated annually when currency weights are adjusted.

*Major Currency Index* (March 1973=100): This index serves purposes similar to the G-10 index, namely, it is a measure of the competitiveness of U.S. goods and a gauge of financial pressure on the dollar. The index includes countries whose currencies are traded in deep and relatively liquid financial markets and for which information on short- and long-term interests rates is readily available. A benefit of this country group is that it excludes economies that have been subject to high inflation. The large depreciation of those currencies would mask movement of the dollar's value against that of other currencies. As of October 1998, this index includes the currencies of the following countries: Canada, Euro area (Germany, France, Italy, the Netherlands, Belgium, Luxembourg, Spain, Ireland, Austria, Finland, and Portugal), Japan, the United Kingdom, Switzerland, Australia, and Sweden.

*Other Important Trading Partners (OITP) Index* (January 1997=100): This index captures the competitiveness of U.S. goods in key emerging markets in Latin America, Asia, the Middle East, and Eastern Europe. Because of the episodes of hyperinflation that some of the countries have experienced, this index is more useful for analysis of short-term exchange rate movements. The countries that make up this index include, as of October 1998, Mexico, China, Taiwan, South Korea, Singapore, Hong Kong, Malaysia, Brazil, Thailand, Indonesia, the Philippines, Russia, India, Saudi Arabia, Israel, Argentina, Venezuela, Chile, and Colombia.

*G-10 Index* (March 1973=100): This measure is an index of the weighted average exchange value of the U.S. dollar against the currencies of other G-10 (industrialized) countries, which are Belgium, Canada, France, Germany, Italy, Japan, the Netherlands, Sweden, Switzerland, and the United Kingdom. This index was revised in August 1978. Unlike the previous three indexes, the weights on this index were fixed, and annual revisions were not necessary. These data are from the Federal Reserve and were published weekly in the H.10 release. The Federal Reserve ceased to calculate this index as of December 1998.

Foreign exchange rates include market, official, principal, and secondary rates as published by the IMF. The primary rates used were market and official rates. For the Democratic Republic of the Congo and Malawi, 1997 values are estimated using three quarters of data.

The **CFA Franc** is used in Benin, Burkina Faso, Cameroon, Central African Republic, Chad, Republic of the Congo, Cote D'Ivoire, Equitorial Guinea, Gabon, Mali, Niger, Senegal, and Togo.

The **East Caribbean Dollar** is used in Antigua and Barbuda, Dominica, Grenada, St. Kitts and Nevis, St. Lucia, and St. Vincent and the Grenadines.

For the following countries or currencies, end of year values were used when annual averages were unavailable: Barbados, Belarus, Belize, East Caribbean Dollar, Egypt, El Salvador, Liberia, Libya, Netherlands Antillies, Oman, Panama, and the Syrian Arab Republic.

## DATA AVAILABILITY

The source for all of the national currency exchange rates is *International Financial Statistics*, International Monetary Fund. The data are reprinted by permission. Source for the trade weighted indexes is the Federal Reserve. These indexes may be found on the Federal Reserve Bank of St. Louis web site, <www.stls.frb.org/fred/data/exchange.html>. Additional currency exchange rate information is available from the Federal Reserve web site <www.federalreserve.com>, for daily, monthly, and annual data.

# PART B.
# U.S. FOREIGN TRADE IN SERVICES

Source: Bureau of Economic Analysis

### DATA NOTES

Data in this section are for private service transactions.

The data cover what are referred to as "cross-border" transactions, that is, transactions between residents of the United States and residents of another country. (In this context, "residents" includes businesses as well as individuals.) The transactions may be between independent entities (unaffiliated), or may be trade within a multinational company (affiliated). In both cases, the transactions are included in the international transactions accounts of both countries, as an export for the seller's country and an import for the buyer's country.

Transactions with foreigners by foreign affiliates of U.S. companies are transactions between two foreign entities and are not considered U.S. international transactions. Transactions between U.S. residents and U.S. affiliates of foreign companies are domestic transactions within the United States and do not enter into the international transactions accounts.

Since 1989, a majority of U.S. purchases of services from foreign entities have been purchases from foreign affiliates in the United States, that is, transactions that are not included in the international trade data. In some recent years, sales of services to foreigners by foreign affiliates of U.S. firms have about equaled U.S. cross-border sales. (For more information, see "U.S. International Sales and Purchases of Private Services: Cross-Border Transactions in 1997 and Sales by Affiliates in 1996," *Survey of Current Business*, October 1998.)

### DEFINITIONS

*Travel:* This category covers purchases of goods and services by U.S. persons traveling abroad and by foreign persons traveling in the United States for business or personal reasons for less than 1 year. The types of goods and services most likely to be purchased are lodging, food, recreation and entertainment, local transportation, and gifts. U.S. travel transactions with both Canada and Mexico include border transactions, which often involve stays of less than 24 hours.

*Passenger fares:* This category covers fares paid by residents of one country to airline and vessel operators that reside in another country. Exports consist of fares received by U.S. operators for transporting foreign residents between the United States and a foreign country and between foreign countries. Imports consist of fares paid to foreign operators by U.S. residents for travel to and from the United States.

*Other transportation:* This category covers primarily transactions for freight and port services for the transportation of goods by ocean, air, and truck to and from the United States. Freight receipts of U.S. carriers are for transporting U.S. goods exports and for transporting goods between two foreign points; freight payments to foreign carriers are for transporting U.S. goods imports. Port services receipts are the value of the goods and services procured by foreign carriers in both U.S. sea- and airports; port services payments are the value of goods and services procured by U.S. carriers in foreign sea- and airports.

*Royalties and license fees:* This category covers transactions with foreign residents that involve patented and unpatented techniques, processes, formulas, and other intangible property rights used in the production of goods; transactions involving copyrights, trademarks, franchises, broadcast rights, and other intangible rights; the rights to distribute, use, and reproduce computer software; and the rights to sell products under a particular trademark, brand name, or signature.

*Other private services:* This category consists of a variety of services: education; financial services; insurance; telecommunications; business, professional, and technical services; and other affiliated and unaffiliated services.

*Education* receipts consist of expenditures for tuition and living expenses by foreign students enrolled in U.S. colleges and universities; payments consist of tuition and living expenses of U.S. students for study abroad.

*Financial services* covers a variety of services, including funds management, credit card services, explicit fees and commissions on transactions in securities, fees on credit-related activities, and other miscellaneous financial services; implicit fees paid and received on bond trading are also covered.

*Insurance* includes premiums earned and paid for primary insurance and for reinsurance; losses paid by U.S. insurers and losses recovered from foreign insurers are netted against the premiums. Primary insurance consists of life insurance, accident and health insurance, and property and casualty insurance. Each type of primary insurance may be reinsured; reinsurance is the ceding of a portion of a premium to another insurer, who then assumes a corresponding portion of the risk. Reinsurance is one way of providing coverage for events with so high a degree of risk or liability that a single insurer is unwilling or unable to underwrite insurance against their occurrence.

*Telecommunications* consists of settlements between U.S. and foreign communications companies for the transmission of messages between the United States and other countries; channel leasing; telex, telegram, and other jointly provided (basic) services; value-added serv-

ices, such as electronic mail and video conferencing; and telecommunications support services.

*Business, professional, and technical services* cover a wide variety of services, including accounting, auditing, and bookkeeping services; advertising; agricultural services; computer and data processing services; construction, engineering, architectural, and mining services; database and other information services; industrial engineering; installation, maintenance, and repair of equipment; legal services; mailing, reproduction, and commercial art; management of health care facilities; management, consulting, and public relations services; medical services; miscellaneous disbursements; operational leasing; personnel supply services; research, development, and testing services; sports and performing arts; training services; and other business, professional, and technical services. *Other business, professional, and technical services* consist of language translation services, security services, collection services, actuarial services, salvage services, satellite photography services, oil spill and toxic waste clean-up services, and merchanting (purchase and resale of goods to unaffiliated foreign persons) services.

## DATA AVAILABILITY

The most recent data are published in the October 1998 *Survey of Current Business.* Data are also available on the BEA web site or may be purchased on diskette.

## Table B-1.
## U.S. Private Services Transactions by Type, 1986–1997

### DATA NOTES

*Other unaffiliated service exports* include mainly expenditures of foreign governments and international organizations in the United States. Imports include mainly wages of foreign residents temporarily employed in the United States and of Canadian and Mexican commuters in the U.S. border areas.

## Table B-2.
## U.S. Private Services Transactions by Destination, 1986–1997

### DATA NOTES

The *European Union* is composed of Belgium, Denmark, France, Germany, Greece, Ireland, Italy, Luxembourg, the Netherlands, Portugal, Spain, the United Kingdom, Austria, Finland, and Sweden. The last three countries joined the union on January 1, 1995. The European Union totals prior to 1995 do not include these three countries.

*Eastern Europe* is composed of Albania, Armenia, Azerbaijan, Belarus, Bulgaria, the Czech Republic, Estonia, Georgia, Hungary, Kazakhstan, Kyrgyzstan, Latvia, Lithuania, Moldova, Poland, Romania, Russia, Slovakia, Tajikistan, Turkmenistan, Ukraine, and Uzbekistan.

## Table B-3: U.S. Travel, Passenger Fares, and Other Transportation Receipts, 1994–1997

## Table B-4: Travel, Passenger Fares, and Other Transportation Payments, 1994–97

### DATA NOTES
Other port services receipts and payments for Canada are shown below, in millions of dollars:

### Other Port Services Receipts and Payments, Canada, 1994–97

(millions of dollars)

| Year | Receipts | Payments |
|------|----------|----------|
| 1994 | 145 | 77 |
| 1995 | 149 | 77 |
| 1996 | 160 | 82 |
| 1997 | 153 | 84 |

## Table B-11.
## U.S. Business, Professional, and Technical Service Receipts, 1994–1997

## Table B-12.
## U.S. Business, Professional, and Technical Service Payments, 1994–1997

### DATA NOTES
*Receipts for engineering, architectural, construction, and mining services* are published net of merchandise exports, which are included in merchandise trade in the U.S. international transactions accounts, and net of outlays abroad for wages, services, materials, and other expenses. Gross receipts and the deductions taken to arrive at net receipts are shown below for 1994–1997.

### Engineering, Architechtural, Construction, and Mining Service Receipts, 1994–97

(millions of dollars)

| Year | Gross operating revenue | Merchandise exports | Foreign expenses | Net receipts |
|------|------------------------|---------------------|------------------|--------------|
| 1994 | 4 834 | 690 | 1 670 | 2 474 |
| 1995 | 4 788 | 787 | 1 451 | 2 550 |
| 1996 | 6 931 | 1 535 | 1 836 | 3 560 |
| 1997 | 8 513 | 1 788 | 2 641 | 4 084 |

*Payments for engineering, architectural, construction, and mining services* are not published net of merchandise imports and outlays for wages and other expenses. Data are not collected for merchandise imports and wages and other expenses, and no estimates are made because they are believed to be small.

*Other receipts and payments* consist of accounting, auditing, and bookkeeping services; agricultural services; mailing, reproduction, and commercial art; management of health care facilities; medical services; miscellaneous disbursements; operational leasing; personnel supply services; sports and performing arts; training services; and other business, professional, and technical services. *Other business, professional, and technical services* consist of language translation services, security services, collection services, actuarial services, salvage services, satellite

# PART C.
# U.S. FOREIGN TRADE IN GOODS

photography services, oil spill and toxic waste clean-up services, and merchanting services.

The export statistics are initially collected and compiled by the Bureau of the Census into the approximately 8,000 commodity classifications contained in Schedule B, *Statistical Classification of Domestic and Foreign Commodities Exported from the United States.* Schedule B is a U.S. Bureau of the Census publication and is based on the Harmonized Commodity Description and Coding System (Harmonized System).

The import statistics are initially collected and compiled in terms of the approximately 14,000 commodity classifications in the *Harmonized Tariff Schedule of the United States Annotated for Statistical Reporting Purposes.*

Related to the Harmonized System is the Standard International Trade Classification (SITC). This is an international statistical classification of the commodities in world trade, maintained by the United Nations. These uniform classifications facilitate the international comparison of trade-by-commodity data.

The data in Table C-3 are based on Standard Industrial Classification product codes. The data are converted from the Harmonized System by the Bureau of the Census. These classifications may differ from the SIC industry classifications on which many domestic economic reports are based. The SIC industry codes classify establishments by type of activity. Each establishment is coded based on its principal activity. However, one establishment sometimes may produce more than one type of product. Exports and imports are classified by product irrespective of whether the product was produced in an establishment primarily producing this product. Product classifications approximate industry classifications but are not a precise match.

The new North American Industry Classification System (NAICS) is being adopted by Canada, Mexico, and United States, and, in the United States, it is replacing the SIC. The first data on an NAICS basis are being released during 1999, and NAICS will be fully implemented around 2004 or later. Bernan Press, in cooperation with the National Technical Information Service, is the official publisher and distributor of the manual, *North American Industry Classification System, United States, 1997,* Executive Office of the President, Office of Management and Budget. Tables matching NAICS to the SIC are included, as is a complete index. The manual is available in hardcover, softcover, or CD-ROM by calling Bernan (1-800-865-3457) or placing an order through the Bernan internet site, <www.bernan.com>.

## Table C-1.
## U.S. Foreign Trade in Goods, 1970–1998

Source: Bureau of the Census; data compiled OTEA.

### DATA NOTES
Census data concordances link the 1980–1992 trade figures into time series that are as consistent as possible. Data for 1970 to 1979 are not linked and are from published sources. Import values are based on transaction prices whenever possible (f.a.s. from 1974 to 1979, and customs basis thereafter), maintaining a consistent data series over time. Import data before 1974 do not exist on a transaction price basis. Imports for 1991 include revisions for passenger cars, trucks, petroleum, and petroleum products not included elsewhere. *Total goods* include military grant aid and trade between the U.S. Virgin Islands and foreign countries. For all categories other than total goods, data for 1970 to 1980 exclude trade between the U.S. Virgin Islands and foreign countries.

*Manufactured goods* include commodity sections 5 through 9 under Schedules A and E for 1970 to 1982, and SITC revision 3 for 1983 to present. Manufactures include undocumented exports to Canada, nonmonetary gold (excluding gold ore, scrap, and base bullion), and special category shipments.

*Agricultural products* from 1983 forward utilize the latest Census definition that excludes manufactured goods that were previously classified as manufactured agricultural products.

*Mineral fuels* include commodity section 3 under SITC revision 1 for 1970 to 1976, SITC revision 2 for 1977 to 1982, and SITC revision 3 from 1983 forward. This category includes petroleum, petroleum products, and natural gas and related products.

### DATA AVAILABILITY
This table, formerly published by OTEA in *Foreign Trade Highlights*, now may be found on the OTEA web site.

## Table C-2.
## U.S. Foreign Trade in Goods by End-Use Category, 1978–1998

Source: Bureau of the Census; data compiled by OTEA.

### DATA NOTES
Data in this table are classified in accordance with the use for which the goods are intended.

*Foods, feeds, and beverages* include alcoholic beverages, animal feeds, bakery products, corn, dairy products, eggs, fish, shellfish, fruits, frozen juices, meat, poultry, nonagricultural foods, nuts, oilseeds, food oils, rice, sorghum, barley, oats, soybeans, vegetables, wheat, and other foods.

*Industrial supplies and materials* include aluminum and alumina; chemical fertilizers; inorganic and organic chemicals; other chemicals; coal and other fuels; copper; cotton fiber cloth; raw cotton; crude oil; electric energy; finished metal shapes; finished textile supplies; fuel oil; natural gas; plate and sheet glass; hair; waste materials; hides and skins; industrial rubber products; iron and steel products; leather and furs; logs and lumber; manmade cloth; metallurgical grade coal; manufactured mineral supplies; natural gas liquids; newsprint; nonferrous metals; nonmetallic minerals; nonmonetary gold; nontextile floor tiles; nuclear fuel materials; petroleum products; plastic materials; precious metals; pulpwood and woodpulp; shingles, molding, and wallboard; steelmaking materials; primary synthetic rubber; audio and video tapes; unmanufactured tobacco; manufactured wood supplies; and other industrial supplies.

*Capital goods, except automotive* include agricultural machinery and equipment; business machines and equipment; civilian aircraft; commercial vessels; computer accessories; computers; drilling and oilfield equipment; electric apparatus; engines for civilian aircraft; excavating machinery; food and tobacco machinery; generators, accessories; industrial engines; other industrial machines; laboratory testing instruments; marine engines and parts; materials handling equipment; measuring, testing, and control instruments; medicinal equipment; metalworking machine tools; nonfarm tractors and parts; parts for civilian aircraft; photographic and service industry machinery; pulp and paper machinery; railway transportation equipment; semiconductors; nonmilitary spacecraft; specialized mining; telecommunications equipment; textile sewing machines; vessels, except scrap; and wood, glass, and plastic.

*Automotive vehicles, engines, and parts* include semis and heavy trucks, as well as automobiles and light trucks. Vehicles for both commercial and personal use are included.

*Consumer goods* include textile apparel and household goods; nontextile apparel and household goods; artwork, antiques, and stamps; books and printed matter; cookware, cutlery, and tools; furniture and household goods; gem diamonds; glassware and chinaware; household appliances; jewelry; musical instruments; numismatic coins; nursery stock; other household goods; pharmaceutical preparations; pleasure boats and motors; records, tapes, and disks; rugs; sports apparel and gear; stereo equipment; manufactured tobacco; toiletries and cosmetics; toys, games, and sporting goods; TVs and VCRs; and writing and art supplies.

### DATA AVAILABILITY
Data are available from the OTEA web site. More detailed data are released each month in the joint Census-BEA release (FT900). Historical data for recent years are available from the Census Bureau web site. Current data for the six main categories are also published monthly by BEA in the *Survey of Current Business*.

## Table C-3.
## U.S. Foreign Trade by Industry, 1991–1997

Source: Bureau of the Census, ; data compiled by OTEA.

## DATA NOTES

Data are on a Census basis, exports are on an f.a.s. value basis, and imports are on a customs value basis. The data are classified on the basis of SIC product codes as explained above.

## DATA AVAILABILITY

This compilation, formerly published by OTEA in *Foreign Trade Highlights*, now may be found on the OTEA web site.

## Table C-4.
### U.S. Foreign Trade in Goods, Summary by Region, 1991-1997

## Table C-5.
### U.S. Foreign Trade in Goods by Destination, 1991-1997

Source: Bureau of the Census, data compiled by OTEA.

## DATA NOTES

Data are based on the Harmonized System of commodity classification and converted to other classification systems using recent Census data concordances to produce consistent time series. Therefore, the data in this table will differ from values in other published sources. Manufactured goods are as defined in SITC (revision 3) 5–9. Data in this table are not necessarily revised to reflect revisions in total U.S. exports and imports. (See the general notes for Section C for an explanation of these classification systems.)

Exports are on a Census basis, f.a.s. value. Imports are on a Census basis, customs value. When necessary, country and regional foreign trade data were adjusted to create data series that utilize the same country definitions over time.

## COUNTRY AND REGION NOTES

Effective January 1, 1993, Czechoslovakia ceased to exist and became two countries, the Czech Republic and Slovakia.

In June 1992 the U.S. Bureau of the Census began to report trade figures for the new republics of the former Yugoslavia; therefore, 1992 trade figures do not reflect the entire year for these republics. However, 1992 trade figures for Yugoslavia (former) do reflect the entire year. Yugoslavia (former) consists of Bosnia-Herzegovina, Croatia, Macedonia, Serbia and Montenegro, and Slovenia.

In January 1992 the U.S. Bureau of the Census began to report trade figures for Estonia, Latvia, and Lithuania. In February 1992 the U.S. Bureau of the Census began to report trade figures for the other republics of the former USSR; therefore, 1992 trade figures for the individual republics reflect only February through December 1992 and do not reflect the entire year for these republics. However, the 1992 total trade figure for all the former Soviet republics does combined reflect the entire year.

Effective July 1, 1993, the Census Bureau began collecting data for Eritrea.

*Western Hemisphere* includes all countries of the Western Hemisphere except for the United States.

*North America* includes Canada and Mexico.

*South and Central America and Caribbean* include all the countries listed below in the individual regions.

*Caribbean* countries include the Bahamas, Barbados, Belize, Cayman Islands, Dominican Republic, Guyana, Haiti, Jamaica, Leeward and Windward Islands (i.e., Antigua, British Virgin Islands, Dominica, Grenada, Montserrat, St. Christopher-Nevis and Anguilla, St. Lucia, and St. Vincent), Netherlands Antilles and Aruba, Suriname, Trinidad and Tobago, and Turks and Caicos Islands.

*Central American* countries consist of Costa Rica, El Salvador, Guatemala, Honduras, Nicaragua, and Panama.

*South America* includes Argentina, Bolivia, Brazil, Chile, Colombia, Ecuador, Paraguay, Peru, Uruguay, and Venezuela.

*Europe* consists of Western Europe and Eastern Europe.

*Western Europe* includes the European Union (EU) and non-EU Western Europe.

The *European Union* includes Austria, Belgium, Luxembourg, Denmark, Finland, France, Germany (both East and West), Greece, Ireland, Italy, the Netherlands, Portugal (including the Azores and the Madeira Islands), Spain (including Spanish Africa and the Canary Islands), Sweden, and the United Kingdom.

*Western Europe, except European Union* includes Cyprus, Gibraltar, Iceland, Malta, Norway, Switzerland, Turkey, Yugoslavia (former), and, after 1987, other non-EU Western Europe (Andorra, Faroe Islands, Liechtenstein, Monaco, San Marino, Svalbard and Jan Mayen Island, and Vatican City).

*Eastern Europe and former Soviet republics* include Albania, Bulgaria, the Czech Republic and Slovakia (former Czechoslovakia), Hungary, Poland, Romania, and the former Soviet republics.

The *former Soviet republics* consist of Armenia, Azerbaijan, Belarus, Estonia, Georgia, Kazakhstan, Kyrgyzstan, Latvia, Lithuania, Russia, Tajikistan, Turkmenistan, Ukraine, and Uzbekistan.

*Asia, including Middle East,* includes Afghanistan, Bangladesh, Bhutan, Brunei, Burma, Cambodia, China, Hong Kong, India, Indonesia, Japan, Laos, Macao, Malaysia, Maldive Islands, Mongolia, Nepal, North Korea, Pakistan, the Philippines, Singapore, South Korea, Sri Lanka, Taiwan, Thailand, Vietnam, and the Middle East.

The *Middle East* includes Bahrain, Iran, Iraq, Israel (including the Gaza Strip and the West Bank), Jordan, Kuwait, Lebanon, the Neutral Zone, Oman, Qatar, Saudi Arabia, Syria, the United Arab Emirates, and the Yemen Arab Republic.

*Australia and Oceania* consist of Australia, Australian island dependencies (i.e., Christmas Island, Cocos Island, Heard and McDonald Islands, and Norfolk Island),

French Pacific Islands (i.e., French Polynesia, New Caledonia, and Wallis and Futuna), New Zealand, New Zealand island dependencies (i.e., Cook Islands, Niue, and Tokelau Islands), Papua New Guinea, Southern Pacific Islands (i.e., Kiribati, Pitcairn Island, Solomon Islands, Tuvalu, and Vanuatu), Former Trust Territory (i.e., Federated States of Micronesia, Marshall Islands, and Palau), Western Samoa, and other Pacific islands NEC (i.e., Fiji, Nauru, and Tonga).

*Africa* consists of all the countries on the continent. French Indian Ocean areas include Reunion and French Southern and Antarctic Lands. Western Africa NEC includes Cape Verde, Guinea-Bissau, and Sao Tome and Principe. In January 1993 the U.S. Bureau of the Census began to report trade figures for Eritrea.

*The Association of Southeast Asian Nations (ASEAN)* members are Burma, Brunei, Indonesia, Laos, Malaysia, the Philippines, Singapore, Thailand, and Vietnam. Burma and Laos joined in 1997; however, Cambodia did not join, as expected, in 1997.

*Asia–Pacific Economic Cooperation (APEC)* countries are Australia, Brunei, Canada, Chile, China, Hong Kong, Indonesia, Japan, Malaysia, Mexico, New Zealand, Papua New Guinea, Philippines, Singapore, South Korea, Taiwan, Thailand, and the United States. Peru, Russia, and Vietnam joined APEC in 1998, this data does not include these countries.

*Caribbean Basin Initiative* countries consist of the Caribbean countries and the Central American countries.

### DATA AVAILABILITY
Full data are available from the OTEA web site. Monthly data for a large number of countries are available from the Census web site or may be found in the FT900 report.

**State and Metropolitan Area Exporter Location (EL) Data**

Source: Bureau of the Census; compiled by OTEA.

# PART D.
# STATE EXPORTS OF GOODS

# PART E.
# METROPOLITAN AREA EXPORTS OF GOODS

### DATA NOTES
All of the state and metropolitan area data shown have been compiled from the Census Bureau's Exporter Location series by the Office of Trade and Economic Analysis, International Trade Administration, U.S. Department of Commerce. All of the state and metropolitan area export data are based on f.a.s. value. All state and metropolitan area data exclude timing adjustments and the Canada adjustment. A timing adjustment is an adjustment to a previous period's data because the data were not reported in a timely manner; the Canada adjustment is for inland freight that is sometimes included in Canadian exports. All figures are based on initial, unrevised data.

The EL series show export sales by exporters of record located in the state or metropolitan area listed. Typically, the EL data reflect the point of sale, that is, the marketing origin of the exports. This is not necessarily the location where the goods are produced. *Thus, the EL series provide an approximation, but not a complete and reliable record, of the production origin of U.S. exports.* The data are best viewed as a measure of international sales activity. They should be interpreted with caution as a measure of export-related production or jobs.

About three-fourths of manufacturing exports are generated by manufacturers who do their own exporting. For these shipments the production origin and the sales origin are generally, but not always, the same. For the remaining one-fourth of manufactured exports and most nonmanufactured exports, the seller (the exporter of record) is not the producer. The production may or may not have occurred in the same state or metropolitan area. Overall, Census Bureau research suggests that, for manufacturing establishments, the zip code location of the exporter of record is the same as the physical location of production for about 88 percent of the value of exports.

The data measure final sales of goods leaving the country. Even where the final product was produced in the same location as the sale, it may contain raw materials and intermediate products produced elsewhere.

In some cases, the exporter of record may be a headquarters or central office that may or may not engage in international marketing activity. Thus, the significance of a "headquarters effect" is unclear.

There are significant differences between the EL series and the alternative Origin of Movement (OM) state export series, also prepared by the Bureau of the Census. Data from these two series cannot be compared to each other. The OM series measures the transportation origin of exports, which inflates the exports of states with major shipping ports. Also, the OM series is available only for states, while the EL series can show both states and metropolitan areas.

The export figures shown in these tables for states and metropolitan areas can be used together. That is, it is possible to use the data for a metropolitan area to estimate its share of the state's export sales.

When calculating these data, the Census Bureau was unable to allocate about 7.5 percent of exports to any local jurisdiction because of faulty reporting of zip codes by exporters. Thus, it can be inferred that export totals for at least some of the metropolitan areas are understated. Further, improvements in reporting may cause one-time statistical "gains" in exports, simply because the data become available. As an example, Detroit, Michigan, showed a $10.7 billion, or 65 percent, gain in 1994. On closer inspection, it was found that as much as $6 billion of this may have been due to better reporting on export declarations.

Commodity categories shown in state and metropolitan tables are based on SIC product codes. (See the general notes for Section C for an explanation of SIC and other classifications.) Manufactured goods that cannot be classified by type—for example, those with incomplete data—are labeled "unidentified manufactures."

*Metropolitan areas.* In general, a metropolitan statistical area (MSA) is a geographic area consisting of a large population nucleus together with adjacent communities that have a high degree of economic and social integration with that nucleus. Except in New England, MSAs consist of groups of adjacent counties. MSAs are defined by the U.S. Office of Management and Budget based on a specified set of criteria. These definitions are used for statistical purposes throughout the federal government. The metropolitan areas presented in this book conform to this official definition. Metropolitan complexes with populations of one million or more may be divided into primary metropolitan statistical areas (PMSAs). When PMSAs are defined, the larger metropolitan area of which they are components is designated a consolidated metropolitan statistical area (CMSA). The metropolitan area data tables cover both MSAs and PMSAs. CMSAs are excluded.

The metropolitan area export data were tabulated based on the five-digit zip codes entered by businesses on the export declarations. Zip codes that cross from a metropolitan area into an adjacent rural area were assigned to the metro area. Where two adjacent metropolitan areas share the same zip code, the zip code was assigned to a catch-all "crossover" category. The crossover category accounted for 2.9 percent of total goods exports in 1997.

### DATA AVAILABILITY
All data are available on the OTEA web site.

## Table D-1.
## State Exports of Goods, 1987 and 1991–1997

### DATA NOTES
All figures reflect sales by exporters of record located in the jurisdictions shown. The location from which exports are sold is not always the same as the one at which the goods were produced. The category "Unallocated" represents exports that, because of faulty reporting of the zip code of the exporter, cannot be allocated to any state.

## Table D-2.
## State Exports of Goods by Destination, 1993–1997

## Table D-3.
## State Exports of Goods by Destination and Industry, 1993–1997

### DATA NOTES
*Central and South America and Caribbean* include the following country categories. *Central America* includes Costa Rica, El Salvador, Guatemala, Honduras,

Nicaragua, and Panama. *South America* includes Argentina, Bolivia, Brazil, Chile, Colombia, Ecuador, Paraguay, Peru, Uruguay, and Venezuela. *The Caribbean* includes the Bahamas, Barbados, Belize, Cayman Islands, Dominican Republic, Guyana, Haiti, Jamaica, Leeward and Windward Islands (i.e., Antigua, British Virgin Islands, Dominica, Grenada, Montserrat, St. Christopher-Nevis and Anguilla, St. Lucia, and St. Vincent), Netherlands Antilles and Aruba, Suriname, Trinidad and Tobago, and Turks and Caicos Islands.

*European Union* includes Austria, Belgium, Luxembourg, Denmark, Finland, France, Germany, Greece, Ireland, Italy, the Netherlands, Portugal, Spain, Sweden, and the United Kingdom.

The *Asian 10* include China, Hong Kong, Indonesia, Japan, Malaysia, the Philippines, Singapore, South Korea, Taiwan, and Thailand.

The *African 8* include Angola, Ethiopia, Ghana, Ivory Coast, Kenya, Nigeria, South Africa, and Zimbabwe.

*Developing Countries* include all export destinations except Australia, Canada, EU and non-EU Western Europe, Japan, New Zealand, and South Africa.

## Table E-1.
## Metropolitan Area Exports of Goods, 1993–1997

### DATA NOTES
Out of a total of 335 metropolitan areas, this table shows the 256 for which export data are available. Data are not available for the other metropolitan areas for one of two reasons. One reason is that there is no export business reported from that area. The other reason is that the federal government restricts disclosure of confidential business data of individual companies. If an individual company could be identified by the data, then the data are suppressed. This practice prevents publication of data for some relatively large metropolitan areas.

## Table E-2.
## Metropolitan Area Exports of Goods by Industry, 1993–1997

### DATA NOTES
This table includes 43 of the 50 largest exporters. Some metropolitan tables may show two or more classifications combined. This method prevents disclosure of data on individual firms, while still providing a sense of the exports from these classifications. Other metropolitan areas could not be shown because of the disclosure restrictions.

## Table E-3.
## Metropolitan Area Exports of Goods by Destination, 1993–1997

### DATA NOTES
This table shows 181 metropolitan areas. As in the previous tables, some metropolitan areas could not be shown because of the disclosure restrictions.

# INDEX

(Numbers in italics indicate figures of tables.)